ARCTIC OCEAN
Barents Sea
RUSSIA
NORWAY
SWEDEN
FINLAND
ESTONIA
LATVIA
LITHUANIA
Baltic Sea
BELARUS
POLAND
UKRAINE
CZECHIA
SLOVAKIA
AUSTRIA
HUNGARY
MOLDOVA
ROMANIA
BULGARIA
Black Sea
GEORGIA
ARMENIA
AZERBAIJAN
Caspian Sea
GREECE
TURKEY
MALTA
TUNISIA
CYPRUS
LEBANON
ISRAEL
SYRIA
IRAQ
IRAN
JORDAN
KUWAIT
QATAR
BAHRAIN
U.A.E.
SAUDI ARABIA
OMAN
YEMEN
LIBYA
EGYPT
Red Sea
KAZAKHSTAN
Aral Sea
Lake Balkhash
UZBEKISTAN
TURKMENISTAN
KYRGYZSTAN
TAJIKISTAN
AFGHANISTAN
PAKISTAN
MONGOLIA
Lake Baikal
CHINA
NEPAL
BHUTAN
BANGLADESH
INDIA
Arabian Sea
Bay of Bengal
MYANMAR (BURMA)
LAOS
VIETNAM
THAILAND
CAMBODIA
Hainan
South China Sea
PHILIPPINES
Philippine Sea
Taiwan
East China Sea
Yellow Sea
NORTH KOREA
SOUTH KOREA
Sea of Japan (East Sea)
JAPAN
Sea of Okhotsk
Kurile Islands
Bering Sea
Arctic Circle
PACIFIC OCEAN
Tropic of Cancer
Northern Marianas Islands (to US)
Guam (to US)
MARSHALL ISLANDS
FEDERATED STATES OF MICRONESIA
PALAU
NAURU
Equator
KIRIBATI
PAPUA NEW GUINEA
New Guinea
TUVALU
SOLOMON ISLANDS
Wallis and Futuna (to France)
VANUATU
Coral Sea
Coral Sea Islands (to Australia)
New Caledonia (to France)
FIJI
Tropic of Capricorn
Andaman Islands (to India)
SRI LANKA
Nicobar Islands (to India)
MALDIVES
MALAYSIA
BRUNEI
SINGAPORE
Sumatra
Borneo
Moluccas
INDONESIA
Java Sea
Java
Flores Sea
TIMOR-LESTE
INDIAN OCEAN
SEYCHELLES
COMOROS
Mayotte (to France)
MAURITIUS
Réunion (to France)
MADAGASCAR
AUSTRALIA
Tasmania
Tasman Sea
NEW ZEALAND
CHAD
SUDAN
ERITREA
DJIBOUTI
Socotra (to Yemen)
SOUTH SUDAN
ETHIOPIA
SOMALIA
CENTRAL AFRICAN REPUBLIC
CAMEROON
GABON
CONGO
DEMOCRATIC REPUBLIC OF THE CONGO
UGANDA
KENYA
Lake Victoria
RWANDA
BURUNDI
TANZANIA
ANGOLA
ZAMBIA
MALAWI
MOZAMBIQUE
ZIMBABWE
NAMIBIA
BOTSWANA
ESWATINI
LESOTHO
SOUTH AFRICA
SOUTHERN OCEAN
Antarctic Circle
ANTARCTICA

acrobat

gecko
reel
amber
sunflower
laptop
poisonous
fly mushroom
fishhook
zebra
digital camera
ZOOM LENS 4x
5
racing car

cupola

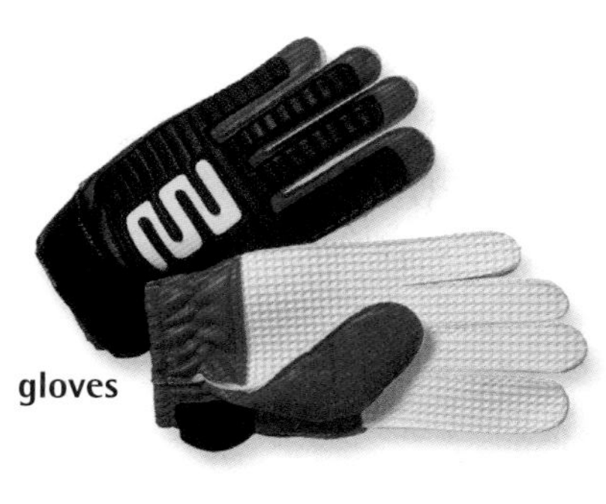
gloves

hamburger

beetle

Merriam-Webster Children's Dictionary

cane toad

catcher

forget-me-not

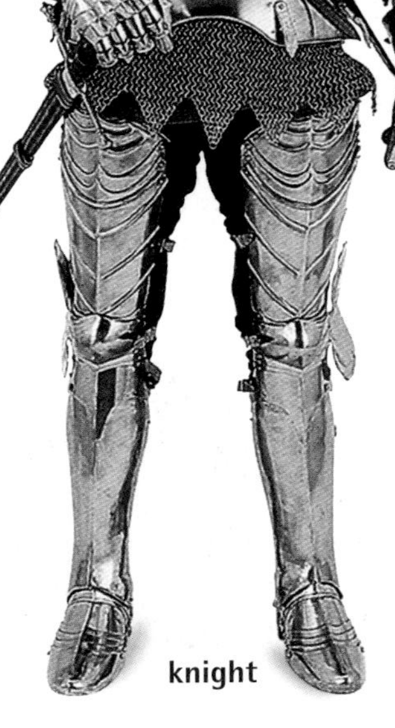
knight

Third Edition

DK Delhi
Senior Editor Virien Chopra
Project Art Editor Mansi Agrawal
Assistant Editor Sai Prasanna
Senior Jacket Designer Suhita Dharamjit
DTP Designer Bimlesh Tiwari
Pre-production Manager Balwant Singh
Production Manager Pankaj Sharma
Managing Editor Kingshuk Ghoshal
Managing Art Editor Govind Mittal

DK London
Senior Editor Carron Brown
Project Art Editor Gregory McCarthy
Senior Cartographic Editor Simon Mumford
US Executive Editor Lori Cates Hand
Jacket Design Development Manager Sophia MTT
Senior Producer, Pre-production Jacqueline Street-Elkayam
Senior Producer Jude Crozier
Managing Editor Francesca Baines
Managing Art Editor Philip Letsu
Publisher Andrew Macintyre
Associate Publishing Director Liz Wheeler
Art Director Karen Self
Publishing Director Jonathan Metcalf

For Merriam-Webster, Incorporated
Senior Editor Linda Picard Wood
Project Editors Anne P. Bello, Daniel B. Brandon, Christopher C. Conner, Ilya A. Davidovich, Joshua S. Guenter, Daniel J. Hopkins, Joan I. Narmontas, Thomas Pitoniak, James L. Rader, Donna L. Rickerby, Paul S. Wood
Data-Entry Staff Mary M. Dunn, E. Louise Langford, Stacy-Ann S. Lall

First Edition
For DK Publishing

Senior Editor Monica Byles
Project Editors Samantha Gray, Ranjana Saklani
Editors Azza Brown, Lucy Hurst, Atanu Raychaudhuri, Dawn Rowley
Managing Editor Jayne Parsons
Editorial Directors Anita Roy, Sue Unstead
Senior Production Controller Kate Oliver
Picture Research Frances Vargo
DTP Designers Nomazwe Madonko, Sunil Sharma

Senior Art Editor Esther van der Werf
Project Art Editors Tina Borg, Shuka Jain
Designers Ruth Jones, Prabal Mandal, Shefali Upadhyay, Clair Watson
Managing Art Editor Gillian Shaw
Art Directors Linda Cole, Alpana Khare
Production Assistant Shivani Pandey
DK Picture Library Martin Copeland, Charlotte Oster, Romaine Werblow

For Merriam-Webster, Incorporated

Senior Editor Children's Dictionaries Victoria Neufeldt
Director of Editorial Operations Madeline L. Novak
Project Editors Daniel J. Hopkins, Linda Picard Wood

This American Edition, 2019
First American Edition, 2000
Published in the United States by DK Publishing, 1450 Broadway, Suite 801, New York, NY 10018
and Merriam-Webster, Incorporated, 47 Federal Street, Springfield, MA 01102

21 22 23 24 25 10 9 8 7 6 5
005–316689–Dec/2019

Published in Great Britain by Dorling Kindersley Limited.

A catalog record for this book is available from the Library of Congress.
ISBN 978-1-4654-8882-4

Printed and bound in Latvia

For the curious
www.dk.com

CONTENTS

Preface

THE VOLUME YOU ARE HOLDING IS THE FRUIT OF an extraordinary collaboration between two companies with formidable reputations – Merriam-Webster, certainly America's most eminent publisher of dictionaries, and Dorling Kindersley, whose books are renowned for their ability to make information visually exciting and accessible to readers of all ages.

Designed for children ages 8 and up, *The DK Merriam-Webster Children's Dictionary* combines vibrant pictures from the Dorling Kindersley archive with authoritative text from Merriam-Webster. But this is no mere dictionary with illustrations. The thinking behind the selection of each individual picture has been as exacting as it has been for the choice of words. If we had added images only for their decorative value, this book would not serve as much more than a dictionary with pretty pictures. Instead, the choosing of images has been directed by their accuracy, usefulness, and potential for bringing unfamiliar subjects to life, and by their capacity to expand a word definition, illuminate the obscure, or cast light on those areas where the possibilities of verbal description are stretched to the limit. Special features have also been created to provide a wide range of themes with additional information: labels placed around images pinpoint individual features and expand the reader's vocabulary; diagrams, models, and cross sections enhance understanding and add detail to a host of topics; and collections of images establish the range of objects within a single theme.

These features combine to offer an exciting way to improve spelling, grammar, vocabulary, and understanding of our language – producing a handsome resource that children will look forward to using at home and at school.

Enjoy this dictionary, both as a remarkable work of the English language and as a colorful parade of words and illustrations. It has been a privilege to work with our colleagues at Merriam-Webster in creating it for your family's use.

parachute

NEAL PORTER
VICE PRESIDENT & PUBLISHER (1996–2000)
DORLING KINDERSLEY PUBLISHING, INC.

crane

drums

pink grapefruit

THE DK MERRIAM-WEBSTER CHILDREN'S DICTIONARY is written, designed, and illustrated for students in the elementary grades. It is meant to be a young student's first real dictionary. It has many of the features that appear in larger dictionaries that grown-ups use. Yet the definitions are in plain language that is easy to understand.

covered wagon

The text of the dictionary comes from Merriam-Webster and is based on the same information that goes into other Merriam-Webster dictionaries, including *Merriam-Webster's Collegiate Dictionary*. Dorling Kindersley created the design and illustrations that make this book a pleasure to browse and that help expand a student's understanding of words and their definitions.

Students using this dictionary will discover a world of information between its covers. They will learn about the meanings of words and how to spell and pronounce them. They will find out about synonyms, and they will discover the interesting histories of many words. There are examples to show how words are used, and thousands of illustrations and diagrams to provide additional information on many interesting topics. There are also special sections about nations and places around the world.

The dictionary includes entries for 35,000 words and phrases. They include all the words that students ordinarily use in talking and in writing and that they are likely to encounter in schoolwork and outside reading.

A dictionary is a very special book. In fact, it can become one of the most important books a student owns. It is not meant to be looked at once and then put away. Instead, it is a book that should be picked up often. The more a student uses this dictionary, the more it will become like a good friend — someone to go to whenever there is a question about words and someone who can always be relied upon for trustworthy answers.

JOHN MORSE
PRESIDENT & PUBLISHER (1980–2016)
MERRIAM-WEBSTER, INC.

identical twins

fire engine

How to Use Your Dictionary

THE FOLLOWING PAGES will help you understand all the features and conventions used in the *DK Merriam-Webster Children's Dictionary*, from the structure and content of individual word entries to a complete list of pronunciation symbols. The dictionary itself appears on pages 28–922, and is followed by an illustrated reference section, which includes maps of the world, listings of presidents and vice presidents of the USA, a guide to common abbreviations used in English, as well as a comprehensive picture index.

Letter information
The start of each letter has an explanation describing the different sounds that a letter can make.

Alphabet
The color-coded alphabet helps users find their way through the dictionary.

Alphabet locators
Alphabet sections are easily located using the color coding.

380 |

A B C D E F G H I

Hh

Sounds of H: The sound of the letter **H** is heard in ***hope*** and ***behave***. In some words, **H** is silent, such as in ***hour***, ***ghost***, ***rhyme***, and ***oh***. Letter **H** also combines with a number of other letters to make different sounds. **H** combines with **C** to make the sound heard in ***chat***, and with **G** to make the **F** sound heard in ***cough***. (**G** and **H** together are also sometimes silent, as in ***though***.) **H** also combines with **S** to make the sound heard in ***show***, with **T** to make the sounds heard in ***the*** and ***think***, and with **P** to make the **F** sound heard in ***photo***. **W** and **H** together, as in ***which***, can be pronounced in two ways. Some people pronounce it with a silent **H**, so that ***which*** sounds like "witch". Other people pronounce it with the **H** sound first, so that ***which*** is pronounced \'hwich\.

h \'āch\ *n, pl* **h's** *or* **hs** \'ā-chəz\ *often cap*
the eighth letter of the English alphabet
ha *or* **hah** \'hä\ *interj*
used to show surprise or joy
hab•it \'ha-bət\ *n*
1 usual way of behaving ⟨We're studying the *habits* of wild birds.⟩
3 a way of acting or doing that has become fixed by being repeated often
4 characteristic way of growing ⟨These are trees of spreading *habit*.⟩
hab•it•able \'ha-bə-tə-bəl\ *adj*
suitable or fit to live in ⟨a *habitable* house⟩
hab•i•tat \'ha-bə-ˌtat\ *n*
the place where a plant or animal grows or lives in nature
hab•i•ta•tion \ˌha-bə-'tā-shən\ *n*
1 the act of living in a place ⟨The house is fit for *habitation*.⟩
2 a place to live
ha•bit•u•al \hə-'bi-chə-wəl\ *adj*
1 occurring regularly or repeatedly : being or done by habit ⟨*habitual* kindness⟩
2 doing or acting by force of habit ⟨*habitual* liars⟩
3 REGULAR 1 ⟨Salad is my *habitual* lunch.⟩
ha•bit•u•al•ly \-wə-lē\ *adv*
ha•ci•en•da \ˌhä-sē-'en-də\ *n*
a large estate especially in a Spanish-speaking country
[1]**hack** \'hak\ *vb* **hacked**; **hack•ing**
1 to cut with repeated chopping blows
2 to cough in a short broken way
3 to write computer programs for enjoyment
4 to gain access to a computer illegally
[2]**hack** *n*
a short broken cough
[3]**hack** *n*
1 a horse let out for hire or used for varied work
2 a person who works for pay at a routine writing job
3 a person who does work that is not good or original and especially a writer who is not very good
hack•er \'ha-kər\ *n*
1 HACK 3
2 an expert at programming and solving problems with a computer
3 a person who illegally gains access to a computer system
hack•les \'ha-kəlz\ *n pl*
hairs (as on the neck of a dog) that can be made to stand up
hack•ney \'hak-nē\ *n, pl* **hack•neys**
a horse for ordinary riding or driving
hack•saw \'hak-ˌsȯ\ *n*
▼ a saw with small teeth used for cutting hard materials (as metal)

hacksaw

had *past and past participle of* HAVE
had•dock \'ha-dək\ *n, pl* **haddock** *or* **haddocks**
▼ a fish of the northern Atlantic Ocean that is related to the cod and is often used for food

haddock

hadn't \'ha-dᵊnt\ had not
haf•ni•um \'haf-nē-əm\ *n*
a gray metallic chemical element
hag \'hag\ *n*
1 WITCH 1
2 an ugly old woman
hag•gard \'ha-gərd\ *adj*
having a hungry, tired, or worried look ⟨a *haggard* face⟩

\ā\ take \ä\ cot, cart \aü\ out \ch\ chin \e\ pet \ē\ easy \g\ go \i\ tip \ī\ life \j\ job

frog 1
Frogs generally have squat bodies, smooth skin, strongly muscled hind legs for leaping, and webbed feet. Most frogs reproduce in water, and lay eggs that develop into larvae known as tadpoles. Frogs are the most commonly found amphibians in the world, living in habitats ranging from moist areas such as lakes, marshes, and rain forests to dry regions such as mountains and deserts.

green tree frog

poison dart frog

European common frog

tomato frog

Features
Features give more detailed explanations, and often use larger illustrations or a series of images to aid understanding. Labels help identify individual details or parts of the topic being illustrated.

Picture index

A picture index on pages 956–959 provides a quick reference to entries that are illustrated throughout the dictionary.

Guide words

The right-hand page heading identifies the last word entry to appear on that page; the left-hand heading identifies the first entry to appear.

▶ **Word History** In the Christian calendar the first day of November is All Saints' Day, which honors all the saints in heaven. The usual earlier name for this day in English was *All Hallows Day* or *All Hallow Day*, and the previous evening (October 31) was called *All Hallows Eve* or *All Hallow Even*. (The word *hallow*, related to *holy*, meant "saint.") In Scotland *All Hallow Even* was contracted to *Hallow-e'en*, now spelled *Halloween*.

hallow | 381

hag•gle \'ha-gəl\ *vb* **hag•gled; hag•gling**
to argue especially over a price
hag•gler \'ha-glər\ *n*
hah *variant of* HA
ha–ha \hä-'hä\ *interj*
used to show amusement or scorn
hai•ku \'hī-,kü\ *n, pl* **haiku**
a Japanese poem or form of poetry without rhyme having three lines with the first and last lines having five syllables and the middle having seven
¹hail \'hāl\ *n*
1 small lumps of ice and snow that fall from the clouds sometimes during thunderstorms
2 ¹VOLLEY 1 ⟨a *hail* of bullets⟩
²hail *vb* **hailed; hail•ing**
1 to fall as hail ⟨It's *hailing* hard.⟩
2 to pour down like hail
³hail *vb* **hailed; hailing**
1 GREET 1, WELCOME
2 to call out to ⟨I'll *hail* a taxi.⟩
hail from to come from (a place)
hail•stone \'hāl-,stōn\ *n*
a lump of hail
hail•storm \'hāl-,stȯrm\ *n*
a storm that brings hail
hair \'her\ *n*
1 a threadlike growth from the skin of a person or animal ⟨She pulled out a *hair*.⟩
2 a covering or growth of hairs ⟨I got my *hair* cut.⟩
3 something (as a growth on a leaf) like an animal hair
4 a very small distance or amount ⟨I won by a *hair*.⟩
haired \'herd\ *adj*
hair•less \'her-ləs\ *adj*
hair•like \-,līk\ *adj*
hair•cut \'her-,kət\ *n*
the act, process, or result of cutting the hair
hair•do \'her-,dü\ *n, pl* **hairdos**
a way of arranging a person's hair
hair•dress•er \'her-,dre-sər\ *n*
▶ a person who styles or cuts hair
hair•dress•ing *n*
hair•pin \'her-,pin\ *n*
a pin in the shape of a U for holding the hair in place
hair–rais•ing \'her-,rā-ziŋ\ *adj*
causing terror, excitement, or great surprise
hair•style \'her-,stīl\ *n*
HAIRDO
hairy \'her-ē\ *adj* **hair•i•er; hair•i•est**
covered with hair
hair•i•ness *n*
ha•lal \hə-'läl\ *adj*
1 fit for eating under Islamic law ⟨*halal* meat⟩
2 selling or serving food fit for eating under Islamic law ⟨*halal* restaurants⟩

¹hale \'hāl\ *adj*
strong and healthy
²hale *vb* **haled; hal•ing**
to force to go ⟨The judge *haled* them into court.⟩

half–dollar 1

¹half \'haf, 'häf\ *n, pl* **halves** \'havz, 'hävz\
1 one of two equal parts into which something can be divided ⟨Cut it in *half*.⟩
2 a part of something that is about equal to the remainder ⟨*half* the distance⟩
3 one of a pair
²half *adj*
1 being one of two equal parts ⟨Add a *half* cup of milk.⟩
2 amounting to about a half ⟨a *half* smile⟩
³half *adv*
1 to the extent of half ⟨*half* full⟩
2 not completely ⟨She was *half* asleep.⟩
half•back \'haf-,bak, 'häf-\ *n*
1 a football player who runs with the ball and blocks
2 a player positioned behind the forward line in some games (as soccer)

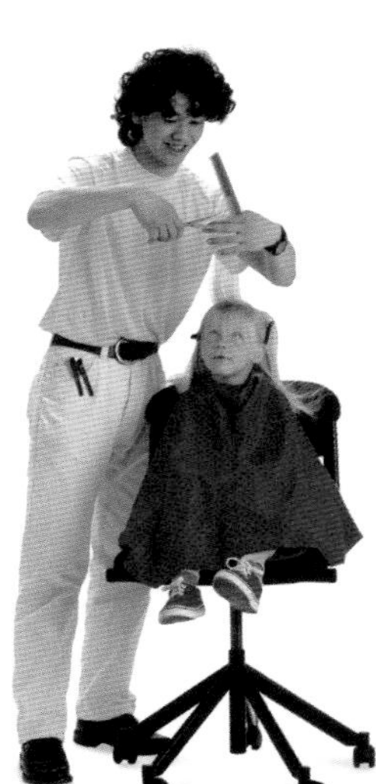

hairdresser: a hairdresser cutting hair

half brother *n*
a brother by one parent only
half–dol•lar \'haf-'dä-lər, 'häf-\ *n*
1 ◀ a coin representing 50 cents
2 the sum of 50 cents
half•heart•ed \'haf-'här-təd, 'häf-\ *adj*
lacking enthusiasm or interest ⟨There was only *halfhearted* applause.⟩
half•heart•ed•ly *adv*
half–knot \'haf-,nät, 'häf-\ *n*
▼ a knot in which two rope ends are wrapped once around each other and which is used to start other knots

a b c d e f g **h** i

\ŋ\ sing \ō\ bone \ȯ\ saw \ȯi\ coin \th\ thin \t͟h\ this \ü\ food \u̇\ foot \y\ yet

Language paragraphs

Some entries include short paragraphs providing word histories or synonyms. Word histories give fascinating information about the origins of words, and trace the development of meanings; synonyms provide cross-reference to similar words, and help to expand vocabulary.

Quick-reference Guide to Word Entries

¹hail \'hāl\ *n*
1 small lumps of ice and snow that fall from the clouds sometimes during thunderstorms
2 ¹VOLLEY 1 ⟨a *hail* of bullets⟩
²hail *vb* **hailed; hail•ing**
1 to fall as hail ⟨It's *hailing* hard.⟩
2 to pour down like hail
³hail *vb* **hailed; hailing**
1 GREET 1, WELCOME
2 to call out to ⟨I'll *hail* a taxi.⟩
hail from to come from (a place)
hail•stone \'hāl-,stōn\ *n*
a lump of hail
hail•storm \'hāl-,stȯrm\ *n*
a storm that brings hail
hair \'her\ *n*
1 a threadlike growth from the skin of a person or animal ⟨She pulled out a *hair*.⟩
2 a covering or growth of hairs ⟨I got my *hair* cut.⟩
3 something (as a growth on a leaf) like an animal hair
4 a very small distance or amount ⟨I won by a *hair*.⟩
haired \'herd\ *adj*
hair•less \'her-ləs\ *adj*
hair•like \-,līk\ *adj*

Numerals denote words that are spelled the same but have different functions or origins

Cross-reference directs the reader to a word that has the same meaning

Dark numbers introduce different senses of the same word

Dots in entry words show where words can be broken at the end of a line

For a fuller explanation, and examples of all the elements found in a word entry, see pages 10–25.

Functional label indicates the part of speech (such as noun, verb)

Pronunciation guide

Examples of usage show the word in action

Derived words help the reader increase word power

Pronunciation symbols

An easy-reference guide to letter pronunciation runs across the bottom of each spread.

Key to Using Your Dictionary

1. Main Entry Words

saber–toothed tiger *n*
a very large extinct cat of prehistoric times with long sharp curved upper canine teeth
^{2}**safe** *n*
▲ a metal box with a lid that is used for keeping something (as money) safe

2. End-of-line Divisions

sat•is•fac•tion \ˌsa-təs-ˈfak-shən\ *n* ...

3. Pronunciation Symbols

saun•ter \ˈsȯn-tər\ *vb* **saun•tered**; **saun•ter•ing**
to walk in a slow relaxed way **:** STROLL

4. Variant Spellings

^{2}**racket** *or* **rac•quet** *n* ...

5. Functional Labels

sea•coast \ˈsē-ˌkōst\ *n*
the shore of the sea

6. Homographs

^{1}**seal** \ˈsēl\ *n*
1 a sea mammal that swims ...
^{2}**seal** *n*
1 something that closes tightly ...
^{3}**seal** *vb* **sealed**; **seal•ing**
1 to close tightly ...

7. Inflected Forms

dish \ˈdish\ *n*
1 ▼ a usually round shallow container used for cooking or serving food
2 dish•es *pl* all items (as plates and silverware) used for cooking and eating food ⟨Would you do the *dishes*?⟩
^{2}**shade** *vb* **shad•ed**; **shad•ing**

8. Usage Labels

^{1}**co•lo•nial** \kə-ˈlō-nē-əl\ *adj*
1 of, relating to, or characteristic of a colony
2 *often cap* of or relating to the original 13 colonies that formed the United States

9. Definitions

skim \ˈskim\ *vb* **skimmed**; **skim•ming**
1 to clean a liquid of scum or floating substance : remove (as cream or film) from the top part of a liquid
2 to read or examine quickly and not thoroughly ...

10. Synonyms and Cross-references

slav•ery \ˈslā-və-rē, ˈslāv-rē\ *n*
1 the state of being owned by another person **:** BONDAGE
2 the custom or practice of owning slaves
3 hard tiring labor **:** DRUDGERY

11. Verbal Illustrations

si•lent \ˈsī-lənt\ *adj*
1 not speaking ⟨He stood *silent* for a moment, and then answered.⟩
2 not talkative ⟨a *silent* person⟩
3 free from noise or sound **:** STILL ⟨Except for a ticking clock the house was *silent*.⟩
4 done or felt without being spoken ⟨*silent* reading⟩ ⟨*silent* prayer⟩ ...

12. Run-in Entries

sol•stice \ˈsäl-stəs, ˈsōl-, ˈsȯl-\ *n*
the time of the year when the sun passes overhead the farthest north (**summer solstice,** about June 22) or south (**winter solstice,** about December 22) of the equator

13. Usage Notes

cas•ta•net \ˌka-stə-ˈnet\ *n*
► a rhythm instrument that consists of two small flat round parts fastened to the thumb and clicked by the fingers — usually used in pl.

14. Undefined Run-on Entries

[1]**sour** \ˈsau̇r\ *adj* ...
sour•ly *adv*
sour•ness *n*

15. Synonym Paragraphs

splen•did \ˈsplen-dəd\ *adj*
1 impressive in beauty, excellence, or magnificence ⟨You did a *splendid* job.⟩ ⟨a *splendid* palace⟩ ...

► **Synonyms** SPLENDID, GLORIOUS, and SUPERB mean very impressive. SPLENDID is used for something far above the ordinary in excellence or magnificence. ⟨What a *splendid* idea!⟩ ⟨She wore a *splendid* jewel.⟩ ...

16. Defined Run-on Phrases

choke \ˈchōk\ *vb* **choked; chok•ing**
1 to keep from breathing in a normal way by cutting off the supply of air ⟨Many people were *choked* by thick smoke.⟩ ...
choke down to eat with difficulty ⟨I *choked down* a bite.⟩
choke up to become too emotional to speak

17. Word History Paragraphs

sur•ly \ˈsər-lē\ *adj* **sur•li•er; sur•li•est**
mean and rude **:** UNFRIENDLY ⟨a *surly* neighbor⟩

► **Word History** To a noble person it might seem natural to link together high birth and good manners, but the word *surly* is evidence that other people have not always thought this way. In Middle English the word was spelled *sirly,* which made more obvious its ...

18. Guide Words

leap year

leap year *n*
a year of 366 days with February 29 as the extra day

Using Your Dictionary

1. Main Entry Words

When you open your dictionary to just about any page, you will find a list of words down the left-hand column printed in heavy black **boldface** type. Each of these is followed by information that explains or tells something about the word. The boldface word or phrase together with the explanation is a **dictionary entry**, and the boldface word itself is the **entry word** or **main entry**.

> **s** \ˈes\ *n, pl* **s's** *or* **ss** \ˈes-əz\
> *often cap*
> **1** the 19th letter of the English alphabet
> **2** a grade rating a student's work as satisfactory
> [3]**-s** *vb suffix*
> used to form the third person singular present of most verbs that do not end in *s, z, sh, ch, x,* or *y* following a consonant ⟨fall*s*⟩ ⟨take*s*⟩ ⟨play*s*⟩
> **saber-toothed tiger** *n*
> a very large extinct cat of prehistoric times with long sharp curved upper canine teeth
> [2]**safe** *n*
> a metal box with a lock that is used for keeping something (as money) safe
> [1]**safe•guard** \ˈsāf-ˌgärd\ *n*
> something that protects and gives safety ⟨Drink water as a *safeguard* against dehydration.⟩
> **safety pin** *n*
> a pin that is bent back to form a spring and has a guard that covers the point

The main entry may take many forms. It may be a single letter like **s** or a single word like **safe**. It may be an abbreviation like **oz.** It may also be a compound made up of two or more words written together **(safeguard)** or as separate words **(safety pin)** or with a hyphen **(saber-toothed tiger)**. Sometimes an entry will be made up of all capital letters **(IOU** or **TV)** or of a letter and number **(3D)** or even of a letter and a word **(T-shirt)**.

Finally some entries are only parts of words. The entry **-s** is one of these, and the entries **bi-** and **-graph**, shown below, are two more examples.

Such entries all begin or end with a hyphen. They are the building blocks of our language, for they are used to create many new words.

> **bi-** *prefix*
> **1** two ⟨*bi*ped⟩
> **2** coming or occurring every two ⟨*bi*ennial⟩
> **3** into two parts ⟨*bi*sect⟩
> **4** twice : doubly : on both sides
> **-graph** \ˌgraf\ *n suffix*
> **1** something written ⟨para*graph*⟩
> **2** instrument for making or sending records ⟨tele*graph*⟩

For example, **bi-** ("two") when combined with **cycle** gives us **bicycle** (literally "two wheels"). The word part **-graph** ("something written") combines with other word parts to give us such words as **autograph** and **paragraph**. The hyphen with the entry word is only there to show you where the word part is attached to other word parts. The entry **bi-** goes at the beginning of a word and is called a **prefix**. The entry **-graph** goes at the end of a word and is called a **suffix**.

Now that you know the kinds of entries you will find in your dictionary, you should know how the entries are arranged so you can find them easily and quickly.

All of the words in your dictionary are arranged in alphabetical order. To find a word, you simply look it up by the way it is spelled. Since **a** comes before **b** and **b** comes before **c** in the alphabet, you know that all of the words beginning with **a** will come before all of those beginning with **b**, the **b** words will all come before the **c** words, and so on all the way through the dictionary.

But merely grouping together all of the words that begin with the letter **a** would not help you find a particular word, like **alphabet**, very quickly. Well, alphabetical order also applies within each letter grouping. After all of the words are arranged by first letter, they are further grouped alphabetically by second letter. Then those words with the same first and second letters are arranged in alphabetical order by third letter and so on until every word has its own special place in the dictionary. So if you should want to look up the words **brat**, **bite**, and **bad**, you know that **bad** will come first, then **bite**, and finally **brat** because **a** comes first in the alphabet and **i** comes ahead of **r**. The words **chop**, **chute**, **chili**, **chalk**, and **cheese** all begin with the letters **ch**, so their third letters must be used in ordering them: **chalk**, **cheese**, **chili**, **chop**, and **chute**.

Now when we arrange words in alphabetical order, we do not count spaces or hyphens between words. The words are arranged just as if the space or hyphen were not there. So you will find these words that begin **doub–** arranged in the dictionary in just the order you see them here.

> [4]**double** *n* ...
> **double bass** *n* ...
> **dou•ble–cross** \ˌdəb-əl-ˈkrȯs\ *vb* ...
> **dou•ble•head•er** \ˌdəb-əl-ˈhed-ər\ *n* ...

Some of the main entries in the *DK Merriam-Webster Children's Dictionary* are groups of letters that are not pronounced like ordinary words. But these entries, like **DDT** and **TV**, are still words, and they are arranged among the other words using the same rule of alphabetical order. Thus you will find **TV** between **tuxedo** and **twain**, because **v**, the second letter in **TV**, comes after **u** and before **w**.

Whenever the main entry has a number in it, like **3D**, it is arranged just as if the number were spelled out. You will find **3D** between the words **three-dimensional** and [2]**three** just as if it were spelled **three D**.

2. End-of-line Divisions

Most of the entry words in your dictionary are shown with dots at different places in the word. These dots are not a part of the spelling of the word but are there to show you end-of-line divisions – places where you can put a hyphen if you have to break up a word because there is room for only part of it at the end of a line.

> **sat•is•fac•tion** \ˌsa-təs-ˈfak-shən\ *n* ...

In the example shown above, the word is normally written **satisfaction**, but if you have to divide it at the end of a line, the dots show you three places where you can put a hyphen.

> **sat-**
> **isfaction**
> **satis-**
> **faction**
> **satisfac-**
> **tion**

Words should not be divided so that only one letter comes at the end of a line or at the beginning of the next line.

> [1]**aban•don** \ə-ˈban-dən\ *vb* ...
> **ba•nana** \bə-ˈna-nə\ *n* ...

For this reason no dot is shown after the first letter of the word **abandon** or before the last letter of the word **banana**. Thus, end-of-line divisions do not always separate the syllables of a word. Syllables are shown only in the pronunciation, explained in the next section.

When two or more main entries have the same spelling and the same end-of-line divisions, the dots are shown only in the first of these entries.

> [1]**mo•tion** \ˈmō-shən\ *n* ...
> [2]**motion** *vb* ...

3. Pronunciation Symbols

The English language is used in two different ways, in speaking and writing. Although the language is the same in both uses, writing and speaking are quite different from each other. Speech is made up of sounds and writing uses marks made on paper.

It is often hard to tell from the written spelling how to pronounce a word. Different letters may be used to spell the same sound, as in the words *right* and *write* or *sea* and *see*. One letter or a group of letters may be used to spell different sounds, like the letter **a** in the words *bat, car, late, any,* and *above*. There are also many words that have two or more pronunciations.

In order to show the sounds of words in this book, we use special **pronunciation symbols**. Each pronunciation symbol stands for one important sound in English. Most of the symbols look like letters of the regular alphabet. However, do not think of pronunciation symbols as letters. Learn the sound each symbol stands for. When you see a symbol, think of its sound. Pronunciation symbols are always written between slant lines \ˌlīk-ˈt͟his\ so you will know that they are not regular letters. To see how a pronunciation is given in an actual entry, look at the example **saunter** here.

> **saun•ter** \ˈsȯn-tər\ *vb* **saun•tered; saun•ter•ing**
> to walk in a slow relaxed way **:** STROLL

A list of all the pronunciation symbols is printed on page 26. A shorter list is printed across the bottom of facing pages in the dictionary. In both lists the symbols are followed by words containing the sound of each symbol. The boldface letters in these words stand for the same sound as the symbol. If you say the sample word in your regular voice, you will hear the sound that the symbol stands for.

We use hyphens with the pronunciation symbols to show the syllables of a word, as in these examples.

> **beast** \'bēst\ *n* ...
> *(1 syllable)*
> **bed•side** \'bed-,sīd\ *n* ...
> *(2 syllables)*
> [1]**cast•away** \'ka-stə-,wā\ *adj* ...
> *(3 syllables)*
> **op•ti•mism** \'äp-tə-,mi-zəm\ *n* ...
> *(4 syllables)*

Of course, the syllables of words are not separated when we speak. One sound in a word follows right after another without pause.

Notice in the last two examples given above, **castaway** and **optimism**, that the number and position of the hyphens are not the same as the number and position of the dots in the entry words. The dots in the entry words are not meant to show the syllables in the word. Only the hyphens that you see in the pronunciation part of the entry will show you where the syllables are.

Some syllables of a word are spoken with greater force, or **stress**, than others. Three kinds of stress are shown in this dictionary. **Primary stress**, or **strong stress**, is shown by a high mark \'\ placed *before* a syllable. **Secondary stress**, or **medium stress**, is shown by a low mark \,\ before a syllable. The third kind of stress is **weak stress**. There is no mark before syllables with weak stress. Each of these kinds of stress is shown in the pronunciation for **penmanship**.

> **pen•man•ship** \'pen-mən-,ship\ *n* ...

The first syllable has primary stress. The second syllable has weak stress. The third syllable has secondary stress. If you say the word to yourself, you will hear each kind of stress.

Many words are pronounced in two, three, or even more different ways. Two or more pronunciations for an entry are separated by commas. Look at the example **ration**.

> [1]**ra•tion** \'ra-shən, 'rā-shən\ *n* ...

The order in which different pronunciations are given does not mean that the pronunciation placed first is somehow better or more correct than the others. All the pronunciations that are shown in your dictionary are used by large numbers of educated people, and you will be correct whichever one you use. When you are learning a new word, you should choose the pronunciation that sounds most natural to you.

Sometimes when a second or third pronunciation is shown, only part of the pronunciation of a word changes. When this happens, we may show only the part that changes. To get the full second or third pronunciation of a word, just add the part that changes to the part that does not change.

> **greasy** \'grē-sē, -zē\ *adj* ...
> **pa•ja•mas** \pə-'jä-məz, -'ja-\ *n pl* ...

The second pronunciation of **greasy** is \'grē-zē\ and the second pronunciation of **pajamas** is \pə-'ja-məz\.

If two or more entries are spelled the same and have the same pronunciation and end-of-line division, we show the pronunciation only for the first of these entries.

> [1]**se•cure** \si-'kyu̇r\ *adj* ...
> [2]**secure** *vb* ...

Many compound entries are made up of two or three separate words. If we do not show a pronunciation for all or part of such an entry, the missing pronunciation is the same as that for the individual word or words.

> **milk shake** *n*
> a drink made of milk, a flavoring syrup, and ice cream that is shaken or mixed thoroughly
> [1]**milk** \'milk\ *n* ...
> [1]**shake** \'shāk\ *vb* ...

No pronunciation is shown for the example **milk shake**. This means the two words are pronounced just like the separate entries **milk** and **shake**.

When a boldface word appears without a definition at the end of a main entry, sometimes we show only part of the pronunciation. This means the rest of the word is pronounced the same as part of the main entry.

post•pone \pōst-'pōn\ *vb* ...
post•pone•ment \-mənt\ *n*

In the example **postpone** the complete pronunciation of **postponement** is \pōst-'pōn-ment\. Some of these entries will show no pronunciation at all. In these cases the pronunciation of the compound is the same as the pronunciation of the main entry plus the pronunciation of the word ending, which is found at its own alphabetical place in the dictionary.

¹re•mote \ri-'mōt\ *adj* ...
re•mote•ly *adv*
re•mote•ness *n*

In the example **remote**, the entry **remotely** is pronounced \ri-'mōt-lē\ and **remoteness** is pronounced \ri-'mōt-nəs\.

4. Variant Spellings

After the main entry word you may see a second or third spelling, also in boldface type. Additional spellings are called **variant spellings** or simply **variants**.

²racket *or* **rac•quet** *n* ...

Variant spellings are usually separated by *or*. The *or* tells you that both spellings are common in good usage.

Usually we show variants in alphabetical order when one form is not used much more often than another. This is the case with the entry **racket** *or* **racquet**. If, however, one form does seem to be preferred, we show that one first. This sometimes means that variants will be out of alphabetical order.

ca•liph *or* **ca•lif** \'kā-ləf\ *n* ...

In the example **caliph** *or* **calif** this is the case, since in strict alphabetical order the **calif** spelling would come first. The order of the variants tells you that the spelling **caliph** is used a little more often than **calif**.

Keep in mind that all of the variants shown in this dictionary are correct. However, you should pick one form and use it in all of your writing.

Occasionally you will see a variant spelling shown after the word *also*. Look at the example **bonny**.

bon•ny *also* **bon•nie** \'bä-nē\ *adj* ...

The *also* tells you that the next spelling is much less common in ordinary usage than the first, although it is still a correct spelling.

When variant spellings are shown at the beginning of the entry, all of the variants are used in all meanings. If one variant form is shown at a particular definition, however, that spelling is more common for that meaning.

disk *or* **disc** \'disk\ *n*
1 something that is or appears to be flat and round
2 *usually disc* CD
3 a round, thin, flat plate ...
4 *usually disc* a phonograph record
disk•like \-,līk\ *adj*

The information at the entry for **disk** *or* **disc** tells you that both spellings are used for both meanings. The form **disk** is more often used for meanings **1** and **3** (remember that when variants are not in alphabetical order you know the first one is used more often). The label *usually disc* at meanings **2** and **4** tells you that **disc** is more common than **disk** for those meanings.

5. Functional Labels

Words are used in many different ways in a sentence. You know, for example, that if a word is used as the name of something (**car**, **house**, **rainbow**), it is called a **noun**. If it describes some action or state of being (**run**, **stand**, **live**), the word is a **verb**. Words that show a quality of something (**tall**, **short**, **fast**) are **adjectives**, and words that tell how, when, or where something happens (**quickly**, **very**, **yesterday**, **here**) are adverbs. Pronouns (**them**, **you**, **that**) are words which substitute for nouns, and **conjunctions** (**and**, **but**, **yet**) join two words or groups of words. **Prepositions** (**to**, **for**, **by**) combine with nouns and pronouns to form phrases that answer such questions as where?, how?, and which?, and **interjections** (**hi**, **hey**, **ouch**) stand alone and often show a feeling or a reaction to something rather than a meaning.

To show you how the various entry words are used, or how they function in a sentence, we use **functional labels** before the definitions. These labels are usually abbreviations in slanting *italic* type, and they come right after the pronunciation — when one is shown — or immediately after the entry word.

> **sea•coast** \ˈsē-ˌkōst\ *n*
> the shore of the sea

The eight most common functions, known as **parts of speech**, are shown in the examples below.

> **cat** \ˈkat\ *n* ...
> ^{2}**fish** *vb* ...
> **hos•tile** \ˈhä-st^{ə}l\ *adj* ...
> ^{2}**just** *adv* ...
> ^{1}**none** \ˈnən\ *pron* ...
> ^{2}**since** *conj* ...
> ^{2}**under** *prep* ...
> ^{3}**why** *interj* ...

In addition to these parts of speech, a few other special functional labels are used in this book. Abbreviations are indicated by a label.

> **AK** *abbr* Alaska

The words **the**, **a**, and **an** are used before nouns to show that a certain one or any one of a certain group is being talked about. Because the word **the** points out a certain one, it is called a **definite article**. The words **a** and **an**, which refer to any one of many, are called **indefinite articles**.

The prefixes and suffixes that we talked about in the section on main entries are also indicated by a functional label. Often it will be combined with a part-of-speech label when the suffix or prefix always makes one kind of word.

> **-g•ra•phy** \grə-fē\ *n suffix* ...

In the example, **-graphy** always combines with other words or word parts to form nouns (**photography**, **biography**), so its functional label is *noun suffix*.

There are a few special verbs that sometimes are used to help other verbs, such as **may** in a question like "May I go with you?" These special verbs are shown with the italic functional label *helping verb*.

> **may** \ˈmā\ *helping verb, past* **might** \ˈmīt\; *present sing & pl* **may** ...

6. Homographs

Often you will find two, three, or more main entries that come one after another and are spelled exactly alike.

> ^{1}**seal** \ˈsēl\ *n*
> **1** a sea mammal that swims with flippers, lives mostly in cold regions, bears young on land, feeds on fish and other sea animals (as squid), and is sometimes hunted for its fur, hide, or oil
> **2** the soft fur of a seal
> ^{2}**seal** *n*
> **1** something that closes tightly ⟨The *seal* on the package is broken.⟩
> **2** the condition of having a tight seal ⟨Caulk gives the window a *seal.*⟩
> **3** ▶ an official mark stamped or pressed on something
> **4** a device with a cut or raised design or figure that can be stamped or pressed into wax or paper
> **5** a stamp that may be used to close a letter or package ⟨Christmas *seals*⟩
> **6** something (as a pledge) that makes safe or secure ⟨The deal was made under *seal* of secrecy.⟩
> ^{3}**seal** *vb* **sealed**; **seal•ing**
> **1** to close tightly or completely to prevent anyone or anything from moving in or out
> **2** to put an official mark on
> **seal•er** *n*

Although these words look alike, they are different words because they come from different sources and so have different meanings or because they are used in different ways in the sentence.

These similar entries are called **homographs** (from **homo-** "the same" and **-graph** "something written" — in this case "words written in the same way"). Each homograph has a small raised number before it. This number is used only in the dictionary entry to show you that these are different words. The number is not used when you write the word.

Let's look closely at the homographs for **seal** to see just why they are different. The first entry, a noun, is defined as "a sea mammal." The second **seal** entry is also a noun, but this meaning, "something that closes tightly," is completely different from the meaning of the first entry. The third homograph of **seal** is certainly related to the second, but [3]**seal** is a verb, and since it has a different use in the sentence, we show it as a different entry word.

7. Inflected Forms

Whenever we talk about more than one of something, we have to use a special form of a noun. If we want to say that an action is taking place now or has happened already, we need a different form of the verb for each meaning. To say that this is bigger, smaller, or quicker than that, we have to use a special form of an adjective or adverb. These special forms usually involve a change in spelling. These forms are called **inflected forms** or **inflections** of the words.

> **dish** \\'dish\\ *n*
> 1 ▼ a usually round shallow container used for cooking or serving food
> 2 **dish•es** *pl* all items (as plates and silverware) used for cooking and eating food ⟨Would you do the *dishes*?⟩
> 3 the food in a container for serving or eating ⟨a *dish* of strawberries⟩
> 4 food that is prepared in a particular way ⟨an Italian *dish*⟩
> 5 a round shallow object ⟨a radar *dish*⟩
> [2]**shade** *vb* **shad•ed**; **shad•ing**
> 1 to shelter from light or heat ⟨I *shaded* my eyes with a hand.⟩
> 2 to mark with or turn a darker color ⟨The *shaded* parts of the graph show growth.⟩ ⟨Her face *shaded* purple with embarrassment.⟩
> **shady** \\'shā-dē\\ *adj* **shad•i•er**; **shad•i•est**
> 1 sheltered from the sun's rays
> 2 producing shade ⟨a *shady* tree⟩
> 3 not right or honest ⟨*shady* business deals⟩

Nouns show more than one by means of **plural** forms – "washing the *dishes*." Verbs can be made to show that something is happening now by the use of the **present participle** form – "that tree is *shading* our flowers" – or that something happened before but is not happening now by use of the **past tense** or the **past participle** forms – "I *shaded* my eyes; we have *shaded* parts of the drawing to show shadows." The **third person singular present tense** form of verbs shows what he, she, or it is doing now – "this umbrella *shades* us from the sun." Adjectives and adverbs show how one thing is compared with another or with all others of the same kind by **comparative** and **superlative** forms – "this spot is *shadier* than that, but over there is the *shadiest* spot in the garden."

For most words inflected forms are made in a regular way. That is, plurals usually are formed simply by adding **-s** or **-es** to the base word (*shade* → *shades*; *box* → *boxes*); verb inflections are formed by adding **-ed** for the past tense and past participle (*walk* → *walked*), **-ing** for the present participle (*walk* → *walking*), and **-s** or **-es** for the third person singular present tense form (*walk* → *walks*; *wash* → *washes*). Comparative and superlative forms of adjectives and adverbs are considered regular if they are formed by adding **-er** and **-est** to the base word or if the words *more* and *most* are used (*high* → *higher, highest*; *natural* → *more natural, most natural*).

We do not show most regular noun inflections in this dictionary since they should give you no problems in spelling.

> **bri•gade** \\bri-'gād\\ *n*
> 1 a body of soldiers consisting of two or more regiments ...

When you see entries like the example **brigade**, you will know that the inflected forms are regular. **Brigade** becomes **brigades** in the plural.

We do show you noun inflections, however, when they are formed in any way other than by simply adding a suffix. If the base word is changed in any way when the suffix is added or if there are variant inflected forms, these forms are shown.

> **proph•e•cy** \\'prä-fə-sē\\ *n*, *pl* **proph•e•cies** ...
> [1]**beef** \\'bēf\\ *n*, *pl* **beefs** \\'bēfs\\ *or* **beeves** \\'bēvz\\ ...

We also show inflections for a word when no suffix is added

> **deer** \ˈdir\ *n, pl* **deer ...**

and for any words that have regular inflections when we think you might have questions about how they are formed.

> **chim•ney** \ˈchim-nē\ *n, pl* **chimneys ...**

Nouns are usually entered in the *DK Merriam-Webster Children's Dictionary* in the singular form, that is, in the form that means only one of something. And these words can either be used as a singular or be made into plural nouns. However, there are some entries that are used only in the plural. These are shown by the special label *n pl.*

> **aus•pic•es** \ˈȯ-spə-səz\ *n pl*
> support and guidance of a sponsor <A concert was given under the *auspices* of the school.>

Some words that end in an *-s*, like **calisthenics**, may be thought of as singular in some uses and as plural in others.

> **cal•is•then•ics** \ˌka-ləs-ˈthen-iks\ *n pl*
> exercises (as push-ups and jumping jacks) to develop strength and flexibility that are done without special equipment

If you use this word for the form of exercise, for example, you might think of it as singular, like this – "Calisthenics is important for strengthening muscles." But if you think of the various exercises themselves, you might think of the word as a plural and use a plural verb, like this – "I think the calisthenics are very hard to do." At entries for words like **calisthenics**, we show a *n pl* label and add an explanation at the end of the definition indicated by the word **Hint** telling you that the word can be used as a singular or as a plural.

> **Hint:** Calisthenics can be used as a singular or as a plural in writing and speaking.

There are a few entries in this dictionary that have unusual plural uses at individual meanings.

> [1]**dart** \ˈdärt\ *n*
> **1** ▶ a small pointed object that is meant to be thrown
> **2 darts** *pl* a game in which darts are thrown at a target
> **3** a quick sudden movement
> **4** a fold sewn into a piece of clothing

These special uses we show by a *pl* label at the individual definitions. In the **dart** example, the *pl* label at meaning **2** tells you that the spelling is **darts** and it is plural in use. If the plural form has already been shown in boldface at the beginning of the entry, we show it in italic type before the individual definition.

Sometimes a noun entry will show variant plural forms, but only one of these variants is used in a particular meaning. To show this situation, we place the plural form after the *pl* label at the individual meaning.

> [1]**hose** \ˈhōz\ *n, pl* **hose** *or* **hos•es**
> **1** *pl hose* STOCKING 1, SOCK
> **2** ▶ a flexible tube for carrying fluid

This is shown in the example **hose**, where the *pl hose* label tells you that the plural form for this meaning is **hose** but the use is usually singular.

Occasionally you will see a noun entry where you think an inflected form should be shown but it is not. Words like **diplomacy** are not used as plurals, so no plural form is shown.

> **di•plo•ma•cy** \də-ˈplō-mə-sē\ *n*
> **1** the work of keeping good relations between the governments of different countries
> **2** skill in dealing with people

For verb inflections only the past tense (the **-ed** form) and the present participle (the **-ing** form) are normally shown. The past participle is shown only when it is different from the past tense form. When it is shown, it comes between the past tense and present participle.

> **laze** \ˈlāz\ *vb* **lazed; laz•ing**
> to spend time relaxing <We *lazed* the day away.>
> [1]**freeze** \ˈfrēz\ *vb* **froze** \ˈfrōz\; **fro•zen** \ˈfrō-z^{ə}n\; **freez•ing**
> **1** to harden into or be hardened into a solid (as ice) by loss of heat <*freeze* blueberries> ...

The third person singular present tense form (he *likes*, she *knows*, it *seems*) is the most regular of the verb inflections. For most verbs it is formed simply by adding **-s** or **-es** to the base word – even for verbs whose other inflections are not regular. We show this inflection only when we think its spelling or pronunciation might present a problem. When it is shown, this form comes after the present participle form.

> **go** \ˈgō\ *vb* **went** \ˈwent\; **gone** \ˈgȯn\;
> **go•ing** \ˈgō-iŋ\; **goes ...**

For adjectives and adverbs, we show the comparative when it is formed by adding **-er**, and the superlative when it is formed by adding **-est**. In some cases, the spelling of the base word is changed when the suffix is added. If no inflected form is shown, that usually means that the comparative and superlative forms use the words *more* and *most*. In other cases, no inflected form is shown because the adjective or adverb is rarely or never inflected.

> [1]**fast** \ˈfast\ *adj* **fast•er**; **fast•est**
> **1** moving, operating, or acting quickly ⟨a *fast* train⟩ ⟨a *fast* thinker⟩ ...
> [1]**fun•ny** \ˈfə-nē\ *adj* **fun•ni•er**; **fun•ni•est**
> **1** causing laughter **:** full of humor ⟨a *funny* story⟩
> **2** STRANGE 2 ⟨a *funny* noise⟩
> **af•ford•able** \ə-ˈfȯr-də-bəl\ *adj*
> within someone's ability to pay
> **:** reasonably priced ⟨an *affordable* bike⟩
> **abed** \ə-ˈbed\ *adv or adj*
> in bed ⟨*abed* and asleep⟩ ⟨He was found still *abed* in the middle of the day.⟩

No inflected form is shown at **affordable** because the comparative and superlative forms are formed with the words *more* or *most*. No inflected form is shown at **abed** because it is not inflected.

8. Usage Labels

In addition to functional labels at individual entries we use another kind of italic label to give you information about how a word is used. These **usage labels** come after the functional labels or, if they apply only to a particular meaning, just before the beginning of the definition.

> [1]**co•lo•nial** \kə-ˈlō-nē-əl\ *adj*
> **1** of, relating to, or characteristic of a colony
> **2** *often cap* of or relating to the original 13 colonies that formed the United States

One of the things the usage label may tell you is whether or not a particular word is sometimes written with a capital letter. Whenever a word is always or usually written with a capital letter, it has a capital letter in the main entry.

> **Thurs•day** \ˈthərz-dā,-dē\ *n*
> the fifth day of the week

But some words are written with a small letter or a capital letter about equally often. These entries have an italic label *often cap*. Other words are written with a capital letter in some meanings and not in others. These words are usually shown in the dictionary with a small first letter. The italic label tells you when the word is always spelled with a capital letter (*cap*) or very frequently spelled with a capital letter (*often cap*).

> [4]**host** *n, often cap*
> the bread used in Christian Communion
> **earth** \ˈərth\ *n*
> **1** ▶ *often cap* the planet that we live on
> **2** land as distinguished from sea and air ⟨Snow fell to *earth*.⟩
> **3** [2]SOIL 1 ⟨a mound of *earth*⟩
> **french fry** *n, often cap 1st F*
> ◀ a strip of potato fried in deep fat

In the example [4]**host**, the label tells you that sometimes the word is spelled with a capital letter and sometimes not. In the example **earth**, the word is often written with a capital letter (notice the *often cap* label) when the meaning is **1** but with a small letter when the meaning is **2** or **3**.

See if you can tell what the label at the entry **french fry** means. Would you expect to see the word sometimes spelled **French fry**?

Another thing the usage labels can tell you is whether a word or a particular meaning is most commonly used in a limited area of the English-speaking world.

> ^{2}**lift** *n*
> **1** the action or an instance of picking up and raising ⟨He showed his surprise with a *lift* of his eyebrows.⟩
> **2** an improved mood or condition
> **3** a ride in a vehicle ⟨She gave me a *lift* to school.⟩
> **4** *chiefly British* ELEVATOR 1
> **5** an upward force (as on an airplane wing) that opposes the pull of gravity

In the sample entry **lift** you will see that meaning **4** is labeled *chiefly British*. This means that the word in this meaning is used more often in Great Britain than in the United States.

You also find a few entries with the usage label *sometimes offensive*. This tells you that the word is one that you may read or hear, but that offends some people. A note indicated by the word **Hint** will also appear at such an entry to give you further guidance.

> **Es•ki•mo** \ˈe-skə-ˌmō\ *n, pl* **Es•ki•mos**
> *sometimes offensive*
> a member of a group of peoples of Alaska, northern Canada, Greenland, and eastern Siberia
> **Hint:** In the past, this word was not considered offensive. Some people, however, now prefer *Inuit*.

9. Definitions

> **skim** \ˈskim\ *vb* **skimmed**; **skim•ming**
> **1** to clean a liquid of scum or floating substance : remove (as cream or film) from the top part of a liquid
> **2** to read or examine quickly and not thoroughly ⟨I *skimmed* the newspaper.⟩
> **3** to skip (a stone) along the surface of water
> **4** to pass swiftly or lightly over

The definitions are what many people consider the most important part of the dictionary, because meanings are what people usually think of when they think of a dictionary.

All of the definitions in this dictionary start on a new line under the main entry words. Most of the words entered in this book have more than one meaning and therefore they have more than one definition. These separate meanings are shown by boldface numbers. **Skim** has four numbered meanings.

We have arranged the definitions in your dictionary with the most basic meaning first. This allows you to see, just by reading the entry, how a word has grown in use from the first meaning to the last.

Let's look at meaning number **1** of **skim**. This meaning first came into use in English many centuries ago, and through the years it gained a more specific use, that of taking the cream off milk. This specific use is shown as the second definition at meaning **1**. The second definition does not change the original meaning. It only adds a little.

Meaning **2** of **skim** seems to have come into use as a figure of speech. If you think of a spoon barely touching the surface of water or milk or going just under the surface to scoop off something, you realize that the scoop is only taking off what can be seen on the surface. Most of the liquid remains behind. By first applying the word **skim** to reading or examining something and only getting what could be seen "on the surface" without going more deeply into the work, someone was using **skim** as a figure of speech. As more and more people used the word in this way, it came to have a set meaning.

Meaning **3**, which developed after meanings **1** and **2**, seems to have come from the first meaning in a similar way. This time, though, the idea of "just touching" a surface was the one that carried over to the act of causing rocks or other objects to bounce along the surface of a lake.

Can you guess at how meaning **4** came into use? Here it seems the meaning moved one more step away, from the idea of "just touching the surface" to that of "just missing the surface."

With the entry **skim**, you can see just how the word grew from one meaning to four. And the arrangement of the four meanings lets you follow that growth.

There may be times when you will look up a word and not be sure which of several meanings is the right one for the use you are checking. The way to tell which is the right definition is to substitute each definition in place of your word in the sentence until you find the one that is right.

Suppose you were reading the sentence "I just skimmed the book" and you were not certain what *skim* meant. By reading the definitions of **skim** in the sentence you would be able to find the right meaning by substitution. You know that "I just removed cream from the top of the book" certainly is not correct, and it is most unlikely that the writer was "throwing a book so that it skipped across the surface of water" or "passing swiftly over the book." But when you substitute meaning **2** in the sentence, you get a sentence that makes sense. "I was just reading or examining the book quickly and not thoroughly." This is using the method of substitution to find the right meaning.

10. Synonyms and Cross-references

slav•ery \'slā-və-rē, 'slāv-rē\ *n*
1 the state of being owned by another person **:** BONDAGE
2 the custom or practice of owning slaves
3 hard tiring labor **:** DRUDGERY

In the entry **slavery** meanings **1** and **3** both have two definitions. The second definition in each case is a single word that means the same thing as the entry word **slavery** for that particular use. These words with the same meaning as the entry word are called **synonyms**. All synonyms in the *DK Merriam-Webster Children's Dictionary* are written in small capital letters. Any word in small capital letters is a **cross-reference**, referring you to another place in the book. In the case of these synonyms, the small capitals tell you to look at the entry for that word for a full explanation of the meaning or use.

You can see that **bondage** is a synonym of the first meaning of **slavery** ("the state of being owned by another person") and **drudgery** is a synonym of the third meaning ("hard tiring labor"). If you turn to the entry for **drudgery**, for example, you will find a definition that matches the definition for meaning **3** of **slavery**.

Sometimes an entry is defined only by a synonym.

northern lights *n pl*
AURORA BOREALIS
au•ro•ra bo•re•al•is \ə-ˌrȯr-ə-ˌbȯr-ē-'al-əs\ *n*
▶ broad bands of light that have a magnetic and electrical source and that appear in the sky at night especially in the arctic regions

Look at the example **northern lights**. The cross-reference AURORA BOREALIS tells you to look at the entry **aurora borealis** for a definition. The definition at **aurora borealis** is the same as it would be for **northern lights**, since both words mean the same thing. When using synonymous cross-references, we have always put the full definition at the most common of the synonyms.

Sometimes you will see a number used as part of the cross-reference, as in the first meaning given for **accord**.

¹ac•cord \ə-'kȯrd\ *vb* **ac•cord•ed; ac•cord•ing**
1 ¹GIVE 3 ⟨The teacher *accorded* them special privileges.⟩
2 to be in harmony **:** AGREE ⟨Your story of the accident *accords* with theirs.⟩

The cross-reference to ¹GIVE 3 tells you to look at meaning number **3** of the entry **¹give** for a definition that fits this meaning of **accord**.

Because the definition of the synonym must also be a good definition of the entry word, both the entry word and the synonym will always have the same part of speech. Thus, if the synonym of a verb is an entry with two or more homographs, you will always know that the right entry will be the homograph that is a verb. Nevertheless, your dictionary helps you by showing the proper homograph number at the cross-reference when necessary.

The cross-reference at **accord** tells you that meaning **3** of the first homograph of **give** is the synonym, because **accord** is a verb and only the first homograph of **give** is a verb.

The cross-reference printed in small capital letters is also used at certain entries that are variants or inflected forms of another entry.

caught *past and past participle of* CATCH

In the example **caught** the cross-reference tells you that you will find a definition or explanation at the entry shown in small capital letters.

11. Verbal Illustrations

si•lent \'sī-lənt\ *adj*
1 not speaking ⟨He stood *silent* for a moment, and then answered.⟩
2 not talkative ⟨a *silent* person⟩
3 free from noise or sound **:** STILL ⟨Except for a ticking clock the house was *silent.*⟩
4 done or felt without being spoken ⟨*silent* reading⟩ ⟨*silent* prayer⟩
5 making no mention ⟨They were *silent* about their plan.⟩
6 not in operation ⟨*silent* factories⟩
7 not pronounced ⟨The letter **e** in "came" is *silent.*⟩
8 made without spoken dialogue ⟨*silent* movies⟩
si•lent•ly *adv*

At times you may look up a word in your dictionary and understand the definition but still not be sure about the right way to use the word. Sometimes the several meanings are similar but the ways in which the word is actually used in a sentence are quite different. To help you better understand these more difficult words and usages, we have given along with some definitions a brief phrase or sentence called a **verbal illustration**. It shows you a typical use of the word. Most of the definitions at **silent** have verbal illustrations to show how the word is used in each of those meanings. A verbal illustration is always placed after the definition, it is enclosed in pointed brackets, and it has the entry word, or an inflection of it, printed in italic type.

Some verbal illustrations are full sentences. But sometimes the meaning of a word can be easily illustrated with just a few words. In such a case, a verbal illustration might be just a short phrase. You will be able to tell the difference because in illustrations that are full sentences, the first word is capitalized, and it ends with punctuation, just like in writing. When the verbal illustration is just a phrase, the first word is not capitalized and there is no punctuation.

12. Run-in Entries

Sometimes you will see boldface words in the middle of a definition. These are called **run-in entries**. Run-in entries are themselves defined by part of the main definition.

> **sol•stice** \ˈsäl-stəs, ˈsōl-, ˈsȯl-\ *n*
> the time of the year when the sun passes overhead the farthest north (**summer solstice,** about June 22) or south (**winter solstice,** about December 22) of the equator

Within the main entry **solstice** the run-in entry **summer solstice** is being defined as "the time of the year when the sun passes overhead the farthest north of the equator," and **winter solstice** is being defined as "the time of the year when the sun passes overhead the farthest south of the equator."

13. Usage Notes and Hints

The italic usage labels that come before definitions are one way we give you information on the usage of the entry word, and the verbal illustrations after the definitions are another way. In the *DK Merriam-Webster Children's Dictionary* we give information on usage in still another way – **usage notes** that follow definitions. Usage notes are short phrases that are separated from the definition by a dash. They tell you how or when the entry word is used.

> **cas•ta•net** \ˈka-stə-ˈnet\ *n*
> ▶ a rhythm instrument that consists of two small flat round parts fastened to the thumb and clicked by the fingers – usually used in pl.
> **²cheer** *vb* ...
> **2** to grow or be cheerful – usually used with *up* ...

The note at **castanet** tells you that the word is usually used as a plural, **castanets**, although it is defined as a singular. This information is different from what would be given if the word had been entered as **castanets** or shown as **castanets** *pl* just before the definition. In both of those cases, you would be told that the word is defined as plural and is always plural in this use. Do you see how the note "usually used in pl." is different? It tells you that the word is singular – it is defined as a singular and may sometimes be used as singular – but is most often used in the plural form and with a plural verb.

Usage notes like the one at **cheer** tell you what words are usually used with the entry word in a sentence. In this case, the expression is usually *cheer up*.

In a few entries we use a usage note in place of a definition. This is done when the way the word is used is more important than what the word means.

> **²both** *conj*
> used before two words or phrases connected with ***and*** to stress that each is included ⟨*both* New York and London⟩

We also use a usage note in place of a definition for all interjections, which usually express a feeling or reaction to something rather than a meaning.

> **hal•le•lu•jah** \ˌha-lə-ˈlü-yə\ *interj*
> used to express praise, joy, or thanks

Still another way we give information about the usage of a word is by a **Hint**. A **Hint** is a sentence or paragraph that follows a definition. **Hints** provide a variety of types of information about how or when an entry word is used. In the section called Inflected Forms, we explained that at some entries a **Hint** tells you that a word can be used as a singular or as a plural. In the section called Usage Labels, we explained that at some entries a Hint tells you that a word might be offensive. At other entries, a **Hint** may tell you other things about the entry word.

¹fa•ther \'fä-thər\ *n*
1 a male parent …
6 PRIEST
Hint: This sense of *father* is used especially to address a priest or as a priest's title.
thou \'thau̇\ *pron*
YOU
Hint: *Thou* is a very old word that still appears in books and sayings from long ago. People also use it to imitate that old way of speaking.
scat \'skat\ *vb* **scat•ted**; **scat•ting**
to go away quickly
Hint: *Scat* is often used as a command to frighten away an animal. ⟨*Scat!* Go away, cat!⟩

Hints help you to be careful about your choice of words, and to use the words you choose correctly.

14. Undefined Run-on Entries

¹sour \'sau̇r\ *adj* **sour•er**; **sour•est**
1 having an acid or tart taste ⟨a *sour* fruit⟩
2 having spoiled : not fresh ⟨*sour* milk⟩
3 suggesting decay ⟨a *sour* smell⟩
4 not pleasant or friendly ⟨a *sour* look⟩
sour•ly *adv* ⟨He spoke *sourly.*⟩
sour•ness *n*

The boldface words at the end of the entry **sour** are **undefined run-on entries**. Each of these run-on entries is shown without a definition. You can easily discover the meaning of any of these words by simply combining the meaning of the base word (the main entry) and that of the suffix. For example, **sourly** is simply **sour** plus **-ly** ("in a specified manner") and so means "in a sour manner," and **sourness** is **sour** plus **-ness** ("state : condition") and so means "the state or condition of being sour."

We have run on only words whose meanings you should have no trouble figuring out. Whenever a word derived from a main entry has a meaning that is not easily understandable from the meanings of the two parts, we have entered and defined it at its own alphabetical place.

15. Synonym Paragraphs

At the end of certain entries, you will see a special kind of cross-reference like the one at **sparkle**.

¹spar•kle \'spär-kəl\ *vb* **spar•kled**; **spar•kling**
1 to give off small flashes of light ⟨The diamond *sparkled.*⟩
2 to be lively or bright ⟨The conversation *sparkled.*⟩ ⟨His eyes *sparkled.*⟩
synonyms see GLEAM

The direction "**synonyms** see GLEAM" means "for a discussion of synonyms that includes **sparkle**, see the entry **gleam**."

At several entries in the *DK Merriam-Webster Children's Dictionary* like **gleam** and **splendid**, shown here, there are short discussions of the differences between certain synonyms.

splen•did \'splen-dəd\ *adj*
1 impressive in beauty, excellence, or magnificence ⟨You did a *splendid* job.⟩ ⟨a *splendid* palace⟩
2 having or showing splendor **:** BRILLIANT
3 EXCELLENT ⟨We had a *splendid* time.⟩
splen•did•ly *adv*

▶ **Synonyms** SPLENDID, GLORIOUS, and SUPERB mean very impressive. SPLENDID is used for something far above the ordinary in excellence or magnificence. ⟨What a *splendid* idea!⟩ ⟨She wore a *splendid* jewel.⟩ GLORIOUS is used for something that is radiant with light or beauty. ⟨I watched the *glorious* sunset.⟩ SUPERB is used of the highest possible point of magnificence or excellence. ⟨The food was *superb.*⟩

These discussions are called **synonym paragraphs**. Synonyms can often be substituted freely for one another in a sentence because they mean basically the same thing. But some words that are synonyms because they mean nearly the same thing cannot always be substituted for one another. They may differ slightly in what they suggest to the reader – in the image they call to mind. These suggested meanings are what make one synonym a better choice than another in certain situations.

In the synonym paragraphs we indicate these little differences between synonyms. Any of the three words in the paragraph following the entry **splendid** might be satisfactory in the examples given to indicate something impressive. But through long usage people have come to think of the word **glorious** as more suited to describing something where light or beauty is involved, while **splendid** and **superb** are used of other things. And something described as **superb** is often thought of as more wonderful than something merely **splendid**.

16. Defined Run-on Phrases

The last kind of boldface entry you will find in your dictionary is the **defined run-on phrase**. These phrases are groups of words that, when used together, have a special meaning that is more than just the sum of the ordinary meanings of each word.

choke \ˈchōk\ *vb* **choked**; **chok•ing**
1 to keep from breathing in a normal way by cutting off the supply of air ⟨Many people were *choked* by thick smoke.⟩
2 to have the trachea blocked entirely or partly ⟨He nearly *choked* on a bone.⟩
3 to slow or prevent the growth or action of ⟨The flowers were *choked* by weeds.⟩
4 to block by clogging ⟨Leaves *choked* the sewer.⟩
choke down to eat with difficulty ⟨I *choked down* a bite.⟩
choke up to become too emotional to speak

The **defined run-on phrases** are placed at the end of the entry that is the first major word of the phrase. Normally this will be the first noun or verb rather than an adjective or preposition. The phrases run on at **choke** all begin with the entry word **choke**. But some run-on phrases will not have the major word at the beginning. Keep in mind that the phrase will be entered at the first major word in the phrase. This word is usually a noun or a verb. Where do you think you would find the phrases **do away with**, **in the doghouse**, and **on fire**? If you said at the verb **do**, at the noun **doghouse**, and at the noun **fire**, then you understand how we enter phrases.

Where to find the phrase **get wind of** may puzzle you at first, since it contains both a verb (**get**) and a noun (**wind**). But if you remember that the phrase will be entered at the *first* major word, in this case the verb **get**, you should have no trouble finding the phrases entered in this dictionary.

17. Word History Paragraphs

sur•ly \ˈsər-lē\ *adj* **sur•li•er**; **sur•li•est**
mean and rude : UNFRIENDLY ⟨a *surly* neighbor⟩

► **Word History** To a noble person it might seem natural to link together high birth and good manners, but the word *surly* is evidence that other people have not always thought this way. In Middle English the word was spelled *sirly*, which made more obvious its derivation from *sir*, the traditional title of respect. *Sirly* had much the same meaning as *lordly* does today, that is, "proud, haughty." Although its meaning has evolved to "rude" or "unfriendly," *surly* still refers to a way of acting that is quite the opposite of good-mannered.

One of the important jobs of people who study words and write dictionaries is finding out where the words we use every day in English came from. Some of our words are made up by people using the language today. For example, scientists often make up names for the new elements they discover and the new drugs they create.

But most of the words in the English language have a long history. They usually can be traced back to other words in languages older than English. Many of these languages, like ancient Greek and Latin, are no longer spoken today. The study of the origins of words can be fascinating, for many of our words have very interesting stories behind them.

In this dictionary, we share with you some of the interesting stories of word origins and trace the development of meanings in special short **word history paragraphs**.

18. Guide Words

To save you from having to search up and down page after page looking for the word you want, we have printed a **guide word** at the top of each outside column of two facing pages. The guide word on the left-hand page is the first main entry word on the left page and the guide word on the right-hand page is the last main entry word on the right page. So the two guide words tell you the first and last entries on the two facing pages. By looking at the guide words and thinking about whether the word you are hunting will fit in alphabetically between them, you can quickly move from page to page until you find the right one. Say, for example, you are looking up the word **length** and you have already turned to the section of words that begin with the letter **l**. You next would look at the guide words at the top of the pages. Let's take two pairs of pages, pages 478 and 479 and pages 480 and 481, as a sample to see how the system works.

leap year — *first main entry at top of left-hand page, page 478*

leap year *n*
a year of 366 days with February 29 as the extra day

last main entry at bottom of right-hand page, page 479 — **legislator**

leg•is•la•tor \ˈle-jə-ˌslā-ˌtȯr, -ˌslā-tər\ *n*
a person who makes laws and is a member of a legislature

On pages 478 and 479 in this sample are the guide words **leap year** and **legislator**. You can see that **length** (len-) comes after the last guide word, **legislature** (leg-), so the page you want must be farther along.

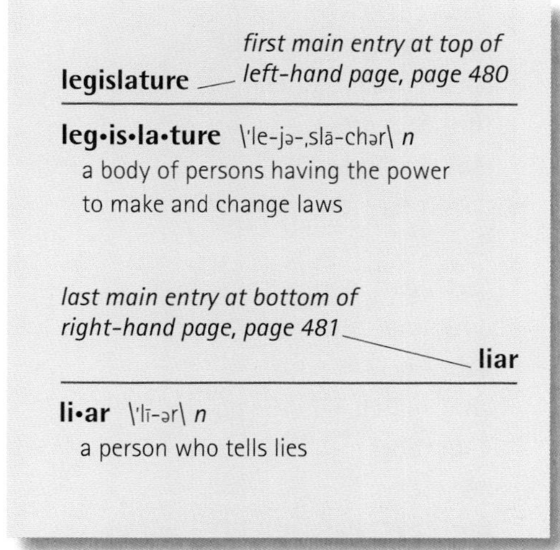

legislature — *first main entry at top of left-hand page, page 480*

leg•is•la•ture \ˈle-jə-ˌslā-chər\ *n*
a body of persons having the power to make and change laws

last main entry at bottom of right-hand page, page 481 — **liar**

li•ar \ˈlī-ər\ *n*
a person who tells lies

The guide words on pages 480 and 481 are **legislature** and **liar**. You can see that **length** (leng-) comes after **legislature** (leg-) and before **liar** (lia-), so you know the word you are looking for will be found on one of these two pages.

Pronunciation Symbols and Abbreviations

Pronunciation Symbols

ə	(called *schwa* \ˈshwä\) banana, collide, abut; in stressed syllables as in humdrum, mother, abut
ᵊ	battle, mitten, eaten
ər	further, learner
a	mat, mad, gag
ā	day, fade, mate, vacation
ä	bother, cot
är	cart, heart, park
au̇	now, loud, out
b	baby, rib
ch	chin, match, nature \ˈna-cher\
d	did, ladder
e	bed, pet
er	fair, bear, share
ē	beat, easy, me, carefree
f	fifty, cuff, phone
g	go, dig, bigger
h	hat, ahead
hw	whale as pronounced by those who do not pronounce *whale* and *wail* the same
i	bid, tip, banish, active
ir	near, deer, pier
ī	side, site, buy
j	job, gem, judge
k	kick, cook, ache
l	lily, pool, cold
m	murmur, dim, lamp
n	no, own
ŋ	sing \ˈsiŋ\, singer \ˈsiŋ-er\, finger \ˈfiŋ-ger\, ink \ˈiŋk\
ō	bone, know, soap
ȯ	saw, all, moth, taut
ȯi	coin, destroy
ȯr	door, more, boar
p	pepper, lip
r	red, rarity, rhyme, car
s	source, less
sh	shy, mission, machine, special
t	tie, attack, hot, water
th	thin, ether
t͟h	this, either
ü	rule, youth, few \ˈfyü\, union \ˈyün-yən\
u̇	pull, wood, foot, cure \ˈkyu̇r\
u̇r	tour, insure
v	give, vivid
w	we, away
y	yet, you, cue \ˈkyü\, union \ˈyün-yen\
yü	youth, union, cue, few, music
yu̇	cure, fury
z	zone, raise
zh	vision , azure \ˈa-zhər\
\ \	slant lines used to mark the beginning and end of a pronunciation: \ˈpen\
ˈ	mark at the beginning of a syllable with primary (strongest) stress: \ˈpen-mən\
ˌ	mark at the beginning of a syllable with secondary (next-strongest) stress: \ˈpen-mən-ˌship\
-	a hyphen separates syllables in pronunciations
,	a comma separates pronunciation variants: \ˈrüm, ˈru̇m\

Abbreviations

abbr	abbreviation
adj	adjective
adv	adverb
cap	capitalized
conj	conjunction
interj	interjection
n	noun
n pl	noun plural
pl	plural
prep	preposition
pron	pronoun
sing	singular
vb	verb

THE ILLUSTRATED DICTIONARY

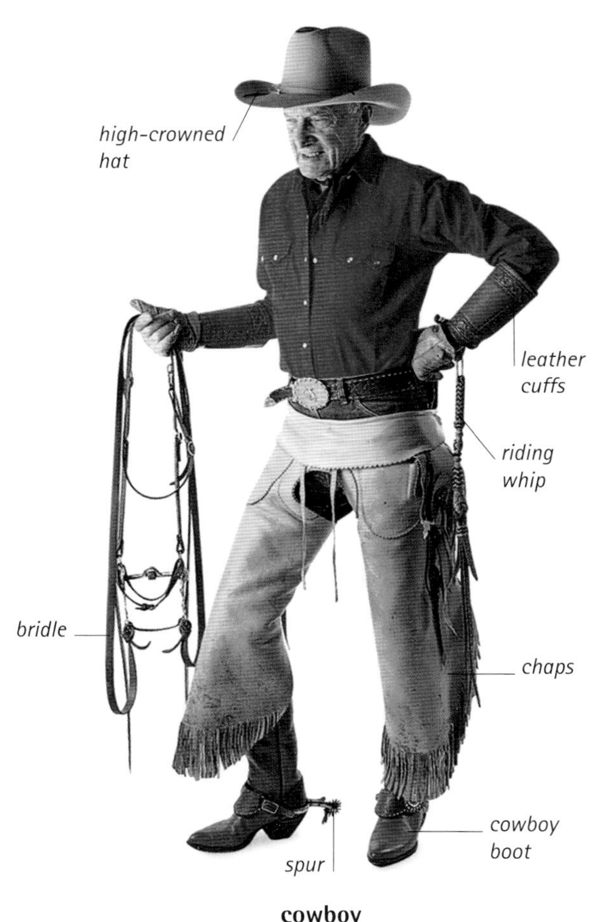

cowboy

Sounds of A: The letter **A** makes several sounds. The short **A** is the sound heard in ***apple***, while the long **A** is the sound heard in the word ***lake***. The long **A** is indicated in pronunciations by the symbol ā. Letter **A** also makes the schwa sound, which is indicated by the symbol ə, in words like ***ability*** and ***comma***. The sound of **A** that is heard in ***watch*** is indicated by ä, and the sound of **A** that is heard in ***cart*** is indicated by är. In ***call*** and ***law***, letter **A** makes a sound indicated by the symbol ȯ.

[1]**a** \'ā\ *n, pl* **a's** *or* **as** \'āz\ *often cap*
1 the first letter of the English alphabet
2 a grade that shows a student's work is excellent
3 a musical note referred to by the letter A

[2]**a** \ə, 'ā\ *indefinite article*
1 someone or something being mentioned for the first time ⟨There's *a* dog in the yard.⟩
2 the same ⟨two of *a* kind⟩
3 [1]ANY 1 ⟨It's hard for *a* person to understand.⟩
4 for or from each ⟨an apple *a* day⟩ ⟨The new theater charges ten dollars *a* person.⟩
5 [2]ONE 1 ⟨*a* dozen doughnuts⟩ ⟨*a* week⟩ ⟨This is *a* third the size of that.⟩
Hint: *A* is used before words that do not begin with a vowel sound.

a– \ə\ *prefix*
1 on : in : at ⟨*a*bed⟩
2 in (such) a state, condition, or manner ⟨*a*fire⟩ ⟨*a*loud⟩
3 in the act or process of ⟨gone *a*-hunting⟩

aard•vark \'ärd-,värk\ *n*
an African animal with a long snout and a long sticky tongue that feeds mostly on ants and termites and is active at night

AB *abbr* Alberta

ab– *prefix*
from : differing from ⟨*ab*normal⟩

aback \ə-'bak\ *adv*
by surprise ⟨He was taken *aback* by the change in plan.⟩

aba•cus \'a-bə-kəs\ *n, pl* **aba•ci** \'a-bə-,sī\ *or* **aba•cus•es**
▼ an instrument for doing arithmetic by sliding counters along rods or in grooves

abacus

ab•a•lo•ne \,a-bə-'lō-nē\ *n*
▼ a shellfish that is a mollusk which has a flattened shell with a pearly lining

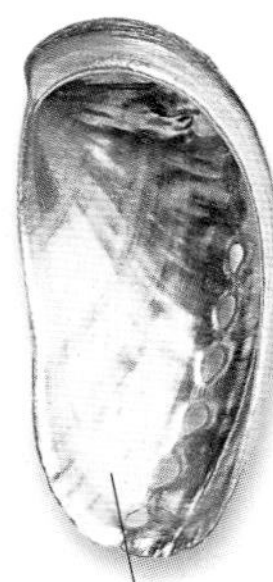

mother-of-pearl lining

abalone

[1]**aban•don** \ə-'ban-dən\ *vb* **aban•doned**; **aban•don•ing**
1 to leave and never return to : give up completely ⟨They had to *abandon* the sinking ship.⟩
2 to stop having or doing ⟨Never *abandon* hope.⟩ ⟨She *abandoned* writing her book.⟩
aban•don•ment \-mənt\ *n*

► **Synonyms** ABANDON, DESERT, and FORSAKE mean to give up completely. ABANDON is used when someone has no interest in what happens to the person or thing he or she has given up. ⟨She *abandoned* the wrecked car on the side of the road.⟩ DESERT is used when a person leaves something to which he or she has a duty or responsibility. ⟨He *deserted* his family.⟩ FORSAKE is used when a person is leaving someone or something for which he or she once had affection. ⟨Don't *forsake* old friends in times of trouble.⟩

[2]**abandon** *n*
a feeling of complete freedom ⟨Grandpa drove with reckless *abandon*.⟩

aban•doned \ə-'ban-dənd\ *adj*
given up : left empty or unused ⟨*abandoned* houses⟩

abash \ə-'bash\ *vb* **abashed**; **abash•ing**
EMBARRASS

abate \ə-'bāt\ *vb* **abat•ed**; **abat•ing**
to make or become less ⟨The flood *abated* slowly.⟩
abate•ment \-mənt\ *n*

ab•bess \'a-bəs\ *n*
the head of an abbey for women

ab•bey \'a-bē\ *n, pl* **abbeys**
1 MONASTERY, CONVENT
2 ► a church that is connected to buildings where nuns or monks live

ab•bot \'a-bət\ *n*
the head of an abbey for men

abbr *abbr* abbreviation

ab•bre•vi•ate \ə-'brē-vē-,āt\ *vb* **ab•bre•vi•at•ed**; **ab•bre•vi•at•ing**
to make briefer : SHORTEN

ab•bre•vi•a•tion \ə-,brē-vē-'ā-shən\ *n*
a shortened form of a word or phrase

ab•di•cate \'ab-di-,kāt\ *vb* **ab•di•cat•ed**; **ab•di•cat•ing**
to give up a position of power or authority ⟨The ruler was forced to *abdicate*.⟩
ab•di•ca•tion \,ab-di-'kā-shən\ *n*

ab•do•men \'ab-də-mən, ab-'dō-\ *n*
1 the part of the body between the chest and the hips including the cavity containing the stomach and other digestive organs
2 ► the hind part of the body of an arthropod (as an insect)

abdomen

abdomen 2

ab•dom•i•nal \ab-'dä-mə-nᵊl\ *adj*
relating to or located in the abdomen ⟨*abdominal* muscles⟩

abbey 2: 9th-century abbey in Brantôme, France

ab•duct \ab-ˈdəkt\ *vb* **ab•duct•ed**; **ab•duct•ing**
to take a person away by force : KIDNAP
ab•duc•tion \ab-ˈdək-shən\ *n*

abed \ə-ˈbed\ *adv or adj*
in bed ⟨*abed* and asleep⟩ ⟨He was found still *abed* in the middle of the day.⟩

ab•er•ra•tion \ˌa-bə-ˈrā-shən\ *n*
an instance of being different from what is normal or usual ⟨The poor test grade was an *aberration* for her.⟩

ab•hor \ab-ˈhȯr\ *vb* **ab•horred**; **ab•hor•ring**
to dislike very much : LOATHE ⟨I *abhor* her phony friendliness.⟩

ab•hor•rent \ab-ˈhȯr-ənt\ *adj*
causing or deserving strong dislike ⟨an *abhorrent* crime⟩

abide \ə-ˈbīd\ *vb* **abode** \-ˈbōd\ *or* **abid•ed**; **abid•ing**
1 to put up with patiently : TOLERATE ⟨They won't *abide* bad behavior.⟩
2 [1]LAST 1, ENDURE ⟨His love for his work *abided* until he died.⟩
3 to stay or live in a place
abide by to accept the terms of : OBEY ⟨She was forced to *abide by* the rules.⟩

abil•i•ty \ə-ˈbi-lə-tē\ *n, pl* **abil•i•ties**
1 power to do something ⟨The cleaner has the *ability* to kill germs.⟩
2 natural talent or acquired skill ⟨great musical *ability*⟩

▶ **Synonyms** ABILITY and TALENT mean physical or mental power to do or accomplish something. ABILITY may be used of an inborn power to do something especially well. ⟨Many athletes have the *ability* to run fast.⟩ TALENT is used for an unusual ability to create things. ⟨You should develop your *talent* for writing short stories.⟩

-abil•i•ty *also* **-ibil•i•ty** \ə-ˈbi-lə-tē\ *n suffix, pl* **-abil•i•ties** *also* **-ibil•i•ties**
ability, fitness, or tendency to act or be acted upon in (such) a way ⟨cap*ability*⟩ ⟨vis*ibility*⟩

ab•ject \ˈab-ˌjekt\ *adj*
1 very bad or severe ⟨*abject* poverty⟩
2 low in spirit, strength, or hope ⟨an *abject* coward⟩
ab•ject•ly *adv*

ablaze \ə-ˈblāz\ *adj*
1 on fire ⟨The forest was *ablaze*.⟩
2 glowing with light, color, or emotion ⟨The garden was *ablaze* with blossoms.⟩

able \ˈā-bəl\ *adj* **abler** \-blər\; **ablest** \-bləst\
1 having enough power, resources, or skill to do something ⟨Are you *able* to swim?⟩
2 having the freedom or opportunity to do something ⟨I'll come when I'm *able*.⟩
3 having or showing much skill ⟨an *able* dancer⟩

▶ **Synonyms** ABLE and CAPABLE mean having the power to do or accomplish. ABLE may be used for someone who has exceptional skill and has done well in the past. ⟨She is an *able* surgeon with years of experience.⟩ CAPABLE is usually used to describe someone who has the characteristics suitable for a particular kind of work. ⟨The recruits soon proved to be *capable* soldiers.⟩

-able *also* **-ible** \ə-bəl\ *adj suffix*
1 capable of, fit for, or worthy of being ⟨lov*able*⟩ ⟨flex*ible*⟩
2 tending or likely to ⟨change*able*⟩
-ably *also* **-ibly** \ə-blē\ *adv suffix*

able–bod•ied \ˌā-bəl-ˈbä-dēd\ *adj*
physically fit

ably \ˈā-blē\ *adv*
in a skillful way ⟨She danced *ably*.⟩

ab•nor•mal \ab-ˈnȯr-məl\ *adj*
differing from the normal usually in a noticeable way ⟨an *abnormal* growth⟩
ab•nor•mal•ly *adv*

ab•nor•mal•i•ty \ˌab-nər-ˈma-lə-tē\ *n*, *pl* **ab•nor•mal•i•ties**
something that is not usual, expected, or normal ⟨The X-ray showed no *abnormalities*.⟩

[1]**aboard** \ə-ˈbȯrd\ *adv*
on, onto, or within a ship, train, bus, or airplane ⟨No one *aboard* was injured.⟩

[2]**aboard** *prep*
on or into especially for passage ⟨Go *aboard* ship.⟩

[1]**abode** *past of* ABIDE

[2]**abode** \ə-ˈbōd\ *n*
the place where someone stays or lives

abol•ish \ə-ˈbä-lish\ *vb* **abol•ished**; **abol•ish•ing**
to do away with : put an end to ⟨*abolish* discrimination⟩

ab•o•li•tion \ˌa-bə-ˈli-shən\ *n*
a complete elimination of ⟨the *abolition* of war⟩

ab•o•li•tion•ist \ˌa-bə-ˈli-shə-nist\ *n*
a person favoring the abolition of slavery

A–bomb \ˈā-ˌbäm\ *n*
ATOMIC BOMB

abom•i•na•ble \ə-ˈbä-mə-nə-bəl\ *adj*
1 deserving or causing disgust ⟨*abominable* treatment of animals⟩
2 very disagreeable or unpleasant ⟨an *abominable* odor⟩
abom•i•na•bly \-blē\ *adv*

abom•i•na•tion \ə-ˌbä-mə-ˈnā-shən\ *n*
something that causes disgust

ab•orig•i•nal \ˌa-bə-ˈri-jə-nᵊl\ *adj*
1 being the first of its kind in a region ⟨*aboriginal* plants⟩
2 ▼ of or relating to the original people living in a region

ab•orig•i•ne \ˌa-bə-ˈri-jə-nē\ *n*, *pl* **ab•orig•i•nes**
a member of the original people living in a region
: NATIVE

aboriginal 2:
Australian aboriginal pendant

abound \ə-ˈbau̇nd\ *vb* **abound•ed**; **abound•ing**
1 to be plentiful : TEEM ⟨Salmon *abound* in the river.⟩
2 to be fully supplied ⟨The book *abounds* with pictures.⟩

[1]**about** \ə-ˈbau̇t\ *adv*
1 ALMOST, NEARLY ⟨*about* an hour ago⟩
2 on all sides : AROUND ⟨Bees were swarming *about*.⟩
3 in the opposite direction ⟨The ship came *about*.⟩
4 on the verge of ⟨I was *about* to call you.⟩

[2]**about** *prep*
1 having to do with ⟨The story is *about* dogs.⟩
2 on every side of : AROUND ⟨There are trees *about* the house.⟩
3 over or in different parts of ⟨He traveled *about* the country.⟩
4 near or not far from in time ⟨*about* the middle of the month⟩

[1]**above** \ə-ˈbəv\ *adv*
in or to a higher place ⟨Stars shine *above*.⟩

[2]**above** *prep*
1 higher than : OVER ⟨*above* the clouds⟩
2 too good for ⟨You're not *above* that kind of work.⟩
3 more than ⟨I won't pay *above* ten dollars.⟩
4 to a greater degree than ⟨She values her family *above* all else.⟩
5 having more power or importance than ⟨A captain is *above* a lieutenant.⟩

[3]**above** *adj*
said or written earlier ⟨Read the *above* definition.⟩

[1]**above•board** \ə-ˈbəv-ˌbȯrd\ *adv*
in an honest open way ⟨All business is done *aboveboard*.⟩

[2]**aboveboard** *adj*
free from tricks and secrecy ⟨an *aboveboard* sale⟩

ab•ra•ca•dab•ra \ˌa-brə-kə-ˈda-brə\ *n*
a magical charm or word

abrade \ə-ˈbrād\ *vb* **abrad•ed**; **abrad•ing**
to wear away or irritate by rubbing ⟨The rough fabric *abraded* his skin.⟩

[1]**abra•sive** \ə-ˈbrā-siv\ *n*
a substance for grinding, smoothing, or polishing

[2]**abrasive** *adj*
1 causing damage or wear by rubbing
2 very unpleasant or irritating ⟨an *abrasive* voice⟩

abreast \ə-ˈbrest\ *adv or adj*
1 right beside one another ⟨Cars traveled three *abreast*.⟩
2 up to a certain level of knowledge ⟨I try to keep *abreast* of the news.⟩

abridge \ə-ˈbrij\ *vb* **abridged**; **abridg•ing**
to shorten by leaving out some parts ⟨*abridge* a dictionary⟩

abridg•ment *or* **abridge•ment** \ə-ˈbrij-mənt\ *n*
a shortened form of a written work

abroad \ə-ˈbrȯd\ *adv or adj*
1 over a wide area ⟨The tree's branches are spread *abroad*.⟩
2 in the open : OUTDOORS ⟨Few people are *abroad* at this early hour.⟩
3 in or to a foreign country ⟨travel *abroad*⟩
4 known to many people ⟨The rumor soon got *abroad*.⟩

abrupt \ə-ˈbrəpt\ *adj*
1 happening without warning : SUDDEN ⟨The meeting came to an *abrupt* end.⟩
2 [1]STEEP 1 ⟨an *abrupt* drop⟩

3 rudely brief ⟨an *abrupt* reply⟩
abrupt•ly *adv*
abrupt•ness *n*

ab•scess \'ab-ˌses\ *n*
a collection of pus with swollen and red tissue around it
ab•scessed \-ˌsest\ *adj*

ab•sence \'ab-səns\ *n*
1 a failure to be present at a usual or expected place
2 ²LACK, WANT ⟨There was an *absence* of affection between members of the family.⟩

ab•sent \'ab-sənt\ *adj*
1 not present ⟨I missed a field trip when I was *absent.*⟩
2 not existing ⟨Trees were *absent* from the desert landscape.⟩
3 showing a lack of attention ⟨an *absent* stare⟩

ab•sen•tee \ˌab-sən-'tē\ *n*
a person who is not present

ab•sent•mind•ed \ˌab-sənt-'mīn-dəd\ *adj*
tending to forget or not pay attention ⟨Two *absentminded* students forgot their homework today.⟩
ab•sent•mind•ed•ly *adv*
ab•sent•mind•ed•ness *n*

ab•so•lute \'ab-sə-ˌlüt\ *adj*
1 ¹TOTAL 1, COMPLETE ⟨*absolute* darkness⟩
2 not limited in any way ⟨*absolute* power⟩
3 free from doubt : CERTAIN ⟨*absolute* proof⟩
ab•so•lute•ly *adv*

ab•solve \əb-'zälv, -'sälv\ *vb* **ab•solved**; **ab•solv•ing**
to make free from guilt or responsibility ⟨He was *absolved* of wrongdoing.⟩

ab•sorb \əb-'sȯrb, -'zȯrb\ *vb* **ab•sorbed**; **ab•sorb•ing**
1 ▼ to take in or swallow up ⟨A sponge *absorbs* water.⟩
2 to hold the complete attention of ⟨She was *absorbed* by the movie.⟩
3 to receive without giving back ⟨The walls of the theater *absorb* sound.⟩

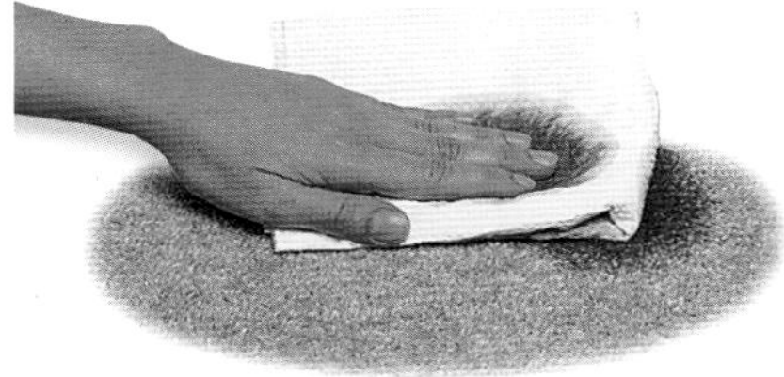

absorb 1:
a towel absorbs spilled liquid

ab•sor•ben•cy \əb-'sȯr-bən-sē, -'zȯr-\ *n*
the quality or state of being able to draw in or soak up

ab•sor•bent \əb-'sȯr-bənt, -'zȯr-\ *adj*
able to draw in or soak up ⟨*absorbent* paper towels⟩

ab•sorp•tion \əb-'sȯrp-shən, -'zȯrp-\ *n*
1 the process of drawing in or soaking up : absorbing or being absorbed ⟨the *absorption* of water by soil⟩
2 complete attention

ab•stain \əb-'stān\ *vb* **ab•stained**; **ab•stain•ing**
to choose not to do or have something ⟨*abstain* from voting⟩
ab•stain•er *n*

ab•sti•nence \'ab-stə-nəns\ *n*
an avoidance by choice especially of certain foods or of liquor

¹ab•stract \'ab-ˌstrakt\ *adj*
1 hard to understand ⟨*abstract* problems⟩
2 relating to general ideas or qualities rather than specific people, things, or actions ⟨"Honesty" is an *abstract* word.⟩
ab•stract•ly *adv*

²ab•stract \'ab-ˌstrakt\ *n*
²SUMMARY

³ab•stract \ab-'strakt\ *vb* **ab•stract•ed**; **ab•stract•ing**
1 to take away : SEPARATE ⟨Certain information was *abstracted* from the records.⟩
2 SUMMARIZE

ab•strac•tion \ab-'strak-shən\ *n*
1 the act of summarizing : the state of being summarized
2 a thought or thoughts about general qualities or ideas rather than people or things

ab•surd \əb-'sərd, -'zərd\ *adj*
completely foolish, unreasonable, or untrue : RIDICULOUS ⟨His claims are *absurd.*⟩
ab•surd•ly *adv*

▶ **Synonyms** ABSURD, FOOLISH, and SILLY mean not showing good sense. ABSURD is used when something is not in keeping with common sense, good reasoning, or accepted ideas. ⟨The notion that horses can talk is *absurd.*⟩ FOOLISH is used when something is not thought of by others as wise or sensible. ⟨You would be *foolish* to invest your money in that.⟩ SILLY is used when something makes no sense and has no purpose. ⟨They had a *silly* argument over who ate the most.⟩

ab•sur•di•ty \əb-'sər-də-tē, -'zər-\ *n*, *pl* **ab•sur•di•ties**
1 the fact of being ridiculous ⟨the *absurdity* of the situation⟩
2 something that is ridiculous ⟨Every day there is some new *absurdity* to deal with.⟩

abun•dance \ə-'bən-dəns\ *n*
a large quantity : PLENTY

abun•dant \ə-'bən-dənt\ *adj*
more than enough : PLENTIFUL ⟨*abundant* rainfall⟩
abun•dant•ly *adv*

¹abuse \ə-'byüs\ *n*
1 wrong or unfair treatment or use ⟨*abuse* of power⟩
2 the act or practice of improperly using or of using in harmful amounts ⟨drug *abuse*⟩
3 harmful treatment of a person or an animal
4 harsh insulting language
5 a dishonest practice ⟨election *abuses*⟩

²abuse \ə-'byüz\ *vb* **abused**; **abus•ing**
1 to treat in a cruel or harmful way ⟨*abuse* an animal⟩
2 to use wrongly : MISUSE ⟨*abuse* privileges⟩
3 to use improperly or in harmful amounts ⟨*abuse* drugs⟩
4 to blame or scold rudely

abu•sive \ə-'byü-siv, -ziv\ *adj*
1 using or involving harmful treatment
2 using harsh insulting language ⟨*abusive* comments⟩

abut \ə-'bət\ *vb* **abut•ted**; **abut•ting**
to touch along an edge

abys•mal \ə-'biz-məl\ *adj*
extremely bad ⟨an *abysmal* report card⟩

abyss \ə-'bis\ *n*
a gulf so deep or space so great that it cannot be measured

AC *abbr*
1 air-conditioning
2 alternating current
3 area code

ac•a•dem•ic \ˌa-kə-'de-mik\ *adj*
1 of or relating to schools and education
2 having no practical importance ⟨Your question of whether it's better to fly or drive is purely *academic* since we're not going anywhere.⟩
ac•a•dem•i•cal•ly \-mi-kə-lē\ *adv*

academy 3: the Honolulu Academy of Arts

acad•e•my \ə-'ka-də-mē\ *n, pl* **acad•e•mies**
1 a private high school
2 a high school or college where special subjects are taught ⟨a military *academy*⟩
3 ▲ an organization which supports art, science, or literature

► **Word History** In ancient Greece, a philosopher named Plato started a school at a public exercise field. The field and nearby groves of trees were named for a hero of Greek legend. The English word *academy* came from the name of the hero for whom Plato's school was named.

ac•cede \ak-'sēd\ *vb* **ac•ced•ed**; **ac•ced•ing**
to agree to ⟨They *acceded* to our demands.⟩

ac•cel•er•ate \ak-'se-lə-,rāt\ *vb* **ac•cel•er•at•ed**; **ac•cel•er•at•ing**
1 to move or cause to move faster ⟨The car *accelerated* going downhill.⟩
2 to cause to happen more quickly ⟨Using plant food *accelerates* growth.⟩

ac•cel•er•a•tion \ak-,se-lə-'rā-shən\ *n*
the act or process of speeding up

ac•cel•er•a•tor \ak-'se-lə-,rā-tər\ *n*
a pedal in an automobile for controlling the speed of the motor

[1]**ac•cent** \'ak-,sent, ak-'sent\ *vb* **ac•cent•ed**; **ac•cent•ing**
1 to give a greater force or stress
2 to mark with a written or printed accent

[2]**ac•cent** \'ak-,sent\ *n*
1 a way of pronouncing words shared by the people of a particular country or region
2 greater stress or force given to a syllable of a word in speaking or to a beat in music
3 a mark (as ' or ,) used in writing or printing to show the place of greater stress on a syllable

ac•cen•tu•ate \ak-'sen-chə-,wāt\ *vb* **ac•cen•tu•at•ed**; **ac•cen•tu•at•ing**
to make more noticeable ⟨Your blue shirt *accentuates* your eyes.⟩

ac•cept \ik-'sept, ak-\ *vb* **ac•cept•ed**; **ac•cept•ing**
1 to receive or take willingly ⟨*accept* a gift⟩ ⟨*accept* as a member⟩
2 to agree to ⟨He *accepted* my invitation.⟩
3 to stop resisting ⟨*accept* change⟩
4 to admit deserving ⟨*accept* blame⟩ ⟨*accept* responsibility⟩

ac•cept•able \ik-'sep-tə-bəl, ak-\ *adj*
1 worthy of being accepted ⟨an *acceptable* excuse⟩
2 ADEQUATE 2 ⟨He plays an *acceptable* game of tennis.⟩
ac•cept•ably \-blē\ *adv*

ac•cep•tance \ik-'sep-təns, ak-\ *n*
1 the act of accepting
2 the quality or state of being accepted or acceptable

[1]**ac•cess** \'ak-,ses\ *n*
1 the right or ability to approach, enter, or use ⟨Only a few have *access* to the secret information.⟩
2 a way or means of approaching ⟨*access* to the sea⟩

[2]**access** *vb* **ac•cessed**; **ac•cess•ing**
to get at : get access to

ac•ces•si•ble \ak-'se-sə-bəl\ *adj*
1 able to be reached ⟨The resort is *accessible* by train.⟩
2 able to be used or obtained ⟨The book is *accessible* in your school library.⟩

accessory 2
Fashion accessories add color and style to an outfit.

accompanist: a tenor (right) with an accompanist

ac•ces•sion \ak-ˈse-shən\ *n*
the rise to a position of power ⟨*accession* to the throne⟩

ac•ces•so•ry \ik-ˈse-sə-rē, ak-\ *n, pl* **ac•ces•so•ries**
1 a person who helps another in doing wrong ⟨an *accessory* to theft⟩
2◀ an object or device not necessary in itself but adding to the beauty or usefulness of something else

ac•ci•dent \ˈak-sə-dənt, -sə-ˌdent\ *n*
1 something that happens by chance or from unknown causes and that often causes injury or damage : MISHAP ⟨an automobile *accident*⟩
2 [1]CHANCE 1 ⟨We met by *accident*.⟩

ac•ci•den•tal \ˌak-sə-ˈden-tᵊl\ *adj*
1 happening by chance or unexpectedly ⟨an *accidental* discovery⟩
2 not happening or done on purpose ⟨an *accidental* shooting⟩
ac•ci•den•tal•ly *adv*

[1]**ac•claim** \ə-ˈklām\ *vb* **ac•claimed**; **ac•claim•ing**
[1]PRAISE 1 ⟨The book was *acclaimed* by the critics.⟩

[2]**acclaim** *n*
[2]PRAISE 1

ac•cli•mate \ə-ˈklī-mət, ˈa-klə-ˌmāt\ *vb* **ac•cli•mat•ed**; **ac•cli•mat•ing**
to adjust or change to fit a new climate or new surroundings ⟨He had trouble *acclimating* to the hot weather.⟩

ac•cli•ma•tize \ə-ˈklī-mə-ˌtīz\ *vb* **ac•cli•ma•tized**; **ac•cli•ma•tiz•ing**
ACCLIMATE

ac•com•mo•date \ə-ˈkä-mə-ˌdāt\ *vb* **ac•com•mo•dat•ed**; **ac•com•mo•dat•ing**
1 to provide with a place to stay or sleep ⟨*accommodate* guests⟩
2 to provide with something needed : help out ⟨My teacher will change her schedule to *accommodate* her students.⟩
3 to have room for ⟨The bus *accommodates* 40 people.⟩

ac•com•mo•dat•ing \ə-ˈkä-mə-ˌdā-tiŋ\ *adj*
ready to help

ac•com•mo•da•tion \ə-ˌkä-mə-ˈdā-shən\ *n*
1 *accommodations pl* a place where travelers can sleep and find other services
2 something supplied that is useful or handy ⟨Campsite *accommodations* include a fireplace.⟩

ac•com•pa•ni•ment \ə-ˈkəm-pə-nē-mənt\ *n*
music played in support of someone singing or playing an instrument

ac•com•pa•nist \ə-ˈkəm-pə-nist\ *n*
▲ a musician who plays in support of someone else who is singing or playing an instrument

ac•com•pa•ny \ə-ˈkəm-pə-nē\ *vb* **ac•com•pa•nied**; **ac•com•pa•ny•ing**
1 to go with as a companion ⟨Four adults *accompanied* the children on their field trip.⟩
2 to play a musical accompaniment for
3 to go or occur with ⟨Heavy winds *accompanied* the rain.⟩

ac•com•plice \ə-ˈkäm-pləs\ *n*
a partner in wrongdoing

ac•com•plish \ə-ˈkäm-plish\ *vb* **ac•com•plished**; **ac•com•plish•ing**
to succeed in doing or reaching ⟨The club *accomplished* its goal of raising money.⟩

ac•com•plished \ə-ˈkäm-plisht\ *adj*
skilled through practice or training : EXPERT ⟨an *accomplished* dancer⟩

ac•com•plish•ment \ə-ˈkäm-plish-mənt\ *n*
1 the act of successfully doing or reaching
2 something successfully done or reached especially through effort
3 an ability or skill gained by practice or training

[1]**ac•cord** \ə-ˈkȯrd\ *vb* **ac•cord•ed**; **ac•cord•ing**
1 [1]GIVE 3 ⟨The teacher *accorded* them special privileges.⟩
2 to be in harmony : AGREE ⟨Your story of the accident *accords* with theirs.⟩

[2]**accord** *n*
1 AGREEMENT 1, HARMONY ⟨They acted in *accord* with their parents' wishes.⟩
2 willingness to act or to do something ⟨They went to the library of their own *accord*.⟩
3 AGREEMENT 3, TREATY

ac•cor•dance \ə-ˈkȯr-dᵊns\ *n*
AGREEMENT 1 ⟨He took his medicine in *accordance* with the directions.⟩

ac•cord•ing•ly \ə-ˈkȯr-diŋ-lē\ *adv*
1 in the necessary way : in the way called for ⟨Knowing my limits, I ran *accordingly*.⟩
2 as a result : SO ⟨He wants to slim down. *Accordingly*, he's changing his habits.⟩

ac•cord•ing to *prep*
1 in agreement with ⟨Everything was done *according to* the rules.⟩
2 as stated by ⟨*According to* the weather report, it's going to rain.⟩

ac•cor•di•on \ə-ˈkȯr-dē-ən\ *n*
▼ a portable keyboard musical instrument played by forcing air from a bellows past metal reeds

accordion: a boy playing an accordion

ac•cost \ə-ˈkȯst\ *vb* **ac•cost•ed**; **ac•cost•ing**
to approach and speak to in a demanding or aggressive way

[1]ac•count \ə-ˈkau̇nt\ *n*
1 a record of money received and money paid out
2 an arrangement with a bank to hold money and keep records of transactions
3 an arrangement for regular dealings with a business
4 an arrangement in which a person uses the Internet or e-mail services of a particular company
5 a statement of explanation or of reasons or causes ⟨I gave an *account* of my actions.⟩
6 a statement of facts or events : REPORT
7 [2]WORTH 1, IMPORTANCE ⟨It's of little *account* to them what I think.⟩
on account of for the sake of : because of ⟨We left *on account of* the rain.⟩
on someone's account because of someone

[2]account *vb* **ac•count•ed**; **ac•count•ing**
to think of as ⟨He *accounted* himself lucky.⟩
account for 1 to take into consideration ⟨She didn't *account for* the extra costs.⟩
2 to give an explanation ⟨How do you *account for* your success?⟩
3 to be the cause of ⟨The flu *accounts for* many absences.⟩
4 to make up or form ⟨Women *account for* half the employees.⟩

ac•count•able \ə-ˈkau̇n-tə-bəl\ *adj*
1 required to explain actions or decisions ⟨The mayor is *accountable* to voters.⟩
2 RESPONSIBLE 1 ⟨You're *accountable* for your mistakes.⟩

ac•coun•tant \ə-ˈkau̇n-tᵊnt\ *n*
someone whose job is keeping the financial records of a person or a business

ac•count•ing \ə-ˈkau̇n-tiŋ\ *n*
the work of keeping the financial records of a person or a business

ac•cu•mu•late \ə-ˈkyü-myə-ˌlāt\ *vb* **ac•cu•mu•lat•ed**; **ac•cu•mu•lat•ing**
1 COLLECT 3, GATHER ⟨*accumulate* proof⟩
2 to increase in quantity or number ⟨My money is *accumulating*.⟩

ac•cu•mu•la•tion \ə-ˌkyü-myə-ˈlā-shən\ *n*
1 an act of collecting or gathering ⟨an *accumulation* of snow⟩
2 COLLECTION 2 ⟨an *accumulation* of junk⟩

ac•cu•ra•cy \ˈa-kyə-rə-sē\ *n*
freedom from mistakes

ac•cu•rate \ˈa-kyə-rət\ *adj*
free from mistakes ⟨an *accurate* answer⟩
synonyms see CORRECT
ac•cu•rate•ly *adv*

ac•cursed \ə-ˈkərst, -ˈkər-səd\ *or* **ac•curst** \-ˈkərst\ *adj*
1 being under a curse
2 greatly disliked ⟨this *accursed* place⟩

ac•cu•sa•tion \ˌa-kyə-ˈzā-shən\ *n*
a claim that someone has done something bad or illegal

ac•cuse \ə-ˈkyüz\ *vb* **ac•cused**; **ac•cus•ing**
to blame for something wrong or illegal
ac•cus•er *n*

ac•cus•tom \ə-ˈkə-stəm\ *vb* **ac•cus•tomed**; **ac•cus•tom•ing**
to cause (someone) to get used to something ⟨We tried to *accustom* the children to rising early in the morning.⟩

ac•cus•tomed \ə-ˈkə-stəmd\ *adj*
1 CUSTOMARY 2, USUAL ⟨their *accustomed* lunch hour⟩
2 familiar with ⟨*accustomed* to city life⟩

[1]ace \ˈās\ *n*
1 ▶ a playing card with one figure in its center
2 [2]EXPERT ⟨a flying *ace*⟩

▶ **Word History** An Old French word referring to the side of a die with one spot came from a Latin word *as*, the name of a small coin, perhaps because a throw of "one" in a gambling game was only worth a single *as*. The English word *ace* was borrowed from the Old French word. Later, *ace* was extended in meaning from the side of a die with one spot to a playing card with a single mark. Other meanings have come from this sense.

[2]ace *adj*
of the very best kind ⟨an *ace* reporter⟩

[1]ache \ˈāk\ *vb* **ached**; **ach•ing**
1 to suffer a dull continuous pain ⟨My muscles *ached* from shoveling snow.⟩
2 to desire very much : YEARN ⟨She *aches* for someone to talk to.⟩

[2]ache *n*
a dull continuous pain

achieve \ə-ˈchēv\ *vb* **achieved**; **achiev•ing**
1 to get by means of hard work ⟨She *achieved* a perfect score.⟩
2 to become successful ⟨Our school provides us with the skills to *achieve* in college.⟩
synonyms see REACH

achieve•ment \ə-ˈchēv-mənt\ *n*
1 the state of having gotten through great effort ⟨*achievement* of a goal⟩
2 something gotten especially by great effort

[1]ac•id \ˈa-səd\ *adj*
1 having a taste that is sour, bitter, or stinging
2 harsh or critical in tone ⟨*acid* remarks⟩
3 of, relating to, or like an acid ⟨an *acid* solution⟩
ac•id•ly *adv*

[2]acid *n*
▶ a chemical compound that tastes sour and forms a water solution which turns blue litmus paper red

acid•i•ty \ə-ˈsi-də-tē\ *n, pl* **acid•i•ties**
the quality, state, or degree of being acid

[1]ace 1: the four aces from a pack of playing cards

ac•knowl•edge \ik-ˈnä-lij, ak-\ *vb* **ac•knowl•edged**; **ac•knowl•edg•ing**
1 to admit the truth or existence of ⟨They *acknowledged* their mistake.⟩
2 to make known that something has been received or noticed ⟨He refuses to *acknowledge* my generosity.⟩
3 to recognize the rights or authority of ⟨They *acknowledged* her as captain.⟩
4 to express thanks or appreciation for

ac•knowl•edged \ik-ˈnä-lijd, ak-\ *adj*
generally accepted

^{2}acid

Acids dissolve in water to form sharp-tasting solutions. Alkalies dissolve in water to form soapy solutions. The strength of a solution is measured by its value on a scale of acidity or alkalinity. Litmus paper is used to test for levels of acidity and alkalinity.

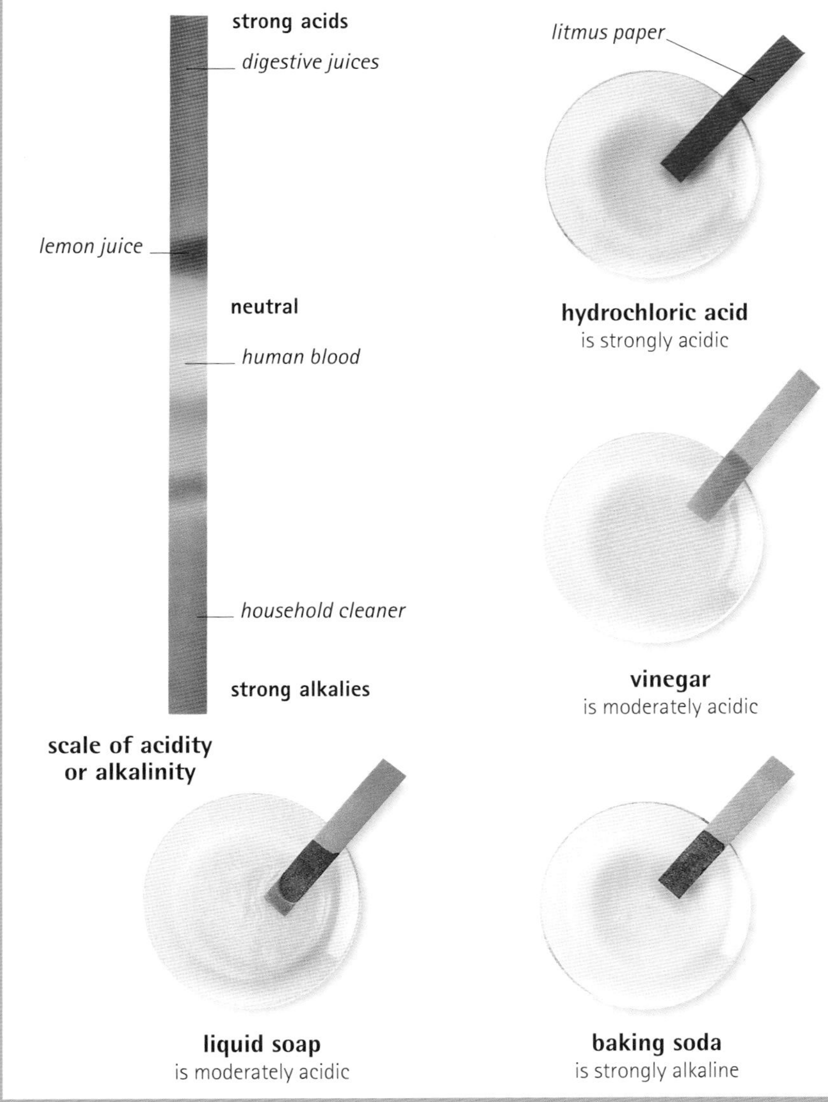

hydrochloric acid is strongly acidic

vinegar is moderately acidic

liquid soap is moderately acidic

baking soda is strongly alkaline

ac•knowl•edg•ment *or* **ac•knowl•edge•ment** \ik-ˈnä-lij-mənt, ak-\ *n*
1 an act of admitting the truth or existence of
2 an act of praising or thanking for some deed or achievement
3 a usually written statement saying that a letter or message was received

ac•ne \ˈak-nē\ *n*
a skin condition in which pimples and blackheads are present

acorn \ˈā-ˌkȯrn, -kərn\ *n*
the nut of the oak tree

acous•tic \ə-ˈkü-stik\ *or* **acous•ti•cal** \-sti-kəl\ *adj*
1 of or relating to hearing or sound
2 not having the sound changed by electrical devices 〈an *acoustic* guitar〉

acous•tics \ə-ˈkü-stiks\ *n pl*
the qualities in a room that affect how well a person in it can hear

ac•quaint \ə-ˈkwānt\ *vb* **ac•quaint•ed**; **ac•quaint•ing**
1 to cause to know personally 〈They became *acquainted* at school.〉
2 to make familiar 〈The supervisor *acquainted* them with their duties.〉

ac•quain•tance \ə-ˈkwān-tᵊns\ *n*
1 a person someone knows slightly
2 personal knowledge 〈He has some *acquaintance* with car repair.〉

ac•qui•esce \ˌa-kwē-ˈes\ *vb* **ac•qui•esced**; **ac•qui•esc•ing**
to accept, agree, or give consent by keeping silent or by not making objections 〈They *acquiesced* to the demands.〉

ac•qui•es•cence \ˌa-kwē-ˈe-sᵊns\ *n*
the act of agreeing, accepting, or giving consent

ac•quire \ə-ˈkwīr\ *vb* **ac•quired**; **ac•quir•ing**
to get especially through effort : GAIN 〈*acquire* a skill〉

ac•qui•si•tion \ˌa-kwə-ˈzi-shən\ *n*
1 the act of gaining especially through effort 〈the *acquisition* of knowledge〉
2 something gained especially through effort 〈the museum's new *acquisitions*〉

ac•quit \ə-ˈkwit\ *vb* **ac•quit•ted**; **ac•quit•ting**
1 to declare innocent of a crime or of wrongdoing
2 to behave in a certain way 〈You are to *acquit* yourselves as young ladies and gentlemen.〉

ac•quit•tal \ə-ˈkwi-tᵊl\ *n*
the act of declaring someone innocent of a crime or wrongdoing

acre \ˈā-kər\ *n*
a measure of land area equal to 43,560 square feet (about 4047 square meters)

acre•age \ˈā-kə-rij, ˈā-krij\ *n*
area in acres

ac•rid \ˈa-krəd\ *adj*
1 sharp or bitter in taste or odor
2 very harsh or unpleasant 〈an *acrid* manner〉

ac•ro•bat \ˈa-krə-ˌbat\ *n*
▶ a person skillful at performing stunts like jumping, balancing, tumbling, and swinging from a bar

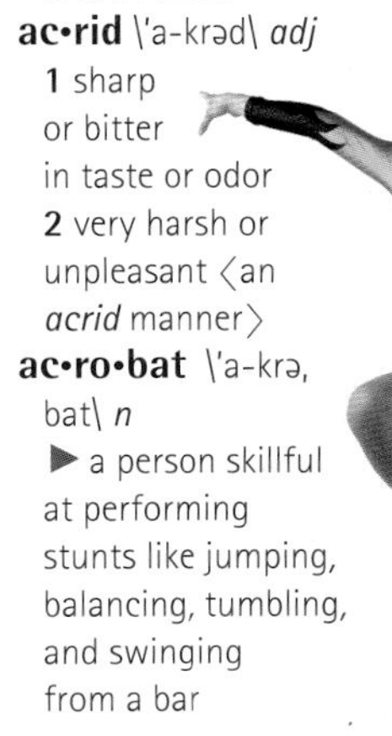

acrobat: two young acrobats displaying acrobatics

A B C D E F G H I J K L M N O P Q R S T U V W X Y Z

ac•ro•bat•ic \ˌa-krə-ˈba-tik\ *adj*
relating to acrobats or acrobatics

ac•ro•bat•ics \ˌa-krə-ˈba-tiks\ *n pl*
1 the art or performance of an acrobat
2 difficult or dangerous stunts
Hint: *Acrobatics* can be used as a singular or a plural in writing and speaking. 〈*Acrobatics* is taught at clown school.〉 〈The *acrobatics* were amazing.〉

ac•ro•nym \ˈa-krə-ˌnim\ *n*
a word formed from the first letter or letters of the words of a compound term 〈The word "radar" is an *acronym* for "radio detecting and ranging."〉

¹across \ə-ˈkrȯs\ *adv*
1 from one side to the other 〈They reached *across* and shook hands.〉
2 a measurement from one side to another 〈The lake is a mile *across*.〉
3 on the opposite side 〈Watch me till I get *across*.〉

²across *prep*
1 to or on the opposite side of 〈The chicken ran *across* the street.〉 〈My grandparents live *across* the street.〉
2 so as to pass, go over, or intersect at an angle 〈Lay one stick *across* another.〉
3 in every part of 〈The story spread all *across* town.〉

¹act \ˈakt\ *n*
1 something that is done : DEED 〈an *act* of bravery〉
2 a law made by a governing body
3 a main division of a play
4 one of the performances in a show 〈a juggling *act*〉
5 an insincere way of behaving 〈Her crying was just an *act*.〉

²act *vb* **act•ed**; **act•ing**
1 to do something : MOVE 〈It's important to *act* quickly in an emergency.〉
2 to behave oneself in a certain way 〈He's been *acting* strangely.〉
3 to perform as a character in a play 〈Both stars agreed to *act* in the movie.〉
4 to perform a certain function 〈She'll *act* as our guide.〉
5 to have a result : make something happen : WORK 〈The medicine *acts* on the heart.〉
synonyms see IMPERSONATE
act up to behave badly

act•ing \ˈak-tiŋ\ *adj*
serving for a short time only or in place of another 〈Teachers met with the *acting* principal.〉

ac•tion \ˈak-shən\ *n*
1 the process by which something produces a change in another thing 〈the *action* of acid on metal〉
2 the doing of something 〈*Action* is needed on this problem.〉
3 something done 〈The mayor's first *action* was to call a meeting.〉
4 the way something runs or works 〈the toy car's spinning *action*〉
5 combat in war

action figure *n*
▼ a model often of a superhero used as a toy

action figure: Robin, Batman, and Superman

ac•ti•vate \ˈak-tə-ˌvāt\ *vb* **ac•ti•vat•ed**; **ac•ti•vat•ing**
to start working or cause to start working 〈*Activate* the alarm.〉

ac•tive \ˈak-tiv\ *adj*
1 producing or involving action or movement 〈Cats are most *active* at night.〉
2 showing that the subject of a sentence is the doer of the action represented by the verb 〈The word "hit" in "they hit the ball" is *active*.〉
3 quick in physical movement : LIVELY 〈an *active* child〉
4 taking part in an action or activity 〈She is *active* in school athletics.〉
ac•tive•ly *adv*

ac•tiv•i•ty \ak-ˈti-və-tē\ *n*, *pl* **ac•tiv•i•ties**
1 energetic action 〈There is always *activity* around the holidays.〉
2 something done especially for relaxation or fun

ac•tor \ˈak-tər\ *n*
▶ a person who acts especially in a play or movie

ac•tress \ˈak-trəs\ *n*
a woman or girl who acts especially in a play or movie

ac•tu•al \ˈak-chə-wəl\ *adj*
really existing or happening : not false 〈The movie is based on *actual* events.〉
synonyms see REAL

ac•tu•al•ly \ˈak-chə-wə-lē\ *adv*
in fact : REALLY 〈It's not a lie. It *actually* happened.〉

acute \ə-ˈkyüt\ *adj* **acut•er**; **acut•est**
1 ▶ measuring less than 90 degrees 〈*acute* angles〉
2 marked by or showing an ability to understand things that are not obvious 〈an *acute* observation〉
3 SEVERE 2, SHARP 〈*acute* pain〉
4 developing quickly and lasting only a short time 〈*acute* illness〉
5 CRITICAL 4, URGENT 〈an *acute* shortage of food〉
6 very strong and sensitive 〈an *acute* sense of smell〉
acute•ly *adv*
acute•ness *n*

ad \ˈad\ *n*
ADVERTISEMENT

A.D. *abbr* in the year of our Lord
Hint: *A.D.* is an abbreviation for the Latin phrase *anno Domini*, which means "in the year of our Lord."

ad•age \ˈa-dij\ *n*
an old familiar saying : PROVERB

ad•a•mant \ˈa-də-mənt\ *adj*
not giving in 〈I tried to change her mind, but she was *adamant*.〉

Ad•am's apple \ˈa-dəmz-\ *n*
the lump formed in the front of a person's neck by cartilage in the throat

actor: actors performing in a play

acute 1:
an acute angle

adapt \ə-ˈdapt\ *vb* **adapt•ed**; **adapt•ing**
1 to change behavior so that it is easier to function in a particular place or situation ⟨He easily *adapted* to high school.⟩
2 to make or become suitable or able to function ⟨The camera was *adapted* for underwater use.⟩

adapt•able \ə-ˈdap-tə-bəl\ *adj*
capable of changing or being changed to better suit a situation

ad•ap•ta•tion \ˌa-ˌdap-ˈtā-shən\ *n*
1 the act or process of changing to better suit a situation
2 a body part or feature or a behavior that helps a living thing survive and function better in its environment

add \ˈad\ *vb* **add•ed**; **add•ing**
1 to combine numbers into a single sum
2 to join or unite to something ⟨They plan to *add* a room to the house.⟩
3 to cause to have ⟨Parsley *adds* color to the dish.⟩
4 to say something more ⟨The teacher *added,* "It's not only wrong, it's foolish."⟩
add up
1 to be added together to equal the expected amount
2 to make sense ⟨Something about his story doesn't *add up.*⟩

ad•dend \ˈa-ˌdend\ *n*
a number that is to be added to another number

ad•den•dum \ə-ˈden-dəm\ *n, pl* **ad•den•da** \ə-ˈden-də\
something added (as to a book)

ad•der \ˈa-dər\ *n*
1 ► a poisonous snake of Europe or Africa
2 a harmless North American snake

ad•dict \ˈa-ˌdikt\ *n*
1 a person who is not able to stop taking drugs ⟨a heroin *addict*⟩
2 a person who likes or enjoys something excessively ⟨a chocolate *addict*⟩

ad•dict•ed \ə-ˈdik-təd\ *adj*
1 unable to stop using a drug ⟨*addicted* to cocaine⟩
2 having an unusually great need to do or have something ⟨He's *addicted* to playing video games.⟩
ad•dic•tion \ə-ˈdik-shən\ *n*

ad•di•tion \ə-ˈdi-shən\ *n*
1 the act or process of adding numbers to obtain their sum
2 something added ⟨an *addition* to a house⟩
in addition as something more
in addition to along with or together with ⟨There was ice cream *in addition to* cake and pie.⟩

ad•di•tion•al \ə-ˈdi-shə-nᵊl\ *adj*
[1]EXTRA ⟨We needed *additional* time to finish.⟩
ad•di•tion•al•ly \-ē\ *adv*

ad•di•tive \ˈa-də-tiv\ *n*
a substance added to another in small amounts

ad•dle \ˈa-dᵊl\ *vb* **ad•dled**; **ad•dling**
to make or become confused ⟨She was *addled* by the many detours.⟩

[1]**ad•dress** \ə-ˈdres\ *vb* **ad•dressed**; **ad•dress•ing**
1 to put directions for delivery on ⟨*address* a letter⟩
2 to speak or write to
3 to use a specified name or title when speaking or writing to (someone) ⟨The children *address* me as "sir."⟩
4 to deal with : give attention to ⟨*address* a problem⟩

[2]**ad•dress** \ə-ˈdres, ˈa-ˌdres\ *n*
1 the place where a person can usually be reached ⟨a business *address*⟩
2 the directions for delivery placed on mail
3 the symbols (as numerals or letters) that identify the location where particular information (as a home page) is stored on a computer especially on the Internet
4 a formal speech ⟨The president will give an *address* at the ceremony.⟩
5 the name of a computer account from which e-mail can be sent or received

ad•dress•ee \ˌa-ˌdres-ˈē\ *n*
the person to whom something is addressed

ad•e•noids \ˈa-dᵊ-ˌnȯidz\ *n pl*
fleshy growths near the opening of the nose into the throat

ad•ept \ə-ˈdept\ *adj*
very good at something ⟨*adept* at swimming⟩
adept•ly *adv*
adept•ness *n*

► **Word History** Several centuries ago, at the beginnings of modern science, some people claimed to have found the trick of turning common metals to gold. The Latin word *adeptus,* meaning "someone who has attained something," was even used to describe a person who could perform this feat. The English word *adept,* which means "skilled at something," came from this Latin word. Certainly, a person who could make gold in this way would have to be highly skilled.

ad•e•quate \ˈa-di-kwət\ *adj*
1 [1]ENOUGH ⟨Be sure you have *adequate* time to get ready.⟩
2 good enough ⟨The lunch provides *adequate* nutrition.⟩
ad•e•quate•ly *adv*

adder 1:
a puff adder

ad•here \ad-ˈhir\ *vb* **ad•hered**; **ad•her•ing**
1 to stick tight : CLING ⟨The stamps *adhered* to the envelope.⟩
2 to act in the way that is required by ⟨*adhere* to the rules⟩

ad•her•ence \ad-ˈhir-əns\ *n*
the act of doing what is required by ⟨*adherence* to the terms of a contract⟩

A

ad•her•ent \ad-ˈhir-ənt\ *n*
a person who is loyal to a belief, an organization, or a leader

ad•he•sion \ad-ˈhē-zhən\ *n*
the act or state of sticking ⟨They tested the *adhesion* of the paint to the wall.⟩

[1]**ad•he•sive** \ad-ˈhē-siv, -ziv\ *adj*
tending to stick : STICKY ⟨*adhesive* bandages⟩

[2]**adhesive** *n*
▼ a substance that is used to make things stick together

[2]**adhesive:** a bottle of glue

adj *abbr* adjective

ad•ja•cent \ə-ˈjā-sᵊnt\ *adj*
next to or near something ⟨My sister sleeps in the *adjacent* room.⟩

ad•jec•ti•val \ˌa-jik-ˈtī-vəl\ *adj*
of, relating to, or functioning as an adjective ⟨an *adjectival* phrase⟩
ad•jec•ti•val•ly *adv*

ad•jec•tive \ˈa-jik-tiv\ *n*
a word that says something about a noun or pronoun ⟨In the phrases "good people," "someone good," "it's good to be here," and "they seem very good" the word "good" is an *adjective.*⟩

ad•join \ə-ˈjȯin\ *vb* **ad•joined**; **ad•join•ing**
to be next to or in contact with ⟨The two rooms *adjoin* each other.⟩

ad•journ \ə-ˈjərn\ *vb* **ad•journed**; **ad•journ•ing**
to bring or come to a close for a period of time ⟨*adjourn* a meeting⟩
ad•journ•ment \-mənt\ *n*

ad•just \ə-ˈjəst\ *vb* **ad•just•ed**; **ad•just•ing**
1 to change (something) in a minor way to make it work better
2 to change the position of (something) ⟨He *adjusted* his glasses.⟩
3 to become used to ⟨He *adjusted* to a new school.⟩

ad•just•able \ə-ˈjə-stə-bəl\ *adj*
▼ possible to change to make work or be positioned better ⟨*adjustable* shelves⟩

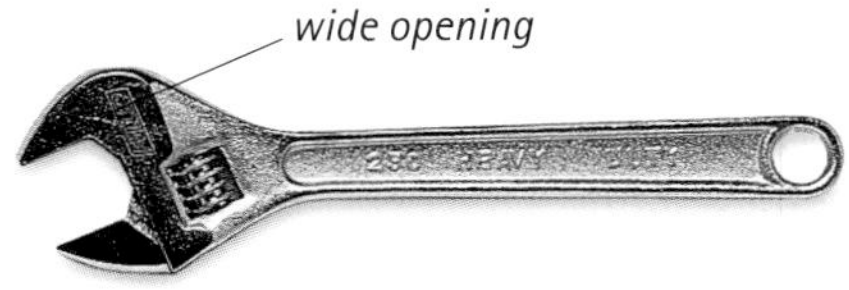

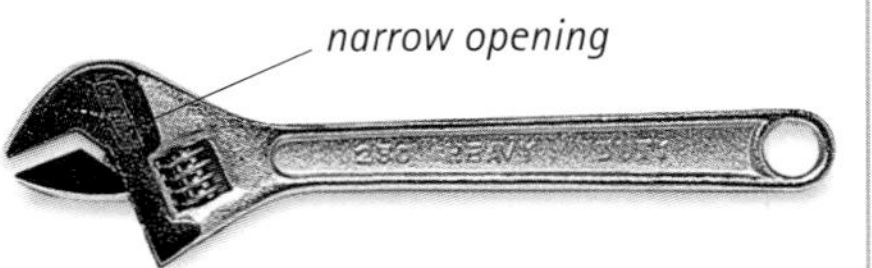

adjustable: an adjustable wrench

ad•just•ment \ə-ˈjəst-mənt\ *n*
1 a small change that improves something or makes it work better
2 the act or process of changing or adjusting
3 the decision about and payment of a claim or debt

ad•ju•tant \ˈa-jə-tənt\ *n*
an officer who assists the officer in command

ad–lib \ˈad-ˈlib\ *vb* **ad–libbed**; **ad–lib•bing**
to make up something and especially music or spoken lines during a performance : IMPROVISE

ad•min•is•ter \əd-ˈmi-nə-stər\ *vb* **ad•min•is•tered**; **ad•min•is•ter•ing**
1 to be in charge of : MANAGE ⟨She *administers* an athletic program.⟩
2 to give out as deserved ⟨*administer* justice⟩
3 to give officially ⟨*administer* an oath⟩ ⟨The teacher *administered* the test.⟩
4 to give or supply as treatment ⟨*administer* medicine⟩

ad•min•is•tra•tion \əd-ˌmi-nə-ˈstrā-shən\ *n*
1 the act or process of administering ⟨*administration* of the oath⟩
2 the work involved in managing something
3 the people who direct the business of something (as a city or school)
4 a government department ⟨the Food and Drug *Administration*⟩

ad•min•is•tra•tive \əd-ˈmi-nə-ˌstrā-tiv\ *adj*
of or assisting in administration

ad•min•is•tra•tor \əd-ˈmi-nə-ˌstrā-tər\ *n*
a person who administers business, school, or government affairs

ad•mi•ra•ble \ˈad-mə-rə-bəl, ˈad-mrə-bəl\ *adj*
deserving great respect and approval ⟨He showed *admirable* courage.⟩
ad•mi•ra•bly \-blē\ *adv*

ad•mi•ral \ˈad-mə-rəl, -mrəl\ *n*
a high-ranking commissioned officer in the navy or coast guard

▶ **Word History** The word *admiral* looks a lot like the word *admire.* The two words, though, are not related. *Admire* came from a Latin verb that meant "to marvel at." *Admiral* came from an Arabic title that meant "commander." It may have been part of a phrase that meant "commander of the sea."

ad•mi•ral•ty \ˈad-mə-rəl-tē, -mrəl-\ *adj*
of or relating to conduct on the sea ⟨*admiralty* law⟩

ad•mi•ra•tion \ˌad-mə-ˈrā-shən\ *n*
a feeling of great respect and approval

ad•mire \əd-ˈmīr\ *vb* **ad•mired**; **ad•mir•ing**
to think very highly of : feel admiration for
ad•mir•er *n*

ad•mis•si•ble \əd-ˈmi-sə-bəl\ *adj*
able to be or deserving to be admitted or allowed : ALLOWABLE ⟨The jury listened to all of the *admissible* evidence.⟩

ad•mis•sion \əd-ˈmi-shən\ *n*
1 acknowledgment by someone of something about him or her that has not been proved ⟨an *admission* of guilt⟩
2 the right or permission to enter ⟨*admission* to college⟩
3 the price of entrance

ad•mit \əd-ˈmit\ *vb* **ad•mit•ted**; **ad•mit•ting**
1 to make known usually with some unwillingness
2 to allow to enter : let in ⟨No one under 18 is *admitted.*⟩
3 [1]PERMIT 2, ALLOW ⟨This law *admits* no exceptions.⟩

ad•mit•tance \əd-ˈmi-tᵊns\ *n*
permission to enter

ad•mon•ish \ad-ˈmä-nish\ *vb* **ad•mon•ished**; **ad•mon•ish•ing**
1 to criticize or warn gently but seriously ⟨The principal *admonished* a student for talking.⟩
2 to give friendly advice or encouragement ⟨I *admonished* them to keep trying.⟩

ad•mo•ni•tion \ˌad-mə-ˈni-shən\ *n*
a gentle or friendly criticism or warning ⟨an *admonition* against false pride⟩

ado \ə-ˈdü\ *n*
foolish or unnecessary trouble, activity, or excitement

ado•be \ə-ˈdō-bē\ *n*
1 brick made of earth or clay dried in the sun
2 ▼ a building made of adobe

ad•o•les•cence \ˌa-də-ˈle-sᵊns\ *n*
the period of life between childhood and adulthood

ad•o•les•cent \ˌa-də-ˈle-sᵊnt\ *n*
a person who is no longer a child but not yet an adult

adopt \ə-ˈdäpt\ *vb* **adopt•ed**; **adopt•ing**
1 to legally take a child of other parents to raise
2 to take up as someone's own ⟨After moving to Quebec, he *adopted* French as his language.⟩
3 to accept and put into action ⟨The state *adopted* a law requiring drivers to wear seat belts.⟩

adop•tion \ə-ˈdäp-shən\ *n*
the act of adopting : the state of being adopted

ador•able \ə-ˈdȯr-ə-bəl\ *adj*
CHARMING, LOVELY ⟨an *adorable* baby⟩
ador•ably \-blē\ *adv*

ad•o•ra•tion \ˌa-də-ˈrā-shən\ *n*
deep love

adore \ə-ˈdȯr\ *vb* **adored**; **ador•ing**
1 ^{2}WORSHIP 1
2 to be very fond of

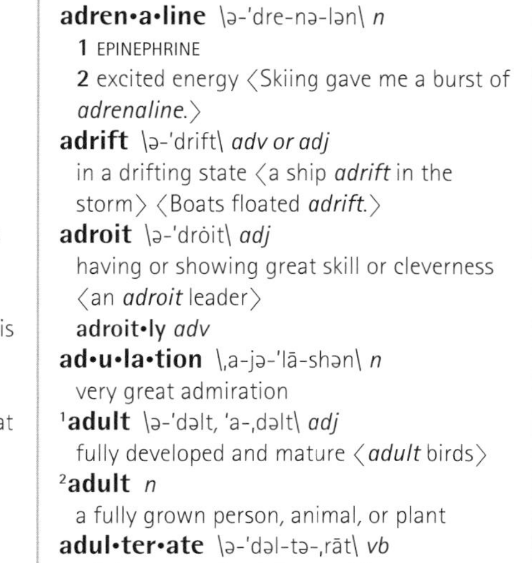

adorn \ə-ˈdȯrn\ *vb* **adorned**; **adorn•ing**
to make more attractive by adding something ⟨Paintings *adorn* the walls.⟩

adorn•ment \ə-ˈdȯrn-mənt\ *n*
something added to make a person or thing more attractive

adren•a•line \ə-ˈdre-nə-lən\ *n*
1 EPINEPHRINE
2 excited energy ⟨Skiing gave me a burst of *adrenaline*.⟩

adrift \ə-ˈdrift\ *adv or adj*
in a drifting state ⟨a ship *adrift* in the storm⟩ ⟨Boats floated *adrift*.⟩

adroit \ə-ˈdrȯit\ *adj*
having or showing great skill or cleverness ⟨an *adroit* leader⟩
adroit•ly *adv*

ad•u•la•tion \ˌa-jə-ˈlā-shən\ *n*
very great admiration

^{1}**adult** \ə-ˈdəlt, ˈa-ˌdəlt\ *adj*
fully developed and mature ⟨*adult* birds⟩

^{2}**adult** *n*
a fully grown person, animal, or plant

adul•ter•ate \ə-ˈdəl-tə-ˌrāt\ *vb* **adul•ter•at•ed**; **adul•ter•at•ing**
to make impure or weaker by adding something different or of poorer quality ⟨The company *adulterated* its orange juice with water and sugar.⟩

adult•hood \ə-ˈdəlt-ˌhu̇d\ *n*
the period of being an adult

adv *abbr* adverb

adobe 2: an adobe house

^{1}**ad•vance** \əd-ˈvans\ *vb* **ad•vanced**; **ad•vanc•ing**
1 to move forward ⟨*Advance* your piece five spaces on your next turn.⟩
2 to help the progress of ⟨Laws were passed that *advance* freedom.⟩
3 to raise to a higher rank : PROMOTE ⟨She was *advanced* from teller to assistant bank manager.⟩
4 to give ahead of time ⟨My boss *advanced* me 100 dollars from my wages.⟩
5 PROPOSE 1 ⟨The candidate *advanced* a new plan.⟩

^{2}**advance** *n*
1 a forward movement ⟨Troops tried to halt the enemy's *advance*.⟩
2 progress in development : IMPROVEMENT ⟨*advances* in medicine⟩
3 a rise in price, value, or amount
4 a first step or approach ⟨friendly *advances*⟩
5 money given ahead of the usual time ⟨I asked for an *advance* on my salary.⟩
in advance before an expected event ⟨You knew a week *in advance* about the test.⟩

ad•vanced \əd-ˈvanst\ *adj*
1 being far along in years or progress ⟨an *advanced* civilization⟩
2 being beyond the elementary or introductory level ⟨*advanced* mathematics⟩

ad•vance•ment \əd-ˈvan-smənt\ *n*
1 the action of moving forward in position or progress : the state of being moved forward in position or progress ⟨the *advancement* of science⟩
2 the act of raising to a higher rank or position : the result of being raised to a higher rank or position

ad•van•tage \əd-ˈvan-tij\ *n*
1 something that benefits the one it belongs to ⟨Speed is an *advantage* in sports.⟩
2 the fact of being in a better position or condition ⟨His great height is an *advantage* in basketball.⟩
3 personal benefit or gain ⟨It's to your own *advantage* to study.⟩

ad•van•ta•geous \ˌad-vən-ˈtā-jəs, -ˌvan-\ *adj*
giving a benefit especially that others do not have : giving an advantage ⟨A college degree is *advantageous* when job hunting.⟩
ad•van•ta•geous•ly *adv*

ad•vent \ˈad-ˌvent\ *n*
the arrival or coming of something ⟨the *advent* of spring⟩

ad•ven•ture \əd-ˈven-chər\ *n*
1 an action that involves unknown dangers and risks
2 an unusual experience

A B C D E F G H I J K L M N O P Q R S T U V W X Y Z

ad•ven•tur•er \əd-ˈven-chər-ər\ *n*
a person who seeks dangerous or exciting experiences

ad•ven•ture•some \əd-ˈven-chər-səm\ *adj*
likely to take risks : DARING

ad•ven•tur•ous \əd-ˈven-chə-rəs\ *adj*
1 ready to take risks or to deal with new or unexpected problems ⟨*adventurous* explorers⟩
2 DANGEROUS 1, RISKY ⟨an *adventurous* voyage⟩

► **Synonyms** ADVENTUROUS, VENTURESOME, and DARING mean taking risks that are not necessary. ADVENTUROUS is used for a person who goes in search of adventure in spite of the possible dangers. ⟨*Adventurous* youngsters went on a hike through the forest.⟩ VENTURESOME is used of a person willing to take many chances. ⟨*Venturesome* explorers searched for lost treasure.⟩ DARING is used when someone is fearless and willing to take unnecessary risks. ⟨Early pilots were especially *daring.*⟩

ad•verb \ˈad-ˌvərb\ *n*
a word used to modify a verb, an adjective, or another adverb and often used to show degree, manner, place, or time ⟨The words "almost" and "very" in "at almost three o'clock on a very hot day" are *adverbs.*⟩

ad•ver•bi•al \ad-ˈvər-bē-əl\ *adj*
of, relating to, or used as an adverb
ad•ver•bi•al•ly *adv*

ad•ver•sary \ˈad-vər-ˌser-ē\ *n, pl* **ad•ver•sar•ies**
OPPONENT, ENEMY

ad•verse \ad-ˈvərs\ *adj*
1 acting against or in an opposite direction ⟨*adverse* winds⟩
2 not helping or favoring ⟨*adverse* circumstances⟩
ad•verse•ly *adv*

ad•ver•si•ty \ad-ˈvər-sə-tē\ *n, pl* **ad•ver•si•ties**
hard times : MISFORTUNE

ad•ver•tise \ˈad-vər-ˌtīz\ *vb* **ad•ver•tised**; **ad•ver•tis•ing**
1 to call to public attention to persuade to buy ⟨*advertise* a car⟩
2 to announce publicly ⟨The fund raising event was *advertised* on TV.⟩
synonyms see DECLARE
ad•ver•tis•er *n*

ad•ver•tise•ment \ˌad-vər-ˈtīz-mənt, ad-ˈvər-təz-\ *n*
► a notice or short film advertising something

ad•ver•tis•ing \ˈad-vər-ˌtī-ziŋ\ *n*
1 speech, writing, pictures, or films meant to persuade people to buy something
2 the business of preparing advertisements

ad•vice \əd-ˈvīs\ *n*
suggestions about a decision or action ⟨He took his father's *advice* on buying a car.⟩

ad•vis•able \əd-ˈvī-zə-bəl\ *adj*
reasonable or wise to do ⟨It is not *advisable* to look directly at the sun.⟩

ad•vise \əd-ˈvīz\ *vb* **ad•vised**; **ad•vis•ing**
1 to give suggestions about a decision or action : give advice to
2 to give information about something ⟨Passengers were *advised* of bad flying conditions.⟩
ad•vis•er *or* **ad•vi•sor** \-ˈvī-zər\ *n*

ad•vi•so•ry \əd-ˈvī-zə-rē, -ˈvīz-rē\ *adj*
having the power or right to advise ⟨an *advisory* committee⟩

[1]ad•vo•cate \ˈad-və-kət, -ˌkāt\ *n*
1 a person who argues for or supports an idea or plan ⟨peace *advocates*⟩
2 a person who argues for another especially in court

[2]ad•vo•cate \ˈad-və-ˌkāt\ *vb* **ad•vo•cat•ed**; **ad•vo•cat•ing**
to speak in favor of : argue for ⟨*advocate* change⟩

adze *also* **adz** \ˈadz\ *n, pl* **adz•es**
► a cutting tool that has a thin curved blade at right angles to the handle and is used for shaping wood

adze: an 18th-century adze

ae•on *or* **eon** \ˈē-ən, ˈē-ˌän\ *n*
a very long period of time

aer- *or* **aero-** *prefix*
air : atmosphere : gas ⟨*aer*ate⟩ ⟨*aero*sol⟩ ⟨*aero*space⟩

aer•ate \ˈer-ˌāt\ *vb* **aer•at•ed**; **aer•at•ing**
1 to supply or cause to be filled with air ⟨*aerate* the soil⟩
2 to supply (blood) with oxygen by breathing
aer•a•tor \-ˌā-tər\ *n*

aer•a•tion \er-ˈā-shən\ *n*
the process of supplying or filling with air or gas

[1]ae•ri•al \ˈer-ē-əl, ā-ˈir-ē-əl\ *adj*
1 performed or occurring in the air ⟨We were amazed by the *aerial* stunts of the circus performers.⟩
2 of aircraft ⟨*aerial* navigation⟩
3 taken from, used in, or performed using an airplane ⟨*aerial* camera⟩ ⟨*aerial* warfare⟩

[2]aer•i•al \ˈer-ē-əl\ *n*
ANTENNA 2

aero•nau•ti•cal \ˌer-ə-ˈnȯ-ti-kəl\ *adj*
of or relating to aeronautics ⟨*aeronautical* engineer⟩

aero•nau•tics \ˌer-ə-ˈnȯ-tiks\ *n*
a science dealing with the building and flying of aircraft

aero•sol \ˈer-ə-ˌsäl, -ˌsȯl\ *n*
1 ► a substance (as an insect repellent or medicine) that is released from a container as a spray of tiny solid or liquid particles in gas

advertisement: advertisements in Times Square, New York City

2 a container (as a can) that dispenses a substance as a spray

[1]aero•space \'er-ō-ˌspās\ *n*
1 the earth's atmosphere and the space beyond
2 a science dealing with aerospace

[2]aerospace *adj*
relating to aerospace, to the vehicles used in aerospace or their manufacture, or to travel in aerospace ⟨*aerospace* research⟩ ⟨an *aerospace* museum⟩

aes•thet•ic \es-'the-tik\ *adj*
relating to beauty and what is beautiful ⟨They made *aesthetic* improvements to the building.⟩
aes•thet•i•cal•ly \-i-kə-lē\ *adv*

[1]afar \ə-'fär\ *adv*
from, at, or to a great distance ⟨wandered *afar*⟩

aerosol 1:
an aerosol being sprayed

[2]afar *n*
a long way off ⟨There came a voice from *afar.*⟩

af•fa•ble \'a-fə-bəl\ *adj*
friendly and easy to talk to ⟨He's an *affable* dinner host.⟩
af•fa•bly \-blē\ *adv*

af•fair \ə-'fer\ *n*
1 **affairs** *pl* work or activities done for a purpose : BUSINESS ⟨government *affairs*⟩
2 something that relates to or involves someone ⟨His problem is no *affair* of mine.⟩
3 a social event or activity

[1]af•fect \ə-'fekt\ *vb* **af•fect•ed**; **af•fect•ing**
to pretend that a false behavior or feeling is natural or genuine ⟨She *affected* surprise upon hearing the news.⟩

[2]affect *vb* **affected**; **affecting**
1 to have an effect on ⟨I hope this disagreement won't *affect* our friendship.⟩ ⟨The oceans are *affected* by the moon.⟩
2 to cause strong emotions in
3 to cause illness in ⟨Rabies can *affect* dogs and cats.⟩

af•fect•ed \ə-'fek-təd\ *adj*
not natural or genuine ⟨*affected* manners⟩
af•fect•ed•ly *adv*

af•fec•tion \ə-'fek-shən\ *n*
a feeling of liking and caring for someone or something ⟨He shows great *affection* for his grandchildren.⟩

af•fec•tion•ate \ə-'fek-shə-nət\ *adj*
feeling or showing a great liking for a person or thing : LOVING ⟨an *affectionate* friend⟩
af•fec•tion•ate•ly *adv*

af•fi•da•vit \ˌa-fə-'dā-vət\ *n*
a written statement signed by a person who swears that the information is true

af•fil•i•ate \ə-'fi-lē-ˌāt\ *vb* **af•fil•i•at•ed**; **af•fil•i•at•ing**
to associate as a member or partner ⟨The spokesperson has long been *affiliated* with the charity.⟩

af•fin•i•ty \ə-'fi-nə-tē\ *n*, *pl* **af•fin•i•ties**
a strong liking for or attraction to someone or something ⟨They had much in common and felt a close *affinity.*⟩

af•firm \ə-'fərm\ *vb* **af•firmed**; **af•firm•ing**
to declare that something is true ⟨The man *affirms* that he is innocent.⟩

af•fir•ma•tion \ˌa-fər-'mā-shən\ *n*
an act of saying or showing that something is true

[1]af•fir•ma•tive \ə-'fər-mə-tiv\ *adj*
1 saying or showing that the answer is "yes" ⟨He gave an *affirmative* answer.⟩
2 being positive or helpful ⟨Take an *affirmative* approach to the problem.⟩

[2]affirmative *n*
1 an expression (as the word *yes*) of agreement
2 the side that supports or votes for something

[1]af•fix \ə-'fiks\ *vb* **af•fixed**; **af•fix•ing**
1 to attach firmly ⟨*Affix* the stamp to the envelope.⟩
2 to add to something else ⟨He *affixed* his signature to the letter.⟩

[2]af•fix \'a-ˌfiks\ *n*
a letter or group of letters (as a prefix or suffix) that comes at the beginning or end of a word and has a meaning of its own

af•flict \ə-'flikt\ *vb* **af•flict•ed**; **af•flict•ing**
to cause pain or unhappiness to ⟨An unusual illness *afflicted* the young girl.⟩

af•flic•tion \ə-'flik-shən\ *n*
1 the state of being affected by something that causes pain or unhappiness ⟨his *affliction* with polio⟩
2 something that causes pain or unhappiness ⟨Chicken pox is an *affliction* caused by a virus.⟩

af•flu•ence \'a-ˌflü-əns\ *n*
the state of having much money and expensive things : WEALTH

af•flu•ent \'a-ˌflü-ənt\ *adj*
having plenty of money and expensive things : WEALTHY ⟨an *affluent* family⟩

af•ford \ə-'fȯrd\ *vb* **af•ford•ed**; **af•ford•ing**
1 to be able to do or bear without serious harm ⟨You cannot *afford* to waste your strength.⟩
2 to be able to pay for ⟨I can't *afford* a new car.⟩
3 to supply or provide someone with ⟨Tennis *affords* good exercise.⟩

af•ford•able \ə-'fȯr-də-bəl\ *adj*
within someone's ability to pay : reasonably priced ⟨an *affordable* bike⟩

[1]af•front \ə-'frənt\ *vb* **af•front•ed**; **af•front•ing**
to insult openly : OFFEND

[2]affront *n*
an act or statement that insults or offends someone

Af•ghan \'af-ˌgan\ *n*
1 a person born or living in Afghanistan
2 ▼ *not cap* a blanket or shawl made of wool or cotton knitted or crocheted into patterns

afghan 2:
a baby wrapped in an afghan

afield \ə-'fēld\ *adv*
1 to, in, or into the countryside
2 away from home ⟨People came from as far *afield* as Canada.⟩
3 out of a usual, planned, or proper course ⟨His question led the discussion far *afield.*⟩

afire \ə-'fīr\ *adj*
1 being on fire ⟨The house was *afire.*⟩
2 in a state of great excitement or energy ⟨His mind was *afire* with ideas.⟩

aflame \ə-'flām\ *adj*
burning with flames

afloat: a boat afloat on water

afloat \ə-'flōt\ *adv or adj*
▲ carried on or as if on water ⟨The boat stayed *afloat* through the storm.⟩

aflut•ter \ə-'flə-tər\ *adj*
1 flapping quickly ⟨The flags were *aflutter* in the breeze.⟩
2 very excited and nervous

afoot \ə-'fůt\ *adv or adj*
1 on foot ⟨traveled *afoot*⟩
2 happening now : going on ⟨We sensed that there was trouble *afoot.*⟩

afore•men•tioned \ə-'fȯr-,men-chənd\ *adj*
mentioned before ⟨The *aforementioned* book is my favorite.⟩

afore•said \ə-'fȯr-,sed\ *adj*
named before ⟨the *aforesaid* persons⟩

afraid \ə-'frād\ *adj*
1 filled with fear ⟨She was *afraid* of snakes.⟩
2 filled with concern or regret ⟨I'm *afraid* I won't be able to go.⟩
3 having a dislike for something ⟨They're not *afraid* to work hard.⟩

afresh \ə-'fresh\ *adv*
again from the beginning ⟨Let's start *afresh.*⟩

[1]Af•ri•can \'a-fri-kən\ *n*
a person born or living in Africa

[2]African *adj*
of or relating to Africa or African people ⟨*African* history⟩ ⟨*African* wildlife⟩

African–American *n*
an American having African and especially black African ancestors
African–American *adj*

African violet *n*
▼ a tropical African plant often grown for its showy white, pink, or purple flowers and its velvety leaves

African violet

Af•ro–Amer•i•can \,a-frō-ə-'mer-ə-kən\ *n*
AFRICAN–AMERICAN
Afro–American *adj*

aft \'aft\ *adv*
toward or at the back part of a ship or the tail of an aircraft ⟨We stood on the ship's deck facing *aft.*⟩

[1]af•ter \'af-tər\ *adv*
following in time or place : at a later time ⟨He ate and left immediately *after.*⟩

[2]after *prep*
1 behind in time or place ⟨They got there *after* me.⟩ ⟨*after* lunch⟩
2 for the reason of catching, seizing, or getting ⟨Run *after* the ball.⟩ ⟨They're going *after* the championship.⟩
3 following in order or in a series ⟨The number 20 comes before 21 and *after* 19.⟩
4 following the actions or departure of ⟨Don't expect me to clean up *after* you.⟩
5 with the name of ⟨He's named *after* his father.⟩

[3]after *conj*
following the time when ⟨I opened the door *after* she knocked.⟩

af•ter•ef•fect \'af-tər-ə-,fekt\ *n*
an effect that follows its cause after some time has passed

af•ter•glow \'af-tər-,glō\ *n*
1 a glow remaining (as in the sky after sunset) where a light has disappeared
2 a pleasant feeling that remains after some good experience ⟨the *afterglow* of victory⟩

af•ter•life \'af-tər-,līf\ *n*
an existence after death

af•ter•math \'af-tər-,math\ *n*
1 a result or consequence ⟨She felt tired as an *aftermath* of the long race.⟩
2 the period of time following a bad and usually destructive event ⟨the *aftermath* of a hurricane⟩

af•ter•noon \,af-tər-'nün\ *n*
the part of the day between noon and evening

af•ter•thought \'af-tər-,thȯt\ *n*
something done or said that was not thought of originally ⟨A bow was added to the present as an *afterthought.*⟩

af•ter•ward \'af-tər-wərd\ *or* **af•ter•wards** \-wərdz\ *adv*
at a later time ⟨He found out the truth long *afterward.*⟩

again \ə-'gen\ *adv*
1 for another time : once more ⟨did it *again*⟩
2 on the other hand ⟨You might, but then *again*, you might not.⟩
3 in addition ⟨half as much *again*⟩

against \ə-'genst\ *prep*
1 opposed to ⟨Everyone was *against* her idea.⟩
2 not agreeing with or allowed by ⟨*against* the law⟩
3 as protection from ⟨We built a shelter *against* the cold.⟩
4 in or into contact with ⟨The ball bounced *against* the wall.⟩
5 in a direction opposite to ⟨*against* the wind⟩
6 before the background of ⟨green trees *against* a blue sky⟩

agape \ə-ˈgāp\ *adj*
having the mouth open in wonder, surprise, or shock ⟨He stood there with mouth *agape.*⟩

ag•ate \ˈa-gət\ *n*
▶ a mineral that is a form of quartz with colors arranged in stripes or patches and that is used especially in jewelry

aga•ve \ə-ˈgä-vē\ *n*
▼ a plant that has sword-shaped leaves with spiny edges and is sometimes grown for its large stalks of flowers

agave

[1]age \ˈāj\ *n*
1 the amount of time during which someone or something has lived or existed ⟨The child was six years of *age.*⟩
2 the time of life when a person receives some right or capacity ⟨The voting *age* is 18.⟩
3 the later part of life ⟨His mind was active in *age* as in youth.⟩
4 the condition of being old ⟨The building is showing signs of *age.*⟩
5 a period of time associated with a person or thing ⟨the *age* of dinosaurs⟩
6 a long period of time ⟨It's been *ages* since we last saw you.⟩
synonyms see PERIOD

[2]age *vb* **aged** \ˈājd\; **ag•ing** *or* **age•ing**
1 to become old or older ⟨As he *aged,* he grew more forgetful.⟩
2 to cause to become old or to appear to be old ⟨Her troubles have *aged* her.⟩
3 to remain or cause to remain undisturbed until fit for use : MATURE ⟨The cheese must *age.*⟩

-age \ij\ *n suffix*
1 total amount : collection ⟨mile*age*⟩
2 action : process ⟨cover*age*⟩
3 result of ⟨coin*age*⟩
4 rate of ⟨shrink*age*⟩
5 house or place of ⟨orphan*age*⟩
6 state : condition ⟨block*age*⟩
7 fee : charge ⟨post*age*⟩

aged \ˈā-jəd *for 1,* ˈājd *for 2*\ *adj*
1 very old ⟨an *aged* oak⟩ ⟨an *aged* man⟩

agate

2 having reached a specified age ⟨a child *aged* ten⟩

age•less \ˈāj-ləs\ *adj*
1 not growing old or showing the effects of age ⟨an *ageless* face⟩
2 lasting forever : TIMELESS ⟨an *ageless* story⟩

agen•cy \ˈā-jən-sē\ *n, pl* **agen•cies**
1 a person or thing through which power is used or something is achieved ⟨Through the *agency* of his former school, he reunited with some old friends.⟩
2 a business that provides a particular service ⟨an advertising *agency*⟩
3 a part of a government that is responsible for providing a particular service or performing a specific function ⟨law enforcement *agencies*⟩

agen•da \ə-ˈjen-də\ *n*
a list of things to be done or talked about

agent \ˈā-jənt\ *n*
1 something that produces an effect ⟨cleansing *agents*⟩
2 a person who acts or does business for another ⟨a travel *agent*⟩

ag•gra•vate \ˈa-grə-ˌvāt\ *vb* **ag•gra•vat•ed; ag•gra•vat•ing**
1 to make worse or more serious ⟨*aggravate* an injury⟩ ⟨Don't *aggravate* an already bad situation.⟩
2 to make angry usually by bothering again and again ⟨All of these delays really *aggravate* me.⟩

ag•gra•va•tion \ˌa-grə-ˈvā-shən\ *n*
1 an act or the result of making worse or more serious ⟨All that walking resulted in *aggravation* of an existing knee injury.⟩
2 something that annoys or bothers someone

[1]ag•gre•gate \ˈa-gri-ˌgāt\ *vb* **ag•gre•gat•ed; ag•gre•gat•ing**
to collect or gather into a mass or whole ⟨The particles of sand *aggregated* into giant dunes.⟩

[2]ag•gre•gate \ˈa-gri-gət\ *n*
1 a mass or body of units or parts ⟨The rock is an *aggregate* of several minerals.⟩
2 the whole sum or amount ⟨They won by an *aggregate* of 30 points.⟩

ag•gre•ga•tion \ˌa-gri-ˈgā-shən\ *n*
1 the collecting of units or parts into a mass or whole ⟨The formation of a blood clot begins with the *aggregation* of platelets.⟩
2 a group, body, or mass composed of many distinct parts ⟨A galaxy is an *aggregation* of stars, gas, and dust.⟩

ag•gres•sion \ə-ˈgre-shən\ *n*
1 angry or violent behavior or feelings ⟨Young children must learn to use words rather than physical *aggression.*⟩
2 hostile action made without reasonable cause ⟨military *aggression*⟩

ag•gres•sive \ə-ˈgre-siv\ *adj*
1 showing a readiness to fight or argue ⟨an *aggressive* dog⟩ ⟨*aggressive* behavior⟩
2 engaging in hostile action without reasonable cause ⟨an *aggressive* nation⟩
3 being forceful in getting things done ⟨an overly *aggressive* salesperson⟩
ag•gres•sive•ly *adv*
ag•gres•sive•ness *n*

ag•gres•sor \ə-ˈgre-sər\ *n*
a person or a country that engages in hostile action without reasonable cause

ag•grieved \ə-ˈgrēvd\ *adj*
1 having or showing a troubled or unhappy mind ⟨She answered with an *aggrieved* tone.⟩
2 having cause for complaint especially from unfair treatment ⟨The judge ordered payment to the *aggrieved* party.⟩

aghast \ə-ˈgast\ *adj*
struck with terror, surprise, or horror ⟨The news left her *aghast.*⟩

ag•ile \ˈa-jəl\ *adj*
1 able to move quickly and easily ⟨an *agile* athlete⟩
2 having a quick mind ⟨an *agile* thinker⟩
ag•ile•ly *adv*

agil•i•ty \ə-ˈji-lə-tē\ *n*
the ability to move quickly and easily

aging *present participle of* AGE

ag•i•tate \ˈa-jə-ˌtāt\ *vb* **ag•i•tat•ed; ag•i•tat•ing**
1 to move or stir up ⟨The water was *agitated* by wind.⟩
2 to disturb, excite, or anger ⟨She was *agitated* by the bad news.⟩
3 to try to stir up public feeling ⟨*agitate* for change⟩
ag•i•ta•tor \-tā-tər\ *n*

ag•i•ta•tion \ˌa-jə-ˈtā-shən\ *n*
the act of agitating : the state of being agitated ⟨*agitation* of the water's surface⟩ ⟨He spoke with increasing *agitation* about the situation.⟩

aglow \ə-ˈglō\ *adj*
1 glowing with light or color ⟨The room was *aglow* with candlelight.⟩
2 feeling or showing excitement and happiness ⟨Her parents were *aglow* with pride.⟩

ago \ə-ˈgō\ *adv*
before this time ⟨a week *ago*⟩

agog \ə-ˈgäg\ *adj*
full of excitement ⟨The children were all *agog* over their new toys.⟩

ag•o•nize \ˈa-gə-ˌnīz\ *vb* **ag•o•nized**; **ag•o•niz•ing**
to think or worry very much about something

ag•o•ny \ˈa-gə-nē\ *n, pl* **ag•o•nies**
great physical pain or emotional distress

agree \ə-ˈgrē\ *vb* **agreed**; **agree•ing**
1 to give approval or permission ⟨*agree* to a plan⟩
2 to have the same opinion ⟨We don't *agree* about everything.⟩
3 ADMIT 1 ⟨He finally *agreed* that I was right.⟩
4 to be alike ⟨Their stories don't *agree*.⟩
5 to come to an understanding ⟨They *agreed* on a price.⟩
6 to be fitting or healthful ⟨The climate *agrees* with you.⟩

agree•able \ə-ˈgrē-ə-bəl\ *adj*
1 pleasing to the mind or senses ⟨an *agreeable* taste⟩
2 willing to do, allow, or approve something ⟨She's *agreeable* to my idea.⟩
3 of a kind that can be accepted ⟨Is the schedule *agreeable*?⟩
agree•ably \-blē\ *adv*

agree•ment \ə-ˈgrē-mənt\ *n*
1 the act or fact of having the same opinion or an understanding ⟨There is widespread *agreement* on the matter.⟩
2 the act or fact of giving approval or permission ⟨Any changes to the rules require the *agreement* of all the players.⟩
3 an arrangement by which people agree about what is to be done

ag•ri•cul•tur•al \ˌa-gri-ˈkəl-chə-rəl, -ˈkəlch-rəl\ *adj*
relating to or used in farming or agriculture ⟨*agricultural* land⟩

ag•ri•cul•ture \ˈa-gri-ˌkəl-chər\ *n*
▼ the cultivating of the soil, producing of crops, and raising of livestock

aground \ə-ˈgrau̇nd\ *adv or adj*
on or onto the shore or the bottom of a body of water ⟨The ship ran *aground* during the storm.⟩

aha \ä-ˈhä\ *interj*
used to express discovery or understanding ⟨*Aha*! I knew it was you!⟩

ahead \ə-ˈhed\ *adv or adj*
1 in or toward the front ⟨The road stretched *ahead* for many miles.⟩
2 into or for the future ⟨You should think *ahead*.⟩

ahead of *prep*
1 in front of ⟨He stood *ahead of* me in line.⟩
2 earlier than ⟨They arrived *ahead of* us.⟩
3 having a lead over ⟨The other team is *ahead of* us by two points.⟩

ahoy \ə-ˈhȯi\ *interj*
used in calling out to a passing ship or boat ⟨Ship *ahoy*!⟩

[1]aid \ˈād\ *vb* **aid•ed**; **aid•ing**
to provide what is useful or necessary : HELP

[2]aid *n*
1 the act of helping
2 help given ⟨The teacher sought the *aid* of several students for the project.⟩
3 someone or something that is of help or assistance ⟨The compass is an *aid* to navigation.⟩

aide \ˈād\ *n*
a person who acts as an assistant ⟨a teacher's *aide*⟩

AIDS \ˈādz\ *n*
a serious disease of the human immune system in which large numbers of the cells that help the body fight infection are destroyed by the HIV virus carried in the blood and other fluids of the body

AIDS virus *n*
HIV

agriculture
People have grown crops and raised animals for thousands of years all over the world. Today, some of the main agricultural products of the US are cow's milk, corn, and soybeans.

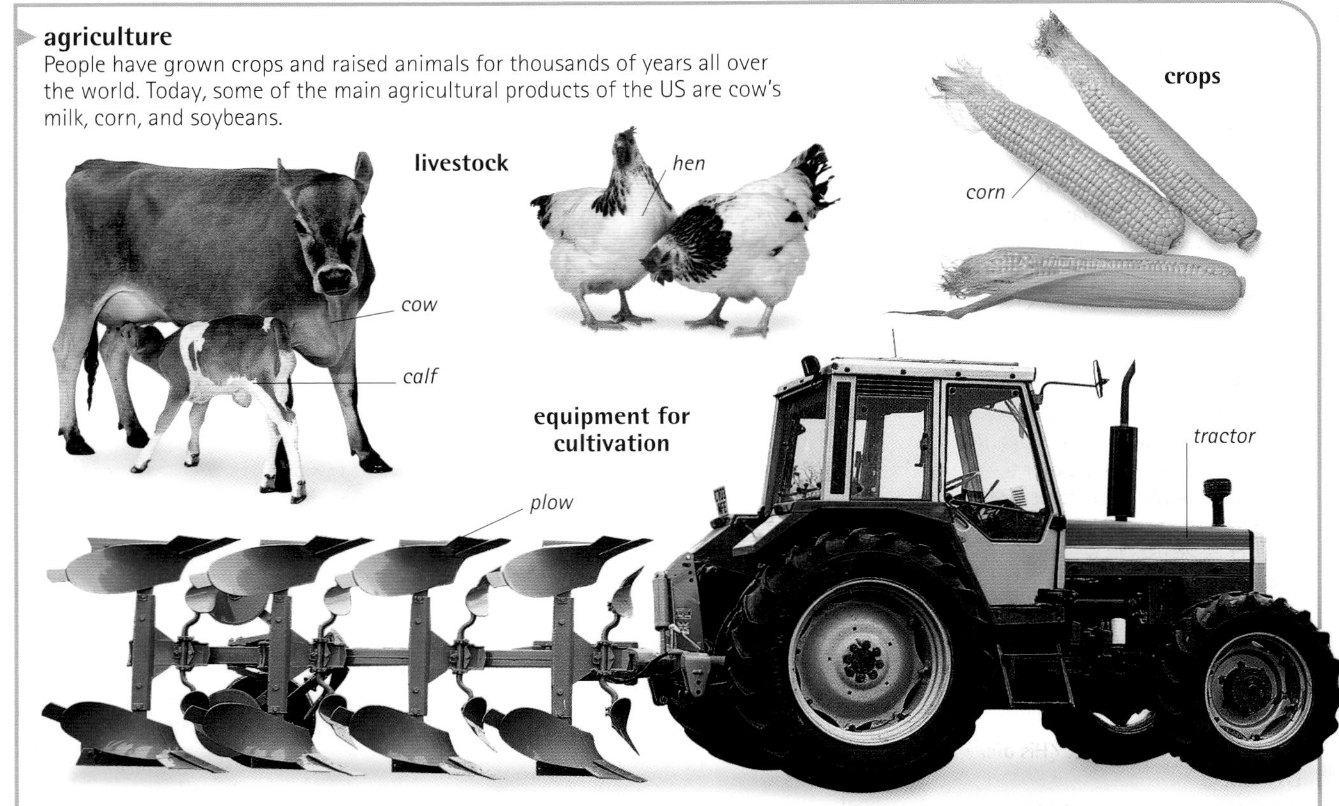

ail \'āl\ *vb* **ailed**; **ail•ing**
1 to be wrong with ⟨What *ails* you?⟩
2 to suffer especially with ill health ⟨She has been *ailing* for years.⟩

ail•ment \'āl-mənt\ *n*
a sickness or disease

¹aim \'ām\ *vb* **aimed**; **aim•ing**
1 to point a weapon toward an object
2 INTEND ⟨We *aim* to please.⟩
3 to direct toward an object or goal ⟨He *aimed* the stone at the tree.⟩ ⟨The exercise is *aimed* at improving balance.⟩

▶ **Word History** Both *aim* and *estimate* come from a Latin verb *aestimare*, meaning "to value" or "to estimate." Through sound changes over the centuries *aestimare* became in Old French *esmer*, which meant "to aim, direct, or adjust," as well as "to appreciate" and "to estimate." English borrowed the word *aim* from the Old French word, and then took the word *estimate* directly from Latin.

²aim *n*
1 the ability to hit a target ⟨His *aim* was excellent.⟩
2 the pointing of a weapon at a target ⟨She took careful *aim*.⟩
3 a goal or purpose ⟨Our *aim* is to win.⟩

aim•less \'ām-ləs\ *adj*
lacking a goal or purpose ⟨an *aimless* existence⟩ ⟨*aimless* conversations⟩
aim•less•ly *adv*

ain't \'ānt\
1 am not : are not : is not
2 have not : has not
Hint: Most people feel that *ain't* is not proper English. When you are trying to speak or write your best, you should avoid using *ain't*. Most people who use *ain't* use it especially when they are talking in a casual way, or in familiar expressions like "you *ain't* seen nothing yet." Authors use it especially when a character is talking to help you understand what the character is like.

¹air \'er\ *n*
1 the invisible mixture of odorless tasteless gases that surrounds the earth
2 the space or sky that is filled with air ⟨The balloon rose up into the *air*.⟩
3 air that is compressed ⟨I filled the car's tires with *air*.⟩
4 outward appearance : a quality that a person or thing has ⟨He has an *air* of mystery about him.⟩
5 AIRCRAFT ⟨travel by *air*⟩
6 AVIATION 1
7 a radio or television broadcast ⟨He gave a speech on the *air*.⟩
8 *airs pl* an artificial way of acting ⟨put on *airs*⟩

²air *vb* **aired**; **air•ing**
1 to place in the air for cooling, freshening, or cleaning ⟨*air* blankets⟩
2 to make known in public ⟨*air* complaints⟩

air bag *n*
an automobile safety device consisting of a bag that inflates to cushion a rider in an accident

air base *n*
a base for military aircraft

air•borne \'er-ˌbȯrn\ *adj*
moving through the air ⟨*airborne* dust particles⟩ ⟨The plane was *airborne*.⟩

air–con•di•tion \ˌer-kən-'dish-ən\ *vb* **air–con•di•tioned**; **air–con•di•tion•ing**
to equip with a device for cleaning air and controlling its humidity and temperature
air con•di•tion•er *n*
air–con•di•tion•ing *n*

air•craft \'er-ˌkraft\ *n, pl* **aircraft**
▲ a vehicle (as an airplane or helicopter) that can travel through the air and that is supported either by its own lightness or by the action of the air against its surfaces

airport
The buildings of a large international airport are like a city. The main terminal contains an area for passengers checking in, baggage handling facilities, shops, and restaurants. Passengers wait for flights near the arrival and departure gates.

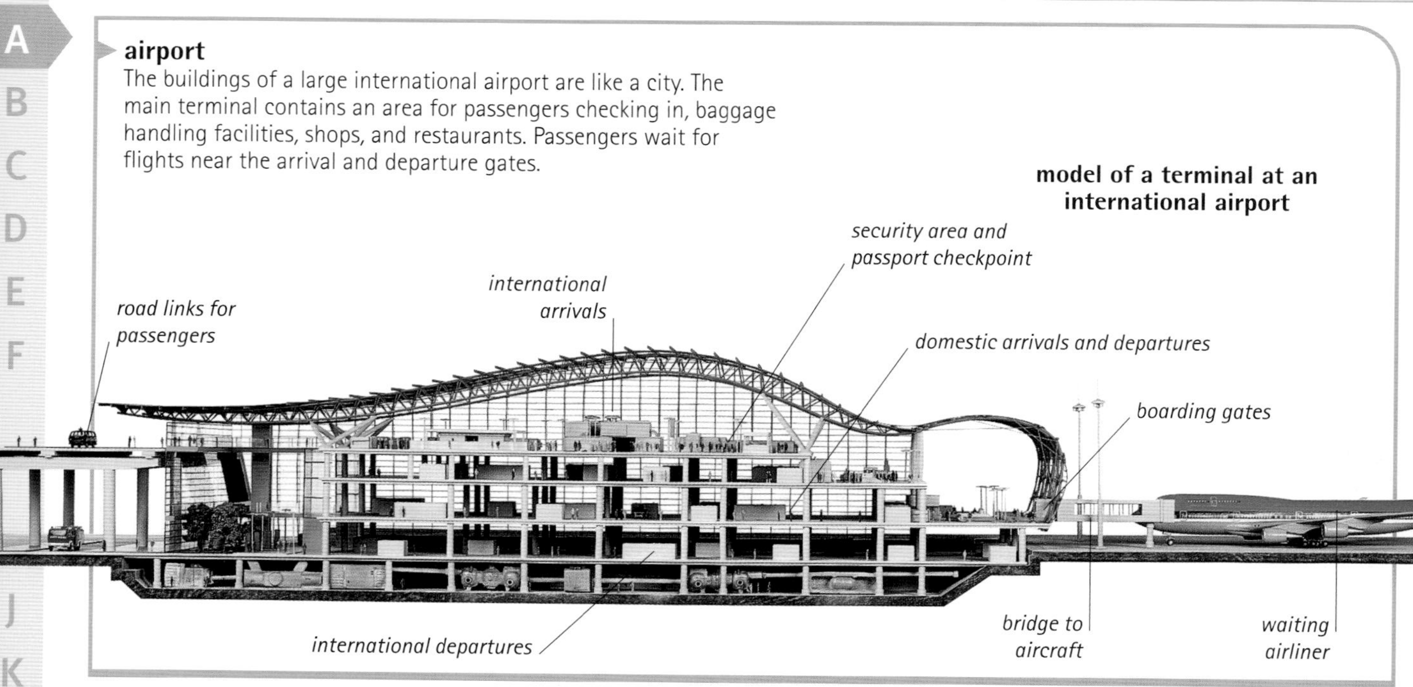

air•field \'er-ˌfēld\ *n*
a field or airport where airplanes take off and land

air force *n*
the military organization of a nation for air warfare

air•lift \'er-ˌlift\ *vb* **air•lift•ed**; **air•lift•ing**
to move people or cargo by aircraft usually to or from an area that cannot be reached otherwise ⟨Food was *airlifted* to the earthquake victims.⟩
airlift *n*

air•line \'er-ˌlīn\ *n*
a company that owns and operates many airplanes which are used for carrying passengers and cargo to different places

air•lin•er \'er-ˌlī-nər\ *n*
a large airplane used for carrying passengers

[1]**air•mail** \'er-'māl\ *n*
1 the system of carrying mail by airplanes
2 mail carried by airplanes

[2]**airmail** *vb* **air•mailed**; **air•mail•ing**
to send by airmail

air•man \'er-mən\ *n, pl* **air•men** \-mən\
1 an enlisted person in the air force in one of the ranks below sergeant
2 [1]PILOT 1, AVIATOR

airman basic *n*
an enlisted person of the lowest rank in the air force

airman first class *n*
an enlisted person in the air force ranking just below that of sergeant

air•plane \'er-ˌplān\ *n*
an aircraft with wings which do not move, that is heavier than air, is driven by a propeller or jet engine, and is supported by the action of the air against its wings

air•port \'er-ˌpȯrt\ *n*
▲ a place where aircraft land and take off and where there are usually buildings for passengers to wait in and for aircraft and equipment to be kept

air sac *n*
one of the small pouches in the lungs where oxygen and carbon dioxide are exchanged

air•ship \'er-ˌship\ *n*
an aircraft lighter than air that is kept in the air by one or more compartments filled with gas and that has an engine and steering

air•strip \'er-ˌstrip\ *n*
a runway without places (as hangars) for the repair of aircraft or shelter of passengers or cargo

air•tight \'er-'tīt\ *adj*
so tightly sealed that no air can get in or out ⟨Store the cookies in an *airtight* container.⟩

air•wave \'er-ˌwāv\ *n*
the radio waves used to broadcast radio and television programs — usually used in pl.

air•way \'er-ˌwā\ *n*
1 the passage through which air moves from the nose or mouth to the lungs in breathing
2 a route along which airplanes regularly fly
3 AIRLINE

airy \'er-ē\ *adj* **air•i•er**; **air•i•est**
1 open to the air : BREEZY ⟨an *airy* room⟩
2 high in the air ⟨the bird's *airy* perch⟩
3 having a light or careless quality that shows a lack of concern
4 like air in lightness and delicacy ⟨*airy* feathers⟩
air•i•ly \'er-ə-lē\ *adv*

aisle \'īl\ *n*
1 a passage between sections of seats (as in a church or theater)
2 a passage between shelves (as in a supermarket)

ajar \ə-'jär\ *adv or adj*
slightly open ⟨I left the door *ajar.*⟩

AK *abbr* Alaska

aka *abbr* also known as

akim•bo \ə-'kim-bō\ *adv or adj*
1 with the hands on the hips and the elbows turned outward ⟨She stood with arms *akimbo.*⟩
2 set in a bent position ⟨He sat with legs *akimbo.*⟩

akin \ə-'kin\ *adj*
1 related by blood ⟨They discovered that they were *akin*—cousins, in fact.⟩
2 SIMILAR ⟨Your hobbies are *akin* to mine.⟩

AL *abbr* Alabama

[1]**-al** \əl, l\ *adj suffix*
of, relating to, or showing ⟨fiction*al*⟩

[2]-al *n suffix*
action : process 〈rehears*al*〉

Ala. *abbr* Alabama

al•a•bas•ter \'a-lə-,ba-stər\ *n*
a smooth usually white stone used for carving

à•la•carte \,ä-lə-'kärt, ,a-lə-\ *adv or adj*
with a separate price for each item on the menu 〈an *à la carte* dinner〉

alac•ri•ty \ə-'la-krə-tē\ *n*
a cheerful readiness to do something 〈He accepted the challenge with *alacrity.*〉

[1]alarm \ə-'lärm\ *n*
1 a warning of danger 〈The dog's barking gave the *alarm.*〉
2 a device (as a bell) that warns or signals people 〈a car *alarm*〉
3 ALARM CLOCK 〈Set the *alarm* for six o'clock.〉
4 the feeling of fear caused by a sudden sense of danger 〈She was filled with *alarm* on hearing the crash downstairs.〉

[2]alarm *vb* **alarmed**; **alarm•ing**
to cause to feel a sense of danger : worry or frighten

alarm clock *n*
▶ a clock that can be set to sound an alarm at a desired time

alas \ə-'las\ *interj*
used to express unhappiness, pity, disappointment, or worry 〈*Alas*, it was too late!〉

al•ba•tross \'al-bə-,tròs\ *n*
a very large seabird with webbed feet

al•be•it \òl-'bē-ət\ *conj*
even though : ALTHOUGH 〈The movie was entertaining, *albeit* long.〉

al•bi•no \al-'bī-nō\ *n, pl* **al•bi•nos**
1 ▼ a person or an animal that has little or no coloring matter in skin, hair, and eyes
2 a plant with little or no coloring matter

albino 1

al•bum \'al-bəm\ *n*
1 a book with blank pages in which to put a collection (as of photographs, stamps, or autographs)
2 one or more recordings (as on tape or disk) produced as a single collection

al•bu•men \al-'byü-mən\ *n*
1 the white of an egg
2 ALBUMIN

al•bu•min \al-'byü-mən\ *n*
any of various proteins that dissolve in water and occur in blood, the whites of eggs, and in plant and animal tissues

al•che•my \'al-kə-mē\ *n*
a science that was used in the Middle Ages with the goal of changing ordinary metals into gold

al•co•hol \'al-kə-,hòl\ *n*
1 a colorless flammable liquid that in one form is the substance in liquors (as beer, wine, or whiskey) that can make a person drunk
2 a drink containing alcohol

alarm clock

[1]al•co•hol•ic \,al-kə-'hò-lik, -'hä-\ *adj*
1 of, relating to, or containing alcohol 〈*alcoholic* drinks〉
2 affected with alcoholism

[2]alcoholic *n*
a person affected with alcoholism

al•co•hol•ism \'al-kə-,hò-,liz-əm\ *n*
continued, uncontrolled, and greater than normal use of alcoholic drinks accompanied by physical and mental dependence on alcohol

al•cove \'al-,kōv\ *n*
a small part of a room set back from the rest of it

al•der \'òl-dər\ *n*
a shrub or small tree that is related to the birch and usually grows in moist soil (as near a river or pond)

al•der•man \'òl-dər-mən\ *n*
a member of a lawmaking body in a city

ale \'āl\ *n*
an alcoholic drink made from malt and flavored with hops that is usually more bitter than beer

[1]alert \ə-'lərt\ *adj*
1 watchful and ready especially to meet danger
2 quick to understand and act 〈An *alert* reader noticed the error in grammar.〉
alert•ly *adv*
alert•ness *n*

[2]alert *n*
1 an alarm or signal of danger 〈The police issued an *alert.*〉
2 the period during which an alert is in effect 〈We stayed indoors during the *alert.*〉
on the alert watchful against danger

[3]alert *vb* **alert•ed**; **alert•ing**
to make aware of a need to get ready or take action : WARN 〈The siren *alerted* us that a tornado was approaching.〉

al•fal•fa \al-'fal-fə\ *n*
▶ a plant with purple flowers that is related to the clovers and is grown as a food for horses and cattle

alfalfa flowers

al•ga \'al-gə\ *n, pl* **al•gae** \'al-,jē\
▼ any of a large group of simple plants and plant-like organisms (as a seaweed) that usually grow in water and produce chlorophyll like plants but do not produce seeds

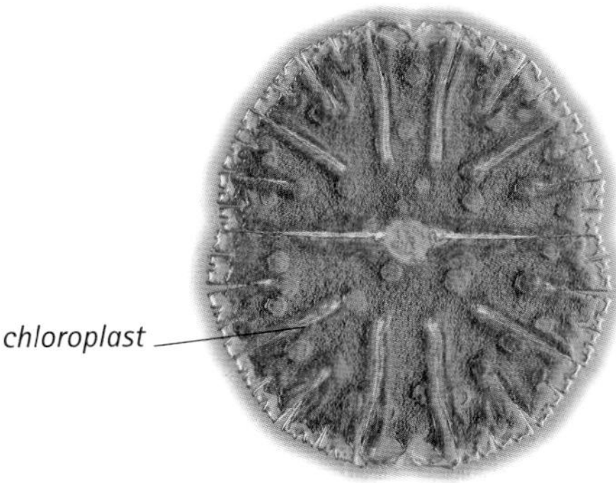

alga: magnified view of a single-celled green alga

al•ge•bra \'al-jə-brə\ *n*
▼ a branch of mathematics in which symbols (as letters and numbers) are combined according to the rules of arithmetic

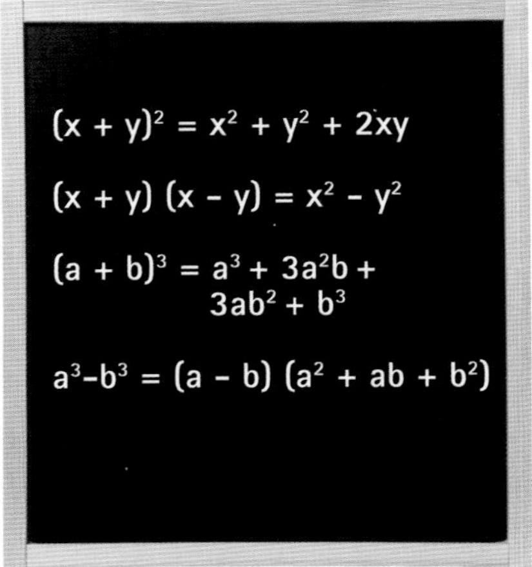

algebra:
calculations in algebra

Al•gon•qui•an \al-'gän-kwē-ən\ *or* **Al•gon•quin** \-kwən\ *n*
1 a group of American Indian people of southeastern Ontario and southern Quebec or their language
Hint: The word is usually *Algonquin* in this sense.
2 a family of American Indian languages spoken by people from Newfoundland and Labrador to North Carolina and westward into the Great Plains
3 a member of the group of people speaking Algonquian languages
Hint: The word is usually *Algonquian* in senses 2 and 3.

[1]ali•as \'ā-lē-əs\ *adv*
otherwise known as ⟨Samuel Clemens, *alias* Mark Twain, wrote many stories about life on the Mississippi.⟩

[2]alias *n*
a false name ⟨The criminal used several *aliases*.⟩

al•i•bi \'a-lə-,bī\ *n, pl* **al•i•bis**
1 the explanation given by a person accused of a crime that he or she was somewhere else when the crime was committed
2 an excuse intended to avoid blame ⟨She made up an *alibi* for why she was late.⟩

[1]alien \'ā-lē-ən, 'āl-yən\ *adj*
1 different from what is familiar ⟨Keeping their hands clean was an *alien* idea to the young boys.⟩
2 from another country and not a citizen of the country of residence : FOREIGN ⟨an *alien* resident⟩
3 from somewhere other than the planet earth ⟨an *alien* spaceship⟩

[2]alien *n*
1 a resident who was born elsewhere and is not a citizen of the country in which he or she now lives
2 a being that comes from somewhere other than the planet earth

alien•ate \'ā-lē-ə-,nāt, 'āl-yə-\ *vb* **alien•at•ed**; **alien•at•ing**
to cause (a person who used to be friendly or loyal) to become unfriendly or disloyal

[1]alight \ə-'līt\ *vb* **alight•ed**; **alight•ing**
1 to get down : DISMOUNT ⟨The riders *alighted* from their horses.⟩
2 to come down from the air and settle ⟨Butterflies *alighted* on the flowers.⟩

[2]alight *adj*
full of light : lighted up ⟨The sky was *alight* with stars.⟩ ⟨His face was *alight* with excitement.⟩

align \ə-'līn\ *vb* **aligned**; **align•ing**
to arrange things so that they form a line or are in proper position ⟨He *aligned* the two holes so he could put the screw through them.⟩

align•ment \ə-'līn-mənt\ *n*
▼ the state of being arranged in a line or in proper position ⟨The machine was not working properly because its parts were out of *alignment*.⟩

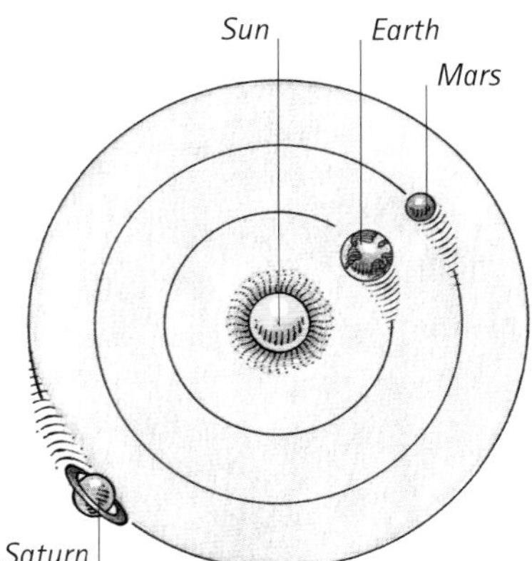

alignment: a diagram showing the alignment of the Earth and Mars on one side of the Sun and the planet Saturn on the other

[1]alike \ə-'līk\ *adv*
in the same way ⟨The two friends think *alike*.⟩

[2]alike *adj*
being like each other : similar in appearance, nature, or form ⟨All the shapes are *alike*.⟩

al•i•men•ta•ry canal \,a-lə-'men-tə-rē-, -'men-trē-\ *n*
DIGESTIVE TRACT

alimentary tract *n*
DIGESTIVE TRACT

al•i•mo•ny \'a-lə-,mō-nē\ *n*
money for living expenses paid regularly by one spouse to another after their legal separation or divorce

alive \ə-'līv\ *adj*
1 having life : not dead
2 still in force, existence, or operation ⟨The thought kept our hopes *alive*.⟩ ⟨They keep the old traditions *alive*.⟩
3 aware of the existence of ⟨He was *alive* to the danger.⟩
4 filled with life and activity ⟨The city streets were *alive* with shoppers.⟩

al•ka•li \'al-kə-,lī\ *n, pl* **al•ka•lies** *or* **al•ka•lis**
1 a substance that has a bitter taste and reacts with an acid to form a salt : BASE
2 a salt or a mixture of salts sometimes found in large amounts in the soil of dry regions

al•ka•line \'al-kə-,līn, -lən\ *adj*
1 having the properties of an alkali ⟨*alkaline* solutions⟩
2 containing an alkali ⟨Some plants grow better in *alkaline* soils.⟩

al•ka•lin•i•ty \,al-kə-'li-nə-tē\ *n*
the quality, state, or degree of being alkaline

[1]all \'ȯl\ *adj*
1 every one of ⟨*All* students can go.⟩
2 the whole of ⟨He sat up *all* night.⟩
3 the whole number of ⟨after *all* these years⟩
4 any whatever ⟨beyond *all* doubt⟩
5 the greatest possible ⟨Her story was told in *all* seriousness.⟩

[2]all *adv*
1 COMPLETELY ⟨He sat *all* alone.⟩ ⟨I'm *all* finished.⟩
2 so much ⟨He is *all* the better for being put in another class.⟩
3 [1]VERY 1 ⟨The child was *all* excited.⟩
4 for each side ⟨The score is two *all*.⟩

[3]all *pron*
1 the whole number or amount ⟨I ate *all* of the candy.⟩
2 EVERYTHING ⟨*All* is lost.⟩
3 the only thing ⟨*All* I know is I'm done.⟩

Al•lah \'ä-lə, ä-'lä\ *n*
God as named in Islam

all–around \,ȯl-ə-'rau̇nd\ *also* **all–round** \'ȯl-'rau̇nd\ *adj*
1 having many good aspects ⟨an *all-around* good neighbor⟩
2 skillful or useful in many ways ⟨an *all-around* athlete⟩

al•lay \ə-'lā\ *vb* **al•layed**; **al•lay•ing**
1 to make less severe ⟨*allay* pain⟩
2 to put to rest ⟨*allay* fears⟩

all but *adv*
very nearly : ALMOST

al•le•ga•tion \ˌa-li-ˈgā-shən\ *n*
a statement that usually accuses someone of wrongdoing often without proof

al•lege \ə-ˈlej\ *vb* **al•leged; al•leg•ing**
to state as fact but without proof

al•le•giance \ə-ˈlē-jəns\ *n*
loyalty and service to a group, country, or idea 〈I pledge *allegiance* to my country.〉
synonyms see LOYALTY

al•le•lu•ia \ˌa-lə-ˈlü-yə\ *interj*
HALLELUJAH

al•ler•gen \ˈa-lər-jən\ *n*
▶ a substance that causes an allergic reaction

al•ler•gic \ə-ˈlər-jik\ *adj*
of, relating to, causing, or affected by allergy 〈*allergic* to peanuts〉 〈an *allergic* reaction〉

al•ler•gist \ˈa-lər-jist\ *n*
a medical doctor who specializes in treating allergies

al•ler•gy \ˈa-lər-jē\ *n, pl* **al•ler•gies**
a condition in which a person is made sick by something that is harmless to most people

al•le•vi•ate \ə-ˈlē-vē-ˌāt\ *vb* **al•le•vi•at•ed; al•le•vi•at•ing**
to make less painful, difficult, or severe

al•ley \ˈa-lē\ *n, pl* **al•leys**
1 a narrow passageway between buildings
2 a special narrow wooden floor on which balls are rolled in bowling

all fours *n pl*
all four legs of a four-legged animal or both legs and both arms of a person

al•li•ance \ə-ˈlī-əns\ *n*
1 a relationship in which people, groups, or countries agree to work together 〈The environmental groups formed an *alliance.*〉
2 an association of people, groups, or nations working together for a specific purpose 〈the Arts *Alliance*〉

al•lied \ə-ˈlīd, ˈa-ˌlīd\ *adj*
1 being connected or related in some way 〈chemistry and *allied* subjects〉
2 joined in a relationship in which people, groups, or countries work together

al•li•ga•tor \ˈa-lə-ˌgā-tər\ *n*
▶ a large short-legged reptile that has a long body, thick skin, a long broad snout, and sharp teeth and is related to the crocodile and lizards

al•lit•er•a•tion \ə-ˌli-tə-ˈrā-shən\ *n*
the repetition of a sound at the beginning of two or more neighboring words (as in *a babbling brook*)

al•lo•cate \ˈa-lə-ˌkāt\ *vb* **al•lo•cat•ed; al•lo•cat•ing**
1 to divide and give out for a special reason or to particular people or things 〈Funds were *allocated* among the clubs.〉
2 to set apart for a particular purpose 〈Part of the classroom was *allocated* for reading.〉

all•o•sau•rus \ˌa-lə-ˈsȯr-əs\ *n*
a large meat-eating dinosaur related to the tyrannosaur

al•lot \ə-ˈlät\ *vb* **al•lot•ted; al•lot•ting**
to give out as a share or portion 〈She finished the test in the time *allotted.*〉

al•lot•ment \ə-ˈlät-mənt\ *n*
1 the act of giving out as a share or portion 〈His *allotment* of time for a turn was fair.〉
2 an amount of something that is given out as a share or portion

all–out \ˈȯl-ˈau̇t\ *adj*
as great as possible 〈an *all-out* effort〉

al•low \ə-ˈlau̇\ *vb* **al•lowed; al•low•ing**
1 to give permission to 〈Mom *allowed* us to stay up late.〉
2 to fail to prevent 〈Don't *allow* the dog to roam.〉
3 to assign as a share or suitable amount (as of time or money) 〈Mom *allowed* us an hour to play.〉
4 to accept as true : CONCEDE 〈I'm willing to *allow* that he may be right.〉
5 to consider when making a decision or a calculation 〈Our plans didn't *allow* for the possibility of rain.〉
6 to make it possible to have or do something 〈Your shoes should be big enough to *allow* for growth.〉

al•low•able \ə-ˈlau̇-ə-bəl\ *adj*
not forbidden 〈Parking on the street is *allowable* only on weekends.〉

alligator

A B C D E F G H I J K L M N O P Q R S T U V W X Y Z

al•low•ance \ə-ˈlau̇-əns\ *n*
1 an amount of money given regularly for a specific purpose
2 a share given out 〈an *allowance* of time〉
3 the act of considering things that could affect a result

al•loy \ˈa-ˌlȯi, ə-ˈlȯi\ *n*
▼ a substance made of two or more metals melted together

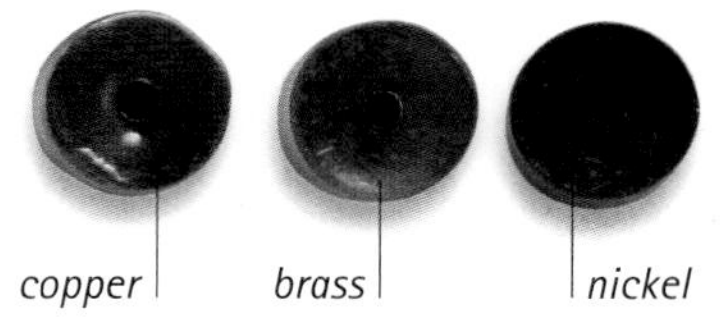

alloy: three metal-plated beads coated with the alloys copper, brass, and nickel

[1]all right *adv*
1 fairly well : well enough 〈She does *all right* in school.〉
2 used to show agreement, acceptance, annoyance, reluctance, pleasure, or excitement 〈Well, *all right*. Go if you must.〉 〈You got the job? *All right*!〉

[2]all right *adj*
1 not ill, hurt, or unhappy : WELL 〈Did you cut yourself? No, I'm *all right*.〉
2 used to tell someone not to be concerned 〈Calm down. Everything is *all right*.〉
3 within acceptable limits of behavior 〈Is it *all right* if I take another cookie?〉
4 suitable or appropriate 〈Is this movie *all right* for children?〉
5 fairly good 〈As an artist, he's *all right*.〉

all–round *variant of* ALL–AROUND

All Saints' Day *n*
November 1 observed as a church holy day in honor of the Christian saints

all–star \ˈȯl-ˈstär\ *adj*
made up mainly or entirely of outstanding participants 〈an *all-star* team〉

all–terrain vehicle *n*
a small open vehicle with three or four wheels for use on rough ground

al•lude \ə-ˈlüd\ *vb* **al•lud•ed**; **al•lud•ing**
to talk about or hint at without mentioning directly 〈The poem *alludes* to a myth.〉

[1]al•lure \ə-ˈlu̇r\ *vb* **al•lured**; **al•lur•ing**
to try to attract or influence by offering what seems to be a benefit or pleasure

[2]allure *n*
power to attract 〈the *allure* of the islands〉

al•lu•sion \ə-ˈlü-zhən\ *n*
a statement that refers to something without mentioning it directly

[1]al•ly \ˈa-ˌlī, ə-ˈlī\ *n, pl* **al•lies**
a person, group, or nation associated or united with another in a common purpose

[2]al•ly \ə-ˈlī, ˈa-ˌlī\ *vb* **al•lied**; **al•ly•ing**
to form a connection between : join in an alliance 〈He *allied* himself with supporters of the new law.〉

al•ma•nac \ˈȯl-mə-ˌnak, ˈal-\ *n*
a book containing a calendar of days, weeks, and months and usually facts about weather and astronomy and information of general interest

al•mighty \ȯl-ˈmī-tē\ *adj, often cap*
having absolute power over all 〈*Almighty* God〉

al•mond \ˈä-mənd, ˈa-\ *n*
a nut that is the edible kernel of a small tree related to the peach tree

al•most \ˈȯl-ˌmōst\ *adv*
only a little less than : very nearly 〈We're *almost* finished.〉

alms \ˈämz, ˈälmz\ *n, pl* **alms**
money given to help the poor : CHARITY

aloft \ə-ˈlȯft\ *adv*
1 at or to a great height 〈Wind carried my balloon *aloft*.〉
2 in the air : in flight
3 at, on, or to the top of the mast or the higher rigging of a ship

[1]alone \ə-ˈlōn\ *adj*
1 separated from others
2 not including anyone or anything else 〈Food *alone* is not enough for health.〉

► **Synonyms** ALONE, SOLITARY, and LONELY mean separated from others. ALONE is used when a person is entirely without company. 〈I was left *alone* in the room.〉 SOLITARY may be used to emphasize the fact of being the only one. 〈The old tree had but a *solitary* apple.〉 LONELY is used when someone longs for company. 〈I felt *lonely* after my friends left.〉

[2]alone *adv*
1 and nothing or no one else 〈You *alone* are responsible.〉
2 without company or help 〈We thought we could do it *alone*.〉

[1]along \ə-ˈlȯŋ\ *prep*
1 on or near in a lengthwise direction 〈Walk *along* the trail.〉
2 at a point on 〈He stopped *along* the way.〉

[2]along *adv*
1 farther forward or on 〈Move *along*.〉
2 as a companion, associate, or useful item 〈I brought a friend *along*.〉
3 at an advanced point 〈The project is pretty well *along*.〉

all along all the time 〈I knew it was you *all along*.〉

[1]along•side \ə-ˈlȯŋ-ˌsīd\ *adv*
along or by the side 〈Walk *alongside* your sister.〉

[2]alongside *prep*
parallel to 〈Bring the boats *alongside* the dock.〉

[1]aloof \ə-ˈlüf\ *adv*
at a distance 〈stood *aloof*〉

[2]aloof *adj*
not friendly or outgoing 〈a shy *aloof* manner〉

aloud \ə-ˈlau̇d\ *adv*
in a voice that can be clearly heard 〈read *aloud*〉

al•paca \al-ˈpa-kə\ *n*
▼ a long-necked South American animal related to the vicuña and llama that is raised for its long woolly hair which is woven into warm strong cloth

al•pha•bet \ˈal-fə-ˌbet\ *n*
the letters used in writing a language arranged in their regular order

al•pha•bet•i•cal \ˌal-fə-ˈbe-ti-kəl\ *or* **al•pha•bet•ic** \-tik\ *adj*
arranged in the order of the letters of the alphabet
— **al•pha•bet•i•cal•ly** *adv*

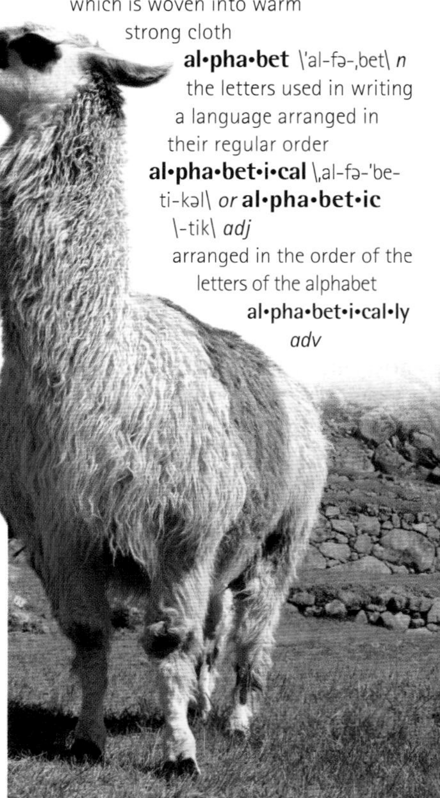

alpaca

al•pha•bet•ize \ˈal-fə-bə-ˌtīz\ *vb* **al•pha•bet•ized**; **al•pha•bet•iz•ing**
to arrange in alphabetical order

al•ready \ȯl-ˈre-dē\ *adv*
1 before a certain time : by this time 〈I had *already* left when you called.〉
2 so soon 〈Are they here *already*?〉

al•so \'ȯl-sō\ *adv*
in addition : TOO

alt. *abbr*
1 alternate
2 altitude

Alta *abbr* Alberta

al•tar \'ȯl-tər\ *n*
1 a platform or table used as a center of worship
2 a usually raised place on which sacrifices are offered

al•ter \'ȯl-tər\ *vb* **al•tered**; **al•ter•ing**
to change partly but not completely
synonyms see CHANGE

al•ter•ation \,ȯl-tə-'rā-shən\ *n*
1 the act or process of changing something ⟨She began *alteration* of the design.⟩
2 the result of changing : MODIFICATION

[1]**al•ter•nate** \'ȯl-tər-nət\ *adj*
1 occurring or following by turns ⟨*alternate* sunshine and rain⟩
2 arranged one above, beside, or next to another ⟨*alternate* layers of cake and filling⟩
3 every other : every second ⟨We meet on *alternate* days.⟩
al•ter•nate•ly *adv*

[2]**al•ter•nate** \'ȯl-tər-,nāt\ *vb* **al•ter•nat•ed**; **al•ter•nat•ing**
to take place or cause to take place by turns ⟨She *alternated* between running and lifting weights.⟩

[3]**al•ter•nate** \'ȯl-tər-nət\ *n*
a person named to take the place of another whenever necessary

alternating current *n*
an electric current that reverses its direction of flow regularly many times per second

al•ter•na•tion \,ȯl-tər-'nā-shən\ *n*
the act, process, or result of taking place by turns ⟨*alternation* of light and dark⟩

[1]**al•ter•na•tive** \ȯl-'tər-nə-tiv\ *adj*
offering or expressing a choice ⟨*alternative* plans⟩
al•ter•na•tive•ly *adv*

[2]**alternative** *n*
1 a chance to choose between two things ⟨I moved, since I had no *alternative*.⟩
2 one of the things between which a choice is to be made ⟨As it got dark, our best *alternative* was to find shelter.⟩

alternative energy *n*
usable power (as heat or electricity) that comes from a renewable or green resource

al•though \ȯl-'t͟hō\ *conj*
1 in spite of the fact that ⟨*Although* you say it, you don't mean it.⟩
2 [1]BUT 1 ⟨I think it's this way, *although* I could be wrong.⟩

al•ti•tude \'al-tə-,tüd, -,tyüd\ *n*
1 height above a certain level and especially above sea level
2 the perpendicular distance from the base of a geometric figure to the vertex or to the side parallel to the base
synonyms see HEIGHT

al•to \'al-tō\ *n, pl* **altos**
1 the lowest female singing voice
2 the second highest part in harmony that has four parts
3 a singer or an instrument having an alto range or part

al•to•geth•er \,ȯl-tə-'ge-t͟hər\ *adv*
1 COMPLETELY ⟨I'm not *altogether* sure.⟩
2 with everything taken into consideration ⟨*Altogether* our school is one of the best.⟩
3 when everything is added together ⟨How much rain will we get *altogether*?⟩

al•um \'a-ləm\ *n*
either of two aluminum compounds that are used especially in medicine (as to stop bleeding)

alu•mi•num \ə-'lü-mə-nəm\ *n*
▼ a silver-white light metallic chemical element that is easily shaped, conducts electricity well, resists weathering, and is the most plentiful metal in the earth's crust

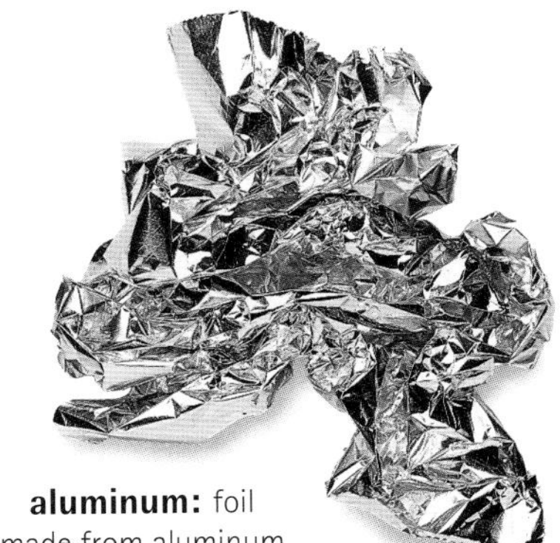
aluminum: foil made from aluminum

alum•na \ə-'ləm-nə\ *n, pl* **alum•nae** \-,nē\
a girl or woman who has attended or has graduated from a school, college, or university

alum•nus \ə-'ləm-nəs\ *n, pl* **alum•ni** \-,nī\
a person who has attended or has graduated from a school, college, or university

al•ways \'ȯl-wēz, -wəz, -wāz\ *adv*
1 at all times ⟨My dad *always* knows the answer.⟩
2 throughout all time : FOREVER ⟨I'll remember it *always*.⟩
3 often, frequently, or repeatedly ⟨People *always* forget my name.⟩

am *present first person sing of* BE

Am. *abbr*
1 America
2 American

a.m., A.M. *abbr* before noon
Hint: The abbreviation *a.m.* is short for the Latin phrase *ante meridiem*, which means "before noon."

amass \ə-'mas\ *vb* **amassed**; **amass•ing**
to collect or gather together ⟨The businessman was able to *amass* a fortune.⟩

[1]**am•a•teur** \'am-ə-,tər, -,chər\ *n*
1 a person who takes part in sports or occupations for pleasure and not for pay
2 a person who takes part in something without having experience or skill in it
am•a•teur•ish \,am-ə-'tər-ish, -'chər-\ *adj*

► **Word History** The English word *amateur* came from a French word which in turn came from a Latin word that meant "lover." In English, amateurs are so called because they do something for the love of doing it and not for pay.

[2]**amateur** *adj*
not professional ⟨*amateur* athletes⟩

amaze \ə-'māz\ *vb* **amazed**; **amaz•ing**
to surprise or puzzle very much ⟨His skill with the ball *amazed* us.⟩
synonyms see SURPRISE

amaze•ment \ə-'māz-mənt\ *n*
great surprise

am•bas•sa•dor \am-'ba-sə-dər\ *n*
a person sent as the chief representative of his or her government in another country
am•bas•sa•dor•ship \-,ship\ *n*

am•ber \'am-bər\ *n*
1 ▼ a hard yellowish to brownish clear substance that is a fossil resin from trees long dead and that can be polished and used in making ornamental objects (as beads)
2 a dark orange yellow : the color of honey

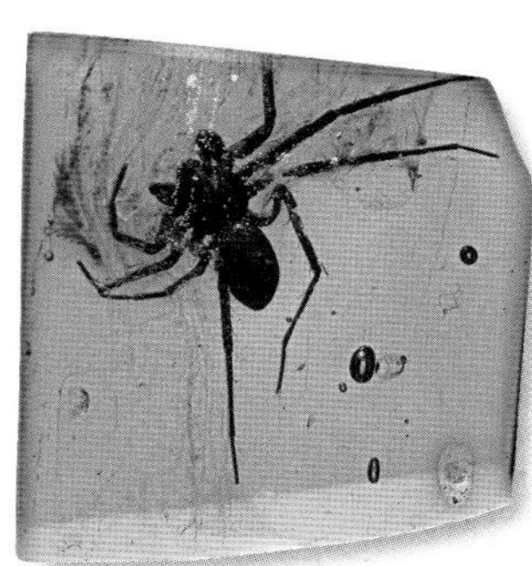
amber 1: amber containing a fossilized spider

a b c d e f g h i j k l m n o p q r s t u v w x y z

A B C D E F G H I J K L M N O P Q R S T U V W X Y Z

ambi- *prefix*
both

am•bi•dex•trous \ˌam-bi-ˈdek-strəs\ *adj*
using both hands with equal ease ⟨an *ambidextrous* basketball player⟩
am•bi•dex•trous•ly *adv*

am•bi•gu•i•ty \ˌam-bə-ˈgyü-ə-tē\ *n*, *pl* **am•bi•gu•i•ties**
something that can be understood in more than one way ⟨The message was filled with confusing *ambiguities.*⟩

am•bi•tious \am-ˈbi-shəs\ *adj*
1 possessing a desire for success, honor, or power
2 not easily done or achieved ⟨She has an *ambitious* plan to become a doctor.⟩
am•bi•tious•ly *adv*

am•ble \ˈam-bəl\ *vb* **am•bled**; **am•bling**
to walk at a slow easy pace

am•bu•lance \ˈam-byə-ləns\ *n*
▼ a vehicle used to carry a sick or injured person

amend•ment \ə-ˈmend-mənt\ *n*
a change in wording or meaning especially in a law, bill, or motion

amends \ə-ˈmendz\ *n pl*
something done or given by a person to make up for a loss or injury he or she has caused ⟨He was sorry for ruining the garden and promised to make *amends.*⟩
Hint: *Amends* can be used as a singular, but is more common as a plural.

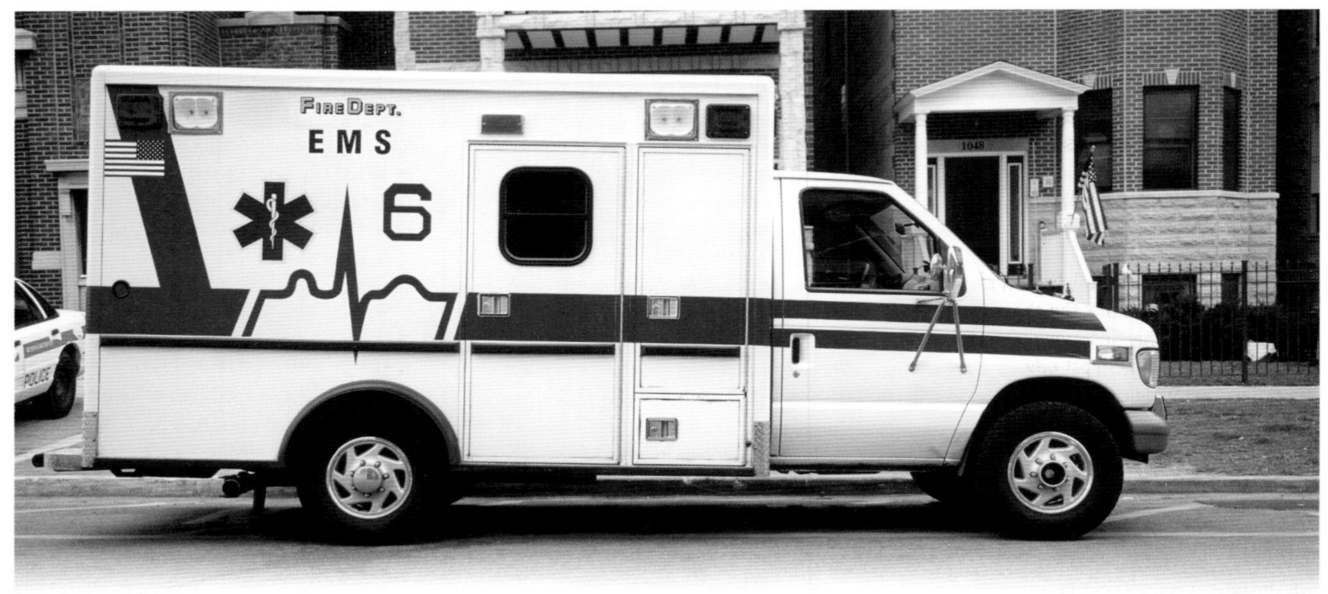

ambulance

am•big•u•ous \am-ˈbi-gyə-wəs\ *adj*
able to be understood in more than one way ⟨an *ambiguous* explanation⟩
am•big•u•ous•ly *adv*

am•bi•tion \am-ˈbi-shən\ *n*
1 a desire for success, honor, or power
2 something a person hopes to do or achieve ⟨My *ambition* is to become a jet pilot.⟩
3 the drive to do things and be active ⟨I'm tired and have no *ambition.*⟩

▶ **Word History** Like the candidates of today, some men ran for public office in ancient Rome by going around and asking people to vote for them. The Latin word for this practice, *ambitio,* came from a verb meaning "to go around." Since looking for votes showed "a desire for power or honor," the Latin word took on that meaning. The English word *ambition* came from the Latin word.

[1]am•bush \ˈam-ˌbu̇sh\ *vb* **am•bushed**; **am•bush•ing**
to attack by surprise from a hidden place

[2]ambush *n*
1 a hidden place from which a surprise attack can be made
2 a surprise attack made from a hidden place

amen \ˈā-ˈmen, ˈä-\ *interj*
1 used at the end of a prayer
2 used to express agreement ⟨When I said we could use a bit of luck, he replied, "*Amen!*"⟩

ame•na•ble \ə-ˈmē-nə-bəl, -ˈme-\ *adj*
readily giving in or agreeing ⟨The builders were *amenable* to our wishes.⟩

amend \ə-ˈmend\ *vb* **amend•ed**; **amend•ing**
1 to change for the better : IMPROVE ⟨He tried to *amend* the situation by apologizing.⟩
2 to change the wording or meaning of : ALTER ⟨Congress voted to *amend* the law.⟩

ame•ni•ty \ə-ˈmen-ə-tē, -ˈmē-\ *n*, *pl* **ame•ni•ties**
1 the quality or characteristic of being pleasant or agreeable
2 *amenities pl* something that makes life easier or more pleasant ⟨Our hotel has many *amenities.*⟩

Amer. *abbr*
1 America
2 American

[1]Amer•i•can \ə-ˈmer-ə-kən\ *n*
1 a citizen of the United States
2 a person born or living in North or South America

[2]American *adj*
1 of or relating to the United States or its citizens
2 of or relating to North or South America or their residents

American Indian *n*
a member of any of the first groups of people to live in North and South America

AmerInd *abbr* American Indian

am•e•thyst \'a-mə-thəst\ *n*
▶ a clear purple or bluish violet quartz used as a gem

amethyst

▶ **Word History** People once believed that amethysts could cure drunkenness. The ancient Greeks gave the stone a name that reflected this belief. The Greek name was formed from a prefix that meant "not" and a verb that meant "to be drunk." This verb came from a Greek word that meant "wine." The English word *amethyst* came from the Greek name for the stone.

ami•a•ble \'ā-mē-ə-bəl\ *adj*
having a friendly and pleasant manner
ami•a•bly \-blē\ *adv*

am•i•ca•ble \'a-mi-kə-bəl\ *adj*
showing kindness or goodwill
am•i•ca•bly \-blē\ *adv*

amid \ə-'mid\ *or* **amidst** \-'midst\ *prep*
in or into the middle of ⟨The champ advanced *amid* cheering crowds.⟩

amid•ships \ə-'mid-,ships\ *adv*
in or near the middle of a ship

ami•no acid \ə-'mē-nō-\ *n*
any of various acids containing carbon and nitrogen that are building blocks of protein and are made by living plant or animal cells or are obtained from the diet

[1]**amiss** \ə-'mis\ *adv*
in the wrong way ⟨Don't take his criticism *amiss.*⟩

[2]**amiss** *adj*
not right : WRONG ⟨I feel certain something is *amiss.*⟩

am•i•ty \'a-mə-tē\ *n*
a feeling of friendship

am•me•ter \'am-,ēt-ər\ *n*
an instrument for measuring electric current in amperes

am•mo•nia \ə-'mō-nyə\ *n*
1 a colorless gas that is a compound of nitrogen and hydrogen, has a sharp smell and taste, can be easily made liquid by cold and pressure, and is used in cleaning products and in making fertilizers and explosives
2 a solution of ammonia and water

am•mu•ni•tion \,am-yə-'ni-shən\ *n*
objects fired from weapons

am•ne•sia \am-'nē-zhə\ *n*
abnormal and usually complete loss of memory

amoe•ba \ə-'mē-bə\ *n, pl* **amoe•bas** *or* **amoe•bae** \-bē\
a tiny water animal that is a single cell which flows about and takes in food

amok *or* **amuck** \ə-'mək, -'mäk\ *adv*
in a wild or uncontrolled manner
Hint: This adverb is usually used in the phrase "run amok" or "run amuck."

among \ə-'məŋ\ *also* **amongst** \-'məŋst\ *prep*
1 in or through the middle of ⟨My ball landed *among* the trees.⟩ ⟨Disease spread *among* members of the class.⟩
2 in the presence of : WITH ⟨You're *among* friends.⟩
3 through all or most of ⟨There is discontent *amongst* voters.⟩
4 in shares to each of ⟨The candy was divided *among* the friends.⟩
5 in the number or group of being considered or compared ⟨*among* the best⟩ ⟨He was *among* her biggest fans.⟩
synonyms see BETWEEN

[1]**amount** \ə-'maùnt\ *vb* **amount•ed**; **amount•ing**
1 to add up ⟨The bill *amounted* to ten dollars.⟩
2 to be the same in meaning or effect ⟨Giving up would *amount* to failure.⟩

[2]**amount** *n*
the total number or quantity

am•pere \'am-,pir\ *n*
a unit for measuring the strength of an electric current

am•per•sand \'am-pər-,sand\ *n*
a character & standing for the word *and*

am•phet•amine \am-'fe-tə-,mēn, -mən\ *n*
a drug that makes the nervous system more active

am•phib•i•an \am-'fi-bē-ən\ *n*
1 ▼ any of a group of cold-blooded vertebrate animals (as frogs and toads) that have gills and live in water as larvae but breathe air as adults
2 an airplane designed to take off from and land on either land or water

am•phib•i•ous \am-'fi-bē-əs\ *adj*
1 able to live both on land and in water ⟨*amphibious* animals⟩
2 meant to be used on both land and water ⟨*amphibious* vehicles⟩
3 made by land, sea, and air forces acting together ⟨*amphibious* attack⟩

amphibian 1
Amphibians have skin that dries out quickly, so many species live in damp conditions. Some, however, have adapted to life in desert habitats.

A B C D E F G H I J K L M N O P Q R S T U V W X Y Z

amphitheater
The ancient Greeks built elegant amphitheaters, where shows were staged for thousands of people. Amphitheaters are still used today for open-air performances in many parts of the world.

am•phi•the•ater \'am-fə-,thē-ə-tər\ *n*
▲ an arena with seats rising in curved rows around an open space

am•ple \'am-pəl\ *adj* **am•pler**; **am•plest**
enough or more than enough of what is needed ⟨*ample* time⟩
am•ply \-plē\ *adv*

am•pli•fi•er \'am-plə-,fī-ər\ *n*
a device that increases the strength of electric signals so that sounds played through an electronic system are louder

am•pli•fy \'am-plə-,fī\ *vb* **am•pli•fied**; **am•pli•fy•ing**
1 to make louder or greater ⟨You can *amplify* your voice by using a megaphone.⟩
2 to give more information about ⟨*amplify* a statement⟩
am•pli•fi•ca•tion \,am-plə-fə-'kā-shən\ *n*

am•pu•tate \'am-pyə-,tāt\ *vb* **am•pu•tat•ed**; **am•pu•tat•ing**
to cut off (a part of a person's body)

amt. *abbr* amount

amuck *variant of* AMOK

am•u•let \'am-yə-lət\ *n*
► a small object worn as a charm against evil

amuse \ə-'myüz\ *vb* **amused**; **amus•ing**
1 to entertain with something pleasant
2 to please the sense of humor of ⟨The children found his silly jokes *amusing*.⟩

► **Synonyms** AMUSE and ENTERTAIN mean to cause the time to pass in an agreeable way. AMUSE is used for holding someone's interest with something that is pleasant or humorous. ⟨The toy *amused* the child for hours.⟩ ENTERTAIN is used vwhen something special is done to provide a person with amusement. ⟨Celebrities *entertained* the troops.⟩

amuse•ment \ə-'myüz-mənt\ *n*
1 something that amuses or entertains ⟨games and other *amusements*⟩
2 the feeling of being amused or entertained ⟨reading for *amusement*⟩

amulet: an ancient Egyptian amulet

amusement park *n*
► a place for entertainment having games and rides

an \ən, an\ *indefinite article* [2]A
Hint: *An* is used before words beginning with a vowel sound. ⟨*an* oak⟩ ⟨*an* hour⟩

[1]**-an** \ən\ *or* **-ian** *also* **-ean** \ē-ən, yən, ən\ *n suffix*
1 one that belongs to ⟨Americ*an*⟩
2 one skilled in or specializing in ⟨magic*ian*⟩

[2]**-an** *or* **-ian** *also* **-ean** *adj suffix*
1 of or relating to ⟨Americ*an*⟩
2 like : resembling

an•a•bol•ic steroid \,a-nə-'bä-lik-\ *n*
a hormone used in medicine to help tissue grow that is sometimes abused by athletes to increase muscle size and strength despite possible harmful effects (as stunted growth in teenagers)

an•a•con•da \,a-nə-'kän-də\ *n*
▼ a large South American snake that coils around and crushes its prey

anaconda

an•al \'ā-nᵊl\ *adj*
relating to the anus

anal•o•gous \ə-'na-lə-gəs\ *adj*
showing analogy : SIMILAR

anal•o•gy \ə-'na-lə-jē\ *n, pl* **anal•o•gies**
1 a comparison of things based on ways they are alike
2 the act of comparing things that are alike in some way ⟨explain by *analogy*⟩

anal•y•sis \ə-'na-lə-səs\ *n, pl* **anal•y•ses** \-,sēz\
1 an examination of something to find out how it is made or works or what it is
2 an explanation of the nature and meaning of something ⟨*analysis* of the news⟩

an•a•lyst \'a-nə-ləst\ *n*
a person who studies or analyzes something

an•a•lyt•ic \,a-nə-'li-tik\ *or* **an•a•lyt•i•cal** \,a-nə-'li-ti-kəl\ *adj*
of, relating to, or skilled in the careful study of something ⟨an *analytic* mind⟩
an•a•lyt•i•cal•ly *adv*

amusement park: a Ferris wheel at an amusement park

an•a•lyze \ˈa-nə-ˌlīz\ *vb* **an•a•lyzed**; **an•a•lyz•ing**
1 to examine something to find out what it is or what makes it work ⟨The bacteria were *analyzed* under a powerful microscope.⟩
2 to study carefully to understand the nature or meaning of ⟨*analyze* a problem⟩

an•a•tom•i•cal \ˌa-nə-ˈtä-mi-kəl\ *or* **an•a•tom•ic** \-ˈtäm-ik\ *adj*
of or relating to the structural makeup of living things

anat•o•my \ə-ˈna-tə-mē\ *n*, *pl* **anat•o•mies**
1 a science that has to do with the structure of living things
2 the structural makeup especially of a person or animal ⟨the *anatomy* of the cat⟩

-ance \əns\ *n suffix*
1 action or process ⟨perform*ance*⟩
2 quality or state ⟨resembl*ance*⟩
3 amount or degree ⟨clear*ance*⟩

an•ces•tor \ˈan-ˌse-stər\ *n*
1 a person from whom someone is descended
2 something from which something else develops

an•ces•tral \an-ˈse-strəl\ *adj*
of, relating to, or coming from an ancestor ⟨They visited their *ancestral* home.⟩

an•ces•try \ˈan-ˌse-strē\ *n*, *pl* **an•ces•tries**
a person's ancestors

[1]**an•chor** \ˈaŋ-kər\ *n*
1 a heavy device attached to a ship by a cable or chain and used to hold the ship in place when thrown overboard
2 someone or something that provides strength and support ⟨He is the family's *anchor.*⟩

[2]**anchor** *vb* **an•chored**; **an•chor•ing**
1 to hold or become held in place with an anchor ⟨*anchor* a ship⟩
2 to fasten tightly ⟨The cables are *anchored* to the bridge.⟩

an•chor•age \ˈaŋ-kə-rij\ *n*
a place where boats can be anchored

[1]**an•cient** \ˈān-shənt\ *adj*
1 very old ⟨*ancient* customs⟩
2 of or relating to a time long past or to those living in such a time ⟨*ancient* Egypt⟩

[2]**ancient** *n*
1 a very old person
2 **ancients** *pl* the civilized peoples of ancient times and especially of Greece and Rome

-an•cy \ən-sē, -ᵊn-sē\ *n suffix*, *pl* **-an•cies**
quality or state ⟨buoy*ancy*⟩

and \ənd, and\ *conj*
1 added to ⟨2 *and* 2 make 4.⟩
2 AS WELL AS ⟨ice cream *and* cake⟩ ⟨strong *and* healthy⟩
3 used to describe an action that is repeated or that occurs for a long time ⟨The dog barked *and* barked.⟩
4 used to indicate the purpose of an action ⟨Please try *and* call.⟩
and so forth and others or more of the same kind ⟨He collects model cars, trains, planes, *and so forth.*⟩
and so on and so forth ⟨Young cats are called kittens, young dogs are puppies, *and so on.*⟩

and•iron \ˈan-ˌdī-ərn\ *n*
one of a pair of metal supports for firewood in a fireplace

an•ec•dote \ˈa-nik-ˌdōt\ *n*
a short story about something interesting or funny in a person's life

ane•mia \ə-ˈnē-mē-ə\ *n*
a sickness in which there is too little blood or too few red blood cells or too little hemoglobin in the blood

an•e•mom•e•ter \ˌa-nə-ˈmä-mə-tər\ *n*
▶ an instrument for measuring the speed of the wind

anemometer: a hand-held mechanical anemometer

anem•o•ne \ə-ˈne-mə-nē\ *n*
1 a plant that blooms in spring and is often grown for its large white or colored flowers
2 SEA ANEMONE

an•es•the•sia \ˌa-nəs-ˈthē-zhə\ *n*
loss of feeling in all or part of the body with or without loss of consciousness

[1]**an•es•thet•ic** \ˌa-nəs-ˈthe-tik\ *adj*
of, relating to, or capable of producing loss of feeling in all or part of the body

[2]**anesthetic** *n*
something that produces loss of feeling in all or part of the body

anew \ə-ˈnü, -ˈnyü\ *adv*
1 over again ⟨begin *anew*⟩
2 in a new or different form ⟨I'll tear down and build *anew.*⟩

a b c d e f g h i j k l m n o p q r s t u v w x y z

A B C D E F G H I J K L M N O P Q R S T U V W X Y Z

an•gel \'ān-jəl\ *n*
1 a spiritual being serving God especially as a messenger
2 a person who is very good, kind, or beautiful

[1]an•ger \'aŋ-gər\ *vb* **an•gered**; **an•ger•ing**
to make strongly displeased : make angry

[2]anger *n*
a strong feeling of displeasure or annoyance and often of active opposition to an insult, injury, or injustice

▶ **Synonyms** ANGER, RAGE, and FURY mean the feelings brought about by great displeasure. ANGER can be used of either a strong or a mild feeling. 〈I was able to hide my *anger*.〉 RAGE is used of strong violent feeling that is difficult to control. 〈He was screaming with *rage*.〉 FURY is used of overwhelming rage that may cause a person to become violent. 〈In their *fury* the people smashed windows.〉

[1]an•gle \'aŋ-gəl\ *n*
1 ▼ the figure formed by two lines meeting at a point
2 POINT OF VIEW 〈Let's consider the problem from a new *angle*.〉
3 a sharp corner 〈an *angle* of a building〉
4 the slanting direction in which something is positioned 〈The road goes off on an *angle*.〉

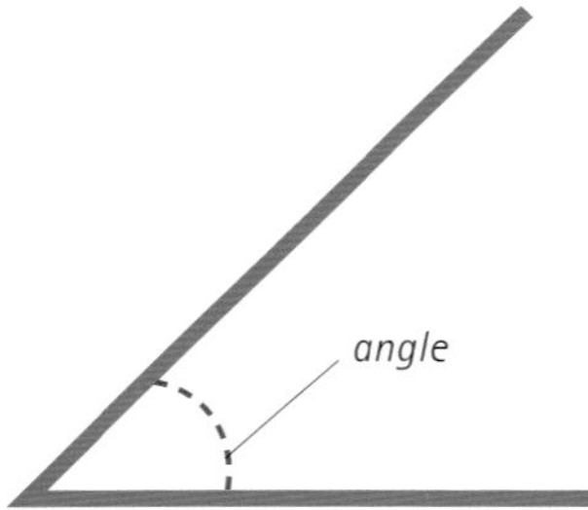

[1]angle 1: an angle between two straight lines

[2]angle *vb* **an•gled**; **an•gling** to turn, move, or point in a direction that is not straight or flat 〈The spotlight was *angled* down toward the floor.〉

[3]angle *vb* **an•gled**; **an•gling**
1 to fish with hook and line
2 to try to get something in a sly way 〈He's always *angling* for a compliment.〉

an•gler \'aŋ-glər\ *n*
a person who fishes with hook and line especially for pleasure

an•gling \'aŋ-gliŋ\ *n*
fishing with hook and line for pleasure

An•glo- \'aŋ-glō\ *prefix*
1 English
2 English and

[1]An•glo–Sax•on \,aŋ-glō-'sak-sən\ *n*
1 ▶ a member of the German people who conquered England in the fifth century A.D.
2 a person whose ancestors were English

[2]Anglo–Saxon *adj*
relating to the Anglo-Saxons

an•go•ra \aŋ-'gȯr-ə\ *n*
▼ cloth or yarn made from the long soft silky hair of a special usually white domestic rabbit (**Angora rabbit**) or from the long shiny wool of a goat (**Angora goat**)

angora
Fibers are collected from the coats of Angora rabbits or goats. The fibers are spun and dyed to make soft yarn.

Angora rabbit

angora yarn

an•gry \'aŋ-grē\ *adj* **an•gri•er**; **an•gri•est**
feeling or showing great annoyance or displeasure : feeling or showing anger
an•gri•ly \-grə-lē\ *adv*

an•guish \'aŋ-gwish\ *n*
great physical or emotional pain

an•guished \'aŋ-gwisht\ *adj*
full of physical or emotional pain 〈an *anguished* cry〉

an•gu•lar \'aŋ-gyə-lər\ *adj*
1 having angles or sharp corners
2 lean and bony 〈an *angular* face〉

an•i•mal \'a-nə-məl\ *n*
1 any member of the kingdom of living things (as earthworms, crabs, birds, and people) that differ from plants typically in being able to move about, in not having cell walls made of cellulose, and in depending on plants and other animals as sources of food
2 any of the animals lower than humans in the natural order

[1]Anglo–Saxon 1: a 9th-century jewel made by Anglo-Saxons

3 MAMMAL 〈the birds and *animals*〉

animal kingdom *n*
a basic group of natural objects that includes all living and extinct animals

[1]an•i•mate \'a-nə-mət\ *adj*
having life

[2]an•i•mate \'a-nə-,māt\ *vb* **an•i•mat•ed**; **an•i•mat•ing**
1 to give life or energy to 〈Her performance *animates* the movie.〉
2 to make appear to move 〈*animate* a cartoon〉

an•i•mat•ed \'a-nə-,mā-təd\ *adj*
1 full of life and energy : LIVELY 〈an *animated* discussion〉
2 appearing to be alive or moving 〈*animated* cartoon characters〉

an•i•ma•tion \,a-nə-'mā-shən\ *n*
1 a lively or excited quality 〈She spoke with *animation* about her trip.〉
2 a way of making a movie by using slightly different pictures that when shown quickly in a series create the appearance of movement

an•i•ma•tor \'a-nə-,mā-tər\ *n*
a person who creates animated movies and cartoons

an•i•me \'a-nə-,mā, 'ä-nē-\ *n*
a style of animation created in Japan that uses colorful images, strong characters, and action-filled plots

an•i•mos•i•ty \,a-nə-'mä-sə-tē\ *n*, *pl* **an•i•mos•i•ties**
[1]DISLIKE, HATRED

an•kle \'aŋ-kəl\ *n*
1 the joint between the foot and the leg
2 the area containing the ankle joint

ankylosaur: model of a North American ankylosaur, *Euoplocephalus*

bony plate

an•klet \'aŋ-klət\ *n*
1 something (as an ornament) worn around the ankle
2 a short sock reaching just above the ankle

an•ky•lo•saur \'aŋ-kə-lō-,sȯr\ *n*
▲ a plant-eating dinosaur with bony plates covering the back

an•nals \'a-nᵊlz\ *n pl*
1 a record of events arranged in yearly sequence
2 historical records **:** HISTORY

an•neal \ə-'nēl\ *vb* **an•nealed**; **an•neal•ing**
to heat (as glass or steel) and then cool so as to toughen and make less brittle

[1]**an•nex** \ə-'neks, 'a-,neks\ *vb* **an•nexed**; **an•nex•ing**
to add (something) to something else usually so as to become a part of it ⟨I *annexed* a postscript to my letter.⟩ ⟨The United States *annexed* Texas and it became a state.⟩

[2]**an•nex** \'a-,neks\ *n*
a building or part of a building attached to or near another building and considered part of it ⟨a school *annex*⟩

an•nex•ation \,a-,nek-'sā-shən\ *n*
the act of adding new territory

an•ni•hi•late \ə-'nī-ə-,lāt\ *vb* **an•ni•hi•lat•ed**; **an•ni•hi•lat•ing**
to destroy entirely **:** put completely out of existence
an•ni•hi•la•tion \-,nī-ə-'lā-shən\ *n*

an•ni•ver•sa•ry \,a-nə-'vərs-ə-rē, -'vərs-rē\ *n*, *pl* **an•ni•ver•sa•ries**
a date remembered or celebrated every year because of something special that happened on it in an earlier year ⟨a wedding *anniversary*⟩

an•nounce \ə-'naůns\ *vb* **an•nounced**; **an•nounc•ing**
1 to make known publicly ⟨The principal will *announce* her plan to retire.⟩
2 to give notice of the arrival, presence, or readiness of ⟨*announce* dinner⟩
synonyms see DECLARE

an•nounce•ment \ə-'naůn-smənt\ *n*
1 the act of making known publicly
2 a public notice making something known ⟨a wedding *announcement*⟩

an•nounc•er \ə-'naůn-sər\ *n*
a person who gives information on television or radio

an•noy \ə-'nȯi\ *vb* **an•noyed**; **an•noy•ing**
to cause to feel slightly angry or irritated

▶ **Synonyms** ANNOY, PESTER, and TEASE mean to disturb and upset a person. ANNOY is used for bothering someone to the point of anger. ⟨I am *annoyed* by your bad behavior.⟩ PESTER is used for bothering someone over and over. ⟨Stop *pestering* me for more money.⟩ TEASE often is used for continually tormenting someone until that person is provoked or upset. ⟨They *teased* the child to the point of tears.⟩

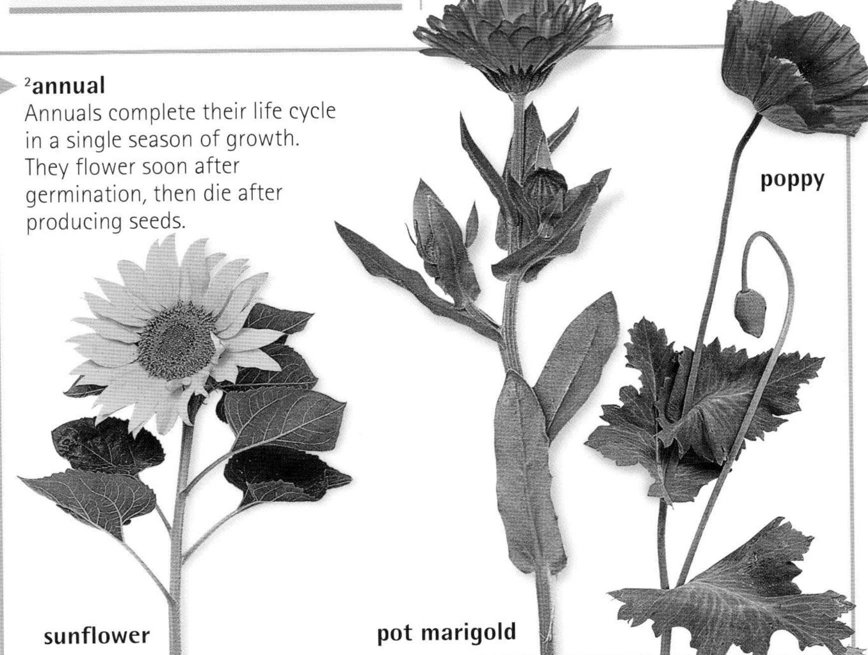

▶ [2]**annual**
Annuals complete their life cycle in a single season of growth. They flower soon after germination, then die after producing seeds.

an•noy•ance \ə-'nȯi-əns\ *n*
1 slight anger or irritation ⟨I can sense your *annoyance* with me.⟩
2 a source or cause of slight anger or irritation ⟨The dog's constant barking was an *annoyance*.⟩

an•noy•ing \ə-'nȯi-iŋ\ *adj*
causing slight anger or irritation ⟨an *annoying* habit⟩
an•noy•ing•ly *adv*

[1]**an•nu•al** \'an-yə-wəl\ *adj*
1 coming, happening, done, made, or given once a year ⟨The library holds an *annual* book sale.⟩
2 completing the life cycle in one growing season ⟨*annual* plants⟩
an•nu•al•ly *adv*

[2]**annual** *n*
▼ an annual plant

annual ring *n*
the layer of wood produced by one year's growth of a woody plant (as in the trunk of a tree)

an•nu•ity \ə-'nü-ə-tē, -'nyü-\ *n*, *pl* **an•nu•ities**
a sum of money paid yearly or at other regular intervals

A B C D E F G H I J K L M N O P Q R S T U V W X Y Z

an•nul \ə-'nəl\ *vb* **an•nulled; an•nul•ling**
to cancel by law **:** take away the legal force of ⟨*annul* a marriage⟩
an•nul•ment \-mənt\ *n*

an•ode \'a-,nōd\ *n*
1 the positive electrode of an electrolytic cell
2 the negative end of a battery that is delivering electric current
3 the electron-collecting electrode of an electron tube

anoint \ə-'nȯint\ *vb* **anoint•ed; anoint•ing**
1 to rub or cover with oil or grease
2 to put oil on as part of a religious ceremony

anom•a•lous \ə-'nä-mə-ləs\ *adj*
not regular or usual ⟨*anomalous* test results⟩

anom•a•ly \ə-'nä-mə-lē\ *n, pl* **anom•a•lies**
something different, abnormal, strange, or not easily described

anon. *abbr* anonymous

anon•y•mous \ə-'nä-nə-məs\ *adj*
1 not named or identified ⟨an *anonymous* caller⟩
2 made or done by someone unknown ⟨an *anonymous* phone call⟩
anon•y•mous•ly *adv*

[1]an•oth•er \ə-'nə-t͟hər\ *adj*
1 some other ⟨Choose *another* day to go.⟩
2 one more ⟨We need *another* cup.⟩

[2]another *pron*
1 one more ⟨He hit one homer in the first game and *another* in the second.⟩
2 someone or something different ⟨Complaining is one thing, but finding a solution is *another*.⟩

ans. *abbr* answer

[1]an•swer \'an-sər\ *n*
1 something said or written in reply (as to a question)
2 a solution of a problem ⟨Money is not the *answer* to improving this situation.⟩

[2]answer *vb* **an•swered; an•swer•ing**
1 to speak or write in order to satisfy a question
2 to write a response to a letter or e-mail
3 to pick up (a ringing telephone)
4 to open (a door) when someone knocks on it
5 to react to something with an action ⟨*answer* a job ad⟩
6 to take responsibility ⟨The camp director *answered* for the children's safety.⟩
answer back to reply rudely

an•swer•able \'an-sə-rə-bəl\ *adj*
1 RESPONSIBLE 1 ⟨You are *answerable* for your actions.⟩
2 possible to answer ⟨an *answerable* question⟩

answering machine *n*
a machine that receives telephone calls and records messages from callers

ant \'ant\ *n*
▼ a small insect related to the bees and wasps that lives in colonies and forms nests in the ground or in wood in which it stores food and raises its young

ants

ant. *abbr* antonym

ant– *see* ANTI–

[1]–ant \ənt\ *n suffix*
1 one that does or causes a certain thing ⟨deodor*ant*⟩
2 thing that is acted upon in a certain way

[2]–ant *adj suffix*
1 doing a certain thing or being a certain way ⟨observ*ant*⟩
2 causing a certain action

an•tag•o•nism \an-'ta-gə-,ni-zəm\ *n*
a strong feeling of dislike or disagreement

an•tag•o•nist \an-'ta-gə-nəst\ *n*
a person who is against something or someone else **:** OPPONENT

an•tag•o•nis•tic \an-,ta-gə-'ni-stik\ *adj*
showing dislike or opposition **:** HOSTILE, UNFRIENDLY

an•tag•o•nize \an-'ta-gə-,nīz\ *vb* **an•tag•o•nized; an•tag•o•niz•ing**
to stir up dislike or anger in ⟨The bully *antagonizes* younger kids.⟩

ant•arc•tic \ant-'ärk-tik, -'är-tik\ *adj, often cap*
▼ of or relating to the south pole or to the region around it ⟨*antarctic* explorers⟩

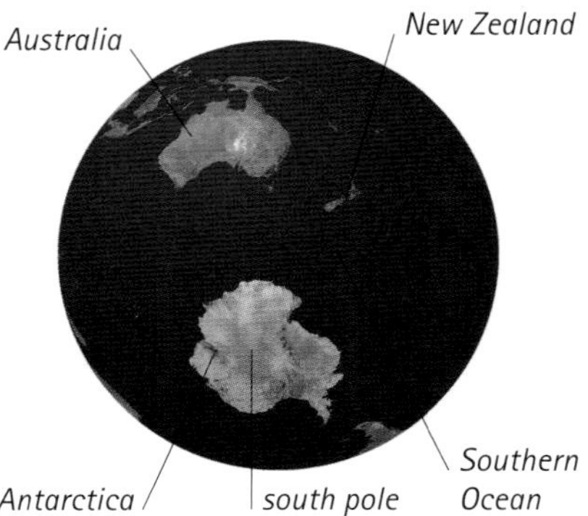

antarctic: map of the world showing the antarctic region

ante– \'an-ti\ *prefix*
1 before in time **:** earlier
2 in front of ⟨*ante*room⟩

ant•eat•er \'ant-,ē-tər\ *n*
► an animal that has a long nose and long sticky tongue and feeds chiefly on ants and termites

an•te•lope \'an-tə-,lōp\ *n*
an animal chiefly of Africa and southwest Asia that resembles a deer and has horns that extend upward and backward

an•ten•na \an-'te-nə\ *n*
1 ▼ *pl* **an•ten•nae** \-'te-nē\ one of two or four threadlike movable feelers on the head of insects and crustaceans (as lobsters)
2 *pl* **an•ten•nas** a metallic device (as a rod or wire) for sending or receiving radio waves

antenna 1: antennae of a butterfly

► **Word History** In Greece more than two thousand years ago, the philosopher and naturalist Aristotle wrote a description of insects' feelers. He used the Greek word *keraia*, which is derived from the word *keras*, "horn," as a name for the feelers. The word *keraia* in Greek also means "sail yard," the long piece of wood that spreads and supports the sails on a ship. Centuries later, when Aristotle's work was translated into Latin, the Latin word for a sail yard, *antenna*, was used to translate *keraia*. English later borrowed the word *antenna* from Latin.

an•te•room \'an-ti-,rüm, -,ru̇m\ *n*
a room used as an entrance to another

an•them \'an-thəm\ *n*
1 a sacred song usually sung by a church choir
2 a patriotic song

an•ther \'an-thər\ *n*
the enlargement at the tip of a flower's stamen that contains pollen

ant•hill \'ant-,hil\ *n*
a mound made by ants in digging their nest

anteater: a giant anteater

an•thol•o•gy \an-ˈthä-lə-jē\ *n, pl* **an•thol•o•gies**
a collection of writings (as stories and poems)

an•thra•cite \ˈan-thrə-ˌsīt\ *n*
a hard glossy coal that burns without much smoke

an•thrax \ˈan-ˌthraks\ *n*
a serious bacterial disease of warm-blooded animals (as sheep) that can affect humans

an•thro•pol•o•gy \ˌan-thrə-ˈpä-lə-jē\ *n*
a science that studies people and especially their origins, societies, and cultures

anti- \ˈan-ti, ˈan-ˌtī\ *or* **ant-** \ant\ *prefix*
1 opposite in kind, position, or action ⟨*anti*cyclone⟩
2 hostile toward ⟨*anti*social⟩

an•ti•bi•ot•ic \ˌan-ti-bī-ˈä-tik\ *n*
a substance produced by living things and especially by bacteria and fungi that is used to kill or prevent the growth of harmful germs

[1]antique: an antique chair

an•ti•body \ˈan-ti-ˌbä-dē\ *n, pl* **an•ti•bod•ies**
a substance produced by special cells of the body that counteracts the effects of a disease germ or its poisons

an•tic \ˈan-tik\ *n*
a wildly playful or funny act or action ⟨The kitten entertained us with his *antics*.⟩

an•tic•i•pate \an-ˈti-sə-ˌpāt\ *vb* **an•tic•i•pat•ed; an•tic•i•pat•ing**
1 to think of ahead of time : EXPECT ⟨I don't *anticipate* any problems.⟩
2 to look forward to ⟨We're *anticipating* your visit.⟩

an•tic•i•pa•tion \an-ˌti-sə-ˈpā-shən\ *n*
1 excitement about something that's going to happen
2 the act of preparing for something

an•ti•cy•clone \ˌan-ti-ˈsī-ˌklōn\ *n*
a system of winds that is like a cyclone but that rotates about a center of high atmospheric pressure instead of low

an•ti•dote \ˈan-ti-ˌdōt\ *n*
something used to reverse or prevent the action of a poison

an•ti•freeze \ˈan-ti-ˌfrēz\ *n*
a substance added to the water in an automobile radiator to prevent its freezing

an•ti•mo•ny \ˈan-tə-ˌmō-nē\ *n*
a silvery white metallic chemical element

an•tip•a•thy \an-ˈti-pə-thē\ *n, pl* **an•tip•a•thies**
a strong feeling of dislike

an•ti•per•spi•rant \ˌan-ti-ˈpər-spə-rənt, -sprənt\ *n*
a substance that is used to prevent sweating

an•ti•quat•ed \ˈan-tə-ˌkwā-təd\ *adj*
very old and no longer useful or popular

[1]an•tique \an-ˈtēk\ *n*
◀ an object (as a piece of furniture) made at an earlier time

[2]antique *adj*
belonging to or like a former style or fashion ⟨*antique* lamps⟩

an•tiq•ui•ty \an-ˈti-kwə-tē\ *n*
1 ancient times ⟨The town dates from *antiquity*.⟩
2 very great age ⟨a castle of great *antiquity*⟩

[1]an•ti•sep•tic \ˌan-tə-ˈsep-tik\ *adj*
killing or preventing the growth or action of germs that cause decay or sickness ⟨Iodine is *antiseptic*.⟩

[2]antiseptic *n*
a substance that helps stop the growth or action of germs

an•ti•so•cial \ˌan-ti-ˈsō-shəl, ˌan-ˌtī-\ *adj*
1 violent or harmful to people ⟨Crime is *antisocial*.⟩
2 UNFRIENDLY 1 ⟨She's not *antisocial*, just shy.⟩

an•tith•e•sis \an-ˈti-thə-səs\ *n, pl* **an•tith•e•ses** \-ə-ˌsēz\
the exact opposite ⟨Poverty is the *antithesis* of wealth.⟩

an•ti•tox•in \ˌan-ti-ˈtäk-sən\ *n*
a substance that is formed in the blood of one exposed to a disease and that prevents or acts against that disease

ant•ler \ˈant-lər\ *n*
▼ a bony branching structure that grows from the head of a deer or related animal (as a moose) and that is cast off and grown anew each year
— **ant•lered** \-lərd\ *adj*

antler: antlers of a deer

ant lion *n*
▼ an insect having a larva form with long jaws that digs a cone-shaped hole in which it waits for prey (as ants)

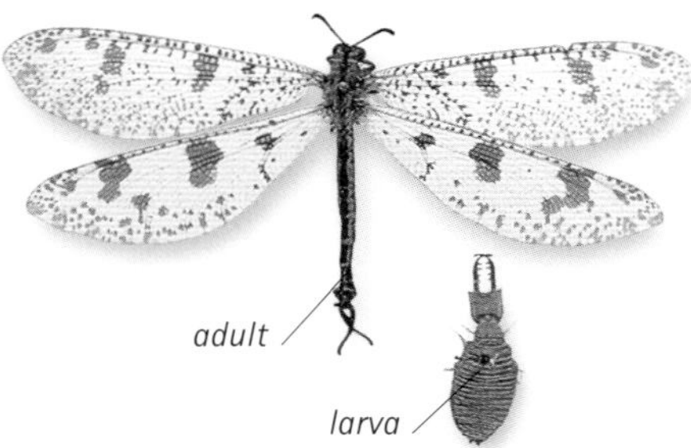

ant lion

an•to•nym \'an-tə-,nim\ *n*
a word of opposite meaning ⟨The words "hot" and "cold" are *antonyms.*⟩

ant•sy \'ant-sē\ *adj* **ant•si•er; ant•si•est**
impatient and unable to keep still

anus \'ā-nəs\ *n*
the lower opening of the digestive tract

an•vil \'an-vəl\ *n*
an iron block on which pieces of metal are hammered into shape

anx•i•ety \aŋ-'zī-ə-tē\ *n, pl* **anx•i•eties**
fear or nervousness about what might happen

anx•ious \'aŋk-shəs\ *adj*
1 afraid or nervous about what may happen ⟨I was *anxious* about her health.⟩
2 causing or showing fear or nervousness ⟨an *anxious* moment⟩
3 wanting very much : EAGER ⟨She is *anxious* to get home.⟩
synonyms see EAGER
anx•ious•ly *adv*

[1]**any** \'e-nē\ *adj*
1 whichever one of ⟨Ask directions from *any* person you meet.⟩
2 of whatever number or amount ⟨Do you need *any* help?⟩

[2]**any** *pron*
1 any one or ones of the people or things in a group ⟨Are *any* of you ready?⟩
2 any amount ⟨Is there *any* left?⟩

[3]**any** *adv*
to the least amount or degree ⟨You can't get it *any* cleaner.⟩ ⟨It's not *any* good.⟩

any•body \'e-nē-,bä-dē, -bə-dē\ *pron*
any person : ANYONE

any•how \'e-nē-,hau̇\ *adv*
1 in any way, manner, or order ⟨Why should I care about what he does *anyhow?*⟩
2 ANYWAY 1 ⟨I don't agree, but *anyhow* it's her decision.⟩

any•more \,e-nē-'mȯr\ *adv*
NOWADAYS ⟨We never see them *anymore.*⟩

any•one \'e-nē-,wən\ *pron*
any person

any•place \'e-nē-,plās\ *adv*
ANYWHERE

any•thing \'e-nē-,thiŋ\ *pron*
a thing of any kind ⟨She didn't do *anything* all day.⟩

any•way \'e-nē-,wā\ *adv*
1 without regard to other considerations ⟨He knew it was a lie, but he said it *anyway.*⟩
2 as an additional consideration or thought ⟨It's too expensive, and *anyway,* you have one just like it.⟩

3 into parts : to pieces ⟨He took the clock *apart.*⟩
4 one from another ⟨I can't tell the twins *apart.*⟩
5 as something separated : SEPARATELY ⟨The price was considered *apart* from other points.⟩

apart•ment \ə-'pärt-mənt\ *n*
a room or set of rooms rented as a home

apartment building *n*
▼ a large building having several apartments

apartment house *n*
APARTMENT BUILDING

apartment building: outside view of an apartment building

any•where \'e-nē-,hwer, -,wer\ *adv*
in, at, or to any place

aor•ta \ā-'ȯr-tə\ *n*
the main artery that carries blood from the heart for distribution to all parts of the body

Apache \ə-'pa-chē\ *n, pl* **Apache** *or* **Apach•es**
1 a member of an American Indian people of the southwestern United States
2 any of the languages of the Apache people

apart \ə-'pärt\ *adv*
1 away from each other ⟨Our parents kept me and my sister *apart.*⟩
2 separated by an amount of time ⟨The girls were born two years *apart.*⟩

ap•a•thy \'a-pə-thē\ *n*
lack of feeling or of interest : INDIFFERENCE
ap•a•the•tic \,a-pə-'the-tik\ *adj*

apato•sau•rus \ə-,pa-tə-'sȯr-əs\ *n*
BRONTOSAURUS

[1]**ape** \'āp\ *n*
► any of a group of tailless animals (as gorillas or chimpanzees) that are primates most closely related to humans
ape•like \'āp-,līk\ *adj*

[2]**ape** *vb* **aped; ap•ing**
to imitate (someone) awkwardly ⟨He *aped* the singer's style.⟩

ap•er•ture \'a-pər-,chu̇r\ *n*
an opening or open space : HOLE

apex \'ā-ˌpeks\ *n, pl* **apex•es** *or* **api•ces** \'ā-pə-ˌsēz\
1 the highest point : PEAK ⟨the *apex* of a mountain⟩
2 the most successful time ⟨He was at the *apex* of his career.⟩

aphid \'ā-fəd\ *n*
a small insect that sucks the juices of plants

apiece \ə-'pēs\ *adv*
for each one ⟨They cost 25 cents *apiece.*⟩

aplomb \ə-'pläm\ *n*
confidence and skill shown especially in a difficult situation

apol•o•get•ic \ə-ˌpä-lə-'je-tik\ *adj*
sorry for having done or said something wrong ⟨was *apologetic* about the error⟩
apol•o•get•i•cal•ly \-ti-kə-lē\ *adv*

apol•o•gize \ə-'pä-lə-ˌjīz\ *vb* **apol•o•gized**; **apol•o•giz•ing**
to express regret for having done or said something wrong

apol•o•gy \ə-'pä-lə-jē\ *n, pl* **apol•o•gies**
an expression of regret for having done or said something wrong

apos•tle \ə-'pä-səl\ *n*
one of the twelve close followers of Jesus Christ

apos•tro•phe \ə-'pä-strə-fē\ *n*
a mark ' used to show that letters or figures are missing (as in "can't" for "cannot" or "'76" for "1776") or to show the possessive case (as in "Mike's") or the plural of letters or figures (as in "cross your t's")

apoth•e•cary \ə-'pä-thə-ˌker-ē\ *n, pl* **apoth•e•car•ies**
PHARMACIST

app \'ap\ *n*
a computer program that performs a special function : APPLICATION 6

ap•pall \ə-'pȯl\ *vb* **ap•palled**; **ap•pall•ing**
to cause to feel shock, horror, or disgust

ap•pall•ing *adj*
being shocking and terrible ⟨He suffered *appalling* injuries.⟩

ap•pa•ra•tus \ˌa-pə-'ra-təs, -'rā-\ *n, pl* **ap•pa•ra•tus•es** *or* **apparatus**
▶ the equipment or material for a particular use or job ⟨laboratory *apparatus*⟩

glass tube

clamp

apparatus: laboratory apparatus

ap•par•el \ə-'per-əl\ *n*
things that are worn : CLOTHING

ap•par•ent \ə-'per-ənt\ *adj*
1 clear to the understanding : EVIDENT ⟨It was *apparent* that we could not win.⟩
2 open to view : VISIBLE ⟨On a clear night many stars are *apparent.*⟩
3 appearing to be real or true ⟨The *apparent* theft of my lunch made me angry.⟩
ap•par•ent•ly *adv*

ap•pa•ri•tion \ˌa-pə-'ri-shən\ *n*
1 GHOST
2 an unusual or unexpected sight

▶ **[1]ape**
Like their human relatives, apes have large brains and are among the most intelligent creatures on earth. Apes spend much of their time in trees, although most species can walk upright on two legs.

a b c d e f h i j k l m n o p q r t u v w x y z

[1]ap•peal \ə-ˈpēl\ *n*
1 the power to cause enjoyment **:** ATTRACTION 〈the *appeal* of music〉
2 the act of asking for something badly needed or wanted **:** PLEA 〈an *appeal* for funds〉
3 a legal action by which a case is brought to a higher court for review

[2]appeal *vb* **ap•pealed; ap•peal•ing**
1 to be pleasing or attractive
2 to ask for something badly needed or wanted 〈They *appealed* to the boss for more money.〉
3 to take action to have a case or decision reviewed by a higher court

ap•pear \ə-ˈpir\ *vb* **ap•peared; ap•pear•ing**
1 to come into sight 〈Stars *appeared* in the sky.〉
2 to present oneself 〈*appear* in court〉
3 SEEM 1 〈The runner in the lead *appears* to be tired.〉
4 to come before the public 〈The book *appeared* last year.〉
5 to come into existence 〈The first dinosaurs *appeared* around 215 million years ago.〉

ap•pear•ance \ə-ˈpir-əns\ *n*
1 the way something looks 〈The room has a cool *appearance*.〉
2 the act or an instance of appearing 〈His sudden *appearance* startled us.〉

ap•pease \ə-ˈpēz\ *vb* **ap•peased; ap•peas•ing**
1 to make calm or quiet 〈*appease* their anger〉
2 to make less severe 〈*appeased* his hunger〉

ap•pend \ə-ˈpend\ *vb* **ap•pend•ed; ap•pend•ing**
to add as something extra 〈*append* a postscript〉

ap•pend•age \ə-ˈpen-dij\ *n*
▼ something (as a leg) attached to a larger or more important thing

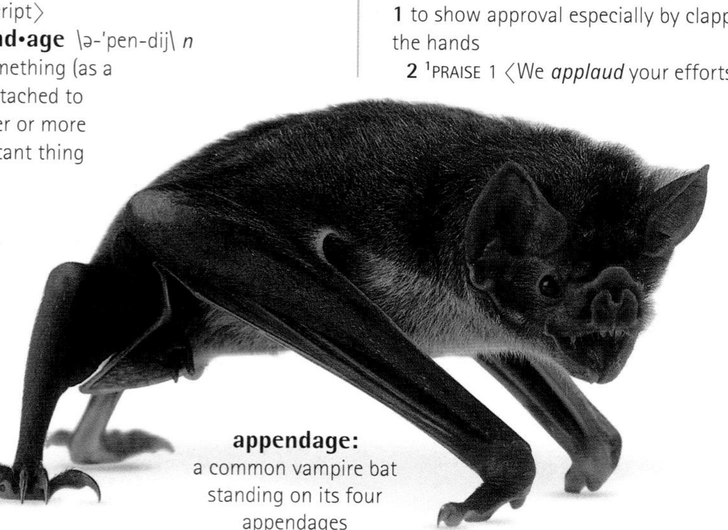

appendage: a common vampire bat standing on its four appendages

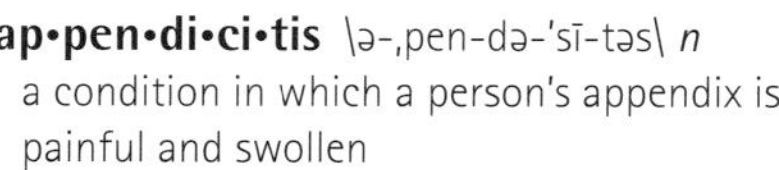

ap•pen•di•ci•tis \ə-ˌpen-də-ˈsī-təs\ *n*
a condition in which a person's appendix is painful and swollen

ap•pen•dix \ə-ˈpen-diks\ *n, pl* **ap•pen•dix•es** *or* **ap•pen•di•ces** \-də-ˌsēz\
1 a part of a book giving added and helpful information (as notes or tables)
2 a small tubelike part growing out from the large intestine

ap•pe•tite \ˈa-pə-ˌtīt\ *n*
1 a natural desire especially for food
2 a desire or liking for something 〈an *appetite* for adventure〉

ap•pe•tiz•er \ˈa-pə-ˌtī-zər\ *n*
▼ a food or drink served before a meal

appetizer

ap•pe•tiz•ing \ˈa-pə-ˌtī-ziŋ\ *adj*
pleasing to the appetite 〈an *appetizing* smell〉

ap•plaud \ə-ˈplȯd\ *vb* **ap•plaud•ed; ap•plaud•ing**
1 to show approval especially by clapping the hands
2 [1]PRAISE 1 〈We *applaud* your efforts.〉

ap•plause \ə-ˈplȯz\ *n*
approval shown especially by clapping the hands

ap•ple \ˈa-pəl\ *n*
▼ a round or oval fruit with red, yellow, or green skin and white flesh that grows on a spreading tree related to the rose

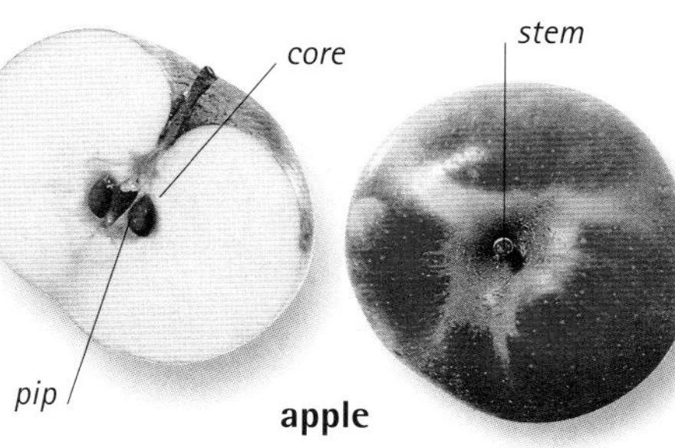

apple

ap•ple•sauce \ˈa-pəl-ˌsȯs\ *n*
a sweet sauce made from cooked apples

ap•pli•ance \ə-ˈplī-əns\ *n*
► a piece of household equipment that performs a particular job

ap•pli•ca•ble \ˈa-pli-kə-bəl\ *adj*
capable of being put to use or put into practice 〈the *applicable* law〉

ap•pli•cant \ˈa-pli-kənt\ *n*
a person who applies for something (as a job)

ap•pli•ca•tion \ˌa-plə-ˈkā-shən\ *n*
1 the act or an instance of applying 〈*application* of the rules〉 〈One *application* of paint should cover the wall well enough.〉
2 something put or spread on a surface 〈The nurse put cold *applications* on the sprained ankle.〉
3 [1]REQUEST 1 〈an *application* for a job〉
4 a document used to make a request for something 〈You have to fill out an *application*.〉
5 ability to be put to practical use 〈The tool has a number of *applications*.〉
6 a computer program (as a word processor or browser)

ap•pli•ca•tor \ˈa-plə-ˌkā-tər\ *n*
a device for applying a substance (as medicine or polish)

ap•ply \ə-ˈplī\ *vb* **ap•plied; ap•ply•ing**
1 to request especially in writing 〈*apply* for a job〉
2 to lay or spread on 〈*apply* a coat of paint〉
3 to place in contact 〈*apply* heat〉
4 to have relation or a connection 〈This law *applies* to everyone.〉
5 to put to use 〈I *applied* my knowledge.〉
6 to give full attention 〈I *applied* myself to my work.〉

appliance
Household appliances save time in running a household. Many modern appliances, such as all of the examples shown here, run on electricity.

washing machine

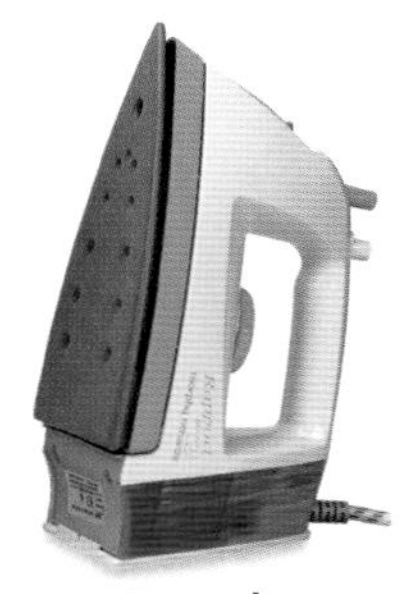
steam iron

refrigerator

hair dryer

coffee maker

vacuum cleaner

ap•point \ə-ˈpȯint\ *vb* **ap•point•ed**; **ap•point•ing**
1 to choose for some duty, job, or office 〈The school board *appointed* three new teachers.〉
2 to decide on usually from a position of authority 〈The teacher *appointed* a time for our meeting.〉

ap•point•ment \ə-ˈpȯint-mənt\ *n*
1 an agreement to meet at a fixed time 〈an eight-o'clock doctor's *appointment*〉
2 the act of choosing for a position or office or of being chosen for a position or office 〈She became less popular after her *appointment* as director.〉
3 a position or office to which a person is named 〈her *appointment* as ambassador〉
4 *appointments pl* FURNISHINGS

ap•po•si•tion \ˌa-pə-ˈzi-shən\ *n*
a grammatical construction in which a noun is followed by another that explains it 〈In "my friend the doctor," the word "doctor" is in *apposition* with "friend."〉

ap•pos•i•tive \ə-ˈpä-zə-tiv\ *n*
the second of a pair of nouns in apposition 〈In "my friend the doctor," the word "doctor" is an *appositive*.〉

ap•prais•al \ə-ˈprā-zəl\ *n*
an act or instance of setting a value on 〈*appraisal* of the property〉

ap•praise \ə-ˈprāz\ *vb* **ap•praised**; **ap•prais•ing**
to set a value on 〈*appraise* a diamond〉

ap•pre•cia•ble \ə-ˈprē-shə-bəl\ *adj*
large enough to be noticed or measured 〈an *appreciable* change〉
ap•pre•cia•bly \-blē\ *adv*

ap•pre•ci•ate \ə-ˈprē-shē-ˌāt\ *vb* **ap•pre•ci•at•ed**; **ap•pre•ci•at•ing**
1 to be grateful for 〈We *appreciate* your help.〉
2 to admire greatly and with understanding 〈He *appreciates* poetry.〉
3 to be fully aware of 〈I *appreciate* how important this is.〉
4 to increase in number or value

Synonyms APPRECIATE, TREASURE, and CHERISH mean to think very much of something. APPRECIATE is used when a person understands and enjoys the true worth of something. 〈I can *appreciate* good music.〉 TREASURE is often used of something of great sentimental value that is thought of as precious and is kept in a safe place. 〈Parents *treasure* gifts that their children make.〉 CHERISH is used when a person loves and cares for something very much and often for a long time. 〈We *cherished* their friendship for many years.〉

ap•pre•ci•a•tion \ə-ˌprē-shē-ˈā-shən\ *n*
1 a feeling of being grateful 〈Let me express my *appreciation* for your help.〉
2 awareness or understanding of worth or value 〈She studied art *appreciation*.〉
3 a rise in value

ap•pre•cia•tive \ə-ˈprē-shə-tiv\ *adj*
having or showing gratitude ⟨an *appreciative* smile⟩
ap•pre•cia•tive•ly *adv*

ap•pre•hend \ˌa-pri-ˈhend\ *vb*
ap•pre•hend•ed; **ap•pre•hend•ing**
1 [1]ARREST 1 ⟨Police *apprehended* the burglar.⟩
2 to look forward to with fear and uncertainty
3 UNDERSTAND 1 ⟨*apprehend* the meaning⟩

ap•pre•hen•sion \ˌa-pri-ˈhen-shən\ *n*
1 [2]ARREST
2 fear of or uncertainty about what may be coming ⟨They approached the old house with *apprehension*.⟩
3 an understanding of something

ap•pre•hen•sive \ˌa-pri-ˈhen-siv\ *adj*
fearful of what may be coming ⟨He was *apprehensive* about the surgery.⟩
ap•pre•hen•sive•ly *adv*

[1]**ap•pren•tice** \ə-ˈpren-təs\ *n*
a person who is learning a trade or art by experience under a skilled worker

[2]**apprentice** *vb* **ap•pren•ticed**; **ap•pren•tic•ing**
to set at work as an apprentice

ap•pren•tice•ship \ə-ˈpren-təs-ˌship\ *n*
1 service as an apprentice
2 the period during which a person serves as an apprentice

[1]**ap•proach** \ə-ˈprōch\ *vb* **ap•proached**; **ap•proach•ing**
1 to come near or nearer **:** draw close ⟨This train is *approaching* the station.⟩ ⟨The temperature is *approaching* 90 degrees.⟩
2 to begin to deal with ⟨*approach* a problem⟩
3 to start talking to for a specific purpose ⟨How can I *approach* the teacher about having cheated?⟩

[2]**approach** *n*
1 an act or instance of drawing near ⟨the *approach* of summer⟩ ⟨The cat made a cautious *approach*.⟩
2 a way of doing or thinking about something **:** a way of dealing with something
3 a path or road to get to a place

ap•proach•able \ə-ˈprō-chə-bəl\ *adj*
easy to meet or deal with

[1]**ap•pro•pri•ate** \ə-ˈprō-prē-ət\ *adj*
especially fitting or suitable ⟨The movie is *appropriate* for small children.⟩
ap•pro•pri•ate•ly *adv*
ap•pro•pri•ate•ness *n*

[2]**ap•pro•pri•ate** \ə-ˈprō-prē-ˌāt\ *vb*
ap•pro•pri•at•ed; **ap•pro•pri•at•ing**
1 to take possession of especially in an illegal or unfair way
2 to set apart for a certain purpose or use ⟨The school *appropriated* funds for new books.⟩

ap•pro•pri•a•tion \ə-ˌprō-prē-ˈā-shən\ *n*
1 an act or instance of taking especially illegally or unfairly
2 the act or an instance of setting apart for a special purpose
3 a sum of money set apart for a special purpose

ap•prov•al \ə-ˈprü-vəl\ *n*
1 the belief that something is good or acceptable
2 permission to do something

ap•prove \ə-ˈprüv\ *vb* **ap•proved**; **ap•prov•ing**
1 to think of as good ⟨I don't *approve* of the way those children behave.⟩
2 to accept as satisfactory ⟨The school committee *approved* the new curriculum.⟩

[1]**ap•prox•i•mate** \ə-ˈpräk-sə-mət\ *adj*
nearly correct or exact ⟨the *approximate* cost⟩
ap•prox•i•mate•ly *adv*

[2]**ap•prox•i•mate** \ə-ˈpräk-sə-ˌmāt\ *vb*
ap•prox•i•mat•ed; **ap•prox•i•mat•ing**
to come near in position, value, or characteristics **:** APPROACH ⟨*approximating* the distance⟩ ⟨He tried to *approximate* the singer's style.⟩

ap•prox•i•ma•tion \ə-ˌpräk-sə-ˈmā-shən\ *n*
1 an estimate or figure that is not intended to be exact
2 an act or the result of coming near or close

appt. *abbr* appointment

Apr. *abbr* April

apri•cot \ˈa-prə-ˌkät, ˈā-\ *n*
a small oval orange-colored fruit that looks like the related peach and plum

> ▶ **Word History** The Romans seem to have thought that apricots were "early-ripening peaches," since that is the literal meaning of the Latin name for the fruit: *persica praecocia*. The second word in this phrase was borrowed by the Greeks, in the form *praikokion*, as their name for the fruit. When the Arabs entered the Mediterranean Sea region in the early Middle Ages, they in turn borrowed the Greek word as *barqūq*, and Arabic *al-barqūq*, "the apricot," is the ultimate source of the English word *apricot*.

April \ˈā-prəl\ *n*
the fourth month of the year

apron \ˈā-prən\ *n*
1 ▶ a piece of cloth worn on the front of the body to keep clothing from getting dirty
2 a paved area for parking or handling airplanes

apron 1

apt \ˈapt\ *adj*
1 having a tendency **:** LIKELY ⟨He is *apt* to become angry over small things.⟩
2 just right **:** SUITABLE ⟨an *apt* reply⟩
3 quick to learn ⟨a student *apt* in arithmetic⟩
apt•ly *adv*
apt•ness *n*

ap•ti•tude \ˈap-tə-ˌtüd, -ˌtyüd\ *n*
1 natural ability **:** TALENT ⟨He has an *aptitude* for music.⟩
2 capacity to learn ⟨a test of *aptitude*⟩

aqua \ˈä-kwə, ˈa-\ *n*
a light greenish blue **:** the color of water in a swimming pool

aqua•ma•rine \ˌä-kwə-mə-ˈrēn, ˌa-\ *n*
▼ a transparent gem that is blue, blue-green, or green

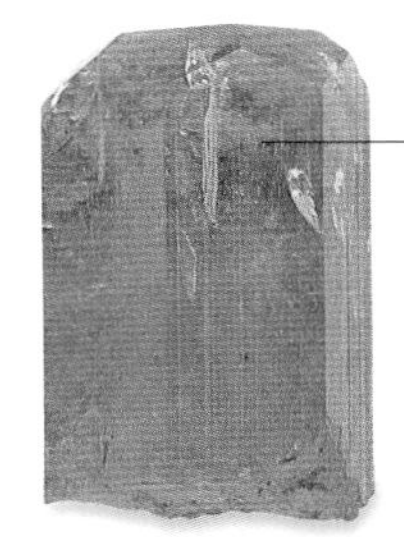

uncut aquamarine

cut aquamarine

aquamarine

aquar•i•um \ə-ˈkwer-ē-əm\ *n*
1 a container (as a tank or bowl) in which fish and other water animals and plants can live
2 a building in which water animals or water plants are exhibited

Aquar•i•us \ə-ˈkwer-ē-əs\ *n*
1 a constellation between Capricorn and Pisces imagined as a man pouring water
2 the eleventh sign of the zodiac or a person born under this sign

aquat•ic \ə-ˈkwä-tik, -ˈkwa-\ *adj*
growing, living, or done in water ⟨*aquatic* animals⟩

aq•ue•duct \ˈa-kwə-ˌdəkt\ *n*
an artificial channel used to carry water over a valley

aque•ous \'ā-kwē-əs, 'a-\ *adj*
made of, by, or with water ⟨an *aqueous* solution⟩

AR *abbr* Arkansas

-ar \ər\ *adj suffix*
of or relating to ⟨molecul*ar*⟩

Ar•ab \'er-əb\ *n*
a person born or living in the Arabian Peninsula of southwestern Asia
Arab *adj*

[1]**Ara•bi•an** \ə-'rā-bē-ən\ *n*
ARAB

[2]**Arabian** *adj*
of or relating to Arabs or to the Arabian Peninsula of southwestern Asia

[1]**Ar•a•bic** \'er-ə-bik\ *n*
a language spoken in the Arabian Peninsula of southwestern Asia, Iraq, Jordan, Lebanon, Syria, Egypt, and parts of northern Africa

[2]**Arabic** *adj*
of or relating to the Arabian Peninsula of southwestern Asia, the Arabs, or Arabic

Arabic numeral *n*
one of the number symbols 1, 2, 3, 4, 5, 6, 7, 8, 9, and 0

ar•a•ble \'er-ə-bəl\ *adj*
fit for or cultivated by plowing : suitable for producing crops ⟨*arable* land⟩

Arap•a•ho *or* **Arap•a•hoe** \ə-'ra-pə-,hō\ *n, pl* **Arapaho** *or* **Arapahos** *or* **Arapahoe** *or* **Arapahoes**
1 a member of an American Indian people of the plains region of the United States and Canada
2 the language of the Arapaho people

ar•bi•trary \'är-bə-,trer-ē\ *adj*
1 made, chosen, or acting without thought of what is fair or right ⟨*arbitrary* decisions⟩ ⟨an *arbitrary* ruler⟩
2 seeming to have been made or chosen by chance ⟨We were given an *arbitrary* list of books to choose from.⟩
ar•bi•trari•ly \,är-bə-'trer-ə-lē\ *adv*
ar•bi•trar•i•ness \'är-bə-,trer-ē-nəs\ *n*

ar•bi•trate \'är-bə-,trāt\ *vb* **ar•bi•trat•ed**; **ar•bi•trat•ing**
1 to settle a disagreement after hearing the arguments of both sides ⟨She agreed to *arbitrate* their dispute.⟩
2 to refer a dispute to others for settlement

ar•bi•tra•tion \,är-bə-'trā-shən\ *n*
the settling of a disagreement in which both sides present their arguments to a third person or group for decision

ar•bi•tra•tor \'är-bə-,trā-tər\ *n*
a person chosen to settle differences in a disagreement

ar•bor \'är-bər\ *n*
a shelter shaped like an arch over which vines grow

ar•bo•re•al \är-'bȯr-ē-əl\ *adj*
1 living in or often found in trees ⟨Koalas are *arboreal* animals.⟩
2 of or relating to a tree ⟨the forest's *arboreal* beauty⟩

archaeology
In archaeology, experts investigate remains such as tools, ornaments, and buildings to learn about the lives of ancient peoples.

gold mask

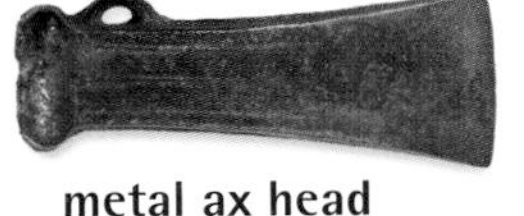

metal ax head

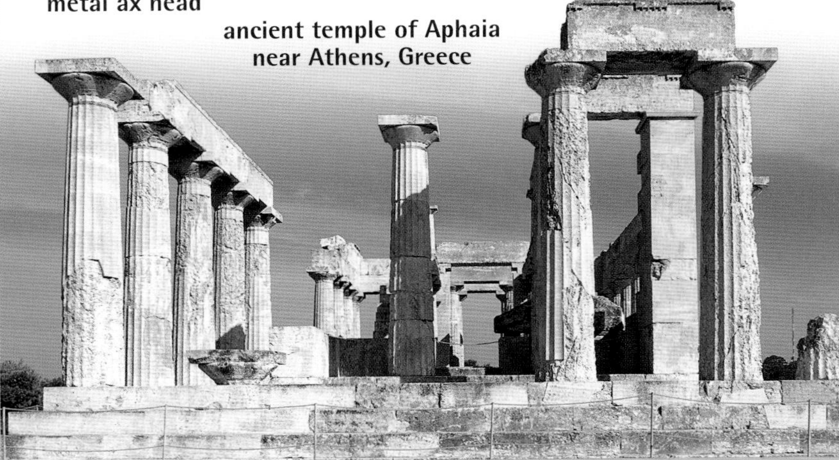

ancient temple of Aphaia near Athens, Greece

ar•bo•re•tum \,är-bə-'rē-təm\ *n, pl* **ar•bo•re•tums** *or* **ar•bo•re•ta** \-'rē-tə\
a place where trees and plants are grown to be studied

[1]**arc** \'ärk\ *n*
1 a glowing light across a gap in an electric circuit or between electrodes
2 a part of a curved line between any two points on it

[2]**arc** *vb* **arced** \'ärkt\; **arc•ing** \'är-kiŋ\
1 to form an electric arc
2 to follow a curved course ⟨A missile *arced* across the sky.⟩

ar•cade \är-'kād\ *n*
1 a row of arches supported by columns
2 an arched or covered passageway between two rows of shops
3 a place with electronic games that are operated by coins or tokens

[1]**arch 1:** a triumphal arch in Madrid, Spain

[1]**arch** \'ärch\ *n*
1 ▲ a usually curved part of a structure that is over an opening and serves as a support (as for the wall above the opening)
2 something that has a curved shape like an arch ⟨the *arch* of the foot⟩
arched \'ärcht\ *adj*

[2]**arch** *vb* **arched**; **arch•ing**
1 to form or shape into an arch : CURVE ⟨The cat *arched* her back.⟩
2 to cover with an arch ⟨Tree branches *arched* the narrow road.⟩

[3]**arch** *adj*
1 [2]CHIEF 2, PRINCIPAL ⟨an *arch* opponent⟩
2 being clever and mischievous ⟨an *arch* look⟩
arch•ly *adv*

ar•chae•ol•o•gy *or* **ar•che•ol•o•gy** \,är-kē-'ä-lə-jē\ *n*
◀ a science that deals with past human life and activities as shown by objects (as pottery, tools, and statues) left by ancient peoples

ar•cha•ic \är-ˈkā-ik\ *adj*
of, relating to, or existing from an earlier time 〈*archaic* words〉 〈*archaic* customs〉

arch•an•gel \ˈärk-ˌān-jəl\ *n*
a chief angel

arch•bish•op \ˈärch-ˈbi-shəp\ *n*
the bishop of highest rank in a group of dioceses

ar•cher \ˈär-chər\ *n*
a person who shoots with a bow and arrow

ar•chery \ˈär-chə-rē, ˈärch-rē\ *n*
the sport or practice of shooting with bow and arrows

ar•chi•pel•a•go \ˌär-kə-ˈpe-lə-ˌgō, ˌär-chə-\ *n, pl* **ar•chi•pel•a•goes** *or* **ar•chi•pel•a•gos**
a group of islands

ar•chi•tect \ˈär-kə-ˌtekt\ *n*
a person who designs buildings

ar•chi•tec•ture \ˈär-kə-ˌtek-chər\ *n*
1 ▼ the art of designing buildings 〈studying *architecture*〉
2 a style of building 〈a church of modern *architecture*〉
ar•chi•tec•tur•al *adj*
ar•chi•tec•tur•al•ly *adv*

ar•chive \ˈär-ˌkīv\ *n*
a place in which public records or historical papers are saved

arch•way \ˈärch-ˌwā\ *n*
1 a passage under an arch
2 an arch over a passage

-archy \ˌär-kē, *in a few words also* ər-kē\ *n suffix, pl* **-archies**
rule : government 〈mon*archy*〉

arc•tic \ˈärk-tik, ˈär-tik\ *adj*
1 ▶ *often cap* of or relating to the north pole or to the region around it 〈*arctic* explorers〉
2 very cold 〈*arctic* temperatures〉

▶ **Word History** The Big Dipper is a group of stars in the northern sky. It is part of a larger group of stars that ancient people thought looked like a large bear. The ancient Greeks gave the group of stars the name *arktos*, "bear." The English word *arctic* came from the Greek name for this group of stars that contains the Big Dipper. Because when we look at the Big Dipper we are looking toward the north, the word *arctic* refers to the region around the north pole.

ar•dent \ˈär-d^{ə}nt\ *adj*
showing or having warmth of feeling : PASSIONATE 〈She's an *ardent* supporter of education.〉
ar•dent•ly *adv*

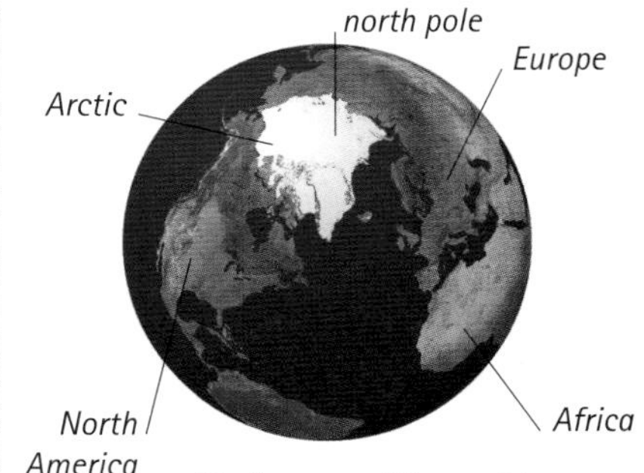

arctic 1: map of the world showing the arctic region

ar•dor \ˈär-dər\ *n*
1 warmth of feeling 〈the *ardor* of young love〉
2 great eagerness : ZEAL

ar•du•ous \ˈär-jə-wəs\ *adj*
DIFFICULT 1 〈an *arduous* climb〉
ar•du•ous•ly *adv*

are *present second person sing or present pl of* BE

ar•ea \ˈer-ē-ə\ *n*
1 REGION 1 〈a farming *area*〉
2 the amount of surface included within limits 〈the *area* of a triangle〉
3 a part of the surface of something
4 a field of activity or study 〈the *area* of medicine〉

▶ **architecture 1**
Architecture is the art of drawing plans for the construction of new buildings or for changes to existing ones. Many modern buildings, such as the one shown here, are built using concrete, glass, and steel.

The Casino de Montreal in Montreal, Canada

area code *n*
a usually three-digit number that represents a telephone service area in a country

are•na \ə-ˈrē-nə\ *n*
1 an enclosed area used for public entertainment ⟨a skating *arena*⟩
2 a building containing an enclosed area used for public entertainment
3 a field of activity ⟨the political *arena*⟩

▶ **Word History** In ancient Rome gladiators fought in big outdoor theaters. These theaters had a large open space in the middle covered with sand. The Latin word for this space, *harena,* meant literally "sand." The English word *arena* came from this Latin word.

aren't \ˈärnt, ˈär-ənt\
are not

ar•gue \ˈär-gyü\ *vb* **ar•gued; ar•gu•ing**
1 to discuss some matter usually with different points of view ⟨His parents *argue* about politics.⟩
2 to give reasons for or against something ⟨The Senator *argued* in favor of lower taxes.⟩
3 to persuade by giving reasons ⟨No one can *argue* me out of doing this.⟩
4 to disagree or fight using angry words **:** QUARREL ⟨They *argue* about everything.⟩
synonyms see DISCUSS
ar•gu•er *n*

ar•gu•ment \ˈär-gyə-mənt\ *n*
1 an angry disagreement **:** QUARREL
2 a reason for or against something ⟨There's a strong *argument* for changing the law.⟩
3 a discussion in which reasons for and against something are given

ar•id \ˈer-əd\ *adj*
not having enough rainfall to support agriculture

Ar•ies \ˈer-ˌēz, ˈer-ē-ˌēz,\ *n*
1 a constellation between Pisces and Taurus imagined as a ram
2 the first sign of the zodiac or a person born under this sign

aright \ə-ˈrīt\ *adv*
in a correct way ⟨She tried to set things *aright.*⟩

arise \ə-ˈrīz\ *vb* **arose** \-ˈrōz\; **aris•en** \-ˈri-zᵊn\; **aris•ing** \-ˈrī-ziŋ\
1 to move upward ⟨Mist *arose* from the valley.⟩
2 to get up from sleep or after lying down
3 to come into existence ⟨A dispute *arose.*⟩

ar•is•toc•ra•cy \ˌer-ə-ˈstä-krə-sē\ *n, pl* **ar•is•toc•ra•cies**
1 a government that is run by a small class of people
2 an upper class that is usually based on birth and is richer and more powerful than the rest of a society
3 people thought of as being better than the rest of the community

aris•to•crat \ə-ˈri-stə-ˌkrat, ˈer-ə-stə-\ *n*
a member of an aristocracy

aris•to•crat•ic \ə-ˌri-stə-ˈkra-tik, ˌer-ə-stə-\ *adj*
of or relating to the aristocracy or aristocrats
aris•to•crat•i•cal•ly \-ti-kə-lē\ *adv*

arith•me•tic \ə-ˈrith-mə-ˌtik\ *n*
1 a science that deals with the addition, subtraction, multiplication, and division of numbers
2 an act or method of adding, subtracting, multiplying, or dividing
arith•met•ic \ˌer-ith-ˈme-tik\ *or* **ar•ith•met•i•cal** \-ti-kəl\ *adj*

ar•ith•met•ic mean \ˌer-ith-ˈme-tik-\ *n*
a quantity formed by adding quantities together and dividing by their number ⟨The *arithmetic mean* of 6, 4, and 5 is 5.⟩

Ariz. *abbr* Arizona

ark \ˈärk\ *n, often cap*
1 the ship in which an ancient Hebrew of the Bible named Noah and his family were saved from a great flood that God sent down on the world because of its wickedness
2 a cabinet in a synagogue for the scrolls of the Torah

Ark. *abbr* Arkansas

¹arm \ˈärm\ *n*
1 ▶ a human upper limb especially between the shoulder and wrist
2 something like an arm in shape or position ⟨an *arm* of the sea⟩ ⟨the *arm* of a chair⟩
3 SLEEVE 1
4 ¹POWER 1 ⟨the long *arm* of the law⟩
5 a foreleg of a four-footed animal

²arm *vb* **armed; arm•ing**
1 to provide with weapons
2 to provide with a way of fighting, competing, or succeeding ⟨She *armed* her lawyer with facts.⟩

³arm *n*
1 WEAPON, FIREARM
2 a branch of an army or of the military forces
3 **arms** *pl* the designs on a shield or flag of a family or government
4 **arms** *pl* actual fighting **:** WARFARE ⟨a call to *arms*⟩

ar•ma•da \är-ˈmä-də, -ˈmā-\ *n*
a large fleet of warships

ar•ma•dil•lo \ˌär-mə-ˈdi-lō\ *n, pl* **ar•ma•dil•los**
▼ a small burrowing animal found from Texas to Argentina that has the head and body protected by small bony plates

armadillo

ar•ma•ment \ˈär-mə-mənt\ *n*
1 the military strength and equipment of a nation
2 the supply of materials for war
3 the process of preparing for war ⟨the country's long *armament*⟩

ar•ma•ture \ˈär-mə-chər\ *n*
the part of an electric motor or generator that turns in a magnetic field

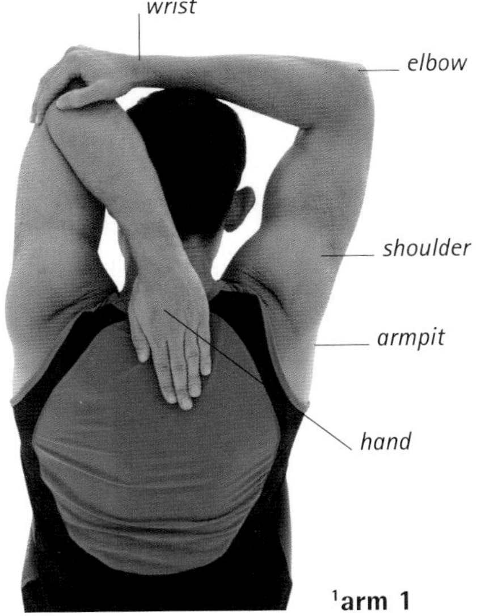

¹arm 1

arm•chair \ˈärm-ˌcher\ *n*
a chair with armrests

¹armed \ˈärmd\ *adj*
1 carrying weapons ⟨*armed* bandits⟩
2 involving the use of weapons ⟨an *armed* robbery⟩

²armed *adj*
having arms of a specified kind or number ⟨hairy-*armed*⟩ ⟨one-*armed*⟩

armed forces *n pl*
the military, naval, and air forces of a nation

arm•ful \ˈärm-ˌfu̇l\ *n, pl* **arm•fuls** \-ˌfu̇lz\ *or* **arms•ful** \ˈärmz-ˌfu̇l\
as much as a person's arm can hold

ar•mi•stice \ˈär-mə-stəs\ *n*
a pause in fighting brought about by agreement between the two sides

ar•mor \ˈär-mər\ *n*
1 ▶ a covering (as of metal) to protect the body in battle
2 a hard covering that provides protection ⟨A turtle's shell is its *armor.*⟩
3 armored forces and vehicles (as tanks)

ar•mored \ˈär-mərd\ *adj*
protected by or equipped with armor ⟨*armored* cars⟩

ar•mory \ˈär-mə-rē\ *n, pl* **ar•mor•ies**
1 a supply of weapons
2 a place where weapons are kept and where soldiers are often trained
3 a place where weapons are made

arm•pit \ˈärm-ˌpit\ *n*
the hollow under a person's arm where the arm joins the shoulder

ar•my \ˈär-mē\ *n, pl* **ar•mies**
1 a large body of soldiers trained for land warfare
2 *often cap* the complete military organization of a nation for land warfare
3 a great number of people or things ⟨an *army* of volunteers⟩

aro•ma \ə-ˈrō-mə\ *n*
a noticeable and pleasant smell

ar•o•mat•ic \ˌer-ə-ˈma-tik\ *adj*
of, relating to, or having a noticeable and pleasant smell ⟨*aromatic* spices⟩

arose *past of* ARISE

[1]around \ə-ˈrau̇nd\ *adv*
1 in circumference ⟨The tree is five feet *around.*⟩
2 in or along a curving course ⟨The road goes *around* the lake.⟩
3 on all sides ⟨Papers were lying *around.*⟩
4 NEARBY ⟨Stay *around* a while.⟩
5 in close so as to surround ⟨People gathered *around* to see.⟩
6 in many different directions or places ⟨He likes to travel *around* from state to state.⟩
7 to each in turn ⟨Pass the candy *around.*⟩
8 in an opposite direction ⟨Turn *around.*⟩
9 almost but not exactly : APPROXIMATELY ⟨The price is *around* five dollars.⟩

[2]around *prep*
1 in a curving path along the outside boundary of ⟨He walked *around* the house and peeked in the windows.⟩
2 on every side of ⟨A crowd gathered *around* the winner.⟩
3 on or to another side of ⟨*around* the corner⟩

armor 1

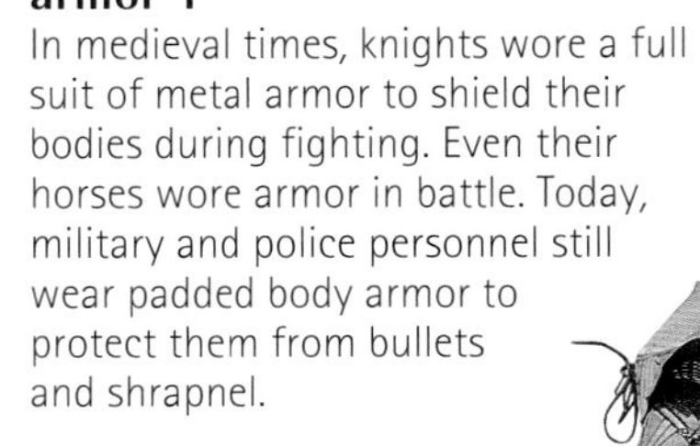

In medieval times, knights wore a full suit of metal armor to shield their bodies during fighting. Even their horses wore armor in battle. Today, military and police personnel still wear padded body armor to protect them from bullets and shrapnel.

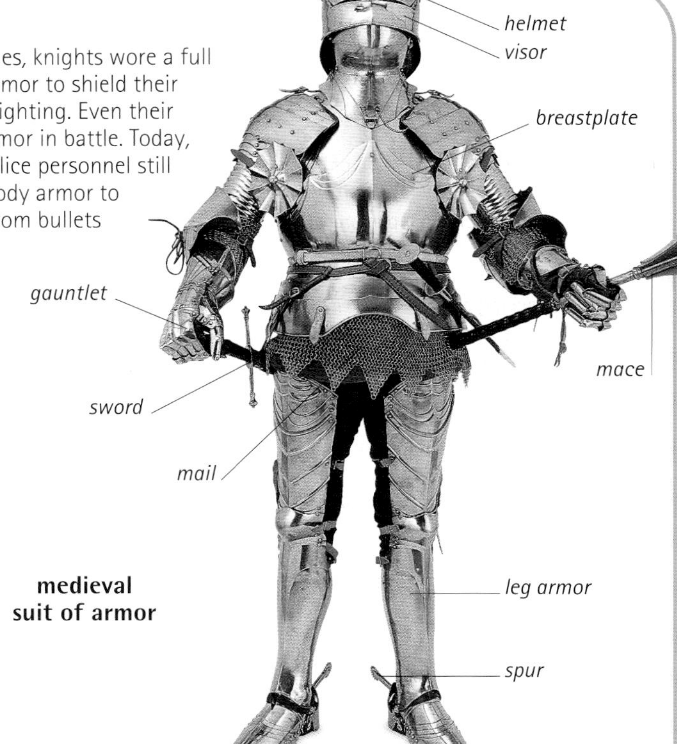

medieval suit of armor

4 here and there in ⟨She plans to travel *around* the country.⟩
5 near in number, time, or amount ⟨They left *around* three o'clock.⟩
6 in the area near to ⟨Fish are plentiful *around* the reefs.⟩

arouse \ə-ˈrau̇z\ *vb* **aroused**; **arous•ing**
1 to awaken from sleep
2 to cause to feel ⟨*arouse* anger⟩
3 to cause to become active or upset ⟨*arouse* the opposition⟩

ar•range \ə-ˈrānj\ *vb* **ar•ranged**; **ar•rang•ing**
1 to put in order and especially a particular order ⟨The books were *arranged* by subject.⟩
2 to make plans for ⟨*arrange* a meeting⟩
3 to come to an agreement about : SETTLE ⟨*arrange* a truce⟩
4 to write or change (a piece of music) to suit particular voices or instruments
ar•rang•er *n*

ar•range•ment \ə-ˈrānj-mənt\ *n*
1 the act of putting things in order : the order in which things are put ⟨the *arrangement* of furniture in a room⟩
2 something made by putting things together and organizing them ⟨a flower *arrangement*⟩
3 preparation or planning done in advance ⟨Have you made *arrangements* for the trip?⟩
4 a usually informal agreement ⟨a business *arrangement*⟩
5 a piece of music written or changed to suit particular voices or instruments

ar•rant \ˈer-ənt\ *adj*
of the worst kind ⟨*arrant* nonsense⟩

[1]ar•ray \ə-ˈrā\ *vb* **ar•rayed**; **ar•ray•ing**
1 to place in order ⟨Soldiers *arrayed* themselves for review.⟩ ⟨The table was *arrayed* with all sorts of delicacies.⟩
2 to dress especially in fine or beautiful clothing

[2]array *n*
1 an impressive group ⟨You can choose from an *array* of colors.⟩
2 a group of persons (as soldiers) in a certain order
3 fine or beautiful clothing ⟨They were dressed in magnificent *array.*⟩
4 regular order or arrangement
5 a group of mathematical elements (as numbers or letters) arranged in rows and columns

ar•rears \ə-ˈrirz\ *n pl*
1 the state of being behind in paying debts ⟨He is two months in *arrears* with the rent.⟩
2 unpaid and overdue debts ⟨She's been trying to pay off the *arrears.*⟩

A B C D E F G H I J K L M N O P Q R S T U V W X Y Z

[1]**ar•rest** \ə-ˈrest\ *vb* **ar•rest•ed; ar•rest•ing**
1 to take or keep control over (someone) by authority of law ⟨She was *arrested* on suspicion of robbery.⟩
2 to stop the progress or movement of : CHECK ⟨*arrest* a disease⟩
3 to attract and hold the attention of

[2]**arrest** *n*
the act of taking or holding a person by authority of law

ar•riv•al \ə-ˈrī-vəl\ *n*
1 the act of reaching a place
2 the time when something begins or happens ⟨the *arrival* of spring⟩
3 a person or thing that has come to a place

ar•rive \ə-ˈrīv\ *vb* **ar•rived; ar•riv•ing**
1 to reach the place started out for ⟨We *arrived* home at six o'clock.⟩
2 COME 4 ⟨The time to leave finally *arrived.*⟩
3 to be born ⟨The baby *arrived* at noon on Monday.⟩
arrive at to reach by effort or thought ⟨*arrive at* a decision⟩

ar•ro•gance \ˈer-ə-gəns\ *n*
a person's sense of his or her own importance that shows itself in a proud and insulting way

ar•ro•gant \ˈer-ə-gənt\ *adj*
showing the attitude of a person who is overly proud of himself or herself or of his or her own opinions
ar•ro•gant•ly *adv*

ar•row \ˈer-ō\ *n*
1 ▼ a weapon that is shot from a bow and Is usually a stick with a point at one end and feathers at the other
2 a mark to show direction ⟨Follow the *arrows* on the signs.⟩

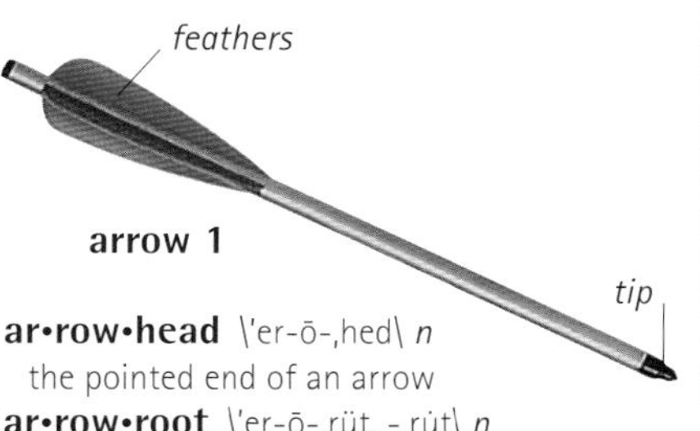

arrow 1

ar•row•head \ˈer-ō-ˌhed\ *n*
the pointed end of an arrow

ar•row•root \ˈer-ō-ˌrüt, -ˌru̇t\ *n*
an edible starch obtained from the roots of a tropical plant

ar•se•nal \ˈärs-nəl, ˈär-sə-\ *n*
a place where military equipment is made and stored

ar•se•nic \ˈärs-nik, ˈär-sə-\ *n*
a solid poisonous chemical element that is usually gray and snaps easily

ar•son \ˈär-sᵊn\ *n*
the illegal burning of a building or other property

art \ˈärt\ *n*
1 ▼ works (as pictures, poems, or songs) made through use of the imagination and creative skills by artists ⟨the *art* of the Renaissance⟩
2 the methods and skills used for creative visual works (as painting, sculpting, and drawing) ⟨a teacher of *art*⟩
3 an activity (as painting, music, or writing) whose purpose is making things that are beautiful to look at, listen to, or read ⟨the performing *arts*⟩
4 skill that comes through experience or study ⟨the *art* of making friends⟩
5 an activity that requires skill ⟨Cooking is an *art.*⟩

ar•tery \ˈär-tə-rē\ *n, pl* **ar•ter•ies**
1 one of the branching tubes that carry blood from the heart to all parts of the body
2 a main road or waterway

art 1
Painting, film, music, and literature are all forms of art, created by artists to entertain or instruct their audience.

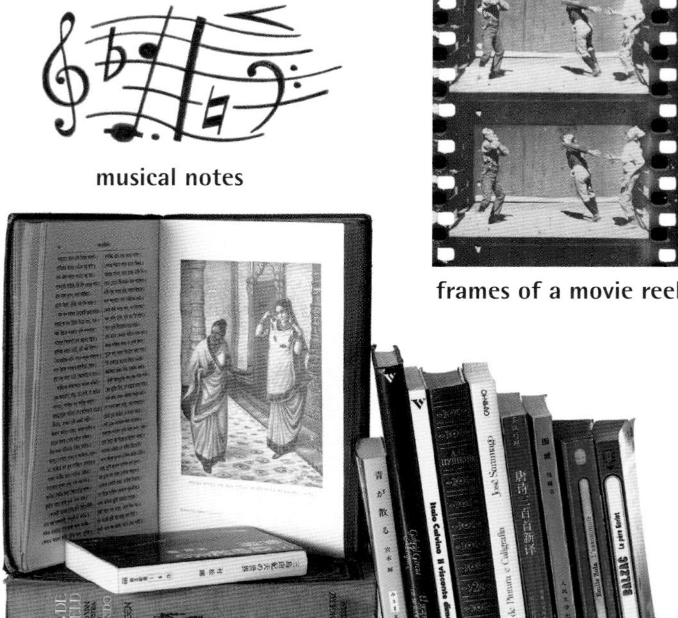

musical notes

frames of a movie reel

printed books

an oil painting:
Nicolas-Guy Brenet's *Flight into Egypt*

art•ful \'ärt-fəl\ *adj*
1 done with or showing art or skill ⟨*artful* writing⟩
2 clever at taking advantage ⟨an *artful* salesman⟩
art•ful•ly \-fə-lē\ *adv*

ar•thri•tis \är-'thrī-təs\ *n*
a condition in which the joints are painful and swollen

ar•thro•pod \'är-thrə-,päd\ *n*
▶ any of a large group of animals (as crabs, insects, and spiders) with jointed limbs and a body made up of segments

ar•ti•choke \'är-tə-,chōk\ *n*
▼ the immature flower head of a Mediterranean plant that is cooked and eaten as a vegetable

artichoke

ar•ti•cle \'är-ti-kəl\ *n*
1 a piece of writing other than fiction or poetry that forms a separate part of a publication (as a magazine or newspaper)
2 one of a class of things ⟨*articles* of clothing⟩
3 a word (as *a*, *an*, or *the*) used with a noun to limit it or make it clearer
4 a separate part of a document

[1]**ar•tic•u•late** \är-'ti-kyə-lət\ *adj*
1 clearly understandable ⟨an *articulate* essay⟩
2 able to express oneself clearly and well ⟨an *articulate* speaker⟩
ar•tic•u•late•ly *adv*

[2]**ar•tic•u•late** \är-'ti-kyə-,lāt\ *vb*
ar•tic•u•lat•ed; **ar•tic•u•lat•ing**
to speak or pronounce clearly

ar•tic•u•la•tion \är-,ti-kyə-'lā-shən\ *n*
the making of articulate sounds (as in speaking)

ar•ti•fice \'är-tə-fəs\ *n*
a clever trick or device ⟨She used every *artifice* to avoid work.⟩

ar•ti•fi•cial \,är-tə-'fi-shəl\ *adj*
1 made by humans ⟨an *artificial* lake⟩
2 not natural in quality ⟨an *artificial* smile⟩
3 made to seem like something natural ⟨*artificial* flowers⟩ ⟨*artificial* flavoring⟩
ar•ti•fi•cial•ly *adv*

artificial respiration *n*
the forcing of air into and out of the lungs of a person whose breathing has stopped

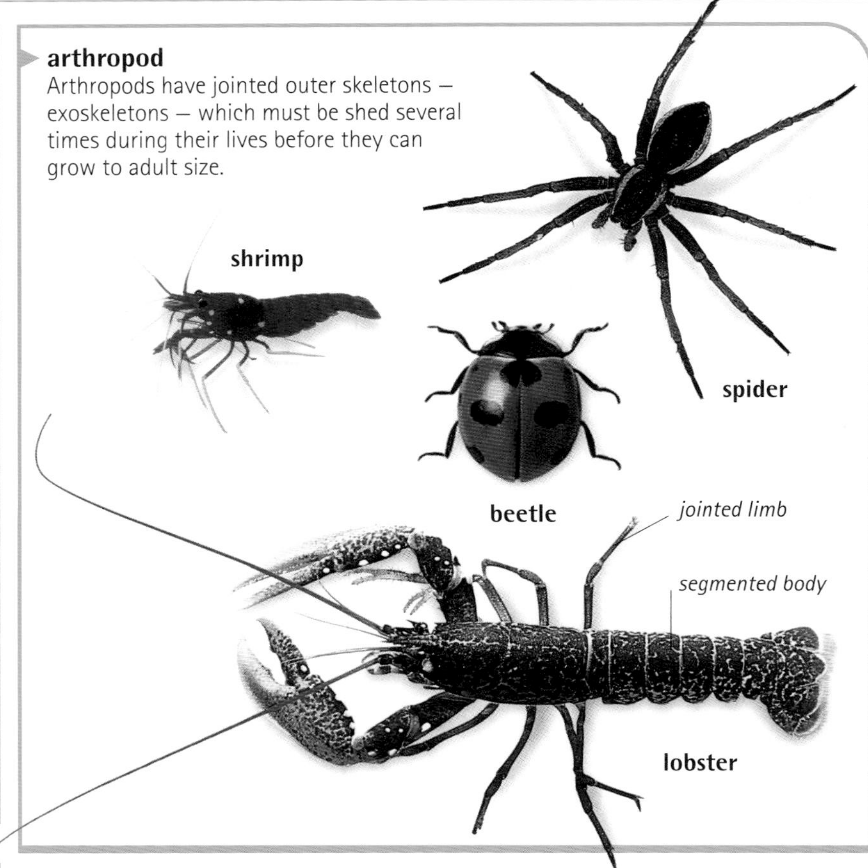

arthropod
Arthropods have jointed outer skeletons — exoskeletons — which must be shed several times during their lives before they can grow to adult size.

ar•til•lery \är-'ti-lə-rē\ *n*
1 ▼ large firearms (as cannon or rockets)
2 a branch of an army armed with artillery

ar•ti•san \'är-tə-zən\ *n*
a person who makes things by using skill with the hands

art•ist \'är-tist\ *n*
1 a person skilled in one of the arts (as painting, music, or writing)
2 a person who is very good at something

ar•tis•tic \är-'tis-tik\ *adj*
1 relating to art or artists
2 having or showing skill and imagination
ar•tis•ti•cal•ly \-sti-kə-lē\ *adv*

[1]**-ary** \,er-ē, ə-rē\ *n suffix, pl* **-ar•ies**
thing or person belonging to or connected with ⟨bound*ary*⟩

[2]**-ary** *adj suffix*
of, relating to, or connected with ⟨legend*ary*⟩

[1]**as** \əz, az\ *adv*
1 to the same degree or amount ⟨*as* good as gold⟩
2 for example ⟨various trees, *as* oaks and maples⟩

[2]**as** *conj*
1 in equal amount or degree with ⟨cold *as* ice⟩
2 in the way that ⟨Do *as* I say.⟩ ⟨You can come and go *as* you please.⟩

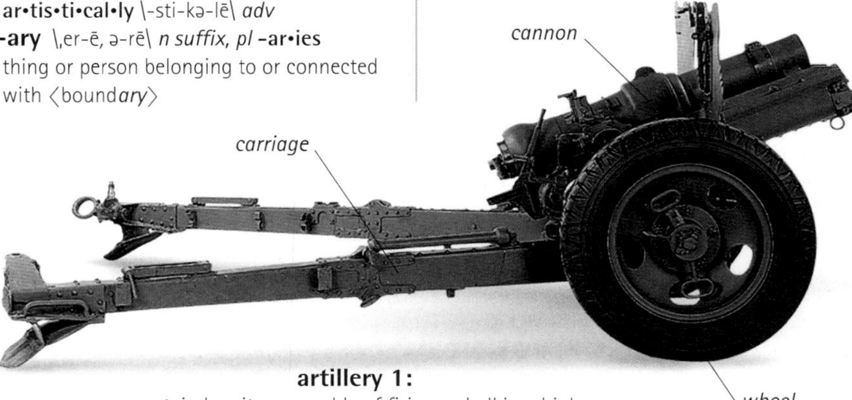

artillery 1:
a mountain howitzer, capable of firing a shell in a high arc

3 at the same time that 〈They sang *as* they marched.〉
4 for the reason that : BECAUSE 〈I stayed home, *as* I had no car.〉

[3]**as** *pron*
1 [1]THAT 1, WHO, WHICH 〈She was a kind soul such *as* I'd never known before.〉 〈He has the same name *as* my cousin does.〉
2 a fact that 〈You are happy, *as* we all know.〉 〈*As* I said before, you must leave.〉

[4]**as** *prep*
1 [4]LIKE 1 〈I went dressed *as* a princess.〉
2 in the position or role of 〈He works *as* a firefighter.〉

as•bes•tos \as-'bes-təs, az-\ *n*
a grayish mineral that separates easily into long flexible fibers and has been used especially in the past in making fireproof materials

as•cend \ə-'send\ *vb* **as•cend•ed**; **as•cend•ing**
1 to go or move up 〈We *ascended* the hill.〉
2 to rise to a higher or more powerful position 〈Abraham Lincoln *ascended* to the presidency in 1861.〉

► **Synonyms** ASCEND, MOUNT, and CLIMB mean to move upward or toward the top. ASCEND is used for a gradual upward movement. 〈We slowly *ascended* the staircase.〉 MOUNT is used for reaching the very top of something. 〈Soldiers *mounted* the hill and placed a flag there.〉 CLIMB is used when effort and often the hands and feet are needed to move up something. 〈Explorers *climbed* the rugged mountain.〉

as•cen•sion \ə-'sen-shən\ *n*
the act or process of moving or rising up especially to a higher or more powerful position 〈*ascension* to the throne〉

as•cent \ə-'sent\ *n*
1 ► the act of rising or climbing upward 〈The hikers began their *ascent* of the mountain.〉
2 the act of rising to a higher or more powerful position
3 an upward slope or path

as•cer•tain \ˌa-sər-'tān\ *vb* **as•cer•tained**; **as•cer•tain•ing**
to find out with certainty 〈Police tried to *ascertain* the cause of the accident.〉

as•cribe \ə-'skrīb\ *vb* **as•cribed**; **as•crib•ing**
to think of as coming from a specified cause, source, or author 〈They *ascribed* his success to nothing more than good luck.〉

asex•u•al \'ā-'sek-shə-wəl\ *adj*
formed by, characterized by, or being a process of reproduction (as the dividing of one cell into two cells) that does not involve the combining of male and female germ cells
asex•u•al•ly \-wə-lē\ *adv*

[1]**ash** \'ash\ *n*
a tree that has seeds with a winglike part, bark with grooves, and hard strong wood

[2]**ash** *n*
1 the solid matter left when something is completely burned 〈cigarette *ashes*〉 〈Wind blew the *ash* left by our fire.〉
2 *ashes pl* the last remains of the dead human body

ashamed \ə-'shāmd\ *adj*
1 feeling shame, guilt, or disgrace 〈I'm *ashamed* of my behavior.〉
2 kept from doing something by fear of shame or embarrassment 〈He was *ashamed* to beg.〉

ash•en \'a-shən\ *adj*
1 of the color of ashes
2 very pale 〈She was *ashen* with fear.〉

ashore \ə-'shȯr\ *adv*
on or to the shore 〈We collected seashells that the waves had washed *ashore*.〉

ashy \'a-shē\ *adj* **ash•i•er**; **ash•i•est**
1 of or relating to ashes
2 very pale 〈an *ashy* face〉

[1]**Asian** \'ā-zhən\ *adj*
of or relating to Asia or its people 〈*Asian* cities〉 〈*Asian* cooking〉

[2]**Asian** *n*
a person born or living in Asia

Asian–Amer•i•can \-ə-'mer-ə-kən\ *n*
an American who has Asian ancestors

aside \ə-'sīd\ *adv*
1 to or toward the side 〈stepped *aside*〉
2 out of the way especially for future use 〈She's putting money *aside* for a car.〉
3 not included or considered 〈All kidding *aside*, we think you did a great job.〉

aside from *prep*
with the exception of 〈*Aside from* a few pieces of bread, the food is gone.〉

ascent 1

a b c d e f g h i j k l m n o p q r s t u v w x y z

A B C D E F G H I J K L M N O P Q R S T U V W X Y Z

as if *conj*
1 the way it would be if ⟨It's *as if* we'd never left.⟩
2 as someone would do if ⟨They acted *as if* they knew me.⟩
3 [2]THAT 1 ⟨It seemed *as if* the day would never end.⟩

ask \'ask\ *vb* **asked**; **ask•ing**
1 to seek information by posing a question ⟨She *asked* if I was worried.⟩ ⟨They *asked* about our trip.⟩
2 to make a request ⟨Did you *ask* for help?⟩
3 to set as a price ⟨I'm *asking* ten dollars for my skates.⟩
4 INVITE 1 ⟨I *asked* some friends to my party.⟩
5 to behave as if seeking a result ⟨You're *asking* for trouble.⟩

askance \ə-'skans\ *adv*
1 with a side glance ⟨She did not turn her head but watched him *askance.*⟩
2 with distrust or disapproval ⟨We looked *askance* at the strangers.⟩

askew \ə-'skyü\ *adv or adj*
not straight : at an angle ⟨pictures hanging *askew*⟩

aslant \ə-'slant\ *adv or adj*
in a slanting direction ⟨with head *aslant*⟩

[1]**asleep** \ə-'slēp\ *adj*
1 being in a state of sleep
2 having no feeling ⟨My foot is *asleep.*⟩

[2]**asleep** *adv*
into a state of sleep ⟨I fell *asleep* during the movie.⟩

as of *prep*
[1]ON 8, AT ⟨We begin work *as of* Tuesday.⟩

as•par•a•gus \ə-'sper-ə-gəs\ *n*
► a vegetable that is the young shoots of a garden plant related to the lilies that lives for many years

► **Word History** The word *asparagus* is borrowed from the ancient Greeks' name for the plant, *asparagos,* which could also just refer to the young shoot of any plant. This word is probably related to a Greek verb *spharageitai,* meaning "it's full to bursting," which might describe a fast-growing plant shoot. But to English speakers the word has sometimes seemed odd and a little difficult to say. In the American countryside people have turned *asparagus* into "aspergrass" or "aspirin grass" or—the most popular—"sparrow grass." These expressions are easier to say and tickle our sense of humor a bit.

as•pect \'a-,spekt\ *n*
1 the appearance of something : LOOK ⟨The old house took on a dark and lonely *aspect* at night.⟩
2 a certain way in which something appears or may be thought of ⟨We considered every *aspect* of the question.⟩
3 a position facing a certain direction ⟨The house has a southern *aspect.*⟩

as•pen \'a-spən\ *n*
► a poplar tree whose leaves move easily in the breeze

aspen leaves

as•phalt \'as-,fólt\ *n*
1 a dark-colored substance obtained from natural deposits in the earth or from petroleum
2 any of various materials made of asphalt that are used for pavements and as a waterproof cement

as•phyx•i•ate \as-'fik-sē-,āt\ *vb* **as•phyx•i•at•ed**; **as•phyx•i•at•ing**
to cause (as a person) to become unconscious or die by cutting off the normal taking in of oxygen whether by blocking breathing or by replacing the oxygen of the air with another gas

as•pi•ra•tion \,a-spə-'rā-shən\ *n*
1 a strong desire to achieve something ⟨She left home with *aspirations* for a better life.⟩
2 something that someone wants very much to achieve ⟨Fame has always been his *aspiration.*⟩

asparagus

as•pire \ə-'spīr\ *vb* **as•pired**; **as•pir•ing**
to very much want to have or achieve something ⟨*aspire* to greatness⟩

as•pi•rin \'a-sprən, 'a-spə-rən\ *n*
a white drug used to relieve pain and fever

ass \'as\ *n*
1 ► an animal that looks like but is smaller than the related horse and has shorter hair in the mane and tail and longer ears : DONKEY
2 a stupid or stubborn person
Hint: This sense of the word is often considered impolite, and you may offend people by using it.

as•sail \ə-'sāl\ *vb* **as•sailed**; **as•sail•ing**
1 to attack violently or angrily with blows or words ⟨His plan was *assailed* by critics.⟩
2 to be troubled or bothered by ⟨*assailed* by doubts⟩ ⟨A horrible odor *assailed* my nose.⟩

as•sail•ant \ə-'sā-lənt\ *n*
a person who attacks someone violently

as•sas•sin \ə-'sa-,sᵊn\ *n*
someone who kills another person usually for pay or from loyalty to a cause

as•sas•si•nate \ə-'sa-sə-,nāt\ *vb* **as•sas•si•nat•ed**; **as•sas•si•nat•ing**
to murder a usually important person by a surprise or secret attack
synonyms see KILL

as•sas•si•na•tion \ə-,sa-sə-'nā-shən\ *n*
the act of murdering a usually important person by a surprise or secret attack

[1]**as•sault** \ə-'sólt\ *n*
1 a violent or sudden attack ⟨a military *assault* on the castle⟩
2 an unlawful attempt or threat to harm someone

[2]**assault** *vb* **as•sault•ed**; **as•sault•ing**
to violently attack ⟨Enemy forces *assaulted* the city.⟩

as•sem•blage \ə-'sem-blij\ *n*
a collection of persons or things ⟨an *assemblage* of parents and teachers⟩

as•sem•ble \ə-'sem-bəl\ *vb* **as•sem•bled**; **as•sem•bling**
1 to collect in one place or group ⟨She *assembled* all her trophies for display.⟩
2 to fit together the parts of ⟨*assemble* a toy⟩
3 to meet together in one place ⟨The class *assembled* in the cafeteria.⟩
synonyms see GATHER
as•sem•bler *n*

as•sem•bly \ə-'sem-blē\ *n, pl* **as•sem•blies**
1 a group of people gathered together ⟨an *assembly* of citizens⟩ ⟨a school *assembly*⟩

ass 1

2 *cap* a group of people who make and change laws for a government or organization
3 the act of gathering together ⟨The right of *assembly* is protected by the First Amendment to the United States Constitution.⟩
4 the act of connecting together the parts of ⟨This toy requires no *assembly.*⟩
5 a collection of parts that make up a complete unit

assembly line *n*
▼ an arrangement for assembling a product mechanically in which work passes from one operation to the next in a direct line until the product is finished

[1]as•sent \ə-ˈsent\ *vb* **as•sent•ed; as•sent•ing**
to agree to or approve of something

as•ser•tion \ə-ˈsər-shən\ *n*
1 the act of stating clearly and strongly or making others aware ⟨the *assertion* of his innocence⟩
2 something stated as if certain

as•ser•tive \ə-ˈsər-tiv\ *adj*
having a bold or confident manner ⟨an *assertive* attitude⟩

as•sess \ə-ˈses\ *vb* **as•sessed; as•sess•ing**
1 to make a judgment about ⟨The school *assessed* the students' progress each year.⟩
2 to decide on the rate, value, or amount of (as for taxation) ⟨The jury *assessed* damages of $5000.⟩ ⟨The house was *assessed* at $140,000.⟩
3 to put a charge or tax on ⟨The city *assessed* all car owners a fee.⟩
as•ses•sor \-ər\ *n*

2 to give out to : PROVIDE ⟨Each student is *assigned* a locker.⟩
3 to give a particular quality, value, or identity to ⟨*Assign* a number to each picture.⟩

as•sign•ment \ə-ˈsīn-mənt\ *n*
1 the act of giving out or assigning ⟨the *assignment* of seats⟩
2 something (as a job or task) that is given out ⟨a homework *assignment*⟩

as•sim•i•late \ə-ˈsi-mə-ˌlāt\ *vb* **as•sim•i•lat•ed; as•sim•i•lat•ing**
1 to become or cause to become part of a different group or country ⟨She was completely *assimilated* into her new country.⟩
2 to take in and make part of a larger thing ⟨The body *assimilates* nutrients in food.⟩
3 to learn thoroughly ⟨*assimilate* new ideas⟩

assembly line: an asssembly line at a car manufacturing plant

[2]assent *n*
an act of agreeing to or approving of something

as•sert \ə-ˈsərt\ *vb* **as•sert•ed; as•sert•ing**
1 to state clearly and strongly ⟨*assert* an opinion⟩
2 to make others aware of ⟨*assert* your independence⟩
3 to speak or act in a way that demands attention or recognition ⟨If you want people to listen, you have to *assert* yourself.⟩

as•set \ˈa-ˌset\ *n*
1 someone or something that provides a benefit ⟨Your sense of humor is an *asset.*⟩ ⟨She is an *asset* to the class.⟩
2 *assets pl* all the property belonging to a person or an organization

as•sid•u•ous \ə-ˈsi-jə-wəs\ *adj*
showing great care, attention, and effort ⟨They were *assiduous* in gathering evidence.⟩
as•sid•u•ous•ly *adv*

as•sign \ə-ˈsīn\ *vb* **as•signed; as•sign•ing**
1 to give out as a job or responsibility ⟨Our teacher *assigned* homework in math.⟩

as•sim•i•la•tion \ə-ˌsi-mə-ˈlā-shən\ *n*
the act or process of assimilating

[1]as•sist \ə-ˈsist\ *vb* **as•sist•ed; as•sist•ing**
to give support or help ⟨He *assisted* his mother in preparing dinner.⟩

[2]assist *n*
an act of supporting or helping ⟨I finished my chores with an *assist* from my friends.⟩

as•sis•tance \ə-ˈsi-stəns\ *n*
1 the act of helping ⟨I need *assistance* in moving the boxes.⟩
2 the help given ⟨financial *assistance*⟩

A B C D E F G H I J K L M N O P Q R S T U V Z

[1]**as•sis•tant** \ə-ˈsi-stənt\ *adj*
acting as a helper to another ⟨an *assistant* manager⟩

[2]**assistant** *n*
a person who assists another

assn. *abbr* association

[1]**as•so•ci•ate** \ə-ˈsō-shē-ˌāt\ *vb* **as•so•ci•at•ed; as•so•ci•at•ing**
1 to join or come together as partners, friends, or companions ⟨He *associates* with some interesting people.⟩
2 to connect in thought ⟨I *associate* hot chocolate with winter.⟩

[2]**as•so•ciate** \ə-ˈsō-shē-ət, -shət\ *adj*
having a rank or position that is below the highest level ⟨an *associate* member of the club⟩

[3]**as•so•ciate** \ə-ˈsō-shē-ət, -shət\ *n*
a person who you work with or spend time with ⟨business *associates*⟩

as•so•ci•a•tion \ə-ˌsō-sē-ˈā-shən, -shē-\ *n*
1 a connection or relationship between things or people ⟨She studied the *association* between sugar intake and cavity formation.⟩
2 an organization of persons having a common interest ⟨an athletic *association*⟩
3 a feeling, memory, or thought connected with a person, place, or thing ⟨His grandparents' old house had happy *associations* for him.⟩

as•so•cia•tive \ə-ˈsō-shē-ˌā-tiv, -shə-tiv\ *adj*
relating to or being a property of a mathematical operation (as addition or multiplication) in which the result does not depend on how the elements are grouped ⟨The *associative* property of addition states that (2 + 3) + 1 and 2 + (3 + 1) will both have a sum of 6.⟩

as•sort \ə-ˈsȯrt\ *vb* **as•sort•ed; as•sort•ing**
to sort into groups of like kinds ⟨They *assorted* the marbles by color.⟩

as•sort•ed \ə-ˈsȯr-təd\ *adj*
1 ▼ made up of various kinds ⟨*assorted* chocolates⟩

assorted 1:
assorted chocolates

aster

2 suited to one another : matching or fitting together ⟨a well *assorted* pair⟩

as•sort•ment \ə-ˈsȯrt-mənt\ *n*
1 the act of sorting into groups
2 a group or collection of various or different things or persons ⟨an *assortment* of snacks⟩

asst. *abbr* assistant

as•suage \ə-ˈswāj\ *vb* **as•suaged; as•suag•ing**
to make less severe or intense ⟨*assuage* pain⟩ ⟨*assuaged* her grief⟩

as•sume \ə-ˈsüm\ *vb* **as•sumed; as•sum•ing**
1 to begin to take on or perform ⟨*assume* responsibility⟩ ⟨*assumed* the presidency⟩
2 to take or begin to have ⟨The problem *assumes* greater importance now.⟩
3 to pretend to have or be
4 to accept as true ⟨I *assume* you're right.⟩

as•sump•tion \ə-ˈsəmp-shən\ *n*
1 the act of taking on ⟨the *assumption* of power⟩
2 something accepted as true ⟨I'm making plans on the *assumption* that you will be here.⟩

as•sur•ance \ə-ˈshu̇r-əns\ *n*
1 the act of making sure or confident ⟨You have my *assurance* that it's true.⟩
2 the state of being sure or confident ⟨I lent him money with *assurance* that I would be repaid.⟩
3 SELF-CONFIDENCE

as•sure \ə-ˈshu̇r\ *vb* **as•sured; as•sur•ing**
1 to give certainty, confidence, or comfort to ⟨He *assured* the children all was well.⟩ ⟨She *assured* herself that the doors were locked.⟩
2 to inform positively ⟨I *assure* you that you won't be disappointed.⟩
3 to provide a guarantee of ⟨*assure* their safety⟩ ⟨Hard work *assures* success.⟩

as•sured \ə-ˈshu̇rd\ *adj*
1 made sure or certain ⟨Our success is by no means *assured*.⟩
2 very confident ⟨an *assured* manner⟩
as•sured•ly \-ˈshu̇r-əd-lē\ *adv*

as•ter \ˈa-stər\ *n*
◀ any of various herbs related to the daisies that have leafy stems and white, pink, purple, or yellow flower heads which bloom in the fall

as•ter•isk \ˈa-stə-ˌrisk\ *n*
a symbol * used in printing or in writing especially to refer a reader to a note usually at the bottom of a page

astern \ə-ˈstərn\ *adv*
1 in, at, or toward the back of a boat or ship : in, at, or toward the stern ⟨The island lay *astern*.⟩
2 in a reverse direction : BACKWARD ⟨The ship went full speed *astern*.⟩

as•ter•oid \ˈa-stə-ˌrȯid\ *n*
▼ one of thousands of rocky objects that move in orbits mostly between those of Mars and Jupiter and have diameters from a fraction of a mile to nearly 500 miles (800 kilometers)

asteroid

asth•ma \ˈaz-mə\ *n*
a lung disorder that causes periods of wheezing, coughing, and difficulty with breathing

as to *prep*
1 with respect to : ABOUT ⟨I'm confused *as to* what happened.⟩
2 ACCORDING TO 1 ⟨The flowers were graded *as to* color.⟩

as•ton•ish \ə-ˈstä-nish\ *vb* **as•ton•ished**; **as•ton•ish•ing**
to strike with sudden wonder or surprise ⟨I was *astonished* to find a meteorite in my backyard.⟩
synonyms see SURPRISE

as•ton•ish•ment \ə-ˈstä-nish-mənt\ *n*
great surprise or wonder : AMAZEMENT ⟨We watched in *astonishment.*⟩

as•tound \ə-ˈstau̇nd\ *vb* **as•tound•ed**; **as•tound•ing**
to fill with puzzled wonder ⟨The magician will *astound* you.⟩

astray \ə-ˈstrā\ *adv or adj*
1 off the right path or route ⟨Our rocket went *astray* after liftoff.⟩
2 in or into error ⟨Their plans have gone *astray.*⟩

astride \ə-ˈstrīd\ *prep*
with one leg on each side of ⟨He sat *astride* his horse.⟩

as•trin•gent \ə-ˈstrin-jənt\ *n*
a substance that is able to shrink or tighten body tissues
astringent *adj*

astro- \ˈa-strə, -strō\ *prefix*
star : heavens : astronomical

as•trol•o•gy \ə-ˈsträ-lə-jē\ *n*
the study of the supposed influences of the stars and planets on people's lives and behavior

as•tro•naut \ˈa-strə-ˌnȯt\ *n*
▼ a person who travels beyond the earth's atmosphere : a traveler in a spacecraft

as•tro•nau•tics \ˌa-strə-ˈnȯ-tiks\ *n*
the science of the construction and operation of spacecraft

as•tron•o•mer \ə-ˈsträ-nə-mər\ *n*
a person who is a specialist in astronomy

astronaut: an astronaut on the moon

astronomy
Astronomy is the study of what exists in the universe outside the earth's atmosphere. Modern astronomers learn about the universe using powerful ground-based telescopes, space probes, and satellites.

telescope

star chart showing constellations

as•tro•nom•i•cal \ˌa-strə-ˈnä-mi-kəl\ *or* **as•tro•nom•ic** \-ik\ *adj*
1 of or relating to astronomy ⟨*astronomical* research⟩
2 extremely or unbelievably large ⟨The cost was *astronomical.*⟩
as•tro•nom•i•cal•ly *adv*

as•tron•o•my \ə-ˈsträ-nə-mē\ *n*
▲ a science concerned with objects and matter outside the earth's atmosphere and of their motions and makeup

as•tute \ə-ˈstüt, -ˈstyüt\ *adj*
very alert and aware : CLEVER ⟨an *astute* observer⟩
as•tute•ly *adv*

asun•der \ə-ˈsən-dər\ *adv*
into parts ⟨torn *asunder*⟩

as well as *conj*
and in addition ⟨brave *as well as* loyal⟩

asy•lum \ə-ˈsī-ləm\ *n*
1 a place of protection and shelter ⟨They sought *asylum* from the storm.⟩
2 protection given especially to political refugees
3 a place for the care of the poor or the physically or mentally ill
Hint: Sense 3 is somewhat old-fashioned.

asym•met•ri•cal \ˌā-sə-ˈme-tri-kəl\ *adj*
having two sides or halves that are not the same : not symmetrical

at \ət, at\ *prep*
1 used to indicate a particular place or time ⟨They're *at* the door.⟩ ⟨Be here *at* six.⟩
2 used to indicate the person or thing toward which an action, motion, or feeling is directed or aimed ⟨swinging *at* the ball⟩ ⟨laughed *at* me⟩
3 used to indicate position or condition ⟨*at* rest⟩
4 used to tell how or why ⟨sold *at* auction⟩ ⟨angry *at* his answer⟩
5 used to indicate time, age, or position on a scale ⟨ate *at* noon⟩ ⟨temperature *at* 90 degrees⟩

ate *past of* EAT

[1]-ate \ət, ˌāt\ *n suffix*
one acted upon in such a way ⟨duplic*ate*⟩

[2]-ate *n suffix*
office : rank : group of persons holding such an office or rank

[3]-ate *adj suffix*
marked by having ⟨vertebr*ate*⟩

[4]-ate \ˌāt\ *vb suffix*
1 cause to be changed or affected by ⟨pollin*ate*⟩
2 cause to become ⟨activ*ate*⟩
3 furnish with ⟨aer*ate*⟩

athe•ist \ˈā-thē-ist\ *n*
a person who believes there is no God

ath•lete \ˈath-ˌlēt\ *n*
a person who is trained in or good at games and exercises that require physical skill, endurance, and strength

A B C D E F G H I J K L M N O P Q R S T U V W X Y Z

athletics

Athletics involve a variety of exercises, sports, or games requiring physical skills that are engaged in by athletes. Some athletes compete for medals, or titles, while many people practice athletics for personal fitness.

shot

shot put is a field event in which a heavy metallic ball – the shot – is "put" with a single pushing action.

long jump is a field event in which the athlete runs and then jumps from a mark on a board at the end of the run-up, landing into the sand. The jump is measured from the mark to the nearest part of the sand touched by the athlete on landing.

tennis is a racket sport played between two players (singles) or between two teams of two players (doubles). The players use a stringed racket to strike a hollow rubber ball covered with felt over a net into the opponent's court.

weight training is a system of physical conditioning that involves lifting weights. Different muscles are worked, building muscle mass to increase strength. Weight training also improves physical endurance. This woman is strengthening her triceps by moving a weight from a position parallel to the floor to a position perpendicular to the floor.

athlete's foot *n*
a fungus infection of the foot marked by blisters, itching, and cracks between and under the toes

ath•let•ic \ath-'le-tik\ *adj*
1 of, relating to, or characteristic of athletes or athletics ⟨an *athletic* event⟩
2 used by athletes ⟨*athletic* equipment⟩
3 active in sports or exercises ⟨She's very *athletic*.⟩
4 strong and muscular ⟨an *athletic* build⟩

ath•let•ics \ath-'le-tiks\ *n pl*
◀ games, sports, and exercises requiring strength, endurance, and skill
Hint: *Athletics* can be used as a singular or a plural in writing and speaking. ⟨*Athletics* is an important part of their curriculum.⟩ ⟨*Athletics* are helpful in staying fit.⟩

-ation \'ā-shən\ *n suffix*
1 action or process ⟨comput*ation*⟩
2 something connected with an action or process ⟨discolor*ation*⟩

-ative \ə-tiv, ˌā-\ *adj suffix*
1 of, relating to, or connected with ⟨authorit*ative*⟩
2 designed to do something ⟨inform*ative*⟩
3 tending to ⟨talk*ative*⟩

at•las \'at-ləs\ *n*
a book of maps

ATM \ˌā-ˌtē-'em\ *n*
a computerized machine that performs basic banking functions (as cash withdrawals)

at•mo•sphere \'at-mə-ˌsfir\ *n*
1 ▶ the whole mass of air that surrounds the earth
2 the gas surrounding a heavenly body (as a planet) ⟨The *atmosphere* of Mars is made up mostly of carbon dioxide.⟩
3 the air in a particular place
4 a surrounding influence or set of conditions ⟨an *atmosphere* of excitement⟩

at•mo•spher•ic \ˌat-mə-'sfir-ik, -'sfer-\ *adj*
of or relating to the atmosphere ⟨*atmospheric* gases⟩

▶ **atmosphere 1**
The earth's atmosphere is divided into layers. Each layer has its own composition of gases and temperature level.

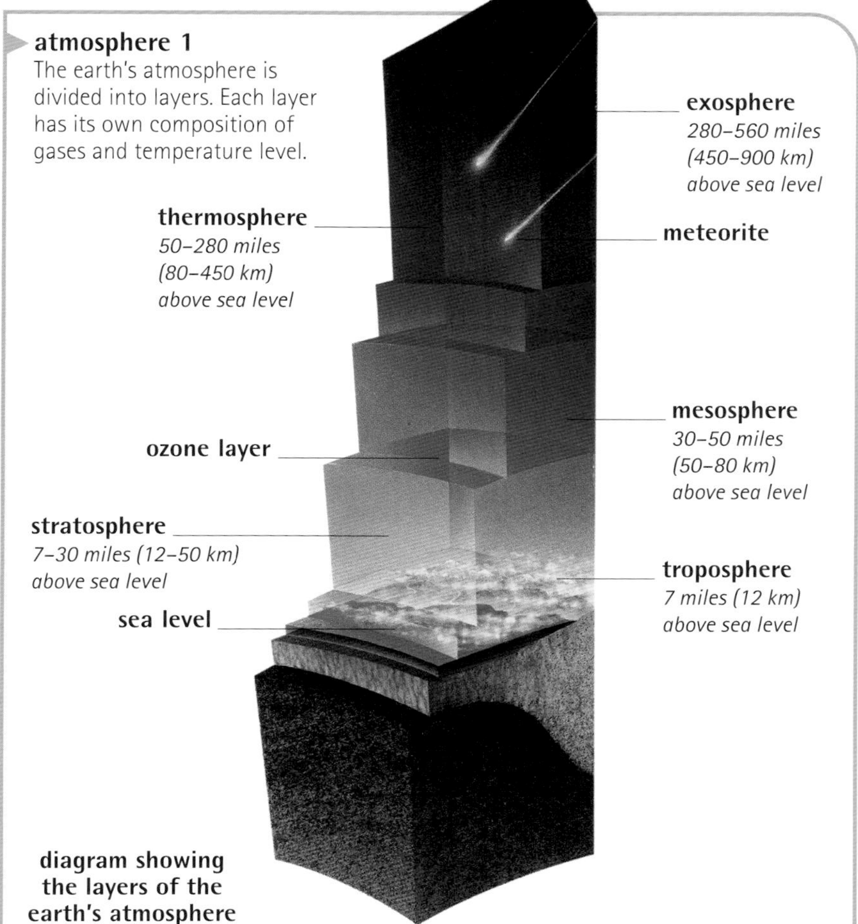

diagram showing the layers of the earth's atmosphere

atoll \'a-ˌtȯl, -ˌtäl\ *n*
▼ a ring-shaped coral island consisting of a coral reef surrounding a lagoon

at•om \'a-təm\ *n*
1 ▶ the smallest particle of an element that can exist alone or in combination ⟨carbon *atoms*⟩
2 a tiny particle : BIT ⟨There's not an *atom* of truth to what he said.⟩

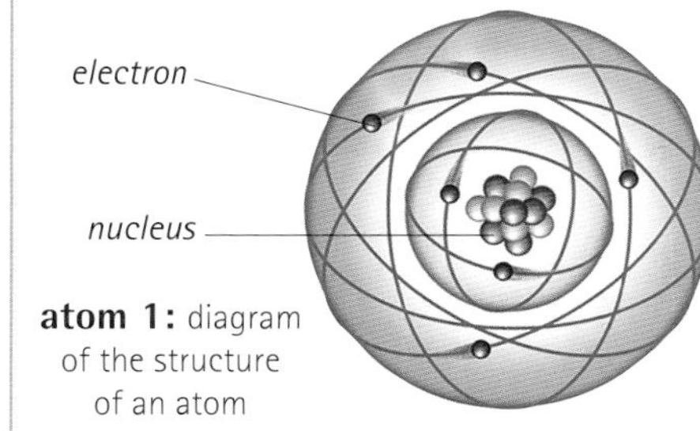

atom 1: diagram of the structure of an atom

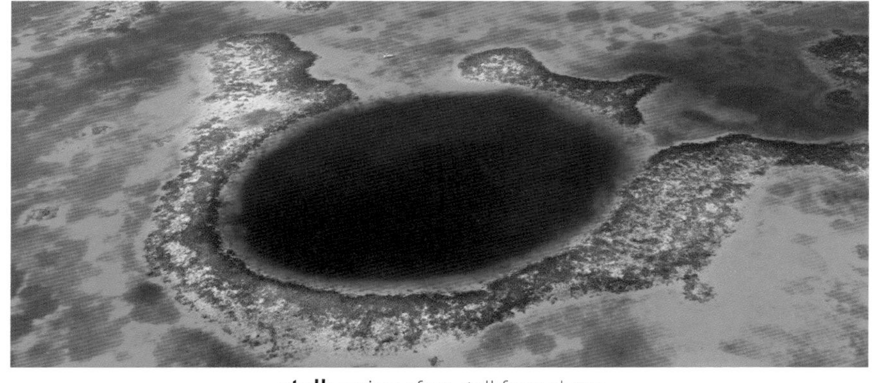

atoll: a view of an atoll from above

▶ **Word History** The English word *atom* came from a Greek word *atomos*, meaning "not able to be divided." Ancient Greek philosophers believed that matter consisted of the very smallest particles, atoms, which could not be further divided. Modern science revived the atom idea, but it was discovered that even atoms could be split, and that doing so produced great amounts of energy.

atom·ic \ə-ˈtä-mik\ *adj*
1 of or relating to atoms ⟨*atomic* physics⟩
2 NUCLEAR 3 ⟨*atomic* energy⟩

atomic bomb *n*
a bomb whose great power is due to the sudden release of the energy in the nuclei of atoms

at·om·iz·er \ˈa-tə-ˌmī-zər\ *n*
▼ a device for spraying a liquid (as a perfume or disinfectant)

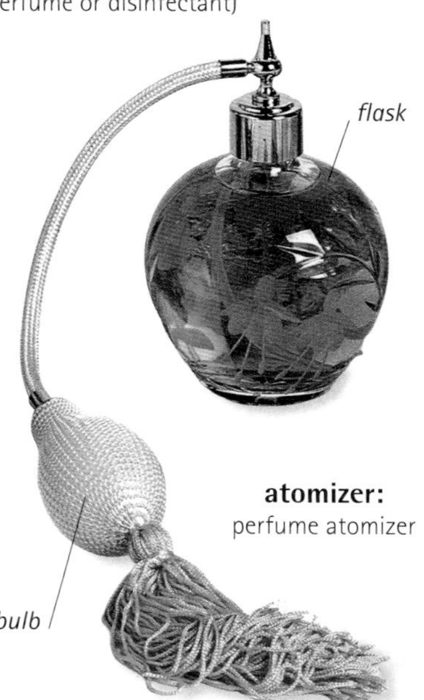

atomizer: perfume atomizer

atone \ə-ˈtōn\ *vb* **atoned**; **aton·ing**
to do something to make up for a wrong

atone·ment \ə-ˈtōn-mənt\ *n*
a making up for an offense or injury

atop \ə-ˈtäp\ *prep*
on top of ⟨The castle sits *atop* a cliff.⟩

atri·um \ˈā-trē-əm\ *n*
► the part of the heart that receives blood from the veins

atro·cious \ə-ˈtrō-shəs\ *adj*
1 extremely brutal, cruel, or wicked ⟨an *atrocious* crime⟩
2 very bad ⟨*atrocious* weather⟩ ⟨*atrocious* manners⟩
atro·cious·ly *adv*

atroc·i·ty \ə-ˈträ-sə-tē\ *n, pl* **atroc·i·ties**
an extremely cruel or terrible act, object, or situation ⟨the *atrocities* of war⟩

at sign *n*
the symbol @ used especially as part of an e-mail address

at·tach \ə-ˈtach\ *vb* **at·tached**; **at·tach·ing**
1 to fasten or join one thing to another ⟨The boy *attached* a bell to his bicycle.⟩
2 to bind by feelings of affection
3 to think of as belonging to something ⟨*Attach* no importance to his remark.⟩

at·tach·ment \ə-ˈtach-mənt\ *n*
1 connection by feelings of affection or regard ⟨The children had a strong *attachment* to their grandmother.⟩
2 an extra part that can be attached to a machine or tool ⟨vacuum cleaner *attachments*⟩
3 a connection by which one thing is joined to another
4 a document or file that is sent with e-mail

[1]at·tack \ə-ˈtak\ *vb* **at·tacked**; **at·tack·ing**
1 to take strong action against : try to hurt, injure, or destroy ⟨Troops *attacked* the fortress at dawn.⟩
2 to use harsh words against : criticize harshly ⟨People *attacked* the plan as being too complicated.⟩
3 to begin to affect or to act upon harmfully ⟨A disease *attacked* our crops.⟩
4 to start to work on in a determined and eager way ⟨She *attacked* the problem.⟩
at·tack·er *n*

[2]attack *n*
1 a violent, harmful, or destructive act against someone or something ⟨a shark *attack*⟩
2 strong criticism ⟨a verbal *attack*⟩
3 the setting to work on some undertaking ⟨They made a new *attack* on the problem.⟩
4 a sudden short period of suffering from an illness or of being affected by a strong emotion ⟨an asthma *attack*⟩ ⟨an *attack* of nerves⟩

at·tain \ə-ˈtān\ *vb* **at·tained**; **at·tain·ing**
1 to accomplish or achieve ⟨*attain* a goal⟩
2 to come into possession of : OBTAIN ⟨*attain* knowledge⟩
3 to reach or come to gradually : arrive at ⟨*attain* the top of the hill⟩
at·tain·able \ə-ˈtā-nə-bəl\ *adj*

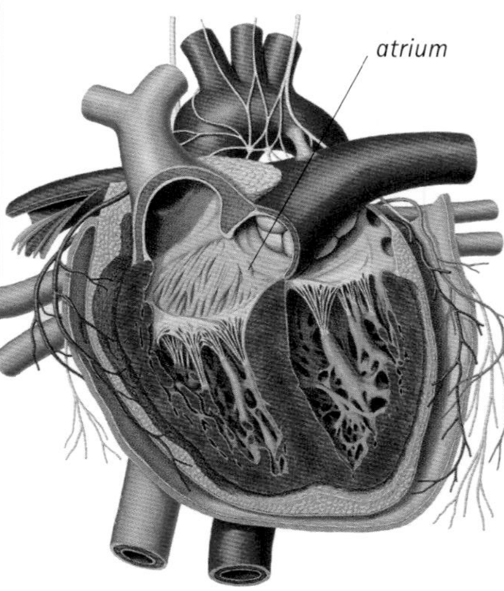

atrium: an illustration of a heart showing the atrium

at·tain·ment \ə-ˈtān-mənt\ *n*
1 the act of obtaining or doing something difficult : the state of having obtained or done something difficult ⟨*attainment* of a goal⟩
2 ACHIEVEMENT 2 ⟨scientific *attainments*⟩

[1]at·tempt \ə-ˈtempt\ *vb* **at·tempt·ed**; **at·tempt·ing**
to try to do, accomplish, or complete ⟨*attempt* to win⟩

[2]attempt *n*
the act or an instance of trying to do something

at·tend \ə-ˈtend\ *vb* **at·tend·ed**; **at·tend·ing**
1 to go to or be present at ⟨*attend* school⟩ ⟨*attend* a party⟩
2 to look after : take charge of ⟨The hotel staff *attended* to my every need.⟩
3 to direct attention ⟨*attend* to business⟩
4 to pay attention to
5 to go with especially as a servant or companion ⟨Servants *attended* the king.⟩
6 to care for ⟨Nurses *attend* the sick.⟩

at·ten·dance \ə-ˈten-dəns\ *n*
1 presence at a place ⟨*Attendance* is required.⟩
2 a record of how often a person is present at a place ⟨These students have perfect *attendance*.⟩
3 the number of people present

[1]at·ten·dant \ə-ˈten-dənt\ *n*
1 a person who goes with or serves another ⟨the king's *attendants*⟩
2 an employee who waits on or helps customers ⟨a parking *attendant*⟩

[2]attendant *adj*
coming with or following closely as a result ⟨heavy rain and its *attendant* flooding⟩

at·ten·tion \ə-ˈten-shən\ *n*
1 the act or the power of fixing the mind on something : careful listening or watching ⟨Pay *attention* to what happens next.⟩
2 notice, interest, or awareness ⟨attract *attention*⟩
3 careful thinking about something so as to be able to take action on it ⟨This matter requires immediate *attention*.⟩
4 special care or treatment ⟨His scrape did not require medical *attention*.⟩
5 an act of kindness or politeness
6 the way a soldier stands with the body stiff and straight, heels together, and arms at the sides

at·ten·tive \ə-ˈten-tiv\ *adj*
1 paying attention ⟨an *attentive* listener⟩
2 very thoughtful about the needs of others
at·ten·tive·ly *adv*
at·ten·tive·ness *n*

at•test \ə-ˈtest\ *vb* **at•test•ed; at•test•ing**
to show or give proof of : say to be true ⟨I can *attest* to his innocence.⟩

at•tic \ˈa-tik\ *n*
a room or a space just under the roof of a building

[1]at•tire \ə-ˈtīr\ *vb* **at•tired; at•tir•ing**
to dress especially in special or fine clothes ⟨The groom was *attired* in a tuxedo.⟩

[2]attire *n*
CLOTHING ⟨beach *attire*⟩

at•ti•tude \ˈa-tə-ˌtüd, -ˌtyüd\ *n*
1 a feeling or way of thinking that affects a person's behavior ⟨a positive *attitude*⟩
2 a way of positioning the body or its parts ⟨He bowed in an *attitude* of respect.⟩

at•tor•ney \ə-ˈtər-nē\ *n, pl* **at•tor•neys**
a person and usually a lawyer who acts for another in business or legal matters

at•tract \ə-ˈtrakt\ *vb* **at•tract•ed; at•tract•ing**
1 to draw by appealing to interest or feeling ⟨*attract* visitors⟩ ⟨Her smile *attracted* me.⟩
2 to draw to or toward something else ⟨A magnet *attracts* iron.⟩

at•trac•tion \ə-ˈtrak-shən\ *n*
1 a feeling of interest in something or someone ⟨a romantic *attraction*⟩
2 the act or power of drawing toward something ⟨magnetic *attraction*⟩
3 something that interests or pleases ⟨tourist *attractions*⟩

at•trac•tive \ə-ˈtrak-tiv\ *adj*
1 having the power or quality of drawing interest ⟨an *attractive* offer⟩
2 having a pleasing appearance ⟨an *attractive* home⟩
at•trac•tive•ly *adv*
at•trac•tive•ness *n*

[1]at•tri•bute \ˈa-trə-ˌbyüt\ *n*
a quality belonging to a particular person or thing ⟨Patience is a good *attribute* for a teacher.⟩

[2]at•trib•ute \ə-ˈtri-byət\ *vb* **at•trib•ut•ed; at•trib•ut•ing**
1 to explain as the cause of ⟨We *attribute* their success to hard work.⟩
2 to think of as likely to be a quality of a person or thing ⟨Some people *attribute* stubbornness to mules.⟩

atty. *abbr* attorney

ATV \ˌā-ˌtē-ˈvē\ *n*
ALL-TERRAIN VEHICLE

atyp•i•cal \ˈā-ˈti-pi-kəl\ *adj*
not usual or normal : not typical ⟨an *atypical* case⟩
atyp•i•cal•ly *adv*

au•burn \ˈȯ-bərn\ *adj*
of a reddish brown color ⟨*auburn* hair⟩

[1]auc•tion \ˈȯk-shən\ *n*
a public sale at which things are sold to those who offer to pay the most

[2]auction *vb* **auc•tioned; auc•tion•ing**
to sell at an auction ⟨*auction* a house⟩

auc•tion•eer \ˌȯk-shə-ˈnir\ *n*
a person who runs an auction

au•da•cious \ȯ-ˈdā-shəs\ *adj*
1 very bold and daring : FEARLESS ⟨an *audacious* scheme⟩
2 disrespectful of authority : INSOLENT ⟨an *audacious* radio personality⟩
au•da•cious•ly *adv*

au•dac•i•ty \ȯ-ˈdas-ə-tē\ *n*
a bold and daring quality that is sometimes shocking or rude ⟨She had the *audacity* to show up uninvited.⟩

au•di•ble \ˈȯ-də-bəl\ *adj*
loud enough to be heard
au•di•bly \-blē\ *adv*

au•di•ence \ˈȯ-dē-əns\ *n*
1 ▶ a group that listens or watches (as at a play or concert)
2 a chance to talk with a person of very high rank ⟨She was granted an *audience* with the queen.⟩
3 those people who give attention to something said, done, or written ⟨Adventure stories appeal to a wide *audience*.⟩

[1]au•dio \ˈȯ-dē-ˌō\ *adj*
1 of or relating to sound or its reproduction
2 relating to or used in the transmitting or receiving of sound (as in radio or television)

[2]audio *n*
1 the transmitting, receiving, or reproducing of sound
2 the section of television equipment that deals with sound

audio book *n*
a recording of a book being read

au•dio•tape \ˈȯ-dē-ō-ˌtāp\ *n*
a magnetic tape recording of sound

au•dio•vi•su•al \ˌȯ-dē-ō-ˈvi-zhə-wəl\ *adj*
of, relating to, or using both sound and sight ⟨*audiovisual* teaching aids⟩

[1]au•dit \ˈȯ-dət\ *n*
a thorough check of business accounts

[2]audit *vb* **au•dit•ed; au•dit•ing**
to thoroughly check the business records of

audience 1: an audience at a music concert

[1]au•di•tion \ȯ-ˈdi-shən\ *n*
a short performance to test the talents of someone (as a singer, dancer, or actor)

[2]audition *vb* **au•di•tioned; au•di•tion•ing**
to test or try out in a short performance ⟨He *auditioned* for a part in the play.⟩ ⟨They *auditioned* her for the lead role.⟩

au•di•tor \ˈȯ-də-tər\ *n*
a person who checks the accuracy of business accounts

au•di•to•ri•um \ˌȯ-də-ˈtȯr-ē-əm\ *n*
1 the part of a building where an audience sits
2 ◀ a large room where people gather as an audience

au•di•to•ry \ˈȯ-də-ˌtȯr-ē\ *adj*
of or relating to hearing ⟨an *auditory* nerve⟩

Aug. *abbr* August

au•ger \ˈȯ-gər\ *n*
a tool used for boring holes

auditorium 2: model of an auditorium in a 19th-century theater

\ŋ\ sing \ō\ bone \ȯ\ saw \ȯi\ coin \th\ thin \t͟h\ this \ü\ food \u̇\ foot \y\ yet \yü\ few \yu̇\ cure \zh\ vision

aught \'ȯt\ *n*
ZERO 1

aug•ment \ȯg-'ment\ *vb* **aug•ment•ed**; **aug•ment•ing**
to increase in size, amount, or degree ⟨He works a second job to *augment* his income.⟩

au•gust \ȯ-'gəst\ *adj*
being grand and noble : MAJESTIC ⟨an *august* university⟩

Au•gust \'ȯ-gəst\ *n*
the eighth month of the year

► **Word History** The first Roman calendar began the year with March. The sixth month was the one we now know as August. The first Latin name given to this month was *Sextilis,* derived from *sextus,* "sixth." The Romans renamed the month after the first Roman emperor, Caesar Augustus, who first took power on August 19, 43 B.C. Hence the English word *August* came from the emperor's Latin name, which means literally "worthy of respect."

auk \'ȯk\ *n*
a black-and-white diving seabird of cold parts of the northern hemisphere

aunt \'ant, 'änt\ *n*
1 a sister of a person's parent
2 the wife of a person's uncle

au•ra \'ȯr-ə\ *n*
a feeling that seems to be given off by a person or thing ⟨There is an *aura* of mystery about the house.⟩

au•ral \'ȯr-əl\ *adj*
of or relating to the ear or sense of hearing
au•ral•ly *adv*

au•ri•cle \'ȯr-i-kəl\ *n*
ATRIUM

au•ro•ra bo•re•al•is \ə-,rȯr-ə-,bȯr-ē-'a-ləs\ *n*
► broad bands of light that have a magnetic and electrical source and that appear in the sky at night especially in the arctic regions

aus•pic•es \'ȯ-spə-səz\ *n pl*
support and guidance of a sponsor ⟨A concert was given under the *auspices* of the school.⟩

aus•pi•cious \ȯ-'spi-shəs\ *adj*
promising success ⟨an *auspicious* beginning⟩
aus•pi•cious•ly *adv*

aus•tere \ȯ-'stir\ *adj*
1 seeming or acting serious and unfriendly ⟨an *austere* family⟩
2 [1]PLAIN 1 ⟨an *austere* room⟩
aus•tere•ly *adv*

aus•ter•i•ty \ȯ-'ster-ə-tē\ *n*
lack of all luxury

[1]**Aus•tra•lian** \ȯ-'strāl-yən\ *adj*
of or relating to Australia or the Australians

[2]**Australian** *n*
a person born or living in Australia

aut- \ȯt\ *or* **au•to-** \'ȯ-tə, 'ȯ-tō\ *prefix*
1 self : same one ⟨*auto*biography⟩
2 automatic

au•then•tic \ə-'then-tik, ȯ-\ *adj*
being really what it seems to be : GENUINE ⟨an *authentic* signature⟩
au•then•ti•cal•ly \-i-kə-lē\ *adv*

au•then•ti•cate \ə-'then-ti-,kāt\ *vb* **au•then•ti•cat•ed**; **au•then•ti•cat•ing**
to prove or serve as proof that something is authentic

au•thor \'ȯ-thər\ *n*
a person who writes something (as a novel)

au•thor•i•ta•tive \ə-'thȯr-ə-,tā-tiv\ *adj*
having or coming from authority ⟨an *authoritative* order⟩
au•thor•i•ta•tive•ly *adv*

au•thor•i•ty \ə-'thȯr-ə-tē\ *n, pl* **au•thor•i•ties**
1 power to exercise control
2 a person looked to as an expert ⟨She's a leading *authority* on fitness.⟩
3 people having powers to make decisions and enforce rules and laws ⟨State *authorities* are investigating the disputed election.⟩
4 a fact or statement used to support a position ⟨What is your *authority* for this argument?⟩

doing certain actions (as saying a word or rocking the body) over and over again

au•to \'ȯ-tō\ *n, pl* **au•tos**
[1]AUTOMOBILE

auto- see AUT-

au•to•bi•og•ra•phy \,ȯ-tə-bī-'ä-grə-fē\ *n, pl* **au•to•bi•og•ra•phies**
the biography of a person written by that person

[1]**au•to•graph** \'ȯ-tə-,graf\ *n*
a person's signature written by hand

[2]**autograph** *vb* **au•to•graphed**; **au•to•graph•ing**
to write a person's own signature in or on ⟨*autograph* a book⟩

au•to•mate \'ȯ-tə-,māt\ *vb* **au•to•mat•ed**; **au•to•mat•ing**
to run or operate something using machines instead of people ⟨*automate* a factory⟩

au•to•mat•ic \,ȯ-tə-'ma-tik\ *adj*
1 INVOLUNTARY ⟨*automatic* blinking of eyelids⟩
2 being a machine or device that allows something to work without being directly controlled by a person ⟨an *automatic* washer⟩
au•to•mat•i•cal•ly \-ti-kə-lē\ *adv*

aurora borealis in the night sky

au•tho•rize \'ȯ-thə-,rīz\ *vb* **au•tho•rized**; **au•tho•riz•ing**
1 to give power to : give authority to ⟨Their guardian is *authorized* to act for them.⟩
2 to give legal or official approval to ⟨Who *authorized* the closing of school?⟩

au•thor•ship \'ȯ-thər-,ship\ *n*
the profession of writing

au•tism \'ȯ-,ti-zəm\ *n*
a condition that is characterized especially by problems in interacting and communicating with other people and by

au•to•ma•tion \,ȯ-tə-'mā-shən\ *n*
1 the method of making a machine, a process, or a system work without being directly controlled by a person
2 automatic working of a machine, process, or system by mechanical or electronic devices that take the place of humans

au•to•mo•bile \,ȯ-tə-mō-'bēl, 'ȯ-tə-mō-,bēl\ *n*
► a usually four-wheeled vehicle that runs on its own power and is designed to carry passengers

automobile

The first mass-produced automobiles were produced in the US about one hundred years ago. The US now manufactures almost 12 million automobiles each year.

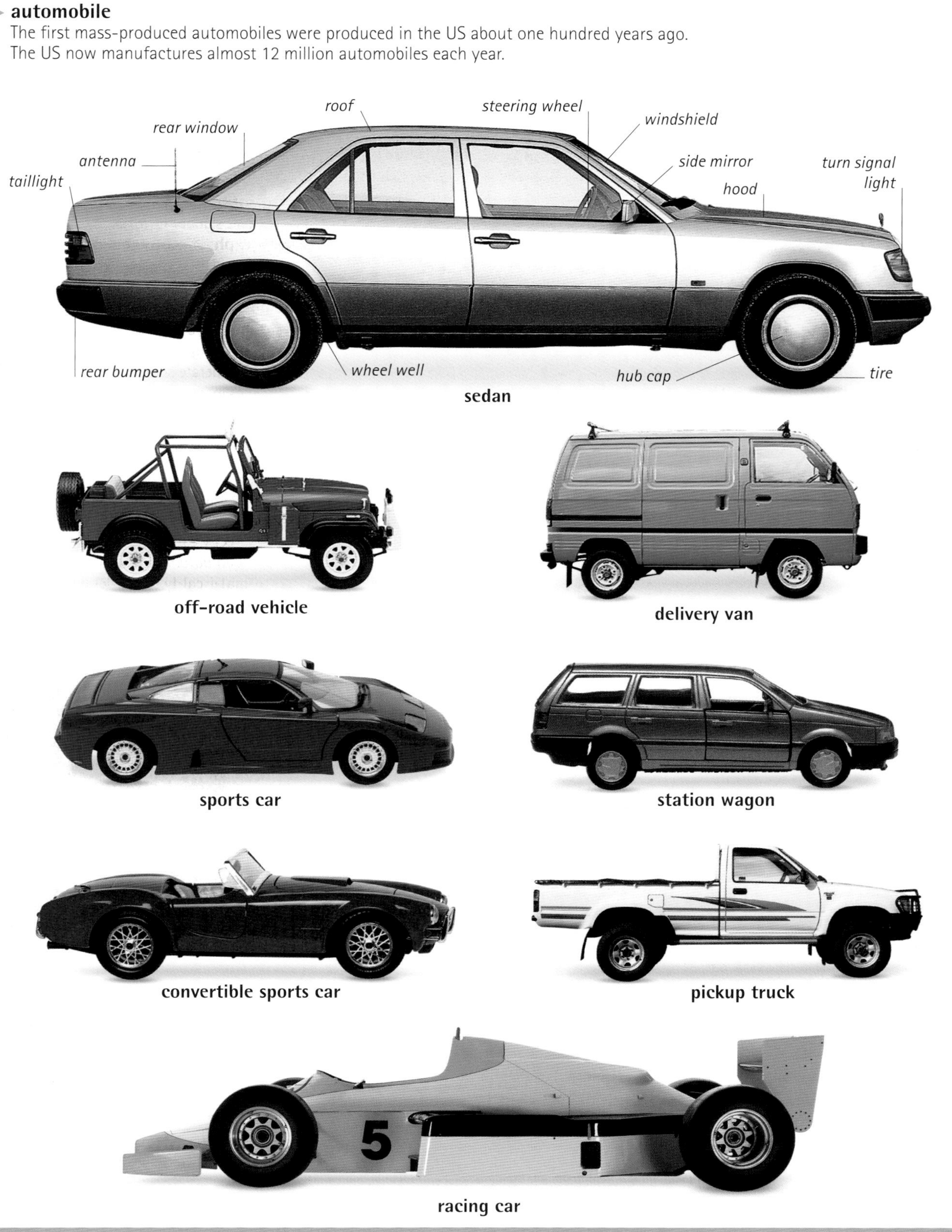

sedan

off-road vehicle

delivery van

sports car

station wagon

convertible sports car

pickup truck

racing car

au•to•mo•tive \ˌȯ-tə-ˈmō-tiv\ *adj*
of or relating to automobiles ⟨an *automotive* parts store⟩

au•tumn \ˈȯ-təm\ *n*
the season between summer and winter

au•tum•nal \ȯ-ˈtəm-nəl\ *adj*
of or relating to autumn

[1]**aux•il•ia•ry** \ȯg-ˈzi-lyə-rē, -ˈzi-lə-rē, -ˈzil-rē\ *adj*
available to provide something extra ⟨an *auxiliary* engine⟩

[2]**auxiliary** *n, pl* **aux•il•ia•ries**
1 a group that provides assistance
2 HELPING VERB

aviary: birds in an aviary

[1]**avail** \ə-ˈvāl\ *vb* **availed**; **avail•ing**
1 to be of use or help
2 to make use of ⟨Many employees *availed* themselves of the free health services.⟩

[2]**avail** *n*
help toward reaching a goal : USE ⟨Our work was of little *avail.*⟩

avail•able \ə-ˈvā-lə-bəl\ *adj*
1 SUITABLE, USABLE ⟨She used every *available* excuse to get out of work.⟩
2 possible to get : OBTAINABLE ⟨*available* supplies⟩
avail•abil•i•ty \ə-ˌvā-lə-ˈbi-lə-tē\ *n*

av•a•lanche \ˈa-və-ˌlanch\ *n*
a large mass of snow and ice or of earth or rock sliding down a mountainside or over a cliff

av•a•rice \ˈa-və-rəs, ˈav-rəs\ *n*
strong desire for riches : GREED

av•a•ri•cious \ˌa-və-ˈri-shəs\ *adj*
greedy for riches
av•a•ri•cious•ly *adv*

ave. *abbr* avenue

avenge \ə-ˈvenj\ *vb* **avenged**; **aveng•ing**
to take revenge for ⟨*avenge* a wrong⟩
aveng•er *n*

av•e•nue \ˈa-və-ˌnü, -ˌnyü\ *n*
1 a wide street
2 a way of reaching a goal ⟨She saw the job as an *avenue* to success.⟩

[1]**av•er•age** \ˈa-və-rij, ˈav-rij\ *n*
1 a number that is calculated by adding quantities together and dividing the total by the number of quantities : ARITHMETIC MEAN ⟨An *average* of 20 students are in each class.⟩
2 something usual in a group, class, or series ⟨His grades have been better than *average.*⟩

[2]**average** *adj*
1 equaling or coming close to an average ⟨The *average* age of students in my class is eleven.⟩
2 being ordinary or usual ⟨the *average* person⟩

[3]**average** *vb* **av•er•aged**; **av•er•ag•ing**
1 to amount to usually ⟨We *averaged* ten miles a day.⟩
2 to find the average of ⟨Our teacher *averaged* our test scores.⟩

averse \ə-ˈvərs\ *adj*
having a feeling of dislike ⟨He is *averse* to exercise.⟩

aver•sion \ə-ˈvər-zhən\ *n*
1 a strong dislike
2 something strongly disliked

avert \ə-ˈvərt\ *vb* **avert•ed**; **avert•ing**
1 to turn away ⟨When asked if he had lied, he *averted* his eyes.⟩
2 to keep from happening ⟨*avert* disaster⟩

avi•ary \ˈā-vē-ˌer-ē\ *n, pl* **avi•ar•ies**
◀ a place (as a large cage or a building) where birds are kept

avi•a•tion \ˌā-vē-ˈā-shən\ *n*
1 the flying of aircraft
2 the designing and making of aircraft

avi•a•tor \ˈā-vē-ˌā-tər\ *n*
the pilot of an aircraft

av•id \ˈa-vəd\ *adj*
very eager ⟨an *avid* football fan⟩
av•id•ly *adv*

av•o•ca•do \ˌa-və-ˈkä-dō, ˌäv-\ *n, pl* **av•o•ca•dos**
▼ a usually green fruit that is shaped like a pear or an egg, grows on a tropical American tree, and has a rich oily flesh

avocado

av•o•ca•tion \ˌa-və-ˈkā-shən\ *n*
an interest or activity that is not a regular job : HOBBY

avoid \ə-ˈvȯid\ *vb* **avoid•ed**; **avoid•ing**
1 to keep away from ⟨Are you *avoiding* me?⟩
2 to keep from happening ⟨*avoid* mistakes⟩
3 to keep from doing or being

avoid•ance \ə-ˈvȯi-dᵊns\ *n*
the act of avoiding something ⟨*avoidance* of trouble⟩

avow \ə-ˈvau̇\ *vb* **avowed**; **avow•ing**
to declare openly and frankly

avow•al \ə-ˈvau̇-əl\ *n*
an open declaration

await \ə-ˈwāt\ *vb* **await•ed**; **await•ing**
1 to wait for ⟨*await* a train⟩
2 to be ready or waiting for ⟨Dinner was *awaiting* them on their arrival.⟩

[1]**awake** \ə-ˈwāk\ *vb* **awoke** \-ˈwōk\; **awo•ken** \-ˈwō-kən\ *or* **awaked** \-ˈwākt\; **awak•ing**
1 to stop sleeping : wake up
2 to make or become conscious or aware of something ⟨They finally *awoke* to the danger.⟩

[2]**awake** *adj*
not asleep

awak•en \ə-ˈwā-kən\ *vb* **awak•ened**; **awak•en•ing**
[1]AWAKE

[1]**award** \ə-ˈwȯrd\ *vb* **award•ed**; **award•ing**
1 to give as deserved or needed ⟨*award* a medal⟩ ⟨*award* a scholarship⟩
2 to give by official decision ⟨*award* a contract⟩

[2]**award** *n*
something (as a prize) that is given in recognition of good work or a good act

aware \ə-ˈwer\ *adj*
having or showing understanding or knowledge : CONSCIOUS ⟨Aren't you *aware* of what's happening?⟩
aware•ness *n*

awash \ə-ˈwȯsh, -ˈwäsh\ *adj*
flooded or covered with water or other liquid ⟨The ship began to sink, her decks already *awash.*⟩

[1]**away** \ə-ˈwā\ *adv*
1 from this or that place ⟨Go *away*!⟩
2 in another place or direction ⟨turn *away*⟩
3 out of existence ⟨The echo died *away.*⟩
4 from someone's possession ⟨He gave *away* a fortune.⟩
5 without stopping or slowing down ⟨talk *away*⟩
6 at or to a great distance in space or time : FAR ⟨*away* back in 1910⟩

[2]**away** *adj*
1 ABSENT 1 ⟨I wasn't planning to be *away* from home.⟩
2 DISTANT 1 ⟨The lake is ten miles *away.*⟩

[1]**awe** \ˈȯ\ *n*
a feeling of mixed fear, respect, and wonder

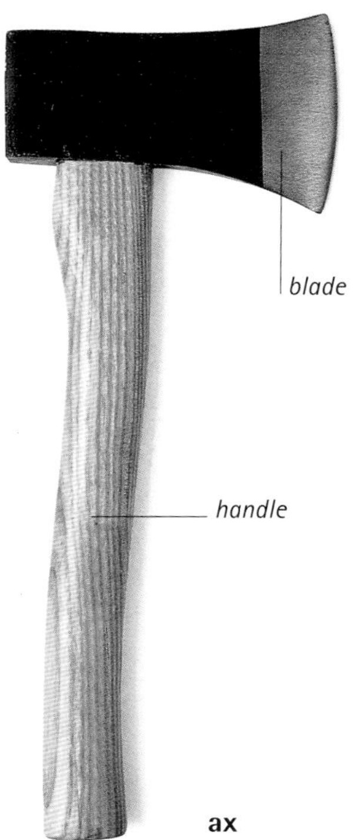

ax

[2]**awe** *vb* **awed**; **aw•ing**
to fill with respect, fear, and wonder

awe•some \ˈȯ-səm\ *adj*
1 causing a feeling of respect, fear, and wonder ⟨an *awesome* view of the canyon⟩
2 extremely good ⟨He made an *awesome* catch.⟩

awe•struck \ˈȯ-ˌstrək\ *adj*
filled with awe ⟨Her first visit to the big city left her *awestruck.*⟩

[1]**aw•ful** \ˈȯ-fəl\ *adj*
1 very bad or unpleasant ⟨an *awful* cold⟩
2 very much ⟨We have an *awful* lot to do.⟩
3 causing fear or terror ⟨an *awful* roar⟩

[2]**awful** *adv*
AWFULLY ⟨That's an *awful* dangerous stunt.⟩

aw•ful•ly \ˈȯ-flē, *especially for 2* -fə-lē\ *adv*
1 to a very great degree : VERY ⟨After the race I was *awfully* tired.⟩
2 in a disagreeable or unpleasant manner ⟨He sings *awfully.*⟩

awhile \ə-ˈhwīl, ə-ˈwīl\ *adv*
for a while : for a short time ⟨Sit down and rest *awhile.*⟩

awk•ward \ˈȯ-kwərd\ *adj*
1 not graceful : CLUMSY ⟨an *awkward* dancer⟩
2 likely to embarrass ⟨an *awkward* question⟩
3 difficult to use or handle ⟨*awkward* tools⟩
awk•ward•ly *adv*
awk•ward•ness *n*

awl \ˈȯl\ *n*
a pointed tool for making small holes (as in leather or wood)

aw•ning \ˈȯ-niŋ\ *n*
a cover (as of canvas) that shades or shelters like a roof

awoke *past of* AWAKE

awoken *past participle of* AWAKE

awry \ə-ˈrī\ *adv or adj*
1 turned or twisted to one side : ASKEW ⟨His hat was all *awry.*⟩
2 out of the right course : AMISS ⟨The plans had gone *awry.*⟩

ax *or* **axe** \ˈaks\ *n*
◀ a tool that has a heavy head with a sharp edge fixed to a handle and is used for chopping and splitting wood

ax•i•om \ˈak-sē-əm\ *n*
1 MAXIM
2 a statement thought to be clearly true

ax•is \ˈak-səs\ *n, pl* **ax•es** \ˈak-ˌsēz\
1 a straight line about which a body or a geometric figure rotates or may be thought of as rotating ⟨the earth's *axis*⟩
2 a line of reference used to assign numbers to locations in a geometric plane

ax•le \ˈak-səl\ *n*
a pin or shaft on or with which a wheel or pair of wheels turns

ax•on \ˈak-ˌsän\ *n*
a long fiber that carries impulses away from a nerve cell

[1]**aye** \ˈī\ *adv*
[1]YES 1 ⟨*Aye, aye,* sir.⟩

[2]**aye** \ˈī\ *n*
a yes vote or voter ⟨The *ayes* outnumber the nays.⟩

AZ *abbr* Arizona

aza•lea \ə-ˈzāl-yə\ *n*
▼ a usually small bush that has flowers of many colors which are shaped like funnels

azure \ˈa-zhər\ *n*
the blue color of the clear daytime sky

azalea

Bb

Sounds of B: The letter **B** makes one main sound, the sound heard in the words ***bubble*** and *knob*. The letter **B** is often silent when it follows an **M**, as in *climbing* and *thumb*, and when it comes before a **T**, as in *debt* and *doubted*.

b \'bē\ *n, pl* **b's** *or* **bs** \'bēz\ *often cap*
1 the second letter of the English alphabet
2 a grade that shows a student's work is good
3 a musical note referred to by the letter B

[1]baa \'ba, 'bä\ *n*
the cry of a sheep

[2]baa *vb* **baaed**; **baa•ing**
to make the cry of a sheep

[1]bab•ble \'ba-bəl\ *vb* **bab•bled**; **bab•bling** \'ba-bə-liŋ, 'ba-bliŋ\
1 to make meaningless sounds
2 to talk foolishly
3 to make the sound of a brook

[2]babble *n*
1 talk that is not clear
2 the sound of a brook

babe \'bāb\ *n*
[1]BABY 1 ⟨a newborn *babe*⟩

ba•boon \ba-'bün\ *n*
▼ a large monkey of Africa and Asia with a doglike face

baboons

[1]ba•by \'bā-bē\ *n, pl* **babies**
1 a very young child
2 a very young animal
3 the youngest of a group
4 a childish person
ba•by•ish \'bā-bē-ish\ *adj*

[2]baby *adj*
1 [1]YOUNG 1 ⟨a *baby* deer⟩
2 very small ⟨Take *baby* steps.⟩

[3]baby *vb* **ba•bied**; **ba•by•ing**
to treat as a baby : to be overly kind to ⟨He's 15. Stop *babying* him.⟩

ba•by•hood \'bā-bē-,hu̇d\ *n*
the time in a person's life when he or she is a baby

ba•by•sit \'bā-bē-,sit\ *vb* **ba•by•sat** \-,sat\; **ba•by•sit•ting**
to care for a child while the child's parents are away

ba•by•sit•ter \'bā-bē-,si-tər\ *n*
a person who cares for a child while the child's parents are away

baby tooth *n*
MILK TOOTH

bach•e•lor \'ba-chə-lər, 'bach-lər\ *n*
a man who is not married
bach•e•lor•hood \-,hu̇d\ *n*

[1]back \'bak\ *n*
1 the rear part of the human body from the neck to the end of the spine : the upper part of the body of an animal
2 the part of something that is opposite or away from the front part
3 a player in a team game who plays behind the forward line of players
backed \'bakt\ *adj*

[2]back *adv*
1 to, toward, or at the rear ⟨The crowd moved *back*.⟩
2 in or to a former time, state, or place ⟨knew him years *back*⟩ ⟨I'll be right *back*.⟩
3 under control ⟨I kept *back* my anger.⟩
4 in return or reply ⟨Please write *back*.⟩ ⟨Give me *back* my bike.⟩
back and forth
1 toward the back and then toward the front
2 between two places or people ⟨They sailed *back and forth* across the lake.⟩

[3]back *adj*
1 located at the back ⟨the *back* door⟩
2 far from a central or main area ⟨*back* roads⟩
3 not yet paid : OVERDUE ⟨He owes *back* rent.⟩
4 published at an earlier time

[4]back *vb* **backed**; **back•ing**
1 to give support or help to : UPHOLD ⟨Which candidate are you *backing*?⟩
2 to move backward
back•er *n*
back down *or* **back off** to stop arguing or fighting for something
back out to decide not to do something after agreeing to do it
back up
1 to move backward
2 to block or become blocked
3 to give help or support to
4 to make a copy of (as a computer file) to protect it from being lost

back•bone \'bak-'bōn\ *n*
1 the column of bones in the back enclosing and protecting the spinal cord : SPINAL COLUMN
2 the strongest part of something ⟨He is the *backbone* of the family.⟩
3 strength of character

[1]back•fire \'bak-,fīr\ *vb* **back•fired**; **back•fir•ing**
1 to have a result opposite to what was planned ⟨The joke *backfired*.⟩
2 to make a loud engine noise caused by fuel igniting at the wrong time

[2]backfire *n*
1 a loud engine noise caused by fuel igniting at the wrong time
2 a fire that is set to stop the spread of a forest fire or a grass fire by burning off a strip of land ahead of it

back•ground \'bak-,grau̇nd\ *n*
1 the scenery or ground that is behind a main figure or object
2 a position that attracts little attention
3 the total of a person's experience, knowledge, and education

[1]back•hand \'bak-,hand\ *n*
1 ▶ a stroke in sports played with a racket that is made with the back of the hand turned in the direction in which the hand is moving
2 a catch (as in baseball) made with the arm across the body and the palm turned away from the body

[2]backhand *adv or adj*
with a backhand ⟨caught *backhand*⟩

back•hand•ed \'bak-,han-dəd\ *adj*
1 using or done with a backhand ⟨a *backhanded* catch⟩
2 not sincere ⟨*backhanded* praise⟩

back•pack \'bak-,pak\ *n*
▶ a bag worn on the back for carrying things

back•side \'bak-,sīd\ *n*
1 RUMP 1
2 the part of the body on which a person sits

back•stage \'bak-'stāj\ *adv or adj*
in or to the area behind the stage

back•stop \'bak-,stäp\ *n*
a fence behind the catcher to keep a baseball from rolling away

back•track \'bak-,trak\ *vb* **back•tracked**; **back•track•ing**
to go back over a course or a path

back•up \'bak-,əp\ *n*
1 a person who takes the place of or supports another ⟨The guard called for a *backup.*⟩
2 a situation in which the flow of something becomes blocked
3 a copy of information stored on a computer

[1]backhand 1: a girl using a backhand

backpack: a girl with a backpack

[1]back•ward \'bak-wərd\ *or* **back•wards** \-wərdz\ *adv*
1 toward the back ⟨look *backward*⟩
2 with the back first ⟨ride *backward*⟩
3 opposite to the usual way ⟨count *backward*⟩

[2]backward *adj*
1 turned toward the back
2 done backward ⟨a *backward* flip⟩
3 less advanced in development

back•woods \'bak-'wu̇dz\ *n pl*
wooded or partly cleared areas away from cities

back•yard \'bak-'yärd\ *n*
an area in the back of a house

ba•con \'bā-kən\ *n*
salted and smoked meat from the sides and the back of a pig

bac•te•ri•al \bak-'tir-ē-əl\ *adj*
relating to or caused by bacteria

bac•te•ri•um \bak-'tir-ē-əm\ *n, pl* **bac•te•ria** \-ē-ə\
any of a group of single-celled microscopic organisms that are important to humans because of their chemical activities and as causes of disease

bad \'bad\ *adj* **worse** \'wərs\; **worst** \'wərst\
1 not good : POOR ⟨*bad* weather⟩ ⟨*bad* work⟩
2 not favorable ⟨a *bad* report⟩
3 not fresh or sound ⟨*bad* meat⟩
4 not good or right : EVIL ⟨a *bad* person⟩
5 not behaving properly ⟨a *bad* dog⟩
6 not enough ⟨*bad* lighting⟩
7 UNPLEASANT ⟨*bad* news⟩
8 HARMFUL ⟨*bad* for the health⟩
9 SERIOUS 2, SEVERE ⟨a *bad* cold⟩ ⟨in *bad* trouble⟩
10 not correct ⟨*bad* spelling⟩
11 not cheerful or calm ⟨a *bad* mood⟩
12 not healthy ⟨*bad* teeth⟩ ⟨He felt *bad* from a cold.⟩
13 SORRY 1 ⟨I felt *bad* about my mistake.⟩
14 not skillful
bad•ness *n*

▶ **Synonyms** BAD, EVIL, and WICKED mean not doing or being what is right. BAD is used of anyone or anything that a person might dislike or find fault with. ⟨He had to stay after school for *bad* behavior.⟩ EVIL is a more powerful word than *bad* and is used for something of bad moral character. ⟨Criminals were planning *evil* deeds.⟩ WICKED is used of someone or something that is truly and deliberately bad. ⟨He was a very *wicked* ruler who caused many people harm.⟩

bade *past of* BID

badge \'baj\ *n*
▶ something worn to show that a person belongs to a certain group or rank

badge: a sheriff's badge

[1]bad•ger \'ba-jər\ *n*
a furry burrowing animal with short thick legs and long claws on the front feet

[2]badger *vb* **bad•gered**; **bad•ger•ing**
to annoy again and again

bad•ly \'bad-lē\ *adv* **worse** \'wərs\; **worst** \'wərst\
1 in a bad manner
2 very much ⟨I *badly* wanted to win.⟩

bad•min•ton \'bad-,min-t^{ə}n\ *n*
a game in which a shuttlecock is hit back and forth over a net by players using light rackets

baf•fle \'ba-fəl\ *vb* **baf•fled**; **baf•fling** \'ba-fə-liŋ, 'ba-fliŋ\
to completely confuse
baffled *adj*

[1]bag \'bag\ *n*
1 a container made of flexible material (as paper or plastic)
2 [1]PURSE 1, HANDBAG
3 SUITCASE

[2]bag *vb* **bagged**; **bag•ging**
1 to swell out : BULGE
2 to put into a bag ⟨*bagging* groceries⟩
3 to kill or capture in hunting ⟨*bag* a deer⟩

bagel: a bagel with filling

ba•gel \'bā-gəl\ *n*
▲ a bread roll shaped like a ring

bag•gage \'ba-gij\ *n*
the bags, suitcases, and personal belongings of a traveler

bag•gy \'ba-gē\ *adj* **bag•gi•er**; **bag•gi•est**
hanging loosely or puffed out like a bag ⟨*baggy* pants⟩

bag•pipe \'bag-ˌpīp\ *n*
a musical instrument played especially in Scotland that consists of a tube, a bag for air, and pipes from which the sound comes

[1]**bail** \'bāl\ *vb* **bailed**; **bail•ing**
to dip and throw out water (as from a boat)
bail out to jump out of an airplane

[2]**bail** *n*
money given to free a prisoner until his or her trial

[3]**bail** *vb* **bailed**; **bailing**
to get the release of (a prisoner) by giving money as a guarantee of the prisoner's return for trial

[1]**bait** \'bāt\ *n*
something that is used to attract fish or animals so they can be caught

[2]**bait** *vb* **bait•ed**; **bait•ing**
1 to put something (as food) on or in to attract and catch fish or animals ⟨*bait* a trap⟩
2 to torment by mean or unjust attacks ⟨They *baited* him by using a nickname he hated.⟩

bake \'bāk\ *vb* **baked**; **bak•ing**
1 to cook or become cooked in a dry heat especially in an oven
2 to dry or harden by heat ⟨*bake* clay⟩

bak•er \'bā-kər\ *n*
a person who bakes and sells bread, cakes, or pastry

baker's dozen *n*
[2]THIRTEEN

bak•ery \'bā-kə-rē, 'bā-krē\ *n, pl* **bak•er•ies**
a place where bread, cakes, and pastry are made or sold

baking powder *n*
a powder used to make the dough rise in making baked goods (as cakes)

baking soda *n*
a white powder used especially in baking to make dough rise and in medicine to reduce stomach acid

[1]**bal•ance** \'ba-ləns\ *n*
1 a steady position or condition ⟨The gymnast kept her *balance*.⟩
2 something left over : REMAINDER
3 ▼ an instrument for weighing
4 a state in which things occur in equal or proper amounts ⟨a *balance* of work and fun⟩
5 the amount of money in a bank account
6 an amount of money still owed

feathers
pebbles

[1]**balance 3:** weighing scales

► **Word History** The first meaning of the word *balance* was "an instrument used to weigh things." Some weighing instruments have two small pans on either side, into which equal amounts must be placed to keep the beam that holds the pans from tipping. The English word *balance* came from a Latin word that meant literally "having two pans." This Latin word, *bilanx*, is a compound of *bi-*, "two," and *lanx*, "dish, pan of a pair of scales."

[2]**balance** *vb* **bal•anced**; **bal•anc•ing**
1 to make or keep steady : keep from falling
2 to make the two sides of (an account) add up to the same total
3 to be or make equal in weight, number, or amount

bal•co•ny \'bal-kə-nē\ *n, pl* **bal•co•nies**
1 a platform enclosed by a low wall or a railing built out from the side of a building
2 a platform inside a theater extending out over part of the main floor

bald \'bȯld\ *adj* **bald•er**; **bald•est**
1 lacking a natural covering (as of hair)
2 lacking extra details or exaggeration ⟨a *bald* statement⟩
bald•ness *n*

bald eagle *n*
► a North American eagle that when full-grown has white head and neck feathers

[1]**bale** \'bāl\ *n*
a large bundle of goods tightly tied for storing or shipping ⟨a *bale* of cotton⟩

[2]**bale** *vb* **baled**; **bal•ing**
to press together and tightly tie or wrap into a large bundle
bal•er *n*

ba•leen \bə-'lēn\ *n*
a tough material that hangs down from the upper jaw of whales without teeth and is used by the whale to filter small ocean animals out of seawater

balk \'bȯk\ *vb* **balked**; **balk•ing**
1 to stop short and refuse to go
2 to refuse to do something often suddenly ⟨He *balked* at paying the bill.⟩

balky \'bȯ-kē\ *adj* **balk•i•er**; **balk•i•est**
likely to stop or refuse to go ⟨a *balky* engine⟩

[1]**ball** \'bȯl\ *n*
1 something round or roundish ⟨a *ball* of yarn⟩
2 a round or roundish object used in a game or sport
3 a game or sport (as baseball) played with a ball
4 a solid usually round shot for a gun
5 the rounded bulge at the base of the thumb or big toe ⟨the *ball* of the foot⟩
6 a pitched baseball that is not hit and is not a strike

[2]**ball** *vb* **balled**; **ball•ing**
to make or come together into a ball ⟨He *balled* his fists.⟩

[3]**ball** *n*
1 a large formal party for dancing
2 a good time ⟨I had a *ball* at the wedding.⟩

bal•lad \'ba-ləd\ *n*
1 a short poem suitable for singing that tells a story in simple language
2 a simple song
3 a slow usually romantic song

bald eagle

ball–and–socket joint *n*
a joint (as in the shoulder) in which a rounded part can move in many directions in a socket

bal•last \'ba-ləst\ *n*
1 heavy material used to make a ship steady or to control the rising of a balloon
2 gravel or broken stone laid in a foundation for a railroad or used in making concrete

ball bearing *n*
1 a bearing in which the revolving part turns on metal balls that roll easily in a groove
2 one of the balls in a ball bearing

bal•le•ri•na \,ba-lə-'rē-nə\ *n*
► a female ballet dancer

bal•let \'ba-,lā, ba-'lā\ *n*
1 a stage dance that tells a story in movement and pantomime
2 a group that performs ballets

[1]**bal•loon** \bə-'lün\ *n*
1 a bag that rises and floats above the ground when filled with heated air or with a gas that is lighter than air
2 a toy or decoration consisting of a rubber bag that can be blown up with air or gas
3 an outline containing words spoken or thought by a character (as in a cartoon)

[2]**balloon** *vb* **bal•looned**; **bal•loon•ing**
to swell or puff out

bal•lot \'ba-lət\ *n*
1 a printed sheet of paper used in voting
2 the action or a system of voting
3 the right to vote
4 the number of votes cast

► **Word History** Long ago, the Italian city of Venice was a republic. The people of Venice had secret voting. They used balls with different colors or marks to vote. The Italian word for a ball used to vote, *ballotta*, meant literally "little ball." The English word *ballot* came from this Italian word. Anything used to cast a secret vote, such as a piece of paper, can be called a *ballot*.

ball•park \'bȯl-,pärk\ *n*
► a park in which baseball games are played

ball•point \'bȯl-,pȯint\ *n*
a pen whose writing point is a small metal ball that rolls ink on a writing surface

ball•room \'bȯl-,rüm, -,ru̇m\ *n*
a large room for dances

balm \'bäm, 'bälm\ *n*
a greasy substance used for healing or protecting the skin ⟨lip *balm*⟩

ballerina

balmy \'bä-mē, 'bäl-mē\ *adj* **balm•i•er**; **balm•i•est**
warm, calm, and pleasant ⟨a *balmy* breeze⟩

bal•sa \'bȯl-sə\ *n*
the very light but strong wood of a tropical American tree

bal•sam \'bȯl-səm\ *n*
1 a material with a strong pleasant smell that oozes from some plants
2 a fir tree that yields balsam

bal•us•ter \'ba-lə-stər\ *n*
a short post that supports the upper part of a railing

bal•us•trade \'ba-lə-,strād\ *n*
a row of balusters topped by a rail to serve as an open fence (as along the side of a bridge or a balcony)

bam•boo \bam-'bü\ *n*
a tall treelike tropical grass with a hard hollow jointed stem that is used in making furniture and in building

[1]**ban** \'ban\ *vb* **banned**; **ban•ning**
to forbid especially by law or social pressure ⟨Smoking was *banned.*⟩

[2]**ban** *n*
an official order forbidding something

ba•nana \bə-'na-nə\ *n*
a fruit that is shaped somewhat like a finger, is usually yellow when ripe, and grows in bunches on a large treelike tropical plant with very large leaves

[1]**band** \'band\ *n*
1 a strip of material that holds together or goes around something else
2 a strip of something that is different from what it goes around or across ⟨a hat *band*⟩
3 a range of frequencies (as of radio waves)

[2]**band** *vb* **band•ed**; **band•ing**
1 to put a strip of material on or around **:** tie together with a band ⟨The envelopes are *banded* in packs of 50.⟩
2 to unite in a group

[3]**band** *n*
1 a group of persons or animals ⟨a *band* of outlaws⟩
2 a group of musicians performing together

[1]**ban•dage** \'ban-dij\ *n*
a strip of material used to cover and wrap up wounds

ballpark

[2]ban·dage *vb* **ban·daged; ban·dag·ing**
to cover or wrap up (a wound) with a strip of material

ban·dan·na *or* **ban·dana** \ban-ˈda-nə\ *n*
a large handkerchief usually with a colorful design printed on it

ban·dit \ˈban-dət\ *n*
a criminal who attacks and steals from travelers and is often a member of a group

band·stand \ˈband-ˌstand\ *n*
an outdoor platform used for band concerts

band·wag·on \ˈband-ˌwa-gən\ *n*
1 a wagon carrying musicians in a parade
2 a candidate, side, or movement that attracts growing support

[1]bang \ˈbaŋ\ *vb* **banged; bang·ing**
to beat, strike, or shut with a loud noise ⟨*bang* a drum⟩ ⟨*bang* a door⟩

[2]bang *n*
1 a sudden loud noise
2 a hard hit or blow ⟨a *bang* on the head⟩
3 [2]THRILL 1 ⟨I got a *bang* out of it.⟩

[3]bang *n*
hair cut short across the forehead — usually used in pl.

ban·ish \ˈba-nish\ *vb* **ban·ished; ban·ish·ing**
1 to force to leave a country
2 to cause to go away ⟨*banish* fears⟩

ban·ish·ment \ˈba-nish-mənt\ *n*
an act of forcing or of being forced to leave a country

ban·is·ter \ˈba-nə-stər\ *n*
1 one of the slender posts used to support the handrail of a staircase
2 a handrail and its supporting posts
3 the handrail of a staircase

ban·jo \ˈban-jō\ *n, pl* **banjos**
◀ a musical instrument with a round body, long neck, and four or five strings

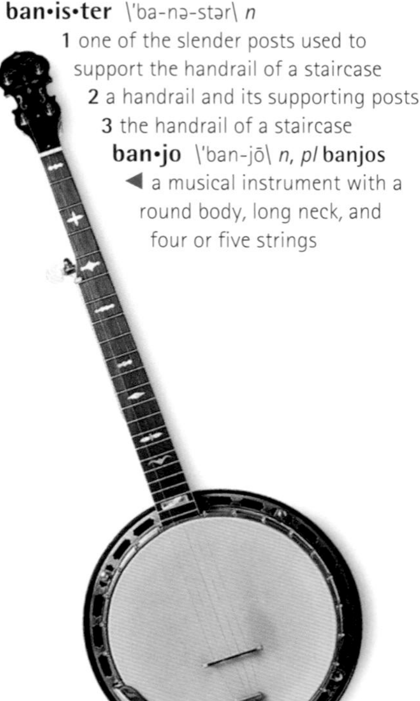

banjo

[1]bank \ˈbaŋk\ *n*
1 a mound or ridge especially of earth ⟨a *bank* of snow⟩
2 the side of a hill
3 the higher ground at the edge of a river, lake, or sea ⟨the *banks* of the river⟩
4 something shaped like a mound ⟨a *bank* of clouds⟩
5 an undersea elevation : SHOAL

[2]bank *vb* **banked; bank·ing**
1 to build (a curve) in a road or track with a slope upward from the inside edge
2 to heap up in a mound or pile ⟨Wind *banked* snow against the door.⟩
3 to raise a pile or mound around ⟨*bank* a stone wall⟩
4 to tilt to one side when turning

[3]bank *n*
1 a business where people deposit and withdraw their money and borrow money
2 a small closed container in which money may be saved
3 a storage place for a reserve supply ⟨a blood *bank*⟩

[4]bank *vb* **banked; bank·ing**
1 to have an account in a bank ⟨We *bank* locally.⟩
2 to deposit in a bank ⟨*bank* ten dollars⟩

[5]bank *n*
a group or series of objects arranged together in a row ⟨a *bank* of seats⟩

bank·er \ˈbaŋ-kər\ *n*
a person who is engaged in the business of a bank

bank·ing \ˈbaŋ-kiŋ\ *n*
the business of a bank or banker

[1]bank·rupt \ˈbaŋk-ˌrəpt\ *adj*
not having enough money to pay debts

[2]bankrupt *vb* **bank·rupt·ed; bank·rupt·ing**
to cause to not have enough money to pay debts

[3]bankrupt *n*
a person or business that does not have enough money to pay debts

bank·rupt·cy \ˈbaŋk-ˌrəpt-sē\ *n, pl* **bank·rupt·cies**
the state of not having enough money to pay debts

ban·ner \ˈba-nər\ *n*
1 [1]FLAG
2 a piece of cloth with a design, a picture, or some writing on it

ban·quet \ˈbaŋ-kwət\ *n*
a formal dinner for many people usually to celebrate a special event

ban·tam \ˈban-təm\ *n*
a miniature breed of domestic chicken often raised for exhibiting in shows

[1]ban·ter \ˈban-tər\ *n*
good-natured teasing and joking

[2]banter *vb* **ban·tered; ban·ter·ing**
to tease or joke with in a friendly way

bap·tism \ˈbap-ˌti-zəm\ *n*
the act or ceremony of baptizing

bap·tize \bap-ˈtīz, ˈbap-ˌtīz\ *vb* **bap·tized; bap·tiz·ing**
1 to dip in water or sprinkle water on as a part of the ceremony of receiving into the Christian church
2 to give a name to as in the ceremony of baptism : CHRISTEN

[1]bar \ˈbär\ *n*
1 a usually slender rigid piece (as of wood or metal) that has a specific use (as for a lever or barrier)
2 a rectangular solid piece or block of something ⟨a *bar* of soap⟩
3 a counter on which alcoholic drinks are served
4 a place of business for the sale of alcoholic drinks
5 a part of a place of business where a particular food or drink is served ⟨a snack *bar*⟩
6 something that blocks the way
7 a submerged or partly submerged bank along a shore or in a river
8 a court of law
9 the profession of law
10 a straight stripe, band, or line longer than it is wide
11 a vertical line across a musical staff marking equal measures of time
12 [1]MEASURE 6

[2]bar *vb* **barred; bar·ring**
1 to fasten with a bar ⟨*Bar* the doors!⟩
2 to block off ⟨Our path was *barred* by a chain.⟩
3 to shut out ⟨*barred* from the meeting⟩

[3]bar *prep*
with the exception of ⟨She is the best reader in the class, *bar* none.⟩

barb \ˈbärb\ *n*
a sharp point that sticks out and backward (as from the tip of an arrow or fishhook)
barbed \ˈbärbd\ *adj*

bar·bar·i·an \bär-ˈber-ē-ən\ *n*
an uncivilized person

bar·bar·ic \bär-ˈber-ik\ *adj*
1 BARBAROUS
2 showing a lack of restraint ⟨*barbaric* power⟩

bar·ba·rous \ˈbär-bə-rəs, -brəs\ *adj*
1 not civilized
2 CRUEL 2, HARSH ⟨*barbarous* treatment⟩
3 very offensive ⟨*barbarous* language⟩

[1]bar•be•cue \'bär-bi-ˌkyü\ *vb* **bar•be•cued**; **bar•be•cu•ing**
to cook over hot coals or on an open fire often in a highly seasoned sauce

[2]barbecue *n*
1 an often portable grill
2 an outdoor meal or party at which food is cooked over hot coals or an open fire

barbed wire *n*
wire that has sharp points and is often used for fences

bar•ber \'bär-bər\ *n*
a person whose business is cutting hair and shaving and trimming beards

bar code *n*
a group of thick and thin lines placed on a product that represents computerized information about the product (as price)

bard \'bärd\ *n*
1 a person in ancient societies skilled at composing and singing songs about heroes
2 POET

[1]bare \'ber\ *adj* **bar•er**; **bar•est**
1 having no covering : NAKED ⟨*bare* feet⟩ ⟨The trees were *bare* of leaves.⟩
2 [1]EMPTY 1 ⟨The cupboard was *bare*.⟩
3 having nothing left over or added : MERE ⟨the *bare* necessities⟩
4 BALD 2 ⟨the *bare* facts⟩
synonyms see NAKED

[2]bare *vb* **bared**; **bar•ing**
UNCOVER 2 ⟨The wolf *bared* its teeth.⟩

bare•back \'ber-ˌbak\ *adv or adj*
on the bare back of a horse : without a saddle

bare•foot \'ber-ˌfu̇t\ *adv or adj*
with the feet bare

bare•ly \'ber-lē\ *adv*
1 almost not
2 with nothing to spare : by a narrow margin ⟨I'd *barely* enough to eat.⟩ ⟨She *barely* passed the test.⟩

barf \'bärf\ *vb* **barfed**; **barf•ing**
[2]VOMIT

[1]bar•gain \'bär-gən\ *n*
1 an agreement settling what each person is to give and receive in a business deal ⟨He made a *bargain* to mow his neighbor's lawn for five dollars.⟩
2 something bought or offered for sale at a good price

[2]bargain *vb* **bar•gained**; **bar•gain•ing**
to talk over the terms of a purchase or agreement

[1]barge \'bärj\ *n*
a broad boat with a flat bottom used chiefly in harbors and on rivers and canals

[2]barge *vb* **barged**; **barg•ing**
to move or push in a fast and often rude way ⟨He *barged* through the crowd.⟩

bar graph *n*
a chart that uses parallel bars whose lengths are in proportion to the numbers represented

bari•tone \'ber-ə-ˌtōn\ *n*
1 a male singing voice between bass and tenor in range
2 a singer having a baritone voice

[1]bark \'bärk\ *vb* **barked**; **bark•ing**
1 to make the short loud cry of a dog or like a dog's
2 to shout or speak sharply ⟨The captain *barked* orders at the soldiers.⟩

[2]bark *n*
the sound made by a barking dog or a similar sound

[3]bark *n*
▶ the outside covering of the trunk, branches, and roots of a tree

[4]bark *or* **barque** \'bärk\ *n*
1 a small sailing boat
2 a three-masted ship with foremast and mainmast square-rigged

[5]bark *vb* **barked**; **barking**
to rub or scrape the skin off ⟨He *barked* his shins.⟩

bark•er \'bär-kər\ *n*
a person who stands at the entrance to a show and tries to attract people to it

bar•ley \'bär-lē\ *n*
a cereal grass grown for its grain which is used mostly to feed farm animals or make malt

bar mitz•vah \bär-'mits-və\ *n*, *often cap B & M*
1 a Jewish boy who at 13 years of age takes on religious responsibilities
2 the ceremony recognizing a boy as a bar mitzvah

barn \'bärn\ *n*
▼ a building used for storing grain and hay and for housing farm animals

bar•na•cle \'bär-ni-kəl\ *n*
a small saltwater animal that is a crustacean and becomes permanently attached (as to rocks or the bottoms of boats) as an adult

barn•yard \'bärn-ˌyärd\ *n*
a usually fenced area next to a barn

[3]bark: bark peeling off a birch tree

ba•rom•e•ter \bə-'rä-mə-tər\ *n*
an instrument that measures air pressure and is used to forecast changes in the weather

bar•on \'ber-ən\ *n*
a man who is a member of the lowest rank of British nobility

bar•on•ess \'ber-ə-nəs\ *n*
1 the wife or widow of a baron
2 a woman who is a member of the lowest rank of British nobility

bar•on•et \'ber-ə-nət\ *n*
the holder of a rank of honor below a baron but above a knight

ba•ro•ni•al \bə-'rō-nē-əl\ *adj*
of, relating to, or suitable for a baron

barn

barque *variant of* [4]BARK

bar•rack \'ber-ək, -ik\ *n*
a building or group of buildings in which soldiers live — usually used in pl.

bar•ra•cu•da \,ber-ə-'kü-də\ *n*
any of several large fierce marine fishes of warm seas that have strong jaws and sharp teeth

bar•rage \bə-'räzh\ *n*
1 continuous artillery or machine-gun fire directed upon a narrow strip of ground
2 a great amount of something that comes quickly and continuously ⟨a *barrage* of commercials⟩

[1]**bar•rel** \'ber-əl\ *n*
1 ▼ a round container often with curved sides that is longer than it is wide and has flat ends

[1]**barrel 1:** a wooden barrel

2 the amount contained in a full barrel
3 something shaped like a cylinder ⟨the *barrel* of a gun⟩

[2]**barrel** *vb* **bar•reled** *or* **bar•relled**; **bar•rel•ing** *or* **bar•rel•ling**
to move at a high speed

bar•ren \'ber-ən\ *adj*
1 unable to produce seed, fruit, or young ⟨*barren* plants⟩
2 growing only poor or few plants ⟨*barren* soil⟩

bar•rette \bä-'ret, bə-\ *n*
a clasp or bar used to hold hair in place

[1]**bar•ri•cade** \'ber-ə-,kād\ *vb* **bar•ri•cad•ed**; **bar•ri•cad•ing**
to block off with a temporary barrier

[2]**barricade** *n*
a temporary barrier for protection against attack or for blocking the way

bar•ri•er \'ber-ē-ər\ *n*
1 something (as a fence) that blocks the way
2 something that keeps apart or makes progress difficult ⟨a language *barrier*⟩

barrier island *n*
a long broad sandy island parallel to a shore that is built up by the action of waves, currents, and winds

barrier reef *n*
a coral reef parallel to the shore and separated from it by a lagoon

bar•ring *prep*
aside from the possibility of ⟨*Barring* an emergency, I'll be there.⟩

bar•row \'ber-ō\ *n*
1 WHEELBARROW
2 PUSHCART

[1]**bar•ter** \'bär-tər\ *vb* **bar•tered**; **bar•ter•ing**
to trade by exchanging one thing for another without the use of money
bar•ter•er \'bär-tər-ər\ *n*

[2]**barter** *n*
the trade of one thing for another without the use of money

[1]**base** \'bās\ *n*
1 a thing or a part on which something rests ⟨the *base* of a statue⟩
2 a starting place or goal in various games
3 any of the four stations a runner in baseball must touch in order to score
4 the main place or starting place of an action or operation ⟨The company's *base* is in New York.⟩
5 a place where a military force keeps its supplies or from which it starts its operations ⟨an air force *base*⟩
6 a line or surface of a geometric figure upon which an altitude is or is thought to be constructed ⟨*base* of a triangle⟩
7 the main substance in a mixture
8 a number with reference to which a system of numbers is constructed
9 a chemical substance (as lime or ammonia) that reacts with an acid to form a salt and turns red litmus paper blue

basil

[2]**base** *vb* **based**; **bas•ing**
to use as a main place of operation or action
base on *or* **base upon** to make or form from a starting point ⟨The movie is *based on* a true story.⟩

[3]**base** *adj* **bas•er**; **bas•est**
1 of low value and not very good in some ways ⟨*base* metals⟩
2 not honorable

base•ball \'bās-,bȯl\ *n*
1 ▶ a game played with a bat and ball by two teams of nine players on a field with four bases that mark the course a runner must take to score
2 the ball used in the game of baseball

base•board \'bās-,bȯrd\ *n*
a thin line of boards running along the bottom of the walls of a room

base•ment \'bā-smənt\ *n*
the part of a building that is partly or entirely below ground level

bash \'bash\ *vb* **bashed**; **bash•ing**
to hit very hard

bash•ful \'bash-fəl\ *adj*
1 uneasy in the presence of others
2 showing shyness ⟨a *bashful* smile⟩
synonyms see SHY

[1]**ba•sic** \'bā-sik\ *adj*
1 relating to or forming the basis or most important part of something ⟨the *basic* principles of science⟩
2 relating to or characteristic of a chemical base ⟨a *basic* compound⟩
ba•si•cal•ly \-si-kə-lē\ *adv*

[2]**basic** *n*
something that is one of the simplest and most important parts of something

ba•sil \'ba-zəl, 'bā-\ *n*
◀ a fragrant mint used in cooking

ba•sin \'bā-s[ə]n\ *n*
1 a wide shallow usually round dish or bowl
2 the amount that a basin holds
3 the land drained by a river and its branches
4 a partly enclosed area of water for anchoring ships

ba•sis \'bā-səs\ *n, pl* **ba•ses** \-,sēz\
something on which another thing is based or established **:** FOUNDATION ⟨The story has its *basis* in fact.⟩

bask \'bask\ *vb* **basked**; **bask•ing**
1 to lie or relax in a warm place ⟨Reptiles often *bask* in the sun.⟩
2 to take pleasure or derive enjoyment ⟨They *basked* in their success.⟩

baseball 1

This competitive sport is played by two teams who take turns at bat and in the field. The pitcher throws the ball and the batter attempts to hit it. If he or she hits the ball and it is not caught by a player on the opposing team, the batter runs to each base in sequence to reach home plate. When each team has had a turn at bat, this is known as an inning. A standard game lasts for nine innings.

face mask

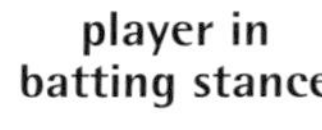

player in batting stance

baseball

glove

bat

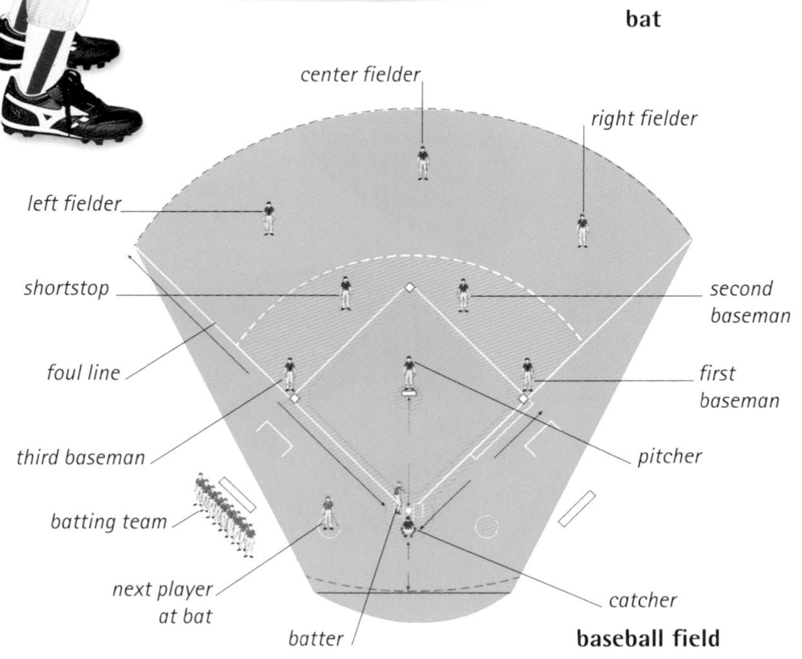

baseball field

basket 1

bas•ket \ˈba-skit\ *n*

1 ▲ a container usually made by weaving together materials (as reeds, straw, or strips of wood)

2 the contents of a basket 〈a *basket* of berries〉

3 a net hanging from a metal ring through which a ball is shot in basketball

4 a shot that scores in basketball

bas•ket•like \-ˌlīk\ *adj*

bas•ket•ball \ˈba-skit-ˌbȯl\ *n*

1 a game in which two teams try to throw a ball through a hanging net

2 ▼ the ball used in basketball

basketball 2

bas•ket•ry \ˈba-ski-trē\ *n*

1 the making of objects (as baskets) by weaving or braiding long slender pieces of material (as reed or wood)

2 objects made of interwoven material

bas mitzvah *variant of* BAT MITZVAH

[1]**bass** \ˈbas\ *n, pl* **bass** *or* **bass•es**

any of numerous freshwater or saltwater fishes that are caught for sport and food

[2]**bass** \ˈbās\ *n*

1 a tone of low pitch

2 the lowest part in harmony that has four parts

3 the lower half of the musical pitch range

4 the lowest male singing voice

5 a singer or an instrument having a bass range or part

[3]**bass** *adj*

having a very low sound or range 〈*bass* drums〉

bas•soon \bə-ˈsün, ba-\ *n*
a woodwind instrument with two bound reeds and with a usual range two octaves lower than an oboe

► **Word History** The bassoon usually plays the lowest part among the woodwinds in an orchestra. The English word came from the French name for the instrument, *basson,* which in turn came from the Italian name, *bassone.* Not surprisingly, *bassone* is derived from Italian *basso,* "bass."

[1]**baste** \ˈbāst\ *vb* **bast•ed**; **bast•ing**
to sew with long loose stitches so as to hold the cloth temporarily in place

[2]**baste** *vb* **bast•ed**; **bast•ing**
to moisten (as with melted fat or juices) while roasting 〈*baste* a turkey〉

[1]**bat** \ˈbat\ *n*
1 a sharp blow or slap 〈a *bat* on the ear〉
2 an implement used for hitting the ball in various games
3 a turn at batting 〈You're next at *bat.*〉

[2]**bat** *vb* **bat•ted**; **bat•ting**
1 to strike with or as if with a bat
2 to take a turn at bat 〈Have you *batted* yet?〉

[3]**bat** *n*
▼ any of a group of mammals that fly by means of long front limbs modified into wings

batch \ˈbach\ *n*
1 an amount used or made at one time 〈a *batch* of cookies〉
2 a group of persons or things 〈a *batch* of presents〉

bate \ˈbāt\ *vb* **bat•ed**; **bat•ing**
to reduce the force or intensity of 〈We listened with *bated* breath.〉

bath \ˈbath, ˈbäth\ *n, pl* **baths** \ˈbat͟hz, ˈbät͟hz\
1 an act of washing the body usually in a bathtub 〈took a *bath*〉
2 water for bathing 〈draw a *bath*〉
3 a place, room, or building where people may bathe 〈ancient Roman *baths*〉
4 BATHROOM
5 BATHTUB

bathe \ˈbāt͟h\ *vb* **bathed**; **bath•ing**
1 to take a bath
2 to give a bath to 〈*bathe* the baby〉
3 to go swimming
4 to apply a liquid to for washing or rinsing 〈*bathe* the eyes〉
5 to cover with or as if with a liquid 〈The room was *bathed* in sunlight.〉
bath•er *n*

bathing suit *n*
SWIMSUIT

bath•robe \ˈbath-ˌrōb, ˈbäth-\ *n*
► a robe that is worn especially before or after a bath

bath•room \ˈbath-ˌrüm, ˈbäth-, -ˌru̇m\ *n*
a room containing a sink and toilet and usually a bathtub or shower

bath•tub \ˈbath-ˌtəb, ˈbäth-\ *n*
a tub in which to take a bath

bat mitz•vah \bät-ˈmits-və\ *also* **bas mitz•vah** \bäs-\ *n, often cap B & M*
1 a Jewish girl who at twelve or more years of age takes on religious responsibilities
2 the ceremony recognizing a girl as a bat mitzvah

ba•ton \bə-ˈtän, ba-\ *n*
1 a thin stick with which a leader directs an orchestra or band
2 a rod with a ball at one or both ends that is carried by a person leading a marching band

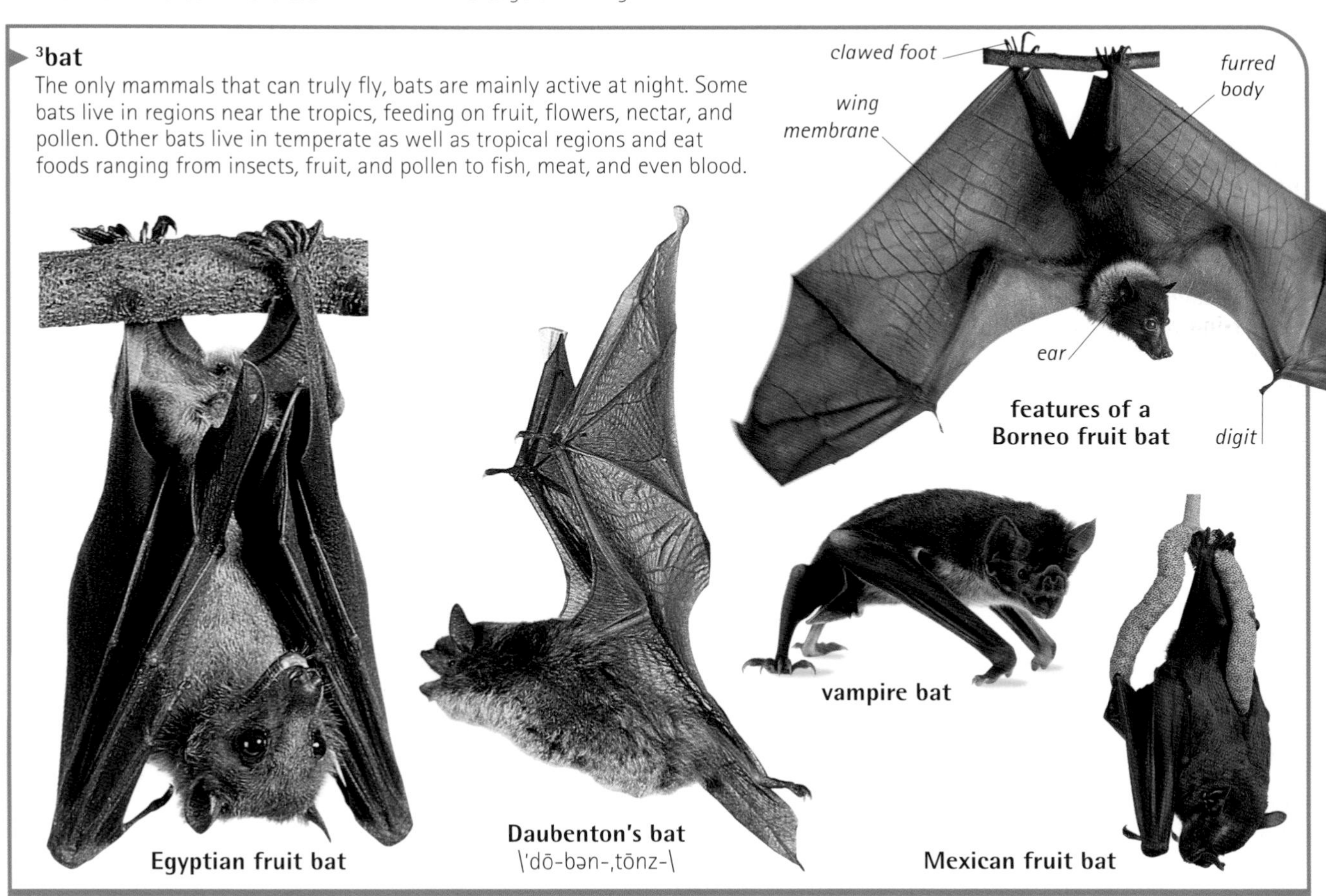

Egyptian fruit bat

Daubenton's bat \ˈdō-bən-ˌtōnz-\

Mexican fruit bat

bathrobe

3 a stick that is passed from one runner to the next in a relay race

bat•tal•ion \bə-ˈtal-yən\ *n*
a part of an army consisting of two or more companies

bat•ten \ˈba-tᵊn\ *vb* **bat•tened**; **bat•ten•ing**
1 to secure by or as if by fastening — often used with *down* ⟨Everything on the ship's deck was *battened* down.⟩
2 to prepare for possible trouble or difficulty — often used with *down* ⟨People *battened* down in preparation for winter.⟩

[1]**bat•ter** \ˈba-tər\ *vb* **bat•tered**; **bat•ter•ing**
1 to beat with repeated violent blows ⟨Waves *battered* the shore.⟩
2 to damage by blows or hard use

[2]**batter** *n*
a mixture made chiefly of flour and a liquid that is cooked and eaten ⟨pancake *batter*⟩

[3]**batter** *n*
the player whose turn it is to bat

bat•tered \ˈba-tərd\ *adj*
worn down or injured by hard use ⟨She wore a *battered* old hat.⟩

bat•ter•ing ram \ˈba-tə-riŋ-\ *n*
1 an ancient military machine that consisted of a heavy beam with an iron tip swung back and forth in order to batter down walls
2 a heavy metal bar with handles used (as by firefighters) to break down doors or walls

bat•tery \ˈba-tə-rē\ *n*, *pl* **bat•ter•ies**
1 two or more big military guns that are controlled as a unit
2 ▶ an electric cell or connected electric cells for providing electric current ⟨a flashlight *battery*⟩
3 a number of similar items or devices grouped together ⟨a *battery* of tests⟩
4 an unlawful touching or use of force on a person against his or her will

battery 2

bat•ting \ˈba-tiŋ\ *n*
sheets of soft material (as cotton or wool) used mostly for stuffing quilts or packaging goods

[1]**bat•tle** \ˈba-tᵊl\ *n*
1 a fight between armies, warships, or airplanes
2 a fight between two persons or animals
3 a long or hard struggle or contest ⟨the *battle* against hunger⟩
4 WARFARE 1, COMBAT

[2]**battle** *vb* **bat•tled**; **bat•tling**
1 to engage in fighting
2 to try to stop or defeat ⟨*battling* a forest fire⟩

bat•tle–ax *or* **bat•tle–axe** \ˈba-tᵊl-ˌaks\ *n*
an ax with a broad blade formerly used as a weapon

bat•tle•field \ˈba-tᵊl-ˌfēld\ *n*
a place where a military battle is fought or was once fought

bat•tle•ground \ˈba-tᵊl-ˌgrau̇nd\ *n*
BATTLEFIELD

bat•tle•ment \ˈba-tᵊl-mənt\ *n*
a low wall (as at the top of a castle) with openings to shoot through

bat•tle•ship \ˈba-tᵊl-ˌship\ *n*
▼ a large warship with heavy armor and large guns

person forced to face pursuers when it is impossible to escape ⟨Hunters brought the wild boar to *bay.*⟩
3 the position of someone or something held off or kept back ⟨He kept the hounds at *bay.*⟩ ⟨She held her fear at *bay.*⟩

[4]**bay** *n*
a part of a large body of water extending into the land

[5]**bay** *n*
the laurel or a related tree or shrub

bay•ber•ry \ˈbā-ˌber-ē\ *n*, *pl* **bay•ber•ries**
a shrub with leathery leaves and clusters of small berries covered with grayish white wax

[1]**bay•o•net** \ˈbā-ə-nət, ˌbā-ə-ˈnet\ *n*
a weapon like a dagger made to fit on the end of a rifle

[2]**bayonet** *vb* **bay•o•net•ted**; **bay•o•net•ting**
to stab with a bayonet

bay•ou \ˈbī-ü, -ō\ *n*
a body of water (as a creek) that flows slowly through marshy land

battleship: the Royal Navy cruiser HMS *Belfast*

bat•ty \ˈba-tē\ *adj* **bat•ti•er**; **bat•ti•est**
CRAZY 1

[1]**bawl** \ˈbȯl\ *vb* **bawled**; **bawl•ing**
1 to shout or cry loudly
2 to weep noisily
bawl out to scold severely

[2]**bawl** *n*
a loud cry

[1]**bay** \ˈbā\ *n*
1 a reddish-brown horse with black mane, tail, and lower legs
2 a reddish brown

[2]**bay** *vb* **bayed**; **bay•ing**
to bark or bark at with long deep tones

[3]**bay** *n*
1 a deep bark
2 the position of an animal or a

bay window \ˈbā-\ *n*
a large window or a set of windows that sticks out from the wall of a building

ba•zaar \bə-ˈzär\ *n*
1 a marketplace (as in southwestern Asia and northern Africa) that has rows of small shops
2 a place where many kinds of goods are sold
3 a fair for the sale of goods especially for charity

ba•zoo•ka \bə-ˈzü-kə\ *n*
a portable gun that rests on a person's shoulder and consists of a tube open at both ends that shoots an explosive rocket

BC *abbr* British Columbia

B.C. *abbr* before Christ

[1]bead 1: a string of beads

be \bē\ *vb, past first person & third person sing* **was** \wəz, ˈwəz, wäz\; *second person sing* **were** \wər, ˈwər\; *pl* **were**; *past subjunctive* **were**; *past participle* **been** \bin\; *present participle* **be•ing** \ˈbē-iŋ\; *present first person sing* **am** \əm, am\; *second person sing* **are** \ər, är\; *third person sing* **is** \iz, əz\; *pl* **are**; *present subjunctive* **be**
1 to equal in meaning or identity 〈She *is* my neighbor.〉
2 to have a specified character, quality, or condition 〈The leaves *are* green.〉 〈How *are* you? I *am* fine.〉
3 to belong to the group or class of 〈Apes *are* mammals.〉
4 to exist or live 〈Once there *was* a brave knight.〉
5 to occupy a place, situation, or position 〈The book *is* on the table.〉
6 to take place 〈The concert *was* last night.〉
7 [1]COST 1
8 used as a helping verb with other verbs 〈The ball *was* thrown.〉

be- *prefix*
1 on : around : over
2 provide with or cover with : dress up with 〈*be*whiskered〉
3 about : to : upon 〈*be*moan〉
4 make : cause to be 〈*be*little〉 〈*be*friend〉

[1]beach \ˈbēch\ *n*
a sandy or gravelly part of the shore of an ocean or a lake

[2]beach *vb* **beached**; **beach•ing**
to run or drive ashore 〈*beach* a boat〉

bea•con \ˈbē-kən\ *n*
1 a guiding or warning light or fire on a high place
2 a radio station that sends out signals to guide aircraft
3 someone or something that guides or gives hope to others 〈These countries are *beacons* of democracy.〉

[1]bead \ˈbēd\ *n*
1 ◀ a small piece of solid material with a hole through it by which it can be strung on a thread
2 a small round drop of liquid 〈a *bead* of sweat〉

▶ **Word History** In medieval English the word *bede*, from which our word *bead* descends, meant "a prayer." Then, as now, people sometimes used strings of little balls to keep track of their prayers. Each little ball stood for a prayer. In time the word that meant "prayer" came to be used for the little balls themselves. Now any small object that can be strung on a string is called a *bead*.

[2]bead *vb* **bead•ed**; **bead•ing**
to decorate or cover with beads 〈a *beaded* dress〉 〈His face was *beaded* with sweat.〉

beady \ˈbē-dē\ *adj* **bead•i•er**; **bead•i•est**
like a bead especially in being small, round, and shiny 〈*beady* eyes〉

bea•gle \ˈbē-gəl\ *n*
▼ a small hound with short legs and a smooth coat

beagle

beak \ˈbēk\ *n*
1 the bill of a bird 〈an eagle's *beak*〉
2 a part shaped like or resembling a bird's bill
beaked \ˈbēkt\ *adj*

bea•ker \ˈbē-kər\ *n*
a cup or glass with a wide mouth and usually a lip for pouring that is used especially in science laboratories for holding and measuring liquids

[1]beam \ˈbēm\ *n*
1 a long heavy piece of timber or metal used as a main horizontal support of a building or a ship 〈a ceiling *beam*〉
2 a ray of light
3 a radio wave sent out from an airport to guide pilots

[2]beam *vb* **beamed**; **beam•ing**
1 to send out beams of light
2 to smile with joy
3 to aim a radio broadcast by use of a special antenna

bean \ˈbēn\ *n*
1 ▶ the edible seed or pod of a bushy or climbing garden plant related to the peas and clovers
2 a seed or fruit like a bean 〈coffee *beans*〉

[1]bear \ˈber\ *n, pl* **bears**
1 ▼ *or pl* **bear** a large heavy mammal with long shaggy hair and a very short tail

[1]bear 1

2 a person resembling a bear in size or behavior

[2]bear *vb* **bore** \ˈbȯr\; **borne** \ˈbȯrn\; **bear•ing**
1 [1]SUPPORT 1 〈*bear* weight〉
2 to move while holding up and supporting : CARRY 〈They came *bearing* gifts.〉
3 to hold in the mind 〈She *bears* a grudge.〉
4 to put up with 〈I can't *bear* the suspense.〉
5 to assume or accept 〈*bear* the blame〉
6 to have as a feature or characteristic 〈She *bears* a resemblance to her sister.〉
7 give birth to 〈*bear* children〉
8 [1]PRODUCE 1 〈trees *bearing* fruit〉 〈*bear* interest〉
9 to move or lie in the indicated direction 〈*Bear* right at the fork.〉
10 to have a relation to the matter at hand 〈These facts don't *bear* on the question.〉
bear down on to push or lean down on 〈*Bear down* hard *on* your pencil.〉
bear in mind to think of especially as a warning 〈*Bear in mind* that you only get one chance.〉

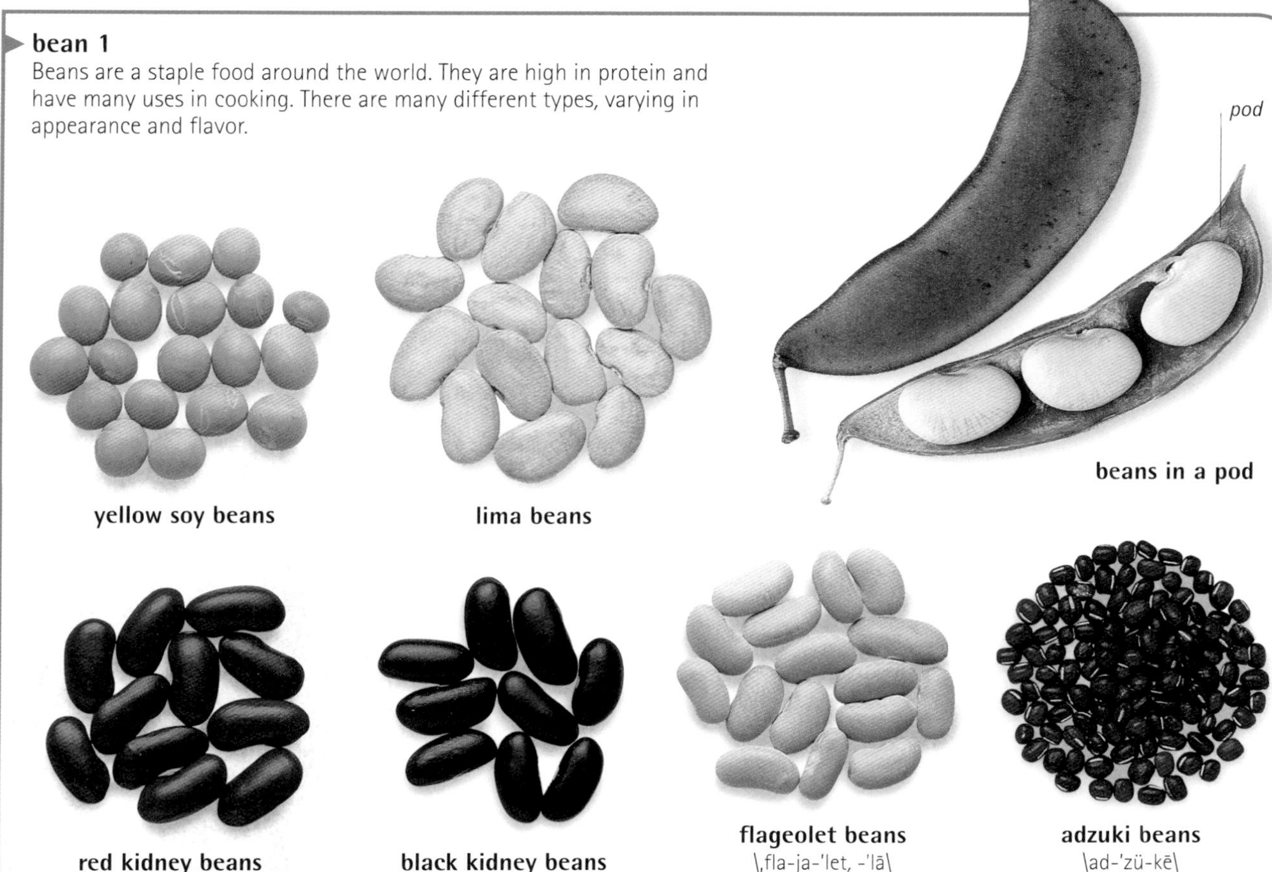

bear up to have strength or courage ⟨She's *bearing up* under the stress.⟩
bear with to be patient with ⟨*Bear with* me.⟩

bear•able \ˈber-ə-bəl\ *adj*
possible to put up with

beard \ˈbird\ *n*
1 the hair that grows on a man's face often not including the mustache
2 a hairy growth or tuft (as on the chin of a goat)
beard•ed *adj*

bear•er \ˈber-ər\ *n*
1 someone or something that bears, supports, or carries ⟨She was the *bearer* of bad news.⟩
2 a person who has a check or an order for payment

bear•ing \ˈber-iŋ\ *n*
1 the manner in which a person carries or conducts himself or herself ⟨a man of kingly *bearing*⟩
2 a part of a machine in which another part turns
3 the position or direction of one point with respect to another or to the compass
4 a determination of position ⟨take a *bearing*⟩
5 bearings *pl* understanding of position or situation ⟨I lost my *bearings.*⟩
6 a relation or connection ⟨Personal feelings had no *bearing* on our decision.⟩

beast \ˈbēst\ *n*
1 a mammal with four feet (as a bear or deer) especially as distinguished from human beings ⟨*beasts* of the forest⟩
2 a wild animal that is large, dangerous, or unusual
3 a farm animal especially when kept for work ⟨Oxen are used as *beasts* of burden.⟩
4 a horrid person

beast•ly \ˈbēst-lē\ *adj*
very unpleasant : HORRIBLE ⟨*beastly* behavior⟩

[1]**beat** \ˈbēt\ *vb* **beat; beat•en** \ˈbē-tᵊn\ *or* **beat; beat•ing**
1 to hit or strike again and again ⟨*beat* a drum⟩ ⟨waves *beating* the shore⟩
2 to hit repeatedly in order to cause pain or injury ⟨They *beat* him with sticks.⟩ — often used with *up*
3 to mix by stirring rapidly ⟨*beat* eggs⟩
4 to win against : DEFEAT ⟨*beat* the enemy⟩
5 to come, arrive, or act before ⟨I *beat* him to the finish line.⟩
6 [1]THROB 3, PULSATE ⟨Her heart was still *beating.*⟩
7 to flap against ⟨wings *beating* the air⟩
8 to move with an up and down motion : FLAP ⟨The bird *beat* its wings.⟩
9 to do or be better than ⟨You can't *beat* that for fun.⟩
10 to be beyond the understanding of ⟨It *beats* me how she does it.⟩
11 to make by walking or riding over ⟨*beat* a path⟩
beat•er *n*
beat it to go away quickly

[2]**beat** *n*
1 a blow or a stroke made again and again
2 a single pulse (as of the heart)
3 a sound produced by or as if by beating ⟨the *beat* of drums⟩
4 a measurement of time in music : an accent or regular pattern of accents in music or poetry
5 an area or place regularly visited or traveled through as part of a job ⟨a police officer's *beat*⟩

[3]beat *adj*
very tired

beat•en \'bē-tᵊn\ *adj*
1 worn smooth by passing feet ⟨a *beaten* path⟩
2 having lost all hope or spirit

beat–up \'bēt-,əp\ *adj*
badly worn or damaged by use or neglect ⟨a *beat-up* old car⟩

beau•te•ous \'byü-tē-əs\ *adj*
BEAUTIFUL

beau•ti•cian \byü-'ti-shən\ *n*
a person who gives beauty treatments (as to skin and hair)

beau•ti•ful \'byü-ti-fəl\ *adj*
1 having qualities of beauty : giving pleasure to the mind or senses ⟨a *beautiful* child⟩ ⟨a *beautiful* song⟩
2 very good : EXCELLENT ⟨*beautiful* weather⟩
beau•ti•ful•ly *adv*

► **Synonyms** BEAUTIFUL, PRETTY, and HANDSOME mean pleasing or delightful in some way. BEAUTIFUL is used of whatever is most pleasing to the senses or the mind. ⟨We saw a *beautiful* sunset.⟩ ⟨It was a *beautiful* story about faith.⟩ PRETTY is usually used of something that is small or dainty. ⟨She held a *pretty* little doll.⟩ HANDSOME is used of something that is well formed and therefore pleasing to look at. ⟨The mayor sat at a *handsome* desk.⟩

beau•ti•fy \'byü-tə-,fī\ *vb* **beau•ti•fied**; **beau•ti•fy•ing**
to make beautiful ⟨We *beautified* the room with flowers.⟩

beau•ty \'byü-tē\ *n, pl* **beauties**
1 the qualities of a person or a thing that give pleasure to the senses or to the mind ⟨the *beauty* of the landscape⟩
2 a beautiful or excellent person or thing ⟨That car is a real *beauty*.⟩

bea•ver \'bē-vər\ *n*
▼ an animal that has thick brown fur, webbed hind feet, and a broad flat tail, that cuts down trees with its teeth, and that builds dams and houses of sticks and mud in water

beaver

be•cause \bi-'kȯz, -'kəz\ *conj*
for the reason that ⟨I ran *because* I was scared.⟩
because of for the reason of ⟨The game was canceled *because of* rain.⟩

beck•on \'be-kən\ *vb* **beck•oned**; **beck•on•ing**
1 to call or signal by a motion (as a wave or nod) ⟨They *beckoned* to us to come over.⟩
2 to appear inviting ⟨New adventures were *beckoning*.⟩

be•come \bi-'kəm\ *vb* **be•came** \-'kām\; **become**; **be•com•ing**
1 to come or grow to be ⟨He *became* president.⟩ ⟨It's *becoming* cold.⟩ ⟨A tadpole *becomes* a frog.⟩
2 to be suitable to especially in a pleasing way ⟨Look for clothes that *become* you.⟩
become of to happen to ⟨What has *become of* my friend?⟩

be•com•ing \bi-'kə-miŋ\ *adj*
having a flattering effect ⟨*becoming* clothes⟩

[1]bed \'bed\ *n*
1 a piece of furniture on which a person sleeps or rests
2 a place for sleeping or resting ⟨Deer made a *bed* in the grass.⟩
3 sleep or a time for sleeping ⟨She reads before *bed*.⟩
4 a piece of ground prepared for growing plants
5 the bottom of something ⟨the *bed* of a river⟩
6 [1]LAYER 1 ⟨a thick *bed* of rock⟩

[2]bed *vb* **bed•ded**; **bed•ding**
to put or go to bed

bed•bug \'bed-,bəg\ *n*
a small wingless insect that sucks blood and is sometimes found in houses and especially in beds

bed•clothes \'bed-,klōz, -klōthz\ *n pl*
coverings (as sheets and blankets) for a bed

bed•ding \'be-diŋ\ *n*
1 BEDCLOTHES
2 material for a bed

be•deck \bi-'dek\ *vb* **be•decked**; **be•deck•ing**
to dress up or decorate with showy things ⟨*bedecked* with ribbon⟩

be•dev•il \bi-'de-vəl\ *vb* **be•dev•iled**; **be•dev•il•ing**
to trouble or annoy again and again ⟨*bedeviled* by problems⟩

bed•lam \'bed-ləm\ *n*
a place, scene, or state of uproar and confusion

be•drag•gled \bi-'dra-gəld\ *adj*
limp, wet, or dirty from or as if from rain or mud ⟨*bedraggled* hair⟩

bed•rid•den \'bed-,ri-dᵊn\ *adj*
forced to stay in bed by sickness or weakness ⟨*bedridden* patients⟩

bed•rock \'bed-,räk\ *n*
the solid rock found under surface materials (as soil)

bed•room \'bed-,rüm, -,ru̇m\ *n*
a room used for sleeping

bed•side \'bed-,sīd\ *n*
the place next to a bed

bed•spread \'bed-,spred\ *n*
a decorative top covering for a bed

bed•stead \'bed-,sted\ *n*
the framework of a bed

bed•time \'bed-,tīm\ *n*
time to go to bed

bee \'bē\ *n*
1 ▼ an insect with four wings that is related to the wasps, gathers pollen and nectar from flowers from which it makes beebread and honey for food, and usually lives in large colonies
2 a gathering of people to do something together or engage in a competition ⟨a spelling *bee*⟩

bee 1: a honeybee

bee•bread \'bē-,bred\ *n*
a bitter yellowish brown food material prepared by bees from pollen and stored in their honeycomb

beech \'bēch\ *n*
a tree with smooth gray bark, deep green leaves, and small edible nuts

[1]beef \'bēf\ *n, pl* **beefs** \'bēfs\ *or* **beeves** \'bēvz\
1 the meat of a steer, cow, or bull
2 a steer, cow, or bull especially when fattened for food
3 *pl beefs* COMPLAINT 2

[2]beef *vb* **beefed**; **beef•ing**
COMPLAIN ⟨He's always *beefing* about something.⟩

beetle 1
The beetle is an insect that can be found in nearly all parts of the world. There are hundreds of thousands of different types, and they live in habitats that range from scorching deserts to muddy ponds and cold mountaintops. Some beetles eat plants, while others feed on dead animals. Many beetles are brilliantly colored or patterned.

weevil  | **stag beetle** 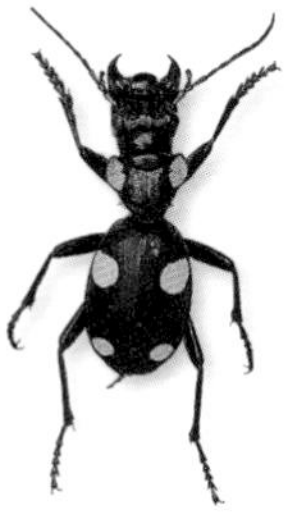 | **tiger beetle** 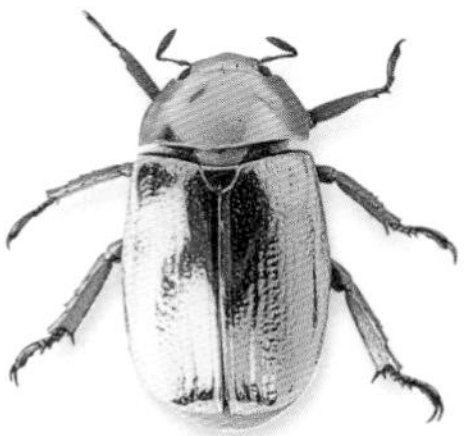 | **golden beetle** 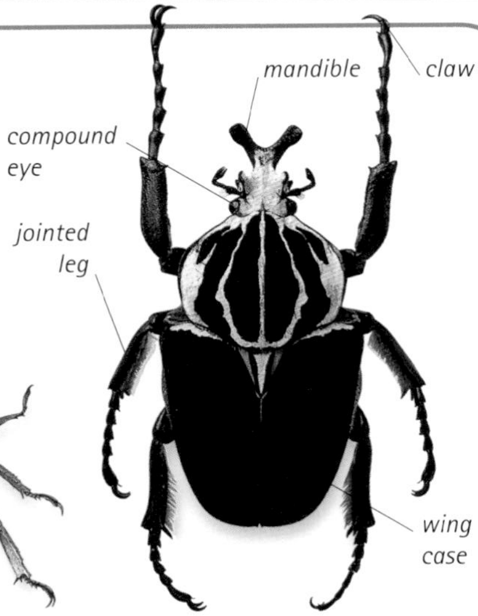 | **features of a Goliath beetle** \gə-ˈlī-əth\

dung beetle  | **tortoise beetle**  | **jewel beetle**  | **leaf beetle**  | **long-horned beetle**

beef up to add weight, strength, or power to ⟨The coach *beefed up* the team's defense.⟩

bee•hive \ˈbē-ˌhīv\ *n*
HIVE

bee•line \ˈbē-ˌlīn\ *n*
a straight direct course

been *past participle of* BE

[1]**beep** \ˈbēp\ *n*
a sound that signals or warns

[2]**beep** *vb* **beeped**; **beep•ing**
to make or cause to make a sound that signals or warns ⟨The alarm is *beeping.*⟩

beer \ˈbir\ *n*
an alcoholic drink made from malt and flavored with hops

bees•wax \ˈbēz-ˌwaks\ *n*
wax made by bees and used by them in building honeycomb

beet \ˈbēt\ *n*
1 a leafy plant with a thick juicy root that is used as a vegetable or as a source of sugar
2 the root of a beet plant

bee•tle \ˈbē-tᵊl\ *n*
1 ▲ any of a group of insects with four wings the outer pair of which are stiff cases that cover the others when folded
2 an insect that looks like a beetle

▶ **Word History** Beetles are not usually stinging insects, at least in the cooler climates of North America and Europe, but Old English *bitela*, the ancestor of our modern word *beetle*, means literally "biter." Actually, the speakers of Old English seem to have applied *bitela* to several not very beetle-like insects, such as cockroaches, which snack on our belongings—so the biting in question may be eating rather than defense. A related Old English word for an insect that has not survived into modern English is *hrædbita* literally "quick-biter."

beeves *pl of* BEEF

be•fall \bi-ˈfȯl\ *vb* **be•fell** \-ˈfel\; **be•fall•en** \-ˈfȯ-lən\; **be•fall•ing**
to happen to

be•fit \bi-ˈfit\ *vb* **be•fit•ted**; **be•fit•ting**
to be suitable to or proper for ⟨Wear clothes *befitting* the occasion.⟩

[1]**be•fore** \bi-ˈfȯr\ *adv*
1 at an earlier time ⟨I've been here *before.*⟩
2 AHEAD ⟨go on *before*⟩

[2]**before** *prep*
1 in front of ⟨He stood *before* a mirror.⟩
2 earlier than ⟨You got there *before* me.⟩
3 before in order ⟨Your name is listed *before* mine.⟩
4 in the presence of ⟨She spoke *before* a crowd.⟩

[3]**before** *conj*
1 ahead of the time when ⟨Wash *before* you eat.⟩
2 sooner or quicker than ⟨I'll be done *before* you know it.⟩
3 more willingly than ⟨I'd starve *before* I'd steal.⟩
4 until the time that ⟨It wasn't long *before* he caught on.⟩

be•fore•hand \bi-ˈfȯr-ˌhand\ *adv*
at an earlier or previous time ⟨They decided *beforehand* to leave early.⟩

be•friend \bi-ˈfrend\ *vb* **be•friend•ed**; **be•friend•ing**
to act as a friend to

be•fud•dle \bi-ˈfə-dᵊl\ *vb* **be•fud•dled**; **be•fud•dling**
CONFUSE 1

beg \ˈbeg\ *vb* **begged**; **beg•ging**
1 to ask for money, food, or help as charity 〈*beg* in the streets〉
2 to ask as a favor in an earnest or polite way : PLEAD

beg•gar \ˈbe-gər\ *n*
a person who lives by begging

be•gin \bi-ˈgin\ *vb* **be•gan** \-ˈgan\; **be•gun** \-ˈgən\; **be•gin•ning**
1 to do the first part of an action 〈Please *begin* writing.〉
2 to come into existence 〈Our problems were just *beginning*.〉
3 to start to have a feeling or thought 〈I *began* to feel sick.〉
4 to have a starting point 〈The alphabet *begins* with the letter A.〉
5 to do or succeed in the least degree 〈I can't *begin* to explain.〉

be•gin•ner \bi-ˈgi-nər\ *n*
a person who is doing something for the first time

be•gin•ning \bi-ˈgi-niŋ\ *n*
1 the point at which something begins 〈the *beginning* of the year〉
2 the first part 〈the *beginning* of the song〉

be•gone \bi-ˈgȯn\ *vb*
to go away
Hint: This word is used as a command. 〈*Begone*, you rascal!〉

be•go•nia \bi-ˈgōn-yə\ *n*
▼ a plant with a juicy stem, ornamental leaves, and bright waxy flowers

begonia

be•grudge \bi-ˈgrəj\ *vb* **be•grudged**; **be•grudg•ing**
to give or allow reluctantly 〈He *begrudged* the time spent away from home.〉

be•guile \bi-ˈgīl\ *vb* **be•guiled**; **be•guil•ing**
1 ²TRICK, DECEIVE 〈He was *beguiled* with lies.〉
2 to cause time to pass pleasantly
3 to attract or interest by or as if by charm 〈The scenery *beguiled* us.〉

be•half \bi-ˈhaf, -ˈhäf\ *n*
a person's interest or support 〈He argued in my *behalf*.〉
on behalf of *or* **in behalf of**
1 in the interest of 〈I speak *in behalf of* my friend.〉
2 as a representative of 〈I accepted the award *on behalf of* the whole class.〉

be•have \bi-ˈhāv\ *vb* **be•haved**; **be•hav•ing**
1 to act in a particular manner 〈The children *behaved* well at the party.〉
2 to act in a proper or acceptable way 〈Tell them to *behave*.〉
3 to act or function in a particular way 〈We're studying how metals *behave* under pressure.〉

be•hav•ior \bi-ˈhāv-yər\ *n*
1 the manner in which a person acts 〈Students are rewarded for good *behavior*.〉
2 the whole activity of something and especially a living being 〈Scientists observed the elephant's *behavior*.〉

be•head \bi-ˈhed\ *vb* **be•head•ed**; **be•head•ing**
to cut off the head of

¹**be•hind** \bi-ˈhīnd\ *adv*
1 in a place that is being or has been left 〈You can leave your books *behind*.〉
2 in, to, or toward the back 〈look *behind*〉 〈fall *behind*〉
3 not up to the general level 〈*behind* in math〉
4 not keeping up to a schedule 〈*behind* in his payments〉

²**behind** *prep*
1 at or to the back of 〈*behind* the door〉
2 not up to the level of 〈Sales are *behind* those of last year.〉
3 out of the thoughts of 〈Let's put our troubles *behind* us.〉
4 responsible for 〈Who's *behind* these pranks?〉
5 in support of 〈We're *behind* you all the way!〉

be•hold \bi-ˈhōld\ *vb* **be•held** \-ˈheld\; **be•hold•ing**
to look upon : SEE 〈There I *beheld* a wondrous sight.〉
be•hold•er *n*

be•hold•en \bi-ˈhol-dən\ *adj*
owing the return of a gift or favor 〈I'm not *beholden* to anyone for my success.〉

be•hoove \bi-ˈhüv\ *vb* **be•hooved**; **be•hoov•ing**
to be necessary or proper for

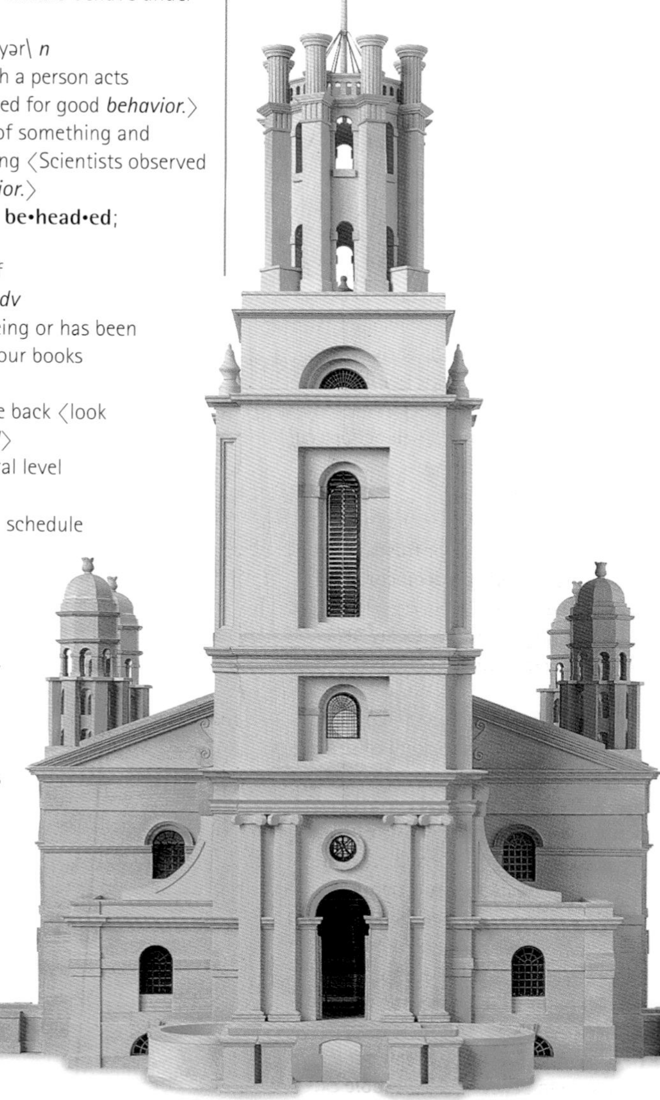

belfry: a model of a church with a belfry

beige \'bāzh\ *n*
a yellowish brown
beige *adj*

be•ing \'bē-iŋ\ *n*
1 the state of having life or existence ⟨He explained how the myth came into *being.*⟩
2 a living thing
3 an entity believed to be divine

be•la•bor \bi-'lā-bər\ *vb* **be•la•bored; be•la•bor•ing**
to keep explaining or insisting on to excess ⟨*belabor* an argument⟩

be•lat•ed \bi-'lā-təd\ *adj*
happening or coming very late or too late ⟨*belated* birthday wishes⟩
be•lat•ed•ly *adv*

[1]**belch** \'belch\ *vb* **belched; belch•ing**
1 to force out gas suddenly from the stomach through the mouth usually with a sound
2 to throw out or be thrown out with force ⟨Smoke *belched* from the chimney.⟩

[2]**belch** *n*
a forcing out of gas from the stomach through the mouth

bel•fry \'bel-frē\ *n, pl* **belfries**
◀ a tower or room in a tower for a bell or set of bells

[1]**Bel•gian** \'bel-jən\ *adj*
of or relating to Belgium or the Belgians

[2]**Belgian** *n*
a person born or living in Belgium

be•lie \bi-'lī\ *vb* **be•lied; be•ly•ing**
1 to give a false idea of ⟨Her youthful appearance *belies* her age.⟩
2 to show to be false ⟨Their actions *belie* their claim of innocence.⟩

be•lief \bə-'lēf\ *n*
1 a feeling of being sure that a person or thing exists or is true or trustworthy ⟨*belief* in ghosts⟩ ⟨*belief* in democracy⟩
2 religious faith
3 something believed ⟨It's my *belief* that our team really won.⟩

► **Synonyms** BELIEF and FAITH mean agreement with the truth of something. BELIEF is used when there is some kind of evidence for believing even though the believer is not always sure of the truth. ⟨The story strengthened my *belief* in ghosts.⟩ FAITH is used when the believer is certain even if there is no evidence or proof. ⟨Even after the robbery, I kept my *faith* in the goodness of people.⟩ **Synonyms** see in addition OPINION.

be•liev•able \bə-'lē-və-bəl\ *adj*
possible to believe ⟨a *believable* excuse⟩

be•lieve \bə-'lēv\ *vb* **be•lieved; be•liev•ing**
1 to have faith or confidence in the existence or worth of ⟨I don't *believe* in ghosts.⟩ ⟨He *believes* in daily exercise.⟩
2 to accept as true
3 to accept the word of ⟨They didn't *believe* me.⟩
4 to hold an opinion : THINK ⟨I *believe* I'll have more time later.⟩

be•liev•er \bə-'lē-vər\ *n*
someone who has faith or confidence in the existence or worth of something ⟨a *believer* in the value of hard work⟩ ⟨a *believer* in God⟩

be•lit•tle \bi-'li-tᵊl\ *vb* **be•lit•tled; be•lit•tling**
to make (a person or a thing) seem small or unimportant

bell \'bel\ *n*
1 a hollow metallic device that is shaped somewhat like a cup and makes a ringing sound when struck
2 DOORBELL
3 the stroke or sound of a bell that tells the hour
4 the time indicated by the stroke of a bell
5 a half-hour period of watch on shipboard
6 something shaped like a bell ⟨the *bell* of a trumpet⟩

bell•boy \'bel-,bȯi\ *n*
BELLHOP

belle \'bel\ *n*
an attractive and popular girl or woman

bell•hop \'bel-,häp\ *n*
► a hotel or club employee who takes guests to rooms, moves luggage, and runs errands

bel•lied \'be-lēd\ *adj*
having a belly of a certain kind ⟨a large-*bellied* man⟩

[1]**bel•lig•er•ent** \bə-'li-jə-rənt\ *adj*
1 carrying on war
2 feeling or showing readiness to fight ⟨*belligerent* remarks⟩

[2]**belligerent** *n*
1 a nation at war
2 a person taking part in a fight

bell jar *n*
a usually glass vessel shaped like a bell and used to cover objects, hold gases, or keep a vacuum

[1]**bel•low** \'be-lō\ *vb* **bel•lowed; bel•low•ing**
1 to shout in a deep voice ⟨He *bellowed* for them to stop.⟩
2 to make a deep and loud sound ⟨a bull *bellowing*⟩

[2]**bellow** *n*
a loud deep sound ⟨an angry *bellow*⟩

bel•lows \'be-lōz, -ləz\ *n pl*
a device that produces a strong current of air when its sides are pressed together
Hint: *Bellows* can be used as a singular or a plural in writing and speaking. ⟨The *bellows* were used to start the fire.⟩ ⟨The *bellows* is on the hearth.⟩

bel•ly \'be-lē\ *n, pl* **bellies**
1 the front part of the body between the chest and the hips
2 the under part of an animal's body
3 [1]STOMACH 1 ⟨My *belly* was full.⟩
4 a space inside something ⟨cargo stored in the ship's *belly*⟩

► **Word History** Our words *bellows* and *belly* both come from an Old English word *belg,* meaning "bag" or "purse." The plural from *belga* was also used with the meaning "bellows." It was probably a shortening of the compound word *blæstbelga,* literally, "blow-bags." It is *belga* that ultimately gives us the modern word *bellows.* The singular *belg* gives us the modern word *belly,* though the use of a word meaning "bag" for "stomach" only arose in English of the later Middle Ages, after the end of the Old English period.

bellhop: a hotel bellhop

a b c d e f g h i j k l m n o p q r s t u v w x y z

belly button *n*
NAVEL

be•long \bə-ˈlȯŋ\ *vb* **be•longed**; **be•long•ing**
1 to be in a proper place ⟨This book *belongs* on the top shelf.⟩
2 to be the property of a person or group of persons ⟨The money *belongs* to me.⟩
3 to be a part of : be connected with : go with ⟨These pieces *belong* to that game.⟩

be•long•ings \bə-ˈlȯŋ-iŋz\ *n pl*
the things that belong to a person ⟨They gathered their *belongings* and left.⟩

be•lov•ed \bə-ˈlə-vəd, -ˈləvd\ *adj*
greatly loved : very dear

[1]**be•low** \bə-ˈlō\ *adv*
1 in or to a lower place ⟨The pencil rolled off the desk and fell on the floor *below.*⟩
2 below zero ⟨The temperature was ten *below.*⟩

[2]**below** *prep*
1 in or to a lower place than : BENEATH ⟨The sun sank *below* the horizon.⟩ ⟨Vines grew *below* the window.⟩
2 at the bottom of : directly underneath ⟨a caption *below* the picture⟩
3 lower in number, size, or amount ⟨temperatures *below* average⟩

[1]**belt** \ˈbelt\ *n*
1 a strip of flexible material (as leather or cloth) worn around a person's body for holding in or supporting something (as clothing or weapons) or for ornament
2 a flexible endless band running around wheels or pulleys and used for moving or carrying something ⟨a fan *belt* on a car⟩
3 a region suited to or producing something or having some special feature ⟨the corn *belt*⟩
belt•ed \ˈbel-təd\ *adj*

[2]**belt** *vb* **belt•ed**; **belt•ing**
1 to put a belt on or around ⟨He *belted* the child into the car seat.⟩
2 to hit hard ⟨The batter *belted* the ball over the fence.⟩
3 to sing in a loud and forceful way ⟨*belt* out a song⟩

belying *present participle of* BELIE

be•moan \bi-ˈmōn\ *vb* **be•moaned**; **be•moan•ing**
to express sadness, distress, or displeasure over

be•muse \bi-ˈmyüz\ *vb* **be•mused**; **be•mus•ing**
to cause to be confused and often also somewhat amused ⟨He was *bemused* by all the attention he was receiving.⟩

bench \ˈbench\ *n*
1 ▼ a long seat for two or more persons ⟨a park *bench*⟩
2 a long table for holding work and tools ⟨a carpenter's *bench*⟩
3 the position or rank of a judge

bench 1: a park bench

[1]**bend** \ˈbend\ *vb* **bent** \ˈbent\; **bend•ing**
1 to make, be, or become curved or angular rather than straight or flat ⟨*Bend* the wire into a circle.⟩
2 to move out of a straight line or position ⟨*Bend* over and pick it up.⟩
3 to not follow or tell exactly ⟨*bend* the rules⟩ ⟨*bend* the truth⟩

[2]**bend** *n*
something that is bent : a curved part of something ⟨a *bend* in the river⟩

[1]**be•neath** \bi-ˈnēth\ *adv*
1 in a lower place ⟨the mountains and the town *beneath*⟩
2 directly under ⟨Look at the picture and read what is *beneath.*⟩

[2]**beneath** *prep*
1 in or to a lower position than : BELOW ⟨The sun sank *beneath* the horizon.⟩
2 directly under (something or someone) ⟨the ground *beneath* our feet⟩
3 not worthy of ⟨She thinks this work is *beneath* her.⟩

bene•dic•tion \ˌbe-nə-ˈdik-shən\ *n*
1 a short blessing said especially at the end of a religious service
2 an expression of good wishes

ben•e•fac•tor \ˈbe-nə-ˌfak-tər\ *n*
someone who helps another especially by giving money

ben•e•fi•cial \ˌbe-nə-ˈfi-shəl\ *adj*
producing good results or effects : HELPFUL ⟨*beneficial* new medicines⟩

ben•e•fi•cia•ry \ˌbe-nə-ˈfi-shē-ˌer-ē\ *n*, *pl* **ben•e•fi•cia•ries**
a person who benefits or will benefit from something

[1]**ben•e•fit** \ˈbe-nə-ˌfit\ *n*
1 a good or helpful result or effect ⟨the *benefits* of fresh air⟩
2 useful assistance : HELP
3 money paid in time of death, sickness, or unemployment or in old age (as by an insurance company)

[2]**benefit** *vb* **ben•e•fit•ed**; **ben•e•fit•ing**
1 to be useful or profitable to ⟨The changes will *benefit* everyone.⟩
2 to be helped ⟨He'll *benefit* from new experiences.⟩

be•nev•o•lence \bə-ˈne-və-ləns\ *n*
KINDNESS 1, GENEROSITY

be•nev•o•lent \bə-ˈne-və-lənt\ *adj*
1 having a desire to do good : KINDLY
2 marked by or suggestive of a kindly feeling
be•nev•o•lent•ly *adv*

be•nign \bi-ˈnīn\ *adj*
1 marked by gentleness and kindness ⟨a *benign* mood⟩
2 not causing death or serious harm ⟨a *benign* growth on the skin⟩
be•nign•ly *adv*

[1]bent \'bent\ *adj*
1 changed by bending : CROOKED ⟨a *bent* pin⟩
2 strongly favorable to : quite determined ⟨She was *bent* on going anyway.⟩

[2]bent *n*
a natural talent or interest ⟨Some students have a scientific *bent*.⟩

be•queath \bi-'kwēth, -'kwēth\ *vb* **be•queathed; be•queath•ing**
1 to give or leave by means of a will ⟨I *bequeath* this ring to my sister.⟩
2 to hand down ⟨These stories were *bequeathed* to us by our ancestors.⟩

be•quest \bi-'kwest\ *n*
1 the act of leaving property by means of a will
2 something given or left by a will

be•rate \bi-'rāt\ *vb* **be•rat•ed; be•rat•ing**
to scold in a loud and angry way

be•reaved \bi-'rēvd\ *adj*
grieving over the death of a loved one ⟨a *bereaved* widow⟩

be•reft \bi-'reft\ *adj*
1 not having something needed, wanted, or expected ⟨The lost cat was *bereft* of a home.⟩
2 BEREAVED ⟨a *bereft* mother⟩

be•ret \bə-'rā\ *n*
a soft round flat cap without a visor

berg \'bərg\ *n*
ICEBERG

beri•beri \ˌber-ē-'ber-ē\ *n*
a disease marked by weakness, wasting, and damage to nerves and caused by a lack of the vitamin thiamine in the diet

ber•ry \'ber-ē\ *n, pl* **berries**
1 a small juicy and usually edible fruit (as a strawberry)
2 ▼ a fruit (as a grape or tomato) in which the ripened ovary wall is fleshy
3 a dry seed (as of the coffee plant)

ber•serk \bər-'sərk, -'zərk\ *adj*
out of control especially due to extreme anger or excitement

berth \'bərth\ *n*
1 a place in the water where a ship stops and stays when anchored or at a wharf
2 a bed on a ship or train
3 an amount of distance kept for the sake of safety ⟨We gave the haunted house a wide *berth*.⟩

be•seech \bi-'sēch\ *vb* **be•sought** \-'sȯt\ *or* **be•seeched; be•seech•ing**
to ask in a serious and emotional way

be•set \bi-'set\ *vb* **be•set; be•set•ting**
1 to attack violently
2 SURROUND 1
3 to cause problems or difficulties for ⟨Doubts *beset* him.⟩

be•side \bi-'sīd\ *prep*
1 at or by the side of ⟨Come, sit *beside* me.⟩
2 compared with ⟨He looks small *beside* you.⟩
3 [1]BESIDES
4 not relating to ⟨That remark is *beside* the point.⟩

[1]be•sides \bi-'sīdz\ *prep*
1 in addition to ⟨*Besides* cookies, they also baked a cake.⟩
2 other than ⟨There's no one here *besides* me.⟩

[2]besides *adv*
in addition : ALSO ⟨We had pretzels and fruit and juice *besides*.⟩

be•siege \bi-'sēj\ *vb* **be•sieged; be•sieg•ing**
1 to surround with armed forces for the purpose of capturing
2 to crowd around ⟨The movie star was *besieged* by photographers.⟩
3 to overwhelm with questions or requests ⟨The president was *besieged* for an answer.⟩

[1]best \'best\ *adj, superlative of* GOOD
1 better than all others ⟨He's the *best* speller in the class.⟩
2 most appropriate, useful, or helpful ⟨This is the *best* way to solve the problem.⟩
best part [3]MOST ⟨It rained for the *best part* of their vacation.⟩

berry 2
A wide variety of flowering plants produce berries which have soft flesh and usually plentiful seeds. Many berries are cultivated for human consumption, but in the natural world their juicy flesh is eaten by animals and the seeds are dispersed to produce new plants.

A B C D E F G H I J K L M N O P Q R S T U V W X Y Z

²best *adv, superlative of* WELL
1 in a way that is better than all the others ⟨This dessert is *best* eaten hot.⟩
2 ²MOST 1 ⟨She's *best* able to do the work.⟩

³best *n*
1 a person or thing or part of a thing that is better than all the others ⟨You're the *best*!⟩
2 someone's greatest effort ⟨Do your *best*.⟩

⁴best *vb* **best•ed**; **best•ing**
to do better than : defeat or outdo ⟨He *bested* us in every game.⟩

be•stir \bi-ˈstər\ *vb* **be•stirred**; **be•stir•ring**
to stir up : rouse to action ⟨a candidate *bestirring* supporters⟩

be•stow \bi-ˈstō\ *vb* **be•stowed**; **be•stow•ing**
to give as a gift or honor ⟨*bestowing* an award⟩

¹bet \ˈbet\ *n*
1 an agreement requiring the person who guesses wrong about the result of a contest or the outcome of an event to give something to the person who guesses right
2 the money or thing risked in a bet
3 a choice made by considering what might happen ⟨It's a safe *bet* that they will win.⟩

²bet *vb* **bet** *or* **bet•ted**; **bet•ting**
1 to risk in a bet ⟨*bet* a dollar⟩
2 to make a bet with ⟨I *bet* you he'll win.⟩
3 to be sure enough to make a bet ⟨I *bet* she knows the answer.⟩

bet. *abbr* between

be•tray \bi-ˈtrā\ *vb* **be•trayed**; **be•tray•ing**
1 to give over to an enemy by treason or treachery ⟨*betray* a fort⟩
2 to be unfaithful to ⟨*betray* a friend⟩ ⟨*betrayed* our trust⟩
3 to reveal or show without meaning to ⟨*betray* fear⟩
4 to tell in violation of a trust ⟨*betray* a secret⟩

be•troth \bi-ˈtrōth, -ˈtȯth\ *vb* **be•trothed**; **be•troth•ing**
to promise to marry or give in marriage

be•troth•al \bi-ˈtrō-thəl, -ˈtrȯ-\ *n*
an engagement to be married

¹bet•ter \ˈbe-tər\ *adj, comparative of* GOOD
1 more satisfactory or skillful than another
2 improved in health ⟨I was sick but now I'm *better*.⟩
better part more than half ⟨We waited the *better part* of an hour.⟩

²better *vb* **bet•tered**; **bet•ter•ing**
to make or become more satisfactory ⟨They are trying to *better* their performance.⟩

³better *adv, comparative of* WELL
1 in a superior or more excellent way ⟨He sings *better* than I do.⟩
2 to a higher or greater degree ⟨She knows the story *better* than I do.⟩

⁴better *n*
1 something that is more satisfactory ⟨This is a change for the *better*.⟩
2 ADVANTAGE 2, VICTORY ⟨She got the *better* of her opponent.⟩

bet•ter•ment \ˈbe-tər-mənt\ *n*
the act or result of making something more satisfactory : IMPROVEMENT

bet•tor *or* **bet•ter** \ˈbe-tər\ *n*
someone that bets

beverage:
a cup of coffee

¹be•tween \bi-ˈtwēn\ *prep*
1 in the time or space that separates ⟨*between* nine and ten o'clock⟩ ⟨*between* the two desks⟩
2 functioning to separate or tell apart ⟨What are the differences *between* soccer and football?⟩
3 by the efforts of each of ⟨*Between* us we can get the job done.⟩
4 by comparing ⟨You must choose *between* two things.⟩
5 shared by ⟨There's a strong bond *between* parent and child.⟩
6 in shares to each of ⟨She divided the money *between* the two children.⟩
7 to and from ⟨He travels *between* New York and Chicago every week.⟩

²between *adv*
in a position between others

be•twixt \bi-ˈtwikst\ *prep*
BETWEEN 1

¹bev•el \ˈbe-vəl\ *n*
a slant or slope of one surface or line against another

► **Word History** At first the word *bevel* was used for a certain kind of angle. This was the angle formed by two surfaces that are not at right angles. Look at the opening of such an angle. You may be able to imagine that it looks like an open mouth. The English word *bevel* came from an Old French word *baïf* that meant "with open mouth." This word was formed from the Old French verb *baer*, "to yawn."

²bevel *vb* **bev•eled** *or* **bev•elled**; **bev•el•ing** *or* **bev•el•ling**
to cut or shape (an edge or surface) at an angle or slant

bev•er•age \ˈbe-və-rij, ˈbev-rij\ *n*
◄ a liquid for drinking

be•ware \bi-ˈwer\ *vb*
to be cautious or careful ⟨*beware* of the dog⟩ ⟨He told them to *beware*.⟩
Hint: *Beware* is used only in the forms *beware* or *to beware*.

be•whis•kered \bi-ˈhwi-skərd, -ˈwi-\ *adj*
having whiskers

be•wil•der \bi-ˈwil-dər\ *vb* **be•wil•dered**; **be•wil•der•ing**
CONFUSE 1
be•wil•der•ment \-mənt\ *n*

be•witch \bi-ˈwich\ *vb* **be•witched**; **be•witch•ing**
1 to gain an influence over by means of magic or witchcraft
2 to attract or delight as if by magic

¹be•yond \bē-ˈänd\ *adv*
on or to the farther side

²beyond *prep*
1 on the other side of ⟨*beyond* the sea⟩
2 out of the limits or range of ⟨*beyond* help⟩

bi- *prefix*
1 two ⟨*bi*ped⟩
2 coming or occurring every two ⟨*bi*ennial⟩
3 into two parts ⟨*bi*sect⟩
4 twice : doubly : on both sides

¹bi•as \ˈbī-əs\ *n*
1 a seam, cut, or stitching running in a slant across cloth
2 a favoring of some ideas or people over others : PREJUDICE

²bias *vb* **bi•ased** *or* **bi•assed**; **bi•as•ing** *or* **bi•as•sing**
to give a prejudiced outlook to

bib \'bib\ *n*
1 ▶ a cloth or plastic shield fastened under the chin (as of a young child) to protect the clothes
2 the upper part of an apron or of overalls

Bi•ble \'bī-bəl\ *n*
1 the book of sacred writings accepted by Christians as coming from God
2 a book containing the sacred writings of a religion

bib•li•cal \'bi-bli-kəl\ *adj*
relating to, taken from, or found in the Bible

bib•li•og•ra•phy \,bi-blē-'ä-grə-fē\ *n, pl* **bib•li•og•ra•phies**
1 a list of materials (as books or magazine articles) used in the preparation of a written work or mentioned in a text

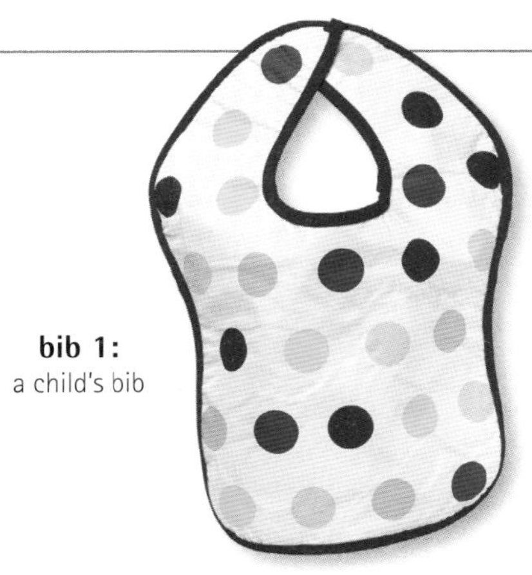

bib 1: a child's bib

2 a list of writings about an author or a subject
bib•lio•graph•ic \bi-blē-ə-'gra-fik\ *also* **bib•lio•graph•i•cal** \-fi-kəl\ *adj*

bi•car•bon•ate of soda \bī-'kär-bə-nət-, -,nāt-\ *n*
BAKING SODA

bi•ceps \'bī-,seps\ *n, pl* **biceps** *also* **bi•ceps•es**
a large muscle of the front of the upper arm

bick•er \'bi-kər\ *vb* **bick•ered**; **bick•er•ing**
to quarrel in an irritating way especially over unimportant things

bi•cus•pid \bī-'kə-spəd\ *n*
either of the two teeth with double points on each side of each jaw of a person

¹bi•cy•cle \'bī-,si-kəl\ *n*
▼ a light vehicle having two wheels one behind the other, handlebars, a seat, and pedals by which it is made to move

¹bicycle
The bicycle is one of the most popular modes of transportation in the world. The types available today are much more sophisticated than early examples such as the penny-farthing. They range from simple, gearless models to specially equipped multi-geared racing and mountain bicycles for competitive sports and cycling in rough terrain.

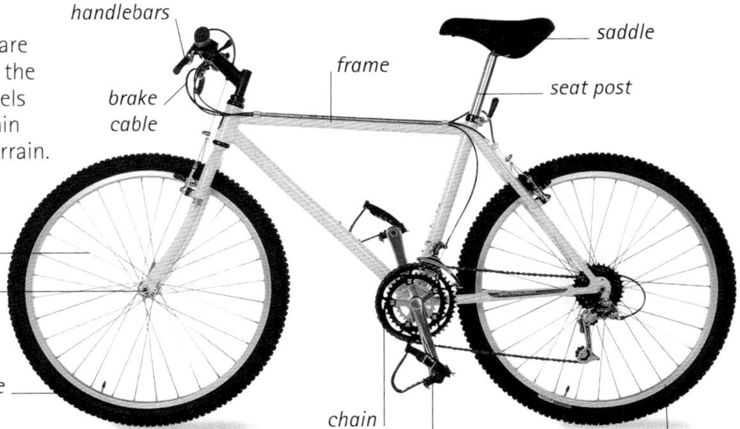

handlebars
saddle
frame
seat post
brake cable
spoke
wheel hub
tire
chain ring
pedal
metal wheel rim
training wheels

child's bicycle

features of a mountain bicycle

streamlined frame

penny-farthing was a 19th-century bicycle

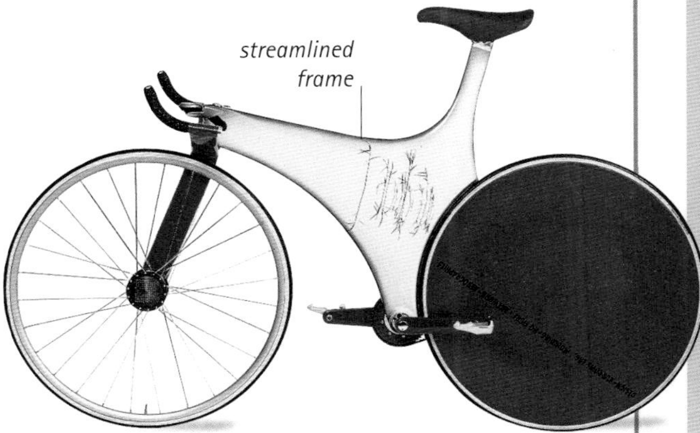

time-trial bicycle

a b c d e f g h i j k l m n o p q r s t u v w x y z

[2]bicycle *vb* **bi•cy•cled; bi•cy•cling** \'bī-,si-kə-liŋ, -,si-kliŋ\
to ride a bicycle

bi•cy•clist \'bī-,si-kləst\ *n*
a person who rides a bicycle

[1]bid \'bid\ *vb* **bade** \'bad\ *or* **bid; bid•den** \'bi-dᵊn\ *or* **bid; bid•ding**
1 [1]ORDER 2, COMMAND ⟨Do as I *bid* you.⟩
2 to express to ⟨We *bade* our guests good-bye.⟩
3 to make an offer for something (as at an auction) ⟨I *bid* $25 for a painting.⟩
bid•der *n*

[2]bid *n*
1 an offer to pay a certain sum for something or to do certain work at a stated fee
2 an attempt to win, achieve, or attract ⟨They made a strong *bid* for the championship.⟩

bide \'bīd\ *vb* **bode** \'bōd\ *or* **bid•ed** \'bī-dəd\; **bid•ed; bid•ing**
to wait or wait for ⟨*bide* a while⟩

[1]bi•en•ni•al \bī-'e-nē-əl\ *adj*
1 occurring every two years ⟨a *biennial* celebration⟩
2 growing stalks and leaves one year and flowers and fruit the next before dying
bi•en•ni•al•ly \-ē-ə-lē\ *adv*

[2]biennial *n*
a biennial plant

bier \'bir\ *n*
a stand on which a corpse or coffin is placed

big \'big\ *adj* **big•ger; big•gest**
1 large in size ⟨a *big* house⟩ ⟨a *big* man⟩
2 large in number or amount ⟨a *big* group⟩
3 of great importance ⟨*big* news⟩
4 of great strength or force ⟨a *big* storm⟩
big•ness *n*

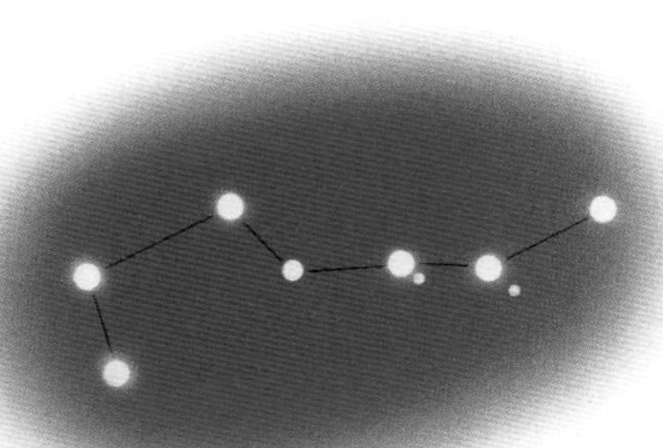

Big Dipper

Big Dipper *n*
▲ a group of seven stars in the northern sky arranged in a form like a dipper with the two stars that form the side opposite the handle pointing to the North Star

big•horn \'big-,hȯrn\ *n*
▼ a grayish brown wild sheep of mountainous western North America

bighorn

big•ot \'bi-gət\ *n*
a person who hates or refuses to accept the members of a particular group
big•ot•ed \-gə-təd\ *adj*

big•ot•ry \'bi-gə-trē\ *n*
acts or beliefs characteristic of a bigot

big tree *n*
GIANT SEQUOIA

[1]bike \'bīk\ *n*
1 [1]BICYCLE
2 MOTORCYCLE

[2]bike *vb* **biked; bik•ing**
[2]BICYCLE

bik•er \'bī-kər\ *n*
a person who rides a bicycle or motorcycle

bile \'bīl\ *n*
a thick bitter yellow or greenish fluid produced by the liver to aid in digestion of fats in the small intestine

bi•lin•gual \,bī-'liŋ-gwəl, -gyə-wəl\ *adj*
1 using or expressed in two languages ⟨a *bilingual* dictionary⟩
2 able to speak two languages

[1]bill \'bil\ *n*
1 ▶ the jaws of a bird together with their horny covering
2 a part of an animal (as a turtle) that resembles the bill of a bird
billed \'bild\ *adj*

[2]bill *n*
1 a draft of a law presented to a legislature for consideration ⟨The representative introduced a *bill* in Congress.⟩
2 a record of goods sold, services performed, or work done with the cost involved ⟨a telephone *bill*⟩
3 a piece of paper money ⟨a dollar *bill*⟩
4 a sign or poster advertising something

[3]bill *vb* **billed; bill•ing**
to send a bill to ⟨I was *billed* for the repairs.⟩

bill•board \'bil-,bȯrd\ *n*
a flat surface on which outdoor advertisements are displayed

bill•fold \'bil-,fōld\ *n*
WALLET

bil•liards \'bil-yərdz\ *n*
a game played by driving solid balls with a cue into each other or into pockets on a large rectangular table

bil•lion \'bil-yən\ *n*
1 a thousand millions
2 a very large number ⟨*billions* of stars⟩

[1]bil•lionth \'bil-yənth\ *adj*
being last in a series of a billion

[2]billionth *n*
number 1,000,000,000 in a series

Bill of Rights *n*
the first ten amendments to the United States Constitution

[1]bil•low \'bi-lō\ *n*
1 a large wave
2 a moving cloud or mass (as of smoke or flame)

[2]billow *vb* **bil•lowed; bil•low•ing**
1 to rise or roll in large waves ⟨the *billowing* ocean⟩
2 to move as a large cloud or mass ⟨Smoke *billowed* from the chimney.⟩
3 to bulge or swell out ⟨Sails *billowed* in the breeze.⟩

bil•lowy \'bi-lə-wē\ *adj*
1 full of large waves ⟨the *billowy* sea⟩
2 bulging or puffing out ⟨a *billowy* skirt⟩

bil•ly club \'bi-lē-\ *n*
NIGHTSTICK

billy goat *n*
a male goat

bin \'bin\ *n*
a box or enclosed place used for storage ⟨a laundry *bin*⟩

[1]bill 1

bi•na•ry \ˈbī-nə-rē\ *adj*
of, relating to, or being a number system with a base of 2 ⟨1 and 0 are *binary* digits.⟩

¹bind \ˈbīnd\ *vb* **bound** \ˈbau̇nd\; **bind•ing**
1 to tie or wrap securely (as with rope)
2 to hold or restrict by force or obligation ⟨The oath *binds* you.⟩
3 to wrap or cover with a bandage
4 to cause to be joined together closely ⟨Their common interest *binds* them together.⟩
5 to put a cover or binding on (a book)

²bind *n*
a difficult situation

bind•er \ˈbīn-dər\ *n*
1 a person who binds books
2 a cover for holding together loose sheets of paper
3 a machine that cuts grain and ties it into bundles

bind•ing \ˈbīn-diŋ\ *n*
1 the cover and the fastenings of a book
2 a narrow strip of fabric used along the edge of an article of clothing
3 a device that attaches a boot to a ski

¹binge \ˈbinj\ *n*
an act of doing something (as eating) to excess in a short time

²binge *vb* **binge•ing** *or* **bing•ing; binged**
to do something (as eat) to excess in a short time

bin•go \ˈbiŋ-gō\ *n*
a game in which players match numbered squares on a card with numbers that are called out until someone wins by matching five squares in a row

bin•oc•u•lar \bī-ˈnä-kyə-lər, bə-\ *adj*
of, using, or suited for the use of both eyes

bin•oc•u•lars \bə-ˈnä-kyə-lərz, bī-\ *n pl*
▼a hand-held instrument for seeing at a distance that is made up of two telescopes usually having prisms and a focusing device

binoculars

bio- *prefix*
life : living organisms ⟨*bio*diversity⟩

bio•de•grad•able \ˌbī-ō-di-ˈgrā-də-bəl\ *adj*
possible to break down into very small harmless parts by the action of living things (as bacteria) ⟨*biodegradable* bags⟩

bio•die•sel \ˌbī-ō-ˈdē-zəl, -səl\ *n*
a fuel that is similar to diesel fuel and is usually derived from plants

bio•di•ver•si•ty \ˌbī-ō-də-ˈvər-sə-tē, -dī-\ *n*
the existence of many different kinds of plants and animals in an environment

bi•og•ra•pher \bī-ˈä-grə-fər\ *n*
someone who tells the account of a real person's life

bio•graph•i•cal \ˌbī-ə-ˈgra-fi-kəl\ *adj*
of or relating to an account of a real person's life

bi•og•ra•phy \bī-ˈä-grə-fē\ *n*, *pl* **bi•og•ra•phies**
an account of a real person's life

bi•o•log•i•cal \ˌbī-ə-ˈlä-ji-kəl\ *adj*
1 of or relating to biology or to life and living things ⟨*biological* activity⟩
2 related by birth

bi•ol•o•gist \bī-ˈä-lə-jəst\ *n*
a person specializing in biology

bi•ol•o•gy \bī-ˈä-lə-jē\ *n*
a science that deals with living things and their relationships, distribution, and behavior

bi•ome \ˈbī-ˌōm\ *n*
a major type of community of distinctive plants and animals living together in a particular climate and physical environment

bio•tech•nol•o•gy \ˌbī-ō-tek-ˈnä-lə-jē\ *n*
the use of techniques from genetics to combine inherited characteristics selected from different kinds of organisms into one organism in order to produce useful products (as drugs)

bi•ped \ˈbī-ˌped\ *n*
a two-footed animal

bi•plane \ˈbī-ˌplān\ *n*
▼an airplane with two wings on each side usually placed one above the other

biplane
Many early airplanes were constructed from wood and canvas, with two pairs of wings braced with wires, because these were stronger and more stable than a single pair. Although monoplanes were in use before 1910, biplanes continued to dominate airplane design until the 1930s.

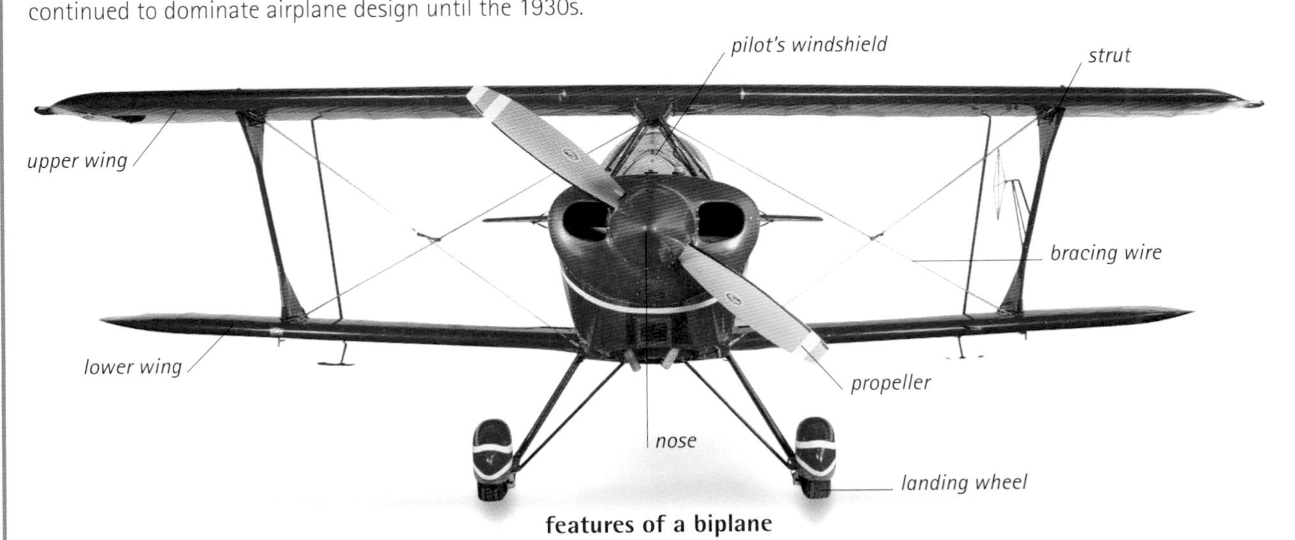

features of a biplane

bird
All birds have a body covered with feathers, a pair of wings, a beak, and scaly legs and feet. They reproduce by laying eggs. Instead of teeth, birds have a special grinding organ called a gizzard. There are many bird species around the world, adapted to life in a wide range of habitats.

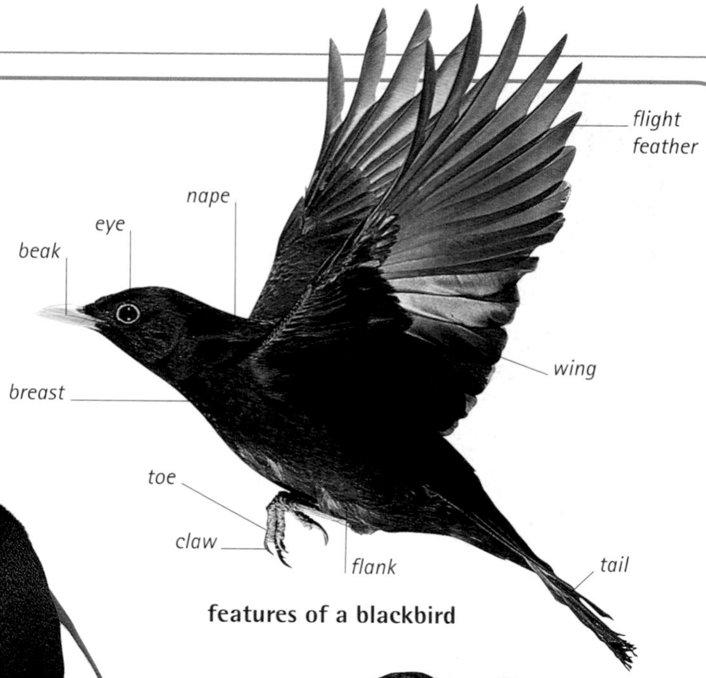

features of a blackbird

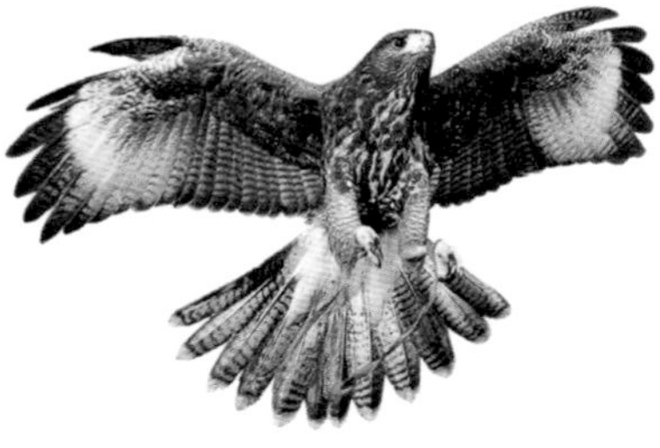

hawk

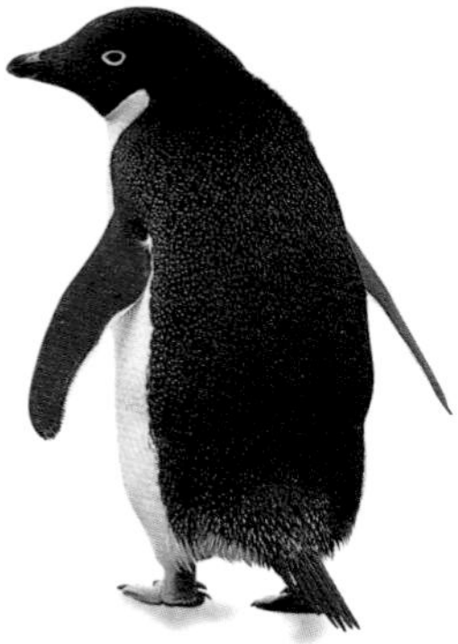

Adélie penguin

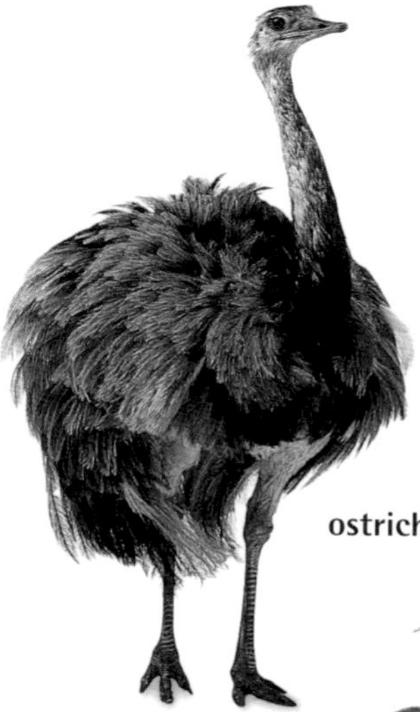

ostrich

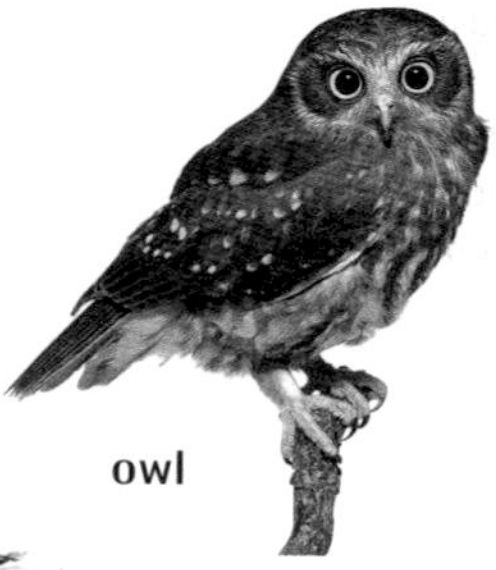

owl

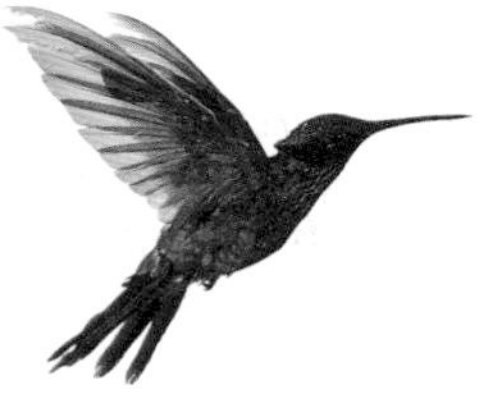

hummingbird

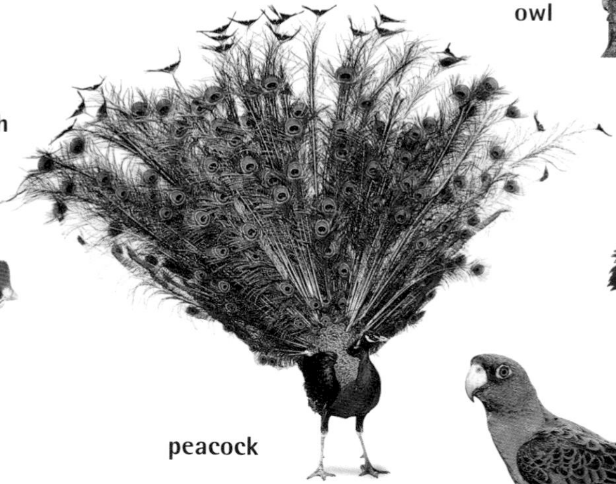

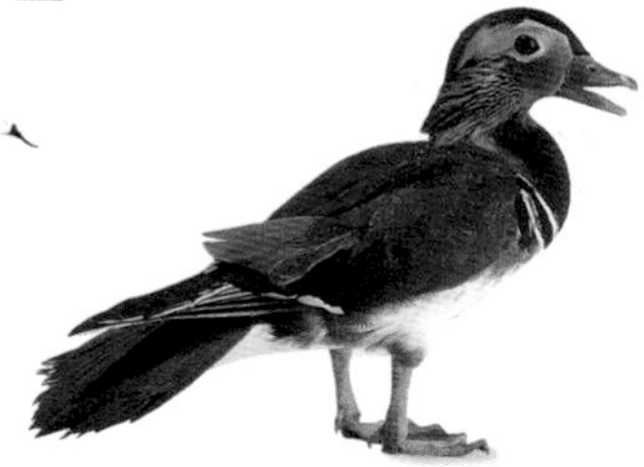

mandarin duck

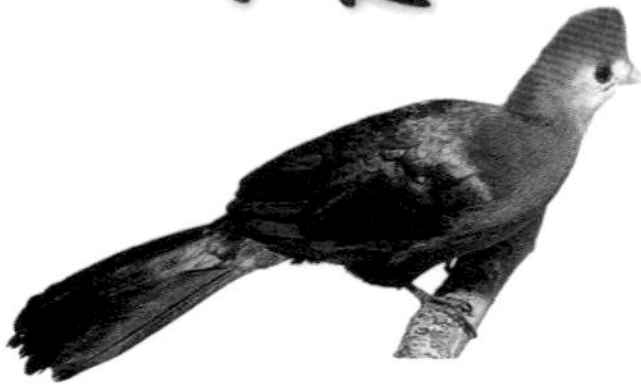

peacock

turaco
\'tür-ə-kō\

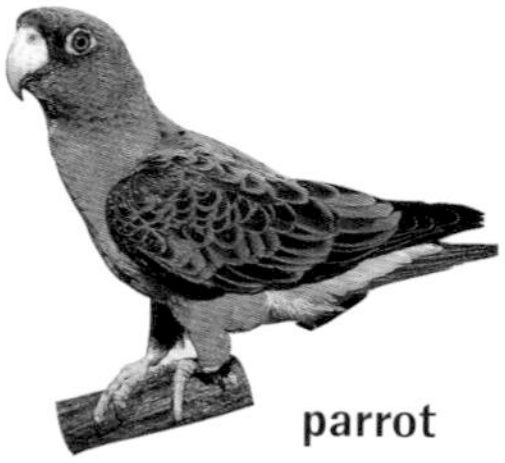

parrot

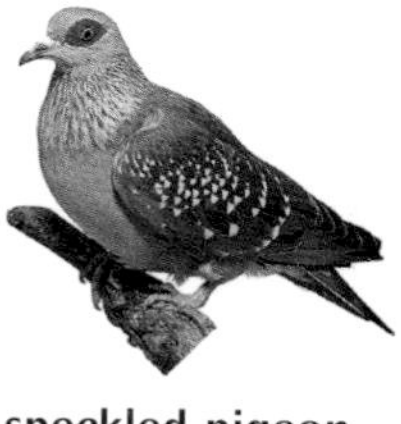

speckled pigeon

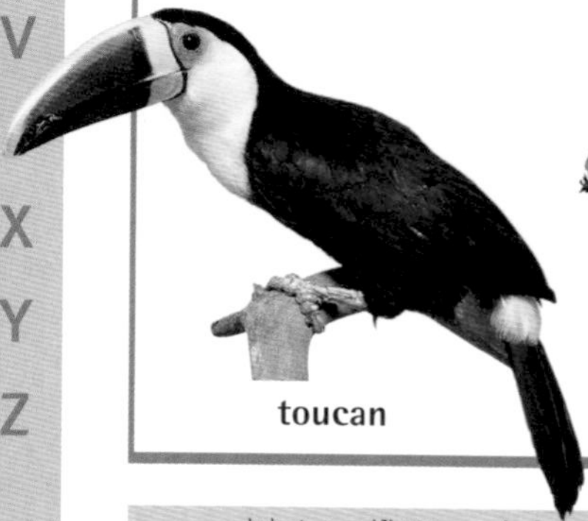

toucan

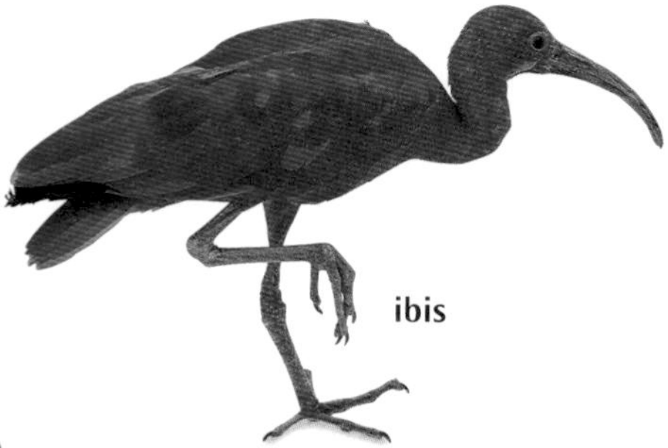

ibis

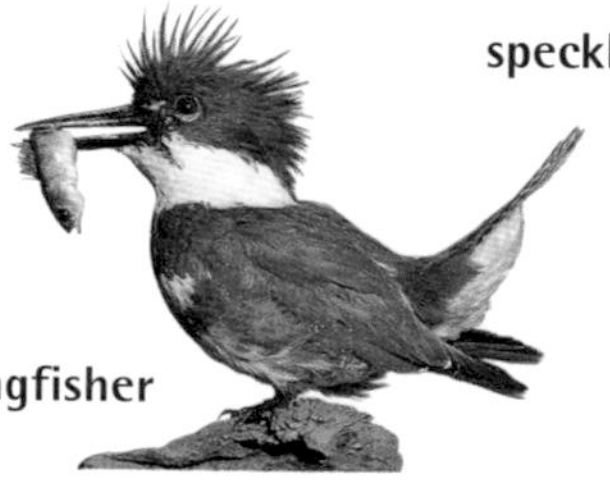

kingfisher

birch

birch \ˈbərch\ *n*
▲ a tree with hard wood and a smooth bark that can be peeled off in thin layers

bird \ˈbərd\ *n*
◀ an animal that lays eggs and has wings and a body covered with feathers

bird•bath \ˈbərd-ˌbath, -ˌbäth\ *n*
a basin for birds to bathe in

bird•house \ˈbərd-ˌhau̇s\ *n*
an artificial nesting place (as a wooden box) for birds

bird of prey *n, pl* **birds of prey**
a bird (as an eagle or owl) that feeds almost entirely on meat taken by hunting

bird's–eye \ˈbərdz-ˌī\ *adj*
seen from above as if by a flying bird ⟨a *bird's-eye* view of the city⟩

birth \ˈbərth\ *n*
1 the coming of a new individual from the body of its parent
2 the act of bringing into life
3 LINEAGE 1 ⟨a person of noble *birth*⟩
4 ORIGIN 3 ⟨the *birth* of the solar system⟩

birth•day \ˈbərth-ˌdā\ *n*
1 the day or anniversary of someone's birth
2 a day of beginning ⟨Our town just celebrated its 150th *birthday.*⟩

birth defect *n*
a physical defect that a person is born with and that may be inherited or caused by something in the environment

birth•mark \ˈbərth-ˌmärk\ *n*
an unusual mark or blemish on the skin at birth

birth•place \ˈbərth-ˌplās\ *n*
the place where a person was born or where something began ⟨the *birthplace* of freedom⟩

birth•right \ˈbərth-ˌrīt\ *n*
a right belonging to a person because of his or her birth

birth•stone \ˈbərth-ˌstōn\ *n*
a gemstone associated with the month of a person's birth

bis•cuit \ˈbi-skət\ *n*
a small light bread

bi•sect \ˈbī-ˌsekt\ *vb* **bi•sect•ed; bi•sect•ing**
1 to divide into two equal parts
2 INTERSECT

► **Word History** When you bisect something you are cutting it in two. The word *bisect* itself will tell you that. The word was formed in English, but it came from two Latin elements. The *bi-* came from a Latin prefix meaning "two." The *-sect* came from a Latin verb *secare* meaning "to cut."

bish•op \ˈbi-shəp\ *n*
1 a member of the clergy of high rank
2 ▼ a piece in the game of chess

bishop 2

► **Word History** The original duty of a bishop was to watch over the members of a church as a shepherd watches over a flock. Appropriately, the word *bishop* comes ultimately from a Greek word, *episkopos,* that means literally "overseer": the prefix *epi-* means "on" or "over," and the second part *-skopos* means "watcher." The pronunciation of the word was changed when it was borrowed from Greek into Latin, and further changed when it was borrowed into Old English. In Old English it was spelled *bisceop* but probably sounded quite a bit like the modern word *bishop.*

bis•muth \ˈbiz-məth\ *n*
a heavy grayish white metallic chemical element that is used in alloys and in medicines

bi•son \ˈbī-s^{ə}n, -z^{ə}n\ *n, pl* **bison**
► a large animal with short horns and a shaggy mane that is related to the cows and oxen

[1]bit \ˈbit\ *n*
1 a small piece or quantity ⟨a *bit* of food⟩
2 a short time ⟨Rest a *bit.*⟩
a bit [1]SOMEWHAT ⟨I was *a bit* tired.⟩
bit by bit by small steps or amounts : GRADUALLY ⟨*Bit by bit,* the truth came out.⟩

[2]bit *n*
1 a part of a bridle that is put in the horse's mouth
2 the cutting or boring edge or part of a tool

[3]bit *n*
a unit of computer information that represents the selection of one of two possible choices (as *on* or *off*)

bitch \ˈbich\ *n*
a female dog

[1]bite \ˈbīt\ *vb* **bit** \ˈbit\; **bit•ten** \ˈbi-t^{ə}n\; **bit•ing** \ˈbī-tiŋ\
1 to seize, grip, or cut into with or as if with teeth ⟨*bite* an apple⟩
2 to wound or sting usually with a stinger or fang
3 to take a bait ⟨The fish are *biting.*⟩

[2]bite *n*
1 an act of seizing or cutting into with the teeth ⟨three quick *bites*⟩
2 a wound made by biting : STING
3 the amount of food taken at a bite
4 a sharp or biting sensation ⟨The pepper has a *bite.*⟩

bit•ing \ˈbī-tiŋ\ *adj*
causing intense discomfort ⟨*biting,* cold winds⟩

bit•ter \ˈbi-tər\ *adj* **bit•ter•er; bit•ter•est**
1 sharp, biting, and unpleasant to the taste
2 unhappy and angry because of unfair treatment ⟨a *bitter* former friend⟩
3 hard to put up with ⟨a *bitter* defeat⟩
4 caused by anger, distress, or sorrow ⟨*bitter* tears⟩
5 very harsh or sharp : BITING ⟨a *bitter* wind⟩
bit•ter•ly *adv*
bit•ter•ness *n*

bison

bit•tern \'bi-tərn\ *n*
a brownish marsh bird which has a loud booming cry

[1]bit•ter•sweet \'bi-tər-,swēt\ *n*
1 ▼ a poisonous vine originally of Europe and Asia with purple flowers and red berries
2 a poisonous North American woody climbing plant with orange seed capsules that open when ripe to reveal red seeds

berry

[1]bittersweet 1

[2]bittersweet *adj*
being partly bitter or sad and partly sweet or happy ⟨*bittersweet* memories⟩

bi•tu•mi•nous coal \bə-'tü-mə-nəs-, -'tyü-\ *n*
a soft coal that smokes a lot when burned

bi•zarre \bə-'zär\ *adj*
very strange or odd

blab \'blab\ *vb* **blabbed**; **blab•bing**
1 to reveal a secret
2 to talk too much

[1]black \'blak\ *adj* **black•er**; **black•est**
1 of the color of coal : colored black
2 very dark ⟨a *black* night⟩
3 *often cap* of or relating to any peoples having dark skin and especially any of the original peoples of Africa south of the Sahara
4 of or relating to Americans having ancestors from Africa south of the Sahara
5 WICKED 1 ⟨a *black* deed⟩
6 very sad or gloomy ⟨in a *black* mood⟩
7 UNFRIENDLY 1 ⟨a *black* look⟩
black•ish *adj*
black•ness *n*

[2]black *n*
1 the color of coal : the opposite of white
2 black clothing ⟨He is dressed in *black*.⟩
3 a person belonging to a race of people having dark skin
4 an American having black African ancestors : AFRICAN-AMERICAN
5 total or near total darkness ⟨the *black* of night⟩
in the black making a profit

[3]black *vb* **blacked**; **black•ing**
BLACKEN 1
black out to lose consciousness or the ability to see for a short time

black–and–blue \,bla-kən-'blü\ *adj*
darkly discolored (as from a bruise)

black•ber•ry \'blak-,ber-ē\ *n*, *pl* **black•ber•ries**
the black or dark purple sweet juicy berry of a prickly plant related to the raspberry

black•bird \'blak-,bərd\ *n*
▶ any of several birds of which the males are mostly black

black•board \'blak-,bȯrd\ *n*
a hard smooth dark surface used for writing or drawing on with chalk

black•en \'bla-kən\ *vb* **black•ened**; **black•en•ing**
1 to make or become dark or black
2 [1]SPOIL 2 ⟨The scandal will *blacken* his reputation.⟩

black–eyed Su•san \,bla-,kīd-'sü-zᵊn\ *n*
▼ a daisy with yellow or orange petals and a dark center

black–eyed Susan

black•head \'blak-,hed\ *n*
a darkened bit of oily material that blocks the opening of a gland in the skin

black hole *n*
a heavenly body with such strong gravity that light cannot escape it and that is thought to be caused by the collapse of a massive star

[1]black•mail \'blak-,māl\ *n*
1 the act of forcing someone to do or pay something by threatening to reveal a secret
2 something (as money) obtained by threatening to reveal a secret

[2]blackmail *vb* **black•mailed**; **black•mail•ing**
to threaten with the revealing of a secret unless money is paid
black•mail•er *n*

blackbird

black•out \'blak-,au̇t\ *n*
1 a period of darkness enforced as a protection against enemy attack by airplanes during a war
2 a period of darkness caused by power failure
3 a temporary loss of vision or consciousness

black•smith \'blak-,smith\ *n*
a person who makes things out of iron by heating and hammering it

black•snake \'blak-,snāk\ *n*
either of two harmless snakes of the United States with blackish skins

black•top \'blak-,täp\ *n*
a black material used especially to pave roads

black widow *n*
▶ a poisonous spider the female of which is black with a red mark shaped like an hourglass on the underside of the abdomen

blad•der \'bla-dər\ *n*
1 an organ in the body resembling a pouch into which urine passes from the kidneys and is temporarily stored until discharged from the body
2 a container that can be filled with air or gas

blade \'blād\ *n*
1 a leaf of a plant and especially of a grass
2 the broad flat part of a leaf
3 something that widens out like the blade of a leaf ⟨the *blade* of a propeller⟩
4 the cutting part of a tool, machine, or weapon ⟨a knife *blade*⟩
5 SWORD
6 the runner of an ice skate
blad•ed \'blā-dəd\ *adj*

[1]blame \'blām\ *vb* **blamed**; **blam•ing**
1 to find fault with
2 to hold responsible ⟨He *blamed* me for everything.⟩
3 to place responsibility for ⟨Don't *blame* it on us.⟩

[2]blame *n*
1 responsibility for something that fails or is wrong ⟨They took *blame* for the defeat.⟩
2 expression of disapproval ⟨He received both praise and *blame*.⟩
blame•less \'blām-ləs\ *adj*

blame•wor•thy \'blām-,wər-t͟hē\ *adj*
deserving blame

blanch \'blanch\ *vb* **blanched**; **blanch•ing**
1 [1]BLEACH, WHITEN
2 to scald so as to remove the skin from ⟨*Blanch* the tomatoes.⟩
3 to turn pale

bland \'bland\ *adj* **bland•er**; **bland•est**
1 not interesting or exciting ⟨a *bland* story⟩
2 not having much flavor ⟨a *bland* soup⟩
3 not showing emotion ⟨a *bland* face⟩

[1]blank \'blaŋk\ *adj*
1 not having any writing or marks ⟨a *blank* sheet of paper⟩
2 having empty spaces to be filled in ⟨a *blank* job application⟩
3 not showing emotion or understanding ⟨a *blank* look⟩

black widow

[2]blank *n*
1 an empty space in a line of writing or printing
2 a paper with empty spaces to be filled in
3 a cartridge loaded with powder but no bullet
4 events or a time that cannot be remembered ⟨Everything after the accident is a *blank*.⟩

[1]blan•ket \'blaŋ-kət\ *n*
1 a heavy woven covering used especially for beds
2 a covering layer ⟨a *blanket* of snow⟩

[2]blanket *vb* **blank•et•ed**; **blank•et•ing**
to cover with or as if with a blanket ⟨Snow *blanketed* the ground.⟩

[1]blare \'bler\ *vb* **blared**; **blar•ing**
1 to sound loud and harsh ⟨I heard the sirens *blare*.⟩
2 to present in a harsh noisy manner ⟨Loudspeakers *blared* advertisements.⟩

[2]blare *n*
a harsh loud noise

[1]blast \'blast\ *n*
1 the sound made by a wind instrument ⟨the *blast* of a whistle⟩
2 EXPLOSION 1
3 a strong gust of wind ⟨icy *blasts* of winter⟩
4 a stream of air or gas forced through an opening
5 a very enjoyable experience ⟨The party was a *blast*.⟩

[2]blast *vb* **blast•ed**; **blast•ing**
1 to break to pieces by an explosion : SHATTER ⟨*blast* rock⟩
2 to hit with great force ⟨He *blasted* a home run.⟩
3 [1]SHOOT 2
4 to hit (someone or something) with something (as air or water) that is moving forcefully ⟨I *blasted* the flames with water.⟩
5 to make a loud unpleasant sound ⟨a television *blasting*⟩
6 to strongly criticize ⟨The mayor was *blasted* for ignoring the problem.⟩
blast off to take off ⟨The rocket *blasted off*.⟩

blast•off \'blast-,ȯf\ *n*
an instance of taking off (as of a rocket)

bla•tant \'blā-tᵊnt\ *adj*
completely obvious in a disagreeable way ⟨a *blatant* lie⟩

[1]blaze \'blāz\ *n*
1 an intense and dangerous fire
2 great brightness and heat ⟨the *blaze* of the sun⟩
3 a bright display ⟨a *blaze* of color⟩
4 OUTBURST 1 ⟨a *blaze* of anger⟩

[2]blaze *vb* **blazed**; **blaz•ing**
1 to burn brightly ⟨A fire was *blazing*.⟩
2 to shine as if on fire ⟨Her eyes *blazed* with anger.⟩

[3]blaze *n*
1 a white stripe down the center of an animal's face
2 a mark made on a tree to show a trail

[4]blaze *vb* **blazed**; **blaz•ing**
to show a path by making marks on trees ⟨*blaze* a trail⟩

bldg. *abbr* building

[1]bleach \'blēch\ *vb* **bleached**; **bleach•ing**
to make white by removing the color or stains from

[2]bleach *n*
a chemical used for bleaching

bleach•er \'blē-chər\ *n*
one of a set of open seats arranged like steps for sitting on while watching a game or performance — usually used in pl.

bleak \'blēk\ *adj* **bleak•er**; **bleak•est**
1 open to wind or weather ⟨a *bleak* coast⟩
2 being cold and raw or cheerless ⟨a *bleak* wind⟩ ⟨a *bleak* landscape⟩
3 not hopeful or encouraging ⟨The future looks *bleak*.⟩
bleak•ly *adv*
bleak•ness *n*

[1]bleat \'blēt\ *vb* **bleat•ed**; **bleat•ing**
to make the cry of a sheep, goat, or calf

[2]bleat *n*
the sound made by a sheep, goat, or calf

bleed \'blēd\ *vb* **bled** \'bled\; **bleed•ing**
1 to lose or shed blood
2 to feel pain or pity ⟨My heart *bleeds* for the victims of the fire.⟩
3 to draw a liquid or gas from ⟨*bleed* a tire⟩
4 to spread into something else ⟨colors *bleeding*⟩

[1]blem•ish \'blem-ish\ *n*
a mark that makes something imperfect : an unwanted mark on a surface

[2]blemish *vb* **blem•ished**; **blem•ish•ing**
to spoil by or as if by an ugly mark ⟨A scratch *blemished* the table.⟩

[1]blend \'blend\ *vb* **blend•ed**; **blend•ing**
1 to mix so completely that the separate things mixed cannot be told apart
2 to exist agreeably with each other ⟨She chose soft colors that *blend* well.⟩
synonyms see MIX
blend in to look like part of something ⟨He tried to *blend in* with the group.⟩

[2]blend *n*
1 a thorough mixture : a product made by blending
2 a word formed by combining parts of two or more other words so that they overlap ⟨The word "smog" is a *blend* of "smoke" and "fog."⟩

blend•er \'blen-dər\ *n*
► an appliance used to chop, mix, blend, and liquefy

blender

[2]blindfold: a girl with a blindfold

bless \'bles\ *vb* **blessed** \'blest\ *also* **blest**; **bless•ing**
1 to make holy by a religious ceremony or words ⟨*bless* an altar⟩
2 to ask the favor or protection of God for ⟨*Bless* the children of the world.⟩
Hint: The phrase *bless you* is used to wish good health especially to someone who has just sneezed.
3 to praise or honor as holy ⟨*bless* the Lord⟩
4 to give happiness or good fortune to ⟨He is *blessed* with good health.⟩

bless•ed \'ble-səd, 'blest\ *adj*
1 HOLY 1
2 enjoying happiness
bless•ed•ness \'ble-səd-nəs\ *n*

bless•ing \'ble-siŋ\ *n*
1 the act of someone who blesses
2 APPROVAL ⟨The marriage has my *blessing.*⟩
3 something that makes a person happy or content ⟨We enjoy the *blessings* of peace.⟩
4 a short prayer

blew *past of* BLOW

[1]blight \'blīt\ *n*
a disease that makes plants dry up and die

[2]blight *vb* **blight•ed**; **blight•ing**
to injure or destroy by or as if by a blight ⟨Huge signs *blighted* the landscape.⟩

blimp \'blimp\ *n*
an airship filled with gas like a balloon

[1]blind \'blīnd\ *adj* **blind•er**; **blind•est**
1 unable or nearly unable to see
2 lacking in judgment or understanding ⟨He is *blind* to his own faults.⟩
3 UNQUESTIONING ⟨*blind* faith⟩
4 closed at one end ⟨a *blind* alley⟩
blind•ly *adv*
blind•ness *n*

[2]blind *vb* **blind•ed**; **blind•ing**
1 to cause the permanent loss of sight in
2 to make it impossible to see well for a short time ⟨Our driver was *blinded* by the sun.⟩

[3]blind *n*
1 a device to reduce sight or keep out light ⟨window *blinds*⟩
2 a place of hiding ⟨a duck *blind*⟩

[4]blind *adv*
with only instruments as guidance ⟨Fog made it necessary to fly *blind.*⟩

[1]blind•fold \'blīnd-ˌfōld\ *vb* **blind•fold•ed**; **blind•fold•ing**
to cover the eyes of with a piece of cloth

[2]blindfold *n*
◀ a covering over the eyes

blind•man's buff \ˌblīnd-ˌmanz-'bəf\ *n*
a game in which a blindfolded player tries to catch and identify one of the other players

blink \'bliŋk\ *vb* **blinked**; **blink•ing**
1 to shut and open the eyes quickly
2 to shine with a light that goes or seems to go on and off ⟨lights *blinking*⟩

blink•er \'bliŋ-kər\ *n*
a light that blinks to indicate that a vehicle will be turning

bliss \'blis\ *n*
great happiness : JOY
bliss•ful \-fəl\ *adj*
bliss•ful•ly \-fə-lē\ *adv*

[1]blis•ter \'bli-stər\ *n*
1 a small raised area of the skin filled with a watery liquid
2 a swelling (as in paint) that looks like a blister of the skin

[2]blister *vb* **blis•tered**; **blis•ter•ing**
1 to develop a blister or blisters ⟨My heel *blistered* on the hike.⟩
2 to cause blisters on ⟨Tight shoes can *blister* your feet.⟩

blithe \'blīth, 'blīth\ *adj* **blith•er**; **blith•est**
free from worry : MERRY, CHEERFUL
blithe•ly *adv*

bliz•zard \'bli-zərd\ *n*
a long heavy snowstorm

bloat \'blōt\ *vb* **bloat•ed**; **bloat•ing**
to make swollen with or as if with fluid

blob \'bläb\ *n*
a small lump or drop of something thick

[1]block \'bläk\ *n*
1 a solid piece of some material usually with one or more flat sides ⟨a *block* of ice⟩
2 an area of land surrounded by four streets in a city
3 the length of one side of a city block
4 a number of things thought of as forming a group or unit ⟨a *block* of seats⟩
5 a large building divided into separate houses or shops ⟨an apartment *block*⟩
6 an action that stops or slows down an opponent (as in football)
7 something that prevents a person from thinking about certain things ⟨a mental *block*⟩
8 something that stops or makes passage or progress difficult : OBSTRUCTION
9 a case enclosing one or more pulleys

[2]block *vb* **blocked**; **block•ing**
1 to stop or make passage through or through to difficult : OBSTRUCT ⟨A gate *blocked* the entrance.⟩
2 to stop or make the passage of difficult ⟨Opponents *blocked* the bill in Congress.⟩
3 to make an opponent's movement (as in football) difficult

[1]block•ade \blä-'kād\ *vb* **block•ad•ed**; **block•ad•ing**
to close off a place to prevent the coming in or going out of people or supplies

[2]blockade *n*
the closing off of a place (as by warships) to prevent the coming in or going out of people or supplies

block and tackle *n*
an arrangement of pulleys in blocks with rope or cable for lifting or hauling

block•house \'bläk-ˌhaůs\ *n*
a building (as of heavy timbers or of concrete) built with holes in its sides through which people inside may fire out at an enemy

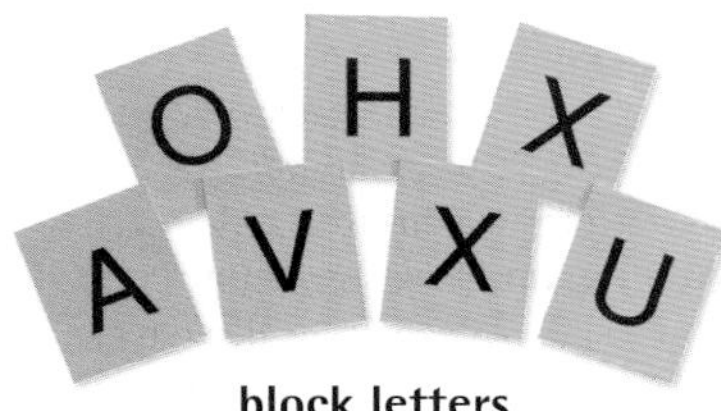

block letters

block letter *n*
▲ a capital letter often printed by hand that has all lines of equal thickness

[1]blog \'blȯg, 'bläg\ *n*
a Web site on which someone writes about personal opinions, activities, and experiences

[2]blog *vb* **blogged**; **blog•ging**
to write a blog
blog•ger *n*

[1]blond *or* **blonde** \'bländ\ *adj* **blond•er**; **blond•est**
1 of a golden or pale yellowish brown color ⟨*blond* hair⟩
2 having hair of a light color ⟨a *blond* boy⟩

[2]blond *or* **blonde** *n*
someone with golden or pale yellowish brown hair

blood \'bləd\ *n*
1 the red fluid that circulates in the heart, arteries, capillaries, and veins of persons and animals and that brings nourishment and oxygen to and carries away waste products from all parts of the body

2 relationship through a common ancestor : KINSHIP 〈She is my aunt by marriage, not by *blood.*〉
blood•ed \'blə-dəd\ *adj*

blood•cur•dling \'bləd-,kərd-liŋ\ *adj* causing great horror or fear 〈a *bloodcurdling* scream〉

blood•hound \'bləd-,hau̇nd\ *n* ▼ a large hound with long drooping ears, a wrinkled face, and a very good sense of smell

bloodhound

blood pressure *n* pressure of the blood on the walls of blood vessels and especially arteries

blood•shed \'bləd-,shed\ *n* serious injury or death caused by violence

blood•shot \'bləd-,shät\ *adj* red and sore 〈*bloodshot* eyes〉

blood•stream \'bləd-,strēm\ *n* the circulating blood in the living body

blood•suck•er \'bləd-,sə-kər\ *n* an animal (as a leech) that sucks blood
blood•suck•ing \-,sə-kiŋ\ *adj*

blood•thirsty \'bləd-,thər-stē\ *adj* eager to kill or hurt

blood vessel *n* ► an artery, vein, or capillary of the body

bloody \'blə-dē\ *adj* **blood•i•er; blood•i•est**
1 bleeding or covered with blood 〈a *bloody* nose〉 〈a *bloody* bandage〉
2 causing or accompanied by bloodshed 〈a *bloody* fight〉

[1]**bloom** \'blüm\ *n*
1 [1]FLOWER 1
2 the period or state of producing flowers 〈The bushes are in *bloom.*〉
3 a condition or time of beauty, freshness, and strength 〈the *bloom* of youth〉
4 the rosy color of the cheek

[2]**bloom** *vb* **bloomed; bloom•ing**
1 to produce flowers
2 to change, grow, or develop fully

[1]**blos•som** \'blä-səm\ *n*
1 [1]FLOWER 1 〈cherry *blossoms*〉
2 [1]BLOOM 2 〈The tree is in full *blossom.*〉

[2]**blossom** *vb* **blos•somed; blos•som•ing**
1 [2]BLOOM 1
2 to appear, change, grow, or develop

[1]**blot** \'blät\ *n*
1 a spot or stain of dirt or ink
2 a mark of shame or dishonor 〈The lie was a *blot* on my record.〉

[2]**blot** *vb* **blot•ted; blot•ting**
1 [2]SPOT 1
2 to dry by pressing with paper or cloth
blot out
1 to make (something) difficult to see 〈Clouds *blotted out* the sun.〉
2 to destroy completely

blotch \'bläch\ *n*
1 a blemish on the skin
2 a large irregular spot of color or ink
blotched \'blächt\ *adj*

blotchy \'blä-chē\ *adj* **blotch•i•er; blotch•i•est** marked with irregular spots

blot•ter \'blä-tər\ *n* a piece of blotting paper

blot•ting paper \'blä-tiŋ-\ *n* a soft spongy paper used to absorb wet ink

blouse \'blau̇s\ *n*
1 a loose garment for women covering the body from the neck to the waist
2 the jacket of a uniform

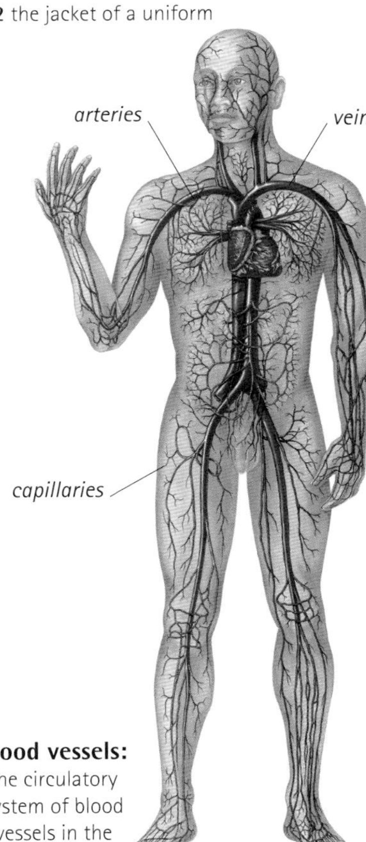

blood vessels: the circulatory system of blood vessels in the human body

[1]**blow** \'blō\ *vb* **blew** \'blü\; **blown** \'blōn\; **blow•ing**
1 to move or be moved usually with speed and force 〈Wind is *blowing* from the north.〉 〈The door *blew* shut.〉
2 to move in or with the wind 〈Dust *blew* through the cracks.〉
3 to send forth a strong stream of air from the mouth or from a bellows 〈If you are cold, *blow* on your hands.〉
4 to make a sound or cause to sound by blowing 〈The whistle *blows* loudly.〉 〈*Blow* your horn.〉
5 to clear by forcing air through 〈*Blow* your nose.〉
6 to shape by forcing air into 〈The workers showed how they *blow* glass.〉
7 to enter or leave very quickly 〈She *blew* into the room.〉
8 to fail in performing or keeping 〈The actor *blew* his lines.〉 〈The team *blew* a big lead.〉
blow•er \'blō-ər\ *n*
blow over to pass without effect 〈His anger will *blow over.*〉
blow up
1 EXPLODE 1
2 to fill with a gas 〈*blow up* a balloon〉

[2]**blow** *n* a blowing of wind : GALE

[3]**blow** *n*
1 a hard hit with a part of the body or an object 〈a hammer's *blow*〉 〈a *blow* to the head〉
2 a sudden happening that causes suffering or loss 〈The dog's death was a severe *blow.*〉

blow•gun \'blō-,gən\ *n* a tube from which a dart may be shot by the force of the breath

blow•torch \'blō-,tȯrch\ *n* a small portable burner in which the flame is made hotter by a blast of air or oxygen

[1]**blub•ber** \'blə-bər\ *vb* **blub•bered; blub•ber•ing**
1 to weep noisily
2 to utter while weeping 〈"I'm sorry," he *blubbered.*〉

[2]**blubber** *n* the fat of various sea mammals (as whales and seals) from which oil can be obtained

[1]**blue** \'blü\ *n*
1 the color of the clear daytime sky
2 blue clothing or cloth
3 SKY 1
4 SEA 1
blu•ish *adj*
out of the blue suddenly and unexpectedly

[2]**blue** *adj* **blu•er; blu•est**
1 of the color of the sky : of the color blue ⟨*blue* ink⟩
2 SAD 1 ⟨Why are you so *blue*?⟩

blue•bell \'blü-,bel\ *n*
▶ a plant with blue or purplish flowers shaped like bells

bluebell

blue•ber•ry \'blü-,ber-ē\ *n, pl* **blue•ber•ries**
a sweet blue or blackish berry that grows on a bush and has many small soft seeds

blue•bird \'blü-,bərd\ *n*
▶ a small North American songbird that is blue above and reddish brown or pale blue below

blue•bot•tle \'blü-,bä-tᵊl\ *n*
▼ a large blue hairy fly

bluebottle

blue cheese *n*
cheese ripened by and full of greenish blue mold

blue•fish \'blü-,fish\ *n*
a saltwater fish that is bluish above with silvery sides and is often used for food

blue•grass \'blü-,gras\ *n*
1 a grass with bluish green stems
2 a type of traditional American music that is played on stringed instruments

blue jay \'blü-,jā\ *n*
a crested and mostly blue North American bird related to the crows

blue jeans *n pl*
pants made of blue denim

blue•print \'blü-,print\ *n*
1 a photographic print made with white lines on a blue background and showing how something will be made
2 a detailed plan of something to be done

blue ribbon *n*
a decorative ribbon colored blue that is given to the winner in a competition

blues \'blüz\ *n pl*
1 low spirits ⟨He was suffering from the *blues*.⟩
2 a style of music that was created by African-Americans and that expresses feelings of sadness

blue whale *n*
a very large whale that is generally considered the largest living animal

[1]**bluff** \'bləf\ *adj*
1 rising steeply with a broad front ⟨a *bluff* shoreline⟩
2 frank and outspoken in a rough but good-natured way

[2]**bluff** *n*
a high steep bank : CLIFF

[3]**bluff** *vb* **bluffed; bluff•ing**
to deceive or frighten by pretending to have more strength or confidence than is really true

bluebird

[4]**bluff** *n*
an act or instance of pretending to have more strength, confidence, or ability than is really true

[1]**blun•der** \'blən-dər\ *vb* **blun•dered; blun•der•ing**
1 to move in a clumsy way
2 to make a mistake

[2]**blunder** *n*
a bad or stupid mistake
synonyms see ERROR

blun•der•buss \'blən-dər-,bəs\ *n*
a short gun that has a barrel which is larger at the end and that was used long ago for shooting at close range without taking exact aim

[1]**blunt** \'blənt\ *adj* **blunt•er; blunt•est**
1 having a thick edge or point : DULL ⟨a *blunt* knife⟩
2 speaking or spoken in plain language without thought for other people's feelings ⟨*blunt* remarks⟩
blunt•ly *adv*

[2]**blunt** *vb* **blunt•ed; blunt•ing**
to make or become less sharp

[1]**blur** \'blər\ *n*
1 something that cannot be seen clearly ⟨The ball was moving so fast, all I saw was a *blur*.⟩
2 something that is difficult to remember ⟨By now, my summer vacation is a *blur*.⟩

[2]**blur** *vb* **blurred; blur•ring**
1 to make unclear or hard to see or remember
2 to make or become unclear or confused

blur•ry \'blər-ē\ *adj* **blur•ri•er; blur•ri•est**
not in sharp focus ⟨The picture is *blurry*.⟩

blurt \'blərt\ *vb* **blurt•ed; blurt•ing**
to say or tell suddenly and without thinking ⟨"I know the secret," she *blurted*.⟩

[1]**blush** \'bləsh\ *vb* **blushed; blush•ing**
1 to become red in the face from shame, confusion, or embarrassment
2 to feel ashamed or embarrassed ⟨I *blush* to admit the truth.⟩

[2]**blush** *n, pl* **blush•es**
1 a reddening of the face from shame, confusion, or embarrassment
2 a rosy color

[1]**blus•ter** \'blə-stər\ *vb* **blus•tered; blus•ter•ing**
1 to talk or act in a noisy boastful way
2 to blow hard and noisily

[2]**bluster** *n*
noisy violent action or speech

blvd. *abbr* boulevard

boa \'bō-ə\ *n*
▼ a large snake (as a python) that coils around and crushes its prey

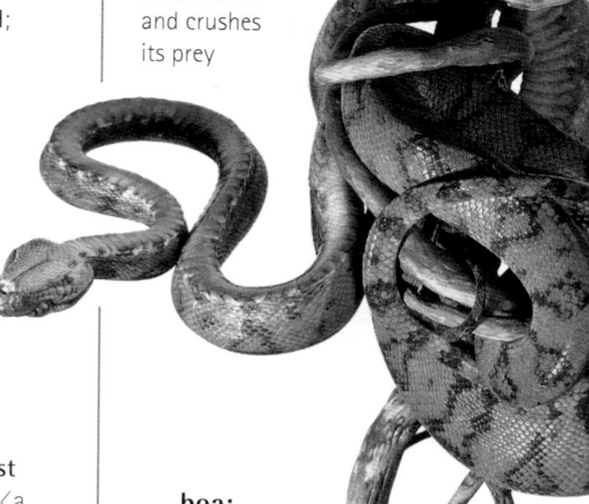

boa:
a boa constrictor

boar \'bȯr\ *n*
1 a male pig
2 WILD BOAR

¹board \'bȯrd\ *n*
1 a sawed piece of lumber that is much broader and longer than it is thick
2 a usually rectangular piece of rigid material used for some special purpose ⟨a diving *board*⟩ ⟨a game *board*⟩
3 BLACKBOARD
4 a number of persons having authority to manage or direct something ⟨the school *board*⟩
5 meals given at set times for a price ⟨He paid $20 a week for room and *board.*⟩
6 **boards** *pl* the low wooden wall enclosing a hockey rink
7 a sheet of insulating material carrying electronic parts (as for a computer)
on board ¹ABOARD

²board *vb* **board•ed**; **board•ing**
1 to go aboard ⟨We *boarded* the plane in New York.⟩
2 to cover with boards ⟨The windows were *boarded* up.⟩
3 to give or get meals and a place to live for a price

board•er \'bȯr-dər\ *n*
a person who pays for meals and a place to live at another's house

board•ing•house \'bȯr-diŋ-ˌhau̇s\ *n*
a house at which people are given meals and often a place to live

boarding school *n*
a school at which most of the students live during the school year

board•walk \'bȯrd-ˌwȯk\ *n*
a walk made of planks especially along a beach

¹boast \'bōst\ *vb* **boast•ed**; **boast•ing**
1 to express too much pride in a person's own qualities, possessions, or achievements ⟨Players on the other team *boasted* of their strength.⟩
2 to have and be proud of having ⟨Our school *boasts* more top students than any other in the city.⟩

²boast *n*
1 an act of expressing too much pride in a person's own qualities, possessions, or achievements
2 a cause for pride
boast•ful \'bōst-fəl\ *adj*
boast•ful•ly *adv*

¹boat \'bōt\ *n*
1 ▼ a small vessel driven on the water by oars, paddles, sails, or a motor
2 ¹SHIP 1

²boat *vb* **boat•ed**; **boat•ing**
to use a boat
boat•er *n*

▶ **¹boat 1**
Simple boats have served to transport people and goods across water for centuries. Today boats can be specially equipped for specific purposes, including recreation, competitive racing, rescue missions, towing larger vessels, and even as permanent homes.

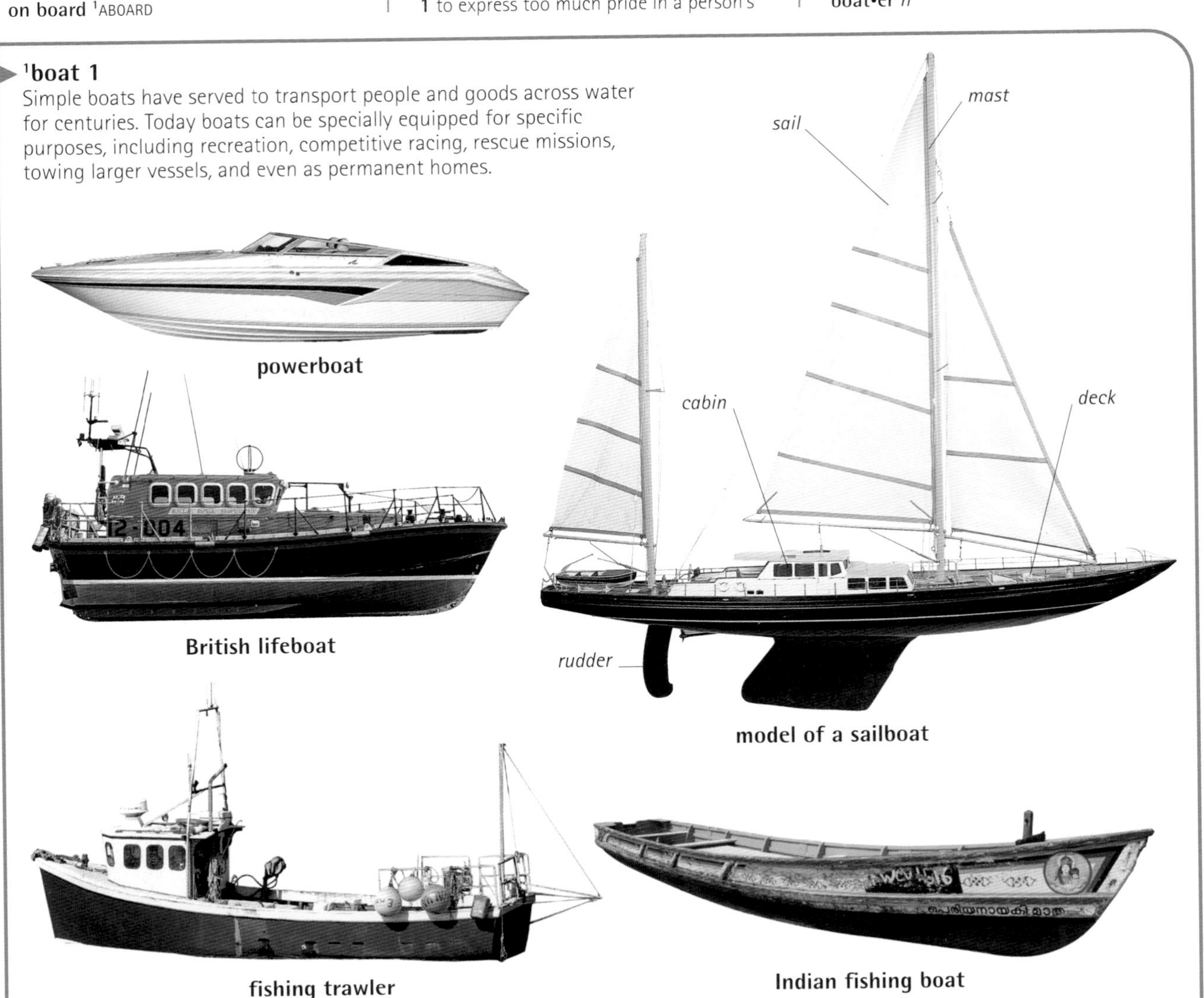

powerboat

British lifeboat

model of a sailboat

fishing trawler

Indian fishing boat

boat•house \'bōt-,hau̇s\ *n*
a house or shelter for boats

boat•man \'bōt-mən\ *n*, *pl* **boat•men** \-mən\
► a person who works on, handles, or operates boats

boat•swain \'bō-s^{ə}n\ *n*
a warrant officer on a warship or a petty officer on a commercial ship who has charge of the hull, anchors, boats, and rigging

[1]bob \'bäb\ *vb* **bobbed**; **bob•bing**
1 to move or cause to move with a short jerky up-and-down motion
2 to try to seize something with the teeth ⟨*bob* for apples⟩

[2]bob *n*
a short jerky up-and-down motion

[3]bob *n*
1 a float used to buoy up the baited end of a fishing line
2 a woman's or child's short haircut

[4]bob *vb* **bobbed**; **bob•bing**
1 to cut (hair) in the style of a bob
2 to cut shorter ⟨*bob* a dog's tail⟩

bob•by pin \'bä-bē-\ *n*
a flat metal hairpin with the two ends pressed close together

bob•cat \'bäb-,kat\ *n*
▼ a North American wildcat that is a small rusty brown type of lynx

bobcat

bob•o•link \'bäb-ə-,liŋk\ *n*
a North American songbird related to the blackbirds

bob•sled \'bäb-,sled\ *n*
a racing sled made with two sets of runners, a hand brake, and often a steering wheel

bob•tail \'bäb-,tāl\ *n*
1 a short tail : a tail cut short
2 an animal (as a dog) with a short tail

bob•white \bäb-'hwīt, -'wīt\ *n*
► a North American quail with gray, white, and reddish brown coloring

boatman: a boatman rowing his boat

[1]bode \'bōd\ *vb* **bod•ed**; **bod•ing**
to be a sign of (a future event) ⟨This could *bode* difficulty for all of us.⟩

[2]bode *past of* BIDE

bod•ice \'bä-dəs\ *n*
the upper part of a dress

[1]bodi•ly \'bä-də-lē\ *adj*
of or relating to the body ⟨*bodily* functions⟩

[2]bodily *adv*
1 by the body ⟨Police removed them *bodily*.⟩
2 as a whole ⟨a house moved *bodily*⟩

body \'bä-dē\ *n*, *pl* **bod•ies**
1 the physical whole of a live or dead person or animal ⟨the human *body*⟩
2 the main part of a person, animal, or plant : TRUNK 6
3 PERSON : ⟨all a *body* could want⟩
4 the main or central part ⟨the *body* of a letter⟩
5 the main part of a motor vehicle
6 a group of persons or things united for some purpose ⟨a *body* of troops⟩
7 a mass or portion of something distinct from other masses ⟨a *body* of water⟩

bod•ied \'bäd-ēd\ *adj*

bobwhite

body•guard \'bä-dē-,gärd\ *n*
a person or a group of persons whose duty it is to protect someone

[1]bog \'bäg, 'bȯg\ *n*
wet spongy ground that is usually acid and found next to a body of water (as a pond)

[2]bog *vb* **bogged**; **bog•ging**
to sink or stick fast in or as if in a bog ⟨The car *bogged* down in the road.⟩ ⟨I got *bogged* down in my work.⟩

bo•gey *also* **bo•gie** *or* **bo•gy** *n*, *pl* **bogeys** *or* **bogies**
1 \'bu̇-gē, 'bō-\ GHOST, GOBLIN
2 \'bō-gē, 'bu̇-gē\ something a person is afraid of without reason

bo•gus \'bō-gəs\ *adj*
not genuine

[1]boil \'bȯil\ *n*
a red painful lump in the skin that contains pus and is caused by infection

[2]boil *vb* **boiled**; **boil•ing**
1 to heat or become heated to the temperature at which bubbles form and rise to the top ⟨*boil* water⟩
2 to cook or become cooked in boiling water ⟨*boil* eggs⟩ ⟨Let the stew *boil* slowly.⟩
3 to feel angry or upset ⟨The crowd *boiled* in frustration.⟩

[3]boil *n*
the state of something that is boiling ⟨Bring the water to a *boil*.⟩

boil•er \'bȯi-lər\ *n*
1 a container in which something is boiled
2 a tank heating and holding water
3 a strong metal container used in making steam (as to heat buildings)

boiling point *n*
1 the temperature at which a liquid boils
2 the point at which a person or people might do or say something out of anger

bois•ter•ous \'bȯi-stə-rəs, -strəs\ *adj*
being rough and noisy ⟨a *boisterous* class⟩
bois•ter•ous•ly *adv*

bold \'bōld\ *adj* **bold•er; bold•est**
1 willing to meet danger or take risks : DARING ⟨*bold* knights⟩
2 not polite and modest : FRESH ⟨a *bold* remark⟩
3 showing or calling for courage or daring ⟨a *bold* plan⟩
4 standing out prominently ⟨She has a face with *bold* features.⟩
5 being or set in boldface
synonyms see BRAVE
bold•ly *adv*
bold•ness *n*

bold•face \'bōld-,fās\ *n*
a heavy black type
bold–faced \-,fāst\ *adj*

boll \'bōl\ *n*
the usually roundish pod of some plants ⟨cotton *bolls*⟩

boll weevil *n*
a grayish or brown insect that lays its eggs in cotton bolls

bo•lo•gna \bə-'lō-nē\ *n*
a large smoked sausage usually made of beef, veal, and pork

¹bol•ster \'bōl-stər\ *n*
a long pillow or cushion sometimes used to support bed pillows

²bolster *vb* **bol•stered; bol•ster•ing**
to support with or as if with a bolster ⟨We tried to *bolster* their courage.⟩

¹bolt \'bōlt\ *n*
1 a stroke of lightning : THUNDERBOLT
2 a sliding bar used to fasten a door
3 the part of a lock worked by a key
4 a metal pin or rod with a head at one end and a screw thread at the other that is used to hold something in place
5 a roll of cloth or wallpaper

²bolt *vb* **bolt•ed; bolt•ing**
1 to move suddenly and rapidly ⟨She *bolted* from the room.⟩
2 to run away ⟨The horse shied and *bolted.*⟩
3 to fasten with a bolt ⟨Be sure to *bolt* the door.⟩
4 to swallow hastily or without chewing

¹bomb \'bäm\ *n*
1 a hollow case or shell filled with explosive material
2 a container in which something (as an insecticide) is stored under pressure and from which it is released in a fine spray
3 something that is a complete failure ⟨The new movie was a *bomb.*⟩

²bomb *vb* **bombed; bomb•ing**
1 to attack with bombs
2 to fail completely ⟨His comedy act *bombed.*⟩

bom•bard \bäm-'bärd\ *vb* **bom•bard•ed; bom•bard•ing**
1 to attack with heavy fire from big guns : SHELL ⟨*bombard* a fort⟩
2 to hit or attack again and again ⟨We were *bombarded* by ads.⟩

bomb•er \'bä-mər\ *n*
▼ an airplane specially made for dropping bombs

bomber: model of a bomber

bo•na fide \'bō-nə-,fīd, 'bä-\ *adj*
GENUINE 1 ⟨I have a *bona fide* excuse.⟩

bon•bon \'bän-,bän\ *n*
a candy with a soft coating and a creamy center

¹bond \'bänd\ *n*
1 something that binds
2 the condition of being held together ⟨The glue forms a strong *bond.*⟩
3 a force or influence that brings or holds together ⟨a *bond* of friendship⟩
4 a chain or rope used to prevent someone from moving or acting freely
5 a promise to do something ⟨My word is my *bond.*⟩
6 a legal agreement in which a person agrees to pay a sum of money if he or she fails to do a certain thing
7 a government or business certificate promising to pay a certain sum by a certain day

²bond *vb* **bond•ed; bond•ing**
1 to stick or cause to stick together
2 to form a close relationship ⟨The girls quickly *bonded.*⟩

bond•age \'bän-dij\ *n*
the state of being a slave

¹bone \'bōn\ *n*
1 any of the hard pieces that form the skeleton of most animals ⟨the *bones* of the arm⟩
2 the hard material of which the skeleton of most animals is formed ⟨a piece of *bone*⟩
bone•less \-ləs\ *adj*

²bone *vb* **boned; bon•ing**
to remove the bones from ⟨*bone* a fish⟩

bone marrow *n*
▶ a soft tissue rich in blood vessels that fills the spaces of most bones and includes one type that is red and produces red blood cells and white blood cells and another type that is yellow and contains fat

bon•fire \'bän-,fīr\ *n*
a large fire built outdoors

bong \'bäŋ, 'bȯŋ\ *n*
a deep sound like that of a large bell

bongos

bon•go \'bäŋ-gō, 'bȯŋ-gō\ *n, pl* **bongos** *also* **bongoes**
▲ either of a pair of small drums of different sizes that are joined together and played with the hands

bon•net \'bä-nət\ *n*
a child's or woman's hat usually tied under the chin by ribbons or strings

bon•ny *also* **bon•nie** \'bä-nē\ *adj* **bon•ni•er; bon•ni•est** *chiefly British*
HANDSOME 1, BEAUTIFUL

bo•nus \'bō-nəs\ *n*
something given to somebody (as a worker) in addition to what is usual or owed

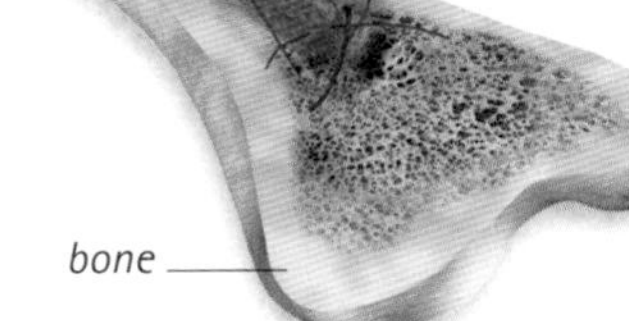

bone marrow

bony \ˈbō-nē\ *adj* **bon•i•er**; **bon•i•est**
1 of or relating to bone ⟨a *bony* growth⟩
2 like bone especially in hardness ⟨*bony* material⟩
3 having bones and especially large or noticeable bones ⟨a *bony* fish⟩ ⟨*bony* hands⟩
4 very thin ⟨He is tall and *bony*.⟩

[1]boo \ˈbü\ *interj*
used to express disapproval or to startle or frighten

[2]boo *n, pl* **boos**
a cry expressing disapproval

[3]boo *vb* **booed**; **boo•ing**
to express disapproval of with boos

boo•by–trap \ˈbü-bē-ˌtrap\ *vb* **boo•by–trapped**; **boo•by–trap•ping**
to set up as a booby trap

boo•by trap \ˈbü-bē-\ *n*
1 a hidden bomb that explodes when the object connected to it is touched
2 a trap set for an unsuspecting person

[1]book \ˈbu̇k\ *n*
1 a set of sheets of paper bound together
2 a long written work ⟨a *book* about birds⟩
3 a large division of a written work ⟨the *books* of the Bible⟩
4 a pack of small items bound together ⟨a *book* of matches⟩
5 the records of a business's accounts — often used in pl. ⟨a credit on the *books*⟩

[2]book *vb* **booked**; **book•ing**
to reserve for future use ⟨He *booked* rooms at the hotel.⟩

book•case \ˈbu̇k-ˌkās\ *n*
a set of shelves to hold books

book•end \ˈbu̇k-ˌend\ *n*
a support at the end of a row of books to keep them standing up

book•keep•er \ˈbu̇k-ˌkē-pər\ *n*
a person who keeps financial records for a business

book•keep•ing \ˈbu̇k-ˌkē-piŋ\ *n*
the work of keeping business records

book•let \ˈbu̇k-lət\ *n*
a little book usually having paper covers and few pages

book•mark \ˈbu̇k-ˌmärk\ *n*
1 ▶ something placed in a book to show the page the reader wants to return to
2 something on a computer screen that serves as a shortcut (as to a Web site)

bookmark 1

book•mo•bile \ˈbu̇k-mō-ˌbēl\ *n*
a truck with shelves of books that is a traveling library

book•worm \ˈbu̇k-ˌwərm\ *n*
a person who reads a lot

[1]boom \ˈbüm\ *vb* **boomed**; **boom•ing**
1 to make a deep, hollow, and loud sound ⟨The cannon *boomed*.⟩
2 to increase or develop rapidly ⟨Business *boomed* last year.⟩

[2]boom *n*
1 a deep, hollow, and loud sound
2 a rapid increase in activity or popularity ⟨a sales *boom*⟩

[3]boom *n*
1 a long pole attached to the bottom of a sail
2 a long beam sticking out from the mast of a derrick to support or guide something that is being lifted
3 a long pole for holding a microphone

boom box *n*
a large portable radio and CD or tape player

boo•mer•ang \ˈbü-mə-ˌraŋ\ *n*
▼ a curved club that can be thrown so as to return to the thrower

boomerang

▶ **Word History** The word *boomerang* was taken from a language called Dharuk, spoken by the native Australian people who lived around what is today Sydney, Australia, when the first Europeans landed there in 1788. Many Dharuk speakers died of smallpox, brought by European colonists, and the language was almost completely out of use by about 1850. Curiously, the earliest record of Dharuk, taken down in 1790, incorrectly described *boomerang* as a kind of wooden sword.

boom•ing \ˈbü-miŋ\ *adj*
1 making a deep sound ⟨a *booming* voice⟩
2 forcefully or powerfully done ⟨a *booming* hit⟩

boon \ˈbün\ *n*
1 something asked or granted as a favor
2 something pleasant or helpful that comes at just the right time ⟨The rain was a *boon* to the farmers.⟩

[1]boost \ˈbüst\ *vb* **boost•ed**; **boost•ing**
1 to raise or push up from below ⟨He *boosted* me through the window.⟩
2 to make bigger or greater ⟨*boost* production⟩
boost•er *n*

[2]boost *n*
a push up : an act of boosting ⟨Give me a *boost*.⟩

[1]boot \ˈbüt\ *n*
▶ a covering usually of leather or rubber for the foot and part of the leg

[1]boot: a pair of cowboy boots

[2]boot *vb* **boot•ed**; **boot•ing**
[1]KICK 1

boo•tee *or* **boo•tie** \ˈbü-tē\ *n*
an infant's knitted sock

booth \ˈbüth\ *n, pl* **booths** \ˈbüthz\
1 a partly enclosed area or small building used for a particular purpose ⟨a ticket *booth*⟩
2 a table in a restaurant between two benches with high backs

boo•ty \ˈbü-tē\ *n*
1 goods seized from an enemy in war or by robbery : PLUNDER
2 a valuable gain or prize

[1]bop \ˈbäp\ *vb* **bopped**; **bop•ping**
[1]HIT 1 ⟨She *bopped* him with her purse.⟩

[2]bop *n*
[2]HIT 1 ⟨a *bop* on the head⟩

[1]bor•der \ˈbȯr-dər\ *n*
1 a boundary especially of a country or state
2 the outer edge of something ⟨the *border* of the woods⟩
3 a decorative strip on or near the edge of something

[2]border *vb* **bor•dered**; **bor•der•ing**
1 to put a border on ⟨*Border* the garden with flowers.⟩
2 to be close or next to ⟨The United States *borders* on Canada.⟩

bor•der•line \ˈbȯr-dər-ˌlīn\ *adj*
not quite average, standard, or normal ⟨She's a *borderline* student for advanced math.⟩

[1]bore \ˈbȯr\ *vb* **bored**; **bor•ing**
1 to make a hole in especially with a drill ⟨*bore* a piece of wood⟩
2 to make by piercing or drilling ⟨*bore* a hole⟩
bor•er *n*

²bore *n*
1 a hole made by boring
2 a space (as in a gun barrel) shaped like a cylinder
3 the diameter of a hole or cylinder

³bore *past of* BEAR

⁴bore *n*
an uninteresting person or thing

⁵bore *vb* **bored**; **bor•ing**
to make tired and restless by being uninteresting ⟨This long-winded story *bores* me.⟩

bore•dom \'bȯr-dəm\ *n*
the state of being bored

bo•ric acid \'bȯr-ik-\ *n*
a weak acid containing boron used to kill germs

bor•ing \'bȯr-iŋ\ *adj*
dull and uninteresting

born \'bȯrn\ *adj*
1 brought into life by birth
2 brought into existence ⟨when the universe was *born*⟩
3 having a certain characteristic from or as if from birth ⟨a *born* leader⟩

borne *past participle of* BEAR

bo•ron \'bȯr-,än\ *n*
a powdery or hard solid chemical element that is used especially in making glass and detergents

bor•ough \'bər-ō\ *n*
1 a town, village, or part of a large city that has its own government
2 one of the five political divisions of New York City

bor•row \'bär-ō\ *vb* **bor•rowed**; **bor•row•ing**
1 to take and use something with the promise of returning it
2 to use something begun or thought up by another : ADOPT ⟨*borrow* an idea⟩
3 to adopt into one language from another ⟨Many English words are *borrowed* from French.⟩
bor•row•er \'bär-ə-wər\ *n*

¹bos•om \'bu̇z-əm\ *n*
1 the front of the human chest
2 the breasts of a woman

²bosom *adj*
very close ⟨*bosom* friends⟩

¹boss \'bȯs\ *n*
1 the person at a job who tells workers what to do
2 the head of a group (as a political organization)

²boss *vb* **bossed**; **boss•ing**
to give orders to ⟨Don't *boss* me around.⟩

bossy \'bȯ-sē\ *adj* **boss•i•er**; **boss•i•est**
liking to order people around

bo•tan•i•cal \bə-'ta-ni-kəl\ *adj*
of or relating to the study of plants

bot•a•nist \'bä-tə-nist\ *n*
a person specializing in botany

bot•a•ny \'bä-tə-nē, 'bät-nē\ *n*
a branch of biology dealing with plants

¹botch \'bäch\ *vb* **botched**; **botch•ing**
to do clumsily and unskillfully : BUNGLE ⟨*botch* a job⟩

²botch *n*
a badly done job ⟨He made a *botch* of it.⟩

¹both \'bōth\ *pron*
each one of two things or people : the two ⟨*both* of us⟩

²both *conj*
used before two words or phrases connected with *and* to stress that each is included ⟨*both* New York and London⟩

³both *adj*
the two ⟨*Both* books are mine.⟩

¹both•er \'bä-t͟h-ər\ *vb* **both•ered**; **both•er•ing**
1 to trouble (someone) in body or mind : ANNOY ⟨*bothered* by flies⟩
2 to cause to worry ⟨Your illness *bothers* me.⟩
3 to take the time or trouble ⟨Don't *bother* to dress up.⟩
4 to intrude upon : INTERRUPT ⟨Don't *bother* me while I'm on the phone.⟩

²bother *n*
1 someone or something that is annoying ⟨This project is such a *bother*.⟩
2 COMMOTION
3 a state of worry or annoyance ⟨It's not worth the *bother*.⟩

both•er•some \'bä-t͟hər-səm\ *adj*
ANNOYING

¹bot•tle \'bä-tᵊl\ *n*
1 ▼ a container (as of glass or plastic) usually having a narrow neck and mouth and no handle
2 the quantity held by a bottle

¹bottle 1: glass bottles

²bottle *vb* **bot•tled**; **bot•tling**
1 to put into a bottle
2 to shut up as if in a bottle ⟨She *bottles* up her feelings.⟩

bot•tle•neck \'bä-tᵊl-,nek\ *n*
a place or condition where improvement or movement is held up

bot•tom \'bä-təm\ *n*
1 the lowest part of something ⟨the *bottom* of the stairs⟩ ⟨the *bottom* of the bowl⟩
2 the under surface of something ⟨There's gum on the *bottom* of my shoe.⟩
3 a supporting surface or part : BASE ⟨chair *bottoms*⟩
4 the lowest or worst level or position ⟨She graduated at the *bottom* of her class.⟩
5 clothing that covers the lower part of the body ⟨pajama *bottoms*⟩
6 the bed of a body of water ⟨the lake *bottom*⟩
7 low land along a river ⟨Mississippi River *bottoms*⟩
8 the most basic part ⟨Let's get to the *bottom* of the problem.⟩
9 the second half of an inning of baseball

bot•tom•less \'bä-təm-ləs\ *adj*
1 having no bottom
2 very deep ⟨a *bottomless* pit⟩

bough \'bau̇\ *n*
a usually large or main branch of a tree

bought *past and past participle of* BUY

bouil•lon \'bü-,yän, 'bu̇l-,yän, 'bu̇l-yən\ *n*
a clear soup or stock made from meat or vegetables

boul•der \'bōl-dər\ *n*
a very large rounded piece of rock

bou•le•vard \'bu̇-lə-,värd\ *n*
a wide usually major street often having strips with trees, grass, or flowers planted along its center or sides

¹bounce \'bau̇ns\ *vb* **bounced**; **bounc•ing**
1 to spring back or up after hitting a surface ⟨The ball *bounced* into the street.⟩
2 to cause to spring back ⟨*bounce* a ball⟩
3 to jump or move up and down ⟨*bouncing* on a bed⟩ ⟨Her curls *bounced* as she walked.⟩
4 to leap suddenly

²bounce *n*
1 the action of springing back after hitting something
2 a sudden leap
bouncy *adj*

¹bound \'bau̇nd\ *adj*
going or intending to go ⟨homeward *bound*⟩

²bound *n*
1 a boundary line
2 a point or line beyond which a person or thing cannot go ⟨The ball has to stay within these *bounds*.⟩

³bound *past and past participle of* BIND

[4]**bound** *vb* **bound•ed**; **bound•ing**
to form the boundary of ⟨The farm is *bounded* by a river on one side.⟩

[5]**bound** *adj*
1 tied or fastened with or as if with bands
2 required by law or duty
3 under the control of something ⟨*bound* by the spell⟩
4 covered with binding ⟨a *bound* book⟩
5 firmly determined ⟨We were *bound* we would succeed.⟩
6 very likely : CERTAIN ⟨It is *bound* to rain.⟩

[6]**bound** *n*
a leap or long jump

[7]**bound** *vb* **bounded**; **bounding**
to make a long leap or move in leaps

bound•ary \'bau̇n-də-rē, 'bau̇n-drē\ *n*, *pl* **bound•aries**
something that points out or shows a limit or end : a dividing line

bound•less \'bau̇nd-ləs\ *adj*
having no limits ⟨*boundless* energy⟩

boun•te•ous \'bau̇n-tē-əs\ *adj*
1 GENEROUS 1 ⟨a *bounteous* host⟩
2 given in plenty : ABUNDANT ⟨a *bounteous* harvest⟩

boun•ti•ful \'bau̇n-ti-fəl\ *adj*
1 giving freely or generously ⟨this *bountiful* land⟩
2 PLENTIFUL 1 ⟨a *bountiful* feast⟩

boun•ty \'bau̇n-tē\ *n*, *pl* **boun•ties**
1 GENEROSITY 1 ⟨acts of *bounty*⟩
2 things given in generous amounts ⟨the *bounty* of nature⟩
3 money given as a reward

bou•quet \bō-'kā, bü-\ *n*
▼ a bunch of flowers

bouquet

bout \'bau̇t\ *n*
1 a contest of skill or strength ⟨a wrestling *bout*⟩
2 [2]ATTACK 4, OUTBREAK ⟨a bad *bout* of the flu⟩

bou•tique \bü-'tēk\ *n*
a small fashionable shop

[1]**bow** \'bau̇\ *vb* **bowed**; **bow•ing**
1 to bend the head or body as an act of politeness or respect
2 to stop resisting : YIELD ⟨He *bowed* to pressure to resign.⟩

[2]**bow** *n*
the act of bending the head or body to express politeness or respect

[3]**bow** \'bō\ *n*
1 ► a weapon used for shooting arrows and usually made of a strip of wood bent by a cord connecting the two ends
2 something shaped in a curve
3 a knot made with one or more loops ⟨Tie the ribbon in a *bow*.⟩
4 a rod with horsehairs stretched from end to end used for playing a stringed instrument (as a violin)

grip
bowstring
[3]bow 1

[4]**bow** \'bō\ *vb* **bowed**; **bow•ing**
to bend or cause to bend into a curve ⟨The wall *bows* out.⟩

[5]**bow** \'bau̇\ *n*
the forward part of a ship

bow•el \'bau̇-əl\ *n*
1 INTESTINE — usually used in pl.
2 a part of the intestine ⟨the large *bowel*⟩

bow•er \'bau̇-ər\ *n*
a shelter in a garden made of boughs of trees or vines

[1]**bowl** \'bōl\ *n*
1 a round hollow dish without handles
2 the contents of a bowl ⟨I ate a *bowl* of cereal.⟩
3 something in the shape of a bowl (as part of a spoon or pipe)

[2]**bowl** *vb* **bowled**; **bowl•ing**
1 to play a game of bowling
2 to move rapidly and smoothly ⟨The car *bowled* down the hill.⟩
bowl over
1 to hit and push down while moving quickly
2 to surprise or impress very much

bow•legged \'bō-'le-gəd, -'legd\ *adj*
having the legs bowed outward

bow•line \'bō-lən\ *n*
a knot used for making a loop that will not slip

bowl•ing \'bō-liŋ\ *n*
a game in which large heavy balls are rolled so as to knock down pins

bow•sprit \'bau̇-,sprit, 'bō-\ *n*
a large spar sticking out forward from the bow of a ship

bow•string \'bō-,striŋ\ *n*
the cord connecting the two ends of a bow

[1]**box** \'bäks\ *n*
an evergreen shrub or small tree used for hedges

[2]**box** *n*
1 a container usually having four sides, a bottom, and a cover
2 the contents of a box ⟨Don't eat the whole *box* of candy!⟩
3 a four-sided shape on a piece of paper or computer screen ⟨Put an X in the *box*.⟩
4 an enclosed place for one or more persons ⟨a penalty *box*⟩

[3]**box** *vb* **boxed**; **box•ing**
to enclose in or as if in a box

[4]**box** *vb* **boxed**; **boxing**
to fight with the fists

box•car \'bäks-,kär\ *n*
a roofed freight car usually having sliding doors in the sides

box elder *n*
a North American maple with leaves divided into several leaflets

[1]**boxer** \'bäk-sər\ *n*
a person who engages in the sport of boxing

[2]**boxer** *n*
► a compact dog of German origin that is of medium size with a square build and has a short and often tan coat

[2]boxer

► **Word History** The word *boxer*, as well as the dog breed itself, is of German origin; the dog was first bred in the city of Munich in the 1890s. Scholars of word origins have assumed that the German noun *Boxer* is in its turn borrowed from English *boxer*, "a man who fights with his fists," but its exact origin is somewhat mysterious. The boxer is not an aggressive dog, but the breed's ancestors may have been used for bullbaiting, a sport in which chained bulls were set upon by fierce dogs. There is some evidence that *Boxer* was a name given to such a dog.

box•ing \'bäk-siŋ\ *n*
the sport of fighting with the fists

box office *n*
a place where tickets to public entertainments (as sports or theatrical events) are sold

boy \'bȯi\ *n*
1 a male child from birth to young manhood
2 SON 1 ⟨She has two *boys*.⟩
3 a male servant

[1]**boy•cott** \'bȯi-,kät\ *vb* **boy•cot•ted**; **boy•cot•ting**
to join with others in refusing to deal with someone (as a person, organization, or country) as a way of protesting or forcing changes

[2]**boycott** *n*
the process or an instance of joining with others in refusing to deal with someone (as a person, organization, or country) as a way of protesting or forcing changes

boy•friend \'bȯi-,frend\ *n*
a man or boy involved in a romantic relationship

boy•hood \'bȯi-,hu̇d\ *n*
the time or condition of being a boy

boy•ish \'bȯi-ish\ *adj*
relating to or having qualities often felt to be typical of boys

Boy Scout *n*
a member of a scouting program (as the Boy Scouts of America)

bp *abbr* birthplace

Br. *abbr*
1 Britain
2 British

bra \'brä\ *n*
a woman's undergarment for breast support

[1]**brace** \'brās\ *vb* **braced**; **brac•ing**
1 to make strong, firm, or steady
2 to get ready ⟨They *braced* for a storm.⟩

[2]**brace** *n*
1 something that adds strength or support ⟨a neck *brace*⟩
2 **brac•es** *pl* a usually wire device worn to correct the position of teeth
3 one of a pair of marks { } used to connect words or items to be considered together
4 two of a kind ⟨a *brace* of quail⟩
5 a tool with a U-shaped bend that is used to turn wood-boring bits

brace•let \'brā-slət\ *n*
a decorative band or chain usually worn on the wrist or arm

brack•en \'bra-kən\ *n*
a large branching fern

[1]**brack•et** \'bra-kət\ *n*
1 a support for a weight (as a shelf) that is usually attached to a wall
2 one of a pair of marks [ ] (**square brackets**) used to enclose letters or numbers or in mathematics to enclose items to be treated together
3 one of a pair of marks < > (**angle brackets**) used to enclose letters or numbers
4 [1]GROUP 1, CATEGORY ⟨an age *bracket*⟩

[2]**bracket** *vb* **brack•et•ed**; **brack•et•ing**
1 to place within brackets
2 to put into the same class : GROUP

brack•ish \'bra-kish\ *adj*
somewhat salty ⟨*brackish* water⟩

brad \'brad\ *n*
a thin nail with a small usually indented head

brag \'brag\ *vb* **bragged**; **brag•ging**
to speak in a way that shows too much pride : BOAST
brag•ger \'bra-gər\ *n*

brag•gart \'bra-gərt\ *n*
a person who boasts a lot

[1]**braid** \'brād\ *vb* **braid•ed**; **braid•ing**
to weave three strands together ⟨She *braided* her hair.⟩

[2]**braid**

[2]**braid** *n*
◀ a length of cord, ribbon, or hair formed of three or more strands woven together

braille \'brāl\ *n, often cap*
a system of printing for the blind in which the letters are represented by raised dots

▶ **Word History** Born in France in 1809, Louis Braille became completely blind at the age of five due to an accident. A brilliant student, he worked on a system of reading raised dots by touch while still a teenager. The writing and printing system named after him was not widely adopted until after his death in 1852.

[1]**brain** \'brān\ *n*
1 ▼ the part of the nervous system that is inside the skull, consists of grayish nerve cells and whitish nerve fibers, and is the organ of thought and the central control point for the nervous system
2 the ability to think : INTELLIGENCE
3 someone who is very smart

▶ [1]**brain 1**
The brain monitors and regulates actions and reactions in the body. The brain stem controls breathing and heart rate. The cerebrum is the center of thinking, while the cerebellum coordinates movement and balance. The thalamus directs nerve impulses to specialized areas and the hypothalamus produces hormones for the nervous system.

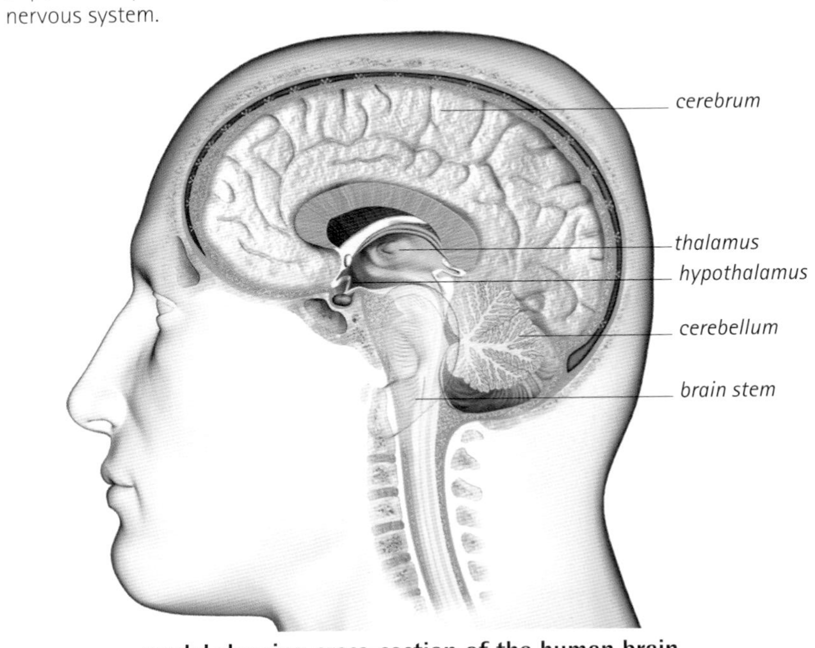

model showing cross-section of the human brain

[2]brain *vb* **brained**; **brain•ing**
to hit on the head very hard ⟨He was *brained* by a falling tree branch.⟩

brain•storm \ˈbrān-ˌstȯrm\ *n*
a sudden inspiration or idea

brainy \ˈbrā-nē\ *adj* **brain•i•er**; **brain•i•est**
very smart

[1]brake \ˈbrāk\ *n*
a device for slowing or stopping motion (as of a wheel) usually by friction

[2]brake *vb* **braked**; **brak•ing**
to slow or stop by using a brake ⟨I had to *brake* suddenly.⟩

brake•man \ˈbrāk-mən\ *n*, *pl* **brake•men** \-mən\
a crew member on a train who inspects the train and helps the conductor

bramble

bram•ble \ˈbram-bəl\ *n*
▲ a rough prickly bush or vine — usually used in pl. ⟨blackberry *brambles*⟩

bran \ˈbran\ *n*
the broken coat of the seed of cereal grain separated (as by sifting) from the flour or meal

[1]branch \ˈbranch\ *n*
1 a part of a tree that grows out from the trunk or from a main division of the trunk
2 something extending from a main line or body like a branch ⟨a *branch* of a railroad⟩
3 a division or subordinate part of something ⟨a *branch* of government⟩ ⟨The bank opened a new *branch*.⟩
branched \ˈbrancht\ *adj*

[2]branch *vb* **branched**; **branch•ing**
to spread or divide into smaller or attached parts : send out a branch

▶ **brass 2**
Brass instruments were originally made from brass, but are now formed from a variety of materials. While they come in many shapes and sizes, all have a mouthpiece, a hollow tube, and a flared bell. To produce different notes, a player adjusts lip tension on the mouthpiece or alters the length of the tube through which air passes. This is done using either a valve system or sliding sections.

third piston valve
second piston valve
first piston valve
little finger support
tuning slide
flared bell
mouthpiece
first valve slide
second valve slide
finger ring
third valve slide

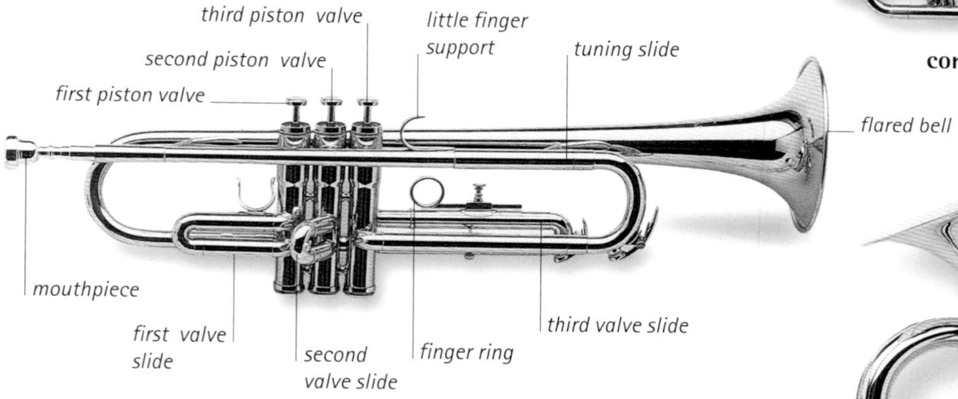

features of a trumpet

cornet

tuba

tenor horn

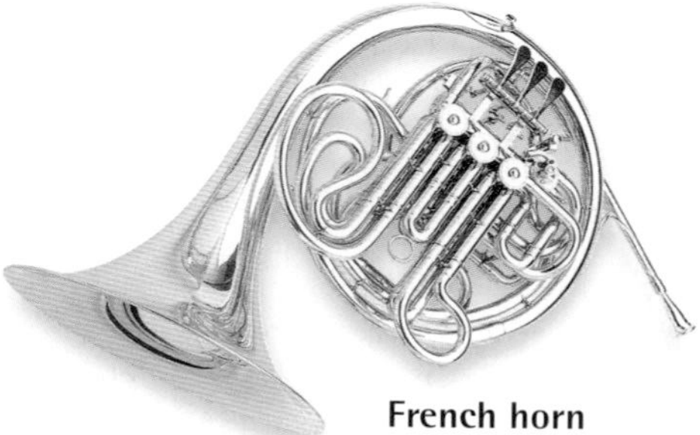

French horn

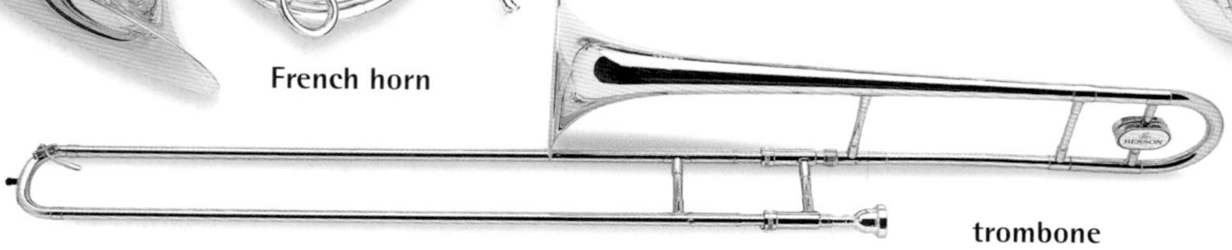

trombone

[1]brand \'brand\ *n*
1 a mark made by burning (as on cattle) or by stamping or printing (as on manufactured goods) to show ownership, maker, or quality
2 a category of goods identified by a name as being made by a certain company ⟨a *brand* of jeans⟩
3 TRADEMARK
4 a particular type ⟨a *brand* of humor⟩
5 a mark of disgrace

[2]brand *vb* **brand•ed**; **brand•ing**
1 put a mark on to show ownership ⟨*brand* cattle⟩
2 to show or claim (something) to be bad or wrong ⟨Opponents *branded* the experiment a failure.⟩

bran•dish \'bran-dish\ *vb* **bran•dished**; **bran•dish•ing**
to wave or shake in a threatening manner

brand–new \'brand-'nü, -'nyü\ *adj*
completely new

bran•dy \'bran-dē\ *n, pl* **brandies**
an alcoholic liquor made from wine or fruit juice

brass \'bras\ *n*
1 an alloy made by combining copper and zinc
2◀ the musical instruments of an orchestra or band that are usually made of brass and include the cornets, trumpets, trombones, French horns, and tubas

brat \'brat\ *n*
a naughty annoying child

[1]brave \'brāv\ *adj* **brav•er**; **brav•est**
feeling or showing no fear
brave•ly *adv*

▶ **Synonyms** BRAVE, COURAGEOUS, and BOLD mean showing no fear. BRAVE is used of a person who has or shows no fear when faced with danger or difficulty. ⟨The *brave* crew tried to save the ship.⟩ COURAGEOUS is used of a person who is always prepared to meet danger or difficulty. ⟨The early astronauts were *courageous* in facing the dangers of space travel.⟩ BOLD is used of a person who welcomes dangerous situations. ⟨The *bold* explorers went in search of adventure.⟩

[2]brave *vb* **braved**; **brav•ing**
to face or handle without fear

[3]brave *n*
an American Indian warrior

brav•ery \'brā-və-rē, 'brāv-rē\ *n*
COURAGE

[1]brawl \'bról\ *vb* **brawled**; **brawl•ing**
to quarrel or fight noisily

[2]brawl *n*
a noisy quarrel or fight

brawn \'brón\ *n*
muscular strength

brawny \'bró-nē\ *adj* **brawn•i•er**; **brawn•i•est**
having large strong muscles ⟨a *brawny* football player⟩

[1]bray \'brā\ *vb* **brayed**; **bray•ing**
to make the loud harsh cry of a donkey

[2]bray *n*
the loud harsh cry of a donkey

bra•zen \'brā-zᵊn\ *adj*
1 made of brass
2 sounding loud and usually harsh ⟨*brazen* voices⟩
3 done or acting in a very bold and shocking way without shame

Bra•zil nut \brə-'zil-\ *n*
▼ a dark three-sided nut with a white kernel

Brazil nut

[1]breach \'brēch\ *n*
1 a failure to act in a promised or required way ⟨a *breach* of contract⟩
2 an opening made by breaking ⟨a *breach* in the dam⟩

[2]breach *vb* **breached**; **breach•ing**
1 to fail to do as promised or required by ⟨*breach* an agreement⟩
2 to make a break in

[1]bread \'bred\ *n*
1 a baked food made from flour or meal
2 FOOD 1 ⟨our daily *bread*⟩

[2]bread *vb* **bread•ed**; **bread•ing**
to cover with bread crumbs

breadth \'bredth\ *n*
1 distance measured from side to side
2 SCOPE 2 ⟨the *breadth* of the investigation⟩

[1]break \'brāk\ *vb* **broke** \'brōk\; **bro•ken** \'brō-kən\; **break•ing**
1 to separate into parts especially suddenly or forcibly ⟨*break* a stick⟩ ⟨*break* into groups⟩
2 to cause (a bone) to separate into two or more pieces
3 to stop working or cause to stop working because of damage or wear ⟨I *broke* my watch.⟩
4 to fail to keep ⟨*broke* the law⟩ ⟨*break* a promise⟩
5 to force a way ⟨They *broke* out of jail.⟩
6 to cut into and turn over ⟨*break* the soil⟩
7 to go through : PENETRATE ⟨*break* the skin⟩
8 [2]TAME ⟨*break* a wild horse⟩
9 to do better than ⟨*broke* the school record⟩
10 to interrupt or put an end to : STOP ⟨A shout *broke* the silence.⟩ ⟨Let's *break* for lunch.⟩
11 to reduce the force of ⟨*break* a fall⟩
12 to develop or burst out suddenly ⟨Day is *breaking*.⟩ ⟨They *broke* into laughter.⟩
13 to make known ⟨*broke* the news⟩
14 SOLVE ⟨*break* a code⟩
15 [1]CHANGE 4 ⟨*break* a ten-dollar bill⟩
16 to run or flee suddenly ⟨*break* for cover⟩
break down
1 to stop working properly ⟨The car *broke down*.⟩
2 to separate or become separated into simpler substances : DECOMPOSE
3 to be overcome by emotion ⟨*broke down* in tears⟩
4 to knock down ⟨*break down* a door⟩
break out
1 to develop a skin rash
2 to start up suddenly ⟨A fight *broke out*.⟩
break up
1 to separate into parts ⟨The meteor *broke up* in the earth's atmosphere.⟩
2 to bring or come to an end ⟨The party *broke up* late.⟩
3 to end a romantic relationship

[2]break *n*
1 an act of breaking ⟨at *break* of day⟩
2 something produced by breaking ⟨a bad *break* in the leg⟩
3 a period of time when an activity stops ⟨Let's take a *break*.⟩
4 an accidental event ⟨a lucky *break*⟩

break•down \'brāk-,daůn\ *n*
1 a failure to function properly
2 a sudden failure of mental or physical health

brea•ker \'brā-kər\ *n*
1 a person or thing that breaks something ⟨a circuit *breaker*⟩
2 a wave that breaks on shore

[1]break•fast \'brek-fəst\ *n*
▼ the first meal of the day

[1]breakfast:
a large traditional breakfast

A B C D E F G H I J K L M N O P Q R S T U V W X Y Z

[1]bridge 1
There are a number of ways to construct a bridge to make it strong enough to support its own weight as well as that of the vehicles crossing it. Most modern bridges are built using a combination of concrete and steel for strength and flexibility.

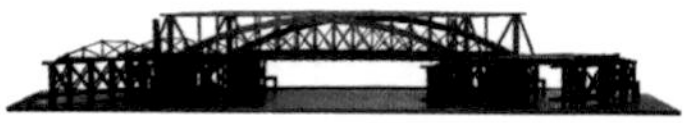

model of an arch bridge

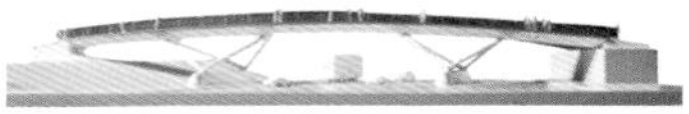

model of a beam bridge

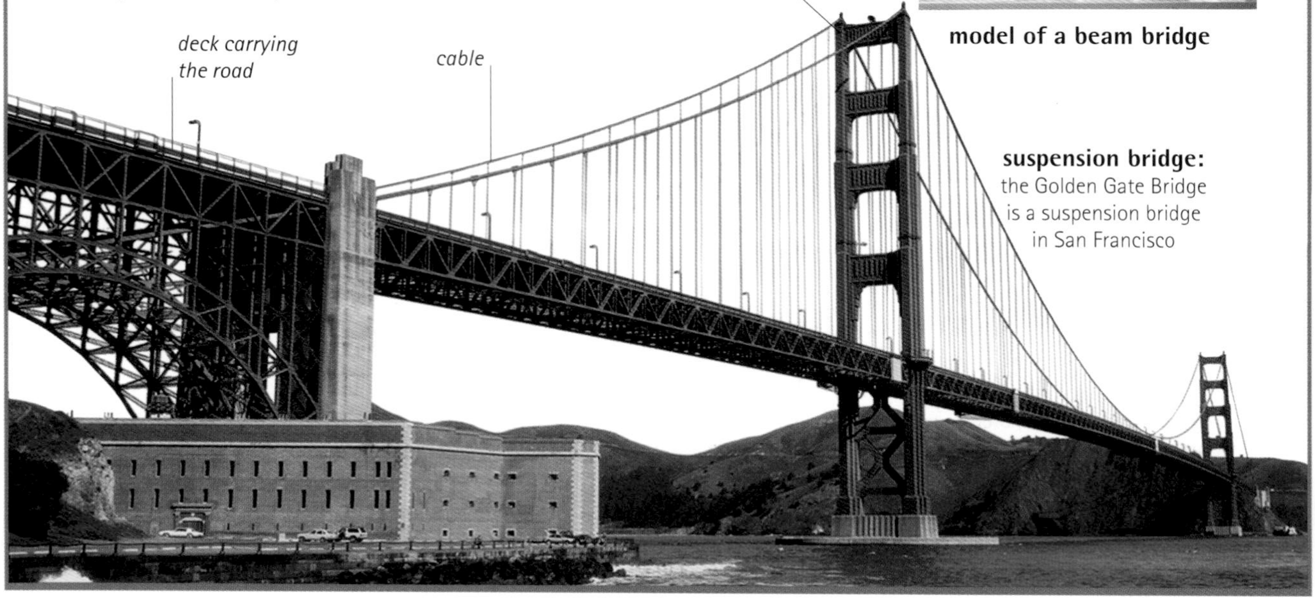
support tower
deck carrying the road
cable

suspension bridge: the Golden Gate Bridge is a suspension bridge in San Francisco

[2]breakfast *vb* **break•fast•ed**; **break•fast•ing**
to eat breakfast

break•neck \ˈbrāk-ˌnek\ *adj*
very fast or dangerous ⟨*breakneck* speed⟩

break•through \ˈbrāk-ˌthrü\ *n*
a sudden advance or successful development ⟨a *breakthrough* in medical research⟩

break•wa•ter \ˈbrāk-ˌwȯ-tər, -ˌwä-\ *n*
an offshore wall to protect a beach or a harbor from the sea

breast \ˈbrest\ *n*
1 either of the two enlarged soft parts on a woman's chest that contain a gland that produces milk when she has a baby
2 the front part of the body between the neck and the stomach ⟨He held the treasure to his *breast*.⟩
3 the front part of a bird's body below the neck
breast•ed \ˈbre-stəd\ *adj*

breast•bone \ˈbrest-ˈbōn\ *n*
a flat narrow bone in the middle of the chest to which the ribs are connected

breast–feed \ˈbrest-ˈfēd\ *vb* **breast–fed** \-ˈfed\; **breast–feed•ing**
to feed (a baby) from a mother's breast

breast•plate \ˈbrest-ˌplāt\ *n*
a piece of armor for covering the breast

breast•work \ˈbrest-ˌwərk\ *n*
a wall thrown together to serve as a defense in battle

breath \ˈbreth\ *n*
1 ability to breathe : ease of breathing ⟨I lost my *breath* for a moment.⟩
2 air taken in or sent out by the lungs ⟨Hold your *breath*.⟩ ⟨It's so cold I can see my *breath*.⟩
3 a slight breeze ⟨a *breath* of wind⟩
out of breath breathing very rapidly as a result of hard exercise
under someone's breath very quietly ⟨speaking *under his breath*⟩

breathe \ˈbrēth\ *vb* **breathed**; **breath•ing**
1 to draw air into and expel it from the lungs
2 to take in by inhaling ⟨*breathed* in the delicious smell⟩
3 [1]LIVE 1
4 [1]SAY 1, UTTER ⟨Don't *breathe* a word of this.⟩

breath•er \ˈbrē-thər\ *n*
a pause for rest

breath•less \ˈbreth-ləs\ *adj*
1 panting from exertion
2 filled with excitement or tension ⟨a *breathless* silence⟩
breath•less•ly *adv*

breath•tak•ing \ˈbreth-ˌtā-kiŋ\ *adj*
very exciting or beautiful

breech•es \ˈbri-chəz\ *n pl*
1 ▼ short pants fastening below the knee
2 PANTS

breeches

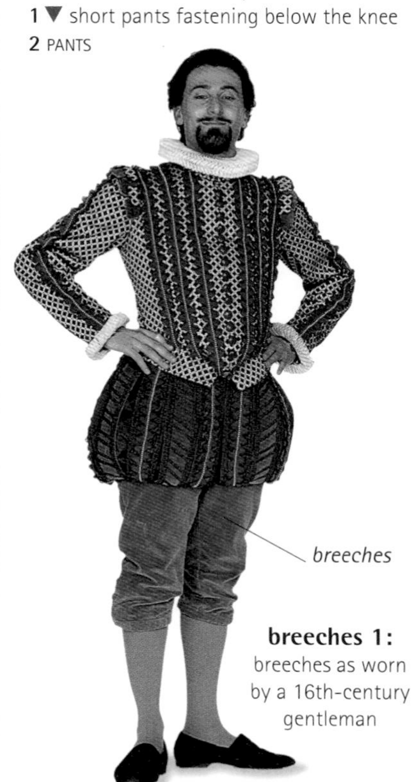

breeches 1: breeches as worn by a 16th-century gentleman

[1]**breed** \'brēd\ *vb* **bred** \'bred\; **breed•ing**
1 to produce or increase (animals or plants) by sexual reproduction 〈Ranchers *breed* cattle for market.〉
2 to produce offspring by sexual reproduction 〈Mosquitoes *breed* in damp areas.〉
3 to bring up : TRAIN 〈I was born and *bred* in this town.〉
4 to bring about : CAUSE 〈Poverty *breeds* despair.〉
breed•er *n*

[2]**breed** *n*
1 a kind of animal or plant that is found only under human care and is different from related kinds 〈a *breed* of long-haired dogs〉
2 [1]CLASS 6, KIND

breed•ing \'brē-diŋ\ *n*
training especially in manners

breeze \'brēz\ *n*
1 a gentle wind
2 something that is easy to do 〈The test was a *breeze*.〉

breezy \'brē-zē\ *adj* **breez•i•er**; **breez•i•est**
1 somewhat windy
2 lively and somewhat carefree 〈a *breezy* reply〉
breez•i•ly \-zə-lē\ *adv*

breth•ren \'breth-rən\ *pl of* BROTHER
Hint: *Brethren* is used chiefly in formal situations.

breve \'brēv, 'brev\ *n*
a mark ˘ placed over a vowel to show that the vowel is short

brev•i•ty \'bre-və-tē\ *n*
the condition of being short or brief 〈The concert's *brevity* disappointed fans.〉

[1]**brew** \'brü\ *vb* **brewed**; **brew•ing**
1 to make (beer) from water, malt, and hops
2 to prepare by soaking in hot water 〈*brew* tea〉
3 [2]PLAN 2 〈He's *brewing* mischief.〉
4 to start to form 〈A storm is *brewing*.〉
brew•er *n*

[2]**brew** *n*
something made by brewing

brew•ery \'brü-ə-rē\ *n, pl* **brew•er•ies**
a place where malt liquors are brewed

bri•ar *also* **bri•er** \'brī-ər\ *n*
a plant (as the rose or blackberry) with a thorny or prickly stem

[1]**bribe** \'brīb\ *n*
something given or promised to a person in order to influence dishonestly a decision or action

[2]**bribe** *vb* **bribed**; **brib•ing**
to influence or try to influence dishonestly by giving or promising something

brib•ery \'brī-bə-rē\ *n, pl* **brib•er•ies**
the act of giving or taking a bribe

[1]**brick** \'brik\ *n*
1 a building or paving material made from clay molded into blocks and baked
2 a block made of brick

[2]**brick** *vb* **bricked**; **brick•ing**
to close, face, or pave with bricks

brick•lay•er \'brik-,lā-ər\ *n*
a person who builds or paves with bricks

brid•al \'brī-dᵊl\ *adj*
of or relating to a bride or a wedding

bride \'brīd\ *n*
a woman just married or about to be married

bride•groom \'brīd-,grüm\ *n*
a man just married or about to be married

brides•maid \'brīdz-,mād\ *n*
a woman who attends a bride at her wedding

[1]**bridge** \'brij\ *n*
1 ◀ a structure built over something (as water, a low place, or a railroad) so people can cross
2 the place on a ship where the ship is steered
3 something that joins or connects : something like a bridge 〈the *bridge* of the nose〉 〈a *bridge* between cultures〉

[2]**bridge** *vb* **bridged**; **bridg•ing**
to make a bridge over or across 〈*bridge* a gap〉

[3]**bridge** *n*
a card game for four players in two teams

[1]**bri•dle** \'brī-dᵊl\ *n*
a device for controlling a horse made up of a set of straps enclosing the head, a bit, and a pair of reins

[2]**bridle** *vb* **bri•dled**; **bri•dling** \'brīd-liŋ, 'brī-dᵊl-iŋ\
1 to put a bridle on 〈*bridle* a horse〉
2 RESTRAIN 2 〈He tried to *bridle* his anger.〉
3 to hold the head high and draw in the chin as an expression of resentment

[1]**brief** \'brēf\ *adj* **brief•er**; **brief•est**
not very long : SHORT 〈a *brief* explanation〉
brief•ly *adv*

[2]**brief** *vb* **briefed**; **brief•ing**
to give information or instructions to 〈The captain *briefed* the crew on the plan.〉

brief•case \'brēf-,kās\ *n*
a flat case for carrying papers or books

briefs \'brēfs\ *n pl*
short snug underpants

brier *variant of* BRIAR

brig \'brig\ *n*
▼ a square-rigged sailing ship with two masts

bri•gade \bri-'gād\ *n*
1 a body of soldiers consisting of two or more regiments
2 a group of persons organized for acting together 〈a fire *brigade*〉

▶ **brig**
A brig was a merchant ship of the 18th and 19th centuries. This model is shown fully rigged with extra "studding" sails to give more power with a light wind blowing from behind.

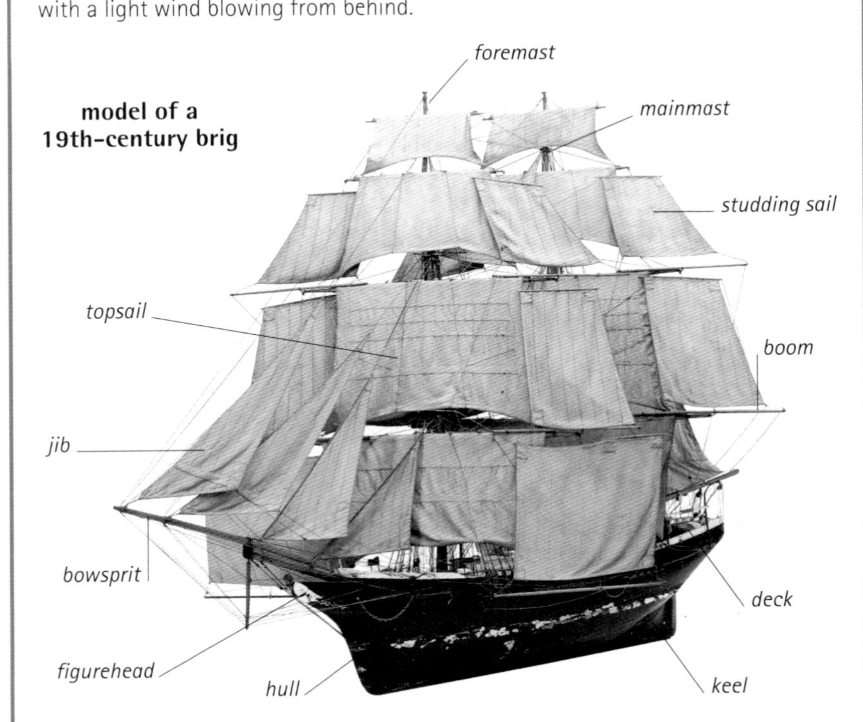

A B C D E F G H I J K L M N O P Q R S T U V W X Y Z

brig•a•dier general \ˌbri-gə-ˈdir-\ *n*
a commissioned officer in the army, air force, or marine corps ranking above a colonel

bright \ˈbrīt\ *adj*
1 giving off or filled with much light ⟨a *bright* fire⟩ ⟨a *bright* room⟩
2 very clear or vivid in color ⟨a *bright* red⟩
3 INTELLIGENT 1, CLEVER ⟨a *bright* child⟩
4 CHEERFUL 1 ⟨a *bright* smile⟩
5 likely to be good ⟨a *bright* future⟩
bright•ly *adv*
bright•ness *n*

► **Synonyms** BRIGHT, RADIANT, and BRILLIANT mean shining or glowing with light. BRIGHT can be used of something that produces or reflects a great amount of light. ⟨*Bright* stars shone overhead.⟩ ⟨A *bright* full moon filled the sky.⟩ RADIANT is more often used of something that sends forth its own light. ⟨The sun is a *radiant* body.⟩ BRILLIANT is used of something that shines with a sparkling or flashing light. ⟨The case was filled with *brilliant* diamonds.⟩

bright•en \ˈbrī-tᵊn\ *vb* **bright•ened**; **bright•en•ing**
1 to add more light to ⟨Candlelight *brightened* the room.⟩
2 to make or become cheerful ⟨You *brightened* my day.⟩

bril•liance \ˈbril-yəns\ *n*
great brightness

bril•liant \ˈbril-yənt\ *adj*
1 flashing with light : very bright ⟨*brilliant* jewels⟩
2 very impressive ⟨a *brilliant* career⟩
3 very smart or clever ⟨a *brilliant* student⟩
synonyms see BRIGHT
bril•liant•ly *adv*

¹brim \ˈbrim\ *n*
1 the edge or rim of something hollow ⟨The cup was filled to the *brim*.⟩
2 ▼ the part of a hat that sticks out around the lower edge

¹brim 2

²brim *vb* **brimmed**; **brim•ming**
to be or become full to overflowing ⟨*brimming* with happiness⟩

brin•dled \ˈbrin-dᵊld\ *adj*
having dark streaks or spots on a gray or brownish background ⟨a *brindled* cow⟩

brine \ˈbrīn\ *n*
1 a mixture of salty water used especially to preserve or season food ⟨pickle *brine*⟩
2 the salty water of the ocean

bring \ˈbriŋ\ *vb* **brought** \ˈbrȯt\; **bring•ing**
1 to cause to come by carrying or leading : take along ⟨Students were told to *bring* lunches.⟩ ⟨*Bring* all your friends!⟩
2 to cause to reach a certain state or take a certain action ⟨*Bring* the water to a boil.⟩ ⟨I couldn't *bring* myself to say it.⟩
3 to cause to arrive or exist ⟨Their cries *brought* help.⟩ ⟨The storm *brought* snow and ice.⟩
4 to sell for ⟨The house *brought* a high price.⟩
bring•er *n*
bring about to cause to happen
bring back to cause to return to a person's memory ⟨Seeing him *brought* it all *back* to me.⟩
bring forth to cause to happen or exist ⟨Her statement *brought forth* protest.⟩
bring on to cause to happen to ⟨You've *brought* these problems *on* yourself.⟩
bring out
1 to produce and make available ⟨The manufacturer *brought out* a new model.⟩
2 to cause to appear ⟨His friends *bring out* the best in him.⟩
bring to to bring back from unconsciousness
bring up
1 to bring to maturity through care and education ⟨*bring up* a child⟩
2 to mention when talking ⟨*bring up* a subject⟩

brink \ˈbriŋk\ *n*
1 the edge at the top of a steep place
2 a point of beginning ⟨on the *brink* of disaster⟩

briny \ˈbrī-nē\ *adj* **brin•i•er**; **brin•i•est**
SALTY

brisk \ˈbrisk\ *adj*
1 done or spoken with quickness and energy ⟨a *brisk* walk⟩
2 quick and efficient ⟨a *brisk* voice⟩
3 very refreshing ⟨*brisk* fall weather⟩
brisk•ly *adv*

¹bris•tle \ˈbri-səl\ *n*
1 a short stiff hair ⟨a hog's *bristle*⟩
2 ▼ a stiff hair or something like a hair fastened in a brush

²bristle *vb* **bris•tled**; **bris•tling**
1 to rise up and stiffen like bristles ⟨Her evil laugh makes your hair *bristle*.⟩

¹bristle 2

2 to show signs of anger ⟨She *bristled* at the insult.⟩
3 to be covered with ⟨He wore a costume *bristling* with feathers.⟩

bris•tly \ˈbris-lē\ *adj* **bris•tli•er**; **bris•tli•est**
of, like, or having many bristles ⟨*bristly* whiskers⟩

Brit. *abbr*
1 Britain
2 British

britch•es \ˈbri-chəz\ *n pl*
1 BREECHES 1
2 PANTS

¹Brit•ish \ˈbri-tish\ *adj*
of or relating to Great Britain (England, Scotland, and Wales) or the British

²British *n pl*
the people of Great Britain

brit•tle \ˈbri-tᵊl\ *adj* **brit•tler**; **brit•tlest**
hard but easily broken ⟨*brittle* glass⟩
brit•tle•ness *n*

► **Synonyms** BRITTLE, CRISP, and FRAGILE mean easily broken. BRITTLE is used of something that is hard and dry. ⟨*Brittle* twigs snapped under our feet.⟩ CRISP is used of something hard and dry but also fresh. ⟨These crackers are no longer *crisp*.⟩ FRAGILE is used of anything so delicate that it may be broken easily. ⟨He held a piece of *fragile* china.⟩

bro *abbr* brother

broach \ˈbrōch\ *vb* **broached**; **broach•ing**
to bring up as a subject for discussion ⟨She *broached* an idea.⟩

broad \ˈbrȯd\ *adj* **broad•er**; **broad•est**
1 not narrow : WIDE ⟨a *broad* stripe⟩
2 extending far and wide : SPACIOUS ⟨*broad* prairies⟩
3 ¹COMPLETE 1, FULL ⟨*broad* daylight⟩
4 not limited ⟨a *broad* variety⟩
5 covering only the main points : GENERAL ⟨The inspector gave a *broad* outline of the problem.⟩
broad•ly *adv*

broad•band \'brȯd-,band\ *n*
a high-speed electronic network that carries more than one type of communication (as Internet and cable television signals)

[1]broad•cast \'brȯd-,kast\ *vb* **broadcast; broad•cast•ing**
1 to send out by radio or television from a transmitting station ⟨The speech will be *broadcast.*⟩
2 to make widely known ⟨It's a secret, so don't *broadcast* it.⟩
3 to scatter far and wide ⟨The farm workers *broadcast* seed by hand.⟩
broad•cast•er *n*

[2]broadcast *n*
1 an act of broadcasting
2 a radio or television program

broad•cloth \'brȯd-,klȯth\ *n*
a fine cloth with a firm smooth surface

broad•en \'brȯ-dᵊn\ *vb* **broad•ened; broad•en•ing**
to make or become wide or wider

broad–mind•ed \'brȯd-'mīn-dəd\ *adj*
willing to consider unusual or different opinions, beliefs, and practices

[1]broad•side \'brȯd-,sīd\ *n*
a firing of all of the guns that are on the same side of a ship

[2]broadside *adv*
1 with one side forward ⟨turned *broadside*⟩
2 from the side ⟨I hit the other car *broadside.*⟩

broad•sword \'brȯd-,sȯrd\ *n*
a sword having a broad blade

bro•cade \brō-'kād\ *n*
► a cloth with a raised design woven into it
bro•cad•ed *adj*

broc•co•li \'brä-kə-lē, 'brä-klē\ *n*
▼ a vegetable that has green stalks and green or purplish clustered flower buds

broccoli

brogue \'brōg\ *n*
an Irish or Scottish accent

broil \'brȯil\ *vb* **broiled; broil•ing**
1 to cook or be cooked directly over or under a heat source
2 to make or feel extremely hot ⟨Players were *broiling* in the bright sun.⟩

broil•er \'brȯi-lər\ *n*
a young chicken suitable for broiling

[1]broke *past of* BREAK

[2]broke \'brōk\ *adj*
having no money

[1]broken *past participle of* BREAK

brocade

[2]bro•ken \'brō-kən\ *adj*
1 separated into parts or pieces ⟨*broken* glass⟩ ⟨a *broken* bone⟩
2 not working properly ⟨a *broken* camera⟩
3 having gaps or breaks ⟨a *broken* line⟩
4 not kept or followed ⟨a *broken* promise⟩
5 imperfectly spoken ⟨*broken* English⟩

bro•ken•heart•ed \,brō-kən-'här-təd\ *adj*
very sad

bro•ker \'brō-kər\ *n*
a person who acts as an agent for others in the buying or selling of property

bro•mine \'brō-,mēn\ *n*
a chemical element that is a deep red liquid giving off an irritating smelly vapor

bron•chi•al \'bräŋ-kē-əl\ *adj*
of or relating to either of the two branches (**bronchial tubes**) of the trachea that carry air into the lungs

bron•chi•tis \brän-'kī-təs\ *n*
a sore raw state of the bronchial tubes

bron•co \'bräŋ-kō\ *n, pl* **bron•cos**
MUSTANG

bron•to•sau•rus \,brän-tə-'sȯr-əs\ *n*
a huge plant-eating dinosaur with a long neck and tail and four thick legs

[1]bronze \'bränz\ *n*
1 ► an alloy of copper and tin and sometimes other elements
2 a yellowish brown color
3 a medal made of bronze given to the third place winner in a competition

[2]bronze *adj*
1 made of bronze
2 having a yellowish brown color

[1]bronze 1: hand mirror in bronze

brooch \'brōch, 'brüch\ *n*
a piece of jewelry fastened to clothing with a pin

[1]brood \'brüd\ *vb* **brood•ed; brood•ing**
1 to sit on eggs to hatch them
2 to cover (young) with the wings for warmth and protection
3 to think long and anxiously about something ⟨She *brooded* over her mistake.⟩

[2]brood *n*
1 ▼ the young of birds hatched at the same time ⟨a *brood* of chicks⟩
2 a group of young children or animals having the same mother

[2]brood 1

brood•er \'brü-dər\ *n*
a building or a compartment that can be heated and is used for raising young fowl

brook \'brük\ *n*
a small stream

broom \'brüm, 'brům\ *n*
1 ► a brush with a long handle used for sweeping
2 a plant with long slender branches along which grow many yellow flowers

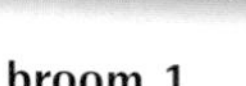
broom 1

broom•stick \'brüm-,stik, 'brům-\ *n*
the handle of a broom

bros *abbr* brothers

broth \'bròth\ *n*
the liquid in which a meat, fish, or vegetable has been cooked

broth•er \'brə-thər\ *n, pl* **brothers** *also* **breth•ren** \'breth-rən\
1 a male person or animal related to another person or animal by having one or both parents in common
2 a fellow member of an organization

broth•er•hood \'brə-thər-,hůd\ *n*
1 the state of being a brother
2 a group of people who are engaged in the same business or have a similar interest
3 feelings of friendship, support, and understanding between people

broth•er–in–law \'brə-thər-ən-,lò\ *n, pl* **broth•ers–in–law**
1 the brother of a person's husband or wife
2 the husband of a person's sister

broth•er•ly \'brə-thər-lē\ *adj*
1 of or relating to brothers
2 [2]KIND 1, AFFECTIONATE

brought *past and past participle of* BRING

brow \'braů\ *n*
1 EYEBROW
2 FOREHEAD
3 the upper edge of a steep slope

[1]**brown** \'braůn\ *adj*
1 of the color of coffee : colored brown
2 having a dark or tanned complexion

[2]**brown** *n*
a color like that of coffee or chocolate
brown•ish \'braů-nish\ *adj*

[3]**brown** *vb* **browned**; **brown•ing**
to make or become brown ⟨Her skin was *browned* by the sun.⟩

brown•ie \'braů-nē\ *n*
1 a small square piece of chewy chocolate cake
2 *cap* a member of a program of the Girl Scouts for girls in the first through third grades in school
3 a cheerful elf believed to perform helpful services at night

brown sugar *n*
▼ sugar that contains molasses

brown sugar

browse \'braůz\ *vb* **browsed**; **brows•ing**
1 to read or look in a casual way ⟨We went in the shop to *browse*.⟩
2 to nibble young shoots and foliage ⟨*browsing* deer⟩

brows•er \'braů-zər\ *n*
1 a person or animal that browses
2 a computer program providing access to sites on the World Wide Web

bru•in \'brü-ən\ *n*
[1]BEAR 1

[1]**bruise** \'brüz\ *vb* **bruised**; **bruis•ing**
to injure the flesh (as by a blow) without breaking the skin

[2]**bruise** *n*
a black-and-blue spot on the body or a dark spot on fruit caused by an injury or damage

brunch \'brənch\ *n*
a meal that combines breakfast and lunch and is usually eaten in late morning

bru•net *or* **bru•nette** \brü-'net\ *adj*
having dark brown or black hair and dark eyes
Hint: The word is usually spelled *brunet* when used of a boy or man and *brunette* when used of a girl or woman.
brunet *or* **brunette** *n*

brunt \'brənt\ *n*
the main force or stress (as of an attack) ⟨The coast received the *brunt* of the storm.⟩

[1]**brush** \'brəsh\ *n*
1 a tool made of bristles set in a handle and used for cleaning, smoothing, or painting
2 an act of smoothing or scrubbing with a brush
3 a light stroke ⟨a *brush* of the hand⟩
4 a bushy tail

[2]**brush** *vb* **brushed**; **brush•ing**
1 to scrub or smooth with a brush ⟨*Brush* your hair.⟩
2 to remove with or as if with a brush ⟨I *brushed* up the dirt.⟩
3 to pass lightly across ⟨A twig *brushed* my cheek.⟩

[3]**brush** *n*
1 branches and twigs cut from trees
2 a heavy growth of small trees and bushes

[4]**brush** *n*
a brief fight or quarrel

brush•wood \'brəsh-,wůd\ *n*
[3]BRUSH

brusque \'brəsk\ *adj*
so abrupt and frank in manner or speech as to be impolite ⟨a *brusque* doctor⟩ ⟨a *brusque* reply⟩
brusque•ly *adj*
brusque•ness *n*

brus•sels sprouts \,brə-səlz-\ *n pl*
▼ *often cap B* small leafy heads resembling tiny cabbages and eaten as a vegetable

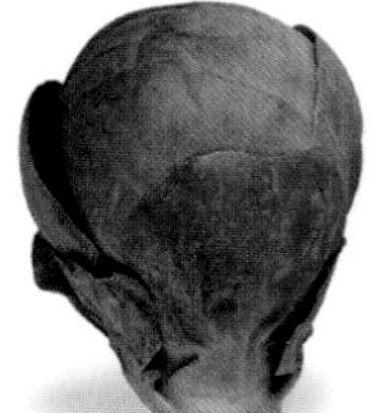

brussels sprouts

bru•tal \'brü-tᵊl\ *adj*
cruel and harsh ⟨*brutal* treatment⟩
bru•tal•ly *adv*

bru•tal•i•ty \brü-'ta-lə-tē\ *n, pl* **bru•tal•i•ties**
1 the quality of being cruel and harsh
2 a cruel and harsh act or course of action ⟨the *brutalities* of prison⟩

[1]**brute** \'brüt\ *adj*
typical of beasts : like that of a beast ⟨We used *brute* force to open the door.⟩

[2]**brute** *n*
1 a four-footed animal especially when wild
2 a cruel or rough person

brut•ish \'brü-tish\ *adj*
being unfeeling and stupid

BSA *abbr* Boy Scouts of America

BTW *abbr* by the way

bu. *abbr* bushel

[1]**bub•ble** \'bə-bəl\ *n*
1 a tiny round body of air or gas in a liquid ⟨*bubbles* in boiling water⟩
2 a round body of air within a solid ⟨a *bubble* in glass⟩
3 a thin film of liquid filled with air or gas ⟨soap *bubbles*⟩
bub•bly \'bə-blē\ *adj*

[2]bubble *vb* **bub•bled; bub•bling**
1 to form or produce bubbles
2 to flow with a gurgle ⟨The brook *bubbles* over rocks.⟩

bu•bon•ic plague \bü-ˈbä-nik, byü-\ *n*
a dangerous disease which is spread by rats and in which fever, weakness, and swollen lymph nodes are present

buc•ca•neer \ˌbə-kə-ˈnir\ *n*
PIRATE

[1]buck \ˈbək\ *n*
1 the male of an animal (as a deer or rabbit) the female of which is called *doe*
2 DOLLAR ⟨The cost is ten *bucks.*⟩
3 [1]MAN 1, FELLOW

► **Word History** The word *buck* in the sense "dollar" was originally short for *buckskin,* in other words, the skin of a male deer. In colonial America, especially in the southeastern colonies, American Indians hunted deer and prepared their hides to trade for European goods. "Bucks," or buckskins, became a means of calculating the value of goods, and the word was transferred to the dollar when the deerskin trade came to an end.

[2]buck *vb* **bucked; buck•ing**
1 to spring or jump upward with head down and back arched ⟨When he heard the explosion, the horse *bucked.*⟩
2 to charge or push against ⟨Our boat was *bucking* the waves.⟩
3 to go against **:** OPPOSE ⟨We decided to *buck* the trend and wear ties.⟩
buck up to become more confident

buck•board \ˈbək-ˌbȯrd\ *n*
a lightweight carriage with four wheels that has a seat supported by a springy platform

buck•et \ˈbə-kət\ *n*
1 a usually round container with a handle for holding or carrying liquids or solids
2 a large container that is part of a machine and is used for collecting, scooping, or carrying
3 BUCKETFUL

buck•et•ful \ˈbə-kət-ˌfu̇l\ *n,* *pl* **buck•et•fuls** \-ˌfu̇lz\ *or* **buck•ets•ful** \ˈbə-kəts-ˌfu̇l\
1 as much as a bucket will hold
2 a large quantity ⟨He won a *bucketful* of money.⟩

buck•eye \ˈbək-ˌī\ *n*
► a tree with showy clusters of flowers and large brown inedible nutlike seeds

[1]buck•le \ˈbə-kəl\ *n*
a fastening device which is attached to one end of a belt or strap and through which the other end is passed and held

[2]buckle *vb* **buck•led; buck•ling**
1 to fasten with a buckle
2 to bend, crumple, or give way ⟨The pavement *buckled* in the heat.⟩
buckle down to start to work hard
buckle up to fasten your seatbelt

buck•skin \ˈbək-ˌskin\ *n*
► a soft flexible leather usually having a suede finish

buck•wheat \ˈbək-ˌhwēt, -ˌwēt\ *n*
a plant with pinkish white flowers that is grown for its dark triangular seeds which are used as a cereal grain

[1]bud \ˈbəd\ *n*
1 a small growth at the tip or on the side of a stem that later develops into a flower, leaf, or branch
2 a flower that has not fully opened
3 an early stage of development ⟨Let's nip this problem in the *bud.*⟩

[2]bud *vb* **bud•ded; bud•ding**
1 to form or put forth a small growth that develops into a flower, leaf, or branch ⟨The trees *budded* early this spring.⟩
2 to reproduce by asexual means by forming a small growth that pinches off and develops into a new organism ⟨a *budding* yeast cell⟩

buckeye: a flower cluster from a buckeye

buckskin: a buckskin jacket of the Algonquin people

Bud•dha \ˈbü-də, ˈbu̇-\ *n*
1 the founder of Buddhism originally known as Siddhartha Gautama
2 a statue that represents Buddha

Bud•dhism \ˈbü-ˌdi-zəm, ˈbu̇-\ *n*
a religion of eastern and central Asia based on the teachings of Gautama Buddha
Bud•dhist \ˈbü-dəst, ˈbu̇d-\ *n*

bud•dy \ˈbə-dē\ *n, pl* **buddies**
a close friend

budge \ˈbəj\ *vb* **budged; budg•ing**
1 to move or cause to move especially slightly
2 to give in ⟨He wouldn't *budge* in his decision.⟩

[1]bud•get \ˈbə-jət\ *n*
1 a statement of estimated income and expenses for a period of time
2 a plan for using money

[2]budget *vb* **bud•get•ed; bud•get•ing**
1 to include in a plan for using money ⟨It's important to *budget* money for food.⟩
2 to plan for efficient use ⟨*Budget* your time wisely.⟩

[1]buff \ˈbəf\ *n*
1 a pale orange yellow
2 a stick or wheel with a soft surface for applying polish
3 [3]FAN

[2]buff *vb* **buffed; buff•ing**
to polish with or as if with a buff

buf•fa•lo \ˈbə-fə-ˌlō\ *n, pl* **buffalo** *or* **buf•fa•loes**
any of several wild oxen and especially the American bison

buffalo wing *n*
a deep-fried chicken wing coated with a spicy sauce and usually served with blue cheese dressing

A B C D E F G H I J K L M N O P Q R S T U V W X Y Z

[1]buf•fet \'bə-fət\ *vb* **buf•fet•ed**; **buf•fet•ing**
to pound repeatedly : BATTER ⟨Waves *buffeted* our little boat.⟩

[2]buf•fet \ˌbə-'fā, bü-\ *n*
1 a cabinet or set of shelves for the display of dishes and silver : SIDEBOARD
2 a meal set out on a buffet or table from which people may serve themselves

buf•foon \bə-'fün\ *n*
a foolish or stupid person

[1]bug \'bəg\ *n*
1 any of a large group of insects that have four wings, suck liquid food (as plant juices or blood), and have young which resemble the adults but lack wings
2 an insect or other small creeping or crawling animal
3 FLAW ⟨a *bug* in the computer system⟩

[2]bug *vb* **bugged**; **bug•ging**
1 [1]BOTHER 1, ANNOY
2 to stick out — often used with *out*

bug•gy \'bə-gē\ *n*, *pl* **buggies**
▼ a light carriage that is usually drawn by one horse

bu•gle \'byü-gəl\ *n*
an instrument like a simple trumpet used chiefly for giving military signals

[1]build \'bild\ *vb* **built** \'bilt\; **build•ing**
1 to make by putting together parts or materials
2 to produce or create gradually by effort ⟨It takes time to *build* a winning team.⟩
3 to grow or increase to a high point or level ⟨Excitement was *building*.⟩

▶ **Synonyms** BUILD, CONSTRUCT, and ERECT mean to make a structure. BUILD is used for putting together several parts or materials to form something. ⟨Workers are *building* the house.⟩ CONSTRUCT is used for the designing of something and the process of fitting its parts together. ⟨Engineers *constructed* a system of dams across the river.⟩ ERECT is used for the idea of building something that stands up. ⟨The tower was *erected* many years ago.⟩

[2]build *n*
the shape and size of a person's or animal's body

build•er \'bil-dər\ *n*
a person whose business is the construction of buildings

build•ing \'bil-diŋ\ *n*
1 ▶ a permanent structure built as a dwelling, shelter, or place for human activities or for storage ⟨an office *building*⟩
2 the art, work, or business of assembling materials into a structure

built–in \'bil-'tin\ *adj*
forming a permanent part of a structure ⟨*built-in* bookcases⟩

bulb \'bəlb\ *n*
1 LIGHT BULB
2 a dormant stage of a plant that is formed underground and consists of a very short stem with one or more flower buds surrounded by special thick leaves
3 a plant structure (as a tuber) that is somewhat like a bulb
4 a rounded object or part ⟨the *bulb* of a thermometer⟩

buggy

bul•bous \'bəl-bəs\ *adj*
round or swollen ⟨a *bulbous* nose⟩

[1]bulge \'bəlj\ *vb* **bulged**; **bulg•ing**
to swell or curve outward ⟨Muscles *bulged* from his shirt.⟩

building 1:
the Empire State Building in New York City

[2]bulge *n*
a swelling part : a part that sticks out

bulk \'bəlk\ *n*
1 greatness of size or volume ⟨The chair is hard to move because of its *bulk*.⟩
2 the largest or chief part ⟨I've already finished the *bulk* of my homework.⟩
in bulk in large amounts ⟨The restaurant buys rice *in bulk*.⟩

bulk•head \'bəlk-ˌhed\ *n*
a wall separating sections in a ship

bulky \'bəl-kē\ *adj* **bulk•i•er**; **bulk•i•est**
1 great in size or volume
2 being large and awkward to handle

bull \'bu̇l\ *n*
an adult male ox or an adult male of certain other large animals (as the elephant and the whale)

bull•dog \'bu̇l-ˌdȯg\ *n*
a dog of English origin with short hair and a stocky powerful build

bull•doz•er \'bu̇l-ˌdō-zər\ *n*
▶ a motor vehicle with tracks instead of tires and a large wide blade for pushing (as in clearing land of trees)

bul•let \'bu̇-lət\ *n*
► a small piece of metal made to be shot from a firearm

bullet

bul•le•tin \'bu̇-lə-tən\ *n*
a short public notice usually coming from an informed or official source

bulletin board *n*
a board for posting bulletins and announcements

bul•let•proof \'bu̇-lət-,prüf\ *adj*
impenetrable to bullets

bull•fight \'bu̇l-,fīt\ *n*
a public entertainment popular especially in Spain in which a person (**bull•fight•er**) displays skill in escaping the charges of a bull and usually kills it with a sword

bull•finch \'bu̇l-,finch\ *n*
► a European songbird that has a thick bill and a red breast

bull•frog \'bu̇l-,frȯg, -,fräg\ *n*
a large heavy deep-voiced frog

bull•head \'bu̇l-,hed\ *n*
any of various fishes with large heads

bul•lion \'bu̇l-yən\ *n*
gold or silver metal in bars or blocks

bull•ock \'bu̇-lək\ *n*
1 a young bull
2 [2]STEER

bull's–eye \'bu̇lz-,ī\ *n*
1 the center of a target
2 a shot that hits the center of a target

[1]bul•ly \'bu̇-lē\ *n, pl* **bul•lies**
someone who is cruel, insulting, or threatening to another and often to one who is smaller, weaker, or in some way vulnerable

[2]bully *vb* **bul•lied**; **bul•ly•ing**
to be cruel, insulting, or threatening to another and often to one who is smaller, weaker, or in some way vulnerable

bul•rush \'bu̇l-,rəsh\ *n*
any of several large rushes or sedges that grow in wet places

bul•wark \'bu̇l-wərk\ *n*
1 a solid structure like a wall built for defense against an enemy
2 something that defends or protects

[1]bum \'bəm\ *n*
1 a person who avoids work
2 [2]TRAMP 1, HOBO

[2]bum *vb* **bummed**; **bum•ming**
to obtain by asking or begging ⟨Can I *bum* a dollar from you?⟩

bum•ble \'bəm-bəl\ *vb* **bum•bled**; **bum•bling**
to act, move, or speak in a clumsy way

bum•ble•bee \'bəm-bəl-,bē\ *n*
a large hairy bee that makes a loud humming sound

[1]bump \'bəmp\ *n*
1 a rounded swelling of flesh as from an injury
2 a small raised area on a surface
3 a sudden heavy impact or jolt

bullfinch

[2]bump *vb* **bumped**; **bump•ing**
1 to strike or knock against something ⟨Open your eyes before you *bump* into something.⟩
2 to move along unevenly : JOLT

bulldozer

[1]bump•er \'bəm-pər\ *n*
a bar across the front or back of a motor vehicle intended to lessen shock or damage from collision

[2]bum•per \'bəm-pər\ *adj*
larger or finer than usual ⟨a *bumper* crop of corn⟩

bumpy \'bəm-pē\ *adj* **bump•i•er**; **bump•i•est**
1 having or covered with bumps ⟨a *bumpy* road⟩ ⟨*bumpy* skin⟩
2 having sudden up-and-down movements ⟨a *bumpy* ride⟩

bun \'bən\ *n*
a sweet or plain round roll

[1]bunch \'bənch\ *n*
1 a number of things of the same kind growing together ⟨a *bunch* of grapes⟩
2 [1]GROUP 1 ⟨a *bunch* of children⟩

[2]bunch *vb* **bunched**; **bunch•ing**
to gather in a bunch

[1]bun•dle \'bən-dᵊl\ *n*
► a number of things fastened, wrapped, or gathered closely together

[1]bundle: a bundle of cinnamon sticks

[2]bundle *vb* **bun•dled**; **bun•dling**
1 to fasten, tie, or wrap a group of things together
2 to move or push into or out of a place quickly ⟨We were immediately *bundled* off the plane.⟩
bundle up to dress warmly

bung \'bəŋ\ *n*
a stopper that closes or covers a hole in a barrel

bun•ga•low \'bəŋ-gə-,lō\ *n*
a house with a main level and a smaller second level above

bun•gle \'bəŋ-gəl\ *vb* **bun•gled**; **bun•gling**
to act, do, make, or work badly ⟨*bungled* the job⟩
bun•gler *n*

bun•ion \'bən-yən\ *n*
a sore reddened swelling of the first joint of a big toe

[1]bunk \'bəŋk\ *n*
1 BUNK BED
2 a built-in bed (as on a ship or train)
3 a sleeping place

[2]bunk *vb* **bunked**; **bunk•ing**
to stay overnight

A B C D E F G H I J K L M N O P Q R S T U V W X Y Z

bunk bed *n*
one of two single beds usually placed one above the other

bun•ny \'bə-nē\ *n, pl* **bunnies**
RABBIT

bunt \'bənt\ *vb* **bunt•ed**; **bunt•ing**
to hit a baseball lightly so that the ball rolls for a short distance
bunt *n*

[1]**bun•ting** \'bən-tiŋ\ *n*
► a bird similar to a sparrow in size and habits but having a stout bill

[1]**bunting:** an indigo bunting

[2]**bunting** *n*
flags or decorations made of a thin cloth

[1]**buoy** \'bü-ē, 'bȯi\ *n*
1 a floating object anchored in a body of water to mark a channel or to warn of danger
2 LIFE BUOY

[2]**buoy** *vb* **buoyed**; **buoy•ing**
1 to keep from sinking : keep afloat
2 to brighten the mood of ⟨*buoyed* by the hope of success⟩

buoy•an•cy \'bȯi-ən-sē, 'bü-yən-\ *n*
1 the power of rising and floating (as on water or in air) ⟨Cork has *buoyancy* in water.⟩
2 the power of a liquid to hold up a floating body ⟨Seawater has *buoyancy.*⟩

buoy•ant \'bȯi-ənt, 'bü-yənt\ *adj*
1 able to rise and float in the air or on the top of a liquid ⟨*buoyant* cork⟩
2 able to keep a body afloat
3 LIGHTHEARTED, CHEERFUL

bur *or* **burr** \'bər\ *n*
a rough or prickly covering or shell of a seed or fruit

[1]**bur•den** \'bər-d[ə]n\ *n*
1 something carried : LOAD
2 something that is hard to endure ⟨a heavy *burden* of sorrow⟩
3 the capacity of a ship for carrying cargo

[2]**burden** *vb* **bur•dened**; **bur•den•ing**
1 to have a heavy load or put a heavy load on
2 to cause to have to deal with ⟨He is *burdened* with responsibilities.⟩

bur•den•some \'bər-d[ə]n-səm\ *adj*
so heavy or hard to take as to be a burden

bur•dock \'bər-,däk\ *n*
a tall weed related to the thistles that has prickly purplish heads of flowers

bu•reau \'byu̇r-ō\ *n*
1 a low chest of drawers for use in a bedroom
2 a division of a government department ⟨the Federal *Bureau* of Investigation⟩
3 a business office that provides services ⟨a travel *bureau*⟩

► **Word History** A chest of drawers and an office, which are two of the meanings of the word *bureau,* do not seem to have much of a connection. In French, from which we have borrowed the word, *bureau* originally referred to a piece of rough cloth used to protect the surface of a desk. But its meaning expanded so that it could also refer to the desk itself, and to the room containing the desk, that is, an office. On some bureaus with lots of drawers the writing surface could be raised and closed to form a slanting top. In the United States a chest of drawers without any writing surface came to be called a *bureau.*

bur•ger \'bər-gər\ *n*
1 HAMBURGER 1
2 a sandwich like a hamburger ⟨a turkey *burger*⟩

bur•glar \'bər-glər\ *n*
a person who commits burglary

bur•glary \'bər-glə-rē\ *n, pl* **bur•glar•ies**
the act of breaking into a building especially at night with the intent to commit a crime (as theft)

buri•al \'ber-ē-əl\ *n*
the act of placing a dead body in a grave or tomb

bur•lap \'bər-,lap\ *n*
a rough cloth made usually from jute or hemp and used mostly for bags

bur•ly \'bər-lē\ *adj* **bur•li•er**; **bur•li•est**
strongly and heavily built ⟨a *burly* truck driver⟩

[1]**burn** \'bərn\ *vb* **burned** \'bərnd\ *or* **burnt** \'bərnt\; **burn•ing**
1 to be on fire or to set on fire ⟨a candle *burning*⟩
2 to destroy or be destroyed by fire or heat ⟨The building *burned* to the ground.⟩
3 to make or produce by fire or heat ⟨Sparks *burned* a hole in my shirt.⟩
4 to give light ⟨lanterns *burning*⟩
5 to injure or affect by or as if by fire or heat ⟨I *burned* my finger.⟩ ⟨The hot peppers *burned* my throat.⟩
6 to ruin by cooking too long or with too much heat
7 to feel or cause to feel as if on fire ⟨*burning* with fever⟩
8 to feel a strong emotion ⟨*burn* with anger⟩
9 to record music or data on a computer disk ⟨*burn* a CD⟩
10 to get a sunburn

[2]**burn** *n*
an injury produced by burning or by something rubbing away the skin ⟨a rope *burn*⟩

burn•er \'bər-nər\ *n*
the part of a stove or furnace where the flame or heat is produced

bur•nish \'bər-nish\ *vb* **bur•nished**; **bur•nish•ing**
to make shiny

[1]**burp** \'bərp\ *vb* **burped**; **burp•ing**
1 [1]BELCH 1
2 to help (a baby) let out gas from the stomach especially by patting or rubbing the baby's back

[2]**burp** *n*
[2]BELCH

burr *variant of* BUR

bur•ro \'bər-ō\ *n, pl* **burros**
a small donkey often used to carry loads

[1]**bur•row** \'bər-ō\ *n*
► a hole in the ground made by an animal (as a rabbit or fox) for shelter or protection

[2]**burrow** *vb* **bur•rowed**; **bur•row•ing**
1 to hide in or as if in a burrow
2 to make a burrow
3 to proceed by or as if by digging ⟨He *burrowed* through his suitcase.⟩

[1]**burst** \'bərst\ *vb* **burst**; **burst•ing**
1 to break open or in pieces (as by an explosion from within) ⟨bombs *bursting* in air⟩ ⟨buds *bursting* open⟩
2 to suddenly show emotion ⟨He *burst* into tears.⟩
3 to come or go suddenly ⟨He *burst* into the room.⟩
4 to be filled to the maximum ⟨The puppy is *bursting* with energy.⟩

[2]**burst** *n*
a sudden release or effort ⟨a *burst* of laughter⟩ ⟨a *burst* of energy⟩

bury \'ber-ē\ *vb* **bur•ied**; **bury•ing**
1 to place in the ground and cover over for concealment ⟨The pirates *buried* their treasure.⟩
2 to put (a dead body) in a grave or tomb
3 to cover with something ⟨The snowstorm *buried* my car.⟩
4 to cover up : HIDE ⟨I was so ashamed that I *buried* my face in my hands.⟩

bus \'bəs\ *n, pl* **bus•es** *or* **bus•ses**
a large motor vehicle for carrying passengers

[1]burrow
A burrow protects animals against predators and against extremes of weather. In a burrow dug by moles, as shown here, different tunnels provide access to the surface or to the breeding nest beneath the molehill. They may also be used for food storage.

model of a mole's burrow

bus•boy \'bəs-,bȯi\ *n*
a person hired by a restaurant to clear and set tables

bush \'bu̇sh\ *n*
1 a usually low shrub with many branches
2 a stretch of uncleared or lightly settled country

bush•el \'bu̇-shəl\ *n*
a unit of measure (as of grain, produce, or seafood) equal to four pecks or 32 quarts (about 35 liters)

bushy \'bu̇-shē\ *adj* **bush•i•er**; **bush•i•est**
1 being thick and spreading ⟨a *bushy* beard⟩ ⟨a *bushy* tail⟩
2 overgrown with bushes ⟨a *bushy* yard⟩

busi•ness \'biz-nəs\ *n*
1 the activity of making, buying, and selling goods or services ⟨We're open for *business.*⟩
2 a commercial enterprise ⟨She's starting a new *business.*⟩
3 the normal activity of a person or group ⟨Learning is the *business* of a student.⟩
4 personal concerns ⟨It's none of your *business.*⟩
5 [1]MATTER 1 ⟨Cleaning up the mess was an unpleasant *business.*⟩

busi•ness•man \'biz-nəs-,man\ *n*, *pl* **busi•ness•men** \-,men\
a man in business especially as an owner or a manager

busi•ness•wom•an \'biz-nəs-,wu̇-mən\ *n*, *pl* **busi•ness•wom•en** \-,wi-mən\
a woman in business especially as an owner or a manager

[1]bust \'bəst\ *n*
1 a piece of sculpture representing the upper part of the human figure including the head and neck
2 a woman's bosom

[2]bust *vb* **bust•ed**; **bust•ing**
1 to hit with the fist
2 [1]BREAK 1

[1]bus•tle \'bə-səl\ *vb* **bus•tled**; **bus•tling**
to move about in a busy or noisy way

[2]bustle *n*
busy or noisy activity

[1]busy \'bi-zē\ *adj* **busi•er**; **busi•est**
1 actively at work
2 being used ⟨I tried to call, but the line was *busy.*⟩
3 full of activity ⟨a *busy* day⟩
busi•ly \'bi-zə-lē\ *adv*

[2]busy *vb* **bus•ied**; **busy•ing**
to make busy ⟨I *busied* myself with chores.⟩

busy•body \'bi-zē-,bä-dē\ *n*, *pl* **busy•bod•ies**
a person who is too interested in the affairs of other people

[1]but \bət\ *conj*
1 yet nevertheless ⟨She fell *but* wasn't hurt.⟩
2 while just the opposite ⟨I ski *but* you don't.⟩
3 except that : UNLESS ⟨It never rains *but* it pours.⟩

[2]but *prep*
other than : EXCEPT ⟨everyone *but* you⟩

[3]but *adv*
[2]ONLY 1 ⟨We have *but* one choice.⟩

[1]butch•er \'bu̇-chər\ *n*
1 a person whose business is killing animals for sale as food
2 a dealer in meat
3 a person who kills in large numbers or in a brutal manner

[2]butcher *vb* **butch•ered**; **butch•er•ing**
1 to kill and prepare (an animal) for food
2 [2]MASSACRE
3 to make a mess of : BOTCH

but•ler \'bət-lər\ *n*
the chief male servant of a household

[1]butt \'bət\ *n*
a target of ridicule or hurtful humor ⟨He became the *butt* of their jokes.⟩

[2]butt *n*
1 the part of the body on which a person sits
2 the thicker or bottom end of something ⟨the *butt* of a rifle⟩
3 an unused remainder ⟨a cigarette *butt*⟩

[3]butt *vb* **butt•ed**; **butt•ing**
to strike or thrust with the head or horns
butt in to intrude on someone else's activity or conversation

[4]butt *n*
a blow or thrust with the head or horns

butte \'byüt\ *n*
an isolated hill with steep sides

[1]but•ter \'bə-tər\ *n*
1 a solid yellowish fatty food obtained from cream or milk by churning
2 a food that is made of cooked and crushed nuts or fruit and that can be spread ⟨apple *butter*⟩ ⟨peanut *butter*⟩

[2]butter *vb* **but•tered**; **but•ter•ing**
to spread with or as if with butter

a b c d e f g h i j k l m n o p q r s t u v w x y z

A B C D E F G H I J K L M N O P Q R S T U V W X Y Z

butterfly
There are many species of butterfly, identifiable by their wing markings. Adult butterflies fly during the day and feed on nectar from flowers. Each butterfly starts life as an egg, which soon hatches into a caterpillar. This feeds and grows, then wraps itself in a silky cocoon, finally emerging as an adult butterfly.

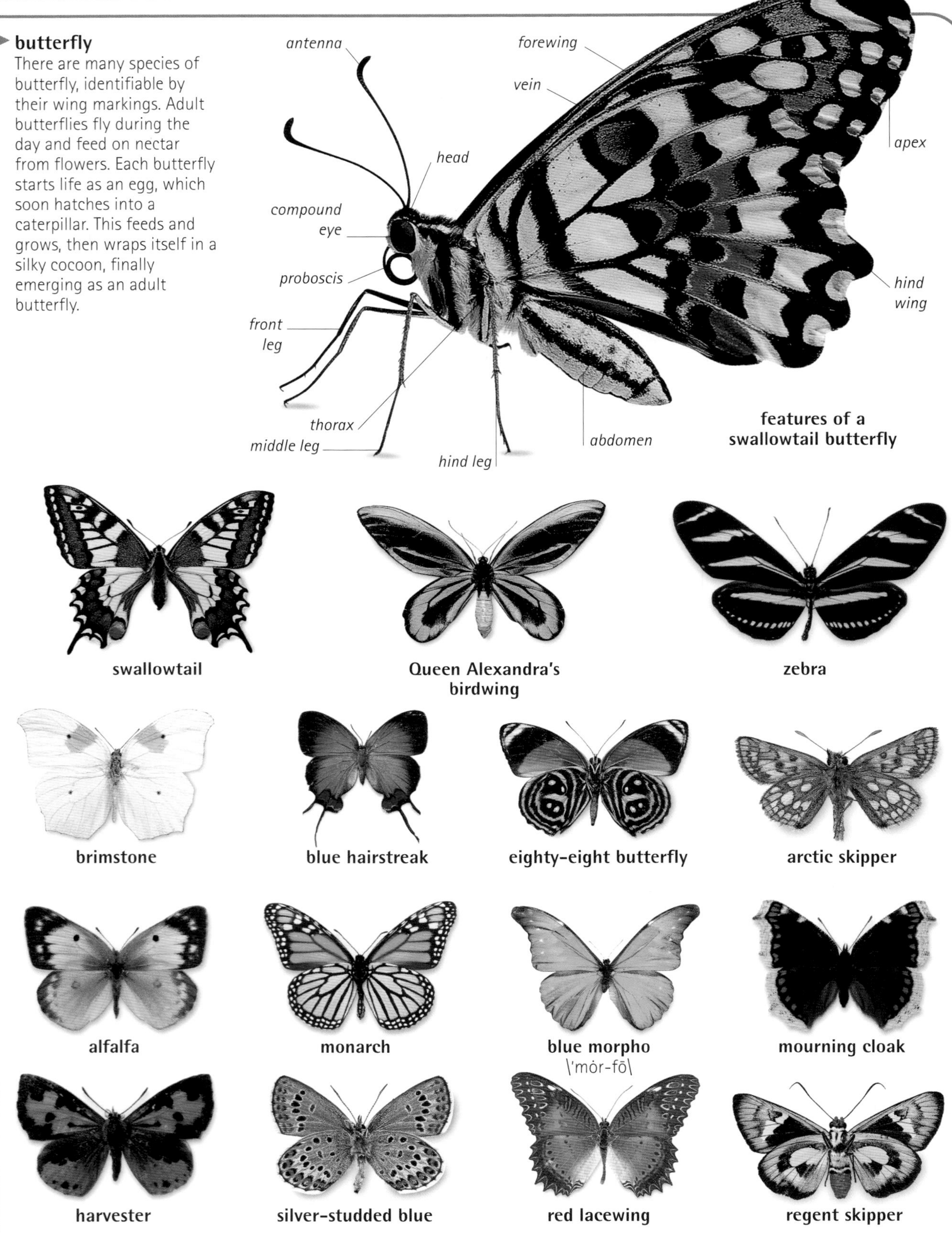

features of a swallowtail butterfly

swallowtail

Queen Alexandra's birdwing

zebra

brimstone

blue hairstreak

eighty-eight butterfly

arctic skipper

alfalfa

monarch

blue morpho \ˈmȯr-fō\

mourning cloak

harvester

silver-studded blue

red lacewing

regent skipper

buttercup

but•ter•cup \'bə-tər-,kəp\ *n*
▲ a common wildflower with bright yellow blossoms

but•ter•fat \'bə-tər-,fat\ *n*
the natural fat of milk that is the chief ingredient of butter

but•ter•fly \'bə-tər-,flī\ *n, pl* **but•ter•flies**
◀ an insect that has a slender body and large colored wings covered with tiny overlapping scales and that flies mostly in the daytime

but•ter•milk \'bə-tər-,milk\ *n*
the liquid left after churning butter from milk or cream

but•ter•nut \'bə-tər-,nət\ *n*
an eastern North American tree that has sweet egg-shaped nuts

but•ter•scotch \'bə-tər-,skäch\ *n*
a candy made from sugar, corn syrup, and water

but•tock \'bə-tək\ *n*
1 the back of the hip which forms one of the rounded parts on which a person sits
2 buttocks *pl* RUMP 1

1**but•ton** \'bə-tᵊn\ *n*
1 a small ball or disk used for holding parts of a garment together or as an ornament
2 a small often round part of a machine that makes the machine do something when pushed

2**button** *vb* **but•toned; but•ton•ing**
to close or fasten with buttons

but•ton•hole \'bə-tᵊn-,hōl\ *n*
a slit or loop for fastening a button

but•ton•wood \'bə-tᵊn-,wu̇d\ *n*
SYCAMORE 2

1**but•tress** \'bə-trəs\ *n*
1 a structure built against a wall or building to give support and strength
2 something that supports, props, or strengthens

2**buttress** *vb* **but•tressed; but•tress•ing**
to support or strengthen : to support with or as if with a buttress

bux•om \'bək-səm\ *adj*
having a healthy plump form

1**buy** \'bī\ *vb* **bought** \'bȯt\; **buy•ing**
to get by paying for : PURCHASE
buy•er *n*

2**buy** *n*
1BARGAIN 2 ⟨I got a good *buy* at the grocery store.⟩

1**buzz** \'bəz\ *vb* **buzzed; buzz•ing**
1 to make a low humming sound like that of bees
2 to be filled with a low hum or murmur ⟨The room *buzzed* with excitement.⟩
3 to fly an airplane low over

2**buzz** *n*
a low humming sound

buzzard: a turkey vulture, also called a turkey buzzard

buz•zard \'bə-zərd\ *n*
▲ a usually large bird of prey that flies slowly

buzz•er \'bə-zər\ *n*
an electric signaling device that makes a buzzing sound

1**by** \bī\ *prep*
1 close to : NEAR ⟨His dog stood *by* the door.⟩
2 so as to go on ⟨We went *by* the back road.⟩ ⟨I prefer to travel *by* bus.⟩
3 so as to go through ⟨The burglar left *by* the back window.⟩
4 so as to pass ⟨A policeman drove *by* the house.⟩
5 AT 1, DURING ⟨I travel *by* night.⟩
6 no later than ⟨Be sure to leave *by* noon.⟩
7 with the use or help of ⟨She won *by* cheating.⟩
8 through the action of ⟨It was seen *by* the others.⟩
9 ACCORDING TO 1 ⟨Play *by* the rules.⟩
10 with respect to ⟨He is a lawyer *by* profession.⟩ ⟨She is a Canadian *by* birth.⟩
11 to the amount of ⟨The youngest runner won *by* a mile.⟩
12 used to join two or more measurements ⟨a room 14 feet wide *by* 20 feet long⟩ or to join the numbers in a statement of multiplication or division ⟨Divide 8 *by* 4.⟩

2**by** *adv*
1 near at hand ⟨Stand *by*.⟩
2 4PAST ⟨in days gone *by*⟩ ⟨We walked right *by*.⟩
by and by after a while ⟨We left *by and by*.⟩

1**by•gone** \'bī-,gȯn\ *adj*
gone by : PAST ⟨He lived in a *bygone* time.⟩

2**by•gone** *n*
an event that is over and done with ⟨Let *bygones* be *bygones*.⟩

1**by•pass** \'bī-,pas\ *n*
a road serving as a substitute route around a blocked or crowded area

2**bypass** *vb* **by•passed; by•pass•ing**
1 to make a detour around
2 AVOID 1, FORGO ⟨No one is allowed to *bypass* the required classes.⟩

by–prod•uct \'bī-,prä-dəkt\ *n*
something produced (as in manufacturing) in addition to the main product

by•stand•er \'bī-,stan-dər\ *n*
a person present or standing near but taking no part in what is going on

byte \'bīt\ *n*
a group of eight bits that a computer handles as a unit

by•way \'bī-,wā\ *n*
a road that is not used very much

Sounds of C: Most of the time, the letter **C** sounds like a **K**, as in *cat* and *concrete*. When it comes before an **E**, **I**, or **Y**, though, **C** usually sounds like an **S**, as in *cent*, *city*, and *emergency*. In some words, such as *ocean* and *magician*, **C** sounds like **SH**. **C** and **H** together usually make the sound heard in *cheek* and *inch*. **C** sometimes makes this **CH** sound all by itself, as in *cello*. Occasionally, **CH** sounds like **K**, as in *character* and *ache*, or less often like **SH**, as in *machine*. **C** and **K** together sound like **K**, as in *stick*. In words like *scene*, **C** is silent.

c \'sē\ *n, pl* **c's** *or* **cs** \'sēz\ *often cap*
1 the third letter of the English alphabet
2 the number 100 in Roman numerals
3 a musical note referred to by the letter C
4 a grade that shows a student's work is fair or average

C *abbr*
1 Celsius
2 centigrade

c. *abbr*
1 carat
2 cent
3 centimeter
4 century
5 chapter
6 cup

CA *abbr* California

cab \'kab\ *n*
1 a light closed carriage pulled by a horse
2 TAXICAB
3 the covered compartment for the engineer and the controls of a locomotive or for the operator of a truck, tractor, or crane

ca•bana \kə-'ba-nyə, -nə\ *n*
a shelter usually with an open side used by people at a beach or swimming pool

cab•bage \'ka-bij\ *n*
▶ a garden plant related to the turnips that has a round firm head of leaves used as a vegetable

cab•in \'ka-bən\ *n*
1 a small simple dwelling usually having only one story ⟨a log *cabin*⟩
2 a private room on a ship
3 a place below deck on a small boat for passengers or crew
4 a part of an airplane for cargo, crew, or passengers

cab•i•net \'ka-bə-nət, 'kab-nət\ *n*
1 a case or cupboard with shelves or drawers for storing or displaying things ⟨a medicine *cabinet*⟩
2 a group of people who act as advisers (as to the head of a country) ⟨a member of the President's *cabinet*⟩

[1]ca•ble \'kā-bəl\ *n*
1 a very strong rope, wire, or chain
2 ▼ a bundle of wires to carry electric current
3 TELEGRAM
4 CABLE TELEVISION

plastic insulator

copper wires

[1]cable 2: an electric cable

[2]cable *vb* **ca•bled; ca•bling**
to send a message by telegraph ⟨She *cabled* the news to her parents.⟩

cable television *n*
a television system in which paying customers receive the television signals over electrical wires

ca•boose \kə-'büs\ *n*
a car usually at the rear of a freight train for the use of the train crew

▶ **Word History** *Caboose* is now a railroading word, but its origins lie at sea. When it first appeared in English, in the 1700s, *caboose* referred to a kitchen—or in sailors' language, a galley—on a ship used in trading. (A train's caboose serves the needs of the crew, just as the galley of a ship does.) The ship's caboose was at first a sort of cabin enclosing a cooking fire on the ship's deck. *Caboose* was borrowed from Dutch *kabuis* or *kombuis*, perhaps a compound word with *huis*, "house," as its second part.

ca•cao \kə-'kau̇, kə-'kā-ō\ *n, pl* **cacaos**
a South American tree with fleshy yellow pods that contain fatty seeds from which chocolate is made

cabbage

A leafy vegetable, cabbages are produced all year round. Most are round in shape, with leaves that are held loosely, or tightly curled around the heart, which is the central cluster of small leaves at the stalk. Cabbages may be white, red, or green. The leaves can be smooth or crinkled.

roundhead cabbage

crinkled cabbage

Chinese cabbage

[1]cache \ˈkash\ *n*
1 a place for hiding, storing, or preserving treasure or supplies ⟨The hole in the wall is my *cache*.⟩
2 something hidden or stored in a cache ⟨a *cache* of money⟩

[2]cache *vb* **cached**; **cach•ing**
to put or store so as to be safe or hidden **:** place in a cache ⟨The coins were *cached* in a teapot.⟩

[1]cack•le \ˈka-kəl\ *vb* **cack•led**; **cack•ling**
1 to make the noise or cry a hen makes especially after laying an egg
2 to laugh or chatter noisily

[2]cackle *n*
a sound made by a hen or like that made by a hen ⟨a *cackle* of laughter⟩

cac•tus \ˈkak-təs\ *n, pl* **cac•ti** \-ˌtī, -tē\ *or* **cac•tus•es**
▼ any of a large group of flowering plants of dry regions that have thick juicy stems and branches with scales or spines

cactus

ca•dav•er \kə-ˈda-vər\ *n*
CORPSE

[1]cad•die *or* **cad•dy** \ˈka-dē\ *n, pl* **cad•dies**
a person who carries a golfer's clubs

[2]caddie *or* **caddy** *vb* **cad•died**; **cad•dy•ing**
to carry a golfer's clubs

cad•dis fly \ˈka-dəs-\ *n*
an insect that has four wings and a larva which lives in water in a silk case covered especially with bits of wood, gravel, sand, or plant matter

ca•dence \ˈkā-dᵊns\ *n*
a regular beat or rhythm ⟨We heard the steady *cadence* of the drums.⟩

ca•det \kə-ˈdet\ *n*
a student in a military school or college

ca•fé *also* **ca•fe** \ka-ˈfā, kə-\ *n*
a small restaurant serving usually simple meals

caf•e•te•ria \ˌka-fə-ˈtir-ē-ə\ *n*
a place where people get food at a counter and carry it to a table for eating ⟨a school *cafeteria*⟩

caf•feine \ka-ˈfēn, ˈka-ˌfēn\ *n*
a substance found especially in coffee and tea that makes a person feel more awake

[1]cage \ˈkāj\ *n*
1 ► a box or enclosure that has large openings covered usually with wire net or bars and is used for keeping birds or animals ⟨a hamster *cage*⟩
2 an enclosure like a cage in shape or purpose ⟨a bank teller's *cage*⟩

[2]cage *vb* **caged**; **cag•ing**
to put or keep in or as if in a cage ⟨She *caged* the birds together.⟩

ca•gey \ˈkā-jē\ *adj* **ca•gi•er**; **ca•gi•est**
1 unwilling to act or speak in a direct or open way ⟨He was *cagey* about his intentions.⟩
2 clever in a tricky way ⟨a *cagey* opponent⟩

ca•hoot \kə-ˈhüt\ *n*
a secret partnership — usually used in pl. ⟨They were in *cahoots* with the thieves.⟩

ca•jole \kə-ˈjōl\ *vb* **ca•joled**; **ca•jol•ing**
to coax or persuade especially by flattery or false promises ⟨She *cajoled* me into accompanying her.⟩

[1]cake \ˈkāk\ *n*
1 ▼ a baked food made from a sweet batter or dough ⟨chocolate *cake*⟩
2 a usually flat round piece of food that is baked or fried ⟨a crab *cake*⟩ ⟨rice *cakes*⟩
3 a substance hardened or molded into a solid piece ⟨a *cake* of soap⟩

[1]cake 1:
cherry and chocolate cake

[2]cake *vb* **caked**; **cak•ing**
1 ENCRUST ⟨His clothes were *caked* with dust.⟩
2 to become dry and hard ⟨The mud had *caked* on her boots.⟩

Cal. *abbr* California

cal•a•mine \ˈka-lə-ˌmīn\ *n*
a skin lotion used especially to reduce itching (as from an insect bite or poison ivy)

ca•lam•i•ty \kə-ˈla-mə-tē\ *n, pl* **ca•lam•i•ties**
1 great distress or misfortune

[1]cage 1: a bird cage

2 an event that causes great harm and suffering **:** DISASTER
— **ca•lam•i•tous** \-təs\ *adj*

cal•ci•um \ˈkal-sē-əm\ *n*
a silvery soft metallic chemical element that is essential for strong healthy bones

calcium carbonate *n*
a solid substance that is found as limestone and marble and in plant ashes, bones, and shells

cal•cu•late \ˈkal-kyə-ˌlāt\ *vb* **cal•cu•lat•ed**; **cal•cu•lat•ing**
1 to find by adding, subtracting, multiplying, or dividing **:** COMPUTE ⟨*calculate* an average⟩
2 [1]ESTIMATE ⟨She *calculated* the risk.⟩
3 to plan by careful thought **:** INTEND ⟨Her remark was *calculated* to shock her listeners.⟩

> ► **Word History** In Latin the word *calculus* meant "pebble." Because the Romans used pebbles to do addition and subtraction on a counting board, the word became associated with computation, and the phrase *ponere calculos*, literally, "to place pebbles," was used to mean "to carry out a computation." Latin words coming from *calculus* include *calculator*, "person able to do arithmetic," and *calculare*, "to reckon," from which we get the word *calculate*.

cal•cu•lat•ing \ˈkal-kyə-ˌlā-tiŋ\ *adj*
carefully thinking about and planning actions for selfish or improper reasons ⟨a cold and *calculating* criminal⟩

cal•cu•la•tion \ˌkal-kyə-ˈlā-shən\ *n*
the process or result of adding, subtracting, multiplying, or dividing ⟨Careful *calculation* is required to determine the answer.⟩ ⟨Our *calculations* indicate a slight increase.⟩

cal•cu•la•tor \'kal-kyə-,lā-tər\ *n*
1 a person who calculates
2 ▼ a usually small electronic device for solving mathematical problems

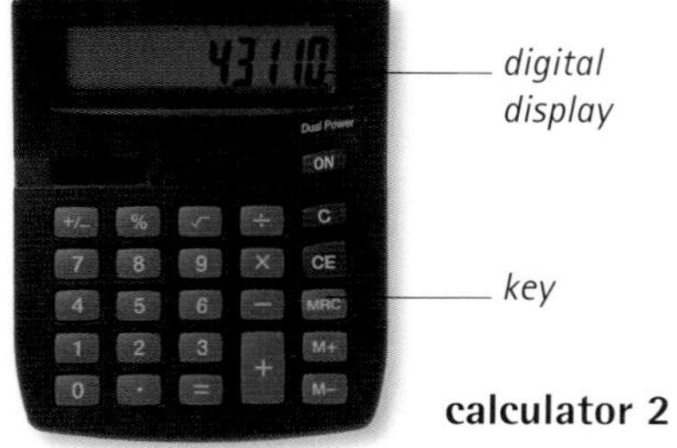

calculator 2

cal•cu•lus \'kal-kyə-ləs\ *n*
an advanced branch of mathematics that deals mostly with rates of change and with finding lengths, areas, and volumes

caldron *variant of* CAULDRON

cal•en•dar \'ka-lən-dər\ *n*
1 a chart showing the days, weeks, and months of the year
2 a schedule of planned events or activities ⟨the town's recreation *calendar*⟩

[1]**calf** \'kaf, 'käf\ *n, pl* **calves** \'kavz, 'kävz\
1 a young cow
2 the young of various large animals (as the elephant, moose, or whale)

[2]**calf** *n, pl* **calves**
the muscular back part of the leg below the knee

calf•skin \'kaf-,skin, 'käf-\ *n*
leather made from the skin of a calf

cal•i•ber *or* **cal•i•bre** \'ka-lə-bər\ *n*
1 level of excellence, skill, or importance
2 the diameter of a bullet or of the hole in the barrel of a gun

cal•i•co \'ka-li-,kō\ *n, pl* **cal•i•coes** *or* **cal•i•cos**
1 a cotton cloth especially with a colored pattern printed on one side
2 a blotched or spotted animal (as a cat)

Calif. *abbr* California

cal•i•per \'ka-lə-pər\ *n*
an instrument with two adjustable legs used to measure the thickness of objects or the distance between surfaces — usually used in pl. ⟨a pair of *calipers*⟩

ca•liph *or* **ca•lif** \'kā-ləf\ *n*
an important Muslim political and religious leader

cal•is•then•ics \,ka-ləs-'the-niks\ *n pl*
exercises (as push-ups and jumping jacks) to develop strength and flexibility that are done without special equipment
Hint: *Calisthenics* can be used as a singular or as a plural in writing and speaking. ⟨*Calisthenics* is an important form of exercise.⟩ ⟨This morning's *calisthenics* were tough.⟩

[1]**call** \'kȯl\ *vb* **called**; **call•ing**
1 to speak in a loud clear voice
2 to announce or read (something) loudly ⟨He *called* the roll.⟩
3 to tell, order, or ask to come ⟨Please *call* everyone to dinner.⟩
4 to give the order for ⟨*call* a meeting⟩
5 to utter a cry ⟨birds *calling*⟩
6 to get in touch with by telephone ⟨He *calls* home every day.⟩
7 to make a short visit ⟨She *called* at a neighbor's house.⟩
8 [2]NAME 1 ⟨I *called* the cat "Patches."⟩
9 to address someone or something as ⟨What did you *call* me?⟩
10 to regard as being of a certain kind ⟨Would you *call* that generous?⟩
11 to say or guess what the result will be ⟨The election is too close to *call*.⟩
12 to estimate as being ⟨Let's *call* it even.⟩
13 SUSPEND 4, END ⟨The game was *called* on account of rain.⟩
call for
1 to require as necessary or suitable ⟨We'll do whatever is *called for*.⟩
2 to make a request or demand ⟨The newspaper *called for* an investigation.⟩
call off
1 CANCEL 2 ⟨The party was *called off*.⟩
2 to cause or tell to stop attacking or chasing
call on
1 to ask for an answer from
2 [1]VISIT 1 ⟨*call on* a friend⟩
call out
1 to speak in a loud voice
2 to announce or read (something) loudly ⟨I *called out* the winners.⟩
3 to order (a group of people) to come or go somewhere ⟨*call out* the troops⟩
call to mind to cause to be thought of or remembered

[2]**call** *n*
1 a loud shout or cry
2 a cry of an animal
3 a loud sound or signal ⟨a bugle *call*⟩
4 a public request or command ⟨The group renewed their *calls* for change.⟩
5 [1]REQUEST 1 ⟨I got *calls* for an encore.⟩
6 a short visit
7 something called or announced ⟨That was the last *call* for passengers to board.⟩
8 the act of calling on the telephone
9 DECISION 1 ⟨It was a tough *call* to make.⟩
10 the attraction or appeal of a particular place or condition ⟨*call* of the wild⟩

call•er \'kȯ-lər\ *n*
someone who calls

cal•li•gra•phy \kə-'li-grə-fē\ *n*
1 beautiful artistic handwriting
2 the art of producing beautiful handwriting

call•ing \'kȯ-liŋ\ *n*
a profession especially that a person feels strongly about

cal•lous \'ka-ləs\ *adj*
feeling or showing no sympathy for others

cal•lus \'ka-ləs\ *n, pl* **cal•lus•es**
a hard thickened area on the skin and especially on the hands and feet

[1]**calm** \'käm, 'kälm\ *n*
1 a period or condition of freedom from storm, wind, or rough water

camel
There are two camel species: the dromedary and the Bactrian. The dromedary has one hump, while the Bactrian camel has two. The hump serves a useful purpose — storing fat for times when the camel's food of desert plants becomes scarce. As the fat is used up, the hump shrinks.

dromedary **Bactrian camel**

2 a quiet and peaceful state ⟨We enjoyed the *calm* of the countryside.⟩

[2]**calm** *vb* **calmed**; **calm•ing**
to make or become less active or disturbed — often used with *down* ⟨The music *calmed* her.⟩ ⟨The winds *calmed* down overnight.⟩

[3]**calm** *adj* **calm•er**; **calm•est**
1 not stormy or windy ⟨a *calm* night⟩
2 not excited or upset ⟨a *calm* reply⟩ ⟨Please remain *calm.*⟩
calm•ly *adv*
calm•ness *n*

▶ **Synonyms** CALM, PEACEFUL, and TRANQUIL mean quiet and free from disturbance. CALM is used when someone is not excited or upset even when there is cause for it. ⟨They stayed *calm* during the fire.⟩ PEACEFUL is used when someone or something has reached a quiet state after some period of disturbance. ⟨The storm is over and the lake is *peaceful* again.⟩ TRANQUIL is used for a total or lasting state of rest. ⟨They stopped at a *tranquil* garden.⟩

cal•o•rie \'ka-lə-rē, 'kal-rē\ *n*
1 a unit for measuring heat equal to the amount of heat required to raise the temperature of one gram of water one degree Celsius
2 a unit of heat used to indicate the amount of energy foods produce in the human body that is equal to 1000 calories

calve \'kav, 'käv\ *vb* **calved**; **calv•ing**
to give birth to a calf ⟨The cow *calved* in the barn.⟩

calves *pl of* CALF

ca•lyp•so \kə-'lip-sō\ *n*, *pl* **calypsos**
a lively folk song or style of singing of the West Indies

ca•lyx \'kā-liks\ *n*, *pl* **ca•lyx•es** *or* **ca•ly•ces** \-lə-ˌsēz\
the usually green outer part of a flower consisting of sepals

cam•bi•um \'kam-bē-əm\ *n*, *pl* **cam•bi•ums** *or* **cam•bia** \-bē-ə\
soft tissue in woody plants from which new wood and bark grow

cam•cord•er \'kam-ˌkȯr-dər\ *n*
a small video camera

came *past of* COME

cam•el \'ka-məl\ *n*
◀ a large hoofed animal that has one or two large humps on its back and is used in the deserts of Asia and Africa for carrying passengers and loads

▶ **camera 1**

Cameras can record images either digitally or on light-sensitive film. While many cameras adjust focus and lighting levels automatically, single-lens reflex — SLR — cameras must be set by hand, giving greater control to the photographer.

cam•era \'kam-rə\ *n*
1▲ a device that has a lens on one side to let light in and is used for taking pictures
2 the part of a television sending device in which the image to be sent out is formed

▶ **Word History** The word *camera* is short for *camera obscura*, which in Latin means "dark room." A camera obscura is a darkened enclosure—which can be as small as a box or as large as a room —into which light is admitted through a very small hole. Because of the way in which light beams cross rather than scatter, an upside-down image of whatever is outside the enclosure is projected on the surface opposite the hole. The image can be made brighter by passing the light through a lens. The first photographic camera was simply a camera obscura with the image projected on light-sensitive chemicals.

[1]**cam•ou•flage** \'ka-mə-ˌfläzh, -ˌfläj\ *n*
1 the hiding or disguising of something by covering it up or changing the way it looks ⟨The leopard has spots for *camouflage.*⟩
2 something (as color or shape) that protects an animal from attack by making it difficult to see in the area around it

[2]**camouflage** *vb* **cam•ou•flaged**; **cam•ou•flag•ing**
to hide or disguise by covering or making harder to see

[1]**camp** \'kamp\ *n*
1 a place where temporary shelters are erected ⟨The hikers set up *camp* for the night.⟩
2 a place or program for recreation or instruction usually during the summer

[2]**camp** *vb* **camped**; **camp•ing**
1 to make or occupy a camp ⟨The travelers *camped* under a large tree.⟩
2 to sleep outdoors usually in a tent ⟨We *camped* out overnight.⟩

[1]**cam•paign** \kam-'pān\ *n*
1 a series of activities meant to produce a particular result ⟨an election *campaign*⟩
2 a series of military operations in a certain area or for a certain purpose

[2]**campaign** *vb* **cam•paigned**; **cam•paign•ing**
to take part in a series of activities meant to produce a particular result ⟨They *campaigned* for a new library.⟩
cam•paign•er *n*

camp•er \'kam-pər\ *n*
1 a person who sleeps outdoors (as in a tent)
2 a type of vehicle or special trailer that people can live and sleep in when they are traveling or camping
3 a young person who goes to a camp during the summer

Camp Fire Girl *n*
a member of a national organization for girls from ages 5 to 18

camp•ground \'kamp-,graund\ *n*
▼ an area used for a camp or for camping

campground:
tents set up on a campground

cam•phor \'kam-fər\ *n*
a white fragrant solid that comes from the wood and bark of a tall Asian tree (**camphor tree**) and is used mostly in medicine, in making plastics, and to repel moths

camp•site \'kamp-,sīt\ *n*
a place used for camping ⟨This *campsite* has a picnic table and grill.⟩

cam•pus \'kam-pəs\ *n*
the grounds and buildings of a college or school

[1]**can** \kən, 'kan\ *helping verb, past* **could** \kəd, 'kůd\; *present sing & pl* **can**
1 know how to ⟨We *can* read.⟩
2 be able to ⟨I *can* hear you.⟩
3 be permitted by conscience or feeling to ⟨They *can* hardly blame me.⟩
4 have permission to ⟨You *can* go now.⟩
5 to be possible ⟨*Can* he still be alive?⟩

[2]**can** \'kan\ *n*
1 a metal container usually shaped like a cylinder ⟨a soda *can*⟩
2 the contents of a can ⟨Add a *can* of tomatoes.⟩

[3]**can** \'kan\ *vb* **canned**; **can•ning**
to prepare for later use by sealing in an airtight can or jar ⟨Let's *can* peaches for winter.⟩

Can., Canad. *abbr*
1 Canada
2 Canadian

[1]**Ca•na•di•an** \kə-'nā-dē-ən\ *adj*
of or relating to Canada or its people

[2]**Canadian** *n*
a person born or living in Canada

ca•nal \kə-'nal\ *n*
1 an artificial waterway for boats or for irrigation of land
2 ▶ a tubelike passage in the body ⟨The ear *canal* leads from the opening of the ear to the eardrum.⟩

ca•nary \kə-'ner-ē\ *n, pl* **ca•nar•ies**
a small usually yellow songbird often kept in a cage

can•cel \'kan-səl\ *vb* **can•celed** *or* **can•celled**; **can•cel•ing** *or* **can•cel•ling**
1 to take back : stop from being in effect ⟨She *canceled* the order.⟩
2 to cause to not happen
3 to be equal in force or importance but have opposite effect ⟨The disadvantages of the plan *canceled* out the advantages.⟩
4 to remove (a common divisor) from numerator and denominator : remove (equivalents) on opposite sides of an equation
5 to cross out or strike out with a line ⟨He *canceled* what he had written.⟩
6 to mark (as a postage stamp) so as to make impossible to use again

can•cel•la•tion \,kan-sə-'lā-shən\ *n*
1 an act of causing something to end or no longer be in effect ⟨*cancellation* of a game⟩
2 a mark that makes something impossible to use again ⟨the *cancellation* on a postage stamp⟩

can•cer \'kan-sər\ *n*
a serious sometimes deadly disease characterized by the growth of abnormal cells that form tumors which may damage or destroy normal body tissue

can•de•la•bra \,kan-də-'lä-brə, -'la-\ *n*
◀ a candlestick or lamp that has several branches for lights

candelabra

can•de•la•brum \,kan-də-'lä-brəm, -'la-\ *n, pl* **can•de•la•bra** \-'lä-brə, -'la-\ *also* **can•de•la•brums**
CANDELABRA

can•did \'kan-dəd\ *adj*
1 marked by or showing honesty : FRANK ⟨a *candid* discussion⟩

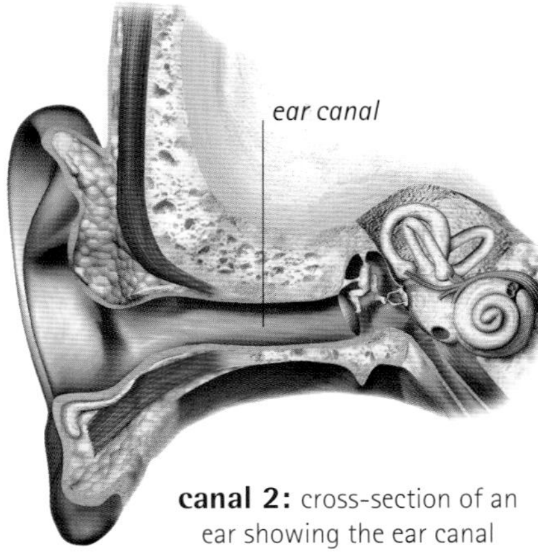

canal 2: cross-section of an ear showing the ear canal

2 relating to photography of people acting naturally without being posed ⟨a *candid* picture⟩
can•did•ly *adv*

can•di•da•cy \'kan-də-də-sē\ *n, pl* **can•di•da•cies**
the position of a person who is trying to be elected : the state of being a candidate ⟨He announced his *candidacy* for governor.⟩

can•di•date \'kan-də-,dāt\ *n*
1 a person who is trying to be elected ⟨a presidential *candidate*⟩
2 a person who is being considered for a position or honor ⟨a job *candidate*⟩

▶ **Word History** A person campaigning for public office in ancient Rome traditionally wore a toga that had been whitened with chalk when he greeted voters in the Forum. Hence the Latin word for an office seeker came to be *candidatus*, literally meaning "wearing white"; this word itself comes from the adjective *candidus*, "white, bright." In the 1600s the word *candidatus* was borrowed into English to denote someone aspiring to an office, job, or honor.

can•died \'kan-dēd\ *adj*
cooked in or coated with sugar ⟨*candied* ginger⟩

[1]**can•dle** \'kan-dᵊl\ *n*
▶ a stick of tallow or wax containing a wick and burned to give light

[2]**candle** *vb* **can•dled**; **can•dling**
to examine (an egg) by holding between the eye and a light
can•dler *n*

can•dle•light \'kan-dəl-,līt\ *n*
the light of a candle ⟨They dined by *candlelight*.⟩

can•dle•stick \'kan-dəl-,stik\ *n*
a holder for a candle

can•dor \'kan-dər\ *n*
sincere and honest expression ⟨She spoke with *candor* about the problem.⟩

[1]**can•dy** \'kan-dē\ *n, pl* **can•dies**
a sweet made of sugar often with flavoring and filling

[2]**candy** *vb* **can•died**; **can•dy•ing**
to coat or become coated with sugar often by cooking

cane \'kān\ *n*
1 an often hollow, slender, and somewhat flexible plant stem
2 a tall woody grass or reed (as sugarcane)
3 a rod made especially of wood or metal that often has a curved handle and is used to help someone walk
4 a rod for beating

[1]candle
In the days before electricity, candles provided a common means of lighting after dark. Today, they are still popular, especially for table settings. There are many styles to choose from, in different sizes, shapes, and colors.

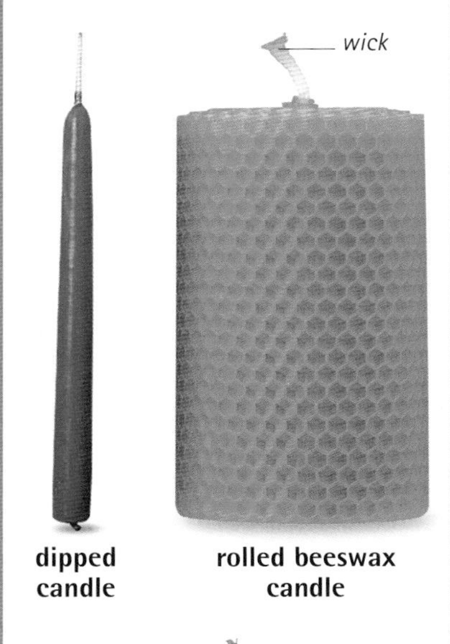

dipped candle
rolled beeswax candle
novelty candle

[1]**ca•nine** \'kā-,nīn\ *n*
1 a pointed tooth next to the incisors
2 a domestic dog or a related animal (as a wolf or fox)

[2]**canine** *adj*
1 of or relating to the domestic dog or a related animal ⟨*canine* behavior⟩
2 like or typical of a dog ⟨*canine* loyalty⟩

can•is•ter \'ka-nə-stər\ *n*
a small box or can for holding a dry product ⟨*canisters* of flour⟩

can•ker sore \'kaŋ-kər-\ *n*
a small painful sore of the mouth

can•nery \'ka-nə-rē\ *n, pl* **can•ner•ies**
a factory where foods are canned

can•ni•bal \'ka-nə-bəl\ *n*
1 a human being who eats human flesh
2 an animal that eats other animals of its own kind

[2]**canoe** *vb* **ca•noed**; **ca•noe•ing**
to travel or carry in a canoe ⟨We *canoed* across the lake.⟩
ca•noe•ist \-'nü-ist\ *n*

can•on \'ka-nən\ *n*
1 a rule or law of a church
2 an accepted rule ⟨He follows the *canons* of good taste.⟩

can•o•py \'ka-nə-pē\ *n, pl* **can•o•pies**
1 a covering fixed over a bed or throne or carried on poles (as over a person of high rank)
2 something that hangs over and shades or shelters something else
3 the uppermost spreading layer of a forest

can't \'kant, 'känt, 'kānt\
can not ⟨I *can't* see in the dark.⟩

can•ta•loupe \'kan-tə-,lōp\ *n*
a melon usually with a hard rough skin and reddish orange flesh

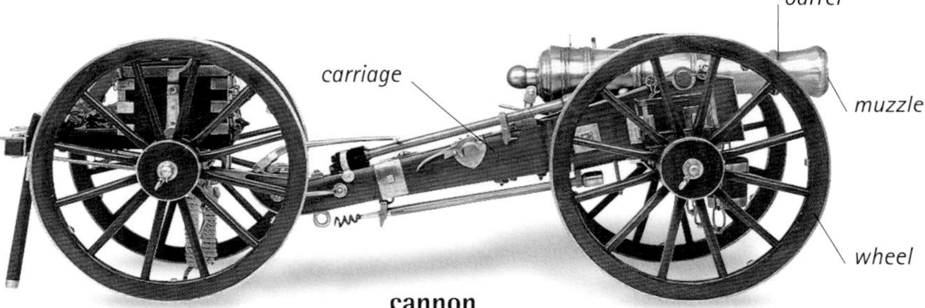

cannon

can•non \'ka-nən\ *n, pl* **cannons** *or* **cannon**
▲ a large heavy weapon consisting mostly of a metal tube that is mounted on wheels and is used for firing cannonballs

can•non•ball \'ka-nən-,bȯl\ *n*
1 a usually round solid missile (as of stone or metal) for firing from a cannon
2 a jump into water made with the arms holding the knees tight against the chest

can•not \'ka-,nät, kə-'nät\
can not ⟨We *cannot* attend the party.⟩

can•ny \'ka-nē\ *adj* **can•ni•er**; **can•ni•est**
clever especially in taking advantage of opportunities : SHREWD ⟨a *canny* decision⟩ ⟨*canny* shoppers⟩
can•ni•ly \'ka-nə-lē\ *adv*

[1]**ca•noe** \kə-'nü\ *n*
► a long light narrow boat with pointed ends and curved sides that is usually moved by a paddle

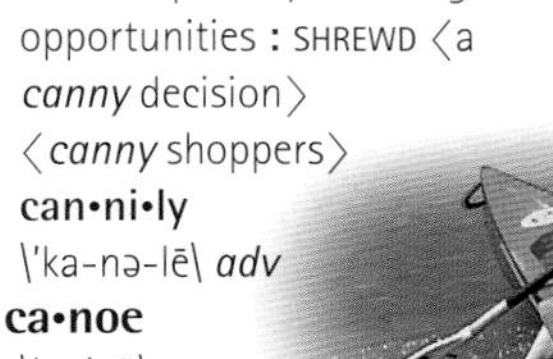

[1]**canoe:** passengers paddling a canoe

can•tan•ker•ous \kan-'taŋ-kə-rəs\ *adj*
CRABBY, QUARRELSOME

can•ta•ta \kən-'tä-tə\ *n*
a piece of music that features solos, duets, and choruses with instrumental accompaniment and is sometimes based on a poem, play, or story

can•teen \kan-'tēn\ *n*
1 a store (as in a camp or factory) in which food, drinks, and small supplies are sold
2 a place of recreation and entertainment for people in military service
3 a small container for carrying water or another liquid ⟨a hiker's *canteen*⟩

[1]can•ter \'kan-tər\ *n*
a horse's gait resembling but slower than a gallop

[2]canter *vb* **can•tered**; **can•ter•ing**
to run with a movement that resembles but is slower than a gallop

can•ti•le•ver \'kan-tə-,lē-vər, -,le-\ *n*
1 a beam or similar support fastened (as by being built into a wall) only at one end ⟨The balcony is supported by wooden *cantilevers.*⟩
2 either of two structures that stick out from piers toward each other and when joined form a span in a bridge (**cantilever bridge**)

can•to \'kan-,tō\ *n, pl* **can•tos**
one of the major divisions of a long poem

can•ton \'kan-t^{ə}n, 'kan-,tän\ *n*
a division of a country (as Switzerland)

can•tor \'kan-tər\ *n*
a synagogue official who sings religious music and leads the congregation in prayer

can•vas \'kan-vəs\ *n*
1 a strong cloth of hemp, flax, or cotton ⟨*canvas* bags⟩
2 a specially prepared piece of cloth used as a surface for painting

can•vas•back \'kan-vəs-,bak\ *n*
▼ a North American wild duck with reddish brown head and grayish back

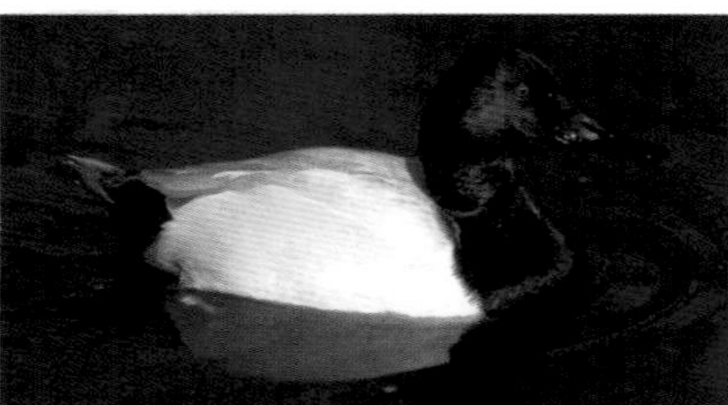

canvasback

can•vass \'kan-vəs\ *vb* **can•vassed**; **can•vass•ing**
to go to (people) to ask for votes, contributions, or orders for goods or to determine public opinion
can•vass•er *n*

can•yon \'kan-yən\ *n*
▶ a deep valley with steep sides and often a stream flowing through it

[1]cap \'kap\ *n*
1 a head covering and especially one having a visor and no brim
2 something that serves as a cover or protection for something ⟨a bottle *cap*⟩
3 a part that forms the top of something ⟨a mushroom *cap*⟩
4 an upper limit ⟨a *cap* on spending⟩
5 a paper or metal container holding a small explosive charge ⟨The toy pistol shoots *caps.*⟩

[2]cap *vb* **capped**; **cap•ping**
1 to cover or provide with a top or cover ⟨Please remember to *cap* the marker.⟩ ⟨The mountaintops are *capped* with snow.⟩
2 to bring to a high point or end ⟨He *capped* off the show with a song.⟩
3 to match or follow with something equal or better ⟨She *capped* his joke with one of her own.⟩
4 to put an upper limit on ⟨Attendance is *capped* at 80 participants.⟩

cap. *abbr*
1 capital
2 capitalize
3 capitalized

ca•pa•bil•i•ty \,kā-pə-'bi-lə-tē\ *n, pl* **ca•pa•bil•i•ties**
ABILITY 1 ⟨That job is beyond my *capability.*⟩

ca•pa•ble \'kā-pə-bəl\ *adj*
1 having the qualities or abilities that are needed to do or accomplish something ⟨You are *capable* of better work.⟩
2 able to do something well ⟨a *capable* actress⟩
synonyms see ABLE
ca•pa•bly \-blē\ *adv*

ca•pa•cious \kə-'pā-shəs\ *adj*
able to hold a great deal ⟨a *capacious* pocket⟩

ca•pac•i•ty \kə-'pa-sə-tē\ *n, pl* **ca•pac•i•ties**
1 ability to contain or deal with something ⟨The room has a large seating *capacity.*⟩ ⟨Factories are working to *capacity.*⟩
2 mental or physical power ⟨You have the *capacity* to do better.⟩
3 VOLUME 3 ⟨The tank has a ten-gallon *capacity.*⟩
4 ROLE 1, STATUS ⟨In your *capacity* as team captain, you can set a good example.⟩

[1]cape \'kāp\ *n*
a point of land that juts out into the sea or into a lake

[2]cape *n*
a sleeveless garment worn so as to hang over the shoulders, arms, and back

[1]ca•per \'kā-pər\ *vb* **ca•pered**; **ca•per•ing**
to leap about in a lively way

[2]caper *n*
1 a playful or mischievous trick
2 a lively leap or spring
3 an illegal or questionable act

[1]cap•il•lary \'ka-pə-,ler-ē\ *adj*
1 having a long slender form and a small inner diameter ⟨a *capillary* tube⟩
2 of or relating to capillary action or a capillary

[2]capillary *n, pl* **cap•il•lar•ies**
one of the slender hairlike tubes that are the smallest blood vessels and connect arteries with veins

capillary action *n*
the action by which the surface of a liquid where it is in contact with a solid (as in a capillary tube) is raised or lowered

[1]cap•i•tal \'ka-pə-t^{ə}l, 'kap-t^{ə}l\ *adj*
1 being like the letters A, B, C, etc. rather than a, b, c, etc.
2 being the location of a government ⟨Columbus is the *capital* city of Ohio.⟩
3 punishable by or resulting in death ⟨a *capital* crime⟩ ⟨*capital* punishment⟩

canyon: a view of the Grand Canyon West, Nevada

4 of or relating to accumulated wealth
5 EXCELLENT 〈a *capital* idea〉

[2]capital *n*
1 a capital letter 〈Begin each sentence with a *capital*.〉
2 a capital city 〈Name the *capital* of North Dakota.〉
3 the money and property that a person owns
4 profitable use 〈They made *capital* out of my weakness.〉

[3]capital *n*
the top part of an architectural column

cap•i•tal•ism \'ka-pə-tə-,liz-əm\ *n*
a system under which the ownership of land and wealth is for the most part in the hands of private individuals

cap•i•tal•ist \'ka-pə-tə-list\ *n*
1 a person who has usually a lot of money which is used to make more money
2 a person who supports capitalism

cap•i•tal•ize \'ka-pə-tə-,līz\ *vb* **cap•i•tal•ized**; **cap•i•tal•iz•ing**
1 to write with a beginning capital letter or in all capital letters
2 to provide money needed to start or develop (a business)
3 to gain by turning something to advantage 〈The winner *capitalized* on his opponent's mistakes.〉
cap•i•tal•i•za•tion \,ka-pə-tə-lə-'zā-shən\ *n*

cap•i•tol \'ka-pə-tᵊl, 'kap-tᵊl\ *n*
1 the building in which a state legislature meets
2 *cap* the building in Washington, D.C., in which the United States Congress meets

▶ **Word History** The word *capitol* is pronounced the same as *capital*, and the two words seem to have linked meanings: the building called the *Capitol* is located in our nation's *capital*. Curiously, their origins are quite different, though both come from Latin. *Capital* is from *capitalis*, which means literally "of the head" and in later Latin came to mean "chief" or "principal." *Capitol* is from the *Capitolium*, a hill at the center of ancient Rome that held a fortress and an important temple to the god Jupiter.

ca•pon \'kā-,pän\ *n*
a castrated male chicken

ca•price \kə-'prēs\ *n*
a sudden change in feeling, opinion, or action : WHIM

ca•pri•cious \kə-'pri-shəs\ *adj*
1 moved or controlled by a sudden desire 〈a *capricious* shopper〉
2 likely to change suddenly 〈*capricious* weather〉
ca•pri•cious•ly *adv*

cap•size \'kap-,sīz\ *vb* **cap•sized**; **cap•siz•ing**
to turn over : UPSET 〈Sit down or you'll *capsize* the canoe.〉

cap•stan \'kap-stən\ *n*
a device that consists of a drum to which a rope is fastened and that is used especially on ships for raising the anchor

cap•sule \'kap-səl\ *n*
1 a case enclosing the seeds or spores of a plant
2 a small case of material that contains medicine to be swallowed
3 ▶ a closed compartment for travel in space

Capt. *abbr*
captain

[1]cap•tain \'kap-tən\ *n*
1 the commanding officer of a ship
2 a leader of a group : someone in command 〈the *captain* of a football team〉
3 an officer of high rank in a police or fire department
4 a commissioned officer in the navy or coast guard ranking above a commander
5 a commissioned officer in the army, air force, or marine corps ranking below a major

[2]captain *vb* **cap•tained**; **cap•tain•ing**
to be captain of 〈She *captains* the team.〉

cap•tion \'kap-shən\ *n*
a comment or title that goes with a picture

cap•ti•vate \'kap-tə-,vāt\ *vb* **cap•ti•vat•ed**; **cap•ti•vat•ing**
to fascinate by some special charm 〈The play is *captivating* audiences.〉

[1]cap•tive \'kap-tiv\ *adj*
1 taken and held prisoner
2 kept within bounds or under control 〈*captive* animals〉
3 as a prisoner 〈I was taken *captive*.〉
4 unable to avoid watching or listening to something 〈a *captive* audience〉

[2]captive *n*
someone who is held prisoner

cap•tiv•i•ty \kap-'ti-və-tē\ *n*
the state of being held prisoner

cap•tor \'kap-tər\ *n*
someone who has captured a person or thing

[1]cap•ture \'kap-chər\ *vb* **cap•tured**; **cap•tur•ing**
1 to take and hold especially by force 〈The eagle *captured* its prey.〉
2 to win and get through effort 〈The candidate *captured* half the vote.〉
3 to get and hold
4 to put into a lasting form 〈She *captured* the scene in a photo.〉
synonyms see CATCH

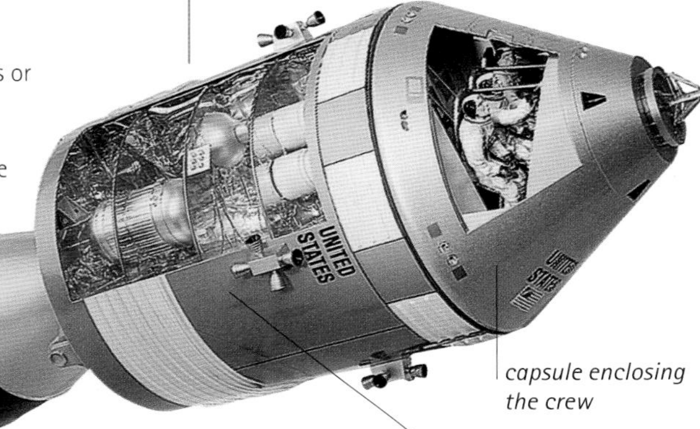

capsule 3: the capsule of a model spacecraft showing the interior

[2]capture *n*
the act of taking and holding especially by force

car \'kär\ *n*
1 a vehicle that moves on wheels
2 a separate section of a train
3 the part of an elevator that holds passengers

ca•rafe \kə-'raf\ *n*
▶ a bottle that has a wide mouth and is used to hold water or beverages

carafe

car•a•mel \'kär-məl, 'ker-ə-məl\ *n*
1 a firm chewy candy
2 burnt sugar used for coloring and flavoring

car•at \'ker-ət\ *n*
a unit of weight for gemstones (as diamonds) equal to 200 milligrams

car•a•van \'ker-ə-,van\ *n*
1 a group (of people or animals) traveling together on a long journey
2 a group of vehicles traveling together one behind the other

car•a•vel \'ker-ə-,vel\ *n*
▶ a small sailing ship of the 15th and 16th centuries with a broad bow and high stern and three or four masts

car•a•way \'ker-ə-,wā\ *n*
the dried seeds of a white-flowered plant that are used especially in seasoning foods

car•bine \'kär-,bēn, -,bīn\ *n*
a short light rifle

car•bo•hy•drate \,kär-bō-'hī-,drāt\ *n*
a substance (as a starch or sugar) that is rich in energy and is made up of carbon, hydrogen, and oxygen

car•bon \'kär-bən\ *n*
a chemical element occurring as diamond and graphite, in coal and petroleum, and in plant and animal bodies

car•bon•ate \'kär-bə-,nāt\ *vb*
car•bon•at•ed; **car•bon•at•ing**
to fill with carbon dioxide which escapes in the form of bubbles ⟨a *carbonated* soft drink⟩

carbon di•ox•ide \-dī-'äk-,sīd\ *n*
a heavy colorless gas that is formed by burning fuels, by the breakdown or burning of animal and plant matter, and by the act of breathing and that is absorbed from the air by plants in photosynthesis

carbon footprint *n*
the amount of greenhouse gases and especially carbon dioxide given off by something (as a person's activities) during a given period

carbon mon•ox•ide \-mə-'näk-,sīd\ *n*
a colorless odorless very poisonous gas formed by incomplete burning of carbon

car•bu•re•tor \'kär-bə-,rā-tər\ *n*
the part of an engine in which liquid fuel (as gasoline) is mixed with air to make it burn easily

car•cass \'kär-kəs\ *n*
the body of a dead animal

caravel:
model of a 15th-century Spanish caravel

card \'kärd\ *n*
1 a decorated piece of thick paper that contains a greeting or is used to write a message ⟨birthday *card*⟩ ⟨note *card*⟩
2 a thick stiff piece of paper or plastic that contains information about a person or business ⟨I lost my library *card*.⟩
3 PLAYING CARD
4 *cards pl* a game played with playing cards
5 TRADING CARD
6 CREDIT CARD
7 a thin hard board that has small electronic devices on it and that can be added to a computer to make the computer perform different tasks ⟨a video *card*⟩

card•board \'kärd-,bȯrd\ *n*
a stiff material made of wood pulp that has been pressed and dried

car•di•ac \'kär-dē-,ak\ *adj*
of, relating to, or affecting the heart

[1]**car•di•nal** \'kärd-nəl, 'kär-də-\ *n*
1 a high official of the Roman Catholic Church ranking next below the pope
2 a bright red songbird with a crest and a whistling call

[2]**cardinal** *adj*
of first importance : MAIN, PRINCIPAL

cardinal number *n*
a number (as 1, 5, 22) that is used in simple counting and shows how many

cardinal point *n*
one of the four chief points of the compass which are north, south, east, west

car•dio•pul•mo•nary re•sus•ci•ta•tion \,kär-dē-ō-'pu̇l-mə-,ner-ē-\ *n*
▼ a method used in an emergency to save the life of a person whose heart has stopped beating that involves breathing into the victim's mouth to force air into the lungs and pressing on the victim's chest to cause blood to flow through the body

▶ **cardiopulmonary resuscitation** or CPR is an emergency medical procedure for a person whose heart has stopped. It is used to supply the blood with oxygen so as to keep the vital organs alive.

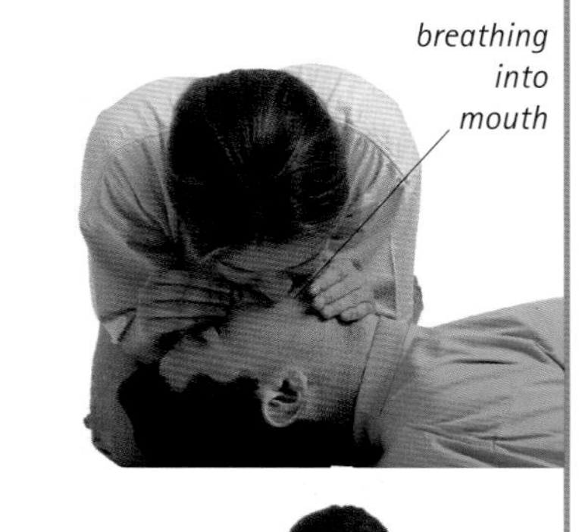

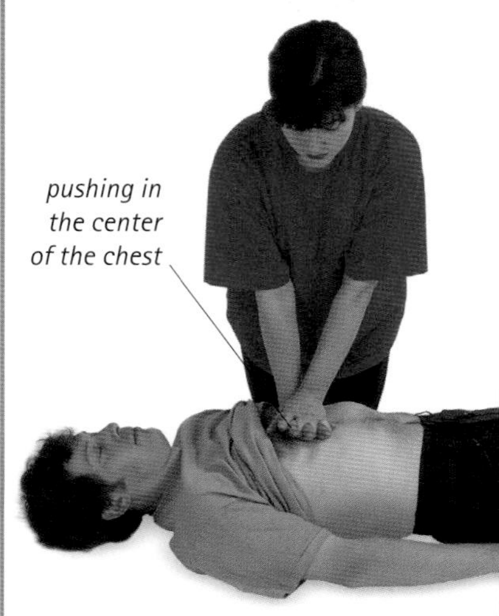

[1]**care** \'ker\ *n*
1 close attention ⟨Use *care* when driving.⟩
2 CHARGE 1 ⟨under a doctor's *care*⟩
3 proper maintenance of something
4 a feeling of concern or worry

[2]**care** *vb* **cared**; **car•ing**
1 to feel interest or concern ⟨We *care* about what happens to you.⟩

2 to provide help, protection, or supervision to : look after ⟨His job is to *care* for the sick.⟩
3 to have a liking or desire ⟨Do you *care* for more tea?⟩

ca•reen \kə-ˈrēn\ *vb* **ca•reened**; **ca•reen•ing**
to go at high speed without control

ca•reer \kə-ˈrir\ *n*
1 a period of time spent in a job or profession ⟨She had a long *career* in medicine.⟩
2 a job followed as a life's work ⟨He made teaching his *career.*⟩

care•free \ˈker-ˌfrē\ *adj*
free from care or worry ⟨*Carefree* children skipped through the park.⟩

care•ful \ˈker-fəl\ *adj*
1 using care ⟨a *careful* driver⟩
2 made, done, or said with care ⟨*careful* planning⟩ ⟨She gave a *careful* answer.⟩
care•ful•ly \-fə-lē\ *adv*

► **Synonyms** CAREFUL and CAUTIOUS mean taking care to avoid trouble. CAREFUL is used for a person who is able to prevent mistakes or accidents by being alert. ⟨Be *careful* when you paint the fence.⟩ CAUTIOUS is used for a person who takes care to avoid further problems or difficulties. ⟨A *cautious* driver will drive slowly in bad weather.⟩

care•less \ˈker-ləs\ *adj*
1 not taking proper care ⟨a *careless* worker⟩
2 done, made, or said without being careful ⟨a *careless* mistake⟩
3 CAREFREE
care•less•ly *adv*
care•less•ness *n*

[1]**ca•ress** \kə-ˈres\ *n*
a tender or loving touch or hug

[2]**caress** *vb* **ca•ressed**; **ca•ress•ing**
to touch in a tender or loving way

care•tak•er \ˈker-ˌtā-kər\ *n*
a person who takes care of property for someone else

car•go \ˈkär-gō\ *n, pl* **cargoes** *or* **cargos**
the goods carried by a ship, airplane, or vehicle

car•i•bou \ˈker-ə-ˌbü\ *n*
► a large deer of northern and arctic regions that has antlers in both the male and female
Hint: The word *caribou* is used especially to refer to these animals when they live in North America. The word *reindeer* is usually used for these animals when they live in Europe and Asia.

car•ies \ˈker-ēz\ *n, pl* **caries**
a decayed condition of a tooth or teeth

car•il•lon \ˈker-ə-ˌlän, -lən\ *n*
a set of bells sounded by hammers controlled by a keyboard

car•nage \ˈkär-nij\ *n*
[1]SLAUGHTER 3

car•na•tion \kär-ˈnā-shən\ *n*
▼ a fragrant usually white, pink, or red garden or greenhouse flower

carnation: a variegated carnation

car•ne•lian \kär-ˈnēl-yən\ *n*
► a hard reddish quartz used as a gem

car•ni•val \ˈkär-nə-vəl\ *n*
1 a form of entertainment that travels from town to town and includes rides and games
2 an organized program of entertainment or exhibition : FESTIVAL ⟨a winter *carnival*⟩

car•ni•vore \ˈkär-nə-ˌvȯr\ *n*
an animal that feeds on meat

car•niv•o•rous \kär-ˈni-və-rəs\ *adj*
feeding on animal flesh or tissue ⟨Wolves are *carnivorous* animals.⟩

[1]**car•ol** \ˈker-əl\ *n*
a usually religious song of joy

[2]**carol** *vb* **car•oled** *or* **car•olled**; **car•ol•ing** *or* **car•ol•ling**
1 to sing in a joyful manner
2 to sing carols and especially Christmas carols
car•ol•er *or* **car•ol•ler** *n*

[1]**car•om** \ˈker-əm\ *n*
the act of bouncing back at an angle

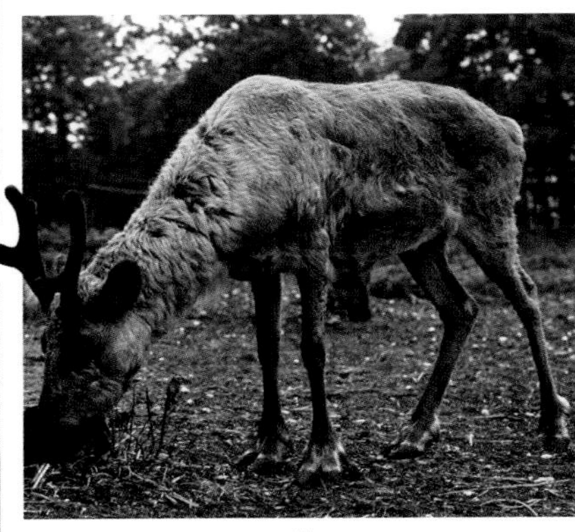

caribou

[2]**carom** *vb* **car•omed**; **car•om•ing**
to hit and bounce back at an angle ⟨The puck *caromed* off his stick toward the goal.⟩

car•ou•sel \ˌker-ə-ˈsel\ *n*
MERRY-GO-ROUND

[1]**carp** \ˈkärp\ *vb* **carped**; **carp•ing**
to complain in an annoying way

[2]**carp** *n*
a freshwater fish that lives a long time and is often used for food

car•pel \ˈkär-pəl\ *n*
the female reproductive structure of a flower that encloses the ovules ⟨The pistil of a flower can be made up of a single *carpel* or a group of *carpels* fused together.⟩

car•pen•ter \ˈkär-pən-tər\ *n*
a worker who builds or repairs wooden things

car•pen•try \ˈkär-pən-trē\ *n*
the skill or work of building or repairing wooden things

uncut carnelian

cut carnelian

carnelian

[1]**car•pet** \ˈkär-pət\ *n*
1 a heavy woven fabric used especially as a floor covering
2 a covering like a carpet ⟨a *carpet* of grass⟩

[2]**carpet** *vb* **car•pet•ed**; **car•pet•ing**
to cover with or as if with a carpet ⟨The ground was *carpeted* with moss.⟩

car pool *n*
an arrangement by a group of automobile owners in which each takes turns driving his or her own car and giving the others a ride

car•riage \ˈker-ij\ *n*
1 a vehicle with wheels used for carrying people
2 a support with wheels used for carrying a load ⟨a gun *carriage*⟩
3 a movable part of a machine that carries or supports some other moving part
4 the manner of holding the body : POSTURE

car•ri•er \ˈker-ē-ər\ *n*
1 a person or thing that carries ⟨a mail *carrier*⟩
2 a person or business that transports passengers or goods or provides a certain service
3 a person, animal, or plant that carries disease germs without showing symptoms and passes them on to others

A B C D E F G H I J K L M N O P Q R S T U V W X Y Z

car•ri•on \ˈker-ē-ən\ *n*
dead and decaying flesh

car•rot \ˈker-ət\ *n*
a long orange root of a garden plant that is eaten as a vegetable

car•ry \ˈker-ē\ *vb* **car•ried; car•ry•ing**
1 to take or transfer from one place to another ⟨Can you *carry* a package?⟩ ⟨You might need to *carry* a number in addition.⟩
2 to contain and direct the course of ⟨The pipe is *carrying* water to the sea.⟩
3 to wear or have on or within the body ⟨*carry* money⟩ ⟨She is *carrying* an unborn child.⟩
4 to have as an element, quality, or part ⟨Does the camera *carry* a guarantee?⟩
5 to have for sale ⟨The market *carries* fresh fish.⟩
6 to go over or travel a distance ⟨His voice *carried* across the river.⟩
7 [1]SUPPORT 1, BEAR ⟨The building has pillars that *carry* an arch.⟩
8 [1]WIN 3 ⟨He will *carry* the election.⟩
9 to hold or bear the body or some part of it ⟨*Carry* your head high.⟩
10 to sing in correct pitch ⟨Can you *carry* a tune?⟩
11 to present to the public ⟨The story was *carried* on the evening news.⟩ ⟨The paper *carries* weather reports.⟩
carry away to cause strong feeling in ⟨The music *carried* her *away*.⟩
carry on
1 to behave in an improper or excited manner
2 MANAGE 1 ⟨They *carry on* a business.⟩
3 to continue in spite of difficulties ⟨The scientists *carried on* even without their equipment.⟩
carry out to put into action or effect

car seat *n*
a seat for a small child that attaches to an automobile seat and holds the child safely

[1]cart \ˈkärt\ *n*
1 ▶ a heavy vehicle with two wheels usually drawn by horses and used for hauling
2 a light vehicle pushed or pulled by hand

[2]cart *vb* **cart•ed; cart•ing**
1 to carry in a cart
2 CARRY 1
cart•er *n*

car•ti•lage \ˈkär-tə-lij\ *n*
tough flexible tissue that makes up most of the skeleton of vertebrates during early development and except for in a few places in the body (as the nose or outer ear) is replaced by bone

car•ti•lag•i•nous \ˌkär-tə-ˈla-jə-nəs\ *adj*
relating to or made of cartilage ⟨*Cartilaginous* tissue is found in the outer ear and the nose.⟩

car•ton \ˈkär-tᵊn\ *n*
a cardboard container

car•toon \kär-ˈtün\ *n*
1 a movie or television program made by photographing a series of drawings
2 ▼ a drawing (as in a newspaper) making people or objects look funny or foolish
3 COMIC STRIP

cartoon 2: cartoon of a boy looking at a hovering seagull through binoculars

car•toon•ist \kär-ˈtü-nist\ *n*
a person who draws cartoons

car•tridge \ˈkär-trij\ *n*
1 a case or shell containing gunpowder and shot or a bullet for use in a firearm
2 a container that is inserted into a machine to make it work ⟨an ink *cartridge*⟩

cart•wheel \ˈkärt-ˌhwēl, -ˌwēl\ *n*
a handspring made to the side with arms and legs sticking out

carve \ˈkärv\ *vb* **carved; carv•ing**
1 to cut with care ⟨He *carved* a block of wood to use as a bowl.⟩
2 to make or get by cutting ⟨Artists were *carving* ice sculptures.⟩
3 to slice and serve (meat) ⟨Would you *carve* the turkey?⟩
carv•er *n*

carv•ing \ˈkär-viŋ\ *n*
1 the art or act of a person who carves
2 an object or design that has been carved

[1]cas•cade \ka-ˈskād\ *n*
▶ a steep usually small waterfall

[2]cascade *vb* **cas•cad•ed; cas•cad•ing**
to flow or fall rapidly and in large quantity ⟨Tears *cascaded* from the baby's eyes.⟩

[1]case \ˈkās\ *n*
1 a particular instance, situation, or example ⟨a *case* of injustice⟩
2 a situation or an object that calls for investigation or action (as by the police)
3 a question to be settled in a court of law
4 a form of a noun, pronoun, or adjective showing its grammatical relation to other words ⟨The word "child's" in "the child's toy" is in the possessive *case*.⟩
5 the actual situation ⟨I was called greedy, but that is not the *case*.⟩
6 a convincing argument ⟨A *case* could be made for promoting her.⟩
7 an instance of disease, injury, or discomfort ⟨a *case* of chicken pox⟩
in any case no matter what has happened or been said ⟨He couldn't find the keys and *in any case* there was no gas in the car.⟩
in case for the purpose of being ready for something that might happen ⟨Take an umbrella *in case* it rains.⟩

[2]case *n*
1 a container (as a box) for holding something
2 a box and its contents ⟨a *case* of books⟩
3 an outer covering

[1]cart 1: a horse pulling a cart

[1]cascade at Krka National Park, Croatia

ca•sein \kā-'sēn\ *n*
a whitish to yellowish protein that is found in milk and cheese and is used in making paints, plastics, and adhesives

case•ment \'kā-smənt\ *n*
1 a window sash opening on hinges
2 a window with a casement

[1]**cash** \'kash\ *n*
1 money in the form of coins or bills
2 money or its equivalent (as a check) paid for goods at the time of purchase or delivery

[2]**cash** *vb* **cashed**; **cash•ing**
to give or get cash for 〈The bank refused to *cash* his check.〉

cash•ew \'ka-shü\ *n*
a curved edible nut that comes from a tropical American tree

cash•ier \ka-'shir\ *n*
a person who is responsible for giving out or taking in money (as in a bank or store)

cash•mere \'kazh-,mir, 'kash-\ *n*
a soft yarn or fabric once made from the fine wool of an Indian goat but now often from sheep's wool

cash register *n*
a machine used in a business to calculate the amount of cash due for a sale and having a drawer to hold money

cas•ing \'kā-siŋ\ *n*
something that covers or encloses 〈sausage *casings*〉

cask \'kask\ *n*
1 a container that is shaped like a barrel and is usually used for liquids
2 the amount contained in a cask

cas•ket \'ka-skət\ *n*
1 COFFIN
2 ▶ a small box for storage or safekeeping (as for jewels)

cas•se•role \'ka-sə-,rōl\ *n*
1 a mix of food baked and served in a deep dish
2 a deep dish in which food can be baked and served

cas•sette \kə-'set\ *n*
1 ▶ a container that holds audiotape or videotape and in which the tape passes from one reel to another when being played
2 a container holding photographic film or plates that can be easily loaded into a camera

[1]**cast** \'kast\ *vb* **cast**; **cast•ing**
1 [1]THROW 1 〈*cast* a stone〉 〈*cast* a fishing line〉
2 to direct to or toward something or someone 〈*cast* a glance〉
3 to send out or forward 〈*cast* a shadow〉 〈*cast* light〉
4 to put under the influence of 〈*cast* a spell〉 〈The news *cast* gloom over the party.〉
5 to throw out, off, or away : SHED 〈Snakes *cast* their skins.〉
6 to make (a vote) formally
7 to assign a part or role to 〈I was *cast* as the hero in the play.〉
8 to give shape to liquid material by pouring it into a mold and letting it harden 〈The statue was *cast* in bronze.〉

[2]**cast** *n*
1 an act of throwing 〈He caught a fish on his first *cast.*〉
2 the characters or the people acting in a play or story
3 a stiff dressing (as of plaster) hardened around a part of the body to allow a broken bone to heal 〈I had a *cast* on my leg.〉
4 a hint of color 〈a bluish *cast*〉
5 the container used to give a shape to the thing made in it

casket 2

cassette 1

6 something formed by casting in a mold or form 〈a bronze *cast* of a statue〉
7 the distance to which a thing can be thrown
8 [2]SHAPE 1 〈His face has a rugged *cast.*〉
9 something (as the skin of an insect or the waste of an earthworm) that is shed or thrown out or off

cas•ta•net \,ka-stə-'net\ *n*
▶ a rhythm instrument that consists of two small flat round parts fastened to the thumb and clicked by the fingers — usually used in pl.

castanet

[1]**cast•away** \'ka-stə-,wā\ *adj*
1 thrown away
2 cast adrift or ashore

[2]**castaway** *n*
a person who is stranded in a place where there are no other people (as because of a shipwreck)

caste \'kast\ *n*
1 one of the classes into which the Hindu people of India were formerly divided
2 a division or class of society based on wealth, rank, or occupation
3 social rank : PRESTIGE

cast•er \'ka-stər\ *n*
one of a set of small wheels on a piece of furniture that makes it easier to move

cas•ti•gate \'ka-stə-,gāt\ *vb* **cas•ti•gat•ed**; **cas•ti•gat•ing**
to punish or criticize harshly

cast•ing \'ka-stiŋ\ *n*
1 the act or action of someone or something that casts
2 something that is cast in a mold 〈a bronze *casting*〉
3 [2]CAST 9

cast iron *n*
a hard and brittle alloy of iron, carbon, and silicon shaped by being poured into a mold while melted

cat 1

The domestic cat is most likely descended from a small wildcat of northern Africa and southwestern Asia. They are popular pets, being both affectionate toward people and skillful hunters, adept at controlling pests. Cats mostly search for their prey at night and can see well in low light levels, focusing on their prey from a distance. Excellent hearing and whiskers that are sensitive to touch also help them to find their way. There are more than 100 recognized breeds and varieties as well as non-pedigree types.

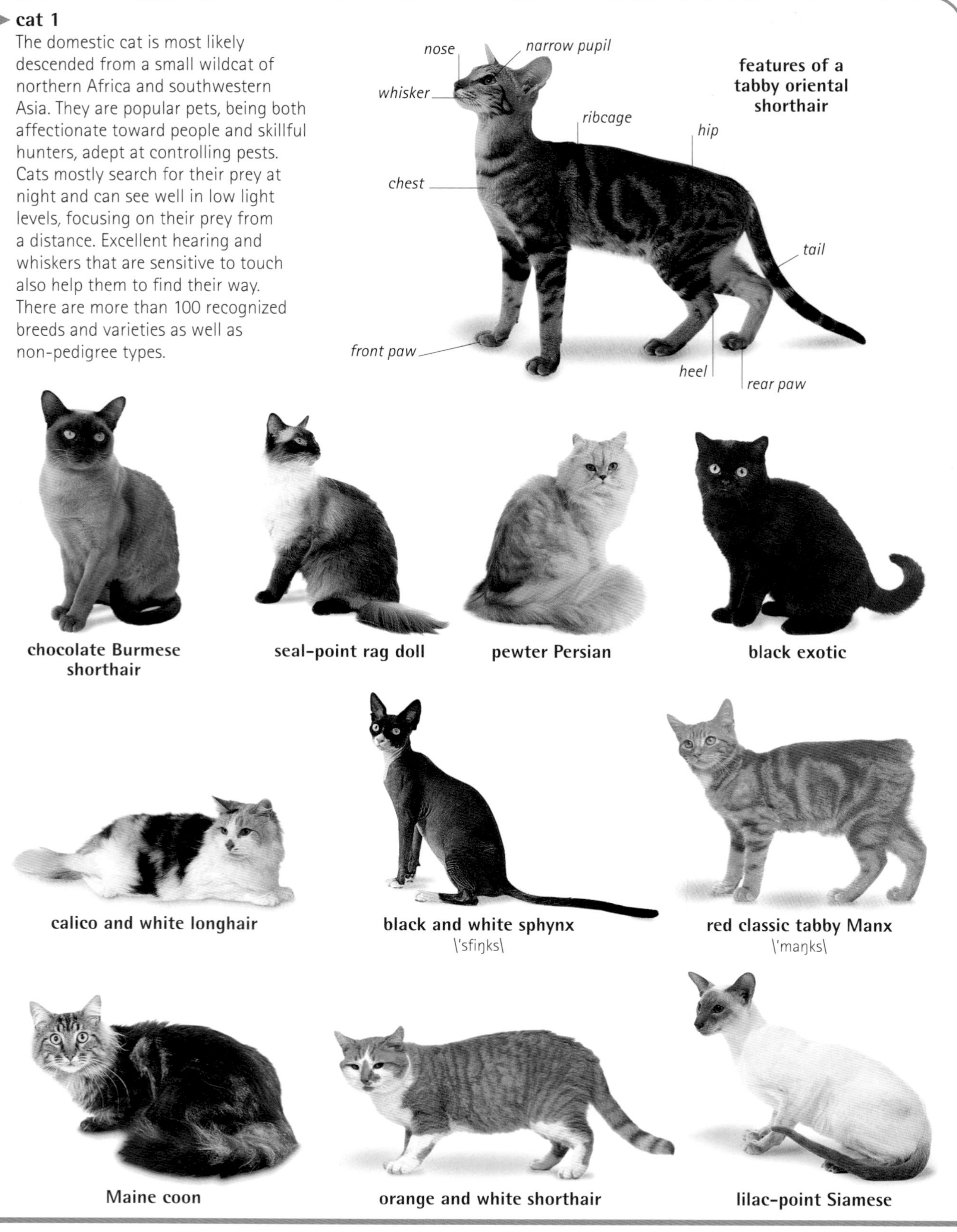

features of a tabby oriental shorthair

chocolate Burmese shorthair

seal-point rag doll

pewter Persian

black exotic

calico and white longhair

black and white sphynx \ˈsfiŋks\

red classic tabby Manx \ˈmaŋks\

Maine coon

orange and white shorthair

lilac-point Siamese

castle 1

cas•tle \'ka-səl\ *n*
1 ▲ a large building or group of buildings usually having high walls with towers that was built in the past to protect against attack
2 a large or impressive house

cast•off \'kast-,ȯf\ *n*
a person or thing that has been thrown aside or rejected

cast–off \'kast-,ȯf\ *adj*
thrown away or aside ⟨She wore *cast-off* clothes.⟩

cas•tor oil \'ka-stər-\ *n*
a thick yellowish liquid that comes from the seeds (**castor beans**) of a tropical herb and is used as a lubricant and as a strong laxative

cas•trate \'ka-,strāt\ *vb* **cas•trat•ed**; **cas•trat•ing**
to remove the sex glands of

ca•su•al \'kazh-wəl, 'ka-zhə-wəl, 'ka-zhəl\ *adj*
1 happening unexpectedly or by chance : not planned or foreseen ⟨a *casual* meeting⟩
2 occurring without regularity : OCCASIONAL ⟨*casual* visits⟩
3 showing or feeling little concern : NONCHALANT ⟨This is awful! How can you be so *casual* about it?⟩
4 meant for informal use ⟨Wear *casual* clothing for the tour.⟩
ca•su•al•ly *adv*

ca•su•al•ty \'ka-zhəl-tē\ *n*, *pl* **ca•su•al•ties**
1 a person who is hurt or killed in a war, disaster, or accident
2 a person or thing injured, lost, or destroyed ⟨The old tree was a *casualty* of the storm.⟩

cat \'kat\ *n*
1 ◀ a common furry meat-eating animal kept as a pet or for catching mice and rats
2 any of a family of mammals (as the lion, tiger, and leopard) to which the domestic cat belongs

[1]cat•a•log *or* **cat•a•logue** \'ka-tə-,lȯg\ *n*
1 a book containing brief descriptions of things that can be purchased or signed up for ⟨a garden supply *catalog*⟩ ⟨a college course *catalogue*⟩
2 a list of names, titles, or articles arranged by some system

[2]catalog *or* **catalogue** *vb* **cat•a•loged** *or* **cat•a•logued**; **cat•a•log•ing** *or* **cat•a•logu•ing**
1 to make a catalog of
2 to enter in a catalog
cat•a•log•er *or* **cat•a•logu•er** *n*

ca•tal•pa \kə-'tal-pə\ *n*
a tree of North America and Asia with broad leaves, showy flowers, and long pods

[1]cat•a•pult \'ka-tə-,pəlt\ *n*
1 ▶ an ancient military machine for hurling stones and arrows
2 a device for launching an airplane from the deck of a ship

[2]catapult *vb* **cat•a•pult•ed**; **cat•a•pult•ing**
1 to throw by or as if by a catapult
2 to quickly advance ⟨The movie role *catapulted* her to fame.⟩

cat•a•ract \'ka-tə-,rakt\ *n*
1 a clouding of the lens of the eye or of the cover around the lens that blocks the passage of light
2 a large waterfall
3 a sudden rush or flow like a waterfall

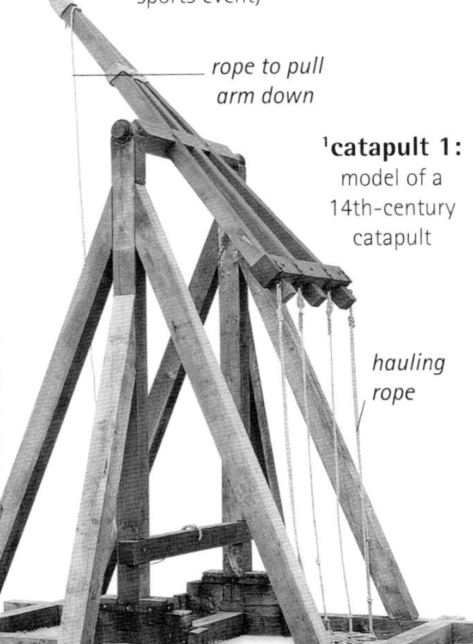

[1]catapult 1: model of a 14th-century catapult

ca•tas•tro•phe \kə-'ta-strə-fē\ *n*
1 a sudden disaster ⟨The oil spill was an environmental *catastrophe*.⟩
2 complete failure : FIASCO ⟨The party was a *catastrophe*.⟩

cat•bird \'kat-,bərd\ *n*
a dark gray songbird that has a call like a cat's meow

cat•boat \'kat-,bōt\ *n*
a sailboat with a single mast set far forward and a single large sail with a long boom

cat•call \'kat-,kȯl\ *n*
a sound like the cry of a cat or a noise expressing disapproval (as at a sports event)

[1]catch \ˈkach, ˈkech\ *vb* **caught** \ˈkȯt\; **catch•ing**
1 to capture and hold ⟨*catch* a ball⟩ ⟨*catch* fish⟩
2 to discover unexpectedly ⟨A policeman *caught* them breaking the window.⟩
3 to stop suddenly before doing something ⟨I *caught* myself before blurting out the secret.⟩
4 to take hold of ⟨As I was falling, Grandma *caught* my arm.⟩
5 to become affected by ⟨*catch* fire⟩ ⟨*catch* a cold⟩
6 to take or get briefly or quickly ⟨He *caught* a glimpse of the actor.⟩
7 to be in time for ⟨I'll *catch* the next bus.⟩
8 to grasp by the senses or the mind ⟨I didn't *catch* what you said.⟩
9 to play catcher on a baseball team
10 to get tangled ⟨She *caught* her sleeve on a nail.⟩
11 to hold firmly : FASTEN ⟨The lock will not *catch.*⟩
12 to recover by resting ⟨I need to *catch* my breath.⟩
catch on
1 to realize something ⟨I finally *caught on* that he was teasing me.⟩
2 to become popular ⟨The new toy *caught on* quickly.⟩
catch up to move or progress fast enough to join another

▶ **Synonyms** CATCH, CAPTURE, and TRAP mean to get possession or control of by or as if by seizing. CATCH is used for the act of trying to seize something or someone that is moving or hiding. ⟨*Catch* that dog!⟩ CAPTURE is used when there is a struggle or some other kind of difficulty. ⟨Police officers *captured* the robbers as they tried to flee.⟩ TRAP is used when there is use of a device that catches and holds the prey. ⟨He made a living by *trapping* animals.⟩

[2]catch *n*
1 something caught : the amount caught at one time ⟨a large *catch* of fish⟩
2 the act of catching ⟨The shortstop made a great *catch.*⟩
3 a pastime in which a ball is thrown and caught
4 something that checks, fastens, or holds immovable ⟨a *catch* on a door⟩
5 a hidden difficulty ⟨Dad got a raise, but there's a *catch*. He needs more training.⟩

catch•er \ˈka-chər, ˈke-\ *n*
1 someone or something that catches
2 ▶ a baseball player who plays behind home plate

catch•ing \ˈka-chiŋ, ˈke-\ *adj*
1 INFECTIOUS 1, CONTAGIOUS ⟨Is her illness *catching?*⟩
2 likely to spread as if infectious ⟨The laughter was *catching.*⟩

catchy \ˈka-chē, ˈke-\ *adj* **catch•i•er; catch•i•est**
likely to attract and be remembered ⟨a *catchy* tune⟩

cat•e•chism \ˈka-tə-ˌki-zəm\ *n*
1 a series of questions and answers used in giving religious instruction
2 a set of formal questions

cat•e•go•ry \ˈka-tə-ˌgȯr-ē\ *n*, *pl* **cat•e•go•ries**
a basic division or grouping of things ⟨He competed in the junior *category.*⟩

ca•ter \ˈkā-tər\ *vb* **ca•tered; ca•ter•ing**
1 to provide a supply of food ⟨*cater* for parties⟩
2 to supply what is needed or wanted
ca•ter•er *n*

cat•er•pil•lar \ˈka-tər-ˌpi-lər, ˈka-tə-ˌpi-\ *n*
a wormlike often hairy larva of an insect and usually a butterfly or moth

▶ **Word History** Our common word for a butterfly or moth larva first appeared in the 1400s as *catirpel*. It is almost certainly borrowed from a medieval French word which we know only in modern French dialects as *catepeleuse*, literally, "hairy cat." Similar applications of a name for a furry animal to fuzzy larvae are English *woolly bear* and French *chenille*, "caterpillar," descended from Latin *canicula*, "little dog."

catcher 2

cat•fish \ˈkat-ˌfish\ *n*
▼ a fish with a large head and feelers about the mouth

catfish: spotted talking catfish

cat•gut \ˈkat-ˌgət\ *n*
a tough cord made from intestines of animals (as sheep) and used for strings of musical instruments and rackets and for sewing in surgery

ca•the•dral \kə-ˈthē-drəl\ *n*
the principal church of a district headed by a bishop

cath•o•lic \ˈkath-lik, ˈka-thə-\ *adj*
1 including many different things or types
2 *cap* of or relating to the Roman Catholic church

Catholic *n*
a member of the Roman Catholic church

cat•kin \ˈkat-kən\ *n*
a flower cluster (as of the willow and birch) in which the flowers grow in close circular rows along a slender stalk

cat•nap \ˈkat-ˌnap\ *n*
a very short light nap

cat•nip \ˈkat-ˌnip\ *n*
a plant that is a mint with a smell especially attractive to cats

catsup *variant of* KETCHUP

cat•tail \ˈkat-ˌtāl\ *n*
a tall plant with long flat leaves and tall furry stalks that grows in marshy areas

cat•tle \ˈka-tᵊl\ *n*, *pl* **cattle**
domestic animals with four feet and especially cows, bulls, and calves

cat•walk \ˈkat-ˌwȯk\ *n*
a narrow walk or way (as along a bridge)

caught *past and past participle of* CATCH

caul•dron *also* **cal•dron** \ˈkȯl-drən\ *n*
a large kettle

cau•li•flow•er \ˈkȯ-li-ˌflau̇-ər, ˈkä-\ *n*
a vegetable that is a white head of undeveloped flowers and is related to the cabbage

[1]caulk \ˈkȯk\ *vb* **caulked; caulk•ing**
to fill up a crack, seam, or joint so as to make it watertight

[2]caulk *also* **caulk•ing** \ˈkȯ-kiŋ\ *n*
material used to fill up a crack, seam, or joint so as to make it watertight

[1]cause \ˈkȯz\ *n*
1 a person or thing that brings about a result ⟨Carelessness is the *cause* of many accidents.⟩

2 a good or good enough reason for something ⟨His return was a *cause* for rejoicing.⟩
3 something supported or deserving support ⟨a worthy *cause*⟩

[2]cause *vb* **caused; caus•ing**
to make happen or exist ⟨You'll *cause* an accident.⟩

[2]cavalier *adj*
1 easy and lighthearted in manner
2 having or showing no concern for a serious or important matter ⟨He has a *cavalier* attitude about money.⟩

cav•al•ry \'ka-vəl-rē\ *n, pl* **cav•al•ries**
a unit of troops mounted on horseback or moving in motor vehicles

[1]cave: a natural cave at Gran Canaria, Spain

[3]cause \'kȯz, 'kəz\ *conj*
BECAUSE

cause•way \'kȯz-,wā\ *n*
a raised road or way across wet ground or water

caus•tic \'kȯ-stik\ *adj*
1 capable of eating away by chemical action : CORROSIVE
2 very harsh and critical ⟨*caustic* remarks⟩

[1]cau•tion \'kȯ-shən\ *n*
1 care taken to avoid trouble or danger : PRECAUTION ⟨They approached the dog with *caution.*⟩
2 WARNING ⟨a word of *caution*⟩

[2]caution *vb* **cau•tioned; cau•tion•ing**
to warn about danger

cau•tious \'kȯ-shəs\ *adj*
showing or using care to avoid trouble or danger
synonyms see CAREFUL
cau•tious•ly *adv*

cav•al•cade \,ka-vəl-'kād\ *n*
1 a procession especially of riders or carriages
2 a dramatic series (as of related events)

[1]cav•a•lier \,ka-və-'lir\ *n*
1 a mounted soldier
2 a brave and courteous gentleman

[1]cave \'kāv\ *n*
▲ a large hollow place formed by natural processes in the side of a hill or cliff or underground

[2]cave *vb* **caved; cav•ing**
to fall or cause to fall in or down : COLLAPSE ⟨The mine *caved* in.⟩

cave•man \'kāv-,man\ *n, pl* **cave•men** \-,men\
a person living in a cave especially during the Stone Age

cav•ern \'ka-vərn\ *n*
a cave often of large or unknown size

cav•ern•ous \'ka-vər-nəs\ *adj*
1 having caverns or hollow places
2 like a cavern in being large and hollow ⟨a *cavernous* cellar⟩

cav•i•ty \'ka-və-tē\ *n, pl* **cav•i•ties**
1 a small hole formed in a tooth by decay
2 a hollow place ⟨The explosion left a *cavity* in the ground.⟩

ca•vort \kə-'vȯrt\ *vb* **ca•vort•ed; ca•vort•ing**
to move or hop about in a lively way

[1]caw \'kȯ\ *n*
the cry of a crow or a raven

[2]caw *vb* **cawed; caw•ing**
to make the sound of a crow or raven

cay \'kē, 'kā\ *n*
[4]KEY

cay•enne pepper \,kī-'en-, ,kā-'en-\ *n*
dried ripe hot peppers ground and used to add flavor to food

CD \,sē-'dē\ *n*
a small plastic disk on which information (as music or computer data) is recorded

CD–ROM \,sē-,dē-'räm\ *n*
a CD that contains computer data that cannot be changed

cease \'sēs\ *vb* **ceased; ceas•ing**
to come or bring to an end : STOP ⟨The talking *ceased.*⟩

cease•less \'sēs-ləs\ *adj*
occurring without stop or over and over again

ce•cro•pia moth \si-'krō-pē-ə-\ *n*
▼ a colorful moth that is the largest moth of North America

cecropia moth

ce•dar \'sē-dər\ *n*
a tree having cones and a strong wood with a pleasant smell

cede \'sēd\ *vb* **ced•ed; ced•ing**
to give up especially by treaty ⟨The land was *ceded* to another country.⟩

ceil•ing \'sē-liŋ\ *n*
1 the overhead inside surface of a room
2 the greatest height at which an airplane can fly properly
3 the height above the ground of the bottom of the lowest layer of clouds
4 an upper limit ⟨a *ceiling* on prices⟩

► **Word History** As we now *line* a coat with a *lining,* we also used to *ceil* a room with a *ceiling.* The verb *ceil,* however, is now very seldom used on its own. Originally to *ceil* was to cover the surfaces of a room—both above and on the sides—with a coating of plaster or with carved panels. *Ceiling* could once mean nearly the same as "paneling," but the only sense we now use refers only to what is overhead in a room.

cel•e•brate \'se-lə-,brāt\ *vb* **cel•e•brat•ed**; **cel•e•brat•ing**
1 to observe (a holiday or important occasion) in some special way
2 to perform (a religious ceremony)
3 [1]PRAISE 1 ⟨We should *celebrate* the freedoms we have.⟩

cel•e•brat•ed \'se-lə-,brā-təd\ *adj*
widely known and praised ⟨a *celebrated* author⟩

cel•e•bra•tion \,se-lə-'brā-shən\ *n*
1 the act of doing something to observe a special occasion
2 the activities or ceremonies for observing a special occasion

ce•leb•ri•ty \sə-'le-brə-tē\ *n*, *pl* **ce•leb•ri•ties**
1 FAME
2 a famous person

celery

cel•ery \'se-lə-rē, 'sel-rē\ *n*
◀ a vegetable that has crisp light green leafstalks that are eaten raw or cooked

ce•les•tial \sə-'les-chəl\ *adj*
1 of, relating to, or suggesting heaven
2 of or relating to the sky ⟨a *celestial* chart⟩

cell \'sel\ *n*
1 a very small room (as in a prison or a monastery)
2 the basic structural unit of living things that is made up of cytoplasm enclosed by a membrane and that typically includes a nucleus and other smaller parts (as mitochondria or chloroplasts) which perform specific functions necessary for life
3 a small enclosed part or division (as in a honeycomb)
4 a container with substances which can produce an electric current by chemical action
5 a device that converts light (as sunlight) that falls on it into electrical energy that is used as a power source
6 CELL PHONE
celled \'seld\ *adj*

cel•lar \'se-lər\ *n*
a room or set of rooms below the surface of the ground : BASEMENT

cell membrane *n*
the thin outside layer that surrounds the cytoplasm of a cell and controls the movement of materials into and out of the cell

cel•lo \'che-lō\ *n*, *pl* **cel•los**
a large stringed instrument of the violin family that plays the bass part

cel•lo•phane \'se-lə-,fān\ *n*
a thin clear material made from cellulose and used as a wrapping

cell phone *n*
▶ a portable telephone that connects to other telephones by radio through a system of transmitters each of which covers a limited geographical area

cell phone

cel•lu•lar \'sel-yə-lər\ *adj*
1 of, relating to, or made up of cells ⟨*cellular* tissue⟩
2 of, relating to, or being a cell phone

cel•lu•lose \'sel-yə-,lōs\ *n*
a substance that is the chief part of the cell walls of plants and is used in making various products (as paper and rayon)

cell wall *n*
the firm outer nonliving layer that surrounds the cell membrane and encloses and supports the cells of most plants, bacteria, and fungi

Cel•si•us \'sel-sē-əs\ *adj*
relating to or having a thermometer scale on which the interval between the freezing point and the boiling point of water is divided into 100 degrees with 0 representing the freezing point and 100 the boiling point

[1]ce•ment \si-'ment\ *n*
1 a powder that is made mainly from compounds of aluminum, calcium, silicon, and iron heated together and then ground and mixed with water to make mortar and concrete
2 [2]CONCRETE, MORTAR
3 a substance used to make things stick together firmly

[2]cement *vb* **ce•ment•ed**; **ce•ment•ing**
1 to join together with or as if with cement
2 to make stronger ⟨The experience *cemented* their friendship.⟩

ce•men•tum \si-'men-təm\ *n*
a thin bony layer covering the part of a tooth inside the gum

cem•e•tery \'se-mə-,ter-ē\ *n*, *pl* **cem•e•ter•ies**
a place where dead people are buried : GRAVEYARD

Ce•no•zo•ic \,sē-nə-'zō-ik, ,se-\ *n*
an era of geological history lasting from 70 million years ago to the present time in which there has been a rapid evolution of mammals and birds and of flowering plants

[1]cen•sor \'sen-sər\ *n*
an official who checks writings or movies to take out things considered offensive or immoral

[2]censor *vb* **cen•sored**; **cen•sor•ing**
to examine (as a book) to take out things considered offensive or immoral

cen•sor•ship \'sen-sər-,ship\ *n*
the system or practice of examining writings or movies and taking out things considered offensive or immoral

[1]cen•sure \'sen-shər\ *n*
1 the act of finding fault with or blaming
2 an official criticism

[2]censure *vb* **cen•sured**; **cen•sur•ing**
to find fault with especially publicly

cen•sus \'sen-səs\ *n*
a count of the number of people in a country, city, or town

cent \'sent\ *n*
1 a hundredth part of the unit of the money system in a number of different countries ⟨In the United States 100 *cents* equal one dollar.⟩
2 a coin, token, or note representing one cent

cent. *abbr*
1 centigrade
2 century

cen•taur \'sen-,tȯr\ *n*
a creature in Greek mythology that is part man and part horse

cen•ten•ni•al \sen-'te-nē-əl\ *n*
a 100th anniversary or a celebration of it
centennial *adj*

[1]cen•ter \'sen-tər\ *n*
1 the middle part of something ⟨the *center* of a room⟩
2 a person or thing characterized by a particular concentration or activity ⟨She likes to be the *center* of attention.⟩
3 a place used for a particular purpose ⟨day care *center*⟩
4 the middle point of a circle or a sphere equally distant from every point on the circumference or surface
5 a player occupying a middle position on a basketball, football, hockey, lacrosse, or soccer team

[2]center *vb* **cen•tered**; **cen•ter•ing**
1 to place or fix at or around a center or central area ⟨Can you *center* the picture on the wall?⟩

2 to collect or concentrate at or around one point, group, or person 〈His life *centers* around his family.〉

center of gravity *n, pl* **centers of gravity**
the point at which the entire weight of a body may be thought of as centered so that if supported at this point the body would balance perfectly

cen•ter•piece \'sen-tər-ˌpēs\ *n*
a piece put in the center of something and especially a decoration (as flowers) for a table

centi- *prefix*
hundredth part 〈*centi*meter〉 — used in terms of the metric system

cen•ti•grade \'sen-tə-ˌgrād\ *adj*
CELSIUS

cen•ti•gram \'sen-tə-ˌgram\ *n*
a unit of weight equal to 1/100 gram

cen•ti•li•ter \'sen-tə-ˌlē-tər\ *n*
a unit of liquid capacity equal to 1/100 liter

cen•ti•me•ter \'sen-tə-ˌmē-tər\ *n*
a unit of length equal to 1/100 meter

cen•ti•pede \'sen-tə-ˌpēd\ *n*
an animal that is an arthropod with a long somewhat flattened body with one pair of legs on most of its many body sections

cen•tral \'sen-trəl\ *adj*
1 located or placed at, in, or near the center 〈*central* Australia〉
2 most important : CHIEF 〈The *central* character of the story is an orphan.〉
cen•tral•ly *adv*

[1]**Central American** *adj*
of or relating to Central America or the Central Americans

[2]**Central American** *n*
a person born or living in Central America

centrifugal force: centrifugal force holds the car on the track

cereal 1
Cereals are one of the world's most important food crops. The ripe seed, or grain, is harvested to make foods such as breakfast cereals, pasta, bread, and cakes. The stems can be used to weave baskets or, when dried, to provide straw for animal bedding and fodder.

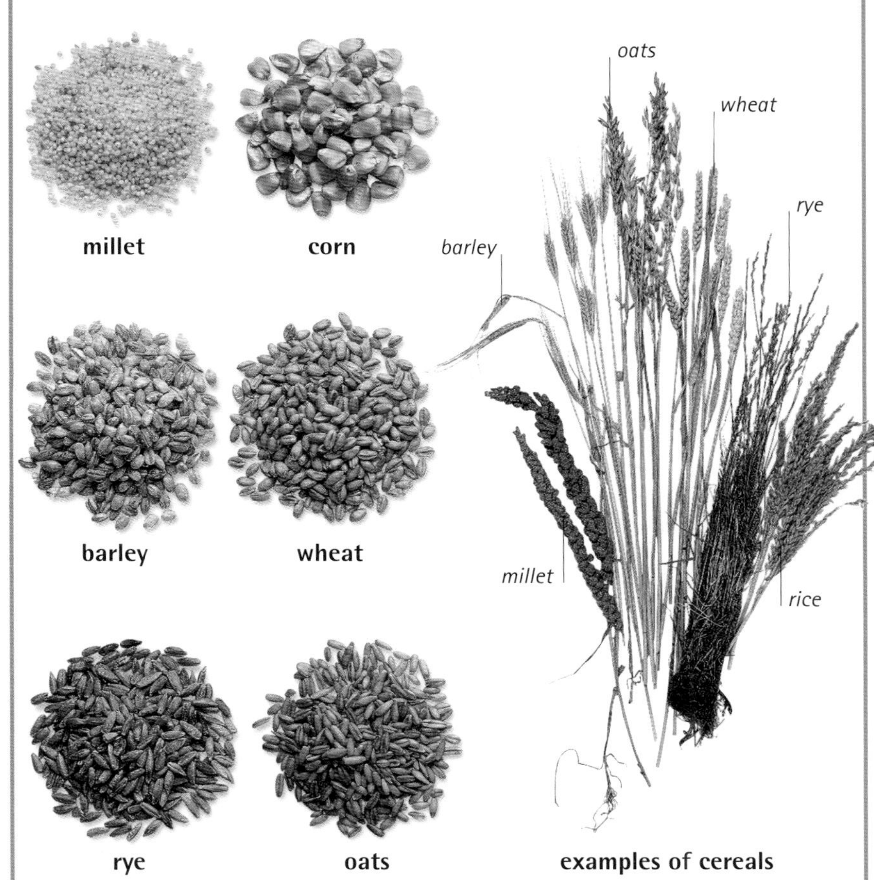

examples of cereals

central angle *n*
an angle with its vertex at the center of a circle and with sides that are radii of the circle

cen•tral•ize \'sen-trə-ˌlīz\ *vb* **cen•tral•ized**; **cen•tral•iz•ing**
to bring to a central point or under a single control 〈The school system *centralized* student records at the main office.〉

central processing unit *n*
PROCESSOR 3

cen•tre *chiefly British variant of* CENTER

cen•trif•u•gal force \sen-'tri-fyə-gəl-\ *n*
◀ the force that tends to cause a thing or parts of a thing to go outward from a center of rotation

cen•tu•ry \'sen-chə-rē, 'sench-rē\ *n, pl* **cen•tu•ries**
a period of 100 years

ce•ram•ic \sə-'ra-mik\ *n*
1 *ceramics pl* the art of making things (as pottery or tiles) of baked clay
2 a product made by baking clay

cereal \'sir-ē-əl\ *n*
1 ▲ a plant (as a grass) that produces grain for food
2 a food prepared from grain 〈breakfast *cereals*〉

▶ **Word History** In Roman mythology Ceres was the goddess of agriculture. A Latin word *Cerealis*, "of Ceres," was formed from her name. Since Ceres was in charge of grain and grain plants, *Cerealis* came to mean "of grain" as well. The English word *cereal* came from this Latin word.

cer•e•bel•lum \ˌser-ə-ˈbe-ləm\ *n, pl* **cer•e•bel•lums** *or* **cer•e•bel•la** \-ˈbe-lə\
the lower back part of the brain whose chief functions are controlling the coordination of muscles and keeping the body in proper balance

ce•re•bral \sə-ˈrē-brəl, ˈser-ə-brəl\ *adj*
1 of or relating to the brain or mind
2 of, relating to, or affecting the cerebrum

ce•re•brum \sə-ˈrē-brəm, ˈser-ə-brəm\ *n, pl* **ce•re•brums** *or* **ce•re•bra** \-brə\
the enlarged front and upper part of the brain that is the center of thinking

[1]cer•e•mo•ni•al \ˌser-ə-ˈmō-nē-əl\ *adj*
of, used in, or being a ceremony ⟨*ceremonial* drums⟩ ⟨a *ceremonial* dinner⟩
cer•e•mo•ni•al•ly *adv*

[2]ceremonial *n*
a special ceremony

cer•e•mo•ni•ous \ˌser-ə-ˈmō-nē-əs\ *adj*
1 [1]CEREMONIAL ⟨a *ceremonious* occasion⟩
2 [1]FORMAL 1
cer•e•mo•ni•ous•ly *adv*

cer•e•mo•ny \ˈser-ə-ˌmō-nē\ *n, pl* **cer•e•mo•nies**
1 an act or series of acts performed in some regular way according to fixed rules especially as part of a social or religious event ⟨the marriage *ceremony*⟩
2 very polite behavior : FORMALITY ⟨"Who are you?" the lady demanded without *ceremony*.⟩

[1]cer•tain \ˈsər-t^{ə}n\ *adj*
1 without any doubt : SURE ⟨Are you *certain* you saw her?⟩
2 known to be true ⟨It's *certain* that they were here.⟩
3 known but not named ⟨A *certain* person told me.⟩
4 being fixed or settled ⟨a *certain* percentage of the profit⟩
5 bound by the way things are ⟨Our plan is *certain* to succeed.⟩
6 sure to have an effect ⟨a *certain* cure⟩

[2]certain *pron*
known ones that are not named ⟨*Certain* of the students could work harder.⟩

cer•tain•ly \ˈsər-t^{ə}n-lē\ *adv*
1 without fail ⟨I will *certainly* help.⟩
2 without doubt ⟨You *certainly* don't look your age.⟩

cer•tain•ty \ˈsər-t^{ə}n-tē\ *n, pl* **cer•tain•ties**
1 something that is sure ⟨Victory was a *certainty*.⟩
2 the quality or state of being sure ⟨She answered with *certainty*.⟩

cer•tif•i•cate \sər-ˈti-fi-kət\ *n*
1 a written or printed statement that is proof of some fact
2 a paper showing that a person has met certain requirements
3 a paper showing ownership

chain saw

cer•ti•fy \ˈsər-tə-ˌfī\ *vb* **cer•ti•fied**; **cer•ti•fy•ing**
1 to show to be true or as claimed by a formal or official statement ⟨Only the teacher can *certify* test scores.⟩
2 to guarantee the quality, fitness, or value of officially ⟨*certified* milk⟩ ⟨*certify* a check⟩
3 to show to have met certain requirements ⟨His school needs to *certify* him for graduation.⟩

ces•sa•tion \se-ˈsā-shən\ *n*
a coming to a stop

ch. *abbr*
1 chapter
2 church

chafe \ˈchāf\ *vb* **chafed**; **chaf•ing**
1 to become irritated or impatient ⟨Some of the guests *chafed* at the sleeping arrangements.⟩
2 to rub so as to wear away or make sore ⟨Chains *chafed* the skin of the animal's legs.⟩

[1]chaff \ˈchaf\ *n*
1 the husks of grains and grasses separated from the seed in threshing
2 something worthless

[2]chaff *vb* **chaffed**; **chaff•ing**
to tease in a friendly way

cha•grin \shə-ˈgrin\ *n*
a feeling of being annoyed by failure or disappointment

[1]chain \ˈchān\ *n*
1 ▶ a series of connected links or rings usually of metal ⟨She wore a gold *chain* around her neck.⟩
2 a series of things joined together as if by links ⟨a *chain* of mountains⟩ ⟨a *chain* of events⟩
3 a group of businesses that have the same name and sell the same products or services ⟨a *chain* of grocery stores⟩

[2]chain *vb* **chained**; **chain•ing**
to fasten, bind, or connect with or as if with a chain ⟨I *chained* my bike to a tree.⟩

chain reaction *n*
a series of events in which each event causes the next one

chain saw *n*
◀ a portable saw that cuts using teeth that are linked together to form a continuous chain

chair \ˈcher\ *n*
1 ▶ a seat for one person usually having a back and four legs
2 a person who leads a meeting, group, or event

chair•man \ˈcher-mən\ *n, pl* **chair•men** \-mən\
1 CHAIR 2
2 a person who is in charge of a company
chair•man•ship \-ˌship\ *n*

chair•per•son \ˈcher-ˌpər-s^{ə}n\ *n*
CHAIR 2

chair•wom•an \ˈcher-ˌwu̇-mən\ *n, pl* **chair•wom•en** \-ˌwi-mən\
1 a woman who leads a meeting, group, or event : CHAIR
2 a woman who is in charge of a company

cha•let \sha-ˈlā\ *n*
1 a Swiss dwelling with a steep roof that sticks far out past the walls
2 a cottage or house built to look like a Swiss chalet

chal•ice \ˈcha-ləs\ *n*
GOBLET

[1]chalk \ˈchȯk\ *n*
1 a soft white, gray, or buff limestone made up mainly of the shells of tiny saltwater animals
2 a material like chalk especially when used for writing or drawing

[2]chalk *vb* **chalked**; **chalk•ing**
to rub, mark, write, or draw with chalk
chalk up
1 to attribute to a supposed cause or source ⟨Her mistakes can be *chalked up* to inexperience.⟩
2 to earn or achieve ⟨The business *chalked up* large profits.⟩

chalk•board \ˈchȯk-ˌbȯrd\ *n*
BLACKBOARD

[1]chain 1

chair 1

From earliest civilized times, chairs have been used for relaxation and as seating around tables. Today, there are many different styles of chair to suit a range of of functions within the office, home, and garden. Chairs may be simple, or padded and upholstered. Not always strictly practical, chairs reflect contemporary styles of fashion.

beach chair

dining chair

office chair

armchair

baby's
high chair

chalky \'chȯ-kē\ *adj* **chalk•i•er; chalk•i•est**
1 made of or like chalk ⟨*chalky* rock⟩
2 very pale ⟨His face was *chalky* from fright.⟩

¹chal•lenge \'cha-lənj\ *vb* **chal•lenged; chal•leng•ing**
1 to object to as bad or incorrect : DISPUTE ⟨The coach *challenged* the referee's call.⟩
2 to confront or defy boldly ⟨He *challenged* them to prove him wrong.⟩
3 to invite or dare to take part in a contest ⟨Are you *challenging* us to a race?⟩
4 to be difficult enough to be interesting to : test the skill or ability of ⟨This puzzle will *challenge* you.⟩
5 to halt and demand identification from ⟨The guard *challenged* the stranger.⟩
chal•leng•er *n*

²challenge *n*
1 an objection to something as not being true, genuine, correct, or proper or to a person (as a juror) as not being correct, qualified, or approved
2 a call or dare for someone to compete in a contest or sport
3 a difficult task or problem ⟨Memorizing the poem was a *challenge*.⟩
4 an order to stop and provide identification

challenged *adj*
having a disability or deficiency

cham•ber \'chām-bər\ *n*
1 an enclosed space, cavity, or compartment ⟨the *chambers* of the heart⟩
2 a room in a house and especially a bedroom
3 a room used for a special purpose ⟨the pyramid's burial *chamber*⟩
4 a meeting hall of a government body ⟨the Senate *chamber*⟩
5 a room where a judge conducts business outside of the courtroom
6 a group of people organized into a lawmaking body ⟨The Senate and the House of Representatives make up the two *chambers* of the United States legislature.⟩
7 a board or council of volunteers (as businessmen)
cham•bered \-bərd\ *adj*

cham•ber•lain \'chām-bər-lən\ *n*
1 a chief officer in the household of a ruler or noble
2 TREASURER ⟨city *chamberlain*⟩

cham•ber•maid \'chām-bər-ˌmād\ *n*
a maid who takes care of bedrooms (as in a hotel)

chamber music *n*
instrumental music to be performed in a room or small hall

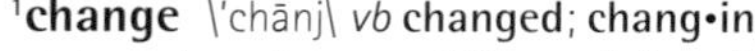

cha•me•leon \kə-ˈmēl-yən\ *n*
▼ a lizard that has the ability to change the color of its skin

chameleon

▶ **Word History** Many of the lizards of the Old World must have looked quite startling. They may even have reminded the ancients of small lions. The Greeks gave these strange-looking lizards the name *chamaileōn*, a compound of *chamai*, "on the ground," and *leōn*, "lion." The English word *chameleon* came from the Greek word.

cham•ois \ˈsha-mē\ *n*, *pl* **cham•ois** \-mē, -mēz\
1 ▼ a goatlike animal of the mountains of Europe and Asia
2 a soft yellowish leather made from the skin of the chamois or from sheepskin

chamois 1

[1]**champ** \ˈchamp\ *vb* **champed**; **champ•ing**
to bite and chew noisily ⟨a horse *champing* its bit⟩
champing at the bit waiting in an impatient way ⟨We were *champing at the bit* to begin.⟩

[2]**champ** *n*
1 [1]CHAMPION 2
2 [1]CHAMPION 3

[1]**cham•pi•on** \ˈcham-pē-ən\ *n*
1 a person who fights or speaks for another person or in favor of a cause ⟨a *champion* of equal rights⟩
2 a person accepted as better than all others in a sport or in a game of skill
3 the winner of first place in a competition

[2]**champion** *vb* **cham•pi•oned**; **cham•pi•on•ing**
to fight or speak publicly in support of ⟨*championing* a cause⟩

cham•pi•on•ship \ˈcham-pē-ən-ˌship\ *n*
1 the position or title of best or winning player or team in a sport or game of skill ⟨The skier was defending her *championship*.⟩
2 a contest held to determine the best or winning player or team in a sport or game

[1]**chance** \ˈchans\ *n*
1 the happening of events that is not planned or controlled ⟨They met by *chance*.⟩
2 OPPORTUNITY 1 ⟨I had a *chance* to travel.⟩
3 [1]RISK 1, GAMBLE ⟨take *chances*⟩
4 the possibility that something will happen ⟨There's a slight *chance* of rain.⟩
5 a ticket in a raffle ⟨He bought five *chances*.⟩

[2]**chance** *vb* **chanced**; **chanc•ing**
1 to take place without planning : to happen by luck
2 to find or meet unexpectedly ⟨I *chanced* on a bargain.⟩
3 to accept the danger of : RISK ⟨He couldn't *chance* another injury.⟩

[3]**chance** *adj*
happening without being planned ⟨a *chance* meeting⟩

chan•cel•lor \ˈchan-sə-lər, ˈchan-slər\ *n*
1 a high government official (as in Germany)
2 the head of a university

chan•de•lier \ˌshan-də-ˈlir\ *n*
▶ a lighting fixture with several branches that usually hangs from the ceiling

chandelier: a black metal ornate chandelier

[1]**change** \ˈchānj\ *vb* **changed**; **chang•ing**
1 to make or become different ⟨*changing* autumn leaves⟩ ⟨I like how you've *changed* this room.⟩
2 to give a different position, course, or direction to ⟨I *changed* my plans.⟩
3 to put one thing in the place of another : SWITCH ⟨Our teacher made us *change* places.⟩
4 to give or receive an equal amount of money in usually smaller units of value or in the money of another country ⟨Can you *change* a ten-dollar bill?⟩
5 to put fresh clothes or covering on ⟨*change* a bed⟩
6 to put on different clothes ⟨We always *change* for dinner.⟩
change hands to pass from one person's possession or ownership to another's ⟨The restaurant has *changed hands*.⟩

▶ **Synonyms** CHANGE, ALTER, and VARY mean to make or become different. CHANGE may be used for making such a difference in a thing that it becomes something else. ⟨They've *changed* the house into a restaurant.⟩ CHANGE may also be used for substituting one thing for another. ⟨We *changed* our seats for better ones.⟩ ALTER is used for making a small difference in something. ⟨He *altered* the picture by adding color.⟩ VARY is used for making a difference in order to break away from a routine. ⟨The boss *varied* our tasks.⟩

[2]**change** *n*
1 the act, process, or result of making or becoming different ⟨There's been a *change* in plans.⟩ ⟨a *change* of seasons⟩
2 something that is different from what is usual or expected ⟨The trip was a welcome *change* from our routine.⟩
3 a fresh set of clothes ⟨Pack several *changes* for your vacation.⟩
4 money in small units of value received in exchange for an equal amount in larger units ⟨Do you have *change* for a ten-dollar bill?⟩
5 money returned when a payment is more than the amount due ⟨Don't forget your *change*.⟩
6 money in coins ⟨I have two dollars in *change*.⟩

change•able \ˈchān-jə-bəl\ *adj*
able or likely to become different ⟨*changeable* weather⟩

[1]**chan•nel** \ˈcha-nᵊl\ *n*
1 the bed of a stream
2 the deeper part of a waterway (as a river or harbor)
3 a strait or a narrow sea ⟨the English *Channel*⟩
4 a passage (as a tube) through which something flows ⟨an irrigation *channel*⟩
5 a long groove
6 a means by which something is passed or carried from one place or person to another ⟨*channels* of trade⟩ ⟨a *channel* of communication⟩
7 a band of frequencies used by a single radio or television station in broadcasting ⟨What's on this *channel*?⟩

[2]**channel** *vb* **chan•neled** *or* **chan•nelled**; **chan•nel•ing** *or* **chan•nel•ling**
to direct into or through a passage or channel ⟨Water was *channeled* into the pond.⟩

[1]**chant** \ˈchant\ *vb* **chant•ed**; **chant•ing**
1 to sing using a small number of musical tones
2 to recite or speak in a rhythmic usually loud way ⟨The crowd began *chanting* her name.⟩

[2]**chant** *n*
1 a melody in which several words or syllables are sung on one tone
2 something spoken in a rhythmic usually loud way

Chanukah *variant of* HANUKKAH

cha•os \ˈkā-ˌäs\ *n*
complete confusion and disorder

cha•ot•ic \kā-ˈä-tik\ *adj*
in a state of or characterized by complete confusion and disorder ⟨a *chaotic* scene⟩

[1]**chap** \ˈchap\ *vb* **chapped**; **chap•ping**
to open in slits : CRACK ⟨My lips always *chap* in the winter.⟩

[2]**chap** *n*
[1]FELLOW 1 ⟨He's a friendly *chap*.⟩

chap•el \ˈcha-pəl\ *n*
1 ▶ a building or a room or place for prayer or special religious services
2 a religious service or assembly held in a school or college

[1]**chap•er•one** *or* **chap•er•on** \ˈsha-pə-ˌrōn\ *n*
a person who goes with and is responsible for a group of young people

[2]**chaperone** *or* **chaperon** *vb* **chap•er•oned**; **chap•er•on•ing**
to go with and supervise a group of young people : act as a chaperone ⟨Several parents *chaperoned* the school dance.⟩

chap•lain \ˈcha-plən\ *n*
a member of the clergy who performs religious services for a special group (as the army)

chaps \ˈshaps, ˈchaps\ *n pl*
leather coverings for the legs worn over pants ⟨a cowboy's *chaps*⟩

chap•ter \ˈchap-tər\ *n*
1 a main division of a book or story
2 a local branch of a club or organization ⟨the charity's Springfield *chapter*⟩

char \ˈchär\ *vb* **charred**; **char•ring**
to burn slightly

char•ac•ter \ˈker-ək-tər\ *n*
1 a mark, sign, or symbol (as a letter or figure) used in writing or printing
2 the group of qualities that make a person, group, or thing different from others ⟨The town has special *character*.⟩
3 a distinguishing feature : CHARACTERISTIC ⟨the plant's bushy *character*⟩
4 a person who says or does funny or unusual things ⟨Your friend is quite a *character*.⟩
5 a person in a story or play
6 the usually good opinions that most people have about a particular person : REPUTATION ⟨She made an attack on his *character*.⟩
7 moral excellence ⟨She is a person of *character* known for her honesty.⟩

[1]**char•ac•ter•is•tic** \ˌker-ək-tə-ˈri-stik\ *n*
a special quality or appearance that makes an individual or a group different from others ⟨physical *characteristics*⟩ ⟨Gentleness is a *characteristic* of this dog breed.⟩

[2]**characteristic** *adj*
serving to distinguish an individual or a group : typical of a person, thing, or group ⟨He replied with *characteristic* good humor.⟩
char•ac•ter•is•ti•cal•ly \ˌker-ək-tə-ˈris-ti-kə-lē\ *adv*

chapel 1: a chapel in Santa Fe, New Mexico

char•ac•ter•ize \ˈker-ək-tə-ˌrīz\ *vb* **char•ac•ter•ized**; **char•ac•ter•iz•ing**
1 to describe the special qualities of ⟨I would *characterize* this as a positive change.⟩
2 to be a typical or distinguishing quality of ⟨Mystery and intrigue *characterize* this story.⟩

char•coal \ˈchär-ˌkōl\ *n*
a black or dark absorbent fuel made by heating wood in the absence of air

[1]**charge** \ˈchärj\ *n*
1 the responsibility of managing, controlling, or caring for ⟨She has *charge* of the building.⟩ ⟨He took *charge* of the planning.⟩
2 a task or duty given to a person : OBLIGATION ⟨Grooming the animals was his *charge*.⟩
3 a person or thing given to someone to look after
4 the price asked especially for a service
5 an amount listed as a debt on an account ⟨*charges* on a phone bill⟩
6 ACCUSATION ⟨a *charge* of mutiny⟩
7 an instruction or command based on authority ⟨a judge's *charge* to a jury⟩
8 the amount of an explosive material (as dynamite) used in a single blast
9 an amount of electricity ⟨an electrical *charge*⟩
10 a rushing attack ⟨the soldiers' *charge*⟩
11 the signal for attack ⟨Sound the *charge*!⟩
synonyms see PRICE

[2]**charge** *vb* **charged**; **charg•ing**
1 to give an electric charge to ⟨*charge* a device⟩
2 to refill (as an exhausted battery) with available energy
3 to give a task, duty, or responsibility to ⟨I was *charged* with supervising the children.⟩
4 to instruct or command with authority
5 to accuse especially formally ⟨He was *charged* with speeding.⟩
6 to rush toward or against ⟨The bull *charged* the matador.⟩
7 to ask for payment from ⟨You *charged* me too much.⟩
8 to ask or set as a price or fee ⟨The garage *charged* 100 dollars for repairs.⟩
9 to enter as a debt or responsibility on a record ⟨The purchase was *charged* to her account.⟩

charg•er \ˈchär-jər\ *n*
1 a device that restores energy to an exhausted battery
2 a cavalry horse

char•i•ot \'cher-ē-ət\ *n*
▶ a vehicle of ancient times that had two wheels, was pulled by horses, and was used in battle and in races and parades

chariot: an ancient Roman chariot

char•i•ta•ble \'cher-ə-tə-bəl\ *adj*
1 freely giving money or help to needy persons : GENEROUS
2 given for the needy : of service to the needy ⟨*charitable* donations⟩ ⟨*charitable* organizations⟩
3 kindly especially in judging other people

char•i•ty \'cher-ə-tē\ *n, pl* **char•i•ties**
1 love for others
2 kindliness especially in judging others
3 the giving of aid to the needy
4 aid (as food or money) given to those in need
5 an organization for helping the needy

char•la•tan \'shär-lə-tən\ *n*
a person who falsely pretends to know or be something ⟨The *charlatan* sold useless medicinal potions.⟩

char•ley horse \'chär-lē-,hȯrs\ *n*
a painful cramp in a muscle (as of the leg)

[1]**charm** \'chärm\ *n*
1 an action, word, or phrase believed to have magic powers
2 something believed to keep away evil and bring good luck
3 a small decorative object worn on a chain or bracelet
4 a quality that attracts and pleases ⟨The café has old-fashioned *charm.*⟩

[2]**charm** *vb* **charmed**; **charm•ing**
1 to affect or influence by or as if by a magic spell ⟨He *charmed* the group into supporting him.⟩
2 FASCINATE 2, DELIGHT ⟨She was *charmed* by the idea.⟩
3 to attract by being graceful, beautiful, or welcoming ⟨I was *charmed* by the inn.⟩
4 to protect by or as if by a charm ⟨She leads a *charmed* life.⟩

charm•ing \'chär-miŋ\ *adj*
very pleasing ⟨a *charming* young man⟩

[1]**chart** \'chärt\ *n*
1 a sheet giving information in a table or lists or by means of diagrams ⟨a seating *chart*⟩ ⟨a growth *chart*⟩
2 a map showing features (as coasts, currents, and depths of water) of importance to sailors
3 ▼ a diagram of an area showing information other than natural features

[2]**chart** *vb* **chart•ed**; **chart•ing**
1 to make a map or chart of ⟨*chart* the seas⟩ ⟨They *charted* their results.⟩
2 to make a plan for ⟨We *charted* our next move.⟩

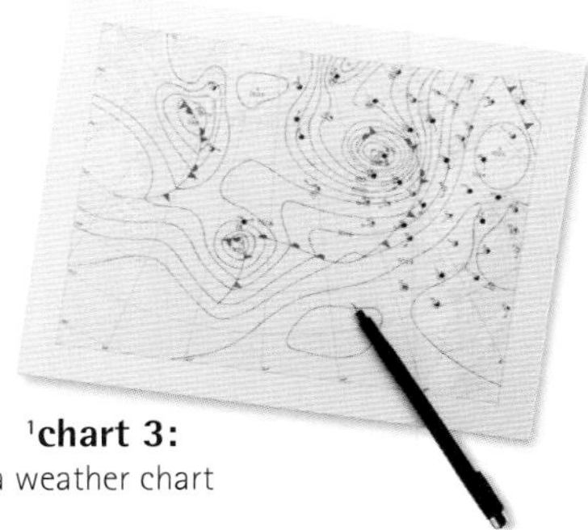
[1]**chart 3:** a weather chart

[1]**char•ter** \'chär-tər\ *n*
1 an official document setting out the rights and duties of a group ⟨The settlers were granted a *charter* by the king.⟩
2 a document which declares that a city, town, school, or corporation has been established ⟨our town's *charter*⟩
3 a document that describes the basic laws or principles of a group ⟨the charity's *charter*⟩

[2]**charter** *vb* **char•tered**; **char•ter•ing**
1 to grant a charter to ⟨The city was *chartered* in 1853.⟩
2 to hire (as a bus or an aircraft) for temporary use ⟨*charter* a plane⟩

charter school *n*
a public school that is established by a charter describing its programs and goals and is supported by taxes but does not have to be run according to many of the rules of a city or state

[1]**chase** \'chās\ *n*
the act of following quickly in order to capture or catch up with : PURSUIT ⟨Police caught the bank robbers after a *chase.*⟩

[2]**chase** *vb* **chased**; **chas•ing**
1 to follow quickly in order to catch up with or capture ⟨*chase* a thief⟩ ⟨*chase* a bus⟩
2 to drive away or out ⟨She *chased* the rabbit away.⟩

▶ **Synonyms** CHASE, PURSUE, and FOLLOW mean to go after someone or something. CHASE is used of someone or something moving swiftly in order to catch up with something. ⟨The children *chased* the ball.⟩ PURSUE is used of a long, continual chase. ⟨They *pursued* the enemy for miles.⟩ FOLLOW does not suggest speed or a desire to actually catch up with something. ⟨This dog *followed* me home.⟩

chasm \'ka-zəm\ *n*
a deep split or gap in the earth

chas•sis \'cha-sē, 'sha-\ *n, pl* **chas•sis** \-sēz\
the supporting frame of a structure (as an automobile or television)

chaste \'chāst\ *adj* **chast•er**; **chast•est**
1 pure in thought and act : MODEST
2 simple or plain in design

chas•ten \'chā-sᵊn\ *vb* **chas•tened**; **chas•ten•ing**
to correct by punishment : DISCIPLINE

chas•tise \cha-'stīz\ *vb* **chas•tised**; **chas•tis•ing**
1 to punish severely (as by whipping)
2 to criticize harshly ⟨The boy was *chastised* for his behavior.⟩
chas•tise•ment \-mənt\ *n*

chas•ti•ty \'cha-stə-tē\ *n*
the quality or state of being pure in thought and act

[1]**chat** \'chat\ *vb* **chat•ted**; **chat•ting**
1 to talk in a friendly way about things that are not serious
2 to talk over the Internet by sending messages back and forth in a chat room

[2]**chat** *n*
1 a light friendly conversation
2 a talk held over the Internet by people using a chat room

chat room *n*
a Web site or computer program that allows people to send messages to each other instantly over the Internet

châ•teau \sha-'tō\ *n, pl* **châ•teaus** \-'tōz\ *or* **châ•teaux** \-'tō, -'tōz\
▶ a castle or a large house especially in France

A B C D E F G H I J K L M N O P Q R S T U V W X Y Z

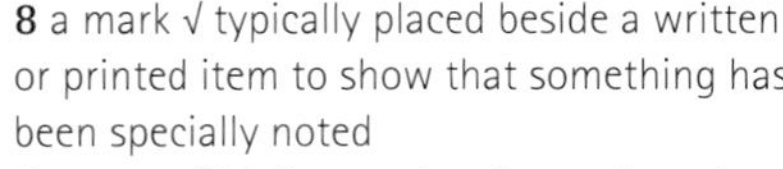

¹chat•ter \ˈcha-tər\ *vb* **chat•tered**; **chat•ter•ing**
1 to talk fast without thinking or without stopping ⟨My brothers *chattered* during the entire trip.⟩
2 to make quick sounds that suggest speech but lack meaning ⟨Monkeys *chattered* in the trees.⟩
3 to make clicking sounds by hitting together again and again ⟨My teeth are *chattering* from the cold.⟩

²chatter *n*
1 the act or sound of chattering ⟨the *chatter* of squirrels⟩ ⟨the *chatter* of teeth⟩
2 quick or unimportant talk

chat•ter•box \ˈcha-tər-ˌbäks\ *n*
a person who talks a lot

chat•ty \ˈcha-tē\ *adj* **chat•ti•er**; **chat•ti•est**
1 tending to talk a lot : TALKATIVE
2 having the style and manner of friendly conversation ⟨a *chatty* letter⟩

chauf•feur \ˈshō-fər, shō-ˈfər\ *n*
a person hired to drive people around in a car

¹cheap \ˈchēp\ *adj* **cheap•er**; **cheap•est**
1 not costing much ⟨I bought the *cheapest* cereal in the store.⟩
2 charging low prices ⟨a *cheap* hotel⟩
3 worth little : of low quality ⟨*cheap* perfume⟩
4 gained without much effort ⟨a *cheap* victory⟩
5 having little self-respect ⟨I feel *cheap* from lying to my mother.⟩
6 not willing to share or spend money : STINGY ⟨She was too *cheap* to pay for dinner.⟩
cheap•ly *adv*

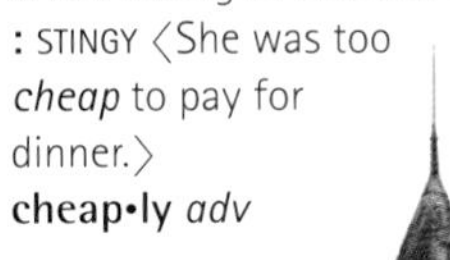

²cheap *adv*
at low cost ⟨They'll build you a house *cheap*.⟩

cheap•en \ˈchē-pən\ *vb* **cheap•ened**; **cheap•en•ing**
to cause to be of lower quality, value, or importance ⟨Products are *cheapened* by poor workmanship.⟩

cheap•skate \ˈchēp-ˌskāt\ *n*
a stingy person

¹cheat \ˈchēt\ *vb* **cheat•ed**; **cheat•ing**
1 to use unfair or dishonest methods to gain an advantage ⟨*cheat* on a test⟩
2 to take something away from or keep from having something by dishonest tricks
cheat•er \ˈchē-tər\ *n*

²cheat *n*
a dishonest person

¹check \ˈchek\ *n*
1 a sudden stopping of progress : PAUSE ⟨The anchor gave a *check* to the ship's motion.⟩
2 something that delays, stops, or holds back ⟨The new penalty will serve as a *check* on pollution.⟩
3 EXAMINATION 1, INVESTIGATION ⟨a safety *check*⟩
4 a written order telling a bank to pay out money from a person's account to the one named on the order
5 a ticket or token showing a person's ownership, identity, or claim to something ⟨a baggage *check*⟩
6 a slip of paper showing the amount due
7 a pattern in squares ⟨The shirt has a blue and red *check*.⟩
8 a mark √ typically placed beside a written or printed item to show that something has been specially noted
9 an act of hitting or stopping a player in hockey
10 a situation in chess in which a player's king can be captured on the opponent's next turn
in check under control ⟨Try to keep your emotions *in check*.⟩

²check *vb* **checked**; **check•ing**
1 to slow or bring to a stop ⟨A bandage *checked* the bleeding.⟩
2 to hold back or under control ⟨You must *check* your temper.⟩
3 to make sure that something is correct or satisfactory ⟨Don't forget to *check* your spelling.⟩
4 to get information by examining ⟨He *checked* his watch.⟩
5 to mark with a check ⟨*Check* the correct answer.⟩
6 to leave or accept for safekeeping or for shipment ⟨*check* baggage⟩
7 to stop or hit (a player) in hockey
check out
1 to look at ⟨*Check out* his new car.⟩
2 to borrow from a library ⟨She *checked out* two books.⟩
3 to pay for purchases

checked \ˈchekt\ *adj*
CHECKERED

check•er•board \ˈche-kər-ˌbȯrd\ *n*
a board marked with 64 squares in two colors and used for games (as checkers)

check•ered \ˈche-kərd\ *adj*
having a pattern made up of squares of different colors

check•ers \ˈche-kərz\ *n*
a game played on a checkerboard by two players each having twelve pieces

checking account *n*
an account in a bank from which the depositor can draw money by writing checks

check•mate \ˈchek-ˌmāt\ *n*
a situation in chess in which a player loses because the player's king is in a position from which it cannot escape capture

check•up \ˈchek-ˌəp\ *n*
1 INSPECTION, EXAMINATION
2 a general physical examination made by a doctor or veterinarian

cheek \ˈchēk\ *n*
1 the side of the face below the eye and above and to the side of the mouth
2 disrespectful speech or behavior

cheeky \ˈchē-kē\ *adj* **cheek•i•er**; **cheek•i•est**
showing disrespect : RUDE

château

A B C D E F G H I J K L M N O P Q R S T U V W X Y Z

[1]cheep \'chēp\ *vb* **cheeped**; **cheep•ing**
[3]PEEP, CHIRP ⟨The chicks were *cheeping* for food.⟩

[2]cheep *n*
[1]CHIRP

[1]cheer \'chir\ *n*
1 a happy feeling : good spirits ⟨full of *cheer*⟩
2 something that gladdens ⟨words of *cheer*⟩
3 a shout of praise or encouragement ⟨The crowd let out a *cheer*.⟩

[2]cheer *vb* **cheered**; **cheer•ing**
1 to give hope to or make happier : COMFORT ⟨Signs of spring *cheered* her.⟩
2 to grow or be cheerful — usually used with *up*
3 to urge on especially with shouts or cheers ⟨They *cheered* the team to victory.⟩
4 to shout with joy, approval, or enthusiasm ⟨We *cheered* when he crossed the finish line.⟩

cheer•ful \'chir-fəl\ *adj*
1 feeling or showing happiness
2 causing good feelings or happiness ⟨*cheerful* news⟩
3 pleasantly bright ⟨a sunny *cheerful* room⟩
cheer•ful•ly \-fə-lē\ *adv*
cheer•ful•ness *n*

cheer•less \'chir-ləs\ *adj*
offering no happiness or cheer : GLOOMY ⟨a *cheerless* room⟩

cheery \'chir-ē\ *adj* **cheer•i•er**; **cheer•i•est**
merry and bright in manner or effect : CHEERFUL ⟨a *cheery* voice⟩ ⟨a *cheery* welcome⟩
cheer•i•ly \-ə-lē\ *adv*
cheer•i•ness \-ē-nəs\ *n*

cheese \'chēz\ *n*
▼ the curd of milk pressed for use as food

cheese•cloth \'chēz-,klȯth\ *n*
a thin loosely woven cotton cloth

cheesy \'chē-zē\ *adj* **chees•i•er**; **chees•i•est**
1 resembling cheese especially in appearance or smell ⟨a *cheesy* texture⟩
2 containing cheese ⟨a *cheesy* sauce⟩
3 of poor quality : lacking style or good taste

chee•tah \'chē-tə\ *n*
▼ a long-legged spotted African and formerly Asian animal of the cat family that is the fastest animal on land

chef \'shef\ *n*
1 a professional cook who is usually in charge of a kitchen in a restaurant
2 [1]COOK ⟨My mom is a great *chef*.⟩

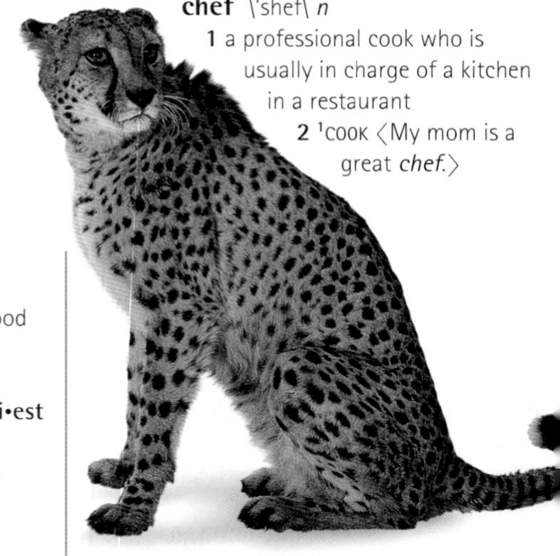

cheetah

cheese

Cheese is made from curdled milk or cream. The solid curds produced are put into molds to ripen. The time a cheese is left to mature and the type of milk used determine its texture and flavor. Hard cheese is matured for a long time, while soft cheese is ripened only briefly. Most cheese is produced from cow's milk, but milk from goats and sheep is also used.

Parmesan \'pär-mə-,zän\ is a very hard cheese

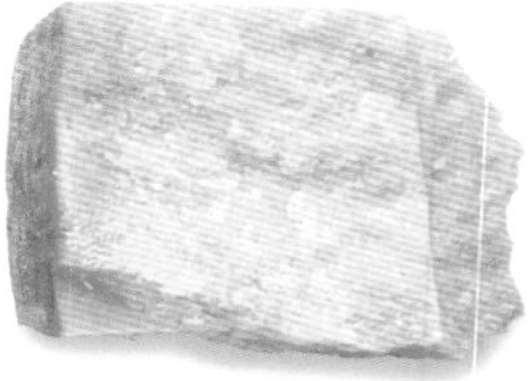

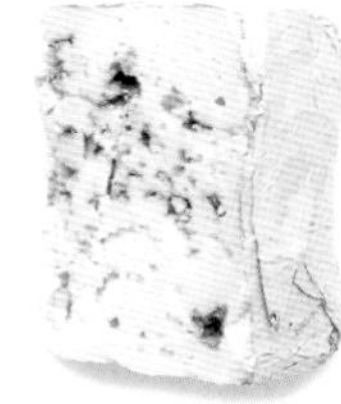
blue cheese has veins of greenish-blue mold

mozzarella \,mät-sə-'rel-ə\ is a soft cheese

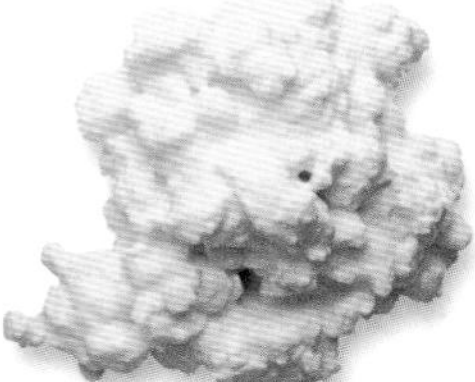
cottage cheese is a very soft cheese

Edam \'ē-dəm\ is a hard cheese

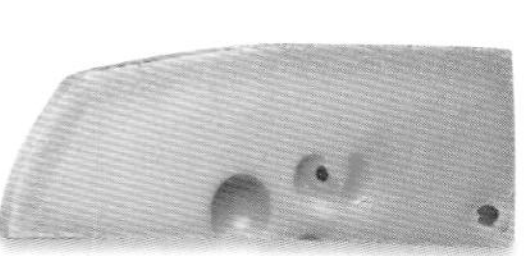
Swiss cheese is a hard cheese with large holes

Brie \'brē\ is a soft cheese

Monterey Jack \'män-tə-,rā-'jak\ is a semisoft cheese

cheddar \'ched-ər\ is a hard cheese

feta \'fe-tə\ is a crumbly goat cheese

[1]chem•i•cal \'ke-mi-kəl\ *adj*
of or relating to chemistry or chemicals
chem•i•cal•ly *adv*

[2]chemical *n*
any substance (as an acid) that is formed when two or more other substances act upon one another or that is used to produce a change in another substance

chem•ist \'ke-mist\ *n*
a person trained or engaged in chemistry

chem•is•try \'ke-mə-strē\ *n*
1 a science that deals with the composition and properties of substances and of the changes they undergo
2 chemical composition and properties ⟨the *chemistry* of food⟩

cher•ish \'cher-ish\ *vb* **cher•ished**; **cher•ish•ing**
1 to hold dear **:** feel or show affection for ⟨*cherish* a friend⟩
2 to remember or hold in a deeply felt way ⟨She *cherishes* the memory.⟩
synonyms see APPRECIATE

Cher•o•kee \'cher-ə-kē\ *n, pl* **Cherokee** *or* **Cherokees**
1 a member of an American Indian people originally of Tennessee and North Carolina
2 the language of the Cherokee people

cherry 1

cher•ry \'cher-ē\ *n, pl* **cherries**
1 ▲ the small round yellow to deep red smooth-skinned fruit of a tree that is related to the plum tree
2 a medium red

cher•ub \'cher-əb\ *n*
1 a beautiful child usually with wings in paintings and drawings
2 a cute chubby child

chess \'ches\ *n*
► a game for two players in which each player moves 16 pieces according to fixed rules across a checkerboard and tries to place the opponent's king in a position from which it cannot escape

chest \'chest\ *n*
1 a container (as a box or case) for storing, safekeeping, or shipping ⟨tool *chest*⟩ ⟨treasure *chest*⟩
2 the front part of the body enclosed by the ribs and breastbone
3 a fund of public money ⟨a community *chest* to benefit the needy⟩
chest•ed \'che-stəd\ *adj*

chest•nut \'ches-,nət\ *n*
1 a sweet edible nut that grows in burs on a tree related to the beech
2 a reddish brown

chev•ron \'shev-rən\ *n*
a sleeve badge of one or more bars or stripes usually in the shape of an upside-down V indicating the wearer's rank (as in the armed forces)

[1]chew \'chü\ *vb* **chewed**; **chew•ing**
to crush or grind with the teeth ⟨*chewing* food⟩

[2]chew *n*
1 the act of crushing or grinding with the teeth
2 something that a person or animal chews ⟨a dog's rawhide *chew*⟩

chew•ing gum \'chü-iŋ-\ *n*
a sweetened and flavored soft material (as of chicle) that is chewed but not swallowed

chewy \'chü-ē\ *adj* **chew•i•er**; **chew•i•est**
requiring a lot of chewing ⟨*chewy* cookies⟩

Chey•enne \shī-'an, -'en\ *n, pl* **Cheyenne** *or* **Chey•ennes**
1 a member of an American Indian people of the western plains ranging between the Arkansas and Missouri rivers
2 the language of the Cheyenne people

[1]chic \'shēk\ *n*
fashionable style

[2]chic *adj* **chic•er**; **chic•est**
STYLISH, FASHIONABLE ⟨*chic* clothes⟩

Chi•ca•na \chi-'kä-nə\ *n*
an American woman or girl of Mexican ancestry

chess: pieces laid out on a chessboard

[1]Chi•ca•no \chi-'kä-nō\ *n, pl* **Chicanos**
an American of Mexican ancestry

[2]Chicano *adj*
of or relating to Chicanos ⟨*Chicano* artists⟩

chick \'chik\ *n*
▼ a baby bird and especially a baby chicken

chick

chick•a•dee \'chi-kə-dē\ *n*
a small mostly grayish bird with the top of the head black

[1]chick•en \'chi-kən\ *n*
1 a bird that is commonly raised by people for its eggs and meat **:** a hen or rooster
2 the meat of a chicken used as food
3 COWARD

[2]chicken *adj*
COWARDLY 1 ⟨He's too *chicken* to go on the rollercoaster.⟩

chicken out *vb* **chick•ened out**; **chick•en•ing out**
to become too scared to do something

chicken pox *n*
a contagious illness especially of children in which there is fever and the skin breaks out in watery blisters

chick•pea \'chik-,pē\ *n*
an edible roundish pale yellow seed from the pod of an Asian plant that is cooked and eaten as a vegetable

chi•cle \'chi-kəl, -klē\ *n*
a gum obtained from the sap of a tropical American tree and used in making chewing gum

chide \'chīd\ *vb* **chid•ed**; **chid•ing**
to scold gently

[1]chief \'chēf\ *n*
the head of a group **:** LEADER ⟨the *chief* of police⟩
in chief in the highest ranking position or place ⟨editor *in chief*⟩

[2]chief *adj*
1 highest in rank or authority ⟨*chief* executive⟩
2 most important **:** MAIN ⟨a *chief* reason⟩

chief•ly \'chē-flē\ *adv*
1 above all **:** most importantly ⟨We're *chiefly* concerned with safety.⟩
2 for the most part ⟨Owls are active *chiefly* at night.⟩

chief master sergeant *n*
a noncommissioned officer in the air force ranking above a senior master sergeant

chief petty officer *n*
a petty officer in the navy or coast guard ranking below a senior chief petty officer

chief•tain \'chēf-tən\ *n*
a chief especially of a band, tribe, or clan

chief warrant officer *n*
a warrant officer in any of the three top grades

chig•ger \'chi-gər\ *n*
the six-legged larva of a mite that clings to the skin and causes itching

chil•blain \'chil-,blān\ *n*
a red swollen itchy condition caused by cold that occurs especially on the hands or feet

child \'chīld\ *n, pl* **chil•dren** \'chil-drən\
1 an unborn or recently born person
2 a young person of either sex between infancy and youth
3 a son or daughter of any age ⟨My *children* are grown now.⟩

child•birth \'chīld-,bərth\ *n*
the act or process of giving birth to a child

child•hood \'chīld-,hu̇d\ *n*
the period of life between infancy and youth

child•ish \'chīl-dish\ *adj*
1 of, like, or thought to be suitable to children ⟨*childish* laughter⟩
2 showing the less pleasing qualities (as silliness) often thought to be those of children ⟨a *childish* prank⟩

child•like \'chīld-,līk\ *adj*
1 like that of a child ⟨a *childlike* voice⟩
2 showing the more pleasing qualities (as innocence and trustfulness) often thought to be those of children ⟨*childlike* wonder⟩

child•proof \'chīld-,prüf\ *adj*
1 made to prevent opening by children ⟨a *childproof* bottle⟩
2 made safe for children ⟨a *childproof* house⟩

chili *also* **chile** *or* **chil•li** \'chi-lē\ *n, pl* **chil•ies** *also* **chil•es** *or* **chil•is** *or* **chil•lies**
1 ► a small pepper with a very hot flavor
2 a spicy stew of ground beef and chilies usually with beans

chili 1

[1]chill \'chil\ *n*
1 coldness that is unpleasant but not extreme ⟨There was a *chill* in the autumn air.⟩
2 a feeling of coldness accompanied by shivering ⟨She has a fever and *chills.*⟩
3 a feeling of coldness caused by fear ⟨The grisly sight gave me the *chills.*⟩

[2]chill *adj*
1 unpleasantly cold : RAW ⟨a *chill* wind⟩
2 not friendly ⟨a *chill* greeting⟩

[3]chill *vb* **chilled; chill•ing**
1 to make or become cold or chilly ⟨The wind *chilled* us to the bone.⟩
2 to make cool especially without freezing ⟨*Chill* the pudding for dessert.⟩
3 to cause to feel cold from fear ⟨This ghost story will *chill* you.⟩

chill•ing \'chi-liŋ\ *adj*
very upsetting or frightening ⟨a *chilling* story⟩

chilly \'chi-lē\ *adj* **chill•i•er; chill•i•est**
noticeably cold ⟨a *chilly* morning⟩

[1]chime \'chīm\ *vb* **chimed; chim•ing**
1 to make sounds like a bell
2 to call or indicate by chiming ⟨The clock *chimed* midnight.⟩
chime in to interrupt or join in a conversation

[2]chime *n*
1 a set of bells tuned to play music ⟨door *chimes*⟩
2 the sound from a set of bells — usually used in pl. ⟨the *chimes* of a church bell⟩

chim•ney \'chim-nē\ *n, pl* **chimneys**
a structure that allows smoke to escape (as from a fireplace) and that is often made of brick

chimney sweep *n*
a person who cleans soot from chimneys

chimney swift *n*
► a small dark gray bird with long narrow wings that often builds its nest inside chimneys

chimp \'chimp\ *n*
CHIMPANZEE

chim•pan•zee \,chim-,pan-'zē, chim-'pan-zē\ *n*
an African ape that lives mostly in trees and is smaller than the related gorilla

chin \'chin\ *n*
the part of the face below the mouth and including the point of the lower jaw

chi•na \'chī-nə\ *n*
1 PORCELAIN
2 dishes of pottery or porcelain for use as tableware

chinchilla

chin•chil•la \chin-'chi-lə\ *n*
▲ a South American animal that is a rodent resembling a squirrel and is often raised for its soft silvery gray fur

[1]Chi•nese \chī-'nēz\ *adj*
of or relating to China, the Chinese people, or the languages of China

[2]Chinese *n, pl* **Chinese**
1 a person born or living in China
2 a group of related languages used in China

chink \'chiŋk\ *n*
a narrow slit or crack (as in a wall)

[1]chip \'chip\ *n*
1 a small piece cut or broken off ⟨wood *chips*⟩ ⟨a *chip* of glass⟩
2 a thin crisp piece of food and especially potato ⟨tortilla *chips*⟩
3 a small bit of candy used in baking ⟨chocolate *chips*⟩

chimney swift

4 a flaw left after a small piece has been broken off ⟨There's a *chip* in the rim of that cup.⟩
5 INTEGRATED CIRCUIT
6 a small slice of silicon containing a number of electronic circuits (as for a computer)

[2]**chip** *vb* **chipped**; **chip•ping**
1 to cut or break a small piece from ⟨I fell and *chipped* my tooth.⟩
2 to break off in small pieces ⟨We *chipped* the ice from the windshield.⟩

chip•munk \'chip-,məŋk\ *n*
a small striped animal related to the squirrel

[1]**chirp** \'chərp\ *n*
the short high-pitched sound made by crickets and some small birds

[2]**chirp** *vb* **chirped**; **chirp•ing**
to make a short high-pitched sound ⟨We heard insects *chirping*.⟩

[1]**chis•el** \'chi-zəl\ *n*
▼ a metal tool with a sharp edge at the end of a usually flat piece used to chip away stone, wood, or metal

[1]**chisel**

[2]**chisel** *vb* **chis•eled** *or* **chis•elled**; **chis•el•ing** *or* **chis•el•ling**
to cut, shape, or carve with a chisel ⟨A name was *chiseled* into stone.⟩

chit•chat \'chit-,chat\ *n*
friendly conversation

chiv•al•rous \'shi-vəl-rəs\ *adj*
1 of or relating to a knight or knighthood ⟨*chivalrous* adventures⟩
2 having or showing honor, generosity, and courtesy ⟨a *chivalrous* and kind man⟩
3 showing special courtesy and regard to women ⟨*chivalrous* behavior⟩

chiv•al•ry \'shi-vəl-rē\ *n*
1 the system, spirit, ways, or customs of knighthood
2 very honorable and courteous behavior

chlo•rine \'klȯr-,ēn, -ən\ *n*
a chemical element that is a greenish yellow irritating gas of strong odor used as a bleach and as a disinfectant to purify water

chlo•ro•form \'klȯr-ə-,fȯrm\ *n*
a colorless heavy liquid used especially to dissolve fatty substances

chlo•ro•phyll \'klȯr-ə-,fil\ *n*
the green coloring matter found mainly in the chloroplasts of plants that absorbs energy from sunlight to produce carbohydrates from carbon dioxide and water during photosynthesis

chlo•ro•plast \'klȯr-ə-,plast\ *n*
one of the tiny parts in a plant cell that contains chlorophyll and is the place where photosynthesis occurs

chock–full \'chäk-'fu̇l\ *adj*
very full ⟨This Web site is *chock-full* of good information.⟩

choc•o•late \'chä-kə-lət, 'chä-klət, 'chȯ-\ *n*
1 a food prepared from ground roasted cacao beans
2 ▼ a candy made or coated with chocolate
3 a beverage of chocolate in water or milk
chocolate *adj*

chocolate 2

▶ **Word History** The word *chocolate*, like *chili* and *tomato*, comes from an American Indian language called Nahuatl, which was spoken in central Mexico at the time of the Spanish conquest. The Nahuatl word *chocolātl* looks like a compound, but its parts are not known for certain, and this has led to much discussion about its origin. One interesting idea is that the real source is *chicolātl*, a Nahuatl dialect word, made from *chicolli*, "hook"—here referring to the small hooked stick used to beat chocolate and hot water to a froth—and *ātl*, "liquid, water."

Choc•taw \'chäk-,tȯ\ *n, pl* **Choctaw** *or* **Choc•taws**
1 a member of an American Indian people of Mississippi, Alabama, and Louisiana
2 the language of the Choctaw people

[1]**choice** \'chȯis\ *n*
1 the act of picking between two or more possibilities ⟨You have some *choices* to make.⟩
2 the power of choosing : OPTION ⟨If I had a *choice*, I'd stay here.⟩
3 a person or thing chosen ⟨This restaurant was a good *choice*.⟩ ⟨She's my first *choice* for the job.⟩
4 a range of possibilities to choose from ⟨The menu offers a lot of *choice*.⟩

[2]**choice** *adj* **choic•er**; **choic•est**
of very good quality ⟨the *choicest* fruits⟩

choir \'kwīr\ *n*
1 an organized group of singers especially in a church
2 the part of a church set aside for the singers

choke \'chōk\ *vb* **choked**; **chok•ing**
1 to keep from breathing in a normal way by cutting off the supply of air ⟨Many people were *choked* by thick smoke.⟩
2 to have the trachea blocked entirely or partly ⟨He nearly *choked* on a bone.⟩
3 to slow or prevent the growth or action of ⟨The flowers were *choked* by weeds.⟩
4 to block by clogging ⟨Leaves *choked* the sewer.⟩
choke down to eat with difficulty ⟨I *choked down* a bite.⟩
choke up to become too emotional to speak

choke•cher•ry \'chōk-,cher-ē\ *n, pl* **choke•cher•ries**
a wild cherry tree with clusters of bitter reddish black fruits

chol•era \'kä-lə-rə\ *n*
a serious disease that causes severe vomiting and diarrhea

choose \'chüz\ *vb* **chose** \'chōz\; **cho•sen** \'chō-zᵊn\; **choos•ing**
1 to select freely and after careful thought ⟨*choose* a leader⟩
2 to decide what to do ⟨We *chose* to leave.⟩
3 to see fit ⟨Do as you *choose*.⟩

▶ **Synonyms** CHOOSE, ELECT, and SELECT mean to decide upon one possibility from among several. CHOOSE is used for making a decision after careful thought. ⟨She *chose* to follow the right course.⟩ ELECT may be used for the deliberate picking of one thing over another. ⟨Voters *elect* one candidate for president.⟩ SELECT is used when there are many things from which to choose. ⟨Customers may *select* from a variety of goods.⟩

choosy \'chü-zē\ *adj* **choos•i•er**; **choos•i•est**
careful in making choices ⟨a *choosy* shopper⟩

[1]**chop** \'chäp\ *vb* **chopped**; **chop•ping**
1 to cut by striking especially over and over with something sharp ⟨*Chop* down the tree with an ax.⟩
2 to cut into small pieces : MINCE ⟨*chop* onions⟩

[2]chop *n*
1 a sharp downward blow or stroke (as with an ax)
2 a small cut of meat often including a part of a rib 〈a pork *chop*〉

chop•per \ˈchä-pər\ *n*
1 someone or something that chops 〈a food *chopper*〉
2 HELICOPTER

chop•py \ˈchä-pē\ *adj* **chop•pi•er**; **chop•pi•est**
1 rough with small waves 〈*choppy* water〉
2 marked by sudden stops and starts : not smooth 〈He spoke in quick, *choppy* sentences.〉

chops \ˈchäps\ *n pl*
the fleshy covering of the jaws 〈The fox was licking his *chops*.〉

chop•stick \ˈchäp-ˌstik\ *n*
► one of two thin sticks used chiefly in Asian countries to pick up and eat food

chopsticks

cho•ral \ˈkȯr-əl\ *adj*
of or relating to a choir or chorus 〈*choral* music〉

cho•rale \kə-ˈral\ *n*
1 a hymn sung by the choir or congregation at a church service
2 CHORUS 1

[1]chord \ˈkȯrd\ *n*
a group of tones sounded together to form harmony

[2]chord *n*
a straight line joining two points on a curve

chore \ˈchȯr\ *n*
1 a small job that is done regularly 〈a household *chore*〉 〈Milking the cows is one of my *chores* on the farm.〉
2 a dull, unpleasant, or difficult task 〈Washing windows is such a *chore*.〉

cho•re•og•ra•phy \ˌkȯr-ē-ˈä-grə-fē\ *n*
1 the art of arranging the movements of dancers for a performance and especially a ballet
2 the arrangement of a dance 〈The *choreography* for the video won an award.〉
cho•re•og•ra•pher \-fər\ *n*

chor•tle \ˈchȯr-tᵊl\ *vb* **chor•tled**; **chor•tling**
to chuckle in amusement or joy 〈He *chortled* with delight.〉

[1]cho•rus \ˈkȯr-əs\ *n*
1 a group of singers : CHOIR
2 a group of dancers and singers (as in a musical comedy)
3 a part of a song or hymn that is repeated every so often : REFRAIN
4 a song meant to be sung by a group : group singing
5 sounds uttered by a group of persons or animals together

[2]chorus *vb* **cho•rused**; **cho•rus•ing**
to speak, sing, or sound at the same time or together 〈The class *chorused* "Good morning!"〉

chose *past of* CHOOSE

[1]chosen *past participle of* CHOOSE

[2]cho•sen \ˈchō-zᵊn\ *adj*
1 carefully selected 〈his *chosen* profession〉
2 picked to be shown favor or given special privilege 〈Only a *chosen* few were asked to join.〉

chow•der \ˈchau̇-dər\ *n*
a soup or stew made of fish, clams, or a vegetable usually simmered in milk

Christ \ˈkrīst\ *n*
JESUS CHRIST

chris•ten \ˈkri-sᵊn\ *vb* **chris•tened**; **chris•ten•ing**
1 BAPTIZE 1
2 to name at baptism 〈The parents *christened* the baby Robin.〉
3 [2]NAME 1
4 to name or dedicate (as a ship) in a ceremony

chris•ten•ing \ˈkri-sniŋ, ˈkri-sᵊn-iŋ\ *n*
BAPTISM

[1]Chris•tian \ˈkris-chən\ *n*
1 a person who believes in Jesus Christ and follows his teachings
2 a member of a Christian church

[2]Christian *adj*
1 of or relating to Jesus Christ or the religion based on his teachings
2 of or relating to people who follow the teachings of Jesus Christ 〈a *Christian* nation〉
3 being what a person who practices Christianity should be or do 〈*Christian* behavior toward others〉

Chris•tian•i•ty \ˌkris-chē-ˈa-nə-tē\ *n*
the religion based on the teachings of Jesus Christ

Christian name *n*
the personal name given to a person at birth or christening

Christ•mas \ˈkris-məs\ *n*
December 25 celebrated in honor of the birth of Jesus Christ

Christ•mas•tide \ˈkris-məs-ˌtīd\ *n*
the season of Christmas

Christmas tree *n*
► a usually evergreen tree decorated at Christmas

chro•mat•ic scale \krō-ˈma-tik-\ *n*
a musical scale that has all half steps

chrome \ˈkrōm\ *n*
1 CHROMIUM
2 something plated with an alloy of chromium

chro•mi•um \ˈkrō-mē-əm\ *n*
a bluish white metallic chemical element used especially in alloys

chro•mo•some \ˈkrō-mə-ˌsōm\ *n*
one of the rod-shaped or threadlike structures of a cell nucleus that contain genes and divide when the cell divides

chron•ic \ˈkrä-nik\ *adj*
1 continuing for a long time or returning often 〈a *chronic* disease〉
2 happening or done frequently or by habit 〈a *chronic* complainer〉 〈*chronic* tardiness〉
chron•i•cal•ly \-ni-kə-lē\ *adv*

[1]chron•i•cle \ˈkrä-ni-kəl\ *n*
an account of events in the order that they happened : HISTORY

[2]chronicle *vb* **chron•i•cled**; **chron•i•cling**
to record in the order of occurrence 〈This chapter *chronicles* the events leading to the American Revolution.〉

Christmas tree

chron•o•log•i•cal \ˌkrä-nə-ˈlä-ji-kəl\ *adj*
arranged in or according to the order of time ⟨She wrote a *chronological* account of their journey.⟩
chron•o•log•i•cal•ly *adv*

chrys•a•lis \ˈkris-ə-ləs\ *n*
1 a moth or butterfly pupa that is enclosed in a hardened protective case
2 the hardened protective case made by and enclosing a moth or butterfly pupa

chry•san•the•mum \kri-ˈsan-thə-məm\ *n*
a plant related to the daisies that has brightly colored flower heads

chub•by \ˈchə-bē\ *adj* **chub•bi•er**; **chub•bi•est**
somewhat fat ⟨a *chubby* baby⟩

chuck \ˈchək\ *vb* **chucked**; **chuck•ing**
1 to give a pat or tap to ⟨He *chucked* me under the chin.⟩
2 [1]TOSS 1 ⟨I *chucked* it out the window.⟩

[1]**chuck•le** \ˈchə-kəl\ *vb* **chuck•led**; **chuck•ling**
to laugh in a quiet way

[2]**chuckle** *n*
a low quiet laugh

chuck wagon *n*
► a wagon carrying a stove and food for cooking

chug \ˈchəg\ *vb* **chugged**; **chug•ging**
to move with repeated low sounds like that of a steam engine ⟨The old car *chugged* along.⟩

[1]**chum** \ˈchəm\ *n*
a close friend : PAL

[2]**chum** *vb* **chummed**; **chum•ming**
to spend time with as a friend ⟨She likes to *chum* around with older students.⟩

chum•my \ˈchə-mē\ *adj* **chum•mi•er**; **chum•mi•est**
very friendly ⟨He slapped me on the back in a *chummy* way.⟩

chunk \ˈchəŋk\ *n*
a short thick piece ⟨a *chunk* of ice⟩

chunky \ˈchəŋ-kē\ *adj* **chunk•i•er**; **chunk•i•est**
1 heavy, thick, and solid ⟨*chunky* jewelry⟩
2 having a short and thick body ⟨a *chunky* wrestler⟩
3 containing many solid pieces ⟨*chunky* peanut butter⟩

church \ˈchərch\ *n*
1 a building for public worship and especially Christian worship
2 *often cap* an organized body of religious believers ⟨What *church* do you belong to?⟩
3 public worship ⟨I'm going to *church*.⟩

church•yard \ˈchərch-ˌyärd\ *n*
an area of land that belongs to and usually surrounds a church and that is often used as a burial ground

[1]**churn** \ˈchərn\ *n*
a container in which milk or cream is stirred or shaken in making butter

[2]**churn** *vb* **churned**; **churn•ing**
1 to stir or shake in a churn (as in making butter)
2 to stir or shake forcefully ⟨The boat's motor *churned* up the mucky water.⟩
3 to feel the effects of an emotion (as fear) ⟨My stomach *churned* as I stood on the stage.⟩
4 to move by or as if by forceful stirring action ⟨Steamboats *churned* up and down the river.⟩

chute \ˈshüt\ *n*
1 a tube or passage down or through which people slide or things are slid or dropped ⟨a laundry *chute*⟩ ⟨Children slid down the *chute*.⟩
2 [1]PARACHUTE

ci•ca•da \sə-ˈkā-də\ *n*
▼ an insect that has transparent wings and a stout body and the males of which make a loud buzzing noise

cicada

-cide \ˌsīd\ *n suffix*
1 killer ⟨insecti*cide*⟩
2 killing ⟨homi*cide*⟩

ci•der \ˈsī-dər\ *n*
the juice pressed out of fruit (as apples) and used especially as a drink and in making vinegar

ci•gar \si-ˈgär\ *n*
a small roll of tobacco leaf for smoking

cig•a•rette \ˌsi-gə-ˈret\ *n*
a small roll of cut tobacco wrapped in paper for smoking

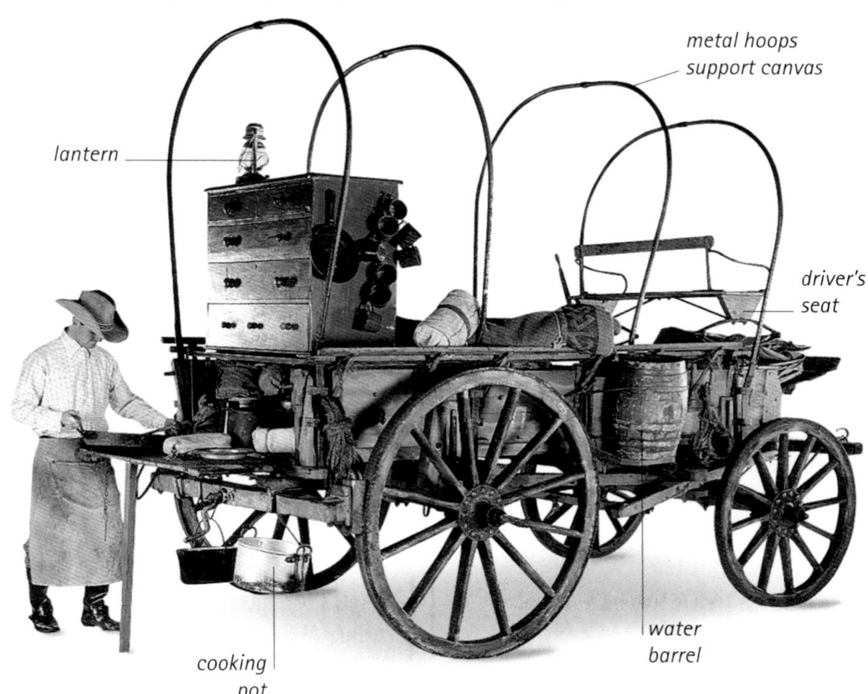

chuck wagon

cil•i•um \ˈsi-lē-əm\ *n, pl* **cil•ia** \ˈsi-lē-ə\
a tiny hairlike structure on the surface of some cells

[1]**cinch** \ˈsinch\ *n*
1 a sure or an easy thing ⟨This game is a *cinch* to learn.⟩
2 GIRTH 2

[2]**cinch** *vb* **cinched**; **cinch•ing**
to fasten (as a belt or strap) tightly

cin•cho•na \siŋ-ˈkō-nə\ *n*
a South American tree whose bark yields quinine

cin•der \ˈsin-dər\ *n*
1 a piece of partly burned coal or wood that is not burning
2 EMBER
3 *cinders pl* [2]ASH 1

cin•e•ma \ˈsi-nə-mə\ *n*
1 a movie theater ⟨What's playing at the *cinema*?⟩
2 the movie industry ⟨She had a long career in the *cinema*.⟩

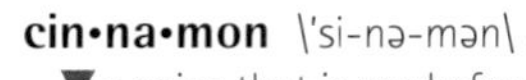

cin•na•mon \'si-nə-mən\ *n*
▼a spice that is made from the fragrant bark of a tropical Asian tree and is used especially in cooking and baking

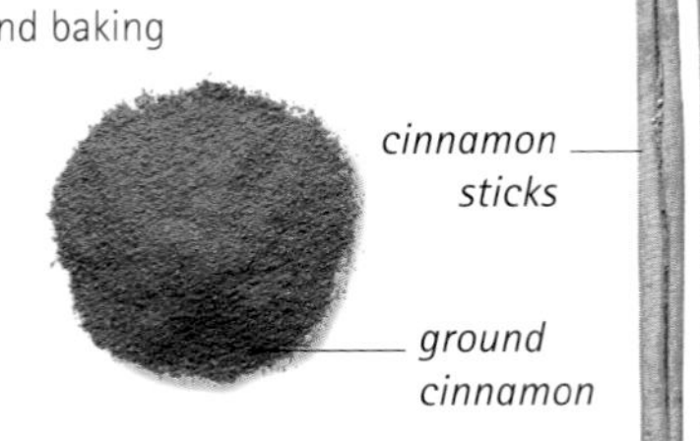

cinnamon

[1]ci•pher \'sī-fər\ *n*
1 ZERO 1
2 a method of secret writing or the alphabet or letters and symbols used in such writing
3 a message in code

[2]cipher *vb* **ci•phered**; **ci•pher•ing**
to use figures in doing a problem in arithmetic : CALCULATE

[1]cir•cle \'sər-kəl\ *n*
1 a line that is curved so that its ends meet and every point on the line is the same distance from the center
2 something in the form of a circle or part of a circle ⟨We gathered in a *circle* around the fireplace.⟩
3 [1]CYCLE 2, ROUND ⟨The wheel has come full *circle*.⟩
4 a group of people sharing a common interest ⟨a reading *circle*⟩ ⟨a *circle* of friends⟩

[2]circle *vb* **cir•cled**; **cir•cling**
1 to form or draw a circle around ⟨*Circle* the correct answers.⟩
2 to move or revolve around ⟨Satellites *circle* the earth.⟩
3 to move in or as if in a circle ⟨Vultures *circled* overhead.⟩

cir•cuit \'sər-kət\ *n*
1 a boundary line around an area
2 an enclosed space
3 movement around something ⟨The earth makes a *circuit* around the sun.⟩
4 a regular tour of service (as by a judge) around an assigned territory : a course so traveled
5 a series of performances, competitions, or appearances held at many different places ⟨the pro tennis *circuit*⟩
6 the complete path of an electric current
7 a group of electronic parts

circuit breaker *n*
a switch that automatically stops the flow of electric current if a circuit becomes overloaded

[1]cir•cu•lar \'sər-kyə-lər\ *adj*
1 shaped like a circle or part of a circle : ROUND ⟨a *circular* track⟩
2 passing or going around in a circle ⟨a *circular* motion⟩
3 not said in simple or sincere language ⟨a *circular* explanation⟩

[2]circular *n*
a printed notice or advertisement given or sent to many people

cir•cu•late \'sər-kyə-,lāt\ *vb* **cir•cu•lat•ed**; **cir•cu•lat•ing**
1 to move around in a course ⟨Blood *circulates* in the body.⟩
2 to pass or be passed from place to place or from person to person ⟨The rumor *circulated* around the school.⟩

cir•cu•la•tion \,sər-kyə-'lā-shən\ *n*
1 movement through something ⟨A fan will improve the *circulation* of air in the room.⟩
2 passage from place to place or person to person ⟨coins in *circulation*⟩
3 the average number of copies (as of a newspaper) sold in a given period

cir•cu•la•to•ry \'sər-kyə-lə-,tȯr-ē\ *adj*
of or relating to circulation and especially the circulation of blood in the body

circulatory system *n*
▼ the system of the body that circulates blood and lymph and includes the heart and blood vessels

circum– *prefix*
around : about ⟨*circum*navigate⟩

cir•cum•fer•ence \sər-'kəm-fə-rəns, -fərns\ *n*
1 the line that goes around a circle
2 a boundary line enclosing an area ⟨A fence marks the *circumference* of the yard.⟩
3 the distance around something

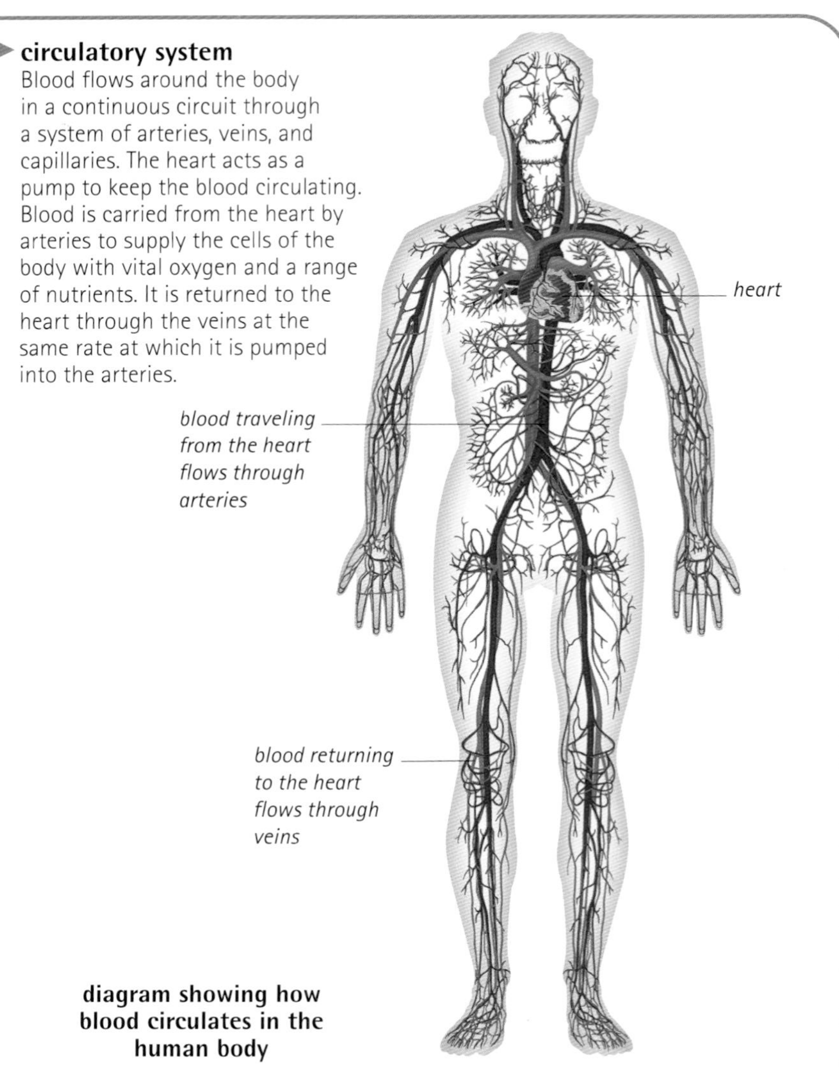

circulatory system
Blood flows around the body in a continuous circuit through a system of arteries, veins, and capillaries. The heart acts as a pump to keep the blood circulating. Blood is carried from the heart by arteries to supply the cells of the body with vital oxygen and a range of nutrients. It is returned to the heart through the veins at the same rate at which it is pumped into the arteries.

diagram showing how blood circulates in the human body

circus

The modern-style traveling circus dates from the mid-18th century and is still a popular form of family entertainment. Performances are traditionally held in a huge tent called the big top, with each act introduced by a ringmaster. Early circuses commonly featured performing wild animals, but today concern for animal welfare has led to the development of people-only circuses.

cir•cum•nav•i•gate \ˌsər-kəm-ˈna-və-ˌgāt\ *vb* **cir•cum•nav•i•gat•ed; cir•cum•nav•i•gat•ing**
to go completely around (as the earth) especially by water

cir•cum•po•lar \ˌsər-kəm-ˈpō-lər\ *adj*
1 continually visible above the horizon ⟨a *circumpolar* star⟩
2 surrounding or found near a pole of the earth

cir•cum•stance \ˈsər-kəm-ˌstans\ *n*
1 a fact or event that affects a situation ⟨Illness is the only *circumstance* that will excuse your absence.⟩
2 *circumstances pl* conditions at a certain time or place ⟨Under the *circumstances*, I think we did well.⟩
3 *circumstances pl* the way something happens ⟨Please explain the *circumstances* of the accident.⟩
4 *circumstances pl* the conditions in which someone lives ⟨He lives in easy *circumstances.*⟩
5 an uncontrollable event or situation ⟨a victim of *circumstance*⟩

cir•cum•vent \ˌsər-kəm-ˈvent\ *vb* **cir•cum•vent•ed; cir•cum•vent•ing**
to avoid the force or effect of by cleverness ⟨They tried to *circumvent* the rules.⟩

cir•cus \ˈsər-kəs\ *n*
▲ a traveling show that often takes place under a tent and that usually includes acts performed by acrobats, clowns, and trained animals

cir•rus \ˈsir-əs\ *n, pl* **cir•ri** \ˈsir-ī\
a thin white cloud of tiny ice crystals that forms at a very high altitude

cis•tern \ˈsi-stərn\ *n*
an artificial reservoir or tank for storing water usually underground

cit•a•del \ˈsi-tə-dᵊl, -ˌdel\ *n*
a fortress that sits high above a city

ci•ta•tion \sī-ˈtā-shən\ *n*
1 an official order to appear in court
2 an act or instance of quoting
3 QUOTATION
4 a formal public statement praising a person for doing something good ⟨a *citation* for bravery⟩

cite \ˈsīt\ *vb* **cit•ed; cit•ing**
1 to order to appear in court ⟨She was *cited* for reckless driving.⟩
2 to quote as an example, authority, or proof ⟨He *cites* several experts in his report.⟩
3 to refer to especially in praise ⟨The school was *cited* as a model for others.⟩

cit•i•zen \ˈsi-tə-zən\ *n*
1 a person who lives in a particular place ⟨the *citizens* of Boston⟩
2 a person who legally belongs to, gives allegiance to, and has the rights and protections of a country

A B C D E F G H I J K L M N O P Q R S T U V W X Y Z

cit•i•zen•ry \'si-tə-zən-rē\ *n*
all the citizens of a place

cit•i•zen•ship \'si-tə-zən-,ship\ *n*
1 the state of being a citizen ⟨He was granted *citizenship* in the United States.⟩
2 the behavior expected of a person as a member of a community ⟨good *citizenship*⟩

cit•ron \'si-trən\ *n*
1 a citrus fruit like the smaller lemon and having a thick rind that is preserved for use in cakes and puddings
2 a small hard watermelon used especially in pickles and preserves

cit•rus \'si-trəs\ *n, pl* **citrus** *or* **cit•rus•es**
► a juicy fruit (as a lemon, orange, or grapefruit) with a thick rind that comes from a tree or shrub that grows in warm regions

city \'si-tē\ *n, pl* **cit•ies**
1 a place in which people live and work that is larger than a town
2 the people of a city ⟨The whole *city* was excited about the football game.⟩

city hall *n*
the main administrative building of a city

civ•ic \'si-vik\ *adj*
of or relating to a citizen, a city, or citizenship ⟨*civic* pride⟩ ⟨*civic* duty⟩

civ•ics \'si-viks\ *n*
the study of the rights and duties of citizens and of how government works

civ•il \'si-vəl\ *adj*
1 of or relating to citizens ⟨*civil* rights⟩
2 of or relating to matters within a country
3 of or relating to the regular business of citizens or government that is not connected to the military or a religion
4 polite without being friendly
5 relating to laws about private rights rather than criminal laws ⟨She brought a *civil* lawsuit against the maker of the defective car.⟩
civ•il•ly *adv*

► **Synonyms** CIVIL, POLITE, and COURTEOUS mean following the rules of good behavior. CIVIL is used for showing only enough proper behavior to avoid being actually rude. ⟨I know you're angry but try to be *civil*.⟩ POLITE is used of good manners and thoughtfulness. ⟨The host was *polite* and made us feel at home.⟩ COURTEOUS is usually used for a politeness that is somewhat dignified. ⟨The salesclerks were trained to be *courteous* always.⟩

¹ci•vil•ian \sə-'vil-yən\ *n*
a person who is not a member of a military, police, or firefighting force

²civilian *adj*
of or relating to people who are not members of a military, police, or firefighting force ⟨After serving in the army, he got a *civilian* job.⟩

ci•vil•i•ty \sə-'vi-lə-tē\ *n, pl* **ci•vil•i•ties**
1 polite behavior
2 a polite act or thing to say ⟨He offered no *civilities*, not even a hello.⟩

civ•i•li•za•tion \,si-və-lə-'zā-shən\ *n*
1 an advanced stage (as in art, science, and government) in the development of society
2 the way of life of a people ⟨Greek *civilization*⟩
3 all the societies of the world ⟨the end of *civilization*⟩

civ•i•lize \'si-və-,līz\ *vb* **civ•i•lized**; **civ•i•liz•ing**
to cause to have a more advanced or modern way of living

civil service *n*
the branch of a government that takes care of the business of running the government and its programs but that does not include the legislature, the military, or the courts

civil war *n*
a war between opposing groups of citizens of the same country

¹clack \'klak\ *vb* **clacked**; **clack•ing**
1 to talk rapidly and without stopping
2 to make or cause to make a short sharp sound

²clack *n*
1 rapid continuous talk ⟨The disc jockey's *clack* went on all morning.⟩
2 a sound of clacking ⟨the *clack* of a typewriter⟩

¹clad *past and past participle of* CLOTHE

²clad \'klad\ *adj*
1 being covered ⟨copper-*clad* pots⟩

2 being dressed ⟨The children were *clad* in their best clothes.⟩

[1]claim \'klām\ *vb* **claimed**; **claim•ing**
1 to ask for as something that is a right or is deserved ⟨*claim* an inheritance⟩ ⟨Be sure to *claim* credit for your idea.⟩
2 to take as the rightful owner ⟨I *claimed* my luggage at the airport.⟩
3 to state as a fact **:** insist to be true
4 to cause the end or death of ⟨The disease *claimed* many lives.⟩

[2]claim *n*
1 a demand for something owed or believed to be owed ⟨an insurance *claim*⟩
2 a right to something ⟨He has a *claim* to the family fortune.⟩
3 something (as an area of land) claimed as someone's own ⟨a prospector's *claim*⟩
4 a statement that others may dispute ⟨Do you believe his outrageous *claims*?⟩

clam \'klam\ *n*
▼ a shellfish that lives in sand or mud and has a soft body surrounded by a hinged shell with two parts and that is often eaten as food

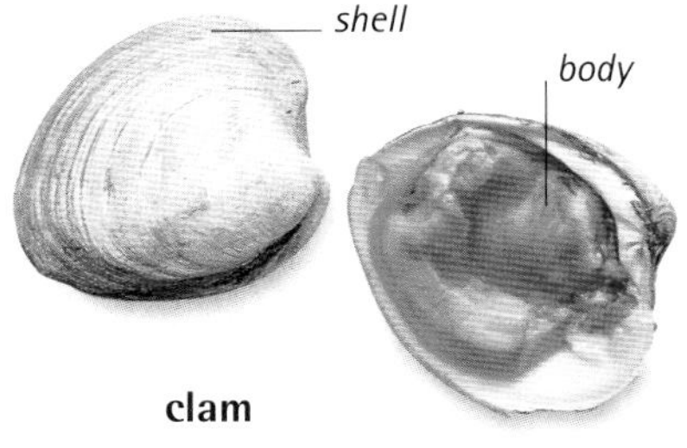

clam

clam•bake \'klam-,bāk\ *n*
an outdoor party where clams and other foods are cooked usually on heated rocks covered by seaweed

clam•ber \'klam-bər\ *vb* **clam•bered**; **clam•ber•ing**
to climb in an awkward way (as by scrambling)

clam•my \'kla-mē\ *adj* **clam•mi•er**; **clam•mi•est**
unpleasantly damp, sticky, and cool ⟨*clammy* skin⟩

[1]clam•or \'kla-mər\ *n*
1 a noisy shouting
2 a loud continuous noise ⟨the *clamor* of a storm⟩
3 strong and loud demand ⟨There was a public *clamor* for change.⟩

[2]clamor *vb* **clam•ored**; **clam•or•ing**
to make a loud noise or demand ⟨Fans *clamored* for the star's autograph.⟩

[1]clamp \'klamp\ *n*
▶ a device that holds or presses parts together firmly

[2]clamp *vb* **clamped**; **clamp•ing**
to fasten or to hold tightly with or as if with a clamp

clan \'klan\ *n*
1 a group (as in the Scottish Highlands) made up of households whose heads claim to have a common ancestor
2 a large family

[1]clang \'klaŋ\ *vb* **clanged**; **clang•ing**
to make or cause to make the loud ringing sound of metal hitting something ⟨The pots *clanged* together.⟩

[2]clang *n*
a loud ringing sound like that made by pieces of metal striking together

[1]clank \'klaŋk\ *vb* **clanked**; **clank•ing**
1 to make or cause to make a clank or series of clanks ⟨The radiator hissed and *clanked*.⟩
2 to move with a clank ⟨The old pickup *clanked* down the road.⟩

[2]clank *n*
a sharp short ringing sound ⟨the *clank* of chains⟩

[1]clap \'klap\ *vb* **clapped**; **clap•ping**
1 to hit (the palms of the hands) together usually more than once
2 to hit or touch with the open hand ⟨He *clapped* his friend on the shoulder.⟩
3 to hit together noisily ⟨She *clapped* the two boards together.⟩ ⟨The door *clapped* shut.⟩
4 to put or place quickly or with force ⟨He *clapped* his hat on his head.⟩

[2]clap *n*
1 a loud sharp sound ⟨a *clap* of thunder⟩
2 a hard or a friendly slap ⟨a *clap* on the back⟩

clap•board \'kla-bərd, -,bȯrd\ *n*
a narrow board thicker at one edge than at the other used as siding for a building

clap•per \'kla-pər\ *n*
the part hanging inside a bell that hits the sides to make the bell ring

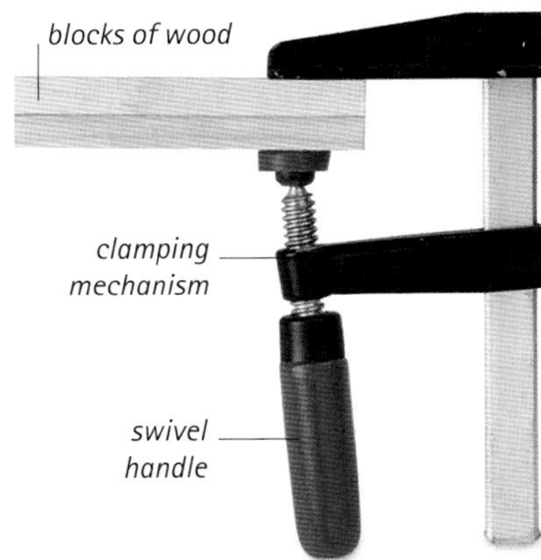

[1]clamp: a carpenter's clamp

clar•i•fy \'kler-ə-,fī\ *vb* **clar•i•fied**; **clar•i•fy•ing**
1 to make or to become pure or clear ⟨*clarify* a liquid⟩
2 to make or become more easily understood ⟨*clarify* a statement⟩

clar•i•net \,kler-ə-'net\ *n*
▼ a woodwind instrument with a single reed, a straight body formed like a tube, and keys

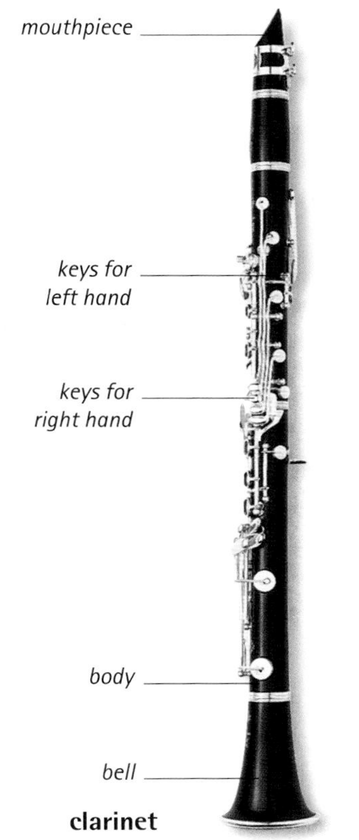

clarinet

clar•i•ty \'kler-ə-tē\ *n*
clear quality or state ⟨the *clarity* of the water⟩ ⟨You can adjust the picture for greater *clarity*.⟩ ⟨She remembered her dream with *clarity*.⟩

[1]clash \'klash\ *vb* **clashed**; **clash•ing**
1 to make or cause to make the loud sound of metal objects hitting ⟨*clashing* cymbals⟩
2 to come into conflict ⟨Protesters *clashed* with the police.⟩
3 to not go together well ⟨Their personalities *clashed*.⟩ ⟨Your shirt and tie *clash*.⟩

[2]clash *n*
1 a loud sharp sound usually of metal striking metal ⟨the *clash* of swords⟩
2 a struggle or strong disagreement

[1]clasp \'klasp\ *n*
1 a device for holding together objects or parts of something
2 a firm hold with the hands or arms

[2]clasp *vb* **clasped**; **clasp•ing**
1 to fasten with or as if with a clasp ⟨She *clasped* her purse shut.⟩
2 to hold firmly with the hands or arms ⟨She *clasped* her hands together.⟩

[1]class \'klas\ *n*
1 ▼ a group of students who are taught together regularly ⟨I'm the youngest in my *class.*⟩

[1]class 1: a class being instructed in ballet

2 one of the meetings of students being taught ⟨I'm late for *class.*⟩
3 a course of instruction ⟨a *class* in science⟩
4 a group of students who graduate together ⟨the senior *class*⟩
5 a group of people in a society who are at the same level of wealth or social status ⟨the working *class*⟩
6 a group of related living things (as plants or animals) that ranks above the order and below the phylum or division in scientific classification ⟨Birds and mammals form two separate *classes* in the animal kingdom.⟩
7 a category (as of goods or services) based on quality

[2]class *vb* **classed**; **class•ing**
CLASSIFY

[1]clas•sic \'kla-sik\ *adj*
1 serving as a model of the best of its kind ⟨It's a *classic* story for children.⟩
2 fashionable year after year ⟨a *classic* style⟩
3 of or relating to the ancient Greeks and Romans or their culture ⟨*classic* sculptures⟩
4 being typical of its kind ⟨a *classic* mistake⟩

[2]classic *n*
1 a written work or author of ancient Greece or Rome
2 a great work of art ⟨a *classic* of literature⟩
3 something long regarded as outstanding of its kind ⟨a *classic* car⟩

clas•si•cal \'kla-si-kəl\ *adj*
1 of a kind that has long been considered great ⟨*classical* ballet⟩
2 of or relating to the ancient Greek and Roman world and especially to its language and arts
3 relating to music in a European tradition that includes opera and symphony and that is generally considered more serious than other kinds of music
4 concerned with a general study of the arts and sciences ⟨a *classical* education⟩

clas•si•fi•ca•tion \ˌkla-sə-fə-'kā-shən\ *n*
1 the act of arranging into groups of similar things
2 an arrangement into groups of similar things ⟨a *classification* of plants⟩

clas•si•fied \'kla-sə-ˌfīd\ *adj*
1 arranged in groups with other similar things ⟨a *classified* advertisement⟩
2 kept secret from all but a few people in government ⟨*classified* information⟩

clas•si•fy \'kla-sə-ˌfī\ *vb* **clas•si•fied**; **clas•si•fy•ing**
to arrange in groups based on similarities ⟨Our librarians *classify* books by subject.⟩

class•mate \'klas-ˌmāt\ *n*
a member of the same class in a school or college

class•room \'klas-ˌrüm, -ˌru̇m\ *n*
a room where classes are held in a school

[1]clat•ter \'kla-tər\ *vb* **clat•tered**; **clat•ter•ing**
1 to make or cause to make a rattling sound ⟨Dishes *clattered* in the kitchen.⟩
2 to move or go with a rattling sound ⟨The cart *clattered* down the road.⟩

[2]clatter *n*
1 a rattling sound (as of hard objects striking together) ⟨the *clatter* of pots and pans⟩
2 COMMOTION

clause \'klȯz\ *n*
1 a separate part of a document (as a will)
2 a group of words having its own subject and predicate ⟨The sentence "When it rained they went inside" is made up of two *clauses*: "when it rained" and "they went inside."⟩

clav•i•cle \'kla-vi-kəl\ *n*
COLLARBONE

[1]claw \'klȯ\ *n*
1 a sharp usually thin and curved nail on the finger or toe of an animal (as a cat or bird)
2 the end of a limb of some animals (as an insect, scorpion, or lobster) that is pointed or used for grasping

[2]claw *vb* **clawed**; **claw•ing**
to scratch, seize, or dig with claws or fingers ⟨They *clawed* a hole in the beach sand.⟩

clay \'klā\ *n*
1 ▼ an earthy material that is sticky and easily molded when wet and hard when baked
2 a substance like clay that is used for modeling

clay 1: clay is used to make pots

[1]clean \'klēn\ *adj* **clean•er**; **clean•est**
1 free of dirt or pollution ⟨*clean* air⟩ ⟨Put on a *clean* shirt.⟩
2 not yet used ⟨Use a *clean* sheet of paper.⟩
3 not involving or showing involvement with anything wrong or illegal ⟨good, *clean* fun⟩ ⟨I've got a *clean* record.⟩

A B C D E F G H I J K L M N O P Q R S T U V W X Y Z

4 not offensive 〈a *clean* joke〉
5 THOROUGH 1 〈She made a *clean* break with the past.〉
6 having a simple graceful form : TRIM 〈The ship has *clean* lines.〉
7 ¹SMOOTH 1 〈The knife made a *clean* cut.〉
clean•ly \'klēn-lē\ *adv*

²clean *adv*
all the way : COMPLETELY 〈The nail went *clean* through.〉 〈Birds picked the bones *clean*.〉

³clean *vb* **cleaned**; **clean•ing**
to make or become free of dirt or disorder 〈I *cleaned* my room.〉 〈Please *clean* up for supper.〉
clean•er *n*

clean•li•ness \'klen-lē-nəs\ *n*
the condition of being clean : the habit of keeping clean

cleanse \'klenz\ *vb* **cleansed**; **cleans•ing**
to make clean 〈*Cleanse* the wound with soap and water.〉

cleans•er \'klen-zər\ *n*
a substance (as a scouring powder) used for cleaning

¹clear \'klir\ *adj* **clear•er**; **clear•est**
1 easily heard, seen, noticed, or understood 〈a *clear* definition〉 〈The differences were *clear*.〉 〈She spoke in a *clear* voice.〉
2 free of clouds, haze, or mist 〈a *clear* day〉
3 free from feelings of guilt 〈a *clear* conscience〉
4 easily seen through 〈*clear* water〉
5 free from doubt or confusion : SURE 〈Are you *clear* on what you need to do?〉
6 free of blemishes 〈*clear* skin〉
7 not blocked 〈a *clear* path〉 〈a *clear* view〉
8 BRIGHT 1, LUMINOUS 〈*clear* sunlight〉
clear•ly *adv*
clear•ness *n*

²clear *vb* **cleared**; **clear•ing**
1 to free of things blocking 〈I *cleared* my throat.〉
2 to make or become free of clouds, haze, or mist 〈The sky *cleared*.〉
3 to get rid of : REMOVE 〈Please *clear* dishes from the table.〉
4 to go over or by without touching 〈The ball I hit *cleared* the fence.〉
5 to go away : DISPERSE 〈The crowd *cleared* rapidly.〉
6 EXPLAIN 1 〈We tried to *clear* the matter up.〉
7 to free from blame 〈The judge *cleared* my name.〉
8 to approve or be approved by 〈Our plane was *cleared* to land.〉 〈Our proposal *cleared* the committee.〉
9 to make as profit 〈We *cleared* 85 dollars on the sale.〉

³clear *adv*
1 in a way that is easy to hear 〈loud and *clear*〉
2 all the way 〈I could hear you *clear* across the room.〉

clear•ance \'klir-əns\ *n*
1 the act or process of removing something
2 the distance by which one object avoids hitting or touching another
3 official permission 〈The plane has *clearance* to land.〉

clear•ing \'klir-iŋ\ *n*
an open area of land in which there are no trees 〈We found a *clearing* in the forest.〉

cleat \'klēt\ *n*
1 a wooden or metal device used to fasten a line or a rope
2 ► a strip or projection fastened to the bottom of a shoe to prevent slipping
3 *pl* shoes equipped with cleats

cleat

cleat 2: cleats on a shoe's sole

cleav•age \'klē-vij\ *n*
1 the tendency of a rock or mineral to split readily in one or more directions
2 the action of splitting
3 the state of being split

¹cleave \'klēv\ *vb* **cleaved** *or* **clove** \'klōv\; **cleav•ing**
to cling to a person or thing closely 〈The child *cleaved* to his mother.〉

²cleave *vb* **cleaved** *also* **cleft** \'kleft\ *or* **clove** \'klōv\; **cleaved** *also* **cleft** *or* **clo•ven** \'klō-vən\; **cleav•ing**
to divide by or as if by a cutting blow : SPLIT 〈The ax *cleaved* the log in two.〉

cleav•er \'klē-vər\ *n*
▼ a heavy knife used for cutting up meat

cleaver

clef \'klef\ *n*
a sign placed on the staff in writing music to show what pitch is represented by each line and space

¹cleft \'kleft\ *n*
1 a space or opening made by splitting or cracking : CREVICE
2 ¹NOTCH 1

²cleft *adj*
partly split or divided

clem•en•cy \'kle-mən-sē\ *n, pl* **clemencies**
1 MERCY 1
2 an act of mercy

clench \'klench\ *vb* **clenched**; **clench•ing**
1 to hold tightly : CLUTCH 〈She *clenched* a pen in her hand.〉
2 to set or close tightly 〈*clench* your teeth〉

cler•gy \'klər-jē\ *n, pl* **clergies**
the group of religious officials (as priests, ministers, and rabbis) specially prepared and authorized to lead religious services

cler•gy•man \'klər-ji-mən\ *n, pl* **cler•gy•men** \-mən\
a member of the clergy

cler•i•cal \'kler-i-kəl\ *adj*
1 relating to the clergy 〈The minister wore his *clerical* collar.〉
2 relating to a clerk or office worker 〈the *clerical* staff〉

¹clerk \'klərk\ *n*
1 a person whose job is to keep records or accounts
2 a salesperson in a store

²clerk *vb* **clerked**; **clerk•ing**
to act or work as a clerk

clev•er \'kle-vər\ *adj* **clev•er•er**; **clev•er•est**
1 having a quick inventive mind 〈a *clever* designer〉
2 showing intelligence, wit, or imagination 〈a *clever* joke〉 〈a *clever* idea〉
3 showing skill in using the hands
synonyms see INTELLIGENT
clev•er•ly *adv*
clev•er•ness *n*

¹click \'klik\ *vb* **clicked**; **click•ing**
1 to make or cause to make a slight sharp noise 〈He has a habit of *clicking* his tongue.〉
2 to fit in or work together smoothly 〈By the middle of the season the team *clicked*.〉
3 to select or make a selection especially on a computer by pressing a button on a control device (as a mouse) 〈*Click* on the icon to open the program.〉

²click *n*
a slight sharp noise

click•er \'kli-kər\ *n*
REMOTE CONTROL 1

cli•ent \'klī-ənt\ *n*
a person who uses the professional advice or services of another

cliff: jagged edges of a cliff on the shore of the Atlantic Ocean in Cornwall, England

cli•en•tele \ˌklī-ən-ˈtel\ *n*
a group of clients

cliff \ˈklif\ *n*
▲ a high steep surface of rock

cli•mate \ˈklī-mət\ *n*
the average weather conditions of a place over a period of years

cli•max \ˈklī-ˌmaks\ *n*
the most interesting, exciting, or important time or part of something ⟨a story's *climax*⟩

[1]**climb** \ˈklīm\ *vb* **climbed**; **climb•ing**
1 to move in a way that involves going up or down ⟨He *climbed* over the fence.⟩ ⟨They *climbed* out the window.⟩
2 to go up or down on often with the help of the hands ⟨*climb* stairs⟩ ⟨*climb* a ladder⟩
3 to rise little by little to a higher point ⟨Smoke was *climbing* in the air.⟩
4 to go upward in growing (as by winding around something) ⟨a *climbing* vine⟩
5 to increase in amount, value, or level ⟨The temperature is *climbing*.⟩
synonyms see ASCEND
climb•er \ˈklī-mər\ *n*

[2]**climb** *n*
1 a place where climbing is necessary
2 the act of climbing ⟨It's a tiring *climb* to the top.⟩

clime \ˈklīm\ *n*
CLIMATE

clinch \ˈklinch\ *vb* **clinched**;**clinch•ing**
to show to be certain or true ⟨She presented facts that *clinched* the argument.⟩

cling \ˈkliŋ\ *vb* **clung** \ˈkləŋ\; **cling•ing**
1 to hold fast by grasping or winding around ⟨To avoid falling, *cling* to the railing.⟩
2 to remain close ⟨He *clings* to the family.⟩
3 to hold fast or stick closely to a surface ⟨These wet socks are *clinging* to my feet.⟩
4 to continue to believe in ⟨We *clung* to the hope that we'd be rescued.⟩

clin•ic \ˈkli-nik\ *n*
1 a place where people can receive medical treatment usually for minor ailments
2 a group meeting for teaching a certain skill and working on individual problems ⟨a reading *clinic*⟩

[1]**clink** \ˈkliŋk\ *vb* **clinked**; **clink•ing**
to make or cause to make a slight short sound like that of metal being struck

[2]**clink** *n*
a slight sharp ringing sound

[1]**clip** \ˈklip\ *n*
a device that holds or hooks

[2]**clip** *vb* **clipped**; **clip•ping**
to fasten with a clip ⟨Remember to *clip* the papers together.⟩

[3]**clip** *vb* **clipped**; **clip•ping**
1 to shorten or remove by cutting ⟨*clip* a hedge⟩ ⟨We *clipped* a leaf to examine it.⟩
2 to cut off or trim the hair or wool of
3 to cut out or off ⟨He *clipped* articles from the newspaper.⟩

[4]**clip** *n*
1 a sharp blow
2 a rapid pace ⟨My horse moved along at a good *clip*.⟩
3 a short section of a recording ⟨a film *clip*⟩

clip•board \ˈklip-ˌbȯrd\ *n*
1 a small board with a clip at the top for holding papers
2 a part of computer memory that is used to store data (as items to be copied to another file) temporarily

clip•per \ˈkli-pər\ *n*
1 clippers *pl* a device used for clipping ⟨hair *clippers*⟩ ⟨nail *clippers*⟩
2 ▼ a fast sailing ship with three tall masts and large square sails
3 a person who clips

clipper 2:
model of a 19th-century clipper

clip•ping \ˈkli-piŋ\ *n*
something cut out or off ⟨grass *clippings*⟩ ⟨a magazine *clipping*⟩

clique \ˈklēk, ˈklik\ *n*
a small group of friends who are not friendly to others

[1]**cloak** \ˈklōk\ *n*
1 a long loose outer garment
2 something that hides or covers ⟨A *cloak* of secrecy surrounded the meeting.⟩

[2]**cloak** *vb* **cloaked**; **cloak•ing**
to cover or hide completely ⟨Night *cloaked* the fields in darkness.⟩

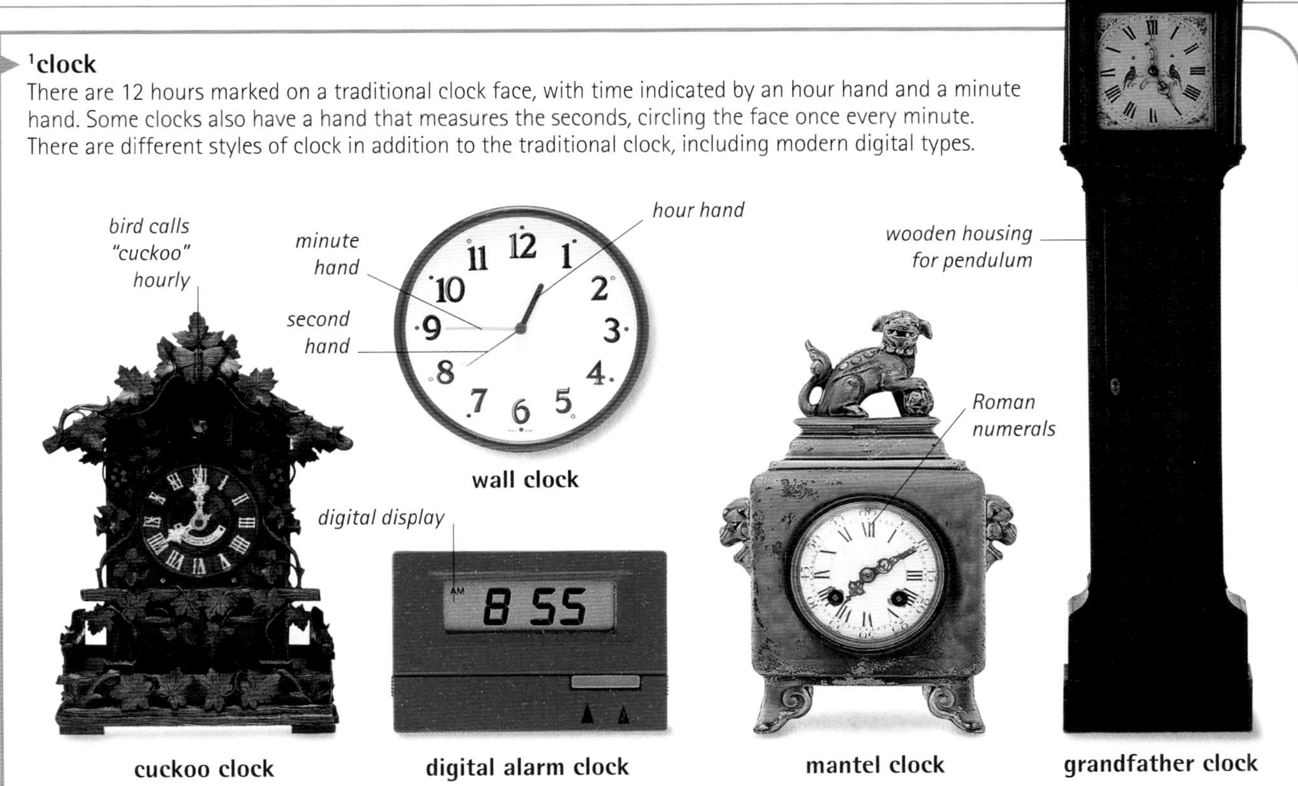

wall clock

cuckoo clock

digital alarm clock

mantel clock

grandfather clock

cloak•room \'klōk-,rüm, -,ru̇m\ *n*
a room (as in a school) in which coats and hats may be kept

clob•ber \'klä-bər\ *vb* **clob•bered**; **clob•ber•ing**
1 to hit with force ⟨He *clobbered* a ball to the outfield.⟩
2 to defeat very easily

¹clock \'kläk\ *n*
▲ a device for measuring or telling the time and especially one not meant to be worn or carried by a person
around the clock at every hour of the day ⟨The store is open *around the clock.*⟩

²clock *vb* **clocked**; **clock•ing**
1 to measure the amount of time it takes to do something ⟨We ran while the coach *clocked* us.⟩
2 to show (as time or speed) on a recording device

clock•wise \'kläk-,wīz\ *adv or adj*
in the direction in which the hands of a clock turn

clock•work \'kläk-,wərk\ *n*
machinery that makes the parts of a device move
like clockwork in a very regular or exact way ⟨He stops in every day *like clockwork.*⟩

clod \'kläd\ *n*
1 a lump or mass especially of earth or clay
2 a clumsy or stupid person

¹clog \'kläg\ *vb* **clogged**; **clog•ging**
to make passage through difficult or impossible : PLUG ⟨Snow *clogged* the roads.⟩

²clog *n*
1 something that hinders or holds back ⟨There's a *clog* in the drain.⟩
2 a shoe having a thick usually wooden sole

clois•ter \'klȯi-stər\ *n*
1 MONASTERY, CONVENT
2 a covered passage with arches along or around the walls of a courtyard

clomp \'klämp, 'klȯmp\ *vb* **clomped**; **clomp•ing**
to walk with loud heavy steps

clop \'kläp\ *n*
a sound like that of a hoof against pavement

¹close \'klōz\ *vb* **closed**; **clos•ing**
1 to cover the opening of ⟨I *closed* the box.⟩
2 to change the position of so as to prevent passage through an opening : SHUT ⟨Please *close* the door.⟩
3 to bring or come to an end ⟨I *closed* my account.⟩ ⟨After a long discussion, the meeting *closed.*⟩
4 to end the operation of for a period of time or permanently ⟨The school was *closed* for summer.⟩
5 to bring the parts or edges of together ⟨*close* a book⟩ ⟨*Close* your eyes.⟩
6 ¹APPROACH 1
7 ¹DECREASE ⟨I ran faster and the gap between us *closed.*⟩
close in to come or move nearer or closer ⟨A storm *closed in.*⟩ ⟨Let's go before night *closes in.*⟩

²close \'klōz\ *n*
the point at which something ends ⟨the *close* of business⟩

³close \'klōs\ *adj* **clos•er**; **clos•est**
1 not far apart in space, time, degree, or effect ⟨His house is *close* to the border.⟩ ⟨It's *close* to nine o'clock.⟩
2 very similar ⟨The material is a *close* match with the curtains.⟩
3 almost reaching a particular condition ⟨Illness brought her *close* to death.⟩
4 having a strong liking each one for the other ⟨*close* friends⟩
5 strict and careful in attention to details ⟨*close* examination⟩
6 decided by a narrow margin ⟨It was a *close* election.⟩
7 ¹SHORT 1 ⟨a *close* haircut⟩
8 having little extra space ⟨We all fit, but it was *close.*⟩
9 kept secret or tending to keep secrets
10 lacking fresh or moving air ⟨a *close* room⟩
close•ly *adv*
close•ness *n*

[4]close \ˈklōs\ *adv* **clos•er; clos•est**
a short distance or time away 〈Stay *close* so you don't get lost.〉 〈The time drew *closer.*〉

close call \ˈklōs-\ *n*
a barely successful escape from a difficult or dangerous situation

closed \ˈklōzd\ *adj*
not open 〈a *closed* door〉

clos•et \ˈklä-zət\ *n*
a small room for clothing or for supplies for the house 〈a clothes *closet*〉

close–up \ˈklōs-ˌəp\ *n*
a photograph taken at close range

clo•sure \ˈklō-zhər\ *n*
1 an act of closing 〈The weather forced a *closure* of the schools.〉
2 the condition of being closed 〈*Closure* of the business has hurt the workers.〉

[1]clot \ˈklät\ *n*
a lump made by some substance getting thicker and sticking together 〈a blood *clot*〉

[2]clot *vb* **clot•ted; clot•ting**
to become thick and partly solid

cloth \ˈklȯth\ *n, pl* **cloths** \ˈklȯt͟hz, ˈklȯths\
1 a woven or knitted material (as of cotton or nylon)
2 a piece of cloth for a certain use
3 TABLECLOTH

clothe \ˈklōt͟h\ *vb* **clothed** *or* **clad** \ˈklad\; **cloth•ing**
1 to cover with or as if with clothing
2 to provide with clothes 〈Kind neighbors fed and *clothed* the homeless family.〉

clothes \ˈklōz, ˈklōt͟hz\ *n pl*
CLOTHING

clothes•pin \ˈklōz-ˌpin, ˈklōt͟hz-\ *n*
a small object used for holding clothes in place on a line

cloth•ing \ˈklō-t͟hiŋ\ *n*
the things people wear to cover their bodies

[1]cloud \ˈklau̇d\ *n*
1 ▶ a visible mass of tiny bits of water or ice hanging usually high in the sky
2 a visible mass of small particles in the air 〈a *cloud* of dust〉
3 a large number of things that move together in a group 〈a *cloud* of mosquitoes〉
4 an overwhelming feeling 〈The news cast a *cloud* of gloom.〉
5 the computers and connections that support cloud computing
cloud•less \-ləs\ *adj*

[2]cloud *vb* **cloud•ed; cloud•ing**
1 to make or become cloudy 〈The sky *clouded* up.〉
2 to have a bad effect on 〈Involvement in the crime *clouded* his future.〉
3 to make confused 〈Doubts *clouded* her judgment.〉

cloud•burst \ˈklau̇d-ˌbərst\ *n*
a sudden heavy rainfall

cloud computing *n*
the practice of storing regularly used data on computers that can be accessed through the Internet

cloudy \ˈklau̇-dē\ *adj* **cloud•i•er; cloud•i•est**
1 covered over by clouds 〈a *cloudy* sky〉
2 not clear 〈a *cloudy* liquid〉
cloud•i•ness *n*

[1]clout \ˈklau̇t\ *n*
1 a blow especially with the hand
2 the power to influence or control situations

[2]clout *vb* **clout•ed; clout•ing**
to hit hard

[1]clove \ˈklōv\ *n*
▶ the dried flower bud of a tropical tree used in cooking as a spice

[1]clove

[2]clove *past of* CLEAVE

cloven *past participle of* [2]CLEAVE

cloven hoof *n*
a hoof (as of a sheep or cow) with the front part divided into two sections

clo•ver \ˈklō-vər\ *n*
a small plant that has leaves with three leaflets and flowers in dense heads and is sometimes grown for hay or pasture

[1]clown \ˈklau̇n\ *n*
1 a performer (as in a circus) who entertains by playing tricks and who usually wears comical clothes and makeup
2 someone who does things to make people laugh

[2]clown *vb* **clowned; clown•ing**
to act in a funny or silly way : act like a clown

▶ **[1]cloud 1**
Clouds form when air containing water vapor rises and cools, changing into tiny water droplets or ice crystals. Clouds are grouped by their altitude and appearance, although this varies according to where they are in the world, the season, and the time of the day. Low-lying clouds, such as cumulus, nimbostratus, and stratus, form at less than $1\frac{1}{2}$ miles (2 km) above sea level. Mid-level clouds, such as altocumulus and cumulonimbus, lie at $1\frac{1}{4}$–3 miles (2–5 km) in altitude. High-level cirrus clouds are wispy, and form at 3–$7\frac{1}{2}$ miles (5–12 km) above ground.

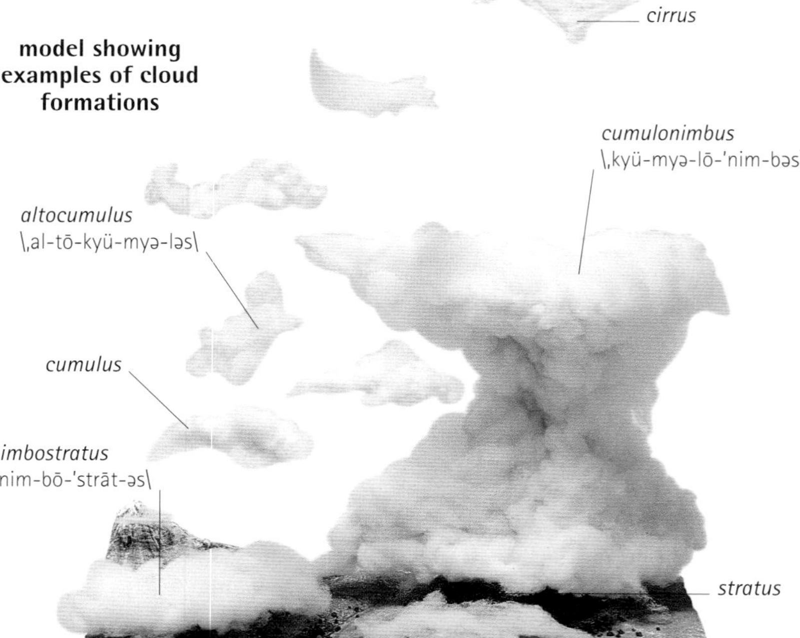

model showing examples of cloud formations

A B C D E F G H I J K L M N O P Q R S T U V W X Y Z

¹club 2: a golfer hitting a shot with a club

¹club \'kləb\ *n*
1 a heavy usually wooden stick used as a weapon
2 ▲ a stick or bat used to hit a ball in various games ⟨golf *club*⟩
3 a group of people associated because of a shared interest
4 the meeting place of a club

²club *vb* **clubbed; club•bing**
to beat or strike with or as if with a club

club•house \'kləb-,haủs\ *n*
1 a building used by a club
2 locker rooms used by an athletic team

¹cluck \'klək\ *vb* **clucked; cluck•ing**
to make the low sound of or like a hen

²cluck *n*
the sound made by a hen

clue \'klü\ *n*
something that helps a person to find something or to solve a mystery

► **Word History** The word *clue* was originally an alternate spelling of *clew*, meaning "a ball of thread or yarn." Our usual modern sense of *clue*, "something that helps solve a mystery," grows out of the image of a ball of thread that helps a person to find a way out of a maze. Of stories containing this image, the best known is the Greek myth of Theseus and Ariadne. Ariadne gave the hero Theseus a ball of thread that he unraveled as he searched the labyrinth, or huge maze, of her father, King Minos. After killing the monster in the labyrinth, Theseus retraced his steps by rewinding the thread.

¹clump \'kləmp\ *n*
1 a group of things clustered together ⟨a *clump* of bushes⟩
2 a cluster or lump of something ⟨A *clump* of mashed potatoes fell on his lap.⟩
3 a heavy tramping sound

²clump *vb* **clumped; clump•ing**
1 to form or cause to form a clump or clumps
2 to walk with loud heavy steps : CLOMP

clum•sy \'kləm-zē\ *adj* **clum•si•er; clum•si•est**
1 lacking skill or grace in movement ⟨*clumsy* fingers⟩
2 awkwardly or carelessly made or done ⟨a *clumsy* apology⟩ ⟨a *clumsy* error⟩
3 awkward to handle ⟨a *clumsy* package⟩
clum•si•ly \-zə-lē\ *adv*
clum•si•ness \-zē-nəs\ *n*

¹coach 1: model of a 19th-century coach

clung *past and past participle of* CLING

clunk \'kləŋk\ *n*
a loud dull sound

¹clus•ter \'klə-stər\ *n*
a number of similar things growing or grouped closely together : BUNCH ⟨a *cluster* of houses⟩ ⟨a flower *cluster*⟩

²cluster *vb* **clus•tered; clus•ter•ing**
to grow, collect, or assemble in a bunch

¹clutch \'kləch\ *vb* **clutched; clutch•ing**
1 to grasp or hold tightly with or as if with the hands or claws
2 to make a grab ⟨He began *clutching* at the falling child.⟩

²clutch *n*
1 control or power someone has over someone else — usually used in pl.
2 a coupling for connecting and disconnecting a driving and a driven part in machinery
3 a lever or pedal operating a clutch

³clutch *n*
1 a group of eggs that is laid by a bird at one time
2 a small group of things or people

¹clut•ter \'klə-tər\ *vb* **clut•tered; clut•ter•ing**
to fill or cover with scattered things

²clutter *n*
a collection of scattered things

cm *abbr* centimeter

CO *abbr* Colorado

co. *abbr*
1 company
2 county

co- *prefix*
1 with : together : joint : jointly ⟨*co*operate⟩
2 in or to the same degree
3 fellow : partner ⟨*co*author⟩

¹coach \'kōch\ *n*
1 ▼ a large carriage that has four wheels and a raised seat outside in front for the driver and is drawn by horses
2 a person who instructs or trains a performer or team
3 a person who teaches students individually
4 a railroad passenger car without berths
5 the least expensive seats on an airplane or a train

²coach *vb* **coached; coach•ing**
to teach and train

coach•man \'kōch-mən\ *n, pl* **coach•men** \-mən\
a person whose business is driving a coach or carriage

co•ag•u•late \kō-'a-gyə-,lāt\ *vb* **co•ag•u•lat•ed; co•ag•u•lat•ing**
to gather into a thick compact mass : CLOT ⟨The blood *coagulated*.⟩

coal \ˈkōl\ *n*
1 a piece of glowing or charred wood : EMBER
2 ▶ a black solid mineral substance that is formed by the partial decay of plant matter under the influence of moisture and often increased pressure and temperature within the earth and is mined for use as a fuel

coarse \ˈkȯrs\ *adj* **coars•er**; **coars•est**
1 having a harsh or rough quality ⟨*coarse* dry skin⟩ ⟨a *coarse* fabric⟩
2 made up of large particles ⟨*coarse* sand⟩
3 crude in taste, manners, or language
4 of poor or ordinary quality
coarse•ly *adv*
coarse•ness *n*

coars•en \ˈkȯr-sᵊn\ *vb* **coars•ened**; **coars•en•ing**
to make or become rough or rougher ⟨His hands were *coarsened* by hard labor.⟩

[1]**coast** \ˈkōst\ *n*
the land near a shore

[2]**coast** *vb* **coast•ed**; **coast•ing**
1 to move downhill by the force of gravity
2 to sail close to shore along a coast

coast•al \ˈkō-stᵊl\ *adj*
of, relating to, or located on, near, or along a coast ⟨*coastal* trade⟩

coast•er \ˈkō-stər\ *n*
1 a ship that sails or trades along a coast
2 a small mat on which a glass is placed to protect the surface of a table

coast guard *n*
a military force that guards a coast and helps people on boats and ships that are in trouble

[1]**coat** \ˈkōt\ *n*
1 an outer garment worn especially for warmth
2 the outer covering (as fur or feathers) of an animal
3 a layer of material covering a surface ⟨a *coat* of paint⟩
coat•ed \-əd\ *adj*

[2]**coat** *vb* **coat•ed**; **coat•ing**
to cover with a coat or covering

coat•ing \ˈkō-tiŋ\ *n*
[1]COAT 3, COVERING ⟨The stairs have a *coating* of ice.⟩

coat of arms *n, pl* **coats of arms**
▶ a special group of pictures or symbols belonging to a person, family, or group and shown on a shield

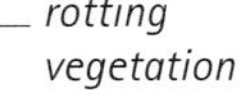
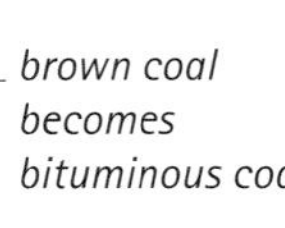

coal 2: layers showing how coal forms over millions of years

coat of mail *n, pl* **coats of mail**
a garment of metal scales or rings worn long ago as armor

co•au•thor \ˈkō-ˈȯ-thər\ *n*
an author who works with another author

coax \ˈkōks\ *vb* **coaxed**; **coax•ing**
1 to influence by gentle urging, special attention, or flattering ⟨She *coaxed* her kitty out of the tree.⟩
2 to get or win by means of gentle urging or flattery ⟨He *coaxed* a raise from the boss.⟩

cob \ˈkäb\ *n*
1 a male swan
2 CORNCOB

co•balt \ˈkō-ˌbȯlt\ *n*
a tough shiny silvery white metallic chemical element found with iron and nickel

coat of arms

cob•bled \ˈkä-bəld\ *adj*
paved or covered with cobblestones ⟨*cobbled* streets⟩

cob•bler \ˈkä-blər\ *n*
1 a person who mends or makes shoes
2 a fruit pie with a thick upper crust and no bottom crust that is baked in a deep dish

cob•ble•stone \ˈkä-bəl-ˌstōn\ *n*
a rounded stone used especially in the past to pave streets

co•bra \ˈkō-brə\ *n*
◀ a very poisonous snake of Asia and Africa that puffs out the skin around its neck into a hood when threatened

cob•web \ˈkäb-ˌweb\ *n*
1 SPIDERWEB
2 tangles of threads of old spiderwebs usually covered with dirt and dust

cobra

co•caine \kō-ˈkān\ *n*
a habit-forming drug obtained from the leaves of a South American shrub and sometimes used as a medicine to deaden pain

coc•cus \ˈkä-kəs\ *n, pl* **coc•ci** \ˈkä-ˌkī, -ˌkē; ˈkäk-ˌsī, -ˌsē\
a bacterium shaped like a ball

co•chlea \ˈkō-klē-ə, ˈkä-\ *n, pl* **co•chle•as** *or* **co•chle•ae** \-ˌē, -ˌī\
a coiled tube in the inner part of the ear that contains the endings of the nerve which carries information about sound to the brain

[1]**cock** \ˈkäk\ *n*
1 a male bird : ROOSTER
2 a faucet or valve for controlling the flow of a liquid or a gas

[2]**cock** *vb* **cocked**; **cock•ing**
1 to turn or tip upward or to one side ⟨The puppy *cocked* her head when she heard your voice.⟩
2 to set or draw back in readiness for some action ⟨Watch how I *cock* my arm to throw.⟩
3 to draw back the hammer of (a gun) in readiness for firing

[3]**cock** *n*
the act of tipping or turning at an angle : TILT ⟨a *cock* of the head⟩

cock•a•too \ˈkä-kə-ˌtü\ *n, pl* **cock•a•toos**
a large, noisy, and usually brightly colored crested parrot mostly of Australia

cock•eyed \ˈkäk-ˌīd\ *adj*
1 tilted to one side
2 FOOLISH ⟨a *cockeyed* plan⟩

cock•le \'kä-kəl\ *n*
an edible shellfish with a shell that has two parts and is shaped like a heart

cock•le•bur \'kä-kəl-,bər, 'kə-\ *n*
▼ a plant with prickly fruit that is related to the thistles

cocklebur: the prickly fruit of a cocklebur

cock•le•shell \'kä-kəl-,shel\ *n*
a shell of a cockle

cock•pit \'käk-,pit\ *n*
1 an open space in the deck from which a small boat (as a yacht) is steered
2 ▼ a space in an airplane for the pilot

cockpit 2

cock•roach \'käk-,rōch\ *n*
a black or brown insect that is active chiefly at night and can be a troublesome pest in homes

cocky \'kä-kē\ *adj* **cock•i•er**; **cock•i•est**
very sure of oneself : boldly self-confident

co•coa \'kō-kō\ *n*
1 a brown powder that is made from the roasted seeds (**cocoa beans**) of the cacao tree after some of its fat is removed and that is used to make chocolate
2 a hot drink made from cocoa powder mixed with water or milk

co•co•nut \'kō-kə-nət, -,nət\ *n*
a large nutlike fruit that has a thick husk with white flesh and a watery liquid inside it and that grows on a tall tropical palm (**coconut palm**)

co•coon \kə-'kün\ *n*
the silky covering which moth caterpillars make around themselves and in which they are protected while changing into a moth

cod \'käd\ *n, pl* **cod**
a large fish found in the deep colder parts of the northern Atlantic Ocean and often used for food

COD *abbr*
1 cash on delivery
2 collect on delivery

cod•dle \'kä-dᵊl\ *vb* **cod•dled**; **cod•dling**
to treat with too much care : PAMPER

[1]**code** \'kōd\ *n*
1 a system of rules or principles ⟨a *code* of conduct⟩
2 a system of signals or letters and symbols with special meanings used for sending messages
3 a collection of laws ⟨criminal *code*⟩
4 GENETIC CODE
5 a set of instructions for a computer

[2]**code** *vb* **cod•ed**; **cod•ing**
to put in the form of a code

cod•fish \'käd-,fish\ *n, pl* **codfish** *or* **cod•fish•es**
COD

cod•ger \'kä-jər\ *n*
an odd or cranky man

co•erce \kō-'ərs\ *vb* **co•erced**; **co•erc•ing**
[2]FORCE 1, COMPEL ⟨He was *coerced* into giving up his lunch money.⟩

cof•fee \'kȯ-fē\ *n*
1 a drink made from the roasted and ground seeds (**coffee beans**) of a tropical plant
2 the roasted seeds of the coffee plant when whole or ground

coffee table *n*
a low table usually placed in front of a sofa

cof•fer \'kȯ-fər\ *n*
a box used especially for holding money and valuables

cof•fin \'kȯ-fən\ *n*
a box or case to hold a dead body for burial

cog \'käg\ *n*
a tooth on the rim of a wheel or gear

cog•i•tate \'kä-jə-,tāt\ *vb* **cog•i•tat•ed**; **cog•i•tat•ing**
to think over : PONDER ⟨The book left her *cogitating* about the author's life.⟩

cog•i•ta•tion \,kä-jə-'tā-shən\ *n*
careful consideration

cog•wheel \'käg-,hwēl, -,wēl\ *n*
a wheel with cogs on the rim

co•her•ent \kō-'hir-ənt, -'her-\ *adj*
1 logical and well-organized ⟨a *coherent* speech⟩
2 to be able to speak well ⟨The accident left her shaken but *coherent*.⟩

co•he•sion \kō-'hē-zhən\ *n*
1 the action of sticking together
2 the force of attraction between the molecules in a mass

[1]**coil** \'kȯil\ *n*
1 a circle, a series of circles, or a spiral made by coiling
2 a long thin piece of material that is wound into circles

[2]**coil** *vb* **coiled**; **coil•ing**
1 to wind into rings or a spiral ⟨*coil* a rope⟩
2 to form or lie in a coil ⟨The cat *coiled* up before the fireplace.⟩

[1]**coin** \'kȯin\ *n*
1 ▼ a piece of metal put out by government authority as money
2 metal money

[2]**coin** *vb* **coined**; **coin•ing**
1 to make coins especially by stamping pieces of metal : MINT
2 to make metal (as gold or silver) into coins
3 to make up (a new word or phrase)

coin•age \'kȯi-nij\ *n*
1 the act or process of making coins
2 money in the form of coins
3 a word or phrase that has recently been invented

a dime is a 10-cent coin

a penny is a 1-cent coin

a nickel is a 5-cent coin

a quarter is a 25-cent coin

[1]**coin 1:** a range of US coins

co•in•cide \ˌkō-ən-ˈsīd\ *vb* **co•in•cid•ed; co•in•cid•ing**
1 to happen at the same time ⟨The band's performance is scheduled to *coincide* with the fireworks.⟩
2 to agree exactly ⟨Their goals *coincided.*⟩
3 to occupy the same space ⟨The edges of the wallpaper must *coincide.*⟩

co•in•ci•dence \kō-ˈin-sə-dəns\ *n*
1 a situation in which things happen at the same time without planning ⟨It was a *coincidence* that we chose the same week for vacation.⟩
2 a condition of coming together in space or time ⟨The *coincidence* of the two events was eerie.⟩

coke \ˈkōk\ *n*
gray lumps of fuel made by heating soft coal in a closed chamber until some of its gases have passed off

col. *abbr* column

[1]**cold** \ˈkōld\ *adj* **cold•er; cold•est**
1 having a low temperature or one much below normal ⟨a *cold* day⟩
2 suffering from lack of warmth ⟨I feel *cold.*⟩
3 cooled after being cooked ⟨We ate *cold* chicken.⟩
4 served at a low temperature or with ice ⟨Have a *cold* drink.⟩
5 lacking warmth of feeling : UNFRIENDLY ⟨She's been *cold* to me ever since our disagreement.⟩
cold•ly *adv*
cold•ness *n*
in cold blood with planning beforehand

[2]**cold** *n*
1 a condition of low temperature : cold weather ⟨I can't stand the *cold.*⟩
2 the bodily feeling produced by lack of warmth : CHILL ⟨He was shivering with *cold.*⟩
3 COMMON COLD

cold–blood•ed \ˈkōld-ˈblə-dəd\ *adj*
1 having a body temperature that varies with the temperature of the environment ⟨Frogs are *cold-blooded* animals.⟩
2 lacking or showing a lack of normal human feelings ⟨a *cold-blooded* criminal⟩

cold cuts *n pl*
slices of cold cooked meats

col•i•se•um \ˌkä-lə-ˈsē-əm\ *n*
▼ a large structure (as a stadium) for athletic contests or public entertainment

col•lab•o•rate \kə-ˈla-bə-ˌrāt\ *vb* **col•lab•o•rat•ed; col•lab•o•rat•ing**
1 to work with others (as in writing a book)
2 to cooperate with an enemy force that has taken over a person's country

col•lage \kə-ˈläzh\ *n*
a work of art made by gluing pieces of different materials to a flat surface

[1]**col•lapse** \kə-ˈlaps\ *vb* **col•lapsed; col•laps•ing**
1 to break down completely : fall in ⟨He escaped from the mine before it *collapsed.*⟩
2 to completely relax ⟨I *collapsed* onto the sofa.⟩
3 to suffer a physical or mental breakdown ⟨She *collapsed* from exhaustion.⟩
4 to fail or stop working suddenly ⟨The ancient civilization *collapsed.*⟩
5 to fold together ⟨The umbrella *collapses* to a small size.⟩

[2]**collapse** *n*
the act or an instance of breaking down ⟨The building is in danger of *collapse.*⟩

coliseum: the Coliseum in Rome, Italy, built nearly 2,000 years ago

Col. *abbr*
1 colonel
2 Colorado

col– see COM–

co•la \ˈkō-lə\ *n, pl* **co•las**
a sweet brown carbonated soft drink that contains flavoring from the nut of a tropical tree

col•an•der \ˈkä-lən-dər, ˈkə-\ *n*
a bowl-shaped utensil with small holes for draining foods

cole•slaw \ˈkōl-ˌslȯ\ *n*
a salad made with chopped raw cabbage

co•le•us \ˈkō-lē-əs\ *n*
a plant grown as a houseplant or a garden plant for its many-colored leaves

col•ic \ˈkä-lik\ *n*
1 sharp pain in the intestines
2 a condition in which a healthy baby is uncomfortable and cries for long periods of time
col•icky \ˈkä-lə-kē\ *adj*

col•laps•ible \kə-ˈlap-sə-bəl\ *adj*
capable of collapsing or possible to collapse ⟨a *collapsible* table⟩

[1]**col•lar** \ˈkä-lər\ *n*
1 the part of a piece of clothing that fits around a person's neck
2 a band of material worn around an animal's neck
3 a ring used to hold something (as a pipe) in place
col•lar•less \-ləs\ *adj*

[2]collar *vb* **col•lared; col•lar•ing**
to seize by or as if by the collar
: CAPTURE, GRAB

col•lar•bone \'kä-lər-,bōn\ *n*
a bone of the shoulder joined to the breastbone and the shoulder blade

col•league \'kä-,lēg\ *n*
an associate in a profession : a fellow worker

col•lect \kə-'lekt\ *vb* **col•lect•ed; col•lect•ing**
1 to gather from a number of sources 〈*collect* stamps〉 〈She *collected* stories from all over the world.〉
2 to receive payment for 〈Our landlord is here to *collect* the rent money.〉
3 to bring or come together into one body or place 〈Our teacher *collected* our homework papers.〉
4 to gain or regain control of 〈After losing my way, I had to stop and *collect* my thoughts.〉
5 to increase in amount 〈Dust *collected* on the furniture.〉
6 to get and bring **synonyms** see GATHER

col•lect•ed \kə-'lek-təd\ *adj*
[3]CALM 2

col•lect•ible \kə-'lek-tə-bəl\ *adj*
considered valuable by collectors
collectible *n*

col•lec•tion \kə-'lek-shən\ *n*
1 the act or process of gathering together 〈*collection* of trash〉
2 a group of things that have been gathered 〈A *collection* of tools cluttered the garage.〉
3 a group of objects gathered for study or exhibition or as a hobby
4 the act of gathering money (as for charitable purposes)
5 money gathered for a charitable purpose

col•lec•tive \kə-'lek-tiv\ *adj*
1 having to do with a number of persons or things thought of as a whole 〈*collective* nouns〉
2 done or shared by a number of persons as a group 〈Neighbors made a *collective* effort to pick up litter.〉
col•lec•tive•ly *adv*

col•lec•tor \kə-'lek-tər\ *n*
1 a person or thing that collects 〈stamp *collector*〉
2 a person whose business it is to collect money 〈a bill *collector*〉

col•lege \'kä-lij\ *n*
a school that offers more advanced classes than a high school

col•le•giate \kə-'lē-jət\ *adj*
1 having to do with a college 〈*collegiate* studies〉
2 of, relating to, or characteristic of college students 〈*collegiate* humor〉

col•lide \kə-'līd\ *vb* **col•lid•ed; col•lid•ing**
1 to strike against each other with strong force
2 [1]CLASH 2 〈Their different goals *collided.*〉

col•lie \'kä-lē\ *n*
a large usually long-haired dog of Scottish origin that has been used to herd sheep

col•li•sion \kə-'li-zhən\ *n*
an act or instance of colliding

col•lo•qui•al \kə-'lō-kwē-əl\ *adj*
used in or suited to familiar and informal conversation 〈*colloquial* language〉

col•lo•qui•al•ism \kə-'lō-kwē-ə-,li-zəm\ *n*
a word or expression used in or suited to familiar and informal conversation

co•logne \kə-'lōn\ *n*
a perfumed liquid made up of alcohol and fragrant oils

[1]co•lon \'kō-lən\ *n*
the main part of the large intestine

[2]colon *n*
a punctuation mark : used mostly to call attention to what follows (as a list, explanation, or quotation)

col•o•nel \'kər-n^{ə}l\ *n*
a commissioned officer in the army, air force, or marine corps ranking above a major and below a general

[1]co•lo•nial \kə-'lō-nē-əl\ *adj*
1 of, relating to, or characteristic of a colony
2 *often cap* of or relating to the original 13 colonies that formed the United States

[2]colonial *n*
a member of or a person living in a colony

col•o•nist \'kä-lə-nəst\ *n*
1 a person living in a colony
2 a person who helps to found a colony

col•o•nize \'kä-lə-,nīz\ *vb* **col•o•nized; col•o•niz•ing**
1 to establish a colony in or on
2 to settle in a colony

col•on•nade \,kä-lə-'nād\ *n*
a row of columns usually supporting a roof

col•o•ny \'kä-lə-nē\ *n*, *pl* **col•o•nies**
1 a distant territory belonging to or under the control of a nation
2 a group of people sent out by a government to a new territory
3 a group of living things of one kind living together 〈a *colony* of ants〉
4 a group of people with common qualities or interests located in close association 〈an art *colony*〉

[1]col•or \'kə-lər\ *n*
1 ◀ the appearance of a thing apart from size and shape when light strikes it 〈Red is the *color* of blood.〉
2 skin tone as a mark of race 〈You cannot discriminate on the basis of *color.*〉
3 the rosy tint of a light-skinned person's face
4 [2]BLUSH 1 〈Her embarrassment showed in the *color* rising in her face.〉
5 **colors** *pl* an identifying flag
6 [1]INTEREST 2 〈Details added *color* to his story.〉

▶ [1]color 1
The color of an object is the way in which our eyes interpret light reflecting from it. In painting, the main, or primary, colors are red, blue, and yellow. If these three colors are combined, they create black. Mixing two primary colors makes the secondary colors orange, green, and violet. Further combinations make many more shades of color.

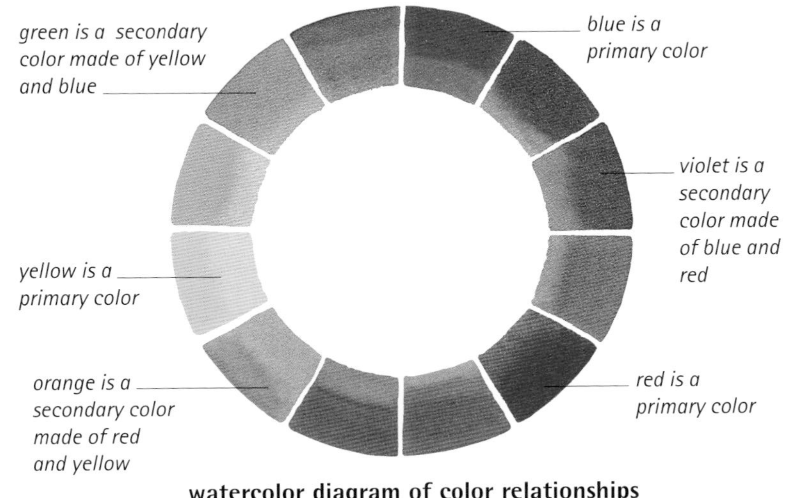

watercolor diagram of color relationships

[2]color *vb* **col•ored; col•or•ing**
1 to give color to
2 to change the color of ⟨She *colored* her hair.⟩
3 to fill in the outlines of a shape or picture with color
4 to take on or change color : BLUSH ⟨He *colored* in anger.⟩
5 [2]INFLUENCE ⟨I won't let these rumors *color* my opinion.⟩

col•or•ation \ˌkə-lə-ˈrā-shən\ *n*
use or arrangement of colors or shades : COLORING ⟨The monarch butterfly is well-known for its orange and black *coloration.*⟩

color–blind \ˈkə-lər-ˌblīnd\ *adj*
unable to see the difference between certain colors

col•ored \ˈkə-lərd\ *adj*
having color ⟨*colored* glass⟩ ⟨brightly-*colored* birds⟩

col•or•ful \ˈkə-lər-fəl\ *adj*
1 having bright colors
2 full of variety or interest ⟨She is a *colorful* person.⟩

col•or•ing \ˈkə-lə-riŋ\ *n*
1 the act of applying colors ⟨His favorite activities are doing puzzles and *coloring.*⟩
2 something that produces color ⟨This cookie has no artificial *coloring.*⟩
3 the effect produced by the use of color ⟨His paintings are famous for their bright *coloring.*⟩
4 natural color ⟨The cat has beautiful *coloring.*⟩
5 COMPLEXION ⟨That red shirt looks great with your *coloring.*⟩

coloring book *n*
a book of drawings made in solid lines for coloring

col•or•less \ˈkə-lər-ləs\ *adj*
1 having no color
2 WAN 1, PALE
3 [1]DULL 3 ⟨Her face had a *colorless* expression.⟩

co•los•sal \kə-ˈlä-səl\ *adj*
very large : HUGE ⟨a *colossal* success⟩ ⟨She gave the ball a *colossal* heave.⟩

col•our *chiefly British variant of* COLOR

colt \ˈkōlt\ *n*
a young male horse

col•um•bine \ˈkä-ləm-ˌbīn\ *n*
▶ a plant that has leaves with three parts and showy flowers usually with five petals that are thin and pointed

columbine

col•umn \ˈkä-ləm\ *n*
1 one of two or more vertical sections of a printed page ⟨Read the article in the left *column.*⟩
2 a group of items shown one under the other down a page ⟨a *column* of figures⟩
3 a regular feature in a newspaper or magazine ⟨a sports *column*⟩
4▼ a pillar used to support a building
5 something that is tall or thin in shape or arrangement ⟨a *column* of smoke⟩
6 a long straight row ⟨a *column* of soldiers⟩

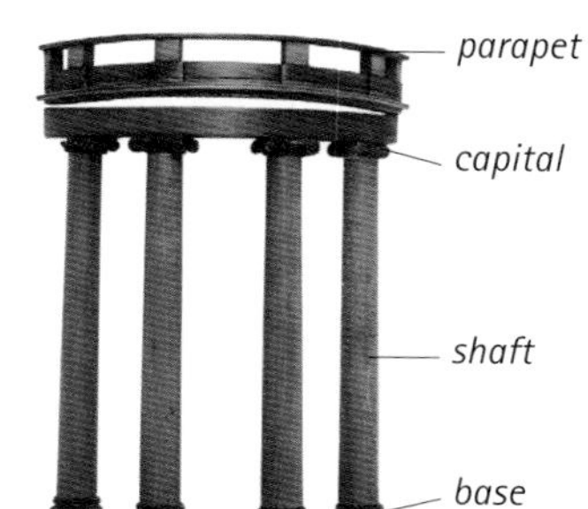

column 4: architect's model of columns supporting a parapet

col•um•nist \ˈkä-ləm-nəst, -lə-məst\ *n*
a writer of a column in a newspaper or magazine

com *abbr* commercial organization

com– *or* **col–** *or* **con–** *prefix*
with : together : jointly ⟨*com*press⟩ — usually *com–* before *b, p,* or *m, col–* before *l* and *con–* before other sounds

co•ma \ˈkō-mə\ *n*
a condition resembling deep sleep that is caused by sickness or injury

Co•man•che \kə-ˈman-chē\ *n, pl* **Comanche** *or* **Co•man•ches**
1 a member of an American Indian people ranging from Wyoming and Nebraska into New Mexico and northwestern Texas
2 the language of the Comanche people

[1]comb \ˈkōm\ *n*
1 a toothed implement used to smooth and arrange the hair or worn in the hair to hold it in place
2 a soft fleshy part on top of the head of a chicken or some related birds
3 HONEYCOMB

[2]comb *vb* **combed; comb•ing**
1 to smooth, arrange, or untangle with a comb
2 to search over or through carefully ⟨Police *combed* the building in search of evidence.⟩

[1]com•bat \ˈkäm-ˌbat\ *n*
1 a fight or contest between individuals or groups
2 active military fighting ⟨Five soldiers were wounded in *combat.*⟩

[2]com•bat \kəm-ˈbat, ˈkäm-ˌbat\ *vb* **com•bat•ed** *or* **com•bat•ted; com•bat•ing** *or* **com•bat•ting**
to fight with : fight against : OPPOSE ⟨*combat* disease⟩

com•bat•ant \kəm-ˈba-tᵊnt, ˈkäm-bə-tənt\ *n*
a person who takes part in a combat

com•bi•na•tion \ˌkäm-bə-ˈnā-shən\ *n*
1 a result or product of combining or being combined ⟨I succeeded by a *combination* of hard work and luck.⟩
2 a series of numbers or letters that is used to open a lock

combination lock *n*
▶ a lock with one or more dials or rings marked usually with numbers which are used to open the lock by moving them in a certain order to certain positions

combination lock

[1]com•bine \käm-ˈbīn\ *vb* **com•bined; com•bin•ing**
1 to mix together so as to make or to seem one thing ⟨Combine the ingredients in a large bowl.⟩
2 to be or cause to be together for a purpose ⟨The two groups *combined* to work for reform.⟩

[2]com•bine \ˈkäm-ˌbīn\ *n*
1 a union of persons or groups that work together to achieve a common goal
2 a machine that harvests and threshes grain

com•bus•ti•ble \kəm-ˈbə-stə-bəl\ *adj*
catching fire or burning easily

com•bus•tion \kəm-ˈbəs-chən\ *n*
the process of burning

come \ˈkəm, kəm\ *vb* **came** \ˈkām\; **come; com•ing** \ˈkəm-iŋ\
1 to move toward : APPROACH ⟨*Come* here.⟩
2 to go or travel to a place ⟨I'll be *coming* home for the weekend.⟩
3 ORIGINATE 2, ARISE ⟨They *come* from a good family.⟩
4 to reach the point of being or becoming ⟨The water *came* to a boil.⟩ ⟨The rope *came* untied.⟩
5 to add up : AMOUNT ⟨The bill *comes* to ten dollars.⟩
6 to happen or occur ⟨This couldn't have *come* at a better time.⟩
7 to be available ⟨These books *come* in four bindings.⟩
8 [1]REACH 3 ⟨The water *came* to our knees.⟩
come about : HAPPEN 1 ⟨How did it *come about* that he got lost?⟩
come across to meet or find by chance ⟨I *came across* an interesting article.⟩

come along
1 to go somewhere with someone
2 to make progress ⟨She's not better yet, but she's *coming along.*⟩
3 to appear or occur as a possibility ⟨Don't marry the first person who *comes along.*⟩
come by
1 to make a visit to ⟨*Come by* my desk when you can.⟩
2 ACQUIRE ⟨A reliable used car is hard to *come by.*⟩
come down to fall sick ⟨He *came down* with a cold.⟩
come over to affect suddenly and strangely ⟨I'm sorry I yelled. I don't know what *came over* me.⟩
come to to become conscious again ⟨He fainted but *came to* after several minutes.⟩
come upon to meet or find by chance ⟨I *came upon* a stray dog.⟩

co•me•di•an \kə-ˈmē-dē-ən\ *n*
1 a performer who makes people laugh
2 an amusing person

com•e•dy \ˈkä-mə-dē\ *n, pl* **com•e•dies**
1 an amusing play that has a happy ending
2 an amusing and often ridiculous event

come•ly \ˈkəm-lē\ *adj* **come•li•er**; **come•li•est**
physically attractive

com•et \ˈkä-mət\ *n*
▼ a small bright heavenly body that develops a cloudy tail as it moves in an orbit around the sun

▶ **Word History** The tail of a comet looks rather like long hair streaming behind the head. The ancient Greeks named comets with the word *komētēs,* which means literally "long-haired." This word comes from the noun *komē,* "hair on one's head" or "shock of hair." The English word *comet* came from the Greek name for comets.

comet

[1]com•fort \ˈkəm-fərt\ *vb* **com•fort•ed**; **com•fort•ing**
to ease the grief or trouble of ⟨*comfort* the sick⟩

[2]comfort *n*
1 acts or words that bring relief from grief or trouble
2 the feeling of being cheered
3 something that makes a person comfortable ⟨the *comforts* of home⟩

com•fort•able \ˈkəm-fər-tə-bəl, ˈkəmf-tər-bəl\ *adj*
1 giving physical ease ⟨a *comfortable* chair⟩
2 more than what is needed ⟨a *comfortable* income⟩
3 physically at ease
com•fort•ably \-blē\ *adj*

com•fort•er \ˈkəm-fər-tər\ *n*
1 a person or thing that gives relief to someone suffering grief or trouble
2 [1]QUILT

com•ic \ˈkä-mik\ *adj*
1 of, relating to, or characteristic of comedy
2 [1]FUNNY 1

com•i•cal \ˈkä-mi-kəl\ *adj*
[1]FUNNY 1, RIDICULOUS ⟨a *comical* sight⟩
com•i•cal•ly *adv*

comic book *n*
a magazine made up of a series of comic strips

comic strip *n*
▼ a series of cartoons that tell a story or part of a story

[2]command *n*
1 an order given ⟨Obey her *command.*⟩
2 the authority, right, or power to command : CONTROL ⟨The troops are under my *command.*⟩
3 the ability to control and use : MASTERY ⟨She has a good *command* of the language.⟩
4 the people, area, or unit (as of soldiers and weapons) under a commander
5 a position from which military operations are directed

com•man•dant \ˈkä-mən-ˌdant, -ˌdänt\ *n*
an officer who is in charge of a group of soldiers

com•mand•er \kə-ˈman-dər\ *n*
a commissioned officer in the navy or coast guard ranking above a lieutenant and below a captain

commander in chief *n, pl* **commanders in chief**
a person who holds supreme command of the armed forces of a nation

com•mand•ment \kə-ˈmand-mənt\ *n*
1 something given as a command
2 one of ten rules given by God that are mentioned in the Bible

com•man•do \kə-ˈman-dō\ *n, pl* **com•man•dos** *or* **com•man•does**
1 a unit of troops trained for making surprise raids into enemy territory
2 a member of a commando

comic strip

com•ma \ˈkä-mə\ *n*
a punctuation mark , used chiefly to show separation of words or word groups within a sentence

[1]com•mand \kə-ˈmand\ *vb* **com•mand•ed**; **com•mand•ing**
1 to order with authority ⟨The king *commanded* them to leave.⟩
2 to have power or control over : be commander of ⟨He *commands* an army.⟩
3 to demand as right or due : EXACT ⟨A piano teacher *commands* a high fee.⟩
4 to survey from a good position ⟨The fort is on a hill that *commands* a view of the city.⟩

command sergeant major *n*
a noncommissioned officer in the army ranking above a first sergeant

com•mem•o•rate \kə-ˈme-mə-ˌrāt\ *vb* **com•mem•o•rat•ed**; **com•mem•o•rat•ing**
1 to observe with a ceremony ⟨*commemorate* an anniversary⟩
2 to serve as a memorial of ⟨The statue *commemorates* the battle.⟩

com•mem•o•ra•tion \kə-ˌme-mə-ˈrā-shən\ *n*
1 the act of commemorating
2 something (as a ceremony) that commemorates

com•mence \kə-ˈmens\ *vb* **com•menced**; **com•menc•ing**
BEGIN 1, START

a b c d e f g h i j k l m n o p q r s t u v w x y z

com•mence•ment \kə-ˈmens-mənt\ *n*
1 graduation exercises
2 the act or the time of beginning 〈We look forward to *commencement* of the school year.〉

com•mend \kə-ˈmend\ *vb* **com•mend•ed**; **com•mend•ing**
1 to give into another's care : ENTRUST
2 to speak or write of with approval : PRAISE 〈The police officers were *commended* for bravery.〉

com•mend•able \kə-ˈmen-də-bəl\ *adj*
deserving praise or approval

com•men•da•tion \ˌkä-mən-ˈdā-shən\ *n*
1 [2]PRAISE 1, APPROVAL
2 an expression of approval 〈The worker's supervisor wrote her a *commendation*.〉

[1]com•ment \ˈkä-ˌment\ *n*
1 an expression of opinion either in speech or writing 〈The most frequent *comment* was that service was slow.〉
2 mention of something that deserves notice 〈I'd like to make a few general *comments* before we begin class.〉

[2]comment *vb* **com•ment•ed**; **com•ment•ing**
to make a statement about someone or something : make a comment

com•men•ta•tor \ˈkä-mən-ˌtā-tər\ *n*
a person who describes or analyzes a news, sports, or entertainment event (as over radio or on television)

com•merce \ˈkä-mərs, -ˌmərs\ *n*
the buying and selling of goods especially on a large scale and between different places : TRADE

[1]com•mer•cial \kə-ˈmər-shəl\ *n*
an advertisement broadcast on radio or television

[2]commercial *adj*
1 having to do with the buying and selling of goods and services
2 used to earn a profit 〈a *commercial* jet〉
com•mer•cial•ly *adv*

com•mer•cial•ize \kə-ˈmər-shə-ˌlīz\ *vb* **com•mer•cial•ized**; **com•mer•cial•iz•ing**
to handle with the idea of making a profit 〈*commercializing* a holiday〉

[1]com•mis•sion \kə-ˈmi-shən\ *n*
1 an order granting the power to perform various acts or duties : the right or duty to be performed
2 a certificate that gives military or naval rank and authority : the rank and authority given 〈He received his *commission* in the army as a captain.〉
3 authority to act as agent for another : a task or piece of business entrusted to an agent
4 a group of persons given orders and authority to perform specified duties 〈a housing *commission*〉
5 an act of doing something wrong 〈the *commission* of a crime〉
6 a fee paid to an agent for taking care of a piece of business

[2]commission *vb* **com•mis•sioned**; **com•mis•sion•ing**
1 to give a commission to
2 to put (a ship) into service

commissioned officer \kə-ˌmi-shənd-\ *n*
an officer in the armed forces who ranks above the enlisted persons or warrant officers and who is appointed by the President

com•mis•sion•er \kə-ˈmi-shə-nər, -ˈmish-nər\ *n*
1 a member of a commission
2 an official who is the head of a government department

com•mit \kə-ˈmit\ *vb* **com•mit•ted**; **com•mit•ting**
1 to bring about : PERFORM 〈*commit* a crime〉
2 to make secure or put in safekeeping : ENTRUST
3 to place in or send to a prison or mental hospital
4 to pledge to do some particular thing 〈When asked if he would volunteer, he wouldn't *commit* himself.〉
com•mit•ment \-mənt\ *n*

com•mit•tee \kə-ˈmi-tē\ *n*
a group of persons appointed or elected to study a problem, plan an event, or perform a specific duty

com•mod•i•ty \kə-ˈmä-də-tē\ *n*, *pl* **com•mod•i•ties**
something produced by agriculture, mining, or manufacture

com•mo•dore \ˈkä-mə-ˌdȯr\ *n*
an officer of high rank in the navy

[1]com•mon \ˈkä-mən\ *adj*
1 affecting, belonging to, needed by, or used by everybody 〈for the *common* good〉 〈a *common* room〉
2 shared by two or more individuals or by the members of a family or group 〈a *common* ancestor〉
3 [1]GENERAL 1 〈*common* knowledge〉
4 occurring, appearing, or used frequently 〈a *common* sight〉 〈a *common* name〉
5 not above the average in rank or status 〈a *common* soldier〉
6 not privileged or elite
7 expected from polite and decent people 〈*common* courtesy〉
in common shared together 〈We have a lot *in common*.〉

▶ **Synonyms** COMMON, ORDINARY, and FAMILIAR mean occurring often. COMMON is used for something that is of the everyday sort and frequently occurs. 〈Fishing boats are a *common* sight around here.〉 ORDINARY is used when something is of the usual standard. 〈I had an *ordinary* day.〉 FAMILIAR is used of something that is well-known and easily recognized. 〈That song is *familiar*.〉

[2]common *n*
land (as a park) owned and used by a community

common cold *n*
▼ a contagious illness which causes the lining of the nose and throat to be sore, swollen, and red and in which there is usually much mucus and coughing and sneezing

common cold:
a girl suffering from the common cold

common denominator *n*
a common multiple of the denominators of a number of fractions

com•mon•er \ˈkä-mə-nər\ *n*
a person who is not privileged or high in social status

common multiple *n*
a multiple of each of two or more numbers

common noun *n*
a noun that names a class of persons or things or any individual of a class and that may occur with a limiting modifier (as *a*, *the*, *some*, or *every*) 〈The words "child," "city," and "day" are *common nouns*.〉

[1]com•mon•place \ˈkä-mən-ˌplās\ *adj*
often seen or met with : ORDINARY 〈He draws *commonplace* objects, like fences.〉

[2]**commonplace** *n*
something that is often seen or met with ⟨Crowds are a *commonplace* of city life.⟩

common sense *n*
ordinary good sense and judgment
com•mon•sense \'kä-mən-'sens\ *adj*

com•mon•wealth \'kä-mən-,welth\ *n*
1 a political unit (as a nation or state)
2 one of four states of the United States—Kentucky, Massachusetts, Pennsylvania, or Virginia

com•mo•tion \kə-'mō-shən\ *n*
noisy excitement and confusion : TURMOIL

com•mune \kə-'myün\ *vb* **com•muned**; **com•mun•ing**
to be in close accord or communication with someone or something ⟨He enjoys walking in the woods and *communing* with nature.⟩

com•mu•ni•ca•ble \kə-'myü-ni-kə-bəl\ *adj*
able to be passed to another person ⟨a *communicable* disease⟩

com•mu•ni•cate \kə-'myü-nə-,kāt\ *vb* **com•mu•ni•cat•ed**; **com•mu•ni•cat•ing**
1 to get in touch
2 to make known ⟨I *communicated* my needs to the nurse.⟩
3 to pass (as a disease) from one to another : SPREAD

com•mu•ni•ca•tion \kə-,myü-nə-'kā-shən\ *n*
1 the exchange (as by speech or letter) of information between persons
2 information exchanged
3 ▼ **communications** *pl* a system of sending information
4 **communications** *pl* a system of routes for transportation

com•mu•nion \kə-'myü-nyən\ *n*
1 a close relationship ⟨in *communion* with nature⟩
2 *cap* a Christian ceremony commemorating with bread and wine the last supper of Jesus Christ
3 a body of Christians having similar beliefs

com•mu•nism \'kä-myə-,ni-zəm\ *n*
a social system or theory in which property and goods are held in common

com•mu•nist \'kä-myə-nəst\ *n*
a person who supports communism

communication 3
Modern technology allows information to be communicated and received faster than ever before. Traditional methods of communication include surface mail, but today there are many, swifter options. These include the telephone, fax, computer e-mail, and satellites. In addition, world news is conveyed via radio and television almost as soon as events occur.

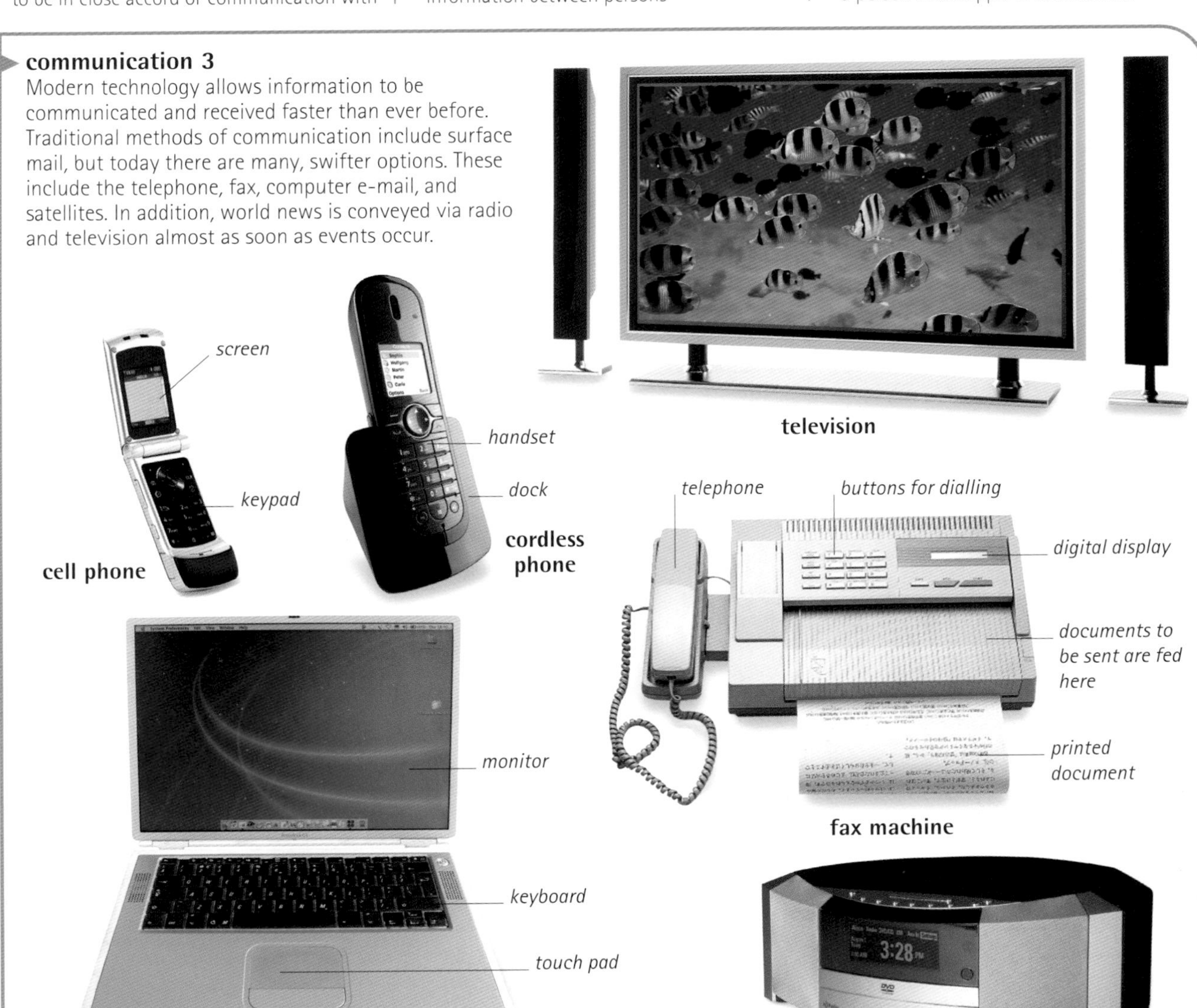

com•mu•ni•ty \kə-ˈmyü-nə-tē\ *n*, *pl* **com•mu•ni•ties**
1 the people living in a certain place (as a village or city) : the area itself
2 a natural group (as of kinds of plants and animals) living together and depending on one another for various necessities of life (as food or shelter)
3 a group of people with common interests 〈the business *community*〉 〈a *community* of artists〉
4 a feeling of caring about others in a group 〈The school fosters a sense of *community*.〉

com•mu•ta•tive \ˈkä-myə-ˌtā-tiv\ *adj*
being a property of a mathematical operation (as addition or multiplication) in which the result does not depend on the order of the elements 〈The *commutative* property of addition states that 1 + 2 and 2 + 1 will both have a sum of 3.〉

com•mute \kə-ˈmyüt\ *vb* **com•mut•ed**; **com•mut•ing**
1 to travel back and forth regularly
2 to change (as a penalty) to something less severe 〈The governor *commuted* the convict's sentence.〉
com•mut•er *n*

[1]**com•pact** \kəm-ˈpakt, ˈkäm-ˌpakt\ *adj*
1 closely united or packed 〈*compact* dirt〉
2 arranged so as to save space 〈a *compact* house〉
synonyms see DENSE
com•pact•ly *adv*
com•pact•ness *n*

[2]**compact** *vb* **com•pact•ed**; **com•pact•ing**
1 to draw together : COMBINE
2 to press together tightly 〈The machine *compacts* the trash.〉

[3]**com•pact** \ˈkäm-ˌpakt\ *n*
1 ▶ a small case for cosmetics
2 a somewhat small automobile

[3]compact 1: a ladies' compact

[4]**com•pact** \ˈkäm-ˌpakt\ *n*
AGREEMENT 3

compact disc *n*
CD

com•pan•ion \kəm-ˈpan-yən\ *n*
1 a person or thing that accompanies another
2 one of a pair of things that go together 〈The book is the *companion* to the TV show.〉
3 a person employed to live with and assist another

com•pan•ion•ship \kəm-ˈpan-yən-ˌship\ *n*
FELLOWSHIP 1, COMPANY

com•pa•ny \ˈkəm-pə-nē, ˈkəmp-nē\ *n*, *pl* **com•pa•nies**
1 an association of persons operating a business
2 the presence of someone who brings comfort 〈I enjoy your *company*.〉
3 a person or thing someone enjoys being with 〈She's good *company*.〉
4 a person's companions or associates 〈You are known by the *company* you keep.〉
5 guests or visitors especially at a person's home 〈We have *company*.〉
6 a group of persons or things
7 a body of soldiers
8 a band of musical or dramatic performers 〈an opera *company*〉

com•pa•ra•ble \ˈkäm-pə-rə-bəl, -prə-bəl\ *adj*
being similar or about the same 〈Every member of the group is *comparable* in age.〉

[1]**com•par•a•tive** \kəm-ˈper-ə-tiv\ *adj*
1 not entirely but more so than others : RELATIVE 〈We live in *comparative* freedom.〉
2 of or relating to the form of an adjective or adverb that shows an increase in the quality that the adjective or adverb expresses 〈"Taller" is the *comparative* form of "tall."〉
com•par•a•tive•ly *adv*

[2]**comparative** *n*
the degree or form in a language that indicates an increase in the quality expressed by an adjective or adverb 〈"Taller" is the *comparative* of "tall."〉

com•pare \kəm-ˈper\ *vb* **com•pared**; **com•par•ing**
1 to point out as similar : LIKEN 〈She *compared* the activity of ants to the behavior of humans.〉
2 to examine for similarity or differences 〈Before buying *compare* the two bicycles.〉
3 to appear in relation to others 〈She *compares* well with the rest of the class.〉
4 to state the positive, comparative, and superlative forms of an adjective or adverb

▶ **Synonyms** COMPARE and CONTRAST mean to look closely at something in order to show likenesses and differences. COMPARE is used for showing the likenesses between two or more things. 〈*Compare* these sofas for size and comfort.〉 CONTRAST is used for showing the differences and especially the characteristics which are opposite. 〈She finds it easy to *contrast* country and city life.〉

com•par•i•son \kəm-ˈper-ə-sən\ *n*
1 the act of examining things to see if they are similar or different : the condition of being examined to find similarity or difference
2 SIMILARITY 〈There's no *comparison* between the two models.〉
3 change in the form and meaning of an adjective or an adverb (as by adding *-er* or *-est* to the word or by adding *more* or *most* before the word) to show different levels of quality, quantity, or relation

com•part•ment \kəm-ˈpärt-mənt\ *n*
1 a small chamber, receptacle, or container 〈The suitcase has *compartments* for personal items.〉
2 one of the separate areas of a train, airplane, or automobile

com•pass \ˈkəm-pəs\ *n*
1 ▼ a device having a magnetic needle that indicates direction on the earth's surface by pointing toward the north

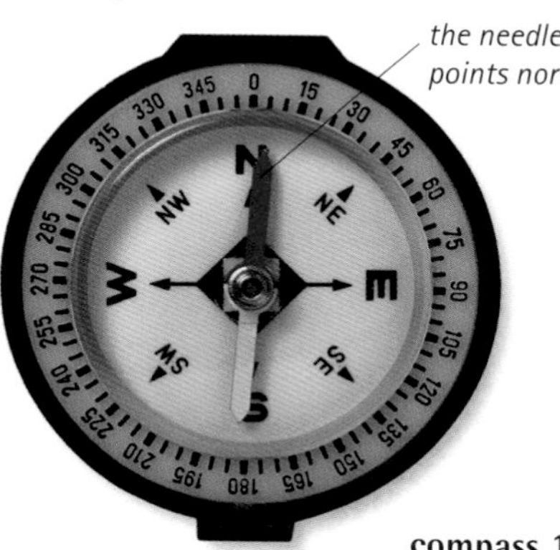

compass 1

2 an instrument for drawing circles or marking measurements consisting of two pointed legs joined at the top by a pivot — usually used in pl.
3 [1]RANGE 2, SCOPE 〈He is within the *compass* of my voice.〉

com•pas•sion \kəm-ˈpa-shən\ *n*
pity for and a desire to help someone

com•pas•sion•ate \kəm-ˈpa-shə-nət\ *adj*
having or showing pity for and desire to help someone

com•pat•i•ble \kəm-ˈpa-tə-bəl\ *adj*
capable of existing together in harmony

com•pa•tri•ot \kəm-ˈpā-trē-ət\ *n*
a person from the same country as someone else

com•pel \kəm-ˈpel\ *vb* **com•pelled**; **com•pel•ling**
1 to make (as a person) do something by the use of physical, moral, or mental pressure : FORCE
2 to make happen by force 〈He *compelled* obedience.〉

com•pen•sate \'käm-pən-,sāt\ *vb* **com•pen•sat•ed; com•pen•sat•ing**
1 to make up for
2 to give money to make up for something ⟨The factory will *compensate* an injured worker.⟩

com•pen•sa•tion \,käm-pən-'sā-shən\ *n*
1 something that makes up for or is given to make up for something else
2 money paid regularly ⟨When the business was struggling, she worked without *compensation*.⟩

com•pete \kəm-'pēt\ *vb* **com•pet•ed; com•pet•ing**
to strive for something (as a prize or a reward) for which another is also striving

com•pe•tence \'käm-pə-təns\ *n*
the quality or state of being capable

com•pe•tent \'käm-pə-tənt\ *adj*
CAPABLE 2, EFFICIENT ⟨a *competent* teacher⟩
com•pe•tent•ly *adv*

com•pe•ti•tion \,käm-pə-'ti-shən\ *n*
1 the act or process of trying to get or win something others are also trying to get or win
2 a contest in which all who take part strive for the same thing
3 all of a person's competitors ⟨He beat the *competiton*.⟩

com•pet•i•tive \kəm-'pe-tə-tiv\ *adj*
characterized by or based on a situation in which more than one person is striving for the same thing ⟨*competitive* sports⟩

com•pet•i•tor \kəm-'pe-tə-tər\ *n*
▼someone or something that is trying to beat or do better than others in a contest or in the selling of goods or services : RIVAL

competitor: competitors jumping over hurdles in a race

com•pile \kəm-'pīl\ *vb* **com•piled; com•pil•ing**
1 to create by gathering things together ⟨She *compiled* a list of names.⟩
2 to put things together in a publication or collection

com•pla•cen•cy \kəm-'plā-sᵊn-sē\ *n*
a feeling of being satisfied with the way things are and not wanting to make them better

com•pla•cent \kəm-'plā-sᵊnt\ *adj*
feeling or showing satisfaction and lack of worry or caution ⟨His team became *complacent* in the second half and lost the game.⟩

com•plain \kəm-'plān\ *vb* **com•plained; com•plain•ing**
to express grief, pain, or discontent : find fault
com•plain•er *n*

com•plaint \kəm-'plānt\ *n*
1 expression of grief, pain, or discontent ⟨He does his work without *complaint*.⟩
2 a cause or reason for expressing grief, pain, or discontent ⟨The noise is my biggest *complaint*.⟩
3 a sickness or disease of the body ⟨a stomach *complaint*⟩
4 a charge of wrongdoing against a person ⟨What's her *complaint* against me?⟩

¹com•ple•ment \'käm-plə-mənt\ *n*
1 something that makes whole or better ⟨The cool salad was the perfect *complement* to the spicy dish.⟩
2 the number or quantity of something that is needed or used ⟨the ship's *complement* of crew⟩

²com•ple•ment \'käm-plə-,ment\ *vb* **com•ple•ment•ed; com•ple•ment•ing**
to serve as something necessary to make whole or better ⟨Find a hat that *complements* your costume.⟩

com•ple•men•ta•ry \,käm-plə-'men-tə-rē\ *adj*
serving to make whole or improve something ⟨Their *complementary* talents make them a great team.⟩

¹com•plete \kəm-'plēt\ *adj*
1 having all necessary parts : not lacking anything ⟨a *complete* set of books⟩
2 entirely done ⟨His training is *complete*.⟩
3 THOROUGH 1 ⟨*complete* darkness⟩
com•plete•ness *n*

²complete *vb* **com•plet•ed; com•plet•ing**
1 to bring to an end : FINISH ⟨*complete* a job⟩
2 to make whole or perfect ⟨He needs six more state flags to *complete* his collection.⟩

com•plete•ly \kəm-'plēt-lē\ *adv*
as much as possible : in every way or detail ⟨Without a map, we got *completely* lost.⟩

com•ple•tion \kəm-'plē-shən\ *n*
the act or process of making whole or finishing : the condition of being whole or finished

com•plex \käm-'pleks, kəm-'pleks, 'käm-,pleks\ *adj*
1 not easy to understand or explain : not simple ⟨*complex* instructions⟩
2 having parts that go together in complicated ways ⟨a *complex* invention⟩

complex fraction *n*
a fraction with a fraction or mixed number in the numerator or denominator or both ⟨5/1¾ is a *complex fraction*.⟩

com•plex•ion \kəm-'plek-shən\ *n*
the color or appearance of the skin and especially of the face ⟨a fair *complexion*⟩

com•plex•i•ty \kəm-'plek-sə-tē\ *n, pl* **com•plex•i•ties**
1 the quality or condition of being difficult to understand or of lacking simplicity ⟨the *complexity* of a problem⟩
2 something difficult to understand or lacking simplicity ⟨the *complexities* of business⟩

com•pli•cate \'käm-plə-,kāt\ *vb* **com•pli•cat•ed; com•pli•cat•ing**
to make or become difficult or lacking in simplicity

com•pli•cat•ed \'käm-plə-,kā-təd\ *adj*
difficult to understand or explain ⟨*complicated* rules⟩

A B C D E F G H I J K L M N O P Q R S T U V W X Y Z

com•pli•ca•tion \ˌkäm-plə-ˈkā-shən\ *n*
something that makes a situation more difficult

[1]**com•pli•ment** \ˈkäm-plə-mənt\ *n*
1 an act or expression of praise, approval, respect, or admiration
2 **compliments** *pl* best wishes ⟨Please accept this with my *compliments.*⟩

[2]**com•pli•ment** \ˈkäm-plə-ˌment\ *vb*
com•pli•ment•ed; **com•pli•ment•ing**
to express praise, approval, respect, or admiration to

▶ **Synonyms** COMPLIMENT, PRAISE, and FLATTER mean to express approval or admiration to someone personally. COMPLIMENT is used of a courteous or pleasant statement of admiration. ⟨He *complimented* students on their neat work.⟩ PRAISE may be used when the statement of approval comes from a person in authority. ⟨The boss *praised* us for doing a good job.⟩ FLATTER is used of complimenting a person too much and especially insincerely. ⟨We *flattered* the teacher in the hope of getting better grades.⟩

com•pli•men•ta•ry \ˌkäm-plə-ˈmen-tə-rē, -ˈmen-trē\ *adj*
1 expressing or containing praise, approval, respect, or admiration ⟨*complimentary* remarks⟩
2 given free as a courtesy or favor ⟨*complimentary* tickets⟩

com•ply \kəm-ˈplī\ *vb* **com•plied**; **com•ply•ing**
to act in agreement with another's wishes or in obedience to a rule ⟨Everyone *complied* with the request.⟩

com•po•nent \kəm-ˈpō-nənt\ *n*
one of the parts or units of a combination, mixture, or system

com•pose \kəm-ˈpōz\ *vb* **com•posed**; **com•pos•ing**
1 to form by putting together ⟨*compose* a team⟩
2 to be the parts or materials of ⟨This cloth is *composed* of silk and wool.⟩
3 to create and write ⟨*compose* a song⟩ ⟨*compose* a letter⟩
4 to make calm : get under control ⟨Although the news is shocking, I'll try to *compose* myself.⟩

com•posed \kəm-ˈpōzd\ *adj*
being calm and in control emotionally ⟨She sat *composed* during the whole interview.⟩

com•pos•er \kəm-ˈpō-zər\ *n*
a writer of music

com•pos•ite \kəm-ˈpä-zət\ *adj*
made up of different parts or elements ⟨Concrete is a *composite* material made up of cement, sand, stone, and water.⟩

composite number *n*
an integer that is a product of two or more whole numbers each greater than 1

com•po•si•tion \ˌkäm-pə-ˈzi-shən\ *n*
1 a short piece of writing done as a school exercise
2 the act of writing words or music
3 the manner in which the parts of a thing are put together : MAKEUP, CONSTITUTION ⟨The president discussed the population's changing *composition.*⟩ ⟨Each rock has a slightly different *composition.*⟩
4 a literary, musical, or artistic production

compost

com•post \ˈkäm-ˌpōst\ *n*
▲ decayed organic material (as of leaves and grass) used to improve soil especially for growing crops

com•po•sure \kəm-ˈpō-zhər\ *n*
calmness especially of mind, manner, or appearance ⟨Throughout the crisis he managed to maintain his *composure.*⟩

[1]**com•pound** \käm-ˈpau̇nd\ *vb*
com•pound•ed; **com•pound•ing**
1 to form by combining separate things ⟨*compound* a medicine⟩
2 to make worse ⟨*compound* a problem⟩
3 to pay (interest) on both an original amount of money and on the interest it has already earned

[2]**com•pound** \ˈkäm-ˌpau̇nd\ *adj*
made of or by the union of two or more parts ⟨a *compound* leaf with three leaflets⟩

[3]**com•pound** \ˈkäm-ˌpau̇nd\ *n*
1 a word made up of parts that are themselves words ⟨The words "rowboat" and "hide-and-seek" are *compounds.*⟩
2 something (as a chemical) that is formed by combining two or more parts or elements

[4]**com•pound** \ˈkäm-ˌpau̇nd\ *n*
an enclosed area containing a group of buildings

com•pre•hend \ˌkäm-pri-ˈhend\ *vb*
com•pre•hend•ed; **com•pre•hend•ing**
1 to understand fully
2 to take in : INCLUDE

com•pre•hen•sion \ˌkäm-pri-ˈhen-shən\ *n*
ability to understand ⟨reading *comprehension*⟩ ⟨beyond *comprehension*⟩

com•pre•hen•sive \ˌkäm-pri-ˈhen-siv\ *adj*
including much : INCLUSIVE ⟨a *comprehensive* course of study⟩ ⟨a *comprehensive* description⟩

[1]**com•press** \kəm-ˈpres\ *vb* **com•pressed**; **com•press•ing**
1 to press or squeeze together ⟨*compressing* his lips⟩
2 to reduce in size, quantity, or volume by or as if by pressure ⟨The pump is for *compressing* air.⟩

[2]**com•press** \ˈkäm-ˌpres\ *n*
▶ a pad (as of folded cloth) applied firmly to a part of the body (as to stop bleeding)

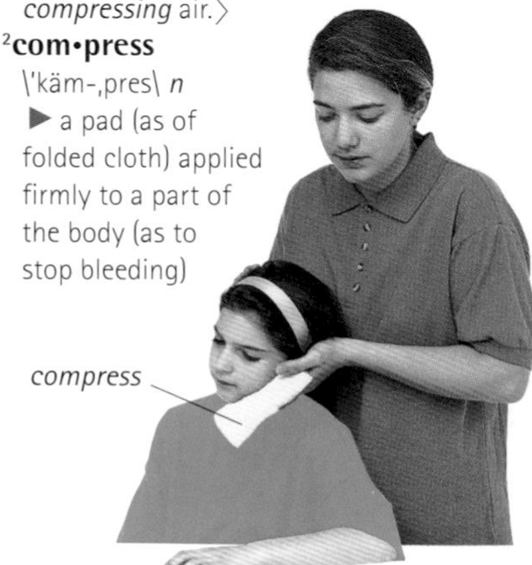

[2]**compress**

com•pres•sion \kəm-ˈpre-shən\ *n*
the act, process, or result of pressing something together

com•pres•sor \kəm-ˈpre-sər\ *n*
a machine for reducing the volume of something (as air) by pressure

com•prise \kəm-ˈprīz\ *vb* **com•prised**; **com•pris•ing**
1 to be made up of : consist of ⟨The play *comprises* three acts.⟩
2 [2]FORM 3 ⟨Nine players *comprise* a baseball team.⟩

[1]**com•pro•mise** \ˈkäm-prə-ˌmīz\ *n*
1 an agreement over a dispute reached by each side changing or giving up some demands ⟨After much argument, they finally reached a *compromise.*⟩
2 something agreed upon as a result of each side changing or giving up some demands ⟨Our *compromise* is to take turns with the toy.⟩

[2]**compromise** *vb* **com•pro•mised; com•pro•mis•ing**
1 to settle by agreeing that each side will change or give up some demands
2 to expose to risk, suspicion, or disgrace ⟨A spy can *compromise* national security.⟩

com•pul•sion \kəm-ˈpəl-shən\ *n*
1 a very strong urge to do something ⟨He felt a *compulsion* to say something.⟩
2 a force that makes someone do something ⟨She was acting under *compulsion*.⟩
3 an act or the state of forcing an action ⟨They got what they wanted through *compulsion*.⟩

com•pul•so•ry \kəm-ˈpəls-rē, -ˈpəl-sə-rē\ *adj*
1 required by or as if by law ⟨*compulsory* education⟩
2 having the power of forcing someone to do something ⟨a *compulsory* law⟩

com•pu•ta•tion \ˌkäm-pyə-ˈtā-shən\ *n*
1 the act or action of determining by use of mathematics
2 a result obtained by using mathematics

com•pute \kəm-ˈpyüt\ *vb* **com•put•ed; com•put•ing**
to find out by using mathematics ⟨*compute* a total⟩

com•put•er \kəm-ˈpyü-tər\ *n*
▼ an automatic electronic machine that can store and process data

com•put•er•ize \kəm-ˈpyü-tə-ˌrīz\ *vb* **com•put•er•ized; com•put•er•iz•ing**
1 to carry out, control, or produce on a computer ⟨*computerize* a billing system⟩
2 to equip with computers ⟨*computerize* a school⟩
3 to put in a form that a computer can use ⟨*computerize* school records⟩

com•rade \ˈkäm-ˌrad, -rəd\ *n*
COMPANION 1

[1]**con** \ˈkän\ *adv*
on the negative side ⟨argue pro and *con*⟩

[2]**con** *n*
an opposing argument, person, or position ⟨She considered the pros and *cons* of the question.⟩

con- see COM-

con•cave \kän-ˈkāv\ *adj*
▼ hollow or rounded inward like the inside of a bowl

concave:
the inside of a bowl is concave

con•ceal \kən-ˈsēl\ *vb* **con•cealed; con•ceal•ing**
1 to hide from sight ⟨The safe was *concealed* behind a large painting.⟩
2 to keep secret ⟨He managed to *conceal* his true identity.⟩

con•ceal•ment \kən-ˈsēl-mənt\ *n*
1 the act of hiding : the state of being hidden ⟨*concealment* of the treasure⟩
2 a hiding place ⟨The animal came out of its *concealment*.⟩

con•cede \kən-ˈsēd\ *vb* **con•ced•ed; con•ced•ing**
1 to admit to be true ⟨The candidate had to *concede* defeat.⟩
2 to grant or yield usually unwillingly ⟨Britain *conceded* the independence of the colonies.⟩

con•ceit \kən-ˈsēt\ *n*
too much pride in a person's own abilities or qualities : excessive self-esteem

con•ceit•ed \kən-ˈsē-təd\ *adj*
VAIN 2

con•ceiv•able \kən-ˈsē-və-bəl\ *adj*
possible to imagine or understand ⟨They serve ice cream in every *conceivable* flavor.⟩

con•ceive \kən-ˈsēv\ *vb* **con•ceived; con•ceiv•ing**
1 to form an idea of : IMAGINE ⟨She is unable to *conceive* how it happened.⟩
2 THINK 1 ⟨He was generally *conceived* of as a genius.⟩

computer

Computers are a fast means of processing information. They perform a wide range of tasks, from air traffic control to weather forecasting. A computer is controlled by a central processing unit — CPU — within the computer's case. Programs, known as software, enable the computer to carry out instructions.

computer and other items of hardware

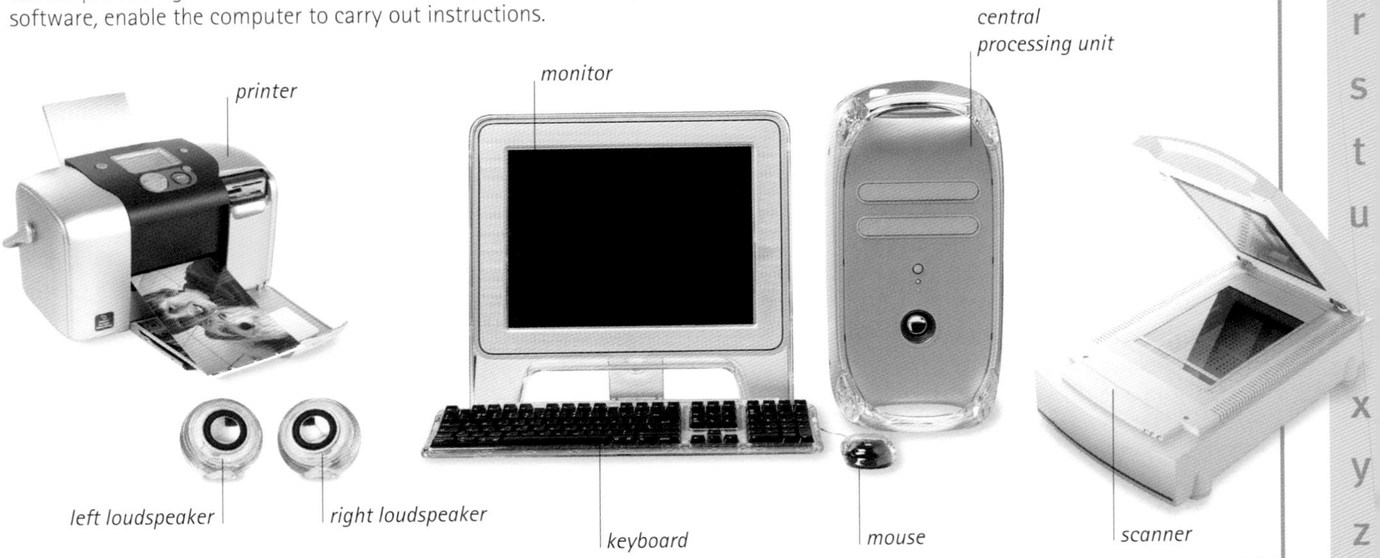

a b c d e f g h i j k l m n o p q r s t u x y z

con•cen•trate \'kän-sən-,trāt\ *vb* **con•cen•trat•ed; con•cen•trat•ing**
1 to focus thought or attention on something
2 to bring or come to or direct toward a common center
3 to make stronger or thicker by removing something (as water) ⟨Simmer the sauce to *concentrate* its flavors.⟩

con•cen•tra•tion \,kän-sən-'trā-shən\ *n*
1 close attention to or thought about a subject ⟨There is a *concentration* on math in the curriculum.⟩
2 the ability to pay close attention ⟨I lost my *concentration* when an ambulance drove past.⟩
3 a large amount of something or a large number of people in one place

con•cept \'kän-,sept\ *n*
something thought of : a general idea ⟨*concepts* of science⟩

[1]**con•cern** \kən-'sərn\ *vb* **con•cerned; con•cern•ing**
1 to relate to : be about ⟨The story *concerns* a young prince.⟩
2 to be of interest or importance to : AFFECT ⟨This problem *concerns* us all.⟩
3 to make worried ⟨Her illness *concerned* my parents.⟩
4 ENGAGE 2, OCCUPY ⟨She *concerns* herself with other people's business.⟩

[2]**concern** *n*
1 a feeling of worry or care about a person or thing ⟨*concern* for the poor⟩ ⟨a cause for *concern*⟩
2 something that causes worry or is regarded as important ⟨The students' safety is her main *concern*.⟩
3 something that relates to or involves a person : AFFAIR ⟨This is not your *concern*.⟩
4 a business organization ⟨a banking *concern*⟩

con•cerned \kən-'sərnd\ *adj*
feeling interest and worry ⟨Teachers met with *concerned* parents.⟩

con•cern•ing \kən-'sər-niŋ\ *prep*
relating to : ABOUT ⟨I received a notice *concerning* the meeting.⟩

con•cert \'kän-sərt, -,sərt\ *n*
► a musical performance by several voices or instruments or by both
in concert : TOGETHER 5 ⟨The staff members are working *in concert* to finish the job.⟩

con•cer•ti•na \,kän-sər-'tē-nə\ *n*
a small musical instrument like an accordion

con•cer•to \kən-'cher-tō\ *n, pl* **con•cer•tos**
a musical composition usually in three parts for orchestra with one or more principal instruments

con•ces•sion \kən-'se-shən\ *n*
1 the act or an instance of giving up or admitting something ⟨a *concession* of defeat⟩
2 something given up ⟨The employees won *concessions* from the company.⟩
3 a right to engage in business given by an authority ⟨a mining *concession*⟩
4 a small business where things are sold (as at a sports facility or public place)

conch \'käŋk, 'känch, 'kȯŋk\ *n, pl* **conchs** \'käŋks, 'kȯŋks\ *or* **conch•es** \'kän-chəz\
▼ a very large sea snail with a tall thick spiral shell

conch: the shell of a conch

con•cil•i•ate \kən-'si-lē-,āt\ *vb* **con•cil•i•at•ed; con•cil•i•at•ing**
1 to bring into agreement : RECONCILE ⟨It's hard to *conciliate* the stories of what happened.⟩
2 to gain or regain the goodwill or favor of ⟨She apologized to *conciliate* an angry friend.⟩

con•cise \kən-'sīs\ *adj*
expressing much in few words ⟨a *concise* description⟩

con•clude \kən-'klüd\ *vb* **con•clud•ed; con•clud•ing**
1 to bring or come to an end : FINISH ⟨*conclude* a speech⟩
2 to decide after a period of thought or research ⟨I *conclude* that I was wrong.⟩
3 to bring about as a result ⟨They would like to *conclude* an agreement on working together.⟩

con•clu•sion \kən-'klü-zhən\ *n*
1 final decision reached by reasoning ⟨I came to the *conclusion* that the plan won't work.⟩
2 the last part of something
3 a final settlement ⟨We had hoped for a quick *conclusion* of the conflict.⟩

con•clu•sive \kən-'klü-siv\ *adj*
DECISIVE 1 ⟨Police found *conclusive* evidence.⟩
con•clu•sive•ly *adv*

con•coct \kən-'käkt, kän-\ *vb* **con•coct•ed; con•coct•ing**
1 to prepare (as food) by putting several different things together
2 to make up : DEVISE ⟨*concoct* a plan⟩

con•cord \'kän-,kȯrd\ *n*
a state of agreement ⟨They lived in peace and *concord*⟩

con•course \'kän-,kȯrs\ *n*
1 a flocking, moving, or flowing together (as of persons or streams) : GATHERING
2 an open space or hall (as in a mall or airport)

[1]**con•crete** \kän-'krēt\ *adj*
1 made of or relating to concrete
2 being specific and useful ⟨a *concrete* example⟩
3 being real and useful ⟨*concrete* evidence⟩

concert: a concert at Symphony Hall in Boston

[2]con•crete \ˈkän-ˌkrēt\ *n*
▼ a hardened mixture of cement, sand, and water with gravel or broken stone used in construction

[2]concrete: a woman shoveling concrete

con•cur \kən-ˈkər\ *vb* **con•curred; con•cur•ring**
1 to act or happen together
2 to be in agreement (as in action or opinion) : ACCORD ⟨The two judges *concurred*.⟩

con•cus•sion \kən-ˈkə-shən\ *n*
injury to the brain caused by a hard hit on the head

con•demn \kən-ˈdem\ *vb* **con•demned; con•demn•ing**
1 to cause to suffer or live in difficult or unpleasant conditions ⟨She was *condemned* to spend her summer in a cast.⟩
2 to sentence to a usually severe punishment
3 to declare to be wrong ⟨School policy *condemns* cheating.⟩
4 to declare to be unfit for use ⟨*condemn* a house⟩

con•dem•na•tion \ˌkän-ˌdem-ˈnā-shən, -dəm-\ *n*
1 CRITICISM 1, DISAPPROVAL
2 the act of condemning or state of being condemned ⟨*condemnation* of the prisoner⟩ ⟨*condemnation* of the building⟩

con•den•sa•tion \ˌkän-ˌden-ˈsā-shən, -dən-\ *n*
1 the act or process of making more compact or concise
2 something that has been made more compact or concise ⟨a *condensation* of the story⟩
3 the conversion of a vapor to a liquid (as by cooling)

con•dense \kən-ˈdens\ *vb* **con•densed; con•dens•ing**
1 to make or become more compact or concise ⟨*Condense* the paragraph into one sentence.⟩
2 to change or cause to change from a vapor to a liquid (as by cooling) ⟨Air *condensed* onto the cold window.⟩

con•de•scend \ˌkän-di-ˈsend\ *vb* **con•de•scend•ed; con•de•scend•ing**
1 to stoop to the level of someone considered less important
2 to grant favors with a show of being better than others ⟨She only *condescended* to speak to me because she needed something.⟩

con•di•ment \ˈkän-də-mənt\ *n*
▼ something added to food to make it taste better ⟨Ketchup and mustard are his favorite *condiments*.⟩

condiments

[1]con•di•tion \kən-ˈdi-shən\ *n*
1 state of physical fitness or readiness for use ⟨The car was in good *condition*.⟩
2 something agreed upon or necessary if some other thing is to take place ⟨You can come on the *condition* that you behave.⟩
3 *conditions pl* the way things are at a certain time or in a certain place
4 state of being ⟨water in a frozen *condition*⟩
5 situation in life ⟨people of humble *condition*⟩

[2]condition *vb* **con•di•tioned; con•di•tion•ing**
1 to put into the proper or desired state
2 to change the habits of usually by training

con•di•tion•al \kən-ˈdi-shə-nᵊl\ *adj*
of or relating to something that will happen only if something else happens ⟨a *conditional* promise⟩

con•do \ˈkän-dō\ *n, pl* **con•dos**
CONDOMINIUM

con•do•min•i•um \ˌkän-də-ˈmi-nē-əm\ *n*
an individually owned unit in a building with many units

con•done \kən-ˈdōn\ *vb* **con•doned; con•don•ing**
to treat (something bad) as acceptable, forgivable, or harmless ⟨I can't *condone* his actions.⟩

con•dor \ˈkän-dər, -ˌdȯr\ *n*
▼ a very large American vulture having a bare head and neck and a frill of feathers on the neck

condor: an Andean condor

[1]con•duct \kən-ˈdəkt\ *vb* **con•duct•ed; con•duct•ing**
1 to plan and put into operation from a position of command : LEAD ⟨*conduct* a business⟩
2 [2]GUIDE 1
3 BEHAVE 1 ⟨She *conducted* herself with courtesy.⟩
4 to direct the performance of (musicians or singers)
5 to have the quality of transmitting light, heat, sound, or electricity

► **Synonyms** CONDUCT, DIRECT, and MANAGE mean to provide the leadership or guidance for something. CONDUCT means leading something in person. ⟨I will *conduct* the meeting.⟩ DIRECT is used for guiding something that needs constant attention. ⟨Our mayor *directed* the building of a new school.⟩ MANAGE means the handling of the small items of something (as a business) or the careful guiding of something to a goal. ⟨He's *managing* the president's reelection campaign.⟩

[2]con•duct \ˈkän-ˌdəkt\ *n*
1 personal behavior
2 the act or way of managing something

con•duc•tion \kən-ˈdək-shən\ *n*
1 the act of transporting something ⟨Pipes are for the *conduction* of water.⟩
2 transmission through a conductor ⟨*conduction* of heat⟩

con•duc•tor \kən-'dək-tər\ *n*
1 a person in charge of a public means of transportation (as a train)
2 ► a person or thing that directs or leads ⟨She is the *conductor* of our school orchestra.⟩
3 a substance or body capable of transmitting light, electricity, heat, or sound ⟨Copper is a good *conductor* of electricity.⟩

cone \'kōn\ *n*
1 a thin crisp cookie shaped to hold ice cream
2 ▼ a scaly structure of certain trees (as the pine or fir) that produces pollen or egg cells and seeds
3 a shape with a circular base and sides that taper evenly to a point
4 a cell of the retina of the eye that is sensitive to colored light

cone 2:
a pine cone

con•fec•tion \kən-'fek-shən\ *n*
a very fancy and usually sweet food

con•fec•tion•er \kən-'fek-shə-nər\ *n*
a maker of or dealer in sweet foods (as candies)

con•fed•er•a•cy \kən-'fe-də-rə-sē\ *n*, *pl* **con•fed•er•a•cies**
1 a league of persons, parties, or states
2 *cap* the eleven southern states that seceded from the United States in 1860 and 1861 to form their own government

[1]**con•fed•er•ate** \kən-'fe-də-rət\ *adj*
1 united in a league
2 *cap* of or relating to the southern Confederacy ⟨Her grandfather collected *Confederate* stamps.⟩

[2]**confederate** *n*
1 a member of a league of persons, parties, or states
2 ACCOMPLICE
3 *cap* a soldier of or a person who sided with the southern Confederacy

con•fer \kən-'fər\ *vb* **con•ferred**; **con•fer•ring**
1 BESTOW, PRESENT ⟨Many honors were *conferred* upon her at graduation.⟩
2 to compare views especially in studying a problem ⟨The umpires decided to *confer* with one another.⟩

conductor 2:
the conductor of an orchestra

con•fer•ence \'kän-fə-rəns, -frəns\ *n*
a meeting for discussion or exchange of opinions

con•fess \kən-'fes\ *vb* **con•fessed**; **con•fess•ing**
1 to tell of doing something wrong or illegal or of something embarrassing : ADMIT ⟨*confessed* to the crime⟩ ⟨*confessed* being jealous⟩
2 to admit committing sins to God or to a priest

con•fes•sion \kən-'fe-shən\ *n*
1 an act of telling of sins or wrong, illegal, or embarrassing acts
2 a written or spoken admission of guilt of a crime

con•fet•ti \kən-'fe-tē\ *n*
► small bits of brightly colored paper made for throwing at celebrations

con•fide \kən-'fīd\ *vb* **con•fid•ed**; **con•fid•ing**
1 to have or show faith ⟨*confide* in a doctor's skill⟩
2 to display trust by telling secrets ⟨She needed to *confide* in a friend.⟩
3 to tell without anyone else knowing ⟨I *confided* the secret to a pal.⟩
4 ENTRUST 2 ⟨The property was *confided* to their care.⟩

con•fi•dence \'kän-fə-dəns\ *n*
1 a feeling of trust or belief ⟨Do you have *confidence* in your partner?⟩
2 SELF-CONFIDENCE
3 reliance on another's secrecy or loyalty ⟨Remember, I told you that in *confidence*.⟩
4 [2]SECRET ⟨Don't betray a *confidence*.⟩

con•fi•dent \'kän-fə-dənt\ *adj*
having or showing sureness and optimism
con•fi•dent•ly *adv*

con•fi•den•tial \ˌkän-fə-'den-shəl\ *adj*
1 [1]SECRET 1 ⟨*confidential* information⟩
2 indicating a need for secrecy ⟨She spoke in a *confidential* tone.⟩
3 trusted with secret matters ⟨a *confidential* assistant⟩
con•fi•den•tial•ly *adv*

con•fine \kən-'fīn\ *vb* **con•fined**; **con•fin•ing**
1 to keep within limits ⟨Her study of bears is *confined* to those in North America.⟩
2 to shut up : IMPRISON
3 to keep indoors ⟨She was *confined* by sickness.⟩
con•fine•ment \-mənt\ *n*

con•fines \'kän-ˌfīnz\ *n pl*
the boundary or limits of something ⟨Stay within the *confines* of the yard.⟩

con•firm \kən-'fərm\ *vb* **con•firmed**; **con•firm•ing**
1 to make sure of the truth of ⟨Their arrest *confirms* my suspicion.⟩
2 to make firm or firmer (as in a habit, in faith, or in intention) : STRENGTHEN ⟨The job at the shelter *confirmed* her intention to become a veterinarian.⟩
3 APPROVE 2, ACCEPT ⟨Senators *confirmed* the treaty.⟩
4 to perform a ceremony admitting a person into a church or synagogue

con•fir•ma•tion \ˌkän-fər-'mā-shən\ *n*
1 an act of ensuring the truth of, strengthening, or approving
2 a religious ceremony admitting a person to full privileges in a church or synagogue
3 something that ensures the truth of, strengthens, or approves ⟨He received a *confirmation* of his order.⟩

confetti

con•firmed \kən-ˈfərmd\ *adj*
unlikely to change ⟨a *confirmed* optimist⟩

con•fis•cate \ˈkän-fə-ˌskāt\ *vb* **con•fis•cat•ed; con•fis•cat•ing**
to seize by or as if by public authority ⟨Police *confiscated* the stolen car.⟩
— **con•fis•ca•tion** \ˌkän-fə-ˈskā-shən\ *n*

con•fla•gra•tion \ˌkän-flə-ˈgrā-shən\ *n*
a large destructive fire

¹con•flict \ˈkän-ˌflikt\ *n*
1 an extended struggle : BATTLE
2 a clashing disagreement (as between ideas or interests)

²con•flict \kən-ˈflikt\ *vb* **con•flict•ed; con•flict•ing**
to be in opposition ⟨Their goals *conflict.*⟩ ⟨The meeting *conflicts* with my appointment.⟩

con•form \kən-ˈfȯrm\ *vb* **con•formed; con•form•ing**
1 to make or be like : AGREE, ACCORD ⟨The weather *conforms* to the recent pattern.⟩
2 COMPLY ⟨Every student needs to *conform* to school rules.⟩

con•for•mi•ty \kən-ˈfȯr-mə-tē\ *n, pl* **con•for•mi•ties**
1 agreement in form, manner, or character ⟨The uniforms ensure *conformity* in dress.⟩
2 action in accordance with some standard or authority ⟨*conformity* to rules of etiquette⟩

con•found \kən-ˈfau̇nd, kän-\ *vb* **con•found•ed; con•found•ing**
CONFUSE 1 ⟨The crime has *confounded* police.⟩

con•front \kən-ˈfrənt\ *vb* **con•front•ed; con•front•ing**
1 to face especially in challenge : OPPOSE ⟨*confront* an enemy⟩
2 to cause to face or meet ⟨His lawyer *confronted* us with the evidence.⟩
— **con•fron•ta•tion** \ˌkän-frən-ˈtā-shən\ *n*

con•fuse \kən-ˈfyüz\ *vb* **con•fused; con•fus•ing**
1 to make uncertain or unable to understand : PERPLEX ⟨The directions *confused* me and I got lost.⟩
2 to fail to tell apart ⟨Teachers always *confused* the twins.⟩

con•fu•sion \kən-ˈfyü-zhən\ *n*
1 difficulty in understanding or in being able to tell one thing from a similar thing
2 a feeling or state of uncertainty

con•geal \kən-ˈjēl\ *vb* **con•gealed; con•geal•ing**
1 to change from a fluid to a solid state by or as if by cold : FREEZE
2 to make or become hard, stiff, or thick

con•ge•nial \kən-ˈjē-nyəl\ *adj*
1 alike or sympathetic in nature, disposition, or tastes
2 existing together in harmony
3 tending to please or satisfy ⟨*congenial* work⟩
4 FRIENDLY 1

con•gest \kən-ˈjest\ *vb* **con•gest•ed; con•gest•ing**
to make too crowded or full : CLOG ⟨More and more cars are *congesting* our highways.⟩

con•gest•ed \kən-ˈje-stəd\ *adj*
blocked or clogged with fluid and especially mucus ⟨a *congested* nose⟩

con•glom•er•ate \kən-ˈglä-mə-rət\ *n*
1 ▶ a mass (as a rock) formed of fragments from various sources
2 a corporation engaging in many different kinds of business

con•grat•u•late \kən-ˈgra-chə-ˌlāt\ *vb* **con•grat•u•lat•ed; con•grat•u•lat•ing**
to express pleasure on account of success or good fortune ⟨I *congratulated* the winner.⟩

con•grat•u•la•tion \kən-ˌgra-chə-ˈlā-shən\ *n*
1 the act of expressing pleasure at another person's success or good fortune
2 an expression of pleasure at another person's success or good fortune — usually used in pl.

con•gre•gate \ˈkäŋ-gri-ˌgāt\ *vb* **con•gre•gat•ed; con•gre•gat•ing**
to collect or gather into a crowd or group : ASSEMBLE ⟨Workers *congregate* around the coffee maker.⟩

con•gre•ga•tion \ˌkäŋ-gri-ˈgā-shən\ *n*
1 ▼ an assembly of persons gathered for religious worship
2 a gathering or collection of people or things
3 the membership of a church or synagogue

con•gress \ˈkäŋ-grəs\ *n*
1 the chief lawmaking body of a republic that in the United States is made up of the Senate and the House of Representatives
2 a formal meeting of delegates for discussion and action : CONFERENCE
— **con•gres•sio•nal** \kən-ˈgre-shə-nᵊl\ *adj*

conglomerate 1

con•gress•man \ˈkäŋ-grəs-mən\ *n, pl* **con•gress•men** \-mən\
a member of a congress and especially of the United States House of Representatives

con•gress•wom•an \ˈkäŋ-grəs-ˌwu̇-mən\ *n, pl* **con•gress•wom•en** \-grəs-ˌwi-mən\
a woman member of a congress and especially of the United States House of Representatives

con•gru•ent \kən-ˈgrü-ənt, ˈkäŋ-grə-wənt\ *adj*
having the same size and shape ⟨*congruent* triangles⟩

congregation 1: a congregation inside a cathedral

con·i·cal \ˈkä-ni-kəl\ *adj*
shaped like a cone ⟨a *conical* hill⟩

co·ni·fer \ˈkä-nə-fər, ˈkō-\ *n*
▼ any of a group of mostly evergreen trees and shrubs (as pines) that typically produce cones and have leaves resembling needles or scales in shape
co·nif·er·ous \kō-ˈni-fə-rəs, kə-\ *adj*

conifer: a branch and cone of an Arizona cypress

conj *abbr* conjunction

[1]**con·jec·ture** \kən-ˈjek-chər\ *n*
[2]GUESS

[2]**conjecture** *vb* **con·jec·tured**; **con·jec·tur·ing**
[1]GUESS 1, SURMISE

con·ju·gate \ˈkän-jə-ˌgāt\ *vb* **con·ju·gat·ed**; **con·ju·gat·ing**
to give the various forms of a verb in order
con·ju·ga·tion \ˌkän-jə-ˈgā-shən\ *n*

con·junc·tion \kən-ˈjəŋk-shən\ *n*
1 a joining together : UNION
2 a word or expression that joins together sentences, clauses, phrases, or words

con·jure \ˈkän-jər, ˈkən-jər\ *vb* **con·jured**; **con·jur·ing**
1 to practice magical arts
2 IMAGINE 1 ⟨*conjure* up an image⟩
3 to produce by or as if by magic

Conn. *abbr* Connecticut

con·nect \kə-ˈnekt\ *vb* **con·nect·ed**; **con·nect·ing**
1 to join or link together ⟨*connect* two wires⟩ ⟨A hallway *connects* the two rooms.⟩
2 to have something to do with ⟨She's not in any way *connected* to the crime.⟩
3 to bring together in thought ⟨I *connect* the smell of barbequed food with summer.⟩
con·nec·tor \-ˈnek-tər\ *n*

con·nec·tion \kə-ˈnek-shən\ *n*
1 the act of linking together ⟨*connection* of the pipes⟩
2 the fact or condition of having a link : RELATIONSHIP ⟨There's no *connection* between the two incidents.⟩
3 a thing that links ⟨hose *connections*⟩ ⟨a telephone *connection*⟩
4 a person having a relationship with another by kinship, friendship, or common interest ⟨He was able to get tickets through his *connections*.⟩
5 a social, professional, or commercial relationship
6 the act or the means of continuing a journey by transferring (as to another train)

con·nois·seur \ˌkä-nə-ˈsər\ *n*
a person qualified to act as a judge in matters involving taste and appreciation

con·quer \ˈkäŋ-kər\ *vb* **con·quered**; **con·quer·ing**
1 to get or gain by force : win by fighting
2 OVERCOME 1 ⟨She worked hard to *conquer* her fears.⟩

con·quer·or \ˈkäŋ-kər-ər\ *n*
a person who gains something by force

con·quest \ˈkän-ˌkwest\ *n*
1 the act or process of getting or gaining especially by force
2 something that is gotten or gained especially by force
synonyms see VICTORY

con·quis·ta·dor \kän-ˈkē-stə-ˌdȯr\ *n*, *pl* **con·quis·ta·do·res** \-ˌkē-stə-ˈdȯr-ēz\ *or* **con·quis·ta·dors**
▼ a leader in the Spanish conquest especially of Mexico and Peru in the 16th century

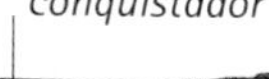

conquistador: a 16th-century beaker showing a Spanish conquistador

con·science \ˈkän-shəns\ *n*
a sense of right and wrong and a feeling that what is right should be done ⟨Her *conscience* told her to tell the truth.⟩

con·sci·en·tious \ˌkän-shē-ˈen-shəs\ *adj*
1 guided by or agreeing with a sense of doing what is right ⟨No *conscientious* person would stand for such unfair actions.⟩
2 using or done with care ⟨*conscientious* teachers⟩ ⟨*conscientious* efforts⟩

con·scious \ˈkän-shəs\ *adj*
1 aware of facts, feelings, or some particular condition or situation
2 known or felt by a person's inner self ⟨*conscious* guilt⟩
3 mentally awake or active ⟨He remained *conscious* following the accident.⟩
4 INTENTIONAL ⟨I made a *conscious* effort to be polite.⟩
con·scious·ly *adv*

con·scious·ness \ˈkän-shəs-nəs\ *n*
1 the condition of being mentally awake and active ⟨Following surgery, she slowly regained *consciousness*.⟩
2 the part of the mind involving thought and awareness ⟨The memory is preserved in my *consciousness*.⟩
3 knowledge of something specified ⟨News reports raised *consciousness* of the problem.⟩

con·se·crate \ˈkän-sə-ˌkrāt\ *vb* **con·se·crat·ed**; **con·se·crat·ing**
to declare to be sacred or holy : set apart for a sacred purpose ⟨*consecrate* a church⟩

con·sec·u·tive \kən-ˈse-kyə-tiv\ *adj*
following one another in order without gaps ⟨It rained for three *consecutive* days.⟩

[1]**con·sent** \kən-ˈsent\ *vb* **con·sent·ed**; **con·sent·ing**
to express willingness or approval : AGREE ⟨The mayor *consented* to speak at our banquet.⟩

[2]**consent** *n*
approval of or agreement with what is done or suggested by another person ⟨You must have a parent's *consent* to go on the trip.⟩

con·se·quence \ˈkän-sə-ˌkwens\ *n*
1 something produced by a cause or following from a condition ⟨Her fear of stairs is a *consequence* of her fall.⟩
2 real importance ⟨His promotion is of no *consequence* to me.⟩

con·se·quent \ˈkän-si-kwənt\ *adj*
following as a result or effect ⟨Weather forecasters predicted heavy rain and *consequent* flooding.⟩

con·se·quent·ly \ˈkän-sə-ˌkwent-lē\ *adv*
as a result ⟨She missed the bus and *consequently* was late.⟩

con·ser·va·tion \ˌkän-sər-ˈvā-shən\ *n*
planned management of something (as natural resources or historic places) to prevent waste, destruction, damage, or neglect

[1]**con·ser·va·tive** \kən-ˈsər-və-tiv\ *adj*
1 favoring a policy of keeping things as they are : opposed to change
2 favoring established styles and standards ⟨He wears *conservative* ties.⟩

3 likely to be lower than what the real amount or number is ⟨a *conservative* estimate⟩
con•ser•va•tive•ly *adv*
²conservative *n*
a person who is opposed to change : a cautious person
con•ser•va•to•ry \kən-ˈsər-və-ˌtȯr-ē\ *n*, *pl* **con•ser•va•to•ries**
1 a place of instruction in some special study (as music)
2 GREENHOUSE
¹con•serve \kən-ˈsərv\ *vb* **con•served**; **con•serv•ing**
1 to prevent the waste of ⟨Close the window to *conserve* heat.⟩
2 to keep in a safe condition : SAVE ⟨We must *conserve* our forests.⟩
²con•serve \ˈkän-ˌsərv\ *n*
▼ a rich fruit preserve

²conserve: blueberry conserve

con•sid•er \kən-ˈsi-dər\ *vb* **con•sid•ered**; **con•sid•er•ing**
1 to think over carefully : PONDER, REFLECT ⟨He should *consider* moving.⟩
2 to treat in a kind or thoughtful way ⟨You never *consider* my feelings.⟩
3 to think of in a certain way : BELIEVE ⟨I *consider* vacation a good time to do some reading.⟩
con•sid•er•able \kən-ˈsi-də-rə-bəl\ *adj*
rather large in extent, amount, or size ⟨a *considerable* distance⟩
con•sid•er•ably \-blē\ *adv*
con•sid•er•ate \kən-ˈsi-də-rət\ *adj*
thoughtful of the rights and feelings of others
con•sid•er•ation \kən-ˌsi-də-ˈrā-shən\ *n*
1 careful thought : DELIBERATION ⟨Give my idea some serious *consideration*.⟩
2 thoughtfulness for other people
3 something that needs to be thought over carefully before deciding or acting
4 a payment made in return for something
con•sid•er•ing \kən-ˈsi-də-riŋ\ *prep*
taking into account ⟨She gets around pretty well *considering* her age.⟩
con•sign \kən-ˈsīn\ *vb* **con•signed**; **con•sign•ing**
1 to send (as goods) to an agent to be sold or cared for
2 to put (something) in a place to store it or get rid of it ⟨She *consigned* her old shoes to the back of a closet.⟩
con•sign•ment \-mənt\ *n*
con•sist \kən-ˈsist\ *vb* **con•sist•ed**; **con•sist•ing**
to be made up or composed ⟨Coal *consists* mostly of carbon.⟩
con•sis•ten•cy \kən-ˈsi-stən-sē\ *n*, *pl* **con•sis•ten•cies**
1 degree of compactness, firmness, or stickiness ⟨Bakers need dough of the right *consistency*.⟩
2 agreement or harmony between parts or elements ⟨The style of furniture lacks *consistency*.⟩
3 a pattern of sticking with one way of thinking or acting ⟨The judge's decisions show *consistency*.⟩
con•sis•tent \kən-ˈsi-stənt\ *adj*
1 always the same ⟨*consistent* behavior⟩
2 being in harmony ⟨A balanced diet is *consistent* with good health.⟩
con•sis•tent•ly *adv*
con•so•la•tion \ˌkän-sə-ˈlā-shən\ *n*
1 something that lessens disappointment, misery, or grief
2 the act of comforting or the state of being comforted
¹con•sole \kən-ˈsōl\ *vb* **con•soled**; **con•sol•ing**
to comfort in a time of grief or distress
²con•sole \ˈkän-ˌsōl\ *n*
1 ► a panel on which are dials and switches for controlling an electronic or mechanical device
2 an electronic system that connects to a display (as a TV) and is used to play video games
3 a cabinet (as for a television) that stands on the floor
4 the part of an organ at which the organist sits and which contains the keyboard and controls
con•sol•i•date \kən-ˈsä-lə-ˌdāt\ *vb* **con•sol•i•dat•ed**; **con•sol•i•dat•ing**
1 to join together into one whole : UNITE ⟨The towns *consolidated* their high schools.⟩
2 STRENGTHEN ⟨The leader *consolidated* his power.⟩
con•so•nant \ˈkän-sə-nənt\ *n*
1 a letter in the English alphabet other than *a*, *e*, *i*, *o*, or *u*
2 a speech sound (as \p\, \n\, or \s\) produced by partly or completely stopping the flow of air breathed out of the mouth
¹con•sort \ˈkän-ˌsȯrt\ *n*
a wife or husband especially of a king or queen
²con•sort \kən-ˈsȯrt\ *vb* **con•sort•ed**; **con•sort•ing**
to spend time with as a companion : ASSOCIATE
con•spic•u•ous \kən-ˈspi-kyə-wəs\ *adj*
1 easily seen ⟨The trail is marked with *conspicuous* flags.⟩
2 attracting attention ⟨I tried not to be too *conspicuous* as I walked in late.⟩
con•spic•u•ous•ly *adv*
con•spir•a•cy \kən-ˈspir-ə-sē\ *n*, *pl* **con•spir•a•cies**
1 a secret agreement to do something harmful or unlawful
2 the act of plotting with others to do something harmful or unlawful
3 a group of conspirators
con•spir•a•tor \kən-ˈspir-ə-tər\ *n*
a person who plots with others to do something harmful or unlawful
con•spire \kən-ˈspīr\ *vb* **con•spired**; **con•spir•ing**
1 to make an agreement with others especially in secret to do an unlawful act
2 to act together ⟨Car problems and the weather *conspired* to spoil our vacation.⟩
con•sta•ble \ˈkän-stə-bəl, ˈkən-\ *n*
a police officer usually of a village or small town
con•stan•cy \ˈkän-stən-sē\ *n*
firmness and loyalty in beliefs or personal relationships

²console 1: a game console

a b c d e f g h i j k l m n o p q r s t u v w x y z

con•stant \ˈkän-stənt\ *adj*
1 remaining steady and unchanged ⟨a *constant* temperature⟩
2 occurring continuously or following one after another ⟨*constant* headaches⟩
3 always faithful and true ⟨*constant* friends⟩
con•stant•ly *adv*

con•stel•la•tion \ˌkän-stə-ˈlā-shən\ *n*
▶ any of 88 named groups of stars forming patterns

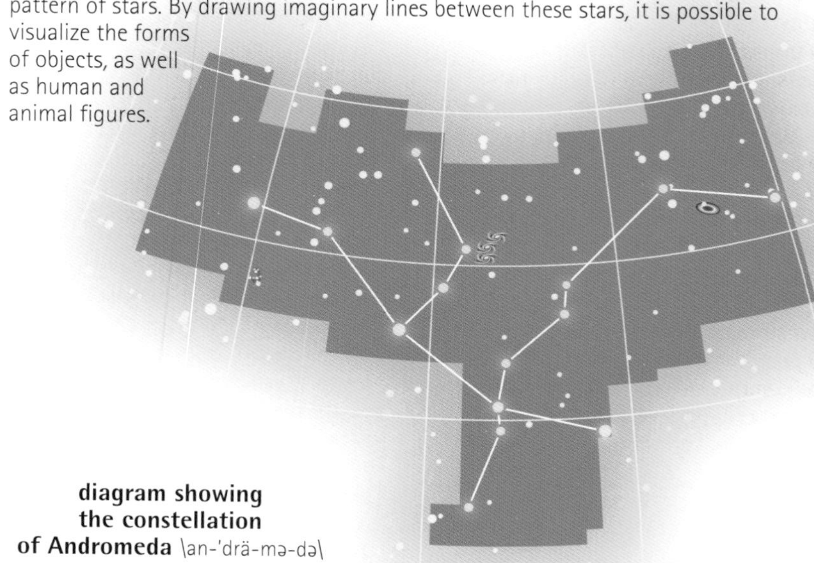

diagram showing the constellation of Andromeda \an-ˈdrä-mə-də\

con•ster•na•tion \ˌkän-stər-ˈnā-shən\ *n*
amazement, alarm, or disappointment that results in a feeling of helplessness or confusion

con•sti•pa•tion \ˌkän-stə-ˈpā-shən\ *n*
difficult or infrequent passage of dry hard material from the bowels

[1]**con•stit•u•ent** \kən-ˈsti-chə-wənt\ *n*
1 one of the parts or materials of which something is made : ELEMENT, INGREDIENT
2 any of the voters who elect a person to represent them

[2]**constituent** *adj*
forming part of a whole

con•sti•tute \ˈkän-stə-ˌtüt, -ˌtyüt\ *vb* **con•sti•tut•ed**; **con•sti•tut•ing**
1 to form the whole of ⟨Twelve months *constitute* a year.⟩
2 to establish or create ⟨A fund has been *constituted* to help needy students.⟩

con•sti•tu•tion \ˌkän-stə-ˈtü-shən, -ˈtyü-\ *n*
1 the physical makeup of an individual
2 the basic structure of something
3 the basic beliefs and laws of a nation, state, or social group by which the powers and duties of the government are established and certain rights are guaranteed to the people or a document that sets forth these beliefs and laws

[1]**con•sti•tu•tion•al** \ˌkän-stə-ˈtü-shə-nᵊl, -ˈtyü-\ *adj*
1 having to do with a person's physical or mental makeup
2 relating to or in agreement with a constitution (as of a nation) ⟨*constitutional* rights⟩

[2]**constitutional** *n*
a walk taken to maintain health

con•strain \kən-ˈstrān\ *vb* **con•strained**; **con•strain•ing**
1 COMPEL 1, FORCE ⟨He was *constrained* to retire because of ill health.⟩
2 to restrict or limit ⟨She felt the rules *constrained* her creativity.⟩

con•straint \kən-ˈstrānt\ *n*
1 control that limits or restricts ⟨The committee refused to act under *constraint*.⟩
2 something that limits or restricts ⟨money *constraints*⟩

con•strict \kən-ˈstrikt\ *vb* **con•strict•ed**; **con•strict•ing**
to make narrower, smaller, or tighter by drawing together : SQUEEZE

con•stric•tion \kən-ˈstrik-shən\ *n*
an act or instance of drawing together

con•stric•tor \kən-ˈstrik-tər\ *n*
▼ a snake (as a boa) that kills its prey by coiling around and crushing it

constrictor: a boa constrictor

con•struct \kən-ˈstrəkt\ *vb* **con•struct•ed**; **con•struct•ing**
to make or form by combining parts ⟨*construct* a bridge⟩
synonyms see BUILD

con•struc•tion \kən-ˈstrək-shən\ *n*
1 the process, art, or manner of building something
2 something built or put together : STRUCTURE ⟨a flimsy *construction*⟩
3 the arrangement of words and the relationship between words in a sentence

construction paper *n*
a thick paper available in many colors for school art work

con•struc•tive \kən-ˈstrək-tiv\ *adj*
helping to develop or improve something ⟨*constructive* criticism⟩
con•struc•tive•ly *adv*

con•strue \kən-ˈstrü\ *vb* **con•strued**; **con•stru•ing**
to understand or explain the sense or intention of ⟨He mistakenly *construed* my actions as unfriendly.⟩

con•sul \ˈkän-səl\ *n*
an official appointed by a government to live in a foreign country in order to look after the commercial interests of citizens of the appointing country

con•sult \kən-ˈsəlt\ *vb* **con•sult•ed**; **con•sult•ing**
1 to seek the opinion or advice of ⟨*consult* a doctor⟩
2 to seek information from ⟨*consult* a dictionary⟩
3 to talk something over ⟨I'll have to *consult* with my lawyer.⟩

A B C D E F G H I J K L M N O P Q R S T U V W X Y Z

con•sul•tant \kən-ˈsəl-tᵊnt\ *n*
a person who gives professional advice or services

con•sul•ta•tion \ˌkän-səl-ˈtā-shən\ *n*
1 a meeting held to talk things over
2 the act of talking things over

con•sume \kən-ˈsüm\ *vb* **con•sumed**; **con•sum•ing**
1 to destroy by or as if by fire
2 to eat or drink up
3 to use up ⟨*consume* electricity⟩ ⟨Our entire day was *consumed* searching for his glasses.⟩
4 to take up the interest or attention of ⟨Curiosity *consumed* the crowd.⟩

con•sum•er \kən-ˈsü-mər\ *n*
a person who buys and uses up goods

con•sump•tion \kən-ˈsəmp-shən\ *n*
1 the act or process of using up something (as food or coal)
2 a wasting away of the body especially from tuberculosis of the lungs

cont. *abbr* continued

[1]**con•tact** \ˈkän-ˌtakt\ *n*
1 a meeting or touching of persons or things
2 communication with other people ⟨Have you been in *contact* with her?⟩ ⟨He has no outside *contact*.⟩
3 a person someone knows who serves as a connection especially in the business or political world ⟨I've got *contacts* in the company.⟩
4 CONTACT LENS

[2]**contact** *vb* **con•tact•ed**; **con•tact•ing**
1 to touch or make touch physically
2 to get in touch or communication with

[3]**contact** *adj*
involving or activated by physical interaction ⟨*contact* sports⟩ ⟨*contact* poisons⟩

contact lens *n*
▼ a thin lens used to correct bad eyesight and worn over the cornea of the eye

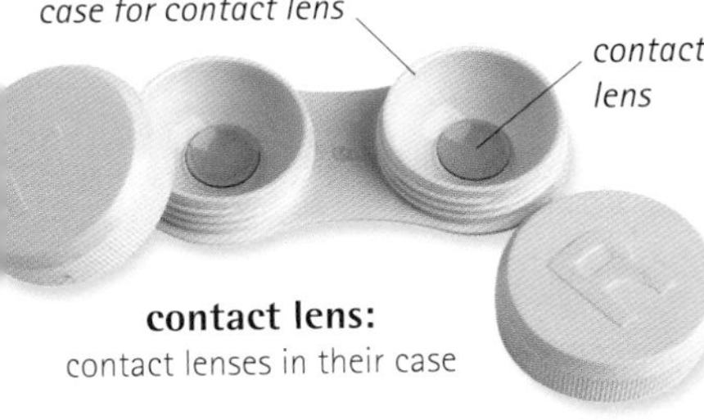

contact lens: contact lenses in their case

con•ta•gion \kən-ˈtā-jən\ *n*
1 the passing of a disease from one individual to another as a result of some contact between them
2 a contagious disease

con•ta•gious \kən-ˈtā-jəs\ *adj*
1 able to be passed from one individual to another through contact ⟨a *contagious* disease⟩
2 having a sickness that can be passed to someone else
3 causing other people to feel or act a similar way ⟨a *contagious* laugh⟩

con•tain \kən-ˈtān\ *vb* **con•tained**; **con•tain•ing**
1 to have within : HOLD ⟨The box *contained* some old books.⟩
2 to consist of or include ⟨The building *contains* classrooms.⟩
3 to keep within limits : RESTRAIN, CHECK ⟨The fire was *contained*.⟩ ⟨I tried to *contain* my anger.⟩

con•tain•er \kən-ˈtā-nər\ *n*
▶ something into which other things can be put (as for storage)

con•tam•i•nate \kən-ˈta-mə-ˌnāt\ *vb* **con•tam•i•nat•ed**; **con•tam•i•nat•ing**
1 to soil, stain, or infect by contact or association ⟨The wound was *contaminated* by bacteria.⟩
2 to make unfit for use by adding something harmful or unpleasant ⟨The water is *contaminated* with chemicals.⟩

con•tem•plate \ˈkän-təm-ˌplāt\ *vb* **con•tem•plat•ed**; **con•tem•plat•ing**
1 to look at with careful and thoughtful attention
2 to think about deeply and carefully
3 to have in mind : plan on ⟨Maybe we should *contemplate* a trip to Europe.⟩

con•tem•pla•tion \ˌkän-təm-ˈplā-shən\ *n*
1 the act of thinking about spiritual things : MEDITATION
2 the act of looking at or thinking about something for some time

[1]**con•tem•po•rary** \kən-ˈtem-pə-ˌrer-ē\ *adj*
1 living or occurring at the same period of time ⟨Mark Twain and Jack London were *contemporary* writers.⟩
2 MODERN 1 ⟨*contemporary* musicians⟩

[2]**contemporary** *n, pl* **con•tem•po•rar•ies**
a person who lives at the same time or is about the same age as another ⟨Mark Twain and Jack London were *contemporaries*.⟩

con•tempt \kən-ˈtempt\ *n*
1 a feeling of disrespect or disapproval of something or someone
2 the state of being despised ⟨He holds them in *contempt*.⟩
3 lack of proper respect for a judge or court ⟨He was fined for *contempt* of court.⟩

con•tempt•ible \kən-ˈtemp-tə-bəl\ *adj*
deserving or causing a person to be despised ⟨a *contemptible* criminal⟩ ⟨a *contemptible* lie⟩

con•temp•tu•ous \kən-ˈtemp-chə-wəs\ *adj*
SCORNFUL ⟨a *contemptuous* smile⟩

con•tend \kən-ˈtend\ *vb* **con•tend•ed**; **con•tend•ing**
1 COMPETE ⟨*contend* for a prize⟩
2 to try hard to deal with ⟨He has many problems to *contend* with.⟩
3 to argue or state earnestly ⟨She *contends* the test was unfair.⟩

container: an airtight container

con•tend•er \kən-ˈten-dər\ *n*
a person who is in competition with others

[1]**con•tent** \ˈkän-ˌtent\ *n*
1 the things that are within — usually used in pl. ⟨the *contents* of a room⟩
2 the subject or topic treated (as in a book) — usually used in pl. ⟨a table of *contents*⟩
3 the important part or meaning (as of a book) ⟨Do you understand the *content* of the paragraph?⟩
4 a certain amount ⟨The soup has a high *content* of salt.⟩

[2]**con•tent** \kən-ˈtent\ *adj*
pleased and satisfied

[3]**content** *vb* **con•tent•ed**; **con•tent•ing**
to make pleased : SATISFY ⟨He *contented* himself with a seat beside the fire.⟩

[4]**content** *n*
freedom from care or discomfort ⟨She fell asleep in complete *content*.⟩

con•tent•ed \kən-ˈten-təd\ *adj*
satisfied or showing satisfaction ⟨a *contented* smile⟩
con•tent•ed•ly *adv*

con•ten•tion \kən-ˈten-chən\ *n*
1 something that is argued ⟨It's my *contention* that watching television is a waste of time.⟩
2 anger and disagreement
3 a state or situation of having a chance to win ⟨She's in *contention* for the gold medal.⟩

con•tent•ment \kən-ˈtent-mənt\ *n*
freedom from worry or restlessness : peaceful satisfaction

[1]**con•test** \ˈkän-ˌtest\ *n*
a struggle for victory : COMPETITION ⟨a pie baking *contest*⟩

[2]**con•test** \kən-ˈtest\ *vb* **con•test•ed**; **con•test•ing**
to make (something) a cause of dispute or fighting ⟨They will *contest* a claim to the fortune.⟩

con•tes•tant \kən-ˈtes-tənt\ *n*
a person who takes part in a competition ⟨He's a *contestant* on a quiz show.⟩

con•text \ˈkän-ˌtekst\ *n*
1 the words that are used with a certain word in writing or speaking ⟨Without the *context*, I don't know what he meant by the word "odd."⟩
2 the situation in which something happens ⟨The book considers her actions in their historical *context*.⟩

con•ti•nent \ˈkän-tə-nənt\ *n*
▼ one of the great divisions of land on the globe—Africa, Antarctica, Asia, Australia, Europe, North America, or South America

con•ti•nen•tal \ˌkän-tə-ˈnen-tᵊl\ *adj*
1 being the mainland part and not including islands ⟨the *continental* United States⟩
2 *often cap* of the colonies later forming the United States ⟨the *Continental* Army⟩

con•tin•gent \kən-ˈtin-jənt\ *adj*
depending on something else that may or may not exist or occur ⟨Our trip is *contingent* on whether we can get tickets.⟩

con•tin•u•al \kən-ˈtin-yə-wəl\ *adj*
1 going on or lasting without stop
2 occurring again and again within short periods of time ⟨Your *continual* interruptions are annoying.⟩
con•tin•u•al•ly *adv*

con•tin•u•ance \kən-ˈtin-yə-wəns\ *n*
the act of going on or lasting for a long time ⟨the long *continuance* of peace⟩

con•tin•u•a•tion \kən-ˌtin-yə-ˈwā-shən\ *n*
1 something that begins where something else ends and follows a similar pattern ⟨the *continuation* of a road⟩
2 the act of beginning again after an interruption ⟨*continuation* of the game⟩

con•tin•ue \kən-ˈtin-yü\ *vb* **con•tin•ued**; **con•tinu•ing**
1 to do or cause to do the same thing without changing or stopping ⟨The weather *continued* hot and sunny.⟩
2 to begin again after stopping ⟨After you left, I *continued* working.⟩

con•ti•nu•i•ty \ˌkän-tə-ˈnü-ə-tē, -ˈnyü-\ *n*, *pl* **con•ti•nu•i•ties**
the quality or state of going on without stop ⟨the *continuity* of care⟩

con•tin•u•ous \kən-ˈtin-yə-wəs\ *adj*
going on without stop ⟨a *continuous* line of traffic⟩
con•tin•u•ous•ly *adv*

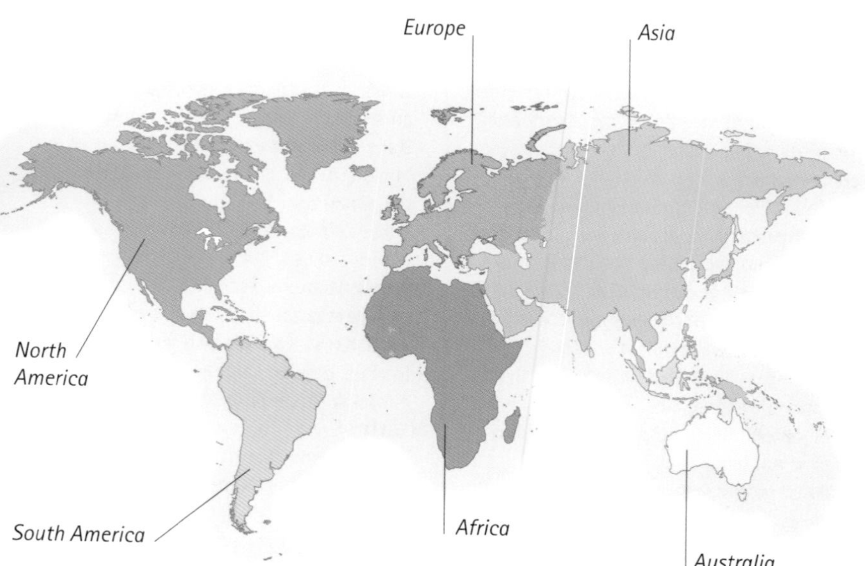

continent: the inhabited continents of the world

con•tort \kən-ˈtȯrt\ *vb* **con•tort•ed**; **con•tort•ing**
to give an unusual appearance or unnatural shape to by twisting ⟨His face *contorted* with anger.⟩

con•tor•tion \kən-ˈtȯr-shən\ *n*
the act or result of twisting out of shape ⟨The heat caused *contortion* of the plastic figure.⟩

con•tour \ˈkän-ˌtu̇r\ *n*
the outline of a figure, body, or surface ⟨the *contour* of the coastline⟩

contra– *prefix*
1 against : contrary : contrasting ⟨*contra*diction⟩
2 pitched below normal bass

con•tra•band \ˈkän-trə-ˌband\ *n*
goods forbidden by law to be owned or to be brought into or out of a country

[1]**con•tract** \ˈkän-ˌtrakt\ *n*
1 a legal agreement
2 a written document that shows the terms and conditions of a legal agreement

[2]**con•tract** \kən-ˈtrakt, *1 is also* ˈkän-ˌtrakt\ *vb* **con•tract•ed**; **con•tract•ing**
1 to agree by contract ⟨The property's owner *contracted* to build a house.⟩
2 to become sick with : CATCH ⟨*contract* pneumonia⟩
3 to draw together and make shorter and broader ⟨*contract* a muscle⟩
4 to make or become smaller : SHRINK ⟨Cold metal *contracts*.⟩
5 to make (as a word) shorter by dropping sounds or letters

con•trac•tion \kən-ˈtrak-shən\ *n*
1 the act, process, or result of making or becoming smaller or shorter and broader ⟨*contraction* of a muscle⟩
2 a short form of a word or word group (as *don't* or *they've*) produced by leaving out a letter or letters

con•tra•dict \ˌkän-trə-ˈdikt\ *vb* **con•tra•dict•ed**; **con•tra•dict•ing**
1 to deny the truth of a statement : say the opposite of what someone else has said
2 to be opposed to ⟨Your actions *contradict* your words.⟩

con•tra•dic•tion \ˌkän-trə-ˈdik-shən\ n
something (as a statement) that is the opposite of or is much different from something else ⟨There were many *contradictions* in her story.⟩

con•tra•dic•to•ry \ˌkän-trə-ˈdik-tə-rē\ *adj*
involving, causing, or being the opposite of or much different something else ⟨*contradictory* reports⟩

con•tral•to \kən-ˈtral-tō\ *n, pl* **con•tral•tos**
1 the lowest female singing voice : ALTO
2 a singer with a low female singing voice

con•trap•tion \kən-ˈtrap-shən\ *n*
GADGET

[1]**con•trary** \ˈkän-ˌtrer-ē\ *n, pl* **con•trar•ies**
something opposite
on the contrary just the opposite : NO ⟨You look tired. *On the contrary,* I'm wide awake.⟩

[2]**con•trary** \ˈkän-ˌtrer-ē, *4 is often* kən-ˈtrer-ē\ *adj*
1 exactly opposite ⟨Their opinion is *contrary* to mine.⟩
2 being against what is usual or expected ⟨Her actions are *contrary* to school policy.⟩
3 not favorable ⟨*contrary* weather⟩
4 unwilling to accept control or advice ⟨a *contrary* child⟩

[1]**con•trast** \kən-ˈtrast\ *vb* **con•trast•ed**; **con•trast•ing**
1 to show noticeable differences ⟨Red *contrasts* with black.⟩
2 to compare two persons or things so as to show the differences between them ⟨*Contrast* the styles of these two authors.⟩
synonyms see COMPARE

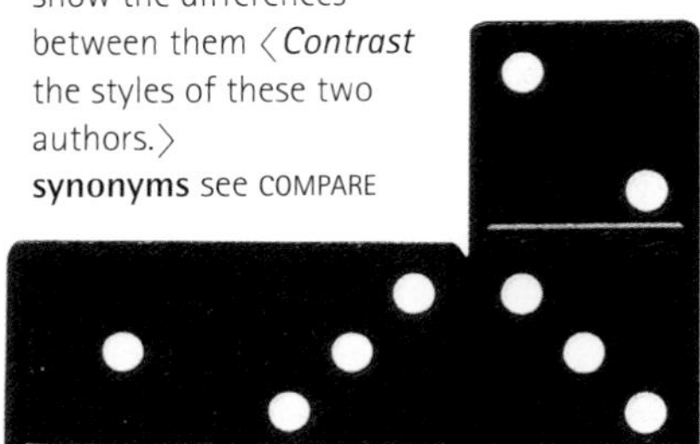

[2]**contrast 2:** the white dots on a domino are in sharp contrast with the black background

[2]**con•trast** \ˈkän-ˌtrast\ *n*
1 something that is different from another ⟨Today's weather is quite a *contrast* to yesterday's.⟩
2 ▲ difference or the amount of difference (as in color or brightness) between parts ⟨a photo with good *contrast*⟩
3 difference or amount of difference between related or similar things ⟨the *contrast* between summer and winter⟩

con•trib•ute \kən-ˈtri-byət, -byüt\ *vb* **con•trib•ut•ed**; **con•trib•ut•ing**
1 to give along with others
2 to have a share in something ⟨You all *contributed* to the success of the project.⟩
3 to supply (as an article) for publication especially in a magazine
con•trib•u•tor \kən-ˈtri-byə-tər\ *n*

con•tri•bu•tion \ˌkän-trə-ˈbyü-shən\ *n*
the act of giving something or something given : DONATION

con•trite \ˈkän-ˌtrīt, kən-ˈtrīt\ *adj*
feeling or showing sorrow for having done something bad or wrong : REPENTANT

con•triv•ance \kən-ˈtrī-vəns\ *n*
something (as a scheme or a mechanical device) produced with skill and cleverness

con•trive \kən-ˈtrīv\ *vb* **con•trived**; **con•triv•ing**
1 [2]PLAN 1, PLOT ⟨We must *contrive* a way to escape.⟩
2 to form or make in some skillful or clever way ⟨He *contrived* a small pipe out of the piece of wood.⟩
3 to manage to bring about or do ⟨She *contrived* to get there on time.⟩

[1]**con•trol** \kən-ˈtrōl\ *vb* **con•trolled**; **con•trol•ling**
1 to have power over ⟨He *controls* the business.⟩
2 to direct the actions or behavior of ⟨Police can *control* a crowd.⟩
3 to keep within bounds : RESTRAIN ⟨Learn to *control* your temper.⟩
4 to direct the function of ⟨How do you *control* this machine?⟩

▶ **Word History** In medieval England, records were kept in a variety of French. In this variety of French, a *contreroule,* or "counter-roll," was a piece of parchment on which payments and receipts were written down. The verb *contrerouler* meant to check the original records against the "counter-roll" to be sure no mistakes were made. These two words were the source of our noun and verb *control.* The sense "checking for mistakes" survives in the way we use *control* to mean something used to check the results of a scientific experiment.

[2]**control** *n*
1 the power or authority to manage ⟨The city wanted local *control* of education.⟩
2 ability to keep within bounds or direct the operation of ⟨The fire is out of *control.*⟩ ⟨He lost *control* of the automobile.⟩
3 SELF-RESTRAINT ⟨She finally lost *control* and started screaming.⟩
4 REGULATION 2 ⟨price *controls*⟩
5 a device used to start, stop, or change the operation of a machine or system ⟨a radio *control*⟩
6 something that is not treated or exposed to testing in an experiment in order to serve as a comparison to others that have undergone treatment or exposure

con•tro•ver•sial \ˌkän-trə-ˈvər-shəl\ *adj*
relating to or causing disagreement or argument ⟨a *controversial* law⟩

con•tro•ver•sy \ˈkän-trə-ˌvər-sē\ *n, pl* **con•tro•ver•sies**
1 an argument that involves many people who strongly disagree about something : DISPUTE
2 [1]QUARREL 1

co•nun•drum \kə-ˈnən-drəm\ *n*
[1]RIDDLE 1

con•va•lesce \ˌkän-və-ˈles\ *vb* **con•va•lesced**; **con•va•lesc•ing**
to regain health and strength gradually after sickness or injury

con•va•les•cence \ˌkän-və-ˈle-sᵊns\ *n*
the period or process of becoming well again after a sickness or injury

[1]**con•va•les•cent** \ˌkän-və-ˈle-sᵊnt\ *adj*
going through or used for the process of becoming well again after a sickness or injury ⟨a *convalescent* patient⟩ ⟨a *convalescent* home⟩

[2]**convalescent** *n*
a person who is in the process of becoming well again after a sickness or injury

convection: heat is transferred in a liquid by convection

con•vec•tion \kən-ˈvek-shən\ *n*
▲ motion in a gas (as air) or a liquid in which the warmer portions rise and the colder portions sink ⟨Heat can be transferred by *convection.*⟩

con•vene \kən-ˈvēn\ *vb* **con•vened**; **con•ven•ing**
to come or bring together as an assembly ⟨The legislature *convened* on Tuesday.⟩ ⟨The teacher *convened* the class.⟩

con•ve•nience \kən-ˈvē-nyəns\ *n*
1 the quality or state of being available, easy to use, useful, or helpful ⟨Shoppers enjoy the *convenience* of an elevator.⟩
2 personal comfort ⟨I thought only of my own *convenience.*⟩
3 OPPORTUNITY 1 ⟨Come at your earliest *convenience.*⟩
4 something that gives comfort or advantage ⟨They live in a house with modern *conveniences.*⟩

A B C D E F G H I J K L M N O P Q R S T U V W X Y Z

con•ve•nient \kən-'vē-nyənt\ *adj*
1 suited to a person's comfort or ease ⟨a *convenient* time⟩ ⟨a *convenient* house⟩
2 suited to a certain situation ⟨a *convenient* excuse⟩
3 easy to get to ⟨There are several *convenient* stores in my neighborhood.⟩
con•ve•nient•ly *adv*

con•vent \'kän-vənt, -ˌvent\ *n*
1 a group of nuns living together
2 a house or a set of buildings occupied by a community of nuns

con•ven•tion \kən-'ven-chən\ *n*
1 a meeting of people for a common purpose ⟨a teachers' *convention*⟩
2 a custom or a way of acting and doing things that is widely accepted and followed ⟨Follow the *conventions* of punctuation in your writing.⟩
3 AGREEMENT 3 ⟨a *convention* among nations⟩

con•ven•tion•al \kən-'ven-shə-nᵊl\ *adj*
1 following the usual or widely accepted way of doing things ⟨a *conventional* wedding ceremony⟩
2 used or accepted through general agreement ⟨*conventional* signs and symbols⟩

con•ver•sa•tion \ˌkän-vər-'sā-shən\ *n*
a talk between two or more people : the act of talking
con•ver•sa•tion•al \-shə-nᵊl\ *adj*

con•verse \kən-'vərs\ *vb* **con•versed**; **con•vers•ing**
to talk to another person or to other people
synonyms see SPEAK

con•ver•sion \kən-'vər-zhən\ *n*
1 the act of changing : the process of being changed ⟨They've finished the *conversion* of the old school into an apartment building.⟩
2 a change of religion

[1]con•vert \kən-'vərt\ *vb* **con•vert•ed**; **con•vert•ing**
1 to change from one form to another
2 to change from one belief, religion, view, or party to another
3 to exchange for an equivalent ⟨I *converted* my dollars into euros.⟩

[2]con•vert \'kän-ˌvərt\ *n*
a person who has been convinced to change to a different belief, religion, view, or party

[1]con•vert•ible \kən-'vərt-ə-bəl\ *adj*
possible to change in form or use

[2]convertible *n*
1 ► an automobile with a top that can be raised, lowered, or removed
2 something that can be changed into a different form

con•vex \kän-'veks, 'kän-ˌveks\ *adj*
rounded like the outside of a ball or circle

con•vey \kən-'vā\ *vb* **con•veyed**; **con•vey•ing**
1 to carry from one place to another : TRANSPORT ⟨Pipes *convey* water.⟩
2 to make known : COMMUNICATE ⟨We use words to *convey* our thoughts.⟩

con•vey•ance \kən-'vā-əns\ *n*
1 the act of carrying from one place to another ⟨the *conveyance* of goods⟩
2 something used to carry goods or passengers

[1]con•vict \kən-'vikt\ *vb* **con•vict•ed**; **con•vict•ing**
to prove or find guilty

[2]con•vict \'kän-ˌvikt\ *n*
a person serving a prison sentence

con•vic•tion \kən-'vik-shən\ *n*
1 a strong belief or opinion ⟨political *convictions*⟩
2 the state of mind of a person who is sure that what he or she believes or says is true ⟨She spoke with *conviction*.⟩
3 the act of proving or finding guilty : the state of being proven guilty ⟨He appealed his *conviction*.⟩

con•vince \kən-'vins\ *vb* **con•vinced**; **con•vinc•ing**
to argue so as to make a person agree or believe ⟨She *convinced* them to go along.⟩

con•vinc•ing \kən-'vin-siŋ\ *adj*
causing someone to believe or agree : PERSUASIVE ⟨*convincing* testimony⟩
con•vinc•ing•ly *adv*

[1]con•voy \'kän-ˌvȯi\ *n, pl* **con•voys**
a group traveling together for protection

[2]con•voy \'kän-ˌvȯi, kən-'vȯi\ *vb* **con•voyed**; **con•voy•ing**
to travel with and protect

con•vulse \kən-'vəls\ *vb* **con•vulsed**; **con•vuls•ing**
to shake violently or with jerky motions ⟨I *convulsed* with laughter.⟩

con•vul•sion \kən-'vəl-shən\ *n*
an attack of powerful involuntary muscular contractions

con•vul•sive \kən-'vəl-siv\ *adj*
causing or marked by violent, frantic, or jerky movement
con•vul•sive•ly *adv*

folding top

[2]convertible 1: a convertible from the 1970s

[1]coo \'kü\ *vb* **cooed**; **coo•ing**
1 to make the soft sound made by doves and pigeons or a similar sound
2 to talk or say fondly or lovingly ⟨"Hush now," she *cooed* to her baby.⟩

[2]coo *n, pl* **coos**
a sound of or similar to that made by doves and pigeons

[1]cook \'ku̇k\ *n*
a person who prepares food for eating

[2]cook *vb* **cooked**; **cook•ing**
1 to prepare food for eating by the use of heat
2 to go through the process of being heated in preparation for being eaten ⟨Dinner is *cooking*.⟩
3 to create through thought and imagination — usually used with *up* ⟨The boys are *cooking* up a scheme to earn money.⟩

cook•book \'ku̇k-ˌbu̇k\ *n*
a book of recipes and directions for the preparation of food

cook•ie \'ku̇-kē\ *n, pl* **cook•ies**
▼ a small sweet cake

cookie: a chocolate-chip cookie

cooking spray *n*
an aerosol that contains vegetable oil and that is sprayed on cooking pans to prevent food from sticking

cook•out \'ku̇k-ˌau̇t\ *n*
an outing at which a meal is cooked and served outdoors

[1]cool \'kül\ *adj* **cool•er**; **cool•est**
1 somewhat cold : not warm ⟨a *cool* day⟩
2 not letting or keeping in heat ⟨*cool* clothes⟩
3 [3]CALM 2 ⟨She's *cool* in a crisis.⟩
4 not friendly or interested : INDIFFERENT ⟨She was *cool* to my suggestion.⟩

5 fashionable, stylish, or attractive in a way that is widely approved of
6 very good : EXCELLENT
cool•ly *adv*
cool•ness *n*

[2]cool *vb* **cooled; cool•ing**
to make or become less warm

[3]cool *n*
1 a time or place that is not warm ⟨the *cool* of the evening⟩
2 a calm state of mind ⟨Keep your *cool.*⟩

cool•er \'kü-lər\ *n*
▼ a container for keeping food or drinks cool

cooler: a cooler with bottles of water

coon \'kün\ *n*
RACCOON

[1]coop \'küp, 'ku̇p\ *n*
▼ a cage or small building for keeping poultry

[2]coop *vb* **cooped; coop•ing**
to restrict to a small space ⟨The children were *cooped* up by bad weather.⟩

[1]coop: a chicken coop

coo•per \'kü-pər, 'ku̇-\ *n*
a worker who makes or repairs wooden casks, tubs, or barrels

co•op•er•ate \kō-'ä-pə-,rāt\ *vb* **co•op•er•at•ed; co•op•er•at•ing**
to act or work together so as to get something done

co•op•er•a•tion \kō-,ä-pə-'rā-shən\ *n*
the act or process of working together to get something done

[1]co•op•er•a•tive \kō-'ä-pə-rə-tiv\ *adj*
1 willing to work with others
2 relating to an organization owned by and operated for the benefit of the people who use its services ⟨a *cooperative* store⟩

[2]cooperative *n*
an organization owned by and operated for the benefit of the people who use its services

[1]co•or•di•nate \kō-'ȯr-də-nət\ *n*
any of a set of numbers used to locate a point on a line or surface or in space

[2]co•or•di•nate \kō-'ȯr-də-,nāt\ *vb* **co•or•di•nat•ed; co•or•di•nat•ing**
to work or cause to work together smoothly ⟨She *coordinated* the field day activities.⟩

co•or•di•na•tion \kō-,ȯr-də-'nā-shən\ *n*
smooth working together (as of parts) ⟨good muscular *coordination*⟩

cop \'käp\ *n*
POLICE OFFICER

cope \'kōp\ *vb* **coped; cop•ing**
to deal with and try to find solutions for problems

copi•er \'kä-pē-ər\ *n*
a machine for making duplicates

co•pi•lot \'kō-,pī-lət\ *n*
a person who assists in flying an airplane

co•pi•ous \'kō-pē-əs\ *adj*
very plentiful : ABUNDANT ⟨She takes *copious* notes in class.⟩
co•pi•ous•ly *adv*

cop•per \'kä-pər\ *n*
1 a tough reddish metallic chemical element that is one of the best conductors of heat and electricity
2 a reddish brown color ⟨*copper* hair⟩

cop•per•head \'kä-pər-,hed\ *n*
▼ a poisonous snake of the eastern and central United States with a reddish brown head

copperhead

cop•pice \'kä-pəs\ *n*
a thicket, grove, or growth of small trees

copse \'käps\ *n*
COPPICE

[1]copy \'kä-pē\ *n, pl* **cop•ies**
1 something that is made to look exactly like something else : DUPLICATE ⟨a *copy* of a letter⟩ ⟨a *copy* of a painting⟩
2 one of the total number of books, magazines, or papers printed at one time ⟨She owns a *copy* of a popular atlas.⟩
3 written material to be published

[2]copy *vb* **cop•ied; copy•ing**
1 to make a duplicate of
2 IMITATE 1 ⟨He's good at *copying* a dancer's steps.⟩

► **Synonyms** COPY, IMITATE, and MIMIC mean to make something so that it resembles something else. COPY means trying to duplicate a thing as much as possible. ⟨*Copy* this drawing exactly.⟩ IMITATE means that a person uses something as an example but does not try to make an exact copy. ⟨They *imitated* the actions of their parents.⟩ MIMIC means carefully copying something (as a person's voice) often for the purpose of making fun of it. ⟨The comedian *mimicked* a popular singer.⟩

copy•cat \'kä-pē-,kat\ *n*
a person who imitates another person

[1]copy•right \'kä-pē-,rīt\ *n*
the legal right to be the only one to reproduce, publish, and sell the contents and form of a literary or artistic work

[2]copyright *vb* **copy•right•ed; copy•right•ing**
to get a copyright on

¹**coral 2:** rose coral

¹**cor•al** \'kȯr-əl\ *n*
1 a tiny soft-bodied animal that typically lives within a stony skeleton grouped in large colonies and that is related to the jellyfish
2 ▲ a piece of stony material consisting of the skeletons of corals
3 a colony of corals : CORAL REEF
4 a dark pink

²**coral** *adj*
1 made of coral ⟨a *coral* deposit⟩
2 of a dark pink color

coral reef *n*
a reef composed of a large colony of corals including the stony skeletons of both living and dead corals

coral snake *n*
a small poisonous tropical American snake ringed with red, black, and yellow or white

cord \'kȯrd\ *n*
1 a covered electrical wire used to connect an electrical appliance with an outlet
2 ▼ material like a small thin rope that is used mostly for tying things
3 an amount of firewood equal to a pile measuring 128 cubic feet (about 3.6 cubic meters)
4 a rib or ridge woven into cloth
5 a ribbed fabric

cord 2

cor•dial \'kȯr-jəl\ *adj*
warm and friendly ⟨a *cordial* host⟩
cor•dial•ly *adv*

cor•di•al•i•ty \'kȯr-jē-'a-lə-tē\ *n*
sincere warmth and kindness

cor•du•roy \'kȯr-də-,rȯi\ *n*
1 a heavy ribbed usually cotton cloth
2 **corduroys** *pl* trousers made of a heavy ribbed cloth

¹**core** \'kȯr\ *n*
1 the usually inedible central part of some fruits (as a pineapple or pear)
2 the central part of a heavenly body (as the earth or sun)
3 the central or most important part of something ⟨the *core* of a problem⟩

²**core** *vb* **cored**; **cor•ing**
to remove the core from ⟨*core* an apple⟩

¹**cork** \'kȯrk\ *n*
1 the light but tough material that is the outer layer of bark of a tree (**cork oak**) and is used especially for stoppers and insulation
2 a stopper for a bottle or jug

²**cork** *vb* **corked**; **cork•ing**
to stop with a stopper ⟨*cork* a bottle⟩

¹**cork•screw** \'kȯrk-,skrü\ *n*
► a pointed spiral piece of metal with a handle that is screwed into corks to pull them from bottles

¹**corkscrew**

²**corkscrew** *adj*
having a spiral shape

cor•mo•rant \'kȯr-mə-rənt\ *n*
a black seabird with webbed feet, a long neck, and a slender hooked beak

¹**corn** \'kȯrn\ *n*
1 a tall American cereal grass plant widely grown for its large ears of starchy grain which come in many varieties
2 the seeds of a corn plant that are used especially as food for humans and animals and are typically yellow or whitish
3 an ear of corn with or without its leafy outer covering ⟨shucking *corn*⟩

²**corn** *n*
a hardening and thickening of the skin (as on a person's toe)

corn bread *n*
bread made with cornmeal

corn•cob \'kȯrn-,käb\ *n*
the woody core on which grains of corn grow

cor•nea \'kȯr-nē-ə\ *n*
the transparent outer layer of the front of the eye covering the pupil and iris

corned beef \'kȯrnd-\ *n*
beef that has been preserved in salt water

¹**cor•ner** \'kȯr-nər\ *n*
1 the point or place where edges or sides meet

¹**corner 2:** a street corner

2 ▲ the place where two streets or passageways meet
3 a position from which escape or retreat is difficult or impossible
4 a place away from ordinary life or business ⟨a quiet *corner* of a big city⟩
cor•nered \-nərd\ *adj*

²**corner** *adj*
1 located at a corner ⟨a *corner* store⟩
2 used or usable in or on a corner ⟨a *corner* bookcase⟩

³**corner** *vb* **cor•nered**; **cor•ner•ing**
to force into a place from which escape is difficult or into a difficult position

cor•net \kȯr-'net\ *n*
a brass musical instrument similar to but shorter than a trumpet

corn•flow•er \'kȯrn-,flau̇-ər\ *n*
a European plant related to the daisies that is often grown for its bright heads of blue, pink, or white flowers

cor•nice \'kȯr-nəs\ *n*
1 an ornamental piece that forms the top edge of the front of a building or pillar
2 an ornamental molding placed where the walls meet the ceiling of a room

corn•meal \'kȯrn-,mēl\ *n*
coarse flour made from ground corn

corn•stalk \'kȯrn-,stȯk\ *n*
a stalk of corn

corn•starch \'kȯrn-,stärch\ *n*
a fine powder made from corn and used to thicken foods when cooking

corn syrup *n*
a syrup made from cornstarch

cor•nu•co•pia \ˌkȯr-nə-ˈkō-pē-ə, -nyə-\ *n*
a container in the shape of a horn overflowing with fruits and flowers used as a symbol of plenty

corny \ˈkȯr-nē\ *adj* **corn•i•er**; **corn•i•est**
so simple, sentimental, or old-fashioned as to be annoying 〈a *corny* joke〉

co•rol•la \kə-ˈrä-lə\ *n*
the part of a flower that is formed by the petals

cor•o•nary \ˈkȯr-ə-ˌner-ē\ *adj*
of or relating to the heart or its blood vessels 〈a *coronary* artery〉

cor•o•na•tion \ˌkȯr-ə-ˈnā-shən\ *n*
the act or ceremony of crowning a king or queen

cor•o•ner \ˈkȯr-ə-nər\ *n*
a public official responsible for determining the causes of deaths which are not due to natural causes

cor•o•net \ˌkȯr-ə-ˈnet\ *n*
1 a small crown worn by a person of noble but less than royal rank
2 an ornamental wreath or band worn around the head

[1]**cor•po•ral** \ˈkȯr-pə-rəl, ˈkȯr-prəl\ *adj*
of or relating to the body 〈*corporal* punishment〉

[2]**corporal** *n*
a noncommissioned officer ranking above a private in the army or above a lance corporal in the marine corps

cor•po•ra•tion \ˌkȯr-pə-ˈrā-shən\ *n*
a business or organization authorized by law to carry on an activity with the rights and duties of a single person

cor•po•re•al \kȯr-ˈpȯr-ē-əl\ *adj*
having, consisting of, or relating to a physical body

corps \ˈkȯr\ *n, pl* **corps** \ˈkȯrz\
1 an organized branch of a country's military forces 〈Marine *Corps*〉
2 a group of persons acting under one authority 〈diplomatic *corps*〉

corpse \ˈkȯrps\ *n*
a dead body

cor•pu•lent \ˈkȯr-pyə-lənt\ *adj*
very fat

cor•pus•cle \ˈkȯr-ˌpə-səl\ *n*
a very small cell (as a red blood cell) that floats freely in the blood

[1]**cor•ral** \kə-ˈral\ *n*
an enclosure for keeping or capturing animals

[2]**corral** *vb* **cor•ralled**; **cor•ral•ling**
1 to confine in or as if in an enclosure 〈*corral* cattle〉
2 to gather or get control over 〈*corralling* votes〉

[1]**cor•rect** \kə-ˈrekt\ *vb* **cor•rect•ed**; **cor•rect•ing**
1 to make or set right 〈Please *correct* any misspelled words.〉
2 to change or adjust so as to bring to some standard or to a required condition 〈My watch was slow, so I *corrected* it.〉 〈Glasses will *correct* your vision.〉
3 to punish in order to improve 〈*correct* a child for bad manners〉
4 to show how a thing can be improved or made right 〈She *corrected* the students' papers.〉

[2]**correct** *adj*
1 free from mistakes : ACCURATE 〈the *correct* answer〉
2 meeting or agreeing with some standard : APPROPRIATE 〈*correct* behavior〉 〈*correct* dress for school〉

cor•rect•ly *adv*

cor•rect•ness *n*

▶ **Synonyms** CORRECT, EXACT, and ACCURATE mean agreeing with a fact, truth, or standard. CORRECT is used for something that contains no errors. 〈Can you give me *correct* directions?〉 EXACT is used for something that agrees very closely with fact or truth. 〈I need the *exact* measurements of the room.〉 ACCURATE is used when great care has been taken to make sure that something agrees with the facts. 〈He gave an *accurate* description of the scene.〉

cor•rec•tion \kə-ˈrek-shən\ *n*
1 the act of making something agree with what is right or standard 〈*correction* of vision〉
2 a change that makes something right 〈I read the teacher's *corrections* on my paper.〉
3 PUNISHMENT 1

cor•rec•tion•al \-shə-nᵊl\ *adj*

cor•re•spond \ˌkȯr-ə-ˈspänd\ *vb* **cor•re•spond•ed**; **cor•re•spond•ing**
1 to be alike : AGREE 〈Her finished sculpture did not *correspond* to how she had imagined it.〉
2 to compare closely 〈The words "give" and "donate" *correspond* in meaning.〉
3 to communicate with a person by exchanging letters

cor•re•spon•dence \ˌkȯr-ə-ˈspän-dəns\ *n*
1 communication by means of letters or e-mail : the letters or e-mail exchanged
2 agreement between certain things 〈Sometimes there is little *correspondence* between the spelling and the pronunciation of a word.〉

cor•re•spon•dent \ˌkȯr-ə-ˈspän-dənt\ *n*
1 a person with whom another person communicates by letter or e-mail
2 a person who sends news stories or comment to a newspaper, magazine, or broadcasting company especially from a distant place

cor•ri•dor \ˈkȯr-ə-dər\ *n*
▼ a passage into which rooms open

cor•rob•o•rate \kə-ˈrä-bə-ˌrāt\ *vb* **cor•rob•o•rat•ed**; **cor•rob•o•rat•ing**
to support with evidence or authority 〈Several witnesses *corroborated* her story.〉

corridor: a corridor in a hotel

cor•rode \kə-ˈrōd\ *vb* **cor•rod•ed**; **cor•rod•ing**
1 to wear away little by little (as by rust or acid)
2 to gradually destroy or weaken ⟨*corroding* traditions⟩

cor•ro•sion \kə-ˈrō-zhən\ *n*
the process or effect of destroying, weakening, or wearing away little by little

cor•ro•sive \kə-ˈrō-siv, -ziv\ *adj*
tending or able to destroy, weaken, or wear away little by little ⟨*corrosive* substances⟩

cor•ru•gat•ed \ˈkȯr-ə-ˌgā-təd\ *adj*
having a wavy surface ⟨*corrugated* tin⟩ ⟨a *corrugated* roof⟩

¹cor•rupt \kə-ˈrəpt\ *vb* **cor•rupt•ed**; **cor•rupt•ing**
1 to change (as in morals, manners, or actions) from good to bad ⟨He believes television can *corrupt* children.⟩
2 to influence a public official in an improper way (as by a bribe)

²corrupt *adj*
1 behaving in a bad or improper way : doing wrong ⟨The *corrupt* judges will accept bribes.⟩
2 morally bad : EVIL ⟨*corrupt* values⟩

cor•rup•tion \kə-ˈrəp-shən\ *n*
1 dishonest or illegal behavior ⟨*corruption* in politics⟩
2 the process of causing someone else to do something wrong
3 the act of changing or damaging something ⟨the *corruption* of an ancient text⟩ ⟨the *corruption* of a computer file⟩

cor•sage \kȯr-ˈsäzh\ *n*
▼ a small bouquet of flowers usually worn on the shoulder

corsage

corse•let *or* **cors•let** \ˈkȯr-slət\ *n*
▶ the body armor worn by a knight especially on the upper part of the body

cor•set \ˈkȯr-sət\ *n*
a tight undergarment worn to support or give shape to waist and hips

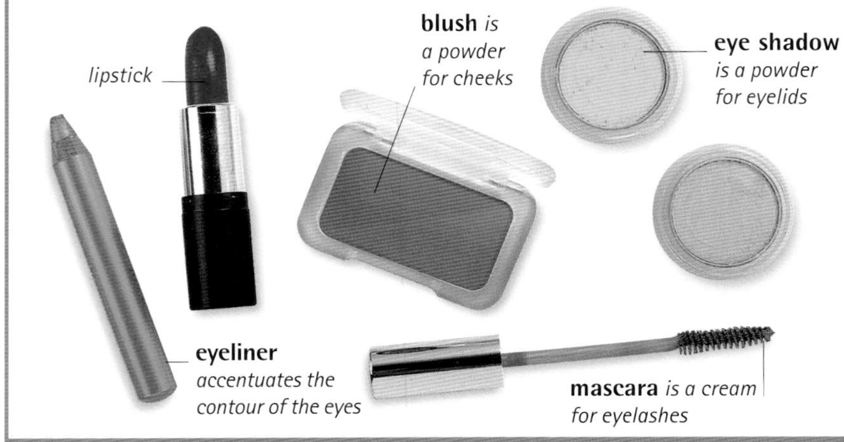

cos•met•ic \käz-ˈmet-ik\ *n*
▲ a material (as a cream, lotion, or powder) used to improve a person's appearance

cos•mic \ˈkäz-mik\ *adj*
of or relating to the whole universe

cosmic ray *n*
a stream of very penetrating particles that enter the earth's atmosphere from outer space at high speed

cos•mo•naut \ˈkäz-mə-ˌnȯt\ *n*
an astronaut in the space program of Russia or the former Soviet Union

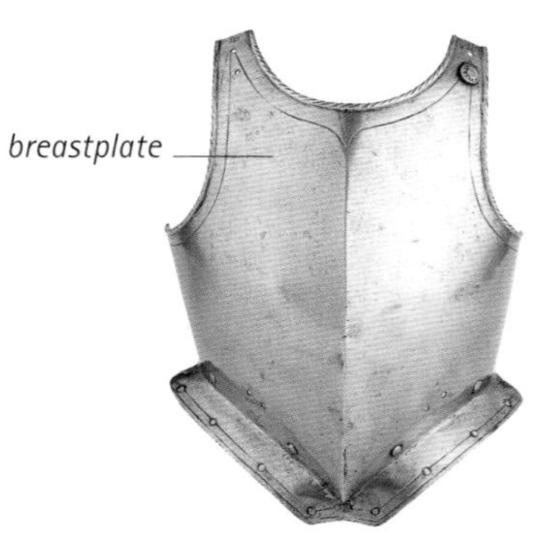

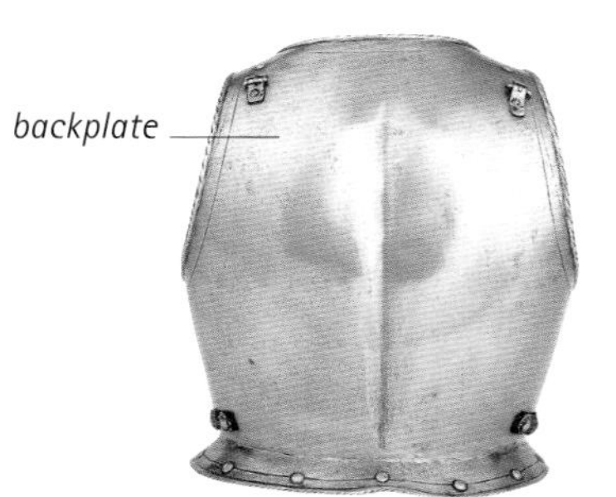

corselet: early 17th-century English corselet

cos•mos \ˈkäz-məs, *1 is also* -ˌmōs, -ˌmäs\ *n*
1 the universe especially as thought of as an orderly system
2 ▼ a tall garden plant related to the daisies that has showy white, pink, or rose-colored flower heads

cosmos 2

¹cost \ˈkȯst\ *vb* **cost**; **cost•ing**
1 to have a price of ⟨He bought a ticket *costing* one dollar.⟩
2 to cause the payment, spending, or loss of ⟨Being lazy *cost* me my job.⟩

²cost *n*
1 the amount paid or charged for something : PRICE
2 loss or penalty involved in gaining something ⟨Losing my friends was the *cost* of moving.⟩
synonyms see PRICE

cost•ly \ˈkȯst-lē\ *adj* **cost•li•er**; **cost•li•est**
1 having a high price or value : EXPENSIVE
2 causing loss or suffering ⟨a *costly* mistake⟩

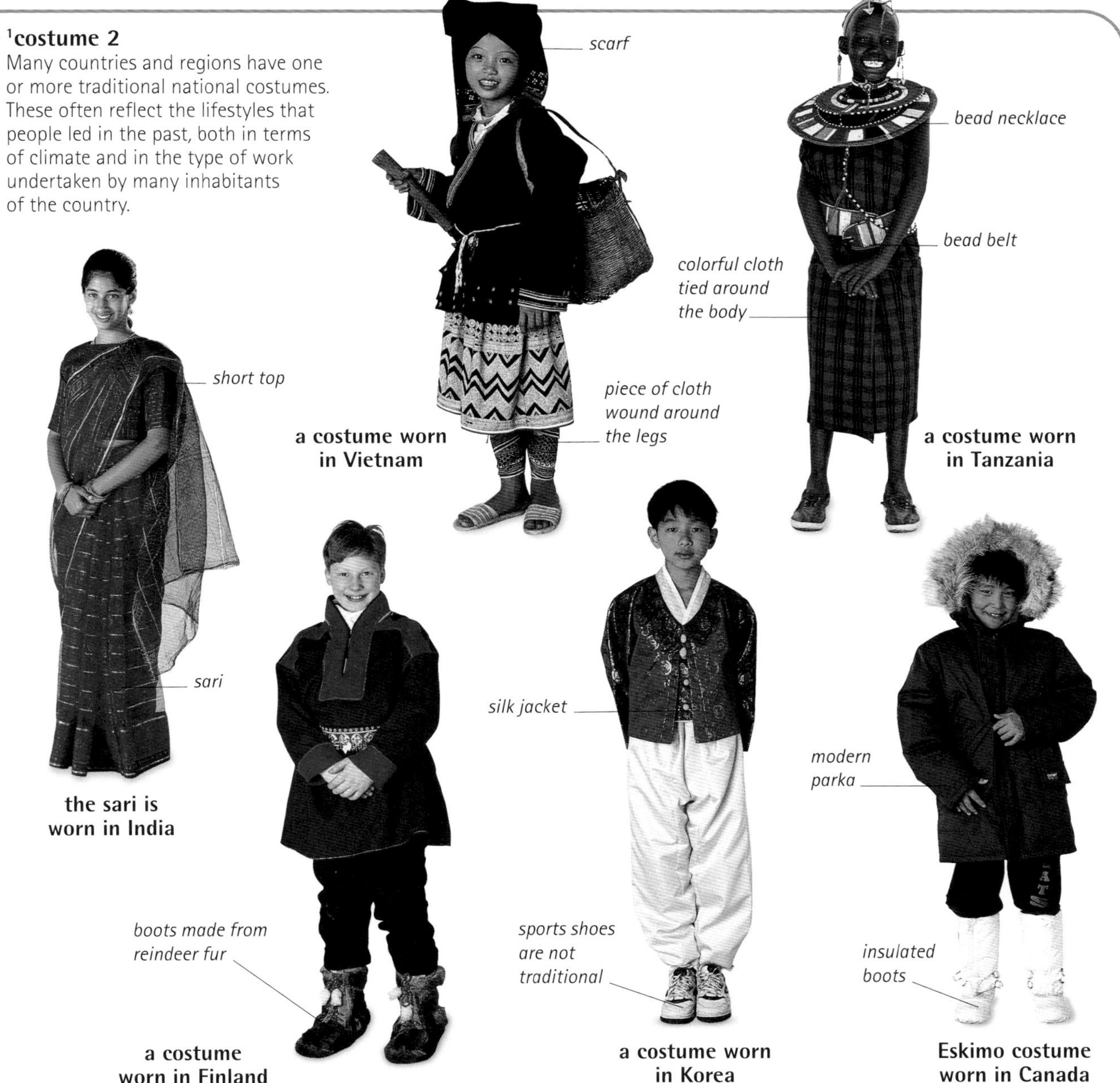

a costume worn in Vietnam

a costume worn in Tanzania

the sari is worn in India

a costume worn in Finland

a costume worn in Korea

Eskimo costume worn in Canada

[1]**cos•tume** \'käs-,tüm, -,tyüm\ *n*
1 special or fancy dress (as for wear on the stage or at a masquerade)
2 ▲ style of clothing, ornaments, and hair used during a certain period, in a certain region, or by a certain class or group ⟨ancient Roman *costume*⟩ ⟨peasant *costume*⟩

[2]**costume** *vb* **cos•tumed**; **cos•tum•ing**
to provide with a special or fancy outfit

cot \'kät\ *n*
a narrow bed often made to fold up

cot•tage \'kät-ij\ *n*
a small house usually in the country or for vacation use

cottage cheese *n*
a very soft white cheese made from soured skim milk

cot•ton \'kä-tᵊn\ *n*
1 a soft fluffy usually white material made up of twisted hairs that surrounds the seeds of a tall plant of warm regions and is spun into thread or yarn
2 thread, yarn, or cloth made from cotton
cotton *adj*

cotton gin *n*
a machine for removing seeds from cotton

cot•ton•mouth \'kä-tᵊn-,maůth\ *n*
WATER MOCCASIN

cot•ton•seed \'kä-tᵊn-,sēd\ *n*
the seed of the cotton plant from which comes an oil used especially in cooking and a protein-rich meal used in livestock feed

cot•ton•tail \'kä-tᵊn-,tāl\ *n*
a small rabbit with a white tail

cot•ton•wood \'kä-tᵊn-,wůd\ *n*
a poplar tree that has seeds with bunches of hairs resembling cotton

a b c d e f g h i j k l m n o p q r s t u v w x y z

couch

cot•y•le•don \ˌkä-tə-ˈlē-dᵊn\ *n*
the first leaf or one of the first leaves of a plant which is usually folded within a seed until germination and which serves as a storehouse of food for the plant

couch \ˈkau̇ch\ *n*
▲ a long piece of furniture that a person can sit or lie on

cougar

cou•gar \ˈkü-gər\ *n*
▲ a large yellowish brown wild animal of North and South America related to the domestic cat

[1]cough \ˈkȯf\ *vb* **coughed**; **cough•ing**
1 to force air from the lungs suddenly with a sharp short noise or series of noises
2 to get rid of by coughing ⟨*cough* up mucus⟩

[2]cough *n*
1 a condition in which there is severe or frequent coughing ⟨She has a bad *cough.*⟩
2 an act or sound of coughing ⟨a dry *cough*⟩

could \kəd, ˈku̇d\ *past of* CAN
1 used as a helping verb in the past ⟨Her daughter *could* read at the age of five.⟩
2 used as a polite form instead of *can* ⟨*Could* you help me?⟩
3 used to say something is possible ⟨You *could* win.⟩ ⟨You *could* have been hurt.⟩

couldn't \ˈku̇-dᵊnt\
could not ⟨I *couldn't* unlock the door.⟩

coun•cil \ˈkau̇n-səl\ *n*
a group of people appointed or elected to make laws or give advice ⟨the city *council*⟩

coun•cil•lor *or* **coun•cil•or** \ˈkau̇n-sə-lər\ *n*
a member of a group of people appointed or elected to make laws or give advice : a member of a council

[1]coun•sel \ˈkau̇n-səl\ *n*
1 advice given ⟨My grandfather's *counsel* was to be patient.⟩
2 *pl* **counsel** a lawyer representing someone in court

[2]counsel *vb* **coun•seled** *or* **coun•selled**; **coun•sel•ing** *or* **coun•sel•ling**
1 to give advice to : ADVISE ⟨She *counseled* him to study harder.⟩
2 to suggest or recommend ⟨The doctor *counseled* rest.⟩

coun•sel•or *or* **coun•sel•lor** \ˈkau̇n-sə-lər\ *n*
1 a person who gives advice
2 a supervisor of campers or activities at a summer camp
3 LAWYER

[1]count \ˈkau̇nt\ *vb* **count•ed**; **count•ing**
1 to add one by one in order to find the total number
2 to name the numbers one by one, by groups, or in order up to a particular point ⟨*Count* to 100 by fives.⟩
3 to include in thinking about ⟨Don't *count* Sunday as a work day.⟩
4 to have value, force, or importance ⟨Every vote *counts.*⟩
5 to consider or judge to be ⟨I *count* myself lucky.⟩

count on
1 to rely or depend on (someone) to do something ⟨I'm *counting on* you to help.⟩
2 to expect (something) to happen ⟨Don't *count on* exams being cancelled.⟩

[2]count *n*
1 the act or process of naming numbers or adding one by one
2 a total arrived at by adding ⟨a vote *count*⟩
3 any one crime that a person is charged with ⟨She is guilty on all *counts.*⟩

[3]count *n*
a European nobleman whose rank is like that of a British earl

count•down \ˈkau̇nt-ˌdau̇n\ *n*
the process of subtracting the time remaining before an event (as the launching of a rocket)

[1]coun•te•nance \ˈkau̇n-tᵊn-əns\ *n*
the human face or its expression ⟨a kind *countenance*⟩

[2]countenance *vb* **coun•te•nanced**; **coun•te•nanc•ing**
to give approval or tolerance to ⟨I will not *countenance* such rude behavior.⟩

[1]counter 1: a counter at a restaurant

[1]count•er \ˈkau̇n-tər\ *n*
1 ▲ a level surface usually higher than a table that is used especially for selling, serving food, displaying things, or working on
2 a piece used in games or to find a total in adding

[2]count•er *n*
1 a person whose job is to determine a total
2 a device for showing a number or amount

[3]coun•ter \ˈkau̇n-tər\ *vb* **coun•tered**; **coun•ter•ing**
1 to say in response to something said ⟨"That's not true!" he *countered.*⟩
2 to act in opposition to : OPPOSE ⟨She *countered* with a move that ended the game.⟩

[4]coun•ter *adv*
in another or opposite direction ⟨He will always go *counter* to advice.⟩

[5]coun•ter *n*
an answering or opposing force or blow

coun•ter- *prefix*
1 opposite ⟨*counter*clockwise⟩
2 opposing
3 like : matching ⟨*counter*part⟩
4 duplicate : substitute

coun•ter•act \ˌkau̇n-tər-ˈakt\ *vb* **coun•ter•act•ed**; **coun•ter•act•ing**
to make (something) have less of an effect or no effect at all ⟨The antidote *counteracts* the poison.⟩

coun•ter•clock•wise \ˌkau̇n-tər-ˈkläk-ˌwīz\ *adv or adj*
in a direction opposite to that in which the hands of a clock move

[1]**coun•ter•feit** \ˈkau̇n-tər-ˌfit\ *adj*
1 made in exact imitation of something genuine and meant to be taken as genuine 〈*counterfeit* money〉
2 not sincere 〈*counterfeit* sympathy〉

[2]**counterfeit** *vb* **coun•ter•feit•ed**; **coun•ter•feit•ing**
1 to imitate or copy especially in order to deceive 〈Modern money is difficult to *counterfeit*.〉
2 PRETEND 2 〈She tried to *counterfeit* enthusiasm.〉
coun•ter•feit•er *n*

[3]**counterfeit** *n*
something made to imitate another thing with the desire to deceive 〈The 100 dollar bill turned out to be a *counterfeit*.〉

coun•ter•part \ˈkau̇n-tər-ˌpärt\ *n*
a person or thing that is very like or equivalent to another person or thing

coun•ter•sign \ˈkau̇n-tər-ˌsīn\ *n*
a secret signal that must be given by a person wishing to pass a guard : PASSWORD

count•ess \ˈkau̇n-təs\ *n*
1 the wife or widow of a count or an earl
2 a woman who holds the rank of a count or an earl in her own right

counting number *n*
NATURAL NUMBER

count•less \ˈkau̇nt-ləs\ *adj*
too many to be counted 〈*countless* grains of sand〉

coun•try \ˈkən-trē\ *n, pl* **coun•tries**
1 ▼ a land lived in by a people with a common government 〈the *countries* of Europe〉
2 REGION 1, DISTRICT 〈good farming *country*〉
3 open rural land away from big towns and cities 〈Take a ride in the *country*.〉
4 the people of a nation 〈a whole *country* in revolt〉

country 1:
map showing the country of Italy

country and western *n*
COUNTRY MUSIC

coun•try•man \ˈkən-trē-mən\ *n, pl* **coun•try•men** \-mən\
1 a person born in the same country as another : a fellow citizen
2 a person living or raised in a place away from big towns and cities

country music *n*
a style of music that developed in the southern and western United States, that is similar to folk music, and that often has lyrics about people who live in the country

coun•try•side \ˈkən-trē-ˌsīd\ *n*
a rural area or its people

coun•ty \ˈkau̇n-tē\ *n, pl* **coun•ties**
a division of a state or country for local government

cou•pé *or* **coupe** \kü-ˈpā, *2 is often* ˈküp\ *n*
1 a carriage with four wheels and an enclosed body seating two persons and with an outside seat for the driver in front
2 an enclosed two-door automobile for two persons

[1]**cou•ple** \ˈkəp-əl\ *n*
1 two people who are married or in a romantic relationship
2 two people or things paired together 〈Line up in *couples*.〉
3 two things that are of the same kind or that are thought of together 〈It cost a *couple* of dollars.〉 〈A *couple* of strange things happened today.〉

[2]**couple** *vb* **cou•pled**; **cou•pling**
1 to join or link together : CONNECT 〈Workers *coupled* freight cars.〉
2 to join in pairs

cou•plet \ˈkə-plət\ *n*
two rhyming lines of verse one after another 〈"The butcher, the baker, / The candlestick maker" is an example of a *couplet*.〉

cou•pling \ˈkə-pliŋ\ *n*
1 the act of bringing or coming together 〈the *coupling* of the freight cars〉
2 ▶ something that connects two parts or things 〈a pipe *coupling*〉

cou•pon \ˈkü-ˌpän, ˈkyü-\ *n*
1 a ticket or form that allows the holder to receive some service, payment, or discount
2 a part of an advertisement meant to be cut out for use as an order blank

cour•age \ˈkər-ij\ *n*
the ability to meet danger and difficulties with firmness

cou•ra•geous \kə-ˈrā-jəs\ *adj*
having or showing the ability to meet danger and difficulties with firmness
synonyms see BRAVE
cou•ra•geous•ly *adv*

cou•ri•er \ˈku̇r-ē-ər, ˈkər-\ *n*
MESSENGER

[1]**course** \ˈkȯrs\ *n*
1 motion from one point to another : progress in space or time 〈The earth makes its *course* around the sun in 365 days.〉 〈During the *course* of a year he meets dozens of people.〉
2 the path over which something moves 〈The ship was blown off *course*.〉
3 a natural channel for water 〈A trail follows the river's *course*.〉
4 a way of doing something 〈Choose a *course* of action.〉
5 the ordinary way something happens over time 〈the *course* of business〉
6 a series of acts or proceedings arranged in regular order 〈a *course* of therapies〉
7 a series of classes in a subject 〈a geography *course*〉
8 a part of a meal served separately 〈We ate a three *course* dinner.〉
of course as might be expected 〈You know, *of course*, that I like you.〉

[2]**course** *vb* **coursed**; **cours•ing**
1 to run through or over
2 to move rapidly : RACE

[1]**court** \ˈkȯrt\ *n*
1 a space arranged for playing a certain game 〈tennis *court*〉 〈basketball *court*〉
2 an official meeting led by a judge for settling legal questions or the place where it is held
3 a judge or the judges presiding in a courtroom 〈The *court* decides issues of law.〉
4 the home of a ruler (as a king)
5 a ruler's assembly of advisers and officers as a governing power

coupling 2: a pipe coupling

6 the family and people who follow a ruler
7 an open space completely or partly surrounded by buildings
8 a short street
9 respect meant to win favor 〈Pay *court* to the king.〉

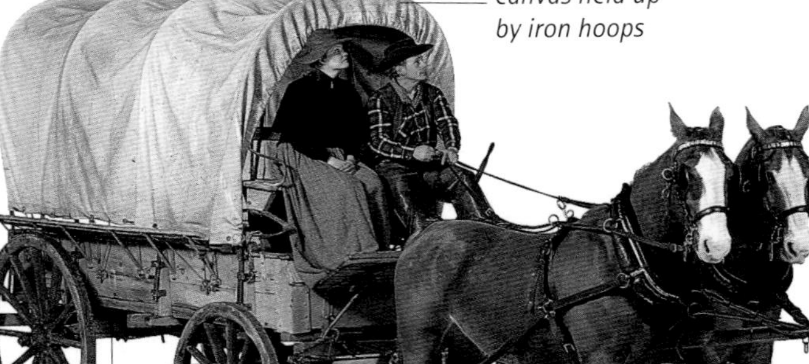

covered wagon

[2]court *vb* **court•ed**; **court•ing**
1 to seek the love or companionship of
2 to try to gain or get the support of : SEEK ⟨Both candidates *courted* new voters.⟩
3 to seem to be asking for : TEMPT ⟨You're *courting* trouble by not fixing your car.⟩

cour•te•ous \ˈkər-tē-əs\ *adj*
showing respect and consideration for others : POLITE
synonyms see CIVIL
cour•te•ous•ly *adv*

cour•te•sy \ˈkər-tə-sē\ *n, pl* **cour•te•sies**
1 the quality or state of being respectful and considerate of others
2 a polite or generous act or expression ⟨Hot meals were served through the *courtesy* of volunteers.⟩
3 something that is a favor and not a right ⟨Transportation is provided as a *courtesy* of the hotel.⟩

court•house \ˈkȯrt-ˌhau̇s\ *n*
1 a building in which courts of law are held
2 a building in which county offices are housed

court•i•er \ˈkȯr-tē-ər\ *n*
a member of a royal court

court•ly \ˈkȯrt-lē\ *adj* **court•li•er**; **court•li•est**
polite and graceful in a formal way ⟨*courtly* manners⟩

court•room \ˈkȯrt-ˌrüm, -ˌru̇m\ *n*
a room in which formal legal meetings and trials take place

court•ship \ˈkȯrt-ˌship\ *n*
the act of seeking the love or companionship of someone

court•yard \ˈkȯrt-ˌyärd\ *n*
[1]COURT 7

cous•in \ˈkə-zᵊn\ *n*
a child of a person's uncle or aunt

cove \ˈkōv\ *n*
a small sheltered inlet or bay

cov•e•nant \ˈkə-və-nənt\ *n*
a formal or serious agreement or promise ⟨the *covenant* of marriage⟩

[1]cov•er \ˈkə-vər\ *vb* **cov•ered**; **cov•er•ing**
1 to place or spread something over ⟨*Cover* the pot.⟩
2 to be spread with or extend over much or all of the surface of ⟨His face is *covered* with freckles.⟩
3 to form a covering over ⟨Snow *covered* the ground.⟩
4 to pass over or through ⟨The bikers *covered* 50 miles a day.⟩
5 to provide protection to or against ⟨Soldiers *covered* the landing with artillery.⟩
6 to maintain a check on by patrolling ⟨Police *cover* the highways.⟩
7 to hide from sight or knowledge ⟨I *covered* my embarrassment.⟩
8 to deal with as a subject ⟨The test will *cover* everything we've studied so far.⟩
9 to have as a field of activity or interest ⟨Our newspaper employs a reporter *covering* the courthouse.⟩
10 to provide insurance for

[2]cover *n*
1 something that protects, shelters, or hides
2 a covering (as a blanket) used on a bed
3 a binding or a protecting case ⟨a book *cover*⟩
4 something that is placed over or about another thing : LID, TOP ⟨a mattress *cover*⟩ ⟨the *cover* of a box⟩

cov•er•age \ˈkə-və-rij, ˈkəv-rij\ *n*
1 insurance against something ⟨fire *coverage*⟩
2 the value or amount of insurance ⟨a thousand dollars' *coverage*⟩
3 treatment of an event or subject ⟨The local radio station has good sports *coverage*.⟩

cov•er•all \ˈkə-vər-ˌȯl\ *n*
an outer garment that combines shirt and pants and is worn to protect a person's regular clothes — usually used in pl.

covered wagon *n*
◀ a large long wagon with a curving canvas top

cov•er•ing \ˈkə-və-ring, ˈkəv-riŋ\ *n*
something that shelters, protects, or conceals

cov•er•let \ˈkə-vər-lət\ *n*
BEDSPREAD

[1]co•vert \ˈkəv-ərt, ˈkō-vərt\ *adj*
made or done secretly ⟨a *covert* glance⟩ ⟨*covert* military operations⟩
co•vert•ly *adv*

[2]covert *n*
1 a hiding place (as a thicket that gives shelter to game animals)
2 one of the small feathers around the bottom of the quills on the wings and tail of a bird

cov•et \ˈkəv-ət\ *vb* **cov•et•ed**; **cov•et•ing**
to wish for greatly or with envy ⟨I admit I *covet* success.⟩ ⟨It's wrong to *covet* a friend's happiness.⟩

cov•et•ous \ˈkə-vət-əs\ *adj*
having or showing too much desire for wealth or possessions or for something belonging to another person

cov•ey \ˈkə-vē\ *n, pl* **coveys**
1 a small flock of birds ⟨a *covey* of quail⟩
2 [1]GROUP 1 ⟨a *covey* of reporters⟩

[1]cow \ˈkau̇\ *n*
▼ the adult female of cattle or of any of various other large animals (as moose or seals)

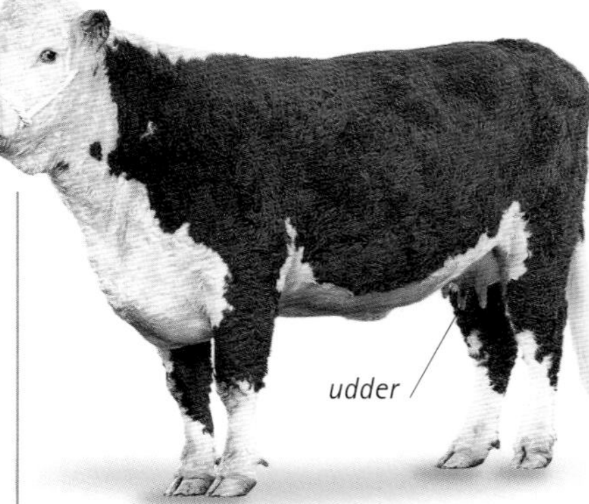

[1]cow

[2]cow *vb* **cowed**; **cow•ing**
to make afraid ⟨They were *cowed* by threats.⟩

cow•ard \ˈkau̇-ərd\ *n*
a person who shows shameful fear

cow•ard•ice \ˈkau̇-ər-dəs\ *n*
shameful fear

cow•ard•ly \ˈkau̇-ərd-lē\ *adj*
1 shamefully fearful ⟨a *cowardly* traitor⟩
2 showing shameful fear
cow•ard•li•ness *n*

cow•bell \ˈkau̇-ˌbel\ *n*
◀ a bell hung around the neck of a cow to tell where it is

cow•bird \ˈkau̇-ˌbərd\ *n*
a small North American blackbird that lays its eggs in the nests of other birds

cow•boy \ˈkau̇-ˌbȯi\ *n*
▶ a man or boy who works on a ranch or performs at a rodeo

cow•catch•er \ˈkau̇-ˌka-chər\ *n*
a strong frame on the front of a railroad engine for moving things blocking the track

cow•er \ˈkau̇-ər\ *vb* **cow•ered**; **cow•er•ing**
to shrink away or crouch down shivering (as from fear) ⟨The thunder made our dog *cower.*⟩

cow•girl \ˈkau̇-ˌgərl\ *n*
a girl or woman who works on a ranch or performs at a rodeo

cow•hand \ˈkau̇-ˌhand\ *n*
a person who works on a cattle ranch

cowbell

cow•herd \ˈkau̇-ˌhərd\ *n*
a person who tends cows

cow•hide \ˈkau̇-ˌhīd\ *n*
1 the hide of cattle or leather made from it
2 a whip of rawhide or braided leather

cowl \ˈkau̇l\ *n*
a hood or long hooded cloak especially of a monk

cow•lick \ˈkau̇-ˌlik\ *n*
a small bunch of hair that sticks out and will not lie flat

cox•swain \ˈkäk-sən, -ˌswān\ *n*
the person who steers or directs the rowers of a boat

coy \ˈkȯi\ *adj*
falsely shy or modest

▶ **Word History** *Coy* now usually means "pretending to be shy," but earlier in the history of English it meant just "shy" as well as "quiet." English borrowed the word from medieval French. In French, it comes, by regular changes in sound, from Latin *quietus,* which—borrowed directly from Latin into English—gives us the word *quiet.*

coy•ote \kī-ˈō-tē, ˈkī-ˌōt\ *n*
a yellowish to reddish gray doglike animal chiefly of western North America that is closely related to but smaller than the wolf

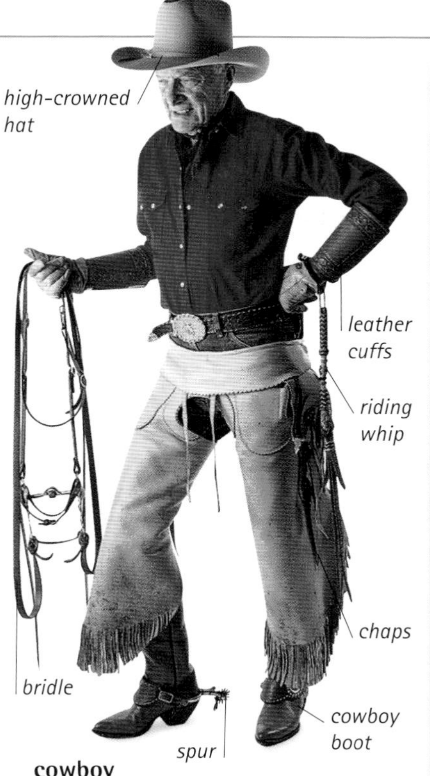

cowboy

[1]co•zy \ˈkō-zē\ *adj* **co•zi•er**; **co•zi•est**
enjoying or providing warmth and comfort ⟨a *cozy* fireplace⟩
co•zi•ly \-zə-lē\ *adv*
co•zi•ness \-zē-nəs\ *n*

[2]cozy *n, pl* **co•zies**
a padded covering for a container (as a teapot) to keep the contents hot

CPR *abbr* cardiopulmonary resuscitation

cpu \ˌsē-ˌpē-ˈyü\ *n, often cap C & P & U*
the part of a computer that does most of the processing of data

[1]crab \ˈkrab\ *n*
▼ a sea animal that is a crustacean related to the lobsters and has a short broad flat shell and a front pair of legs with small claws

[1]crab

[2]crab *n*
a person who is usually grouchy

[3]crab *vb* **crabbed**; **crab•bing**
COMPLAIN

crab apple *n*
1 an apple tree grown for its white, pink, or red flowers or its small usually brightly colored sour fruit
2 the small sour fruit of a crab apple tree

crab•bed \ˈkra-bəd\ *adj*
CRABBY

crab•by \ˈkra-bē\ *adj* **crab•bi•er**; **crab•bi•est**
GROUCHY

crab•grass \ˈkrab-ˌgras\ *n*
▼ a weedy grass with coarse stems that root at the joints

crabgrass: crabgrass in a field

[1]crack \ˈkrak\ *vb* **cracked**; **crack•ing**
1 to break or cause to break with a sudden sharp sound ⟨*crack* an egg⟩
2 to break often without completely separating into parts ⟨The ice *cracked* in several places.⟩
3 to make or cause to make a sound as if breaking ⟨*crack* a whip⟩
4 to open a small amount ⟨*crack* a window⟩
5 to tell (a joke) especially in a clever way
6 to lose self-control ⟨He *cracked* under the strain.⟩
7 to change in tone quality ⟨My voice *cracked* from emotion.⟩
8 to strike or receive a sharp blow
9 SOLVE ⟨I *cracked* the code.⟩
crack up
1 to have a reputation as a result of praise ⟨The show wasn't as good as it was *cracked up* to be.⟩
2 to damage or destroy (a vehicle) by crashing
3 to laugh or cause to laugh ⟨Her costume *cracked* me *up.*⟩

a b c d e f g h i j k l m n o p q r s t u v w x y z

[2]**crack** *n*
1 a narrow break or opening ⟨a *crack* in the glass⟩
2 a sudden sharp noise ⟨a *crack* of thunder⟩
3 a sharp clever remark
4 a broken tone of the voice
5 the beginning moment ⟨I awoke at the *crack* of dawn.⟩
6 a sharp blow
7 [2]ATTEMPT ⟨It was my first *crack* at writing.⟩

[3]**crack** *adj*
of high quality or ability ⟨*crack* troops⟩

crack•er \'kra-kər\ *n*
a dry thin baked food made of flour and water

[1]**crack•le** \'kra-kəl\ *vb* **crack•led**; **crack•ling**
1 to make many small sharp noises
2 to form little cracks in a surface

[2]**crackle** *n*
the noise of repeated small cracks (as of burning wood)

crack–up \'krak-,əp\ *n*
1 BREAKDOWN 2
2 [2]CRASH 3, WRECK ⟨My car received minor damage in the *crack-up.*⟩

[1]**cra•dle** \'krā-dᵊl\ *n*
1 a baby's bed usually on rockers
2 place of beginning ⟨the *cradle* of civilization⟩
3 the earliest period of life ⟨I was pampered from the *cradle.*⟩
4 a framework or support resembling a baby's bed in appearance or use ⟨a phone's *cradle*⟩

[2]**cradle** *vb* **cra•dled**; **cra•dling**
to hold or support in or as if in a cradle ⟨She *cradled* my head in her arms.⟩

[1]**craft** \'kraft\ *n*
1 skill in making things especially with the hands
2 an occupation or trade requiring skill with the hands or as an artist ⟨Carpentry is a *craft.*⟩
3 *pl usually* **craft** a boat especially when of small size
4 *pl usually* **craft** AIRCRAFT
5 skill and cleverness often used to trick people

cranberry: a basket of cranberries

[2]**craft** *vb* **craft•ed**; **craft•ing**
to make or produce with care or skill

crafts•man \'krafts-mən\ *n, pl* **crafts•men** \-mən\
1 a person who works at a trade or handicraft
2 a highly skilled worker

crafty \'kraf-tē\ *adj* **craft•i•er**; **craft•i•est**
skillful at tricking others : CUNNING
craft•i•ly \'kraf-tə-lē\ *adv*
craft•i•ness \-tē-nəs\ *n*

crag \'krag\ *n*
a steep rock or cliff

crag•gy \'kra-gē\ *adj* **crag•gi•er**; **crag•gi•est**
having many steep rocks or cliffs ⟨*craggy* hills⟩

cram \'kram\ *vb* **crammed**; **cram•ming**
1 to stuff or pack tightly
2 to fill full ⟨I *crammed* my suitcase with clothes.⟩
3 to study hard just before a test
synonyms see PACK

[1]**cramp** \'kramp\ *n*
1 a sudden painful tightening of a muscle
2 sharp pain in the abdomen — usually used in pl.

[2]**cramp** *vb* **cramped**; **cramp•ing**
1 to cause or experience a sudden painful muscular tightening in ⟨My hand was *cramping* from all the writing.⟩
2 to hold back from free action or expression : HAMPER ⟨We were *cramped* by all the rules.⟩

cramped \'krampt\ *adj*
1 having too little space ⟨a *cramped* apartment⟩
2 unable to move freely because of lack of space ⟨Everyone in the the boat was *cramped.*⟩

cran•ber•ry \'kran-,ber-ē\ *n, pl* **cran•ber•ries**
◀ a sour bright red berry that is eaten in sauces and jelly and is the fruit of an evergreen swamp plant related to the blueberries

[1]**crane** \'krān\ *n*
1 ▶ a large tall wading bird with a long neck, bill, and legs
2 a machine with a swinging arm for lifting and carrying heavy weights

[2]**crane** *vb* **craned**; **cran•ing**
to stretch the neck to see better ⟨Neighbors *craned* out the window to see the parade.⟩

cra•ni•al \'krā-nē-əl\ *adj*
of or relating to the skull and especially the part enclosing the brain

cra•ni•um \'krā-nē-əm\ *n, pl* **cra•ni•ums** *or* **cra•nia** \-nē-ə\
1 SKULL
2 the part of the skull enclosing the brain

[1]**crank** \'kraŋk\ *n*
1 a bent part with a handle that is turned to start or run machinery
2 a person with strange ideas
3 a cross or irritable person

[2]**crank** *vb* **cranked**; **crank•ing**
1 to start or run by or as if by turning a part with a handle
2 to make or become greater in speed or intensity ⟨*crank* the volume⟩
crank out to produce quickly and often carelessly ⟨You can't just *crank out* a good book.⟩

cranky \'kraŋ-kē\ *adj* **crank•i•er**; **crank•i•est**
easily angered or irritated
crank•i•ness *n*

cran•ny \'kra-nē\ *n, pl* **cran•nies**
1 a small break or slit (as in a cliff)
2 a place that is not generally known or noticed

crap•pie \'krä-pē\ *n*
either of two silvery sunfish that are caught for sport or for food

[1]**crash** \'krash\ *vb* **crashed**; **crash•ing**
1 to break or go to pieces with or as if with violence and noise : SMASH
2 to fall or strike something with noise and damage ⟨A plane *crashed* in the storm.⟩ ⟨The lamp *crashed* to the floor.⟩
3 to hit or cause to hit something with force and noise ⟨The car *crashed* into a tree.⟩
4 to make or cause to make a loud noise ⟨Thunder *crashed* overhead.⟩

[1]**crane 1**

5 to move roughly and noisily ⟨I heard something *crashing* through the woods.⟩
6 to stay for a short time where someone else lives

[2]**crash** *n*
1 a loud sound (as of things smashing)
2 an instance of hitting something with force
3 a collision involving a vehicle ⟨a plane *crash*⟩
4 a sudden weakening or failure (as of a business or prices)

[1]**crate** \'krāt\ *n*
a box or frame of wooden slats or boards for holding and protecting something in shipment

[2]**crate** *vb* **crat•ed**; **crat•ing**
to pack in a wooden box or frame

cra•ter \'krā-tər\ *n*
1 ▼ the area around the opening of a volcano or geyser that is shaped like a bowl

crater 1: a volcanic crater

2 a hole (as in the surface of the earth or moon) formed by an impact (as of a meteorite)

cra•vat \krə-'vat\ *n*
NECKTIE

crave \'krāv\ *vb* **craved**; **crav•ing**
1 to want greatly : long for ⟨*crave* chocolate⟩ ⟨The stray dog *craved* affection.⟩
2 to ask for earnestly
synonyms see DESIRE

cra•ven \'krā-vən\ *adj*
COWARDLY

crav•ing \'krā-viŋ\ *n*
a great desire or longing ⟨I have a *craving* for pizza.⟩

craw \'krȯ\ *n*
1 [1]CROP 3
2 the stomach of an animal

craw•fish \'krȯ-,fish\ *n, pl* **crawfish**
1 CRAYFISH
2 SPINY LOBSTER

[1]**crawl** \'krȯl\ *vb* **crawled**; **crawl•ing**
1 to move slowly with the body close to the ground : move on hands and knees
2 to go very slowly or carefully ⟨Traffic was *crawling* along.⟩
3 to be covered with or have the feeling of being covered with creeping things ⟨The food was *crawling* with flies.⟩

[2]**crawl** *n*
1 the act or motion of going very slowly ⟨Traffic is at a *crawl*.⟩
2 a swimming stroke performed by moving first one arm over the head and then the other while kicking the legs

cray•fish \'krā-,fish\ *n, pl* **crayfish**
1 ▼ a freshwater shellfish that looks like the related lobster but is much smaller
2 SPINY LOBSTER

crayfish 1

[1]**cray•on** \'krā-,än, -ən\ *n*
▼ a stick of colored wax or sometimes chalk used for writing or drawing

[1]**crayon:** wax crayons

[2]**crayon** *vb* **cray•oned**; **cray•on•ing**
to draw or color with a crayon

craze \'krāz\ *n*
something that is very popular for a short while

cra•zy \'krā-zē\ *adj* **cra•zi•er**; **cra•zi•est**
1 having a severe mental illness : INSANE
2 not sensible or logical ⟨a *crazy* idea⟩
3 very excited or pleased ⟨They're *crazy* about their new house.⟩
4 very annoyed ⟨This song makes me *crazy*.⟩
cra•zi•ly \'krā-zə-lē\ *adv*
cra•zi•ness \-zē-nəs\ *n*

[1]**creak** \'krēk\ *vb* **creaked**; **creak•ing**
to make a long scraping or squeaking sound

[2]**creak** *n*
a long squeaking or scraping noise

creaky \'krē-kē\ *adj* **creak•i•er**; **creak•i•est**
making or likely to make a long squeaking or scraping sound ⟨*creaky* stairs⟩

[1]**cream** \'krēm\ *n*
1 the thick yellowish part of milk that contains butterfat
2 a food prepared with cream ⟨*cream* of mushroom soup⟩
3 a very thick liquid used to soften, protect, or heal the skin ⟨hand *cream*⟩
4 the best part ⟨Only the *cream* of the crop get into that college.⟩
5 a pale yellow

[2]**cream** *vb* **creamed**; **cream•ing**
1 to stir (as butter) until smooth and soft
2 to defeat easily and completely ⟨They *creamed* us in the championship game.⟩

cream cheese *n*
a soft white cheese made from whole milk enriched with cream

cream•ery \'krē-mə-rē, 'krēm-rē\ *n, pl* **cream•er•ies**
a place where milk is made into other products (as cream and cheese)

creamy \'krē-mē\ *adj* **cream•i•er; cream•i•est**
1 full of or containing cream ⟨*creamy* salad dressing⟩
2 smooth and soft ⟨*creamy* skin⟩ ⟨*creamy* peanut butter⟩
cream•i•ness *n*

[1]crease \'krēs\ *n*
a line or mark made by folding, pressing, or wrinkling

[2]crease *vb* **creased; creas•ing**
to make a line or lines in or on ⟨I used an iron to *crease* my pants.⟩

cre•ate \krē-'āt\ *vb* **cre•at•ed; cre•at•ing**
to cause to exist : bring into existence : PRODUCE

cre•a•tion \krē-'ā-shən\ *n*
1 the act of bringing the world into existence out of nothing
2 the act of making, inventing, or producing something ⟨the *creation* of a poem⟩
3 something produced by human intelligence or imagination ⟨The artist showed me her *creations.*⟩
4 a wide range of places ⟨The puppy ran all over *creation.*⟩
5 a living thing or living things ⟨There was peace among all *creation.*⟩

cre•a•tive \krē-'ā-tiv\ *adj*
able to invent or produce new and original things
cre•a•tive•ly *adv*
cre•a•tive•ness *n*

cre•a•tor \krē-'ā-tər\ *n*
1 someone that invents or produces
2 *cap* GOD 1

crea•ture \'krē-chər\ *n*
1 a lower animal
2 PERSON 1 ⟨You're the most selfish *creature* I've ever met.⟩
3 an imaginary or strange being

cred•i•ble \'kre-də-bəl\ *adj*
possible to believe : deserving belief ⟨*credible* witnesses⟩
cred•i•bly \-blē\ *adv*

[1]cred•it \'kre-dət\ *n*
1 recognition or honor received for some quality or work ⟨A doctor was given *credit* for the discovery.⟩ ⟨She got extra *credit* for her report.⟩
2 the balance in an account in a person's favor
3 money or goods or services allowed to a person by a bank or business with the expectation of payment later
4 good reputation especially for honesty : high standing
5 a source of honor or pride ⟨You are a *credit* to your school.⟩
6 a unit of schoolwork ⟨I took two *credits* in Spanish.⟩
7 belief or trust in the truth of something ⟨These rumors deserve no *credit.*⟩

[2]credit *vb* **cred•it•ed; cred•it•ing**
1 to give recognition or honor to for something ⟨The team *credited* their coach for the championship.⟩
2 to place something in a person's favor on (a business account) ⟨We will *credit* your account with ten dollars.⟩
3 BELIEVE 2 ⟨Don't *credit* a statement from a stranger.⟩

cred•it•able \'kre-də-tə-bəl\ *adj*
good enough to deserve praise ⟨They made a *creditable* attempt to clean up.⟩

credit card *n*
a card with which a person can buy things and pay for them later

cred•i•tor \'kre-də-tər\ *n*
a person to whom a debt is owed

creed \'krēd\ *n*
1 a statement of the basic beliefs of a religious faith
2 a set of guiding rules or beliefs

creek \'krēk, 'krik\ *n*
▼ a stream of water usually larger than a brook and smaller than a river

creek

Creek \'krēk\ *n*
1 a confederacy of American Indian people once occupying most of Alabama and Georgia
2 the language of the Creek people

creel \'krēl\ *n*
a basket for holding caught fish

[1]creep \'krēp\ *vb* **crept** \'krept\; **creep•ing**
1 to move along with the body close to the ground or floor : move slowly on hands and knees : CRAWL
2 to move or advance slowly, timidly, or quietly
3 to grow or spread along the ground or along a surface ⟨Ivy was *creeping* up a wall.⟩

[2]creep *n*
1 a strange or unlikable person
2 a slow, timid, or quiet movement
3 a feeling of nervousness or fear — usually used in pl. ⟨Spiders give me the *creeps.*⟩

creeper 3

creep•er \'krē-pər\ *n*
1 a person or animal that moves slowly, timidly, or quietly
2 a small bird that creeps about trees and bushes in search of insects
3 ▲ a plant (as ivy) that grows by spreading over a surface

creepy \'krē-pē\ *adj* **creep•i•er; creep•i•est**
1 EERIE ⟨a *creepy* old house⟩
2 annoyingly unpleasant ⟨Dozens of frogs gave me a *creepy* feeling.⟩
creep•i•ness *n*

cre•mate \'krē-,māt\ *vb* **cre•mat•ed; cre•mat•ing**
to burn (as a dead body) to ashes
cre•ma•tion \kri-'mā-shən\ *n*

A B C D E F G H I J K L M N O P Q R S T U V W X Y Z

crepe \'krāp\ *n*
1 a thin crinkled fabric (as of silk or wool)
2 a very thin pancake

crepe paper *n*
paper with a crinkled or puckered look and feel

crept *past and past participle of* CREEP

cre•scen•do \kri-'shen-dō\ *n, pl* **cre•scen•dos**
a gradual increase in the loudness of music

[1]**cres•cent** \'kre-s^{ə}nt\ *n*
1 the shape of the visible part of the moon when it is less than half full
2 something shaped like a crescent moon

[2]**crescent** *adj*
shaped like the crescent moon ⟨*crescent* rolls⟩

cress \'kres\ *n*
▼ a small plant having leaves with a sharp taste that are eaten in salads

cress

crest \'krest\ *n*
1 a showy growth (as of flesh or feathers) on the head of an animal
2 the highest part or point of something ⟨the *crest* of the wave⟩ ⟨the *crest* of a hill⟩
3 an emblem or design used to represent a family, group, or organization
crest•ed \'kres-təd\ *adj*

crest•fall•en \'krest-,fò-lən\ *adj*
feeling disappointment and loss of pride

crev•ice \'kre-vəs\ *n*
a narrow opening (as in the earth) caused by cracking or splitting : FISSURE

crew \'krü\ *n*
1 the group of people who operate a ship, train, or airplane
2 a group of people working together ⟨the news *crew*⟩
3 a gathering of people ⟨Mom feeds a large *crew* on holidays.⟩

crib \'krib\ *n*
1 ▶ a small bed frame with high sides for a child
2 a building or bin for storage ⟨corn *crib*⟩
3 a long open box for feeding animals

[1]**crick•et** \'kri-kət\ *n*
▶ a small leaping insect noted for the chirping sound made by the males rubbing part of the wings together

[2]**cricket** *n*
a game played on a large field with bats, ball, and wickets by two teams of eleven players

[1]**cricket**

cri•er \'krī-ər\ *n*
a person whose job is to call out orders or announcements

crime \'krīm\ *n*
1 the act of doing something forbidden by law or the failure to do an act required by law
2 an act that is foolish or wrong ⟨It's a *crime* to waste food.⟩

[1]**crim•i•nal** \'kri-mə-n^{ə}l\ *adj*
1 being or guilty of an act that is unlawful, foolish, or wrong
2 relating to unlawful acts or their punishment ⟨*criminal* law⟩
crim•i•nal•ly \-n^{ə}l-ē\ *adv*

[2]**criminal** *n*
a person who has committed an unlawful act

crimp \'krimp\ *vb* **crimped**; **crimp•ing**
to make wavy or bent ⟨She *crimped* her hair.⟩

crim•son \'krim-zən\ *n*
a deep purplish red

cringe \'krinj\ *vb* **cringed**; **cring•ing**
1 to shrink in fear : COWER
2 to show disgust or embarrassment at something ⟨He *cringed* at the suggestion of eating liver.⟩

crin•kle \'kriŋ-kəl\ *vb* **crin•kled**; **crin•kling**
1 to form or cause little waves or wrinkles on the surface : WRINKLE
2 [1]RUSTLE 1

crin•kly \'kriŋ-klē\ *adj* **crin•kli•er**; **crin•kli•est**
full of small wrinkles ⟨*crinkly* skin⟩

[1]**crip•ple** \'kri-pəl\ *n, sometimes offensive*
a disabled person who is unable to fully use one or both of his or her arms or legs
Hint: In the past, this word was not considered offensive. In recent years, however, some people have come to find the word hurtful, and you may offend someone by using it.

[2]**cripple** *vb* **crip•pled**; **crip•pling**
1 to cause to lose the use of one or more arms or legs ⟨The accident *crippled* the boy.⟩
2 to make useless or powerless

cri•sis \'krī-səs\ *n, pl* **cri•ses** \'krī-,sēz\
a difficult or dangerous situation that needs serious attention ⟨a medical *crisis*⟩

crib 1

[1]crisp \ˈkrisp\ *adj* **crisp•er; crisp•est**
1 being thin, hard, and easily crumbled ⟨*crisp* potato chips⟩
2 pleasantly firm and fresh ⟨*crisp* celery⟩
3 being clear and brief ⟨a *crisp* reply⟩
4 pleasantly cool and invigorating : BRISK ⟨a *crisp* autumn day⟩
5 having clear details ⟨a *crisp* photo⟩
synonyms see BRITTLE
crisp•ly *adv*
crisp•ness *n*

[2]crisp *vb* **crisped; crisp•ing**
to make or keep something crispy or fresh

crispy \ˈkri-spē\ *adj*
pleasantly thin, dry, and crunchy

criss•cross \ˈkris-ˌkrȯs\ *vb* **criss•crossed; criss•cross•ing**
1 to go from one side of (something) to the other side and come back again ⟨On our trip we *crisscrossed* the state.⟩
2 to mark with or make lines that go across one another

crit•ic \ˈkri-tik\ *n*
1 a person who makes or gives a judgment of the value, worth, beauty, or quality of something ⟨a movie *critic*⟩
2 a person who finds fault or complains

crit•i•cal \ˈkri-ti-kəl\ *adj*
1 likely or eager to find fault
2 consisting of or involving judgment of value, worth, beauty, or quality ⟨*critical* writings⟩
3 using or involving careful judgment ⟨a *critical* examination of a patient⟩
4 extremely important ⟨It is *critical* that you follow the instructions exactly.⟩
crit•i•cal•ly *adv*

crit•i•cism \ˈkri-tə-ˌsi-zəm\ *n*
1 the act of finding fault ⟨His *criticism* of her work made her stop and revise it.⟩
2 a remark that expresses disapproval ⟨I had only one *criticism* about his work.⟩
3 a careful judgment or review especially by a person whose job is to judge the value, worth, beauty, or quality of something

crit•i•cize \ˈkri-tə-ˌsīz\ *vb* **crit•i•cized; crit•i•ciz•ing**
1 to examine and judge
2 to find fault with

crit•ter \ˈkri-tər\ *n*
a small animal

[1]croak \ˈkrōk\ *vb* **croaked; croak•ing**
1 to utter with a rough low voice ⟨"I need water," he *croaked*.⟩
2 to make a deep harsh sound ⟨frogs *croaked*⟩

[2]croak *n*
a hoarse harsh sound or cry

[1]cro•chet \krō-ˈshā\ *vb* **cro•cheted; cro•chet•ing**
to make (something) or create a fabric with a hooked needle by forming and weaving loops in a thread

[2]crochet *n*
▼ work done or a fabric formed by weaving loops in a thread using a hooked needle

[2]crochet: late 19th-century crocheted purse

crock \ˈkräk\ *n*
a thick pot or jar of baked clay

crock•ery \ˈkrä-kə-rē\ *n*
EARTHENWARE

croc•o•dile \ˈkrä-kə-ˌdīl\ *n*
▼ a reptile that resembles the related alligator but that has a long narrow snout

crocodile

▶ **Word History** The word *crocodile* is taken from Greek *krokodeilos,* which is probably a compound of *krokē,* "pebble, stone," and a rare word *drilos,* which may mean "worm." According to the ancient Greek writer Herodotus, some Greeks gave this name to the lizards that lived among the stone walls of their farms. When these Greeks visited Egypt, the enormous reptiles of the Nile River reminded them of the lizards and they applied the same name to them.

cro•cus \ˈkrō-kəs\ *n*
a small plant having grasslike leaves and colorful flowers that bloom in the spring

cro•ny \ˈkrō-nē\ *n, pl* **cro•nies**
a close friend especially of someone in power

[1]crook \ˈkru̇k\ *vb* **crooked** \ˈkru̇kt\; **crook•ing**
[1]BEND 1, CURVE ⟨*crook* your finger⟩

[2]crook *n*
1 a dishonest person (as a thief)
2 a shepherd's staff with one end curved into a hook
3 a curved or hooked part of a thing : BEND

crook•ed \ˈkru̇-kəd\ *adj*
1 having bends and curves ⟨a *crooked* path⟩
2 not set or placed straight ⟨The picture is *crooked*.⟩
3 DISHONEST ⟨*crooked* salesmen⟩
crook•ed•ly *adv*
crook•ed•ness *n*

croon \ˈkrün\ *vb* **crooned; croon•ing**
to hum or sing in a low soft voice

[1]crop \ˈkräp\ *n*
1 a plant or product that is grown and harvested ⟨Corn is their main *crop*.⟩
2 the amount gathered or harvested : HARVEST ⟨a *crop* of wheat⟩
3 an enlargement just above the stomach of a bird or insect in which food is temporarily stored
4 a short riding whip
5 BATCH 2 ⟨a new *crop* of students⟩
6 a close cut of the hair

[2]crop *vb* **cropped; crop•ping**
1 to remove (as by cutting or biting) the upper or outer parts of : TRIM ⟨Sheep were *cropping* clover.⟩
2 to grow or yield a crop (as of grain) : cause (land) to bear a crop
crop up to come or appear when not expected ⟨Problems *crop up* daily.⟩

A B C D E F G H I J K L M N O P Q R S T U V W X Y Z

cro•quet \krō-ˈkā\ *n*
▼ a game in which players hit wooden balls with mallets through a series of wickets set out on a lawn

wooden ball
mallet
wicket
croquet equipment

cro•quette \krō-ˈket\ *n*
a roll or ball of hashed meat, fish, or vegetables fried in deep fat

[1]**cross** \ˈkròs\ *n*
1 a structure, object, or mark consisting of one line or bar extending across another at right angles
2 *often cap* the structure on which Jesus Christ was crucified used as a symbol of Christianity
3 mixture of two different things, types, or qualities ⟨a *cross* of luck and skill⟩
cross to bear a hardship that someone endures for a long time

[2]**cross** *vb* **crossed**; **cross•ing**
1 to move, pass, or extend across or past ⟨Look both ways before you *cross* the street.⟩
2 to place one over the other ⟨*Cross* your fingers!⟩
3 to lie or be situated across ⟨A path *crosses* the front yard.⟩
4 to go across : INTERSECT
5 to turn (the eyes) toward the nose
6 to draw a line across ⟨*Cross* your t's.⟩
7 to act against : OPPOSE ⟨She's tough, and I wouldn't dare to *cross* her.⟩
8 to cause (an animal or plant) to breed with one of another kind : produce hybrids
9 to pass going in opposite directions ⟨Their letters *crossed* in the mail.⟩
cross off to draw a line through (something) ⟨*Cross* my name *off* the list.⟩
cross out to draw a line through (something) to show that it is wrong ⟨I *crossed out* the misspelled word.⟩
cross someone's mind to be thought of by someone ⟨It never *crossed her mind* that she might lose.⟩
cross yourself to touch the forehead, chest, and shoulders as an expression of Christian faith (as in prayer)

[3]**cross** *adj* **cross•er**; **cross•est**
1 hard to get along with : IRRITABLE
2 lying, falling, or passing across ⟨a *cross* street⟩
cross•ly *adv*

cross•bar \ˈkròs-ˌbär\ *n*
a piece or stripe placed crosswise or across something

cross•bones \ˈkròs-ˌbōnz\ *n pl*
two leg or arm bones placed or pictured as lying across each other

cross•bow \ˈkròs-ˌbō\ *n*
▼ a short strip mounted crosswise near the end of a wooden stock that shoots short arrows

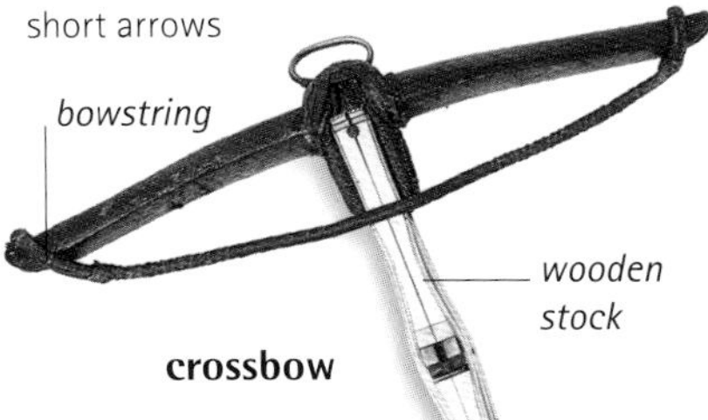

crossbow

cross–ex•am•ine \ˌkròs-ig-ˈza-mən\ *vb* **cross–ex•am•ined**; **cross–ex•am•in•ing**
to question (a witness) in an effort to show that statements or answers given earlier in the legal hearing were false

cross–eyed \ˈkròs-ˈīd\ *adj*
having one or both eyes turned toward the nose

cross•ing \ˈkrò-siŋ\ *n*
1 ▼ a point where a line, track, or street intersects another line, track, or street
2 a place provided for going across a street, railroad tracks, or a stream
3 a voyage across a body of water

crossing 1: intersecting railway lines

cross•piece \ˈkròs-ˌpēs\ *n*
something placed so as to lie across something else

cross–ref•er•ence \ˈkròs-ˈre-fə-rəns, -ˈre-frəns\ *n*
a note (as in a dictionary) that directs a user to information at another place

cross•road \ˈkròs-ˌrōd\ *n*
a place where roads run across each other — usually used in pl.

cross section *n*
1 a cutting made across something (as a log or an apple)
2 a view showing what the inside of something looks like after a cut has been made through it ⟨a *cross section* of a ship⟩
3 a small group that includes examples of the different types of people or things in a larger group ⟨a *cross section* of voters⟩

cross•walk \ˈkròs-ˌwòk\ *n*
a specially marked path for people to walk across a street

cross•wise \ˈkròs-ˌwīz\ *adv*
so as to cross something ⟨The carrots were cut *crosswise.*⟩

cross•word puzzle \ˌkròs-ˌwərd-\ *n*
a puzzle in which words are filled into a pattern of numbered squares in answer to clues so that they read across and down

crotch \ˈkräch\ *n*
1 the part of the body where the legs join together
2 an angle formed by the spreading apart of two legs or branches or of a limb from its trunk ⟨the *crotch* of a tree⟩

crotch•ety \ˈkrä-chə-tē\ *adj*
very grumpy or unpleasant

[1]**crouch** \ˈkrau̇ch\ *vb* **crouched**; **crouch•ing**
to stoop or bend low with the arms and legs close to the body

[2]**crouch** *n*
the position of stooping with the arms and legs close to the body

croup \ˈkrüp\ *n*
an illness that usually affects young children and causes a hoarse cough and difficult breathing

[1]**crow** \ˈkrō\ *n*
1 ▶ a glossy black bird that has a harsh cry
2 *cap* a member of an American Indian people of Montana
3 the language of the Crow people

[1]**crow 1**

a b c d e f g h i j k l m n o p q r s t u v w x y z

A B C D E F G H I J K L M N O P Q R S T U V W X Y Z

[2]crow *vb* **crowed; crow•ing**
1 to make the loud cry of a rooster
2 to make sounds of delight
3 [1]BOAST 1
4 to say with delight ⟨"You should have told me today was your birthday!" she *crowed.*⟩

[3]crow *n*
1 the cry of a rooster
2 a cry of triumph

crow•bar \'krō-,bär\ *n*
a metal bar used as a lever (as for prying things apart)

[1]crowd \'kraůd\ *vb* **crowd•ed; crowd•ing**
1 to push into a small space ⟨After the meeting we all *crowded* into an elevator.⟩
2 to form a tight group ⟨Players *crowded* around the coach.⟩
3 to collect in numbers ⟨People *crowded* at the entrance.⟩
4 to fill or pack by pressing together ⟨Cars *crowded* the roads.⟩

[2]crowd *n*
1 a large number of people in one place
2 the population as a whole : ordinary people ⟨These books appeal to the *crowd.*⟩
3 a group of people who spend time together or have a common interest ⟨She hangs around with a wild *crowd.*⟩

[1]crown \'kraůn\ *n*
1 a royal headdress
2 a wreath or band worn especially as a symbol of victory or honor
3 the top of the head
4 the highest part (as of a tree or mountain)
5 *often cap* royal power or authority, a person having such power, or the government of a country ruled by a king or queen ⟨He pledged his loyalty to the *crown.*⟩
6 any of various coins (as a British coin worth five shillings)
7 the top part of a hat
8 the part of a tooth outside of the gum or an artificial substitute for it
crowned \'kraůnd\ *adj*

[2]crown *vb* **crowned; crown•ing**
1 to place a royal headdress on : give the title of king or queen to
2 to declare officially to be ⟨She was *crowned* champion.⟩
3 to cover or be situated on the top of ⟨Snow *crowned* the mountain.⟩
4 to bring to a conclusion
5 to put an artificial crown on a damaged tooth
6 to hit on the head

crow's nest *n*
▶ a partly enclosed place to stand high on the mast of a ship for use as a lookout

cru•cial \'krü-shəl\ *adj*
1 being a final or very important test or decision : DECISIVE ⟨a *crucial* battle⟩
2 very important : SIGNIFICANT ⟨Water is a *crucial* element in our weather.⟩

cru•ci•ble \'krü-sə-bəl\ *n*
a pot in which metals or other substances are heated to a very high temperature or melted

cru•ci•fix \'krü-sə-,fiks\ *n*
a cross with a figure representing Jesus crucified on it

cru•ci•fix•ion \,krü-sə-'fik-shən\ *n*
1 the act of killing someone by nailing his or her feet and hands to a cross
2 *cap* the crucifying of Jesus on a cross

cru•ci•fy \'krü-sə-,fī\ *vb* **cru•ci•fied; cru•ci•fy•ing**
1 to put to death by nailing or binding the hands and feet to a cross
2 to treat cruelly or harshly ⟨Dishonest judges were *crucified* in the newspapers.⟩

crude \'krüd\ *adj* **crud•er; crud•est**
1 in a natural state and not changed by special treatment : RAW ⟨*crude* oil⟩ ⟨*crude* sugar⟩
2 planned or done in a rough or unskilled way ⟨a *crude* drawing⟩
3 not having or showing good manners : VULGAR ⟨*crude* language⟩
crude•ly *adv*
crude•ness *n*

cru•el \'krü-əl\ *adj* **cru•el•er** *or* **cru•el•ler; cru•el•est** *or* **cru•el•lest**
1 wanting to cause others to suffer ⟨a *cruel* ruler⟩
2 causing or helping to cause suffering ⟨*cruel* punishment⟩ ⟨a *cruel* joke⟩
cru•el•ly *adv*

cru•el•ty \'krü-əl-tē\ *n, pl* **cru•el•ties**
1 the quality or state of causing or wanting to cause suffering ⟨a man of *cruelty*⟩
2 treatment that causes suffering

[1]cruise \'krüz\ *vb* **cruised; cruis•ing**
1 to travel by ship often stopping at a series of ports ⟨They *cruised* along the coast.⟩
2 to travel at a steady pace

[2]cruise *n*
a trip on a ship

cruis•er \'krü-zər\ *n*
1 a police car used for patrolling streets and equipped with radio for communicating with headquarters
2 a warship that is smaller than a battleship
3 a motorboat equipped for living aboard

crumb \'krəm\ *n*
1 a very small piece of food ⟨bread *crumbs*⟩
2 a little bit ⟨She only overheard *crumbs* of their conversation.⟩

crum•ble \'krəm-bəl\ *vb* **crum•bled; crum•bling**
1 to break into small pieces ⟨*crumble* bread⟩
2 to fall to pieces : fall into ruin

crum•bly \'krəm-blē\ *adj* **crum•bli•er; crum•bli•est**
easily broken into small pieces

crum•my \'krə-mē\ *adj* **crum•mi•er; crum•mi•est**
very poor ⟨The worker did a *crummy* job.⟩

crum•ple \'krəm-pəl\ *vb* **crum•pled; crum•pling**
1 to press or crush out of shape ⟨*crumple* paper⟩
2 to become full of wrinkles ⟨My shirt got all *crumpled* in the suitcase.⟩
3 [1]COLLAPSE 1 ⟨At the sight of blood, I *crumpled* to the floor.⟩

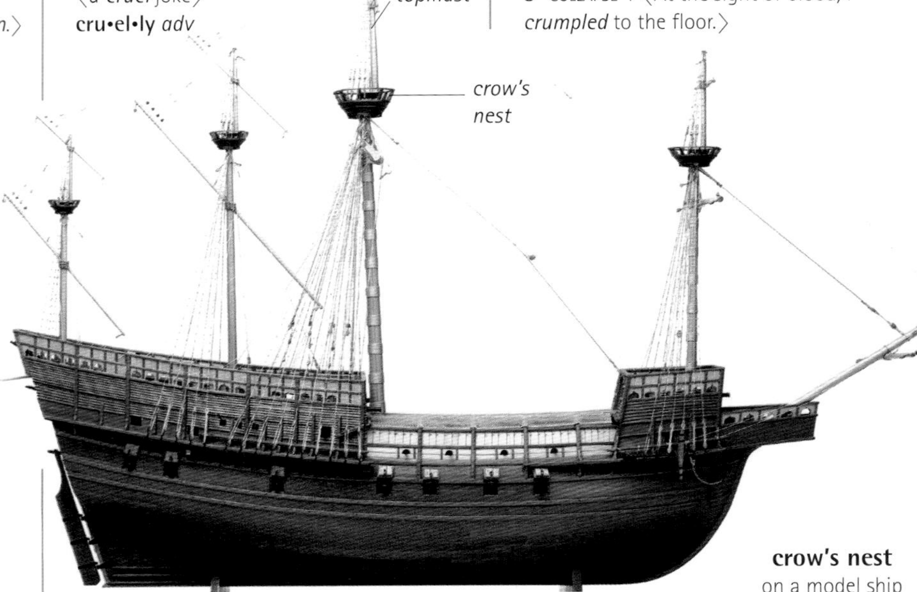

crow's nest
on a model ship

[1]crunch \'krənch\ *vb* **crunched; crunch•ing**
1 to chew or grind with a crushing noise 〈He is *crunching* on hard candy.〉
2 to make the sound of being crushed or squeezed 〈The snow *crunched* underfoot.〉

[2]crunch *n*
an act or sound of crushing 〈She bit into the apple with a loud *crunch*.〉

crunchy \'krən-chē\ *adj* **crunch•i•er; crunch•i•est**
being firm and making a sharp sound when chewed or crushed

[1]cru•sade \krü-'sād\ *n*
1 ▼ *cap* one of the military expeditions made by Christian countries in the eleventh, twelfth, and thirteenth centuries to recover the Holy Land from the Muslims
2 a campaign to get things changed for the better 〈a *crusade* against litter〉

[2]crusade *vb* **cru•sad•ed; cru•sad•ing**
1 to take part in a medieval military expedition to recover the Holy Land
2 to take part in a campaign to make things better
cru•sad•er \krü-'sā-dər\ *n*

[1]crush \'krəsh\ *vb* **crushed; crush•ing**
1 to squeeze together so as to change or destroy the natural shape or condition 〈We *crush* grapes for their juice.〉
2 to break into fine pieces by pressure 〈The machine *crushes* stone.〉
3 OVERWHELM 1 〈*crush* an enemy〉
4 to defeat in spirit 〈The injury *crushed* her hopes of winning.〉

[1]crusade 1: the equipment and costume of a crusader on a crusade

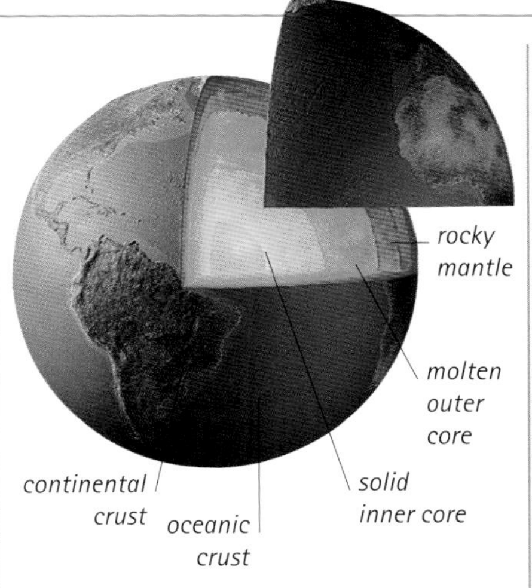

crust 5:
model showing the crust and other layers in the Earth

[2]crush *n*
1 a tightly packed crowd 〈He got caught in the *crush* of holiday shoppers.〉
2 a foolish or very strong liking : INFATUATION

crust \'krəst\ *n*
1 the hardened outside surface of bread
2 a hard dry piece of bread
3 the pastry cover of a pie
4 a hard outer covering or surface layer 〈a *crust* of snow〉
5 ◀ the outer part of the earth

crus•ta•cean \,krəs-'tā-shən\ *n*
▼ any of a large group of mostly water animals (as crabs, lobsters, and shrimps) with a body made of segments, a tough outer shell, two pairs of antennae, and limbs that are jointed

crusty \'krə-stē\ *adj* **crust•i•er; crust•i•est**
1 having a thick or crispy crust 〈*crusty* bread〉
2 [3]CROSS 1 〈a *crusty* reply〉

crustacean
Most crustaceans live in or near seawater. Crabs prefer sandy shores and rock pools, while lobsters search for food along the ocean floor. Shrimps dig into the sand to hide during the day, only coming out at night to hunt for food.

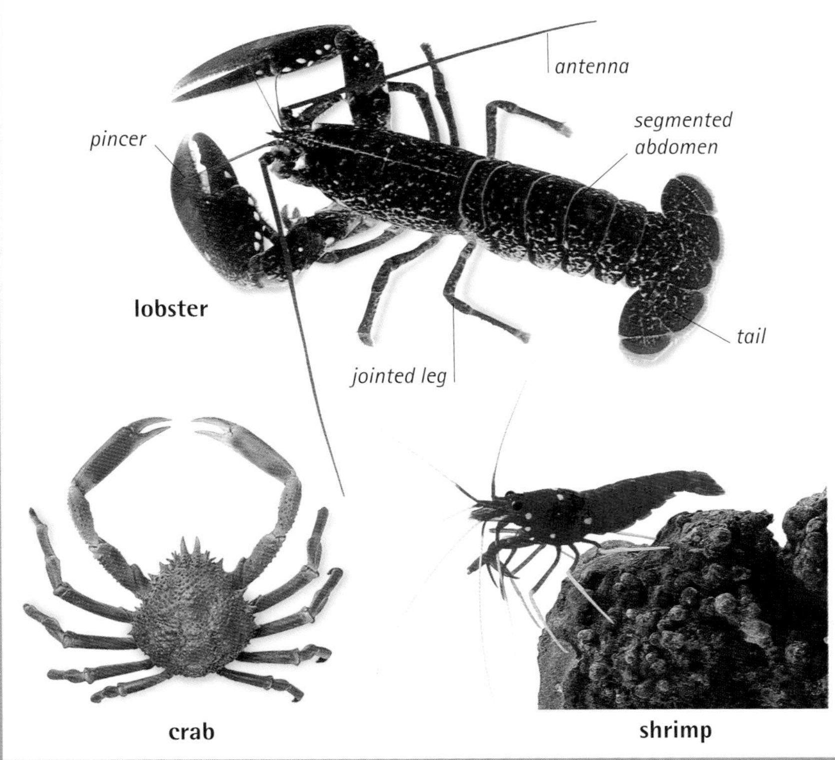

crutch \'krəch\ *n*
1 ▼ a long stick usually made with a piece at the top to fit under the armpit that is used as an aid in walking
2 something that a person depends on to help deal with problems ⟨The child uses his blanket as a *crutch* to feel more secure.⟩

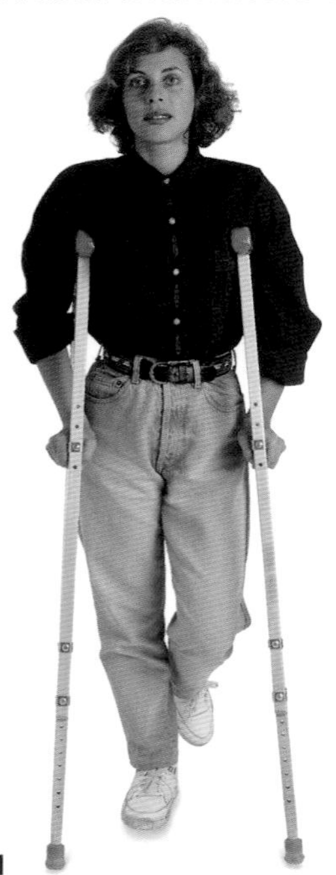
crutch 1

[1]**cry** \'krī\ *vb* **cried**; **cry•ing**
1 to shed tears : WEEP
2 to make a loud call : SHOUT, EXCLAIM ⟨"Wait!" she *cried* as the car drove away.⟩
3 to utter a special sound or call ⟨We could hear gulls *crying* through the fog.⟩

[2]**cry** *n, pl* **cries**
1 a loud call or shout (as of pain, fear, or joy)
2 [1]APPEAL 2 ⟨a *cry* for help⟩
3 an act or period of weeping ⟨When she left, I had a good *cry*.⟩
4 the special sound made by an animal ⟨a hawk's *cry*⟩

cry•ba•by \'krī-,bā-bē\ *n, pl* **cry•ba•bies**
a person who cries easily or who complains often

cryp•tic \'krip-tik\ *adj*
difficult to understand or make sense of ⟨He left a *cryptic* message.⟩

[1]**crys•tal** \'kri-st^{ə}l\ *n*
1 ► quartz that is colorless and clear or nearly so
2 a body formed by a substance hardening so that it has flat surfaces in an even arrangement ⟨an ice *crystal*⟩ ⟨a salt *crystal*⟩
3 a clear colorless glass of very good quality
4 something clear like colorless quartz
5 the clear cover over a clock or watch dial

cub 1
Newborn cubs are nourished by their mother's milk. At this early stage of life, they are helpless and dependent on parental care for survival. Within a few months they are running around and playing. As they continue to grow, they learn how to hunt for food so that they can survive on their own as adults.

tiger cub

fox cub

lion cub

[2]**crystal** *adj*
1 made of or being like a clear colorless glass of very good quality ⟨a *crystal* candy dish⟩
2 [1]CLEAR 4 ⟨a *crystal* sky⟩

crys•tal•line \'kri-stə-lən\ *adj*
1 made of crystal or composed of crystals
2 [1]CLEAR 4

crys•tal•lize \'kri-stə-,līz\ *vb* **crys•tal•lized**; **crys•tal•liz•ing**
1 to form or cause to form crystals or grains
2 to take or cause to take definite form ⟨The plan *crystallized* slowly.⟩

CT *abbr* Connecticut

ct. *abbr*
1 cent
2 court

[1]**crystal 1**

cu. *abbr* cubic

cub \'kəb\ *n*
1 ▲ the young of various animals (as the bear, fox, or lion)
2 CUB SCOUT

cub•by•hole \'kə-bē-,hōl\ *n*
a snug place (as for storing things)

[1]**cube** \'kyüb\ *n*
1 ▼ a solid body having six equal square sides
2 the product obtained by multiplying the square of a number by the number itself ⟨The number 27 is the *cube* of 3.⟩

[2]**cube** *vb* **cubed**; **cub•ing**
1 to take (a number) as a factor three times ⟨The number 3 *cubed* is 27.⟩
2 to cut food into solid squares

[1]**cube 1:**
a solid cube

cu•bic \'kyü-bik\ *adj*
1 having the shape of a cube
2 being the volume of a cube whose edge has a specified length ⟨a *cubic* centimeter⟩

cu•bit \'kyü-bət\ *n*
a unit of length usually equal to about 18 inches (46 centimeters)

Cub Scout *n*
a member of a program of the Boy Scouts for boys in the first through fifth grades in school

cuck•oo \'kü-kü, 'kü-\ *n, pl* **cuckoos**
1 ▼ a grayish brown European bird that lays eggs in the nests of other birds which hatch and raise them
2 the call of the cuckoo

cuckoo 1

cu•cum•ber \'kyü-,kəm-bər\ *n*
▼ a long usually green-skinned vegetable that is used in salads and for making pickles and is the fruit of a vine related to the melons and gourds

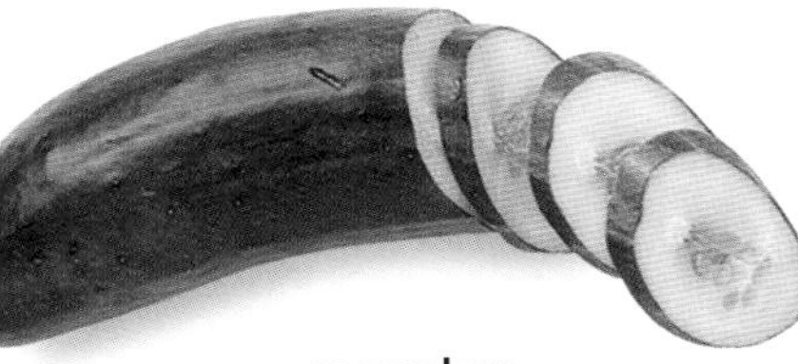
cucumber

cud \'kəd\ *n*
a portion of food brought up from the first stomach compartment of some animals (as the cow and sheep) to be chewed again

cud•dle \'kə-dᵊl\ *vb* **cud•dled**; **cud•dling**
1 to hold close for warmth or comfort or in affection
2 to lie close : NESTLE, SNUGGLE

[1]**cud•gel** \'kə-jəl\ *n*
a short heavy club

[2]**cudgel** *vb* **cud•geled** *or* **cud•gelled**; **cud•gel•ing** *or* **cud•gel•ling**
to beat with or as if with a short heavy club

[1]**cue** \'kyü\ *n*
1 something serving as a signal or suggestion : HINT ⟨The baby's whine is a *cue* she's tired.⟩
2 a word, phrase, or action in a play serving as a signal for the next actor to speak or to do something

[2]**cue** *n*
a straight tapering stick used in playing billiards and pool

[1]**cuff** \'kəf\ *n*
1 a band or turned-over piece at the end of a sleeve
2 the turned-back hem of a pant leg

[2]**cuff** *vb* **cuffed**; **cuff•ing**
to strike especially with or as if with the palm of the hand : SLAP

[3]**cuff** *n*
[2]SLAP 1

cu•li•nary \'kə-lə-,ner-ē, 'kyü-\ *adj*
of or relating to the kitchen or cooking ⟨*culinary* skills⟩

[2]**cull** *n*
something rejected from a group because it is not as good as the rest

cul•mi•nate \'kəl-mə-,nāt\ *vb* **cul•mi•nat•ed**; **cul•mi•nat•ing**
to reach the end or the final result of ⟨Her campaign *culminated* with a victory.⟩

cul•prit \'kəl-prət\ *n*
a person accused of, charged with, or guilty of a crime or fault

cul•ti•vate \'kəl-tə-,vāt\ *vb* **cul•ti•vat•ed**; **cul•ti•vat•ing**
1 to prepare land for the raising of crops ⟨*cultivate* a field⟩
2 to raise or assist the growth of crops by tilling or by labor and care ⟨*cultivate* corn⟩
3 to improve or develop by careful attention, training, or study : devote time and thought to ⟨He's trying to *cultivate* a better attitude.⟩
4 to seek the company and friendship of

cul•ti•vat•ed \'kəl-tə-,vā-təd\ *adj*
1 raised or grown on a farm or under other controlled conditions ⟨*cultivated* fruits⟩
2 having or showing good education and proper manners

cultivation 1: cultivation of a field by plowing

[1]**cull** \'kəl\ *vb* **culled**; **cull•ing**
1 to select from a group ⟨The best poems were *culled* from her collection.⟩
2 to identify and remove less desirable members from ⟨*cull* sheep from a flock⟩

cul•ti•va•tion \,kəl-tə-'vā-shən\ *n*
1 ▲ the act or process of preparing the soil for the raising of crops
2 REFINEMENT 2

cul•ti•va•tor \ˈkəl-tə-ˌvā-tər\ *n*
a tool or machine for loosening the soil between rows of a crop

cul•tur•al \ˈkəl-chə-rəl\ *adj*
1 relating to the habits, beliefs, and traditions of a certain people
2 relating to the arts (as music, dance, or painting)
cul•tur•al•ly *adv*

cul•ture \ˈkəl-chər\ *n*
1 CULTIVATION 1
2 the raising or development (as of a crop or product) by careful attention ⟨grape *culture*⟩
3 the appreciation and knowledge of the arts (as music, dance, and painting)
4 the habits, beliefs, and traditions of a particular people, place, or time ⟨Greek *culture*⟩

cul•tured \ˈkəl-chərd\ *adj*
1 having or showing refinement in taste, speech, or manners
2 produced under artificial conditions ⟨*cultured* pearls⟩

cul•vert \ˈkəl-vərt\ *n*
a drain or waterway crossing under a road or railroad

cum•ber•some \ˈkəm-bər-səm\ *adj*
hard to handle or manage because of size or weight

cu•mu•la•tive \ˈkyü-myə-lə-tiv, -ˌlā-\ *adj*
increasing (as in force, strength, amount, or importance) over time ⟨Rainy weather had a *cumulative* effect on the crops.⟩

cu•mu•lus \ˈkyü-myə-ləs\ *n, pl* **cu•mu•li** \-ˌlī, -ˌlē\
▼ a massive cloud form having a flat base and rounded outlines often piled up like a mountain

cumulus: cumulus clouds gathered in the sky

cu•ne•i•form \kyü-ˈnē-ə-ˌfȯrm\ *adj*
▼ made up of or written with marks or letters shaped like wedges
cuneiform *n*

cuneiform:
cuneiform writing on a tablet from western Asia, dating to about 2500 B.C.

[1]cun•ning \ˈkə-niŋ\ *adj*
1 skillful and clever at using special knowledge or at getting something done ⟨a *cunning* craftsman⟩
2 showing craftiness and trickery ⟨a *cunning* plot⟩ ⟨a *cunning* thief⟩

[2]cunning *n*
1 SKILL 1, DEXTERITY
2 cleverness or skill especially at tricking people in order to get something

[1]cup \ˈkəp\ *n*
1 a container to drink out of in the shape of a small bowl usually with a handle
2 the contents of a small drinking container : CUPFUL ⟨I drank a *cup* of tea.⟩
3 a unit of measure that equals half a pint or eight fluid ounces
4 a trophy in the shape of a cup with two handles
5 something like a small bowl in shape or use

[2]cup *vb* **cupped**; **cup•ping**
1 to curve the hand or hands into the shape of a small bowl
2 to put the hands in a curved shape around ⟨She *cupped* my face.⟩

cup•board \ˈkə-bərd\ *n*
▼ a closet usually with shelves for dishes or food

cupboard

cup•cake \ˈkəp-ˌkāk\ *n*
a small cake baked in a mold shaped like a cup

cup•ful \ˈkəp-ˌfu̇l\ *n, pl* **cup•fuls** \-ˌfu̇lz\ *also* **cups•ful** \ˈkəps-ˌfu̇l\
1 the amount held by a cup ⟨We served forty *cupfuls* of soup.⟩
2 a half pint : eight ounces (about 236 milliliters)

cu•pid \ˈkyü-pəd\ *n*
1 *cap* the god of love in ancient Roman mythology
2 a picture or statue of a naked child with wings holding a bow and arrow and symbolizing love

cu•po•la \ˈkyü-pə-lə\ *n*
1 a small structure built on top of a roof
2 ▶ a rounded roof or ceiling : DOME

cur \ˈkər\ *n*
a worthless or mongrel dog

cur•able \ˈkyu̇r-ə-bəl\ *adj*
possible to bring about recovery from : possible to cure ⟨a *curable* disease⟩

cu•rate \ˈkyu̇r-ət\ *n*
a member of the clergy who assists the rector or vicar of a church

cu•ra•tor \'kyu̇r-,ā-tər, kyu̇-'rā-, 'kyu̇r-ə-\ *n*
a person in charge of a museum or zoo

[1]**curb** \'kərb\ *n*
1 an enclosing border (as of stone or concrete) often along the edge of a street
2 [1]CHECK 2 〈a *curb* on rising prices〉

[2]**curb** *vb* **curbed**; **curb•ing**
to control or limit 〈*curb* spending〉 〈This will *curb* your appetite.〉

curb•ing \'kər-biŋ\ *n*
1 material for making an enclosing border along the edge of a street
2 [1]CURB 1

curd \'kərd\ *n*
the thickened or solid part of milk that separates from the whey after milk sours and is used to make cheese

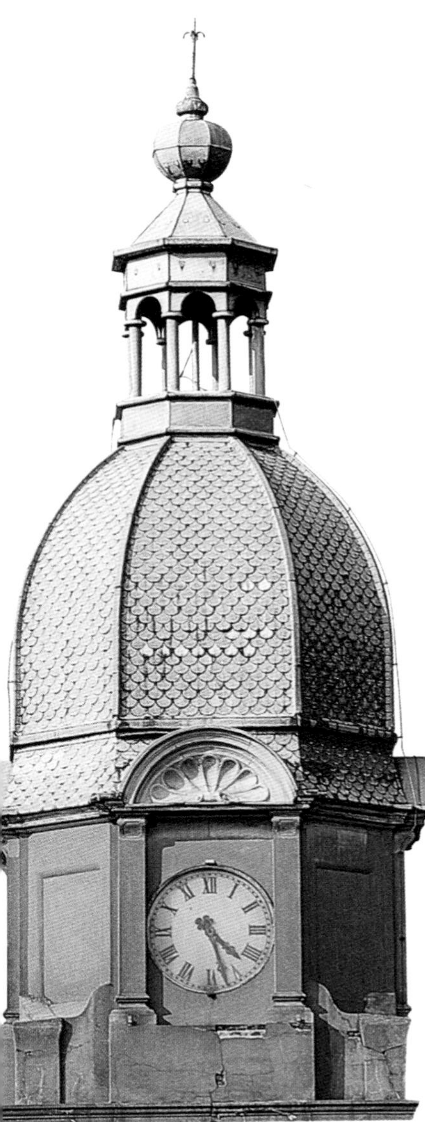

cupola 2

cur•dle \'kər-dᵊl\ *vb* **cur•dled**; **cur•dling**
to thicken or cause to become thickened with or as if with curds 〈The milk *curdled.*〉

[1]**cure** \'kyu̇r\ *n*
1 something (as a drug or medical treatment) that brings about recovery from a disease or illness : REMEDY 〈a *cure* for colds〉

currant 2

2 recovery or relief from a disease 〈His *cure* was complete.〉
3 something that solves a problem or improves a bad situation 〈Money isn't a *cure* for everything.〉

[2]**cure** *vb* **cured**; **cur•ing**
1 to make or become healthy or sound again 〈The doctor pronounced her *cured.*〉
2 to bring about recovery from 〈*cure* a disease〉
3 to prepare by or undergo a chemical or physical process for use or storage 〈*Cure* the pork in brine.〉 〈The pork is *curing.*〉
4 to provide a solution for 〈The threat of having to repeat fifth grade *cured* me of bad study habits.〉

cur•few \'kər-,fyü\ *n*
a rule requiring certain or all people to be off the streets or at home at a stated time

cu•rio \'kyu̇r-ē-,ō\ *n, pl* **cu•ri•os**
a rare or unusual article : CURIOSITY

cu•ri•os•i•ty \,kyu̇r-ē-'ä-sə-tē\ *n, pl* **cu•ri•os•i•ties**
1 an eager desire to learn and often to learn things that are another's concern 〈"What's happening?" he asked with *curiosity.*〉
2 something strange or unusual
3 an object or article valued because it is strange or rare

cu•ri•ous \'kyu̇r-ē-əs\ *adj*
1 eager to learn : INQUISITIVE 〈*Curious* onlookers gathered at the scene.〉
2 showing an eagerness to learn 〈a *curious* expression〉
3 attracting attention by being strange or unusual : ODD
cu•ri•ous•ly *adv*

[1]**curl** \'kərl\ *vb* **curled**; **curl•ing**
1 to twist or form into ringlets 〈*curl* hair〉
2 to take or move in a curved form 〈Smoke was *curling* from the chimney.〉
curl up to arrange the body into a ball 〈She likes to *curl up* in a chair.〉

[2]**curl** *n*
1 a lock of hair that coils : RINGLET
2 something having a spiral or winding form : COIL 〈a *curl* of smoke〉

cur•li•cue \'kər-li-,kyü\ *n*
a fancy shape having curves in it

curly \'kər-lē\ *adj* **curl•i•er**; **curl•i•est**
1 having coils 〈*curly* hair〉
2 having a curved shape 〈a *curly* tail〉

cur•rant \'kər-ənt\ *n*
1 a small seedless raisin used in baking and cooking
2 ◀ a sour red, white, or black edible berry that is often used in making jams and jellies

cur•ren•cy \'kər-ən-sē\ *n, pl* **cur•ren•cies**
1 common use or acceptance 〈The rumor has wide *currency.*〉
2 ▼ money in circulation

currency 2:
denominations of US currency

[1]**cur•rent** \'kər-ənt\ *adj*
1 now passing 〈the *current* month〉
2 occurring in or belonging to the present time 〈*current* events〉
3 generally and widely accepted, used, or practiced 〈*current* customs〉

[2]**current** *n*
1 a body of fluid (as air or water) moving in a specified direction
2 the swiftest part of a stream
3 the general course : TREND 〈The *current* of public opinion is in the mayor's favor.〉
4 a flow of electricity

cur•ric•u•lum \kə-'ri-kyə-ləm\ *n, pl* **cur•ric•u•la** \-lə\ *also* **cur•ric•u•lums**
all the courses of study offered by a school

cur•ry favor \'kər-ē-\ *vb* **cur•ried favor; cur•ry•ing favor**
to try to win approval by saying or doing nice things ⟨She is always *currying favor* with the teacher.⟩

[1]curse \'kərs\ *n*
1 a series of words calling for harm to come to someone
2 a word or an expression used in swearing or in calling for harm to come to someone
3 evil or misfortune that comes as if in answer to someone's request ⟨The land suffered the *curse* of drought.⟩
4 a cause of great harm or evil ⟨All this money has been nothing but a *curse*.⟩

[2]curse *vb* **cursed; curs•ing**
1 to call upon divine power to send harm or evil upon ⟨He *cursed* his enemies.⟩
2 SWEAR 1
3 to bring unhappiness or evil upon : AFFLICT
4 to say or think bad things about (someone or something) ⟨He *cursed* the unfairness of the world.⟩

cur•sive \'kər-siv\ *n*
▼ a type of handwriting in which all the letters of a word are connected to each other
cursive *adj*

cursive: a letter written in cursive

cur•sor \'kər-sər, -,sȯr\ *n*
a symbol (as an arrow or blinking line) on a computer screen that shows where the user is working

cur•so•ry \'kərs-rē, 'kər-sə-rē\ *adj*
done or made quickly ⟨a *cursory* reply⟩

curt \'kərt\ *adj* **curt•er; curt•est**
rudely brief in language ⟨a *curt* answer⟩
curt•ly *adv*

cur•tail \,kər-'tāl\ *vb* **cur•tailed; cur•tail•ing**
to shorten or reduce by cutting off the end or a part of ⟨I had to *curtail* my speech.⟩

theatre curtain with tassels

[1]cur•tain \'kər-tᵊn\ *n*
1 ► a piece of material (as cloth) hung up to darken, hide, divide, or decorate
2 something that covers, hides, or separates like a curtain ⟨a *curtain* of fog⟩

[2]curtain *vb* **cur•tained; cur•tain•ing**
1 to furnish with cloth that darkens, hides, divides, or decorates
2 to hide or shut off

[1]curtain 1

[1]curt•sy *also* **curt•sey** \'kərt-sē\ *vb* **curt•sied** *also* **curt•seyed; curt•sy•ing** *also* **curt•sey•ing**
to lower the body slightly by bending the knees as an act of politeness or respect

[2]curtsy *also* **curtsey** *n, pl* **curtsies** *also* **curtseys**
► an act of politeness or respect made by women and consisting of a slight lowering of the body by bending the knees

cur•va•ture \'kər-və-,chu̇r\ *n*
a part having a somewhat round shape

[1]curve \'kərv\ *vb* **curved; curv•ing**
to turn or cause to turn from a straight line or course ⟨The road *curved* to the left.⟩

[2]curve *n*
1 a smooth rounded line or surface ⟨Slow down! There's a *curve* in the road.⟩
2 something having a somewhat round shape ⟨the *curves* of the body⟩
3 a ball thrown so that it moves away from a straight course

[1]cush•ion \'ku̇-shən\ *n*
1 ▼ a soft pillow or pad to rest on or against
2 something soft like a pad ⟨Moss formed a *cushion* on the ground.⟩
3 something that serves to soften or lessen the effects of something bad or unpleasant

[1]cushion 1: a pair of cushions

[2]cushion *vb* **cush•ioned; cush•ion•ing**
1 to place on or as if on a soft pillow or pad
2 to furnish with a soft pillow or pad
3 to soften or lessen the force or shock of ⟨The soft sand *cushioned* her fall.⟩

cusp \'kəsp\ *n*
a point or pointed end ⟨the *cusp* of a tooth⟩

cus•pid \'kəs-pəd\ *n*
[1]CANINE 1

cuss \'kəs\ *vb* **cussed; cuss•ing**
SWEAR 1

cus•tard \'kə-stərd\ *n*
a sweetened mixture of milk and eggs baked, boiled, or frozen

[2]curtsy: a girl making a curtsy

cus•to•di•an \,kə-'stō-dē-ən\ *n*
a person who guards and protects or takes care of ⟨the school *custodian*⟩

cus•to•dy \'kə-stə-dē\ *n*
1 direct responsibility for care and control ⟨The boy is in the *custody* of his parents.⟩
2 the state of being arrested or held by police ⟨has the suspect in *custody*⟩

[1]**cus•tom** \'kə-stəm\ *n*
1 the usual way of doing things **:** the usual practice
2 customs *pl* duties or taxes paid on imports or exports
3 support given to a business by its customers

[2]**custom** *adj*
1 made or done to personal order ⟨*custom* furniture⟩
2 specializing in work done to personal order ⟨a *custom* printer⟩

cus•tom•ary \'kə-stə-,mer-ē\ *adj*
1 usual in a particular situation or at a particular place or time
2 typical of a particular person ⟨her *customary* cheerfulness⟩

cus•tom•er \'kə-stə-mər\ *n*
a person who buys from or uses the services of a company especially regularly

[1]**cut** \'kət\ *vb* **cut**; **cut•ting**
1 to penetrate or divide with or as if with an edged tool ⟨*cut* a finger⟩
2 to undergo shaping or penetrating with an edged tool ⟨Cheese *cuts* easily.⟩
3 to divide into two or more parts ⟨*cut* a deck of cards⟩ ⟨Would you *cut* the cake?⟩
4 to shorten or remove with scissors, a knife, or clippers
5 to go by a short or direct path or course ⟨We *cut* across the lawn.⟩
6 to destroy the connection of ⟨Soldiers *cut* electricity to the enemy.⟩
7 to intentionally not attend ⟨*cut* class⟩
8 to move quickly or suddenly ⟨The driver *cut* across two lanes of traffic.⟩
9 to make less ⟨*cut* costs⟩
10 to experience the growth of through the gum ⟨The baby is *cutting* teeth.⟩
11 to stop or cause to stop ⟨*Cut* the motor.⟩ ⟨*Cut* that whispering.⟩
12 to cause painful feelings ⟨That remark really *cut*.⟩
13 to shape by carving or grinding ⟨*cut* a gem⟩
14 to remove (something) from a computer document in a way that allows you to move it to another part of the document or to another document

cut back
1 to use less or do less of ⟨I *cut back* on watching TV.⟩
2 to reduce the size or amount of ⟨You'll have to *cut back* on your plans.⟩

cut down
1 to knock down and wound or kill
2 to reduce the size or amount of ⟨The new route *cuts down* our travel time.⟩
3 to use less or do less of ⟨I'm *cutting down* on sweets.⟩

cutout: paper cutouts

cut in INTERRUPT 1

cut into to reduce the amount of ⟨The increase in supply costs *cut into* their profit.⟩

cut off
1 ISOLATE ⟨The flood *cut* us *off* from the rest of the city.⟩
2 DISCONTINUE ⟨His father threatened to *cut off* his allowance.⟩
3 to stop or interrupt while speaking ⟨She always *cuts* me *off* while I'm talking.⟩

cut out
1 to form by removing with scissors, a knife, or a saw
2 to assign through necessity ⟨You've got your work *cut out* for you.⟩
3 to put an end to ⟨*Cut out* that nonsense!⟩

[2]**cut** *n*
1 something (as a gash or wound) produced by a sharp object
2 REDUCTION 1 ⟨He took a *cut* in pay.⟩
3 something resulting from shortening, division, or removal ⟨a *cut* of beef⟩
4 [1]SHARE 1 ⟨They took their *cut* of the winnings.⟩
5 a sharp stroke or blow
6 the way in which a thing is styled, formed, or made ⟨the *cut* of the pants⟩
7 something done or said that hurts someone's feelings

cute \'kyüt\ *adj* **cut•er**; **cut•est**
1 attractive in looks or actions ⟨a *cute* puppy⟩
2 CLEVER 2 ⟨a *cute* story⟩
3 clever in a way that annoys ⟨Don't be *cute* with me!⟩

cu•ti•cle \'kyü-ti-kəl\ *n*
1 an outer layer (as of skin or a leaf) often produced by the cells beneath
2 a dead or hard layer of skin especially around a fingernail

cut•lass \'kət-ləs\ *n*
a short heavy curved sword

cut•lery \'kət-lə-rē\ *n*
1 cutting tools (as knives and scissors)
2 utensils used in cutting, serving, and eating food

cut•let \'kət-lət\ *n*
1 a small thin slice of meat
2 meat, fish, or vegetables pressed into a flat piece, covered with bread crumbs, and fried in oil

cut•out \'kət-,au̇t\ *n*
▲ a shape or picture that is cut from some material (as cardboard or wood)

cut•ter \'kə-tər\ *n*
1 someone or something that cuts ⟨a diamond *cutter*⟩ ⟨a cookie *cutter*⟩
2 a boat used by warships for carrying passengers and stores to and from the shore
3 a small sailing boat with one mast
4 a small military ship ⟨a coast guard *cutter*⟩

cut•ting \'kə-tiŋ\ *n*
a part (as a shoot) of a plant able to grow into a whole new plant

cut•tle•fish \'kə-t^{ə}l-,fish\ *n*
▼ a sea animal with ten arms that is related to the squid and octopus

cut•up \'kət-,əp\ *n*
a person who behaves in a silly way and tries to make other people laugh

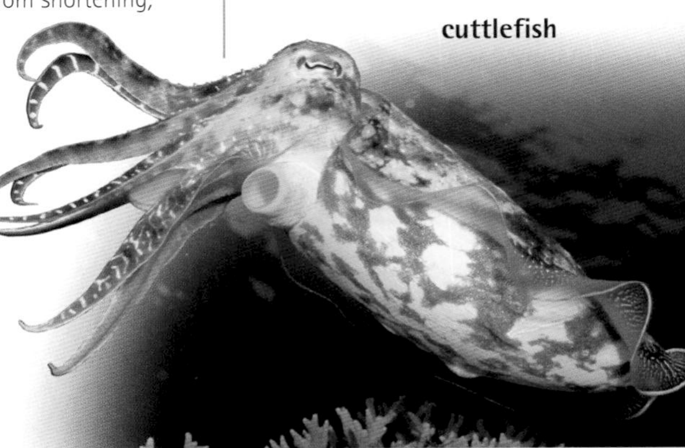
cuttlefish

cut•worm \ˈkət-ˌwərm\ *n*
a moth caterpillar that has a smooth body and feeds on the stems of plants at night

-cy \sē\ *n suffix, pl* **-cies**
1 action : practice ⟨*piracy*⟩
2 rank : office
3 body : class
4 state : quality ⟨accura*cy*⟩ ⟨bankrupt*cy*⟩

cy•a•nide \ˈsī-ə-ˌnīd\ *n*
any of several compounds containing carbon and nitrogen and including two very poisonous substances

cyber- *prefix*
relating to computers or computer networks

cy•ber•bul•ly•ing \ˈsī-bər-ˌbu̇-lē-iŋ\ *n*
the act of bullying someone through electronic means (as by posting mean or threatening messages about the person online)

cy•ber•space \ˈsī-bər-ˌspās\ *n*
the online world of computer networks and especially the Internet

cy•cad \ˈsī-kəd\ *n*
► a tropical plant like a palm but related to the conifers

¹cy•cle \ˈsī-kəl\ *n*
1 a period of time taken up by a series of events or actions that repeat themselves again and again in the same order ⟨the *cycle* of the seasons⟩
2 a complete round or series ⟨The dishwasher started its drying *cycle*.⟩
3 ¹BICYCLE
4 MOTORCYCLE

²cycle *vb* **cy•cled; cy•cling**
to ride a bicycle or motorcycle

cy•clist \ˈsī-kləst\ *n*
a person who rides a bicycle

cy•clone \ˈsī-ˌklōn\ *n*
1 a storm or system of winds that rotates about a center of low atmospheric pressure and that moves forward at a speed of 20 to 30 miles (30 to 50 kilometers) an hour and often brings heavy rain
2 TORNADO

cyl•in•der \ˈsi-lən-dər\ *n*
a long round body whether hollow or solid

cy•lin•dri•cal \sə-ˈlin-dri-kəl\ *adj*
having a long round shape

cycad: a cycad tree

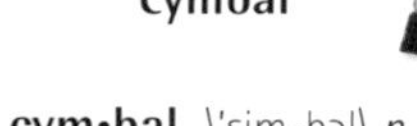

cymbal

cym•bal \ˈsim-bəl\ *n*
▲ a musical instrument in the form of a brass plate that is struck with a drumstick or is used in pairs struck together

cyn•i•cal \ˈsi-nə-kəl\ *adj*
believing that people are selfish and dishonest

cy•press \ˈsī-prəs\ *n*
an evergreen tree or shrub with small overlapping leaves resembling scales

cyst \ˈsist\ *n*
1 an abnormal lump or sac that forms in or on the body
2 a saclike structure with a protective covering or a body (as a spore) with such a covering

cy•to•plasm \ˈsī-tə-ˌpla-zəm\ *n*
the jellylike material that fills most of the space in a cell and surrounds the nucleus

CZ *abbr* Canal Zone

czar \ˈzär\ *n*
a male ruler of Russia before 1917

cza•ri•na \zä-ˈrē-nə\ *n*
1 a female ruler of Russia before 1917
2 the wife of a czar

Sounds of D: The letter **D** makes one main sound, the sound heard in the words ***did*** and ***adult***. At the end of some words, such as the word ***finished***, **D** sounds like a **T**. Letter **D** sometimes sounds like a **J**, as in the word ***procedure***. The combination of **D** and **G** also makes the **J** sound, as in ***bridge***.

d \ˈdē\ *n, pl* **d's** *or* **ds** \ˈdēz\ *often cap*
1 the fourth letter of the English alphabet
2 500 in Roman numerals
3 a grade that shows a student's work is poor
4 a musical note referred to by the letter D

d. *abbr*
1 day
2 dead
3 deceased
4 penny

[1]**dab** \ˈdab\ *n*
1 a small amount ⟨Add a *dab* of butter.⟩
2 a light quick touch

[2]**dab** *vb* **dabbed**; **dab•bing**
1 to strike or touch lightly
2 to apply with light or uneven strokes

dab•ble \ˈda-bəl\ *vb* **dab•bled**; **dab•bling**
1 to wet by splashing : SPATTER
2 to paddle or play in or as if in water ⟨Ducks *dabbled* in the pond.⟩
3 to work without any deep involvement ⟨I just *dabble* with art.⟩
dab•bler \ˈda-blər\ *n*

dace \ˈdās\ *n, pl* **dace**
▼ a small freshwater fish related to the carp

dace

dachshund: a smooth-haired dachshund

dachs•hund \ˈdäks-ˌhu̇nt, ˈdäk-sənt\ *n*
▲ a small dog of German origin with a long body, short legs, and long drooping ears

▶ **Word History** Several centuries ago, the Germans developed a dog with short legs and a long body. These dogs were used to hunt burrowing animals such as badgers. Because of their shape, the dogs could follow a badger right down its hole. The Germans gave these dogs the name *Dachshund*, a compound word formed from *Dachs*, "badger," and *Hund*, "dog." The English word *dachshund* came from this German name.

dad \ˈdad\ *n*
[1]FATHER 1

dad•dy \ˈda-dē\ *n, pl* **daddies**
[1]FATHER 1

dad•dy long•legs \ˌda-dē-ˈlȯŋ-ˌlegz\ *n, pl* **daddy longlegs**
1 a small animal like the related spider but with longer more slender legs
2 a fly with long legs that resembles a large mosquito but does not bite

daf•fo•dil \ˈda-fə-ˌdil\ *n*
▶ a plant that grows from a bulb and has long slender leaves and usually yellow or white flowers with petals whose inner parts are arranged to form a trumpet-shaped tube

daf•fy \ˈda-fē\ *adj* **daf•fi•er**; **daf•fi•est**
silly or oddly funny

daft \ˈdaft\ *adj* **daft•er**; **daft•est**
FOOLISH, CRAZY

dag•ger \ˈda-gər\ *n*
a short knife used for stabbing

dahl•ia \ˈdal-yə, ˈdäl-\ *n*
a plant related to the daisies and grown for its brightly colored flowers

[1]**dai•ly** \ˈdā-lē\ *adj*
1 occurring, done, produced, appearing, or used every day or every weekday ⟨Be sure to get your *daily* exercise.⟩
2 figured by the day ⟨a *daily* wage⟩

[2]**daily** *adv*
every day ⟨She jogs three miles *daily*.⟩

[3]**daily** *n, pl* **dai•lies**
a newspaper published every weekday

[1]**dain•ty** \ˈdān-tē\ *n, pl* **dain•ties**
a delicious food : DELICACY

[2]**dainty** *adj* **dain•ti•er**; **dain•ti•est**
1 tasting good
2 pretty in a delicate way ⟨*dainty* flowers⟩
3 having or showing delicate or finicky taste ⟨He is a *dainty* eater.⟩
dain•ti•ly \ˈdān-tə-lē\ *adv*

dairy \ˈder-ē\ *n, pl* **dair•ies**
1 a place where milk is stored or is made into butter and cheese
2 a farm that produces milk
3 a company or a store that sells milk products

da•is \ˈdā-əs\ *n*
a raised platform (as in a hall or large room) ⟨The guest speaker stood on the *dais*.⟩

daffodil

a b c d e f g h i j k l m n o p q r s t u v w x y z

dai•sy \'dā-zē\ *n, pl* **daisies**
a plant with flower heads consisting of one or more rows of white or colored flowers like petals around a central disk of tiny often yellow flowers closely packed together

► **Word History** The modern English word *daisy* descends from an Old English word *dægesēage* that means literally "day's eye." The yellow center of a daisy looks a bit like the sun, and the sun may be thought of as the bright eye of the day.

Da•ko•ta \də-'kō-tə\ *n, pl* **Da•ko•tas** *also* **Dakota**
1 a member of an American Indian people of the area that is now Minnesota, North Dakota, and South Dakota
2 the language of the Dakota people

dale \'dāl\ *n*
VALLEY

dal•ly \'da-lē\ *vb* **dal•lied**; **dal•ly•ing**
1 to act playfully ⟨Boys and girls *dallied* at the dance.⟩
2 to waste time ⟨I *dallied* at my desk and didn't finish my homework.⟩

dalmatian

3 LINGER 1, DAWDLE ⟨Don't *dally* on your way home.⟩

dal•ma•tian \dal-'mā-shən\ *n, often cap*
▲ a large dog having a short white coat with black or brown spots

¹dam \'dam\ *n*
the female parent of a domestic animal (as a dog or horse)

²dam *n*
► a barrier (as across a stream) to hold back a flow of water

³dam *vb* **dammed**; **dam•ming**
to hold back or block with or as if with a dam ⟨Leaves *dammed* the drains.⟩

¹dam•age \'da-mij\ *n*
1 loss or harm caused by injury to a person's body or property ⟨How much *damage* was done to the car?⟩
2 **damages** *pl* money demanded or paid according to law for injury or damage
synonyms see HARM

²damage *vb* **dam•aged**; **dam•ag•ing**
to cause harm or loss to

dame \'dām\ *n*
a woman of high rank or social position

¹damn \'dam\ *vb* **damned**; **damn•ing**
1 to condemn to everlasting punishment especially in hell
2 to declare to be bad or a failure
3 to swear at : CURSE

²damn *or* **damned** \'damd\ *adj*
1 very bad ⟨the *damn* weather⟩
2 used to make a statement more forceful ⟨These bugs are a *damned* nuisance.⟩
Hint: This word is considered impolite, and you may offend people by using it.

¹damp \'damp\ *n*
1 MOISTURE ⟨The cold and *damp* made me shiver.⟩
2 a harmful gas found especially in coal mines

²damp *vb* **damped**; **damp•ing**
DAMPEN

³damp *adj* **damp•er**; **damp•est**
slightly wet : MOIST
damp•ness *n*

damp•en \'dam-pən\ *vb* **damp•ened**; **damp•en•ing**
1 to make or become slighty wet ⟨Please *dampen* this washcloth.⟩
2 to make dull or less active ⟨A bad start didn't *dampen* our confidence.⟩

damp•er \'dam-pər\ *n*
1 something that discourages or deadens ⟨The rain put a *damper* on our picnic.⟩
2 a valve or movable plate for controlling a flow of air

dam•sel \'dam-zəl\ *n*
GIRL 1, MAIDEN

¹dance \'dans\ *vb* **danced**; **danc•ing**
1 to step or move through a series of movements usually in time to music

► **²dam**
Most dams are built across river valleys to control flooding, create a reservoir for water storage, or provide hydroelectric power. Often constructed from reinforced concrete, dams are designed to suit the size and shape of a valley, and the types of rock and soil present.

Glen Canyon Dam on the Colorado River, Arizona

2 to move about or up and down quickly and lightly ⟨Butterflies *danced* in the garden.⟩
danc•er *n*

[2]dance *n*
1 an act of stepping or moving through a series of movements usually in time to music
2 a social gathering for dancing
3 a set of movements or steps for dancing usually in time to special music ⟨The samba is a popular *dance* of Brazil.⟩
4 the art of dancing ⟨She is studying *dance*.⟩

dan•de•li•on \'dan-də-,lī-ən\ *n*
▼ a weedy plant that has bright yellow flowers with hollow stems and leaves that are sometimes used as food

dandelion

dan•der \'dan-dər\ *n*
1 tiny scales from hair, feathers, or skin that may cause allergic reactions
2 [2]ANGER ⟨The insults got my *dander* up.⟩

dan•druff \'dan-drəf\ *n*
thin dry whitish flakes of dead skin that form on the scalp and come off freely

[1]dan•dy \'dan-dē\ *n, pl* **dandies**
1 a man who is extremely interested in his clothes and appearance
2 something excellent or unusual

[2]dandy *adj* **dan•di•er**; **dan•di•est**
very good ⟨We had a *dandy* time.⟩

Dane \'dān\ *n*
a person born or living in Denmark

dan•ger \'dān-jər\ *n*
1 the state of not being protected from harm or evil : PERIL ⟨With my cat around, the mice are in *danger*.⟩
2 something that may cause injury or harm ⟨Astronauts brave the *dangers* of space travel.⟩

► **Synonyms** DANGER, HAZARD, and RISK mean a chance of loss, injury, or death. DANGER is used for a harm that may or may not be avoided. ⟨This animal is in *danger* of extinction.⟩ HAZARD is usually used for a great danger. ⟨They're trying to reduce the *hazards* of mining.⟩ RISK is used for a chance of danger that a person accepts. ⟨There are *risks* that come with flying a plane.⟩

dan•ger•ous \'dān-jə-rəs, 'dānj-rəs\ *adj*
1 involving possible harm or death : full of danger ⟨*dangerous* work⟩
2 able or likely to injure ⟨A chain saw is a *dangerous* tool.⟩
dan•ger•ous•ly *adv*

dan•gle \'daŋ-gəl\ *vb* **dan•gled**; **dan•gling**
1 to hang loosely especially with a swinging motion
2 to cause to hang loosely ⟨We *dangled* our feet in the water.⟩

[1]Dan•ish \'dā-nish\ *adj*
belonging to or relating to Denmark, the Danes, or the Danish language

[2]Danish *n*
1 the language of the Danes
2 a piece of Danish pastry

Danish pastry

Danish pastry *n*
▲ a pastry made of rich raised dough

dank \'daŋk\ *adj* **dank•er**; **dank•est**
unpleasantly wet or moist ⟨a *dank* cave⟩

dap•per \'da-pər\ *adj*
neat and trim in dress or appearance

dap•ple \'da-pəl\ *vb* **dap•pled**; **dap•pling**
► to mark or become marked with rounded spots of color ⟨a *dappled* horse⟩

[1]dare \'der\ *vb* **dared**; **dar•ing**
1 to have courage enough for some purpose : be bold enough ⟨Try it if you *dare*.⟩ — sometimes used as a helping verb ⟨We *dared* not say a word.⟩
2 to challenge to do something especially as a proof of courage ⟨I *dare* you to jump.⟩
3 to face with courage ⟨They *dared* the dangerous crossing.⟩

[2]dare *n*
a challenge to do something as proof of courage

dare•dev•il \'der-,dev-əl\ *n*
a person who does dangerous things especially for attention

[1]dar•ing \'der-iŋ\ *adj*
ready to take risks : BOLD, VENTURESOME ⟨a *daring* explorer⟩
synonyms see ADVENTUROUS

[2]daring *n*
bold fearlessness : readiness to take chances

[1]dark \'därk\ *adj* **dark•er**; **dark•est**
1 without light or without much light ⟨a *dark* closet⟩
2 not light in color ⟨My dog has a *dark* coat.⟩
3 not bright and cheerful : GLOOMY ⟨Don't look on the *dark* side of things.⟩
4 arising from or characterized by evil ⟨The villain revealed his *dark* side.⟩

[2]dark *n*
1 absence of light : DARKNESS ⟨I'm not afraid of the *dark*.⟩
2 a place or time of little or no light ⟨We got home before *dark*.⟩

Dark Ages *n pl*
the period of European history from about A.D. 476 to about 1000

dark•en \'där-kən\ *vb* **dark•ened**; **dark•en•ing**
1 to make or grow dark or darker
2 to make or become gloomy ⟨Her mood *darkened* with the news.⟩

dark•ly \'därk-lē\ *adv*
1 with a dark or blackish color ⟨a *darkly* painted room⟩
2 with a gloomy or threatening manner or quality ⟨"It's hopeless," he said *darkly*.⟩

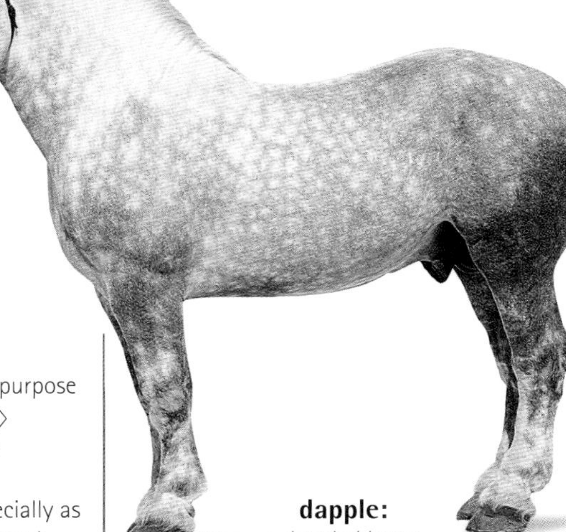

dapple: a dappled horse

dark•ness \'därk-nəs\ *n*
1 absence of light ⟨The room was in *darkness*.⟩
2 NIGHT 1 ⟨We were already in bed when *darkness* fell.⟩
3 ^{2}EVIL 1, WICKEDNESS

speedometer
fuel gauge
air-conditioning vents

dashboard with steering wheel in an automobile

dark•room \'därk-,rüm, -,rům\ *n*
a usually small dark room used in developing photographic plates and film

^{1}**dar•ling** \'där-liŋ\ *n*
1 a dearly loved person
2 ^{1}FAVORITE ⟨He is the *darling* of golf fans.⟩

^{2}**darling** *adj*
1 dearly loved ⟨Come here, *darling* child.⟩
2 very pleasing : CHARMING ⟨a *darling* little house⟩

^{1}**darn** \'därn\ *vb* **darned**; **darn•ing**
to mend by sewing

^{2}**darn** *interj*
used to express anger or annoyance

^{3}**darn** *or* **darned** \'därnd\ *adj*
1 very bad ⟨That *darned* dog!⟩
2 used to make a statement more forceful ⟨a *darn* good meal⟩

darning needle *n*
DRAGONFLY

^{1}**dart** \'därt\ *n*
1 ► a small pointed object that is meant to be thrown
2 **darts** *pl* a game in which darts are thrown at a target
3 a quick sudden movement
4 a fold sewed into a piece of clothing

^{2}**dart** *vb* **dart•ed**; **dart•ing**
to move or shoot out suddenly and quickly ⟨A toad *darted* out its tongue.⟩

^{1}**dash** \'dash\ *vb* **dashed**; **dash•ing**
1 to knock, hurl, or shove violently ⟨The storm *dashed* the boat against a reef.⟩
2 ^{2}SMASH 1 ⟨He *dashed* the plate to pieces.⟩
3 ^{1}SPLASH 2 ⟨She *dashed* water on her face.⟩
4 ^{1}RUIN 2 ⟨Their hopes were *dashed*.⟩
5 to complete or do hastily ⟨He *dashed* off a note before leaving.⟩
6 to move with sudden speed ⟨The boys *dashed* up the stairs.⟩

^{2}**dash** *n*
1 a sudden burst or splash ⟨a *dash* of cold water⟩
2 a punctuation mark — that is used most often to show a break in the thought or structure of a sentence
3 a small amount : TOUCH ⟨Add a *dash* of salt.⟩

^{1}**dart 1:**
dart shown with a target

4 liveliness in style and action ⟨A scarf adds *dash* to the outfit.⟩
5 a sudden rush or attempt ⟨a *dash* for the goal⟩
6 a short fast race ⟨100-yard *dash*⟩
7 a long click or buzz forming a letter or part of a letter (as in Morse code)
8 DASHBOARD

dash•board \'dash-,bȯrd\ *n*
◄ a panel across an automobile or aircraft below the windshield usually containing dials and controls

dash•ing \'da-shiŋ\ *adj*
very attractive ⟨The groom looked *dashing* in his tuxedo.⟩

das•tard•ly \'da-stərd-lē\ *adj*
very mean and tricky ⟨a *dastardly* deed⟩ ⟨They nabbed the *dastardly* traitor.⟩

da•ta \'dā-tə, 'da-tə\ *n pl*
1 facts about something that can be used in calculating, reasoning, or planning
2 information expressed as numbers for use especially in a computer
Hint: *Data* can be used as a singular or a plural. ⟨This *data* is useful.⟩ ⟨These *data* have been questioned.⟩

da•ta•base \'dā-tə-,bās, 'da-\ *n*
a collection of data that is organized especially to be used by a computer

^{1}**date** \'dāt\ *n*
▼ the sweet brownish fruit of an Old World palm (date palm)

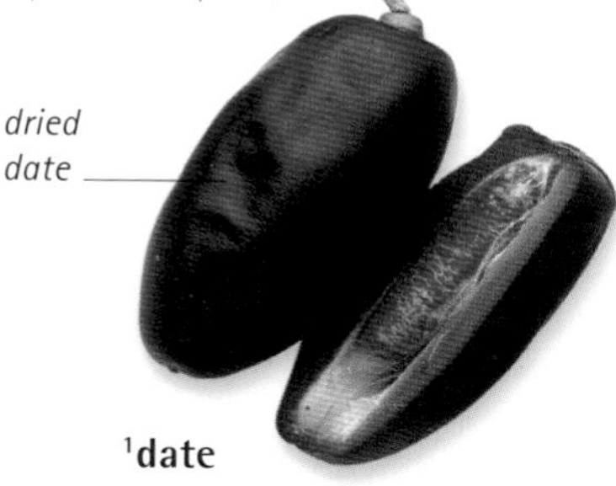

^{1}**date**

► **Word History** The English word for the fruit of the date palm comes by way of French and Latin from a Greek word *daktylos*. The original meaning of this Greek word was "finger," but it was also used for the fruit. A cluster of dates on a palm tree must have looked to someone like the fingers on a hand.

^{2}**date** *n*
1 the day, month, or year on which an event happens or happened ⟨What is your *date* of birth?⟩
2 a statement of time on something (as a coin, letter, book, or building) ⟨Write the *date* on your paper.⟩

A B C D E F G H I J K L M N O P Q R S T U V W X Y Z

3 APPOINTMENT 1
4 an arrangement to meet between two people usually with romantic feelings for each other 〈It's not a *date*—we're just friends.〉
5 either of two people who meet for a usually romantic social engagement 〈Do you have a *date* for the dance?〉

[3]**date** *vb* **dat•ed**; **dat•ing**
1 to write the date on 〈Be sure to *date* the letter.〉
2 to find or show the date or age of 〈Scientists *dated* the fossil.〉
3 to belong to or have survived from a time 〈My house *dates* from colonial times.〉
4 to make or have a date with 〈I'm *dating* him tonight.〉
5 to go together regularly on romantic social engagements 〈They've been *dating* for a year.〉

da•tum \'dā-təm, 'da-, 'dä-\ *n, pl* **da•ta** \-tə\ *or* **da•tums**
a single piece of information : FACT

[1]**daub** \'dȯb\ *vb* **daubed**; **daub•ing**
to cover with something soft and sticky 〈I *daubed* the wound with ointment.〉

[2]**daub** *n*
a small amount of something 〈The child left *daubs* of paint on the easel.〉

daugh•ter \'dȯ-tər\ *n*
1 a female child or offspring
2 a woman or girl associated with or thought of as a child of something (as a country, race, or religion) 〈The book tells the stories of two *daughters* of Africa.〉

daugh•ter–in–law \'dȯ-tər-ən-,lȯ\ *n, pl* **daugh•ters–in–law**
the wife of a person's son

daunt \'dȯnt\ *vb* **daunt•ed**; **daunt•ing**
DISCOURAGE 1, FRIGHTEN 〈The dangers didn't *daunt* them.〉

daunt•ing \'dȯn-tiŋ\ *adj*
likely to discourage or frighten

daunt•less \'dȯnt-ləs\ *adj*
bravely determined 〈The *dauntless* pilot performed dangerous maneuvers.〉

daw•dle \'dȯ-dᵊl\ *vb* **daw•dled**; **daw•dling**
1 to spend time wastefully : DALLY 〈If you *dawdle*, you'll never finish.〉
2 to move slowly and without purpose 〈Don't *dawdle* in the hall.〉

[1]**dawn** \'dȯn\ *vb* **dawned**; **dawn•ing**
1 to begin to grow light as the sun rises 〈Morning *dawned* bright and clear.〉
2 to start becoming plain or clear 〈It *dawned* on us that we were lost.〉

[2]**dawn** *n*
1 the time when the sun comes up in the morning
2 a first appearance : BEGINNING 〈Early rockets marked the *dawn* of the space age.〉

day \'dā\ *n*
1 ▼ the time between sunrise and sunset : DAYLIGHT
2 the time a planet or moon takes to make one turn on its axis 〈A *day* on earth lasts 24 hours.〉
3 a period of 24 hours beginning at midnight 〈The offer expires in ten *days*.〉
4 a specified day or date 〈Tuesday is Election *Day*.〉
5 a particular time : AGE 〈There was no Internet in your grandparent's *day*.〉
6 the time set apart by custom or law for work 〈He works an eight-hour *day*.〉

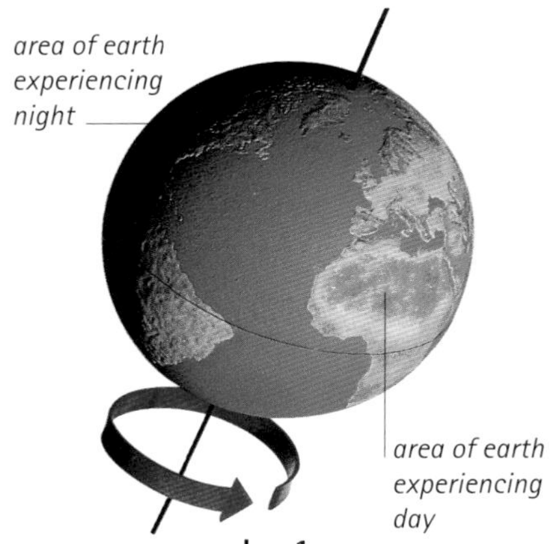

day 1:
model of the earth showing day and night

day•break \'dā-,brāk\ *n*
[2]DAWN 1

day care *n*
a program in which or a place where care is provided during the day for young children

[1]**day•dream** \'dā-,drēm\ *n*
a person's pleasant and usually wishful thoughts about life

[2]**daydream** *vb* **day•dreamed**; **day•dream•ing**
to think pleasant and usually wishful thoughts while awake

day•light \'dā-,līt\ *n*
1 the light of day
2 DAYTIME 〈They travel only during *daylight*.〉
3 [2]DAWN 1

daylight saving time *n*
time usually one hour ahead of standard time

day•time \'dā-,tīm\ *n*
the period of daylight

[1]**daze** \'dāz\ *vb* **dazed**; **daz•ing**
1 to stun by or as if by a blow 〈She was *dazed* by all the questions.〉
2 to dazzle with light 〈Headlights *dazed* the crossing deer.〉

[2]**daze** *n*
a state of not being able to think or act as quickly as normal

daz•zle \'da-zəl\ *vb* **daz•zled**; **daz•zling**
1 to overpower with too much light 〈The desert sunlight *dazzled* us.〉
2 to confuse, surprise, or delight by being or doing something special and unusual 〈The magician's tricks *dazzled* the audience.〉
daz•zling•ly \'daz-liŋ-lē\ *adv*

DC *abbr*
1 *or* **D.C.** District of Columbia
2 direct current

DDS *abbr* doctor of dental surgery

DDT \,dē-,dē-'tē\ *n*
a chemical that was used as an insecticide until it was found to damage the environment

DE *abbr* Delaware

de– *prefix*
1 do the opposite of 〈*de*code〉
2 reverse of 〈*de*segregation〉
3 remove or remove from something 〈*de*forest〉
4 reduce
5 get off of 〈*de*rail〉

dea•con \'dē-kən\ *n*
1 an official in some Christian churches ranking just below a priest
2 a church member in some Christian churches who has special duties

[1]**dead** \'ded\ *adj*
1 no longer living
2 having the look of death 〈a *dead* faint〉
3 [1]NUMB 1
4 very tired 〈That was hard work. I'm *dead*.〉
5 lacking motion, activity, energy, or power to function 〈a *dead* battery〉
6 no longer in use 〈*dead* languages〉
7 no longer active 〈a *dead* volcano〉
8 lacking warmth or vigor 〈Make sure the fire is *dead*.〉
9 not lively 〈This party is *dead*.〉
10 ACCURATE, PRECISE 〈a *dead* shot〉
11 being sudden and complete 〈The ride came to a *dead* stop.〉
12 [1]COMPLETE 1, TOTAL 〈*dead* silence〉
13 facing certain punishment 〈If we get caught, we're *dead*.〉

[2]**dead** *n, pl* **dead**
1 a person who is no longer alive
Hint: This sense of *dead* is usually used for all people who are no longer alive. 〈the living and the *dead*〉
2 the time of greatest quiet or least activity 〈the *dead* of night〉

[3]**dead** *adv*
1 in a whole or complete manner 〈*dead* tired〉
2 suddenly and completely 〈stopped *dead*〉
3 [2]STRAIGHT 2 〈*dead* ahead〉

a b c d e f g h i j k l m n o p q r s t u v w x y z

dead•en \'de-dᵊn\ *vb* **dead•ened**; **dead•en•ing**
to take away some of the force of : make less ⟨Medicine will *deaden* the pain.⟩

dead end *n*
an end (as of a street) with no way out

dead•line \'ded-,līn\ *n*
a date or time by which something must be done

[1]**dead•lock** \'ded-,läk\ *n*
a situation in which a disagreement cannot be ended because neither side will give in

[2]**deadlock** *vb* **dead•locked**; **dead•lock•ing**
to be unable to end a disagreement because neither side will give in

[1]**dead•ly** \'ded-lē\ *adj* **dead•li•er**; **dead•li•est**
1 causing or capable of causing death ⟨*deadly* poisons⟩
2 meaning or hoping to kill or destroy ⟨*deadly* enemies⟩
3 very accurate ⟨He shot the arrow with *deadly* aim.⟩
4 [1]EXTREME 1 ⟨*deadly* seriousness⟩

> ▶ **Synonyms** DEADLY, MORTAL, and FATAL mean causing or capable of causing death. DEADLY is used of something that is certain or very likely to cause death. ⟨The mushroom contains a *deadly* poison.⟩ MORTAL is used of something that already has caused death or is about to cause death. ⟨He received a *mortal* wound in battle.⟩ FATAL is used when death is certain to follow. ⟨The wounds proved to be *fatal*.⟩

[2]**deadly** *adv*
1 in a way suggestive of death ⟨Her face was *deadly* pale.⟩
2 to an extreme degree ⟨*deadly* dull⟩

deaf \'def\ *adj*
1 wholly or partly unable to hear
2 unwilling to hear or listen ⟨She was *deaf* to all suggestions.⟩
deaf•ness *n*

deaf•en \'de-fən\ *vb* **deaf•ened**; **deaf•en•ing**
to make unable to hear ⟨We were *deafened* by the explosion.⟩

[1]**deal** \'dēl\ *n*
1 an indefinite amount ⟨It means a great *deal* to me.⟩
2 ▶ a person's turn to pass out the cards in a card game

[2]**deal** *vb* **dealt** \'delt\; **deal•ing** \'dē-liŋ\
1 to give out as a person's share ⟨It's your turn to *deal* the cards.⟩ ⟨The judge *dealt* out justice to all.⟩
2 [1]GIVE 8, ADMINISTER
3 to have to do ⟨This book *deals* with airplanes.⟩
4 to take action ⟨The sheriff *dealt* with the outlaws.⟩
5 to buy and sell regularly : TRADE ⟨*deals* cars⟩
deal•er \'dē-lər\ *n*

[3]**deal** *n*
1 an agreement to do business ⟨We made a *deal* to trade baseball cards.⟩
2 treatment received ⟨We got a bad *deal* from the ref.⟩
3 an arrangement that is good for everyone involved

deal•ing \'dē-liŋ\ *n*
1 **deal•ings** *pl* friendly or business relations ⟨She has frequent *dealings* with the mayor.⟩
2 a way of acting or doing business ⟨fair *dealing*⟩

dean \'dēn\ *n*
1 a church official in charge of a cathedral
2 the head of a section (as a college) of a university ⟨the *dean* of the medical school⟩
3 an official in charge of students or studies in a school or college ⟨the *dean* of women⟩

[1]**dear** \'dir\ *adj*
1 greatly loved or cared about ⟨a *dear* friend⟩
2 used as a form of address especially in letters ⟨*Dear* Sir⟩
3 having a high price ⟨Fuel is *dear* just now.⟩
4 deeply felt : EARNEST ⟨My *dearest* wish is to see you.⟩
dear•ly *adv*

[2]**dear** *adv*
with love ⟨We held her *dear*.⟩

[3]**dear** *n*
a loved one : DARLING

[1]**deal 2:** a player's deal in a card game

dearth \'dərth\ *n*
SCARCITY, LACK ⟨There was a *dearth* of news.⟩

death \'deth\ *n*
1 the end or ending of life
2 the cause of loss of life ⟨Drinking will be the *death* of him.⟩
3 the state of being dead ⟨He was more famous in *death* than in life.⟩
4 [2]RUIN 1, EXTINCTION ⟨DVDs meant the *death* of videotape.⟩
death•like \-,līk\ *adj*
to death [1]VERY 1, EXTREMELY ⟨We were scared *to death*.⟩

death•bed \'deth-,bed\ *n*
the bed a person dies in
on someone's deathbed very close to death

[1]**death•ly** \'deth-lē\ *adj*
relating to or suggesting death ⟨*deathly* silence⟩

[2]**deathly** *adv*
in a way suggesting death ⟨*deathly* pale⟩

de•bat•able \di-'bā-tə-bəl\ *adj*
possible to question or argue about ⟨The wisdom of his advice is *debatable*.⟩

[1]**debate 1:** two US presidential candidates in a debate

[1]**de•bate** \di-'bāt\ *n*
1 ▲ a discussion or argument carried on between two teams or sides
2 a discussion of issues

[2]**debate** *vb* **de•bat•ed**; **de•bat•ing**
1 to discuss a question by giving arguments on both sides : take part in a debate
2 to consider reasons for and against : give serious and careful thought to
synonyms see DISCUSS
de•bat•er *n*

de•bil•i•tate \di-'bi-lə-,tāt\ *vb* **de•bil•i•tat•ed**; **de•bil•i•tat•ing**
to make feeble : WEAKEN ⟨a *debilitating* disease⟩

de•bil•i•ty \di-ˈbi-lə-tē\ *n, pl* **de•bil•i•ties**
a weakened state especially of health

[1]**deb•it** \ˈde-bət\ *vb* **deb•it•ed; deb•it•ing**
to record as money paid out or as a debt 〈The amount was *debited* on my bank statement.〉

[2]**debit** *n*
an entry in a business record showing money paid out or owed

deb•o•nair \ˌde-bə-ˈner\ *adj*
gracefully charming 〈The *debonair* gentleman charmed everyone.〉

de•bris \də-ˈbrē\ *n, pl* **de•bris** \-ˈbrēz\
the junk or pieces left from something broken down or destroyed

debt \ˈdet\ *n*
1 [1]SIN 1 〈We ask forgiveness of our *debts*.〉
2 something owed to another
3 the condition of owing something 〈I am in *debt* to you for all your help.〉

debt•or \ˈde-tər\ *n*
a person who owes a debt

[1]**de•but** \ˈdā-ˌbyü, dā-ˈbyü\ *n*
1 a first public appearance 〈The singer made his *debut* on TV.〉
2 the formal entrance of a young woman into society

[2]**debut** *vb* **de•but•ing** \ˈdā-ˌbyü-iŋ, dā-ˈbyü-iŋ\; **de•but•ed** \-ˌbyüd, -ˈbyüd\
1 to make a first public appearance 〈A new character *debuted* in today's comic strip.〉
2 to present to the public for the first time 〈The car manufacturer is *debuting* its new models.〉

deb•u•tante \ˈde-byü-ˌtänt\ *n*
a young woman making her debut

Dec. *abbr* December

deca- *or* **dec-** *or* **deka-** *or* **dek-** *prefix*
ten 〈*decagon*〉

de•cade \ˈde-ˌkād, de-ˈkād\ *n*
a period of ten years

deca•gon \ˈde-kə-ˌgän\ *n*
a closed figure having ten angles and ten sides

de•cal \ˈdē-ˌkal\ *n*
a design made to be transferred (as to glass) from specially prepared paper

de•camp \di-ˈkamp\ *vb* **de•camped; de•camp•ing**
1 to pack up gear and leave a camp
2 to go away suddenly

de•cant•er \di-ˈkan-tər\ *n*
► an ornamental glass bottle used especially for serving wine

decanter

de•cap•i•tate \di-ˈka-pə-ˌtāt\ *vb* **de•cap•i•tat•ed; de•cap•i•tat•ing**
to cut off the head of : BEHEAD

[1]**de•cay** \di-ˈkā\ *vb* **de•cayed; de•cay•ing**
1 to break down or cause to break down slowly by natural processes 〈Fruit *decayed* on the ground.〉
2 to slowly worsen in condition 〈The old theater *decayed*.〉

[2]**decay** *n*
1 ▼ the process or result of slowly breaking down by natural processes 〈The *decay* of dead plants enriches the soil.〉
2 a gradual worsening in condition 〈a *decay* in manners〉
3 a natural change of a radioactive element into another form of the same element or into a different element

[2]**decay 1:** the decay of a red pepper

[1]**de•ceased** \di-ˈsēst\ *adj*
no longer living—used of people

[2]**deceased** *n, pl* **deceased**
a dead person

de•ce•dent \di-ˈsē-dᵊnt\ *n*
a dead person

de•ceit \di-ˈsēt\ *n*
1 the act or practice of making someone believe something that is not true : DECEPTION 〈The villain used *deceit* to further his evil plan.〉
2 a statement or act that is meant to fool or trick someone 〈We saw through her *deceit*.〉
3 the quality of being dishonest

de•ceit•ful \di-ˈsēt-fəl\ *adj*
not honest : full of deceit 〈*deceitful* advertising〉

de•ceive \di-ˈsēv\ *vb* **de•ceived; de•ceiv•ing**
1 to cause to believe what is not true : MISLEAD 〈His lies *deceived* me.〉
2 to be dishonest and misleading 〈Appearances can *deceive*.〉

de•cel•er•ate \dē-ˈse-lə-ˌrāt\ *vb* **de•cel•er•at•ed; de•cel•er•at•ing**
to slow down 〈The car slowly *decelerated*.〉

De•cem•ber \di-ˈsem-bər\ *n*
the twelfth month of the year

► **Word History** The earliest Roman calendar had only ten months and began with the month of March. The tenth and last month was called in Latin *December*, a word which combines the Latin words for "ten" (*decem*), "month" (*mens*), and a final word-forming element *-ri-*. The name was kept—and eventually borrowed by English—after December became the last of twelve Roman months.

de•cen•cy \ˈdē-sᵊn-sē\ *n, pl* **de•cen•cies**
a way or habit of behaving with good manners or good morals 〈Show some *decency* and apologize.〉

de•cent \ˈdē-sᵊnt\ *adj*
1 meeting an accepted standard of good taste (as in speech, dress, or behavior) 〈Including them would be the *decent* thing to do.〉
2 being moral and good 〈She was raised by *decent* folks.〉
3 not offensive 〈*decent* language〉
4 fairly good 〈a *decent* salary〉
de•cent•ly *adv*

de•cep•tion \di-ˈsep-shən\ *n*
1 the act of making someone believe something that is not true 〈Magicians are masters of *deception*.〉
2 [1]TRICK 1

de•cep•tive \di-ˈsep-tiv\ *adj*
tending or able to deceive 〈*deceptive* advertisements〉
de•cep•tive•ly *adv*

deci- *prefix*
tenth part 〈*decimeter*〉

deci•bel \ˈde-sə-ˌbel, -bəl\ *n*
a unit for measuring the loudness of sounds

de•cide \di-ˈsīd\ *vb* **de•cid•ed; de•cid•ing**
1 to make a judgment on 〈The judge *decided* the case.〉
2 to bring to an end in a particular way 〈One vote could *decide* the election.〉
3 to make a choice especially after careful thought 〈We *decided* to go.〉

de•cid•ed \di-ˈsī-dəd\ *adj*
1 UNMISTAKABLE 〈The older students had a *decided* advantage.〉
2 free from doubt 〈"I quit!" she said in a *decided* tone.〉
de•cid•ed•ly *adv*

a b c **d** e f g h i j k l m n o p q r s t u v w x y z

A B C D E F G H I J K L M N O P Q R S T U V W X Y Z

deciduous: oak trees are deciduous and lose their leaves in winter

de•cid•u•ous \di-'si-jə-wəs\ *adj*
▲ made up of or having a part that falls off at the end of a period of growth and use ⟨*deciduous* trees⟩

[1]dec•i•mal \'de-sə-məl, 'des-məl\ *adj*
1 based on the number 10 **:** numbered or counting by tens
2 expressed in or including a decimal ⟨The *decimal* form of 1/4 is .25.⟩

[2]decimal *n*
a proper fraction in which the denominator is 10 or 10 multiplied one or more times by itself and is indicated by a point placed at the left of the numerator ⟨the *decimal* .2=2/10, the *decimal* .25=25/100⟩

decimal point *n*
the dot at the left of a decimal (as .05) or between the decimal and whole parts of a mixed number (as 3.125)

dec•i•mate \'de-sə-ˌmāt\ *vb* **dec•i•mated; dec•i•mat•ing**
1 to destroy a large number of ⟨The insects *decimated* large numbers of trees.⟩
2 to severely damage or destroy a large part of

deci•me•ter \'de-sə-ˌmē-tər\ *n*
a unit of length equal to one tenth of a meter

de•ci•pher \dē-'sī-fər\ *vb* **de•ci•phered; de•ci•pher•ing**
1 to translate from secret or mysterious writing **:** DECODE
2 to make out the meaning of something not clear ⟨I can't *decipher* her writing.⟩

de•ci•sion \di-'si-zhən\ *n*
1 the act or result of making a choice especially after careful thought
2 the ability to make choices quickly and confidently ⟨a leader of *decision*⟩

de•ci•sive \di-'sī-siv\ *adj*
1 causing something to end in a certain way ⟨*decisive* proof⟩
2 UNQUESTIONABLE ⟨a *decisive* victory⟩
3 firmly determined ⟨He began in a *decisive* manner.⟩
de•ci•sive•ly *adv*

[1]deck \'dek\ *n*
1 ▼ a floor that goes from one side of a ship to the other
2 something like the deck of a ship ⟨the *deck* of a house⟩
3 a pack of playing cards

[2]deck *vb* **decked; deck•ing**
to dress or decorate especially in a fancy way ⟨The house is *decked* out for the holidays.⟩

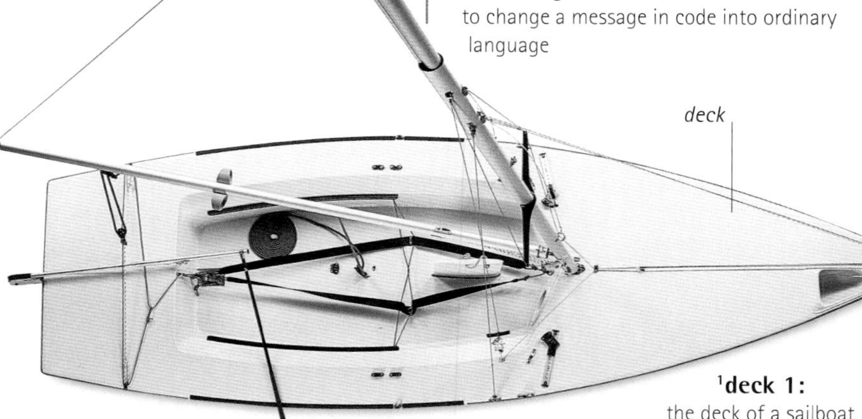

[1]deck 1: the deck of a sailboat

dec•la•ra•tion \ˌde-klə-'rā-shən\ *n*
1 an act of formally or confidently stating something
2 something formally or confidently stated or a document containing such a statement

de•clar•a•tive \di-'kler-ə-tiv\ *adj*
making a statement ⟨a *declarative* sentence⟩

de•clare \di-'kler\ *vb* **de•clared; de•clar•ing**
1 to make known in a clear or formal way ⟨The judges *declared* the race a tie.⟩
2 to state as if certain

▶ **Synonyms** DECLARE, ANNOUNCE, and ADVERTISE mean to make known to the public. DECLARE is used of something that is said very clearly and often in a formal manner. ⟨The governor *declared* a policy change.⟩ ANNOUNCE is used when something of interest is declared for the first time. ⟨Scientists *announced* the discovery of a new planet.⟩ ADVERTISE is used when a statement is repeated over and over and all around. ⟨She *advertised* her grades to the whole class.⟩

[1]de•cline \di-'klīn\ *vb* **de•clined; de•clin•ing**
1 to bend or slope downward ⟨The road *declines* into the valley.⟩
2 to pass toward a lower, worse, or weaker level ⟨Her health *declined.*⟩
3 to refuse to accept, do, or agree ⟨*decline* an invitation⟩ ⟨*decline* to leave⟩

[2]decline *n*
1 a process of becoming worse or weaker in condition
2 a change to a lower state or level ⟨a business *decline*⟩
3 the time when something is nearing its end ⟨the empire's *decline*⟩

de•code \dē-'kōd\ *vb* **de•cod•ed; de•cod•ing**
to change a message in code into ordinary language

de•com•pose \ˌdē-kəm-ˈpōz\ *vb* **de•com•posed; de•com•pos•ing**
1 to break down or be broken down into simpler parts or substances especially by the action of living things (as bacteria and fungi) 〈Leaves *decomposed* on the forest floor.〉
2 to separate a substance into simpler compounds 〈Water can be *decomposed* into hydrogen and oxygen.〉

de•com•pos•er \ˌdē-kəm-ˈpō-zər\ *n*
a living thing (as a bacterium, fungus, or insect) that feeds on and breaks down plant and animal matter into simpler parts or substances

de•com•po•si•tion \ˌdē-ˌkäm-pə-ˈzi-shən\ *n*
the process of breaking down or being broken down into simpler parts or substances especially by the action of living things

dec•o•rate \ˈde-kə-ˌrāt\ *vb* **dec•o•rat•ed; dec•o•rat•ing**
1 to make more attractive by adding beautiful or festive things 〈We *decorated* the room with flowers.〉
2 to award a badge of honor to 〈The soldier was *decorated* for bravery.〉

dec•o•ra•tion \ˌde-kə-ˈrā-shən\ *n*
1 the act of adding things to improve the appearance of something
2 ▼ something that adds beauty
3 a badge of honor

decoration 2: decorations on a Christmas tree

dec•o•ra•tive \ˈde-kə-rə-tiv, ˈde-krə-\ *adj*
serving to improve appearance : ORNAMENTAL

dec•o•ra•tor \ˈde-kə-ˌrā-tər\ *n*
a person who decorates especially the rooms of houses

de•co•rum \di-ˈkȯr-əm\ *n*
proper behavior 〈Grandpa insisted on *decorum* during the ceremony.〉

[1]**de•coy** \di-ˈkȯi, ˈdē-ˌkȯi\ *n*
▼ a person or thing (as an artificial bird) used to lead or lure into a trap or snare

[1]**decoy:** artificial ducks used to attract live ducks toward hunters

[2]**decoy** *vb* **de•coyed; de•coy•ing**
to lure by or as if by a decoy 〈Hunters *decoyed* the ducks to the pond.〉

[1]**de•crease** \di-ˈkrēs\ *vb* **de•creased; de•creas•ing**
to grow less or cause to grow less

[2]**de•crease** \ˈdē-ˌkrēs\ *n*
1 the process of growing less 〈a gradual *decrease* in interest〉
2 the amount by which something grows less

[1]**de•cree** \di-ˈkrē\ *n*
an order or decision given by a person or group in authority

[2]**decree** *vb* **de•creed; de•cree•ing**
to give an order as an authority 〈Mom *decreed* that it was bedtime.〉

de•crep•it \di-ˈkre-pət\ *adj*
broken down with age : WORN-OUT 〈a *decrepit* old house〉

de•cre•scen•do \ˌdā-krə-ˈshen-dō\ *n*
a gradual decrease in the loudness of music

ded•i•cate \ˈde-di-ˌkāt\ *vb* **ded•i•cat•ed; ded•i•cat•ing**
1 to set apart for some purpose : DEVOTE 〈The land was *dedicated* as a nature preserve.〉
2 to commit to a goal or way of life 〈She *dedicated* her life to finding a cure.〉
3 to say or write that something (as a book or song) is written or performed as a compliment to someone

ded•i•ca•tion \ˌde-di-ˈkā-shən\ *n*
1 an act of setting apart for a special purpose 〈The *dedication* of the park will take place today.〉
2 a message at the beginning of a work of art (as a book or a song) saying that it is written or performed to honor someone
3 extreme devotion

de•duce \di-ˈdüs, -ˈdyüs\ *vb* **de•duced; de•duc•ing**
to figure out by using reason or logic 〈What can we *deduce* from the evidence?〉

de•duct \di-ˈdəkt\ *vb* **de•duct•ed; de•duct•ing**
to take away an amount of something : SUBTRACT

de•duc•tion \di-ˈdək-shən\ *n*
1 SUBTRACTION
2 an amount deducted
3 a conclusion reached by reasoning 〈Her *deduction* was based on all the clues.〉

[1]**deed** \ˈdēd\ *n*
1 something that is done : ACT 〈a brave *deed*〉
2 a legal document by which a person transfers land or buildings to another

[2]**deed** *vb* **deed•ed; deed•ing**
to transfer by a deed 〈He *deeded* the house to the new owners.〉

deem \ˈdēm\ *vb* **deemed; deem•ing**
to have as an opinion 〈She *deemed* it wise to wait.〉

[1]**deep** \ˈdēp\ *adj* **deep•er; deep•est**
1 reaching far down below the surface
2 reaching far inward or back from the front or outer part 〈a *deep* cut〉 〈a *deep* closet〉
3 located well below the surface or well within the boundaries of 〈*deep* in the ground〉
4 coming from well within 〈a *deep* sigh〉
5 completely absorbed 〈*deep* in thought〉
6 hard to understand 〈This story is too *deep* for me.〉
7 MYSTERIOUS 〈a *deep*, dark secret〉
8 extreme in degree : HEAVY 〈a *deep* sleep〉
9 dark and rich in color 〈a *deep* red〉
10 low in tone 〈a *deep* voice〉
deep•ly *adv*

[2]**deep** *adv* **deep•er; deep•est**
1 to a great depth : DEEPLY 〈It sank *deeper* in the mud.〉
2 [2]LATE 1 〈She read *deep* into the night.〉

[3]**deep** *n*
1 a very deep place or part 〈the ocean *deeps*〉
2 OCEAN 1 〈Pirates sailed the briny *deep*.〉
3 the middle or most intense part 〈the *deep* of winter〉

deep•en \ˈdē-pən\ *vb* **deep•ened; deep•en•ing**
to make or become deep or deeper 〈I *deepened* the hole.〉

A B C D E F G H I J K L M N O P Q R S T U V W X Y Z

deep fat *n*
hot fat or oil deep enough in a cooking utensil to cover the food to be fried

deep–fry \'dēp-'frī\ *vb* **deep–fried; deep–fry•ing**
to cook in deep fat

deep•ly \'dēp-lē\ *adv*
1 at or to a great depth : far below the surface ⟨The wheels sunk *deeply* in mud.⟩
2 in a high degree : THOROUGHLY ⟨I was *deeply* moved.⟩
3 with intensity of color ⟨She flushed *deeply*.⟩

deer \'dir\ *n, pl* **deer**
▼ a mammal that has cloven hoofs and in the male antlers which are often branched

deer: a female deer

deer•skin \'dir-,skin\ *n*
leather made from the skin of a deer or a garment made of such leather

de•face \di-'fās\ *vb* **de•faced; de•fac•ing**
to damage the face or surface of ⟨Vandals *defaced* the statue.⟩

[1]**de•fault** \di-'fȯlt\ *n*
failure to do something especially that is required by law or duty

[2]**default** *vb* **de•fault•ed; de•fault•ing**
to fail to do something required ⟨He *defaulted* on repaying the money.⟩

[1]**de•feat** \di-'fēt\ *vb* **de•feat•ed; de•feat•ing**
1 to win victory over ⟨The champs *defeated* their rivals handily.⟩
2 to cause to fail or be destroyed ⟨The bill was *defeated* in Congress.⟩

[2]**defeat** *n*
loss of a contest or battle

de•fect \'dē-,fekt, di-'fekt\ *n*
1 something that makes a thing imperfect : FLAW ⟨A slight *defect* lowered the diamond's value.⟩
2 a lack of something needed for perfection ⟨a hearing *defect*⟩

de•fec•tive \di-'fek-tiv\ *adj*
having a defect or flaw ⟨The car's brakes were *defective*.⟩

de•fence *chiefly British variant of* DEFENSE

de•fend \di-'fend\ *vb* **de•fend•ed; de•fend•ing**
1 to protect from danger or attack
2 to act or speak in favor of when others are opposed

▶ **Synonyms** DEFEND, PROTECT, and SAFEGUARD mean to keep safe. DEFEND is used for a danger or an attack that is actual or threatening. ⟨The soldiers *defended* the fort against enemy troops.⟩ PROTECT is used when some kind of shield can prevent possible attack or injury. ⟨*Protect* your eyes with dark glasses.⟩ SAFEGUARD is used when a course of action can protect against a possible danger. ⟨The health rules help *safeguard* the students from disease.⟩

de•fend•er \di-'fen-dər\ *n*
1 a person or thing that protects from danger or attack
2 a player in a sport who tries to keep the other team from scoring

de•fense \di-'fens\ *n*
1 the act of protecting or defending ⟨They were defeated in spite of a brave *defense*.⟩
2 something that defends or protects
3 the players on a team who try to stop the other team from scoring
de•fense•less \-ləs\ *adj*

[1]**de•fen•sive** \di-'fen-siv\ *adj*
1 serving or meant to defend or protect ⟨a *defensive* structure⟩
2 ▶ relating to the attempt to keep an opponent from scoring ⟨a *defensive* play⟩
3 showing a dislike for criticism ⟨She got *defensive* about my suggestion.⟩
de•fen•sive•ly *adv*

[2]**defensive** *n*
a position or attitude that is meant to defend ⟨The criticism put him on the *defensive*.⟩

[1]**de•fer** \di-'fər\ *vb* **de•ferred; de•fer•ring**
to put off to a future time : POSTPONE ⟨The test is *deferred* to next week.⟩

[2]**defer** *vb* **de•ferred; de•fer•ring**
to give in or yield to the opinion or wishes of another

def•er•ence \'de-fə-rəns, 'de-frəns\ *n*
respect and consideration for the wishes of another

de•fer•ment \di-'fər-mənt\ *n*
the act of postponing

de•fi•ance \di-'fī-əns\ *n*
1 a refusal to obey ⟨a *defiance* of the rule⟩
2 a willingness to resist

de•fi•ant \di-'fī-ənt\ *adj*
showing a willingness to resist ⟨a *defiant* child⟩
de•fi•ant•ly *adv*

de•fi•cien•cy \di-'fi-shən-sē\ *n, pl* **de•fi•cien•cies**
the condition of being without something necessary and especially something required for health ⟨a vitamin *deficiency*⟩

[1]**defensive 2:** a defensive action in basketball

de•fi•cient \di-ˈfi-shənt\ *adj*
lacking something necessary for completeness or health ⟨Her diet is *deficient* in proteins.⟩

def•i•cit \ˈde-fə-sət\ *n*
a shortage especially in money

de•fine \di-ˈfīn\ *vb* **de•fined**; **de•fin•ing**
1 to explain the meaning of ⟨*define* a word⟩
2 to make clear especially in outline ⟨Your responsibilities are *defined* in the handout.⟩

def•i•nite \ˈde-fə-nət\ *adj*
1 having certain or distinct limits ⟨a *definite* period of time⟩
2 clear in meaning ⟨a *definite* answer⟩
3 UNQUESTIONABLE ⟨Your grades show a *definite* improvement.⟩
def•i•nite•ly *adv*

definite article *n*
the article *the* used to show that the following noun refers to one or more specific persons or things

def•i•ni•tion \ˌde-fə-ˈni-shən\ *n*
1 a statement of the meaning of a word or a word group
2 clearness of outline or detail

de•flate \di-ˈflāt\ *vb* **de•flat•ed**; **de•flat•ing**
1 ▼ to let the air or gas out of something that has been blown up
2 to reduce in size or importance ⟨His confidence *deflated* when he saw the size of his opponent.⟩

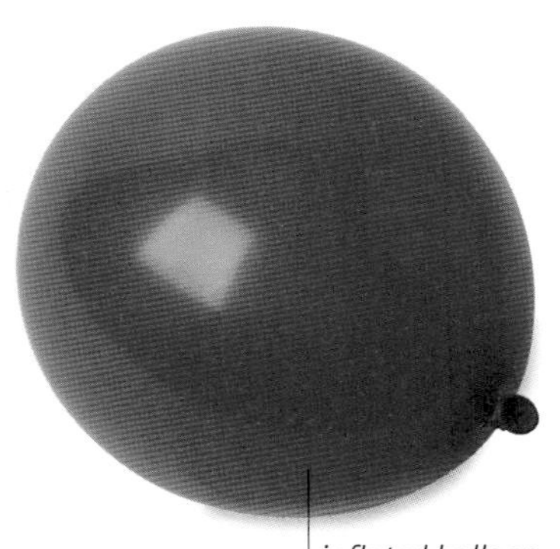
inflated balloon

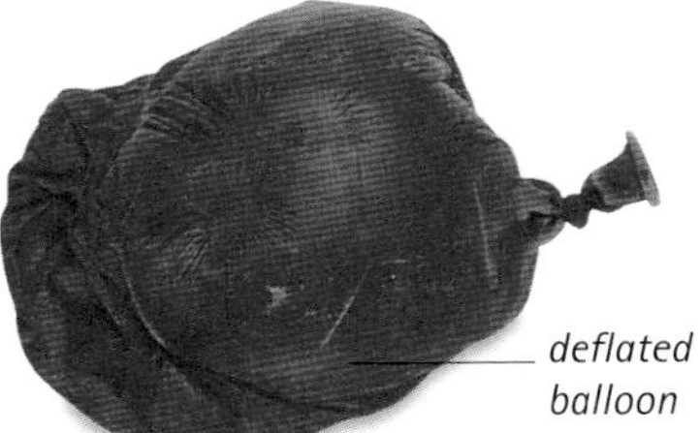
deflated balloon

deflate 1

de•flect \di-ˈflekt\ *vb* **de•flect•ed**; **de•flect•ing**
to change or cause to change direction ⟨The goalie *deflected* the puck.⟩

de•for•est \dē-ˈfȯr-əst\ *vb* **de•for•est•ed**; **de•for•est•ing**
to clear of forests
de•for•es•ta•tion \-ˌfȯr-ə-ˈstā-shən\ *n*

de•form \di-ˈfȯrm\ *vb* **de•formed**; **de•form•ing**
to spoil the form or the natural appearance of

de•for•mi•ty \di-ˈfȯr-mə-tē\ *n*, *pl* **de•for•mi•ties**
1 the condition of having a physical flaw
2 a flaw in something and especially in the body of a person or animal

de•fraud \di-ˈfrȯd\ *vb* **de•fraud•ed**; **de•fraud•ing**
to get something from by trickery

de•frost \di-ˈfrȯst\ *vb* **de•frost•ed**; **de•frost•ing**
1 to thaw out ⟨*defrost* a steak⟩
2 to remove ice from ⟨*defrost* a freezer⟩
de•frost•er *n*

deft \ˈdeft\ *adj* **deft•er**; **deft•est**
quick and skillful in action ⟨He cut hair with *deft* fingers.⟩
deft•ly *adv*

de•funct \di-ˈfəŋkt\ *adj*
no longer existing or being used ⟨The old factory was *defunct.*⟩

de•fy \di-ˈfī\ *vb* **de•fied**; **de•fy•ing**
1 to refuse boldly to obey or yield to ⟨The protesters *defied* orders to leave.⟩
2 to challenge to do something thought to be impossible : DARE ⟨I *defy* you to explain the trick.⟩
3 to resist attempts at : WITHSTAND ⟨The scene *defies* description.⟩

de•grade \di-ˈgrād\ *vb* **de•grad•ed**; **de•grad•ing**
1 to lower in character or dignity ⟨He felt *degraded* by their insults.⟩
2 to break down or separate into simpler parts or substances ⟨Bacteria will *degrade* the spilled pollutant.⟩
3 to reduce from a higher to a lower rank or degree ⟨He was *degraded* to a private by his commander.⟩

de•gree \di-ˈgrē\ *n*
1 a step in a series ⟨His health improved by *degrees.*⟩
2 amount of something as measured by a series of steps ⟨a high *degree* of progress⟩
3 one of the three forms an adjective or adverb may have when it is compared
4 a title given (as to students) by a college or university ⟨She received a *degree* of doctor of medicine.⟩
5 one of the divisions marked on a measuring instrument (as a thermometer)
6 a 360th part of the circumference of a circle
7 a line or space of the staff in music or the difference in pitch between two notes

de•hu•mid•i•fy \ˌdē-hyü-ˈmi-də-ˌfī\ *vb* **de•hu•mid•i•fied**; **de•hu•mid•i•fy•ing**
to take moisture from (as the air)
de•hu•mid•i•fi•er *n*

de•hy•drate \dē-ˈhī-ˌdrāt\ *vb* **de•hy•drat•ed**; **de•hy•drat•ing**
1 to take water from (as foods) ⟨*dehydrate* fruit⟩
2 to lose water or body fluids
de•hy•dra•tion \ˌdē-ˌhī-ˈdrā-shən\ *n*

deign \ˈdān\ *vb* **deigned**; **deign•ing**
to do something a person considers below his or her dignity ⟨The teenager *deigned* to play with his little cousin.⟩

de•i•ty \ˈdē-ə-tē, ˈdā-\ *n*, *pl* **de•i•ties**
1 *cap* GOD 1
2 GOD 2, GODDESS ⟨Roman *deities*⟩

de•ject•ed \di-ˈjek-təd\ *adj*
SAD 1 ⟨We were *dejected* at losing the game.⟩
de•ject•ed•ly *adv*

de•jec•tion \di-ˈjek-shən\ *n*
a feeling of sadness

deka- *or* **dek-** see DECA-

Del. *abbr* Delaware

Del•a•ware \ˈde-lə-ˌwer, -wər\ *n*, *pl* **Delaware** *or* **Del•a•wares**
1 a member of an American Indian people originally of the region from southeastern New York to northern Delaware
2 the language of the Delaware people

[1]**de•lay** \di-ˈlā\ *n*
1 a putting off of something ⟨We began without *delay.*⟩
2 the time during which something is delayed ⟨We will have a *delay* of 30 minutes.⟩

[2]**delay** *vb* **de•layed**; **de•lay•ing**
1 to put off
2 to stop or prevent for a time ⟨Bad weather *delayed* our flight.⟩
3 to move or act slowly ⟨We cannot *delay* any longer.⟩

de•lec•ta•ble \di-ˈlek-tə-bəl\ *adj*
1 very pleasing : DELIGHTFUL
2 DELICIOUS

[1]**del•e•gate** \ˈde-li-gət\ *n*
a person sent with power to act for another or others

[2]**del•e•gate** \'de-lə-,gāt\ *vb* **del•e•gat•ed**; **del•e•gat•ing**
1 to entrust to another ⟨The voters *delegate* power to their elected officials.⟩
2 to make responsible for getting something done ⟨We were *delegated* to clean up.⟩

del•e•ga•tion \,de-lə-'gā-shən\ *n*
1 the act of giving someone authority or responsibility for
2 one or more persons chosen to represent others

de•lete \di-'lēt\ *vb* **de•let•ed**; **de•let•ing**
to take out especially by erasing, crossing out, or cutting ⟨*delete* a sentence⟩ ⟨*delete* a computer file⟩

de•le•tion \di-'lē-shən\ *n*
1 an act of taking out ⟨The *deletion* of the file was a mistake.⟩
2 something taken out

deli \'de-lē\ *n, pl* **del•is**
DELICATESSEN

[1]**de•lib•er•ate** \di-'li-bə-,rāt\ *vb* **de•lib•er•at•ed**; **de•lib•er•at•ing**
to think about carefully

[2]**de•lib•er•ate** \di-'li-bə-rət, -'li-brət\ *adj*
1 showing careful thought ⟨a *deliberate* decision⟩
2 done or said on purpose ⟨a *deliberate* lie⟩
3 slow in action : not hurried ⟨a *deliberate* pace⟩
synonyms see VOLUNTARY
de•lib•er•ate•ly *adv*

de•lib•er•a•tion \di-,li-bə-'rā-shən\ *n*
1 careful thought : CONSIDERATION
2 the quality of being deliberate ⟨He spoke with great *deliberation*.⟩

del•i•ca•cy \'de-li-kə-sē\ *n, pl* **del•i•ca•cies**
1 ▼ something pleasing to eat that is rare or a luxury
2 fineness of structure
3 weakness of body : FRAILTY
4 a need for careful treatment ⟨This is a situation of great *delicacy*.⟩
5 consideration for the feelings of others ⟨She had the *delicacy* to ignore my blunder.⟩

delicacy 1: an appetizer topped with caviar

del•i•cate \'de-li-kət\ *adj*
1 pleasing because of fineness or mildness ⟨a *delicate* flavor⟩ ⟨*delicate* lace⟩
2 able to sense very small differences ⟨a *delicate* instrument⟩
3 calling for skill and careful treatment ⟨a *delicate* operation⟩
4 easily damaged ⟨*delicate* flowers⟩
5 SICKLY 1 ⟨a *delicate* child⟩
6 requiring tact ⟨a *delicate* subject⟩
del•i•cate•ly *adv*

del•i•ca•tes•sen \,de-li-kə-'te-sᵊn\ *n*
▼ a store where prepared foods (as salads and meats) are sold

delicatessen:
processed meats in a delicatessen

de•li•cious \di-'li-shəs\ *adj*
giving great pleasure especially to the taste or smell
de•li•cious•ly *adv*

[1]**de•light** \di-'līt\ *n*
1 great pleasure or satisfaction : JOY ⟨The baby clapped with *delight*.⟩
2 something that gives great pleasure ⟨Visiting with them was a *delight*.⟩

[2]**delight** *vb* **de•light•ed**; **de•light•ing**
1 to take great pleasure ⟨Grandma *delights* in showing us her old photos.⟩
2 to give joy or satisfaction to ⟨The show *delights* all ages.⟩

de•light•ed \di-'lī-təd\ *adj*
very pleased

de•light•ful \di-'līt-fəl\ *adj*
giving delight : very pleasing
de•light•ful•ly \-fə-lē\ *adv*

de•lin•quent \di-'liŋ-kwənt\ *n*
a usually young person who is guilty of improper or illegal behavior

de•lir•i•ous \di-'lir-ē-əs\ *adj*
1 not able to think or speak clearly usually because of a high fever or other illness
2 wildly excited
de•lir•i•ous•ly *adv*

de•lir•i•um \di-'lir-ē-əm\ *n*
1 a condition of mind in which thought and speech are confused usually because of a high fever or other illness
2 wild excitement

de•liv•er \di-'li-vər\ *vb* **de•liv•ered**; **de•liv•er•ing**
1 to take and give to or leave for another ⟨*deliver* a letter⟩ ⟨This restaurant *delivers*.⟩
2 to set free : RESCUE ⟨They were *delivered* from their captors.⟩
3 to give birth to or help in giving birth to ⟨*deliver* a baby⟩
4 [1]SAY 1 ⟨*deliver* a speech⟩
5 to send to an intended target ⟨*deliver* a pitch⟩
6 to do what is expected ⟨He *delivered* on all his promises.⟩
de•liv•er•er *n*

de•liv•er•ance \di-'li-və-rəns, -'li-vrəns\ *n*
a setting free

de•liv•ery \di-'li-və-rē, -'li-vrē\ *n, pl* **de•liv•er•ies**
1 the transfer of something from one place or person to another ⟨*delivery* of the mail⟩
2 a setting free from something that restricts or burdens ⟨We prayed for *delivery* from our troubles.⟩
3 the act of giving birth
4 speaking or manner of speaking (as of a formal speech)
5 the act or way of throwing ⟨an underhand *delivery*⟩

dell \'del\ *n*
a small valley usually covered with trees

del•ta \'del-tə\ *n*
► a piece of land in the shape of a triangle or fan made by deposits of mud and sand at the mouth of a river

de•lude \di-'lüd\ *vb* **de•lud•ed**; **de•lud•ing**
DECEIVE 1, MISLEAD ⟨They were *deluded* by the ad's claims.⟩

[1]**del•uge** \'del-yüj\ *n*
1 a flooding of land by water : FLOOD
2 a drenching rain
3 a sudden huge stream of something ⟨a *deluge* of mail⟩

[2]**deluge** *vb* **del•uged**; **del•ug•ing**
1 [2]FLOOD 1

2 to overwhelm as if with a flood ⟨We were *deluged* by questions.⟩

de•lu•sion \di-'lü-zhən\ *n*
a false belief that continues in spite of the facts

de•luxe \di-'ləks, -'lüks\ *adj*
very fine or luxurious

delve \'delv\ *vb* **delved**; **delv•ing**
1 to dig or work hard with or as if with a shovel
2 to work hard looking for information

[1]de•mand \di-'mand\ *n*
1 a forceful expression of what is desired ⟨a *demand* for money⟩
2 something claimed as owed ⟨He presented a list of *demands*.⟩
3 an expressed desire to own or use something ⟨The *demand* for new cars is up.⟩
4 a seeking or state of being sought after ⟨Good teachers are in great *demand*.⟩

[2]demand *vb* **de•mand•ed**; **de•mand•ing**
1 to claim as a right ⟨I *demand* an apology.⟩
2 to ask earnestly or in the manner of a command ⟨The sentry *demanded* the password.⟩
3 to call for : REQUIRE ⟨The situation *demands* attention.⟩
on demand when requested or needed ⟨Payment is due *on demand*.⟩

de•mand•ing \di-'man-diŋ\ *adj*
requiring or expecting much effort ⟨a *demanding* teacher⟩

[1]de•mean \di-'mēn\ *vb* **de•meaned**; **de•mean•ing**
BEHAVE 2 ⟨He *demeaned* himself like a gentleman.⟩

[2]demean *vb* **de•meaned**; **de•mean•ing**
to lower in character or dignity ⟨She feels that such work *demeans* her.⟩

de•mean•or \di-'mē-nər\ *n*
outward manner or behavior ⟨a gentle *demeanor*⟩

de•ment•ed \di-'men-təd\ *adj*
INSANE 1, MAD

de•mer•it \dē-'mer-ət\ *n*
a mark placed against a person's record for doing something wrong

demi- *prefix*
half or partly

de•mise \di-'mīz\ *n*
1 DEATH 1
2 an ending of existence or activity ⟨the *demise* of a newspaper⟩

de•mo•bi•lize \di-'mō-bə-,līz\ *vb* **de•mo•bi•lized**; **de•mo•bi•liz•ing**
1 to let go from military service
2 to change from a state of war to a state of peace

de•moc•ra•cy \di-'mä-krə-sē\ *n*, *pl* **de•moc•ra•cies**
1 government by the people : majority rule
2 government in which the highest power is held by the people and is usually used through representatives
3 a political unit (as a nation) governed by the people
4 belief in or practice of the idea that all people are socially equal

dem•o•crat \'de-mə-,krat\ *n*
1 a person who believes in or practices democracy
2 *cap* a member of the Democratic party of the United States

dem•o•crat•ic \,de-mə-'kra-tik\ *adj*
1 relating to or favoring political democracy
2 relating to a major political party in the United States that is associated with helping common people
3 believing in or practicing the idea that people are socially equal
dem•o•crat•i•cal•ly \-ti-kə-lē\ *adv*

de•mol•ish \di-'mä-lish\ *vb* **de•mol•ished**; **de•mol•ish•ing**
1 to destroy by breaking apart ⟨*demolish* a building⟩
2 to ruin completely : SHATTER ⟨He *demolished* the speed record.⟩

de•mo•li•tion \,de-mə-'li-shən\ *n*
the act of destroying by breaking apart especially using explosives

de•mon \'dē-mən\ *n*
1 ▼ an evil spirit : DEVIL
2 a person of great energy or enthusiasm ⟨a speed *demon*⟩

demon 1:
a demon mask from Korea

dem•on•strate \'de-mən-,strāt\ *vb* **dem•on•strat•ed**; **dem•on•strat•ing**
1 to show clearly ⟨He *demonstrates* a willingness to change.⟩
2 to prove or make clear by reasoning ⟨Galileo *demonstrated* that the earth revolves around the sun.⟩
3 to explain (as in teaching) by use of examples or experiments ⟨My science project *demonstrates* blood circulation.⟩
4 to show to people the good qualities of an article or a product ⟨*demonstrate* a new car⟩
5 to make a public display (as of feelings or military force) ⟨Marchers *demonstrated* for human rights.⟩

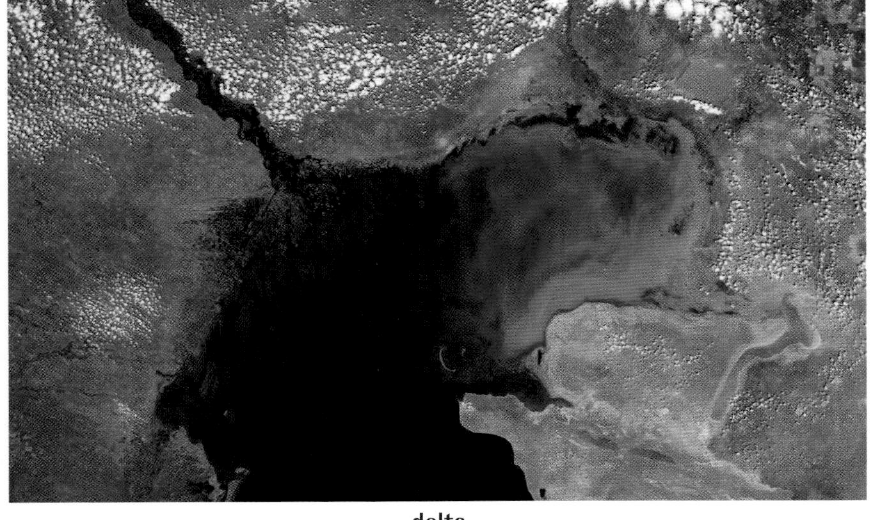

delta

dem•on•stra•tion \ˌde-mən-ˈstā-shən\ *n*
1 an outward expression (as a show of feelings) ⟨a *demonstration* of affection⟩
2 an act or a means of showing ⟨a cooking *demonstration*⟩
3 a showing or using of an article for sale to display its good points
4 a parade or a gathering to show public feeling

de•mon•stra•tive \di-ˈmän-strə-tiv\ *adj*
1 pointing out the one referred to and showing that it differs from others ⟨In "this is my dog" and "that is their dog," "this" and "that" are *demonstrative* pronouns.⟩
2 showing feeling freely ⟨a *demonstrative* person⟩

dem•on•stra•tor \ˈde-mən-ˌstā-tər\ *n*
1 a person who makes or takes part in a demonstration
2 a manufactured article (as an automobile) used for demonstration

de•mor•al•ize \di-ˈmȯr-ə-ˌlīz\ *vb* **de•mor•al•ized**; **de•mor•al•iz•ing**
to weaken the spirit or confidence of

de•mote \di-ˈmōt\ *vb* **de•mot•ed**; **de•mot•ing**
to reduce to a lower grade or rank ⟨He was *demoted* to private.⟩

de•mure \di-ˈmyu̇r\ *adj*
1 proper and reserved in behavior and speech
2 pretending to be proper and reserved : COY
de•mure•ly *adv*

den \ˈden\ *n*
1 ▼ the shelter or resting place of a wild animal ⟨a fox's *den*⟩
2 a quiet or private room in a home
3 a hiding place (as for thieves)

den 1: foxes in their den

den•drite \ˈden-ˌdrīt\ *n*
any of the usually branched fibers that carry nerve impulses toward a nerve cell body

de•ni•al \di-ˈnī-əl\ *n*
1 a refusal to give or agree to something asked for ⟨a *denial* of the request⟩
2 a refusal to admit the truth of a statement ⟨a *denial* of the accusation⟩
3 a refusal to accept or believe in someone or something
4 a cutting down or limiting ⟨a *denial* of his appetite⟩

den•im \ˈde-nəm\ *n*
1 ▼ a firm often coarse cotton cloth
2 **denims** *pl* overalls or pants of usually blue denim

denim 1:
a shirt made of denim

► **Word History** The word *denim* came from a French phrase that meant "serge of Nimes." Serge is a kind of sturdy cloth. Nimes is a city in the southern part of France where making cloth was traditionally a major industry. When the English borrowed the French phrase that meant "serge of Nimes" they made it *serge denim.* Later this phrase was shortened to *denim.*

de•nom•i•na•tion \di-ˌnä-mə-ˈnā-shən\ *n*
1 a value in a series of values (as of money) ⟨She asked for her money in small *denominations.*⟩
2 a name especially for a class of things
3 a religious body made up of a number of congregations having the same beliefs

de•nom•i•na•tor \di-ˈnä-mə-ˌnā-tər\ *n*
the part of a fraction that is below the line ⟨The number 5 is the *denominator* of the fraction 3/5.⟩

de•note \di-ˈnōt\ *vb* **de•not•ed**; **de•not•ing**
1 to serve as a mark or indication of ⟨The hands of a clock *denote* the time.⟩
2 to have the meaning of : MEAN

de•nounce \di-ˈnau̇ns\ *vb* **de•nounced**; **de•nounc•ing**
1 to point out as wrong or evil : CONDEMN
2 to inform against : ACCUSE ⟨I *denounced* him as a traitor.⟩

dense \ˈdens\ *adj* **dens•er**; **dens•est**
1 having its parts crowded together : THICK ⟨*dense* vegetation⟩ ⟨*dense* fog⟩
2 STUPID 1 ⟨I'm not *dense* enough to believe this story.⟩
dense•ly *adv*

► **Synonyms** DENSE, THICK, and COMPACT mean having parts that are gathered tightly together. DENSE is used of something in which the parts are very close together. ⟨They lost their way in the *dense* forest.⟩ THICK is used of something that has many small parts that form a single mass. ⟨He has a *thick* head of hair.⟩ COMPACT is used of something that has a close and firm gathering of parts, especially within a small area. ⟨I live in a *compact* town where everything is within walking distance.⟩

den•si•ty \ˈden-sə-tē\ *n, pl* **den•si•ties**
1 the condition of having parts that are close together ⟨the jungle's *density*⟩
2 the amount of something in a specified volume or area ⟨high population *density*⟩

[1]dent \ˈdent\ *vb* **dent•ed**; **dent•ing**
1 to make a hollow mark in or on ⟨I *dented* my car.⟩
2 to become damaged by a hollow mark

[2]dent *n*
a notch or hollow mark made in a surface by a blow or by pressure

den•tal \ˈden-tᵊl\ *adj*
relating to the teeth or dentistry

dental floss *n*
▼ a special thread used for cleaning between teeth

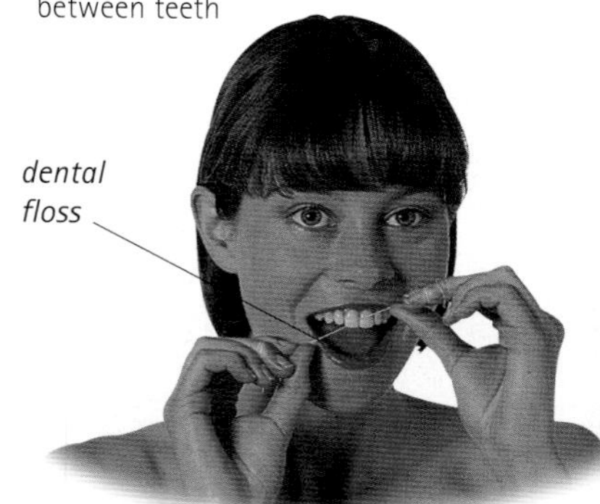

dental floss:
a woman using dental floss

den•tin \ˈden-tᵊn\ *or* **den•tine** \ˈden-ˌtēn\ *n*
a calcium-containing material that is similar to bone but harder and that makes up the main part of a tooth

den•tist \'den-təst\ *n*
a person whose profession is the care, treatment, and repair of the teeth

den•tist•ry \'den-tə-strē\ *n*
the profession or practice of a dentist

de•nude \di-'nüd, -'nyüd\ *vb* **de•nud•ed**; **de•nud•ing**
to make bare 〈The tree was *denuded* of bark.〉

de•ny \di-'nī\ *vb* **de•nied**; **de•ny•ing**
1 to declare not to be true
2 to refuse to grant 〈*deny* a request〉
3 to refuse to admit 〈*deny* guilt〉

de•odor•ant \dē-'ō-də-rənt\ *n*
something used to remove or hide unpleasant odors

de•odor•ize \dē-'ō-də-,rīz\ *vb* **de•odor•ized**; **de•odor•iz•ing**
to remove odor and especially a bad smell from

de•part \di-'pärt\ *vb* **de•part•ed**; **de•part•ing**
1 to go away or go away from : LEAVE
2 to turn away from 〈Do not *depart* from your chosen path.〉
depart this life [1]DIE 1

de•part•ment \di-'pärt-mənt\ *n*
a special part or division of an organization (as a government or college)

department store: a department store in New York City

department store *n*
▲ a store having individual departments for different kinds of goods

de•par•ture \di-'pär-chər\ *n*
1 an act of leaving or setting out
2 an act of turning away or aside (as from a way of doing things) 〈a *departure* from tradition〉

de•pend \di-'pend\ *vb* **de•pend•ed**; **de•pend•ing**
to be subject to determination by the situation 〈"Are you going to the party?" "I don't know. It *depends*."〉
depend on
1 to rely for support 〈Children *depend on* their parents.〉
2 to be determined by or based on a person, action, or condition 〈Success *depends on* hard work.〉
3 [1]TRUST 2, RELY 〈You can *depend on* me to get the job done.〉

de•pend•able \di-'pen-də-bəl\ *adj*
TRUSTWORTHY, RELIABLE 〈a *dependable* car〉

de•pen•dence \di-'pen-dəns\ *n*
1 a condition of being influenced and caused by something else
2 a state of having to rely on someone or something 〈*dependence* on charity〉
3 [2]TRUST 1, RELIANCE
4 addiction to a drug or alcohol

[1]**de•pen•dent** \di-'pen-dənt\ *adj*
1 determined by something or someone else 〈Our plans are *dependent* on the weather.〉
2 relying on someone else for support
3 requiring or addicted to a drug or alcohol

[2]**dependent** *n*
a person who depends upon another for support

de•pict \di-'pikt\ *vb* **de•pict•ed**; **de•pict•ing**
1 to represent by a picture
2 to describe in words

de•pic•tion \di-'pik-shən\ *n*
1 a representation of something using a picture
2 DESCRIPTION 1

de•plete \di-'plēt\ *vb* **de•plet•ed**; **de•plet•ing**
to reduce in amount by using up 〈The soil was *depleted* of minerals.〉

de•plor•able \di-'plȯr-ə-bəl\ *adj*
1 deserving to be deplored : REGRETTABLE 〈a *deplorable* mistake〉
2 very bad : WRETCHED

de•plore \di-'plȯr\ *vb* **de•plored**; **de•plor•ing**
1 to regret strongly
2 to disapprove of

de•port \di-'pȯrt\ *vb* **de•port•ed**; **de•port•ing**
1 BEHAVE 1 〈He *deported* himself well.〉
2 to force (a person who is not a citizen) to leave a country

de•por•ta•tion \,dē-,pȯr-'tā-shən\ *n*
the removal from a country of a person who is not a citizen

de•pose \di-'pōz\ *vb* **de•posed**; **de•pos•ing**
to remove from a high office 〈*depose* a king〉

[1]**de•pos•it** \di-'pä-zət\ *vb* **de•pos•it•ed**; **de•pos•it•ing**
1 to place for or as if for safekeeping 〈I *deposited* money in the bank.〉
2 to give as a pledge that a purchase will be made or a service used 〈He *deposited* ten dollars on a new bicycle.〉
3 to lay down : PUT 〈He *deposited* his books on the table.〉
4 to let fall or sink 〈Layers of mud were *deposited* by flood waters.〉

[2]**deposit** *n*
1 the state of being deposited 〈money on *deposit*〉
2 money that is deposited
3 something given as a pledge or as part payment 〈He put a *deposit* of ten dollars on a new bicycle.〉
4 something laid or thrown down 〈A *deposit* of mud was left by the flood.〉
5 ▼ mineral matter built up in nature

[2]**deposit 5:** a crystal deposit on a rock

a b c d e f g h i j k l m n o p q r s t u v w x y z

de•pos•i•tor \di-ˈpä-zə-tər\ *n*
a person who makes a deposit especially of money in a bank

de•pot *usually* ˈde-ˌpō *for 1 & 2,* ˈdē- *for 3*\ *n*
1 a place where military supplies are kept
2 STOREHOUSE 1
3 a railroad or bus station

de•pre•ci•ate \di-ˈprē-shē-ˌāt\ *vb* **de•pre•ci•at•ed; de•pre•ci•at•ing**
1 BELITTLE ⟨He often *depreciates* his own talent.⟩
2 to lower the price or value of
3 to lose value ⟨New cars *depreciate* rapidly.⟩

de•press \di-ˈpres\ *vb* **de•pressed; de•press•ing**
1 to press down ⟨*Depress* the "enter" key.⟩
2 to make sad or discouraged
3 to lessen the activity or strength of ⟨Bad weather had *depressed* sales.⟩

de•pres•sant \di-ˈpre-sᵊnt\ *n*
a drug that slows the activity of the nervous system

de•pressed \di-ˈprest\ *adj*
1 SAD 1
2 suffering from bad economic times ⟨a *depressed* city⟩

de•pres•sion \di-ˈpre-shən\ *n*
1 an act of pressing down ⟨*depression* of the brake pedal⟩
2 a hollow place or part ⟨My foot made a *depression* in the sand.⟩
3 a feeling of sadness ⟨Your support eased my *depression.*⟩
4 a period of low activity in business with much unemployment

de•pri•va•tion \ˌde-prə-ˈvā-shən, ˌdē-ˌprī-\ *n*
1 a taking or keeping away ⟨a *deprivation* of rights⟩
2 the state of having something taken away ⟨sleep *deprivation*⟩

de•prive \di-ˈprīv\ *vb* **de•prived; de•priv•ing**
to take something away from or keep from having something ⟨The noise *deprived* me of sleep.⟩

de•prived \di-ˈprīvd\ *adj*
not having the things that are needed for a good or healthful life

dept. *abbr* department

depth \ˈdepth\ *n*
1 measurement from top to bottom or from front to back ⟨a cupboard's *depth*⟩
2 a place far below a surface or far inside something (as a sea or a forest) ⟨Some unusual fish live at great *depths.*⟩
3 the middle of time ⟨the *depth* of winter⟩
4 INTENSITY 2 ⟨a *depth* of color⟩
5 ABUNDANCE, COMPLETENESS ⟨The speaker displayed a *depth* of knowledge.⟩

dep•u•tize \ˈde-pyə-ˌtīz\ *vb* **dep•u•tized; dep•u•tiz•ing**
to appoint as deputy

dep•u•ty \ˈde-pyə-tē\ *n, pl* **dep•u•ties**
a person who officially acts for or in place of another

de•rail \di-ˈrāl\ *vb* **de•railed; de•rail•ing**
1 to leave or cause to leave the rails ⟨The train *derailed.*⟩
2 to make progress or success difficult for ⟨Injuries *derailed* his plan for a championship.⟩

der•by \ˈdər-bē\ *n, pl* **der•bies**
1 a race for three-year-old horses usually held every year
2 a race or contest open to anyone ⟨a fishing *derby*⟩
3 ▶ a stiff felt hat with a narrow brim and a rounded top

▶ **Word History** The first horse race called a *Derby* was named after an English nobleman named Edward Stanley, the Earl of Derby (1752–1834). The Earl of Derby instituted the race in 1780, and it continues to be run to the present day in England on the first Wednesday in June. The name *Derby* has become attached to other horse races, such as the Kentucky Derby in the United States, as well as to races and contests that have nothing to do with horses.

[1]**der•e•lict** \ˈder-ə-ˌlikt\ *adj*
1 abandoned by the owner or occupant
2 in poor condition : RUN-DOWN ⟨a *derelict* old building⟩
3 failing to do what should be done ⟨They were *derelict* in their duties.⟩

[2]**derelict** *n*
1 something abandoned (as a boat)
2 [1]BUM 1, VAGRANT

de•ride \di-ˈrīd\ *vb* **de•rid•ed; de•rid•ing**
to laugh at in scorn : make fun of : RIDICULE

de•ri•sion \di-ˈri-zhən\ *n*
a feeling of dislike or disrespect often shown by the use of insults ⟨He was treated with *derision.*⟩

der•i•va•tion \ˌder-ə-ˈvā-shən\ *n*
1 the formation of a word from an earlier word or root
2 ETYMOLOGY
3 ORIGIN 1, SOURCE ⟨She enjoys foods of Mexican *derivation.*⟩
4 an act or process by which one thing is formed from another

[1]**de•riv•a•tive** \di-ˈri-və-tiv\ *n*
1 a word formed from an earlier word or root ⟨"Childhood" is a *derivative* of "child."⟩
2 something that is formed from something else ⟨Gasoline is a *derivative* of petroleum.⟩

[2]**derivative** *adj*
formed from something else ⟨a *derivative* product⟩
de•riv•a•tive•ly *adv*

derby 3

de•rive \di-ˈrīv\ *vb* **de•rived; de•riv•ing**
1 to take or get from a source ⟨I *derive* great pleasure from reading.⟩
2 to come from a certain source ⟨Some modern holidays *derive* from ancient traditions.⟩
3 to trace the origin or source of ⟨We *derive* the word "cherry" from a French word.⟩

der•mal \ˈdər-məl\ *adj*
of or relating to skin

der•mis \ˈdər-məs\ *n*
the inner sensitive layer of the skin

de•rog•a•to•ry \di-ˈrä-gə-ˌtȯr-ē\ *adj*
expressing a low opinion of a person or thing ⟨a *derogatory* remark⟩

der•rick \ˈder-ik\ *n*
1 a machine for moving or lifting heavy weights by means of a long arm fitted with ropes and pulleys
2 a framework or tower over an oil well used to support machinery

de•scend \di-ˈsend\ *vb* **de•scend•ed; de•scend•ing**
1 to come or go down from a higher place or level to a lower one ⟨The elevator *descended.*⟩
2 to move down or down along ⟨*Descending* the cliff was dangerous.⟩
3 to slope or lead downward ⟨The road *descends* to the valley.⟩
4 to come down from an earlier time ⟨The custom *descends* from ancient times.⟩

5 to come down from a source or ancestor : DERIVE ⟨Many words *descend* from Latin.⟩
6 to be handed down to an heir
7 to arrive from or as if from the sky ⟨Locusts *descended* on the crops.⟩ ⟨Holiday shoppers *descended* on the mall.⟩
8 to sink in dignity or respectability : STOOP ⟨I never thought they would *descend* to cheating.⟩
9 to sink to a worse condition ⟨The classroom *descended* into chaos.⟩

de•scen•dant \di-ˈsen-dənt\ *n*
1 someone related to a person or group of people who lived at an earlier time
2 a thing that comes from something that existed at an earlier time

de•scent \di-ˈsent\ *n*
1 ▼ an act of coming or going down in location or condition ⟨The plane began its *descent*.⟩
2 a downward slope ⟨a steep *descent*⟩
3 a person's ancestors ⟨She is of Korean *descent*.⟩

de•scribe \di-ˈskrīb\ *vb* **de•scribed**; **de•scrib•ing**
1 to write or tell about ⟨*Describe* what you saw.⟩
2 to draw the outline of ⟨First, *describe* a circle.⟩
synonyms see REPORT

de•scrip•tion \di-ˈskrip-shən\ *n*
1 a written or spoken statement about something that enables a reader or listener to picture it
2 [1]SORT 1, KIND ⟨People of every *description* were there.⟩

de•scrip•tive \di-ˈskrip-tiv\ *adj*
giving information about what something is like

[1]desert: the landscape of a desert

des•e•crate \ˈde-si-ˌkrāt\ *vb* **des•e•crat•ed**; **des•e•crat•ing**
to treat a sacred place or sacred object shamefully or with great disrespect

de•seg•re•gate \dē-ˈse-gri-ˌgāt\ *vb* **de•seg•re•gat•ed**; **de•seg•re•gat•ing**
to end by law the separation of members of different races ⟨*desegregate* schools⟩

de•seg•re•ga•tion \dē-ˌse-gri-ˈgā-shən\ *n*
the act or process or an instance of ending a law or practice that separates people of different races

[1]des•ert \ˈde-zərt\ *n*
▲ a dry land with few plants and little rainfall

[2]de•sert \di-ˈzərt\ *n*
a reward or punishment that a person deserves ⟨He got his just *deserts*.⟩

[3]de•sert \di-ˈzərt\ *vb* **de•sert•ed**; **de•sert•ing**
1 to leave usually without intending to return
2 to leave a person or a thing that one should stay with ⟨The soldier did not *desert* his post.⟩
3 to fail in time of need ⟨My courage *deserted* me.⟩
synonyms see ABANDON
de•sert•er *n*

de•serve \di-ˈzərv\ *vb* **de•served**; **de•serv•ing**
to have earned because of some act or quality

▶ **Synonyms** DESERVE, MERIT, and EARN mean to be worthy of something. DESERVE is used when a person should rightly receive something good or bad because of his or her actions or character. ⟨A hard worker *deserves* to be rewarded.⟩ MERIT is used when someone or something is especially worthy of reward, punishment, or consideration. ⟨These students *merit* special praise.⟩ EARN is used when a person has spent time and effort and gets what he or she deserves. ⟨You've *earned* a long vacation.⟩

descent 1: skiers making a descent

A B C D E F G H I J K L M N O P Q R S T U V W X Y Z

de•served•ly \di-ˈzər-vəd-lē, -ˈzərvd-lē\ *adv*
as earned by acts or qualities ⟨She was *deservedly* honored.⟩

de•serv•ing \di-ˈzər-viŋ\ *adj*
WORTHY 2 ⟨The scholarship will go to a *deserving* student.⟩

¹de•sign \di-ˈzīn\ *vb* **de•signed; de•sign•ing**
1 to think up and plan out in the mind ⟨Our engineers have *designed* a new engine.⟩
2 to set apart for or have as a special purpose : INTEND ⟨The Web site is *designed* for fun.⟩
3 to make a pattern or sketch of ⟨She *designs* clothes.⟩

²design *n*
1 an arrangement of parts in a structure or a work of art ⟨The *design* of the house suits a large family.⟩
2 the art or process of planning and creating something ⟨His job is Web page *design.*⟩
3 a sketch, model, or plan of something made or to be made ⟨Architects studied the *design* for the building.⟩
4 a decorative pattern
5 ¹PLAN 1, SCHEME
6 a planned intention ⟨They had ambitious *designs* for their children.⟩
7 a secret purpose : PLOT ⟨I know you have *designs* on my money.⟩

des•ig•nate \ˈde-zig-ˌnāt\ *vb* **des•ig•nat•ed; des•ig•nat•ing**
1 to appoint or choose for a special purpose ⟨They *designated* a leader.⟩
2 to call by a name or title ⟨Let's *designate* this angle of the triangle *a*.⟩
3 to mark or point out : INDICATE ⟨These lines *designate* the boundaries.⟩

des•ig•na•tion \ˌde-zig-ˈnā-shən\ *n*
1 an act of choosing to be or do something ⟨Voters approved *designation* of the land as a wildlife refuge.⟩
2 a name, sign, or title that identifies something

de•sign•er \di-ˈzī-nər\ *n*
a person who plans how to make or change something ⟨a house *designer*⟩

de•sir•able \di-ˈzī-rə-bəl\ *adj*
1 having pleasing qualities : ATTRACTIVE ⟨a *desirable* location⟩
2 worth having or seeking

¹de•sire \di-ˈzīr\ *vb* **de•sired; de•sir•ing**
1 to long for : wish for in earnest ⟨Both sides *desire* peace.⟩
2 to express a wish for : REQUEST

²desire *n*
1 a strong wish : LONGING ⟨a *desire* for companionship⟩
2 something longed for ⟨It was his heart's *desire* to return home.⟩

▶ **Synonyms** DESIRE, WISH, and CRAVE mean to want something very much. DESIRE is used when a person has a great feeling for and actually strives to get what is wanted. ⟨The immigrants *desired* a better life.⟩ WISH is used when a person wants something that he or she has little or no chance of getting. ⟨He foolishly sat around and *wished* for wealth.⟩ CRAVE is used for the force of physical or mental needs. ⟨The hungry dogs *craved* food.⟩

de•sist \di-ˈzist, -ˈsist\ *vb* **de•sist•ed; de•sist•ing**
to stop doing something ⟨Please *desist* from making that noise.⟩

desk \ˈdesk\ *n*
1 a piece of furniture with a flat or sloping surface for use in writing or reading
2 a counter at which a person works especially to help customers

desk•top \ˈdesk-ˌtäp\ *n*
1 the top of a desk
2 ▼ a computer that is used on a desk or table and is too big to be moved easily
3 an area on a computer screen in which items are arranged as if they were objects on top of a desk

¹des•o•late \ˈde-sə-lət\ *adj*
1 having no comfort or companionship : LONELY
2 left neglected or in ruins ⟨a *desolate* old house⟩
3 without signs of life : BARREN ⟨a dry, *desolate* land⟩
4 CHEERLESS, GLOOMY ⟨She put aside *desolate* thoughts.⟩
des•o•late•ly *adv*

²des•o•late \ˈde-sə-ˌlāt\ *vb* **des•o•lat•ed; des•o•lat•ing**
to ruin or leave without comfort or companionship

des•o•la•tion \ˌde-sə-ˈlā-shən\ *n*
1 the state of being deserted or ruined
2 sadness resulting from grief or loneliness

¹de•spair \di-ˈsper\ *vb* **de•spaired; de•spair•ing**
to give up or lose all hope or confidence

²despair *n*
1 loss of hope : a feeling of complete hopelessness ⟨He finally gave up in *despair.*⟩
2 a cause of hopelessness

de•spair•ing \di-ˈsper-iŋ\ *adj*
having or showing no hope ⟨a *despairing* voice⟩
de•spair•ing•ly *adv*

des•per•ate \ˈde-spə-rət, -sprət\ *adj*
1 very sad and worried and with little or no hope ⟨People became *desperate* for food.⟩
2 showing great worry and loss of hope ⟨a *desperate* call for help⟩
3 giving little reason to hope : causing despair ⟨a *desperate* situation⟩
4 reckless because of despair : RASH ⟨He made a *desperate* attempt to escape.⟩
5 very severe ⟨The injury is in *desperate* need of attention.⟩

des•per•ate•ly \ˈde-spə-rət-lē, -sprət-lē\ *adv*
1 in a way showing great worry and weakening hope ⟨They *desperately* called for help.⟩
2 in such a way as to leave little hope ⟨He became *desperately* ill.⟩
3 with great intensity ⟨I *desperately* wanted a pony.⟩

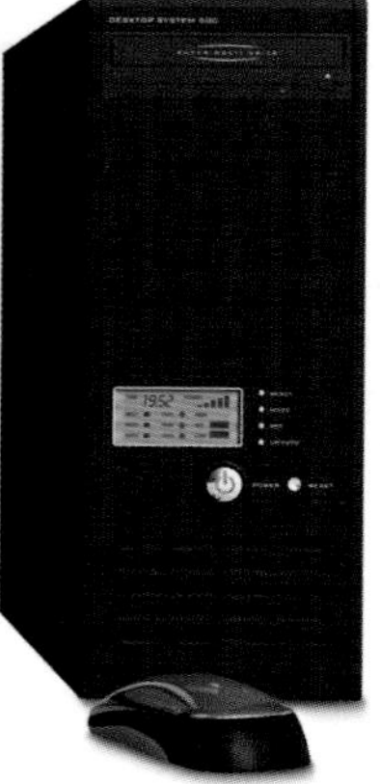

desktop 2

des•per•a•tion \ˌde-spə-ˈrā-shən\ *n*
a condition of hopelessness often leading to recklessness ⟨The robbery was an act of *desperation*.⟩

de•spi•ca•ble \di-ˈspi-kə-bəl, ˈde-spik-\ *adj*
very bad : deserving to be despised ⟨a *despicable* act of cowardice⟩

de•spise \di-ˈspīz\ *vb* **de•spised**; **de•spis•ing**
to feel scorn and dislike for

▶ **Synonyms** DESPISE and SCORN mean to consider a person or thing as not worth noticing or taking an interest in. DESPISE may be used of feeling ranging from strong dislike to true hatred. ⟨I *despise* liars.⟩ SCORN is used of a deep and ready feeling of angry disgust for anything that a person doesn't respect. ⟨The sergeant *scorned* the soldiers who were lazy.⟩

de•spite \di-ˈspīt\ *prep*
in spite of ⟨The quarterback played *despite* an injury.⟩

de•spon•den•cy \di-ˈspän-dən-sē\ *n*
DEJECTION, SADNESS

de•spon•dent \di-ˈspän-dənt\ *adj*
very sad ⟨Left alone, she grew *despondent*.⟩
de•spon•dent•ly *adv*

des•pot \ˈde-spət\ *n*
a ruler having absolute power and authority and especially one who rules cruelly

des•sert \di-ˈzərt\ *n*
a sweet food eaten at the end of a meal

des•ti•na•tion \ˌde-stə-ˈnā-shən\ *n*
a place that a person starts out for or that something is sent to

des•tined \ˈde-stənd\ *adj*
1 certain to do or be something ⟨He was *destined* to be king.⟩
2 going or traveling to a particular place ⟨This train is *destined* for New York.⟩

des•ti•ny \ˈde-stə-nē\ *n, pl* **des•ti•nies**
1 what happens to someone or something in the future ⟨You can decide your own *destiny*.⟩
2 the course of events believed to be controlled by a superhuman power
3 a power that is believed to control the future

des•ti•tute \ˈde-stə-ˌtüt, -ˌtyüt\ *adj*
1 lacking something needed or desirable ⟨The room was *destitute* of comforts.⟩
2 very poor ⟨The charity helps *destitute* people.⟩

des•ti•tu•tion \ˌde-stə-ˈtü-shən, -ˈtyü-\ *n*
the condition of being very poor

de•stroy \di-ˈstrȯi\ *vb* **de•stroyed**; **de•stroy•ing**
1 to put an end to : do away with ⟨*destroy* a building⟩ ⟨*destroy* a dream⟩
2 [1]KILL 1 ⟨Officials *destroyed* the diseased animals.⟩

de•stroy•er \di-ˈstrȯi-ər\ *n*
1 someone or something that ruins or ends something
2 ▼ a small fast warship armed with guns, torpedoes, and sometimes missiles

de•struc•tion \di-ˈstrək-shən\ *n*
1 the act or process of killing, ruining, or putting an end to something ⟨*Destruction* of the old building is underway.⟩
2 the state or fact of being killed, ruined, or brought to an end

de•struc•tive \di-ˈstrək-tiv\ *adj*
1 causing great damage or ruin ⟨a *destructive* storm⟩
2 not positive or helpful ⟨*destructive* criticism⟩

de•tach \di-ˈtach\ *vb* **de•tached**; **de•tach•ing**
to separate from something else or from others especially for a certain purpose ⟨The hood *detaches* from the jacket.⟩
de•tach•able \-ə-bəl\ *adj*

de•tached \di-ˈtacht\ *adj*
1 not joined or connected : SEPARATE ⟨a *detached* garage⟩
2 not taking sides or being influenced by others ⟨They wanted the opinion of a *detached* judge.⟩

destroyer 2

de•tach•ment \di-'tach-mənt\ *n*
1 SEPARATION 1
2 the sending out of a body of troops or ships on a special duty
3 a small unit of troops or ships sent out for a special duty
4 lack of interest in worldly concerns ⟨He maintained an air of cool *detachment.*⟩
5 freedom from the favoring of one side over another ⟨He judged with *detachment.*⟩

[1]**de•tail** \di-'tāl, 'dē-,tāl\ *n*
1 a dealing with something with attention to each item ⟨The story went into *detail.*⟩
2 a small part of something larger : ITEM ⟨Every *detail* of the wedding was perfect.⟩
3 a soldier or group of soldiers picked for special duty

[2]**detail** *vb* **de•tailed**; **de•tail•ing**
1 to report with attention to each item ⟨The letter *detailed* her vacation plans.⟩
2 to select for some special duty

de•tailed \di-'tāld, 'dē-,tāld\ *adj*
including many small items or parts ⟨a *detailed* report⟩

de•tain \di-'tān\ *vb* **de•tained**; **de•tain•ing**
1 to hold or keep in or as if in prison ⟨The suspect was *detained* by police.⟩
2 to stop especially from going on : DELAY ⟨We were *detained* by heavy traffic.⟩

de•tect \di-'tekt\ *vb* **de•tect•ed**; **de•tect•ing**
to learn that something or someone is or was there ⟨He *detected* an odor of smoke.⟩
de•tec•tor \-'tek-tər\ *n*

de•tec•tion \di-'tek-shən\ *n*
the act of learning that something or someone is or was there : DISCOVERY

de•tec•tive \di-'tek-tiv\ *n*
a person (as a police officer) who solves crimes and catches criminals or gathers information that is not easy to get

de•ten•tion \di-'ten-chən\ *n*
1 the act of holding back or delaying : the condition of being held or delayed ⟨The prisoner was held in *detention* before trial.⟩
2 the punishment of being kept after school

de•ter \di-'tər\ *vb* **de•terred**; **de•ter•ring**
1 to cause (someone) not to do something
2 to prevent (something) from happening ⟨Painting the metal will *deter* rust.⟩

de•ter•gent \di-'tər-jənt\ *n*
▶ a substance that cleans

de•te•ri•o•rate \di-'tir-ē-ə-,rāt\ *vb* **de•te•ri•o•rat•ed**; **de•te•ri•o•rat•ing**
to make or become worse or of less value ⟨Their relationship *deteriorated.*⟩ ⟨Rain *deteriorates* wooden structures.⟩

de•ter•mi•na•tion \di-,tər-mə-'nā-shən\ *n*
1 firm or fixed intention ⟨She set out with *determination* to complete the journey.⟩
2 an act of deciding or the decision reached ⟨Has the jury made a *determination?*⟩
3 an act of making sure of the position, size, or nature of something

de•ter•mine \di-'tər-mən\ *vb* **de•ter•mined**; **de•ter•min•ing**
1 to come to a decision ⟨The court will *determine* who wins the case.⟩
2 to learn or find out exactly ⟨Officials *determined* the cause of the accident.⟩
3 to be the cause of or reason for ⟨The weather will *determine* if we eat outside.⟩
4 to fix exactly and with certainty ⟨Her future was *determined.*⟩

de•ter•mined \di-'tər-mənd\ *adj*
1 free from doubt about doing something ⟨He was *determined* to make it home.⟩
2 not weak or uncertain : FIRM ⟨She's making a *determined* effort.⟩

de•ter•min•er \di-'tər-mə-nər\ *n*
a word belonging to a group of noun modifiers that can occur before descriptive adjectives modifying the same noun ⟨"The" in "the red house" is a *determiner.*⟩

de•ter•rent \di-'tər-ənt, -'ter-\ *n*
something that makes someone decide not to do something ⟨The alarm is a *deterrent* against theft.⟩

de•test \di-'test\ *vb* **de•test•ed**; **de•test•ing**
to dislike very much

de•throne \di-'thrōn\ *vb* **de•throned**; **de•thron•ing**
to remove (a king or queen) from power

detergent:
liquid detergent

[1]**de•tour** \'dē-,tu̇r\ *n*
a roundabout way that temporarily replaces part of a regular route

[2]**detour** *vb* **de•toured**; **de•tour•ing**
to go or make go on a different route than usual ⟨All cars were *detoured.*⟩

de•tract \di-'trakt\ *vb* **de•tract•ed**; **de•tract•ing**
to take away (as from value or importance)

det•ri•ment \'de-trə-mənt\ *n*
injury or damage or its cause : HARM

det•ri•men•tal \'de-trə-'men-t^{ə}l\ *adj*
causing damage or injury ⟨the *detrimental* effects of smoking⟩

dev•as•tate \'de-və-,stāt\ *vb* **dev•as•tat•ed**; **dev•as•tat•ing**
1 to destroy entirely or nearly entirely ⟨The forest was *devastated* by fire.⟩
2 to cause to suffer emotionally

dev•as•ta•tion \,de-və-'stā-shən\ *n*
the action of destroying or damaging greatly : the state of being greatly damaged or destroyed ⟨the storm's *devastation*⟩

de•vel•op \di-'ve-ləp\ *vb* **de•vel•oped**; **de•vel•op•ing**
1 to make or become plain little by little : UNFOLD ⟨as the story *develops*⟩
2 to make a photograph from (film) by using special processes and chemicals
3 to bring out the possibilities of : IMPROVE ⟨*develop* an idea⟩
4 to make more available or usable ⟨*develop* land⟩
5 to begin to have gradually ⟨*develop* a cough⟩
6 to begin to exist or be present gradually ⟨A romance *developed* between them.⟩
7 to create over time ⟨*develop* new medicines⟩
8 to grow or cause to grow bigger or more advanced ⟨*develop* muscles⟩
de•vel•op•er *n*

de•vel•oped \di-'ve-ləpt\ *adj*
1 having many large industries and a complex economic system ⟨*developed* nations⟩
2 bigger, more mature, or more advanced ⟨Dogs have a highly *developed* sense of smell.⟩

de•vel•op•ment \di-'ve-ləp-mənt\ *n*
1 the act, process, or result of developing
2 the state of being developed

de•vi•ate \'dē-vē-,āt\ *vb* **de•vi•at•ed**; **de•vi•at•ing**
to follow a course, principle, standard, or topic that is different from usual ⟨He never *deviates* from his daily routine.⟩

de•vice \di-'vīs\ *n*
1 a piece of equipment made for a special purpose ⟨electronic *devices*⟩

2 choice of what to do ⟨We were left to our own *devices.*⟩
3 a thing or act used to deceive : TRICK

dev•il \'de-vəl\ *n*
1 ▼ *often cap* the most powerful spirit of evil
2 an evil spirit : DEMON, FIEND
3 a wicked or cruel person

devil 1: a medieval sculpture of the devil

4 an attractive, mischievous, or unfortunate person ⟨a handsome *devil*⟩ ⟨poor *devils*⟩

dev•iled \'de-vəld\ *adj*
spicy or highly seasoned ⟨*deviled* ham⟩

dev•il•ish \'de-və-lish, 'dev-lish\ *adj*
1 evil and cruel
2 MISCHIEVOUS 1

dev•il•ment \'de-vəl-mənt\ *n*
MISCHIEF 2

de•vi•ous \'dē-vē-əs\ *adj*
1 SNEAKY, DISHONEST
2 not straight : having many twists and turns ⟨a *devious* trail⟩

de•vise \di-'vīz\ *vb* **de•vised; de•vis•ing**
to think up : PLAN, INVENT ⟨We *devised* a plan to win.⟩

de•void \di-'vȯid\ *adj*
completely without ⟨The room was *devoid* of decoration.⟩

de•vote \di-'vōt\ *vb* **de•vot•ed; de•vot•ing**
1 to set apart for a special purpose ⟨The land was *devoted* to wildlife preservation.⟩
2 to give up to entirely or in part ⟨He *devoted* himself to finding a cure.⟩

de•vot•ed \di-'vō-təd\ *adj*
1 completely loyal ⟨*devoted* supporters and admirers⟩
2 AFFECTIONATE, LOVING ⟨a *devoted* parent⟩
de•vot•ed•ly *adv*

de•vo•tion \di-'vō-shən\ *n*
1 deep love or loyalty
2 an act of giving (as effort or time) to something ⟨His *devotion* of many hours of work was rewarded.⟩
3 a religious exercise or practice (as prayers) especially that is private

de•vour \di-'vau̇r\ *vb* **de•voured; de•vour•ing**
1 to eat up hungrily
2 to take in eagerly by the senses or mind ⟨He *devoured* the information.⟩
3 to destroy as if by eating ⟨The buildings were *devoured* by flames.⟩

de•vout \di-'vau̇t\ *adj*
1 deeply religious
2 strongly loyal or devoted ⟨They are *devout* believers in education.⟩
3 warmly sincere and earnest ⟨*devout* thanks⟩
de•vout•ly *adv*

dew \'dü, 'dyü\ *n*
▶ moisture that collects on cool surfaces at night

dew•lap \'dü-,lap, 'dyü-\ *n*
▼ loose skin hanging under the neck of some animals (as cows)

dewlap: a bull with dewlap

dew point *n*
the temperature at which the moisture in the air begins to turn to dew

dewy \'dü-ē, 'dyü-\ *adj* **dew•i•er; dew•i•est**
moist with or as if with dew ⟨*dewy* grass⟩ ⟨*dewy* eyes⟩

dex•ter•i•ty \dek-'ster-ə-tē\ *n, pl* **dex•ter•i•ties**
1 skill and ease in the use of the hands or body
2 the ability to think and act quickly and cleverly

dex•ter•ous \'dek-stə-rəs, -strəs\ *adj*
1 skillful with the hands ⟨a *dexterous* potter⟩
2 CLEVER 2 ⟨a *dexterous* chess player⟩
3 done with skill ⟨The skier made a *dexterous* jump.⟩
dex•ter•ous•ly *adv*

dew: dew drops on a leaf

di•a•be•tes \,dī-ə-'bē-tēz, -'bē-təs\ *n*
a disease in which too little or no insulin is produced or insulin is produced but cannot be used normally resulting in high levels of sugar in the blood

di•a•bet•ic \,dī-ə-'be-tik\ *n*
a person with diabetes

di•a•crit•i•cal mark \,dī-ə-'kri-ti-kəl-\ *n*
a mark that is placed over, under, or through a letter in some languages to show that the letter should be pronounced in a particular way

di•ag•nose \'dī-əg-,nōs\ *vb* **di•ag•nosed; di•ag•nos•ing**
to recognize (as a disease) by signs and symptoms ⟨The test is used for *diagnosing* strep throat.⟩

di•ag•no•sis \,dī-əg-'nō-səs\ *n, pl* **di•ag•no•ses** \-,sēz\
1 the act of recognizing a disease from its signs and symptoms
2 the conclusion that is reached following examination and testing ⟨The *diagnosis* was pneumonia.⟩

¹di•ag•o•nal \dī-'a-gə-nᵊl, -'ag-nəl\ *adj*
1 running from one corner to the opposite corner of a four-sided shape (as a square) ⟨a *diagonal* line⟩
2 running in a slanting direction ⟨*diagonal* stripes⟩
di•ag•o•nal•ly \-nə-lē\ *adv*

A B C D E F G H I J K L M N O P Q R S T U V W X Y Z

²diagonal *n*
a line, direction, or pattern that runs in a slanting direction

¹di•a•gram \'dī-ə-ˌgram\ *n*
a drawing, plan, or chart that makes something clearer or easier to understand

²diagram *vb* **di•a•grammed** *or* **di•a•gramed** \'dī-ə-ˌgramd\; **di•a•gram•ming** *or* **di•a•gram•ing** \-ˌgra-miŋ\
to put in the form of a drawing, plan, or chart

¹di•al \'dī-əl\ *n*
1 ▼ the face of a watch or clock
2 SUNDIAL
3 a usually flat round part of a piece of equipment with numbers or marks to show some measurement usually by means of a pointer 〈the *dial* of a pressure gauge〉
4 a part of a machine or device (as a radio) that may be turned to operate or adjust it

¹dial 1

²dial *vb* **di•aled** *or* **di•alled**; **di•al•ing** *or* **di•al•ling**
to use a knob, button, or other control to operate or select

di•a•lect \'dī-ə-ˌlekt\ *n*
a form of a language that is spoken in a certain region or by a certain group

di•a•logue *also* **di•a•log** \'dī-ə-ˌlȯg\ *n*
1 conversation given in a written story or a play
2 a conversation between two or more people or groups 〈Both sides agreed to a *dialogue* about the issue.〉

di•am•e•ter \dī-'a-mə-tər\ *n*
1 a straight line that runs from one side of a figure and passes through the center 〈Measure the *diameter* of the circle.〉
2 the distance through the center of an object from one side to the other : THICKNESS 〈the *diameter* of a tree trunk〉

di•a•mond \'dī-ə-mənd, 'dī-mənd\ *n*
1 ▼ a very hard mineral that is a form of carbon, is usually nearly colorless, and is used especially in jewelry
2 a flat figure ◊ like one of the surfaces of certain cut diamonds
3 INFIELD 1

diamond 1

di•a•per \'dī-pər, 'dī-ə-pər\ *n*
a piece of absorbent material for a baby worn pulled up between the legs and fastened around the waist

di•a•phragm \'dī-ə-ˌfram\ *n*
1 a muscular wall that separates the lungs from the stomach area and assists in breathing in
2 a thin disk (as in a microphone) that vibrates when sound strikes it

di•ar•rhea \ˌdī-ə-'rē-ə\ *n*
abnormally frequent and watery bowel movements

di•a•ry \'dī-ə-rē, 'dī-rē\ *n, pl* **di•a•ries**
1 a daily written record especially of personal experiences and thoughts
2 a book for keeping a record of experiences and thoughts

¹dice \'dīs\ *n, pl* **dice**
²DIE 1

²dice *vb* **diced**; **dic•ing**
to cut into small cubes 〈*dice* carrots〉

di•cot \ 'dī-ˌkät\ *n* DICOTYLEDON

di•cot•y•le•don \ˌdī-ˌkä-tə-'lē-dᵊn\ *n*
a flowering plant (as an oak or bean plant) having an embryo with two cotyledons

¹dic•tate \'dik-ˌtāt\ *vb* **dic•tat•ed**; **dic•tat•ing**
1 to speak or read for someone else to write down or for a machine to record
2 to say or state with authority : ORDER
3 to make necessary 〈Tradition *dictates* that we go first.〉

²dictate *n*
1 a statement made or direction given with authority : COMMAND
2 a guiding rule or principle

dic•ta•tion \dik-'tā-shən\ *n*
the act of speaking words for someone else to write down or for a machine to record the words spoken

dic•ta•tor \'dik-ˌtā-tər\ *n*
a person who rules with total power and often in a cruel manner
dic•ta•tor•ship \dik-'tā-tər-ˌship\ *n*

dic•tion \'dik-shən\ *n*
1 choice of words especially with regard to correctness, clearness, and effectiveness
2 the ability to say words 〈He has excellent *diction* for his age.〉

dic•tio•nary \'dik-shə-ˌner-ē\ *n, pl* **dic•tio•nar•ies**
1 a book giving the meaning and usually the pronunciation of words listed in alphabetical order
2 a reference book explaining words of a particular subject listed in alphabetical order 〈a medical *dictionary*〉
3 a book listing words of one language in alphabetical order with definitions in another language

did *past of* DO

didn't \'di-dᵊnt\
did not

¹die \'dī\ *vb* **died**; **dy•ing**
1 to stop living
2 to come to an end 〈Their hope has not *died.*〉
3 to want badly 〈I'm *dying* to go.〉
4 to stop working or running 〈The motor *died.*〉
die down to gradually become less strong 〈The wind *died down.*〉
die off to die one after another so fewer and fewer are left 〈Without water, the cattle *died off.*〉
die out to disappear gradually 〈The dinosaurs *died out* millions of years ago.〉

²die 1

²die *n*
1 ▲ *pl* **dice** \'dīs\ a small cube marked on each side with one to six spots and used in games
2 *pl* **dies** \'dīz\ a device for forming or cutting material by pressure

die•sel \'dē-zəl, -səl\ *n*
1 DIESEL ENGINE
2 ▶ a vehicle that has a diesel engine
3 DIESEL FUEL

diesel engine *n*
an engine in which the mixture of air and fuel is compressed until enough heat is created to ignite the mixture that uses diesel fuel instead of gasoline

diesel fuel *n*
a heavy oil used as fuel in diesel engines

[1]**di•et** \'dī-ət\ *n*
1 the food and drink that a person or animal usually takes ⟨a balanced *diet*⟩
2 the kind and amount of food selected or allowed in certain circumstances (as poor health) ⟨a low fat *diet*⟩

[2]**diet** *vb* **di•et•ed**; **di•et•ing**
to eat less or according to certain rules in order to lose weight
di•et•er *n*

[3]**diet** *adj*
reduced in calories ⟨a *diet* soft drink⟩

di•e•tary \'dī-ə-,ter-ē\ *adj*
relating to a diet ⟨special *dietary* needs⟩

di•e•ti•tian *or* **di•e•ti•cian** \,dī-ə-'ti-shən\ *n*
a person trained to give advice about diet and nutrition

dif•fer \'di-fər\ *vb* **dif•fered**; **dif•fer•ing**
1 to be unlike : be different
2 DISAGREE 1 ⟨We *differ* on how best to proceed.⟩

dif•fer•ence \'di-fə-rəns, 'di-frəns\ *n*
1 what makes two or more persons or things not the same ⟨I can't see any *difference* between the two designs.⟩
2 a disagreement about something ⟨They've always had their *differences*.⟩
3 the number that is left after subtracting one number from another ⟨The *difference* between six and four is two.⟩
4 an important change ⟨A tutor has made a *difference* in his grades.⟩

diesel 2:
a locomotive with a diesel engine

dif•fer•ent \'di-fə-rənt, 'di-frənt\ *adj*
1 not of the same kind ⟨They come from *different* backgrounds.⟩
2 not the same ⟨We went to *different* schools.⟩
3 not ordinary ⟨That movie was certainly *different*.⟩
dif•fer•ent•ly *adv*

dif•fer•en•ti•ate \,di-fə-'ren-shē-,āt\ *vb* **dif•fer•en•ti•at•ed**; **dif•fer•en•ti•at•ing**
1 to make or become different ⟨What *differentiates* the cars?⟩
2 to recognize or state the difference between ⟨I can't *differentiate* the two colors.⟩

dif•fer•en•ti•a•tion \,di-fə-,ren-shē-'ā-shən\ *n*
the process of change by which immature living structures develop to maturity

dif•fi•cult \'di-fi-,kəlt\ *adj*
1 not easy : hard to do or make ⟨a *difficult* job⟩
2 hard to deal with ⟨*difficult* circumstances⟩ ⟨a *difficult* child⟩
3 hard to understand ⟨a *difficult* subject⟩

dif•fi•cul•ty \'di-fi-,kəl-tē\ *n*, *pl* **dif•fi•cul•ties**
1 the state of being hard to do ⟨the *difficulty* of a task⟩
2 great effort ⟨He solved the puzzle with *difficulty*.⟩
3 something that makes something hard to do : OBSTACLE ⟨She overcame great *difficulties* to achieve success.⟩
4 a troublesome situation ⟨She saw a way out of the *difficulty*.⟩

dif•fi•dent \'di-fə-dənt\ *adj*
1 lacking confidence
2 cautious about acting or speaking ⟨He was *diffident* about expressing his thoughts.⟩

dif•fuse \di-'fyüz\ *vb* **dif•fused**; **dif•fus•ing**
to spread or allow to spread freely

dif•fu•sion \di-'fyü-zhən\ *n*
1 the act of spreading or allowing to spread freely
2 ▼ the mixing of particles of liquids or gases so that they move from a region of high concentration to one of lower concentration

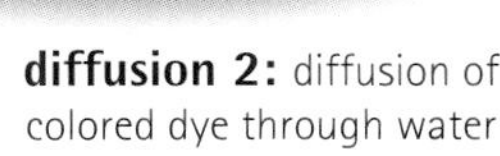

diffusion 2: diffusion of colored dye through water

[1]**dig** \'dig\ *vb* **dug** \'dəg\; **dig•ging**
1 to turn up, loosen, or remove the soil ⟨The dog was *digging* in the garden again.⟩
2 to turn up or remove with a shovel or by similar means ⟨I *dug* into the snow.⟩
3 to form by removing earth ⟨*dig* a hole⟩ ⟨*dig* a cellar⟩
4 to uncover or search by or as if by turning up earth ⟨They *dug* for gold.⟩
5 [1]PROD 1, POKE ⟨He *dug* me in the ribs.⟩
dig in to begin eating ⟨Supper's ready, so *dig in*.⟩
dig into
1 to begin eating ⟨He *dug into* a plate of pasta.⟩
2 to try to discover information ⟨Reporters were *digging into* the story.⟩
dig up
1 to uncover or remove (as from soil) ⟨*dig up* a bush⟩
2 DISCOVER ⟨I *dug up* information about her past.⟩

[2]**dig** *n*
1 [2]POKE ⟨a *dig* in the ribs⟩
2 a place where buried objects are being uncovered ⟨a dinosaur *dig*⟩
3 a project to uncover buried objects ⟨The bones were found during a recent *dig*.⟩
4 a nasty remark ⟨She got in a *dig* about forgetting her birthday.⟩

[1]**di•gest** \'dī-,jest\ *n*
information in shortened form

A B C D E F G H I J K L M N O P Q R S T U V W X Y Z

²di•gest \dī-ˈjest, də-\ *vb* **di•gest•ed; di•gest•ing**
1 to change or become changed into simpler forms that can be used by the body 〈*digest* a meal〉 〈My dinner is still *digesting.*〉
2 to think over and try to understand 〈That's a lot of information to *digest.*〉

di•gest•ible \dī-ˈjes-tə-bəl, də-\ *adj*
possible to digest

di•ges•tion \dī-ˈjes-chən, də-\ *n*
▶ the body's process or power of changing food into simpler forms that can be taken up and used

di•ges•tive \dī-ˈje-stiv, də-\ *adj*
relating to or functioning in the body's process of changing food into simpler forms that can be taken up and used 〈*digestive* processes〉

digestive system *n*
the system of the body that takes in, breaks down, and absorbs food and discharges solid waste and consists of the digestive tract and related glands (as the salivary glands and pancreas)

digestive tract *n*
the tube-shaped passage including the mouth, pharynx, esophagus, stomach, and intestines that is concerned with taking in, breaking down, and absorbing food and discharging solid waste

dig•it \ˈdi-jət\ *n*
1 any of the numerals 1 to 9 and the symbol 0
2 ▼ a finger or toe

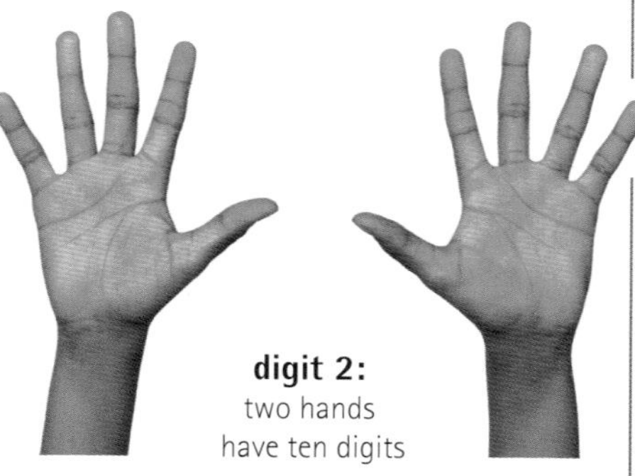

digit 2: two hands have ten digits

dig•i•tal \ˈdi-jə-tᵊl\ *adj*
1 relating to or using calculation directly with digits rather than through measurable physical quantities
2 of or relating to data in the form of numerical digits 〈*digital* images〉 〈*digital* broadcasting〉
3 providing displayed or recorded information in numerical digits from an automatic device 〈a *digital* watch〉
dig•i•tal•ly \-tᵊl-ē\ *adv*

▶ **digestion**
Digestion begins in the mouth, where food is chewed into smaller chunks by the teeth. Saliva helps the tongue and teeth to form the food into a paste, which then travels into the pharynx, through the esophagus, and into the stomach, where it is further broken down by acid digestive fluid. The food now passes into the small intestine, where secretions from the intestine, pancreas, gall bladder (not shown), and liver continue digestion, and nutrients are absorbed into the bloodstream. Any remaining waste is compressed in the large intestine, and expelled from the body via the rectum.

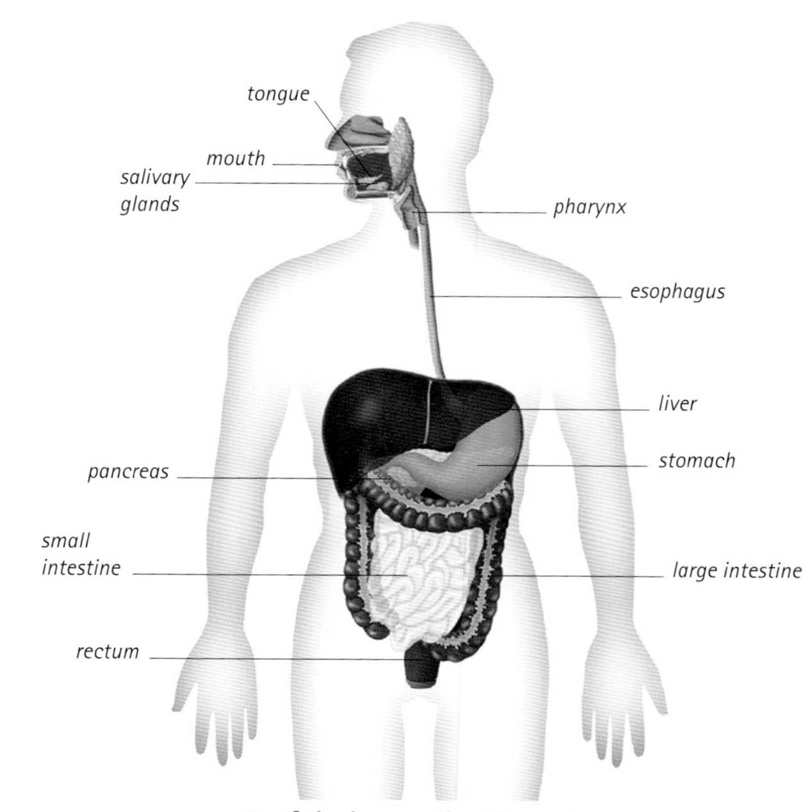

parts of the human digestive system

digital camera *n*
▶ a camera that takes pictures without using film by recording the images as electronic data

dig•ni•fied \ˈdig-nə-ˌfīd\ *adj*
having or showing dignity

dig•ni•fy \ˈdig-nə-ˌfī\ *vb* **dig•ni•fied; dig•ni•fy•ing**
1 to give dignity or importance to 〈She felt formal clothes would *dignify* the occasion.〉
2 to treat with respect or seriousness that is not deserved 〈I'm not going to *dignify* that remark with a response.〉

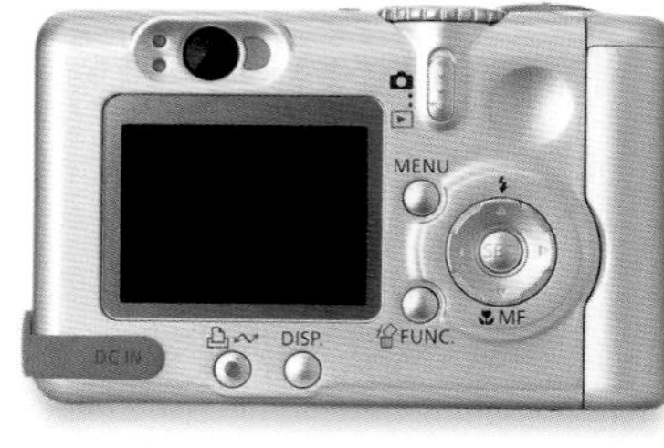

digital camera: front and back views of a digital camera

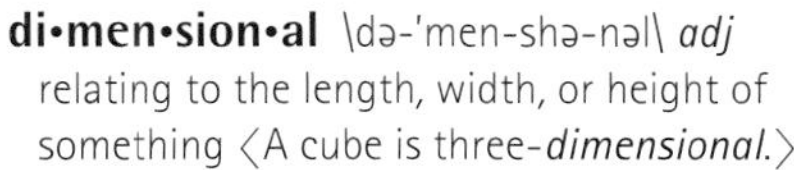

dig•ni•tary \'dig-nə-,ter-ē\ *n*, *pl* **dig•ni•tar•ies**
a person of high position or honor

dig•ni•ty \'dig-nə-tē\ *n*, *pl* **dig•ni•ties**
1 the quality or state of being worthy of honor and respect
2 a serious and admirable look or way of behaving

dike \'dīk\ *n*
1 a long trench dug in the earth to carry water
2 a mound of earth built to control water

di•lap•i•dat•ed \də-'la-pə-,dā-təd\ *adj*
falling apart or ruined from age or from lack of care ⟨a *dilapidated* car⟩

di•late \dī-'lāt\ *vb* **di•lat•ed**; **di•lat•ing**
to make or grow larger or wider ⟨Her pupils *dilated* in the dark.⟩

di•lem•ma \də-'le-mə\ *n*
a situation in which a person has to choose between things that are all bad or unsatisfactory ⟨He was faced with the *dilemma* of having to tell on his best friend, or not telling and getting blamed himself.⟩

dil•i•gence \'di-lə-jəns\ *n*
careful and continued hard work

dil•i•gent \'di-lə-jənt\ *adj*
showing steady and earnest care and hard work ⟨a *diligent* search⟩
dil•i•gent•ly *adv*

dill \'dil\ *n*
▼an herb that is related to the carrot plant and has fragrant leaves and seeds used in flavoring foods and especially pickles

dill

dil•ly•dal•ly \'di-lē-,dalē\ *vb* **dil•ly•dal•lied**; **dil•ly•dal•ly•ing**
to waste time : DAWDLE

di•lute \dī-'lüt, də-\ *vb* **di•lut•ed**; **di•lut•ing** to make thinner or more liquid by adding something

di•lu•tion \dī-'lü-shən, də-\ *n*
1 the act of making thinner or more liquid : the state of being made thinner or more liquid
2 something (as a solution) that has had something added to it to make it thinner or more liquid

[1]**dim** \'dim\ *adj* **dim•mer**; **dim•mest**
1 not bright or distinct : FAINT ⟨a *dim* light⟩
2 not seeing or understanding clearly ⟨*dim* eyes⟩ ⟨a *dim* awareness⟩
dim•ly *adv*
dim•ness *n*

[2]**dim** *vb* **dimmed**; **dim•ming**
to make or become less bright or clear ⟨*Dim* the lights.⟩ ⟨Vision can *dim* with age.⟩

dime

dime \'dīm\ *n*
▲ a United States coin worth ten cents

▶ **Word History** In earlier English, our name for a coin worth a tenth of a dollar meant simply "a tenth part" of something. This word was borrowed from medieval French *dime* or *disme*, with the same meaning. *Dime*, in turn, descends from Latin *decima*, a form of *decimus*, meaning "tenth."

di•men•sion \də-'men-shən\ *n*
the length, width, or height of something

di•men•sion•al \də-'men-shə-nəl\ *adj*
relating to the length, width, or height of something ⟨A cube is three-*dimensional*.⟩

di•min•ish \də-'mi-nish\ *vb* **di•min•ished**; **di•min•ish•ing**
1 to make less or cause to seem less
2 BELITTLE
3 to become gradually less or smaller
di•min•ish•ment \-mənt\ *n*

di•min•u•en•do \də-,min-yə-'wen-dō\ *n*, *pl* **di•min•u•en•dos** *or* **di•min•u•en•does**
DECRESCENDO

di•min•u•tive \də-'min-yə-tiv\ *adj*
very small : TINY

dim•ple \'dim-pəl\ *n*
a slight hollow spot especially in the cheek or chin

din \'din\ *n*
loud confused noise

dine \'dīn\ *vb* **dined**; **din•ing**
to eat dinner ⟨Will you *dine* with us?⟩
dine out to eat at a restaurant

din•er \'dī-nər\ *n*
1 a person eating dinner
2 a railroad dining car or a restaurant that looks like one

di•nette \dī-'net\ *n*
a small room or separate area near a kitchen that is used for dining

ding•dong \'diŋ-,dȯŋ\ *n*
the sound of a bell ringing

din•ghy \'diŋ-ē, 'diŋ-gē\ *n*, *pl* **dinghies**
1▼ a small light rowboat
2 a rubber life raft

din•gy \'din-jē\ *adj* **din•gi•er**; **din•gi•est**
rather dark and dirty ⟨a *dingy* room⟩

din•ky \'diŋ-kē\ *adj* **din•ki•er**; **din•ki•est**
very small and not impressive ⟨a *dinky* car⟩

din•ner \'di-nər\ *n*
1 the main meal of the day
2 a usually large formal event at which a meal is served

dinghy 1: two girls in a dinghy

di•no•saur \'dī-nə-,sȯr\ *n*
▼ any of a group of extinct often very large mostly land-dwelling reptiles that lived millions of years ago

dint \'dint\ *n*
the force or power of something — used in the phrase *by dint of* 〈They succeeded by *dint* of hard work.〉

di•o•cese \'dī-ə-səs, -,sēz\ *n*
the area that is under the authority of a bishop

[1]dip \'dip\ *vb* **dipped; dip•ping**
1 to lower or push briefly into a liquid to wet or coat 〈He *dipped* a chip in the salsa.〉
2 to lift (liquid) out from a container
3 to lower and quickly raise again **:** drop or sink and quickly rise again 〈Temperatures *dipped* below freezing overnight.〉
4 to sink out of sight 〈The sun *dipped* below the horizon.〉
5 to slope downward 〈The road *dips* slightly.〉

[2]dip *n*
1 a short swim
2 something obtained by or as if by a ladle 〈a *dip* of ice cream〉
3 a sauce into which solid food may be dipped 〈chips and *dip*〉
4 a downward slope 〈a *dip* in the road〉
5 a brief decrease 〈a *dip* in prices〉

diph•the•ria \dif-'thir-ē-ə, dip-\ *n*
a contagious disease that often makes breathing and swallowing difficult

diph•thong \'dif-,thȯŋ, 'dip-\ *n*
two vowel sounds joined in one syllable to form one speech sound 〈The sounds of "ou" in "out" and of "oy" in "boy" are *diphthongs*.〉

di•plo•ma \də-'plō-mə\ *n*
a certificate that shows a person has finished a course of study or graduated from a school

di•plo•ma•cy \də-'plō-mə-sē\ *n*
1 the work of keeping good relations between the governments of different countries
2 skill in dealing with people

dip•lo•mat \'di-plə-,mat\ *n*
1 a person whose work is keeping good relations between the governments of different countries
2 a person who is good at dealing with people in a way that avoids bad feelings

dip•lo•mat•ic \,di-plə-'ma-tik\ *adj*
1 of or relating to keeping good relations between the governments of different countries
2 not causing bad feelings 〈a *diplomatic* answer〉 〈a *diplomatic* manager〉
dip•lo•mat•i•cal•ly \-ti-kə-lē\ *adv*

dip•per \'di-pər\ *n*
[1]LADLE

dire \'dīr\ *adj* **dir•er; dir•est**
1 causing horror or worry **:** DREADFUL 〈a *dire* warning〉
2 very urgent or serious 〈in *dire* need〉

[1]di•rect \də-'rekt, dī-\ *vb* **di•rect•ed; di•rect•ing**
1 to cause to point or move in a particular direction 〈*Direct* your light over here.〉
2 to cause to focus on 〈*direct* your attention〉
3 to show or tell the way 〈Signs *directed* us to the exit.〉
4 to put an address on 〈*direct* a letter〉
5 [1]ORDER 2, COMMAND 〈Bake as *directed*.〉

dinosaur

Dinosaurs were a large group of reptiles that roamed the earth until their extinction over 65 million years ago. They may be divided into two groups according to the formation of their hip bones. Lizard-hipped dinosaurs such as *Carnotaurus*, *Deinonychus*, and *Tyrannosaurus* had an arrangement of hip bones similar to that of other reptiles. Bird-hipped dinosaurs, such as the remaining dinosaurs shown here, had an arrangement of hip bones similar to that of modern birds.

examples of dinosaurs

Carnotaurus \,kär-nə-'tȯr-əs\ had broad "horns" over the eyes

Lesothosaurus \lə-,sō-tō-'sȯr-əs\ could run fast to escape predators

Tyrannosaurus

Deinonychus \dī-'nän-i-kəs\ had large claws to slash its prey

6 to manage or control the making or activities of ⟨*direct* a play⟩
synonyms see CONDUCT

[2]direct *adj*
1 going from one point to another without turning or stopping **:** STRAIGHT ⟨a *direct* route⟩
2 coming straight from a cause or source
3 said or done in a clear and honest way ⟨a *direct* answer⟩
4 being in an unbroken family line ⟨a *direct* ancestor⟩
5 [1]EXACT ⟨a *direct* translation⟩ ⟨a *direct* hit⟩
di•rect•ness *n*

[3]direct *adv*
DIRECTLY 1 ⟨We flew *direct* to New York.⟩

direct current *n*
an electric current flowing in one direction only

di•rec•tion \də-ˈrek-shən, dī-\ *n*
1 the path along which something moves, lies, or points ⟨It came from that *direction.*⟩
2 an order or instruction to be followed ⟨Read the *directions* first.⟩
3 instructions on how to get somewhere
4 SUPERVISION, MANAGEMENT

di•rect•ly \də-ˈrekt-lē, dī-\ *adv*
1 in a straight course or line ⟨She sits *directly* across from me.⟩ ⟨The road runs *directly* north.⟩
2 straight to or from a source **:** without interference ⟨I spoke *directly* to the principal.⟩
3 IMMEDIATELY 2 ⟨She began *directly* to work.⟩

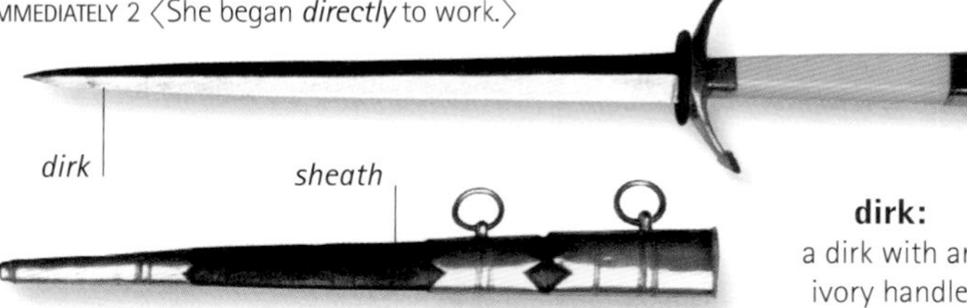

dirk:
a dirk with an ivory handle

direct object *n*
a word that represents the main goal or the result of the action of a verb ⟨The word "me" in "you hit me" is a *direct object.*⟩

di•rec•tor \də-ˈrek-tər, dī-\ *n*
1 a person who manages something ⟨a day care *director*⟩
2 a person in charge of making a movie or play

di•rec•to•ry \də-ˈrek-tə-rē, dī-\ *n, pl* **di•rec•to•ries**
a book containing an alphabetical list of names, addresses, and telephone numbers

di•ri•gi•ble \ˈdir-ə-jə-bəl, də-ˈri-jə-\ *n*
AIRSHIP

dirk \ˈdərk\ *n*
▲ a long dagger with a straight blade

dirt \ˈdərt\ *n*
1 [2]SOIL 1
2 a substance (as mud or dust) that makes things unclean

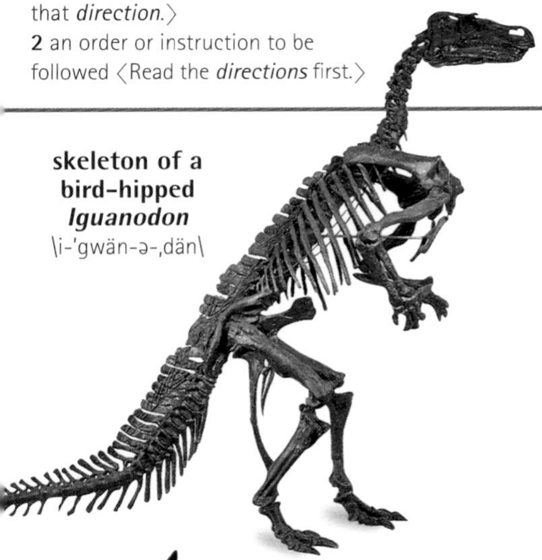

skeleton of a bird-hipped *Iguanodon*
\i-ˈgwän-ə-ˌdän\

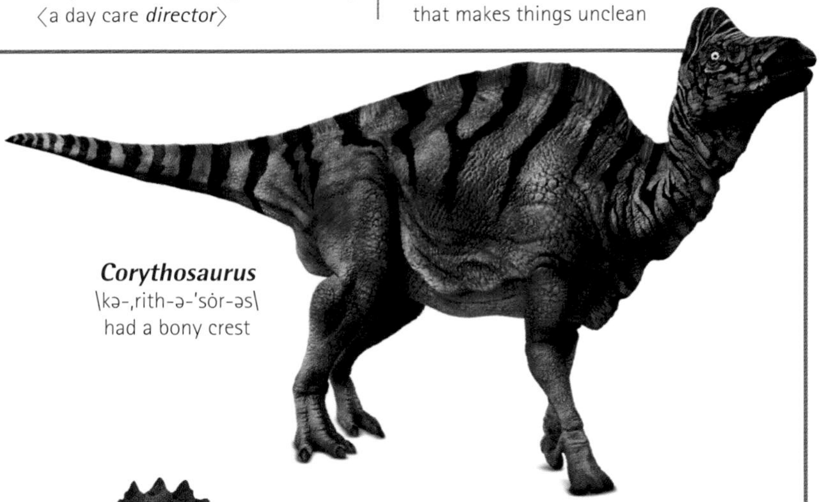

Corythosaurus
\kə-ˌrith-ə-ˈsȯr-əs\
had a bony crest

Stegosaurus

Triceratops

a b c d e f g h i j k l m n o p q r s t w x y z

[1]dirty \'dər-tē\ *adj* **dirt•i•er; dirt•i•est**
1 not clean ⟨*dirty* clothes⟩
2 UNFAIR, MEAN ⟨a *dirty* trick⟩
3 not pleasant but usually necessary ⟨a *dirty* job⟩
4 being vulgar : not decent ⟨*dirty* jokes⟩
5 showing dislike or anger ⟨a *dirty* look⟩
dirt•i•ness *n*

[2]dirty *adv*
in an unfair or dishonest way ⟨She plays *dirty.*⟩

[3]dirty *vb* **dirt•ied; dirty•ing**
to make or become unclean

dis- *prefix*
1 do the opposite of ⟨*dis*assemble⟩
2 deprive of ⟨*dis*arm⟩
3 opposite or absence of ⟨*dis*approval⟩
4 not ⟨*dis*agreeable⟩

dis•abil•i•ty \,di-sə-'bi-lə-tē\ *n, pl* **dis•abil•i•ties**
a condition (as one present at birth or caused by injury) that interferes with or limits a person's ability to engage in certain physical or mental tasks or actions

dis•able \dis-'ā-bəl\ *vb* **dis•abled; dis•abling**
1 to cause (something) to be unable to work in the normal way ⟨He *disabled* the alarm.⟩
2 to impair physically or mentally : to cause disability in ⟨an illness that *disabled* thousands⟩

dis•abled \dis-'ā-bəld\ *adj*
impaired or limited in the ability to engage in certain physical or mental tasks (as due to injury or condition present at birth)

dis•ad•van•tage \,dis-əd-'van-tij\ *n*
a state or condition that favors someone else ⟨Our late start was a *disadvantage* in the race.⟩

dis•ad•van•ta•geous \,dis-,ad-,van-'tā-jəs\ *adj*
making it harder for a person or thing to succeed or do something ⟨The store was in a *disadvantageous* location.⟩

dis•agree \,di-sə-'grē\ *vb* **dis•agreed; dis•agree•ing**
1 to have different ideas or opinions ⟨We *disagreed* over the price.⟩
2 to be unlike each other : be different ⟨Their descriptions *disagree.*⟩
3 to make ill ⟨Fried foods *disagree* with me.⟩

dis•agree•able \,di-sə-'grē-ə-bəl\ *adj*
1 UNPLEASANT ⟨a *disagreeable* taste⟩
2 difficult to get along with

dis•agree•ment \,di-sə-'grē-mənt\ *n*
1 failure to agree ⟨There was *disagreement* over what actually happened.⟩
2 ARGUMENT 1

dis•ap•pear \,di-sə-'pir\ *vb* **dis•ap•peared; dis•ap•pear•ing**
1 to stop being visible : pass out of sight ⟨The sun *disappeared* behind a cloud.⟩
2 to stop existing ⟨Dinosaurs *disappeared* long ago.⟩

dis•ap•pear•ance \,di-sə-'pir-əns\ *n*
the act of passing out of sight or existence

dis•ap•point \,di-sə-'pȯint\ *vb* **dis•ap•point•ed; dis•ap•point•ing**
to fail to satisfy the hope or expectation of ⟨The team *disappointed* its fans.⟩

dis•ap•point•ment \,di-sə-'pȯint-mənt\ *n*
1 unhappiness from the failure of something hoped for or expected to happen
2 someone or something that fails to satisfy hopes or expectations ⟨The movie was a *disappointment.*⟩

dis•ap•prov•al \,di-sə-'prü-vəl\ *n*
the feeling of not liking or agreeing with something or someone

dis•ap•prove \,di-sə-'prüv\ *vb* **dis•ap•proved; dis•ap•prov•ing**
to dislike or be against someone or something ⟨Mom *disapproved* of the TV show.⟩

dis•arm \dis-'ärm\ *vb* **dis•armed; dis•arm•ing**
1 to take weapons from ⟨*Disarm* the prisoner.⟩
2 to reduce the size and strength of the armed forces of a country
3 to make harmless ⟨He *disarmed* the bomb.⟩
4 to end dislike or mistrust : win over ⟨a *disarming* smile⟩
dis•ar•ma•ment \-'är-mə-mənt\ *n*

dis•ar•ray \,dis-ə-'rā\ *n*
a confused or messy condition ⟨The room was in complete *disarray.*⟩

dis•as•sem•ble \,dis-ə-'sem-bəl\ *vb* **dis•as•sem•bled; dis•as•sem•bling**
to take apart ⟨They *disassembled* the toy racetrack.⟩

di•sas•ter \diz-'as-tər, dis-\ *n*
▼ something (as a flood or a tornado) that happens suddenly and causes much suffering or loss

► **Word History** People who experience bad luck are sometimes said to be "star-crossed." This expression comes from the belief that the position of the stars and planets has a direct influence on earthly events. The origins of the word *disaster* can be traced to this same belief. *Disaster* is borrowed from *disastro,* an Italian word formed from the negative prefix *dis-* and the noun *astro,* meaning "star." *Disastro* originally referred to an unfortunate event, such as a military defeat, that took place when certain heavenly bodies were in an unlucky position.

disaster: destruction caused by a hurricane

di•sas•trous \diz-'as-trəs\ *adj*
1 causing great suffering or loss
2 very bad ⟨a *disastrous* performance⟩

dis•band \dis-'band\ *vb* **dis•band•ed; dis•band•ing**
to break up and stop being a group

dis•be•lief \,dis-bə-'lēf\ *n*
refusal or inability to believe

dis•be•lieve \,dis-bə-'lēv\ *vb* **dis•be•lieved; dis•be•liev•ing**
to think not to be true or real ⟨The jury *disbelieved* the story.⟩

dis•burse \dis-'bərs\ *vb* **dis•bursed; dis•burs•ing**
to pay out ⟨All the money was *disbursed.*⟩
dis•burse•ment \-mənt\ *n*

A B C D E F G H I J K L M N O P Q R S T U V W X Y Z

disc *variant of* DISK

[1]**dis•card** \di-ˈskärd\ *vb* **dis•card•ed**; **dis•card•ing**
1 to get rid of as useless or unwanted
2 to throw down an unwanted card from a hand of cards

[2]**dis•card** \ˈdi-ˌskärd\ *n*
something thrown away or rejected

dis•cern \di-ˈsərn, -ˈzərn\ *vb* **dis•cerned**; **dis•cern•ing**
to see, recognize, or understand something

[1]**dis•charge** \dis-ˈchärj\ *vb* **dis•charged**; **dis•charg•ing**
1 to allow to leave or get off ⟨The patient was *discharged* from the hospital.⟩
2 to dismiss from service ⟨*discharge* a worker⟩
3 to free of a load or burden : UNLOAD ⟨*discharge* a ship⟩
4 [1]SHOOT 2 ⟨*discharge* a gun⟩
5 to cause to shoot out of ⟨*discharge* a bullet⟩
6 to pour forth fluid or other contents ⟨The chimney *discharged* smoke.⟩
7 to get rid of by paying or doing ⟨*discharge* a debt⟩ ⟨He *discharged* his responsibilities.⟩

[2]**dis•charge** \ˈdis-ˌchärj\ *n*
1 the release of someone from a place
2 the release from a duty or debt
3 a certificate of release or payment
4 the act of firing a person from a job
5 an end of a person's military service
6 an act of firing off ⟨a gun's *discharge*⟩
7 something that flows out ⟨The *discharge* was coming from a pipe.⟩

dis•ci•ple \di-ˈsī-pəl\ *n*
1 a person who accepts and helps to spread the teachings of another
2 APOSTLE

dis•ci•plin•ary \ˈdi-sə-plə-ˌner-ē\ *adj*
relating to the correction or punishment of bad behavior ⟨*disciplinary* action⟩

[1]**dis•ci•pline** \ˈdi-sə-plən\ *n*
1 PUNISHMENT 1
2 strict training that corrects or strengthens ⟨"Boys need *discipline*," he said.⟩
3 habits and ways of acting that are gotten through practice
4 control that is gained by insisting that rules be followed ⟨The teacher tried to maintain *discipline*.⟩

[2]**discipline** *vb* **dis•ci•plined**; **dis•ci•plin•ing**
1 to punish as a way to bring about good behavior ⟨The principal *disciplined* the troublemakers.⟩
2 to train in self-control or obedience ⟨The diet *disciplines* overeaters.⟩
3 to bring under control ⟨*discipline* troops⟩
synonyms see PUNISH

disc jockey *n*
▼ someone who plays recorded music on the radio or at a party

dis•claim \dis-ˈklām\ *vb* **dis•claimed**; **dis•claim•ing**
to deny being part of or responsible for

[2]**discontent** *adj*
not satisfied ⟨*discontent* customers⟩

dis•con•tent•ed \ˌdis-kən-ˈten-təd\ *adj*
not satisfied

dis•con•tin•ue \ˌdis-kən-ˈtin-yü\ *vb* **dis•con•tin•ued**; **dis•con•tinu•ing**
to bring to an end : STOP

disc jockey: a disc jockey perfoming

dis•close \dis-ˈklōz\ *vb* **dis•closed**; **dis•clos•ing**
to make known : REVEAL ⟨A friend doesn't *disclose* secrets.⟩

dis•clo•sure \dis-ˈklō-zhər\ *n*
1 an act of making known ⟨They demanded full *disclosure* of the facts.⟩
2 something made known

dis•col•or \dis-ˈkə-lər\ *vb* **dis•col•ored**; **dis•col•or•ing**
to change in color especially for the worse

dis•col•or•a•tion \dis-ˌkə-lə-ˈrā-shən\ *n*
1 change of color
2 a spot that is changed in color

dis•com•fort \dis-ˈkəm-fərt\ *n*
the condition of being uncomfortable ⟨The dog whimpered in *discomfort*.⟩

dis•con•cert \ˌdis-kən-ˈsərt\ *vb* **dis•con•cert•ed**; **dis•con•cert•ing**
to make confused and a little upset

dis•con•nect \ˌdis-kə-ˈnekt\ *vb* **dis•con•nect•ed**; **dis•con•nect•ing**
to undo or break the connection of

dis•con•so•late \dis-ˈkän-sə-lət\ *adj*
too sad to be cheered up
dis•con•so•late•ly *adv*

[1]**dis•con•tent** \ˌdis-kən-ˈtent\ *n*
the condition of being dissatisfied

dis•cord \ˈdis-ˌkȯrd\ *n*
lack of agreement or harmony : CONFLICT ⟨Money problems caused family *discord*.⟩

dis•cor•dant \dis-ˈkȯr-dᵊnt\ *adj*
being in disagreement ⟨*discordant* opinions⟩

[1]**dis•count** \ˈdis-ˌkau̇nt\ *n*
an amount taken off a regular price

[2]**dis•count** \ˈdis-ˌkau̇nt, dis-ˈkau̇nt\ *vb* **dis•count•ed**; **dis•count•ing**
1 to lower the amount of a bill, debt, or price
2 to think of as not important or serious ⟨Don't *discount* her idea.⟩

dis•cour•age \dis-ˈkər-ij\ *vb* **dis•cour•aged**; **dis•cour•ag•ing**
1 to make less determined, hopeful, or confident ⟨Yet another failed attempt didn't *discourage* him.⟩
2 to make less likely to happen ⟨The law *discourages* speeding.⟩
3 to try to persuade not to do something
dis•cour•age•ment \-mənt\ *n*

[1]**dis•course** \ˈdis-ˌkȯrs\ *n*
1 CONVERSATION
2 a long talk or essay about a subject

[2]**dis•course** \dis-ˈkȯrs\ *vb* **dis•coursed**; **dis•cours•ing**
to talk especially for a long time

dis•cour•te•ous \dis-ˈkər-tē-əs\ *adj*
not polite : RUDE

A B C D E F G H I J K L M N O P Q R S T U V W X Y Z

dis•cour•te•sy \dis-ˈkər-tə-sē\ *n, pl* **dis•cour•te•sies**
1 rude behavior ⟨She forgave his *discourtesy.*⟩
2 a rude act

dis•cov•er \di-ˈskə-vər\ *vb* **dis•cov•ered**; **dis•cov•er•ing**
to find out, see, or learn of especially for the first time : FIND ⟨Scientists have *discovered* a new species.⟩ ⟨She *discovered* a hole in her shirt.⟩
dis•cov•er•er *n*

dis•cov•ery \di-ˈskəv-ə-rē, -ˈskəv-rē\ *n, pl* **dis•cov•er•ies**
1 an act of finding out or learning of for the first time ⟨Experiments led to their *discovery* of the cure.⟩
2 something found or learned of for the first time ⟨a recent *discovery*⟩

[1]**dis•cred•it** \dis-ˈkre-dət\ *vb* **dis•cred•it•ed**; **dis•cred•it•ing**
1 to cause to seem dishonest or untrue ⟨*discredit* a report⟩
2 to harm the reputation of ⟨The candidates tried to *discredit* each other.⟩

[2]**discredit** *n*
loss of good name or respect

dis•creet \dis-ˈkrēt\ *adj*
careful not to attract attention or let out private information
dis•creet•ly *adv*

dis•crep•an•cy \di-ˈskre-pən-sē\ *n*
a difference between things that are expected to be the same

dis•crete \di-ˈskrēt\ *adj*
[2]SEPARATE 3, DISTINCT ⟨The report is divided into *discrete* sections.⟩

dis•cre•tion \di-ˈskre-shən\ *n*
1 care in not attracting attention or letting out private information ⟨Use *discretion* in dealing with the situation.⟩
2 the power to decide what to do ⟨I'll leave it to your *discretion.*⟩

dis•crim•i•nate \di-ˈskri-mə-ˌnāt\ *vb* **dis•crim•i•nat•ed**; **dis•crim•i•nat•ing**
1 to unfairly treat a person or group differently from other people or groups ⟨It is against the law to *discriminate* on the basis of race.⟩
2 to be able to tell the difference between things ⟨He can *discriminate* among the birds by their calls.⟩

dis•crim•i•na•tion \di-ˌskri-mə-ˈnā-shən\ *n*
1 the practice of unfairly treating a person or group differently from other people or groups of people ⟨The law prohibits *discrimination* against the disabled.⟩
2 the ability to see differences ⟨Police use a dog's *discrimination* of smells.⟩

dis•crim•i•na•to•ry \di-ˈskrim-ə-nə-ˌtȯr-ē\ *adj*
showing discrimination : being unfair ⟨*discriminatory* work policies⟩

dis•cus \ˈdi-skəs\ *n, pl* **dis•cus•es**
▼ an object that is shaped like a disk and hurled for distance in a track-and-field event

discus

discus and a discus thrower

dis•cuss \di-ˈskəs\ *vb* **dis•cussed**; **dis•cuss•ing**
1 to talk about
2 to argue or consider fully and openly

▶ **Synonyms** DISCUSS, ARGUE, and DEBATE mean to talk about something in order to reach a decision or to convince someone of a point of view. DISCUSS is used when there is an exchange of ideas. ⟨We will *discuss* plans for the school picnic.⟩ ARGUE is used when evidence or reasons for or against something are given. ⟨She *argued* for the need for more hospitals.⟩ DEBATE is used when there is an argument between opposing persons or groups according to rules and often before an audience. ⟨The candidates will *debate* on TV.⟩

dis•cus•sion \di-ˈskə-shən\ *n*
conversation for the purpose of understanding or debating a question or subject

[1]**dis•dain** \dis-ˈdān\ *n*
a feeling of dislike for someone or something considered not good enough ⟨She eyed the cramped little home with *disdain.*⟩
dis•dain•ful *adj*
dis•dain•ful•ly \-fə-lē\ *adv*

[2]**disdain** *vb* **dis•dained**; **dis•dain•ing**
1 to feel dislike for something or someone usually for not being good enough ⟨He *disdained* weakness.⟩
2 to refuse because of feelings of dislike ⟨She *disdained* to answer.⟩

dis•ease \di-ˈzēz\ *n*
a change in a living body (as of a person or plant) that prevents it from functioning normally : SICKNESS

dis•eased \-ˈzēzd\ *adj*
having a sickness ⟨a *diseased* tree⟩

dis•em•bark \ˌdi-səm-ˈbärk\ *vb* **dis•em•barked**; **dis•em•bark•ing**
to leave or remove from a ship or airplane

dis•en•fran•chise \ˌdi-sᵊn-ˈfran-ˌchīz\ *vb* **dis•en•fran•chised**; **dis•en•fran•chis•ing**
to deprive of the right to vote
dis•en•fran•chise•ment \-ˈfran-ˌchīz-mənt\ *n*

dis•en•tan•gle \ˌdi-sᵊn-ˈtaŋ-gəl\ *vb* **dis•en•tan•gled**; **dis•en•tan•gling**
UNTANGLE

[1]**dis•fa•vor** \dis-ˈfā-vər\ *n*
1 DISAPPROVAL ⟨She looked with *disfavor* at the mess.⟩
2 the condition of being disliked ⟨The style has fallen into *disfavor.*⟩

[2]**disfavor** *vb* **dis•fa•vored**; **dis•fa•vor•ing**
[2]DISLIKE, DISAPPROVE

dis•fig•ure \dis-ˈfi-gyər\ *vb* **dis•fig•ured**; **dis•fig•ur•ing**
to spoil the looks of

dis•fig•ure•ment \dis-ˈfi-gyər-mənt\ *n*
something that spoils the appearance of a person or thing

dis•fran•chise \dis-ˈfran-ˌchīz\ *vb* **dis•fran•chised**; **dis•fran•chis•ing**
DISENFRANCHISE

[1]**dis•grace** \di-ˈskrās, dis-ˈgrās\ *vb* **dis•graced**; **dis•grac•ing**
to bring shame to ⟨Her behavior *disgraced* the family.⟩

[2]**disgrace** *n*
1 the condition of being looked down on : loss of respect ⟨He resigned in *disgrace.*⟩
2 a cause of shame ⟨You are a *disgrace* to this organization.⟩

dis•grace•ful \-fəl\ *adj*
bringing or deserving shame
dis•grace•ful•ly \-fə-lē\ *adv*

dis•grun•tled \dis-ˈgrən-tᵊld\ *adj*
unhappy and annoyed

[1]**dis•guise** \də-ˈskīz, dis-ˈgīz\ *vb* **dis•guised**; **dis•guis•ing**
1 to change the looks or sound of to avoid being recognized ⟨He *disguised* his voice on the phone.⟩
2 to keep from revealing ⟨She *disguised* her true feelings.⟩

[2]**disguise** *n*
1 clothing worn to avoid being recognized
2 an outward appearance that hides what something really is ⟨a blessing in *disguise*⟩

[1]**dis•gust** \di-ˈskəst, dis-ˈgəst\ *n*
a strong feeling of dislike or annoyance for something considered sickening or bad

[2]**disgust** *vb* **dis•gust•ed**; **dis•gust•ing**
to cause to feel strong dislike or annoyance by being sickening or bad ⟨This greasy food *disgusts* me.⟩
dis•gust•ed•ly *adv*

dis•gust•ing \di-ˈskə-stiŋ, dis-ˈgə-stiŋ\ *adj*
very sickening or bad ⟨a *disgusting* smell⟩

dish \ˈdish\ *n*
1 ▼ a usually round shallow container used for cooking or serving food

dish 1:
a meal served on a dish

2 **dish•es** *pl* all items (as plates and silverware) used for cooking and eating food ⟨Would you do the *dishes*?⟩
3 the food in a container for serving or eating ⟨a *dish* of strawberries⟩
4 food that is prepared in a particular way ⟨an Italian *dish*⟩
5 a round shallow object ⟨a radar *dish*⟩

dis•heart•en \dis-ˈhär-tᵊn\ *vb* **dis•heart•ened**; **dis•heart•en•ing**
DISCOURAGE 1 ⟨She was *disheartened* by the bad news.⟩

di•shev•eled *or* **di•shev•elled** \di-ˈshe-vəld\ *adj*
MESSY 1

dis•hon•est \dis-ˈä-nəst\ *adj*
not honest or trustworthy ⟨*dishonest* advertising⟩
dis•hon•est•ly *adv*

dis•hon•es•ty \dis-ˈä-nə-stē\ *n*
the quality of being untruthful : lack of honesty

[1]**dis•hon•or** \dis-ˈä-nər\ *n*
1 loss of honor or good name ⟨He felt retreat would bring *dishonor*.⟩
2 a cause of disgrace ⟨Her failure was a family *dishonor*.⟩

[2]**dishonor** *vb* **dis•hon•ored**; **dis•hon•or•ing**
to bring shame on : DISGRACE ⟨He *dishonored* his parents.⟩

dis•hon•or•able \dis-ˈä-nə-rə-bəl\ *adj*
SHAMEFUL ⟨*dishonorable* conduct⟩
dis•hon•or•ably \-blē\ *adv*

dis•il•lu•sion \ˌdis-ə-ˈlü-zhən\ *vb* **dis•il•lu•sioned**; **dis•il•lu•sion•ing**
to cause to stop having a mistaken belief that something is good, valuable, or true
dis•il•lu•sion•ment \-mənt\ *n*

dis•in•fect \ˌdi-sᵊn-ˈfekt\ *vb* **dis•in•fect•ed**; **dis•in•fect•ing**
to cleanse of germs that might cause disease

dis•in•fec•tant \ˌdi-sᵊn-ˈfek-tənt\ *n*
something that kills germs

dis•in•her•it \ˌdi-sᵊn-ˈher-ət\ *vb* **dis•in•her•it•ed**; **dis•in•her•it•ing**
to take away the legal right to receive money or property from at death ⟨The millionaire *disinherited* his son.⟩

dis•in•te•grate \dis-ˈin-tə-ˌgrāt\ *vb* **dis•in•te•grat•ed**; **dis•in•te•grat•ing**
to separate or break up into small parts or pieces

dis•in•te•gra•tion \dis-ˌin-tə-ˈgrā-shən\ *n*
the act or process of breaking into small pieces : the condition of being broken into small pieces

dis•in•ter•est•ed \dis-ˈin-trə-stəd, -ˈin-tə-rə-\ *adj*
1 not interested ⟨*disinterested* in sports⟩
2 not influenced by personal feelings or concerns ⟨a *disinterested* judge⟩

dis•joint•ed \dis-ˈjȯin-təd\ *adj*
not clear and orderly ⟨a *disjointed* story⟩
dis•joint•ed•ly *adv*

disk *or* **disc** \ˈdisk\ *n*
1 something that is or appears to be flat and round
2 *usually disc* CD
3 a round, thin, flat plate coated with a magnetic substance on which data for a computer is stored
4 *usually disc* a phonograph record
disk•like \-ˌlīk\ *adj*

disk drive *n*
the part of a computer that moves data to and from a disk

disk•ette \ˌdis-ˈket\ *n*
FLOPPY DISK

[1]**dis•like** \dis-ˈlīk\ *n*
a strong feeling of not liking or approving ⟨She quickly took a *dislike* to the game.⟩

[2]**dislike** *vb* **dis•liked**; **dis•lik•ing**
to not like or approve of

dis•lo•cate \ˈdis-lō-ˌkāt, dis-ˈlō-\ *vb* **dis•lo•cat•ed**; **dis•lo•cat•ing**
to displace a bone from its normal connections with another bone

dis•lo•ca•tion \ˌdis-lō-ˈkā-shən\ *n*
the condition of being moved out of a normal location

dis•lodge \dis-ˈläj\ *vb* **dis•lodged**; **dis•lodg•ing**
to force out of a place of resting, hiding, or defense

dis•loy•al \dis-ˈlȯi-əl\ *adj*
failing to support or be true ⟨*disloyal* friends⟩
synonyms see FAITHLESS

dis•loy•al•ty \dis-ˈlȯi-əl-tē\ *n, pl* **dis•loy•al•ties**
1 lack of faithfulness or support ⟨The king suspected *disloyalty* in his advisor.⟩
2 an act that shows a lack of faithfulness or support ⟨She was hurt by her friend's *disloyalty*.⟩

dis•mal \ˈdiz-məl\ *adj*
very gloomy ⟨*dismal* weather⟩

dis•man•tle \dis-ˈman-tᵊl\ *vb* **dis•man•tled**; **dis•man•tling**
1 to take completely apart (as for storing or repair)
2 to strip of furniture or equipment

[1]**dis•may** \dis-ˈmā\ *vb* **dis•mayed**; **dis•may•ing**
to feel worry, disappointment, fear, or shock

[2]**dismay** *n*
a feeling of fear, disappointment, shock, or worry ⟨We listened with *dismay* to the bad news.⟩

dis•miss \dis-ˈmis\ *vb* **dis•missed**; **dis•miss•ing**
1 to allow or cause to leave ⟨*dismiss* a class⟩
2 to remove from a job or position ⟨She *dismissed* her assistant.⟩
3 to decide not to think about ⟨He *dismissed* the criticism.⟩

dis•miss•al \dis-ˈmi-səl\ *n*
the act of dismissing : the state or fact of being dismissed ⟨The students will have an early *dismissal*.⟩

dis•mount \dis-ˈmau̇nt\ *vb* **dis•mount•ed**; **dis•mount•ing**
to get down from something (as a horse or bicycle)

dis•obe•di•ence \ˌdis-ə-ˈbē-dē-əns\ *n*
an act of failing or refusing to behave as told or taught

dis•obe•di•ent \ˌdis-ə-ˈbē-dē-ənt\ *adj*
not behaving as told or taught ⟨a *disobedient* child⟩
dis•obe•di•ent•ly *adv*

dis•obey \ˌdis-ə-ˈbā\ *vb* **dis•obeyed**; **dis•obey•ing**
to refuse or fail to behave as told or taught

[1]**dis•or•der** \dis-ˈȯr-dər\ *vb* **dis•or•dered**; **dis•or•der•ing**
to disturb the regular or normal arrangement or functioning of ⟨You've *disordered* my papers.⟩

[2]**disorder** *n*
1 a confused or messy state ⟨His room was in complete *disorder*.⟩
2 unruly behavior ⟨Recess monitors prevented any *disorder*.⟩
3 a physical or mental condition that is not normal or healthy ⟨a stomach *disorder*⟩

dis•or•der•ly \dis-ˈȯr-dər-lē\ *adj*
1 not behaving quietly or well **:** UNRULY ⟨*disorderly* students⟩
2 not neat or orderly ⟨a *disorderly* desk⟩

dis•or•ga•ni•za•tion \dis-ˌȯr-gə-nə-ˈzā-shən\ *n*
lack of order

dis•or•ga•nized \dis-ˈȯr-gə-ˌnīzd\ *adj*
1 not having order ⟨a *disorganized* desk⟩
2 not able to manage or plan things well ⟨*disorganized* students⟩

dis•own \dis-ˈōn\ *vb* **dis•owned**; **dis•own•ing**
to refuse to accept any longer a relationship with or connection to ⟨*disowned* her family⟩

dis•par•age \di-ˈsper-ij\ *vb* **dis•par•aged**; **dis•par•ag•ing**
to speak of as unimportant or bad **:** BELITTLE ⟨He *disparaged* the other team.⟩
dis•par•age•ment \-mənt\ *n*

dis•pas•sion•ate \dis-ˈpa-shə-nət\ *adj*
not influenced by strong feeling or personal involvement **:** CALM, IMPARTIAL ⟨a *dispassionate* judgment⟩
dis•pas•sion•ate•ly *adv*

[1]**dis•patch** \di-ˈspach\ *vb* **dis•patched**; **dis•patch•ing**
1 to send away quickly to a certain place or for a certain reason ⟨The general *dispatched* a messenger.⟩
2 to get done quickly ⟨She *dispatched* one job and moved to the next.⟩
3 [1]KILL 1 ⟨*dispatch* a sick animal⟩
dis•patch•er *n*

[2]**dispatch** *n*
1 MESSAGE 1
2 a news story sent in to a newspaper
3 [1]SPEED 1 ⟨You must act with *dispatch*.⟩

dis•pel \di-ˈspel\ *vb* **dis•pelled**; **dis•pel•ling**
to make go away ⟨*dispel* doubts⟩

dis•pense \di-ˈspens\ *vb* **dis•pensed**; **dis•pens•ing**
1 to give out in small amounts ⟨The machine *dispenses* candy.⟩
2 to give out as deserved ⟨The judge *dispensed* justice.⟩
3 to put up or prepare medicine in a form ready for use
dispense with to do or get along without

dis•pens•er \di-ˈspen-sər\ *n*
a container that gives out something in small amounts ⟨a soap *dispenser*⟩

dis•perse \di-ˈspərs\ *vb* **dis•persed**; **dis•pers•ing**
to break up and scatter ⟨The clouds *dispersed*.⟩

dis•pir•it•ed \di-ˈspir-ə-təd\ *adj*
not cheerful or enthusiastic
dis•pir•it•ed•ly *adv*

dis•place \dis-ˈplās\ *vb* **dis•placed**; **dis•plac•ing**
1 to remove from the usual or proper place ⟨The fire *displaced* many forest animals.⟩
2 to take the place of **:** REPLACE ⟨Chess *displaced* checkers as his favorite game.⟩
3 to move out of position ⟨A floating object *displaces* water.⟩
dis•place•ment \-mənt\ *n*

[1]**dis•play** \di-ˈsplā\ *vb* **dis•played**; **dis•play•ing**
1 to put (something) in plain sight ⟨The store *displays* toys in its window.⟩
2 to make clear the existence or presence of **:** show plainly ⟨*display* anger⟩ ⟨She *displayed* a gift for acting.⟩

[2]**display** *n*
1 ▶ a presentation of something ⟨a fireworks *display*⟩
2 an arrangement of something where it can be easily seen ⟨a store *display*⟩
3 an electronic device (as a computer monitor) that shows information

dis•please \dis-ˈplēz\ *vb* **dis•pleased**; **dis•pleas•ing**
to cause to feel unhappy or unsatisfied

dis•plea•sure \dis-ˈple-zhər\ *n*
a feeling of dislike and irritation **:** DISSATISFACTION

dis•pos•able \dis-ˈpō-zə-bəl\ *adj*
made to be thrown away after use ⟨*disposable* diapers⟩

dis•pos•al \dis-ˈpō-zəl\ *n*
1 ▶ the act of getting rid of ⟨trash *disposal*⟩
2 right or power to use **:** CONTROL ⟨I have money at my *disposal*.⟩

disposal 1: trash disposal

dis•pose \dis-ˈpōz\ *vb* **dis•posed**; **dis•pos•ing**
to put in place **:** ARRANGE ⟨Campsites were *disposed* around the lake.⟩
dispose of
1 to finish with ⟨The matter was quickly *disposed of*.⟩
2 to get rid of

dis•posed \di-ˈspōzd\ *adj*
1 having the desire or tendency to ⟨Come along if you feel so *disposed*.⟩
2 feeling or thinking in a particular way about ⟨They're favorably *disposed* toward the idea.⟩

dis•po•si•tion \ˌdis-pə-ˈzi-shən\ *n*
1 a person's usual attitude or mood ⟨has a nasty *disposition*⟩
2 TENDENCY 1, LIKING ⟨She has a *disposition* to complain.⟩
3 ARRANGEMENT 1

[2]**display 1:** a fireworks display

dis•pro•por•tion \ˌdis-prə-ˈpȯr-shən\ *n*
a marked difference in the size, number, or amount of something as compared to another thing

dis•prove \dis-ˈprüv\ *vb* **dis•proved**; **dis•prov•ing**
to show to be false or wrong ⟨Scientists *disproved* the theory.⟩

¹dis•pute \di-ˈspyüt\ *vb* **dis•put•ed**; **dis•put•ing**
1 to question or deny the truth or rightness of ⟨No one ever *disputed* the story.⟩
2 ARGUE 1 ⟨We *disputed* over who won.⟩
3 to fight over ⟨The two nations *disputed* the territory.⟩

²dispute *n*
1 ¹DEBATE 3 ⟨It is a fact beyond *dispute*.⟩
2 ¹QUARREL 1

dis•qual•i•fy \dis-ˈkwä-lə-ˌfī\ *vb* **dis•qual•i•fied**; **dis•qual•i•fy•ing**
to make or declare not fit to have, do, or take part in ⟨The judges *disqualified* the runner from the race.⟩

¹dis•qui•et \dis-ˈkwī-ət\ *vb* **dis•qui•et•ed**; **dis•qui•et•ing**
to make uneasy or worried ⟨We were *disquieted* by strange noises in the house.⟩

²disquiet *n*
an uneasy feeling

¹dis•re•gard \ˌdis-ri-ˈgärd\ *vb* **dis•re•gard•ed**; **dis•re•gard•ing**
to pay no attention to ⟨Please *disregard* the last announcement.⟩
synonyms see NEGLECT

²disregard *n*
the act of paying no attention to ⟨He treated the rules with complete *disregard*.⟩

dis•re•pair \ˌdis-ri-ˈper\ *n*
the condition of needing to be fixed ⟨The house was in *disrepair*.⟩

dis•rep•u•ta•ble \dis-ˈre-pyə-tə-bəl\ *adj*
not respectable or honest ⟨*disreputable* business practices⟩

dis•re•pute \ˌdis-ri-ˈpyüt\ *n*
the state of not being respected or trusted by most people ⟨The doctor's methods have fallen into *disrepute*.⟩

dis•re•spect \ˌdis-ri-ˈspekt\ *n*
lack of respect : DISCOURTESY
dis•re•spect•ful *adj*
dis•re•spect•ful•ly \-fə-lē\ *adv*

dis•rupt \dis-ˈrəpt\ *vb* **dis•rupt•ed**; **dis•rupt•ing**
1 to cause disorder in ⟨*disrupted* the class⟩
2 to interrupt the normal course of ⟨Barking dogs *disrupted* my sleep.⟩
dis•rup•tion \dis-ˈrəp-shən\ *n*
dis•rup•tive \-ˈrəp-tiv\ *adj*

dis•sat•is•fac•tion \di-ˌsa-təs-ˈfak-shən\ *n*
a feeling of unhappiness or disapproval

dis•sat•is•fy \di-ˈsa-təs-ˌfī\ *vb* **dis•sat•is•fied**; **dis•sat•is•fy•ing**
to fail to give what is desired or expected ⟨He was *dissatisfied* by the poor service.⟩

dis•sect \di-ˈsekt\ *vb* **dis•sect•ed**; **dis•sect•ing**
to cut or take apart especially for examination

dis•sec•tion \di-ˈsek-shən\ *n*
the act of cutting something or taking something apart for examination

dis•sen•sion \di-ˈsen-shən\ *n*
difference in opinion

¹dis•sent \di-ˈsent\ *vb* **dis•sent•ed**; **dis•sent•ing**
DISAGREE 1 ⟨Mom suggested eating out, but Dad *dissented*.⟩
dis•sent•er *n*

²dissent *n*
difference of opinion ⟨The class voted without *dissent* for a field trip.⟩

dis•ser•vice \di-ˈsər-vəs\ *n*
a harmful, unfair, or unjust act ⟨I have done you a *disservice* by blaming you.⟩

dis•sim•i•lar \di-ˈsi-mə-lər\ *adj*
DIFFERENT 1

dis•si•pate \ˈdi-sə-ˌpāt\ *vb* **dis•si•pat•ed**; **dis•si•pat•ing**
1 to cause to break up and disappear : DISPERSE ⟨The wind *dissipated* the clouds.⟩
2 to scatter or waste foolishly : SQUANDER

dis•si•pat•ed \ˈdi-sə-ˌpā-təd\ *adj*
indulging in bad, foolish, or harmful activities ⟨a spoiled, *dissipated* young man⟩

dis•si•pa•tion \ˌdi-sə-ˈpā-shən\ *n*
1 the act of causing to break up and disappear ⟨the *dissipation* of the fog⟩
2 indulgence in too much pleasure

dis•solve \di-ˈzälv\ *vb* **dis•solved**; **dis•solv•ing**
1 to become part of a liquid ⟨Sugar *dissolves* in water.⟩
2 to bring to an end : TERMINATE ⟨The businessmen *dissolved* their partnership.⟩
3 to fade away as if by melting or breaking up ⟨His anger quickly *dissolved*.⟩
4 to be overcome by a strong feeling ⟨He *dissolved* into tears.⟩

dis•so•nance \ˈdi-sə-nəns\ *n*
an unpleasant combination of musical sounds

dis•suade \di-ˈswād\ *vb* **dis•suad•ed**; **dis•suad•ing**
to persuade or advise not to do something

dis•tance \ˈdi-stəns\ *n*
1 how far from each other two points or places are
2 a point or place that is far away ⟨He saw a light in the *distance*.⟩
3 the quality or state of not being friendly ⟨There was a cold *distance* in his voice.⟩

dis•tant \ˈdi-stənt\ *adj*
1 existing or happening at a place far away ⟨a *distant* planet⟩ ⟨*distant* thunder⟩
2 far away in time ⟨the *distant* future⟩
3 not closely related ⟨*distant* cousins⟩
4 ¹COLD 5, UNFRIENDLY ⟨a *distant* manner⟩
dis•tant•ly *adv*

dis•taste \dis-ˈtāst\ *n*
¹DISLIKE

dis•taste•ful \dis-ˈtāst-fəl\ *adj*
UNPLEASANT ⟨a *distasteful* subject⟩

dis•tend \di-ˈstend\ *vb* **dis•tend•ed**; **dis•tend•ing**
EXPAND 2, SWELL ⟨Illness can cause the stomach to *distend*.⟩

dis•till *also* **dis•til** \di-ˈstil\ *vb* **dis•tilled**; **dis•till•ing**
to make (a liquid) pure by heating it until it becomes a gas and then cooling it until it becomes a liquid ⟨*distill* water⟩
dis•till•er *n*

dis•til•la•tion \ˌdi-stə-ˈlā-shən\ *n*
▼ the process of heating a liquid until it gives off a gas and then cooling the gas until it becomes liquid

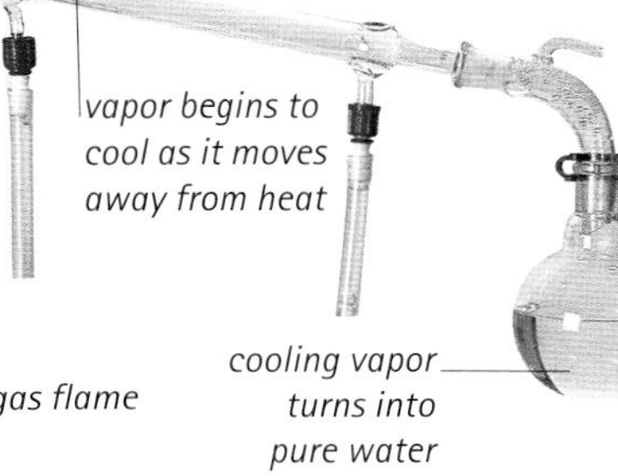

distillation:
experiment showing how pure water is distilled from a liquid mixture

dis•tinct \di-ˈstiŋkt\ *adj*
1 different from each other ⟨*distinct* species⟩
2 easy to notice or understand ⟨I detected the *distinct* smell of smoke.⟩
dis•tinct•ly *adv*

dis•tinc•tion \di-ˈstiŋk-shən\ *n*
1 DIFFERENCE 1 ⟨the *distinction* between right and wrong⟩
2 the act of seeing or pointing out a difference ⟨He made a *distinction* between the two words.⟩
3 great worth : EXCELLENCE ⟨a writer of *distinction*⟩
4 something that makes a person or thing special or different ⟨Our house has the *distinction* of being the oldest one in town.⟩

dis•tinc•tive \di-ˈstiŋk-tiv\ *adj*
1 clearly marking a person or a thing as different from others ⟨a *distinctive* walk⟩
2 having or giving a special look or way ⟨*distinctive* clothes⟩
dis•tinc•tive•ly *adv*

dis•tin•guish \di-ˈstiŋ-gwish\ *vb* **dis•tin•guished**; **dis•tin•guish•ing**
1 to recognize one thing from others by some mark or quality ⟨He *distinguished* the sound of the piano in the orchestra.⟩
2 to hear or see clearly ⟨You can't *distinguish* the details in this photo.⟩
3 to know the difference ⟨Can you *distinguish* between right and wrong?⟩
4 to set apart as different or special ⟨She *distinguished* herself by heroic actions.⟩

dis•tin•guish•able \di-ˈstiŋ-gwi-shə-bəl\ *adj*
possible to recognize or tell apart from others

dis•tin•guished \di-ˈstiŋ-gwisht\ *adj*
widely known and admired ⟨a *distinguished* scientist⟩

dis•tort \di-ˈstȯrt\ *vb* **dis•tort•ed**; **dis•tort•ing**
1 to twist out of shape
2 to change so as to make untrue or inaccurate ⟨Reports *distorted* the facts.⟩

dis•tor•tion \di-ˈstȯr-shən\ *n*
the act of twisting out of shape or making inaccurate : the state of being twisted out of shape or made inaccurate ⟨a *distortion* of the facts⟩ ⟨a facial *distortion*⟩

dis•tract \di-ˈstrakt\ *vb* **dis•tract•ed**; **dis•tract•ing**
to draw a person's thoughts or attention to something else ⟨The TV *distracts* me when I'm studying.⟩

dis•trac•tion \di-ˈstrak-shən\ *n*
1 something that makes it hard to pay attention ⟨One robber created a *distraction* and the other grabbed the money.⟩
2 the act of having thoughts or attention drawn away : the state of drawing thoughts or attention away
3 a state of being annoyed or upset ⟨Her whining drove me to *distraction*.⟩
4 something that amuses or entertains ⟨The game was a good *distraction* during the long car ride.⟩

dis•traught \di-ˈstrȯt\ *adj*
very upset

[1]**dis•tress** \di-ˈstres\ *n*
1 physical or mental pain or suffering
2 a state of danger or desperate need ⟨The ship was in *distress*.⟩

[2]**distress** *vb* **dis•tressed**; **dis•tress•ing**
to upset or cause to worry ⟨The news *distressed* her.⟩
dis•tress•ing•ly \di-ˈstre-siŋ-lē\ *adv*

dis•trib•ute \di-ˈstri-ˌbyüt, -byət\ *vb* **dis•trib•ut•ed**; **dis•trib•ut•ing**
1 to give out to or deliver to ⟨They *distribute* pay on Friday.⟩
2 to divide among many or several ⟨The aid is *distributed* among the poor.⟩
3 to spread out so as to cover something ⟨Make sure the paint is *distributed* evenly.⟩

dis•tri•bu•tion \ˌdi-strə-ˈbyü-shən\ *n*
1 the act of giving out or delivering to or dividing among ⟨the weekly *distribution* to the poor⟩
2 the way things are divided or spread out ⟨She studies the *distribution* of wildcats in the area.⟩
3 something given out or delivered to or divided among

dis•trib•u•tive \di-ˈstri-byü-tiv, -byə-\ *adj*
1 of or relating to the act of giving or spreading out
2 producing the same answer when operating on the sum of several numbers as when operating on each and collecting the results ⟨Multiplication is *distributive*.⟩

dis•trib•u•tor \di-ˈstri-byü-tər, -byə-\ *n*
a person or company that supplies stores or businesses with goods

dis•trict \ˈdi-ˌstrikt\ *n*
1 an area or section (as of a city or nation) set apart for some purpose ⟨our school *district*⟩
2 an area or region with some special feature ⟨the city's shopping *district*⟩

[1]**dis•trust** \dis-ˈtrəst\ *n*
a lack of belief or confidence in : SUSPICION ⟨They eyed each other with *distrust*.⟩
dis•trust•ful *adj*

[2]**distrust** *vb* **dis•trust•ed**; **dis•trust•ing**
to have no belief or confidence in ⟨I *distrust* the ad's claims.⟩

dis•turb \di-ˈstərb\ *vb* **dis•turbed**; **dis•turb•ing**
1 to interfere with : INTERRUPT ⟨Don't *disturb* him while he's working.⟩
2 to change the position or arrangement of
3 [1]UPSET 1, WORRY ⟨I am very *disturbed* by your behavior.⟩
4 to make confused or disordered ⟨*disturb* the peace⟩

dis•tur•bance \di-ˈstər-bəns\ *n*
1 the act of interrupting, changing the arrangement of, or upsetting : the state of being interrupted, changed in arrangement, or upset ⟨Fish can feel any *disturbances* in the water.⟩
2 [2]DISORDER 2, COMMOTION ⟨I reported a *disturbance* to the police.⟩

dis•turbed \di-ˈstərbd\ *adj*
showing signs of mental or emotional illness ⟨He works with emotionally *disturbed* patients.⟩

dis•use \dis-ˈyüs\ *n*
lack of use

dis•used \dis-ˈyüzd\ *adj*
not used any more

[1]**ditch** \ˈdich\ *n*
▼ a long narrow channel or trench dug in the earth

[1]**ditch**

[2]**ditch** *vb* **ditched**; **ditch•ing**
1 to get rid of ⟨He *ditched* the old car.⟩
2 to end a relationship with ⟨She *ditched* her friends.⟩

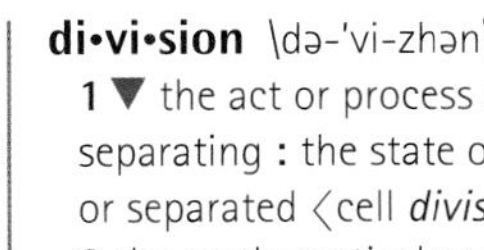

[2]dive 1:
sequence showing a dive

dith•er \'di-t͟hər\ *n*
a very nervous or excited state ⟨The bride's parents were all in a *dither.*⟩

dit•ty \'di-tē\ *n, pl* **ditties**
a short simple song

[1]dive \'dīv\ *vb* **dived** *or* **dove** \'dōv\; **div•ing**
1 to plunge into water headfirst
2 to swim underwater especially while using special equipment
3 SUBMERGE 1 ⟨The submarine *dived.*⟩
4 to fall fast ⟨The temperature is *diving.*⟩
5 to descend in an airplane at a steep angle
6 to move forward suddenly into or at something ⟨We *dove* for cover.⟩
div•er *n*

[2]dive *n*
1 ▲ an act of plunging headfirst into water
2 an act of swimming underwater especially while using special equipment
3 an act of submerging a submarine
4 a quick drop (as of prices)
5 a sudden movement forward into or at something ⟨He made a *dive* for the door.⟩

di•verse \dī-'vərs, də-\ *adj*
1 different from each other : UNLIKE ⟨She met people with *diverse* interests.⟩
2 made up of people or things that are different from each other ⟨Her speech was heard by a *diverse* audience.⟩

di•ver•si•fy \də-'vər-sə-,fī, dī-\ *vb* **di•ver•si•fied; di•ver•si•fy•ing**
to change to include many different things ⟨The cafeteria has *diversified* its menu choices.⟩

di•ver•sion \də-'vər-zhən, dī-\ *n*
1 an act or instance of changing the direction or use of ⟨*diversion* of the river⟩
2 something that relaxes, distracts, or entertains ⟨The city offers many *diversions* for visitors.⟩

di•ver•si•ty \də-'vər-sə-tē, dī-\ *n, pl* **di•ver•si•ties**
the condition or fact of being different ⟨The island has great *diversity* in its plant life.⟩

di•vert \də-'vərt, dī-\ *vb* **di•vert•ed; di•vert•ing**
1 to turn from one path or to use another ⟨Police *diverted* traffic.⟩
2 to turn the attention away : DISTRACT
3 to give pleasure to : AMUSE ⟨Paint and paper *diverted* the children.⟩

di•vide \də-'vīd\ *vb* **di•vid•ed; di•vid•ing**
1 to separate into two or more parts or pieces ⟨She *divided* the pie into eight pieces.⟩
2 to give out in shares ⟨I *divided* the money between us.⟩
3 to be or make different in opinion or interest ⟨The country was *divided* over the issue.⟩
4 to subject to or perform mathematical division ⟨*Divide* 10 by 2.⟩
5 to branch off : FORK ⟨The road *divides* here.⟩
synonyms see SEPARATE
di•vid•er \də-'vī-dər\ *n*

div•i•dend \'di-və-,dend\ *n*
1 a number to be divided by another number
2 an amount of a company's profits that is paid to the owners of its stock

div•i•na•tion \,di-və-'nā-shən\ *n*
the art or practice of using signs and omens or magic powers to foretell the future

[1]di•vine \də-'vīn\ *adj*
1 of or relating to God or a god ⟨*divine* will⟩
2 being in praise of God : RELIGIOUS, HOLY ⟨*divine* worship⟩
3 like a god ⟨The pharaohs of ancient Egypt were considered *divine.*⟩
4 very good
di•vine•ly *adv*

[2]divine *vb* **di•vined; di•vin•ing**
1 to discover or understand something by using intuition
2 to foretell the future by using signs and omens or magic powers

di•vin•i•ty \də-'vi-nə-tē\ *n, pl* **di•vin•i•ties**
1 the quality or state of being God or a god
2 a god or goddess ⟨the *divinities* of ancient Greece⟩
3 the study of religion

di•vis•i•ble \də-'vi-zə-bəl\ *adj*
possible to divide or separate ⟨Nine is *divisible* by three.⟩

di•vi•sion \də-'vi-zhən\ *n*
1 ▼ the act or process of dividing or separating : the state of being divided or separated ⟨cell *division*⟩
2 the mathematical process of finding out how many times one number is contained in another
3 something that divides, separates, or marks off ⟨The river is the *division* between the two towns.⟩
4 one of the parts or groups that make up a whole
5 a large military unit
6 a level of competitors ⟨He finished third in his weight *division.*⟩
7 a group of plants that ranks above the class and below the kingdom and in scientific classification is typically equal to a phylum

whole apple

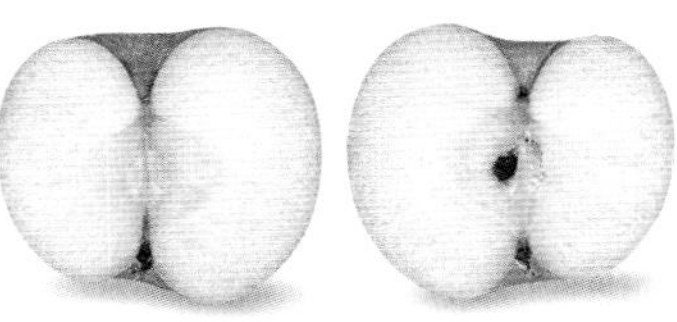

two halves

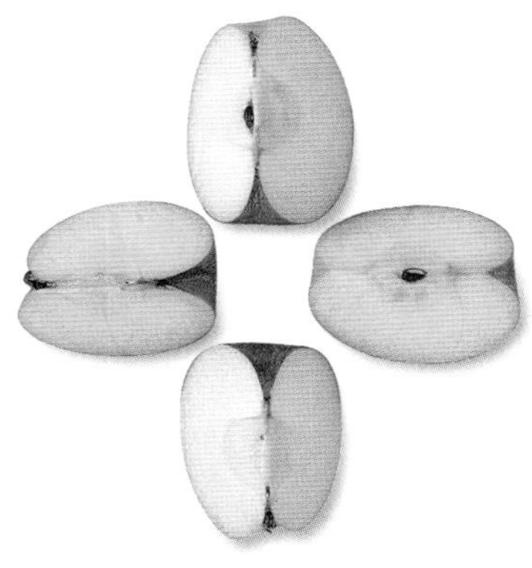

four quarters

division 1: the division of a whole apple into halves and quarters

di•vi•sor \də-'vī-zər\ *n*
the number by which a dividend is divided

[1]di•vorce \də-'vȯrs\ *n*
a legal ending of a marriage

[2]divorce *vb* **di•vorced; di•vorc•ing**
to end a marriage legally : get a divorce

di•vulge \də-ˈvəlj, dī-\ *vb* **di•vulged**; **di•vulg•ing**
to make known to others : REVEAL, DISCLOSE ⟨*divulge* a secret⟩

diz•zy \ˈdi-zē\ *adj* **diz•zi•er**; **diz•zi•est**
1 having the feeling of spinning
2 causing a feeling of spinning ⟨*dizzy* heights⟩
3 overwhelmed with emotion ⟨*dizzy* with joy⟩
diz•zi•ness \ˈdi-zē-nəs\ *n*

DMD *abbr* doctor of dental medicine

DNA \ˌdē-ˌen-ˈā\ *n*
▶a complicated organic acid that carries genetic information in the chromosomes

[1]**do** \dü\ *vb* **did** \did\; **done** \ˈdən\; **do•ing** \ˈdü-iŋ\; **does** \ˈdəz\
1 to cause (as an act or action) to happen : PERFORM ⟨Tell me what to *do*.⟩ ⟨*Do* me a favor.⟩
2 [2]ACT 2, BEHAVE ⟨*Do* as I say, not as I *do*.⟩
3 to make progress : SUCCEED ⟨He is *doing* well in school.⟩
4 to finish working on — used in the past participle ⟨My project is almost *done*.⟩
5 to put forth : EXERT ⟨Just *do* your best.⟩
6 to work on, prepare, produce, or put in order ⟨*Do* your homework.⟩ ⟨This artist *does* beautiful landscapes.⟩
7 to work at as a paying job ⟨What does she *do* for a living?⟩
8 to serve the purpose : SUIT ⟨This will *do* very well.⟩
9 to have an effect ⟨A vacation would *do* you some good.⟩
10 to travel at a speed of ⟨*doing* 50 miles per hour⟩
11 used as a helping verb (1) before the subject in a question ⟨*Do* you work?⟩, (2) in a negative statement ⟨I *do* not know.⟩, (3) for emphasis ⟨I think you *do* know.⟩, and (4) as a substitute for a predicate that has already been stated ⟨You work harder than I *do*.⟩
do away with
1 to get rid of
2 [1]KILL 1

[2]**do** \ˈdō\ *n*
the first note of the musical scale

DOB *abbr* date of birth

doc•ile \ˈdä-səl\ *adj*
easily taught, led, or managed ⟨a *docile* horse⟩
doc•ile•ly *adv*

[1]**dock** \ˈdäk\ *vb* **docked**; **dock•ing**
1 to cut off the end of ⟨*dock* a horse's tail⟩
2 to take away a part of ⟨His pay was *docked*.⟩

▶ **DNA**
Stored in the cells of all living things are chromosomes, made up of long spirals of DNA. Each molecule of DNA consists of many genes, responsible for characteristics such as hair and eye color.

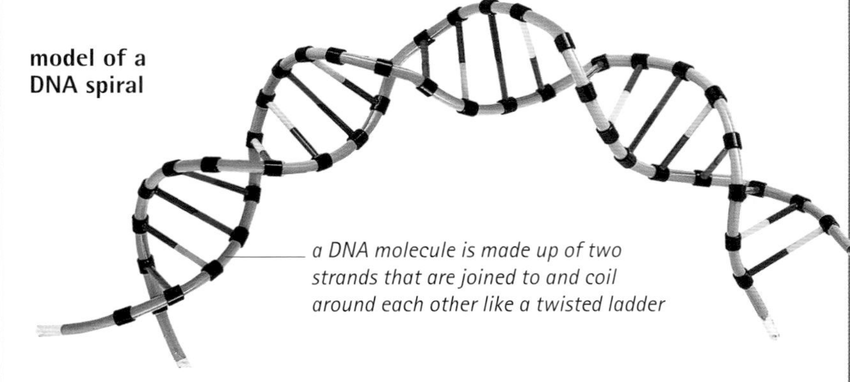

[2]**dock** *n*
1 an artificial basin for ships that has gates to keep the water in or out
2 a waterway usually between two piers to receive ships
3 a wharf or platform for loading or unloading materials

[3]**dock** *vb* **docked**; **dock•ing**
1 to haul or guide into a dock
2 to come or go into a dock
3 to join (as two spacecraft) mechanically while in space

[1]**doc•tor** \ˈdäk-tər\ *n*
a person (as a physician or veterinarian) skilled and specializing in the art of healing

[2]**doctor** *vb* **doc•tored**; **doc•tor•ing**
1 to use remedies on or for ⟨*doctor* a wound⟩
2 to practice medicine

doc•trine \ˈdäk-trən\ *n*
something (as a rule or principle) that is taught, believed in, or considered to be true

[1]**doc•u•ment** \ˈdä-kyə-mənt\ *n*
1 a written or printed paper that gives information about or proof of something ⟨Your birth certificate is a legal *document*.⟩
2 a computer file containing data entered by a user

[2]**document** *vb* **doc•u•ment•ed**; **doc•u•ment•ing**
1 to record (as on paper or in film) the details about ⟨Scientists *documented* the medical study.⟩
2 to prove through usually written records

doc•u•men•ta•ry \ˌdä-kyə-ˈmen-tə-rē, -ˈmen-trē\ *n, pl* **doc•u•men•ta•ries**
a film that tells the facts about something

[1]**dodge** \ˈdäj\ *n*
1 a sudden movement to one side
2 a trick done to avoid something

[2]**dodge** *vb* **dodged**; **dodg•ing**
1 to move suddenly aside or to and fro ⟨We *dodged* through the crowd.⟩
2 to avoid especially by moving quickly ⟨*dodge* a punch⟩
3 EVADE ⟨I *dodged* the question.⟩
dodg•er *n*

dodge ball *n*
a game in which players try to knock other players out of the game by hitting them with a ball

do•do \ˈdō-dō\ *n, pl* **do•does** *or* **do•dos**
a large heavy bird unable to fly that once lived on some of the islands of the Indian Ocean

doe \ˈdō\ *n*
the female of an animal (as a deer or kangaroo) the male of which is called *buck*

do•er \ˈdü-ər\ *n*
a person who tends to act rather than talk or think about things

does *present third person sing of* DO

doesn't \ˈdə-zᵊnt\
does not

doff \ˈdäf, ˈdȯf\ *vb* **doffed**; **dof•fing**
to take off ⟨He politely *doffed* his cap.⟩

[1]**dog** \ˈdȯg\ *n*
1 ▶ a domestic animal that eats meat and is closely related to the wolves
2 any of the group of mammals (as wolves, foxes, and jackals) to which the domestic dog belongs
3 PERSON 1 ⟨You lucky *dog*!⟩
dog•like \ˈdȯ-ˌglīk\ *adj*

A B C D E F G H I J K L M N O P Q R S T U V W X Y Z

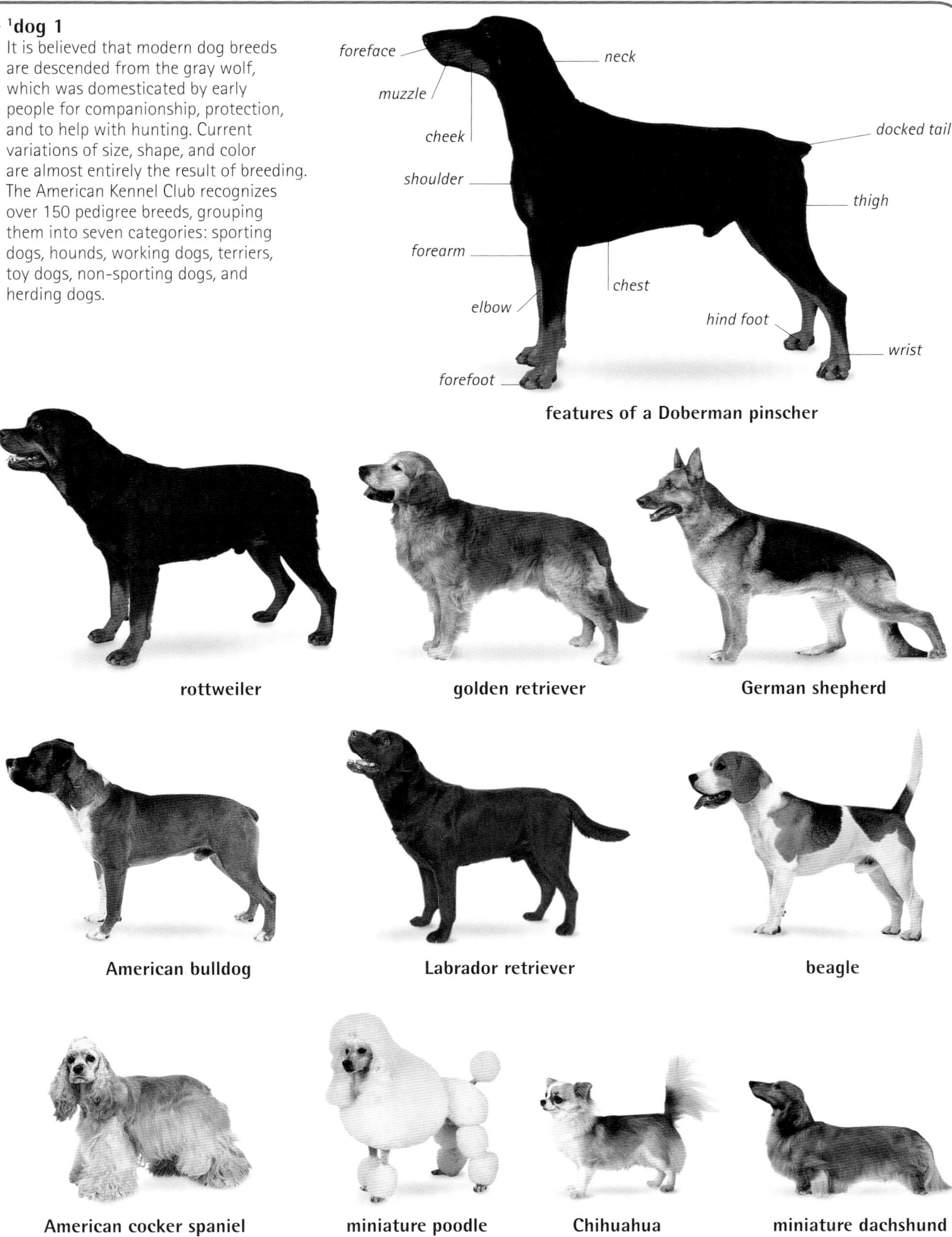

¹dog 1
It is believed that modern dog breeds are descended from the gray wolf, which was domesticated by early people for companionship, protection, and to help with hunting. Current variations of size, shape, and color are almost entirely the result of breeding. The American Kennel Club recognizes over 150 pedigree breeds, grouping them into seven categories: sporting dogs, hounds, working dogs, terriers, toy dogs, non-sporting dogs, and herding dogs.
foreface
neck
muzzle
cheek
docked tail
shoulder
thigh
forearm
chest
elbow
hind foot
wrist
forefoot
features of a Doberman pinscher
rottweiler
golden retriever
German shepherd
American bulldog
Labrador retriever
beagle
American cocker spaniel
miniature poodle
Chihuahua
miniature dachshund

dogsled: a dogsled being pulled by dogs

[2]**dog** *vb* **dogged**; **dog•ging**
1 to hunt, track, or follow like a hound ⟨I *dogged* them all the way.⟩
2 PESTER
3 to cause problems for ⟨Injuries *dogged* the team.⟩

dog•catch•er \'dȯg-ˌka-chər\ *n*
an official paid to catch and get rid of stray dogs

dog days *n pl*
the hot period between early July and early September

▶ **Word History** The brightest star in the sky is Sirius, also known as the Dog Star. Sirius was given this name by the ancients because it was considered the hound of the hunter Orion, whose constellation was nearby. The Dog Star was regarded by the ancient Greeks as the bringer of scorching heat, because its early-morning rising coincided with the hottest summer days of July and August. The Greek writer Plutarch called this time *hēmerai kynades*, literally, "dog days"—the days of the Dog Star—and by way of Latin this phrase was translated into English as *dog days*.

dog–eared \'dȯg-ˌird\ *adj*
having a lot of pages with corners turned over ⟨a *dog-eared* book⟩

dog•fish \'dȯg-ˌfish\ *n*
▼ a small shark often seen near shore

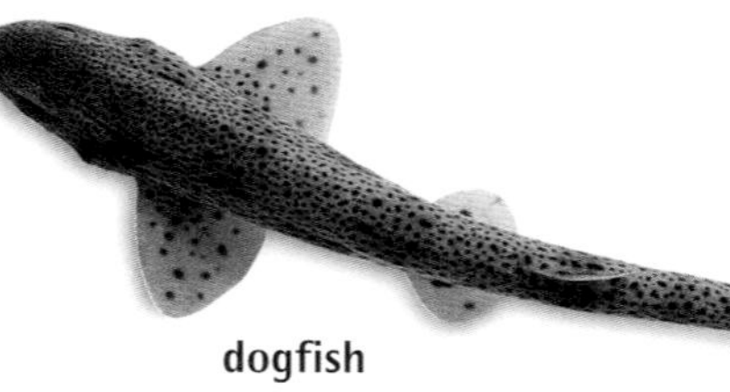
dogfish

dog•ged \'dȯ-gəd\ *adj*
stubbornly determined ⟨He continued his *dogged* search for the truth.⟩
dog•ged•ly *adv*

dog•gy *or* **dog•gie** \'dȯ-gē\ *n*, *pl* **doggies**
a usually small or young dog

dog•house \'dȯg-ˌhau̇s\ *n*
a shelter for a dog
in the doghouse in trouble over some wrongdoing

dog•ma \'dȯg-mə\ *n*
1 something firmly believed ⟨She repeated medical *dogma* against eating sugar.⟩
2 a belief or set of beliefs taught by a church

dog•sled \'dȯg-ˌsled\ *n*
▲ a sled pulled by dogs

dog•wood \'dȯg-ˌwu̇d\ *n*
▼ a shrub or small tree with clusters of small flowers often surrounded by four showy leaves that look like petals

dogwood: dogwood flowers

doi•ly \'dȯi-lē\ *n*, *pl* **doilies**
a small often lacy cloth or paper used to protect the surface of furniture

do•ing \'dü-iŋ\ *n*
1 the act of performing : ACTION ⟨It will take some *doing* to beat us.⟩
2 doings *pl* things that are done or that go on ⟨He asked about all the *doings* back home.⟩

dol•drums \'dōl-drəmz, 'däl-, 'dȯl-\ *n pl*
1 a spell of sadness
2 a period of no activity or improvement ⟨Her business was in the *doldrums*.⟩
3 a part of the ocean near the equator known for its calms

[1]**dole** \'dōl\ *n*
1 an act of giving out food, clothing, or money to the needy
2 something given out to the needy especially at regular times

[2]**dole** *vb* **doled**; **dol•ing**
to give out ⟨Food was *doled* out to the poor.⟩

dole•ful \'dōl-fəl\ *adj*
very sad ⟨a *doleful* day⟩
dole•ful•ly \-fə-lē\ *adv*

doll \'däl\ *n*
1 a child's toy in the form of a baby or small person
2 a kind or loveable person

dol•lar \'dä-lər\ *n*
any of various coins or pieces of paper money (as of the United States or Canada) equal to 100 cents

▶ **Word History** In the early 1500s, much of the silver used to mint coins in Europe came from the mountains on the current border of Germany and the Czech Republic. A mine in these mountains near the town of Sankt Joachimstal produced a coin called in German the *Joachimstaler*, or *Taler* for short. In the Dutch form *daler*, this word was borrowed into English and applied to similar silver coins. One such coin was the Spanish peso, which circulated in England's North American colonies. When the newly independent American colonies settled on an official money unit in 1785, they chose the name *dollar* after this familiar coin.

dolly \'dä-lē\ *n*, *pl* **dollies**
1 DOLL 1
2 a platform on a roller or on wheels for moving heavy things

dol•phin \'däl-fən, 'dȯl-\ *n*
1 ▶ a small whale with teeth and a long nose

2 either of two large fish usually of warm seas that are often used for food

-dom \dəm\ *n suffix*
1 the area ruled by ⟨king*dom*⟩
2 state or fact of being ⟨free*dom*⟩
3 the group having a certain office, occupation, interest, or character

do•main \dō-'mān\ *n*
1 land under the control of a ruler or a government
2 a field of knowledge or activity
3 DOMAIN NAME

domain name *n, pl* **domain names**
the characters (as Merriam-Webster.com) that form the main part of an Internet address

dome \'dōm\ *n*
1 ▶ a rounded top or roof that looks like half of a ball
2 a rounded structure

dome 1: the dome of a planetarium

domed \'dōmd\ *adj*
having a rounded shape like a dome

do•mes•tic \də-'me-stik\ *adj*
1 relating to a household or a family
2 relating to, made in, or done in a person's own country ⟨The president spoke about *domestic* issues.⟩
3 living with or under the care of human beings : TAME ⟨*domestic* animals⟩
do•mes•ti•cal•ly \-sti-kə-lē\ *adv*

do•mes•ti•cate \də-'me-sti-,kāt\ *vb* **do•mes•ti•cat•ed; do•mes•ti•cat•ing**
to bring under the control of and make usable by humans

do•mi•cile \'dä-mə-,sīl\ *n*
a place where someone lives

dom•i•nance \'dä-mə-nəns\ *n*
the state or fact of being in control of or having more power than another

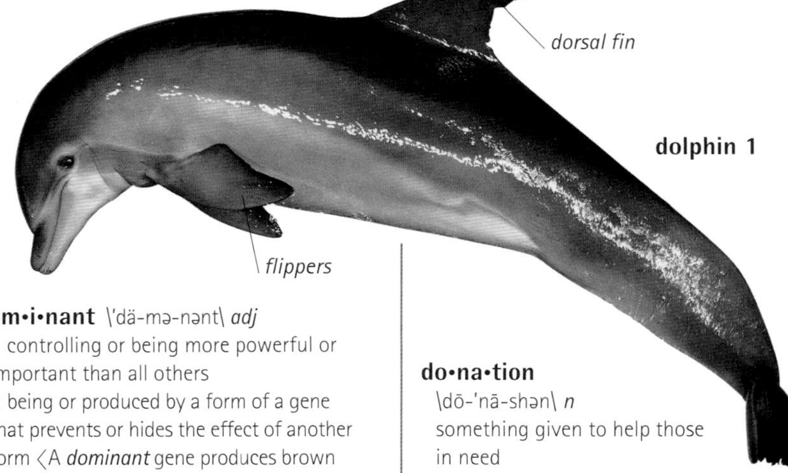

dolphin 1

dom•i•nant \'dä-mə-nənt\ *adj*
1 controlling or being more powerful or important than all others
2 being or produced by a form of a gene that prevents or hides the effect of another form ⟨A *dominant* gene produces brown eye color.⟩

dom•i•nate \'dä-mə-,nāt\ *vb* **dom•i•nat•ed; dom•i•nat•ing**
to have a commanding position or controlling power over ⟨The mountain *dominates* the landscape.⟩

do•min•ion \də-'min-yən\ *n*
1 ruling or controlling power : SOVEREIGNTY
2 a territory under the control of a ruler

dom•i•no \'dä-mə-,nō\ *n, pl* **dom•i•noes** *or* **dom•i•nos**
one of a set of flat oblong dotted pieces used in playing a game (**dominoes**)

don \'dän\ *vb* **donned; don•ning**
to put on ⟨*don* a cap⟩

do•nate \'dō-,nāt\ *vb* **do•nat•ed; do•nat•ing**
to give as a way of helping people in need : CONTRIBUTE ⟨*donate* money⟩ ⟨*donate* blood⟩
synonyms see GIVE

do•na•tion \dō-'nā-shən\ *n*
something given to help those in need

[1]**done** *past participle of* DO

[2]**done**
1 used to say that something has ended ⟨My work is never *done.*⟩ ⟨Are you *done* with the scissors?⟩
2 cooked completely or enough ⟨The cake is *done.*⟩
3 socially acceptable or fashionable ⟨You can't behave like that. It is simply not *done!*⟩
done for doomed to failure, defeat, punishment, or death

don•key \'däŋ-kē, 'dəŋ-, 'dȯŋ-\ *n, pl* **donkeys**
▼ an animal related to but smaller than the horse that has short hair in mane and tail and very large ears

donkey

do•nor \'dō-nər\ *n*
a person who makes a donation

don't \'dōnt\ do not

[1]**doo•dle** \'dü-dᵊl\ *vb* **doo•dled; doo•dling**
to scribble or sketch often while thinking about something else

[2]**doodle** *n*
a scribble or sketch done often while thinking about something else

[1]doom \'düm\ *n*
1 terrible or unhappy ending or happening
2 DEATH 1 ⟨Prepare to meet your *doom.*⟩

[2]doom *vb* **doomed; doom•ing**
to make sure that something bad will happen ⟨The plan was *doomed* to failure.⟩

dooms•day \'dümz-,dā\ *n*
the day the world ends or is destroyed

door \'dȯr\ *n*
1 a usually swinging or sliding frame or barrier by which an entrance (as into a house) is closed and opened
2 a part of a piece of furniture that swings or slides open or shut ⟨the dryer *door*⟩
3 DOORWAY

door•bell \'dȯr-,bel\ *n*
a bell or set of chimes that is rung usually by pushing a button beside an outside door

doorman: a doorman at a hotel

door•man \'dȯr-,man, -mən\ *n*, *pl* **door•men** \-,men\
▲ a person whose job is to help people at the door of a building

door•step \'dȯr-,step\ *n*
a step or a series of steps in front of an outside door

door•way \'dȯr-,wā\ *n*
the opening or passage that a door closes

dope \'dōp\ *n*
1 an illegal drug
2 a stupid person
3 INFORMATION ⟨What's the *dope* on the new kid?⟩

dop•ey \'dō-pē\ *adj* **dop•i•er; dop•i•est**
1 lacking alertness and activity : SLUGGISH
2 STUPID 2 ⟨a *dopey* remark⟩

dorm \'dȯrm\ *n*
DORMITORY

dor•mant \'dȯr-mənt\ *adj*
not active for the time being ⟨The plants are *dormant* for the winter.⟩

dor•mer \'dȯr-mər\ *n*
a window placed upright in a sloping roof or the structure containing it

dor•mi•to•ry \'dȯr-mə-,tȯr-ē\ *n*, *pl* **dor•mi•to•ries**
1 a building at a school with rooms where students live ⟨a college *dormitory*⟩
2 a large room for several people to sleep

dor•mouse \'dȯr-,maůs\ *n*, *pl* **dor•mice** \-,mīs\
a small European animal that resembles a mouse but has a bushy tail, lives mostly in trees, and is active at night

dor•sal \'dȯr-səl\ *adj*
▼ relating to or being on or near the surface of the body that in humans is the back but in most animals is the upper surface ⟨a fish's *dorsal* fin⟩

dorsal: dorsal fin of a fish

do•ry \'dȯr-ē\ *n*, *pl* **dories**
▶ a boat with a flat bottom, high sides that flare out, and a sharp bow

[1]dose \'dōs\ *n*
a measured amount to be used at one time ⟨a *dose* of medicine⟩

[2]dose *vb* **dosed; dos•ing**
to give medicine to

[1]dot \'dät\ *n*
1 a small point, mark, or spot
2 a certain point in time ⟨noon on the *dot*⟩
3 a short click forming a letter or part of a letter (as in Morse code)

[2]dot *vb* **dot•ted; dot•ting**
to mark with or as if with small spots ⟨*Dot* your *i's.*⟩

dote \'dōt\ *vb* **dot•ed; dot•ing**
to give a lot of love or attention to ⟨They *doted* on their grandchild.⟩

doth \'dəth\ *archaic present third person sing of* DO
⟨The wind *doth* blow.⟩
Hint: *Doth* is a very old word that still appears in books and sayings from long ago. People also use it today to imitate that old way of speaking.

[1]dou•ble \'də-bəl\ *adj*
1 being twice as great or as many ⟨I made a *double* batch of cookies.⟩
2 made up of two parts or members ⟨This egg has a *double* yolk.⟩
3 having two very different aspects ⟨She serves a *double* role as teacher and friend.⟩
4 made for two ⟨a *double* bed⟩
5 extra large in size or amount ⟨*double* roses⟩

[2]double *vb* **dou•bled; dou•bling**
1 to make or become twice as great or as many : multiply by two ⟨You'll need to *double* the recipe.⟩
2 to fold usually in the middle ⟨*Double* your paper.⟩
3 to bend over at the waist ⟨He *doubled* over in laughter.⟩
4 CLENCH 2 ⟨I *doubled* my fist.⟩
5 to turn sharply and go back over the same path ⟨The squirrel *doubled* back instead of crossing the street.⟩
6 to have another use or job ⟨The table *doubled* as his desk.⟩

[3]double *adv*
1 two times the amount ⟨The last test question counts *double.*⟩

dory: a Portuguese dory

2 two together ⟨You'll have to sleep *double.*⟩

[4]**double** *n*

1 something that is twice the usual size or amount ⟨The waiter charged me *double.*⟩

2 a hit in baseball that allows the batter to reach second base

3 someone or something that is very like another ⟨You're a *double* for your sister.⟩

on the double very quickly

double bass *n*

▶ an instrument of the violin family that is the largest member and has the deepest tone

dou•ble–cross \ˌdə-bəl-ˈkrȯs\ *vb* **dou•ble–crossed**; **dou•ble–cross•ing**

BETRAY 2

dou•ble–cross•er *n*

dou•ble•head•er \ˌdə-bəl-ˈhe-dər\ *n*

two games played one right after the other on the same day

dou•ble–joint•ed \ˌdə-bəl-ˈjȯin-təd\ *adj*

having a joint that permits unusual freedom of movement of the parts that are joined

double play *n*

a play in baseball by which two base runners are put out

dou•blet \ˈdə-blət\ *n*

a close-fitting jacket worn by men in Europe especially in the 16th century

dou•ble–talk \ˈdə-bəl-ˌtȯk\ *n*

language that seems to make sense but is actually a mixture of sense and nonsense

dou•bly \ˈdə-blē\ *adv*

to two times the amount or degree ⟨*doubly* glad⟩

[1]**doubt** \ˈdau̇t\ *vb* **doubt•ed**; **doubt•ing**

1 to be uncertain about ⟨I *doubt* everything he says.⟩

2 to lack confidence in ⟨I'm starting to *doubt* my own judgment.⟩

3 to consider unlikely ⟨I *doubt* I can go tonight.⟩

[2]**doubt** *n*

1 a feeling of being uncertain ⟨Their predicament filled her with *doubt.*⟩

2 a reason for disbelief

3 the condition of being undecided ⟨Our plans are now in *doubt.*⟩

4 a lack of trust ⟨I have my *doubts* about this explanation.⟩

doubt•ful \ˈdau̇t-fəl\ *adj*

1 undecided or unsure about something ⟨I'm *doubtful* we'll make it on time.⟩

2 not likely to be true ⟨a *doubtful* claim⟩

3 not likely to be good ⟨*doubtful* quality⟩

4 not certain in outcome ⟨a *doubtful* future⟩

doubt•ful•ly \-fə-lē\ *adv*

double bass

doubt•less \ˈdau̇t-ləs\ *adv*

without doubt or with very little doubt ⟨She was *doubtless* the smartest girl in her class.⟩ ⟨There will *doubtless* be some problems.⟩

dough \ˈdō\ *n*

1 a thick mixture usually mainly of flour and liquid that is baked ⟨bread *dough*⟩

2 MONEY 1

dough•nut \ˈdō-ˌnət\ *n*

a small ring of sweet dough fried in fat

dour \ˈdau̇r, ˈdu̇r\ *adj*

looking or being serious and unfriendly ⟨a *dour* old man⟩ ⟨a *dour* expression⟩

douse \ˈdau̇s\ *vb* **doused**; **dous•ing**

1 to stick into water ⟨He *doused* his head in the stream.⟩

2 to throw a liquid on ⟨The chef *doused* the shrimp in sauce.⟩

3 to put out : EXTINGUISH ⟨*douse* a light⟩

[1]**dove** \ˈdəv\ *n*

▶ a bird that is related to the pigeon but usually of somewhat smaller size

[2]**dove** *past and past participle of* DIVE

dowdy \ˈdau̇-dē\ *adj* **dowd•i•er**; **dowd•i•est**

1 not neatly or well dressed or cared for ⟨She plays a *dowdy* old woman in the movie.⟩

2 not stylish ⟨a *dowdy* dress⟩

dow•el \ˈdau̇-əl\ *n*

a pin or peg used for fastening together two pieces of wood

[1]**down** \ˈdau̇n\ *adv*

1 toward or in a lower position ⟨He jumped up and *down.*⟩

2 to a lying or sitting position ⟨Please sit *down.*⟩

3 toward or to the ground, floor, or bottom ⟨She fell *down.*⟩

4 below the horizon ⟨The sun went *down.*⟩

5 to or toward the south ⟨We're heading *down* to Florida.⟩

6 in or into the stomach ⟨They gulped *down* lunch.⟩

7 as a down payment ⟨I paid five dollars *down.*⟩

8 on paper ⟨Write this *down.*⟩

9 to a lower level or rate ⟨Turn the volume *down.*⟩ ⟨Slow *down.*⟩

10 to a weaker or worse condition ⟨The quality of their food has gone *down.*⟩

11 from a past time ⟨These stories were handed *down.*⟩

12 to or in a state of less activity ⟨Everyone quiet *down,* please.⟩

13 in a way that limits movement ⟨Tie the load *down.*⟩

[2]**down** *prep*

1 from a higher to a lower point of something ⟨She climbed *down* the ladder.⟩

2 along the course or path of ⟨We walked *down* the beach.⟩

[3]**down** *vb* **downed**; **down•ing**

1 to go or cause to go or come to the ground ⟨Wind *downed* the power line.⟩

2 EAT 1 ⟨They *downed* their lunch.⟩

3 [1]DEFEAT 2 ⟨Voters *downed* the new law.⟩

[1]**dove:** a pink-spotted fruit-dove

[4]down *adj*
1 in a low position ⟨The window shades are *down.*⟩
2 directed or going downward ⟨the *down* escalator⟩
3 at a lower level ⟨Sales were *down.*⟩
4 having a lower score ⟨Our team is *down* by two.⟩
5 SAD 1 ⟨You look so *down.* What's wrong?⟩
6 not working ⟨The system is *down.*⟩
7 finished or completed ⟨I have two *down,* and two to go.⟩
8 learned completely ⟨I have the dance steps *down.*⟩

[5]down *n*
a low or falling period ⟨Life has its ups and *downs.*⟩

[6]down *n*
a high area of land with low hills and no trees — usually used in pl. ⟨the grassy *downs*⟩

[7]down *n*
1 ▼ soft fluffy feathers ⟨goose *down*⟩
2 small soft hairs ⟨the *down* of a peach⟩

[7]down 1: down on a duckling

down•beat \'dau̇n-ˌbēt\ *n*
the first beat of a measure of music

down•cast \'dau̇n-ˌkast\ *adj*
1 SAD 1 ⟨a *downcast* face⟩
2 directed down ⟨*downcast* eyes⟩

down•fall \'dau̇n-ˌfȯl\ *n*
a sudden fall (as from power, happiness, or a high position) or the cause of such a fall ⟨the *downfall* of the Roman Empire⟩ ⟨Greed proved to be his *downfall.*⟩
down•fall•en \-ˌfȯl-ən\ *adj*

[1]down•grade \'dau̇n-ˌgrād\ *n*
a downward slope (as of a road) ⟨I lost my brakes on the *downgrade.*⟩

[2]downgrade *vb* **down•grad•ed; down•grad•ing**
to lower in grade, rank, position, or standing ⟨The hurricane was *downgraded* to a tropical storm.⟩

down•heart•ed \'dau̇n-'här-təd\ *adj*
SAD 1

[1]down•hill \'dau̇n-'hil\ *adv*
1 toward the bottom of a hill ⟨Our bikes coasted *downhill.*⟩
2 toward a worse condition ⟨Her career is heading *downhill.*⟩

[2]down•hill \'dau̇n-ˌhil\ *adj*
1 sloping downward ⟨a *downhill* path⟩
2 having to do with skiing down mountains

down•load \'dau̇n-ˌlōd\ *vb* **down•load•ed; down•load•ing**
to move from a usually larger computer system to another computer system ⟨*download* music⟩

down payment *n*
a part of a price paid when something is bought with an agreement to pay the rest later

down•pour \'dau̇n-ˌpȯr\ *n*
a heavy rain

[1]down•right \'dau̇n-ˌrīt\ *adv*
REALLY 2, VERY ⟨That was *downright* stupid.⟩

[2]downright *adj*
[2]OUTRIGHT 1, ABSOLUTE ⟨a *downright* lie⟩

[1]down•stairs \'dau̇n-'sterz\ *adv*
down the stairs : on or to a lower floor ⟨The children are playing *downstairs.*⟩

[2]down•stairs \'dau̇n-ˌsterz\ *adj*
situated on a lower floor or on the main or first floor ⟨the *downstairs* bathroom⟩

[3]down•stairs \'dau̇n-'sterz\ *n pl*
the lower floor of a building

down•stream \'dau̇n-'strēm\ *adv*
in the direction a stream is flowing ⟨paddling *downstream*⟩

[1]down•town \ˌdau̇n-'tau̇n, 'dau̇n-ˌtau̇n\ *n*
the main or central part of a city or town

[2]down•town \ˌdau̇n-'tau̇n\ *adv*
to or toward the main or central part of a city or town ⟨walked *downtown*⟩

[1]down•ward \'dau̇n-wərd\ *or* **down•wards** \-wərdz\ *adv*
from a higher place, amount, or level to a lower one ⟨The company's sales continue to go *downward.*⟩

[2]downward *adj*
going or moving from a higher place, amount, or level to a lower one ⟨a *downward* slope⟩

down•wind \'dau̇n-'wind\ *adv or adj*
in the direction the wind is blowing ⟨sailing *downwind*⟩ ⟨the *downwind* side⟩

downy \'dau̇-nē\ *adj* **down•i•er; down•i•est**
1 like small soft feathers ⟨The flower has *downy* petals.⟩
2 covered or filled with small soft feathers or hairs ⟨*downy* chicks⟩

dow•ry \'dau̇-rē\ *n, pl* **dowries**
property that in some cultures a woman gives to her husband in marriage

doz. *abbr* dozen

[1]doze \'dōz\ *vb* **dozed; doz•ing**
to sleep lightly
doze off to fall asleep ⟨I *dozed off* on the ride home.⟩

[2]doze *n*
a light sleep

doz•en \'də-zᵊn\ *n, pl* **dozens** *or* **dozen**
▼ a group of twelve

dozen: twelve green apples

Dr. *abbr* doctor

drab \'drab\ *adj* **drab•ber; drab•best**
1 not bright or interesting : DULL ⟨a *drab* apartment⟩
2 grayish brown in color
drab•ly *adv*
drab•ness *n*

[1]draft \'draft, 'dräft\ *n*
1 a version of something written or drawn (as an essay, document, or plan) that has or will have more than one version ⟨I finished the rough *draft* of my report.⟩
2 a current of air
3 a device to regulate an air supply (as in a fireplace)
4 the act of pulling or hauling : the thing or amount pulled ⟨a beast of *draft*⟩
5 the act or an instance of drinking or inhaling : the portion drunk or inhaled at one time ⟨He took a *draft* of his drink.⟩
6 the act of drawing out liquid (as from a cask) : a portion of liquid drawn out ⟨a *draft* of beer⟩
7 the depth of water a ship needs in order to float
8 the practice of ordering people into military service
9 the practice of choosing someone to play on a professional sports team
10 an order made by one person or organization to another to pay money to a third person or organization

²draft *adj*
1 used for pulling loads ⟨a *draft* animal⟩
2 not in final form ⟨a *draft* report⟩
3 ready to be drawn from a container ⟨*draft* beer⟩

³draft *vb* **draft•ed**; **draft•ing**
1 to write or draw a version of something (as an essay or plan) that usually needs more work
2 to choose someone to do something ⟨Mom *drafted* us to clean the garage.⟩
3 to pick especially for required military service

drafty \'draf-tē, 'dräf-\ *adj* **draft•i•er**; **draft•i•est**
having usually cool air moving through ⟨a *drafty* hall⟩

¹drag \'drag\ *n*
1 something used for pulling along (as a device used underwater to catch something)
2 something without wheels (as a heavy sled for carrying loads) that is pulled along or over a surface
3 something that slows down motion
4 a dull or unpleasant event, person, or thing

²drag *vb* **dragged**; **drag•ging**
1 to pull slowly or heavily ⟨I *dragged* my trunk across the room.⟩
2 to move with slowness or difficulty ⟨She *dragged* herself out of bed.⟩
3 to move or cause to move along on the ground ⟨You're *dragging* your scarf.⟩ ⟨Your scarf is *dragging*.⟩
4 to bring by or as if by force ⟨He *dragged* us to the store.⟩
5 to pass or cause to pass slowly ⟨The hot day *dragged* on.⟩
6 to hang or lag behind ⟨The runner *dragged* behind the others.⟩
7 to search or fish by pulling something (as a net) under water

drag•net \'drag-,net\ *n*
1 ► a net that is pulled along the bottom of a body of water in order to catch or find something
2 a series of actions by police for catching a criminal

dragnet 1

metal bead

dragon:
a model of a dragon

drag•on \'dra-gən\ *n*
▲ an imaginary animal usually pictured as a huge serpent or lizard with wings and large claws

drag•on•fly \'dra-gən-,flī\ *n*, *pl* **drag•on•flies**
► a large insect with a long slender body and four wings

drag race *n*
a race between vehicles to see who can increase speed most quickly over a short distance

¹drain \'drān\ *vb* **drained**; **drain•ing**
1 to remove (liquid) from something by letting it flow away or out ⟨We need to *drain* water from the pool.⟩
2 to slowly make or become dry or empty ⟨*drain* a swamp⟩
3 to flow into, away from, or out of something ⟨The water slowly *drained*.⟩
4 to slowly disappear ⟨His anger *drained* away.⟩
5 to tire out ⟨She was *drained* by the busy weekend.⟩

²drain *n*
1 something used to remove a liquid ⟨the tub's *drain*⟩
2 something that slowly empties of or uses up ⟨The long trip was a *drain* on Grandma's strength.⟩

drain•age \'drā-nij\ *n*
the act or process of removing a liquid ⟨*Drainage* of the flooded area has begun.⟩

drain•pipe \'drān-,pīp\ *n*
a pipe for removing water

drake \'drāk\ *n*
a male duck

dra•ma \'drä-mə, 'dra-\ *n*
1 a written work that tells a story through action and speech and is acted out : a usually serious play, movie, or television production
2 the art or profession of creating or putting on plays
3 an exciting or emotional situation or event

dra•mat•ic \drə-'ma-tik\ *adj*
1 having to do with drama ⟨a *dramatic* actor⟩
2 attracting attention ⟨He made a *dramatic* entrance.⟩
3 sudden and extreme ⟨a *dramatic* change⟩
dra•mat•i•cal•ly \-ti-kə-lē\ *adv*

dra•ma•tist \'dra-mə-təst, 'drä-\ *n*
PLAYWRIGHT

dragonfly:
an adult dragonfly

dra•ma•tize \'dra-mə-,tīz, 'drä-\ *vb* **dram•a•tized**; **dram•a•tiz•ing**
1 to make into a play, movie, or other show ⟨The TV show *dramatized* the musician's life.⟩
2 to present in a way that attracts attention ⟨The accident *dramatized* the need for greater safety measures.⟩
dra•ma•ti•za•tion \,dra-mə-tə-'zā-shən, ,drä-\ *n*

drank *past and past participle of* DRINK

¹drape \'drāp\ *vb* **draped**; **drap•ing**
1 to decorate or cover with or as if with folds of cloth
2 to arrange or hang in flowing lines ⟨The veil *draped* over her head.⟩

²drape *n*, *pl* **drapes**
DRAPERY 1

drawbridge: a drawbridge on the Chicago River

drap•ery \'drā-pə-rē, 'drā-prē\ *n*, *pl* **drap•er•ies**
1 long heavy curtains
2 a decorative fabric hung in loose folds

dras•tic \'dra-stik\ *adj*
severe in effect : HARSH 〈a *drastic* change〉
dras•ti•cal•ly \-sti-kə-lē\ *adv*

draught \'draft, 'dräft\ *chiefly British variant of* DRAFT

[1]**draw** \'drȯ\ *vb* **drew** \'drü\; **drawn** \'drȯn\; **draw•ing**
1 to cause to move by pulling 〈*Draw* the curtains, please.〉 〈She *drew* a chair up to the table.〉
2 to create a picture of by making lines on a surface 〈I *drew* a map on the chalkboard.〉
3 to bring or pull out 〈*Draw* your sword!〉
4 to move in a particular direction 〈He *drew* back in horror.〉
5 to bend (a bow) by pulling back the string
6 to move or go slowly or steadily 〈Spring is *drawing* near.〉
7 ATTRACT 2 〈The fair *drew* a crowd.〉 〈He didn't want to *draw* attention to himself.〉
8 to get as a response 〈The speech *drew* cheers.〉
9 to bring or get from a source 〈*draw* blood〉
10 INHALE 1 〈*Draw* a deep breath.〉
11 to let air flow through 〈The fireplace is *drawing* well.〉
12 WITHDRAW 1 〈I *drew* money from the bank.〉
13 to take or get at random 〈We *drew* names from a hat.〉
14 to think of after considering information 〈*draw* a conclusion〉
15 to write out in proper form 〈The lawyer *drew* up her will.〉
draw on
1 to make use of something 〈The story *draws on* old legends.〉
2 to come closer 〈Night *draws on.*〉

drawer 1: cutlery in a drawer

draw out
1 to make last longer 〈Questions *drew out* the meeting.〉
2 to cause to talk freely 〈Her friendliness *drew out* the new student.〉
draw up
1 to bring or come to a stop 〈The car *drew up* to the door.〉
2 to straighten up 〈He *drew* himself *up* to his full height.〉

[2]**draw** *n*
1 the act or the result of pulling out 〈The outlaw was quick on the *draw*.〉
2 a tie game or contest
3 something or someone that attracts people

draw•back \'drȯ-,bak\ *n*
an unwanted feature or characteristic

draw•bridge \'drȯ-,brij\ *n*
▲ a bridge that moves up, down, or to the side to allow boats or vehicles to pass

draw•er \'drȯ-ər, 'drȯr\ *n*
1 ◀ a box that slides in and out of a piece of furniture and is used for storage 〈a desk *drawer*〉
2 **drawers** *pl* UNDERPANTS

draw•ing \'drȯ-iŋ\ *n*
1 a picture created by making lines on a surface
2 the act or art of creating a picture, plan, or sketch by making lines on a surface
3 an act or instance of picking something at random

drawing room *n*
a formal room for entertaining company

[1]**drawl** \'drȯl\ *vb* **drawled**; **drawl•ing**
to speak slowly with vowel sounds that are longer than usual

[2]**drawl** *n*
a way of speaking with vowel sounds that are longer than usual

drawn \'drȯn\ *adj*
looking very thin and tired especially from worry, pain, or illness

draw•string \'drȯ-,striŋ\ *n*
▶ a string at the top of a bag or on clothing that can be pulled to close or tighten

[1]dread \'dred\ *vb* **dread•ed**; **dread•ing**
1 to fear or dislike greatly ⟨He can't swim and *dreads* going into the water.⟩
2 to be very unwilling to face ⟨I *dread* Monday.⟩

[2]dread *n*
great fear especially of something that will or might happen

[3]dread *adj*
causing great fear or anxiety ⟨a *dread* disease⟩

dread•ful \'dred-fəl\ *adj*
1 causing fear ⟨a *dreadful* storm⟩
2 very unpleasant ⟨a *dreadful* cold⟩

dread•ful•ly \'dred-fə-lē\ *adv*
1 [1]VERY 1 ⟨I'm *dreadfully* sorry.⟩
2 very badly ⟨The play went *dreadfully.*⟩

[1]dream \'drēm\ *n*
1 a series of thoughts or visions that occur during sleep
2 [1]DAYDREAM
3 something very pleasing
4 a goal that is wished for

[2]dream *vb* **dreamed** \'dremt, 'drēmd\ *or* **dreamt** \'dremt\; **dream•ing** \'drē-miŋ\
1 to have a series of thoughts or visions while sleeping
2 to spend time having daydreams
3 to think of as happening or possible ⟨I *dream* of a better world.⟩
dream•er \'drē-mər\ *n*
dream up to think of or invent ⟨Did you *dream up* this plan?⟩

dreamy \'drē-mē\ *adj* **dream•i•er**; **dream•i•est**
1 appearing to be daydreaming ⟨He had a *dreamy* look on his face.⟩
2 seeming like a dream ⟨The old castle looked *dreamy* in the fog.⟩
3 quiet and relaxing ⟨*dreamy* music⟩
dream•i•ly \-mə-lē\ *adv*

drea•ry \'drir-ē\ *adj* **drea•ri•er**; **drea•ri•est**
dull and depressing ⟨a *dreary*, rainy Monday⟩
drea•ri•ly \'drir-ə-lē\ *adv*
drea•ri•ness \'drir-ē-nəs\ *n*

[1]dredge \'drej\ *vb* **dredged**; **dredg•ing**
to dig or gather with or as if with a device dragged along the bottom of a body of water ⟨*dredged* the river⟩ ⟨*dredging* for oysters⟩
dredg•er *n*

[2]dredge *n*
1 a heavy iron frame with a net attached to be dragged along the bottom of a body of water
2 a machine or boat used in dragging along the bottom of a body of water
3 a machine for removing earth usually by buckets on an endless chain or by a suction tube

dregs \'dregz\ *n pl*
1 solids that sink to the bottom of a liquid ⟨*dregs* of coffee⟩
2 the worst or most useless part ⟨the *dregs* of society⟩

drench \'drench\ *vb* **drenched**; **drench•ing**
to make completely wet ⟨We had pancakes *drenched* in syrup.⟩

[1]dress \'dres\ *vb* **dressed**; **dress•ing**
1 to put clothes on
2 to put on clothes in a particular way ⟨Be sure to *dress* warmly.⟩
3 to wear formal or fancy clothes ⟨Do I have to *dress* for dinner?⟩
4 to apply medicine or bandages to ⟨*dress* a wound⟩
5 to trim or decorate for display ⟨*dress* a store window⟩
6 to prepare for cooking or eating ⟨*dress* a chicken⟩ ⟨*dress* the salad⟩
dress up
1 to put on formal or fancy clothes
2 to put on a costume

[2]dress *n*
1 a piece of clothing for a woman or girl that has a top part that covers the upper body and that is connected to a skirt covering the lower body
2 CLOTHING

[3]dress *adj*
proper for a formal event ⟨*dress* clothes⟩

[1]dress•er \'dre-sər\ *n*
a piece of furniture that has drawers for storing clothes and that sometimes has a mirror

[2]dresser *n*
a person who dresses in a certain way ⟨a sloppy *dresser*⟩ ⟨a stylish *dresser*⟩

dress•ing \'dre-siŋ\ *n*
1 a sauce put on a salad
2 a seasoned mixture used as a stuffing ⟨turkey with *dressing*⟩
3 material (as ointment or gauze) used to cover an injury
4 the act of putting on clothes

dressy \'dre-sē\ *adj* **dress•i•er**; **dress•i•est**
1 requiring fancy clothes ⟨a *dressy* event⟩
2 proper for formal events ⟨*dressy* clothes⟩

drew *past of* DRAW

[1]drib•ble \'dri-bəl\ *vb* **drib•bled**; **drib•bling**
1 to fall or let fall in small drops : TRICKLE ⟨Water *dribbled* out of the crack.⟩
2 to let saliva or other liquid drip or trickle from the mouth
3 to move forward by bouncing, tapping, or kicking ⟨*dribble* a basketball⟩

[2]dribble *n*
1 a trickling flow
2 ▼ the act of moving a ball or puck forward by bouncing, kicking, or tapping it

drawstring: a 19th-century embroidered bag with a drawstring

[2]dribble 2: players practicing a dribble

drier *variant of* DRYER

[1]drift \'drift\ *n*
1 the slow movement of something carried by wind or water
2 a pile of something that has been blown by the wind 〈a *drift* of snow〉
3 a course something appears to be taking 〈the *drift* of the conversation〉
4 the meaning of something said or implied 〈I don't get your *drift.*〉

[2]drift *vb* **drift•ed**; **drift•ing**
1 to move slowly on wind or water
2 to be piled up by wind or water 〈*drifting* sand〉
3 to move along or change without effort or purpose 〈She *drifts* from job to job.〉 〈He *drifted* in and out of sleep.〉
drift•er *n*

drift•wood \'drift-,wu̇d\ *n*
wood carried by water

[1]drill \'dril\ *vb* **drilled**; **drill•ing**
1 to make holes in with a drill
2 to teach by repeating a lesson or exercise again and again
drill•er *n*

[2]drill 1: an electric drill

[2]drill *n*
1 ▲ a tool for making holes in hard substances
2 the training of soldiers (as in marching)
3 instruction in a subject or physical training that is practiced repeatedly

[3]drill *n*
a special machine for making holes or furrows and planting seeds in them

[4]drill *vb* **drilled**; **drill•ing**
to sow seeds with or as if with a special machine

drily *variant of* DRYLY

[1]drink \'driŋk\ *vb* **drank** \'draŋk\; **drunk** \'drəŋk\; **drink•ing**
1 to swallow liquid
2 to absorb a liquid 〈Plants *drink* up water.〉
3 to drink alcoholic beverages
4 to take in through the senses 〈He *drank* in the beautiful scenery.〉
drink•er *n*

[2]drink *n*
1 a liquid safe for swallowing 〈Food and *drink* will be provided.〉
2 an amount of liquid swallowed 〈a *drink* of water〉
3 alcoholic beverages

drink•able \'driŋ-kə-bəl\ *adj*
suitable or safe for drinking

[1]drip \'drip\ *vb* **dripped**; **drip•ping**
1 to fall in drops 〈Sap *dripped* from the trees.〉
2 to let fall drops of liquid 〈My wet clothes *dripped* on the floor.〉
3 to have or show a large amount of something 〈The popcorn was *dripping* with butter.〉 〈Her voice *dripped* with spite.〉

[2]drip *n*
1 the act of falling in drops 〈The barrel caught the *drip* of rain from the roof.〉
2 a drop of liquid that falls 〈a *drip* of paint〉
3 the sound made by falling drops

[1]drive \'drīv\ *vb* **drove** \'drōv\; **driv•en** \'dri-vən\; **driv•ing** \'drī-viŋ\
1 to direct the movement of 〈*drive* a car〉
2 to go or carry in a vehicle 〈*drive* into town〉 〈Mom *drove* me to school.〉
3 to move using force
4 to push in with force 〈*drive* a nail〉
5 to set or keep in motion or operation 〈The machines are *driven* by electricity.〉
6 to carry through 〈*drive* a bargain〉
7 to force to work or to act 〈The peasants were *driven* by hunger to steal.〉
8 to bring into a particular condition 〈That noise is *driving* me crazy!〉
driv•er \'drī-vər\ *n*

[2]drive *n*
1 a trip in a vehicle
2 DRIVEWAY
3 an often scenic public road
4 an organized effort to achieve a goal 〈a fund-raising *drive*〉
5 a strong natural need or desire 〈the *drive* to eat〉
6 energy and determination to succeed
7 an act of leading animals in a group to another place 〈a cattle *drive*〉
8 the means for making a machine or machine part move
9 a device in a computer that can read information off and copy information onto disks or tape 〈a disk *drive*〉

drive–in \'drīv-,in\ *n*
a restaurant or theater that serves customers while they stay in their vehicles

drive–through \'drīv-,thrü\ *adj*
DRIVE-UP

drive–up \'drīv-,əp\ *adj*
set up to allow customers to be served while they stay in their vehicles

drive•way \'drīv-,wā\ *n*
▼ a private road leading from the street to a house or garage

[1]driz•zle \'dri-zəl\ *n*
a fine misty rain

[2]drizzle *vb* **driz•zled**; **driz•zling**
to rain in very small drops

driveway: driveway at Glamis Castle, Scotland

droll \'drōl\ *adj* **droller**; **droll•est**
having an odd or amusing quality ⟨a *droll* expression⟩

drom•e•dary \'drä-mə-,der-ē\ *n, pl* **drom•e•dar•ies**
▼ the camel of western Asia and northern Africa that has only one hump

4 a small amount ⟨I'll have just a *drop* of tea.⟩
5 the distance of a fall ⟨a 20-foot *drop*⟩
6 a decrease in amount or quality ⟨a *drop* in sales⟩
7 an act of delivering something **:** a place where something is left to be picked up ⟨a mail *drop*⟩

dromedary

drop•per \'drä-pər\ *n*
▼ a short tube with a rubber bulb used to measure out liquids by drops

dropper:
a bottle of eye drops

drought \'drau̇t\ *n*
a long period of time during which there is very little or no rain

[1]**drove** \'drōv\ *n*
a large group of animals or people moving or acting together ⟨*droves* of shoppers⟩

[2]**drove** *past of* DRIVE

drown \'drau̇n\ *vb* **drowned**; **drown•ing**
1 to die or cause to die from being underwater and unable to breathe
2 to cover with a liquid ⟨She *drowns* her salad with dressing.⟩
3 to overpower especially with noise
4 to make helpless or overwhelmed ⟨*drowning* in work⟩

[1]**drowse** \'drau̇z\ *vb* **drowsed**; **drows•ing**
to sleep lightly

[2]**drowse** *n*
a light sleep **:** DOZE

drowsy \'drau̇-zē\ *adj* **drows•i•er**; **drows•i•est**
1 ready to fall asleep
2 causing sleepiness ⟨*drowsy* music⟩
drows•i•ly \-zə-lē\ *adv*
drows•i•ness \-zē-nəs\ *n*

drub \'drəb\ *vb* **drubbed**; **drub•bing**
1 to beat severely
2 to defeat completely

drub•bing \'drə-biŋ\ *n*
a bad defeat ⟨The team took a *drubbing*.⟩

drudge \'drəj\ *n*
a person who does hard or dull work

drudg•ery \'drə-jə-rē\ *n, pl* **drudg•er•ies**
hard or dull work

[1]**drug** \'drəg\ *n*
1 a substance used as a medicine or in making medicines
2 a substance (as cocaine or marijuana) that may harm or addict a user

[1]**drone** \'drōn\ *n*
a male bee

[2]**drone** *vb* **droned**; **dron•ing**
to make or to speak with a low dull tone or hum ⟨The speaker *droned* on and on.⟩

[3]**drone** *n*
a low dull tone or hum

[1]**drool** \'drül\ *vb* **drooled**; **drool•ing**
to let saliva drip from the mouth

[2]**drool** *n*
saliva that drips from the mouth

[1]**droop** \'drüp\ *vb* **drooped**; **droop•ing**
1 to sink, bend, or hang down ⟨The flowers *drooped* in the hot sun.⟩
2 to become sad or weak ⟨My spirits *drooped*.⟩

[2]**droop** *n*
the condition of hanging or bending down ⟨The dog's tail had a sad *droop*.⟩

[1]**drop** \'dräp\ *n*
1 a small amount of liquid that falls in a rounded shape
2 *drops pl* liquid medicine measured by drops ⟨ear *drops*⟩
3 something (as a small round candy) that is shaped like a liquid drop

[2]**drop** *vb* **dropped**; **drop•ping**
1 to fall or let fall often by accident ⟨I *dropped* my ice cream cone!⟩
2 to go down suddenly ⟨The cliff *drops* straight down.⟩
3 to go or make lower ⟨The temperature *dropped*.⟩ ⟨He *dropped* his voice.⟩
4 to become less or make less ⟨Business has *dropped*.⟩
5 LOSE 5
6 DISAPPEAR 1 ⟨They *dropped* out of sight.⟩
7 to stop or let end ⟨Let the matter *drop*.⟩
8 QUIT ⟨Don't *drop* out of school.⟩
9 to make a brief visit ⟨We *dropped* in on a friend.⟩
10 to deliver with a quick stop ⟨Mom *dropped* us off at school.⟩
11 SEND 1 ⟨*Drop* me a note about it.⟩
drop off to fall asleep

drop–down \'dräp-,dau̇n\ *adj*
PULL-DOWN

drop•let \'drä-plət\ *n*
a tiny drop

drop•out \'dräp-,au̇t\ *n*
a person who quits school or a training program

[2]drug *vb* **drugged**; **drug•ging**
1 to poison with or as if with a drug
2 to make sleepy or unconscious with drugs

drug•gist \'drə-gəst\ *n*
a person who prepares and sells drugs and medicines : PHARMACIST

drug•store \'drəg-,stȯr\ *n*
▼ a retail store where medicines and often other items are sold : PHARMACY

drugstore

[1]drum \'drəm\ *n*
1 ► a musical instrument usually consisting of a metal or wooden round frame with flat ends covered by tightly stretched skin
2 a tapping sound : a sound of or like a drum
3 an object shaped like a cylinder ⟨an oil *drum*⟩

[2]drum *vb* **drummed**; **drum•ming**
1 to beat or play a drum
2 to make a tapping sound : make a sound like a drum ⟨The rain *drummed* on the roof.⟩
3 to beat or tap in a rhythmic way ⟨She *drummed* her fingers.⟩
drum•mer \'drə-mər\ *n*
drum into to force (something) to be learned by repeating it over and over ⟨He *drummed* the lesson *into* our heads.⟩
drum out of to force to leave (a place or organization) ⟨They *drummed* him *out of* the club.⟩
drum up to gather or create by hard work ⟨We need to *drum up* new business.⟩

[1]drum 1:
a drum set

drum major *n*
the marching leader of a band or drum corps

drum ma•jor•ette \,drəm-,mā-jə-'ret\ *n*
a girl who is the leader of a marching band or drum corps

drum•stick \'drəm-,stik\ *n*
1 a stick for beating a drum
2 the lower section of the leg of a bird eaten for food

[1]drunk *past participle of* DRINK

[2]drunk \'drəŋk\ *adj* **drunk•er**; **drunk•est**
1 being so much under the influence of alcohol that normal thinking and acting become difficult or impossible
2 controlled by a strong feeling ⟨*drunk* with power⟩

[3]drunk *n*
DRUNKARD

drunk•ard \'drəŋ-kərd\ *n*
a person who is often drunk

drunk•en \'drəŋ-kən\ *adj*
1 [2]DRUNK 1
2 resulting from being drunk ⟨a *drunken* sleep⟩
drunk•en•ly *adv*
drunk•en•ness *n*

[1]dry \'drī\ *adj* **dri•er**; **dri•est**
1 not wet or moist ⟨*dry* clothes⟩
2 having little or no rain ⟨a *dry* climate⟩
3 not being in or under water ⟨*dry* land⟩
4 having little natural moisture ⟨a *dry* throat⟩
5 no longer liquid or sticky ⟨The paint is *dry*.⟩
6 containing no liquid ⟨a *dry* creek⟩
7 not giving milk ⟨a *dry* cow⟩
8 not producing desired results ⟨a *dry* spell⟩
9 not producing a wet substance from the body ⟨a *dry* cough⟩ ⟨*dry* sobs⟩
10 funny but expressed in a serious way ⟨He has a *dry* sense of humor.⟩
11 UNINTERESTING ⟨a *dry* lecture⟩
12 not sweet ⟨*dry* wines⟩
dry•ly *or* **dri•ly** *adv*
dry•ness *n*

[2]dry *vb* **dried**; **dry•ing**
to remove or lose any moisture

dry cell *n*
a small cell producing electricity by means of chemicals in a sealed container

dry–clean \'drī-,klēn\ *vb* **dry–cleaned**; **dry–clean•ing**
to clean (fabrics) with chemicals instead of water

dry cleaner *n*
a person whose business is cleaning fabrics with chemicals instead of water

dry cleaning *n*
1 the cleaning of fabrics with a substance other than water
2 an item that has been dry-cleaned

dry•er *also* **dri•er** \'drī-ər\ *n*
a device for removing moisture by using heat or air ⟨a clothes *dryer*⟩

dry ice *n*
solidified carbon dioxide used chiefly to keep something very cold

DST *abbr* daylight saving time

du•al \'dü-əl, 'dyü-\ *adj*
1 having two different parts or aspects ⟨The tool has a *dual* purpose.⟩
2 having two like parts ⟨The car has *dual* airbags.⟩

[1]dub \'dəb\ *vb* **dubbed**; **dub•bing**
1 to make a knight of
2 [2]NAME 1, NICKNAME ⟨The football player was *dubbed* "The Bulldozer."⟩

[2]dub *vb* **dubbed**; **dub•bing**
to add (a different language or sound effects) to a film or broadcast

du•bi•ous \'dü-bē-əs, 'dyü-\ *adj*
1 causing doubt : UNCERTAIN ⟨Our plans are *dubious* at this point.⟩
2 feeling doubt ⟨I was *dubious* about our chances.⟩
3 QUESTIONABLE 1 ⟨a *dubious* excuse⟩
du•bi•ous•ly *adv*

duch•ess \'də-chəs\ *n*
1 the wife or widow of a duke
2 a woman who has the same rank as a duke

[1]**duck** \'dək\ *n*
▼ a swimming bird that has a broad flat bill and is smaller than the related goose and swan

[1]**duck:** a male mallard duck

[2]**duck** *vb* **ducked**; **duck•ing**
1 to push under water for a moment ⟨The swan *ducked* its head.⟩
2 to lower the head or body suddenly ⟨You have to *duck* through the doorway.⟩
3 to avoid by moving quickly ⟨He *ducked* the punch.⟩
4 to avoid a duty, question, or responsibility

duck•bill \'dək-ˌbil\ *n*
PLATYPUS

duck•ling \'dək-liŋ\ *n*
a young duck

duct \'dəkt\ *n*
a pipe, tube, or vessel that carries something ⟨air-conditioning *ducts*⟩ ⟨tear *ducts*⟩

duct tape *n*
a wide sticky usually silver tape made of cloth

dud \'dəd\ *n*
1 a complete failure ⟨The party was a *dud.*⟩
2 a bomb or missile that fails to explode
3 **duds** *pl* CLOTHING

dude \'düd, 'dyüd\ *n*
1 a person from the eastern United States in the West
2 [1]MAN 1, GUY

[1]**due** \'dü, 'dyü\ *adj*
1 required or expected to happen or be done ⟨This assignment is *due* tomorrow.⟩
2 owed or deserved ⟨Payment is *due.*⟩ ⟨Treat your teacher with *due* respect.⟩
3 in a proper or necessary amount ⟨I will give your idea *due* consideration.⟩
due to because of

[2]**due** *n*
1 something that should be given ⟨Give the man his *due*, he's a fighter.⟩
2 **dues** *pl* a regular or legal charge or fee

[3]**due** *adv*
DIRECTLY 1 ⟨*due* north⟩

[1]**du•el** \'dü-əl, 'dyü-\ *n*
1 a fight between two persons especially that is fought by agreement with weapons in front of other people
2 a contest between two opponents

[2]**duel** *vb* **du•eled** *or* **du•elled**; **du•el•ing** *or* **du•el•ling**
to take part in an agreed-upon fight with weapons

du•et \dü-'et, dyü-\ *n*
1 a piece of music for two performers
2 two people performing music together

dug *past and past participle of* DIG

dug•out \'dəg-ˌau̇t\ *n*
1 a low shelter facing a baseball diamond and containing the players' bench
2 a shelter dug in a hillside or in the ground
3 a boat made by hollowing out a log

duke \'dük, 'dyük\ *n*
a man of the highest rank of the British nobility

[1]**dull** \'dəl\ *adj* **dull•er**; **dull•est**
1 not sharp in edge or point : BLUNT ⟨a *dull* knife⟩
2 not shiny or bright ⟨The old trophy had a *dull* finish.⟩
3 not interesting : BORING ⟨a *dull* movie⟩
4 not clear and ringing ⟨a *dull* sound⟩
5 not sharp or intense ⟨I have a *dull* ache in my arm.⟩
6 slightly grayish ⟨a *dull* red⟩
7 CLOUDY 1, OVERCAST ⟨a *dull* sky⟩
8 slow in understanding things : not smart
9 without energy or spirit ⟨She was feeling *dull.*⟩
10 slow in action : SLUGGISH ⟨Business was *dull.*⟩
dull•ness *n*
dul•ly *adv*

[2]**dull** *vb* **dulled**; **dull•ing**
to make or become less sharp, bright, or intense ⟨Medicine *dulled* the pain.⟩

du•ly \'dü-lē, 'dyü-\ *adv*
in a due or appropriate manner, time, or degree ⟨Preparations were *duly* made.⟩

dumb \'dəm\ *adj* **dumb•er**; **dumb•est**
1 lacking the power of human speech ⟨*dumb* animals⟩
2 *often offensive* lacking the ability to speak
Hint: In the past, this word was not considered offensive when used in this way. In recent years, however, many people have come to find it hurtful, and you may offend someone by using it.
3 temporarily unable to speak (as from shock or surprise)
4 STUPID 1, FOOLISH ⟨There are no *dumb* questions.⟩
dumb•ly *adv*

dumb•found \ˌdəm-'fau̇nd\ *vb* **dumb•found•ed**; **dumb•found•ing**
to make speechless with surprise

dum•my \'də-mē\ *n, pl* **dummies**
1 something shaped like a human ⟨a clothes store *dummy*⟩
2 a doll used in a ventriloquist's act
3 a stupid person

[1]**dump** \'dəmp\ *vb* **dumped**; **dump•ing**
1 to let fall in a heap ⟨He *dumped* his clothes on the bed.⟩
2 to get rid of ⟨You can't just *dump* trash anywhere.⟩

[2]**dump** *n*
1 a place for getting rid of trash
2 a place for storage of military materials or the materials stored ⟨an ammunition *dump*⟩
3 a messy or shabby place

dump•ling \'dəmp-liŋ\ *n*
1 ▼ a small amount of dough cooked by boiling or steaming
2 a dessert of fruit wrapped in dough

dumps \'dəmps\ *n pl*
a sad mood ⟨down in the *dumps*⟩

dumpy \'dəm-pē\ *adj* **dump•i•er**; **dump•i•est**
having a short and round body

dumpling 1:
a bowl of dumpling soup

dun \'dən\ *n*
a slightly brownish dark gray

dunce \'dəns\ *n*
a stupid person

dune: a dune by the seaside

dune \'dün, 'dyün\ *n*
▲ a hill or ridge of sand piled up by the wind

dung \'dəŋ\ *n*
solid waste matter from an animal

dun•ga•ree \ˌdəŋ-gə-'rē\ *n*
1 a heavy cotton cloth **:** DENIM
2 ▼ **dungarees** *pl* clothes made of denim

dungaree 2: a girl wearing blue dungarees

dun•geon \'dən-jən\ *n*
a dark usually underground prison

dunk \'dəŋk\ *vb* **dunked**; **dunk•ing**
1 to dip into liquid ⟨I like to *dunk* my cookies in milk.⟩
2 to jump and push the ball down through the basket in basketball

duo \'dü-ō, 'dyü-\ *n, pl* **du•os**
1 two people who are usually seen together
2 DUET

[1]dupe \'düp, 'dyüp\ *n*
a person who has been or is easily deceived or cheated

[2]dupe *vb* **duped**; **dup•ing**
[2]TRICK ⟨Don't be *duped* into giving them money.⟩

du•plex \'dü-ˌpleks, 'dyü-\ *n*
a house with two separate living spaces

[1]du•pli•cate \'dü-pli-kət, 'dyü-\ *adj*
exactly the same as another ⟨*duplicate* copies⟩

[2]du•pli•cate \'dü-pli-ˌkāt, 'dyü-\ *vb* **du•pli•cat•ed**; **du•pli•cat•ing**
to make an exact copy of

[3]du•pli•cate \'dü-pli-kət, 'dyü-\ *n*
a thing that is exactly like another

du•pli•ca•tion \ˌdü-pli-'kā-shən, ˌdyü-\ *n*
1 the act or process of copying ⟨He sent the paper out for *duplication*.⟩
2 the state of being copied

du•ra•bil•i•ty \ˌdu̇r-ə-'bi-lə-tē, ˌdyu̇r-\ *n*
ability to last or to stand hard or continued use

du•ra•ble \'du̇r-ə-bəl, 'dyu̇r-\ *adj*
able to last a long time

du•ra•tion \du̇-'rā-shən, dyu̇-\ *n*
the time during which something exists or lasts

dur•ing \ˌdu̇r-iŋ, ˌdyu̇r-\ *prep*
1 throughout the course of ⟨I swim every day *during* the summer.⟩
2 at some point in the course of ⟨You may call me *during* the day.⟩

dusk \'dəsk\ *n*
the time when the sky is getting dark at night

dusky \'də-skē\ *adj* **dusk•i•er**; **dusk•i•est**
1 somewhat dark in color ⟨a *dusky* bird⟩
2 somewhat dark **:** DIM ⟨a *dusky* room⟩

[1]dust \'dəst\ *n*
1 fine dry powdery particles (as of earth) **:** a fine powder that often builds up on furniture
2 a fine powder made from a particular substance or from something that has disintegrated ⟨gold *dust*⟩
3 the surface of the ground ⟨The horses pawed at the *dust*.⟩

[2]dust *vb* **dust•ed**; **dust•ing**
1 to make free of dust **:** brush or wipe away dust ⟨*dust* furniture⟩
2 to sprinkle with or as if with fine particles ⟨*Dust* the pan with flour.⟩
dust•er \'də-stər\ *n*

dust•pan \'dəst-ˌpan\ *n*
a flat pan shaped like a shovel into which dirt from the floor is swept

dust storm *n*
a very strong wind carrying dust across a dry region

dusty \'də-stē\ *adj* **dust•i•er**; **dust•i•est**
1 filled or covered with dust
2 resembling dust ⟨*dusty* soil⟩

[1]Dutch \'dəch\ *adj*
of or relating to the Netherlands, its people, or their language

[2]Dutch *n*
1 Dutch *pl* the people of the Netherlands
2 the language of the people of the Netherlands

du•ti•ful \'dü-ti-fəl, 'dyü-\ *adj*
doing or showing the willingness to do what is expected or required ⟨a *dutiful* child⟩
du•ti•ful•ly \-fə-lē\ *adv*

du•ty \'dü-tē, 'dyü-\ *n, pl* **duties**
1 something a person feels he or she ought to do because it is morally right ⟨Dad says it's his *duty* to take care of Grandma.⟩
2 something a person is required to do by law ⟨jury *duty*⟩
3 an action done as part of a job or position ⟨a principal's *duties*⟩
4 the time during which a person must do his or her job ⟨The police officer was on *duty*.⟩
5 active military service ⟨He returned from *duty* overseas.⟩
6 a tax especially on imports into a country
synonyms see TASK

DVD \ˌdē-ˌvē-ˈdē\ *n, pl* DVDs
a plastic disk that is used to store information (as computer data or a movie) and is read using a laser

DVR \ˌdē-ˌvē-ˈär\ *n, pl* DVRs
a machine that is used to make and watch recordings of television programs

¹dwarf \ˈdwȯrf\ *n, pl* **dwarfs** \ˈdwȯrfs\ *also* **dwarves** \ˈdwȯrvz\
1 ▼ a person, animal, or plant much smaller than normal size

¹dwarf 1: a dwarf tree, pruned to restrict its growth

2 a creature in legends that is usually pictured as a small person who is skilled at some craft

²dwarf *vb* **dwarfed; dwarf•ing**
to cause to appear smaller

³dwarf *adj*
of less than the usual size 〈*dwarf* pine trees〉

dwarf planet *n*
a heavenly body similar to a planet but too small to clear other objects from its orbit

dwell \ˈdwel\ *vb* **dwelt** \ˈdwelt\ *or* **dwelled** \ˈdweld\; **dwell•ing**
1 to live in a place : RESIDE
2 to keep the attention directed 〈Try not to *dwell* on your mistakes.〉
dwell•er *n*

dwell•ing \ˈdwe-liŋ\ *n*
a shelter in which a person or an animal lives

dwin•dle \ˈdwin-dəl\ *vb* **dwin•dled; dwin•dling**
to make or become less or smaller 〈The crowd *dwindled.*〉

¹dye \ˈdī\ *n*
► a substance used to change the color of something 〈hair *dye*〉

²dye *vb* **dyed; dye•ing**
to change the color of something using a substance

dying *present participle of* DIE

dy•nam•ic \dī-ˈna-mik\ *adj*
always active, energetic, or changing 〈a *dynamic* city〉

¹dy•na•mite \ˈdī-nə-ˌmīt\ *n*
an explosive used in blasting

²dynamite *vb* **dy•na•mit•ed; dy•na•mit•ing**
to blow up with dynamite

dy•na•mo \ˈdī-nə-ˌmō\ *n, pl* **dy•na•mos**
1 GENERATOR
2 an energetic person

¹dye: experiment showing how dye colors paper

dy•nas•ty \ˈdī-nə-stē\ *n, pl* **dy•nas•ties**
a series of rulers of the same family

dys•en•tery \ˈdi-sᵊn-ˌter-ē\ *n*
a disease marked especially by severe often bloody diarrhea

dys•lex•ia \dis-ˈlek-sē-ə\ *n*
a learning disability in which a person usually has a problem in reading, spelling, and writing
dys•lex•ic \-ˈlek-sik\ *adj*

Sounds of E: The letter **E** makes a number of sounds. The sound heard in the words *fresh* and *melt* is the short **E**. The long **E** is heard in words like *me* and *complete*. The sound of the long **E** is indicated by the symbol ē. Letter **E** also makes the schwa sound, which is indicated by the symbol ə, in words like *angel* and *bulletin*. In *pretty*, **E** sounds like a short **I**. **E** makes a variety of sounds when combined with other letters, such as the long **A** sound in *vein*, *prey*, and *steak*. The combination **EW** can often sound just like the long **U**, like in *few* or *grew*. Sometimes **E** is silent, especially at the end of a word, such as in *note*.

e \ˈē\ *n, pl* **e's** *or* **es** \ˈēz\ *often cap*
1 the fifth letter of the English alphabet
2 a grade that shows a student's work is failing
3 a musical note referred to by the letter E

E *abbr*
1 east
2 eastern
3 excellent

ea. *abbr* each

[1]**each** \ˈēch\ *adj*
every one of two or more individuals considered separately ⟨read *each* book⟩

[2]**each** *pron*
each one ⟨We *each* took a turn.⟩

[3]**each** *adv*
to or for each : APIECE ⟨We were given two presents *each*.⟩ ⟨They cost 50 cents *each*.⟩

each other *pron*
each of two or more in a shared action or relationship ⟨They greeted *each other*.⟩

ea•ger \ˈē-gər\ *adj*
very excited and interested
ea•ger•ly *adv*
ea•ger•ness *n*

► **Synonyms** EAGER, ANXIOUS, and KEEN mean having or showing a strong desire or interest. EAGER is used when there is much enthusiasm and often impatience. ⟨*Eager* travelers waited for their train.⟩ ANXIOUS is used when there is fear of failure or disappointment. ⟨I was *anxious* to learn who won.⟩ KEEN is used when there is great interest and readiness to act. ⟨The new scouts are *keen* to learn.⟩

ea•gle \ˈē-gəl\ *n*
► a large bird of prey noted for keen sight and powerful flight

ea•glet \ˈē-glət\ *n*
a young eagle

► **eagle**

There are more than 50 species of eagle found around the world. Related to the hawks, they are powerful predators who use their keen eyesight to locate their prey of small mammals, fish, reptiles, and other birds. They dive through the air and grasp the victim with their talons, later using their hooked beaks to devour the flesh.

tawny eagle

white-bellied sea eagle

powerful wing
hooked bill
broad wingspread
talon
long tail feathers

features of a golden eagle

[1]ear 1
The ear is used for hearing and balance. The outermost part of the ear receives sound waves which travel through the auditory canal and cause the eardrum and parts of the middle ear to vibrate. The vibrations reach the inner ear where they convert into nerve impulses which travel to the brain.

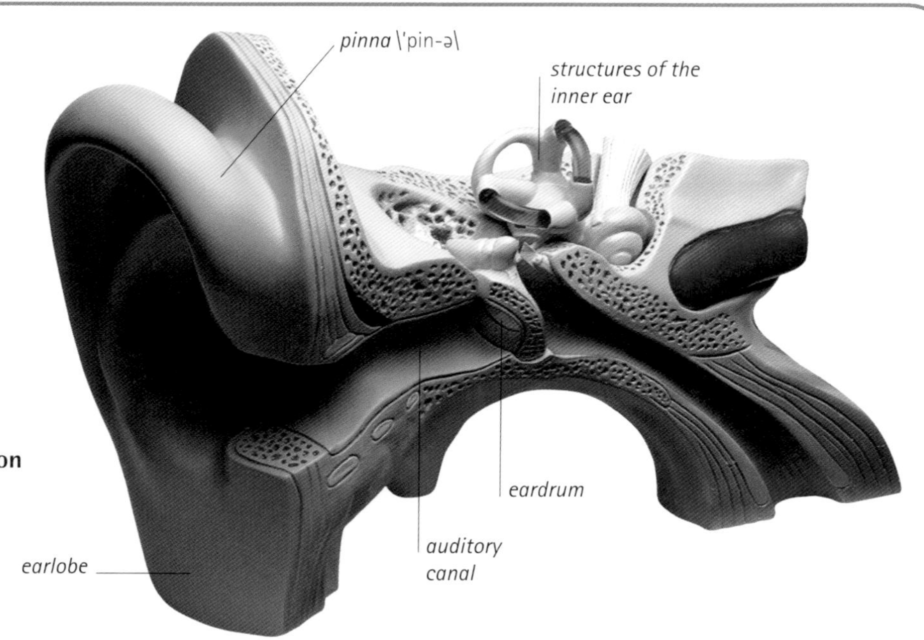

model of the human ear in cross-section

-ean see **-an**

[1]ear \'ir\ *n*
1 ▲ the organ of hearing and balance of vertebrates that in most mammals is made up of an outer part that collects sound, a middle part that carries sound, and an inner part that receives sound and sends nerve signals to the brain
2 the outer part of the ear ⟨She pulled on his *ear.*⟩
3 the sense of hearing ⟨a good *ear* for music⟩
4 willing or sympathetic attention ⟨The coach had every player's *ear.*⟩
eared \'ird\ *adj*

[2]ear *n*
▶ the seed-bearing head of a cereal grass ⟨an *ear* of corn⟩

corn silk

[2]ear: an ear of corn

ear•ache \'ir-,āk\ *n*
an ache or pain in the ear

ear•drum \'ir-,drəm\ *n*
the membrane that separates the outer and middle parts of the ear and vibrates when sound waves strike it

earl \'ərl\ *n*
a member of the British nobility who ranks below a marquess and above a viscount

[1]ear•ly \'ər-lē\ *adv* **ear•li•er**; **ear•li•est**
1 at or near the beginning of a period of time ⟨woke up *early*⟩ ⟨*early* in my career⟩
2 before the usual or expected time ⟨arrived *early*⟩

[2]early *adj* **ear•li•er**; **ear•li•est**
occurring near the beginning or before the usual time ⟨*early* morning⟩

ear•muff \'ir-,məf\ *n*
one of a pair of coverings joined by a flexible band and worn to protect the ears from cold or noise

earn \'ərn\ *vb* **earned**; **earn•ing**
1 to get for work done ⟨She *earns* her pay.⟩
2 to deserve as a result of labor or service ⟨He *earned* good grades.⟩
synonyms see DESERVE

ear•nest \'ər-nəst\ *adj*
not light or playful
synonyms see SERIOUS
ear•nest•ly *adv*
ear•nest•ness *n*

earn•ings \'ər-niŋz\ *n pl*
money received as wages or gained as profit

earphones

ear•phone \'ir-,fōn\ *n*
▲ a device that converts electrical energy into sound and is worn over the opening of the ear or inserted into it

ear•ring \'ir-,riŋ\ *n*
▼ an ornament worn on the ear

earring: a pair of earrings

ear•shot \'ir-,shät\ *n*
the range within which a person's voice can be heard

A B C D E F G H I J K L M N O P Q R S T U V W X Y Z

earth \'ərth\ *n*
1 ▶ *often cap* the planet that we live on
2 land as distinguished from sea and air ⟨Snow fell to *earth*.⟩
3 ²SOIL 1 ⟨a mound of *earth*⟩

earth•en \'ər-thən\ *adj*
made of earth or of baked clay ⟨an *earthen* dam⟩ ⟨an *earthen* jar⟩

earth•en•ware \'ər-thən-,wer\ *n*
things (as dishes) made of baked clay

earth•ly \'ərth-lē\ *adj*
1 having to do with or belonging to the earth
2 IMAGINABLE, POSSIBLE ⟨It's of no *earthly* use.⟩

earth•quake \'ərth-,kwāk\ *n*
a shaking or trembling of a portion of the earth

earth•worm \'ərth-,wərm\ *n*
▼ a worm that has a long body made up of similar segments and lives in damp soil

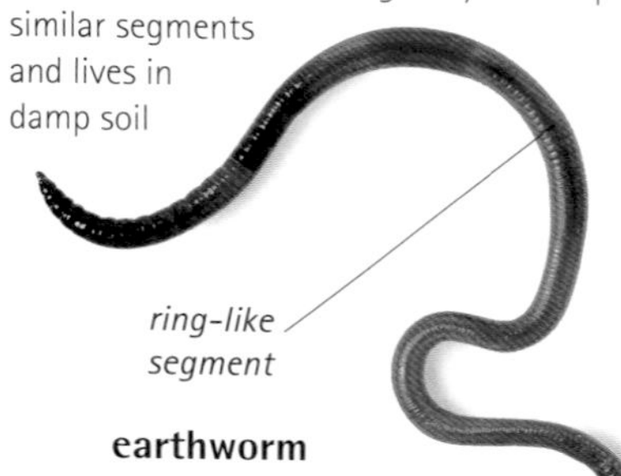

earthworm

earthy \'ər-thē\ *adj* **earth•i•er**; **earth•i•est**
1 of or like earth ⟨an *earthy* smell⟩ ⟨*earthy* colors⟩
2 open and direct ⟨Voters like the mayor's *earthy* manner.⟩
3 not polite : CRUDE ⟨*earthy* humor⟩

ear•wax \'ir-,waks\ *n*
a yellowish brown waxy substance made by glands in the canal of the outer part of the ear

ear•wig \'ir-,wig\ *n*
an insect with long slender feelers and a part at the end of its body that pinches and is used for self-defense

¹ease \'ēz\ *n*
1 freedom from pain or trouble : comfort of body or mind ⟨a life of *ease*⟩
2 lack of difficulty ⟨I completed the task with *ease*.⟩
3 freedom from any feeling of difficulty or embarrassment

²ease *vb* **eased**; **eas•ing**
1 to free from discomfort or worry : RELIEVE ⟨This medicine will *ease* the pain.⟩
2 to make less tight : LOOSEN ⟨She *eased* up on the rope.⟩
3 to move very carefully

ea•sel \'ē-zəl\ *n*
a frame for supporting an artist's painting

▶ **earth 1**
The earth is the fifth largest planet in the solar system, and the only planet known to sustain life. It is made up of four main layers: the inner core, outer core, mantle, and crust, and is surrounded by the atmosphere.

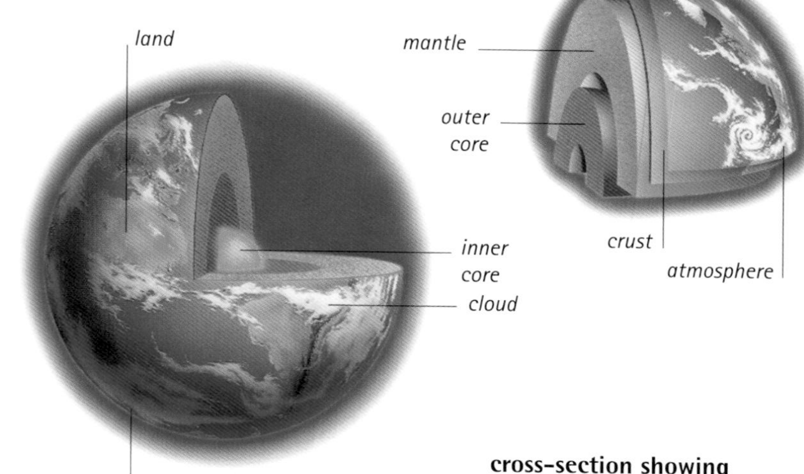

cross-section showing the structure of the earth

▶ **Word History** Our word *easel* is borrowed from the Dutch word *ezel*, which means literally "donkey." A donkey is used for carrying loads, and an artist's easel, like an obedient animal, does the work of supporting an artist's canvas. If this comparison seems at all odd, we should recall that *horse* in English is used in a similar way, as in the compound *sawhorse*, a frame that supports wood for cutting.

eas•i•ly \'ē-zə-lē, 'ēz-lē\ *adv*
1 without difficulty ⟨I won the race *easily*.⟩
2 without doubt : by far ⟨You're *easily* the best person for the job.⟩

¹east \'ēst\ *n*
1 the direction of sunrise : the compass point opposite to west
2 *cap* regions or countries east of a certain point

²east *adj*
placed toward, facing, or coming from the east ⟨the *east* end⟩ ⟨an *east* wind⟩

³east *adv*
to or toward the east ⟨traveled *east*⟩

Eas•ter \'ē-stər\ *n*
a Christian holy day that celebrates the Resurrection

east•er•ly \'ē-stər-lē\ *adv or adj*
1 toward the east ⟨They sailed *easterly*.⟩ ⟨They sailed in an *easterly* direction.⟩
2 from the east ⟨an *easterly* wind⟩

east•ern \'ē-stərn\ *adj*
1 lying toward or coming from the east
2 *often cap* of, relating to, or like that of the East

east•ward \'ēs-twərd\ *adv or adj*
toward the east

¹easy \'ē-zē\ *adj* **eas•i•er**; **eas•i•est**
1 not hard to do or get : not difficult ⟨an *easy* lesson⟩
2 not hard to please ⟨an *easy* teacher⟩
3 free from pain, trouble, or worry ⟨She had an *easy* life.⟩
4 COMFORTABLE 1 ⟨an *easy* chair⟩
5 showing ease : NATURAL ⟨an *easy* manner⟩

²easy *adv*
1 EASILY ⟨Our team should win *easy*.⟩
2 slowly and carefully or calmly ⟨*Easy* does it.⟩
3 without much punishment ⟨You got off *easy*.⟩

eat \'ēt\ *vb* **ate** \'āt\; **eat•en** \'ē-tᵊn\; **eat•ing**
1 to chew and swallow food
2 to take a meal ⟨Let's *eat* at home.⟩
3 to destroy as if by eating : CORRODE ⟨Acids *ate* away the metal.⟩
eat•er *n*

eat•able \'ē-tə-bəl\ *adj*
fit to be eaten : EDIBLE

eave \'ēv\ *n*
the lower edge of a roof that sticks out past the wall — usually used in pl.

eaves•drop \'ēvz-,dräp\ *vb* **eaves•dropped**;

eaves•drop•ping
to listen secretly to private conversation

[1]**ebb** \'eb\ *n*
1 the flowing out of the tide
2 a low point or condition

[2]**ebb** *vb* **ebbed**; **ebb•ing**
1 to flow out or away : RECEDE
2 [1]DECLINE 2, WEAKEN

[1]**eb•o•ny** \'e-bə-nē\ *n*, *pl* **eb•o•nies**
a hard heavy blackish wood that comes from tropical trees

[2]**ebony** *adj*
1 made of or like ebony 〈an *ebony* table〉
2 very dark or black

e-book \'ē-,bu̇k\ *n*
a book that is read on a computer, e-reader, or other electronic device

[1]**ec•cen•tric** \ik-'sen-trik, ek-\ *adj*
1 acting or thinking in a strange way
2 not of the usual or normal kind 〈*eccentric* behavior〉

[2]**eccentric** *n*
a person who behaves strangely

[1]**echo** \'e-kō\ *n*, *pl* **ech•oes**
the repetition of a sound caused by the reflection of sound waves

[2]**echo** *vb* **ech•oed**; **echo•ing**
1 to send back or repeat a sound
2 to repeat another's words

echo•lo•ca•tion \,e-kō-lō-'kā-shən\ *n*
a method for locating objects that is used by various animals (as bats and dolphins) and that involves sending out sound waves which are reflected back from the objects to the sender as echoes

éclair \ā-'kler\ *n*
a long thin pastry filled with whipped cream or custard

▶ **Word History** *Éclair* came from a French word with the same spelling that first meant "lightning." We don't know why the *éclair* was named after lightning. Perhaps it was because it is so light, or perhaps because an *éclair* is likely to be eaten in a flash.

eclec•tic \e-'klek-tik, i-\ *adj*
including things taken from many different sources 〈an *eclectic* mix of music〉

[1]**eclipse** \i-'klips\ *n*
1 a complete or partial hiding of the sun caused by the moon's passing between the sun and the earth
2 a darkening of the moon caused by its entering the shadow of the earth
3 the hiding of any heavenly body by another

[2]**eclipse** *vb* **eclipsed**; **eclips•ing**
1 to cause an eclipse of 〈The sun was *eclipsed* by the moon.〉
2 to be or do much better than : OUTSHINE

eco•log•i•cal \,ē-kə-'lä-ji-kəl, ,e-kə-\ *adj*
of or relating to the science of ecology or the patterns of relationships between living things and their environment

ecol•o•gist \i-'kä-lə-jəst\ *n*
a person specializing in ecology

ecol•o•gy \i-'kä-lə-jē\ *n*
1 a branch of science concerned with the relationships between living things and their environment
2 the pattern of relationships between living things and their environment

eco•nom•ic \,e-kə-'nä-mik, ,ē-\ *adj*
1 of or relating to the study of economics
2 relating to or based on the making, selling, and using of goods and services

eco•nom•i•cal \,e-kə-'nä-mi-kəl, ,ē-\ *adj*
1 using what is available without waste
2 costing little to use 〈*economical* cars〉
eco•nom•i•cal•ly *adv*

▶ **Synonyms** ECONOMICAL, THRIFTY, and SPARING mean careful in the use of money or goods. ECONOMICAL means using things in the best possible way without waste. 〈She's an *economical* cook who feeds us well.〉 THRIFTY is used when someone manages things well and is industrious. 〈The *thrifty* business owner saved money.〉 SPARING is used when someone spends or uses as little as possible. 〈He's *sparing* in giving tips.〉

eco•nom•ics \,e-kə-'nä-miks, ,ē-\ *n pl*
the science concerned with the making, selling, and using of goods and services
Hint: *Economics* can be used as a singular or a plural in writing or speaking.

econ•o•mize \i-'kä-nə-,mīz\ *vb* **econ•o•mized**; **econ•o•miz•ing**
1 to be thrifty
2 to use less of 〈*economize* on fuel〉

econ•o•my \i-'kä-nə-mē\ *n*, *pl* **econ•o•mies**
1 the way in which goods and services are made, sold, and used in a country or area
2 the careful use of money and goods

eco•sys•tem \'ē-kō-,si-stəm, 'e-\ *n*
▼ the whole group of living and nonliving things that make up an environment and affect each other

ec•sta•sy \'ek-stə-sē\ *n*, *pl* **ec•sta•sies**
very great happiness or delight

ec•stat•ic \ek-'sta-tik\ *adj*
very happy or excited

ec•ze•ma \ig-'zē-mə, 'eg-zə-mə, 'ek-sə-mə\ *n*
a skin disease in which the skin is red and itchy and has scaly or crusty patches

▶ **ecosystem**
A typical ecosystem includes sunlight, water, plants, animals, and microorganisms. Sunlight and water help plants to grow, and the plants in turn offer food and protection to the animals. These feed on the plants or other animals, while the microorganisms help to break down decaying material.

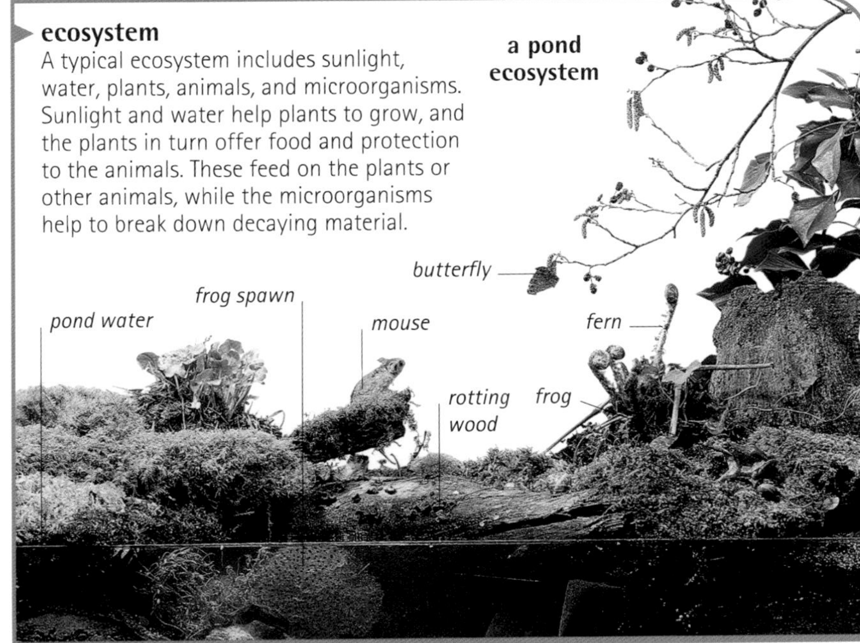

A B C D E F G H I J K L M N O P Q R S T U V W X Y Z

[1]-ed \d *after a vowel or b, g, j, l, m, n, ŋ, r, th, v, z, zh;* əd, id *after d, t;* t *after other sounds*\ *vb suffix or adj suffix*
1 used to form the past participle of verbs ⟨fad*ed*⟩ ⟨tri*ed*⟩
2 having : showing ⟨cultur*ed*⟩
3 having the characteristics of ⟨dogg*ed*⟩

[2]-ed *vb suffix*
used to form the past tense of verbs ⟨judg*ed*⟩ ⟨deni*ed*⟩ ⟨dropp*ed*⟩

[1]ed•dy \'e-dē\ *n, pl* **eddies**
a current of air or water running against the main current or in a circle

[2]eddy *vb* **ed•died; ed•dy•ing**
to move in a circle : to form an eddy

[1]edge \'ej\ *n*
1 the line where a surface ends : MARGIN, BORDER ⟨He sat on the *edge* of the stage.⟩
2 ▼ the cutting side of a blade
edged \'ejd\ *adj*
on edge NERVOUS 1, TENSE

[1]edge 2:
the sharp edge of a knife

[2]edge *vb* **edged; edg•ing**
1 to give a border to ⟨The sleeve was *edged* with lace.⟩
2 to move slowly and gradually

edge•wise \'ej-,wīz\ *adv*
SIDEWAYS 2

ed•i•ble \'e-də-bəl\ *adj*
fit or safe to eat

edict \'ē-,dikt\ *n*
a command or law given or made by an authority (as a ruler)

ed•i•fice \'e-də-fəs\ *n*
a large or impressive building

ed•it \'e-dət\ *vb* **ed•it•ed; ed•it•ing**
1 to correct, revise, and get ready for publication : collect and arrange material to be printed ⟨I'm *editing* a book of poems.⟩
2 to be in charge of the publication of something (as an encyclopedia or a newspaper) that is the work of many writers

edi•tion \i-'di-shən\ *n*
1 the form in which a book is published ⟨a paperback *edition*⟩
2 the whole number of copies of a book, magazine, or newspaper published at one time ⟨the third *edition*⟩
3 one of several issues of a newspaper for a single day ⟨the evening *edition*⟩

ed•i•tor \'e-də-tər\ *n*
a person whose job is to correct and revise writing so it can be published

[1]ed•i•to•ri•al \,e-də-'tȯr-ē-əl\ *adj*
of or relating to an editor or editing ⟨an *editorial* office⟩

[2]editorial *n*
a newspaper or magazine article that gives the opinions of its editors or publishers

ed•u•cate \'e-jə-,kāt\ *vb* **ed•u•cat•ed; ed•u•cat•ing**
1 to provide schooling for ⟨Her parents are *educating* her at home.⟩
2 to develop the mind and morals of especially by formal instruction : TEACH ⟨Teachers work hard to *educate* their students.⟩
3 to provide with necessary information ⟨The public should be *educated* about how to save energy.⟩
ed•u•ca•tor \'e-jə-,kā-tər\ *n*

ed•u•cat•ed \'e-jə-,kā-təd\ *adj*
1 having an education and especially a good education
2 based on some knowledge ⟨an *educated* guess⟩

ed•u•ca•tion \,e-jə-'kā-shən\ *n*
1 the act or process of teaching or of being taught ⟨the *education* of students⟩
2 knowledge, skill, and development gained from study or training
3 the study of the methods and problems of teaching ⟨He's taking courses in *education.*⟩

ed•u•ca•tion•al \,e-jə-'kā-shə-nᵊl\ *adj*
1 having to do with education
2 offering information or something of value in learning ⟨an *educational* film⟩

[1]-ee \'ē, ,ē\ *n suffix*
1 person who receives or benefits from a specified thing or action ⟨address*ee*⟩
2 person who does a specified thing ⟨escap*ee*⟩

[2]-ee *n suffix*
1 a certain and especially a small kind of ⟨boot*ee*⟩
2 one like or suggesting ⟨goat*ee*⟩

eel \'ēl\ *n*
a long fish that looks like a snake and has smooth slimy skin

-eer \'ir\ *n suffix*
person who is concerned with or conducts or produces as a profession ⟨auction*eer*⟩

ee•rie \'ir-ē\ *adj* **ee•ri•er; ee•ri•est**
causing fear and uneasiness : STRANGE ⟨an *eerie* coincidence⟩

ef•face \i-'fās\ *vb* **ef•faced; ef•fac•ing**
to cause to fade or disappear

[1]ef•fect \i-'fekt\ *n*
1 an event, condition, or state of affairs that is produced by a cause : INFLUENCE
2 the act of making a certain impression ⟨The tears were only for *effect.*⟩
3 EXECUTION 2, OPERATION ⟨The law went into *effect* today.⟩
4 **effects** *pl* personal property or possessions ⟨household *effects*⟩
5 something created in film, television, or radio to imitate something real ⟨sound *effects*⟩
in effect in actual fact ⟨The suggestion was *in effect* an order.⟩

[2]effect *vb* **ef•fect•ed; ef•fect•ing**
to make happen : bring about ⟨*effect* a change⟩

ef•fec•tive \i-'fek-tiv\ *adj*
1 producing or able to produce a desired effect ⟨*effective* medicines⟩
2 IMPRESSIVE ⟨an *effective* speech⟩
3 being in operation ⟨The rule is *effective* immediately.⟩
ef•fec•tive•ly *adv*
ef•fec•tive•ness *n*

ef•fec•tu•al \i-'fek-chə-wəl\ *adj*
producing or able to produce a desired effect ⟨an *effectual* remedy⟩
ef•fec•tu•al•ly *adv*

ef•fi•cien•cy \i-'fi-shən-sē\ *n, pl* **ef•fi•cien•cies**
the ability to do something or produce something without waste

ef•fi•cient \i-'fi-shənt\ *adj*
capable of bringing about a desired result with little waste (as of time or energy) ⟨an *efficient* worker⟩
ef•fi•cient•ly *adv*

ef•fort \'e-fərt\ *n*
1 hard physical or mental work : EXERTION ⟨The job took great *effort.*⟩
2 a serious attempt : TRY
3 something produced by work ⟨This picture is not one of my better *efforts.*⟩

ef•fort•less \'e-fərt-ləs\ *adj*
showing or needing little or no effort ⟨She made an *effortless* catch.⟩
ef•fort•less•ly *adv*

e.g. *abbr* for example
Hint: The abbreviation *e.g.* is short for the Latin phrase *exempli gratia*, meaning "for example."

[1]egg \'eg, 'āg\ *n*
1 ▶ an oval or rounded body surrounded by a shell or membrane by which some animals (as birds, fish, insects, and reptiles) reproduce and from which the young hatches out
2 EGG CELL
3 the contents of the egg of a bird and especially a chicken that is eaten as food

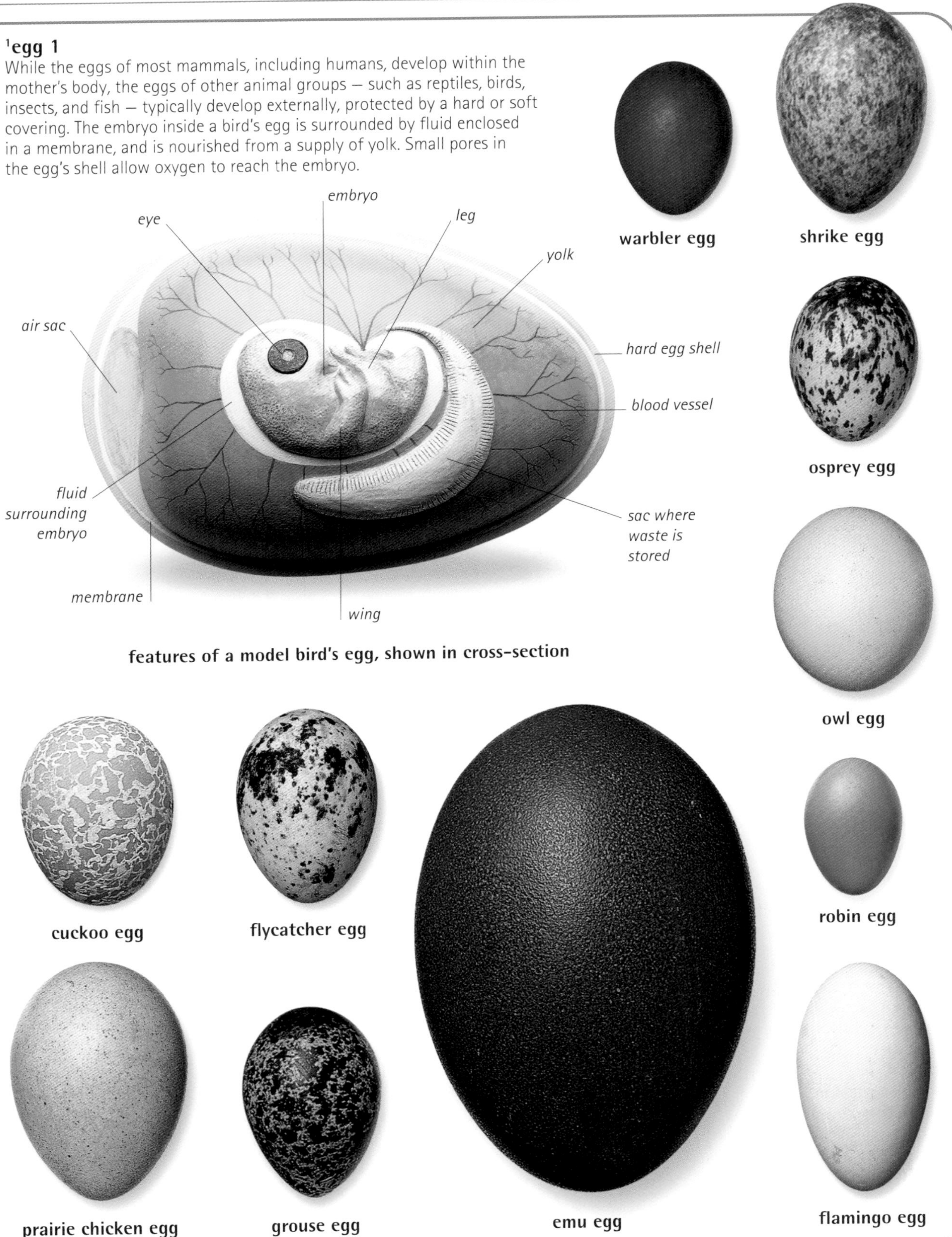

features of a model bird's egg, shown in cross-section

a b c d e f g h i j k l m n o p q r s t u v w x y z

A B C D E F G H I J K L M N O P Q R S T U V W X Y Z

[2]egg *vb* **egged**; **egg•ing**
to urge or encourage to do usually something foolish or dangerous

egg cell *n*
a female reproductive cell of animals and plants that can unite with a sperm cell to form a new individual

egg•nog \'eg-,näg, 'āg-\ *n*
a drink made of eggs beaten with sugar, milk or cream, and often alcoholic liquor

egg•plant \'eg-,plant, 'āg-\ *n*
▼ an oval vegetable with a usually glossy purplish skin and white flesh

eggplant

egg•shell \'eg-,shel, 'āg-\ *n*
the shell of an egg

egret \'ē-grət, i-'gret\ *n*
a heron with usually white feathers

[1]Egyp•tian \i-'jip-shən\ *adj*
of or relating to Egypt or the Egyptians

[2]Egyptian *n*
1 a person who is born or lives in Egypt
2 the language of the ancient Egyptians

ei•der \'ī-dər\ *n*
a large duck of northern seas with very soft down

[1]eight \'āt\ *n*
1 one more than seven : two times four : 8
2 the eighth in a set or series

[2]eight *adj*
being one more than seven

[1]eigh•teen \ā-'tēn, 'āt-,tēn\ *n*
one more than 17 : three times six : 18

[2]eighteen *adj*
being one more than 17

[1]eigh•teenth \ā-'tēnth, 'āt-'tēnth\ *adj*
coming right after 17th

[2]eighteenth *n*
number 18 in a series

[1]eighth \'ātth\ *adj*
coming right after seventh

[2]eighth *n*
1 number eight in a series
2 one of eight equal parts ⟨an *eighth* of a mile⟩

[1]eight•i•eth \'ā-tē-əth\ *adj*
coming right after 79th

[2]eightieth *n*
number 80 in a series

[1]eighty \'ā-tē\ *adj*
eight times ten : 80

[2]eighty *n*
being eight times ten

[1]ei•ther \'ē-thər, 'ī-\ *adj*
1 [1]EACH ⟨There are flowers on *either* side of the road.⟩
2 being one or the other ⟨You can take *either* road.⟩

[2]either *pron*
the one or the other ⟨She hadn't told *either* of her parents.⟩

[3]either *conj*
used before words or phrases the last of which follows "or" to show that they are choices or possibilities ⟨You can *either* go or stay.⟩

[4]either *adv*
ALSO — used after a negative statement ⟨The car is reliable and not expensive *either.*⟩

ejac•u•late \i-'jak-yə-,lāt\ *vb* **ejac•u•lat•ed**; **ejac•u•lat•ing**
EXCLAIM

eject \i-'jekt\ *vb* **eject•ed**; **eject•ing**
to force or push out ⟨He was *ejected* from the meeting.⟩ ⟨The machine *ejected* the tape.⟩

eke out \'ēk-'au̇t\ *vb* **eked out**; **ek•ing out**
1 to get with great effort ⟨They *eked out* a living from the farm.⟩
2 to add to bit by bit ⟨She *eked out* her income with odd jobs.⟩

elderberry 1: elderberry flowers

[1]elab•o•rate \i-'la-bə-rət, -'la-brət\ *adj*
made or done with great care or with much detail ⟨an *elaborate* ceremony⟩
elab•o•rate•ly *adv*

[2]elab•o•rate \i-'la-bə-,rāt\ *vb* **elab•o•rat•ed**; **elab•o•rat•ing**
1 to give more details about ⟨Would you *elaborate* on what happened?⟩
2 to work out in detail

elapse \i-'laps\ *vb* **elapsed**; **elaps•ing**
to slip past : go by ⟨Nearly a year *elapsed* before his return.⟩

[1]elas•tic \i-'la-stik\ *adj*
capable of returning to original shape or size after being stretched, pressed, or squeezed together

[2]elastic *n*
1 RUBBER BAND
2 material that can be stretched

elas•tic•i•ty \i-,la-'sti-sə-tē\ *n*
the quality or state of being easily stretched

elate \i-'lāt\ *vb* **elat•ed**; **elat•ing**
to fill with joy or pride ⟨Winning the game *elated* our fans.⟩

ela•tion \i-'lā-shən\ *n*
the quality or state of being filled with joy or pride

[1]el•bow \'el-,bō\ *n*
1 ▶ the joint or the region of the joint of the arm or of the same part of an animal's front legs
2 a part (as of a pipe) bent like an elbow

[2]elbow *vb* **el•bowed**; **el•bow•ing**
1 to jab with an elbow
2 to push or force a way with or as if with the elbows

[1]el•der \'el-dər\ *n*
ELDERBERRY 1

[2]elder *adj*
being older than another person

[3]elder *n*
1 a person who is older
2 a person having authority because of age and experience ⟨*elders* of the village⟩
3 an official in some churches

el•der•ber•ry \'el-dər-,ber-ē\ *n*, *pl* **el•der•ber•ries**
1 ◀ a shrub or small tree with clusters of small white flowers and a black or red berrylike fruit
2 the fruit of the elderberry

el•der•ly \'el-dər-lē\ *adj*
somewhat old

el•dest \'el-dəst\ *adj*
being oldest of a group of people ⟨her *eldest* child⟩

[1]elect \i-'lekt\ *vb* **elect•ed**; **elect•ing**
1 to select by vote ⟨*elect* a senator⟩

2 to make a choice ⟨The team *elected* to kick off.⟩
synonyms see CHOOSE

[2]**elect** *adj*
chosen for office but not yet holding office ⟨the president-*elect*⟩

elec•tion \i-ˈlek-shən\ *n*
an act of choosing or the fact of being chosen especially by vote

elec•tive \i-ˈlek-tiv\ *adj*
chosen or filled by election ⟨an *elective* official⟩ ⟨an *elective* position⟩

electr- *or* **electro-** *prefix*
1 electricity ⟨*electro*lysis⟩
2 electric ⟨*electr*ode⟩
3 electric and ⟨*electro*magnetic⟩

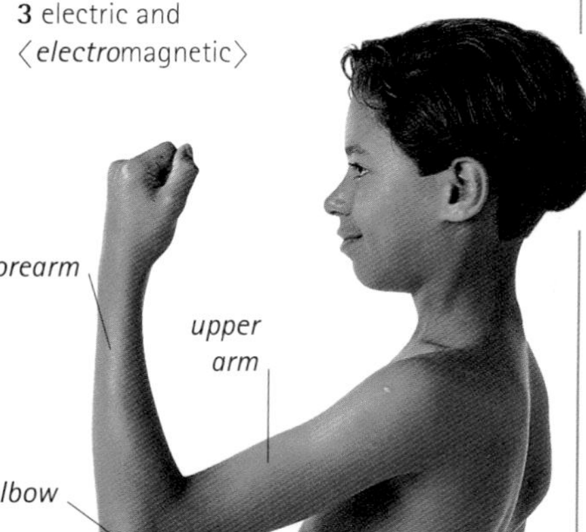

[1]**elbow 1:** a boy's elbow

elec•tric \i-ˈlek-trik\ *adj*
1 *or* **elec•tri•cal** \-tri-kəl\ of or relating to electricity or its use ⟨an *electric* current⟩ ⟨*electrical* engineering⟩
2 heated, moved, made, or run by electricity ⟨an *electric* heater⟩ ⟨an *electric* locomotive⟩
3 giving off sounds through an electronic amplifier ⟨an *electric* guitar⟩
4 having a thrilling effect ⟨The singer gave an *electric* performance.⟩
elec•tri•cal•ly *adv*

▶ **Word History** People in ancient Greece found that if they rubbed a piece of amber it would attract light things like straws and feathers. The rubbing gave the amber an electric charge. We owe the English word *electric* to this property of amber. Our word came from a Greek word *ēlektron* that meant "amber."

electric eel *n*
▶ a large South American eel-shaped fish with organs that can give an electric shock

elec•tri•cian \i-ˌlek-ˈtri-shən\ *n*
a person who installs, operates, or repairs electrical equipment

elec•tric•i•ty \i-ˌlek-ˈtri-sə-tē\ *n*
1 an important form of energy that is found in nature but that can be artificially produced by rubbing together two unlike things (as glass and silk), by the action of chemicals, or by means of a generator
2 electric current

electric eel

elec•tri•fy \i-ˈlek-trə-ˌfī\ *vb* **elec•tri•fied**; **elec•tri•fy•ing**
1 to charge with electricity ⟨an *electrified* fence⟩
2 to equip for use of or supply with electric power ⟨Remote regions are still not *electrified*.⟩
3 [1]THRILL ⟨Her performance *electrified* the audience.⟩

elec•tro•cute \i-ˈlek-trə-ˌkyüt\ *vb* **elec•tro•cut•ed**; **elec•tro•cut•ing**
to kill by an electric shock
elec•tro•cu•tion \-ˌlek-trə-ˈkyü-shən\ *n*

elec•trode \i-ˈlek-ˌtrōd\ *n*
a conductor (as a metal or carbon) used to make electrical contact with a part of an electrical circuit that is not metallic

elec•trol•y•sis \i-ˌlek-ˈträ-lə-səs\ *n*
◀ the producing of chemical changes by passage of an electric current through a liquid

elec•tro•lyte \i-ˈlek-trə-ˌlīt\ *n*
1 a substance (as an acid or salt) that when dissolved (as in water) conducts an electric current
2 a substance (as sodium or calcium) that is an ion in the body regulating the flow of nutrients into and waste products out of cells

▶ **electrolysis**
In electrolysis, an electric current passed through a liquid solution causes chemical changes to substances in the solution. In the experiment shown here, copper is drawn from a chemical solution to coat the surface of a key.

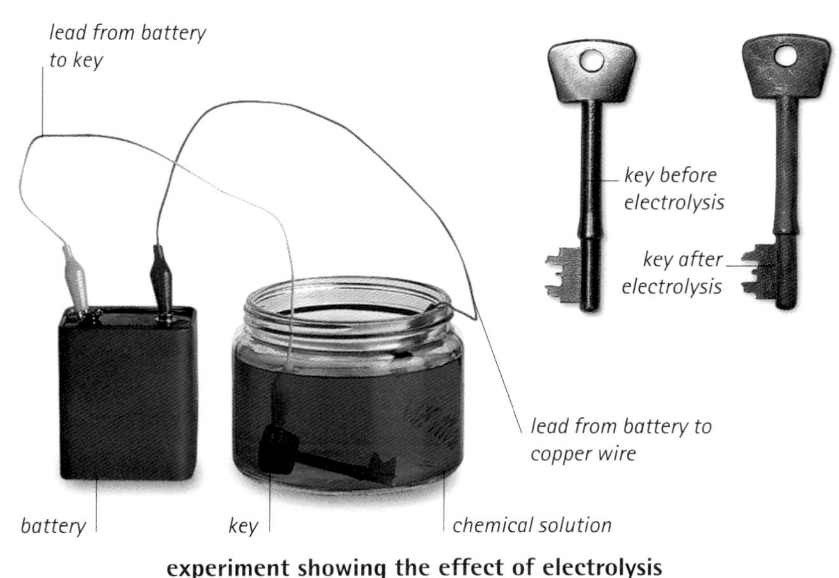

experiment showing the effect of electrolysis

elec•tro•lyt•ic \i-ˌlek-trə-ˈli-tik\ *adj*
of or relating to electrolysis or an electrolyte ⟨an *electrolytic* cell⟩

elec•tro•mag•net \i-ˌlek-trō-ˈmag-nət\ *n*
a piece of iron encircled by a coil of wire through which an electric current is passed to magnetize the iron

elec•tro•mag•net•ic \i-ˌlek-trō-mag-ˈne-tik\ *adj*
of or relating to a magnetic field produced by an electric current

electromagnetic wave *n*
a wave (as a radio wave or wave of light) that travels at the speed of light and consists of a combined electric and magnetic effect

elec•tron \i-ˈlek-ˌträn\ *n*
a very small particle that has a negative charge of electricity and travels around the nucleus of an atom

elec•tron•ic \i-ˌlek-ˈträ-nik\ *adj*
1 relating to or using the principles of electronics ⟨an *electronic* device⟩
2 operating by means of or using a computer ⟨*electronic* banking⟩
elec•tron•i•cal•ly *adv*

electronic mail *n*
[1]E-MAIL

elec•tron•ics \i-ˌlek-ˈträ-niks\ *n*
a science that deals with the giving off, action, and effects of electrons in vacuums, gases, and semiconductors and with devices using such electrons

electron tube *n*
▼a device in which conduction of electricity by electrons takes place through a vacuum or a gas within a sealed container and which has various uses (as in radio and television)

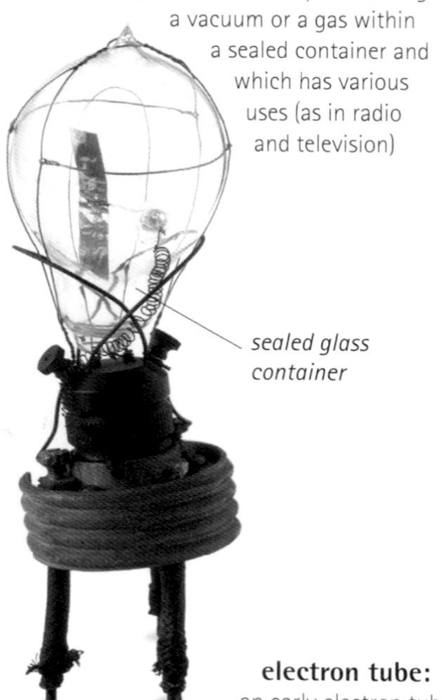

electron tube:
an early electron tube

el•e•gance \ˈe-li-gəns\ *n*
1 gracefulness of style or movement
2 tasteful luxury ⟨The hotel was known for its *elegance*.⟩

el•e•gant \ˈe-li-gənt\ *adj*
showing good taste **:** having or showing beauty and refinement ⟨an *elegant* room⟩
el•e•gant•ly *adv*

el•e•ment \ˈe-lə-mənt\ *n*
1 any of more than 100 substances that cannot by ordinary chemical means be separated into different substances ⟨Gold and carbon are *elements*.⟩
2 one of the parts of which something is made up ⟨There is an *element* of risk in surfing.⟩

elephant
The African elephant and the Asian elephant (also called the Indian elephant) are the largest land animals on earth, and the last two living species of a group of animals with a long, flexible snout. Elephants are intelligent and sociable creatures. Females and calves live in family herds, led by an older female, while males past puberty form their own herds or travel alone. Elephants feed on vegetation such as grass and leaves.

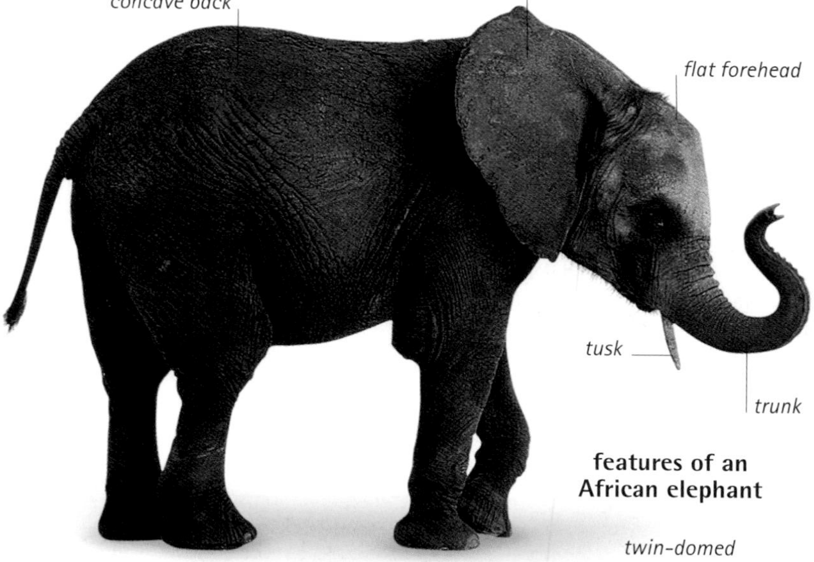

concave back
large ear
flat forehead
tusk
trunk

features of an African elephant

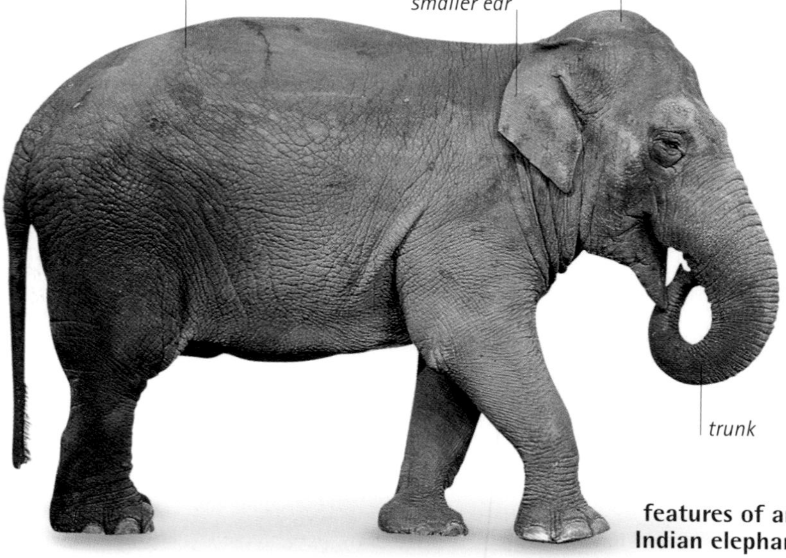

convex back
smaller ear
twin-domed forehead
trunk

features of an Indian elephant

3 the simplest principles of a subject of study 〈the *elements* of arithmetic〉
4 a member of a mathematical set
5 the state or place natural to or suited to a person or thing 〈At school I was in my *element*.〉
6 **elements** *pl* the forces of nature

el•e•men•ta•ry \ˌe-lə-ˈmen-tə-rē, -ˈmen-trē\ *adj*
1 relating to the beginnings or simplest principles of a subject 〈*elementary* arithmetic〉
2 relating to or teaching the basic subjects of education 〈*elementary* school〉

el•e•phant \ˈe-lə-fənt\ *n*
◀ a huge typically gray mammal of Africa or Asia with the nose drawn out into a long trunk and two large curved tusks

el•e•vate \ˈe-lə-ˌvāt\ *vb* **el•e•vat•ed**; **el•e•vat•ing**
to lift up : RAISE

l•e•va•tion \ˌe-lə-ˈvā-shən\ *n*
1 height especially above sea level : ALTITUDE
2 a raised place (as a hill)
3 the act of raising : the condition of being raised
synonyms see HEIGHT

l•e•va•tor \ˈe-lə-ˌvā-tər\ *n*
1 a floor or little room that can be raised or lowered for carrying people or goods from one level to another
2 a device (as an endless belt) for raising material
3 GRAIN ELEVATOR

elev•en \i-ˈle-vən\ *n*
1 one more than ten : 11
2 the eleventh in a set or series

eleven *adj*
being one more than ten

elev•enth \i-ˈle-vənth\ *adj*
coming right after tenth

eleventh *n*
number eleven in a series

lf \ˈelf\ *n, pl* **elves** \ˈelvz\
an often mischievous fairy

lf•in \ˈel-fən\ *adj*
relating to elves

l•i•gi•ble \ˈe-li-jə-bəl\ *adj*
qualified to be chosen, to participate, or to receive 〈You're *eligible* for a loan.〉

lim•i•nate \i-ˈli-mə-ˌnāt\ *vb* **elim•i•nat•ed**; **elim•i•nat•ing**
to get rid of : do away with

lim•i•na•tion \i-ˌli-mə-ˈnā-shən\ *n*
1 the act or process of excluding or getting rid of
2 a getting rid of waste from the body

elk \ˈelk\ *n*
1 ▼ a large deer of North America, Europe, and Asia with curved antlers having many branches
2 the moose of Europe and Asia

elk 1

el•lipse \i-ˈlips\ *n*
a shape that looks like a flattened circle

el•lip•ti•cal \i-ˈlip-ti-kəl\ *or* **el•lip•tic** \-tik\ *adj*
having the shape of an ellipse 〈an *elliptical* orbit〉

elm \ˈelm\ *n*
▶ a tall shade tree with a broad rather flat top and spreading branches

elm

el•o•cu•tion \ˌe-lə-ˈkyü-shən\ *n*
the art of reading or speaking clearly and effectively in public

elon•gate \i-ˈlȯŋ-ˌgāt\ *vb* **elon•gat•ed**; **elon•gat•ing**
to make or grow longer

elope \i-ˈlōp\ *vb* **eloped**; **elop•ing**
to run away to be married
elope•ment \-mənt\ *n*

el•o•quence \ˈe-lə-kwəns\ *n*
1 speaking or writing that is forceful and convincing
2 the ability to speak or write with force and in a convincing way

el•o•quent \ˈe-lə-kwənt\ *adj*
1 having or showing clear and forceful expression 〈an *eloquent* speaker〉 〈an *eloquent* plan〉
2 clearly showing some feeling or meaning 〈an *eloquent* look〉
el•o•quent•ly *adv*

[1]**else** \ˈels\ *adv*
1 in a different way or place or at a different time 〈How *else* could it be done?〉
2 if the facts are or were different : if not 〈Hurry or *else* you'll be late.〉

[2]**else** *adj*
1 being other and different 〈Ask someone *else*.〉
2 being in addition 〈What *else* can I bring?〉

else•where \ˈels-ˌhwer, -ˌwer\ *adv*
in or to another place 〈If it's not here it must be *elsewhere*.〉

elude \i-ˈlüd\ *vb* **elud•ed**; **elud•ing**
to avoid or escape by being quick, skillful, or tricky

elu•sive \i-ˈlü-siv\ *adj*
1 hard to find or capture 〈*elusive* treasure〉 〈an *elusive* thief〉
2 hard to understand or define 〈an *elusive* idea〉

elves *pl of* ELF

em- see **en-**

¹e-mail \'ē-,māl\ *n*
1 a system for sending messages between computers
2 ▼ a message sent electronically from one computer to another

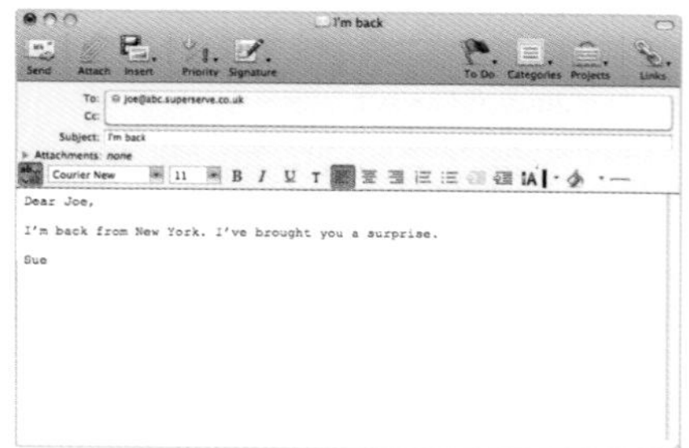

¹e-mail 2

²e-mail \'ē-,māl\ *vb* **e-mailed**; **e-mail•ing**
to send e-mail or as e-mail ⟨She *e-mailed* her friends.⟩

em•a•nate \'e-mə-,nāt\ *vb* **em•a•nat•ed**; **em•a•nat•ing**
1 to come out from a source ⟨Heat *emanated* from the fire.⟩
2 to give off or out ⟨The teacher's face *emanated* kindness.⟩

eman•ci•pate \i-'man-sə-,pāt\ *vb* **eman•ci•pat•ed**; **eman•ci•pat•ing**
to set free from control or slavery : LIBERATE
eman•ci•pa•tor \-,pā-tər\ *n*

eman•ci•pa•tion \i-,man-sə-'pā-shən\ *n*
an act of setting someone free from control or slavery

em•balm \im-'bäm, -'bälm\ *vb* **em•balmed**; **em•balm•ing**
to treat a dead body so as to preserve it from decay
em•balm•er *n*

em•bank•ment \in-'baŋk-mənt\ *n*
► a raised bank or wall to carry a roadway or hold back water

em•bar•go \im-'bär-gō\ *n, pl* **em•bar•goes**
an order of a government forbidding ships engaged in trade from leaving its ports ⟨an oil *embargo*⟩

em•bark \im-'bärk\ *vb* **em•barked**; **em•bark•ing**
1 to go on or put on board a ship or an airplane ⟨The last of the passengers *embarked*.⟩
2 to begin a project or task ⟨She *embarked* on a new career.⟩

em•bar•rass \im-'ber-əs\ *vb* **em•bar•rassed**; **em•bar•rass•ing**
to cause to feel confused and foolish in front of other people

em•bar•rass•ment \im-'ber-əs-mənt\ *n*
1 something that causes a person or group to feel foolish ⟨The poor test scores were an *embarrassment* to the school.⟩
2 the condition of feeling foolish in front of others

emblem from a US Army officer's cap in World War II (1941–45)

em•bas•sy \'em-bə-sē\ *n, pl* **em•bas•sies**
1 a group of people led by an ambassador who represent their country in a foreign country
2 the building where an ambassador lives or works

em•bed \im-'bed\ *vb* **em•bed•ded**; **em•bed•ding**
to enclose in or as if in a surrounding substance ⟨Workers *embedded* the posts in concrete.⟩

em•bel•lish \im-'be-lish\ *vb* **em•bel•lished**; **em•bel•lish•ing**
DECORATE 1 ⟨Artwork *embellished* the book.⟩
em•bel•lish•ment \-mənt\ *n*

em•ber \'em-bər\ *n*
a glowing piece of coal or wood in the ashes from a fire

em•bez•zle \im-'be-zəl\ *vb* **em•bez•zled**; **em•bez•zling**
to steal (money or property) despite being entrusted to take care of it

em•bit•ter \im-'bi-tər\ *vb* **em•bit•tered**; **em•bit•ter•ing**
to make sad and angry : make bitter

em•blem \'em-bləm\ *n*
◄ an object or an image used to suggest a thing that cannot be pictured ⟨The flag is the *emblem* of our nation.⟩

► **Synonyms** EMBLEM, SYMBOL, and TOKEN mean a visible thing that stands for something that cannot be pictured. EMBLEM is usually used of an object or a picture that stands for a group such as a family, an organization, or a nation. ⟨The eagle is one of our national *emblems*.⟩ SYMBOL may be used of anything that is understood as a sign for something else. ⟨The lion is the *symbol* of courage.⟩ TOKEN is used of an object or act that shows the existence of something else. ⟨This gift is a *token* of our love.⟩

em•body \im-'bä-dē\ *vb* **em•bod•ied**; **em•body•ing**
1 to give form to ⟨The poet *embodied* her ideas in words.⟩
2 to represent in visible form ⟨The firefighters *embodied* courage during the disaster.⟩
3 to make something a body or system or part of a body or system ⟨The basic law of the United States is *embodied* in its constitution.⟩

embankment: a tree-lined path along an embankment

em•boss \im-ˈbäs, -ˈbȯs\ *vb* **em•bossed**; **em•boss•ing**
to decorate with a raised pattern or design

[1]**em•brace** \im-ˈbrās\ *vb* **em•braced**; **em•brac•ing**
1 to hold in the arms : HUG
2 to surround on all sides ⟨Low hills *embraced* the valley.⟩
3 to accept readily or gladly ⟨She is always ready to *embrace* an opportunity.⟩
4 INCLUDE ⟨Mathematics *embraces* arithmetic, algebra, and geometry.⟩

[2]**embrace** *n*
an act of holding in the arms : HUG

em•broi•der \im-ˈbrȯi-dər\ *vb* **em•broi•dered**; **em•broi•der•ing**
1 to make with needlework ⟨She *embroidered* her initials.⟩
2 to decorate with needlework ⟨I'm *embroidering* a tablecloth.⟩
3 to make more interesting by exaggerating or adding details

em•broi•dery \im-ˈbrȯi-də-rē\ *n*, *pl* **em•broi•der•ies**
1 ▶ needlework done to decorate cloth
2 the act or art of embroidering

em•bryo \ˈem-brē-ˌō\ *n*, *pl* **em•bry•os**
1 ▼ an unborn human or animal in the earliest stages of growth when its basic structures are being formed
2 a tiny young plant inside a seed

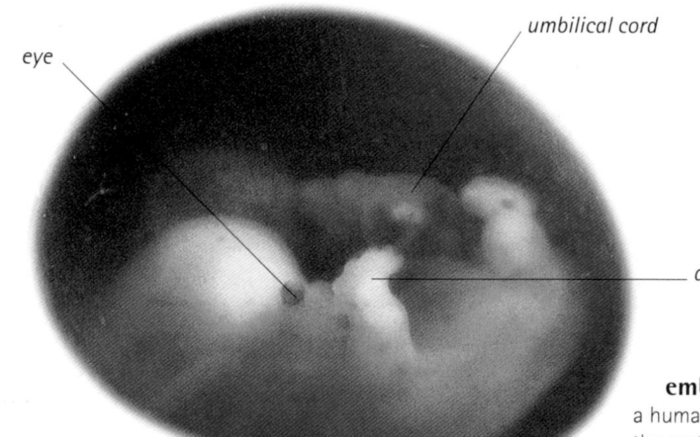

embryo 1: a human embryo in the mother's uterus

em•er•ald \ˈe-mə-rəld, ˈem-rəld\ *n*
a gemstone of a rich green color

emerald *adj*
brightly or richly green

emerge \i-ˈmərj\ *vb* **emerged**; **emerg•ing**
1 to come out or into view
2 to become known ⟨The facts of the case began to *emerge*.⟩

emer•gen•cy \i-ˈmər-jən-sē\ *n*, *pl* **emer•gen•cies**
an unexpected situation that requires immediate action ⟨a medical *emergency*⟩

emergency room *n*
a room in a hospital with doctors, nurses, and medical equipment for treating people who need medical care immediately

embroidery 1: a bag with embroidery

em•ery \ˈe-mə-rē, ˈem-rē\ *n*, *pl* **em•er•ies**
a mineral used as a powder for polishing and grinding

em•i•grant \ˈe-mi-grənt\ *n*
a person who leaves one country or region to live in another

em•i•grate \ˈe-mə-ˌgrāt\ *vb* **em•i•grat•ed**; **em•i•grat•ing**
to leave one country or region to live in another ⟨My grandparents *emigrated* from China.⟩

em•i•gra•tion \ˌe-mə-ˈgrā-shən\ *n*
the act of leaving one region or country to live in another

em•i•nence \ˈe-mə-nəns\ *n*
1 the condition of being well-known and respected
2 a piece of high ground : HILL

em•i•nent \ˈe-mə-nənt\ *adj*
successful, well-known, and respected ⟨an *eminent* physician⟩

em•is•sary \ˈe-mə-ˌser-ē\ *n*, *pl* **em•is•sar•ies**
a person sent on a mission to represent someone else

emis•sion \ē-ˈmi-shən\ *n*
1 the act of giving off ⟨The energy plant is reducing the *emission* of harmful gases.⟩
2 something that is given off

emit \ē-ˈmit\ *vb* **emit•ted**; **emit•ting**
to send out from a source ⟨*emit* light⟩

emo•tion \i-ˈmō-shən\ *n*
strong feeling (as anger, love, joy, or fear) often accompanied by a physical reaction ⟨She flushed with *emotion*.⟩

emo•tion•al \i-ˈmō-shə-nᵊl\ *adj*
1 relating to a person's feelings ⟨an *emotional* upset⟩
2 likely to show or express feelings ⟨He gets *emotional* at weddings.⟩
3 expressing strong feelings ⟨an *emotional* speech⟩
emo•tion•al•ly *adv*

em•pa•thize \ˈem-pə-ˌthīz\ *vb* **em•pa•thized**; **em•pa•thiz•ing**
to share the same feelings as another person : to feel empathy

em•pa•thy \ˈem-pə-thē\ *n*
the understanding and sharing of the emotions and experiences of another person ⟨He has great *empathy* toward the poor.⟩

em•per•or \ˈem-pər-ər\ *n*
a man who rules an empire

em•pha•sis \ˈem-fə-səs\ *n*, *pl* **em•pha•ses** \-ˌsēz\
1 a forcefulness in the way something is said or written that gives it special attention or importance
2 special force given to one or more words or syllables in speaking or reading ⟨In the word "vacation," the *emphasis* is on the second syllable.⟩
3 special attention or importance given to something

em•pha•size \ˈem-fə-ˌsīz\ *vb* **em•pha•sized**; **em•pha•siz•ing**
to give special attention or importance to ⟨He *emphasized* the word "maybe."⟩

A B C D E F G H I J K L M N O P Q R S T U V W X Y Z

em•phat•ic \im-ˈfa-tik\ *adj*
spoken or done forcefully ⟨She shook her head in *emphatic* refusal.⟩
em•phat•ic•al•ly *adv*

em•phy•se•ma \ˌem-fə-ˈzē-mə, -ˈsē-mə\ *n*
a disease in which the lungs become stretched and inefficient

em•pire \ˈem-ˌpīr\ *n*
1 a group of territories or peoples under one ruler ⟨the Roman *empire*⟩
2 a country whose ruler is called an emperor

[1]**em•ploy** \im-ˈplȯi\ *vb* **em•ployed**; **em•ploy•ing**
1 to give a job to **:** use the services of ⟨The company *employs* over 500 workers.⟩
2 to make use of ⟨They *employ* traditional methods of farming.⟩

[2]**employ** *n*
the state of being hired for a job by ⟨The gentleman is in the *employ* of a large bank.⟩

em•ploy•ee \im-ˌplȯi-ˈē\ *n*
a person who is paid to work for another

em•ploy•er \im-ˈplȯi-ər\ *n*
a person or business that pays others for their services

em•ploy•ment \im-ˈplȯi-mənt\ *n*
1 the act of using something ⟨The artist is known for her *employment* of unusual materials.⟩
2 JOB 1, OCCUPATION ⟨I am seeking *employment* in your area.⟩
3 the act of hiring a person to do work

em•pow•er \im-ˈpau̇-ər\ *vb* **em•pow•ered**; **em•pow•er•ing**
to give authority or legal power to ⟨She *empowered* her lawyer to act on her behalf.⟩

em•press \ˈem-prəs\ *n*
1 a woman who rules an empire
2 the wife of an emperor

[1]**emp•ty** \ˈemp-tē\ *adj* **emp•ti•er**; **emp•ti•est**
1 containing nothing ⟨an *empty* box⟩
2 not occupied or lived in **:** VACANT ⟨an *empty* house⟩ ⟨an *empty* seat⟩
3 not sincere or meaningful ⟨an *empty* threat⟩
emp•ti•ness *n*

▶ **Synonyms** EMPTY and VACANT both mean not having anything inside. EMPTY is used for a thing that has nothing in it at all. ⟨He threw away the *empty* bag.⟩ It may also be used instead of *vacant*. ⟨The house sat *empty* until a new family moved in.⟩ VACANT is the opposite of *occupied* and is used of something that is not occupied usually only for a while. ⟨That apartment is *vacant* right now.⟩

[2]**empty** *vb* **emp•tied**; **emp•ty•ing**
1 to remove the contents of ⟨Please *empty* the wastebasket.⟩
2 to remove all of (something) from a container ⟨*Empty* the flour into the bin.⟩
3 to become unoccupied ⟨The school quickly *emptied*.⟩
4 to flow into ⟨The river *empties* into the gulf.⟩

emp•ty–hand•ed \ˌemp-tē-ˈhan-dəd\ *adj*
1 not carrying or bringing anything
2 having gotten or gained nothing ⟨He left the contest *empty-handed*.⟩

EMT \ˌē-ˌem-ˈtē\ *n, pl* **EMTs** *or* **EMT's**
a person that is trained to give emergency medical care to a patient before and on the way to a hospital

emu \ˈē-ˌmyü\ *n*
▼ a large fast-running Australian bird that cannot fly

em•u•late \ˈem-yə-ˌlāt\ *vb* **em•u•lat•ed**; **em•u•lat•ing**
to try hard to be like or do better than **:** IMITATE ⟨She grew up *emulating* her sports heroes.⟩

em•u•la•tion \ˌem-yə-ˈlā-shən\ *n*
an attempt to be like or do better than others

[1]**-en** \ən, -n\ *also* **-n** \n\ *adj suffix*
made of **:** consisting of ⟨earth*en*⟩ ⟨wool*en*⟩

[2]**-en** *vb suffix*
1 become or cause to be ⟨sharp*en*⟩
2 cause or come to have ⟨length*en*⟩

en•able \i-ˈnā-bəl\ *vb* **en•abled**; **en•abling**
to give strength, power, or ability to **:** make able

en•act \i-ˈnakt\ *vb* **en•act•ed**; **en•act•ing**
1 to perform or act out ⟨Two students *enacted* the story for the class.⟩
2 to make into law ⟨*enact* legislation⟩
en•act•ment \-mənt\ *n*

[1]**enam•el** \i-ˈna-məl\ *vb* **enam•eled** *or* **enam•elled**; **enam•el•ing** *or* **enam•el•ling**
to cover or decorate with a smooth hard glossy coating ⟨*enamel* a pot⟩

[2]**enamel** *n*
1 ▶ a glassy substance used to coat the surface of metal, glass, and pottery
2 the hard outer surface of the teeth
3 a paint that dries to form a hard glossy coat

emu

emul•si•fy \i-ˈməl-sə-ˌfī\ *vb* **emul•si•fied**; **emul•si•fy•ing**
to combine two liquids to make an emulsion

emul•sion \i-ˈməl-shən\ *n*
two liquids mixed together so that tiny drops of one liquid are scattered throughout the other

en- *also* **em-** *prefix*
1 put or go into or onto ⟨*en*case⟩ ⟨*en*throne⟩
2 cause to be ⟨*en*rich⟩
3 provide with ⟨*em*power⟩
Hint: In all senses *en-* is usually *em-* before *b, m,* or *p.*

en•camp•ment \in-ˈkamp-mənt\ *n*
1 the act of making a camp
2 [1]CAMP 1

en•case \in-ˈkās\ *vb* **en•cased**; **en•cas•ing**
to cover or surround **:** enclose in or as if in a case

-ence \əns, -ns\ *n suffix*
1 action or process ⟨refer*ence*⟩
2 quality or state ⟨exist*ence*⟩ ⟨confid*ence*⟩

en•chant \in-ˈchant\ *vb* **en•chant•ed**; **en•chant•ing**
1 to put under a spell by or as if by magic **:** BEWITCH

2 to please greatly : DELIGHT 〈The story *enchanted* us.〉
en•chant•ment \-mənt\ *n*

en•chant•ing \in-ˈchan-tiŋ\ *adj*
very attractive : CHARMING 〈an *enchanting* smile〉

en•chant•ress \in-ˈchan-trəs\ *n*
a woman who casts magic spells : WITCH, SORCERESS

en•cir•cle \in-ˈsər-kəl\ *vb* **en•cir•cled**; **en•cir•cling**
1 to make a circle around : SURROUND 〈A deep moat *encircles* the castle.〉
2 to go completely around 〈The dogs *encircled* the sheep.〉

²enamel 1: a bird-shaped brooch with enamel

en•close \in-ˈklōz\ *vb* **en•closed**; **en•clos•ing**
1 to close in : SURROUND 〈The porch is *enclosed* with glass.〉
2 to hold in : CONFINE 〈He *enclosed* the animals in a pen.〉
3 to put in the same package or envelope with something else

▶ **Synonyms** ENCLOSE, ENVELOP, and FENCE mean to surround something and close it off. ENCLOSE is used of putting up barriers (as walls) or a cover around something so as to give it protection or privacy. 〈A high hedge *encloses* the garden.〉 ENVELOP is used of surrounding something completely by a soft layer or covering to hide or protect it. 〈Clouds *enveloped* the peaks of the mountains.〉 FENCE is used of surrounding something with or as if with a fence so that nothing may enter or leave. 〈A stone wall *fences* in the yard.〉

en•clo•sure \in-ˈklō-zhər\ *n*
1 the act of closing in or surrounding 〈*enclosure* of the animals〉
2 ▶ a space that is closed in 〈The sheep escaped their *enclosure*.〉
3 the act of including with a letter or package 〈*enclosure* of a photo〉
4 something included with a letter or package

en•com•pass \in-ˈkəm-pəs\ *vb* **en•com•passed**; **en•com•pass•ing**
1 to cover or surround : ENCIRCLE 〈Mountains *encompass* the peaceful valley.〉
2 INCLUDE

en•core \ˈän-ˌkȯr\ *n*
1 a demand by an audience for a performance to continue or be repeated
2 a further appearance or performance given in response to applause

¹en•coun•ter \in-ˈkau̇n-tər\ *vb* **en•coun•tered**; **en•coun•ter•ing**
1 to meet face-to-face or by chance 〈I *encountered* an old friend.〉
2 to experience or face often unexpectedly 〈Have you *encountered* any difficulty?〉

²encounter *n*
1 a meeting face-to-face and often by chance
2 an often unexpected experience

en•cour•age \in-ˈkər-ij\ *vb* **en•cour•aged**; **en•cour•ag•ing**
1 make more determined, hopeful, or confident : HEARTEN
2 to give help or support to : AID 〈Warm weather *encourages* plant growth.〉
en•cour•ag•ing•ly *adv*

enclosure 2:
a baby giraffe in its enclosure

en•cour•age•ment \in-ˈkər-ij-mənt\ *n*
1 something that gives hope, determination, or confidence 〈Winning was just the *encouragement* she needed.〉
2 the act of giving hope or confidence to 〈His teacher's *encouragement* helped his grades.〉

en•croach \in-ˈkrōch\ *vb* **en•croached**; **en•croach•ing**
1 to take over the rights or property of another little by little or in secret 〈The prince *encroached* on the king's authority.〉
2 to go beyond the usual or proper limits 〈Cities have *encroached* upon wildlife habitats.〉

en•crust \in-ˈkrəst\ *vb* **en•crust•ed**; **en•crust•ing**
to cover with or as if with a crust

en•cum•ber \in-ˈkəm-bər\ *vb* **en•cum•bered**; **en•cum•ber•ing**
1 to weigh down : BURDEN 〈Their heavy coats *encumbered* the children.〉
2 to cause problems or delays for : HINDER 〈Bad weather *encumbered* the building project.〉

-en•cy \ən-sē, ᵊn-sē\ *n suffix, pl* **-en•cies**
quality or state 〈inconsist*ency*〉 〈urg*ency*〉

en•cy•clo•pe•dia \in-ˌsī-klə-ˈpē-dē-ə\ *n*
▼ a book or a set of books containing information on all branches of learning in articles arranged alphabetically by subject

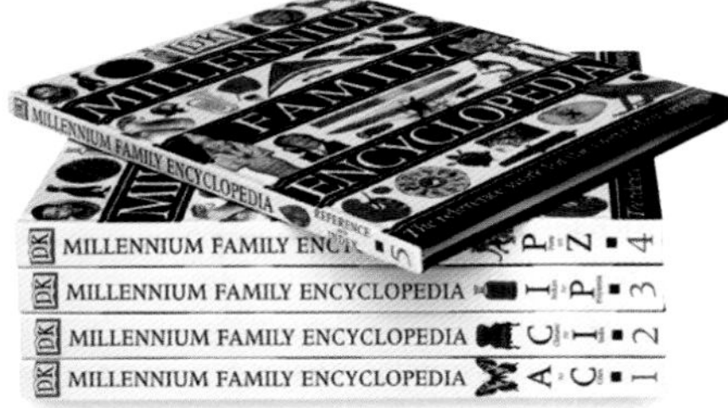

encyclopedia: a set of encyclopedias

▶ **Word History** If you read an entire encyclopedia, you might learn something about nearly everything, and, suitably, the original sense of the word *encyclopedia* was "general education" or "education in all branches of knowledge." *Encyclopedia* is formed from two Greek words, *enkyklios*, meaning "circular, recurrent, ordinary," and *paideia*, "education." *Paideia* is itself a derivative of *pais*, "child."

A B C D E F G H I J K L M N O P Q R S T U V W X Y Z

¹end \'end\ *n*
1 the part near the boundary of an area ⟨I live in the city's north *end*.⟩
2 the point where something stops or ceases to exist ⟨That's the *end* of the story.⟩
3 the first or last part of a thing ⟨She knotted the *end* of the rope.⟩
4 DEATH 1, DESTRUCTION ⟨a tragic *end*⟩
5 PURPOSE, GOAL ⟨It achieves the same *end*.⟩
6 a player in football positioned at the end of the line of scrimmage
7 a part of an undertaking ⟨He kept his *end* of the agreement.⟩

²end *vb* **end•ed**; **end•ing**
to bring or come to an end : STOP, FINISH ⟨I wish vacation would never *end*.⟩ ⟨He *ended* the discussion.⟩
end up to reach or come to a place, condition, or situation unexpectedly ⟨I *ended up* getting lost.⟩

en•dan•ger \in-'dān-jər\ *vb* **en•dan•gered**; **en•dan•ger•ing**
to expose to possible harm : RISK

en•dan•gered \in-'dān-jərd\ *adj*
close to becoming extinct : dying out

en•dear \in-'dir\ *vb* **en•deared**; **en•dear•ing**
to make beloved or admired ⟨His kind nature *endeared* him to all.⟩

en•dear•ment \in-'dir-mənt\ *n*
a word or an act that shows love or affection

¹en•deav•or \in-'de-vər\ *vb* **en•deav•ored**; **en•deav•or•ing**
to make an effort : try hard

²endeavor *n*
a serious effort or attempt

end•ing \'en-diŋ\ *n*
the final part : END

end•less \'end-ləs\ *adj*
1 lasting or taking a long time
2 joined at the ends : CONTINUOUS
end•less•ly *adv*

en•do•crine gland \'en-də-krən-, -,krīn-\ *n*
▶ any of several glands (as the thyroid or pituitary gland) that release hormones directly into the blood

en•do•plasmic re•tic•u•lum \,en-de-'plaz-mik-ri-'ti-kye-lem\ *n*
a system of cavities and tiny connecting canals that occupy much of the cytoplasm of the cell and functions especially in the movement of materials within the cell

en•dorse \in-'dȯrs\ *vb* **en•dorsed**; **en•dors•ing**
1 to show support or approval for ⟨*endorse* an idea⟩
2 to sign the back of to receive payment ⟨*endorse* a check⟩
en•dorse•ment \-mənt\ *n*

en•dow \in-'dau̇\ *vb* **en•dowed**; **en•dow•ing**
1 to provide with money for support ⟨The millionaire *endowed* a scholarship.⟩
2 to provide with something freely or naturally ⟨Humans are *endowed* with reason.⟩

en•dow•ment \in-'dau̇-mənt\ *n*
1 the act of providing money for support
2 money provided for support ⟨The college has a large *endowment*.⟩

end•point \'end-,pȯint\ *n*
either of two points that mark the ends of a line segment or a point that marks the end of a ray

en•dur•ance \in-'du̇r-əns, -'dyu̇r-\ *n*
the ability to put up with strain, suffering, or hardship

en•dure \in-'du̇r, -'dyu̇r\ *vb* **en•dured**; **en•dur•ing**
1 to continue to exist over a long time : LAST ⟨This tradition has *endured* for centuries.⟩
2 to experience without giving in ⟨They had to *endure* hardship to survive.⟩
3 to put up with ⟨He could not *endure* another minute of waiting.⟩

en•e•my \'e-nə-mē\ *n, pl* **en•e•mies**
1 a person who hates another : a person who attacks or tries to harm another
2 a country or group of people with which another country or group is at war or a person belonging to such a country or group
3 something that harms or threatens ⟨Drought is the farmer's *enemy*.⟩

en•er•get•ic \,e-nər-'je-tik\ *adj*
having or showing the ability to be active ⟨*energetic* dancers⟩
en•er•get•i•cal•ly \-ti-kə-lē\ *adv*

en•er•gize \'e-nər-,jīz\ *vb* **en•er•gized**; **en•er•giz•ing**
to give the ability to be active to : give energy to

en•er•gy \'e-nər-jē\ *n, pl* **en•er•gies**
1 ability to be active : strength of body or mind to do things or to work
2 strong action or effort ⟨He puts a lot of *energy* into his work.⟩
3 usable power or the resources (as oil) used to produce usable power

▶ **endocrine gland**
The endocrine glands are situated in different parts of the body. Together with related organs they form the endocrine system. The endocrine glands secrete hormones into the bloodstream. Hormones are needed for healthy growth and for the body to work properly.

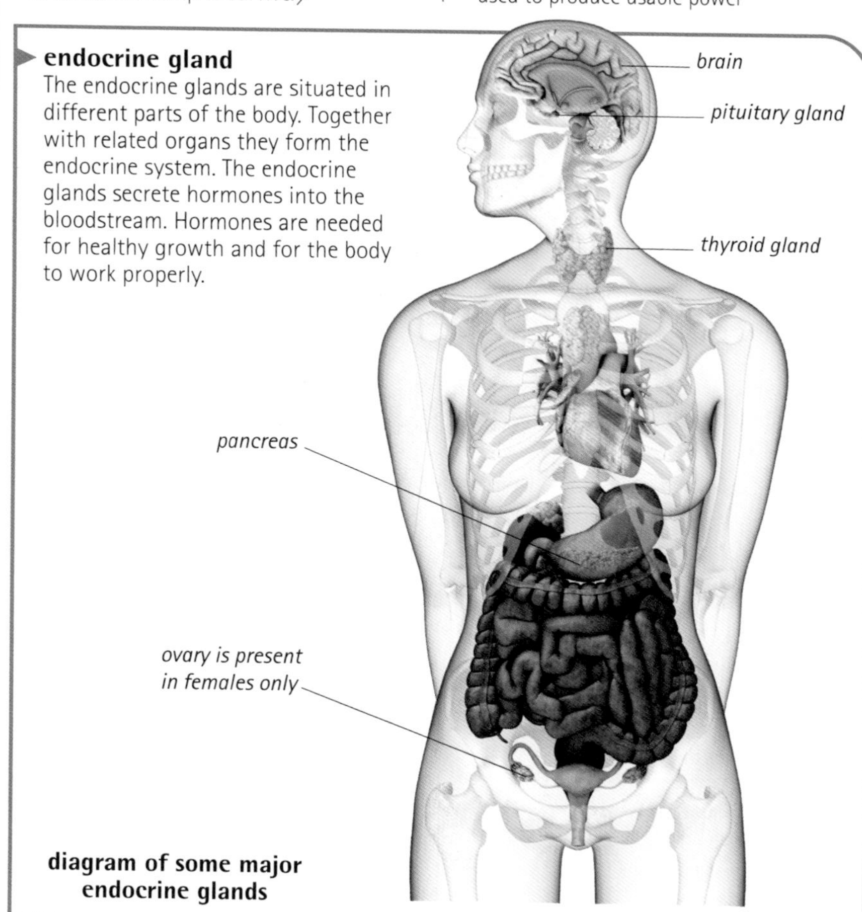

diagram of some major endocrine glands

energy pyramid *n*
a triangle-shaped diagram that represents the amount of energy in an ecosystem that is transferred from one level of food chain or food web to the next

en•fold \in-ˈfōld\ *vb* **en•fold•ed**; **en•fold•ing**
1 to wrap up ⟨He carefully *enfolded* the infant in a blanket.⟩
2 [1]EMBRACE 1

en•force \in-ˈfȯrs\ *vb* **en•forced**; **en•forc•ing**
1 to make happen ⟨*enforce* obedience⟩
2 to carry out or make effective ⟨*enforce* a law⟩
en•force•ment \-mənt\ *n*

Eng. *abbr*
1 England
2 English

en•gage \in-ˈgāj\ *vb* **en•gaged**; **en•gag•ing**
1 to catch and keep fixed (as someone's attention) ⟨The story *engaged* my interest.⟩
2 to take part in or cause to take part in something ⟨He *engages* in many school activities.⟩
3 to enter into contest or battle with ⟨Soldiers *engaged* the enemy.⟩
4 to arrange for the services or use of : EMPLOY ⟨I suggest you *engage* a lawyer.⟩ ⟨I've *engaged* a room at the hotel.⟩
5 MESH ⟨The gears *engaged.*⟩

en•gaged \in-ˈgājd\ *adj*
1 busy with an activity ⟨She is *engaged* in full-time research.⟩
2 promised to be married

en•gage•ment \in-ˈgāj-mənt\ *n*
1 the act of becoming engaged to be married : the state of being engaged to be married
2 EMPLOYMENT 3 ⟨a speaking *engagement*⟩
3 APPOINTMENT 1
4 a fight between armed forces : BATTLE

en•gag•ing \in-ˈgā-jiŋ\ *adj*
attractive or interesting ⟨an *engaging* story⟩ ⟨an *engaging* smile⟩

en•gine \ˈen-jən\ *n*
1 a mechanical tool or device ⟨tanks, planes, and other *engines* of war⟩
2 ▼ a machine for driving or operating something especially by using the energy of steam, gasoline, or oil ⟨a diesel *engine*⟩
3 LOCOMOTIVE

▶ **Word History** The English word *engine* came from the Latin word *ingenium,* meaning "natural talent." At first the word *engine* meant "skill" or "cleverness." In time the word came to be used for things that are products of human skills and cleverness — tools and machines, for example.

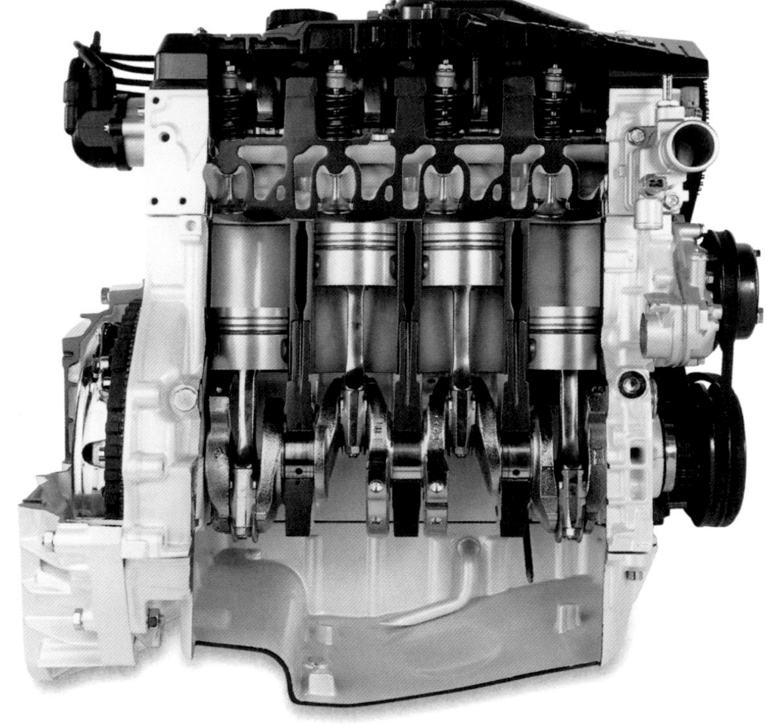

engine 2:
cross-section view of a car engine

[1]engineer 1: an engineer examining a piece of machinery

[1]en•gi•neer \ˌen-jə-ˈnir\ *n*
1 ▲ a person who designs and builds machinery or technical equipment : a person who studies or works in a branch of engineering ⟨an electrical *engineer*⟩
2 a person who runs or is in charge of a railroad engine or other machinery or technical equipment

[2]engineer *vb* **en•gi•neered**; **en•gi•neer•ing**
1 to plan, build, or manage as an engineer ⟨They *engineered* a faster race car.⟩
2 to plan out in a skillful or clever way : CONTRIVE

en•gi•neer•ing \ˌen-jə-ˈnir-iŋ\ *n*
the application of science to the goal of creating useful machines (as automobiles) or structures (as roads and dams) ⟨industrial *engineering*⟩

[1]En•glish \ˈiŋ-glish\ *adj*
of or relating to England, its people, or the English language ⟨*English* literature⟩ ⟨*English* customs⟩

[2]English *n*
1 the language of England, the United States, and some other countries now or at one time under British rule
2 English *pl* the people of England
3 English language or literature as a subject in school

English horn *n*
▶ a woodwind instrument that is similar to an oboe but is longer and has a deeper tone

en•grave \in-ˈgrāv\ *vb* **en•graved**; **en•grav•ing**
1 to cut or carve (as letters or designs) on a hard surface ⟨The jeweler *engraved* the ring with her initials.⟩
2 to print from a cut surface ⟨an *engraved* invitation⟩
en•grav•er *n*

English horn

a b c d e f g h i j k l m n o p q r s t u v w x y z

ensemble: a dance ensemble

en•grav•ing \in-ˈgrā-viŋ\ *n*
1 the art of cutting something especially into the surface of wood, stone, or metal
2 a print made from a cut surface

en•gross \in-ˈgrōs\ *vb* **en•grossed**; **en•gross•ing**
to take the attention of completely ⟨He was *engrossed* in a book.⟩

en•gulf \in-ˈgəlf\ *vb* **en•gulfed**; **en•gulf•ing**
1 to flow over and cover or surround ⟨The town was *engulfed* by the flood.⟩
2 to be overwhelmed by ⟨He was *engulfed* by fear.⟩

en•hance \in-ˈhans\ *vb* **en•hanced**; **en•hanc•ing**
to make greater or better

enig•ma \i-ˈnig-mə\ *n*
someone or something that is hard to understand ⟨Why she quit the team is an *enigma* to me.⟩

en•joy \in-ˈjȯi\ *vb* **en•joyed**; **en•joy•ing**
1 to get pleasure from ⟨I *enjoy* camping.⟩
2 to have the use or benefit of ⟨We all *enjoy* good health.⟩

en•joy•able \in-ˈjȯi-ə-bəl\ *adj*
providing pleasure ⟨an *enjoyable* trip⟩

en•joy•ment \in-ˈjȯi-mənt\ *n*
1 the action or condition of getting pleasure or satisfaction from something ⟨The land is set aside for public *enjoyment*.⟩
2 something that gives pleasure ⟨life's simple *enjoyments*⟩
synonyms see PLEASURE

en•large \in-ˈlärj\ *vb* **en•larged**; **en•larg•ing**
to make or grow larger : EXPAND

en•large•ment \in-ˈlärj-mənt\ *n*
1 an act of making or growing larger
2 the state of having been made or having grown larger
3 a larger copy of a photograph

en•light•en \in-ˈlī-tᵊn\ *vb* **en•light•ened**; **en•light•en•ing**
to give knowledge or understanding to

en•list \in-ˈlist\ *vb* **en•list•ed**; **en•list•ing**
1 to join the armed forces as a volunteer
2 to get the help of ⟨Let's *enlist* our family in painting the house.⟩
en•list•ment \-mənt\ *n*

en•list•ed \in-ˈli-stəd\ *adj*
serving in the armed forces in a rank below a commissioned officer or warrant officer

en•liv•en \in-ˈlī-vən\ *vb* **en•liv•ened**; **en•liv•en•ing**
to put life or spirit into ⟨Games *enlivened* the party.⟩

en•mi•ty \ˈen-mə-tē\ *n, pl* **en•mi•ties**
hatred especially when shared : ILL WILL

enor•mous \i-ˈnȯr-məs\ *adj*
unusually great in size, number, or degree ⟨an *enormous* animal⟩ ⟨an *enormous* problem⟩
enor•mous•ly *adv*

[1]enough \i-ˈnəf\ *adj*
equal to the needs or demands ⟨Do we have *enough* time?⟩

[2]enough *adv*
in the amount necessary or to the degree necessary ⟨Are you warm *enough*?⟩

[3]enough *pron*
a number or amount that provides what is needed ⟨There is *enough* for everyone.⟩

en•quire *chiefly British variant of* INQUIRE

en•rage \in-ˈrāj\ *vb* **en•raged**; **en•rag•ing**
to fill with rage : ANGER

en•rich \in-ˈrich\ *vb* **en•riched**; **en•rich•ing**
1 to make rich or richer
2 to improve the quality of food by adding vitamins and minerals ⟨*enriched* flour⟩
3 to make more fertile ⟨Farmers *enrich* soil with fertilizer.⟩

en•roll \in-ˈrōl\ *vb* **en•rolled**; **en•roll•ing**
1 to include (as a name) on a roll or list
2 to take in as a member
3 to become a member : JOIN

en•roll•ment \in-ˈrōl-mənt\ *n*
1 the act of becoming a member or being made a member
2 the number of members

en route \än-ˈrüt\ *adv*
on or along the way ⟨I finished my homework *en route* to school.⟩

en•sem•ble \än-ˈsäm-bəl\ *n*
◀ a group of people or things making up a complete unit ⟨a musical *ensemble*⟩ ⟨She wore a three-piece *ensemble*.⟩

en•sign \ˈen-sən, *1 is also* -ˌsīn\ *n*
1 a flag flown as the symbol of nationality
2 a commissioned officer of the lowest rank in the navy or coast guard

en•slave \in-ˈslāv\ *vb* **en•slaved**; **en•slav•ing**
to make a slave of

en•sue \in-ˈsü\ *vb* **en•sued**; **en•su•ing**
to come after in time or as a result : FOLLOW ⟨The show ended, and a long standing ovation *ensued*.⟩

en•sure \in-ˈshu̇r\ *vb* **en•sured**; **en•sur•ing**
to make sure, certain, or safe : GUARANTEE ⟨The crossing guard *ensures* our safety as we cross the street.⟩

en•tan•gle \in-ˈtaŋ-gəl\ *vb* **en•tan•gled**; **en•tan•gling**
1 to make tangled or confused ⟨Don't *entangle* the ropes.⟩
2 to catch in a tangle ⟨Birds were *entangled* in the net.⟩

en•ter \ˈen-tər\ *vb* **en•tered**; **en•ter•ing**
1 to come or go in or into ⟨*enter* a room⟩ ⟨*enter* middle age⟩
2 to stab into : PIERCE ⟨The thorn *entered* my thumb.⟩
3 to put into a list or book : write down ⟨The teacher *entered* my name on the roster.⟩
4 to put in or into ⟨*Enter* the data into the computer.⟩
5 to become a member of ⟨I *entered* a fitness club.⟩
6 to become a participant in or take an interest in ⟨*enter* a race⟩ ⟨*enter* politics⟩
7 enroll in : begin attending ⟨*enter* kindergarten⟩

en•ter•prise \ˈen-tər-ˌprīz\ *n*
1 a project or undertaking that is difficult, complicated, or risky
2 willingness to engage in daring or difficult action
3 a business organization or activity

en•ter•pris•ing \ˈen-tər-ˌprī-ziŋ\ *adj*
bold and energetic in trying or

experimenting ⟨A few *enterprising* pioneers founded a new town.⟩

en•ter•tain \ˌen-tər-ˈtān\ *vb* **en•ter•tained**; **en•ter•tain•ing**
1 to host a social event ⟨My parents *entertain* often.⟩
2 to have as a guest ⟨*entertain* friends⟩
3 to perform for or provide amusement for ⟨Comedians *entertained* the crowd.⟩
4 to have in mind ⟨She *entertained* thoughts of quitting.⟩
synonyms see AMUSE

en•ter•tain•er \ˌen-tər-ˈtā-nər\ *n*
a person who performs for public entertainment

en•ter•tain•ment \ˌen-tər-ˈtān-mənt\ *n*
1 the act of amusing or entertaining
2 something (as a show) that is a form of amusement or recreation

en•thrall \in-ˈthrȯl\ *vb* **en•thralled**; **en•thrall•ing**
to hold the attention of completely ⟨The show *enthralls* audiences.⟩

en•throne \in-ˈthrōn\ *vb* **en•throned**; **en•thron•ing**
1 to place on a throne ⟨*enthrone* a king⟩
2 to seat or put in a place to indicate authority or value ⟨The trophy was *enthroned* on his bookcase.⟩

en•thu•si•asm \in-ˈthü-zē-ˌaz-əm, -ˈthyü-\ *n*
strong feeling in favor of something ⟨*enthusiasm* for sports⟩

en•thu•si•ast \in-ˈthü-zē-ˌast, -ˈthyü-\ *n*
a person who is very excited about or interested in something ⟨a fishing *enthusiast*⟩

en•thu•si•as•tic \in-ˌthü-zē-ˈa-stik, -ˌthyü-\ *adj*
feeling strong excitement about something : full of enthusiasm

en•thu•si•as•ti•cal•ly \in-ˌthü-zē-ˈa-sti-kə-lē, -ˌthyü-\ *adv*
with strong excitement ⟨cheering *enthusiastically*⟩

en•tice \in-ˈtīs\ *vb* **en•ticed**; **en•tic•ing**
to attract by raising hope or desire : TEMPT ⟨Glittery window displays *enticed* shoppers.⟩

en•tire \in-ˈtīr\ *adj*
complete in all parts or respects ⟨the *entire* day⟩ ⟨He had *entire* control of the project.⟩
en•tire•ly *adv*

en•tire•ty \in-ˈtī-rə-tē, -ˈtīr-tē\ *n*
the whole or total amount ⟨the *entirety* of the treasure⟩

en•ti•tle \in-ˈtī-tᵊl\ *vb* **en•ti•tled**; **en•ti•tling**
1 to give a title to
2 to give a right or claim to ⟨Buying a ticket *entitles* you to a seat.⟩

en•trails \ˈen-ˌtrālz, -trəlz\ *n pl*
the internal parts of an animal

envelope containing a letter

[1]**en•trance** \ˈen-trəns\ *n*
1 the act of going in ⟨He waited for the right moment to make his *entrance*.⟩
2 a door, gate, or way for going in
3 permission to join, participate in, or attend

[2]**en•trance** \in-ˈtrans\ *vb* **en•tranced**; **en•tranc•ing**
1 to put into a trance
2 to fill with delight and wonder

en•trap \in-ˈtrap\ *vb* **en•trapped**; **en•trap•ping**
to catch in or as if in a trap

en•treat \in-ˈtrēt\ *vb* **en•treat•ed**; **en•treat•ing**
to ask in a serious and urgent way

en•treaty \in-ˈtrē-tē\ *n, pl* **en•treat•ies**
a serious and urgent request

en•trust \in-ˈtrəst\ *vb* **en•trust•ed**; **en•trust•ing**
1 to give care of something to ⟨They *entrusted* me with their money.⟩
2 to give to another with confidence ⟨I'll *entrust* the job to you.⟩

en•try \ˈen-trē\ *n, pl* **en•tries**
1 the act of going in : ENTRANCE ⟨Her *entry* surprised us.⟩
2 the right to go in or join ⟨He was denied *entry* into the club.⟩
3 a place (as a hall or door) through which entrance is made
4 the act of making a written record of something ⟨She was hired to do data *entry*.⟩
5 something written down as part of a list or a record ⟨dictionary *entries*⟩
6 a person or thing taking part in a contest ⟨the winning *entry*⟩

en•twine \in-ˈtwīn\ *vb* **en•twined**; **en•twin•ing**
to twist or twine together or around

enu•mer•ate \i-ˈnü-mə-ˌrāt, -ˈnyü-\ *vb* **enu•mer•at•ed**; **enu•mer•at•ing**
1 [1]COUNT 1
2 to name one after another : LIST

enun•ci•ate \ē-ˈnən-sē-ˌāt\ *vb* **enun•ci•at•ed**; **enun•ci•at•ing**
1 to make known publicly
2 to pronounce words or parts of words

enun•ci•a•tion \ē-ˌnən-sē-ˈā-shən\ *n*
clearness of pronunciation

en•vel•op \in-ˈve-ləp\ *vb* **en•vel•oped**; **en•vel•op•ing**
to put a covering completely around : wrap up or in
synonyms see ENCLOSE

en•ve•lope \ˈen-və-ˌlōp, ˈän-\ *n*
◀ a flat usually paper container (as for a letter)

en•vi•ous \ˈen-vē-əs\ *adj*
feeling or showing unhappiness over someone else's good fortune and a desire to have the same
en•vi•ous•ly *adv*

en•vi•ron•ment \in-ˈvī-rən-mənt, -ˈvī-ərn-mənt\ *n*
1 a person's physical surroundings ⟨He lives in a comfortable rural *environment*.⟩
2 the surrounding conditions or forces (as soil, climate, and living things) that influence a plant's or animal's characteristics and ability to survive
3 the social and cultural conditions that affect the life of a person or community ⟨a happy home *environment*⟩

en•voy \ˈen-ˌvȯi, ˈän-\ *n*
1 a representative sent by one government to another
2 MESSENGER

[1]**en•vy** \ˈen-vē\ *n, pl* **envies**
1 a feeling of unhappiness over another's good fortune together with a desire to have the same good fortune ⟨He was filled with *envy* on seeing her success.⟩
2 a person or a thing that is envied

[2]**envy** *vb* **en•vied**; **en•vy•ing**
to feel unhappiness over the good fortune of (someone) and desire the same good fortune : feel envy toward or because of ⟨I *envy* you for your talent.⟩

en•zyme \ˈen-ˌzīm\ *n*
a substance produced by body cells that helps bring about or speed up bodily chemical activities (as the digestion of food) without being destroyed in so doing

eon *variant of* AEON

[1]**ep•ic** \ˈe-pik\ *n*
a long poem that tells the story of a hero's deeds

[2]**epic** *adj*
1 telling a great and heroic story ⟨an *epic* poem⟩
2 heroic or impressive because of great size or effort

[1]**ep•i•dem•ic** \ˌe-pə-ˈde-mik\ *n*
1 a rapidly spreading outbreak of disease
2 something harmful that spreads or develops rapidly ⟨a crime *epidemic*⟩

a b c d **e** f g h i j k l m n o p q r s t u v w x y z

[2]epidemic *adj*
spreading widely and affecting many people at the same time ⟨an *epidemic* disease⟩

epi•der•mis \ˌe-pə-ˈdər-məs\ *n*
1 a thin outer layer of skin covering the dermis
2 any of various thin outer layers of plants or animals

ep•i•lep•sy \ˈe-pə-ˌlep-sē\ *n*
a disorder of the nervous system that causes people to have seizures

ep•i•neph•rine \ˌe-pə-ˈne-frən\ *n*
a hormone that causes blood vessels to narrow and the blood pressure to increase

ep•i•sode \ˈe-pə-ˌsōd\ *n*
1 an event or one of a series of events that stands out clearly ⟨Let's forget the whole *episode*.⟩
2 one in a series of connected stories or performances

ep•i•taph \ˈe-pə-ˌtaf\ *n*
▶ a brief statement on a tombstone in memory of a dead person

ep•och \ˈe-pək\ *n*
a period that is important or memorable

epitaph: an epitaph written in Hebrew

[1]equal \ˈē-kwəl\ *adj*
1 exactly the same in number, amount, degree, rank, or quality
2 the same for each person ⟨*equal* rights⟩
3 having enough strength, ability, or means ⟨He's *equal* to the task.⟩
synonyms see SAME
equal•ly \ˈē-kwə-lē\ *adv*

[2]equal *vb* **equaled** *or* **equalled**; **equal•ing** *or* **equal•ling**
to be the same in number, amount, degree, rank, or quality as

[3]equal *n*
someone or something that is as good or valuable as another

equal•i•ty \i-ˈkwä-lə-tē\ *n, pl* **equal•i•ties**
the condition or state of being the same in number, amount, degree, rank, or quality

equal•ize \ˈē-kwə-ˌlīz\ *vb* **equal•ized**; **equal•iz•ing**
to make even or equal

equa•tion \i-ˈkwā-zhən\ *n*
1 a statement of the equality of two mathematical expressions
2 an expression representing a chemical reaction by means of chemical symbols

equa•tor \i-ˈkwā-tər\ *n*
▶ an imaginary circle around the earth everywhere equally distant from the north pole and the south pole

equa•to•ri•al \ˌē-kwə-ˈtȯr-ē-əl, ˌe-kwə-\ *adj*
relating to or lying near the equator

eques•tri•an \i-ˈkwe-strē-ən\ *adj*
relating to the act of riding horses

equi•lat•er•al \ˌē-kwə-ˈla-tə-rəl, ˌe-kwə-\ *adj*
having all sides or faces equal ⟨an *equilateral* triangle⟩

equi•lib•ri•um \ˌē-kwə-ˈli-brē-əm, ˌe-kwə-\ *n*
1 a state of balance between opposing forces or actions
2 the normal balanced state of the body that is maintained by the inner part of the ear and that keeps a person or animal from falling

equi•nox \ˈē-kwə-ˌnäks, ˈe-kwə-\ *n*
either of the two times each year (as in spring around March 21 and in fall around September 23) when the sun's center crosses the equator and day and night are everywhere of equal length

equip \i-ˈkwip\ *vb* **equipped**; **equip•ping**
to provide with necessary supplies or features

equip•ment \i-ˈkwip-mənt\ *n*
supplies or tools needed for a special purpose

[1]equiv•a•lent \i-ˈkwi-və-lənt\ *adj*
alike or equal in number, value, or meaning

[2]equivalent *n*
something like or equal to something else in number, value, or meaning

[1]-er \ər\ *adj suffix or adv suffix*
used to form the comparative degree of adjectives and adverbs of one syllable ⟨hott*er*⟩ ⟨dri*er*⟩ and of some adjectives and adverbs of two or more syllables ⟨shallow*er*⟩ ⟨earli*er*⟩

[2]-er \ər\ *also* **-ier** \ē-ər, yər\ *or* **-yer** \yər\ *n suffix*
1 a person whose work or business is connected with ⟨hatt*er*⟩ ⟨law*yer*⟩
2 a person or thing belonging to or associated with ⟨old-tim*er*⟩
3 a native of : resident of ⟨New York*er*⟩
4 a person or thing that has
5 a person or thing that produces ⟨thrill*er*⟩
6 a person or thing that performs a specified action ⟨report*er*⟩
7 a person or thing that is a suitable object of a specified action ⟨broil*er*⟩
8 a person or thing that is ⟨foreign*er*⟩

era \ˈer-ə, ˈir-ə\ *n*
1 a period of time starting from some special date or event or known for a certain feature ⟨the computer *era*⟩
2 an important period of history

erad•i•cate \i-ˈra-də-ˌkāt\ *vb* **erad•i•cat•ed**; **erad•i•cat•ing**
to destroy completely

erase \i-ˈrās\ *vb* **erased**; **eras•ing**
1 to cause to disappear by rubbing or scraping ⟨*erase* a chalk mark⟩
2 to remove marks from ⟨*erase* a chalkboard⟩
3 to remove recorded matter from
eras•er \i-ˈrā-sər\ *n*

era•sure \i-ˈrā-shər\ *n*
an act of erasing

[1]ere \ˈer\ *prep*
[2]BEFORE 2

[2]ere *conj*
[3]BEFORE 3

e-read•er \ˈē-ˌrē-dər\ *n*
an electronic device used for reading e-books and similar material

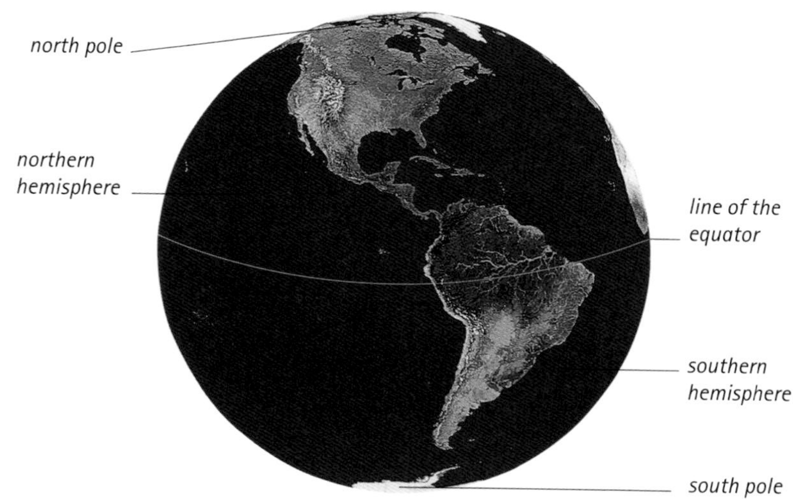

equator encircling the earth

¹erect \i-ˈrekt\ *adj*
straight up and down
⟨an *erect* tree⟩

²erect *vb* **erect•ed**; **erect•ing**
1 to put up by fitting together materials or parts ⟨*erect* a tent⟩
2 to set or place straight up ⟨*erect* a flagpole⟩
synonyms see BUILD
erec•tor \i-ˈrek-tər\ *n*

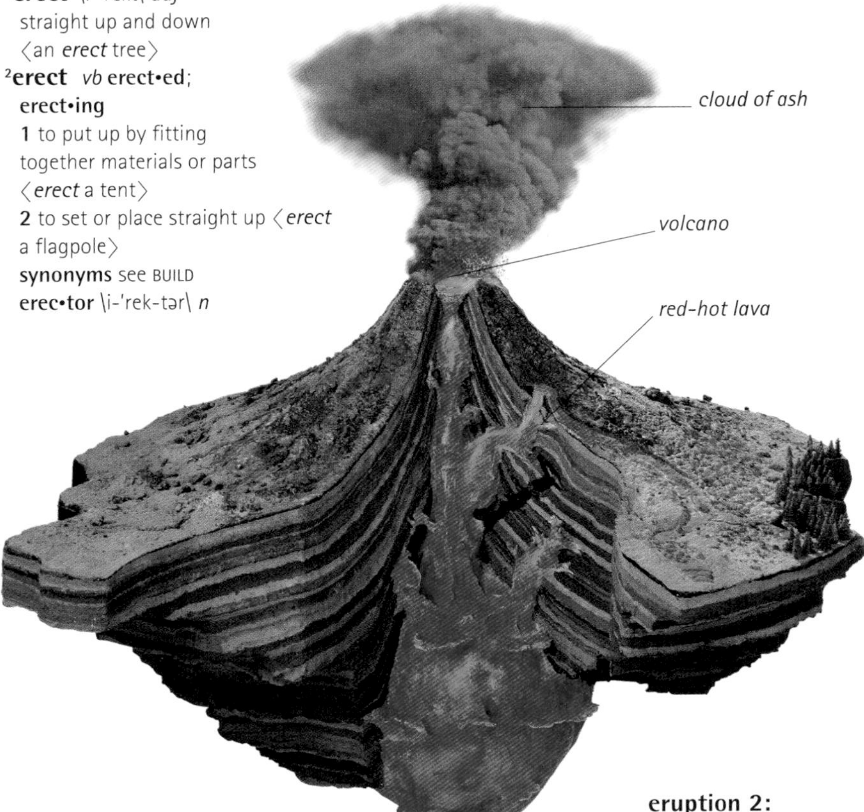

eruption 2: cross-section model of a volcanic eruption

er•mine \ˈər-mən\ *n*
a weasel of northern regions having white fur in winter with a tail tipped in black

erode \i-ˈrōd\ *vb* **erod•ed**; **erod•ing**
to wear away : destroy by wearing away ⟨Waves *erode* the shore.⟩

ero•sion \i-ˈrō-zhən\ *n*
the act of wearing away or eroding : the state of being eroded

err \ˈer, ˈər\ *vb* **erred**; **err•ing**
to make a mistake

er•rand \ˈer-ənd\ *n*
1 a short trip made to do or get something
2 the purpose of a short trip

er•rant \ˈer-ənt\ *adj*
1 wandering in search of adventure ⟨an *errant* knight⟩
2 straying from a proper course

er•rat•ic \i-ˈra-tik\ *adj*
not following a regular, usual, or expected course ⟨The butterfly's flight was *erratic*.⟩

er•ro•ne•ous \i-ˈrō-nē-əs\ *adj*
INCORRECT 1

er•ror \ˈer-ər\ *n*
a failure to be correct or accurate : MISTAKE

▶ **Synonyms** ERROR, MISTAKE, and BLUNDER mean an act or statement that is not right or true or proper. ERROR is used for failure to follow a model correctly. ⟨There was an *error* in the addition.⟩ MISTAKE is used when someone misunderstands something or does not intend to do wrong. ⟨I took someone else's coat by *mistake*.⟩ BLUNDER is used for a really bad mistake made because of a lack of knowledge, intelligence, caution, or care. ⟨The actors made several *blunders* during the play.⟩

erupt \i-ˈrəpt\ *vb* **erupt•ed**; **erupt•ing**
1 to send out lava, rocks, and ash in a sudden explosion ⟨The volcano *erupted*.⟩
2 to burst out in a sudden explosion ⟨Lava *erupted* from the volcano.⟩
3 to happen, begin, or appear suddenly

erup•tion \i-ˈrəp-shən\ *n*
1 an instance of a volcano erupting
2 ▲ the bursting out of material from a volcano
3 the sudden occurrence or appearance of something

-ery \ə-rē, rē\ *n, suffix pl* **-er•ies**
1 qualities considered as a group : character : -NESS
2 art : practice ⟨trick*ery*⟩
3 place of doing, keeping, producing, or selling ⟨fish*ery*⟩ ⟨bak*ery*⟩
4 collection ⟨fin*ery*⟩
5 state or condition ⟨slav*ery*⟩

¹-es \əz, iz *after* s, z, sh, ch; z *after* v *or a vowel*\ *n pl suffix*
used to form the plural of most nouns that end in *s* ⟨glass*es*⟩, *z* ⟨buzz*es*⟩, *sh* ⟨bush*es*⟩, *ch* ⟨peach*es*⟩, or a final *y* that changes to *i* ⟨ladi*es*⟩ and of some nouns ending in *f* that changes to *v* ⟨loav*es*⟩

²-es *vb suffix*
used to form the third person singular present of most verbs that end in *s* ⟨bless*es*⟩, *z* ⟨fizz*es*⟩, *sh* ⟨blush*es*⟩, *ch* ⟨catch*es*⟩, or a final *y* that changes to *i* ⟨deni*es*⟩

es•ca•la•tor \ˈe-skə-ˌlā-tər\ *n*
▼ a moving stairway for going from one level (as of a building) to another

escalator: a girl riding an escalator

a b c d e f g h i j k l m n o p q r s t u v w x y z

es•ca•pade \ˈe-skə-ˌpād\ *n*
a daring or reckless adventure

[1]**es•cape** \i-ˈskāp\ *vb* **es•caped; es•cap•ing**
1 to get away : get free or clear ⟨Everyone *escaped* from the burning building.⟩
2 to keep free of : AVOID ⟨She managed to *escape* injury.⟩
3 to fail to be noticed or remembered by ⟨The name *escapes* me.⟩
4 to leak out ⟨Gas is *escaping* from the tank.⟩

► **Word History** Picture a person who is held by a cape or cloak. The person may be able to slip out of the garment and so escape. The word *escape* is based on such a picture. *Escape* came from an Old French verb *escaper* or *eschaper*. This word in turn came ultimately from the Latin words *ex*, "out of," and *cappa*, "head covering, cloak."

[2]**escape** *n*
1 the act of getting away ⟨a narrow *escape*⟩
2 a way of getting away ⟨The window was his only *escape*.⟩

es•cap•ee \i-ˌskā-ˈpē\ *n*
a person who escapes

[1]**es•cort** \ˈe-ˌskȯrt\ *n*
1 a person or group that accompanies someone to give protection or show courtesy ⟨a police *escort*⟩
2 the man who goes with a woman to a social event

[2]**es•cort** \i-ˈskȯrt\ *vb* **es•cort•ed; es•cort•ing**
to accompany someone to protect or show courtesy

[1]**-ese** \ˈēz\ *adj suffix*
of, relating to, or coming from a certain place or country ⟨Japan*ese*⟩

[2]**-ese** *n suffix, pl* **-ese**
1 native or resident of a specified place or country ⟨Chin*ese*⟩
2 language of a particular place, country, or nationality

Es•ki•mo \ˈe-skə-ˌmō\ *n, pl* **Es•ki•mos**
sometimes offensive
a member of a group of peoples of Alaska, northern Canada, Greenland, and eastern Siberia
Hint: In the past, this word was not considered offensive. Some people, however, now prefer *Inuit*.

ESL *abbr* English as a second language

esoph•a•gus \i-ˈsä-fə-gəs\ *n, pl* **esoph•a•gi** \-ˌgī, -ˌjī\
a muscular tube that leads from the mouth through the throat to the stomach

esp. *abbr* especially

es•pe•cial \i-ˈspe-shəl\ *adj*
more than usual : SPECIAL
es•pe•cial•ly *adv*

es•pi•o•nage \ˈe-spē-ə-ˌnäzh\ *n*
the practice of spying : the use of spies

es•py \i-ˈspī\ *vb* **es•pied; es•py•ing**
to catch sight of

-ess \əs\ *n suffix*
female ⟨godd*ess*⟩

es•say \ˈe-ˌsā\ *n*
a piece of writing that tells a person's thoughts or opinions about a subject

es•say•ist \ˈe-ˌsā-ist\ *n*
a writer of essays

es•sence \ˈe-sᵊns\ *n*
1 the basic part of something ⟨Freedom is the *essence* of democracy.⟩
2 a substance made from a plant or drug and having its special qualities
3 [1]PERFUME 1

[1]**es•sen•tial** \i-ˈsen-shəl\ *adj*
1 extremely important or necessary ⟨It is *essential* that we all meet here.⟩
2 forming or belonging to the basic part of something ⟨Free speech is an *essential* right of citizenship.⟩
es•sen•tial•ly *adv*

[2]**essential** *n*
something that is basic or necessary ⟨I only packed the bare *essentials* for the trip.⟩

-est \əst\ *adj suffix or adv suffix*
used to form the superlative of adjectives and adverbs of one syllable ⟨fatt*est*⟩ ⟨lat*est*⟩ and of some adjectives and adverbs of two or more syllables ⟨lucki*est*⟩ ⟨often*est*⟩

es•tab•lish \i-ˈsta-blish\ *vb* **es•tab•lished; es•tab•lish•ing**
1 to bring into being : FOUND ⟨They *established* a colony.⟩
2 to put beyond doubt : PROVE ⟨She *established* her innocence.⟩

es•tab•lish•ment \i-ˈsta-blish-mənt\ *n*
1 the act of founding or of proving
2 a place where people live or do business

es•tate \i-ˈstāt\ *n*
1 the property of all kinds that a person leaves at death
2 ▼ a mansion on a large piece of land
3 [1]STATE 1 ⟨the low *estate* of the poor⟩

[1]**es•teem** \i-ˈstēm\ *n*
respect and affection ⟨Her work with children has won her *esteem*.⟩

[2]**esteem** *vb* **es•teemed; es•teem•ing**
to think favorably of ⟨He was *esteemed* as a man of generosity.⟩

estate 2: front view of an estate

[1]es•ti•mate \'e-stə-,māt\ *vb* **es•ti•mat•ed; es•ti•mat•ing**
to give or form a general idea of (as the value, size, or cost of something)

[2]es•ti•mate \'e-stə-mət\ *n*
1 an opinion or judgment especially of the value or quality of something ⟨In my *estimate*, the product is poorly made.⟩
2 an approximation of the size or cost of something

es•ti•ma•tion \,e-stə-'mā-shən\ *n*
1 the act of making a judgment especially of value, size, or cost ⟨an *estimation* of expenses⟩
2 OPINION 2

es•tu•ary \'es-chə-,wer-ē\ *n, pl* **es•tu•ar•ies**
an arm of the sea at the lower end of a river

et al. *abbr* and others
Hint: The abbreviation *et al.* is short for the Latin phrase *et alia*, meaning "and others."

etc. *abbr* et cetera

et cet•era \et-'se-tə-rə, -'se-trə\
and others of the same kind : and so forth : and so on

etch \'ech\ *vb* **etched; etch•ing**
to produce designs or figures on metal or glass by using acid to eat into the surface

etch•ing \'e-chiŋ\ *n*
1 ▼ the art or process of producing drawings or pictures by printing from etched plates
2 a picture made from an etched plate

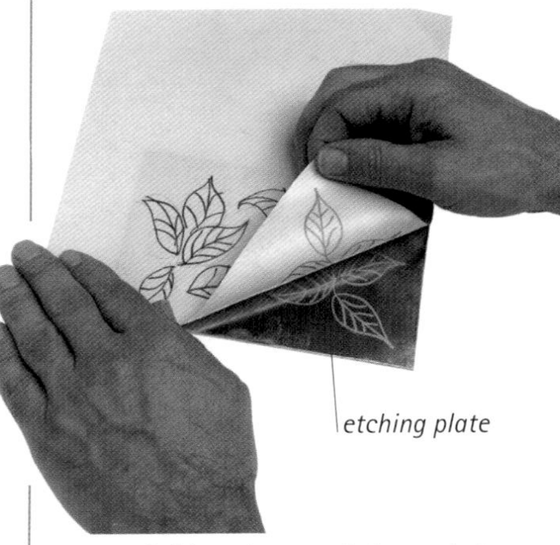

etching 1: paper being peeled back from an etched plate

eter•nal \i-'tər-nᵊl\ *adj*
1 lasting forever : having no beginning and no end
2 continuing without interruption : seeming to last forever ⟨*eternal* patience⟩

eter•ni•ty \i-'tər-nə-tē\ *n, pl* **eter•ni•ties**
1 time without end
2 the state after death
3 a period of time that seems endless ⟨I waited an *eternity*.⟩

-eth see **-th**

ether \'ē-thər\ *n*
a light flammable liquid used to dissolve fats and especially in the past as an anesthetic

ethe•re•al \i-'thir-ē-əl\ *adj*
1 suggesting heaven or the heavens ⟨*ethereal* music⟩
2 very delicate : AIRY

eth•i•cal \'e-thi-kəl\ *adj*
1 involving questions of right and wrong : relating to ethics ⟨*ethical* issues⟩
2 following accepted rules of behavior ⟨We expect *ethical* treatment of animals.⟩

eth•ics \'e-thiks\ *n pl*
1 a branch of philosophy dealing with what is morally right or wrong
2 the rules of moral behavior governing an individual or a group
Hint: *Ethics* can be used as a singular or a plural in writing and speaking.

eth•nic \'eth-nik\ *adj*
of or relating to groups of people with common characteristics and customs ⟨*ethnic* food⟩
eth•ni•cal•ly \-ni-kə-lē\ *adv*

et•i•quette \'e-ti-kət, -,ket\ *n*
the rules governing the proper way to behave or to do something

-ette \'et\ *n suffix*
1 little one ⟨kitchen*ette*⟩
2 female ⟨drum major*ette*⟩

et•y•mol•o•gy \,e-tə-'mä-lə-jē\ *n, pl* **et•y•mol•o•gies**
the history of a word shown by tracing it or its parts back to the earliest known forms and meanings both in its own language and any other language from which it may have been taken

eu•ca•lyp•tus \,yü-kə-'lip-təs\ *n, pl* **eu•ca•lyp•ti** \-,tī\ *or* **eu•ca•lyp•tus•es**
a tree mainly of Australia that is widely grown for its timber, gums, and oils

eu•gle•na \yu̇-'glē-nə\ *n*
▼ a tiny green single-celled organism that lives in fresh water and moves about by means of a flagellum

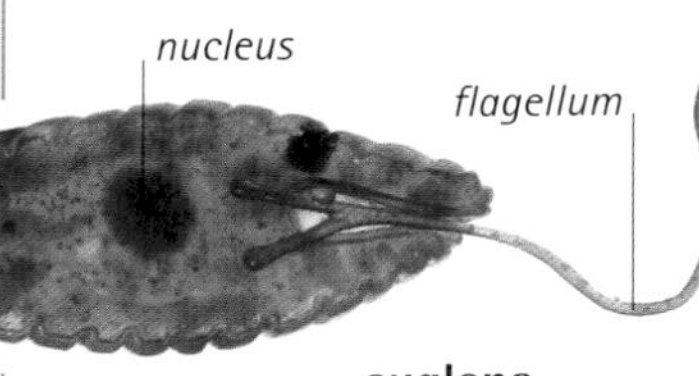

euglena

eu•ro \'yu̇r-ō\ *n, pl* **euros**
▼ a coin or bill used by many countries of the European Union

euro: denominations of the euro currency

[1]Eu•ro•pe•an \,yu̇r-ə-'pē-ən\ *adj*
of or relating to Europe or the people of Europe ⟨*European* history⟩

[2]European *n*
a native or resident of Europe

a b c d e f g h i j k l o p q r s t u v w x y z

evac•u•ate \i-ˈva-kyə-ˌwāt\ *vb* **evac•u•at•ed; evac•u•at•ing**
1 to leave or cause to leave a place of danger
2 to make empty : empty out
3 to discharge waste matter from the body

evade \i-ˈvād\ *vb* **evad•ed; evad•ing**
to get away from or avoid meeting directly ⟨*evade* a question⟩

eval•u•ate \i-ˈval-yə-ˌwāt\ *vb* **eval•u•at•ed; eval•u•at•ing**
to judge the value or condition of

eval•u•a•tion \i-ˌval-yə-ˈwā-shən\ *n*
the act or result of judging the condition or value of ⟨an *evaluation* of the patient⟩

evan•ge•list \i-ˈvan-jə-ləst\ *n*
a Christian preacher who tries to change or increase religious feelings

evap•o•rate \i-ˈva-pə-ˌrāt\ *vb* **evap•o•rat•ed; evap•o•rat•ing**
1 to change into vapor ⟨The liquid *evaporated* quickly.⟩
2 to remove some of the water from something (as by heating) ⟨*evaporate* milk⟩
3 to disappear without being seen to go ⟨Their savings quickly *evaporated.*⟩

evap•o•ra•tion \i-ˌva-pə-ˈrā-shən\ *n*
the process of changing from a liquid to a vapor

eve \ˈēv\ *n*
1 EVENING
2 the evening or day before a special day ⟨Christmas *eve*⟩
3 the period just before an important event

[1]**even** \ˈē-vən\ *adj*
1 having a flat, smooth, or level surface ⟨*even* ground⟩
2 being on the same line or level ⟨Water is *even* with the rim of a glass.⟩
3 staying the same over a period of time ⟨*even* breathing⟩
4 equal in size, number, or amount ⟨The bread was cut in *even* slices.⟩
5 not giving an advantage to one side : FAIR ⟨an *even* trade⟩
6 able to be divided by two into two equal whole numbers ⟨Fourteen is *even*, but fifteen is odd.⟩
synonyms see LEVEL
even•ly *adv*
even•ness *n*

[2]**even** *adv*
1 used to stress a highly unlikely condition or instance ⟨*Even* a child can do it.⟩
2 to a greater extent or degree : STILL ⟨*even* better⟩
3 so much as ⟨She didn't *even* offer to help.⟩
4 INDEED ⟨We were willing, *even* eager, to help.⟩
5 at the very time ⟨It's happening *even* as we speak.⟩

[3]**even** *vb* **evened; even•ing**
to make or become smooth or equal ⟨I *evened* out the rug.⟩ ⟨Let's *even* the score.⟩

eve•ning \ˈēv-niŋ\ *n*
the final part of the day and early part of the night

evening star *n*
a bright planet (as Venus) seen in the western sky after sunset

event \i-ˈvent\ *n*
1 something important or notable that happens ⟨historical *events*⟩
2 a social occasion (as a party)
3 the fact of happening ⟨in the *event* of rain⟩
4 a contest in a program of sports ⟨Olympic *events*⟩
synonyms see INCIDENT

event•ful \i-ˈvent-fəl\ *adj*
1 full of important happenings ⟨an *eventful* vacation⟩
2 very important ⟨an *eventful* decision⟩

even•tu•al \i-ˈven-chə-wəl\ *adj*
coming at some later time ⟨*eventual* success⟩
even•tu•al•ly *adv*

ev•er \ˈe-vər\ *adv*
1 at any time ⟨Has this *ever* been done?⟩
2 in any way ⟨How can I *ever* thank you?⟩
3 ALWAYS 1 ⟨*ever* faithful⟩

ev•er•glade \ˈe-vər-ˌglād\ *n*
a swampy grassland

[1]**ev•er•green** \ˈe-vər-ˌgrēn\ *n*
▼ a plant (as a pine or a laurel) having leaves that stay green through more than one growing season

[1]**evergreen:** a squat evergreen plant

[2]**evergreen** *adj*
having leaves that stay green through more than one growing season

ev•er•last•ing \ˌe-vər-ˈla-stiŋ\ *adj*
1 lasting forever : ETERNAL ⟨*everlasting* fame⟩
2 going on for a long time ⟨Stop that *everlasting* noise!⟩

ev•ery \ˈev-rē\ *adj*
1 including each of a group or series without leaving out any ⟨I heard *every* word you said!⟩
2 at regularly spaced times or distances ⟨He stopped *every* few feet.⟩

ev•ery•body \ˈev-ri-ˌbə-dē, -ˌbä-\ *pron*
every person

ev•ery•day \ˌev-rē-ˌdā\ *adj*
used or suitable for every day : ORDINARY ⟨*everyday* clothing⟩

ev•ery•one \ˈev-rē-wən, -ˌwən\ *pron*
every person

ev•ery•thing \ˈev-rē-ˌthiŋ\ *pron*
all that exists or is important ⟨*Everything* is all ready.⟩

ev•ery•where \ˈev-rē-ˌhwer, -ˌwer\ *adv*
in or to every place ⟨I looked *everywhere.*⟩

evict \i-ˈvikt\ *vb* **evict•ed; evict•ing**
to force (someone) to leave a place

ev•i•dence \ˈe-və-dəns\ *n*
1 a sign which shows that something exists or is true : INDICATION ⟨They found *evidence* of a robbery.⟩
2 material presented to a court to help find the truth about something

ev•i•dent \ˈe-və-dənt\ *adj*
clear to the sight or to the mind : PLAIN
ev•i•dent•ly \-dənt-lē, -ˌdent-\ *adv*

[1]**evil** \ˈē-vəl\ *adj*
1 morally bad : WICKED ⟨an *evil* influence⟩
2 causing harm : tending to injure ⟨an *evil* spell⟩
synonyms see BAD

[2]**evil** *n*
1 something that brings sorrow, trouble, or destruction ⟨the *evils* of poverty⟩
2 the fact of suffering or wrongdoing ⟨We must rid the world of *evil.*⟩
3 bad behavior or moral state : WICKEDNESS

evoke \i-ˈvōk\ *vb* **evoked; evok•ing**
to bring to mind

evo•lu•tion \ˌe-və-ˈlü-shən, ˌē-və-\ *n*
1 ► the theory that the various kinds of existing animals and plants have come from kinds that existed in the past
2 the process of development of an animal or a plant

evolve \i-ˈvälv\ *vb* **evolved; evolv•ing**
to change or develop gradually

ewe and her lamb

ewe \'yü\ *n*
▲ a female sheep

ex– \'eks\ *prefix*
former ⟨*ex*-president⟩

[1]**ex•act** \ig-'zakt\ *adj*
completely correct or precise : ACCURATE ⟨an *exact* copy⟩ ⟨the *exact* time⟩
synonyms see CORRECT
ex•act•ly *adv*
ex•act•ness *n*

[2]**exact** *vb* **ex•act•ed**; **ex•act•ing**
to demand and get by force or threat ⟨They *exacted* terrible revenge.⟩

ex•act•ing \ig-'zak-tiŋ\ *adj*
expecting a lot from a person ⟨an *exacting* teacher⟩

ex•ag•ger•ate \ig-'za-jə-,rāt\ *vb*
ex•ag•ger•at•ed; **ex•ag•ger•at•ing**
to describe as larger or greater than what is true

ex•ag•ger•a•tion \ig-,za-jə-'rā-shən\ *n*
1 the act of describing as larger or greater than what is true
2 a statement that has been enlarged beyond what is true

ex•alt \ig-'zȯlt\ *vb* **ex•alt•ed**; **ex•alt•ing**
1 to raise to a higher level ⟨The king *exalted* his loyal servant to a councillor.⟩
2 to praise highly

ex•am \ig-'zam\ *n*
EXAMINATION

ex•am•i•na•tion \ig-,za-mə-'nā-shən\ *n*
1 ► the act of checking closely and carefully ⟨The doctor performed an *examination* of the patient.⟩
2 a test given to determine progress, fitness, or knowledge ⟨a college entrance *examination*⟩

ex•am•ine \ig-'za-mən\ *vb* **ex•am•ined**; **ex•am•in•ing**
1 to look at or check carefully ⟨He had his eyes *examined*.⟩
2 to question closely ⟨The police *examined* a witness.⟩

ex•am•ple \ig-'zam-pəl\ *n*
1 something to be imitated : MODEL ⟨Try to set a good *example*.⟩
2 a sample of something taken to show what the whole is like : INSTANCE
3 a problem to be solved to show how a rule works ⟨an *example* in arithmetic⟩
4 something that is a warning to others ⟨Let his punishment be an *example* to you.⟩
synonyms see MODEL

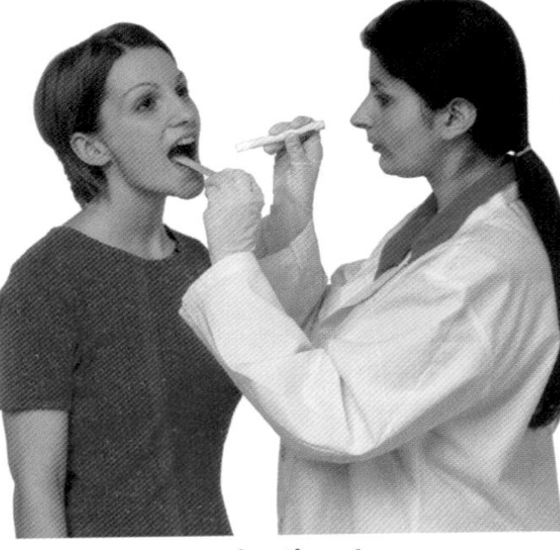

examination 1:
a doctor giving a patient an examination

ex•as•per•ate \ig-'za-spə-,rāt\ *vb*
ex•as•per•at•ed; **ex•as•per•at•ing**
to make angry

ex•as•per•a•tion \ig-,za-spə-'rā-shən\ *n*
extreme annoyance : ANGER

► **evolution 1**
Evolution is a theory that explains the process by which all living things slowly develop new features over time. From studying fossil remains, for example, scientists believe that the modern elephant may have evolved from a much smaller ancestor, belonging to or resembling the genus *Moeritherium*, which has long been extinct.

the modern elephant with some extinct relatives

Moeritherium \,mir-ə-'thir-ē-əm\ died out about 35 million years ago

Phiomia \fī-'ō-mē-ə\ died out more than 24 million years ago

Gomphotherium \,gäm-fō-'thir-ē-əm\ died out about 20 million years ago

Deinotherium \,dī-nə-'thir-ē-əm\ died out about 2 million years ago

elephant is a modern-day species

ex•ca•vate \'ek-skə-,vāt\ *vb* **ex•ca•vat•ed**; **ex•ca•vat•ing**
1 to expose to view by digging away a covering ⟨They've *excavated* an ancient city.⟩
2 to hollow out : form a hole in ⟨Workers *excavated* the side of a hill.⟩
3 to make by hollowing out ⟨We must *excavate* a tunnel.⟩
4 to dig out and remove ⟨Miners *excavate* diamonds.⟩

ex•ca•va•tion \,ek-skə-'vā-shən\ *n*
1 the act of excavating
2 a hollow place formed by excavating

ex•ceed \ik-'sēd\ *vb* **ex•ceed•ed**; **ex•ceed•ing**
1 to be greater than ⟨The cost must not *exceed* 100 dollars.⟩
2 to go or be beyond the limit of ⟨Don't *exceed* the speed limit.⟩

ex•ceed•ing•ly \ik-'sē-diŋ-lē\ *adv*
to a very great degree ⟨He's *exceedingly* happy.⟩

ex•cel \ik-'sel\ *vb* **ex•celled**; **ex•cel•ling**
to do better than others : SURPASS ⟨She *excelled* at running.⟩

ex•cel•lence \'ek-sə-ləns\ *n*
high quality

ex•cel•lent \'ek-sə-lənt\ *adj*
very good of its kind ⟨*excellent* advice⟩
ex•cel•lent•ly *adv*

[1]**ex•cept** \ik-'sept\ *prep*
1 not including ⟨We're open every day *except* Sundays.⟩
2 other than : BUT ⟨She told everyone *except* me.⟩

[2]**except** *conj*
if it were not for the fact that : ONLY ⟨I'd go, *except* it's too far.⟩

[3]**except** *vb* **ex•cept•ed**; **ex•cept•ing**
to leave out from a number or a whole : EXCLUDE ⟨Children are *excepted* from the requirements.⟩

ex•cep•tion \ik-'sep-shən\ *n*
1 someone or something that is not included ⟨I returned all the books with one *exception*.⟩
2 a case to which a rule does not apply ⟨We'll make an *exception* this time.⟩
3 an objection or a reason for objecting — usually used with *take* ⟨He took *exception* to the change.⟩

ex•cep•tion•al \ik-'sep-shə-nᵊl\ *adj*
1 being unusual ⟨an *exceptional* amount⟩
2 better than average : SUPERIOR
ex•cep•tion•al•ly *adv*

[1]**ex•cess** \ik-'ses, 'ek-,ses\ *n*
1 a state of being more than enough ⟨Don't eat to *excess*.⟩
2 the amount by which something is or has too much

[2]**excess** *adj*
more than is usual or acceptable

ex•ces•sive \ik-'se-siv\ *adj*
being too much ⟨*excessive* talking⟩
ex•ces•sive•ly *adv*

[1]**ex•change** \iks-'chānj\ *n*
1 an act of giving or taking of one thing in return for another : TRADE ⟨a fair *exchange*⟩
2 a place where goods or services are exchanged
3 the act of giving and receiving between two groups ⟨an *exchange* of ideas⟩

[2]**exchange** *vb* **ex•changed**; **ex•chang•ing**
to give or take one thing in return for another : TRADE, SWAP

ex•cit•able \ik-'sī-tə-bəl\ *adj*
easily excited

ex•cite \ik-'sīt\ *vb* **ex•cit•ed**; **ex•cit•ing**
1 to stir up feeling in ⟨The announcement *excited* the children.⟩
2 to increase the activity of ⟨This chemical *excites* nerve cells.⟩

ex•cit•ed \ik-'sī-təd\ *adj*
very enthusiastic and eager ⟨She is *excited* about the trip.⟩
ex•ci•ted•ly *adv*

ex•cite•ment \ik-'sīt-mənt\ *n*
1 something that stirs up feelings of great enthusiasm and interest ⟨The game was filled with *excitement*.⟩
2 a feeling of great enthusiasm and interest : the state of being excited ⟨The children squealed in *excitement*.⟩

ex•cit•ing \ik-'sī-tiŋ\ *adj*
producing excitement ⟨an *exciting* adventure⟩

ex•claim \ik-'sklām\ *vb* **ex•claimed**; **ex•claim•ing**
to speak or cry out suddenly or with strong feeling

ex•cla•ma•tion \,ek-sklə-'mā-shən\ *n*
a sharp or sudden cry or expression of strong feeling

exclamation point *n*
a punctuation mark ! used to show force in speaking or strong feeling

ex•clam•a•to•ry \ik-'sklam-ə-,tȯr-ē\ *adj*
containing or using exclamation ⟨*exclamatory* outbursts⟩

ex•clude \ik-'sklüd\ *vb* **ex•clud•ed**; **ex•clud•ing**
to shut out : keep out ⟨Don't *exclude* your little sister from the game.⟩

ex•clu•sion \ik-'sklü-zhən\ *n*
the act of shutting or keeping out : the state of being shut or kept out

ex•clu•sive \ik-'sklü-siv, -ziv\ *adj*
1 excluding or trying to exclude others ⟨an *exclusive* neighborhood⟩
2 [4]SOLE 2 ⟨Residents have *exclusive* use of the beach.⟩
3 ENTIRE, COMPLETE ⟨Please give me your *exclusive* attention.⟩
ex•clu•sive•ly *adv*

ex•crete \ik-'skrēt\ *vb* **ex•cret•ed**; **ex•cret•ing**
to separate and give off cellular waste matter from the body usually as urine or sweat

ex•cre•tion \ik-'skrē-shən\ *n*
1 the act or process of separating and giving off cellular waste matter from the body ⟨*excretion* of urine⟩
2 waste material given off from the body

ex•cre•to•ry \'ek-skrə-,tȯr-ē\ *adj*
of or relating to excretion : used in excreting ⟨The kidneys and bladder are part of the *excretory* system.⟩

ex•cur•sion \ik-'skər-zhən\ *n*
1 ▼ a brief trip for pleasure
2 a trip at special reduced rates

excursion 1: a family on an excursion

ex•cus•able \ik-ˈskyü-zə-bəl\ *adj* possible to excuse ⟨Minor mistakes are *excusable.*⟩

¹ex•cuse \ik-ˈskyüz\ *vb* **ex•cused; ex•cus•ing**
1 to make apology for ⟨I *excused* myself for being late.⟩
2 to overlook or pardon as of little importance ⟨Please *excuse* my clumsiness.⟩
3 to let off from doing something ⟨He was *excused* from chores for a week.⟩
4 to be an acceptable reason for ⟨Nothing *excuses* bad manners.⟩

²ex•cuse \ik-ˈskyüs\ *n*
1 a reason given for having done something wrong ⟨What's your *excuse* for being so late?⟩
2 something that is an acceptable reason for or justifies ⟨There is no *excuse* for bad behavior.⟩
3 a reason for doing something ⟨That's a good *excuse* for a party.⟩

ex•e•cute \ˈek-sə-ˌkyüt\ *vb* **ex•e•cut•ed; ex•e•cut•ing**
1 to kill according to a legal order
2 to put into effect : perform or carry out ⟨*execute* a plan⟩
3 to make according to a design ⟨The painting was *executed* in bright colors.⟩

ex•e•cu•tion \ˌek-sə-ˈkyü-shən\ *n*
1 the act of killing someone as a legal penalty
2 the act of doing or performing something ⟨*execution* of a plan⟩

¹ex•ec•u•tive \ig-ˈze-kyə-tiv\ *adj*
1 fitted for or relating to the managing or directing of things ⟨*executive* skills⟩
2 relating to the carrying out of the law and the conduct of public affairs ⟨the *executive* branch of government⟩

²executive *n*
1 a person who manages or directs ⟨a sales *executive*⟩
2 the executive branch of a government

ex•em•pli•fy \ig-ˈzem-plə-ˌfī\ *vb* **ex•em•pli•fied; ex•em•pli•fy•ing** to serve as an example of ⟨Salad *exemplifies* a healthy menu choice.⟩

¹ex•empt \ig-ˈzempt\ *adj* free or released from some requirement that other persons must meet or deal with ⟨I'm *exempt* from the test.⟩

²exempt *vb* **ex•empt•ed; ex•empt•ing** to release from a requirement that others must meet

ex•emp•tion \ig-ˈzemp-shən\ *n* freedom from having to do something that other people are required to do

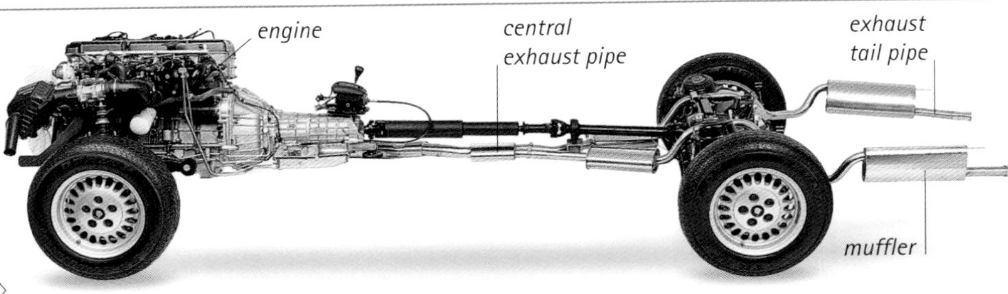

²exhaust 2: features of an automobile dual exhaust system

¹ex•er•cise \ˈek-sər-ˌsīz\ *n*
1 the act of putting into use, action, or practice ⟨the *exercise* of patience⟩
2 ▶ bodily activity for the sake of improving physical fitness
3 a school lesson or other task performed to develop skill : practice work : DRILL ⟨math *exercises*⟩
4 **exercises** *pl* a program of songs, speeches, and announcements of awards and honors ⟨graduation *exercises*⟩

¹exercise 2: a man jogging for exercise

²exercise *vb* **ex•er•cised; ex•er•cis•ing**
1 to put into use : EXERT ⟨He's *exercising* his authority.⟩
2 to take part in bodily activity for the sake of improving physical fitness
3 to use again and again to train or develop ⟨*exercise* a muscle⟩

ex•ert \ig-ˈzərt\ *vb* **ex•ert•ed; ex•ert•ing**
1 to put forth (as strength) : bring into use ⟨He *exerted* force to open the jar.⟩
2 to make an effort ⟨She *exerts* herself to help others.⟩

ex•er•tion \ig-ˈzər-shən\ *n*
1 the act of putting into use ⟨They won by the *exertion* of great effort.⟩
2 use of strength or ability ⟨The game requires physical *exertion.*⟩

ex•hale \eks-ˈhāl\ *vb* **ex•haled; ex•hal•ing**
1 to breathe out
2 to send forth : give off ⟨The pipe *exhaled* thick smoke.⟩

¹ex•haust \ig-ˈzȯst\ *vb* **ex•haust•ed; ex•haust•ing**
1 to tire out : FATIGUE ⟨Hard work will *exhaust* you.⟩
2 to use up completely ⟨We've *exhausted* our supplies.⟩
3 to try out all of ⟨We *exhausted* all options.⟩

²exhaust *n*
1 the gas that escapes from an engine
2 ▲ a system of pipes through which exhaust escapes

ex•haus•tion \ig-ˈzȯs-chən\ *n*
1 the condition of being very tired
2 the act of using up completely ⟨*exhaustion* of a water supply⟩

¹ex•hib•it \ig-ˈzi-bət\ *vb* **ex•hib•it•ed; ex•hib•it•ing**
1 to show by outward signs : REVEAL ⟨The child *exhibited* interest in music.⟩
2 to put on display ⟨I'm *exhibiting* my art.⟩
synonyms see SHOW

²exhibit *n*
1 an article or collection shown in an exhibition ⟨a museum *exhibit*⟩
2 an object or document presented as evidence in a court of law

ex•hi•bi•tion \ˌek-sə-ˈbi-shən\ *n*
1 the act of showing ⟨an *exhibition* of courage⟩
2 a public showing (as of athletic skill or works of art)

ex•hil•a•rate \ig-ˈzi-lə-ˌrāt\ *vb* **ex•hil•a•rat•ed; ex•hil•a•rat•ing** to make cheerful or excited

ex•hort \ig-ˈzȯrt\ *vb* **ex•hort•ed; ex•hort•ing** to try to influence by words or advice : urge strongly

¹ex•ile \ˈeg-ˌzīl, ˈek-ˌsīl\ *n*
1 the situation of a person who is forced to leave his or her own country ⟨He's living in *exile.*⟩
2 the period of time someone is forced to live away from his or her country ⟨a 20 year *exile*⟩
3 a person who is forced to leave his or her own country

[2]exile *vb* **ex•iled**; **ex•il•ing**
to force (someone) to leave his or her own country

ex•ist \ig-ˈzist\ *vb* **ex•ist•ed**; **ex•ist•ing**
1 to have actual being : be real ⟨Do unicorns *exist*?⟩
2 to be found : OCCUR ⟨Problems *exist* in every neighborhood.⟩
3 to continue to live ⟨She barely earned enough to *exist*.⟩

ex•is•tence \ig-ˈzi-stəns\ *n*
1 the fact or the condition of being or of being real ⟨The blue whale is the largest animal in *existence*.⟩
2 the state of being alive : LIFE

[1]ex•it \ˈeg-zət, ˈek-sət\ *n*
1 the act of going out of or away from a place : DEPARTURE ⟨He made his *exit*.⟩
2 a way of getting out of a place

[2]exit *vb* **ex•it•ed**; **ex•it•ing**
LEAVE 5, DEPART

ex•o•dus \ˈek-sə-dəs\ *n*
the departure of a large number of people at the same time

ex•or•bi•tant \ig-ˈzȯr-bə-tənt\ *adj*
more than what is fair, reasonable, or expected ⟨*exorbitant* prices⟩

exo•sphere \ˈek-sō-ˌsfir\ *n*
the outermost region of the atmosphere

ex•ot•ic \ig-ˈzä-tik\ *adj*
1 very different, strange, or unusual
2 introduced from another country : not native ⟨*exotic* plants⟩

ex•pand \ik-ˈspand\ *vb* **ex•pand•ed**; **ex•pand•ing**
1 to grow or increase in size, number, or amount ⟨The airport is *expanding*.⟩
2 to open wide : UNFOLD ⟨The eagle's wings *expanded*.⟩
3 to take up or cause to take up more space ⟨Metals *expand* under heat.⟩
4 to speak or write about in greater detail ⟨Would you *expand* on that idea?⟩

ex•panse \ik-ˈspans\ *n*
a wide area or stretch ⟨an *expanse* of desert⟩

ex•pan•sion \ik-ˈspan-shən\ *n*
the act of growing or increasing : ENLARGEMENT

ex•pect \ik-ˈspekt\ *vb* **ex•pect•ed**; **ex•pect•ing**
1 to think that something probably will be or happen ⟨They *expect* rain.⟩
2 to await the arrival of ⟨We're *expecting* guests.⟩
3 to consider to be obliged ⟨I *expect* you to pay your debts.⟩
4 to consider reasonable, due, or necessary ⟨I *expect* your attention.⟩

ex•pec•tant \ik-ˈspek-tənt\ *adj*
1 looking forward to or waiting for something
2 awaiting the birth of a child ⟨an *expectant* mother⟩

ex•pec•ta•tion \ˌek-ˌspek-ˈtā-shən\ *n*
1 the state of looking forward to or waiting for something ⟨The crowd waited in *expectation* for her.⟩
2 something expected ⟨The *expectation* was for a win.⟩

ex•pe•di•ent \ik-ˈspē-dē-ənt\ *adj*
providing a quick and easy way to accomplish something ⟨an *expedient* solution⟩
ex•pe•di•ent•ly *adv*

ex•pe•di•tion \ˌek-spə-ˈdi-shən\ *n*
1 a journey for a particular purpose ⟨a scientific *expedition*⟩
2 a group of people traveling for exploration or adventure

ex•pel \ik-ˈspel\ *vb* **ex•pelled**; **ex•pel•ling**
1 to force to leave ⟨He was *expelled* from school.⟩
2 to force out ⟨*expel* air from lungs⟩

ex•pend \ik-ˈspend\ *vb* **ex•pend•ed**; **ex•pend•ing**
1 to pay out : SPEND
2 to use up ⟨He *expended* a lot of energy.⟩

ex•pen•di•ture \ik-ˈspen-di-chər\ *n*
1 the act of spending (as money, time, or energy)
2 something that is spent ⟨Keep a record of your *expenditures*.⟩

ex•pense \ik-ˈspens\ *n*
1 something spent or required to be spent : COST
2 a cause for spending ⟨A car can be a great *expense*.⟩

ex•pen•sive \ik-ˈspen-siv\ *adj*
COSTLY 1

[1]ex•pe•ri•ence \ik-ˈspir-ē-əns\ *n*
1 the process of living through an event or events ⟨You learn by *experience*.⟩
2 the skill or knowledge gained by actually doing a thing ⟨The job requires someone with *experience*.⟩
3 something that someone has actually done or lived through ⟨She told us about her *experience* flying a plane.⟩

[2]experience *vb* **ex•pe•ri•enced**; **ex•pe•ri•enc•ing**
to undergo or live through : have experience of

ex•pe•ri•enced \ik-ˈspir-ē-ənst\ *adj*
made skillful or wise from having lived through or undergone something ⟨an *experienced* sailor⟩

[1]ex•per•i•ment \ik-ˈsper-ə-mənt\ *n*
▼ a trial or test made to find out about something

[1]experiment: an experiment to measure the density of different liquids and the weight of different objects

[2]ex•per•i•ment \ik-ˈsper-ə-ˌment\ *vb* **ex•per•i•ment•ed**; **ex•per•i•ment•ing**
to try or test a new way, idea, or activity : to make experiments

ex•per•i•men•tal \ik-ˌsper-ə-ˈmen-tᵊl\ *adj*
relating to, based on, or used for experiment ⟨He's trying an *experimental* treatment for the disease.⟩

[1]ex•pert \ˈek-ˌspərt, ik-ˈspərt\ *adj*
showing special skill or knowledge gained from experience or training ⟨*expert* advice⟩ ⟨an *expert* salesperson⟩
ex•pert•ly *adv*

[2]ex•pert \ˈek-ˌspərt\ *n*
a person with special skill or knowledge of a subject

ex•per•tise \ˌek-spər-ˈtēz, -ˈtēs\ *n*
the skill or knowledge of an expert

ex•pi•ra•tion \ˌek-spə-ˈrā-shən\ *n*
1 the end of something that lasts for a certain period of time ⟨*expiration* of a coupon⟩
2 the act of breathing out

ex•pire \ik-ˈspīr\ *vb* **ex•pired**; **ex•pir•ing**
1 to come to an end ⟨Your membership *expired*.⟩
2 [1]DIE 1
3 to breathe out : EXHALE

ex•plain \ik-ˈsplān\ *vb* **ex•plained**; **ex•plain•ing**
1 to make clear : CLARIFY ⟨Let me *explain* how it works.⟩
2 to give the reasons for or cause of ⟨Please *explain* why you're late.⟩

ex•pla•na•tion \ˌek-splə-ˈnā-shən\ *n*
1 the act or process of making clear or giving reasons for
2 a statement that makes something clear or gives reasons for something

ex•plan•a•to•ry \ik-ˈspla-nə-ˌtȯr-ē\ *adj* giving explanation ⟨*explanatory* notes⟩

ex•plic•it \ik-ˈspli-sət\ *adj* so clear in statement that there is no doubt about the meaning ⟨*explicit* instructions⟩

ex•plode \ik-ˈsplōd\ *vb* **ex•plod•ed**; **ex•plod•ing**
1 to burst or cause to burst with violence and noise ⟨The bomb *exploded*.⟩
2 to suddenly show or say with great emotion ⟨He *exploded* with anger.⟩

[1]**ex•ploit** \ˈek-ˌsplȯit\ *n* an exciting or daring act

[2]**ex•ploit** \ik-ˈsplȯit\ *vb* **ex•ploit•ed**; **ex•ploit•ing**
1 to get the value or use out of ⟨*exploit* an opportunity⟩
2 to take unfair advantage of ⟨He had a reputation for *exploiting* his workers.⟩

ex•plo•ra•tion \ˌek-splə-ˈrā-shən\ *n* the act or an instance of searching through or into

ex•plore \ik-ˈsplȯr\ *vb* **ex•plored**; **ex•plor•ing**
1 to search through or into : study closely ⟨Doctors *explored* the spread of the disease.⟩
2 to go into or through for purposes of discovery or adventure ⟨*explore* a cave⟩
ex•plor•er \ik-ˈsplȯr-ər\ *n*

ex•plo•sion \ik-ˈsplō-zhən\ *n*
1 a sudden and noisy bursting (as of a bomb) : the act of exploding
2 a sudden outburst of feeling

[1]**ex•plo•sive** \ik-ˈsplō-siv, -ziv\ *adj*
1 able to cause explosion ⟨the *explosive* power of gunpowder⟩
2 tending to show anger easily : likely to explode ⟨an *explosive* temper⟩
ex•plo•sive•ly *adv*

[2]**explosive** *n* a substance that is used to cause an explosion

ex•po•nent \ik-ˈspō-nənt\ *n* a numeral written above and to the right of a number to show how many times the number is to be used as a factor ⟨The *exponent* 3 in 10^3 indicates 10 × 10 × 10.⟩

[1]**ex•port** \ek-ˈspȯrt\ *vb* **ex•port•ed**; **ex•port•ing** to send a product to another country to sell it

[2]**ex•port** \ˈek-ˌspȯrt\ *n*
1 something that is sent to another country to be sold ⟨Oil is Saudi Arabia's most important *export*.⟩
2 the act of sending a product to another country to be sold

ex•pose \ik-ˈspōz\ *vb* **ex•posed**; **ex•pos•ing**
1 to leave without protection, shelter, or care : subject to a harmful condition ⟨The plants were *exposed* to an early frost.⟩
2 to cause to be affected or influenced by something ⟨She *exposed* her students to music of different countries.⟩
3 to let light strike the photographic film or plate in taking a picture
4 to make known : REVEAL ⟨Reporters *exposed* a dishonest scheme.⟩

ex•po•si•tion \ˌek-spə-ˈzi-shən\ *n*
1 an explanation of something
2 a public exhibition

ex•po•sure \ik-ˈspō-zhər\ *n*
1 the fact or condition of being subject to some effect or influence ⟨*exposure* to germs⟩ ⟨*exposure* to great art⟩
2 the condition that results from being unprotected especially from severe weather (as extreme cold) ⟨The child suffered from *exposure*.⟩
3 an act of making something public ⟨They were stopped by the *exposure* of the plot.⟩
4 the act of letting light strike a photographic film or the time during which light strikes a film
5 a section of a roll of film for one picture
6 position with respect to direction ⟨The room has a southern *exposure*.⟩

ex•pound \ik-ˈspau̇nd\ *vb* **ex•pound•ed**; **ex•pound•ing** EXPLAIN 1, INTERPRET ⟨Let me *expound* my theory.⟩

[1]**ex•press** \ik-ˈspres\ *vb* **ex•pressed**; **ex•press•ing**
1 to make known especially in words ⟨I *expressed* my surprise.⟩
2 to represent by a sign or symbol ⟨The amount was *expressed* as a percentage.⟩
3 to send by a quick method of delivery

[2]**express** *adj*
1 clearly stated ⟨an *express* order⟩
2 of a certain sort ⟨I came for an *express* purpose.⟩
3 sent or traveling at high speed ⟨*express* mail⟩

[3]**express** *vb*
1 a system for the quick transportation of goods ⟨Send your package by *express*.⟩
2 a vehicle (as a train or elevator) run at special speed with few or no stops

ex•pres•sion \ik-ˈspre-shən\ *n*
1 the act or process of making known especially in words
2 a meaningful word or saying ⟨Grandpa uses old-fashioned *expressions*.⟩
3 the look on someone's face ⟨She had a pleased *expression*.⟩
4 a way of speaking, singing, or playing that shows mood or feeling ⟨She read her lines with *expression*.⟩

ex•pres•sive \ik-ˈspre-siv\ *adj*
1 showing emotions : full of expression ⟨*expressive* eyes⟩
2 making something known ⟨Her story is *expressive* of her mood.⟩
ex•pres•sive•ly *adv*

ex•press•ly \ik-ˈspres-lē\ *adv* for the stated purpose : ESPECIALLY ⟨We came *expressly* to see her.⟩

ex•press•way \ik-ˈspres-ˌwā\ *n* ▼a highway for rapid traffic

expressway: a six-lane expressway

ex•pul•sion \ik-'spəl-shən\ *n*
the act of forcing to leave : the state of being forced to leave

ex•qui•site \ek-'skwi-zət, 'ek-skwi-\ *adj*
1 finely made or done ⟨*exquisite* workmanship⟩
2 very pleasing (as through beauty) ⟨*exquisite* roses⟩
3 INTENSE 1, EXTREME ⟨*exquisite* pain⟩

ex•tend \ik-'stend\ *vb* **ex•tend•ed**; **ex•tend•ing**
1 to hold out ⟨*extend* a hand⟩
2 to stretch out or across something ⟨A bridge *extends* across the stream.⟩
3 to make longer ⟨*extend* a visit⟩
4 [1]STRETCH 2 ⟨*extend* a sail⟩
5 ENLARGE ⟨*extend* the meaning of a word⟩

ex•ten•sion \ik-'sten-shən\ *n*
1 the act of making something longer or greater ⟨*extension* of the sail⟩
2 an increase in length or time
3 ▼ a part forming an addition or enlargement

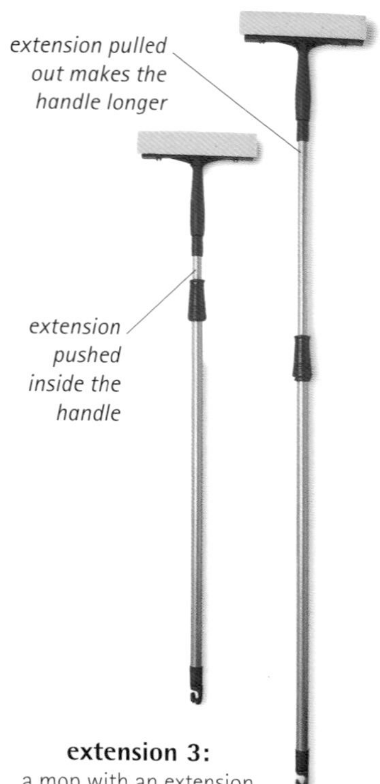

extension 3: a mop with an extension

ex•ten•sive \ik-'sten-siv\ *adj*
including or affecting many things ⟨The storm caused *extensive* damage.⟩

ex•tent \ik-'stent\ *n*
1 the distance or range that is covered or affected by something
2 the point, degree, or limit to which something reaches or extends ⟨the *extent* of our property⟩

[1]**ex•te•ri•or** \ek-'stir-ē-ər\ *adj*
EXTERNAL

[2]**exterior** *n*
1 an external part or surface ⟨the building's *exterior*⟩
2 the way someone appears ⟨His tough *exterior* hides a soft heart.⟩

ex•ter•mi•nate \ik-'stər-mə-,nāt\ *vb* **ex•ter•mi•nat•ed**; **ex•ter•mi•nat•ing**
to get rid of completely : wipe out ⟨*exterminate* cockroaches⟩
ex•ter•mi•na•tion \-,stər-mə-'nā-shən\ *n*

ex•ter•nal \ek-'stər-nᵊl\ *adj*
situated on or relating to the outside : OUTSIDE

ex•tinct \ik-'stiŋkt\ *adj*
1 no longer active ⟨an *extinct* volcano⟩
2 no longer existing ⟨Dinosaurs are *extinct*.⟩

ex•tinc•tion \ik-'stiŋk-shən\ *n*
the state of being, becoming, or making extinct

ex•tin•guish \ik-'stiŋ-gwish\ *vb* **ex•tin•guished**; **ex•tin•guish•ing**
1 to cause to stop burning
2 to cause to die out ⟨More bad news *extinguished* all hope.⟩
ex•tin•guish•er *n*

ex•tol \ik-'stōl\ *vb* **ex•tolled**; **ex•tol•ling**
to praise highly : GLORIFY

[1]**ex•tra** \'ek-strə\ *adj*
being more than what is usual, expected, or due ⟨I need *extra* help.⟩

[2]**extra** *adv*
beyond the usual size, amount, or extent ⟨*extra* large eggs⟩ ⟨I took an *extra* long walk.⟩

[3]**extra** *n*
1 something additional ⟨The vacation package included some nice *extras*.⟩
2 an added charge
3 a special edition of a newspaper
4 a person hired for a group scene (as in a movie)

extra- *prefix*
outside : beyond

[1]**ex•tract** \ik-'strakt\ *vb* **ex•tract•ed**; **ex•tract•ing**
1 to remove by pulling ⟨*extract* a tooth⟩
2 to get out by pressing, distilling, or by a chemical process ⟨*extract* juice⟩
3 to choose and take out for separate use ⟨He *extracted* a few lines from a poem.⟩

[2]**ex•tract** \'ek-,strakt\ *n*
1 a selection from a writing
2 ▶ a product obtained by pressing, distilling, or by a chemical process ⟨vanilla *extract*⟩

ex•trac•tion \ik-'strak-shən\ *n*
1 the act of pulling out ⟨the *extraction* of a tooth⟩
2 ORIGIN 2, DESCENT ⟨of French *extraction*⟩

ex•tra•cur•ric•u•lar \,ek-strə-kə-'ri-kyə-lər\ *adj*
relating to activities (as athletics) that are offered by a school but are not part of the course of study

ex•traor•di•nary \ik-'strȯr-də-,ner-ē, ,ek-strə-'ȯr-\ *adj*
so unusual as to be remarkable ⟨She has *extraordinary* talent.⟩
ex•traor•di•nari•ly \ik-,strȯr-də-'ner-ə-lē, ,ek-strə-,ȯr-də-'ner-\ *adv*

ex•trav•a•gance \ik-'stra-və-gəns\ *n*
1 the wasteful or careless spending of money
2 something that is wasteful especially of money ⟨A new car is an *extravagance* he can't afford.⟩
3 the quality or fact of being wasteful especially of money

ex•trav•a•gant \ik-'stra-və-gənt\ *adj*
1 going beyond what is reasonable or suitable ⟨*extravagant* praise⟩
2 wasteful especially of money
ex•trav•a•gant•ly *adv*

[1]**ex•treme** \ik-'strēm\ *adj*
1 very great in degree or severity ⟨*extreme* heat⟩ ⟨*extreme* poverty⟩
2 farthest away ⟨the *extreme* edge⟩
3 more demanding or dangerous than normal ⟨*extreme* sports⟩
ex•treme•ly *adv*

[2]**extreme** *n*
1 something as far as possible from a center or from its opposite ⟨*extremes* of heat and cold⟩
2 the greatest possible degree : MAXIMUM ⟨He pushed the athletes to the *extreme*.⟩

ex•trem•i•ty \ik-'strem-ə-tē\ *n*, *pl* **ex•trem•i•ties**
1 the farthest limit, point, or part ⟨the *extremity* of the island⟩
2 an end part (as a foot) of a limb of the body
3 an extreme degree (as of emotion)

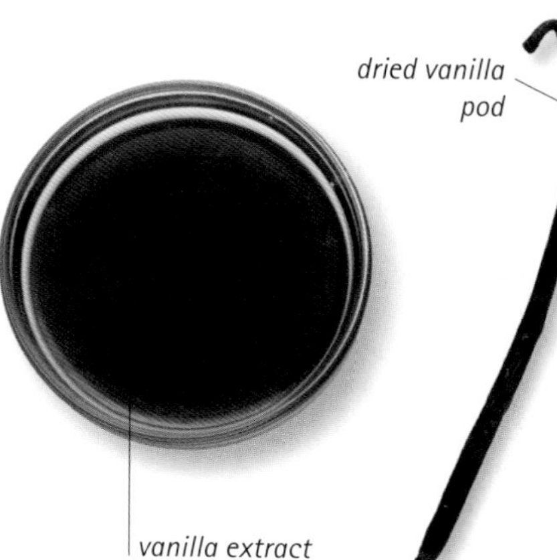

[2]**extract 2:** vanilla extract

▶ [1]eye 1

The human eye lies in a bony socket in the skull. Light rays enter the pupil, and are focused by the cornea and lens to form upside-down images on the retina. The images are then transmitted as impulses along the optic nerve to the brain, which interprets them so that they appear right way up.

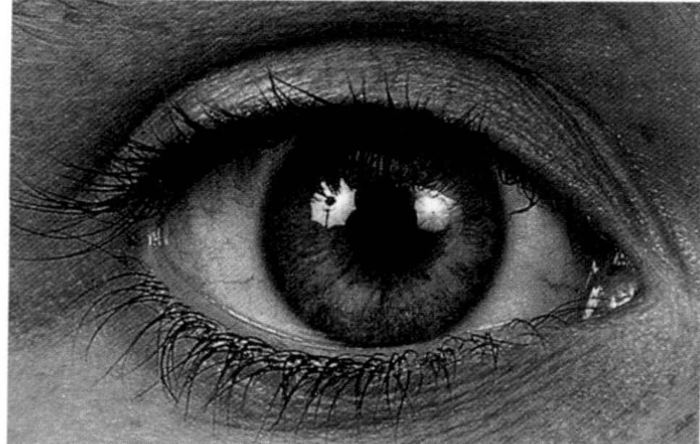

front view of the human eye

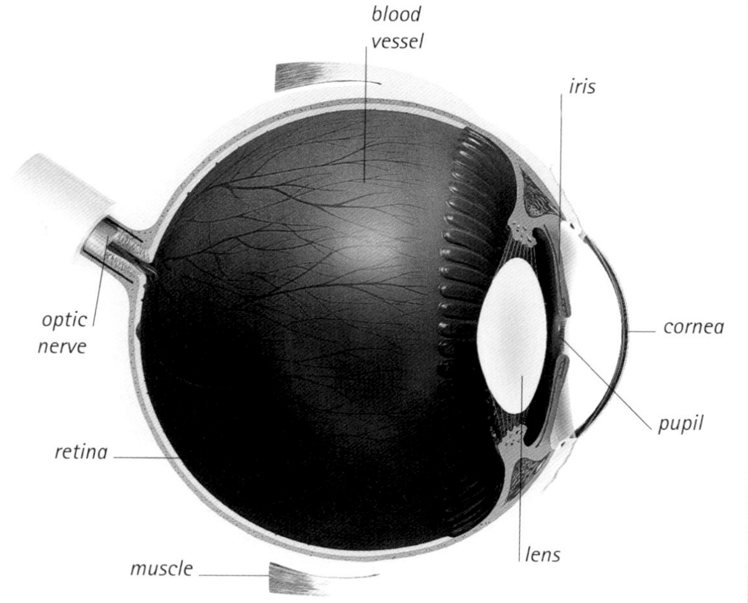

model of a human eye in cross-section

ex•tri•cate \'ek-strə-,kāt\ *vb* **ex•tri•cat•ed**; **ex•tri•cat•ing**
to free from a trap or difficulty

ex•u•ber•ant \ig-'zü-bə-rənt\ *adj*
filled with energy and enthusiasm
ex•u•ber•ance \-bə-rəns\ *n*

ex•ult \ig-'zəlt\ *vb* **ex•ult•ed**; **ex•ult•ing**
to feel or show great happiness : REJOICE

▶ **Word History** When we exult we feel like jumping for joy. At first the English word *exult* meant "to jump for joy." *Exult* came from a Latin word *exsultare* that meant literally "to jump up." This word was formed from the prefix *ex-*, meaning "out," and the verb *saltare*, meaning "to jump."

ex•ul•tant \ig-'zəl-tᵊnt\ *adj*
very happy and excited
ex•ul•tant•ly *adv*

-ey see **-y**

[1]**eye** \'ī\ *n*
1 ▲ the organ of seeing that in vertebrates is a round organ filled with a jellylike material, is located in a bony cavity in the skull, and has a lens which focuses light on the retina
2 the eye along with its surrounding parts (as the eyelids)
3 the colored surface of the iris ⟨He has blue *eyes*.⟩
4 the ability to see ⟨I have good *eyes*.⟩
5 the ability to recognize or appreciate ⟨He has a good *eye* for color.⟩
6 [2]GLANCE ⟨It caught my *eye*.⟩
7 close attention : WATCH ⟨Keep an *eye* on dinner.⟩
8 JUDGMENT 1 ⟨They are guilty in the *eyes* of the law.⟩
9 something like or suggesting an eye ⟨the *eye* of a needle⟩
10 the center of something ⟨the *eye* of a hurricane⟩
eyed \'īd\ *adj*
eye•less \'ī-ləs\ *adj*

[2]**eye** *vb* **eyed**; **eye•ing** *or* **ey•ing**
to look at : watch closely ⟨They *eyed* the stranger suspiciously.⟩

eye•ball \'ī-,bȯl\ *n*
the whole eye

eye•brow \'ī-,brau̇\ *n*
the arch or ridge over the eye : the hair on the ridge over the eye

eye•drop•per \'ī-,drä-pər\ *n*
DROPPER

eye•glass \'ī-,glas\ *n*
1 a glass lens used to help a person to see clearly
2 **eyeglasses** *pl* GLASS 3

eye•lash \'ī-,lash\ *n*
one of the hairs that grow along the top of the eyelid

eye•let \'ī-lət\ *n*
1 ▶ a small hole (as in cloth or leather) for a lace or rope
2 GROMMET

eye•lid \'ī-,lid\ *n*
the thin movable fold of skin and muscle that can be closed over the eyeball

eye•piece \'ī-,pēs\ *n*
the lens or combination of lenses at the eye end of an optical instrument (as a microscope or telescope)

eye•sight \'ī-,sīt\ *n*
[1]SIGHT 4, VISION

eye•sore \'ī-,sȯr\ *n*
something that looks ugly ⟨That empty building is an *eyesore*.⟩

eye•tooth \'ī-'tüth\ *n*, *pl* **eye•teeth** \-'tēth\
a canine tooth of the upper jaw

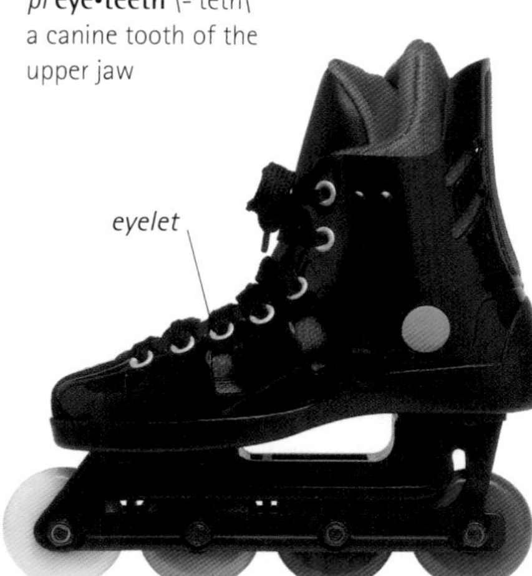

eyelet 1:
eyelets on an in-line skate

Ff

Sounds of F: The letter **F** makes one main sound, the sound heard in the words *fun* and *wolf.* In the word *of,* the letter **F** sounds like a **V**.

f \'ef\ *n, pl* **f's** *or* **fs** \'efs\ *often cap*
1 the sixth letter of the English alphabet
2 a grade that shows a student's work is failing
3 a musical note referred to by the letter F

F *abbr*
1 Fahrenheit
2 false

f. *abbr* female

fa \'fä\ *n*
the fourth note of the musical scale

fa•ble \'fā-bəl\ *n*
1 a story that is not true
2 a story in which animals speak and act like people and which is usually meant to teach a lesson

fab•ric \'fa-brik\ *n*
1 CLOTH 1
2 the basic structure ⟨the *fabric* of society⟩

fab•u•lous \'fa-byə-ləs\ *adj*
1 extremely good ⟨a *fabulous* trip⟩
2 very great in amount or size ⟨*fabulous* wealth⟩
3 told in or based on fable ⟨*fabulous* creatures⟩
fab•u•lous•ly *adv*

fa•cade \fə-'säd\ *n*
▶ the face or front of a building

¹face \'fās\ *n*
1 the front part of the head
2 an expression of the face ⟨a sad *face*⟩
3 outward appearance ⟨It looks easy on the *face* of it.⟩
4 a funny or silly expression
5 an expression showing displeasure
6 ¹RESPECT 1 ⟨He was afraid of losing *face.*⟩
7 a front, upper, or outer surface
8 one of the flat surfaces that bound a solid ⟨a *face* of a cube⟩

²face *vb* **faced; fac•ing**
1 to have the front or face toward ⟨The house *faces* east.⟩
2 to cover the front or surface of ⟨The building will be *faced* with marble.⟩
3 to oppose with determination ⟨*face* danger⟩

face–off \'fās-,ȯf\ *n*
1 a method of beginning play (as in hockey or lacrosse) in which the puck or ball is dropped between two opposing players
2 a clashing of forces or ideas ⟨a *face-off* between enemies⟩

fac•et \'fa-sət\ *n*
▶ one of the small flat surfaces on a cut gem

fa•ce•tious \fə-'sē-shəs\ *adj*
intended or trying to be funny ⟨a *facetious* remark⟩
fa•ce•tious•ly *adv*

face–to–face \,fās-tə-,fās\ *adv or adj*
within each other's presence ⟨spoke *face-to-face*⟩ ⟨a *face-to-face* meeting⟩

fa•cial \'fā-shəl\ *adj*
of or relating to the face ⟨*facial* hair⟩

fa•cil•i•tate \fə-'si-lə-,tāt\ *vb*
fa•cil•i•tat•ed; fa•cil•i•tat•ing
to make easier

facet: facets of a diamond

fa•cil•i•ty \fə-'si-lə-tē\ *n, pl* **fa•cil•i•ties**
1 something built for a particular purpose ⟨a sports *facility*⟩
2 something that makes an action, operation, or activity easier ⟨Our hotel room had cooking *facilities.*⟩
3 ease in doing something ⟨She handled the job with *facility.*⟩

facade of a 19th-century building in New York City

fac•sim•i•le \fak-ˈsi-mə-lē\ *n*, *pl* **fac•sim•i•les**
1 an exact copy
2 a system of sending and reproducing printed matter or pictures by means of signals sent over telephone lines

fact \ˈfakt\ *n*
1 something that really exists or has occurred ⟨Space travel is now a *fact.*⟩
2 a true piece of information
in fact in truth : ACTUALLY ⟨She got there early and *in fact* she was earliest.⟩

[1]**fac•tor** \ˈfak-tər\ *n*
1 something that helps produce a result ⟨Price was a *factor* in my decision.⟩
2 any of the numbers that when multiplied together form a product ⟨The *factors* of 6 are 1, 2, 3, and 6.⟩

[2]**factor** *vb* **fac•tored; fac•tor•ing**
1 to be considered in making a judgment ⟨Class participation will *factor* into your grade.⟩
2 to find the factors of a number

fac•to•ry \ˈfak-tə-rē, ˈfak-trē\ *n*, *pl* **fac•to•ries**
▶ a place where products are manufactured

fac•tu•al \ˈfak-chə-wəl\ *adj*
relating to or based on facts ⟨a *factual* report⟩
fac•tu•al•ly *adv*

fac•ul•ty \ˈfak-əl-tē\ *n*, *pl* **fac•ul•ties**
1 ability to do something : TALENT ⟨He has a *faculty* for making friends.⟩
2 one of the powers of the mind or body ⟨the *faculty* of hearing⟩
3 the teachers in a school or college

fad \ˈfad\ *n*
something that is very popular for a short time
synonyms see FASHION

fade \ˈfād\ *vb* **fad•ed; fad•ing**
1 to lose or cause to lose brightness of color
2 to dry up : WITHER ⟨The flowers were *fading.*⟩
3 to grow dim or faint ⟨The path *faded* out.⟩ ⟨Her memory *faded.*⟩

Fahr•en•heit \ˈfar-ən-ˌhīt\ *adj*
relating to or having a temperature scale on which the boiling point of water is at 212 degrees above the zero of the scale and the freezing point is at 32 degrees above zero

[1]**fail** \ˈfāl\ *vb* **failed; fail•ing**
1 to be unsuccessful ⟨He *failed* the test.⟩
2 to grade as not passing ⟨My teacher *failed* me.⟩
3 to stop functioning ⟨The engine *failed.*⟩
4 to be or become absent or not enough ⟨The water supply *failed.*⟩
5 to become bankrupt ⟨The business *failed.*⟩
6 [1]NEGLECT 2 ⟨Don't *fail* to ask if you need my help.⟩
7 DISAPPOINT, DESERT ⟨I need your help. Please don't *fail* me.⟩
8 to lose strength : WEAKEN ⟨She's *failing* in health.⟩
9 to fall short ⟨One drink *failed* to satisfy my thirst.⟩
10 to die away ⟨The family line *failed.*⟩

[2]**fail** *n*
FAILURE 2 ⟨We met daily without *fail.*⟩

fail•ing \ˈfā-liŋ\ *n*
a weakness or flaw in a person's character, behavior, or ability

factory: engines being assembled in an automobile factory

fail•ure \ˈfāl-yər\ *n*
1 a lack of success ⟨The experiment resulted in *failure.*⟩
2 the act of neglecting or forgetting to do or perform ⟨I was disappointed by his *failure* to keep a promise.⟩
3 an instance of not working properly ⟨power *failure*⟩ ⟨a *failure* of memory⟩
4 a loss of the ability to work normally ⟨heart *failure*⟩
5 someone or something that has not succeeded ⟨The new show was a *failure.*⟩
6 an instance of falling short ⟨crop *failure*⟩
7 BANKRUPTCY

[1]**faint** \ˈfānt\ *adj* **faint•er; faint•est**
1 not clear or plain : DIM ⟨*faint* handwriting⟩
2 weak or dizzy and likely to collapse ⟨I feel *faint.*⟩
3 lacking strength ⟨a *faint* attempt⟩ ⟨a *faint* breeze⟩
faint•ly *adv*
faint•ness *n*

[2]**faint** *vb* **faint•ed; faint•ing**
to suddenly lose consciousness

[3]**faint** *n*
an act or condition of suddenly losing consciousness

faint•heart•ed \ˈfānt-ˈhär-təd\ *adj*
COWARDLY 1

[1]**fair** \ˈfer\ *adj* **fair•er; fair•est**
1 not favoring one over another ⟨Everyone received *fair* treatment.⟩
2 observing the rules ⟨*fair* play⟩
3 neither good nor bad ⟨He's only a *fair* singer.⟩
4 not stormy or cloudy ⟨*fair* weather⟩
5 not dark ⟨*fair* hair⟩
6 attractive in appearance : BEAUTIFUL ⟨our *fair* city⟩
7 being within the foul lines ⟨a *fair* ball⟩
fair•ness *n*

[2]**fair** *adv*
according to the rules ⟨play *fair*⟩

[3]**fair** *n*
1 a large public event at which farm animals and products are shown and entertainment, amusements, and food are provided ⟨a county *fair*⟩
2 an event at which people gather to buy, sell, or get information ⟨a job *fair*⟩ ⟨a book *fair*⟩
3 a sale of articles for charity ⟨a church *fair*⟩

fair•ground \ˈfer-ˌgraủnd\ *n*
an area set aside for fairs, circuses, or exhibitions

fair•ly \ˈfer-lē\ *adv*
1 in a just and proper manner ⟨I was treated *fairly.*⟩
2 very close to ⟨He was *fairly* bursting with pride.⟩
3 for the most part : RATHER ⟨It's a *fairly* easy job.⟩

a b c d e f g h i j k l m n o p q r s t u v w x y z

fair•way \'fer-,wā\ *n*
the mowed part of a golf course between a tee and a green

[1]**fairy** \'fer-ē\ *n, pl* **fair•ies**
▼ an imaginary magical creature who has the form of a tiny human being

> ▶ **Word History** In Greek and Roman myth, the Fates were three goddesses who set the course of human life. There was nothing especially magical or charming about the Fates. Yet the Latin word *Fata*, "Fate," is the ultimate source of the English word *fairy*: *Fata* became Old French *fee*, which was borrowed into English as *faie* or *fay*. (*Fairy*, which originally meant "fairyland," is a derivative of *fay*.) In a few fairy tales, such as "Sleeping Beauty," fairies maintain the ability to strongly influence the destiny of humans.

[1]**fairy:** a girl dressed as a fairy

[2]**fairy** *adj*
relating to or like a fairy 〈a *fairy* princess〉

fairy•land \'fer-ē-,land\ *n*
1 an imaginary place where fairies live
2 a beautiful or magical place

fairy tale *n*
a simple children's story about magical creatures

faith \'fāth\ *n*
1 strong belief or trust 〈I have *faith* in our leaders.〉
2 belief in God
3 a system of religious beliefs : RELIGION 〈people of all *faiths*〉
4 loyalty to duty or to a person or thing 〈The team's true fans keep the *faith*.〉
synonyms see BELIEF

faith•ful \'fāth-fəl\ *adj*
1 firm in devotion or support 〈a *faithful* friend〉
2 RELIABLE 〈a *faithful* worker〉
3 true to the facts : ACCURATE 〈The model was a *faithful* copy of my grandfather's car.〉
faith•ful•ly \-fə-lē\ *adv*
faith•ful•ness *n*

> ▶ **Synonyms** FAITHFUL, LOYAL, and TRUE mean firm in devotion to something. FAITHFUL is used of someone who has a firm and constant devotion to something to which he or she is united by or as if by a promise or pledge. 〈Always be *faithful* to your duty.〉 LOYAL is used of someone who firmly refuses to desert or betray someone or something. 〈Most volunteers are *loyal* to their country.〉 TRUE is used of a person who is personally devoted to someone or something. 〈She was a *true* friend who would help in time of need.〉

faith•less \'fāth-ləs\ *adj*
not worthy of trust : DISLOYAL

> ▶ **Synonyms** FAITHLESS, DISLOYAL, and TRAITOROUS mean not being true to something that has a right to a person's loyalty. FAITHLESS is used when a person breaks a promise or pledge to remain loyal to someone or something. 〈Our *faithless* friends left us at the first sign of trouble.〉 DISLOYAL is used when a person is unfaithful to someone or something that has the right to expect loyalty. 〈The *disloyal* citizens will be punished.〉 TRAITOROUS is used for actual treason or a betrayal of trust. 〈The *traitorous* soldier was giving secrets to the enemy.〉

[1]**fake** \'fāk\ *adj*
not true or real 〈The *fake* spider frightened me.〉

[2]**fake** *n*
a person or thing that is not really what is pretended 〈The diamond is a *fake*.〉

[3]**fake** *vb*
faked; **fak•ing**
1 PRETEND 2 〈*faking* surprise〉
2 to change or treat in a way that gives a false effect 〈She *faked* the test results.〉
3 to imitate in order to deceive 〈*fake* a signature〉

fal•con \'fal-kən, 'fȯl-\ *n*
1 a hawk trained for use in hunting small game
2 ▶ any of several small hawks with long wings and swift flight

falcon 2: a Lanner falcon

fal•con•ry \'fal-kən-rē, 'fȯl-\ *n*
the sport of hunting with a falcon

[1]**fall** \'fȯl\ *vb* **fell** \'fel\; **fall•en** \'fȯ-lən\; **fall•ing**
1 to come or go down freely by the force of gravity 〈An apple *fell* from the tree.〉
2 to come as if by falling 〈Night *fell* before we got home.〉
3 to become lower (as in degree or value) 〈The temperature *fell* ten degrees.〉
4 to topple from an upright position 〈The tree *fell*.〉
5 to collapse wounded or dead 〈Too many soldiers have *fallen* in battle.〉
6 to become captured 〈The city *fell* to the enemy.〉
7 to occur at a certain time 〈This year my birthday *falls* on a Monday.〉
8 to pass from one condition of body or mind to another 〈*fall* asleep〉 〈*fall* ill〉
fall back [2]RETREAT 1
fall short to fail to be as good or successful as expected 〈The sequel to my favorite movie *fell short*.〉

[2]**fall** *n*
1 the act or an instance of going or coming down by the force of gravity 〈a *fall* from a horse〉
2 AUTUMN
3 a thing or quantity that falls 〈a heavy *fall* of snow〉
4 a loss of greatness : DOWNFALL 〈the *fall* of an empire〉
5 WATERFALL — usually used in pl. 〈Niagara *Falls*〉
6 a decrease in size, amount, or value 〈a *fall* in prices〉
7 the distance something falls 〈a *fall* of three feet〉

fal•la•cy \'fa-lə-sē\ *n, pl* **fal•la•cies**
1 a false or mistaken idea
2 false reasoning

fall•out \'fȯl-,au̇t\ *n*
1 the usually radioactive particles falling through the atmosphere as a result of a nuclear explosion
2 the bad result of something ⟨He suffered the *fallout* from his poor decision.⟩

fal•low \'fa-lō\ *adj*
not tilled or planted ⟨*fallow* fields⟩

fallow deer *n*
▼a small European deer with broad antlers and a pale yellowish coat spotted with white in summer

2 the quality or state of being not true or genuine ⟨The jury will determine the truth or *falsity* of the statement.⟩

fal•ter \'fȯl-tər\ *vb* **fal•tered**; **fal•ter•ing**
1 to move unsteadily : WAVER
2 to hesitate in speech
3 to hesitate in purpose or action

fame \'fām\ *n*
the fact or condition of being known or recognized by many people

famed \'fāmd\ *adj*
known widely and well : FAMOUS ⟨a *famed* artist⟩

fa•mil•ial \fə-'mil-yəl\ *adj*
relating to or typical of a family

fam•i•ly \'fa-mə-lē, 'fam-lē\ *n, pl* **fam•i•lies**
1 a social group made up of parents and their children
2 a group of people who come from the same ancestor ⟨You resemble your mother's side of the *family*.⟩
3 a group of people living together : HOUSEHOLD
4 a group of things sharing certain characteristics ⟨a *family* of languages⟩
5▼ a group of related living things (as plants or animals) that ranks above the genus and below the order in scientific classification ⟨Domestic cats, lions, and tigers are some of the members of the cat *family*.⟩

fallow deer

family 5:
three members of the rose family

false \'fȯls\ *adj* **fals•er**; **fals•est**
1 not true, genuine, or honest ⟨*false* testimony⟩ ⟨*false* documents⟩ ⟨*false* teeth⟩
2 not faithful or loyal ⟨*false* friends⟩
3 not based on facts or sound judgment ⟨a *false* feeling of security⟩
4 CARELESS 2
false•ly *adv*

false *adv*
in a dishonest or misleading manner ⟨He spoke *false*.⟩

alse•hood \'fȯls-,hu̇d\ *n*
1 ^{3}LIE
2 the habit of lying ⟨His *falsehood* ruined our friendship.⟩

al•si•fy \'fȯl-sə-,fī\ *vb* **fal•si•fied**; **fal•si•fy•ing**
to change in order to deceive ⟨They were caught *falsifying* their records.⟩

al•si•ty \'fȯl-sə-tē\ *n, pl* **fal•si•ties**
1 ^{3}LIE

fa•mil•iar \fə-'mil-yər\ *adj*
1 often seen, heard, or experienced ⟨She read us a *familiar* story.⟩
2 closely acquainted : INTIMATE ⟨*familiar* friends⟩
3 having a good knowledge of ⟨Parents should be *familiar* with their children's schools.⟩
4 INFORMAL 1 ⟨He spoke in a *familiar* way.⟩
5 too friendly or bold
synonyms see COMMON

fa•mil•iar•i•ty \fə-,mil-'yer-ə-tē, -,mil-ē-'er-\ *n, pl* **fa•mil•iar•i•ties**
1 close friendship : INTIMACY
2 good knowledge of something ⟨His *familiarity* with the trail was a big advantage to us.⟩
3 INFORMALITY

fa•mil•iar•ize \fə-'mil-yə-,rīz\ *vb* **fa•mil•iar•ized**; **fa•mil•iar•iz•ing**
to make knowledgeable about ⟨He *familiarized* his students with the library.⟩

fam•ine \'fa-mən\ *n*
a very great shortage of food that affects many people over a wide area

fam•ish \'fa-mish\ *vb* **fam•ished**; **fam•ish•ing**
STARVE

fam•ished \'fa-misht\ *adj*
very hungry

fa•mous \'fā-məs\ *adj*
very well-known

fa•mous•ly \'fā-məs-lē\ *adv*
very well ⟨We got along *famously*.⟩

safety cage

rotating blade

[1]fan \ˈfan\ *n*
1 ▶ a machine or device that is used for producing a current of air
2 something having the shape of a half circle
fan•like \-ˌlīk\ *adj*

[1]fan 1: an electric fan

[2]fan *vb* **fanned**; **fan•ning**
1 to direct a current of air upon with a fan
2 to strike out in baseball

[3]fan *n*
an enthusiastic follower or admirer

[1]fa•nat•ic \fə-ˈna-tik\ *adj*
very or overly enthusiastic or devoted

▶ **Word History** In Latin the adjective *fanaticus*, a derivative of *fanum*, "temple," meant literally "of a temple," though the more common sense was "inspired by a god" or "frenzied." The word was borrowed into English as *fanatic* in the 1500s with this sense. In the following century the word was applied to members of certain Protestant groups who argued for their beliefs—in the view of most people—with excessive enthusiasm, acting as if they were divinely inspired. Eventually, *fanatic* was applied to anyone who showed extreme devotion to a cause.

[2]fanatic *n*
a very enthusiastic supporter or admirer

fan•ci•ful \ˈfan-si-fəl\ *adj*
1 showing free use of the imagination ⟨He gave his children *fanciful* names.⟩
2 coming from the imagination ⟨a *fanciful* tale⟩
fan•ci•ful•ly \-fə-lē\ *adv*

[1]fan•cy \ˈfan-sē\ *adj* **fan•ci•er**; **fan•ci•est**
1 not plain or ordinary ⟨a *fancy* dress⟩
2 being above the average (as in quality or price) ⟨*fancy* fruits⟩
3 done with great skill and grace ⟨*fancy* diving⟩
fan•ci•ly \ˈfan-sə-lē\ *adv*
fan•ci•ness \-sē-nəs\ *n*

[2]fancy *n, pl* **fan•cies**
1 IMAGINATION 1 ⟨a flight of *fancy*⟩
2 LIKING ⟨She took a *fancy* to her new neighbors.⟩
3 IDEA 2, NOTION

[3]fancy *vb* **fan•cied**; **fan•cy•ing**
1 to have a liking for ⟨I've never *fancied* Halloween.⟩
2 IMAGINE 1

fang \ˈfaŋ\ *n*
1 one of the long sharp teeth by which an animal seizes and holds its prey
2 one of the usually two long hollow or grooved teeth by which a poisonous snake injects its poison
fanged \ˈfaŋd\ *adj*

fan•ny \ˈfa-nē\ *n*
a person's rear

fan•tas•tic \fan-ˈta-stik\ *adj*
1 produced by or like something produced by the imagination ⟨a *fantastic* scheme⟩
2 extremely good ⟨That was a *fantastic* meal.⟩
3 barely believable ⟨We moved at a *fantastic* speed.⟩
fan•tas•ti•cal•ly \-sti-kə-lē\ *adv*

fan•ta•sy \ˈfan-tə-sē, -zē\ *n, pl* **fan•ta•sies**
1 IMAGINATION 1 ⟨The plan was a product of pure *fantasy*.⟩
2 something produced by the imagination ⟨His *fantasy* is to win a million dollars.⟩

FAQ \ˈfak, ˌef-ˌā-ˈkyü\ *abbr*
frequently asked question, frequently asked questions — used to refer to a list of questions and answers to typical questions that users of a Web site might have

[1]far \ˈfär\ *adv* **far•ther** \ˈfär-t͟hər\ *or* **fur•ther** \ˈfər-\; **far•thest** \ˈfär-t͟həst\ *or* **fur•thest** \ˈfər-\
1 at or to a great distance in space or time ⟨*far* from home⟩ ⟨*far* into the night⟩
2 to a great extent : MUCH ⟨*far* better⟩
3 to or at a definite distance or point ⟨I walked as *far* as I could.⟩
4 to an advanced point ⟨A smart student can go *far*.⟩
by far by a great extent or degree ⟨better *by far*⟩

[2]far *adj* **far•ther** *or* **fur•ther**; **far•thest** *or* **fur•thest**
1 very distant in space or time ⟨a *far* country⟩
2 the more distant of two ⟨the *far* side of the stream⟩
3 [1]LONG 2 ⟨a *far* journey⟩

far•away \ˈfär-ə-ˌwā\ *adj*
1 [1]REMOTE 1, DISTANT ⟨*faraway* lands⟩
2 appearing as if lost in a daydream ⟨He had a *faraway* look in his eyes.⟩

farce \ˈfärs\ *n*
something that is ridiculous ⟨Instead of being fair, the trial was a *farce*.⟩

[1]fare \ˈfer\ *vb* **fared**; **far•ing**
to get along : SUCCEED ⟨Businesses at that location don't *fare* very well.⟩

[2]fare *n*
1 the money a person pays to travel (as on a bus)
2 a person paying a fare
3 FOOD 1 ⟨Mexican *fare*⟩

[1]fare•well \fer-ˈwel\ *n*
[2]GOOD-BYE

[2]fare•well \ˈfer-ˌwel\ *adj*
relating to a time or act of leaving : FINAL

far•fetched \ˈfär-ˈfecht\ *adj*
not likely to be true ⟨a *farfetched* tale⟩

[1]farm \ˈfärm\ *n*
1 ▼ a piece of land used for raising crops or animals
2 an area of water where fish or shellfish are grown

[2]farm *vb* **farmed**; **farm•ing**
1 to use for raising crops or animals ⟨They *farm* the land.⟩
2 to work on or run a farm
farm•er *n*

[1]farm 1: a farmer working on his farm

farm•hand \'färm-,hand\ *n*
a farm worker

farm•ing \'fär-miŋ\ *n*
the occupation or business of running a farm

farm•yard \'färm-,yärd\ *n*
the yard around or enclosed by farm buildings

far–off \'fär-'ȯf\ *adj*
distant in time or space

far–reach•ing \'fär-'rē-chiŋ\ *adj*
having a wide range, influence, or effect ⟨*far-reaching* changes⟩

far•sight•ed \'fär-'sī-təd\ *adj*
1 able to see distant things more clearly than near ones
2 able to judge how something will work out in the future
far•sight•ed•ness *n*

[1]**far•ther** \'fär-t͟hər\ *adv*
1 at or to a greater distance or more advanced point ⟨They drove *farther* north.⟩
2 more completely ⟨The class grew interested as she explained her idea *farther*.⟩

[2]**farther** *adj*
more distant ⟨the *farther* hill⟩

far•thest \'fär-t͟həst\ *adj*
most distant ⟨the *farthest* end of the beach⟩

farthest *adv*
1 to or at the greatest distance in space or time ⟨She ran *farthest*.⟩
2 to the most advanced point

fas•ci•nate \'fa-sə-,nāt\ *vb* **fas•ci•nat•ed**; **fas•ci•nat•ing**
1 to seize and hold the attention of
2 to attract greatly

fas•ci•nat•ing \'fa-sə-,nā-tiŋ\ *adj*
extremely interesting or charming ⟨a *fascinating* story⟩

fas•ci•na•tion \,fa-sə-'nā-shən\ *n*
a great interest in or attraction to something

fas•cism \'fa-,shi-zəm\ *n, often cap*
a political system headed by a dictator in which the government controls business and labor and opposition is not permitted

fas•cist \'fa-shəst\ *n, often cap*
a person who supports or practices fascism

[1]**fash•ion** \'fa-shən\ *n*
1 ▼ the popular style of a thing at a certain time or among a certain group
2 MANNER 2, WAY

[1]fashion 1:
a couple dressed in the fashion of the 1920s

► **Synonyms** FASHION, STYLE, and FAD mean the way that up-to-date people do things. FASHION is used of any custom (as a way of dressing or behaving) that is widely accepted at any one time or place. ⟨It was once the *fashion* for everyone to wear hats.⟩ STYLE may suggest a fashion that is approved of by people with taste. ⟨The house was decorated in the latest *style*.⟩ FAD is used for something that is very popular and often only for a short time. ⟨Beach tennis may be just a *fad*.⟩

[2]**fashion** *vb* **fash•ioned**; **fash•ion•ing**
to give shape or form to

fash•ion•able \'fa-shə-nə-bəl, 'fash-nə-\ *adj*
following the current fashion or style ⟨*fashionable* clothes⟩
fash•ion•ably \-blē\ *adv*

[1]**fast** \'fast\ *adj* **fast•er**; **fast•est**
1 moving, operating, or acting quickly ⟨a *fast* train⟩ ⟨a *fast* thinker⟩
2 taking a short time ⟨a *fast* trip⟩
3 indicating ahead of the correct time ⟨The clock is *fast*.⟩
4 firmly placed ⟨The plant's roots were *fast* in the ground.⟩
5 not likely to fade ⟨*fast* colors⟩
6 totally loyal ⟨*fast* friends⟩

► **Synonyms** FAST, RAPID, and SWIFT mean moving, proceeding, or acting with great speed. FAST is used of the thing that moves. ⟨He rode a *fast* horse.⟩ RAPID is used of the speedy movement itself. ⟨The horse moved at a *rapid* pace.⟩ SWIFT suggests ease of movement along with great speed. ⟨A *swift* horse can easily jump the fence.⟩

[2]**fast** *adv* **fast•er**; **fast•est**
1 with great speed ⟨Don't walk so *fast*!⟩
2 to the full extent : SOUND ⟨*fast* asleep⟩
3 in a firm or fixed way ⟨The rear wheels were stuck *fast* in the mud.⟩

[3]**fast** *vb* **fast•ed**; **fast•ing**
1 to go without eating
2 to eat in small amounts or only certain foods

[4]**fast** *n*
1 the act of going without food
2 a time when no food is eaten

fas•ten \'fa-sᵊn\ *vb* **fas•tened**; **fas•ten•ing**
1 to attach or join by or as if by pinning, tying, or nailing ⟨She *fastened* the papers together.⟩
2 to make firm and secure ⟨*Fasten* your seat belt.⟩
3 to become fixed or joined ⟨The dress *fastens* in the back.⟩
fas•ten•er *n*

fas•ten•ing \'fa-sᵊn-iŋ\ *n*
something that holds another thing shut or in the right position

fast food \'fast-,füd\ *n*
food that is prepared and served quickly
fast–food *adj*

fast–for•ward \,fast-'fȯr-wərd\ *vb* **fast–for•ward•ed**; **fast–for•ward•ing**
to advance a recording (as of music or video) at a faster rate than normal

fas•tid•i•ous \fa-'sti-dē-əs\ *adj*
hard to please : very particular ⟨a *fastidious* dresser⟩

[1]**fat** \'fat\ *adj* **fat•ter; fat•test**
1 having much body fat ⟨a *fat* pig⟩
2 [1]THICK 1 ⟨a *fat* book⟩
3 richly rewarding or profitable ⟨He signed a *fat* contract.⟩
4 swollen up ⟨I fell and got a *fat* lip.⟩
fat•ness *n*

[2]**fat** *n*
1 animal or plant tissue containing much greasy or oily material
2 any of numerous compounds of carbon, hydrogen, and oxygen that make up most of animal or plant fat and that are important to nutrition as sources of energy
3 a solid fat as distinguished from an oil
4 the best or richest part ⟨the *fat* of the land⟩

fa•tal \'fā-t[ə]l\ *adj*
1 causing death : MORTAL ⟨*fatal* injuries⟩
2 causing ruin or failure ⟨a *fatal* mistake⟩ **synonyms** see DEADLY
fa•tal•ly *adv*

fa•tal•i•ty \fā-'ta-lə-tē\ *n, pl* **fa•tal•i•ties**
a death resulting from a disaster or accident

fate \'fāt\ *n*
1 a power beyond human control that is believed to determine what happens : DESTINY ⟨It was *fate* that brought them together.⟩
2 something that happens as though determined by fate : FORTUNE
3 final outcome ⟨Voters will decide the *fate* of the election.⟩

fate•ful \'fāt-fəl\ *adj*
having serious results ⟨a *fateful* decision⟩

[1]**fa•ther** \'fä-thər\ *n*
1 a male parent
2 *cap* GOD 1
3 ANCESTOR 1
4 a person who cares for another as a father might
5 a person who invents or begins something ⟨the *father* of modern science⟩
6 PRIEST
Hint: This sense of *father* is used especially to address a priest or as a priest's title.
fa•ther•hood \-,hu̇d\ *n*
fa•ther•less \-ləs\ *adj*

fault 4: aerial view of the San Andreas Fault in California

[2]**father** *vb* **fa•thered; fa•ther•ing**
1 to become the father of
2 to care for as a father
3 to be the founder, producer, or author of ⟨He *fathered* a new style of music.⟩

fa•ther–in–law \'fä-thər-ən-,lȯ\ *n, pl* **fa•thers–in–law**
the father of a person's husband or wife

fa•ther•land \'fä-thər-,land\ *n*
the land of a person's birth

fa•ther•ly \'fä-thər-lē\ *adj*
of or like a father ⟨He gave me *fatherly* advice.⟩

[1]**fath•om** \'fa-thəm\ *n*
a unit of length equal to six feet (about 1.8 meters) used chiefly in measuring the depth of water

[2]**fathom** *vb* **fath•omed; fath•om•ing**
1 to understand the reason for something ⟨I couldn't *fathom* how he escaped punishment.⟩
2 to measure the depth of water by means of a special line

[1]**fa•tigue** \fə-'tēg\ *n*
1 a state of being very tired
2 **fa•tigues** *pl* the uniform worn by members of the military for physical labor

[2]**fatigue** *vb* **fa•tigued; fa•tigu•ing**
to tire by work or exertion ⟨a *fatiguing* hike⟩

fat•ten \'fa-t[ə]n\ *vb* **fat•tened; fat•ten•ing**
to make or become fat

fat•ty \'fa-tē\ *adj* **fat•ti•er; fat•ti•est**
containing or like fat

fau•cet \'fȯ-sət\ *n*
a fixture for controlling the flow of a liquid (as from a pipe or cask)

fault \'fȯlt\ *n*
1 a weakness in character : FAILING ⟨Forgetfulness is my worst *fault.*⟩
2 responsibility for something wrong ⟨Why should he take the blame when it wasn't his *fault?*⟩
3 FLAW, IMPERFECTION ⟨She bought the jacket even though it had a *fault.*⟩
4◀ a crack in the earth's crust along which movement occurs
at fault responsible for something wrong

fault•less \'fȯlt-ləs\ *adj*
[1]PERFECT 1

faulty \'fȯl-tē\ *adj* **fault•i•er; fault•i•est**
having a fault, flaw, or weakness : IMPERFECT

faun \'fȯn\ *n*
▶ a Roman god of country life represented as part goat and part man

faun: an ancient Roman statue of a faun

fau•na \'fȯ-nə\ *n*
the animal life typical of a region, period, or special environment ⟨the island's *fauna*⟩

[1]**fa•vor** \'fā-vər\ *n*
1 an act of kindness ⟨Do me a *favor.*⟩
2 APPROVAL 1, LIKING ⟨They look with *favor* on protecting wildlife.⟩
3 a preference for one side over another ⟨The umpire showed *favor* toward the champs.⟩
4 a small gift or decorative item ⟨party *favors*⟩
in favor of
1 wanting or approving of ⟨All *in favor of* going say aye.⟩

2 in support of ⟨The judge ruled *in favor of* the defendant.⟩

[2]favor *vb* **fa•vored**; **fa•vor•ing**
1 to prefer especially unfairly ⟨My mom always *favors* my little brother.⟩
2 to approve of ⟨The president *favors* a bill to cut taxes.⟩
3 to present with ⟨The author *favored* us with a copy of her book.⟩
4 to make possible or easier ⟨Winds *favored* the ship's journey east.⟩
5 to look like ⟨He *favors* his mother.⟩

fa•vor•able \'fā-və-rə-bəl, 'fāv-rə-\ *adj*
1 showing approval ⟨a *favorable* opinion⟩
2 tending to help ⟨*favorable* weather⟩
fa•vor•ably \-blē\ *adv*

[1]fa•vor•ite \'fā-və-rət, 'fāv-rət\ *n*
a person or a thing that is liked more than others

[2]favorite *adj*
most liked ⟨Pizza is my *favorite* food.⟩

fa•vor•it•ism \'fā-və-rə-,ti-zəm, 'fāv-rə-\ *n*
the unfair treatment of some people better than others

[1]fawn \'fȯn\ *n*
1 a young deer
2 a light grayish brown

[2]fawn *vb* **fawned**; **fawn•ing**
1 to show affection — used especially of a dog
2 to try to win favor by acting as if someone is superior ⟨Fans *fawned* over the actor.⟩

[1]fax \'faks\ *n*
1 FACSIMILE 2
2 a machine used to send or receive material by facsimile
3 something sent or received by facsimile

[2]fax *vb* **faxed**; **fax•ing**
to send material by facsimile

faze \'fāz\ *vb* **fazed**; **faz•ing**
to cause to hesitate or feel fear ⟨Nothing *fazes* her.⟩

FBI *abbr* Federal Bureau of Investigation

[1]fear \'fir\ *vb* **feared**; **fear•ing**
to be afraid of : feel fear

[2]fear *n*
a strong unpleasant feeling caused by being aware of danger or expecting something bad to happen

fear•ful \'fir-fəl\ *adj*
1 causing fear ⟨the *fearful* roar of a lion⟩
2 filled with fear ⟨I was *fearful* of failing the test.⟩
3 showing or caused by fear ⟨a *fearful* expression⟩
fear•ful•ly \-fə-lē\ *adv*
fear•ful•ness *n*

fear•less \'fir-ləs\ *adj*
not afraid : BRAVE
fear•less•ly *adv*
fear•less•ness *n*

fear•some \'fir-səm\ *adj*
very frightening ⟨a *fearsome* growl⟩

fea•si•ble \'fē-zə-bəl\ *adj*
possible to do or accomplish ⟨a *feasible* goal⟩

[1]feast \'fēst\ *n*
1 ▼ a very large or fancy meal
2 a holy day observed by members of a religion

[1]feast 1

[2]feast *vb* **feast•ed**; **feast•ing**
1 to eat well
2 [2]DELIGHT 1 ⟨She *feasted* her eyes on the decorations.⟩

feat \'fēt\ *n*
an act showing courage, strength, or skill

[1]feath•er \'fe-thər\ *n*
▼ one of the light horny growths that make up the outer covering of a bird
feath•ered \-thərd\ *adj*

[1]feather
Unique to adult birds, feathers are lightweight and waterproof, and are kept in condition by regular preening. In flight, wing feathers increase lift, while tail feathers help with balance and maneuvering. Fluffy body feathers insulate the bird against extremes of weather. Many birds have colorful feathers to attract a mate, while others have feathers that provide protective camouflage.

quill

wing feather
of a macaw

inner wing feather
of an owl

outer wing feather
of a parakeet

tail feather
of a parrot

body feathers
of a parrot

[2]feather *vb* **feath•ered; feath•er•ing**
1 to provide or decorate with feathers
2 to grow or form feathers

feath•ery \'fe-thə-rē\ *adj*
1 like a feather or tuft of feathers
2 covered with feathers

[1]fea•ture \'fē-chər\ *n*
1 a part (as the nose or the mouth) of the face
2 something especially noticeable ⟨a safety *feature*⟩
3 MOVIE 1
4 a special story in a newspaper or magazine

[2]feature *vb* **fea•tured; fea•tur•ing**
1 to have as a characteristic ⟨The TV *features* a flat screen.⟩
2 to give special prominence to ⟨The newspaper *featured* a story about the election.⟩
3 to play an important part ⟨A bus tour *featured* in our trip.⟩

Feb. *abbr* February

Feb•ru•ary \'fe-byə-ˌwer-ē, 'fe-brə-, 'fe-bə-\ *n*
the second month of the year

▶ **Word History** In the ancient Roman calendar March was originally the first month of the year and hence February was the last. The last weeks of the year were a time when people made up for their wrongdoing to the gods and purifications were performed. These rituals were called *februa* in Latin, and from them the month took its name, *Februarius*. English has taken the name from Latin.

fe•ces \'fē-ˌsēz\ *n pl*
body waste that passes out from the intestine

fed•er•al \'fe-də-rəl, 'fe-drəl\ *adj*
relating to a nation formed by the union of several parts

fed•er•a•tion \ˌfe-də-'rā-shən\ *n*
a union of organizations or states ⟨a wildlife *federation*⟩

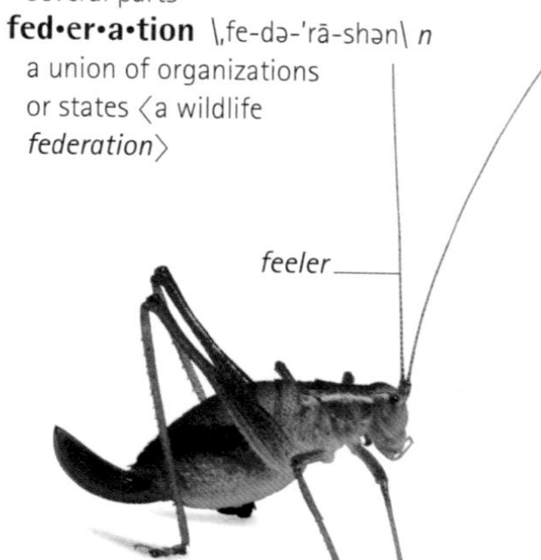

feelers of a speckled bush cricket

fee \'fē\ *n*
1 an amount of money that must be paid ⟨A *fee* is charged to get into the park.⟩
2 a charge for services ⟨a doctor's *fee*⟩

fee•ble \'fē-bəl\ *adj* **fee•bler** \-blər\; **fee•blest** \-bləst\
1 lacking in strength or endurance ⟨a *feeble* old dog⟩
2 not effective or sufficient ⟨a *feeble* attempt⟩ ⟨Her *feeble* cry could not be heard.⟩
synonyms see WEAK
fee•ble•ness \-bəl-nəs\ *n*
fee•bly \-blē\ *adv*

[1]feed \'fēd\ *vb* **fed** \'fed\; **feed•ing**
1 to give food to or give as food ⟨*fed* the dog⟩ ⟨She *fed* cereal to the baby.⟩
2 to take food into the body : EAT ⟨cattle *feeding* on hay⟩
3 to supply with something necessary (as to growth or operation) ⟨It's important to *feed* plants with fertilizer.⟩ ⟨Two streams *feed* the lake.⟩
feed•er *n*

[2]feed *n*
food especially for livestock

feed•back \'fēd-ˌbak\ *n*
helpful information or criticism given to someone to indicate what can be done to improve something

[1]feel \'fēl\ *vb* **felt** \'felt\; **feel•ing**
1 to be aware of through physical contact ⟨*feel* cold⟩
2 to examine or search for by touching ⟨The doctor *felt* for broken bones.⟩
3 to be conscious of ⟨He *felt* a fear of the dark.⟩
4 to seem especially to the touch ⟨This cloth *feels* like silk.⟩
5 to sense a physical, mental, or emotional state ⟨*felt* sick⟩ ⟨*felt* confused and angry⟩
6 to have sympathy ⟨I *feel* for you.⟩
7 BELIEVE 4, THINK ⟨Say what you *feel*.⟩
feel like to have an urge or desire to ⟨Do you *feel like* taking a walk?⟩

[2]feel *n*
1 SENSATION 2, FEELING ⟨He likes the *feel* of the sun on his skin.⟩
2 the quality of something as learned through or as if through touch ⟨The sweater had a scratchy *feel* to it.⟩

feel•er \'fē-lər\ *n*
◀ a long flexible structure (as an insect's antenna) that is an organ of touch

feel•ing \'fē-liŋ\ *n*
1 the sense by which a person knows whether things are hard or soft, hot or cold, heavy or light
2 a sensation of temperature or pressure ⟨a *feeling* of cold⟩ ⟨a *feeling* of pain⟩
3 a state of mind ⟨a *feeling* of joy⟩
4 **feelings** *pl* the state of a person's emotions ⟨You hurt her *feelings*.⟩
5 an opinion, belief, or expectation ⟨I have the *feeling* we've met before.⟩

feet *pl of* FOOT

feign \'fān\ *vb* **feigned; feign•ing**
PRETEND 2 ⟨*feigning* sickness⟩

[1]feint \'fānt\ *n*
a pretended blow or attack at one point or in one direction to take attention away from the point or direction the attack or blow is really coming from

[2]feint *vb* **feint•ed; feint•ing**
to make a feint ⟨The boxer *feinted* right, then struck with his left.⟩

fe•lic•i•ty \fə-'li-sə-tē\ *n*
great happiness

[1]fe•line \'fē-ˌlīn\ *adj*
1 of or relating to the domestic cat or a related animal (as a lion) ⟨*feline* anatomy⟩
2 like or like that of a cat ⟨*feline* movements⟩

[2]feline *n*
CAT

[1]fell \'fel\ *vb* **felled; fell•ing**
to cut or knock down ⟨I *felled* a tree.⟩

[2]fell *past of* FALL

[1]fel•low \'fe-lō\ *n*
1 a male person
2 COMPANION 1, COMRADE

[2]fellow *adj*
belonging to the same group or class ⟨my *fellow* Americans⟩

fel•low•ship \'fe-lō-ˌship\ *n*
1 friendly relationship existing among persons
2 a group with similar interests

fel•on \'fe-lən\ *n*
[2]CRIMINAL

fel•o•ny \'fe-lə-nē\ *n, pl* **fel•o•nies**
a very serious crime

[1]felt: a hat made of felt

[1]felt \'felt\ *n*
▲ a soft heavy cloth made by rolling and pressing fibers together

[2]felt *past and past participle of* FEEL

A B C D E F G H I J K L M N O P Q R S T U V W X Y Z

fem. *abbr* feminine

[1]fe•male \'fē-,māl\ *adj*
1 of, relating to, or being the sex that bears young or lays eggs
2 having a pistil but no stamens ⟨a *female* plant⟩
3 of or characteristic of women or girls

[2]female *n*
1 a woman or a girl
2 a person or animal that can bear young or lay eggs
3 a plant with a pistil but no stamens

fem•i•nine \'fe-mə-nən\ *adj*
1 of the female sex
2 characteristic of or relating to women ⟨a *feminine* style⟩

fem•i•nism \'fe-mə-,ni-zəm\ *n*
1 the belief that women and men should have equal rights and opportunities
2 organized activity on behalf of women's rights and interests
fem•i•nist \-nist\ *n or adj*

fe•mur \'fē-mər\ *n, pl* **fe•murs** *or* **fem•o•ra** \'fe-mə-rə\
the long leg bone that extends from the hip to the knee

[1]fence \'fens\ *n*
a barrier (as of wood or wire) to prevent escape or entry or to mark a boundary

[2]fence *vb* **fenced**; **fenc•ing**
1 to enclose with a fence ⟨*fence* a yard⟩
2 to fight with swords : to practice the sport of fencing
synonyms see ENCLOSE
fenc•er *n*

fenc•ing \'fen-siŋ\ *n*
▼ the sport of having a pretended fight with blunted swords

fender: fender of an Auburn 851 Speedster

fend \'fend\ *vb* **fend•ed**; **fend•ing**
1 to drive away or repel ⟨I tried to *fend* off an attack.⟩
2 to get along without help ⟨You'll have to *fend* for yourself.⟩

fend•er \'fen-dər\ *n*
▲ the part of a motor vehicle or bicycle that covers a wheel

fe•ral \'fir-əl, 'fer-\ *adj*
having escaped from the care of people and become wild ⟨*feral* pigs⟩

[1]fer•ment \fər-'ment\ *vb* **fer•ment•ed**; **fer•ment•ing**
to go through a chemical change that results in the production of alcohol

[2]fer•ment \'fər-,ment\ *n*
1 something (as yeast) that causes fermentation
2 an excited state

fer•men•ta•tion \,fər-mən-'tā-shən\ *n*
a chemical breaking down of a substance (as sugar) that is controlled by an enzyme, usually does not require oxygen, and typically results in the production of alcohol and carbon dioxide

fern \'fərn\ *n*
► a plant that produces spores instead of seeds and no flowers and whose leaves are usually divided into many parts
fern•like \-,līk\ *adj*

fern: leaves of a fern

fe•ro•cious \fə-'rō-shəs\ *adj*
FIERCE 1, SAVAGE ⟨a *ferocious* storm⟩ ⟨a *ferocious* roar⟩
fe•ro•cious•ly *adv*

fe•roc•i•ty \fə-'rä-sə-tē\ *n, pl* **fe•roc•i•ties**
the quality or state of being fierce or savage

[1]fer•ret \'fer-ət\ *n*
a domesticated animal with usually white or light brown or gray fur that originates from the European polecat

► **Word History** The ferret is a domesticated breed of the European polecat. For centuries the ferret has been used in Europe for hunting rats and sometimes rabbits. But both the wild polecat and his domestic relative have a rather bad reputation as chicken thieves. Appropriately, then, the ferret is, according to the history of its name, a "little thief." Medieval English *ferret* (or *furet*) is borrowed from French *furet,* which ultimately goes back to Latin *fur,* "thief."

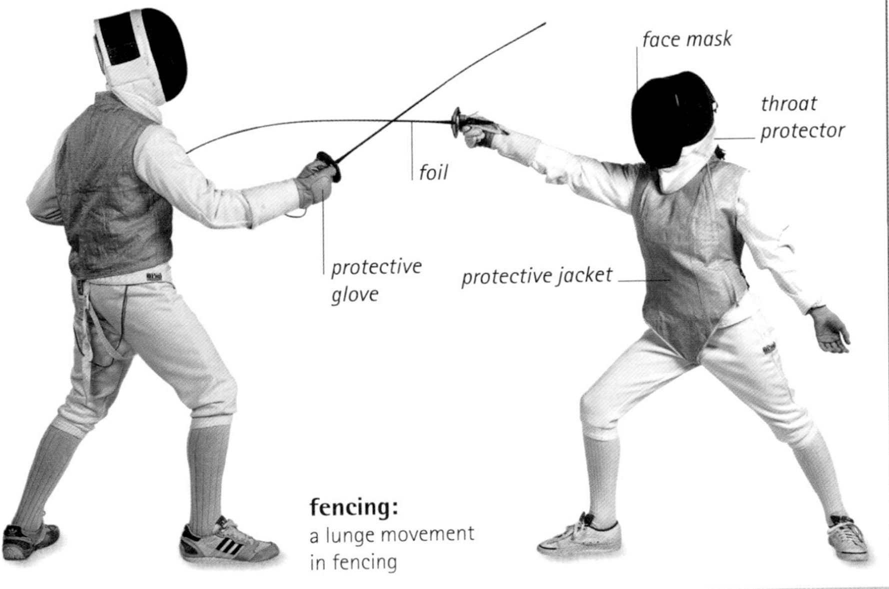

fencing: a lunge movement in fencing

ferryboat

[2]**ferret** *vb* **fer•ret•ed**; **fer•ret•ing**
to find by eager searching 〈Could you *ferret* out the answer?〉

Fer•ris wheel \'fer-əs-\ *n*
an amusement park ride consisting of a large vertical wheel that is moved by a motor and has seats around its rim

[1]**fer•ry** \'fer-ē\ *vb* **fer•ried**; **fer•ry•ing**
1 to carry by boat over a body of water
2 to cross a body of water by a ferryboat
3 to transport for a short distance

[2]**ferry** *n, pl* **fer•ries**
1 FERRYBOAT
2 a place where persons or things are ferried

fer•ry•boat \'fer-ē-,bōt\ *n*
▲ a boat used to carry passengers, vehicles, or goods

fer•tile \'fər-tᵊl\ *adj*
1 producing many plants or crops 〈*fertile* fields〉
2 producing many ideas 〈a *fertile* mind〉
3 capable of developing and growing 〈a *fertile* egg〉

fer•til•i•ty \,fər-'ti-lə-tē\ *n*
the condition of being fertile 〈soil *fertility*〉

fer•til•iza•tion \,fər-tə-lə-'zā-shən\ *n*
1 an act or process of making fertile 〈*fertilization* of a new lawn〉
2 ▶ the joining of an egg cell and a sperm cell to form the first stage of an embryo

fer•til•ize \'fər-tə-,līz\ *vb* **fer•til•ized**; **fer•til•iz•ing**
to make fertile or more fertile 〈a *fertilized* egg〉 〈Workers *fertilized* the garden with nutrients.〉

fer•til•iz•er \'fər-tə-,lī-zər\ *n*
material added to soil to make it more fertile

fer•vent \'fər-vənt\ *adj*
felt very strongly 〈*fervent* gratitude〉
fer•vent•ly *adv*

fer•vor \'fər-vər\ *n*
strong feeling or expression

fes•ter \'fe-stər\ *vb* **fes•tered**; **fes•ter•ing**
to become painfully red and sore and usually full of pus 〈The wound *festered*.〉

fes•ti•val \'fe-stə-vəl\ *n*
1 a time or event of celebration 〈a harvest *festival*〉
2 a program of cultural events or entertainment 〈a jazz *festival*〉

fes•tive \'fe-stiv\ *adj*
1 having to do with a feast or festival
2 very merry and joyful 〈*festive* decorations〉

fes•tiv•i•ty \fe-'sti-və-tē\ *n, pl* **fes•tiv•i•ties**
1 festive activity 〈holiday *festivities*〉
2 celebration and enjoyment 〈a feeling of *festivity*〉

[1]**fes•toon** \fe-'stün\ *n*
a chain or strip hanging between two points as decoration

[2]**festoon** *vb* **fes•tooned**; **fes•toon•ing**
to hang or form festoons or other decorations on

fetch \'fech\ *vb* **fetched**; **fetch•ing**
1 to go after and bring back
2 to bring as a price : sell for 〈The artwork will *fetch* a high price.〉

▶ **fertilization 2**
In mammals, fertilization takes place when a male reproductive cell, or sperm cell, penetrates and unites with the female reproductive cell, or egg cell. The genes from each one combine, so that the fertilized egg develops into a new individual with characteristics inherited from both parents.

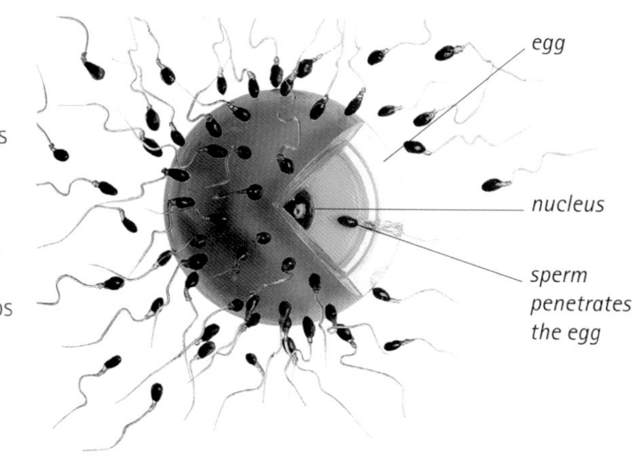

model in cross-section showing fertilization of an egg

fetch•ing \'fe-chiŋ\ *adj*
very attractive

[1]fet•ter \'fe-tər\ *n*
1 a chain for the feet
2 something that holds back : RESTRAINT

[2]fetter *vb* **fet•tered; fet•ter•ing**
1 to chain the feet of
2 to keep from moving or acting freely ⟨He was *fettered* by many responsibilities.⟩

fe•tus \'fē-təs\ *n*
an animal not yet born or hatched but more developed than an embryo

[1]feud \'fyüd\ *n*
a long bitter quarrel between two people, families, or groups

[2]feud *vb* **feud•ed; feud•ing**
to carry on a long bitter quarrel

feu•dal \'fyü-dᵊl\ *adj*
relating to feudalism

feu•dal•ism \'fyü-də-,liz-əm\ *n*
a social system existing in medieval Europe in which people worked and fought for nobles who gave them protection and land in return

fe•ver \'fē-vər\ *n*
1 a body temperature that is higher than normal
2 a disease involving fever

fe•ver•ish \'fē-və-rish\ *adj*
1 having a fever ⟨a *feverish* child⟩
2 characteristic of or relating to a fever ⟨a *feverish* nightmare⟩
3 showing great emotion or activity : HECTIC
fe•ver•ish•ly *adv*

few \'fyü\ *pron*
not many people or things ⟨*Few* were prepared to perform⟩

few *adj* **few•er; few•est**
not many but some ⟨I caught a *few* fish.⟩ ⟨They had *few* complaints.⟩

few *n*
a small number of people or things ⟨A *few* of the students are new.⟩

ew•er \'fyü-ər\ *pron*
a smaller number ⟨*Fewer* got injured this year.⟩

ez \'fez\ *n, pl* **fez•zes**
▶ a round red felt hat that usually has a tassel but no brim

i•an•cé \,fē-,än-'sā\ *n*
a man that a woman is engaged to be married to

i•an•cée \,fē-,än-'sē\ *n*
a woman that a man is engaged to be married to

i•as•co \fē-'a-skō\ *n, pl* **fi•as•coes**
a complete failure ⟨The party was a *fiasco.*⟩

[1]fib \'fib\ *n*
a lie about something unimportant

[2]fib *vb* **fibbed; fib•bing**
to tell a lie about something unimportant
fib•ber *n*

fi•ber \'fī-bər\ *n*
1 ▶ a thread or a structure or object resembling a thread
2 plant material that cannot be digested

fiber 1: raw jute fibers

fi•ber•glass \'fī-bər-,glas\ *n*
glass in the form of fibers used in various products (as filters and insulation)

fiber op•tics \-'äp-tiks\ *n pl*
▶ thin transparent fibers of glass or plastic that transmit light throughout their length

fi•brous \'fī-brəs\ *adj*
containing, made of, or like fibers ⟨*fibrous* roots⟩

fib•u•la \'fi-byə-lə\ *n, pl* **fib•u•lae** \-,lē, -,lī\ *or* **fib•u•las**
the outer and smaller of the two bones between the knee and ankle

-fication \fə-'kā-shən\ *n suffix*
the act or process of or the result of ⟨ampli*fication*⟩

fick•le \'fi-kəl\ *adj*
changing often : not reliable ⟨*fickle* friends⟩ ⟨*fickle* weather⟩
fick•le•ness *n*

fic•tion \'fik-shən\ *n*
1 something told or written that is not fact

fez: a man wearing a fez

2 a made-up story
3 works of literature that are not true stories

fic•tion•al \'fik-shə-nᵊl\ *adj*
not real or true : MADE-UP ⟨a *fictional* character⟩

fic•ti•tious \fik-'ti-shəs\ *adj*
not real ⟨a *fictitious* country⟩

[1]fid•dle \'fi-dᵊl\ *n*
VIOLIN

[2]fiddle *vb* **fid•dled; fid•dling**
1 to play on a fiddle
2 to move the hands or fingers restlessly ⟨She kept *fiddling* with her ring.⟩
3 to spend time in aimless activity ⟨They *fiddled* around and accomplished nothing.⟩
4 to change or handle in a useless way ⟨He *fiddled* with the controls.⟩
5 to handle in a harmful or foolish way : TAMPER ⟨Someone has been *fiddling* with the lock.⟩
fid•dler \'fid-lər\ *n*

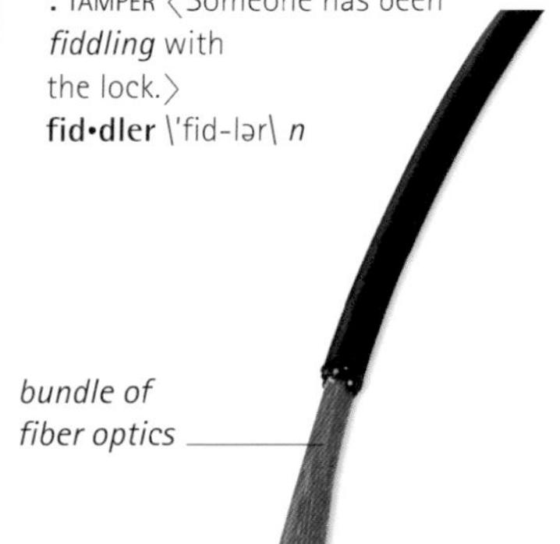

fiber optics: fiber optics encased in plastic

fi•del•i•ty \fə-'de-lə-tē, fī-\ *n*
1 LOYALTY ⟨They swore *fidelity* to the king.⟩
2 ACCURACY ⟨I described the scene with *fidelity.*⟩

fidg•et \'fi-jət\ *vb* **fidg•et•ed; fidg•et•ing**
to move in a restless or nervous way

fidg•ety \'fi-jə-tē\ *adj*
nervous and restless

fief \'fēf\ *n*
an estate of land given to a vassal by a feudal lord

[1]field \'fēld\ *n*
1 a piece of open, cleared, or cultivated land
2 a piece of land put to a special use or giving a special product ⟨a ball *field*⟩ ⟨an oil *field*⟩
3 an area of activity or influence ⟨the *field* of science⟩
4 a background on which something is drawn, painted, or mounted ⟨The United States flag has white stars on a blue *field.*⟩

[2]field *adj*
relating to a field ⟨*field* work⟩

[3]field *vb* **field•ed**; **field•ing**
to catch or stop and throw a ball

field day *n*
a day of outdoor sports, activities, and athletic competitions

field•er \'fēl-dər\ *n*
a baseball player other than the pitcher or catcher on the team that is not at bat

field glasses *n pl*
binoculars without prisms

field goal *n*
a score in football made by kicking the ball through the goal during ordinary play

field hockey *n*
hockey played on a field

field trip *n*
a visit to a place (such as a museum) made by students to learn about something

fiend \'fēnd\ *n*
1 DEMON 1, DEVIL
2 a very wicked or cruel person
3 [2]FANATIC ⟨a golf *fiend*⟩
fiend•ish \'fēn-dish\ *adj*
fiend•ish•ly *adv*

fierce \'firs\ *adj* **fierc•er**; **fierc•est**
1 likely to attack ⟨a *fierce* animal⟩
2 having or showing very great energy or enthusiasm ⟨She plays the game with *fierce* determination.⟩
3 wild or threatening in appearance ⟨He brandished a *fierce* sword.⟩
4 characterized by extreme force, intensity, or anger ⟨a *fierce* fight⟩ ⟨*fierce* winds⟩
fierce•ly *adv*
fierce•ness *n*

fi•ery \'fī-ə-rē, 'fīr-ē\ *adj* **fi•er•i•er**; **fi•er•i•est**
1 marked by fire ⟨a *fiery* explosion⟩
2 hot or glowing like a fire
3 full of spirit ⟨a *fiery* speech⟩
4 easily angered

fi•es•ta \fē-'e-stə\ *n*
▼ a celebration especially in Spain and Latin America that commemorates a saint

fife \'fīf\ *n*
a small musical instrument like a flute that produces a shrill sound

[1]fif•teen \fif-'tēn, 'fif-,tēn\ *adj*
being one more than 14

[2]fifteen *n*
one more than 14 : three times five : 15

[1]fif•teenth \fif-'tēnth, 'fif-,tēnth\ *adj*
coming right after 14th

[2]fifteenth *n*
number 15 in a series

[1]fifth \'fifth\ *adj*
coming right after fourth

[2]fifth *n*
1 number five in a series ⟨The school year began on the *fifth* of September.⟩
2 one of five equal parts ⟨I spent a *fifth* of my allowance.⟩

[1]fif•ti•eth \'fif-tē-əth\ *adj*
coming right after 49th

[2]fiftieth *n*
number 50 in a series

[1]fif•ty \'fif-tē\ *adj*
being five times ten

[2]fifty *n*
five times ten : 50

fiesta: The Cockerel Festival (Fiesta del Gallo) in Spain

A B C D E F G H I J K L M N O P Q R S T U V W X Y Z

fig \'fig\ *n*
a sweet fruit that is oblong or shaped like a pear and is often eaten dried

[1]fight \'fīt\ *vb* **fought** \'fȯt\; **fight•ing**
1 to struggle in battle or in physical combat
2 to argue angrily : QUARREL
3 to try hard ⟨She *fought* to stay awake.⟩
4 to struggle against ⟨*fight* discrimination⟩
fight•er *n*

[2]fight *n*
1 a meeting in battle or in physical combat
2 [1]QUARREL 1
3 strength or desire for fighting ⟨After being wrongly blamed, I was full of *fight*.⟩

fig•ment \'fig-mənt\ *n*
something imagined or made up ⟨I thought I saw her, but it must have been a *figment* of my imagination.⟩

fig•u•ra•tive \'fi-gyə-rə-tiv\ *adj*
expressing one thing in terms normally used for another ⟨The word "foot" is *figurative* in "the foot of the mountain."⟩
fig•u•ra•tive•ly *adv*

[1]fig•ure \'fi-gyər\ *n*
1 a symbol (as 1, 2, 3) that stands for a number : NUMERAL
2 figures *pl* ARITHMETIC 2 ⟨She has a good head for *figures*.⟩
3 value or price expressed in figures
4 the shape or outline of something or someone
5 the shape of the body especially of a person ⟨a slender *figure*⟩
6 an illustration in a printed text
7 [1]PATTERN 1 ⟨cloth with red *figures*⟩
8 a well-known or important person

[2]figure *vb* **fig•ured**; **fig•ur•ing**
1 CALCULATE 1 ⟨Can you *figure* the cost?⟩
2 BELIEVE 4, DECIDE ⟨I *figured* we'd win.⟩
figure on
1 to make plans based on ⟨*Figure on* 20 guests.⟩
2 to rely on
3 to have in mind ⟨I *figured on* going home.⟩
figure out
1 to discover or solve by thinking ⟨I *figured out* how to do this.⟩
2 to find a solution for ⟨Can you *figure out* these math problems?⟩

fig•ure•head \'fi-gyər-,hed\ *n*
1 a carved figure on the bow of a ship
2 a person who is called the head of something but who has no real power

figure of speech *n, pl* **figures of speech**
an expression (as a simile or a metaphor) that uses words in other than a plain or literal way

fil•a•ment \'fi-lə-mənt\ *n*
1 a fine thread ⟨a *filament* of silk⟩
2 a fine wire (as in a light bulb) that is made to glow by the passage of an electric current
3 the stalk of a plant stamen that bears the anther

fil•bert \'fil-bərt\ *n*
the hazel or its nut

filch \'filch\ *vb* **filched**; **filch•ing**
to steal in a sneaky way

[1]file \'fīl\ *n*
a tool with sharp ridges or teeth for smoothing hard substances

[2]file *vb* **filed**; **fil•ing**
to rub, smooth, or cut away with a file

[3]file *vb* **filed**; **fil•ing**
1 to arrange in an orderly way ⟨He *filed* the cards in alphabetical order.⟩
2 to enter or record officially ⟨*file* a claim⟩

[4]file 1

[4]file *n*
1 ▲ a device (as a folder or cabinet) for storing papers or records in an orderly way
2 a collection of papers or records kept in a file
3 a collection of data treated as a unit by a computer

[5]file *n*
a row of persons or things arranged one behind the other ⟨Please walk in single *file*.⟩

[6]file *vb* **filed**; **fil•ing**
to walk in a row ⟨The entire class *filed* out of the building.⟩

fil•ial \'fi-lē-əl, 'fil-yəl\ *adj*
relating to or suitable for a son or daughter

fil•i•gree \'fi-lə-,grē\ *n*
▼ decoration made of fine wire

filigree: brooch with filigree

Fil•i•pi•no \,fi-lə-'pē-nō\ *n*
1 a person born or living in the Philippines
2 the language of the Philippines

[1]fill \'fil\ *vb* **filled**; **fill•ing**
1 to make or become full ⟨Please *fill* the tank.⟩ ⟨The pail *filled* slowly.⟩
2 to use up all the space or time in ⟨Meetings *filled* his schedule.⟩ ⟨Cars *filled* the street.⟩
3 to spread through ⟨Laughter *filled* the room.⟩
4 to stop up : PLUG ⟨The dentist *filled* a tooth.⟩
5 to do the duties of ⟨Who *fills* the office of class president?⟩
6 to hire a person for ⟨*fill* a position⟩
7 to supply according to directions ⟨I need to *fill* a prescription.⟩
8 to succeed in meeting or satisfying ⟨You *fill* all requirements.⟩
fill in
1 to insert information ⟨*Fill in* the blanks.⟩
2 to provide information ⟨*Fill* me *in* on what's happening.⟩
3 to take another's place ⟨Can you *fill in* while I'm away?⟩
fill out
1 to increase in size and fullness ⟨The smaller plants are *filling out*.⟩
2 to complete by providing information ⟨Please *fill out* a form.⟩

[2]fill *n*
1 all that is wanted ⟨I ate my *fill*.⟩
2 material for filling something

fill•er \'fi-lər\ *n*
a material used for filling

fil•let \'fi-lət, fi-'lā\ *n*
a piece of boneless meat or fish

fill•ing \'fi-liŋ\ *n*
a substance used to fill something else ⟨a *filling* for a tooth⟩ ⟨pie *filling*⟩

filling station *n*
GAS STATION

fil•ly \'fi-lē\ *n, pl* **fillies**
a young female horse

finch: finches perched side by side

[1]**film** \'film\ *n*
1 a roll of material prepared for taking pictures
2 MOVIE 1
3 a thin coating or layer

[2]**film** *vb* **filmed**; **film•ing**
1 to make a movie
2 to photograph on a film

filmy \'fil-mē\ *adj* **film•i•er**; **film•i•est**
very thin and light ⟨*filmy* curtains⟩

[1]**fil•ter** \'fil-tər\ *n*
1 a device or a mass of material (as sand or paper) with tiny openings through which a gas or liquid is passed to remove something ⟨The *filter* removes dust from the air.⟩
2 ► a transparent material that absorbs light of some colors and is used for changing light (as in photography)

[2]**filter** *vb* **fil•tered**; **fil•ter•ing**
1 to pass through a filter ⟨*filter* water⟩
2 to remove by means of a filter ⟨Sand helps *filter* impurities from water.⟩

filth \'filth\ *n*
disgusting dirt

filthy \'fil-thē\ *adj* **filth•i•er**; **filth•i•est**
extremely dirty
filth•i•ness *n*

fil•tra•tion \fil-'trā-shən\ *n*
the process of filtering

fin \'fin\ *n*
1 any of the thin parts that stick out from the body of a water animal and especially a fish and are used in moving or guiding the body through the water
2 something shaped like an animal's fin ⟨the *fins* of a missile⟩

[1]**fi•nal** \'fī-nᵊl\ *adj*
1 coming or happening at the end ⟨*final* exams⟩
2 not to be changed ⟨The decision of the judges is *final.*⟩
synonyms see LAST
fi•nal•ly *adv*

[2]**final** *n*
1 the last match or game of a tournament
2 a final examination in a course

fi•na•le \fə-'na-lē\ *n*
the close or end of something (as a musical work)

fi•nal•i•ty \fī-'na-lə-tē\ *n*
the condition of being final or complete ⟨the *finality* of the decision⟩

fi•nal•ize \'fī-nə-,līz\ *vb* **fi•nal•ized**; **fi•nal•iz•ing**
to put in a final or finished form

[1]**fi•nance** \fə-'nans, 'fī-,nans\ *n*
1 **finances** *pl* money available to a government, business, or individual
2 the system that includes the circulation of money, the providing of banks and credit, and the making of investments

► [1]**filter 2**
When a photographer places a filter over a camera lens, only light of a similar color can pass through to the film. This can dramatically alter the look of a picture, as shown below.

photo taken without filter

yellow filter

orange filter

blue filter

a vase photographed using three different color filters

[2]**finance** *vb* **fi•nanced**; **fi•nanc•ing**
to provide money for ⟨She *financed* the trip herself.⟩

fi•nan•cial \fə-'nan-shəl, fī-\ *adj*
having to do with money or finance ⟨a *financial* expert⟩ ⟨*financial* aid⟩
fi•nan•cial•ly *adv*

fin•an•cier \,fi-nən-'sir\ *n*
a specialist in finance and especially in the financing of businesses

finch \'finch\ *n*
◄ a songbird (as a sparrow, bunting, or canary) with a short bill used for eating seeds

[1]**find** \'fīnd\ *vb* **found** \'faủnd\; **find•ing**
1 to come upon by chance ⟨He *found* a dime.⟩
2 to come upon or get by searching, study, or effort ⟨She finally *found* the answer.⟩ ⟨I *found* some free time.⟩
3 to make a decision about ⟨The jury *found* her guilty.⟩
4 to know by experience ⟨I *find* this Web site useful.⟩
5 to gain or regain the use of ⟨I *found* my voice again.⟩
6 to become aware of being in a place, condition, or activity
find•er *n*
find fault to criticize in an unfavorable way
find out to learn by studying, watching, or searching ⟨I *found out* the secret.⟩

[2]**find** *n*
a usually valuable item or person found

find•ing \'fīn-diŋ\ *n*
1 the decision of a court
2 the results of an investigation

[1]**fine** \'fīn\ *n*
a sum of money to be paid as a punishment

[2]**fine** *vb* **fined**; **fin•ing**
to punish by requiring payment of a sum of money

[3]**fine** *adj* **fin•er**; **fin•est**
1 very good in quality or appearance ⟨a *fine* swimmer⟩ ⟨a *fine* garden⟩
2 SATISFACTORY ⟨That's *fine* with me.⟩
3 very small or thin ⟨*fine* print⟩
4 made up of very small pieces ⟨*fine* sand⟩
fine•ly *adv*
fine•ness *n*

[4]**fine** *adv*
very well ⟨I'm doing *fine.*⟩

fin•ery \'fī-nə-rē\ *n, pl* **fin•er•ies**
stylish or showy clothes and jewelry

[1]**fin•ger** \'fiŋ-gər\ *n*
1 one of the five divisions of the end of the hand including the thumb
2 something that resembles a finger ⟨a *finger* of land⟩
3 the part of a glove into which a finger goes

fire engine

[2]**finger** *vb* **fin•gered; fin•ger•ing**
to touch with the fingers : HANDLE

fin•ger•nail \'fiŋ-gər-ˌnāl\ *n*
the hard covering at the end of a finger

[1]**fin•ger•print** \'fiŋ-gər-ˌprint\ *n*
▶ the unique pattern of marks made by pressing the tip of a finger on a surface

[1]**fingerprint**

[2]**fingerprint** *vb* **fin•ger•print•ed; fin•ger•print•ing**
to obtain fingerprints in order to identify a person

fin•icky \'fi-ni-kē\ *adj*
very hard to please : FUSSY

[1]**fin•ish** \'fi-nish\ *vb* **fin•ished; fin•ish•ing**
1 to bring or come to an end : COMPLETE
2 to use up completely ⟨I *finished* the pie.⟩
3 to end a competition in a certain position ⟨I *finished* third in the race.⟩
4 to put a final coat or surface on ⟨He *finished* the wood table with varnish.⟩

[2]**finish** *n*
1 [1]END 2, CONCLUSION ⟨The race had a close *finish*.⟩
2 the final treatment or coating of a surface or the appearance given by such a treatment ⟨The table has a shiny *finish*.⟩

finish line *n*
a line marking the end of a racecourse

fi•nite \'fī-ˌnīt\ *adj*
having definite limits ⟨I was given a *finite* number of choices.⟩

[1]**fink** \'fiŋk\ *n*
1 a person who is disliked
2 a person who tattles

[2]**fink** *vb* **finked; fink•ing**
to tell on : TATTLE

Finn \'fin\ *n*
a person born or living in Finland

finned \'find\ *adj*
having fins

[1]**Finn•ish** \'fi-nish\ *adj*
relating to Finland, its people, or the Finnish language

[2]**Finnish** *n*
the language of the Finns

fiord *variant of* FJORD

fir \'fər\ *n*
a tall evergreen tree related to the pine that yields useful lumber

[1]**fire** \'fīr\ *n*
1 the light and heat and especially the flame produced by burning
2 fuel that is burning in a controlled setting (as in a fireplace)
3 the destructive burning of something (as a building)
4 the shooting of weapons ⟨rifle *fire*⟩
5 ENTHUSIASM
on fire actively burning
under fire
1 exposed to the firing of enemy guns
2 under attack

[2]**fire** *vb* **fired; fir•ing**
1 [1]SHOOT 2 ⟨*fire* a gun⟩
2 to dismiss from employment ⟨He was *fired* from his job.⟩
3 EXCITE 1, STIR ⟨It's a story to *fire* the imagination.⟩
4 to subject to great heat ⟨*fire* pottery⟩
5 to set off : EXPLODE ⟨*fire* a firecracker⟩
6 to set on fire ⟨They carelessly *fired* the barn.⟩

fire alarm *n*
an alarm sounded to signal that a fire has broken out

fire•arm \'fīr-ˌärm\ *n*
a weapon from which a shot is discharged by gunpowder
Hint: *Firearm* is usually used for a small weapon

fire•crack•er \'fīr-ˌkra-kər\ *n*
a paper tube containing an explosive to be set off for amusement

fire drill *n*
a practice drill in getting out of a building in case of fire

fire engine *n*
▲ a truck equipped to fight fires

fire escape *n*
a stairway that provides a way of escape from a building in case of fire

fire extinguisher *n*
▼ something (as a container filled with chemicals) used to put out a fire

fire•fight•er \'fīr-ˌfī-tər\ *n*
a person whose job is to put out fires
fire•fight•ing \-iŋ\ *n*

fire extinguisher

fire•fly \'fīr-,flī\ *n, pl* **fire•flies**
a small beetle producing a soft light

fire•house \'fīr-,hau̇s\ *n*
FIRE STATION

fire•man \'fīr-mən\ *n, pl* **fire•men** \-mən\
1 FIREFIGHTER
2 a person who tends a fire (as in a large furnace)

fire•place \'fīr-,plās\ *n*
▼ a structure with a hearth on which an open fire can be built (as for heating)

fireplace

fire•proof \'fīr-'prüf\ *adj*
not easily burned : made safe against fire

fire•side \'fīr-,sīd\ *n*
1 a place near the hearth
2 [1]HOME 1

fire station *n*
a building housing fire engines and usually firefighters

fire•wood \'fīr-,wu̇d\ *n*
wood cut for fuel

fire•work \'fīr-,wərk\ *n*
1 a device that makes a display of light or noise by the burning of explosive or flammable materials
2 **fireworks** *pl* a display of fireworks

[1]**firm** \'fərm\ *adj* **firm•er; firm•est**
1 having a solid compact texture 〈*firm* ground〉
2 STRONG 1, VIGOROUS 〈a *firm* grip〉
3 not likely to be changed 〈a *firm* price〉
4 not easily moved or shaken : FAITHFUL 〈a *firm* believer〉 〈*firm* friends〉
5 showing certainty or determination 〈*firm* control〉
synonyms see HARD
firm•ly *adv*
firm•ness *n*

[2]**firm** *vb* **firmed; firm•ing**
1 to make or become hard or solid 〈Gently *firm* the soil.〉 〈The jelly *firms* quickly.〉
2 to make more secure or strong 〈She *firmed* her grip on the racquet.〉
3 to put into final form 〈We need to *firm* our plans.〉

[3]**firm** *n*
BUSINESS 2 〈an insurance *firm*〉

[1]**first** \'fərst\ *adj*
coming before all others in time, order, or importance 〈*first* prize〉 〈*first* base〉

[2]**first** *adv*
1 before any other 〈I got home *first*.〉
2 for the first time 〈We *first* met here.〉

[3]**first** *n*
1 number one in a series
2 something or someone that comes before all others
3 the winning place in a competition
at first in the beginning 〈I hated dance lessons *at first*.〉

first aid *n*
care or treatment given to an ill or injured person in an emergency

fishhook: a fishhook for fly fishing

first–class \'fərst-'klas\ *adj*
1 relating to the best group in a classification
2 EXCELLENT

first•hand \'fərst-'hand\ *adj or adv*
coming right from the original source 〈*firsthand* information〉

first lieutenant *n*
a commissioned officer in the army, air force, or marine corps ranking above a second lieutenant

first person *n*
a set of words or forms (as pronouns or verb forms) referring to the person speaking or writing them

first–rate \'fərst-'rāt\ *adj*
EXCELLENT

first re•spond•er \-ri-'spän-dər\ *n*
a person (as a police officer or an EMT) who is responsible for going immediately to the scene of an accident or emergency to provide help

first sergeant *n*
1 a noncommissioned officer serving as the chief assistant to a military commander
2 a noncommissioned officer ranking above a sergeant first class in the army or above a gunnery sergeant in the marine corps

firth \'fərth\ *n*
a narrow arm of the sea

[1]**fish** \'fish\ *n, pl* **fish** *or* **fish•es**
1 ▶ any of a large group of vertebrate animals that live in water, breathe with gills, and usually have fins and scales
2 an animal that lives in water — usually used in combination 〈star*fish*〉
fish•like \-,līk\ *adj*

[2]**fish** *vb* **fished; fish•ing**
1 to catch or try to catch fish
2 to search for something by or as if by feeling 〈I *fished* in my bag for a pen.〉

fish•er•man \'fi-shər-mən\ *n, pl* **fish•er•men** \-mən\
a person who fishes

fish•ery \'fi-shə-rē\ *n, pl* **fish•er•ies**
1 the business of catching, processing, and selling fish
2 a place for catching fish 〈saltwater *fisheries*〉

fish•hook \'fish-,hu̇k\ *n*
◀ a hook used for catching fish

fishy \'fi-shē\ *adj* **fish•i•er; fish•i•est**
1 of or like fish 〈a *fishy* odor〉
2 causing doubt or suspicion : QUESTIONABLE 〈The story sounds *fishy* to me.〉

fis•sion \'fi-shən\ *n*
1 a method of reproduction in which a living cell or body divides into two or more parts each of which grows into a whole new individual
2 ▼ the process of splitting an atomic nucleus with the release of large amounts of energy

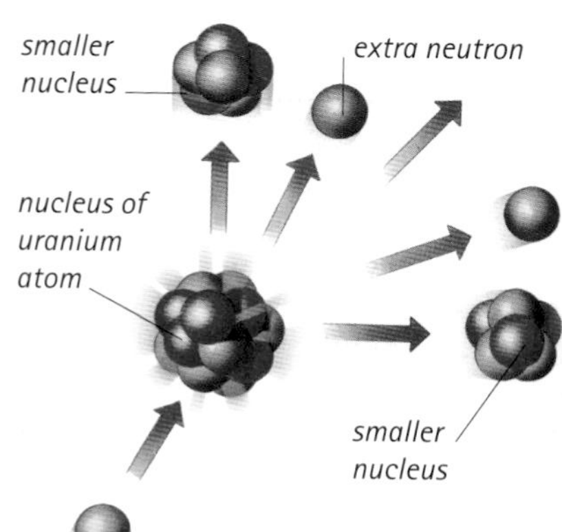

fission 2:
the nucleus of an uranium atom splits into two smaller nuclei and extra neutrons

[1]fish 1

Fish are cold-blooded animals that live in water. They use their fins and tail to move around, and breathe through their gills. Fish are commonly divided into three main groups: bony, cartilaginous, and jawless fish. Most fish are bony fish and have a bony skeleton. Cartilaginous fish, such as sharks, have a skeleton made of cartilage. Jawless fish, such as lampreys, usually also have a cartilaginous skeleton, but are named for their sucker-like mouth.

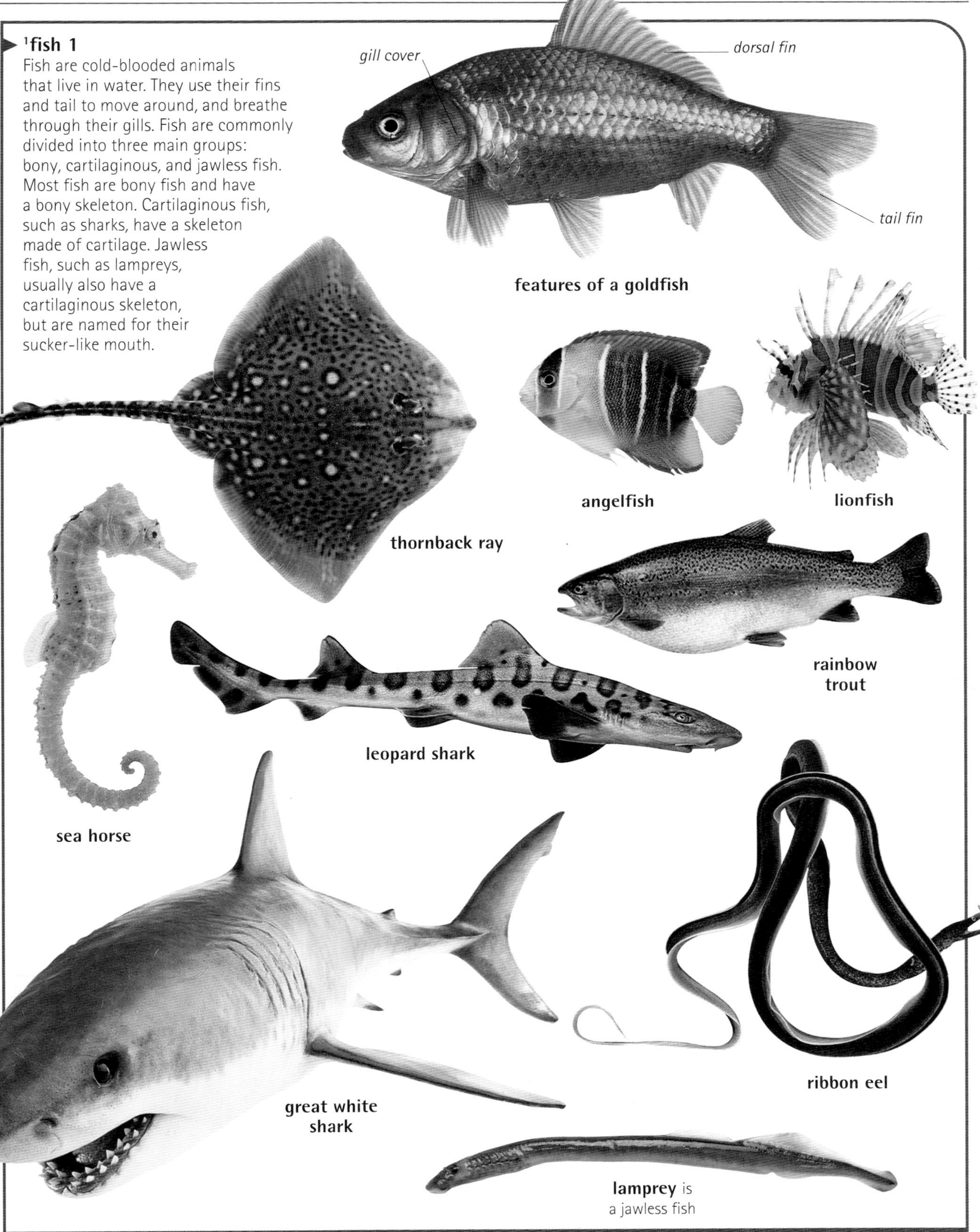

features of a goldfish

thornback ray

angelfish

lionfish

rainbow trout

sea horse

leopard shark

ribbon eel

great white shark

lamprey is a jawless fish

a b c d e f g h i j k l m n o p q r s t u v w x y z

fis•sure \'fi-shər\ *n*
a narrow opening or crack

fist \'fist\ *n*
the hand with the fingers bent tight into the palm

[1]**fit** \'fit\ *adj* **fit•ter; fit•test**
1 good enough : suitable for ⟨*fit* to eat⟩
2 physically healthy
3 made ready ⟨The sailors were getting the ship *fit* for sea.⟩
fit•ness *n*

[2]**fit** *n*
a sudden attack or outburst ⟨a *fit* of anger⟩ ⟨a *fit* of coughing⟩

[3]**fit** *vb* **fit•ted; fit•ting**
1 to be the right shape or size ⟨This shirt doesn't *fit* any more.⟩
2 to bring to the right shape or size ⟨I had the suit *fitted*.⟩
3 to find room or time for ⟨Can you *fit* this in your bag?⟩ ⟨The doctor can *fit* you in.⟩
4 to go into a particular place ⟨Will we all *fit* in your car?⟩
5 to be suitable for or to ⟨I dressed to *fit* the occasion.⟩
6 EQUIP ⟨They *fitted* the ship with new engines.⟩

[4]**fit** *n*
the way something fits ⟨a tight *fit*⟩

fit•ful \'fit-fəl\ *adj*
not regular or steady ⟨*fitful* sleep⟩
fit•ful•ly *adv*

[1]**fit•ting** \'fi-tiŋ\ *adj*
[1]APPROPRIATE, SUITABLE ⟨a *fitting* memorial⟩
fit•ting•ly *adv*

[2]**fitting** *n*
a small part that goes with something larger ⟨a pipe *fitting*⟩

[1]**five** \'fīv\ *adj*
being one more than four ⟨*five* weeks⟩

[2]**five** *n*
1 one more than four : 5
2 the fifth in a set or series

[1]**fix** \'fiks\ *vb* **fixed; fix•ing**
1 [1]REPAIR 1 ⟨Dad *fixed* the broken gate.⟩
2 to make firm or secure ⟨We *fixed* the tent pegs in the ground.⟩
3 to hold or direct steadily ⟨*Fix* your eyes on this.⟩
4 to set definitely : ESTABLISH ⟨Let's *fix* the date of the meeting.⟩
5 to get ready : PREPARE ⟨*fix* dinner⟩
6 to cause to chemically change into an available and useful form ⟨These soil bacteria *fix* nitrogen.⟩
fix•er \'fik-sər\ *n*

[2]**fix** *n*
1 an unpleasant or difficult position ⟨Losing his library book left him in a *fix*.⟩
2 something that solves a problem ⟨a quick *fix*⟩

fixed \'fikst\ *adj*
1 not changing : SET
2 firmly placed ⟨A mirror is *fixed* to the wall.⟩ ⟨That day is *fixed* in my memory.⟩
fix•ed•ly \'fik-səd-lē\ *adv*

fixed star *n*
a star so distant that its motion can be measured only by very careful observations over long periods

fix•ture \'fiks-chər\ *n*
something (as a light or sink) attached as a permanent part ⟨bathroom *fixtures*⟩

[1]**fizz** \'fiz\ *vb* **fizzed; fizz•ing**
to make a hissing or bubbling sound

[2]**fizz** *n*
1 a hissing or bubbling sound
2 a bubbling drink

fiz•zle \'fi-zəl\ *vb* **fiz•zled; fiz•zling**
to fail after a good start

fjord *or* **fiord** \fē-'ȯrd\ *n*
▼ a narrow inlet of the sea between cliffs or steep slopes

FL, Fla. *abbr* Florida

flab \'flab\ *n*
excess body fat

flab•ber•gast \'fla-bər-ˌgast\ *vb* **flab•ber•gast•ed; flab•ber•gast•ing**
to greatly surprise : ASTONISH

flab•by \'fla-bē\ *adj* **flab•bi•er; flab•bi•est**
not hard and firm : SOFT ⟨*flabby* muscles⟩
flab•bi•ness *n*

[1]**flag** \'flag\ *n*
▼ a piece of cloth with a special design or color that is used as a symbol (as of a nation) or as a signal

[1]**flag:** the Canadian national flag

[2]**flag** *vb* **flagged; flag•ging**
to signal to stop

[3]**flag** *vb* **flagged; flag•ging**
to become weak

fla•gel•lum \flə-'je-ləm\ *n, pl* **fla•gel•la** \-'je-lə\
a structure resembling a whip that sticks out from a cell and by which some tiny organisms (as bacteria) move

fjord: aerial view of the Geiranger Fjord, Norway

flag•man \'flag-mən\ *n, pl* **flag•men** \-mən\
a person who signals with a flag

flag•on \'fla-gən\ *n*
a container for liquids usually having a handle, spout, and lid

flag•pole \'flag-,pōl\ *n*
a pole on which to raise a flag

fla•grant \'flā-grənt\ *adj*
so bad as to be impossible to overlook ⟨a *flagrant* lie⟩
fla•grant•ly *adv*

flag•ship \'flag-,ship\ *n*
the ship carrying the commander of a group of ships and flying a flag that tells the commander's rank

flag•staff \'flag-,staf\ *n, pl* **flag•staffs**
FLAGPOLE

[1]**flail** \'flāl\ *vb* **flailed**; **flail•ing**
1 to wave the arms or legs wildly
2 to swing something with a violent motion

[2]**flail** *n*
▶ a tool for threshing grain by hand

[2]**flail:** a 19th-century wooden flail from Russia

flair \'fler\ *n*
1 natural ability ⟨She has a *flair* for acting.⟩
2 [1]STYLE 4 ⟨a dress with *flair*⟩

[1]**flake** \'flāk\ *n*
a small thin flat piece

[2]**flake** *vb* **flaked**; **flak•ing**
to form or separate into small thin flat pieces

flaky \'flā-kē\ *adj* **flak•i•er**; **flak•i•est**
tending to break apart into small thin flat pieces ⟨a *flaky* pie crust⟩
flak•i•ness *n*

flam•boy•ant \flam-'bȯi-ənt\ *adj*
having a noticeable or showy quality
flam•boy•ant•ly *adv*

[1]**flame** \'flām\ *n*
1 the glowing gas that makes up part of a fire ⟨the *flame* of a candle⟩
2 a state of burning brightly ⟨The sticks burst into *flame*.⟩
3 strongly felt emotion

[2]**flame** *vb* **flamed**; **flam•ing**
to burn with or as if with a flame ⟨a torch *flaming*⟩

flame•throw•er \'flām-,thrō-ər\ *n*
a weapon that shoots a burning stream of fuel

fla•min•go \flə-'miŋ-gō\ *n, pl* **fla•min•gos** *or* **fla•min•goes**
▶ a large pale pink to reddish waterbird with very long neck and legs and a broad bill bent downward at the end

▶ **Word History** The English word *flamingo* came from the bird's Spanish name, which was originally spelled *flamengo* and is now *flamenco*. In Spanish *flamenco* literally means "Fleming," which is a name for the Dutch-speaking inhabitants of Belgium. Spaniards conventionally thought of Flemings as fair, but with ruddy faces, and this is probably why they gave this name to the pinkish birds—though no one knows for certain.

flamingo

flam•ma•ble \'fla-mə-bəl\ *adj*
capable of being easily set on fire and of burning quickly

[1]**flank** \'flaŋk\ *n*
1 the area on the side of an animal between the ribs and the hip
2 [1]SIDE 3 ⟨the mountain's *flank*⟩
3 the right or left side of a formation (as of soldiers)

[2]**flank** *vb* **flanked**; **flank•ing**
1 to be located at the side of
2 to attack or threaten the side of ⟨We've *flanked* the enemy troops.⟩

flan•nel \'fla-nᵊl\ *n*
a soft cloth made of wool or cotton

[1]**flap** \'flap\ *n*
1 something broad and flat or flexible that hangs loose ⟨Tape the box *flaps* closed.⟩
2 the motion or sound made by something broad and flexible (as a sail or wing) moving back and forth
3 an upset or worried state of mind ⟨Don't get in a *flap* over nothing.⟩

[2]**flap** *vb* **flapped**; **flap•ping**
to move with a beating or fluttering motion ⟨Birds *flapped* their wings.⟩

flap•jack \'flap-,jak\ *n*
PANCAKE

[1]**flare** \'fler\ *vb* **flared**; **flar•ing**
1 to burn with an unsteady flame
2 to shine or burn suddenly or briefly ⟨A match *flared* in the darkness.⟩
3 to become angry or active ⟨She *flared* up at the remarks.⟩ ⟨His asthma has *flared* up.⟩
4 to spread outward ⟨Her nostrils *flared*.⟩

[2]**flare** *n*
1 a sudden blaze of light ⟨the *flare* of a match⟩
2 a blaze of light used to signal, light up something, or attract attention
3 a device or material used to produce a flare ⟨The emergency kit included *flares*.⟩
4 a sudden outburst ⟨She displayed a *flare* of anger.⟩
5 a spreading outward **:** a part that spreads outward ⟨the *flare* of a skirt⟩

[1]**flash** \'flash\ *vb* **flashed**; **flash•ing**
1 to shine or give off bright light suddenly ⟨Lightning *flashed* in the sky.⟩
2 to appear quickly or suddenly ⟨A message *flashed* on the screen.⟩
3 to come or pass very suddenly ⟨A car *flashed* by.⟩
4 to show briefly ⟨The officer *flashed* his badge.⟩

[2]**flash** *n*
1 ▼ a sudden burst of or as if of light ⟨a *flash* of lightning⟩ ⟨a *flash* of brilliance⟩
2 a very short time ⟨I'll be back in a *flash*.⟩

[3]**flash** *adj* beginning suddenly and lasting only a short time ⟨*flash* floods⟩

[2]**flash 1:** a flash of lightning in the sky

flash•light \'flash-ˌlīt\ *n*
▼a small portable electric light that runs on batteries

flashlight

flashy \'fla-shē\ *adj* **flash•i•er; flash•i•est**
GAUDY, SHOWY ⟨*flashy* clothes⟩

flask \'flask\ *n*
a container like a bottle with a flat or rounded body

[1]**flat** \'flat\ *adj* **flat•ter; flat•test**
1 having a smooth level surface ⟨a *flat* rock⟩
2 spread out on or along a surface ⟨He was lying *flat* on his back.⟩
3 having a broad smooth surface and little thickness ⟨A CD is *flat*.⟩
4 very clear and definite ⟨a *flat* refusal⟩
5 not changing in amount ⟨I charge a *flat* rate.⟩
6 not showing active business ⟨Sales are *flat*.⟩
7 [1]DULL 3 ⟨a *flat* story⟩ ⟨She spoke in a *flat*, tired voice.⟩
8 having lost air ⟨a *flat* tire⟩
9 no longer having bubbles ⟨*flat* ginger ale⟩
10 lower than the true musical pitch
11 lower by a half step in music
12 not shiny ⟨*flat* paint⟩
synonyms see LEVEL
flat•ly *adv*

[2]**flat** *n*
1 a level area of land : PLAIN
2 a flat part or surface ⟨the *flat* of the hand⟩
3 a note or tone that is a half step lower than the note named
4 a sign ♭ meaning that the pitch of a musical note is to be lower by a half step
5 a tire that has lost air

[3]**flat** *adv*
1 on or against a flat surface ⟨lie *flat*⟩
2 without any time more or less : EXACTLY ⟨ten seconds *flat*⟩
3 below the true musical pitch

flat•boat \'flat-ˌbōt\ *n*
a large boat with a flat bottom and square ends

flat•car \-ˌkär\ *n*
a railroad car without sides or a roof that is used to carry freight

flat•fish \'flat-ˌfish\ *n*
a fish (as the flounder) that has a flat body and swims on its side with both eyes on the upper side

flat–out \'flat-ˌau̇t\ *adj*
1 [2]OUT-RIGHT 1
2 greatest possible ⟨a *flat-out* effort⟩

flat out *adv*
1 in a very clear manner ⟨I told him *flat out* to leave.⟩
2 at top speed ⟨We worked *flat out* to finish.⟩

flat–pan•el \'flat-'pa-nᵊl\ *adj*
relating to a thin flat video display ⟨a *flat-panel* computer screen⟩

flat•ten \'fla-tᵊn\ *vb* **flat•tened; flat•ten•ing**
to make or become flat

flat•ter \'fla-tər\ *vb* **flat•tered; flat•ter•ing**
1 to praise but not sincerely ⟨"You haven't changed since the day we met," Grandpa *flattered* Grandma.⟩
2 to cause to feel pleased by showing respect or admiration ⟨I was *flattered* to be asked to sing at the wedding.⟩
3 to show as favorably as possible ⟨This picture *flatters* me.⟩
4 to make look more attractive ⟨That dress *flatters* you.⟩
synonyms see COMPLIMENT
flat•ter•er *n*

flat•tery \'fla-tə-rē\ *n, pl* **flat•ter•ies**
praise that is not deserved or meant

flaunt \'flȯnt\ *vb* **flaunt•ed; flaunt•ing**
1 to wave or flutter in a showy way ⟨The flag *flaunts* in the breeze.⟩
2 to show in a way that attracts attention ⟨They like to *flaunt* their money.⟩

[1]**fla•vor** \'flā-vər\ *n*
1 the quality of something that affects the sense of taste ⟨I like the spicy *flavor* of Indian food.⟩
2 a substance added to food to give it a desired taste ⟨artificial *flavors*⟩

[2]**flavor** *vb* **fla•vored; fla•vor•ing**
to give or add something to produce a taste ⟨The chef *flavored* the sauce with peppers.⟩
flavored *adj*

fla•vor•ing \'flā-və-riŋ, 'flāv-riŋ\ *n*
[1]FLAVOR 2

flaw \'flȯ\ *n*
a small fault or weakness ⟨There is a *flaw* in the plan.⟩
flaw•less \-ləs\ *adj*

flax \'flaks\ *n*
a plant with blue flowers that is grown for its fiber from which rope and linen is made and for its seed from which oil and livestock feed are obtained

flax•en \'flak-sən\ *adj*
having a light yellow color ⟨*flaxen* hair⟩

flax•seed \'flak-ˌsēd\ *n*
the seed of flax from which linseed oil comes

flay \'flā\ *vb* **flayed; flay•ing**
1 to strip off the skin or surface of
2 to beat severely

flea \'flē\ *n*
a small bloodsucking insect that has no wings and a hard body

[1]**fleck** \'flek\ *vb* **flecked; fleck•ing**
to mark with small streaks or spots ⟨The bananas were *flecked* with brown.⟩

[2]**fleck** *n*
1 [1]SPOT 1, MARK
2 a small bit

fledg•ling \'flej-liŋ\ *n*
a young bird that has just grown the feathers needed to fly

flee \'flē\ *vb* **fled** \'fled\; **flee•ing**
to run away or away from ⟨Animals *fled* the fire.⟩

[1]**fleece** \'flēs\ *n*
▼the woolly coat of an animal and especially a sheep

[2]**fleece** *vb* **fleeced; fleec•ing**
to rob or cheat by trickery

[1]fleece: a farmer shearing fleece from a sheep

A B C D E F G H I J K L M N O P Q R S T U V W X Y Z

fleecy \'flē-sē\ *adj* **fleec•i•er**; **fleec•i•est**
covered with, made of, or similar to fleece ⟨a soft *fleecy* sweater⟩ ⟨*fleecy* clouds⟩

¹fleet \'flēt\ *n*
1 a group of warships under one commander
2 a country's navy
3 a group of ships or vehicles that move together or are owned by one company ⟨a fishing *fleet*⟩ ⟨a *fleet* of taxis⟩

²fleet *adj* **fleet•er**; **fleet•est**
very swift ⟨a *fleet* runner⟩
fleet•ly *adv*

fleet•ing \'flē-tiŋ\ *adj*
passing by quickly ⟨a *fleeting* instant⟩

flesh \'flesh\ *n*
1 the soft parts of an animal's or person's body
2 the part of an animal that is eaten : MEAT
3 a soft edible plant part

fleshy \'fle-shē\ *adj* **flesh•i•er**; **flesh•i•est**
1 like or consisting of flesh ⟨a *fleshy* snout⟩
2 ¹FAT 1

flew *past of* FLY

flex \'fleks\ *vb* **flexed**; **flex•ing**
1 to bend especially again and again ⟨Can you *flex* your fingers?⟩
2 to move or tense (a muscle)

flex•i•bil•i•ty \ˌflek-sə-'bi-lə-tē\ *n*
the quality or state of being easy to bend

flex•i•ble \'flek-sə-bəl\ *adj*
1 possible or easy to bend ⟨*flexible* plastic⟩
2 easily changed ⟨a *flexible* schedule⟩

¹flick \'flik\ *n*
a light snapping stroke ⟨the *flick* of a switch⟩

²flick *vb* **flicked**; **flick•ing**
to strike or move with a quick motion ⟨He *flicked* the bug off his arm.⟩ ⟨The snake *flicked* its tongue.⟩

¹flick•er \'fli-kər\ *vb* **flick•ered**; **flick•er•ing**
1 to burn unsteadily ⟨a *flickering* candle⟩
2 to appear briefly ⟨A smile *flickered* across her face.⟩
3 to move quickly

²flicker *n*
1 a quick small movement ⟨a *flicker* of the eyelids⟩
2 a quick movement of light

³flicker *n*
a large North American woodpecker

fli•er *or* **fly•er** \'flī-ər\ *n*
1 a person or thing that flies
2 usually flyer : a printed sheet containing information or advertising that is given to many people

¹flight \'flīt\ *n*
1 an act of passing through the air by the use of wings ⟨the *flight* of a bee⟩
2 a passing through the air or space ⟨a balloon *flight*⟩ ⟨the *flight* of a space shuttle⟩
3 a trip by an airplane or spacecraft ⟨a *flight* to Chicago⟩ ⟨a *flight* to Mars⟩
4 a group of similar things flying through the air together ⟨a *flight* of ducks⟩
5 an extraordinary display ⟨a *flight* of imagination⟩
6 a series of stairs from one level or floor to the next

²flight *n*
the act of running away

flight•less \'flīt-ləs\ *adj*
unable to fly ⟨Penguins are *flightless* birds.⟩

flighty \'flī-tē\ *adj* **flight•i•er**; **flight•i•est**
1 easily excited or frightened : SKITTISH ⟨a *flighty* horse⟩
2 not steady or serious ⟨a *flighty* temper⟩

flim•sy \'flim-zē\ *adj* **flim•si•er**; **flim•si•est**
not strong or solid ⟨a *flimsy* cardboard box⟩ ⟨a *flimsy* excuse⟩

flinch \'flinch\ *vb* **flinched**; **flinch•ing**
to draw back from or as if from pain or fear

¹fling \'fliŋ\ *vb* **flung** \'fləŋ\; **fling•ing**
1 to throw hard or without care ⟨She *flung* the junk out the window.⟩
2 to move forcefully ⟨He *flung* his arms around her.⟩

²fling *n*
1 an act of throwing hard or without care
2 a time of freedom for pleasure ⟨The trip was our last *fling* of the summer.⟩
3 a brief try

flint \'flint\ *n*
a very hard stone that produces a spark when struck by steel

flint•lock \'flint-ˌläk\ *n*
▼ an old-fashioned firearm using a piece of flint for striking a spark to fire the charge

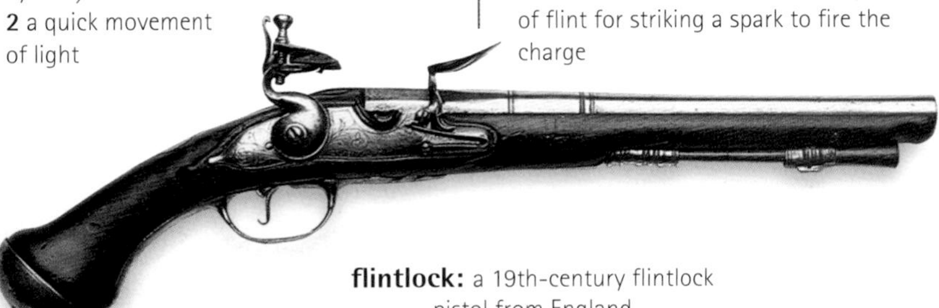

flintlock: a 19th-century flintlock pistol from England

¹flip \'flip\ *vb* **flipped**; **flip•ping**
to move or turn by or as if by tossing ⟨*flip* a coin⟩ ⟨*flip* a switch⟩

²flip *n*
1 a quick turn, toss, or movement ⟨the *flip* of a coin⟩
2 a somersault in the air

flip•pant \'fli-pənt\ *adj*
not respectful or serious ⟨a *flippant* response⟩
flip•pant•ly *adv*

flip•per \'fli-pər\ *n*
1 ▼ a broad flat limb (as of a seal or whale) used for swimming
2 a flat rubber shoe with the front widened into a paddle for use in swimming

flipper 1: a California sea lion with flippers

¹flirt \'flərt\ *vb* **flirt•ed**; **flirt•ing**
to show a romantic interest in someone just for fun

²flirt *n*
a person who flirts a lot

flit \'flit\ *vb* **flit•ted**; **flit•ting**
to move, pass, or fly quickly from one place or thing to another ⟨Hummingbirds *flitted* from flower to flower.⟩

¹float \'flōt\ *n*
1 something that rests in or on the surface of a liquid
2 an inflated support for a person in water
3 a light object that holds up the baited end of a fishing line
4 a platform anchored near a shore for the use of swimmers or boats
5 a structure that holds up an airplane in water
6 a soft drink with ice cream floating in it ⟨a root beer *float*⟩
7 a vehicle with a platform used to carry an exhibit in a parade

[2]float *vb* **float•ed**; **float•ing**
1 to rest on the surface of a liquid ⟨Cork *floats* in water.⟩
2 to be carried along by or as if by moving water or air ⟨The raft *floated* downstream.⟩ ⟨Leaves *floated* down.⟩
3 to cause to rest on or be carried by water ⟨Lumberjacks *float* logs down the river.⟩

[1]flock \'fläk\ *n*
1 a group of animals living or kept together ⟨a *flock* of geese⟩
2 a group someone watches over ⟨the minister's *flock*⟩
3 a large number ⟨a *flock* of tourists⟩

[2]flock *vb* **flocked**; **flock•ing**
to gather or move in a crowd

floe \'flō\ *n*
a sheet or mass of floating ice

flog \'fläg\ *vb* **flogged**; **flog•ging**
to beat severely with a rod or whip

[1]flood \'fləd\ *n*
1 a huge flow of water that rises and spreads over the land
2 the flowing in of the tide
3 a very large number or amount ⟨a *flood* of mail⟩

[2]flood *vb* **flood•ed**; **flood•ing**
1 to cover or become filled with water
2 to fill as if with a flood ⟨Sunlight *flooded* her room.⟩

flood•light \'fləd-,līt\ *n*
a light that shines brightly over a wide area

flood•plain \'fləd-,plān\ *n*
low flat land along a stream that is flooded when the stream overflows

flood•wa•ter \'fləd-,wȯ-tər, -,wä-\ *n*
the water of a flood

[1]floor \'flȯr\ *n*
1 the part of a room on which people stand
2 the lower inside surface of a hollow structure ⟨the *floor* of a car⟩
3 the area of ground at the bottom of something ⟨the ocean *floor*⟩
4 a story of a building ⟨the fourth *floor*⟩

[2]floor *vb* **floored**; **floor•ing**
1 to cover or provide with a floor ⟨The kitchen was *floored* with tile.⟩
2 to knock down ⟨The punch *floored* him.⟩

floor•ing \'flȯr-iŋ\ *n*
1 [1]FLOOR 1
2 material for floors

[1]flop \'fläp\ *vb* **flopped**; **flop•ping**
1 to flap about ⟨A fish *flopped* all over the deck.⟩
2 to drop or fall limply ⟨He *flopped* into the chair.⟩
3 [1]FAIL 1

[2]flop *n*
1 the act or sound of flapping about or falling limply ⟨My backpack hit the ground with a *flop*.⟩
2 FAILURE 1 ⟨The show was a *flop*.⟩

flop•py \'flä-pē\ *adj* **flop•pi•er**; **flop•pi•est**
being soft and flexible ⟨a big *floppy* hat⟩

floppy disk *n*
a small flexible plastic disk with a magnetic coating on which computer data can be stored

flo•ra \'flȯr-ə\ *n*
the plant life typical of a region, period, or special environment

flo•ral \'flȯr-əl\ *adj*
of or relating to flowers

flor•id \'flȯr-əd\ *adj*
1 very fancy or flowery in style ⟨*florid* writing⟩
2 having a reddish color ⟨a *florid* face⟩

flo•rist \'flȯr-əst\ *n*
a person who sells flowers and houseplants

[1]floss \'fläs, 'flȯs\ *n*
1 DENTAL FLOSS
2 soft thread used in embroidery
3 fluffy material full of fibers

[2]floss *vb* **flossed**; **floss•ing**
to use dental floss on

flo•til•la \flō-'ti-lə\ *n*
a fleet of usually small ships

[1]flounce \'flau̇ns\ *vb* **flounced**; **flounc•ing**
1 to move with exaggerated motions
2 *chiefly British* to walk in a way that shows anger ⟨He *flounced* out of the room.⟩

[2]flounce *n*
a strip of fabric or ruffle attached by one edge ⟨a *flounce* on a skirt⟩
flouncy *adj*

[1]floun•der \'flau̇n-dər\ *n*
a flatfish used for food

[2]flounder *vb* **floun•dered**; **floun•der•ing**
1 to struggle to move or get footing ⟨The horses were *floundering* in the mud.⟩
2 to behave or do something in a clumsy way ⟨I *floundered* through the speech.⟩

flour \'flau̇r\ *n*
▶ finely ground wheat or other food product ⟨whole wheat *flour*⟩ ⟨potato *flour*⟩

[1]flour•ish \'flər-ish\ *vb* **flour•ished**; **flour•ish•ing**
1 to grow well : THRIVE ⟨Plants *flourish* in this rich soil.⟩
2 to do well : enjoy success ⟨This style of art *flourished* in the 1920s.⟩
3 to make sweeping movements with ⟨He *flourished* a sword.⟩

[2]flourish *n*
1 a fancy bit of decoration added to something ⟨He added a *flourish* to his signature.⟩
2 a sweeping motion ⟨She removed her hat with a *flourish*.⟩

flout \'flau̇t\ *vb* **flout•ed**; **flout•ing**
to ignore in an open and disrespectful way ⟨The children *flouted* the rules.⟩

[1]flow \'flō\ *vb* **flowed**; **flow•ing**
1 to move in or as if in a stream ⟨The river *flows* to the sea.⟩ ⟨She felt relief *flow* through her.⟩
2 to glide along smoothly ⟨Traffic is *flowing* on the highway.⟩
3 to hang loose and waving ⟨Her hair *flowed* down.⟩

[2]flow *n*
1 an act of moving in or as if in a stream ⟨a *flow* of tears⟩ ⟨a *flow* of praise⟩
2 the rise of the tide ⟨the ebb and *flow* of the tide⟩
3 a smooth even movement : STREAM ⟨the *flow* of conversation⟩ ⟨a *flow* of information⟩
4 an amount or mass of something moving in a stream ⟨blood *flow*⟩

[1]flow•er \'flau̇-ər\ *n*
1 ▶ a plant part that produces seed
2 a small plant grown chiefly for its showy flowers
3 the state of bearing flowers ⟨in full *flower*⟩
4 the best part or example ⟨in the *flower* of youth⟩
flow•ered \-ərd\ *adj*
flow•er•less \-ər-ləs\ *adj*

▶ flour
Wheat flour is a staple food of western culture. It contains a protein (called gluten) that, when mixed with water, becomes elastic and gives dough its structure. The dough can then be baked into bread, crackers, and other products.

[1]flower 1
A flower is the reproductive part of a flowering plant. It may contain the male reproductive organs (filaments and pollen-bearing anthers), or the female organs (stigma, style, and ovule-bearing ovaries), or both. Pollination takes place when pollen is transferred from the anthers to the stigma within the same flower, or to another flower by the action of wind, insects, or birds.

[2]**flower** *vb* **flow•ered; flow•er•ing**
[2]BLOOM 1

flower head *n*
▼ a tight cluster of small flowers that are arranged so that the whole looks like a single flower

flowering plant *n*
a seed plant whose seeds are produced in the ovary of a flower

flower head:
a bluish-purple rounded flower head

flow•ery \ˈflau̇-ə-rē\ *adj* **flow•er•i•er; flow•er•i•est**
1 full of or covered with flowers
2 full of fancy words ⟨*flowery* language⟩

flown *past participle of* FLY

flu \ˈflü\ *n*
1 INFLUENZA
2 any of several virus diseases something like a cold

fluc•tu•ate \ˈflək-chə-ˌwāt\ *vb* **fluc•tu•at•ed; fluc•tu•at•ing**
to change continually and especially up and down ⟨The temperature *fluctuated.*⟩

flue \ˈflü\ *n*
an enclosed passage for smoke or air

flu•en•cy \ˈflü-ən-sē\ *n*
the ability to speak easily and well

flu•ent \ˈflü-ənt\ *adj*
1 able to speak easily and well ⟨He was *fluent* in Spanish.⟩
2 smooth and correct ⟨She speaks *fluent* German.⟩
flu•ent•ly \-ənt-lē\ *adv*

[1]**fluff** \ˈfləf\ *n*
something light and soft ⟨*Fluff* stuck out of the torn cushion.⟩

[2]**fluff** *vb* **fluffed; fluff•ing**
to make or become fuller, lighter, or softer ⟨She *fluffed* up her pillow.⟩

fluffy \ˈflə-fē\ *adj* **fluff•i•er; fluff•i•est**
1 having, covered with, or similar to down ⟨a *fluffy* little chick⟩
2 being or looking light and soft ⟨*fluffy* scrambled eggs⟩ ⟨*fluffy* clouds⟩

[1]**flu•id** \ˈflü-əd\ *adj*
1 capable of flowing like a liquid or gas ⟨*fluid* lava⟩
2 having a graceful or flowing style or appearance ⟨a dancer's *fluid* movement⟩
flu•id•ly *adv*

[2]**fluid** *n*
something that tends to flow and take the shape of its container

fluid ounce *n*
a unit of liquid capacity equal to 1/16 of a pint (about 29.6 milliliters)

flung *past and past participle of* FLING

flunk \ˈfləŋk\ *vb* **flunked; flunk•ing**
[1]FAIL 1 ⟨I *flunked* the test.⟩

fluo•res•cent \flu̇-ˈre-sᵊnt, flō-\ *adj*
1 giving out visible light when exposed to external radiation ⟨a *fluorescent* substance⟩ ⟨a *fluorescent* coating⟩
2 producing visible light by means of a fluorescent coating ⟨a *fluorescent* bulb⟩
3 extremely bright or glowing ⟨*fluorescent* colors⟩

fluo•ri•date \ˈflu̇r-ə-ˌdāt, ˈflȯr-\ *vb* **fluo•ri•dat•ed; fluo•ri•dat•ing**
to add a fluoride to

fluo•ride \ˈflȯr-ˌīd, ˈflu̇r-\ *n*
a compound of fluorine ⟨Many toothpastes contain *fluoride* to help prevent tooth decay.⟩

fluo•rine \ˈflu̇r-ˌēn, ˈflȯr-\ *n*
a yellowish flammable irritating gaseous chemical element

flur•ry \ˈflər-ē\ *n, pl* **flurries**
1 a gust of wind
2 a brief light snowfall
3 a brief outburst

[1]**flush** \ˈfləsh\ *vb* **flushed; flush•ing**
to cause to leave a hiding place ⟨The hunting dogs were *flushing* birds.⟩

[2]**flush** *n*
1 an act of pouring water over or through ⟨Give the toilet a *flush.*⟩
2 [2]BLUSH 1
3 a sudden or strong feeling ⟨a *flush* of relief⟩

[3]**flush** *vb* **flushed; flush•ing**
1 [1]BLUSH 1 ⟨He *flushed* with embarrassment.⟩
2 to pour water over or through ⟨*Flush* your eye with water.⟩

[4]**flush** *adj*
even or level with another surface ⟨The cabinet should be *flush* with the wall.⟩

[5]**flush** *adv*
so as to be even or level with another surface ⟨Pound the nails *flush* with the floor.⟩

[1]**flus•ter** \ˈflə-stər\ *vb* **flus•tered; flus•ter•ing**
to make nervous and confused : UPSET

[2]**fluster** *n*
a state of nervous confusion

flute \ˈflüt\ *n*
▼ a woodwind instrument in the form of a slender tube open at one end that is played by blowing across a hole near the closed end

flute

[1]**flut•ter** \ˈflə-tər\ *vb* **flut•tered; flut•ter•ing**
1 to move the wings rapidly without flying or in making short flights ⟨Butterflies *fluttered* over the garden.⟩
2 to move with a quick flapping motion ⟨Flags *fluttered* in the wind.⟩
3 to move about excitedly

[2]**flutter** *n*
1 an act of moving or flapping quickly ⟨a *flutter* of wings⟩
2 a state of excitement ⟨The contestants were all in a *flutter.*⟩

[1]**fly** \ˈflī\ *vb* **flew** \ˈflü\; **flown** \ˈflōn\; **fly•ing**
1 to move in or pass through the air with wings ⟨Birds and airplanes *fly.*⟩
2 to move through the air or before the wind ⟨Paper was *flying* in all directions.⟩
3 to float or cause to float, wave, or soar in the wind ⟨*fly* a kite⟩ ⟨*fly* a flag⟩
4 to run away : FLEE
5 to pass or move swiftly ⟨Time *flies.*⟩ ⟨Cars were *flying* past us.⟩
6 to operate or travel in an aircraft ⟨*fly* a jet⟩ ⟨I'm *flying* home for the holidays.⟩
7 to become suddenly emotional ⟨He *flew* into a rage.⟩

²fly *n, pl* **flies**
1 a flap of material to cover a fastening in a garment
2 a layer of fabric that goes over the top of a tent
3 a baseball hit very high

³fly *n, pl* **flies**
1 ▶ any of a large group of mostly stout-bodied two-winged insects (as the housefly)
2 a winged insect
Hint: This sense of *fly* is usually used in combination ⟨dragon*fly*⟩ ⟨fire*fly*⟩
3 a fishhook made to look like an insect

fly•catch•er \'flī-ˌka-chər, -ˌke-\ *n*
a small bird that eats flying insects

flyer *variant of* FLIER

flying fish *n*
▼ a fish with large fins that let it jump from the water and move for a distance through the air

flying fish

fly•way \'flī-ˌwā\ *n*
a route regularly followed by migratory birds

¹foal \'fōl\ *n*
a young animal of the horse family especially when less than one year old

²foal *vb* **foaled**; **foal•ing**
to give birth to a baby horse ⟨The mare will *foal* soon.⟩

¹foam \'fōm\ *n*
a mass of tiny bubbles that forms in or on the surface of a liquid

²foam *vb* **foamed**; **foam•ing**
to produce or form a mass of tiny bubbles ⟨Baking soda will *foam* when you add vinegar.⟩

foamy \'fō-mē\ *adj* **foam•i•er**; **foam•i•est**
covered with or looking like foam
foam•i•ness *n*

fo•cal \'fō-kəl\ *adj*
1 of, relating to, or having a focus
2 having central or great importance ⟨She is a *focal* character in the story.⟩

▶ **³fly 1**
Flies make up a huge group of insects with large compound eyes, and feet with sticky pads and claws that allow them to walk on any surface. The larvae of flies are called maggots.

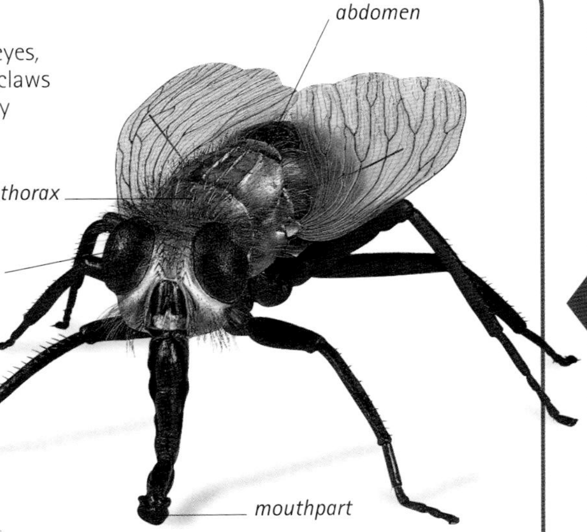

abdomen
thorax
compound eye with many light-sensing units
mouthpart

features of a greenbottle fly \'grēn-ˌbät-l-\

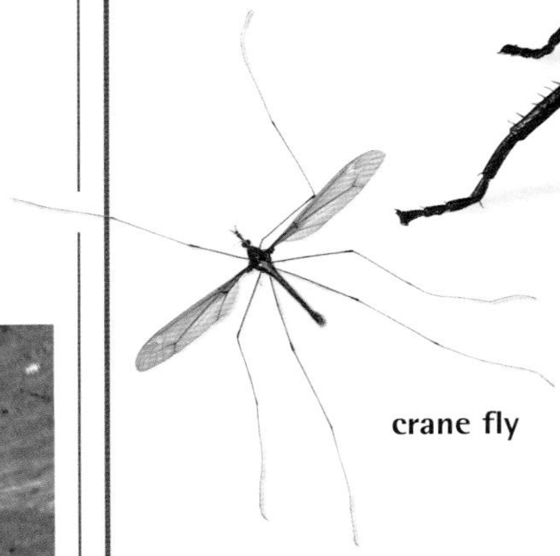

crane fly

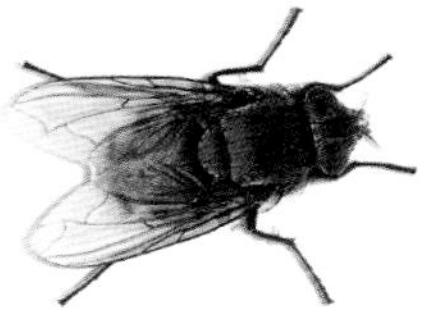

housefly

robber fly

hoverfly \'hə-vər-ˌflī\

¹fo•cus \'fō-kəs\ *n, pl* **fo•ci** \'fō-ˌsī\ *also* **fo•cus•es**
1 a point at which rays (as of light, heat, or sound) meet after being reflected or bent : the point at which an image is formed
2 the distance from a lens or mirror to a focus
3 an adjustment that gives clear vision
4 a center of activity or interest

▶ **Word History** The Latin word *focus* meant "hearth, fireplace." In the scientific Latin of the 1600s, *focus* referred to the point at which rays of light gathered by a lens come together. Since rays of sunlight when directed by a magnifying glass can produce enough heat to ignite paper, their meeting point is aptly described with a word that means "fireplace." Other senses arose from this sense of *focus*.

²focus *vb* **fo•cused** *also* **fo•cussed**; **fo•cus•ing** *also* **fo•cus•sing**
1 to bring or come to a focus ⟨*focus* rays of light⟩
2 to adjust the focus of ⟨He *focused* his binoculars.⟩
3 to direct or cause to direct at ⟨*Focus* your attention on your work.⟩

fod•der \'fä-dər\ *n*
▼ coarse dry food (as cornstalks) for livestock

fodder

foe \'fō\ *n*
an enemy of a person or a country

[1]fog \'fȯg, 'fäg\ *n*
1 tiny drops of water floating in the air at or near the ground
2 a confused state of mind ⟨I woke up in a *fog*.⟩

[2]fog *vb* **fogged; fog•ging**
to cover or become covered with tiny drops of water

fog•gy \'fȯ-gē, 'fä-\ *adj* **fog•gi•er; fog•gi•est**
1 filled with fog ⟨a *foggy* morning⟩
2 unsure or confused ⟨My memory is *foggy*.⟩

fog•horn \'fȯg-,hȯrn, 'fäg-\ *n*
a loud horn sounded in foggy weather to give warning

foi•ble \'fȯi-bəl\ *n*
an unimportant weakness or failing ⟨silly human *foibles*⟩

[1]foil \'fȯil\ *vb* **foiled; foil•ing**
to prevent from achieving a goal ⟨Police *foiled* the bank robbery.⟩

[2]foil *n*
a very thin sheet of metal ⟨aluminum *foil*⟩

[3]foil *n*
a fencing sword having a light flexible blade with a blunt point

[1]fold \'fōld\ *n*
an enclosure for sheep

[2]fold *vb* **fold•ed; fold•ing**
1 to lay one part over or against another part ⟨*fold* a blanket⟩
2 to clasp together ⟨*fold* your hands⟩
3 [1]EMBRACE 1 ⟨She *folded* the child in her arms.⟩

[3]fold *n*
1 an act or the result of laying one part over or against another ⟨With just a few *folds* he made a paper airplane.⟩
2 a part laid over another part ⟨the *folds* of the curtain⟩
3 ▼ a bend produced in a rock layer by pressure

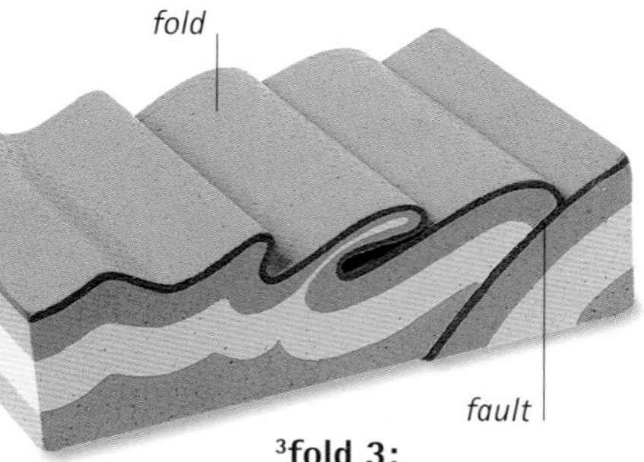

[3]fold 3:
model showing how folds of rock form mountain ridges

-fold \,fōld\ *suffix*
1 multiplied by a specified number : times
Hint: *-fold* is used in adjectives ⟨a twelve*fold* increase⟩ and adverbs ⟨repay ten*fold*⟩.
2 having so many parts ⟨a three*fold* problem⟩

fold•er \'fōl-dər\ *n*
1 a folded cover or large envelope for loose papers ⟨a manila *folder*⟩
2 a folded printed sheet ⟨a travel *folder*⟩
3 a part of a computer operating system used to organize files

fo•li•age \'fō-lē-ij\ *n*
the leaves of a plant

[1]folk \'fōk\ *n, pl* **folk** *or* **folks**
1 persons of a certain kind or group ⟨the old *folk*⟩ ⟨rich *folks*⟩
2 *folks pl* people in general ⟨Most *folks* agree with me.⟩
3 *folks pl* family members and especially parents

[2]folk *adj*
created by the common people ⟨a *folk* dance⟩ ⟨*folk* music⟩

folk•lore \'fōk-,lȯr\ *n*
traditional customs, beliefs, stories, and sayings

folk•sing•er \'fōk-,siŋ-ər\ *n*
a person who sings songs (**folk songs**) created by and long sung among the common people

folk•tale \'fōk-,tāl\ *n*
a story made up and handed down by the common people

fol•low \'fä-lō\ *vb* **fol•lowed; fol•low•ing**
1 to go or come after or behind ⟨The dog *followed* the children home.⟩ ⟨Dessert *followed* dinner.⟩
2 to come after in time or place ⟨Spring *follows* winter.⟩
3 to go on the track of ⟨Police *followed* a clue.⟩
4 to go along or beside ⟨*Follow* that path.⟩
5 to be led or guided by : OBEY ⟨*Follow* the instructions.⟩
6 to result from ⟨Panic *followed* the fire.⟩
7 to work in or at something as a way of life ⟨He *followed* the sea.⟩
8 to watch or pay attention to ⟨Just *follow* the bouncing ball.⟩
9 UNDERSTAND 1 ⟨I'm not *following* this story.⟩
synonyms see CHASE
fol•low•er \'fäl-ə-wər\ *n*

follow suit
1 to play a card that belongs to the same *suit* (as hearts) as the one first played

▶ food 1
Foods contain many chemicals that allow the body to function. Some foods are most important as sources of energy, while others help the body fight infection or keep fluid levels in balance. A healthy diet includes food from all six main food groups: the bread, cereal, rice, and pasta group, which forms the base of the diet; the vegetables group; the fruit group; the meat, poultry, fish, beans, eggs, and nuts group; the milk, yogurt, and cheese group; and lastly, the group of fats, oils, and sugars, which should be eaten sparingly.

a plate of healthy food

2 to do the same thing someone else has just done
follow through to complete something started 〈*follow through* on a promise〉
follow up to take additional similar or related action 〈I *followed up* my letter with a phone call.〉

[1]fol•low•ing \'fä-lə-wiŋ\ *adj*
coming just after 〈the *following* page〉

[2]following *n*
a group of fans or supporters

[3]following *prep*
right after 〈Questions will be taken *following* the presentation.〉

fol•ly \'fä-lē\ *n, pl* **follies**
1 lack of good sense
2 a foolish act or idea

fond \'fänd\ *adj* **fond•er**; **fond•est**
1 having a liking or love 〈She's *fond* of candy.〉
2 AFFECTIONATE, LOVING 〈a *fond* farewell〉
3 strongly wished for 〈a *fond* dream〉
fond•ly *adv*
fond•ness *n*

fon•dle \'fän-dᵊl\ *vb* **fon•dled**; **fon•dling**
to touch or handle in a tender or loving manner

[1]font \'fänt\ *n*
1 ▼ a basin to hold water for baptism
2 SOURCE 1 〈a *font* of information〉

[2]font *n*
a set of letters, numbers, and punctuation marks that are all one size and style

font 1: a baptismal font, dating from 1437

food \'füd\ *n*
1 ◀ the material that people and animals eat : material containing carbohydrates, fats, proteins, and supplements (as minerals and vitamins) that is taken in by and used in the living body for growth and repair and as a source of energy for activities
2 inorganic substances (as nitrate and carbon dioxide) taken in by green plants and used to build organic nutrients
3 organic materials (as sugar and starch) formed by plants and used in their growth and activities
4 solid food as distinguished from drink

▶ food chain
This simplified food chain is shown in the form of a pyramid with the owl, the highest member of the food chain, at the top. The owl would eat the weasels, voles, and mice in the levels below it. The weasels, in turn, would eat the mice and voles, while the mice and voles, at the bottom of the chain, would eat plants and insects. The chart shows that it takes several weasels to feed a single owl, and many more mice and voles to feed the weasels, as well as the owl.

a simple food chain

the owl represents the single predator at the top of the food chain

weasel

vole

mouse

food chain *n*
▲ a sequence of organisms in which each depends on the next and usually lower member as a source of food

food•stuff \'füd-,stəf\ *n*
▼ a substance that is used as food

foodstuff: foodstuffs in a store

food web *n*
the whole group of interacting food chains in a community

[1]fool \'fül\ *n*
1 a person without good sense or judgment
2 JESTER

▶ **Word History** In Latin the word *follis* meant "bag" or (in the plural form *folles*) "bellows." In the late stage of Latin that developed into French, *follis* also took on the meaning "person without sense," whose head seemed, like a bag or bellows, to be full of nothing but air. *Follis* became Old French *fol*, which was borrowed into English as *fol*, later spelled *fool*.

[2]fool *vb* **fooled**; **fool•ing**
1 to speak or act in a playful way or in fun : JOKE 〈We were only *fooling*.〉
2 [2]TRICK 〈Don't let them *fool* you.〉
3 to spend time in an aimless way 〈We *fooled* around in the playground before school.〉
4 to play with or handle something carelessly 〈Don't *fool* with my science project.〉

a b c d e f g h i j k l m n o p q r s t u v w x y z

fool•har•dy \'fül-ˌhär-dē\ *adj*
foolishly adventurous : RECKLESS ⟨a *foolhardy* action⟩

fool•ish \'fü-lish\ *adj*
showing or resulting from lack of good sense ⟨a *foolish* man⟩ ⟨a *foolish* choice⟩
synonyms see ABSURD
fool•ish•ly *adv*
fool•ish•ness *n*

fool•proof \'fül-'prüf\ *adj*
done, made, or planned so well that nothing can go wrong ⟨a *foolproof* recipe⟩

[1]**foot** \'fu̇t\ *n, pl* **feet** \'fēt\
1 the end part of the leg of an animal or person : the part of an animal on which it stands or moves
2 a unit of length equal to twelve inches (about .3 meter)
3 the lowest or end part of something ⟨*foot* of a hill⟩ ⟨*foot* of the bed⟩
on foot by walking ⟨They traveled *on foot.*⟩

[2]**foot** *vb* **foot•ed; foot•ing**
1 [1]WALK 1
2 [1]PAY 2 ⟨I'll *foot* the bill.⟩

foot•ball \'fu̇t-ˌbȯl\ *n*
1 ▶ a game played with an oval ball on a large field by two teams of eleven players that move the ball by kicking, passing, or running with it
2 the ball used in football

foot•ed \'fu̇-təd\ *adj*
1 having a foot or feet ⟨a *footed* goblet⟩
2 having such or so many feet ⟨four-*footed* animals⟩

foot•fall \'fu̇t-ˌfȯl\ *n*
the sound of a footstep

foot•hill \'fu̇t-ˌhil\ *n*
a hill at the bottom of higher hills

foot•hold \'fu̇t-ˌhōld\ *n*
a place where the foot may be put (as for climbing)

foot•ing \'fu̇-tiŋ\ *n*
1 a firm position or placing of the feet ⟨I lost my *footing* and slipped.⟩
2 FOOTHOLD
3 position as compared to others ⟨We all started on the same *footing.*⟩
4 social relationship ⟨We're on a good *footing* with our neighbors.⟩

foot•lights \'fu̇t-ˌlīts\ *n pl*
a row of lights set across the front of a stage floor

foot•man \'fu̇t-mən\ *n, pl* **foot•men** \-mən\
a male servant who performs various duties (as letting visitors in and serving food)

foot•note \'fu̇t-ˌnōt\ *n*
a note at the bottom of a page

foot•path \'fu̇t-ˌpath, -ˌpäth\ *n*
a path for walkers

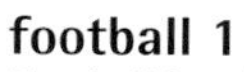

▶ football 1

Football is a highly physical game played by two teams, each of 11 players. All players wear protective equipment and are allowed to throw, kick, or run with the ball. Points are scored for touchdowns and for kicking the ball through the goalposts.

features of a football field

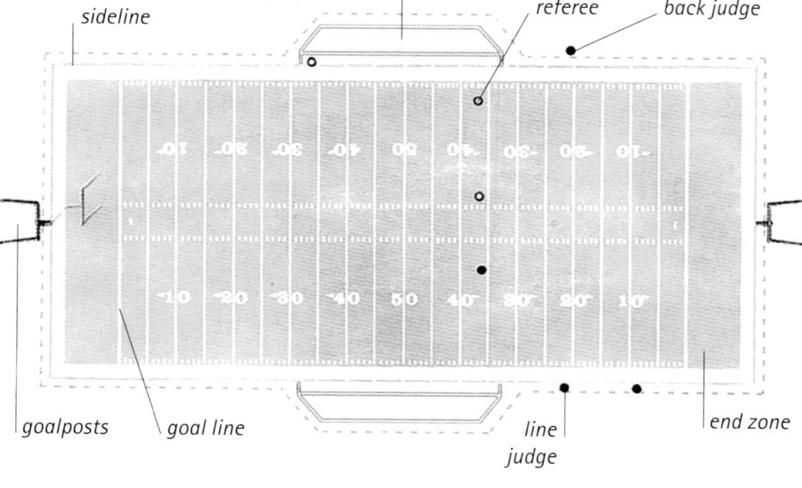

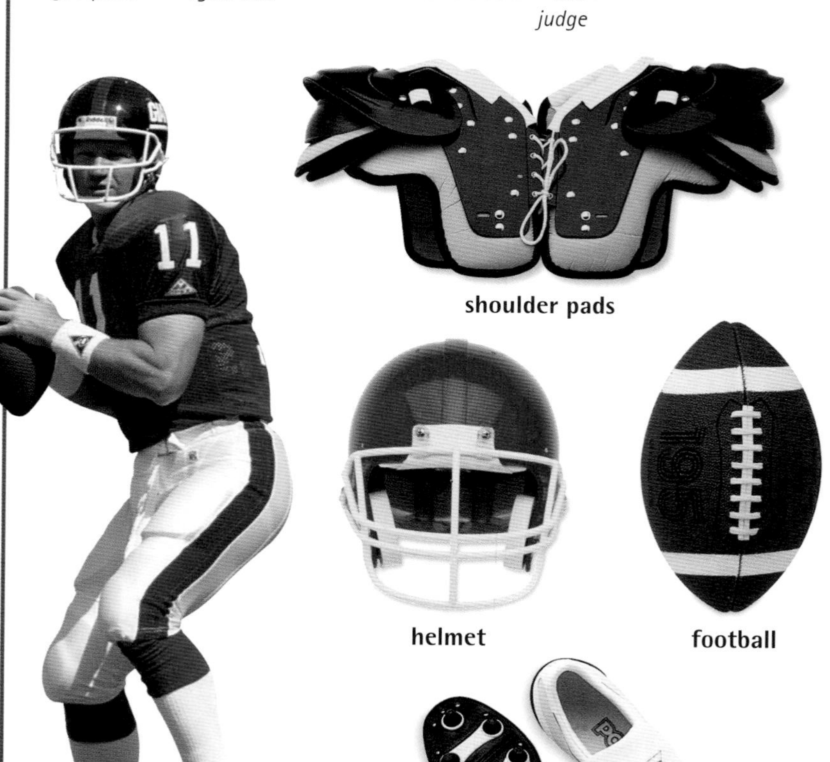

shoulder pads

helmet

football

quarterback

football cleats

foot•print \ˈfu̇t-ˌprint\ *n*
▶ a track left by a foot

footprint

foot•step \ˈfu̇t-ˌstep\ *n*
1 a step of the foot ⟨Don't take another *footstep*!⟩
2 the distance covered by a step ⟨The bathroom is only a few *footsteps* away.⟩
3 FOOTPRINT
4 the sound of a foot taking a step ⟨We heard *footsteps*.⟩
5 a way of life or action ⟨He followed in his father's *footsteps*.⟩

foot•stool \ˈfu̇t-ˌstül\ *n*
a low stool for the feet

foot•work \ˈfu̇t-ˌwərk\ *n*
the skill with which the feet are moved ⟨a dancer's fancy *footwork*⟩

[1]**for** \fər, ˈfȯr\ *prep*
1 by way of getting ready ⟨Did you wash up *for* supper?⟩
2 toward the goal or purpose of ⟨I'm studying *for* the test.⟩ ⟨I've saved *for* a new bike.⟩
3 in order to reach ⟨She left *for* home.⟩
4 as being ⟨eggs *for* breakfast⟩ ⟨Do you take me *for* a fool?⟩
5 because of ⟨They cried *for* joy.⟩
6 used to show who or what is to receive something ⟨There's a letter *for* you.⟩
7 in order to help, serve, or defend ⟨Let me hold that *for* you.⟩ ⟨They fought *for* their country.⟩
8 directed at : AGAINST ⟨a cure *for* cancer⟩
9 in exchange as equal to ⟨How much *for* a ticket?⟩

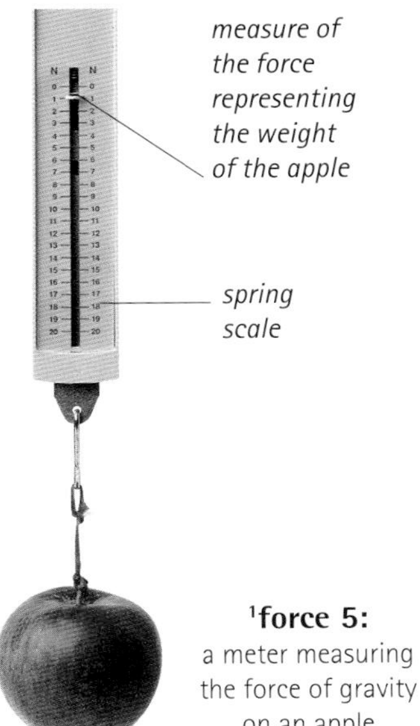

[1]**force 5:**
a meter measuring the force of gravity on an apple

10 with regard to : CONCERNING ⟨a talent *for* music⟩
11 taking into account ⟨You're tall *for* your age.⟩
12 through the period of ⟨He slept *for* ten hours.⟩
13 to a distance of ⟨You can see *for* miles.⟩
14 suitable to ⟨It is not *for* you to choose.⟩
15 in favor of ⟨I voted *for* her.⟩
16 in place of or on behalf of ⟨I speak *for* the group.⟩
17 [2]AFTER 5 ⟨He was named *for* his father.⟩

[2]**for** *conj*
BECAUSE ⟨I know you did it, *for* I saw you.⟩

[1]**for•age** \ˈfȯr-ij\ *n*
food (as grass) for browsing or grazing animals

[2]**forage** *vb* **for•aged**; **for•ag•ing**
1 to nibble or eat grass or other plants ⟨Cows *foraged* in the field.⟩
2 [1]SEARCH 1 ⟨We *foraged* for firewood.⟩

for•bear \fȯr-ˈber\ *vb* **for•bore** \-ˈbȯr\; **for•borne** \-ˈbȯrn\; **for•bear•ing**
1 to hold back ⟨He *forbore* from hitting the bully back.⟩
2 to be patient when annoyed or troubled

for•bid \fər-ˈbid\ *vb* **for•bade** \-ˈbad\; **for•bid•den** \-ˈbi-dᵊn\; **for•bid•ding**
to order not to do something ⟨I *forbid* you to go!⟩

for•bid•ding \fər-ˈbi-diŋ\ *adj*
tending to frighten or discourage ⟨a *forbidding* old house⟩

[1]**force** \ˈfȯrs\ *n*
1 power that has an effect on something ⟨the *force* of the wind⟩ ⟨the *force* of her personality⟩
2 the state of existing and being enforced ⟨That law is still in *force*.⟩
3 a group of people available for a particular purpose ⟨a police *force*⟩ ⟨the work *force*⟩
4 power or violence used on a person or thing ⟨He opened the door by *force*.⟩
5◀ an influence (as a push or pull) that tends to produce a change in the speed or direction of motion of something ⟨the *force* of gravity⟩

[2]**force** *vb* **forced**; **forc•ing**
1 to make someone or something do something ⟨*forced* them to work⟩
2 to get, make, or move by using physical power ⟨Police *forced* their way into the room.⟩
3 to break open using physical power ⟨We *forced* the door.⟩
4 to speed up the development of ⟨I'm *forcing* flower bulbs.⟩

force•ful \ˈfȯrs-fəl\ *adj*
having much strength : VIGOROUS ⟨*forceful* action⟩ ⟨a *forceful* speech⟩
force•ful•ly \-fə-lē\ *adv*
force•ful•ness *n*

for•ceps \ˈfȯr-səps\ *n*, *pl* **forceps**
▼ an instrument for grasping, holding, or pulling on things especially in delicate operations (as by a jeweler or surgeon)

forceps:
a pair of surgical forceps

forc•ible \ˈfȯr-sə-bəl\ *adj*
1 got, made, or done by physical power ⟨a *forcible* entrance⟩
2 showing a lot of strength or energy ⟨*forcible* statements⟩
forc•ibly \-blē\ *adv*

[1]**ford** \ˈfȯrd\ *n*
▼ a shallow place in a body of water that may be crossed by wading

[1]**ford:** a woman crossing a ford

[2]**ford** *vb* **ford•ed**; **ford•ing**
to cross by wading ⟨We had to *ford* a stream.⟩

[1]**fore** \ˈfȯr\ *adv*
in or toward the front ⟨The plane's exits are located *fore* and aft.⟩

[2]**fore** *adj*
being or coming before in time, place, or order ⟨the ship's *fore* hold⟩

[3]**fore** *n*
[1]FRONT 1 ⟨the ship's *fore*⟩

[4]fore *interj*
used by a golfer to warn someone within range of a hit ball

fore- *prefix*
1 earlier : beforehand 〈*fore*see〉
2 at the front : in front 〈*fore*leg〉
3 front part of something specified 〈*fore*arm〉

fore–and–aft \ˌfȯr-ə-ˈnaft\ *adj*
being in line with the length of a ship 〈*fore-and-aft* sails〉

fore•arm \ˈfȯr-ˌärm\ *n*
the part of the arm between the elbow and the wrist

fore•bear \ˈfȯr-ˌber\ *n*
ANCESTOR 1

fore•bod•ing \fȯr-ˈbō-diŋ\ *n*
a feeling that something bad is going to happen

[1]fore•cast \ˈfȯr-ˌkast\ *vb* **forecast**; **fore•cast•ing**
to predict often after thought and study of available evidence
synonyms see FORETELL
fore•cast•er *n*

[2]forecast *n*
a prediction of something in the future

fore•cas•tle \ˈfōk-səl\ *n*
1 the forward part of the upper deck of a ship
2 quarters for the crew in the forward part of a ship

fore•fa•ther \ˈfȯr-ˌfä-thər\ *n*
ANCESTOR 1

fore•fin•ger \ˈfȯr-ˌfing-gər\ *n*
INDEX FINGER

fore•foot \ˈfȯr-ˌfu̇t\ *n, pl* **fore•feet** \-ˌfēt\
one of the front feet of an animal with four feet

fore•front \ˈfȯr-ˌfrənt\ *n*
the most important part or position

forego *variant of* FORGO

fore•go•ing \fȯr-ˈgō-iŋ\ *adj*
going before : already mentioned 〈the *foregoing* examples〉

fore•gone conclusion \ˈfȯr-ˌgȯn-\ *n*
something felt to be sure to happen

fore•ground \ˈfȯr-ˌgrau̇nd\ *n*
the part of a picture or scene that seems to be nearest to and in front of the person looking at it

fore•hand \ˈfȯr-ˌhand\ *n*
▶ a stroke in sports played with a racket made with the palm of the hand turned in the direction in which the hand is moving

fore•head \ˈfȯr-əd, ˈfȯr-ˌhed\ *n*
the part of the face above the eyes

for•eign \ˈfȯr-ən\ *adj*
1 located outside of a place or country and especially outside of a person's own country 〈a *foreign* nation〉
2 belonging to a place or country other than the one under consideration 〈Do you speak a *foreign* language?〉
3 relating to or having to do with other nations 〈*foreign* trade〉
4 not normally belonging or wanted where found 〈*foreign* material in food〉

for•eign•er \ˈfȯr-ə-nər\ *n*
a person who is from a foreign country

fore•leg \ˈfȯr-ˌleg\ *n*
a front leg of an animal

fore•limb \ˈfȯr-ˌlim\ *n*
an arm, fin, wing, or leg that is located toward the front of the body

fore•man \ˈfȯr-mən\ *n, pl* **fore•men** \-mən\
the leader of a group of workers

fore•mast \ˈfȯr-ˌmast, -məst\ *n*
the mast nearest the bow of the ship

[1]fore•most \ˈfȯr-ˌmōst\ *adj*
first in time, place, or order : most important

[2]foremost *adv*
in the first place 〈The park puts safety *foremost*.〉

fore•noon \ˈfȯr-ˌnün\ *n*
MORNING

fore•run•ner \ˈfȯr-ˌrə-nər\ *n*
someone or something that comes before especially as a sign of the coming of another

forehand: a tennis player performing a forehand

fore•see \fȯr-ˈsē\ *vb* **fore•saw** \-ˈsȯ\; **fore•seen** \-ˈsēn\; **fore•see•ing**
to see or know about beforehand 〈I didn't *foresee* the accident.〉

fore•shad•ow \fȯr-ˈsha-dō\ *vb* **fore•shad•owed**; **fore•shad•ow•ing**
to give a hint of beforehand

fore•sight \ˈfȯr-ˌsīt\ *n*
1 the ability to see what will or might happen in the future
2 care for the future : PRUDENCE 〈She had the *foresight* to save for college.〉

for•est \ˈfȯr-əst\ *n*
▶ a growth of trees and underbrush covering a large area
for•est•ed \-əs-təd\ *adj*

fore•stall \fȯr-ˈstȯl\ *vb* **fore•stalled**; **fore•stall•ing**
to keep out, interfere with, or prevent by steps taken in advance 〈*forestalling* problems〉

forest ranger *n*
a person in charge of managing and protecting part of a public forest

for•est•ry \ˈfȯr-ə-strē\ *n*
the science and practice of caring for forests
for•est•er \-stər\ *n*

fore•tell \fōr-ˈtel\ *vb* **fore•told** \-ˈtōld\; **fore•tell•ing**
to tell of a thing before it happens

> ▶ **Synonyms** FORETELL, PREDICT, and FORECAST mean to tell about or announce something before it happens. FORETELL is used when the future is revealed especially by extraordinary powers. 〈The wizards *foretold* a great war.〉 PREDICT is used for a fairly exact statement that is the result of the gathering of information and the use of scientific methods. 〈Scientists can sometimes *predict* earthquakes.〉 FORECAST is often used when a person has weighed evidence and is telling what is most likely to happen. 〈Experts are *forecasting* snow.〉

fore•thought \ˈfōr-ˌthȯt\ *n*
careful thinking or planning for the future

for•ev•er \fə-ˈre-vər\ *adv*
1 for a limitless time 〈Nothing lasts *forever*.〉
2 at all times 〈She is *forever* bothering the teacher.〉

fore•warn \fȯr-ˈwȯrn\ *vb* **fore•warned**; **fore•warn•ing**
to warn in advance

forest: a view of the Chattahoochee National Forest in Georgia, USA

fore•word \'fȯr-ˌwərd\ *n*
PREFACE

[1]**for•feit** \'fȯr-fət\ *vb* **for•feit•ed**; **for•feit•ing**
to lose or lose the right to as punishment for a fault, error, or crime

[2]**forfeit** *n*
something or the right to something lost as punishment for a fault, error, or crime

[1]**forge** \'fȯrj\ *vb* **forged**; **forg•ing**
1 to shape and work metal by heating and hammering
2 to bring into existence ⟨*forging* friendships⟩
3 to produce something that is not genuine : COUNTERFEIT ⟨The check was *forged.*⟩
forg•er *n*

[2]**forge** *n*
▶ a furnace or a place with a furnace where metal is shaped by heating and hammering

[3]**forge** *vb* **forged**; **forg•ing**
to move forward slowly but steadily ⟨We *forged* through the storm.⟩

[2]**forge:** a blacksmith at work in a traditional forge

forg•ery \'fȯr-jə-rē\ *n, pl* **forg•er•ies**
1 the crime of falsely making or changing a written paper or signing someone else's name
2 something that is falsely made or copied ⟨This signature is a *forgery.*⟩

for•get \fər-'get\ *vb* **for•got** \-'gät\; **for•got•ten** \-'gä-tᵊn\ *or* **for•got**; **for•get•ting**
1 to be unable to think of or remember ⟨I *forgot* your name.⟩
2 to fail by accident to do (something) : OVERLOOK ⟨I *forgot* to pay the bill.⟩

for•get•ful \fər-'get-fəl\ *adj*
forgetting easily
for•get•ful•ness *n*

for•get–me–not \fər-'get-mē-ˌnät\ *n*
▼ a small low plant with usually bright blue or white flowers

forget-me-not

for•give \fər-'giv\ *vb* **for•gave** \-'gāv\; **for•giv•en** \-'gi-vən\; **for•giv•ing**
to stop feeling angry at or hurt by ⟨Please *forgive* me—I didn't mean it.⟩

for•give•ness \fər-'giv-nəs\ *n*
the act of ending anger at ⟨She asked for his *forgiveness.*⟩

for•giv•ing \fər-'gi-viŋ\ *adj*
willing or ready to excuse an error or offense

for•go *also* **fore•go** \fȯr-'gō\ *vb* **for•went** *also* **fore•went** \-'went\; **for•gone** *also* **fore•gone** \-'gȯn\; **for•going** *also* **fore•going**
to give up the use or enjoyment of ⟨Don't *forgo* this opportunity.⟩

[1]**fork** \'fȯrk\ *n*
1 ▶ an implement having a handle and two or more prongs for taking up (as in eating), pitching, or digging
2 a forked part or tool
3 the place where something (as a road) divides
4 one of the parts into which something divides or branches ⟨the left *fork*⟩

[2]**fork** *vb* **forked**; **fork•ing**
1 to divide into branches ⟨Drive to where the road *forks.*⟩
2 to pitch or lift with a fork

forked \'fȯrkt, 'fȯr-kəd\ *adj*
having one end divided into two or more branches

for•lorn \fər-'lȯrn\ *adj*
sad from being left alone
for•lorn•ly *adv*

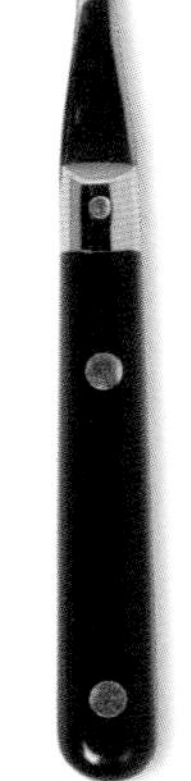

[1]**fork 1:** a table fork

A B C D E F G H I J K L M N O P Q R S T U V W X Y Z

[1]form \'fȯrm\ *n*
1 [1]SORT 1, KIND ⟨Coal is one *form* of carbon.⟩
2 the shape and structure of something ⟨We saw the bear's huge *form.*⟩
3 a printed sheet with blank spaces for information ⟨Fill out the *form.*⟩
4 a way of doing something ⟨There are different *forms* of worship.⟩
5 one of the different pronunciations, spellings, or inflections a word may have ⟨The plural *form* of "lady" is "ladies."⟩
6 a mold in which concrete is placed to set

[2]form *vb* **formed; form•ing**
1 to give form or shape to ⟨Practice *forming* the letter R.⟩
2 DEVELOP 5 ⟨He *formed* good study habits.⟩
3 to come or bring together in making ⟨The students *formed* a line.⟩
4 to take shape **:** come into being ⟨Fog *forms* in the valleys.⟩ ⟨Ideas were *forming* in her mind.⟩
synonyms see MAKE

[1]for•mal \'fȯr-məl\ *adj*
1 following established form, custom, or rule ⟨She wrote a *formal* apology.⟩
2 acquired by attending classes in a school ⟨a *formal* education⟩
3 requiring proper clothing and manners ⟨a *formal* dance⟩
4 suitable for a proper occasion ⟨*formal* attire⟩
for•mal•ly *adv*

[2]formal *n*
a social gathering that requires proper clothing and behavior

for•mal•i•ty \fȯr-'ma-lə-tē\ *n, pl* **for•mal•i•ties**
1 the quality or state of being formal ⟨the *formality* of the occasion⟩
2 an established way of doing something ⟨wedding *formalities*⟩

[1]for•mat \'fȯr-,mat\ *n*
the general organization or arrangement of something

[2]format *vb* **for•mat•ted; for•mat•ting**
1 to organize or arrange in a certain way
2 to prepare for storing computer data ⟨*format* a disk⟩

for•ma•tion \fȯr-'mā-shən\ *n*
1 a creation or development of something ⟨the *formation* of good habits⟩
2 something that is formed or created ⟨a cloud *formation*⟩
3 an arrangement of something ⟨battle *formation*⟩ ⟨punt *formation*⟩

for•mer \'fȯr-mər\ *adj*
coming before in time ⟨a *former* president⟩

for•mer•ly \'fȯr-mər-lē\ *adv*
at an earlier time ⟨They were *formerly* friends.⟩

for•mi•da•ble \'fȯr-mə-də-bəl\ *adj*
1 causing fear or awe ⟨a *formidable* enemy⟩
2 offering serious difficulties ⟨a *formidable* task⟩
3 large or impressive in size or extent ⟨a *formidable* waterfall⟩
for•mi•da•bly *adv*

form•less \'fȯrm-ləs\ *adj*
having no regular form or shape

for•mu•la \'fȯr-myə-lə\ *n*
1 a direction giving amounts of the substances for the preparation of something (as a medicine)
2 an established form or method ⟨a *formula* for success⟩
3 ▼ a milk mixture or substitute for feeding a baby
4 a general fact or rule expressed in symbols ⟨We learned a *formula* for finding the size of an angle.⟩
5 an expression in symbols giving the makeup of a substance ⟨The chemical *formula* for water is H_2O.⟩

formula 3: baby milk formula

for•mu•late \'fȯr-myə-,lāt\ *vb* **for•mu•lat•ed; for•mu•lat•ing**
to create, invent, or produce by careful thought and effort ⟨*formulate* a medicine⟩ ⟨*formulate* an answer⟩

for•sake \fər-'sāk\ *vb* **for•sook** \-'su̇k\; **for•sak•en** \-'sā-kən\; **for•sak•ing**
to give up or leave entirely ⟨Don't *forsake* your friends.⟩
synonyms see ABANDON

for•syth•ia \fər-'si-thē-ə\ *n*
a bush often grown for its bright yellow flowers that appear in early spring

fort \'fȯrt\ *n*
▼ a strong or fortified place

forte \'fȯrt, 'fȯr-,tā\ *n*
something in which a person shows special ability ⟨Music is my *forte.*⟩

forth \'fȯrth\ *adv*
1 onward in time, place, or order ⟨from that time *forth*⟩
2 out into view

fort: a 14th-century fort in Spain

forth•com•ing \fȯrth-ˈkə-miŋ\ *adj*
1 about to appear or to be made available
2 being candid or forthright

forth•right \ˈfȯrth-ˌrīt\ *adj*
going straight to the point clearly and firmly
forth•right•ly *adv*

forth•with \fȯrth-ˈwith, -ˈwith\ *adv*
without delay : IMMEDIATELY ⟨left *forthwith*⟩

[1]**for•ti•eth** \ˈfȯr-tē-əth\ *adj*
coming right after 39th

[2]**fortieth** *n*
number 40 in a series

for•ti•fi•ca•tion \ˌfȯr-tə-fə-ˈkā-shən\ *n*
1 the act of making stronger or enriching
2 something built to strengthen or protect

for•ti•fy \ˈfȯr-tə-ˌfī\ *vb* **for•ti•fied**; **for•ti•fy•ing**
1 to make strong ⟨Calcium *fortifies* bones.⟩
2 to add material to (something) to strengthen or improve it ⟨The cereal was *fortified* with vitamins.⟩

for•ti•tude \ˈfȯr-tə-ˌtüd, -ˌtyüd\ *n*
strength of mind that lets a person meet danger, pain, or hardship with courage

fort•night \ˈfȯrt-ˌnīt\ *n*
two weeks

for•tress \ˈfȯr-trəs\ *n*
a place that is protected against attack

for•tu•nate \ˈfȯr-chə-nət\ *adj*
1 bringing a good result ⟨a *fortunate* discovery⟩
2 having good luck : LUCKY
for•tu•nate•ly *adv*

for•tune \ˈfȯr-chən\ *n*
1 a large sum of money
2 what happens to a person : good or bad luck
3 what is to happen to someone in the future ⟨I had my *fortune* told.⟩
4 WEALTH 1

for•tune–tell•er \ˈfȯr-chən-ˌte-lər\ *n*
a person who claims to foretell future events

[1]**for•ty** \ˈfȯr-tē\ *adj*
being four times ten

[2]**forty** *n*
four times ten : 40

for•ty–nin•er \ˈfȯr-tē-ˈnī-nər\ *n*
a person in the California gold rush of 1849

fo•rum \ˈfȯr-əm\ *n*
1 the marketplace or public place of an ancient Roman city serving as the center for public business
2 a place or opportunity for discussion

[1]**for•ward** \ˈfȯr-wərd\ *adj*
1 near, at, or belonging to the front part ⟨a ship's *forward* deck⟩
2 moving, tending, or leading to a position in front ⟨He made a sudden *forward* movement.⟩
3 lacking proper modesty or reserve

[2]**forward** *or* **for•wards** \ˈfȯr-wərdz\ *adv*
to or toward what is in front ⟨Everyone moved *forward*.⟩

[3]**forward** *vb* **for•ward•ed**; **for•ward•ing**
1 to send on or ahead ⟨*forward* a letter⟩
2 to help onward : ADVANCE ⟨*forward* a cause⟩

[4]**forward** *n*
a player at or near the front of his or her team or near the opponent's goal

fos•sil \ˈfä-səl\ *n*
▼ a trace or print or the remains of a plant or animal of a past age preserved in earth or rock

fossil fuel *n*
a fuel (such as coal, oil, or natural gas) formed in the earth from dead plants or animals

► **fossil**
Fossils are the remains of plants and animals that were quickly buried under sediment such as sand or mud so that decay was prevented or slowed. Most fossils form when minerals dissolved in water seep into and replace the remains. Remains may often leave an impression in soft material such as mud, which then slowly hardens into stone. Sometimes whole creatures are frozen in ice, encased in amber, or preserved in tar.

fossil of a beetle preserved in sand and tar

impression of a leaf in stone formed from mud

mineral fossil of an ammonite \ˈa-mə-ˌnīt\

impression of a sea urchin in sandstone

a spider in amber

[1]fos•ter \'fȯ-stər\ *adj*
giving, receiving, or offering parental care even though not related by blood or legal ties ⟨a *foster* parent⟩ ⟨a *foster* child⟩ ⟨a *foster* home⟩

[2]foster *vb* **fos•tered**; **fos•ter•ing**
1 to give parental care to
2 to help the growth and development of

fought *past and past participle of* FIGHT

[1]foul \'fau̇l\ *adj* **foul•er**; **foul•est**
1 disgusting in looks, taste, or smell ⟨*foul* breath⟩
2 full of or covered with something that pollutes ⟨*foul* air⟩
3 being vulgar or insulting ⟨*foul* language⟩
4 being wet and stormy ⟨*foul* weather⟩
5 very unfair ⟨She would even use *foul* methods to get what she wanted.⟩
6 very unpleasant or bad ⟨a *foul* mood⟩
7 breaking a rule in a game or sport ⟨The boxer was warned for using a *foul* punch.⟩
8 being outside the foul lines ⟨He hit a *foul* ball.⟩

[2]foul *n*
1 a ball in baseball that is batted outside the foul lines
2 an act of breaking the rules in a game or sport

[3]foul *vb* **fouled**; **foul•ing**
1 to make or become foul or filthy ⟨*foul* the air⟩ ⟨*foul* a stream⟩
2 to make a foul in a game

foul line *n*
either of two straight lines running from the rear corner of home plate through first and third base to the boundary of a baseball field

[1]found *past and past participle of* FIND

[2]found \'fau̇nd\ *vb* **found•ed**; **found•ing**
to begin or create : ESTABLISH ⟨This town was *founded* in 1886.⟩

foun•da•tion \fau̇n-'dā-shən\ *n*
1 the support upon which something rests ⟨the *foundation* of a building⟩ ⟨the *foundations* of our legal system⟩
2 the act of beginning or creating ⟨He has taught here since the school's *foundation*.⟩

[1]found•er \'fau̇n-dər\ *n*
a person who creates or establishes something ⟨the country's *founders*⟩

[2]foun•der \'fau̇n-dər\ *vb* **found•ered**; **found•er•ing**
[1]SINK 1 ⟨a *foundering* ship⟩

found•ry \'fau̇n-drē\ *n, pl* **foundries**
a building or factory where metal goods are made

fount \'fau̇nt\ *n*
SOURCE 1 ⟨She was a *fount* of knowledge about wildlife.⟩

foun•tain \'fau̇n-tᵊn\ *n*
1 an artificial stream or spray of water (as for drinking or ornament) or the device from which it comes
2 SOURCE 1 ⟨He was a *fountain* of wisdom.⟩
3 a spring of water coming from the earth

fountain pen *n*
▼ a pen with ink inside that is fed as needed to the writing point

foxy \'fäk-sē\ *adj* **fox•i•er**; **fox•i•est**
very clever ⟨a *foxy* trick⟩

foy•er \'fȯi-ər, 'fȯi-,ā\ *n*
1 a lobby especially in a theater
2 an entrance hall

fr. *abbr* from

Fr. *abbr* father

fra•cas \'frā-kəs, 'fra-\ *n*
a noisy quarrel : BRAWL

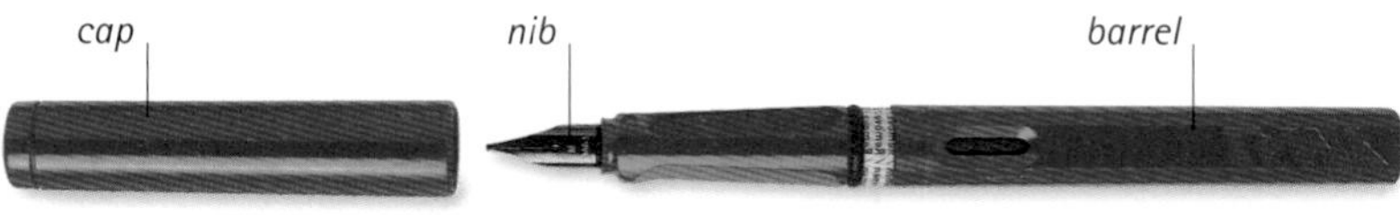

fountain pen

[1]four \'fȯr\ *adj*
being one more than three

[2]four *n*
1 one more than three : two times two : 4
2 the fourth in a set or series

four•fold \'fȯr-,fōld\ *adj*
being four times as great or as many ⟨a *fourfold* increase⟩

four•score \'fȯr-,skȯr\ *adj*
[2]EIGHTY

four•some \'fȯr-səm\ *adj*
a group of four persons or things

[1]four•teen \fȯr-'tēn, 'fȯrt-,tēn\ *adj*
being one more than 13

[2]fourteen *n*
one more than 13 : two times seven : 14

[1]four•teenth \fȯr-'tēnth, 'fȯrt-,tēnth\ *adj*
coming right after 13th

[2]fourteenth *n*
number 14 in a series

[1]fourth \'fȯrth\ *adj*
coming right after third

[2]fourth *n*
1 number four in a series
2 one of four equal parts

Fourth of July *n*
INDEPENDENCE DAY

fowl \'fau̇l\ *n, pl* **fowl** *or* **fowls**
1 BIRD ⟨wild *fowls*⟩
2 a common domestic rooster or hen
3 the meat of a domestic fowl used as food

fox \'fäks\ *n*
1 ► a wild animal closely related to the wolf that has a sharp snout, pointed ears, and a long bushy tail
2 *cap* a member of an American Indian people formerly living in what is now Wisconsin

frac•tion \'frak-shən\ *n*
1 a number (as 1/2, 2/3, 17/100) that indicates one or more equal parts of a whole or group and that may be considered as indicating also division of the number above the line by the number below the line
2 a part of a whole : FRAGMENT ⟨I sold the car for a *fraction* of what I paid for it.⟩

frac•tion•al \'frak-shə-nᵊl\ *adj*
1 of, relating to, or being a fraction ⟨*fractional* numbers⟩
2 fairly small ⟨*fractional* improvement⟩

[1]frac•ture \'frak-chər\ *n*
the result of breaking : damage or an injury caused by breaking ⟨a bone *fracture*⟩

[2]fracture *vb* **frac•tured**; **frac•tur•ing**
[1]BREAK 2 ⟨*fracture* a rib⟩

frag•ile \'fra-jəl\ *adj*
easily broken or hurt : DELICATE ⟨a *fragile* dish⟩ ⟨a *fragile* child⟩
synonyms see BRITTLE

fox 1

frag•ment \ˈfrag-mənt\ *n*
a broken or incomplete part

fra•grance \ˈfrā-grəns\ *n*
a sweet or pleasant smell

fra•grant \ˈfrā-grənt\ *adj*
sweet or pleasant in smell
fra•grant•ly *adv*

frail \ˈfrāl\ *adj*
very delicate or weak ⟨a *frail* little child⟩
synonyms see WEAK

frail•ty \ˈfrāl-tē\ *n, pl* **frailties**
1 the quality or state of being weak
2 a weakness of character ⟨human *frailty*⟩

[1]**frame** \ˈfrām\ *vb* **framed**; **fram•ing**
1 to enclose in or as if in a frame ⟨*frame* a picture⟩ ⟨Curls *framed* his face.⟩
2 to produce (something) in written or spoken words ⟨*frame* a constitution⟩
3 to make appear guilty ⟨He's being *framed* for the crime.⟩
fram•er *n*

[2]**frame** *n*
1 the structure of an animal and especially a human body : PHYSIQUE ⟨a muscular *frame*⟩

rafter

[2]**frame 2:**
the wooden frame of a house under construction

2 ▲ an arrangement of parts that give form or support to something ⟨the *frame* of a house⟩
3 an open case or structure for holding or enclosing something ⟨window *frame*⟩

[3]**frame** *adj*
having a wooden frame ⟨a *frame* house⟩

frame of mind *n*
a particular state or mood

frame•work \ˈfrām-ˌwərk\ *n*
a basic supporting part or structure

franc \ˈfraŋk\ *n*
any of various coins or bills used or once used in countries where French is widely spoken

Fran•co– \ˈfraŋ-kō\ *prefix*
1 French and
2 French

frank \ˈfraŋk\ *adj*
free in or characterized by freedom in expressing feelings and opinions
frank•ly *adv*
frank•ness *n*

frank•furt•er \ˈfraŋk-fər-tər\ *or* **frank•furt** \-fərt\ *n*
▶ a cooked sausage : HOT DOG

frank•in•cense \ˈfraŋ-kən-ˌsens\ *n*
a fragrant plant gum that is burned for its sweet smell

fran•tic \ˈfran-tik\ *adj*
1 feeling or showing fear and worry ⟨a *frantic* search⟩
2 having wild and hurried activity ⟨They made a *frantic* attempt to finish.⟩
fran•ti•cal•ly \-ti-kə-lē\ *adv*

fra•ter•nal \frə-ˈtər-nᵊl\ *adj*
1 having to do with brothers
2 made up of members banded together like brothers ⟨a *fraternal* organization⟩

fraternal twin *n*
either of a pair of twins that are produced from different fertilized eggs and may not have the same sex or appearance

fra•ter•ni•ty \frə-ˈtər-nə-tē\ *n, pl* **fra•ter•ni•ties**
a club of boys or men (as in a college)

fraud \ˈfrȯd\ *n*
1 TRICKERY, DECEIT ⟨They got the money by *fraud.*⟩
2 an act of deceiving : TRICK ⟨Investigators uncovered the *fraud.*⟩
3 a person who pretends to be what he or she is not

fraud•u•lent \ˈfrȯ-jə-lənt\ *adj*
based on or done by deceit ⟨a *fraudulent* claim⟩
fraud•u•lent•ly *adv*

bun
mustard
frankfurter
sausage

fraught \ˈfrȯt\ *adj*
full of some quality ⟨The situation is *fraught* with danger.⟩

[1]**fray** \ˈfrā\ *n*
[2]FIGHT 1, BRAWL

[2]**fray** *vb* **frayed**; **fray•ing**
to wear into shreds

fraz•zle \ˈfra-zəl\ *n*
a tired or nervous condition ⟨I'm worn to a *frazzle.*⟩

[1]**freak** \ˈfrēk\ *n*
a strange, abnormal, or unusual person, thing, or event
freak•ish *adj*
freaky *adj*

[2]**freak** *adj*
not likely ⟨a *freak* accident⟩

[3]**freak** *vb* **freaked**; **freak•ing**
1 to make (someone) upset — usually used with *out* ⟨That creepy movie *freaked* me *out.*⟩
2 to become upset — often used with *out* ⟨He saw the spider and *freaked out.*⟩

[1]**freck•le** \ˈfre-kəl\ *n*
▼ a small brownish spot on the skin

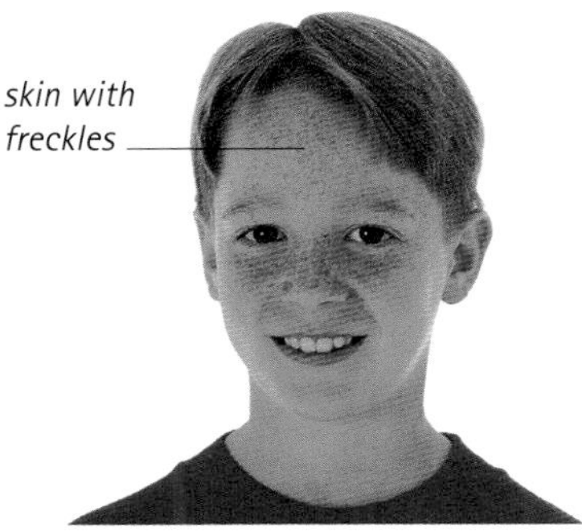

[1]**freckle:** a boy with freckles on his face

[2]**freckle** *vb* **freck•led**; **freck•ling**
to mark or become marked with freckles or spots ⟨His face was tanned and *freckled* by the sun.⟩

[1]free \'frē\ *adj* **fre•er** \'frē-ər\; **fre•est** \'frē-əst\
1 given without charge 〈a *free* ticket〉
2 having liberty : not being a slave or prisoner 〈*free* citizens〉
3 not controlled by a harsh ruler or harsh laws 〈a *free* country〉
4 not physically held by something
5 not having or suffering from something unpleasant, unwanted, or painful 〈*free* from worry〉
6 not held back by fear or uncertainty : OPEN 〈Feel *free* to ask questions.〉
7 not blocked : CLEAR 〈The road was *free* of traffic.〉
8 not required to be doing something 〈Come visit me when you're *free.*〉
9 not used or occupied 〈a *free* seat〉
10 not combined 〈*free* oxygen〉
free•ly *adv*

[2]free *vb* **freed**; **free•ing**
to let go or set free : RELEASE

[3]free *adv*
1 in a free manner : FREELY 〈They let their dog run *free.*〉
2 without charge 〈Buy two, get one *free.*〉

freed•man \'frēd-mən\ *n, pl* **freed•men** \-mən\
a person freed from slavery

free•dom \'frē-dəm\ *n*
1 the condition of having liberty 〈The slaves won their *freedom.*〉
2 ability to move or act as desired 〈*freedom* of choice〉 〈*freedom* of movement〉
3 release from something unpleasant 〈*freedom* from care〉
4 the quality of being very frank : CANDOR 〈spoke with *freedom*〉
5 a political right 〈*freedom* of speech〉

free•hand \'frē-ˌhand\ *adj or adv*
done without mechanical aids 〈a *freehand* drawing〉

free•man \'frē-mən\ *n, pl* **free•men** \-mən\
a free person : a person who is not a slave

free•stand•ing \'frē-'stan-diŋ\ *adj*
standing alone free of attachment or support 〈a *freestanding* wall〉

free•way \'frē-ˌwā\ *n*
an expressway that can be used without paying tolls

free will *n*
a person's own choice or decision 〈She confessed of her own *free will.*〉

[1]freeze \'frēz\ *vb* **froze** \'frōz\; **fro•zen** \'frō-zᵊn\; **freez•ing**
1 to harden into or be hardened into a solid (as ice) by loss of heat 〈*freeze* blueberries〉 〈The river *froze* over.〉
2 to be uncomfortably cold 〈It's *freezing* in here. I'm *frozen.*〉
3 to damage by cold 〈The plants were *frozen* by heavy frost.〉

french fry: a plate of french fries

4 to clog or become clogged by ice 〈Water pipes *froze* overnight.〉
5 to become completely still 〈I was so startled, I *froze.*〉

[2]freeze *n*
1 a period of freezing weather : cold weather
2 the state of being frozen 〈in a deep *freeze*〉

freez•er \'frē-zər\ *n*
a compartment or room used to freeze food or keep it frozen

freezing point *n*
the temperature at which a liquid becomes solid

[1]freight \'frāt\ *n*
1 ▼ goods or cargo carried by a ship, train, truck, or airplane
2 the carrying (as by truck) of goods from one place to another 〈The order was shipped by *freight.*〉
3 the amount paid (as to a shipping company) for carrying goods
4 a train that carries freight

[2]freight *vb* **freight•ed**; **freight•ing**
to send by train, truck, airplane, or ship

freight•er \'frā-tər\ *n*
a ship or airplane used to carry freight

[1]French \'french\ *adj*
of or relating to France, its people, or the French language

[2]French *n*
1 **French** *pl* the people of France
2 the language of the French people

french fry *n, often cap 1st F*
◀ a strip of potato fried in deep fat

French horn *n*
▼ a circular brass musical instrument with a large opening at one end and a mouthpiece shaped like a small funnel

French horn

fren•zied \'fren-zēd\ *adj*
very excited and upset

fren•zy \'fren-zē\ *n, pl* **frenzies**
great and often wild or disorderly activity

[1]freight 1: freight being loaded onto a cargo plane

frigate 2: model of a frigate

fre•quen•cy \'frē-kwən-sē\ *n, pl* **fre•quen•cies**
1 frequent repetition 〈Rain fell with *frequency.*〉
2 rate of repetition 〈She went with increasing *frequency.*〉
3 the number of waves of sound or energy that pass by a point every second 〈Tune the stereo to receive a specific *frequency* of radio waves.〉
friend•less \-ləs\ *adj*

[1]**fre•quent** \frē-'kwent\ *vb* **fre•quent•ed; fre•quent•ing**
to visit often 〈We *frequent* the beach during summer.〉

[2]**fre•quent** \'frē-kwənt\ *adj*
happening often 〈I made *frequent* trips to town.〉
fre•quent•ly *adv*

fresh \'fresh\ *adj* **fresh•er; fresh•est**
1 not salt 〈*fresh* water〉
2 PURE 1, BRISK 〈*fresh* air〉 〈a *fresh* breeze〉
3 not frozen, canned, or pickled 〈*fresh* vegetables〉
4 not stale, sour, or spoiled 〈*fresh* bread〉
5 not dirty or rumpled 〈a *fresh* shirt〉
6 [1]NEW 4 〈Let's make a *fresh* start.〉
7 newly made or received 〈a *fresh* wound〉 〈*fresh* news〉
8 rude and disrespectful 〈*fresh* talk〉
fresh•ly *adv*
fresh•ness *n*

fresh•en \'fre-shən\ *vb* **fresh•ened; fresh•en•ing**
to make or become fresh 〈I took a shower to *freshen* up.〉 〈Wind *freshened* the air.〉

fresh•man \'fresh-mən\ *n, pl* **fresh•men** \-mən\
a first year student in high school or college

fresh•wa•ter \ˌfresh-'wȯ-tər, -ˌwä-\ *adj*
relating to or living in fresh water 〈*freshwater* fish〉

[1]**fret** \'fret\ *vb* **fret•ted; fret•ting**
[1]WORRY 1

[2]**fret** *n*
an irritated or worried state

fret•ful \'fret-fəl\ *adj*
irritated and worried 〈a *fretful* passenger〉
fret•ful•ly \-fə-lē\ *adv*

Fri. *abbr* Friday

fri•ar \'frī-ər\ *n*
a member of a Roman Catholic religious order for men

fric•tion \'frik-shən\ *n*
1 the rubbing of one thing against another
2 resistance to motion between bodies in contact 〈Oiling the parts of the machine reduces *friction.*〉
3 disagreement among persons or groups

Fri•day \'frī-ˌdā, 'frī-dē\ *n*
the sixth day of the week

[1]**friend** \'frend\ *n*
1 a person who has a strong liking for and trust in another person
2 a person who is not an enemy 〈*friend* or foe〉
3 a person who helps or supports something 〈She was a *friend* to environmental causes.〉
friend•less \-ləs\ *adj*

[2]**friend** *vb* **friend•ed; friend•ing**
to include (someone) in a list of designated friends on a social networking site

friend•ly \'frend-lē\ *adj* **friend•li•er; friend•li•est**
1 having or showing the kindness and warmth of a friend 〈a *friendly* neighbor〉 〈a *friendly* smile〉
2 being other than an enemy
3 easy or suitable for 〈a kid-*friendly* restaurant〉
friend•li•ness *n*

friend•ship \'frend-ˌship\ *n*
1 the state of being friends
2 a warm and kind feeling or attitude

frieze \'frēz\ *n*
a band or stripe (as around a building) used as a decoration

frig•ate \'fri-gət\ *n*
1 a square-rigged warship
2 ▲ a modern warship that is smaller than a destroyer

fright \'frīt\ *n*
1 sudden terror : great fear
2 something that frightens or is ugly or shocking 〈You look a *fright*! What happened?〉

fright•en \'frī-tᵊn\ *vb* **fright•ened; fright•en•ing**
to make afraid : TERRIFY
fright•en•ing•ly *adv*

fright•ful \'frīt-fəl\ *adj*
1 causing fear or alarm 〈a *frightful* scream〉
2 SHOCKING 1, OUTRAGEOUS 〈a *frightful* mess〉
fright•ful•ly \-fə-lē\ *adv*

frig•id \'fri-jəd\ *adj*
1 freezing cold
2 not friendly 〈a *frigid* stare〉

frill \'fril\ *n*
1 [2]RUFFLE
2 something added mostly for show

frilly \'fri-lē\ *adj* **frill•i•er; frill•i•est**
having ruffles 〈*frilly* clothes〉

[1]**fringe** \'frinj\ *n*
1 a border or trimming made by or made to look like the loose ends of the cloth
2 a narrow area along the edge

[2]**fringe** *vb* **fringed; fring•ing**
1 to decorate with a fringe
2 to go along or around 〈A hedge *fringed* the yard.〉

frisk \'frisk\ *vb* **frisked; frisk•ing**
1 to move around in a lively or playful way
2 to search (a person) quickly for something that may be hidden

frisky \'fris-kē\ *adj* **frisk•i•er; frisk•i•est**
PLAYFUL 1, LIVELY 〈*frisky* kittens〉

[1]**frit•ter** \'fri-tər\ *n*
a small amount of fried batter often containing fruit or meat 〈clam *fritters*〉

[2]**fritter** *vb* **frit•tered; frit•ter•ing**
to waste on unimportant things 〈He *frittered* away his money.〉

fri•vol•i•ty \fri-'vä-lə-tē\ *n, pl* **fri•vol•i•ties**
a lack of seriousness

friv•o•lous \'fri-və-ləs\ *adj*
1 of little importance 〈a *frivolous* matter〉
2 lacking in seriousness 〈a *frivolous* conversation〉

frizzy \'fri-zē\ *adj* **frizz•i•er; frizz•i•est**
very curly 〈*frizzy* hair〉

fro \'frō\ *adv*
in a direction away 〈She nervously walked to and *fro.*〉

frock \'fräk\ *n*
a woman's or girl's dress

frog \'fròg, 'fräg\ *n*
1 ▲ a tailless animal that is an amphibian with smooth moist skin and webbed feet that spends more of its time in water than the related toad
2 an ornamental fastening for a garment

[1]**frol•ic** \'frä-lik\ *vb* **frol•icked**; **frol•ick•ing**
to play about happily : ROMP ⟨The dog *frolicked* in the snow.⟩

[2]**frolic** *n*
[1]FUN 1

frol•ic•some \'frä-lik-səm\ *adj*
very lively and playful ⟨*frolicsome* ponies⟩

from \frəm, 'frəm, 'främ\ *prep*
1 used to show a starting point ⟨a letter *from* home⟩ ⟨School starts a week *from* today.⟩ ⟨He spoke *from* the heart.⟩
2 used to show a point of separation ⟨The balloon escaped *from* her grasp.⟩
3 used to show a material, source, or cause ⟨The doll was made *from* rags.⟩ ⟨The author read *from* his book.⟩ ⟨He's suffering *from* a cold.⟩

frond \'fränd\ *n*
a large leaf (as of a palm or fern) or leaflike structure (as of a seaweed) with many divisions

[1]**front** \'frənt\ *n*
1 the forward part or surface ⟨the *front* of a shirt⟩ ⟨I stood at the *front* of the line.⟩
2 a region in which active warfare is taking place
3 the boundary between bodies of air at different temperatures ⟨a cold *front*⟩
in front of directly before or ahead of ⟨She sat *in front of* me.⟩

[2]**front** *vb* **front•ed**; **front•ing**
[2]FACE 1 ⟨Their cottage *fronts* the lake.⟩

[3]**front** *adj*
situated at the front ⟨*front* legs⟩ ⟨the *front* door⟩

fron•tal \'frən-tᵊl\ *adj*
of or directed at a front ⟨a *frontal* attack⟩

[1]**fron•tier** \,frən-'tir\ *n*
1 a border between two countries
2 the edge of the settled part of a country

[2]**frontier** *adj*
of, living in, or situated in the frontier ⟨*frontier* towns⟩ ⟨*frontier* families⟩

fron•tiers•man \,frən-'tirz-mən\ *n*, *pl* **fron•tiers•men** \-mən\
a person living on the frontier

[1]**frost** \'fròst\ *n*
1 a covering of tiny ice crystals on a cold surface formed from the water vapor in the air
2 temperature cold enough to cause freezing

[2]**frost** *vb* **frost•ed**; **frost•ing**
1 to cover with frosting ⟨*frost* a cake⟩
2 to cover or become covered with frost

frost•bite \'fròst-,bīt\ *n*
slight freezing of a part of the body (as the feet or hands) or the damage to body tissues caused by such freezing

frost•ing \'frò-stiŋ\ *n*
1 ICING
2 a dull finish on glass

frosty \'frò-stē\ *adj* **frost•i•er**; **frost•i•est**
1 covered with frost ⟨a *frosty* window⟩
2 cold enough to produce frost ⟨a *frosty* evening⟩

[1]**froth** \'fròth\ *n*
bubbles formed in or on liquids

[2]**froth** *vb* **frothed**; **froth•ing**
to produce or form bubbles in or on a liquid

frothy \'frò-thē, -t͟hē\ *adj* **froth•i•er**; **froth•i•est**
full of or made up of small bubbles ⟨*frothy* waves⟩

[1]**frown** \'fraun\ *vb* **frowned**; **frown•ing**
1 to have a serious facial expression (as in anger or thought)
2 to look with disapproval

[2]**frown** *n*
a serious facial expression that shows anger, unhappiness, or deep thought

froze *past of* FREEZE

frozen *past participle of* FREEZE

fru•gal \'frü-gəl\ *adj*
1 careful in spending or using supplies
2 simple and without unnecessary things ⟨a *frugal* meal⟩
fru•gal•ly *adv*

[1]**fruit** \'früt\ *n*
1 a usually soft and juicy plant part (as rhubarb, a strawberry, or an orange) that is often eaten as a dessert and is distinguished from a vegetable
2 ▶ a product of fertilization in a seed plant that consists of the ripened ovary of a flower with its included seeds ⟨Apples, cucumbers, nuts, and blueberries are all *fruits*.⟩
3 [2]RESULT 1, PRODUCT ⟨You can enjoy the *fruits* of your labors.⟩
fruit•ed \-əd\ *adj*

[1]fruit 2
A fruit develops from the ovary of a flower that has been pollinated, and is the part of a plant that contains the seeds. There are two main types of fruit: dry fruits, and succulent fruits, which are juicy and colorful. Of the succulent fruits, some have a single, large seed in a hard case — the stone — while others have many tiny seeds.
sequence showing the development of a melon
pollinated flower
remains of flower
ovary swells
melon grows and ripens
examples of succulent fruits with a stone, or pit
plum
cherries
nectarine
peach
examples of succulent fruits with many seeds
lemon
blackberries
gooseberries
pear
examples of dry fruits
honesty
beech nuts
maple
love-in-a-mist

A B C D E F G H I J K L M N O P Q R S T U V W X Y Z

[2]fruit *vb* **fruit•ed; fruit•ing**
to bear or cause to bear fruit

fruit•cake \ˈfrüt-ˌkāk\ *n*
▼ a rich cake containing nuts, dried or candied fruits, and spices

fruitcake

fruit•ful \ˈfrüt-fəl\ *adj*
1 very productive ⟨a *fruitful* soil⟩
2 bringing results ⟨a *fruitful* idea⟩
fruit•ful•ly \-fə-lē\ *adv*

fruit•less \ˈfrüt-ləs\ *adj*
1 not bearing fruit ⟨*fruitless* trees⟩
2 UNSUCCESSFUL ⟨a *fruitless* search⟩
fruit•less•ly *adv*

fruity \ˈfrü-tē\ *adj* **fruit•i•er; fruit•i•est**
relating to or suggesting fruit ⟨a *fruity* smell⟩

frus•trate \ˈfrə-ˌstrāt\ *vb* **frus•trat•ed; frus•trat•ing**
1 to cause to feel angry or discouraged ⟨The delays *frustrated* passengers.⟩
2 to prevent from succeeding ⟨Police *frustrated* the robbery.⟩
3 [1]DEFEAT 2 ⟨The bad weather *frustrated* their plans for the beach.⟩

frus•trat•ing \ˈfrə-ˌstrā-tiŋ\ *adj*
causing feelings of disappointment and defeat

frus•tra•tion \ˌfrə-ˈstrā-shən\ *n*
DISAPPOINTMENT 1, DEFEAT

[1]fry \ˈfrī\ *vb* **fried; fry•ing**
to cook in fat

[2]fry *n, pl* **fries**
FRENCH FRY

[3]fry *n, pl* **fry**
a recently hatched or very young fish — usually used in pl. ⟨The salmon *fry* were released into the river.⟩

ft. *abbr*
1 feet
2 foot
3 fort

fudge \ˈfəj\ *n*
► a soft creamy candy ⟨chocolate *fudge*⟩

fullback 1: a fullback in action in a football game

[1]fu•el \ˈfyü-əl\ *n*
a substance (as oil or gasoline) that can be burned to produce heat or power

[2]fuel *vb* **fu•eled** *or* **fu•elled; fu•el•ing** *or* **fu•el•ling**
to supply with or take on fuel

[1]fu•gi•tive \ˈfyü-jə-tiv\ *adj*
running away or trying to escape ⟨a *fugitive* prisoner⟩

fudge: squares of fudge

[2]fugitive *n*
a person who is running away

[1]-ful \fəl\ *adj suffix*
1 full of ⟨joy*ful*⟩
2 characterized by ⟨peace*ful*⟩
3 having the qualities of ⟨master*ful*⟩
4 tending or given to ⟨mourn*ful*⟩

[2]-ful \ˌfu̇l\ *n suffix*
number or quantity that fills or would fill ⟨spoon*ful*⟩

ful•crum \ˈfu̇l-krəm, ˈfəl-\ *n, pl* **fulcrums** *or* **ful•cra** \-krə\
the support on which a lever turns in lifting something

ful•fill *or* **ful•fil** \fu̇l-ˈfil\ *vb* **ful•filled; ful•fill•ing**
1 to make real ⟨*fulfill* a dream⟩
2 SATISFY 4 ⟨*fulfill* a requirement⟩
ful•fill•ment \-mənt\ *n*

[1]full \ˈfu̇l\ *adj* **full•er; full•est**
1 containing as much or as many as possible or normal ⟨a *full* glass⟩ ⟨a *full* bus⟩

2 ¹COMPLETE 1 ⟨I waited a *full* hour.⟩
3 not limited in any way ⟨*full* power⟩
4 plump and rounded in outline ⟨a *full* face⟩
5 having much material ⟨a *full* skirt⟩
full•ness *n*

²full *adv*
1 ¹VERY 1 ⟨You know *full* well you're wrong.⟩
2 COMPLETELY ⟨Fill the glass *full.*⟩

³full *n*
1 the highest state, extent, or degree ⟨I enjoyed school to the *full.*⟩
2 the complete amount ⟨paid in *full*⟩

full•back \'fu̇l-,bak\ *n*
1 ◀ a football player who runs with the ball and blocks
2 a player in games like soccer and field hockey who is usually positioned near the goal

full-grown \'fu̇l-'grōn\ *adj*
having reached full growth or development

full moon *n*
▶ the moon with its whole disk lighted

full-time \'fu̇l-'tīm\ *adj*
working or involving the full number of hours considered normal or standard ⟨a *full-time* painter⟩ ⟨a *full-time* job⟩

ful•ly \'fu̇-lē\ *adv*
1 COMPLETELY ⟨He *fully* recovered.⟩
2 at least ⟨*Fully* half of them are here.⟩

¹fum•ble \'fəm-bəl\ *vb* **fum•bled; fum•bling**
1 to feel about for or handle something in a clumsy way ⟨He *fumbled* in his pockets.⟩
2 to lose hold of the ball in football

²fumble *n*
an act of losing hold of the ball in football

¹fume \'fyüm\ *n*
▼ a disagreeable smoke, vapor, or gas — usually used in pl. ⟨noxious *fumes*⟩

²fume *vb* **fumed; fum•ing**
1 to give off a disagreeable smoke, vapor, or gas
2 to be angry
3 to say something in an angry way

¹fun \'fən\ *n*
1 someone or something that provides amusement or enjoyment ⟨They were *fun* to play with.⟩
2 a good time : AMUSEMENT ⟨We had a lot of *fun.*⟩ ⟨She made up stories for *fun.*⟩
3 words or actions to make someone or something an object of ridicule ⟨He made *fun* of my singing.⟩

²fun *adj*
1 providing fun ⟨a *fun* trip⟩
2 full of fun ⟨We had a *fun* time together.⟩

function key *n*
any of a set of keys on a computer keyboard with special functions

fund \'fənd\ *n*
1 a sum of money for a special purpose ⟨a book *fund*⟩
2 **funds** *pl* available money ⟨I'm out of *funds* until I get paid.⟩
3 ¹STOCK 1, SUPPLY ⟨a *fund* of knowledge⟩

¹fun•da•men•tal \,fən-də-'men-tᵊl\ *adj*
being or forming a foundation : BASIC, ESSENTIAL ⟨The discovery was *fundamental* to modern science.⟩ ⟨our *fundamental* rights⟩
fun•da•men•tal•ly *adv*

full moon: a full moon seen from Monument Valley in Utah

¹fume: fumes being emitted after an experiment

¹func•tion \'fəŋk-shən\ *n*
1 the action for which a person or thing is designed or used : PURPOSE ⟨What *function* does this tool serve?⟩
2 a large important ceremony or social affair
3 a mathematical relationship that assigns exactly one element of one set to each element of the same or another set

²function *vb* **func•tioned; func•tion•ing**
to serve a certain purpose : WORK ⟨The new machine *functions* well.⟩ ⟨The couch can also *function* as a bed.⟩

²fundamental *n*
a basic part ⟨the *fundamentals* of math⟩

fu•ner•al \'fyü-nə-rəl, 'fyün-rəl\ *n*
the ceremonies held for a dead person (as before burial)

fun•gal \'fəŋ-gəl\ *or* **fun•gous** \-gəs\ *adj*
of, relating to, or caused by a fungus ⟨a *fungal* infection⟩

fun•gi•cide \'fən-jə-,sīd\ *n*
a substance used to kill fungi
fun•gi•cid•al \,fən-jə-'sī-dᵊl\ *adj*

A B C D E F G H I J K L M N O P Q R S T U V W X Y Z

fungus
Fungi absorb nutrients from dead or living organic matter, and most reproduce by spores. Fungi vary in size from microscopic, single-celled organisms such as yeast, to large, globe-shaped puffballs. Spores are often formed in special structures called fruiting bodies which include the familiar mushrooms. While some fungi are important sources of food and antibiotics, others can be poisonous or cause diseases in plants.

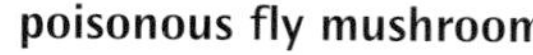

poisonous fly mushroom

edible oyster mushrooms

truffle is an edible fungus

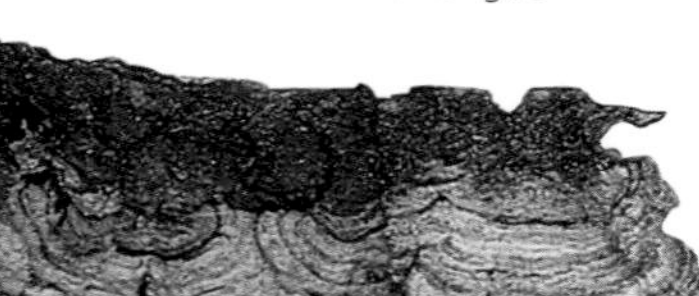

bracket fungus has a shape like a shelf

mold on stale bread

puffball is a globe-shaped fungus

fun•gus \ˈfəŋ-gəs\ *n, pl* **fun•gi** \ˈfən-ˌjī, -ˌgī\ *also* **fun•gus•es**
▲ any member of the kingdom of living things (as mushrooms, molds, and rusts) that have no chlorophyll, must live in or on plants, animals, or decaying material, and were formerly considered plants

funk \ˈfəŋk\ *n*
a sad or worried state ⟨Bad luck left him in a *funk.*⟩

fun•nel \ˈfə-nᵊl\ *n*
1 a utensil usually shaped like a hollow cone with a tube extending from the point and used to catch and direct a downward flow
2 a large pipe for the escape of smoke or for ventilation (as on a ship)

fun•nies \ˈfə-nēz\ *n pl*
comic strips or a section of a newspaper containing comic strips

¹fun•ny \ˈfə-nē\ *adj* **fun•ni•er; fun•ni•est**
1 causing laughter : full of humor ⟨a *funny* story⟩
2 STRANGE 2 ⟨a *funny* noise⟩

²funny *adv*
in an odd or peculiar way ⟨She looked at me *funny.*⟩

fur \ˈfər\ *n*
1 ▼ the hairy coat of a mammal especially when fine, soft, and thick

fur 1: a cat with orange fur

2 a piece of the pelt of an animal
3 an article of clothing made with fur
furred \ˈfərd\ *adj*

▶ **Word History** Though we think of fur as part of the animal that wears it, the history of the word *fur* begins with clothing rather than animals. Middle English *furre,* "fur trim or lining for a garment," was shortened from the synonymous word *furour,* or else derived from a verb *furren,* "to trim or line (a garment) with animal skin." This verb was borrowed from medieval French *fourrer,* with the identical meaning. *Fourrer* is a derivative of *fuerre,* meaning "sheath, wrapper," since lining a garment provides a sort of warm wrapper for its wearer.

fu•ri•ous \ˈfyu̇r-ē-əs\ *adj*
1 very angry

2 very active or fast ⟨a *furious* pace⟩
3 very powerful or violent ⟨a *furious* storm⟩
fu•ri•ous•ly *adv*

furl \'fərl\ *vb* **furled; furl•ing**
to wrap or roll close to or around something ⟨*furl* a flag⟩

fur•long \'fər-ˌlȯŋ\ *n*
a unit of length equal to 220 yards (about 201 meters)

fur•lough \'fər-lō\ *n*
a leave of absence from duty

fur•nace \'fər-nəs\ *n*
▶ an enclosed structure in which heat is produced (as for heating a house or melting metals)

fur•nish \'fər-nish\ *vb*
fur•nished; fur•nish•ing
1 to provide with furniture ⟨*furnish* a house⟩
2 to provide with what is needed ⟨The cave *furnished* us with shelter.⟩
3 to supply to someone or something ⟨We'll *furnish* food for the party.⟩

fur•nish•ings \'fər-ni-shiŋz\ *n pl*
articles of furniture for a room or building

fur•ni•ture \'fər-ni-chər\ *n*
movable articles used to furnish a room

[1]fur•row \'fər-ō\ *n*
1 ▼ a trench made by or as if by a plow
2 a narrow groove : WRINKLE

[2]furrow *vb* **fur•rowed; fur•row•ing**
to make wrinkles or grooves in ⟨He *furrowed* his brow.⟩

furnace: molten iron being poured from a furnace

fur•ry \'fər-ē\ *adj* **fur•ri•er; fur•ri•est**
1 covered with fur ⟨*furry* paws⟩
2 like fur ⟨*furry* slippers⟩

[1]fur•ther \'fər-t͟hər\ *adv*
1 [1]FARTHER 1 ⟨We walked *further* into the forest.⟩
2 [2]BESIDES, ALSO ⟨I understand *further* that it is not your fault.⟩
3 to a greater degree or extent ⟨Her anger increased *further*.⟩

[2]further *vb* **fur•thered; fur•ther•ing**
to help forward : PROMOTE ⟨Training will *further* your career.⟩

[3]further *adj*
1 [2]FARTHER ⟨Our property extends to the *further* tree.⟩
2 going or extending beyond : ADDITIONAL ⟨*further* study⟩

fur•ther•more \'fər-t͟hər-ˌmȯr\ *adv*
MOREOVER ⟨They came. *Furthermore* they came on time.⟩

fur•thest \'fər-t͟həst\ *adv or adj*
FARTHEST ⟨Of all of us, he rode his bike *furthest*.⟩ ⟨She lives in the *furthest* part of town.⟩

fur•tive \'fər-tiv\ *adj*
done in a sneaky or sly manner ⟨a *furtive* look⟩
fur•tive•ly *adv*

fu•ry \'fyu̇r-ē\ *n, pl* **furies**
1 violent anger : RAGE
2 wild and dangerous force ⟨the *fury* of the storm⟩
synonyms see ANGER

[1]fuse \'fyüz\ *vb* **fused; fus•ing**
1 to change into a liquid or to a plastic state by heat
2 to unite by or as if by melting together

[2]fuse *n*
a device having a metal wire or strip that melts and interrupts an electrical circuit when the current becomes too strong

[3]fuse *n*
1 a cord that is set afire to ignite an explosive by carrying fire to it
2 a device for setting off a bomb or torpedo

[1]furrow 1: a farmer using a tractor to plow a furrow in a field

fuselage: the fuselage of a passenger jet

fu•se•lage \'fyü-sə-,läzh, -zə-\ *n*
▲ the part of an airplane that holds the crew, passengers, and cargo

fu•sion \'fyü-zhən\ *n*
1 an act of fusing or melting together
2 union by or as if by melting
3 union of atomic nuclei to form heavier nuclei resulting in the release of enormous quantities of energy

[1]**fuss** \'fəs\ *n*
1 unnecessary activity or excitement often over something unimportant
2 [2]PROTEST 1 ⟨He took the medicine without any *fuss.*⟩
3 a great show of interest ⟨Everyone made a *fuss* over the baby.⟩

[2]**fuss** *vb* **fussed; fuss•ing**
to get excited or upset especially over something unimportant

fussy \'fə-sē\ *adj* **fuss•i•er; fuss•i•est**
1 inclined to complain or whine ⟨a *fussy* child⟩
2 hard to please ⟨His cat is *fussy* about food.⟩
3 overly decorated and complicated

fu•tile \'fyü-tᵊl\ *adj*
having no result or effect ⟨Their efforts to win were *futile.*⟩
fu•tile•ly *adv*

fu•til•i•ty \fyü-'ti-lə-tē\ *n*
the quality or state of being ineffective ⟨She knew the *futility* of trying to argue with him.⟩

[1]**fu•ture** \'fyü-chər\ *adj*
coming after the present ⟨*future* events⟩

[2]**future** *n*
1 the period of time that is to come ⟨What will happen in the *future?*⟩
2 the chance of future success ⟨You have a bright *future.*⟩

fuzz \'fəz\ *n*
fine light hairs or fibers

fuzzy \'fə-zē\ *adj* **fuzz•i•er; fuzz•i•est**
1 covered with or looking like short fine hairs or fibers ⟨a *fuzzy* baby bird⟩
2 not clear ⟨a *fuzzy* memory⟩
fuzz•i•ness \'fə-zē-nəs\ *n*

-fy \,fī\ *vb suffix* **-fied; -fy•ing**
1 make : form into ⟨solidi*fy*⟩
2 provide with the characteristics of ⟨beauti*fy*⟩

Gg

Sounds of G: The letter **G** makes two main sounds. One of those sounds is heard in words like *gum* and *finger*. In other words, **G** sounds like a **J**, as in the words *giraffe* and *cage*. Sometimes **G** makes an **H** sound, as in *Gila monster*. And sometimes **G** is silent, especially when it comes before an **N**, as in the words *gnaw* and *sign*. When **G** follows an **N**, it often makes the sound heard in *sing* and in the many other words ending in *-ing*. This sound is indicated by the symbol ŋ. In a few words, **G** makes the sound heard in *collage*, *beige*, and the way some people say *garage*. This sound is indicated by the symbol zh. **G** and **H** combined sometimes make an **F** sound, as in *tough* and *cough*. Sometimes they are silent, as in *light* and *through*. And sometimes only the **G** is heard, as in *ghost* and *ghastly*.

g \'jē\ *n, pl* **g's** *or* **gs** \'jēz\ *often cap*
1 the seventh letter of the English alphabet
2 the musical note referred to by the letter G
3 a unit of force equal to the force of gravity on a body ⟨The pilot experienced five *G's* during the sudden turn.⟩

G *abbr* good

g. *abbr* gram

GA, Ga. *abbr* Georgia

[1]**gab** \'gab\ *vb* **gabbed**; **gab•bing**
to talk in a relaxed way about unimportant things : CHAT

[2]**gab** *n*
talk about unimportant things

gab•ar•dine \'ga-bər-,dēn\ *n*
a firm cloth with a hard smooth finish

[1]**gab•ble** \'ga-bəl\ *vb* **gab•bled**; **gab•bling**
to talk in a fast or foolish way or in a way that is hard to understand

[2]**gabble** *n*
talk that is fast or foolish or hard to understand

gab•by \'ga-bē\ *adj* **gab•bi•er**; **gab•bi•est**
fond of talking a lot : TALKATIVE ⟨a *gabby* friend⟩

ga•ble \'gā-bəl\ *n*
▶ the triangular part of an outside wall of a building formed by the sides of a sloping roof
ga•bled \'gā-bəld\ *adj*

gad \'gad\ *vb* **gad•ded**; **gad•ding**
to wander or roam from place to place

gad•about \'ga-də-,bau̇t\ *n*
a person who goes to many different places for enjoyment

gad•fly \'gad-,flī\ *n, pl* **gad•flies**
1 a large biting fly
2 a person who annoys others especially with constant criticism

gad•get \'ga-jət\ *n*
a small useful device that is often interesting, unfamiliar, or unusual

[1]**gag** \'gag\ *vb* **gagged**; **gag•ging**
1 to stop from speaking or crying out by or as if by covering or blocking the mouth
2 to vomit or feel like vomiting ⟨The horrible smell almost made me *gag*.⟩
3 CHOKE 2 ⟨He *gagged* on his hot dog.⟩

[2]**gag** *n*
1 something covering or blocking the mouth especially to prevent speaking or crying out
2 something said or done to make other people laugh

gage *variant of* GAUGE

gable: a Norwegian church with gables

gag•gle \'ga-gəl\ *n*
1 ▶ a group of animals and especially a flock of geese
2 a group of people ⟨a *gaggle* of tourists⟩

gai•ety \'gā-ə-tē\ *n, pl* **gai•eties**
1 happy and lively activity : MERRYMAKING
2 bright spirits or manner ⟨The bad news ended their *gaiety*.⟩

gai•ly \'gā-lē\ *adv*
1 in a merry or lively way ⟨Children were playing *gaily*.⟩
2 in a bright or showy way ⟨The performers were *gaily* dressed.⟩

[1]**gain** \'gān\ *n*
1 something valuable or desirable that is obtained or acquired : PROFIT ⟨financial *gains*⟩
2 an increase in amount, size, or degree

[2]**gain** *vb* **gained**; **gain•ing**
1 to get or win often by effort ⟨You *gain* knowledge by study.⟩ ⟨He exercised to *gain* strength.⟩
2 to get or acquire in a natural or gradual way ⟨He *gained* ten pounds.⟩
3 to increase in ⟨The car *gained* speed.⟩
4 to get to : REACH ⟨The swimmer *gained* the shore.⟩
5 to get an advantage : PROFIT ⟨We all *gained* from the lesson.⟩
synonyms see REACH

gain•ful \'gān-fəl\ *adj*
producing gain : making money ⟨She found *gainful* employment.⟩

gait \'gāt\ *n*
a way of walking or running

gal. *abbr* gallon

[1]**ga•la** \'gā-lə, 'ga-lə, 'gä-\ *n*
a large showy celebration ⟨We attended our town's 100th anniversary *gala*.⟩

[2]**gala** *adj*
being or resembling a large showy celebration ⟨*gala* events⟩

ga•lac•tic \gə-'lak-tik\ *adj*
of or relating to a galaxy ⟨*galactic* light⟩

gaggle 1: a gaggle of geese

A B C D E F G H I J K L M N O P Q R S T U V W X Y Z

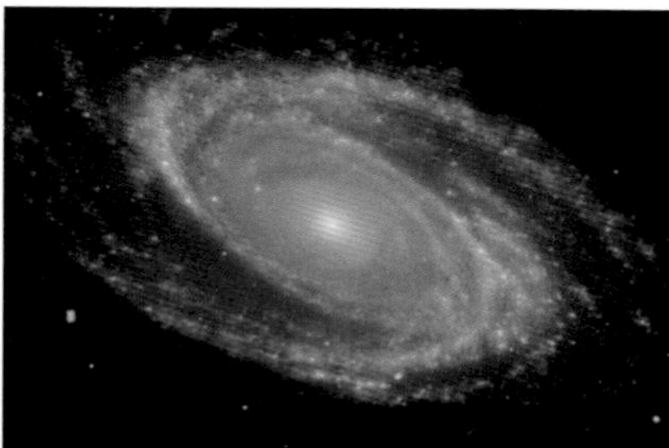

galaxy 2: a spiral galaxy

gal•axy \'ga-lək-sē\ *n, pl* **gal•ax•ies**
1 MILKY WAY GALAXY
2 ▲ one of the very large groups of stars, gas, and dust that make up the universe

► **Word History** The band of light that crosses a clear night sky is caused by many faint stars. We call this band the *Milky Way* because it looks a bit like a stream of milk. The stars of the Milky Way belong to our galaxy, the Milky Way galaxy. The idea that the Milky Way looks like milk is much older than the English language, however. The ancient Greek name for this star system, *galaxias*, was formed from the Greek word *gala*, "milk." The English word *galaxy* was borrowed from the Greek name.

gale \'gāl\ *n*
1 a strong wind
2 a wind of from about 32 to 63 miles per hour (about 51 to 101 kilometers per hour)
3 an outburst of amusement ⟨*gales* of laughter⟩

ga•le•na \gə-'lē-nə\ *n*
► a bluish gray mineral that is the ore from which lead is obtained

galena

[1]gall \'gȯl\ *n*
1 extreme boldness or rudeness ⟨She had the *gall* to return my gift.⟩
2 bile especially when obtained from an animal for use in the arts or medicine

[2]gall *n*
a sore spot (as on a horse's back) caused by rubbing

[3]gall *vb* **galled**; **gall•ing**
1 to make sore by rubbing
2 to annoy or make angry ⟨His selfishness just *galls* me.⟩

[4]gall *n*
an abnormal swelling or growth on a twig or leaf

gal•lant \'ga-lənt\ *adj*
1 showing courage : very brave ⟨a *gallant* soldier⟩
2 CHIVALROUS 2 ⟨a *gallant* knight⟩
3 \gə-'lant, -'länt\ very polite to women ⟨He offered her his seat in a *gallant* gesture.⟩
4 splendid or stately ⟨a *gallant* ship⟩
5 showy in dress or in the way of acting ⟨He was a *gallant* figure in his uniform.⟩
gal•lant•ly *adv*

gal•lant•ry \'ga-lən-trē\ *n*
1 courageous behavior : BRAVERY
2 polite attention shown to women

gall•blad•der \'gȯl-,bla-dər\ *n*
a small sac in which bile from the liver is stored

gal•le•on \'ga-lē-ən\ *n*
a large sailing ship used by the Spanish from the 1400s to the 1700s

gal•lery \'ga-lə-rē, 'gal-rē\ *n, pl* **gal•ler•ies**
1 a long narrow room or hall
2 an indoor structure (as in a theater or church) built out from one or more walls
3 a room or building in which people look at works of art
4 the highest balcony of seats in a theater or the people who sit there
5 a passage (as in wood) made by an animal and especially an insect

gal•ley \'ga-lē\ *n, pl* **galleys**
1 a large low ship of olden times moved by oars and sails
2 the kitchen especially of a ship or an airplane

gal•li•vant \'ga-lə-,vant\ *vb* **gal•li•vant•ed**; **gal•li•vant•ing**
to travel from place to place doing things for pleasure ⟨*gallivanting* around town⟩

[2]gallop 1: a horse at a gallop

gal•lon \'ga-lən\ *n*
a unit of liquid capacity equal to four quarts (about 3.8 liters)

[1]gal•lop \'ga-ləp\ *vb* **gal•loped**; **gal•lop•ing**
1 to run or cause to run at a gallop
2 to ride on a galloping horse

[2]gallop *n*
1 ▲ the fast springing way an animal with four feet and especially a horse runs when all four of its feet leave the ground at the same time
2 a ride or run on a galloping horse

gal•lows \'ga-lōz\ *n, pl* **gallows** *or* **gal•lows•es**
a structure from which criminals are hanged

ga•lore \gə-'lȯr\ *adj*
in large amounts
Hint: *Galore* is used after the word it modifies. ⟨The ride has thrills *galore.*⟩

ga•losh \gə-'läsh\ *n*
a high shoe worn over another shoe to keep the foot dry especially in snow or wet weather — usually used in pl.

ga•lumph \gə-ˈləmf\ *vb* **ga•lumphed; ga•lumph•ing**
to move in a loud and clumsy way

gal•va•nize \ˈgal-və-ˌnīz\ *vb* **gal•va•nized; gal•va•niz•ing**
1 to excite about something so that action is taken
2 to coat with zinc for protection

[1]**gam•ble** \ˈgam-bəl\ *vb* **gam•bled; gam•bling**
1 to play a game in which something (as money) can be won or lost : BET
2 to take a chance ⟨I *gambled* on not being seen.⟩
gam•bler \ˈgam-blər\ *n*

[2]**gamble** *n*
something that could produce a good or bad result : RISK

gam•bol \ˈgam-bəl\ *vb* **gam•boled** *or* **gam•bolled; gam•bol•ing** *or* **gam•bol•ling**
to run or play happily : FROLIC ⟨Children *gamboled* on the lawn.⟩

[1]**game** \ˈgām\ *n*
1 a contest or sport played according to rules with the players in direct opposition to each other
2 the manner of playing in a game or contest ⟨She has improved her *game*.⟩
3 playful activity : something done for amusement ⟨The children were happy at their *games*.⟩
4 animals hunted for sport or for food
5 the meat from animals hunted for food

[2]**game** *adj* **gam•er; gam•est**
1 willing or ready to do something ⟨I'm *game* to try a new restaurant.⟩
2 full of spirit or eagerness ⟨She remained *game* to the end.⟩
3 relating to or being animals that are hunted ⟨the *game* laws⟩ ⟨*game* birds⟩

game•keep•er \ˈgām-ˌkē-pər\ *n*
a person in charge of the breeding and protection of game animals or birds on private land

game•ly \ˈgām-lē\ *adv*
with spirit and courage ⟨She'd already lost the race but *gamely* continued running.⟩

gam•ing \ˈgā-miŋ\ *n*
the practice of gambling

gam•ma ray \ˈga-mə-\ *n*
a ray that is like an X-ray but of higher energy and that is given off especially by a radioactive substance

gamy \ˈgā-mē\ *adj* **gam•i•er; gam•i•est**
having the flavor or smell of meat from wild animals especially when slightly spoiled

[1]**gan•der** \ˈgan-dər\ *n*
a male goose

[2]**gander** *n*
a look or glance

gang \ˈgaŋ\ *n*
1 a group of people working or going about together
2 a group of people acting together to do something illegal ⟨a *gang* of thieves⟩
3 a group of friends ⟨I invited the *gang* over.⟩

gan•gli•on \ˈgaŋ-glē-ən\ *n, pl* **gan•glia** \-glē-ə\
a mass of nerve cells especially outside the brain or spinal cord

gan•gly \ˈgaŋ-glē\ *adj* **gan•gli•er; gan•gli•est**
tall, thin, and awkward ⟨a *gangly* teenager⟩

gang•plank \ˈgaŋ-ˌplaŋk\ *n*
a movable bridge from a ship to the shore

gan•grene \ˈgaŋ-ˌgrēn\ *n*
death of body tissue when the blood supply is cut off

gang•ster \ˈgaŋ-stər\ *n*
a member of a gang of criminals

gang up *vb* **ganged up; gang•ing up**
to join together as a group especially to attack, oppose, or criticize

gang•way \ˈgaŋ-ˌwā\ *n*
1 a passage into, through, or out of an enclosed space
2 GANGPLANK

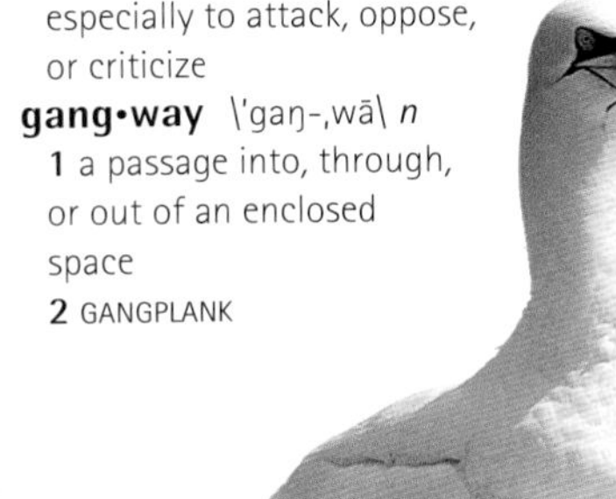
gannet

gan•net \ˈga-nət\ *n*
▲ a large bird that eats fish and spends much time far from land

gan•try \ˈgan-trē\ *n, pl* **gantries**
1 a structure over railroad tracks for holding signals
2 a movable structure for preparing a rocket for launching

gap \ˈgap\ *n*
1 an opening made by a break or rupture ⟨She squeezed through a *gap* in the fence.⟩
2 an opening between mountains
3 a hole or space where something is missing ⟨There are some *gaps* in his story.⟩

[1]**gape** \ˈgāp\ *vb* **gaped; gap•ing**
1 to stare with the mouth open in surprise or wonder
2 to open or part widely ⟨a *gaping* wound⟩

[2]**gape** *n*
an act or instance of opening or staring with the mouth open ⟨He ignored everyone's stunned *gapes*.⟩

ga•rage \gə-ˈräzh, -ˈräj\ *n*
1 a building or part of a building where vehicles are kept when not in use
2 a shop where vehicles are repaired

[1]**garb** \ˈgärb\ *n*
style or kind of clothing ⟨medieval *garb*⟩

[2]**garb** *vb* **garbed; garb•ing**
CLOTHE 1 ⟨She was plainly *garbed*.⟩

gar•bage \ˈgär-bij\ *n*
1 material (as waste food) that has been thrown out
2 something that is worthless, useless, or untrue ⟨Don't watch *garbage* on television.⟩

gar•ble \ˈgär-bəl\ *vb* **gar•bled; gar•bling**
to change or twist the meaning or sound of ⟨He *garbled* the message.⟩

▶ **Word History** At first the word *garble* meant "to sift" or "to sort or pick out." If you pick out a few misleading parts of a message and report only those parts, you distort the message, and so *garble* came to mean "to distort." It is the meaning "sift," however, that reflects the origin of *garble*. The English word *garble* came from an old Italian verb *garbellare* that meant "to sift." This word came in turn from an Arabic word *gharbala* that meant "sieve." The Arabs took this word ultimately from a Latin word *cribellum* that meant "sieve."

[1]**gar•den** \ˈgär-dᵊn\ *n*
1 a piece of ground in which fruits, flowers, or vegetables are grown
2 a public area for the showing of plants

[2]**garden** *vb* **gar•dened; gar•den•ing**
to make or work in a garden

gar•den•er \ˈgär-də-nər, ˈgärd-nər\ *n*
a person who works in a garden especially for pay

gar•de•nia \gär-ˈdē-nyə\ *n*
a large white or yellowish flower with a fragrant smell

gar•gan•tuan \gär-ˈgan-chə-wən\ *adj*
extremely large or great : HUGE

[1]**gar•gle** \ˈgär-gəl\ *vb* **gar•gled; gar•gling**
to rinse the throat with a liquid kept in motion by air forced through it from the lungs

a b c d e f g h i j k l m n o p q r s t u v w x y z

gargoyles on a cathedral in Paris, France

[2]gargle *n*
1 a liquid used for rinsing the throat and mouth
2 a sound like that of gargling

gar•goyle \'gär-ˌgȯil\ *n*
▲ a strange or frightening human or animal figure that sticks out from the roof of a building and often serves as a waterspout

gar•ish \'ger-ish\ *adj*
too bright or showy : GAUDY 〈She was dressed in *garish* colors.〉
gar•ish•ly *adv*

[1]gar•land \'gär-lənd\ *n*
▼ a wreath or rope of material (as leaves or flowers)

[1]garland

[2]garland *vb* **gar•land•ed; gar•land•ing**
to form into or decorate with a garland 〈Flowers *garlanded* her head.〉

gar•lic \'gär-lik\ *n*
a plant related to the onion and grown for its bulbs that have a strong smell and taste and are used to flavor foods

gar•ment \'gär-mənt\ *n*
an article of clothing

gar•ner \'gär-nər\ *vb* **gar•nered; gar•ner•ing**
1 to collect or gather 〈The scientist *garnered* more evidence to support his theory.〉
2 to acquire or earn 〈The band *garnered* a large following.〉

gar•net \'gär-nət\ *n*
▼ a deep red mineral used as a gem

garnet

[1]gar•nish \'gär-nish\ *vb* **gar•nished; gar•nish•ing**
to add decorations or seasoning (as to food)

[2]garnish *n*
something used to add decoration or flavoring (as to food)

gar•ret \'ger-ət\ *n*
a room or unfinished part of a house just under the roof

[1]gar•ri•son \'ger-ə-sən\ *n*
1 a military camp, fort, or base
2 the soldiers stationed at a garrison

[2]garrison *vb* **gar•ri•soned; gar•ri•son•ing**
1 to station troops in 〈The fort was only temporarily *garrisoned*.〉
2 to send (troops) to live in and defend 〈It became necessay to *garrison* troops in the town.〉

gar•ru•lous \'ger-ə-ləs\ *adj*
very talkative

gar•ter \'gär-tər\ *n*
a band worn to hold up a stocking or sock

garter snake *n*
any of numerous harmless American snakes with stripes along the back

[1]gas \'gas\ *n, pl* **gas•es**
1 a substance (as oxygen or hydrogen) having no fixed shape and tending to expand without limit
2 NATURAL GAS
3 a gas or a mixture of gases used to make a person unconscious (as for an operation)
4 a substance that poisons the air or makes breathing difficult
5 GASOLINE
6 a gaseous product of digestion or the discomfort caused by it

[2]gas *vb* **gassed; gas•sing; gas•ses**
1 to poison with gas
2 to supply with gas 〈*Gas* up the car.〉

gas•eous \'ga-sē-əs, 'ga-shəs\ *adj*
1 having the form of gas
2 of or relating to gas 〈*gaseous* odors〉

[1]gash \'gash\ *n*
a long deep cut

[2]gash *vb* **gashed; gash•ing**
to make a long deep cut in 〈The knife slipped and *gashed* her finger.〉

gas mask *n*
▼ a mask connected to a chemical air filter and used to protect the face and lungs from harmful gases

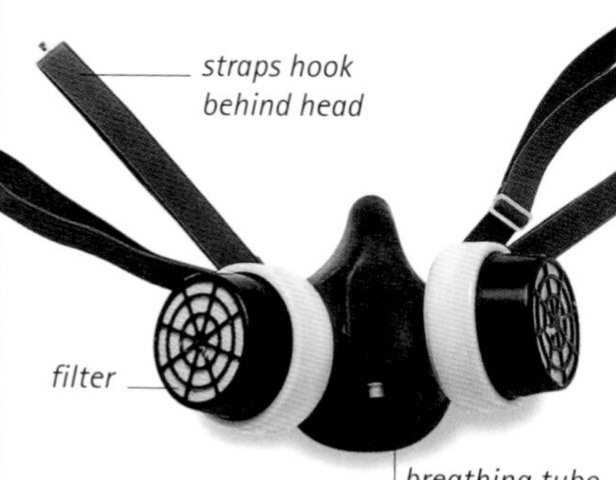

gas mask: a gas mask used for protection from airborne pollutants

gas•o•line \'ga-sə-ˌlēn, ˌga-sə-'lēn\ *n*
a flammable liquid made especially from natural gas found in the earth and from petroleum and used mostly as an automobile fuel

[1]gasp \'gasp\ *vb* **gasped; gasp•ing**
1 to breathe in suddenly and loudly with the mouth open because of surprise, shock, or pain 〈They *gasped* at the sight of the treasure.〉
2 to breathe with difficulty : PANT 〈The runners were *gasping* after the race.〉
3 to utter with quick difficult breaths 〈"I think we're lost," she *gasped*.〉

[2]gasp *n*
1 the act of breathing in suddenly or with difficulty 〈I heard the crowd's loud *gasp*.〉
2 something gasped 〈He let out a *gasp* of surprise.〉

gas station *n*
▶ a place for servicing motor vehicles especially with gasoline and oil

gas•tric juice \'ga-strik-\ *n*
an acid liquid made by the stomach that helps to digest food

gate \ˈgāt\ *n*
1 an opening in a wall or fence
2 a part of a barrier (as a fence) that opens and closes like a door
3 a door, valve, or other device for controlling the flow of water or other fluids ⟨canal *gates*⟩
4 an area at an airport where passengers arrive and leave

gate•house \ˈgāt-ˌhau̇s\ *n*
a small building near a gate

gate•keep•er \ˈgāt-ˌkē-pər\ *n*
a person who guards a gate

gate•way \ˈgāt-ˌwā\ *n*
1 an opening for a gate ⟨a stone *gateway*⟩
2 a passage into or out of a place or condition ⟨Determination is the *gateway* to success.⟩

[1]**gath•er** \ˈga-t͟hər\ *vb* **gath•ered**; **gath•er•ing**
1 to pick up and collect ⟨They *gathered* wood for the fire.⟩
2 to choose and collect ⟨*gather* fruit⟩ ⟨I'm *gathering* facts for my report.⟩
3 to come together in a group or around a center of attraction ⟨A crowd *gathered* on the sidewalk.⟩
4 to gain little by little ⟨*gather* speed⟩
5 to bring or call forth (as strength or courage) from within
6 to get an idea : CONCLUDE ⟨I *gather* you don't agree.⟩
7 to draw together in or as if in folds ⟨She *gathered* her cloak about her.⟩

▶ **Synonyms** GATHER, COLLECT, and ASSEMBLE mean to come or bring together. GATHER is used for the coming or bringing together of different kinds of things. ⟨They *gathered* all the goods in the house and sold them.⟩ COLLECT is used for a careful or orderly gathering of things that are often of one kind. ⟨It's fun to *collect* coins.⟩ ASSEMBLE is used for a gathering of units into an orderly whole. ⟨The choir *assembled* and started to sing.⟩

[2]**gather** *n*
the result of gathering cloth : PUCKER

gath•er•ing \ˈga-t͟hə-riŋ\ *n*
an occasion when people come together as a group ⟨a family *gathering*⟩

gaudy \ˈgȯ-dē\ *adj* **gaud•i•er**; **gaud•i•est**
too bright and showy ⟨*gaudy* jewelry⟩

[1]**gauge** *also* **gage** \ˈgāj\ *n*
1 a measurement (as the distance between the rails of a railroad or the size of a shotgun barrel's inner diameter) according to some standard ⟨a standard *gauge* railway⟩
2 an instrument for measuring, testing, or registering ⟨a rain *gauge*⟩ ⟨a steam *gauge*⟩

[2]**gauge** *also* **gage** *vb* **gauged** *also* **gaged**; **gaug•ing** *also* **gag•ing**
1 to measure exactly ⟨*gauge* rainfall⟩
2 to make a judgment about ⟨It was hard to *gauge* his moods.⟩

gaunt \ˈgȯnt\ *adj* **gaunt•er**; **gaunt•est**
very thin and bony (as from illness or hunger) ⟨a *gaunt* face⟩

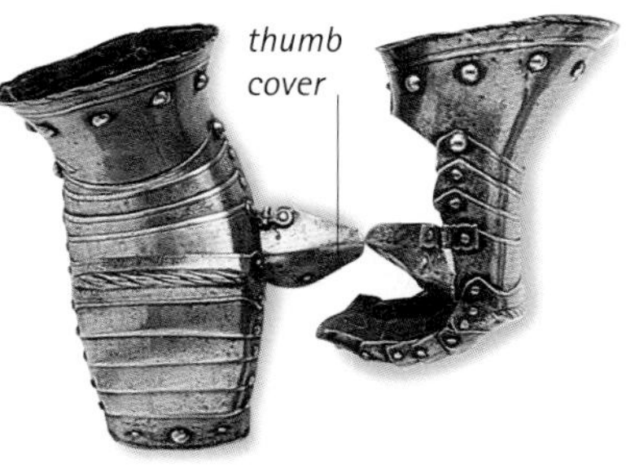

gauntlet 1:
gauntlets from a 16th-century suit of armor

gaunt•let \ˈgȯnt-lət\ *n*
1 ▲ a glove made of small metal plates and worn with a suit of armor
2 a glove with a wide cuff that protects the wrist and part of the arm

gauze \ˈgȯz\ *n*
1 a thin fabric that allows light to pass through it
2 loosely woven cotton used as a bandage

gauzy \ˈgȯ-zē\ *adj* **gauz•i•er**; **gauz•i•est**
thin and transparent like gauze ⟨*gauzy* curtains⟩

gave *past of* GIVE

gav•el \ˈga-vəl\ *n*
a mallet with which the person in charge raps to get people's attention in a meeting or courtroom

gawk \ˈgȯk\ *vb* **gawked**; **gawk•ing**
to stare stupidly ⟨She stood there *gawking* at the celebrities.⟩

gawky \ˈgȯ-kē\ *adj* **gawk•i•er**; **gawk•i•est**
awkward and clumsy ⟨a tall *gawky* boy⟩

gay \ˈgā\ *adj* **gay•er**; **gay•est**
1 MERRY 1, HAPPY ⟨*gay* and carefree children⟩
2 cheerful and lively ⟨They played a *gay* tune.⟩
3 brightly colored ⟨a *gay* dress⟩

[1]**gaze** \ˈgāz\ *vb* **gazed**; **gaz•ing**
to fix the eyes in a long steady look ⟨She *gazed* at the stars.⟩

▶ **Synonyms** GAZE, STARE, and GLARE mean to look at with concentration. GAZE is used of a long and fixed look. ⟨They stood *gazing* at the sunset.⟩ STARE is used of an often curious, rude, or absentminded gaze with eyes wide open. ⟨He *stared* in surprise at the strange creature.⟩ GLARE means an angry stare. ⟨The teacher *glared* at the naughty children.⟩

gas station

gazebo: gazebos are often found in parks, gardens, or public areas

[2]gaze *n*
a long steady look

ga•ze•bo \gə-ˈzē-bō\ *n, pl* **ga•ze•bos**
▲ a small building (as in a garden or park) that is usually open on the sides

ga•zelle \gə-ˈzel\ *n*
▼ a swift graceful antelope of Africa and Asia

gazelle

ga•zette \gə-ˈzet\ *n*
1 NEWSPAPER
2 a journal giving official information

gaz•et•teer \ˌga-zə-ˈtir\ *n*
a geographical dictionary

ga•zil•lion \gə-ˈzil-yən\ *n*
an extremely large number ⟨There were *gazillions* of mosquitoes.⟩
gazillion *adj*

GB *abbr* gigabyte

[1]gear \ˈgir\ *n*
1 EQUIPMENT ⟨camping *gear*⟩
2 a group of parts that has a specific function in a machine ⟨steering *gear*⟩
3 a toothed wheel : COGWHEEL
4 the position the gears of a machine are win when they are ready to work ⟨in *gear*⟩
5 one of the adjustments in a motor vehicle that determine the direction of travel and the relative speed between the engine and the motion of the vehicle ⟨reverse *gear*⟩
6 working order or condition ⟨He got his career in *gear.*⟩

[2]gear *vb* **geared; gear•ing**
1 to make ready for operation ⟨We need to *gear* up for production.⟩
2 to be or make suitable ⟨The book is *geared* to children.⟩

gear•shift \ˈgir-ˌshift\ *n*
a mechanism by which gears are connected and disconnected

gecko \ˈge-ˌkō\ *n, pl* **geck•os** *or* **geck•oes**
▼ a small tropical lizard that eats insects and is usually active at night

gecko

gee \ˈjē\ *interj*
used to show surprise, enthusiasm, or disappointment ⟨*Gee,* what fun!⟩ ⟨*Gee,* that's bad news.⟩

geese *pl of* GOOSE

Gei•ger counter \ˈgī-gər-\ *n*
an instrument for detecting the presence of cosmic rays or radioactive substances

[1]gel \ˈjel\ *n*
a thick jellylike substance

[2]gel *vb* **gelled; gel•ling**
to change into a thick jellylike substance ⟨The mixture will *gel* as it cools.⟩

gel•a•tin \ˈje-lə-tᵊn\ *n*
1 a gummy or sticky protein obtained by boiling animal tissues and used especially as food
2 an edible jelly made with gelatin

ge•lat•i•nous \jə-ˈlat-nəs, -ˈla-tə-\ *adj*
resembling gelatin or jelly ⟨The mushrooms had a *gelatinous* texture.⟩

gem \ˈjem\ *n*
1 ► a usually valuable stone cut and polished for jewelry
2 something prized as being beautiful or perfect ⟨The old house is a real *gem.*⟩

Gem•i•ni \ˈje-mə-nē, -ˌnī\ *n*
1 a constellation between Taurus and Cancer usually pictured as twins sitting together
2 the third sign of the zodiac or a person born under this sign

gem•stone \ˈjem-ˌstōn\ *n*
a stone that when cut and polished can be used in jewelry

gen. *abbr* general

gen•der \ˈjen-dər\ *n*
the state of being male or female : SEX

gene \ˈjēn\ *n*
a unit of DNA that is usually located on a chromosome and that controls the development of one or more traits and is the basic unit by which genetic information is passed from parent to offspring

ge•ne•al•o•gy \ˌjē-nē-ˈä-lə-jē\ *n, pl* **ge•ne•al•o•gies**
1 a line of ancestors of a person or family or a history of such a line of ancestors
2 the study of family lines of ancestors

genera *pl of* GENUS

gem 1
The characteristics that define a gem are a beautiful color, ability to reflect light, rarity, and durability. Most gems, including rubies and emeralds, are minerals that have formed crystals within the earth's crust. Organic gems, such as jet, amber, and pearls, are produced by plants and animals. Mineral gems are usually cut with facets, while organic gems are mostly carved and polished.

features of a cut amethyst

examples of gems

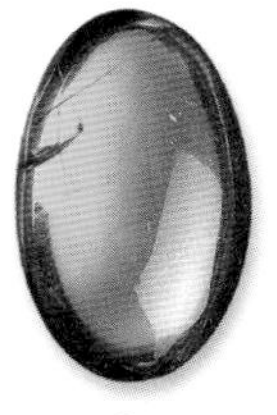
amber

aquamarine

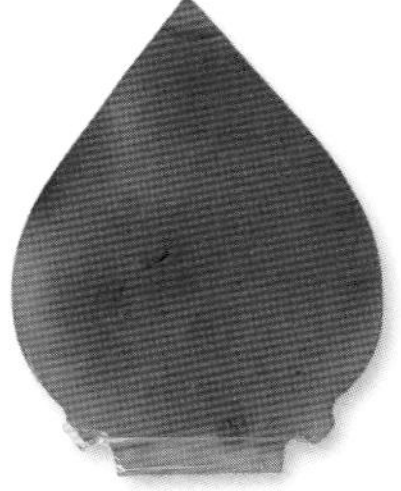
carnelian

diamond

emerald

garnet

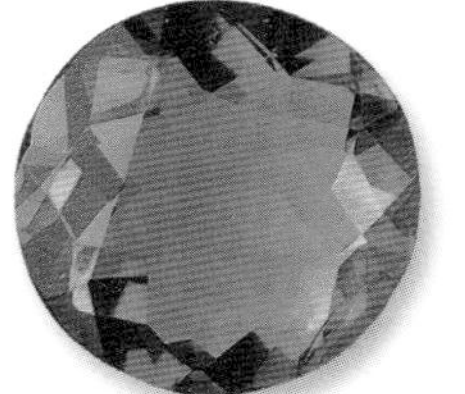
girasole
\ˈjir-ə-ˌsōl\

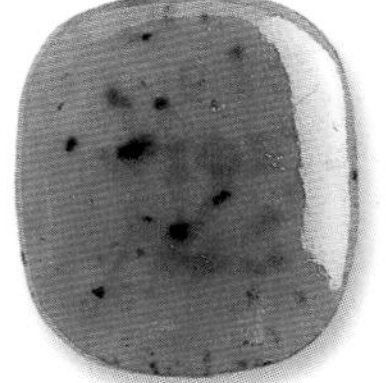
jade

jet

malachite
\ˈmal-ə-ˌkīt\

milky quartz

opal

pearl

peridot
\ˈper-ə-ˌdät\

rock crystal

ruby

sapphire

sardonyx
\sär-ˈdä-niks\

sodalite
\ˈsō-də-ˌlīt\

turquoise

[1]**gen•er•al** \ˈje-nə-rəl, ˈjen-rəl\ *adj*
1 having to do with the whole : applying to more than just a small area or group ⟨It's a matter of *general* interest.⟩
2 not specific or detailed ⟨The book is a good *general* introduction to football.⟩
3 involving or including many or most people ⟨Her plans won *general* acceptance.⟩
4 not specialized ⟨a *general* store⟩

[2]**general** *n*
a military officer ranking above a colonel
in general for the most part ⟨*In general*, I like school.⟩

gen•er•al•iza•tion \ˌje-nə-rə-lə-ˈzā-shən\ *n*
1 the act of forming conclusions from a small amount of information
2 a general statement : a conclusion based on only a small number of items or instances

gen•er•al•ize \ˈje-nə-rə-ˌlīz, ˈjen-rə-\ *vb* **gen•er•al•ized; gen•er•al•iz•ing**
to draw or state a general conclusion from a number of different items or instances

gen•er•al•ly \ˈje-nə-rə-lē, ˈjen-rə-\ *adv*
1 for the most part ⟨*Generally*, I don't enjoy horror movies.⟩
2 in most cases : USUALLY

gen•er•ate \ˈje-nə-ˌrāt\ *vb* **gen•er•at•ed; gen•er•at•ing**
to cause to come into being ⟨*generate* electricity⟩ ⟨*generate* excitement⟩

gen•er•a•tion \ˌje-nə-ˈrā-shən\ *n*
1 those being a single step in a line originating from one ancestor ⟨This family has lived in town for four *generations*.⟩
2 a group of individuals born and living at about the same time ⟨the younger *generation*⟩
3 the act or process of producing or creating something ⟨the *generation* of heat⟩

gen•er•a•tor \ˈje-nə-ˌrā-tər\ *n*
a machine that produces electricity

gen•er•os•i•ty \ˌje-nə-ˈrä-sə-tē\ *n*
1 willingness to give or to share ⟨He shows *generosity* to those in need.⟩
2 an act of unselfish giving ⟨Her *generosity* was appreciated.⟩

gen•er•ous \ˈje-nə-rəs, ˈjen-rəs\ *adj*
1 freely giving or sharing ⟨She was *generous* with her time.⟩
2 providing more than enough of what is needed : ABUNDANT ⟨a *generous* supply⟩
gen•er•ous•ly *adv*

ge•net•ic \jə-ˈne-tik\ *adj*
of or relating to genes or genetics

genetic code *n*
the arrangement of chemical groups within the genes which specify particular kinds of amino acids used to make proteins

ge•net•i•cist \jə-ˈne-tə-səst\ *n*
a person specializing in genetics

ge•net•ics \jə-ˈne-tiks\ *n*
the scientific study of how the characteristics of living things are controlled by genes

ge•nial \ˈjēn-yəl\ *adj*
cheerful and pleasant ⟨a *genial* host⟩
ge•nial•ly \ˈjēn-yə-lē\ *adv*

ge•nial•i•ty \ˌjē-nē-ˈa-lə-tē, jēn-ˈya-\ *n*
a cheerful and pleasant way of acting ⟨Her *geniality* put the guests at ease.⟩

ge•nie \ˈjē-nē\ *n*
a magic spirit believed to take human form and serve the person who calls it

gen•i•tal \ˈje-nə-tᵊl\ *adj*
of or relating to reproduction or the sexual organs

ge•nius \ˈjēn-yəs\ *n*
1 a very smart or gifted person
2 great natural ability ⟨He has artistic *genius*.⟩
3 a very clever or smart quality

gent \ˈjent\ *n*
[1]MAN 1, FELLOW ⟨a delightful old *gent*⟩

gen•teel \jen-ˈtēl\ *adj*
1 relating to the upper classes ⟨She was born into a *genteel* family.⟩
2 having an elegant, tasteful, or polite quality ⟨*genteel* behavior⟩

gen•tian \ˈjen-chən\ *n*
▼ a plant with smooth leaves and usually blue flowers

gentian

[1]**gen•tile** \ˈjen-ˌtīl\ *n, often cap*
a person who is not Jewish

[2]**gentile** *adj, often cap*
of or relating to people who are not Jewish

gen•til•i•ty \jen-ˈti-lə-tē\ *n*
1 high social status
2 a quality of elegance and politeness

gen•tle \ˈjen-tᵊl\ *adj* **gen•tler; gen•tlest**
1 having or showing a kind and quiet nature : not harsh, stern, or violent
2 not hard or forceful ⟨a *gentle* wind⟩
3 not strong or harsh in quality or effect ⟨a *gentle* soap⟩
4 not steep or sharp ⟨*gentle* hills⟩
gen•tle•ness \ˈjen-tᵊl-nəs\ *n*
gen•tly \ˈjent-lē\ *adv*

gen•tle•folk \ˈjen-tᵊl-ˌfōk\ *n pl*
GENTRY

gen•tle•man \ˈjen-tᵊl-mən\ *n, pl* **gen•tle•men** \-mən\
1 a man with very good manners
2 a man of any social position
Hint: This word is used especially in polite speech or when speaking to a group of men. ⟨Good evening, ladies and *gentlemen*.⟩
3 a man of high social status ⟨He's a *gentleman* by birth.⟩
gen•tle•man•ly *adj*

gen•tle•wom•an \ˈjen-tᵊl-ˌwu̇-mən\ *n, pl* **gen•tle•wom•en** \-ˌwi-mən\
1 a woman of good birth and position
2 a woman with very good manners : LADY

gen•try \ˈjen-trē\ *n*
people of high social status

gen•u•flect \ˈjen-yə-ˌflekt\ *vb* **gen•u•flect•ed; gen•u•flect•ing**
to kneel on one knee and rise again as an act of deep respect (as in a church)

gen•u•ine \ˈjen-yə-wən\ *adj*
1 actual, real, or true : not false or fake
2 sincere and honest ⟨She showed *genuine* interest.⟩
gen•u•ine•ly *adv*

ge•nus \ˈjē-nəs\ *n, pl* **gen•era** \ˈje-nə-rə\
a group of related living things (as plants or animals) that ranks below the family in scientific classification and is made up of one or more species

geo- *prefix*
1 earth : soil ⟨*geo*chemistry⟩
2 geographical

geo•cach•ing \ˈjē-ō-ˌka-shiŋ\ *n*
a game in which players are given the geographical coordinates of a cache of items which they search for with a GPS device

geo•chem•is•try \ˌjē-ō-ˈke-mə-strē\ *n*
a science that deals with the chemical composition of and chemical changes in the earth's crust

ge•ode \ˈjē-ˌōd\ *n*
a stone with a hollow space inside lined with crystals or mineral matter

geog. *abbr*
1 geographic
2 geographical
3 geography

geo•graph•ic \ˌjē-ə-ˈgra-fik\ *or* **geo•graph•i•cal** \-i-kəl\ *adj*
of or relating to geography ⟨a large *geographic* area⟩

ge•og•ra•phy \jē-ˈä-grə-fē\ *n*
1 a science that deals with the location of living and nonliving things on earth and the way they affect one another

2 the natural features of an area

geo•log•ic \\ˌjē-ə-ˈlä-jik\\ *or* **geo•log•i•cal** \\-ji-kəl\\ *adj*
of or relating to geology ⟨*geologic* formations⟩

ge•ol•o•gist \\jē-ˈä-lə-jəst\\ *n*
a person specializing in geology

ge•ol•o•gy \\jē-ˈä-lə-jē\\ *n*
1 a science that deals with the history of the earth and its life especially as recorded in rocks
2 the geologic features (as mountains or plains) of an area

geo•mag•net•ic \\ˌjē-ō-mag-ˈne-tik\\ *adj*
of or relating to the magnetism of the earth ⟨the *geomagnetic* field⟩

geo•met•ric \\ˌjē-ə-ˈme-trik\\ *adj*
1 of or relating to geometry
2 consisting of points, lines, and angles

ge•om•e•try \\jē-ˈä-mə-trē\\ *n*
a branch of mathematics that deals with points, lines, angles, surfaces, and solids

geo•sci•ence \\ˌjē-ō-ˈsī-əns\\ *n*
the sciences (as geology) dealing with the earth

geranium

ge•ra•ni•um \\jə-ˈrā-nē-əm\\ *n*
▲ a plant often grown for its bright flowers

► **Word History** Many of the plants of the geranium family have long, thin, pointed fruits that look a bit like the bill of a bird. The ancient Greeks thought that the fruit of the wild geranium looked like the bill of a crane, and so gave the plant the name *geranion*, literally, "little crane." The English word *geranium* came from this Greek name.

ger•bil \\ˈjər-bəl\\ *n*
► a small Old World leaping desert animal that is a rodent and is often kept as a pet

germ \\ˈjərm\\ *n*
1 a source from which something develops ⟨the *germ* of an idea⟩
2 a microorganism (as a bacterium) that causes disease
3 a bit of living matter (as a cell) capable of forming a new individual or one of its parts

[1]Ger•man \\ˈjər-mən\\ *n*
1 a person born or living in Germany
2 the language spoken mainly in Germany, Austria, and parts of Switzerland

[2]German *adj*
of or relating to Germany, the Germans, or the German language

ger•ma•ni•um \\jər-ˈmā-nē-əm\\ *n*
a white hard brittle element used as a semiconductor

German shepherd *n*
► a large dog of German origin that is often used in police work and as a guide dog for the blind

germ cell *n*
a cell (as an egg or sperm cell) that contributes to the formation of a new individual

ger•mi•nate \\ˈjər-mə-ˌnāt\\ *vb* **ger•mi•nat•ed**; **ger•mi•nat•ing**
to begin to grow : SPROUT ⟨She patiently waited for the seeds to *germinate*.⟩

ger•mi•na•tion \\ˌjər-mə-ˈnā-shən\\ *n*
a beginning of development (as of a seed)

ges•tic•u•late \\je-ˈsti-kyə-ˌlāt\\ *vb* **ges•tic•u•lat•ed**; **ges•tic•u•lat•ing**
to make gestures especially when speaking

[1]ges•ture \\ˈjes-chər\\ *n*
1 a movement of the body (as the hands and arms) that expresses an idea or a feeling
2 something said or done that shows a particular feeling ⟨He invited her in a *gesture* of friendship.⟩

gerbil

[2]gesture *vb* **ges•tured**; **ges•tur•ing**
to make or direct with a gesture ⟨She *gestured* for us to join her.⟩

get \\ˈget\\ *vb* **got** \\ˈgät\\; **got** *or* **got•ten** \\ˈgä-t^{ə}n\\; **get•ting** \\ˈge-tiŋ\\
1 to gain possession of (as by receiving, earning, buying, or winning) ⟨Everyone *gets* a present.⟩ ⟨I *got* new clothes.⟩
2 to obtain by request or as a favor ⟨Did you *get* permission?⟩
3 to come to have ⟨I *got* a good night's sleep.⟩

German shepherd

4 [1]CATCH 5 ⟨He *got* pneumonia.⟩
5 ARRIVE 1 ⟨We *got* home early.⟩
6 GO 1, MOVE ⟨*Get* out of my way!⟩
7 BECOME 1 ⟨Don't *get* angry.⟩ ⟨It's *getting* warmer.⟩
8 to cause to be ⟨I *got* my feet wet.⟩
9 PREPARE 2 ⟨You relax while I *get* dinner.⟩
10 IRRITATE 1 ⟨Don't let his teasing *get* to you.⟩
11 [1]HIT 1 ⟨The snowball *got* him on the head.⟩
12 to find out by calculation ⟨Did you *get* the answer yet?⟩
13 to hear correctly ⟨Sorry, I didn't *get* your name.⟩
14 UNDERSTAND 1 ⟨Oh, now I *get* it.⟩
15 PERSUADE ⟨I *got* him to move over.⟩

get ahead to achieve success (as in business)

get along
1 to approach old age ⟨She's *getting along* in years.⟩
2 to stay friendly ⟨The boys *got along* well.⟩
3 to manage with little ⟨They *get along* on a small income.⟩

A B C D E F G H I J K L M N O P Q R S T U V W X Y Z

get around
1 to become known by many people ⟨The rumor quickly *got around.*⟩
2 to avoid having to deal with ⟨He found a way to *get around* the rules.⟩
3 to do or give attention to eventually ⟨I'll *get around* to it.⟩
get at
1 to reach with or as if with the hand ⟨I can't *get at* the switch.⟩
2 to deal with ⟨There's lots to do so let's *get at* it.⟩
3 to say or suggest in an indirect way ⟨Just what are you *getting at?*⟩
get away to avoid being caught ⟨The robber *got away.*⟩
get away with to not be punished for ⟨You won't *get away with* lying.⟩
get back at to get revenge on ⟨I'll *get back at* him for what he did.⟩
get by
1 to manage with little ⟨We can *get by* with what we have.⟩
2 to do well enough to avoid failure ⟨I'm just *getting by* in this class.⟩
get even to get revenge ⟨Are you going to forgive her, or *get even?*⟩
get into to become deeply interested in ⟨She's really *gotten into* music.⟩

geyser: a geyser in Yellowstone National Park, Wyoming

get it to receive punishment ⟨You're going to *get it* when Mom gets home.⟩
get off
1 to start out on a journey ⟨They *got off* on their trip.⟩
2 to escape punishment or harm ⟨He *got off* with just a warning.⟩
get on
1 to approach old age ⟨My grandparents are *getting on.*⟩
2 to start or continue doing ⟨Come on, let's *get on* with it.⟩
3 to stay friendly ⟨The neighbors all *got on* fine.⟩
get out
1 [1]ESCAPE 1 ⟨Everyone *got out* alive.⟩
2 to become known ⟨The secret *got out.*⟩
get over
1 to stop feeling unhappy about
2 to recover from ⟨I finally *got over* my cold.⟩
get up
1 to arise from bed
2 [1]STAND 1
3 to find the ability ⟨I couldn't *get up* the nerve to speak.⟩
get wind of to become aware of : hear about

get•away \ˈge-tə-ˌwā\ *n*
1 [2]ESCAPE 1 ⟨We made our *getaway* under cover of darkness.⟩
2 a place suitable for vacation ⟨a tropical *getaway*⟩
3 a usually short vacation

get–to•geth•er \ˈget-tə-ˌge-t͟hər\ *n*
an informal social gathering

get•up \ˈget-ˌəp\ *n*
[1]OUTFIT 1, COSTUME

gey•ser \ˈgī-zər\ *n*
◀ a spring that now and then shoots up hot water and steam

ghast•ly \ˈgast-lē\ *adj* **ghast•li•er; ghast•li•est**
1 very shocking or horrible ⟨a *ghastly* crime⟩ ⟨a *ghastly* mistake⟩
2 like a ghost : PALE ⟨a *ghastly* face⟩

ghet•to \ˈge-tō\ *n, pl* **ghettos** *or* **ghettoes**
a part of a city in which members of a particular group live in poor conditions

ghost \ˈgōst\ *n*
the spirit of a dead person thought of as living in an unseen world or as appearing to living people

giant sequoia: a person climbing a giant sequoia tree

ghost•ly \ˈgōst-lē\ *adj* **ghost•li•er; ghost•li•est**
of, relating to, or like a ghost

ghost town *n*
a town where all the people have left

ghoul \ˈgül\ *n*
1 an evil being of legend that robs graves and feeds on dead bodies
2 someone whose activities suggest those of a ghoul : an evil or frightening person

GI \ˌjē-ˈī\ *n*
a member of the United States armed forces

[1]**gi•ant** \ˈjī-ənt\ *n*
1 an imaginary person of great size and strength
2 a person or thing that is very large, successful, or powerful

[2]**giant** *adj*
much larger than ordinary : HUGE

giant panda *n*
PANDA 2

giant sequoia *n*
▲ an evergreen tree of California that has needles for leaves and can sometimes grow

to over 270 feet (about 82 meters) in height

gib·ber·ish \'ji-bə-rish\ *n*
confused meaningless talk

gib·bon \'gi-bən\ *n*
▼ a small tailless ape of southeastern Asia that has long arms and legs and lives mostly in trees

[1]**gibe** *or* **jibe** \'jīb\ *vb*
gibed; gib·ing
to speak or tease with words that are insulting or scornful

[2]**gibe** *or* **jibe** *n*
an insulting or scornful remark : JEER

[1]**gilt** \'gilt\ *n*
gold or something resembling gold applied to a surface ⟨The vase was covered with *gilt*.⟩

[2]**gilt** *n*
a young female pig

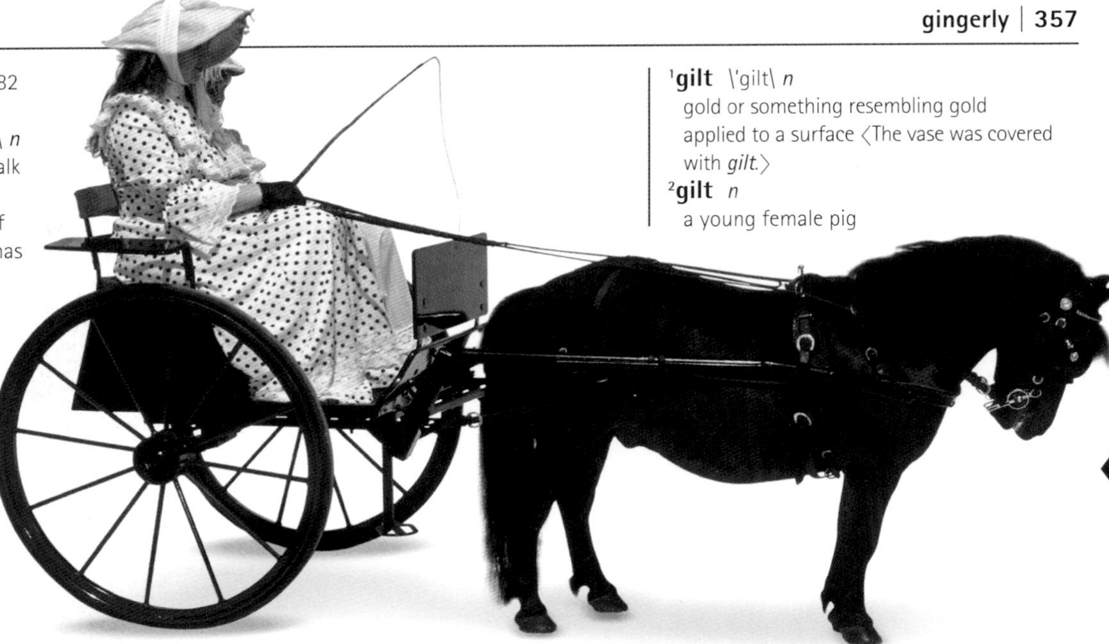

gig 2: a girl driving a gig

gibbon

gib·lets \'ji-bləts\ *n pl*
the edible inner organs (as the heart and liver) of a bird (as a turkey)

gid·dy \'gi-dē\ *adj* **gid·di·er; gid·di·est**
1 having a feeling of whirling or spinning about : DIZZY
2 causing dizziness ⟨a *giddy* height⟩
3 playful and silly ⟨*giddy* children⟩
4 feeling and showing great happiness and joy
gid·di·ness *n*

gift \'gift\ *n*
1 a special ability : TALENT ⟨a *gift* for music⟩
2 something given : [1]PRESENT

gift card *n*
a card that is worth a certain amount of money and given to someone to use at a store or restaurant

gift certificate *n*
a certificate that is worth a certain amount of money and given to someone to use at a store or restaurant

gift·ed \'gif-təd\ *adj*
having great natural ability ⟨a *gifted* athlete⟩

gig \'gig\ *n*
1 a long light boat for a ship's captain
2 ▲ a light carriage having two wheels and pulled by a horse

giga·byte \'ji-gə-ˌbīt, 'gi-\ *n*
a unit of computer information storage capacity equal to 1,073,741,824 bytes

gi·gan·tic \jī-'gan-tik\ *adj*
extremely large or great (as in size, weight, or strength)

[1]**gig·gle** \'gi-gəl\ *vb* **gig·gled; gig·gling**
to laugh with repeated short high sounds that sound childlike

[2]**giggle** *n*
a light silly laugh

Gi·la monster \'hē-lə-\ *n*
► a large black and orange poisonous lizard of the southwestern United States

gild \'gild\ *vb* **gild·ed** *or* **gilt** \'gilt\; **gild·ing**
to cover with a thin coating of gold ⟨*gilded* doors⟩

[1]**gill** \'jil\ *n*
a unit of liquid capacity equal to a quarter of a pint (about 120 milliliters)

[2]**gill** \'gil\ *n*
an organ (as of a fish) for taking oxygen from water

gim·let \'gim-lət\ *n*
a small pointed tool for making holes

gim·mick \'gi-mik\ *n*
a method or trick that is designed to get people's attention or to sell something

[1]**gin** \'jin\ *n*
COTTON GIN

[2]**gin** *vb* **ginned; gin·ning**
to separate seeds from cotton in a cotton gin

[3]**gin** *n*
a strong alcoholic liquor flavored with juniper berries

gin·ger \'jin-jər\ *n*
a hot spice obtained from the root of a tropical plant and used especially to season foods

Gila monster

ginger ale *n*
a soft drink flavored with ginger

gin·ger·bread \'jin-jər-ˌbred\ *n*
a dark cake flavored with ginger and molasses

gin·ger·ly \'jin-jər-lē\ *adv*
with great caution or care ⟨She *gingerly* picked up the broken glass.⟩

A B C D E F G H I J K L M N O P Q R S T U V W X Y Z

giraffe

gin•ger•snap \'jin-jər-,snap\ *n*
a thin hard cookie flavored with ginger

ging•ham \'giŋ-əm\ *n*
a cotton cloth that is often plaid or checked

gi•nor•mous \'jī-'nȯr-məs\ *adj*
extremely large

gi•raffe \jə-'raf\ *n*
▲ a spotted mammal of Africa with a very long neck that feeds mostly on the leaves of trees and is the tallest living land animal

gird \'gərd\ *vb* **gird•ed** *or* **girt** \'gərt\; **gird•ing**
1 to encircle or fasten with or as if with a belt or cord
2 to prepare for conflict or for some difficult task

gird•er \'gər-dər\ *n*
a horizontal main supporting beam ⟨a *girder* of a bridge⟩

[1]gir•dle \'gər-dᵊl\ *n*
1 something (as a belt or sash) that encircles or binds
2 a tight undergarment worn below the waist by women

[2]girdle *vb* **gir•dled**; **gir•dling**
1 to bind with or as if with a girdle, belt, or sash : ENCIRCLE
2 to strip a ring of bark from a tree trunk

girl \'gərl\ *n*
1 a female child or young woman
2 a female servant
3 GIRLFRIEND 2

girl•friend \'gərl-,frend\ *n*
1 a female friend
2 a regular female companion of a boy or man

girl•hood \'gərl-,hu̇d\ *n*
the state or time of being a girl

girl•ish \'gər-lish\ *adj*
having the characteristics of a girl

Girl Scout *n*
a member of the Girl Scouts of the United States of America

girth \'gərth\ *n*
1 the measure or distance around something ⟨the *girth* of a tree⟩
2 a band put around the body of an animal to hold something (as a saddle) on its back

gist \'jist\ *n*
the main point of a matter ⟨He spoke so fast, I only got the *gist* of the story.⟩

[1]give \'giv\ *vb* **gave** \'gāv\; **giv•en** \'giv-ən\; **giv•ing**
1 to hand over to be kept : PRESENT ⟨He *gave* her a present.⟩
2 to cause to have ⟨Don't *give* me trouble.⟩
3 to let someone or something have ⟨*give* permission⟩
4 to offer for consideration or acceptance ⟨Can you *give* an example?⟩
5 [2]UTTER ⟨*give* a yell⟩ ⟨*give* a speech⟩
6 FURNISH 2, PROVIDE ⟨*give* support⟩ ⟨The candle *gives* light.⟩ ⟨I'm *giving* a party.⟩
7 [1]PAY 1 ⟨She *gave* me 20 dollars for my old skates.⟩
8 to deliver by some bodily action ⟨I *gave* her a hug.⟩
9 to yield as a product : PRODUCE ⟨Two plus two *gives* four.⟩
10 to yield slightly ⟨The mattress *gave* under our weight.⟩

give in to stop trying to fight ⟨I begged Mom for permission till she *gave in*.⟩

give out
1 TELL 6 ⟨Don't *give out* your phone number.⟩
2 to stop working ⟨The car finally *gave out*.⟩

give up
1 to let go of ⟨He *gave up* his seat to an elderly woman.⟩
2 QUIT ⟨Oh, I *give up* trying to reason with you.⟩

give way
1 to break down : COLLAPSE ⟨The bridge *gave way*.⟩
2 to be unable to resist ⟨No one *gave way* to fear.⟩

▶ **Synonyms** GIVE, PRESENT, and DONATE mean to hand over to someone without looking for a return. GIVE can be used of anything that is delivered in any way. ⟨Please *give* me your coat.⟩ ⟨I *gave* a friend a gift.⟩ PRESENT is used when something is given with some ceremony. ⟨They *presented* a trophy to the winner.⟩ DONATE is used for giving to a charity. ⟨Some kind person *donated* the toys.⟩

glacier: a glacier in Banff National Park, Canada

[2]**give** *n*
the ability to be bent or stretched ⟨The rope was tight, but still had some *give*.⟩

giv•en \'gi-vən\ *adj*
1 being likely to have or do something ⟨They are *given* to quarreling.⟩
2 decided on beforehand ⟨We meet at a *given* time.⟩

given name *n*
a first name

giz•zard \'gi-zərd\ *n*
a large muscular part of the digestive tract (as of a bird) in which food is churned and ground into small bits

gla•cial \'glā-shəl\ *adj*
1 of or relating to glaciers ⟨*glacial* ice⟩
2 very cold
3 very slow ⟨a *glacial* pace⟩

gla•cier \'glā-shər\ *n*
▼ a large body of ice moving slowly down a slope or over a wide area of land

glad \'glad\ *adj* **glad•der**; **glad•dest**
1 being happy and joyful ⟨She was *glad* to be home.⟩
2 bringing or causing joy ⟨*glad* news⟩
3 very willing ⟨I'd be *glad* to help.⟩
glad•ly *adv*
glad•ness *n*

glad•den \'gla-dᵊn\ *vb* **glad•dened**; **glad•den•ing**
to make glad

glade \'glād\ *n*
a grassy open space in a forest

gladiator: the equipment and costume of a gladiator

glad•i•a•tor \'gla-dē-,ā-tər\ *n*
▲ a man in ancient Rome who took part in fights as public entertainment

glad•i•o•lus \,gla-dē-'ō-ləs\ *n*, *pl* **glad•i•o•li** \-lē, -,lī\ *or* **gladiolus** *also* **glad•i•o•lus•es**
a plant with long stiff pointed leaves and stalks of brightly colored flowers

glam•or•ous \'gla-mə-rəs\ *adj*
very exciting and attractive ⟨*glamorous* travel⟩ ⟨a *glamorous* actress⟩

glam•our \'gla-mər\ *n*
romantic, exciting, and often misleading attractiveness

► **Word History** In the Middle Ages words like Latin *grammatica* and Middle English *gramer*, "grammar," meant not only the study of language and literature, but all sorts of learning. Since almost all learning was expressed in Latin, which most people did not understand, it was commonly believed that subjects such as magic and astrology were also part of "grammar." People became suspicious of students of "grammar," who were thought to practice the dark arts. In Scotland in the 1700s the word *glamer* or *glamour*, an altered form of *grammar*, meant "a magic spell." As *glamour* passed into more general English, it lost this sense and just came to mean "a mysterious attractiveness."

[1]**glance** \'glans\ *vb* **glanced**; **glanc•ing**
1 to strike at an angle and fly off to one side ⟨The ball *glanced* off a tree.⟩
2 to give a quick look ⟨She *glanced* at her watch.⟩

[2]**glance** *n*
a quick look

gland \'gland\ *n*
a cluster of cells or an organ in the body that produces a substance (as saliva, sweat, wor bile) to be used by the body or given off from it

glan•du•lar \'glan-jə-lər\ *adj*
of or relating to glands ⟨*glandular* secretions⟩

[1]**glare** \'gler\ *vb* **glared**; **glar•ing**
1 to shine with a harsh bright light
2 to look fiercely or angrily
synonyms see GAZE

[2]**glare** *n*
1 a harsh bright light
2 a fierce or angry look

glar•ing \'gler-iŋ\ *adj*
1 so bright as to be harsh ⟨*glaring* sunlight⟩
2 very noticeable ⟨a *glaring* error⟩

glass \'glas\ *n*
1 a hard brittle usually transparent substance commonly made from sand heated with chemicals
2 a drinking container made of glass
3 **glasses** *pl* a pair of glass or plastic lenses held in a frame and used to help a person see clearly or to protect the eyes
4 the contents of a glass ⟨a *glass* of milk⟩

glass•blow•ing \'glas-,blō-iŋ\ *n*
▼ the art of shaping a mass of melted glass by blowing air into it through a tube

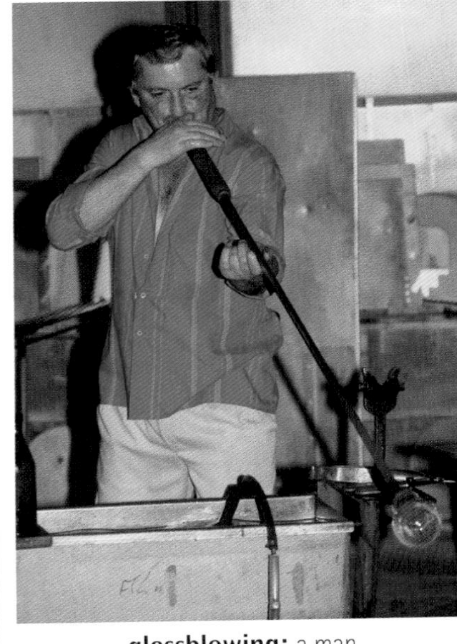

glassblowing: a man practicing the art of glassblowing

glass•ful \ˈglas-ˌfu̇l\ *n*
the amount a glass will hold

glass•ware \ˈglas-ˌwer\ *n*
articles made of glass

glassy \ˈgla-sē\ *adj* **glass•i•er; glass•i•est**
1 smooth and shiny like glass
2 not shiny or bright ⟨*glassy* eyes⟩

[1]glaze \ˈglāz\ *vb* **glazed; glaz•ing**
1 to cover with a smooth or glossy coating ⟨*glaze* pottery⟩
2 to become dull ⟨His eyes *glazed* over with boredom.⟩

[2]glaze *n*
a glassy surface or coating

[1]gleam \ˈglēm\ *n*
1 a faint, soft, or reflected light ⟨the first *gleam* of dawn⟩
2 a bright or shining look ⟨She had a *gleam* in her eyes.⟩
3 a short or slight appearance ⟨a *gleam* of hope⟩

[2]gleam *vb* **gleamed; gleam•ing**
1 to shine with a soft light
2 to give out gleams of light

> ▶ **Synonyms** GLEAM, SPARKLE, and GLITTER mean to send forth light. GLEAM is used when light shines through something else or is reflected or shines against a dark background. ⟨The lighthouse *gleamed* through the fog.⟩ SPARKLE is used for something that has several changing points of light. ⟨Water *sparkled* in the sunlight.⟩ GLITTER is used for a brilliant sparkling of light. ⟨The jewels *glittered* brightly.⟩

glean \ˈglēn\ *vb* **gleaned; glean•ing**
1 to gather from a field what is left by the harvesters
2 to gather (as information) little by little with patient effort

glee \ˈglē\ *n*
great joy : DELIGHT
glee•ful *adj*
glee•ful•ly *adv*

glen \ˈglen\ *n*
a narrow hidden valley

glib \ˈglib\ *adj* **glib•ber; glib•best**
speaking or spoken carelessly and often insincerely ⟨a *glib* answer⟩
glib•ly *adv*

[1]glide \ˈglīd\ *vb* **glid•ed; glid•ing**
to move with a smooth continuous motion

[2]glide *n*
the act or action of moving with a smooth continuous motion

cockpit
rudder
vertical stabilizer

glider

glid•er \ˈglī-dər\ *n*
▲ an aircraft without an engine that glides on air currents

[1]glim•mer \ˈgli-mər\ *vb* **glim•mered; glim•mer•ing**
to shine faintly and unsteadily

[2]glimmer *n*
1 a faint unsteady light
2 a faint suggestion ⟨a *glimmer* of trouble⟩
3 a small amount ⟨a *glimmer* of hope⟩

[1]glimpse \ˈglimps\ *vb* **glimpsed; glimps•ing**
to catch a quick view of

[2]glimpse *n*
a short hurried look

[1]glint \ˈglint\ *vb* **glint•ed; glint•ing**
to shine with tiny bright flashes

[2]glint *n*
a brief flash

glis•ten \ˈgli-sᵊn\ *vb* **glis•tened; glis•ten•ing**
to shine with a soft reflected light

glitch \ˈglich\ *n*
a usually minor problem

[1]glit•ter \ˈgli-tər\ *vb* **glit•tered; glit•ter•ing**
to sparkle brightly
synonyms see GLEAM

[2]glitter *n*
1 sparkling brightness
2 ▼ small glittering objects used for decoration

[2]glitter 2: a star with glitter

glit•tery \ˈgli-tə-rē\ *adj*

gloat \ˈglōt\ *vb* **gloat•ed; gloat•ing**
to talk or think about something with mean or selfish satisfaction

glob \ˈgläb\ *n*
a roundish drop of something soft or wet : BLOB ⟨a *glob* of whipped cream⟩

glob•al \ˈglō-bəl\ *adj*
1 in or having to do with the whole earth
2 shaped like a globe

global warming *n*
a warming of the earth's atmosphere and oceans that is thought to be a result of air pollution

globe 3

globe \ˈglōb\ *n*
1 a round object : BALL, SPHERE
2 EARTH 1
3 ▲ a round model of the earth used like a map

glob•ule \ˈglä-byül\ *n*
a small round mass

glock•en•spiel \ˈglä-kən-ˌspēl\ *n*
▶ a portable musical instrument with a series of metal bars played with hammers

gloom \ˈglüm\ *n*
1 partial or complete darkness
2 a sad mood

gloomy \ˈglü-mē\ *adj* **gloom•i•er; gloom•i•est**
1 partly or completely dark
2 SAD 1, BLUE
3 causing feelings of sadness ⟨a *gloomy* story⟩
4 not hopeful or promising
gloom•i•ly \-mə-lē\ *adv*

glo•ri•fy \'glȯr-ə-ˌfī\ *vb* **glo•ri•fied**; **glo•ri•fy•ing**
1 to honor or praise as divine : WORSHIP

glove: a soccer goalkeeper's gloves

2 to give honor and praise to ⟨*glorify* a hero⟩
3 to show in a way that looks good ⟨*glorify* war⟩

glo•ri•ous \'glȯr-ē-əs\ *adj*
1 having or deserving praise or admiration ⟨*glorious* deeds⟩
2 having great beauty or splendor ⟨*glorious* music⟩
3 DELIGHTFUL ⟨*glorious* weather⟩
synonyms see SPLENDID
glo•ri•ous•ly *adv*

¹glo•ry \'glȯr-ē\ *n, pl* **glories**
1 praise, honor, and admiration given to a person by others
2 something that brings honor, praise, or fame ⟨The pyramids are some of the *glories* of ancient Egypt.⟩
3 BRILLIANCE, SPLENDOR ⟨the *glory* of the sunrise⟩

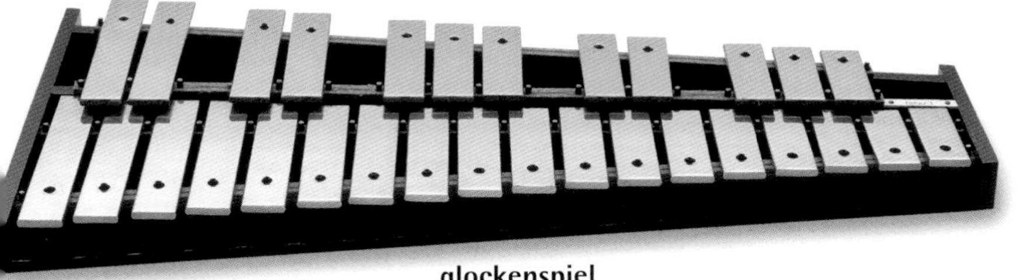

glockenspiel

²glory *vb* **glo•ried**; **glo•ry•ing**
to rejoice proudly : be proud or boastful ⟨He *glories* in the attention he gets.⟩

¹gloss \'gläs, 'glȯs\ *n*
1 brightness from a smooth surface : SHEEN
2 a falsely attractive surface appearance

²gloss *vb* **glossed**; **glos•sing**
1 to shine the surface of
2 to explain as if unimportant ⟨He *glossed* over a mistake.⟩

glos•sa•ry \'glä-sə-rē, 'glȯ-\ *n, pl* **glos•sa•ries**
a list that provides definitions for the difficult or unusual words used in a book

glossy \'glä-sē, 'glȯ-\ *adj* **gloss•i•er**; **gloss•i•est**
smooth and shining on the surface ⟨Crows are *glossy* black birds.⟩

glove \'gləv\ *n*
◀ a covering for the hand having a separate section for each finger
gloved \'gləvd\ *adj*

¹glow \'glō\ *vb* **glowed**; **glow•ing**
1 to shine with or as if with great heat ⟨Fire *glowed* in the fireplace.⟩
2 to shine with steady light ⟨Candles *glowed* in the dark.⟩
3 to have a warm reddish color (as from exercise)
4 to look happy, excited, or healthy ⟨His eyes *glowed* with pride.⟩

²glow *n*
1 light such as comes from something that is very hot but not flaming
2 brightness or warmth of color ⟨There was a rosy *glow* in the sky.⟩
3 a feeling of physical warmth (as from exercise)
4 a warm and pleasant feeling ⟨She felt a *glow* of happiness.⟩

glow•er \'glau̇-ər\ *vb* **glow•ered**; **glow•er•ing**
to stare angrily : SCOWL

glow•worm \'glō-ˌwərm\ *n*
an insect or insect larva that gives off light

glu•cose \'glü-ˌkōs\ *n*
a sugar in plant saps and fruits that is the usual form in which carbohydrate is taken in by the animal body and used as a source of energy

¹glue \'glü\ *n*
a substance used to stick things tightly together
glu•ey \'glü-ē\ *adj*

²glue *vb* **glued**; **glu•ing**
to stick with or as if with glue

glum \'gləm\ *adj* **glum•mer**; **glum•mest**
gloomy and sad ⟨a *glum* expression⟩
glum•ly *adv*

¹glut \'glət\ *vb* **glut•ted**; **glut•ting**
1 to make very full
2 to flood with goods so that supply is greater than demand ⟨The market is *glutted* with new cars.⟩

²glut *n*
too much of something

glu•ti•nous \'glü-tə-nəs\ *adj*
like glue : STICKY ⟨*glutinous* oatmeal⟩

glut•ton \'glə-tᵊn\ *n*
a person or animal that overeats
glut•ton•ous \'glə-tə-nəs\ *adj*

glut•tony \'glə-tə-nē\ *n, pl* **glut•ton•ies**
the act or habit of eating or drinking too much

gly•co•gen \'glī-kə-jən\ *n*
a white tasteless starchy substance that is the main form in which glucose is stored in the body

gm *abbr* gram

gnarled \'närld\ *adj*
being twisted, rugged, or full of knots ⟨a *gnarled* old oak tree⟩

gnarly \'när-lē\ *adj* **gnarl•i•er**; **gnarl•i•est**
GNARLED

gnash \'nash\ *vb* **gnashed**; **gnash•ing**
to strike or grind (the teeth) together ⟨He *gnashed* his teeth in anger.⟩

gnat \'nat\ *n*
a very small usually biting fly

gnaw \'nȯ\ *vb* **gnawed**; **gnaw•ing**
to bite so as to wear away : bite or chew upon ⟨The dog *gnawed* a bone.⟩

gnome \'nōm\ *n*
an imaginary dwarf believed to live inside the earth and guard treasure

gnu \'nü, 'nyü\ *n, pl* **gnu** *or* **gnus**
WILDEBEEST

go \'gō\ *vb* **went** \'went\; **gone** \'gȯn\; **go•ing** \'gō-iŋ\; **goes**
1 to move or travel from one place to or toward another ⟨We *went* home.⟩
2 to move away : LEAVE ⟨The crowd has *gone*.⟩
3 to lead in a certain direction ⟨This road *goes* to the lake.⟩
4 to be sent ⟨The invitation *went* by e-mail.⟩
5 to become lost, used, or spent ⟨Our money was all *gone*.⟩
6 to pass by : ELAPSE ⟨Three hours had *gone* by.⟩
7 to continue its course or action : RUN ⟨Some machines *go* by electricity.⟩
8 to be able to fit in or through a space ⟨No more can *go* in this suitcase.⟩
9 to make its own special sound ⟨A kitten *goes* like this.⟩
10 to be suitable : MATCH ⟨The scarf *goes* with the coat.⟩
11 to reach some state ⟨Try to *go* to sleep.⟩ ⟨The tire *went* flat.⟩

go off
1 EXPLODE 1 〈A bomb *went off.*〉
2 to begin to make a usual noise 〈I woke up when the alarm *went off.*〉
3 to proceed as expected 〈The ceremony *went off* despite bad weather.〉
go on
1 to continue as time passes 〈You can't *go on* being late like this!〉
2 to continue talking 〈I'm sorry for the interruption. Please *go on.*〉
go out
1 to leave home
2 to stop burning 〈Make sure the candle doesn't *go out.*〉
go through [2]EXPERIENCE 〈She has *gone through* hard times.〉

[1]goad \'gōd\ *n*
1 a pointed rod used to keep an animal moving
2 something that urges or forces someone to act

[2]goad *vb* **goad•ed**; **goad•ing**
to urge or force a person or an animal to act

goal \'gōl\ *n*
1 PURPOSE 〈What is your *goal* in life?〉
2 an area or object into which a ball or puck must be driven in various games in order to score
3 ▼ a scoring of one or more points by driving a ball or puck into a goal
4 the point at which a race or journey is to end
5 an area to be reached safely in certain games

goal•ie \'gō-lē\ *n*
GOALKEEPER

goal•keep•er \'gōl-,kē-pər\ *n*
a player who defends a goal

goal line *n*
a line that must be crossed to score a goal

goal•post \'gōl-,pōst\ *n*
one of two upright posts often with a crossbar that serve as the goal in various games

goal•tend•er \'gōl-,ten-dər\ *n*
GOALKEEPER

goat \'gōt\ *n*
▶ an animal that has hollow horns that curve backward, is related to the sheep, and is often raised for its milk, wool, and meat
goat•like \-,līk\ *adj*

goa•tee \gō-'tē\ *n*
a small beard trimmed to a point

goat•herd \'gōt-,hərd\ *n*
a person who tends goats

goat•skin \'gōt-,skin\ *n*
the skin of a goat or leather made from it

gob \'gäb\ *n*
[1]LUMP 1 〈a *gob* of mud〉

[1]gob•ble \'gä-bəl\ *vb* **gob•bled**; **gob•bling**
to eat fast or greedily 〈We *gobbled* up our lunch.〉

[2]gobble *vb* **gob•bled**; **gob•bling**
to make the call of a turkey or a similar sound

[3]gobble *n*
the loud harsh call of a turkey

go–be•tween \'gō-bə-,twēn\ *n*
a person who acts as a messenger or peacemaker

gob•let \'gä-blət\ *n*
a drinking glass with a foot and stem

gob•lin \'gä-blən\ *n*
an ugly and often evil imaginary creature

god \'gäd\ *n*
1 *cap* the Being worshipped as the creator and ruler of the universe
2 a being believed to have more than human powers 〈Ancient peoples worshipped many *gods.*〉
3 an object worshipped as divine

god•child \'gäd-,chīld\ *n*, *pl* **god•chil•dren** \-,chil-drən\
a person for whom another person acts as a sponsor at baptism

goat: a domestic goat

god•daugh•ter \'gäd-,dȯ-tər\ *n*
a girl or woman for whom another person acts as a sponsor at baptism

god•dess \'gä-dəs\ *n*
a female god

god•fa•ther \'gäd-,fä-thər\ *n*
a boy or man who is a sponsor for someone at baptism

god•like \'gäd-,līk\ *adj*
like or suitable for God or a god

god•ly \'gäd-lē\ *adj* **god•li•er**; **god•li•est**
DEVOUT 1, PIOUS

god•moth•er \'gäd-,mə-thər\ *n*
a girl or woman who is a sponsor for someone at baptism

god•par•ent \'gäd-,per-ənt\ *n*
a sponsor at baptism

goal 3: a goal in a soccer game

god•send \'gäd-ˌsend\ *n*
some badly needed thing that comes unexpectedly 〈The new job was a *godsend.*〉

god•son \'gäd-ˌsən\ *n*
a boy or man for whom another person acts as a sponsor at baptism

God•speed \ˌgäd-'spēd\ *n*
a wish for success given to a person who is going away

goes *present third person sing of* GO

go–get•ter \'gō-ˌge-tər\ *n*
a person determined to succeed

gog•gle \'gä-gəl\ *vb* **gog•gled**; **gog•gling**
to stare with bulging or rolling eyes

gog•gles \'gä-gəlz\ *n pl*
protective glasses set in a flexible frame (as of plastic) that fits snugly against the face

go•ings–on \ˌgō-iŋz-'ón, -'än\ *n pl*
things that happen 〈There are strange *goings-on* in that old house.〉

goi•ter \'gȯi-tər\ *n*
a swelling on the front of the neck caused by enlargement of the thyroid gland

gold \'gōld\ *n*
1 a soft yellow metallic chemical element used especially in coins and jewelry
2 gold coins
3 a medal awarded as the first prize in a competition
4 a deep yellow

gold•en \'gōl-dən\ *adj*
1 like, made of, or containing gold
2 having the deep yellow color of gold 〈*golden* flowers〉
3 very good or desirable 〈a *golden* opportunity〉
4 very prosperous and happy 〈a *golden* age〉

gold•en•rod \'gōl-dən-ˌräd\ *n*
a plant with tall stiff stems topped with clusters of tiny yellow flowers

gold•finch \'gōld-ˌfinch\ *n*
1 a small European bird with a yellow patch on each wing
2 a small mostly yellow American bird

gold•fish \'gōld-ˌfish\ *n*
a small usually golden yellow or orange fish often kept in aquariums or ponds

gold•smith \'gōld-ˌsmith\ *n*
a person who makes or sells items of gold

golf \'gälf, 'gȯlf\ *n*
▶ a game played by hitting a small ball with special clubs into each of nine or 18 holes in as few strokes as possible

golf•er \'gäl-fər, 'gȯl-\ *n*
a person who plays golf

▶ **golf**

Starting from a tee, golfers aim to hit a ball into a series of 9 or 18 holes positioned some distance apart. The object is to hit the ball along a strip of grass, avoiding areas of rough and bunkers, to reach a putting green and sink the ball into a hole, all using as few strokes as possible. Golfers use a range of clubs for different purposes.

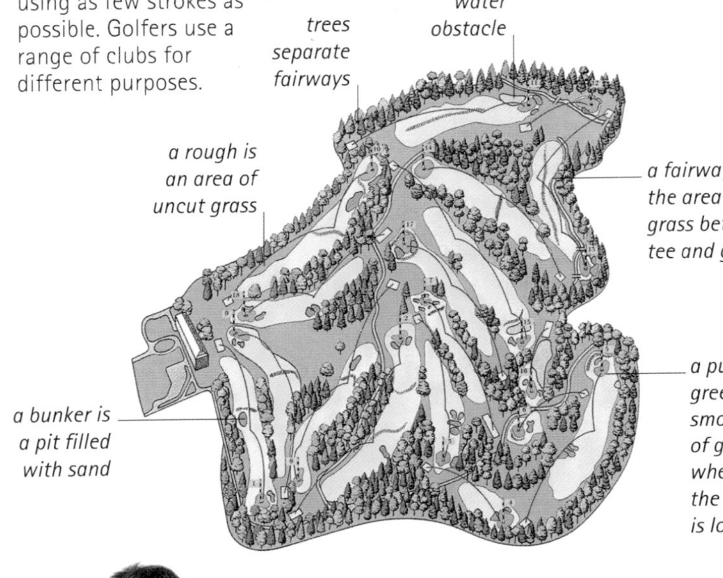

diagram of a golf course

golf ball

tees

golf shoe

golfer preparing to swing at the ball

golf bag

gondola 1

oar

gon•do•la \'gän-də-lə, *2 and 3 also* gän-'dō-lə\ *n*
1 ▲ a long narrow boat used in the canals of Venice, Italy
2 a railroad freight car with no top
3 an enclosure that hangs from a balloon or cable and carries passengers or instruments

[1]gone *past participle of* GO

[2]gone \'gȯn\ *adj*
1 no longer present ⟨By the time I arrived, they were *gone.*⟩
2 no longer existing ⟨Those days are *gone.*⟩
3 [1]DEAD 1

gon•er \'gȯ-nər\ *n*
someone or something with no chance of surviving or succeeding

gong \'gäŋ, 'gȯŋ\ *n*
▼ a metallic disk that produces a harsh ringing tone when struck

gong: a girl beating a gong

[1]good \'gu̇d\ *adj* **bet•ter** \'be-tər\; **best** \'best\
1 better than average ⟨*good* work⟩
2 SKILLFUL ⟨a *good* dancer⟩
3 behaving well ⟨a *good* child⟩
4 PLEASANT 1, ENJOYABLE ⟨We had a *good* time.⟩
5 HEALTHFUL ⟨Eat a *good* breakfast.⟩
6 of a favorable character or tendency ⟨*good* news⟩
7 suitable for a use : SATISFACTORY ⟨You need *good* light for reading.⟩
8 DESIRABLE 1, ATTRACTIVE ⟨a *good* job⟩
9 showing good sense or judgment ⟨*good* advice⟩
10 closely following a standard of what is correct or proper ⟨*good* manners⟩
11 RELIABLE ⟨a *good* neighbor⟩
12 HELPFUL, KIND ⟨How *good* of you to wait!⟩
13 being honest and upright ⟨She comes from a *good* family.⟩
14 being at least the amount mentioned ⟨We waited a *good* hour.⟩
15 CONSIDERABLE ⟨I need a *good* deal more.⟩
as good as ALMOST ⟨The job is *as good as* done.⟩

[2]good *n*
1 WELFARE 1, BENEFIT ⟨Homework is for your own *good.*⟩
2 the good part of a person or thing ⟨I believe there is *good* in all of us.⟩
3 something right or good ⟨*Good* will come of this.⟩
4 **goods** *pl* products that are made for sale ⟨canned *goods*⟩
5 **goods** *pl* personal property ⟨He sold all his worldly *goods.*⟩

[1]good–bye *or* **good–by** \gu̇d-'bī\ *interj*
used to express good wishes to someone who is leaving

[2]good–bye *or* **good–by** *n*
a remark made when someone is leaving

good–heart•ed \'gu̇d-'här-təd\ *adj*
kind and generous
good–heart•ed•ly *adv*

good–hu•mored \'gu̇d-'hyü-mərd, -'yü-\ *adj*
GOOD-NATURED
good–hu•mored•ly *adv*

good•ly \'gu̇d-lē\ *adj* **good•li•er**; **good•li•est**
1 of pleasing appearance
2 LARGE, CONSIDERABLE ⟨a *goodly* amount⟩

good–na•tured \'gu̇d-'nā-chərd\ *adj*
having or showing a pleasant disposition
good–na•tured•ly *adv*

good•ness \'gu̇d-nəs\ *n*
1 the quality or state of being good
2 excellence of morals and behavior

good–sized \'gu̇d-'sīzd\ *adj*
fairly large

good–tem•pered \'gu̇d-'tem-pərd\ *adj*
not easily angered or upset

good•will \'gu̇d-'wil\ *n*
kind feelings or attitude

goody \'gu̇-dē\ *n, pl* **good•ies**
1 something especially good to eat
2 something that is very attractive or desirable ⟨Toys, games, and other *goodies* are on sale.⟩

goo•ey \'gü-ē\ *adj* **goo•i•er**; **goo•i•est**
wet and sticky

[1]goof \'güf\ *n*
1 a stupid or silly person
2 [2]BLUNDER

[2]goof *vb* **goofed**; **goof•ing**
1 to spend time foolishly ⟨He *goofed* off instead of studying.⟩
2 to spend time doing silly or playful things ⟨He *goofed* around with the dogs.⟩
3 to make a blunder

goofy \'gü-fē\ *adj* **goof•i•er**; **goof•i•est**
SILLY 1

goo•gle \'gü-gəl\ *vb* **goo•gled**; **goo•gling**
to use the Google search engine to obtain information about (as a person) on the Internet

goose \'güs\ *n, pl* **geese** \'gēs\
1 ▼ a waterbird with webbed feet that is related to the smaller duck and the larger swan
2 a female goose

goose 1

3 the meat of a goose used as food

goose•ber•ry \'güs-ˌber-ē, 'güz-\ *n, pl* **goose•ber•ries**
▼ the sour berry of a thorny bush related to the currant

gooseberries

goose bumps *n pl*
a roughness of the skin caused by cold, fear, or a sudden feeling of excitement

goose•flesh \'güs-ˌflesh\ *n*
GOOSE BUMPS

goose pimples *n pl*
GOOSE BUMPS

go•pher \'gō-fər\ *n*
1 a burrowing animal that is about the size of a large rat and has strong claws on the forefeet and a large fur-lined pouch on the outside of each cheek
2 a striped ground squirrel of North American prairies
3 a burrowing land tortoise of the southern United States

[1]gore \'gȯr\ *n*
1 blood from a wound or cut
2 violence and bloodshed ⟨The movie had a lot of *gore*.⟩

[2]gore *vb* **gored; gor•ing**
to pierce or wound with a pointed object (as a horn or spear)

[1]gorge \'gȯrj\ *n*
a narrow steep-walled canyon or part of a canyon

[2]gorge *vb* **gorged; gorg•ing**
to eat greedily

gor•geous \'gȯr-jəs\ *adj*
very beautiful
gor•geous•ly *adv*
gor•geous•ness *n*

go•ril•la \gə-'ri-lə\ *n*
▼ a very large ape of the forests of central Africa that lives mostly on the ground

▶ **Word History** In the sixth century B.C. the navigator Hanno, from the city of Carthage, made a trip around the west coast of Africa. An account of his journey disappeared, though a Greek translation survives. Near the furthest point on their voyage Hanno and his men came upon an island "full of wild people, the greater part of whom were females, hairy on their bodies, whom our interpreters called Gorillas." When the great ape we know as the gorilla was first described by scientists in the 1800s, it was given the Latin name *Gorilla gorilla* in recollection of Hanno's description—though exactly what Hanno saw in Africa we will never know.

gory \'gȯr-ē\ *adj* **gor•i•er; gor•i•est**
1 covered with blood
2 having or showing much violence and bloodshed

gorilla

gos•ling \'gäz-liŋ\ *n*
a young goose

gos•pel \'gä-spəl\ *n*
1 *often cap* the teachings of Jesus Christ and the apostles
2 something told or accepted as being absolutely true

gos•sa•mer \'gä-sə-mər, -zə-\ *n*
a film of cobwebs floating in the air

[1]gos•sip \'gä-səp\ *n*
1 a person who repeats stories about other people
2 talk or rumors involving the personal lives of other people

▶ **Word History** At first the word *gossip*, from Old English *godsibb*, meant "godparent." Later it came to mean "close friend" as well. Close friends, of course, share secrets. *Gossip* has come to mean anyone, friend or not, who shares the secrets of others.

[2]gossip *vb* **gos•siped; gos•sip•ing**
to talk about the personal lives of other people

got *past and past participle of* GET

gotten *past participle of* GET

[1]gouge \'gau̇j\ *n*
1 ▼ a chisel with a curved blade for scooping or cutting holes
2 a hole or groove made by cutting or scraping

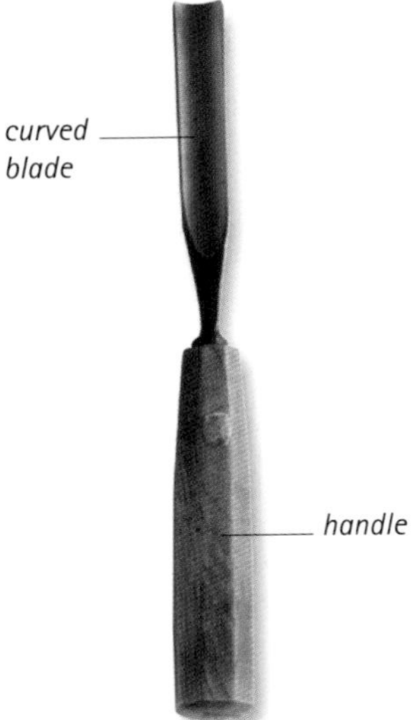

[1]gouge 1

[2]gouge *vb* **gouged; goug•ing**
to make a hole or groove in something by cutting or scraping

a b c d e f g h i j k l m n o p q r s t u v w x y z

gourd \'gȯrd\ *n*
▼ an inedible fruit with a hard rind and many seeds that grows on a vine, is related to the pumpkin and melon, and is often used for decoration or for making objects (as bowls)

gourd: a container made from a gourd that is used for storing liquids

gour•met \'gu̇r-ˌmā\ *n*
a person who appreciates fine food and drink

gov. *abbr* governor

gov•ern \'gə-vərn\ *vb* **gov•erned**; **gov•ern•ing**
1 ²RULE 1
2 to influence the actions and conduct of : CONTROL ⟨Let your good judgment *govern* your decision.⟩
3 to serve as a rule for ⟨Laws *governing* the Internet are changing.⟩

gov•ern•ess \'gə-vər-nəs\ *n*
a woman who teaches and trains a child especially in a private home

gov•ern•ment \'gə-vərn-mənt, -vər-mənt\ *n*
1 control and direction of public business (as of a city or a nation) ⟨The city was hurt by years of weak *government*.⟩
2 a system of control : an established form of political rule ⟨a democratic *government*⟩
3 the people making up a governing body
gov•ern•men•tal \ˌgə-vərn-'men-tᵊl, -vər-'men-tᵊl\ *adj*

gov•er•nor \'gə-vər-nər, 'gə-və-nər\ *n*
a person who governs and especially the elected head of a state of the United States

gov•er•nor•ship \'gə-vər-nər-ˌship, 'gə-və-nər-\ *n*
1 the office or position of governor
2 the term of office of a governor

govt. *abbr* government

gown \'gau̇n\ *n*
1 ► a dress suitable for special occasions
2 a loose robe ⟨graduation *gown*⟩

gown 1: a woman wearing an evening gown

GPS \ˌjē-ˌpē-'es\ *n*
a radio system that uses signals from satellites to determine the user's location and give directions to other places

¹grab \'grab\ *vb* **grabbed**; **grab•bing**
to grasp or seize suddenly

²grab *n*
a sudden attempt to grasp or seize

¹grace \'grās\ *n*
1 a short prayer at a meal
2 beauty and ease of movement
3 pleasant, controlled, and polite behavior ⟨social *graces*⟩ ⟨She handled the situation with *grace*.⟩
4 GOODWILL, FAVOR ⟨They were saved by the *grace* of God.⟩
5 the condition of being in favor ⟨He tried to get in their good *graces*.⟩

²grace *vb* **graced**; **grac•ing**
1 to do credit to : HONOR ⟨Will you *grace* us with your presence?⟩
2 to make more attractive : ADORN ⟨A fountain *graces* the garden.⟩

grace•ful \'grās-fəl\ *adj*
showing grace or beauty in form or action ⟨*graceful* dancers⟩
grace•ful•ly \-fə-lē\ *adv*

gra•cious \'grā-shəs\ *adj*
1 being kind and courteous ⟨a *gracious* hostess⟩
2 GRACEFUL ⟨a *gracious* mansion⟩
gra•cious•ly *adv*
gra•cious•ness *n*

grack•le \'gra-kəl\ *n*
► a large blackbird with shiny feathers that show changeable green, purple, and bronze colors

¹grade \'grād\ *n*
1 a division of a school course representing a year's work ⟨He's in the fourth *grade*.⟩
2 the group of pupils in a school grade ⟨Fifth *grade* is holding a bake sale.⟩
3 a mark or rating especially in school ⟨I got a *grade* of A on the test.⟩
4 a position in a scale of rank, quality, or order ⟨a social *grade*⟩
5 a class of things that are of the same rank, quality, or order
6 the degree of slope (as of a road)

²grade *vb* **grad•ed**; **grad•ing**
1 to give a grade to as an indication of achievement ⟨The teacher *graded* my report a B.⟩
2 to give a rating to ⟨I'd *grade* the movie a ten.⟩
3 to arrange in grades according to some quality ⟨The eggs were *graded* by size.⟩
4 to make level or evenly sloping ⟨*grade* a highway⟩

grad•er \'grā-dər\ *n*
1 a student in a specified grade
2 a person who assigns grades
3 a machine used for leveling earth

grade school *n*
a school including the first six or the first eight grades

grad•u•al \'gra-jə-wəl\ *adj*
moving or happening by steps or degrees
grad•u•al•ly *adv*

¹grad•u•ate \'gra-jə-wət\ *n*
a person who has completed the required course of study in a college or school

²grad•u•ate \'gra-jə-ˌwāt\ *vb* **grad•u•at•ed**; **grad•u•at•ing**
to finish a course of study : become a graduate

grad•u•a•tion \ˌgra-jə-'wā-shən\ *n*
1 the act or process of finishing a course of study
2 COMMENCEMENT 1

Graeco- see GRECO-

grackle

graf•fi•ti \grə-ˈfē-tē\ *n*
▶ writing or drawing made on a public structure without permission

¹graft \ˈgraft\ *n*
1 ▼ a plant that has a twig or bud from another plant attached to it so they are joined and grow together
2 something (as a piece of skin or a plant bud) that is joined to something similar so as to grow together
3 something (as money or advantage) gotten in a dishonest way and especially by betraying a public trust

¹graft 1: a graft of apple tree twigs

²graft *vb* **graft•ed; graft•ing**
1 to attach a twig or bud from one plant to another plant so they are joined and grow together
2 to join one thing to another as if by grafting ⟨*graft* skin⟩
3 to gain dishonestly
graft•er *n*

grain \ˈgrān\ *n*
1 the edible seed or seeds of some grasses (as wheat, corn, or oats) or a few other plants (as buckwheat)
2 plants that produce grain
3 a small hard particle ⟨a *grain* of sand⟩
4 a tiny amount ⟨a *grain* of truth⟩
5 a unit of weight equal to 0.0648 gram
6 the arrangement of fibers in wood
grained \ˈgrānd\ *adj*

grain elevator *n*
a tall building for storing grain

gram \ˈgram\ *n*
a unit of mass in the metric system equal to 1/1000 kilogram

-gram \ˌgram\ *n suffix*
drawing : writing : record ⟨tele*gram*⟩

gram•mar \ˈgra-mər\ *n*
1 the rules of how words are used in a language
2 speech or writing judged according to the rules of grammar

graffiti: walls covered with graffiti

gram•mat•i•cal \grə-ˈma-ti-kəl\ *adj*
of, relating to, or following the rules of grammar
gram•mat•i•cal•ly *adv*

gra•na•ry \ˈgrā-nə-rē, ˈgra-\ *n, pl* **gra•na•ries**
a building in which grain is stored

grand \ˈgrand\ *adj* **grand•er; grand•est**
1 higher in rank than others : FOREMOST ⟨the *grand* prize⟩
2 great in size
3 COMPREHENSIVE, INCLUSIVE ⟨a *grand* total⟩
4 IMPRESSIVE ⟨a *grand* view⟩
5 very good ⟨*grand* weather⟩
grand•ly *adv*

grand•child \ˈgrand-ˌchīld, ˈgran-\ *n, pl* **grand•chil•dren** \-ˌchil-drən\
a child of a person's son or daughter

grand•daugh•ter \ˈgran-ˌdȯ-tər\ *n*
a daughter of a person's son or daughter

gran•deur \ˈgran-jər\ *n*
impressive greatness ⟨the *grandeur* of the mountains⟩

grand•fa•ther \ˈgrand-ˌfä-t͟hər, ˈgran-\ *n*
1 the father of someone's father or mother
2 ANCESTOR

grandfather clock *n*
a tall clock standing directly on the floor

gran•di•ose \ˈgran-dē-ˌōs\ *adj*
overly grand or exaggerated ⟨a *grandiose* plan⟩

grand•ma \ˈgra-ˌmȯ, ˈgra-ˌmä, ˈgran-ˌmȯ, ˈgran-ˌmä\ *n*
GRANDMOTHER 1

grand•moth•er \ˈgrand-ˌmə-t͟hər, ˈgran-\ *n*
1 the mother of someone's father or mother
2 a female ancestor

grand•pa \ˈgram-ˌpȯ, ˈgram-ˌpä, ˈgran-\ *n*
GRANDFATHER 1

grand•par•ent \ˈgrand-ˌper-ənt\ *n*
a parent of someone's father or mother

grand•son \ˈgrand-ˌsən, ˈgran-\ *n*
a son of someone's son or daughter

grand•stand \ˈgrand-ˌstand, ˈgran-\ *n*
a usually roofed structure at a racecourse or stadium for spectators

granite: a rough piece of granite

gran•ite \ˈgra-nət\ *n*
▲ a very hard rock that is used for buildings and for monuments

gran•ny \ˈgra-nē\ *n, pl* **gran•nies**
GRANDMOTHER 1

gra•no•la \grə-ˈnō-lə\ *n*
a mixture of oats and other ingredients (as raisins, coconut, or nuts) that is eaten especially for breakfast or as a snack

[1]grant \'grant\ *vb* **grant•ed**; **grant•ing**
1 to agree to do, give, or allow ⟨I'll *grant* you three wishes.⟩
2 to give as a favor or right
3 to give legally or formally
4 to admit to or agree with ⟨I'll *grant* you that it's a little expensive.⟩

[2]grant *n*
1 the act of giving or agreeing to
2 something given ⟨a land *grant*⟩

grape \'grāp\ *n*
a juicy berry that has a smooth green, dark red, or purple skin and grows in clusters on a woody vine (**grapevine**)

grape•fruit \'grāp-,früt\ *n*
▶ a large fruit with a yellow skin that is related to the orange and lemon

grapefruit: a pink grapefruit

[1]graph \'graf\ *n*
a diagram that by means of dots and lines shows a system of relationships between things ⟨a temperature *graph*⟩

[2]graph *vb* **graphed**; **graph•ing**
to show something using a graph

-graph \,graf\ *n suffix*
1 something written ⟨para*graph*⟩
2 instrument for making or sending records ⟨tele*graph*⟩

[1]graph•ic \'gra-fik\ *adj*
1 being written, drawn, printed, or engraved
2 described in very clear detail ⟨She gave a *graphic* account of an accident.⟩
3 of or relating to the pictorial arts or to printing

[2]graphic *n*
1 a picture, map, or graph used for illustration
2 graphics *pl* a pictorial image or series of images displayed on a computer screen

graphic novel *n*
a work of fiction or nonfiction that tells a story using comic strips and that is published as a book

graph paper *n*
paper covered with lines that form small uniform squares for drawing graphs

graph•ite \'gra-,fīt\ *n*
a soft black form of carbon used in making lead pencils and as a lubricant

-g•ra•phy \grə-fē\ *n suffix, pl* **-g•ra•phies**
writing or picturing in a special way, by a special means, or of a special thing ⟨photo*graphy*⟩

grapple *vb* **grap•pled**; **grap•pling**
1 to seize with an instrument (as a hook)
2 to seize and struggle with another
3 to deal with ⟨*grapple* with a problem⟩

[1]grasp \'grasp\ *vb* **grasped**; **grasp•ing**
1 to seize and hold with or as if with the hand ⟨*grasp* a bat⟩ ⟨*grasp* an opportunity⟩
2 to make the motion of seizing ⟨She *grasped* at branches as she fell.⟩
3 UNDERSTAND 1 ⟨He quickly *grasped* the idea.⟩
synonyms see TAKE

[2]grasp *n*
1 a grip of the hand ⟨a firm *grasp*⟩
2 [2]CONTROL 1, HOLD ⟨a tyrant's *grasp*⟩
3 the power of seizing and holding **:** REACH ⟨He put the tools beyond the child's *grasp*.⟩
4 [1]UNDERSTANDING 1 ⟨a good *grasp* of math⟩

grasp•ing \'gra-spiŋ\ *adj*
GREEDY 1

grass \'gras\ *n*
1 ▼ any of a large group of green plants with jointed stems, long slender leaves, and stalks of clustered flowers
2 plants eaten by grazing animals
3 land (as a lawn) covered with growing grass
grass•like \-,līk\ *adj*

▶ **grass 1**
There are about 9,000 species of grass, growing in a wide range of habitats throughout the world. Grasses are pollinated by the wind, and so have no need of showy flowers to attract insects. Instead, their small flowers produce many grains of pollen that are easily blown by the wind.

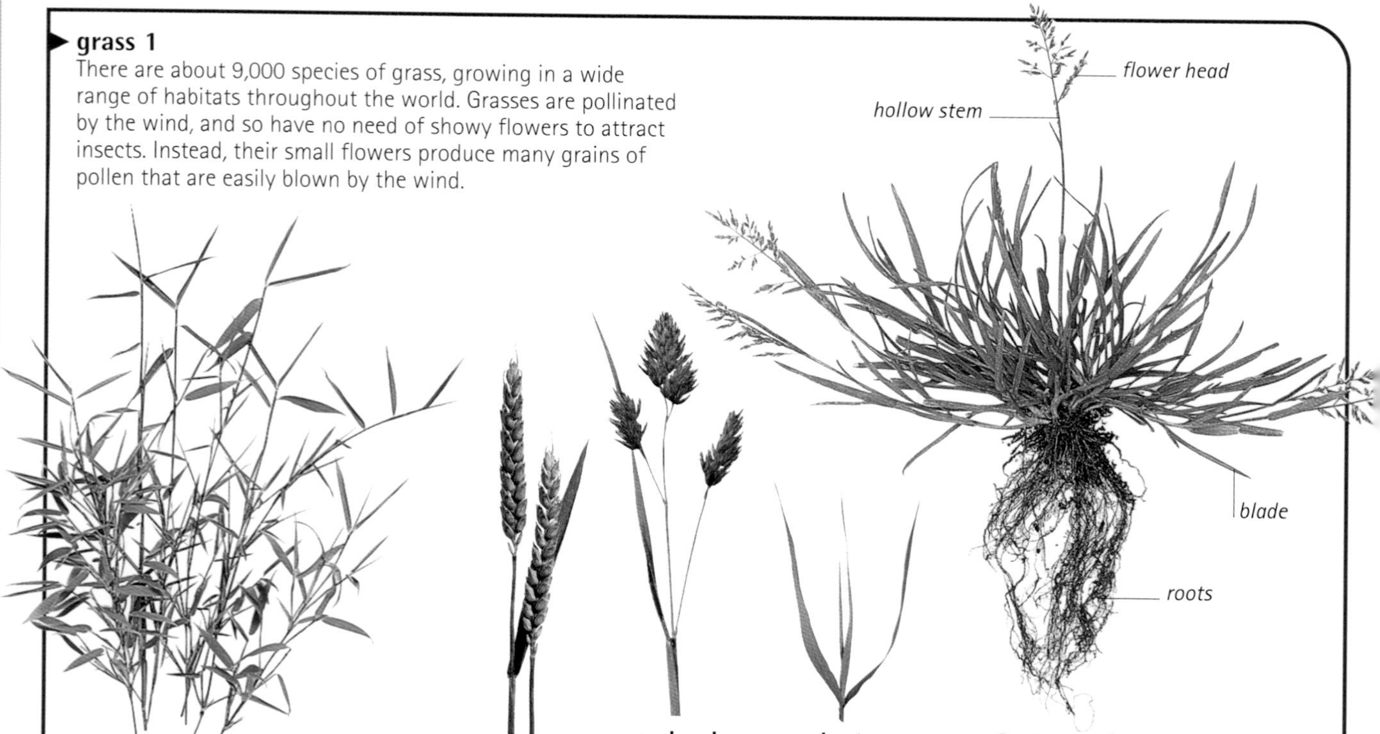

flower head
hollow stem
blade
roots

bamboo **wheat** **orchard grass** **giant reed** **features of meadow grass**

grass•hop•per \'gras-ˌhä-pər\ *n*
▼ a common leaping insect that feeds on plants

wing
hind leg
eye
antenna

grasshopper leaping from a plant

grass•land \'gras-ˌland\ *n*
land covered with herbs (as grass and clover) rather than shrubs and trees

grassy \'gra-sē\ *adj* **grass•i•er**; **grass•i•est**
like or covered with grass ⟨a *grassy* field⟩

[1]**grate** \'grāt\ *vb* **grat•ed**; **grat•ing**
1 to break into small pieces by rubbing against something rough ⟨*grate* cheese⟩
2 to grind or rub against something with a harsh noise
3 to have an irritating effect ⟨His voice *grates* on me.⟩

[2]**grate** *n*
1 a frame containing parallel or crossed bars (as in a window)
2 a frame of iron bars to hold a fire

grate•ful \'grāt-fəl\ *adj*
1 feeling or showing thanks ⟨I'm *grateful* for your help.⟩
2 providing pleasure or comfort
grate•ful•ly \-fə-lē\ *adv*

grat•er \'grā-tər\ *n*
▶ a device with a rough surface for grating ⟨a cheese *grater*⟩

grater: a cheese grater

grat•i•fi•ca•tion \ˌgra-tə-fə-'kā-shən\ *n*
1 the act of giving pleasure or satisfaction to : the state of being pleased or satisfied
2 something that pleases or satisfies

grat•i•fy \'gra-tə-ˌfī\ *vb*
grat•i•fied; **grat•i•fy•ing**
1 to give pleasure or satisfaction to ⟨The loud applause *gratified* her.⟩
2 to do or give whatever is wanted by

grat•ing \'grā-tiŋ\ *n*
[2]GRATE 1

grat•i•tude \'gra-tə-ˌtüd, -ˌtyüd\ *n*
a feeling of appreciation or thanks

[1]**grave** \'grāv\ *n*
a hole in the ground for burying a dead body

[2]**grave** *adj* **grav•er**; **grav•est**
1 very serious : IMPORTANT ⟨*grave* danger⟩ ⟨a *grave* discussion⟩
2 serious in appearance or manner ⟨a *grave* voice⟩
grave•ly *adv*

grav•el \'gra-vəl\ *n*
small pieces of rock and pebbles larger than grains of sand

grav•el•ly \'gra-və-lē\ *adj*
1 containing or made up of gravel ⟨*gravelly* soil⟩
2 sounding rough ⟨a *gravelly* voice⟩

grave•stone \'grāv-ˌstōn\ *n*
a monument on a grave

grave•yard \'grāv-ˌyärd\ *n*
CEMETERY

grav•i•tate \'gra-və-ˌtāt\ *vb*
grav•i•tat•ed; **grav•i•tat•ing**
to move or be drawn toward something

grav•i•ta•tion \ˌgra-və-'tā-shən\ *n*
1 GRAVITY 1
2 movement to or toward something

grav•i•ty \'gra-və-tē\ *n, pl* **grav•i•ties**
1 a force of attraction that tends to draw particles or bodies together
2 ▼ the attraction of bodies by the force of gravity toward the center of the earth
3 great seriousness

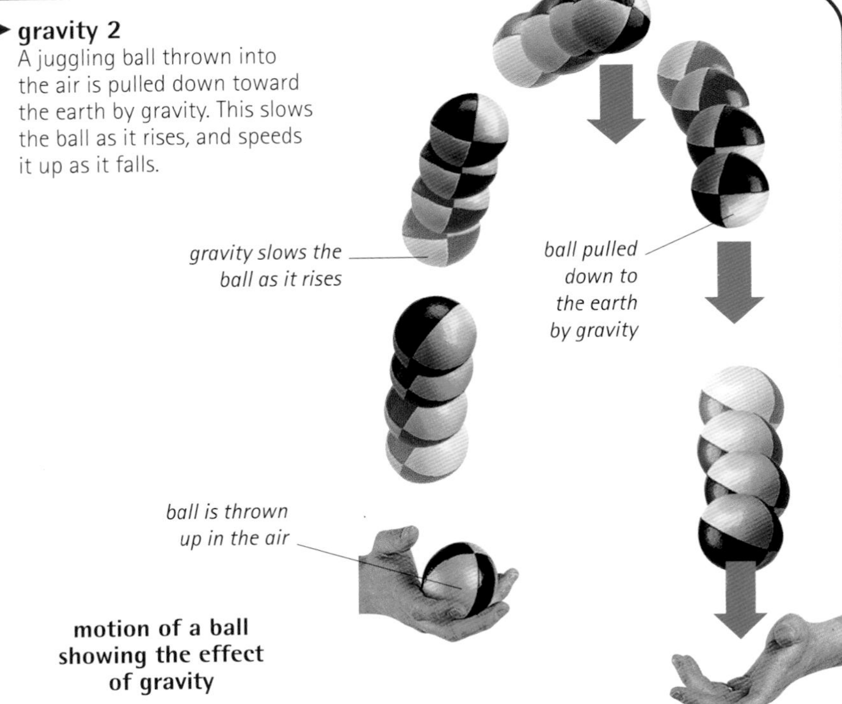

▶ **gravity 2**
A juggling ball thrown into the air is pulled down toward the earth by gravity. This slows the ball as it rises, and speeds it up as it falls.

motion of a ball showing the effect of gravity

gra•vy \'grā-vē\ *n, pl* **gravies**
a sauce made from the juice of cooked meat

[1]**gray** *also* **grey** \'grā\ *adj* **gray•er** *also* **grey•er**; **gray•est** *also* **grey•est**
1 of a color that is a blend of black and white 〈a *gray* stone〉
2 having gray hair 〈a *gray* old man〉
3 lacking cheer or brightness 〈a *gray* day〉
gray•ness *n*

[2]**gray** *also* **grey** *n*
a color that is a blend of black and white

[3]**gray** *also* **grey** *vb* **grayed** *also* **greyed**; **gray•ing** *also* **grey•ing**
to make or become gray 〈*graying* hair〉

gray•ish \'grā-ish\ *adj*
somewhat gray

[1]**graze** \'grāz\ *vb* **grazed**; **graz•ing**
1 to eat grass 〈The cattle *grazed*.〉
2 to supply with grass or pasture

[2]**graze** *vb* **grazed**; **graz•ing**
1 to rub lightly in passing : barely touch
2 to scrape by rubbing against something

[3]**graze** *n*
a scrape or mark caused by scraping against something

[1]**grease** \'grēs\ *n*
1 melted animal fat
2 oily material
3 a thick lubricant

[2]**grease** \'grēs, 'grēz\ *vb* **greased**; **greas•ing**
to coat or lubricate with an oily material

grease•paint \'grēs-,pānt\ *n*
actors' makeup

greasy \'grē-sē, -zē\ *adj* **greas•i•er**; **greas•i•est**
1 covered with an oily material 〈*greasy* hands〉
2 like or full of fat 〈*greasy* french fries〉

great \'grāt\ *adj* **great•er**; **great•est**
1 very large in size : HUGE 〈a *great* mountain〉
2 large in amount 〈a *great* crowd〉
3 [1]LONG 2 〈a *great* while〉
4 much beyond the ordinary 〈a *great* success〉
5 IMPORTANT 1, DISTINGUISHED 〈a *great* artist〉
6 very talented or successful 〈She's *great* at diving.〉
7 very good 〈We had a *great* time.〉
great•ly *adv*

great–grand•child \'grāt-'grand-,chīld, -'gran-\ *n, pl* **great–grand•chil•dren** \-,chil-drən\
a grandson (**great–grandson**) or granddaughter (**great–granddaughter**) of someone's son or daughter

great–grand•par•ent \'grāt-'grand-,per-ənt, -'gran-\ *n*
a grandfather (**great–grandfather**) or grandmother (**great–grandmother**) of someone's father or mother

grebe \'grēb\ *n*
a swimming and diving bird related to the loons

Gre•cian \'grē-shən\ *adj*
[2]GREEK

Gre•co– *or* **Grae•co–** \'grē-kō\ *prefix*
1 Greece : Greeks
2 Greek and

greed \'grēd\ *n*
selfish desire for more than is needed

greedy \'grē-dē\ *adj* **greed•i•er**; **greed•i•est**
1 having or showing a selfish desire for more than is needed
2 having a strong desire to eat or drink
3 very eager to have something 〈She's *greedy* for power.〉
greed•i•ly \'grē-də-lē\ *adv*

[1]**Greek** \'grēk\ *n*
1 a person born or living in Greece
2 the language of the Greeks

[2]**Greek** *adj*
of or relating to Greece, its people, or the Greek language

[1]**green** \'grēn\ *adj* **green•er**; **green•est**
1 of the color of grass : colored green 〈a *green* shirt〉
2 covered with green plant growth 〈*green* fields〉
3 made of green plants or of the leafy parts of plants 〈a *green* salad〉
4 not ripe 〈*green* bananas〉
5 not fully processed, treated, or seasoned 〈*green* lumber〉
6 lacking training or experience 〈*green* troops〉
7 JEALOUS 2 〈*green* with envy〉
8 supporting the protection of or helping to protect the environment 〈*green* activists〉 〈*green* household products〉

[2]**green** *n*
1 a color between blue and yellow : the color of growing grass
2 **greens** *pl* leafy parts of plants used for food
3 a grassy plain or plot 〈the village *green*〉

green bean *n*
a young long green pod of a bean plant eaten as a vegetable

green•ery \'grē-nə-rē\ *n, pl* **green•er•ies**
green plants or foliage

green•horn \'grēn-,hȯrn\ *n*
a person who is new at something

[1]**green•house** \'grēn-,haůs\ *n*
◀ a building with clear walls and roof (as of glass) for growing plants

[2]**greenhouse** *adj*
relating to, causing, or caused by the greenhouse effect 〈*greenhouse* gases〉

greenhouse effect *n*
▶ warming of the lower atmosphere of the earth that occurs when radiation from the sun is absorbed by the earth and then given off again and absorbed by carbon dioxide and water vapor in the atmosphere

green•ish \'grē-nish\ *adj*
somewhat green

green thumb *n*
a talent for growing plants

greet \'grēt\ *vb* **greet•ed**; **greet•ing**
1 to speak to in a friendly polite way upon arrival : WELCOME

greenhouse: flowers in a greenhouse

detonator

explosive chamber

fuse

grenade: cross-section of a grenade

2 to respond to in a certain way ⟨Audience members *greeted* the speech with boos.⟩
3 to present itself to ⟨A pretty scene *greeted* them.⟩
greet•er *n*

greet•ing \ˈgrē-tiŋ\ *n*
1 an expression of pleasure on meeting or seeing someone
2 an expression of good wishes

gre•gar•i•ous \gri-ˈger-ē-əs\ *adj*
1 enjoying the company of other people
2 tending to live in a flock, herd, or community rather than alone ⟨*gregarious* insects⟩

gre•nade \grə-ˈnād\ *n*
◀ a small bomb designed to be thrown by hand or fired (as by a rifle)

grew *past of* GROW

grey *variant of* GRAY

grey•hound \ˈgrā-ˌhau̇nd\ *n*
▶ a tall swift dog with a smooth coat and good eyesight

grid \ˈgrid\ *n*
1 a network of horizontal and perpendicular lines (as for locating places on a map)
2 a frame with bars running across it that is used to cover an opening
3 a group of electrical conductors that form a network

grid•dle \ˈgri-dᵊl\ *n*
a flat surface or pan for cooking food

grid•iron \ˈgrid-ˌī-ərn\ *n*
1 a grate for cooking food over a fire
2 a football field

grief \ˈgrēf\ *n*
1 very deep sorrow
2 a cause of sorrow ⟨The dog was nothing but *grief* to its owner.⟩
3 things that cause problems ⟨I've had enough *grief* for one day.⟩
4 an unfortunate happening ⟨The boat came to *grief* on the rocks.⟩
synonyms see SORROW

▶ **greenhouse effect**
The sun's heat is directed toward the earth, but not all of the reflected heat escapes from the atmosphere, so that the earth becomes warmer. Many scientists studying the effect think it is worsened by the buildup of pollution, which traps even more of the sun's heat. These scientists think that as the climate grows warmer, weather patterns will change, and different parts of the world will experience droughts, storms, and floods.

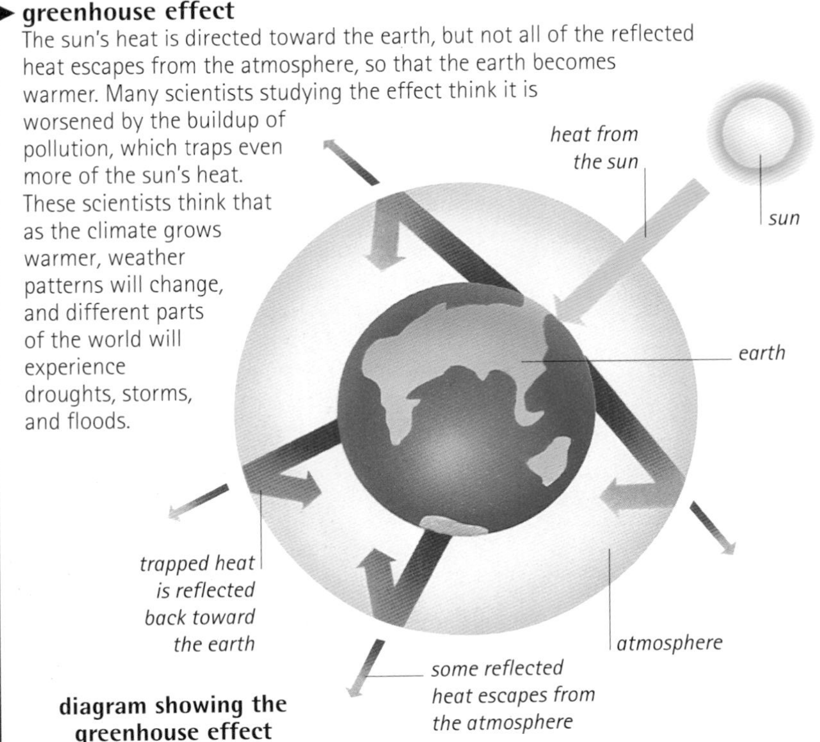

diagram showing the greenhouse effect

griev•ance \ˈgrē-vəns\ *n*
a reason for complaining

grieve \ˈgrēv\ *vb* **grieved**; **griev•ing**
1 to feel or show grief ⟨a *grieving* widow⟩
2 to cause grief to

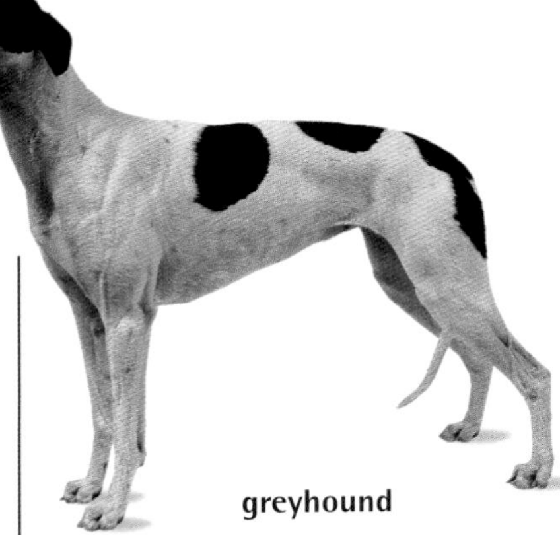

greyhound

griev•ous \ˈgrē-vəs\ *adj*
1 causing suffering or pain ⟨a *grievous* injury⟩
2 SERIOUS 2, GRAVE ⟨a *grievous* error⟩

grif•fin *or* **grif•fon** *also* **gryph•on** \ˈgri-fən\ *n*
▼ an imaginary animal that is half eagle and half lion

griffin: carved stone relief of a griffin

▶ **Word History** The word *griffin* is borrowed, through medieval French and Latin, from the ancient Greek word *gryps*. The image of an animal combining features of a lion and a bird of prey was borrowed by the Greeks from the ancient Near Eastern world. The word *gryps* may have been borrowed as well, as it resembles *karību*, a word for winged lions in Akkadian, the language of ancient Babylonia and Assyria. On the other hand, *gryps* may have been influenced by Greek *gyps*, "vulture," and *grypos*, "curved, bent" (of a bird's beak or claws).

[1]grill \'gril\ *vb* **grilled**; **grill•ing**
1 to cook or be cooked on a frame of bars over fire
2 to question intensely

[2]grill *n*
1 a frame of bars on which food is cooked over a fire
2 a cooking device equipped with a frame of bars ⟨a portable gas *grill*⟩
3 a dish of grilled or broiled food ⟨a seafood *grill*⟩
4 a usually casual restaurant

grille *or* **grill** \'gril\ *n*
an often ornamental arrangement of bars forming a barrier or screen

grim \'grim\ *adj* **grim•mer**; **grim•mest**
1 [1]SAVAGE 2, CRUEL
2 harsh in action or appearance : STERN ⟨a *grim* look⟩
3 GLOOMY 3, DISMAL ⟨*grim* news⟩
4 showing firmness and seriousness ⟨*grim* determination⟩
5 FRIGHTFUL 1 ⟨a *grim* tale⟩
grim•ly *adv*

[1]gri•mace \'gri-məs, gri-'mās\ *n*
a twisting of the face (as in disgust or pain)

[2]grimace *vb* **gri•maced**; **gri•mac•ing**
to twist the face ⟨He *grimaced* in pain.⟩

grime \'grīm\ *n*
dirt rubbed into a surface

grimy \'grī-mē\ *adj* **grim•i•er**; **grim•i•est**
[1]DIRTY 1

[1]grin \'grin\ *vb* **grinned**; **grin•ning**
to smile broadly showing teeth

[2]grin *n*
a broad smile that shows teeth

[1]grind \'grīnd\ *vb* **ground** \'grau̇nd\; **grind•ing**
1 to make or be made into powder or small pieces by rubbing ⟨The mill *grinds* wheat into flour.⟩
2 to wear down, polish, or sharpen by friction ⟨*grind* an ax⟩
3 to rub together with a scraping noise ⟨*grind* the teeth⟩
4 to operate or produce by or as if by turning a crank

[2]grind *n*
1 an act of sharpening or reducing to powder
2 steady hard work ⟨the daily *grind*⟩

grind•stone \'grīnd-,stōn\ *n*
a flat round stone that turns to sharpen or shape things

[1]grip \'grip\ *vb* **gripped**; **grip•ping**
1 to grab or hold tightly
2 to hold the interest of ⟨The story *grips* the reader.⟩

[2]grip *n*
1 a strong grasp
2 strength in holding : POWER ⟨the *grip* of winter⟩
3 [1]UNDERSTANDING 1 ⟨I finally have a *grip* on division.⟩
4 SELF-CONTROL ⟨Calm down and get a *grip*.⟩
5 [1]HANDLE

[1]gripe \'grīp\ *vb* **griped**; **grip•ing**
COMPLAIN

[2]gripe *n*
COMPLAINT 1

grippe \'grip\ *n*
a disease like or the same as influenza

gris•ly \'griz-lē\ *adj* **gris•li•er**; **gris•li•est**
HORRIBLE 1, GRUESOME ⟨a *grisly* murder⟩

grist \'grist\ *n*
grain to be ground or that is already ground

gris•tle \'gri-səl\ *n*
CARTILAGE
gris•tly \'gris-lē\ *adj*

grist•mill \'grist-,mil\ *n*
a mill for grinding grain

[1]grit \'grit\ *n*
1 rough hard bits especially of sand
2 strength of mind or spirit

[2]grit *vb* **grit•ted**; **grit•ting**
[1]GRIND 3, GRATE

grits \'grits\ *n pl*
coarsely ground hulled grain

grit•ty \'gri-tē\ *adj* **grit•ti•er**; **grit•ti•est**
1 containing or like rough hard bits especially of sand
2 showing toughness and courage
3 harshly realistic ⟨a *gritty* story⟩

griz•zled \'gri-zəld\ *adj*
1 streaked or mixed with gray ⟨*grizzled* hair⟩
2 having gray hair

grizzly bear *n*
▶ a large powerful brown bear of western North America

[1]groan \'grōn\ *vb* **groaned**; **groan•ing**
1 to make or say with a moan ⟨"Not a test," she *groaned*.⟩
2 to creak under a strain ⟨The stairs *groaned* under his weight.⟩

[2]groan *n*
a low moaning sound

gro•cer \'grō-sər\ *n*
a person who sells food and household supplies

gro•cery \'grō-sə-rē, 'grōs-rē\ *n*, *pl* **gro•cer•ies**
1 *groceries pl* food and household supplies sold at a store
2 ▶ a store that sells food and household supplies

grog•gy \'grä-gē\ *adj* **grog•gi•er**; **grog•gi•est**
weak, dazed, and unsteady ⟨The medicine made me *groggy*.⟩

groin \'grȯin\ *n*
the fold or area where the abdomen joins the thigh

grom•met \'grä-mət\ *n*
a metal or plastic ring to strengthen or protect a small hole

[1]groom \'grüm\ *n*
1 a man who has just been or is about to be married
2 a person in charge of horses

[2]groom *vb* **groomed**; **groom•ing**
1 to make neat and attractive ⟨*groom* a dog⟩
2 to prepare for a purpose ⟨His family is *grooming* him to take over their business.⟩

[1]groove \'grüv\ *n*
1 a long narrow cut in a surface
2 [1]ROUTINE 1

grizzly bear

grocery 2: a man buying food at a grocery

[2]**groove** *vb* **grooved**; **groov•ing**
to make a long narrow cut in

grope \'grōp\ *vb* **groped**; **grop•ing**
1 to move along by feeling with the hands ⟨He *groped* along the dark hallway.⟩
2 to seek by or as if by feeling around ⟨She *groped* for the light switch.⟩ ⟨He was *groping* for an answer.⟩

gros•beak \'grōs-,bēk\ *n*
▶ a finch with a strong conical bill

grosbeak: a Japanese grosbeak

[1]**gross** \'grōs\ *adj* **gross•er**; **gross•est**
1 noticeably bad : GLARING ⟨a *gross* error⟩
2 DISGUSTING ⟨a *gross* habit⟩
3 consisting of a whole before anything is subtracted ⟨*gross* earnings⟩
4 showing poor manners : VULGAR

[2]**gross** *n*
the whole before anything is deducted

[3]**gross** *n, pl* **gross**
twelve dozen

gro•tesque \grō-'tesk\ *adj*
unnatural in an odd or ugly way

grot•to \'grä-tō\ *n, pl* **grottoes**
1 [1]CAVE, CAVERN
2 an artificial structure like a cave

[1]**grouch** \'grau̇ch\ *n*
a person who is irritable or complains a lot

[2]**grouch** *vb* **grouched**; **grouch•ing**
COMPLAIN

grouchy \'grau̇-chē\ *adj* **grouch•i•er**; **grouch•i•est**
tending to be irritable or to complain a lot

[1]**ground** \'grau̇nd\ *n*
1 the surface of the earth ⟨Leaves fell to the *ground*.⟩
2 [2]SOIL 1, EARTH
3 the bottom of a body of water ⟨The boat struck *ground*.⟩
4 an area of land ⟨sacred *ground*⟩
5 an area used for some purpose ⟨a hunting *ground*⟩
6 grounds *pl* the land around and belonging to a building ⟨the school *grounds*⟩
7 BACKGROUND 1
8 a reason for a belief, action, or argument ⟨What is the *ground* for your complaint?⟩
9 an area of knowledge ⟨We covered a lot of *ground* in class.⟩
10 a level of achievement or success ⟨The company is losing *ground*.⟩
11 grounds *pl* material in a liquid that settles to the bottom ⟨coffee *grounds*⟩

[2]**ground** *vb* **ground•ed**; **ground•ing**
1 to provide a reason for ⟨The practices are *grounded* in tradition.⟩
2 to instruct in basic knowledge or understanding
3 to run or cause to run aground ⟨*ground* a ship⟩
4 to connect electrically with the ground
5 to prevent (a plane or pilot) from flying
6 to prohibit from taking part in certain activities as punishment ⟨My parents *grounded* me for a week.⟩

[3]**ground** *past and past participle of* GRIND

ground•hog \'grau̇nd-,hȯg, -,häg\ *n*
WOODCHUCK

ground•less \'grau̇nd-ləs\ *adj*
having no real reason ⟨*groundless* fears⟩

ground•work \'grau̇nd-,wərk\ *n*
something upon which further work or progress is based

[1]**group** \'grüp\ *n*
1 a number of persons or things considered as a unit
2 a number of persons or things that are considered related in some way ⟨an age *group*⟩ ⟨a food *group*⟩
3 a small band ⟨a rock *group*⟩

[2]**group** *vb* **grouped**; **group•ing**
to arrange in, put into, or form a unit or group

[1]**grouse** \'grau̇s\ *n, pl* **grouse**
▼ a brownish bird mostly of wooded areas that feeds especially on the ground and is sometimes hunted for food or sport

[1]**grouse**

[2]**grouse** *vb* **groused**; **grous•ing**
COMPLAIN

grove \'grōv\ *n*
a small forest or group of planted trees

grov•el \'grä-vəl, 'grə-\ *vb* **grov•eled** *or* **grov•elled**; **grov•el•ing** *or* **grov•el•ling**
1 to kneel, lie, or crawl on the ground (as in fear)
2 to act toward someone in a weak or humble way ⟨He *groveled* before the king.⟩

grow \'grō\ *vb* **grew** \'grü\; **grown** \'grōn\; **grow•ing**
1 to spring up and develop to maturity
2 to be able to live and develop ⟨Most algae *grow* in water.⟩
3 to be related in some way by reason of growing ⟨The tree branches have *grown* together.⟩
4 [1]INCREASE, EXPAND ⟨The city is *growing* rapidly.⟩
5 BECOME 1 ⟨Grandma is *growing* old.⟩
6 to cause to grow : RAISE ⟨I *grow* tomatoes.⟩
grow•er *n*
grow on to become more appealing over time
grow up to become an adult

growing pains *n pl*
pains that occur in the legs of growing children but have not been proven to be caused by growth

[1]**growl** \'grau̇l\ *vb* **growled**; **growl•ing**
1 to make a deep threatening sound ⟨The dog *growled.*⟩
2 to make a low rumbling noise ⟨My stomach is *growling.*⟩
3 to complain or say in an angry way

[2]**growl** *n*
1 a deep threatening sound (as of an animal)
2 a grumbling or muttered complaint

grown \'grōn\ *adj*
having reached full growth : MATURE

[1]**grown–up** \'grōn-,əp\ *adj*
[1]ADULT

[2]**grown–up** *n*
an adult person

growth \'grōth\ *n*
1 a stage or condition in increasing, developing, or maturing ⟨The tree reached its full *growth.*⟩
2 a natural process of increasing in size or developing ⟨*growth* of a crystal⟩
3 a gradual increase ⟨the *growth* of wealth⟩
4 something (as a covering of plants) produced by growing

[1]**grub** \'grəb\ *vb* **grubbed**; **grub•bing**
1 to root out by digging ⟨*grub* out potatoes⟩
2 to work hard

[2]**grub** *n*
1 a soft thick wormlike larva (as of a beetle)
2 FOOD 1

grub•by \'grə-bē\ *adj* **grub•bi•er**; **grub•bi•est**
[1]DIRTY 1

[1]**grudge** \'grəj\ *vb* **grudged**; **grudg•ing**
BEGRUDGE

[2]**grudge** *n*
a feeling of anger or dislike toward someone that lasts a long time

gru•el \'grü-əl\ *n*
a thin porridge

gru•el•ing *or* **gru•el•ling** \'grü-ə-liŋ\ *adj*
calling for great effort ⟨a *grueling* job⟩

grue•some \'grü-səm\ *adj*
causing horror or disgust

gruff \'grəf\ *adj* **gruff•er**; **gruff•est**
rough in speech or manner ⟨a *gruff* reply⟩
gruff•ly *adv*
gruff•ness *n*

[1]**grum•ble** \'grəm-bəl\ *vb* **grum•bled**; **grum•bling**
1 to complain in a low voice
2 [1]RUMBLE

[1]**guard 1:**
a security guard

[2]**grumble** *n*
1 the act of complaining in a low voice
2 [2]RUMBLE

grumpy \'grəm-pē\ *adj* **grump•i•er**; **grump•i•est**
GROUCHY, CROSS
grump•i•ly \-pə-lē\ *adv*
grump•i•ness *n*

guava

[1]**grunt** \'grənt\ *vb* **grunt•ed**; **grunt•ing**
to make a short low sound

[2]**grunt** *n*
a short low sound (as of a pig)

gryphon *variant of* GRIFFIN

GSA *abbr* Girl Scouts of America

GSUSA *abbr* Girl Scouts of the United States of America

gt. *abbr* great

GU *abbr* Guam

[1]**guar•an•tee** \,ger-ən-'tē, ,gär-\ *n*
1 a promise that something will be or will happen as stated
2 something given as a promise of payment : SECURITY

[2]**guarantee** *vb* **guar•an•teed**; **guar•an•tee•ing**
1 to make a promise about the condition or occurrence of something ⟨The dealer *guarantees* the car for one year.⟩
2 to promise to be responsible for the debt or duty of another person ⟨He will *guarantee* his son's loan.⟩

guar•an•tor \,ger-ən-'tȯr, ,gär-\ *n*
a person who gives a guarantee

[1]**guard** \'gärd\ *n*
1 ◀ a person or a body of persons that guards against injury or danger
2 the act or duty of keeping watch
3 a device giving protection ⟨a mouth *guard*⟩

[2]**guard** *vb* **guard•ed**; **guard•ing**
1 to protect from danger : DEFEND
2 to watch over so as to prevent escape
3 to keep careful watch for in order to prevent ⟨I try to *guard* against mistakes.⟩

guard•ed \'gär-dəd\ *adj*
CAUTIOUS ⟨a *guarded* answer⟩

guard•house \'gärd-,hau̇s\ *n*
1 a building used as a headquarters by soldiers on guard duty
2 a military jail

guard•ian \'gär-dē-ən\ *n*
1 a person who guards or looks after something : CUSTODIAN
2 a person who legally has the care of another person or of another person's property
guard•ian•ship \-,ship\ *n*

guards•man \'gärdz-mən\ *n*, *pl* **guards•men** \-mən\
a member of a national guard, coast guard, or other similar military body

gua•va \'gwä-və\ *n*
◀ the sweet fruit of a tropical American tree that has yellow or pink pulp

guide dog:
a guide dog for the blind

gu•ber•na•to•ri•al \ˌgü-bər-nə-'tȯr-ē-əl, ˌgyü-\ *adj*
relating to a governor

guer•ril•la *or* **gue•ril•la** \gə-'ri-lə\ *n*
a member of a group carrying on warfare but not part of a regular army

[1]**guess** \'ges\ *vb* **guessed**; **guess•ing**
1 to form an opinion or give an answer about from little or no information ⟨*Guess* what I got for my birthday.⟩
2 to solve correctly mainly by chance ⟨I *guessed* the riddle.⟩
3 THINK 1, SUPPOSE
guess•er *n*

[2]**guess** *n*
an opinion or answer that is reached with little information or by chance

guess•work \'ges-ˌwərk\ *n*
work done or results gotten by guessing

guest \'gest\ *n*
1 a person invited to visit or stay in someone's home
2 a person invited to a special place or event ⟨a wedding *guest*⟩
3 a customer at a hotel, motel, inn, or restaurant

[1]**guf•faw** \ˌgə-'fȯ\ *n*
a burst of loud laughter

[2]**guffaw** *vb* **guf•fawed**; **guf•faw•ing**
to laugh noisily

guid•ance \'gī-dᵊns\ *n*
help, instruction, or assistance

[1]**guide** \'gīd\ *n*
someone or something (as a book) that leads, directs, or shows the right way

[2]**guide** *vb* **guid•ed**; **guid•ing**
1 to show the way to ⟨She'll *guide* you on your tour.⟩
2 to direct or control the course of ⟨The coach *guided* the team to victory.⟩
3 [1]DIRECT 6, INSTRUCT ⟨Let your conscience *guide* you.⟩

guide•book \'gīd-ˌbu̇k\ *n*
a book of information for travelers

guide dog *n*
◀ a dog trained to lead a person who is blind

guide•line \'gīd-ˌlīn\ *n*
a rule about how something should be done

guide•post \'gīd-ˌpōst\ *n*
a post with signs giving directions for travelers

guide word *n*
either of the terms at the head of a page of an alphabetical reference work (as a dictionary) usually showing the first and last entries on the page

guild \'gild\ *n*
an association of people with common interests or aims

guile \'gīl\ *n*
the use of clever and often dishonest methods

[1]**guil•lo•tine** \'gi-lə-ˌtēn\ *n*
a machine for cutting off a person's head with a heavy blade that slides down two grooved posts

[2]**guillotine** *vb* **guil•lo•tined**; **guil•lo•tin•ing**
to cut off a person's head with a guillotine

guilt \'gilt\ *n*
1 responsibility for having done something wrong and especially something against the law ⟨He admitted his *guilt*.⟩
2 a feeling of shame or regret as a result of bad conduct
guilt•less \-ləs\ *adj*

guilty \'gil-tē\ *adj* **guilt•i•er**; **guilt•i•est**
1 responsible for having done wrong
2 suffering from or showing bad feelings about having done wrong ⟨I feel *guilty* about lying.⟩
guilt•i•ly \-tə-lē\ *adv*

guin•ea \'gi-nē\ *n*
an old British gold coin

guinea fowl *n*
▶ a dark gray African bird that is sometimes raised for food

guinea pig *n*
a small stocky South American animal that is a rodent with short ears and a very short tail and is often kept as a pet

electric guitar

an acoustic guitar is not electronically amplified

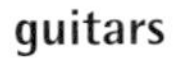

guitars

guise \'gīz\ *n*
1 a style of dress
2 outward appearance

gui•tar \gə-'tär\ *n*
▲ a musical instrument with six strings played by plucking or strumming

gulch \'gəlch\ *n*
a small narrow valley with steep sides

guinea fowl

a b c d e f g h i j k n o p q r s t u v w x y z

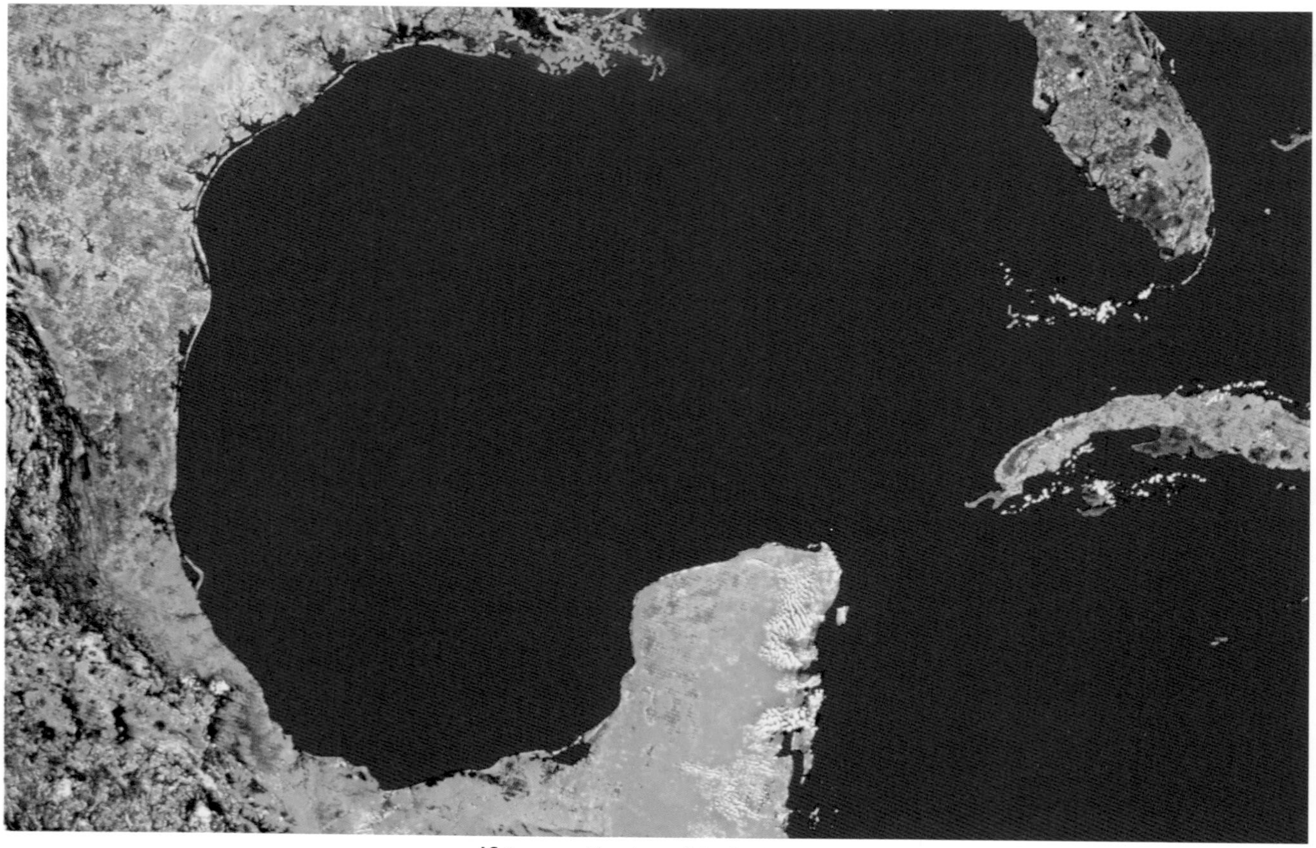

gulf 1: a satellite view of the Gulf of Mexico

gulf \ˈgəlf\ *n*
1 ▲ a part of an ocean or sea that extends into the land ⟨the *Gulf* of Mexico⟩
2 a deep split or gap in the earth
3 a wide separation

gull \ˈgəl\ *n*
▼ a waterbird with webbed feet that is usually gray and white in color and has a thick strong bill

gul•let \ˈgə-lət\ *n*
THROAT 1, ESOPHAGUS

gull

gull•ible \ˈgə-lə-bəl\ *adj*
easily fooled or cheated

gul•ly \ˈgə-lē\ *n, pl* **gullies**
a trench worn in the earth by running water

¹gulp \ˈgəlp\ *vb* **gulped**; **gulp•ing**
1 to swallow in a hurry or in large amounts at a time
2 to breathe in deeply
3 to keep back as if by swallowing ⟨He *gulped* down a sob.⟩
4 to say in a nervous way ⟨"Oops," she *gulped.*⟩

²gulp *n*
1 the act of swallowing or breathing deeply
2 a large swallow

¹gum \ˈgəm\ *n*
the flesh at the roots of the teeth

²gum *n*
1 CHEWING GUM
2 a sticky substance obtained from plants that hardens on drying
3 a substance like a plant gum (as in stickiness)

³gum *vb* **gummed**; **gum•ming**
1 to smear, stick together, or clog with or as if with gum
2 to cause not to work properly ⟨*gum* up the works⟩

gum•bo \ˈgəm-ˌbō\ *n, pl* **gum•bos**
a rich soup usually thickened with okra

gum•drop \ˈgəm-ˌdräp\ *n*
▼ a candy usually made from corn syrup and gelatin

gumdrop: gumdrops in different colors

gum•my \ˈgə-mē\ *adj* **gum•mi•er**; **gum•mi•est**
consisting of or covered with gum or a sticky or chewy substance

gump•tion \ˈgəmp-shən\ *n*
COURAGE

¹gun \ˈgən\ *n*
1 a weapon that fires bullets or shells
2 CANNON

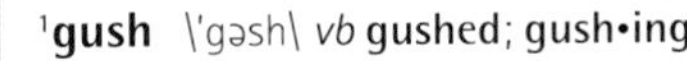

[1]gun 3: a glue gun used in construction work

3 ▲ something like a gun in shape or function ⟨a glue *gun*⟩
4 a discharge of a gun ⟨The runners waited for the *gun.*⟩

[2]gun *vb* **gunned**; **gun•ning**
to open the throttle of quickly so as to increase speed ⟨*gun* the engine⟩

gun•boat \'gən-,bōt\ *n*
a small armed ship for use near a coast

gun•fire \'gən-,fīr\ *n*
the firing of guns

gunk \'gəŋk\ *n*
a dirty, greasy, or sticky substance
gunky \'gəŋ-kē\ *adj*

gun•man \'gən-mən\ *n, pl* **gun•men** \-mən\
a criminal armed with a gun

gun•ner \'gə-nər\ *n*
a person who operates a gun

gun•nery \'gə-nə-rē\ *n*
the use of guns

gunnery sergeant *n*
a noncommissioned officer in the marines ranking above a staff sergeant

gun•pow•der \'gən-,paů-dər\ *n*
an explosive powder used in guns and blasting

gun•shot \'gən-,shät\ *n*
1 a shot from a gun
2 the distance that can be reached by a gun

gun•wale \'gə-nᵊl\ *n*
the upper edge of a ship's side

guppy

gup•py \'gə-pē\ *n, pl* **guppies**
▲ a small tropical fish often kept as an aquarium fish

[1]gur•gle \'gər-gəl\ *vb* **gur•gled**; **gur•gling**
1 to flow in a bubbling current ⟨a *gurgling* stream⟩
2 to sound like a liquid flowing with a bubbling current

[2]gurgle *n*
a sound of or like liquid flowing with a bubbling current

[1]gush \'gəsh\ *vb* **gushed**; **gush•ing**
1 to flow or pour out in large amounts ⟨Water *gushed* from the fountain.⟩
2 to act or speak in a very affectionate or enthusiastic way

[2]gush *n*
a sudden free pouring out ⟨a *gush* of tears⟩

gust \'gəst\ *n*
1 a sudden brief rush of wind
2 a sudden outburst ⟨a *gust* of laughter⟩

gusty \'gə-stē\ *adj* **gust•i•er**; **gust•i•est**
WINDY

[1]gut \'gət\ *n*
1 the inner parts of an animal ⟨a frog's *guts*⟩
2 a person's stomach : BELLY
3 the digestive tract or a part of it (as the intestine)
4 the inner parts ⟨the *guts* of the machine⟩
5 CATGUT
6 *guts pl* COURAGE

[2]gut *vb* **gut•ted**; **gut•ting**
1 to remove the inner organs from ⟨*gut* a fish⟩
2 to destroy the inside of ⟨Fire *gutted* the building.⟩

gut•ter \'gə-tər\ *n*
1 a trough along the eaves of a house to catch and carry off water
2 a low area (as at the side of a road) to carry off surface water

[1]guy \'gī\ *n*
1 [1]FELLOW 1
2 PERSON 1

► **Word History** In England, November 5 is celebrated as Guy Fawkes Day. The day is named after a man named Guy Fawkes who was arrested in London for having planted barrels of gunpowder under the houses of Parliament as part of a plot to blow up the buildings. The failure of this plot is still celebrated with bonfires and the burning of rag and straw images of Guy Fawkes. The rag and straw images came to be called *guys*. Later, the word *guy* was extended to similar images, and then to a person of strange appearance. In the United States, the word has come to mean simply "man," "fellow," or "person."

[2]guy *n*
a rope, chain, rod, or wire (**guy wire**) attached to something to steady it

guz•zle \'gə-zəl\ *vb* **guz•zled**; **guz•zling**
to drink greedily

gym \'jim\ *n*
GYMNASIUM

gym•na•si•um \jim-'nā-zē-əm\ *n*
▼ a room or building for sports events or exercise

gymnasium: a woman exercising in a gymnasium

gymnastics

Three main types of gymnastics are popular: rhythmic gymnastics, artistic gymnastics, and sports acrobatics. In rhythmic gymnastics, girls and women work with a small hand apparatus, such as a ball, hoop, or ribbon. Artistic gymnastics, for both sexes, involves work on an apparatus such as vaulting horse or a bar, as well as on the floor. Balance positions are a major part of sports acrobatics, in which both sexes take part.

gym•nast \'jim-,nast, -nəst\ *n*
a person who is skilled in gymnastics

gym•nas•tic \jim-'na-stik\ *adj*
of or relating to gymnastics

gym•nas•tics \jim-'na-stiks\ *n*
◀ physical exercises for developing skill, strength, and control in the use of the body or a sport in which such exercises are performed

Gyp•sy \'jip-sē\ *n, pl* **Gyp•sies**
sometimes offensive
a member of a group of people coming from India to Europe long ago and living a wandering way of life

▶ **Word History** Gypsies probably first reached England in the later 1400s. An early example of their language, which is called Romany, was taken down in 1547. The English thought that these strangers had come from Egypt and gave them the name *Egyptian.* In time the word was shortened and altered to *Gypsy.*

gypsy moth

gypsy moth *n*
▲ a moth whose caterpillar does great damage to trees by eating the leaves

gy•rate \'jī-,rāt\ *vb* **gy•rat•ed**; **gy•rat•ing**
to move back and forth with a circular motion ⟨The child made the top *gyrate.*⟩
gy•ra•tion \jī-'rā-shən\ *n*

gy•ro•scope \'jī-rə-,skōp\ *n*
▶ a wheel mounted to spin rapidly so that its axis is free to turn in various directions

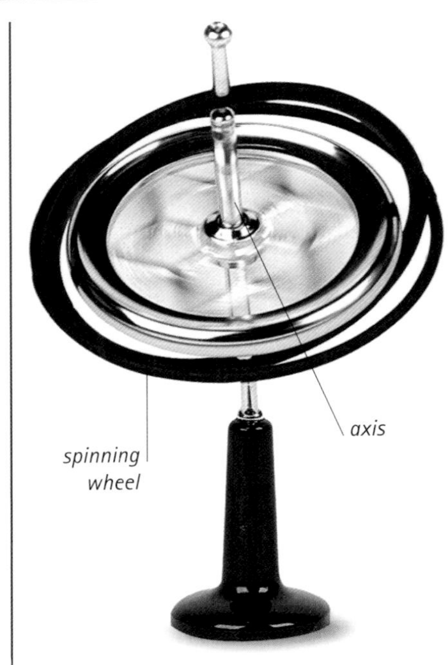

gyroscope

Sounds of H: The sound of the letter **H** is heard in ***hope*** and ***behave***. In some words, **H** is silent, such as in ***hour***, ***ghost***, ***rhyme***, and ***oh***. Letter **H** also combines with a number of other letters to make different sounds. **H** combines with **C** to make the sound heard in ***chat***, and with **G** to make the **F** sound heard in ***cough***. (**G** and **H** together are also sometimes silent, as in ***though***.) **H** also combines with **S** to make the sound heard in ***show***, with **T** to make the sounds heard in ***the*** and ***think***, and with **P** to make the **F** sound heard in ***photo***. **W** and **H** together, as in ***which***, can be pronounced in two ways. Some people pronounce it with a silent **H**, so that *which* sounds like "witch". Other people pronounce it with the **H** sound first, so that *which* is pronounced \'hwich\.

h \'āch\ *n, pl* **h's** *or* **hs** \'ā-chəz\ *often cap*
the eighth letter of the English alphabet

ha *or* **hah** \'hä\ *interj*
used to show surprise or joy

hab•it \'ha-bət\ *n*
1 usual way of behaving 〈We're studying the *habits* of wild birds.〉
2 ▼ clothing worn for a special purpose 〈a riding *habit*〉

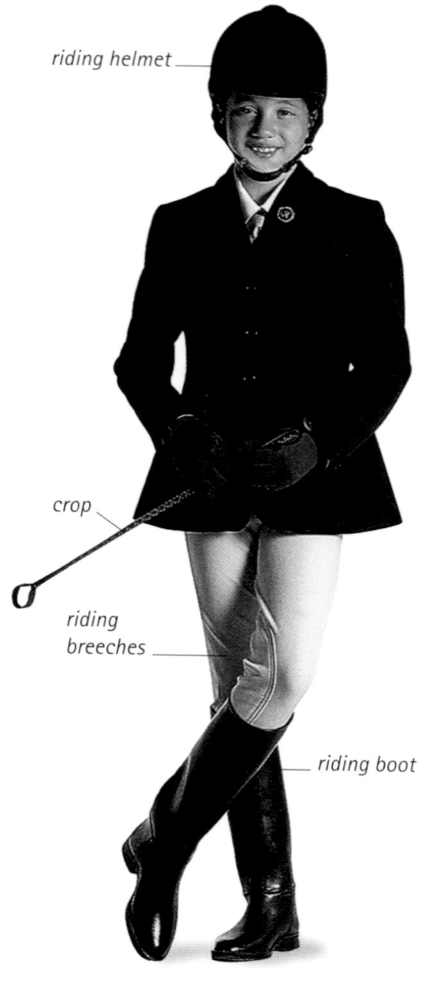

habit 2: a riding habit

3 a way of acting or doing that has become fixed by being repeated often
4 characteristic way of growing 〈These are trees of spreading *habit*.〉

hab•it•able \'ha-bə-tə-bəl\ *adj*
suitable or fit to live in 〈a *habitable* house〉

hab•i•tat \'ha-bə-ˌtat\ *n*
the place where a plant or animal grows or lives in nature

hab•i•ta•tion \ˌha-bə-'tā-shən\ *n*
1 the act of living in a place 〈The house is fit for *habitation*.〉
2 a place to live

ha•bit•u•al \hə-'bi-chə-wəl\ *adj*
1 occurring regularly or repeatedly : being or done by habit 〈*habitual* kindness〉
2 doing or acting by force of habit 〈*habitual* liars〉
3 REGULAR 1 〈Salad is my *habitual* lunch.〉
ha•bit•u•al•ly \-wə-lē\ *adv*

ha•ci•en•da \ˌhä-sē-'en-də\ *n*
a large estate especially in a Spanish-speaking country

[1]**hack** \'hak\ *vb* **hacked**; **hack•ing**
1 to cut with repeated chopping blows
2 to cough in a short broken way
3 to write computer programs for enjoyment
4 to gain access to a computer illegally

[2]**hack** *n*
a short broken cough

[3]**hack** *n*
1 a horse let out for hire or used for varied work
2 a person who works for pay at a routine writing job
3 a person who does work that is not good or original and especially a writer who is not very good

hack•er \'ha-kər\ *n*
1 HACK 3
2 an expert at programming and solving problems with a computer
3 a person who illegally gains access to a computer system

hack•les \'ha-kəlz\ *n pl*
hairs (as on the neck of a dog) that can be made to stand up

hack•ney \'hak-nē\ *n, pl* **hack•neys**
a horse for ordinary riding or driving

hack•saw \'hak-ˌsȯ\ *n*
▼ a saw with small teeth used for cutting hard materials (as metal)

hacksaw

had *past and past participle of* HAVE

had•dock \'ha-dək\ *n, pl* **haddock** *or* **haddocks**
▼ a fish of the northern Atlantic Ocean that is related to the cod and is often used for food

haddock

hadn't \'ha-dᵊnt\ had not

haf•ni•um \'haf-nē-əm\ *n*
a gray metallic chemical element

hag \'hag\ *n*
1 WITCH 1
2 an ugly old woman

hag•gard \'ha-gərd\ *adj*
having a hungry, tired, or worried look 〈a *haggard* face〉

hag•gle \'ha-gəl\ *vb* **hag•gled**; **hag•gling**
to argue especially over a price
hag•gler \'ha-glər\ *n*

hah *variant of* HA

ha–ha \hä-'hä\ *interj*
used to show amusement or scorn

hai•ku \'hī-,kü\ *n, pl* **haiku**
a Japanese poem or form of poetry without rhyme having three lines with the first and last lines having five syllables and the middle having seven

¹hail \'hāl\ *n*
1 small lumps of ice and snow that fall from the clouds sometimes during thunderstorms
2 ¹VOLLEY 1 ⟨a *hail* of bullets⟩

²hail *vb* **hailed**; **hail•ing**
1 to fall as hail ⟨It's *hailing* hard.⟩
2 to pour down like hail

³hail *vb* **hailed**; **hailing**
1 GREET 1, WELCOME
2 to call out to ⟨I'll *hail* a taxi.⟩
hail from to come from (a place)

hail•stone \'hāl-,stōn\ *n*
a lump of hail

hail•storm \'hāl-,stȯrm\ *n*
a storm that brings hail

hair \'her\ *n*
1 a threadlike growth from the skin of a person or animal ⟨She pulled out a *hair.*⟩
2 a covering or growth of hairs ⟨I got my *hair* cut.⟩
3 something (as a growth on a leaf) like an animal hair
4 a very small distance or amount ⟨I won by a *hair.*⟩
haired \'herd\ *adj*
hair•less \'her-ləs\ *adj*
hair•like \-,līk\ *adj*

hair•cut \'her-,kət\ *n*
the act, process, or result of cutting the hair

hair•do \'her-,dü\ *n, pl* **hairdos**
a way of arranging a person's hair

hair•dress•er \'her-,dre-sər\ *n*
▶ a person who styles or cuts hair
hair•dress•ing *n*

hair•pin \'her-,pin\ *n*
a pin in the shape of a U for holding the hair in place

hair–rais•ing \'her-,rā-ziŋ\ *adj*
causing terror, excitement, or great surprise

hair•style \'her-,stīl\ *n*
HAIRDO

hairy \'her-ē\ *adj* **hair•i•er**; **hair•i•est**
covered with hair
hair•i•ness *n*

ha•lal \hə-'läl\ *adj*
1 fit for eating under Islamic law ⟨*halal* meat⟩
2 selling or serving food fit for eating under Islamic law ⟨*halal* restaurants⟩

¹hale \'hāl\ *adj*
strong and healthy

²hale *vb* **haled**; **hal•ing**
to force to go ⟨The judge *haled* them into court.⟩

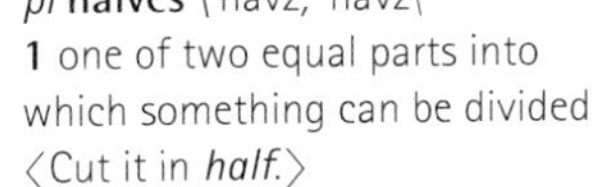

half-dollar 1

¹half \'haf, 'häf\ *n, pl* **halves** \'havz, 'hävz\
1 one of two equal parts into which something can be divided ⟨Cut it in *half.*⟩
2 a part of something that is about equal to the remainder ⟨*half* the distance⟩
3 one of a pair

²half *adj*
1 being one of two equal parts ⟨Add a *half* cup of milk.⟩
2 amounting to about a half ⟨a *half* smile⟩

³half *adv*
1 to the extent of half ⟨*half* full⟩
2 not completely ⟨She was *half* asleep.⟩

half•back \'haf-,bak, 'häf-\ *n*
1 a football player who runs with the ball and blocks
2 a player positioned behind the forward line in some games (as soccer)

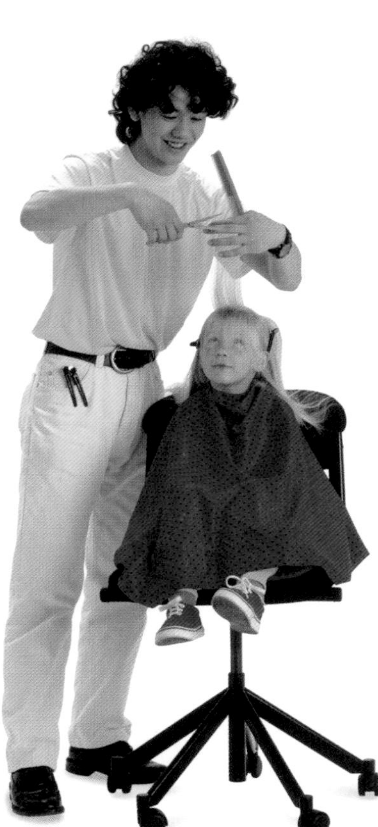
hairdresser: a hairdresser cutting hair

half brother *n*
a brother by one parent only

half–dol•lar \'haf-'dä-lər, 'häf-\ *n*
1 ◀ a coin representing 50 cents
2 the sum of 50 cents

half•heart•ed \'haf-'här-təd, 'häf-\ *adj*
lacking enthusiasm or interest ⟨There was only *halfhearted* applause.⟩
half•heart•ed•ly *adv*

half–knot \'haf-,nät, 'häf-\ *n*
▼ a knot in which two rope ends are wrapped once around each other and which is used to start other knots

half-knot

half–life \'haf-,līf, 'häf-\ *n, pl* **half–lives** \-,līvz\
the time required for half of the atoms of a radioactive substance to change composition

half sister *n*
a sister by one parent only

half•time \'haf-,tīm, 'häf-\ *n*
a period of rest between the halves of a game (as basketball)

¹half•way \'haf-'wā, 'häf-\ *adv*
at or to half the distance

²halfway *adj*
1 midway between two points ⟨Stop at the *halfway* mark.⟩
2 PARTIAL 1 ⟨a *halfway* attempt⟩

half–wit \'haf-,wit, 'häf-\ *n*
a very stupid person
half–wit•ted \-'wi-təd\ *adj*

hal•i•but \'ha-lə-bət\ *n, pl* **halibut** *or* **halibuts**
a very large saltwater flatfish often used for food

hall \'hȯl\ *n*
1 a passage in a building that leads to rooms : CORRIDOR
2 an entrance room
3 AUDITORIUM
4 a large building used for public purposes ⟨city *hall*⟩
5 a building or large room set apart for a special purpose

hal•le•lu•jah \,ha-lə-'lü-yə\ *interj*
used to express praise, joy, or thanks

hal•low \'ha-lō\ *vb* **hal•lowed**; **hal•low•ing**
to set apart for holy purposes : treat as sacred ⟨This ground is *hallowed.*⟩

Hal•low•een \ˌha-lə-ˈwēn, ˌhä-\ *n*
▼ October 31 celebrated especially by wearing costumes and trick-or-treating

► **Word History** In the Christian calendar the first day of November is All Saints' Day, which honors all the saints in heaven. The usual earlier name for this day in English was *All Hallows Day* or *All Hallow Day,* and the previous evening (October 31) was called *All Hallows Eve* or *All Hallow Even.* (The word *hallow,* related to *holy,* meant "saint.") In Scotland *All Hallow Even* was contracted to *Hallow-e'en,* now spelled *Halloween.*

hal•lu•ci•na•tion \hə-ˌlü-sə-ˈnā-shən\ *n*
the seeing of objects or the experiencing of feelings that are not real but are usually the result of mental disorder or the effect of a drug

hal•lu•ci•no•gen \hə-ˈlü-sə-nə-jən\ *n*
a drug that causes hallucinations
hal•lu•ci•no•gen•ic \hə-ˌlü-sə-nə-ˈje-nik\ *adj*

hall•way \ˈhȯl-ˌwā\ *n*
HALL 1, CORRIDOR

ha•lo \ˈhā-lō\ *n, pl* **halos** *or* **haloes**
1 a bright circle around the head of a person (as in a painting) that signifies holiness
2 a circle of light around the sun or moon caused by tiny ice crystals in the air

halter 1

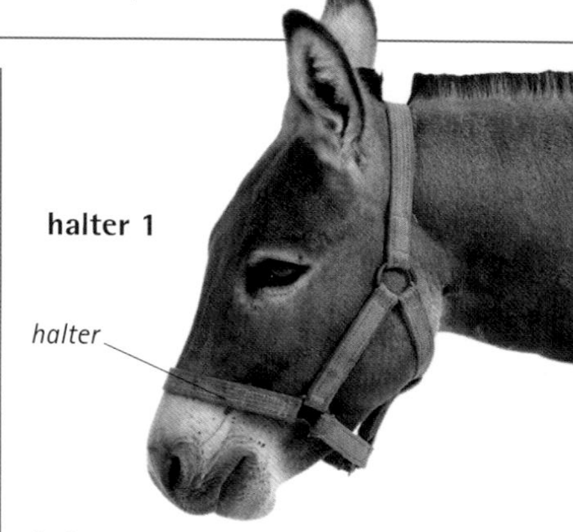

[1]**halt** \ˈhȯlt\ *vb* **halt•ed; halt•ing**
1 to stop or cause to stop marching or traveling
2 [2]END ⟨*halt* work⟩

► **Halloween**
The festival of Halloween is based on the old belief that ghosts and witches haunt the earth on the last night of October. Today, Halloween is often celebrated by dressing up in scary or fantastic costumes and masks. Children visit their neighbors' homes to play trick or treat, and jack-o'-lanterns are placed in windows, traditionally to keep away evil spirits.

monster

fairy princess

witch

cowboy

jack-o'-lantern

children wearing Halloween costumes

²halt *n*
¹END 2 ⟨Call a *halt* to the fighting.⟩

hal•ter \'hȯl-tər\ *n*
1 ◀ a set of straps placed around an animal's head so the animal can be led or tied
2 an article of clothing worn on a woman's upper body and held in place by straps around the neck and back

halve \'hav, 'häv\ *vb* **halved**; **halv•ing**
1 to divide into two equal parts ⟨I *halved* an apple.⟩
2 to reduce to one half ⟨He *halved* the recipe.⟩

halves *pl of* HALF

hal•yard \'hal-yərd\ *n*
a rope for raising or lowering a sail

ham \'ham\ *n*
1 a cut of meat consisting of a thigh of pork
2 an operator of an amateur radio station
3 a showy performer ⟨I know she likes attention, but what a *ham*!⟩

ham•burg•er \'ham-,bər-gər\ *or* **ham•burg** \-,bərg\ *n*
1 ▼ a sandwich made of a patty of ground beef in a split bun
2 ground beef

hamburger 1

ham•let \'ham-lət\ *n*
a small village

¹ham•mer \'ha-mər\ *n*
1 a tool consisting of a head fastened to a handle and used for pounding something (as a nail)
2 something like a hammer in shape or action ⟨an auctioneer's *hammer*⟩
3 ▶ a heavy metal ball with a flexible handle thrown for distance in a track-and-field contest (*hammer* throw)

²hammer *vb* **ham•mered**; **ham•mer•ing**
1 to strike with a hammer
2 to fasten or build (as by nailing) with a hammer ⟨*Hammer* the lid shut.⟩
3 to hit something hard and repeatedly ⟨She *hammered* on the door.⟩
4 to beat hard ⟨His heart *hammered*.⟩
hammer out to produce or bring about by persistent effort

ham•mer•head \'ha-mər-,hed\ *n*
a shark that has a wide flattened head with the eyes spaced widely apart

ham•mock \'ha-mək\ *n*
a swinging bed made of fabric or netting attached on either end to an upright object (as a tree)

¹ham•per \'ham-pər\ *vb* **ham•pered**; **ham•per•ing**
to keep from moving or acting freely ⟨Snow *hampered* traffic.⟩

²hamper *n*
a large basket usually with a cover ⟨a clothes *hamper*⟩

ham•ster \'ham-stər\ *n*
a stocky rodent with a short tail and large cheek pouches

¹hammer 3: a man participating in the hammer throw

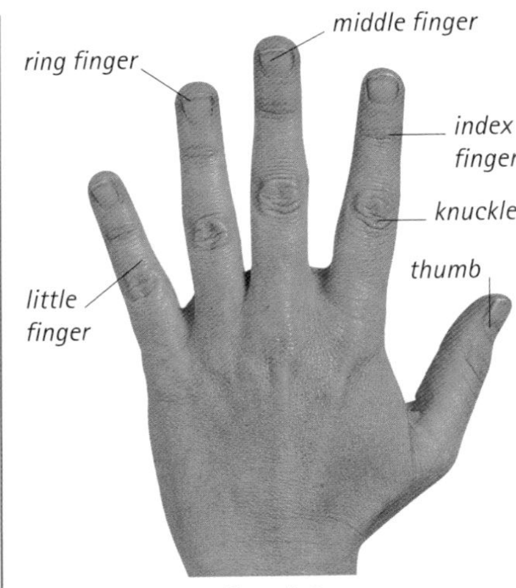

¹hand 1

¹hand \'hand\ *n*
1 ▲ the body part at the end of the human arm that includes the fingers and thumb
2 a bodily structure (as the hind foot of an ape) like the human hand in function or form
3 a pointer on a clock or watch
4 ²HELP 1, ASSISTANCE ⟨I gave her a *hand* loading the truck.⟩
5 ²CONTROL 1 ⟨The fort is in the *hands* of the enemy.⟩
6 one side of a problem ⟨On the one *hand* we could stay. On the other *hand* we could go.⟩
7 an outburst of applause ⟨Give them a *hand*.⟩
8 the cards held by a player in a card game
9 a hired worker **:** LABORER
10 a promise of marriage
11 HANDWRITING
12 ABILITY 1 ⟨I tried my *hand* at painting.⟩
13 a unit of measure equal to four inches (about ten centimeters) ⟨The horse is 15 *hands* high.⟩
14 a part or share in doing something ⟨She had a *hand* in the crime.⟩
at hand near in time or place ⟨The hour is *at hand*.⟩
by hand without the use of automation **:** using the hands
in hand in someone's possession or control ⟨Map *in hand*, he's ready to go.⟩ ⟨I've got the situation well *in hand*.⟩
on hand
1 available for use ⟨Keep some extra batteries *on hand*.⟩
2 ³PRESENT 2
out of hand out of control ⟨The party got *out of hand*.⟩

a b c d e f g h i j k l m n o p q r s t u v w x y z

²hand *vb* **hand•ed; hand•ing**
to give or pass with the hand

hand•bag \'hand-,bag\ *n*
a bag used for carrying money and small personal articles

hand•ball \'hand-,bȯl\ *n*
a game played by hitting a small ball against a wall or board with the hand

hand•bill \'hand-,bil\ *n*
a printed sheet (as of advertising) distributed by hand

hand•book \'hand-,bu̇k\ *n*
a book of facts usually about one subject

hand•car \'hand-,kär\ *n*
a small railroad car that is made to move by hand or by a small motor

¹hand•cuff \'hand-,kəf\ *n*
▶ a metal ring that can be locked around a person's wrist — usually used in pl.

²handcuff *vb* **hand•cuffed; hand•cuff•ing**
to put handcuffs on

hand•ed \'han-dəd\ *adj*
using a particular hand or number of hands ⟨left-*handed*⟩ ⟨a one-*handed* catch⟩

hand•ful \'hand-,fu̇l\ *n, pl* **handfuls** \-,fu̇lz\ *or* **hands•ful** \'handz-,fu̇l\
1 as much or as many as the hand will grasp
2 a small amount or number

¹hand•i•cap \'han-di-,kap\ *n*
1 a disadvantage that makes progress or success difficult
2 a contest in which someone more skilled is given a disadvantage and someone less skilled is given an advantage
3 the disadvantage or advantage given in a contest

▶ Word History *Handicap,* probably short for "hand in cap," was originally a sort of game in which two people would try to trade things of unequal value. A third person would be appointed as umpire to set an extra amount that would even out the value of the items. Some money would then be put in a cap, and the traders would signal agreement or disagreement with the bargain by putting their hands in the cap and taking them out full or empty. Later, horse races were arranged by such rules, with the umpire deciding how much extra weight the better horse should carry. The word *handicap* was eventually extended to other contests, and also came to mean the advantage or disadvantage given to a contestant.

handicap *vb* **hand•i•capped; hand•i•cap•ping**
to put at a disadvantage

hand•i•craft \'han-di-,kraft\ *n*
1 an activity or craft (as weaving or pottery making) that requires skill with the hands
2 ▶ an article made by skillful use of the hands

hand•i•ly \'han-də-lē\ *adv*
in a handy manner : EASILY ⟨Our team won *handily.*⟩

hand•i•work \'han-di-,wərk\ *n*
work done by the hands

hand•ker•chief \'hang-kər-chəf\ *n, pl* **hand•ker•chiefs** \-chəfs\
a small usually square piece of cloth used for wiping the face, nose, or eyes

¹handcuff

¹han•dle \'han-dəl\ *n*
the part by which something (as a dish or tool) is picked up or held
han•dled \-dəld\ *adj*

²handle *vb* **han•dled; han•dling**
1 to touch, feel, hold, or move with the hand
2 to manage or control especially with the hands ⟨He knows how to *handle* a motorcycle.⟩
3 MANAGE 1, DIRECT ⟨His wife *handles* the money.⟩
4 to deal with or act on
5 to deal or trade in ⟨This store *handles* electronics.⟩
6 to put up with ⟨I can't *handle* this heat.⟩
han•dler \'hand-lər\ *n*

han•dle•bars \'han-dəl-,bärz\ *n pl*
▼ a bar (as on a bicycle) that has a handle at each end and is used for steering

handlebars: handlebars on a bicycle

handicraft 2: woven handicrafts

hand•made \'hand-'mād\ *adj*
made by hand rather than by machine ⟨a *handmade* rug⟩

hand–me–downs \'hand-mē-,dau̇nz\ *n pl*
used clothes

hand•out \'hand-,au̇t\ *n*
something (as food, clothing, or money) given to a poor person

hand•rail \'hand-,rāl\ *n*
▼ a rail to be grasped by the hand for support

handrail: a staircase with a handrail

hands down \'handz-'dau̇n\ *adv*
without question : EASILY ⟨He won the race *hands down.*⟩

hand•shake \'hand-,shāk\ *n*
a clasping of hands by two people (as in greeting)

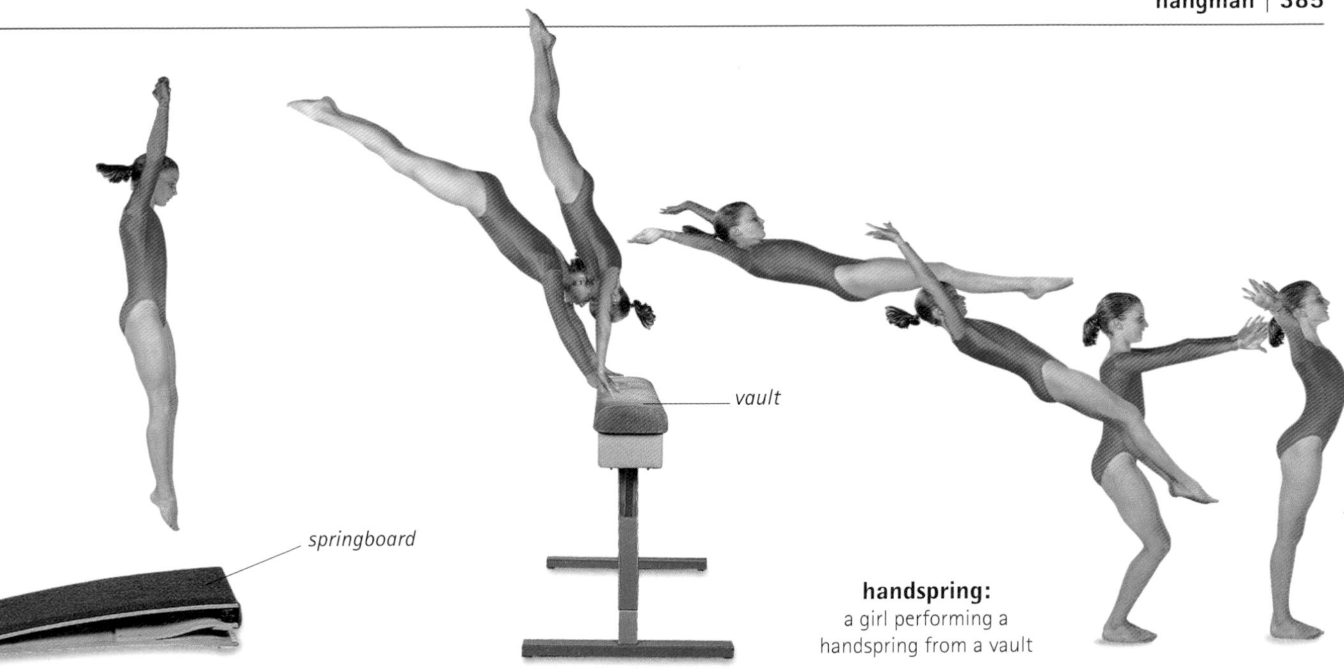

handspring: a girl performing a handspring from a vault

hand•some \'han-səm\ *adj* **hand•som•er; hand•som•est**
1 having a pleasing and impressive appearance ⟨a *handsome* dog⟩
2 CONSIDERABLE ⟨a *handsome* profit⟩
3 more than enough ⟨We left a *handsome* tip.⟩
synonyms see BEAUTIFUL
hand•some•ly *adv*

hand•spring \'hand-,spriŋ\ *n*
▲ a movement in which a person turns the body forward or backward in a full circle from a standing position and lands first on the hands and then on the feet

hand•stand \'hand-,stand\ *n*
an act of balancing on the hands with the body and legs straight up

hand–to–hand \,han-tə-'hand\ *adj*
involving bodily contact ⟨*hand-to-hand* combat⟩

hand•writ•ing \'hand-,rī-tiŋ\ *n*
a person's writing

handy \'han-dē\ *adj* **hand•i•er; hand•i•est**
1 very useful or helpful ⟨a *handy* tool⟩
2 within easy reach ⟨Keep a towel *handy.*⟩
3 clever or skillful especially with the hands

[1]**hang** \'haŋ\ *vb* **hung** \'həŋ\ *also* **hanged; hang•ing**
1 to fasten or be fastened to something without support from below ⟨I helped Mom *hang* curtains.⟩
2 to kill or be killed by suspending (as from a gallows) by a rope tied around the neck
3 to cause to droop ⟨The dog *hung* her head.⟩
hang around
1 to be or stay (somewhere) without doing much ⟨They like to *hang around* the mall.⟩
2 to pass time without doing much ⟨We *hung around* until dark.⟩
hang on
1 to hold or grip something tightly
2 to wait or stop briefly
3 to be determined or decided by ⟨The decision *hangs on* one vote.⟩
hang out to pass time without doing much
hang up
1 to place on a hook or hanger
2 to end a telephone connection

[2]**hang** *n*
1 the way in which a thing hangs ⟨The skirt has a graceful *hang.*⟩
2 skill to do something ⟨Skating was tricky, but I got the *hang* of it.⟩

han•gar \'haŋ-ər\ *n*
▼ a shelter for housing and repairing aircraft

hang•er \'haŋ-ər\ *n*
a device on which something hangs ⟨a clothes *hanger*⟩

hang•man \'haŋ-mən\ *n, pl* **hang•men** \-mən\
a person who hangs criminals

hangar

¹harbor 1: a harbor in Hawaii

hang•nail \'haŋ-,nāl\ *n*
a bit of skin hanging loose at the side or base of a fingernail

► **Word History** *Hangnail* is an alteration of an earlier word *angnail* (or *agnail*), which did not at first mean what we now call a hangnail. The Old English ancestor of the word was *angnægl*, "corn on the foot," with the second part, *nægl*, referring not to a toenail but rather to the nail we drive in with a hammer, the head of an iron nail being likened to a hard corn. By the 1500s the association of *-nail* with the body's nails led to a new sense for *angnail*, "sore around a fingernail or toenail." In the next century, *ang-* was altered to *hang-*, and the main sense came to be "bit of loose skin at the side or root of a fingernail."

hang•out \'haŋ-,aủt\ *n*
a favorite place for spending time

han•ker \'haŋ-kər\ *vb* **han•kered**; **han•ker•ing**
to have a great desire 〈I'm *hankering* for chocolate.〉

han•som \'han-səm\ *n*
a light covered carriage that has two wheels and a driver's seat elevated at the rear

Ha•nuk•kah *also* **Cha•nu•kah** \'hä-nə-kə\ *n*
a Jewish holiday lasting eight days in November or December and marked by the lighting of candles

hap•haz•ard \hap-'ha-zərd\ *adj*
marked by lack of plan, order, or direction 〈We took a *haphazard* route.〉
hap•haz•ard•ly *adv*

hap•less \'ha-pləs\ *adj*
UNFORTUNATE 1 〈The *hapless* runner tripped during the race.〉

hap•pen \'ha-pən\ *vb* **hap•pened**; **hap•pen•ing**
1 to take place 〈Stop crying and tell me what *happened*.〉
2 to occur or come about by chance 〈It just so *happens* I know them.〉
3 to do or be by chance 〈I *happened* to overhear this.〉
4 to come especially by way of injury or harm 〈Nothing will *happen* to you.〉

hap•pen•ing \'ha-pə-niŋ, 'hap-niŋ\ *n*
something that occurs 〈It was a week of strange *happenings*.〉

hap•py \'ha-pē\ *adj* **hap•pi•er**; **hap•pi•est**
1 feeling or showing pleasure : GLAD 〈I'm *happy* you came.〉
2 enjoying a condition or situation : CONTENT 〈They were *happy* together.〉
3 JOYFUL 〈She talked in a *happy* way.〉
4 FORTUNATE 1, LUCKY 〈Meeting him was a *happy* occurrence.〉
5 being suitable for something 〈a *happy* choice〉
hap•pi•ly \'ha-pə-lē\ *adv*
hap•pi•ness \'ha-pē-nəs\ *n*

hap•py–go–lucky \,ha-pē-gō-'lə-kē\ *adj*
free from care

ha•rangue \hə-'raŋ\ *n*
a scolding speech or writing

ha•rass \hə-'ras, 'her-əs\ *vb* **ha•rassed**; **ha•rass•ing**
1 to annoy again and again
2 to make repeated attacks against an enemy
ha•rass•ment \-mənt\ *n*

¹har•bor \'här-bər\ *n*
1 ◄ a part of a body of water (as a sea or lake) so protected as to be a place of safety for ships : PORT
2 a place of safety and comfort : REFUGE

²harbor *vb* **har•bored**; **har•bor•ing**
1 to give shelter to 〈They *harbored* the escaped prisoner.〉
2 to have or hold in the mind 〈For years she *harbored* the desire to travel.〉

¹hard \'härd\ *adj* **hard•er**; **hard•est**
1 not easily cut, pierced, or divided : not soft
2 difficult to do or to understand 〈a *hard* job〉 〈That book contains some *hard* words.〉
3 DILIGENT, ENERGETIC 〈I'm a *hard* worker.〉
4 difficult to put up with : SEVERE 〈a *hard* winter〉 〈a *hard* life〉
5 sounding as the letter *c* in *cold* and the letter *g* in *geese*
6 carried on with steady and earnest effort 〈hours of *hard* study〉
7 UNFEELING 〈He's a *hard* boss.〉
8 high in alcoholic content 〈*hard* drinks〉
9 containing substances that prevent lathering with soap 〈*hard* water〉
hard•ness \'härd-nəs\ *n*

► **Synonyms** HARD, FIRM, and SOLID mean having a structure that can stand up against pressure. HARD is used of something that does not easily bend, stretch, or dent. 〈Steel is *hard*.〉 FIRM is used of something that is flexible but also tough or compact. 〈Exercise makes *firm* muscles.〉 SOLID is used of something that has a fixed structure and is heavy and compact all the way through. 〈They built a *solid* wall of bricks.〉

²hard *adv* **hard•er**; **hard•est**
1 with great effort or energy 〈I ran as *hard* as I could.〉
2 in a forceful way 〈The wind blew *hard*.〉
3 with pain, bitterness, or resentment 〈She took the defeat *hard*.〉

hard copy *n*
a copy of information (as from computer storage) produced on paper in normal size ⟨I need a *hard copy* of the e-mail message.⟩

hard disk *n*
1 a rigid metal disk used to store computer data
2 HARD DRIVE

hard drive *n*
a data storage device of a computer containing one or more hard disks

hard•en \'här-dᵊn\ *vb* **hard•ened**; **hard•en•ing**
1 to make or become hard or harder ⟨By now the cement has *hardened.*⟩
2 to make or become hardy or strong
3 to make or become stubborn or unfeeling ⟨She *hardened* her heart and refused to forgive him.⟩

hard•head•ed \'härd-'he-dəd\ *adj*
1 STUBBORN 1
2 using or showing good judgment ⟨a *hardheaded* businessman⟩

hard•heart•ed \'härd-'här-təd\ *adj*
showing or feeling no pity : UNFEELING

hard•ly \'härd-lē\ *adv*
only just : BARELY

hard•ship \'härd-,ship\ *n*
something (as a loss or injury) that is hard to bear

hard•ware \'härd-,wer\ *n*
1 things (as tools, cutlery, or parts of machines) made of metal
2 equipment or parts used for a particular purpose ⟨The computer system needs *hardware* such as monitors and keyboards.⟩

hard•wood \'härd-,wu̇d\ *n*
1 the usually hard wood of a tree (as a maple or oak) with broad leaves as distinguished from the wood of a tree (as a pine) with leaves that are needles
2 a tree that produces hardwood

har•dy \'här-dē\ *adj* **har•di•er**; **har•di•est**
1 able to withstand weariness, hardship, or severe weather
2 BOLD 1, BRAVE ⟨*hardy* heroes⟩
har•di•ly \'här-də-lē\ *adv*
har•di•ness \'här-dē-nəs\ *n*

hare \'her\ *n*
a gnawing animal that resembles the related rabbit but is usually larger and tends to live by itself

hare•brained \'her-'brānd\ *adj*
FOOLISH

hark \'härk\ *vb* **harked**; **hark•ing**
LISTEN 1
hark back to recall or cause to recall something earlier

[1]harm \'härm\ *n*
physical or mental damage : INJURY ⟨The storm did little *harm* to the sheltered beach.⟩

► **Synonyms** HARM, INJURY, and DAMAGE mean an act that causes loss or pain. HARM can be used of anything that causes suffering or loss. ⟨The frost did great *harm* to the crops.⟩ INJURY is likely to be used of something that has as a result the loss of health or success. ⟨She suffered an *injury* to the eyes.⟩ DAMAGE stresses the idea of loss (as of value or fitness). ⟨The fire caused much *damage* to the furniture.⟩

[2]harm *vb* **harmed**; **harm•ing**
to cause hurt, injury, or damage to ⟨Too much sun can *harm* your skin.⟩

harm•ful \'härm-fəl\ *adj*
causing or capable of causing harm : INJURIOUS
harm•ful•ly \-fə-lē\ *adv*

harm•less \'härm-ləs\ *adj*
not harmful
harm•less•ly *adv*

harmonica

har•mon•i•ca \här-'mä-ni-kə\ *n*
▲ a small musical instrument held in the hand and played by the mouth

har•mo•ni•ous \här-'mō-nē-əs\ *adj*
1 showing agreement in action or feeling ⟨a *harmonious* family⟩
2 combining so as to produce a pleasing result ⟨*harmonious* colors⟩
3 having a pleasant sound : MELODIOUS ⟨*harmonious* voices⟩
har•mo•ni•ous•ly *adv*

har•mo•nize \'här-mə-,nīz\ *vb* **har•mo•nized**; **har•mo•niz•ing**
1 to play or sing in harmony
2 to go together in a pleasing way : be in harmony

har•mo•ny \'här-mə-nē\ *n*, *pl* **har•mo•nies**
1 the playing of musical tones together in chords
2 a pleasing arrangement of parts ⟨a *harmony* of colors⟩
3 AGREEMENT 1, ACCORD ⟨The committee worked in *harmony.*⟩

[1]har•ness \'här-nəs\ *n*
the straps and fastenings placed on an animal so it can be controlled or prepared to pull a load

[2]harness *vb* **har•nessed**; **har•ness•ing**
1 to put straps and fastenings on ⟨I *harnessed* the horses.⟩
2 to put to work : UTILIZE ⟨Wind can be *harnessed* to generate power.⟩

[1]harp \'härp\ *n*
▼ a musical instrument consisting of a triangular frame set with strings that are plucked by the fingers

[2]harp *vb* **harped**; **harp•ing**
to call attention to something over and over again ⟨The teacher *harped* on her mistake.⟩

[1]har•poon \här-'pün\ *n*
a barbed spear used especially for hunting whales and large fish

[2]harpoon *vb* **har•pooned**; **har•poon•ing**
to strike with a barbed spear

[1]harp

harp•si•chord \'härp-sə-ˌkȯrd\ *n*
▶ a keyboard instrument similar to a piano with strings that are plucked

[1]**har•row** \'her-ō\ *n*
a farming tool with metal teeth or disks for breaking up and smoothing soil

[2]**harrow** *vb* **har•rowed; har•row•ing**
1 to cultivate with a harrow
2 [2]DISTRESS

har•row•ing \'her-ə-wiŋ\ *adj*
very distressing or painful ⟨a *harrowing* experience⟩

har•ry \'her-ē\ *vb* **har•ried; har•ry•ing**
HARASS

harsh \'härsh\ *adj* **harsh•er; harsh•est**
1 causing physical discomfort ⟨a *harsh* climate⟩
2 having an unpleasant or harmful effect ⟨a *harsh* sound⟩ ⟨*harsh* colors⟩
3 severe or cruel ⟨*harsh* punishment⟩
harsh•ly *adv*
harsh•ness *n*

[1]**har•vest** \'här-vəst\ *n*
1 the gathering of a crop
2 the season when crops are gathered
3 a ripe crop

[2]**harvest** *vb* **har•vest•ed; har•vest•ing**
1 to gather in a crop
2 to gather or collect for use

har•vest•er \'här-və-stər\ *n*
1 a person who gathers crops or other natural products ⟨oyster *harvesters*⟩
2 ▶ a machine for harvesting field crops

has *present third person sing of* HAVE

[1]**hash** \'hash\ *n*
1 cooked meat and vegetables chopped together and browned
2 [1]MESS 1 ⟨He made a *hash* of the project.⟩

harpsichord

hasp

harvester 2: a harvester in a wheat field

[2]**hash** *vb* **hashed; hash•ing**
1 to talk about : DISCUSS —used with *over* or *out* ⟨Let's *hash* out this problem.⟩
2 to chop into small pieces

hash•tag \'hash-ˌtag\ *n*
a word or phrase that starts with the symbol # and that briefly indicates what a message (such as a tweet) is about

hasn't \'ha-zᵊnt\ has not

hasp \'hasp\ *n*
▼ a fastener (as for a door) consisting of a hinged metal strap that fits over a metal loop and is held by a pin or padlock

[1]**has•sle** \'ha-səl\ *n*
1 something that annoys or bothers
2 an argument or fight

[2]**hassle** *vb* **has•sled; has•sling**
to annoy continuously : HARASS

has•sock \'ha-sək\ *n*
a firm stuffed cushion used as a seat or leg rest

haste \'hāst\ *n*
1 quickness of motion or action : SPEED ⟨He left in *haste*.⟩
2 hasty action ⟨*Haste* makes waste.⟩

has•ten \'hā-sᵊn\ *vb* **has•tened; has•ten•ing**
to move or cause to move or act fast : HURRY ⟨I *hastened* to the exit.⟩

hasty \'hā-stē\ *adj* **hast•i•er; hast•i•est**
1 done or made in a hurry ⟨a *hasty* trip⟩
2 made, done, or decided without proper care and thought ⟨a *hasty* decision⟩
hast•i•ly \-stə-lē\ *adv*

hat \'hat\ *n*
a covering for the head having a crown and usually a brim

[1]hatch \'hach\ *n*
1 an opening in the deck of a ship or in the floor or roof of a building
2 a small door or opening (as in an airplane) ⟨an escape *hatch*⟩
3 the cover for such an opening

[2]hatch *vb* **hatched**; **hatch•ing**
1 to come out of an egg ⟨The chicks were *hatching.*⟩
2 to break open and give forth young ⟨The eggs will soon *hatch.*⟩
3 to develop usually in secret ⟨They *hatched* an evil plan.⟩

hatch•ery \'ha-chə-rē\ *n, pl* **hatch•er•ies**
a place for hatching eggs ⟨a fish *hatchery*⟩

hatch•et \'ha-chət\ *n*
▼ a small ax with a short handle

hatchet

hatch•way \'hach-,wā\ *n*
a hatch usually having a ladder or stairs

[1]hate \'hāt\ *n*
deep and bitter dislike

[2]hate *vb* **hat•ed**; **hat•ing**
to feel great dislike toward
hate someone's guts to hate someone very much

hate•ful \'hāt-fəl\ *adj*
1 full of hate
2 very bad or evil : causing or deserving hate ⟨a *hateful* crime⟩

ha•tred \'hā-trəd\ *n*
[1]HATE

hat•ter \'ha-tər\ *n*
a person who makes, sells, or cleans and repairs hats

haugh•ty \'hȯ-tē\ *adj* **haugh•ti•er**; **haugh•ti•est**
having or showing a proud and superior attitude ⟨a *haughty* princess⟩
haugh•ti•ly \'hȯ-tə-lē\ *adv*
haugh•ti•ness \'hȯ-tē-nəs\ *n*

[1]haul \'hȯl\ *vb* **hauled**; **haul•ing**
1 to pull or drag with effort
2 to transport in a vehicle ⟨*haul* freight⟩

[2]haul *n*
1 the act of pulling or hauling ⟨They got closer with each *haul.*⟩
2 an amount collected ⟨a burglar's *haul*⟩
3 the distance or route traveled or over which a load is moved ⟨It's a long *haul* to the beach.⟩

haunch \'hȯnch\ *n*
1 HINDQUARTER ⟨The dog sat on its *haunches.*⟩
2 the upper part of a person's thigh together with the back part of the hip

[1]haunt \'hȯnt\ *vb* **haunt•ed**; **haunt•ing**
1 to visit or live in as a ghost ⟨Spirits *haunt* the house.⟩
2 to visit often
3 to come to mind frequently ⟨The song *haunts* me.⟩

[2]haunt *n*
a place often visited

have \'hav, həv, əv, *in sense 3 before "to" usually* 'haf\ *vb, past & past participle* **had** \'had, həd, əd\; *present participle* **hav•ing** \'ha-viŋ\; *present third person sing* **has** \'has, həz, əz\
1 to hold or own ⟨I *have* the tickets.⟩
2 to possess as a characteristic ⟨She *has* red hair.⟩
3 to eat or drink ⟨Let's *have* dinner.⟩ ⟨I *had* some water.⟩
4 to consist of or contain ⟨April *has* 30 days.⟩
5 to be affected by ⟨I *have* a cold.⟩
6 to plan, organize, and run (an event) ⟨We're *having* a party.⟩
7 to give birth to ⟨She *had* twins.⟩
8 to cause to be ⟨How often do you *have* your hair cut?⟩
9 to stand in some relationship to ⟨I *have* many friends.⟩
10 to perform a function or engage in an activity ⟨He *had* a fight with his best friend.⟩
11 EXPERIENCE ⟨I *had* fun.⟩
12 to hold in the mind ⟨I *have* an idea.⟩
13 OBTAIN, GAIN, GET ⟨It's the best car to be *had.*⟩
14 to cause to ⟨I'll *have* them call you.⟩
15 [1]PERMIT 1 ⟨We'll *have* none of that.⟩
16 [2]TRICK ⟨We've been *had.*⟩
17 used as a helping verb with the past participle of another verb ⟨My friend *has* gone home.⟩
18 to be forced or feel obliged ⟨They *have* to stay.⟩
19 [2]EXERCISE 1, USE ⟨*have* mercy⟩
had better *or* **had best** would be wise to ⟨You *had better* finish your homework.⟩
have to do with
1 to be about ⟨That book *has to do with* trucks.⟩
2 to be involved in or responsible for ⟨Luck *had* nothing *to do with* her success.⟩

ha•ven \'hā-vən\ *n*
a safe place

haven't \'ha-vənt\ have not

hav•er•sack \'ha-vər-,sak\ *n*
a bag worn over one shoulder for carrying supplies

hav•oc \'ha-vək\ *n*
1 wide destruction ⟨The storm wreaked *havoc.*⟩
2 great confusion and lack of order

Ha•wai•ian \hə-'wä-yən\ *n*
1 a person born or living in Hawaii
2 the language of the Hawaiians

[1]hawk \'hȯk\ *n*
▼ a bird of prey that has a strong hooked bill and sharp curved claws and is smaller than most eagles

[1]hawk: a Harris's Hawk

[2]hawk *vb* **hawked**; **hawk•ing**
to offer for sale by calling out ⟨*hawk* newspapers⟩
hawk•er *n*

[3]hawk *vb* **hawked**; **hawking**
to make a harsh coughing sound in clearing the throat

haw•ser \'hȯ-zər\ *n*
a large rope for towing or tying up a ship

haw•thorn \'hȯ-,thȯrn\ *n*
▼ a thorny shrub or small tree with shiny leaves, white, pink, or red flowers, and small red fruits

hawthorn: flowers from a hawthorn

[1]hay \'hā\ *n*
any of various herbs (as grasses) cut and dried for use as food for animals ⟨bales of *hay*⟩

[2]hay *vb* **hayed**; **hay•ing**
to cut plants for hay

hay fever *n*
an allergy to pollen that is usually marked by sneezing, a runny or stuffed nose, and itchy and watering eyes

hay•loft \'hā-,lȯft\ *n*
a loft in a barn or stable for storing hay

hay•mow \'hā-,mau̇\ *n*
HAYLOFT

hay•stack \'hā-,stak\ *n*
a large pile of hay stored outdoors

hay•wire \'hā-,wīr\ *adj*
1 working badly or in an odd way ⟨The TV went *haywire*.⟩
2 emotionally or mentally out of control : CRAZY ⟨After losing, she went *haywire*.⟩

[1]haz•ard \'ha-zərd\ *n*
a source of danger ⟨a fire *hazard*⟩
synonyms see DANGER

▶ **Word History** English *hazard* was originally the name of a game of chance played with dice. The English word was taken from a medieval French word *hasard*, which in turn came by way of Spanish from an Arabic phrase *az zahr*, "the die" (that is, "one of the dice").

[2]hazard *vb* **haz•ard•ed**; **haz•ard•ing**
to offer something (such as a guess or an opinion) at the risk of being wrong

haz•ard•ous \'ha-zər-dəs\ *adj*
DANGEROUS 1

haze \'hāz\ *n*
fine dust, smoke, or fine particles of water in the air

ha•zel \'hā-zəl\ *n*
1 a shrub or small tree that bears an edible nut
2 a color that combines light brown with green and gray ⟨*hazel* eyes⟩

ha•zel•nut \'hā-zəl-,nət\ *n*
the nut of a hazel

hazy \'hā-zē\ *adj* **haz•i•er**; **haz•i•est**
1 partly hidden or darkened by dust, smoke, or fine particles of water in the air
2 not clear in thought or meaning : VAGUE ⟨a *hazy* memory⟩

H–bomb \'āch-,bäm\ *n*
HYDROGEN BOMB

he \'hē, ē\ *pron*
1 that male one ⟨Ask your brother if *he* wants to go.⟩
2 that person or one
Hint: This sense is used in a general way when the sex of the person is unknown. ⟨Tell whoever is yelling that *he* should stop.⟩

[1]head \'hed\ *n*
1 the part of the body containing the brain, eyes, ears, nose, and mouth
2 [1]MIND 1 ⟨Mom has a good *head* for figures.⟩
3 control of the mind or feelings ⟨He kept his *head* during the emergency.⟩
4 the side of a coin or medal usually thought of as the front
5 DIRECTOR 1, LEADER
6 each person among a number ⟨Count *heads* to make sure everyone is here.⟩
7 *pl* **head** a unit of number ⟨They own 100 *head* of cattle.⟩
8 something like a head in position or use ⟨the *head* of a bed⟩
9 the place where a stream begins
10 a tight mass of plant parts (as leaves or flowers) ⟨a *head* of cabbage⟩
11 a part of a machine, tool, or weapon that performs the main work ⟨*head* of a spear⟩ ⟨shower *head*⟩
12 a place of leadership or honor ⟨He is at the *head* of his class.⟩
13 CLIMAX, CRISIS ⟨Events came to a *head*.⟩
over someone's head beyond someone's understanding

[2]head *adj*
1 [2]CHIEF 1 ⟨He's the *head* coach.⟩
2 located at the front ⟨We sat at the *head* table.⟩
3 coming from in front ⟨We sailed into a *head* wind.⟩

[3]head *vb* **head•ed**; **head•ing**
1 to be the leader of ⟨She *headed* the investigation.⟩
2 to go or cause to go in a certain direction ⟨Let's *head* for home.⟩
3 to be first or get in front of ⟨He *heads* the list of candidates.⟩
4 to provide with or form a head ⟨This cabbage *heads* early.⟩

head•ache \'hed-,āk\ *n*
1 pain in the head
2 something that annoys or confuses ⟨This traffic is a real *headache*.⟩

head•band \'hed-,band\ *n*
a band worn on or around the head

head•board \'hed-,bȯrd\ *n*
a vertical board at the head of a bed

head•dress \'hed-,dres\ *n*
a covering or ornament for the head

head•ed \'he-dəd\ *adj*
having such a head or so many heads ⟨bald-*headed*⟩ ⟨a two-*headed* ax⟩

head•first \'hed-'fərst\ *adv*
with the head in front ⟨He fell *headfirst* down the stairs.⟩

head•gear \'hed-,gir\ *n*
something worn on the head

head•ing \'he-diŋ\ *n*
something (as a title or an address) at the top or beginning (as of a letter)

head•land \'hed-lənd\ *n*
▶ a point of high land sticking out into the sea

head•light \'hed-,līt\ *n*
a light at the front of a vehicle

head•line \'hed-,līn\ *n*
a title of an article in a newspaper

[1]head•long \'hed-'lȯŋ\ *adv*
1 HEADFIRST ⟨The boys dove *headlong* into a pile of leaves.⟩
2 without waiting to think things through ⟨Don't rush *headlong* into marriage.⟩

[2]headlong \'hed-,lȯŋ\ *adj*
1 [1]RASH, IMPULSIVE
2 plunging headfirst ⟨He made a *headlong* run for the exit.⟩

head•mas•ter \'hed-,ma-stər\ *n*
a man who heads the staff of a private school

head•mis•tress \'hed-,mi-strəs\ *n*
a woman who heads the staff of a private school

head–on \'hed-'ȯn, -'än\ *adv or adj*
with the front hitting or facing an object ⟨She ran *head-on* into a tree.⟩

head•phone \'hed-,fōn\ *n*
▶ an earphone held over the ear by a band worn on the head

head•quar•ters \'hed-,kwȯr-tərz\ *n pl*
a place from which something is controlled or directed
Hint: *Headquarters* can be used as a singular or a plural in writing and speaking. ⟨Company *headquarters* is in Chicago.⟩ ⟨Where are the campaign *headquarters*?⟩

head•stall \'hed-,stȯl\ *n*
an arrangement of straps or rope that fits around the head of an animal and forms part of a bridle or halter

head•stand \'hed-,stand\ *n*
the act of standing on the head with support from the hands

head start *n*
an advantage given at the beginning (as to a school child or a runner)

head•stone \'hed-,stōn\ *n*
a stone that marks a grave

head•strong \'hed-,strȯŋ\ *adj*
very stubborn

head•wait•er \'hed-'wā-tər\ *n*
the head of the staff of a restaurant

head•wa•ters \'hed-,wȯ-tərz, -,wä-\ *n pl*
the beginning and upper part of a stream

headphones

head•way \'hed-,wā\ *n*
1 movement in a forward direction (as of a ship)
2 [1]PROGRESS 2

heal \'hēl\ *vb* **healed**; **heal•ing**
to make or become healthy or well again ⟨The cut *healed* slowly.⟩
heal•er *n*

health \'helth\ *n*
1 the condition of being free from illness or disease
2 the overall condition of the body ⟨He is in good *health*.⟩

health•ful \'helth-fəl\ *adj*
good for the health

healthy \'hel-thē\ *adj* **health•i•er**; **health•i•est**
1 being sound and well : not sick
2 showing good health ⟨a *healthy* complexion⟩
3 aiding or building up health ⟨*healthy* exercise⟩
4 rather large in extent or amount ⟨They made a *healthy* profit.⟩
health•i•ly \-thə-lē\ *adv*

[1]heap \'hēp\ *n*
1 a large messy pile ⟨His dirty clothes were in a *heap*.⟩
2 a large number or amount ⟨We had *heaps* of fun.⟩

[2]heap *vb* **heaped**; **heap•ing**
1 to make into a pile : throw or lay in a heap
2 to provide in large amounts ⟨Praise was *heaped* on the cook.⟩
3 to fill to capacity ⟨He *heaped* a plate with food.⟩

hear \'hir\ *vb* **heard** \'hərd\; **hear•ing** \'hir-iŋ\
1 to take in through the ear ⟨I *hear* laughter.⟩
2 to have the power of hearing ⟨He doesn't *hear* well.⟩
3 to gain knowledge of by hearing ⟨I *hear* he's moving to another state.⟩
4 to listen to with care and attention ⟨Wait till you *hear* both sides of the story.⟩
hear•er \'hir-ər\ *n*

headland: a headland jutting out into the sea at Cape Promthep in Phuket, Thailand

A B C D E F G H I J K L M N O P Q R S T U V W X Y Z

hear•ing \ˈhir-iŋ\ *n*
1 the act or power of taking in sound through the ear : the sense by which a person hears
2 EARSHOT ⟨I yelled, but he was out of *hearing.*⟩
3 a chance to be heard or known ⟨Give both sides a fair *hearing.*⟩
4 a meeting at which arguments or testimony is heard ⟨a court *hearing*⟩

hearing aid *n*
▼ an electronic device worn in or behind the ear of a person with poor hearing to make sounds louder

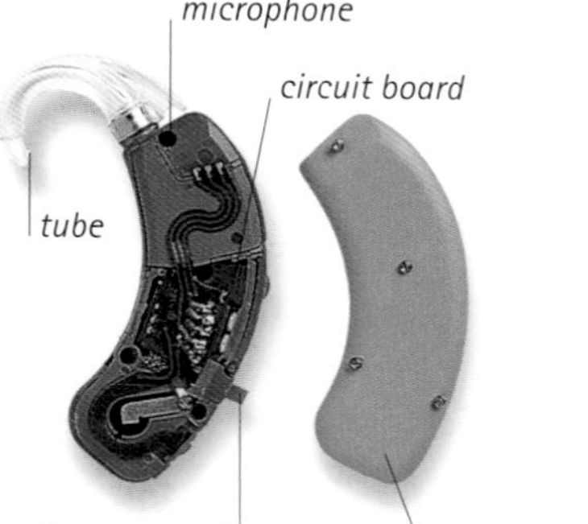

hearing aid: a hearing aid worn behind the ear

hear•ken \ˈhär-kən\ *vb* **hear•kened**; **hear•ken•ing**
LISTEN 1

hear•say \ˈhir-ˌsā\ *n*
something heard from another : RUMOR

hearse \ˈhərs\ *n*
a vehicle for carrying a dead person to the grave

heart \ˈhärt\ *n*
1 ▶ a hollow muscular organ of the body that expands and contracts to move blood through the arteries and veins
2 something shaped like a heart ⟨a Valentine's *heart*⟩
3 a part near the center or deep into the interior ⟨They reached the *heart* of the desert.⟩
4 the most essential part ⟨That's the *heart* of the problem.⟩
5 human feelings ⟨Speak from your *heart.*⟩
6 courage or enthusiasm ⟨I don't have the *heart* to tell them what happened.⟩
by heart so as to be able to repeat from memory

heart•ache \ˈhärt-ˌāk\ *n*
[1]SORROW 1

heart•beat \ˈhärt-ˌbēt\ *n*
a single contracting and expanding of the heart

hearth 2: logs on a hearth

heart•break \ˈhärt-ˌbrāk\ *n*
very great or deep grief

heart•break•ing \ˈhärt-ˌbrā-kiŋ\ *adj*
causing great sorrow

heart•bro•ken \ˈhärt-ˌbrō-kən\ *adj*
overcome by sorrow

heart•en \ˈhär-tᵊn\ *vb* **heart•ened**; **heart•en•ing**
to give new hope or courage to

heart•felt \ˈhärt-ˌfelt\ *adj*
deeply felt : SINCERE ⟨I gave her a *heartfelt* apology.⟩

hearth \ˈhärth\ *n*
1 an area (as of brick) in front of a fireplace
2 ◀ the floor of a fireplace

hearth•stone \ˈhärth-ˌstōn\ *n*
a stone forming a hearth

heart•i•ly \ˈhär-tə-lē\ *adv*
1 with sincerity or enthusiasm ⟨I agree *heartily.*⟩
2 COMPLETELY ⟨I am *heartily* sick of this arguing.⟩

heart•less \ˈhärt-ləs\ *adj*
UNFEELING, CRUEL

heart•sick \ˈhärt-ˌsik\ *adj*
very sad

heart•wood \ˈhärt-ˌwu̇d\ *n*
the usually dark wood in the center of a tree

hearty \ˈhär-tē\ *adj* **heart•i•er**; **heart•i•est**
1 friendly and enthusiastic ⟨a *hearty* welcome⟩

▶ **heart 1**
A hollow muscle in the middle of the chest, the heart acts as a pump that beats rhythmically to send blood around the body. It is divided lengthways by a muscular wall, and each side is separated by a valve into an upper atrium and lower ventricle. Blood is squeezed through the upper chambers and ventricles when the heart muscle contracts.

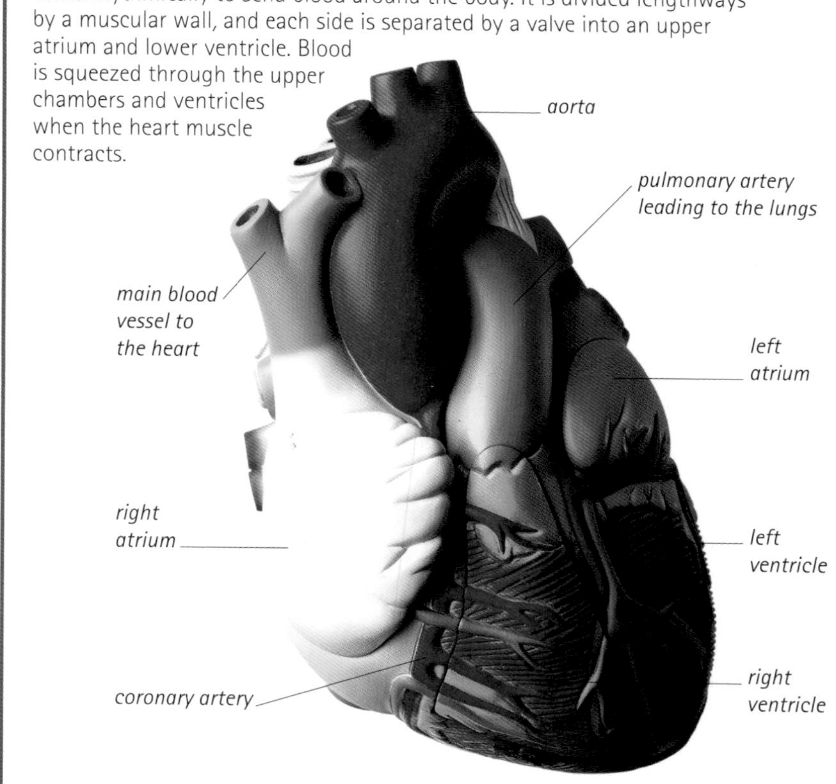

model of the human heart

2 strong, healthy, and active ⟨*hearty* young men⟩
3 having a good appetite ⟨*hearty* eaters⟩
4 large and plentiful ⟨a *hearty* meal⟩
heart•i•ness *n*

[1]**heat** \'hēt\ *vb* **heat•ed**; **heat•ing**
to make or become warm or hot

[2]**heat** *n*
1 a condition of being hot : WARMTH ⟨We enjoyed the *heat* of the fire.⟩
2 hot weather ⟨*heat* and humidity⟩
3 a form of energy that causes an object to rise in temperature
4 strength of feeling or force of action ⟨In the *heat* of anger, I said some cruel things.⟩
5 a single race in a contest that includes two or more races

heather

heat•ed \'hē-təd\ *adj*
1 HOT 1 ⟨*heated* water⟩
2 ANGRY ⟨*heated* words⟩
heat•ed•ly *adv*

heat•er \'hē-tər\ *n*
a device for heating

heath \'hēth\ *n*
1 a low, woody, and often evergreen plant that grows chiefly on poor wet soil
2 a usually open level area of land on which heaths can grow

[1]**hea•then** \'hē-t͟hən\ *adj*
1 relating to people who do not know about and worship the God of the Bible
2 not civilized

[2]**heathen** *n, pl* **heathens** *or* **heathen**
1 a person who does not know about and worship the God of the Bible : PAGAN
2 an uncivilized person

heath•er \'he-t͟hər\ *n*
▲ an evergreen heath of northern and mountainous areas with pink flowers and needlelike leaves

[1]**heave** \'hēv\ *vb* **heaved** *or* **hove** \'hōv\; **heav•ing**
1 to raise with an effort ⟨Help me *heave* this box onto the truck.⟩
2 HURL, THROW ⟨He *heaved* rocks into the water.⟩
3 to utter with an effort ⟨She *heaved* a sigh of relief.⟩
4 to rise and fall again and again ⟨The runner's chest was *heaving*.⟩
5 to be thrown or raised up ⟨Frost caused the ground to *heave*.⟩

[2]**heave** *n*
1 an effort to lift or raise
2 a forceful throw
3 an upward motion (as of the chest in breathing or of waves in motion)

heav•en \'he-vən\ *n*
1 SKY 1 — usually used in pl. ⟨stars in the *heavens*⟩
2 *often cap* a place where good people are believed in some religions to be rewarded with eternal life after death
3 *cap* GOD 1 ⟨Thank *Heaven* you're all right.⟩
4 a place or condition of complete happiness

heav•en•ly \'he-vən-lē\ *adj*
1 occurring or situated in the sky ⟨The sun, moon, and stars are *heavenly* bodies.⟩
2 [1]DIVINE 1 ⟨*heavenly* angels⟩
3 entirely delightful ⟨*heavenly* weather⟩

heavi•ly \'he-və-lē\ *adv*
1 with or as if with weight ⟨Bear down *heavily* on your pen.⟩
2 in a slow and difficult way ⟨He's breathing *heavily*.⟩
3 very much ⟨The house was *heavily* damaged.⟩

heavy \'he-vē\ *adj* **heavi•er**; **heavi•est**
1 having great weight
2 unusually great in amount, force, or effect ⟨*heavy* rain⟩ ⟨*heavy* sleep⟩ ⟨*heavy* damage⟩
3 made with thick strong material ⟨*heavy* rope⟩
4 dense and thick ⟨*heavy* eyebrows⟩
5 hard to put up with ⟨a *heavy* responsibility⟩
6 sad or troubled ⟨It's with a *heavy* heart that I leave you.⟩
7 having little strength or energy ⟨My legs grew *heavier* with every step.⟩
heavi•ness *n*

[1]**He•brew** \'hē-brü\ *adj*
of or relating to the Hebrew peoples or the Hebrew language

[2]**Hebrew** *n*
1 a member of any of a group of peoples of the ancient kingdom of Israel descended from Jacob of the Bible
2 ▼ the language of the ancient Hebrews or a later form of it

[2]**Hebrew 2:**
a traditional Jewish scroll with Hebrew script

¹hedge: a hedge in front of a house

hec•tic \ˈhek-tik\ *adj*
filled with excitement, activity, or confusion ⟨We had a *hectic* day of shopping.⟩

hecto- *prefix*
hundred ⟨*hecto*meter⟩

hec•to•me•ter \ˈhek-tə-ˌmē-tər\ *n*
a unit of length in the metric system equal to 100 meters

he'd \ˈhēd, ēd\
he had : he would

¹hedge \ˈhej\ *n*
▲ a fence or boundary made up of a thick growth of shrubs or low trees

²hedge *vb* **hedged**; **hedg•ing**
1 to surround or protect with a thick growth of shrubs or low trees ⟨The yard is *hedged* by shrubs.⟩
2 to avoid giving a direct or exact answer or promise

hedge•hog \ˈhej-ˌhȯg, -ˌhäg\ *n*
1 ▼ a mammal of Europe, Asia, and Africa that eats insects, has sharp spines mixed with the hair on its back, and is able to roll itself up into a ball when threatened
2 PORCUPINE

hedgehog 1

hedge•row \ˈhej-ˌrō\ *n*
a row of shrubs or trees around a field

¹heed \ˈhēd\ *vb* **heed•ed**; **heed•ing**
to pay attention to : MIND ⟨*Heed* my warning.⟩

²heed *n*
ATTENTION 1 ⟨pay *heed* to a warning⟩
heed•ful *adj*

heed•less \ˈhēd-ləs\ *adj*
not careful or attentive : CARELESS
heed•less•ly *adv*

¹heel \ˈhēl\ *n*
1 the back part of the human foot behind the arch and below the ankle
2 the part of an animal's limb corresponding to a person's heel
3 ▼ a part (as of a stocking or shoe) that covers or supports the human heel
4 one of the crusty ends of a loaf of bread
5 a rear, low, or bottom part
6 a mean selfish person

²heel *vb* **heeled**; **heel•ing**
to lean to one side ⟨The boat was *heeling* in the wind.⟩

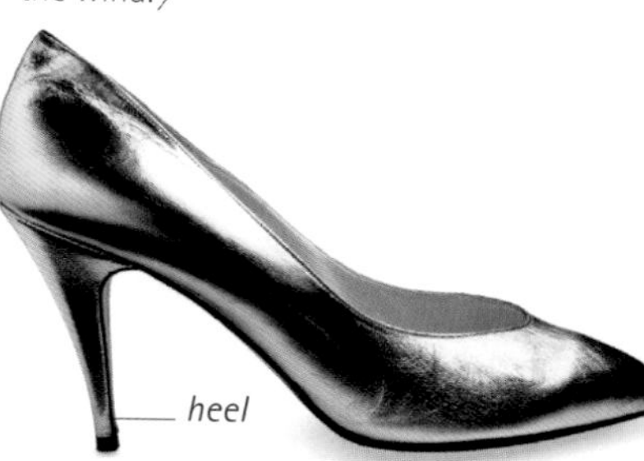

¹heel 3: heel of a shoe

heft \ˈheft\ *vb* **heft•ed**; **heft•ing**
to lift something up ⟨She *hefted* her suitcase onto the train.⟩

hefty \ˈhef-tē\ *adj* **heft•i•er**; **heft•i•est**
1 HEAVY 1
2 very forceful ⟨He opened the door with a *hefty* shove.⟩

heif•er \ˈhe-fər\ *n*
▶ a young cow

height \ˈhīt\ *n*
1 the distance from the bottom to the top of something standing upright
2 distance upward
3 the highest point or greatest degree ⟨She was at the *height* of her career.⟩

▶ **Synonyms** HEIGHT, ALTITUDE, and ELEVATION mean distance upward. HEIGHT may be used in measuring something from bottom to top. ⟨The wall is ten feet in *height*.⟩ ALTITUDE is used in measuring the distance above a fixed level. ⟨A plane was flying at a low *altitude*.⟩ ELEVATION is used in measuring the height to which something is raised. ⟨The *elevation* of the tower is 300 feet.⟩

height•en \ˈhī-tᵊn\ *vb* **height•ened**; **height•en•ing**
to make greater : INCREASE ⟨The film *heightened* their interest in Alaska.⟩

Heim•lich maneuver \ˈhīm-lik-\ *n*
the use of upward pressure to the area directly above the navel of a choking person to force out an object blocking the trachea

heir \ˈer\ *n*
1 a person who inherits or has the right to inherit property after the death of its owner
2 a person who has legal claim to a title or a throne when the person holding it dies

heir•ess \ˈer-əs\ *n*
a girl or a woman who is an heir

heir•loom \ˈer-ˌlüm\ *n*
a piece of personal property handed down in a family from one generation to another

held *past and past participle of* HOLD

he•li•cop•ter \ˈhe-lə-ˌkäp-tər, ˈhē-\ *n*
▶ an aircraft supported in the air by horizontal propellers

he•li•port \ˈhe-lə-ˌpȯrt, ˈhē-\ *n*
a place for a helicopter to land and take off

heifer

he•li•um \'hē-lē-əm\ *n*
a very light gaseous chemical element that is found in various natural gases, will not burn, and is used in balloons

hell \'hel\ *n*
1 a place where evil people are believed in some religions to suffer after death
2 a place or state of misery or wickedness ⟨After the injury, life was *hell.*⟩

he'll \'hēl, ēl\
he shall : he will

hell•ish \'he-lish\ *adj*
extremely bad ⟨*hellish* violence⟩

hel•lo \hə-'lō, he-\ *interj*
used as a greeting or to express surprise

helm \'helm\ *n*
1 ▶ a lever or wheel for steering a ship
2 a position of control

hel•met \'hel-mət\ *n*
▼ a protective covering for the head

helmet: a field hockey goalkeeper's helmet

[1]**help** \'help\ *vb* **helped**; **help•ing**
1 to provide with what is useful in achieving an end
2 to give relief from pain or disease ⟨Did the medicine *help*?⟩
3 PREVENT 1 ⟨I couldn't *help* laughing.⟩
4 [1]SERVE 1 ⟨*Help* yourself to more.⟩
help•er \'hel-pər\ *n*

helm 1: helm from an antique ship

[2]**help** *n*
1 an act or instance of helping : AID ⟨I need your *help.*⟩
2 the fact of being useful or helpful ⟨She's not much *help.*⟩
3 the ability to be helped ⟨We are beyond *help.*⟩
4 a person or a thing that helps ⟨You've been a real *help.*⟩
5 a body of hired helpers

help•ful \'help-fəl\ *adj*
providing help ⟨a *helpful* idea⟩
help•ful•ly \-fə-lē\ *adv*

help•ing \'hel-piŋ\ *n*
a serving of food

helping verb *n*
a verb (as *am, may,* or *will*) that is used with another verb to express person, number, mood, or tense

help•less \'help-ləs\ *adj*
without help or defense ⟨a *helpless* infant⟩
help•less•ly *adv*
help•less•ness *n*

hel•ter–skel•ter \ˌhel-tər-'skel-tər\ *adv*
1 in a confused and reckless manner ⟨Children raced *helter-skelter* through the house.⟩
2 in great disorder ⟨Toys were thrown *helter-skelter* around the room.⟩

[1]**hem** \'hem\ *n*
a border of a cloth article made by folding back an edge and sewing it down

[2]**hem** *vb* **hemmed**; **hem•ming**
1 to finish with or make a hem ⟨I *hemmed* my skirt.⟩
2 SURROUND 1 ⟨Our yard is *hemmed* in by trees.⟩

hemi– *prefix*
half ⟨*hemi*sphere⟩

hemi•sphere \'he-mə-ˌsfir\ *n*
1 one of the halves of the earth as divided by the equator or by a meridian
2 a half of a sphere
3 either the left or the right half of the cerebrum
hemi•spher•ic \ˌhem-ə-'sfir-ik, -'sfer-\ *or* **hemi•spher•i•cal** \-'sfir-i-kəl, -'sfer-\ *adj*

▶ **helicopter**
The most versatile of all flying machines, helicopters have spinning rotor blades powered by an engine. Unlike airplanes, they can fly backward and sideways as well as forward, hover in the air, rise directly upward on takeoff, and land without a runway. They have many uses, including airlift rescue and monitoring ground situations such as highway traffic.

features of a helicopter

hem•lock \'hem-ˌläk\ *n*
1 an evergreen tree related to the pine
2 a poisonous plant with small white flowers and leaves divided into many parts

he•mo•glo•bin \'hē-mə-ˌglō-bən\ *n*
a protein of red blood cells that contains iron and carries oxygen from the lungs to the tissues and carbon dioxide from the tissues to the lungs

hem•or•rhage \'he-mə-rij\ *n*
a large loss of blood

hemp \'hemp\ *n*
a tall Asian plant grown for its tough woody fiber that is used especially in making rope and for its flowers and leaves that yield drugs (as marijuana)

hen \'hen\ *n*
1 a female domestic fowl
2 a female bird

hence \'hens\ *adv*
1 from this place 〈It's a day's journey *hence.*〉
2 from this time
3 as a result : THEREFORE

hence•forth \'hens-ˌfȯrth\ *adv*
from this time on

hench•man \'hench-mən\ *n, pl* **hench•men** \-mən\
a trusted follower or supporter and especially someone who performs unpleasant or illegal tasks

hep•a•ti•tis \ˌhe-pə-'tī-təs\ *n*
a disease which is caused by a virus and in which the liver is damaged and there is yellowing of the skin and fever

hepta- *or* **hept-** *prefix*
seven 〈*hepta*gon〉

hep•ta•gon \'hep-tə-ˌgän\ *n*
a closed geometric figure having seven angles and seven sides

¹her \'hər, ər\ *adj*
relating to or belonging to a certain woman, girl, or female animal 〈*her* book〉 〈*her* paw〉

²her *pron, objective case of* SHE

¹her•ald \'her-əld\ *n*
1 an official messenger
2 a person who brings news or announces something

²herald *vb* **her•ald•ed; her•ald•ing**
1 to give notice of : ANNOUNCE
2 FORETELL

her•ald•ry \'her-əl-drē\ *n*
the art or science of tracing and recording family history and creating coats of arms

herb \'ərb, 'hərb\ *n*
1 a plant with soft stems that die down at the end of the growing season
2 ▶ a plant or plant part used in medicine or in seasoning foods

▶ herb 2
Many of the most popular herbs are used for seasoning food. These are known as culinary — or cooking — herbs, and they are generally available fresh or dried. All herbs have their own distinctive taste and aroma, so that different types are preferred for flavoring particular foods. Some culinary herbs are added during cooking, while others are eaten fresh in salads or used to decorate meals or drinks.

basil

coriander \'kōr-ē-ˌan-dər\

rosemary

oregano \ə-'reg-ə-ˌnō\

fennel \'fen-əl\

peppermint

thyme

tarragon \'tar-ə-gən\

sage

parsley

[1]herd: a herd of elephants

her•bi•vore \'hər-bə-,vȯr, 'ər-\ *n*
an animal that feeds on plants

her•biv•o•rous \,hər-'bi-və-rəs, ,ər-'bi-\ *adj*
feeding on plants

[1]herd \'hərd\ *n*
▲ a number of animals of one kind kept or living together 〈a *herd* of cows〉

[2]herd *vb* **herd•ed; herd•ing**
to gather and move as a group 〈*herd* cattle〉
herd•er \'hərd-ər\ *n*

herds•man \'hərdz-mən\ *n*, *pl* **herds•men** \-mən\
a person who owns or watches over a flock or herd

[1]here \'hir\ *adv*
1 in or at this place 〈Stand *here.*〉
2 at this time : happening now 〈Summer is *here* at last.〉
3 to or into this place : HITHER 〈Come *here.*〉

[2]here *n*
this place 〈Get away from *here.*〉

here•abouts \'hir-ə-,bau̇ts\ *or* **here•about** \-,bau̇t\ *adv*
near or around this place

[1]here•af•ter \hir-'af-tər\ *adv*
1 after this 〈We will *hereafter* have a shorter recess.〉
2 in some future time or state

[2]hereafter *n*
1 [2]FUTURE 1
2 life after death

here•by \hir-'bī\ *adv*
by means of this

he•red•i•tary \hə-'re-də-,ter-ē\ *adj*
1 capable of being passed from parent to offspring 〈*hereditary* disease〉
2 received or passing from an ancestor to an heir

he•red•i•ty \hə-'re-də-tē\ *n*, *pl* **he•red•i•ties**
the passing on of characteristics (as the color of the eyes or hair) from parents to offspring

here•in \hir-'in\ *adv*
in this 〈A map is included *herein.*〉

her•e•sy \'her-ə-sē\ *n*, *pl* **her•e•sies**
1 the holding of religious beliefs opposed to church doctrine : such a belief
2 belief or opinion opposed to a generally accepted view

her•e•tic \'her-ə-,tik\ *n*
a person who believes or teaches something opposed to accepted beliefs (as of a church)

here•to•fore \'hir-tə-,fȯr\ *adv*
up to this time 〈Our school has *heretofore* never closed.〉

here•up•on \'hir-ə-,pȯn, -,pän\ *adv*
right after this 〈He finished the race and *hereupon* collapsed.〉

here•with \hir-'wi<u>th</u>, -'with\ *adv*
with this

her•i•tage \'her-ə-tij\ *n*
the traditions, achievements, and beliefs that are part of the history of a group of people

her•mit \'hər-mət\ *n*
a person who lives apart from others especially for religious reasons

hermit crab *n*
▼ a small crab that lives in the empty shells of mollusks (as snails)

hermit crab

he•ro \'hir-ō, 'hē-rō\ *n*, *pl* **heroes**
1 a person admired for great deeds or fine qualities 〈We study *heroes* of our nation's history.〉
2 a person who shows great courage 〈The firefighters were *heroes.*〉
3 the chief male character in a story, play, or poem

he•ro•ic \hi-'rō-ik\ *adj*
1 of or relating to heroism or heroes 〈*heroic* tales〉
2 COURAGEOUS, DARING 〈a *heroic* rescue〉
he•ro•ical•ly \-i-kə-lē\ *adv*

her•o•in \'her-ə-wən\ *n*
a very harmful illegal drug that is highly addictive and is made from morphine

her•o•ine \'her-ə-wən\ *n*
1 a woman admired for great deeds or fine qualities
2 the chief female character in a story, poem, or play

her•o•ism \'her-ə-,wi-zəm\ *n*
1 behavior showing great courage especially for a noble purpose 〈the *heroism* of soldiers〉
2 the qualities of a hero 〈We honor the *heroism* of our forefathers.〉

her•on \'her-ən\ *n*
a wading bird that has long legs, a long neck, a long thin bill, and large wings

her•ring \'her-iŋ\ *n*
a fish of the northern Atlantic Ocean that is often used for food

hers \'hərz\ *pron*
that which belongs to her 〈This book is *hers.*〉

her•self \hər-'self, ər-\ *pron*
her own self 〈She hurt *herself.*〉 〈She *herself* did it.〉

a b c d e f g h i j k l m n o p q r s t u v w x y z

he's \ˈhēz, ēz\
he is : he has ⟨*He's* the one.⟩ ⟨*He's* been sick.⟩

hes•i•tan•cy \ˈhe-zə-tən-sē\ *n*
the quality or state of being unwilling to do something because of doubt or nervousness

hes•i•tant \ˈhe-zə-tənt\ *adj*
feeling or showing unwillingness to do something because of doubt or nervousness ⟨I was *hesitant* to join in.⟩
hes•i•tant•ly *adv*

hes•i•tate \ˈhe-zə-ˌtāt\ *vb* **hes•i•tat•ed**; **hes•i•tat•ing**
1 to pause before doing something ⟨He *hesitated* before crossing the stream.⟩
2 to be unwilling to do something because of doubt or nervousness ⟨Don't *hesitate* to ask for help.⟩
hes•i•ta•tion \ˌhez-ə-ˈtā-shən\ *n*

hew \ˈhyü\ *vb* **hewed** *or* **hewn** \ˈhyün\; **hew•ing**
1 to chop down ⟨*hew* trees⟩
2 to shape by cutting with an ax ⟨*hew* logs⟩

hex \ˈheks\ *n*
a harmful spell : JINX

hexa- *or* **hex-** *prefix*
six ⟨*hexa*gon⟩

hexa•gon \ˈhek-sə-ˌgän\ *n*
a closed geometric figure having six angles and six sides
hex•ag•o•nal \hek-ˈsag-ən-l\ *adj*

hey \ˈhā\ *interj*
used to call attention or to express surprise or joy

hey•day \ˈhā-ˌdā\ *n*
the time of greatest strength, popularity, or success

hi \ˈhī\ *interj*
used especially as a greeting

HI *abbr* Hawaii

hi•ber•nate \ˈhī-bər-ˌnāt\ *vb* **hi•ber•nat•ed**; **hi•ber•nat•ing**
to pass all or part of the winter in an inactive state in which the body temperature drops and breathing slows
hi•ber•na•tor \-ˌnāt-ər\ *n*

hi•ber•na•tion \ˌhī-bər-ˈnā-shən\ *n*
▼ the act of passing all or part of the winter in an inactive state

hibernation: a squirrel in hibernation

hickory: a hickory tree

[1]hic•cup \ˈhi-ˌkəp\ *n*
a gulping sound caused by sudden movements of muscles active in breathing

[2]hiccup *vb* **hic•cuped** *also* **hic•cupped**; **hic•cup•ing** *also* **hic•cup•ping**
to make a gulping sound caused by sudden movements of muscles active in breathing

hick•o•ry \ˈhi-kə-rē, ˈhi-krē\ *n*, *pl* **hick•o•ries**
▲ a tall tree that has strong tough wood and bears an edible nut (**hickory nut**) in a hard shell

[1]hide \ˈhīd\ *vb* **hid** \ˈhid\; **hid•den** \ˈhi-dᵊn\ *or* **hid**; **hid•ing** \ˈhī-diŋ\
1 to put or stay out of sight
2 to keep secret ⟨We *hid* the truth.⟩
3 to screen from view ⟨Clouds *hid* the sun.⟩

[2]hide *n*
the skin of an animal

hide–and–go–seek \ˌhī-dᵊn-gō-ˈsēk\ *n*
HIDE-AND-SEEK

hide–and–seek \ˌhī-dᵊn-ˈsēk\ *n*
a game in which one player covers his or her eyes and after giving the others time to hide goes looking for them

hide•away \ˈhī-də-ˌwā\ *n*
[1]RETREAT 3, HIDEOUT

hid•eous \ˈhi-dē-əs\ *adj*
very ugly or disgusting : FRIGHTFUL
hid•eous•ly *adv*

hide•out \ˈhīd-ˌaüt\ *n*
a secret place for hiding (as from the police)

hi•ero•glyph•ic \ˌhī-ə-rə-ˈgli-fik\ *n*
▶ any of the symbols in the picture writing of ancient Egypt

hig•gle•dy–pig•gle•dy \ˌhi-gəl-dē-ˈpi-gəl-dē\ *adv or adj*
in a messy way : TOPSY-TURVY ⟨Clothes were scattered *higgledy-piggledy.*⟩ ⟨Their apartment was *higgledy-piggledy.*⟩

[1]high \ˈhī\ *adj* **high•er**; **high•est**
1 extending to a great distance above the ground ⟨*high* mountains⟩
2 having a specified elevation : TALL ⟨The building is 50 stories *high.*⟩
3 of greater degree, size, amount, or cost than average ⟨*high* temperatures⟩ ⟨*high* speed⟩
4 having great force ⟨*high* winds⟩
5 pitched or sounding above some other sound ⟨a *high* note⟩ ⟨a *high* voice⟩
6 very serious ⟨*high* crimes⟩
7 of the best quality ⟨*high* art⟩
8 rich in quality ⟨*high* living⟩

▶ **Synonyms** HIGH, TALL, and LOFTY mean above the usual level in height. HIGH is used of height that is measured from the ground or some other standard. ⟨A *high* fence surrounds the yard.⟩ TALL is used of something that is considered high when compared to others of the same kind. ⟨He's *tall* for his age.⟩ LOFTY is used of something that rises to a grand or impressive height. ⟨They soared over *lofty* mountains.⟩

[2]high *adv* **higher**; **highest**
at or to a high place or degree ⟨She jumped *higher* than the others.⟩

[3]high *n*
1 a high point or level ⟨Prices reached a new *high.*⟩
2 a region of high barometric pressure ⟨A strong *high* brought clear skies.⟩
3 the arrangement of gears in an automobile giving the highest speed of travel

on high in the sky : up above 〈clouds *on high*〉

high•brow \'hī-,braů\ *n*
a person of great learning or culture

high five *n*
a show of celebration by two people slapping each other's hands in the air

high–hand•ed \'hī-'han-dəd\ *adj*
having or showing no regard for the rights, concerns, or feelings of others

hieroglyphic: an ancient Egyptian door plate inscribed with hieroglyphics

high•land \'hī-lənd\ *n*
high or hilly country

[1]**high•light** \'hī-,līt\ *n*
a very interesting event or detail 〈He mentioned the *highlights* of his trip.〉

[2]**highlight** *vb* **high•light•ed**; **high•light•ing**
1 EMPHASIZE 〈The speech *highlighted* the problems we face.〉
2 to be an interesting event or detail 〈Dinner *highlighted* the evening.〉
3 to mark with a highlighter 〈*Highlight* your spelling words on the page.〉
4 to cause (something on a computer screen) to be displayed in a way that stands out

high•light•er \'hī-,lī-tər\ *n*
a pen with a wide felt tip and brightly colored ink for marking text on a page so that it stands out clearly

high•ly \'hī-lē\ *adv*
1 to a high degree : very much 〈He's a *highly* respected citizen.〉
2 with much approval

high•ness \'hī-nəs\ *n*
1 the quality or state of being high 〈*highness* of temperature〉
2 used as a title for a person of very high rank 〈Her Royal *Highness*, the Queen〉

high–rise \'hī-'rīz\ *adj*
having many stories 〈a *high-rise* building〉

high school *n*
a school usually including the ninth to twelfth or tenth to twelfth grades

high seas *n pl*
the part of a sea or ocean that is away from land

high–spir•it•ed \'hī-'spir-ə-təd\ *adj*
LIVELY 1

high–strung \'hī-'strəŋ\ *adj*
very sensitive or nervous 〈a *high-strung* horse〉

high tech \-'tek\ *n*
technology involving the production or use of advanced or sophisticated devices
high–tech *adj*

high tide *n*
the tide when the water is at its greatest height

high•way \'hī-,wā\ *n*
a main road

high•way•man \'hī-,wā-mən\ *n*, *pl* **high•way•men** \-mən\
a man who robbed travelers on a road in past centuries

hi•jack \'hī-,jak\ *vb* **hi•jacked**; **hi•jack•ing**
1 to stop and steal or steal from a moving vehicle
2 to take control of (an aircraft) by force
high•jack•er *n*

[1]**hike** \'hīk\ *vb* **hiked**; **hik•ing**
to take a long walk especially for pleasure or exercise
hik•er *n*

[2]**hike** *n*
a long walk especially for pleasure or exercise

hi•lar•i•ous \hi-'ler-ē-əs\ *adj*
very funny
hi•lar•i•ous•ly *adv*

hi•lar•i•ty \hi-'ler-ə-tē\ *n*
noisy fun or laughter

hill \'hil\ *n*
1 a usually rounded elevation of land lower than a mountain
2 a surface that slopes 〈Our driveway is a long *hill*.〉
3 a heap or mound of something 〈a *hill* of snow〉

hill•bil•ly \'hil-,bi-lē\ *n*, *pl* **hill•bil•lies**
a person from a backwoods area

hill•ock \'hi-lək\ *n*
a small hill

hill•side \'hil-,sīd\ *n*
the part of a hill between the top and the foot

hill•top \'hil-,täp\ *n*
the highest part of a hill

hilly \'hi-lē\ *adj* **hill•i•er**; **hill•i•est**
having many hills 〈a *hilly* city〉

hilt \'hilt\ *n*
a handle especially of a sword or dagger

him \'him, im\ *pron*, *objective case of* HE

him•self \him-'self, im-\ *pron*
his own self 〈He hurt *himself*.〉 〈He *himself* did it.〉

hind \'hīnd\ *adj*
being at the end or back : REAR 〈*hind* legs〉

hin•der \'hin-dər\ *vb* **hin•dered**; **hin•der•ing**
to make slow or difficult 〈Snow and high winds *hindered* our progress.〉

hind•quar•ter \'hīnd-,kwȯr-tər\ *n*
the back half of a side of the body or carcass of a four-footed animal

hin•drance \'hin-drəns\ *n*
someone or something that makes a situation more difficult

hind•sight \'hīnd-,sīt\ *n*
understanding of something only after it has happened

Hin•du \'hin-,dü\ *n*
a person who follows Hinduism

Hin•du•ism \'hin-,dü-,i-zəm\ *n*
a set of cultural and religious beliefs and practices that originated in India

[1]**hinge** \'hinj\ *n*
▼ a jointed piece on which a door, gate, or lid turns or swings

[1]**hinge:** a cupboard hinge

[2]hinge *vb* **hinged; hing•ing**
to attach by or provide with hinges
hinge on to be determined or decided by ⟨Our plans *hinge on* the weather.⟩

[1]hint \'hint\ *n*
1 information that helps a person guess an answer or do something more easily
2 a small amount ⟨a *hint* of garlic⟩

[2]hint *vb* **hint•ed; hint•ing**
to suggest something without plainly asking or saying it ⟨I *hinted* that I need help.⟩

hin•ter•land \'hin-tər-,land\ *n*
a region far from cities

hip \'hip\ *n*
the part of the body that curves out below the waist on each side

hip–hop \'hip-,häp\ *n*
1 rap music
2 the culture associated with rap music

hip•pie *or* **hip•py** \'hi-pē\ *n, pl* **hippies**
a usually young person who rejects the values and practices of society and opposes violence and war

hip•po \'hi-pō\ *n, pl* **hip•pos**
HIPPOPOTAMUS

hip•po•pot•a•mus \,hi-pə-'pä-tə-məs\ *n, pl* **hip•po•pot•a•mus•es** *or* **hip•po•pot•a•mi** \-,mī\
▼ a large African animal with thick hairless brownish gray skin, a big head, and short legs that eats plants and spends most of its time in rivers

▶ **Word History** The bulky African mammal that spends its daytime hours sunk up to its eyes in a river owes its English name to the ancient Greeks. The historian Herodotus called the animal, which he may have seen in Egypt, *ho hippos ho potamios*, "the river horse." Later Greek writers reduced this description to *hippopotamos* (which looks as if it should mean "horse river"). Despite its name, the hippopotamus is more closely related to hogs than horses.

hippopotamus

hire \'hīr\ *vb* **hired; hir•ing**
1 [1]EMPLOY 1 ⟨The company *hired* new workers.⟩
2 to get the temporary use of in return for pay ⟨They *hired* a hall for the party.⟩
3 to take a job ⟨He *hired* out as a cook.⟩

[1]his \hiz, iz\ *adj*
relating to or belonging to a certain man, boy, or male animal ⟨*his* desk⟩ ⟨*his* tail⟩

[2]his \'hiz\ *pron*
that which belongs to him ⟨The book is *his.*⟩

[1]His•pan•ic \hi-'span-ik\ *adj*
of or relating to people of Latin-American origin

[2]Hispanic *n*
a person of Latin-American origin

[1]hiss \'his\ *vb* **hissed; hiss•ing**
1 to make a sound like a long \s\
2 to show dislike or disapproval by hissing
3 to say (something) in a loud or angry whisper ⟨"Keep your voice down!" he *hissed.*⟩

[2]hiss *n*
a sound like a long \s\ sometimes used as a sign of dislike or disapproval ⟨the *hiss* of steam⟩ ⟨The *hiss* from the audience became louder.⟩

hist. *abbr*
1 historian
2 historical
3 history

his•to•ri•an \hi-'stòr-ē-ən\ *n*
a person who studies or writes about history

his•tor•ic \hi-'stòr-ik\ *adj*
famous in history

his•tor•i•cal \hi-'stòr-i-kəl\ *adj*
1 relating to or based on history ⟨*historical* writings⟩
2 known to be true ⟨*historical* fact⟩
his•tor•i•cal•ly *adv*

his•to•ry \'hi-stə-rē\ *n, pl* **his•to•ries**
1 events of the past and especially those relating to a particular place or subject ⟨European *history*⟩
2 a branch of knowledge that records and explains past events
3 a written report of past events ⟨She wrote a *history* of the Internet.⟩
4 an established record of past events ⟨His criminal *history* is well-known.⟩

[1]hit \'hit\ *vb* **hit; hit•ting**
1 to strike or be struck by (someone or something) forcefully
2 to cause or allow (something) to come into contact with something ⟨He *hit* his head on the door.⟩
3 to affect or be affected by in a harmful or damaging way ⟨He was *hit* hard by the loss.⟩
4 OCCUR 1 ⟨The storm *hit* without warning.⟩
5 to come upon by chance ⟨She *hit* upon the right answer.⟩
6 to arrive at ⟨Prices *hit* a new high.⟩
hit•ter *n*

[2]hit *n*
1 a blow striking an object aimed at ⟨Bombers scored a direct *hit.*⟩
2 something very successful ⟨The show is a *hit.*⟩
3 a batted baseball that enables the batter to reach base safely
4 a match in a computer search ⟨The search produced over a thousand *hits.*⟩

hit–and–run \,hi-tᵊn-'rən\ *adj*
being or involving a driver who does not stop after being in an automobile accident

[1]hitch \'hich\ *vb* **hitched; hitch•ing**
1 to fasten by or as if by a hook or knot ⟨*Hitch* the horses to the wagon.⟩
2 HITCHHIKE
3 to pull or lift (something) with a quick movement

[2]hitch *n*
1 an unexpected stop or problem
2 a jerky movement or pull ⟨He gave his pants a *hitch.*⟩
3 a knot used for a temporary fastening

hitch•hike \'hich-,hīk\ *vb* **hitch•hiked; hitch•hik•ing**
to travel by getting free rides in passing vehicles
hitch•hik•er *n*

hith•er \'hi-t͟hər\ *adv*
to this place ⟨Come *hither.*⟩

hith•er•to \'hi-t͟hər-,tü\ *adv*
up to this time

HIV \,āch-,ī-'vē\ *n*
a virus that causes AIDS by destroying large numbers of cells that help the human body fight infection

hive \'hīv\ *n*
1 a container for housing honeybees

2 the usually aboveground nest of bees
3 a colony of bees
4 a place filled with busy people

hives \ˈhīvz\ *n*
an allergic condition in which the skin breaks out in large red itching patches

[1]hoard \ˈhȯrd\ *n*
a supply usually of something of value stored away or hidden

[2]hoard *vb* **hoard•ed**; **hoard•ing**
to gather and store away ⟨Squirrels *hoard* nuts for winter.⟩
hoard•er *n*

hoarse \ˈhȯrs\ *adj* **hoars•er**; **hoars•est**
1 harsh in sound ⟨a *hoarse* voice⟩
2 having a rough voice ⟨I was *hoarse* from talking too much.⟩
hoarse•ly *adv*
hoarse•ness *n*

hoary \ˈhȯr-ē\ *adj* **hoar•i•er**; **hoar•i•est**
1 very old ⟨a *hoary* tale⟩
2 having gray or white hair ⟨a *hoary* head⟩

[1]hoax \ˈhōks\ *vb* **hoaxed**; **hoax•ing**
to trick into thinking something is true or real when it isn't

[2]hoax *n*
1 an act meant to fool or deceive
2 something false passed off as real

[1]hob•ble \ˈhä-bəl\ *vb* **hob•bled**; **hob•bling**
to walk slowly and with difficulty

[2]hobble *n*
a slow and difficult way of walking

hob•by \ˈhä-bē\ *n, pl* **hobbies**
an interest or activity engaged in for pleasure

hob•by•horse \ˈhä-bē-ˌhȯrs\ *n*
a stick that has an imitation horse's head and that a child pretends to ride

hob•gob•lin \ˈhäb-ˌgä-blən\ *n*
1 a mischievous elf
2 BOGEY 2

ho•bo \ˈhō-bō\ *n, pl* **hoboes**
[1]VAGRANT

hock \ˈhäk\ *n*
1 a small piece of meat from the leg of a pig ⟨ham *hocks*⟩
2 the part of the rear leg of a four-footed animal that is like a human ankle

hock•ey \ˈhä-kē\ *n*
▼ a game played on ice or in a field by two teams who try to drive a puck or ball through a goal by hitting it with a stick

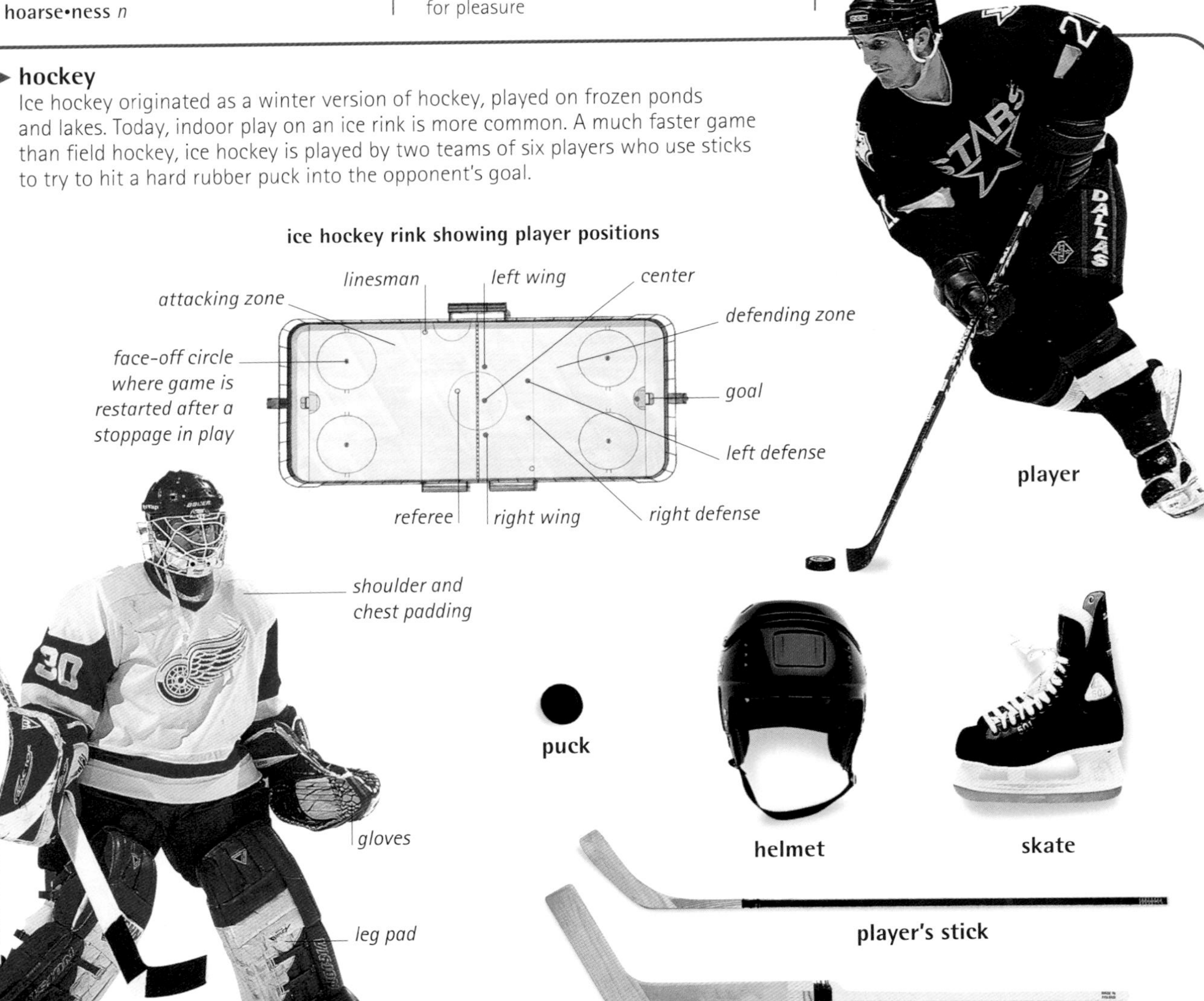

a b c d e f g h i j k l m n o p q r s t u v w x y z

hodge•podge \'häj-ˌpäj\ *n*
a disorderly mixture

[1]hoe \'hō\ *n*
▼a tool with a long handle and a thin flat blade used for weeding and cultivating

[1]hoe

[2]hoe *vb* **hoed**; **hoe•ing**
to weed or loosen the soil around plants with a hoe

[1]hog \'hȯg, 'häg\ *n*
1 a usually large adult pig
2 a greedy or dirty person

[2]hog *vb* **hogged**; **hog•ging**
to take or use in a way that keeps others from having or using ⟨Stop *hogging* the ball.⟩

ho•gan \'hō-ˌgän\ *n*
▼a Navajo Indian dwelling made of logs and mud with a door traditionally facing east

hog•gish \'hȯ-gish, 'hä-\ *adj*
very selfish or greedy
hog•gish•ly *adv*

hogs•head \'hȯgz-ˌhed, 'hägz-\ *n*
1 a very large cask
2 a unit of liquid measure equal to 63 gallons (about 238 liters)

[1]hoist \'hȯist\ *vb* **hoist•ed**; **hoist•ing**
to lift up especially with a pulley
synonyms see LIFT

[2]hoist *n*
a device used for lifting heavy loads

[1]hold \'hōld\ *vb* **held** \'held\; **hold•ing**
1 to have or keep a grip on ⟨*hold* a book⟩ ⟨She *held* the child's hand.⟩
2 to take in and have within : CONTAIN ⟨This jar *holds* a quart.⟩
3 [1]SUPPORT 1 ⟨The floor will *hold* ten tons.⟩
4 to carry on by group action ⟨The club *held* a meeting.⟩
5 to have as a position of responsibility ⟨She *holds* the office of treasurer.⟩
6 to continue in the same way or state : LAST ⟨According to the forecast, good weather will *hold*.⟩
7 to remain fast or fastened ⟨The lock *held*.⟩
8 to have or keep possession or control of ⟨Soldiers *held* the fort.⟩
9 to have in mind ⟨They *hold* different opinions.⟩
10 to limit the movement or activity of : RESTRAIN ⟨A nut *holds* the bolt.⟩ ⟨Please *hold* the dogs.⟩
11 to continue in a condition or position ⟨Can you *hold* still a minute?⟩
12 to continue moving on (a course) without change
13 to make accept a legal or moral duty ⟨They *held* me to my promise.⟩
14 CONSIDER 3, REGARD ⟨He is widely *held* to be a genius.⟩
hold•er \'hōl-dər\ *n*
hold out
1 to continue to be present or exist ⟨My money *held out* until I got paid.⟩
2 to refuse to yield or agree ⟨The soldiers *held out* until help arrived.⟩
hold up
1 [2]DELAY 2 ⟨Police are *holding up* traffic.⟩
2 to rob while threatening with a weapon

[2]hold *n*
1 the act or way of holding : GRIP ⟨He had a tight *hold* on the rope.⟩
2 a note or rest in music kept up longer than usual

[3]hold *n*
1 the part of a ship below the decks in which cargo is stored
2 the cargo compartment of an airplane

hold•up \'hōld-ˌəp\ *n*
1 robbery by an armed robber
2 [1]DELAY ⟨Why aren't we moving? What's the *holdup*?⟩

hole \'hōl\ *n*
1 an opening into or through something ⟨There's a *hole* in the roof.⟩
2 a hollowed out place ⟨I dug a *hole*.⟩
3 DEN 1, BURROW ⟨a mouse *hole*⟩

hole up *vb* **holed up**; **hol•ing up**
to take shelter ⟨During the storm they *holed up* in the basement.⟩

hol•i•day \'hä-lə-ˌdā\ *n*
1 a special day of celebration during which schools and businesses are often closed
2 *chiefly British* [1]VACATION

ho•li•ness \'hō-lē-nəs\ *n*
1 the quality or state of being holy ⟨the *holiness* of saints⟩
2 used as a title for persons of high religious position ⟨His *Holiness* the Pope⟩

[1]hol•ler \'hä-lər\ *vb* **hol•lered**; **hol•ler•ing**
to cry out : SHOUT

[2]holler *n*
[2]SHOUT, CRY

[1]hol•low \'hä-lō\ *adj* **hol•low•er**; **hol•low•est**
1 having a space inside : not solid ⟨a *hollow* chocolate egg⟩
2 curved inward : SUNKEN ⟨*hollow* cheeks⟩
3 suggesting a sound made in an empty place ⟨a *hollow* roar⟩
4 not sincere ⟨a *hollow* promise⟩
hol•low•ly *adv*

holly: holly leaves and berries

[2]hollow *n*
1 a low spot in a surface
2 a small valley
3 an empty space within something ⟨Owls live in the *hollow* of the tree.⟩

[3]hollow *vb* **hol•lowed**; **hol•low•ing**
to make or become hollow ⟨The canoe was made by *hollowing* out a log.⟩

hol•ly \'hä-lē\ *n, pl* **hollies**
▲an evergreen tree or shrub that has shiny leaves with prickly edges and red berries

hogan: cross-section model of a traditional hogan

hollyhock: hollyhock flowers

hol•ly•hock \'hä-lē-ˌhäk\ *n*
▲ a plant with large rounded leaves and tall stalks of bright showy flowers

ho•lo•caust \'hä-lə-ˌkȯst, 'hō-lə-\ *n*
1 a complete destruction especially by fire
2 *often cap* the killing of civilians and especially Jews by the Nazis during World War II

ho•lo•gram \'hō-lə-ˌgram, 'hä-\ *n*
a three-dimensional picture made by laser light reflected onto a photographic substance without the use of a camera

hol•ster \'hōl-stər\ *n*
a usually leather case in which a pistol is carried or worn

ho•ly \'hō-lē\ *adj* **ho•li•er**; **ho•li•est**
1 set apart for the service of God or of a divine being : SACRED ⟨a *holy* temple⟩
2 being a deity ⟨the *holy* Lord God⟩
3 used in exclamations to indicate surprise or excitement ⟨*Holy* mackerel! You won!⟩

holy day *n*
a day set aside for special religious observance

hom- *or* **homo-** *prefix*
one and the same : similar : alike ⟨*homo*graph⟩

hom•age \'ä-mij, 'hä-\ *n*
1 a feudal ceremony in which a person pledges loyalty to a lord and becomes a vassal
2 [1]RESPECT 1 ⟨We paid *homage* to our ancestors.⟩

[1]**home** \'hōm\ *n*
1 the house or apartment where a person lives
2 the place where a person was born or grew up
3 HABITAT ⟨The Arctic is the *home* of polar bears.⟩
4 a place for the care of people unable to care for themselves ⟨an orphans' *home*⟩
5 a family living together ⟨She comes from a good *home*.⟩
6 [1]HOUSE 1 ⟨There are new *homes* for sale.⟩
7 the goal or point to be reached in some games
at home relaxed and comfortable ⟨Make yourself *at home*.⟩

[2]**home** *adv*
1 to or at home ⟨It feels good to be *home*.⟩
2 to the final place or limit ⟨Use a hammer to drive the nail *home*.⟩

home•com•ing \'hōm-ˌkə-miŋ\ *n*
a return home

home•land \'hōm-ˌland\ *n*
the country a person comes from

home•less \'hōm-ləs\ *adj*
having no home or permanent residence
home•less•ness *n*

home•like \'hōm-ˌlīk\ *adj*
like a home (as in comfort and kindly warmth) ⟨a *homelike* atmosphere⟩

home•ly \'hōm-lē\ *adj* **home•li•er**; **home•li•est**
1 not pretty or handsome ⟨a *homely* face⟩
2 suggesting home life ⟨*homely* comforts⟩

home•made \'hōm-'mād\ *adj*
made in the home ⟨*homemade* bread⟩

home•mak•er \'hōm-ˌmā-kər\ *n*
a person who manages a household especially as a wife and mother
home•mak•ing \-ˌmā-kiŋ\ *n*

home page *n*
▶ the page of a World Wide Web site that is seen first and that usually contains links to the other pages of the site or to other sites

home plate *n*
the base that a baseball runner must touch to score

hom•er \'hō-mər\ *n*
HOME RUN

home•room \'hōm-ˌrüm, -ˌrům\ *n*
a classroom where students of the same class report at the start of each day

home run *n*
a hit in baseball that enables the batter to go around all the bases and score

home•school \'hōm-ˌskül\ *vb* **home•schooled**; **home•school•ing**
to teach school subjects to at home ⟨She *homeschools* her third-grade son.⟩

home•school•er \'hōm-ˌskü-lər\ *n*
1 a person who teaches school subjects to children at home
2 a child who is taught school subjects at home

home•sick \'hōm-ˌsik\ *adj*
longing for home and family
home•sick•ness *n*

home•spun \'hōm-ˌspən\ *adj*
1 made at home
2 made of a loosely woven fabric originally made from yarn spun at home
3 not fancy : SIMPLE ⟨*homespun* humor⟩

[1]**home•stead** \'hōm-ˌsted\ *n*
1 a home and the land around it
2 a piece of land gained from United States public lands by living on and farming it

[2]**homestead** *vb* **home•stead•ed**; **home•stead•ing**
to acquire or settle on public land for use as a homestead
home•stead•er \'hōm-ˌste-dər\ *n*

home•town \'hōm-'tau̇n\ *n*
the city or town where a person was born or grew up

home•ward \'hōm-wərd\ *or* **home•wards** \-wərdz\ *adv or adj*
toward home ⟨We headed *homeward*.⟩

home•work \'hōm-ˌwərk\ *n*
work (as school lessons) to be done at home

hom•ey \'hō-mē\ *adj* **hom•i•er**; **hom•i•est**
HOMELIKE

ho•mi•cide \'hä-mə-ˌsīd, 'hō-mə-\ *n*
a killing of one human being by another

hom•ing pigeon \'hō-miŋ-\ *n*
a racing pigeon trained to return home

hom•i•ny \'hä-mə-nē\ *n*
kernels of corn that have the outer covering removed by processing and that are eaten cooked as a cereal or vegetable

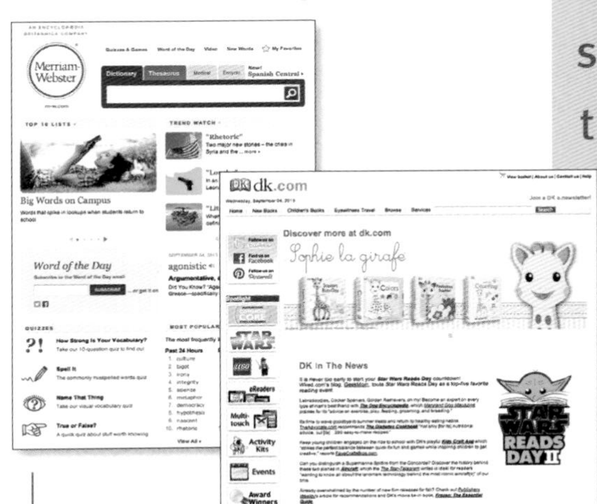

home page: the Merriam-Webster and DK home pages

honeybee

For centuries, people have built hives for honeybees. Modern hives have removable frames to make the collection of honey easier. A modern hive contains only three types of honeybee — the queen, male drones, and female workers. The queen lays all the eggs from which new larvae hatch, while the drones exist only to mate with the queen. The workers build the honeycomb and take care of the queen and larvae.

queen

frame from a hive

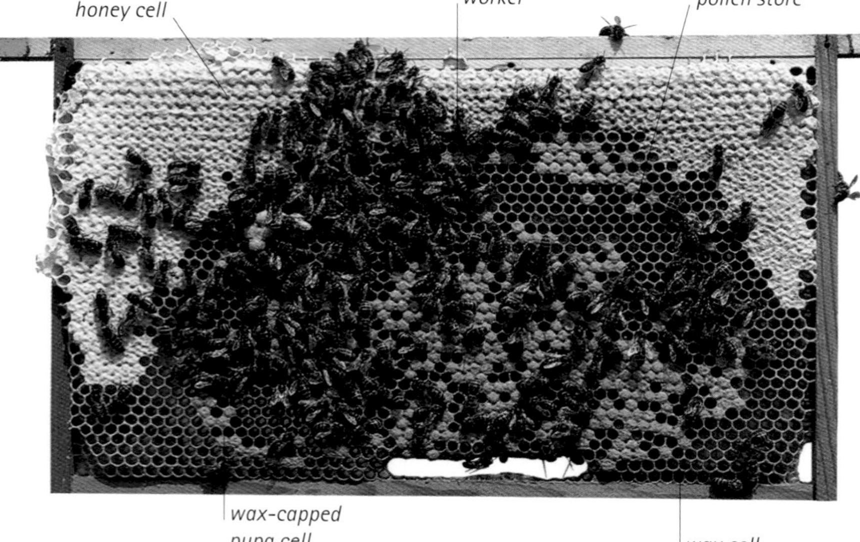

drone

worker

homo– see HOM–

ho•mog•e•nize \hō-ˈmä-jə-ˌnīz, hə-\ *vb* **ho•mog•e•nized**; **ho•mog•e•niz•ing**
to reduce the particles within a liquid (as milk or paint) to the same size and spread them evenly in the liquid

ho•mo•graph \ˈhä-mə-ˌgraf, ˈhō-mə-\ *n*
one of two or more words spelled alike but different in meaning or origin or pronunciation ⟨The noun "conduct" and the verb "conduct" are *homographs.*⟩

hom•onym \ˈhä-mə-ˌnim, ˈhō-mə-\ *n*
1 HOMOPHONE
2 HOMOGRAPH
3 one of two or more words spelled and pronounced alike but different in meaning ⟨The noun "bear" and the verb "bear" are *homonyms.*⟩

ho•mo•phone \ˈhä-mə-ˌfōn, ˈhō-mə-\ *n*
one of two or more words pronounced alike but different in meaning or origin or spelling ⟨The words "to," "too," and "two" are *homophones.*⟩

hone \ˈhōn\ *vb* **honed**; **hon•ing**
to sharpen with or as if with a fine abrasive stone

hon•est \ˈä-nəst\ *adj*
1 not engaging in or involving cheating, stealing, or lying ⟨an *honest* citizen⟩ ⟨an *honest* living⟩
2 not marked by lies or trickery : STRAIGHTFORWARD ⟨an *honest* answer⟩
3 being just what is indicated : REAL, GENUINE ⟨He did an *honest* day's work.⟩
synonyms see UPRIGHT

hon•est•ly \ˈä-nəst-lē\ *adv*
1 without cheating or lying : in an honest manner ⟨They made their money *honestly.*⟩
2 in a real and sincere way ⟨She was *honestly* scared.⟩
3 used to stress the truth or sincerity of what is being said ⟨*Honestly,* I don't know how you do it.⟩
4 used to show annoyance or disapproval ⟨Is that your excuse? *Honestly*!⟩

hon•es•ty \ˈä-nə-stē\ *n*
the quality or state of being truthful and fair

hon•ey \ˈhə-nē\ *n*
1 a sweet sticky material made by bees from the nectar of flowers and stored by them in a honeycomb for food
2 [1]DARLING 1

hon•ey•bee \ˈhə-nē-ˌbē\ *n*
▲ a bee whose honey is used by people as food

hon•ey•comb \ˈhə-nē-ˌkōm\ *n*
a mass of wax cells built by honeybees in their nest to contain young bees and stores of honey

hon•ey•dew melon \ˈhə-nē-ˌdü-, -ˌdyü-\ *n*
▼ a pale melon with greenish sweet flesh and smooth skin

honeydew melon

¹hon•ey•moon \'hə-nē-ˌmün\ *n*
1 a trip taken by a recently married couple
2 a period of harmony especially just after marriage

²honeymoon *vb* **hon•ey•mooned**; **hon•ey•moon•ing**
to go on a trip right after marrying
hon•ey•moon•er *n*

hon•ey•suck•le \'hə-nē-ˌsə-kəl\ *n*
a climbing vine or a bush with fragrant white, yellow, or red flowers

¹honk \'häŋk, 'hȯŋk\ *vb* **honked**; **honk•ing**
to make a sound like the cry of a goose

²honk *n*
1 the cry of a goose
2 a loud sound like the cry of a goose ⟨the *honk* of a horn⟩

¹hon•or \'ä-nər\ *n*
1 good character as judged by other people : REPUTATION
2 outward respect : RECOGNITION ⟨The dinner is in *honor* of the new coach.⟩
3 PRIVILEGE 1 ⟨You will have the *honor* of leading the parade.⟩
4 used especially as a title for an official of high rank ⟨Please welcome His *Honor*, the mayor.⟩
5 a person whose character and accomplishments bring respect or fame ⟨You are an *honor* to your profession.⟩
6 evidence or a symbol of great respect ⟨She's won many national *honors*.⟩
7 high moral standards of behavior

²honor *vb* **hon•ored**; **hon•or•ing**
1 ²RESPECT 1 ⟨*Honor* your parents.⟩
2 to recognize and show admiration for publicly ⟨He was *honored* at a special ceremony.⟩
3 to live up to or fulfill the requirements of ⟨She didn't *honor* her promise.⟩

hon•or•able \'ä-nə-rə-bəl, 'än-rə-bəl\ *adj*
1 bringing about or deserving honor ⟨It's an *honorable* achievement.⟩
2 observing ideas of honor or reputation ⟨They're seeking an *honorable* peace.⟩
3 having high moral standards of behavior : ETHICAL, UPRIGHT ⟨She is too *honorable* to stoop to cheating.⟩
hon•or•ably \-blē\ *adv*

hon•or•ary \'ä-nə-ˌrer-ē\ *adj*
given or done as an honor ⟨They made him an *honorary* member of the club.⟩

hon•our *chiefly British variant of* HONOR

hood \'hu̇d\ *n*
1 a covering for the head and neck and sometimes the face
2 the movable covering for an automobile engine
3 a cover that is used especially to protect or shield something ⟨a lens *hood*⟩
hood•ed \'hu̇-dəd\ *adj*

-hood \ˌhu̇d\ *n suffix*
1 state : condition : quality : nature ⟨child*hood*⟩ ⟨likeli*hood*⟩
2 instance of a specified state or quality ⟨false*hood*⟩
3 individuals sharing a specified state or character ⟨man*hood*⟩

hood•lum \'hüd-ləm, 'hu̇d-\ *n*
a tough and violent criminal : THUG

hood•wink \'hu̇d-ˌwiŋk\ *vb* **hood•winked**; **hood•wink•ing**
to mislead by trickery

hoof \'hu̇f, 'hüf\ *n, pl* **hooves** \'hu̇vz, 'hüvz\ *or* **hoofs**
1 ▼ a covering of tough material that protects the ends of the toes of some animals (as horses, oxen, or pigs)
2 a foot (as of a horse) covered by a hoof
hoofed \'hu̇ft, 'hüft\ *adj*

¹hook \'hu̇k\ *n*
1 ► a curved device (as a piece of bent metal) for catching, holding, or pulling something ⟨coat *hook*⟩ ⟨crochet *hook*⟩
2 something curved or bent like a hook ⟨a *hook* of land⟩
by hook or by crook in any way : fairly or unfairly

¹hook 1

²hook *vb* **hooked**; **hook•ing**
1 to bend in the shape of a hook ⟨He *hooked* his thumbs in his belt.⟩
2 to catch or fasten with a hook ⟨I *hooked* a fish.⟩
3 CONNECT 1 ⟨She *hooked* the hose to the faucet.⟩

hooked \'hu̇kt\ *adj*
1 shaped like or provided with a hook ⟨a *hooked* beak⟩
2 fascinated by or fond of something ⟨He's *hooked* on computer games.⟩

hook•worm \'hu̇k-ˌwərm\ *n*
a small worm that lives in the intestines and makes people sick by sucking their blood

hooky *also* **hook•ey** \'hu̇-kē\ *n*
TRUANT ⟨She played *hooky* from work.⟩

hoof 1
There are two types of hoofed mammals: those with an uneven number of one or three toes, and those with an even number of two or four. Uneven-toed mammals include zebras, horses, and rhinoceroses, and even-toed mammals include cattle, pigs, sheep, giraffes, hippopotamuses, and camels. Hooves, such as those of cattle, that have two toes with a small gap in between, are known as cloven hooves.

hoop \'hüp, 'hu̇p\ *n*
1 a circular figure or object ⟨an embroidery *hoop*⟩
2 a circular band used for holding together the strips that make up the sides of a barrel or tub
3 a circle or series of circles of flexible material (as wire) used for holding a woman's skirt out from the body

hoo•ray \hu̇-'rā\ *also* **hur•rah** \hu̇-'rȯ, -'rä\ *or* **hur•ray** \-'rā\ *interj*
used to express joy, approval, or encouragement

[1]**hoot** \'hüt\ *vb* **hoot•ed**; **hoot•ing**
1 to utter a loud shout or laugh
2 to make the noise of an owl or a similar cry
3 to express by hoots ⟨The crowd *hooted* disapproval.⟩

[2]**hoot** *n*
1 the sound made by an owl
2 a loud laugh or shout
3 the least bit ⟨She doesn't care a *hoot* about sports.⟩

[1]**hop** \'häp\ *vb* **hopped**; **hop•ping**
1 to move by short quick jumps
2 to jump on one foot
3 to jump over ⟨We *hopped* the puddle.⟩
4 to get on, in, or aboard by or as if by hopping ⟨Quick, *hop* the bus.⟩
5 to make a quick trip especially by air ⟨Let's *hop* down to Atlanta.⟩

[2]**hop** *n*
1 a short quick jump especially on one leg
2 a short trip especially by air

[3]**hop** *n*
1 a twining vine whose greenish flowers look like small cones
2 *hops pl* the dried flowers of the hop plant used chiefly in making beer and ale

[1]**hope** \'hōp\ *vb* **hoped**; **hop•ing**
to desire especially with expectation that the wish will be granted ⟨I *hope* she remembers I'm coming.⟩

[2]**hope** *n*
1 desire together with the expectation of getting what is wanted
2 a chance or likelihood for something desired ⟨There isn't much *hope* of winning.⟩
3 something wished for ⟨My *hope* is that we'll all do well.⟩
4 someone or something that may be able to help

hope•ful \'hōp-fəl\ *adj*
1 full of hope
2 giving hope : PROMISING ⟨a *hopeful* sign⟩
hope•ful•ly \-fə-lē\ *adv*

hope•less \'hō-pləs\ *adj*
1 having no hope ⟨He feels *hopeless* about the future.⟩
2 offering no hope ⟨The situation looks *hopeless*.⟩
hope•less•ly *adv*
hope•less•ness *n*

Ho•pi \'hō-pē\ *n, pl* **Hopi** *or* **Ho•pis**
1 a member of an American Indian people of northeastern Arizona
2 the language of the Hopi people

hop•per \'hä-pər\ *n*
1 someone or something that hops
2 an insect that moves by leaping
3 a container used for pouring material (as grain or coal) into a machine or a bin
4 a railroad car for materials that are transported in large quantities

hop•scotch \'häp-,skäch\ *n*
a game in which a player tosses a stone into sections of a figure drawn on the ground and hops through the figure and back to pick up the stone

horde \'hȯrd\ *n*
MULTITUDE, SWARM ⟨a *horde* of ants⟩

ho•ri•zon \hə-'rī-zᵊn\ *n*
1 the line where the earth or sea seems to meet the sky
2 the limit of a person's outlook or experience ⟨Reading broadens our *horizons*.⟩

[1]**hor•i•zon•tal** \,hȯr-ə-'zän-tᵊl\ *adj*
lying flat or level : parallel to the horizon
hor•i•zon•tal•ly *adv*

[2]**horizontal** *n*
something (as a line or plane) that is parallel to the horizon

hor•mone \'hȯr-,mōn\ *n*
any of various chemical substances produced by body cells and released especially into the blood and having a specific effect on cells or organs of the body usually at a distance from the place of origin

horn \'hȯrn\ *n*
1 ▼ one of the hard bony growths on the head of many hoofed animals (as cattle, goats, or sheep)
2 the tough material of which horns and hooves are composed ⟨The knife handle was made of *horn*.⟩
3 a brass musical instrument (as a trumpet or French horn)
4 a usually electrical device that makes a noise like that of a horn ⟨Drivers were blowing their *horns*.⟩
5 something shaped like or made from a horn ⟨Each soldier carried a *horn* of powder.⟩
6 a musical or signaling instrument made from an animal's horn
horned \'hȯrnd\ *adj*
horn•less \'hȯrn-ləs\ *adj*

horn 1: a goat with large horns

horned toad *n*
a small harmless lizard with a wide flattened body like a toad and hard pointed growths on the skin

hor•net \'hȯr-nət\ *n*
a large wasp that can give a severe sting

horn of plenty *n, pl* **horns of plenty**
CORNUCOPIA

horny \'hȯr-nē\ *adj* **horn•i•er**; **horn•i•est**
1 made of horn
2 hard and rough ⟨*horny* hands⟩

horo•scope \'hȯr-ə-,skōp, 'här-\ *n*
1 a diagram of the positions of the planets and signs of the zodiac used in astrology
2 a prediction based on astrology

hor•ren•dous \hȯ-'ren-dəs, hä-, hə-\ *adj*
very bad

hor•ri•ble \'hȯr-ə-bəl\ *adj*
1 causing horror : TERRIBLE ⟨a *horrible* crash⟩
2 very unpleasant ⟨a *horrible* smell⟩
hor•ri•bly \-blē\ *adv*

hor•rid \'hȯr-əd\ *adj*
1 HORRIBLE 1 ⟨They live in *horrid* poverty.⟩
2 very unpleasant : DISGUSTING ⟨He drank the *horrid* medicine.⟩

hor•ri•fy \'hȯr-ə-,fī\ *vb* **hor•ri•fied**; **hor•ri•fy•ing**
to cause to feel great fear, dread, or shock

hor•ror \'hȯr-ər\ *n*
1 great fear, dread, or shock ⟨The survivors were filled with *horror*.⟩
2 a quality or thing that causes horror ⟨They witnessed the *horror* of war.⟩

horse \'hȯrs\ *n*
1 ► a large hoofed animal that feeds especially on grasses and is used as a work animal and for riding
2 a frame that supports something (as wood while being cut)
3 a piece of gymnasium equipment used for vaulting exercises
from the horse's mouth from the original source

horse 1

The first horses evolved millions of years ago, with separate breeds developing in different habitats. Once horses were tamed, certain characteristics were encouraged by breeding from the best animals. Today there are more than 300 breeds of domestic horse. They can broadly be divided into three main types — light horses, heavy horses, and ponies, which are the smallest variety. Various breeds are suited to specific purposes, such as riding, racing, and harness work.

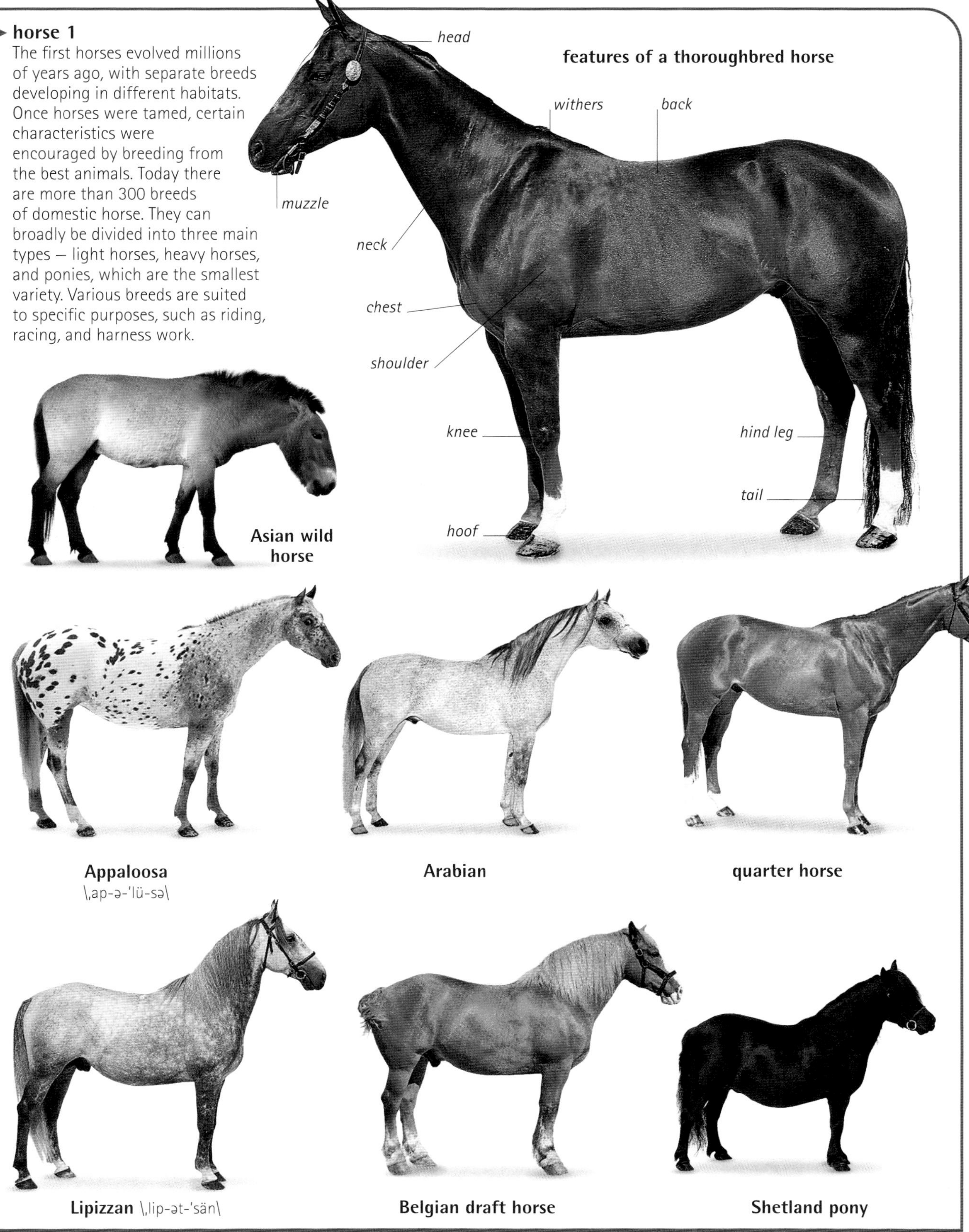

Asian wild horse

Appaloosa \ˌap-ə-ˈlü-sə\

Arabian

quarter horse

Lipizzan \ˌlip-ət-ˈsän\

Belgian draft horse

Shetland pony

A B C D E F G H I J K L M N O P Q R S T U V W X Y Z

[1]horse•back \'hȯrs-ˌbak\ *n*
the back of a horse 〈They're traveling on *horseback.*〉

[2]horseback *adv*
on horseback 〈We rode *horseback.*〉

horse chestnut *n*
▼ a shiny large brown nut that is unfit to eat and is the fruit of a tall tree native to Europe

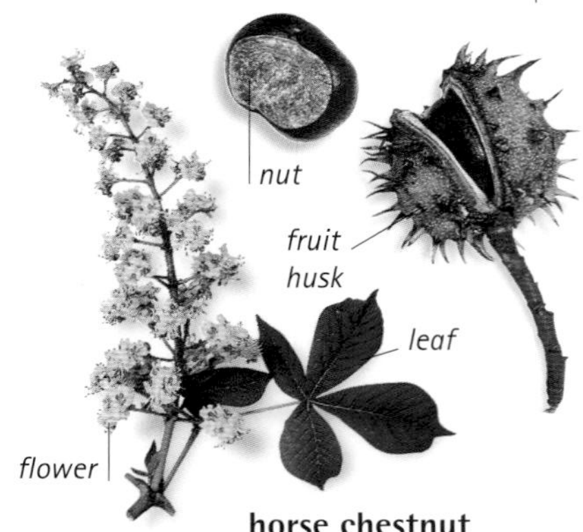

horse chestnut

horse•fly \'hȯrs-ˌflī\ *n, pl* **horse•flies**
a large fly that has bulging eyes and of which the female delivers a painful bite to suck the blood of people and animals

horse•hair \'hȯrs-ˌher\ *n*
1 the hair of a horse especially from the mane or tail
2 a cloth made from horsehair

horse•man \'hȯrs-mən\ *n, pl* **horse•men** \-mən\
1 a horseback rider
2 a person skilled in handling horses
horse•man•ship \-ˌship\ *n*

horse•play \'hȯrs-ˌplā\ *n*
rough play

horse•pow•er \'hȯrs-ˌpau̇-ər\ *n*
a unit of power that equals the work done in lifting 550 pounds one foot in one second

horse•rad•ish \'hȯrs-ˌra-dish\ *n*
a sharp-tasting relish made from the root of a tall white-flowered plant

horse•shoe \'hȯrs-ˌshü\ *n*
1 ▼ a protective iron plate that is nailed to the rim of a horse's hoof
2 something shaped like a horseshoe
3 horseshoes *pl* a game in which horseshoes are tossed at a stake in the ground

horseshoe 1

horse•tail \'hȯrs-ˌtāl\ *n*
a plant that produces spores and has small leaves resembling scales

horse•whip \'hȯrs-ˌwip, 'hȯrs-ˌhwip\ *vb* **horse•whipped; horse•whip•ping**
to beat severely with a whip made to be used on a horse

horse•wom•an \'hȯrs-ˌwu̇-mən\ *n, pl* **horse•wom•en** \-ˌwi-mən\
a woman skilled in riding on horseback or in handling horses

hors•ey *also* **horsy** \'hȯr-sē\ *adj* **hors•i•er; hors•i•est**
of or relating to horses or horsemen and horsewomen

[1]hose \'hōz\ *n, pl* **hose** *or* **hos•es**
1 *pl hose* STOCKING 1, SOCK
2 ▶ a flexible tube for carrying fluid

[1]hose 2:
a fire fighter with a hose

[2]hose *vb* **hosed; hos•ing**
to spray, water, or wash with a hose 〈Can you *hose* off the car?〉

ho•siery \'hō-zhə-rē\ *n*
clothing (as stockings or socks) that is worn on the legs and feet

hos•pi•ta•ble \hä-'spi-tə-bəl, 'hä-spi-\ *adj*
1 friendly and generous to guests and visitors
2 willing to deal with something new 〈They were *hospitable* to the changes.〉
hos•pi•ta•bly \-blē\ *adv*

hos•pi•tal \'hä-ˌspi-tᵊl\ *n*
a place where the sick and injured are given medical care

hos•pi•tal•i•ty \ˌhä-spə-'ta-lə-tē\ *n*
friendly and generous treatment of guests

hos•pi•tal•ize \'hä-ˌspi-tə-ˌlīz\ *vb* **hos•pi•tal•ized; hos•pi•tal•iz•ing**
to place in a hospital for care and treatment
hos•pi•tal•iza•tion \ˌhä-ˌspi-tə-lə-'zā-shən\ *n*

[1]host \'hōst\ *n*
1 a person who receives or entertains guests
2 a living animal or plant on or in which a parasite lives

[2]host *vb* **host•ed; host•ing**
to serve as host to or at 〈*host* friends〉 〈*hosting* a party〉

[3]host *n*
MULTITUDE 〈We faced a *host* of problems.〉

[4]host *n, often cap*
the bread used in Christian Communion

hos•tage \'hä-stij\ *n*
a person who is captured by someone who demands that certain things be done before the captured person is freed

hos•tel \'hä-stᵊl\ *n*
a place providing inexpensive lodging usually for young travelers

host•ess \'hō-stəs\ *n*
a woman who receives or entertains guests

hos•tile \'hä-stᵊl\ *adj*
1 belonging to or relating to an enemy 〈They entered *hostile* territory.〉
2 UNFRIENDLY 1 〈He moved to get away from *hostile* neighbors.〉

hos•til•i•ty \hä-'sti-lə-tē\ *n, pl* **hos•til•i•ties**
1 an unfriendly or hostile state, attitude, or action 〈They showed no *hostility* toward strangers.〉
2 *hostilities pl* acts of warfare

hot \'hät\ *adj* **hot•ter; hot•test**
1 having a high temperature 〈a *hot* stove〉 〈a *hot* day〉
2 having or causing the sensation of an uncomfortably high degree of body heat
3 having a flavor that is spicy or full of pepper 〈*hot* mustard〉
4 currently popular 〈the *hottest* fashions〉
5 close to something sought 〈Keep looking, you're getting *hot.*〉
6 easily excited 〈a *hot* temper〉
7 marked by or causing anger or strong feelings 〈a *hot* issue〉
8 very angry
9 recently stolen

10 recently made or received ⟨*hot* news⟩
11 RADIOACTIVE
hot•ly *adv*
hot•ness *n*

hot•cake \'hät-,kāk\ *n*
PANCAKE

hot dog \'hät-,dȯg\ *n*
a frankfurter cooked and then served in a long split roll

ho•tel \hō-'tel\ *n*
a place that provides lodging and meals for the public : INN

hot•head \'hät-,hed\ *n*
a person who is easily excited or angered
hot•head•ed \-'hed-əd\ *adj*

hot•house \'hät-,hau̇s\ *n*
a heated building enclosed by glass for growing plants

hot•line \'hät-,līn\ *n*
a direct telephone line for getting help in an emergency

hot plate \'hät-,plāt\ *n*
a small portable appliance for heating or cooking

hot rod *n*
an automobile rebuilt for high speed and fast acceleration

hot water *n*
a difficult or distressing situation

[1]hound \'hau̇nd\ *n*
▼ a dog with drooping ears that is used in hunting and follows game by the sense of smell

[2]hound *vb* **hound•ed**; **hound•ing**
to hunt, chase, or annoy without ceasing

hour \'au̇r\ *n*
1 one of the 24 divisions of a day : 60 minutes
2 the time of day ⟨The *hour* is now half past five.⟩
3 a fixed or particular time ⟨school *hours*⟩ ⟨He helped in our *hour* of need.⟩
4 the distance that can be traveled in an hour ⟨She lives three *hours* from here.⟩

hour•glass \'au̇r-,glas\ *n*
▶ a device for measuring time in which sand takes an hour to run from the upper into the lower part of a glass container

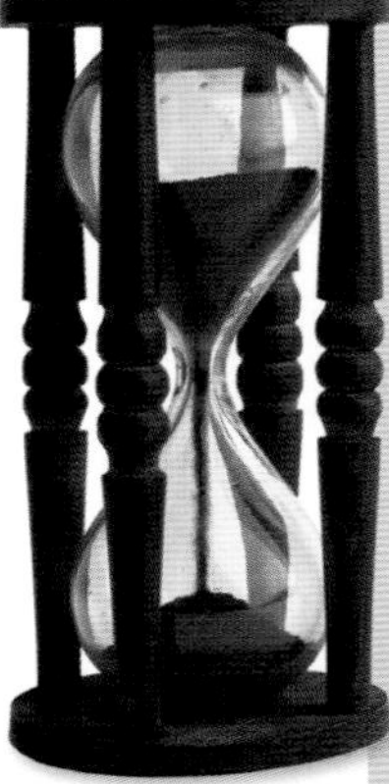
hourglass

[1]hound

Hounds, the oldest variety of dog, were originally bred to catch game birds and animals. In many hounds, the keen sense of smell common to all dogs is extremely well-developed. Other hounds have great stamina and keen vision to chase and pursue game. The greyhound is believed to be the fastest of all dogs and can run up to 40 miles (65 kilometers) per hour.

features of an Irish wolfhound

Afghan hound

bloodhound

wire-haired dachshund

greyhound

basset \'ba-sət\ **hound**

American foxhound \'fäks-,hau̇nd\

[1]hour•ly \ˈau̇r-lē\ *adv*
at or during every hour ⟨Planes leave *hourly* for Miami.⟩

[2]hourly *adj*
1 occurring every hour ⟨*hourly* departures⟩
2 figured by the hour ⟨an *hourly* wage⟩

[1]house \ˈhau̇s\ *n, pl* **hous•es** \ˈhau̇-zəz\
1 a place built for people to live in
2 something (as a nest or den) used by an animal for shelter
3 a building in which something is kept ⟨a carriage *house*⟩
4 [1]HOUSEHOLD ⟨Her noise woke up the whole *house.*⟩
5 a body of persons assembled to make the laws for a country ⟨The United States Congress is made up of two *houses.*⟩
6 a business firm ⟨a publishing *house*⟩
7 the audience in a theater or concert hall
8 FAMILY 2 ⟨the *house* of Windsor⟩
on the house free of charge ⟨Dessert is *on the house.*⟩

[2]house \ˈhau̇z\ *vb* **housed**; **hous•ing**
1 to provide with living quarters or shelter
2 CONTAIN 2 ⟨All three movies are *housed* in a single set.⟩

house•boat \ˈhau̇s-ˌbōt\ *n*
a roomy pleasure boat fitted for use as a place to live

house•boy \ˈhau̇s-ˌbȯi\ *n*
a boy or man hired to do housework

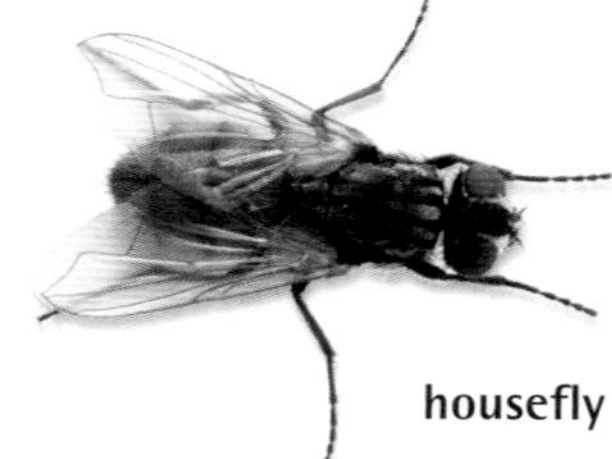
housefly

house•fly \ˈhau̇s-ˌflī\ *n, pl* **house•flies**
▲ a fly that is common in houses and may carry disease germs

[1]house•hold \ˈhau̇s-ˌhōld\ *n*
all the people in a family or group who live together in one house

[2]household *adj*
1 of or relating to a house or a household ⟨*household* chores⟩
2 FAMILIAR 1 ⟨a *household* name⟩

house•hold•er \ˈhau̇s-ˌhōl-dər\ *n*
a person who lives in a dwelling alone or as the head of a household

house•keep•er \ˈhau̇s-ˌkē-pər\ *n*
a person employed to take care of a house

house•keep•ing \ˈhau̇s-ˌkē-piŋ\ *n*
the care and management of a house or the rooms of a hotel

house•maid \ˈhau̇s-ˌmād\ *n*
a woman or girl hired to do housework

house•moth•er \ˈhau̇s-ˌmə-t͟hər\ *n*
a woman who acts as hostess, supervisor, and often housekeeper in a residence for young people

House of Representatives *n*
the lower house of a legislature (as the United States Congress)

house•plant \ˈhau̇s-ˌplant\ *n*
▶ a plant grown or kept indoors

house•top \ˈhau̇s-ˌtäp\ *n*
[1]ROOF 1

house•warm•ing \ˈhau̇s-ˌwȯr-miŋ\ *n*
a party to celebrate moving into a new home

house•wife \ˈhau̇s-ˌwīf\ *n, pl* **house•wives** \-ˌwīvz\
a married woman in charge of a household

house•work \ˈhau̇s-ˌwərk\ *n*
the labor involved in housekeeping

hous•ing \ˈhau̇-ziŋ\ *n*
1 dwellings provided for a number of people ⟨The college built new *housing* for its students.⟩
2 something that covers or protects

hove *past and past participle of* HEAVE

hov•el \ˈhə-vəl, ˈhä-\ *n*
a small poorly built usually dirty house

hov•er \ˈhə-vər, ˈhä-\ *vb* **hov•ered**; **hov•er•ing**
1 to fly or float in the air without moving far in any direction ⟨Bees *hovered* around the hive.⟩
2 to stay near a place ⟨Waiters *hovered* about.⟩

[1]how \ˈhau̇\ *adv*
1 in what way : by what means ⟨*How* do you work this thing?⟩ ⟨*How* did they get here?⟩
2 for what reason ⟨*How* can you treat me so badly?⟩
3 to what degree, number, or amount ⟨*How* cold is it?⟩
4 in what state or condition ⟨*How* are you?⟩
how about what do you say to or think of ⟨*How about* a soda?⟩
how come [1]WHY
how do you do HELLO

[2]how *conj*
in what manner or condition ⟨We're studying *how* plants grow.⟩ ⟨I asked them *how* they were.⟩

how•ev•er \hau̇-ˈe-vər\ *adv*
1 to whatever degree or extent ⟨Finish the job *however* long it takes.⟩
2 in whatever way ⟨*However* you want to do it is fine.⟩
3 in spite of that ⟨The car was old. It did, *however,* get us home.⟩

[1]howl \ˈhau̇l\ *vb* **howled**; **howl•ing**
1 to make a loud long mournful cry or sound ⟨Wolves *howled* at the moon.⟩ ⟨Wind was *howling* through the trees.⟩
2 to cry out loudly (as with pain or amusement)

houseplant: a rubber plant

[2]howl *n*
1 a loud long mournful sound made by dogs and related animals (as wolves)
2 a long loud cry (as of distress, disappointment, or rage)

hr. *abbr* hour

H.S. *abbr* high school

ht. *abbr* height

HTML \ˌāch-(ˌ)tē-(ˌ)em-ˈel\ *n*
a computer language that is used to create pages on the World Wide Web that can include text, pictures, sound, video, and hyperlinks to other Web pages

hub \ˈhəb\ *n*
1 the center of a wheel, propeller, or fan
2 a center of activity ⟨The port is the island's *hub.*⟩

hub•bub \ˈhə-ˌbəb\ *n*
UPROAR

huck•le•ber•ry \ˈhə-kəl-ˌber-ē\ *n, pl* **huck•le•ber•ries**
a dark edible berry like a blueberry but with hard rather large seeds

huck•ster \ˈhək-stər\ *n*
PEDDLER, HAWKER

[1]hud•dle \ˈhə-dᵊl\ *vb* **hud•dled**; **hud•dling**
1 to crowd, push, or pile together ⟨People *huddled* in a doorway until the rain stopped.⟩
2 to get together to talk something over
3 to sit or lie in a curled or bent position

[2]huddle *n*
1 a closely packed group ⟨Sheep stood in a *huddle.*⟩
2 a private meeting or conference
3 a brief gathering of football players to hear instructions for the next play

hue \ˈhyü\ *n*
1 [1]COLOR 1 ⟨Flowers of every *hue* blossomed.⟩
2 a shade of a color

[1]huff \ˈhəf\ *vb* **huffed**; **huff•ing**
1 to give off puffs (as of air or steam)

2 to do or say in a way that shows anger 〈He *huffed* out of the room.〉

[2]huff *n*
a fit of anger or temper 〈We argued and she left in a *huff.*〉

huffy \'hə-fē\ *adj* **huff•i•er; huff•i•est**
easily offended or angered : PETULANT
huff•i•ly \'hə-fə-lē\ *adv*

[1]hug \'həg\ *vb* **hugged; hug•ging**
1 to clasp in the arms : EMBRACE
2 to keep close to 〈The ship *hugged* the coast.〉

[2]hug *n*
[2]EMBRACE

huge \'hyüj, 'yüj\ *adj* **hug•er; hug•est**
great in size or degree : VAST
huge•ly *adv*

hulk \'həlk\ *n*
1 a person or thing that is bulky or clumsy
2 ▼ an abandoned wreck or shell of something (as a ship)

hulk 2: a hulk on a beach

hulk•ing \'həl-kiŋ\ *adj*
very large or heavy

[1]hull \'həl\ *n*
1 the outside covering of a fruit or seed
2 the frame or body of a ship or boat

[2]hull *vb* **hulled; hull•ing**
to remove the outer covering of (a fruit or seed) 〈*hull* peas〉

hul•la•ba•loo \'hə-lə-bə-,lü\ *n, pl* **hul•la•ba•loos**
a confused noise : UPROAR, COMMOTION

[1]hum \'həm\ *vb* **hummed; hum•ming**
1 to utter a sound like a long \m\
2 to make the buzzing noise of a flying insect
3 to make musical tones with closed lips
4 to give forth a low murmur of sounds 〈The street was *humming* with activity.〉
5 to be very busy or active 〈The mall *hummed* with shoppers.〉

[2]hum *n*
1 a low continuous noise 〈the *hum* of bees〉
2 musical tones voiced without words

[1]hu•man \'hyü-mən, 'yü-\ *adj*
1 of, being, or characteristic of people as distinct from animals 〈the *human* body〉
2 having the form or characteristics of people 〈The expression on the dog's face was almost *human.*〉

[2]human *n*
HUMAN BEING
hu•man•like \'hyü-mən-,līk, 'yü-\ *adj*

human being *n*
a man, woman, or child : PERSON

hu•mane \hyü-'mān, yü-\ *adj*
having sympathy and consideration for people or animals
hu•mane•ly *adv*

[1]hu•man•i•tar•i•an \hyü-,ma-nə-'ter-ē-ən, yü-\ *n*
a person who works to improve the lives and living conditions of other people

[2]humanitarian *adj*
relating to or characteristic of people who work to improve the lives and living conditions of other people 〈*humanitarian* efforts〉

hu•man•i•ty \hyü-'ma-nə-tē, yü-\ *n, pl* **hu•man•i•ties**
1 the quality or state of being human 〈Old enemies were joined by their common *humanity* in combating the disease.〉
2 the human race 〈These discoveries will benefit *humanity.*〉
3 *humanities pl* studies (as literature, history, and art) concerned primarily with human culture
4 KINDNESS 1, SYMPATHY

hu•man•ly \'hyü-mən-lē, 'yü-\ *adv*
within the range of human ability 〈The task is not *humanly* possible.〉

[1]hum•ble \'həm-bəl\ *adj* **hum•bler; hum•blest**
1 not regarding others as inferior : not overly proud : MODEST 〈She is *humble* despite her great success.〉
2 expressed in a way that does not show too much pride 〈*humble* apologies〉
3 low in rank or condition 〈They are people of *humble* origin.〉
hum•bly \-blē\ *adv*

[2]humble *vb* **hum•bled; hum•bling**
1 to make modest 〈The failure *humbled* him.〉
2 to easily and unexpectedly defeat 〈Our surprise attack *humbled* the enemy.〉

hum•bug \'həm-,bəg\ *n*
1 FRAUD 3
2 NONSENSE

hum•ding•er \'həm-'diŋ-ər\ *n*
something striking or extraordinary

hum•drum \'həm-,drəm\ *adj*
not interesting 〈a *humdrum* day〉

hu•mer•us \'hyü-mə-rəs\ *n, pl* **hu•meri** \-,rī, -,rē\
► the long bone of the upper arm or forelimb that extends from the shoulder to the elbow

humerus

humerus

hu•mid \'hyü-məd, 'yü-\ *adj*
MOIST 〈a *humid* climate〉

hu•mid•i•fy \hyü-'mi-də-,fī, yü-\ *vb* **hu•mid•i•fied; hu•mid•i•fy•ing**
to make (as the air of a room) more moist
hu•mid•i•fi•er *n*

hu•mid•i•ty \hyü-'mi-də-tē, yü-\ *n, pl* **hu•mid•i•ties**
the degree of wetness especially of the atmosphere

hu•mil•i•ate \hyü-'mi-lē-,āt, yü-\ *vb* **hu•mil•i•at•ed; hu•mil•i•at•ing**
to cause (someone) to feel very ashamed or foolish 〈My brother *humiliates* me with my nickname, Stinky.〉

hu•mil•i•a•tion \hyü-ˌmi-lē-ˈā-shən, yü-\ *n*
1 the state of being made to feel ashamed or foolish 〈He covered his face in *humiliation.*〉
2 an instance of being made to feel ashamed or foolish

hu•mil•i•ty \hyü-ˈmi-lə-tē, yü-\ *n*
the quality of being humble 〈She accepted the award with *humility.*〉

hum•ming•bird \ˈhə-miŋ-ˌbərd\ *n*
▼ a tiny brightly colored American bird whose wings make a humming sound in flight

hummingbird

hum•mock \ˈhə-mək\ *n*
a rounded mound of earth : KNOLL

[1]**hu•mor** \ˈhyü-mər, ˈyü-\ *n*
1 the amusing quality of something 〈She couldn't see the *humor* of the situation.〉
2 the ability to see or tell the amusing quality of things 〈He's got a good sense of *humor.*〉
3 state of mind : MOOD 〈in a bad *humor*〉
hu•mor•less \-ləs\ *adj*

[2]**humor** *vb* **hu•mored; hu•mor•ing**
to give in to the wishes of 〈I *humored* her and listened to her ridiculous idea.〉

hu•mor•ist \ˈhyü-mə-rist, ˈyü-\ *n*
a person who writes or talks in a humorous way

hu•mor•ous \ˈhyü-mə-rəs, ˈyü-\ *adj*
full of humor : FUNNY
hu•mor•ous•ly *adv*

hu•mour *chiefly British variant of* HUMOR

hump \ˈhəmp\ *n*
1 a rounded bulge or lump (as on the back of a camel)
2 a difficult part (as of a task) 〈With that done, we're over the *hump.*〉
humped \ˈhəmpt\ *adj*

hump•back \ˈhəmp-ˌbak\ *n*
1 a humped or crooked back
2 HUMPBACK WHALE
hump•backed \-ˈbakt\ *adj*

humpback whale *n*
a large whale that is black above and white below and has very long flippers

hu•mus \ˈhyü-məs, ˈyü-\ *n*
the dark rich part of earth formed from decaying plant or animal material

[1]**hunch** \ˈhənch\ *vb* **hunched; hunch•ing**
1 to bend the body into an arch or hump 〈Don't *hunch* over when you walk.〉
2 to draw up close together or into an arch 〈The cat *hunched* its back.〉

[2]**hunch** *n*
a strong feeling about what will happen 〈I have a *hunch* she will forgive him.〉

hunch•back \ˈhənch-ˌbak\ *n*
1 HUMPBACK 1
2 a person with a humped or crooked back

[1]**hun•dred** \ˈhən-drəd\ *n*
1 ten times ten : 100
2 a very large number 〈He walked this route *hundreds* of times.〉

[2]**hundred** *adj*
being 100 〈a *hundred* years〉

[1]**hun•dredth** \ˈhən-drədth\ *adj*
coming right after 99th

[2]**hundredth** *n*
number 100 in a series

hung *past and past participle of* HANG

[1]**hun•ger** \ˈhəŋ-gər\ *n*
1 a desire or a need for food
2 a strong desire 〈a *hunger* for knowledge〉

[2]**hunger** *vb* **hun•gered; hun•ger•ing**
1 to feel a desire or need for food
2 to have a strong desire 〈He *hungered* to return home.〉

hun•gry \ˈhəŋ-grē\ *adj* **hun•gri•er; hun•gri•est**
1 feeling or showing hunger
2 having a strong desire 〈She was *hungry* for power.〉
hun•gri•ly \-grə-lē\ *adv*

hunk \ˈhəŋk\ *n*
a large lump or piece

hun•ker \ˈhəŋ-kər\ *vb* **hun•kered; hun•ker•ing**
[1]CROUCH 〈She *hunkered* in the tall grass.〉
hunker down to settle in for a long time 〈He *hunkered down* for the winter.〉

[1]**hunt** \ˈhənt\ *vb* **hunt•ed; hunt•ing**
1 to chase after in order to capture or kill 〈*hunt* deer〉
2 to try to find 〈I *hunted* for my key.〉
synonyms see SEEK
hunting *n*

[2]**hunt** *n*
1 an instance or the practice of chasing to capture or kill
2 an act of searching

hunt•er \ˈhən-tər\ *n*
1 a person who hunts wild animals
2 a dog or horse used or trained for hunting
3 a person who searches for something 〈a bargain *hunter*〉

hunts•man \ˈhənt-smən\ *n, pl* **hunts•men** \-smən\
HUNTER 1

[1]**hur•dle** \ˈhər-dᵊl\ *n*
1 ▼ a barrier to be jumped in a race
2 *hurdles pl* a race in which runners must jump over barriers
3 OBSTACLE 〈He overcame many *hurdles* to become successful.〉

[1]**hurdle 1:** an athlete leaping over a hurdle

[2]**hurdle** *vb* **hur•dled; hur•dling**
1 to leap over while running
2 OVERCOME 1 〈You have obstacles to *hurdle* before graduating.〉

hurl \ˈhərl\ *vb* **hurled; hurl•ing**
to throw with force 〈We *hurled* buckets of water on the flames.〉
synonyms see THROW

hurrah, hurray *variant of* HOORAY

hur•ri•cane \ˈhər-ə-ˌkān, ˈhər-i-kən\ *n*
a tropical cyclone with winds of 74 miles (119 kilometers) per hour or greater usually accompanied by rain, thunder, and lightning

▶ **Word History** The word *hurricane* is borrowed by way of Spanish from the language of the Taino Indians who, prior to the Spanish conquest of the New World, lived in great numbers on Hispaniola (modern Haiti and the Dominican Republic) and other islands of the West Indies. Other English words owed to their language are *barbecue, hammock, maize,* and *potato.*

hur•ried \ˈhər-ēd\ *adj*
1 going or working with speed : FAST ⟨a *hurried* waitress⟩
2 done in a hurry ⟨a *hurried* dinner⟩
hur•ried•ly *adv*

[1]**hur•ry** \ˈhər-ē\ *vb* **hur•ried**; **hur•ry•ing**
1 to carry or cause to go with haste ⟨She is not someone who can be *hurried*.⟩
2 to move or act with haste ⟨She *hurried* off to school.⟩
3 to speed up ⟨Mechanics *hurried* the repair job.⟩

[2]**hurry** *n*
a need to act or move more quickly than usual : RUSH

[1]**hurt** \ˈhərt\ *vb* **hurt**; **hurt•ing**
1 to feel or cause pain ⟨My feet *hurt*.⟩ ⟨These shoes *hurt*.⟩
2 to do harm to : DAMAGE ⟨The drought has *hurt* crops.⟩
3 to cause to be sad
4 to make poorer or more difficult ⟨The fumble *hurt* our team's chance of winning.⟩

[2]**hurt** *n*
1 an injury or wound to the body
2 mental or emotional pain

[3]**hurt** *adj*
physically or emotionally injured ⟨a *hurt* toe⟩ ⟨*hurt* feelings⟩

hurt•ful \ˈhərt-fəl\ *adj*
causing injury or suffering ⟨*hurtful* gossip⟩

hur•tle \ˈhər-tᵊl\ *vb* **hur•tled**; **hur•tling**
to move or fall with great speed or force ⟨Rocks *hurtled* down the hill.⟩

[1]**hus•band** \ˈhəz-bənd\ *n*
a male partner in a marriage

[2]**husband** *vb* **hus•band•ed**; **hus•band•ing**
to manage with thrift : use carefully ⟨I've learned to *husband* my money.⟩

hus•band•ry \ˈhəz-bən-drē\ *n*
1 the management or wise use of resources : THRIFT
2 the raising and management of plants or animals for food

[1]**hush** \ˈhəsh\ *vb* **hushed**; **hush•ing**
to make or become quiet, calm, or still : SOOTHE ⟨He *hushed* the baby.⟩

[2]**hush** *n*
[1]QUIET ⟨A *hush* fell over the room.⟩

hush–hush \ˈhəsh-ˌhəsh\ *adj*
[1]SECRET 1, CONFIDENTIAL ⟨Their plans are *hush-hush*.⟩

[1]**husk** \ˈhəsk\ *n*
the outer covering of a fruit or seed

[2]**husk** *vb* **husked**; **husk•ing**
to remove the outer covering from (a fruit or seed) ⟨*husk* corn⟩
husk•er *n*

[2]**husky:** a pack of huskies

[1]**hus•ky** \ˈhəs-kē\ *adj* **hus•ki•er**; **hus•ki•est**
HOARSE 2 ⟨a *husky* voice⟩
hus•ki•ly \-kə-lē\ *adv*
hus•ki•ness \-kē-nəs\ *n*

[2]**husky** *n, pl* **huskies**
▲ a strong dog with a thick coat often used to pull sleds in arctic regions

[3]**husky** *adj* **hus•ki•er**; **hus•ki•est**
1 STRONG 1, BURLY ⟨*husky* football players⟩
2 larger than average
hus•ki•ness *n*

[1]**hus•tle** \ˈhə-səl\ *vb* **hus•tled**; **hus•tling**
1 to push, crowd, or force forward roughly ⟨Officers *hustled* the prisoner to jail.⟩
2 to move or work rapidly and tirelessly ⟨They're *hustling* to get the job done.⟩ ⟨He *hustled* back to class.⟩

[2]**hustle** *n*
energetic activity ⟨The *hustle* and bustle of the school day began.⟩

hut \ˈhət\ *n*
a small roughly made and often temporary dwelling

hutch \ˈhəch\ *n*
1 a low cupboard usually having open shelves on top
2 a pen or coop for an animal

hy•a•cinth \ˈhī-ə-sinth\ *n*
a plant often grown for its stalks of fragrant flowers shaped like bells

[1]**hy•brid** \ˈhī-brəd\ *n*
1 an animal or plant whose parents differ in some hereditary characteristic or belong to different groups (as breeds or species)
2 something that is of mixed origin or composition ⟨The car is a *hybrid* that runs on gas or electricity.⟩

[2]**hybrid** *adj*
of mixed origin : of or relating to a hybrid ⟨*hybrid* species⟩

hydr- *or* **hydro-** *prefix*
1 water ⟨*hydro*electric⟩
2 hydrogen ⟨*hydro*carbon⟩

hy•drant \ˈhī-drənt\ *n*
▼ a pipe with a spout through which water may be drawn ⟨a fire *hydrant*⟩

hydrant: a fire hydrant

hy•drau•lic \hī-ˈdrȯ-lik\ *adj*
1 operated, moved, or brought about by means of water ⟨*hydraulic* pressure⟩
2 operated by liquid forced through a small hole or through a tube ⟨*hydraulic* brakes⟩
hy•drau•li•cal•ly \-li-kə-lē\ *adv*

hy•dro•car•bon \ˌhī-drə-ˈkär-bən\ *n*
a substance containing only carbon and hydrogen

hy•dro•chlo•ric acid \ˌhī-drə-ˈklȯr-ik-\ *n*
a strong acid formed by dissolving in water a gas made up of hydrogen and chlorine

hy•dro•elec•tric \ˌhī-drō-i-ˈlek-trik\ *adj*
relating to or used in the making of electricity by waterpower ⟨*hydroelectric* power⟩

hy•dro•gen \'hī-drə-jən\ *n*
a colorless, odorless, and tasteless flammable gas that is the lightest of the chemical elements

> ▶ **Word History** When hydrogen is burned it combines with oxygen to make water. That fact accounts for the name of this gas. The word *hydrogen* was formed from two Greek roots. The first, *hydro-*, means "water," and the second, *-gen*, means "giving rise to, producing."

hydrogen bomb *n*
a bomb whose great power is due to the sudden release of energy when the central portions of hydrogen atoms unite

hydrogen peroxide *n*
a liquid chemical containing hydrogen and oxygen and used for bleaching and as an antiseptic

hy•dro•plane \'hī-drə-ˌplān\ *n*
▶ a speedboat whose hull is completely or partly raised as it glides over water

hydroplane

hy•e•na \hī-'ē-nə\ *n*
a large doglike mammal of Asia and Africa that lives on flesh

hy•giene \'hī-ˌjēn\ *n*
1 a science that deals with the bringing about and keeping up of good health
2 conditions or practices (as of cleanliness) necessary for health ⟨He has good personal *hygiene.*⟩

hy•gien•ic \ˌhī-jē-'e-nik, hī-'je-nik\ *adj*
of, relating to, or leading toward health or hygiene ⟨*hygienic* conditions⟩

hy•gien•ist \hī-'jē-nist\ *n*
a person skilled in hygiene and especially in a specified branch of hygiene ⟨a dental *hygienist*⟩

hy•grom•e•ter \hī-'grä-mə-tər\ *n*
▶ an instrument for measuring the humidity of the air

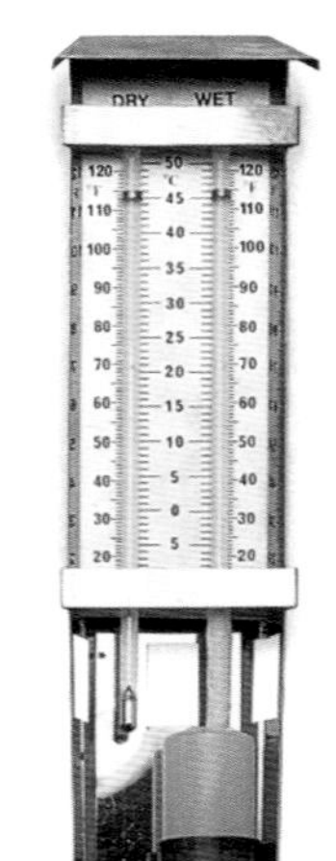

hygrometer

hymn \'him\ *n*
a song of praise especially to God

hym•nal \'him-nəl\ *n*
a book of hymns

hyper- *prefix*
excessively ⟨*hyper*sensitive⟩

hy•per•ac•tive \ˌhī-pər-'ak-tiv\ *adj*
extremely or overly active

hy•per•link \'hī-pər-ˌliŋk\ *n*
an electronic link that allows a computer user to move directly from a marked place in a hypertext document to another in the same or a different document
hyperlink *vb*

hy•per•sen•si•tive \ˌhī-pər-'sen-sə-tiv\ *adj*
very sensitive ⟨These plants are *hypersensitive* to cold.⟩

hy•per•ten•sion \ˌhī-pər-'ten-shən\ *n*
a medical condition marked by abnormally high blood pressure

hy•per•text \'hī-pər-ˌtekst\ *n*
an arrangement of the information in a computer database that allows the user to get other information by clicking on text displayed on the screen

hy•per•ven•ti•late \ˌhī-pər-'ven-tə-ˌlāt\ *vb* **hy•per•ven•ti•lat•ed**; **hy•per•ven•ti•lat•ing**
to breathe very quickly and deeply

hy•pha \'hī-fə\ *n, pl* **hy•phae** \-ˌfē\
one of the fine threads that make up the body of a fungus

¹hy•phen \'hī-fən\ *n*
a mark - used to divide or to compound words or word elements

²hyphen *vb* **hy•phened**; **hy•phen•ing**
HYPHENATE

hy•phen•ate \'hī-fə-ˌnāt\ *vb* **hy•phen•at•ed**; **hy•phen•at•ing**
to connect or mark with a hyphen

hyp•no•sis \hip-'nō-səs\ *n*
a state which resembles sleep but is produced by a person who can then make suggestions to which the person in this state can respond

hyp•not•ic \hip-'nä-tik\ *adj*
1 of or relating to hypnosis ⟨a *hypnotic* state⟩
2 having an effect like that of hypnosis ⟨a *hypnotic* rhythm⟩

hyp•no•tism \'hip-nə-ˌti-zəm\ *n*
the act or practice of producing a state like sleep in a person in which he or she will respond to suggestions made by the hypnotist

hyp•no•tist \'hip-nə-təst\ *n*
a person who hypnotizes others

hyp•no•tize \'hip-nə-ˌtīz\ *vb* **hyp•no•tized**; **hyp•no•tiz•ing**
to affect by or as if by hypnotism ⟨Her beautiful voice *hypnotized* the audience.⟩

hy•poc•ri•sy \hi-'pä-krə-sē\ *n, pl* **hy•poc•ri•sies**
the quality of acting in a way that goes against claimed beliefs or feelings

hyp•o•crite \'hi-pə-ˌkrit\ *n*
a person who acts in a way that goes against what he or she claims to believe or feel ⟨She's a *hypocrite* who complains about litter and then litters herself.⟩
hyp•o•crit•i•cal \ˌhi-pə-'kri-ti-kəl\ *adj*

hy•po•der•mic needle \ˌhī-pə-'dər-mik-\ *n*
1 ¹NEEDLE 5
2 a small syringe used with a hollow needle to inject material (as a vaccine) into or beneath the skin

hypodermic syringe *n*
HYPODERMIC NEEDLE 2

hy•pot•e•nuse \hī-'pä-tə-ˌnüs, -ˌnyüz\ *n*
the side of a right triangle that is opposite the right angle

hy•poth•e•sis \hī-'pä-thə-səs\ *n, pl* **hy•poth•e•ses** \-ə-ˌsēz\
something not proved but assumed to be true for purposes of argument or further study or investigation

hy•po•thet•i•cal \ˌhī-pə-'the-ti-kəl\ *adj*
1 involving or based on a hypothesis
2 imagined as an example for further thought ⟨a *hypothetical* situation⟩
hy•po•thet•i•cal•ly *adv*

hys•te•ria \hi-'ster-ē-ə\ *n*
a state in which emotions (as fear or joy) are so strong that a person acts in an uncontrolled way

hys•ter•i•cal \hi-'ster-i-kəl\ *adj*
1 feeling or showing extreme and uncontrolled emotion ⟨*hysterical* laughter⟩ ⟨We didn't know how to calm the *hysterical* girl.⟩
2 very funny ⟨Your joke was *hysterical.*⟩
hys•ter•i•cal•ly *adv*

hys•ter•ics \hi-'ster-iks\ *n pl*
an outburst of uncontrollable laughing or crying
Hint: *Hysterics* can be used as a singular or a plural in writing and speaking.

Ii

Sounds of I: The letter **I** makes a number of sounds. The sound heard in *pin* and *still* is the short **I**. The long **I** is heard in words like *file* and *time*. The sound of long **I** is indicated by the symbol ī. Letter **I** also makes the schwa sound, which is indicated by the symbol ə, in words like *giraffe*, and *stencil*. **I** sometimes sounds like a long **E**, such as in *ski* and *marine*, and like a **Y** in words like *onion* and *million*. **I** makes different sounds when combined with other letters, such as the long **E** sound in *piece* and *debris*, and the schwa sound in *special*, *spaniel*, and *notion*. In some words **I** is silent, such as in *juice*.

i \ˈī\ *n, pl* **i's** *or* **is** \ˈīz\ *often cap*
1 the ninth letter of the English alphabet
2 the number one in Roman numerals

I \ˈī, ə\ *pron*
the person speaking or writing ⟨*I* am here.⟩

IA, Ia. *abbr* Iowa

-ial \ē-əl, yəl, əl\ *adj suffix*
[1]-AL ⟨aer*ial*⟩

-ian see -AN

ibex \ˈī-ˌbeks\ *n, pl* **ibex** *or* **ibex•es**
▼ a wild goat that lives mostly in high mountains of Europe, Asia, and northeastern Africa and has large horns that curve backward

ibex: a Spanish ibex

-ibility see -ABILITY

ibis \ˈī-bəs\ *n, pl* **ibis** *or* **ibis•es**
a tall bird related to the herons with long legs and a slender bill that curves down

-ible see -ABLE

-ic \ik\ *adj suffix*
1 of, relating to, or having the form of : being ⟨hero*ic*⟩
2 coming from, consisting of, or containing ⟨aquat*ic*⟩
3 in the manner of ⟨aristocrat*ic*⟩
4 making use of ⟨electron*ic*⟩
5 characterized by : exhibiting ⟨nostalg*ic*⟩
6 affected with ⟨aller*gic*⟩

-ical \i-kəl\ *adj suffix*
-IC ⟨symmetr*ical*⟩

[1]**ice** \ˈīs\ *n*
1 frozen water
2 a sheet of frozen water ⟨She skated out onto the *ice*.⟩
3 a substance like ice ⟨Ammonia *ice* is found in the rings of Saturn.⟩
4 a frozen dessert usually made with sweetened fruit juice

[2]**ice** *vb* **iced**; **ic•ing**
1 to coat or become coated with ice ⟨The roads *iced* up.⟩
2 to chill with ice ⟨*Ice* the glasses.⟩
3 to cover with icing

ice age *n*
a period of time during which much of the earth is covered with glaciers

ice•berg \ˈīs-ˌbərg\ *n*
a large mass of ice that has broken away from a glacier and is floating in the ocean

ice•bound \ˈīs-ˌbau̇nd\ *adj*
surrounded or blocked by ice

ice•box \ˈīs-ˌbäks\ *n*
REFRIGERATOR

ice•break•er \ˈīs-ˌbrā-kər\ *n*
1 ▼ a ship equipped to make and keep open a channel through ice
2 something said or done that helps people relax and begin talking in a social situation ⟨The party game was a good *icebreaker*.⟩

ice cap *n*
a large more or less level glacier flowing outward in all directions from its center

ice–cold \ˈīs-ˈkōld\ *adj*
very cold ⟨*ice-cold* drinks⟩

ice skate: a girl wearing ice skates

ice cream *n*
a frozen food containing sweetened and flavored cream or butterfat

ice hockey *n*
hockey played on ice

ice–skate \ˈīs-ˌskāt\ *vb* **ice–skat•ed**; **ice–skat•ing**
to skate on ice
ice skat•er *n*

ice skate *n*
▲ a shoe with a special blade on the bottom that is used for skating on ice

ici•cle \ˈī-ˌsi-kəl\ *n*
a hanging piece of ice formed from dripping water as it freezes

icebreaker 1: model of a Finnish icebreaker

ic•ing \'ī-siŋ\ *n*
a sweet coating for baked goods (as cakes)

icon \'ī-,kän\ *n*
1 a widely known symbol ⟨The Statue of Liberty has become an *icon* of freedom.⟩
2 a person who is very successful or admired ⟨a pop *icon*⟩
3 a religious image usually painted on a small wooden panel
4 a small picture or symbol on a computer screen that represents a function that the computer can perform

-ics \iks\ *n suffix*
1 study : knowledge : skill : practice ⟨electron*ics*⟩
2 characteristic actions or qualities ⟨acrobat*ics*⟩

ICU *abbr* intensive care unit

icy \'ī-sē\ *adj* **ic•i•er**; **ic•i•est**
1 covered with, full of, or being ice ⟨*icy* roads⟩
2 very cold ⟨an *icy* wind⟩
3 UNFRIENDLY 1 ⟨an *icy* look⟩
ic•i•ly \'ī-sə-lē\ *adv*

ID *abbr*
1 Idaho
2 identification

I'd \'īd\ I had : I would ⟨*I'd* better go.⟩ ⟨*I'd* do it.⟩

idea \ī-'dē-ə\ *n*
1 a thought or plan about what to do ⟨Surprising her was a bad *idea*.⟩
2 something imagined or pictured in the mind
3 an understanding of something ⟨I have no *idea* what you mean.⟩
4 a central meaning or purpose ⟨The *idea* of the game is to keep from getting caught.⟩
5 an opinion or belief ⟨What gave you that *idea*?⟩

[1]**ide•al** \ī-'dē-əl\ *adj*
having no flaw : PERFECT ⟨*ideal* weather⟩
ide•al•ly *adv*

[2]**ideal** *n*
1 a standard of perfection, beauty, or excellence ⟨He couldn't live up to his own *ideals*.⟩
2 someone who deserves to be imitated or admired ⟨She considered the older woman her *ideal*.⟩
synonyms see MODEL

iden•ti•cal \ī-'den-ti-kəl\ *adj*
1 being one and the same ⟨We saw the *identical* movie last week.⟩
2 being exactly alike or equal ⟨They wore *identical* dresses.⟩
synonyms see SAME
iden•ti•cal•ly \-kə-lē\ *adv*

identical twin: a pair of identical twins

identical twin *n*
▲ either one of a pair of twins of the same sex that come from a single fertilized egg and are physically similar

iden•ti•fi•ca•tion \ī-,den-tə-fə-'kā-shən\ *n*
1 an act of finding out the identity of ⟨the *identification* of leaves⟩
2 something that shows or proves identity

iden•ti•fy \ī-'den-tə-,fī\ *vb* **iden•ti•fied**; **iden•ti•fy•ing**
1 to find out or show the identity of
2 to feel empathy for ⟨I *identified* with her problem.⟩
3 to think of as joined or associated with ⟨These groups are *identified* with conservation.⟩

iden•ti•ty \ī-'den-tə-tē\ *n, pl* **iden•ti•ties**
1 the set of qualities and beliefs that make one person or group different from others : INDIVIDUALITY ⟨Children establish their own *identities*.⟩
2 the fact of being the same person or thing as claimed ⟨Can you prove your *identity*?⟩
3 the fact or condition of being exactly alike : SAMENESS

id•i•o•cy \'i-dē-ə-sē\ *n, pl* **id•i•o•cies**
1 the condition of being very stupid or foolish
2 something very stupid or foolish

id•i•om \'i-dē-əm\ *n*
an expression that cannot be understood from the meanings of its separate words but must be learned as a whole ⟨The expression "give up," meaning "surrender," is an *idiom*.⟩

id•i•o•syn•cra•sy \,i-dē-ə-'siŋ-krə-sē\ *n, pl* **id•i•o•syn•cra•sies**
an unusual way of behaving or thinking that is characteristic of a person ⟨I know my friend's habits and *idiosyncracies*.⟩

id•i•ot \'i-dē-ət\ *n*
a silly or foolish person

id•i•ot•ic \,i-dē-'ä-tik\ *adj*
FOOLISH ⟨an *idiotic* story⟩

[1]**idle** \'ī-dᵊl\ *adj* **idler** \'īd-lər\; **idlest** \'īd-ləst\
1 not working or in use ⟨*idle* workers⟩ ⟨*idle* farmland⟩
2 LAZY 1
3 not based on anything real or serious ⟨an *idle* threat⟩
idle•ness \'ī-dᵊl-nəs\ *n*
idly \'īd-lē\ *adv*

[2]**idle** *vb* **idled**; **idling** \'īd-liŋ\
1 to spend time doing nothing ⟨I *idled* away the afternoon.⟩
2 to run without being connected for doing useful work ⟨The engine is *idling*.⟩

idol \'ī-dᵊl\ *n*
1 an image worshipped as a god
2 a much loved or admired person or thing ⟨a movie *idol*⟩

idol•ize \'ī-də-,līz\ *vb* **idol•ized**; **idol•iz•ing**
to love or admire greatly : make an idol of ⟨The boy *idolized* his father.⟩

i.e. *abbr* that is
Hint: The abbreviation *i.e.* is short for the Latin phrase *id est*, meaning "that is."

-ie *also* **-y** \ē\ *n suffix, pl* **-ies**
little one ⟨lass*ie*⟩

-ier see [2]-ER

if \'if, əf\ *conj*
1 in the event that ⟨*If* it rains we'll stay home.⟩
2 WHETHER 1 ⟨See *if* they have left.⟩
3 used to introduce a wish ⟨*If* only it would rain.⟩

-ify \ə-,fī\ *vb suffix* **-ified**; **-ify•ing** -FY

ig•loo \'i-glü\ *n, pl* **igloos**
a house often made of blocks of snow and shaped like a dome

ig•ne•ous \'ig-nē-əs\ *adj*
▶ formed by hardening of melted mineral material within the earth ⟨*igneous* rock⟩

igneous: pink granite is an igneous rock

ig•nite \ig-'nīt\ *vb* **ig•nit•ed**; **ig•nit•ing**
1 to set on fire : LIGHT ⟨*ignite* newspaper⟩
2 to catch fire

ig•ni•tion \ig-ˈni-shən\ *n*
1 the act of causing something to start burning
2 the process or means (as an electric spark) of causing the fuel in an engine to burn so that the engine begins working
3 a device that is used to start a motor vehicle 〈Put the key in the *ignition.*〉

ig•no•min•i•ous \ˌig-nə-ˈmi-nē-əs\ *adj*
DISGRACEFUL 〈an *ignominious* defeat〉

ig•no•rance \ˈig-nə-rəns\ *n*
a lack of knowledge, understanding, or education : the state of being ignorant

ig•no•rant \ˈig-nə-rənt\ *adj*
1 having little or no knowledge : not educated
2 not knowing : UNAWARE 〈They're *ignorant* of the facts.〉
3 resulting from or showing lack of knowledge 〈It was an *ignorant* mistake.〉
ig•no•rant•ly *adv*

ig•nore \ig-ˈnȯr\ *vb* **ig•nored; ig•nor•ing**
to pay no attention to 〈I *ignored* her rude remark.〉

igua•na \i-ˈgwä-nə\ *n*
▼a large tropical American lizard with a ridge of tall scales along its back

iguana: a common iguana

IL *abbr* Illinois

il- see **in-**

¹ill \ˈil\ *adj* **worse** \ˈwərs\; **worst** \ˈwərst\
1 not in good health : SICK 〈an *ill* person〉
2 not normal or sound 〈*ill* health〉
3 meant to do harm : EVIL 〈*ill* deeds〉
4 causing suffering or distress 〈*ill* weather〉
5 not helpful 〈He was plagued by *ill* luck.〉
6 not kind or friendly 〈*ill* intentions〉
7 not right or proper 〈*ill* manners〉

²ill *adv* **worse; worst**
1 with displeasure or anger 〈The remark was *ill* received.〉
2 in a harsh or unkind way 〈The animals were *ill* treated.〉
3 SCARCELY 1, HARDLY 〈He can *ill* afford it.〉
4 in a bad or faulty way 〈They're *ill*-prepared to face the winter.〉

³ill *n*
1 the opposite of good 〈Things will change for good or *ill.*〉
2 a sickness or disease 〈childhood *ills*〉
3 ¹TROUBLE 2 〈society's *ills*〉

illumination: the illumination of the Sydney Opera House at night

Ill. *abbr* Illinois

I'll \ˈīl\ I shall : I will 〈*I'll* be back.〉

il•le•gal \i-ˈlē-gəl\ *adj*
not allowed by the laws or rules
il•le•gal•ly \i-ˈlē-gə-lē\ *adv*

il•leg•i•ble \i-ˈle-jə-bəl\ *adj*
impossible or very hard to read 〈His handwriting is *illegible.*〉
il•leg•i•bly \-blē\ *adv*

il•le•git•i•mate \ˌi-li-ˈji-tə-mət\ *adj*
not accepted by the law as rightful 〈an *illegitimate* ruler〉

il•lic•it \i-ˈli-sət\ *adj*
not permitted : UNLAWFUL

il•lit•er•a•cy \i-ˈli-tə-rə-sē\ *n*
the state or condition of being unable to read or write

¹il•lit•er•ate \i-ˈli-tə-rət\ *adj*
unable to read or write

²illiterate *n*
a person who is unable to read or write

ill–na•tured \ˈil-ˈnā-chərd\ *adj*
having or showing an unfriendly nature 〈an *ill-natured* remark〉

ill•ness \ˈil-nəs\ *n*
1 an unhealthy condition of the body or mind 〈Germs can cause *illness.*〉
2 a specific sickness or disease 〈Colds are a common *illness.*〉

il•log•i•cal \i-ˈlä-ji-kəl\ *adj*
not using or following good reasoning 〈an *illogical* argument〉
il•log•i•cal•ly *adv*

ill–tem•pered \ˈil-ˈtem-pərd\ *adj*
having or showing a bad temper

il•lu•mi•nate \i-ˈlü-mə-ˌnāt\ *vb*
il•lu•mi•nat•ed; il•lu•mi•nat•ing
1 to supply with light : light up 〈Candles *illuminated* the room.〉
2 to make clear : EXPLAIN

il•lu•mi•na•tion \i-ˌlü-mə-ˈnā-shən\ *n*
▲the action of lighting something : the state of being lighted

ill–use \ˈil-ˈyüz\ *vb* **ill–used; ill–us•ing**
to treat badly

il•lu•sion \i-ˈlü-zhən\ *n*
1 something that is false or unreal but seems to be true or real 〈The video game creates the *illusion* of flying.〉
2 a mistaken idea

il•lu•so•ry \i-ˈlü-sə-rē\ *adj*
based on something that is not true or real : DECEPTIVE 〈an *illusory* hope〉

il•lus•trate \ˈi-lə-ˌstrāt\ *vb* **il•lus•trat•ed; il•lus•trat•ing**
1 to supply with pictures or diagrams meant to explain or decorate 〈*illustrate* a book〉
2 to make clear by using examples 〈She *illustrated* her point with stories.〉
3 to serve as an example 〈The results *illustrate* the need for planning.〉

il•lus•tra•tion \ˌi-lə-ˈstrā-shən\ *n*
1 a picture or diagram that explains or decorates 〈The dictionary has color *illustrations.*〉
2 an example or instance used to make something clear 〈The speech included *illustrations* of his successes.〉
3 the action of illustrating : the condition of being illustrated 〈He finished the *illustration* of the book.〉

il•lus•tra•tive \i-ˈlə-strə-tiv\ *adj*
serving as an example 〈an *illustrative* story〉

il•lus•tra•tor \ˈi-lə-ˌstrā-tər\ *n*
an artist who makes illustrations (as for books)

il•lus•tri•ous \i-ˈlə-strē-əs\ *adj*
admired and respected because of greatness or achievement : EMINENT

ill will *n*
unfriendly feeling

IM \ˈī-ˈem\ *vb* **IM'd**; **IM•'ing**
1 to send an instant message to
2 to communicate by instant message

image 1: the mirror shows an image of the flowers in the vase

im- see IN-

I'm \ˈīm\
I am ⟨*I'm* here.⟩

im•age \ˈi-mij\ *n*
1 ▲ a picture or reflection of something produced by a device (as a mirror or lens) ⟨We watched the *images* on the screen.⟩
2 someone who looks very much like another ⟨She is the *image* of her mother.⟩
3 the thought of how something looks
4 a representation (as a picture or statue) of something
5 an idea of what someone or something is like ⟨He has an *image* as a troublemaker.⟩

im•ag•ery \ˈi-mij-rē, -mi-jə-\ *n*
pictures or photographs of something ⟨satellite *imagery*⟩

imag•in•able \i-ˈma-jə-nə-bəl\ *adj*
possible to imagine

imag•i•nary \i-ˈma-jə-ˌner-ē\ *adj*
existing only in the imagination : not real

imag•i•na•tion \i-ˌma-jə-ˈnā-shən\ *n*
1 the act, process, or power of forming a mental picture of something not present and especially of something a person has not known or experienced
2 creative ability ⟨a writer's *imagination*⟩
3 a creation of the mind ⟨Is it just my *imagination* or are we moving?⟩

imag•i•na•tive \i-ˈma-jə-nə-tiv\ *adj*
1 relating to or showing imagination ⟨an *imaginative* story⟩
2 having a lively imagination ⟨an *imaginative* artist⟩

imag•ine \i-ˈma-jən\ *vb* **imag•ined**; **imag•in•ing**
1 to form a mental picture of : use the imagination ⟨*Imagine* yourself grown up.⟩
2 THINK 1 ⟨I *imagine* you're right.⟩

imag•in•ings \i-ˈma-jə-niŋz\ *n pl*
products of the imagination ⟨Her mind was filled with strange *imaginings*.⟩

im•be•cile \ˈim-bə-səl\ *n*
IDIOT, FOOL

im•i•tate \ˈi-mə-ˌtāt\ *vb* **im•i•tat•ed**; **im•i•tat•ing**
1 to follow as a pattern, model, or example ⟨He tried to *imitate* the older boys.⟩
2 to be or appear like : RESEMBLE ⟨The vinyl *imitates* leather.⟩
3 to copy exactly : MIMIC ⟨She can *imitate* bird calls.⟩
synonyms see COPY

[1]**im•i•ta•tion** \ˌi-mə-ˈtā-shən\ *n*
1 the act of copying someone or something ⟨She does great *imitations* of celebrities.⟩
2 [1]COPY 1

[2]**imitation** *adj*
made to look like something else and especially something valuable ⟨*imitation* pearls⟩

im•i•ta•tive \ˈi-mə-ˌtā-tiv\ *adj*
made or done to be like something or someone else ⟨*imitative* sounds⟩

im•mac•u•late \i-ˈma-kyə-lət\ *adj*
1 perfectly clean
2 having no flaw or error ⟨He has an *immaculate* driving record.⟩
im•mac•u•late•ly *adv*

im•ma•te•ri•al \ˌi-mə-ˈtir-ē-əl\ *adj*
not important : INSIGNIFICANT ⟨The new evidence is *immaterial*.⟩

im•ma•ture \ˌi-mə-ˈtu̇r, -ˈtyu̇r, -ˈchu̇r\ *adj*
1 not yet fully grown or ripe ⟨an *immature* bird⟩ ⟨*immature* fruit⟩
2 acting in or exhibiting a childish manner ⟨an *immature* teenager⟩ ⟨*immature* behavior⟩
im•ma•ture•ly *adv*

im•mea•sur•able \i-ˈme-zhə-rə-bəl\ *adj*
very great in size or amount
im•mea•sur•ably \-blē\ *adv*

im•me•di•ate \i-ˈmē-dē-ət\ *adj*
1 happening without any delay ⟨I need *immediate* help.⟩
2 occurring or existing now ⟨There is no *immediate* danger.⟩
3 having importance now ⟨Our *immediate* concern is getting help.⟩
4 not far away in time or space ⟨the *immediate* future⟩ ⟨the *immediate* area⟩
5 being next in line or nearest in relationship ⟨my *immediate* family⟩
6 having nothing between ⟨The room is to your *immediate* right.⟩

im•me•di•ate•ly \i-ˈmē-dē-ət-lē\ *adv*
1 with nothing between
2 right away ⟨Come here *immediately*!⟩

im•mense \i-ˈmens\ *adj*
very great in size or amount : HUGE
im•mense•ly *adv*

im•men•si•ty \i-ˈmen-sə-tē\ *n*, *pl* **im•men•si•ties**
extremely great size, amount, or extent

im•merse \i-ˈmərs\ *vb* **im•mersed**; **im•mers•ing**
1 ▼ to plunge into something (as a fluid) that surrounds or covers
2 to become completely involved with ⟨She was *immersed* in a good book.⟩

immerse 1:
a swimmer immersed in water

im•mi•grant \ˈi-mi-grənt\ *n*
a person who comes to a country to live

im•mi•grate \ˈi-mə-ˌgrāt\ *vb* **im•mi•grat•ed**; **im•mi•grat•ing**
to come into a foreign country to live

im•mi•gra•tion \ˌi-mə-ˈgrā-shən\ *n*
an act or instance of coming into a foreign country to live

im•mi•nent \ˈi-mə-nənt\ *adj*
being about to happen ⟨*imminent* danger⟩

im•mo•bile \i-ˈmō-bəl\ *adj*
unable to move or be moved

im•mo•bi•lize \im-ˈō-bə-ˌlīz\ *vb* **im•mo•bi•lized**; **im•mo•bi•liz•ing**
to keep from moving : make immovable

im•mod•est \i-ˈmä-dəst\ *adj*
1 not proper in thought, conduct, or dress ⟨*immodest* behavior⟩
2 being vain or showing vanity ⟨He was *immodest* to call himself a hero.⟩

immune system
The human immune system responds to any threat to the body's health. White blood cells cluster in the lymph nodes and spleen or travel in a clear fluid, lymph, which circulates around the body. As the lymph is filtered by the lymph nodes and the blood is filtered by the spleen, white blood cells recognize and attack infectious agents such as bacteria and viruses. The tonsils and adenoids serve to trap infectious agents that enter the body through the mouth and nose.

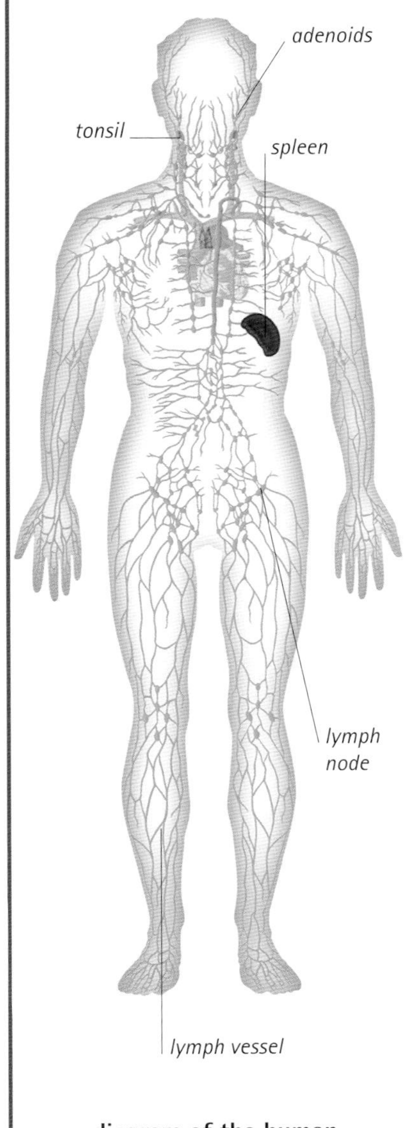

diagram of the human immune system

im•mor•al \i-ˈmȯr-əl\ *adj*
not following principles of right and wrong : WICKED, BAD

im•mo•ral•i•ty \ˌi-mȯ-ˈra-lə-tē\ *n, pl* **im•mo•ral•i•ties**
the quality or state of being without principles of right and wrong

[1]**im•mor•tal** \i-ˈmȯr-tᵊl\ *adj*
living or lasting forever

[2]**immortal** *n*
1 a being that lives forever : a god or goddess
2 a person of lasting fame ⟨baseball *immortals*⟩

im•mor•tal•i•ty \ˌi-mȯr-ˈta-lə-tē\ *n*
1 the quality or state of living forever : endless life ⟨She wished for *immortality.*⟩
2 lasting fame or glory

im•mov•able \i-ˈmü-və-bəl\ *adj*
1 impossible to move : firmly fixed in place
2 not able to be changed or persuaded ⟨He is *immovable* in his beliefs.⟩

im•mune \i-ˈmyün\ *adj*
1 having a high degree of resistance to an illness or disease
2 of, relating to, or involving the body's immune system ⟨an *immune* response⟩
3 not influenced or affected by something ⟨She is *immune* to criticism.⟩
4 not subject to something : EXEMPT ⟨They are *immune* from punishment.⟩

immune system *n*
◀ the system of the body that fights infection and disease and that includes especially the white blood cells and antibodies and the organs that produce them

im•mu•ni•ty \i-ˈmyü-nə-tē\ *n, pl* **im•mu•ni•ties**
1 freedom from an obligation or penalty to which others are subject
2 the power to resist infection whether natural or acquired (as by vaccination)

im•mu•ni•za•tion \ˌi-myə-nə-ˈzā-shən\ *n*
treatment (as with a vaccine) to produce immunity to a disease

im•mu•nize \ˈi-myə-ˌnīz\ *vb* **im•mu•nized; im•mu•niz•ing**
to make immune especially by vaccination

imp \ˈimp\ *n*
1 a small demon
2 a mischievous child

[1]**im•pact** \ˈim-ˌpakt\ *n*
1 ▶ a striking of one body against another : COLLISION ⟨The meteor's *impact* left a crater.⟩
2 a strong effect ⟨warned of the economic *impact*⟩

[2]**im•pact** \im-ˈpakt\ *vb* **im•pact•ed; im•pact•ing**
1 to have a strong and often bad effect on ⟨This change will *impact* all schools.⟩
2 to hit with great force

im•pair \im-ˈper\ *vb* **im•paired; im•pair•ing**
to lessen in function, ability, or quality : weaken or make worse

im•paired \im-ˈperd\ *adj*
lessened in function or ability ⟨visually *impaired* people⟩

im•pale \im-ˈpāl\ *vb* **im•paled; im•pal•ing**
to pierce with something pointed

im•part \im-ˈpärt\ *vb* **im•part•ed; im•part•ing**
1 to give or grant from or as if from a supply ⟨The sun *imparts* warmth.⟩
2 to make known ⟨She *imparted* the news.⟩

im•par•tial \im-ˈpär-shəl\ *adj*
not favoring one side over another : FAIR ⟨an *impartial* referee⟩
im•par•tial•ly *adv*

im•par•tial•i•ty \im-ˌpär-shē-ˈa-lə-tē\ *n*
the quality or state of being fair and just ⟨The judge maintained *impartiality.*⟩

im•pass•able \im-ˈpa-sə-bəl\ *adj*
impossible to pass, cross, or travel

im•pas•sioned \im-ˈpa-shənd\ *adj*
showing very strong feeling ⟨an *impassioned* speech⟩

im•pas•sive \im-ˈpa-siv\ *adj*
not feeling or showing emotion ⟨an *impassive* face⟩
im•pas•sive•ly *adv*

im•pa•tience \im-ˈpā-shəns\ *n*
1 the quality of not wanting to put up with or wait for something or someone : lack of patience
2 restless or eager desire

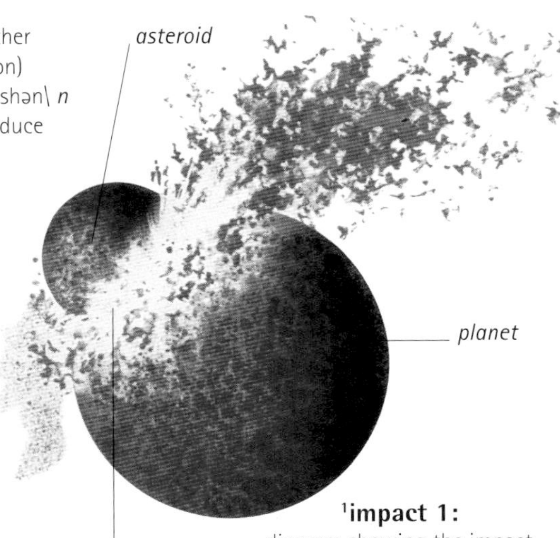

[1]**impact 1:** diagram showing the impact between an asteroid and a planet

im•pa•tient \im-'pā-shənt\ *adj*
1 not wanting to put up with or wait for something or someone
2 showing a lack of patience ⟨an *impatient* reply⟩
3 restless and eager ⟨We're *impatient* to go.⟩
im•pa•tient•ly *adv*

im•peach \im-'pēch\ *vb* **im•peached**; **im•peach•ing**
to charge a public official formally with misconduct in office

im•pec•ca•ble \im-'pe-kə-bəl\ *adj*
free from fault or error ⟨He had *impeccable* manners.⟩

im•pede \im-'pēd\ *vb* **im•ped•ed**; **im•ped•ing**
to interfere with the movement or progress of

im•ped•i•ment \im-'pe-də-mənt\ *n*
1 something that interferes with movement or progress
2 a condition that makes it difficult to speak normally

im•pel \im-'pel\ *vb* **im•pelled**; **im•pel•ling**
to urge or force into action ⟨I felt *impelled* to speak up.⟩

im•pend•ing \im-'pen-diŋ\ *adj*
happening or likely to happen soon ⟨an *impending* storm⟩

im•pen•e•tra•ble \im-'pe-nə-trə-bəl\ *adj*
1 impossible to pass through or see through ⟨*impenetrable* walls⟩ ⟨*impenetrable* darkness⟩
2 impossible to understand ⟨an *impenetrable* mystery⟩

im•per•a•tive \im-'per-ə-tiv\ *adj*
1 expressing a command, request, or strong encouragement ⟨"Come here!" is an *imperative* sentence.⟩
2 URGENT 1 ⟨It is *imperative* that you see a doctor.⟩

im•per•cep•ti•ble \ˌim-pər-'sep-tə-bəl\ *adj*
not noticeable by the senses or by the mind : very small or gradual ⟨*imperceptible* changes⟩
im•per•cep•ti•bly \-blē\ *adv*

im•per•fect \im-'pər-fikt\ *adj*
having a fault of some kind : not perfect
im•per•fect•ly *adv*

im•per•fec•tion \ˌim-pər-'fek-shən\ *n*
1 the quality or state of having faults or defects : lack of perfection
2 a small flaw or fault

im•pe•ri•al \im-'pir-ē-əl\ *adj*
of or relating to an empire or its ruler ⟨the *imperial* palace⟩

im•per•il \im-'per-əl\ *vb* **im•per•iled** *or* **im•per•illed**; **im•per•il•ing** *or* **im•per•il•ling**
to place in great danger

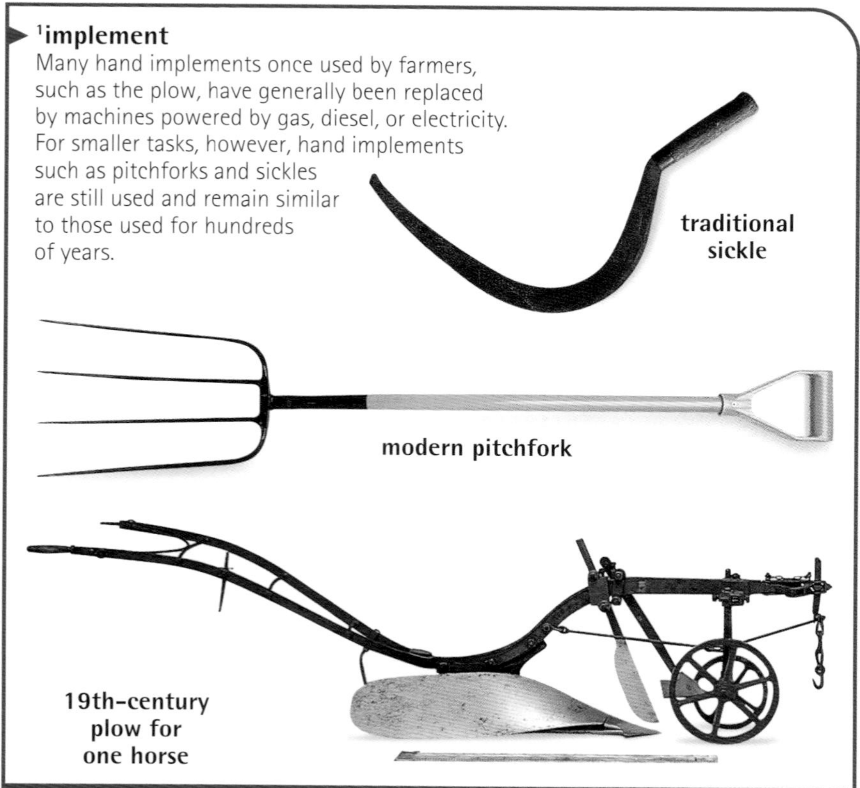

¹implement
Many hand implements once used by farmers, such as the plow, have generally been replaced by machines powered by gas, diesel, or electricity. For smaller tasks, however, hand implements such as pitchforks and sickles are still used and remain similar to those used for hundreds of years.

im•per•son•al \im-'pər-sə-nəl\ *adj*
1 not caring about individual persons or their feelings ⟨She disliked the large *impersonal* city.⟩
2 not showing or involving personal feelings ⟨We discussed the weather and other *impersonal* topics.⟩

im•per•son•ate \im-'pər-sə-ˌnāt\ *vb* **im•per•son•at•ed**; **im•per•son•at•ing**
to pretend to be another person

▶ **Synonyms** IMPERSONATE, PLAY, and ACT mean to pretend to be somebody else. IMPERSONATE is used when someone tries to look and sound like another person as much as possible. ⟨You're good at *impersonating* celebrities.⟩ PLAY is used when someone takes a part in a play, movie, or TV show. ⟨You can *play* the part of the spy.⟩ ACT may be used in situations other than performing in a drama or pretending to be a person. ⟨*Act* like you're a dog.⟩

im•per•son•a•tion \im-ˌpər-sə-'nā-shən\ *n*
the act of pretending to be another person

im•per•ti•nence \im-'pər-tə-nəns\ *n*
the quality or state of being very rude or disrespectful

im•per•ti•nent \im-'pər-tə-nənt\ *adj*
very rude : having or showing a lack of respect ⟨an *impertinent* question⟩

im•per•turb•able \ˌim-pər-'tər-bə-bəl\ *adj*
hard to disturb or upset : very calm ⟨an *imperturbable* teacher⟩

im•per•vi•ous \im-'pər-vē-əs\ *adj*
1 not letting something enter or pass through ⟨The coat is *impervious* to rain.⟩
2 not bothered or affected by something ⟨He's *impervious* to their criticism.⟩

im•pet•u•ous \im-'pe-chə-wəs\ *adj*
acting or done quickly and without thought : IMPULSIVE ⟨an *impetuous* decision⟩

imp•ish \'im-pish\ *adj*
playful and mischievous ⟨an *impish* glance⟩
imp•ish•ly *adv*

im•pla•ca•ble \im-'pla-kə-bəl, -'plā-\ *adj*
impossible to please, satisfy, or change ⟨*implacable* enemies⟩

im•plant \im-'plant\ *vb* **im•plant•ed**; **im•plant•ing**
to set securely or deeply

¹im•ple•ment \'im-plə-mənt\ *n*
◀ an object (as a tool) intended for a certain use ⟨farm *implements*⟩

[2]**im•ple•ment** \'im-plə-ˌment\ *vb* **im•ple•ment•ed; im•ple•ment•ing**
to begin to do or use something ⟨They're *implementing* the plan.⟩

im•pli•cate \'im-plə-ˌkāt\ *vb* **im•pli•cat•ed; im•pli•cat•ing**
to show to be connected or involved ⟨He's been *implicated* in the crime.⟩

im•pli•ca•tion \ˌim-plə-'kā-shən\ *n*
1 the fact or state of being involved in or connected to something
2 a possible future effect or result ⟨Consider the *implications* of your actions.⟩
3 something that is suggested

im•plic•it \im-'pli-sət\ *adj*
1 understood though not put clearly into words ⟨an *implicit* warning⟩
2 not affected by doubt : ABSOLUTE ⟨He had my *implicit* trust.⟩
im•plic•it•ly *adv*

im•plore \im-'plȯr\ *vb* **im•plored; im•plor•ing**
to make a very serious or emotional request to or for ⟨I *implored* him not to go.⟩
im•plor•ing•ly *adv*

im•ply \im-'plī\ *vb* **im•plied; im•ply•ing**
to express indirectly : suggest rather than say plainly

im•po•lite \ˌim-pə-'līt\ *adj*
not polite
im•po•lite•ly *adv*

[1]**im•port** \im-'pȯrt\ *vb* **im•port•ed; im•port•ing**
to bring (as goods) into a country usually for selling

[2]**im•port** \'im-ˌpȯrt\ *n*
1 IMPORTANCE ⟨This is a problem of great *import*.⟩
2 something brought into a country ⟨My car is an *import* from Italy.⟩

im•por•tance \im-'pȯr-tᵊns\ *n*
the quality or state of being important ⟨The discovery is of great *importance*.⟩

im•por•tant \im-'pȯr-tᵊnt\ *adj*
1 having serious meaning or worth ⟨Graduation is an *important* event in your life.⟩
2 having power or authority ⟨an *important* leader⟩
im•por•tant•ly *adv*

im•por•ta•tion \ˌim-ˌpȯr-'tā-shən\ *n*
the act or practice of bringing into a country ⟨*importation* of goods⟩

im•por•tune \ˌim-pər-'tün, -'tyün\ *vb* **im•por•tuned; im•por•tun•ing**
to beg or urge in a repeated or annoying way ⟨Salesmen *importuned* us to buy.⟩

im•pose \im-'pōz\ *vb* **im•posed; im•pos•ing**
1 to establish or apply as a charge or penalty ⟨The judge *imposed* a fine.⟩
2 to force someone to accept or put up with ⟨Don't *impose* your beliefs on me.⟩
3 to ask for more than is fair or reasonable : take unfair advantage ⟨Guests *imposed* on his good nature.⟩

im•pos•ing \im-'pō-ziŋ\ *adj*
impressive because of size, dignity, or magnificence

im•pos•si•bil•i•ty \im-ˌpä-sə-'bi-lə-tē\ *n, pl* **im•pos•si•bil•i•ties**
1 something that cannot be done or occur ⟨Time travel is an *impossibility*.⟩
2 the quality or state of being impossible

im•pos•si•ble \im-'pä-sə-bəl\ *adj*
1 incapable of being or of occurring : not possible ⟨The noise makes it *impossible* to concentrate.⟩
2 very difficult ⟨These math problems are *impossible*!⟩
3 very bad or unpleasant ⟨She is *impossible* to deal with.⟩
im•pos•si•bly \-blē\ *adv*

im•pos•tor *or* **im•pos•ter** \im-'pä-stər\ *n*
a person who deceives others by pretending to be someone else

im•pos•ture \im-'päs-chər\ *n*
the act of deceiving others by pretending to be someone else

im•po•tence \'im-pə-təns\ *n*
the quality or state of lacking power or strength

im•po•tent \'im-pə-tənt\ *adj*
lacking in power, ability, or strength ⟨an *impotent* medicine⟩

im•pound \im-'paund\ *vb* **im•pound•ed; im•pound•ing**
to shut up in or as if in an enclosed place ⟨*impound* cattle⟩

im•pov•er•ish \im-'pä-və-rish\ *vb* **im•pov•er•ished; im•pov•er•ish•ing**
1 to make poor ⟨The greedy tyrant *impoverished* his people.⟩
2 to use up the strength or richness of ⟨*impoverished* soil⟩

im•prac•ti•ca•ble \im-'prak-ti-kə-bəl\ *adj*
difficult to put into practice or use ⟨an *impracticable* plan⟩

im•prac•ti•cal \im-'prak-ti-kəl\ *adj*
1 not suitable for a situation : not practical ⟨Small cars are *impractical* for large families.⟩
2 not capable of dealing sensibly with matters that require action ⟨an *impractical* dreamer⟩

im•pre•cise \ˌim-pri-'sīs\ *adj*
not clear or exact

im•preg•na•ble \im-'preg-nə-bəl\ *adj*
not able to be captured by attack : UNCONQUERABLE

im•press \im-'pres\ *vb* **im•pressed; im•press•ing**
1 to produce by stamping, pressing, or printing ⟨*impress* a design⟩
2 to affect strongly or deeply and especially favorably ⟨Her talent *impressed* me.⟩
3 to give a clear idea of ⟨She *impressed* on us her concerns.⟩

impression 1:
an impression of a bull left by a seal

im•pres•sion \im-'pre-shən\ *n*
1 ▲ something (as a design) made by pressing or stamping a surface ⟨The tires made *impressions* in the mud.⟩
2 the effect that something or someone has on a person's thoughts or feelings ⟨She shared her *impressions* of the city.⟩
3 an idea or belief that is usually uncertain
4 an imitation of a famous person done for entertainment

im•pres•sion•able \im-'pre-shə-nə-bəl\ *adj*
easy to impress or influence ⟨*impressionable* teenagers⟩

im•pres•sive \im-'pre-siv\ *adj*
having the power to impress the mind or feelings especially in a positive way ⟨an *impressive* speech⟩
im•pres•sive•ly *adv*

[1]**im•print** \im-'print\ *vb* **im•print•ed; im•print•ing**
1 to make a mark by pressing against a surface : STAMP ⟨The design was *imprinted* on paper.⟩
2 to fix firmly in the mind or memory ⟨This day is *imprinted* in my memory.⟩

[2]**im•print** \'im-ˌprint\ *n*
a mark made by pressing against a surface ⟨The tires left an *imprint*.⟩

im•pris•on \im-'pri-zᵊn\ *vb* **im•pris•oned; im•pris•on•ing**
to put in prison

im•pris•on•ment \im-'pri-zᵊn-mənt\ *n*
the act of putting in prison : the state of being put or kept in prison

im•prob•a•bil•i•ty \im-ˌprä-bə-ˈbi-lə-tē\ *n*
the quality or state of being unlikely

im•prob•a•ble \im-ˈprä-bə-bəl\ *adj*
not likely : not probable ⟨*improbable* stories⟩
im•prob•a•bly \-blē\ *adv*

im•promp•tu \im-ˈprämp-tü, -tyü\ *adj*
not prepared ahead of time : made or done without preparation ⟨an *impromptu* speech⟩

im•prop•er \im-ˈprä-pər\ *adj*
not proper, right, or suitable ⟨He used *improper* grammar.⟩
im•prop•er•ly *adv*

improper fraction *n*
a fraction whose numerator is equal to or larger than the denominator ⟨13/4 is an *improper fraction*.⟩

im•prove \im-ˈprüv\ *vb* **im•proved**; **im•prov•ing**
to make or become better ⟨Her writing has greatly *improved*.⟩

im•prove•ment \im-ˈprüv-mənt\ *n*
1 the act or process of making something better
2 increased value or excellence ⟨I've noticed *improvement* in your work.⟩
3 an addition or change that makes something better or more valuable ⟨We made *improvements* to our house.⟩

im•pro•vi•sa•tion \im-ˌprä-və-ˈzā-shən\ *n*
1 the act or art of speaking or performing without practicing or preparing ahead of time
2 something that is improvised

im•pro•vise \ˈim-prə-ˌvīz\ *vb* **im•pro•vised**; **im•pro•vis•ing**
1 to speak or perform without preparing ahead of time ⟨I *improvised* a song on the spot.⟩
2 to make, invent, or arrange by using whatever is available

im•pu•dence \ˈim-pyə-dəns\ *n*
behavior or speech that is bold and disrespectful

im•pu•dent \ˈim-pyə-dənt\ *adj*
bold and disrespectful : very rude ⟨an *impudent* remark⟩ ⟨an *impudent* child⟩
im•pu•dent•ly *adv*

im•pulse \ˈim-ˌpəls\ *n*
1 a force that starts a body into motion
2 the motion produced by a starting force
3 a strong sudden desire to do something ⟨She resisted the *impulse* to shout.⟩
4 NERVE IMPULSE

im•pul•sive \im-ˈpəl-siv\ *adj*
1 acting or tending to act suddenly and without careful thought
2 resulting from a sudden impulse ⟨an *impulsive* decision⟩
im•pul•sive•ly *adv*

im•pure \im-ˈpyu̇r\ *adj*
1 not pure : UNCLEAN, DIRTY ⟨*impure* water⟩
2 mixed with something else that is usually not as good ⟨*impure* gold⟩

im•pu•ri•ty \im-ˈpyu̇r-ə-tē\ *n*, *pl* **im•pu•ri•ties**
1 the quality or state of being impure
2 something that is or makes something else impure ⟨*Impurities* in the gold were detected.⟩

[1]in \ˈin, ən\ *prep*
1 located or positioned within ⟨The house is *in* the country.⟩
2 INTO 1 ⟨We ran *in* the house.⟩
3 DURING ⟨It's warmer *in* the summer.⟩
4 WITH 2 ⟨I wrote *in* pencil.⟩
5 used to show a state or condition ⟨You're *in* luck!⟩ ⟨We're *in* trouble.⟩
6 used to show manner or purpose ⟨I'm *in* a hurry.⟩ ⟨He laughed *in* reply.⟩
7 INTO 2 ⟨It broke *in* pieces.⟩

[2]in \ˈin\ *adv*
1 to or toward the inside ⟨I went *in* and closed the door.⟩
2 to or toward some particular place ⟨We flew *in* yesterday.⟩
3 [1]NEAR 1 ⟨Play close *in*.⟩
4 into the midst of something ⟨Mix *in* the flour.⟩
5 to or at its proper place ⟨Can you fit this piece *in*?⟩
6 on the inner side : WITHIN ⟨Everyone is *in*.⟩
7 present and available for use ⟨All the votes are *in*.⟩
in for sure to experience ⟨He was *in for* a surprise.⟩

[3]in \ˈin\ *adj*
1 being inside or within ⟨the *in* part⟩
2 headed or bound inward ⟨the *in* train⟩
3 FASHIONABLE

IN *abbr* Indiana

in. *abbr* inch

[1]in- *or* **il-** *or* **im-** *or* **ir-** *prefix*
not : NON-, UN- — usually *il-* before *l* ⟨*il*logical⟩, *im-* before *b*, *m*, or *p* ⟨*im*moral⟩ ⟨*im*practical⟩, *ir-* before *r* ⟨*ir*reconcilable⟩ and *in-* before other sounds ⟨*in*complete⟩

[2]in- *or* **il-** *or* **im-** *or* **ir-** *prefix*
1 in : within : into : toward : on — usually *il-* before *l* ⟨*il*luminate⟩, *im-* before *b*, *m*, or *p* ⟨*im*port⟩, *ir-* before *r* ⟨*ir*radiate⟩, and *in-* before other sounds ⟨*in*fect⟩
2 EN- 2 ⟨*im*peril⟩

in•abil•i•ty \ˌi-nə-ˈbi-lə-tē\ *n*
the condition of being unable to do something : lack of ability ⟨He laughed at my *inability* to sing.⟩

in•ac•ces•si•bil•i•ty \ˌi-nik-ˌse-sə-ˈbi-lə-tē\ *n*
the quality or state of being hard or impossible to reach or get hold of

in•ac•ces•si•ble \ˌi-nik-ˈse-sə-bəl\ *adj*
hard or impossible to reach or get hold of ⟨an *inaccessible* island⟩

in•ac•cu•ra•cy \in-ˈak-yə-rə-sē\ *n*, *pl* **in•ac•cu•ra•cies**
1 lack of correctness or exactness ⟨I pointed out the *inaccuracy* of his statement.⟩
2 ERROR, MISTAKE ⟨Your report contains *inaccuracies*.⟩

in•ac•cu•rate \i-ˈna-kyə-rət\ *adj*
not correct or exact ⟨He made *inaccurate* claims.⟩
in•ac•cu•rate•ly *adv*

in•ac•tion \i-ˈnak-shən\ *n*
lack of action or activity

in•ac•tive \i-ˈnak-tiv\ *adj*
not active or in use ⟨an *inactive* volcano⟩ ⟨*inactive* mines⟩

in•ac•tiv•i•ty \ˌi-nak-ˈti-və-tē\ *n*
the state or condition of not acting or moving : lack of activity ⟨His job involves hours of *inactivity*.⟩

in•ad•e•qua•cy \i-ˈna-di-kwə-sē\ *n*, *pl* **in•ad•e•qua•cies**
the condition of being not enough or not good enough

in•ad•e•quate \i-ˈna-di-kwət\ *adj*
not enough or not good enough ⟨an *inadequate* supply⟩ ⟨an *inadequate* excuse⟩

in•ad•ver•tent \ˌi-nəd-ˈvər-tᵊnt\ *adj*
not intended or deliberate : ACCIDENTAL ⟨an *inadvertent* mistake⟩
in•ad•ver•tent•ly *adv*

in•ad•vis•able \ˌi-nəd-ˈvī-zə-bəl\ *adj*
not wise to do : not advisable ⟨It's *inadvisable* to drive during the storm.⟩

in•alien•able \i-ˈnāl-yə-nə-bəl\ *adj*
impossible to take away or give up ⟨Our citizens have certain *inalienable* rights.⟩

inane \i-ˈnān\ *adj*
silly and pointless ⟨*inane* remarks⟩

in•an•i•mate \i-ˈna-nə-mət\ *adj*
not living ⟨Stones are *inanimate* objects.⟩

in•ap•pro•pri•ate \ˌi-nə-ˈprō-prē-ət\ *adj*
not right or suited for some purpose or situation ⟨*inappropriate* language⟩
in•ap•pro•pri•ate•ly *adv*

in•ar•tic•u•late \i-när-ˈti-kyə-lət\ *adj*
1 not able to express ideas or feelings clearly and easily ⟨an *inarticulate* speaker⟩
2 not understandable as spoken words ⟨an *inarticulate* mumble⟩

in•as•much as \ˌi-nəz-ˈmə-chəz\ *conj*
considering that : BECAUSE ⟨We're lucky *inasmuch as* no one was hurt.⟩

A B C D E F G H I J K L M N O P Q R S T U V W X Y Z

in•at•ten•tion \ˌi-nə-ˈten-shən\ *n*
failure to pay attention

in•at•ten•tive \ˌi-nə-ˈten-tiv\ *adj*
not paying attention ⟨an *inattentive* student⟩
in•at•ten•tive•ly *adv*

in•au•di•ble \i-ˈnȯ-də-bəl\ *adj*
impossible to hear ⟨an *inaudible* whisper⟩
in•au•di•bly \-blē\ *adv*

in•au•gu•ral \i-ˈnȯ-gyə-rəl\ *adj*
occuring as part of an inauguration ⟨an *inaugural* speech⟩

in•au•gu•rate \i-ˈnȯ-gyə-ˌrāt\ *vb*
in•au•gu•rat•ed; **in•au•gu•rat•ing**
1 to introduce into office with suitable ceremonies ⟨He was *inaugurated* as president.⟩
2 to celebrate the opening of ⟨The town *inaugurated* a new library.⟩
3 to bring about the beginning of ⟨The company will *inaugurate* a new plan.⟩

in•au•gu•ra•tion \i-ˌnȯ-gyə-ˈrā-shən\ *n*
an act or ceremony of introducing into office ⟨a president's *inauguration*⟩

in•born \ˈin-ˈbȯrn\ *adj*
existing from the time someone is born : natural or instinctive ⟨She has an *inborn* talent for music.⟩

in•breed \ˈin-ˈbrēd\ *vb* **in•bred** \-ˈbred\; **in•breed•ing**
to breed with closely related individuals

inc. *abbr*
1 incomplete
2 incorporated

in•can•des•cent \ˌin-kən-ˈde-sᵊnt\ *adj*
white or glowing with great heat

incandescent lamp *n*
LIGHT BULB

in•ca•pa•ble \in-ˈkā-pə-bəl\ *adj*
not able to do something ⟨Penguins are *incapable* of flight.⟩

[1]**in•cense** \ˈin-ˌsens\ *n*
► material used to produce a strong and pleasant smell when burned

[2]**in•cense** \in-ˈsens\ *vb* **in•censed**; **in•cens•ing**
to make very angry

in•cen•tive \in-ˈsen-tiv\ *n*
something that makes a person try or work hard or harder

in•ces•sant \in-ˈse-sᵊnt\ *adj*
going on and on : not stopping or letting up ⟨*incessant* chatter⟩
in•ces•sant•ly *adv*

[1]**inch** \ˈinch\ *n*
a unit of length equal to 1/36 yard (2.54 centimeters)

[2]**inch** *vb* **inched**; **inch•ing**
to move a little bit at a time

inch•worm \ˈinch-ˌwərm\ *n*
▼ a small caterpillar that is a larva of moths and moves by bringing forward the hind part of the body and then extending forward the front part of the body

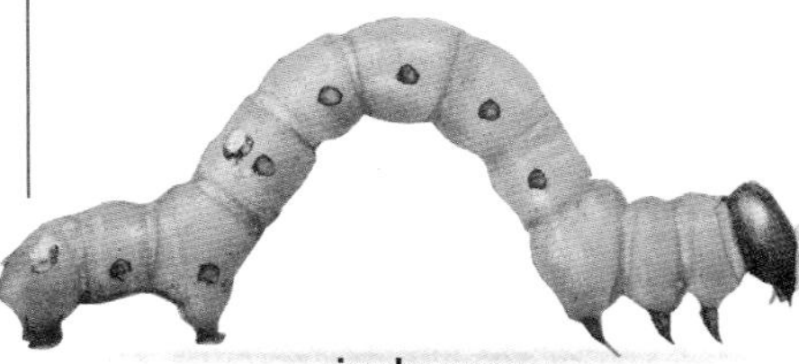
inchworm

in•ci•dent \ˈin-sə-dənt\ *n*
an often unimportant happening that may form a part of a larger event

► **Synonyms** INCIDENT, OCCURRENCE, and EVENT mean something that happens. INCIDENT is used for something that is brief and unimportant. ⟨Except for one *incident*, the trip was fun.⟩ OCCURRENCE may be used for something that is not planned or expected. ⟨Such *occurrences* can't be predicted.⟩ EVENT is often used of something that is important. ⟨They discussed the big *events* of last year.⟩

in•ci•den•tal \ˌin-sə-ˈden-tᵊl\ *adj*
happening as an unimportant part of something else ⟨*incidental* expenses⟩

in•ci•den•tal•ly \ˌin-sə-ˈden-tᵊl-ē\ *adv*
1 as a matter of less interest or importance
2 used to introduce a statement that provides additional information or changes the subject ⟨I'll call your mother. *Incidentally*, how is she?⟩

in•cin•er•ate \in-ˈsi-nə-ˌrāt\ *vb*
in•cin•er•at•ed; **in•cin•er•at•ing**
to burn to ashes

in•cin•er•a•tor \in-ˈsi-nə-ˌrā-tər\ *n*
a furnace or a container for burning waste materials

in•cise \in-ˈsīz\ *vb* **in•cised**; **in•cis•ing**
to cut into : CARVE, ENGRAVE ⟨A design was *incised* in clay.⟩

in•ci•sion \in-ˈsi-zhən\ *n*
an act of cutting into something or the cut or wound that results

in•ci•sor \in-ˈsī-zər\ *n*
a tooth (as any of the four front teeth of the human upper or lower jaw) for cutting

in•cite \in-ˈsīt\ *vb* **in•cit•ed**; **in•cit•ing**
to stir up usually harmful or violent action or feeling

in•clem•ent \in-ˈkle-mənt\ *adj*
STORMY 1 ⟨*inclement* weather⟩

in•cli•na•tion \ˌin-klə-ˈnā-shən\ *n*
1 an act or the action of bending or leaning
2 a usually favorable feeling toward something ⟨His *inclination* was to walk rather than drive.⟩
3 [2]SLANT, TILT ⟨a steep *inclination*⟩

[1]**in•cline** \in-ˈklīn\ *vb* **in•clined**; **in•clin•ing**
1 to cause to bend or lean ⟨She *inclined* her head.⟩
2 [2]SLOPE, LEAN

[2]**in•cline** \ˈin-ˌklīn\ *n*
[1]SLOPE 2 ⟨a steep *incline*⟩

[1]**incense:** incense sticks being offered at a temple in China

in•clined \in-ˈklīnd\ *adj*
1 having a desire ⟨I'm not *inclined* to go.⟩
2 having a tendency ⟨She's *inclined* to fret.⟩
3 having a slope ⟨an *inclined* surface⟩

inclined plane *n*
a flat surface that makes an angle with the line of the horizon

in•clude \in-ˈklüd\ *vb* **in•clud•ed**; **in•clud•ing**
to take in or have as part of a whole ⟨Dinner *includes* dessert.⟩

in•clu•sion \in-ˈklü-zhən\ *n*
1 an act taking in as part of a whole : the state of being taken in as part of a whole ⟨She suggested *inclusion* of an entry.⟩
2 something taken in as part of a whole

in•clu•sive \in-ˈklü-siv, -ziv\ *adj*
1 covering everything or all important points ⟨an *inclusive* price⟩
2 including the stated limits and all in between ⟨from ages three to ten *inclusive*⟩

in•cog•ni•to \ˌin-ˌkäg-ˈnē-tō, in-ˈkäg-nə-ˌtō\ *adv or adj*
with someone's identity kept secret ⟨He's traveling *incognito*.⟩

in•co•her•ence \ˌin-kō-ˈhir-əns\ *n*
the quality or state of not being connected in a clear or logical way

in•co•her•ent \ˌin-kō-ˈhir-ənt\ *adj*
not connected in a clear or logical way ⟨The patient's speech was *incoherent*.⟩
in•co•her•ent•ly *adv*

in•come \ˈin-ˌkəm\ *n*
a gain usually measured in money that comes in from labor, business, or property

income tax *n*
a tax on the income of a person or business

in•com•ing \ˈin-ˌkə-miŋ\ *adj*
arriving at a destination ⟨an *incoming* train⟩

in•com•pa•ra•ble \in-ˈkäm-pə-rə-bəl\ *adj*
better than any other
in•com•pa•ra•bly \-blē\ *adv*

in•com•pat•i•bil•i•ty \ˌin-kəm‚pa-tə-ˈbi-lə-tē\ *n, pl* **in•com•pat•i•bil•i•ties**
the quality or state of being incompatible ⟨software *incompatibility*⟩

in•com•pat•i•ble \ˌin-kəm-ˈpa-tə-bəl\ *adj*
1 not able to exist together without trouble or conflict ⟨*incompatible* workers⟩
2 not able to be used together ⟨This game is *incompatible* with that system.⟩

in•com•pe•tence \in-ˈkäm-pə-təns\ *n*
the inability to do a good job

in•com•pe•tent \in-ˈkäm-pə-tənt\ *adj*
not able to do a good job
in•com•pe•tent•ly *adv*

in•com•plete \ˌin-kəm-ˈplēt\ *adj*
not finished : not complete
in•com•plete•ly *adv*

in•com•pre•hen•si•ble \ˌin-ˌkäm-pri-ˈhen-sə-bəl\ *adj*
impossible to understand
in•com•pre•hen•si•bly \-blē\ *adv*

in•con•ceiv•able \ˌin-kən-ˈsē-və-bəl\ *adj*
impossible to imagine or believe

in•con•gru•ous \in-ˈkäŋ-grə-wəs\ *adj*
not harmonious, suitable, or proper ⟨*incongruous* colors⟩

in•con•sid•er•ate \ˌin-kən-ˈsi-də-rət\ *adj*
careless of the rights or feelings of others

in•con•sis•ten•cy \ˌin-kən-ˈsi-stən-sē\ *n, pl* **in•con•sis•ten•cies**
1 the quality or state of not being in agreement or not being regular ⟨The team's biggest problem is *inconsistency*.⟩
2 something that is not in agreement or not regular ⟨There are *inconsistencies* in her story.⟩

in•con•sis•tent \ˌin-kən-ˈsi-stənt\ *adj*
1 not being in agreement ⟨Their stories are *inconsistent*.⟩
2 not staying the same in thoughts or practices ⟨His grades are *inconsistent*.⟩

in•con•sol•a•ble \ˌin-kən-ˈsō-lə-bəl\ *adj*
very sad and not able to be comforted
in•con•sol•a•bly \-blē\ *adv*

in•con•spic•u•ous \ˌin-kən-ˈspi-kyə-wəs\ *adj*
not easily seen or noticed
in•con•spic•u•ous•ly *adv*

[1]in•con•ve•nience \ˌin-kən-ˈvē-nyəns\ *n*
1 trouble or difficulty : lack of convenience ⟨The delay caused great *inconvenience*.⟩
2 something that causes trouble or difficulty ⟨These changes are such an *inconvenience*.⟩

[2]inconvenience *vb* **in•con•ve•nienced**; **in•con•ve•nienc•ing**
to cause difficulties for ⟨Will a visit *inconvenience* you?⟩

in•con•ve•nient \ˌin-kən-ˈvē-nyənt\ *adj*
causing trouble or difficulty : not convenient ⟨That time is *inconvenient* for me.⟩
in•con•ve•nient•ly *adv*

in•cor•po•rate \in-ˈkȯr-pə-ˌrāt\ *vb* **in•cor•po•rat•ed**; **in•cor•po•rat•ing**
1 to join or unite closely into a single mass or body ⟨The plan *incorporated* all our ideas.⟩
2 to form into a corporation

in•cor•rect \ˌin-kə-ˈrekt\ *adj*
1 not accurate or true : not correct : WRONG ⟨an *incorrect* answer⟩
2 not proper ⟨*incorrect* behavior⟩
in•cor•rect•ly *adv*

[1]in•crease \in-ˈkrēs\ *vb* **in•creased**; **in•creas•ing**
to make or become greater ⟨Skill *increases* with practice.⟩

[2]in•crease \ˈin-ˌkrēs\ *n*
an addition or enlargement in size, extent, or quantity ⟨He received a pay *increase*.⟩

in•creas•ing•ly \in-ˈkrē-siŋ-lē\ *adv*
more and more ⟨The path became *increasingly* rough.⟩

in•cred•i•ble \in-ˈkre-də-bəl\ *adj*
1 too strange or unlikely to be believed ⟨It was an *incredible* story.⟩
2 extremely or amazingly good, great, or large ⟨*incredible* strength⟩
in•cred•i•bly \-blē\ *adv*

in•cred•u•lous \in-ˈkre-jə-ləs\ *adj*
feeling or showing disbelief : SKEPTICAL
in•cred•u•lous•ly *adv*

in•crim•i•nate \in-ˈkri-mə-ˌnāt\ *vb* **in•crim•i•nat•ed**; **in•crim•i•nat•ing**
to make (someone) appear guilty of or responsible for something

in•cu•bate \ˈiŋg-kyə-ˌbāt\ *vb* **in•cu•bat•ed**; **in•cu•bat•ing**
1 to sit upon eggs to hatch them by warmth
2 to keep under conditions good for hatching or development

in•cu•ba•tion \ˌiŋg-kyə-ˈbā-shən\ *n*
1 the act or process of incubating ⟨*incubation* of eggs⟩
2 the period of time between infection with germs and the appearance of symptoms of illness or disease

in•cu•ba•tor \ˈiŋg-kyə-ˌbā-tər\ *n*
1 a device that provides enough heat to hatch eggs artificially
2 ▼ a device to help the growth of tiny newborn babies

in•cum•bent \in-ˈkəm-bənt\ *n*
the holder of an office or position ⟨The *incumbent* was reelected.⟩

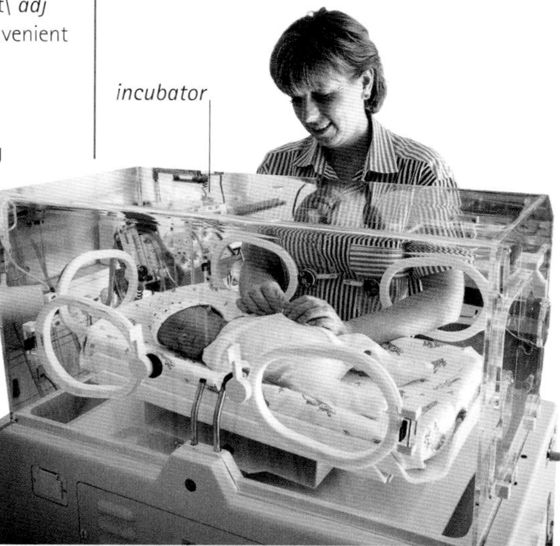

incubator 2: a hospital incubator for a premature baby

in•cur \in-ˈkər\ *vb* **in•curred; in•cur•ring**
to experience as a result of a person's own actions ⟨Because of his behavior he *incurred* suspicion.⟩

in•cur•able \in-ˈkyu̇r-ə-bəl\ *adj*
impossible to cure ⟨an *incurable* disease⟩
in•cur•ably \-blē\ *adv*

Ind. *abbr*
1 Indian
2 Indiana

in•debt•ed \in-ˈde-təd\ *adj*
being in debt : owing something
in•debt•ed•ness *n*

in•de•cen•cy \in-ˈdē-sᵊn-sē\ *n*, *pl* **in•de•cen•cies**
1 offensive quality : lack of decency
2 an act or word that is offensive

in•de•cent \in-ˈdē-sᵊnt\ *adj*
not decent : COARSE, VULGAR

in•de•ci•sion \ˌin-di-ˈsi-zhən\ *n*
difficulty in making a decision

in•de•ci•sive \ˌin-di-ˈsī-siv\ *adj*
1 not decisive or final ⟨an *indecisive* battle⟩
2 finding it hard to make decisions ⟨an *indecisive* person⟩
in•de•ci•sive•ly *adv*

in•deed \in-ˈdēd\ *adv*
TRULY ⟨They were, *indeed*, lost.⟩

in•de•fen•si•ble \ˌin-di-ˈfen-sə-bəl\ *adj*
impossible to defend

in•def•i•nite \in-ˈde-fə-nət\ *adj*
1 not certain in amount or length ⟨We're stuck here for an *indefinite* period.⟩
2 not clear in meaning or details ⟨She is *indefinite* about her plans.⟩
in•def•i•nite•ly *adv*

indefinite article *n*
either of the articles *a* or *an* used to show that the following noun refers to any person or thing of the kind named

in•del•i•ble \in-ˈde-lə-bəl\ *adj*
1 impossible to erase, remove, or forget ⟨He made an *indelible* impression on me.⟩
2 making marks not easily removed ⟨*indelible* ink⟩
in•del•i•bly \-blē\ *adv*

in•del•i•cate \in-ˈde-li-kət\ *adj*
not polite or proper ⟨an *indelicate* remark⟩
in•del•i•cate•ly *adv*

in•dent \in-ˈdent\ *vb* **in•dent•ed; in•dent•ing**
to set in from the margin ⟨*Indent* the first line of your paragraph.⟩

in•den•ta•tion \ˌin-ˌden-ˈtā-shən\ *n*
1 a blank or empty space at the beginning of a written or printed line or paragraph
2 a cut or dent in something

in•den•tured \ˌin-ˈden-chərd\ *adj*
required by contract to work for a certain period of time

in•de•pen•dence \ˌin-də-ˈpen-dəns\ *n*
the quality or state of not being under the control of, reliant on, or connected with someone or something else

Independence Day *n*
July 4 observed by Americans as a legal holiday in honor of the adoption of the Declaration of Independence in 1776

[1]**in•de•pen•dent** \ˌin-də-ˈpen-dənt\ *adj*
1 not under the control or rule of another ⟨an *independent* country⟩
2 not connected with something else : SEPARATE ⟨an *independent* grocery store⟩
3 not depending on anyone else for money to live on
4 thinking freely : not looking to others for guidance
in•de•pen•dent•ly *adv*

[2]**independent** *n*
an independent person

in•de•scrib•able \ˌin-di-ˈskrī-bə-bəl\ *adj*
impossible to describe ⟨*indescribable* joy⟩
in•de•scrib•ably \-blē\ *adv*

in•de•struc•ti•ble \ˌin-di-ˈstrək-tə-bəl\ *adj*
impossible to destroy ⟨an *indestructible* toy⟩

[1]**in•dex** \ˈin-ˌdeks\ *n*, *pl* **in•dex•es** *or* **in•di•ces** \ˈin-də-ˌsēz\
1 a list of names or topics (as in a book) given in alphabetical order and showing where each is to be found
2 POINTER 1 ⟨the *index* on a scale⟩
3 [1]SIGN 3, INDICATION ⟨Prices are an *index* of business conditions.⟩

[2]**index** *vb* **in•dexed; in•dex•ing**
1 to provide (as a book) with an index
2 to list in an index ⟨The topics are *indexed*.⟩

index finger *n*
the finger next to the thumb

[1]**In•di•an** \ˈin-dē-ən\ *n*
1 a person born or living in India
2 AMERICAN INDIAN

▶ **Word History** Once the name *India* was not used just for the land that we now call *India*. The whole of the distant East was often called *India*. Columbus went west hoping to sail to the far East. When he reached the West Indies, islands in the Caribbean, he thought that he had come to the outer islands of "India," the far East. That is why the people that he found there were given the name *Indian*.

Indian corn 2

[2]**Indian** *adj*
1 of or relating to India or its peoples
2 of or relating to the American Indians or their languages

Indian corn *n*
1 [1]CORN
2 ▲ corn that is of a variety having seeds of various colors (as reddish brown, dark purple, and yellow) and is typically used for ornamental purposes

Indian pipe *n*
a waxy white leafless woodland herb with a single drooping flower

Indian summer *n*
a period of mild weather in late autumn or early winter

in•di•cate \ˈin-də-ˌkāt\ *vb* **in•di•cat•ed; in•di•cat•ing**
1 to point out or point to
2 to state or express briefly

in•di•ca•tion \ˌin-də-ˈkā-shən\ *n*
1 the act of pointing out or stating briefly
2 something that points out or suggests something

in•dic•a•tive \in-ˈdi-kə-tiv\ *adj*
1 pointing out or showing something ⟨Fever is *indicative* of illness.⟩
2 of or relating to the verb form that is used to state a fact that can be known or proved ⟨In "I am here," the verb "am" is in the *indicative* mood.⟩

in•di•ca•tor \ˈin-də-ˌkā-tər\ *n*
1 a sign that shows or suggests the condition or existence of something
2 a pointer on a dial or scale
3 [1]DIAL 3, GAUGE

a b c d e f g h i j k l m n o p q r s t u v w x y z

indices *pl of* INDEX

in•dict \in-ˈdīt\ *vb* **in•dict•ed; in•dict•ing**
to formally charge with an offense or crime
in•dict•ment \-ˈdīt-mənt\ *n*

in•dif•fer•ence \in-ˈdi-fə-rəns, -ˈdi-frəns\ *n*
lack of interest or concern ⟨He treated the matter with *indifference*.⟩

in•dif•fer•ent \in-ˈdi-fə-rənt, -ˈdi-frənt\ *adj*
1 not interested or concerned about something
2 neither good nor bad ⟨an *indifferent* performance⟩
in•dif•fer•ent•ly *adv*

in•di•gest•ible \ˌin-dī-ˈje-stə-bəl, -də-\ *adj*
not capable of being broken down and used by the body as food : not easy to digest ⟨*indigestible* seeds⟩

in•di•ges•tion \ˌin-dī-ˈjes-chən, -də-\ *n*
discomfort caused by slow or painful digestion

in•dig•nant \in-ˈdig-nənt\ *adj*
filled with or expressing anger caused by something unjust or unworthy
in•dig•nant•ly *adv*

in•dig•na•tion \ˌin-dig-ˈnā-shən\ *n*
anger caused by something unjust or unworthy

in•dig•ni•ty \in-ˈdig-nə-tē\ *n, pl* **in•dig•ni•ties**
1 an act that injures a person's dignity or self-respect ⟨She remembers every insult, every *indignity*.⟩
2 treatment that shows a lack of respect ⟨He suffered the *indignity* of being fired.⟩

in•di•go \ˈin-di-ˌgō\ *n, pl* **in•di•gos** *or* **in•di•goes**
1 ▼ a blue dye made artificially or obtained especially formerly from plants (**indigo plants**)
2 a deep purplish blue

indigo 1:
a bottle of indigo

in•di•rect \ˌin-də-ˈrekt, -dī-\ *adj*
1 not straight or direct ⟨an *indirect* route⟩
2 not straightforward ⟨an *indirect* answer⟩
3 not having a plainly seen connection ⟨an *indirect* cause⟩
in•di•rect•ly *adv*
in•di•rect•ness *n*

indirect object *n*
an object that represents the person or thing that receives what is being given or done ⟨The word "me" in "you gave me the book" is an *indirect object*.⟩

in•dis•creet \ˌin-di-ˈskrēt\ *adj*
not having or showing good judgment : revealing things that should not be revealed
in•dis•creet•ly *adv*

in•dis•cre•tion \ˌin-di-ˈskre-shən\ *n*
1 lack of good judgment or care in acting or saying things
2 a thoughtless or careless act or remark

in•dis•crim•i•nate \ˌin-di-ˈskri-mə-nət\ *adj*
not done in a careful way : wrongly causing widespread harm ⟨They objected to the *indiscriminate* use of pesticides.⟩

in•dis•pens•able \ˌin-di-ˈspen-sə-bəl\ *adj*
extremely important or necessary : ESSENTIAL ⟨*indispensable* workers⟩

in•dis•posed \ˌin-di-ˈspōzd\ *adj*
1 slightly ill
2 not willing ⟨I'm *indisposed* to permit this.⟩

in•dis•put•able \ˌin-di-ˈspyü-tə-bəl, in-ˈdi-spyə-\ *adj*
impossible to question or doubt ⟨*indisputable* proof⟩
in•dis•put•ably \-blē\ *adv*

in•dis•tinct \ˌin-di-ˈstiŋt\ *adj*
not easily seen, heard, or recognized ⟨*indistinct* voices⟩
in•dis•tinct•ly *adv*

in•dis•tin•guish•able \ˌin-di-ˈstiŋ-gwi-shə-bəl\ *adj*
impossible to recognize as different

[1]in•di•vid•u•al \ˌin-də-ˈvi-jə-wəl\ *adj*
1 relating to a single member of a group ⟨*individual* needs⟩
2 intended for one person ⟨an *individual* pizza⟩
3 [1]PARTICULAR 1, SEPARATE ⟨Each *individual* case is different.⟩
4 having a special quality : DISTINCTIVE ⟨an *individual* style⟩
in•di•vid•u•al•ly *adv*

[2]individual *n*
1 a single member of a group
2 a single human being

in•di•vid•u•al•i•ty \ˌin-də-ˌvi-jə-ˈwa-lə-tē\ *n*
the qualities that make one person or thing different from all others

in•di•vis•i•ble \ˌin-də-ˈvi-zə-bəl\ *adj*
impossible to divide or separate ⟨The two friends were *indivisible*.⟩
in•di•vis•i•bly \-blē\ *adv*

in•doc•tri•nate \in-ˈdäk-trə-ˌnāt\ *vb* **in•doc•tri•nat•ed; in•doc•tri•nat•ing**
to teach especially the ideas, opinions, or beliefs of a certain group

in•do•lence \ˈin-də-ləns\ *n*
the quality of being lazy

in•do•lent \ˈin-də-lənt\ *adj*
LAZY 1, IDLE

in•dom•i•ta•ble \in-ˈdä-mə-tə-bəl\ *adj*
impossible to defeat ⟨an *indomitable* spirit⟩

in•door \ˈin-ˈdȯr\ *adj*
done, used, or belonging within a building ⟨an *indoor* job⟩ ⟨ an *indoor* pool⟩

in•doors \ˈin-ˈdȯrz\ *adv*
in or into a building ⟨These games are played *indoors*.⟩

in•du•bi•ta•ble \in-ˈdü-bə-tə-bəl, -ˈdyü-\ *adj*
being beyond question or doubt
in•du•bi•ta•bly \-blē\ *adv*

in•duce \in-ˈdüs, -ˈdyüs\ *vb* **in•duced; in•duc•ing**
1 to cause to do something ⟨Her pleas *induced* us to give.⟩
2 to bring about ⟨Warm milk *induces* sleepiness.⟩
3 to produce (as an electric current) by induction

in•duce•ment \in-ˈdüs-mənt, -ˈdyüs-\ *n*
something that causes someone to do something

in•duct \in-ˈdəkt\ *vb* **in•duct•ed; in•duct•ing**
1 to take in as a member of a military service
2 to place in office
3 to officially introduce (someone) as a member

in•duc•tion \in-ˈdək-shən\ *n*
1 the act or process of placing someone in a new job or position ⟨*induction* into the Hall of Fame⟩
2 the production of an electrical or magnetic effect through the influence of a nearby magnet, electrical current, or electrically charged body

in•dulge \in-ˈdəlj\ *vb* **in•dulged; in•dulg•ing**
1 to give in to the desires of ⟨Grandparents often *indulge* their grandchildren.⟩
2 to give in to a desire for something ⟨For my birthday, I *indulged* in a day off.⟩

in•dul•gence \in-ˈdəl-jəns\ *n*
1 the practice of allowing enjoyment of whatever is desired ⟨He lives a life of *indulgence*.⟩
2 an act of doing what is desired
3 something that a person enjoys or desires ⟨Chocolate is an *indulgence*.⟩

in•dul•gent \in-ˈdəl-jənt\ *adj*
feeling or showing a willingness to allow enjoyment of whatever is wanted : LENIENT ⟨*indulgent* parents⟩
in•dul•gent•ly *adv*

in•dus•tri•al \in-ˈdə-strē-əl\ *adj*
1 of, relating to, or engaged in industry ⟨*industrial* work⟩
2 having highly developed industries ⟨*industrial* nations⟩
in•dus•tri•al•ly *adv*

in•dus•tri•al•ist \in-ˈdə-strē-ə-list\ *n*
a person who owns or engages in the management of an industry

in•dus•tri•al•i•za•tion \in-ˌdə-strē-ə-lə-ˈzā-shən\ *n*
the process of developing industries : the state of having industry developed

in•dus•tri•al•ize \in-ˈdə-strē-ə-ˌlīz\ *vb*
in•dus•tri•al•ized; in•dus•tri•al•iz•ing
to develop industries

in•dus•tri•ous \in-ˈdə-strē-əs\ *adj*
working hard and steadily ⟨*industrious* students⟩
in•dus•tri•ous•ly *adv*

in•dus•try \ˈin-də-strē\ *n, pl* **in•dus•tries**
1 ▶ businesses that provide a certain product or service ⟨the oil *industry*⟩ ⟨the shipping *industry*⟩
2 manufacturing activity ⟨In May, *industry* slowed down.⟩
3 the habit of working hard and steadily

-ine \ˌīn, ən, ˌēn\ *adj suffix*
of, relating to, or like ⟨alkal*ine*⟩

in•ed•i•ble \in-ˈe-də-bəl\ *adj*
not fit for eating

in•ef•fec•tive \ˌi-nə-ˈfek-tiv\ *adj*
not having the desired effect ⟨The medicine was *ineffective*.⟩
in•ef•fec•tive•ly *adv*

in•ef•fec•tu•al \ˌi-nə-ˈfek-chə-wəl\ *adj*
not producing the proper or desired effect
in•ef•fec•tu•al•ly *adv*

in•ef•fi•cien•cy \ˌi-nə-ˈfi-shən-sē\ *n, pl* **in•ef•fi•cien•cies**
the state or an instance of being ineffective or inefficient

in•ef•fi•cient \ˌi-nə-ˈfi-shənt\ *adj*
1 not effective : INEFFECTUAL ⟨an *inefficient* repair⟩
2 not capable of bringing about a desired result with little waste ⟨*inefficient* workers⟩
in•ef•fi•cient•ly *adv*

in•elas•tic \ˌin-ə-ˈlas-tik\ *adj*
not elastic

in•el•i•gi•ble \i-ˈne-lə-jə-bəl\ *adj*
not qualified to be chosen or used ⟨He was *ineligible* for financial aid.⟩

in•ept \i-ˈnept\ *adj*
1 not suited to the occasion ⟨an *inept* remark⟩
2 lacking in skill or ability ⟨an *inept* painter⟩
in•ept•ly *adv*
in•ept•ness *n*

in•equal•i•ty \ˌi-ni-ˈkwä-lə-tē\ *n, pl* **in•equal•i•ties**
the quality of being unequal or uneven : lack of equality ⟨The laws are aimed to end educational *inequality*.⟩

in•ex•cus•able \ˌi-nik-ˈskyü-zə-bəl\ *adj*
not to be excused ⟨Waste is *inexcusable*.⟩
in•ex•cus•ably \-blē\ *adv*

in•ex•haust•ible \ˌi-nig-ˈzȯ-stə-bəl\ *adj*
plentiful enough not to give out or be used up ⟨an *inexhaustible* supply⟩

in•ex•o•ra•ble \i-ˈnek-sə-rə-bəl\ *adj*
RELENTLESS ⟨We cannot stop the *inexorable* passing of time.⟩
in•ex•o•ra•bly \-blē\ *adv*

in•ex•pen•sive \ˌi-nik-ˈspen-siv\ *adj*
[1]CHEAP 1

industry 1: an oil refinery processes products for the oil industry

in•ert \i-ˈnərt\ *adj*
unable or slow to move or react ⟨*inert* gas⟩
in•ert•ness *n*

in•er•tia \i-ˈnər-shə\ *n*
1 a property of matter by which it remains at rest or in motion in the same straight line unless acted upon by some external force
2 a tendency not to move or change ⟨He stayed at the job mostly because of his *inertia*.⟩

in•es•cap•able \ˌi-nə-ˈskā-pə-bəl\ *adj*
INEVITABLE ⟨She came to the *inescapable* conclusion that he was right.⟩

in•ev•i•ta•bil•i•ty \i-ˌne-və-tə-ˈbi-lə-tē\ *n*
the quality or state of being sure to happen ⟨the *inevitability* of change⟩

in•ev•i•ta•ble \i-ˈne-və-tə-bəl\ *adj*
sure to happen : CERTAIN
in•ev•i•ta•bly \-blē\ *adv*

in•ex•act \ˌi-nig-ˈzakt\ *adj*
INACCURATE ⟨an *inexact* measurement⟩

in•ex•pe•ri•ence \ˌi-nik-ˈspir-ē-əns\ *n*
lack of experience

in•ex•pe•ri•enced \ˌi-nik-ˈspir-ē-ənst\ *adj*
having little or no experience

in•ex•pli•ca•ble \ˌi-nik-ˈspli-kə-bəl, i-ˈnek-spli-\ *adj*
impossible to explain or account for ⟨an *inexplicable* mystery⟩
in•ex•pli•ca•bly \-blē\ *adv*

in•ex•press•ible \ˌi-nik-ˈspre-sə-bəl\ *adj*
being beyond the power to express : INDESCRIBABLE ⟨*inexpressible* happiness⟩
in•ex•press•ibly \-blē\ *adv*

in•fal•li•ble \in-ˈfa-lə-bəl\ *adj*
1 not capable of being wrong ⟨an *infallible* memory⟩
2 certain to succeed : SURE ⟨an *infallible* remedy⟩
in•fal•li•bly \-blē\ *adv*

in•fa•mous \'in-fə-məs\ *adj*
1 having an evil reputation ⟨an *infamous* murderer⟩
2 [1]EVIL 1, BAD ⟨an *infamous* crime⟩
in•fa•mous•ly *adv*

in•fa•my \'in-fə-mē\ *n, pl* **in•fa•mies**
1 an evil reputation ⟨He earned *infamy* for his crimes.⟩
2 an evil or terrible act ⟨The people suffered the *infamies* of their ruler.⟩

in•fan•cy \'in-fən-sē\ *n, pl* **in•fan•cies**
1 the first stage of a child's life : early childhood
2 a beginning or early period of existence ⟨The program is in its *infancy*.⟩

[1]in•fant \'in-fənt\ *n*
1 ► a child in the first period of life : BABY
2 [2]MINOR

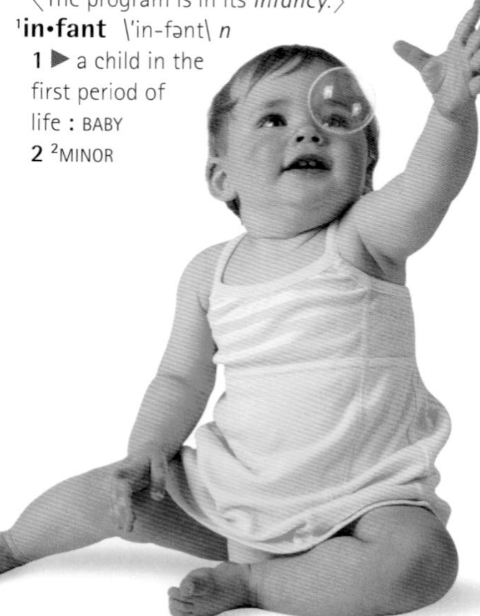

[1]infant 1

► **Word History** To the parent of a crying infant unable to say what the problem is, the etymology of *infant* might seem very appropriate. In Latin the adjective *infans* literally meant "not speaking, incapable of speech." The noun *infans* referred to a very young child who had not yet learned to talk. Later, however, the scope of *infans* was broadened to include any child, no matter how talkative. When the word was adopted from Latin into French, and then into English, the broader usage was carried over also. Over time, English went back to the earlier Latin sense, restricting *infant* to a child still young enough to be called a baby.

[2]infant *adj*
1 of or relating to infancy
2 intended for young children ⟨*infant* clothes⟩

in•fan•tile \'in-fən-,tīl\ *adj*
CHILDISH 2 ⟨*infantile* behavior⟩

in•fan•try \'in-fən-trē\ *n, pl* **in•fan•tries**
a branch of an army composed of soldiers trained to fight on foot

in•fat•u•at•ed \in-'fa-chə-,wā-təd\ *adj*
having a foolish or very strong love or admiration

in•fat•u•a•tion \in-,fa-chə-'wā-shən\ *n*
the state of having a foolish or very strong love or admiration

in•fect \in-'fekt\ *vb* **in•fect•ed**; **in•fect•ing**
1 to pass on or introduce a germ, illness, or disease to : to cause sickness in ⟨Don't *infect* me with your cold.⟩ ⟨The bacteria can *infect* wounds.⟩
2 to cause to share similar feelings ⟨Her enthusiasm *infects* the other players.⟩

in•fec•tion \in-'fek-shən\ *n*
1 the act or process of passing on or introducing a germ, illness, or disease to : the state of being infected
2 any disease caused by germs ⟨an ear *infection*⟩

in•fec•tious \in-'fek-shəs\ *adj*
1 passing from one to another in the form of a germ ⟨an *infectious* illness⟩
2 easily spread to others ⟨an *infectious* laugh⟩

in•fer \in-'fər\ *vb* **in•ferred**; **in•fer•ring**
1 to arrive at as a conclusion based on known facts ⟨I *inferred* he was sick from his cough.⟩
2 [1]GUESS 1 ⟨From the look on her face, I *inferred* she was lying.⟩
3 [2]HINT, SUGGEST

in•fer•ence \'in-fə-rəns\ *n*
1 the act or process of reaching a conclusion about something from known facts
2 a conclusion or opinion reached based on known facts

[1]in•fe•ri•or \in-'fir-ē-ər\ *adj*
1 situated lower down (as in place or importance) ⟨an *inferior* court⟩
2 of little or less importance, value, or merit ⟨He always felt *inferior* to his brother.⟩
3 of poor quality ⟨an *inferior* education⟩

[2]inferior *n*
a less important person or thing

in•fe•ri•or•i•ty \in-,fir-ē-'ȯr-ə-tē\ *n*
1 the state of being of lower importance, value, or quality
2 a sense of being less important or valuable

in•fer•nal \in-'fər-nᵊl\ *adj*
1 very bad or unpleasant ⟨Stop that *infernal* noise!⟩
2 of or relating to hell

in•fer•tile \in-'fər-tᵊl\ *adj*
not fertile ⟨*infertile* soil⟩

in•fest \in-'fest\ *vb* **in•fest•ed**; **in•fest•ing**
to spread or swarm in or over in a harmful manner

in•fi•del \'in-fə-dᵊl, -fə-,del\ *n*
a person who does not believe in a certain religion

in•field \'in-,fēld\ *n*
1 ▼ the diamond-shaped part of a baseball field inside the bases and home plate
2 the players in the infield

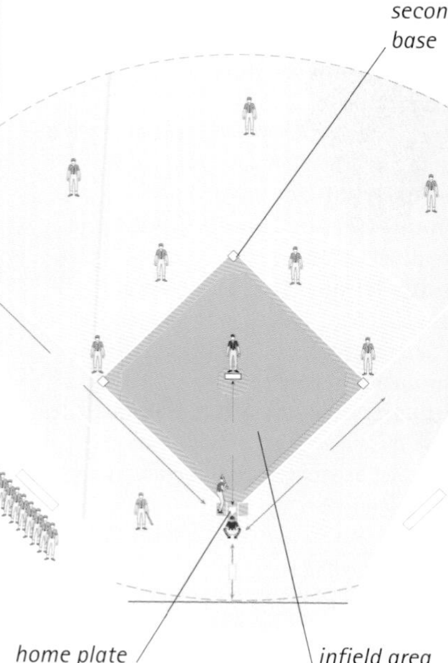

infield 1: diagram showing the infield area on a baseball field

in•field•er \'in-,fēl-dər\ *n*
a baseball player who plays in the infield

in•fi•nite \'in-fə-nət\ *adj*
1 having no limits of any kind ⟨the *infinite* universe⟩
2 seeming to be without limits ⟨She took *infinite* care when handling chemicals.⟩
in•fi•nite•ly *adv*

in•fin•i•tes•i•mal \in-,fi-nə-'te-sə-məl\ *adj*
extremely small ⟨The chance of winning is *infinitesimal*.⟩

in•fin•i•tive \in-'fi-nə-tiv\ *n*
a verb form serving as a noun or as a modifier and at the same time taking objects and adverbial modifiers ⟨In the sentence "I have nothing to do," "to do" is an *infinitive*.⟩

in•fin•i•ty \in-'fi-nə-tē\ *n, pl* **in•fin•i•ties**
1 the quality of being without limits ⟨the *infinity* of space⟩

2 a space, quantity, or period of time that is without limit

in•firm \in-'fərm\ *adj*
weak or frail in body

in•fir•ma•ry \in-'fər-mə-rē\ *n*, *pl* **in•fir•ma•ries**
a place for the care and housing of sick people

in•fir•mi•ty \in-'fər-mə-tē\ *n*, *pl* **in•fir•mi•ties**
the condition of being weak or frail (as from age or illness)

in•flame \in-'flām\ *vb* **in•flamed**; **in•flam•ing**
1 to make more active, excited, angry, or violent ⟨His words *inflamed* the crowd.⟩
2 to cause to redden or grow hot (as from anger)
3 to make or become sore, red, and swollen

in•flam•ma•ble \in-'fla-mə-bəl\ *adj*
1 FLAMMABLE
2 easily inflamed : EXCITABLE ⟨an *inflammable* temper⟩

in•flam•ma•tion \ˌin-flə-'mā-shən\ *n*
a bodily response to injury or disease in which heat, redness, and swelling are present

in•flam•ma•to•ry \in-'fla-mə-ˌtȯr-ē\ *adj*
1 tending to excite anger or disorder ⟨an *inflammatory* speech⟩
2 causing or having inflammation ⟨an *inflammatory* disease⟩

in•flat•able \in-'flā-tə-bəl\ *adj*
possible to fill with air or gas ⟨an *inflatable* life raft⟩

in•flate \in-'flāt\ *vb* **in•flat•ed**; **in•flat•ing**
1 to swell or fill with air or gas ⟨*inflate* a balloon⟩
2 to cause to increase beyond proper limits ⟨Prices have been *inflated.*⟩

in•fla•tion \in-'flā-shən\ *n*
1 an act of filling with air or gas : the state of being filled with air or gas ⟨*inflation* of a balloon⟩
2 a continual rise in the price of goods and services

in•flect \in-'flekt\ *vb* **in•flect•ed**; **in•flect•ing**
1 to change a word by inflection
2 to change the pitch of the voice

in•flec•tion \in-'flek-shən\ *n*
1 a change in the pitch of a person's voice
2 a change in a word that shows a grammatical difference (as of number, person, or tense)

in•flex•i•ble \in-'flek-sə-bəl\ *adj*
1 not easily bent or twisted
2 not easily influenced or persuaded ⟨an *inflexible* judge⟩
3 not easily changed ⟨*inflexible* rules⟩

in•flict \in-'flikt\ *vb* **in•flict•ed**; **in•flict•ing**
1 to give by or as if by striking ⟨*inflict* a wound⟩
2 to cause to be put up with ⟨*inflict* punishment⟩

in•flo•res•cence \ˌin-flə-'re-sᵊns\ *n*
◀ the arrangement of flowers on a stalk

[1]**in•flu•ence** \'in-ˌflü-əns\ *n*
1 the act or power of causing an effect or change without use of direct force or authority ⟨He used his *influence* to get the opposing sides to come to an agreement.⟩
2 a person or thing that has an indirect but usually important effect ⟨She's a bad *influence* on him.⟩

[2]**influence** *vb* **in•flu•enced**; **in•flu•enc•ing**
to affect or change in an indirect but usually important way

in•flu•en•tial \ˌin-flü-'en-shəl\ *adj*
having the power to cause change : having influence

in•flu•en•za \ˌin-flü-'en-zə\ *n*
a very contagious virus disease like a severe cold with fever

▶ **Word History** The Italian word *influenza* was, like English *influence*, a term originally used in astrology. The effect that the stars and planets had on humans was attributed to the "inflow" (the literal meaning of *influence*) of an invisible liquid from the heavens. In the Middle Ages the Italian word was applied more narrowly to outbreaks of disease supposedly brought about by unusual positions of the planets. In the 1600s and 1700s *influenza* came to refer specifically to the disease we now call by this name.

in•form \in-'fȯrm\ *vb* **in•formed**; **in•form•ing**
1 to let a person know something ⟨I *informed* him of the changes.⟩
2 to give information so as to accuse or cause suspicion
in•form•er *n*

in•for•mal \in-'fȯr-məl\ *adj*
1 not requiring serious or formal behavior or dress ⟨an *informal* party⟩
2 suitable for ordinary or everyday use ⟨an *informal* dining area⟩
in•for•mal•ly *adv*

in•for•mal•i•ty \ˌin-fȯr-'ma-lə-tē\ *n*, *pl* **in•for•mal•i•ties**
the quality or state of being informal

in•form•ant \in-'fȯr-mənt\ *n*
a person who gives information especially to accuse or cause suspicion about someone

a b c d e f g h i j k l m n o p q r s t u v w x y z

in•for•ma•tion \ˌin-fər-ˈmā-shən\ *n*
knowledge obtained from investigation, study, or instruction : facts or details about a subject

▶ **Synonyms** INFORMATION, KNOWLEDGE, and LEARNING mean what is or can be known. INFORMATION may be used of a collection of facts gathered from many places. ⟨The book has a lot of *information* about baseball.⟩ KNOWLEDGE is used for facts and ideas acquired by study, observation, or experience. ⟨She has a *knowledge* of birds.⟩ LEARNING is used of knowledge acquired by long and careful study. ⟨The *learning* of a lifetime is in that book.⟩

information superhighway *n*
INTERNET

information technology *n*
the technology involving the development, maintenance, and use of computers and software for the processing and distribution of information

in•for•ma•tive \in-ˈfȯr-mə-tiv\ *adj*
giving knowledge or information

in•frac•tion \in-ˈfrak-shən\ *n*
VIOLATION ⟨an *infraction* of the rules⟩

in•fra•red \ˌin-frə-ˈred\ *adj*
being, relating to, or producing rays like light but lying outside the visible spectrum at its red end

in•fre•quent \in-ˈfrē-kwənt\ *adj*
1 seldom happening : RARE
2 not placed, made, or done at frequent intervals ⟨The bus made *infrequent* stops.⟩
in•fre•quent•ly *adv*

in•fringe \in-ˈfrinj\ *vb* **in•fringed**; **in•fring•ing**
1 to fail to obey or act in agreement with : VIOLATE ⟨*infringe* a law⟩
2 to go further than is right or fair to another : ENCROACH
in•fringe•ment \-mənt\ *n*

in•fu•ri•ate \in-ˈfyu̇r-ē-ˌāt\ *vb* **in•fu•ri•at•ed**; **in•fu•ri•at•ing**
to make furious : ENRAGE

in•fuse \in-ˈfyüz\ *vb* **in•fused**; **in•fus•ing**
1 to put in as if by pouring ⟨The leader *infused* spirit into the group.⟩
2 to steep without boiling ⟨*infuse* tea⟩
in•fu•sion \in-ˈfyü-zhən\ *n*

¹-ing \iŋ\ *n suffix*
1 action or process ⟨meet*ing*⟩
2 product or result of an action or process ⟨engrav*ing*⟩ ⟨earn*ings*⟩
3 something used in or connected with making or doing ⟨bedd*ing*⟩ ⟨roof*ing*⟩

²-ing *vb suffix or adj suffix*
used to form the present participle ⟨sail*ing*⟩ and sometimes to form adjectives that do not come from a verb ⟨hulk*ing*⟩

in•ge•nious \in-ˈjēn-yəs\ *adj*
showing ingenuity : CLEVER ⟨an *ingenious* idea⟩
in•ge•nious•ly *adv*

in•ge•nu•ity \ˌin-jə-ˈnü-ə-tē, -ˈnyü-\ *n*, *pl* **in•ge•nu•ities**
skill or cleverness in discovering, inventing, or planning

in•gen•u•ous \in-ˈjen-yə-wəs\ *adj*
showing innocence and childlike honesty
in•gen•u•ous•ly *adv*

in•got \ˈiŋ-gət\ *n*
▶ a mass of metal cast into a shape that is easy to handle or store

in•gra•ti•ate \in-ˈgrā-shē-ˌāt\ *vb* **in•gra•ti•at•ed**; **in•gra•ti•at•ing**
to gain favor for by effort ⟨He *ingratiates* himself with teachers by being helpful.⟩

in•gra•ti•at•ing \in-ˈgrā-shē-ˌā-tiŋ\ *adj*
1 PLEASING ⟨an *ingratiating* smile⟩
2 intended to gain someone's favor
in•gra•ti•at•ing•ly *adv*

in•grat•i•tude \in-ˈgra-tə-ˌtüd, -ˌtyüd\ *n*
lack of gratitude

in•gre•di•ent \in-ˈgrē-dē-ənt\ *n*
one of the substances that make up a mixture

in•hab•it \in-ˈha-bət\ *vb* **in•hab•it•ed**; **in•hab•it•ing**
to live or dwell in

in•hab•i•tant \in-ˈha-bə-tənt\ *n*
a person or animal that lives in a place

in•ha•la•tion \ˌin-hə-ˈlā-shən, ˌi-nə-\ *n*
the act or an instance of breathing or drawing in by breathing

in•hale \in-ˈhāl\ *vb* **in•haled**; **in•hal•ing**
1 to draw in by breathing
2 to breathe in

medicine canister

mouthpiece

inhaler

in•hal•er \in-ˈhā-lər\ *n*
▲ a device used for breathing medicine into the lungs ⟨An *inhaler* is used to treat asthma.⟩

in•her•ent \in-ˈhir-ənt, -ˈher-\ *adj*
belonging to or being a part of the nature of a person or thing ⟨She has an *inherent* sense of fairness.⟩
in•her•ent•ly *adv*

ingot:
a grid of rusted copper ingots

inherit \in-ˈher-ət\ *vb* **in•her•it•ed**; **in•her•it•ing**
1 to get by legal right from a person at his or her death
2 to get by heredity ⟨I *inherited* red hair.⟩

in•her•i•tance \in-ˈher-ə-təns\ *n*
1 the act of getting by legal right from a person at his or her death or through heredity
2 something gotten by legal right from a person at his or her death

in•hib•it \in-ˈhi-bət\ *vb* **in•hib•it•ed**; **in•hib•it•ing**
to prevent or hold back from doing something

in•hos•pi•ta•ble \ˌin-ˌhä-ˈspi-tə-bəl, in-ˈhä-spi-\ *adj*
not friendly or generous : not showing hospitality ⟨He's *inhospitable* to strangers.⟩
in•hos•pi•ta•bly \-blē\ *adv*

in•hu•man \in-ˈhyü-mən, -ˈyü-\ *adj*
1 lacking pity or kindness
2 unlike what might be expected by a human ⟨an *inhuman* scream⟩

in•hu•mane \ˌin-hyü-ˈmān, -yü-\ *adj*
not kind or humane ⟨*inhumane* treatment⟩

in•hu•man•i•ty \ˌin-hyü-ˈma-nə-tē\ *n*, *pl* **in•hu•man•i•ties**
a cruel act or attitude

in•iq•ui•ty \i-ˈnik-wə-tē\ *n*, *pl* **in•iq•ui•ties**
an evil or unfair act

¹ini•tial \i-ˈni-shəl\ *n*
1 the first letter of a name
2 a large letter beginning a text or a paragraph

²initial *adj*
occurring at or marking the beginning
ini•tial•ly \-shə-lē\ *adv*

[3]initial *vb* **ini•tialed** *or* **ini•tialled; ini•tial•ing** *or* **ini•tial•ling**
to mark with the first letter or letters of a name

ini•ti•ate \i-'ni-shē-,āt\ *vb* **ini•ti•at•ed; ini•ti•at•ing**
1 to set going : BEGIN 〈Scientists *initiated* an experiment.〉
2 to admit into a club by special ceremonies
3 to teach (someone) the basic facts about something 〈She was *initiated* into the management of money.〉

ini•ti•a•tion \i-,ni-shē-'ā-shən\ *n*
1 the act or an instance of initiating : the process of being initiated 〈the *initiation* of treatment〉 〈*initiation* into the club〉
2 the ceremonies with which a person is admitted into a club

ini•tia•tive \i-'ni-shə-tiv\ *n*
1 a first step or movement 〈I took the *initiative* and called first.〉
2 energy shown in getting action started 〈He's a person of great *initiative*.〉

in•ject \in-'jekt\ *vb* **in•ject•ed; in•ject•ing**
1 to force a fluid (as a medicine) into by using a special needle
2 to introduce as something needed or additional 〈He tried to *inject* confidence into his brother.〉

in•jec•tion \in-'jek-shən\ *n*
▼ an act or instance of forcing a fluid (as a medicine) into a part of the body by using a special needle 〈Insulin can be given by *injection*.〉

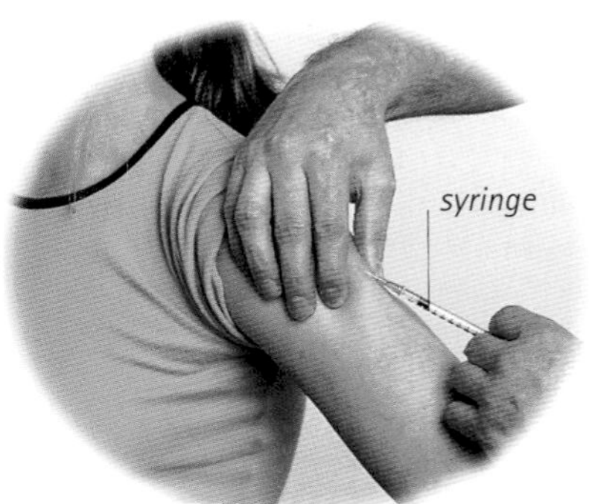

injection: a girl receiving an injection

in•junc•tion \in-'jəŋk-shən\ *n*
a court order commanding or forbidding the doing of some act

in•jure \'in-jər\ *vb* **in•jured; in•jur•ing**
to cause pain or harm to 〈Two people were *injured* in the accident.〉 〈The criticism *injured* my pride.〉

in•ju•ri•ous \in-'jür-ē-əs\ *adj*
causing injury or harm

in•ju•ry \'in-jə-rē\ *n, pl* **in•ju•ries**
1 hurt, damage, or loss suffered 〈She suffered an *injury* to her arm.〉 〈These tools can cause *injury*.〉
2 an act that damages or hurts
synonyms see HARM

in•jus•tice \in-'jə-stəs\ *n*
1 unfair treatment : violation of a person's rights
2 an act of unfair treatment 〈This punishment is an *injustice*.〉

ink \'iŋk\ *n*
a liquid material used for writing or printing

ink–jet \'iŋk-'jet\ *adj*
relating to or being a printer in which droplets of ink are sprayed onto the paper

in•kling \'iŋ-kliŋ\ *n*
a vague notion : HINT

ink•stand \'iŋk-,stand\ *n*
a small stand for holding ink and pens

ink•well \'iŋk-,wel\ *n*
a container for ink

inky \'iŋ-kē\ *adj* **ink•i•er; ink•i•est**
1 consisting of or like ink 〈*inky* darkness〉
2 soiled with or as if with ink

in•laid \'in-'lād\ *adj*
1 set into a surface in a decorative pattern 〈an *inlaid* design〉
2 decorated with a design or material set into a surface 〈an *inlaid* table〉

[1]in•land \'in-,land, -lənd\ *adj*
of or relating to the part of a country away from the coast 〈*inland* towns〉

[2]inland *n*
the part of a country away from the coast or boundaries

[3]inland *adv*
into or toward the area away from a coast 〈The storm moved *inland*.〉

in–law \'in-,ló\ *n*
a relative by marriage and especially the mother or father of a person's husband or wife

[1]in•lay \'in-'lā\ *vb* **in•laid** \-'lād\; **in•lay•ing**
to set into a surface for decoration or strengthening

[2]in•lay \'in-,lā\ *n*
inlaid work : material used in inlaying

in•let \'in-,let\ *n*
1 a small or narrow bay
2 an opening through which air, gas, or liquid can enter something

in–line skate \'in-'līn-\ *n*
a roller skate whose wheels are set in a line one behind the other

in•mate \'in-,māt\ *n*
a person confined in an institution (as a hospital or prison)

in•most \'in-,mōst\ *adj*
INNERMOST

inn \'in\ *n*
▼ a house that provides a place to sleep and food for travelers

in•ner \'i-nər\ *adj*
1 located farther in 〈an *inner* chamber〉
2 of or relating to the mind or spirit 〈*inner* strength〉

inn: a traditional English inn

A B C D E F G H I J K L M N O P Q R S T U V W X Y Z

inner ear *n*
▶ the inner part of the ear that is located in a bony cavity and plays a key role in hearing and keeping the body properly balanced

in•ner•most \'i-nər-,mōst\ *adj*
farthest inward ⟨the *innermost* rooms⟩

in•ning \'i-niŋ\ *n*
a division of a baseball game that consists of a turn at bat for each team

inn•keep•er \'in-,kē-pər\ *n*
the person who runs an inn

in•no•cence \'i-nə-səns\ *n*
the quality or state of being free from sin or guilt ⟨The evidence proved his *innocence*.⟩

in•no•cent \'i-nə-sənt\ *adj*
1 free from sin : PURE ⟨She's as *innocent* as a baby.⟩
2 free from guilt or blame ⟨He is *innocent* of the charges.⟩
3 free from evil influence or effect : HARMLESS ⟨*innocent* fun⟩
in•no•cent•ly *adv*

in•noc•u•ous \i-'nä-kyə-wəs\ *adj*
not harmful ⟨*innocuous* chemicals⟩
in•noc•u•ous•ly *adv*

in•no•va•tion \,i-nə-'vā-shən\ *n*
1 a new idea, method, or device : NOVELTY
2 the introduction of something new ⟨Consumers are looking for *innovation*.⟩

in•nu•mer•a•ble \i-'nü-mə-rə-bəl, -'nyü-\ *adj*
too many to be counted ⟨*innumerable* stars⟩

in•oc•u•late \i-'nä-kyə-,lāt\ *vb* **in•oc•u•lat•ed**; **in•oc•u•lat•ing**
to inject a material (as a vaccine) into to protect against or treat a disease

▶ **Word History** Similar to the way that we use "eye" for the undeveloped bud on a potato, the Romans used the Latin word *oculus*, "eye," to mean "bud of a plant." Having learned that the *oculus* or bud from one plant can be grafted onto another, the Romans derived the verb *inoculare* from *oculus* to refer to the process of grafting. English borrowed this verb as *inoculate* with the same meaning. Introducing a small amount of material to make a person immune to a disease is like implanting a bud, so the verb *inoculate* was also used for this procedure.

in•oc•u•la•tion \i-,nä-kyə-'lā-shən\ *n*
an act or instance of injecting a material (as a vaccine) into to protect against or treat a disease

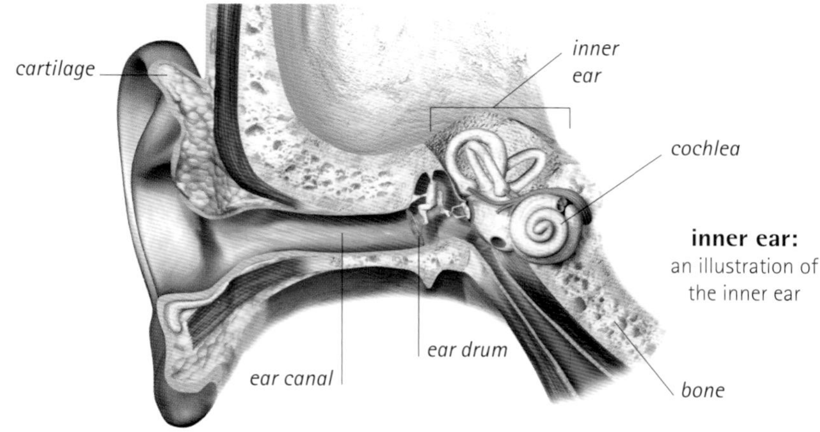

inner ear: an illustration of the inner ear

in•of•fen•sive \,i-nə-'fen-siv\ *adj*
not likely to offend or bother anyone ⟨an *inoffensive* joke⟩

in•op•por•tune \in-,ä-pər-'tün, -'tyün\ *adj*
INCONVENIENT ⟨She always calls at the most *inopportune* time.⟩

[1]**in•put** \'in-,pu̇t\ *n*
1 something (as power, a signal, or data) that is put into a machine or system
2 the point at which an input is made
3 the act of or process of putting in ⟨the *input* of data⟩

[2]**input** *vb* **in•put•ted** *or* **input**; **in•put•ting**
to enter (as data) into a computer

in•quest \'in-,kwest\ *n*
an official investigation especially into the cause of a death

in•quire \in-'kwīr\ *vb* **in•quired**; **in•quir•ing**
1 to ask or ask about ⟨I *inquired* about the schedule.⟩
2 to make an investigation ⟨The committee *inquired* into the matter.⟩
3 to ask a question ⟨"Can I help you?" she *inquired*.⟩
in•quir•er *n*
in•quir•ing•ly *adv*

in•qui•ry \'in-,kwī-rē, -kwə-\ *n, pl* **in•qui•ries**
1 the act of asking a question or seeking information ⟨On further *inquiry*, we learned his name.⟩
2 a request for information ⟨The *inquiry* is confidential.⟩
3 a thorough examination ⟨an official *inquiry*⟩

in•quis•i•tive \in-'kwi-zə-tiv\ *adj*
1 in search of information ⟨*inquisitive* reporters⟩
2 overly curious
in•quis•i•tive•ly *adv*

in•sane \in-'sān\ *adj*
1 not normal or healthy in mind
2 used by or for people who are insane ⟨an *insane* asylum⟩
3 very foolish or unreasonable
in•sane•ly *adv*

in•san•i•ty \in-'sa-nə-tē\ *n*
the condition of being abnormal or unhealthy in mind

in•sa•tia•ble \in-'sā-shə-bəl\ *adj*
impossible to satisfy ⟨*insatiable* thirst⟩

in•scribe \in-'skrīb\ *vb* **in•scribed**; **in•scrib•ing**
1 to write, engrave, or print as a lasting record ⟨His name is *inscribed* on the monument.⟩
2 to write, engrave, or print something on or in ⟨*inscribe* a book⟩

in•scrip•tion \in-'skrip-shən\ *n*
words or a name inscribed on a surface

in•sect \'in-,sekt\ *n*
1 ▶ any of a group of small and often winged animals that are arthropods having six jointed legs and a body formed of a head, thorax, and abdomen ⟨Flies, bees, and lice are true *insects*.⟩
2 an animal (as a spider or a centipede) similar to the true insects
Hint: This meaning is not scientifically accurate but may be encountered in common everyday use.

▶ **Word History** The distinct parts into which insects' bodies are divided—head, thorax, and abdomen—inspired the Greek name used for them by the philosopher Aristotle: *entomon*, the "notched" or "segmented" animal. (*Entomon* is a noun derived from the verb *entemnein*, "to cut up" or "to cut into.") The Romans used *insectum*, a literal translation of Greek *entomon*, as their name for the creatures, and this Latin word has provided us with the ordinary English word for insects.

in•sec•ti•cide \in-'sek-tə-,sīd\ *n*
a chemical used to kill insects

insect 1

Insects have six jointed legs and a jointed body made up of three sections: the head, thorax, and abdomen. They may have one or two pairs of wings, a single pair of antennae, and compound eyes. Insects do not have an internal skeleton like mammals, but usually have a hard outer skeleton. Many pass through a larval stage before changing into their adult form.

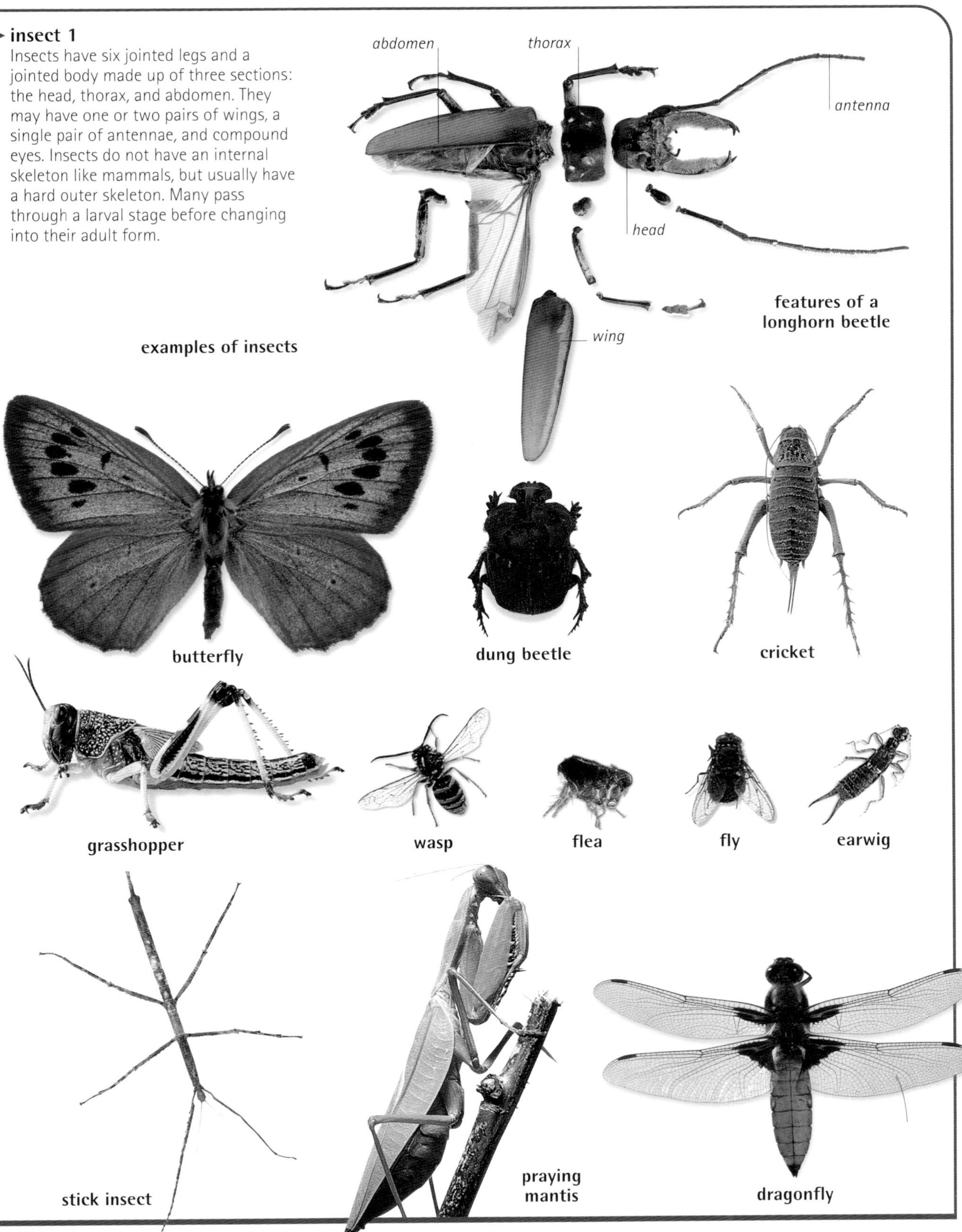

a b c d e f g h i j k l m n o p q r s t u v w x y z

A B C D E F G H I J K L M N O P Q R S T U V W X Y Z

in•se•cure \ˌin-si-ˈkyu̇r\ *adj*
1 not safe or secure ⟨*insecure* property⟩
2 not confident

in•se•cu•ri•ty \ˌin-si-ˈkyu̇r-ə-tē\ *n*
the quality or state of being not safe or not confident

in•sen•si•ble \in-ˈsen-sə-bəl\ *adj*
1 not able to feel ⟨*insensible* to pain⟩
2 not aware of or caring about something ⟨They seemed *insensible* to the danger.⟩

in•sen•si•tive \in-ˈsen-sə-tiv\ *adj*
1 lacking feeling : not sensitive ⟨He's *insensitive* to pain.⟩
2 not caring or showing concern about the problems or feelings of others
in•sen•si•tive•ly *adv*

in•sen•si•tiv•i•ty \in-ˌsen-sə-ˈti-və-tē\ *n*
lack of feeling ⟨*insensitivity* to pain⟩

in•sep•a•ra•ble \in-ˈse-pə-rə-bəl\ *adj*
impossible to separate ⟨*inseparable* companions⟩

[1]in•sert \in-ˈsərt\ *vb* **in•sert•ed**; **in•sert•ing**
to put in or into ⟨*Insert* a coin in the slot.⟩

[2]in•sert \ˈin-ˌsərt\ *n*
something that is or is meant to be inserted ⟨an advertising *insert*⟩

in•ser•tion \in-ˈsər-shən\ *n*
1 the act or process of putting in or into ⟨The lock opened upon *insertion* of a key.⟩
2 [2]INSERT

[1]in•set \ˈin-ˌset\ *n*
a smaller thing that is inserted into a larger thing ⟨The Ohio map has an *inset* showing Columbus in detail.⟩

[2]inset *vb* **in•set** *or* **in•set•ted**; **in•set•ting**
[1]INSERT 2

[1]in•side \in-ˈsīd, ˈin-ˌsīd\ *n*
1 an inner side, surface, or space : INTERIOR ⟨the *inside* of a box⟩
2 the inner parts of a person or animal — usually used in pl.

[2]inside *adv*
1 on the inner side ⟨I cleaned my car *inside* and out.⟩
2 in or into the interior ⟨Go *inside*.⟩

[3]inside *adj*
1 relating to or being on or near the inside ⟨an *inside* wall⟩
2 relating or known to a certain few people ⟨*inside* information⟩

[4]inside *prep*
1 to or on the inside of ⟨They are *inside* the house.⟩
2 before the end of : WITHIN ⟨I'll finish *inside* an hour.⟩

inside out *adv*
1 in such a way that the inner surface becomes the outer ⟨Your shirt is *inside out*.⟩
2 in or into a confused or disorganized state ⟨The room was turned *inside out*.⟩

in•sid•er \in-ˈsī-dər\ *n*
a member of a group or organization who has information about it

in•sight \ˈin-ˌsīt\ *n*
1 the ability to understand a person or a situation very clearly
2 the understanding of the truth of a situation

in•sig•nia \in-ˈsig-nē-ə\ *n, pl* **insignia** *or* **in•sig•ni•as**
▼ an emblem of a certain office, authority, or honor

insignia:
an insignia on the cap of a US Navy officer

in•sig•nif•i•cance \ˌin-sig-ˈni-fi-kəns\ *n*
the quality or state of being unimportant

in•sig•nif•i•cant \ˌin-sig-ˈni-fi-kənt\ *adj*
not important ⟨an *insignificant* change⟩
in•sig•nif•i•cant•ly *adv*

in•sin•cere \ˌin-sin-ˈsir\ *adj*
not expressing or showing true feelings : not sincere or honest
in•sin•cere•ly *adv*

in•sin•cer•i•ty \ˌin-sin-ˈser-ə-tē\ *n*
lack of honesty in showing feelings

in•sin•u•ate \in-ˈsin-yə-ˌwāt\ *vb* **in•sin•u•at•ed**; **in•sin•u•at•ing**
1 [2]HINT, IMPLY ⟨She *insinuated* that I had cheated.⟩
2 to bring or get in little by little or in a secret way ⟨He *insinuated* himself into the group.⟩

in•sip•id \in-ˈsi-pəd\ *adj*
1 having little taste or flavor : TASTELESS
2 not interesting or challenging : DULL

in•sist \in-ˈsist\ *vb* **in•sist•ed**; **in•sist•ing**
1 to make a demand ⟨She *insisted* I stay.⟩
2 to say (something) in a forceful way that doesn't allow for disagreement ⟨She *insists* the money is hers.⟩
insist on *also* **insist upon** to express or show a belief in the importance of something ⟨He *insists on* doing it his way.⟩

in•sis•tence \in-ˈsi-stəns\ *n*
the quality or state of being demanding about something

in•sis•tent \in-ˈsi-stənt\ *adj*
demanding that something happen or that someone act in a certain way ⟨He was *insistent* that I stay overnight.⟩
in•sis•tent•ly *adv*

in•so•lence \ˈin-sə-ləns\ *n*
lack of respect for rank or authority

in•so•lent \ˈin-sə-lənt\ *adj*
showing lack of respect for rank or authority
in•so•lent•ly *adv*

in•sol•u•ble \in-ˈsäl-yə-bəl\ *adj*
1 having no solution or explanation ⟨an *insoluble* problem⟩
2 difficult or impossible to dissolve ⟨*insoluble* in water⟩

in•som•nia \in-ˈsäm-nē-ə\ *n*
difficulty in sleeping

in•spect \in-ˈspekt\ *vb* **in•spect•ed**; **in•spect•ing**
1 to examine closely ⟨Doctors *inspected* the injury.⟩
2 to view and examine in an official way ⟨The president *inspected* the troops.⟩

in•spec•tion \in-ˈspek-shən\ *n*
the act of examining closely or officially

in•spec•tor \in-ˈspek-tər\ *n*
a person who makes inspections

in•spi•ra•tion \ˌin-spə-ˈrā-shən\ *n*
1 the act or power of arousing the mind or the emotions ⟨the *inspiration* of music⟩
2 a clever idea
3 something that moves someone to act, create, or feel an emotion ⟨Mountains were the painter's *inspiration*.⟩

in•spire \in-ˈspīr\ *vb* **in•spired**; **in•spir•ing**
1 to move or guide by divine influence
2 to move (someone) to act, create, or feel emotions : AROUSE ⟨The Senator's comments *inspired* me to write a letter.⟩
3 to cause something to occur or to be created or done

in•sta•bil•i•ty \ˌin-stə-ˈbi-lə-tē\ *n*
the quality or state of being unstable

in•stall \in-ˈstȯl\ *vb* **in•stalled**; **in•stall•ing**
1 to put in office with ceremony ⟨At the next meeting we'll be *installing* new officers.⟩
2 to put in place for use or service ⟨Smoke detectors were *installed* in every apartment.⟩

in•stal•la•tion \ˌin-stə-ˈlā-shən\ *n*
1 the act of putting something in place for use : the state of being put in place for use
2 something put in place for use

[1]in•stall•ment \in-ˈstȯl-mənt\ *n*
INSTALLATION 1

[2]installment *n*
one of several parts of something (as a book) presented over a period of time

in•stance \ˈin-stəns\ *n*
1 a particular occurrence of something : EXAMPLE ⟨an *instance* of true bravery⟩

2 a certain point or situation in a process or series of events ⟨In most *instances*, the medicine helps.⟩

[1]**in•stant** \ˈin-stənt\ *n*
a very short time : MOMENT

[2]**instant** *adj*
1 happening or done right away ⟨The play was an *instant* success.⟩
2 partially prepared by the manufacturer to make final preparation easy ⟨*instant* pudding⟩ ⟨*instant* coffee⟩

in•stan•ta•neous \ˌin-stən-ˈtā-nē-əs\ *adj*
happening or done very quickly
: happening in an instant
in•stan•ta•neous•ly *adv*

in•stant•ly \ˈin-stənt-lē\ *adv*
without delay : IMMEDIATELY

instant mes•sag•ing \-ˈme-si-jiŋ\ *n*
a system for sending messages quickly over the Internet from one computer to another

in•stead \in-ˈsted\ *adv*
as a substitute

in•stead of \in-ˈste-dəv\ *prep*
in place of : as a substitute for ⟨I had milk *instead of* juice.⟩

in•step \ˈin-ˌstep\ *n*
the arched middle part of the human foot between the ankle and the toes

in•sti•gate \ˈin-stə-ˌgāt\ *vb* **in•sti•gat•ed**; **in•sti•gat•ing**
to cause to happen or begin ⟨He *instigated* the fight.⟩

in•still \in-ˈstil\ *vb* **in•stilled**; **in•still•ing**
to put into the mind little by little ⟨She *instilled* in her son a love of books.⟩

in•stinct \ˈin-ˌstiŋkt\ *n*
1 an act or course of action in response to a stimulus that is automatic rather than learned ⟨It's a cat's *instinct* to hunt.⟩
2 a way of knowing something without learning or thinking about it ⟨Her *instincts* told her to wait.⟩
3 a natural ability

in•stinc•tive \in-ˈstiŋk-tiv\ *adj*
of or relating to instinct : resulting from instinct ⟨*instinctive* behavior⟩
in•stinc•tive•ly *adv*

[1]**in•sti•tute** \ˈin-stə-ˌtüt, -ˌtyüt\ *vb* **in•sti•tut•ed**; **in•sti•tut•ing**
1 to begin or establish ⟨The library *instituted* new rules.⟩
2 to give a start to ⟨Police *instituted* an investigation.⟩

[2]**institute** *n*
1 an organization for the promotion of a cause ⟨an *institute* for scientific research⟩
2 a place for study usually in a special field ⟨an art *institute*⟩

in•sti•tu•tion \ˌin-stə-ˈtü-shən, -ˈtyü-\ *n*
1 the beginning or establishment of something ⟨the *institution* of new rules⟩
2 an established custom, practice, or law ⟨Turkey dinners are a Thanksgiving *institution*.⟩
3 an established organization ⟨business *institutions*⟩

in•struct \in-ˈstrəkt\ *vb* **in•struct•ed**; **in•struct•ing**
1 to give knowledge to : TEACH ⟨A tutor *instructs* him in math.⟩
2 to give information to ⟨I *instructed* him that school was closed.⟩
3 to give directions or commands to ⟨She *instructed* us to stay seated.⟩
synonyms see TEACH

in•struc•tion \in-ˈstrək-shən\ *n*
1 **instructions** *pl* a specific rule or command ⟨I left *instructions* that I was not to be disturbed.⟩
2 **instructions** *pl* an outline of how something is to be done ⟨Follow the *instructions* on the box.⟩
3 the act or practice of teaching ⟨Students receive *instruction* in history.⟩

in•struc•tive \in-ˈstrək-tiv\ *adj*
helping to give knowledge or information

in•struc•tor \in-ˈstrək-tər\ *n*
TEACHER

in•stru•ment \ˈin-strə-mənt\ *n*
1 ▼ a tool or device for doing a particular kind of work ⟨a dentist's *instruments*⟩
2 a device used to produce music
3 a way of getting something done ⟨Curiosity is an *instrument* of discovery.⟩
4 a legal document (as a deed)
5 a device that measures something (as altitude or temperature)

▶ **Synonyms** INSTRUMENT, TOOL, and UTENSIL mean a device for doing work. INSTRUMENT is used for a device that can be used to do complicated work. ⟨The surgeon's *instruments* were sterilized.⟩ TOOL is used for a device used for a particular job and often suggests that a special skill is needed to use it. ⟨A carpenter's *tools* include hammers and saws.⟩ UTENSIL is used for a simple device used in jobs around the house. ⟨They bought kitchen *utensils*.⟩

▶ **instrument 1**
Instruments are devices which enable a person to perform a particular task. A pair of compasses ensure that a perfect circle can be drawn. A microscope allows doctors and other scientists to view tiny things. Doctors also use a stethoscope to hear sounds inside the body, such as the beating of the heart.

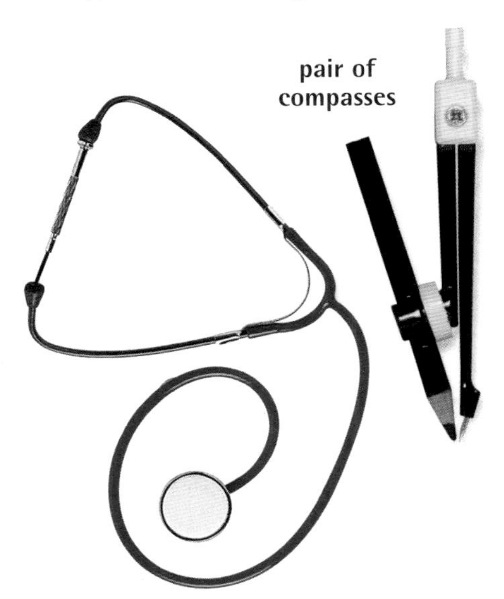

pair of compasses

stethoscope

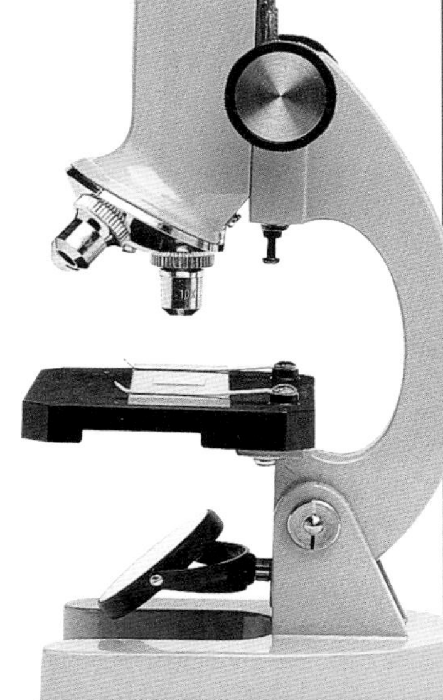

microscope

in•stru•men•tal \\,in-strə-'men-tᵊl\\ *adj*
1 acting to get something done ⟨He was *instrumental* in organizing the club.⟩
2 relating to or done with an instrument ⟨*instrumental* navigation⟩
3 played on an instrument rather than sung ⟨*instrumental* music⟩

in•sub•or•di•nate \\,in-sə-'bȯr-də-nət\\ *adj*
not obeying authority : DISOBEDIENT

in•sub•or•di•na•tion \\,in-sə-,bȯr-də-'nā-shən\\ *n*
failure to obey authority

in•sub•stan•tial \\,in-səb-'stan-chəl\\ *adj*
not large or important ⟨Her contribution was *insubstantial.*⟩

in•suf•fer•able \\in-'sə-fə-rə-bəl\\ *adj*
impossible to bear ⟨*insufferable* behavior⟩
in•suf•fer•ably \\-blē\\ *adv*

in•suf•fi•cient \\,in-sə-'fi-shənt\\ *adj*
not enough : not sufficient ⟨There was *insufficient* time to finish.⟩
in•suf•fi•cient•ly *adv*

in•su•late \\'in-sə-,lāt\\ *vb* **in•su•lat•ed**; **in•su•lat•ing**
1 to separate from others : ISOLATE ⟨At home he *insulates* himself from the city.⟩
2 to separate a conductor of electricity, heat, or sound from other conductors by means of something that does not allow the passage of electricity, heat, or sound ⟨*insulated* electrical wire⟩

in•su•la•tion \\,in-sə-'lā-shən\\ *n*
1 material that is used to stop the passage of electricity, heat, or sound from one conductor to another
2 the act of insulating : the state of being insulated ⟨*insulation* of wires⟩

in•su•la•tor \\'in-sə-,lā-tər\\ *n*
a material (as rubber or glass) that is a poor conductor of electricity, heat, or sound

in•su•lin \\'in-sə-lən\\ *n*
a hormone made by the pancreas that helps the cells in the body take up glucose from the blood and that is used to treat diabetes

[1]**in•sult** \\in-'səlt\\ *vb* **in•sult•ed**; **in•sult•ing**
to treat or speak to with disrespect

[2]**in•sult** \\'in-,səlt\\ *n*
an act or statement showing disrespect

in•sur•ance \\in-'shu̇r-əns\\ *n*
1 an agreement by which a person pays a company and the company promises to pay money if the person becomes injured or dies or to pay for the value of property lost or damaged
2 the amount for which something is insured
3 the business of insuring persons or property

in•sure \\in-'shu̇r\\ *vb* **in•sured**; **in•sur•ing**
1 to give or get insurance on or for ⟨I *insured* my car.⟩
2 to make certain ⟨I want to *insure* your safety.⟩
in•sur•er *n*

in•sur•gent \\in-'sər-jənt\\ *n*
a person who revolts : REBEL

in•sur•rec•tion \\,in-sə-'rek-shən\\ *n*
an act or instance of rebelling against a government

in•tact \\in-'takt\\ *adj*
not broken or damaged : not touched especially by anything that harms ⟨The storm left our house *intact.*⟩

in•take \\'in-,tāk\\ *n*
1 the act of taking in ⟨the *intake* of oxygen⟩
2 something taken in ⟨Limit your daily sugar *intake.*⟩
3 a place where liquid or air is taken into something (as a pump)

in•tan•gi•ble \\in-'tan-jə-bəl\\ *adj*
1 not capable of being touched ⟨Light is *intangible.*⟩
2 not having physical substance ⟨Goodwill is an *intangible* asset.⟩

in•te•ger \\'in-ti-jər\\ *n*
a number that is a natural number (as 1, 2, or 3), the negative of a natural number (as -1, -2, -3), or 0

in•te•gral \\'in-ti-grəl\\ *adj*
very important and necessary : needed to make something complete ⟨an *integral* part⟩

in•te•grate \\'in-tə-,grāt\\ *vb* **in•te•grat•ed**; **in•te•grat•ing**
1 to form into a whole : UNITE ⟨Her music *integrates* jazz and rock.⟩
2 to make a part of a larger unit ⟨They help *integrate* immigrants into the community.⟩
3 DESEGREGATE ⟨The schools are being *integrated.*⟩

integrated circuit *n*
▼ a tiny group of electronic devices and their connections that is produced in or on a small slice of material (as silicon)

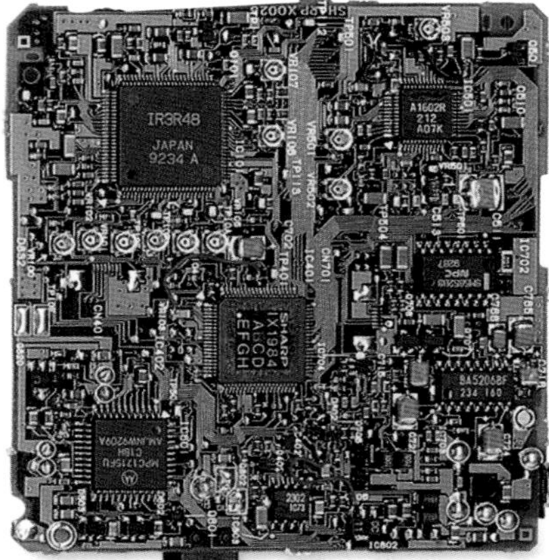

integrated circuit

in•te•gra•tion \\,in-tə-'grā-shən\\ *n*
1 the act or process of uniting different things
2 the practice of uniting people from different races in an attempt to give people equal rights ⟨racial *integration*⟩

in•teg•ri•ty \\in-'te-grə-tē\\ *n*
1 total honesty and sincerity ⟨a person of *integrity*⟩
2 the condition of being free from damage or defect ⟨The building has structural *integrity.*⟩

in•tel•lect \\'in-tə-,lekt\\ *n*
1 the ability to think and understand ⟨She has a superior *intellect.*⟩
2 a person with great powers of thinking and reasoning

[1]**in•tel•lec•tu•al** \\,in-tə-'lek-chə-wəl\\ *adj*
1 of or relating to thought or understanding ⟨*intellectual* development⟩
2 interested in serious study and thought ⟨an *intellectual* person⟩
3 requiring study and thought ⟨an *intellectual* challenge⟩
in•tel•lec•tu•al•ly \\-wə-lē\\ *adv*

[2]**intellectual** *n*
a person who takes pleasure in serious study and thought

in•tel•li•gence \\in-'te-lə-jəns\\ *n*
1 the ability to learn and understand ⟨The test measures *intelligence.*⟩
2 secret information collected about an enemy or a possible enemy

in•tel•li•gent \\in-'te-lə-jənt\\ *adj*
1 having or showing serious thought and good judgment ⟨an *intelligent* student⟩ ⟨an *intelligent* decision⟩
2 able to learn and understand ⟨Is there *intelligent* life on other planets?⟩
in•tel•li•gent•ly *adv*

▶ **Synonyms** INTELLIGENT, CLEVER, and BRILLIANT mean having a good amount of mental ability. INTELLIGENT is used of a person who can handle new situations and solve problems. ⟨We need an *intelligent* person to run the company.⟩ CLEVER is used of a person who learns very quickly. ⟨The *clever* youngster learned the trick in a few minutes.⟩ BRILLIANT is used of a person whose mental ability is much greater than normal. ⟨A *brilliant* doctor discovered the cure for that disease.⟩

in•tel•li•gi•ble \\in-'te-lə-jə-bəl\\ *adj*
possible to understand ⟨Her message was barely *intelligible.*⟩
in•tel•li•gi•bly \\-blē\\ *adv*

in•tem•per•ance \in-'tem-pə-rəns\ *n*
lack of self-control (as in satisfying an appetite)

in•tem•per•ate \in-'tem-pə-rət\ *adj*
1 not moderate or mild ⟨*intemperate* weather⟩
2 having or showing a lack of self-control (as in the use of alcoholic beverages)

in•tend \in-'tend\ *vb* **in•tend•ed**; **in•tend•ing**
to have in mind as a purpose or goal : PLAN ⟨I *intend* to do better next time.⟩ ⟨I didn't *intend* to hurt you.⟩

in•tense \in-'tens\ *adj*
1 very great in degree : EXTREME ⟨*intense* heat⟩
2 done with great energy, enthusiasm, or effort ⟨*intense* concentration⟩
3 having very strong feelings ⟨an *intense* person⟩
in•tense•ly *adv*

in•ten•si•fy \in-'ten-sə-,fī\ *vb* **in•ten•si•fied**; **in•ten•si•fy•ing**
to make or become stronger or more extreme

in•ten•si•ty \in-'ten-sə-tē\ *n*, *pl* **in•ten•si•ties**
1 strength or force ⟨the sun's *intensity*⟩
2 the degree or amount of a quality or condition ⟨This storm is of a lower *intensity*.⟩

interaction 1

[1]in•ten•sive \in-'ten-siv\ *adj*
1 involving special effort or concentration ⟨*intensive* study⟩
2 giving emphasis ⟨The pronoun "myself" in "I myself did it" is *intensive*.⟩

[2]intensive *n*
a word that emphasizes or stresses something ⟨"Quite" is an *intensive* in "*quite* a musician."⟩

intensive care *n*
constant observation and treatment of very ill patients in a special unit of a hospital

[1]in•tent \in-'tent\ *n*
1 what someone plans to do or accomplish : PURPOSE ⟨Upsetting her was not my *intent*.⟩
2 MEANING 2 ⟨What is the author's *intent*?⟩

[2]intent *adj*
1 showing concentration or great attention ⟨an *intent* gaze⟩
2 showing great determination ⟨They were *intent* on going.⟩
in•tent•ly *adv*

in•ten•tion \in-'ten-shən\ *n*
1 a determination to act in a particular way ⟨She announced her *intention* to run for president.⟩
2 an aim or plan ⟨It's his *intention* to win.⟩

in•ten•tion•al \in-'ten-shə-nəl\ *adj*
done in a deliberate way : not accidental ⟨an *intentional* error⟩
synonyms see VOLUNTARY
in•ten•tion•al•ly *adv*

in•ter \in-'tər\ *vb* **in•terred**; **in•ter•ring**
BURY 2

inter- *prefix*
1 between : among : together ⟨*inter*mingle⟩
2 mutual : mutually ⟨*inter*relation⟩
3 located, occurring, or carried on between ⟨*inter*national⟩

in•ter•act \,in-tər-'akt\ *vb* **in•ter•act•ed**; **in•ter•act•ing**
1 to talk or do things with other people ⟨The neighbors don't *interact*.⟩
2 to act upon or together with something else ⟨The chemicals *interacted* to produce smoke.⟩

in•ter•ac•tion \,in-tər-'ak-shən\ *n*
1 ◀ the act of talking or doing things with other people ⟨Board games encourage *interaction*.⟩
2 the action or influence of things on one another ⟨*interaction* of the heart and lungs⟩

in•ter•ac•tive \,in-tər-'ak-tiv\ *adj*
designed to be used in a way that involves the frequent participation of a user ⟨*interactive* Web sites⟩
in•ter•ac•tive•ly *adv*

in•ter•cede \,in-tər-'sēd\ *vb* **in•ter•ced•ed**; **in•ter•ced•ing**
1 to try to help settle differences between unfriendly individuals or groups ⟨I *interceded* to stop the argument.⟩
2 to plead for the needs of someone else

in•ter•cept \,in-tər-'sept\ *vb* **in•ter•cept•ed**; **in•ter•cept•ing**
1 to take, seize, or stop before reaching an intended destination ⟨*intercept* a message⟩
2 to catch (a football) passed by a member of the opposing team

[1]in•ter•change \,in-tər-'chānj\ *vb* **in•ter•changed**; **in•ter•chang•ing**
to put each in the place of the other : EXCHANGE ⟨You can *interchange* the two signs.⟩

[2]in•ter•change \'in-tər-,chānj\ *n*
1 an act or instance of sharing or exchanging things ⟨an *interchange* of ideas⟩
2 ▼ an area where highways meet and it is possible to move from one to the other without stopping

in•ter•change•able \,in-tər-'chān-jə-bəl\ *adj*
capable of being used in place of each other ⟨The parts are *interchangeable*.⟩
in•ter•change•ably \-blē\ *adv*

[2]interchange 2

A B C D E F G H I J K L M N O P Q R S T U V W X Y Z

▶ intercom
With an intercom, the person who receives a call hears the caller's voice through a loudspeaker or telephone, and may see his or her face on a video screen. Intercoms are sometimes used to provide security in buildings. The receiver of a call presses a button to open the door, allowing the caller into the building.

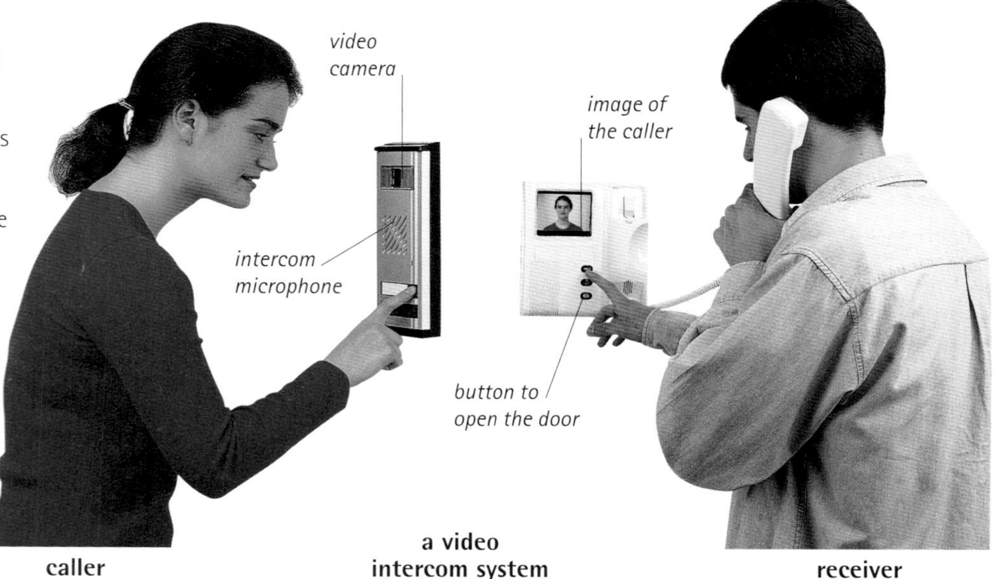

a video intercom system

in•ter•com \ˈin-tər-ˌkäm\ *n*
▲ a communication system with a microphone and loudspeaker at each end

in•ter•course \ˈin-tər-ˌkōrs\ *n*
dealings between persons or groups ⟨Social *intercourse* requires communication.⟩

in•ter•de•pen•dence \ˌin-tər-di-ˈpen-dəns\ *n*
the quality or state of depending on one another

in•ter•de•pen•dent \ˌin-tər-di-ˈpen-dənt\ *adj*
depending on one another

[1]**in•ter•est** \ˈin-trəst, ˈin-tə-rəst\ *n*
1 a feeling of concern or curiosity about or desire to be involved with something ⟨an *interest* in music⟩ ⟨We lost *interest* in the game.⟩
2 a quality that makes something more appealing or interesting ⟨Personal stories add *interest* to the book.⟩
3 something that a person enjoys learning about or doing ⟨Sports is one of his many *interests*.⟩
4 something that provides help or benefit to a person or group ⟨It's in your *interest* to study.⟩
5 the money paid by a borrower for the use of borrowed money
6 the profit made on money that is invested
7 a right, title, or legal share in something ⟨They bought out his *interest* in the company.⟩
8 **interests** *pl* a group financially interested in an industry or business ⟨mining *interests*⟩

[2]**interest** *vb* **in•ter•est•ed**; **in•ter•est•ing**
1 to persuade to become involved in ⟨Can I *interest* you in joining us?⟩
2 to arouse and hold the concern, curiosity, or attention of ⟨This movie doesn't *interest* me.⟩

in•ter•est•ed \ˈin-trə-stəd, ˈin-tə-rə-\ *adj*
wanting to learn more about or become involved with something ⟨an *interested* listener⟩

in•ter•est•ing \ˈin-trə-stiŋ, ˈin-tə-rə-\ *adj*
holding the attention : not dull or boring ⟨an *interesting* story⟩
in•ter•est•ing•ly *adv*

in•ter•fere \ˌin-tər-ˈfir\ *vb* **in•ter•fered**; **in•ter•fer•ing**
1 to get in the way of as an obstacle ⟨Hills *interfere* with the radio signal.⟩
2 to become involved in the concerns of others when such involvement is not wanted ⟨Stop *interfering* in my private matters.⟩
synonyms see MEDDLE

in•ter•fer•ence \ˌin-tər-ˈfir-əns\ *n*
1 something that gets in the way as an obstacle
2 involvement in the concerns of others when such involvement is not wanted ⟨The young couple disliked their parents' *interference*.⟩

in•ter•im \ˈin-tə-rəm\ *n*
a period of time between events ⟨He studied during the *interim* between tests.⟩

[1]**in•te•ri•or** \in-ˈtir-ē-ər\ *adj*
1 being or occurring inside something : INNER ⟨*interior* walls⟩
2 far from the border or shore : INLAND

[2]**interior** *n*
1 the inner part of something
2 the inland part ⟨the island's *interior*⟩

interj *abbr* interjection

in•ter•ject \ˌin-tər-ˈjekt\ *vb* **in•ter•ject•ed**; **in•ter•ject•ing**
to put between or among other things ⟨I *interjected* a remark.⟩

in•ter•jec•tion \ˌin-tər-ˈjek-shən\ *n*
1 a word or cry (as "ouch") expressing sudden or strong feeling
2 the act of inserting or including something

in•ter•lace \ˌin-tər-ˈlās\ *vb* **in•ter•laced**; **in•ter•lac•ing**
to unite by or as if by lacing together

in•ter•lock \ˌin-tər-ˈläk\ *vb* **in•ter•locked**; **in•ter•lock•ing**
to connect or lock together

in•ter•lop•er \ˌin-tər-ˈlō-pər\ *n*
a person present in a situation or place where he or she is not wanted

in•ter•lude \ˈin-tər-ˌlüd\ *n*
1 a period of time or event that comes between others ⟨After a short *interlude*, he returned to the team.⟩
2 an entertainment between the acts of a play
3 a musical composition between parts of a longer composition or of a drama

in•ter•mar•riage \ˌin-tər-ˈmer-ij\ *n*
marriage between members of different groups

in•ter•mar•ry \ˌin-tər-ˈmer-ē\ *vb* **in•ter•mar•ried**; **in•ter•mar•ry•ing**
to marry a member of a different group

in•ter•me•di•ary \ˌin-tər-ˈmē-dē-ˌer-ē\ *n*, *pl* **in•ter•me•di•ar•ies**
GO-BETWEEN

[1]**in•ter•me•di•ate** \ˌin-tər-ˈmē-dē-ət\ *adj*
being or occurring in the middle of a series or between extremes ⟨The car was of *intermediate* size.⟩
in•ter•me•di•ate•ly *adv*

[2]**intermediate** *n*
someone or something that is in the middle of a series or between extremes ⟨Instruction is offered for beginners and *intermediates*.⟩

in•ter•ment \in-ˈtər-mənt\ *n*
BURIAL

in•ter•mi•na•ble \in-ˈtər-mə-nə-bəl\ *adj*
having or seeming to have no end
in•ter•mi•na•bly \-blē\ *adv*

in•ter•min•gle \ˌin-tər-ˈmiŋ-gəl\ *vb* **in•ter•min•gled**; **in•ter•min•gling**
to mix together

in•ter•mis•sion \ˌin-tər-ˈmi-shən\ *n*
a pause or short break (as between acts of a play)

in•ter•mit•tent \ˌin-tər-ˈmi-tᵊnt\ *adj*
starting, stopping, and starting again ⟨*intermittent* rain⟩
in•ter•mit•tent•ly *adv*

[1]**in•tern** \ˈin-ˌtərn\ *vb* **in•terned**; **in•tern•ing**
to force to stay within a place (as a prison) especially during a war
in•tern•ment \in-ˈtərn-mənt\ *n*

[2]**in•tern** \ˈin-ˌtərn\ *n*
▶a student or recent graduate in a special field of study (as medicine or teaching) who works for a period of time to gain practical experience
in•tern•ship \-ˌship\ *n*

in•ter•nal \in-ˈtər-nᵊl\ *adj*
1 being within something : INNER ⟨The core is part of the earth's *internal* structure.⟩
2 occurring or located within the body ⟨The heart is an *internal* organ.⟩
3 existing or occurring within a country ⟨*internal* affairs⟩
in•ter•nal•ly *adv*

in•ter•na•tion•al \ˌin-tər-ˈna-shə-nᵊl\ *adj*
1 involving two or more nations : occurring between nations ⟨*international* trade⟩
2 active or known in many nations ⟨an *international* celebrity⟩
in•ter•na•tion•al•ly *adv*

In•ter•net \ˈin-tər-ˌnet\ *n*
a communications system that connects computers and databases all over the world

in•ter•pose \ˌin-tər-ˈpōz\ *vb* **in•ter•posed**; **in•ter•pos•ing**
1 to put between two or more things ⟨He *interposed* himself between the fighting boys.⟩
2 to introduce between parts of a conversation ⟨May I *interpose* a question?⟩

in•ter•pret \in-ˈtər-prət\ *vb* **in•ter•pret•ed**; **in•ter•pret•ing**
1 to explain the meaning of ⟨She claims to *interpret* dreams.⟩
2 to understand in a particular way
3 to bring out the meaning of ⟨An actor *interprets* a role.⟩

in•ter•pret•er \in-ˈtər-prə-tər\ *n*
a person who turns spoken words of one language into a different language

in•ter•pre•ta•tion \in-ˌtər-prə-ˈtā-shən\ *n*
1 the way something is explained or understood ⟨What's your *interpretation* of the results?⟩
2 a particular way of performing something (as a dramatic role)

in•ter•pre•tive \in-ˈtər-prə-tiv\ *adj*
designed or serving to explain the meaning of something

in•ter•ra•cial \ˌin-tər-ˈrā-shəl\ *adj*
of or involving members of different races ⟨*interracial* harmony⟩

in•ter•re•late \ˌin-tər-ri-ˈlāt\ *vb* **in•ter•re•lat•ed**; **in•ter•re•lat•ing**
to bring into or have a connection with each other ⟨The book *interrelates* two stories.⟩

in•ter•ro•gate \in-ˈter-ə-ˌgāt\ *vb* **in•ter•ro•gat•ed**; **in•ter•ro•gat•ing**
to question thoroughly ⟨Police *interrogated* a suspect.⟩

in•ter•ro•ga•tion \in-ˌter-ə-ˈgā-shən\ *n*
the act of questioning thoroughly

in•ter•rog•a•tive \ˌin-tə-ˈrä-gə-tiv\ *adj*
having the form or force of a question ⟨an *interrogative* sentence⟩

in•ter•rupt \ˌin-tə-ˈrəpt\ *vb* **in•ter•rupt•ed**; **in•ter•rupt•ing**
1 to stop or hinder by breaking in ⟨Don't *interrupt* our conversation.⟩
2 to break the sameness or course of ⟨A loud crash *interrupted* the silence.⟩

in•ter•rup•tion \ˌin-tə-ˈrəp-shən\ *n*
an act of stopping or hindering by breaking in

in•ter•scho•las•tic \ˌin-tər-skə-ˈla-stik\ *adj*
existing or carried on between schools ⟨*interscholastic* sports⟩

in•ter•sect \ˌin-tər-ˈsekt\ *vb* **in•ter•sect•ed**; **in•ter•sect•ing**
to cut or divide by passing through or across : CROSS ⟨One line *intersects* the other.⟩

in•ter•sec•tion \ˌin-tər-ˈsek-shən\ *n*
1 the act or process of crossing or passing across ⟨the *intersection* of line A and line B⟩
2 the place or point where two or more things (as streets) meet or cross each other
3 the set of mathematical elements common to two or more sets

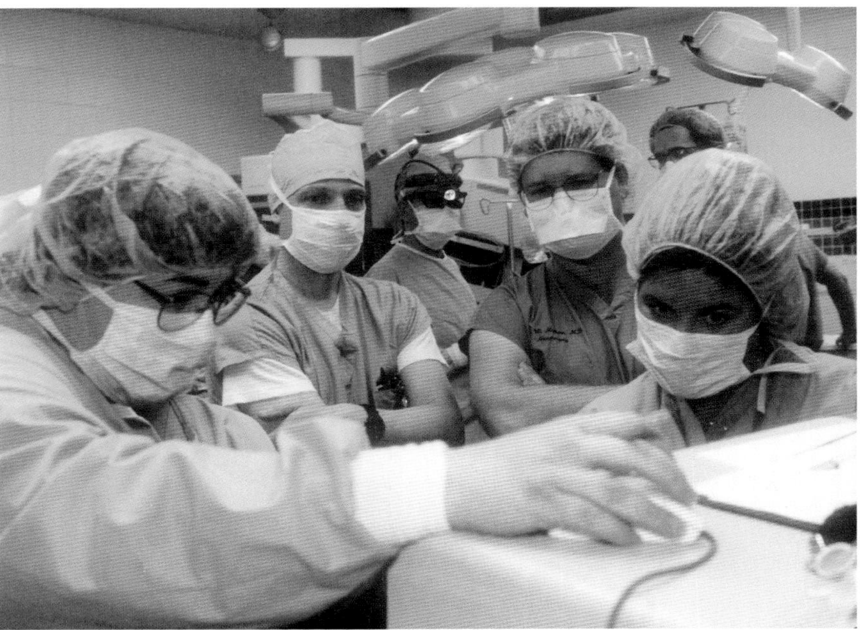

[2]**intern:** medical interns receiving training

in•ter•sperse \ˌin-tər-ˈspərs\ *vb* **in•ter•spersed; in•ter•spers•ing**
1 to put (something) here and there among other things ⟨The publisher *interspersed* pictures throughout the book.⟩
2 to put things at various places in or among ⟨Sunshine was *interspersed* with clouds.⟩

in•ter•state \ˌin-tər-ˈstāt\ *adj*
existing or occurring between two or more states ⟨an *interstate* highway⟩

in•ter•stel•lar \ˌin-tər-ˈste-lər\ *adj*
existing or taking place among the stars ⟨*interstellar* gases⟩

in•ter•twine \ˌin-tər-ˈtwīn\ *vb* **in•ter•twined; in•ter•twin•ing**
to twist or weave together

in•ter•val \ˈin-tər-vəl\ *n*
1 a period of time between events or states ⟨There was a short *interval* between shows.⟩
2 a space between things ⟨Signs were posted at regular *intervals.*⟩
3 the difference in pitch between two tones

in•ter•vene \ˌin-tər-ˈvēn\ *vb* **in•ter•vened; in•ter•ven•ing**
1 to come or occur between events, places, or points of time ⟨One week *intervened* between games.⟩
2 to interfere with something so as to stop, settle, or change ⟨I *intervened* in their quarrel.⟩

in•ter•ven•tion \ˌin-tər-ˈven-shən\ *n*
the act or fact of taking action about something in order to have an effect on its outcome ⟨The dispute required *intervention.*⟩

[1]in•ter•view \ˈin-tər-ˌvyü\ *n*
1 ▶ a meeting at which people talk to each other in order to ask questions and get information ⟨a job *interview*⟩
2 an account of an interview ⟨We saw the *interview* on TV.⟩

[2]interview *vb* **in•ter•viewed; in•ter•view•ing**
to question and talk with to get information
in•ter•view•er *n*

[1]interview 1:
a reporter carrying out an interview

in•ter•weave \ˌin-tər-ˈwēv\ *vb* **in•ter•wove** \-ˈwōv\; **in•ter•wo•ven** \-ˈwō-vən\; **in•ter•weav•ing**
1 to twist or weave together
2 to blend together ⟨The story *interweaves* love and tragedy.⟩

in•tes•ti•nal \in-ˈte-stə-n^{ə}l\ *adj*
of, relating to, or affecting the intestine ⟨an *intestinal* illness⟩

in•tes•tine \in-ˈte-stən\ *n*
▶ the lower part of the digestive canal that is a long tube made up of the small intestine and large intestine and in which most of the digestion and absorption of food occurs and through which waste material passes to be discharged

in•ti•ma•cy \ˈin-tə-mə-sē\ *n, pl* **in•ti•ma•cies**
1 a state marked by emotional closeness ⟨the *intimacy* of old friends⟩
2 a quality suggesting closeness or warmth ⟨the cafe's *intimacy*⟩
3 something that is very personal or private ⟨They shared little *intimacies* in their letters.⟩

[1]in•ti•mate \ˈin-tə-ˌmāt\ *vb* **in•ti•mat•ed; in•ti•mat•ing**
to say indirectly : hint at ⟨She *intimated* that I should go.⟩

[2]in•ti•mate \ˈin-tə-mət\ *adj*
1 very personal or private ⟨*intimate* thoughts⟩
2 marked by very close association ⟨*intimate* friends⟩

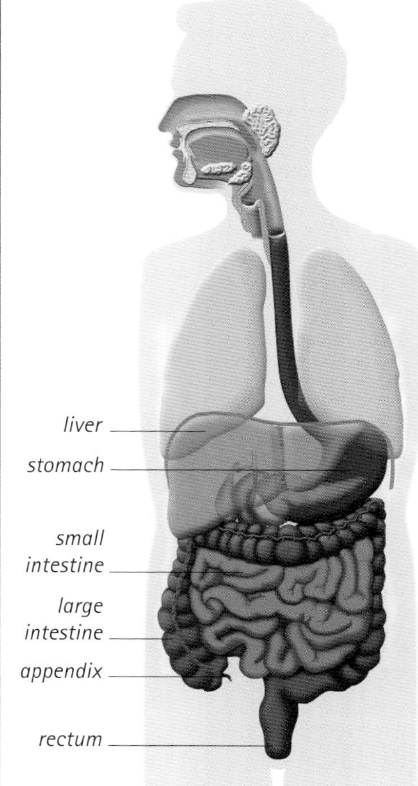

intestine:
model of the human intestine

3 suggesting closeness or warmth : COZY ⟨an *intimate* restaurant⟩
in•ti•mate•ly *adv*

[3]in•ti•mate \ˈin-tə-mət\ *n*
a very close and trusted friend

in•tim•i•date \in-ˈti-mə-ˌdāt\ *vb* **in•tim•i•dat•ed; in•tim•i•dat•ing**
to frighten especially by threats

in•tim•i•da•tion \in-ˌti-mə-ˈdā-shən\ *n*
the act of making frightened by or as if by threats ⟨He got his way by *intimidation.*⟩

in•to \ˈin-tə, -tü\ *prep*
1 to the inside of ⟨I ran *into* the house.⟩
2 to the state, condition, position, or form of ⟨She got *into* mischief.⟩ ⟨Cut the cake *into* pieces.⟩ ⟨It slipped *into* place.⟩
3 so as to hit : AGAINST ⟨He ran *into* the wall.⟩
4 in the direction of ⟨Don't look *into* the sun.⟩
5 used to indicate division ⟨Two goes *into* six three times.⟩

in•tol•er•a•ble \in-ˈtä-lə-rə-bəl\ *adj*
UNBEARABLE ⟨*intolerable* heat⟩
in•tol•er•a•bly \-blē\ *adv*

in•tol•er•ance \in-ˈtä-lə-rəns\ *n*
1 the quality or state of being unable or unwilling to put up with ⟨an *intolerance* to bright light⟩

A B C D E F G H I J K L M N O P Q R S T U V W X Y Z

2 a reluctance to grant rights to other people 〈religious *intolerance*〉

in•tol•er•ant \in-ˈtä-lə-rənt\ *adj*
1 not able or willing to put up with 〈She was *intolerant* of failure.〉
2 not willing to grant rights to some people 〈an *intolerant* government〉

in•to•na•tion \ˌin-tə-ˈnā-shən\ *n*
the rise and fall in pitch of the voice in speech

in•tox•i•cate \in-ˈtäk-sə-ˌkāt\ *vb* **in•tox•i•cat•ed; in•tox•i•cat•ing**
1 to affect by alcohol or a drug especially so that normal thinking and acting becomes difficult or impossible : make drunk
2 to make wildly excited or enthusiastic

in•tox•i•ca•tion \in-ˌtäk-sə-ˈkā-shən\ *n*
1 the condition of being drunk
2 an unhealthy state that is or is like a poisoning 〈carbon monoxide *intoxication*〉

in•tra•mu•ral \ˌin-trə-ˈmyu̇r-əl\ *adj*
being or occurring within the limits of a school 〈*intramural* sports〉

intrans. *abbr* intransitive

in•tran•si•tive \in-ˈtran-sə-tiv, -ˈtran-zə-\ *adj*
not having or containing a direct object 〈In "the bird flies," the word "flies" is an *intransitive* verb.〉

in•trep•id \in-ˈtre-pəd\ *adj*
feeling no fear : BOLD

in•tri•ca•cy \ˈin-tri-kə-sē\ *n*, *pl* **in•tri•ca•cies**
1 the quality or state of being complex or having many parts
2 something that is complex or has many parts

in•tri•cate \ˈin-tri-kət\ *adj*
1 ▶ having many closely combined parts or elements 〈an *intricate* design〉
2 very difficult to follow or understand 〈an *intricate* plot〉
in•tri•cate•ly *adv*

¹in•trigue \in-ˈtrēg\ *vb* **in•trigued; in•trigu•ing**
1 to arouse the interest or curiosity of 〈The mystery *intrigues* me.〉
2 ²PLOT 1, SCHEME 〈His enemies *intrigued* against him.〉

²in•trigue \ˈin-ˌtrēg, in-ˈtrēg\ *n*
a secret and complex plot

in•tro•duce \ˌin-trə-ˈdüs, -ˈdyüs\ *vb* **in•tro•duced; in•tro•duc•ing**
1 to cause to be acquainted : make known 〈Our new neighbor *introduced* herself.〉
2 to bring into practice or use 〈My teacher *introduced* a new rule.〉
3 to make available for sale for the first time 〈New fashions were *introduced*.〉
4 to bring forward for discussion or consideration 〈Her lawyer *introduced* new evidence.〉
5 to put in : INSERT 〈New computers have been *introduced* into the office.〉

in•tro•duc•tion \ˌin-trə-ˈdək-shən\ *n*
1 the part of a book that leads up to and explains what will be found in the main part
2 the act of causing a person to meet another person
3 the action of bringing into use, making available, or presenting for consideration or discussion
4 something introduced or added 〈The plant is a new *introduction* to the garden.〉

in•tro•duc•to•ry \ˌin-trə-ˈdək-tə-rē\ *adj*
serving to introduce : PRELIMINARY 〈an *introductory* lesson〉

in•trude \in-ˈtrüd\ *vb* **in•trud•ed; in•trud•ing**
1 to force in, into, or on especially where not right or proper 〈She *intruded* into our conversation.〉
2 to come or go in without an invitation or right
in•trud•er *n*

in•tru•sion \in-ˈtrü-zhən\ *n*
1 the act of going or forcing in without being wanted
2 something that goes in or interferes without being wanted 〈The phone call was an unwelcome *intrusion*.〉

in•tu•i•tion \ˌin-tü-ˈi-shən, -tyü-\ *n*
1 the ability to know something without having proof
2 something known without proof 〈I had an *intuition* you'd come.〉

In•u•it \ˈi-nü-wət, -nyü-\ *n*, *pl* **Inuit** *or* **In•u•its**
1 a member of the Eskimo people of the arctic regions of North America
2 any of the languages of the Inuit people

in•un•date \ˈin-ən-ˌdāt\ *vb* **in•un•dat•ed; in•un•dat•ing**
to cover with or as if with a flood 〈I'm *inundated* by mail.〉

in•vade \in-ˈvād\ *vb* **in•vad•ed; in•vad•ing**
1 to enter by force to conquer or plunder
2 to show lack of respect for 〈She *invaded* their privacy.〉
in•vad•er *n*

¹in•val•id \in-ˈva-ləd\ *adj*
having no force or effect

²in•va•lid \ˈin-və-ləd\ *n*
a person suffering from sickness or disability

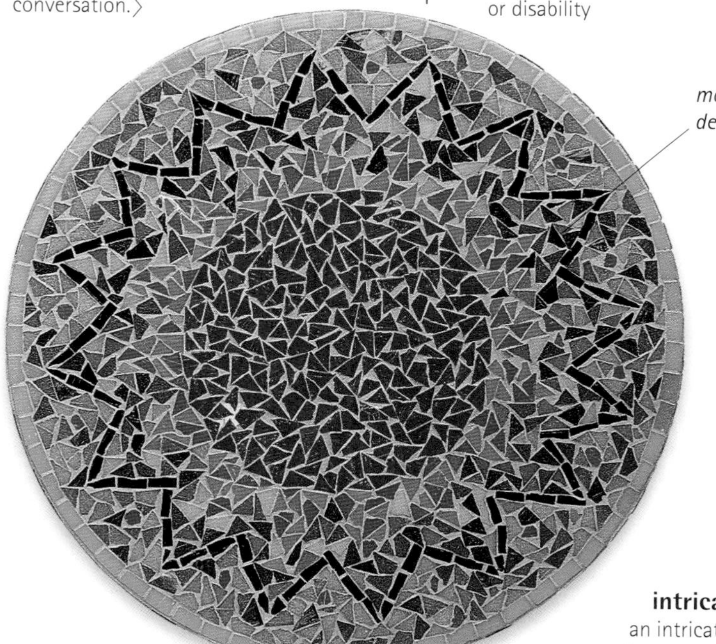

intricate 1: an intricate mosaic design on a table top

in•val•i•date \in-ˈva-lə-ˌdāt\ *vb* **in•val•i•dat•ed; in•val•i•dat•ing**
to weaken or destroy the effect of 〈The phony signature *invalidated* the contract.〉

in•valu•able \in-ˈval-yə-wə-bəl\ *adj*
PRICELESS

in•vari•able \in-ˈver-ē-ə-bəl\ *adj*
not changing or capable of change 〈an *invariable* routine〉
in•vari•ably \-ˈver-ē-ə-blē\ *adv*

in•va•sion \in-ˈvā-zhən\ *n*
an act of invading

a b c d e f g h i j k l m n o p q r s t u v w x y z

A B C D E F G H I J K L M O P Q R S T U V W X Y Z

▶ invention 1

An invention is something that has been thought of and created for the first time by a human being. It can be a simple idea like the wheel, or a complex one such as television. Some inventions dramatically change the way in which people live.

steam engines
were invented in the 1700s

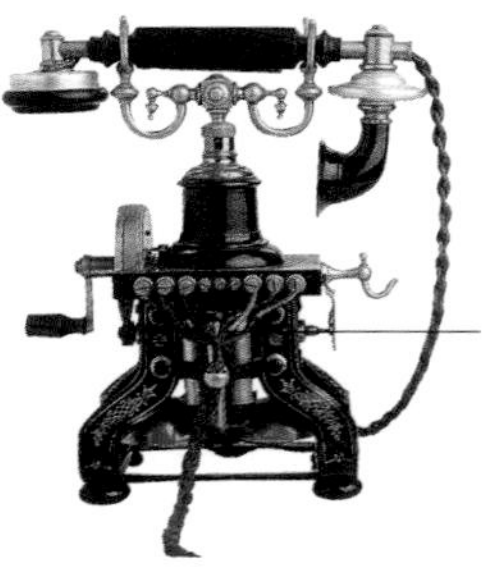

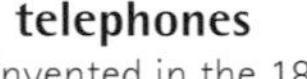

telephones
were invented in the 1870s

phonographs
were invented in the 1880s

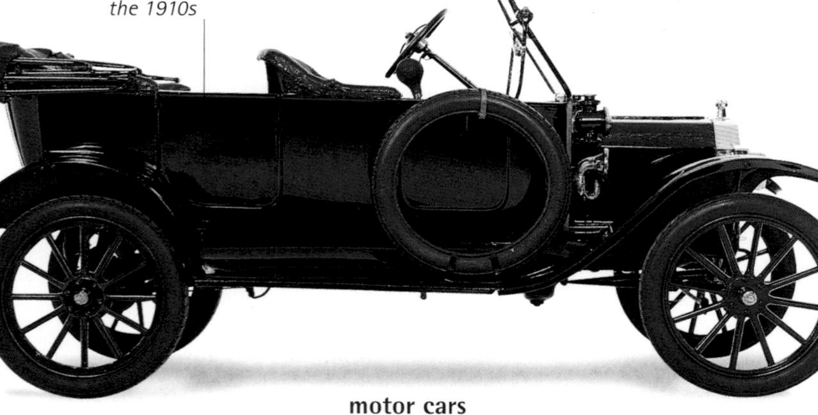

motor cars
were invented in the 1880s

desktop computers
were invented in the 1970s

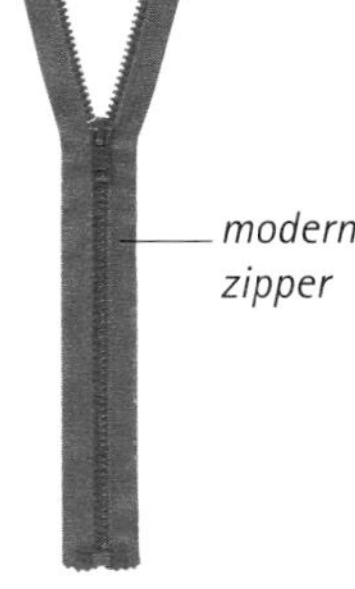

zippers
were invented in the 1890s

in•vent \in-ˈvent\ *vb* **in•vent•ed; in•vent•ing**
1 to create or produce for the first time 〈Thomas Edison *invented* the light bulb.〉
2 to think up **:** make up 〈She *invented* an excuse for being late.〉
in•ven•tor \-ˈvent-ər\ *n*

in•ven•tion \in-ˈven-shən\ *n*
1 ◀ an original device or process
2 ³LIE 〈The story was just an *invention*.〉
3 the act or process of inventing
4 the ability to think of new ideas 〈He was a man of *invention*.〉

in•ven•tive \in-ˈven-tiv\ *adj*
CREATIVE

¹in•ven•to•ry \ˈin-vən-ˌtȯr-ē\ *n, pl* **in•ven•to•ries**
1 a supply of goods 〈*Inventory* is low.〉
2 a list of items (as goods on hand)
3 the act or process of making a list of items

²inventory *vb* **in•ven•to•ried; in•ven•to•ry•ing**
to make a complete list of 〈Store workers *inventoried* the stock.〉

in•verse \in-ˈvərs\ *adj*
1 opposite in order, nature, or effect 〈an *inverse* relationship〉
2 being a mathematical operation that is opposite in effect to another operation 〈Multiplication is the *inverse* operation of division.〉
in•verse•ly *adv*

in•vert \in-ˈvərt\ *vb* **in•vert•ed; in•vert•ing**
1 to turn inside out or upside down 〈*Invert* the bowl onto a plate.〉
2 to reverse the order or position of 〈*invert* numbers〉

¹in•ver•te•brate \in-ˈvər-tə-brət\ *adj*
having no backbone 〈an *invertebrate* animal〉

²invertebrate *n*
▶ an animal (as a worm or a crab) that does not have a backbone

¹in•vest \in-ˈvest\ *vb* **in•vest•ed; in•vest•ing**
to give power or authority to

²invest *vb* **in•vest•ed; in•vest•ing**
1 to put out money in order to gain profit 〈She *invested* in a business.〉
2 to put out (as effort) in support of a usually worthy cause 〈We *invested* time in the project.〉
in•ves•tor \-ˈves-tər\ *n*

in•ves•ti•gate \in-ˈve-stə-ˌgāt\ *vb* **in•ves•ti•gat•ed; in•ves•ti•gat•ing**
to study by close examination and questioning 〈Police are *investigating* the crime.〉
in•ves•ti•ga•tor \-ˌgā-tər\ *n*

in•ves•ti•ga•tion \in-ˌve-stə-ˈgā-shən\ *n*
the act or process of studying by close examination and questioning

in•vest•ment \in-ˈvest-mənt\ *n*
1 the act of putting out money in order to gain a profit
2 a sum of money invested
3 a property in which money is invested

in•vig•o•rate \in-ˈvi-gə-ˌrāt\ *vb* **in•vig•o•rat•ed; in•vig•o•rat•ing**
to give life and energy to ⟨The swim was *invigorating.*⟩

in•vin•ci•bil•i•ty \in-ˌvin-sə-ˈbi-lə-tē\ *n*
the quality or state of being impossible to defeat

in•vin•ci•ble \in-ˈvin-sə-bəl\ *adj*
impossible to defeat

in•vi•o•la•ble \in-ˈvī-ə-lə-bəl\ *adj*
1 too sacred to be broken or denied ⟨an *inviolable* oath⟩
2 impossible to harm or destroy by violence ⟨an *inviolable* fortress⟩

in•vis•i•bil•i•ty \in-ˌvi-zə-ˈbi-lə-tē\ *n*
the quality or state of being impossible to see

in•vis•i•ble \in-ˈvi-zə-bəl\ *adj*
impossible to see ⟨Sound waves are *invisible.*⟩
in•vis•i•bly \-blē\ *adv*

in•vi•ta•tion \ˌin-və-ˈtā-shən\ *n*
1 a written or spoken request for someone to go somewhere or do something
2 the act of inviting

in•vite \in-ˈvīt\ *vb* **in•vit•ed; in•vit•ing**
1 to ask (someone) to go somewhere or do something ⟨I *invited* them to dinner.⟩
2 [1]WELCOME 2 ⟨We *invite* suggestions.⟩
3 to tend to bring on ⟨Such behavior *invites* trouble.⟩

in•vit•ing \in-ˈvī-tiŋ\ *adj*
ATTRACTIVE 1
in•vit•ing•ly *adv*

in•voice \ˈin-ˌvȯis\ *n*
a list of goods shipped usually showing the price and the terms of sale

in•voke \in-ˈvōk\ *vb* **in•voked; in•vok•ing**
1 to ask for aid or protection (as in prayer)
2 to call forth by magic ⟨*invoke* spirits⟩
3 to appeal to as an authority or for support

[2]invertebrate
There are two main groups of animals: vertebrates, which have backbones, and the larger group, invertebrates, which do not. Animals without backbones include mollusks, worms, insects, spiders, and crustaceans. Insects, such as beetles, form the largest group of invertebrates.

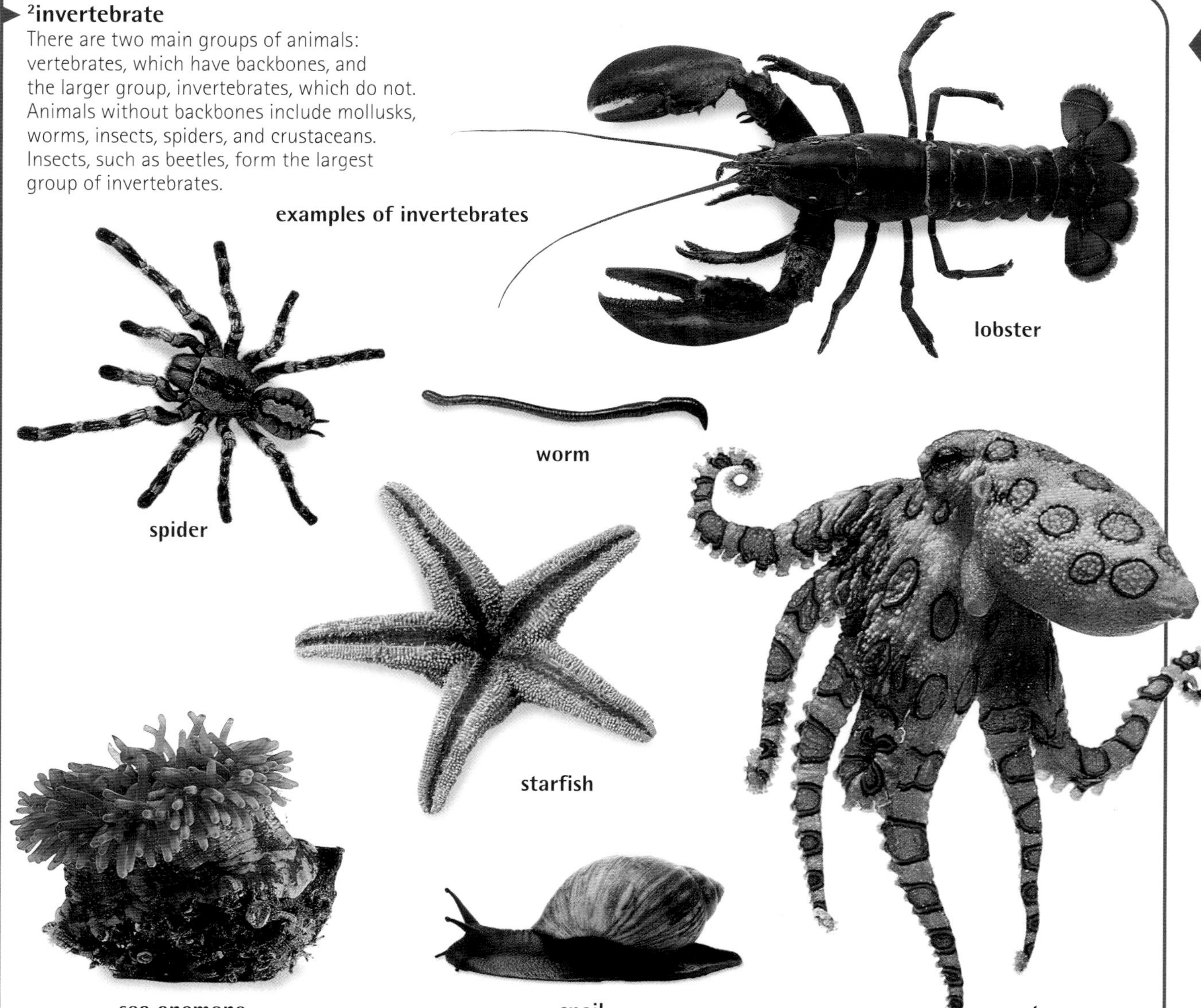

A B C D E F G H I J K L M N O P Q R S T U V W X Y Z

in•vol•un•tary \in-'vä-lən-,ter-ē\ *adj*
1 not done consciously ⟨an *involuntary* whimper⟩
2 not done by choice ⟨*involuntary* labor⟩
in•vol•un•tari•ly \,in-,vä-lən-'ter-ə-lē\ *adv*

in•volve \in-'välv, -'vȯlv\ *vb* **in•volved**; **in•volv•ing**
1 to draw into a situation : ENGAGE ⟨The teacher *involved* her students in the project.⟩
2 to take part in ⟨I'm not *involved* in the planning.⟩
3 INCLUDE ⟨The accident *involved* three cars.⟩
4 to be accompanied by ⟨The plan *involves* some risk.⟩
5 to have or take the attention of completely ⟨He was deeply *involved* in his work.⟩
in•volve•ment \-mənt\ *n*

in•volved \in-'välvd, -'vȯlvd\ *adj*
very complicated ⟨He told a long *involved* story.⟩

in•vul•ner•a•ble \in-'vəl-nə-rə-bəl\ *adj*
1 impossible to injure or damage
2 safe from attack

[1]**in•ward** \'in-wərd\ *adj*
1 toward the inside or center ⟨an *inward* curve⟩
2 of or concerning the mind or spirit ⟨He felt *inward* joy.⟩

[2]**inward** *or* **in•wards** \-wərdz\ *adv*
1 toward the inside or center ⟨The door opens *inward.*⟩
2 toward the mind or spirit ⟨I turned my thoughts *inward.*⟩

in•ward•ly \'in-wərd-lē\ *adv*
1 in a way that is not openly shown or stated : PRIVATELY ⟨suffering *inwardly*⟩ ⟨She cursed *inwardly.*⟩
2 on the inside ⟨bleeding *inwardly*⟩

iodine 2

io•dine \'ī-ə-,dīn, -dᵊn\ *n*
1 a chemical element found in seawater and seaweeds and used especially in medicine and photography
2 ▲ a solution of iodine in alcohol used to kill germs

iris 2

io•dize \'ī-ə-,dīz\ *vb* **io•dized**; **io•diz•ing**
to add iodine to

ion \'ī-ən, 'ī-,än\ *n*
an atom or group of atoms that carries an electric charge

-ion *n suffix*
1 act or process ⟨construct*ion*⟩
2 result of an act or process ⟨regulat*ion*⟩ ⟨erupt*ion*⟩
3 state or condition ⟨perfect*ion*⟩

ion•ize \'ī-ə-,nīz\ *vb* **ion•ized**; **ion•iz•ing**
to change into ions

ion•o•sphere \ī-'ä-nə-,sfir\ *n*
the part of the earth's atmosphere beginning at an altitude of about 30 miles (50 kilometers) and extending outward that contains electrically charged particles

io•ta \ī-'ō-tə\ *n*
a tiny amount ⟨I don't care an *iota.*⟩

IOU \,ī-ō-'yü\ *n*
a written promise to pay a debt

-ious *adj suffix*
-OUS ⟨capac*ious*⟩

IQ \,ī-'kyü\ *n*
a number that represents a person's level of intelligence based on the score of a special test

ir- see **in-**

[1]**Iraqi** \i-'rä-kē\ *n, pl* **Iraqis**
a person born or living in Iraq

[2]**Iraqi** *adj*
of or relating to Iraq or its people

iras•ci•ble \i-'ra-sə-bəl\ *adj*
easily angered

irate \ī-'rāt\ *adj*
ANGRY ⟨*Irate* fans booed loudly.⟩

ire \'īr\ *n*
[2]ANGER, WRATH ⟨He directed his *ire* at me.⟩

ir•i•des•cence \,ir-ə-'de-sᵊns\ *n*
a shifting and constant change of colors producing rainbow effects

ir•i•des•cent \,ir-ə-'de-sᵊnt\ *adj*
having iridescence

irid•i•um \i-'ri-dē-əm\ *n*
a hard brittle heavy metallic chemical element

iris \'ī-rəs\ *n*
1 the colored part around the pupil of an eye
2 ◀ a plant with long pointed leaves and large usually brightly colored flowers

[1]**Irish** \'ī-rish\ *adj*
of or relating to Ireland, its people, or the Irish language

[2]**Irish** *n*
1 **Irish** *pl* the people of Ireland
2 a language of Ireland

irk \'ərk\ *vb* **irked**; **irk•ing**
ANNOY ⟨That noise *irks* me.⟩

irk•some \'ərk-səm\ *adj*
causing annoyance ⟨an *irksome* habit⟩

[1]**iron** \'ī-ərn\ *n*
1 a heavy silvery white metallic chemical element that rusts easily, is strongly attracted by magnets, occurs in meteorites and combined in minerals, and is necessary for transporting oxygen in the blood
2 ▼ a device that is heated and used for making cloth smooth

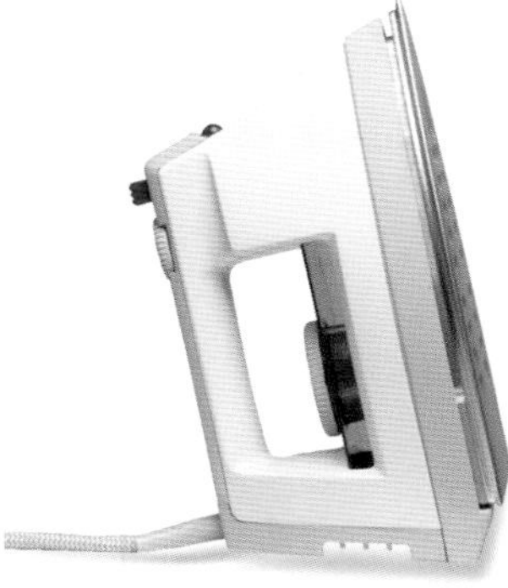
[1]**iron 2**

3 a device that is heated to perform a task ⟨a soldering *iron*⟩
4 **irons** *pl* handcuffs or chains used to bind or to hinder movement

[2]**iron** *adj*
1 made of iron
2 strong and healthy ⟨He has an *iron* constitution.⟩
3 not giving in ⟨an *iron* will⟩

[3]iron *vb* ironed; iron•ing
to press with a heated iron

iron•ic \ī-ˈrä-nik\ *also* **iron•i•cal** \-ni-kəl\ *adj*
relating to, containing, or showing irony ⟨It was *ironic* that the robber's car crashed into the police station.⟩
iron•i•cal•ly \-i-kə-lē\ *adv*

ir•rec•on•cil•able \i-ˌre-kən-ˈsī-lə-bəl\ *adj*
impossible to bring into agreement or harmony ⟨Their *irreconcilable* differences might lead to war.⟩

ir•re•deem•able \ˌir-i-ˈdē-mə-bəl\ *adj*
impossible to save or help ⟨an *irredeemable* gambler⟩

ironworks 2: workers working on molten steel in an ironworks

iron•work \ˈī-ərn-ˌwərk\ *n*
1 things made of iron
2 ▲ **ironworks** *pl* a mill where iron or steel is smelted or heavy iron or steel products are made

iro•ny \ˈī-rə-nē\ *n, pl* **iro•nies**
1 the use of words that mean the opposite of what is really meant
2 a result opposite to what was expected

Ir•o•quois \ˈir-ə-ˌkwȯi\ *n, pl* **Ir•o•quois** \-ˌkwȯi, -ˌkwȯiz\
a member of any of the peoples of an American Indian confederacy that existed originally in central New York state

ir•ra•di•ate \i-ˈrā-dē-ˌāt\ *vb* **ir•ra•di•at•ed**; **ir•ra•di•at•ing**
1 to cast rays of light on
2 to treat by exposure to radiation (as X-rays)

ir•ra•di•a•tion \i-ˌrā-dē-ˈā-shən\ *n*
exposure to radiation

ir•ra•tio•nal \i-ˈra-shə-nᵊl\ *adj*
1 not able to reason ⟨The fever made him *irrational.*⟩
2 not based on reason ⟨*irrational* fears⟩
ir•ra•tio•nal•ly *adv*

ir•re•fut•able \ˌir-i-ˈfyü-tə-bəl, i-ˈre-fyə-\ *adj*
impossible to prove wrong : INDISPUTABLE ⟨*irrefutable* proof⟩

ir•reg•u•lar \i-ˈreg-yə-lər\ *adj*
1 not following custom or rule ⟨Her methods are most *irregular.*⟩
2 not following the usual manner of inflection ⟨The verb "sell" is *irregular* because its past tense is "sold," not "selled."⟩
3 not straight, smooth, or even ⟨an *irregular* coastline⟩
4 not continuous or coming at set times ⟨He works *irregular* hours.⟩
ir•reg•u•lar•ly *adv*

ir•reg•u•lar•i•ty \i-ˌre-gyə-ˈler-ə-tē\ *n, pl* **ir•reg•u•lar•i•ties**
1 the quality or state of being unusual, uneven, or happening at different times
2 something that is unusual, uneven, or happening at different times

ir•rel•e•vance \i-ˈre-lə-vəns\ *n*
the quality or state of having no relation or importance to what is being considered

ir•rel•e•vant \i-ˈre-lə-vənt\ *adj*
having no importance or relation to what is being considered ⟨What's that got to do with it? That's *irrelevant.*⟩

ir•rep•a•ra•ble \i-ˈre-pə-rə-bəl\ *adj*
impossible to get back or to make right ⟨A storm did *irreparable* damage to the beach.⟩
ir•rep•a•ra•bly \-blē\ *adv*

ir•re•place•able \ˌir-i-ˈplā-sə-bəl\ *adj*
too valuable or too rare to be replaced ⟨The stolen art is *irreplaceable.*⟩

ir•re•press•ible \ˌir-i-ˈpre-sə-bəl\ *adj*
impossible to repress or control ⟨an *irrepressible* chuckle⟩

ir•re•proach•able \ˌir-i-ˈprō-chə-bəl\ *adj*
not deserving of criticism : without fault ⟨*irreproachable* manners⟩

ir•re•sist•ible \ˌir-i-ˈzi-stə-bəl\ *adj*
impossible to resist ⟨an *irresistible* temptation⟩
ir•re•sist•ibly \-blē\ *adv*

ir•res•o•lute \i-ˈre-zə-ˌlüt\ *adj*
uncertain how to act or proceed
ir•res•o•lute•ly *adv*

ir•re•spec•tive of \ˌir-i-ˈspek-tiv-\ *prep*
without regard to ⟨The contest is open to anyone *irrespective of* age.⟩

ir•re•spon•si•bil•i•ty \ˌir-i-ˌspän-sə-ˈbil-ət-ē\ *n*
the quality or state of not being responsible

ir•re•spon•si•ble \ˌir-i-ˈspän-sə-bəl\ *adj*
having or showing little or no sense of responsibility ⟨You're too *irresponsible* for a pet.⟩
ir•re•spon•si•bly \-ˈspän-sə-blē\ *adv*

ir•re•triev•able \ˌir-i-ˈtrē-və-bəl\ *adj*
impossible to get back ⟨The lost data is *irretrievable.*⟩
ir•re•triev•ably \-blē\ *adv*

ir•rev•er•ence \i-ˈre-və-rəns\ *n*
lack of respect

ir•rev•er•ent \i-ˈre-və-rənt\ *adj*
not respectful
ir•rev•er•ent•ly *adv*

ir•re•vers•i•ble \ˌir-i-ˈvər-sə-bəl\ *adj*
impossible to change back to a previous condition : impossible to reverse ⟨*irreversible* harm⟩

ir•rev•o•ca•ble \i-ˈre-və-kə-bəl\ *adj*
impossible to take away or undo ⟨an *irrevocable* decision⟩
ir•rev•o•ca•bly \-blē\ *adv*

ir•ri•gate \ˈir-ə-ˌgāt\ *vb* **ir•ri•gat•ed**; **ir•ri•gat•ing**
1 to supply (as land) with water by artificial means ⟨*irrigate* crops⟩
2 to clean with a flow of liquid ⟨*irrigate* a wound⟩

ir•ri•ga•tion \ˌir-ə-ˈgā-shən\ *n*
an act or process of supplying with water or cleaning with a flow of liquid

ir•ri•ta•bil•i•ty \ˌir-ə-tə-ˈbi-lə-tē\ *n*
the quality of easily becoming angry or annoyed

ir•ri•ta•ble \ˈir-ə-tə-bəl\ *adj*
easily made angry or annoyed 〈Hunger makes me *irritable.*〉
ir•ri•ta•bly \-blē\ *adv*

ir•ri•tant \ˈir-ə-tənt\ *n*
1 something that is annoying
2 something that causes soreness or sensitivity

ir•ri•tate \ˈir-ə-ˌtāt\ *vb* **ir•ri•tat•ed**; **ir•ri•tat•ing**
1 ANNOY 〈His constant chatter *irritates* me.〉
2 to make sensitive or sore 〈The harsh soap *irritated* my skin.〉

ir•ri•ta•tion \ˌir-ə-ˈtā-shən\ *n*
1 the act of making annoyed or sore and sensitive : the state of being annoyed or sore and sensitive 〈*irritation* of the skin〉
2 IRRITANT 1

is *present third person sing of* BE

-ish \ish\ *adj suffix*
1 of, relating to, or being 〈Finn*ish*〉
2 characteristic of 〈boy*ish*〉
3 somewhat 〈purpl*ish*〉
4 about (as an age or a time)

Is•lam \is-ˈläm, iz-\ *n*
a religion based on belief in Allah as the only God and in Muhammad the prophet of God
Is•lam•ic \is-ˈlä-mik, iz-\ *adj*

is•land \ˈī-lənd\ *n*
1 ▼ an area of land surrounded by water and smaller than a continent
2 something like an island in its isolation 〈We have a counter *island* in our kitchen.〉

is•land•er \ˈī-lən-dər\ *n*
a person who lives on an island

isle \ˈīl\ *n*
a usually small island

is•let \ˈī-lət\ *n*
a small island

-ism \ˌi-zəm\ *n suffix*
1 act : practice : process 〈bapt*ism*〉 〈critic*ism*〉
2 manner of action or behavior like that of a specified person or thing 〈hero*ism*〉
3 state : condition 〈alcohol*ism*〉
4 teachings : theory : system 〈social*ism*〉

isn't \ˈi-zᵊnt\
is not

iso•bar \ˈī-sə-ˌbär\ *n*
a line on a map to indicate areas having the same atmospheric pressure

iso•late \ˈī-sə-ˌlāt\ *vb* **iso•lat•ed**; **iso•lat•ing**
to place or keep apart from others 〈*Isolate* any diseased plants.〉

iso•la•tion \ˌī-sə-ˈlā-shən\ *n*
the act of keeping apart from others : the condition of being kept apart from others

isos•ce•les triangle \ī-ˈsä-sə-ˌlēz-\ *n*
a triangle having two sides of equal length

ISP *abbr* Internet service provider

[1]Is•rae•li \iz-ˈrā-lē\ *adj*
of or relating to the country of Israel or its people

[2]Israeli *n*
a person born or living in the country of Israel

Is•ra•el•ite \ˈiz-rē-ə-ˌlīt\ *n*
a person born or living in the ancient kingdom of Israel

island 1: an island in the Caribbean Sea

is•su•ance \ˈi-shü-əns\ *n*
the act of making something available or distributing something : the act of issuing

[1]is•sue \ˈi-shü\ *n*
1 something that is discussed or disputed
2 the version of a newspaper or magazine that is published at a particular time
3 the action of going, coming, or flowing out 〈That is the river's place of *issue.*〉
4 OFFSPRING, PROGENY
5 a giving off (as of blood) from the body
6 the act of bringing out, offering, or making available 〈The post office announced the *issue* of new stamps.〉

[2]issue *vb* **is•sued**; **is•su•ing**
1 to go, come, or flow out 〈Smoke *issued* from the chimney.〉
2 to distribute officially 〈Police are *issuing* tickets.〉
3 to announce officially 〈A storm warning has been *issued.*〉
4 to send out for sale or circulation

-ist \əst\ *n suffix*
1 performer of a specified action 〈cycl*ist*〉 : maker : producer 〈novel*ist*〉
2 a person who plays a specified musical instrument or operates a specified mechanical device 〈pian*ist*〉 〈motor*ist*〉
3 a person who specializes in a specified art or science or skill 〈geolog*ist*〉
4 a person who follows or favors a specified teaching, practice, system, or code of behavior 〈optim*ist*〉

isth•mus \ˈi-sməs\ *n*
► a narrow strip of land separating two bodies of water and connecting two larger areas of land

[1]it \ˈit, ət\ *pron*
1 the thing, act, or matter about which these words are spoken or written
2 the whole situation 〈How's *it* going?〉
3 used as a subject of a verb that expresses a condition or action without a doer 〈*It*'s cold outside.〉

[2]it \ˈit\ *n*
the player who has to do something special in a children's game 〈Once you get tagged, you're *it.*〉

IT *abbr*
information technology

ital. *abbr*
1 italic
2 italicized

[1]Ital•ian \i-ˈtal-yən\ *n*
1 a person born or living in Italy
2 the language of the Italians

[2]Italian *adj*
of or relating to Italy, its people, or the Italian language

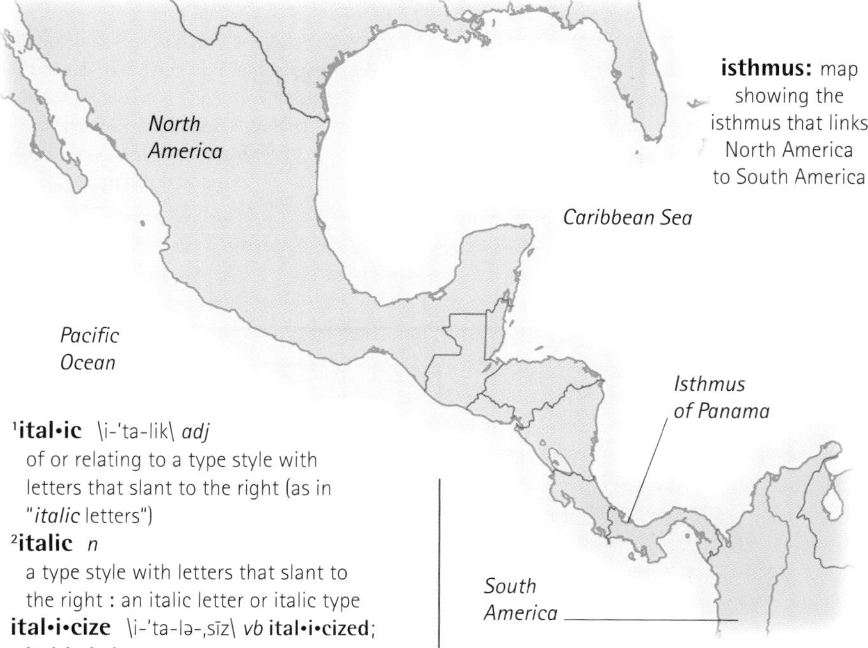

isthmus: map showing the isthmus that links North America to South America

[1]ital•ic \i-'ta-lik\ *adj*
of or relating to a type style with letters that slant to the right (as in "*italic* letters")

[2]italic *n*
a type style with letters that slant to the right : an italic letter or italic type

ital•i•cize \i-'ta-lə-ˌsīz\ *vb* **ital•i•cized**; **ital•i•ciz•ing**
1 to print in italics
2 UNDERLINE 1

[1]itch \'ich\ *vb* **itched**; **itch•ing**
1 to have or produce an unpleasant feeling that causes a desire to scratch ⟨My nose *itches.*⟩
2 to have a strong desire ⟨He was *itching* to go on vacation.⟩

[2]itch *n*
1 an unpleasant feeling that causes a desire to scratch
2 a skin disorder in which an itch is present
3 a restless usually constant desire ⟨an *itch* to travel⟩

itchy \'i-chē\ *adj* **itch•i•er**; **itch•i•est**
having, feeling, or causing a desire to scratch ⟨an *itchy* sweater⟩

it'd \'i-təd\
it had : it would ⟨During the night *it'd* gotten cool.⟩ ⟨He promised *it'd* be fun.⟩

-ite \ˌīt\ *n suffix*
1 native : resident ⟨suburban*ite*⟩
2 descendant
3 adherent : follower

item \'ī-təm\ *n*
1 a single thing in a list, account, or series
2 a brief piece of news

item•ize \'ī-tə-ˌmīz\ *vb* **item•ized**; **item•iz•ing**
to set down one by one : LIST

itin•er•ant \ī-'ti-nə-rənt\ *adj*
traveling from place to place

-itis \'ī-təs\ *n suffix*
inflammation of ⟨tonsill*itis*⟩

it'll \'i-tᵊl\
it shall : it will ⟨*It'll* be illegal from now on.⟩

its \'its\ *adj*
relating to or belonging to it or itself ⟨The fox licked *its* sore paw.⟩

it's \'its\
1 it is ⟨*It's* a shame.⟩
2 it has ⟨*It's* been years since we visited.⟩

it•self \it-'self\ *pron*
that identical one ⟨The cat gave *itself* a bath.⟩ ⟨This *itself* is a good enough reason.⟩

-ity \ə-tē\ *n suffix, pl* **-ities**
quality : state : degree ⟨similar*ity*⟩

-ive \iv\ *adj suffix*
that does or tends to do a specified action ⟨explos*ive*⟩

I've \'īv\
I have ⟨*I've* been here.⟩

ivo•ry \'ī-və-rē, 'īv-rē\ *n, pl* **ivo•ries**
1 ▶ a hard creamy-white material that forms the tusks of mammals (as elephants)
2 a creamy white color

ivory 1: a 6th-century Italian horn made of carved ivory

ivy \'ī-vē\ *n, pl* **ivies**
1 a climbing vine with evergreen leaves and black berries often found growing on buildings
2 a climbing plant that resembles ivy

-i•za•tion \ə-'zā-shən, ī-'zā-shən\ *n suffix*
action : process : state ⟨fertil*ization*⟩

-ize \ˌīz\ *vb suffix* **-ized**; **-iz•ing**
1 cause to be or be like : form or cause to be formed into ⟨crystall*ize*⟩
2 cause to experience a specified action ⟨hypnot*ize*⟩
3 saturate, treat, or combine with
4 treat like ⟨idol*ize*⟩
5 engage in a specified activity

a b c d e f g h i j k l m n o p q r s t u v w x y z

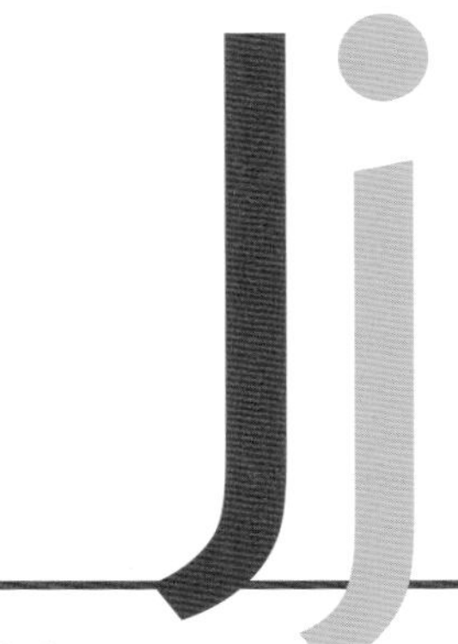

Sounds of J: The sound of the letter **J** is heard in *jet* and *conjure*. In some words, **J** sounds like a **Y**, such as in *hallelujah*. **J** sometimes sounds like an **H**, as in *Navajo*, in words that come from Spanish.

j \ˈjā\ *n, pl* **j's** *or* **js** \ˈjāz\ *often cap*
the tenth letter of the English alphabet

[1]**jab** \ˈjab\ *vb* **jabbed; jab•bing**
to poke quickly or suddenly with or as if with something sharp

[2]**jab** *n*
a quick or sudden poke

[1]**jab•ber** \ˈja-bər\ *vb* **jab•bered; jab•ber•ing**
to talk too fast or not clearly enough to be understood

[2]**jabber** *n*
[2]CHATTER 2

[1]**jack** \ˈjak\ *n*
1 ▼ a device for lifting something heavy a short distance
2 a playing card with the picture of a young man

jack-in-the-box

3 a small six-pointed usually metal object used in a children's game (**jacks**)
4 a socket used with a plug to connect one electric circuit with another

[1]**jack 1:** a jack for lifting a car

[2]**jack** *vb* **jacked; jack•ing**
to move or lift with a special device ⟨We need to *jack* up the car.⟩

jack•al \ˈja-kəl\ *n*
a wild dog of Africa and Asia like but smaller than a wolf

jack•ass \ˈjak-ˌas\ *n*
1 a donkey and especially a male donkey
2 a stupid person

jack•daw \ˈjak-ˌdȯ\ *n*
a black and gray European bird related to but smaller than a crow

jack•et \ˈja-kət\ *n*
1 a short coat
2 an outer cover or casing ⟨a book *jacket*⟩

jack–in–the–box \ˈjak-ən-t͟hə-ˌbäks\ *n, pl* **jack–in–the–box•es** *or* **jacks–in–the–box** \ˈjak-sən-\
◀ a small box out of which a toy figure springs when the lid is raised

jack–in–the–pul•pit \ˌjak-ən-t͟hə-ˈpu̇l-ˌpit\ *n, pl* **jack–in–the–pul•pits** *or* **jacks–in–the–pul•pit** \ˌjak-sən-\
a plant that grows in moist shady woods and has a stalk of tiny yellowish flowers protected by a leaf bent over like a hood

[1]**jack•knife** \ˈjak-ˌnīf\ *n, pl* **jack•knives** \-ˌnīvz\
▼ a knife that has a folding blade or blades and can be put in a pocket

[1]**jackknife**

[2]**jackknife** *vb* **jack•knifed; jack•knif•ing**
to double up like a jackknife

jack–of–all–trades \ˌjak-əv-ˌȯl-ˈtrādz\ *n, pl* **jacks–of–all–trades** \ˌjaks-əv-\
a person who can do several kinds of work fairly well

jack–o'–lan•tern \ˈja-kə-ˌlan-tərn\ *n*
a pumpkin with its insides scooped out and cut to look like a human face

jack•pot \ˈjak-ˌpät\ *n*
1 a large amount of money to be won
2 a large and often unexpected success or reward

jack•rab•bit \ˈjak-ˌra-bət\ *n*
a large hare of North America that has very long ears and long hind legs

jade: an 18th-century jade mask from Mexico

jade \ˈjād\ *n*
▲ a usually green mineral used for jewelry and carvings

jag•ged \ˈja-gəd\ *adj*
having a sharply uneven edge or surface

jag•uar \ˈjag-ˌwär\ *n*
► a large yellowish brown black-spotted animal of the cat family found chiefly from Mexico to Argentina

[1]**jail** \ˈjāl\ *n*
PRISON

[2]**jail** *vb* **jailed**; **jail•ing**
to shut up in or as if in a prison

jail•break \ˈjāl-ˌbrāk\ *n*
escape from prison by force

jail•er *also* **jail•or** \ˈjā-lər\ *n*
a person responsible for the operation of a prison

ja•lopy \jə-ˈlä-pē\ *n, pl* **ja•lop•ies**
a worn old automobile

[1]**jam** \ˈjam\ *vb* **jammed**; **jam•ming**
1 to crowd, squeeze, or wedge into a tight position ⟨Fans *jammed* the auditorium.⟩
2 to put into action hard or suddenly ⟨He *jammed* his hands into his pockets.⟩ ⟨She *jammed* on the brakes.⟩
3 to hurt by pressure ⟨I *jammed* a finger in the car door.⟩
4 to be or cause to be stuck or unable to work because a part is wedged tight ⟨Paper *jammed* the copier.⟩
5 to cause interference in (radio or television signals)

[2]**jam** *n*
a food made by boiling fruit with sugar until it is thick

[3]**jam** *n*
1 a crowded mass of people or things that blocks something ⟨a traffic *jam*⟩
2 a difficult situation

jamb \ˈjam\ *n*
a vertical piece forming the side of an opening (as for a doorway)

jam•bo•ree \ˌjam-bə-ˈrē\ *n*
1 a large party or celebration
2 a national or international camping assembly of Boy Scouts

Jan. *abbr* January

[1]**jan•gle** \ˈjaŋ-gəl\ *vb* **jan•gled**; **jan•gling**
to make or cause to make a sound like the harsh ringing of a bell ⟨He *jangled* his keys.⟩

[2]**jangle** *n*
a harsh often ringing sound

jan•i•tor \ˈjan-ət-ər\ *n*
a person who takes care of a building (as a school)

[2]**Japanese** *n, pl* **Japanese**
1 a person born or living in Japan
2 the language of the Japanese

Japanese beetle *n*
a small glossy green or brown Asian beetle now found in the United States that as a grub feeds on roots and as an adult eats leaves and fruits

[1]**jar** \ˈjär\ *n*
1 a usually glass or pottery container with a wide mouth
2 the contents of a jar ⟨We ate a *jar* of pickles.⟩

[2]**jar** *vb* **jarred**; **jar•ring**
1 to shake or cause to shake hard
2 to have a disagreeable effect

[3]**jar** *n*
1 [2]JOLT 1
2 [2]SHOCK 1

jaguar

Jan•u•ary \ˈjan-yə-ˌwer-ē\ *n*
the first month of the year

► **Word History** The Latin month name *Januarius*, from which we get the word *January*, was associated by the ancient Romans with their god *Janus*. *Janus* was a god of doorways and gates (in Latin, *janua*), and also of beginnings, so the name seems appropriate for the first month of the year. Curiously, however, the early Roman calendar began with March, not January, so the origin of the Latin name is somewhat mysterious.

[1]**Jap•a•nese** \ˌja-pə-ˈnēz\ *adj*
of or relating to Japan, its people, or the Japanese language

jar•gon \ˈjär-gən, -ˌgän\ *n*
1 the special vocabulary of an activity or group ⟨sports *jargon*⟩
2 language that is not clear and is full of long words

jas•mine \ˈjaz-mən\ *n*
a usually climbing plant of warm regions with fragrant flowers

jas•per \ˈjas-pər\ *n*
▼ an opaque usually red, green, brown, or yellow stone used for making decorative objects

jasper

jaunt *n*
a short pleasure trip

jaun•ty \'jȯn-tē\ *adj* **jaun•ti•er**; **jaun•ti•est**
lively in manner or appearance ⟨He approached with a *jaunty* walk.⟩
jaun•ti•ly \'jȯn-tə-lē\ *adv*
jaun•ti•ness \'jȯn-tē-nəs\ *n*

jav•e•lin \'jav-lən, 'ja-və-lən\ *n*
1 a light spear
2 ▶ a slender rod thrown for distance in a track-and-field contest (**javelin throw**)

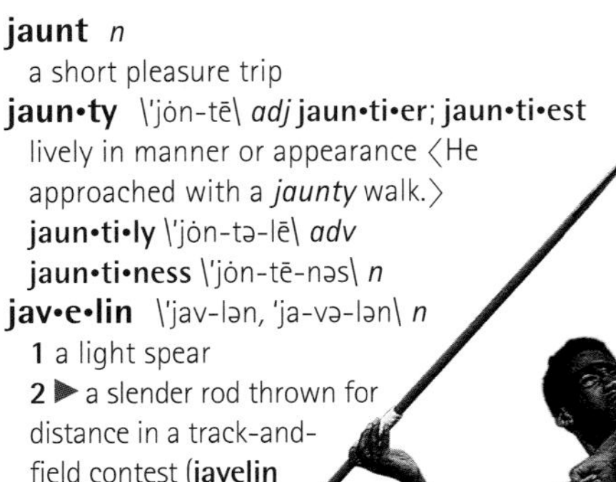

javelin 2:
an athlete throwing a javelin

jaw \'jȯ\ *n*
1 either of an upper or lower bony structure that supports the soft parts of the mouth and usually bears teeth on its edge and of which the lower part is movable
2 a part of an invertebrate animal (as an insect) that resembles or does the work of a human jaw
3 one of a pair of moving parts that open and close for holding or crushing something ⟨Tighten the *jaws* of the vise.⟩

jaw•bone \'jȯ-ˌbōn\ *n*
JAW 1

jay \'jā\ *n*
▼ a usually blue bird related to the crow that has a loud call

jay:
a blue jay

jay•walk \'jā-ˌwȯk\ *vb* **jay•walked**; **jay•walk•ing**
to cross a street in a place or in a way that is against traffic regulations
jay•walk•er *n*

jazz \'jaz\ *n*
a type of American music with lively rhythms and melodies that are often made up by musicians as they play

jeal•ous \'je-ləs\ *adj*
1 feeling anger because of the belief that a loved one might be unfaithful ⟨a *jealous* husband⟩
2 feeling a mean anger toward someone because he or she is more successful
3 CAREFUL 1, WATCHFUL ⟨We are *jealous* of our rights.⟩
jeal•ous•ly *adv*

jeal•ou•sy \'je-lə-sē\ *n, pl* **jeal•ou•sies**
1 a feeling of unhappiness and anger caused by a belief that a loved one might be unfaithful
2 a feeling of unhappiness caused by wanting what someone else has

jeans \'jēnz\ *n pl*
pants made of denim

▶ **Word History** The "Jean" in *jeans*, if we follow it back far enough, was the name of a city, not a person. Several centuries ago *jean* was an adjective describing a kind of fustian (a heavy cotton and linen cloth). *Jean fustian* was originally imported from the Italian city of Genoa, which in medieval English was called *Gene*. Eventually the word *jean* alone became the name of a kind of cloth, and then an article made from the cloth.

jeep \'jēp\ *n*
▼ a small motor vehicle used by the United States military for travel on rough surfaces

[1]**jeer** \'jir\ *vb* **jeered**; **jeer•ing**
1 to speak or cry out in scorn
2 to scorn or mock with taunts

[2]**jeer** *n*
a scornful remark or sound : TAUNT

Je•ho•vah \ji-'hō-və\ *n*
GOD 1

jell \'jel\ *vb* **jelled**; **jell•ing**
1 to become as firm as jelly : SET
2 to take shape ⟨After much thought an idea *jelled*.⟩

jel•lied \'je-lēd\ *adj*
made into or as part of a jelly ⟨*jellied* meats⟩

jeep:
a US Army jeep from the 1940s

jel•ly \ˈje-lē\ *n, pl* **jellies**
a soft springy food made from fruit juice boiled with sugar, from meat juices, or from gelatin
jel•ly•like \-ˌlīk\ *adj*

jelly bean *n*
a chewy bean-shaped candy

jel•ly•fish \ˈje-lē-ˌfish\ *n*
▼ a free-swimming sea animal related to the corals that has a nearly transparent jellylike body shaped like a saucer and tentacles with stinging cells

jellyfish

jen•net \ˈje-nət\ *n*
a female donkey

jeop•ar•dize \ˈje-pər-ˌdīz\ *vb* **jeop•ar•dized; jeop•ar•diz•ing**
to put in danger ⟨A poor diet can *jeopardize* your health.⟩

jeop•ar•dy \ˈje-pər-dē\ *n*
DANGER 1 ⟨The wrong choice could put your future in *jeopardy*.⟩

► **Word History** In French *jeu parti* means literally "divided game." This phrase was used in medieval France for situations involving alternative possibilities, such as a chess game where a player could not be sure which of two plays would be better. In this sense *jeu parti* was borrowed into English as *jeopardie*. It came to be applied to any situation involving equal chances for success or failure. Gradually, the element of risk or danger in such a choice became the word's meaning.

[1]**jerk** \ˈjərk\ *vb* **jerked; jerk•ing**
1 to give a quick sharp pull or twist to ⟨She *jerked* the dog's leash.⟩
2 to move in a quick motion ⟨He *jerked* his head.⟩

[2]**jerk** *n*
1 a short quick pull or jolt
2 a foolish person

jer•kin \ˈjər-kən\ *n*
a short sleeveless jacket

jerky \ˈjər-kē\ *adj* **jerk•i•er; jerk•i•est**
moving with sudden starts and stops ⟨a *jerky* ride⟩

jer•sey \ˈjər-zē\ *n, pl* **jerseys**
1 a knitted cloth (as of cotton) used mostly for making clothing
2 ► a shirt made of knitted fabric and especially one worn by a sports team

[1]**jest** \ˈjest\ *n*
1 a comic act or remark : JOKE
2 a playful mood or manner ⟨He spoke of his adventure in *jest*.⟩

[2]**jest** *vb* **jest•ed; jest•ing**
to make comic remarks : JOKE

jest•er \ˈjes-tər\ *n*
a person formerly kept in royal courts to amuse people

Je•sus \ˈjē-zəs\ *n*
JESUS CHRIST

Jesus Christ *n*
the founder of the Christian religion

[1]**jet** \ˈjet\ *n*
1 a rush of liquid, gas, or vapor through a narrow opening or a nozzle
2 JET AIRPLANE
3 a nozzle for a rush of gas or liquid
4 JET ENGINE

[2]**jet** *adj*
of a very dark black color ⟨*jet* hair⟩

[3]**jet** *n*
1 a black mineral that is often used for jewelry
2 a very dark black

[4]**jet** *vb* **jet•ted; jet•ting**
to come forcefully from a narrow opening ⟨Water *jetted* from the nozzle.⟩

jet airplane *n*
▼ an airplane powered by a jet engine

jet engine *n*
an engine in which fuel burns to produce a rush of heated air and gases that shoot out from the rear and drive the engine forward

jet plane *n*
JET AIRPLANE

jet–pro•pelled \ˌjet-prə-ˈpeld\ *adj*
driven forward or onward by a jet engine

jersey 2: a sports jersey

jet•sam \ˈjet-səm\ *n*
goods thrown overboard to lighten a ship in danger of sinking

jet stream *n*
high-speed winds blowing from a westerly direction several miles above the earth's surface

jet•ti•son \ˈje-tə-sən\ *vb* **jet•ti•soned; jet•ti•son•ing**
to throw out especially from a ship or an airplane

jet•ty \ˈje-tē\ *n, pl* **jetties**
1 a pier built to change the path of the current or tide or to protect a harbor
2 a landing wharf

Jew \ˈjü\ *n*
a person who is a descendant of the ancient Hebrews or whose religion is Judaism

jew•el \ˈjü-əl\ *n*
1 GEM 1
2 an ornament of precious metal often set with gemstones and worn on the body
3 a person who is greatly admired

jet airplane: a passenger plane

a b c d e f g h i j k l m n o p q r s t u v w x y z

jewelry

Decorative objects such as rings, brooches, necklaces, and earrings have been treasured since earliest times. The first jewelry was created using readily available elements such as carved bone or wood. Later pieces were made from gold and other metals, sometimes set with precious stones. Modern jewelry is made from a broad variety of materials, including plated metals, plastic, and enamel.

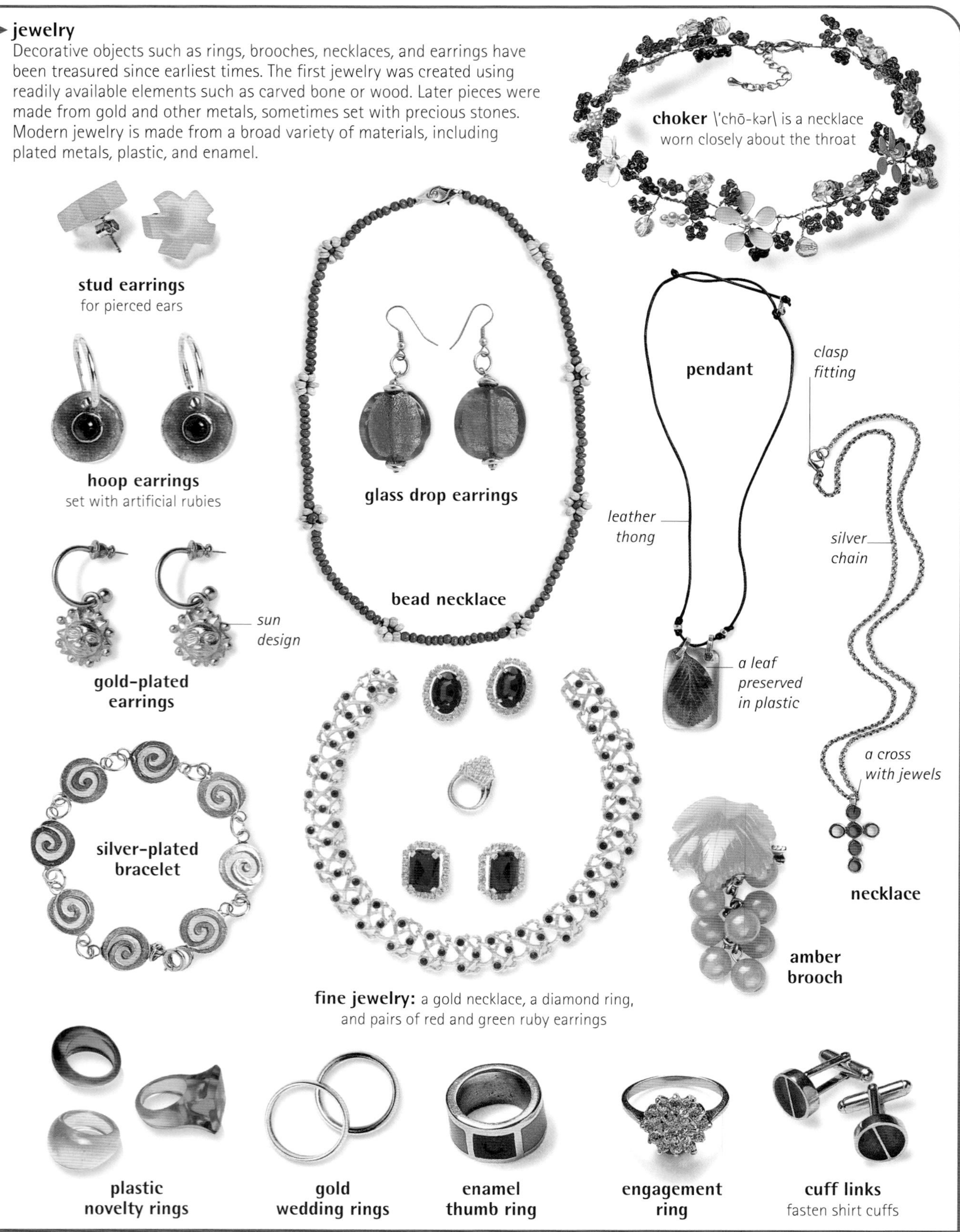

choker \ˈchō-kər\ is a necklace worn closely about the throat

stud earrings for pierced ears

hoop earrings set with artificial rubies

glass drop earrings

pendant

bead necklace

gold-plated earrings

silver-plated bracelet

necklace

amber brooch

fine jewelry: a gold necklace, a diamond ring, and pairs of red and green ruby earrings

plastic novelty rings

gold wedding rings

enamel thumb ring

engagement ring

cuff links fasten shirt cuffs

jew•el•er *or* **jew•el•ler** \ˈjü-ə-lər\ *n*
a person who makes or buys and sells jewelry and related articles (as silverware)

jew•el•ry \ˈjü-əl-rē\ *n*
◀ ornamental pieces (as rings or necklaces) worn on the body

Jew•ish \ˈjü-ish\ *adj*
of or relating to Jews or Judaism

jib \ˈjib\ *n*
a three-cornered sail extending forward from the foremast

[1]**jibe** *variant of* GIBE

[2]**jibe** \ˈjīb\ *vb* **jibed**; **jib•ing**
to be in agreement

jif•fy \ˈji-fē\ *n, pl* **jiffies**
MOMENT 1 ⟨I'll be there in a *jiffy.*⟩

[1]**jig** \ˈjig\ *n*
1 a lively dance
2 music for a lively dance
3 a dishonest act

[2]**jig** *vb* **jigged**; **jig•ging**
1 to dance a jig
2 to move with quick sudden motions ⟨He *jigged* his fishing line.⟩

jig•gle \ˈji-gəl\ *vb* **jig•gled**; **jig•gling**
to move or cause to move with quick little jerks ⟨Try not to *jiggle* the camera.⟩

jig•saw \ˈjig-ˌsȯ\ *n*
a machine saw used to cut curved and irregular lines or openwork patterns

jigsaw puzzle *n*
▼ a puzzle of many small pieces of a picture that must be fitted together

jigsaw puzzle

jim•my \ˈji-mē\ *vb* **jim•mied**; **jim•my•ing**
to force open with or as if with a short crowbar

jim•son•weed \ˈjim-sən-ˌwēd\ *n*
a poisonous weedy plant with bad-smelling leaves and large white or purple flowers

[1]**jin•gle** \ˈjiŋ-gəl\ *vb* **jin•gled**; **jin•gling**
to make or cause to make a light clinking sound ⟨Coins *jingled* in his pocket.⟩

[2]**jingle** *n*
1 a light clinking sound
2 a short catchy verse or song used to help sell a product

[1]**jinx** \ˈjiŋks\ *n, pl* **jinx•es**
something or someone that brings bad luck

[2]**jinx** *vb* **jinxed**; **jinx•ing**
to bring bad luck to

jit•ters \ˈji-tərz\ *n pl*
extreme nervousness

jit•tery \ˈji-tə-rē\ *adj*
1 very nervous ⟨I get *jittery* before a test.⟩
2 showing nervousness ⟨*jittery* handwriting⟩

job \ˈjäb\ *n*
1 work done regularly for pay ⟨My mom has a good *job.*⟩
2 a special duty or function ⟨It's my *job* to wash dishes.⟩
3 a piece of work usually done on order at an agreed rate ⟨Carpenters did the repair *job.*⟩
4 something produced by or as if by work ⟨I can do a better *job.*⟩
synonyms see TASK
job•less \-ləs\ *adj*

jock \ˈjäk\ *n*
ATHLETE

jock•ey \ˈjä-kē\ *n, pl* **jockeys**
1 ▶ a professional rider in a horse race
2 OPERATOR 1

[1]**jog** \ˈjäg\ *vb* **jogged**; **jog•ging**
1 to go or cause to go at a slow run ⟨The dog *jogged* along.⟩
2 to run slowly (as for exercise)
3 to give a slight shake or push to : NUDGE ⟨I *jogged* her awake.⟩
4 to make more alert ⟨Let me *jog* your memory.⟩
jog•ger *n*

[2]**jog** *n*
1 a slow run
2 a slight shake or push
3 a slow jerky gait (as of a horse)

[3]**jog** *n*
a short change in direction ⟨We came to a *jog* in a road.⟩

jog•gle \ˈjä-gəl\ *vb* **jog•gled**; **jog•gling**
to shake or cause to shake slightly

john•ny•cake \ˈjä-nē-ˌkāk\ *n*
a bread made of cornmeal, milk, flour, and eggs

join \ˈjȯin\ *vb* **joined**; **join•ing**
1 to come into the company of
2 to take part in a group activity ⟨We all *joined* in the chorus.⟩
3 to come, bring, or fasten together
4 to become a member of ⟨I'm *joining* the club.⟩
5 to come or bring into close association ⟨Both schools *joined* together to raise funds.⟩
6 to combine the elements of ⟨*Join* the two sets.⟩
7 ADJOIN ⟨The two rooms *join.*⟩

[1]**joint** \ˈjȯint\ *n*
1 a point where two bones of the skeleton come together usually in a way that allows motion ⟨The knee is a *joint.*⟩
2 a place where two things or parts are joined ⟨The pipe has a leaky *joint.*⟩
3 a part of a plant stem where a leaf or branch develops
4 a business establishment ⟨a fried chicken *joint*⟩
joint•ed \ˈjȯin-təd\ *adj*

jockey 1:
a jockey mounted on a horse

[2]**joint** *adj*
1 joined together ⟨The *joint* effect of wind and rain caused erosion.⟩
2 done by or shared by two or more ⟨a *joint* bank account⟩
joint•ly *adv*

joist \ˈjȯist\ *n*
any of the small timbers or metal beams laid crosswise in a building to support a floor or ceiling

A B C D E F G H I J K L M N O P Q R S T U V W X Y Z

[1]joke \'jōk\ *n*
1 something said or done to cause laughter or amusement ⟨They hid his shoes as a *joke.*⟩
2 a very short story with a funny ending that is a surprise ⟨The boys sat around telling *jokes.*⟩
3 something not worthy of being taken seriously ⟨Her excuse was a *joke.*⟩

[2]joke *vb* **joked; jok•ing**
1 to say or do something to cause laughter or amusement
2 to make funny remarks

jok•er \'jō-kər\ *n*
1 a person who says or does things to make others laugh
2 ▼ an extra card used in some card games

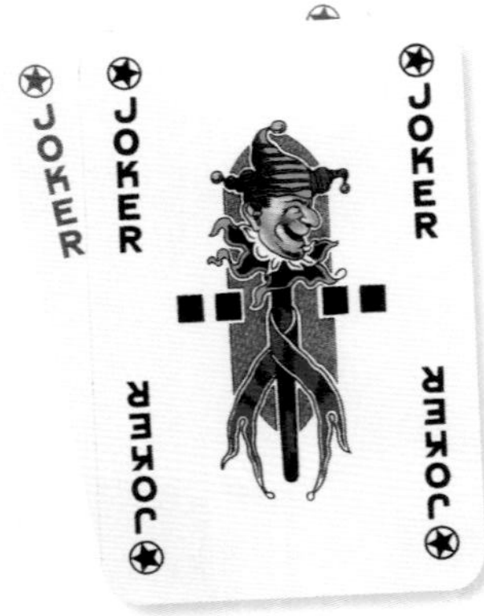

joker 2

jok•ing•ly \'jō-kiŋ-lē\ *adv*
in a manner that is not meant to be taken seriously ⟨He *jokingly* told us to leave.⟩

jol•li•ty \'jä-lə-tē\ *n*
the state of being happy and cheerful

[1]jol•ly \'jä-lē\ *adj* **jol•li•er; jol•li•est**
full of fun or joy

[2]jolly *adv*
[1]VERY 1 ⟨We had a *jolly* good time.⟩

[1]jolt \'jōlt\ *vb* **jolt•ed; jolt•ing**
1 to move or cause to move with a sudden jerky motion ⟨The train *jolted* to a stop.⟩
2 to cause to be upset ⟨The bad news *jolted* us.⟩

[2]jolt *n*
1 an abrupt jerky and usually powerful blow or movement
2 a sudden shock or surprise

jon•quil \'jän-kwəl, 'jäŋ-\ *n*
a plant related to the daffodil but with fragrant yellow or white flowers with a short central tube

josh \'jäsh\ *vb* **joshed; josh•ing**
to make humorous remarks or tease in a good-natured way

jos•tle \'jä-səl\ *vb* **jos•tled; jos•tling**
to push roughly

[1]jot \'jät\ *n*
the least bit ⟨I don't care a *jot.*⟩

[2]jot *vb* **jot•ted; jot•ting**
to write briefly or in a hurry

jounce \'jaùns\ *vb* **jounced; jounc•ing**
to move, fall, or bounce so as to shake

jour•nal \'jər-nᵊl\ *n*
1 a brief record (as in a diary) of daily happenings
2 a magazine that reports on things of special interest to a particular group
3 a daily newspaper

jour•nal•ism \'jər-nə-,li-zəm\ *n*
1 the business of collecting and editing news (as for newspapers, radio, or television)
2 writing of general or popular interest

jour•nal•ist \'jər-nə-list\ *n*
an editor or reporter of the news

[1]jour•ney \'jər-nē\ *n, pl* **jour•neys**
an act of traveling from one place to another

> ▶ **Synonyms** JOURNEY, TRIP, and TOUR mean travel from one place to another. JOURNEY usually means traveling a long distance and often in dangerous or difficult circumstances. ⟨They made the long *journey* across the desert.⟩ TRIP can be used when the traveling is brief, swift, or ordinary. ⟨We took our weekly *trip* to the store.⟩ TOUR is used for a journey with several stops that ends at the place where it began. ⟨Sightseers took a *tour* of the city.⟩

[2]journey *vb* **jour•neyed; jour•ney•ing**
to travel to a distant place

jour•ney•man \'jər-nē-mən\ *n, pl* **jour•ney•men** \-mən\
a worker who has learned a trade and usually works for another person by the day

[1]joust \'jaùst\ *vb* **joust•ed; joust•ing**
to take part in a combat on horseback with a lance

[2]joust *n*
▼ a combat on horseback between two knights with lances

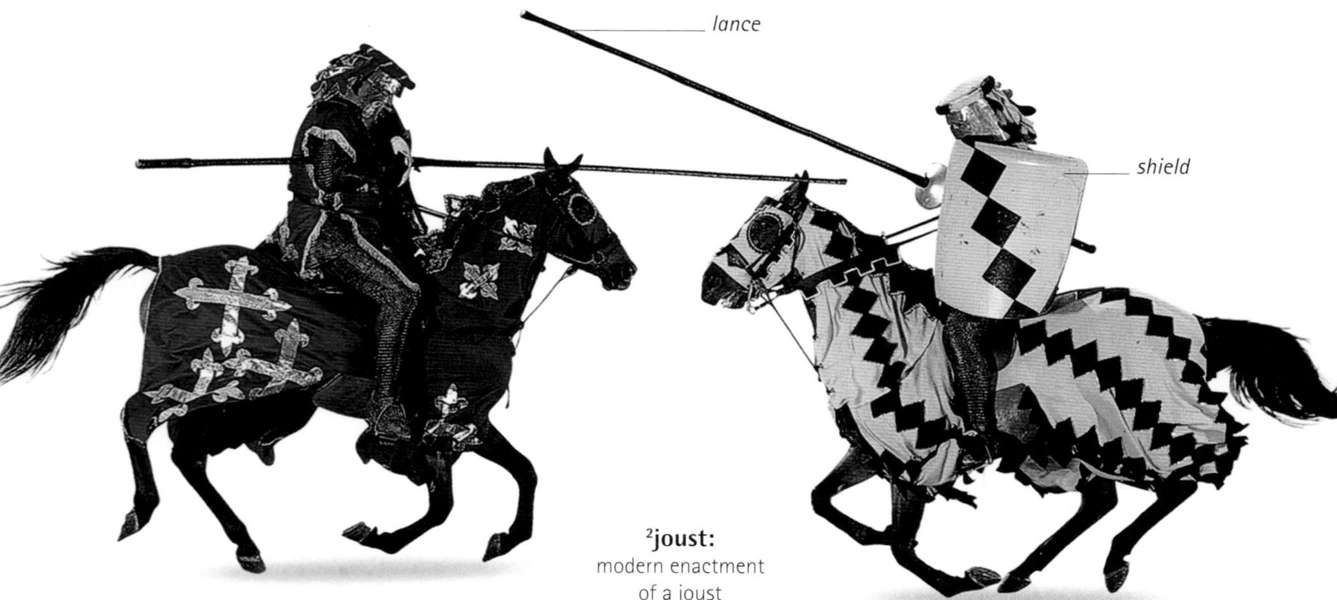

[2]joust: modern enactment of a joust

jo•vial \ˈjō-vē-əl\ *adj*
[1]JOLLY
jo•vial•ly *adv*

[1]jowl \ˈjau̇l\ *n*
loose flesh hanging from the lower jaw, cheeks, and throat

[2]jowl *n*
1 an animal's jaw and especially the lower jaw
2 CHEEK 1

joy \ˈjȯi\ *n*
1 a feeling of pleasure or happiness that comes from success, good fortune, or a sense of well-being
2 something that gives pleasure or happiness
synonyms see PLEASURE

joy•ful \ˈjȯi-fəl\ *adj*
feeling, causing, or showing pleasure or happiness ⟨a *joyful* family reunion⟩
joy•ful•ly \-fə-lē\ *adv*
joy•ful•ness *n*

joy•ous \ˈjȯi-əs\ *adj*
JOYFUL ⟨The baby's birth was a *joyous* occasion.⟩
joy•ous•ly *adv*
joy•ous•ness *n*

joy•stick \ˈjȯi-ˌstik\ *n*
a control lever (as for a computer display or an airplane) capable of motion in two or more directions

Jr. *abbr* junior

ju•bi•lant \ˈjü-bə-lənt\ *adj*
expressing great joy especially with shouting : noisily happy

ju•bi•la•tion \ˌjü-bə-ˈlā-shən\ *n*
the act of rejoicing : the state of being noisily happy

ju•bi•lee \ˈjü-bə-ˌlē, ˌjü-bə-ˈlē\ *n*
1 a 50th anniversary
2 a time of celebration

► **Word History** In ancient Hebrew tradition every 50th year was a time of restoration, when slaves were freed and lands restored to their former owners. This year took its Hebrew name, *yōbhēl,* from the ram's horn trumpets sounded to proclaim its coming. When the Hebrew scriptures were translated into Greek, *yōbhēl* was rendered as *iōbēlaios.* Under the influence of the Latin verb *jubilare,* "to let out joyful shouts," the Greek word became *jubilaeus* in Latin, from which it came into English in the 1300s.

judo: children performing an exercise in judo

Ju•da•ism \ˈjü-dē-ˌi-zəm, ˈjü-də-\ *n*
a religion developed among the ancient Hebrews that stresses belief in one God and faithfulness to the laws of the Torah

[1]judge \ˈjəj\ *vb* **judged; judg•ing**
1 to form an opinion after careful consideration ⟨I *judged* the distance badly.⟩
2 to act with authority to reach a decision (as in a trial)
3 THINK 1
4 to form an opinion of in comparison with others ⟨She *judged* pies at the fair.⟩

[2]judge *n*
1 a public official whose duty is to decide questions brought before a court
2 a person appointed to decide in a contest or competition
3 a person with the experience to give a meaningful opinion : CRITIC

judg•ment *or* **judge•ment** \ˈjəj-mənt\ *n*
1 a decision or opinion (as of a court) given after careful consideration
2 an opinion or estimate formed by examining and comparing ⟨This one's the best in my *judgment.*⟩
3 the ability for reaching a decision after careful consideration ⟨I trust your *judgment.*⟩

ju•di•cial \jü-ˈdi-shəl\ *adj*
1 of courts or judges ⟨the *judicial* branch⟩
2 ordered or done by a court ⟨*judicial* review⟩
ju•di•cial•ly *adv*

ju•di•cious \jü-ˈdi-shəs\ *adj*
having, using, or showing good judgment : WISE
ju•di•cious•ly *adv*

ju•do \ˈjü-dō\ *n*
◄ a sport developed in Japan in which opponents try to throw or pin each other to the ground

jug \ˈjəg\ *n*
a large deep usually earthenware or glass container with a narrow mouth and a handle

jug•gle \ˈjə-gəl\ *vb* **jug•gled; jug•gling**
1 ▼ to keep several things moving in the air at the same time
2 to work or do (several things) at the same time ⟨She *juggles* work and school.⟩
jug•gler \ˈjəg-lər\ *n*

juggle 1: an entertainer juggling clubs

juice \ˈjüs\ *n*
1 the liquid part that can be squeezed out of vegetables and fruit
2 the liquid part of meat

juicy \ˈjü-sē\ *adj* **juic•i•er; juic•i•est**
having much liquid ⟨a *juicy* pear⟩
juic•i•ness *n*

Ju•ly \jü-ˈlī\ *n*
the seventh month of the year

▶ **Word History** In the earliest Roman calendar the year began with March, and the fifth month was the one we now call *July.* The original name of this month in Latin was in fact *Quintilis,* from the word *quintus,* "fifth." After the death of the statesman Julius Caesar, who was born in this month, the Romans renamed it *Julius* in his honor. English *July* comes ultimately from Latin *Julius.*

[1]**jum•ble** \ˈjəm-bəl\ *n*
a disorderly mass or pile

[2]**jumble** *vb* **jum•bled; jum•bling**
to mix in a confused mass

jum•bo \ˈjəm-bō\ *adj*
very large ⟨*jumbo* eggs⟩

[1]**jump** \ˈjəmp\ *vb* **jumped; jump•ing**
1 to spring into the air : LEAP
2 to pass over or cause to pass over with or as if with a leap ⟨Our dog tried to *jump* the fence.⟩
3 to make a sudden movement ⟨The sudden noise made me *jump.*⟩
4 to make a sudden attack
5 to have or cause a sudden sharp increase ⟨Food prices have *jumped.*⟩
6 to make a hasty judgment
jump the gun
1 to start in a race before the starting signal
2 to do something before the proper time

[2]**jump** *n*
1 an act or instance of leaping ⟨He made a running *jump.*⟩
2 a sudden involuntary movement : START ⟨He gave a *jump* when she came in.⟩
3 a sharp sudden increase ⟨a *jump* in temperature⟩
4 an initial advantage ⟨We got the *jump* on the other team.⟩

jum•per \ˈjəm-pər\ *n*
1 someone or something that jumps
2 a sleeveless dress worn usually with a blouse

jumping jack *n*
an exercise in which a person who is standing jumps to a position with legs and arms spread out and then jumps back to the original position

jump•suit \ˈjəmp-ˌsüt\ *n*
a one-piece garment consisting of a shirt with attached pants or shorts

jumpy \ˈjəm-pē\ *adj* **jump•i•er; jump•i•est**
NERVOUS 2

jun *abbr* junior

jun•co \ˈjəŋ-kō\ *n, pl* **juncos** *or* **juncoes**
a small mostly gray North American bird usually having a pink bill

junc•tion \ˈjəŋk-shən\ *n*
1 a place or point where two or more things meet
2 an act of joining

junc•ture \ˈjəŋk-chər\ *n*
an important or particular point or stage in a process or activity

June \ˈjün\ *n*
the sixth month of the year

▶ **Word History** The word *June* came from Latin *Junius,* the Roman name of the month. *Junius* is in turn derived from *Juno,* a goddess special to women who was worshipped in ancient Italy.

jun•gle \ˈjəŋ-gəl\ *n*
1 a thick or tangled growth of tropical plants ⟨The explorers hacked at the *jungle* to clear a path.⟩
2 a large area of land usually in a tropical region covered with a thick tangled growth of plants

jungle gym *n*
▶ a structure of bars for children to climb on

[1]**ju•nior** \ˈjün-yər\ *adj*
1 being younger — used to distinguish a son from a father with the same name ⟨John Doe, *Junior*⟩
2 lower in rank ⟨a *junior* associate⟩
3 of or relating to students in the next-to-last year at a high school, college, or university ⟨the *junior* class⟩

[2]**junior** *n*
1 a person who is younger or lower in rank than another ⟨He is two years my *junior.*⟩
2 a student in the next-to-last year at a high school, college, or university

junior high school *n*
a school usually including seventh, eighth, and ninth grades

ju•ni•per \ˈjü-nə-pər\ *n*
▼ an evergreen tree or shrub related to the pines but having tiny cones resembling berries

juniper: a juniper branch

jungle gym: children playing on a jungle gym

[1]**junk** \ˈjəŋk\ *n*
1 things that have been thrown away or are of little value or use
2 a poorly made product
3 something of little meaning, worth, or significance 〈There's nothing but *junk* on TV tonight.〉

[2]**junk** *vb* **junked**; **junk•ing**
to get rid of as worthless : SCRAP 〈I'm *junking* this car.〉

[3]**junk** *n*
▶ an Asian sailing boat that is high in the front

[3]**junk:** model of a traditional junk

junk food *n*
food that is high in calories but low in nutritional content

junky \ˈjəŋ-kē\ *adj* **junk•i•er**; **junk•i•est**
of poor quality

Ju•pi•ter \ˈjü-pə-tər\ *n*
▼ the planet that is fifth in order of distance from the sun and is the largest of the planets with a diameter of about 89,000 miles (140,000 kilometers)

the Great Red Spot is thought to consist of swirling gases

Jupiter

ju•ror \ˈju̇r-ər\ *n*
a member of a jury

ju•ry \ˈju̇r-ē\ *n, pl* **juries**
1 a group of citizens chosen to hear and decide the facts of a case in a court of law
2 a committee that judges and awards prizes (as at an exhibition)

[1]**just** \ˈjəst\ *adj*
1 being what is deserved 〈a *just* punishment〉
2 having a foundation in fact or reason : REASONABLE 〈a *just* decision〉
3 agreeing with a standard of correctness 〈a *just* price〉
4 morally right or good 〈a *just* cause〉 〈a *just* man〉
synonyms see UPRIGHT
just•ly *adv*

[2]**just** *adv*
1 to an exact degree or in an exact manner 〈The shirt fits *just* right.〉 〈You look *just* like your father.〉
2 very recently 〈She *just* got here.〉
3 by a very small amount : with nothing to spare 〈We *just* managed to fit in his car.〉
4 by a very short distance 〈My best friend lives *just* east of here.〉
5 nothing other than 〈He's *just* a child.〉
6 [1]VERY 2 〈My new job is *just* wonderful.〉

jus•tice \ˈjəs-təs\ *n*
1 fair treatment 〈Everyone deserves *justice*.〉
2 [2]JUDGE 1
3 the process or result of using laws to fairly judge people accused of crimes
4 the quality of being fair or just 〈They were treated with *justice*.〉

jus•ti•fi•ca•tion \ˌjəs-tə-fə-ˈkā-shən\ *n*
1 the act or an instance of proving to be just, right, or reasonable
2 sufficient reason to show that an action is correct or acceptable

jus•ti•fy \ˈjəs-tə-ˌfī\ *vb* **jus•ti•fied**; **jus•ti•fy•ing**
to prove or show to be just, right, or reasonable 〈How can you *justify* your actions?〉
jus•ti•fi•able \-ə-bəl\ *adj*
jus•ti•fi•ably \-blē\ *adv*

jut \ˈjət\ *vb* **jut•ted**; **jut•ting**
to extend or cause to extend above or beyond a surrounding area 〈A rock *juts* out.〉

jute \ˈjüt\ *n*
▼ a strong glossy fiber from a tropical plant used chiefly for making sacks and twine

jute: twine made from jute

[1]**ju•ve•nile** \ˈjü-və-ˌnīl, -və-nᵊl\ *adj*
1 not fully grown or developed 〈a *juvenile* bird〉
2 of or designed for young people 〈a *juvenile* magazine〉
3 having or showing a lack of emotional maturity 〈*juvenile* pranks〉

[2]**juvenile** *n*
a young person : YOUTH

Sounds of K: The letter K makes only one sound, heard in *kite* and *take*. K is sometimes silent, especially before an N, as in *knee* and *knight*.

k \ˈkā\ *n, pl* **k's** *or* **ks** \ˈkāz\
often cap
1 the eleventh letter of the English alphabet
2 ¹THOUSAND 1
3 KILOBYTE

kale \ˈkāl\ *n*
▼ a hardy cabbage with wrinkled leaves that do not form a head

kale: a leaf of curly kale

ka•lei•do•scope \kə-ˈlī-də-ˌskōp\ *n*
1 ► a tube that contains bits of colored glass or plastic and two mirrors at one end and that shows many different patterns as it is turned
2 a changing pattern or scene

► **Word History** If you look into a kaleidoscope you will see changing shapes and pretty colors. The name of the device may seem strange, but it will make sense to a person who knows Greek. *Kaleidoscope* was made up out of two Greek words, *kalos*, "beautiful," and *eidos*, "shape." Added to those is the English word-forming element *-scope*, "something for viewing" (itself from a Greek element *-skopion*).

Kan. *abbr* Kansas

kan•ga•roo \ˌkaŋ-gə-ˈrü\ *n, pl* **kan•ga•roos**
► a leaping mammal of Australia and nearby islands that feeds on plants and has long powerful hind legs, a thick tail used as a support in standing or walking, and in the female a pouch on the abdomen in which the young are carried

Kans. *abbr* Kansas

ka•o•lin \ˈkā-ə-lən\ *n*
a very pure white clay used in making porcelain

kar•a•o•ke \ˌker-ē-ˈō-kē, kə-ˈrō-kē\ *n*
a form of entertainment in which a device plays music to which a person sings along

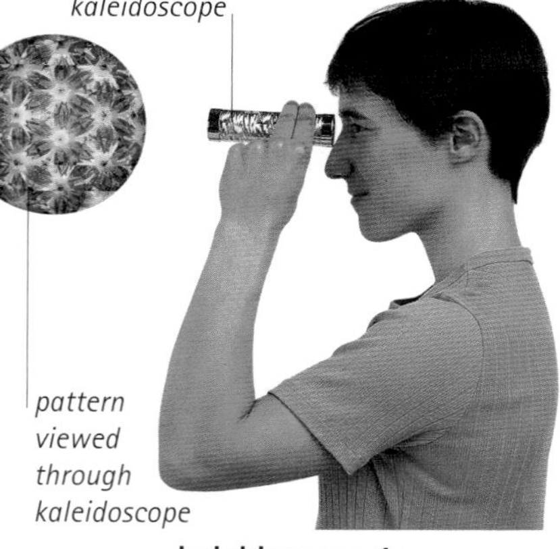

kaleidoscope 1: a girl looking into a kaleidoscope

kar•at \ˈker-ət\ *n*
a unit of fineness for gold 〈14-*karat* gold〉

ka•ra•te \kə-ˈrä-tē\ *n*
an art of self-defense developed in Japan in which an attacker is defeated by kicks and punches

ka•ty•did \ˈkā-tē-ˌdid\ *n*
a large green American grasshopper with males that make shrill noises

kangaroo: a red kangaroo

► **Word History** Some people like to pretend that the sounds insects make are words. When a male katydid rubs his front wings together, it makes a rough noise. Some think it sounds as if he says, "Katy did, Katy didn't," over and over. That is how the katydid got its name.

kay•ak \ˈkī-ˌak\ *n*
a small boat that is pointed at both ends, holds one or two people, and is moved by a paddle with two blades

ka•zoo \kə-ˈzü\ *n, pl* **ka•zoos**
a toy musical instrument which produces a buzzing tone when a person hums into the mouth hole

KB *abbr* kilobyte

keel \ˈkēl\ *n*
a long heavy piece of wood or metal that runs along and usually sticks out from the center of the bottom of a ship

keel over *vb* **keeled over; keel•ing over**
to fall suddenly (as in a faint)

keen \ˈkēn\ *adj* **keen•er; keen•est**
1 having a fine edge or point : SHARP 〈a *keen* knife〉

2 having or showing mental sharpness ⟨a *keen* observation⟩
3 very sensitive (as in seeing, smelling, or hearing) ⟨*keen* eyesight⟩
4 full of enthusiasm : EAGER
5 seeming to cut or sting ⟨a *keen* wind⟩
synonyms see EAGER
keen•ly *adv*
keen•ness *n*

[1]**keep** \'kēp\ *vb* **kept** \'kept\; **keep•ing**
1 to remain or cause to remain in a given place, situation, or condition ⟨*Keep* off the grass.⟩ ⟨She *kept* us waiting.⟩
2 to put in a specified place for storage ⟨Where do you *keep* the sugar?⟩
3 PROTECT ⟨I'll *keep* you from harm.⟩
4 to continue doing something ⟨Snow *kept* falling.⟩
5 to continue to have in possession or power ⟨Did you *keep* the money you found?⟩
6 to prevent from leaving : DETAIN ⟨The criminal was *kept* in jail.⟩
7 to hold back ⟨Can you *keep* a secret?⟩
8 to be faithful to : FULFILL ⟨I *kept* my promise.⟩
9 to act properly in relation to ⟨Remember to *keep* the Sabbath.⟩
10 to take care of : TEND
11 to have available for service or at someone's disposal ⟨Grandpa wants to *keep* a car.⟩
12 to preserve a record in ⟨He began to *keep* a diary.⟩
13 to continue in an unspoiled condition ⟨Buy food that *keeps* well.⟩
14 [1]REFRAIN ⟨They seem unable to *keep* from talking.⟩
keep an eye on [1]WATCH 3 ⟨Please *keep an eye on* the baby until I get back.⟩
keep up
1 to continue without interruption ⟨The rain *kept up* all night.⟩
2 to stay even with others (as in a race)
3 to stay well informed about something
4 MAINTAIN 2 ⟨They *keep up* the yard.⟩

[2]**keep** *n*
1 the strongest part of a castle in the Middle Ages
2 the necessities of life ⟨Their father could not earn the family's *keep*.⟩
for keeps
1 with the understanding that a person or group may keep what is won ⟨We'll play marbles *for keeps*.⟩
2 for a long time : PERMANENTLY ⟨He stayed angry *for keeps*.⟩

keep•er \'kē-pər\ *n*
a person who watches, guards, or takes care of something

keep•ing \'kē-piŋ\ *n*
1 watchful attention : CARE
2 a proper or fitting relationship : HARMONY ⟨He wrote a report in *keeping* with the facts.⟩

keep•sake \'kēp-ˌsāk\ *n*
something kept or given to be kept in memory of a person, place, or happening

keg \'keg\ *n*
1 a small barrel holding 30 gallons (about 114 liters)
2 the contents of a keg ⟨a *keg* of root beer⟩

kelp \'kelp\ *n*
a large brown seaweed

ken•nel \'ke-nᵊl\ *n*
1 a shelter for a dog
2 ▼ a place where dogs or cats are bred or housed

ker•nel \'kər-nᵊl\ *n*
1 the inner softer part of a seed, fruit stone, or nut
2 the whole grain or seed of a cereal plant ⟨a *kernel* of corn⟩
3 a very small amount

ker•o•sene \'ker-ə-ˌsēn\ *n*
a thin oil obtained from petroleum and used as a fuel and solvent

ketch \'kech\ *n*
a fore-and-aft rigged ship with two masts

ketch•up \'ke-chəp, 'ka-\ *also* **cat•sup** \'ke-chəp, 'ka-; 'kat-səp\ *n*
a thick seasoned sauce made from tomatoes

ket•tle \'ke-tᵊl\ *n*
1 a pot for boiling liquids
2 TEAKETTLE

kennel 2

kept *past and past participle of* KEEP

ker•chief \'kər-chəf\ *n, pl* **kerchiefs**
a square of cloth worn as a head covering or as a scarf

► **Word History** Look at the history of the word *kerchief* and you will see that it is a fine word for something that covers the head. The English word comes from an Old French compound made up of two words, *cuer*, "it covers," and *chef*, "head."

ket•tle•drum \'ke-tᵊl-ˌdrəm\ *n*
► a large brass or copper drum that has a rounded bottom and can be varied in pitch

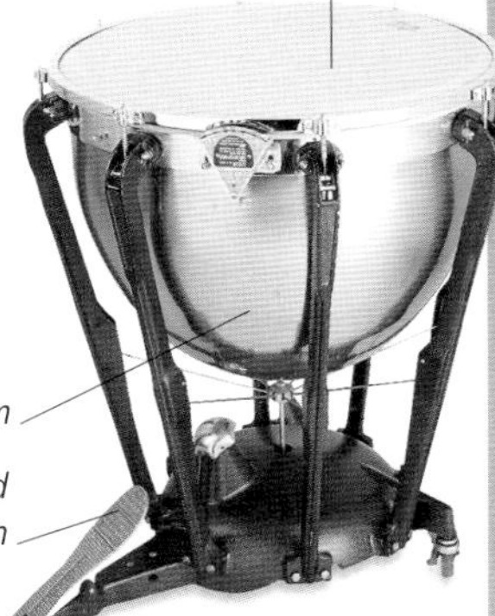

kettledrum

[1]**key** \'kē\ *n*
1 an instrument by which the bolt of a lock (as on a door) is turned or by which an engine is started
2 a device having the form or function of a key ⟨Can you wind the clock with the *key?*⟩
3 the thing that is necessary or most important in doing something ⟨To learn a skill, practice is the *key.*⟩
4 something (as a map legend) that gives an explanation : SOLUTION
5 one of the levers with a flat surface that is pressed with a finger to activate a mechanism of a machine or instrument ⟨computer *keys*⟩
6 a system of seven musical tones arranged in relation to a keynote from which the system is named

[2]**key** *vb* **keyed; key•ing**
1 to regulate the musical pitch of
2 to bring into harmony
3 to record or enter by operating the keys of a machine

[3]**key** *adj*
of great importance : most important ⟨She is one of our *key* players.⟩

[4]**key** *n*
a low island or reef ⟨the Florida *Keys*⟩

key•board \'kē-,bȯrd\ *n*
1 a row of keys by which a musical instrument (as a piano) is played
2 ▼ a portable electronic musical instrument with a row of keys like that of a piano
3 the whole arrangement of keys (as on a computer or typewriter)

key

keyboard 2

key•hole \'kē-,hōl\ *n*
a hole for receiving a key

key•note \'kē-,nōt\ *n*
1 the first tone of a scale fundamental to harmony
2 the fundamental fact, idea, or mood

key•stone \'kē-,stōn\ *n*
1 ▶ the wedge-shaped piece at the top of an arch that locks the other pieces in place
2 something on which other things depend for support

kg *abbr* kilogram

kha•ki \'ka-kē, 'kä-\ *n*
1 a light yellowish brown cloth used especially for military uniforms
2 **kha•kis** *pl* a pair of pants made of khaki
3 a light yellowish brown

[1]**kick** \'kik\ *vb* **kicked; kick•ing**
1 to hit with the foot ⟨*kick* a ball⟩
2 to move the legs forcefully
3 to put an end to ⟨*kick* a habit⟩
kick•er *n*
kick off
1 to start play in a game (as in football or soccer) by kicking the ball
2 BEGIN 1 ⟨The fair *kicks off* with a parade.⟩

[2]**kick** *n*
1 a blow with the foot
2 the act of hitting a ball with the foot
3 a feeling or source of pleasure ⟨He gets a *kick* out of racing.⟩
4 a usually sudden strong interest

kick•ball \'kik-,bȯl\ *n*
a game similar to baseball played with a large rubber ball that is kicked instead of hit with a bat

kick•off \'kik-,ȯf\ *n*
a kick that puts the ball into play (as in football or soccer)

kick•stand \'kik-,stand\ *n*
a metal bar or rod attached to a two-wheeled vehicle (as a bicycle) that is used to prop the vehicle up when it is not in use

[1]**kid** \'kid\ *n*
1 CHILD
2 a young goat or a related animal
3 the flesh, fur, or skin of a young goat or related animal or something (as leather) made from one of these

decorative keystone

keystone 1: a keystone on a building in New York City

[2]**kid** *vb* **kid•ded; kid•ding**
1 to deceive or trick as a joke
2 [1]TEASE 1
kid•der *n*

kid•nap \'kid-,nap\ *vb* **kid•napped** \-,napt\; **kid•nap•ping**
to carry away a person by force or by fraud and against his or her will
kid•nap•per *n*

kid•ney \'kid-nē\ *n, pl* **kid•neys**
▶ either of a pair of organs near the backbone that give off waste from the body in the form of urine and in humans are bean-shaped

kidney bean *n*
the large usually dark red edible seed of a bean plant

[1]**kill** \'kil\ *vb* **killed; kill•ing**
1 to end the life of : SLAY
2 to put an end to ⟨Aspirin will *kill* this headache.⟩
3 to use up ⟨We still have time to *kill.*⟩
4 [1]DEFEAT 2 ⟨Senators may *kill* a proposed law.⟩
5 to cause to become very tired ⟨These long hours are *killing* me.⟩

▶ **Synonyms** KILL, MURDER, and ASSASSINATE mean to take the life of. KILL doesn't specify the manner of death and can apply to the death of anything. ⟨An early frost *killed* the crops.⟩ ⟨There was a person *killed* in the accident.⟩ MURDER is used for the deliberate and unlawful killing of a person. ⟨He was arrested for *murdering* a rival.⟩ ASSASSINATE is usually used for the murder of an important person often for political reasons. ⟨There was a secret plan to *assassinate* the candidate.⟩

[2]**kill** *n*
1 an act of taking the life of a person or animal ⟨The tiger moved in for the *kill.*⟩
2 an animal whose life has been taken ⟨A lion is devouring its *kill.*⟩

kill•deer \'kil-,dir\ *n*
a grayish brown North American bird that has a high-pitched mournful call

▶ **Word History** Killdeers are not vicious birds. They have no particular hatred for deer, but to some people the cry of these birds must have sounded like "Kill deer! Kill deer! Kill deer!" That is why the bird got its unusual name.

▶ kidney

Humans have a pair of kidneys at the back of the abdomen. The kidneys maintain correct levels of water and salt in the body, filter toxic substances from the blood, and excrete excess water and waste in the form of urine, which drains to the bladder.

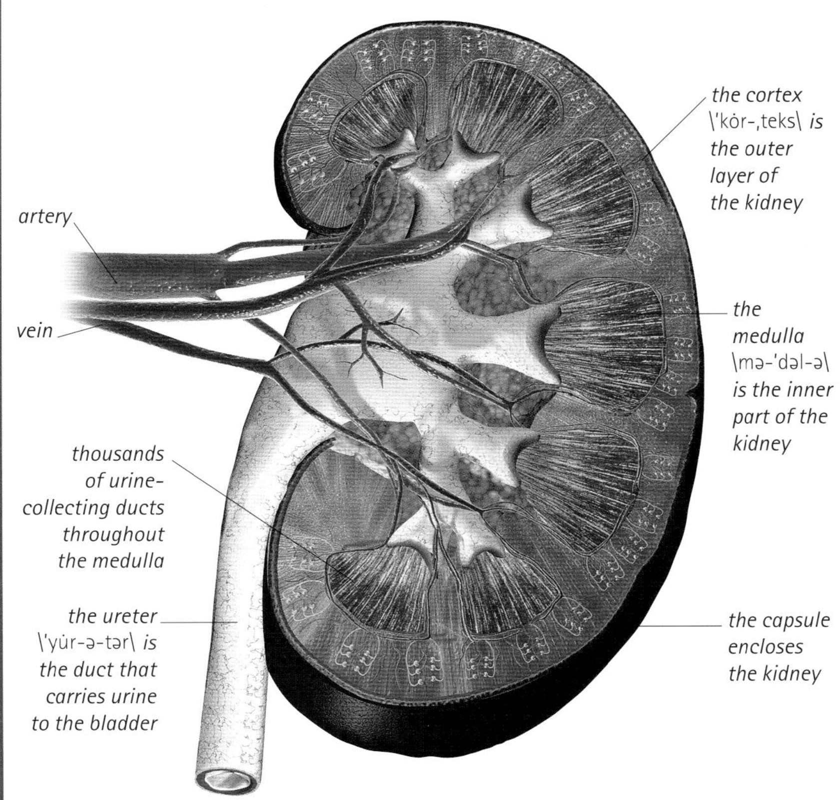

model of the human kidney in cross-section

[1]kill•er \'ki-lər\ *n*
someone or something that takes the life of a person or animal

[2]killer *adj*
1 very impressive or effective ⟨a *killer* smile⟩
2 very difficult ⟨a *killer* exam⟩
3 causing death or ruin

killer whale *n*
▶ a toothed whale that is mostly black above and white below and feeds especially on fish, squid, birds, and sea mammals (as seals)

kill•joy \'kil-,jȯi\ *n*
a person who spoils the pleasure of others

kiln \'kiln, 'kil\ *n*
▶ a furnace or oven in which something (as pottery) is hardened, burned, or dried

ki•lo \'kē-lō\ *n, pl* **kilos**
KILOGRAM

killer whale: a killer whale jumping in the air

kilo- *prefix*
thousand ⟨*kilo*meter⟩

ki•lo•byte \'ki-lə-,bīt\ *n*
a unit of computer information storage equal to 1024 bytes

ki•lo•gram \'ki-lə-,gram\ *n*
a metric unit of weight equal to 1000 grams

ki•lo•me•ter \ki-'lä-mə-tər, 'ki-lə-,mē-tər\ *n*
a metric unit of length equal to 1000 meters

kilo•watt \'ki-lə-,wät\ *n*
a unit of electrical power equal to 1000 watts

kilt \'kilt\ *n*
a knee-length pleated skirt usually of tartan worn by men in Scotland

kil•ter \'kil-tər\ *n*
proper condition ⟨The TV is out of *kilter.*⟩

ki•mo•no \kə-'mō-nō\ *n, pl* **ki•mo•nos**
1 a loose robe with wide sleeves that is traditionally worn with a broad sash as an outer garment by a Japanese person
2 a loose dressing gown worn chiefly by women

kin \'kin\ *n*
1 a person's relatives
2 KINSMAN

-kin \kən\ *also* **-kins** \kənz\ *n suffix*
little ⟨lamb*kin*⟩

kiln: a kiln stacked with pottery, ready for firing

[1]kind \'kīnd\ *n*
a group of persons or things that belong together or have something in common ⟨All *kinds* of people came.⟩ ⟨What *kind* of car does she drive?⟩

[2]kind *adj* **kind•er; kind•est**
1 wanting or liking to do good and to bring happiness to others : CONSIDERATE ⟨a *kind* woman⟩
2 showing or growing out of gentleness or goodness of heart ⟨a *kind* act⟩

kin•der•gar•ten \'kin-dər-ˌgär-tᵊn\ *n*
► a school or a class for very young children
kin•der•gart•ner \-ˌgärt-nər\ *n*

kind•heart•ed \'kīnd-'här-təd\ *adj*
having or showing a kind and sympathetic nature ⟨a *kindhearted* man⟩

kin•dle \'kin-dᵊl\ *vb* **kin•dled; kin•dling**
1 to set on fire : LIGHT
2 to stir up : EXCITE ⟨*kindle* an interest⟩

kin•dling \'kind-liŋ\ *n*
material that burns easily and is used for starting a fire

[1]**kind•ly** \'kīnd-lē\ *adj* **kind•li•er; kind•li•est**
1 [2]KIND 1
2 pleasant or wholesome in nature ⟨a *kindly* climate⟩
kind•li•ness *n*

[2]**kindly** *adv*
1 in a sympathetic manner ⟨The principal treated him *kindly*.⟩
2 in a willing manner ⟨We didn't take *kindly* to the change in schedule.⟩
3 in an appreciative manner ⟨I would take it *kindly* if you could help me.⟩
4 in an obliging manner

kind•ness \'kīnd-nəs\ *n*
1 the quality or state of being gentle and considerate ⟨She helps out of *kindness*.⟩
2 a kind deed : FAVOR

kind of *adv*
SOMEWHAT ⟨It's *kind of* dark in here.⟩

[1]**kin•dred** \'kin-drəd\ *adj*
alike in nature or character

[2]**kindred** *n*
1 a group of related individuals
2 a person's relatives

ki•net•ic \kə-'ne-tik, kī-\ *adj*
relating to the motions of objects and the forces associated with them ⟨*kinetic* energy⟩

kin•folk \'kin-ˌfōk\ *n*
[2]KINDRED 2

king \'kiŋ\ *n*
1 a male ruler of a country who usually inherits his position and rules for life
2 a person or thing that is better or more important than all others ⟨the *king* of jazz⟩
3 the chief piece in the game of chess
4 a playing card bearing the picture of a king
5 a piece in checkers that has reached the opponent's back row

king•dom \'kiŋ-dəm\ *n*
1 a country whose ruler is a king or queen
2 one of the three basic divisions (**animal kingdom, plant kingdom, mineral kingdom**) into which natural objects are commonly grouped
3 a group of related living things (as plants, animals, or bacteria) that ranks above the phylum and division in scientific classification and is the highest and broadest group

kindergarten: students in a kindergarten class

king•fish•er \'kiŋ-ˌfi-shər\ *n*
a crested bird with a short tail, long sharp bill, and bright feathers

king•let \'kiŋ-lət\ *n*
► a small active bird especially of wooded areas

kinglet: a golden-crowned kinglet

king•ly \'kiŋ-lē\ *adj*
1 suited to a king ⟨a *kingly* feast⟩
2 of a king ⟨*kingly* power⟩

king–size \'kiŋ-ˌsīz\ *or* **king–sized** \-ˌsīzd\ *adj*
unusually large ⟨a *king-size* sandwich⟩

kink \'kiŋk\ *n*
1 a short tight twist or curl (as in a thread or hose)
2 [1]CRAMP 1 ⟨I've got a *kink* in my back.⟩
3 an imperfection that makes something hard to use or work
kinky \'kiŋk-ē\ *adj*

-kins see -KIN

kin•ship \'kin-ˌship\ *n*
the quality or state of being related

kins•man \'kinz-mən\ *n, pl* **kins•men** \-mən\
a relative usually by birth

kins•wom•an \'kinz-ˌwu̇-mən\ *n, pl* **kins•wom•en** \-ˌwim-ən\
a woman who is a relative usually by birth

ki•osk \'kē-ˌäsk\ *n*
1 a small light structure with one or more open sides used especially to sell merchandise or services
2 a small structure that provides information and services on a computer

[1]**kiss** \'kis\ *vb* **kissed; kiss•ing**
1 to touch with the lips as a mark of love or greeting
2 to touch gently or lightly ⟨Branches *kissed* the ground below.⟩

[2]**kiss** *n*
1 a loving touch with the lips
2 a gentle touch or contact

kiss•er \'ki-sər\ *n*
1 a person who kisses
2 a person's face ⟨punched in the *kisser*⟩

[1]**kit** \'kit\ *n*
1 a set of articles for personal use ⟨a travel *kit*⟩
2 a set of tools or supplies ⟨a first-aid *kit*⟩
3 a set of parts to be put together ⟨a model-airplane *kit*⟩

[2]**kit** *n*
a young fur-bearing animal ⟨a fox *kit*⟩

kitch•en \'ki-chən\ *n*
a room in which food is prepared and cooking is done

A B C D E F G H I J K L M N O P Q R S T U V W X Y Z

kitch•en•ette \ˌki-chə-'net\ *n*
a small kitchen

kitchen garden *n*
a piece of land where vegetables are grown for household use

kite \'kīt\ *n*
1 ► a toy that consists of a light covered frame for flying in the air at the end of a long string
2 a small hawk with long narrow wings and deeply forked tail that feeds mostly on insects and small reptiles

kith \'kith\ *n*
familiar friends and neighbors or relatives ⟨We invited our *kith* and kin to the party.⟩

kit•ten \'ki-tᵊn\ *n*
a young cat
kit•ten•ish \'ki-tᵊn-ish\ *adj*

kit•ty \'ki-tē\ *n, pl* **kitties**
CAT 1, KITTEN

ki•wi \'kē-wē\ *n*
1 ▼ a grayish brown bird of New Zealand that is unable to fly
2 KIWIFRUIT

kiwi 1

ki•wi•fruit \-ˌfrüt\ *n*
the fruit of a Chinese vine having a fuzzy brown skin and slightly tart green flesh

► **Word History** The tart green fruit that goes by the name *kiwifruit* or often just *kiwi* is not eaten by the bird called the *kiwi* (whose name comes from Maori, the language of the native people of New Zealand). But the kiwi is closely associated with New Zealand, and when kiwifruit grown in that country was first widely exported in the 1960s, it was chosen as a pleasant-sounding name. The older name for the fruit was "Chinese gooseberry," which suggests a fruit much smaller in size than the kiwi.

► **kite 1**
Kites were probably invented by the Chinese over 2,500 years ago to spy on the enemy and carry archers over their opponents in battle. Modern kites are flown for pleasure or sport, and may have a light wooden frame, covered with nylon fabric or paper. Once launched, a kite is lifted by the wind and controlled by a person holding the end of a long line.

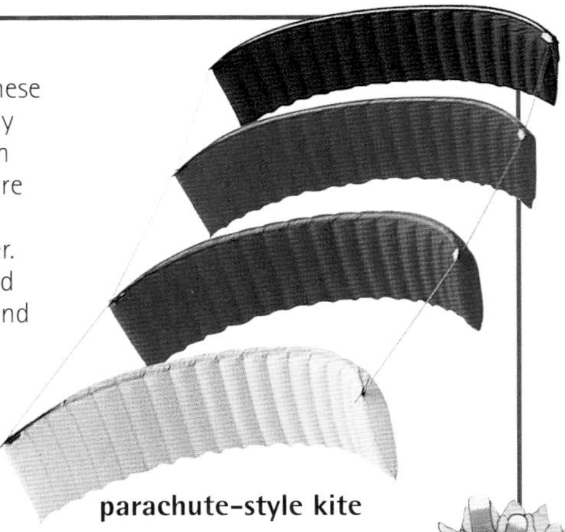

parachute-style kite

novelty kite

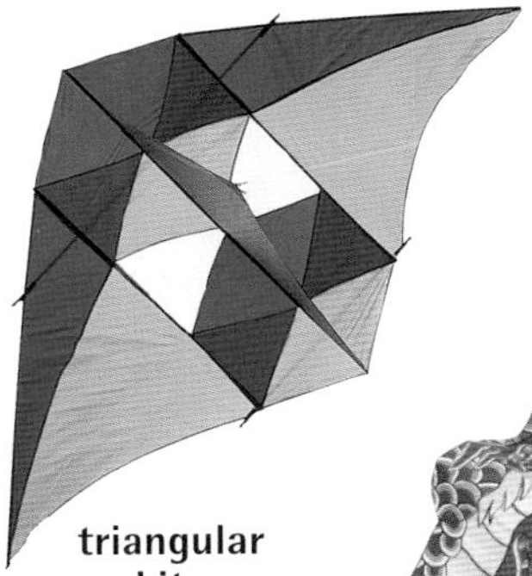

triangular kite

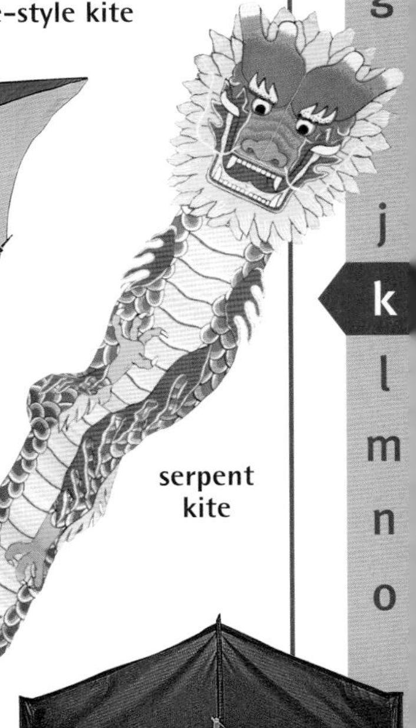

serpent kite

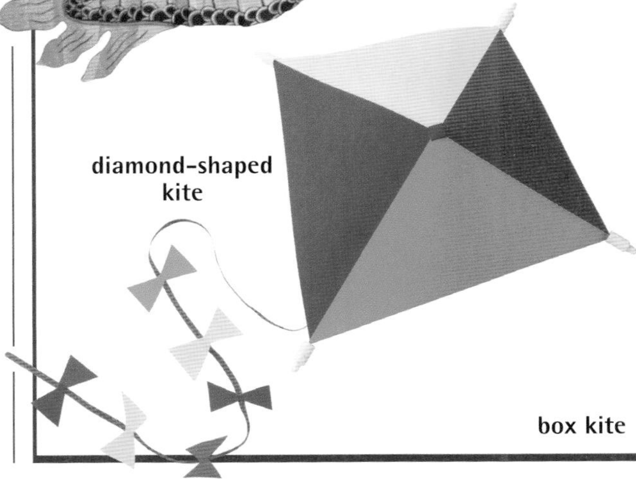

diamond-shaped kite

box kite

klutz \ˈkləts\ *n*
a clumsy person

km *abbr* kilometer

knack \ˈnak\ *n*
1 a natural ability : TALENT ⟨She has a *knack* for making friends.⟩
2 a clever or skillful way of doing something : TRICK

knap•sack \ˈnap-ˌsak\ *n*
a bag for carrying things on the shoulders or back

knave \ˈnāv\ *n*
1 RASCAL 2
2 [1]JACK 2

knead \ˈnēd\ *vb* **knead•ed**; **knead•ing**
1 to work and press into a mass with or as if with the hands ⟨We had to *knead* the dough before baking.⟩
2 [2]MASSAGE
knead•er *n*

knee \ˈnē\ *n*
1 the joint or region in which the thigh and lower leg come together
2 the part of a garment covering the knee
3 [1]LAP ⟨She sat on my *knee.*⟩

knee•cap \ˈnē-ˌkap\ *n*
a thick flat movable bone forming the front part of the knee

kneel \ˈnēl\ *vb* **knelt** \ˈnelt\ *or* **kneeled** \ˈnēld\; **kneel•ing**
to bend the knee : support the body on the knees

knell \ˈnel\ *n*
1 a stroke or sound of a bell especially when rung slowly for a death, funeral, or disaster
2 an indication of the end or failure of something

knew *past of* KNOW

knick•ers \ˈni-kərz\ *n pl*
loose-fitting short pants gathered at the knee

knick•knack \ˈnik-ˌnak\ *n*
a small ornamental object

[1]**knife** \ˈnīf\ *n, pl* **knives** \ˈnīvz\
1 a cutting instrument consisting of a sharp blade fastened to a handle
2 a cutting blade in a machine

[2]**knife** *vb* **knifes**; **knifed**; **knif•ing**
to stab, slash, or wound with a knife

[1]**knight** \ˈnīt\ *n*
1 ▶ a warrior of the Middle Ages who fought on horseback, served a king, held a special military rank, and swore to behave in a noble way
2 a man honored for merit by a king or queen of England and ranking below a baronet
3 one of the pieces in the game of chess
knight•ly *adj*

[2]**knight** *vb* **knight•ed**; **knight•ing**
to honor a man for merit by granting him the title of knight

knight•hood \ˈnīt-ˌhu̇d\ *n*
the rank, dignity, or profession of a knight

knit \ˈnit\ *vb* **knit** *or* **knit•ted**; **knit•ting**
1 to form a fabric or garment by interlacing yarn or thread in connected loops with needles (**knitting needles**) ⟨*knit* a sweater⟩
2 [2]WRINKLE ⟨The suspicious teacher *knit* his brow.⟩
3 to draw or come together closely as if knitted : unite firmly
knit•ter *n*

knob \ˈnäb\ *n*
1 a small rounded handle
2 a rounded switch on an electronic device
3 a rounded lump ⟨Her dog has a *knob* of a tail.⟩
4 a rounded hill

[1]**knight 1:**
a man dressed as a 14th-century knight preparing for battle

knob•by \ˈnä-bē\ *adj* **knob•bi•er**; **knob•bi•est**
1 covered with small rounded lumps ⟨*knobby* branches⟩
2 forming rounded lumps ⟨*knobby* knees⟩

[1]**knock** \ˈnäk\ *vb* **knocked**; **knock•ing**
1 to strike in order to get someone's attention ⟨I *knocked* before entering.⟩
2 to bump against something without intending to
3 to make a pounding noise ⟨The car's engine began *knocking.*⟩
4 to find fault with ⟨Don't *knock* it till you try it.⟩
5 to hit forcefully ⟨He *knocked* the ball out of the park.⟩
knock down
1 to strike to the ground with or as if with a sharp blow
2 to take apart
knock off to stop doing something ⟨Hey, I don't like that, so *knock it off!*⟩
knock over to cause to fall

[2]**knock** *n*
1 a pounding noise
2 a sharp blow ⟨a *knock* on the head⟩
3 a difficult or painful experience ⟨You learn from life's *knocks.*⟩

knock•er \ˈnä-kər\ *n*
▶ a device made like a hinge and fastened to a door for use in knocking

knocker:
a brass door knocker

knock–kneed \ˈnäk-ˈnēd\ *adj*
having the legs curved inward at the knees

knoll \ˈnōl\ *n*
a small round hill

[1]**knot** \ˈnät\ *n*
1 ▶ a section of rope or string that has been tied together to form a lump or knob or to keep something secure
2 [2]TANGLE 1
3 a painful or uncomfortable area in a body part ⟨I had *knots* in my stomach.⟩
4 a cluster of persons or things
5 the inner end of a woody branch enclosed in a plant stem or a section of this in sawed lumber
6 one nautical mile per hour (about two kilometers per hour)

▶ [1]knot 1

There are many types of knot, tied either from single or double lengths of thread, twine, or rope. Each knot has a different purpose – some are used to prevent lines from sliding, or to add weight to a line, while others are used to tie sails, to join two ropes together, or to tether animals.

hitch knot

overhand knot is used to prevent the end of a rope from fraying

square knot

bend knot is used to fasten one rope to another

butterfly knot is used to secure ropes linking rock climbers

[2]knot *vb* **knot•ted; knot•ting**
1 to tie together in a way that cannot be easily untied
2 to become tense or tight ⟨My stomach *knotted* while I waited for the dentist.⟩

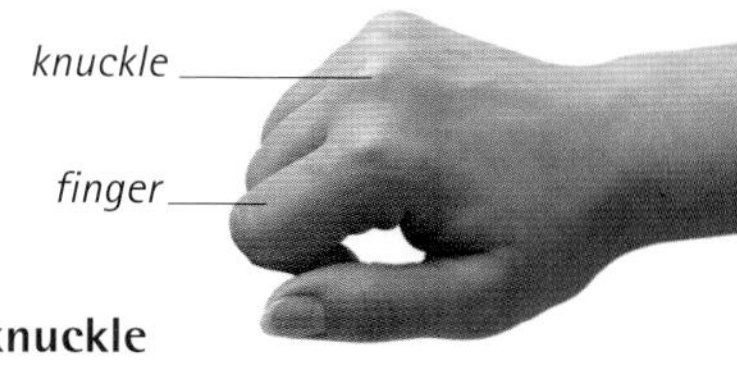

knuckle

knot•hole \'nät-ˌhōl\ *n*
a hole in wood where a knot has come out

knot•ty \'nä-tē\ *adj* **knot•ti•er; knot•ti•est**
1 full of lumps, knobs, tangles, or hard spots ⟨*knotty* muscles⟩ ⟨*knotty* wood⟩
2 DIFFICULT 3 ⟨a *knotty* problem⟩

know \'nō\ *vb* **knew** \'nü, 'nyü\; **known** \'nōn\; **know•ing**
1 to recognize the identity of ⟨I *know* that guy!⟩
2 to be aware of the truth of ⟨We *know* that the earth is round.⟩
3 to have a practical understanding of ⟨Her little sister already *knows* how to read.⟩
4 to have information or knowledge ⟨He *knows* all about cars.⟩
5 to be or become aware ⟨The president *knew* about the problem.⟩
6 to be acquainted or familiar with ⟨A taxi driver *knows* the city well.⟩
7 to have understanding of ⟨It's important to *know* yourself.⟩ ⟨I don't *know* why this happens.⟩
8 to recognize the nature of ⟨We *knew* them to be honest.⟩

know–how \'nō-ˌhau̇\ *n*
knowledge of how to get things done ⟨The job takes a certain amount of *know-how.*⟩

know•ing \'nō-iŋ\ *adj*
1 having or showing special knowledge, information, or intelligence
2 shrewdly and keenly alert
know•ing•ly *adv*

know–it–all \'nō-ət-ˌȯl\ *n*
a person who always claims to know everything

knowl•edge \'nä-lij\ *n*
1 understanding and skill gained by experience ⟨He has a *knowledge* of carpentry.⟩
2 the state of being aware of something or of having information ⟨He borrowed my camera without my *knowledge.*⟩
3 range of information or awareness
4 something learned and kept in the mind : LEARNING
synonyms see INFORMATION

knowl•edge•able \'nä-li-jə-bəl\ *adj*
having or showing understanding and skill gained through experience or education

known \'nōn\ *adj*
generally recognized ⟨She's a *known* liar.⟩

knuck•le \'nə-kəl\ *n*
◀ the rounded lump formed by the ends of two bones (as of a finger) where they come together in a joint

ko•ala \kō-'ä-lə\ *n*
▼ a tailless Australian animal with thick fur and big hairy ears, sharp claws for climbing, and a pouch like the kangaroo's for carrying its young

▶ **Word History** The word *koala* was taken from a language called Dharuk, spoken by the native Australian people who lived around what is today Sydney, Australia, when the first Europeans landed there in 1788. The word was first written *koolah*, which was probably closer to the way it was pronounced in Dharuk. The spelling *koala*—which came to be read as three syllables rather than two—may originally have been someone's misspelling of the word.

koala

kohl•ra•bi \kōl-'rä-bē\ *n*
a cabbage that does not form a head but has a fleshy roundish edible stem

Ko•mo•do dragon \kə-'mō-dō-\ *n*
a lizard of Indonesia that is the largest of all known lizards and may grow to be 10 feet (3 meters) long

kook \'kük\ *n*
a person who acts in a strange or insane way
kooky \'kü-kē\ *adj*

kook•a•bur•ra \'kü-kə-ˌbər-ə\ *n*
▼ an Australian bird that has a call resembling loud laughter

kookaburra

Ko•ran \kə-'ran, -'rän\ *n*
a book of sacred writings accepted by Muslims as revealed to Muhammad by Allah

¹Ko•re•an \kə-'rē-ən\ *n*
1 a person born or living in North Korea or South Korea
2 the language of the Koreans

²Korean *adj*
of or relating to North Korea or South Korea, the Korean people, or their language

ko•sher \'kō-shər\ *adj*
1 accepted by Jewish law as fit for use 〈*kosher* food〉
2 selling or serving food that is accepted as fit for use according to Jewish law

kow•tow \'kaů-'taů, 'kaů-ˌtaů\ *vb*
kow•towed; kow•tow•ing
to obey a person in a position of power in a way that seems weak **:** show overly respectful attention

krill \'kril\ *n*
▼ tiny floating sea animals that resemble shrimp and are a chief food source of some whales

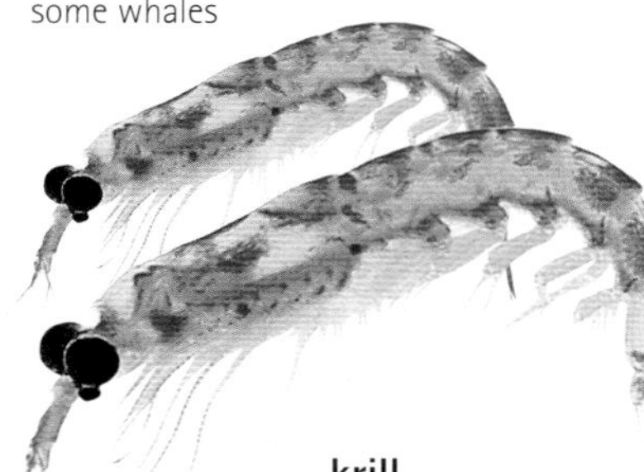

krill

KS *abbr* Kansas

kud•zu \'kůd-zü\ *n*
a fast-growing Asian vine that is grown for hay and to control erosion and is often a serious weed in the southeastern United States

kum•quat \'kəm-ˌkwät\ *n*
▶ a small citrus fruit that has a sweet rind and sour pulp and is used mostly in preserves

kumquat

kung fu \ˌkəŋ-'fü, ˌkůŋ-\ *n*
an art of self-defense without weapons that was developed in China

Kwan•zaa \'kwän-zə\ *n*
an African-American cultural festival held from December 26 to January 1

KY, Ky. *abbr* Kentucky

L

Sounds of L: The sound of the letter **L** is heard in *leaf* and *whale.* In some words that come from Spanish, two **L**s together make a **Y** sound, as in *tortilla.* **L** is sometimes silent, as in *talk* and *half.*

l \'el\ *n, pl* **l's** *or* **ls** \'elz\ *often cap*
1 the twelfth letter of the English alphabet
2 50 in Roman numerals

L *abbr*
1 large
2 left
3 liter

la \'lä\ *n*
the sixth note of the musical scale

LA, La. *abbr* Louisiana

lab \'lab\ *n*
LABORATORY

[1]la•bel \'lā-bəl\ *n*
1 ▼ a slip (as of paper or cloth) attached to something to identify or describe it
2 a word or phrase that describes or names something or someone ⟨a part-of-speech *label*⟩

[1]label 1: labels in potted plants

[2]label *vb* **la•beled** *or* **la•belled**; **la•bel•ing** *or* **la•bel•ling**
1 to put a word or words on (something) to identify or describe it ⟨Be sure to *label* your belongings.⟩
2 to name or describe with or as if with a label

[1]la•bor \'lā-bər\ *n*
1 usually hard physical or mental effort
2 something that has to be done : TASK ⟨The children went about their daily *labors.*⟩
3 work for which someone is paid ⟨The bill included parts and *labor.*⟩
4 workers considered as a group ⟨There's a shortage of skilled *labor.*⟩
5 the process by which or time during which a woman gives birth

▶ **Synonyms** LABOR and WORK mean action involving effort or exertion. WORK can apply to either mental or physical effort and may involve something that is enjoyable but tiring. ⟨Decorating the gym was hard *work.*⟩ LABOR suggests great or unpleasant usually physical exertion. ⟨She dreaded the dull *labor* of cleaning.⟩

[2]labor *vb* **la•bored**; **la•bor•ing**
1 to work hard : TOIL ⟨Workers *labored* in the field.⟩
2 to move slowly and with great effort ⟨The truck *labored* up the hill.⟩

lab•o•ra•to•ry \'la-brə-ˌtȯr-ē, 'la-bə-rə-\ *n, pl* **lab•o•ra•to•ries**
▼ a room or building in which scientific experiments and tests are done

Labor Day *n*
the first Monday in September observed as a legal holiday in honor of working people

la•bored \'lā-bərd\ *adj*
produced or done with effort or difficulty ⟨*labored* breathing⟩

la•bor•er \'lā-bər-ər\ *n*
a person who does physical work for pay ⟨a farm *laborer*⟩

la•bo•ri•ous \lə-'bȯr-ē-əs\ *adj*
requiring much effort ⟨Rebuilding was a slow and *laborious* task.⟩
la•bo•ri•ous•ly *adv*

labor union *n*
an organization of workers formed to help them get better pay and working conditions

la•bour *chiefly British variant of* LABOR

lab•y•rinth \'la-bə-ˌrinth\ *n*
a place that has many confusing paths and passages

[1]lace \'lās\ *vb* **laced**; **lac•ing**
to fasten or join with or as if with a cord or string ⟨*Lace* your shoes.⟩

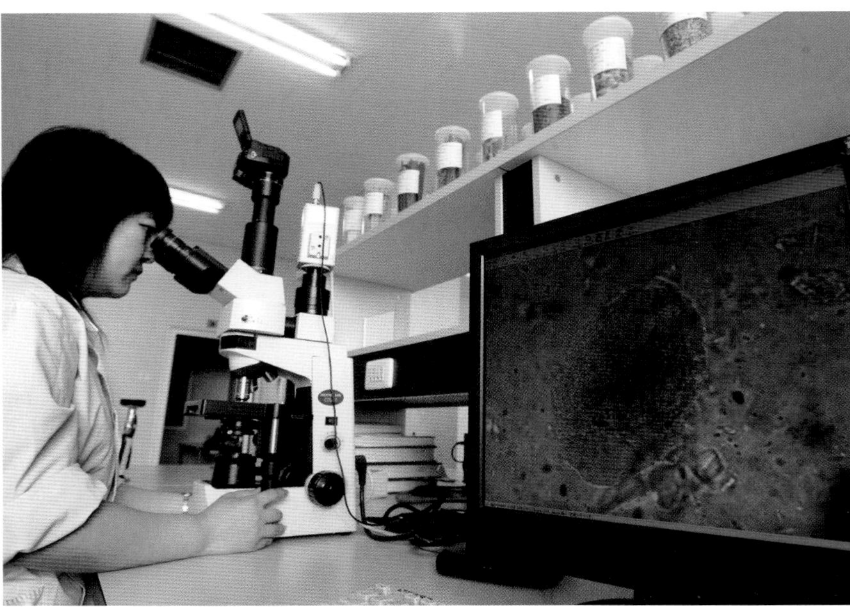

laboratory: a woman conducting an experiment in a laboratory

²lace *n*
1 a cord or string for pulling and holding together opposite edges (as of a shoe)
2 ▼ a very delicate fabric made with patterns of holes

²lace 2: a scarf of lace from Spain

lac•er•ate \'la-sə-,rāt\ *vb* **lac•er•at•ed; lac•er•at•ing**
to injure by cutting or tearing deeply or roughly ⟨a *lacerated* knee⟩

lac•er•a•tion \,la-sə-'rā-shən\ *n*
a deep or jagged cut or tear of the flesh

¹lack \'lak\ *vb* **lacked; lack•ing**
1 to be missing ⟨Something is *lacking* in the soup.⟩
2 to need or be without something ⟨I *lack* the necessary money.⟩

²lack *n*
the fact or state of not having any or enough of something ⟨a *lack* of time⟩

ladder

¹lac•quer \'la-kər\ *n*
a material like varnish that dries quickly into a shiny layer (as on wood or metal)

²lacquer *vb* **lac•quered; lac•quer•ing**
to coat with lacquer

la•crosse \lə-'kròs\ *n*
▼ a game played on a field using a long-handled stick with a shallow net for catching, throwing, and carrying the ball

lac•tose \'lak-,tōs\ *n*
a sugar that is found in milk

lacy \'lā-sē\ *adj* **lac•i•er; lac•i•est**
resembling or made of lace ⟨a *lacy* curtain⟩ ⟨*lacy* flower petals⟩

lad \'lad\ *n*
BOY 1, YOUTH

lad•der \'la-dər\ *n*
◀ a device used for climbing usually consisting of two long pieces of wood, rope, or metal joined at short distances by horizontal pieces on which a person may step

lad•die \'la-dē\ *n*
a young boy

lad•en \'lā-dᵊn\ *adj*
heavily loaded ⟨The truck was *laden* with gravel.⟩

¹la•dle \'lā-dᵊl\ *n*
a large and deep spoon with a long handle that is used especially for serving liquids ⟨a soup *ladle*⟩

²ladle *vb* **la•dled; la•dling**
to take up and carry in a ladle

la•dy \'lā-dē\ *n, pl* **la•dies**
1 a woman of high social position
2 a woman or girl who behaves in a polite way

▶ lacrosse

In the sport of lacrosse, players use a stick with a net to throw, catch, and carry the ball. They can also roll or kick the ball in any direction. The players try to score a goal by aiming the ball into the other team's net. Women's lacrosse teams are made up of 12 players, whereas men's teams have 10 players.

women's lacrosse field

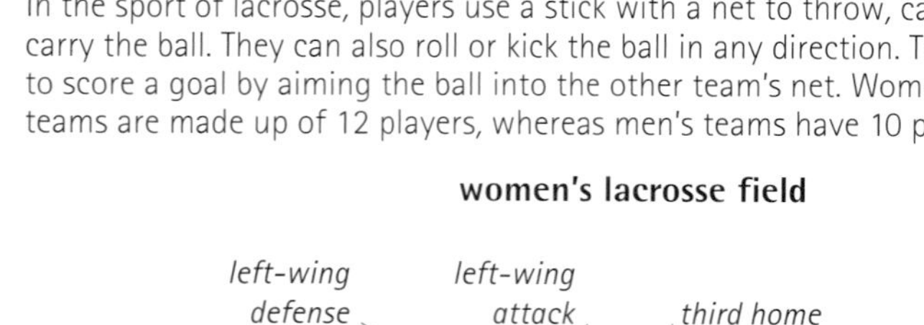

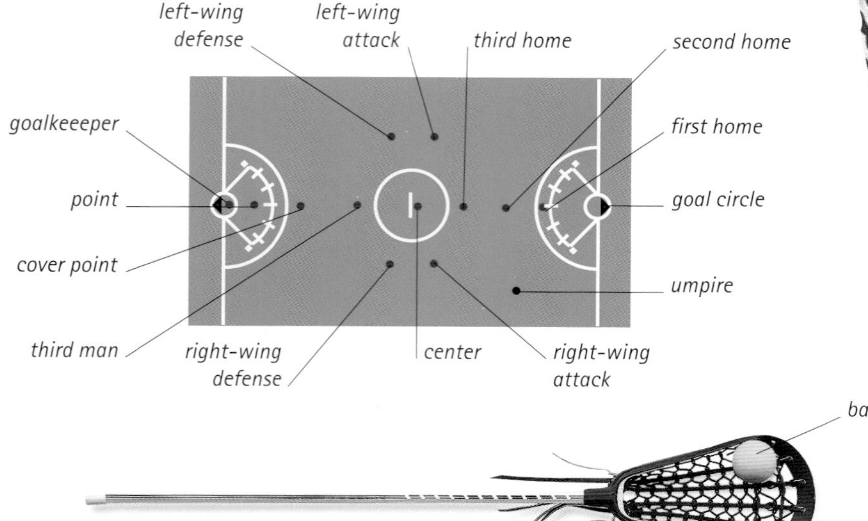

lacrosse stick

player

3 WOMAN 1 ⟨The *lady* behind me was first.⟩
4 WIFE
5 a British noblewoman — used as a title ⟨*Lady* Jane Grey⟩

► **Word History** *Lady* was actually formed as a compound word, though its nature has been completely disguised by centuries of sound change. The Old English ancestor of *lady* was *hlǣfdige*, "female head of the household." This compound is made up of *hlāf*, "loaf, bread," and *-dige*, which is thought to mean "kneader," and is akin to Old English *dāg*, "dough." Why the "kneader of dough" was thought to be the most important woman in the household we are not quite sure.

la•dy•bird \ˈlā-dē-ˌbərd\ *n* LADYBUG

la•dy•bug \ˈlā-dē-ˌbəg\ *n* ► a small rounded beetle that is often brightly colored and spotted and feeds mostly on other insects (as aphids)

ladybug

la•dy•like \ˈlā-dē-ˌlīk\ *adj* suitable to a woman or girl who behaves in a polite way ⟨*ladylike* behavior⟩

la•dy•ship \ˈlā-dē-ˌship\ *n* the rank of a lady — used as a title ⟨Her *Ladyship* is not at home.⟩

lady's slipper *or* **lady slipper** *n* a North American wild orchid with flowers resembling a slipper

¹lag \ˈlag\ *n* a space of time between two events ⟨We resumed work after a short *lag*.⟩

²lag *vb* **lagged**; **lag•ging** to move or advance slowly or more slowly than others ⟨Work *lagged* behind schedule.⟩

¹lag•gard \ˈla-gərd\ *adj* slow to act, move, or respond ⟨He was *laggard* about repaying the debt.⟩

²laggard *n* a person who does not go or move as quickly as others

la•goon \lə-ˈgün\ *n* a shallow channel or pond near or connected to a larger body of water

laid *past and past participle of* LAY

lain *past participle of* LIE

lair \ˈler\ *n* the den or resting place of a wild animal

lake in Misty Fjords National Monument, Alaska

lake \ˈlāk\ *n* ▲ a large inland body of standing water

¹lamb \ˈlam\ *n*
1 ▼ a young sheep usually less than one year old
2 the meat of a lamb used as food

¹lamb 1

²lamb *vb* **lambed**; **lamb•ing** to give birth to a lamb

lamb•kin \ˈlam-kən\ *n* a young lamb

¹lame \ˈlām\ *adj* **lam•er**; **lam•est**
1 not able to get around without pain or difficulty ⟨a *lame* horse⟩
2 injured or sore so that walking or movement is painful or difficult ⟨a *lame* leg⟩
3 not very convincing or effective ⟨a *lame* excuse⟩
lame•ly *adv*
lame•ness *n*

²lame *vb* **lamed**; **lam•ing** to make or become unable to get around without pain and difficulty ⟨*lamed* in a fall⟩

¹la•ment \lə-ˈment\ *vb* **la•ment•ed**; **la•ment•ing**
1 to mourn aloud : WAIL
2 to express great sorrow or regret for ⟨He *lamented* the disappearance of his dog.⟩

²lament *n*
1 a crying out in great sorrow
2 a sad song or poem

la•men•ta•ble \lə-ˈmen-tə-bəl, ˈla-mən-\ *adj* REGRETTABLE ⟨a *lamentable* accident⟩

lam•en•ta•tion \ˌla-mən-ˈtā-shən\ *n*
1 great sorrow
2 an expression of great sorrow ⟨Mourners uttered *lamentations*.⟩

lam•i•nat•ed \ˈla-mə-ˌnā-təd\ *adj* made of thin layers of material firmly joined together ⟨*laminated* wood⟩

lamp \ˈlamp\ *n* ► a device for producing light ⟨a kerosene *lamp*⟩ ⟨an electric *lamp*⟩

lam•prey \ˈlam-prē\ *n, pl* **lampreys** a water animal that looks like an eel but has a sucking mouth with no jaws

lamp

[1]lance \'lans\ *n*
▶ a weapon with a long handle and a sharp steel head used by knights on horseback

[2]lance *vb* **lanced**; **lanc•ing**
to cut open with a small sharp instrument 〈The doctor *lanced* the boil.〉

lance corporal *n*
an enlisted person in the marine corps ranking above a private first class

[1]lance: a 15th-century painting of a knight on horseback holding a lance

[1]land \'land\ *n*
1 the solid part of the surface of the earth
2 an area of ground or soil of a particular kind 〈fertile *land*〉
3 a part of the earth's surface marked off by boundaries 〈They bought some *land*.〉
4 a country or nation 〈your native *land*〉
5 the people of a country 〈All the *land* rose in rebellion.〉
land•less \-ləs\ *adj*

[2]land *vb* **land•ed**; **land•ing**
1 to go ashore or cause to go ashore from a ship 〈The troops *landed* on the island.〉
2 to come down or bring down and settle on a surface 〈The airplane *landed*.〉
3 to hit or come to a surface 〈I fell and *landed* on my back.〉
4 to be or cause to be in a particular place or condition 〈He *landed* in jail.〉
5 to catch and bring in 〈*land* a fish〉
6 to succeed in getting 〈*land* a job〉

land•fill \'land-,fil\ *n*
1 a system of garbage and trash disposal in which waste is buried between layers of earth
2 an area built up by such a landfill

land•hold•er \'land-,hōl-dər\ *n*
LANDOWNER

land•ing \'lan-diŋ\ *n*
1 ▶ the act of returning to a surface after a flight or voyage 〈The plane made a smooth *landing*.〉
2 a place for unloading or taking on passengers and cargo
3 a level area at the top of a flight of stairs or between two flights of stairs

landing field *n*
a field where aircraft land and take off

landing strip *n*
AIRSTRIP

land•la•dy \'land-,lā-dē\ *n, pl* **land•la•dies**
1 a woman who owns land or houses that she rents
2 a woman who runs an inn or rooming house

land•locked \'land-,läkt\ *adj*
1 shut in or nearly shut in by land 〈a *landlocked* harbor〉
2 kept from leaving fresh water by some barrier 〈*landlocked* salmon〉

land•lord \'land-,lȯrd\ *n*
1 a person who owns land or houses and rents them to other people
2 a person who runs an inn or rooming house

land•lub•ber \'land-,lə-bər\ *n*
a person who lives on land and knows little or nothing about the sea

land•mark \'land-,märk\ *n*
1 something (as a building, a large tree, or a statue) that is easy to see and can help a person find the way to a place near it
2 ▶ a building of historical importance
3 a very important event or achievement 〈The case was a *landmark* in legal history.〉

land•mass \'land-,mas\ *n*
a very large area of land

land mine *n*
a mine placed just below the surface of the ground and designed to be exploded by the weight of vehicles or troops passing over it

land•own•er \'land-,ō-nər\ *n*
a person who owns land

[1]land•scape \'land-,skāp\ *n*
1 a picture of natural scenery 〈He enjoys painting *landscapes*.〉
2 the land that can be seen in one glance

[2]landscape *vb* **land•scaped**; **land•scap•ing**
to improve the natural beauty of a piece of land

land•slide \'land-,slīd\ *n*
1 the sudden and rapid downward movement of a mass of rocks or earth on a steep slope
2 the material that moves in a landslide
3 the winning of an election by a very large number of votes

lane \'lān\ *n*
1 a narrow path or road (usually between fences, hedges, or buildings)

landing 1: a plane making a landing

landmark 2: the Washington Monument in Washington, D.C.

2 a special route (as for ships)
3 a strip of road used for a single line of traffic
4 a long narrow wooden floor used for bowling
5 a narrow course of a track or swimming pool in which a competitor must stay during a race

lan•guage \'laŋ-gwij\ *n*
1 the words and expressions used and understood by a large group of people ⟨the English *language*⟩
2 spoken or written words of a particular kind ⟨She used simple and clear *language*.⟩
3 a means of expressing ideas or feelings ⟨sign *language*⟩
4 a formal system of signs and symbols that is used to carry information ⟨a computer *language*⟩
5 the special words used by a certain group or in a certain field ⟨the *language* of science⟩
6 the study of languages

lan•guid \'laŋ-gwəd\ *adj*
1 having very little strength, energy, or spirit ⟨a pale *languid* boy⟩
2 having a slow and relaxed quality ⟨a *languid* pace⟩
lan•guid•ly *adv*

lan•guish \'laŋ-gwish\ *vb* **lan•guished**; **lan•guish•ing**
1 to be or become weak, dull, or listless
2 to continue for a long time without activity or progress in an unpleasant or unwanted situation ⟨The innocent man *languished* in prison.⟩

lank \'laŋk\ *adj* **lank•er**; **lank•est**
1 not well filled out : THIN ⟨*lank* cattle⟩
2 hanging straight and limp in an unattractive way ⟨*lank* hair⟩

lanky \'laŋ-kē\ *adj* **lank•i•er**; **lank•i•est**
very tall and thin ⟨a *lanky* teenager⟩

lan•tern \'lan-tərn\ *n*
a usually portable lamp with a protective covering

lan•yard \'lan-yərd\ *n*
1 a short rope or cord used as a fastening on ships
2 a cord worn around the neck to hold something (as a knife or whistle)
3 a strong cord with a hook at one end used in firing a cannon

[1]lap \'lap\ *n*
the front part of a person between the hips and the knees when seated

[2]lap *vb* **lapped**; **lap•ping**
OVERLAP

[3]lap *n*
1 a part of something that overlaps another part
2 one time around or over a course (as of a racetrack or swimming pool)
3 a stage in a trip

[4]lap *vb* **lapped**; **lap•ping**
1 to scoop up food or drink with the tongue ⟨The dog *lapped* up the water.⟩
2 to splash gently ⟨Waves *lapped* at the shore.⟩

lap•dog \'lap-,dȯg\ *n*
a dog small enough to be held in a person's lap

la•pel \lə-'pel\ *n*
the fold of the front of a coat or jacket below the collar

[1]lapse \'laps\ *n*
1 a slight error usually caused by lack of attention or forgetfulness ⟨a *lapse* in manners⟩ ⟨*lapses* in judgment⟩
2 a change that results in a worse condition ⟨She suffered a *lapse* in confidence.⟩
3 a passage of time ⟨He returned after a *lapse* of two years.⟩

[2]lapse *vb* **lapsed**; **laps•ing**
1 to slip, pass, or fall gradually ⟨The conversation *lapsed* into silence.⟩
2 to come to an end : CEASE ⟨The car insurance *lapsed*.⟩

lap•top \'lap-,täp\ *n*
▼ a small portable computer that can run on battery power and has the main parts (as keyboard and display screen) combined into a single unit

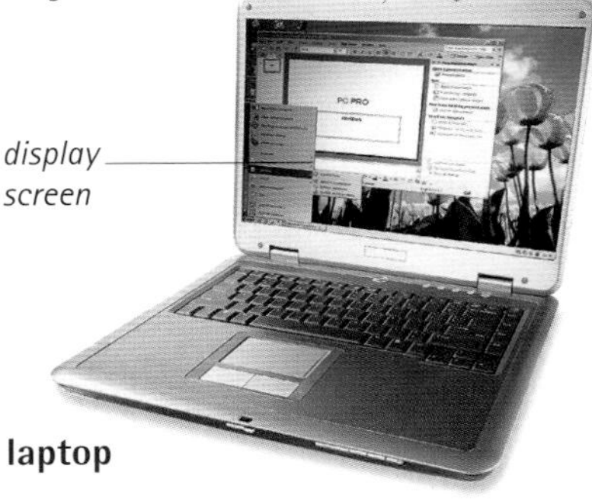

laptop

lar•board \'lär-bərd\ *n*
[3]PORT

lar•ce•ny \'lär-sə-nē\ *n, pl* **lar•ce•nies**
the unlawful taking of personal property without the owner's consent : THEFT

► **Word History** In Latin, the language of ancient Rome, the word *latro* referred to a soldier who fought for pay rather than from a sense of duty. Because such soldiers had a poor reputation, the meaning of the word came to be "robber" or "bandit," and the word derived from it, *latrocinium*, meant "act of robbery." *Latrocinium* became *larecin*, "theft," in medieval French, and this word was borrowed into English as *larceny*.

larch \'lärch\ *n*
a tree related to the pine that sheds its needles each fall

lard \'lärd\ *n*
a soft white fat from fatty tissue of the hog

lar•der \'lär-dər\ *n*
a place where food is kept

large \'lärj\ *adj* **larg•er**; **larg•est**
more than most others of a similar kind in amount or size : BIG ⟨a *large* room⟩ ⟨a *large* city⟩
large•ness *n*
at large
1 not captured or locked up ⟨The bank robbers are still *at large*.⟩
2 as a group or a whole ⟨the public *at large*⟩
3 representing a whole state or district ⟨a delegate-*at-large*⟩

large intestine *n*
the wide lower part of the intestine from which water is absorbed and in which feces are formed

large•ly \ˈlärj-lē\ *adv*
MOSTLY, CHIEFLY

lar•i•at \ˈler-ē-ət\ *n*
▼ a long light rope used to catch livestock or tie up grazing animals

lariat: a man holding a lariat

[1]lark \ˈlärk\ *n*
a usually brownish bird of Europe and Asia that has a pleasant song

[2]lark *n*
something done for fun or adventure ⟨She entered the contest on a *lark*.⟩

lark•spur \ˈlärk-ˌspər\ *n*
▼ a tall plant that is often grown for its stalks of showy blue, purple, pink, or white flowers

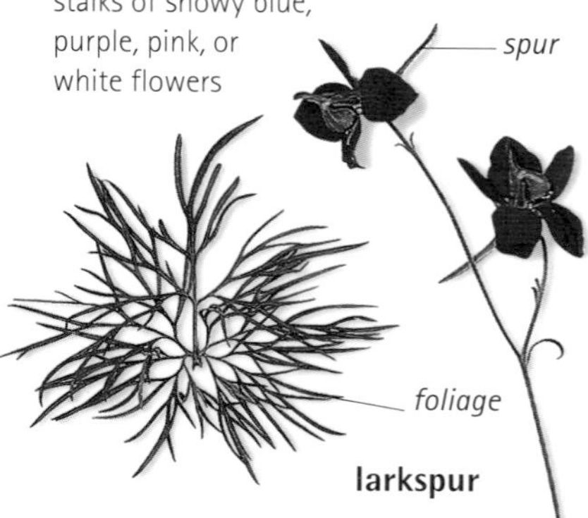

larkspur

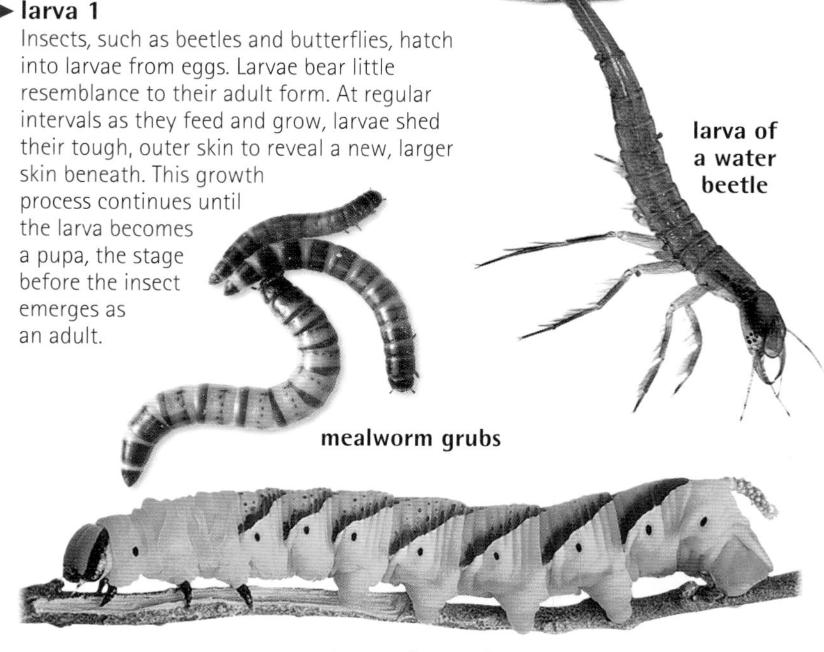

▶ larva 1
Insects, such as beetles and butterflies, hatch into larvae from eggs. Larvae bear little resemblance to their adult form. At regular intervals as they feed and grow, larvae shed their tough, outer skin to reveal a new, larger skin beneath. This growth process continues until the larva becomes a pupa, the stage before the insect emerges as an adult.

lar•va \ˈlär-və\ *n, pl* **lar•vae** \-vē\
1 ▲ a young wingless form (as a grub or caterpillar) of many insects that hatches from an egg
2 an early form of any animal (as a frog) that at birth or hatching is very different from its parents

▶ Word History To biologists in the 1700s, the adult was the only genuine form of an insect. The stages that come between the egg and the adult in many insects' lives were considered somehow unreal, or at best disguises. These stages were named with the Latin words *pupa*, "doll," and *larva*, which in the Latin of the ancient Romans was a sort of ghostly demon or a mask representing a demon. Although to modern biologists larvae such as caterpillars are as real as adults, the traditional terms *larva* and *pupa* remain with us.

lar•yn•gi•tis \ˌler-ən-ˈjī-təs\ *n*
swelling and irritation of the larynx in which the voice becomes hoarse or weak and the throat sore

lar•ynx \ˈler-iŋks\ *n, pl* **la•ryn•ges** \lə-ˈrin-ˌjēz\ *or* **lar•ynx•es**
the upper part of the trachea that contains the vocal cords

la•sa•gna \lə-ˈzän-yə\ *n*
▼ layers of broad flat noodles baked with a sauce usually of tomatoes, cheese, and meat or vegetables

lasagna: a piece of lasagna on a plate

la•ser \ˈlā-zər\ *n*
a device that produces a very powerful beam of light

laser printer *n*
a printer for computer output that produces high-quality images formed by a laser

[1]lash \ˈlash\ *vb* **lashed**; **lash•ing**
1 to hit with a whip ⟨The rider *lashed* his horse.⟩
2 to move forcefully from side to side ⟨The animal *lashed* his tail about.⟩
3 to hit with force ⟨Rain *lashed* the windows.⟩

4 to make a sudden and angry attack against ⟨He *lashed* out at his critics.⟩

²lash *n*
1 a blow with a whip or switch
2 the flexible part of a whip
3 EYELASH

³lash *vb* **lashed**; **lashing**
to tie or tie down with a rope or chain ⟨*Lash* the canoe to the roof of the car.⟩

lash•ing \ˈla-shiŋ\ *n*
something used for tying, wrapping, or fastening

lass \ˈlas\ *n*
GIRL 1

lass•ie \ˈla-sē\ *n*
a young girl

¹las•so \ˈla-sō, la-ˈsü\ *vb* **las•soed**; **las•so•ing**
to catch with a rope having a slipknot ⟨Cowboys *lassoed* a calf.⟩

²lasso *n, pl* **lassos** *or* **lassoes**
a rope with a slipknot that is used for catching animals

¹last \ˈlast\ *vb* **last•ed**; **last•ing**
1 to go on ⟨The game *lasted* two hours.⟩
2 to stay in good condition ⟨These sneakers won't *last*.⟩
3 to be enough for the needs of ⟨We have food to *last* the week.⟩
4 to be able to continue in a particular condition ⟨Are you too hungry to *last* till lunch?⟩

²last *adv*
1 after any others in time or order ⟨She spoke *last*.⟩
2 most recently ⟨They were *last* seen here.⟩

³last *adj*
1 following all the rest : FINAL ⟨I was the *last* one out.⟩
2 most recent ⟨*last* week⟩
3 lowest in rank or position ⟨Our team was *last* in the league.⟩
4 most unlikely ⟨You're the *last* person I thought I'd see.⟩

▶ **Synonyms** LAST and FINAL mean following all the others. LAST is used for something at the end of a series but it does not always mean that the series is complete or permanently ended. ⟨I spent my *last* dollar on a ticket.⟩ FINAL is used for something that positively closes a series and forever settles the matter. ⟨This is the *final* game of the championship.⟩

⁴last *n*
a person or thing that is last ⟨That order was my *last*.⟩

at last *or* **at long last** after a long period of time : FINALLY ⟨We're finished *at last*!⟩

last•ing \ˈlas-tiŋ\ *adj*
continuing for a long while ⟨a *lasting* impression⟩

last•ly \ˈlast-lē\ *adv*
at the end ⟨*Lastly*, I would like to thank you all.⟩

¹latch \ˈlach\ *n*
a movable piece that holds a door, gate, or window closed

²latch *vb* **latched**; **latch•ing**
to close or fasten with a latch

¹late \ˈlāt\ *adj* **lat•er**; **lat•est**
1 coming or occurring after the usual or proper time ⟨a *late* spring⟩
2 coming or occurring toward the end ⟨He married in his *late* twenties.⟩
3 having died or recently left a certain position ⟨the *late* president⟩
4 RECENT 2 ⟨a *late* discovery⟩
late•ness *n*

²late *adv* **lat•er**; **lat•est**
1 after the usual or proper time ⟨We arrived *late*.⟩
2 near the end of something ⟨We'll see you *late* next week.⟩
of late LATELY ⟨I have not seen him *of late*.⟩

late•com•er \ˈlāt-ˌkə-mər\ *n*
a person who arrives late

late•ly \ˈlāt-lē\ *adv*
not long ago : RECENTLY

la•tent \ˈlā-tᵊnt\ *adj*
present but not visible or active ⟨a *latent* infection⟩

lat•er•al \ˈla-tə-rəl\ *adj*
being on or directed toward the side ⟨*lateral* movement⟩
lat•er•al•ly *adv*

la•tex \ˈlā-ˌteks\ *n*
1 a milky plant juice that is the source of rubber
2 a mixture of water and tiny particles of rubber or plastic used especially in paints

lath \ˈlath\ *n, pl* **laths** \ˈlat͟hz, ˈlaths\
a thin strip of wood used (as in a wall) as a base for plaster

lathe \ˈlāt͟h\ *n*
a machine in which a piece of material (as wood) is held and turned while being shaped by a tool

¹lath•er \ˈla-t͟hər\ *n*
1 the foam made by stirring soap and water together
2 foam from sweating (as on a horse)

²lather *vb* **lath•ered**; **lath•er•ing**
1 to spread soapy foam over ⟨He *lathered* his hair.⟩
2 to form a foam ⟨This soap *lathers* well.⟩

¹Lat•in \ˈla-tᵊn\ *adj*
1 of or relating to the language of the ancient Romans ⟨*Latin* grammar⟩
2 of or relating to the countries or people of Latin America

²Latin *n*
1 the language of the ancient Romans
2 a member of a people whose language and customs have descended from the ancient Romans
3 a person born or living in Latin America

La•ti•na \lə-ˈtē-nə\ *n*
a woman or girl born or living in Latin America or of Latin-American origin living in the United States

Lat•in–Amer•i•can \ˌla-tᵊn-ə-ˈmer-ə-kən\ *adj*
of or relating to Latin America or its people

Latin American *n*
a person born or living in Latin America

La•ti•no \lə-ˈtē-nō\ *n, pl* **Latinos**
a person born or living in Latin America or of Latin-American origin living in the United States

lat•i•tude \ˈla-tə-ˌtüd, -ˌtyüd\ *n*
1 the distance north or south of the equator measured in degrees
2 a region marked by its distance north or south of the equator ⟨cold *latitudes*⟩
3 freedom to act or speak as desired ⟨Students weren't given much *latitude* in deciding what to study.⟩

lat•ter \ˈla-tər\ *adj*
1 coming or occurring near the end ⟨We are in the *latter* stages of the work.⟩
2 relating to or being the last thing or person mentioned ⟨Of cake or pie, I'll choose the *latter*.⟩

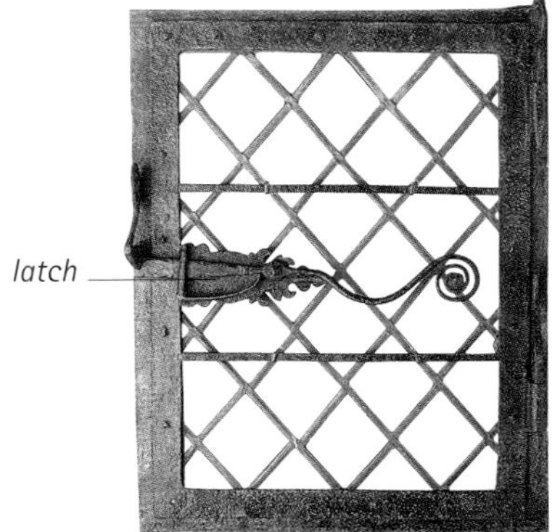

lattice 2: a 16th-century window from England

lat•tice \ˈla-təs\ *n*
1 a structure made of thin strips of wood or metal that cross each other
2 ▲ a window or gate having a lattice

a b c d e f g h i j k l m n o p q r s t u v w x y z

[2]launch: the launch of NASA's Saturn V rocket

[1]laugh \'laf, 'läf\ *vb* **laughed**; **laugh•ing**
to show amusement, joy, or scorn by smiling and making sounds (as chuckling) in the throat

[2]laugh *n*
the act or sound of laughing

laugh•able \'la-fə-bəl, 'lä-\ *adj*
causing or likely to cause laughter or scorn 〈His attempt at skating was *laughable.*〉
laugh•ably \-blē\ *adv*

laugh•ing•ly \'la-fiŋ-lē, 'lä-\ *adv*
with laughter 〈She *laughingly* recalled the dog's antics.〉

laugh•ing•stock \'la-fiŋ-,stäk, 'lä-\ *n*
a person or thing that is made fun of

laugh•ter \'laf-tər, 'läf-\ *n*
the action or sound of laughing

[1]launch \'lónch\ *vb* **launched**; **launch•ing**
1 to throw or spring forward : HURL 〈*launch* a spear〉
2 to send off especially with force 〈*launch* a spacecraft〉
3 to set afloat 〈*launch* a ship〉
4 to give a start to : BEGIN 〈*launch* a plan〉

[2]launch *n*
▲ an act of launching 〈a rocket *launch*〉

[3]launch *n*
a small open or partly covered motorboat

launch•pad \'lónch-,pad\ *n*
a nonflammable platform from which a rocket can be launched

laun•der \'lón-dər\ *vb* **laun•dered**; **laun•der•ing**
to wash or wash and iron clothes or household linens
laun•der•er *n*

laun•dry \'lón-drē\ *n, pl* **laundries**
1 clothes or household linens that need to be washed or that have been washed
2 a place where clothes and household linens are washed and dried

lau•rel \'lór-əl\ *n*
1 a small evergreen European tree with shiny pointed leaves used in ancient times to crown victors (as in sports)
2 a tree or shrub (as the American **mountain laurel**) that resembles the European laurel
3 a crown of laurel used as a mark of honor

la•va \'lä-və, 'la-\ *n*
▼ melted rock coming from a volcano or after it has cooled and hardened

lava:
a block of hardened lava

lav•a•to•ry \'la-və-,tór-ē\ *n, pl* **lav•a•to•ries**
1 a small sink (as in a bathroom)
2 a room for washing that usually has a toilet
3 TOILET 1

lav•en•der \'la-vən-dər\ *n*
1 a European mint with narrow leaves and stalks of small sweet-smelling pale violet flowers
2 a pale purple

[1]lav•ish \'la-vish\ *adj*
1 giving or involving a large amount : EXTRAVAGANT 〈The lobby contained a *lavish* display of flowers.〉
2 spent, produced, or given in large amounts 〈She received *lavish* praise.〉
lav•ish•ly *adv* 〈The book is *lavishly* illustrated.〉

► **Word History** *Lavish* comes from an older English noun *lavish* that meant "plenty." This noun probably came from a medieval French word *lavasse,* "a heavy rain." This French word is derived from a verb *laver,* "to wash," which goes back to Latin *lavare.* Other English words that ultimately trace back to *lavare* are *lavatory* and *laundry.*

[2]lavish *vb* **lav•ished**; **lav•ish•ing**
to spend, use, or give in large amounts 〈They *lavished* attention on the children.〉

law \ˈlȯ\ *n*
1 a rule of conduct or action that a nation or a group of people agrees to follow
2 a whole collection of established rules ⟨the *law* of the land⟩
3 a rule or principle that always works the same way under the same conditions ⟨the *law* of gravity⟩
4 a bill passed by a legislature
5 [2]POLICE 1
6 the profession of a lawyer

law–abid•ing \ˈlȯ-ə-ˌbī-diŋ\ *adj*
obeying the law ⟨a *law-abiding* citizen⟩

law•break•er \ˈlȯ-ˌbrā-kər\ *n*
a person who breaks the law

law•ful \ˈlȯ-fəl\ *adj*
1 permitted by law ⟨*lawful* conduct⟩
2 recognized by law ⟨She's the property's *lawful* owner.⟩
law•ful•ly \-fə-lē\ *adv*

law•less \ˈlȯ-ləs\ *adj*
1 having no laws **:** not based on or controlled by law ⟨a *lawless* frontier town⟩
2 uncontrolled by law **:** UNRULY ⟨a *lawless* mob⟩
law•less•ness *n*

law•mak•er \ˈlȯ-ˌmā-kər\ *n*
someone who takes part in writing and passing laws **:** LEGISLATOR
law•mak•ing \-ˌmā-kiŋ\ *adj or n*

lawn \ˈlȯn, ˈlän\ *n*
ground (as around a house) covered with grass that is kept mowed

lawn mower *n*
▼ a machine used to mow the grass on lawns

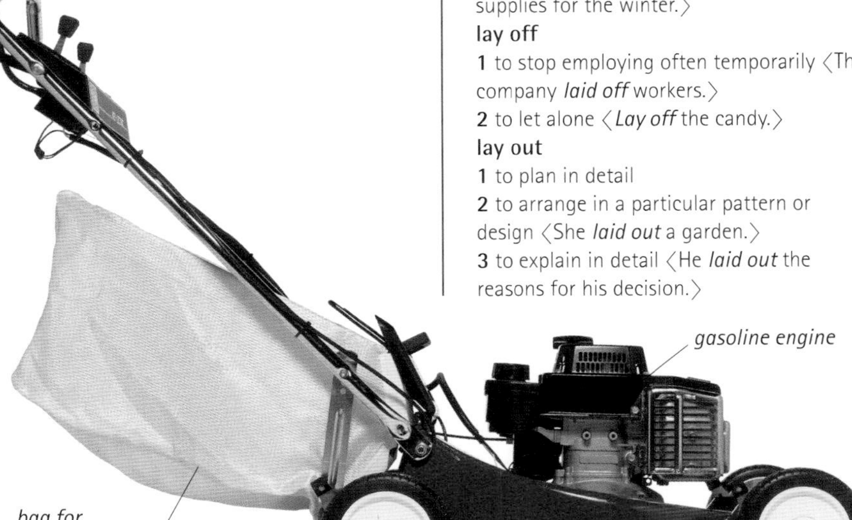

lawn mower: a gasoline-powered lawn mower

lawn tennis *n*
TENNIS

law•suit \ˈlȯ-ˌsüt\ *n*
a process by which a dispute between people or organizations is decided in court

law•yer \ˈlȯ-yər, ˈlȯi-ər\ *n*
a person whose profession is to handle lawsuits for people or to give advice about legal rights and duties

lax \ˈlaks\ *adj*
1 not firm or tight **:** LOOSE ⟨The straps were *lax*.⟩
2 not stern or strict ⟨*lax* discipline⟩
lax•ness *n*

[1]**lax•a•tive** \ˈlak-sə-tiv\ *adj*
tending to relieve constipation

[2]**laxative** *n*
a medicine that relieves constipation

[1]**lay** \ˈlā\ *vb* **laid** \ˈlād\; **lay•ing**
1 to put or set down ⟨I *laid* my hat on the table.⟩
2 to bring down (as with force) ⟨Crops were *laid* flat by the wind.⟩
3 to produce an egg
4 BURY 1
5 to place in position on or along a surface ⟨*lay* tracks⟩
6 PREPARE 1, ARRANGE ⟨*lay* a trap⟩
7 to bring into contact with ⟨He *laid* the watch to his ear.⟩
8 to place a burden, charge, or penalty ⟨*lay* a tax⟩ ⟨He didn't know where to *lay* blame.⟩
lay down to declare forcefully ⟨*lay down* the law⟩
lay eyes on to catch sight of **:** SEE
lay in to store for later use ⟨They *laid in* supplies for the winter.⟩
lay off
1 to stop employing often temporarily ⟨The company *laid off* workers.⟩
2 to let alone ⟨*Lay off* the candy.⟩
lay out
1 to plan in detail
2 to arrange in a particular pattern or design ⟨She *laid out* a garden.⟩
3 to explain in detail ⟨He *laid out* the reasons for his decision.⟩
lay up
1 to store up
2 to disable or confine with illness or injury

[2]**lay** *n*
the way a thing lies in relation to something else ⟨the *lay* of the land⟩

[3]**lay** *past of* LIE

[1]**lay•er** \ˈlā-ər\ *n*
1 ▼ one thickness of something laid over another ⟨a *layer* of rock⟩
2 a person who lays something
3 a bird that lays eggs

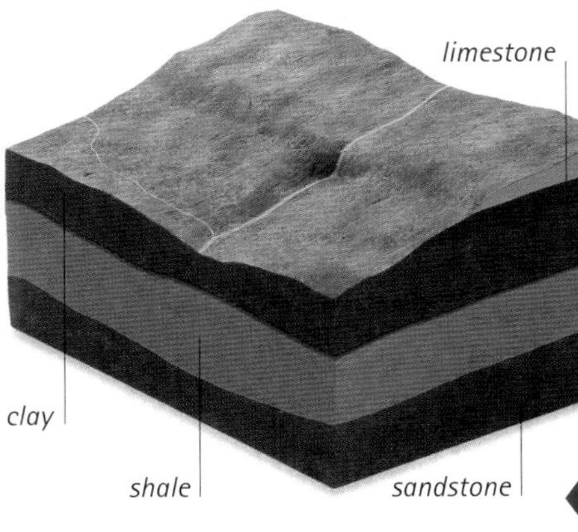

[1]**layer 1:** a cross-section showing rock layers

[2]**layer** *vb* **lay•ered**; **lay•er•ing**
to form or arrange one thickness of something over another

lay•man \ˈlā-mən\ *n, pl* **lay•men** \-mən\
1 a person who is not a member of the clergy
2 a person who is not a member of a certain profession

lay•out \ˈlā-ˌau̇t\ *n*
the design or arrangement of something ⟨the *layout* of the park⟩

lay•per•son \ˈlā-ˌpər-sᵊn\ *n*
LAYMAN 1

laze \ˈlāz\ *vb* **lazed**; **laz•ing**
to spend time relaxing ⟨We *lazed* the day away.⟩

la•zy \ˈlā-zē\ *adj* **la•zi•er**; **la•zi•est**
1 not liking or willing to act or work
2 not having much activity ⟨a *lazy* summer day⟩
3 moving slowly **:** SLUGGISH ⟨a *lazy* stream⟩
la•zi•ly \-zə-lē\ *adv*
la•zi•ness \-zē-nəs\ *n*

lb *abbr* pound
Hint: The abbreviation *lb* is short for the Latin word *libra,* meaning "pound."

leach *vb* **leached**; **leach•ing**
to remove or remove from by the action of a liquid passing through a substance ⟨Water *leaches* minerals from soil.⟩ ⟨The soil was *leached* by the constant rain.⟩

a b c d e f g h i j k l m n o p q r s t u v w x y z

[1]lead \'lēd\ *vb* **led** \'led\; **lead•ing**
1 to guide on a way often by going ahead ⟨You *lead* and we will follow.⟩
2 to be at the head or front part of ⟨She *led* the parade.⟩
3 to direct or guide the actions of ⟨*lead* an orchestra⟩
4 to be best, first, or ahead ⟨The champs *led* by 15 points.⟩
5 to go through : LIVE ⟨They *lead* a happy life.⟩
6 to reach or go in a certain direction ⟨This road *leads* to town.⟩

[2]lead *n*
1 position at the front ⟨He took the *lead.*⟩
2 the amount or distance that a person or thing is ahead ⟨The team had a ten point *lead.*⟩
3 the main role in a movie or play
4 something serving as an indication or clue
5 the first part of a news story

[3]lead \'led\ *n*
1 a heavy soft gray metallic element that is easily bent and shaped
2 a long thin piece of graphite used in pencils
3 AMMUNITION ⟨a shower of *lead*⟩

lead•en \'le-dᵊn\ *adj*
1 made of lead
2 feeling heavy and difficult to move ⟨*leaden* feet⟩
3 of a dull gray color ⟨a *leaden* sky⟩

lead•er \'lē-dər\ *n*
someone or something that leads or is able to lead ⟨a political *leader*⟩
lead•er•ship \-,ship\ *n*

[1]leaf \'lēf\ *n, pl* **leaves** \'lēvz\
1 ▼ one of the usually flat green parts that grow from a plant stem and that functions mainly in making food by photosynthesis
2 FOLIAGE ⟨The trees are in full *leaf.*⟩
3 a single sheet of a book containing a page on each side
4 a part that can be added to or removed from a table top
leaf•less \'lēf-ləs\ *adj*
leaf•like \'lēf-,līk\ *adj*

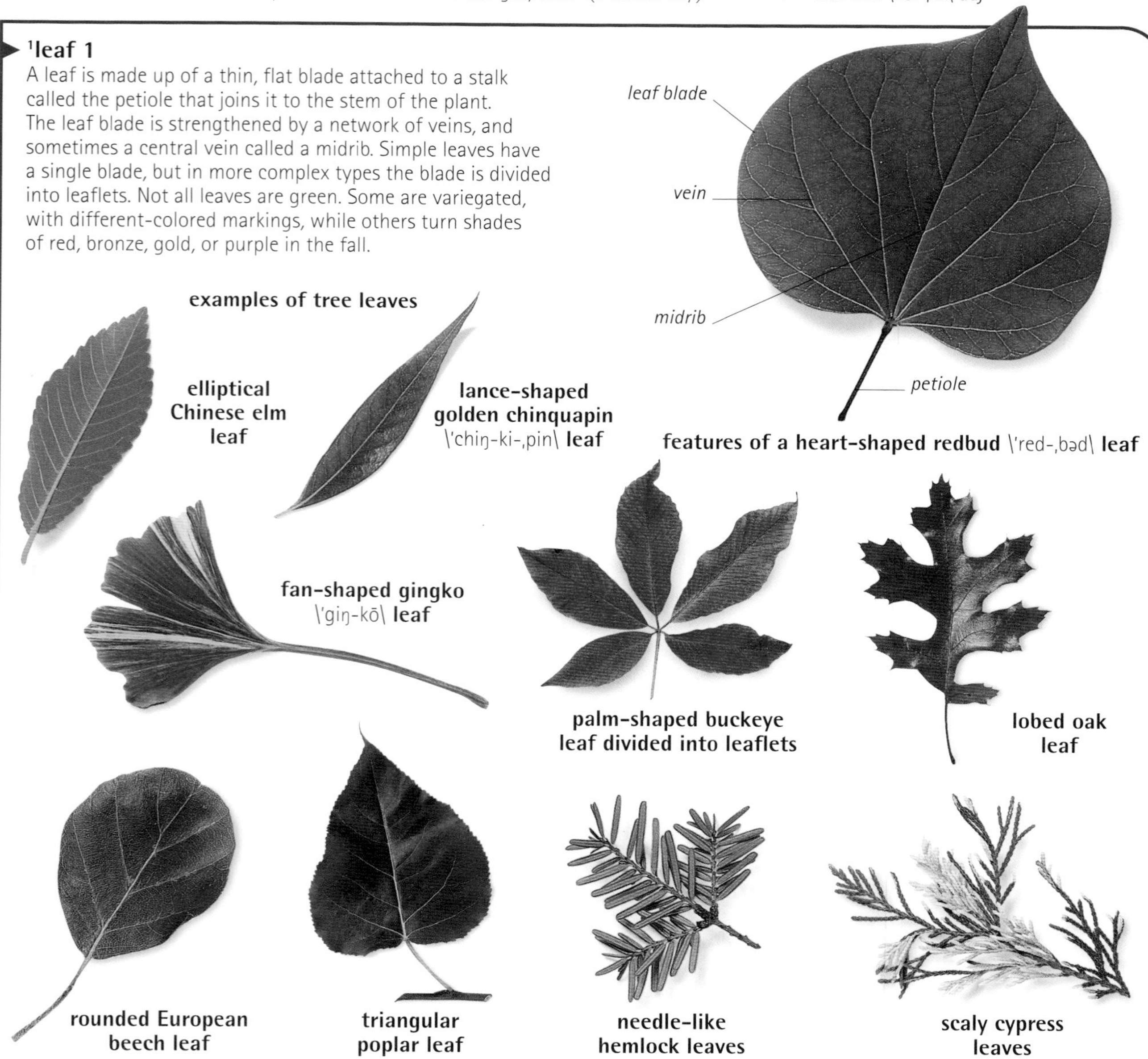

▶ **[1]leaf 1**
A leaf is made up of a thin, flat blade attached to a stalk called the petiole that joins it to the stem of the plant. The leaf blade is strengthened by a network of veins, and sometimes a central vein called a midrib. Simple leaves have a single blade, but in more complex types the blade is divided into leaflets. Not all leaves are green. Some are variegated, with different-colored markings, while others turn shades of red, bronze, gold, or purple in the fall.

[2]leaf *vb* **leafed; leaf•ing**
1 to grow leaves ⟨The trees will *leaf* out in the spring.⟩
2 to turn the pages of a book

leaf•let \ˈlēf-lət\ *n*
1 a printed and often folded sheet of paper that is usually given to people at no cost ⟨an advertising *leaflet*⟩
2 one of the divisions of a leaf which is made up of two or more smaller parts
3 a young or small leaf

leaf•stalk \ˈlēf-ˌstȯk\ *n*
a slender plant part that supports a leaf

leafy \ˈlē-fē\ *adj* **leaf•i•er; leaf•i•est**
having, covered with, or resembling leaves ⟨*leafy* vegetables⟩

[1]league \ˈlēg\ *n*
1 a group of nations working together for a common purpose
2 an association of persons or groups with common interests or goals ⟨a softball *league*⟩
3 an unofficial association or agreement ⟨He was in *league* with the thieves.⟩
4 a class or category of a certain quality or type ⟨When it comes to playing chess, I am not in the same *league* as the experienced players.⟩

[2]league *n*
any of several old units of distance from about 2.4 to 4.6 miles (3.9 to 7.4 kilometers)

[1]leak \ˈlēk\ *vb* **leaked; leak•ing**
1 to enter or escape or let enter or escape through an opening usually by accident ⟨Fumes were *leaking* in.⟩
2 to let a substance or light in or out through an opening ⟨The roof was *leaking.*⟩
3 to make or become known ⟨Don't *leak* this secret.⟩

[2]leak *n*
1 a crack or hole that accidentally lets something pass in or out ⟨I fixed the boat's *leak.*⟩
2 the accidental or secret passing of information ⟨a security *leak*⟩
3 an act or instance of leaking ⟨a slow *leak*⟩

leak•age \ˈlē-kij\ *n*
the act or process of entering or escaping through a crack or hole : LEAK ⟨*leakage* of water⟩

leaky \ˈlē-kē\ *adj* **leak•i•er; leak•i•est**
letting fluid in or out through a crack or hole ⟨a *leaky* roof⟩

[1]lean \ˈlēn\ *vb* **leaned; lean•ing**
1 to bend or tilt from an upright position ⟨*Lean* the ladder against the wall.⟩ ⟨I *leaned* forward.⟩
2 to bend and rest on ⟨You can *lean* on me.⟩
3 DEPEND 1
4 to tend or move toward in opinion, taste, or desire ⟨She *leans* towards city life.⟩

[2]lean *adj* **lean•er; lean•est**
1 having too little flesh : SKINNY ⟨*lean* cattle⟩
2 having little body fat ⟨a *lean* athlete⟩
3 containing very little fat ⟨*lean* meat⟩
4 not large or plentiful ⟨a *lean* harvest⟩
lean•ness *n*

▶ **Synonyms** LEAN, THIN, and SKINNY mean not having a great amount of flesh. LEAN is used of a lack of unnecessary flesh and may also be used for the tough, muscular frame of an athlete. ⟨He has the *lean* body of a runner.⟩ THIN can describe a person having not much flesh or fat and often having an amount less than is desirable for good health. ⟨She's a *thin* and sickly child.⟩ SKINNY suggests a bony, noticeably thin appearance that may indicate poor nourishment. ⟨We found a *skinny* stray cat.⟩

lean–to \ˈlēn-ˌtü\ *n, pl* **lean–tos**
1 a building that has a roof with only one slope and is usually joined to another building
2 a rough shelter that has a roof with only one slope and is held up by posts, rocks, or trees

[1]leap \ˈlēp\ *vb* **leaped** *or* **leapt** \ˈlēpt, ˈlept\; **leap•ing** \ˈlē-piŋ\
1 to jump or cause to jump from a surface ⟨Fish *leaped* out of the water.⟩
2 to move, act, or pass quickly ⟨He *leaped* out of bed.⟩
leap•er \ˈlē-pər\ *n*

[2]leap *n*
1 an act of springing up or over : JUMP
2 a place that is jumped over or from ⟨She took the *leap* with great care.⟩
3 the distance that is jumped ⟨a five foot *leap*⟩

leap•frog \ˈlēp-ˌfrȯg, -ˌfräg\ *n*
▼ a game in which one player bends down and another player leaps over the first player

leapfrog: two girls playing leapfrog

leap year *n*
a year of 366 days with February 29 as the extra day

learn \ˈlərn\ *vb* **learned** \ˈlərnd\ *also* **learnt** \ˈlərnt\; **learn•ing**
1 to get knowledge of or skill in by study, instruction, or experience 〈I'm *learning* a foreign language.〉
2 MEMORIZE 〈Actors have to *learn* their lines.〉
3 to become able through practice 〈Babies *learn* to walk.〉
4 to come to realize and understand 〈You must *learn* right from wrong.〉
5 to find out 〈I finally *learned* what had happened.〉
6 to gain knowledge 〈The children were eager to *learn*.〉
learn•er *n*

learned \ˈlər-nəd\ *adj*
having or showing knowledge or learning 〈a *learned* opinion〉

learn•ing \ˈlər-niŋ\ *n*
1 the act of a person who gains knowledge or skill
2 knowledge or skill gained from teaching or study 〈They're people of great *learning*.〉
synonyms see INFORMATION

learning disability *n*
any of various conditions (as dyslexia) that make learning difficult
learning disabled *adj*

[1]lease \ˈlēs\ *n*
1 an agreement by which a person exchanges property (as a car or house) for a period of time in return for payment or services
2 a piece of property that is leased

[2]lease *vb* **leased**; **leas•ing**
to give or get the use of (property) in return for payment or services

[1]leash \ˈlēsh\ *n*
► a line for holding or controlling an animal

[1]leash:
a woman holding a dog on a leash

[2]leash *vb* **leashed**; **leash•ing**
to put on a line for holding or controlling 〈All dogs must be *leashed*.〉

leather: a satchel made of leather

[1]least \ˈlēst\ *adj, superlative of* [1]LITTLE
smallest in size or degree 〈The *least* noise startles her.〉

[2]least *n*
the smallest or lowest amount or degree 〈I don't mind in the *least*.〉
at least
1 not less or fewer than 〈Read *at least* 20 pages.〉
2 in any case 〈*At least* you have a choice.〉

[3]least *adv, superlative of* [2]LITTLE
in or to the smallest degree 〈You arrived when I *least* expected you.〉

least common denominator *n*
the least common multiple of the denominators of two or more fractions

least common multiple *n*
the smallest number that is a multiple of each of two or more numbers

leath•er \ˈle-t͟hər\ *n*
◄ animal skin that is prepared for use

leath•ery \ˈle-t͟hə-rē\ *adj*
like leather 〈*leathery* skin〉

[1]leave \ˈlēv\ *vb* **left** \ˈleft\; **leav•ing**
1 to go away from 〈Please *leave* the room.〉
2 to cause to remain behind on purpose or without meaning to 〈Oh, no, I *left* my mittens at school.〉 〈*Leave* your money at home.〉
3 to cause or allow to be or remain in a certain condition 〈*Leave* the door open.〉
4 to cause to remain as a trace, mark, or sign 〈The cut *left* a scar.〉
5 to have as a remainder 〈Taking 7 from 10 *leaves* 3.〉
6 to allow to be under another's control 〈*Leave* everything to me.〉
7 to cause to be available 〈*Leave* room for dessert.〉
8 to give by will 〈She *left* property to the children.〉
9 to give up 〈He *left* school before graduating.〉
10 DELIVER 1 〈She *left* the package on the way home.〉

[2]leave *n*
1 permitted absence from duty or work 〈The soldiers were off on *leave*.〉
2 the act of going away and saying good-bye 〈I had to take *leave* of a friend.〉
3 PERMISSION 〈I asked *leave* to speak.〉

leaved \ˈlēvd\ *adj*
having leaves 〈a broad-*leaved* tree〉

leav•en \ˈle-vən\ *vb* **leav•ened**; **leav•en•ing**
to cause to rise by adding something (as baking powder) that produces a gas 〈*leavened* bread〉

leaves *pl of* LEAF

leav•ings \ˈlē-viŋz\ *n pl*
things remaining 〈the *leavings* of dinner〉

[1]lec•ture \ˈlek-chər\ *n*
1 a talk or speech that teaches something
2 a serious talk or scolding

[2]lecture *vb* **lec•tured; lec•tur•ing**
1 to give a talk or speech that teaches something
2 to give a serious or angry talk to 〈Dad *lectured* us about studying.〉
lec•tur•er *n*

led *past and past participle of* LEAD

LED \ˌel-ˌē-ˈdē\ *n*
an electronic device that emits light when power is supplied to it

ledge \ˈlej\ *n*
1 a piece projecting from a top or an edge like a shelf 〈a window *ledge*〉
2 a flat surface that sticks out from a wall of rock

[1]lee \ˈlē\ *n*
1 a protecting shelter
2 the side (as of a ship) sheltered from the wind

[2]lee *adj*
of or relating to the side sheltered from the wind

leech \ˈlēch\ *n*
1 ▼ a bloodsucking worm related to the earthworm
2 a person who stays around other people and uses them for personal gain

► **Word History** Originally the English word *leech* meant "doctor." Centuries ago doctors thought that a good way to cure sick people was to make them bleed. The blood of a sick person supposedly had harmful things in it that would flow away with the blood. To take bad blood out of sick people, early doctors often used little worms that suck blood. *Leech*, the word for a doctor, came to be used for these worms as well.

leech 1

leek \ˈlēk\ *n*
a vegetable having leaves and thick stems which taste like a mild onion

[1]leer \ˈlir\ *vb* **leered; leer•ing**
to look with an unpleasant, mean, or eager glance

[2]leer *n*
an unpleasant, mean, or eager glance

leery \ˈlir-ē\ *adj*
SUSPICIOUS 2, WARY

[1]lee•ward \ˈlē-wərd\ *n*
the side that is sheltered from the wind 〈Sail to the *leeward* of the buoy.〉

[2]leeward *adj*
located on the side that is sheltered from the wind 〈the *leeward* side of the house〉

[1]left \ˈleft\ *adj*
1 located on the same side of the body as the heart 〈the *left* leg〉
2 located nearer to the left side of the body than to the right 〈the *left* side of the road〉
left *adv*

[2]left *n*
the left side : a part or location on or toward the left side 〈Read from *left* to right.〉

[3]left *past and past participle of* LEAVE

left–hand \ˈleft-ˈhand\ *adj*
1 located on the left side 〈the *left-hand* corner of the paper〉
2 LEFT-HANDED

left–hand•ed \ˈleft-ˈhan-dəd\ *adj*
1 using the left hand better or more easily than the right 〈a *left-handed* person〉
2 done or made with or for the left hand 〈a *left-handed* pitch〉 〈a *left-handed* glove〉

left•over \ˈleft-ˌō-vər\ *n*
something (as food) left over

lefty \ˈlef-tē\ *n, pl* **left•ies**
a left-handed person

leg \ˈleg\ *n*
1 ▼ one of the limbs of an animal or person that support the body and are used in walking and running
2 the part of the leg between the knee and the foot
3 something like a leg in shape or use 〈the *legs* of a table〉
4 the part of a garment that covers the leg
5 a stage or part of a journey 〈We started the first *leg* of our trip.〉

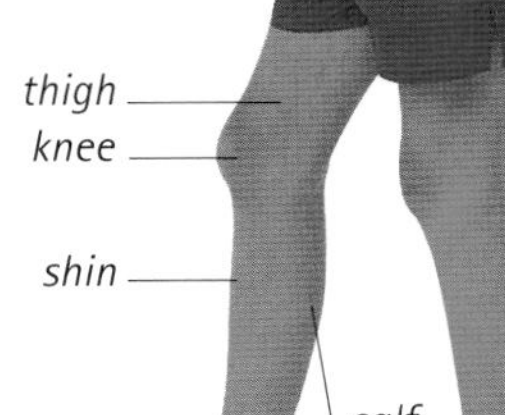

leg 1

leg•a•cy \ˈle-gə-sē\ *n, pl* **leg•a•cies**
1 property (as money) left to a person by a will
2 something (as memories or knowledge) that comes from the past or a person of the past 〈the poet's *legacy*〉

le•gal \ˈlē-gəl\ *adj*
1 of or relating to law or lawyers 〈*legal* books〉
2 based on law 〈a *legal* right〉
3 allowed by law or rules 〈*legal* conduct〉 〈a *legal* play in a game〉
le•gal•ly *adv*

le•gal•ize \ˈlē-gə-ˌlīz\ *vb* **le•gal•ized; le•gal•iz•ing**
to make allowable by law 〈*legalized* gambling〉
le•gal•iza•tion \ˌlē-gə-lə-ˈzā-shən\ *n*

leg•end \ˈle-jənd\ *n*
1 an old story that is widely believed but cannot be proved to be true
2 a person or thing that is very famous for having special qualities or abilities 〈a baseball *legend*〉
3 a list of symbols used (as on a map)

leg•end•ary \ˈle-jən-ˌder-ē\ *adj*
1 told about in legends 〈a *legendary* city〉
2 very famous because of special qualities or abilities 〈a *legendary* musician〉

leg•ged \ˈle-gəd, ˈlegd\ *adj*
having legs especially of a certain kind or number 〈four-*legged*〉

leg•ging \ˈle-gən, ˈle-giŋ\ *n*
an outer covering for the leg usually of cloth or leather 〈a pair of *leggings*〉

leg•i•ble \ˈle-jə-bəl\ *adj*
clear enough to be read 〈*legible* writing〉
leg•i•bly \-blē\ *adv*

le•gion \ˈlē-jən\ *n*
1 a group of from 3000 to 6000 soldiers that made up the chief army unit in ancient Rome
2 ARMY 1
3 a very great number 〈She has a *legion* of admirers.〉

leg•is•late \ˈle-jə-ˌslāt\ *vb* **leg•is•lat•ed; leg•is•lat•ing**
to make laws

leg•is•la•tion \ˌle-jə-ˈslā-shən\ *n*
1 the action of making laws
2 the laws that are made

leg•is•la•tive \ˈle-jə-ˌslā-tiv\ *adj*
1 having the power or authority to make laws 〈the *legislative* branch of government〉
2 of or relating to the action or process by which laws are made 〈*legislative* history〉

leg•is•la•tor \ˈle-jə-ˌslā-ˌtȯr, -ˌslā-tər\ *n*
a person who makes laws and is a member of a legislature

A B C D E F G H I J K L M N O P Q R S T U V W X Y Z

leg•is•la•ture \ˈle-jə-ˌslā-chər\ *n*
a body of persons having the power to make and change laws

le•git•i•mate \li-ˈji-tə-mət\ *adj*
1 accepted by the law as rightful : LAWFUL ⟨a *legitimate* heir⟩
2 being right or acceptable ⟨a *legitimate* excuse⟩
le•git•i•mate•ly *adv*

leg•less \ˈleg-ləs\ *adj*
having no legs

le•gume \ˈle-ˌgyüm\ *n*
any of a large group of plants (as peas, beans, and clover) with fruits that are pods which split into two parts and root nodules containing bacteria that fix nitrogen

lei•sure \ˈlē-zhər\ *n*
free time
at leisure *or* **at someone's leisure**
1 in a way that is not hurried
2 when there is free time available
3 not busy

lei•sure•ly \ˈlē-zhər-lē\ *adj*
UNHURRIED ⟨a *leisurely* walk⟩

lem•on \ˈle-mən\ *n*
1 ▼ an oval yellow fruit with a sour juice that is related to the orange and grows on a small spiny tree
2 something unsatisfactory : DUD

lemon 1

lem•on•ade \ˌle-mə-ˈnād\ *n*
a drink made of lemon juice, sugar, and water

lend \ˈlend\ *vb* **lent** \ˈlent\; **lend•ing**
1 [2]LOAN
2 to give usually for a time ⟨Volunteers *lent* help to flood victims.⟩
3 to add something that improves or makes more attractive ⟨Tomato *lends* color to a salad.⟩
lend•er *n*

length \ˈleŋth\ *n*
1 the measured distance from one end to the other of the longer or longest side of an object
2 a measured distance ⟨The road is three miles in *length*.⟩
3 amount of time something takes ⟨The movie is two hours in *length*.⟩
4 a piece of something that is long ⟨She bought a *length* of pipe.⟩
5 the distance from top to bottom of an article of clothing ⟨knee-*length* pants⟩
6 the sound of a vowel or syllable as it is affected by the time needed to pronounce it
at length
1 very fully ⟨We discussed the problem *at length*.⟩
2 at the end : FINALLY

length•en \ˈleŋ-thən\ *vb* **length•ened**; **length•en•ing**
to make or become longer ⟨*lengthen* a dress⟩

length•ways \ˈleŋth-ˌwāz\ *adv*
LENGTHWISE

length•wise \ˈleŋth-ˌwīz\ *adj or adv*
in the direction of the length ⟨a *lengthwise* fold⟩ ⟨Fold the paper *lengthwise*.⟩

lengthy \ˈleŋ-thē\ *adj* **length•i•er**; **length•i•est**
very long ⟨a *lengthy* argument⟩

le•nient \ˈlē-nē-ənt, ˈlēn-yənt\ *adj*
being kind and patient : not strict ⟨a *lenient* teacher⟩
le•nient•ly *adv*

lens \ˈlenz\ *n*
1 a clear curved piece of material (as glass) used to bend the rays of light to form an image
2 a clear part of the eye behind the pupil and iris that focuses rays of light on the retina to form clear images

len•til \ˈlen-t^{ə}l\ *n*
► the flattened round edible seed of a plant originally of southwestern Asia

Leo \ˈlē-ō\ *n*
1 a constellation between Cancer and Virgo imagined as a lion
2 the fifth sign of the zodiac or a person born under this sign

leopard

leop•ard \ˈle-pərd\ *n*
▲ a large animal of the cat family found in Asia and Africa that has a brownish buff coat with black spots and is an excellent climber

leop•ard•ess \ˈle-pər-dəs\ *n*
a female leopard

le•o•tard \ˈlē-ə-ˌtärd\ *n*
a tight one-piece garment worn by a dancer or acrobat

le•sion \ˈlē-zhən\ *n*
an abnormal spot or area of the body caused by sickness or injury

[1]**less** \ˈles\ *adj, comparative of* [1]LITTLE
1 being fewer ⟨*Less* than ten people showed up.⟩
2 not so much : a smaller amount of ⟨We need *less* talk and more action.⟩

[2]**less** *adv, comparative of* [2]LITTLE
not so much or so well ⟨This quiz is *less* difficult than the last.⟩

[3]**less** *n*
1 a smaller number or amount ⟨They made do with *less*.⟩
2 something that is not as important ⟨You're lucky. I've been grounded for *less*.⟩

[4]**less** *prep*
[1]MINUS 1 ⟨Your cost is the regular price *less* a discount.⟩

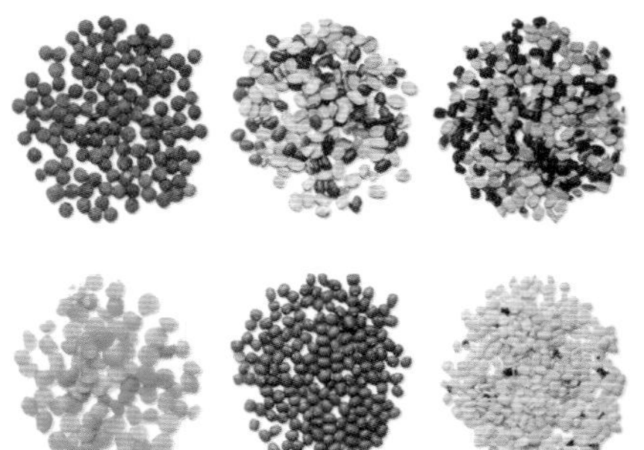
lentil: different types of lentils

-less \ləs\ *adj suffix*
1 not having ⟨friend*less*⟩
2 not able to be acted on or to act in a specified way ⟨cease*less*⟩

less•en \'le-sᵊn\ *vb* **less•ened; less•en•ing**
to make or become fewer or smaller in amount

¹less•er \'le-sər\ *adj*
of smaller size or importance

²lesser *adv*
²LESS ⟨*lesser*-known writers⟩

les•son \'le-sᵊn\ *n*
1 something learned or taught ⟨Travels to other countries taught him valuable *lessons.*⟩
2 a single class or part of a course of instruction ⟨music *lessons*⟩

lest \'lest\ *conj*
for fear that

let \'let\ *vb* **let; let•ting**
1 to allow or permit to ⟨*Let* them go.⟩
2 to allow to go or pass ⟨*Let* me through.⟩
3 to cause to : MAKE ⟨*Let* it be known that I'm not going to confess.⟩
4 ²RENT 2 ⟨rooms to *let*⟩
5 used as a warning ⟨Just *let* him try to do it again!⟩
let alone to leave undisturbed
let down DISAPPOINT ⟨Don't *let* me *down.*⟩
let go
1 to relax or release a grip ⟨Please *let go* of my arm.⟩
2 to dismiss from employment
3 to fail to take care of ⟨They *let* the garden *go.*⟩
let on to admit or reveal
let up
1 to slow down
2 ¹STOP 4, CEASE ⟨The rain has finally *let up.*⟩

-let \lət\ *n suffix*
1 small one ⟨book*let*⟩
2 something worn on ⟨ank*let*⟩

let•down \'let-ˌdau̇n\ *n*
DISAPPOINTMENT 2

let's \'lets\
let us ⟨*Let's* go!⟩

¹let•ter \'le-tər\ *n*
1 one of the marks that are symbols for speech sounds in writing or print and that make up the alphabet
2 ▶ a written or printed communication (as one sent through the mail)
3 **letters** *pl* LITERATURE 2
4 the strict or outward meaning ⟨the *letter* of the law⟩
5 the initial of a school awarded to a student usually for athletic achievement

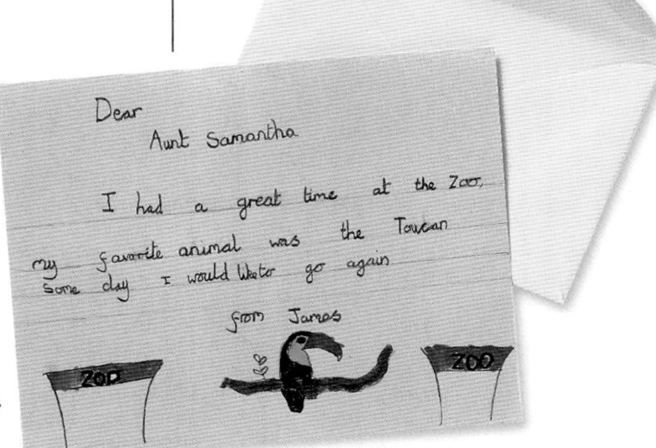

¹letter 2: a thank-you letter from a young child

²letter *vb* **let•tered; let•ter•ing**
to mark with symbols for speech sounds

letter carrier *n*
a person who delivers mail

let•ter•head \'le-tər-ˌhed\ *n*
the name and address of an organization that is printed at the top of a piece of paper used as official stationery

let•ter•ing \'le-tə-riŋ\ *n*
symbols for speech sounds written on something ⟨The sign has fancy *lettering.*⟩

let•tuce \'le-təs\ *n*
▶ a garden plant that has large crisp leaves eaten especially in salads

▶ **Word History** Many kinds of lettuce have a milky white juice. Lettuce owes its name to this fact. The Latin name for lettuce, *lactuca,* from which we get English *lettuce* (through medieval French *letuse*), came from the Latin word for milk, *lac.*

leu•ke•mia \lü-'kē-mē-ə\ *n*
a serious disease in which too many white blood cells are formed

le•vee \'le-vē\ *n*
a bank built along a river to prevent flooding

¹lev•el \'le-vəl\ *n*
1 a horizontal line or surface usually at a named height ⟨Hold it at eye *level.*⟩
2 a step or stage in height, position, or rank ⟨She rose to the *level* of manager.⟩
3 a device used (as by a carpenter) to find a horizontal line or surface

²level *vb* **lev•eled** *or* **lev•elled; lev•el•ing** *or* **lev•el•ling**
to make or become horizontal, flat, or even

³level *adj*
1 having a flat even surface
2 ¹HORIZONTAL
3 of the same height or rank : EVEN
4 steady and cool in judgment ⟨The rescuers kept *level* heads.⟩

lettuce: a head of iceberg lettuce

▶ **Synonyms** LEVEL, FLAT, and EVEN mean having a surface without bends, curves, or interruptions. LEVEL is used especially for a surface or a line that does not slant up or down. ⟨We traveled a *level* road between two hills.⟩ FLAT is used for a surface that is free from curves or bumps or hollows whether or not it is parallel to the ground. ⟨I need a *flat* work surface.⟩ EVEN is used when there is a lack of breaks or bumps in a line or surface. ⟨Dad trimmed the hedge to make it *even.*⟩

¹le•ver \'le-vər, 'lē-\ *n*
1 a bar used to pry or move something
2 a stiff bar for lifting a weight at one point of its length by pressing or pulling at a second point while the bar turns on a support
3 a bar or rod used to run or adjust something ⟨a gearshift *lever*⟩

²lever *vb* **le•vered; le•ver•ing**
to raise or move with a bar

lev•i•tate \'le-və-ˌtāt\ *vb* **lev•i•tat•ed; lev•i•tat•ing**
to rise or make rise up in the air

¹levy \'le-vē\ *n, pl* **lev•ies**
something (as taxes) collected by authority of the law

²levy *vb* **lev•ied; levy•ing**
to collect legally ⟨*levy* taxes⟩

li•a•ble \'lī-ə-bəl\ *adj*
1 LIKELY 1 ⟨It's *liable* to rain.⟩
2 judged by law to be responsible for something ⟨We are *liable* for damage that we do.⟩
3 not sheltered or protected (as from danger or accident) ⟨*liable* to injury⟩

li•ar \'lī-ər\ *n*
a person who tells lies

[1]li•bel \'lī-bəl\ *n*
the publication of a false statement that hurts a person's reputation

[2]libel *vb* **li•beled** *or* **li•belled**; **li•bel•ing** *or* **li•bel•ling**
to hurt a person's reputation by publishing a false statement
li•bel•er *or* **li•bel•ler** *n*

lib•er•al \'li-bə-rəl, 'li-brəl\ *adj*
1 not stingy : GENEROUS ⟨She made a *liberal* donation.⟩
2 not strict ⟨That's a *liberal* interpretation of the rule.⟩
3 BROAD 4 ⟨I got a *liberal* education.⟩
lib•er•al•ly *adv*

lib•er•ate \'li-bə-,rāt\ *vb* **lib•er•at•ed**; **lib•er•at•ing**
to set free

lib•er•ty \'li-bər-tē\ *n, pl* **lib•er•ties**
1 the state of being free : FREEDOM
2 freedom to do as desired ⟨Give the child some *liberty*.⟩
3 the state of not being busy : LEISURE
4 a political right
5 an action that is too free ⟨The movie takes *liberties* with the truth.⟩
at liberty able to act or speak freely ⟨I'm not *at liberty* to discuss the project.⟩

Li•bra \'lē-brə, 'lī-\ *n*
1 a constellation between Virgo and Scorpio imagined as a pair of scales
2 the seventh sign of the zodiac or a person born under this sign

li•brar•i•an \lī-'brer-ē-ən\ *n*
a person in charge of a library

li•brary \'lī-,brer-ē\ *n, pl* **li•brar•ies**
1 a place where literary or reference materials (as books, manuscripts, recordings, or films) are kept for use but are not for sale
2 a collection of literary or reference materials ⟨They have a large personal *library*.⟩

lice *pl of* LOUSE

[1]li•cense *or* **li•cence** \'lī-sᵊns\ *n*
1 permission to do something granted especially by qualified authority ⟨a *license* to sell food⟩
2 a paper, card, or tag showing legal permission ⟨a driver's *license*⟩
3 freedom of action that is carried too far

[2]license *also* **licence** *vb* **li•censed** *also* **li•cenced**; **li•cens•ing** *also* **li•cenc•ing**
to grant formal permission

li•chen \'lī-kən\ *n*
► a plantlike organism made up of an alga and a fungus growing together

[1]lick \'lik\ *vb* **licked**; **lick•ing**
1 to pass the tongue over ⟨I *licked* the spoon.⟩
2 to touch or pass over like a tongue ⟨They saw flames *licking* a wall.⟩
3 to hit again and again : BEAT
4 to get the better of : DEFEAT
lick•ing *n*

[2]lick *n*
1 the act of passing the tongue over
2 a small amount ⟨My sister never did a *lick* of work.⟩
3 a place (**salt lick**) where salt is found or provided for animals

lick•e•ty–split \,li-kə-tē-'split\ *adv*
at top speed

lic•o•rice \'li-kə-rish, -rəs\ *n*
1 the dried root of a European plant or a juice from it used in medicine and in candy
2 candy flavored with licorice

lid \'lid\ *n*
1 a movable cover ⟨the *lid* of a box⟩
2 EYELID
lid•ded \'li-dəd\ *adj*
lid•less \'lid-ləs\ *adj*

[1]lie \'lī\ *vb* **lay** \'lā\; **lain** \'lān\; **ly•ing** \'lī-iŋ\
1 to stretch out or be stretched out ⟨He *lay* on the ground.⟩
2 to be spread flat so as to cover ⟨There was snow *lying* on the fields.⟩
3 to be located or placed ⟨Ohio *lies* east of Indiana.⟩
4 to be or stay ⟨A key *lies* under the mat.⟩

[2]lie *vb* **lied**; **ly•ing**
to say something that is not true in order to deceive someone

[3]lie *n*
something said or done in the hope of deceiving : an untrue statement

liege \'lēj\ *n*
a lord in the time of the Middle Ages

lieu•ten•ant \lü-'te-nənt\ *n*
1 an official who acts for a higher official
2 FIRST LIEUTENANT
3 SECOND LIEUTENANT
4 a commissioned officer in the navy or coast guard ranking above a lieutenant junior grade

lichen: lichen growing on a rock

lieutenant junior grade *n*
a commissioned officer in the navy or coast guard ranking above an ensign

life \'līf\ *n, pl* **lives** \līvz\
1 the state characterized by the ability to get and use energy, reproduce, grow, and respond to change : the quality that plants and animals lose when they die
2 the period during which a person or thing is alive or exists
3 all the experiences that make up the existence of a person : the course of existence ⟨I never heard of such a thing in my *life*!⟩
4 existence as a living being ⟨He saved my *life*.⟩
5 a way of living ⟨We studied the *life* of the ant.⟩
6 the time when something can be used or enjoyed ⟨the *life* of a battery⟩
7 energy and spirit ⟨They gave the party some *life*.⟩
8 BIOGRAPHY

life belt *n*
a life preserver worn like a belt

life•boat \'līf-,bōt\ *n*
a sturdy boat (as one carried by a ship) for use in an emergency

life buoy *n*
▼ a life preserver in the shape of a ring

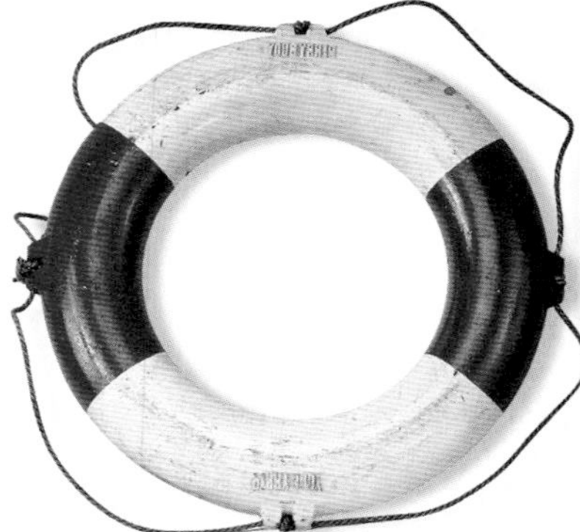
life buoy

life•guard \'līf-,gärd\ *n*
a person employed at a beach or swimming pool to protect swimmers from drowning

life jacket *n*
a life preserver in the form of a vest

life•less \'līf-ləs\ *adj*
1 having no living things ⟨a *lifeless* planet⟩
2 dead or appearing to be dead
3 lacking spirit, interest, or energy ⟨a *lifeless* house⟩

life•like \'līf-,līk\ *adj*
very like something that is alive

A B C D E F G H I J K L M N O P Q R S T U V W X Y Z

life•long \'līf-,lȯŋ\ *adj*
continuing through life ⟨a *lifelong* friendship⟩

life preserver *n*
a device (as a life jacket or life buoy) designed to save a person from drowning by keeping the person afloat

life raft *n*
a small usually rubber boat for use by people forced into the water when a larger boat sinks

life•sav•er \'līf-,sā-vər\ *n*
someone or something that provides greatly needed help

life–size \'līf-'sīz\ *or* **life–sized** \-'sīzd\ *adj*
of natural size : having the same size as the original ⟨a *life-size* portrait⟩

life•style \'līf-'stīl\ *n*
the usual way of life of a person, group, or society ⟨an active *lifestyle*⟩

life•time \'līf-,tīm\ *n*
LIFE 2

life vest *n*
LIFE JACKET

[1]**lift** \'lift\ *vb* **lift•ed**; **lift•ing**
1 to raise from a lower to a higher position, rate, or amount
2 to rise from the ground
3 to move upward and disappear or become scattered ⟨The haze *lifted.*⟩

▶ **Synonyms** LIFT, RAISE, and HOIST mean to move from a lower to a higher place or position. LIFT is used for the act of a bringing up especially from the ground. ⟨*Lift* those boxes onto the table.⟩ RAISE is used when there is a suitable or intended higher position to which something is brought. ⟨*Raise* the flag a little higher.⟩ HOIST means use of pulleys to increase the force applied in raising something very heavy. ⟨*Hoist* the crates onto the ship.⟩

[2]**lift** *n*
1 the action or an instance of picking up and raising ⟨He showed his surprise with a *lift* of his eyebrows.⟩
2 an improved mood or condition
3 a ride in a vehicle ⟨She gave me a *lift* to school.⟩
4 *chiefly British* ELEVATOR 1
5 an upward force (as on an airplane wing) that opposes the pull of gravity

lift•off \'lift-,ȯf\ *n*
a vertical takeoff (as by a rocket)

lig•a•ment \'li-gə-mənt\ *n*
a tough band of tissue that holds bones together or keeps an organ in place in the body

[1]**light** \'līt\ *n*
1 the bright form of energy given off by something (as the sun) that makes it possible to see
2 a source (as a lamp) of light
3 DAYLIGHT 1
4 public knowledge ⟨Facts were brought to *light* during the trial.⟩
5 understanding that comes from information someone has provided ⟨The explanation shed *light* on the problem.⟩

[2]**light** *adj* **light•er**; **light•est**
1 having light : BRIGHT ⟨a *light* room⟩
2 not dark or deep in color

[3]**light** *vb* **lit** \'lit\ *or* **light•ed**; **light•ing**
1 to make or become bright
2 to burn or cause to burn ⟨*light* a match⟩ ⟨*light* the fire⟩

[4]**light** *adj*
1 having little weight : not heavy ⟨a *light* suitcase⟩
2 less in amount or force than usual ⟨a *light* breeze⟩ ⟨a *light* touch⟩
3 not hard to bear, do, pay, or digest ⟨*light* punishment⟩
4 active in motion ⟨I felt *light* on my feet.⟩
5 free from care : HAPPY ⟨a *light* heart⟩
6 not dense and thick ⟨*light* clouds⟩
7 intended mainly to entertain ⟨*light* reading⟩
light•ly *adv*
light•ness *n*

[5]**light** *adv*
with little baggage ⟨I prefer to travel *light.*⟩

[6]**light** *vb* **lit** \'lit\ *or* **light•ed**; **light•ing**
1 [2]PERCH, SETTLE ⟨We saw a bird *light* on a twig.⟩
2 to come by chance ⟨In time I *lit* on a solution.⟩

light bulb *n*
a lamp in which a glow is produced by the heating of a wire by an electric current

[1]**light•en** \'lī-tᵊn\ *vb* **light•ened**; **light•en•ing**
to make or become lighter, brighter, or clearer
light•en•er *n*

[2]**lighten** *vb* **lightened**; **lightening**
1 to make or become less heavy
2 to make less sad or serious ⟨A joke *lightened* the mood.⟩
light•en•er *n*

light•face \'līt-,fās\ *n*
a type having thin lines

light•heart•ed \'līt-'här-təd\ *adj*
free from worry
light•heart•ed•ly *adv*
light•heart•ed•ness *n*

light•house \'līt-,hau̇s\ *n*
▼ a tower that produces a powerful glow to guide sailors at night or in poor visibility

lighthouse: Boston Harbor Light, first built in 1716

light•ing \'līt-iŋ\ *n*
supply of light or of lights ⟨The only *lighting* came through a small window.⟩

light•ning \'līt-niŋ\ *n*
the flashing of light caused by the passing of electricity from one cloud to another or between a cloud and the earth

lightning bug *n*
FIREFLY

light•weight \'līt-,wāt\ *adj*
having less than the usual or expected weight

light–year \'līt-,yir\ *n*
a unit of length in astronomy equal to the distance that light travels in one year or about 5.88 trillion miles (9.46 trillion kilometers)

lik•able *or* **like•able** \'lī-kə-bəl\ *adj*
having pleasant or attractive qualities : easily liked

[1]**like** \'līk\ *vb* **liked**; **lik•ing**
1 ENJOY 1 ⟨My family *likes* games.⟩
2 to feel toward : REGARD ⟨How do you *like* this snow?⟩
3 CHOOSE 3, PREFER ⟨The children did as they *liked*.⟩

[2]**like** *n*
LIKING, PREFERENCE ⟨His *likes* and dislikes are different from hers.⟩

[3]**like** *adj*
SIMILAR, ALIKE ⟨The twins are very *like*.⟩

[4]**like** *prep*
1 similar or similarly to ⟨They act *like* fools.⟩
2 typical of ⟨It is just *like* them to forget.⟩
3 likely to ⟨It looks *like* rain.⟩
4 such as ⟨Choose a color *like* red.⟩
5 close to ⟨The temperature reached something *like* 100 degrees.⟩

[5]**like** *n*
[3]EQUAL, COUNTERPART ⟨We never saw their *like* before.⟩

[6]**like** *conj*
1 AS IF 1 ⟨It looks *like* it might rain.⟩
2 in the same way that : AS ⟨My sister sounds just *like* I do.⟩
3 such as ⟨She often forgets *like* she did yesterday.⟩

-like *adj suffix*
resembling or characteristic of ⟨dog*like*⟩ ⟨a balloon-*like* figure⟩

like•li•hood \'lī-klē-,hùd\ *n*
PROBABILITY 1 ⟨In all *likelihood* we will go.⟩

[1]**like•ly** \'lī-klē\ *adj*
1 very possibly going to happen ⟨That glass is *likely* to fall.⟩
2 seeming to be the truth : BELIEVABLE ⟨That is the most *likely* explanation.⟩
3 giving hope of turning out well : PROMISING ⟨They found a *likely* spot for a picnic.⟩
synonyms see POSSIBLE

[2]**likely** *adv*
without great doubt

lik•en \'lī-kən\ *vb* **lik•ened**; **lik•en•ing**
to describe as similar to : COMPARE ⟨They *liken* their car to a taxi.⟩

like•ness \'līk-nəs\ *n*
1 the state of being similar : RESEMBLANCE
2 a picture of a person : PORTRAIT

like•wise \'līk-,wīz\ *adv*
1 in similar manner ⟨Your sister is helping and you should do *likewise*.⟩
2 ALSO ⟨The new rules will affect you *likewise*.⟩

lik•ing \'lī-kiŋ\ *n*
a feeling of being pleased with someone or something ⟨The soup was too spicy for my *liking*.⟩

li•lac \'lī-,läk, -,lak, -lək\ *n*
1 ▼ a bush having clusters of fragrant pink, purple, or white flowers
2 a medium purple

lilac 1: flowers of a common lilac

lilt \'lilt\ *vb* **lilt•ed**; **lilt•ing**
to sing or play in a lively cheerful manner

lily \'li-lē\ *n, pl* **lil•ies**
a plant (as the **Easter lily** or the **tiger lily**) that grows from a bulb and has a leafy stem and showy funnel-shaped flowers

lily of the valley *n, pl* **lilies of the valley**
a small plant related to the lilies that has usually two leaves and a stalk of fragrant flowers shaped like bells

li•ma bean \'lī-mə-\ *n*
▶ the edible seed of a bean plant that is usually pale green or white

seed

lima bean

limb \'lim\ *n*
1 any of the paired parts (as an arm, wing, or leg) of an animal that stick out from the body and are used mostly in moving and grasping
2 a large branch of a tree
limbed \'limd\ *adj*
limb•less \'lim-ləs\ *adj*

[1]**lim•ber** \'lim-bər\ *adj*
bending easily

[2]**limber** *vb* **lim•bered**; **lim•ber•ing**
to make or become limber ⟨Before a race, I *limber* up with exercises.⟩

[1]**lime** \'līm\ *n*
a small greenish yellow fruit that is related to the lemon and orange

[2]**lime** *n*
a white substance made by heating limestone or shells and used in making plaster and cement and in farming

[3]**lime** *vb* **limed**; **lim•ing**
to treat or cover with a white substance made from limestone or shells

lime•light \'līm-,līt\ *n*
the center of public attention

lim•er•ick \'li-mə-rik\ *n*
a funny poem with five lines

lime•stone \'līm-,stōn\ *n*
▼ a rock formed chiefly from animal remains (as shells or coral) that is used in building and gives lime when burned

limestone

[1]**lim•it** \'li-mət\ *n*
1 a point beyond which it is impossible to go ⟨She runs often, but she knows her *limits*.⟩
2 an amount or number that is the lowest or highest allowed
3 a boundary line ⟨the city *limits*⟩

[2]**limit** *vb* **lim•it•ed**; **lim•it•ing**
to place a control on the size or extent of something ⟨I need to *limit* expenses.⟩

lim•i•ta•tion \,li-mə-'tā-shən\ *n*
1 an act or instance of controlling the size or extent of something
2 something that controls size or extent

lim•it•ed \'li-mə-təd\ *adj*
small in number

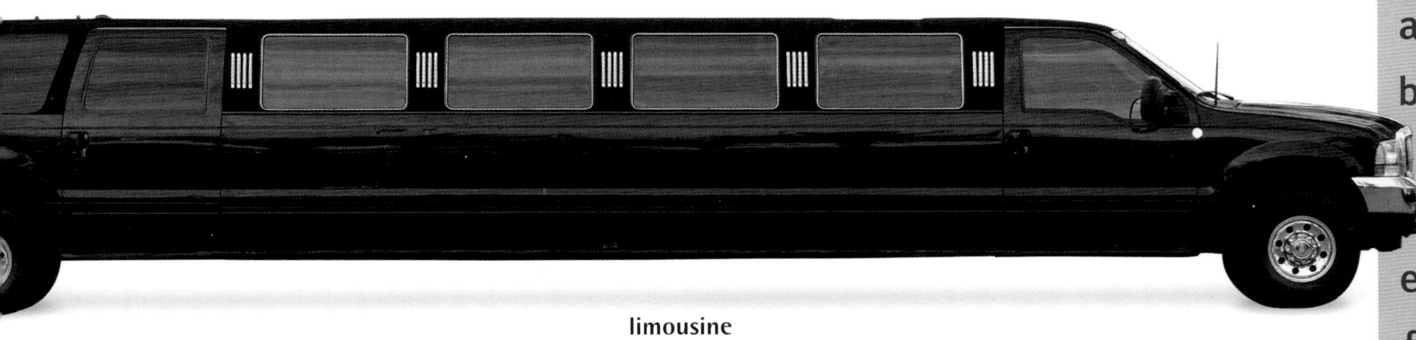

limousine

lim•it•less \'li-mət-ləs\ *adj*
having no boundaries : very numerous or large ⟨The possibilities are *limitless.*⟩

lim•ou•sine \'li-mə-,zēn, ,li-mə-'zēn\ *n*
▲ a large luxurious automobile often driven by a chauffeur

[1]**limp** \'limp\ *vb* **limped**; **limp•ing**
to walk in a slow or uneven way because of an injury to a foot or leg

[2]**limp** *n*
a slow or uneven way of walking caused by an injury to a leg or foot

[3]**limp** *adj*
not firm or stiff
limp•ly *adv*

lim•pid \'lim-pəd\ *adj*
perfectly clear ⟨*limpid* water⟩

lin•den \'lin-dən\ *n*
a shade tree with heart-shaped leaves and drooping clusters of yellowish white flowers

[1]**line** \'līn\ *n*
1 ▶ a long thin cord or rope ⟨fishing *lines*⟩ ⟨Hang your clothes on the *line.*⟩
2 a long narrow mark
3 an arrangement of people or things in a row
4 a row of letters, words, or musical notes across a page or column
5 the boundary or limit of a place ⟨the town *line*⟩
6 FAMILY 2 ⟨He comes from a long *line* of farmers.⟩
7 a way of behaving or thinking ⟨He took a firm *line* with his son.⟩
8 [1]OUTLINE 1, CONTOUR ⟨The sailboat has beautiful *lines.*⟩
9 an area of activity or interest ⟨What *line* of work are you in?⟩
10 the position of military forces who are facing the enemy
11 a pipe carrying a fluid (as steam, water, or oil)
12 an outdoor wire carrying electricity or a telephone signal
13 lines *pl* the words of a part in a play
14 the path along which something moves or is directed ⟨It's in my *line* of vision.⟩
15 the track of a railway
16 AGREEMENT 1, HARMONY ⟨They tried to bring their ideas into *line.*⟩
17 a system of transportation ⟨a bus *line*⟩
18 the football players whose positions are along the line of scrimmage
19 a geometric element produced by moving a point
20 a plan for making or doing something ⟨I wrote a story along these *lines.*⟩

[2]**line** *vb* **lined**; **lin•ing**
1 to indicate with or draw a long narrow mark
2 to place or be placed in a row along ⟨Shops *line* the street.⟩
line up
1 to gather or arrange in a row or rows ⟨The children *lined up.*⟩
2 to put into alignment ⟨Make sure the pieces *line up.*⟩

[1]**line 1:** clothes hanging on lines

[3]**line** *vb* **lined**; **lin•ing**
to cover the inner surface of ⟨*line* a coat⟩

lin•eage \'li-nē-ij\ *n*
1 the ancestors from whom a person is descended
2 people descended from the same ancestor

lin•ear \'li-nē-ər\ *adj*
1 made up of, relating to, or like a line : STRAIGHT
2 involving a single dimension

lin•en \'li-nən\ *n*
1 smooth strong cloth or yarn made from flax
2 household articles (as tablecloths or sheets) or clothing that were once often made of linen

line of scrimmage *n*
an imaginary line in football parallel to the goal lines and running through the place where the ball is laid before each play begins

li•ner \'lī-nər\ *n*
something that covers or is used to cover the inner surface of another thing

line segment *n*
SEGMENT 3

line•up \'līn-,əp\ *n*
1 a list of players taking part in a game (as baseball)
2 a row of persons arranged especially for police identification

-ling \liŋ\ *n suffix*
1 one associated with ⟨nest*ling*⟩
2 young, small, or minor one ⟨duck*ling*⟩

lin•ger \'liŋ-gər\ *vb* **lin•gered**; **lin•ger•ing**
1 to be slow in leaving : DELAY ⟨We *lingered* at the park.⟩
2 to continue to exist as time passes

lin•guist \'liŋ-gwist\ *n*
1 a person skilled in languages
2 a person who specializes in the study of human speech

lin•guis•tics \liŋ-'gwis-tiks\ *n*
the study of human speech including the nature, structure, and development of language or of a language or group of languages

A B C D E F G H I J K L M N O P Q R S T U V W X Y Z

lin•i•ment \'li-nə-mənt\ *n*
a liquid medicine rubbed on the skin to ease pain

lin•ing \'lī-niŋ\ *n*
material that covers an inner surface ⟨a coat *lining*⟩

¹link \'liŋk\ *n*
1 a single ring of a chain
2 something that connects : CONNECTION ⟨Is there a *link* between dinosaurs and birds?⟩
3 HYPERLINK

²link *vb* **linked**; **link•ing**
1 to physically join or connect ⟨The towns are *linked* by a road.⟩
2 to show or suggest a connection ⟨A gang was *linked* to the crime.⟩

linking verb *n*
an intransitive verb that connects a subject with a word or words in the predicate ⟨The words "look" in "you look tired" and "are" in "my favorite fruits are apples and oranges" are *linking verbs.*⟩

li•no•leum \lə-'nō-lē-əm, -'nōl-yəm\ *n*
a floor covering with a canvas back and a surface of hardened linseed oil and cork dust

lin•seed \'lin-,sēd\ *n*
FLAXSEED

linseed oil *n*
a yellowish oil obtained from flaxseed

lint \'lint\ *n*
1 loose bits of thread
2 COTTON 1

► **Word History** *Lint* is usually something we try to get rid of—from our clothes, or from the lint filters of clothes dryers. Centuries ago, however, soft bits of fuzz and fluff—in Middle English *lint* or *lynet*—were considered useful as a dressing for wounds, and were collected by scraping the fuzz off linen cloth. The origin of the word *lint* is uncertain, though it surely has some relationship to Middle English *lin*, "flax" or "cloth made from flax, linen."

lin•tel \'lin-tᵊl\ *n*
a horizontal piece or part across the top of an opening (as of a door) to carry the weight of the structure above it

li•on \'lī-ən\ *n*
► a large meat-eating animal of the cat family that has a brownish buff coat, a tufted tail, and in the male a shaggy mane and that lives in Africa and southern Asia

li•on•ess \'lī-ə-nəs\ *n*
a female lion

lip \'lip\ *n*
1 either of the two folds of flesh that surround the mouth
2 the edge of a hollow container (as a jar) especially where it is slightly spread out
3 an edge (as of a wound) like or of flesh
4 an edge that sticks out ⟨the *lip* of a roof⟩
lipped \'lipt\ *adj*

lip•stick \'lip-,stik\ *n*
▼ a waxy solid colored cosmetic for the lips usually in stick form

lipstick

liq•ue•fy \'li-kwə-,fī\ *vb* **liq•ue•fied**; **liq•ue•fy•ing**
to make or become liquid

¹liq•uid \'li-kwəd\ *adj*
1 flowing freely like water ⟨*liquid* detergent⟩
2 neither solid nor gaseous
3 clear and smooth or shining ⟨*liquid* eyes⟩
4 made up of or easily changed into cash ⟨*liquid* investments⟩

²liquid *n*
a substance that flows freely like water

liq•uor \'li-kər\ *n*
a strong alcoholic beverage

¹lisp \'lisp\ *vb* **lisped**; **lisp•ing**
to pronounce the sounds \s\ and \z\ as \th\ and \th\

²lisp *n*
the act or habit of pronouncing the sounds \s\ and \z\ as \th\ and \th\

¹list \'list\ *n*
a series of items written, mentioned, or considered one following another

²list *vb* **list•ed**; **list•ing**
to put in a series of items

³list *vb* **listed**; **listing**
to lean to one side ⟨The ship is badly *listing.*⟩

⁴list *n*
a leaning over to one side

lis•ten \'li-sᵊn\ *vb* **lis•tened**; **lis•ten•ing**
1 to pay attention in order to hear ⟨Are you *listening* to me?⟩
2 to hear and consider seriously ⟨He *listened* to his father's advice.⟩
lis•ten•er \'lis-nər, 'li-sᵊn-ər\ *n*

list•less \'list-ləs\ *adj*
too tired or too little interested to want to do things
list•less•ly *adv*
list•less•ness *n*

lit *past and past participle of* LIGHT

li•ter \'lē-tər\ *n*
a metric unit of liquid capacity equal to 1.057 quarts

lit•er•al \'li-tə-rəl\ *adj*
1 following the ordinary or usual meaning of the words ⟨I'm using the word in its *literal*, not figurative, sense.⟩
2 true to fact ⟨She gave a *literal* account of what she saw.⟩
lit•er•al•ly *adv*
lit•er•al•ness *n*

lit•er•ary \'li-tə-,rer-ē\ *adj*
of or relating to literature

lion: a family of lions

lit•er•ate \'li-tə-rət\ *adj*
1 able to read and write
2 having gotten a good education

lit•er•a•ture \'li-tə-rə-ˌchu̇r\ *n*
1 written works considered as having high quality and ideas of lasting and widespread interest
2 written material ⟨travel *literature*⟩

lithe \'līth, 'līth\ *adj*
1LIMBER, SUPPLE ⟨*lithe* dancers⟩

lith•o•sphere \'li-thə-ˌsfir\ *n*
the outer part of the solid earth

lit•mus paper \'lit-məs-\ *n*
paper treated with coloring matter that turns red in the presence of an acid and blue in the presence of a base

1lit•ter \'li-tər\ *n*
1 ▼ the young born to an animal at a single time ⟨a *litter* of pigs⟩
2 a messy collection of things scattered about : TRASH
3 material used to soak up the urine and feces of animals

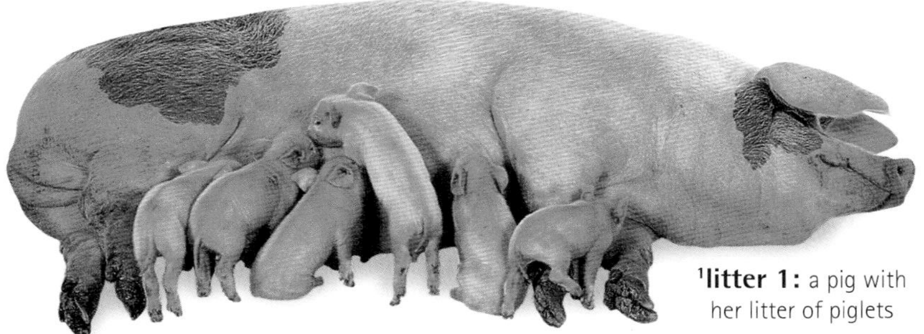

1litter 1: a pig with her litter of piglets

4 a covered and curtained couch having poles and used for carrying a single passenger
5 a stretcher for carrying a sick or wounded person

► **Word History** The different meanings of the word *litter* all grew out of the basic notion "bed." In Old French, *litiere*, a derivative of *lit*, "bed," could refer to a sleeping place in a general way, but it was more typically applied to either a curtained portable couch, or to straw spread on the ground as a sleeping place for animals. In borrowing the word, English kept both usages and added new ones. The "bedding for animals" sense was extended to the offspring of an animal such as a dog. In a different direction, *litter* became not just straw for animal bedding, but straw or similar material spread around for any purpose, and by the 1700s any odds and ends of rubbish lying scattered about.

2litter *vb* **lit•tered; lit•ter•ing**
1 to throw or leave trash on the ground
2 to cover in an untidy way ⟨Leaves *littered* the yard.⟩

lit•ter•bug \'li-tər-ˌbəg\ *n*
a person who carelessly scatters trash in a public area

1lit•tle \'li-tᵊl\ *adj* **lit•tler** \'lit-lər\ *or* **less** \'les\; **lit•tlest** \'lit-ləst\ *or* **least** \'lēst\
1 small in size ⟨a *little* house⟩
2 small in quantity ⟨They had *little* food to eat.⟩
3 1YOUNG 1 ⟨*little* children⟩
4 short in duration or extent ⟨We had a *little* chat.⟩
5 small in importance ⟨It's a *little* problem.⟩
6 1NARROW 3

2little *adv* **less** \'les\; **least** \'lēst\
in a very small quantity or degree ⟨The history is *little* known.⟩
little by little by small steps or amounts : GRADUALLY

3little *n*
a small amount or quantity

Little Dipper *n*
a group of seven stars in the northern sky arranged in a form like a dipper with the North Star forming the tip of the handle

little finger *n*
the shortest finger of the hand farthest from the thumb

lit•ur•gy \'li-tər-jē\ *n, pl* **lit•ur•gies**
a religious rite or body of rites
li•tur•gi•cal \lə-'tər-ji-kəl\ *adj*

1live \'liv\ *vb* **lived; liv•ing**
1 to be alive
2 to continue in life ⟨My grandmother *lived* to the age of 98.⟩
3 DWELL 1
4 to spend life ⟨Let them *live* in peace.⟩
live it up to live with great enthusiasm and excitement
live up to to be good enough to satisfy expectations

2live \'līv\ *adj*
1 having life : ALIVE
2 broadcast at the time of production ⟨a *live* television program⟩
3 charged with an electric current ⟨a *live* wire⟩
4 burning usually without flame ⟨*live* coals⟩
5 not exploded ⟨a *live* bomb⟩

live•li•hood \'līv-lē-ˌhu̇d\ *n*
2LIVING 3

live•long \'liv-ˌlȯŋ\ *adj*
during all of ⟨We worked the *livelong* day.⟩

live•ly \'līv-lē\ *adj* **live•li•er; live•li•est**
1 full of life : ACTIVE ⟨a *lively* puppy⟩
2 showing or resulting from active thought ⟨a *lively* imagination⟩
3 full of spirit or feeling : ANIMATED ⟨*lively* music⟩
live•li•ness *n*

liv•en \'lī-vən\ *vb* **liv•ened; liv•en•ing**
to make or become lively
Hint: *Liven* is often used with *up*.

live oak \'līv-\ *n*
any of several American oaks that have evergreen leaves

liv•er \'li-vər\ *n*
a large gland in the body that has a rich blood supply, secretes bile, and helps in storing some nutrients and in forming some body wastes

liv•er•ied \'li-və-rēd\ *adj*
wearing a special uniform ⟨a *liveried* servant⟩

liv•er•wort \'li-vər-ˌwərt, -ˌwȯrt\ *n*
▼ a flowerless plant that resembles a moss

liverwort: a clump of liverwort

liv•ery \'li-və-rē, 'liv-rē\ *n, pl* **liv•er•ies**
1 a special uniform worn by the servants of a wealthy household
2 the business of keeping horses and vehicles for hire : a place (**livery stable**) that keeps horses and vehicles for hire

lives *pl of* LIFE

live•stock \'līv-ˌstäk\ *n*
animals (as cows, horses, and pigs) kept or raised especially on a farm and for profit

lizard
More than half of the world's reptiles are lizards, and they live in habitats as varied as mountains, seashores, deserts, and rain forests. Cold-blooded reptiles, many lizards enjoy basking in the sun — although there are also lizards that live underground or prefer to be active at night. Some lizards eat plants, but most feed on small animals such as insects. Lizards vary greatly in size, and there are even species, such as glass snakes, that have no legs and resemble snakes.

features of a chameleon

examples of lizards

green iguana
from tropical America eats plants, although its young also eat insects

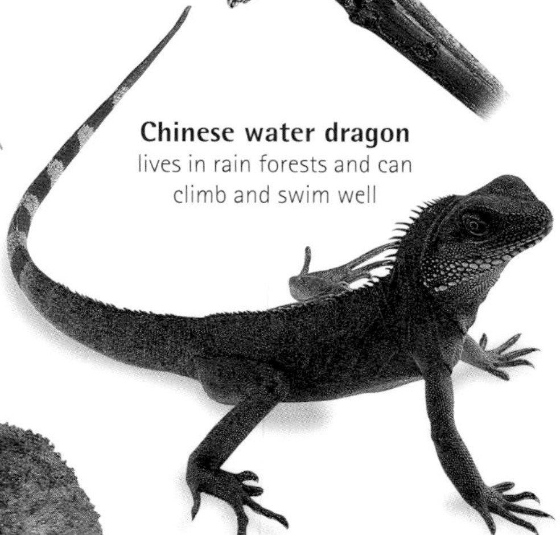

Chinese water dragon
lives in rain forests and can climb and swim well

bearded dragon
lives in the deserts of Australia and obtains water from food and dew

green anole \ə-ˈnō-lē\ **lizard**
from the southeastern US displays its inflated dewlap to other males who threaten its territory

frilled \ˈfrild\ **lizard**
from Australia tries to scare off predators by erecting a large fan of skin

basilisk \ˈba-sə-ˌlisk\ **lizard**
from tropical America can run across water on its hind legs

savannah monitor lizard
from Africa has a forked tongue and sometimes lives in termite mounds

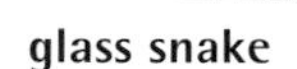

glass snake
is found in Africa, Asia, Europe, and southern US, and is a lizard without legs

live wire *n*
an alert active person

liv•id \'li-vəd\ *adj*
1 very angry
2 pale as ashes ⟨Her face was *livid* with fear.⟩
3 discolored by bruising

[1]liv•ing \'li-viŋ\ *adj*
1 not dead : ALIVE ⟨We're his closest *living* relatives.⟩
2 true to life ⟨You are the *living* image of your parents.⟩

[2]living *n*
1 the condition of being alive
2 conduct or manner of life ⟨healthy *living*⟩
3 what a person has to have to meet basic needs ⟨She made a *living* as a cook.⟩

living room *n*
a room in a house for general family use

liz•ard \'li-zərd\ *n*
◀ a reptile with movable eyelids, ears that are outside the body, and usually four legs

lla•ma \'lä-mə\ *n*
▼ a South American hoofed animal that has a long neck, is related to the camel, and is sometimes used to carry loads and as a source of wool

llama: a man from Peru with a llama

lo \'lō\ *interj*
used to call attention or to show wonder or surprise ⟨*Lo*, an angel appears.⟩

[1]load \'lōd\ *n*
1 something lifted up and carried : BURDEN
2 the quantity of material put into a device at one time ⟨He washed a *load* of clothes.⟩
3 a large number or amount
4 a mass or weight supported by something
5 something that causes worry or sadness
6 a charge for a firearm

lobby: a hotel lobby

[2]load *vb* **load•ed**; **load•ing**
1 to put a load in or on ⟨They *loaded* the truck.⟩
2 to supply abundantly ⟨Newspapers *loaded* her with praise.⟩
3 to put something into a device so it can be used ⟨You have to *load* film into the camera.⟩
load•er *n*

[1]loaf \'lōf\ *n, pl* **loaves** \'lōvz\
1 a usually oblong mass of bread
2 a dish (as of meat) baked in an oblong form

[2]loaf *vb* **loafed**; **loaf•ing**
to spend time idly or lazily ⟨During vacation I will *loaf* on the beach.⟩
loaf•er *n*

loam \'lōm\ *n*
a soil having the appropriate amount of silt, clay, and sand for good plant growth

loamy \'lō-mē\ *adj* **loam•i•er**; **loam•i•est**
made up of or like rich soil

[1]loan \'lōn\ *n*
1 money given with the understanding that it will be paid back
2 something given for a time to a borrower ⟨That's not mine, it's a *loan*.⟩
3 permission to use something for a time

[2]loan *vb* **loaned**; **loan•ing**
to give to another for temporary use with the understanding that the same or a like thing will be returned ⟨*loan* a book⟩ ⟨*loan* money⟩

loath *also* **loth** \'lōth, 'lō<u>th</u>\ *adj*
not willing

loathe \'lō<u>th</u>\ *vb* **loathed**; **loath•ing**
to dislike greatly

loathing *n*
very great dislike

loath•some \'lōth-səm, 'lō<u>th</u>-\ *adj*
very unpleasant : OFFENSIVE

loaves *pl of* LOAF

[1]lob \'läb\ *vb* **lobbed**; **lob•bing**
to send (as a ball) in a high arc by hitting or throwing easily

[2]lob *n*
an act of throwing or hitting (as a ball) in a high arc

lob•by \'lä-bē\ *n, pl* **lobbies**
▲ a hall or entry especially when large enough to serve as a waiting room ⟨a hotel *lobby*⟩

lobe \'lōb\ *n*
a rounded part ⟨a *lobe* of a leaf⟩ ⟨the *lobe* of the ear⟩
lobed \'lōbd\ *adj*

lob•ster \'läb-stər\ *n*
a large edible sea animal that is a crustacean with five pairs of legs of which the first pair usually has large claws

[1]lo•cal \'lō-kəl\ *adj*
of, in, or relating to a particular place ⟨*local* kids⟩ ⟨*local* business⟩ ⟨*local* news⟩
lo•cal•ly *adv*

[2]local *n*
1 a public vehicle (as a bus or train) that makes all or most stops on its run
2 a branch (as of a lodge or labor union) in a particular place

local area network *n*
a computer network that covers a small area (as an office building or a home)

lo•cal•i•ty \lō-'ka-lə-tē\ *n, pl* **lo•cal•i•ties**
a place and its surroundings

lo•cal•ize \'lō-kə-,līz\ *vb* **lo•cal•ized**; **lo•cal•iz•ing**
to keep or be kept in a certain area

A B C D E F G H I J K L M N O P Q R S T U V W X Y Z

lo•cate \'lō-,kāt\ *vb* **lo•cat•ed**; **lo•cat•ing**
1 to find the position of ⟨Try to *locate* your neighborhood on the map.⟩
2 to settle or establish in a particular place ⟨The city *located* the new stadium downtown.⟩

lo•ca•tion \lō-'kā-shən\ *n*
1 the act or process of establishing in or finding a particular place ⟨Fog made *location* of the ship difficult.⟩
2 ¹PLACE 5, POSITION

¹lock \'läk\ *n*
a small bunch of hair or of fiber (as cotton or wool)

²lock *n*
1 a fastening (as for a door) in which a bolt is operated (as by a key)
2 the device for exploding the charge or cartridge of a firearm
3 ▼ an enclosure (as in a canal) with gates at each end used in raising or lowering boats as they pass from level to level

³lock *vb* **locked**; **lock•ing**
1 to fasten with or as if with a lock
2 to shut in or out by or as if by means of a lock
3 to make unable to move by linking parts together

lock•er \'lä-kər\ *n*
a cabinet, compartment, or chest for personal use or for storing frozen food at a low temperature

locker room *n*
a room where sports players change clothes and store equipment in lockers

lock•et \'lä-kət\ *n*
a small ornamental case usually worn on a chain

lock•jaw \'läk-,jȯ\ *n*
TETANUS

lock•smith \'läk-,smith\ *n*
a worker who makes or repairs locks

lock•up \'läk-,əp\ *n*
PRISON

²lock 3: locks on a waterway

lo•co•mo•tion \,lō-kə-'mō-shən\ *n*
the act or power of moving from place to place

lo•co•mo•tive \,lō-kə-'mō-tiv\ *n*
a vehicle that moves under its own power and is used to haul cars on a railroad

lo•cust \'lō-kəst\ *n*
1 ▼ a grasshopper that moves in huge swarms and eats up the plants in its path
2 CICADA
3 a tree with hard wood, leaves with many leaflets, and drooping flower clusters

locust 1

lode•stone \'lōd-,stōn\ *n*
a magnetic rock

¹lodge \'läj\ *vb* **lodged**; **lodg•ing**
1 to provide a temporary living or sleeping space for ⟨They *lodged* guests for the night.⟩
2 to use a place for living or sleeping ⟨We *lodged* in motels.⟩
3 to become stuck or fixed ⟨The arrow *lodged* in a tree.⟩
4 ³FILE 2 ⟨I'm *lodging* a complaint.⟩

²lodge *n*
1 a house set apart for residence in a special season or by an employee on an estate ⟨a hunting *lodge*⟩ ⟨the caretaker's *lodge*⟩
2 a den or resting place of an animal ⟨a beaver's *lodge*⟩
3 the meeting place of a social organization

lodg•er \'lä-jər\ *n*
a person who lives in a rented room in another's house

lodging \'lä-jiŋ\ *n*
1 a temporary living or sleeping place
2 **lodgings** *pl* a room or rooms in the house of another person rented as a place to live

loft \'lȯft\ *n*
1 an upper room or upper story of a building
2 a balcony in a church
3 an upper part of a barn

lofty \'lȯf-tē\ *adj* **loft•i•er**; **loft•i•est**
1 rising to a great height ⟨*lofty* trees⟩
2 of high rank or admirable quality ⟨*lofty* lineage⟩ ⟨He set *lofty* goals.⟩
3 showing a proud and superior attitude
synonyms see HIGH
loft•i•ly \-tə-lē\ *adv*
loft•i•ness \-tē-nəs\ *n*

[1]**log** \'lȯg, 'läg\ *n*
1 ▶ a large piece of a cut or fallen tree
2 a long piece of a tree trunk ready for sawing
3 the record of a ship's voyage or of an aircraft's flight ⟨the captain's *log*⟩
4 a record of performance, events, or daily activities ⟨a computer *log*⟩

[2]**log** *vb* **logged**; **log•ging**
1 to engage in cutting trees for timber
2 to make an official record of
log off *or* **log out** to end the connection of a computer to a system or network
log on *or* **log in** to start the connection of a computer to a system or network

log•ger•head \'lȯ-gər-ˌhed, 'lä-\ *n*
a very large sea turtle found in the warmer parts of the Atlantic Ocean

log•ic \'lä-jik\ *n*
1 a proper or reasonable way of thinking about something : sound reasoning ⟨There's no *logic* in what you said.⟩
2 a science that deals with the rules and processes used in sound thinking and reasoning

log•i•cal \'lä-ji-kəl\ *adj*
1 according to a proper or reasonable way of thinking ⟨a *logical* argument⟩
2 according to what is reasonably expected ⟨the *logical* result⟩
log•i•cal•ly *adv*

-logy *n suffix*
area of knowledge : science ⟨bio*logy*⟩

loin \'lȯin\ *n*
1 the part of the body between the hip and the lower ribs
2 a piece of meat (as beef) from the loin of an animal

loi•ter \'lȯi-tər\ *vb* **loi•tered**; **loi•ter•ing**
1 to hang around somewhere for no good reason
2 to dawdle on the way to somewhere ⟨Don't *loiter* on your way home.⟩
loi•ter•er *n*

loll \'läl\ *vb* **lolled**; **loll•ing**
1 to hang loosely : DROOP ⟨His head *lolled* to one side.⟩
2 to lie around lazily ⟨We *lolled* by the pool.⟩

lol•li•pop *or* **lol•ly•pop** \'lä-lē-ˌpäp\ *n*
a round piece of hard candy on the end of a stick

lone \'lōn\ *adj*
1 having no companion ⟨a *lone* traveler⟩
2 situated by itself ⟨a *lone* outpost⟩

lone•ly \'lōn-lē\ *adj* **lone•li•er**; **lone•li•est**
1 LONE 1 ⟨I saw a *lonely* figure in the distance.⟩
2 not often visited ⟨a *lonely* spot⟩
3 sad from being alone : LONESOME ⟨a *lonely* child⟩
4 producing sad feelings from being alone ⟨I spent a *lonely* evening at home.⟩
synonyms see ALONE
lone•li•ness *n*

[1]**log 1:** stacks of logs at a sawmill

lone•some \'lōn-səm\ *adj*
1 sad from being without companions
2 not often visited or traveled over ⟨the *lonesome* frontier⟩

[1]**long** \'lȯŋ\ *adj* **lon•ger** \'lȯŋ-gər\; **lon•gest** \'lȯŋ-gəst\
1 of great length from end to end : not short ⟨a *long* hallway⟩
2 lasting for some time : not brief ⟨a *long* friendship⟩ ⟨a *long* wait⟩
3 being more than the usual length ⟨a *long* book⟩
4 having a stated length (as in distance or time) ⟨40 feet *long*⟩ ⟨an hour *long*⟩
5 of, relating to, or being one of the vowel sounds \ā, ē, ī, ō, ü\ and sometimes \ä\ and \ȯ\

[2]**long** *adv*
1 for or during a long time ⟨Were you away *long*?⟩
2 for the whole length of ⟨I slept all night *long*.⟩
3 at a distant point of time ⟨*long* ago⟩

[3]**long** *n*
a long time ⟨They'll be here before *long*.⟩

[4]**long** *vb* **longed**; **long•ing**
to wish for something very much ⟨He *longed* to see his family again.⟩
synonyms see YEARN

long division *n*
division in arithmetic that involves several steps that are written out

long•hand \'lȯŋ-ˌhand\ *n*
HANDWRITING

long•horn \'lȯŋ-ˌhȯrn\ *n*
▼ a cow with very long horns that was once common in the southwestern United States

long–horned \'lȯŋ-'hȯrnd\ *adj*
having long horns or antennae ⟨a *long-horned* beetle⟩

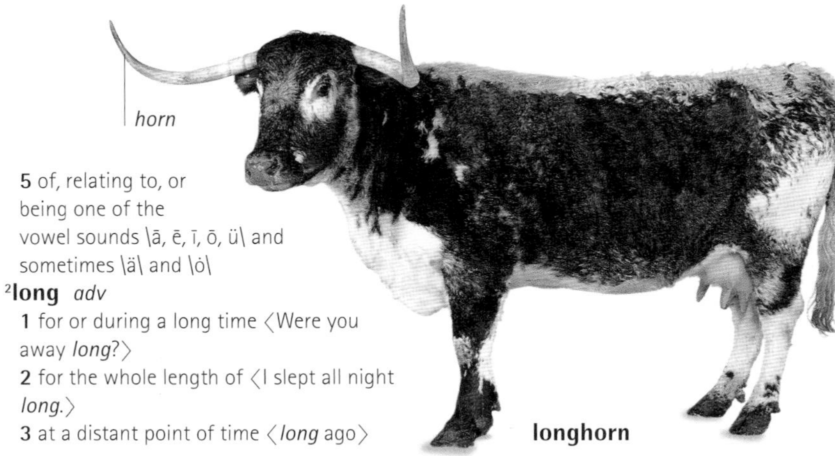

longhorn

long•house \'lȯŋ-ˌhau̇s\ *n*
a long dwelling especially of the Iroquois for several families

long•ing \'lȯŋ-iŋ\ *n*
a very strong desire
long•ing•ly *adv*

lon•gi•tude \'län-jə-ˌtüd, -ˌtyüd\ *n*
distance measured in degrees east or west of an imaginary line that runs from the north pole to the south pole and passes through Greenwich, England

lon•gi•tu•di•nal \ˌlän-jə-'tü-dᵊn-əl, -'tyü-\ *adj*
placed or running lengthwise 〈*longitudinal* stripes〉
lon•gi•tu•di•nal•ly *adv*

long–lived \'lȯŋ-'livd, -'līvd\ *adj*
living or lasting for a long time 〈a *long-lived* disagreement〉

long–range \'lȯŋ-'rānj\ *adj*
1 involving a long period of time 〈*long-range* planning〉
2 capable of traveling or being used over great distances 〈*long-range* rockets〉

long–wind•ed \'lȯŋ-'win-dəd\ *adj*
using or having too many words 〈a *long-winded* explanation〉 〈a *long-winded* speaker〉

¹look \'lu̇k\ *vb* **looked**; **look•ing**
1 to use the power of vision : SEE 〈*Look* before you cross.〉
2 to direct the attention or eyes 〈*Look* in the mirror.〉 〈*Look* at the map.〉
3 SEEM 1 〈That *looks* dangerous.〉
4 to have an appearance that is suitable 〈He *looks* his age.〉
5 ²FACE 1 〈The house *looks* east.〉
look after to take care of 〈*Look after* the children.〉
look down on to regard as bad or inferior
look out to be careful
look up
1 to search for in a reference book 〈*Look* it *up* in the dictionary.〉
2 to get better 〈Your chances are *looking up*.〉
look up to ²RESPECT 1

²look *n*
1 an act of looking 〈We took a *look* around.〉
2 the expression on a person's face or in a person's eyes 〈The child had a mischievous *look*.〉
3 looks *pl* physical appearance 〈good *looks*〉
4 appearance that suggests what something is or means 〈The cloth has a *look* of leather.〉

looking glass *n*
¹MIRROR 1

lookout 2: a lookout over Vancouver, British Columbia, Canada

look•out \'lu̇k-ˌau̇t\ *n*
1 a careful watch for something expected or feared 〈Be on the *lookout* for trouble.〉
2 ▲ a high place from which a wide view is possible
3 a person who keeps watch

¹loom \'lüm\ *n*
▼ a frame or machine for weaving cloth

²loom *vb* **loomed**; **loom•ing**
1 to come into sight suddenly and often with a large, strange, or frightening appearance 〈mountains *loom* ahead.〉
2 to be about to happen 〈A battle is *looming*.〉

loon \'lün\ *n*
a large diving bird that eats fish and has a black head and a black back spotted with white

¹loom: a North African woman weaving cloth on a traditional loom

¹loop \'lüp\ *n*
1 an almost oval form produced when something flexible and thin (as a wire or a rope) crosses over itself
2 something (as a figure or bend) suggesting a flexible loop 〈Her letters have large *loops*.〉

²loop *vb* **looped**; **loop•ing**
1 to make a circle or loop in 〈*Loop* your shoelace.〉
2 to form a circle or loop 〈The road *loops* around the park.〉

loop•hole \'lüp-ˌhōl\ *n*
a way of avoiding something 〈a *loophole* in the law〉

[1]loose \'lüs\ *adj* **loos•er; loos•est**
1 not tightly fixed or fastened ⟨a *loose* board⟩
2 not pulled tight ⟨a *loose* belt⟩
3 not tied up or shut in ⟨a *loose* horse⟩
4 not brought together in a bundle or binding ⟨*loose* sheets of paper⟩
5 having parts that are not held or squeezed tightly together ⟨*loose* gravel⟩
6 not exact or precise ⟨a *loose* translation⟩
loose•ly *adv*
loose•ness *n*

[2]loose *vb* **loosed; loos•ing**
1 to make less tight ⟨He *loosed* the knot.⟩
2 to set free ⟨They *loosed* the dogs.⟩

loose–leaf \'lüs-'lēf\ *adj*
arranged so that pages can be put in or taken out ⟨a *loose-leaf* notebook⟩

loos•en \'lü-sᵊn\ *vb* **loos•ened; loos•en•ing**
to make or become less tight or firmly fixed ⟨Can you *loosen* this screw?⟩ ⟨His grip *loosened*.⟩

[1]loot \'lüt\ *n*
something stolen or taken by force

[2]loot *vb* **loot•ed; loot•ing**
[1]PLUNDER
loot•er *n*

[1]lope \'lōp\ *n*
an effortless way of moving with long smooth steps

[2]lope *vb* **loped; lop•ing**
to go or run in an effortless way with long smooth steps

lop•sid•ed \'läp-'sī-dəd\ *adj*
uneven in position, size, or amount ⟨a *lopsided* score⟩ ⟨a *lopsided* smile⟩

[1]lord \'lȯrd\ *n*
1 a person having power and authority over others
2 *cap* GOD 1
3 *cap* JESUS CHRIST
4 a British nobleman or bishop — used as a title ⟨*Lord* Cornwallis⟩

► **Word History** *Lord* was first formed as a compound word, though its nature has been made unclear by centuries of sound change. The Old English ancestor of *lord* was *hlāford*, "head of the household"; this compound is made up of *hlāf*, "loaf, bread," and *weard*, "keeper, guard." Old English speakers seem to have thought of the most important male in the house as the "keeper of the bread."

[2]lord *vb* **lord•ed; lord•ing**
to act in a proud or bossy way toward others ⟨He's older, and always *lords* it over us.⟩

lord•ship \'lȯrd-,ship\ *n*
the rank or dignity of a lord — used as a title ⟨His *Lordship* is not at home.⟩

lore \'lȯr\ *n*
common or traditional knowledge or belief

lose \'lüz\ *vb* **lost** \'lȯst\; **los•ing** \'lü-ziŋ\
1 to be unable to find or have at hand ⟨I *lost* my keys.⟩
2 to become deprived of ⟨She *lost* her job.⟩
3 to become deprived of by death ⟨She *lost* her grandfather.⟩
4 to fail to use : WASTE ⟨There's no time to *lose*.⟩
5 to fail to win ⟨They *lost* the game.⟩
6 to fail to keep ⟨She *lost* her balance.⟩ ⟨He *lost* control.⟩
los•er *n*

lotus: a bright pink lotus flower

loss \'lȯs\ *n*
1 the act or fact of losing something ⟨a *loss* of courage⟩
2 harm or distress that comes from losing something or someone ⟨We all felt the *loss* when he left.⟩
3 something that is lost ⟨weight *loss*⟩
4 failure to win ⟨It was the team's first *loss*.⟩
at a loss unsure of how to proceed

lost *adj*
1 unable to find the way ⟨a *lost* puppy⟩
2 unable to be found ⟨*lost* luggage⟩
3 not used, won, or claimed ⟨a *lost* opportunity⟩
4 no longer possessed or known ⟨a *lost* art⟩ ⟨long *lost* cousins⟩
5 fully occupied ⟨*lost* in thought⟩
6 not capable of succeeding ⟨a *lost* cause⟩

lot \'lät\ *n*
1 an object used in deciding something by chance or the use of such an object to decide something
2 FATE 2 ⟨It was their *lot* to be poor.⟩
3 a piece or plot of land ⟨a vacant *lot*⟩
4 a large number or amount ⟨*lots* of books⟩ ⟨a *lot* of help⟩

loth *variant of* LOATH

lo•tion \'lō-shən\ *n*
a creamy liquid preparation used on the skin especially for healing or as a cosmetic

lot•tery \'lä-tə-rē\ *n, pl* **lot•ter•ies**
a way of raising money in which many tickets are sold and a few of these are drawn to win prizes

lo•tus \'lō-təs\ *n*
◄ any of various water lilies

[1]loud \'lau̇d\ *adj* **loud•er; loud•est**
1 not low, soft, or quiet in sound : NOISY ⟨*loud* music⟩ ⟨a *loud* cry⟩
2 not quiet or calm in expression ⟨a *loud* complaint⟩
3 too bright or showy to be pleasing ⟨*loud* clothes⟩
loud•ly *adv*
loud•ness *n*

[2]loud *adv*
in a loud manner ⟨Don't talk so *loud*!⟩

loud•speak•er \'lau̇d-'spē-kər\ *n*
▼ an electronic device that makes sound louder

loudspeakers on either side of a stereo unit

A B C D E F G H I J K L M N O P Q R S T U V W X Y Z

²lounge 1: a hotel lounge

¹lounge \ˈlau̇nj\ *vb* **lounged**; **loung•ing**
to stand, sit, or lie in a relaxed manner ⟨I *lounged* on the sofa all afternoon.⟩

²lounge *n*
1 ▲ a room with comfortable furniture for relaxing
2 a long chair or couch

louse \ˈlau̇s\ *n, pl* **lice** \ˈlīs\
1 a small, wingless, and usually flat insect that lives on the bodies of warm-blooded animals
2 an insect or related arthropod that resembles a body louse and feeds on plant juices or decaying matter

lousy \ˈlau̇-zē\ *adj* **lous•i•er**; **lous•i•est**
1 BAD 1 ⟨I had a *lousy* time.⟩
2 deserving disgust or contempt ⟨That *lousy* liar!⟩

lov•able \ˈlə-və-bəl\ *adj*
deserving to be loved : having attractive or appealing qualities ⟨a *lovable* child⟩

¹love \ˈləv\ *n*
1 strong and warm affection (as of a parent for a child)
2 a great liking ⟨The children have a *love* for reading.⟩
3 a beloved person

²love *vb* **loved**; **lov•ing**
1 to feel strong affection for ⟨He *loves* his family.⟩
2 to like very much ⟨She *loves* to ski.⟩
lov•er *n*

love•ly \ˈləv-lē\ *adj* **love•li•er**; **love•li•est**
1 very attractive or beautiful ⟨You look *lovely* in that outfit.⟩
2 very pleasing ⟨We had a *lovely* time.⟩
love•li•ness *n*

lov•ing \ˈlə-viŋ\ *adj*
feeling or showing love or great care ⟨a *loving* glance⟩
lov•ing•ly *adv*

¹low \ˈlō\ *vb* **lowed**; **low•ing**
to make the sound of a cow : MOO

²low *n*
the mooing of a cow

³low *adj* **low•er**; **low•est**
1 not high or tall ⟨a *low* building⟩
2 lying or going below the usual level ⟨*low* ground⟩ ⟨a *low* bow⟩
3 not loud : SOFT ⟨a *low* whisper⟩
4 deep in pitch ⟨a *low* voice⟩
5 not cheerful : SAD ⟨*low* spirits⟩
6 less than usual (as in quantity or value) ⟨*low* prices⟩ ⟨*low* temperatures⟩
7 less than enough ⟨Our supply is getting *low*.⟩
8 not strong ⟨*low* winds⟩
9 not favorable : POOR ⟨I have a *low* opinion of him.⟩
low•ness *n*

⁴low *n*
1 a point or level that is the least in degree, size, or amount ⟨The temperature hit a *low* of ten degrees.⟩
2 a region of reduced barometric pressure
3 the arrangement of gears in an automobile that gives the slowest speed of travel

⁵low *adv* **low•er**; **low•est**
so as to be low ⟨fly *low*⟩ ⟨sing *low*⟩

¹low•er \ˈlō-ər\ *adj*
1 located below another or others of the same kind ⟨a *lower* floor⟩
2 located toward the bottom part of something ⟨the *lower* back⟩
3 placed below another or others in rank or order ⟨a *lower* court⟩
4 less advanced or developed ⟨*lower* animals⟩

²lower *vb* **low•ered**; **low•er•ing**
1 to move to a level or position that is below or less than an earlier one ⟨The sun *lowered* in the west.⟩
2 to let or pull down ⟨He *lowered* a flag.⟩
3 to make or become less (as in value, amount, or volume) ⟨The store *lowered* the price.⟩
4 to reduce the height of ⟨We'll *lower* the fence.⟩

low•er•case \ˌlō-ər-ˈkās\ *adj*
having the form a, b, c, rather than A, B, C
lowercase *n*

lowest common denominator *n*
LEAST COMMON DENOMINATOR

lowest common multiple *n*
LEAST COMMON MULTIPLE

low•land \ˈlō-lənd\ *n*
low flat country

lowly \ˈlō-lē\ *adj* **low•li•er**; **low•li•est**
of low rank or importance: HUMBLE ⟨a *lowly* servant⟩

loy•al \ˈlȯi-əl\ *adj*
having or showing true and constant support for someone or something ⟨*loyal* fans⟩
synonyms see FAITHFUL
loy•al•ly *adv*

loy•al•ist \ˈlȯi-ə-ləst\ *n*
a person who is loyal to a political cause, government, or leader especially in times of revolt

loy•al•ty \'lȯi-əl-tē\ *n, pl* **loy•al•ties**
the quality or state of being true and constant in support of someone or something

▶ **Synonyms** LOYALTY and ALLEGIANCE mean faithfulness owed by duty or by a pledge or promise. LOYALTY is used of a very personal or powerful kind of faithfulness. ⟨I felt great *loyalty* to my teammates.⟩ ALLEGIANCE is used of a duty to something other than a person, especially to a government or idea. ⟨I pledge *allegiance* to the flag.⟩

loz•enge \'lä-zᵊnj\ *n*
a small candy often containing medicine

LSD \ˌel-ˌes-'dē\ *n*
a dangerous drug that causes hallucinations

Lt. *abbr* lieutenant

ltd. *abbr* limited

lu•bri•cant \'lü-bri-kənt\ *n*
something (as oil or grease) that makes a surface smooth or slippery

lu•bri•cate \'lü-brə-ˌkāt\ *vb* **lu•bri•cat•ed**; **lu•bri•cat•ing**
to apply oil or grease to in order to make smooth or slippery

lu•bri•ca•tion \ˌlü-brə-'kā-shən\ *n*
the act or process of making something smooth or slippery

lu•cid \'lü-səd\ *adj*
1 having or showing the ability to think clearly ⟨*lucid* behavior⟩
2 easily understood ⟨*lucid* writing⟩
lu•cid•ly *adv*

luck \'lək\ *n*
1 something that happens to a person by or as if by chance ⟨He cursed his *luck*.⟩
2 the accidental way things happen ⟨Our meeting happened by pure *luck*.⟩
3 good fortune ⟨We had *luck* fishing.⟩

luck•i•ly \'lə-kə-lē\ *adv*
by good luck ⟨*Luckily* no one was hurt.⟩

lucky \'lə-kē\ *adj* **luck•i•er**; **luck•i•est**
1 helped by luck : FORTUNATE ⟨a *lucky* person⟩
2 happening because of good luck ⟨a *lucky* hit⟩
3 thought of as bringing good luck ⟨a *lucky* charm⟩

lu•di•crous \'lü-də-krəs\ *adj*
funny because of being ridiculous : ABSURD
lu•di•crous•ly *adv*

lug \'ləg\ *vb* **lugged**; **lug•ging**
to pull or carry with great effort ⟨I *lugged* my bag to the bus.⟩

lug•gage \'lə-gij\ *n*
suitcases for a traveler's belongings : BAGGAGE

luke•warm \'lük-'wȯrm\ *adj*
1 slightly warm ⟨*lukewarm* water⟩
2 not very interested or eager ⟨We got a *lukewarm* response.⟩

¹lull \'ləl\ *vb* **lulled**; **lull•ing**
to make or become sleepy or less watchful ⟨They were *lulled* into believing his promises.⟩ ⟨He was *lulled* to sleep by the rocking of the boat.⟩

²lull *n*
a period of calm or inactivity

lul•la•by \'lə-lə-ˌbī\ *n, pl* **lul•la•bies**
a song for helping a child fall asleep

¹lum•ber \'ləm-bər\ *vb* **lum•bered**; **lum•ber•ing**
to move in a slow or awkward way ⟨An elephant *lumbered* along the road.⟩

²lumber *n*
timber especially when sawed into boards

lum•ber•jack \'ləm-bər-ˌjak\ *n*
a person whose job is cutting down trees for wood

lum•ber•yard \'ləm-bər-ˌyärd\ *n*
a place where lumber is kept for sale

lu•mi•nous \'lü-mə-nəs\ *adj*
giving off light ⟨the *luminous* dial of a watch⟩
lu•mi•nous•ly *adv*

¹lump \'ləmp\ *n*
1 a small piece or chunk ⟨a *lump* of coal⟩
2 a swelling or growth ⟨She got a *lump* on her forehead.⟩
3 a tight feeling in the throat caused by emotion

²lump *vb* **lumped**; **lump•ing**
1 to group together
2 to form into lumps ⟨The gravy *lumped*.⟩

³lump *adj*
not divided into parts ⟨a *lump* sum⟩

lumpy \'ləm-pē\ *adj* **lump•i•er**; **lump•i•est**
having or full of lumps ⟨a *lumpy* mattress⟩

lu•nar \'lü-nər\ *adj*
1 of or relating to the moon ⟨*lunar* rock⟩
2 measured by the revolutions of the moon ⟨a *lunar* month⟩

¹lu•na•tic \'lü-nə-ˌtik\ *adj*
INSANE 1

²lunatic *n*
1 an insane person
2 a person who behaves very foolishly ⟨That *lunatic* went through a red light.⟩

¹lunch \'lənch\ *n*
1 a light meal especially when eaten in the middle of the day ⟨It's time for *lunch*.⟩
2 food prepared for lunch ⟨You're eating my *lunch*!⟩

²lunch *vb* **lunched**; **lunch•ing**
to eat lunch

lun•cheon \'lən-chən\ *n*
1 ¹LUNCH 1
2 a formal lunch

lunch•room \'lənch-ˌrüm, -ˌru̇m\ *n*
▼ a room (as in a school) where lunch may be eaten

lunchroom: students eating their lunch in a lunchroom

► lung
The lungs supply the body with oxygen and eliminate the waste product carbon dioxide. Air is delivered into the lungs via the trachea (windpipe); this branches into 2 main bronchi (air passages), with one bronchus supplying each lung. The main bronchi divide again into smaller bronchi and then into bronchioles, which lead to air passages that open out into grape-like sacs called alveoli.

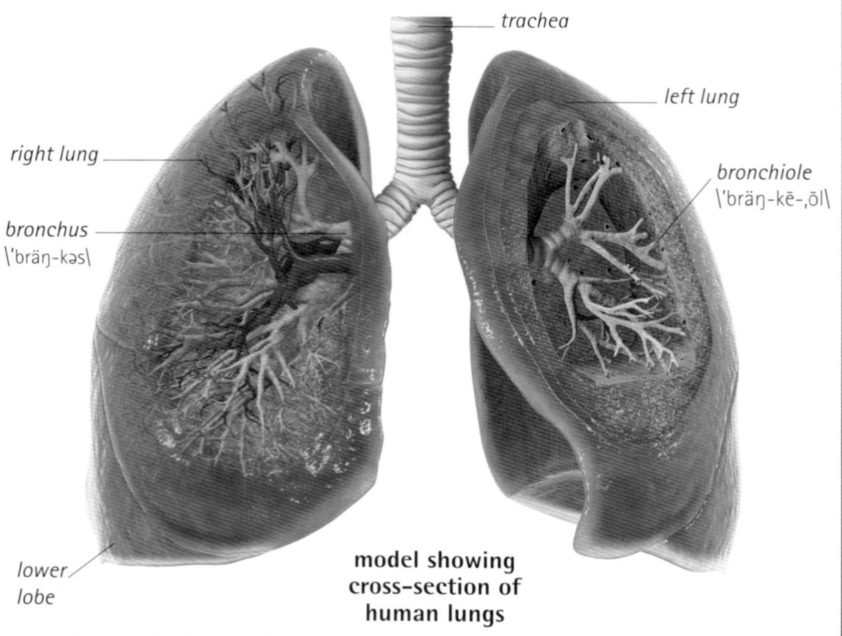

model showing cross-section of human lungs

lung \'ləŋ\ *n*
▲ either of two organs in the chest that are like bags and are the main breathing structure in animals that breathe air

[1]lunge \'lənj\ *n*
a sudden movement forward ⟨She made a *lunge* for the ball.⟩

[2]lunge *vb* **lunged**; **lung•ing**
to move or reach forward in a sudden forceful way ⟨She *lunged* across the table.⟩

lung•fish \'ləŋ-,fish\ *n*
▼ a fish that breathes with structures like lungs as well as with gills

lungfish: an African lungfish

lu•pine \'lü-pən\ *n*
a plant related to the clovers that has tall spikes of showy flowers

[1]lurch \'lərch\ *n*
a sudden swaying, tipping, or jerking movement

[2]lurch *vb* **lurched**; **lurch•ing**
to move with a sudden swaying, tipping, or jerking motion

[1]lure \'lu̇r\ *n*
1 something that attracts or tempts
2 an artificial bait for catching fish

[2]lure *vb* **lured**; **lur•ing**
to tempt by offering pleasure or gain ⟨Men were *lured* by tales of treasure.⟩

lu•rid \'lu̇r-əd\ *adj*
1 causing shock or disgust ⟨a *lurid* story⟩
2 glowing with an overly bright color ⟨*lurid* neon lights⟩
lu•rid•ly *adv*

lurk \'lərk\ *vb* **lurked**; **lurk•ing**
to hide in or about a place

lus•cious \'lə-shəs\ *adj*
1 having a delicious taste or smell ⟨*luscious* fruits⟩
2 delightful to hear, see, or feel ⟨a *luscious* singing voice⟩

lush \'ləsh\ *adj* **lush•er**; **lush•est**
1 characterized by full and healthy growth ⟨*lush* grass⟩
2 covered with a thick growth of healthy plants ⟨a *lush* tropical island⟩
3 LUXURIOUS 1 ⟨a *lush* hotel lobby⟩
lush•ly *adv*
lush•ness *n*

lust \'ləst\ *n*
a strong longing ⟨She has a *lust* for adventure.⟩

lus•ter *or* **lus•tre** \'ləs-tər\ *n*
the shiny quality of a surface that reflects light ⟨a pearl's *luster*⟩

lus•trous \'ləs-trəs\ *adj*
having a shiny quality ⟨a *lustrous* marble counter⟩

lusty \'lə-stē\ *adj*
lust•i•er; **lust•i•est**
full of strength and energy ⟨*lusty* cheers⟩

lute \'lüt\ *n*
► a musical instrument with a pear-shaped body and usually paired strings played with the fingers

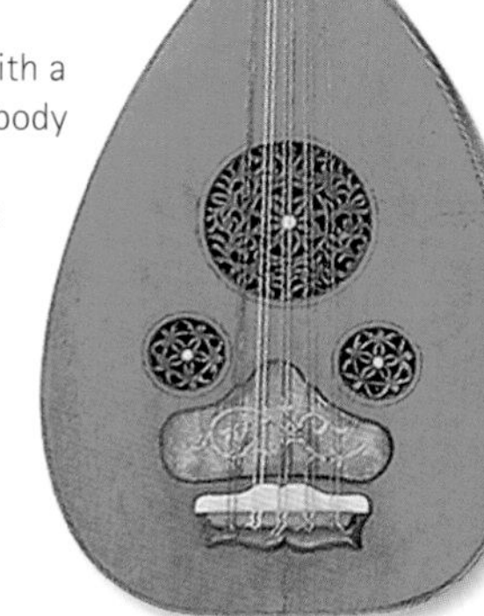

lute

lux•u•ri•ant
\,ləg-'zhu̇r-ē-ənt, ,lək-'shu̇r-\ *adj*
1 having heavy and thick growth ⟨a *luxuriant* forest⟩
2 LUXURIOUS 1
⟨a *luxuriant* restaurant⟩

lux•u•ri•ous \,ləg-'zhu̇r-ē-əs, ,lək-'shu̇r-\ *adj*
1 very fine and comfortable **:** having an appealing rich quality ⟨a *luxurious* home⟩
2 feeling or showing a desire for fine and expensive things ⟨He has *luxurious* tastes.⟩
lux•u•ri•ous•ly *adv*

lux•u•ry \'lək-shə-rē, 'ləg-zhə-\ *n*, *pl* **lux•u•ries**
1 very rich, pleasant, and comfortable surroundings ⟨They live in *luxury*.⟩
2 something desirable but expensive or hard to get ⟨Fresh strawberries are a *luxury* in winter.⟩
3 something adding to pleasure or comfort but not absolutely necessary ⟨That new car is a *luxury* I can't afford.⟩

[1]**-ly** \lē\ *adj suffix*
1 like : similar to ⟨father*ly*⟩
2 happening in each specified period of time : every ⟨hour*ly*⟩

[2]**-ly** *adv suffix*
1 in a specified manner ⟨slow*ly*⟩
2 from a specified point of view ⟨grammatical*ly*⟩

lye \'lī\ *n*
a dangerous compound that is used in cleaning and in making soap

lying *present participle of* LIE

lymph \'limf\ *n*
a clear liquid like blood without the red blood cells that nourishes the tissues and carries off wastes

lym•phat•ic \lim-'fa-tik\ *adj*
relating to or carrying lymph ⟨a *lymphatic* duct⟩

lymph node *n*
one of the small rounded bits of tissue in the body through which lymph passes to be filtered

lym•pho•cyte \'lim-fə-ˌsīt\ *n*
any of the white blood cells of the immune system that play a role in recognizing and destroying foreign cells, particles, or substances that have invaded the body

lynx \'liŋks\ *n, pl* **lynx** *or* **lynx•es**
▼ any of several wildcats with rather long legs, a short tail, and often ears with tufts of long hairs at the tip

lynx

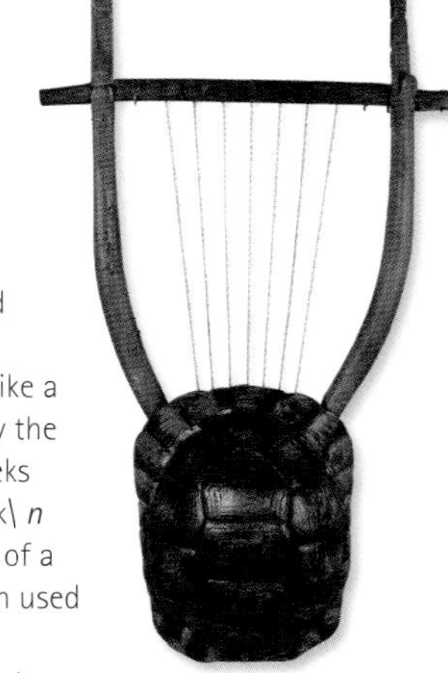
lyre

lyre \'līr\ *n*
▲ a stringed musical instrument like a harp used by the ancient Greeks

[1]**lyr•ic** \'lir-ik\ *n*
1 the words of a song — often used in pl.
2 a poem that expresses feelings in a way that is like a song

[2]**lyric** *adj*
expressing personal emotion in a way that is like a song ⟨*lyric* poetry⟩

ly•so•some \'lī-sə-ˌsōm\ *n*
a tiny saclike part in a cell that contains enzymes which can break down materials (as food products and waste)

Mm

Sounds of M: The letter M makes only one sound, the sound heard in *may* and *came*.

m \'em\ *n, pl* **m's** *or* **ms** \'emz\ *often cap*
1 the 13th letter of the English alphabet
2 1000 in Roman numerals

m. *abbr*
1 male
2 meter
3 mile

ma \'mä, 'mȯ\ *n, often cap*
[1]MOTHER 1

MA *abbr* Massachusetts

ma'am \'mam\ *n*
MADAM

mac•ad•am \mə-'ka-dəm\ *n*
a road surface made of small closely packed broken stone

ma•caque \mə-'kak, -'käk\ *n*
▼ a monkey mostly found in Asia that often has a short tail

macaque: a Sri Lankan macaque

mac•a•ro•ni \,ma-kə-'rō-nē\ *n*
pasta in the shape of little curved tubes

ma•caw \mə-'kȯ\ *n*
▶ a large parrot of Central and South America with a long tail, a harsh voice, and bright feathers

macaw: a scarlet macaw

[1]**mace** \'mās\ *n*
a spice made from the dried outer covering of the nutmeg

[2]**mace** *n*
1 a decorated pole carried by an official as a sign of authority
2 a heavy spiked club used as a medieval weapon

ma•chete \mə-'she-tē\ *n*
a large heavy knife used for cutting sugarcane and underbrush and as a weapon

ma•chine \mə-'shēn\ *n*
1 a device with moving parts that does some desired work when it is provided with power ⟨a sewing *machine*⟩
2 VEHICLE 1 ⟨a flying *machine*⟩

machine gun *n*
a gun that fires bullets continuously and rapidly

ma•chin•ery \mə-'shē-nə-rē, -'shēn-rē\ *n*
1 a group of devices with moving parts that are used to perform specific jobs
2 the working parts of a device used to perform a particular job
3 the people and equipment by which something is done ⟨the *machinery* of government⟩

machine shop *n*
a workshop in which metal articles are put together

ma•chin•ist \mə-'shē-nist\ *n*
a person who makes or works on machines

mack•er•el \'ma-kə-rəl, 'mak-rəl\ *n, pl* **mackerel** *or* **mackerels**
▶ a fish of the North Atlantic that is green above with blue bars and silvery below and is often used as food

mackerel

mack•i•naw \'ma-kə-,nȯ\ *n*
a short heavy woolen coat

ma•cron \'mā-,krän\ *n*
a mark ¯ placed over a vowel to show that the vowel is long

mad \'mad\ *adj*
mad•der; **mad•dest**
1 ANGRY ⟨He's *mad* at his brother.⟩
2 INSANE 1 ⟨I think the whole world has gone *mad.*⟩
3 done or made without thinking ⟨a *mad* promise⟩
4 INFATUATED ⟨She is *mad* about horses.⟩
5 having rabies ⟨a *mad* dog⟩
6 marked by intense and often disorganized activity ⟨At the end of the game, there was a *mad* scramble.⟩
mad•ly *adv*
mad•ness *n*
like mad with a great amount of energy or speed ⟨The crowd cheered *like mad.*⟩ ⟨He ran *like mad.*⟩

mad•am \'ma-dəm\ *n, pl* **mes•dames** \mā-'däm, -'dam\
used without a name as a form of polite address to a woman ⟨May I help you, *madam?*⟩

ma•dame \mə-'dam, ma-'dam, *before a surname also* 'ma-dəm\ *n, pl* **mes•dames** *or* **ma•dames** \mā-'däm, -'dam\
used as a title that means *Mrs.* for a married woman who is not of an English-speaking nationality

mad•cap \'mad-,kap\ *adj*
RECKLESS, WILD ⟨a *madcap* adventure⟩

mad•den \'ma-dᵊn\ *vb* **mad•dened**; **mad•den•ing**
to make angry

mad•den•ing \ˈma-dᵊn-iŋ\ *adj*
very annoying 〈Her constant chatter is *maddening.*〉

made *past and past participle of* MAKE

made–up \ˈmād-ˈəp\ *adj*
created from the imagination 〈a *made-up* excuse〉

mad•house \ˈmad-ˌhau̇s\ *n*
a place or scene of complete confusion or noisy excitement

mad•man \ˈmad-ˌman, -mən\ *n, pl* **mad•men** \-mən\
a man who is or acts as if insane

mag•a•zine \ˈma-gə-ˌzēn\ *n*
1 a publication issued at regular intervals (as weekly or monthly)
2 a storehouse or warehouse for military supplies
3 a container in a gun for holding cartridges

▶ **Word History** The English word *magazine* came from a French word with the same spelling that in turn came from an Arabic word *makhāzin.* Both the French and the Arabic words meant "a place where things are stored." At first the English word had the same meaning, and it is still used in this sense. However, a later sense is now more common—that of a collection of written pieces printed at set times, the suggestion being that such collections are "storehouses of knowledge."

ma•gen•ta \mə-ˈjen-tə\ *n*
a deep purplish red

mag•got \ˈma-gət\ *n*
a legless grub that is the larva of a fly (as a housefly)

[1]**mag•ic** \ˈma-jik\ *n*
1 the power to control natural forces possessed by certain persons (as wizards and witches) in folk tales and fiction
2 the art or skill of performing tricks or illusions for entertainment
3 a power that seems mysterious 〈The team lost its *magic.*〉
4 something that charms 〈They calmed us with the *magic* of their singing.〉

[2]**magic** *adj*
1 having or seeming to have the power to make impossible things happen 〈She chanted the *magic* words.〉
2 of or relating to the power to make impossible things happen 〈*magic* tricks〉
3 giving a feeling of enchantment 〈It was a *magic* moment.〉

mag•i•cal \ˈma-ji-kəl\ *adj*
[2]MAGIC

ma•gi•cian \mə-ˈji-shən\ *n*
a person skilled in performing tricks or illusions

mag•is•trate \ˈma-jə-ˌstrāt\ *n*
1 a chief officer of government
2 a local official with some judicial power

mag•ma \ˈmag-mə\ *n*
molten rock within the earth

mag•na•nim•i•ty \ˌmag-nə-ˈni-mə-tē\ *n*
the quality of being generous and noble

mag•nan•i•mous \mag-ˈna-nə-məs\ *adj*
generous and noble
mag•nan•i•mous•ly *adv*

mag•ne•sium \mag-ˈnē-zē-əm, -ˈnē-zhəm\ *n*
a silvery white metallic chemical element that is lighter than aluminum and is used in lightweight alloys

mag•net \ˈmag-nət\ *n*
▶ a piece of material (as of iron, steel, or alloy) that is able to attract iron

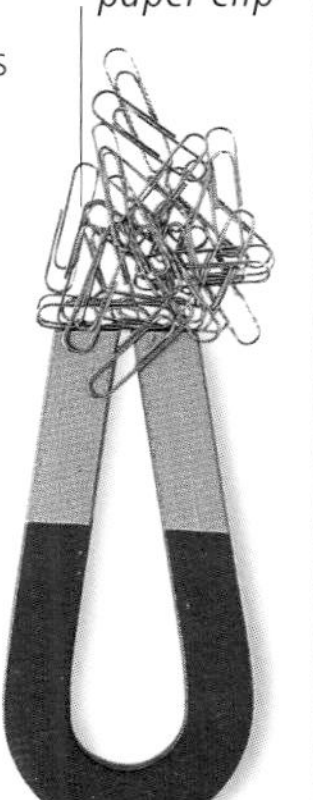

magnet

mag•net•ic \mag-ˈne-tik\ *adj*
1 acting like a magnet
2 of or relating to the earth's magnetic field
3 having a great power to attract people 〈a *magnetic* personality〉

magnetic field *n*
the portion of space near a magnetic object within which magnetic forces can be detected

magnetic needle *n*
a narrow strip of magnetized steel that is free to swing around to show the direction of the earth's magnetic field

magnetic pole *n*
1 either of the poles of a magnet
2 either of two small regions of the earth which are located near the north and south poles and toward which a compass needle points

magnetic tape *n*
a thin ribbon of plastic coated with a magnetic material on which information (as sound) may be stored

mag•ne•tism \ˈmag-nə-ˌti-zəm\ *n*
1 a magnet's power to attract
2 the power to attract others : personal charm

mag•ne•tize \ˈmag-nə-ˌtīz\ *vb* **mag•ne•tized; mag•ne•tiz•ing**
to cause to be magnetic

mag•nif•i•cence \mag-ˈni-fə-səns\ *n*
impressive beauty or greatness 〈The room's *magnificence* awed me.〉

mag•nif•i•cent \mag-ˈni-fə-sənt\ *adj*
very beautiful or impressive 〈a *magnificent* view〉
mag•nif•i•cent•ly *adv*

mag•ni•fy \ˈmag-nə-ˌfī\ *vb* **mag•ni•fied; mag•ni•fy•ing**
1 to enlarge in fact or appearance 〈A microscope *magnifies* an object seen through it.〉
2 to cause to seem greater or more important : EXAGGERATE 〈The problem has been *magnified* by rumors.〉

magnifying glass *n*
a lens that makes something seen through it appear larger than it actually is

mag•ni•tude \ˈmag-nə-ˌtüd, -ˌtyüd\ *n*
greatness of size or importance

mag•no•lia \mag-ˈnōl-yə\ *n*
▼ a tree or tall shrub having showy white, pink, yellow, or purple flowers that appear in early spring

magnolia: magnolia flowers

a b c d e f g h i j k l **m** n o p q r s t u v w x y z

magpie

mag•pie \ˈmag-ˌpī\ *n*
▲ a noisy black-and-white bird related to the jays

Ma•hi•can \mə-ˈhē-kən\ *or* **Mo•hi•can** \mō-, mə-\ *n, pl* **Ma•hi•can** *or* **Ma•hi•cans** *or* **Mo•hi•can** *or* **Mo•hi•cans**
1 a member of an American Indian people of northeastern New York
2 the language of the Mahican people

ma•hog•a•ny \mə-ˈhä-gə-nē\ *n, pl* **ma•hog•a•nies**
a strong reddish brown wood that is used especially for furniture and is obtained from several tropical trees

maid \ˈmād\ *n*
1 [1]MAIDEN
2 a female servant

[1]**maid•en** \ˈmā-dᵊn\ *n*
an unmarried girl or woman

[2]**maiden** *adj*
1 UNMARRIED
2 [1]FIRST ⟨This is our *maiden* voyage to Europe.⟩

maid•en•hair fern \ˈmā-dᵊn-ˌher-\ *n*
► a fern with slender stems and delicate leaves

maiden name *n*
a woman's last name before she is married

maidenhair fern

maid of honor *n, pl* **maids of honor**
a woman who stands with the bride at a wedding

[1]**mail** \ˈmāl\ *n*
1 letters and packages sent from one person to another through the post office
2 the system used for sending and delivering letters and packages
3 [1]E-MAIL 2

[2]**mail** *vb* **mailed; mail•ing**
to send letters and packages through the post office

[3]**mail** *n*
a fabric made of metal rings linked together and used as armor

mail•box \ˈmāl-ˌbäks\ *n*
1 ► a public box in which to place outgoing letters
2 a private box (as on a house) for the delivery of incoming letters

mailbox 1

mail carrier *n*
LETTER CARRIER

mail•man \ˈmāl-ˌman\ *n, pl* **mail•men** \-ˌmen\
LETTER CARRIER

maim \ˈmām\ *vb* **maimed; maim•ing**
to injure badly or cripple by violence

[1]**main** \ˈmān\ *adj*
first in size, rank, or importance : CHIEF ⟨Go in the *main* entrance.⟩ ⟨What's the *main* reason?⟩
main•ly *adv*

[2]**main** *n*
1 the chief part : essential point ⟨The new workers are in the *main* well trained.⟩
2 a principal line, tube, or pipe of a utility system ⟨water *main*⟩ ⟨gas *main*⟩
3 HIGH SEAS
4 physical strength : FORCE

main•land \ˈmān-ˌland\ *n*
a continent or the largest part of a continent as distinguished from an offshore island or islands

main•mast \ˈmān-ˌmast, -məst\ *n*
the principal mast of a sailing ship

main•sail \ˈmān-ˌsāl, -səl\ *n*
the principal sail on the mainmast

main•spring \ˈmān-ˌspriŋ\ *n*
the principal spring in a mechanical device (as a watch or clock)

main•stay \ˈmān-ˌstā\ *n*
1 the large strong rope from the maintop of a ship usually to the foot of the foremast
2 a chief support ⟨the *mainstay* of the family⟩

main•tain \mān-ˈtān\ *vb* **main•tained; main•tain•ing**
1 to carry on : CONTINUE ⟨After many years they still *maintain* a correspondence.⟩
2 to keep in a particular or desired state ⟨Eat properly to *maintain* good health.⟩
3 to insist to be true ⟨She *maintains* her innocence.⟩
4 to provide for : SUPPORT ⟨I *maintained* my family by working two jobs.⟩

main•te•nance \ˈmān-tə-nəns\ *n*
1 the act of keeping or providing for : the state of being kept or provided for ⟨One of government's jobs is the *maintenance* of law and order.⟩ ⟨We collected money for the family's *maintenance*.⟩
2 UPKEEP ⟨Workers in charge of *maintenance* painted the building.⟩

main•top \ˈmān-ˌtäp\ *n*
a platform around the head of a mainmast

maize \ˈmāz\ *n*
[1]CORN

Maj. *abbr* major

ma•jes•tic \mə-ˈje-stik\ *adj*
very impressive and beautiful or dignified ⟨*majestic* mountains⟩
ma•jes•ti•cal•ly \-sti-kə-lē\ *adv*

maj•es•ty \ˈma-jə-stē\ *n, pl* **maj•es•ties**
1 used as a title for a king, queen, emperor, or empress
2 the quality or state of being impressive and dignified
3 royal dignity or authority

[1]**ma•jor** \ˈmā-jər\ *adj*
1 great or greater in number, quantity, rank, or importance ⟨A new car is a *major* expense.⟩
2 of or relating to a musical scale of eight notes with half steps between the third and fourth and between the seventh and eighth notes and with whole steps between all the others

[2]**major** *n*
a commissioned officer in the army, air force, or marine corps ranking above a captain

ma•jor•i•ty \mə-ˈjȯr-ə-tē\ *n, pl* **ma•jor•i•ties**
1 a number greater than half of a total
2 a group or party that makes up the greater part of a whole body of people ⟨The *majority* chose a leader.⟩
3 the amount by which a number is more than half the total ⟨She won the election by a *majority* of 200 votes.⟩
4 the age at which a person has the full rights of an adult

[1]**make** \ˈmāk\ *vb* **made** \ˈmād\; **mak•ing**
1 to form or put together out of material or parts ⟨Do you know how to *make* a dress?⟩
2 to cause to exist or occur ⟨Don't *make* trouble.⟩ ⟨It *makes* a funny noise.⟩
3 to prepare food or drink ⟨She *made* breakfast for us.⟩
4 to cause to be or become ⟨Your visit *made* them happy.⟩

5 COMPEL 1 ⟨Grandma will *make* them go to bed.⟩
6 to arrange the blankets and sheets on (a bed) so that the mattress is covered
7 to combine to produce ⟨Two and two *make* four.⟩
8 GET 1, GAIN ⟨We *made* a profit on the sale.⟩ ⟨Does she *make* friends easily?⟩
9 [1]REACH 2 ⟨We *made* it home.⟩
10 [1]DO 1, PERFORM ⟨I'm *making* a speech.⟩ ⟨He *made* a gesture.⟩
11 to act so as to be ⟨*Make* sure you have your toothbrush.⟩
mak•er \'mā-kər\ *n*
make believe to act as if something known to be imaginary is real or true
make fun of to cause to be the target of laughter in an unkind way
make good FULFILL 1, COMPLETE ⟨I *made good* my promise.⟩
make out
1 to write out ⟨I'll *make out* a list.⟩
2 UNDERSTAND 1 ⟨I can't *make out* what this says.⟩
3 IDENTIFY 1 ⟨I can't *make out* who it is.⟩
4 [1]FARE ⟨How did you *make out* on your tests?⟩
make up
1 to create from the imagination ⟨He *made up* a story.⟩
2 [2]FORM 3, COMPOSE ⟨Eleven players *make up* the team.⟩
3 to do something to correct or repay a wrong ⟨Volunteer work *made up* for their mischief.⟩
4 to become friendly again ⟨They quarreled but later *made up*.⟩
5 to put on makeup
6 DECIDE 1 ⟨I've finally *made up* my mind.⟩

► **Synonyms** MAKE, FORM, and MANUFACTURE mean to cause to come into being. MAKE is a word that can be used of many kinds of creation. ⟨She knows how to *make* a chair.⟩ ⟨They *made* many friends.⟩ FORM is used when the thing brought into being has a design or structure. ⟨The colonies *formed* a new nation.⟩ MANUFACTURE is used for the act of making something in a fixed way and usually by machinery. ⟨The company *manufactures* cars.⟩

[2]make *n*
[1]BRAND 2 ⟨What *make* of car did you buy?⟩
[1]make–be•lieve \'māk-bə-ˌlēv\ *n*
something that is imagined to be real or true
[2]make–believe *adj*
not real : IMAGINARY ⟨She plays with *make-believe* friends.⟩

mall 1: interior of a shopping mall

make•shift \'māk-ˌshift\ *adj*
serving as a temporary substitute ⟨I used my jacket as a *makeshift* pillow.⟩
make•up \'māk-ˌəp\ *n*
1 any of various cosmetics (as lipstick or powder)
2 the way the parts or elements of something are put together or joined
3 materials used in changing a performer's appearance (as for a play or other entertainment)
mal- *prefix*
1 bad : badly ⟨*mal*treat⟩
2 abnormal : abnormally ⟨*mal*formation⟩
mal•ad•just•ed \ˌma-lə-'jə-stəd\ *adj*
not able to deal with other people in a normal or healthy way ⟨a *maladjusted* person⟩
mal•a•dy \'ma-lə-dē\ *n, pl* **mal•a•dies**
a disease or disorder of the body or mind
ma•lar•ia \mə-'ler-ē-ə\ *n*
a serious disease with chills and fever that is spread by the bite of a mosquito
[1]male \'māl\ *n*
1 a man or a boy
2 a person or animal that produces germ cells (as sperm) that fertilize the eggs of a female
3 a plant with stamens but no pistil
[2]male *adj*
1 of, relating to, or being the sex that fertilizes the eggs of a female
2 bearing stamens but no pistil ⟨a *male* flower⟩
3 of or characteristic of men or boys ⟨a *male* singing voice⟩
ma•lev•o•lent \mə-'le-və-lənt\ *adj*
having or showing a desire to cause harm to another person
mal•for•ma•tion \ˌmal-fȯr-'mā-shən\ *n*
something that is badly or wrongly formed

mal•ice \'ma-ləs\ *n*
a desire to cause harm to another person
ma•li•cious \mə-'li-shəs\ *adj*
feeling or showing a desire to cause harm to another person ⟨*malicious* gossip⟩
ma•li•cious•ly *adv*
[1]ma•lign \mə-'līn\ *adj*
MALICIOUS
[2]malign *vb* **ma•ligned**; **ma•lign•ing**
to say evil things about : SLANDER
ma•lig•nant \mə-'lig-nənt\ *adj*
1 MALICIOUS
2 likely to cause death : DEADLY
ma•lig•nant•ly *adv*
mall \'mȯl\ *n*
1 ▲ a large building or group of buildings containing a variety of shops
2 a public area for pedestrians

► **Word History** In Italy in the 1500s a popular game similar to croquet was known as *pallamaglio*, from *palla*, "ball," and *maglio*, "mallet." The game (and word) was adopted by the French as *pallemalle* and in the 1600s by the English as *pall-mall*. The alley on which the game was played came to be known as a *mall*. One of the best known of these alleys, covered with sand and crushed shells, was located in London's St. James Park and was known as "The Mall." After the game lost favor, the Mall at St. James, as it continued to be called, was turned into a fashionable walkway with trees and flowers. Similar open-air places came to be called *malls* also. In the 20th century the word was applied to other public spaces, including the shopping complexes we now know as *malls*.

mammal
Mammals live in a wide range of habitats throughout the world. All mammals are warm-blooded and have some amount of hair on the body. There are three main types of mammals: egg-laying mammals such as the platypus and echidna; marsupials such as the kangaroo; and the largest group, mammals whose young grow inside the mother's body, fed by nutrients that pass through the placenta.

mal•lard \ˈma-lərd\ *n*
▶ a common wild duck of the northern hemisphere that is the ancestor of the domestic ducks

mal•lea•ble \ˈma-lē-ə-bəl, ˈmal-yə-bəl\ *adj*
capable of being extended or shaped with blows from a hammer

mal•let \ˈma-lət\ *n*
1 a hammer with a barrel-shaped head of wood or soft material
2 a club with a short thick head and a long thin handle ⟨a croquet *mallet*⟩

mal•low \ˈma-lō\ *n*
▼ a tall plant with usually large white, rose, or purplish flowers with five petals

mallow

mal•nu•tri•tion \ˌmal-nu̇-ˈtri-shən, -nyu̇-\ *n*
a condition of weakness and poor health that results from not eating enough food or from eating food without the proper nutrients

malt \ˈmȯlt\ *n*
1 grain and especially barley soaked in water until it has sprouted
2 MALTED MILK

malt•ed milk \ˈmȯl-təd-\ *n*
a beverage made by dissolving a powder made from dried milk and cereals in milk

mal•treat \mal-ˈtrēt\ *vb* **mal•treat•ed**; **mal•treat•ing**
to treat in a rough or unkind way : ABUSE

ma•ma *also* **mam•ma** *or* **mom•ma** \ˈmä-mə\ *n*
[1]MOTHER 1

mam•mal \ˈma-məl\ *n*
◀ a warm-blooded animal (as a dog, mouse, bear, whale, or human being) with a backbone that feeds its young with milk produced by the mother and has skin usually more or less covered with hair

mallard

[1]**mam•moth** \ˈma-məth\ *n*
a very large hairy extinct elephant with long tusks that curve upward

[2]**mammoth** *adj*
very large : HUGE ⟨a *mammoth* iceberg⟩

[1]**man** \ˈman\ *n, pl* **men** \ˈmen\
1 an adult male human being
2 a human being : PERSON
3 the human race : MANKIND
4 [1]HUSBAND ⟨I now pronounce you *man* and wife.⟩
5 an adult male servant or employee
6 one of the pieces with which various games (as chess and checkers) are played
7 a member of the group to which human beings belong including both modern humans and extinct related forms

[2]**man** *vb* **manned**; **man•ning**
to work at or do the work of operating ⟨We rode while students *manned* the oars.⟩

Man. *abbr* Manitoba

man•age \ˈma-nij\ *vb* **man•aged**; **man•ag•ing**
1 to look after and make decisions about ⟨*manage* money⟩ ⟨A local woman will *manage* the new hotel.⟩
2 to succeed in doing : accomplish what is desired ⟨They *managed* to win.⟩
synonyms see CONDUCT
man•age•able \ˈma-ni-jə-bəl\ *adj*

man•age•ment \ˈma-nij-mənt\ *n*
1 the act of looking after and making decisions about something
2 the people who look after and make decisions about something

man•ag•er \ˈma-ni-jər\ *n*
1 a person who is in charge of a business or part of a business
2 a person who directs the training and performance of a sports team

man•a•tee \ˈma-nə-ˌtē\ *n*
a mainly tropical water-dwelling mammal that eats plants and has a rounded tail

man•da•rin \ˈman-də-rən\ *n*
1 a public official of the Chinese Empire
2 *cap* the chief dialect of China

man•date \ˈman-ˌdāt\ *n*
1 an order from a higher court to a lower court
2 a command or instruction from an authority
3 the instruction given by voters to their elected representatives

man•da•tory \ˈman-də-ˌtȯr-ē\ *adj*
required by law or by a command ⟨Student attendance is *mandatory*.⟩

man•di•ble \ˈman-də-bəl\ *n*
1 a lower jaw often with its soft parts
2 either the upper or lower part of the bill of a bird
3 either of a pair of mouth parts of some invertebrates (as an insect) that are usually used for biting

man•do•lin \ˌman-də-ˈlin, ˈman-də-lən\ *n*
▶ a musical instrument with four pairs of strings played by plucking

mane \ˈmān\ *n*
long heavy hair growing about the neck and head of some animals (as a horse or lion)
maned \ˈmānd\ *adj*

[1]**ma•neu•ver** \mə-ˈnü-vər, -ˈnyü-\ *n*
1 skillful action or management ⟨The driver avoided an accident by a quick *maneuver*.⟩
2 a training exercise by armed forces
3 a planned movement of troops or ships

[2]**maneuver** *vb* **ma•neu•vered**; **ma•neu•ver•ing**
1 to guide skillfully ⟨Our captain *maneuvered* the boat safely into the harbor.⟩
2 to move troops or ships where they are needed
ma•neu•ver•abil•i•ty \mə-ˌnü-və-rə-ˈbi-lə-tē, -ˌnyü-\ *n*
ma•neu•ver•able \-ˈnü-və-rə-bəl, -ˈnyü-\ *adj*

mandolin

man•ga \ˈmäŋ-gə\ *n*
a Japanese comic book or graphic novel

man•ga•nese \'maŋ-gə-ˌnēz\ *n*
a grayish white brittle metallic chemical element that resembles iron

mange \'mānj\ *n*
a contagious skin disease usually of domestic animals in which there is itching and loss of hair

man•ger \'mān-jər\ *n*
an open box in which food for farm animals is placed

man•gle \'maŋ-gəl\ *vb* **man•gled**; **man•gling**
1 to injure badly by cutting, tearing, or crushing
2 to spoil while making or performing ⟨If she's nervous, she'll *mangle* the speech.⟩

man•go \'maŋ-gō\ *n, pl* **man•goes** *or* **man•gos**
▼ a tropical fruit with yellowish red skin and juicy mildly tart yellow flesh

mango

mangy \'mān-jē\ *adj* **mang•i•er**; **mang•i•est**
1 affected with mange ⟨a *mangy* dog⟩
2 SHABBY 1 ⟨a *mangy* old rug⟩
3 SEEDY 2 ⟨a *mangy* restaurant⟩

man•hole \'man-ˌhōl\ *n*
a covered hole (as in a street) large enough to let a person pass through

man•hood \'man-ˌhu̇d\ *n*
1 qualities (as strength and courage) believed to be typical of men
2 the state of being an adult human male
3 adult human males

ma•nia \'mā-nē-ə, -nyə\ *n*
extreme enthusiasm

ma•ni•ac \'mā-nē-ˌak\ *n*
1 a person who is or behaves as if insane
2 a person who is extremely enthusiastic about something

[1]**man•i•cure** \'ma-nə-ˌkyu̇r\ *n*
a treatment for the care of the hands and fingernails

[2]**manicure** *vb* **man•i•cured**; **man•i•cur•ing**
to give a beauty treatment to the hands and fingernails

mannequin: clothes displayed on mannequins

man•i•cur•ist \'ma-nə-ˌkyu̇r-ist\ *n*
a person whose job is the treatment of hands and fingernails

[1]**man•i•fest** \'ma-nə-ˌfest\ *adj*
easy to detect or recognize : OBVIOUS ⟨Their relief was *manifest.*⟩

[2]**manifest** *vb* **man•i•fest•ed**; **man•i•fest•ing**
to show plainly

man•i•fes•ta•tion \ˌma-nə-fə-'stā-shən\ *n*
1 the act of showing plainly ⟨It was his only *manifestation* of concern.⟩
2 something that makes clear : EVIDENCE ⟨Crocuses are an early *manifestation* of spring.⟩

man•i•fold \'ma-nə-ˌfōld\ *adj*
of many and various kinds ⟨*manifold* blessings⟩

ma•nip•u•late \mə-'ni-pyə-ˌlāt\ *vb* **ma•nip•u•lat•ed**; **ma•nip•u•lat•ing**
1 to operate, use, or move with the hands or by mechanical means ⟨She learned to *manipulate* the levers of the machine.⟩
2 to manage skillfully and especially with intent to deceive ⟨The candidates tried to *manipulate* public opinion.⟩

man•kind *n*
1 \'man-'kīnd\ human beings
2 \-ˌkīnd\ men as distinguished from women

man•ly \'man-lē\ *adj* **man•li•er**; **man•li•est**
having or showing qualities (as strength or courage) often felt to be proper for a man ⟨a *manly* voice⟩
man•li•ness *n*

man–made \'man-'mād\ *adj*
made by people rather than nature ⟨a *man-made* lake⟩

man•na \'ma-nə\ *n*
1 food which according to the Bible was supplied by a miracle to the Israelites in the wilderness
2 a usually sudden and unexpected source of pleasure or gain

man•ne•quin \'ma-ni-kən\ *n*
▲ a form representing the human figure used especially for displaying clothes

man•ner \'ma-nər\ *n*
1 the way something is done or happens ⟨She worked in a quick *manner.*⟩
2 a way of acting ⟨He has a gentle *manner.*⟩
3 **manners** *pl* behavior toward or in the presence of other people ⟨They have good *manners* in a restaurant.⟩
4 [1]SORT 1

man•nered \'ma-nərd\ *adj*
having manners of a specified kind ⟨mild-*mannered*⟩ ⟨well-*mannered*⟩

man•ner•ism \'ma-nə-ˌri-zəm\ *n*
a habit (as of looking or moving in a certain way) that occurs commonly in a person's behavior

man•ner•ly \'ma-nər-lē\ *adj*
showing good manners

man–of–war \ˌma-nəv-'wȯr\ *n, pl* **men–of–war** \me-\
WARSHIP

man•or \'ma-nər\ *n*
a large estate

man•sion \'man-shən\ *n*
a large fine house

man•slaugh•ter \'man-ˌslȯ-tər\ *n*
the unintentional but unlawful killing of a person

man•ta ray \'man-tə-\ *n*
a very large ray of warm seas that has fins that resemble wings

man•tel \'man-tᵊl\ *n*
a shelf above a fireplace

man•tel•piece \'man-tᵊl-,pēs\ *n*
1 a shelf above a fireplace along with side pieces
2 MANTEL

man•tis \'man-təs\ *n, pl* **man•tis•es** *also* **man•tes** \'man-,tēz\
PRAYING MANTIS

man•tle \'man-tᵊl\ *n*
1 a loose sleeveless outer garment
2 something that covers or wraps ⟨The town was covered with a *mantle* of snow.⟩
3 the part of the earth's interior beneath the crust and above the central core
4 a fold of the body wall of a mollusk that produces the shell material

¹man•u•al \'man-yə-wəl\ *adj*
1 of or relating to hard physical work ⟨*manual* labor⟩
2 operated by the hands ⟨a *manual* gearshift⟩
3 of or with the hands ⟨*manual* skill⟩
man•u•al•ly *adv*

²manual *n*
HANDBOOK ⟨a scout *manual*⟩

¹man•u•fac•ture \,man-yə-'fak-chər\ *vb* **man•u•fac•tured; man•u•fac•tur•ing**
1 to make from raw materials by hand or machinery
2 to create using the imagination often in order to deceive ⟨He *manufactures* excuses for being absent.⟩
synonyms see MAKE
man•u•fac•tur•er *n*

²manufacture *n*
1 the making of products by hand or machinery
2 PRODUCTION 2 ⟨the *manufacture* of blood in the body⟩

ma•nure \mə-'nu̇r, -'nyu̇r\ *n*
material (as animal wastes) used to fertilize land

man•u•script \'man-yə-,skript\ *n*
1 ► a document written by hand especially before the development of printing ⟨An ancient *manuscript* was found in the church.⟩
2 the original copy of a writer's work before it is printed

¹many \'me-nē\ *adj* **more** \'mȯr\; **most** \'mōst\
1 amounting to a large number ⟨We had *many* children to play with.⟩
2 being one of a large but not definite number ⟨There was *many* a day when she felt lonely.⟩

²many *pron*
a large number of people or things ⟨Some stayed, but *many* left.⟩

manuscript 1: a decorated medieval Armenian manuscript

► **¹map 1**
There are a number of different types of maps produced to serve a range of functions. For example, city maps show the streets and landmarks of towns and cities, road maps show major and minor roads with their intersections, and satellite maps record the earth's surface. City and road maps are used for finding routes, with city maps giving detailed information on local facilities such as railroad stations.

regional map places the area in context
commuter train station
parking
water taxi boarding point
tourist information

map showing the location of tourist sites in Miami

³many *n*
a large number ⟨*Many* of our friends left.⟩

¹map \'map\ *n*
1 ▲ a picture or chart that shows the features of an area ⟨a street *map*⟩ ⟨a *map* of Africa⟩
2 a picture or chart of the sky showing the position of stars and planets

► **Word History** In the Latin of ancient Rome the word *mappa* was applied to a rectangular piece of cloth used as a towel, napkin, or small tablecloth. After the fall of the Roman Empire people still employed Latin as a written language, and *mappa* then seems to have been applied by land surveyors to squares of cloth on which they plotted land holdings. Eventually any representation of part of the earth's surface was called *mappa*, and this word was borrowed from Latin into English.

²map *vb* **mapped; map•ping**
1 to make a map of ⟨Astronomers are working to *map* the heavens.⟩
2 to plan in detail ⟨We *mapped* out our strategy.⟩

ma•ple \'mā-pəl\ *n*
► a tree having deeply notched leaves, seeds with a winglike part, and hard pale wood and including some whose sap is evaporated to a sweet syrup (**maple syrup**) and a brownish sugar (**maple sugar**)

maple: a leaf from a maple

mar *vb* **marred; mar•ring**
to ruin the beauty or perfection of : SPOIL

Mar. *abbr* March

ma•ra•ca \mə-'rä-kə, -'ra-\ *n*
a musical rhythm instrument made of a dried gourd with seeds or pebbles inside that is usually played in pairs by shaking

mar•a•thon \'mer-ə-,thän\ *n*
1 a long-distance running race
2 a long hard contest

ma•raud \mə-'rȯd\ *vb* **ma•raud•ed; ma•raud•ing**
to roam about and raid in search of things to steal
ma•raud•er *n*

mar•ble \'mär-bəl\ *n*
1 a type of limestone that is capable of taking a high polish and is used in architecture and sculpture
2 ▶ a little ball (as of glass) used in a children's game (**marbles**)

marble 2: glass marbles

[1]march \'märch\ *vb* **marched**; **march•ing**
1 to move or cause to move along with a steady regular step especially with others ⟨Our band will *march* in a parade.⟩
2 to make steady progress ⟨Science *marches* on.⟩
march•er *n*

[2]march *n*
1 the action of moving along with a steady regular step especially with others
2 an organized walk by a large group of people to support or protest something
3 the distance covered in marching ⟨a long day's *march*⟩
4 a regular and organized way that soldiers walk
5 a musical piece in a lively rhythm with a strong beat that is suitable to march to

March \'märch\ *n*
the third month of the year

> ▶ **Word History** The English word *March* came from the Latin name for the month, Martius, which in turn came from *Mars*, the name of the Roman god of war and farming. The planet Mars also got its name from this god.

mar•chio•ness \'mär-shə-nəs\ *n*
1 the wife or widow of a marquess
2 a woman who holds the rank of a marquess in her own right

mare \'mer\ *n*
an adult female horse or related animal (as a zebra or donkey)

mar•ga•rine \'mär-jə-rən\ *n*
a food product made usually from vegetable oils and skim milk and used as a spread or for cooking

mar•gin \'mär-jən\ *n*
1 the part of a page or sheet outside the main body of print or writing
2 [1]BORDER 2
3 an extra amount (as of time or money) allowed for use if needed ⟨We have a *margin* of five minutes before the bus leaves.⟩
4 a measurement of difference ⟨They lost by a small *margin*.⟩

mari•gold \'mer-ə-,gōld\ *n*
a plant grown for its usually yellow, orange, or brownish red flowers

mar•i•jua•na \,mer-ə-'wä-nə\ *n*
dried leaves and flowers of the hemp plant smoked as a drug

ma•ri•na \mə-'rē-nə\ *n*
a dock or basin providing a place to anchor motorboats and yachts

[1]ma•rine \mə-'rēn\ *adj*
1 of or relating to the sea ⟨*marine* animals⟩
2 of or relating to the navigation of the sea : NAUTICAL ⟨*marine* charts⟩
3 of or relating to soldiers in the United States Marine Corps ⟨*marine* barracks⟩

[2]marine *n*
1 a soldier of the United States Marine Corps
2 the ships of a country

mar•i•ner \'mer-ə-nər\ *n*
SEAMAN 1, SAILOR

mar•i•o•nette \,mer-ē-ə-'net\ *n*
▼ a puppet moved by attached strings

marionette

mar•i•tal \'mer-ə-tᵊl\ *adj*
of or relating to marriage

mar•i•time \'mer-ə-,tīm\ *adj*
1 of or relating to ocean navigation or trade ⟨*maritime* law⟩
2 bordering on or living near the sea ⟨*maritime* nations⟩

[1]mark \'märk\ *n*
1 a blemish (as a scratch or stain) made on a surface ⟨There were tire *marks* on the lawn.⟩
2 a written or printed symbol ⟨a punctuation *mark*⟩
3 something that shows that something else exists : SIGN, INDICATION ⟨They traded T-shirts as a *mark* of friendship.⟩
4 something aimed at : TARGET
5 a grade or score showing the quality of work or conduct ⟨He gets good *marks* in school.⟩
6 something designed or serving to record position ⟨high-water *mark*⟩
7 the starting line of a race

[2]mark *vb* **marked**; **mark•ing**
1 to indicate a location ⟨He *marked* his place in the book.⟩
2 to set apart by a line or boundary ⟨We tried to *mark* off a baseball diamond.⟩
3 to make a shape, symbol, or word on ⟨I'll *mark* the top with a cross.⟩
4 to decide and show the value or quality of : GRADE ⟨Teachers *mark* tests.⟩
5 to be an important characteristic of ⟨The disease is *marked* by fever.⟩
6 to take notice of ⟨You'll be sorry, *mark* my words.⟩
mark•er *n*

marked \'märkt\ *adj*
1 having notes or information written on it
2 NOTICEABLE ⟨Her father speaks with a *marked* accent.⟩
3 showing identification ⟨a *marked* police car⟩

[1]mar•ket \'mär-kət\ *n*
1 ▼ a public place where people gather to buy and sell things
2 a store where foods are sold to the public ⟨a meat *market*⟩
3 a region in which something can be sold ⟨*markets* for American cotton⟩
4 an opportunity for selling something ⟨There's no *market* for snowplows in Florida.⟩

[2]market *vb* **mar•ket•ed**; **mar•ket•ing**
to sell or promote the sale of ⟨The shop *markets* local vegetables.⟩

[1]market 1: a market for fresh produce

▶ marsupial

Newborn marsupials wriggle their way to a nipple usually within a pouch by using their well-developed forelimbs to grasp their mother's fur. The young suckle milk and continue to grow until they are ready to fend for themselves. Marsupials are found in Australia, New Guinea, North America, and South America.

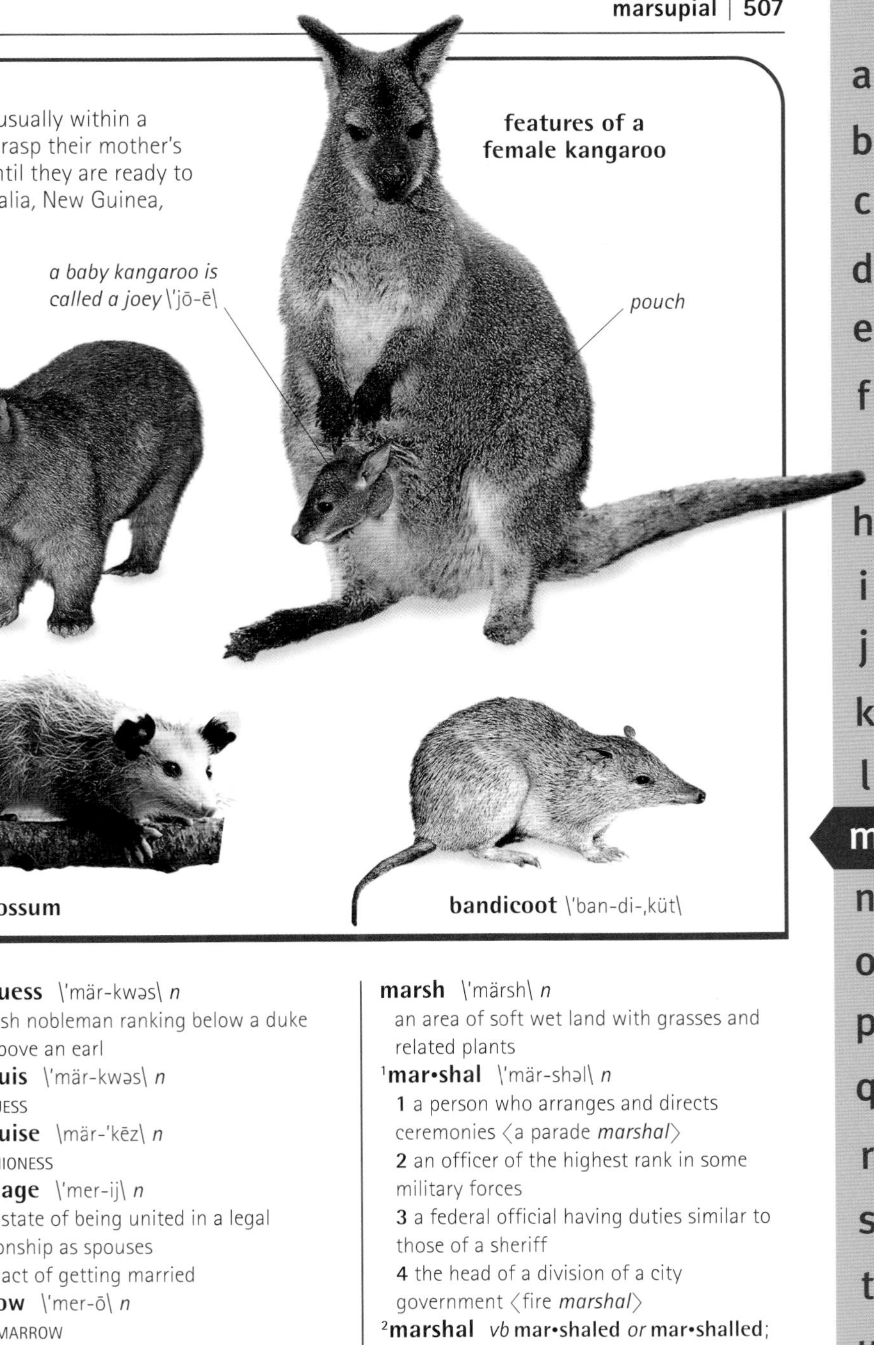

mar•ket•place \'mär-kət-ˌplās\ *n*
a location where public sales are held

mark•ing \'mär-kiŋ\ *n*
1 a shape, symbol, or word on something
2 the arrangement or pattern of contrasting colors on an animal

marks•man \'märks-mən\ *n*, *pl* **marks•men** \-mən\
a person who shoots well
marks•man•ship \-ˌship\ *n*

mar•ma•lade \'mär-mə-ˌlād\ *n*
a jam containing pieces of fruit and fruit rind ⟨orange *marmalade*⟩

mar•mo•set \'mär-mə-ˌset\ *n*
a small monkey of South and Central America with soft fur and a bushy tail

mar•mot \'mär-mət\ *n*
a stocky burrowing animal with short legs and a bushy tail that is related to the squirrels

¹ma•roon \mə-'rün\ *vb* **ma•rooned**; **ma•roon•ing**
to abandon in a place that is difficult to escape from

²maroon *n*
a dark red

mar•quess \'mär-kwəs\ *n*
a British nobleman ranking below a duke and above an earl

mar•quis \'mär-kwəs\ *n*
MARQUESS

mar•quise \mär-'kēz\ *n*
MARCHIONESS

mar•riage \'mer-ij\ *n*
1 the state of being united in a legal relationship as spouses
2 the act of getting married

mar•row \'mer-ō\ *n*
BONE MARROW

mar•ry \'mer-ē\ *vb* **mar•ried**; **mar•ry•ing**
1 to take for husband or wife ⟨She *married* her high school sweetheart.⟩
2 to become joined in marriage
3 to join in marriage ⟨They were *married* by a priest.⟩
4 to give in marriage ⟨They *married* off all their children.⟩

Mars \'märz\ *n*
the planet that is fourth in order of distance from the sun, is known for its redness, and has a diameter of about 4200 miles (6800 kilometers)

marsh \'märsh\ *n*
an area of soft wet land with grasses and related plants

¹mar•shal \'mär-shəl\ *n*
1 a person who arranges and directs ceremonies ⟨a parade *marshal*⟩
2 an officer of the highest rank in some military forces
3 a federal official having duties similar to those of a sheriff
4 the head of a division of a city government ⟨fire *marshal*⟩

²marshal *vb* **mar•shaled** *or* **mar•shalled**; **mar•shal•ing** *or* **mar•shal•ling**
to arrange in order ⟨*marshal* troops⟩

marsh•mal•low \'märsh-ˌme-lō, -ˌma-\ *n*
a soft spongy sweet food made from corn syrup, sugar, and gelatin

marshy \'mär-shē\ *adj* **marsh•i•er**; **marsh•i•est**
like or containing soft wet land

mar•su•pi•al \mär-'sü-pē-əl\ *n*
▲ a mammal (as a kangaroo or opossum) that does not develop a true placenta and usually has a pouch on the female's abdomen in which the young develop and are carried

marten

mart \'märt\ *n*
a trading place : MARKET

mar•ten \'mär-tᵊn\ *n*
▲ a slender animal related to the weasel that has soft gray or brown fur and often climbs trees

mar•tial \'mär-shəl\ *adj*
having to do with or suitable for war 〈*martial* music〉 〈*martial* courage〉

martial art *n*
any of several forms of combat and self-defense (as karate or judo) that are widely practiced as sports

mar•tin \'mär-tᵊn\ *n*
1 a European swallow with a forked tail
2 ▶ any of several birds (as the North American **purple martin**) resembling or related to the true martin

martin 2:
a purple martin

Mar•tin Lu•ther King Day \'mär-tᵊn-'lü-thər-\ *n*
the third Monday in January observed as a legal holiday in the United States

[1]**mar•tyr** \'mär-tər\ *n*
a person who suffers greatly or dies rather than give up his or her religion or principles

[2]**martyr** *vb* **mar•tyred**; **mar•tyr•ing**
to put to death for refusing to give up a belief

[1]**mar•vel** \'mär-vəl\ *n*
something that causes wonder or astonishment

[2]**marvel** *vb* **mar•veled** *or* **mar•velled**; **mar•vel•ing** *or* **mar•vel•ling**
to feel astonishment or wonder 〈I *marvel* at your skill.〉

mar•vel•ous *or* **mar•vel•lous** \'mär-və-ləs\ *adj*
1 causing wonder or astonishment 〈*marvelous* adventures〉
2 of the finest kind or quality 〈a *marvelous* dinner〉
mar•vel•ous•ly *adv*

masc. *abbr* masculine

mas•cot \'mas-,kät, -kət\ *n*
a person, animal, or object adopted as the symbol of a group (as a school or sports team) and believed to bring good luck

mas•cu•line \'mas-kyə-lən\ *adj*
1 of the male sex
2 characteristic of or relating to men : MALE 〈a *masculine* voice〉

[1]**mash** \'mash\ *vb* **mashed**; **mash•ing**
to make into a soft mass

[2]**mash** *n*
1 a mixture of ground feeds used for feeding livestock
2 a mass of something made soft by beating or crushing
3 a wet mixture of crushed malt or grain used to make alcoholic drinks

[1]**mask** \'mask\ *n*
1 a cover for the face or part of the face used for disguise or protection 〈a Halloween *mask*〉 〈a catcher's *mask*〉
2 something that disguises or conceals 〈She visited under a *mask* of friendship.〉

[2]**mask** *vb* **masked**; **mask•ing**
CONCEAL, DISGUISE 〈She found it difficult to *mask* her anger.〉

ma•son \'mā-sᵊn\ *n*
a person who builds or works with stone or brick

ma•son•ry \'mā-sᵊn-rē\ *n, pl* **ma•son•ries**
1 something built of stone or brick
2 the work done using stone or brick
3 the art, trade, or occupation of a mason

masque \'mask\ *n*
an old form of dramatic entertainment in which the actors wore masks

[1]**mas•quer•ade** \,ma-skə-'rād\ *n*
1 a party (as a dance) at which people wear masks and costumes
2 the act of pretending to be something different

[2]**masquerade** *vb* **mas•quer•ad•ed**; **mas•quer•ad•ing**
1 to wear a disguise
2 to pretend to be something different : POSE 〈He was *masquerading* as a policeman.〉
mas•quer•ad•er *n*

[1]**mass** \'mas\ *n*
1 a large quantity or number 〈A great *mass* of people pushed through the gate.〉
2 an amount of something that holds or clings together 〈a *mass* of clouds〉
3 large size : BULK 〈an elephant's huge *mass*〉
4 the principal part main body 〈The great *mass* of voters supported change.〉
5 **masses** *pl* the body of ordinary or common people 〈She was a hero to the *masses*.〉

[2]**mass** *vb* **massed**; **mass•ing**
to collect into a large body

[3]**mass** *n, often cap*
a religious service in which communion is celebrated

Mass. *abbr* Massachusetts

[1]**mas•sa•cre** \'ma-sə-kər\ *n*
the violent and cruel killing of a large number of people

[2]**massacre** *vb* **mas•sa•cred**; **mas•sa•cring**
to kill a large number of people in a violent and cruel manner

[1]**mas•sage** \mə-'säzh\ *n*
a soothing treatment of the body done by rubbing, kneading, and tapping

[2]**massage** *vb* **mas•saged**; **mas•sag•ing**
to give a soothing treatment to (the body) by rubbing, stroking, or pressing with the hands

mas•sive \'ma-siv\ *adj*
very large, heavy, and solid 〈a *massive* ship〉

mast \'mast\ *n*
a long pole that rises from the bottom of a ship and supports the sails and rigging
mast•ed \'mas-təd\ *adj*

[1]**mas•ter** \'ma-stər\ *n*
1 someone having authority over another person, an animal, or a thing 〈the slave's *master*〉 〈the *master* of a ship〉
2 a male teacher
3 an artist or performer of great skill 〈He is a *master* at making desserts.〉
4 used as a title for a young boy too young to be called *mister* 〈*Master* Timothy Roe〉

[2]**master** *vb* **mas•tered**; **mas•ter•ing**
1 to get control of 〈You must *master* your fear.〉
2 to become skillful at 〈I managed to *master* arithmetic.〉

mas•ter•ful \'ma-stər-fəl\ *adj*
1 tending to take control : displaying authority
2 having or showing great skill 〈a *masterful* sailor〉

mas•ter•ly \'ma-stər-lē\ *adj*
showing exceptional knowledge or skill 〈a *masterly* performance〉

mas•ter•piece \'ma-stər-ˌpēs\ *n*
something done or made with exceptional skill

master sergeant *n*
a noncommissioned officer in the army ranking above a sergeant first class or in the air force ranking above a technical sergeant or in the marines ranking above a gunnery sergeant

mas•tery \'ma-stə-rē\ *n*
1 complete control ⟨The wrestler gained *mastery* over all of his opponents.⟩
2 a very high level of skill or knowledge

mast•head \'mast-ˌhed\ *n*
the top of a ship's mast

mas•ti•cate \'ma-stə-ˌkāt\ *vb*
mas•ti•cat•ed; mas•ti•cat•ing
: [1]CHEW

mas•tiff \'ma-stəf\ *n*
a very large powerful dog with a smooth coat

[1]mat \'mat\ *n*
1 a piece of material used as a floor or seat covering or in front of a door to wipe the shoes on
2 a decorative piece of material used under dishes or vases
3 a pad or cushion for gymnastics or wrestling
4 something made up of many tangled strands ⟨a *mat* of hair⟩

[2]mat *vb* **mat•ted; mat•ting**
to form into a tangled mass

mat•a•dor \'ma-tə-ˌdȯr\ *n*
► a bullfighter who plays the most important human part in a bullfight

[1]match \'mach\ *n*
1 a person or thing that is equal to or as good as another ⟨We are a *match* for our opponents.⟩
2 a contest between two individuals or teams ⟨a tennis *match*⟩
3 a thing that is exactly like another thing ⟨I'm trying to find a *match* for this sock.⟩
4 two people or things that go well together ⟨The curtains and carpet are a good *match*.⟩
5 MARRIAGE 1 ⟨Your parents made a good *match*.⟩

[2]match *vb* **matched; match•ing**
1 to be the same or suitable to one another ⟨The colors of our shirts *match*.⟩
2 to choose something that is the same as another or goes with it ⟨Try to *match* this material.⟩
3 to place in competition ⟨The game *matched* the two former champions.⟩
4 to be as good as ⟨You'll never *match* her at golf.⟩

[3]match *n*
a short slender piece of material tipped with a mixture that produces fire when scratched

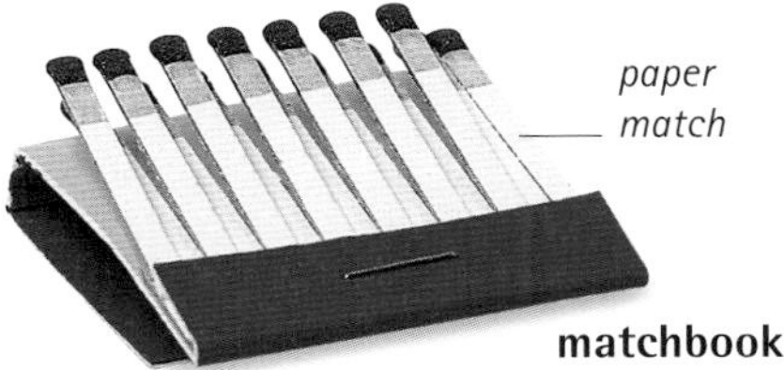

matchbook

match•book \'mach-ˌbu̇k\ *n*
▲ a small folder containing rows of paper matches

match•less \'mach-ləs\ *adj*
having no equal better than any other of the same kind

[1]mate \'māt\ *n*
1 COMPANION 1, COMRADE
2 *chiefly British* [1]CHUM, FRIEND
Hint: British speakers often use *mate* as a familiar form of address. ⟨Good night, *mate*!⟩
3 either member of a breeding pair of animals
4 an officer on a ship used to carry passengers or freight who ranks below the captain
5 either member of a married couple
6 either of two objects that go together ⟨I lost the *mate* to this glove.⟩

[2]mate *vb* **mat•ed; mat•ing**
1 to join as married partners
2 to come or bring together for breeding ⟨These birds *mate* for life.⟩

[1]ma•te•ri•al \mə-'tir-ē-əl\ *adj*
1 of, relating to, or made of matter : PHYSICAL ⟨the *material* world⟩
2 of or relating to a person's bodily needs or wants ⟨Money buys *material* comforts.⟩
3 having real importance ⟨Those facts aren't *material* to the case.⟩
ma•teri•al•ly *adv*

[2]material *n*
1 the elements, substance, or parts of which something is made or can be made ⟨We purchased bricks and other building *material*.⟩
2 equipment needed for doing something ⟨writing *materials*⟩

ma•te•ri•al•ize \mə-'tir-ē-ə-ˌlīz\ *vb*
ma•te•ri•al•ized; ma•te•ri•al•iz•ing
1 to appear suddenly ⟨As soon as I arrived, my friends *materialized*.⟩
2 to become actual fact ⟨Their hopes never *materialized*.⟩
3 to cause to take on a physical form ⟨She claimed she could *materialize* the spirits of the dead.⟩

ma•ter•nal \mə-'tər-nᵊl\ *adj*
1 of or relating to a mother ⟨*maternal* instincts⟩
2 related through the mother ⟨*maternal* grandparents⟩
ma•ter•nal•ly *adv*

matador: a Spanish matador in traditional costume

ma•ter•ni•ty \mə-ˈtər-nə-tē\ *n*
the state of being a mother

math \ˈmath\ *n*
MATHEMATICS

math•e•mat•i•cal \ˌma-thə-ˈma-ti-kəl\ *adj*
1 of or relating to numbers, quantities, measurements, and the relations between them : of or relating to mathematics
2 [1]EXACT ⟨*mathematical* precision⟩
math•e•mat•i•cal•ly *adv*

math•e•ma•ti•cian \ˌma-thə-mə-ˈti-shən\ *n*
a specialist in mathematics

math•e•mat•ics \ˌma-thə-ˈma-tiks\ *n*
the science that studies and explains numbers, quantities, measurements, and the relations between them

mat•i•nee *or* **mat•i•née** \ˌma-tə-ˈnā\ *n*
a musical or dramatic performance in the afternoon

ma•tri•arch \ˈmā-trē-ˌärk\ *n*
a woman who is the head of a family, group, or state

mat•ri•mo•ni•al \ˌma-trə-ˈmō-nē-əl\ *adj*
of or relating to marriage

mat•ri•mo•ny \ˈma-trə-ˌmō-nē\ *n*
MARRIAGE 1

ma•tron \ˈmā-trən\ *n*
1 a married woman usually of high social position
2 a woman who is in charge of women or children (as in a school or police station)

[1]**mat•ter** \ˈma-tər\ *n*
1 something to be dealt with or considered ⟨I have a serious *matter* to discuss with you.⟩
2 PROBLEM 2, DIFFICULTY ⟨What's the *matter*?⟩
3 the substance that things are made of and that takes up space and has weight
4 material substance of a certain kind or function ⟨coloring *matter*⟩ ⟨plant *matter*⟩
5 PUS
6 a small quantity or amount ⟨The difference is a *matter* of ten cents.⟩
as a matter of fact ACTUALLY ⟨Hello. *As a matter of fact* I just tried to call you.⟩
no matter it makes no difference
no matter what regardless of the costs or consequences

[2]**matter** *vb* **mat•tered**; **mat•ter•ing**
to be of importance ⟨It does not *matter* whether you call or write.⟩

mat•ter–of–fact \ˌma-tər-ə-ˈfakt\ *adj*
sticking to or concerned with fact and usually not showing emotion ⟨He gave a *matter-of-fact* answer.⟩
mat•ter–of–fact•ly \-ˈfakt-lē\ *adv*

mat•ting \ˈma-tiŋ\ *n*
rough fabric used as a floor covering

mat•tress \ˈma-trəs\ *n*
a springy pad for use on a bed

[1]**ma•ture** \mə-ˈtu̇r, -ˈtyu̇r, -ˈchu̇r\ *adj*
ma•tur•er; **ma•tur•est**
1 fully grown or developed : ADULT, RIPE ⟨*mature* fruit⟩ ⟨*mature* fish⟩
2 having or showing the qualities of an adult person ⟨a *mature* outlook⟩
3 due for payment ⟨a *mature* loan⟩

[2]**mature** *vb* **ma•tured**; **ma•tur•ing**
1 to reach full development
2 to become due for payment ⟨The bond *matures* in ten years.⟩

ma•tu•ri•ty \mə-ˈtu̇r-ə-tē, -ˈtyu̇r-, -ˈchu̇r-\ *n*
the condition of being fully developed

[1]**maul** \ˈmȯl\ *n*
a heavy hammer used especially for driving wedges or posts

[2]**maul** *vb* **mauled**; **maul•ing**
1 to attack and injure by biting, cutting, or tearing flesh
2 to handle roughly

mauve \ˈmōv, ˈmȯv\ *n*
a medium purple, violet, or lilac

maxi– *prefix*
very long or large

max•il•la \mak-ˈsi-lə\ *n*, *pl* **max•il•lae** \-lē\
1 an upper jaw especially of a mammal
2 either of the pair of mouth parts next behind the mandibles of an arthropod (as an insect or a crustacean)

max•im \ˈmak-səm\ *n*
a short saying (as "live and let live") expressing a general truth or rule of conduct

max•imize \ˈmak-sə-ˌmīz\ *vb*
max•i•mized; **max•i•miz•ing**
1 to increase (something) as much as possible ⟨*maximize* profits⟩
2 to make the most of ⟨I want to *maximize* this opportunity.⟩
3 to increase the size of (a program's window) to fill a computer screen

[1]**max•i•mum** \ˈmak-sə-məm\ *n*, *pl* **max•i•ma** \-sə-mə\ *or* **maximums**
the highest value : greatest amount ⟨We had to pay the *maximum*.⟩

[2]**maximum** *adj*
as great as possible in amount or degree ⟨We work with *maximum* efficiency.⟩

meadowlark

[3]**maximum** *adv*
at the most

may \ˈmā\ *helping verb, past* **might** \ˈmīt\; *present sing & pl* **may**
1 have permission to ⟨You *may* go.⟩
2 be in some degree likely to ⟨You *may* be right.⟩
3 used to express a wish ⟨*May* the best man win.⟩
4 used to express purpose ⟨We exercise so that we *may* be strong.⟩

May \ˈmā\ *n*
the fifth month of the year

> ▶ **Word History** The English word *May* came from *Maius*, the Latin name for the same month. The Latin name came from *Maia*, a Roman goddess. Every year on the first of May, the ancient Romans made offerings to this goddess.

may•be \ˈmā-bē\ *adv*
possibly but not certainly

mayn't \ˈmā-ənt, mānt\ may not

may•on•naise \ˈmā-ə-ˌnāz\ *n*
▼ a creamy dressing usually made of egg yolk, oil, and vinegar or lemon juice

mayonnaise

may•or \ˈmā-ər\ *n*
an official elected to serve as head of a city, town, or borough

maze \ˈmāz\ *n*
a confusing arrangement of paths or passages

MB *abbr*
1 Manitoba
2 megabyte

MD, Md. *abbr* Maryland

M.D. *abbr* doctor of medicine

me \ˈmē\ *pron, objective case of* I

ME, Me. *abbr* Maine

mead•ow \ˈme-dō\ *n*
▶ usually moist and low grassland

mead•ow•lark \ˈme-dō-ˌlärk\ *n*
◀ a songbird that has brownish upper parts and a yellow breast

mea•ger *or* **mea•gre** \ˈmē-gər\ *adj*
1 not enough in quality or amount
2 having little flesh : THIN

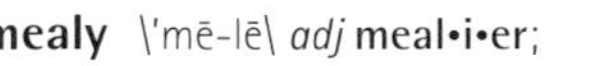

[1]meal \'mēl\ *n*
1 the food eaten or prepared for eating at one time
2 the act or time of eating

[2]meal *n*
coarsely ground seeds of a cereal grass and especially of corn

► **Word History** You might assume that the *meal* of "three meals a day" and the *meal* of "ground meal" have a common origin, since both words have to do with food. Surprisingly, this is not the case. The *meal* of "ground meal" comes from Old English *melu*, a word akin to Latin *molere*, "to grind," and *molina*, "mill." The meal of "three meals a day," however, is from Old English *mǣl* or *mēl*, "measure, appointed time, meal time."

mealy \'mē-lē\ *adj* **meal•i•er**; **meal•i•est**
soft, dry, and crumbly ⟨a *mealy* potato⟩
meal•i•ness *n*

[1]mean \'mēn\ *vb* **meant** \'ment\; **mean•ing** \'mē-niŋ\
1 to represent or have as a definite explanation or idea : SIGNIFY ⟨What does this word *mean*?⟩
2 to be a sign of ⟨Those clouds *mean* rain.⟩
3 to have in mind as a purpose : INTEND ⟨I *mean* to win.⟩ ⟨He *meant* to be funny.⟩
4 to intend for a particular use ⟨It's a book *meant* for children.⟩
5 to have importance to ⟨Your visit *meant* a lot to me.⟩

[2]mean *adj* **mean•er**; **mean•est**
1 deliberately unkind ⟨That was a *mean* trick.⟩
2 STINGY 1
3 low in quality, worth, or dignity ⟨That was no *mean* achievement.⟩
4 EXCELLENT ⟨He plays a *mean* guitar.⟩
mean•ly *adv*
mean•ness *n*

[3]mean *adj*
occurring or being in a middle position : AVERAGE ⟨the *mean* temperature⟩

[4]mean *n*
1 a middle point or something (as a place, time, number, or rate) that falls at or near a middle point : MODERATION
2 ARITHMETIC MEAN
3 **means** *pl* something that helps a person to get what he or she wants ⟨Use every *means* you can think of to find it.⟩
4 **means** *pl* WEALTH 1 ⟨a person of *means*⟩
by all means CERTAINLY 1
by any means in any way ⟨I was not a good student *by any means*.⟩
by means of through the use of
by no means certainly not

me•an•der \mē-'an-dər\ *vb* **me•an•dered**; **me•an•der•ing**
1 to follow a winding course ⟨A brook *meanders* through the fields.⟩
2 to wander without a goal or purpose ⟨He *meandered* around town.⟩

mean•ing \'mē-niŋ\ *n*
1 the idea that is represented by a word, phrase, or statement
2 the idea a person intends to express by something said or done ⟨What is the *meaning* of this behavior?⟩
3 the reason or explanation for something
4 the quality of communicating something or of being important ⟨He gave me a look full of *meaning*.⟩

mean•ing•ful \'mē-niŋ-fəl\ *adj*
having a meaning or purpose
mean•ing•ful•ly \-fə-lē\ *adv*

mean•ing•less \'mē-niŋ-ləs\ *adj*
having no meaning or importance

[1]mean•time \'mēn-,tīm\ *n*
1 the time between events or points of time ⟨You'll go again but in the *meantime* rest.⟩
2 a time during which more than one thing is being done ⟨He napped, and in the *meantime* I worked.⟩

[2]meantime *adv*
in the time between events or points of time or during which more than one thing is being done ⟨She worked and *meantime* raised a family.⟩

[1]mean•while \'mēn-,hwīl, -,wīl\ *n*
[1]MEANTIME

[2]meanwhile *adv*
1 [2]MEANTIME
2 at the same time

meadow: a meadow with flowers

A B C D E F G H I J K L M N O P Q R S T U V W X Y Z

mea•sles \ˈmē-zəlz\ *n*
1 a contagious disease in which there are fever and red spots on the skin
2 any of several diseases (as **German measles**) resembling true measles

mea•sly \ˈmēz-lē\ *adj*
mea•sli•er; mea•sli•est
so small or unimportant as to be rejected with scorn

mea•sur•able \ˈme-zhə-rə-bəl\ *adj*
capable of having the size, extent, amount, or significance determined ⟨a *measurable* rainfall⟩ ⟨a *measurable* improvement⟩
mea•sur•ably \-blē\ *adv*

[1]**mea•sure** \ˈme-zhər\ *n*
1 EXTENT 2, DEGREE, AMOUNT ⟨Our plan did succeed in large *measure*.⟩
2 the size, capacity, or quantity of something that has been determined ⟨Use equal *measures* of flour and milk.⟩
3 something (as a yardstick or cup) used in determining size, capacity, or quantity
4 a unit used in determining size, capacity, or quantity ⟨An inch is a *measure* of length.⟩
5 a system of determining size, capacity, or quantity ⟨liquid *measure*⟩
6 the notes and rests between bar lines on a musical staff
7 a way of accomplishing something ⟨a safety *measure*⟩ ⟨The new law is a *measure* to save energy.⟩
for good measure as something added or extra ⟨We gave the wall another coat of paint *for good measure*.⟩

[2]**measure** *vb* **mea•sured; mea•sur•ing**
1 to find out the size, extent, or amount of ⟨You should *measure* the cloth before cutting.⟩
2 to separate out a fixed amount ⟨She *measured* the rice.⟩
3 [1]ESTIMATE ⟨I had to *measure* the distance with my eye.⟩
4 to bring into comparison ⟨Why don't you *measure* your skill against mine?⟩
5 to give a determination of size, capacity, or quantity : INDICATE ⟨A thermometer *measures* temperature.⟩
6 to have as its size, capacity, or quantity ⟨The cloth *measures* ten meters.⟩
measure up to satisfy needs or requirements ⟨They did not *measure up* to expectations.⟩

mea•sure•ment \ˈme-zhər-mənt\ *n*
1 the act of determining size, capacity, or quantity ⟨The instruments provide accurate *measurement*.⟩
2 the extent, size, capacity, or amount of something as has been determined

mechanic: a mechanic repairing a mountain bike

meat \ˈmēt\ *n*
1 the flesh of an animal used as food
Hint: The word *meat* often does not include the flesh of fish or seafood.
2 solid food as distinguished from drink
3 the part of something that can be eaten ⟨nut *meats*⟩
4 the most important part : SUBSTANCE ⟨Get to the *meat* of the story.⟩
meat•less \-ləs\ *adj*

meat•ball \ˈmēt-ˌbȯl\ *n*
a small round lump of chopped or ground meat

me•chan•ic \mi-ˈka-nik\ *n*
▲ a person who makes or repairs machines

me•chan•i•cal \mi-ˈka-ni-kəl\ *adj*
1 of or relating to machinery ⟨He has *mechanical* skill.⟩
2 made or operated by a machine ⟨a *mechanical* toy⟩
3 done or produced as if by a machine ⟨They sing in a *mechanical* way.⟩
me•chan•i•cal•ly *adv*

me•chan•ics \mi-ˈka-niks\ *n pl*
1 a science dealing with the action of forces on objects
2 the way something works or things are done ⟨the *mechanics* of a watch⟩ ⟨the *mechanics* of writing⟩
Hint: *Mechanics* can be used as a singular or as a plural in writing and speaking.

mech•a•nism \ˈme-kə-ˌni-zəm\ *n*
1 a piece of machinery
2 ▶ the parts by which a machine operates ⟨the *mechanism* of a watch⟩
3 the parts or steps that make up a process or activity ⟨the *mechanism* of government⟩

mech•a•nize \ˈme-kə-ˌnīz\ *vb*
mech•a•nized; mech•a•niz•ing
1 to cause to be done by machines rather than humans or animals
2 to equip with machinery

med•al \ˈme-dᵊl\ *n*
a piece of metal often in the form of a coin with design and words in honor of a special event, a person, or an achievement

me•dal•lion \mə-ˈdal-yən\ *n*
1 a large medal
2 a decoration shaped like a large medal

mechanism 2:
mechanism of a watch

med•dle \'me-dᵊl\ *vb* **med•dled**; **med•dling**
to be overly interested or involved in someone else's business

▶ **Synonyms** MEDDLE, INTERFERE, AND TAMPER mean to get involved with something that is someone else's business. MEDDLE is used for intruding in an inconsiderate and annoying fashion. ⟨Don't *meddle* in her personal problems.⟩ INTERFERE is used for getting in the way of or disturbing someone or something whether intentionally or not. ⟨I tried to give advice without *interfering*.⟩ TAMPER is used for intruding or experimenting in a way that is wrong or uncalled-for and likely to be harmful. ⟨Someone had *tampered* with the lock.⟩

med•dle•some \'me-dᵊl-səm\ *adj*
intruding in another person's business in an inconsiderate and annoying way

me•dia \'mē-dē-ə\ *n*
the system and organizations of communication through which information is spread to the public
Hint: *Media* can be used as a singular or a plural in writing and speaking.

me•di•an \'mē-dē-ən\ *n*
a value in a series arranged from smallest to largest below and above which there are an equal number of values or which is the average of the two middle values if there is no one middle value ⟨The *median* of the set 1, 3, 7, 12, 19 is 7.⟩

med•i•cal \'me-di-kəl\ *adj*
of or relating to the science or practice of medicine ⟨*medical* care⟩
med•i•cal•ly *adv*

med•i•cate \'me-də-,kāt\ *vb* **med•i•cat•ed**; **med•i•cat•ing**
1 to treat with medicine
2 to add medicinal material to

med•i•ca•tion \,me-də-'kā-shən\ *n*
MEDICINE 1

me•dic•i•nal \mə-'di-sᵊn-əl\ *adj*
used or likely to prevent, cure, or relieve disease ⟨*medicinal* ingredients⟩
me•dic•i•nal•ly *adv*

med•i•cine \'me-də-sən\ *n*
1 ▶ something (as a pill or liquid) used to prevent, cure, or relieve a disease
2 a science dealing with the prevention, cure, or relief of disease

medicine dropper *n*
DROPPER 2

medicine man *n*
a person especially among American Indian groups believed to have magic powers to cure illnesses and keep away evil spirits

me•di•eval *also* **me•di•ae•val** \,mē-dē-'ē-vəl, ,me-\ *adj*
of or relating to the Middle Ages

me•di•o•cre \,mē-dē-'ō-kər\ *adj*
not very good ⟨a *mediocre* restaurant⟩

med•i•tate \'me-də-,tāt\ *vb* **med•i•tat•ed**; **med•i•tat•ing**
1 to consider carefully : PLAN
2 to spend time in quiet thinking : REFLECT

med•i•ta•tion \,me-də-'tā-shən\ *n*
the act or an instance of planning or thinking quietly

Med•i•ter•ra•nean \,me-də-tə-'rā-nē-ən, -'rān-yən\ *adj*
of or relating to the Mediterranean Sea or to the lands or peoples surrounding it

[1]**me•di•um** \'mē-dē-əm\ *n, pl* **me•di•ums** *or* **me•dia** \-dē-ə\
1 something that is in a middle position (as in size)
2 the thing by which or through which something is done ⟨Writing is a *medium* of communication.⟩
3 the substance in which something lives or acts ⟨the *medium* of air⟩
4 *pl usually media* a form or system of communication, information, or entertainment
5 a person through whom other persons try to communicate with the spirits of the dead

[2]**medium** *adj*
intermediate in amount, quality, position, or degree ⟨*medium* size⟩

med•ley \'med-lē\ *n, pl* **medleys**
1 MIXTURE 2, JUMBLE ⟨a *medley* of tastes⟩
2 a musical selection made up of a series of different songs or parts of different compositions

me•dul•la ob•lon•ga•ta \mə-'də-lə-,ä-,blȯŋ-'gä-tə\ *n*
the part of the brain that joins the spinal cord and is concerned especially with control of involuntary activities (as breathing and beating of the heart) necessary for life

meek \'mēk\ *adj* **meek•er**; **meek•est**
having or showing a quiet, gentle, and humble nature ⟨a *meek* child⟩ ⟨a *meek* reply⟩
meek•ly *adv*
meek•ness *n*

▶ **medicine 1**
Medicines are used to treat a wide variety of ailments, from minor complaints such as a sore throat to life-threatening conditions such as heart disease. A common method for taking medicines is to swallow them in tablet, capsule, or syrup form. Other medicines are given by injection using a syringe, inhaled through the nose or mouth, introduced in liquid form through a dropper to the eye or ear, or absorbed through the skin as cream or ointment.

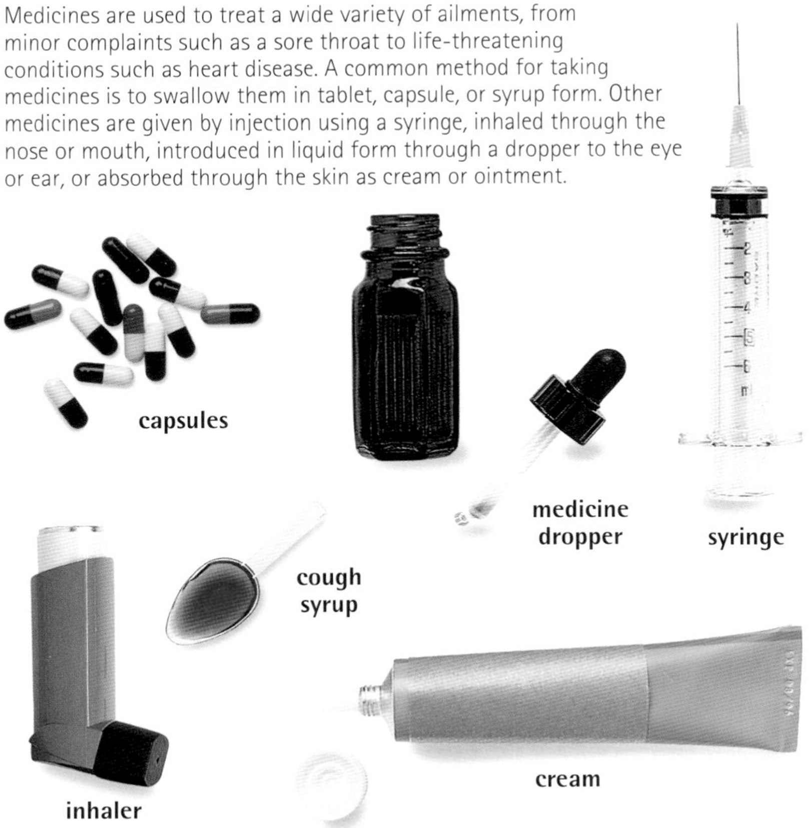

capsules

medicine dropper

syringe

cough syrup

inhaler

cream

megaphone:
a woman speaking through a megaphone

[1]meet \ˈmēt\ *vb* **met** \ˈmet\; **meet•ing**
1 to get to know : become acquainted ⟨They *met* at a party.⟩
2 to come upon or across ⟨He *met* a friend while shopping.⟩
3 to be at a place to greet or keep an appointment ⟨Please *meet* me at the airport.⟩ ⟨We *met* in the park for lunch.⟩
4 to approach from the opposite direction ⟨When you *meet* another car, keep to the right.⟩
5 to touch and join or cross ⟨The town is located where two rivers *meet.*⟩
6 to experience something ⟨He *met* his first major disappointment.⟩
7 to hold a gathering or assembly
8 to be sensed by ⟨What lovely sounds *meet* the ears!⟩
9 to deal with ⟨You must *meet* problems as they appear.⟩
10 to fulfill the requirements of : SATISFY ⟨I will be unable to *meet* your demands.⟩

[2]meet *n*
a meeting for sports competition ⟨a track *meet*⟩

meet•ing \ˈmē-tiŋ\ *n*
1 the act of persons or things that come together ⟨a chance *meeting*⟩
2 a gathering of people for a particular purpose ⟨The club holds weekly *meetings.*⟩

meet•ing•house \ˈmē-tiŋ-ˌhau̇s\ *n*
a building used for public assembly and especially for Protestant worship

mega•byte \ˈme-gə-ˌbīt\ *n*
a unit of computer information storage capacity equal to 1,048,576 bytes

mega•phone \ˈme-gə-ˌfōn\ *n*
▲ a device shaped like a cone that is used to direct the voice and increase its loudness

[1]mel•an•choly \ˈme-lən-ˌkä-lē\ *adj*
SAD 1 ⟨I'll be *melancholy* if you go.⟩

[2]melancholy *n*
a sad or gloomy mood

[1]mel•low \ˈme-lō\ *adj*
1 fully ripe or mature ⟨a *mellow* peach⟩
2 made mild by age
3 being clear, full, and pure : not harsh ⟨a *mellow* sound⟩ ⟨a *mellow* color⟩
4 very calm and relaxed
mel•low•ness *n*

[2]mellow *vb* **mel•lowed**; **mel•low•ing**
to make or become mild or relaxed especially over time

me•lod•ic \mə-ˈlä-dik\ *adj*
MELODIOUS

me•lo•di•ous \mə-ˈlō-dē-əs\ *adj*
having a pleasant musical sound
me•lo•di•ous•ly *adv*

melo•dra•mat•ic \ˌme-lə-drə-ˈma-tik\ *adj*
extremely or overly emotional ⟨a *melodramatic* scream⟩

mel•o•dy \ˈme-lə-dē\ *n, pl* **mel•o•dies**
1 pleasing arrangement of sounds
2 a series of musical notes or tones arranged in a definite pattern of pitch and rhythm
3 the main part in a musical composition

mel•on \ˈme-lən\ *n*
a usually large fruit (as a watermelon or cantaloupe) that grows on a vine and has juicy sweet flesh and a hard rind

melt \ˈmelt\ *vb* **melt•ed**; **melt•ing**
1 to change from a solid to a liquid usually through the action of heat ⟨Snow *melts.*⟩ ⟨I'm *melting* butter.⟩
2 to grow less : DISAPPEAR ⟨Clouds *melted* away.⟩
3 to make or become gentle : SOFTEN ⟨The kittens *melted* her heart.⟩
4 to lose clear outline ⟨He *melted* into the fog.⟩

melting point *n*
the temperature at which a solid melts

mem•ber \ˈmem-bər\ *n*
1 someone or something that is part of a group
2 a part (as an arm or leg) of a person or animal
3 a part of a structure ⟨A supporting *member* of the roof gave way.⟩

mem•ber•ship \ˈmem-bər-ˌship\ *n*
1 the state or fact of belonging to a group
2 the whole number of individuals that make up a group

mem•brane \ˈmem-ˌbrān\ *n*
a thin soft flexible layer especially of animal or plant tissue ⟨mucous *membranes*⟩

mem•bra•nous \ˈmem-brə-nəs\ *adj*
made of or like membrane ⟨*membranous* body tissue⟩

me•men•to \mi-ˈmen-tō\ *n, pl* **me•men•tos** *or* **me•men•toes**
something that serves as a reminder ⟨She collected *mementos* on her trip.⟩

mem•o•ra•ble \ˈme-mə-rə-bəl, ˈmem-rə-bəl\ *adj*
worth remembering : not easily forgotten ⟨a *memorable* experience⟩
mem•o•ra•bly \-blē\ *adv*

mem•o•ran•dum \ˌme-mə-ˈran-dəm\ *n, pl* **mem•o•ran•dums** *or* **mem•o•ran•da** \-də\
1 an informal report or message
2 a written reminder

[1]me•mo•ri•al \mə-ˈmȯr-ē-əl\ *n*
◀ something by which the memory of a person or an event is kept alive
: MONUMENT ⟨the Lincoln *Memorial*⟩

[2]memorial *adj*
serving to honor the memory of a person or event ⟨a *memorial* service⟩

[1]memorial:
the Lincoln Memorial in Washington, D.C.

Memorial Day *n*
a legal holiday in remembrance of war dead observed on the last Monday in May in most states of the United States

mem•o•rize \'me-mə-ˌrīz\ *vb* **mem•o•rized; mem•o•riz•ing**
to learn by heart

mem•o•ry \'me-mə-rē, 'mem-rē\ *n, pl* **mem•o•ries**
1 the power or process of remembering
2 the store of things learned and kept in the mind
3 the act of remembering and honoring ⟨The statue is in *memory* of a great soldier.⟩
4 something remembered ⟨a pleasant *memory*⟩
5 the time within which past events are remembered ⟨What happened is not within the *memory* of any living person.⟩
6 a device or part in a computer which can receive and store information for use when wanted ⟨random access *memory*⟩
7 capacity for storing information ⟨The computer has 512 megabytes of *memory*.⟩

men *pl of* MAN

[1]**men•ace** \'me-nəs\ *n*
1 DANGER 2 ⟨That vicious dog is a *menace*.⟩
2 an annoying person

[2]**menace** *vb* **men•aced; men•ac•ing**
to threaten harm to ⟨The pirates *menaced* the ship's passengers.⟩

me•nag•er•ie \mə-'na-jə-rē\ *n*
a collection of wild animals kept especially to be shown to the public

[1]**mend** \'mend\ *vb* **mend•ed; mend•ing**
1 IMPROVE, CORRECT ⟨I suggest you *mend* your ways.⟩
2 to put into good shape or working order again ⟨Can you *mend* a torn sleeve?⟩
3 to improve in health : HEAL ⟨Your injury will soon *mend*.⟩
mend•er *n*

▶ **Synonyms** MEND, PATCH, and REPAIR mean to take something that has been damaged and make it usable again. MEND is used for making something that has been broken or damaged once again whole or fit for use. ⟨Fishermen were *mending* their nets.⟩ PATCH is used for mending a hole or tear by using the same or similar material. ⟨*Patch* the hole with concrete.⟩ PATCH may also be used for a hurried, careless job. ⟨Just *patch* the roof for now.⟩ REPAIR is used for a skillful mending of a complicated thing. ⟨The mechanic *repaired* our car.⟩

[2]**mend** *n*
a place where something has been fixed so that it is usable again
on the mend getting better ⟨Her broken leg is *on the mend*.⟩

men•folk \'men-ˌfōk\ *or* **men•folks** \-ˌfōks\ *n pl*
the men of a family or community

men•ha•den \men-'hā-dᵊn\ *n, pl* **menhaden**
a fish of the Atlantic coast of the United States that is related to the herring and is a source of oil and fertilizer

me•nial \'mē-nē-əl, -nyəl\ *adj*
of or relating to boring or unpleasant work that does not require special skill ⟨*menial* tasks⟩

men–of–war *pl of* MAN–OF–WAR

me•no•rah \mə-'nōr-ə\ *n*
▼ a holder for candles used in Jewish worship

menorah

men•stru•a•tion \ˌmen-strə-'wā-shən, men-'strā-shən\ *n*
a discharge of bloody fluid from the uterus that usually happens each month

-ment \mənt\ *n suffix*
1 result, goal, or method of a specified action ⟨entertain*ment*⟩
2 action : process ⟨develop*ment*⟩
3 place of a specified action ⟨encamp*ment*⟩
4 state : condition ⟨amaze*ment*⟩

men•tal \'men-tᵊl\ *adj*
1 of or relating to the mind ⟨*mental* abilities⟩ ⟨*mental* illness⟩
2 done in the mind ⟨*mental* arithmetic⟩
3 intended for the care of persons affected by a disorder of the mind ⟨a *mental* hospital⟩
men•tal•ly *adv*

men•tal•i•ty \men-'ta-lə-tē\ *n*
1 mental ability
2 a particular way of thinking : OUTLOOK

men•thol \'men-ˌthȯl\ *n*
a white crystalline soothing substance from oils of mint

[1]**men•tion** \'men-shən\ *n*
a short statement calling attention to something or someone

[2]**mention** *vb* **men•tioned; men•tion•ing**
to refer to or speak about briefly ⟨He barely *mentioned* our help.⟩

menu \'men-yü\ *n*
1 a list of dishes that may be ordered in a restaurant
2 the dishes or kinds of food served at a meal
3 a list shown on a computer screen from which a user can select an operation for the computer to perform

▶ **Word History** The word *menu* can be traced to the Latin adjective *minutus*, meaning "small." From *minutus* came the French adjective *menu*, the meanings of which include "small" and "detailed." The use of *menu* as a noun meaning "a list of dishes" came from the "detailed" sense of the adjective, since menus are to different degrees detailed lists of foods.

[1]**me•ow** \mē-'au̇\ *n*
the cry of a cat

[2]**meow** *vb* **me•owed; me•ow•ing**
to make the cry of a cat

mer•can•tile \'mər-kən-ˌtēl, -ˌtīl\ *adj*
of or relating to merchants or trade ⟨a rich *mercantile* family⟩

[1]**mer•ce•nary** \'mər-sə-ˌner-ē\ *n, pl* **mer•ce•nar•ies**
a soldier paid by a foreign country to fight in its army

[2]**mercenary** *adj*
1 doing something only for the pay or reward
2 greedy for money

mer•chan•dise \'mər-chən-ˌdīz, -ˌdīs\ *n*
goods that are bought and sold

mer•chant \'mər-chənt\ *n*
1 a person who buys and sells goods especially on a large scale or with foreign countries
2 STOREKEEPER 1

merchant marine *n*
1 the trading ships of a nation
2 the people who work in trading ships

mer•ci•ful \'mər-si-fəl\ *adj*
having or showing mercy or compassion ⟨a *merciful* ruler⟩
mer•ci•ful•ly \-fə-lē\ *adv*

mer•ci•less \'mər-si-ləs\ *adj*
having no mercy or pity ⟨*merciless* honesty⟩
mer•ci•less•ly *adv*

mercury 3: the planet Mercury

mer•cu•ry \ˈmər-kyə-rē\ *n*
1 a heavy silvery white poisonous metallic chemical element that is liquid at ordinary temperatures
2 the column of mercury in a thermometer or barometer
3 ▲ *cap* the planet that is nearest the sun and has a diameter of about 3,000 miles (4,700 kilometers)

mer•cy \ˈmər-sē\ *n, pl* **mer•cies**
1 kind and forgiving treatment of someone (as a wrongdoer or an opponent) ⟨The prisoners were shown *mercy.*⟩
2 kindness or help given to an unfortunate person ⟨an act of *mercy*⟩
3 a kind sympathetic disposition : willingness to forgive, spare, or help
4 a blessing as an act of divine love ⟨the *mercies* of God⟩
5 a fortunate happening ⟨It's a *mercy* that we arrived in time.⟩
at the mercy of completely without protection from

mere \ˈmir\ *adj, superlative* **mer•est**
nothing more than ⟨*mere* rumors⟩ ⟨a *mere* child⟩

mere•ly \ˈmir-lē\ *adv*
nothing else than : JUST

merge \ˈmərj\ *vb* **merged**; **merg•ing**
to be or cause to be combined or blended into a single unit

merg•er \ˈmər-jər\ *n*
the combination of two or more businesses into one

me•rid•i•an \mə-ˈri-dē-ən\ *n*
1 any imaginary semicircle on the earth's surface reaching from the north pole to the south pole
2 a representation of a meridian on a map or globe numbered according to degrees of longitude

me•ringue \mə-ˈraŋ\ *n*
a light mixture of beaten egg whites and sugar used especially as a topping for pies or cakes

me•ri•no \mə-ˈrē-nō\ *n, pl* **me•ri•nos**
1 a sheep of a breed that produces a heavy fleece of white fine wool
2 a fine wool and cotton yarn

[1]mer•it \ˈmer-ət\ *n*
1 the condition or fact of deserving reward or punishment ⟨Students are graded according to *merit.*⟩
2 [2]WORTH 1, VALUE ⟨The suggestion has great *merit.*⟩
3 a quality worthy of praise : VIRTUE ⟨the *merit* of honesty⟩

[2]merit *vb* **mer•it•ed**; **mer•it•ing**
to be worthy of or have a right to ⟨Both ideas *merit* further consideration.⟩
synonyms see DESERVE

mer•i•to•ri•ous \ˌmer-ə-ˈtȯr-ē-əs\ *adj*
deserving reward or honor : PRAISEWORTHY ⟨*meritorious* conduct⟩

mer•maid \ˈmər-ˌmād\ *n*
an imaginary sea creature usually shown with a woman's head and body and a fish's tail

mer•man \ˈmər-ˌman\ *n, pl* **mer•men** \-ˌmen\
an imaginary sea creature usually shown with a man's head and body and a fish's tail

mer•ri•ment \ˈmer-i-mənt\ *n*
laughter and enjoyment

mer•ry \ˈmer-ē\ *adj* **mer•ri•er**; **mer•ri•est**
1 full of joy and good cheer ⟨a *merry* man⟩
2 full of festive celebration and enjoyment ⟨a *merry* Christmas⟩
mer•ri•ly \ˈmer-ə-lē\ *adv*

mer•ry–go–round \ˈmer-ē-gō-ˌrau̇nd\ *n*
▼ a round platform that spins and has seats and figures of animals on which people sit for a ride

mer•ry•mak•er \ˈmer-ē-ˌmā-kər\ *n*
a person taking part in joyful celebration

mer•ry•mak•ing \ˈmer-ē-ˌmā-kiŋ\ *n*
fun and enjoyment joyful celebration

me•sa \ˈmā-sə\ *n*
a hill with a flat top and steep sides

mesdames *pl of* MADAM, MADAME, *or* MRS.

[1]mesh \ˈmesh\ *n*
1 a material of open texture with evenly spaced holes ⟨wire *mesh*⟩
2 one of the spaces formed by the threads of a net or the wires of a sieve or screen
3 the coming or fitting together (as of the teeth of two sets of gears)

[2]mesh *vb* **meshed**; **mesh•ing**
to fit or join together ⟨The gear teeth must *mesh.*⟩

mes•mer•ize \ˈmez-mə-ˌrīz\ *vb* **mes•mer•ized**; **mes•mer•iz•ing**
to hold the complete attention of : FASCINATE ⟨The children were *mesmerized* by the fireworks.⟩

Mes•o•zo•ic \ˌme-zə-ˈzō-ik, -sə-\ *n*
an era of geological history which extends from the Paleozoic to the Cenozoic and in which dinosaurs are present and the first birds, mammals, and flowering plants appear

mes•quite \mə-ˈskēt\ *n*
a spiny shrub or small tree of the southwestern United States and Mexico

[1]mess \ˈmes\ *n*
1 a dirty or untidy state ⟨They left things in a *mess.*⟩
2 something in a dirty or untidy state ⟨Your hair is a *mess.*⟩
3 a difficult situation ⟨How do you get into these *messes?*⟩
4 a group of people (as military personnel) who regularly eat together
5 a place (as in the military) where meals are served ⟨the officers' *mess*⟩

[2]mess *vb* **messed**; **mess•ing**
1 to make dirty or untidy ⟨They *messed* the place up.⟩
2 to make mistakes in or mix up ⟨She *messed* up the speech.⟩

merry-go-round

▶ metal 1

Some metals are valued for their beauty and rarity, others for their usefulness. Precious metals such as gold, silver, and platinum are commonly made into jewelry, while more readily available metals such as aluminum, lead, and tin are used to make a range of practical items. Metals may also be combined to make an alloy — brass, for example, is a combination of copper and zinc.

gold

platinum

silver

lead pellets

3 to become confused or make an error ⟨I *messed* up the first time.⟩
4 to use or do in an aimless way ⟨I *messed* around on the computer all afternoon.⟩
5 to handle in a careless way ⟨Stop *messing* with my camera.⟩
6 to deal with in a way that may cause anger or trouble ⟨Don't *mess* with them.⟩

mes•sage \'me-sij\ *n*
1 the exchange of information in writing, in speech, or by signals
2 an underlying theme or idea

message board *n*
a public computer system on the Internet that allows people to read and leave messages for other users

mes•sen•ger \'me-s^{ə}n-jər\ *n*
a person who carries a message or does an errand

Messrs. *pl of* MR.

messy \'me-sē\ *adj* **mess•i•er; mess•i•est**
1 not clean or tidy ⟨a *messy* room⟩
2 causing or making a mess ⟨*messy* food⟩
3 not careful or precise ⟨*messy* writing⟩
mess•i•ness \'me-sē-nəs\ *n*

met *past and past participle of* MEET

met•a•bol•ic \,me-tə-'bä-lik\ *adj*
of or relating to metabolism

me•tab•o•lism \mə-'ta-bə-,li-zəm\ *n*
the processes by which a living organism uses food to obtain energy and build tissue and disposes of waste material

met•al \'me-t^{ə}l\ *n*
1 ▲ a substance (as gold, tin, copper, or bronze) that has a more or less shiny appearance, is a good conductor of electricity and heat, and usually can be made into a wire or hammered into a thin sheet
2 METTLE ⟨The soldiers showed their *metal.*⟩

me•tal•lic \mə-'ta-lik\ *adj*
1 relating to, being, or resembling a metal
2 containing or made of metal ⟨*metallic* objects⟩
3 having a harsh sound

met•al•lur•gi•cal \,me-t^{ə}l-'ər-ji-kəl\ *adj*
of or relating to metallurgy

met•al•lur•gy \'me-t^{ə}l-,ər-jē\ *n*
the science of obtaining metals from their ores and preparing them for use

meta•mor•phic \,me-tə-'mȯr-fik\ *adj*
formed by the action of pressure, heat, and water that results in a more compact form ⟨a *metamorphic* rock⟩

meta•mor•pho•sis \,me-tə-'mȯr-fə-səs\ *n, pl* **meta•mor•pho•ses** \-fə-,sēz\
1 a great change in appearance or character
2 the process of great and usually rather sudden change in the form and habits of some animals during transformation from an immature stage (as a caterpillar or tadpole) to an adult stage (as a butterfly or frog)

met•a•phor \'me-tə-,fȯr\ *n*
a figure of speech comparing two unlike things without using *like* or *as* ⟨"Their cheeks were roses" is a *metaphor* while "their cheeks were like roses" is a simile.⟩

mete \'mēt\ *vb* **met•ed; met•ing**
to distribute as deserved ⟨The judge will *mete* out punishment.⟩

me•te•or \'mē-tē-ər\ *n*
▶ one of the small pieces of matter in the solar system that enter the earth's atmosphere where friction may cause them to glow and form a streak of light

me•te•or•ic \,mē-tē-'ȯr-ik\ *adj*
1 of or relating to a meteor ⟨*meteoric* impacts⟩
2 like a meteor in speed or in sudden and temporary success ⟨a *meteoric* career⟩

me•te•or•ite \'mē-tē-ə-,rīt\ *n*
a meteor that reaches the surface of the earth

me•te•o•rol•o•gist \,mē-tē-ə-'rä-lə-jəst\ *n*
a person who specializes in meteorology

me•te•o•rol•o•gy \,mē-tē-ə-'rä-lə-jē\ *n*
a science that deals with the atmosphere, weather, and weather forecasting

^{1}me•ter \'mē-tər\ *n*
1 a planned rhythm in poetry that is usually repeated
2 the repeated pattern of musical beats in a measure

^{2}meter *n*
a measure of length on which the metric system is based and which is equal to about 39.37 inches

^{3}meter *n*
an instrument for measuring and sometimes recording the amount of something ⟨a gas *meter*⟩

-meter *n suffix*
instrument for measuring ⟨thermo*meter*⟩

meth•od \'me-thəd\ *n*
1 a certain way of doing something ⟨She uses her own *method* of teaching.⟩
2 careful arrangement ⟨His work lacks *method.*⟩

me•thod•i•cal \mə-'thä-di-kəl\ *adj*
1 done or arranged in a planned way : using a careful and orderly procedure ⟨a *methodical* search⟩
2 following a planned and orderly way of doing something especially out of habit ⟨He was a slow and *methodical* worker.⟩
me•thod•i•cal•ly *adv*

me•tic•u•lous \mə-'tik-yə-ləs\ *adj*
showing extreme or excessive care in thinking about or dealing with small details ⟨a *meticulous* description⟩

meteor: a meteor streaking through the sky

met•ric \'me-trik\ *adj*
of, relating to, or based on the metric system ⟨*metric* measurements⟩

met•ri•cal \'me-tri-kəl\ *adj*
of or relating to poetic or musical meter

metric system *n*
a system of weights and measures in which the meter is the unit of length and the kilogram is the unit of weight

metric ton *n*
a unit of weight equal to 1000 kilograms

met•ro•nome \'me-trə-,nōm\ *n*
▼ a device that ticks in a regular pattern to help a musician play a piece of music at the proper speed

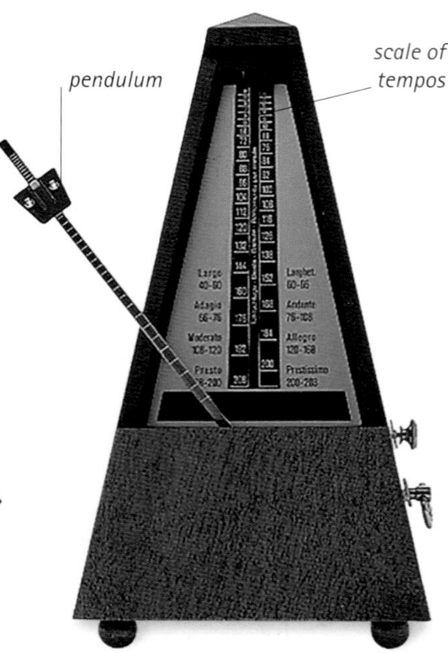

metronome

me•trop•o•lis \mə-'trä-pə-ləs\ *n*
1 the chief or capital city of a country, state, or region
2 a large or important city

met•ro•pol•i•tan \,me-trə-'pä-lə-tən\ *adj*
of, relating to, or like that of a large city ⟨a *metropolitan* area⟩

met•tle \'me-tᵊl\ *n*
strength of spirit : COURAGE

[1]**mew** \'myü\ *vb* **mewed**; **mew•ing**
to make a sound like a meow

[2]**mew** *n*
[1]MEOW

Mex. *abbr*
1 Mexican
2 Mexico

[1]**Mex•i•can** \'mek-si-kən\ *adj*
of or relating to Mexico or its people ⟨*Mexican* food⟩

[2]**Mexican** *n*
a person born or living in Mexico

mg *abbr* milligram

mi \'mē\ *n*
the third note of the musical scale

MI *abbr* Michigan

mi. *abbr*
1 mile
2 miles

mi•ca \'mī-kə\ *n*
a mineral that easily breaks into very thin transparent sheets

mice *pl of* MOUSE

Mich. *abbr* Michigan

micr- *or* **micro-** *prefix*
1 small : tiny ⟨*micro*organism⟩
2 millionth

mi•crobe \'mī-,krōb\ *n*
a very tiny and often harmful living thing : MICROORGANISM

mi•cro•com•put•er \'mī-krō-kəm-,pyü-tər\ *n*
PERSONAL COMPUTER

mi•cro•film \'mī-krə-,film\ *n*
a film on which something (as printing) is recorded in a much smaller size

mi•crom•e•ter \mī-'krä-mə-tər\ *n*
1 an instrument used with a telescope or microscope for measuring very small distances
2 an instrument having a rod moved by fine screw threads and used for making exact measurements

mi•cro•or•gan•ism \,mī-krō-'ȯr-gə-,ni-zəm\ *n*
a living thing (as a bacterium) that can only be seen with a microscope

mi•cro•phone \'mī-krə-,fōn\ *n*
▼ an instrument in which sound is changed into an electrical signal for transmitting or recording (as in radio or television)

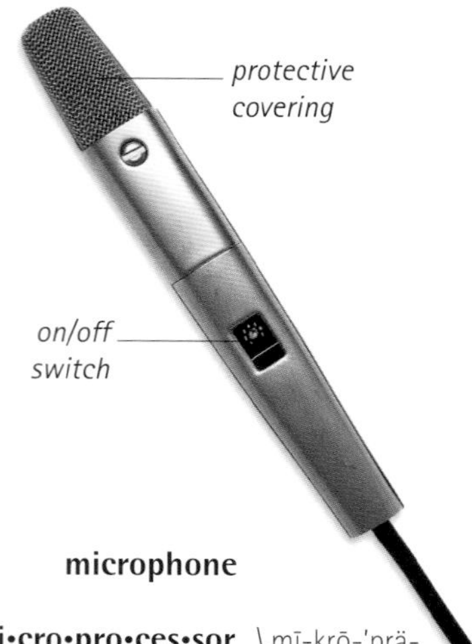

microphone

mi•cro•pro•ces•sor \,mī-krō-'prä-,se-sər, -'prō-\ *n*
a computer processor contained on an integrated-circuit chip

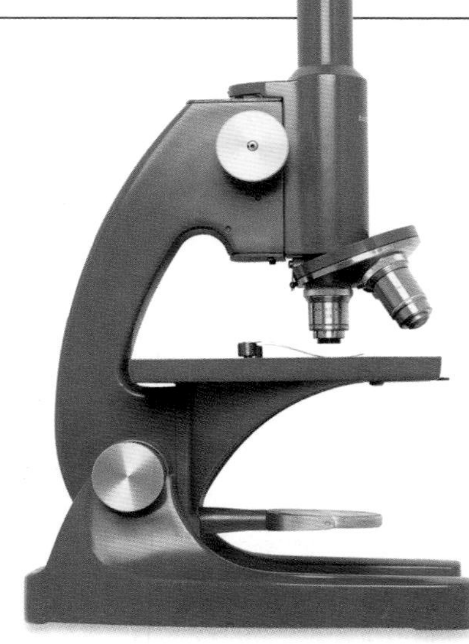
microscope:
side view of a light microscope

mi•cro•scope \'mī-krə-,skōp\ *n*
▲ an instrument with one or more lenses used to help a person to see something very small by making it appear larger

mi•cro•scop•ic \,mī-krə-'skä-pik\ *adj*
1 of, relating to, or conducted with the microscope ⟨a *microscopic* examination⟩
2 so small as to be visible only through a microscope : very tiny ⟨a *microscopic* crack⟩
mi•cro•scop•i•cal•ly \-pi-kə-lē\ *adv*

[1]**mi•cro•wave** \'mī-krō-,wāv\ *n*
1 a radio wave between one millimeter and one meter in wavelength
2 MICROWAVE OVEN

[2]**microwave** *vb* **mi•cro•waved**; **mi•cro•wav•ing**
to cook or heat in a microwave oven

microwave oven *n*
an oven in which food is cooked by the heat produced as a result of penetration of the food by microwaves

[1]**mid** \'mid\ *adj*
being the part in the middle ⟨*mid*-June⟩

[2]**mid** *prep*
AMID ⟨I hid *mid* the bushes.⟩

mid•air \'mid-'er\ *n*
a region in the air some distance above the ground ⟨The bird hovered in *midair.*⟩

mid•day \'mid-,dā\ *n*
NOON

[1]**mid•dle** \'mi-dᵊl\ *adj*
1 equally distant from the ends : CENTRAL ⟨the *middle* aisle⟩
2 being at neither extreme : halfway between two opposite states or conditions ⟨of *middle* size⟩

Middle Ages

The Middle Ages in Europe was the period of history between the Dark Ages following the fall of the Roman Empire, and the Renaissance. In Europe in the Middle Ages, most countries were organized into a feudal system, each ruled by a king who owned most of the land. The king granted land to noblemen — barons and bishops — who, in turn, often divided their lands among lords or knights. At the lowest level of society were the peasants, who worked on land belonging to the local lord. The Catholic Church possessed its own lands and had enormous power.

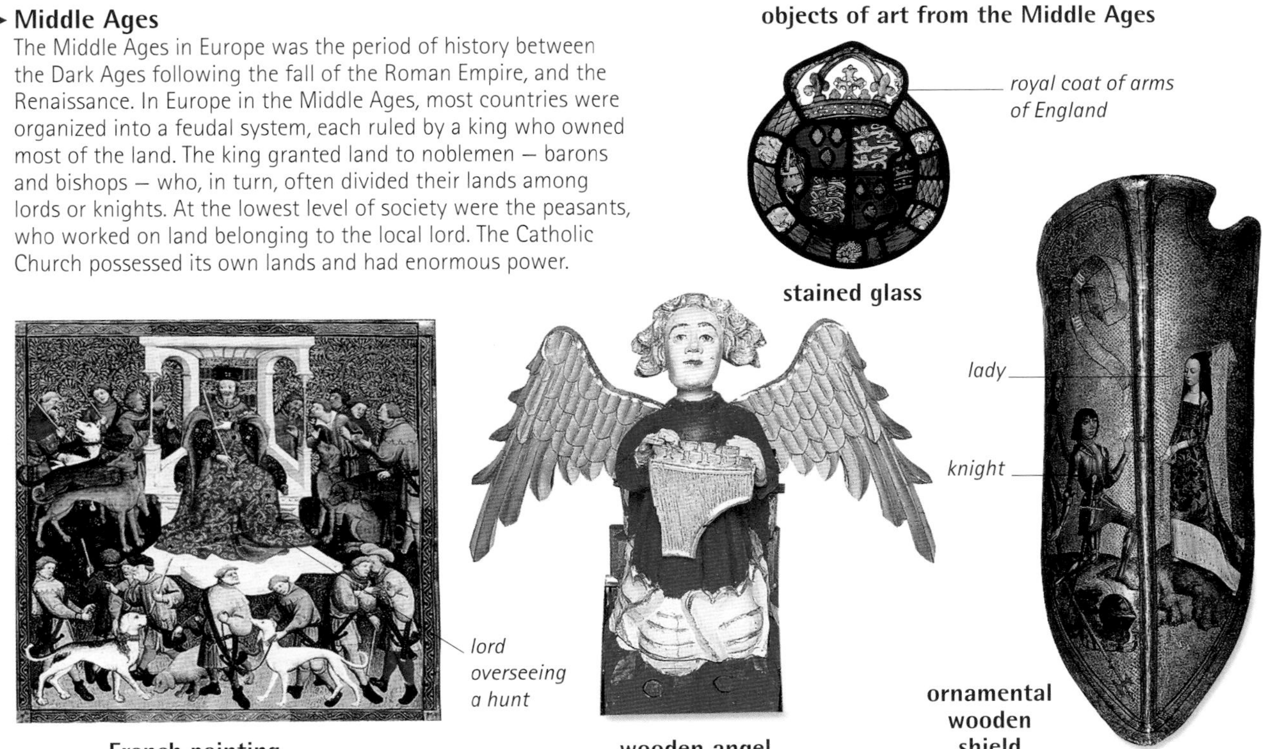

²middle *n*
the part, point, or position that is equally distant from the ends or opposite sides : CENTER ⟨the *middle* of the room⟩

middle age *n*
the period of life from about 45 to about 64 years of age
mid•dle–aged \ˌmi-dᵊl-ˈājd\ *adj*

Middle Ages *n pl*
▲ the period of European history from about A.D. 500 to about 1500

middle class *n*
a social class between that of the wealthy and the poor

Middle English *n*
the English language of the 12th to 15th centuries

middle finger *n*
the long finger that is the middle one of the five fingers of the hand

middle school *n*
a school usually including grades five to eight or six to eight

midge \ˈmij\ *n*
a very small fly : GNAT

¹midg•et \ˈmi-jət\ *n, sometimes offensive*
a person who is much smaller than normal
Hint: In the past, this word was not considered offensive. In recent years, however, some people have come to find the word hurtful, and you may offend someone by using it.

²midget *adj*
much smaller than usual or normal ⟨a *midget* horse⟩

mid•night \ˈmid-ˌnīt\ *n*
twelve o'clock at night

mid•rib \ˈmid-ˌrib\ *n*
the central vein of a leaf

mid•riff \ˈmid-ˌrif\ *n*
the middle part of the human body between the chest and the waist

mid•ship•man \ˈmid-ˌship-mən\ *n, pl* **mid•ship•men** \-mən\
a person who is training to become an officer in the navy

¹midst \ˈmidst\ *n*
1 the middle or central part ⟨in the *midst* of the forest⟩
2 a position among the members of a group ⟨a stranger in our *midst*⟩
3 the condition of being surrounded ⟨in the *midst* of dangers⟩

²midst *prep*
AMID

mid•stream \ˈmid-ˈstrēm\ *n*
the part of a stream farthest from each bank

mid•sum•mer \ˈmid-ˈsə-mər\ *n*
1 the middle of summer
2 the summer solstice

¹mid•way \ˈmid-ˌwā, -ˈwā\ *adv or adj*
in the middle of the way or distance : HALFWAY

²mid•way \ˈmid-ˌwā\ *n*
an area at a fair, carnival, or amusement park for food stands, games, and rides

mid•wife \ˈmid-ˌwīf\ *n, pl* **mid•wives**
a woman who helps other women during childbirth

mid•win•ter \ˈmid-ˈwin-tər\ *n*
1 the middle of winter
2 the winter solstice

mien \ˈmēn\ *n*
a person's appearance or way of acting that shows mood or personality

¹might \ˈmīt\ *past of* MAY
used as a helping verb to show that something is possible but not likely ⟨We *might* arrive before it rains.⟩

²might *n*
power that can be used (as by a person or group) ⟨our army's *might*⟩ ⟨I tried with all my *might*.⟩

might•i•ly \ˈmī-tə-lē\ *adv*
1 very forcefully ⟨He shouted *mightily*.⟩
2 very much ⟨She tried *mightily* to win.⟩

a b c d e f g h i j k l m n o p q r s t u v w x y z

mightn't \'mī-tᵊnt\
might not

[1]**mighty** \'mī-tē\ *adj*
might•i•er; might•i•est
1 having great power or strength ⟨a *mighty* nation⟩
2 done by or showing great power or strength ⟨*mighty* deeds⟩
3 great in size or effect ⟨a *mighty* famine⟩

[2]**mighty** *adv*
[1]VERY 1 ⟨a *mighty* good friend⟩

mi•grant \'mī-grənt\ *n*
a person or animal that migrates

mi•grate \'mī-,grāt\ *vb* **mi•grat•ed; mi•grat•ing**
1 to move from one country or region to another ⟨Families *migrated* west in search of work.⟩
2 to pass from one region to another on a regular basis ⟨Many birds *migrate* south for the winter.⟩

mi•gra•tion \mī-'grā-shən\ *n*
the act or an instance of moving from one place to another often on a regular basis

mi•gra•to•ry \'mī-grə-,tȯr-ē\ *adj*
1 moving from one place to another ⟨*migratory* workers⟩ ⟨*migratory* birds⟩
2 of or relating to migration ⟨a bird's *migratory* route⟩

mike \'mīk\ *n*
MICROPHONE

mild \'mīld\ *adj* **mild•er; mild•est**
1 gentle in personality or behavior ⟨a *mild* young man⟩
2 not strong or harsh in action or effect ⟨*mild* soap⟩
3 not sharp, spicy, or bitter ⟨*mild* cheese⟩
4 not extreme or severe ⟨*mild* weather⟩ ⟨a *mild* headache⟩
mild•ly *adv*
mild•ness *n*

[1]**mil•dew** \'mil-,dü, -,dyü\ *n*
1 ▼ a thin whitish growth produced by a fungus especially on decaying material or on living plants
2 a fungus producing mildew

[1]**mildew 1:** leaves covered with mildew

[2]**mildew** *vb* **mil•dewed; mil•dew•ing**
to become affected with mildew

mile \'mīl\ *n*
1 a measure of distance (**statute mile**) equal to 5280 feet (1609 meters)
2 a measure of distance (**geographical mile** or **nautical mile**) used in air and sea travel equal to about 6076 feet (1852 meters)

> ▶ **Word History** In English we use the word *mile* for two different lengths. Though the ancient Roman mile was not the same as either of these, the English word *mile* comes from the Latin name for the Roman mile. This Latin word, *milia*, came from the phrase *milia passuum*, literally, "thousands of steps." From the Latin word for "thousand," *mille*, we also get the words *mill* (a thousandth of a dollar) and *million* (a thousand thousands).

mile•age \'mī-lij\ *n*
1 distance in miles ⟨What's the *mileage* from here to Chicago?⟩
2 distance covered or traveled in miles ⟨This car has a lot of *mileage*.⟩
3 the average number of miles a car or truck will travel on a gallon of fuel
4 an amount of money given for traveling expenses at a certain rate per mile

mile•stone \'mīl-,stōn\ *n*
1 ▶ a stone by the side of a road showing the distance in miles to a given place
2 an important point in progress or development

milestone 1: an old milestone in London, UK

[1]**mil•i•tary** \'mi-lə-,ter-ē\ *adj*
1 of or relating to soldiers, the army, or war ⟨*military* drills⟩
2 carried on by soldiers : supported by armed forces ⟨a *military* government⟩

[2]**military** *n, pl* **military**
members of the armed forces

mi•li•tia \mə-'li-shə\ *n*
a group of citizens with some military training who are called into service only in emergencies

[1]**milk** \'milk\ *n*
1 a whitish liquid produced and given off by the breasts or udder of a female mammal as food for her young
2 milk from an animal and especially a cow used as food by people
3 a liquid that looks like milk ⟨coconut *milk*⟩

[2]**milk** *vb* **milked; milk•ing**
to draw milk from (as by pressing) ⟨*milk* a cow⟩

milk•man \'milk-,man\ *n, pl* **milk•men** \-,men\
a person who sells or delivers milk

milk shake *n*
a drink made of milk, a flavoring syrup, and ice cream that is shaken or mixed thoroughly

milk tooth *n, pl* **milk teeth**
one of the first and temporary teeth of which humans grow 20

milk•weed \'milk-,wēd\ *n*
a plant with milky juice and clusters of flowers

milky \'mil-kē\ *adj* **milk•i•er; milk•i•est**
1 like milk especially in color ⟨*milky* skin⟩
2 containing or full of milk ⟨*milky* tea⟩

Milky Way *n*
1 a broad band of light that stretches across the sky and is caused by the light of a very great number of faint stars
2 MILKY WAY GALAXY

Milky Way galaxy *n*
the galaxy of which the sun and the solar system are a part and which contains the stars that make up the Milky Way

[1]**mill** \'mil\ *n*
1 a building with machinery for grinding grain into flour
2 a machine or device that prepares a material for use by grinding or crushing ⟨a pepper *mill*⟩
3 a factory using machines to make a product from raw material ⟨a steel *mill*⟩

[2]**mill** *vb* **milled; mill•ing**
1 to subject to processing in a mill ⟨Grain is *milled* into flour.⟩ ⟨The logs are *milled* into lumber.⟩
2 to move about in a circle or in disorder ⟨A crowd was *milling* around before the race.⟩

[3]**mill** *n*
one tenth of a cent

mil•len•ni•um \mə-'le-nē-əm\ *n, pl* **mil•len•nia** \-nē-ə\ *or* **millenniums**
1 a period of 1000 years
2 a 1000th anniversary or its celebration
mil•len•ni•al \-nē-əl\ *adj*

mill•er \'mi-lər\ *n*
a person who works in or runs a mill that grinds grain into flour

mil•let \'mi-lət\ *n*
a grass with small whitish seeds that are used as food for people, livestock, and birds

milli- *prefix*
thousandth 〈*milli*meter〉

mil•li•gram \'mi-lə-,gram\ *n*
a unit of weight equal to 1/1000 gram

mil•li•li•ter \'mi-lə-,lē-tər\ *n*
a unit of capacity equal to 1/1000 liter

mil•li•me•ter \'mi-lə-,mē-tər\ *n*
a unit of length equal to 1/1000 meter

mil•li•ner \'mi-lə-nər\ *n*
a person who makes, decorates, or sells women's hats

[1]**mil•lion** \'mil-yən\ *n*
1 one thousand thousands : 1,000,000
2 a very large number 〈*millions* of mosquitoes〉

[2]**million** *adj*
1 being 1,000,000 〈a *million* dollars〉
2 being very great in number 〈a *million* questions〉

mil•lion•aire \,mil-yə-'ner\ *n*
a person having a million dollars or more

[1]**mil•lionth** \'mil-yənth\ *adj*
being last in a series of a million 〈the *millionth* customer〉

[2]**millionth** *n*
number 1,000,000 in a series

mil•li•pede \'mi-lə-,pēd\ *n*
▼ an animal that is an arthropod with a long roundish body somewhat like that of a centipede but with two pairs of legs on most of its many body sections

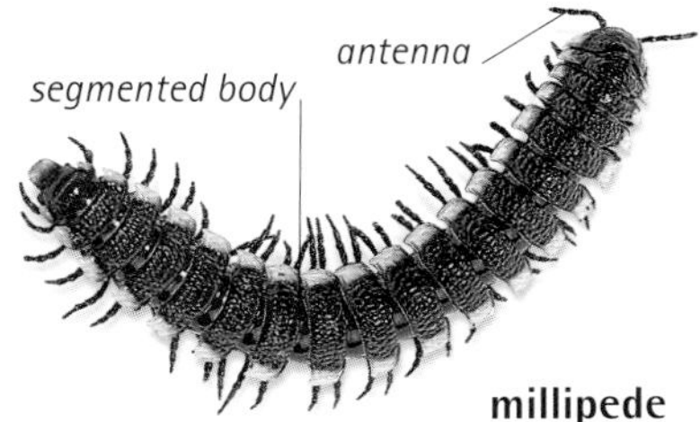

millipede

mill•stone \'mil-,stōn\ *n*
► either of two large circular stones used for grinding grain

mime \'mīm\ *n*
1 the art of showing a character or telling a story using body movements and gestures without words
2 a person who performs mime

mim•eo•graph \'mi-mē-ə-,graf\ *n*
a machine for making copies of typed, written, or drawn matter using a stencil

[1]**mim•ic** \'mi-mik\ *n*
a person or animal that imitates something or someone

minaret: minarets of the New Mosque in Istanbul, Turkey

[2]**mimic** *vb* **mim•icked; mim•ick•ing**
1 to imitate very closely 〈She can *mimic* her favorite actress.〉
2 to make fun of by imitating 〈Stop *mimicking* everything I say.〉
synonyms see COPY

mim•ic•ry \'mi-mi-krē\ *n*
a type of protection from predators in which one animal resembles the coloring, form, or behavior of another animal that is harmful or bad-tasting

min. *abbr* minute

min•a•ret \,mi-nə-'ret\ *n*
▲ a tall slender tower of a mosque with a balcony from which the people are called to prayer

mince \'mins\ *vb* **minced; minc•ing**
1 to cut or chop into very small pieces 〈*minced* onion〉
2 to act or speak in an unnaturally dainty way
3 to phrase comments in such a way as to not cause offense 〈I'll not *mince* words with you; you know you lied.〉

millstone: an ancient millstone inside the Ethnographic Museum in Istria, Croatia

mince•meat \'mins-,mēt\ *n*
a finely chopped mixture (as of raisins, apples, spices, and sometimes meat) that is especially used in pies

[1]**mind** \'mīnd\ *n*
1 the part of a person that thinks, reasons, feels, understands, and remembers
2 MEMORY 1 〈Keep my advice in *mind.*〉
3 INTENTION 1 〈I changed my *mind.*〉
4 a person's view or opinion about something 〈Speak your *mind.*〉

[2]**mind** *vb* **mind•ed; mind•ing**
1 to pay attention to 〈*Mind* what you're doing.〉
2 OBEY 1 〈Be sure to *mind* the teacher.〉
3 to be bothered by 〈Never *mind* that mistake.〉
4 to object to : DISLIKE 〈I don't *mind* the cold.〉
5 to take charge of 〈Please *mind* the children.〉
6 to be careful about 〈You should *mind* what you say.〉
synonyms see OBEY

mind•ed \'mīn-dəd\ *adj*
1 having a particular kind of mind 〈open-*minded*〉
2 greatly interested or concerned about something 〈safety-*minded*〉

mind•ful \'mīnd-fəl\ *adj*
keeping in mind : AWARE

mind•less \'mīnd-ləs\ *adj*
using or requiring little attention or thought 〈*mindless* work〉

[1]mine \'mīn\ *pron*
that which belongs to me 〈That book is *mine*.〉 〈Those books are *mine*.〉

[2]mine *n*
1 a pit or tunnel from which minerals (as coal, gold, or diamonds) are taken
2 an explosive device placed in the ground or water and set to explode when disturbed (as by an enemy soldier, vehicle, or ship)
3 a rich source of supply 〈She was a *mine* of information.〉

[3]mine *vb* **mined**; **min•ing**
1 to dig or work in a mine 〈They *mined* the hills for gold.〉
2 to obtain from a mine 〈*mine* coal〉
3 to place explosive mines in or under 〈*mine* a field〉
min•er *n*

[1]min•er•al \'mi-nə-rəl, 'min-rəl\ *n*
1 ▼ a naturally occurring solid substance (as diamond, gold, or quartz) that is not of plant or animal origin
2 a naturally occurring substance (as ore, coal, salt, or petroleum) obtained from the ground usually for humans to use

[2]mineral *adj*
1 of or relating to minerals 〈a *mineral* deposit〉
2 containing gases or mineral salts 〈*mineral* water〉

mineral kingdom *n*
a basic group of natural objects that includes objects consisting of matter that does not come from plants and animals

min•gle \'miŋ-gəl\ *vb* **min•gled**; **min•gling**
1 to bring or combine together or with something else 〈The story *mingled* fact with fiction.〉
2 to move among others within a group 〈He *mingled* with the crowd.〉

mini– *prefix*
very short or small

[1]min•i•a•ture \'mi-nē-ə-,chu̇r, 'mi-ni-,chu̇r\ *n*
1 a copy of something that is much smaller than the original
2 a very small portrait or painting

▶ **Word History** *Minium* was the Latin name for a red pigment used in ancient times. In the days before printed books, this substance was used to decorate manuscripts. The Latin verb meaning to color with *minium* was *miniare*. In early Italian, its meaning was broadened to mean simply "to decorate a manuscript," and the noun *miniatura* was used to refer to any manuscript illustration, no matter what color. Since the illustrations in manuscripts (called illuminations) are small by comparison with most other paintings, the word *miniature*, borrowed into English from Italian *miniature*, came to mean any small painting, and eventually anything very small.

[2]miniature *adj*
very small represented on a small scale 〈*miniature* books〉 〈a *miniature* breed〉

▶ **[1]mineral 1**
Minerals are solid substances that are found in rocks. Some rocks contain only one mineral, but generally rocks consist of a number of minerals. Different minerals are identified by a variety of factors, including their characteristic crystalline formation and their hardness. Although some can be identified by color, many are white or colorless or, like quartz, occur in a variety of shades.

amethyst

beryl \'ber-əl\

calcite \'kal-,sīt\

corundum \kə-'rən-dəm\

dioptase \dī-'äp-,tās\

malachite \'mal-ə-,kīt\

orpiment \'ȯr-pə-mənt\

pitchblende

proustite \'prü-,stīt\

pyrite \'pī-,rīt\

n•i•mize \ˈmi-nə-ˌmīz\ *vb* **min•i•mized**; **ıin•i•miz•ing**
 to make as small as possible ⟨Safety ıles *minimized* the risks.⟩
 to treat or describe (something) as less nportant than it is ⟨Don't *minimize* the npact of the change.⟩
 to make (a program's window) change to very small form that takes little room on a ɔmputer screen
in•i•mum \ˈmi-nə-məm\ *n*,
/ min•i•mums *or* **min•i•ma** \-mə\
ıe lowest value : the least amount
inimum *adj*
ɛing the least or lowest possible
n•ing \ˈmī-niŋ\ *n*
ıe process or business of digging in mines ı obtain minerals
in•is•ter \ˈmi-nə-stər\ *n*
 a person who performs religious ceremonies ıpecially in Protestant church services
 a government official at the head of a ɛction of government activities

azurite \ˈazh-ə-ˌrīt\

scolecite \ˈskäl-ə-ˌsīt\

minnow 1

3 a person who represents his or her government in a foreign country

[2]**minister** *vb* **min•is•tered**; **min•is•ter•ing**
to give help or care ⟨*minister* to the sick⟩

min•is•try \ˈmi-nə-strē\ *n, pl* **min•is•tries**
1 the office or duties of a religious minister
2 a group of religious ministers : CLERGY
3 a section of a government headed by a minister ⟨the *ministry* of transportation⟩

mink \ˈmiŋk\ *n, pl* **mink** *or* **minks**
1 a small animal related to the weasel that has partly webbed feet, lives around water, and feeds on smaller animals (as frogs, crabs, and mice)
2 the soft thick usually brown fur of a mink

Minn. *abbr* Minnesota

min•now \ˈmi-nō\ *n*
1 ▲ a small freshwater fish (as a shiner) related to the carp
2 a fish that looks like a true minnow

[1]**mi•nor** \ˈmī-nər\ *adj*
1 not great in size, importance, or seriousness ⟨*minor* details⟩ ⟨a *minor* injury⟩
2 of or relating to a musical scale having the third tone lowered a half step

[2]**minor** *n*
a person too young to have the full rights of an adult

mi•nor•i•ty \mə-ˈnȯr-ə-tē\ *n, pl* **mi•nor•i•ties**
1 the state of not being old enough to have the full rights of an adult
2 a number less than half of a total
3 a group that makes up a smaller part of a larger group
4 a part of a population that is in some ways (as in race or religion) different from others

min•strel \ˈmin-strəl\ *n*
1 a musical entertainer in the Middle Ages
2 a member of a group of entertainers who performed black American melodies and jokes with blackened faces in the 19th and early 20th centuries

[1]**mint** \ˈmint\ *n*
1 a fragrant plant (as catnip or peppermint) with square stems
2 a piece of candy flavored with mint

[2]**mint** *n*
1 a place where coins are made from metals
2 a great amount especially of money

[3]**mint** *vb* **mint•ed**; **mint•ing**
to make coins out of metal : COIN ⟨*mint* silver dollars⟩

min•u•end \ˈmin-yə-ˌwend\ *n*
a number from which another number is to be subtracted

min•u•et \ˌmin-yə-ˈwet\ *n*
a slow graceful dance

[1]**mi•nus** \ˈmī-nəs\ *prep*
1 with the subtraction of ⟨7 *minus* 4 is 3.⟩
2 [1]WITHOUT 2 ⟨I went outside *minus* my hat.⟩

[2]**minus** *adj*
1 having a value that is below zero ⟨The temperature was *minus* 15.⟩
2 located in the lower part of a range ⟨a grade of C *minus*⟩

mi•nus•cule \ˈmi-nə-ˌskyül\ *adj*
very small ⟨*minuscule* amounts⟩

minus sign *n*
a sign — used especially in mathematics to indicate subtraction (as in 8−6=2) or a quantity less than zero (as in −15°)

[1]**min•ute** \ˈmi-nət\ *n*
1 a unit of time equal to 60 seconds : the 60th part of an hour
2 MOMENT 1 ⟨Can you wait a *minute*?⟩
3 one of 60 equal parts into which a degree can be divided for measuring angles
4 **minutes** *pl* a brief record of what was said and done during a meeting

[2]mi•nute \mī-'nüt, mə-, -'nyüt\ *adj* **mi•nut•er; mi•nut•est**
1 very small : TINY ⟨*minute* particles of dust⟩
2 marked by or paying attention to small details ⟨a *minute* description⟩
mi•nute•ly *adv*

min•ute•man \'mi-nət-,man\ *n, pl* **min•ute•men** \-,men\
a member of a group of armed men who favored independence of the American colonies and who were ready to fight at a minute's notice immediately before and during the American Revolution

mir•a•cle \'mir-i-kəl\ *n*
1 an extraordinary event taken as a sign of the power of God
2 something (as an event or accomplishment) that is very outstanding, unusual, or wonderful ⟨It will take a *miracle* for us to win.⟩

mi•rac•u•lous \mə-'ra-kyə-ləs\ *adj*
being or being like a miracle : very wonderful or amazing ⟨a *miraculous* recovery⟩
mi•rac•u•lous•ly *adv*

mi•rage \mə-'räzh\ *n*
an illusion sometimes seen at sea, in the desert, or over hot pavement that looks like a pool of water or a mirror in which distant objects are glimpsed

[1]mire \'mīr\ *n*
heavy deep mud

[2]mire *vb* **mired; mir•ing**
to stick or cause to become stuck in or as if in heavy deep mud

[1]mir•ror \'mir-ər\ *n*
1 a piece of glass that reflects images
2 something that gives a true likeness or description

[2]mirror *vb* **mir•rored; mir•ror•ing**
to reflect in or as if in a mirror

mirth \'mərth\ *n*
happiness and laughter : merry behavior

mis- *prefix*
1 in a way that is bad or wrong ⟨*mis*judge⟩
2 bad : wrong ⟨*mis*fortune⟩
3 opposite or lack of ⟨*mis*trust⟩

mis•ad•ven•ture \,mi-səd-'ven-chər\ *n*
an unfortunate or unpleasant event

mis•be•have \,mis-bi-'hāv\ *vb* **mis•be•haved; mis•be•hav•ing**
to behave badly

mis•cal•cu•late \mis-'kal-kyə-,lāt\ *vb* **mis•cal•cu•lat•ed; mis•cal•cu•lat•ing**
to make a mistake in figuring or estimating

mis•car•ry \mis-'ker-ē\ *vb* **mis•car•ried; mis•car•ry•ing**
to go wrong : FAIL ⟨The plan *miscarried.*⟩

mis•cel•la•neous \,mi-sə-'lā-nē-əs, -nyəs\ *adj*
consisting of many things of different sorts

mis•chief \'mis-chəf\ *n*
1 behavior or activity that annoys or bothers but is not meant to cause serious harm
2 injury or damage caused by a person

mis•chie•vous \'mis-chə-vəs\ *adj*
1 causing or likely to cause minor injury or harm ⟨a *mischievous* puppy⟩
2 showing a spirit of irresponsible fun or playfulness ⟨The boy had a *mischievous* look on his face.⟩
3 harming or intended to do harm ⟨*mischievous* gossip⟩
mis•chie•vous•ly *adv*

mis•con•duct \mis-'kän-,dəkt\ *n*
bad behavior

mis•count \mis-'kaůnt\ *vb* **mis•count•ed; mis•count•ing**
to incorrectly determine the total of

mis•cre•ant \'mis-krē-ənt\ *n*
VILLAIN 1, RASCAL

mis•deed \mis-'dēd\ *n*
a bad action

mis•de•mean•or \,mis-di-'mē-nər\ *n*
1 a crime less serious than a felony
2 MISDEED

mis•di•rect \,mis-də-'rekt\ *vb* **mis•di•rect•ed; mis•di•rect•ing**
to send to the wrong place

mi•ser \'mī-zər\ *n*
a stingy person who lives poorly in order to store away money

mis•er•a•ble \'mi-zə-rə-bəl, 'mi-zər-bəl\ *adj*
1 very unhappy or distressed ⟨The stranded passengers were *miserable.*⟩
2 causing great discomfort ⟨a *miserable* cold⟩
3 very unsatisfactory ⟨*miserable* weather⟩
mis•er•a•bly \-blē\ *adv*

mi•ser•ly \'mī-zər-lē\ *adj*
STINGY ⟨a *miserly* neighbor⟩ ⟨a *miserly* contribution⟩

mis•ery \'mi-zə-rē, 'miz-rē\ *n, pl* **mis•er•ies**
great suffering or unhappiness

mis•fit \mis-'fit, 'mis-,fit\ *n*
1 something that is the wrong shape or size or is inappropriate
2 a person who does not seem to belong in a particular group or situation

mis•for•tune \mis-'fȯr-chən\ *n*
1 bad luck
2 an unfortunate situation or event

mis•giv•ing \mis-'gi-viŋ\ *n*
a feeling of distrust or doubt especially about what is going to happen

mis•guid•ed \mis-'gī-dəd\ *adj*
having or resulting from mistaken ideas or values ⟨*misguided* advisers⟩ ⟨a *misguided* attempt⟩

mis•hap \'mis-,hap\ *n*
an unfortunate accident

mis•judge \mis-'jəj\ *vb* **mis•judged; mis•judg•ing**
to make a wrong or unfair judgment or estimate of

mis•lay \mis-'lā\ *vb* **mis•laid** \-'lād\; **mis•lay•ing**
to put in a place later forgotten : LOSE
synonyms see MISPLACE

mis•lead \mis-'lēd\ *vb* **mis•led** \-'led\; **mis•lead•ing**
to cause (someone) to believe something that is not true

mis•place \mis-'plās\ *vb* **mis•placed; mis•plac•ing**
1 to put (something) where it doesn't belong ⟨*misplace* a comma⟩
2 MISLAY

> ▶ **Synonyms** MISPLACE and MISLAY mean to put in the wrong place. MISPLACE may mean to put something in a place that is not its usual location. ⟨Someone seems to have *misplaced* the crayons.⟩ MISPLACE may also mean putting something where it should not have been at all. ⟨I *misplaced* my confidence in them.⟩ MISLAY means not only placing something in the wrong location but also forgetting that location. ⟨I *mislaid* my keys.⟩

mis•print \'mis-,print\ *n*
a mistake in a word that has been printed

mis•pro•nounce \,mis-prə-'naůns\ *vb* **mis•pro•nounced; mis•pro•nounc•ing**
to say or make the sounds of incorrectly ⟨*mispronounce* a word⟩

mis•pro•nun•ci•a•tion \,mis-prə-,nən-sē-'ā-shən\ *n*
the act or state of saying or making the sounds of incorrectly

mis•read \mis-'rēd\ *vb* **mis•read** \-'red\; **mis•read•ing** \-'rēd-iŋ\
1 to incorrectly pronounce or understand something written
2 MISUNDERSTAND ⟨He *misread* the emotion on her face.⟩

mis•rep•re•sent \,mis-,re-pri-'zent\ *vb* **mis•rep•re•sent•ed; mis•rep•re•sent•ing**
to give a false or misleading idea of ⟨The movie *misrepresents* what actually happened.⟩

[1]miss \'mis\ *vb* **missed; miss•ing**
1 to fail to hit, catch, reach, or get ⟨*miss* a target⟩ ⟨*miss* a deadline⟩
2 [1]ESCAPE 2 ⟨She just *missed* being hit by the car.⟩
3 to fail to arrive in time for ⟨Don't *miss* the bus!⟩
4 to feel or notice the absence of ⟨I'm enjoying the trip, but I *miss* my friends.⟩

A B C D E F G H I J K L M N O P Q R S T U V W X Y Z

5 to fail to take ⟨I *missed* my turn.⟩ ⟨Don't *miss* this opportunity.⟩
6 to fail to be present for ⟨*miss* school⟩
7 to fail to hear or see ⟨I *missed* what he said.⟩ ⟨It's huge. You can't *miss* it.⟩

[2]**miss** *n*
failure to hit or catch

[3]**miss** *n*
1 *cap* used as a title before the name of an unmarried woman ⟨*Miss* Smith⟩
2 young lady
Hint: *Miss* is used without a name as a form of polite address to a girl or young woman. ⟨Do you need some help, *miss*?⟩

Miss. *abbr* Mississippi

mis•shap•en \mis-ˈshā-pən\ *adj*
badly shaped

mis•sile \ˈmi-səl\ *n*
▶ an object (as a stone, arrow, bullet, or rocket) that is dropped, thrown, shot, or launched usually so as to strike something at a distance

miss•ing \ˈmi-siŋ\ *adj*
1 ABSENT 1 ⟨Who is *missing*?⟩
2 LOST 2 ⟨a *missing* book⟩

mis•sion \ˈmi-shən\ *n*
1 a task that is assigned or begun
2 a task that is regarded as a very important duty ⟨She thinks of teaching as her *mission*.⟩
3 a group of missionaries
4 a group of people sent by a government to represent it in a foreign country
5 a place where the work of missionaries is carried on

[1]**mis•sion•ary** \ˈmi-shə-ˌner-ē\ *n*, *pl* **mis•sion•ar•ies**
a person sent to a place to spread a religious faith

[2]**missionary** *adj*
relating to efforts to gain new religious followers or to people sent to spread a religion ⟨a *missionary* society⟩

missile: launch of a rocket missile

mis•sive \ˈmi-siv\ *n*
[1]LETTER 2

mis•spell \mis-ˈspel\ *vb* **mis•spelled**; **mis•spell•ing**
to spell in an incorrect way

mis•step \mis-ˈstep\ *n*
1 a wrong movement
2 [2]MISTAKE 2, SLIP

[1]**mist** \ˈmist\ *n*
▼ very tiny drops of water floating in the air or falling as fine rain

[1]**mist:** countryside shrouded in mist

[2]**mist** *vb* **mist•ed**; **mist•ing**
1 to cover or become covered with tiny drops of water
2 to become wet with tears ⟨Her eyes *misted*.⟩
3 to rain very lightly

[1]**mis•take** \mə-ˈstāk\ *vb* **mis•took** \mə-ˈstu̇k\; **mis•tak•en** \mə-ˈstā-kən\; **mis•tak•ing**
1 MISUNDERSTAND ⟨It was easy to *mistake* her message.⟩
2 to fail to recognize correctly ⟨She *mistook* me for someone else.⟩

[2]**mistake** *n*
1 a wrong judgment or action ⟨She was accused by *mistake*.⟩
2 something that is incorrect ⟨Correct the *mistakes* on your paper.⟩
synonyms see ERROR

mis•tak•en \mə-ˈstā-kən\ *adj*
1 being in error : judging wrongly ⟨We were *mistaken* about the time.⟩
2 [1]WRONG 2, INCORRECT ⟨a *mistaken* idea⟩
mis•tak•en•ly *adv*

mis•ter \ˈmi-stər\ *n*
1 *cap* used sometimes in writing instead of the usual *Mr.*
2 SIR 1 ⟨Do you want a paper, *mister*?⟩

mis•tle•toe \ˈmi-səl-ˌtō\ *n*
▼ a plant with waxy white berries that grows on the branches and trunks of trees

mistletoe: a sprig of mistletoe

mis•treat \mis-ˈtrēt\ *vb* **mis•treat•ed**; **mis•treat•ing**
to handle, use, or act toward in a harsh way : ABUSE

mis•tress \ˈmi-strəs\ *n*
1 a female teacher
2 a woman who has control or authority over another person, an animal, or a thing

[1]**mis•trust** \mis-ˈtrəst\ *n*
[1]DISTRUST

[2]**mistrust** *vb* **mis•trust•ed**; **mis•trust•ing**
1 [2]DISTRUST, SUSPECT
2 to lack confidence in ⟨They *mistrust* your abilities.⟩

misty \'mi-stē\ *adj* **mist•i•er; mist•i•est**
1 full of very tiny drops of water ⟨a *misty* valley⟩
2 clouded by tears ⟨I looked at the photo through *misty* eyes.⟩
3 VAGUE 3, INDISTINCT ⟨a *misty* memory⟩
mist•i•ly \-stə-lē\ *adv*

mis•un•der•stand \,mis-,ən-dər-'stand\ *vb* **mis•un•der•stood** \-'stu̇d\; **mis•un•der•stand•ing**
to fail to get the meaning of : fail to understand

mis•un•der•stand•ing \,mis-,ən-dər-'stan-diŋ\ *n*
1 a failure to get the meaning of : a failure to understand
2 ARGUMENT 1, QUARREL

¹mis•use \mis-'yüz\ *vb* **mis•used; mis•us•ing**
1 to put into action or service in a wrong way
2 ²ABUSE 1, MISTREAT

²mis•use \mis-'yüs\ *n*
incorrect or improper handling ⟨He was criticized for *misuse* of public funds.⟩

mite \'mīt\ *n*
1 ▼ a tiny animal that is related to and resembles the spider and often lives as a parasite on plants and other animals
2 a very small person, thing, or amount
a mite ²SOMEWHAT

mite 1: a model of a mite shown many times its natural size

mi•to•chon•dri•on \,mī-tə-'kän-drē-ən\ *n, pl* **mi•to•chon•dria** \-drē-ə\
one of the parts found in the cytoplasm of a cell outside the nucleus that provides the cell with energy released from the breakdown of nutrients

mi•to•sis \mī-'tō-səs\ *n, pl* **mi•to•ses** \-'tō-,sēz\
a process of cell division in which two new nuclei are formed each containing the original number of chromosomes

mitt \'mit\ *n*
1 MITTEN ⟨Use a *mitt* to hold the hot dish.⟩
2 a baseball catcher's or first baseman's glove

mit•ten \'mi-tᵊn\ *n*
a covering for the hand and wrist having a separate division for the thumb only

¹mix \'miks\ *vb* **mixed; mix•ing**
1 to make into one thing by stirring together : BLEND ⟨*Mix* flour and water to make a paste.⟩
2 to become one thing through blending ⟨Oil will not *mix* with water.⟩
3 to make by combining different things
4 to bring together ⟨The book *mixes* funny and serious elements.⟩
5 to feel or act friendly toward ⟨Our families don't *mix*.⟩
mix•er \'mik-sər\ *n*
mix up
1 CONFUSE 1 ⟨I *mix* the sisters *up*.⟩
2 to put in the wrong place with other things ⟨Don't *mix up* the papers.⟩
3 to involve or cause to be involved with a bad situation or group ⟨Don't get *mixed up* in the trouble.⟩

moat: a moat surrounding a 12th-century medieval castle

▶ **Synonyms** MIX and BLEND mean to combine into a whole that is more or less the same all over. MIX is used of a fairly complete combining in which the elements may or may not lose their individual identity. ⟨*Mix* several vegetables for a salad.⟩ ⟨*Mix* apple and grape juice.⟩ BLEND is used when there is a complete uniting of similar things so that the original parts cannot be separated or recognized. ⟨*Blend* milk, eggs, and sugar.⟩

²mix *n*
1 MIXTURE 2
2 a prepared combination of ingredients for making a food ⟨cake *mix*⟩

mixed \'mikst\ *adj*
1 made up of two or more kinds ⟨*mixed* candy⟩
2 made up of both females and males ⟨They sing in a *mixed* choir.⟩
3 made up of parts that are very different from one another ⟨He has *mixed* feelings about moving away.⟩

mixed number *n*
a number (as 1²/₃) made up of a whole number and a fraction

mix•ture \'miks-chər\ *n*
1 the act of combining
2 something combined or being combined ⟨Add water to the *mixture*.⟩
3 two or more substances combined together in such a way that each remains unchanged ⟨Sand and sugar form a *mixture*.⟩
4 a combination of different things

mix–up \'miks-,əp\ *n*
an instance of confusion ⟨There was a *mix-up* about the date.⟩

miz•zen \'mi-zᵊn\ *n*
1 a fore-and-aft sail set on the mizzenmast
2 MIZZENMAST

miz•zen•mast \'mi-zᵊn-,mast, -məst\ *n*
the mast behind or next behind the mainmast

ml *abbr* milliliter
mm *abbr* millimeter
MN *abbr* Minnesota
MO *abbr* Missouri
mo. *abbr* month

¹moan \'mōn\ *n*
1 a long low sound showing pain or grief
2 a long low sound ⟨the engine's *moan*⟩

[2]moan *vb* **moaned; moan•ing**
1 to utter a long low sound
2 COMPLAIN

moat \'mōt\ *n*
◀ a deep wide ditch around the walls of a castle or fort that is usually filled with water

[1]mob \'mäb\ *n*
1 a rowdy excited crowd
2 the people of a society who are poor and uneducated

[2]mob *vb* **mobbed; mob•bing**
to crowd about in an aggressive, excited, or annoying way

[1]mo•bile \'mō-bəl, -,bēl, -,bīl\ *adj*
1 easily moved : MOVABLE
2 changing quickly in expression

[2]mo•bile \'mō-,bēl\ *n*
an artistic structure whose parts can be moved especially by air currents

mobile phone *n*
CELL PHONE

mo•bi•lize \'mō-bə-,līz\ *vb* **mo•bi•lized; mo•bi•liz•ing**
to assemble (as military forces) and make ready for action

moc•ca•sin \'mä-kə-sən\ *n*
1 ▶ a soft shoe with no heel and the sole and sides made of one piece
2 WATER MOCCASIN

moccasin 1: a traditional Iroquois moccasin

[1]mock \'mäk\ *vb* **mocked; mock•ing**
1 to treat with scorn : RIDICULE
2 [2]MIMIC 2

[2]mock *adj*
not real : MAKE-BELIEVE ⟨a *mock* battle⟩

mock•ery \'mä-kə-rē\ *n, pl* **mock•er•ies**
1 [1]RIDICULE
2 a bad imitation : FAKE ⟨a *mockery* of justice⟩

mock•ing•bird \'mä-kiŋ-,bərd\ *n*
▶ a songbird of North America noted for its imitations of other birds

[1]mode \'mōd\ *n*
1 a particular form or variety of something ⟨a *mode* of teaching⟩
2 a way of doing something ⟨a *mode* of travel⟩
3 the most frequent value in a set of values

[2]mode *n*
a popular fashion or style

[1]mod•el \'mä-dᵊl\ *n*
1 a small but exact copy of a thing
2 a pattern or figure of something to be made
3 a person who sets a good example ⟨Their daughter is a *model* of politeness.⟩
4 a person who poses for an artist or photographer
5 a person who wears and displays garments that are for sale
6 a special type of a product ⟨Our car is a recent *model.*⟩

> ▶ **Synonyms** MODEL, EXAMPLE, and IDEAL mean something that serves as guidance or imitation. MODEL is used for a thing or person very worthy of imitation. ⟨That school system can be a *model* for the whole state.⟩ EXAMPLE usually means that the person, act, or conduct is likely to be copied, even though this may not always be a good thing. ⟨Parents are *examples* for their children.⟩ IDEAL is used for something, either real or imagined, considered to be the best of its kind that can exist. ⟨She is the *ideal* of beauty.⟩

[2]model *adj*
1 worthy of being imitated ⟨*model* pupils⟩
2 being a miniature copy ⟨a *model* airplane⟩

[3]model *vb* **mod•eled** *or* **mod•elled; mod•el•ing** *or* **mod•el•ling**
1 to plan or shape after a pattern ⟨This sports car is *modeled* on a racing car.⟩
2 to make a model of ⟨He learned how to *model* a dog in clay.⟩
3 to act or serve as a model

mo•dem \'mō-dəm, -,dem\ *n*
a device that changes electrical signals from one form to another and is used especially to send or receive computer data over a telephone line

[1]mod•er•ate \'mä-də-rət\ *adj*
1 neither too much nor too little ⟨*moderate* heat⟩
2 neither very good nor very bad ⟨*moderate* success⟩
3 not expensive : REASONABLE ⟨*moderate* rates⟩

mockingbird

4 not extreme or excessive ⟨a *moderate* point of view⟩ ⟨a *moderate* eater⟩
mod•er•ate•ly *adv*

[2]mod•er•ate \'mä-də-,rāt\ *vb* **mod•er•at•ed; mod•er•at•ing**
to make or become less extreme or severe

mod•er•a•tion \,mä-də-'rā-shən\ *n*
1 the act of avoiding extreme behavior or belief
2 the condition of being reasonable and not extreme

mod•ern \'mä-dərn\ *adj*
1 of or characteristic of the present time or times not long past ⟨*modern* machinery⟩
2 of a style or way of thinking that is new and different ⟨*modern* ideas⟩
3 having a style that is newer and different from older, more traditional styles ⟨*modern* dance⟩
4 of the period from about 1500 to the present ⟨*modern* history⟩

mod•ern•ize \'mä-dər-,nīz\ *vb* **mod•ern•ized; mod•ern•iz•ing**
to make or become new and different or suitable for the present time

mod•est \'mä-dəst\ *adj*
1 not overly proud or confident : not boastful ⟨a *modest* winner⟩
2 limited in size or amount ⟨*modest* wealth⟩
3 not showy ⟨She lives in a *modest* house.⟩
4 decent in thought, conduct, and dress
mod•est•ly *adv*

mod•es•ty \'mä-də-stē\ *n*
the quality of being decent or not boastful

mod•i•fi•ca•tion \,mä-də-fə-'kā-shən\ *n*
1 the act or process of changing parts of something
2 a slightly changed form

mod•i•fi•er \'mä-də-,fī-ər\ *n*
a word (as an adjective or adverb) used with another word to limit its meaning ⟨In the phrase "very big dog" the words "very" and "big" are *modifiers.*⟩

mod•i•fy \'mä-də-,fī\ *vb* **mod•i•fied; mod•i•fy•ing**
1 to make changes in ⟨*modify* a plan⟩
2 to lower or reduce in amount or scale
3 to limit in meaning : QUALIFY ⟨The word "green" in the phrase "green gloves" *modifies* the word "gloves."⟩

mod•ule \'mä-,jül\ *n*
a part of a space vehicle that can work alone

mo•hair \'mō-,her\ *n*
a fabric or yarn made from the long silky hair of an Asian goat

Mo•hawk \'mō-,hȯk\ *n, pl* **Mohawk** *or* **Mo•hawks**
1 a member of an American Indian people of central New York
2 the language of the Mohawk people

Mo•he•gan \mō-'hē-gən\ *or* **Mo•hi•can** \-kən\ *n, pl* **Mo•he•gan** *or* **Mo•he•gans** *or* **Mohican** *or* **Mo•hi•cans**
a member of an American Indian people of southeastern Connecticut

moist \'mȯist\ *adj*
slightly wet : DAMP
moist•ness *n*

moist•en \'mȯi-sᵊn\ *vb* **moist•ened**; **moist•en•ing**
to make damp

mois•ture \'mȯis-chər\ *n*
a small amount of liquid that makes something slightly wet

mo•lar \'mō-lər\ *n*
a large tooth near the back of the mouth with a broad surface used for grinding

► **Word History** A millstone is a large stone used for grinding grain. We have teeth, called *molars,* that are also used for grinding. The English word *molar* comes from a Latin word *molaris* that is derived from *mola,* "millstone." The English word *mill* comes ultimately from Latin *molina,* which is also derived from *mola.*

mo•las•ses \mə-'la-səz\ *n*
a thick brown syrup that is made from raw sugar

[1]**mold** \'mōld\ *n*
1 a hollow form in which something is shaped ⟨Make a candle by pouring wax in a *mold.*⟩
2 ▼ something shaped in a mold ⟨a *mold* of gelatin⟩

[1]**mold 2:** a mold of gelatin

[2]**mold** *vb* **mold•ed**; **mold•ing**
1 to work and press into shape ⟨We learned how to *mold* clay.⟩
2 to shape in a hollow form
3 to influence or affect the character of ⟨Parents try to *mold* their children into responsible adults.⟩

[3]**mold** *n*
1 an often fuzzy surface growth of fungus on damp or decaying material
2 a fungus that forms mold

► **mollusk**
There are many different types of mollusks, ranging from small snails to large octopuses. Most live in water but some live on land, often along the seashore. The mollusk's soft body is typically protected by a hard shell secreted by the mantle, a thin layer of tissue.

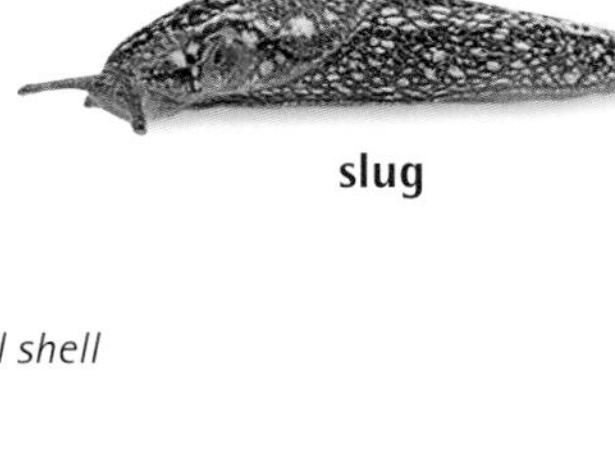

slug

spiral shell
soft body
tentacle
foot

features of a land snail

[4]**mold** *vb* **mold•ed**; **mold•ing**
to become moldy ⟨The old bread began to *mold.*⟩

[5]**mold** *n*
light rich crumbly earth that contains decaying material

mold•ing \'mōl-diŋ\ *n*
a strip of material having a design and used as a decoration (as on a wall or the edge of a table)

moldy \'mōl-dē\ *adj* **mold•i•er**; **mold•i•est**
covered with or containing mold ⟨*moldy* fruit⟩

[1]**mole** \'mōl\ *n*
a small usually brown spot on the skin

[2]**mole** *n*
▼ a small burrowing animal with soft fur and very small eyes

mo•lec•u•lar \mə-'le-kyə-lər\ *adj*
of or relating to a molecule ⟨*molecular* structure⟩

mol•e•cule \'mä-li-ˌkyül\ *n*
the smallest portion of a substance having the properties of the substance ⟨a *molecule* of water⟩

mole•hill \'mōl-ˌhil\ *n*
a little ridge of dirt pushed up by a mole as it burrows underground

mo•lest \mə-'lest\ *vb* **mo•lest•ed**; **mo•lest•ing**
to disturb or injure by interfering

mol•li•fy \'mä-lə-ˌfī\ *vb* **mol•li•fied**; **mol•li•fy•ing**
to soothe in temper or disposition

[2]**mole:** a mole emerging from its burrow

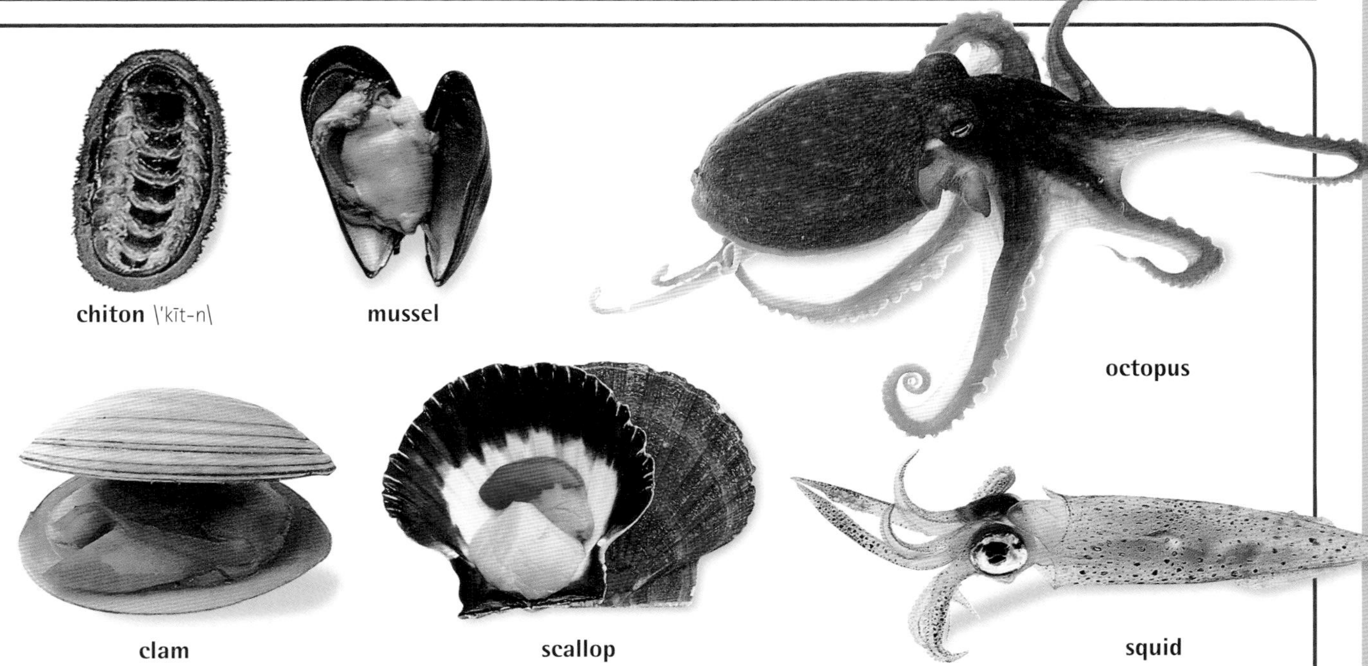

mol•lusk \ˈmä-ləsk\ *n*
▲ an animal (as a clam, snail, or octopus) that lives mostly in water and has a soft body usually enclosed in a shell containing calcium

molt \ˈmōlt\ *vb* **molt•ed**; **molt•ing**
to shed outer material (as hair, shell, or horns) that will be replaced by a new growth

mol•ten \ˈmōl-tᵊn\ *adj*
melted especially by very great heat ⟨*molten* metal⟩

mo•lyb•de•num \mə-ˈlib-də-nəm\ *n*
a white metallic chemical element used in some steel to give greater strength and hardness

mom \ˈmäm, ˈməm\ *n*
[1]MOTHER 1

mo•ment \ˈmō-mənt\ *n*
1 a very brief time ⟨A shooting star lasts only a *moment.*⟩
2 present time ⟨I'm busy at the *moment.*⟩
3 IMPORTANCE ⟨We met to discuss a subject of great *moment.*⟩

mo•men•tary \ˈmō-mən-ˌter-ē\ *adj*
lasting only a very brief time ⟨The loud noise gave us a *momentary* fright.⟩
mo•men•tar•i•ly \ˌmō-mən-ˈter-ə-lē\ *adv*

mo•men•tous \mō-ˈmen-təs\ *adj*
very important ⟨a *momentous* decision⟩

mo•men•tum \mō-ˈmen-təm\ *n*
the force that a moving body has because of its weight and motion

momma *variant of* MAMA

mom•my \ˈmä-mē, ˈmə-\ *n, pl* **mom•mies**
[1]MOTHER 1

Mon. *abbr* Monday

mon– *or* **mono–** *prefix*
one : single : alone ⟨*mono*syllable⟩

mon•arch \ˈmä-nərk, -ˌnärk\ *n*
1 a person who reigns over a kingdom or an empire
2 MONARCH BUTTERFLY

monarch butterfly *n*
▼ a large orange and black American butterfly

mon•ar•chy \ˈmä-nər-kē\ *n, pl* **mon•ar•chies**
1 a state or country having a king or queen
2 a form of government headed by a king or queen

monarch butterfly

mon•as•tery \ˈmä-nə-ˌster-ē\ *n, pl* **mon•as•ter•ies**
a place where a community of monks lives and works

mo•nas•tic \mə-ˈna-stik\ *adj*
of or relating to monks or monasteries ⟨He took *monastic* vows.⟩

Mon•day \ˈmən-ˌdā, -dē\ *n*
the second day of the week

mo•ner•an \mō-ˈnir-ən, mə-\ *n*
any member of the kingdom of living things (as bacteria) consisting of a single simple cell that lacks a nucleus

mon•e•tary \ˈmä-nə-ˌter-ē\ *adj*
of or relating to money

mon•ey \ˈmə-nē\ *n, pl* **moneys** *or* **mon•ies** \-ēz\
1 something (such as coins or bills) used to buy goods and services and to pay people for their work
2 a person's wealth

money order *n*
a piece of paper like a check that can be bought (as at a post office) and that orders payment of a sum of money printed on it to the person named

mon•goose \ˈmän-ˌgüs, ˈmäŋ-ˌgüs\ *n, pl* **mon•goos•es**
a long thin furry animal with sharp claws that eats small animals (as snakes and mice), eggs, and fruit

[1]**mon•grel** \ˈmäŋ-grəl, ˈməŋ-\ *n*
an animal of mixed or uncertain origin

monk: a Buddhist monk with an alms bowl

[2]mongrel *adj*
of mixed or uncertain origin ⟨a *mongrel* dog⟩

[1]mon•i•tor \ˈmä-nə-tər\ *n*
1 a video screen used for display (as of television pictures or computer information)
2 a student in a school picked for a special duty (as keeping order)
3 a person or thing that watches or checks something ⟨a heart *monitor*⟩

[2]monitor *vb* **mon•i•tored; mon•i•tor•ing**
to watch or check for a special reason

monk \ˈməŋk\ *n*
◀ a member of a religious group of men who promise to stay poor, obey the rules of their group, and not get married

[1]mon•key \ˈməŋ-kē\ *n, pl* **monkeys**
▶ a furry animal of warm regions that has a long tail and that along with the apes is most closely related to humans

[2]monkey *vb* **mon•keyed; mon•key•ing**
1 to spend time in an idle or aimless way ⟨We just *monkeyed* around in the gym.⟩
2 to handle secretly or in a careless or incorrect way ⟨*monkeyed* with the car⟩

mon•key•shine \ˈməŋ-kē-ˌshīn\ *n*
PRANK — usually used in pl.

monkey wrench *n*
1 a wrench with one fixed and one adjustable jaw
2 something that disrupts ⟨The storm threw a *monkey wrench* into our plans.⟩

mono– see MON–

mono•cot \ˈmä-nə-ˌkät\ *n*
MONOCOTYLEDON

mono•cot•y•le•don \ˌmä-nə-ˌkä-tə-ˈlē-dᵊn\ *n*
a flowering plant (as a palm tree or grass) having an embryo with a single cotyledon

mono•gram \ˈmä-nə-ˌgram\ *n*
a design usually made by combining two or more of a person's initials

mono•plane \ˈmä-nə-ˌplān\ *n*
▼ an airplane with only one large wing that crosses the body

mo•nop•o•lize \mə-ˈnä-pə-ˌlīz\ *vb* **mo•nop•o•lized; mo•nop•o•liz•ing**
to get or have complete control over ⟨My sister *monopolized* the conversation.⟩

mo•nop•o•ly \mə-ˈnä-pə-lē\ *n, pl* **mo•nop•o•lies**
1 complete ownership or control of the entire supply of goods or a service
2 a person or group having complete control over something
3 complete ownership or control of something

[1]monkey: a De Brazza's \dē-ˈbrä-zäz\ monkey

mono•syl•la•ble \ˈmä-nə-ˌsi-lə-bəl\ *n*
a word of one syllable

mo•not•o•nous \mə-ˈnä-tə-nəs\ *adj*
boring from always being the same
mo•not•o•nous•ly *adv*

mo•not•o•ny \mə-ˈnä-tə-nē\ *n, pl* **mo•not•o•nies**
a boring lack of change

mono•treme \ˈmä-nə-ˌtrēm\ *n*
any of a small group of egg-laying mammals that includes the platypus

mon•soon \män-ˈsün\ *n*
1 a wind in the Indian Ocean and southern Asia that blows from the southwest from April to October and from the northeast from October to April

▶ **monoplane**
The first monoplanes were introduced in the early 20th century. More streamlined in shape than biplanes, they could fly faster and were easier to maneuver. However, their single wings were weak and needed strong wires to brace them to vertical posts called king posts. More powerful, all-metal monoplanes became widespread by the 1930s.

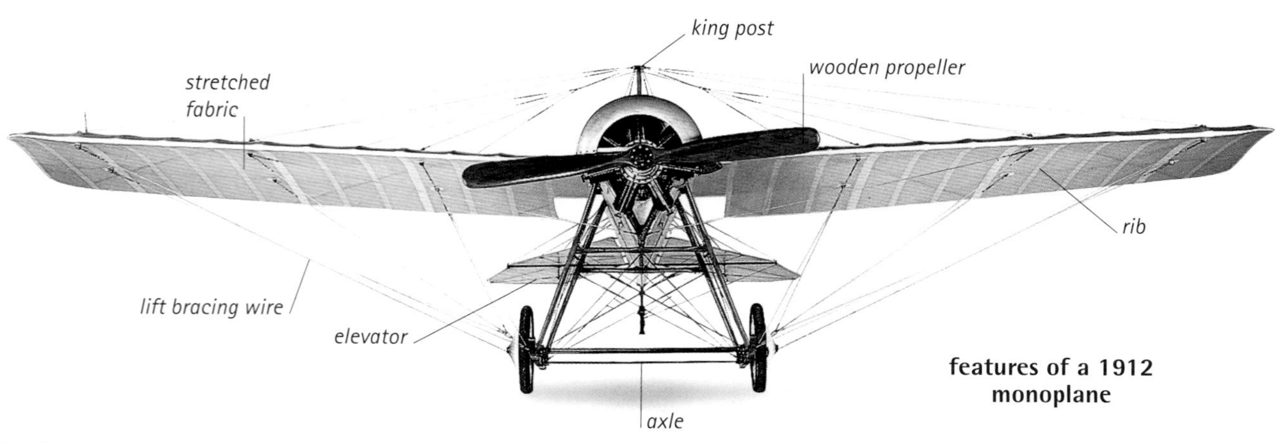

features of a 1912 monoplane

2 the rainy season that comes with the southwest monsoon

mon•ster \ˈmän-stər\ *n*
1 a strange or horrible creature
2 something unusually large
3 an extremely wicked or cruel person

mon•stros•i•ty \män-ˈsträ-sə-tē\ *n, pl* **mon•stros•i•ties**
something that is large and ugly

mon•strous \ˈmän-strəs\ *adj*
1 unusually large : ENORMOUS 〈He has a *monstrous* appetite.〉
2 very bad or wrong 〈a *monstrous* injustice〉
3 having the qualities or appearance of a monster 〈The *monstrous* creature approached.〉
mon•strous•ly *adv*

Mont. *abbr* Montana

month \ˈmənth\ *n*
one of the twelve parts into which the year is divided

[1]**month•ly** \ˈmənth-lē\ *adj*
1 happening, done, or published every month 〈our *monthly* visit〉
2 figured in terms of one month 〈a *monthly* salary〉
3 lasting a month
monthly *adv*

[2]**monthly** *n, pl* **monthlies**
a magazine published every month

mon•u•ment \ˈmän-yə-mənt\ *n*
1 ► a structure (as a building, stone, or statue) made to keep alive the memory of a person or event
2 something that serves as a good reminder or example

[1]**moo** \ˈmü\ *vb* **mooed; moo•ing**
to make the sound of a cow : LOW

[2]**moo** *n, pl* **moos**
the low sound made by a cow

[1]**mood** \ˈmüd\ *n*
an emotional state of mind or feeling 〈I'm in a good *mood* today.〉

[2]**mood** *n*
a set of forms of a verb that show whether the action or state expressed is to be thought of as a fact, a command, or a wish or possibility

moody \ˈmü-dē\ *adj*
mood•i•er; mood•i•est
often feeling or showing a gloomy or a bad frame of mind
mood•i•ly \ˈmü-də-lē\ *adv*
mood•i•ness \ˈmüd-ē-nəs\ *n*

[1]**moon** \ˈmün\ *n*
1 the natural heavenly body that shines by reflecting light from the sun and revolves about the earth in about 29½ days
2 SATELLITE 1

[2]**moon** *vb* **mooned; moon•ing**
[2]DAYDREAM

moon•beam \ˈmün-ˌbēm\ *n*
a ray of light from the moon

moon•light \ˈmün-ˌlīt\ *n*
the light of the moon

moon•lit \ˈmün-ˌlit\ *adj*
lighted by the moon 〈a *moonlit* night〉

moon•shine \ˈmün-ˌshīn\ *n*
1 MOONLIGHT
2 alcoholic liquor produced illegally

moon•stone \ˈmün-ˌstōn\ *n*
a partly transparent shining stone used as a gem

[1]**moor** \ˈmu̇r\ *n*
an area of open land that is too wet or too poor for farming

[2]**moor** *vb* **moored; moor•ing**
to fasten in place with cables, lines, or anchors 〈*moor* a boat〉

moor•ing \ˈmu̇r-iŋ\ *n*
1 a place where a boat can be fastened so it will not float away
2 a chain or line used to hold a boat in place

moor•land \ˈmu̇r-lənd\ *n*
land consisting of ground that is too wet or too poor for farming

moose \ˈmüs\ *n, pl* **moose**
a large animal with broad flattened antlers and humped shoulders that is related to the deer and lives in forests of Canada, the northern United States, Europe, and Asia

[1]**mop** \ˈmäp\ *n*
1 a tool for cleaning floors made of a bundle of cloth or yarn or a sponge fastened to a long handle
2 something that looks like a cloth or yarn mop 〈a *mop* of hair〉

[2]**mop** *vb* **mopped; mop•ping**
to wipe or clean with or as if with a mop 〈He *mopped* the sweat from his forehead with a rag.〉

mope \ˈmōp\ *vb* **moped; mop•ing**
to be in a dull and sad state of mind 〈She *moped* when she didn't get her way.〉

mo•raine \mə-ˈrān\ *n*
a pile of earth and stones left by a glacier

[1]**mor•al** \ˈmȯr-əl\ *adj*
1 concerned with or relating to what is right and wrong in human behavior 〈*moral* problems〉 〈a *moral* judgment〉
2 able to teach a lesson of how people should behave 〈a *moral* story〉
3 [1]GOOD 13, VIRTUOUS 〈They lead a *moral* life.〉
4 able to tell right from wrong 〈Humans are *moral* beings.〉
mor•al•ly *adv*

monument 1: the D.C. World War memorial in Washington, D.C.

[2]moral *n*
 1 the lesson to be learned from a story or experience
 2 **morals** *pl* ways of behaving : moral conduct ⟨They have a high standard of *morals.*⟩
 3 **morals** *pl* teachings or rules of right behavior

mo•rale \mə-ˈral\ *n*
 the condition of the mind or feelings (as in relation to enthusiasm, spirit, or hope) of an individual or group ⟨The team's *morale* is low.⟩

mo•ral•i•ty \mə-ˈra-lə-tē\ *n, pl* **mo•ral•i•ties**
 1 the quality or fact of being in agreement with ideals of right behavior ⟨We discussed the *morality* of lying so a person's feelings aren't hurt.⟩
 2 beliefs about what kind of behavior is good or bad ⟨A society's *morality* may change.⟩

mo•rass \mə-ˈras\ *n*
 MARSH, SWAMP

mo•ray eel \mə-ˈrā-, ˈmȯr-ā-\ *n*
 ▼an often brightly colored eel of warm seas with sharp teeth

moray eel

mor•bid \ˈmȯr-bəd\ *adj*
 1 not healthy or normal ⟨He has a *morbid* fear of snakes.⟩
 2 having or showing an interest in unpleasant or gloomy things ⟨*morbid* thoughts⟩

[1]more \ˈmȯr\ *adj*
 1 greater in amount, number, or size ⟨You like *more* sugar in your tea than I do.⟩
 2 [1]EXTRA, ADDITIONAL ⟨I need *more* time.⟩

[2]more *adv*
 1 in addition ⟨Wait one day *more.*⟩
 2 to a greater extent
 Hint: *More* is often used with an adjective or adverb to form the comparative. ⟨*more* active⟩ ⟨*more* actively⟩

[3]more *n*
 1 a greater amount or number ⟨I got *more* than I expected.⟩
 2 an additional amount ⟨He was too full to eat any *more.*⟩

more•over \mȯr-ˈō-vər\ *adv*
 in addition to what has been said : BESIDES

morn \ˈmȯrn\ *n*
 MORNING

morn•ing \ˈmȯr-niŋ\ *n*
 the early part of the day : the time from sunrise to noon

mosque: the Dome of the Rock mosque in Jerusalem

morning glory *n*
 a vine that climbs by twisting around something and has large trumpet-shaped flowers that close in bright sunshine

morning star *n*
 a bright planet (as Venus) seen in the eastern sky before or at sunrise

mo•ron \ˈmȯr-ˌän\ *n*
 a stupid or foolish person

mo•rose \mə-ˈrōs, mȯ-\ *adj*
 very serious, unhappy, and quiet ⟨She became *morose* and spoke to no one.⟩

mor•phine \ˈmȯr-ˌfēn\ *n*
 a habit-forming drug made from opium and used to relieve pain

mor•row \ˈmär-ō\ *n*
 the next day

Morse code \ˈmȯrs-\ *n*
 a system of sending messages that uses long and short sounds or dots and dashes to represent letters and numbers

mor•sel \ˈmȯr-səl\ *n*
 a small amount : a little piece (as of food)

[1]mor•tal \ˈmȯr-tᵊl\ *adj*
 1 capable of causing death ⟨a *mortal* wound⟩
 2 certain to die ⟨We all are *mortal.*⟩
 3 feeling great and lasting hatred ⟨a *mortal* enemy⟩
 4 very great or overpowering ⟨*mortal* fear⟩
 5 [1]HUMAN 1 ⟨*mortal* power⟩
 synonyms see DEADLY
 mor•tal•ly *adv*

[2]mortal *n*
 a human being

[1]mor•tar \ˈmȯr-tər\ *n*
 1 a strong deep bowl in which substances are pounded or crushed with a pestle
 2 a short light cannon used to shoot shells high into the air

[2]mortar *n*
 a building material made of lime and cement mixed with sand and water that is spread between bricks or stones so as to hold them together when it hardens

[1]mort•gage \ˈmȯr-gij\ *n*
 1 a transfer of rights to a piece of property (as a house) that is usually in return for a loan of money and that is canceled when the loan is paid
 2 the document recording such a transfer

[2]**mortgage** *vb* **mort•gaged**; **mort•gag•ing**
to transfer rights to a piece of property in return for a loan of money with the understanding that the rights end when the loan is paid

mor•ti•fy \'mȯr-tə-ˌfī\ *vb* **mor•ti•fied**; **mor•ti•fy•ing**
to embarrass greatly

mo•sa•ic \mō-'zā-ik\ *n*
a decoration on a surface made by setting small pieces of glass, stone, or tile of different colors into another material to make patterns or pictures

Mos•lem \'mäz-ləm\ *variant of* MUSLIM

mosque \'mäsk\ *n*
◀ a building in which Muslims worship

mos•qui•to \mə-'skē-tō\ *n*, *pl* **mos•qui•toes**
a small fly the female of which punctures the skin of people and animals to suck their blood

moss \'mȯs\ *n*
1 a plant that has no flowers and grows as a small leafy stem in patches like cushions clinging to rocks, bark, or damp ground
2 a plant or plantlike organism (as a lichen) resembling moss

mossy \'mȯ-sē\ *adj* **moss•i•er**; **moss•i•est**
like or covered with moss 〈a *mossy* log〉

[1]**most** \'mōst\ *adj*
1 the majority of : almost all 〈*Most* people believe this.〉
2 greatest in amount or extent 〈The youngest of the group had the *most* courage.〉

[2]**most** *adv*
1 to the greatest or highest level or extent
Hint: *Most* is often used with an adjective or adverb to form the superlative. 〈*most* active〉 〈*most* actively〉
2 [1]VERY 1 〈He is a *most* careful driver.〉

[3]**most** *n*
the greatest amount, number, or part 〈The *most* I can give you is five dollars.〉

most•ly \'mōst-lē\ *adv*
for the greatest part 〈The story was *mostly* untrue.〉

mote \'mōt\ *n*
a small particle : SPECK 〈a *mote* of dust〉

mo•tel \mō-'tel\ *n*
a building or group of buildings for travelers to stay in which the rooms are usually reached directly from an outdoor parking area

moth \'mȯth\ *n*, *pl* **moths** \'mȯt͟hz, 'mȯths\
▼ an insect that usually flies at night and has mostly feathery antennae and stouter body, duller coloring, and smaller wings than the related butterflies

[1]**moth•er** \'mə-t͟hər\ *n*
1 a female parent
2 a nun in charge of a convent
3 [1]CAUSE 1, ORIGIN 〈Necessity is the *mother* of invention.〉
moth•er•hood \-ˌhu̇d\ *n*
moth•er•less \-ləs\ *adj*

▶ **moth**
Unlike butterflies, many moths are drab in color, although there are a number of brilliantly colored types. Moths generally fly at night but there are also many day-flying types. The front and back wings of most moths hook together, the bristles on the underside of the hind wing catching on to a flap on the forewing.

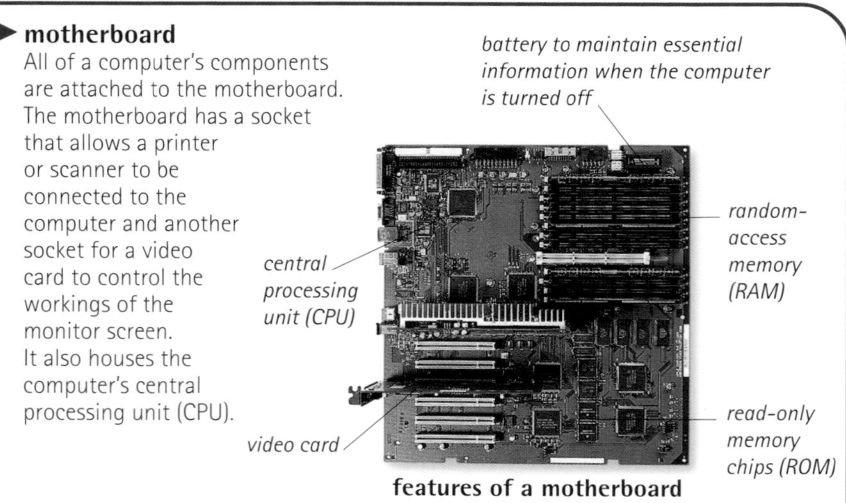

features of a motherboard

[2]**mother** *adj*
1 of or having to do with a mother ⟨*mother* love⟩
2 being in a relation suggesting that of a mother to others ⟨our *mother* country⟩

[3]**mother** *vb* **moth•ered; moth•er•ing**
to be or act as a mother to

moth•er•board \ˈmə-t͟hər-ˌbȯrd\ *n*
▲ the main circuit board especially of a small computer

moth•er–in–law \ˈmə-t͟hər-ən-ˌlȯ\ *n, pl* **mothers–in–law**
the mother of someone's husband or wife

moth•er•ly \ˈmə-t͟hər-lē\ *adj*
1 of or characteristic of a mother ⟨*motherly* affection⟩
2 like a mother ⟨a *motherly* nurse⟩

Mother Nature *n*
nature represented as a woman thought of as the guiding force behind natural events

moth•er–of–pearl \ˌmə-t͟hər-əv-ˈpərl\ *n*
▶ a hard pearly material that lines the shell of some mollusks (as mussels) is often used for ornamental objects and buttons

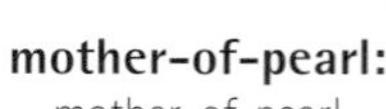
mother-of-pearl: mother-of-pearl lining of an abalone shell

[1]**mo•tion** \ˈmō-shən\ *n*
1 an act or process of changing place or position : MOVEMENT ⟨We felt the swaying *motion* of the train.⟩
2 a movement of the body or its parts ⟨He signaled with a *motion* of his arm.⟩
3 a formal plan or suggestion for action offered according to the rules of a meeting ⟨She made a *motion* to adjourn.⟩
mo•tion•less \-ləs\ *adj*

[2]**motion** *vb* **mo•tioned; mo•tion•ing**
to direct or signal by a movement or sign ⟨He *motioned* them to come.⟩

motion picture *n*
1 a series of pictures projected on a screen rapidly one after another so as to give the appearance of a continuous picture in which the objects move
2 MOVIE 1

mo•ti•vate \ˈmō-tə-ˌvāt\ *vb* **mo•ti•vat•ed; mo•ti•vat•ing**
to give or be a reason for doing something ⟨Prizes *motivated* him to join the contest.⟩

[1]**mo•tive** \ˈmō-tiv\ *n*
a reason for doing something

[2]**motive** *adj*
causing motion ⟨*motive* power⟩

mot•ley \ˈmät-lē\ *adj*
composed of various often unlike kinds or parts ⟨a *motley* collection of junk⟩

[1]**mo•tor** \ˈmō-tər\ *n*
a machine that produces motion or power for doing work ⟨an electric *motor*⟩

[2]**motor** *adj*
1 of, relating to, or designed for use in an automobile ⟨a *motor* trip⟩ ⟨*motor* oil⟩
2 equipped with or driven by a motor
3 causing or controlling movement ⟨*motor* nerves⟩

[3]**motor** *vb* **mo•tored; mo•tor•ing**
[1]DRIVE 2

mo•tor•bike \ˈmō-tər-ˌbīk\ *n*
a small usually lightweight motorcycle

mo•tor•boat \ˈmō-tər-ˌbōt\ *n*
▼ an often small boat driven by a motor

mo•tor•cade \ˈmō-tər-ˌkād\ *n*
a line of motor vehicles traveling as a group ⟨a presidential *motorcade*⟩

mo•tor•car \ˈmō-tər-ˌkär\ *n*
AUTOMOBILE

mo•tor•cy•cle \ˈmō-tər-ˌsī-kəl\ *n*
▶ a motorized vehicle for one or two passengers that has two wheels

mo•tor•ist \ˈmō-tə-rist\ *n*
a person who travels by automobile

mo•tor•ized \ˈmō-tə-ˌrīzd\ *adj*
1 having a motor ⟨a *motorized* wheelchair⟩
2 using motor vehicles for transportation ⟨*motorized* troops⟩

motorboat: a motorboat moored at a dock

motorcycle

Like bicycles, motorcycles have a streamlined frame, a wheel at the front and back, and controls on the handlebars. Like cars, they also have an engine. The first motorcycle was invented in the mid 19th-century. Today, motorcycles are designed for many purposes, including racing and touring, as well as for everyday use. Engine sizes are measured in cubic centimeters (cc), and range from 50cc to more than 1000cc on the most powerful motorcycles.

features of a racing motorbike

1940s motorcycle for military use

1950s motorcycle with a sidecar for a passenger

1960s motorcycle for commuting

1970s motorcycle for touring

1980s motorcycle for touring

1990s 1500cc motorcycle for cruising

motor scooter *n*
a motorized vehicle having two or three wheels like a child's scooter but having a seat

motor vehicle *n*
a motorized vehicle (as an automobile or motorcycle) not operated on rails

mot•tled \'mä-t^{ə}ld\ *adj*
having spots or blotches of different colors 〈*mottled* leaves〉

mot•to \'mä-tō\ *n, pl* **mottoes**
1 a phrase or word inscribed on something (as a coin or public building) to suggest its use or nature
2 a short expression of a guiding rule of conduct 〈The Boy Scout *motto* is "Be prepared."〉

[1]**mound** \'mau̇nd\ *n*
1 a small hill or heap of dirt or stones
2 [1]HEAP 1, PILE 〈a *mound* of dirty laundry〉
3 the slightly raised ground on which a baseball pitcher stands

[2]**mound** *vb* **mound•ed**; **mound•ing**
to make a pile or heap of 〈Snow was *mounded* on both sides of the road.〉

[1]**mount** \'mau̇nt\ *n*
▼ a high hill : MOUNTAIN
Hint: *Mount* is used especially before a proper name 〈*Mount* Everest〉

[2]**mount** *vb* **mount•ed**; **mount•ing**
1 to go up : CLIMB 〈*mount* a ladder〉
2 to get up onto something 〈*mount* a platform〉 〈*mount* a horse〉
3 to increase rapidly in amount 〈His debts were *mounting.*〉
4 to prepare for use or display by fastening in position on a support 〈I *mounted* a picture on cardboard.〉
5 to organize and carry out 〈Police *mounted* a search.〉
synonyms see ASCEND

[3]**mount** *n*
1 a frame or support that holds something 〈a camera lens *mount*〉
2 a horse used for riding

moun•tain \'mau̇n-t^{ə}n\ *n*
1 a raised area of land higher than a hill
2 a great mass or huge number 〈a *mountain* of mail〉

moun•tain•eer \,mau̇n-tə-'nir\ *n*
1 a person who lives in the mountains
2 ▶ a mountain climber

mountain goat *n*
a goatlike animal of the mountains of western North America with a thick white coat and slightly curved black horns

mountain lion *n*
COUGAR

moun•tain•ous \'mau̇n-tə-nəs\ *adj*
1 having many mountains 〈*mountainous* country〉
2 like a mountain in size : HUGE 〈a *mountainous* pile〉

moun•tain•side \'mau̇n-t^{ə}n-,sīd\ *n*
the side of a mountain

mountaineer 2: a mountaineer climbing a rock face on a mountain

moun•tain•top \'mau̇n-t^{ə}n-,täp\ *n*
the highest part of a mountain

mount•ing \'mau̇n-tiŋ\ *n*
a frame or support that holds something 〈a *mounting* for an engine〉

mourn \'mȯrn\ *vb* **mourned**; **mourn•ing**
to feel or show grief or sorrow especially over someone's death
mourn•er *n*

[1]**mount:** Mount Everest

mourn•ful \'mȯrn-fəl\ *adj*
1 full of sorrow or sadness 〈a *mournful* face〉
2 causing sorrow 〈*mournful* news〉
mourn•ful•ly \-fə-lē\ *adv*
mourn•ful•ness *n*

mourn•ing \'mȯr-niŋ\ *n*
1 the act of feeling or expressing sorrow
2 an outward sign (as black clothes or an arm band) of grief for a person's death

mourning dove *n*
▼ a dove of the United States named for its mournful cry

mourning dove

mouse \'mau̇s\ *n, pl* **mice** \'mīs\
1 ▶ a very small furry gnawing animal that is a rodent with a pointed snout and long slender tail
2 a person without spirit or courage
3 *pl also* **mous•es** a small movable device that is connected to a computer and used to move the cursor and select functions on the screen
mouse•like \'mau̇s-,līk\ *adj*

mouse pad *n*
a thin flat pad (as of rubber) on which a computer mouse is used

mous•er \'mau̇-sər\ *n*
a cat good at catching mice

moustache *variant of* MUSTACHE

¹mouth \'mau̇th\ *n, pl* **mouths** \'mau̇thz, 'mau̇ths\
1 the opening through which food passes into the body and which in humans is surrounded on the outside by the lips and contains the tongue and teeth
2 an opening that is like a mouth 〈the *mouth* of a cave〉
3 the place where a stream enters a larger body of water

²mouth \'mau̇th\ *vb* **mouthed; mouth•ing**
1 to form with the lips without speaking 〈The librarian *mouthed* "quiet."〉
2 to repeat without being sincere or without understanding 〈Salesmen *mouthed* meaningless slogans.〉

mouthed \'mau̇thd, 'mau̇tht\ *adj*
having a mouth especially of a specified kind 〈a large-*mouthed* jar〉

mouth•ful \'mau̇th-,fu̇l\ *n*
1 as much as the mouth will hold 〈a *mouthful* of water〉
2 the amount put into the mouth at one time 〈Take another *mouthful.*〉
3 a word or phrase that is very long or difficult to say

mouth•piece \'mau̇th-,pēs\ *n*
the part put to, between, or near the lips 〈the *mouthpiece* of a trumpet〉

mov•able *or* **move•able** \'mü-və-bəl\ *adj*
1 possible to move 〈*movable* desks〉
2 changing date from year to year 〈Thanksgiving is a *movable* holiday.〉

¹move \'müv\ *vb* **moved; mov•ing**
1 to go from one place to another
2 to change the place or position of : SHIFT 〈*Move* your chair closer.〉
3 to set in motion 〈Come on, *move* your feet.〉
4 to cause to act : PERSUADE 〈Your speech *moved* me to change my opinion.〉

mouse 1

5 to affect the feelings of 〈The sad story *moved* me to tears.〉
6 to change position 〈Stop *moving* until I finish cutting your hair.〉
7 to go to a different place to live
8 to suggest according to the rules in a meeting 〈I *move* to adjourn.〉

²move *n*
1 the action of changing position, place, or residence 〈a sudden *move*〉
2 the act of moving a piece in a game
3 the turn of a player to move 〈It's your *move.*〉
4 an action taken to accomplish something 〈a career *move*〉

move•ment \'müv-mənt\ *n*
1 the act or process of moving and especially changing place or position : an instance of moving 〈the *movement* of the planets〉
2 a program or series of acts working toward a desired end 〈a reform *movement*〉
3 a mechanical arrangement (as of wheels) for causing a particular motion (as in a clock or watch)
4 a section of a longer piece of music
5 an emptying of waste matter from the bowels

mov•er \'mü-vər\ *n*
a person or company that moves the belongings of others (as from one home to another)

mov•ie \'mü-vē\ *n*
1 a story represented in motion pictures
2 a showing of a movie — often used in pl. 〈We went to the *movies* last night.〉

mov•ing \'mü-viŋ\ *adj*
1 changing place or position 〈a *moving* target〉
2 causing feelings of sadness or sympathy 〈a *moving* story〉
3 used for transporting belongings from one place to another 〈a *moving* van〉
mov•ing•ly *adv*

moving picture *n*
MOTION PICTURE 1

¹mow \'mau̇\ *n*
the part of a barn where hay or straw is stored

²mow \'mō\ *vb* **mowed; mowed** *or* **mown** \'mōn\; **mow•ing**
1 to cut down with a blade or machine 〈*mow* grass〉
2 to cut the standing plant cover from 〈*mow* the lawn〉
3 to cause to fall in a violent way 〈The team's offense *mowed* down the defensive line.〉
mow•er \'mō-ər\ *n*

mpg *abbr* miles per gallon

mph *abbr* miles per hour

MP3 \,em-,pē-'thrē\ *n*
1 a computer format for creating sound files (as songs) that are much smaller than standard sound files
2 a computer file (such as a song) in the MP3 format

Mr. \'mi-stər\ *n, pl* **Messrs.** \'me-sərz\
used as a title before a man's name 〈*Mr.* Doe〉

Mrs. \'mi-səz, -zəz\ *n, pl* **Mes•dames** \mā-'däm, -'dam\
used as a title before a married woman's name 〈*Mrs.* Doe〉

MS *abbr* Mississippi

Ms. \'miz\ *n*
often used instead of *Miss* or *Mrs.* 〈*Ms.* Jane Doe〉

MT *abbr* Montana

mt. *abbr*
1 mount
2 mountain

[1]much \'məch\ *adj* **more** \'mȯr\; **most** \'mōst\
1 great in amount or extent 〈*much* effort〉
2 great in importance 〈Nothing *much* happened today.〉
3 more than enough 〈That pizza is a bit *much* for one person.〉

[2]much *adv* **more**; **most**
1 to a great or high level or extent 〈He's *much* happier.〉
2 just about 〈She looks *much* the same.〉

[3]much *n*
1 a great amount or part 〈*Much* that was said is true.〉
2 something important or impressive 〈It's not *much* to look at.〉

mu•ci•lage \'myü-sə-lij\ *n*
a water solution of a gum or similar substance used especially to stick things together

muck \'mək\ *n*
1 MUD, MIRE
2 soft moist barnyard manure
3 DIRT 2, FILTH

mu•cous \'myü-kəs\ *adj*
containing or producing mucus 〈a *mucous* membrane〉

mu•cus \'myü-kəs\ *n*
a slippery thick sticky substance that coats, protects, and moistens the linings of body passages and spaces (as of the nose, lungs, and intestines)

mud \'məd\ *n*
soft wet earth or dirt

[1]mud•dle \'mə-dᵊl\ *vb* **mud•dled**; **mud•dling**
1 to be or cause to be confused or bewildered 〈He was *muddled* by too much advice.〉
2 to mix up in a confused manner 〈They *muddled* the story.〉
3 to think or proceed in a confused way 〈I somehow *muddled* through the task.〉

[2]muddle *n*
a state of confusion

[1]mud•dy \'mə-dē\ *adj* **mud•di•er**; **mud•di•est**
1 filled or covered with mud 〈a *muddy* pond〉 〈*muddy* shoes〉
2 looking like mud 〈a *muddy* color〉
3 not clear or bright : DULL 〈*muddy* skin〉
4 being mixed up 〈*muddy* thinking〉

[2]muddy *vb* **mud•died**; **mud•dy•ing**
1 to cover with mud 〈She *muddied* her clothes.〉
2 to make cloudy or dull (as in color)
3 to become or cause to become confused

[1]muff \'məf\ *n*
a soft thick cover into which both hands can be placed to protect them from cold

[2]muff *vb* **muffed**; **muff•ing**
to make a mistake in doing or handling 〈He *muffed* an easy catch.〉

muf•fin \'mə-fən\ *n*
► a bread made of batter containing eggs and baked in a small cup-shaped container

muf•fle \'mə-fəl\ *vb* **muf•fled**; **muf•fling**
1 to deaden the sound of 〈*muffle* a cry〉
2 to wrap up so as to hide or protect 〈She *muffled* the kitten in a blanket.〉

muffins

muf•fler \'mə-flər\ *n*
1 a scarf for the neck
2 a device to deaden the noise of an engine (as of an automobile)

mug \'məg\ *n*
a large drinking cup with a handle

mug•gy \'mə-gē\ *adj* **mug•gi•er**; **mug•gi•est**
being very warm and humid 〈*muggy* weather〉
mug•gi•ness *n*

Mu•ham•mad \mō-'ha-məd, -'hä-; mü-\ *n*
the founder of Islam

mul•ber•ry \'məl-ˌber-ē\ *n, pl* **mul•ber•ries**
► a tree that bears edible usually purple fruit-like berries and has leaves on which silkworms can be fed

[1]mulch \'məlch\ *n*
a material (as straw or bark) spread over the ground especially to protect the roots of plants from heat or cold, to keep soil moist, and to control weeds

[2]mulch *vb* **mulched**; **mulch•ing**
to cover with mulch

mule \'myül\ *n*
1 an animal that is an offspring of a donkey and a horse
2 a stubborn person

mul•ish \'myü-lish\ *adj*
STUBBORN 1
mul•ish•ly *adv*

mull \'məl\ *vb* **mulled**; **mull•ing**
to think about slowly and carefully : PONDER 〈*mull* over an idea〉

mulled \'məld\ *adj*
mixed with sugar and spice and served warm 〈*mulled* cider〉

mul•let \'mə-lət\ *n*
any of various chiefly saltwater fishes some mostly gray (**gray mullets**) and others red or golden (**red mullets**) that are often used as food

multi- \ˌməl-ti\ *prefix*
1 many : much 〈*multi*colored〉
2 more than two 〈*multi*cultural〉
3 many times over

mul•ti•col•ored \ˌməl-ti-'kə-lərd\ *adj*
having, made up of, or including many colors 〈a *multicolored* robe〉

mul•ti•cul•tur•al \ˌməl-ˌtē-'kəl-chə-rəl\ *adj*
relating to or made up of several different cultures 〈a *multicultural* society〉

mul•ti•me•dia \ˌməl-ti-'mē-dē-ə\ *adj*
using or composed of more than one form of communication or expression 〈The museum has a *multimedia* exhibit of photographs, videos, and music.〉

[1]mul•ti•ple \'məl-tə-pəl\ *adj*
being or consisting of more than one 〈We had *multiple* copies of a document.〉

[2]multiple *n*
the number found by multiplying one number by another 〈35 is a *multiple* of 7.〉

mul•ti•pli•cand \ˌməl-tə-plə-'kand\ *n*
a number that is to be multiplied by another number

mul•ti•pli•ca•tion \ˌməl-tə-plə-'kā-shən\ *n*
a short way of finding out what would be the result of adding one number the number of times indicated by a second number 〈The *multiplication* of 7 by 3 is equal to 7 plus 7 plus 7, which gives 21.〉

mulberry: berries on a mulberry tree

mural: part of a mural on the ceiling of the Cunard Building in New York City

mul•ti•pli•er \ˈməl-tə-ˌplī-ər\ *n*
a number by which another number is multiplied

mul•ti•ply \ˈməl-tə-ˌplī\ *vb* **mul•ti•plied**; **mul•ti•ply•ing**
1 to increase in number **:** make or become more numerous ⟨His worries *multiplied.*⟩
2 to find the product of by means of multiplication ⟨*Multiply* 7 by 8.⟩

mul•ti•tude \ˈməl-tə-ˌtüd, -ˌtyüd\ *n*
a great number of people or things

¹mum \ˈməm\ *adj*
SILENT 4 ⟨Keep *mum* about the secret.⟩

²mum *chiefly British variant of* MOM

¹mum•ble \ˈməm-bəl\ *vb* **mum•bled**; **mum•bling**
to speak softly so that words are not clear

²mumble *n*
speech that is not clear enough to be understood

mum•my \ˈmə-mē\ *n, pl* **mummies**
▼ a dead body preserved for burial in the manner of the ancient Egyptians

mumps \ˈməmps\ *n*
a contagious disease marked especially by fever and swelling of the glands around the lower jaw

munch \ˈmənch\ *vb* **munched**; **munch•ing**
to eat or chew especially noisily

mun•dane \ˌmən-ˈdān, ˈmən-ˌdān\ *adj*
1 dull and ordinary ⟨I helped with *mundane* tasks, like doing dishes.⟩
2 relating to ordinary life on earth rather than spiritual things

mu•nic•i•pal \myu̇-ˈni-sə-pəl\ *adj*
of or relating to the government of a town or city ⟨*municipal* buildings⟩

mu•nic•i•pal•i•ty \myu̇-ˌni-sə-ˈpa-lə-tē\ *n, pl* **mu•nic•i•pal•i•ties**
a town or city having its own local government

mu•ni•tion \myu̇-ˈni-shən\ *n*
military equipment and supplies for fighting

mural *n*
◀ a usually large painting on a wall or ceiling

¹mur•der \ˈmər-dər\ *n*
the intentional and unlawful killing of a human being

²murder *vb* **mur•dered**; **mur•der•ing**
1 to kill (someone) intentionally and unlawfully
2 to spoil or ruin by performing or using badly ⟨*murder* a song⟩
synonyms see KILL
mur•der•er *n*

mur•der•ous \ˈmər-də-rəs\ *adj*
1 intending or capable of causing murder
2 very hard to bear or withstand ⟨*murderous* heat⟩

murk \ˈmərk\ *n*
darkness or fog that is hard to see through

murky \ˈmər-kē\ *adj* **murk•i•er**; **murk•i•est**
1 very dark or foggy ⟨*murky* skies⟩
2 CLOUDY 2 ⟨*murky* water⟩
3 not clearly expressed or understood ⟨a *murky* explanation ⟩

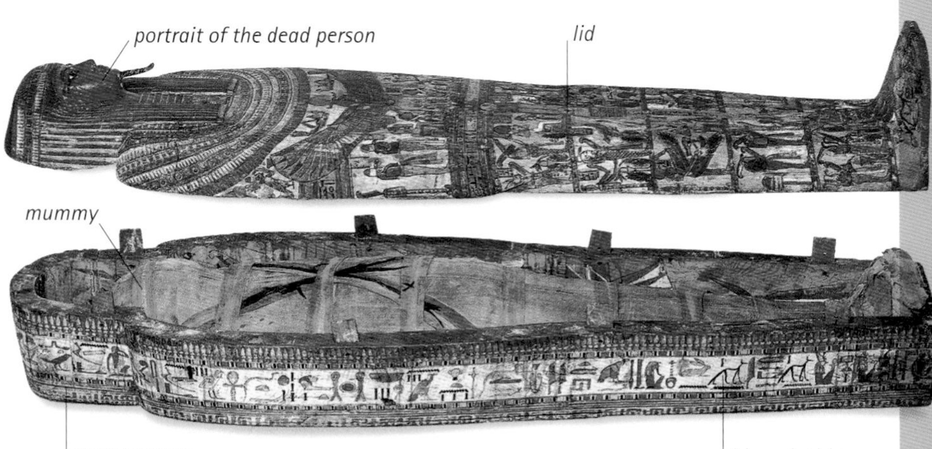

mummy: an ancient Egyptian mummy in its case

[1]mur•mur \'mər-mər\ *n*
1 a low faint sound ⟨the *murmur* of voices⟩
2 a quiet expression of an opinion or feeling ⟨*murmurs* of encouragement⟩

[2]murmur *vb* **mur•mured; mur•mur•ing**
1 to make a low faint sound ⟨The breeze *murmured* in the trees.⟩
2 to say in a voice too quiet to be heard clearly ⟨She *murmured* "thank you" as she left.⟩

mus•cle \'mə-səl\ *n*
1 a tissue of the body consisting of long cells that can contract and produce motion
2 ▼ an organ of the body that is a mass of muscle tissue attached at either end (as to bones) so that it can make a body part move
3 strength of the muscles ⟨He doesn't have the *muscle* to lift that.⟩

▶ **Word History** The English word *muscle* came from a Latin word *musculus* that means literally "small mouse." The movement of the muscles under the skin probably made someone think of a lively mouse.

mus•cle–bound \'mə-səl-,baůnd\ *adj*
having large muscles that do not move and stretch easily

mus•cu•lar \'mə-skyə-lər\ *adj*
1 of, relating to, or done by the muscles ⟨*muscular* strength⟩ ⟨*muscular* activity⟩
2 having large and strong muscles ⟨*muscular* legs⟩ ⟨a *muscular* athlete⟩

muscle 2

There are three types of muscle: skeletal, smooth, and cardiac. Skeletal muscles are attached to the bones by tendons, usually at one end to a bone that moves, and at the other end to one that does not. Smooth muscles are found in the walls of hollow organs and cardiac muscles are found in the heart.

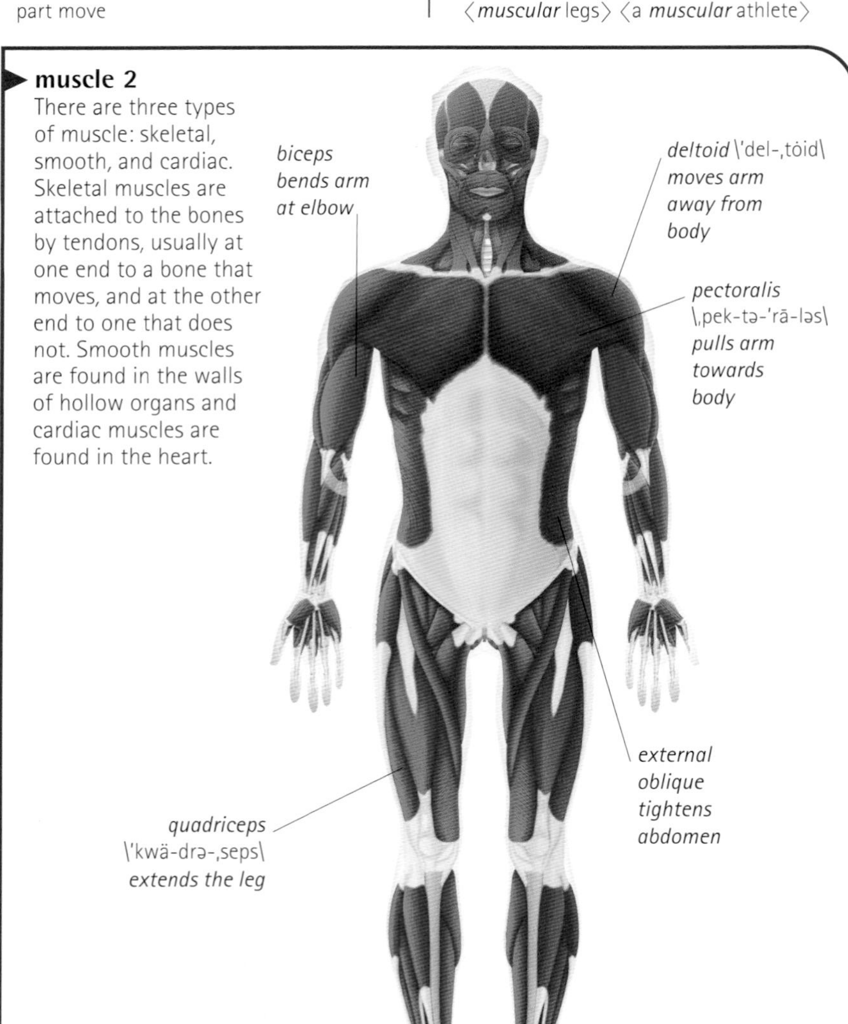

diagram of the skeletal muscular system

muse \'myüz\ *vb* **mused; mus•ing**
to think about carefully or thoroughly : PONDER ⟨She *mused* over what might have been.⟩

mu•se•um \myů-'zē-əm\ *n*
a building in which objects of interest or value are displayed ⟨an art *museum*⟩ ⟨a *museum* of science⟩

[1]mush \'məsh\ *n*
1 cornmeal boiled in water or milk
2 something that is soft and wet and often shapeless ⟨He cooked the vegetables till they were *mush*.⟩

[2]mush *vb* **mushed; mush•ing**
to travel across snow with a sled pulled by dogs

[1]mush•room \'məsh-,rüm, -,rům\ *n*
▶ a part of a fungus that bears spores, grows above ground, and suggests an umbrella in shape

[2]mushroom *vb* **mush•roomed; mush•room•ing**
to appear or develop suddenly or increase rapidly ⟨The town's population has *mushroomed*.⟩

mushy \'mə-shē\ *adj* **mush•i•er; mush•i•est**
1 soft and wet ⟨The rotting apples turned *mushy*.⟩
2 overly romantic or sentimental ⟨*mushy* love songs⟩

mu•sic \'myü-zik\ *n*
1 an arrangement of sounds having melody, rhythm and usually harmony ⟨classical *music*⟩
2 the art of producing pleasing or expressive combinations of tones especially with melody, rhythm, and usually harmony ⟨I want to study *music* in college.⟩
3 a musical composition set down on paper ⟨Bring your *music*.⟩
4 a pleasing sound ⟨Your voice is *music* to my ears.⟩

[1]mu•si•cal \'myü-zi-kəl\ *adj*
1 having to do with music or the writing or performing of music ⟨*musical* instruments⟩
2 pleasing like music ⟨a *musical* voice⟩
3 fond of or talented in music ⟨a *musical* family⟩
4 set to music ⟨a *musical* play⟩
mu•si•cal•ly *adv*

[2]musical *n*
a movie or play that tells a story with both speaking and singing

music box *n*
a box that contains a mechanical device which uses gears like those of a clock to play a tune when the box is open

mu•si•cian \myů-'zi-shən\ *n*
a person who writes, sings, or plays music with skill and especially as a profession

A B C D E F G H I J K L M N O P Q R S T U V W X Y Z

[1]mushroom
Mushrooms are fungi that can be found growing wild mainly in damp woodlands and meadows. They are a popular food around the world, and many edible types are cultivated. To reproduce, mushrooms release spores from flaps called gills, or from hollows called pores, on the underside of their caps.

cap

gills

stem

features of an edible parasol mushroom

crimson wax caps are not edible

smooth lepiotas \ˌle-pē-ˈō-təz\ are poisonous

death caps are very poisonous

shaggymanes are poisonous

morels \mə-ˈrelz\ are a delicacy

porcini have a nutty flavor

musk \ˈməsk\ *n*
a strong-smelling material that is used in perfumes and is obtained from a gland of an Asian deer (**musk deer**) or is prepared artificially

mus•ket \ˈmə-skət\ *n*
a firearm that is loaded through the muzzle and that was once used by soldiers trained to fight on foot

mus•ke•teer \ˌmə-skə-ˈtir\ *n*
a soldier armed with a musket

musk•mel•on \ˈməsk-ˌme-lən\ *n*
a small round to oval melon (as a cantaloupe) with sweet usually green or orange flesh

musk ox *n*
a shaggy animal like an ox found in Greenland and northern North America

musk•rat \ˈməsk-ˌrat\ *n, pl* **muskrat** *or* **musk•rats**
► a North American animal that is a rodent living in or near water and having webbed hind feet, a long scaly tail, and glossy usually dark brown fur

musky \ˈmə-skē\ *adj*
musk•i•er; musk•i•est
having an odor of or resembling musk 〈*musky* perfume〉

Mus•lim \ˈməz-ləm\ *n*
a person whose religion is Islam

muskrat

mus•lin \ˈməz-lən\ *n*
a cotton fabric of plain weave

[1]muss \ˈməs\ *n*
a state of disorder **:** MESS

[2]muss *vb* **mussed; muss•ing**
to make messy or untidy 〈The wind *mussed* my hair.〉

mus•sel \ˈmə-səl\ *n*
1 a saltwater shellfish that has a long dark shell in two parts and is sometimes used as food
2 a freshwater clam of the United States with shells from which mother-of-pearl is obtained

[1]must \ˈməst\ *helping verb, present and past all persons* **must**
1 to be commanded, requested, or urged to 〈You *must* stop the noise at once.〉
2 to be required to 〈A person *must* eat to live.〉
3 to be very likely to 〈It *must* be time.〉 〈I *must* have lost it.〉

[2]**must** *n*
something that is or seems to be required or necessary ⟨Sturdy shoes are a *must* for this hike.⟩

mus•tache *also* **mous•tache** \'mə-,stash, mə-'stash\ *n*
the hair growing on the human upper lip

mus•tang \'mə-,staŋ\ *n*
a small hardy wild horse of the western United States that is descended from horses brought in by the Spaniards

► **Word History** Centuries ago in Spain, stray cattle were rounded up each year and sold. The Spanish word for this roundup of strays, *mesta,* came from a Latin phrase that meant "mixed animals" (*animalia mixta*). From *mesta,* the Spanish made another word, *mestengo,* that meant "a stray animal." In Mexico, this word was used for a kind of wild horse. That is where English *mustang* came from.

mus•tard \'mə-stərd\ *n*
▼ a sharp-tasting yellow powder that is prepared from the seeds of a plant related to the cabbage and is used especially as a seasoning for foods

mustard

[1]**mus•ter** \'mə-stər\ *n*
1 a formal gathering of military troops for inspection
2 an act of careful examination or consideration to determine whether something is acceptable or good enough ⟨Your excuses will not pass *muster.*⟩

[2]**muster** *vb* **mus•tered; mus•ter•ing**
1 to call together (as troops) for roll call or inspection
2 to bring into being or action ⟨*mustering* courage⟩

mustn't \'mə-sᵊnt\ must not

musty \'mə-stē\ *adj* **must•i•er; must•i•est**
smelling of dampness, decay, or lack of fresh air ⟨a *musty* basement⟩

[1]**mu•tant** \'myü-tᵊnt\ *adj*
resulting from genetic mutation ⟨a *mutant* frog⟩

[2]**mutant** *n*
a plant, animal, or microorganism resulting from genetic mutation

mu•tate \'myü-,tāt\ *vb* **mu•tat•ed; mu•tat•ing**
to undergo genetic mutation

mu•ta•tion \myü-'tā-shən\ *n*
a change in a gene or the resulting new trait it produces in an individual

[1]**mute** \'myüt\ *adj* **mut•er; mut•est**
1 unable or unwilling to speak ⟨The shy boy sat *mute* through class.⟩
2 felt or expressed without the use of words ⟨He touched her hand in *mute* sympathy.⟩

[2]**mute** *n*
1 a person who cannot or does not speak
2 ▼ a device on a musical instrument that deadens, softens, or muffles its tone

[3]**mute** *vb* **mut•ed; mut•ing**
to soften or reduce the sound of ⟨We *muted* our voices.⟩

mu•ti•late \'myü-tə-,lāt\ *vb* **mu•ti•lat•ed; mu•ti•lat•ing**
1 to destroy or cut off a necessary part (as a limb) : MAIM
2 to ruin by damaging or changing ⟨He *mutilated* the book with a scissors.⟩ ⟨The actors *mutilated* the play.⟩

mu•ti•neer \,myü-tə-'nir\ *n*
a person who takes part in a mutiny

mu•ti•nous \'myü-tə-nəs\ *adj*
1 involved in turning against a person in charge (as the captain of a ship) ⟨a *mutinous* crew⟩
2 feeling or showing a desire to disobey ⟨*mutinous* grumblings⟩

[1]**mu•ti•ny** \'myü-tə-nē\ *n, pl* **mu•ti•nies**
1 a turning of a group (as of sailors) against a person in charge
2 refusal to obey those in charge

[2]**mutiny** *vb* **mu•ti•nied; mu•ti•ny•ing**
to try to take control away from a person in charge ⟨The sailors were preparing to *mutiny.*⟩

mutt \'mət\ *n*
a dog that is a mix of usually undetermined breeds

mut•ter \'mə-tər\ *vb* **mut•tered; mut•ter•ing**
1 to speak in a low voice with lips partly closed ⟨He *muttered* an apology.⟩
2 to complain in a low voice : GRUMBLE ⟨She *muttered* about the bad food.⟩

mut•ton \'mə-tᵊn\ *n*
the meat of an adult sheep

mu•tu•al \'myü-chə-wəl\ *adj*
1 given and received in equal amount ⟨*mutual* affection⟩
2 having the same relation to one another ⟨They are *mutual* enemies.⟩
3 shared by two or more at the same time ⟨It turns out we have a *mutual* friend.⟩
mu•tu•al•ly *adv*

[2]mute 2:
a mute on a trumpet

[1]**muz•zle** \'mə-zəl\ *n*
1 the nose and mouth of an animal (as a dog)
2 ▼ a covering for the mouth of an animal to prevent it from biting or eating
3 the open end of a gun from which the bullet comes out when the gun is fired

[1]**muzzle 2:**
a muzzle on a German shepherd

[2]**muzzle** *vb* **muz•zled**; **muz•zling**
1 to put a muzzle on ⟨You must *muzzle* your dog.⟩
2 to keep from free expression of ideas or opinions ⟨The dictator *muzzled* the press.⟩

my \'mī, mə\ *adj*
belonging or relating to me or myself ⟨*my* head⟩ ⟨*my* injuries⟩

my•nah *or* **my•na** \'mī-nə\ *n*
▶ an Asian bird that is related to the starling and can be trained to mimic words

[1]**myr•i•ad** \'mir-ē-əd\ *n*
a very large number of things ⟨a *myriad* of possibilities⟩ ⟨*myriads* of stars⟩

[2]**myriad** *adj*
many in number : extremely numerous

myrrh \'mər\ *n*
a sticky brown fragrant material obtained from African and Arabian trees and used especially in perfumes or formerly in incense

myr•tle \'mər-tᵊl\ *n*
1 an evergreen shrub of southern Europe with fragrant flowers
2 [1]PERIWINKLE

my•self \mī-'self, mə-\ *pron*
my own self ⟨I hurt *myself.*⟩ ⟨I *myself* did it.⟩
by myself [1]ALONE 1

mys•te•ri•ous \mi-'stir-ē-əs\ *adj*
strange, unknown, or hard to understand or explain ⟨a *mysterious* noise⟩ ⟨a *mysterious* stranger⟩
mys•te•ri•ous•ly *adv*
mys•te•ri•ous•ness *n*

mys•tery \'mi-stə-rē\ *n, pl* **mys•ter•ies**
1 something that has not been or cannot be explained ⟨Her disappearance remains a *mystery.*⟩ ⟨Their success is a *mystery* to me.⟩
2 a piece of fiction about solving a crime

mys•tic \'mi-stik\ *adj*
1 MYSTICAL
2 relating to magic
3 MYSTERIOUS

mys•ti•cal \'mi-sti-kəl\ *adj*
having a spiritual meaning that is difficult to see or understand ⟨a *mystical* symbol⟩

mynah

mys•ti•fy \'mi-stə-,fī\ *vb* **mys•ti•fied**; **mys•ti•fy•ing**
to confuse or bewilder completely ⟨His strange behavior has *mystified* us.⟩

myth \'mith\ *n*
1 a story often describing the adventures of beings with more than human powers that attempts to explain mysterious events (as the changing of the seasons) or that explains a religious belief or practice
2 such stories as a group
3 a person or thing existing only in the imagination ⟨The dragon is a *myth.*⟩
4 a popular belief that is not true ⟨It's just a *myth* that money can buy happiness.⟩

myth•i•cal \'mi-thi-kəl\ *adj*
1 based on or told of in a myth ⟨a *mythical* hero⟩
2 IMAGINARY ⟨a *mythical* town⟩

my•thol•o•gy \mi-'thä-lə-jē\ *n, pl* **my•thol•o•gies**
a collection of myths ⟨Greek *mythology*⟩

Sounds of N: The letter **N** makes the sound heard in *now* and *canyon*. When **N** is combined with **G**, it makes the sound heard in *king* or in any of the many words ending in -ing. That sound is indicated by the symbol ŋ. In some words, **N** is silent, as in *column*.

n \ˈen\ *n, pl* **n's** *or* **ns** \ˈenz\ *often cap*
the 14th letter of the English alphabet

n *abbr* noun

N *abbr*
1 north
2 northern

-n see -EN

nab \ˈnab\ *vb* **nabbed**; **nab•bing**
[1]ARREST 1

na•cho \ˈnä-chō\ *n, pl* **nachos**
▼ a tortilla chip topped with melted cheese and often additional toppings

nacho: a bowl of nachos

[1]**nag** \ˈnag\ *vb* **nagged**; **nag•ging**
1 to annoy by repeated complaining, scolding, or urging 〈Mom *nagged* me to finish my homework.〉
2 to annoy continually or again and again 〈She was *nagged* by a toothache.〉

[2]**nag** *n*
an old and usually worn-out horse

na•iad \ˈnā-əd\ *n, pl* **na•iads** *or* **na•ia•des** \ˈnā-ə-ˌdēz\
a nymph believed in ancient times to be living in lakes, rivers, and springs

[1]**nail** \ˈnāl\ *n*
1 a tough covering protecting the upper end of each finger and toe
2 a slender pointed piece of metal driven into or through something for fastening

[2]**nail** *vb* **nailed**; **nail•ing**
to fasten with or as if with a nail

na•ive *or* **na•ïve** \nä-ˈēv\ *adj* **na•iv•er**; **na•iv•est**
1 showing lack of experience or knowledge 〈He asked a lot of *naive* questions.〉
2 being simple and sincere
na•ive•ly *adv*

na•ked \ˈnā-kəd\ *adj*
1 having no clothes on : NUDE
2 lacking a usual or natural covering 〈*naked* trees〉
3 not in its case or without a covering 〈a *naked* sword〉 〈a *naked* light bulb〉
4 stripped of anything misleading : PLAIN 〈the *naked* truth〉
5 not aided by an artificial device 〈Bacteria cannot be seen by the *naked* eye.〉
na•ked•ly *adv*
na•ked•ness *n*

► **Synonyms** NAKED and BARE mean being without a natural or usual covering. NAKED is used when there is neither protective nor ornamental covering. 〈She was holding a *naked* baby.〉 BARE is used when there is no unnecessary covering or when all covering has been removed. 〈Let's hang some pictures on the *bare* walls.〉

[1]**name** \ˈnām\ *n*
1 a word or combination of words by which a person or thing is known
2 REPUTATION 2 〈She made a *name* for herself in the restaurant business.〉
3 a word or phrase used to describe and insult someone 〈Stop calling me *names*!〉

[2]**name** *vb* **named**; **nam•ing**
1 to choose a word or words by which something will be known : give a name to 〈They plan to *name* the baby Diana.〉
2 to refer to by the word by which a person or thing is known : call by name 〈Can you *name* all the state capitals?〉
3 to appoint to a job of authority 〈Our principal was *named* superintendent of schools.〉
4 to decide on 〈Have you *named* the date for your wedding?〉
5 [2]MENTION 〈Just *name* your price.〉
6 to choose to be 〈Their son was *named* student of the year.〉

[3]**name** *adj*
well-known because of wide distribution 〈That store doesn't sell *name* brands.〉

name•less \ˈnām-ləs\ *adj*
1 having no name 〈a *nameless* species〉
2 not marked with a name 〈a *nameless* grave〉
3 [1]UNKNOWN, ANONYMOUS 〈My favorite poem is by a *nameless* writer.〉
4 not to be described 〈Upon entering the house he suffered *nameless* fears.〉

name•ly \ˈnām-lē\ *adv*
that is to say 〈We studied the cat family, *namely*, lions, tigers, and related animals.〉

name•sake \ˈnām-ˌsāk\ *n*
a person who has the same name as someone else

nan•ny \ˈna-nē\ *n, pl* **nannies**
a child's nurse

nanny goat *n*
▼ a female goat

nanny goat: a nanny goat with her kid

[1]**nap** \ˈnap\ *n*
a short sleep especially during the day

[2]**nap** *vb* **napped; nap•ping**
1 to sleep briefly especially during the day
2 to be unprepared ⟨When the ball came to her, she was caught *napping.*⟩

[3]**nap** *n*
a hairy or fluffy surface (as on cloth)

nape \ˈnāp\ *n*
the back of the neck

naph•tha \ˈnaf-thə, ˈnap-thə\ *n*
any of various usually flammable liquids prepared from coal or petroleum and used especially to dissolve substances

nap•kin \ˈnap-kən\ *n*
a small piece of cloth or paper used when eating to wipe the lips or fingers and protect the clothes

nar•cis•sus \när-ˈsi-səs\ *n, pl* **narcissus** *or* **nar•cis•sus•es** *or* **nar•cis•si** \-ˈsi-ˌsī, -sē\
a daffodil with flowers that have short trumpet-shaped tubes

[1]**nar•cot•ic** \när-ˈkä-tik\ *n*
an addicting drug that in small doses dulls the senses, relieves pain, and brings on sleep but in larger doses has dangerous effects and that includes some (as morphine) that are used in medicine and others (as heroin) that are used illegally

[2]**narcotic** *adj*
of, relating to, or being a narcotic ⟨*narcotic* drugs⟩ ⟨*narcotic* laws⟩

nar•rate \ˈner-ˌāt, na-ˈrāt\ *vb* **nar•rat•ed; nar•rat•ing**
to tell in full detail ⟨Let me *narrate* the story of my adventure.⟩
synonyms see REPORT
nar•ra•tor \ˈner-ˌā-tər, na-ˈrā-\ *n*

nar•ra•tion \na-ˈrā-shən\ *n*
1 the act or process or an instance of telling in full detail ⟨I enjoyed his *narration* of the story.⟩
2 [1]NARRATIVE

[1]**nar•ra•tive** \ˈner-ə-tiv\ *n*
something (as a story) that is told in full detail

[2]**narrative** *adj*
having the form of a story ⟨a *narrative* poem⟩

[1]**nar•row** \ˈner-ō\ *adj* **nar•row•er; nar•row•est**
1 of slender or less than usual width ⟨a *narrow* strip of grass⟩ ⟨a *narrow* street⟩
2 limited in size or extent ⟨We had a *narrow* range of choices.⟩
3 not broad or open in mind or views ⟨They are *narrow* in their thinking.⟩
4 barely successful : CLOSE ⟨We made a *narrow* escape.⟩
nar•row•ly *adv*
nar•row•ness *n*

[2]**narrow** *vb* **nar•rowed; nar•row•ing**
1 to make or become less wide
2 to limit in number become fewer ⟨The list of candidates has been *narrowed* to ten.⟩

[3]**narrow** *n*
a narrow passage connecting two bodies of water — usually used in pl.

nar•row–mind•ed \ˌner-ō-ˈmīn-dəd\ *adj*
[1]NARROW 3, INTOLERANT
nar•row–mind•ed•ly *adv*
nar•row–mind•ed•ness *n*

nar•whal \ˈnär-ˌhwäl, -ˌwäl\ *n*
▼ an arctic marine animal that is related to dolphins and whales and in the male has a long twisted ivory tusk

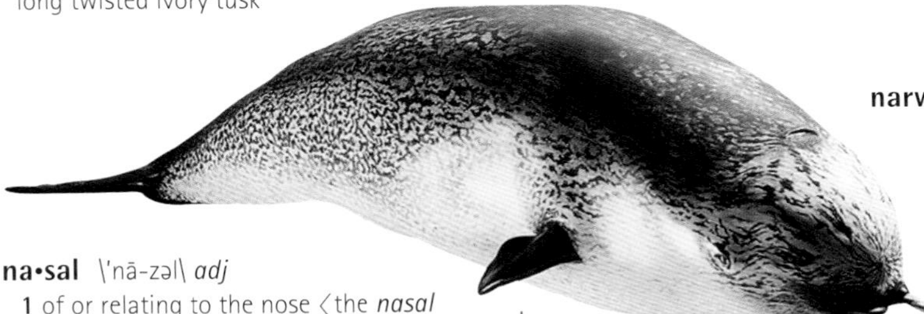
narwhal

na•sal \ˈnā-zəl\ *adj*
1 of or relating to the nose ⟨the *nasal* passages⟩
2 uttered with the nose passage open ⟨The consonants \m\, \n\, and \ŋ\ are *nasal.*⟩
na•sal•ly *adv*

nas•tur•tium \nə-ˈstər-shəm, na-\ *n*
▼ an herb with roundish leaves and red, orange, yellow, or white flowers

nasturtium

nas•ty \ˈna-stē\ *adj* **nas•ti•er; nas•ti•est**
1 [2]MEAN 1 ⟨He has a *nasty* disposition.⟩
2 very unpleasant ⟨*nasty* weather⟩ ⟨a *nasty* taste⟩
3 very serious : HARMFUL ⟨I had a *nasty* fall on the ice.⟩
4 very dirty : FILTHY
5 INDECENT ⟨*nasty* jokes⟩
nas•ti•ly \ˈna-stə-lē\ *adv*
nas•ti•ness \ˈna-stē-nəs\ *n*

na•tion \ˈnā-shən\ *n*
1 COUNTRY 1 ⟨China is a *nation* I'd like to visit.⟩
2 a community of people made up of one or more nationalities usually with its own territory and government
3 NATIONALITY 3

[1]**na•tion•al** \ˈna-shə-nᵊl\ *adj*
of or relating to an entire country ⟨a *national* anthem⟩ ⟨the *national* news⟩
na•tion•al•ly *adv*

[2]**national** *n*
a citizen of a particular country

National Guard *n*
a part of the United States military whose members are recruited by each state, equipped by the federal government, and can be used by either the state or the country

na•tion•al•ism \ˈna-shə-nə-ˌli-zəm\ *n*
devotion to the interests of a certain country and belief that it is better and more important than other countries

na•tion•al•ist \ˈna-shə-nə-list\ *n*
a person who believes that his or her country is better and more important than other countries

na•tion•al•i•ty \ˌna-shə-ˈna-lə-tē\ *n, pl* **na•tion•al•i•ties**
1 the fact or state of belonging to a particular country
2 the state of being a separate country
3 a group of people having a common history, tradition, culture, or language

na•tion•al•ize \ˈna-shə-nə-ˌlīz\ *vb* **na•tion•al•ized; na•tion•al•iz•ing**
to place under government control

na•tion•wide \ˌnā-shən-ˈwīd\ *adj*
extending throughout an entire country ⟨They experienced a *nationwide* drought.⟩

[1]na•tive \ˈnā-tiv\ *adj*
1 born in a certain place or country 〈He's a *native* Belgian.〉
2 belonging to a person because of place of birth 〈His parents speak their *native* language at home.〉
3 living or growing naturally in a certain region 〈*native* plants〉
4 grown, produced, or coming from a certain place 〈*native* tomatoes〉 〈*native* art〉
5 NATURAL 3 〈He's a swimmer with *native* ability.〉

[2]native *n*
1 a person who was born in or comes from a particular place
2 a kind of plant or animal that originally grew or lived in a particular place

Native American *n*
a member of any of the first groups of people to live in North and South America and especially in the United States

Na•tiv•i•ty \nə-ˈti-və-tē\ *n*, *pl* **Na•tiv•i•ties**
the birth of Jesus Christ 〈a *Nativity* scene〉

nat•ty \ˈna-tē\ *adj* **nat•ti•er**; **nat•ti•est**
very neat, trim, and stylish
nat•ti•ly \ˈna-tə-lē\ *adv*

nat•u•ral \ˈna-chə-rəl, ˈnach-rəl\ *adj*
1 found in or produced by nature 〈That's her *natural* hair color.〉 〈a *natural* lake〉
2 being or acting as expected : NORMAL 〈a *natural* reaction〉
3 present or existing at birth : born in a person or animal 〈*natural* instincts〉 〈*natural* curiosity〉
4 having qualities or skills without training or effort 〈She's a *natural* jumper.〉
5 occurring in the normal course of life 〈He died of *natural* causes.〉
6 being simple and sincere 〈She had *natural* manners.〉
7 LIFELIKE 〈The photo is very *natural*.〉
8 not raised or lowered in musical pitch using a sharp or flat

natural gas *n*
a flammable gas mixture from below the earth's surface that is used especially as a fuel

nat•u•ral•ist \ˈna-chə-rə-list, ˈnach-rə-\ *n*
a person who studies nature and especially plants and animals as they live in nature

nat•u•ral•i•za•tion \ˌna-chə-rə-lə-ˈzā-shən, ˌnach-rə-\ *n*
the act or process of making or becoming a citizen

nat•u•ral•ize \ˈna-chə-rə-ˌlīz, ˈnach-rə-\ *vb* **nat•u•ral•ized**; **nat•u•ral•iz•ing**
1 to become or allow to become a citizen
2 to become or cause to become established as if native 〈*naturalize* a plant〉

nat•u•ral•ly \ˈna-chər-ə-lē, ˈnach-rə-lē\ *adv*
1 without anything added or changed : by natural character 〈Fruit is *naturally* sweet.〉
2 in the normal or expected way 〈*Naturally*, you're tired from running.〉
3 because of a quality present at birth 〈Cats are *naturally* curious.〉
4 in a way that is relaxed and normal 〈Just speak *naturally*.〉

natural number *n*
the number 1 or any number obtained by adding 1 to it one or more times

natural resource *n*
▼ something (as water, a mineral, forest, or kind of animal) that is found in nature and is valuable to humans

na•ture \ˈnā-chər\ *n*
1 the physical world and everything in it 〈It is one of the most beautiful creatures found in *nature*.〉
2 natural scenery or surroundings 〈We took a hike to enjoy *nature*.〉
3 the basic character of a person or thing 〈Scientists studied the *nature* of the new substance.〉
4 natural feelings : DISPOSITION, TEMPERAMENT 〈She has a generous *nature*.〉
5 [1]SORT 1, TYPE 〈What is the *nature* of your problem?〉

[1]naught *also* **nought** \ˈnȯt\ *pron*
[1]NOTHING 1 〈Our efforts came to *naught* in the end.〉

[2]naught *also* **nought** *n*
ZERO 1, CIPHER

natural resource
Natural resources are important for the prosperity and political power of a country. If it has many natural resources, such as fish, minerals, or wood, its people may enjoy good food, health, and housing. The country can also trade resources with other nations for materials that are lacking locally.

examples of natural resources

minerals are used to make jewelry, and in manufacturing

fish are used for food

wood is used for fuel, to make furniture, and to build homes

water is used for drinking and irrigating crops, and supports aquatic life

naugh•ty \'nȯ-tē\ *adj* **naugh•ti•er; naugh•ti•est**
behaving in a bad or improper way
naugh•ti•ly \'nȯ-tə-lē\ *adv*
naugh•ti•ness \'nȯ-tē-nəs\ *n*

nau•sea \'nȯ-zē-ə, 'nȯ-shə\ *n*
1 a disturbed and unpleasant condition of the stomach **:** the feeling of being about to vomit
2 deep disgust **:** LOATHING

▶ **Word History** The ancient Greeks were a seafaring people, so feeling motion sickness on board a ship was nothing new to them. In fact the Greek word for "seasickness," *nausia,* was derived from the word *naus,* meaning "ship." Since the main signs of seasickness are an upset stomach and the urge to vomit, *nausia* was applied to stomach discomfort of any origin. The word was borrowed into Latin as *nausea,* and from Latin into English.

nau•se•ate \'nȯ-zē-,āt, 'nȯ-shē-\ *vb* **nau•se•at•ed; nau•se•at•ing**
to cause to feel nausea ⟨That smell *nauseates* me.⟩
nau•se•at•ing *adj*
nau•se•at•ing•ly *adv*

nau•seous \'nȯ-shəs, 'nȯ-zē-əs\ *adj*
1 suffering from nausea
2 causing nausea ⟨a *nauseous* smell⟩

nau•ti•cal \'nȯ-ti-kəl\ *adj*
of or relating to sailors, navigation, or ships

Na•va•jo *also* **Na•va•ho** \'na-və-hō, 'nä-\ *n, pl* **Na•va•jos** *also* **Na•va•hos**
1 a member of an American Indian people of northern New Mexico and Arizona
2 the language of the Navajo people

na•val \'nā-vəl\ *adj*
of or relating to a navy or warships ⟨*naval* vessels⟩

nave \'nāv\ *n*
▶ the long central main part of a church

na•vel \'nā-vəl\ *n*
a hollow or bump in the middle of the stomach that marks the place where the umbilical cord was attached

nav•i•ga•ble \'na-vi-gə-bəl\ *adj*
1 deep enough and wide enough to permit passage of ships ⟨a *navigable* river⟩
2 possible to steer ⟨a *navigable* balloon⟩
nav•i•ga•bil•i•ty \,na-vi-gə-'bi-lə-tē\ *n*

nav•i•gate \'na-və-,gāt\ *vb* **nav•i•gat•ed; nav•i•gat•ing**
1 to travel by water ⟨Explorers *navigated* around the world.⟩
2 to sail or travel over, on, or through ⟨The crew *navigated* the river.⟩
3 to steer a course in a ship or aircraft
4 to steer or direct the course of (as a boat)
5 to find information on the Internet or a Web site

nav•i•ga•tion \,na-və-'gā-shən\ *n*
1 the act or practice of steering, directing the course of, or finding a way through
2 ▲ the science of figuring out the position and course of a ship or aircraft
nav•i•ga•tion•al \-shə-nᵊl\ *adj*

navigation 2: a radar screen being used to direct US military aircraft from an aircraft carrier

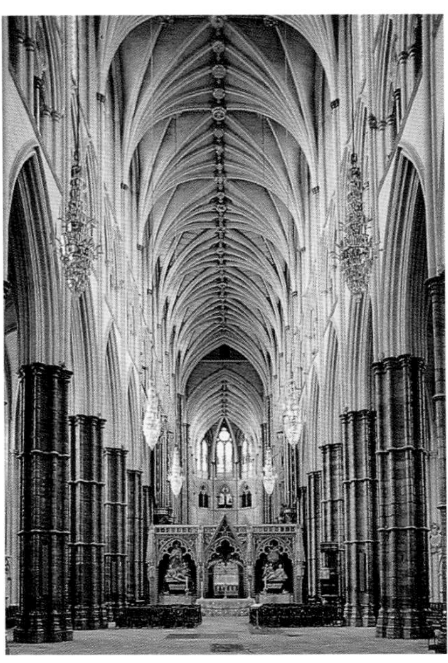

nave of Westminster Abbey, in London, UK

nav•i•ga•tor \'na-və-,gā-tər\ *n*
an officer on a ship or aircraft responsible for directing its course

na•vy \'nā-vē\ *n, pl* **navies**
1 the complete military organization of a nation for warfare at sea
2 a dark blue

[1]**nay** \'nā\ *adv*
[1]NO 2 ⟨Are you coming? *Nay,* I'm not.⟩

[2]**nay** *n, pl* **nays**
1 [3]NO 2 ⟨The final vote was 3 ayes and 6 *nays.*⟩
2 [3]NO 3

Na•zi \'nät-sē\ *n*
a member of a political party controlling Germany from 1933 to 1945

NB *abbr* New Brunswick

NC *abbr* North Carolina

ND, N. Dak. *abbr* North Dakota

NE *abbr*
1 Nebraska
2 northeast

Ne•an•der•thal \nē-'an-dər-,thȯl\ *or* **Ne•an•der•tal** \-,tȯl\ *n*
an ancient human who lived 30,000 to 200,000 years ago

[1]**near** \'nir\ *adv* **near•er; near•est**
1 at, within, or to a short distance or time ⟨Don't go any *nearer.*⟩ ⟨Night drew *near.*⟩
2 ALMOST, NEARLY ⟨The weather was *near* perfect.⟩

[2]**near** *prep*
close to ⟨We'll take a table *near* the window.⟩

[3]**near** *adj* **near•er; near•est**
1 closely related or associated 〈a *near* relative〉
2 not far away in distance or time 〈the *nearest* exit〉 〈the *near* future〉
3 coming close : NARROW 〈a *near* miss〉
4 being the closer of two 〈the *near* side〉
near•ness *n*

[4]**near** *vb* **neared; near•ing**
to come near : APPROACH

near•by \nir-ˈbī\ *adv or adj*
close at hand 〈Bandages are kept *nearby*.〉 〈a *nearby* park〉

near•ly \ˈnir-lē\ *adv*
1 in a close manner or relationship 〈They're *nearly* related.〉
2 almost but not quite 〈We're *nearly* finished.〉
3 to the least extent 〈It's not *nearly* enough.〉

near•sight•ed \ˈnir-ˈsī-təd\ *adj*
able to see things that are close more clearly than distant ones
near•sight•ed•ness *n*

neat \ˈnēt\ *adj* **neat•er; neat•est**
1 showing care and a concern for order 〈a *neat* room〉
2 skillful in a fascinating or entertaining way 〈a *neat* trick〉
neat•ly *adv*
neat•ness *n*

▶ **Word History** The English word *neat* can be traced back to a Latin adjective *nitidus* that meant "shining," "bright," or "clear." The French word *net* that came from this Latin word had the same meanings and came into English as *neat*. English *neat* at first meant "bright" or "clean." Later it was used to mean "simple and in good taste," "skillful," and "tidy."

▶ **Synonyms** NEAT, TIDY, and TRIM mean showing care and a concern for order. NEAT is used when something is clean in addition to being orderly. 〈Your clothes should always be *neat*.〉 TIDY is used for something that is continually kept orderly and neat. 〈I work hard to keep my room *tidy*.〉 TRIM is used when something is orderly and compact. 〈They live in *trim*, comfortable houses.〉

Neb., Nebr. *abbr* Nebraska

neb•u•la \ˈne-byə-lə\ *n, pl* **neb•u•lae** \-ˌlē\ *or* **neb•u•las**
1 ▶ any of many clouds of gas or dust seen in the sky among the stars
2 GALAXY 2

neb•u•lous \ˈne-byə-ləs\ *adj*
not clear : VAGUE

[1]**nec•es•sary** \ˈne-sə-ˌser-ē\ *adj*
needing to be had or done : ESSENTIAL 〈Food is *necessary* to life.〉 〈I got the *necessary* work done first.〉
nec•es•sar•i•ly \ˌne-sə-ˈser-ə-lē\ *adv*

[2]**necessary** *n, pl* **nec•es•sar•ies**
something that is needed

ne•ces•si•tate \ni-ˈse-sə-ˌtāt\ *vb* **ne•ces•si•tat•ed; ne•ces•si•tat•ing**
to make necessary : REQUIRE 〈New achievement tests *necessitated* a curriculum change.〉

ne•ces•si•ty \ni-ˈse-sə-tē\ *n, pl* **ne•ces•si•ties**
1 the state of things that forces certain actions 〈The *necessity* of eating forced her to work.〉
2 very great need 〈Call us for help in case of *necessity*.〉
3 the state of being in need : POVERTY 〈I am forced by *necessity* to beg.〉
4 something that is badly needed 〈He bought a few *necessities* before his trip.〉

neck \ˈnek\ *n*
1 the part of the body between the head and the shoulders
2 the section of a garment covering or nearest to the part connecting the head with the body
3 something that is long and narrow or that connects two larger parts 〈a *neck* of land〉 〈the *neck* of a bottle〉
necked \ˈnekt\ *adj*
neck and neck so nearly equal (as in a race or election) that one cannot be said to be ahead of the other

neck•er•chief \ˈne-kər-chəf\ *n, pl* **neck•er•chiefs** \-chifs, -ˌchēvz\
a square of cloth worn folded around the neck like a scarf

neck•lace \ˈne-kləs\ *n*
a piece of jewelry (as a string of beads) worn around the neck

neck•line \ˈnek-ˌlīn\ *n*
the outline of the neck opening of a garment

neck•tie \ˈnek-ˌtī\ *n*
▶ a narrow length of material worn under the collar and tied in front

necktie

necktie: a man wearing a necktie

nec•tar \ˈnek-tər\ *n*
a sweet liquid produced by plants and used by bees in making honey

nebula 1: the Orion nebula

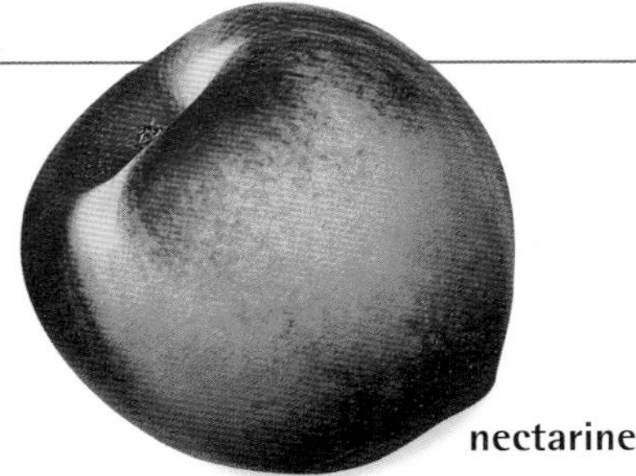
nectarine

nec•tar•ine \ˌnek-tə-ˈrēn\ *n*
▲ a peach with a smooth skin

née *or* **nee** \ˈnā\ *adj*
used to identify a woman by her maiden name ⟨Mrs. Jane Brown, *née* Johnson⟩

[1]need \ˈnēd\ *vb* **need•ed**; **need•ing**
1 to suffer from the lack of something important to life or health ⟨Give to those who *need*.⟩
2 to be necessary ⟨Something *needs* to be done.⟩
3 to be without : REQUIRE ⟨I *need* advice.⟩ ⟨He bought what he *needed*.⟩

[2]need *n*
1 something that must be done : OBLIGATION ⟨An electrician understands the *need* to be careful.⟩
2 a lack of something necessary, useful, or desired ⟨After losing his job, he was in great *need*.⟩
3 something necessary or desired ⟨Our daily *needs* are few.⟩

need•ful \ˈnēd-fəl\ *adj*
[1]NECESSARY

[1]nee•dle \ˈnē-dᵊl\ *n*
1 a small slender pointed usually steel tool used for sewing
2 a slender pointed piece of metal or plastic (used for knitting)
3 a leaf (as of a pine) shaped like a needle
4 a pointer on a dial ⟨The *needle* on her gas gauge read "empty."⟩
5 a slender hollow instrument that has a sharp point and by which material is put into or taken from the body through the skin
nee•dle•like \ˈnē-dᵊl-ˌlīk\ *adj*

[2]needle *vb* **nee•dled**; **nee•dling**
[1]TEASE 1, TAUNT

nee•dle•point \ˈnē-dᵊl-ˌpȯint\ *n*
embroidery done on canvas usually in simple even stitches across counted threads

need•less \ˈnēd-ləs\ *adj*
UNNECESSARY
need•less•ly *adv*

nee•dle•work \ˈnē-dᵊl-ˌwərk\ *n*
1 things made by embroidery, knitting, or needlepoint
2 ▶ the activity or art of making things by embroidery, knitting, or needlepoint

needn't \ˈnē-dᵊnt\ need not

needy \ˈnē-dē\ *adj* **need•i•er**; **need•i•est**
very poor
need•i•ness *n*

ne'er \ˈner\ *adv*
NEVER

ne'er–do–well \ˈner-dü-ˌwel\ *n*
a worthless person who will not work

[1]neg•a•tive \ˈne-gə-tiv\ *adj*
1 emphasizing the bad side of a person, situation, or thing ⟨a *negative* attitude⟩ ⟨Whenever I ask her how she's doing, her reply is *negative*.⟩
2 not positive ⟨His test results came back *negative*.⟩
3 less than zero and shown by a minus sign ⟨−2 is a *negative* number.⟩
4 being the part toward which the electric current flows from the outside circuit ⟨the *negative* pole of a storage battery⟩
5 of, being, or relating to electricity of which the electron is the unit and which is produced in a hard rubber rod that has been rubbed with wool ⟨a *negative* charge⟩
6 having more electrons than protons ⟨a *negative* particle⟩
neg•a•tive•ly *adv*
neg•a•tiv•i•ty \ˌne-gə-ˈti-və-tē\ *n*

[2]negative *n*
1 a part of something which is harmful or bad ⟨Consider the *negatives* of quitting school.⟩
2 an expression (as the word *no*) that denies or says the opposite
3 the side that argues or votes against something
4 a photographic image on film from which a final picture is made

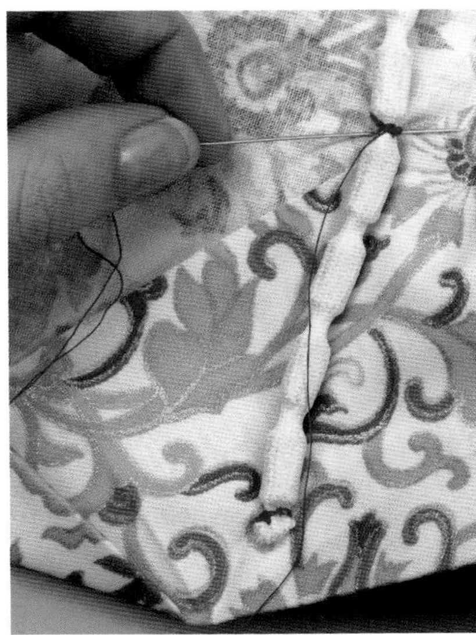
needlework 2

[1]ne•glect \ni-ˈglekt\ *vb* **ne•glect•ed**; **ne•glect•ing**
1 to fail to give the right amount of attention to ⟨The property has been *neglected*.⟩
2 to fail to do or look after especially because of carelessness ⟨She *neglected* to say goodbye.⟩

▶ **Synonyms** NEGLECT and DISREGARD mean to pass over something without giving it any or enough attention. NEGLECT is used when a person does not give, whether deliberately or not, enough attention to something that deserves or requires attention. ⟨You have been *neglecting* your homework.⟩ DISREGARD is used for deliberately overlooking something usually because it is not considered worth noticing. ⟨He *disregarded* the "keep out" sign.⟩

[2]neglect *n*
1 lack of attention or care to something or someone ⟨*neglect* of duty⟩
2 the state of not being looked after or given attention ⟨The house suffers from *neglect*.⟩

ne•glect•ful \ni-ˈglekt-fəl\ *adj*
not looking after or giving attention to : NEGLIGENT

neg•li•gee \ˌne-glə-ˈzhā\ *n*
a woman's loose robe made of thin material

neg•li•gence \ˈne-glə-jəns\ *n*
failure to take proper or normal care of something or someone

neg•li•gent \ˈne-glə-jənt\ *adj*
failing to take proper or normal care of something or someone
neg•li•gent•ly *adv*

neg•li•gi•ble \ˈne-glə-jə-bəl\ *adj*
so small or unimportant as to deserve little or no attention ⟨Crops received a *negligible* amount of rainfall.⟩

ne•go•tia•ble \ni-ˈgō-shə-bəl\ *adj*
1 able to be discussed in order to reach an agreement ⟨a *negotiable* price⟩
2 able to be successfully dealt with or traveled over ⟨*negotiable* roads⟩

ne•go•ti•ate \ni-ˈgō-shē-ˌāt\ *vb* **ne•go•ti•at•ed**; **ne•go•ti•at•ing**
1 to have a discussion with another in order to settle something ⟨We are willing to *negotiate* with the enemy for peace.⟩
2 to arrange for by discussing ⟨I'm trying to *negotiate* a loan.⟩
3 to be successful in getting around, through, or over ⟨Keep your hands on the steering wheel to *negotiate* a turn.⟩
ne•go•ti•a•tor \-ˌā-tər\ *n*

ne•go•ti•a•tion \ni-ˌgō-shē-ˈā-shən\ *n*
the act or process of having a discussion in order to reach an agreement

Ne•gro \ˈnē-ˌgrō\ *n, pl* **Ne•groes** *sometimes offensive*
a member of a race of people native to Africa and classified according to certain physical characteristics (as dark skin)
Hint: In the past, this word was more commonly used. In recent years, however, many people have come to consider the word hurtful, and you may offend someone by using it.

¹neigh \ˈnā\ *vb* **neighed**; **neigh•ing**
to make the long loud cry of a horse

²neigh *n*
the long loud cry of a horse

¹neigh•bor \ˈnā-bər\ *n*
1 a person living near another
2 a person, animal, or thing located near some other person, animal, or thing ⟨The house's nearest *neighbor* is a church.⟩

²neighbor *vb* **neigh•bored**; **neigh•bor•ing**
to be near or next to
neigh•bor•ing *adj*

neigh•bor•hood \ˈnā-bər-ˌhu̇d\ *n*
1 a residential section of a city ⟨They are building a house in our *neighborhood.*⟩
2 the people living near one another
3 a place or region near : VICINITY
4 an amount, size, or range that is close to ⟨It cost in the *neighborhood* of ten dollars.⟩

neigh•bor•ly \ˈnā-bər-lē\ *adj*
familiar and helpful : FRIENDLY
neigh•bor•li•ness *n*

¹nei•ther \ˈnē-t͟hər, ˈnī-\ *conj*
1 not either ⟨His grades were *neither* good nor bad.⟩
2 also not ⟨Our parents did not want to go and *neither* did we.⟩

²neither *pron*
not the one and not the other ⟨*Neither* of the bottles is full.⟩

³neither *adj*
not either ⟨*Neither* answer is correct.⟩

ne•on \ˈnē-ˌän\ *n*
a colorless gaseous chemical element found in very small amounts in the air and used in electric lamps

neo•phyte \ˈnē-ə-ˌfīt\ *n*
1 BEGINNER, NOVICE
2 a new convert

neph•ew \ˈne-fyü\ *n*
a son of a person's brother or sister

Nep•tune \ˈnep-ˌtün, -ˌtyün\ *n*
▶ the planet that is eighth in order of distance from the sun and has a diameter of about 31,000 miles (50,000 kilometers)

▶ **nervous system**
The human body contains an intricate system of nerves which arise in the brain and spinal cord. Electrical signals called nerve impulses are carried between the brain and spinal cord or central nervous system and other regions of the body, such as muscles and organs. Specialized nerves control automatic functions such as breathing or the beating of the heart.

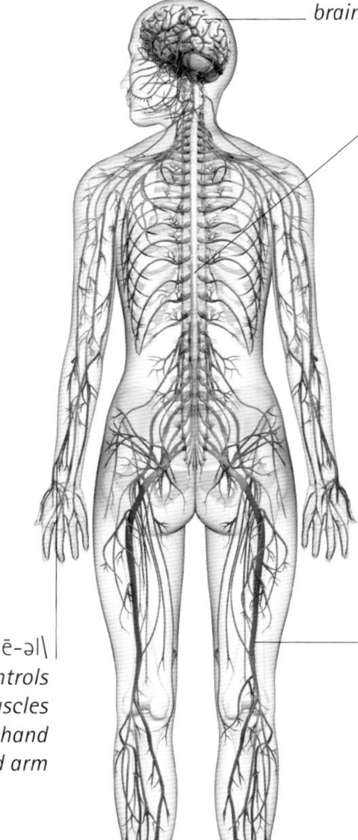

diagram showing the human nervous system

nep•tu•ni•um \nep-ˈtü-nē-əm, -ˈtyü-\ *n*
a radioactive chemical element similar to uranium

nerd \ˈnərd\ *n*
1 a person who is socially awkward, unattractive, or not fashionable
2 a person who is extremely interested in technical or intellectual subjects
nerdy \ˈnər-dē\ *adj*

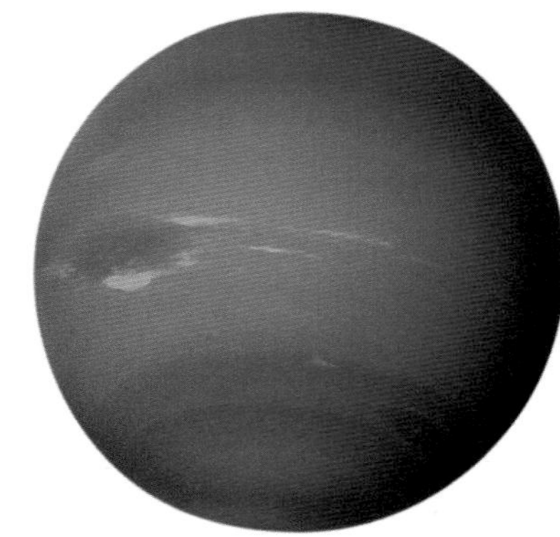

Neptune

nerve \ˈnərv\ *n*
1 a bundle of nerve fibers that carries messages in the form of nerve impulses to or away from the brain and spinal cord
2 COURAGE, BOLDNESS
3 rude or disrespectful boldness ⟨You've got a lot of *nerve* to talk to me that way.⟩
4 nerves *pl* feelings of worry ⟨The groom suffered from *nerves* before the wedding.⟩
5 the sensitive soft inner part of a tooth
nerve•less \-ləs\ *adj*

nerve cell *n*
a cell of the nervous system with fibers that carry nerve impulses

nerve fiber *n*
any of the threadlike extensions (as axons or dendrites) of a nerve cell that carry nerve impulses

nerve impulse *n*
an electrical signal carried by nerve cells which relays information from the body's sense organs to the brain and spinal cord or instructions from the brain and spinal cord to a body part (as a muscle or gland)

ner•vous \'nər-vəs\ *adj*
1 having or showing feelings of worry, fear, or anxiety ⟨Having to give a speech makes me *nervous*.⟩
2 easily becoming worried, frightened, or anxious ⟨She's a *nervous* driver.⟩
3 of, relating to, or made up of nerves or nerve cells ⟨*nervous* tissue⟩
ner•vous•ly *adv*
ner•vous•ness *n*

nervous system *n*
◀ a system of the body that in vertebrates includes the brain, spinal cord, nerves, and sense organs and receives, interprets, and responds to stimuli from inside and outside the body

nervy \'nər-vē\ *adj* **nerv•i•er**; **nerv•i•est**
1 showing calm courage ⟨The team won after a *nervy* performance.⟩
2 showing or acting with disrespectful boldness

-ness \nəs\ *n suffix*
state : condition ⟨good*ness*⟩ ⟨sick*ness*⟩

[1]**nest** \'nest\ *n*
1 ▶ a shelter made by an animal and especially a bird for its eggs and young
2 a place where some animals live and usually lay eggs ⟨a termite's *nest*⟩
3 a cozy place : HOME
4 those living in a nest ⟨a *nest* of robins⟩

[2]**nest** *vb* **nest•ed**; **nest•ing**
to build or live in a nest ⟨*nesting* birds⟩

nes•tle \'ne-səl\ *vb* **nes•tled**; **nes•tling** \'nes-liŋ, -ə-liŋ\
1 to lie close and snug : CUDDLE
2 to be located snugly or in a place not easily noticed ⟨The village *nestles* in a valley.⟩

nest•ling \'nest-liŋ\ *n*
a young bird not yet able to leave the nest

[1]**net** \'net\ *n*
1 ▶ a device made of strands that weave in and out with open spaces between and used to hold or catch something
2 a fabric made of strands of thread, cord, rope, or wire that weave in and out with much open space ⟨a *net* for catching fish⟩

net

3 the object placed between players in some games (as tennis)
4 the area that serves as the goal in some games (as soccer and hockey)
5 *often cap* INTERNET
6 NETWORK 1 ⟨a *net* of passageways⟩
7 something that traps and is difficult to escape from ⟨They were caught in a *net* of lies.⟩

[2]**net** *vb* **net•ted**; **net•ting**
1 to cover with or as if with a net
2 to catch in or as if in a net

[3]**net** *adj*
remaining after all charges or expenses have been subtracted ⟨We made a *net* profit of eight dollars.⟩

[4]**net** *vb* **net•ted**; **net•ting**
to gain or produce as profit : CLEAR ⟨Each sale *nets* ten cents.⟩

net•ting \'ne-tiŋ\ *n*
1 [1]NET 1
2 [1]NET 2

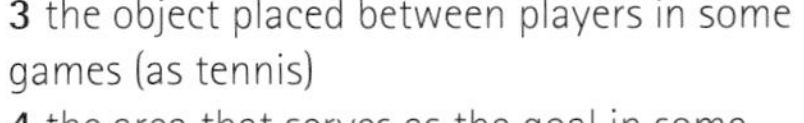

nettle

net•tle \'ne-təl\ *n*
▶ a tall plant with hairs on the leaves that when touched can cause a painful skin rash

net•work \'net-,wərk\ *n*
1 an arrangement of things forming a pattern with spaces between ⟨a *network* of roads⟩
2 a system of computers connected by communications lines
3 a group of connected radio or television stations

neu•ron \'nü-,rän, 'nyü-\ *n*
NERVE CELL

▶ [1]**nest 1**

Birds' nests are built according to the materials available and the predators that threaten the birds' nestlings. Different bird species may raise their young in complex nests woven from grasses, in solid nests constructed from dried mud, or even on tumbled heaps of twigs and feathers.

features of a European buzzard's nest

reed warblers live in Europe and build nests slung between reeds

ovenbirds from South America mold their nests from dried mud

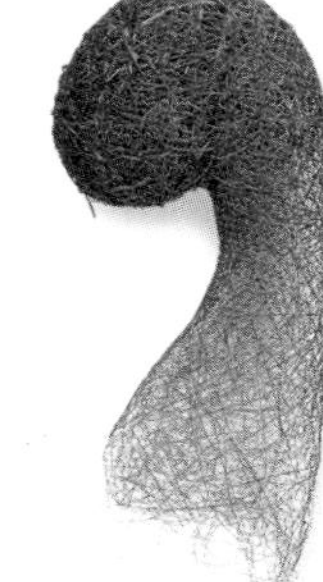

weaverbirds found in West Africa weave nests from grass

A B C D E F G H I J K L M N O P Q R S T U V W X Y Z

neu•ter \'nü-tər, 'nyü-\ *vb* **neu•tered**; **neu•ter•ing**
to remove the sex glands and especially the testes from : CASTRATE ⟨*neuter* a dog⟩

[1]**neu•tral** \'nü-trəl, 'nyü-\ *n*
1 a person or group that does not favor either side in a quarrel, contest, or war
2 a grayish color or color that is not bright
3 a position of gears (as in the transmission of a motor vehicle) in which they are not in contact

[2]**neutral** *adj*
1 not favoring either side in a quarrel, contest, or war
2 of or relating to a country that doesn't favor either side in a dispute ⟨*neutral* territory⟩
3 not strong in opinion or feeling ⟨My feelings toward work are *neutral.*⟩
4 having a color that is not bright : GRAYISH ⟨*neutral* walls⟩
5 neither acid nor basic
6 not electrically charged

neu•tral•i•ty \nü-'tra-lə-tē, nyü-\ *n*
the quality or state of not favoring one side or the other

neu•tral•i•za•tion \,nü-trə-lə-'zā-shən, ,nyü-\ *n*
the act or process of making chemically neutral : the state of being chemically neutral

neu•tral•ize \'nü-trə-,līz, 'nyü-\ *vb* **neu•tral•ized**; **neu•tral•iz•ing**
1 to make chemically neutral ⟨An acid is *neutralized* with lime.⟩
2 to make ineffective ⟨Good pitching will *neutralize* the other team's hitters.⟩

neu•tron \'nü-,trän, 'nyü-\ *n*
a particle that has a mass nearly equal to that of the proton but no electrical charge and that is present in all atomic nuclei except those of hydrogen

Nev. *abbr* Nevada

nev•er \'ne-vər\ *adv*
1 not ever : at no time ⟨He *never* said he was innocent.⟩
2 not to any extent or in any way ⟨*Never* fear, I have the solution.⟩

nev•er•more \,ne-vər-'mȯr\ *adv*
never again

nev•er•the•less \,ne-vər-thə-'les\ *adv*
even so : HOWEVER

[1]**new** \'nü, 'nyü\ *adj* **new•er**; **new•est**
1 recently bought, acquired, or rented ⟨Dad gave me a *new* rug for my *new* apartment.⟩
2 taking the place of someone or something that came before ⟨We got a *new* teacher in March.⟩
3 recently discovered or learned ⟨a *new* planet⟩ ⟨He showed us a *new* trick.⟩
4 beginning as a repeating of a previous thing ⟨a *new* year⟩
5 being in a position, place, or state for the first time ⟨He's a *new* member of the team.⟩ ⟨We met her *new* husband.⟩
6 having recently come into existence ⟨We looked at *new* computers.⟩
7 not used by anyone previously ⟨She traded her used car for a *new* one.⟩
8 not accustomed ⟨He's *new* to the job.⟩
new•ness *n*

newsstand

[2]**new** *adv*
NEWLY, RECENTLY ⟨*new*-mown grass⟩

new•born \'nü-'bȯrn, 'nyü-\ *adj*
1 recently born ⟨a *newborn* calf⟩
2 made new or strong again

new•com•er \'nü-,kə-mər, 'nyü-\ *n*
1 someone or something recently arrived
2 BEGINNER

new•el \'nü-əl, 'nyü-\ *n*
a post at the bottom or at a turn of a stairway

new•fan•gled \'nü-'faŋ-gəld, 'nyü-\ *adj*
of the newest style : NOVEL ⟨He loves these *newfangled* gadgets.⟩

new•ly \'nü-lē, 'nyü-\ *adv*
not long ago : RECENTLY ⟨a *newly* elected governor⟩

new•ly•wed \'nü-lē-,wed, 'nyü-\ *n*
a person recently married ⟨Some *newlyweds* moved in next door.⟩

new moon *n*
1 the moon's phase when its dark side is toward the earth
2 the thin curved outline of the moon seen shortly after sunset for a few days after the new moon

news \'nüz, 'nyüz\ *n*
1 a report of recent events or unknown information ⟨I have good *news*! We won!⟩
2 information or recent events reported in a newspaper or magazine or on a broadcast
3 a broadcast of information on recent events ⟨We saw pictures of a flood on the evening *news.*⟩
4 an event that is interesting enough to be reported

news•boy \'nüz-,bȯi, 'nyüz-\ *n*
a boy or man who delivers or sells newspapers

news•cast \'nüz-,kast, 'nyüz-\ *n*
a radio or television broadcast of information on recent events

news•girl \'nüz-,gərl, 'nyüz-\ *n*
a girl or woman who delivers or sells newspapers

news•man \'nüz-mən, 'nyüz-\ *n, pl* **news•men** \-mən\
a person who gathers or reports information on recent events

news•pa•per \'nüz-,pā-pər, 'nyüz-\ *n*
a paper that is printed and sold usually every day or weekly and that contains information on recent events, articles of opinion, features, and advertising

news•reel \'nüz-,rēl, 'nyüz-\ *n*
a short motion picture made in the past about events at that time

news•stand \'nüz-,stand, 'nyüz-\ *n*
◀ a place where newspapers and magazines are sold

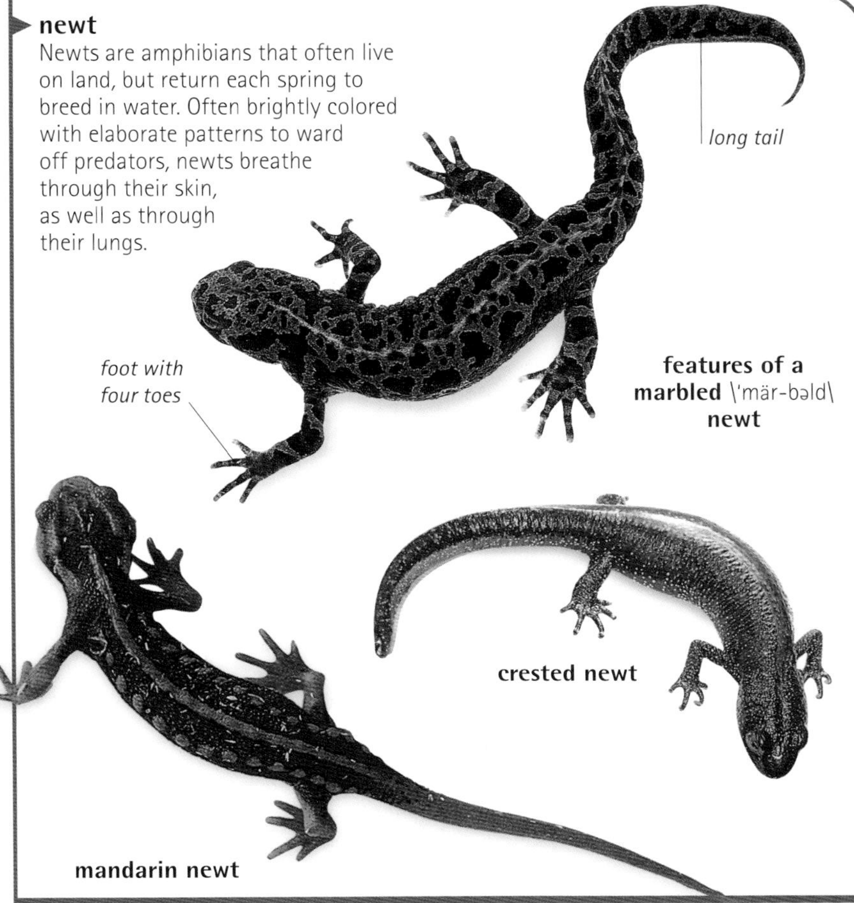

▶ **newt**
Newts are amphibians that often live on land, but return each spring to breed in water. Often brightly colored with elaborate patterns to ward off predators, newts breathe through their skin, as well as through their lungs.

news•wom•an \'nüz-,wu̇-mən\ *n, pl* **news•wom•en** \-,wim-ən\
a woman who gathers or reports information on recent events

New World *n*
the lands in the western hemisphere and especially North and South America

newt \'nüt, 'nyüt\ *n*
▲ a small salamander that often lives on land but lays eggs in water

New Year's Day *n*
January 1 observed as a legal holiday in many countries

[1]**next** \'nekst\ *adj*
coming just before or after 〈Turn to the *next* page.〉

[2]**next** *adv*
1 in the nearest place, time, or order following 〈Do that *next.*〉
2 at the first time after this 〈I'll tell you more when *next* we meet.〉

[3]**next** *n*
a person or thing that immediately follows another person or thing 〈It's one thing after the *next.*〉

next–door \'neks-'dȯr\ *adj*
located in the next building, apartment, or room 〈She is my *next-door* neighbor.〉

next door *adv*
in or to the nearest building, apartment, or room 〈She lives *next door.*〉

[1]**next to** *prep*
1 BESIDE 1 〈I sat *next to* my friend.〉
2 following right after 〈I'd say *next to* chocolate, strawberry ice cream is my favorite.〉

[2]**next to** *adv*
very nearly 〈He ate *next to* nothing.〉

Nez Percé *or* **Nez Perce** \'nez-'pərs\ *n, pl* **Nez Percé** *or* **Nez Perc•és** *or* **Nez Perce** *or* **Nez Perc•es**
1 a member of an American Indian people of Idaho, Washington, and Oregon
2 the language of the Nez Percé people

NH *abbr* New Hampshire

nib \'nib\ *n*
1 a pointed object (as the bill of a bird)
2 the point of a pen

[1]**nib•ble** \'ni-bəl\ *vb* **nib•bled; nib•bling**
to bite or chew gently or bit by bit

[2]**nibble** *n*
a very small amount

nice \'nīs\ *adj* **nic•er; nic•est**
1 PLEASING, PLEASANT 〈*nice* weather〉 〈I had a *nice* time.〉
2 kind, polite, and friendly 〈a *nice* person〉
3 of good quality 〈It's a *nice* place to live.〉
4 done very well 〈*Nice* work!〉
5 well behaved 〈*nice* children〉
nice•ly *adv*
nice•ness *n*

▶ **Word History** The English word *nice* came from an Old French word with the same spelling that meant "foolish." This Old French word came in turn from a Latin word *nescius* that meant "ignorant." At first, English *nice* meant "foolish" or "frivolous." Later it came to mean "finicky" or "fussy." Not until the 1700s did *nice* come to mean "pleasing" or "pleasant."

ni•ce•ty \'nī-sə-tē\ *n, pl* **ni•ce•ties**
1 something dainty, delicate, or of especially good quality
2 a fine detail that is considered part of polite or proper behavior 〈Grandma taught me the *niceties* of setting a table.〉

niche \'nich\ *n*
1 ▼ an open hollow space in a wall (as for a statue)
2 a place, job, or use for which a person or a thing is best fitted 〈She found her *niche* in teaching.〉

niche 1:
a niche for a statue set into a wall

[1]nick \'nik\ *n*
1 a small cut or chip in a surface
2 the last moment 〈We arrived at the dock in the *nick* of time.〉

[2]nick *vb* **nicked; nick•ing**
to make a small cut or chip in

nick•el \'ni-kəl\ *n*
1 a hard silvery white metallic chemical element that can be highly polished, resists weathering, and is used in alloys
2 ▼ a United States coin worth five cents

nickel 2

nick•er \'nik-ər\ *vb* **nick•ered; nick•er•ing**
[1]NEIGH, WHINNY

[1]nick•name \'nik-,nām\ *n*
1 a usually descriptive name used in addition to a person's given name 〈My brother had the *nickname* "Nosy."〉
2 a familiar form of a proper name 〈"Bill" and "Willie" are *nicknames* for "William."〉

▶ **Word History** In the Middle Ages there was an English word *ekename* that meant "an extra name." It was made of a word *eke* that meant "extra part" added to the word *name.* It started with a vowel, so *an* was used with this word instead of *a.* When *an ekename* was said fast, it sounded a bit like *a nekename.* As a result, some people thought the word started with *n* and began to pronounce it *nekename.* They did not know they were taking *n* away from *an,* adding it to *ekename,* and so making a new word. From this new word came the word *nickname* that we use now.

[2]nickname *vb* **nick•named; nick•nam•ing**
to give a usually descriptive name to that is additional to a given name

nic•o•tine \'ni-kə-,tēn\ *n*
a poisonous substance found in small amounts in tobacco

niece \'nēs\ *n*
a daughter of a person's brother or sister

nif•ty \'nif-tē\ *adj* **nif•ti•er; nif•ti•est**
very unusual and attractive 〈a *nifty* outfit〉

nig•gling \'ni-gliŋ\ *adj*
PETTY 1

[1]nigh \'nī\ *adv*
1 near in time or place 〈Autumn is *nigh.*〉
2 ALMOST, NEARLY 〈It was *nigh* impossible to hear them.〉

[2]nigh *adj*
[3]CLOSE 1, NEAR 〈I wandered in the woods *nigh* home.〉

night \'nīt\ *n*
1 the time between dusk and dawn when there is no sunlight
2 the early part of the night : NIGHTFALL 〈We go bowling every Friday *night.*〉
3 the darkness of night 〈His eyes were black as *night.*〉

night•club \'nīt-,kləb\ *n*
a place of entertainment open at night usually serving food and alcoholic beverages and having music for dancing

night crawl•er \'nīt-,krȯ-lər\ *n*
EARTHWORM

night•fall \'nīt-,fȯl\ *n*
the coming of night 〈The travelers arrived at *nightfall.*〉

night•gown \'nīt-,gau̇n\ *n*
a loose garment worn in bed

night•hawk \'nīt-,hȯk\ *n*
a bird that is active at twilight and feeds on insects caught in flight

night•in•gale \'nī-tᵊn-,gāl\ *n*
▶ a reddish brown European bird noted for the sweet song of the male usually heard at night

[1]night•ly \'nīt-lē\ *adj*
happening or done at night or every night 〈a *nightly* newscast〉

[2]nightly *adv*
every night 〈The band performs *nightly.*〉

night•mare \'nīt-,mer\ *n*
1 a frightening dream
2 a horrible experience
night•mar•ish \'nīt-,mer-ish\ *adj*

▶ **Word History** The *-mare* in *nightmare* comes from an Old English word for a kind of evil spirit. Such spirits were believed to bother people who were sleeping.

night•shirt \'nīt-,shərt\ *n*
a long loose shirt worn in bed

night•stick \'nīt-,stik\ *n*
a police officer's club

night•time \'nīt-,tīm\ *n*
NIGHT 1

nil \'nil\ *n*
nothing at all : ZERO

nim•ble \'nim-bəl\ *adj* **nim•bler; nim•blest**
1 quick and light in motion : AGILE 〈a *nimble* dancer〉
2 quick in understanding and learning : CLEVER 〈a *nimble* mind〉
nim•ble•ness *n*
nim•bly \-blē\ *adv*

nim•bus \'nim-bəs\ *n, pl* **nim•bi** \-,bī\ *or* **nim•bus•es**
a rain cloud

[1]nine \'nīn\ *adj*
being one more than eight

[2]nine *n*
1 one more than eight : three times three : 9
2 the ninth in a set or series

[1]nine•teen \nīn-'tēn, nīnt-\ *adj*
being one more than 18

[2]nineteen *n*
one more than 18 : 19

[1]nine•teenth \nīn-'tēnth, nīnt-\ *adj*
coming right after 18th

[2]nineteenth *n*
number 19 in a series

[1]nine•ti•eth \'nīn-tē-əth\ *adj*
coming right after 89th

[2]ninetieth *n*
number 90 in a series

[1]nine•ty \'nīn-tē\ *adj*
being nine times ten

[2]ninety *n*
nine times ten : 90

nightingale

nin•ja \'nin-jə\ *n, pl* **ninja** *also* **nin•jas**
a person trained in ancient Japanese martial arts who works as a spy and assassin especially in the past

[1]ninth \'nīnth\ *adj*
coming right after eighth

[2]ninth *n*
1 number nine in a series
2 one of nine equal parts

[1]nip \'nip\ *vb* **nipped; nip•ping**
1 to bite or pinch lightly 〈The dog *nipped* at my ankles.〉
2 to injure or make numb with cold 〈The cold wind *nipped* our cheeks.〉

3 to remove or cut off by or as if by pinching ⟨*Nip* off the flower bud with your fingers.⟩
4 to move quickly ⟨I *nipped* upstairs to fetch my book.⟩
nip (something) in the bud to stop (something) right away so it does not become a problem

[2]**nip** *n*
a light bite or pinch ⟨The dog gave me a *nip* on the leg.⟩

[3]**nip** *n*
a small amount of liquor

nip and tuck \ˌnip-ən-ˈtək\ *adj or adv*
so close that the lead shifts rapidly from one contestant to another

nip•ple \ˈni-pəl\ *n*
1 the part of the breast or chest from which a baby or young animal sucks milk
2 something (as the mouthpiece of a baby's bottle) like a nipple

nip•py \ˈni-pē\ *adj* **nip•pi•er; nip•pi•est**
CHILLY ⟨a *nippy* day⟩

nit \ˈnit\ *n*
the egg of a louse

ni•trate \ˈnī-ˌtrāt\ *n*
a substance that is made from or similar in composition to nitric acid

ni•tric acid \ˈnī-trik-\ *n*
a strong liquid acid that contains hydrogen, nitrogen, and oxygen and is used in making fertilizers, explosives, and dyes

ni•tro•gen \ˈnī-trə-jən\ *n*
a colorless odorless gaseous chemical element that makes up 78 percent of the atmosphere and forms a part of all living tissues

nitrogen cycle *n*
► a continuous series of natural processes by which nitrogen passes from air to soil to living things and back into the air

nitrogen fix•a•tion \-fik-ˈsā-shən\ *n*
the changing of nitrogen into an available and useful form especially by bacteria (**nitrogen–fixing bacteria**)

ni•tro•glyc•er•in *or* **ni•tro•glyc•er•ine** \ˌnī-trō-ˈgli-sə-rən\ *n*
an oily liquid explosive from which dynamite is made

NJ *abbr* New Jersey

NL *abbr* Newfoundland and Labrador

NM, N. Mex. *abbr* New Mexico

[1]**no** \nō\ *adv*
1 not at all : not any ⟨It was *no* better than I expected it to be.⟩
2 not so — used to express disagreement or refusal ⟨*No*, I'm not hungry.⟩
3 used to express surprise, doubt, or disbelief ⟨*No*—you don't say!⟩

[2]**no** *adj*
1 not any ⟨He has *no* money.⟩
2 hardly any : very little ⟨I finished in *no* time.⟩
3 not a ⟨I'm *no* liar.⟩

[3]**no** *n, pl* **noes** *or* **nos**
1 an act or instance of refusing or denying by the use of the word *no* : DENIAL ⟨I received a firm *no* in reply.⟩
2 a vote or decision against something ⟨There were 100 ayes and only 12 *noes.*⟩
3 *noes or nos pl* persons voting against something ⟨The *noes* raised their hands.⟩

no. *abbr*
1 north
2 number

no•bil•i•ty \nō-ˈbi-lə-tē\ *n, pl* **no•bil•i•ties**
1 the quality or state of having a fine or admirable character
2 high social rank
3 the class or a group of people of high birth or rank

[1]**no•ble** \ˈnō-bəl\ *adj* **no•bler; no•blest**
1 having or showing very fine or admirable qualities ⟨a *noble* deed⟩ ⟨He was a *noble* person of courage and honesty.⟩
2 of very high birth or rank ⟨a *noble* lady⟩
3 grand in appearance ⟨a *noble* cathedral⟩
no•ble•ness *n*
no•bly \-blē\ *adv*

[2]**noble** *n*
a person of high birth or rank

no•ble•man \ˈnō-bəl-mən\ *n, pl* **no•ble•men** \-mən\
a man of high birth or rank

no•ble•wom•an \ˈnō-bəl-ˌwu̇-mən\ *n, pl* **no•ble•wom•en** \-ˌwi-mən\
a woman of high birth or rank

[1]**no•body** \ˈnō-ˌbä-dē, -bə-dē\ *pron*
no person : not anybody ⟨*Nobody* lives in that house.⟩

[2]**nobody** *n, pl* **no•bod•ies**
a person of no importance

noc•tur•nal \näk-ˈtər-nᵊl\ *adj*
1 happening at night ⟨a *nocturnal* journey⟩
2 active at night ⟨*nocturnal* insects⟩

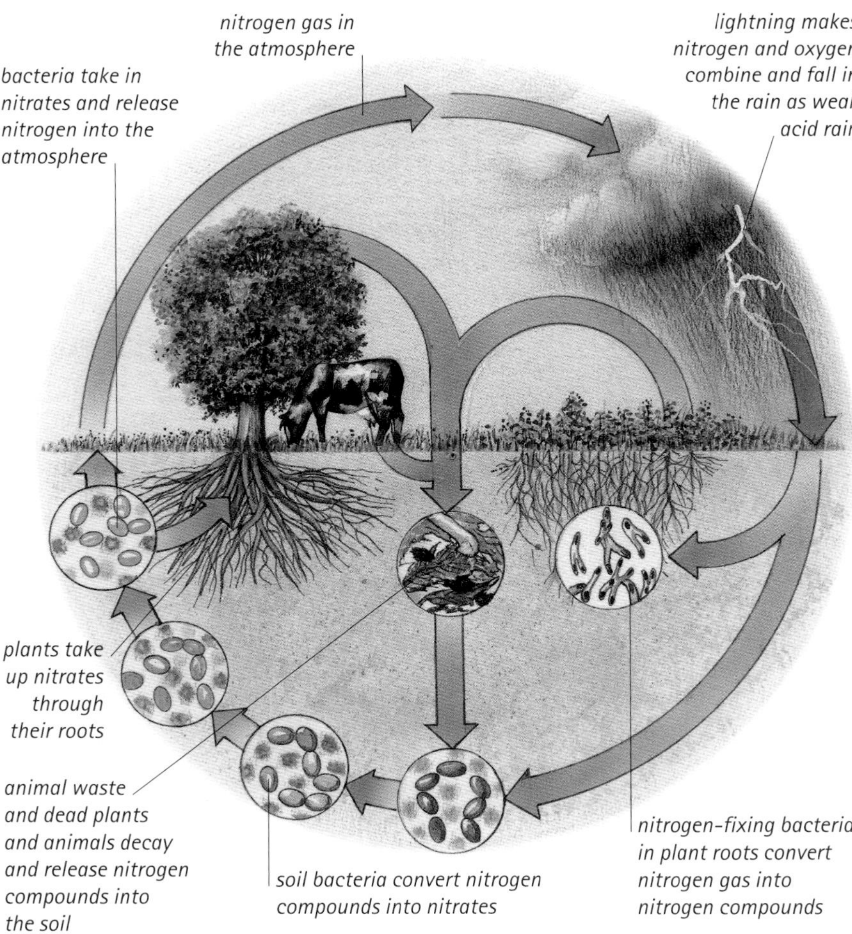

nitrogen cycle: a depiction of the nitrogen cycle, with the blue arrows showing the direction of nitrogen movement

[1]nod \'näd\ *vb* **nod•ded; nod•ding**
1 to bend the head up and down one or more times 〈He *nodded* in agreement.〉
2 to move up and down 〈She *nodded* her head.〉 〈Daisies *nodded* in the breeze.〉
3 to tip the head in a certain direction 〈He *nodded* toward the door.〉
nod off to fall asleep

[2]nod *n*
the action of bending the head up and down

node \'nōd\ *n*
▼ a thickened spot or part (as of a plant stem where a leaf develops)

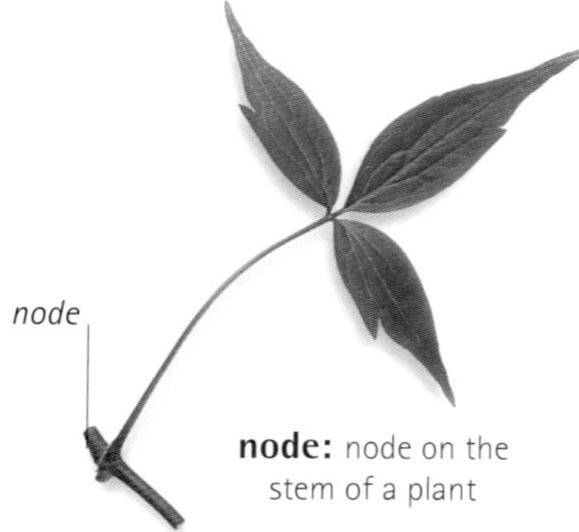

node: node on the stem of a plant

nod•ule \'nä-jül\ *n*
a small roundish lump or mass

no•el \nō-'el\ *n*
1 a Christmas carol
2 *cap* the Christmas season

noes *pl of* NO

nog•gin \'nä-gən\ *n*
a person's head

[1]noise \'nȯiz\ *n*
1 a loud or unpleasant sound
2 [3]SOUND 1 〈the *noise* of the wind〉
noise•less \-ləs\ *adj*
noise•less•ly *adv*

[2]noise *vb* **noised; nois•ing**
to spread by rumor or report 〈The story was *noised* about.〉

noise•mak•er \'nȯiz-,mā-kər\ *n*
a device used to make noise especially at parties

noisy \'nȯi-zē\ *adj* **nois•i•er; nois•i•est**
1 making a lot of noise 〈*noisy* children〉
2 full of noise 〈a *noisy* street〉
nois•i•ly \-zə-lē\ *adv*
nois•i•ness \-zē-nəs\ *n*

[1]no•mad \'nō-,mad\ *n*
1 ▼ a member of a people having no permanent home but moving from place to place usually in search of food or to graze livestock
2 a person who moves often

[2]nomad *adj*
NOMADIC

no•mad•ic \nō-'ma-dik\ *adj*
1 characteristic of or being a nomad or group of nomads 〈*nomadic* herders〉 〈a *nomadic* lifestyle〉
2 roaming about from place to place 〈*nomadic* wolves〉

nom•i•nal \'nä-mə-nᵊl\ *adj*
1 existing as something in name only 〈He was the *nominal* head of the government.〉
2 very small 〈There's just a *nominal* fee.〉
nom•i•nal•ly *adv*

nom•i•nate \'nä-mə-,nāt\ *vb* **nom•i•nat•ed; nom•i•nat•ing**
to choose as a candidate for election, appointment, or honor 〈The parties each *nominate* a candidate for president.〉

nom•i•na•tion \,nä-mə-'nā-shən\ *n*
the act or an instance of choosing as a candidate for election, appointment, or honor 〈The Senate has to approve the *nomination*.〉

nom•i•na•tive \'nä-mə-nə-tiv\ *adj*
being or belonging to the case of a noun or pronoun that is usually the subject of a verb 〈"Mary" in "Mary sees Anne" is in the *nominative* case.〉

nom•i•nee \,nä-mə-'nē\ *n*
someone or something that has been chosen as a candidate for election, appointment, or honor

non- *prefix*
not 〈*non*fiction〉 〈*non*stop〉

non•cha•lance \,nän-shə-'läns\ *n*
the state of being relaxed and free from concern or excitement

[1]nomad 1: a family of Mongolian nomads

non•cha•lant \ˌnän-shə-ˈlänt\ *adj*
showing or having a relaxed manner free from concern or excitement
non•cha•lant•ly \-ˈlänt-lē\ *adv*

non•com•bat•ant \ˌnän-kəm-ˈba-tᵊnt, ˈnän-ˈkäm-bə-tənt\ *n*
1 a member (as a chaplain) of the armed forces whose duties do not include fighting
2 a person who is not in the armed forces : CIVILIAN

non•com•mis•sioned officer \ˌnän-kə-ˈmi-shənd-\ *n*
an officer in the army, air force, or marine corps appointed from among the enlisted persons

non•com•mit•tal \ˌnän-kə-ˈmi-tᵊl\ *adj*
not revealing thoughts or decisions 〈a *noncommittal* answer〉

non•con•form•ist \ˌnän-kən-ˈfȯr-mist\ *n*
a person who does not behave according to generally accepted standards or customs

non•de•script \ˌnän-di-ˈskript\ *adj*
having no special or interesting characteristics : not easily described

[1]**none** \ˈnən\ *pron*
not any : not one 〈*None* of them went.〉 〈*None* of this is necessary.〉

[2]**none** *adv*
1 not at all 〈We arrived *none* too soon.〉
2 in no way 〈It's an old bike but *none* the worse for wear.〉

non•en•ti•ty \nän-ˈen-tə-tē\ *n, pl* **non•en•ti•ties**
someone or something of no importance

[1]**non•es•sen•tial** \ˌnän-i-ˈsen-shəl\ *adj*
not necessary 〈We cut back on *nonessential* purchases.〉

[2]**nonessential** *n*
something that is not necessary

none•the•less \ˌnən-t͟hə-ˈles\ *adv*
NEVERTHELESS

non•fic•tion \ˈnän-ˈfik-shən\ *n*
writing that is about facts or real events

non•flam•ma•ble \ˈnän-ˈfla-mə-bəl\ *adj*
not easily set on fire 〈*nonflammable* fabric〉

non•liv•ing \ˈnän-ˈli-viŋ\ *adj*
not living 〈*nonliving* matter〉

non•par•ti•san \ˈnän-ˈpär-tə-zən\ *adj*
not supporting one party or side over another

non•per•ish•able \ˌnän-ˈper-i-shə-bəl\ *adj*
able to be stored for a long time without spoiling 〈*nonperishable* food items〉

non•plussed \ˈnän-ˈpləst\ *adj*
so surprised or confused as to be at a loss as to what to say, think, or do 〈She was *nonplussed* by his confession.〉

non•poi•son•ous \ˈnän-ˈpȯi-zᵊn-əs\ *adj*
not poisonous 〈*nonpoisonous* snakes〉

non•prof•it \ˈnän-ˈprä-fət\ *adj*
not existing or done to make a profit 〈*nonprofit* organizations〉

non•re•new•able \ˌnän-ri-ˈnü-ə-bəl, -ˈnyü-\ *adj*
not restored or replaced by natural processes in a short period of time 〈Petroleum is a *nonrenewable* resource.〉

[1]**non•res•i•dent** \ˈnän-ˈre-zə-dənt\ *adj*
not living in a certain place 〈a *nonresident* student〉

[2]**nonresident** *n*
a person who does not live in a certain place

non•sec•tar•i•an \ˌnän-sek-ˈter-ē-ən\ *adj*
not limited to a particular religious group

non•sense \ˈnän-ˌsens, -səns\ *n*
foolish or meaningless words, ideas, or actions 〈Don't believe such *nonsense*.〉

non•sen•si•cal \nän-ˈsen-si-kəl\ *adj*
making no sense : ABSURD 〈a *nonsensical* argument〉

non•smok•er \(ˈ)nän-ˈsmō-kər\ *n*
a person who does not smoke tobacco

non•smok•ing \(ˈ)nän-ˈsmō-kiŋ\ *adj*
reserved for the use of nonsmokers 〈I prefer the *nonsmoking* section of the restaurant.〉

non•stan•dard \ˈnän-ˈstan-dərd\ *adj*
different from or lower in quality than what is typical 〈*nonstandard* work〉

non•stop \ˈnän-ˈstäp\ *adv or adj*
without a stop 〈He talked *nonstop*.〉 〈It's a *nonstop* flight.〉

noo•dle \ˈnü-dᵊl\ *n*
▼ a thin often flat strip of fresh or dried dough (as of flour and egg) that is usually boiled

noodle: a dish of noodles

nook \ˈnu̇k\ *n*
1 an inner corner 〈a chimney *nook*〉
2 a sheltered or hidden place 〈a shady *nook*〉

noon \ˈnün\ *n*
the middle of the day : twelve o'clock in the daytime

noon•day \ˈnün-ˌdā\ *n*
NOON, MIDDAY

no one *pron*
[1]NOBODY 〈*No one* was home.〉

noon•time \ˈnün-ˌtīm\ *n*
NOON

noose \ˈnüs\ *n*
a loop that passes through a knot at the end of a line so that it gets smaller when the other end of the line is pulled

nor \nər, ˈnȯr\ *conj*
and not 〈neither young *nor* old〉

norm \ˈnȯrm\ *n*
1 [1]AVERAGE 2
2 a common practice

[1]**nor•mal** \ˈnȯr-məl\ *adj*
1 of the regular or usual kind 〈a *normal* day〉
2 healthy in body or mind 〈a *normal* baby boy〉
synonyms see REGULAR
nor•mal•ly *adv*

> ▶ **Word History** People who work with wood use something called a *square* to make and check right angles. The English word *normal* came from the Latin word for this kind of square, *norma,* which also meant "standard" or "pattern." *Normal* at first meant "forming a right angle." Later *normal* came to mean "by a rule or pattern" or "regular."

[2]**normal** *n*
the usual form, state, level, or amount : AVERAGE 〈Your temperature is *normal*.〉

nor•mal•cy \ˈnȯr-məl-sē\ *n*
NORMALITY

nor•mal•i•ty \nȯr-ˈma-lə-tē\ *n*
the quality or state of being of the regular or usual kind

Nor•man \ˈnȯr-mən\ *n*
1 one of the Scandinavians who conquered Normandy in the tenth century
2 one of the people of mixed Norman and French ancestry who conquered England in 1066

Norse \ˈnȯrs\ *n*
1 *pl* **Norse** the people of Scandinavia
2 *pl* **Norse** the people of Norway
3 any of the languages of the Norse people

[1]**north** \ˈnȯrth\ *adv*
to or toward the north

[2]**north** *adj*
placed toward, facing, or coming from the north 〈the *north* entrance〉 〈a *north* wind〉

[3]north *n*
1 the direction to the left of someone facing east : the compass point opposite to south
2 *cap* regions or countries north of a point that is mentioned or understood

[1]North American *n*
a person born or living in North America

[2]North American *adj*
of or relating to North America or the North Americans ⟨a *North American* tree⟩

north•bound \'nȯrth-ˌbau̇nd\ *adj*
going north ⟨a *northbound* train⟩

[1]north•east \nȯrth-'ēst\ *adv*
to or toward the direction between north and east ⟨We headed *northeast.*⟩

[2]northeast *adj*
placed toward, facing, or coming from the northeast ⟨the *northeast* part of a state⟩

[3]northeast *n*
1 the direction between north and east
2 *cap* regions or countries northeast of a point that is mentioned or understood

north•east•er•ly \nȯrth-'ē-stər-lē\ *adv or adj*
1 from the northeast ⟨*northeasterly* winds⟩
2 toward the northeast ⟨a *northeasterly* direction⟩

north•east•ern \nȯrth-'ē-stərn\ *adj*
1 *often cap* of, relating to, or like that of the Northeast ⟨*northeastern* forests⟩
2 lying toward or coming from the northeast ⟨the *northeastern* corner of the state⟩

north•er•ly \'nȯr-t͟hər-lē\ *adj or adv*
1 from the north ⟨a *northerly* wind⟩
2 toward the north ⟨a *northerly* city⟩ ⟨We sailed *northerly.*⟩

north•ern \'nȯr-t͟hərn\ *adj*
1 *often cap* of, relating to, or like that of the North ⟨*northern* weather⟩
2 lying toward or coming from the north ⟨*northern* Europe⟩

[1]nose 1: a beagle using its nose to sniff a trail

northern lights *n pl*
AURORA BOREALIS

north•land \'nȯrth-ˌland\ *n, often cap*
land in the north : the north of a country or region

north pole *n*
1 *often cap N & P* the most northern point of the earth : the northern end of the earth's axis
2 the end of a magnet that points toward the north when the magnet is free to swing

North Star *n*
the star toward which the northern end of the earth's axis most closely points

north•ward \'nȯrth-wərd\ *adv or adj*
toward the north

[1]north•west \nȯrth-'west\ *adv*
to or toward the direction between north and west ⟨It's *northwest* of here.⟩

[2]northwest *adj*
placed toward, facing, or coming from the northwest ⟨a *northwest* wind⟩

[3]northwest *n*
1 the direction between north and west
2 *cap* regions or countries northwest of a point that is mentioned or understood

north•west•er•ly \nȯrth-'we-stər-lē\ *adv or adj*
1 from the northwest ⟨*northwesterly* breezes⟩
2 toward the northwest ⟨a *northwesterly* direction⟩

north•west•ern \nȯrth-'we-stərn\ *adj*
1 *often cap* of, relating to, or like that of the Northwest ⟨*northwestern* wildflowers⟩
2 lying toward or coming from the northwest ⟨the *northwestern* part of the state⟩

[1]Nor•we•gian \nȯr-'wē-jən\ *adj*
of or relating to Norway, its people, or the Norwegian language

[2]Norwegian *n*
1 a person who is born or lives in Norway
2 the language of the Norwegians

nos *pl of* NO

[1]nose \'nōz\ *n*
1 ◀ the part of the face or head that contains the nostrils
2 the sense or organ of smell ⟨Most dogs have a good *nose.*⟩
3 the front end or part of something ⟨the *nose* of an airplane⟩
4 an ability to discover ⟨She's got a *nose* for news.⟩
nosed \'nōzd\ *adj*

[2]nose *vb* **nosed; nos•ing**
1 to search for or find by smelling ⟨The dog *nosed* around in the garbage.⟩
2 to touch or rub with the nose : NUZZLE ⟨The horse *nosed* my hand.⟩
3 to search for especially in an unwelcome way : PRY ⟨Stop *nosing* around in my business.⟩
4 to move ahead slowly or carefully ⟨The ship *nosed* into its berth.⟩

nose•bleed \'nōz-ˌblēd\ *n*
a bleeding at the nose

nose cone *n*
▼ a protective cone forming the forward end of an airplane, rocket, or missile

nose cone:
nose cone on a model rocket

nose•dive \'nōz-ˌdīv\ *n*
1 a downward plunge (as of an airplane)
2 a sudden sharp drop (as in prices)

nose–dive *vb* **nose–dived; nose–div•ing**
to plunge or drop suddenly or sharply

nos•tal•gia \nä-'stal-jə\ *n*
a longing for something past

nos•tal•gic \nä-'stal-jik\ *adj*
having, showing, or characterized by a longing for something past ⟨*nostalgic* stories⟩

nos•tril \'nä-strəl\ *n*
either of the outer openings of the nose through which people and many animals breathe

nosy *or* **nos•ey** \ˈnō-zē\ *adj* **nos•i•er; nos•i•est**
wanting to know about someone else's business ⟨*nosy* neighbors⟩

not \ˈnät\ *adv*
1 used to make a word or group of words negative ⟨The books are *not* here.⟩
2 used to stand for the negative of a group of words that comes before ⟨It is sometimes hard to see and sometimes *not*.⟩

[1]**no•ta•ble** \ˈnō-tə-bəl\ *adj*
1 deserving special notice : REMARKABLE ⟨a *notable* sight⟩
2 very successful or respected : DISTINGUISHED ⟨a *notable* writer⟩
no•ta•bly \-blē\ *adv*

[2]**notable** *n*
a famous person

no•ta•rize \ˈnō-tə-ˌrīz\ *vb* **no•ta•rized; no•ta•riz•ing**
to sign as a notary public to show that a document is authentic

no•ta•ry public \ˈnō-tə-rē-\ *n, pl* **notaries public** *or* **notary publics**
a public official who witnesses the making of a document (as a will) and signs it to show that it is authentic

no•ta•tion \nō-ˈtā-shən\ *n*
1 the act of noting
2 [2]NOTE 5 ⟨He made *notations* on a paper.⟩
3 ▶ a system of signs, marks, or figures used to give a certain kind of information ⟨musical *notation*⟩ ⟨scientific *notation*⟩

[1]**notch** \ˈnäch\ *n*
1 a cut in the shape of a V in an edge or surface
2 a narrow pass between mountains
3 DEGREE 1, STEP ⟨Turn the radio up a *notch*.⟩

[2]**notch** *vb* **notched; notch•ing**
to make V-shaped cuts in

[1]**note** \ˈnōt\ *vb* **not•ed; not•ing**
1 to notice or observe with care ⟨*Note* the differences between the two paintings.⟩
2 to record in writing ⟨Let me *note* down your address.⟩
3 to make special mention of

[2]**note** *n*
1 a musical sound : TONE
2 a symbol in music that by its shape and position on the staff shows the pitch of a tone and the length of time it is to be held
3 the musical call or song of a bird
4 a quality that shows a feeling ⟨There's a *note* of sadness in your voice.⟩
5 something written down often to aid the memory ⟨I'll make a *note* of the appointment.⟩
6 a printed comment in a book that helps explain part of the text
7 DISTINCTION 3 ⟨artists of *note*⟩
8 a short written message or letter ⟨a thank-you *note*⟩
9 careful notice ⟨Please take *note* of the time.⟩
10 frame of mind : MOOD ⟨She began the day on a happy *note*.⟩
11 a piano key
12 a written promise to pay a debt

note•book \ˈnōt-ˌbu̇k\ *n*
▼ a book of blank pages for writing in

not•ed \ˈnō-təd\ *adj*
well-known and highly regarded ⟨a *noted* scientist⟩

note•wor•thy \ˈnōt-ˌwər-t͟hē\ *adj*
worthy of attention : REMARKABLE ⟨a *noteworthy* event⟩

[1]**noth•ing** \ˈnə-thiŋ\ *pron*
1 not anything : no thing ⟨There's *nothing* in the box.⟩
2 someone or something of no interest, value, or importance ⟨Your opinion is *nothing* to me.⟩

[2]**nothing** *adv*
not at all : in no way ⟨He is *nothing* like his brother.⟩

[3]**nothing** *n*
1 something that does not exist : empty space ⟨The magician made a rabbit appear out of *nothing*.⟩
2 ZERO 1 ⟨The score was ten to *nothing*.⟩
3 someone or something of little or no worth or importance ⟨I'm *nothing* without my friends and family.⟩
noth•ing•ness *n*
for nothing
1 for no reason ⟨We did all that work *for nothing*.⟩
2 for no money

▶ notation 3

To write down the music they create, composers make signs and symbols, called notation, on a staff divided into five parallel lines. The position of each note on, or in the space between, the lines indicate its pitch — how high or low it is to be played. Notation also gives other information, including the length of a pause and the speed at which music is to be played.

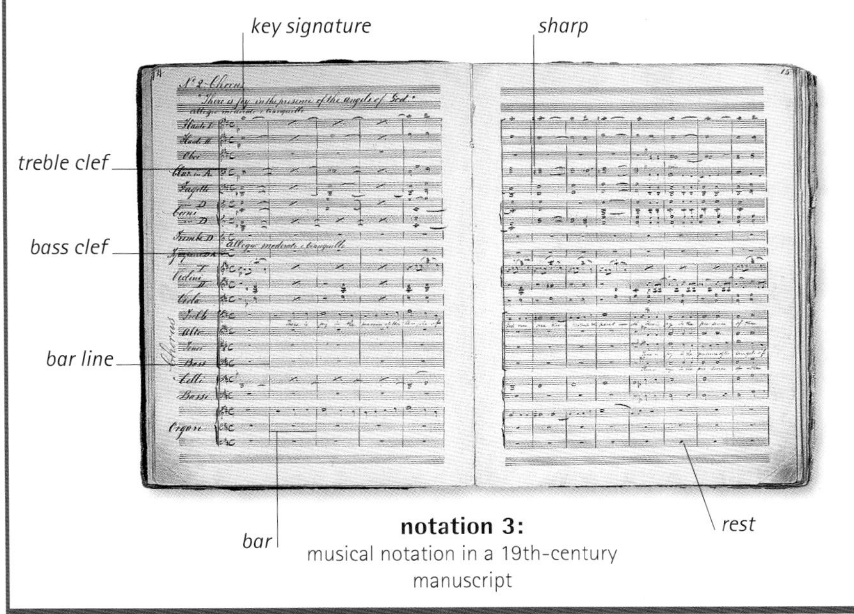

notation 3: musical notation in a 19th-century manuscript

notebook

[1]no•tice \'nō-təs\ *n*
1 WARNING, ANNOUNCEMENT ⟨The schedule may change without *notice*.⟩
2 an indication that an agreement will end at a specified time ⟨I gave my employer *notice*.⟩
3 ATTENTION 1, HEED ⟨Take no *notice* of them.⟩
4 a written or printed announcement ⟨*Notices* were sent to parents about the school trip.⟩
5 a short piece of writing that gives an opinion (as of a book or play) ⟨The new show received good *notices*.⟩

[2]notice *vb* **no•ticed; no•tic•ing**
to become aware of : pay attention to ⟨He didn't *notice* the broken window.⟩

no•tice•able \'nō-tə-sə-bəl\ *adj*
deserving notice : likely to attract attention
no•tice•ably \-blē\ *adv*

> ▶ **Synonyms** NOTICEABLE and OUTSTANDING mean attracting notice or attention. NOTICEABLE is used for something that is likely to be observed. ⟨There's been a *noticeable* improvement in your grades.⟩ OUTSTANDING is used for something that attracts notice because it rises above and is better than others of the same kind. ⟨She's an *outstanding* tennis player.⟩

no•ti•fi•ca•tion \ˌnō-tə-fə-'kā-shən\ *n*
1 the act or an instance of giving notice or information ⟨*Notification* of all winners will occur tomorrow.⟩
2 something written or printed that gives notice ⟨I received *notification* of my acceptance.⟩

no•ti•fy \'nō-tə-ˌfī\ *vb* **no•ti•fied; no•ti•fy•ing**
to give notice to : INFORM ⟨Please *notify* the school of your new address.⟩

no•tion \'nō-shən\ *n*
1 IDEA 2 ⟨I haven't the faintest *notion* what to do.⟩
2 WHIM ⟨We had a sudden *notion* to go swimming.⟩
3 notions *pl* small useful articles (as buttons, needles, and thread)

no•to•ri•e•ty \ˌnō-tə-'rī-ə-tē\ *n*
the state of being widely known especially for some bad characteristic ⟨He gained *notoriety* with the film.⟩

no•to•ri•ous \nō-'tȯr-ē-əs\ *adj*
widely known especially for some bad characteristic ⟨a *notorious* thief⟩
no•to•ri•ous•ly *adv*

[1]not•with•stand•ing \ˌnät-with-'stan-diŋ, -w*i*th-\ *prep*
in spite of ⟨We went *notwithstanding* the weather.⟩

[2]notwithstanding *adv*
NEVERTHELESS

nou•gat \'nü-gət\ *n*
a candy consisting of a sugar paste with nuts or fruit pieces

nought *variant of* NAUGHT

noun \'naůn\ *n*
a word or phrase that is the name of something (as a person, place, or thing) and that is used in a sentence especially as subject or object of a verb or as object of a preposition

nour•ish \'nər-ish\ *vb* **nour•ished; nour•ish•ing**
to cause to grow or live in a healthy state especially by providing with enough good food or nutrients
nour•ish•ing *adj*

nour•ish•ment \'nər-ish-mənt\ *n*
something (as food) that causes growth or health

Nov. *abbr* November

[1]nov•el \'nä-vəl\ *adj*
new and different from what is already known ⟨a *novel* idea⟩

[2]novel *n*
▼ a long story usually about imaginary characters and events

nov•el•ist \'nä-və-list\ *n*
a writer of novels

nov•el•ty \'nä-vəl-tē\ *n, pl* **nov•el•ties**
1 something new or unusual ⟨Grandma remembers when television was a *novelty*.⟩
2 the quality or state of being new or unusual ⟨The toy's *novelty* soon wore off.⟩
3 a small unusual ornament or toy

No•vem•ber \nō-'vem-bər\ *n*
the eleventh month of the year

> ▶ **Word History** The earliest Roman calendar had only ten months and began with the month of March. The ninth month was called in Latin *November*, a word which combines the Latin words for "nine" (*novem*), "month" (*mens*), and a final word-forming element *-ri-*. The name was kept—and eventually borrowed by English—after November became the eleventh of twelve Roman months.

nov•ice \'nä-vəs\ *n*
1 a person who has no previous experience with something : BEGINNER ⟨a *novice* at skiing⟩
2 a new member of a religious community who is preparing to take the vows of religion

[2]novel: a stack of novels

[1]now \ˈnau̇\ *adv*
1 at this time ⟨I am busy *now.*⟩
2 immediately before the present time ⟨They left just *now.*⟩
3 in the time immediately to follow ⟨Can you leave *now*?⟩
4 used to express command or introduce an important point ⟨*Now,* you listen to me.⟩
5 SOMETIMES ⟨*now* one and *now* another⟩
6 in the present circumstances ⟨*Now* what should we do?⟩
7 at the time referred to ⟨*Now* the trouble began.⟩
now and then from time to time : OCCASIONALLY

[2]now *conj*
in view of the fact that : SINCE ⟨*Now* that we're all here, let's begin.⟩

[3]now *n*
the present time ⟨I've been busy up till *now.*⟩

now•a•days \ˈnau̇-ə-ˌdāz\ *adv*
at the present time ⟨No one goes there much *nowadays.*⟩

[1]no•where \ˈnō-ˌhwer, -ˌwer\ *adv*
1 not in or at any place ⟨The book is *nowhere* to be found.⟩
2 to no place ⟨We've gone *nowhere* all week.⟩
3 not at all ⟨That's *nowhere* near enough.⟩

[2]nowhere *n*
a place that does not exist ⟨The sound seems to be coming from *nowhere.*⟩

nox•ious \ˈnäk-shəs\ *adj*
causing harm ⟨*noxious* fumes⟩

noz•zle \ˈnä-zəl\ *n*
► a short tube often used on the end of a hose or pipe to direct or speed up a flow of fluid

nozzle: nozzle on a garden hose

NS *abbr* Nova Scotia

NT *abbr* Northwest Territories

-n't \nt, ᵊnt, ənt\ *adv suffix*
not ⟨is*n't*⟩

NU *abbr* Nunavut

nub \ˈnəb\ *n*
1 a small rounded part that sticks out from something ⟨These shoes have *nubs* on the bottom to prevent slipping.⟩
2 a small piece or end that remains after something has been removed or worn away ⟨a *nub* of pencil⟩

nub•by \ˈnə-bē\ *adj* **nub•bi•er**; **nub•bi•est**
having small knobs or lumps ⟨*nubby* tires⟩

nu•cle•ar \ˈnü-klē-ər, ˈnyü-\ *adj*
1 of, relating to, or being a nucleus (as of a cell)
2 of or relating to the nucleus of the atom ⟨Fission is a *nuclear* reaction.⟩
3 produced by a nuclear reaction ⟨*nuclear* energy⟩
4 of, relating to, or being a weapon whose destructive power comes from an uncontrolled nuclear reaction
5 relating to or powered by nuclear energy ⟨a *nuclear* submarine⟩

nu•cle•us \ˈnü-klē-əs, ˈnyü-\ *n, pl* **nu•clei** \-klē-ˌī\
1 a usually round part of most cells that is enclosed in a double membrane, controls the activities of the cell, and contains the chromosomes
2 the central part of an atom that comprises nearly all of the atomic mass and that consists of protons and neutrons
3 a central point, group, or mass ⟨Those players are the *nucleus* of the team.⟩

nude \ˈnüd, ˈnyüd\ *adj* **nud•er**; **nud•est**
not wearing clothes : NAKED

[1]nudge \ˈnəj\ *vb* **nudged**; **nudg•ing**
1 to touch or push gently ⟨The teacher *nudged* her students back to class.⟩
2 to attract the attention of by touching or pushing gently (as with the elbow) ⟨He *nudged* me and pointed to the huge cake on the table.⟩

[2]nudge *n*
a slight push

nu•di•ty \ˈnü-də-tē, ˈnyü-\ *n*
the state of having no clothes on

nug•get \ˈnə-gət\ *n*
1 ► a solid lump especially of precious metal ⟨a *nugget* of gold⟩
2 a small usually rounded piece of food ⟨chicken *nuggets*⟩

nui•sance \ˈnü-sᵊns, ˈnyü-\ *n*
an annoying or troublesome person, thing, or situation

null \ˈnəl\ *adj*
having no legal force : not binding ⟨The law was declared *null* and void.⟩

[1]numb \ˈnəm\ *adj*
1 unable to feel anything especially because of cold ⟨My toes are *numb.*⟩
2 unable to think, feel, or react normally (as because of great fear, surprise, or sadness) ⟨She was *numb* after hearing the startling news.⟩
numb•ly *adv*
numb•ness *n*

[2]numb *vb* **numbed**; **numb•ing**
to make or become unable to feel pain or touch ⟨The cold *numbed* my face.⟩

[1]num•ber \ˈnəm-bər\ *n*
1 the total of persons, things, or units taken together : AMOUNT ⟨What is the *number* of people in the room?⟩
2 a total that is not specified ⟨I got a *number* of presents on my birthday.⟩
3 a unit belonging to a mathematical system and subject to its rules ⟨Tell me a *number* divisible by 2.⟩
4 a word, symbol, or letter used to represent a mathematical number : NUMERAL ⟨the *number* 5⟩
5 a certain numeral for telling one person or thing from another or from others ⟨a house *number*⟩
6 a quality of a word form that shows whether the word is singular or plural ⟨A verb agrees in *number* with its subject.⟩
7 one of a series ⟨a *number* two pencil⟩
8 a song or dance usually that is part of a larger performance ⟨The band played a catchy *number.*⟩

[2]number *vb* **num•bered**; **num•ber•ing**
1 [1]COUNT 1 ⟨The grains of sand cannot be *numbered.*⟩
2 INCLUDE ⟨I was *numbered* among the guests.⟩
3 to limit to a certain number ⟨Vacation days are *numbered* now.⟩
4 to give a number to ⟨*Number* the pages of your journal.⟩
5 to add up to or have a total of ⟨Our group *numbered* ten in all.⟩

nugget 1: a nugget of platinum

num•ber•less \ˈnəm-bər-ləs\ *adj*
too many to count ⟨the *numberless* stars in the sky⟩

number line *n*
a line in which points are matched to numbers

nu•mer•al \ˈnü-mə-rəl, ˈnyü-\ *n*
a symbol or group of symbols representing a number

nu•mer•a•tor \ˈnü-mə-ˌrā-tər, ˈnyü-\ *n*
the part of a fraction that is above the line ⟨3 is the *numerator* of the fraction 3/5.⟩

nu•mer•i•cal \nü-ˈmer-i-kəl, nyü-\ *adj*
of or relating to numbers : stated in numbers ⟨*numerical* order⟩
nu•mer•i•cal•ly *adv*

nu•mer•ous \ˈnü-mə-rəs, ˈnyü-\ *adj*
consisting of a large number : MANY ⟨She has *numerous* friends.⟩

nun \ˈnən\ *n*
a woman belonging to a religious community and living according to vows

nun•nery \ˈnə-nə-rē\ *n, pl* **nun•ner•ies**
CONVENT

nup•tial \ˈnəp-shəl\ *adj*
of or relating to marriage or a wedding ⟨*nuptial* vows⟩

nup•tials \ˈnəp-shəlz\ *n pl*
WEDDING

[1]**nurse** \ˈnərs\ *n*
1 a person skilled or trained in caring for sick or injured people
2 a woman employed for the care of a young child

► **Word History** The English word *nurse* can be traced back to a Latin word *nutricius* that meant "nourishing" or "feeding." In the past some mothers did not feed their babies at their own breasts but hired someone else to do so. The English word *nurse* was first used for such a woman. Later it came to be used for any woman hired to take care of a young child. The word *nurse* is also used now for a person who takes care of sick or injured people.

[2]**nurse** *vb* **nursed**; **nurs•ing**
1 to feed at the breast : SUCKLE
2 to take care of (as a young child or a sick person) ⟨She *nursed* me back to health.⟩
3 to treat with special care or attention ⟨*Nurse* that ankle until it's all healed.⟩

nurse•maid \ˈnərs-ˌmād\ *n*
[1]NURSE 2

nurs•ery \ˈnər-sə-rē, ˈnərs-rē\ *n, pl* **nurs•er•ies**
1 the room where a baby sleeps
2 a place where small children are temporarily cared for in their parent's absence
3 a place where plants (as trees or shrubs) are grown and usually sold

nursery rhyme *n*
a short rhyme for children that often tells a story

nursery school *n*
[2]PRESCHOOL

[1]**nur•ture** \ˈnər-chər\ *n*
1 the way a person or animal was raised : UPBRINGING
2 something (as food) that is essential to healthy growth and development

[2]**nurture** *vb* **nur•tured**; **nur•tur•ing**
1 to provide with things (as food and protection) essential to healthy growth and development ⟨He was *nurtured* by loving parents.⟩
2 to further the development of ⟨The teacher *nurtured* the students' creativity.⟩

nut \ˈnət\ *n*
1 ▼ a dry fruit or seed with a firm inner kernel and a hard shell
2 the often edible kernel of a nut
3 a small piece of metal with a hole through it that can be screwed onto a bolt for tightening or holding something
4 a foolish or crazy person
5 a person who is very interested in or enthusiastic about something ⟨a sports *nut*⟩
nut•like \-ˌlīk\ *adj*

nut•crack•er \ˈnət-ˌkra-kər\ *n*
a device used for cracking the shells of nuts

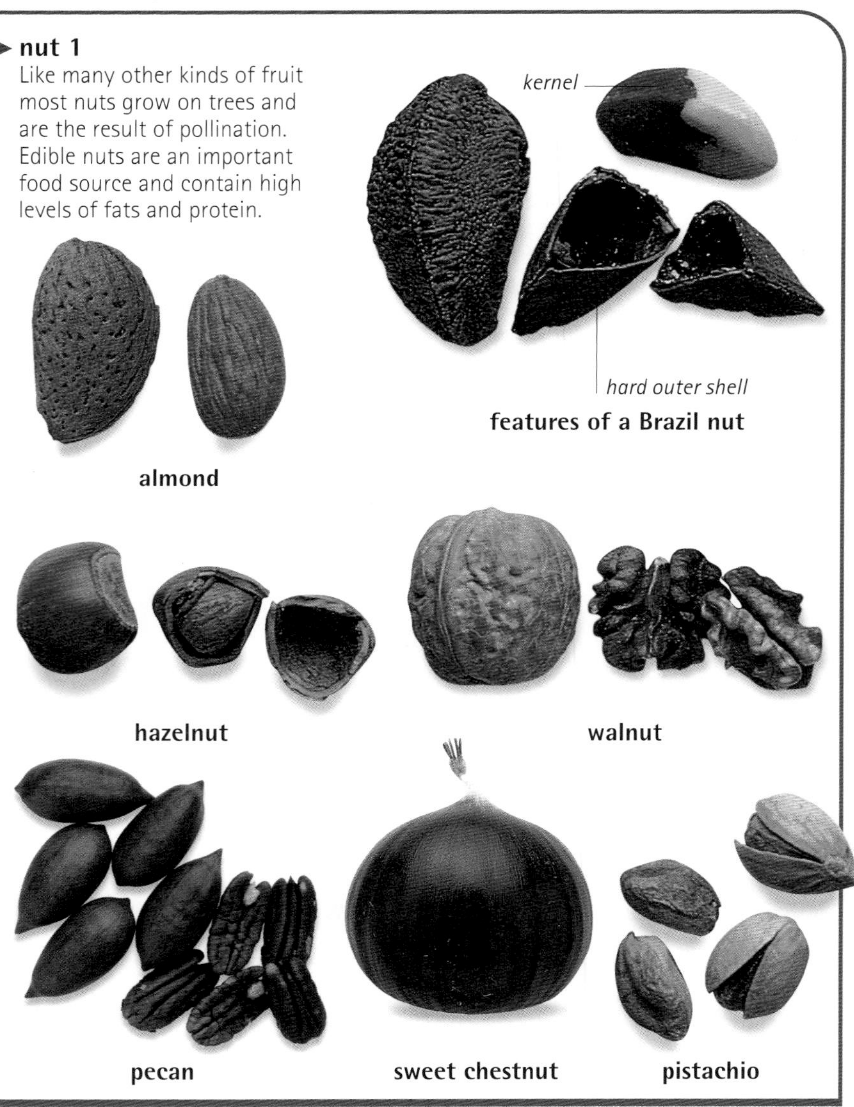

► **nut 1**
Like many other kinds of fruit most nuts grow on trees and are the result of pollination. Edible nuts are an important food source and contain high levels of fats and protein.

nuthatch: a red-breasted nuthatch

nut•hatch \'nət-,hach\ *n*
▲ a small bird that creeps on tree trunks and branches and eats insects

nut•meg \'nət-,meg\ *n*
▶ a spice made from the ground seeds of a small tropical evergreen tree

nu•tri•ent \'nü-trē-ənt, 'nyü-\ *n*
a substance that is needed for healthy growth, development, and functioning 〈Fruits and vegetables have important *nutrients.*〉 〈Plants get *nutrients* from the soil.〉

nu•tri•ment \'nü-trə-mənt, 'nyü-\ *n*
something that nourishes

nu•tri•tion \nü-'tri-shən, nyü-\ *n*
the act or process of nourishing or being nourished : the processes by which a living thing takes in and uses nutrients

nu•tri•tion•al \nü-'tri-shə-nᵊl, nyü-\ *adj*
relating to, providing, or involved in the proper intake of nutrients 〈Avoid foods with little *nutritional* value.〉

nu•tri•tious \nü-'tri-shəs, nyü-\ *adj*
providing nutrients : NOURISHING 〈*nutritious* snacks〉

nu•tri•tive \'nü-trə-tiv, 'nyü-\ *adj*
1 NUTRITIONAL
2 NUTRITIOUS

nuts \'nəts\ *adj*
1 enthusiastic about or interested in something 〈She was *nuts* about horror movies.〉
2 CRAZY 1 〈All this noise is going to make me *nuts.*〉

nut•shell \'nət-,shel\ *n*
the shell of a nut
in a nutshell very briefly 〈And that, *in a nutshell,* is my explanation.〉

nutmeg

nut•ty \'nə-tē\ *adj* **nut•ti•er**; **nut•ti•est**
1 not showing good sense 〈a *nutty* idea〉
2 having a flavor like that of nuts

nuz•zle \'nə-zəl\ *vb* **nuz•zled**; **nuz•zling**
to push or rub with the nose 〈The dog *nuzzled* my leg.〉

NV *abbr* Nevada

NW *abbr* northwest

NY *abbr* New York

ny•lon \'nī-,län\ *n*
▼ a strong man-made material used in the making of fabrics and plastics

nylon: a jacket made of nylon

nymph \'nimf\ *n*
1 one of many goddesses in old legends represented as beautiful young women living in the mountains, forests, and waters
2 an immature insect that differs from the adult chiefly in being of smaller size and having undeveloped wings

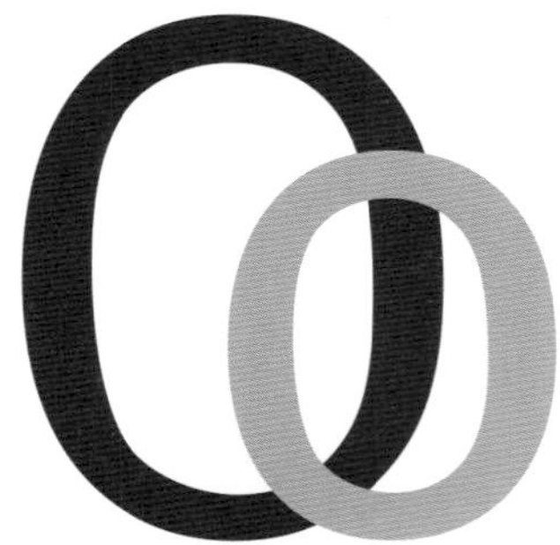

Sounds of O: The letter **O** makes a number of sounds. The sound heard in *stop* and *hot* is called the short **O**, and it is indicated by the symbol ä. The long **O** is heard in *old* and *home*, and it is indicated by the symbol ō. Letter **O** also makes the sound heard in words like *long*, indicated by the symbol ȯ, and the sound heard in words like *corn*, indicated by the symbol ȯr. **O** can also make the schwa sound, indicated by the symbol ə, either by itself or combined with **U**, in words such as *month* and *generous*. When combined with other letters, **O** makes a variety of other sounds, such as the long **O** sound heard in *road* and *toe*, the long **U** sound heard in *food*, *canoe*, and *group*, and the ȯr sound heard in *board*. Combined with **I** or **Y**, **O** makes the sound heard in *coin* and *boy*, which is indicated by the symbol ȯi. Combined with **U**, **O** can also make the sound heard in *about*, which is indicated by the symbol aů. Two **O**s together can also make the sound heard in *foot*, which is indicated by the symbol ů.

o \'ō\ *n, pl* **o's** *or* **os** \'ōz\ *often cap*
1 the 15th letter of the English alphabet
2 ZERO 1

O *variant of* OH

O. *abbr* Ohio

oaf \'ōf\ *n*
a stupid or awkward person
oaf•ish \'ō-fish\ *adj*

oak \'ōk\ *n*
▼ a tree or shrub that produces acorns and has tough wood much used for furniture and flooring

oak: leaves and acorns from an oak

oars for a boat

oak•en \'ō-kən\ *adj*
made of oak ⟨an *oaken* door⟩

oar \'ȯr\ *n*
▲ a long pole that is flat and wide at one end and that is used for rowing or steering a boat

oar•lock \'ȯr-,läk\ *n*
a usually U-shaped device for holding an oar in place

oars•man \'ȯrz-mən\ *n, pl* **oars•men** \-mən\
a person who rows a boat

oa•sis \ō-'ā-səs\ *n, pl* **oa•ses** \-,sēz\
▼ a fertile or green spot in a desert

oat \'ōt\ *n*
1 a cereal grass grown for its loose clusters of seeds that are used for human food and animal feed
2 oats *pl* a crop or the seeds of the oat

oath \'ōth\ *n, pl* **oaths** \'ōthz, 'ōths\
1 a solemn promise to tell the truth or do a specific thing
2 an obscene or impolite word used to express anger or frustration

oat•meal \'ōt-,mēl\ *n*
1 oat seeds that have had the outer covering removed and are ground into meal or flattened into flakes
2 a hot cereal made from meal or flakes of oats

obe•di•ence \ō-'bē-dē-əns\ *n*
the act of obeying : willingness to obey

oasis: an oasis in a desert in southern Peru

obe•di•ent \ō-ˈbē-dē-ənt\ *adj*
willing to do as told by someone in authority : willing to obey
obe•di•ent•ly *adv*

obe•lisk \ˈä-bə-ˌlisk, ˈō-\ *n*
▶ a four-sided pillar that becomes narrower toward the top and ends in a pyramid

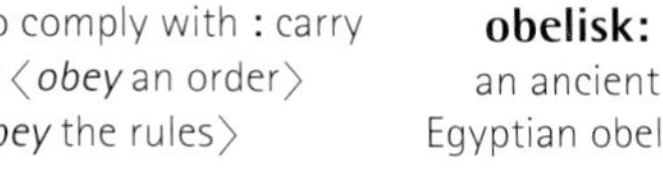

obelisk: an ancient Egyptian obelisk

obese \ō-ˈbēs\ *adj*
very fat
obe•si•ty \ō-ˈbē-sə-tē\ *n*

obey \ō-ˈbā\ *vb* **obeyed**; **obey•ing**
1 to follow the commands or guidance of ⟨Dogs are trained to *obey* their masters.⟩
2 to comply with : carry out ⟨*obey* an order⟩ ⟨*obey* the rules⟩

▶ **Synonyms** OBEY and MIND mean to do what a person says. OBEY is used when someone quickly yields to the authority of another or follows a rule or law. ⟨*Obey* your parents.⟩ ⟨*Obey* all traffic laws.⟩ MIND is used like *obey* especially when speaking to children but it often means paying attention to the wishes or commands of another. ⟨*Mind* what I said about talking.⟩

obit•u•ary \ō-ˈbi-chə-ˌwer-ē\ *n*, *pl* **obit•u•ar•ies**
a notice of a person's death (as in a newspaper)

obj. *abbr*
1 object
2 objective

[1]**ob•ject** \ˈäb-jikt\ *n*
1 something that may be seen or felt ⟨Tables and chairs are *objects*.⟩
2 PURPOSE, AIM ⟨The *object* is to raise money.⟩
3 something that arouses feelings in an observer ⟨That diamond is the *object* of their envy.⟩
4 a noun or a term behaving like a noun that receives the action of a verb or completes the meaning of a preposition

[2]**ob•ject** \əb-ˈjekt\ *vb* **ob•ject•ed**; **ob•ject•ing**
1 to offer or mention as a reason for a feeling of disapproval ⟨She *objected* that the price was too high.⟩
2 to oppose something firmly and usually with words ⟨Residents *object* to the plan.⟩

▶ **Synonyms** OBJECT and PROTEST mean to oppose something by arguing against it. OBJECT is used of a person's great dislike or hatred. ⟨I *object* to being called a liar.⟩ PROTEST is used for the act of presenting objections in speech, writing, or in an organized, public demonstration. ⟨There were several groups *protesting* the building of the airport.⟩

ob•jec•tion \əb-ˈjek-shən\ *n*
1 an act of showing disapproval or great dislike
2 a reason for or a feeling of disapproval

ob•jec•tion•able \əb-ˈjek-shə-nə-bəl\ *adj*
arousing disapproval or great dislike : OFFENSIVE

[1]**ob•jec•tive** \əb-ˈjek-tiv\ *adj*
1 dealing with facts without allowing personal feelings to confuse them ⟨an *objective* report⟩
2 being or belonging to the case of a noun or pronoun that is an object of a transitive verb or a preposition
3 being outside of the mind and independent of it
ob•jec•tive•ly *adv*

[2]**objective** *n*
PURPOSE, GOAL

ob•li•gate \ˈä-blə-ˌgāt\ *vb* **ob•li•gat•ed**; **ob•li•gat•ing**
to make (someone) do something by law or because it is right ⟨The contract *obligates* you to pay monthly.⟩

ob•li•ga•tion \ˌä-blə-ˈgā-shən\ *n*
1 something a person must do because of the demands of a promise or contract ⟨Make sure you know your rights and *obligations* before you sign.⟩
2 something a person feels he or she must do : DUTY ⟨I can't go because of other *obligations*.⟩
3 a feeling of being indebted for an act of kindness

oblige \ə-ˈblīj\ *vb* **obliged**; **oblig•ing**
1 [2]FORCE 1, COMPEL ⟨The soldiers were *obliged* to retreat.⟩
2 to do a favor for or do something as a favor ⟨If you need help, I'll be glad to *oblige*.⟩
3 to earn the gratitude of ⟨You will *oblige* me by coming early.⟩

oblig•ing \ə-ˈblī-jiŋ\ *adj*
willing to do favors
oblig•ing•ly *adv*

oblique \ō-ˈblēk, ə-\ *adj*
having a slanting position or direction : neither perpendicular nor parallel
oblique•ly *adv*

oblit•er•ate \ə-ˈbli-tə-ˌrāt\ *vb* **oblit•er•at•ed**; **oblit•er•at•ing**
to remove, destroy, or hide completely

obliv•i•on \ə-ˈbli-vē-ən\ *n*
1 the state of forgetting or having forgotten or of being unaware or unconscious
2 the state of being forgotten

obliv•i•ous \ə-ˈbli-vē-əs\ *adj*
not being conscious or aware ⟨The boys were *oblivious* to the danger.⟩
obliv•i•ous•ly *adv*

[1]**ob•long** \ˈä-ˌblȯŋ\ *adj*
different from a square, circle, or sphere by being longer in one direction than the other ⟨an *oblong* tablecloth⟩ ⟨an *oblong* melon⟩

[2]**oblong** *n*
a figure or object that is larger in one direction than the other

ob•nox•ious \äb-ˈnäk-shəs, əb-\ *adj*
very disagreeable : HATEFUL
ob•nox•ious•ly *adv*

oboe \ˈō-bō\ *n*
a woodwind instrument with two reeds that is pitched higher than the bassoon and has a distinctive bright sound

▶ **Word History** The oboe, the English horn, and the bassoon belong to the same group of woodwind instruments. Of the three the oboe has the highest pitch. The English word *oboe* comes from the Italian name of the instrument, *oboe*, which in turn comes from the oboe's French name, *hautbois*. The word *hautbois* is a compound made up of *haut*, "high, loud," and *bois*, "wood."

ob•scene \äb-ˈsēn, əb-\ *adj*
very shocking to a person's sense of what is moral or decent

ob•scen•i•ty \äb-ˈse-nə-tē, əb-\ *n*, *pl* **ob•scen•i•ties**
1 the quality or state of being shocking to a person's sense of what is moral or decent
2 something that is shocking to a person's sense of what is moral or decent

[1]**ob•scure** \äb-ˈskyu̇r, əb-\ *adj*
1 not easy to see : FAINT ⟨an *obscure* light⟩
2 hidden from view ⟨an *obscure* village⟩
3 not easily understood or clearly expressed ⟨I struggled with an *obscure* chapter in the book.⟩
4 not outstanding or famous ⟨It was written by an *obscure* poet.⟩

a b c d e f g h i j k l m n o p q r s t u v w x y z

observatory

Observatories are usually built in remote places, far from bright city lights, where astronomers can observe the movements and other features of stars and planets in the sky. Inside an observatory, huge telescopes view the sky through an opening in the roof and computers collect data.

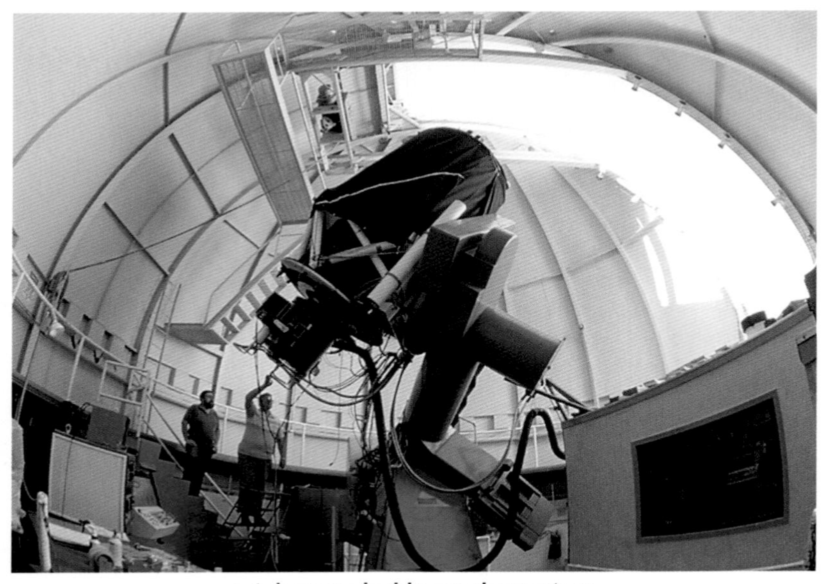

a telescope inside an observatory

²obscure *vb* **ob•scured**; **ob•scur•ing**
to make difficult to see or understand

ob•scu•ri•ty \äb-ˈskyůr-ə-tē, əb-\ *n*, *pl* **ob•scu•ri•ties**
1 the state of being difficult to see or understand
2 the state of being unknown or forgotten ⟨He lived in *obscurity*.⟩
3 something that is difficult to understand ⟨The poems are filled with *obscurities*.⟩

ob•serv•able \əb-ˈzər-və-bəl\ *adj*
NOTICEABLE ⟨Her cat's shape was *observable* under the blanket.⟩
ob•serv•ably \-blē\ *adv*

ob•ser•vance \əb-ˈzər-vəns\ *n*
1 an established practice or ceremony ⟨religious *observances*⟩
2 an act of following a custom, rule, or law ⟨Careful *observance* of the speed limit is a wise idea.⟩

ob•ser•vant \əb-ˈzər-vənt\ *adj*
quick to take notice : WATCHFUL, ALERT
ob•ser•vant•ly *adv*

ob•ser•va•tion \ˌäb-sər-ˈvā-shən, -zər-\ *n*
1 an act or the power of seeing or taking notice of something
2 the gathering of information by noting facts or occurrences ⟨weather *observations*⟩
3 an opinion formed or expressed after watching or noticing ⟨It's not a criticism, just an *observation*.⟩
4 the fact of being watched and studied ⟨The patient was in the hospital for *observation*.⟩

ob•ser•va•to•ry \əb-ˈzər-və-ˌtȯr-ē\ *n*, *pl* **ob•ser•va•to•ries**
▲ a place that has instruments for making observations (as of the stars)

ob•serve \əb-ˈzərv\ *vb* **ob•served**; **ob•serv•ing**
1 to watch carefully ⟨They *observed* her behavior.⟩
2 to act in agreement with : OBEY ⟨Remember to *observe* the law.⟩
3 CELEBRATE 1 ⟨Next Friday we will *observe* a religious holiday.⟩
4 ²REMARK, SAY ⟨The stranger *observed* that it was a fine day.⟩
ob•serv•er *n*

ob•sess \əb-ˈses\ *vb* **ob•sessed**; **ob•sess•ing**
to occupy the thoughts of completely or abnormally ⟨A new scheme *obsesses* him.⟩

ob•ses•sion \əb-ˈse-shən\ *n*
a persistent abnormally strong interest in or concern about someone or something

obsidian

ob•sid•i•an \əb-ˈsi-dē-ən\ *n*
▲ a smooth dark rock formed by the cooling of lava

ob•so•lete \ˌäb-sə-ˈlēt\ *adj*
no longer in use : OUT-OF-DATE ⟨The machinery is now *obsolete*.⟩

ob•sta•cle \ˈäb-stə-kəl\ *n*
something that stands in the way or opposes : HINDRANCE

ob•sti•nate \ˈäb-stə-nət\ *adj*
1 sticking stubbornly to an opinion or purpose
2 difficult to deal with or get rid of ⟨an *obstinate* fever⟩
ob•sti•nate•ly *adv*

ob•struct \əb-ˈstrəkt\ *vb* **ob•struct•ed**; **ob•struct•ing**
1 to block or make passage through difficult ⟨A fallen tree is *obstructing* the road.⟩
2 to be or come in the way of : HINDER ⟨She was uncooperative and *obstructed* the investigation.⟩
3 to make (something) difficult to see

ob•struc•tion \əb-ˈstrək-shən\ *n*
1 an act of blocking or hindering : the state of having something that blocks or hinders
2 something that gets in the way : OBSTACLE

ob•tain \əb-ˈtān\ *vb* **ob•tained**; **ob•tain•ing**
to gain or get hold of with effort ⟨She was able to *obtain* a ticket to the show.⟩ ⟨We *obtained* permission to enter.⟩

ob•tain•able \əb-ˈtā-nə-bəl\ *adj*
possible to get ⟨Tickets were not *obtainable*.⟩

ob•tuse \äb-ˈtüs, -ˈtyüs\ *adj*
1 ▼ measuring more than a right angle
2 not able to understand something obvious

obtuse 1: an obtuse angle

ob•vi•ous \ˈäb-vē-əs\ *adj*
easily found, seen, or understood
ob•vi•ous•ly *adv*
ob•vi•ous•ness *n*

[1]oc•ca•sion \ə-ˈkā-zhən\ *n*
1 a special event ⟨The banquet was an elegant *occasion.*⟩
2 the time of an event ⟨This has happened on more than one *occasion.*⟩
3 a suitable opportunity **:** a good chance ⟨Take the first *occasion* to write.⟩

[2]occasion *vb* **oc•ca•sioned; oc•ca•sion•ing**
to bring about

oc•ca•sion•al \ə-ˈkā-zhə-nᵊl\ *adj*
happening or met with now and then ⟨They went to an *occasional* movie.⟩
oc•ca•sion•al•ly *adv*

oc•cu•pan•cy \ˈä-kyə-pən-sē\ *n, pl* **oc•cu•pan•cies**
the act of using, living in, or taking possession of a place

oc•cu•pant \ˈä-kyə-pənt\ *n*
a person who uses, lives in, or possesses a place

oc•cu•pa•tion \ˌä-kyə-ˈpā-shən\ *n*
1 a person's business or profession ⟨His uncle was a tailor by *occupation.*⟩
2 the act of using or taking possession and control of a place ⟨Human *occupation* of this area began thousands of years ago.⟩

oc•cu•pa•tion•al \ˌä-kyə-ˈpā-shə-nᵊl\ *adj*
relating to a person's business or profession ⟨an *occupational* risk⟩
oc•cu•pa•tion•al•ly *adv*

oc•cu•py \ˈä-kyə-ˌpī\ *vb* **oc•cu•pied; oc•cu•py•ing**
1 to fill up (an extent of time or space) ⟨Sports *occupy* our spare time.⟩
2 to take up the attention or energies of ⟨Reading *occupied* me most of the summer.⟩
3 to live in as an owner or tenant ⟨Her sisters *occupied* the house for three years.⟩
4 to take or hold possession of ⟨Enemy troops *occupied* the town.⟩
5 to perform the functions of ⟨She *occupies* a position of authority.⟩

oc•cur \ə-ˈkər\ *vb* **oc•curred; oc•cur•ring**
1 to come by or as if by chance **:** HAPPEN ⟨Success doesn't just *occur,* it is earned.⟩
2 to come into the mind ⟨It never *occurred* to me to ask.⟩
3 to be found or met with **:** APPEAR ⟨It's a disease that *occurs* among cows.⟩

oc•cur•rence \ə-ˈkər-əns\ *n*
1 something that happens ⟨Lightning is a natural *occurrence.*⟩
2 the action or process of happening
synonyms see INCIDENT

ocean \ˈō-shən\ *n*
1 the whole body of salt water that covers nearly three fourths of the earth
2 ▲ one of the large bodies of water into which the larger body that covers the earth is divided

ocean 2: view of an ocean from an elevation

oce•an•ic \ˌō-shē-ˈa-nik\ *adj*
of or relating to the ocean

ocean•og•ra•phy \ˌō-shə-ˈnä-grə-fē\ *n*
a science that deals with the ocean

oce•lot \ˈä-sə-ˌlät, ˈō-\ *n*
a medium-sized American wildcat that is yellowish brown or grayish and blotched with black

o'•clock \ə-ˈkläk\ *adv*
according to the clock ⟨The time is one *o'clock.*⟩

Oct. *abbr* October

octa- *or* **octo-** *also* **oct-** *prefix*
eight

oc•ta•gon \ˈäk-tə-ˌgän\ *n*
▶ a flat geometric figure with eight angles and eight sides

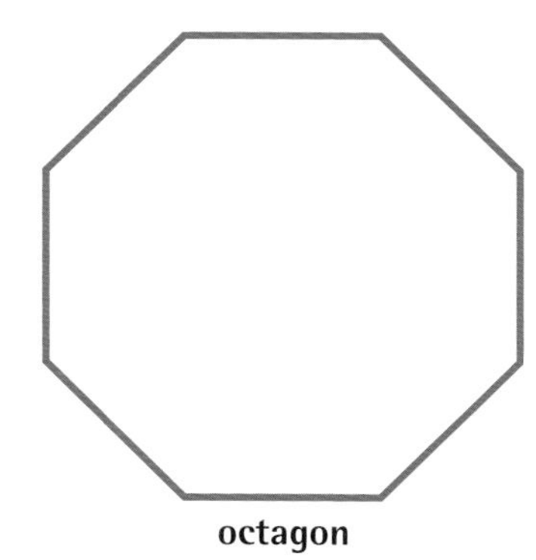

octagon

oc•tag•o•nal \äk-ˈta-gə-nᵊl\ *adj*
having eight sides

oc•tave \ˈäk-tiv\ *n*
1 a space of eight steps between musical notes
2 a tone or note that is eight steps above or below another note or tone

Oc•to•ber \äk-ˈtō-bər\ *n*
the tenth month of the year

▶ **Word History** The earliest Roman calendar had only ten months and began with the month of March. The eighth month was called in Latin *October,* a word that combines the number *octo,* "eight," with the element *-ber* found in *September, November,* and *December.* The name was kept—and eventually borrowed by English—after October became the tenth of twelve Roman months.

oc•to•pus \'äk-tə-pəs\ *n, pl* **oc•to•pus•es** *or* **oc•to•pi** \-tə-ˌpī\
►a marine animal that has a soft rounded body with eight long flexible arms about its base which have sucking disks able to seize and hold things (as prey)

oc•u•lar \'ä-kyə-lər\ *adj*
of or relating to the eye or eyesight ⟨*ocular* diseases⟩

odd \'äd\ *adj* **odd•er**; **odd•est**
1 not usual or common : STRANGE ⟨Walking backward is an *odd* thing to do.⟩
2 not usual, expected, or planned ⟨He does *odd* jobs to earn extra money.⟩ ⟨Finding the passage was an *odd* stroke of luck.⟩
3 not capable of being divided by two without leaving a remainder ⟨The *odd* numbers include 1, 3, 5, 7, etc.⟩
4 not one of a pair or a set ⟨She found an *odd* glove.⟩
5 being or having a number that cannot be divided by two without leaving a remainder ⟨an *odd* year⟩
6 some more than the number mentioned ⟨The ship sank fifty *odd* years ago.⟩
odd•ly *adv*
odd•ness *n*

odd•ball \'äd-ˌbȯl\ *n*
a person who behaves strangely

odd•i•ty \'ä-də-tē\ *n, pl* **odd•i•ties**
1 something strange
2 the quality or state of being strange

odds \'ädz\ *n pl*
1 a difference in favor of one thing over another ⟨She wanted to improve her *odds* of winning.⟩
2 conditions that make something difficult ⟨He overcame great *odds* and succeeded.⟩
3 DISAGREEMENT 1 ⟨Those two are always at *odds* with one another.⟩

odds and ends *n pl*
things left over : miscellaneous things

ode \'ōd\ *n*
a lyric poem that expresses a noble feeling with dignity

odi•ous \'ō-dē-əs\ *adj*
causing hatred or strong dislike worthy of hatred

odom•e•ter \ō-'dä-mə-tər\ *n*
an instrument for measuring the distance traveled (as by a vehicle)

odor \'ō-dər\ *n*
a particular smell ⟨The *odor* of flowers filled my room.⟩
odor•less \'ō-dər-ləs\ *adj*

o'er \'ȯr\ *adv or prep*
OVER ⟨They sailed *o'er* the ocean.⟩

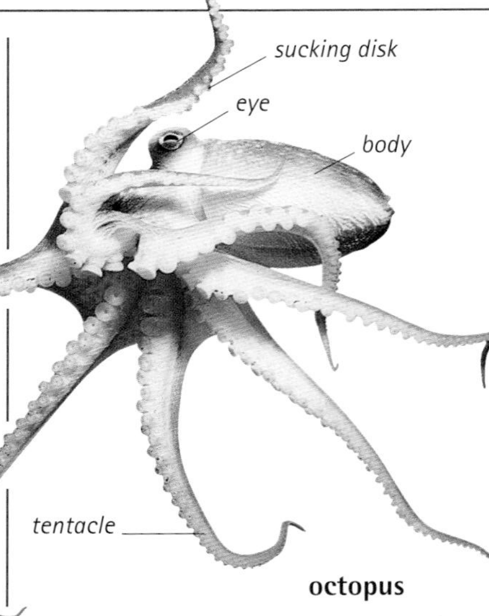

octopus

of \əv, 'əv, 'äv\ *prep*
1 used to join an amount or a part with the whole which includes it ⟨most *of* the children⟩ ⟨the back *of* the closet⟩
2 belonging to, relating to, or connected with ⟨a shirt *of* his⟩ ⟨the top *of* the hill⟩
3 CONCERNING ⟨I heard the news *of* your success.⟩
4 that is ⟨the city *of* Rome⟩
5 made from ⟨a house *of* bricks⟩
6 that has : WITH ⟨a man *of* courage⟩ ⟨a thing *of* no importance⟩
7 used to show what has been taken away ⟨a tree bare *of* leaves⟩ ⟨cured *of* disease⟩
8 used to indicate the reason for ⟨a fear *of* spiders⟩
9 living in ⟨the people *of* China⟩
10 that involves ⟨a test *of* knowledge⟩
11 used to indicate what an amount or number refers to ⟨an acre *of* land⟩
12 used to indicate the point from which someone or something is located ⟨He lives north *of* town.⟩
13 used to indicate the object affected by an action ⟨destruction *of* property⟩

[1]**off** \'ȯf\ *adv*
1 from a place or position ⟨He got angry and marched *off.*⟩
2 from a course : ASIDE ⟨The driver turned *off* onto a side street.⟩
3 so as not to be supported, covering or enclosing, or attached ⟨I jumped *off.*⟩ ⟨The lid blew *off.*⟩ ⟨The handle fell *off.*⟩
4 so as to be discontinued or finished ⟨Turn the radio *off.*⟩ ⟨The couple paid *off* their debts.⟩
5 away from work ⟨I took the day *off.*⟩

[2]**off** *prep*
1 away from the surface or top of ⟨Take those books *off* the table.⟩
2 at the expense of ⟨I lived *off* my parents.⟩
3 released or freed from ⟨The officer was *off* duty.⟩
4 below the usual level of ⟨We can save a dollar *off* the price.⟩
5 away from ⟨The hotel is just *off* the highway.⟩

[3]**off** *adj*
1 not operating or flowing ⟨The radio is *off.*⟩ ⟨The electricity is *off.*⟩
2 not attached to or covering ⟨The lid is *off.*⟩
3 started on the way ⟨They're *off* on a trip.⟩
4 not taking place ⟨The game is *off.*⟩
5 not correct : WRONG ⟨Your guess is way *off.*⟩
6 not as good as usual ⟨He's having an *off* day.⟩
7 provided for ⟨His family is well *off.*⟩
8 small in degree : SLIGHT ⟨There's an *off* chance I'll win.⟩
9 away from home or work ⟨He's *off* fishing.⟩

off. *abbr* office

of•fend \ə-'fend\ *vb* **of•fend•ed**; **of•fend•ing**
1 to hurt the feelings of or insult ⟨She uses language that *offends* people.⟩
2 to do wrong ⟨Is the released prisoner likely to *offend* again?⟩

of•fend•er \ə-'fen-dər\ *n*
a person who does wrong

of•fense *or* **of•fence** \ə-'fens\ *n*
1 something done that hurts feelings or insults
2 WRONGDOING, SIN
3 the act of hurting feelings or insulting
4 a team or the part of a team that attempts to score in a game
5 an act of attacking : ASSAULT

[1]**of•fen•sive** \ə-'fen-siv\ *adj*
1 causing displeasure or resentment ⟨an *offensive* smell⟩ ⟨an *offensive* question⟩
2 of or relating to the attempt to score in a game or contest ⟨the *offensive* team⟩
3 made for or relating to an attack ⟨*offensive* weapons⟩ ⟨an *offensive* strategy⟩
of•fen•sive•ly *adv*
of•fen•sive•ness *n*

[2]**offensive** *n*
[2]ATTACK 1 ⟨The enemy launched an *offensive.*⟩
on the offensive in a situation that calls for opposing action ⟨The soldiers are *on the offensive.*⟩

[1]**of•fer** \'ȯ-fər\ *vb* **of•fered**; **of•fer•ing**
1 to present (something) to be accepted or rejected
2 to declare willingness ⟨We *offered* to help.⟩

3 to present for consideration : SUGGEST ⟨Can I *offer* a suggestion?⟩
4 to make by effort ⟨The local people *offered* no resistance to invaders.⟩
5 to present as an act of worship ⟨We *offered* up prayers.⟩

▶ **Synonyms** OFFER and PRESENT mean to put before another for acceptance. OFFER is used when the thing may be accepted or refused. ⟨He *offered* more coffee to the guests.⟩ PRESENT is used when something is offered with the hope or expectation of its being accepted. ⟨Salesmen *presented* their goods.⟩ ⟨The principal *presented* our diplomas.⟩

²offer *n*
1 an act of presenting (something) to be accepted or rejected
2 an act of declaring willingness ⟨Thanks for your *offer* to help.⟩
3 a price suggested by someone prepared to buy : BID ⟨The *offer* for the house was too low.⟩

of•fer•ing \'ȯ-fə-riŋ, 'ȯf-riŋ\ *n*
1 something presented for acceptance
2 a contribution to the support of a church
3 a sacrifice given as part of worship

off•hand \'ȯf-'hand\ *adv or adj*
without previous thought or preparation ⟨I can't say *offhand* who came.⟩

of•fice \'ȯ-fəs\ *n*
1 a place where business is done or a service is supplied ⟨a doctor's *office*⟩
2 a special duty or position and especially one of authority in government ⟨My uncle wants to run for *office*.⟩

of•fice•hold•er \'ȯ-fəs-,hōl-dər\ *n*
a person who has been elected or appointed to a public position

of•fi•cer \'ȯ-fə-sər\ *n*
1 ▶ a person given the responsibility of enforcing the law ⟨a police *officer*⟩
2 a person who holds a position of authority ⟨an *officer* of the company⟩
3 a person who holds a commission in the military ⟨His father is an *officer* in the navy.⟩

¹of•fi•cial \ə-'fi-shəl\ *n*
a person who holds a position of authority in an organization or government

²official *adj*
1 relating to a position of authority ⟨*official* duties⟩
2 having authority to perform a duty ⟨the *official* referee⟩
3 coming from or meeting the requirements of an authority ⟨an *official* team baseball⟩
4 proper for a person in office ⟨The White House is the President's *official* residence.⟩
of•fi•cial•ly *adv*

of•fi•ci•ate \ə-'fi-shē-,āt\ *vb* **of•fi•ci•at•ed; of•fi•ci•at•ing**
1 to perform a ceremony or duty ⟨A bishop *officiated* at the wedding.⟩
2 to act as an officer : PRESIDE ⟨She *officiated* at the annual meeting.⟩

off•ing \'ȯ-fiŋ\ *n*
the near future or distance ⟨I see trouble in the *offing*.⟩

off–lim•its \'ȯf-'li-məts\ *adj*
not to be entered or used ⟨The couch is *off-limits* to the dog.⟩

off–line \'ȯf-,līn\ *adj or adv*
not connected to or directly controlled by a computer system ⟨*off-line* data storage⟩ ⟨I went *off-line* after sending the e-mail.⟩

off•set \'ȯf-,set\ *vb* **offset; off•set•ting**
to make up for

officer 1:
an officer from the Boston Police

off•shoot \'ȯf-,shüt\ *n*
a branch of a main stem of a plant

¹off•shore \'ȯf-,shȯr\ *adj*
1 coming or moving away from the shore ⟨an *offshore* breeze⟩
2 located off the shore ⟨*offshore* oil⟩

²off•shore \'ȯf-'shȯr\ *adv*
from the shore : at a distance from the shore

offspring:
a dachshund with its offspring

off•spring \'ȯf-,spriŋ\ *n, pl* **offspring** *also* **off•springs**
▲ the young of a person, animal, or plant

off•stage \'ȯf-'stāj\ *adv or adj*
off or away from the stage

oft \'ȯft\ *adv*
OFTEN

of•ten \'ȯ-fən\ *adv*
many times : FREQUENTLY

of•ten•times \'ȯ-fən-,tīmz\ *adv*
OFTEN

ogle \'ō-gəl\ *vb* **ogled; ogling**
to look at in a way that suggests unusual interest or desire

ogre \'ō-gər\ *n*
1 an ugly giant of fairy tales and folklore who eats people
2 a person or object that is frightening or causes strong feelings of dislike

oh *also* **O** \ō, 'ō\ *interj*
1 used to express an emotion (as surprise or pain) ⟨*Oh*, why did I ever come here?⟩
2 used in direct address ⟨*Oh*, children, stop that noise!⟩

OH *abbr* Ohio

¹oil \'ȯil\ *n*
1 any of numerous greasy usually liquid substances from plant, animal, or mineral sources that do not dissolve in water and are used especially as lubricants, fuels, and food
2 PETROLEUM
3 paint made of pigments and oil
4 a painting done in oils

²oil *vb* **oiled; oil•ing**
to rub on or lubricate with a greasy substance

oil•cloth \'ȯil-,klȯth\ *n*
material treated with a greasy substance so as to be waterproof and used for shelf and table coverings

oily \'ȯi-lē\ *adj* **oil•i•er; oil•i•est**
covered with or containing a greasy substance ⟨*oily* rags⟩
oil•i•ness *n*

oint•ment \'ȯint-mənt\ *n*
a thick greasy medicine for use on the skin

Ojib•wa *or* **Ojib•way** *or* **Ojib•we** \ō-'jib-wā\ *n, pl* **Ojibwa** *or* **Ojib•was** *or* **Ojibway** *or* **Ojib•ways** *or* **Ojibwe** *or* **Ojib•wes**
1 a member of an American Indian people originally of Michigan
2 the language of the Ojibwa people

[1]**OK** *or* **okay** \ō-'kā\ *adv or adj*
all right

► **Word History** In the 1830s Boston newspapers were full of abbreviations. Just about anything might be abbreviated. *N.G.* stood for "no go." *A.R.* stood for "all right." Soon some phrases were spelled wrong on purpose and then abbreviated. *K.G.*, for "know go," was used instead of *N.G. O.W.*, "oll wright," was used instead of *A.R. O.K.*, "oll korrect," was used instead of *A.C.* The fad faded, but the one abbreviation *O.K.* caught on and is still widely used.

[2]**OK** *or* **okay** *n*
APPROVAL 2 ⟨I need your *OK* to begin.⟩

[3]**OK** *or* **okay** *vb* **OK'd** *or* **okayed; OK'•ing** *or* **okay•ing**
APPROVE 2, AUTHORIZE

[4]**OK** *abbr* Oklahoma

oka•pi \ō-'kä-pē\ *n*
▼ an animal of the African forests related to the giraffe

okapi

okra:
okra pods

Okla. *abbr* Oklahoma

okra \'ō-krə\ *n*
▲ the green pods of a garden plant that are used as a vegetable especially in soups and stews

[1]**old** \'ōld\ *adj* **old•er; old•est**
1 having lived a long time ⟨an *old* dog⟩
2 showing the effects of time or use ⟨Grandpa wore an *old* coat.⟩
3 having existed for a specified length of time ⟨My brother is three years *old.*⟩
4 dating from the distant past : ANCIENT ⟨an *old* custom⟩
5 having lasted or been such for a long time ⟨She's an *old* friend of mine.⟩
6 FORMER ⟨My *old* neighbors came to visit.⟩

[2]**old** *n*
a distant or earlier time ⟨Life was tough in days of *old.*⟩

old•en \'ōl-dən\ *adj*
of an earlier period

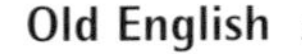

Old English *n*
the language of England from the earliest documents in the seventh century to about 1100

old–fash•ioned \'ōld-'fa-shənd\ *adj*
1 from or like that of an earlier time ⟨an *old-fashioned* hairdo⟩
2 using or preferring ways and traditions of the past

Old French *n*
the French language from the ninth to the thirteenth century

Old Glory *n*
the flag of the United States

old maid *n*
1 an elderly unmarried woman
2 a very neat fussy person
3 a card game in which cards are matched in pairs and the player holding the extra queen at the end loses

old–time \'ōld-'tīm\ *adj*
from or like that of an earlier or distant period ⟨*old-time* music⟩ ⟨*old-time* transportation⟩

old–tim•er \'ōld-'tī-mər\ *n*
1 a person who has been part of an organization (as a business) for a long time
2 an old person

old–world \'ōld-'wərld\ *adj*
having old-fashioned charm

Old World *n*
the lands in the eastern hemisphere and especially Europe but not including Australia

ol•fac•to•ry \äl-'fak-tə-rē, ōl-\ *adj*
of or relating to smelling or the sense of smell ⟨*olfactory* nerves⟩

ol•ive \'ä-liv\ *n*
1 ▼ the oily fruit of an evergreen tree that is eaten both ripe and unripe and is the source of an edible oil (**olive oil**)
2 a yellowish green color

black olive
green olive

olive 1

Olym•pic \ə-ˈlim-pik, ō-\ *adj*
▶ of or relating to the Olympic Games

Olympic Games *n pl*
a series of international athletic contests held as separate winter and summer events in a different country every four years

om•e•let *or* **om•e•lette** \ˈäm-lət, ˈä-mə-lət\ *n*
▼ beaten eggs cooked without stirring until firm and folded in half often with a filling

▶ **Word History** Although the word *omelet* does not have much resemblance to the Latin word *lamina*, the shape of an omelet does resemble a thin plate, which is what *lamina*, the ultimate source of *omelet*, means. The Romans used the noun *lamella*, which is derived from *lamina*, to mean "thin metal plate." *Lamella* became *lemelle* in Old French, then, by a long series of changes, *amelette* or *omelette* by about 1600. The word also took on the additional meaning "dish of beaten eggs," and was borrowed from French into English in the 1600s.

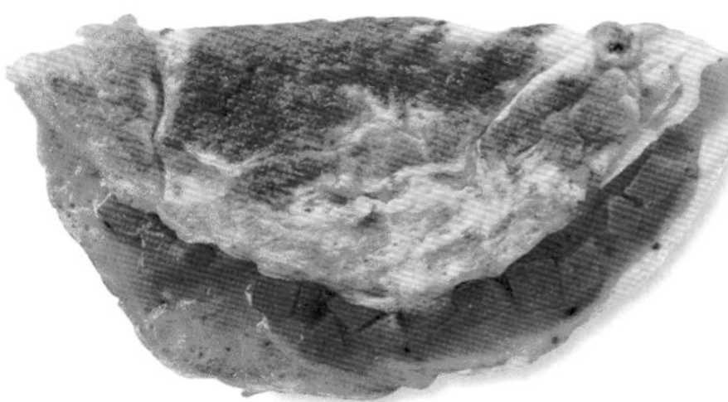

omelet with a cheese and ham filling

omen \ˈō-mən\ *n*
a happening believed to be a sign or warning of a future event

om•i•nous \ˈä-mə-nəs\ *adj*
considered a sign of evil or trouble to come
om•i•nous•ly *adv*

omis•sion \ō-ˈmi-shən\ *n*
1 something left out ⟨There are some *omissions* in the list.⟩
2 the act of leaving out : the state of being left out

omit \ō-ˈmit\ *vb* **omit•ted**; **omit•ting**
1 to leave out : fail to include ⟨Her name was *omitted* from the credits.⟩
2 to leave undone : NEGLECT

om•ni•bus \ˈäm-ni-ˌbəs\ *n*, *pl* **om•ni•bus•es**
BUS

om•nip•o•tent \äm-ˈni-pə-tənt\ *adj*
having power or authority without limit : ALMIGHTY

Olympic: the Olympic flag

om•ni•vore \ˈäm-ni-ˌvȯr\ *n*
an animal that feeds on plants and other animals

om•niv•o•rous \äm-ˈni-və-rəs\ *adj*
feeding on plants and animals

[1]**on** \ˈȯn, ˈän\ *prep*
1 in contact with and supported by ⟨Put the books *on* the table.⟩
2 used to indicate means of being carried ⟨He rode *on* a tractor.⟩
3 used to indicate the location of something ⟨Both bedrooms are *on* the top floor.⟩
4 used to indicate the focus of a certain action ⟨He went down *on* his stomach.⟩ ⟨She chewed *on* gum.⟩ ⟨We called the police *on* him.⟩
5 AGAINST 4 ⟨There were shadows *on* the wall.⟩
6 near or connected with ⟨We stopped in a town *on* the river.⟩
7 [1]TO 1 ⟨Mine is the first house *on* the left.⟩
8 sometime during ⟨We can begin work *on* Monday.⟩
9 in the state or process of ⟨*on* fire⟩ ⟨*on* sale⟩
10 [2]ABOUT 1 ⟨I'm looking for a book *on* minerals.⟩
11 by means of ⟨She likes to talk *on* the phone.⟩

[2]**on** *adv*
1 into operation or a position allowing operation ⟨Turn the light *on*.⟩
2 in or into contact with a surface ⟨Put the kettle *on*.⟩ ⟨She has new shoes *on*.⟩
3 forward in time, space, or action ⟨We finally went *on* home.⟩ ⟨The argument went *on* for weeks.⟩
4 from one to another ⟨Pass the word *on*.⟩

[3]**on** *adj*
1 being in operation ⟨The radio is *on*.⟩
2 placed so as to allow operation ⟨The switch is *on*.⟩
3 taking place ⟨The game is *on*.⟩
4 having been planned ⟨She has nothing *on* for tonight.⟩

ON *abbr* Ontario

[1]**once** \ˈwəns\ *adv*
1 one time only ⟨It happened just *once*.⟩
2 at some time in the past : FORMERLY ⟨It was *once* done that way.⟩
3 at any one time : EVER ⟨She didn't *once* thank me.⟩
once and for all now and for the last time
once in a while from time to time

[2]**once** *n*
one single time ⟨We can make an exception just this *once*.⟩
at once
1 at the same time ⟨I can't understand with both of you talking *at once*.⟩
2 IMMEDIATELY 2 ⟨Leave *at once*.⟩

[3]**once** *conj*
as soon as : WHEN ⟨*Once* you've finished your homework, you may go outside.⟩

once–over \ˌwəns-ˈō-vər\ *n*
a quick glance or examination

on•com•ing \ˈȯn-ˌkə-miŋ, ˈän-\ *adj*
coming nearer ⟨an *oncoming* car⟩

[1]**one** \ˈwən\ *adj*
1 being a single unit or thing ⟨There's *one* catch.⟩
2 being a certain unit or thing ⟨He arrived early *one* morning.⟩
3 being the same in kind or quality ⟨All the members of *one* class will sit together.⟩
4 not specified ⟨We'll meet again *one* day.⟩

[2]**one** *n*
1 the number denoting a single unit : 1
2 the first in a set or series
3 a single person or thing

[3]**one** *pron*
1 a single member or individual ⟨I met *one* of your friends.⟩
2 any person

one another *pron*
EACH OTHER

Onei•da \ō-ˈnī-də\ *n*, *pl* **Oneida** *or* **Onei•das**
1 a member of an American Indian people originally of New York
2 the language of the Oneida people

oner•ous \'ä-nə-rəs, 'ō-\ *adj*
being difficult and unpleasant to do or to deal with

one•self \,wən-'self\ *pron*
a person's own self ⟨Living by *oneself* can be lonely.⟩

one–sid•ed \'wən-'sī-dəd\ *adj*
1 done or occurring on one side only ⟨a *one-sided* decision⟩
2 having one side more developed : LOPSIDED
3 favoring or dominated by one side ⟨a *one-sided* fight⟩

one•time \'wən-,tīm\ *adj*
FORMER

one–way \'wən-'wā\ *adj*
moving or allowing movement in one direction only ⟨*one-way* traffic⟩ ⟨a *one-way* street⟩

on•go•ing \'ón-,gō-iŋ, 'än-\ *adj*
being in progress or movement ⟨The investigation is *ongoing*.⟩

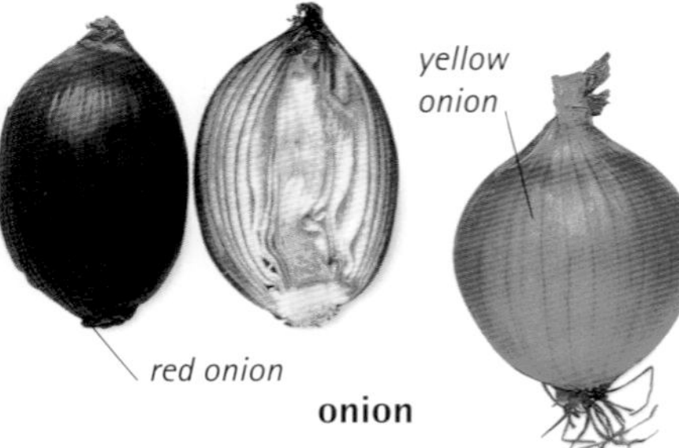

onion

on•ion \'ən-yən\ *n*
▲ the roundish edible bulb of a plant related to the lily that has a sharp odor and taste and is used as a vegetable and to season foods

online \'ón-,līn, 'än-\ *adj or adv*
connected to, directly controlled by, or available through a computer system ⟨an *online* database⟩ ⟨working *online*⟩

on•look•er \'ón-,lu̇-kər, 'än-\ *n*
SPECTATOR

[1]on•ly \'ōn-lē\ *adj*
1 alone in or of a class or kind : SOLE ⟨He is the *only* survivor.⟩
2 best without doubt ⟨You are the *only* person for me.⟩

[2]only *adv*
1 no more than ⟨We lost *only* one game.⟩
2 no one or nothing other than ⟨*Only* you know my secret.⟩ ⟨There may be other methods, but *only* this will do.⟩
3 in no other situation, time, place, or condition except ⟨Use medicine *only* when necessary.⟩
4 in the end ⟨It will *only* make you sick.⟩
5 as recently as ⟨I saw him *only* last week.⟩

[3]only *conj*
except that ⟨I'd like to play, *only* I'm too tired.⟩

on•o•mato•poe•ia \,ä-nə-,ma-tə-'pē-ə\ *n*
the forming of a word (as "buzz" or "hiss") in imitation of a natural sound

on•rush \'ón-,rəsh, 'än-\ *n*
a strong fast movement forward

on•set \'ón-,set, 'än-\ *n*
1 BEGINNING 1 ⟨the *onset* of winter⟩
2 [2]ATTACK 1

on•slaught \'än-,slót, 'ón-\ *n*
a violent attack

Ont. *abbr* Ontario

on•to \'ón-(,)tü, 'än-\ *prep*
to a position on or against ⟨I leaped *onto* the horse.⟩

[1]on•ward \'ón-wərd, 'än-\ *adv*
toward or at a point lying ahead in space or time : FORWARD ⟨The river flows *onward* to the coast.⟩

[2]onward *adj*
directed or moving forward ⟨There's no stopping the *onward* march of time.⟩

oo•dles \'ü-dᵊlz\ *n pl*
a great quantity

[1]ooze \'üz\ *n*
soft mud : SLIME

[2]ooze *vb* **oozed**; **ooz•ing**
to flow or leak out slowly

opal \'ō-pəl\ *n*
▼ a mineral with soft changeable colors that is used as a gem

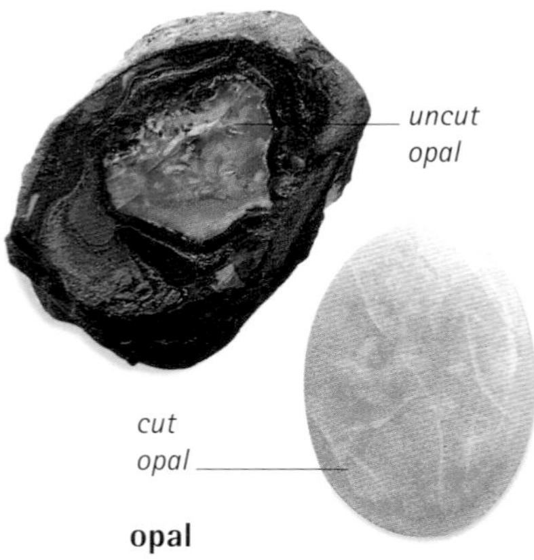

opal

opaque \ō-'pāk\ *adj*
1 not letting light through : not transparent
2 not reflecting light : DULL ⟨an *opaque* paint⟩

[1]open \'ō-pən\ *adj*
1 not shut or blocked : not closed ⟨an *open* window⟩ ⟨*open* books⟩
2 not sealed, locked, or fastened ⟨an *open* zipper⟩ ⟨There's an *open* bottle of ketchup in the refrigerator.⟩
3 easy to enter, get through, or see ⟨*open* country⟩
4 ready to consider appeals or ideas ⟨an *open* mind⟩
5 not drawn together : spread out ⟨an *open* flower⟩ ⟨*open* umbrellas⟩
6 not enclosed or covered ⟨an *open* boat⟩ ⟨an *open* fire⟩
7 not secret : PUBLIC ⟨They have an *open* dislike for one another.⟩
8 to be used, entered, or taken part in by all ⟨an *open* golf tournament⟩ ⟨an *open* meeting⟩
9 not decided or settled ⟨an *open* question⟩
open•ly *adv*
open•ness *n*

[2]open *vb* **opened**; **open•ing**
1 to change or move from a shut condition ⟨Sit down and *open* a book.⟩ ⟨The door *opened*.⟩ ⟨She *opened* her eyes.⟩
2 to clear by or as if by removing something in the way ⟨Workers were sent to *open* a road blocked with snow.⟩
3 to make or become ready for use ⟨They plan to *open* a store.⟩ ⟨The office *opens* at eight.⟩
4 to give access ⟨The rooms *open* onto a hall.⟩
5 BEGIN 1, START ⟨Police have *opened* an investigation.⟩ ⟨They *opened* fire on the enemy.⟩
open•er \'ō-pə-nər, 'ōp-nər\ *n*

[3]open *n*
space that is not enclosed or covered : OUTDOORS ⟨Some slept in a cabin while others slept in the *open*.⟩

open air *n*
space that is not enclosed or covered
open–air *adj*

open–and–shut \,ō-pən-ən-'shət\ *adj*
[1]PLAIN 3, OBVIOUS ⟨The police say it's an *open-and-shut* case.⟩

open•heart•ed \,ō-pən-'här-təd\ *adj*
1 FRANK
2 GENEROUS 1

open house *n*
1 friendly and welcoming treatment to anyone who comes
2 an event in which an organization (as a school) invites the public to see the things that happen there

open•ing \'ō-pə-niŋ, 'ōp-niŋ\ *n*
1 a place that is not enclosed or covered : CLEARING
2 an act of making or becoming ready for use ⟨Neighbors are anxious for the *opening* of a new store.⟩
3 BEGINNING ⟨People who came late missed the *opening* of the speech.⟩
4 [1]OCCASION 3 ⟨He was waiting for an *opening* to tell the joke.⟩

5 a job opportunity ⟨There is an *opening* in the legal department.⟩

open•work \'ō-pən-,wərk\ *n*
something made or work done so as to show spaces through the fabric or material

op•era \'ä-pə-rə, 'ä-prə\ *n*
a play in which the entire text is sung with orchestral accompaniment

op•er•ate \'ä-pə-,rāt\ *vb* **op•er•at•ed**; **op•er•at•ing**
1 to work or cause to work in a proper or particular way ⟨The machine is *operating* smoothly.⟩ ⟨He will learn to *operate* a car.⟩
2 MANAGE 1 ⟨They *operate* a farm.⟩
3 to perform surgery : do an operation on ⟨The doctors *operated* on the patient.⟩

operating system *n*
a program or series of programs that controls the operation of a computer and directs the processing of the user's programs

op•er•a•tion \,ä-pə-'rā-shən\ *n*
1 a set of actions for a particular purpose ⟨a rescue *operation*⟩
2 ► a medical procedure that involves cutting into a living body in order to repair or remove a damaged or diseased part ⟨I need an *operation* to remove my appendix.⟩
3 the process of putting military forces into action ⟨naval *operations*⟩
4 the state of working or being able to work ⟨The factory is now in *operation.*⟩
5 a method or manner of working ⟨The camera is designed for easy *operation.*⟩
6 a process (as addition or multiplication) of getting one mathematical expression from others according to a rule
7 a single step performed by a computer in carrying out a program

op•er•a•tion•al \,ä-pə-'rā-shə-n^{ə}l\ *adj*
ready for use ⟨The new airport is now *operational.*⟩

op•er•a•tor \'ä-pə-,rā-tər\ *n*
1 a person who manages or controls something ⟨a plow *operator*⟩
2 a person in charge of a telephone switchboard
3 a person who is skillful at achieving things by persuasion or deception

op•er•et•ta \,ä-pə-'re-tə\ *n*
a funny play set to music with speaking, singing, and dancing scenes

opin•ion \ə-'pin-yən\ *n*
1 a belief based on experience and on certain facts but not amounting to sure knowledge ⟨In my *opinion* you should take the job.⟩
2 a judgment about a person or thing ⟨She has a high *opinion* of herself.⟩
3 a statement by an expert after careful study ⟨He should get an *opinion* from a lawyer.⟩

► **Synonyms** OPINION and BELIEF mean a judgment that someone thinks is true. OPINION is used when the judgment is not yet final or certain but is founded on some facts. ⟨I soon changed my *opinion* of the plan.⟩ BELIEF is used if the judgment is certain and firm in a person's own mind without regard to the amount or kind of evidence. ⟨It's my *belief* we'll win the election.⟩

opin•ion•at•ed \ə-'pin-yə-,nā-təd\ *adj*
having and expressing very strong ideas and opinions about things

opi•um \'ō-pē-əm\ *n*
a bitter brownish narcotic drug that is the dried juice of a poppy of Europe and Asia

opos•sum \ə-'pä-səm\ *n*
► an American animal related to the kangaroo that has a long pointed snout, lives both on the ground and in trees, and is active at night

op•po•nent \ə-'pō-nənt\ *n*
a person or thing that takes an opposite position in a contest, fight, or controversy

op•por•tu•ni•ty \,ä-pər-'tü-nə-tē, -'tyü-\ *n*, *pl* **op•por•tu•ni•ties**
1 a favorable combination of circumstances, time, and place ⟨He practices guitar at every *opportunity.*⟩
2 a chance for greater success ⟨The new job was a real *opportunity.*⟩

opossum

► **operation 2**
Operations are undertaken when a medical team needs to cut into a patient's body in order to treat a disease or an injury. An operation may also be performed to replace organs such as the liver or kidney, or to deliver a baby. Operations are generally performed in a hospital operating room by surgeons and nurses. An anesthetist \ə-'nes-thə-tist\ controls the supply of anesthetic to the patient to produce loss of feeling in the area of surgery or to make the patient unconscious throughout the procedure.

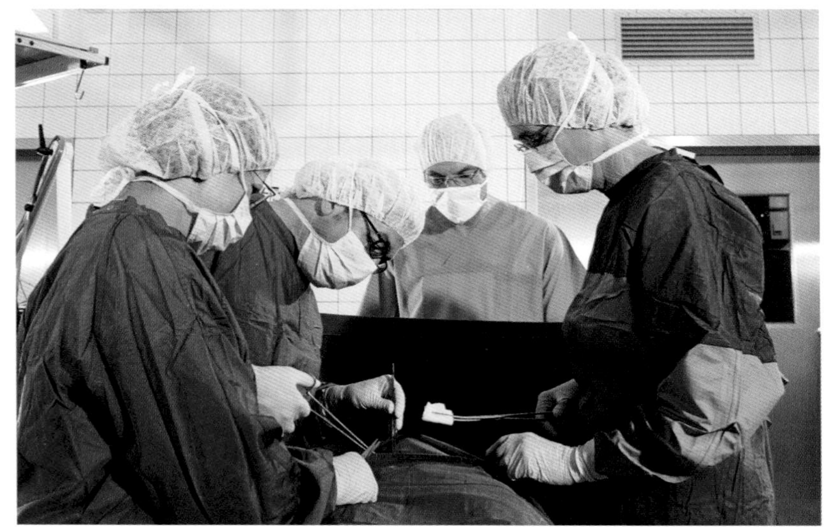
surgeons performing a heart operation on a patient

a b c d e f g h i j k l m n o p q r s t u v w x y z

A B C D E F G H I J K L M N O P Q R S T U V W X Y Z

op•pose \ə-'pōz\ *vb* **op•posed**; **op•pos•ing**
1 to disagree with or disapprove of ⟨They *oppose* the proposed changes.⟩
2 to compete against ⟨She will *oppose* the mayor in November's election.⟩
3 to provide contrast to ⟨Good *opposes* evil.⟩
4 to offer resistance to : try to stop or defeat ⟨The group will *oppose* the new law.⟩

[1]**op•po•site** \'ä-pə-zət\ *adj*
1 being at the other end, side, or corner ⟨We live on *opposite* sides of the street.⟩
2 being as different as possible ⟨They ran in *opposite* directions.⟩
3 being in a position to contrast with or cancel out ⟨Consider the *opposite* side of the question.⟩

[2]**opposite** *n*
either of two persons or things that are as different as possible

[3]**opposite** *adv*
on the other side of someone or something : across from ⟨He lives in the house *opposite* to mine.⟩

[4]**opposite** *prep*
across from (someone or something) ⟨The park is *opposite* our house.⟩

op•po•si•tion \ˌä-pə-'zi-shən\ *n*
1 the state of disagreeing with or disapproving of ⟨He voiced his *opposition.*⟩
2 the action of resisting ⟨The proposal met with fierce *opposition.*⟩
3 a group of people that disagree with, disapprove of, or resist someone or something

op•press \ə-'pres\ *vb* **op•pressed**; **op•press•ing**
1 to control or rule in a harsh or cruel way ⟨The cruel ruler *oppressed* his people.⟩
2 to cause to feel burdened in spirit ⟨Grief *oppressed* the survivors.⟩
op•press•or \-'pre-sər\ *n*

op•pres•sion \ə-'pre-shən\ *n*
cruel or unjust use of power or authority

op•pres•sive \ə-'pre-siv\ *adj*
1 cruel or harsh without just cause ⟨*oppressive* laws⟩
2 very unpleasant or uncomfortable ⟨*oppressive* heat⟩
op•pres•sive•ly *adv*

op•tic \'äp-tik\ *adj*
of or relating to seeing or the eye ⟨the *optic* nerve⟩

op•ti•cal \'äp-ti-kəl\ *adj*
1 relating to the science of optics
2 relating to seeing : VISUAL
3 involving the use of devices that are sensitive to light to get information for a computer ⟨an *optical* scanner⟩

optical fiber *n*
a single fiber used in fiber optics

optical illusion *n*
something that looks different from what it actually is

op•ti•cian \äp-'ti-shən\ *n*
a person who prepares lenses for and sells eyeglasses

op•tics \'äp-tiks\ *n*
a science that deals with the nature and properties of light and the changes that it undergoes and produces

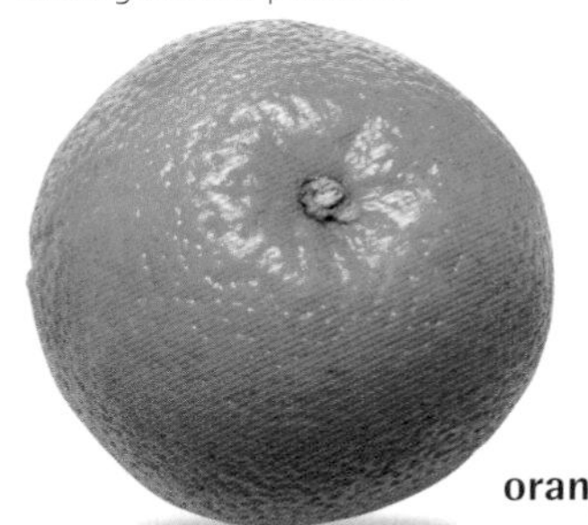
orange 2

op•ti•mism \'äp-tə-ˌmi-zəm\ *n*
a feeling or belief that good things will happen

op•ti•mist \'äp-tə-məst\ *n*
a person who habitually expects good things to happen

op•ti•mis•tic \ˌäp-tə-'mi-stik\ *adj*
expecting good things to happen : HOPEFUL ⟨We are *optimistic* about the future.⟩
op•ti•mis•ti•cal•ly \-sti-kə-lē, -sti-klē\ *adv*

op•ti•mum \'äp-tə-məm\ *adj*
most desirable or satisfactory ⟨The shuttle is launched only under *optimum* conditions.⟩

op•tion \'äp-shən\ *n*
1 the power or right to choose ⟨Children have an *option* between milk or juice.⟩
2 something that can be chosen ⟨Quitting is not an *option.*⟩
3 a right to buy or sell something at a specified price during a specified period ⟨His parents took an *option* on the house.⟩

op•tion•al \'äp-shə-nᵊl\ *adj*
left to choice : not required

op•tom•e•trist \äp-'tä-mə-trəst\ *n*
a person who examines the eyes and prescribes glasses or exercise to improve the eyesight

op•u•lent \'ä-pyə-lənt\ *adj*
having or showing much wealth ⟨*opulent* homes⟩

or \ər, 'ór\ *conj*
used between words or phrases that are choices ⟨juice *or* milk⟩ ⟨pay *or* get out⟩

OR *abbr* Oregon

[1]**-or** \ər\ *n suffix*
someone or something that does a specified thing ⟨act*or*⟩ ⟨elevat*or*⟩

[2]**-or** *n suffix*
condition activity ⟨demean*or*⟩

or•a•cle \'ór-ə-kəl\ *n*
1 a person (as a priestess in ancient Greece) through whom a god is believed to speak
2 the place where a god speaks through a person
3 an answer given by a person through whom a god speaks

oral \'ór-əl\ *adj*
1 [2]SPOKEN 1 ⟨an *oral* agreement⟩
2 of, involving, or given by the mouth ⟨an *oral* medication⟩ ⟨*oral* hygiene⟩
oral•ly *adv*

or•ange \'ór-inj\ *n*
1 a color between red and yellow : the color of a carrot
2 ◀ a sweet juicy citrus fruit with orange colored rind that grows on an evergreen tree with shining leaves and fragrant white flowers

orang•utan \ə-'raŋ-ə-ˌtaŋ, -ˌtan\ *n*
▼ a large ape of Borneo and Sumatra that lives in trees, eats mostly fruit, leaves, and other plant matter, and has very long arms, long reddish brown hair, and a nearly hairless face

► **Word History** Orangutans live in dense tropical forests on the islands of Borneo and Sumatra, part of Indonesia. Like most apes they look a bit like humans. In a language called Malay, spoken by many people of Indonesia as a second language, the apes were given a name formed from Malay *orang*, "man," and *hutan*, "forest"—in other words, "man of the forest." Europeans visiting the islands adopted the word *orangutan*, and it found its way into English.

orangutan

ora•tion \ə-ˈrā-shən\ *n*
an important speech given on a special occasion

or•a•tor \ˈȯr-ə-tər\ *n*
a public speaker noted for skill and power in speaking

or•a•to•ry \ˈȯr-ə-ˌtȯr-ē\ *n*
1 the art of making speeches
2 the style of language used in important speeches

orb \ˈȯrb\ *n*
something in the shape of a ball (as a planet or the eye)

[1]**or•bit** \ˈȯr-bət\ *n*
▶ the path taken by one body circling around another body 〈The earth makes an *orbit* around the sun.〉

[2]**orbit** *vb* **or•bit•ed; or•bit•ing**
1 to move in an orbit around : CIRCLE t〈The moon *orbits* the earth.〉
2 to send up so as to move in an orbit 〈The weather bureau will *orbit* a new satellite.〉

or•ca \ˈȯr-kə\ *n*
KILLER WHALE

or•chard \ˈȯr-chərd\ *n*
a place where fruit trees are grown

or•ches•tra \ˈȯr-kə-strə\ *n*
1 a group of musicians who perform instrumental music using mostly stringed instruments
2 the front part of the main floor in a theater
or•ches•tral \ȯr-ˈke-strəl\ *adj*

▶ **Word History** In ancient Greek plays the chorus danced and sang in a space in front of the stage. The Greek name for this space was *orchēstra,* which came from the verb *orcheisthai,* "to dance." The English word *orchestra* came from the Greek word for the space in front of a stage. At first the English word was used to refer to such a space but is now used to mean "the front part of the main floor." In today's theaters a group of musicians often sits in the space in front of the stage. Such a group, too, came to be called an *orchestra.*

or•chid \ˈȯr-kəd\ *n*
▶ a plant with usually showy flowers with three petals of which the middle petal is enlarged and differs from the others in shape and color

or•dain \ȯr-ˈdān\ *vb* **or•dained; or•dain•ing**
1 [2]DECREE 〈It was *ordained* by law.〉
2 to make a person a Christian minister or priest by a special ceremony

[1]**orbit:** view of planets in their orbits around the sun

or•deal \ȯr-ˈdēl\ *n*
a severe test or experience

[1]**or•der** \ˈȯr-dər\ *vb* **or•dered; or•der•ing**
1 to put into a particular grouping or sequence : ARRANGE 〈Dictionary entries are *ordered* alphabetically.〉
2 to give a command to or for 〈*order* troops into battle〉 〈*order* lunch〉

[2]**order** *n*
1 a certain rule or regulation : COMMAND
2 the arrangement of objects or events in space or time 〈alphabetical *order*〉
3 the way something should be 〈He kept the room in *order.*〉
4 the state of things when law or authority is obeyed
5 good working condition 〈The telephone is out of *order.*〉
6 a statement of what a person wants to buy 〈Place your *order* for a birthday cake.〉
7 goods or items bought or sold
8 a group of people united (as by living under the same religious rules or by loyalty to common needs or duties) 〈He belongs to an *order* of monks.〉
9 **orders** *pl* the office of a person in the Christian ministry 〈holy *orders*〉
10 a group of related living things (as plants or animals) that ranks above the family and below the class in scientific classification
11 a written direction to pay a sum of money
in order that so that
in order to for the purpose of

orchid:
a moth orchid

ordered pair *n*
a pair of numbers that represent the position of a point on a graph or coordinate plane

[1]**or•der•ly** \ˈȯr-dər-lē\ *adj*
1 having a neat arrangement : TIDY 〈an *orderly* room〉
2 obeying commands or rules : well-behaved 〈an *orderly* meeting〉 〈*orderly* children〉

[2]**orderly** *n, pl* **or•der•lies**
1 a soldier who works for an officer especially to carry messages
2 a person who does cleaning and general work in a hospital

or•di•nal \ˈȯr-də-nəl\ *n*
ORDINAL NUMBER

ordinal number *n*
a number that is used to show the place (as first, fifth, 22nd) taken by someone or something in a series

A B C D E F G H I J K L M N O P

or•di•nance \'ȯr-də-nəns\ *n*
a law or regulation especially of a city or town

or•di•nar•i•ly \ˌȯr-də-'ner-ə-lē\ *adv*
in the usual course of events : USUALLY

[1]**or•di•nary** \'ȯr-də-ˌner-ē\ *adj*
1 to be expected : NORMAL, USUAL ⟨This has been an *ordinary* day.⟩
2 neither good nor bad : AVERAGE ⟨They're just *ordinary* people.⟩
3 not very good : MEDIOCRE ⟨She gave a very *ordinary* speech.⟩
synonyms see COMMON

[2]**ordinary** *n*
the conditions or events that are usual or normal ⟨I see nothing out of the *ordinary*.⟩

ord•nance \'ȯrd-nəns\ *n*
1 military supplies (as guns, ammunition, trucks, and tanks)
2 ARTILLERY 1

ore \'ȯr\ *n*
a mineral mined to obtain a substance (as gold) that it contains

Ore., Oreg. *abbr* Oregon

or•gan \'ȯr-gən\ *n*
1 ▼ a musical instrument played by means of one or more keyboards and having pipes sounded by compressed air
2 a part of a person, plant, or animal that is specialized to perform a particular function
3 a way of getting something done ⟨Courts are *organs* of government.⟩

or•gan•elle \ˌȯr-gə-'nel\ *n*
a structure (as a lysosome) in a cell that performs a special function

or•gan•ic \ȯr-'ga-nik\ *adj*
1 relating to or obtained from living things ⟨*organic* matter⟩
2 relating to carbon compounds : containing carbon
3 being, involving, or producing food grown or made without the use of artificial chemicals

or•gan•ism \'ȯr-gə-ˌni-zəm\ *n*
a living thing made up of one or more cells and able to carry on the activities of life (as using energy, growing, or reproducing)

or•gan•ist \'ȯr-gə-nist\ *n*
a person who plays an organ

or•ga•ni•za•tion \ˌȯr-gə-nə-'zā-shən\ *n*
1 the act or process of arranging ⟨He assisted in the *organization* of a new club.⟩
2 the state or way of being arranged ⟨We studied the *organization* of government.⟩
3 a group of people united for a common purpose ⟨a business *organization*⟩

or•ga•nize \'ȯr-gə-ˌnīz\ *vb* **or•ga•nized; or•ga•niz•ing**
1 to arrange by effort and planning ⟨My teacher *organized* a field trip.⟩
2 to put in a certain order ⟨The computer *organized* the documents by date.⟩
3 to make separate parts into one united whole ⟨The players were *organized* into teams.⟩
or•ga•niz•er *n*

ori•ent \'ōr-ē-ˌent\ *vb* **ori•ent•ed; ori•ent•ing**
1 to set or arrange in a position especially so as to be lined up with certain points of the compass ⟨Builders *oriented* the house to face east.⟩
2 to make familiar with an existing situation or environment ⟨Volunteers are needed to *orient* new students.⟩
3 to direct toward the interests of a particular group
ori•en•ta•tion \ˌōr-ē-ən-'tā-shən\ *n*

ori•en•tal \ˌōr-ē-'en-tᵊl\ *adj, often cap*
1 *sometimes offensive* [1]ASIAN
Hint: In the past, this word was not considered offensive when applied to Asian people. In recent years, however, many people have come to find the word hurtful when applied to a person, and you may offend someone by using it in that way.
2 relating to or from the region that includes the countries of eastern Asia (as China, Japan, South Korea, and North Korea)

ori•ga•mi \ˌȯr-ə-'gä-mē\ *n*
▼ the art of folding paper into three-dimensional figures or designs without cutting the paper or using glue

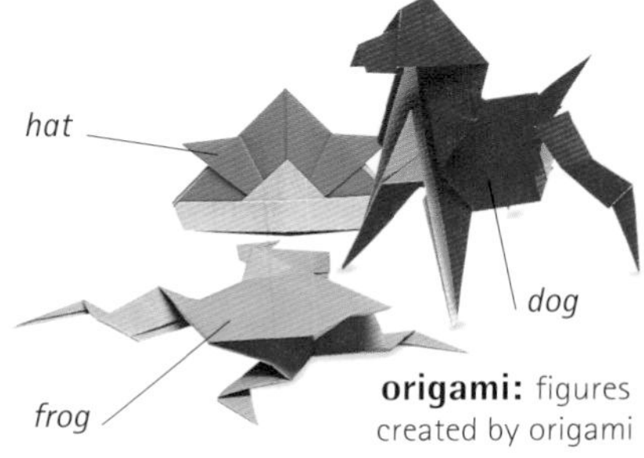

origami: figures created by origami

organ 1: a large church organ

or•i•gin \'ȯr-ə-jən\ *n*
1 basic source or cause ⟨The *origin* of their quarrel is not known.⟩
2 a person's ancestry ⟨They are people of humble *origin*.⟩
3 the rise or beginning from a source ⟨The story has its *origin* in fact.⟩
4 the point where the reference axes meet in a graph or coordinate plane

[1]**orig•i•nal** \ə-'ri-jə-nᵊl\ *adj*
1 of or relating to the source or beginning : FIRST ⟨My room is in the *original* part of an old house.⟩
2 not copied from anything else : not translated : NEW ⟨an *original* painting⟩ ⟨an *original* idea⟩
3 able to think up new things : CREATIVE
orig•i•nal•ly *adv*

[2]**original** *n*
something that is produced by an artist or writer and from which a copy or translation can be made ⟨The paintings are *originals*.⟩ ⟨She read the Russian novel in the *original*.⟩

orig•i•nal•i•ty \ə-ˌri-jə-'na-lə-tē\ *n*
the quality or state of being creative or new and different

orig•i•nate \ə-'ri-jə-ˌnāt\ *vb* **orig•i•nat•ed; orig•i•nat•ing**
1 to bring into being : INVENT, INITIATE

⟨*originate* a new game⟩
2 to come into being ⟨The custom *originated* in ancient times.⟩
orig•i•na•tor \-ˌnā-tər\ *n*

ori•ole \ˈȯr-ē-ˌōl\ *n*
1 an American songbird related to the blackbird that has a bright orange and black male
2 a yellow and black bird of Europe and Asia related to the crow

[1]or•na•ment \ˈȯr-nə-mənt\ *n*
something that adds beauty : DECORATION ⟨a Christmas tree *ornament*⟩

[2]or•na•ment \ˈȯr-nə-ˌment\ *vb* **or•na•ment•ed; or•na•ment•ing**
DECORATE 1

[1]or•na•men•tal \ˌȯr-nə-ˈmen-tᵊl\ *adj*
serving to add beauty : DECORATIVE ⟨The columns are just *ornamental.*⟩

[2]ornamental *n*
a plant grown for its beauty

or•na•men•ta•tion \ˌȯr-nə-mən-ˈtā-shən\ *n*
1 the act or process of decorating : the state of being decorated
2 something that adds beauty

or•nate \ȯr-ˈnāt\ *adj*
decorated in a fancy way ⟨an *ornate* costume⟩ ⟨One of the performers wore a traditional costume with an *ornate* headdress.⟩
or•nate•ly *adv*
or•nate•ness *n*

or•nery \ˈȯr-nə-rē\ *adj* **or•neri•er; or•neri•est**
becoming angry or annoyed easily

[1]or•phan \ˈȯr-fən\ *n*
a child whose parents are dead

[2]orphan *vb* **or•phaned; or•phan•ing**
to leave without parents : cause to become an orphan ⟨She was *orphaned* as a baby.⟩

or•phan•age \ˈȯr-fə-nij\ *n*
a place where children who have lost their parents live and are cared for

ostrich

or•tho•don•tist \ˌȯr-thə-ˈdän-təst\ *n*
a dentist who adjusts badly placed or crooked teeth especially through the use of braces

or•tho•dox \ˈȯr-thə-ˌdäks\ *adj*
1 approved as measuring up to some standard : CONVENTIONAL ⟨The doctor practices *orthodox* medicine.⟩
2 closely following the established beliefs of a religion

[1]-ory *n suffix, pl* **-ories**
place of or for ⟨observat*ory*⟩

[2]-ory *adj suffix*
of, relating to, or associated with ⟨sens*ory*⟩

Osage \ō-ˈsāj, ˈō-ˌsāj\ *n, pl* **Osag•es** *or* **Osage**
1 a member of an American Indian people of Missouri
2 the language of the Osage people

os•cil•late \ˈä-sə-ˌlāt\ *vb* **os•cil•lat•ed; os•cil•lat•ing**
to swing or move back and forth between two points

os•mo•sis \äs-ˈmō-səs, äz-\ *n*
a passing of material and especially water through a membrane (as of a living cell) that will not allow all kinds of molecules to pass

os•prey \ˈäs-prē\ *n, pl* **ospreys**
a large hawk that feeds chiefly on fish

os•ten•si•ble \ä-ˈsten-sə-bəl\ *adj*
seeming to be true : APPARENT ⟨The *ostensible* reason for the call was to chat, but then he asked for money.⟩
os•ten•si•bly \-blē\ *adv*

os•ten•ta•tious \ˌä-stən-ˈtā-shəs\ *adj*
attracting or fond of attracting attention by showing off wealth or cleverness

os•tra•cize \ˈä-strə-ˌsīz\ *vb* **os•tra•cized; os•tra•ciz•ing**
to shut out of a group ⟨After I cheated, I was *ostracized* by the other players.⟩

os•trich \ˈä-strich\ *n*
◀ a very large bird of Africa that often weighs as much as 300 pounds (140 kilograms) and runs very fast but cannot fly

[1]oth•er \ˈə-t͟hər\ *adj*
1 being the one (as of two or more) left ⟨I broke my *other* arm.⟩
2 [1]SECOND 1 ⟨Every *other* page contains an illustration.⟩
3 [1]EXTRA, ADDITIONAL ⟨Some *other* guests are coming.⟩
4 different or separate from those already mentioned ⟨Some people believe it and *other* people don't.⟩

[2]other *n*
a remaining or different one ⟨Lift one foot and then the *other.*⟩ ⟨The *others* will follow us later.⟩

[3]other *pron*
another thing ⟨There's always something or *other* going on.⟩

oth•er•wise \ˈə-t͟hər-ˌwīz\ *adv*
1 in another way ⟨He never treated her *otherwise* than with respect.⟩
2 in different circumstances ⟨Thanks for driving; *otherwise* I couldn't go.⟩
3 in other ways ⟨Trucks aren't allowed but it is an *otherwise* busy street.⟩
4 if not : or else

otter: an Oriental short-clawed otter

ot•ter \ˈä-tər\ *n*
▲ a web-footed animal that lives mostly in the water, feeds on fish, and has dark brown fur

ouch \ˈau̇ch\ *interj*
used especially to express sudden pain

ought \ˈȯt\ *helping verb*
1 used to show duty ⟨You *ought* to obey your parents.⟩
2 used to show what it would be wise to do ⟨You *ought* to take care of that cough.⟩
3 used to show what is naturally expected ⟨They *ought* to be here by now.⟩
4 used to show what is correct ⟨You *ought* to get nine for the answer.⟩

oughtn't \ˈȯ-tᵊnt\
ought not

ounce \ˈau̇ns\ *n*
1 a unit of weight equal to $^{1}/_{16}$ pound (about 28 grams)
2 a unit of liquid capacity equal to $^{1}/_{16}$ pint (about 30 milliliters)

our \är, ˈau̇r\ *adj*
relating to or belonging to us : caused by, produced by, or participated in by us ⟨*our* family⟩ ⟨*our* house⟩ ⟨*our* fault⟩ ⟨*our* field trip⟩

ours \ˈau̇rz, ärz\ *pron*
that which belongs to us ⟨This classroom is *ours.*⟩ ⟨These desks are *ours.*⟩

our•selves \au̇r-ˈselvz, är-\ *pron*
our own selves 〈We amused *ourselves.*〉 〈We did it *ourselves.*〉

-ous \əs\ *adj suffix*
full of : having : resembling 〈danger*ous*〉 〈poison*ous*〉

oust \ˈau̇st\ *vb* **oust•ed**; **oust•ing**
to force or drive out (as from office or from possession of something)

oust•er \ˈau̇-stər\ *n*
the act or an instance of forcing out or of being forced out

[1]out \ˈau̇t\ *adv*
1 in a direction away from the inside, center, or surface 〈The boy looked *out* at the snow.〉
2 away from home, business, or the usual or proper place 〈I went *out* for lunch.〉
3 so as to be used up, completed, or discontinued 〈Our food supply ran *out.*〉 〈The patient filled the form *out.*〉 〈He blew the candle *out.*〉
4 so as to be missing or moved from the usual or proper place 〈You left a comma *out.*〉
5 in or into the open 〈The sun came *out* in the afternoon.〉
6 ALOUD 〈The dog cried *out* in pain.〉
7 beyond control or possession 〈She promised not to let the secret *out.*〉
8 so as to be or make unsuccessful in reaching base in baseball 〈Our catcher threw the runner *out.*〉

[2]out *prep*
1 outward through 〈The boy looked *out* the window.〉
2 outward on or along 〈We drove *out* the road by the river.〉
out of
1 from the inside to the outside of : not in 〈I walked *out of* the room.〉 〈They are *out of* town.〉
2 beyond the limits or range of 〈The bird flew *out of* sight.〉 〈The patient is *out of* danger.〉
3 because of 〈They obeyed *out of* fear.〉
4 in a group of 〈I only got one *out of* five right.〉
5 [1]WITHOUT 2 〈The store is *out of* bread.〉
6 FROM 3 〈We made a table *out of* some boxes.〉

[3]out *adj*
1 no longer in power or use 〈The lights are *out.*〉
2 no longer continuing or taking place 〈The fire is *out.*〉 〈School is *out.*〉
3 not confined : not concealed or covered 〈The secret is *out.*〉 〈The sun is *out.*〉
4 ABSENT 1 〈I can't use a basket with its bottom *out.*〉 〈The teacher is *out* today.〉
5 located outside or at a distance
6 being no longer at bat and not successful in reaching base
7 no longer in fashion
8 OUT-OF-BOUNDS

[4]out *n*
the act of causing a baseball player to be unsuccessful in reaching base

out- *prefix*
in a manner that goes beyond 〈*out*number〉 〈*out*run〉

out–and–out \ˌau̇t-ᵊn-ˈau̇t\ *adj*
THOROUGH 1, TOTAL 〈That's an *out-and-out* lie!〉

outboard motor: a man traveling in a boat powered by an outboard motor

out•board motor \ˈau̇t-ˌbȯrd-\ *n*
▲ a small gasoline engine with an attached propeller that can be fastened to the back end of a small boat

out•break \ˈau̇t-ˌbrāk\ *n*
a sudden occurrence or increase of something 〈an *outbreak* of chicken pox〉

out•build•ing \ˈau̇t-ˌbil-diŋ\ *n*
▼ a building (as a shed or stable) separate from a main building

out•burst \ˈau̇t-ˌbərst\ *n*
1 a sudden expression of strong feeling
2 a sudden increase of activity or growth

outcast *n*
a person who is not accepted by society

out•class \au̇t-ˈklas\ *vb* **out•classed**; **out•class•ing**
to be or do much better than : SURPASS

out•come \ˈau̇t-ˌkəm\ *n*
[2]RESULT 1

out•cry \ˈau̇t-ˌkrī\ *n, pl* **out•cries**
1 a loud and excited shout
2 a strong protest 〈Students raised an *outcry* against the new rules.〉

out•dat•ed \au̇t-ˈdā-təd\ *adj*
not modern or current 〈They replaced their *outdated* machinery.〉

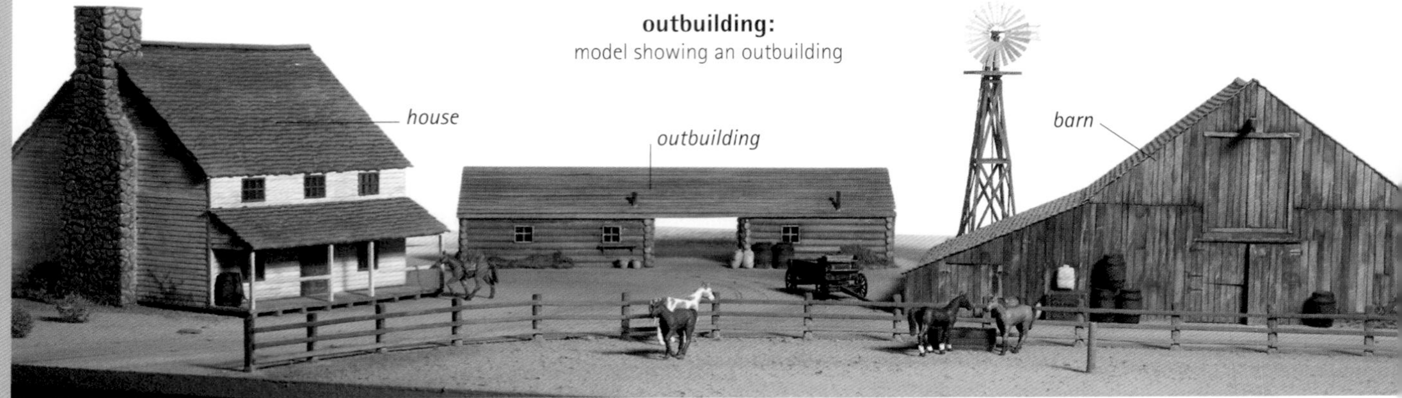

outbuilding:
model showing an outbuilding

A B C D E F G H I J K L M N O P Q R S T U V W X Y Z

out•dis•tance \au̇t-ˈdi-stəns\ *vb* **out•dis•tanced; out•dis•tanc•ing**
to go far ahead of (as in a race)

out•do \au̇t-ˈdü\ *vb* **out•did** \-ˈdid\; **out•done** \-ˈdən\; **out•do•ing** \-ˈdü-iŋ\; **out•does** \-ˈdəz\
to do better than : SURPASS ⟨He always tries to *outdo* everyone.⟩

out•door \ˈau̇t-ˌdȯr\ *adj*
1 used, being, or done outside ⟨an *outdoor* table⟩ ⟨*outdoor* sports⟩
2 preferring to spend time in the open air ⟨an *outdoor* person⟩

¹out•doors \au̇t-ˈdȯrz\ *adv*
outside a building : in or into the open air ⟨She likes to play *outdoors*.⟩

²outdoors *n*
the open air

out•er \ˈau̇-tər\ *adj*
located on the outside or farther out ⟨I peeled off the onion's *outer* skin.⟩

out•er•most \ˈau̇-tər-ˌmōst\ *adj*
farthest out

outer space *n*
the region beyond earth's atmosphere and especially beyond the solar system

out•field \ˈau̇t-ˌfēld\ *n*
the part of a baseball field beyond the infield and between the foul lines

out•field•er \ˈau̇t-ˌfēl-dər\ *n*
▶ a baseball player who plays in the outfield

¹out•fit \ˈau̇t-ˌfit\ *n*
1 a set of clothing worn together
2 the equipment for a special use ⟨a camping *outfit*⟩
3 a group of persons working together or associated in the same activity ⟨I'm working for a landscaping *outfit*.⟩

²outfit *vb* **out•fit•ted; out•fit•ting**
to supply with equipment for a special purpose : EQUIP ⟨Parents need to *outfit* children for school.⟩
out•fit•ter *n*

out•go \ˈau̇t-ˌgō\ *n, pl* **outgoes**
EXPENDITURE 2 ⟨The treasurer told us that income must be greater than *outgo*.⟩

out•go•ing \ˈau̇t-ˌgō-iŋ\ *adj*
1 FRIENDLY 1 ⟨She's an *outgoing* person.⟩
2 leaving a place ⟨an *outgoing* ship⟩
3 retiring from a place or position ⟨the *outgoing* president⟩

out•grow \au̇t-ˈgrō\ *vb* **out•grew** \-ˈgrü\; **out•grown** \-ˈgrōn\; **out•grow•ing**
1 to grow too large or too old for ⟨I *outgrew* my clothes.⟩
2 to grow faster than ⟨One plant *outgrew* all the others.⟩

out•growth \ˈau̇t-ˌgrōth\ *n*
something that grows out of or develops from something else

out•ing \ˈau̇-tiŋ\ *n*
a brief usually outdoor trip for pleasure ⟨We went on an *outing* to the beach.⟩

out•land•ish \au̇t-ˈlan-dish\ *adj*
very strange or unusual : BIZARRE ⟨*outlandish* behavior⟩ ⟨*outlandish* clothes⟩

out•last \au̇t-ˈlast\ *vb* **out•last•ed; out•last•ing**
to last longer than ⟨The boxer *outlasted* his opponent.⟩

¹out•law \ˈau̇t-ˌlȯ\ *n*
a person who has broken the law and is hiding or fleeing to avoid punishment

²outlaw *vb* **out•lawed; out•law•ing**
to make illegal ⟨Dueling was *outlawed*.⟩

out•lay \ˈau̇t-ˌlā\ *n*
an amount of money spent

out•let \ˈau̇t-ˌlet\ *n*
1 a place or opening for letting something out ⟨The lake has several *outlets*.⟩
2 a way of releasing or expressing a feeling or impulse ⟨I needed an *outlet* for my anger.⟩
3 a device (as in a wall) into which the prongs of an electrical plug are inserted for making connection with an electrical circuit

outfielder: an outfielder tries to make a catch during a baseball game

¹outline 2: the sketched outline of a man's head

¹out•line \ˈau̇t-ˌlīn\ *n*
1 a line that traces or forms the outer limits of an object or figure and shows its shape
2 ▲ a drawing or picture or style of drawing in which only the outer edges of an object or figure are shown ⟨*outlines* of animals⟩
3 an often numbered or lettered list of the important parts of something (as an essay)
4 a short treatment of a subject ⟨an *outline* of world history⟩

²outline *vb* **out•lined; out•lin•ing**
1 to draw or trace the outer edges of ⟨*Outline* the circle in gold.⟩
2 to list or describe the main features or parts of ⟨He *outlined* our responsibilities.⟩

out•live \au̇t-ˈliv\ *vb* **out•lived; out•liv•ing**
to live or last longer than ⟨That rule has *outlived* its usefulness.⟩

out•look \ˈau̇t-ˌlu̇k\ *n*
1 a view from a certain place ⟨There are scenic *outlooks* along the highway.⟩
2 a way of thinking about or looking at things ⟨He has a cheerful *outlook*.⟩
3 conditions that seem to lie ahead ⟨What's the *outlook* for business?⟩

out•ly•ing \ˈau̇t-ˌlī-iŋ\ *adj*
being far from a central point : REMOTE ⟨We saw *outlying* parts of the city.⟩

out•mod•ed \au̇t-ˈmō-dəd\ *adj*
no longer in style or in use ⟨an *outmoded* dress⟩ ⟨*outmoded* equipment⟩

out•num•ber \au̇t-ˈnəm-bər\ *vb* **out•num•bered; out•num•ber•ing**
to be more than in number

out–of–bounds \ˌau̇t-əv-ˈbau̇ndz\ *adv or adj*
outside the limits of the playing area in a game or sport

out–of–date \ˌau̇t-əv-ˈdāt\ *adj*
not modern or current

out–of–doors \ˌau̇t-əv-ˈdȯrz\ *n*
²OUTDOORS ⟨She loves to paint the *out-of-doors*.⟩

out of doors *adv*
[1]OUTDOORS ⟨He worked *out of doors.*⟩

out•post \'au̇t-,pōst\ *n*
1 a guard placed at a distance from a military force or camp
2 the place occupied by such a guard
3 an outlying settlement

out•pour•ing \'au̇t-,pȯr-iŋ\ *n*
an act of expressing or giving freely ⟨There was an *outpouring* of sympathy.⟩

[1]**out•put** \'au̇t-,pu̇t\ *n*
1 something produced ⟨The factory increased steel *output.*⟩
2 the information produced by a computer

[2]**output** *vb* **out•put•ted** *or* **out•put**; **out•put•ting**
to produce something ⟨Computers *output* data quickly.⟩

[1]**out•rage** \'au̇t-,rāj\ *n*
1 angry feelings caused by a hurtful, unjust, or insulting act
2 an act that is hurtful or unjust or shows disrespect for a person's feelings

[2]**outrage** *vb* **out•raged**; **out•rag•ing**
1 to cause to feel anger or strong resentment ⟨We were *outraged* by the way we were treated.⟩
2 to cause to suffer great insult

out•ra•geous \au̇t-'rā-jəs\ *adj*
1 extremely annoying, insulting, or shameful ⟨Her lies are *outrageous.*⟩
2 very strange or unusual ⟨They wore *outrageous* costumes.⟩

[1]**out•right** \au̇t-'rīt\ *adv*
1 COMPLETELY ⟨They rejected the idea *outright.*⟩
2 without holding back ⟨He laughed *outright* at the story.⟩
3 quickly and entirely ⟨Fire destroyed the house *outright.*⟩

[2]**out•right** \'au̇t-,rīt\ *adj*
1 complete and total : very clear or obvious ⟨an *outright* lie⟩
2 done, made, or given with no restrictions or exceptions ⟨an *outright* gift⟩

out•run \au̇t-'rən\ *vb* **out•ran** \-'ran\; **out•run**; **out•run•ning**
to run or move faster than

out•sell \au̇t-'sel\ *vb* **out•sold** \-'sōld\; **out•sell•ing**
to sell or be sold more than ⟨Apples *outsold* bananas.⟩

out•set \'au̇t-,set\ *n*
BEGINNING 1, START

out•shine \au̇t-'shīn\ *vb* **out•shone** \-'shōn\; **out•shin•ing**
1 to shine brighter than
2 to do better than : OUTDO

[1]**out•side** \au̇t-'sīd\ *n*
1 an outer side or surface ⟨The *outside* of the house needs painting.⟩
2 the greatest amount or limit : MOST ⟨The job will take a week at the *outside.*⟩

[2]**outside** *adj*
1 of, relating to, or being on the outside ⟨the *outside* edge⟩
2 not belonging to a place or group ⟨*outside* influences⟩
3 barely possible ⟨an *outside* chance⟩

[3]**outside** *adv*
[1]OUTDOORS ⟨Let's play *outside.*⟩

[4]**outside** *prep*
1 on or to the outside of ⟨*outside* the door⟩
2 beyond the limits of ⟨*outside* the law⟩

out•sid•er \au̇t-'sī-dər\ *n*
a person who does not belong to a particular group

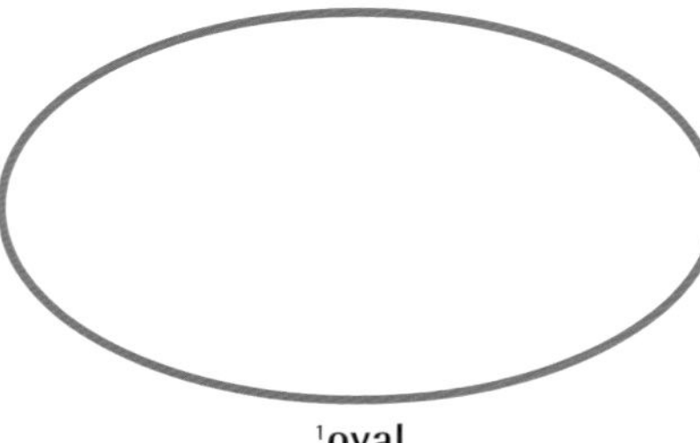

[1]**oval**

out•size \'au̇t-,sīz\ *adj*
unusually large

out•skirts \'au̇t-,skərts\ *n pl*
the area that lies away from the center of a city or town

out•smart \au̇t-'smärt\ *vb* **out•smart•ed**; **out•smart•ing**
to beat or trick by being more clever than

out•spo•ken \au̇t-'spō-kən\ *adj*
talking in a free and honest way : BLUNT ⟨an *outspoken* critic⟩
out•spo•ken•ly *adv*
out•spo•ken•ness *n*

out•spread \au̇t-'spred\ *adj*
spread out completely ⟨*outspread* wings⟩

out•stand•ing \au̇t-'stan-diŋ\ *adj*
1 standing out especially because of excellence ⟨an *outstanding* musician⟩ ⟨an *outstanding* job⟩
2 UNPAID ⟨*outstanding* bills⟩
synonyms see NOTICEABLE
out•stand•ing•ly *adv*

out•stay \au̇t-'stā\ *vb* **out•stayed**; **out•stay•ing**
OVERSTAY

out•stretched \au̇t-'strecht\ *adj*
stretched out ⟨*outstretched* arms⟩

out•strip \au̇t-'strip\ *vb* **out•stripped**; **out•strip•ping**
1 to go faster or farther than ⟨She *outstripped* the other runners.⟩
2 to do better than ⟨We *outstripped* all rivals.⟩

[1]**out•ward** \'au̇t-wərd\ *adj*
1 moving or turned toward the outside or away from a center ⟨an *outward* flow⟩
2 showing on the outside ⟨*outward* signs of fear⟩

[2]**outward** *or* **out•wards** \'au̇t-wərdz\ *adv*
away from a center ⟨The city stretches *outward* for miles.⟩

out•ward•ly \'au̇t-wərd-lē\ *adv*
on the outside : in outward appearance ⟨Though nervous, he remained *outwardly* calm.⟩

out•weigh \au̇t-'wā\ *vb* **out•weighed**; **out•weigh•ing**
to be greater than in weight or importance

out•wit \au̇t-'wit\ *vb* **out•wit•ted**; **out•wit•ting**
OUTSMART

ova *pl of* OVUM

[1]**oval** \'ō-vəl\ *n*
◀ something having the shape of an egg or ellipse ⟨The racetrack is an *oval.*⟩

[2]**oval** *adj*
having the shape of an egg or ellipse : ELLIPTICAL

ova•ry \'ō-və-rē\ *n*, *pl* **ova•ries**
1 one of the usually two organs in the body of female animals in which eggs are produced
2 ▶ the larger rounded lower part of the pistil of a flower that contains the ovules in which the seeds are formed

seed
ovary

ovary 2: cross-section showing the ovary of a rose

ova•tion \ō-'vā-shən\ *n*
an expression of approval or enthusiasm made by clapping or cheering

ov•en \'ə-vən\ *n*
▶ a heated chamber (as in a stove) for baking, heating, or drying

[1]**over** \'ō-vər\ *adv*
1 across a barrier or space ⟨Just climb *over.*⟩ ⟨Can you move *over?*⟩
2 in a direction down or forward and down ⟨It fell *over.*⟩
3 across the brim ⟨The soup boiled *over.*⟩
4 so as to bring the underside up ⟨Turn the cards *over.*⟩
5 from one person or side to another ⟨Hand it *over.*⟩

6 to someone's home ⟨I asked them *over.*⟩
7 beyond a limit ⟨The show ran a minute *over.*⟩
8 more than needed ⟨She has food left *over.*⟩
9 once more : AGAIN ⟨Please do it *over.*⟩
10 [1]OVERNIGHT 1 ⟨Can I sleep *over?*⟩
over and over many times

[2]**over** *prep*
1 above in place : higher than ⟨He towered *over* us.⟩
2 above in power or value ⟨I respect those *over* me.⟩
3 in front of ⟨We have a big lead *over* the others.⟩
4 more than ⟨It costs *over* five dollars.⟩
5 down upon ⟨He hit me *over* the head.⟩
6 all through or throughout ⟨We drove all *over* town.⟩
7 on or along the surface of ⟨Glide *over* the ice.⟩
8 on or to the other side of : ACROSS ⟨Jump *over* the puddle.⟩
9 down from the top or edge of ⟨He fell *over* the edge.⟩
10 having to do with ⟨They are still arguing *over* it.⟩

[3]**over** *adj*
1 being more than needed or expected ⟨The balance was three dollars *over.*⟩
2 brought or come to an end ⟨Those days are *over.*⟩

oven: oven with open door showing uncooked desserts

over- \'ō-vər, ˌō-vər\ *prefix*
more than usual, normal, or proper ⟨*over*load⟩ ⟨*over*size⟩

[1]**over•all** \ˌō-vər-'ȯl\ *adv*
as a whole : in most ways ⟨They did a nice job *overall.*⟩

[2]**overall** *adj*
including everyone or everything ⟨*overall* expenses⟩

over•alls \'ō-vər-ˌȯlz\ *n pl*
loose pants usually with shoulder straps and a piece in front to cover the chest

over•bear•ing \ˌō-vər-'ber-iŋ\ *adj*
acting in a proud or bossy way toward other people

over•board \'ō-vər-ˌbȯrd\ *adv*
1 over the side of a ship into the water ⟨Don't fall *overboard!*⟩
2 to extremes of enthusiasm ⟨He went *overboard* with this party.⟩

over•bur•den \ˌō-vər-'bər-dᵊn\ *vb* **over•bur•dened; over•bur•den•ing**
to burden too heavily

over•cast \'ō-vər-ˌkast\ *adj*
covered with or darkened by clouds

over•charge \ˌō-vər-'chärj\ *vb* **over•charged; over•charg•ing**
to charge too much money

over•coat \'ō-vər-ˌkōt\ *n*
▶ a heavy coat worn over indoor clothing

over•come \ˌō-vər-'kəm\ *vb* **over•came** \-'kām\; **overcome; over•com•ing**
1 to win a victory over : CONQUER ⟨Soldiers *overcame* the enemy.⟩
2 to gain control of through great effort ⟨He *overcame* his fear of heights.⟩
3 to cause to lose physical ability or emotional control ⟨Firefighters were *overcome* by smoke.⟩ ⟨The family was *overcome* by grief.⟩

over•crowd \ˌō-vər-'krau̇d\ *vb* **over•crowd•ed; over•crowd•ing**
to cause to be too crowded ⟨Passengers *overcrowded* the train.⟩

over•do \ˌō-vər-'dü\ *vb* **over•did** \-'did\; **over•done** \-'dən\; **over•do•ing** \-'dü-iŋ\
1 to do too much of ⟨Don't *overdo* it exercising.⟩
2 to use too much of ⟨They *overdid* the decorations.⟩
3 to cook too long ⟨I *overdid* the steak.⟩

over•dose \'ō-vər-ˌdōs\ *n*
too large a dose (as of a drug)

over•dress \ˌō-vər-'dres\ *vb* **over•dressed; over•dress•ing**
to dress in clothes too fancy for an occasion

over•due \ˌō-vər-'dü, -'dyü\ *adj*
1 not paid when due ⟨*overdue* bills⟩
2 delayed beyond an expected time ⟨The plane was an hour *overdue.*⟩
3 more than ready ⟨He is *overdue* for a haircut.⟩

over•eat \ˌō-vər-'ēt\ *vb* **over•ate** \-'āt\; **over•eat•en** \-'ē-tᵊn\; **over•eat•ing**
to eat too much
over•eat•er \ˌō-vər-'ē-tər\ *n*

over•es•ti•mate \ˌō-vər-'e-stə-ˌmāt\ *vb* **over•es•ti•mat•ed; over•es•ti•mat•ing**
to estimate too highly ⟨I *overestimated* the number of guests.⟩

[1]**over•flow** \ˌō-vər-'flō\ *vb* **over•flowed; over•flow•ing**
1 to flow over the top of ⟨The river *overflowed* its banks.⟩
2 to flow over bounds ⟨The creek *overflows* every spring.⟩
3 to fill or become filled beyond capacity ⟨The basket was *overflowing* with candy.⟩
4 to fill a space up and spread beyond its limits ⟨The crowd *overflowed* into the street.⟩

overcoat

[2]**over•flow** \'ō-vər-ˌflō\ *n*
1 a flowing over ⟨Dams couldn't stop the *overflow.*⟩
2 something that flows over or fills a space and spreads beyond its limits

over•grown \ˌō-vər-'grōn\ *adj*
1 grown too big ⟨*overgrown* boys⟩
2 covered with plants that have grown in an uncontrolled way ⟨an *overgrown* path⟩

[1]**over•hand** \'ō-vər-ˌhand\ *adj*
made with the hand brought forward and down from above the shoulder

[2]**overhand** *adv*
with an overhand movement ⟨I threw the ball *overhand.*⟩

[1]**over•hang** \'ō-vər-,haŋ\ *vb* **over•hung** \-,həŋ\; **over•hang•ing**
to stick out or hang over

[2]**overhang** *n*
▶ a part that overhangs ⟨the *overhang* of a roof⟩

[1]**over•haul** \,ō-vər-'hȯl\ *vb* **over•hauled**; **over•haul•ing**
1 to examine thoroughly and make necessary repairs or improvements on ⟨Mechanics *overhauled* the car's engine.⟩
2 to catch up with : OVERTAKE ⟨Police *overhauled* the thieves.⟩

[2]**over•haul** \'ō-vər-,hȯl\ *n*
an instance of overhauling

[1]**over•head** \,ō-vər-'hed\ *adv*
above someone's head : in the sky or space above someone ⟨A chandelier hung directly *overhead.*⟩

[2]**over•head** \'ō-vər-,hed\ *adj*
placed in the space above someone ⟨an *overhead* light⟩

[3]**over•head** \'ō-vər-,hed\ *n*
the general expenses (as for rent or heat) of a business

over•hear \,ō-vər-'hir\ *vb* **over•heard** \-'hərd\; **over•hear•ing** \-'hir-iŋ\
to hear something by accident without the speaker's knowledge

over•heat \,ō-vər-'hēt\ *vb* **over•heat•ed**; **over•heat•ing**
to heat too much : become too hot ⟨The engine *overheated.*⟩

over•joyed \,ō-vər-'jȯid\ *adj*
filled with great joy

[1]**over•land** \'ō-vər-,land\ *adv*
by land rather than by water ⟨travel *overland*⟩

[2]**overland** *adj*
going by land rather than by water ⟨an *overland* route⟩

over•lap \,ō-vər-'lap\ *vb* **over•lapped**; **over•lap•ping**
▼ to place or be placed so that a part of one covers a part of another ⟨The roof shingles *overlap.*⟩

²overhang: the overhang on a stable roof

overlap: wooden shingles overlapping

[1]**over•lay** \,ō-vər-'lā\ *vb* **over•laid** \-'lād\; **over•lay•ing**
to lay or spread over or across ⟨The table top is *overlaid* with ceramic tiles.⟩

[2]**over•lay** \'ō-vər-,lā\ *n*
a usually thin covering that is laid over or across something

over•load \,ō-vər-'lōd\ *vb* **over•load•ed**; **over•load•ing**
to put too great a load on or in

over•look \,ō-vər-'lu̇k\ *vb* **over•looked**; **over•look•ing**
1 to look down upon or provide a view of from above ⟨The house *overlooks* a valley.⟩
2 to fail to see : MISS ⟨The detective *overlooked* an important clue.⟩
3 to pay no attention to : IGNORE ⟨I'll *overlook* the mistake this time.⟩

over•ly \'ō-vər-lē\ *adv*
by too much : to an excessive degree ⟨*overly* worried⟩ ⟨an *overly* long movie⟩

[1]**over•night** \,ō-vər-'nīt\ *adv*
1 during or through the night ⟨Can I stay *overnight?*⟩
2 very quickly or suddenly ⟨He became famous *overnight.*⟩

[2]**overnight** *adj*
1 done or lasting through the night ⟨an *overnight* journey⟩
2 staying for the night ⟨an *overnight* guest⟩
3 for use on short trips ⟨an *overnight* bag⟩
4 happening very quickly or suddenly ⟨an *overnight* success⟩

over•pass \'ō-vər-,pas\ *n*
1 ▶ a crossing (as of two highways or a highway and a railroad) at different levels usually by means of a bridge
2 the upper level of an overpass

over•pop•u•la•tion \,ō-vər-,pä-pyə-'lā-shən\ *n*
the condition of having too many people living in a certain area

over•pow•er \,ō-vər-'pau̇-ər\ *vb* **over•pow•ered**; **over•pow•er•ing**
1 to overcome by greater force : DEFEAT ⟨The enemy was *overpowered.*⟩
2 to affect by being too strong ⟨The odor *overpowered* us.⟩

over•rate \,ō-vər-'rāt\ *vb* **over•rat•ed**; **over•rat•ing**
to value or praise too highly ⟨The restaurant is *overrated.*⟩

over•re•act \,ō-vər-rē-'akt\ *vb* **over•re•act•ed**; **over•re•act•ing**
to respond with an emotion that is too strong or an action that is extreme or unnecessary

over•ride \,ō-vər-'rīd\ *vb* **over•rode** \-'rōd\; **over•rid•den** \-'ri-dᵊn\; **over•rid•ing** \-'rī-diŋ\
to push aside as less important ⟨Don't let anger *override* sense.⟩

over•ripe \,ō-vər-'rīp\ *adj*
passed beyond ripeness toward decay ⟨*overripe* fruit⟩

over•rule \,ō-vər-'rül\ *vb* **over•ruled**; **over•rul•ing**
1 to decide against ⟨The judge *overruled* the objection.⟩
2 to set aside a decision or ruling made by someone having less authority ⟨Mother *overruled* our plans.⟩

over•run \ˌō-vər-ˈrən\ *vb* **over•ran** \-ˈran\; **overrun**; **over•run•ning**
1 to take over and occupy by force ⟨The outpost was *overrun* by the enemy.⟩
2 to run or go past ⟨The runner *overran* second base.⟩
3 to spread over so as to cover ⟨Weeds *overran* the garden.⟩

[1]**over•seas** \ˌō-vər-ˈsēz\ *adv*
to or in a foreign country that is across the sea ⟨I lived *overseas.*⟩

over•size \ˌō-vər-ˈsīz\ *or* **over•sized** \-ˈsīzd\ *adj*
larger than the usual or normal size ⟨an *oversize* package⟩

over•sleep \ˌō-vər-ˈslēp\ *vb* **over•slept** \-ˈslept\; **over•sleep•ing**
to sleep beyond the usual time or beyond the time set for getting up

over•state \ˌō-vər-ˈstāt\ *vb* **over•stat•ed**; **over•stat•ing**
to put in too strong terms : EXAGGERATE ⟨He *overstated* the usefulness of his invention.⟩

overpass 1: an overpass above a freeway

[2]**overseas** *adj*
involving, occurring in, or intended for lands across the sea ⟨*overseas* trade⟩

over•see \ˌō-vər-ˈsē\ *vb* **over•saw** \-ˈsȯ\; **over•seen** \-ˈsēn\; **over•see•ing**
to be in charge of : SUPERVISE

over•seer \ˈō-vər-ˌsir\ *n*
a person who supervises something

over•shad•ow \ˌō-vər-ˈsha-dō\ *vb* **over•shad•owed**; **over•shad•ow•ing**
1 to cast a shadow over : DARKEN
2 to be or become more important than

over•shoe \ˈō-vər-ˌshü\ *n*
a shoe (as of rubber) worn over another for protection

over•shoot \ˌō-vər-ˈshüt\ *vb* **over•shot** \-ˈshät\; **over•shoot•ing**
to miss by going beyond

over•sight \ˈō-vər-ˌsīt\ *n*
1 the act or duty of overseeing : watchful care
2 an error or something forgotten through carelessness or haste

over•sim•pli•fy \ˌō-vər-ˈsim-plə-ˌfī\ *vb* **over•sim•pli•fied**; **over•sim•pli•fy•ing**
to cause (something) to seem simpler than it is ⟨He *oversimplified* a complicated problem.⟩

over•stay \ˌō-vər-ˈstā\ *vb* **over•stayed**; **over•stay•ing**
to stay beyond or longer than ⟨We *overstayed* our welcome.⟩

over•step \ˌō-vər-ˈstep\ *vb* **over•stepped**; **over•step•ping**
to step over or beyond : EXCEED ⟨She *overstepped* her authority.⟩

over•sup•ply \ˌō-vər-sə-ˈplī\ *n*, *pl* **over•sup•plies**
a supply that is too large

overt \ō-ˈvərt, ˈō-vərt\ *adj*
not secret or hidden

over•take \ˌō-vər-ˈtāk\ *vb* **over•took** \-ˈtu̇k\; **over•tak•en** \-ˈtā-kən\; **over•tak•ing**
1 to catch up with and often pass ⟨I *overtook* the runner ahead.⟩
2 to come upon or happen to suddenly or without warning ⟨*overtaken* by rain⟩

[1]**over•throw** \ˌō-vər-ˈthrō\ *vb* **over•threw** \-ˈthrü\; **over•thrown** \-ˈthrōn\; **over•throw•ing**
1 OVERTURN 1 ⟨Wind *overthrew* the flower pots.⟩
2 to cause the fall or end of : DESTROY ⟨Rebels *overthrew* the government.⟩

[2]**over•throw** \ˈō-vər-ˌthrō\ *n*
an act of causing the fall or end of : the state of being overthrown : DEFEAT

over•time \ˈō-vər-ˌtīm\ *n*
1 time spent working that is more than one usually works in a day or a week
2 extra time added to a game when the score is tied at the end of the normal playing time

over•ture \ˈō-vər-ˌchu̇r\ *n*
1 something first offered or suggested with the hope of reaching an agreement ⟨Old enemies made *overtures* of peace.⟩
2 a piece of music played at the beginning of an opera or musical play

over•turn \ˌō-vər-ˈtərn\ *vb* **over•turned**; **over•turn•ing**
1 to turn over or upside down ⟨Waves *overturned* the boat.⟩
2 to reverse or cancel something previously decided or ordered ⟨The judge *overturned* the lower court's ruling.⟩

over•view \ˈō-vər-ˌvyü\ *n*
a short explanation or description : SUMMARY ⟨an *overview* of American history⟩

over•weight \ˌō-vər-ˈwāt\ *adj*
weighing more than is normal, necessary, or allowed ⟨an *overweight* suitcase.⟩

over•whelm \ˌō-vər-ˈhwelm, -ˈwelm\ *vb* **over•whelmed**; **over•whelm•ing**
1 to overcome completely (as with great force or emotion) ⟨The larger army *overwhelmed* the troops.⟩ ⟨She was *overwhelmed* with grief.⟩
2 to cover over completely : SUBMERGE ⟨Waves *overwhelmed* the small boat.⟩

over•whelm•ing \ˌō-vər-ˈhwel-miŋ, -ˈwel-\ *adj*
1 very great or strong ⟨an *overwhelming* majority⟩
2 very difficult or confusing ⟨an *overwhelming* task⟩

[1]**over•work** \ˌō-vər-ˈwərk\ *vb* **over•worked**; **over•work•ing**
1 to work or cause to work too much or too hard ⟨The captain *overworked* the crew.⟩
2 to use too much or too often ⟨*overworked* phrases⟩

[2]**overwork** *n*
too much work

over•wrought \ˌō-vər-ˈrȯt\ *adj*
very excited or upset

ovule \ˈäv-yül, ˈōv-\ *n*
a tiny structure in the ovary of a flower and on the scale of a cone that contains an egg cell and can develop into a seed following fertilization

a b c d e f g h i j k l m n **o** p q r s t u v w x y z

ovum \ˈō-vəm\ *n, pl* **ova** \ˈō-və\
EGG CELL

owe \ˈō\ *vb* **owed**; **ow•ing**
1 to be obligated to pay, give, or return ⟨I still *owe* 100 dollars.⟩ ⟨I don't *owe* any favors to anyone.⟩
2 to be in debt to ⟨You *owe* me money.⟩
3 to have as a result ⟨I *owe* my success to hard work.⟩

owing to *prep*
because of ⟨absent *owing to* illness⟩

owl \ˈau̇l\ *n*
▼ a large bird with big head and eyes, hooked bill, and strong claws that is active at night and feeds on small animals
owl•ish *adj*

owl•et \ˈau̇-lət\ *n*
a young or small owl

[1]**own** \ˈōn\ *adj*
used to show the fact that something belongs to or relates to a particular person or thing and no other ⟨I have my *own* room.⟩

[2]**own** *vb* **owned**; **own•ing**
1 to have or hold as property ⟨She *owns* two cars.⟩
2 to admit that something is true ⟨He *owned* to being scared.⟩

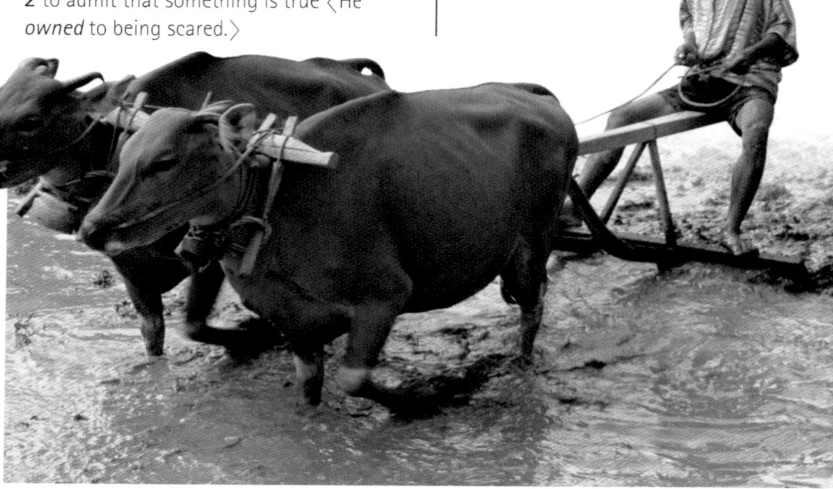

ox 2: a farmer using oxen to plow his field

▶ owl

There are some 130 species of owl, most of which hunt at night. Owls use their large, forward-facing eyes and sharp hearing to locate their prey of small birds, insects, frogs, and rodents — even in total darkness. Special fringed feathers reduce the sound of their flapping wings, allowing owls to swoop down almost silently on their prey.

fringed flight feathers

features of a barn owl

large eye

flat face

tail feather

sharp talon

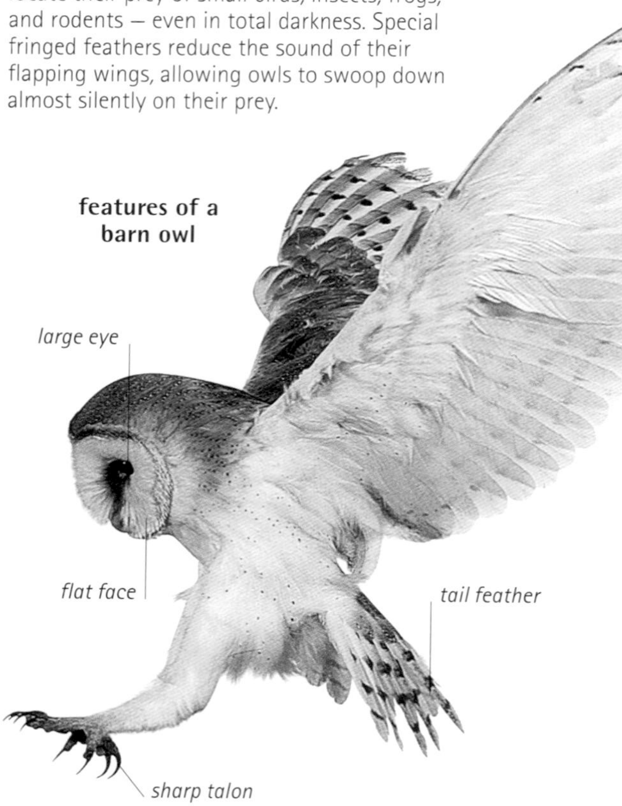

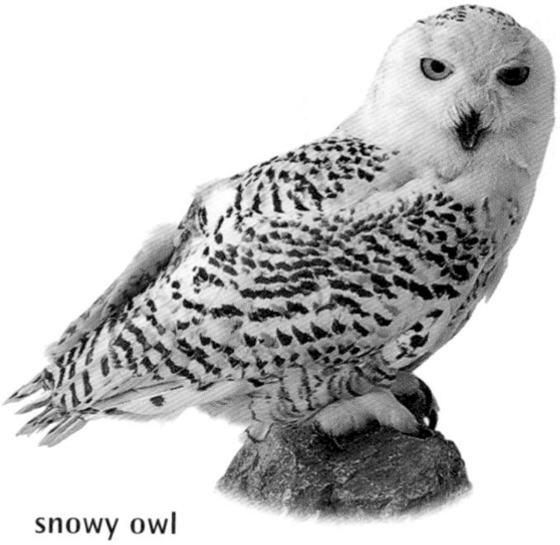

snowy owl

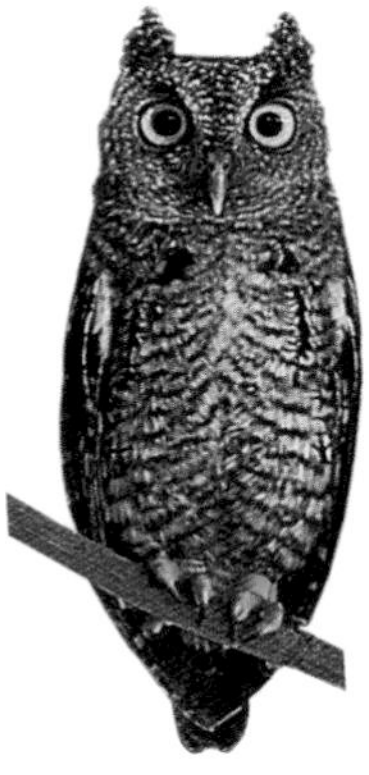

screech owl

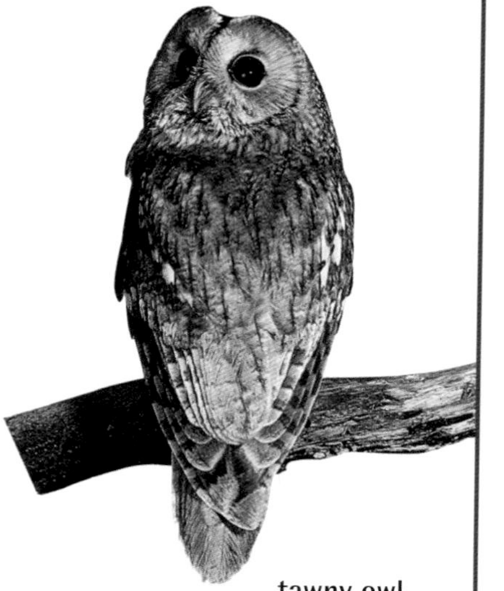

tawny owl

own•er \'ō-nər\ *n*
a person who owns something

own•er•ship \'ō-nər-ˌship\ *n*
the state or fact of owning something ⟨home *ownership*⟩

ox \'äks\ *n, pl* **ox•en** \'äk-sən\ *also* **ox**
1 the male or female of common domestic cattle or a closely related animal (as a yak)
2◀ an adult castrated male ox used especially for hauling loads

ox•bow \'äks-ˌbō\ *n*
▼ a bend in a river in the shape of a U

oxbow

ox•cart \'äks-ˌkärt\ *n*
a cart pulled by oxen

ox•i•da•tion \ˌäk-sə-'dā-shən\ *n*
the process of oxidizing

ox•ide \'äk-ˌsīd\ *n*
a compound of oxygen with another element or group of elements ⟨an iron *oxide*⟩

ox•i•dize \'äk-sə-ˌdīz\ *vb* **ox•i•dized**; **ox•i•diz•ing**
to combine or become combined with oxygen

ox•y•gen \'äk-si-jən\ *n*
a chemical element found in the air as a colorless odorless tasteless gas that is necessary for life

▶ **Word History** People once thought that all acids were formed by adding oxygen to some other substance. This belief turned out not to be true. However, it did give oxygen its name. The first part of the word, *oxy-*, came from Greek *oxys*, meaning "acid" or "sharp." The second part, *-gen*, came from a Greek element meaning "producing" or "giving rise to."

oys•ter \'ȯi-stər\ *n*
▶ a shellfish that lives on stony bottoms (**oyster beds**) in shallow seawater, has a rough grayish shell made up of two hinged parts, and is often used for food

oz. *abbr*
1 ounce
2 ounces

ozone \'ō-ˌzōn\ *n*
a faintly blue form of oxygen that is present in the air in small quantities

ozone layer *n*
a layer of the earth's upper atmosphere that is characterized by high ozone content which blocks most of the sun's ultraviolet radiation from entering the lower atmosphere

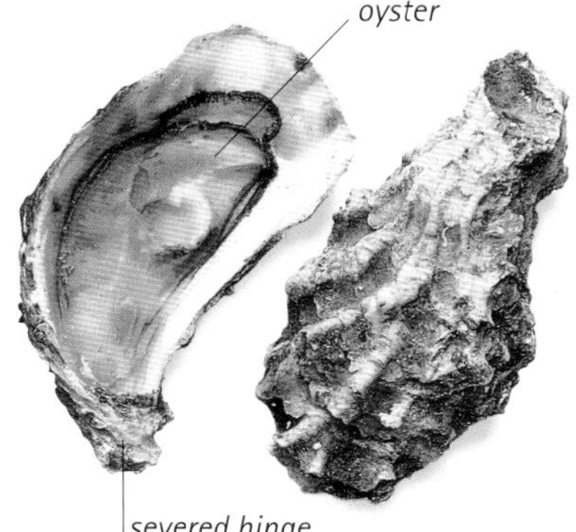

oyster: an oyster in its shell, shown with the shell halves separated

Pp

Sounds of P: The letter **P** makes the sound heard in *pop* and *put*. The combination of **P** and **H** makes the sound of the letter **F**, as in *photo*. In some words, **P** is silent, as in *psychology*.

p \ˈpē\ *n*, *pl* **p's** *or* **ps** \ˈpēz\ *often cap*
the sixteenth letter of the English alphabet

p. *abbr* page

pa \ˈpä, ˈpȯ\ *n*
[1]FATHER 1

PA, Pa. *abbr* Pennsylvania

[1]**pace** \ˈpās\ *n*
1 the speed of moving forward or ahead
2 the speed at which something is done or happens 〈The *pace* of production needs to increase.〉
3 a horse's gait in which the legs on the same side move at the same time
4 a single step or its length

[2]**pace** *vb* **paced**; **pac•ing**
1 to walk back and forth across 〈The nervous man began *pacing* the floor.〉
2 to walk with slow steps
3 to measure by steps 〈We *paced* off the length of the garden.〉
4 to set or regulate the speed at which something is done or happens

pa•cif•ic \pə-ˈsi-fik\ *adj*
1 [3]CALM 1, PEACEFUL 〈*pacific* skies〉
2 loving or wanting peace 〈a *pacific* man〉

pac•i•fy \ˈpa-sə-ˌfī\ *vb* **pac•i•fied**; **pac•i•fy•ing**
to make peaceful or quiet **:** CALM, SOOTHE 〈The babysitter tried to *pacify* the crying baby.〉

[1]**pack** \ˈpak\ *n*
1 a bundle arranged for carrying especially on the back of a person or animal
2 a group of like persons or things 〈a Cub Scout *pack*〉 〈a wolf *pack*〉

[2]**pack** *vb* **packed**; **pack•ing**
1 to put into a container or bundle 〈*Pack* your clothes.〉
2 to put things into 〈Have you *packed* a suitcase?〉
3 to crowd into so as to make full **:** CRAM 〈Students *packed* the auditorium.〉
4 to send away 〈Parents *pack* children off to school.〉
pack•er *n*

> ▶ **Synonyms** PACK, CRAM, and STUFF mean to fill something to its limit or beyond. PACK may be used for the act of filling up tightly in an orderly way. 〈*Pack* a trunk.〉 Or it may mean filling up something too much. 〈People *packed* the room.〉 CRAM usually is used when something has been filled in a forceful, careless, or disorderly way. 〈She *crammed* everything into one small box.〉 STUFF means filling something as much as it will hold and often to the point of bulging. 〈I *stuffed* my bag with apples.〉

pack•age \ˈpa-kij\ *n*
1 a bundle made up for mailing or transporting
2 a container that covers or holds something 〈The ingredients are listed on the *package*.〉
3 something that comes in a container 〈a *package* of gum〉

pack•et \ˈpa-kət\ *n*
a small package

pact \ˈpakt\ *n*
AGREEMENT 3, TREATY

[1]**pad** \ˈpad\ *n*
1 a tablet of writing or drawing paper
2 something soft used for protection or comfort **:** CUSHION
3 one of the cushioned parts of the underside of the feet of some animals (as a dog)
4 ▼ a floating leaf of a water plant (as a water lily)
5 a piece of material that holds ink used in inking rubber stamps

[2]**pad** *vb* **pad•ded**; **pad•ding**
to move with quiet steps

[3]**pad** *vb* **pad•ded**; **pad•ding**
1 to stuff or cover with soft material 〈We made a bed for the dog by *padding* a box.〉
2 to make longer by adding words 〈*pad* a speech〉 〈He likes to *pad* a speech with humorous stories.〉

pad•ding \ˈpa-diŋ\ *n*
soft material used to cover or line a surface

[1]**pad•dle** \ˈpa-dᵊl\ *vb* **pad•dled**; **pad•dling**
1 to move or drive forward with an instrument like an oar or with short quick movements of hands and feet
2 to stir, mix, or beat with a paddle

[1]**pad 4:** water lily pads

paddock 1: horses grazing in a paddock

²paddle *n*
1 an instrument like an oar used in moving and steering a small boat (as a canoe)
2 an implement having a broad flat end and used for beating, mixing, or hitting
3 one of the broad boards at the outer edge of a waterwheel or a paddle wheel

³paddle *vb* **paddled**; **paddling**
to move or splash about in the water

paddle wheel *n*
a wheel with broad boards near its outer edge used to make a boat move

²page 2: a boy dressed as a 15th-century page

pad•dock \ˈpa-dək\ *n*
1 ▲ an enclosed area where animals are put to eat grass or to exercise
2 an enclosed area where racehorses are saddled and paraded

pad•dy \ˈpa-dē\ *n, pl* **paddies**
wet land in which rice is grown

¹pad•lock \ˈpad-ˌläk\ *n*
a removable lock with a curved piece that snaps into a catch

²padlock *vb* **pad•locked**; **pad•lock•ing**
to fasten with a removable lock

¹pa•gan \ˈpā-gən\ *n*
²HEATHEN 1

²pagan *adj*
of or relating to heathens or their worship : HEATHEN 〈a *pagan* temple〉

¹page \ˈpāj\ *n*
1 one side of a printed or written sheet of paper
2 a large section of computer memory
3 the information found at a single World Wide Web address

²page *n*
1 a person employed (as by a hotel or the United States Congress) to carry messages or run errands
2 ◀ a boy being trained to be a knight in the Middle Ages

³page *vb* **paged**; **pag•ing**
to send for or contact someone by a public announcement or by using a pager

pag•eant \ˈpa-jənt\ *n*
1 a grand and fancy public ceremony and display
2 an entertainment made up of scenes based on history or legend 〈a Christmas *pageant*〉
3 a contest in which a group of women or girls are judged 〈a beauty *pageant*〉

pag•er \ˈpā-jər\ *n*
a small electronic device that beeps, vibrates, or flashes when it receives a signal

pa•go•da \pə-ˈgō-də\ *n*
▼ a tower of several stories built as a temple or memorial in eastern or southeastern Asia

pagoda: a pagoda in the city of Harbin, China

paid *past and past participle of* PAY

pail \ˈpāl\ *n*
1 a usually round container with a handle : BUCKET
2 PAILFUL 〈He poured out a *pail* of water.〉

pail•ful \ˈpāl-ˌfu̇l\ *n, pl* **pail•fuls** \-ˌfu̇lz\
the amount a bucket holds

¹pain \ˈpān\ *n*
1 physical suffering that accompanies a bodily disorder (as a disease or an injury) 〈The medicine relieves *pain*.〉
2 a very unpleasant feeling (as a prick or an ache) that is caused especially by something harmful 〈I have a *pain* in my side.〉
3 suffering of the mind or emotions : GRIEF 〈The humiliation brought her great *pain*.〉
4 **pains** *pl* great care or effort 〈My sister took *pains* with the garden.〉
5 someone or something annoying
pain•ful \ˈpān-fəl\ *adj*
pain•ful•ly \-fə-lē\ *adv*
pain•less \-ləs\ *adj*

A B C D E F G H I J K L M N O P Q R S T U V W X Y Z

[2]pain *vb* **pained; pain•ing**
1 to cause physical or mental suffering in or to ⟨It *pains* me to think of it.⟩
2 to give or feel physical or mental suffering

pains•tak•ing \ˈpān-ˌstā-kiŋ\ *adj*
taking or showing great care ⟨*painstaking* work⟩
pains•tak•ing•ly *adv*

[1]paint \ˈpānt\ *vb* **paint•ed; paint•ing**
1 to cover a surface with or as if with paint ⟨I'm *painting* the wall.⟩
2 to make a picture or design by using paints
3 to describe clearly
paint•er *n*

[2]paint *n*
a mixture of coloring matter with a liquid that forms a dry coating when spread on a surface

paint•brush \ˈpānt-ˌbrəsh\ *n*
a tool with bristles that is used to apply paint

paint•ing *n*
1 a work of art made with paint
2 the art or occupation of creating pictures with paint

[1]pair \ˈper\ *n, pl* **pairs** *or* **pair**
1 ▼ two things that match or are meant to be used together ⟨a *pair* of gloves⟩ ⟨a *pair* of draft horses⟩
2 a thing having two similar parts that are connected ⟨a *pair* of scissors⟩
3 two people who are connected in some way or do something together ⟨Those two are quite a *pair*.⟩

[1]pair 1: a pair of horses

[2]pair *vb* **paired; pair•ing**
1 to put in or join in a group of two ⟨The guests *paired* off for dancing.⟩
2 to form a group of two : MATCH ⟨This glove doesn't *pair* with that.⟩

Pai•ute \ˈpī-ˌyüt\ *n*
1 a member of an American Indian people originally of Utah, Arizona, Nevada, and California
2 either of the two languages of the Paiute people

pa•ja•mas \pə-ˈjä-məz, -ˈja-\ *n pl*
clothes usually consisting of pants and top that are worn for sleeping

▶ **Word History** When the English went to India they saw many people wearing light, loose trousers. In Hindi, a major language of northern India, these trousers were called *pājāma*. This word had been borrowed by Hindi speakers from Persian, a language of Iran. In Persian *pājāma* is a compound made up of *pā-*, "foot, leg" and *jāma*, "garment." The English adopted both the word and the loose trousers from Hindi, using the trousers in place of a nightshirt to sleep in.

pal \ˈpal\ *n*
a close friend

pal•ace \ˈpa-ləs\ *n*
1 the home of a ruler
2 a large or splendid house

pal•at•able \ˈpa-lə-tə-bəl\ *adj*
pleasant to the taste

pal•ate \ˈpa-lət\ *n*
1 the top area of the inside of the mouth made up of a bony front part (**hard palate**) and a soft flexible back part (**soft palate**)
2 the sense of taste

[1]pale \ˈpāl\ *adj*
pal•er; pal•est
1 having very light skin
2 having a lighter skin color than normal because of sickness or fear
3 not bright or brilliant ⟨a *pale* star⟩
4 light in color or shade ⟨*pale* pink⟩
pale•ness *n*

[2]pale *vb* **paled; pal•ing**
1 to lose color
2 to make or become less adequate, impressive, or intense ⟨My science project *paled* in comparison to those of the other students.⟩

Pa•leo•zo•ic \ˌpā-lē-ə-ˈzō-ik\ *n*
an era of geological history ending about 280 million years ago which came before the Mesozoic and in which vertebrates and land plants first appeared

pal•ette \ˈpa-lət\ *n*
1 ▶ a thin board or tablet on which a painter puts and mixes colors
2 the set of colors that an artist is using

pal•in•drome \ˈpa-lən-ˌdrōm\ *n*
a word, phrase, sentence, or number that reads the same backward or forward ⟨"Step on no pets" is a *palindrome*.⟩

pal•i•sade \ˌpa-lə-ˈsād\ *n*
1 a fence made of poles to protect against attack
2 a line of steep cliffs

[1]pall \ˈpȯl\ *vb* **palled; pall•ing**
to become dull

[2]pall *n*
1 a heavy cloth covering for a coffin, hearse, or tomb
2 something that makes things gloomy or depressing ⟨The news put a *pall* on the celebration.⟩

pall•bear•er \ˈpȯl-ˌber-ər\ *n*
a person who helps to carry the coffin at a funeral

pal•let \ˈpa-lət\ *n*
1 a mattress of straw
2 a hard temporary bed

pal•lid \ˈpa-ləd\ *adj*
[1]PALE 1

pal•lor \ˈpa-lər\ *n*
paleness of face

[1]palm \ˈpäm, ˈpälm\ *n*
a tropical tree, shrub, or vine with a usually tall stem or trunk topped with large leaves that are shaped like feathers or fans

▶ **Word History** The Latin word *palma* originally meant "front of the hand from the wrist to the fingertips." Because the leaves of palm trees look a little like an outstretched hand, the Latin word also came to mean "palm tree." English has borrowed the word with both meanings, but through different pathways. In the sense "palm tree," Old English borrowed the word directly from Latin. In the sense "palm of the hand," English borrowed the word from Old French *palme*, which Old French had taken from Latin *palma*.

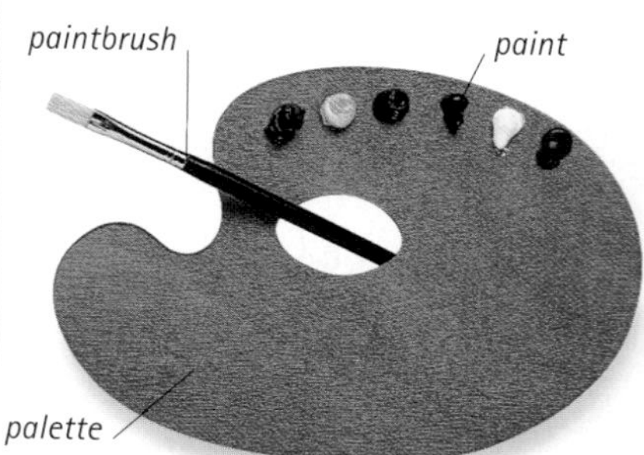

palette 1

[2]palm *n*
1 the under part of the hand between the fingers and the wrist
2 a measure of length based on the width of a palm

[3]palm *vb* **palmed**; **palm•ing**
to hide in the hand ⟨She *palmed* the coin.⟩
palm off to get rid of or pass on in a dishonest way ⟨They tried to *palm off* plastic as real leather.⟩

pal•met•to \pal-ˈme-tō\ *n, pl* **pal•met•tos** *or* **pal•met•toes**
a low-growing palm with leaves shaped like fans

pal•o•mi•no \ˌpa-lə-ˈmē-nō\ *n, pl* **pal•o•mi•nos**
a horse with a light golden coat and a cream or white mane and tail

pal•pi•tate \ˈpal-pə-ˌtāt\ *vb* **pal•pi•tat•ed**; **pal•pi•tat•ing**
[1]THROB 2

pal•sy \ˈpȯl-zē\ *n*
1 PARALYSIS
2 an uncontrollable trembling of the body or a part of the body

pal•try \ˈpȯl-trē\ *adj* **pal•tri•er**; **pal•tri•est**
of little amount, value, or importance ⟨He got a *paltry* raise.⟩

pam•pas \ˈpam-pəz\ *n pl*
▼ wide treeless plains of South America

pam•per \ˈpam-pər\ *vb* **pam•pered**; **pam•per•ing**
to treat (someone or something) with great care and attention

pam•phlet \ˈpam-flət\ *n*
a short publication without a binding : BOOKLET

[1]pan \ˈpan\ *n*
1 a usually shallow open container used for cooking
2 a shallow open tray or container ⟨Put the gold on the *pan* and we'll weigh it.⟩

[2]pan *vb* **panned**; **pan•ning**
to wash earthy material so as to collect bits of metal (as gold)
pan out to give a good result : SUCCEED

pan•cake \ˈpan-ˌkāk\ *n*
▶ a flat cake made of thin batter and cooked on both sides on a griddle

pan•cre•as \ˈpaŋ-krē-əs\ *n*
a large gland near the stomach that produces insulin and a fluid (**pancreatic juice**) with enzymes that aid digestion

pan•cre•at•ic \ˌpaŋ-krē-ˈa-tik\ *adj*
of or relating to the pancreas

pan•da \ˈpan-də\ *n*
1 RED PANDA
2 a large black-and-white animal of central and western China that feeds mostly on the leaves and stems of the bamboo and is related to the bear

▶ **Word History** A picture of a panda—the red panda rather than the panda of China—as well as the word *panda* itself first appeared in Europe in 1825. The French naturalist who published the picture, Frédéric Cuvier, did not tell us where he found the word, but it is assumed to be from a language of Nepal. When the panda of China first became known, it was thought to be a kind of bear. In 1901 scientists decided it was most closely related to the red panda and hence named it "giant panda." Though the kinship between the two animals is now known to be much more distant, the name *panda* is still firmly attached to both animals.

pampas: pampas with grazing sheep in Chile

pan•de•mo•ni•um \ˌpan-də-ˈmō-nē-əm\ *n*
wild uproar ⟨*Pandemonium* broke out with the winning goal.⟩

pane \ˈpān\ *n*
a sheet of glass (as in a window)

pancakes

[1]pan•el \ˈpa-nᵊl\ *n*
1 a usually rectangular section of something (as a door or a wall)
2 a piece of material (as plywood) made to form part of a surface (as of a wall)
3 a board into which instruments or controls are set
4 a group of people appointed for some service ⟨a jury *panel*⟩
5 a group of people taking part in a discussion or answering questions for an audience

[2]panel *vb* **pan•eled** *or* **pan•elled**; **pan•el•ing** *or* **pan•el•ling**
to cover or decorate with sections of material (as wood) ⟨*panel* a wall⟩

pan•el•ing \ˈpa-nᵊl-iŋ\ *n*
sections of material (as wood) joined in a continuous surface and used to cover a wall or ceiling

pang \ˈpaŋ\ *n*
a sudden sharp feeling of physical pain or emotion ⟨hunger *pangs*⟩ ⟨a *pang* or guilt⟩

[1]pan•ic \ˈpa-nik\ *n*
a sudden overpowering fear often without reasonable cause

▶ **Word History** One of the many gods in the mythology of ancient Greece was named Pan. He was the god of shepherds and of woods and pastures. The Greeks believed that he often wandered peacefully through the woods, playing a pipe, but when accidentally awakened from his noontime nap he could give a great shout that would cause flocks to stampede. From this aspect of Pan's nature Greek authors derived the word *panikon*, "sudden fear," the ultimate source of English *panic*.

a b c d e f g h i j k l m n o p q r s t u v w x y z

[2]**panic** *vb* **pan•icked; pan•ick•ing**
to feel or cause to feel sudden overpowering fear

pan•icky \'pa-ni-kē\ *adj*
feeling or overcome with sudden fear

pan•o•rama \ˌpa-nə-'ra-mə, -'rä-\ *n*
a clear complete view in every direction

pan•sy \'pan-zē\ *n, pl* **pansies**
▼ a garden plant related to the violets that has large velvety colorful flowers

pansy

[1]**pant** \'pant\ *vb* **pant•ed; pant•ing**
to breathe hard or quickly ⟨Dogs *pant* when they are hot.⟩

[2]**pant** *n*
a hard or quick breath

pan•ta•loons \ˌpan-tə-'lünz\ *n pl*
PANTS

pan•ther \'pan-thər\ *n*
1 LEOPARD
2 COUGAR
3 JAGUAR

pant•ie *or* **panty** \'pan-tē\ *n, pl* **pant•ies**
a woman's or child's undergarment with short legs or no legs

[1]**pan•to•mime** \'pan-tə-ˌmīm\ *n*
1 the act of showing or explaining something through movements of the body and face instead of by talking
2 a show in which a story is told by using expressions on the face and movements of the body instead of words

[2]**pantomime** *vb* **pan•to•mimed; pan•to•mim•ing**
to tell through movements rather than words

pan•try \'pan-trē\ *n, pl* **pan•tries**
a small room where mainly food is kept

pants \'pants\ *n pl*
a piece of clothing usually reaching from the waist to the ankle and covering each leg separately

pa•pa \'pä-pə\ *n*
[1]FATHER 1

papaw *variant of* PAWPAW

pa•pa•ya \pə-'pī-ə\ *n*
► a yellow fruit that has a sweet flesh and many black seeds and grows on a tropical American tree

[1]**pa•per** \'pā-pər\ *n*
1 a material made from fibers (as of wood or cloth) and in the form of thin sheets or a sheet or piece of such material ⟨Fold the *paper* in half.⟩
2 a piece of paper having something written or printed on it : DOCUMENT
3 NEWSPAPER
4 a piece of written schoolwork
5 WALLPAPER

[2]**paper** *adj*
made of paper ⟨*paper* plates⟩

[3]**paper** *vb* **pa•pered; pa•per•ing**
to cover with wallpaper ⟨*paper* a room⟩

pa•per•back \'pā-pər-ˌbak\ *n*
a book with a flexible paper binding

paper clip *n*
a piece of bent wire used to hold sheets of paper together

pa•per•work \'pā-pər-ˌwərk\ *n*
the documents that are a requirement for or a routine part of something

pa•pery \'pā-pə-rē\ *adj*
very thin or dry

pa•pier–mâ•ché \ˌpā-pər-mə-'shā, ˌpa-ˌpyā-\ *n*
material made of paper mixed with glue and other substances that hardens as it dries

pa•pri•ka \pə-'prē-kə\ *n*
a mild red spice made from dried peppers

pa•py•rus \pə-'pī-rəs\ *n, pl* **pa•py•rus•es** *or* **pa•py•ri** \-rē, -ˌrī\
1 a tall African plant related to the grasses that grows especially in Egypt
2 a material like paper used by ancient people to write on

papaya

par \'pär\ *n*
1 an equal level ⟨They are two people with talents on a *par.*⟩
2 the score set for each hole of a golf course
3 a usual or average level ⟨His grades were below *par.*⟩

par•a•ble \'per-ə-bəl\ *n*
a simple story that teaches a moral lesson

[1]**para•chute** \'per-ə-ˌshüt\ *n*
► a piece of equipment usually made of cloth and attached to someone or something for making a safe jump or drop from an airplane

[2]**parachute** *vb* **para•chut•ed; para•chut•ing**
to transport or come down by parachute

[1]**pa•rade** \pə-'rād\ *n*
1 ▼ a public celebration that includes people moving in order down a street by walking or riding in vehicles or on floats ⟨a circus *parade*⟩ ⟨the Independence Day *parade*⟩
2 the formation of troops before an officer for inspection
3 great show or display

[1]**parade 1:** a parade in Havana, Cuba

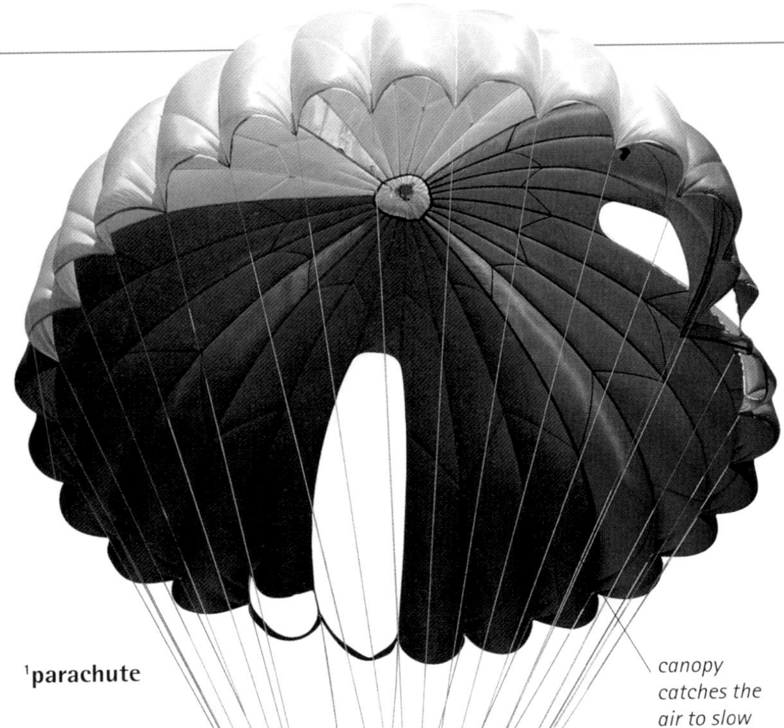

¹parachute

²**parade** *vb* **pa•rad•ed**; **pa•rad•ing**
1 to march in an orderly group
2 to show off
synonyms see SHOW

par•a•dise \'per-ə-,dīs, -,dīz\ *n*
1 a place, state, or time of great beauty or happiness
2 HEAVEN 2
3 the place where Adam and Eve first lived according to the Bible

par•a•dox \'per-ə-,däks\ *n*
1 a statement that seems to say opposite things and yet is perhaps true
2 a person or thing having qualities that seem to be opposite

par•af•fin \'per-ə-fən\ *n*
a white waxy substance obtained from wood, coal, or petroleum and used in coating and sealing and in candles

para•graph \'per-ə-,graf\ *n*
a part of a piece of writing that is made up of one or more sentences and has to do with one topic or gives the words of one speaker

par•a•keet \'per-ə-,kēt\ *n*
a small parrot that has a long tail and is sometimes kept as a caged bird

¹**par•al•lel** \'per-ə-,lel\ *adj*
lying or moving in the same direction but always the same distance apart ⟨*parallel* lines⟩ ⟨Train tracks are *parallel.*⟩

²**parallel** *n*
1 a line or surface that lies at or moves in the same direction as another but is always the same distance from it
2 one of the imaginary circles on the earth's surface running in the same direction as the equator and marking latitude
3 a way in which things are similar ⟨The *parallel* between their lives is obvious.⟩
4 ³EQUAL

³**parallel** *vb* **par•al•leled**; **par•al•lel•ing**
1 to move, run, or extend in the same direction with but always at the same distance from ⟨A road *parallels* the river.⟩
2 to be similar or equal to

par•al•lel•o•gram \,per-ə-'le-lə-,gram\ *n*
a plane figure with four sides whose opposite sides are parallel and equal

pa•ral•y•sis \pə-'ra-lə-səs\ *n*, *pl* **pa•ral•y•ses** \-,sēz\
loss of the ability to move all or part of the body (as from disease or injury)

par•a•lyze \'per-ə-,līz\ *vb* **par•a•lyzed**; **par•a•lyz•ing**
1 to cause to be unable to move all or part of the body
2 to destroy or decrease something's energy or ability to act ⟨The city was *paralyzed* by a heavy snowstorm.⟩

par•a•me•cium \,per-ə-'mē-shē-əm, -sē-əm\ *n*, *pl* **par•a•me•cia** \-shē-ə, -sē-ə\ *also* **par•a•me•ciums**
a tiny living thing found in water that is a single cell shaped like a slipper and moves by means of cilia

para•med•ic \,per-ə-'me-dik\ *n*
a person specially trained to care for a patient before or during the trip to a hospital

par•a•mount \'per-ə-,maůnt\ *adj*
highest in importance or greatness ⟨The children's safety is *paramount.*⟩

para•noid \'per-ə-,nȯid\ *adj*
having unreasonable feelings of suspicion, distrust, and persecution

par•a•pet \'per-ə-pət, -,pet\ *n*
1 a low wall or fence at the edge of a platform, roof, or bridge
2 a wall of earth or stone to protect soldiers

¹**para•phrase** \'per-ə-,frāz\ *vb* **para•phrased**; **para•phras•ing**
to give the meaning of in different words

²**paraphrase** *n*
a way of stating something again by giving the meaning in different words

para•pro•fes•sion•al \,per-ə-prə-'fe-shə-nᵊl\ *n*
a person trained to assist a professional person (as a teacher)

par•a•site \'per-ə-,sīt\ *n*
1 a living thing (as a flea, worm, or fungus) that lives in or on another living thing and gets food and sometimes shelter from it and usually causes harm to it
2 a person who lives at the expense of another

par•a•sit•ic \,per-ə-'si-tik\ *adj*
relating to or having the habit of a parasite : caused by parasites ⟨a *parasitic* worm⟩ ⟨*parasitic* diseases⟩

par•a•sol \'per-ə-,sȯl\ *n*
▼ a light umbrella used as a protection against the sun

parasol

para•troop•er \'per-ə-,trü-pər\ *n*
a soldier trained and equipped to parachute from an airplane

[1]par•cel \'pär-səl\ *n*
1 PACKAGE 1
2 a plot of land

[2]parcel *vb* **par•celed** *or* **par•celled**; **par•cel•ing** *or* **par•cel•ling**
to divide and give out by parts

parcel post *n*
a mail service that handles packages

parch \'pärch\ *vb* **parched**; **parch•ing**
to dry or make dry from heat and lack of moisture

parch•ment \'pärch-mənt\ *n*
1 the skin of a sheep or goat prepared so that it can be written on
2 strong tough paper used in baking and in wrapping food

[1]par•don \'pär-dᵊn\ *n*
1 forgiveness for wrong or rude behavior
2 the act of freeing from legal punishment

[2]pardon *vb* **par•doned**; **par•don•ing**
1 to free from penalty for a fault or crime
2 to allow (a wrong act) to pass without punishment : FORGIVE

pare \'per\ *vb* **pared**; **par•ing**
1 to cut or shave off the outside or the ends of 〈*pare* apples〉
2 to reduce as if by cutting 〈He had to *pare* the cost of his trip.〉

par•ent \'per-ənt\ *n*
1 a father or mother of a child
2 an animal or plant that produces offspring

par•ent•age \'per-ən-tij\ *n*
a line of ancestors

pa•ren•tal \pə-'ren-tᵊl\ *adj*
of or as expected from a mother and father 〈*parental* responsibility〉

pa•ren•the•sis \pə-'ren-thə-səs\ *n*, *pl* **pa•ren•the•ses** \-,sēz\
one of a pair of marks ( ) used to enclose a word or group of words or to group mathematical terms to be dealt with as a unit
par•en•thet•i•cal \-ti-kəl\ *adj*

par•ish \'per-ish\ *n*
1 a section of a church district under the care of a priest or minister
2 the people who attend a particular church
3 a division in the state of Louisiana that is similar to a county in other states

parish house *n*
a building for the educational and social activities of a church

pa•rish•io•ner \pə-'ri-shə-nər\ *n*
a member of a particular church

[1]park \'pärk\ *n*
1 ▼ an area of land set aside for recreation or for its beauty
2 an enclosed field for ball games

[2]park *vb* **parked**; **park•ing**
to stop a vehicle and leave it for a while 〈Never *park* in front of a hydrant.〉

[1]park 1

par•ka \'pär-kə\ *n*
a warm windproof jacket with a hood

park•way \'pärk-,wā\ *n*
a broad landscaped highway

[1]par•ley \'pär-lē\ *n*, *pl* **parleys**
a discussion with an enemy

[2]parley *vb* **par•leyed**; **par•ley•ing**
to hold a discussion of terms with an enemy

par•lia•ment \'pär-lə-mənt\ *n*
an assembly that is the highest legislative body of a country (as the United Kingdom)

par•lor \'pär-lər\ *n*
1 a room for receiving guests and for conversation
2 a usually small place of business 〈beauty *parlor*〉 〈ice cream *parlor*〉

pa•ro•chi•al school \pə-'rō-kē-əl-\ *n*
a private school that is run by a religious body

pa•role \pə-'rōl\ *n*
an early release of a prisoner

par•rot \'per-ət\ *n*
► a brightly colored tropical bird that has a strong hooked bill and is sometimes trained to imitate human speech

[1]par•ry \'per-ē\ *vb* **par•ried**; **par•ry•ing**
1 to turn aside an opponent's weapon or blow
2 to avoid by a skillful answer 〈She *parried* an embarrassing question.〉

[2]parry *n*, *pl* **par•ries**
an act or instance of skillfully avoiding something

pars•ley \'pär-slē\ *n*, *pl* **pars•leys**
a garden plant that has small leaves used to season or decorate various foods

pars•nip \'pär-snəp\ *n*
the long white root of a garden plant that is cooked as a vegetable

par•son \'pär-sᵊn\ *n*
[1]MINISTER 1

par•son•age \'pär-sə-nij\ *n*
a house provided by a church for its pastor to live in

[1]part \'pärt\ *n*
1 one of the sections into which something is divided 〈This is the best *part* of the movie.〉 〈That wasn't *part* of our agreement.〉
2 some of something 〈My dog is *part* husky.〉 〈I spent *part* of my day reading.〉
3 a general area 〈She moved to another *part* of the state.〉
4 a piece of a machine
5 one of the sides or aspects 〈The best *part* of camp is making new friends.〉
6 the role of a character in a play
7 a line along which the hair is divided
8 a person's share or duty 〈I did my *part* for the team.〉

parrot
The majority of parrots are native to forests in the warm parts of the world. Sociable birds, parrots stay with the same mate for life and often gather together in flocks, communicating through noisy calls. Nearly all parrots are plant eaters, feeding on fruits, seeds, nuts, and sometimes nectar from flowers. Most are active by day — flying from tree to tree and using their strong feet and hooked bills to climb along branches — but there are also nocturnal types that stay on the ground.

features of a rainbow lorikeet \'lȯr-ə-ˌkēt\

cockatoo

cockatiel \'käk-ə-tēl\ is a small parrot from Australia with a large crest

budgerigar \'bə-jə-rē-ˌgär\ is a small Australian parrot often kept as a pet

macaw

9 the music for a voice or instrument ⟨the soprano *part*⟩
10 a voice or instrument ⟨four-*part* harmony⟩
11 a piece of a plant or animal body
for the most part with few exceptions : on the whole ⟨They were, *for the most part*, very pleased.⟩

▶ **Synonyms** PART, PORTION, and SECTION mean something less than the whole to which it belongs. PART is used when something is taken away from the whole or thought of as being separate from the rest. ⟨A *part* of the room is used for storage.⟩ PORTION is used when a whole has been divided into assigned parts. ⟨Cut the pie into six *portions*.⟩ SECTION is used if the parts of the whole are recognizable and have been separated by or as if by cutting. ⟨This newspaper has four *sections*.⟩

²part *vb* **part•ed; part•ing**
1 to leave each other ⟨They *parted* at the intersection.⟩
2 to separate the hair by combing on each side of a line
3 to give up possession of ⟨She won't *part* with her money.⟩
4 to hold apart ⟨He *parted* the curtains.⟩
5 to come apart ⟨The crowd *parted* to let us through.⟩
6 to divide into parts
synonyms see SEPARATE

part. *abbr* participle

par•take \pär-'tāk\ *vb* **par•took** \-'tu̇k\; **par•tak•en** \-'tā-kən\; **par•tak•ing** to take a share or part

par•tial \'pär-shəl\ *adj*
1 not complete ⟨a *partial* success⟩ ⟨a *partial* eclipse⟩
2 favoring one side of a question over another ⟨I'm too *partial* to be a fair judge.⟩
3 fond or too fond of someone or something ⟨Grandma is *partial* to ice cream sodas.⟩
par•tial•ly \'pär-shə-lē\ *adv*

par•ti•al•i•ty \ˌpär-shē-'a-lə-tē\ *n* the quality or state of favoring one side over another

par•tic•i•pant \pər-'ti-sə-pənt, pär-\ *n* a person who takes part in something ⟨contest *participants*⟩

par•tic•i•pate \pər-'ti-sə-ˌpāt, pär-\ *vb* **par•tic•i•pat•ed; par•tic•i•pat•ing** to join with others in doing something

par•tic•i•pa•tion \pär-ˌti-sə-'pā-shən\ *n* the act of joining with others in doing something ⟨Class *participation* counts toward your grade.⟩

par•ti•ci•ple \'pär-tə-ˌsi-pəl\ *n* a form of a verb that is used to indicate a past or ongoing action and that can be used like an adjective ⟨The word "smiling" in "the smiling child" is a *participle*.⟩

par•ti•cle \'pär-ti-kəl\ *n* a very small bit or amount of something ⟨a *particle* of sand⟩ ⟨a *particle* of sense⟩

A B C D E F G H I J K L M N O P Q R S T U V W X Y Z

[1]**par·tic·u·lar** \pər-'ti-kyə-lər\ *adj*
1 relating to one person or thing ⟨Each city has its *particular* problems.⟩
2 not usual : SPECIAL ⟨Pay *particular* attention to correct spelling.⟩
3 having strong opinions about what is acceptable ⟨He's very *particular* about food.⟩
4 being one of several ⟨Which *particular* bike would you like?⟩
5 concerned about details ⟨Our teacher is very *particular*.⟩
par·tic·u·lar·ly *adv*
in particular
1 that can be specifically named ⟨I wasn't referring to anyone *in particular*.⟩
2 more specially than others : ESPECIALLY ⟨She loves flowers and roses *in particular*.⟩

[2]**particular** *n*
a single fact or detail ⟨The account was correct in every *particular*.⟩

part·ing \'pär-tiŋ\ *n*
an act of leaving someone ⟨Our *parting* was a sad occasion.⟩

par·ti·san \'pär-tə-zən, -sən\ *n*
a person who strongly supports something or someone ⟨I'm a *partisan* of the governor.⟩
par·ti·san·ship \-,ship\ *n*

[1]**par·ti·tion** \pər-'ti-shən, pär-\ *n*
a wall or screen that separates one area from another

[2]**partition** *vb* **par·ti·tioned**; **par·ti·tion·ing**
to divide into separate shares, parts, or areas ⟨We *partitioned* the basement into three rooms.⟩

part·ly \'pärt-lē\ *adv*
somewhat but not completely ⟨I was *partly* to blame for the argument.⟩

part·ner \'pärt-nər\ *n*
1 a person who does or shares something with another ⟨You are my favorite dancing *partner*.⟩
2 either one of a married couple
3 someone who plays with another person on the same side in a game ⟨a tennis *partner*⟩
4 one of two or more people who run a business together

part·ner·ship \'pärt-nər-,ship\ *n*
an arrangement in which people engage in an activity or business with one another or share something with each other

part of speech *n, pl* **parts of speech**
a class of words (as adjectives, adverbs, conjunctions, interjections, nouns, prepositions, pronouns, or verbs) identified according to the kinds of ideas they express and the work they do in a sentence

party 1: children at a birthday party

partook *past of* PARTAKE

par·tridge \'pär-trij\ *n, pl* **partridge** *or* **par·tridg·es**
a plump grayish brown bird that lives mostly on the ground and is sometimes hunted for food or sport

part–time \'pärt-'tīm\ *adj*
involving fewer than the usual hours ⟨*part-time* work⟩

par·ty \'pär-tē\ *n, pl* **par·ties**
1 ▲ a social gathering or the entertainment provided for it
2 a person or group concerned in some action ⟨He's a *party* to the lawsuit.⟩ ⟨A search *party* was formed.⟩
3 a group of people who take one side of a question or share a set of beliefs ⟨a political *party*⟩

[1]**pass** \'pas\ *vb* **passed**; **pass·ing**
1 [1]MOVE 1, PROCEED ⟨The airplane *passed* out of sight.⟩
2 to go away ⟨The pain will soon *pass*.⟩
3 to go by or move past ⟨*Pass* that car.⟩
4 to go or allow to go across, over, or through ⟨They let me *pass*.⟩
5 to transfer or throw to another person ⟨Please *pass* the salt.⟩ ⟨*Pass* me the football!⟩
6 to go successfully through an examination or inspection
7 to cause or permit to elapse ⟨We *passed* the time playing cards.⟩
8 HAPPEN 1 ⟨The day *passed* without any problems.⟩
9 to move from one place or condition to another ⟨The business has *passed* to new ownership.⟩

10 to be or cause to be approved ⟨The Senate *passed* the bill.⟩
11 to be or cause to be identified or recognized ⟨She tried to *pass* for an expert.⟩
12 [1]DIE 1
pass•er *n*
pass away [1]DIE 1
pass out to become unconscious : FAINT
pass up to let go by : REFUSE ⟨It was an offer too good to *pass up.*⟩

[2]pass *n*
1 an opening or way for going along or through
2 a gap in a mountain range

[3]pass *n*
1 the act or an instance of moving ⟨The plane made two *passes* over the area.⟩
2 the act or an instance of throwing or transferring (as a ball) to another person
3 a written permit to go or come ⟨I got some movie *passes* for my birthday.⟩
4 SITUATION 1 ⟨Things have come to a strange *pass.*⟩

pass•able \ˈpa-sə-bəl\ *adj*
1 fit to be traveled on ⟨*passable* roads⟩
2 barely good enough ⟨I speak *passable* Spanish.⟩
pass•ably \-blē\ *adv*

pas•sage \ˈpa-sij\ *n*
1 a space or path by which something or someone can go through
2 a brief part of a speech or written work
3 the act or process of going from one place or condition to another ⟨Our ship made a smooth *passage.*⟩
4 the act of approving a law
5 a right or permission to go as a passenger ⟨She obtained *passage* aboard the ship.⟩

pas•sage•way \ˈpa-sij-ˌwā\ *n*
a space, road, or way by which a person or thing may move

pas•sen•ger \ˈpa-sᵊn-jər\ *n*
someone riding on or in a vehicle

passenger pigeon *n*
a North American wild pigeon once common but now extinct

pass•er•by \ˌpa-sər-ˈbī\ *n, pl* **pass•ers•by** \-sərz-ˈbī\
someone who goes by

[1]pass•ing \ˈpa-siŋ\ *adj*
1 going by or past ⟨*passing* cars⟩
2 lasting only for a short time ⟨a *passing* fad⟩
3 showing haste or lack of attention ⟨a *passing* glance⟩
4 used for going past ⟨*passing* lanes⟩
5 showing satisfactory work in a test or course of study ⟨a *passing* mark⟩

[2]passing *n*
1 the act of going by or going away ⟨We await the *passing* of winter.⟩
2 DEATH 1

pas•sion \ˈpa-shən\ *n*
1 a strong feeling or emotion ⟨He spoke with *passion.*⟩
2 an object of someone's love, liking, or desire ⟨Art is my *passion.*⟩
3 strong liking or desire : LOVE ⟨She has a *passion* for music.⟩

pas•sion•ate \ˈpa-shə-nət\ *adj*
1 showing or affected by strong feeling ⟨a *passionate* performance⟩
2 easily caused to feel strong emotions ⟨a *passionate* person⟩
pas•sion•ate•ly *adv*

pas•sive \ˈpa-siv\ *adj*
1 not taking an active part ⟨We were *passive* spectators.⟩
2 showing that the person or thing represented by the subject is acted on by the verb ⟨The phrase "were met" in "we were met by our friends" is *passive.*⟩
3 offering no resistance ⟨The captives showed *passive* obedience.⟩
pas•sive•ly *adv*

Pass•over \ˈpas-ˌō-vər\ *n*
a Jewish holiday celebrated in March or April in honor of the freeing of the Hebrews from slavery in Egypt

pass•port \ˈpas-ˌpȯrt\ *n*
▼ a government document needed to enter or leave a country

pass•word \ˈpas-ˌwərd\ *n*
a secret word, phrase, or group of numbers that a person must know to be allowed to enter a place or use a computer system

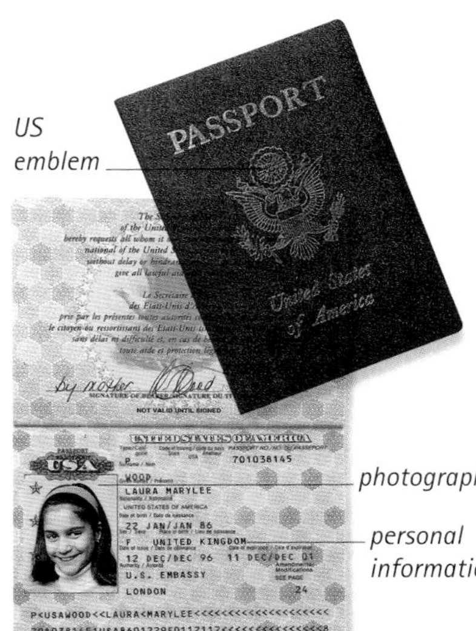

passport: a US passport

[1]past \ˈpast\ *adj*
1 of or relating to a time that has gone by ⟨I've worked for the *past* month.⟩
2 relating to a verb tense that expresses a time gone by
3 no longer serving ⟨a *past* president⟩

[2]past *prep*
1 [2]BEYOND 1 ⟨We left at ten minutes *past* five.⟩
2 going close to and then beyond ⟨She walked *past* my house.⟩

[3]past *n*
1 a former time ⟨In the *past* trains went from here to New York.⟩
2 life or history of a time gone by ⟨We're studying the nation's *past.*⟩

[4]past *adv*
so as to pass by or beyond ⟨A deer ran *past.*⟩

pas•ta \ˈpä-stə\ *n*
1 ▼ a dough of flour, eggs, and water made in different shapes and dried or used fresh
2 a dish of cooked pasta ⟨She ordered *pasta* with sauce.⟩

[1]paste \ˈpāst\ *n*
1 a mixture of flour or starch and water used for sticking things together
2 a soft smooth thick mixture ⟨tomato *paste*⟩ ⟨Mix cement and water into a *paste.*⟩

pasta 1: different shapes of pasta

[2]paste *vb* **past•ed; past•ing**
1 to stick on or together with an adhesive mixture
2 to move (something cut or copied from a computer document) to another place

paste•board \ˈpāst-ˌbȯrd\ *n*
CARDBOARD

[1]pas•tel \pa-ˈstel\ *n*
1 a soft pale color
2 a crayon made by mixing ground coloring matter with a watery solution of a gum
3 a drawing made with pastels

[2]pastel *adj*
1 made with pastels
2 light and pale in color ⟨a *pastel* blouse⟩

pas•teur•i•za•tion \ˌpas-chə-rə-ˈzā-shən, ˌpa-stə-\ *n*
the process of heating a liquid to a temperature to kill germs and then rapidly cooling it

pas•teur•ize \ˈpas-chə-ˌrīz, ˈpa-stə-\ *vb* **pas•teur•ized**; **pas•teur•iz•ing**
to keep a liquid (as milk) for a time at a temperature high enough to kill many harmful germs and then cool it rapidly
pas•teur•iz•er *n*

pas•time \ˈpas-ˌtīm\ *n*
something (as a hobby) that helps to make time pass pleasantly

pas•tor \ˈpa-stər\ *n*
a minister or priest in charge of a church

pas•to•ral \ˈpa-stə-rəl\ *adj*
1 of or relating to peaceful scenes of the countryside
2 of or relating to the pastor of a church

past participle *n*
a word that expresses completed action and is one of the principal parts of a verb ⟨The words "raised" in "many hands were raised" and "thrown" in "the ball has been thrown" are *past participles.*⟩

past•ry \ˈpā-strē\ *n, pl* **past•ries**
1 ▼ sweet baked goods (as pies) made mainly of flour and fat
2 a piece of sweet baked goods

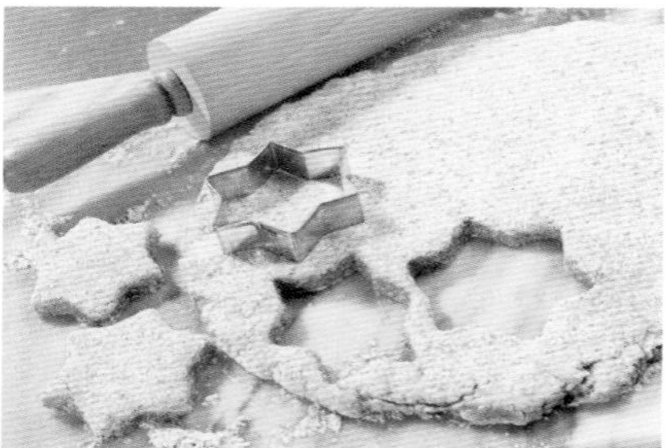

pastry 1: star-shaped pastry pieces ready for baking

past tense *n*
a verb tense used to express an action or state having already taken place or existed ⟨The *past tense* of the verb "run" is "ran."⟩

pas•ture \ˈpas-chər\ *n*
1 plants (as grass) for feeding grazing animals
2 land on which animals graze

[1]**pat** \ˈpat\ *vb* **pat•ted**; **pat•ting**
to tap or stroke gently with the open hand ⟨He stopped to *pat* the dog.⟩

[2]**pat** *n*
1 a light tap with an open hand or a flat instrument ⟨She gave me a *pat* on the head.⟩
2 the sound of a pat or tap
3 a small flat piece (as of butter)

[3]**pat** *adj* **pat•ter**; **pat•test**
1 learned perfectly ⟨I had my lines in the play down *pat.*⟩
2 exactly suitable ⟨a *pat* answer⟩
3 not changing ⟨He stood *pat* against all arguments.⟩

pat. *abbr* patent

[1]**patch** \ˈpach\ *n*
1 a piece of cloth used to mend or cover a torn or worn place
2 a small piece or area different from what is around it ⟨There is a *patch* of snow in the yard.⟩ ⟨Her dog has a *patch* of white on its head.⟩

[2]**patch** *vb* **patched**; **patch•ing**
to mend or cover with a piece of cloth
synonyms see MEND
patch up to resolve by agreement ⟨Let's forget our quarrel and *patch* things *up.*⟩

patch•work \ˈpach-ˌwərk\ *n*
1 ▶ pieces of cloth of different colors and shapes sewed together
2 something made up of different parts ⟨The farm is a *patchwork* of fields.⟩

pa•tel•la \pə-ˈte-lə\ *n, pl* **pa•tel•lae** \-ˈte-lē, -ˈte-ˌlī\ *or* **pa•tel•las**
KNEECAP

[1]**pat•ent** *for 1* ˈpa-tᵊnt *or* ˈpā-, *for 2* ˈpa-\ *adj*
1 OBVIOUS, EVIDENT ⟨a *patent* lie⟩
2 relating to or concerned with patents ⟨*patent* law⟩

[2]**pat•ent** \ˈpa-tᵊnt\ *n*
a document that gives the inventor of something the right to be the only one to make or sell the invention for a certain number of years

[3]**pat•ent** \ˈpa-tᵊnt\ *vb* **pat•ent•ed**; **pat•ent•ing**
to obtain the legal right to be the only one to make or sell an invention

pa•ter•nal \pə-ˈtər-nᵊl\ *adj*
1 of or like that of a father : FATHERLY ⟨*paternal* advice⟩
2 related through the father ⟨my *paternal* cousins⟩
pa•ter•nal•ly *adv*

path \ˈpath, ˈpäth\ *n, pl* **paths** \ˈpat͟hz, ˈpät͟hz\
1 a track made by traveling on foot ⟨We followed a *path* through the woods.⟩
2 the way or track in which something moves or in which something will be encountered ⟨the *path* of a planet⟩
3 a way of life or thought

pa•thet•ic \pə-ˈthe-tik\ *adj*
causing feelings of pity, tenderness, or sorrow
pa•thet•ic•al•ly *adv*

path•way \ˈpath-ˌwā, ˈpäth-\ *n*
PATH 1

pa•tience \ˈpā-shəns\ *n*
the ability to remain calm when dealing with a difficult or annoying situation, task, or person ⟨A person will need *patience* to do this work.⟩

patchwork 1: a section of patchwork

[1]**pa•tient** \ˈpā-shənt\ *adj*
able to or showing the ability to remain calm when dealing with a difficult or annoying situation, task, or person ⟨a *patient* response⟩ ⟨a *patient* teacher⟩
pa•tient•ly *adv*

[2]**patient** *n*
a person under medical care or treatment

pa•tio \ˈpa-tē-ˌō, ˈpä-\ *n, pl* **pa•ti•os**
an open area next to a house that is usually paved

pa•tri•arch \ˈpā-trē-ˌärk\ *n*
1 a man who heads a family, group, or government
2 a respected old man

pa•tri•ot \ˈpā-trē-ət\ *n*
a person who loves his or her country and strongly supports it

pa•tri•ot•ic \ˌpā-trē-ˈä-tik\ *adj*
having or showing love that a person feels for his or her country

pa•tri•ot•ism \ˈpā-trē-ə-ˌti-zəm\ *n*
love that a person feels for his or her country

[1]**pa•trol** \pə-ˈtrōl\ *n*
1 the action of going around an area to make sure that it is safe
2 a person or group going around an area to make sure that it is safe
3 a part of a Boy Scout or Girl Scout troop

[2]**patrol** *vb* **pa•trolled; pa•trol•ling**
to go around an area for the purpose of watching or protecting

pa•trol•man \pə-ˈtrōl-mən\ *n, pl* **pa•trol•men** \-mən\
a police officer who has a regular beat

pa•tron \ˈpā-trən\ *n*
1 a person who gives generous support or approval
2 CUSTOMER

pa•tron•age \ˈpa-trə-nij, ˈpā-trə-\ *n*
1 the help or business given by a supporter
2 a group of customers (as of a shop or theater)
3 the control by officials of giving out jobs, contracts, and favors

pa•tron•ize \ˈpā-trə-ˌnīz, ˈpa-trə-\ *vb* **pa•tron•ized; pa•tron•iz•ing**
1 to act as a supporter of ⟨He *patronizes* the arts.⟩
2 to be a customer of ⟨She prefers to *patronize* a neighborhood store.⟩
3 to treat (a person) as if he or she were not as good or less important

patron saint *n*
a saint to whom a church or society is dedicated

[1]**pat•ter** \ˈpa-tər\ *vb* **pat•tered; pat•ter•ing**
1 to strike again and again with light blows ⟨We could hear rain *pattering* on the roof.⟩
2 to run with quick light steps

[2]**patter** *n*
a series of quick light sounds ⟨We heard the *patter* of little feet.⟩

[1]**pat•tern** \ˈpa-tərn\ *n*
1 the form or figures used in decoration : DESIGN ⟨The cloth has a fancy *pattern*.⟩
2 ▶ a model or guide for making something ⟨Mom used a *pattern* to make the dress.⟩
3 the regular and repeated way in which something is done ⟨Their behavior has fallen into a *pattern*.⟩
4 something worth copying : MODEL

pat•terned \-tərnd\ *adj*

▶ **Word History** In medieval English a person who served as a model to be copied was called a *patron*. Some people began to say *patron* in such a way that the sound of the *r* changed its place. *Patron* soon became *pattern*. After a time *pattern*, the new way of saying the word, was used just for the meaning "a model to be copied." The older *patron* lost that meaning, though it kept its other senses. In this way we got a new word, *pattern*, from an older word, *patron*.

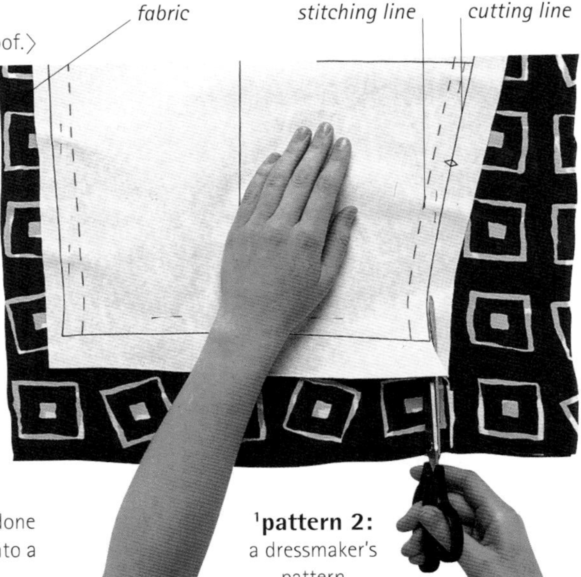

[1]**pattern 2:** a dressmaker's pattern

[2]**pattern** *vb* **pat•terned; pat•tern•ing**
1 to make or develop by following an example ⟨The building was *patterned* on a Greek temple.⟩
2 to have a design

pat•ty \ˈpa-tē\ *n, pl* **pat•ties**
a small flat cake of chopped food ⟨a hamburger *patty*⟩

pau•per \ˈpȯ-pər\ *n*
a very poor person

[1]**pause** \ˈpȯz\ *n*
1 a temporary stop
2 a sign 𝄐 above a musical note or rest to show that the note or rest is to be held longer

[2]**pause** *vb* **paused; paus•ing**
to stop for a time : make a temporary stop

pave \ˈpāv\ *vb* **paved; pav•ing**
to make a hard surface on (as with concrete or asphalt) ⟨A crew *paved* a street.⟩
pave the way to make it easier for something to happen or for someone to do something

pave•ment \ˈpāv-mənt\ *n*
1 a hard surface of concrete or asphalt
2 material used in making a hard surface

pa•vil•ion \pə-ˈvil-yən\ *n*
1 a very large tent
2 a building usually with open sides that is used as a place for entertainment or shelter in a park or garden

pav•ing \ˈpā-viŋ\ *n*
PAVEMENT

[1]**paw:** a kitten cleaning its paws

[1]**paw** \ˈpȯ\ *n*
▲ the foot of a four-footed animal (as a lion, dog, or cat) that has claws

[2]**paw** *vb* **pawed; paw•ing**
1 to touch or hit with a paw ⟨My dog *pawed* the door.⟩
2 to beat or scrape with a hoof ⟨The nervous horse *pawed* the ground.⟩
3 to touch or handle in a clumsy or rude way

[1]**pawn** \ˈpȯn\ *n*
1 the piece of least value in the game of chess
2 a person who has little power and is controlled by a more powerful person or group

[2]**pawn** *vb* **pawned; pawn•ing**
to leave as a guarantee of repayment for a loan ⟨He *pawned* a watch.⟩

pawn•bro•ker \ˈpȯn-ˌbrō-kər\ *n*
a person who lends money in exchange for personal property that can be sold if the money is not repaid

paw•paw *also* **pa•paw** *n*
1 \pə-ˈpȯ\ PAPAYA
2 \ˈpä-pȯ, ˈpȯ\ the greenish or yellow edible fruit of a North American tree with purple flowers

[1]**pay** \'pā\ *vb* **paid** \'pād\; **pay•ing**
1 to give (as money) in return for services received or for something bought ⟨*Pay* the taxi driver.⟩ ⟨I *paid* for a ticket.⟩
2 to give money for (something owed) ⟨I have to *pay* the rent.⟩
3 to get even with ⟨She wants to *pay* them back for the insult.⟩
4 to give or offer freely ⟨*pay* a compliment⟩ ⟨*pay* attention⟩
5 to have a worthwhile result : be worth the effort or pains required ⟨It *pays* to drive carefully.⟩
pay•er *n*
pay off
1 to give all of what is owed ⟨It felt good to *pay off* a debt.⟩
2 to have a good result ⟨Hours of practice *paid off* in a successful show.⟩
pay up to pay in full especially debts that are due

[2]**pay** *n*
1 the act of giving money for something bought or used or for what is owed : PAYMENT
2 SALARY

pay•able \'pā-ə-bəl\ *adj*
that may, can, or must be paid

pay•check \'pā-ˌchek\ *n*
a check given or received as wages or salary

pay•ment \'pā-mənt\ *n*
1 the act of giving money for something bought or for a service used
2 money given to pay a debt ⟨For three years I'll make *payments* on a car.⟩

pay•roll \'pā-ˌrōl\ *n*
1 a list of persons who receive pay
2 the amount of money necessary to pay the employees of a business

PC \ˌpē-'sē\ *n, pl* **PCs** *or* **PC's**
PERSONAL COMPUTER

PDA \ˌpē-ˌdē-'ā\ *n*
a small hand-held computer that is used especially for organizing information (as phone numbers or schedules)

PE *abbr* Prince Edward Island

pea \'pē\ *n, pl* **peas** \'pēz\
1 ▼ a round green seed that is eaten as a vegetable and comes from the pods of a climbing garden plant
2 a plant (as the sweet pea) resembling or related to the garden plant that produces peas

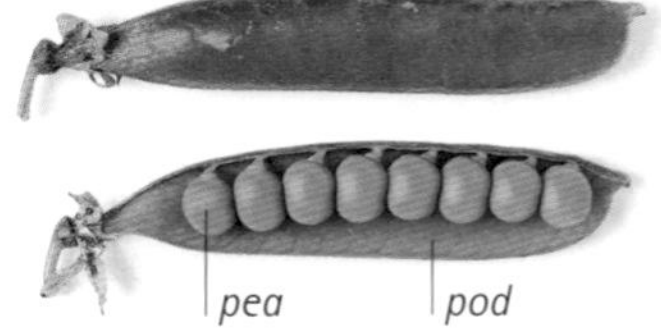

pea 1: peas in a pod

peace \'pēs\ *n*
1 freedom or a period of freedom from public disturbance or war
2 a quiet and calm state of mind
3 agreement and harmony among people
4 an agreement to end a war

peace•able \'pē-sə-bəl\ *adj*
1 PEACEFUL 1
2 PEACEFUL 3

peace•ful \'pēs-fəl\ *adj*
1 not easily moved to argue or fight ⟨a *peaceful* people⟩
2 full of or enjoying quiet, calm, or freedom from disturbance
3 not involving fighting ⟨Try to settle a dispute by *peaceful* means.⟩
synonyms see CALM
peace•ful•ly \-fə-lē\ *adv*
peace•ful•ness *n*

peace•mak•er \'pēs-ˌmā-kər\ *n*
a person who settles an argument or stops a fight

peace pipe *n*
a decorated pipe of the American Indians used for certain ceremonies

peach \'pēch\ *n*
1 ▼ a fruit that is related to the plum and has a sweet juicy yellow or whitish pulp, hairy skin, and a large rough pit
2 a pale yellowish pink color

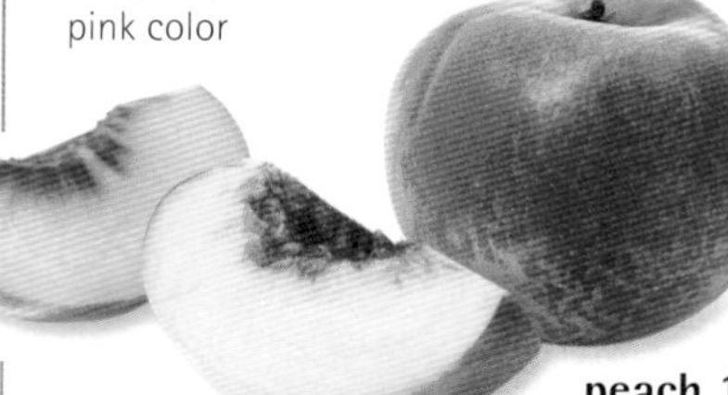
peach 1

▶ **Word History** When the peach, which is native to China, was introduced to the Roman Empire, it was known in Greek as *mēlon Persikon* and in Latin as *malum Persicum.* Both names literally meant "Persian apple." (*Persia* is a traditional name for the Asian country now known as "Iran.") The fruit may not have reached the Mediterranean region directly from Persia, and "Persian" in the name may just mean that people felt it came from somewhere in the east. Latin *malum Persicum* was shortened to *persicum,* which later became *persica.* Latin *persica* developed into *pesche* in Old French, and this word became the source of English *peach.*

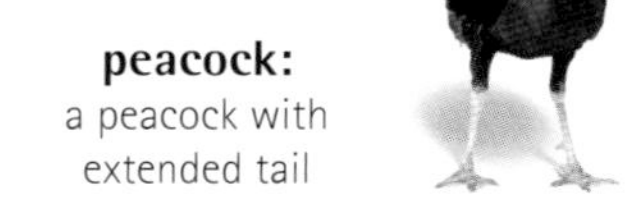
peacock: a peacock with extended tail

pea•cock \'pē-ˌkäk\ *n*
▲ the male of a very large Asian pheasant that can lift up its very long colorful tail and spread it apart like a fan

peak \'pēk\ *n*
1 ▼ a prominent mountain ⟨We saw a snowy *peak* rising from the plain.⟩
2 the pointed top of a hill or mountain ⟨I climbed all the way to the *peak.*⟩
3 a sharp or pointed end ⟨The roof rises to a *peak.*⟩
4 the highest point of development ⟨He is at the *peak* of his career.⟩

[1]**peaked** \'pēkt\ *adj*
having a point or a prominent end

[2]**peak•ed** \'pē-kəd\ *adj*
looking pale and sick

[1]**peal** \'pēl\ *n*
1 the sound of bells
2 a loud sound : a series of loud sounds ⟨a *peal* of thunder⟩

peak 1

[2]**peal** *vb* **pealed; peal•ing**
to make a loud sound and especially the sound of bells.

pea•nut \'pē-ˌnət\ *n*
a nutlike edible seed related to the pea that comes from the tough underground pods of a widely grown plant and that are eaten whole or crushed to form a spread (**peanut butter**) or produce oil for cooking (**peanut oil**)

pear \'per\ *n*
a fruit with pale green or brownish skin and white sweet juicy flesh that is usually larger at the end opposite the stem

pearl \'pərl\ *n*
1 ▼ a smooth rounded shiny usually white body that is formed within the shell of some mollusks (as oysters) usually around an irritating particle which has gotten into the shell
2 MOTHER-OF-PEARL
3 something like a pearl in shape, color, or value

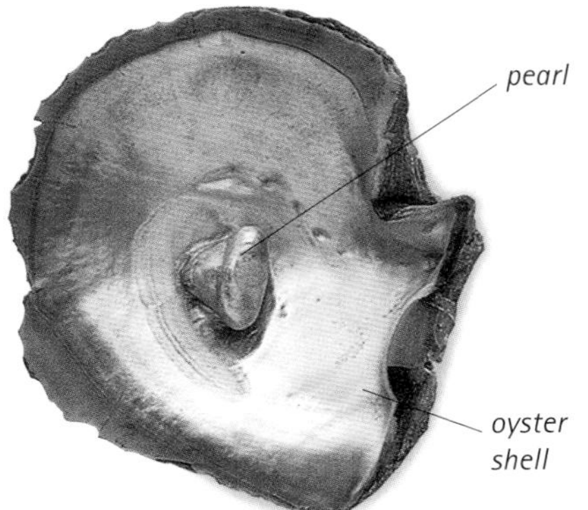

pearl 1: a pearl shown in the oyster shell in which it formed

pearly \'pər-lē\ *adj* **pearl•i•er; pearl•i•est**
resembling a pearl in color, shape, or luster

peas•ant \'pe-zᵊnt\ *n*
a farmer or farm worker of low social class

peat \'pēt\ *n*
a blackish or dark brown material that is the remains of plants partly decayed in water and is dug and dried for use as fuel

peat moss *n*
a spongy brownish moss of wet areas that is often the chief plant making up peat

peb•ble \'pe-bəl\ *n*
a small rounded stone

pe•can \pi-'kän, -'kan; 'pē-ˌkan\ *n*
an oval edible nut related to the walnut that usually has a thin shell and is the fruit of a tall tree of the central and southern United States

peccary: a collared peccary

pec•ca•ry \'pe-kə-rē\ *n, pl* **pec•ca•ries**
▲ a mostly tropical American animal that gathers in herds, is active at night, and looks like but is smaller than the related pig

[1]**peck** \'pek\ *vb* **pecked; peck•ing**
1 to strike or pick up with the beak or a sharp instrument (as a pick) 〈Birds *pecked* the cherries that filled the tree.〉
2 to make by striking with the beak or a sharp instrument 〈Birds *pecked* holes.〉

[2]**peck** *n*
1 a unit of capacity equal to one quarter of a bushel
2 a great deal **:** a large quantity 〈She's in a *peck* of trouble.〉

[3]**peck** *n*
1 the act of striking with the bill or with a sharp instrument
2 a mark made by striking with the bill or with a sharp instrument

pe•cu•liar \pi-'kyül-yər\ *adj*
1 of or limited to only one person, thing, or place 〈It's a custom *peculiar* to England.〉
2 different from the usual **:** ODD
pe•cu•liar•ly *adv*

► **Word History** The word *peculiar* first meant "a person's own." You may have some quality that is just your own. No one else has it. That surely makes it unusual. This is how *peculiar* came to mean "unusual" or "odd."

pe•cu•li•ar•i•ty \pi-ˌkyü-lē-'er-ə-tē\ *n, pl* **pe•cu•li•ar•i•ties**
1 something odd or individual 〈All of us have some *peculiarities.*〉
2 the quality or state of being odd or individual

[1]**ped•al** \'pe-dᵊl\ *n*
a lever worked by the foot or feet

[2]**pedal** *vb* **ped•aled** *also* **ped•alled; ped•al•ing** *also* **ped•al•ling**
to use or work levers with a foot or feet 〈She's learning how to *pedal* a bicycle.〉

ped•dle \'pe-dᵊl\ *vb* **ped•dled; ped•dling**
to go about especially from house to house with goods for sale

ped•dler *also* **ped•lar** \'ped-lər\ *n*
someone who goes about trying to sell things

ped•es•tal \'ped-əs-tᵊl\ *n*
1 ▼ a support or foot of an upright structure (as a column, statue, or lamp)
2 a position of high regard 〈The students put their teacher on a *pedestal.*〉

pe•des•tri•an \pə-'des-trē-ən\ *n*
a person who is walking

pe•di•a•tri•cian \ˌpē-dē-ə-'tri-shən\ *n*
a doctor who specializes in the care of babies and children

pedestal 1: a pedestal supporting a statue of an ancient Roman god

ped•i•cure \'pe-di-,kyu̇r\ *n*
a treatment of the feet, toes, and toenails for beauty or comfort

ped•i•gree \'pe-də-,grē\ *n*
1 a table or list showing the line of ancestors of a person or animal
2 a line of ancestors

pe•dom•e•ter \pi-'dä-mə-tər\ *n*
an instrument that measures the distance a person covers in walking

[1]**peek** \'pēk\ *vb* **peeked**; **peek•ing**
1 to look in a sneaky or cautious way 〈He *peeked* through the bushes.〉
2 to take a quick glance 〈I *peeked* at the next chapter.〉

[2]**peek** *n*
a quick or sly look

[1]**peel** \'pēl\ *vb* **peeled**; **peel•ing**
1 to strip off the skin or bark of 〈I'm *peeling* apples.〉
2 to strip or tear off
3 to come off smoothly or in bits 〈The paint is *peeling.*〉
peel•er \'pē-lər\ *n*

[2]**peel** *n*
an outer covering and especially the skin of a fruit

[1]**peep** \'pēp\ *vb* **peeped**; **peep•ing**
1 to look through or as if through a small hole or a crack : PEEK
2 to look quickly
3 to show slightly 〈There are crocuses *peeping* through the snow.〉

[2]**peep** *n*
1 a quick or sneaky look
2 the first appearance 〈We were at the shore by the *peep* of dawn.〉

[3]**peep** *vb* **peeped**; **peeping**
to make a short high sound such as a young bird makes
peep•er *n*

[4]**peep** *n*
a short high sound

[1]**peer** \'pir\ *vb* **peered**; **peer•ing**
1 to look curiously or carefully
2 to come slightly into view : peep out

[2]**peer** *n*
1 a person of the same rank or kind : EQUAL
2 a member of one of the five ranks (duke, marquis, earl, viscount, and baron) of the British nobility

peer•less \'pir-ləs\ *adj*
having no equal

pee•vish \'pē-vish\ *adj*
complaining a lot : IRRITABLE
pee•vish•ly *adv*
pee•vish•ness *n*

pee•wee \'pē-,wē\ *n*
someone or something that is small

[1]**peg** \'peg\ *n*
1 a small stick or rod (as of wood or metal) used especially to fasten things together or to hang things on
2 a piece driven into the ground to mark a boundary or to hold something 〈He pounded in a *peg* for a tent rope.〉
3 a level in approval or esteem 〈The new kid took that bragger down a *peg.*〉

[2]**peg** *vb* **pegged**; **peg•ging**
1 to mark or fasten with a small stick or rod driven into a surface
2 to work hard 〈I keep *pegging* away at my job.〉

PEI *abbr* Prince Edward Island

pel•i•can \'pe-li-kən\ *n*
► a large bird with webbed feet and a very large bill having a pouch on the lower part used to scoop in fish for food

pel•la•gra \pə-'la-grə, -'lā-\ *n*
a disease caused by a diet containing too little protein and too little of a necessary vitamin

pel•let \'pe-lət\ *n*
1 a little ball (as of food or medicine)
2 a piece of small shot
3 a wad of material (as bones and fur) that cannot be digested and has been thrown up by a bird of prey (as an owl)

pell–mell \'pel-'mel\ *adv*
in a confused or hurried way

[1]**pelt** \'pelt\ *n*
a skin of an animal especially with its fur or wool

[2]**pelt** *vb* **pelt•ed**; **pelt•ing**
1 to hit with repeated blows
2 to repeatedly throw (something) at 〈Children *pelted* each other with snowballs.〉
3 to beat or pound against something again and again 〈Rain *pelted* on the roof.〉

pel•vis \'pel-vəs\ *n*
the bowl-shaped part of the skeleton that includes the hip bones and the lower bones of the backbone

[1]**pen** \'pen\ *n*
an instrument for writing with ink

[2]**pen** *vb* **penned**; **pen•ning**
to write especially with a pen 〈Who *penned* this poem?〉

[3]**pen** *n*
a small enclosure especially for animals

[4]**pen** *vb* **penned**; **pen•ning**
to shut in a small enclosure

pe•nal \'pē-nᵊl\ *adj*
relating to or used for punishment

pe•nal•ize \'pē-nə-,līz, 'pe-\ *vb* **pe•nal•ized**; **pe•nal•iz•ing**
to give a penalty to 〈You'll be *penalized* for cheating.〉

pen•al•ty \'pe-nᵊl-tē\ *n, pl* **pen•al•ties**
1 punishment for doing something wrong
2 a disadvantage given for breaking a rule in a sport or game

pen•ance \'pe-nəns\ *n*
an act showing sorrow or regret for sin

pence *pl of* PENNY

[1]**pen•cil** \'pen-səl\ *n*
a device for writing or drawing consisting of a stick of black or colored material enclosed in wood, plastic, or metal

pelican: a Dalmatian \dal-'mā-shən\ Pelican

[2]**pencil** *vb* **pen•ciled** *or* **pen•cilled**; **pen•cil•ing** *or* **pen•cil•ling**
to write, mark, or draw with a pencil

pen•dant \'pen-dənt\ *n*
a piece of jewelry hanging on a chain or cord that is worn around the neck

[1]**pend•ing** \'pen-diŋ\ *prep*
while waiting for 〈He's in jail *pending* a trial.〉

[2]**pending** *adj*
not yet decided 〈The lawsuit is *pending.*〉

pen•du•lum \'pen-jə-ləm, -dyə-\ *n*
a weight hung from a point so as to swing freely back and forth under the action of gravity

pen•e•trate \'pe-nə-,trāt\ *vb* **pen•e•trat•ed**; **pen•e•trat•ing**
1 to pass into or through 〈A nail *penetrated* the tire.〉
2 to see into or through

pen•e•tra•tion \,pe-nə-'trā-shən\ *n*
1 the act or process of piercing
2 keen understanding

A B C D E F G H I J K L M N O P Q R S T U V W X Y Z

penguin: a penguin diving underwater

pen•guin \'pen-gwən, 'peŋ-\ *n*
▲ a short-legged seabird that cannot fly, uses its stiff wings for swimming, and is found in the colder regions of the southern hemisphere

pen•i•cil•lin \,pe-nə-'si-lən\ *n*
an antibiotic that is produced by a mold and is used against disease-causing bacteria

pen•in•su•la \pə-'nin-sə-lə\ *n*
a piece of land extending out into a body of water

pe•nis \'pē-nəs\ *n, pl* **pe•nis•es** *also* **pe•nes** \-,nēz\
a male organ in mammals through which urine and sperm leave the body

pen•i•tence \'pe-nə-təns\ *n*
deep sadness that a person feels for his or her sins or faults

[1]pen•i•tent \'pe-nə-tənt\ *adj*
feeling or showing sadness for a person's own sins or faults

[2]penitent *n*
a person who feels or shows sorrow for sins or faults

pen•i•ten•tia•ry \,pe-nə-'ten-shə-rē\ *n, pl* **pen•i•ten•tia•ries**
PRISON

pen•knife \'pen-,nīf\ *n, pl* **pen•knives** \-,nīvz\
a small jackknife

pen•man•ship \'pen-mən-,ship\ *n*
style or quality of handwriting

Penn., Penna. *abbr* Pennsylvania

pen name *n*
a false name that an author uses on his or her work

pen•nant \'pe-nənt\ *n*
1 a narrow pointed flag used for identification, signaling, or decoration
2 a flag that serves as the emblem of a championship

pen•ni•less \'pe-ni-ləs\ *adj*
very poor : having no money

pen•ny \'pe-nē\ *n, pl* **pennies** \'pe-nēz\
1 CENT
2 *or pl* **pence** \'pens\ a coin of the United Kingdom equal to 1/100 pound

pen pal *n*
a friend known only through letter writing

[1]pen•sion \'pen-shən\ *n*
a sum paid regularly to a person who has retired from work

[2]pension *vb* **pen•sioned**; **pen•sion•ing**
to grant or give a regularly paid sum to (a person who has retired from work)

pen•sive \'pen-siv\ *adj*
lost in serious or sad thought ⟨a *pensive* mood⟩
pen•sive•ly *adv*

pent \'pent\ *adj*
kept inside : not released ⟨*pent* emotions⟩

penta- *or* **pent-** *prefix*
five

pen•ta•gon \'pen-tə-,gän\ *n*
a flat geometric figure having five angles and five sides

pen•tath•lon \pen-'tath-lən, -,län\ *n*
an athletic contest in which each person participates in five different events

pent•house \'pent-,haùs\ *n*
an apartment on the top floor or roof of a building

pe•on \'pē-,än\ *n*
a person who does hard or dull work for very little money

pe•o•ny \'pē-ə-nē\ *n, pl* **pe•o•nies**
a plant that is widely grown for its large showy white, pink, or red flowers

[1]peo•ple \'pē-pəl\ *n, pl* **people** *or* **peoples**
1 all persons considered together
2 a group of human beings who have something in common ⟨young *people*⟩ ⟨the *people* of Montana⟩
Hint: The word *people* is often used in compounds instead of *persons*. ⟨sales*people*⟩
3 a body of persons making up a race, tribe, or nation ⟨the *peoples* of Asia⟩

[2]people *vb* **peo•pled**; **peo•pling**
1 to fill with human beings or a certain type of human beings
2 to dwell on or in

[1]pep \'pep\ *n*
brisk energy or liveliness

[2]pep *vb* **pepped**; **pep•ping**
to make more lively or energetic ⟨Cool weather *peps* us up.⟩

[1]pep•per \'pe-pər\ *n*
1 a black or white spice that has a sharp flavor and comes from the dried ground-up fruit of an Indian climbing shrub
2 a usually green, red, or yellow vegetable that has a sharp or mildly sweet flavor and grows on a bushy garden plant

[2]pepper *vb* **pep•pered**; **pep•per•ing**
1 to season with or as if with pepper
2 to hit with or as if with a shower of blows or objects ⟨Hail *peppered* the hikers.⟩ ⟨Freckles *peppered* his face.⟩

pep•per•mint \'pe-pər-,mint\ *n*
1 a mint plant with small usually purple flowers that yields an oil used especially to flavor candies
2 a candy flavored with peppermint

pep•per•o•ni \,pe-pə-'rō-nē\ *n*
▼ a spicy dry Italian sausage

pepperoni: sliced pepperoni

pep•py \'pe-pē\ *adj* **pep•pi•er**; **pep•pi•est**
full of brisk energy or liveliness

pep•sin \'pep-sən\ *n*
an enzyme that starts the digestion of proteins in the stomach

A B C D E F G H I J K L M N O P Q R S T U V W X Y Z

per \ˈpər\ *prep*
1 to or for each ⟨It cost us ten dollars *per* day.⟩
2 as directed by ⟨Construction was done *per* instructions.⟩

per an•num \pər-ˈa-nəm\ *adv*
by the year : in or for each year : ANNUALLY

per cap•i•ta \pər-ˈka-pə-tə\ *adv or adj*
by or for each person ⟨What is the *per capita* income?⟩

per•ceive \pər-ˈsēv\ *vb* **per•ceived**; **per•ceiv•ing**
1 to become aware of through the senses and especially through sight
2 to recognize or realize ⟨I *perceived* a change in her attitude.⟩
3 to think of as ⟨The message was *perceived* as a threat.⟩

[1]**per•cent** \pər-ˈsent\ *adj or adv*
out of every hundred : measured by the number of units as compared with one hundred

[2]**percent** *n, pl* **percent**
a part or fraction of a whole expressed in hundredths

per•cent•age \pər-ˈsen-tij\ *n*
1 a part of a whole expressed in hundredths
2 a share of profits

per•cep•ti•ble \pər-ˈsep-tə-bəl\ *adj*
possible to detect ⟨There has been a *perceptible* change.⟩

per•cep•tion \pər-ˈsep-shən\ *n*
1 a judgment resulting from awareness or understanding ⟨Visiting the beautiful park changed her *perception* of the city.⟩
2 the ability to understand (as meanings and ideas) ⟨He's a child of remarkable *perception.*⟩
3 understanding or awareness gained through the use of the senses ⟨depth *perception*⟩

[1]**perch** \ˈpərch\ *n*
1 a place where birds roost
2 a raised seat or position

[2]**perch** *vb* **perched**; **perch•ing**
to sit or rest on a raised seat or position

[3]**perch** *n, pl* **perch** *or* **perch•es**
1 a common yellow and greenish brown fish of North America that is sometimes caught for food or sport
2 any of various fish related to or resembling the North American perch

per•chance \pər-ˈchans\ *adv*
PERHAPS

per•co•late \ˈpər-kə-ˌlāt\ *vb* **per•co•lat•ed**; **per•co•lat•ing**
1 to trickle or cause to trickle through something porous : OOZE ⟨Water *percolated* through sand.⟩

percussion
Percussion instruments may have been the earliest type of musical instrument. Most are used to emphasize rhythm and add impact to music, although some, such as the xylophone, can be tuned to produce separate musical notes.

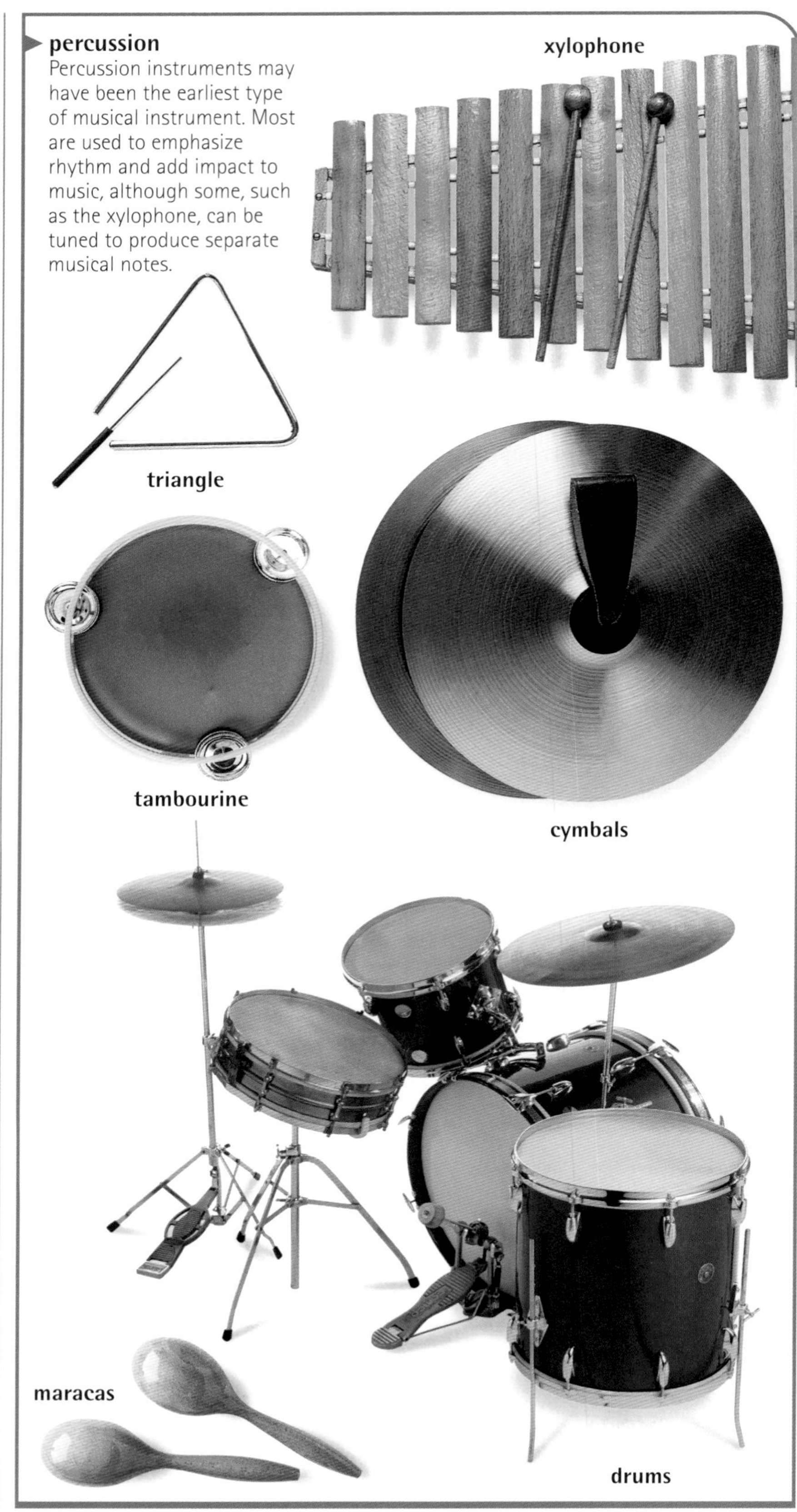

2 to prepare (coffee) by passing hot water through ground coffee beans again and again
per•co•la•tion \ˌpər-kə-ˈlā-shən\ *n*
per•co•la•tor \-ˌlā-tər\ *n*

per•cus•sion \pər-ˈkə-shən\ *n*
◀ the musical instruments (as drums, cymbals, and maracas) that are played by striking or shaking

[1]**pe•ren•ni•al** \pə-ˈre-nē-əl\ *adj*
1 present all through the year ⟨a *perennial* stream⟩
2 living from year to year ⟨a *perennial* plant⟩
3 never ending : CONSTANT ⟨*perennial* joy⟩
4 happening again and again ⟨*perennial* flooding⟩

[2]**perennial** *n*
▶ a plant that lives from year to year

[1]**per•fect** \ˈpər-fikt\ *adj*
1 having no mistake or flaw ⟨a *perfect* plan⟩ ⟨a *perfect* diamond⟩
2 satisfying all requirements ⟨It was the *perfect* ending to a *perfect* day.⟩
3 thoroughly skilled or trained : meeting the highest standards ⟨a *perfect* performance⟩
4 [1]TOTAL 3 ⟨*perfect* silence⟩
per•fect•ly *adv*

[2]**per•fect** \pər-ˈfekt\ *vb* **per•fect•ed**; **per•fect•ing**
to improve (something) so that it has no flaws ⟨Dad *perfected* his golf swing.⟩

per•fec•tion \pər-ˈfek-shən\ *n*
1 a quality or condition that cannot be improved
2 the act of improving something so that it has no flaws
3 excellence or skill without flaw

per•fo•rate \ˈpər-fə-ˌrāt\ *vb* **per•fo•rat•ed**; **per•fo•rat•ing**
to make a hole or many holes through

per•form \pər-ˈfȯrm\ *vb* **per•formed**; **per•form•ing**
1 to carry out : DO ⟨Anyone can *perform* this task.⟩
2 to do something needing special skill ⟨The doctor had to *perform* surgery.⟩
3 to give a public presentation for entertainment ⟨The band *performed* in the park.⟩
per•form•er *n*

per•for•mance \pər-ˈfȯr-məns\ *n*
1 the carrying out of an action ⟨He's in the *performance* of his duty.⟩
2 a public entertainment ⟨We attended a symphony *performance*.⟩

[1]**per•fume** \ˈpər-ˌfyüm\ *n*
1 a liquid used to make a person smell nice
2 a pleasant smell : FRAGRANCE

▶ [2]**perennial**
There are two main types of perennial: herbaceous \ˌhər-ˈbā-shəs, ˌər-ˈbā-shəs\ perennials, which have no woody parts and die down to the ground at the end of each growing season, such as the garden plants shown here, and woody perennials, which have stems that do not die, but add new tissue each season. Woody perennials include shrubs and trees. A perennial typically flowers in the same season each year.

seaside daisy

lily of the valley

daylily \ˈdā-ˌlil-ē\ a popular garden palnt

[2]**per•fume** \pər-ˈfyüm\ *vb* **per•fumed**; **per•fum•ing**
to add a usually pleasant odor to : have the odor of

per•haps \pər-ˈhaps\ *adv*
possibly but not certainly : MAYBE ⟨*Perhaps* we'll go.⟩

per•il \ˈper-əl\ *n*
1 the state of being in great danger ⟨The storm put our ship in *peril*.⟩
2 a cause or source of danger ⟨the *perils* of skydiving⟩

per•il•ous \ˈper-ə-ləs\ *adj*
DANGEROUS 1 ⟨a *perilous* journey⟩
per•il•ous•ly *adv*

pe•rim•e•ter \pə-ˈri-mə-tər\ *n*
1 the whole outer boundary of a figure or area
2 the length of the boundary of a figure

pe•ri•od \ˈpir-ē-əd\ *n*
1 a punctuation mark . used chiefly to mark the end of a declarative sentence or an abbreviation
2 a portion of time set apart by some quality ⟨a *period* of cool weather⟩
3 a portion of time that forms a stage in history ⟨the colonial *period*⟩
4 one of the divisions of a school day ⟨I have math second *period*.⟩
5 a single occurrence of menstruation

▶ **Synonyms** PERIOD and AGE mean a portion of time. PERIOD can be used of any portion of time, no matter how long or short. ⟨We waited a *period* of five minutes.⟩ ⟨A new *period* of space exploration has begun.⟩ AGE is used of a longer period of time that is associated with an important person or outstanding thing. ⟨I'm reading about the *age* of Thomas Jefferson.⟩ ⟨We live in the computer *age*.⟩

pe•ri•od•ic \ˌpir-ē-ˈä-dik\ *adj*
occurring regularly over a period of time

a b c d e f g h i j k l m n o p q r s t u v w x y z

[1]pe•ri•od•i•cal \ˌpir-ē-ˈä-di-kəl\ *adj*
1 PERIODIC
2 published regularly
pe•ri•od•i•cal•ly *adv*

[2]periodical *n*
something (as a magazine) published regularly (as every month)

peri•scope \ˈper-ə-ˌskōp\ *n*
► an instrument containing lenses and mirrors by which a person (as on a submarine) can get a view that would otherwise be blocked

per•ish \ˈper-ish\ *vb* **per•ished**; **per•ish•ing**
to become destroyed : DIE ⟨Dinosaurs *perished* long ago.⟩ ⟨The language slowly *perished.*⟩

per•ish•able \ˈper-i-shə-bəl\ *adj*
likely to spoil or decay ⟨Remember to refrigerate *perishable* foods.⟩

[1]per•i•win•kle \ˈper-i-ˌwiŋ-kəl\ *n*
an evergreen plant that spreads along the ground and has blue or white flowers

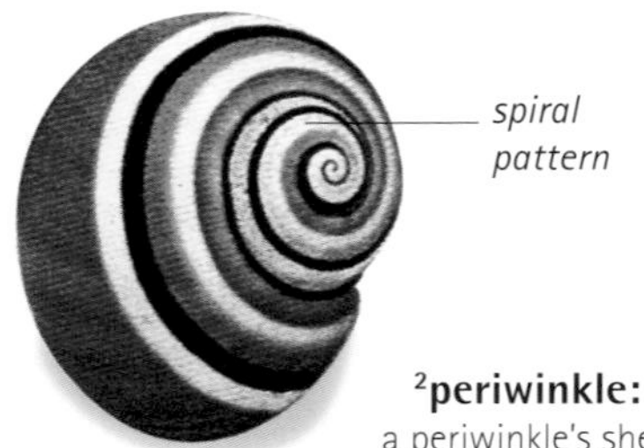

[2]periwinkle: a periwinkle's shell

[2]periwinkle *n*
▲a small snail that lives along rocky seashores

perk \ˈpərk\ *vb* **perked**; **perk•ing**
1 to make or become more lively or cheerful ⟨I *perked* up when I heard the good news.⟩
2 to make fresher in appearance ⟨Let's *perk* the room up with fresh paint.⟩
3 to lift in a quick, alert, or bold way ⟨The dog *perked* its ears.⟩

perky \ˈpər-kē\ *adj* **perk•i•er**; **perk•i•est**
being lively and cheerful

per•ma•nence \ˈpər-mə-nəns\ *n*
the quality or state of lasting forever or for a long time

per•ma•nent \ˈpər-mə-nənt\ *adj*
lasting or meant to last for a long time : not temporary
per•ma•nent•ly *adv*

per•me•able \ˈpər-mē-ə-bəl\ *adj*
having pores or openings that let liquids or gases pass through

per•me•ate \ˈper-mē-ˌāt\ *vb* **per•me•at•ed**; **per•me•at•ing**
1 to pass through something that has pores or small openings or is in a loose form ⟨Water *permeates* sand.⟩
2 to spread throughout ⟨The smell of smoke *permeated* the room.⟩

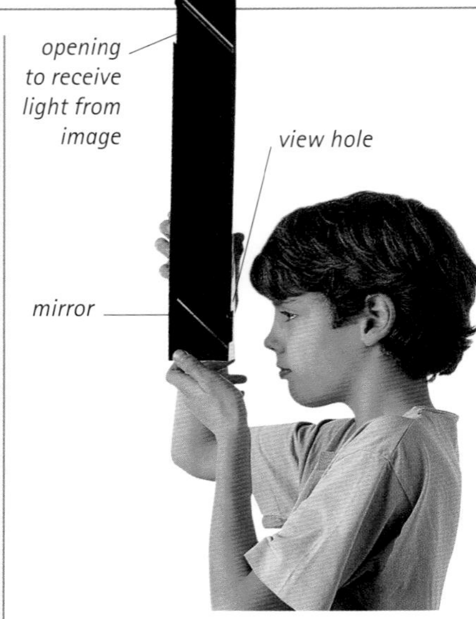

periscope: a boy looking through a periscope in cross-section

per•mis•sion \pər-ˈmi-shən\ *n*
the approval of a person in authority ⟨I have *permission* to leave early.⟩

[1]per•mit \pər-ˈmit\ *vb* **per•mit•ted**; **per•mit•ting**
1 to allow to happen or do : give permission
2 to make possible : give an opportunity ⟨We'll visit the museum if time *permits.*⟩

[2]per•mit \ˈpər-ˌmit\ *n*
a statement of permission (as a license or pass) ⟨You need a parking *permit.*⟩

per•ni•cious \pər-ˈni-shəs\ *adj*
causing great damage or harm ⟨a *pernicious* disease⟩ ⟨a *pernicious* habit⟩

per•ox•ide \pə-ˈräk-ˌsīd\ *n*
HYDROGEN PEROXIDE

[1]per•pen•dic•u•lar \ˌpər-pən-ˈdi-kyə-lər\ *adj*
1 exactly vertical
2 being at right angles to a line or surface ⟨The letter T is made with two *perpendicular* lines.⟩
per•pen•dic•u•lar•ly *adv*

[2]perpendicular *n*
a line, surface, or position at right angles to another line, surface, or position

per•pe•trate \ˈpər-pə-ˌtrāt\ *vb* **per•pe•trat•ed**; **per•pe•trat•ing**
to bring about or carry out : COMMIT ⟨Thieves *perpetrated* the crime.⟩
per•pe•tra•tor \ˈpər-pə-ˌtrā-tər\ *n*

per•pet•u•al \pər-ˈpe-chə-wəl\ *adj*
1 lasting forever or for a very long time ⟨a *perpetual* memorial⟩
2 occurring continually : CONSTANT ⟨*perpetual* arguments⟩
per•pet•u•al•ly *adv*

per•pet•u•ate \pər-ˈpe-chə-ˌwāt\ *vb* **per•pet•u•at•ed**; **per•pet•u•at•ing**
to cause to last a long time

per•plex \pər-ˈpleks\ *vb* **per•plexed**; **per•plex•ing**
to make unable to understand : CONFUSE

per•plexed \pər-ˈplekst\ *adj*
unable to understand something clearly or to think clearly

per•plex•i•ty \pər-ˈplek-sə-tē\ *n, pl* **per•plex•i•ties**
1 a puzzled or anxious state of mind
2 something that puzzles

per•se•cute \ˈpər-si-ˌkyüt\ *vb* **per•se•cut•ed**; **per•se•cut•ing**
to treat continually in a cruel and harmful way

per•se•cu•tion \ˌpər-si-ˈkyü-shən\ *n*
1 the act of continually treating in a cruel and harmful way
2 the state of being continually treated in a cruel and harmful way

per•se•ver•ance \ˌpər-sə-ˈvir-əns\ *n*
the act or power of continuing to do something in spite of difficulties

per•se•vere \ˌpər-sə-ˈvir\ *vb* **per•se•vered**; **per•se•ver•ing**
to keep trying to do something in spite of difficulties ⟨She *persevered* in learning to speak French.⟩

per•sim•mon \pər-ˈsi-mən\ *n*
▼ an orange roundish sweet fruit that grows on a tree of the southeastern United States and Asia and may be very sour when unripe

persimmon

per•sist \pər-ˈsist\ *vb* **per•sist•ed**; **per•sist•ing**
1 to keep on doing or saying something : continue stubbornly ⟨The reporter *persisted* with questions.⟩
2 to last on and on : continue to exist or occur ⟨Rain *persisted* for days.⟩

per•sist•ence \pər-ˈsi-stəns\ *n*
1 the act or fact of stubbornly continuing to do something

2 the act or fact of continuing to exist longer than usual

per•sist•ent \pər-ˈsi-stənt\ *adj*
continuing to act or exist longer than usual ⟨a *persistent* cold⟩
per•sist•ent•ly *adv*

per•son \ˈpər-sᵊn\ *n*
1 a human being considered as an individual ⟨I had never heard a *person* speak Arabic.⟩
Hint: The word *person* is sometimes used in compounds especially to avoid *man* in words that apply to both sexes. ⟨chair*person*⟩
2 the body of a human being ⟨Keep your *person* neat.⟩

per•son•able \ˈpərs-nə-bəl, ˈpər-sə-nə-bəl\ *adj*
pleasing in appearance or manner

per•son•age \ˈpər-sə-nij\ *n*
an important or famous person

per•son•al \ˈpər-sə-nəl\ *adj*
1 of, relating to, or belonging to an individual human being : not public : not general ⟨*personal* property⟩
2 made or done by a particular individual and not by someone acting for him or her ⟨The mayor made a *personal* appearance.⟩
3 of the body ⟨Take precautions for *personal* safety.⟩
4 relating to someone's private matters ⟨May I ask you a *personal* question?⟩
5 intended for or given to one particular individual ⟨I received *personal* service.⟩
6 relating to a particular individual or his or her qualities often in a way that is hurtful ⟨I took the remark as a *personal* insult.⟩
per•son•al•ly *adv*

personal computer *n*
a computer designed for an individual user

per•son•al•i•ty \ˌpər-sə-ˈna-lə-tē\ *n, pl* **per•son•al•i•ties**
1 the qualities (as moods or habits) that make one human being different from others ⟨She has a cheerful *personality.*⟩
2 a human being's pleasing or interesting qualities ⟨He doesn't have much *personality.*⟩
3 a famous person

personal pronoun *n*
a pronoun (as *I, you, it,* or *they*) used instead of a noun that names a definite person or thing

per•son•i•fy \pər-ˈsä-nə-ˌfī\ *vb* **per•son•i•fied; per•son•i•fy•ing**
to think of or represent as a person ⟨The hero is bravery *personified.*⟩

per•son•nel \ˌpər-sə-ˈnel\ *n*
a group of people employed in a business or an organization

per•spec•tive \pər-ˈspek-tiv\ *n*
1 the angle or direction in which a person looks at an object
2 POINT OF VIEW
3 the ability to understand what is important and what isn't ⟨I know you're disappointed, but keep your *perspective.*⟩
4 an accurate rating of what is important and what isn't ⟨Let's keep things in *perspective.*⟩
5 the art of painting or drawing a scene so that objects in it seem to have their right shape and to be the right distance apart

per•spi•ra•tion \ˌpər-spə-ˈrā-shən\ *n*
1 the act or process of perspiring
2 salty liquid given off from skin glands

per•spire \pər-ˈspīr\ *vb* **per•spired; per•spir•ing**
to give off salty liquid through the skin

per•suade \pər-ˈswād\ *vb* **per•suad•ed; per•suad•ing**
to win over to a belief or way of acting : CONVINCE

per•sua•sion \pər-ˈswā-zhən\ *n*
1 the act of convincing
2 the power to convince
3 a way of believing : BELIEF ⟨He and his wife are of the same *persuasion.*⟩

per•sua•sive \pər-ˈswā-siv\ *adj*
able or likely to convince ⟨a *persuasive* salesman⟩
per•sua•sive•ly *adv*
per•sua•sive•ness *n*

pert \ˈpərt\ *adj*
1 rude and disrespectful : FRESH
2 PERKY

per•tain \pər-ˈtān\ *vb* **per•tained; per•tain•ing**
1 to relate to a person or thing ⟨The laws *pertain* to hunting.⟩
2 to belong to as a part, quality, or function ⟨These duties *pertain* to the office of sheriff.⟩

per•ti•nent \ˈpər-tə-nənt\ *adj*
relating to the subject that is being thought about or discussed : RELEVANT ⟨a *pertinent* question⟩

per•turb \pər-ˈtərb\ *vb* **per•turbed; per•turb•ing**
to disturb in mind : trouble greatly

pe•rus•al \pə-ˈrü-zəl\ *n*
the act of reading or reading through carefully

pe•ruse \pə-ˈrüz\ *vb* **pe•rused; pe•rus•ing**
1 READ 1
2 to read through carefully

per•vade \pər-ˈvād\ *vb* **per•vad•ed; per•vad•ing**
to spread through all parts of : PERMEATE ⟨Spicy smells *pervaded* the whole house.⟩

per•verse \pər-ˈvərs\ *adj*
1 stubborn in being against what is right or sensible
2 wrong especially in a way that is strange or offensive

pes•ky \ˈpe-skē\ *adj* **pesk•i•er; pesk•i•est**
TROUBLESOME 1 ⟨*pesky* ants⟩

pe•so \ˈpā-sō\ *n, pl* **pesos**
1 a bill or coin used in one of several Spanish-speaking countries of North and South America
2 a bill or coin used in the Philippines

pes•si•mism \ˈpe-sə-ˌmi-zəm\ *n*
a feeling or belief that things are usually bad or that bad things will happen

pes•si•mist \ˈpe-sə-mist\ *n*
a person who habitually expects bad things to happen or thinks things are bad

pes•si•mis•tic \ˌpe-sə-ˈmi-stik\ *adj*
1 tending to think that bad things will happen
2 having the belief that evil is more common than good

pest \ˈpest\ *n*
1 NUISANCE
2 a plant or animal that is harmful to humans or property
3 PESTILENCE

pes•ter \ˈpe-stər\ *vb* **pes•tered; pes•ter•ing**
to bother again and again
synonyms see ANNOY

pes•ti•cide \ˈpe-stə-ˌsīd\ *n*
a substance used to destroy pests (as insects or weeds)

pes•ti•lence \ˈpe-stə-ləns\ *n*
a contagious usually fatal disease that spreads quickly

pes•tle \ˈpe-səl\ *n*
▼ a tool shaped like a small club for crushing substances in a mortar

pestle: a pestle and mortar used to make ground pepper

¹pet \ˈpet\ *n*
1 a tame animal kept as a companion rather than for work
2 a person who is treated with special kindness or consideration ⟨teacher's *pet*⟩

A B C D E F G H I J K L M N O P Q R S T U V W X Y Z

[2]**pet** *adj*
1 kept or treated as a pet 〈a *pet* rabbit〉
2 showing fondness 〈a *pet* name〉
3 [2]FAVORITE 〈Restoring the old car is my *pet* project.〉

[3]**pet** *vb* **pet•ted**; **pet•ting**
to stroke or pat gently or lovingly

pet•al \ˈpe-təl\ *n*
one of the often brightly colored leaflike outer parts of a flower

pet•i•ole \ˈpe-tē-ˌōl\ *n*
the slender stem of a leaf

pe•tite \pə-ˈtēt\ *adj*
having a small trim figure

[1]**pe•ti•tion** \pə-ˈti-shən\ *n*
1 an earnest appeal
2 a formal written request made to an authority

[2]**petition** *vb* **pe•ti•tioned**; **pe•ti•tion•ing**
to make an often formal request to or for
pe•ti•tion•er *n*

pe•trel \ˈpe-trəl, ˈpē-\ *n*
a small seabird with long wings that flies far from land

pet•ri•fy \ˈpe-trə-ˌfī\ *vb* **pet•ri•fied**; **pet•ri•fy•ing**
1 to change plant or animal matter into stone or something like stone 〈*petrified* wood〉
2 to frighten very much

pe•tro•leum \pə-ˈtrō-lē-əm, -ˈtrōl-yəm\ *n*
a raw oil that is obtained from wells drilled in the ground and that is the source of gasoline, kerosene, and other oils used for fuel

pet•ti•coat \ˈpe-tē-ˌkōt\ *n*
► a skirt worn under a dress or outer skirt

petting zoo *n*
a collection of farm animals or gentle exotic animals for children to pet and feed

pet•ty \ˈpe-tē\ *adj*
pet•ti•er; **pet•ti•est**
1 small and of no importance 〈Don't worry about the *petty* details.〉
2 showing or having a mean narrow-minded attitude
pet•ti•ness \ˈpe-tē-nəs\ *n*

petty officer *n*
an officer in the navy or coast guard appointed from among the enlisted people

pet•u•lance \ˈpe-chə-ləns\ *n*
an irritable temper

pet•u•lant \ˈpe-chə-lənt\ *adj*
often in a bad mood : CROSS

pe•tu•nia \pə-ˈtü-nyə, -ˈtyü-\ *n*
a plant grown for its brightly colored flowers that are shaped like funnels

pew \ˈpyü\ *n*
one of the benches with backs and sometimes doors set in rows in a church

pe•wee \ˈpē-ˌwē\ *n*
a small grayish or greenish brown bird that eats flying insects

pew•ter \ˈpyü-tər\ *n*
1 a metallic substance made mostly of tin sometimes mixed with copper or antimony that is used in making utensils (as pitchers and bowls)
2 utensils made of pewter

pg. *abbr* page

pH \ˈpē-ˈāch\ *n*
a measure of the acidity or alkalinity of a substance 〈Lemon juice has a *pH* of about 2.5.〉 〈Water has a *pH* of 7.〉

phan•tom \ˈfan-təm\ *n*
an image or figure that can be sensed (as with the eyes or ears) but that is not real

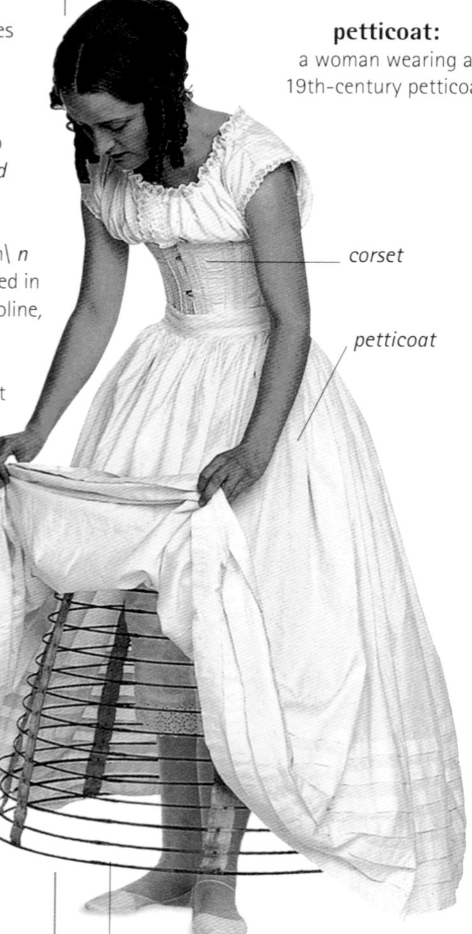

petticoat:
a woman wearing a 19th-century petticoat

pharaoh:
a golden mask representing the face of a young pharaoh

pha•raoh \ˈfer-ō\ *n, often cap*
▲ a ruler of ancient Egypt

phar•ma•cist \ˈfär-mə-səst\ *n*
a person whose job is preparing medicines according to a doctor's prescription

phar•ma•cy \ˈfär-mə-sē\ *n*, *pl* **phar•ma•cies**
a place where medicines are prepared and sold by a pharmacist : DRUGSTORE

phar•ynx \ˈfer-iŋks\ *n, pl* **pha•ryn•ges** \fə-ˈrin-ˌjēz\ *also* **phar•ynx•es**
a tube extending from the back of the nasal passages and mouth to the esophagus that is the passage through which air passes to the larynx and food to the esophagus

phase \ˈfāz\ *n*
1 a step or part in a series of events or actions : STAGE 〈I have completed the first *phase* of my training.〉
2 the way that the moon or a planet looks to the eye at any time in its series of changes with respect to how it shines 〈The new moon and the full moon are two *phases* of the moon.〉

pheas•ant \ˈfe-zᵊnt\ *n*
a large brightly colored bird with a long tail that is related to the chicken and is sometimes hunted for food or sport

phe•nom•e•nal \fi-ˈnä-mə-nᵊl\ *adj*
very remarkable : EXTRAORDINARY 〈He has a *phenomenal* memory.〉

phe•nom•e•non \fi-ˈnä-mə-ˌnän\ *n*, *pl* **phe•nom•e•na** \-nə\ *or* **phe•nom•e•nons**
1 *pl phenomena* an observable fact or event
2 a rare or important fact or event

3 *pl phenomenons* an extraordinary or exceptional person or thing

[1]**-phil** \ˌfil\ *or* **-phile** \ˌfīl\ *n suffix*
a person who loves or is strongly attracted to

[2]**-phil** *or* **-phile** *adj suffix*
having a fondness for or strong attraction to

phil•an•throp•ic \ˌfi-lən-'thrä-pik\ *adj*
for or relating to the act of giving money and time to help needy people : CHARITABLE 〈I do *philanthropic* work.〉

phi•lan•thro•pist \fə-'lan-thrə-pəst\ *n*
a person who gives generously to help other people

phi•lan•thro•py \fə-'lan-thrə-pē\ *n, pl* **phi•lan•thro•pies**
1 desire and active effort to help other people
2 something done or given to help needy people
3 an organization giving or supported by charitable gifts

phil•o•den•dron \ˌfi-lə-'den-drən\ *n*
a plant often grown for its showy usually shiny leaves

phi•los•o•pher \fə-'lä-sə-fər\ *n*
1 a person who studies ideas about knowledge, right and wrong, reasoning, and the value of things
2 a person who takes misfortunes with calmness and courage

phil•o•soph•i•cal \ˌfi-lə-'sä-fi-kəl\ *also* **phil•o•soph•ic** \-'sä-fik\ *adj*
1 of or relating to the study of basic ideas about knowledge, right and wrong, reasoning, and the value of things
2 showing wisdom and calm when faced with misfortune
phil•o•soph•i•cal•ly *adv*

phi•los•o•phy \fə-'lä-sə-fē\ *n, pl* **phi•los•o•phies**
1 the study of the basic ideas about knowledge, right and wrong, reasoning, and the value of things
2 a specific set of ideas of a person or a group 〈Greek *philosophy*〉
3 a set of ideas about how to do something or how to live 〈Live and let live—that's my *philosophy*.〉

phlox \'fläks\ *n, pl* **phlox** *or* **phlox•es**
►a plant grown for its showy clusters of usually white, pink, or purplish flowers

pho•bia \'fō-bē-ə\ *n*
an unreasonable, abnormal, and lasting fear of something

phoe•be \'fē-bē\ *n*
a small grayish brown bird that eats flying insects

phoe•nix \'fē-niks\ *n*
a legendary bird which was thought to live for 500 years, burn itself to death, and rise newborn from the ashes

phon- *or* **phono-** *prefix*
sound : voice : speech 〈*phono*graph〉

[1]**phone** \'fōn\ *n*
[1]TELEPHONE

[2]**phone** *vb* **phoned; phon•ing**
[2]TELEPHONE

pho•neme \'fō-ˌnēm\ *n*
one of the smallest units of speech that distinguish one utterance from another

pho•net•ic \fə-'ne-tik\ *adj*
of or relating to spoken language or speech sounds

pho•nics \'fä-niks\ *n*
a method of teaching beginners to read and pronounce words by learning the usual sound of letters, letter groups, and syllables

pho•no•graph \'fō-nə-ˌgraf\ *n*
►an instrument that reproduces sounds recorded on a grooved disk

[1]**pho•ny** *also* **pho•ney** \'fō-nē\ *adj* **pho•ni•er; pho•ni•est**
not real or genuine 〈a *phony* dollar bill〉

[2]**phony** *also* **phoney** *n, pl* **pho•nies** *also* **pho•neys**
1 a person who is not sincere
2 something that is not real or genuine

phos•pho•rus \'fäs-fə-rəs\ *n*
a white or yellowish waxy chemical element that gives a faint glow in moist air

pho•to \'fō-tō\ *n, pl* **photos**
[1]PHOTOGRAPH

phlox: white and pink phlox flowers

[1]**pho•to•copy** \'fō-tō-ˌkä-pē\ *n*
a copy of usually printed material made using a process in which an image is formed by the action of light on an electrically charged surface

[2]**photocopy** *vb* **pho•to•cop•ied; pho•to•copy•ing**
to make a photocopy of
pho•to•copi•er *n*

horn amplifies sound
record
needle converts uneven grooves in the record into sound

phonograph: an early 20th-century phonograph

[1]**pho•to•graph** \'fō-tə-ˌgraf\ *n*
a picture taken by a camera

[2]**photograph** *vb* **pho•to•graphed; pho•to•graph•ing**
to take a picture of with a camera
pho•tog•ra•pher \fə-'tä-grə-fər\ *n*

pho•to•graph•ic \ˌfō-tə-'gra-fik\ *adj*
obtained by or used in photography

pho•tog•ra•phy \fə-'tä-grə-fē\ *n*
the making of pictures by means of a camera that directs the image of an object onto a surface that is sensitive to light

pho•ton \'fō-ˌtän\ *n*
a tiny particle of light or electromagnetic radiation

pho•to•syn•the•sis \ˌfō-tə-'sin-thə-səs\ *n*
the process by which green plants and a few other organisms (as some protists) form carbohydrates from carbon dioxide and water in the presence of light
pho•to•syn•thet•ic \-sin-'the-tik\ *adj*

[1]phrase \'frāz\ *n*
1 a group of two or more words that express a single idea but do not form a complete sentence ⟨The group of words "out the door" in "they ran out the door" is a *phrase*.⟩
2 a brief expression that is commonly used

[2]phrase *vb* **phrased; phras•ing**
to express in words ⟨The boy was unable to *phrase* his idea.⟩

phy•lum \'fī-ləm\ *n, pl* **phy•la** \-lə\
a group of related living things (as animals or plants) that ranks above the class and below the kingdom in scientific classification

phys ed \'fiz-'ed\ *n*
PHYSICAL EDUCATION

phys•i•cal \'fi-zi-kəl\ *adj*
1 of the body : BODILY
2 existing in a form that can be touched or seen ⟨*physical* objects⟩
3 of or relating to physics
phys•i•cal•ly *adv*

physical education *n*
instruction in the care and development of the body

phy•si•cian \fə-'zi-shən\ *n*
a specialist in healing human disease : a doctor of medicine

phys•i•cist \'fi-zə-səst\ *n*
a person specializing in physics

phys•ics \'fi-ziks\ *n*
a science that deals with the facts about matter and motion and includes the subjects of mechanics, heat, light, electricity, sound, and the atomic nucleus

phys•i•o•log•i•cal \,fi-zē-ə-'lä-ji-kəl\ *or* **phys•i•o•log•ic** \-'lä-jik\ *adj*
of or relating to the processes and activities that keep living things alive ⟨a *physiological* change⟩

phys•i•ol•o•gist \,fi-zē-'ä-lə-jəst\ *n*
a person specializing in physiology

phys•i•ol•o•gy \,fi-zē-'ä-lə-jē\ *n*
1 a branch of biology that deals with the processes and activities that keep living things alive
2 the processes and activities by which a living thing or any part of it functions

phy•sique \fə-'zēk\ *n*
the size and shape of a person's body

pi \'pī\ *n, pl* **pis** \'pīz\
1 the symbol π representing the ratio of the circumference of a circle to its diameter
2 the ratio itself having a value of about 3.1416

pi•a•nist \pē-'a-nist, 'pē-ə-nist\ *n*
a person who plays the piano

piano

The piano allows players to produce a wide range of sounds from very high to very low and from very soft to very loud. There are two main types — the upright piano, not shown, which has a vertical frame, and the grand piano, which has a horizontal frame. In both types, metal strings are stretched taut across the frame. When the player presses a key, a felt-tipped hammer strikes the string, which vibrates to produce a note.

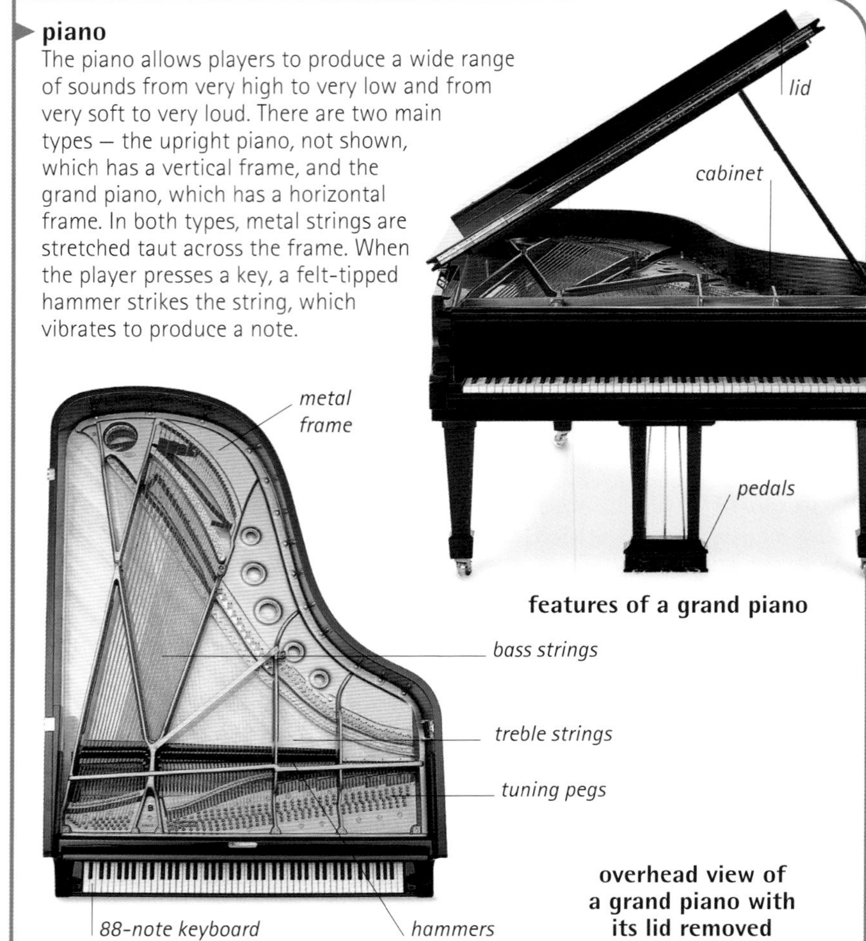

features of a grand piano

overhead view of a grand piano with its lid removed

pi•a•no \pē-'a-nō\ *n, pl* **pianos**
▲ a keyboard instrument having steel wire strings that make a sound when struck by hammers covered with felt

► **Word History** When a harpsichord is played, pressing on the keys causes the strings to be plucked in such a way that loudness and softness cannot be controlled. Around 1700 an Italian instrument maker named Bartolomeo Cristofori invented a mechanism by which the strings of a harpsichord would be struck by felt-covered hammers. This device allowed the performer to play notes with varying degrees of loudness. In Italian this new instrument was called *gravicembalo col piano e forte*, "harpsichord with soft and loud." The name was borrowed into English as *pianoforte* or *fortepiano*, which was eventually shortened to just *piano*.

pic•co•lo \'pi-kə-,lō\ *n, pl* **pic•co•los**
a high-pitched instrument resembling a small flute

[1]pick \'pik\ *vb* **picked; pick•ing**
1 to gather one by one ⟨*Pick* your own strawberries.⟩
2 to remove bit by bit ⟨I *picked* the pepperoni off my pizza.⟩
3 to remove unwanted material from between or inside ⟨He *picked* his teeth.⟩
4 CHOOSE 1, SELECT ⟨*Pick* a card.⟩
5 to walk along slowly and carefully ⟨They *picked* their way through the rubble.⟩
6 to eat sparingly or in a finicky manner ⟨She *picked* at her dinner.⟩
7 to steal from ⟨*pick* a pocket⟩
8 to start (a fight) with someone deliberately
9 to pluck with the fingers or with a pick ⟨*pick* a banjo⟩
10 to unlock without a key ⟨*pick* a lock⟩
pick•er *n*
pick on to single out for mean treatment

A B C D E F G H I J K L M N O P Q R S T U V W X Y Z

pick up
1 to take hold of and lift ⟨She *picked* the book *up.*⟩
2 to clean up : TIDY ⟨*Pick up* your room.⟩
3 to stop for and take along ⟨The bus *picked up* passengers.⟩
4 LEARN 1 ⟨Readers often *pick up* new words from their reading.⟩
5 to get without great effort or by chance ⟨He *picked up* a bad habit.⟩
6 to get by buying ⟨*pick up* a bargain⟩
7 to begin again after a temporary stop ⟨Let's *pick up* our discussion tomorrow.⟩
8 to bring within range of hearing ⟨My radio *picks up* foreign broadcasts.⟩
9 to gain or get back speed or strength ⟨The wind is *picking up.*⟩

[2]**pick** *n*
1 a heavy tool with a wooden handle and a blade pointed at one or both ends for loosening or breaking up soil or rock
2 a slender pointed instrument ⟨ice *pick*⟩
3 a thin piece of metal or plastic used to pluck the strings of a musical instrument
4 the act or opportunity of choosing ⟨I had my *pick* of flavors.⟩
5 [1]CHOICE 3 ⟨Who's your *pick* to win?⟩
6 the best ones ⟨the *pick* of the crop⟩

pick•ax \'pik-,aks\ *n*
[2]PICK 1

pick•er•el \'pi-kə-rəl, 'pik-rəl\ *n, pl* **pickerel** *or* **pick•er•els**
a freshwater fish that resembles but is smaller than the related pike

[1]**pick•et** \'pi-kət\ *n*
1 ▶ a pointed stake or slender post (as for making a fence)
2 a soldier or a group of soldiers assigned to stand guard
3 a person standing or marching near a place (as a factory or store) as part of a strike or protest

[2]**picket** *vb* **pick•et•ed; pick•et•ing**
to stand or march near a place as part of a strike or protest

[1]**pick•le** \'pi-kəl\ *n*
1 a piece of food and especially a cucumber that has been preserved in a solution of salt water or vinegar
2 a mixture of salt and water or vinegar for keeping foods : BRINE
3 a difficult or very unpleasant situation ⟨We were in a *pickle* when we missed our train.⟩

[2]**pickle** *vb* **pick•led; pick•ling**
to soak or keep in a solution of salt water or vinegar

pick•pock•et \'pik-,pä-kət\ *n*
a thief who steals from pockets and purses

pick•up \'pik-,əp\ *n*
a light truck with an open body and low sides

picky \'pi-kē\ *adj* **pick•i•er; pick•i•est**
hard to please ⟨a *picky* eater⟩

[1]**pic•nic** \'pik-,nik\ *n*
1 an outdoor party with food taken along and eaten in the open
2 a pleasant or carefree experience ⟨A broken leg is no *picnic.*⟩

[2]**picnic** *vb* **pic•nicked; pic•nick•ing**
to go on a picnic

pic•to•graph \'pik-tə-,graf\ *n*
1 an ancient or prehistoric drawing or painting on a rock wall
2 a diagram showing information by means of pictures

pic•to•ri•al \pik-'tȯr-ē-əl\ *adj*
1 of or relating to pictures ⟨*pictorial* art⟩
2 having or using pictures ⟨a *pictorial* magazine⟩

[1]**pic•ture** \'pik-chər\ *n*
1 an image of something or someone formed on a surface (as by drawing, painting, printing, or photography)
2 an idea of what someone or something might look like or be like ⟨The book gives a *picture* of frontier life.⟩
3 a perfect example of something ⟨She is the *picture* of health.⟩
4 MOVIE 1
5 an image on the screen of a television set

[1]**picket 1:** a fence made of pickets

[2]**picture** *vb* **pic•tured; pic•tur•ing**
1 to show or represent in a drawing, painting, or photograph ⟨The artist *pictured* her leaning on a fence.⟩
2 to form an idea or mental image of : IMAGINE ⟨I can't *picture* myself skiing.⟩
3 to describe in a particular way

picture graph *n*
PICTOGRAPH 2

pic•tur•esque \,pik-chə-'resk\ *adj*
suggesting a painted scene in being very pretty or charming ⟨a *picturesque* mountain view⟩

pie \'pī\ *n*
▼ a food consisting of a pastry crust and a filling (as of fruit or meat)

pie: a fruit pie

pie•bald \'pī-,bȯld\ *adj*
spotted with two colors and especially black and white ⟨a *piebald* horse⟩

[1]**piece** \'pēs\ *n*
1 a part cut, torn, or broken from something ⟨a *piece* of pie⟩
2 one of a group, set, or mass of things ⟨a *piece* of mail⟩ ⟨a three-*piece* suit⟩
3 a portion marked off ⟨a *piece* of land⟩
4 a single item or example ⟨a *piece* of news⟩
5 a definite amount or size in which something is made or sold ⟨a *piece* of paper⟩
6 something made or written ⟨a *piece* of music⟩
7 a movable object used in playing a board game ⟨a chess *piece*⟩
8 [1]COIN 1 ⟨a fifty-cent *piece*⟩
in one piece not broken, hurt, or damaged

[2]**piece** *vb* **pieced; piec•ing**
to join into a whole : connect the parts or pieces of ⟨I *pieced* a puzzle together.⟩

piece•meal \'pēs-,mēl\ *adv*
one piece at a time : little by little ⟨The repairs were made *piecemeal.*⟩

pier 2: a 19th-century pier in Old Orchard Beach, Maine

pier \'pir\ *n*
1 a support for a bridge
2 ▲ a structure built out into the water as a place for boats to dock or for people to walk or to protect or form a harbor

pierce \'pirs\ *vb* **pierced**; **pierc•ing**
1 to make a hole in or through or as if in or through ⟨I had my ears *pierced.*⟩ ⟨A stab of fear *pierced* his heart.⟩
2 to force or make a way into or through ⟨*pierce* the enemy's line⟩

pierc•ing \'pir-siŋ\ *adj*
1 able to penetrate ⟨a *piercing* wind⟩ ⟨a *piercing* look⟩
2 loud and high-pitched ⟨*piercing* cries⟩

pi•e•ty \'pī-ə-tē\ *n, pl* **pieties**
devotion to God : the state or fact of being pious

pig \'pig\ *n*
1 a hoofed stout-bodied animal with a short tail and legs, thick bristly skin, and a long flattened snout
2 a domestic pig developed from the wild boar and raised for meat
3 a person who has a disagreeable or offensive habit or behavior (as being dirty, rude, or greedy)
4 a metal cast (as of iron) poured directly from the smelting furnace into a mold

pi•geon \'pi-jən\ *n*
a bird with a plump body, short legs, and smooth feathers and especially one that is a variety of the rock dove and is found in cities throughout the world

pi•geon–toed \ˌpi-jən-'tōd\ *adj*
having the toes and front of the foot turned inward

pig•gy•back \'pi-gē-ˌbak\ *adv or adj*
on the back or shoulders ⟨The child wanted a *piggyback* ride.⟩

piggy bank \'pi-gē-\ *n*
▼ a container for keeping coins that is often in the shape of a pig

piggy bank

pig•head•ed \'pig-'he-dəd\ *adj*
very stubborn

pig•let \'pi-glət\ *n*
a baby pig

pig•ment \'pig-mənt\ *n*
1 a substance that gives color to other materials ⟨Red *pigment* is mixed into the ink.⟩
2 natural coloring matter in animals and plants

pig•pen \'pig-ˌpen\ *n*
1 a place where pigs are kept
2 a dirty or messy place

pig•sty \'pig-ˌstī\ *n*
PIGPEN

pig•tail \'pig-ˌtāl\ *n*
a tight braid of hair

[1]**pike** \'pīk\ *n, pl* **pike** *or* **pikes**
a long slender freshwater fish with a large mouth

[2]**pike** *n*
a long wooden pole with a steel point once used as a weapon by soldiers

[3]**pike** *n*
TURNPIKE, ROAD

[1]**pile** \'pīl\ *n*
a large stake or pointed post (as of wood or steel) driven into the ground to support a foundation

[2]**pile** *n*
1 a large number of things that are put one on top of another ⟨a *pile* of stones⟩
2 a great amount ⟨I have *piles* of work.⟩
3 REACTOR

[3]**pile** *vb* **piled**; **pil•ing**
1 to lay or place one on top of another : STACK ⟨*pile* firewood⟩
2 to heap in large amounts ⟨They *piled* a table with food.⟩
3 to move or push forward in a crowd or group ⟨We *piled* into the car.⟩

[4]**pile** *n*
a soft surface of fine short raised threads or fibers ⟨The rug has a thick *pile.*⟩

pil•fer \'pil-fər\ *vb* **pil•fered**; **pil•fer•ing**
to steal small amounts or articles of small value

pil•grim \ˈpil-grəm\ *n*
1 a person who travels to a holy place as an act of religious devotion
2 *cap* one of the English colonists who founded the first permanent settlement in New England at Plymouth in 1620

pil•grim•age \ˈpil-grə-mij\ *n*
a journey made by a pilgrim

pil•ing \ˈpī-liŋ\ *n*
a supporting structure made of large stakes or pointed posts driven into the ground

pill \ˈpil\ *n*
medicine or a food supplement in the form of a small rounded mass to be swallowed whole

[1]**pil•lage** \ˈpi-lij\ *n*
the act of robbing by force especially during a war

[2]**pillage** *vb* **pil•laged**; **pil•lag•ing**
to rob by force especially during a war

pil•lar \ˈpi-lər\ *n*
1 a large post that supports something (as a roof)
2 a single column built as a monument
3 a supporting or important member or part ⟨He was a *pillar* of society.⟩
4 something that resembles a column in shape ⟨*pillars* of smoke⟩

pil•lo•ry \ˈpi-lə-rē\ *n, pl* **pil•lo•ries**
a device once used for punishing someone in public consisting of a wooden frame with holes in which the head and hands can be locked

pil•low \ˈpi-lō\ *n*
a bag filled with soft or springy material used as a cushion usually for the head of a person lying down

pil•low•case \ˈpi-lō-ˌkās\ *n*
a removable covering for a pillow

[1]**pi•lot** \ˈpī-lət\ *n*
1 a person who flies an aircraft
2 a person who steers a ship
3 a person especially qualified to guide ships into and out of a port or in dangerous waters

[2]**pilot** *vb* **pi•lot•ed**; **pi•lot•ing**
1 to fly (an airplane)
2 to steer or guide (a boat)

pi•mien•to \pə-ˈmen-tō, pəm-ˈyen-\ *also* **pi•men•to** \pə-ˈmen-tō\ *n, pl* **pi•mien•tos** *also* **pi•men•tos**
a mildly sweet pepper with thick flesh

pim•ple \ˈpim-pəl\ *n*
a small red swelling of the skin often containing pus
pim•pled \-pəld\ *adj*
pim•ply \-plē\ *adj*

[1]**pin** \ˈpin\ *n*
1 a small pointed piece of wire with a rounded head used especially for fastening pieces of cloth

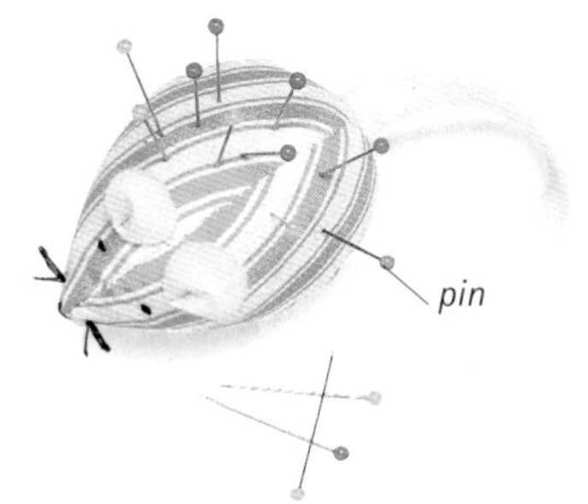

pincushion: a mouse-shaped pincushion

2 something (as an ornament or badge) fastened to the clothing by a pin
3 a slender pointed piece (as of wood or metal) usually having the shape of a cylinder used to fasten articles together or in place
4 one of ten pieces set up as the target in bowling

[2]**pin** *vb* **pinned**; **pin•ning**
1 to fasten or join with a pin
2 to prevent or be prevented from moving ⟨The guards *pinned* his arms to his sides.⟩

pin•a•fore \ˈpi-nə-ˌfōr\ *n*
a sleeveless garment with a low neck worn as an apron or a dress

pi•ña•ta \pēn-ˈyä-tə\ *n*
a decorated container filled with treats (as candy and toys) and hung up to be broken open by a blindfolded person with a stick

pin•cer \ˈpin-chər, ˈpin-sər\ *n*
1 **pincers** *pl* a tool with two handles and two jaws for holding or gripping small objects
2 a part (as the claw of a lobster) resembling a pair of pincers

[1]**pinch** \ˈpinch\ *vb* **pinched**; **pinch•ing**
1 to squeeze between the finger and thumb or between the jaws of an instrument ⟨My aunt *pinched* my cheeks.⟩
2 to squeeze painfully ⟨I *pinched* my finger in a door.⟩
3 to break off by squeezing with the thumb and fingers ⟨*Pinch* off a bit of dough.⟩
4 to cause to look thin or shrunken ⟨a face *pinched* with cold⟩
pinch pennies to be thrifty or stingy

[2]**pinch** *n*
1 a time of emergency ⟨He always helps out in a *pinch*.⟩
2 an act of squeezing skin between the thumb and fingers
3 as much as may be picked up between the finger and the thumb **:** a very small amount ⟨a *pinch* of salt⟩

pinch hitter *n*
1 a baseball player who is sent in to bat for another
2 a person who does another's work in an emergency

pin•cush•ion \ˈpin-ˌku̇-shən\ *n*
◀ a small cushion in which pins may be stuck when not in use

[1]**pine** \ˈpīn\ *n*
an evergreen tree that has cones, narrow needles for leaves, and a wood that ranges from very soft to hard

[2]**pine** *vb* **pined**; **pin•ing**
1 to become thin and weak because of sadness or worry
2 to long for very much ⟨She *pined* for home.⟩
synonyms see YEARN

pine•ap•ple \ˈpī-ˌna-pəl\ *n*
▶ a large fruit that grows on a tropical plant and has a thick skin and sweet juicy yellow flesh

pineapple

pin•feath•er \ˈpin-ˌfe-t͟hər\ *n*
a new feather just breaking through the skin of a bird

pin•ion \ˈpin-yən\ *vb* **pin•ioned**; **pin•ion•ing**
1 to restrain by tying the arms to the body
2 to tie up or hold tightly
3 to prevent a bird from flying especially by cutting off the end of one wing

[1]**pink** \ˈpiŋk\ *n*
a plant with narrow leaves that is grown for its showy pink, red, or white flowers

[2]**pink** *n*
a pale red color

[3]**pink** *adj*
colored a pale red

pink•eye \ˈpiŋk-ˌī\ *n*
a contagious infection that causes the eye and inner part of the eyelid to become red and sore

pin•kie *or* **pin•ky** \ˈpiŋ-kē\ *n, pl* **pinkies**
LITTLE FINGER

pink•ish \ˈpiŋ-kish\ *adj*
somewhat pink

pin•na•cle \ˈpi-nə-kəl\ *n*
1 the peak of a mountain
2 the highest point of development or achievement ⟨Winning the award was the *pinnacle* of her career.⟩
3 a slender tower generally coming to a narrow point at the top

pin•point \ˈpin-ˌpȯint\ *vb* **pin•point•ed**; **pin•point•ing**
to locate or find out exactly

pint \ˈpīnt\ *n*
a unit of liquid capacity equal to one half quart or 16 ounces (about .47 liter)

pin•to \ˈpin-tō\ *n, pl* **pintos**
▶ a horse or pony that has patches of white and another color

pinto

pin•wheel \ˈpin-ˌhwēl, -ˌwēl\ *n*
a toy with fanlike blades at the end of a stick that spin in the wind

[1]**pi•o•neer** \ˌpī-ə-ˈnir\ *n*
1 a person who is one of the first to settle in an area
2 a person who begins or helps develop something new and prepares the way for others to follow 〈They were *pioneers* in the field of medicine.〉

▶**Word History** The source of our word *pioneer* is ultimately Old French *peonier* or *pionier*, a derivative of *peon*, "foot soldier." The word *peonier* also originally meant "foot soldier," but later appeared in the sense "digger" or "excavator," and by the 1300s referred to a soldier who went ahead of the main army and prepared forts for the men who would follow. The word was borrowed by English in the 1500s, and may still apply to troops who build roads and bridges (though *engineer* is the usual term in the United States Army). The word is usually used in the figurative sense of "someone who prepares the way for others."

[2]**pioneer** *vb* **pi•o•neered**; **pi•o•neer•ing**
1 to explore or open up ways or regions for others to follow
2 to begin something new or take part in the early development of something 〈They *pioneered* new scientific techniques.〉

pi•ous \ˈpī-əs\ *adj*
showing devotion to God

[1]**pipe** \ˈpīp\ *n*
1 a long tube or hollow body for carrying a substance (as water, steam, or gas) 〈the exhaust *pipe* of a car〉 〈underground water *pipes*〉
2 a musical instrument or part of a musical instrument consisting of a tube (as of wood or metal) played by blowing or having air passed through it
3 BAGPIPE — usually used in pl.
4 ▼ a tube with a small bowl at one end for smoking tobacco or for blowing bubbles

[1]**pipe 4:** a pipe for smoking tobacco

[2]**pipe** *vb* **piped**; **pip•ing**
1 to move by means of pipes 〈Water was *piped* into the city.〉
2 to play on a pipe 〈The musician *piped* a tune.〉
pip•er *n*
pipe down to stop talking or making noise
pipe up to start talking : say something

pipe•line \ˈpīp-ˌlīn\ *n*
a line of connected pipes with pumps and control devices for carrying liquids or gases over a long distance

pip•ing \ˈpī-piŋ\ *n*
1 a quantity or system of pipes
2 the music of a pipe
3 a high-pitched sound or call 〈the *piping* of frogs〉
4 a narrow fold of material used to decorate edges or seams

pique \ˈpēk\ *vb* **piqued**; **piqu•ing**
1 to stir up : EXCITE 〈The package *piqued* my curiosity.〉
2 to make annoyed or angry

pi•ra•cy \ˈpī-rə-sē\ *n, pl* **pi•ra•cies**
1 robbery of a ship at sea
2 the use of another's work or invention without permission

pi•ra•nha \pə-ˈrä-nə\ *n*
a small South American freshwater fish that has very sharp teeth, often occurs in groups, and may attack human beings and animals in the water

pi•rate \ˈpī-rət\ *n*
a robber of ships at sea : a person who commits piracy

pis *pl of* PI

Pi•sces \ˈpī-sēz\ *n*
1 a constellation between Aquarius and Aries imagined as two fish
2 the twelfth sign of the zodiac or a person born under this sign

pis•ta•chio \pə-ˈsta-shē-ˌō\ *n, pl* **pis•ta•chios**
the greenish edible seed of a small Asian tree

pis•til \ˈpi-stᵊl\ *n*
the part in the center of a flower that is made up of the stigma, style, and ovary and produces the seed

pis•tol \ˈpi-stᵊl\ *n*
a small gun made to be aimed and fired with one hand

pis•ton \ˈpi-stən\ *n*
a disk or short cylinder that slides back and forth inside a larger cylinder and is moved by steam in steam engines and by the explosion of fuel in automobiles

[1]**pit** \ˈpit\ *n*
1 a cavity or hole in the ground usually made by digging 〈a gravel *pit*〉
2 an area set off from and often sunken below surrounding areas 〈a barbecue *pit*〉 〈a theater's orchestra *pit*〉
3 a small hole or dent on a surface
4 pits *pl* something very bad 〈Being sick is the *pits*.〉
pit•ted \ˈpi-təd\ *adj*

[2]**pit** *vb* **pit•ted**; **pit•ting**
1 to make small holes or dents in
2 to set against another in a fight or contest 〈The former teammates were *pitted* against each other.〉

[3]**pit** *n*
a hard seed or stone of a fruit (as a peach or cherry)

[4]**pit** *vb* **pit•ted**; **pit•ting**
to remove the pit from

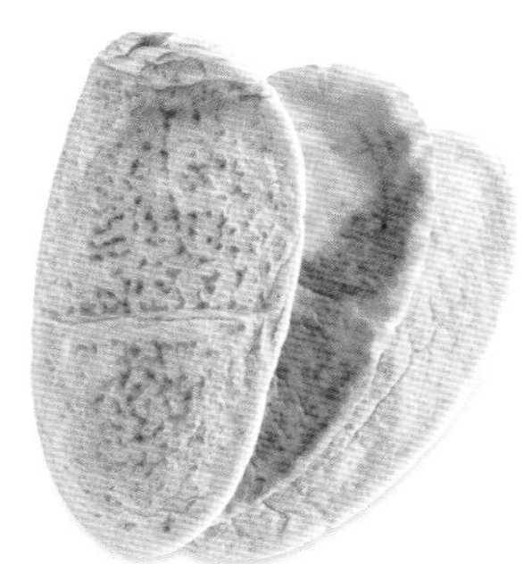
pita

pi•ta \'pē-tə\ *n*
▲ a thin flat bread that can be opened to form a pocket for holding food

[1]pitch \'pich\ *vb* **pitched**; **pitch•ing**
1 to set up and fix firmly in place ⟨We *pitched* a tent.⟩
2 to throw usually toward a certain point ⟨I *pitched* hay onto a wagon.⟩
3 to throw a baseball or softball to a batter
4 to plunge or fall forward
5 [2]SLOPE, SLANT ⟨The roof is steeply *pitched.*⟩
6 to fix or set at a certain highness or lowness ⟨*Pitch* the tune higher.⟩
7 to move in such a way that one end falls while the other end rises ⟨The ship *pitched* in a rough sea.⟩
pitch in to contribute to a common task or goal

[2]pitch *n*
1 highness or lowness of sound
2 amount of slope ⟨The roof has a steep *pitch.*⟩
3 an up-and-down movement ⟨the *pitch* of a ship⟩
4 the throw of a baseball or softball to a batter
5 the amount or level of something (as a feeling) ⟨Excitement reached a high *pitch.*⟩
pitched \'picht\ *adj*

[3]pitch *n*
1 a dark sticky substance left over from distilling tar and used in making roofing paper, in waterproofing seams, and in paving
2 resin from various evergreen trees (as the pine)

pitch–black \'pich-'blak\ *adj*
extremely dark or black ⟨a *pitch-black* night⟩

pitch•blende \'pich-ˌblend\ *n*
a dark mineral that is a source of radium and uranium

pitch–dark \'pich-'därk\ *adj*
extremely dark

[1]pitch•er \'pi-chər\ *n*
► a container usually with a handle and a lip or spout used for holding and pouring out liquids

[2]pitcher *n*
the player who throws the ball to the batter in baseball or softball

pitch•fork \'pich-ˌfȯrk\ *n*
► a tool having a long handle and usually two to five metal prongs that is used especially for lifting and tossing hay or straw

pitchfork

pit•e•ous \'pi-tē-əs\ *adj*
PITIFUL ⟨The dog let out a *piteous* whine.⟩
pit•e•ous•ly *adv*

pit•fall \'pit-ˌfȯl\ *n*
1 a covered or camouflaged pit used to capture animals or people
2 a danger or difficulty that is hidden or is not easily recognized

pith \'pith\ *n*
1 the loose spongy tissue forming the center of the stem in most plants
2 the important part ⟨the *pith* of the problem⟩

piti•able \'pi-tē-ə-bəl\ *adj*
PITIFUL

piti•ful \'pi-ti-fəl\ *adj*
1 deserving or causing feelings of pity ⟨a *pitiful* sight⟩
2 deserving or causing a feeling of dislike or disgust by not being sufficient or good enough ⟨a *pitiful* excuse⟩
piti•ful•ly \-fə-lē, -flē\ *adv*

piti•less \'pi-ti-ləs\ *adj*
having no pity : CRUEL

pi•tu•i•tary gland \pə-'tü-ə-ˌter-ē-, -'tyü-\ *n*
a gland at the base of the brain that produces several hormones of which one affects growth

[1]pity \'pi-tē\ *n*
1 a feeling of sadness or sympathy for the suffering or unhappiness of others
2 something that causes regret or disappointment ⟨What a *pity* that you can't go.⟩

[1]pitcher

[2]pity *vb* **pit•ied**; **pity•ing**
to feel sadness and sympathy for

[1]piv•ot \'pi-vət\ *n*
1 a shaft or pin with a pointed end on which something turns
2 the action or an instance of turning around on a point

[2]pivot *vb* **piv•ot•ed**; **piv•ot•ing**
to turn on or as if on a pivot : turn around on a central point ⟨*pivot* on one foot⟩

pix•el \'pik-səl\ *n*
any of the small parts that make up an image (as on a computer or television screen)

pix•ie *also* **pixy** \'pik-sē\ *n, pl* **pix•ies**
a mischievous elf or fairy

piz•za \'pēt-sə\ *n*
a dish made of flattened bread dough topped usually with tomato sauce and cheese and often meat and vegetables and baked

pk. *abbr*
1 park
2 peck

pkg. *abbr* package

pl. *abbr* plural

plac•ard \'pla-kərd, -ˌkärd\ *n*
a large notice or poster for announcing or advertising something

pla•cate \'plā-ˌkāt, 'pla-\ *vb* **pla•cat•ed**; **pla•cat•ing**
to calm the anger of ⟨The apology did little to *placate* customers.⟩

[1]place \'plās\ *n*
1 an available seat or space : ROOM ⟨Let's make a *place* for the newcomer.⟩ ⟨There's no *place* to sit.⟩
2 a region or space not specified ⟨There's dust all over the *place.*⟩
3 a particular portion of a surface : SPOT
4 a point in a speech or a piece of writing ⟨I lost my *place.*⟩
5 a building or area used for a special purpose ⟨a *place* of worship⟩
6 a certain area or region of the world ⟨It's a nice *place* to visit.⟩
7 a piece of land with a house on it ⟨We own a *place* in the country.⟩
8 position in a scale or series in comparison with another or others ⟨I finished the race in second *place.*⟩
9 usual space or use ⟨Paper towels can take the *place* of linen.⟩
10 the position of a figure in a numeral ⟨The number 128 has three *places.*⟩
11 a public square
12 a short street

[2]place *vb* **placed; plac•ing**
1 to put in or as if in a certain space or position ⟨*Place* the book on my desk.⟩ ⟨They *place* great importance on teamwork.⟩
2 to give an order for ⟨I'd like to *place* an ad in the paper.⟩
3 to appoint to a job or find a job for ⟨He was *placed* in command.⟩
4 to identify by connecting with a certain time, place, or happening ⟨I couldn't quite *place* her face.⟩

place•hold•er \'plās-,hōl-dər\ *n*
a symbol (as *x*, Δ, *) used in mathematics in the place of a numeral

place•kick \'plās-,kik\ *n*
▼ a kick in football made with the ball held in place on the ground

pla•cen•ta \plə-'sen-tə\ *n*
the organ in most mammals by which the fetus is joined to the uterus of the mother and is nourished

place value *n*
the value of the location of a digit in a number ⟨In 125 the location of the digit 2 has a *place value* of ten.⟩

plac•id \'pla-səd\ *adj*
calm and peaceful ⟨a *placid* face⟩ ⟨a *placid* lake⟩

pla•gia•rism \'plā-jə-,ri-zəm\ *n*
an act of copying the ideas or words of another person without giving credit to that person

[1]plague \'plāg\ *n*
1 something that causes much distress ⟨a *plague* of locusts⟩
2 a disease that causes death and spreads quickly to a large number of people
3 BUBONIC PLAGUE

[2]plague *vb* **plagued; plagu•ing**
1 to affect with disease or trouble ⟨Fleas *plague* the poor dog.⟩
2 to cause worry or distress to ⟨I'm *plagued* by guilt.⟩

plaid \'plad\ *n*
1 a pattern consisting of rectangles formed by crossed lines of various widths
2 TARTAN
plaid *adj*

[1]plain \'plān\ *adj* **plain•er; plain•est**
1 having no pattern or decoration ⟨a *plain* jacket⟩
2 not handsome or beautiful
3 not hard to do or understand ⟨The lesson was explained in *plain* words.⟩ ⟨The directions were *plain*.⟩
4 without anything having been added ⟨He eats *plain* yogurt.⟩
5 open and clear to the sight ⟨I left my money in *plain* view.⟩
6 FRANK ⟨The judge is famous for her *plain* speaking.⟩
7 of common or average accomplishments or position : ORDINARY ⟨just *plain* folks⟩
plain•ly *adv*
plain•ness *n*

[2]plain *n*
a large area of level or rolling treeless land

[3]plain *adv*
without any question : to a complete degree

plain•tive \'plān-tiv\ *adj*
showing or suggesting sadness : MOURNFUL ⟨a *plaintive* sigh⟩

placekick

[1]plait \'plāt, 'plat\ *n*
a flat braid (as of hair)

[2]plait *vb* **plait•ed; plait•ing**
1 [1]BRAID
2 to make by braiding ⟨The man was *plaiting* a basket.⟩

[1]plan \'plan\ *n*
1 a method or scheme of acting, doing, or arranging ⟨vacation *plans*⟩
2 a drawing or diagram showing the parts or outline of something

> ▶ **Synonyms** PLAN, PLOT, and SCHEME mean a method of making or doing something or achieving an end. PLAN is used when some thinking was done beforehand often with something written down or pictured. ⟨The builder proposed a *plan* for a new school.⟩ PLOT is used for a complicated, carefully shaped plan of several parts. PLOT can be used of the plan of a story. ⟨It's a mystery story with a good *plot*.⟩ It can also be used of a secret, usually evil plan. ⟨The robbery *plot* was uncovered.⟩ SCHEME is used when there is a tricky plan often for evil reasons. ⟨The *scheme* to cheat people backfired.⟩

[2]plan *vb* **planned; plan•ning**
1 to form a diagram of or for : arrange the parts or details of ahead of time ⟨*plan* a bridge⟩ ⟨*plan* a picnic⟩
2 to have in mind : INTEND

[1]plane \'plān\ *n*
1 AIRPLANE
2 a surface in which if any two points are chosen a straight line joining them lies completely in that surface
3 a level of thought, existence, or development ⟨The two stories are not on the same *plane*.⟩
4 a level or flat surface ⟨a horizontal *plane*⟩

[2]plane *adj*
[1]HORIZONTAL, FLAT ⟨a *plane* surface⟩

[3]plane *n*
▼ a tool that smooths wood by shaving off thin strips

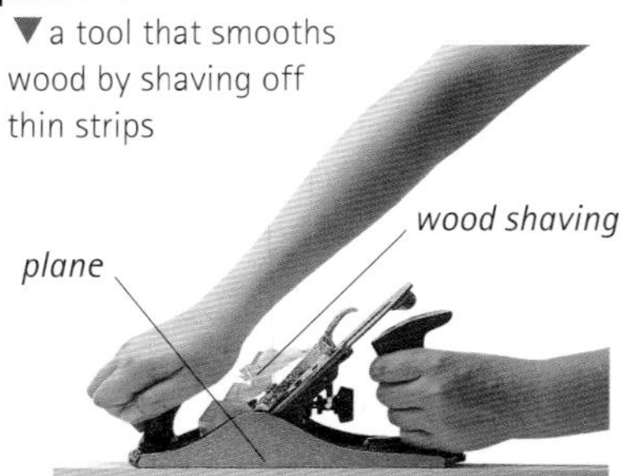

[3]plane

A B C D E F G H I J K L M N O P Q R S T U V W X Y Z

[4]**plane** *vb* **planed**; **plan•ing**
1 to smooth or level off with a tool made for smoothing
2 to remove with or as if with a tool for smoothing wood

plan•et \'pla-nət\ *n*
any large heavenly body that orbits a star (as the sun)

► **Word History** Most stars seem to stay in fixed positions night after night. There are certain heavenly bodies, the planets, that look very much like stars but are not. They seem to wander about among the fixed stars. The ancient Greeks gave them the name *planētes,* meaning "wanderers." The English word *planet* comes from this Greek word.

plan•e•tar•i•um \ˌpla-nə-'ter-ē-əm\ *n*
a building in which there is a device for projecting the images of heavenly bodies on a ceiling shaped like a dome

plan•e•tary \'pla-nə-ˌter-ē\ *adj*
1 of or relating to a planet
2 having a motion like that of a planet

plank \'plaŋk\ *n*
a heavy thick board

plank•ton \'plaŋk-tən\ *n*
the tiny floating plants and animals of a body of water

[1]**plant** \'plant\ *vb* **plant•ed**; **plant•ing**
1 to place in the ground to grow ⟨We'll *plant* seeds in the spring.⟩
2 to fill with seeds or plants ⟨*plant* a garden⟩
3 to set firmly in the ground ⟨They *planted* posts for a fence.⟩
4 to place firmly ⟨He *planted* himself on the couch.⟩
5 to introduce as a thought or idea
6 to place (someone or something) secretly ⟨*plant* a listening device⟩

[2]**plant** *n*
1 any member of the kingdom of many-celled mostly photosynthetic living things (as mosses, ferns, grasses, and trees) that lack a nervous system or sense organs and the ability to move about and that have cellulose cell walls
2 the buildings and equipment of an industrial business or an institution ⟨a power *plant*⟩
plant•like \'plant-ˌlīk\ *adj*

plan•tain \'plan-tᵊn\ *n*
the greenish fruit of a kind of banana plant that is eaten cooked and is larger, less sweet, and more starchy than the ordinary banana

plan•ta•tion \plan-'tā-shən\ *n*
1 a large area of land where crops are grown and harvested
2 a settlement in a new country or region

plant•er \'plan-tər\ *n*
1 someone or something that plants crops
2 a person who owns or runs a plantation
3 a container in which plants are grown

plant kingdom *n*
a basic group of natural objects that includes all living and extinct plants

plant louse *n*
APHID

plaque \'plak\ *n*
1 a flat thin piece (as of metal) with writing on it that serves as a memorial of something
2 a sticky usually colorless thin film on the teeth that is formed by and contains bacteria

plas•ma \'plaz-mə\ *n*
the watery part of blood, lymph, or milk

[1]**plas•ter** \'pla-stər\ *n*
a paste (as of lime, sand, and water) that hardens when it dries and is used for coating walls and ceilings

[2]**plaster** *vb* **plas•tered**; **plas•ter•ing**
1 to cover or smear with or as if with a paste used for coating
2 to paste or fasten on especially so as to cover ⟨He likes to *plaster* a wall with posters.⟩

plaster of par•is \-'per-əs\ *n, often cap 2nd P*
a white powder that mixes with water to form a paste that hardens quickly and is used for casts and molds

[1]**plas•tic** \'pla-stik\ *adj*
1 made of plastic ⟨*plastic* bags⟩ ⟨a *plastic* bucket⟩
2 capable of being molded or modeled ⟨*plastic* clay⟩

[2]**plastic** *n*
► any of various manufactured materials that can be molded into objects or formed into films or fibers

[1]**plate** \'plāt\ *n*
1 a shallow usually round dish
2 a main course of a meal ⟨I ate a *plate* of spaghetti.⟩
3 a thin flat piece of material ⟨steel *plate*⟩
4 HOME PLATE
5 a piece of metal on which something is engraved or molded ⟨a license *plate*⟩
6 an illustration often covering a full page of a book
7 a sheet of glass coated with a chemical sensitive to light for use in a camera

► [2]**plastic**
Since their introduction in the early 20th century, plastics have become some of the most commonly used materials in the world. They are soft or liquid when first made, and can be molded into shape under heat and pressure before they harden. Some plastics, such as those used to make certain plastic bags or bottles, can be recycled.

examples of items made from plastic

plateau: a road running through a plateau in Tibet

²plate *vb* **plat•ed; plat•ing**
to cover with a thin layer of metal (as gold or silver)

pla•teau \pla-'tō\ *n, pl* **plateaus** *or* **pla•teaux** \-'tōz\
▲ a broad flat area of high land

plate•let \'plāt-lət\ *n*
one of the tiny colorless disk-shaped bodies of the blood that assist in blood clotting

plate tec•ton•ics \-tek-'tä-niks\ *n*
a scientific theory that the earth's surface is made of very large sections that move very slowly

plat•form \'plat-,fȯrm\ *n*
1 a level usually raised surface ⟨We hurried to the train *platform.*⟩ ⟨Visitors can observe wildlife from a *platform.*⟩
2 a raised floor or stage for performers or speakers
3 a statement of the beliefs and rules of conduct for which a group stands ⟨The candidates discussed their party's *platform.*⟩
4 an arrangement of computer components that uses a particular operating system

plat•i•num \'pla-tə-nəm\ *n*
a heavy grayish white metallic chemical element

pla•toon \plə-'tün\ *n*
a part of a military company usually made up of two or more squads

platoon sergeant *n*
a noncommissioned officer in the army ranking above a staff sergeant

plat•ter \'pla-tər\ *n*
a large plate used especially for serving meat

platy•pus \'pla-ti-pəs\ *n*
▼ a small water-dwelling mammal of Australia that lays eggs and has webbed feet, dense fur, and a bill that resembles that of a duck

platypus

plau•si•ble \'plȯ-zə-bəl\ *adj*
seeming to be reasonable ⟨a *plausible* excuse⟩
plau•si•bly \-blē\ *adv*

¹play \'plā\ *vb* **played; play•ing**
1 to do activities for enjoyment
2 to take part in a game of ⟨*play* cards⟩
3 to compete against in a game ⟨We are *playing* the Dodgers today.⟩
4 to produce music or sound with ⟨*play* the piano⟩ ⟨*play* a CD⟩
5 to perform the music of ⟨He *played* my favorite tune.⟩
6 to act or present on the stage or screen ⟨She was chosen to *play* Annie.⟩ ⟨What's *playing* at the movies?⟩
7 PRETEND 1 ⟨Let's *play* school.⟩ ⟨The dog *played* dead.⟩
8 to perform (as a trick) for fun
9 ²ACT 2, BEHAVE ⟨She doesn't *play* fair.⟩
10 to handle something idly **:** TOY ⟨Don't *play* with your food!⟩
11 to affect something by performing a function ⟨Luck *played* a part in their winning.⟩
12 to move swiftly or lightly ⟨Leaves *played* in the wind.⟩
synonyms see IMPERSONATE

²play *n*
1 a story performed on stage
2 the action of or a particular action in a game ⟨That was a great *play* by the shortstop.⟩
3 exercise or activity for enjoyment ⟨children at *play*⟩
4 a person's turn to take part in a game ⟨It's your *play.*⟩
5 quick or light movement ⟨We felt the light *play* of a breeze through the room.⟩
6 freedom of motion ⟨There is too much *play* in the steering wheel.⟩
7 a way of acting **:** CONDUCT ⟨fair *play*⟩
8 the state of being active

play•act•ing \'plā-,ak-tiŋ\ *n*
the performance of make-believe roles

play•er \'plā-ər\ *n*
1 a person who participates in a game
2 a person who produces sound on a musical instrument
3 a device that reproduces sounds or video images that have been recorded (as on magnetic tape or a hard drive)

play•ful \'plā-fəl\ *adj*
1 full of energy and a desire for fun 〈a *playful* kitten〉
2 not serious : HUMOROUS 〈a *playful* mood〉
play•ful•ly \-fə-lē\ *adv*
play•ful•ness *n*

play•ground \'plā-,grau̇nd\ *n*
an area used for games and playing

play•house \'plā-,hau̇s\ *n*
1 a small house for children to play in
2 THEATER 1

playing card *n*
▼ any of a set of cards marked to show rank and suit (**spades, hearts, diamonds,** or **clubs**) and used in playing various games

playing cards

play•mate \'plā-,māt\ *n*
a friend with whom a child plays

play–off \'plā-,ȯf\ *n*
a game or series of games to determine a championship or to break a tie

play•pen \'plā-,pen\ *n*
a small enclosure in which a baby is placed to play

play•thing \'plā-,thiŋ\ *n*
[1]TOY 1

play•wright \'plā-,rīt\ *n*
a writer of plays

pla•za \'pla-zə, 'plä-\ *n*
a public square in a city or town

plea \'plē\ *n*
1 an earnest appeal 〈The prisoner made a *plea* for mercy.〉
2 something offered as a defense or excuse

plead \'plēd\ *vb* **plead•ed** *or* **pled** \'pled\; **plead•ing**
1 to ask for in a serious and emotional way : BEG 〈I *pleaded* for help.〉
2 to offer as a defense, an excuse, or an apology 〈To avoid going, I'll *plead* illness.〉
3 to argue for or against : argue in court 〈His lawyer will *plead* the case before a jury.〉
4 to answer to a criminal charge 〈They all *plead* not guilty.〉

pleas•ant \'ple-zᵊnt\ *adj*
1 giving pleasure : AGREEABLE 〈a *pleasant* day〉
2 having pleasing manners, behavior, or appearance 〈a *pleasant* young man〉
pleas•ant•ly *adv*

[1]please \'plēz\ *vb* **pleased**; **pleas•ing**
1 to make happy or satisfied 〈The gift *pleased* him.〉
2 to be willing : LIKE, CHOOSE 〈You can come and go as you *please*.〉

[2]please *adv*
used to show politeness or emphasis in requesting or accepting 〈May I *please* be excused?〉 〈Attention, *please*!〉 〈More milk? Yes, *please*.〉

pleas•ing \'plē-ziŋ\ *adj*
giving pleasure : AGREEABLE
pleas•ing•ly *adv*

plea•sur•able \'ple-zhə-rə-bəl\ *adj*
PLEASANT 1

plea•sure \'ple-zhər\ *n*
1 a feeling of enjoyment or satisfaction 〈I take great *pleasure* in reading.〉
2 recreation or enjoyment 〈Is the trip for business or *pleasure*?〉
3 something that pleases or delights 〈It's been a *pleasure* working with you.〉
4 a particular desire 〈What is your *pleasure*?〉

▶ **Synonyms** PLEASURE, JOY, and ENJOYMENT mean the agreeable feeling that accompanies getting something good or much wanted. PLEASURE is used for a feeling of happiness or satisfaction that may not be shown openly. 〈He took *pleasure* in helping others.〉 JOY is used for a radiant feeling that is very strong. 〈Hers is a life filled with *joy*.〉 ENJOYMENT is used for a conscious reaction to something intended to make a person happy. 〈The songs added to our *enjoyment* of the movie.〉

[1]pleat \'plēt\ *vb* **pleat•ed**; **pleat•ing**
to arrange in folds made by doubling material over on itself

[2]pleat *n*
a fold (as in cloth) made by doubling material over on itself

[1]pledge \'plej\ *n*
1 a promise or agreement that must be kept
2 something handed over to another to ensure that the giver will keep his or her promise or agreement
3 a promise to give money

[2]pledge *vb* **pledged**; **pledg•ing**
1 to promise to give 〈I *pledge* allegiance.〉
2 to cause (someone) to promise something 〈He *pledged* himself to secrecy.〉
3 to give as assurance of a promise (as of repayment of a loan)

plen•ti•ful \'plen-ti-fəl\ *adj*
1 present in large numbers or amount : ABUNDANT 〈*plentiful* rain〉
2 giving or containing a large number or amount 〈Vegetables are a *plentiful* source of vitamins.〉
plen•ti•ful•ly \-fə-lē\ *adv*

plen•ty \'plen-tē\ *n*
a full supply : more than enough

pleu•ri•sy \'plu̇r-ə-sē\ *n*
a sore swollen state of the membrane that lines the chest often with fever, painful breathing, and coughing

plex•us \'plek-səs\ *n, pl* **plex•us•es**
a network usually of nerves or blood vessels

pli•able \'plī-ə-bəl\ *adj*
1 possible to bend without breaking
2 easily influenced 〈a *pliable* teenager〉

pli•ant \'plī-ənt\ *adj*
PLIABLE

pli•ers \'plī-ərz\ *n pl*
▶ small pincers with long jaws used for bending or cutting wire or handling small things

pliers

plight \'plīt\ *n*
a bad condition or state : PREDICAMENT

plod \'pläd\ *vb* **plod•ded**; **plod•ding**
to move or travel slowly but steadily
plod•der *n*

[1]plop \'pläp\ *vb* **plopped**; **plop•ping**
1 to move with or make a sound like that of something dropping into water 〈Ice cubes *plopped* into the glass.〉
2 to sit or lie down heavily 〈She *plopped* into her chair.〉
3 to place or drop heavily 〈He *plopped* the tray down.〉

[2]plop *n*
a sound like something dropping into water

[1]plot \'plät\ *n*
1 a secret usually evil scheme
2 the plan or main story of a play or novel
3 a small area of ground 〈a garden *plot*〉
synonyms see PLAN

[2]plot *vb* **plot•ted**; **plot•ting**
1 to plan or scheme secretly usually to do something bad
2 to make a plan of 〈Have you *plotted* your route?〉
plot•ter *n*

a b c d e f g h i j k l m n o p q r s t u v w x y z

plough *chiefly British variant of* PLOW

plo•ver \'plə-vər, 'plō-\ *n*
a small shorebird having a shorter and stouter bill than the related sandpiper

[1]**plow** \'plaù\ *n*
1 ▼ a farm machine used to dig into, break up, and turn over soil
2 a device (as a snowplow) used to spread or clear away matter on the ground

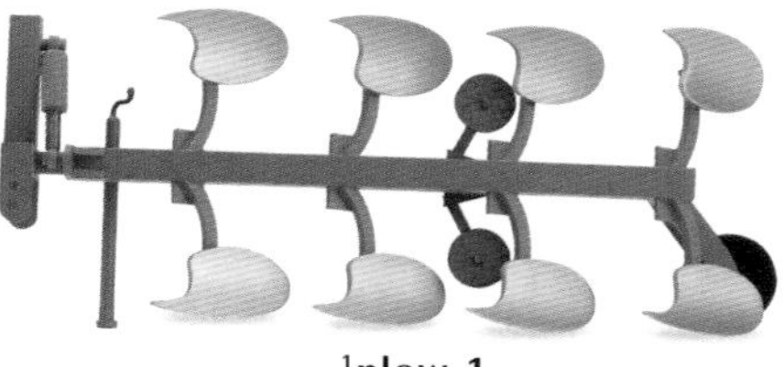
[1]**plow 1**

[2]**plow** *vb* **plowed**; **plow•ing**
1 to dig into, break up, or turn over soil with a plow ⟨*plow* a furrow⟩ ⟨*plow* the soil⟩
2 to move through or continue with force or determination ⟨Our ship *plowed* through the waves.⟩

plow•share \'plaù-,sher\ *n*
the part of a plow that cuts into the earth

ploy \'plòi\ *n, pl* **ploys**
a trick used to make someone do something or get an advantage

pls. *abbr* please

[1]**pluck** \'plək\ *vb* **plucked**; **pluck•ing**
1 to pull off : PICK ⟨*pluck* grapes⟩
2 to remove something (as a hair or feather) with a quick pull
3 to seize and remove quickly : SNATCH
4 to pull at (a string) and let go

[2]**pluck** *n*
1 a sharp pull : TUG
2 COURAGE, SPIRIT

plucky \'plə-kē\ *adj* **pluck•i•er**; **pluck•i•est**
showing courage : BRAVE

[1]**plug** \'pləg\ *n*
1 a device usually on a cord used to make an electrical connection by putting it into another part (as a socket)
2 a piece (as of wood or metal) used to stop up or fill a hole

[2]**plug** *vb* **plugged**; **plug•ging**
1 to connect to an electric circuit ⟨*Plug* in the lamp.⟩
2 to stop or make tight with something that fills a hole
3 to keep steadily at work or in action ⟨I *plugged* away at my homework.⟩

plum \'pləm\ *n*
1 ► a fruit related to the peach and cherry that usually has smooth purple or reddish skin, sweet juicy flesh, and a stony pit
2 a dark reddish purple
3 a choice or desirable thing : PRIZE

plum•age \'plü-mij\ *n*
the feathers of a bird

[1]**plumb** \'pləm\ *n*
a small weight attached to a line and used to show depth or a straight vertical line

[2]**plumb** *vb* **plumbed**; **plumb•ing**
to measure or test with a plumb ⟨They *plumbed* the depth of a well.⟩

[3]**plumb** *adv*
1 exactly straight up and down
2 COMPLETELY ⟨I *plumb* forgot.⟩

plumb•er \'plə-mər\ *n*
a person who installs or repairs plumbing

► **Word History** The word *plumber* originally meant "person who works with lead." It comes from a Latin word *plumbarius* with the same meaning, which is derived from *plumbum,* "lead." In the past water pipes in buildings were often made of lead. The plumbers who put in these pipes and took care of them were workers in lead.

plumb•ing \'plə-miŋ\ *n*
1 a system of pipes and fixtures for supplying and carrying off water in a building
2 the installation or repair of part or all of such a system of pipes and fixtures

plume \'plüm\ *n*
1 a large or showy feather of a bird
2 an ornamental feather or tuft of feathers (as on a hat)
3 something shaped like a large feather ⟨a *plume* of smoke⟩
plumed \'plümd\ *adj*

plum•met \'plə-mət\ *vb* **plum•met•ed**; **plum•met•ing**
to fall straight down ⟨The satellite *plummeted* toward the ocean.⟩

plum 1:
ripe plums

[1]**plump** \'pləmp\ *adj* **plump•er**; **plump•est**
having a pleasingly full rounded shape ⟨*plump* cheeks⟩ ⟨a *plump* turkey⟩
plump•ness *n*

[2]**plump** *vb* **plumped**; **plump•ing**
1 to drop or fall heavily or suddenly ⟨He *plumped* down on the couch.⟩
2 to come out in favor of something ⟨I'm *plumping* for my favorite candidate.⟩

[3]**plump** *adv*
DIRECTLY 1 ⟨He ran *plump* into the wall.⟩

[4]**plump** *vb* **plumped**; **plump•ing**
to make or become rounded or filled out ⟨I *plumped* up the pillows.⟩

[1]**plun•der** \'plən-dər\ *vb* **plun•dered**; **plun•der•ing**
to rob or steal especially openly and by force (as during war)

[2]**plunder** *n*
something stolen by force : LOOT

[1]**plunge** \'plənj\ *vb* **plunged**; **plung•ing**
1 to leap or dive suddenly ⟨She *plunged* into the water.⟩
2 to thrust or force quickly ⟨I *plunged* my arm into the pipe.⟩
3 to suddenly enter or cause to enter a certain situation or state ⟨Foolish investments *plunged* the family into debt.⟩
4 to drop suddenly downward or forward and downward ⟨Cliffs *plunge* to the valley.⟩

[2]**plunge** *n*
a sudden dive, rush, or leap

plung•er \'plən-jər\ *n*
a part that moves up and down usually inside a tube or cylinder to push something out

plunk \'pləŋk\ *vb* **plunked**; **plunk•ing**
1 to lie or sit down suddenly or heavily
2 to drop or place heavily or carelessly ⟨She *plunked* her mug on the table.⟩
3 to make a sound on (an instrument) by pulling the strings or keys

[1]**plu•ral** \'plùr-əl\ *adj*
relating to or being a word form used to show more than one ⟨"Candies" is a *plural* noun.⟩

[2]**plural** *n*
a form of a word used to show that more than one person or thing is meant

[1]**plus** \'pləs\ *adj*
falling high in a certain range ⟨He got a grade of B *plus.*⟩

[2]**plus** *prep*
increased by : with the addition of ⟨4 *plus* 5 equals 9.⟩ ⟨You can come, *plus* your friends.⟩

²plush:
a teddy bear made of plush

¹plush \'pləsh\ *adj* **plush•er**; **plush•est**
1 made of a thick soft fabric
2 very rich and fine 〈a *plush* hotel〉

²plush *n*
▲ a fabric like a very thick soft velvet

plus sign *n*
a sign + used in mathematics to show addition (as in 8+6=14) or a quantity greater than zero (as in +10°)

Plu•to \'plü-tō\ *n*
► a celestial object that orbits the sun at an average distance of 3.7 billion miles (5.9 billion kilometers) and has a diameter of about 1500 miles (2300 kilometers) and is sometimes considered one of the planets

plu•to•ni•um \plü-'tō-nē-əm\ *n*
a radioactive metallic chemical element formed from neptunium and used for releasing atomic energy

¹ply \'plī\ *vb* **plied**; **ply•ing**
1 to use something steadily or forcefully 〈*ply* an ax〉
2 to keep supplying 〈They *plied* their guest with food.〉
3 to work at 〈*ply* a trade〉

²ply *n, pl* **plies**
one of the folds, layers, or threads of which something (as yarn or plywood) is made up

ply•wood \'plī-,wu̇d\ *n*
a strong board made by gluing together thin sheets of wood under heat and pressure

p.m., P.M. *abbr* afternoon
Hint: The abbreviation *p.m.* is short for Latin *post meridiem*, which means "after noon."

pneu•mat•ic \nu̇-'ma-tik, nyu̇-\ *adj*
1 moved or worked by the pressure of air
2 made to hold or be inflated with compressed air 〈a *pneumatic* tire〉

pneu•mo•nia \nu̇-'mō-nyə, nyu̇-'mō-\ *n*
a serious illness affecting the lungs that is marked especially by fever, cough, and difficulty in breathing

P.O. *abbr* post office

¹poach \'pōch\ *vb* **poached**; **poach•ing**
to cook slowly in liquid

²poach *vb* **poached**; **poaching**
to hunt or fish unlawfully

pock \'päk\ *n*
a small swelling like a pimple on the skin (as in smallpox) or the mark it leaves

¹pock•et \'pä-kət\ *n*
1 a small bag sewn into a piece of clothing for carrying small articles
2 a place or thing that is different from the larger place or thing that it is part of 〈They found a *pocket* of gold in the mine.〉
3 a condition of the air (as a down current) that causes an airplane to drop suddenly
4 a bag at the corner or side of a pool table

²pocket *vb* **pock•et•ed**; **pock•et•ing**
1 to put something in a pocket
2 to keep often dishonestly 〈He was tempted to *pocket* the profits.〉

Pluto

³pocket *adj*
POCKET-SIZE 〈a *pocket* dictionary〉

pock•et•book \'pä-kət-,bu̇k\ *n*
1 HANDBAG
2 the amount of money that someone has to spend 〈The price suits my *pocketbook.*〉

pock•et•knife \'pä-kət-,nīf\ *n, pl* **pock•et•knives** \-,nīvz\
a small knife that has one or more blades that fold into the handle

pock•et–size \'pä-kət-,sīz\ *adj*
small enough to fit in a pocket

pock•mark \'päk-,märk\ *n*
1 the mark left by a pock
2 a small hole or dent 〈Rust left *pockmarks* on the car.〉
pock•marked \-,märkt\ *adj*

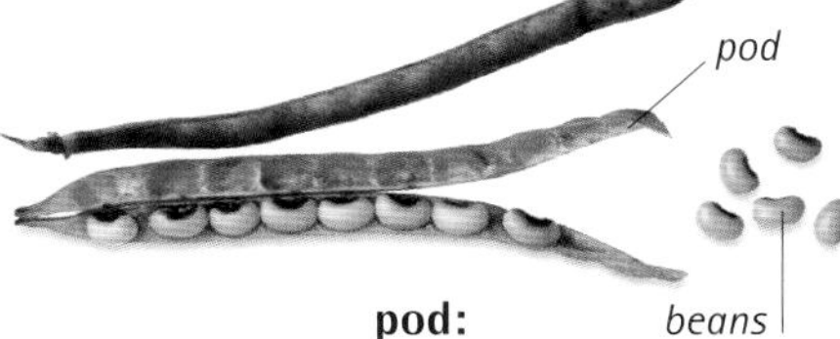
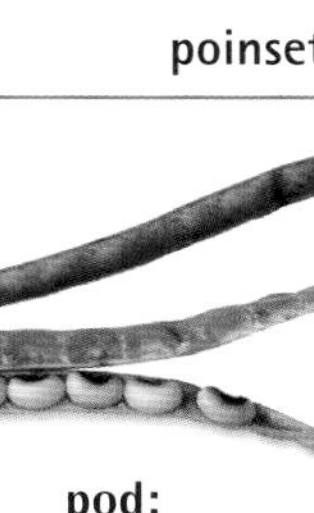

pod:
bean pods

pod \'päd\ *n*
▲ a fruit (as a pea or bean) that is dry when ripe and splits open to free its seeds

pod•cast \'päd-,kast\ *n*
a program (as of music or talk) made available in digital format to be downloaded automatically over the Internet

po•di•um \'pōd-ē-əm\ *n*
1 a raised platform especially for the conductor of an orchestra
2 a stand with a slanted surface (as for holding papers or a book) that a person can stand behind or near when giving a speech

po•em \'pō-əm\ *n*
a piece of writing often having figurative language and lines that have rhythm and sometimes rhyme

po•et \'pō-ət\ *n*
a writer of poems

po•et•ic \pō-'e-tik\ *or* **po•et•i•cal** \-i-kəl\ *adj*
of, relating to, or like that of poets or poetry

po•et•ry \'pō-ə-trē\ *n*
1 writing that usually involves figurative language and lines that have rhythm and sometimes rhyme : VERSE
2 the writings of a poet

po•go stick \'pō-gō-\ *n*
a pole with a strong spring at the bottom and two rests for the feet on which a person stands and bounces

poin•set•tia \pȯin-'se-tē-ə, -'se-tə\ *n*
▼ a tropical plant with showy usually red leaves that grow like petals around its small greenish yellow flowers

poinsettia

A B C D E F G H I J K L M N O P Q R S T U V W X Y Z

[1]point \ˈpȯint\ *n*
1 a separate or particular detail : ITEM ⟨She explained the main *points* of the plan.⟩
2 an individual quality : CHARACTERISTIC ⟨He has many good *points.*⟩
3 the chief idea or meaning ⟨the *point* of a story⟩
4 PURPOSE, AIM ⟨There's no *point* in trying any more.⟩
5 a geometric element that has a position but no dimensions and is pictured as a small dot
6 a particular place or position ⟨We saw *points* of interest in the city.⟩
7 a particular stage or moment ⟨the boiling *point*⟩ ⟨Let's stop at this *point.*⟩
8 the usually sharp end (as of a sword, pin, or pencil)
9 a piece of land that sticks out
10 a dot in writing or printing
11 one of the 32 marks indicating direction on a compass
12 a unit of scoring in a game ⟨I scored fifteen *points.*⟩
point•ed \ˈpȯin-təd\ *adj*
pointy \ˈpȯin-tē\ *adj*

[2]point *vb* **point•ed; point•ing**
1 to show the position or direction of something especially by extending a finger in a particular direction ⟨He *pointed* to the door.⟩
2 to direct someone's attention to ⟨I *pointed* out the mistakes.⟩
3 [1]AIM 1, DIRECT ⟨She *pointed* the telescope toward Mars.⟩ ⟨The arrow *pointed* to the left.⟩
4 to give a sharp end to ⟨*point* a pencil⟩

point–blank *adv*
in a very clear and direct way

point•ed•ly \ˈpȯin-təd-lē\ *adv*
in a way that very clearly expresses a particular meaning or thought ⟨He spoke *pointedly.*⟩

point•er \ˈpȯin-tər\ *n*
1 something that points or is used for pointing
2 a helpful hint ⟨I got a few *pointers* on diving.⟩
3 ▼ a large dog with long ears and short hair that is trained to direct its head and body in the direction of an animal that is being hunted

pointer 3:
a German short-haired pointer

point•less \ˈpȯint-ləs\ *adj*
having no meaning or purpose ⟨a *pointless* story⟩ ⟨*pointless* attempts⟩

point of view *n, pl* **points of view**
a way of looking at or thinking about something

[1]poise \ˈpȯiz\ *vb* **poised; pois•ing**
1 to hold or make steady by balancing ⟨A book was *poised* on her head.⟩
2 to remain in position without moving
3 to be or become ready for something ⟨The company was *poised* for success.⟩

[2]poise *n*
1 the state of being balanced
2 a natural self-confident manner ⟨He spoke with great *poise.*⟩

[1]poi•son \ˈpȯi-zᵊn\ *n*
a substance that by its chemical action can injure or kill a living thing

> ▶ **Word History** Both *poison* and *potion* come from the same Latin word, *potio,* the original meaning of which was just "a drink." Already in Latin, however, *potio* could refer to a drink containing powerful substances that might heal or charm—what we call a *potion.* The Latin word *potio* became *poison* in Old French and began to refer to any powerful substance, whether a drink or not, that might sicken or kill when consumed. *Poison* and later *potion* both came into English from French.

[2]poison *vb* **poi•soned; poi•son•ing**
1 to injure or kill with poison
2 to put poison on or in

poison ivy *n*
1 a usually climbing plant that has leaves with three leaflets and can cause an itchy painful rash when touched
2 a skin rash caused by poison ivy

poison oak *n*
a bush related to poison ivy that can cause an itchy painful rash when touched

poi•son•ous \ˈpȯi-zᵊn-əs\ *adj*
containing poison : having or causing an effect of poison ⟨*poisonous* mushrooms⟩

poison sumac *n*
a shrub or small tree related to poison ivy that can cause an itchy painful rash when touched

[1]poke \ˈpōk\ *vb* **poked; pok•ing**
1 to push something usually thin or sharp into or at ⟨I *poked* the mud with a stick.⟩
2 to make by stabbing or piercing ⟨The pen *poked* a hole in my bag.⟩
3 to thrust or stick out or cause to thrust or stick out ⟨I *poked* my head out of the window.⟩
4 to search through or look around often without purpose ⟨We were *poking* around in the attic.⟩
5 to move slowly or lazily

[2]poke *n*
a quick push with something pointed

[1]pok•er \ˈpō-kər\ *n*
a metal rod used for stirring a fire

[2]po•ker \ˈpō-kər\ *n*
a card game in which players bet on the value of their cards

poky *or* **pok•ey** \ˈpō-kē\ *adj* **pok•i•er; pok•i•est**
1 so slow as to be annoying
2 small and cramped ⟨a *poky* room⟩

po•lar \ˈpō-lər\ *adj*
1 of or relating to the north pole or south pole or nearby regions ⟨*polar* ice caps⟩
2 coming from or being like a polar region ⟨*polar* cold⟩
3 of or relating to a pole of a magnet

polar bear *n*
▶ a large creamy-white bear of arctic regions

[1]pole \ˈpōl\ *n*
a long straight thin piece of material (as wood or metal)

[2]pole *n*
1 either end of the imaginary line on which the earth or another planet turns
2 either of the two ends of a magnet

Pole \ˈpōl\ *n*
a person born or living in Poland

pole•cat \ˈpōl-ˌkat\ *n, pl* **pole•cats** *or* **polecat**
1 a brown or black European animal related to the weasel
2 SKUNK

pole vault *n*
a track-and-field event in which each athlete uses a pole to jump over a high bar

[1]po•lice \pə-ˈlēs\ *vb* **po•liced; po•lic•ing**
to keep order in or among ⟨Officers *police* the city.⟩

[2]police *n, pl* **police**
1 the department of government that keeps order and enforces law, investigates crimes, and makes arrests
2 *police pl* members of a police force

police dog *n*
a dog trained to help police

po•lice•man \pə-ˈlēs-mən\ *n, pl* **po•lice•men** \-mən\
a man who is a police officer

police officer *n*
a member of a police force

po•lice•wom•an \pə-ˈlēs-ˌwu̇-mən\ *n, pl* **po•lice•wom•en** \-ˌwi-mən\
a woman who is a police officer

[1]pol•i•cy \ˈpä-lə-sē\ *n, pl* **pol•i•cies**
a set of guidelines or rules that determine a course of action ⟨What is the store's return *policy*?⟩

[2]policy *n, pl* **pol•i•cies**
a document that contains the agreement made by an insurance company with a person whose life or property is insured

po•lio \ˈpō-lē-ˌō\ *n*
a once common disease often affecting children and sometimes causing paralysis

po•lio•my•eli•tis \ˌpō-lē-ˌō-ˌmī-ə-ˈlī-təs\ *n*
POLIO

[1]pol•ish \ˈpä-lish\ *vb* **pol•ished; pol•ish•ing**
1 to make smooth and shiny usually by rubbing ⟨*polish* silver⟩
2 to improve in manners, condition, or style ⟨I took a few hours to *polish* my speech.⟩
pol•ish•er *n*
polish off to finish completely ⟨We *polished off* the whole cake.⟩

[2]polish *n*
1 a smooth and shiny surface ⟨the *polish* of the table⟩
2 a substance for making a surface smooth and shiny ⟨shoe *polish*⟩ ⟨metal *polish*⟩
3 good manners : REFINEMENT

[1]Pol•ish \ˈpō-lish\ *adj*
of or relating to Poland, the Poles, or Polish

[2]Polish *n*
the language of the Poles

po•lite \pə-ˈlīt\ *adj* **po•lit•er; po•lit•est**
showing courtesy or good manners
synonyms see CIVIL
po•lite•ly *adv*
po•lite•ness *n*

po•lit•i•cal \pə-ˈli-ti-kəl\ *adj*
relating to the government or the way government is carried on ⟨*political* views⟩
po•lit•i•cal•ly *adv*

pol•i•ti•cian \ˌpä-lə-ˈti-shən\ *n*
a person who is active in government usually as an elected official

pol•i•tics \ˈpä-lə-ˌtiks\ *n pl*
1 the activities, actions, and policies that are used to gain and hold power in a government or to influence a government
2 a person's opinions about the management of government
Hint: *Politics* can be used as a singular or a plural in writing and speaking. ⟨*Politics* has always interested me.⟩ ⟨The country's *politics* have changed.⟩

pol•ka \ˈpōl-kə\ *n*
a lively dance for couples or the music for it

polar bear

pol•ka dot \ˈpō-kə-\ *n*
a dot in a pattern of evenly spaced dots (as on fabric)

[1]poll \ˈpōl\ *n*
1 the casting or recording of the votes or opinions of a number of persons ⟨A *poll* showed a decrease in student interest.⟩
2 the place where votes are cast — usually used in pl. ⟨We go to the *polls* tomorrow.⟩

[2]poll *vb* **polled; poll•ing**
to question in order to get information or opinions about something ⟨She *polled* her classmates on their study habits.⟩

pol•lack *or* **pol•lock** \ˈpä-lək\ *n, pl* **pollack** *or* **pollock**
either of two fishes of the northern Atlantic Ocean and the northern Pacific Ocean that are related to the cod and are often used for food

pol•len \ˈpä-lən\ *n*
▼ the very tiny grains produced by the stamens of a flower or special sacs of a male cone that fertilize the seeds and usually appear as fine yellow dust

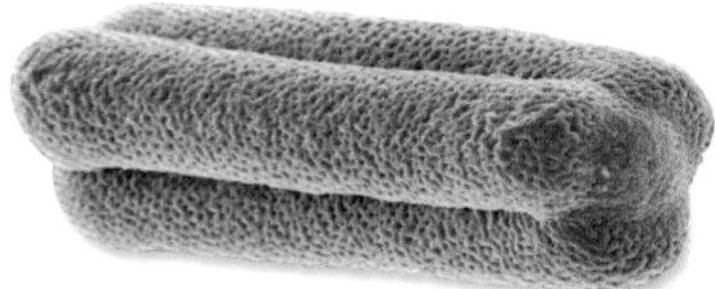

pollen: an enlarged photograph of a pollen grain

pol•li•nate \ˈpä-lə-ˌnāt\ *vb* **pol•li•nat•ed; pol•li•nat•ing**
to transfer or carry pollen from a stamen to a pistil of a flower or from a male cone to a female cone ⟨Bees are *pollinating* the clover.⟩

pol•li•na•tion \ˌpä-lə-ˈnā-shən\ *n*
the transfer of pollen from a stamen to a pistil of a flower or from a male cone to a female cone

pol•lut•ant \pə-ˈlü-tᵊnt\ *n*
a substance that makes something (as air or water) impure and often unsafe

pol•lute \pə-ˈlüt\ *vb* **pol•lut•ed; pol•lut•ing**
to spoil or make impure especially with waste made by humans ⟨Factories *pollute* the stream.⟩
pol•lut•er *n*

pol•lu•tion \pə-ˈlü-shən\ *n*
the action of making something impure and often unsafe or unsuitable for use : the state of being polluted

a b c d e f g h i j k l m n o p q r s t u v w x y z

A B C D E F G H I J K L M N O P Q R S T U V W X Y Z

pol•ly•wog *or* **pol•li•wog** \ˈpä-lē-ˌwäg\ *n*
TADPOLE

po•lo \ˈpō-lō\ *n*
▶ a game played by teams of players on horseback who use long-handled mallets to hit a wooden ball into a goal

poly– *prefix*
many : much : MULTI– ⟨*poly*mer⟩

poly•es•ter \ˈpä-lē-ˌe-stər\ *n*
a synthetic fiber used especially in clothing

poly•gon \ˈpä-li-ˌgän\ *n*
a flat geometric figure having three or more straight sides

poly•mer \ˈpä-lə-mər\ *n*
a chemical compound that is made of small molecules that are arranged in a simple repeating structure to form a larger molecule

pol•yp \ˈpä-ləp\ *n*
▼ a small sea animal (as a coral) having a tubelike body closed and attached to something (as a rock) at one end and opening at the other with a mouth surrounded by tentacles

polyp: polyps clinging to a rock

pome•gran•ate \ˈpä-mə-ˌgra-nət, ˈpäm-ˌgra-\ *n*
a reddish fruit that has a thick leathery skin and many seeds in a pulp of tart flavor and that grows on a tropical Asian tree

pom•mel \ˈpə-məl\ *n*
a rounded knob on the handle of a sword or at the front of a saddle

pomp \ˈpämp\ *n*
a show of wealth and splendor

pom–pom \ˈpäm-ˌpäm\ *n*
1 a small fluffy ball used as decoration especially on clothing
2 a usually brightly colored fluffy ball waved by cheerleaders

pomp•ous \ˈpäm-pəs\ *adj*
having or showing an attitude of someone who thinks he or she is better than other people
pomp•ous•ly *adv*

polo: polo players

pon•cho \ˈpän-chō\ *n, pl* **ponchos**
▼ a garment that is like a blanket with a hole in the middle for the head

poncho: a girl wearing a poncho

pond \ˈpänd\ *n*
a body of water usually smaller than a lake

pon•der \ˈpän-dər\ *vb* **pon•dered**; **pon•der•ing**
to think over carefully ⟨*ponder* a question⟩

pon•der•ous \ˈpän-də-rəs\ *adj*
1 very heavy ⟨a *ponderous* stone⟩
2 slow or clumsy because of weight and size ⟨The elephant moved with *ponderous* steps.⟩
3 unpleasantly dull ⟨a *ponderous* speech⟩
pon•der•ous•ly *adv*

pon•toon \pän-ˈtün\ *n*
a large hollow container filled with air and used to make something (as a boat, plane, or bridge) float

po•ny \ˈpō-nē\ *n, pl* **ponies**
a small horse

pony express *n, often cap P & E*
a rapid postal system that operated across the western United States in 1860–61 by changing horses and riders along the way

po•ny•tail \ˈpō-nē-ˌtāl\ *n*
long hair that is pulled together and banded usually at the back of the head

poo•dle \ˈpü-dᵊl\ *n*
a small or medium-sized dog with a thick curly coat of solid color

[1]**pool** \ˈpül\ *n*
1 a small deep body of usually fresh water
2 something like a pool (as in shape or depth) ⟨The lamp cast a *pool* of light.⟩
3 a small body of standing liquid : PUDDLE ⟨a *pool* of blood⟩
4 SWIMMING POOL

²pool *n*
1 ▶ a game of billiards played on a table with six pockets
2 a supply of people or things available for use ⟨a *pool* of talent⟩

³pool *vb* **pooled**; **pool•ing**
to contribute to a common fund or effort

pooped \'püpt\ *adj*
very tired

poor \'pu̇r\ *adj* **poor•er**; **poor•est**
1 having little money or few possessions
2 less than enough ⟨a *poor* crop⟩
3 worthy of pity ⟨a *poor* lost dog⟩
4 low in quality or condition ⟨*poor* health⟩ ⟨a *poor* performance⟩
poor•ly *adv*

¹pop \'päp\ *vb* **popped**; **pop•ping**
1 to burst or cause to burst with a short loud sound ⟨The balloon *popped.*⟩
2 to cause to open suddenly
3 to go, come, or appear suddenly or unexpectedly ⟨Let's *pop* in for a visit.⟩ ⟨An idea *popped* into my head.⟩
4 to put into or onto quickly or suddenly ⟨I *popped* a grape into my mouth.⟩
5 to stick out ⟨His eyes *popped* in surprise.⟩
6 to shoot with a gun

²pop *n*
1 a short loud sound
2 SODA POP

pop•corn \'päp-,kȯrn\ *n*
1 corn whose kernels burst open when exposed to high heat to form white or yellowish puffy pieces
2 the kernels after popping

pope \'pōp\ *n, often cap*
the head of the Roman Catholic Church

pop•lar \'pä-plər\ *n*
a tree that has rough bark and a white substance resembling cotton around its seeds

pop•py \'pä-pē\ *n, pl* **poppies**
a plant with a hairy stem and showy usually red, yellow, or white flowers

pop•u•lace \'pä-pyə-ləs\ *n*
1 the common people
2 the people who live in a country or area

pop•u•lar \'pä-pyə-lər\ *adj*
1 of or relating to most of the people in a country or area ⟨the *popular* vote⟩
2 enjoyed or approved by many people ⟨a *popular* game⟩
3 frequently encountered or widely accepted ⟨*popular* opinion⟩
pop•u•lar•ly *adv*

pop•u•lar•i•ty \,pä-pyə-'ler-ə-tē\ *n*
the quality or state of being liked, enjoyed, accepted, or practiced by many people

▶ **²pool 1**
Pool is played on a rectangular table with holes, known as pockets, in the corners and in the center of the longest sides. Players use a long wooden stick called a cue to aim a cue ball toward a colored or striped ball to try to hit it into a pocket. Points are scored by hitting designated balls into pockets, and the player or team that scores an agreed number of points first wins.

pool balls

pool table

cue

pop•u•late \'pä-pyə-,lāt\ *vb* **pop•u•lat•ed**; **pop•u•lat•ing**
to fill or provide with people, animals, or things

pop•u•la•tion \,pä-pyə-'lā-shən\ *n*
1 the whole number of people living in a country, city, or area
2 a group of people or animals living in a certain place ⟨the deer *population*⟩

pop•u•lous \'pä-pyə-ləs\ *adj*
having a large population ⟨a *populous* city⟩

¹pop-up \'päp-,əp\ *n*
a window that appears suddenly on a computer screen often for advertising

²pop-up *adj*
1 relating to or having a part or device that pops up ⟨a *pop-up* book⟩
2 appearing suddenly on a computer screen ⟨*pop-up* ads⟩

por•ce•lain \'pȯr-sə-lən\ *n*
a hard white product of baked clay used especially for dishes, tile, and decorative objects

porch \'pȯrch\ *n*
a covered entrance to a building usually with a separate roof

por•cu•pine \'pȯr-kyə-,pīn\ *n*
▶ a gnawing slow-moving animal that is a large rodent and has stiff sharp quills among its hairs

porcupine

▶ **Word History** The porcupine is certainly not a source of pork, but the word *pork* and the *porc-* in the word *porcupine* both come ultimately from Latin *porcus*, "pig, hog." *Porcupine* was modified from a compound word in Romance languages such as medieval French *porc espin*, literally, "spiny pig." (The *espin* part comes from Latin *spina*, "thorn, spine.")

a b c d e f g h i j k l m n o p q r s t u v w x y z

[1]pore \ˈpȯr\ *vb* **pored**; **por•ing**
to read with great attention : STUDY ⟨I *pored* over my book.⟩

[2]pore *n*
a tiny opening (as in the skin or in the soil)

pork \ˈpȯrk\ *n*
the meat of a pig used for food

po•rous \ˈpȯr-əs\ *adj*
1 full of small holes ⟨*porous* wood⟩
2 capable of absorbing liquids ⟨*porous* paper⟩

por•poise \ˈpȯr-pəs\ *n*
1 a small whale with teeth that resembles a dolphin but has a blunt rounded snout
2 DOLPHIN 1

por•ridge \ˈpȯr-ij\ *n*
a soft food made by boiling partly ground grain or a vegetable (as peas) in water or milk until it thickens

[1]port \ˈpȯrt\ *n*
1 a town or city with a harbor where ships load or unload cargo ⟨Miami is a major United States *port.*⟩
2 a place (as a harbor) where ships can find shelter from a storm

[2]port *n*
1 an opening (as in machinery) for gas, steam, or water to go in or out
2 PORTHOLE

[3]port *n*
the left side of a ship or airplane looking forward

por•ta•ble \ˈpȯr-tə-bəl\ *adj*
easy or possible to carry or move about ⟨a *portable* television⟩

por•tal \ˈpȯr-tᵊl\ *n*
a large or fancy door or gate

port•cul•lis \pȯrt-ˈkə-ləs\ *n*
a heavy iron gate that can be lowered to prevent entrance (as to a castle)

por•tend \pȯr-ˈtend\ *vb* **por•tend•ed**; **por•tend•ing**
to give a sign or warning of beforehand ⟨Distant thunder *portended* a storm.⟩

por•tent \ˈpȯr-ˌtent\ *n*
a sign or warning of something usually bad that is going to happen : OMEN

por•ten•tous \pȯr-ˈten-təs\ *adj*
giving a sign or warning of something usually bad that is going to happen ⟨a *portentous* dream⟩

por•ter \ˈpȯr-tər\ *n*
1 a person whose job is to carry baggage (as at a hotel)
2 a person whose job is helping passengers on a train

port•fo•lio \pȯrt-ˈfō-lē-ˌō\ *n, pl* **port•fo•li•os**
1 a flat case for carrying papers or drawings
2 a collection of art (as paintings) presented together in a folder

port•hole \ˈpȯrt-ˌhōl\ *n*
a small window in the side of a ship or airplane

por•ti•co \ˈpȯr-ti-ˌkō\ *n, pl* **por•ti•coes** *or* **por•ti•cos**
▼ a row of columns supporting a roof at the entrance of a building

[1]por•tion \ˈpōr-shən\ *n*
1 a part or share of a whole
2 SERVING ⟨a large *portion* of pasta⟩
synonyms see PART

[2]portion *vb* **por•tioned**; **por•tion•ing**
to divide into parts : DISTRIBUTE ⟨They *portioned* the supplies out equally.⟩

port•ly \ˈpȯrt-lē\ *adj* **port•li•er**; **port•li•est**
having a round and heavy body : somewhat fat

por•trait \ˈpȯr-trət, -ˌtrāt\ *n*
▼ a picture of a person usually showing the face

portrait: a portrait of a woman

por•tray \pȯr-ˈtrā\ *vb* **por•trayed**; **por•tray•ing**
1 to make a portrait of ⟨The artist *portrayed* the young queen.⟩
2 to describe in words or words and images ⟨The story *portrays* frontier life.⟩

portico: a portico of a theater in Paris, France

3 to play the role of ⟨He *portrays* the hero.⟩

por•tray•al \pȯr-ˈtrā-əl\ *n*
the act or result of showing in a portrait or describing in words or images ⟨The movie is an accurate *portrayal* of her life.⟩

[1]Por•tu•guese \ˈpȯr-chə-ˌgēz\ *adj*
of or relating to Portugal, its people, or the Portuguese language

[2]Portuguese *n, pl* **Portuguese**
1 a person born or living in Portugal
2 the language of Portugal and Brazil

[1]pose \ˈpōz\ *vb* **posed**; **pos•ing**
1 to hold or cause to hold a special position of the body ⟨Everyone *posed* for the photo.⟩
2 to be or create ⟨The game *poses* a risk of injury.⟩
3 to ask (a question)
4 to pretend to be someone or something else ⟨The impostor *posed* as royalty.⟩

[2]pose *n*
1 a position of the body held for a special purpose ⟨He's pictured in different *poses.*⟩
2 a pretended attitude ⟨Her friendliness is just a *pose.*⟩

[1]po•si•tion \pə-ˈzi-shən\ *n*
1 the way in which something or someone is placed or arranged ⟨The seat is in the upright *position.*⟩
2 a way of looking at or considering things ⟨What's your *position* on the issue?⟩
3 the place where a person or thing is or should be ⟨Take your *position* on stage.⟩
4 the situation that someone or something is in ⟨Your request puts me in an awkward *position.*⟩
5 the rank or role a person has in an organization or in society
6 JOB 1

[2]position *vb* **po•si•tioned**; **po•si•tion•ing**
to put in a particular place or arrangement ⟨He *positioned* the helmet on his head.⟩

[1]pos•i•tive \ˈpä-zə-tiv\ *adj*
1 fully confident : CERTAIN ⟨I'm *positive* that I will win.⟩
2 having a real or beneficial effect or result ⟨They took *positive* action.⟩ ⟨I had a *positive* experience.⟩
3 beyond doubt : UNQUESTIONABLE ⟨*positive* proof⟩
4 showing acceptance or approval ⟨a *positive* response⟩
5 thinking of good qualities or possibilities : OPTIMISTIC ⟨a *positive* attitude⟩
6 being greater than zero and often shown by a plus sign ⟨2 or +2 is a *positive* number.⟩
7 being or relating to electricity of a kind that is produced in a glass rod rubbed with silk ⟨a *positive* charge⟩
8 having more protons than electrons ⟨a *positive* particle⟩
9 being the part from which the electric current flows to the external circuit ⟨the *positive* pole of a storage battery⟩
10 showing the presence of what is looked for or suspected to be present ⟨The test for strep throat was *positive.*⟩
11 relating to or having the form of an adjective or adverb that shows no degree of comparison
pos•i•tive•ly *adv*

[2]positive *n*
1 a good or useful feature or quality ⟨There are many *positives* of living in the country.⟩
2 the degree or a form of an adjective or adverb that shows no comparison

poss. *abbr* possessive

pos•se \ˈpä-sē\ *n*
a group of people gathered together to make a search and especially in the past to search for a criminal

pos•sess \pə-ˈzes\ *vb* **pos•sessed**; **pos•sess•ing**
1 to have and hold as property : OWN ⟨I *possess* little money.⟩
2 to have as a characteristic or quality ⟨She *possesses* great patience.⟩
3 to enter into and control firmly ⟨He acted as if *possessed* by a demon.⟩
pos•ses•sor \-ər\ *n*

pos•ses•sion \pə-ˈze-shən\ *n*
1 the act or state of possessing or holding as property ⟨The missing items were found in her *possession.*⟩
2 something that is held by someone as property ⟨a valuable *possession*⟩

[1]pos•ses•sive \pə-ˈze-siv\ *adj*
1 being or belonging to the case of a noun or pronoun that shows possession ⟨"His" is a *possessive* pronoun.⟩
2 showing the desire to possess or control : unwilling to share

[2]possessive *n*
a word or form of a word that shows possession

pos•si•bil•i•ty \ˌpä-sə-ˈbi-lə-tē\ *n, pl* **pos•si•bil•i•ties**
1 a chance that something may or may not happen or exist : the state or fact of being possible ⟨There's a *possibility* of rain today.⟩
2 something that may happen or exist ⟨Life on other planets is a *possibility.*⟩

pos•si•ble \ˈpä-sə-bəl\ *adj*
1 able to be done ⟨Call whenever *possible.*⟩
2 able to happen or exist ⟨A storm is *possible.*⟩
3 able or suited to be or to become ⟨I have a *possible* solution.⟩

> ▶ **Synonyms** POSSIBLE and LIKELY mean capable of becoming true or of actually happening. POSSIBLE is used when something may happen or exist under the proper conditions. ⟨It is *possible* that you may get rich.⟩ LIKELY is used when chances are good that something will actually happen but there is no proof it will. ⟨He's *likely* to be late.⟩

pos•si•bly \ˈpä-sə-blē\ *adv*
1 by any possibility ⟨I can't *possibly* go.⟩
2 by nothing more than chance : PERHAPS

pos•sum \ˈpä-səm\ *n*
OPOSSUM

[1]post \ˈpōst\ *n*
a piece of material (as metal or wood) placed firmly in an upright position and used especially as a support or marker

[2]post *vb* **post•ed**; **post•ing**
1 to fasten (as a notice or sign) to a suitable place (as a wall or bulletin board)
2 to make known publicly as if by putting up a notice ⟨Information is *posted* on the Web site.⟩
3 to forbid persons from entering or using by putting up warning notices ⟨Officials *posted* the trout stream.⟩

[3]post *n*
1 *chiefly British* postal service
2 *chiefly British* the mail handled by the post
3 *chiefly British* a single shipment of mail
4 something (as a message) published online

[4]post *vb* **post•ed**; **post•ing**
1 to ride or travel quickly
2 to send by mail
3 to make aware of recent news about something ⟨Keep me *posted.*⟩

[5]post *n*
1 the place where a soldier or guard is stationed
2 a place where a body of troops is stationed
3 a place or office to which a person is appointed ⟨a teaching *post*⟩
4 TRADING POST

[6]post *vb* **post•ed**; **post•ing**
to station in a given place ⟨*post* a guard⟩

post– *prefix*
after : later : following : behind ⟨*post*script⟩

post•age \ˈpō-stij\ *n*
a fee for sending a letter or package by mail

post•al \ˈpō-stᵊl\ *adj*
relating to the post office or the sending and delivery of mail ⟨*postal* rates⟩

postcard 1: two postcards

postal card *n*
1 a blank card with a postage stamp printed on it
2 POSTCARD 1

postal service *n*
a government department in charge of handling the mail

post•card \'pōst-,kärd\ *n*
1 ▲ a card on which a message may be sent by mail without an envelope and that often has a picture on one side
2 POSTAL CARD 1

post•er \'pō-stər\ *n*
a usually large sheet with writing or pictures on it that is displayed as a notice, advertisement, or for decoration

pos•ter•i•ty \pä-'ster-ə-tē\ *n*
all future generations ⟨*Posterity* will remember her as a great leader.⟩

potato chips

post•man \'pōst-mən\ *n, pl* **post•men** \-mən\
LETTER CARRIER

post•mark \'pōst-,märk\ *n*
a mark put on a piece of mail especially for canceling the postage stamp

post•mas•ter \'pōst-,ma-stər\ *n*
a person in charge of a post office

post•mis•tress \'pōst-,mi-strəs\ *n*
a woman in charge of a post office

post office *n*
1 POSTAL SERVICE
2 a place where mail is received, handled, and sent out

post•paid \'pōst-'pād\ *adv*
with postage paid by the sender

post•pone \pōst-'pōn\ *vb* **post•poned**; **post•pon•ing**
to put off until a later time
post•pone•ment \-mənt\ *n*

post•script \'pōst-,skript\ *n*
a note added at the end of a letter, article, or book

pos•ture \'päs-chər\ *n*
the way in which the body is positioned when sitting or standing : the general way of holding the body ⟨an upright *posture*⟩ ⟨a humble *posture*⟩

po•sy \'pō-zē\ *n, pl* **posies**
1 a small bunch of flowers
2 [1]FLOWER 1

[1]**pot** \'pät\ *n*
1 a deep usually rounded container ⟨a cooking *pot*⟩ ⟨a clay flower *pot*⟩
2 the amount a pot will hold ⟨a *pot* of soup⟩

[2]**pot** *vb* **pot•ted**; **pot•ting**
to put or pack in a pot ⟨I'm *potting* up begonias.⟩

pot•ash \'pät-,ash\ *n*
potassium or a compound of potassium

po•tas•si•um \pə-'ta-sē-əm\ *n*
a silvery soft light metallic chemical element found especially in minerals

po•ta•to \pə-'tā-tō\ *n, pl* **po•ta•toes**
the thick edible usually rounded underground tuber of a widely grown South American plant that is eaten as a vegetable

potato chip *n*
◀ a thin slice of potato fried crisp

po•tent \'pō-tᵊnt\ *adj*
1 very effective : STRONG ⟨*potent* medicine⟩
2 having power or authority ⟨a *potent* ruler⟩

[1]**po•ten•tial** \pə-'ten-shəl\ *adj*
existing as a possibility : capable of becoming real ⟨*potential* dangers⟩
po•ten•tial•ly *adv*

[2]**potential** *n*
1 the chance or possibility that something will develop and become real ⟨There is a *potential* for injury.⟩
2 an ability or quality that can lead to success or excellence : PROMISE ⟨She has great *potential* as a musician.⟩

pot•hole \'pät-,hōl\ *n*
a deep round hole (as in a road)

po•tion \'pō-shən\ *n*
a drink that is meant to have a special or magical effect on someone

pot•luck \'pät-'lək\ *n*
a meal to which people bring food to share

pot•ter \'pä-tər\ *n*
a person who makes pottery

pot•tery \'pä-tə-rē\ *n, pl* **pot•ter•ies**
1 the art or craft of making objects (as dishes and vases) out of clay
2 ▼ objects made from clay that is shaped while moist and hardened by heat

▶ pottery 2

Pottery can be made in several ways — for example, from coils or flat slabs of clay, by pressing clay into a mold, or by shaping it on a potter's wheel. This last method involves the potter shaping the wet clay with both hands while the wheel spins, giving the pot an even shape. The pot is then left to dry before it is baked at very high temperatures in an oven called a kiln — this process is known as firing.

pouch \'pau̇ch\ *n*
1 a small bag that can be closed (as with a string)
2 a bag for carrying goods or valuables ⟨a mail *pouch*⟩

3 a pocket of folded skin especially for carrying the young (as on the abdomen of a kangaroo) or for carrying food (as in the cheek of a hamster)
4 a structure of the body in the form of a bag

poul•tice \'pōl-təs\ *n*
a soft and heated preparation usually containing medicine that is spread on cloth and placed on the skin to heal a sore or relieve pain

poul•try \'pōl-trē\ *n*
▶birds (as chickens, turkeys, ducks, and geese) raised for their meat or eggs

pounce \'pau̇ns\ *vb* **pounced; pounc•ing**
1 to suddenly jump toward and seize something with or as if with claws ⟨The cat waited to *pounce*.⟩
2 to act, approach, or attack suddenly or without hesitation ⟨I *pounced* on the opportunity.⟩

[1]pound \'pau̇nd\ *n*
1 a measure of weight equal to 16 ounces (about .45 kilograms)
2 any of several units of money (as of the United Kingdom or Egypt)

[2]pound *n*
a place where stray animals are kept

[3]pound *vb* **pound•ed; pound•ing**
1 to crush or break into very small pieces by beating ⟨The wheat is *pounded* into flour.⟩
2 to hit with force again and again ⟨He *pounded* his fist on the table.⟩ ⟨Waves *pounded* the shore.⟩
3 to move with heavy and loud steps ⟨Horses *pounded* down the track.⟩
4 [1]THROB 2 ⟨My heart was *pounding*.⟩

pour \'pȯr\ *vb* **poured; pour•ing**
1 to flow or cause to flow in or as if in a stream ⟨*Pour* some tea.⟩ ⟨Smoke *poured* out the windows.⟩ ⟨His feelings came *pouring* out.⟩
2 to rain hard
3 to move or come continuously ⟨Money was *pouring* in.⟩

[1]pout \'pau̇t\ *vb* **pout•ed; pout•ing**
1 to show displeasure by pushing out the lips
2 [1]SULK ⟨He *pouts* when he doesn't get his way.⟩

[2]pout *n*
a facial expression that shows displeasure and is made by pushing out the lips

pov•er•ty \'pä-vər-tē\ *n*
the condition of being poor : lack of money or possessions

▶ **poultry**
People have kept poultry for centuries, mainly as a source of meat and eggs, although the feathers of ducks and geese are often used to stuff pillows and quilts. On some modern farms, birds are raised in large numbers in highly controlled conditions to encourage them to grow quickly. Poultry reared in a more natural setting are known as "free range."

[1]pow•der \'pau̇-dər\ *vb* **pow•dered; pow•der•ing**
1 to sprinkle or cover with or as if with fine particles of something ⟨The cookies were *powdered* with sugar.⟩
2 to reduce or change to powder

[2]powder *n*
1 a dry substance made up of fine particles ⟨The stone was crushed into *powder*.⟩
2 something (as a food, medicine, or cosmetic) made in or changed to the form of a powder ⟨garlic *powder*⟩
3 GUNPOWDER

powder horn *n*
a cow or ox horn made into a container for carrying gunpowder

pow•dery \'pau̇-də-rē\ *adj*
1 made of or like powder ⟨*powdery* snow⟩
2 easily crumbled ⟨*powdery* bricks⟩
3 covered or sprinkled with or as if with powder ⟨a *powdery* mountain slope⟩

[1]pow•er \'pau̇-ər\ *n*
1 possession of control, authority, or influence over others
2 a nation that has influence among other nations ⟨a foreign *power*⟩
3 the ability to act or produce an effect ⟨It's in your *power* to change things.⟩
4 the right to do something ⟨the president's *powers*⟩
5 physical might : STRENGTH ⟨The wind grew in *power*.⟩
6 the number of times as shown by an exponent that a number is used as a factor to obtain a product ⟨10^3 is the third *power* of 10 and means $10 \times 10 \times 10$.⟩
7 force or energy used to do work ⟨electric *power*⟩
8 the rate of speed at which work is done
9 the number of times an optical instrument (as a microscope) magnifies the object viewed

[2]power *vb* **pow•ered; pow•er•ing**
to supply with a form of energy ⟨The old train was *powered* by coal.⟩

power plant: steam billowing from the cooling towers of a power plant

pow•er•ful \ˈpau̇-ər-fəl\ *adj*
full of or having power, strength, or influence ⟨*powerful* magnets⟩ ⟨a *powerful* speech⟩
pow•er•ful•ly \-fə-lē\ *adv*

pow•er•house \ˈpau̇-ər-ˌhau̇s\ *n*
1 POWER PLANT
2 a person or thing having unusual strength or energy

pow•er•less \ˈpau̇-ər-ləs\ *adj*
without power, strength, authority, or influence ⟨He was *powerless* to stop them.⟩

power plant *n*
▲ a building in which electric power is generated

pow•wow \ˈpau̇-ˌwau̇\ *n*
1 an American Indian ceremony or social gathering
2 a meeting for discussion

pp. *abbr* pages

PQ *abbr* Province of Quebec

PR *abbr* Puerto Rico

pr. *abbr* pair

prac•ti•ca•ble \ˈprak-ti-kə-bəl\ *adj*
possible to do or put into practice ⟨a *practicable* plan⟩

prac•ti•cal \ˈprak-ti-kəl\ *adj*
1 of or relating to real action rather than ideas or thought ⟨*practical* matters⟩
2 capable of being put to use : reasonable to do or use ⟨*practical* advice⟩ ⟨Those shoes are nice, but these are more *practical*.⟩
3 tending to act according to reason and logic ⟨a *practical* person⟩

practical joke *n*
a joke involving an act rather than words : a trick played on someone
practical joker *n*

prac•ti•cal•ly \ˈprak-ti-kə-lē\ *adv*
1 ALMOST ⟨It rained *practically* all night.⟩
2 in a way that is reasonable or logical ⟨*Practically* speaking, it's too far to drive.⟩

[1]**prac•tice** \ˈprak-təs\ *vb* **prac•ticed**; **prac•tic•ing**
1 to do or work at often so as to learn well or improve ⟨*Practice* the piano daily.⟩
2 to do or perform often or usually ⟨Try to *practice* good manners.⟩
3 to engage in or work at as a profession ⟨*practice* medicine⟩

[2]**practice** *n*
1 the act of doing something again and again in order to learn or improve ⟨Ballet takes a lot of *practice*.⟩
2 a regular event at which something is done again and again to increase skill ⟨soccer *practice*⟩
3 actual performance : USE ⟨I put his advice into *practice*.⟩
4 a usual way of doing something ⟨It's our *practice* to rise early.⟩
5 continuous work in a profession ⟨the *practice* of law⟩

prai•rie \ˈprer-ē\ *n*
a large area of level or rolling grassland

prairie chicken *n*
a grouse of the prairies of the central United States

prairie dog *n*
► a burrowing animal of the prairies of the central and western United States that is related to the squirrel and lives in large colonies

prairie schooner *n*
a long covered wagon used by pioneers to cross the prairies

[1]**praise** \ˈprāz\ *vb* **praised**; **prais•ing**
1 to express approval of ⟨Dad *praised* my good grades.⟩
2 to glorify (God or a saint)
synonyms see COMPLIMENT

[2]**praise** *n*
1 an expression of approval
2 [1]WORSHIP 1 ⟨hymns of *praise*⟩

praise•wor•thy \ˈprāz-ˌwər-t͟hē\ *adj*
deserving praise ⟨a *praiseworthy* goal⟩

prance \ˈprans\ *vb* **pranced**; **pranc•ing**
1 to move by taking high steps ⟨horses *prancing*⟩
2 to walk or move in a lively and proud way ⟨She *pranced* around in her new dress.⟩

prank \ˈpraŋk\ *n*
a mischievous act : PRACTICAL JOKE

prairie dog: a black-tailed prairie dog

[1]prat•tle \ˈpra-tᵊl\ *vb* **prat•tled; prat•tling**
to talk a great deal about unimportant or uninteresting things

[2]prattle *n*
uninteresting or unimportant talk

pray \ˈprā\ *vb* **prayed; pray•ing**
1 to speak to God especially to give thanks or ask for something
2 to hope or wish very much for 〈I *prayed* no one would forget.〉
3 to ask earnestly : BEG 〈Do not leave, I *pray* you.〉

prayer \ˈprer\ *n*
1 words spoken to God 〈a *prayer* for peace〉
2 the act of praying to God 〈We knelt in *prayer.*〉
3 a strong hope or wish 〈It's our *prayer* that you will return safely.〉
4 a set form of words used in praying
5 a religious service that is mostly prayers 〈evening *prayer*〉

praying mantis \ˌprā-iŋ-\ *n*
▶ a large usually green insect that feeds on other insects which are held in the raised front legs

pre- *prefix*
1 earlier than : before 〈*pre*historic〉
2 beforehand 〈*pre*pay〉
3 in front of : front 〈*pre*molar〉

preach \ˈprēch\ *vb* **preached; preach•ing**
1 to give a sermon
2 to urge publicly 〈*preach* patience〉

preach•er \ˈprē-chər\ *n*
1 a person who gives sermons
2 [1]MINISTER 1

pre•am•ble \ˈprē-ˌam-bəl\ *n*
an introduction (as to a law) that often gives the reasons for what follows

pre•car•i•ous \pri-ˈker-ē-əs\ *adj*
not safe, strong, or steady 〈*precarious* balance〉 〈a *precarious* journey〉
pre•car•i•ous•ly *adv*

pre•cau•tion \pri-ˈkȯ-shən\ *n*
something done beforehand to prevent harm or trouble or bring about good results 〈You should take *precautions* against fire.〉

pre•cede \pri-ˈsēd\ *vb* **pre•ced•ed; pre•ced•ing**
to be or go before in importance, position, or time 〈Many failures *preceded* her success.〉

pre•ce•dent \ˈpre-sə-dənt\ *n*
something that can be used as a rule or example to be followed in the future

pre•ced•ing \pri-ˈsē-diŋ\ *adj*
existing or happening before in time or place : PREVIOUS 〈the *preceding* week〉

pre•cinct \ˈprē-ˌsiŋkt\ *n*
1 any of the sections into which a town or city is divided for a particular purpose (as voting or police protection)
2 a surrounding or enclosed area 〈Stay within school *precincts.*〉

pre•cious \ˈpre-shəs\ *adj*
1 very valuable 〈Diamonds and emeralds are *precious* stones.〉
2 greatly loved or valued 〈a *precious* friend〉 〈*precious* memories〉

prec•i•pice \ˈpre-sə-pəs\ *n*
a very steep side of a mountain or cliff

pre•cip•i•tate \pri-ˈsi-pə-ˌtāt\ *vb* **pre•cip•i•tat•ed; pre•cip•i•tat•ing**
1 to cause to happen suddenly or unexpectedly 〈The misunderstanding *precipitated* a quarrel.〉
2 to change from a vapor to a liquid or solid and fall as rain or snow
3 to separate from a solution 〈The procedure called for *precipitating* salt from seawater.〉

praying mantis

pre•cip•i•ta•tion \pri-ˌsi-pə-ˈtā-shən\ *n*
water that falls to the earth as hail, mist, rain, sleet, or snow

pre•cise \pri-ˈsīs\ *adj*
1 exactly stated or explained 〈He gave *precise* instructions.〉
2 very exact : ACCURATE 〈*precise* measurements〉
3 being exactly the one mentioned or indicated and no other 〈At that *precise* moment, the telephone rang.〉
pre•cise•ly *adv*

pre•ci•sion \pri-ˈsi-zhən\ *n*
the quality or state of being precise or exact : ACCURACY 〈The lines were drawn with great *precision.*〉

pre•co•cious \pri-ˈkō-shəs\ *adj*
showing qualities or abilities of an adult at an unusually early age
pre•co•cious•ly *adv*

pred•a•tor \ˈpre-də-tər\ *n*
an animal that lives mostly by killing and eating other animals

pred•a•to•ry \ˈpre-də-ˌtȯr-ē\ *adj*
living by killing and eating other animals 〈An owl is a *predatory* bird.〉

pre•de•ces•sor \ˈpre-də-ˌse-sər, ˈprē-\ *n*
a person who held a job or position before someone else

pre•dic•a•ment \pri-ˈdi-kə-mənt\ *n*
a bad situation

[1]pred•i•cate \ˈpre-di-kət\ *n*
the part of a sentence or clause that tells what is said about the subject 〈"Rang" in "the doorbell rang" is the *predicate.*〉

[2]predicate *adj*
completing the meaning of a linking verb 〈"Sweet" in "the sugar is sweet" is a *predicate* adjective.〉

pre•dict \pri-ˈdikt\ *vb* **pre•dict•ed; pre•dict•ing**
to say that (something) will or might happen in the future 〈*predict* the weather〉
synonyms see FORETELL

pre•dic•tion \pri-ˈdik-shən\ *n*
1 an act of saying what will or might happen in the future 〈*prediction* of earthquakes〉
2 a statement about what will or might happen in the future 〈a weather *prediction*〉

pre•dom•i•nance \pri-ˈdä-mə-nəns\ *n*
the quality or state of being greater than others in number, frequency, strength, influence, or authority 〈a *predominance* of errors〉

pre•dom•i•nant \pri-ˈdä-mə-nənt\ *adj*
greater than others in number, frequency, strength, influence, or authority 〈a *predominant* view〉 〈the *predominant* flavors〉

pre•dom•i•nate \pri-ˈdä-mə-ˌnāt\ *vb* **pre•dom•i•nat•ed; pre•dom•i•nat•ing**
to be greater than others in number, frequency, strength, influence, or authority 〈In this forest, pine trees *predominate.*〉

preen \ˈprēn\ *vb* **preened; preen•ing**
1 to smooth and clean with the bill 〈The sparrow *preened* its feathers.〉
2 to make a person's own appearance neat and tidy 〈He *preened* himself in front of the mirror.〉

pre•fab•ri•cat•ed \prē-ˈfa-bri-ˌkā-təd\ *adj*
made of parts that are made at a factory and can be put together late 〈*prefabricated* houses〉

pref•ace \ˈpre-fəs\ *n*
a section at the beginning that introduces a book or a speech

pre•fer \pri-ˈfər\ *vb* **pre•ferred; pre•fer•ring**
to like better than another or others 〈She *prefers* chocolate ice cream.〉

A B C D E F G H I J K L M N O P Q R S T U V W X Y Z

pref•er•a•ble \'pre-fə-rə-bəl\ *adj*
better or more desireable ⟨the *preferable* choice⟩
pref•er•a•bly \-blē\ *adv*

pref•er•ence \'pre-fə-rəns, 'pref-rəns\ *n*
1 a choosing of or special liking for one person or thing rather than another or others ⟨Buyers are showing a *preference* for small cars.⟩
2 the power or chance to choose : CHOICE ⟨I gave him his *preference.*⟩
3 a person or thing that is liked or wanted more than another ⟨My *preference* is to travel by train.⟩

pre•fix \'prē-,fiks\ *n*
a letter or group of letters that comes at the beginning of a word and has its own meaning

preg•nan•cy \'preg-nən-sē\ *n, pl* **preg•nan•cies**
the state of being pregnant

preg•nant \'preg-nənt\ *adj*
1 ▶ carrying one or more unborn offspring in the body
2 full of meaning ⟨There was a *pregnant* pause before the announcement.⟩

pre•hen•sile \prē-'hen-səl\ *adj*
capable of grasping something by wrapping around it ⟨Some monkeys have a *prehensile* tail.⟩

pre•his•tor•ic \,prē-hi-'stȯr-ik\ *adj*
▼ relating to or existing in the time before written history began ⟨*prehistoric* animals⟩

¹prej•u•dice \'pre-jə-dəs\ *n*
1 a liking or dislike for one rather than another especially without good reason ⟨She has a *prejudice* against department stores.⟩

pregnant 1: a pregnant woman

2 a feeling of unfair dislike directed against an individual or a group because of some characteristic (as race or religion)
3 injury or damage to a person's rights

²prejudice *vb* **prej•u•diced**; **prej•u•dic•ing**
1 to cause to have an unfair dislike of ⟨The incident *prejudiced* them against the company.⟩
2 to cause damage to (as a person's rights) ⟨Newspaper stories *prejudiced* the upcoming trial.⟩

prej•u•diced \'pre-jə-dəst\ *adj*
having or showing an unfair dislike of a person or group because of some characteristic (as race or religion) ⟨a *prejudiced* comment⟩

¹pre•lim•i•nary \pri-'li-mə-,ner-ē\ *n, pl* **pre•lim•i•nar•ies**
something that comes before the main or final part ⟨The athletes competed in the *preliminaries.*⟩

²preliminary *adj*
coming before the main or full part ⟨I won the *preliminary* round.⟩ ⟨The *preliminary* results are promising.⟩

pre•lude \'prel-,yüd, 'prā-,lüd\ *n*
1 something that comes before and prepares for the main or more important parts
2 a short piece of music played at the beginning of something (as an opera or church service)

pre•ma•ture \,prē-mə-'tür, -'tyür, -'chür\ *adj*
happening, coming, or done before the usual or proper time : too early ⟨a *premature* decision⟩ ⟨*premature* infants⟩
pre•ma•ture•ly *adv*

pre•med•i•tate \pri-'me-də-,tāt\ *vb* **pre•med•i•tat•ed**; **pre•med•i•tat•ing**
to think about and plan beforehand

▶ **prehistoric**
Information about prehistoric life comes from fossils, and from objects made by early humans. By examining these, experts can build up a picture of what life was like before systems of writing were developed to record events. Prehistoric people are known to have found food by hunting animals and gathering fruit, seeds, nuts, and wild vegetables. They made simple clothes from animal skins and later from wool, and lived in caves or in shelters they built.

examples of prehistoric objects

cave painting

flint hand ax

carved antler

[1]**pre·mier** \pri-ˈmir, ˈprē-mē-ər\ *adj*
first in importance, excellence, or rank ⟨*premier* scientists⟩

[2]**premier** *n*
PRIME MINISTER

[1]**pre·miere** \pri-ˈmyer, -ˈmir\ *n*
a first showing or performance

[2]**premiere** *vb* **pre·miered**; **pre·mier·ing**
to have a first showing or performance ⟨The movie *premieres* next week.⟩

prem·ise \ˈpre-məs\ *n*
1 a statement or idea taken to be true and on which an argument or reasoning may be based
2 **premises** *pl* a piece of land with the buildings on it

pre·mi·um \ˈprē-mē-əm\ *n*
1 a reward for a special act
2 an amount above the regular or stated price ⟨There is a *premium* for overnight delivery.⟩
3 the amount paid for a contract of insurance ⟨health insurance *premiums*⟩
4 a high or extra value ⟨He put a *premium* on accuracy.⟩

pre·mo·lar \ˈprē-ˈmō-lər\ *n*
a double-pointed tooth that comes between the canines and molars

pre·mo·ni·tion \ˌprē-mə-ˈni-shən, ˌpre-\ *n*
a feeling that something is going to happen

pre·oc·cu·pied \prē-ˈä-kyə-ˌpīd\ *adj*
thinking about or worrying about one thing a great deal

prep *abbr* preposition

prep·a·ra·tion \ˌpre-pə-ˈrā-shən\ *n*
1 the act or process of making or getting ready beforehand ⟨Travel requires a lot of *preparation*.⟩
2 something done to make or get ready ⟨*Preparations* for the move are underway.⟩
3 something made for a special purpose ⟨a *preparation* for burns⟩

pre·par·a·to·ry \pri-ˈper-ə-ˌtȯr-ē\ *adj*
preparing or serving to prepare for something ⟨He attended a *preparatory* school before college.⟩

pre·pare \pri-ˈper\ *vb* **pre·pared**; **pre·par·ing**
1 to make or get ready beforehand ⟨I have to *prepare* for a test.⟩ ⟨Farmers *prepare* the soil for planting.⟩
2 to put together the elements of ⟨*prepare* dinner⟩

pre·pay \ˈprē-ˈpā\ *vb* **pre·paid** \-ˈpād\; **pre·pay·ing**
to pay or pay for beforehand ⟨*prepay* the bill⟩

prep·o·si·tion \ˌpre-pə-ˈzi-shən\ *n*
a word or group of words that combines with a noun or pronoun to form a phrase that usually acts as an adverb, adjective, or noun ⟨"With" in "the house with the red door" is a *preposition*.⟩

prep·o·si·tion·al \ˌpre-pə-ˈzi-shə-nᵊl\ *adj*
relating to or containing a preposition ⟨In "she is from China," "from China" is a *prepositional* phrase.⟩

pre·pos·ter·ous \pri-ˈpä-stə-rəs\ *adj*
making little or no sense : FOOLISH ⟨a *preposterous* excuse⟩

pre·req·ui·site \prē-ˈre-kwə-zət\ *n*
something that is needed beforehand : REQUIREMENT ⟨Citizenship is a *prerequisite* for voting.⟩

pres. *abbr*
1 present
2 president

[1]**pre·school** \ˈprē-ˌskül\ *adj*
relating to the time in a child's life that comes before attendance at school

[2]**preschool** *n*
► a school for children usually under five years old who are too young for kindergarten

[2]**preschool:** children busy in a preschool

pre·school·er \ˈprē-ˈskü-lər\ *n*
a child of preschool age

pre·scribe \pri-ˈskrīb\ *vb* **pre·scribed**; **pre·scrib·ing**
1 to order or direct the use of as a remedy ⟨Did the doctor *prescribe* medicine?⟩
2 to lay down as a rule of action : ORDER ⟨School rules *prescribe* daily physical activity.⟩

pre·scrip·tion \pri-ˈskrip-shən\ *n*
1 a written direction or order for the preparing and use of a medicine
2 a medicine that is ordered by a doctor as a remedy

pres·ence \ˈpre-zᵊns\ *n*
1 the fact or condition of being in a certain place ⟨No one noticed the stranger's *presence*.⟩
2 position close to a person ⟨The child is shy in the *presence* of strangers.⟩
3 a person's appearance or manner ⟨The actor has great *presence* on stage.⟩

presence of mind *n*
ability to think clearly and act quickly in an emergency

[1]**pres·ent** \ˈpre-zᵊnt\ *n*
something given : GIFT ⟨a birthday *present*⟩

[2]**pre·sent** \pri-ˈzent\ *vb* **pre·sent·ed**; **pre·sent·ing**
1 to give with ceremony ⟨Officials *presented* the award.⟩
2 to make a gift to ⟨He *presented* me with a ring.⟩
3 to bring before the public ⟨*present* a play⟩
4 to introduce one person to another ⟨I'd like to *present* my sister.⟩
5 to appear in a particular place ⟨Come out—*present* yourself!⟩
6 to offer to view : SHOW, DISPLAY ⟨You must *present* identification.⟩
7 to come into or cause to come into being ⟨An opportunity *presented* itself.⟩
synonyms see GIVE, OFFER

[3]**pres·ent** \ˈpre-zᵊnt\ *adj*
1 not past or future : now going on ⟨What is your *present* position?⟩
2 being at a certain place and not elsewhere ⟨All students are *present*.⟩
3 pointing out or relating to time that is not past or future

[4]**pres·ent** \ˈpre-zᵊnt\ *n*
the time right now

pre·sent·able \pri-ˈzen-tə-bəl\ *adj*
having a satisfactory or pleasing appearance ⟨Make yourself *presentable*.⟩

pre·sen·ta·tion \ˌprē-ˌzen-ˈtā-shən, ˌpre-zᵊn-\ *n*
1 an act of showing, describing, or explaining something to a group of people
2 an act of giving a gift or award
3 something given

pres·ent·ly \ˈpre-zᵊnt-lē\ *adv*
1 before long : SOON
2 at the present time : NOW ⟨She's *presently* at home.⟩

present participle *n*
the form of a verb that in English is formed with the suffix *-ing* and that expresses present action

present tense *n*
a verb tense that expresses action or state in the present time and is used of what is true at the time of speaking or is always true

pres•er•va•tion \ˌpre-zər-ˈvā-shən\ *n*
the effort of keeping from injury, loss, or decay 〈wildlife *preservation*〉 〈*preservation* of historic buildings〉

pre•ser•va•tive \pri-ˈzər-vət-iv\ *n*
a substance added to food to keep it from spoiling

[1]**pre•serve** \pri-ˈzərv\ *vb* **pre•served**; **pre•serv•ing**
1 to keep or save from injury, loss, or ruin : PROTECT 〈The laws will help *preserve* rain forests.〉
2 to prepare (as by canning or pickling) fruits or vegetables to be kept for future use
3 MAINTAIN 2, CONTINUE 〈*preserve* silence〉
pre•serv•er *n*

[2]**preserve** *n*
1 ▼ fruit cooked in sugar or made into jam or jelly — often used in pl. 〈strawberry *preserves*〉
2 an area where land and animals are protected

[2]**preserve 1:** a jar of peach preserves

pre•side \pri-ˈzīd\ *vb* **pre•sid•ed**; **pre•sid•ing**
to be in charge 〈He *presided* over the meeting.〉 〈She will *preside* over the company.〉

pres•i•den•cy \ˈpre-zə-dən-sē\ *n*, *pl* **pres•i•den•cies**
1 the office of president
2 the term during which a president holds office

pres•i•dent \ˈpre-zə-dənt\ *n*
1 the head of the government and chief executive officer of a modern republic
2 the chief officer of a company, organization, or society 〈a bank *president*〉 〈a college *president*〉

pres•i•den•tial \ˌpre-zə-ˈden-shəl\ *adj*
of or relating to a president or the presidency

[1]**press** \ˈpres\ *vb* **pressed**; **press•ing**
1 to push steadily against 〈*Press* the button.〉
2 to ask or urge strongly
3 to move forward forcefully 〈A crowd *pressed* toward the gate.〉
4 to squeeze so as to force out the juice or contents 〈*press* apples〉
5 to flatten out or smooth by bearing down upon especially by ironing 〈*press* clothes〉

[2]**press** *n*
1 [2]CROWD 1, THRONG 〈He got caught in the *press* of holiday shoppers.〉
2 a machine that uses pressure to shape, flatten, squeeze, or stamp
3 the act of pressing : PRESSURE 〈the *press* of a button〉
4 a printing or publishing business
5 the newspapers and magazines of a country
6 news reporters and broadcasters
7 PRINTING PRESS
8 CLOSET

press•ing \ˈpre-siŋ\ *adj*
needing immediate attention 〈We have *pressing* business.〉

pres•sure \ˈpre-shər\ *n*
1 the action of pushing steadily against
2 a force or influence that cannot be avoided 〈social *pressure*〉
3 the force with which one body presses against another
4 the need to get things done 〈Mom works well under *pressure*.〉

pres•tige \pre-ˈstēzh\ *n*
importance or respect gained through success or excellence

pres•to \ˈpre-stō\ *adv or adj*
suddenly as if by magic 〈You called and *presto*, we're here.〉

pre•sum•ably \pri-ˈzü-mə-blē\ *adv*
it seems likely : PROBABLY 〈Since he likes art, he will *presumably* enjoy the museum.〉

pre•sume \pri-ˈzüm\ *vb* **pre•sumed**; **pre•sum•ing**
1 to undertake without permission or good reason : DARE 〈Don't *presume* to question a judge's decision.〉
2 to suppose to be true without proof 〈A person is *presumed* innocent until proved guilty.〉

pre•sump•tion \pri-ˈzəmp-shən\ *n*
1 behavior or attitude going beyond what is proper
2 a strong reason for believing something to be so
3 something believed to be so but not proved

pre•sump•tu•ous \pri-ˈzəmp-chə-wəs\ *adj*
going beyond what is proper 〈It would be *presumptuous* to ask personal questions.〉
pre•sump•tu•ous•ly *adv*
pre•sump•tu•ous•ness *n*

pre•tend \pri-ˈtend\ *vb* **pre•tend•ed**; **pre•tend•ing**
1 to make believe 〈Let's *pretend* we're riding on a bus.〉
2 to put forward as true something that is not true 〈She will *pretend* friendship.〉
pre•tend•er *n*

pre•tense *or* **pre•tence** \ˈprē-ˌtens, pri-ˈtens\ *n*
1 an act or appearance that looks real but is false 〈He made a *pretense* of studying.〉
2 an effort to reach a certain condition or quality 〈His report makes no *pretense* at completeness.〉

pre•ten•tious \pri-ˈten-shəs\ *adj*
trying to appear better or more important than is really the case 〈a *pretentious* snob〉
pre•ten•tious•ly *adv*
pre•ten•tious•ness *n*

[1]**pret•ty** \ˈpri-tē\ *adj* **pret•ti•er**; **pret•ti•est**
pleasing to the eye or ear especially because of being graceful or delicate 〈a *pretty* face〉 〈a *pretty* tune〉
synonyms see BEAUTIFUL
pret•ti•ly \ˈpri-tə-lē\ *adv*
pret•ti•ness \ˈpri-tē-nəs\ *n*

[2]**pretty** *adv*
in some degree : FAIRLY 〈*pretty* good〉

pret•zel \ˈpret-səl\ *n*
▼ a brown cracker that is salted and is often shaped like a loose knot

pretzel

▶ **Word History** Pretzels have been known in the United States since as early as the 1830s, when the word *pretzel* (borrowed from German *Brezel*) first turns up in writing. In Germany, though, both the hard, knot-shaped bread and the word for it are many centuries older, going back to medieval German *brezitela*. The word is ultimately a borrowing from Latin *brachiatus*, "having branches like arms." Twisted pastries such as pretzels must have been so called because they suggested a pair of folded arms.

pre•vail \pri-ˈvāl\ *vb* **pre•vailed; pre•vail•ing**
1 to succeed in convincing ⟨Students *prevailed* upon the teacher to extend recess.⟩
2 to be or become usual, common, or widespread ⟨West winds *prevail* in that region.⟩
3 to win against opposition ⟨Good will *prevail* over evil.⟩

prev•a•lence \ˈpre-və-ləns\ *n*
the state of happening, being accepted, or being practiced often or over a wide area

prev•a•lent \ˈpre-və-lənt\ *adj*
accepted, practiced, or happening often or over a wide area ⟨*prevalent* beliefs⟩

pre•vent \pri-ˈvent\ *vb* **pre•vent•ed; pre•vent•ing**
1 to keep from happening ⟨Helmets help to *prevent* injuries.⟩
2 to hold or keep back ⟨Bad weather *prevented* us from leaving.⟩
pre•vent•able \pri-ˈven-tə-bəl\ *adj*

pre•ven•tion \pri-ˈven-shən\ *n*
the act or practice of keeping something from happening ⟨the *prevention* of fires⟩

pre•ven•tive \prē-ˈven-tiv\ *adj*
used for keeping something from happening

pre•view \ˈprē-ˌvyü\ *n*
an instance of showing something (as a movie) before others get to see it

pre•vi•ous \ˈprē-vē-əs\ *adj*
going before in time or order : PRECEDING ⟨No *previous* experience is needed.⟩
pre•vi•ous•ly *adv*

[1]prey \ˈprā\ *n*
1 ▶ an animal that is hunted or killed by another animal for food
2 a person that is helpless and unable to escape attack : VICTIM

[1]prey 1: a frog leaping towards its prey

[2]prey *vb* **preyed; prey•ing**
1 to hunt and kill for food ⟨The dogs survived by *preying* on small game.⟩
2 to have a harmful effect ⟨Fears *prey* on my mind.⟩

[1]price \ˈprīs\ *n*
1 the quantity of one thing given or asked for something else : the amount of money paid or to be paid
2 the cost at which something is gotten or done ⟨Giving up privacy is the *price* of fame.⟩
3 a reward for the capture of a criminal

▶ **Synonyms** PRICE, CHARGE, and COST mean the amount asked or given in payment for something. PRICE usually refers to what is asked for goods. ⟨What is the *price* of the car?⟩ CHARGE usually refers to the amount asked for services. ⟨There is a *charge* for the first visit.⟩ COST is usually used to state what is paid for something by the buyer rather than what is asked by the seller. ⟨The *cost* of our dinner seemed very high.⟩

[2]price *vb* **priced; pric•ing**
1 to determine the amount something costs ⟨The house is *priced* too high.⟩
2 to find out how much something costs ⟨I've been *pricing* TVs.⟩

price•less \ˈprīs-ləs\ *adj*
more valuable than any amount of money : not to be bought for any amount of money

[1]prick \ˈprik\ *n*
1 an act of piercing with a small sharp point
2 a feeling of pain that accompanies a piercing of the skin with a sharp point
3 a sudden strong feeling ⟨a *prick* of conscience⟩

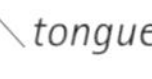

[2]prick *vb* **pricked; prick•ing**
1 to point upward ⟨The horse *pricked* up its ears.⟩
2 to pierce slightly with a sharp point
3 to have or to cause a feeling of or as if of being pierced with a sharp point

prick•er \ˈpri-kər\ *n*
[1]PRICKLE 1, THORN

[1]prick•le \ˈpri-kəl\ *n*
1 a small sharp point (as a thorn)
2 a slight stinging pain

[2]prickle *vb* **prick•led; prick•ling**
[2]PRICK 3

prick•ly \ˈpri-klē\ *adj* **prick•li•er; prick•li•est**
1 having small sharp points ⟨a *prickly* cactus⟩
2 having or causing slight stinging pain ⟨a *prickly* sensation⟩ ⟨*prickly* cold⟩

prickly pear *n*
▼ a cactus with flat branching spiny stems and a sweet fruit shaped like a pear

prickly pear in bloom

[1]pride \ˈprīd\ *n*
1 a reasonable and justifiable feeling of being worthwhile : SELF-RESPECT
2 a feeling of being better than others
3 a sense of pleasure that comes from some act or possession ⟨Parents take *pride* in their children's progress.⟩
4 someone or something that makes someone proud ⟨That car is my *pride* and joy.⟩

[2]pride *vb* **prid•ed; prid•ing**
to feel self-esteem ⟨I *pride* myself on my accurate spelling.⟩

priest \ˈprēst\ *n*
a person who has the authority to lead or perform religious ceremonies

priest•ess \ˈprē-stəs\ *n*
a woman who has the authority to lead or perform religious ceremonies

prim \ˈprim\ *adj* **prim•mer; prim•mest**
very formal and proper
prim•ly *adv*

pri•mar•i•ly \prī-ˈmer-ə-lē\ *adv*
more than anything else : MAINLY

primate

Primates usually gather together in social groups. Most live in trees, although some live on the ground. Almost all have forward-facing eyes, long arms, and fingers that are capable of gripping objects. There are two main groups — more highly developed primates called anthropoids \'an-thrə-ˌpȯidz\, and less developed primates called prosimians \'prō-'si-mē-ənz\. Humans, apes, and monkeys are anthropoids, with large brains and high levels of intelligence. Prosimians, such as bush babies and lemurs \'lē-mərz\, are less intelligent.

features of an orangutan

gibbons move swiftly through the trees, swinging hand over hand

squirrel monkeys live in groups, sometimes of several hundred

baboons are found in the trees and on the ground in open grasslands

tamarins \'ta-mə-rənz\ inhabit the trees of South American forests

bush babies have long hind legs that help them leap from branch to branch

lemurs spend most of their time in trees

gorillas are the largest of the primates, and the males usually weigh over 300 lbs (135 kgs)

[1]pri•ma•ry \'prī-ˌmer-ē, -mə-rē\ *adj*
1 first in time or development ⟨the *primary* grades⟩
2 most important : MAIN ⟨*primary* duties⟩
3 not made or coming from something else : BASIC ⟨the *primary* source of information⟩
4 relating to or being the heaviest of three levels of stress in pronunciation

[2]primary *n, pl* **pri•ma•ries**
an election in which members of a political party nominate candidates for office

primary color *n*
one of the colors red, yellow, or blue which can be mixed together to make other colors

pri•mate \'prī-ˌmāt\ *n*
◀ any of a group of mammals that includes humans together with the apes and monkeys and a few related forms

[1]prime \'prīm\ *n*
the period in life when a person is best in health, looks, or strength

[2]prime *adj*
first in importance, rank, or quality ⟨Spring is a *prime* season to work outdoors.⟩

[3]prime *vb* **primed**; **prim•ing**
1 to put a first color or coating on ⟨*Prime* the wall before painting.⟩
2 to put into working order by filling ⟨*prime* a pump⟩
3 to make (someone or something) ready ⟨The coach is *priming* him to be quarterback.⟩

prime minister *n*
the chief officer of the government in some countries

prime number *n*
a number (as 2, 3, or 5) that results in a whole number from division only when it is divided by itself or by 1

prim•er \'pri-mər\ *n*
1 a small book for teaching children to read
2 a book or other writing that introduces a subject

pri•me•val \prī-'mē-vəl\ *adj*
belonging to the earliest time : PRIMITIVE

prim•i•tive \'pri-mə-tiv\ *adj*
1 of or belonging to very early times ⟨*primitive* cultures⟩
2 of or belonging to an early stage of development ⟨*primitive* tools⟩

primp \'primp\ *vb* **primped**; **primp•ing**
to dress or arrange in a careful or fussy manner

prim•rose \'prim-ˌrōz\ *n*
▶ a small plant with large leaves and showy often yellow or pink flowers

prince \'prins\ *n*
1 MONARCH 1
2 the son of a monarch
3 a nobleman of very high or the highest rank

prince•ly \'prins-lē\ *adj*
1 suitable for a prince ⟨*princely* service⟩
2 very large or impressive ⟨a *princely* sum⟩

prin•cess \'prin-səs, -ˌses\ *n*
a daughter or granddaughter of a monarch : a female member of a royal family

[1]prin•ci•pal \'prin-sə-pəl\ *adj*
highest in rank or importance : CHIEF ⟨My sister had the *principal* part in the school play.⟩
prin•ci•pal•ly *adv*

[2]principal *n*
1 the head of a school
2 a leading or most important person or thing
3 a sum of money that is placed to earn interest, is owed as a debt, or is used as a fund

prin•ci•pal•i•ty \ˌprin-sə-'pa-lə-tē\ *n, pl* **prin•ci•pal•i•ties**
a small territory that is ruled by a prince ⟨the *principality* of Monaco⟩

principal parts *n pl*
the infinitive, the past tense, and the past and present participles of an English verb

prin•ci•ple \'prin-sə-pəl\ *n*
1 a general or basic truth on which other truths or theories can be based ⟨scientific *principles*⟩
2 a rule of conduct based on beliefs of what is right and wrong
3 a law or fact of nature which makes possible the working of a machine or device ⟨the *principle* of magnetism⟩

[1]print \'print\ *n*
1 a mark made on the surface of something ⟨They left *prints* on the window.⟩
2 FOOTPRINT
3 printed matter
4 printed letters ⟨The package has a warning in small *print*.⟩
5 a picture, copy, or design taken from an engraving or photographic negative
6 cloth upon which a design is stamped ⟨a cotton *print*⟩

[2]print *vb* **print•ed**; **print•ing**
1 to write in separate letters ⟨*Print* your name clearly.⟩
2 PUBLISH 1 ⟨Does the college *print* a newspaper?⟩

primrose: flower and leaf of a primrose

3 to make a copy of by pressing paper against an inked surface (as type or an engraving)
4 to make a picture from a photographic negative
print out to produce a paper copy of from a computer

print•er \'prin-tər\ *n*
1 a person or company whose business is making copies of text and images
2 a machine that produces text and images on paper

print•ing \'prin-tiŋ\ *n*
1 the art, practice, or business of making copies of text and images
2 writing that uses separate letters

printing press *n*
a machine that makes copies of text and images

print•out \'print-ˌau̇t\ *n*
a printed copy produced by a computer

[1]pri•or \'prī-ər\ *n*
a monk who is head of a religious house

[2]prior *adj*
1 being or happening before something else ⟨a *prior* date⟩ ⟨*prior* experience⟩
2 being more important than something else ⟨a *prior* claim⟩
prior to [2]BEFORE 2 ⟨The project must be finished *prior to* July.⟩

pri•or•ess \'prī-ə-rəs\ *n, pl* **pri•or•ess•es**
a nun who is head of a religious house

pri•or•i•ty \prī-'ȯr-ə-tē\ *n, pl* **pri•or•i•ties**
a condition of being more important than other things

pri•o•ry \'prī-ə-rē\ *n, pl* **pri•o•ries**
a religious house under the leadership of a prior or prioress

prism \'pri-zəm\ *n*
a transparent object that usually has three sides and bends light so that it breaks up into rainbow colors

pris•on \'pri-zᵊn\ *n*
a place where criminals are locked up

pris•on•er \'pri-zᵊn-ər, 'priz-nər\ *n*
a person who has been captured or locked up

pri•va•cy \'prī-və-sē\ *n*
1 the state of being out of the sight and hearing of other people ⟨I went to my room for some *privacy*.⟩
2 freedom from intrusion ⟨My parents respect my *privacy*.⟩

[1]pri•vate \'prī-vət\ *adj*
1 having to do with or for the use of a single person or group not public ⟨*private* property⟩
2 not holding any public office ⟨a *private* citizen⟩
3 [1]SECRET 1 ⟨*private* meetings⟩
pri•vate•ly *adv*

a b c d e f g h i j k l m n o p q r s t u v w x y z

A B C D E F G H I J K L M N O P Q R S T U V W X Y Z

[2]**private** *n*
an enlisted person of the lowest rank in the marine corps or of either of the two lowest ranks in the army

pri•va•teer \ˌprī-və-ˈtir\ *n*
1 a privately owned armed ship permitted by its government to make war on ships of an enemy country
2 a sailor on a privateer

private first class *n*
an enlisted person in the army or marine corps ranking above a private

priv•et \ˈpri-vət\ *n*
▼ a shrub with small white flowers that is often used for hedges

privet: privet flowers

priv•i•lege \ˈpri-və-lij\ *n*
1 a right or liberty granted as a favor or benefit especially to some and not others
2 an opportunity that is special and pleasant 〈I had the *privilege* of meeting the president.〉

priv•i•leged \ˈpri-və-lijd\ *adj*
having more things and a better chance in life than most people 〈He comes from a *privileged* family.〉

privy \ˈpri-vē\ *n, pl* **priv•ies**
a small building without plumbing used as a toilet

[1]**prize** \ˈprīz\ *n*
1 something won or to be won in a contest
2 something unusually valuable or eagerly sought 〈The *prize* of the greenhouse is the rare orchid.〉

[2]**prize** *adj*
1 outstanding of its kind 〈That's my *prize* baseball card.〉
2 awarded as a prize 〈*prize* money〉
3 awarded a prize 〈a *prize* essay〉

[3]**prize** *vb* **prized**; **priz•ing**
to value highly : TREASURE 〈Abraham Lincoln's autograph is *prized* by collectors.〉

[4]**prize** *n*
something taken (as in war) by force especially at sea

prize•fight•er \ˈprīz-ˌfī-tər\ *n*
▶ a professional boxer

[1]**pro** \ˈprō\ *n, pl* **pros**
an argument or evidence in favor of something 〈We weighed the *pros* and cons of wind power.〉

[2]**pro** *adv*
in favor of something 〈We heard arguments *pro* and con.〉

[3]**pro** *n or adj*
PROFESSIONAL 〈*pro* athletes〉 〈He sank the putt like a *pro*.〉

pro– *prefix*
approving : in favor of

prob•a•bil•i•ty \ˌprä-bə-ˈbi-lə-tē\ *n, pl* **prob•a•bil•i•ties**
1 the chance of happening 〈The *probability* of rain is low.〉
2 something likely 〈Rain is a *probability*.〉
3 a measure of how likely a given event is 〈The *probability* of a coin landing face up is $1/2$.〉

prob•a•ble \ˈprä-bə-bəl\ *adj*
reasonably sure but not certain of happening or being true : LIKELY

prob•a•bly \ˈprä-bə-blē\ *adv*
very likely 〈With dark clouds like those, it will *probably* rain.〉

pro•ba•tion \prō-ˈbā-shən\ *n*
1 the condition of being closely watched and evaluated for a period of time or the period of time during which this happens
2 the early release of a prisoner on certain conditions

prizefighter

[1]**probe** \ˈprōb\ *n*
1 a slender instrument for examining a cavity (as a deep wound)
2 a careful investigation

[2]**probe** *vb* **probed**; **prob•ing**
1 to examine with or as if with an instrument
2 to investigate thoroughly

prob•lem \ˈprä-bləm\ *n*
1 something to be worked out or solved 〈a *problem* in arithmetic〉
2 a person or thing that is hard to understand or deal with 〈He's not the *problem*. His parents are.〉 〈Her behavior is a big *problem*.〉

pro•bos•cis \prə-ˈbä-səs, -ˈbäs-kəs\ *n*
▼ a long flexible hollow body part (as the trunk of an elephant)

proboscis: an elephant's proboscis

pro•ce•dure \prə-ˈsē-jər\ *n*
an action or series of actions for doing or accomplishing something 〈What is the *procedure* for school enrollment?〉

pro•ceed \prō-ˈsēd\ *vb* **pro•ceed•ed**; **pro•ceed•ing**
1 to go forward or onward : ADVANCE 〈The plane stopped in Chicago before *proceeding* to Boston.〉
2 to begin and continue with an action or process 〈After stopping, he *proceeded* to drive on.〉
3 to go or act by an orderly method 〈Did the meeting *proceed* according to plan?〉
4 to come from a source 〈Light *proceeds* from the sun.〉

pro•ceed•ings \prō-ˈsē-diŋz\ *n pl*
things that are said or done 〈The secretary kept a record of the *proceedings*.〉

pro•ceeds \ˈprō-ˌsēdz\ *n pl*
money or profit made 〈the *proceeds* of a sale〉

¹pro•cess \'prä-,ses, 'prō-\ *n*
1 a series of actions, motions, or operations leading to some result ⟨the manufacturing *process*⟩
2 a series of changes that occur naturally ⟨the growth *process*⟩

²process *vb* **pro•cessed**; **pro•cess•ing**
1 to change by a special treatment ⟨The fruit is picked and *processed* for shipment.⟩
2 to take care of according to a routine ⟨His job is to *process* insurance claims.⟩
3 to take in and organize for use ⟨Computers *process* data.⟩

pro•ces•sion \prə-'se-shən\ *n*
a group of individuals moving along in an orderly often ceremonial way ⟨a funeral *procession*⟩

pro•ces•sor \'prä-,se-sər, 'prō-\ *n*
1 a person or machine that changes something by a special treatment or takes care of something according to a routine
2 COMPUTER
3 the part of a computer that operates on data

pro•claim \prō-'klām\ *vb* **pro•claimed**; **pro•claim•ing**
to announce publicly : DECLARE ⟨The president *proclaimed* a holiday.⟩

proc•la•ma•tion \,prä-klə-'mā-shən\ *n*
1 the act of making something known publicly or officially
2 an official formal announcement

pro•cras•ti•nate \prə-'kra-stə-,nāt\ *vb* **pro•cras•ti•nat•ed**; **pro•cras•ti•nat•ing**
to keep putting off something that should be done

► **Word History** To procrastinate is to go against the old saying, "Never put off until tomorrow what you can do today." Appropriately, the word *procrastinate* has the Latin word *cras*, meaning "tomorrow," tucked inside it, because when you procrastinate you often are putting something off until the next day. The source of *procrastinate* is the Latin verb *procrastinare*, formed from the prefix *pro-*, "forward," and the adjective *crastinus*, "of tomorrow," which itself is formed from the adverb *cras*, "tomorrow."

pro•cure \prə-'kyu̇r\ *vb* **pro•cured**; **pro•cur•ing**
OBTAIN ⟨I'm trying to *procure* a ticket to the game.⟩

¹prod \'präd\ *vb* **prod•ded**; **prod•ding**
1 to poke with something ⟨He *prodded* the dog with his foot.⟩
2 to stir or encourage a person or animal to action ⟨She was *prodded* into joining the team.⟩

²prod *n*
1 something used for stirring an animal to action ⟨a cattle *prod*⟩
2 an act of poking
3 a sharp urging or reminder ⟨Sometimes she needs a *prod* to do her homework.⟩

¹prod•i•gal \'prä-di-gəl\ *adj*
carelessly wasteful ⟨a *prodigal* spender⟩

²prodigal *n*
somebody who wastes money carelessly

prod•i•gy \'prä-də-jē\ *n, pl* **prod•i•gies**
1 an unusually talented child
2 an amazing event or action : WONDER

¹pro•duce \prə-'düs, -'dyüs\ *vb* **pro•duced**; **pro•duc•ing**
1 to bring forth : YIELD ⟨This tree *produces* good fruit.⟩
2 ¹MANUFACTURE 1 ⟨This city *produces* steel.⟩
3 to bring to view : EXHIBIT ⟨Can you *produce* evidence to support your claim?⟩
4 to prepare (as a play) for public presentation
pro•duc•er *n*

²pro•duce \'prä-,düs, 'prō-, -,dyüs\ *n*
fresh fruits and vegetables

prod•uct \'prä-dəkt\ *n*
1 the number resulting from the multiplication of two or more numbers ⟨The *product* of 3 and 5 is 15.⟩
2 something resulting from manufacture, labor, thought, or growth

pro•duc•tion \prə-'dək-shən\ *n*
1 something prepared for public presentation ⟨a television *production*⟩
2 the act of manufacturing ⟨*production* of cars⟩
3 the amount brought forth ⟨Miners have increased *production* of coal.⟩

pro•duc•tive \prə-'dək-tiv\ *adj*
1 having the power to yield in large amounts ⟨*productive* soil⟩
2 producing well ⟨I'm most *productive* in the morning.⟩

prof. *abbr* professor

¹pro•fane \prō-'fān\ *adj*
showing disrespect for God or holy things

²profane *vb* **pro•faned**; **pro•fan•ing**
to treat (something sacred) with great disrespect

pro•fan•i•ty \prō-'fa-nə-tē\ *n, pl* **pro•fan•i•ties**
language that is offensive or disrespectful

pro•fess \prə-'fes\ *vb* **pro•fessed**; **pro•fess•ing**
1 to declare openly ⟨Does the boss *profess* confidence in her workers?⟩
2 PRETEND 2 ⟨She *professed* to be my friend.⟩

pro•fes•sion \prə-'fe-shən\ *n*
1 an occupation (as medicine, law, or teaching) that is not mechanical or agricultural and that requires special education
2 an act of publicly declaring or claiming ⟨a *profession* of religious faith⟩
3 the people working in an occupation

¹pro•fes•sion•al \prə-'fe-shə-nᵊl\ *adj*
1 relating to an occupation : of or as an expert ⟨*professional* advice⟩
2 taking part in an activity (as a sport) in order to make money
3 participated in by people who are paid to compete ⟨*professional* sports⟩
4 having or showing a quality appropriate in a profession ⟨He did a very *professional* job.⟩
pro•fes•sion•al•ly *adv*

²professional *n*
1 a person who does a job that requires special education or skill
2 a person who is paid to participate in a sport or activity

pro•fes•sor \prə-'fe-sər\ *n*
a teacher especially of the highest rank at a college or university

prof•fer \'prä-fər\ *vb* **prof•fered**; **prof•fer•ing**
¹OFFER 1

pro•fi•cient \prə-'fi-shənt\ *adj*
very good at doing something ⟨a *proficient* reader⟩
pro•fi•cient•ly *adv*

pro•file \'prō-,fīl\ *n*
1 ▼ something (as a head or a mountain) seen or drawn from the side
2 a level of activity that draws attention ⟨As an actress, she can't avoid a high *profile*.⟩

profile 1: profile of a famous 19th-century English scientist on a medal

[1]**prof•it** \'prä-fət\ *n*
1 the gain after all the expenses are subtracted from the total amount received ⟨Their business shows a *profit* of $100 a week.⟩
2 the gain or benefit from something ⟨She began to see the *profit* of exercising.⟩
prof•it•less \-ləs\ *adj*

[2]**profit** *vb* **prof•it•ed**; **prof•it•ing**
1 to get some good out of something : GAIN ⟨You'll *profit* from the experience.⟩
2 to be of use to (someone) ⟨We finally reached an agreement that *profited* us all.⟩

prof•it•able \'prä-fə-tə-bəl\ *adj*
producing a benefit or monetary gain ⟨a *profitable* business⟩
prof•it•ably \-blē\ *adv*

pro•found \prə-'faund\ *adj*
1 having or showing great knowledge and understanding ⟨a *profound* thinker⟩
2 very deeply felt ⟨*profound* sorrow⟩
pro•found•ly *adv*

pro•fuse \prə-'fyüs\ *adj*
very plentiful
pro•fuse•ly *adv*

pro•fu•sion \prə-'fyü-zhən\ *n*
a plentiful supply : PLENTY

prog•e•ny \'prä-jə-nē\ *n, pl* **prog•e•nies**
human descendants or animal offspring

[1]**pro•gram** \'prō-,gram, -grəm\ *n*
1 a brief statement or written outline (as of a concert, play, ceremony, or religious service)
2 PERFORMANCE 2 ⟨a television *program*⟩
3 a plan of action
4 a set of step-by-step instructions that tell a computer to do something with data

[2]**program** *vb* **pro•grammed** \'prō-,gramd, -grəmd\; **pro•gram•ming**
to give (a computer) a set of instructions : provide with a program

pro•gram•mer \'prō-,gra-mər, -grə-\ *n*
a person who creates and tests programs for computers

[1]**prog•ress** \'prä-grəs, -,gres\ *n*
1 the act of moving toward a goal ⟨The ship made rapid *progress.*⟩
2 gradual improvement ⟨He's not a good reader, but he is making *progress.*⟩
in progress happening at the present time ⟨The trial is *in progress.*⟩

[2]**pro•gress** \prə-'gres\ *vb* **pro•gressed**; **pro•gress•ing**
1 to move forward in place or time : ADVANCE ⟨The story *progresses.*⟩
2 to move toward a higher, better, or more advanced stage

pro•gres•sion \prə-'gre-shən\ *n*
1 the act of advancing or moving forward
2 a continuous and connected series (as of acts, events, or steps)

pro•gres•sive \prə-'gre-siv\ *adj*
1 of, relating to, or showing advancement ⟨a *progressive* city⟩
2 taking place gradually or step by step ⟨a *progressive* disease⟩
3 favoring gradual political change and social improvement by action of the government
pro•gres•sive•ly *adv*

pro•hib•it \prō-'hi-bət\ *vb* **pro•hib•it•ed**; **pro•hib•it•ing**
1 to forbid by authority ⟨Parking is *prohibited.*⟩
2 to make impossible ⟨The high walls *prohibit* escape.⟩

pro•hi•bi•tion \,prō-ə-'bi-shən\ *n*
1 the act of making something illegal or impossible
2 the forbidding by law of the sale or manufacture of alcoholic liquids for use as beverages

[1]**proj•ect** \'prä-,jekt, -jikt\ *n*
1 a plan or scheme to do something ⟨home improvement *projects*⟩
2 a task or problem in school that requires work over a period of time and is often displayed or presented ⟨a science *project*⟩
3 a group of houses or apartment buildings built according to a single plan

[2]**pro•ject** \prə-'jekt\ *vb* **pro•ject•ed**; **pro•ject•ing**
1 to stick out ⟨The rock *projected* above the ground.⟩
2 to cause to fall on a surface ⟨The machine *projects* motion pictures on a screen.⟩
3 to send or throw forward

pro•jec•tile \prə-'jek-təl\ *n*
something (as a bullet or rocket) thrown or shot especially from a weapon

pro•jec•tion \prə-'jek-shən\ *n*
1 something that sticks out
2 the act or process of causing to appear on a surface (as by means of motion pictures or slides)

pro•jec•tor \prə-'jek-tər\ *n*
▼ a machine for producing images on a screen

projector: a projector for showing slides

pro•lif•ic \prə-'li-fik\ *adj*
1 very inventive or productive ⟨a *prolific* writer⟩
2 producing young or fruit in large numbers ⟨a *prolific* fruit tree⟩

pro•long \prə-'lȯŋ\ *vb* **pro•longed**; **pro•long•ing**
to make longer than usual or expected ⟨Medicines *prolonged* his life.⟩

prom \'präm\ *n*
a usually formal dance given by a high school or college class

prom•e•nade \,prä-mə-'nād, -'näd\ *n*
1 a walk or ride for pleasure or to be seen
2 ▼ a place for walking

promenade 2: people walking along a promenade

prom•i•nence \'prä-mə-nəns\ *n*
1 the state of being important, famous, or noticeable ⟨She is a doctor of *prominence*.⟩
2 something (as a mountain) that is conspicuous

prom•i•nent \'prä-mə-nənt\ *adj*
1 important or well-known ⟨*prominent* citizens⟩
2 attracting attention (as by size or position) : CONSPICUOUS ⟨Long hair covers her *prominent* ears.⟩
3 sticking out beyond the surface
prom•i•nent•ly *adv*

[1]**prom•ise** \'prä-məs\ *n*
1 a statement by a person that he or she will do or not do something ⟨I made a *promise* to pay within a month.⟩
2 a cause or ground for hope ⟨These plans give *promise* of success.⟩

[2]**promise** *vb* **prom•ised**; **prom•is•ing**
1 to state that something will or will not be done ⟨I *promise* to clean my room this afternoon.⟩
2 to give reason to expect ⟨Dark clouds *promise* rain.⟩

prom•is•ing \'prä-mə-siŋ\ *adj*
likely to turn out well or be good ⟨a *promising* start⟩

prom•on•to•ry \'prä-mən-,tȯr-ē\ *n*, *pl* **prom•on•to•ries**
a high point of land sticking out into the sea

pro•mote \prə-'mōt\ *vb* **pro•mot•ed**; **pro•mot•ing**
1 to move up in position or rank ⟨Their daughter was *promoted* to the next grade.⟩
2 to help (something) to grow or develop ⟨Good soil *promotes* plant growth.⟩

pro•mo•tion \prə-'mō-shən\ *n*
1 the act of moving up in position or rank ⟨She earned a *promotion* to captain.⟩
2 the act of helping something happen, develop, or increase ⟨*promotion* of business⟩

[1]**prompt** \'prämpt\ *vb* **prompt•ed**; **prompt•ing**
1 to lead to do something ⟨Curiosity *prompted* me to ask the question.⟩
2 to be the cause of ⟨The incident *prompted* an investigation.⟩
3 to remind of something forgotten or poorly learned ⟨Sometimes it's necessary to *prompt* an actor.⟩
prompt•er *n*

[2]**prompt** *adj* **prompt•er**; **prompt•est**
1 quick and ready to act ⟨She's always *prompt* to volunteer.⟩
2 being on time : PUNCTUAL
3 done at once : given without delay ⟨The patient needed *prompt* attention.⟩
synonyms see QUICK
prompt•ly *adv*
prompt•ness *n*

pron *abbr* pronoun

prone \'prōn\ *adj*
1 likely to be or act a certain way ⟨Her dog is *prone* to laziness.⟩
2 lying with the front of the body facing downward

prong \'prȯŋ\ *n*
1 one of the sharp points of a fork
2 a slender part that sticks out (as a point of an antler)

prong•horn \'prȯŋ-,hȯrn\ *n*
► an animal that resembles an antelope and lives mostly in the grasslands and deserts of western North America

pro•noun \'prō-,nau̇n\ *n*
a word used as a substitute for a noun

pro•nounce \prə-'nau̇ns\ *vb* **pro•nounced**; **pro•nounc•ing**
1 to use the voice to make the sounds of ⟨He practiced *pronouncing* Spanish words.⟩
2 to say correctly ⟨I can't *pronounce* your name.⟩
3 to state in an official or solemn way ⟨The judge *pronounced* sentence.⟩

pro•nounced \prə-'nau̇nst\ *adj*
very noticeable ⟨She was walking with a *pronounced* limp.⟩

pro•nounce•ment \prə-'nau̇ns-mənt\ *n*
an official or solemn statement

pro•nun•ci•a•tion \prə-,nən-sē-'ā-shən\ *n*
the act or way of saying a word or words

[1]**proof** \'prüf\ *n*
1 evidence of truth or correctness
2 a printing (as from type) prepared for study and correction
3 a test print made from a photographic negative
4 [1]TEST 2 ⟨Let's put her theory to the *proof*.⟩

[2]**proof** *adj*
able to keep out something that could be harmful ⟨The seal on the bottle is *proof* against tampering.⟩
Hint: The adjective *proof* is usually used in compounds. ⟨water*proof*⟩

proof•read \'prüf-,rēd\ *vb* **proof•read** \-,red\; **proof•read•ing** \-,rē-diŋ\
to read over and fix mistakes in (written or printed matter) ⟨It's a good idea to *proofread* your homework.⟩
proof•read•er *n*

[1]**prop** \'präp\ *vb* **propped**; **prop•ping**
1 to keep from falling or slipping by providing a support under or against
2 to give help, encouragement, or support to

[2]**prop** *n*
something that supports

[3]**prop** *n*
an object used by a performer or actor or used to create a certain effect in a play or movie

pronghorn

pro•pa•gan•da \,prä-pə-'gan-də\ *n*
an organized spreading of often false ideas or the ideas spread in such a way

prop•a•gate \'prä-pə-,gāt\ *vb* **prop•a•gat•ed**; **prop•a•gat•ing**
1 to have or cause to have offspring : MULTIPLY ⟨You can *propagate* apple trees from seed.⟩
2 to cause (as an idea or belief) to spread out and affect a greater number or wider area ⟨The preacher traveled to *propagate* his faith.⟩

prop•a•ga•tion \,prä-pə-'gā-shən\ *n*
the act or process of causing to multiply or spread out ⟨the *propagation* of ideas⟩

pro•pel \prə-'pel\ *vb* **pro•pelled**; **pro•pel•ling**
to push or cause to move usually forward or onward

pro•pel•ler \prə-'pe-lər\ *n*
a device having a hub fitted with blades that is made to turn rapidly by an engine and that causes a ship, power boat, or airplane to move

pro•pen•si•ty \prə-'pen-sə-tē\ *n*
a natural tendency to do or favor something ⟨They have a *propensity* to chatter.⟩

A B C D E F G H I J K L M N O P Q R S T U V W X Y Z

prop•er \'prä-pər\ *adj*
1 correct according to social or moral rules 〈*proper* behavior〉
2 [1]APPROPRIATE, SUITABLE 〈Use the *proper* tool for the job.〉
3 strictly accurate : CORRECT
4 referring to one individual only 〈a *proper* name〉
5 considered in its true or basic meaning 〈Her family lived outside the city *proper*.〉

proper fraction *n*
a fraction in which the numerator is smaller than the denominator

prop•er•ly \'prä-pər-lē\ *adv*
1 in a fit or suitable way 〈Students should dress *properly*.〉
2 according to fact 〈*Properly* speaking, whales are not fish.〉

proper noun *n*
a noun that names a particular person, place, or thing 〈"Tom," "Chicago," and "Friday" are *proper nouns*.〉

prop•er•ty \'prä-pər-tē\ *n, pl* **prop•er•ties**
1 something (as land or money) that is owned 〈That car is my *property*.〉
2 a special quality of a thing 〈Sweetness is a *property* of sugar.〉

proph•e•cy \'prä-fə-sē\ *n, pl* **proph•e•cies**
1 something foretold : PREDICTION
2 the ability to predict what will happen in the future

proph•e•sy \'prä-fə-,sī\ *vb* **proph•e•sied**; **proph•e•sy•ing**
FORETELL, PREDICT

proph•et \'prä-fət\ *n*
1 ▶ someone who declares publicly a message that he or she believes has come from God or a god
2 a person who predicts the future

pro•phet•ic \prə-'fe-tik\ *adj*
1 of or relating to a prophet or prophecy
2 serving to foretell

pro•por•tion \prə-'pȯr-shən\ *n*
1 the size, number, or amount of one thing or group of things as compared to that of another thing or group of things 〈The *proportion* of boys to girls in our class is two to one.〉
2 a balanced or pleasing arrangement 〈The oversize garage is out of *proportion* with the house.〉
3 a statement of the equality of two ratios (as $4/2 = 10/5$)
4 a fair or just share 〈I did my *proportion* of the work.〉
5 size, shape, or extent of something 〈It was a crisis of large *proportions*.〉

pro•por•tion•al \prə-'pȯr-shə-nəl\ *adj*
having a direct relationship to something in size, number, or amount 〈The children received allowances *proportional* to their ages.〉
pro•por•tion•al•ly *adv*

pro•pos•al \prə-'pō-zəl\ *n*
1 an act of stating or putting forward something for consideration
2 something suggested : PLAN
3 an offer of marriage

pro•pose \prə-'pōz\ *vb* **pro•posed**; **pro•pos•ing**
1 to make a suggestion to be thought over and talked about : SUGGEST
2 to make plans : INTEND 〈How do you *propose* to pay for a new bike?〉
3 to make an offer of marriage
4 to suggest (someone) for filling a place or position 〈I *proposed* my teacher for the award.〉

prop•o•si•tion \,prä-pə-'zi-shən\ *n*
1 something suggested for discussion and thought
2 a statement to be proved, explained, or discussed

prophet 1:
a 19th-century book illustration showing the prophet Daniel in the lions' den

pro•pri•e•tor \prə-'prī-ə-tər\ *n*
a person who owns something : OWNER

pro•pri•ety \prə-'prī-ə-tē\ *n, pl* **pro•pri•eties**
1 correctness in manners or behavior 〈He went beyond the bounds of *propriety*.〉
2 the quality or state of being proper
3 *proprieties pl* the rules of correct behavior

pro•pul•sion \prə-'pəl-shən\ *n*
1 the act or process of propelling
2 the force that moves something forward

pros *pl of* PRO

prose \'prōz\ *n*
1 the ordinary language that people use in speaking or writing
2 writing without the repeating rhythm that is used in poetry

pros•e•cute \'prä-si-,kyüt\ *vb* **pros•e•cut•ed**; **pros•e•cut•ing**
1 to carry on a legal action against an accused person to prove his or her guilt
2 to follow up to the end : keep at 〈*prosecute* a war〉

pros•e•cu•tion \,prä-si-'kyü-shən\ *n*
1 the act of carrying on a legal action against a person accused of a crime in court
2 the lawyers in a criminal case trying to prove that the accused person is guilty 〈The *prosecution* will try to prove it was murder.〉

pros•e•cu•tor \'prä-si-,kyü-tər\ *n*
a lawyer in a criminal case who tries to prove that the accused person is guilty

[1]pros•pect \'prä-,spekt\ *n*
1 something that is waited for or expected : POSSIBILITY 〈What are the *prospects* for a good crop this year?〉
2 someone or something that is likely to be successful : a likely candidate 〈a presidential *prospect*〉
3 a wide view 〈The room provides a *prospect* of sea and land.〉

[2]prospect *vb* **pros•pect•ed**; **pros•pect•ing**
to explore especially for mineral deposits

pro•spec•tive \prə-'spek-tiv, 'prä-,spek-\ *adj*
1 likely to become 〈a *prospective* buyer〉
2 likely to come about 〈*prospective* benefits〉

pros•pec•tor \'prä-,spek-tər\ *n*
a person who explores a region in search of valuable minerals (as metals or oil)

pros•per \'prä-spər\ *vb* **pros•pered**; **pros•per•ing**
1 to become successful usually by making money
2 [1]FLOURISH 1, THRIVE

pros•per•i•ty \prä-ˈsper-ə-tē\ *n*
the state of being successful usually by making money

pros•per•ous \ˈprä-spə-rəs\ *adj*
1 having or showing success or financial good fortune
2 strong and healthy in growth ⟨a *prosperous* town⟩

[1]**pros•trate** \ˈprä-ˌstrāt\ *adj*
1 lying with the face turned toward the ground
2 lacking strength or energy ⟨I'm *prostrate* with a cold.⟩

[2]**prostrate** *vb* **pros•trat•ed**; **pros•trat•ing**
1 lie on the ground with the face down ⟨Worshippers *prostrated* themselves on the ground.⟩
2 to bring to a weak and powerless condition ⟨The widow was *prostrated* with grief.⟩

pro•tect \prə-ˈtekt\ *vb* **pro•tect•ed**; **pro•tect•ing**
keep from being harmed especially by covering or shielding : GUARD
synonyms see DEFEND

pro•tec•tion \prə-ˈtek-shən\ *n*
1 the act of shielding from harm : the state of being shielded from harm
2 a person or thing that shields from harm

pro•tec•tive \prə-ˈtek-tiv\ *adj*
giving or meant to keep from harm
pro•tec•tive•ly *adv*
pro•tec•tive•ness *n*

pro•tec•tor \prə-ˈtek-tər\ *n*
a person or thing that shields from harm or is intended to shield from harm

pro•tein \ˈprō-ˌtēn\ *n*
a nutrient found in food (as meat, milk, eggs, and beans) that is made up of many amino acids joined together, is a necessary part of the diet, and is essential for normal cell structure and function

[1]**pro•test** \prə-ˈtest\ *vb* **pro•test•ed**; **pro•test•ing**
1 to complain strongly about : object to ⟨Fans *protested* the umpire's decision.⟩
2 to declare positively : ASSERT ⟨He *protested* his innocence.⟩
synonyms see OBJECT
pro•test•er \prə-ˈte-stər, ˈprō-ˌte-stər\ *n*

[2]**pro•test** \ˈprō-ˌtest\ *n*
1 a complaint or objection against an idea, an act, or a way of doing things
2 an event in which people gather to show disapproval of something

[1]**Prot•es•tant** \ˈprä-tə-stənt\ *n*
a member of one of the Christian churches that separated from the Roman Catholic Church in the 16th century

[2]**Protestant** *adj*
of or relating to Protestants

pro•tist \ˈprō-tist\ *n*
any member of the kingdom of mostly single-celled organisms (as protozoans and algae) that have a nucleus and sometimes form colonies

pro•ton \ˈprō-ˌtän\ *n*
a very small particle that exists in the nucleus of every atom and has a positive charge of electricity

pro•to•plasm \ˈprō-tə-ˌpla-zəm\ *n*
the usually colorless and jellylike living part of cells

pro•to•zo•an \ˌprō-tə-ˈzō-ən\ *n*
a single-celled organism (as an amoeba or paramecium) that is a protist and is capable of movement

pro•tract \prō-ˈtrakt\ *vb* **pro•tract•ed**; **pro•tract•ing**
to make longer : draw out in time or space

pro•trac•tor \prō-ˈtrak-tər\ *n*
▶ an instrument used for drawing and measuring angles

pro•trude \prō-ˈtrüd\ *vb* **pro•trud•ed**; **pro•trud•ing**
to stick out or cause to stick out

proud \ˈpraůd\ *adj* **proud•er**; **proud•est**
1 having great self-respect or dignity ⟨He is too *proud* to beg.⟩
2 having a feeling of pleasure or satisfaction especially with a person's own achievements or with someone else's achievements : very pleased ⟨They were *proud* of their clever child.⟩
3 having or showing a feeling of being better than others : HAUGHTY
proud•ly *adv*

prove \ˈprüv\ *vb* **proved**; **proved** *or* **prov•en** \ˈprü-vən\; **prov•ing**
1 to show the truth or existence of something with facts ⟨I can *prove* he's guilty.⟩
2 to turn out to be ⟨The climb *proved* more difficult than they had expected.⟩
3 to check the correctness of ⟨*prove* the math theory⟩
4 to test by experiment or by a standard

prov•erb \ˈprä-ˌvərb\ *n*
a short well-known saying containing a wise thought : MAXIM, ADAGE ⟨"Haste makes waste" is a *proverb*.⟩

pro•ver•bi•al \prə-ˈvər-bē-əl\ *adj*
1 of a proverb ⟨a *proverbial* expression⟩
2 commonly spoken of ⟨You have the *proverbial* beginner's luck.⟩
pro•ver•bi•al•ly *adv*

pro•vide \prə-ˈvīd\ *vb* **pro•vid•ed**; **pro•vid•ing**
1 to give something that is needed ⟨Volunteers *provide* meals for the poor.⟩
2 to supply something : supply (someone) with something ⟨The room *provides* a view of the city.⟩ ⟨I can't *provide* you with the answer.⟩
3 to make as a condition ⟨The rules *provide* that all players must practice.⟩
pro•vid•er \prə-ˈvī-dər\ *n*

pro•vid•ed \prə-ˈvī-dəd\ *conj*
IF 1 ⟨We'll start now *provided* you agree.⟩

protractor

prov•i•dence \ˈprä-və-dəns\ *n*
1 *often cap* help or care from God or heaven
2 *cap* God as the guide and protector of all human beings
3 PRUDENCE, THRIFT

prov•ince \ˈprä-vəns\ *n*
1 a part of a country having a government of its own (as one of the divisions of Canada)
2 **provinces** *pl* the part or parts of a country far from the capital or chief city
3 an area of activity or authority ⟨the *province* of science⟩

pro•vin•cial \prə-ˈvin-shəl\ *adj*
1 of, relating to, or coming from a province
2 lacking in social graces or sophistication
3 having narrow or limited concerns or interests

[1]**pro•vi•sion** \prə-ˈvi-zhən\ *n*
1 a stock or store of supplies and especially of food — usually used in pl. ⟨We have *provisions* to last us a week.⟩
2 the act of supplying ⟨the *provision* of food⟩
3 [1]CONDITION 2 ⟨the *provisions* of a contract⟩
4 something done beforehand

[2]**provision** *vb* **pro•vi•sioned**; **pro•vi•sion•ing**
to supply with things that are needed

a b c d e f g h i j k l m n o p q r s t u v w x y z

prov•o•ca•tion \,prä-və-'kā-shən\ *n*
something that causes anger or action

pro•voc•a•tive \prə-'vä-kə-tiv\ *adj*
serving or likely to cause a reaction (as interest, curiosity, or anger) ⟨a *provocative* statement⟩
pro•voc•a•tive•ly *adv*

pro•voke \prə-'vōk\ *vb* **pro•voked**; **pro•vok•ing**
1 to cause to become angry ⟨Don't *provoke* your sister.⟩
2 to bring about ⟨The joke *provoked* a smile.⟩

prow \'prau̇\ *n*
▶ the bow of a ship

prow•ess \'prau̇-əs\ *n*
1 great bravery especially in battle
2 very great ability ⟨athletic *prowess*⟩

prowl \'prau̇l\ *vb* **prowled**; **prowl•ing**
to move about quietly and secretly in hunting or searching
prowl•er *n*

proxy \'präk-sē\ *n, pl* **prox•ies**
1 authority to act for another or a paper giving such authority
2 a person with authority to act for another

prude \'prüd\ *n*
a person who cares too much about proper speech and conduct
prud•ish \-ish\ *adj*

pru•dence \'prü-d^{ə}ns\ *n*
careful good judgment that allows someone to avoid danger or risks

pru•dent \'prü-d^{ə}nt\ *adj*
wise and careful in action or judgment
pru•dent•ly *adv*

[1]**prune** \'prün\ *n*
▼ a dried plum

[1]**prune**

[2]**prune** *vb* **pruned**; **prun•ing**
1 to cut off dead or unwanted parts of a bush or tree
2 to cut out useless or unwanted parts (as unnecessary words in something written)

[1]**pry** \'prī\ *vb* **pried**; **pry•ing**
1 to raise or open with a lever
2 to get at with great difficulty ⟨I couldn't *pry* the secret out of him.⟩

prow:
prow of a Portuguese river boat

[2]**pry** *vb* **pried**; **pry•ing**
to be nosy about something

pry•ing \'prī-iŋ\ *adj*
rudely nosy ⟨*prying* questions⟩

P.S. *abbr*
1 postscript
2 public school

psalm \'säm, 'sälm\ *n*
1 a sacred song or poem
2 *cap* one of the hymns that make up the Old Testament Book of Psalms

psy•chi•a•trist \sə-'kī-ə-trəst, sī-\ *n*
a doctor specializing in psychiatry

psy•chi•a•try \sə-'kī-ə-trē, sī-\ *n*
a branch of medicine dealing with problems of the mind, emotions, or behavior

psy•cho•log•i•cal \,sī-kə-'lä-ji-kəl\ *adj*
of or relating to psychology or the mind ⟨*psychological* research⟩ ⟨*psychological* distress⟩

psy•chol•o•gist \sī-'kä-lə-jəst\ *n*
a person specializing in psychology

psy•chol•o•gy \sī-'kä-lə-jē\ *n*
the science that studies the mind and behavior

pt. *abbr*
1 pint
2 point

PTA *abbr* Parent-Teacher Association

ptero•dac•tyl \,ter-ə-'dak-t^{ə}l\ *n*
a very large extinct flying reptile that lived at the same time as the dinosaurs

PTO *abbr* Parent-Teacher Organization

pub \'pəb\ *n*
an establishment where alcoholic drinks are served

pu•ber•ty \'pyü-bər-tē\ *n*
the age at or period during which the body of a boy or girl matures and becomes capable of reproducing

[1]**pub•lic** \'pə-blik\ *adj*
1 open to all ⟨a *public* library⟩
2 of or relating to the people as a whole ⟨*public* opinion⟩
3 known to many people **:** not kept secret ⟨The story became *public.*⟩
4 of, relating to, or working for a government or community ⟨a *public* prosecutor⟩ ⟨My uncle holds *public* office.⟩
5 WELL-KNOWN, PROMINENT ⟨*public* figures⟩
pub•lic•ly *adv*

[2]**public** *n*
1 the people as a whole ⟨The sale is open to the *public.*⟩
2 a group of people having common interests ⟨The author is adored by her *public.*⟩

pub•li•ca•tion \,pə-blə-'kā-shən\ *n*
1 the act or process of producing (a printed work) and selling it to the public
2 a printed work (as a book or magazine) made for sale or distribution

pub•lic•i•ty \,pə-'bli-sə-tē\ *n*
1 attention that is given to someone or something by the media
2 something that attracts the interest of the public ⟨His appearance on TV was good *publicity.*⟩

pub•li•cize \'pə-blə-,sīz\ *vb* **pub•li•cized**; **pub•li•ciz•ing**
to give publicity to

public school *n*
a free school paid for by taxes and run by a local government

pub•lish \'pə-blish\ *vb* **pub•lished**; **pub•lish•ing**
1 to bring printed works (as books) before the public usually for sale
2 to print (as in a magazine or newspaper) ⟨The newspaper *published* her article on dogs.⟩
3 to make widely known
pub•lish•er *n*

puck \'pək\ *n*
a rubber disk used in hockey

[1]**puck•er** \'pə-kər\ *vb* **puck•ered**; **puck•er•ing**
to draw or cause to draw up into folds or wrinkles ⟨The lemon made me *pucker* my lips.⟩

A B C D E F G H I J K L M N O P Q R S T U V W X Y Z

[2]pucker *n*
a fold or wrinkle in a normally even surface

pud•ding \ˈpu̇-diŋ\ *n*
▼ a soft creamy dessert

pudding: a Mexican chocolate pudding

pud•dle \ˈpə-dᵊl\ *n*
a very small pool of liquid

pudgy \ˈpə-jē\ *adj* **pudg•i•er**; **pudg•i•est**
being short and plump : CHUBBY

pueb•lo \ˈpwe-blō\ *n, pl* **pueb•los**
1 ▼ an American Indian village of Arizona or New Mexico made up of groups of stone or adobe houses with flat roofs
2 *cap* a member of any of several American Indian peoples of Arizona or New Mexico

[1]Puer•to Ri•can \ˌpwer-tə-ˈrē-kən, ˌpȯr-\ *adj*
of or relating to Puerto Rico or Puerto Ricans

[2]Puerto Rican *n*
a person born or living in Puerto Rico

[1]puff \ˈpəf\ *vb* **puffed**; **puff•ing**
1 to breathe hard : PANT
2 to send out small whiffs or clouds (as of smoke)
3 to swell up or become swollen with or as if with air ⟨The injured eye *puffed* up.⟩ ⟨I *puffed* out my cheeks.⟩

[2]puff *n*
1 a quick short instance of sending or letting out air, smoke, or steam ⟨We could see *puffs* from a locomotive.⟩
2 a slight swelling
3 a soft pad for putting powder on the skin
4 a light pastry

puf•fin \ˈpə-fən\ *n*
a black-and-white seabird that has a short thick neck and a large bill marked with several colors

puffy \ˈpə-fē\ *adj* **puff•i•er**; **puff•i•est**
1 somewhat swollen ⟨a *puffy* face⟩
2 soft, light, and rounded
3 BREATHLESS 1 ⟨He was still *puffy* after the long run.⟩
4 blowing in puffs ⟨*puffy* smoke⟩

pug \ˈpəg\ *n*
► a small muscular dog having a curled tail and a flattened face with wrinkles

pug nose *n*
a usually short nose turning up at the end

puke \ˈpyük\ *vb* **puked**; **puk•ing**
[2]VOMIT

[1]pull \ˈpu̇l\ *vb* **pulled**; **pull•ing**
1 to use force on so as to cause movement toward the force ⟨*pulled* the rope⟩ ⟨*pulling* a wagon⟩
2 to separate from a firm or a natural attachment ⟨*pull* a tooth⟩ ⟨*pull* weeds⟩
3 [1]MOVE 1 ⟨A train *pulled* out of the station.⟩
4 to draw apart : TEAR, REND ⟨I *pulled* a flower to pieces.⟩
5 to move (something) up or down ⟨*Pull* down the shade.⟩
6 to operate by drawing toward ⟨Going against the current, he had to *pull* the oars harder.⟩
7 to stretch repeatedly ⟨*pull* taffy⟩
pull through to survive a difficult or dangerous period ⟨She was seriously ill, but *pulled through.*⟩

pug

pueblo 1: adobe houses in a pueblo in New Mexico

A B C D E F G H I J K L M N O P Q R S T U V W X Y Z

[2]pull *n*
1 the act or an instance of grasping and causing to move 〈two *pulls* on the cord〉
2 a device for making something move
3 a force that draws one body toward another 〈the *pull* of gravity〉

pull–down \'pu̇l-ˌdau̇n\ *adj*
appearing on a computer screen below a selected item 〈a *pull-down* menu〉

pul•let \'pu̇-lət\ *n*
a young hen

pul•ley \'pu̇-lē\ *n, pl* **pulleys**
▼ a wheel over which a belt, rope, or chain is pulled to lift or lower a heavy object

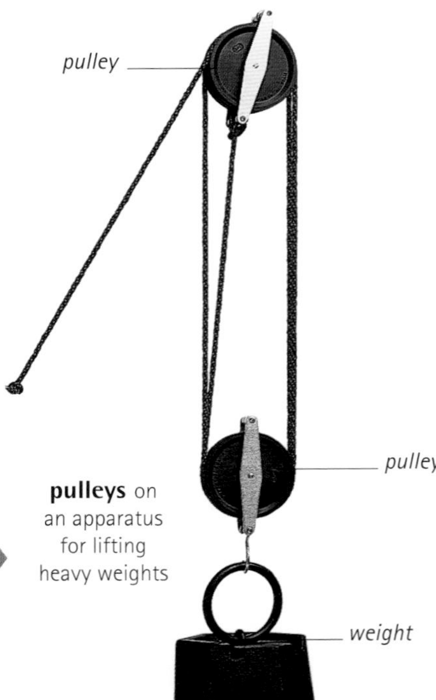

pulleys on an apparatus for lifting heavy weights

pull•over \'pu̇l-ˌō-vər\ *n*
a garment (as a sweater) that is put on by being pulled over the head

pulp \'pəlp\ *n*
1 the soft juicy or moist part of a fruit or vegetable 〈the *pulp* of an orange〉
2 the part of a fruit or vegetable that is left after the liquid has been squeezed from it
3 a material prepared usually from wood or rags and used in making paper
4 the soft sensitive tissue inside a tooth
5 a seriously injured or damaged state 〈He was beaten to a *pulp.*〉

pul•pit \'pu̇l-ˌpit\ *n*
1 a raised place in which a clergyman stands while preaching or conducting a religious service
2 the profession of preachers

pul•sate \'pəl-ˌsāt\ *vb* **pul•sat•ed; pul•sat•ing**
to have or show strong regular beats

pulse \'pəls\ *n*
1 a strong regular beat 〈the music's *pulse*〉
2 the beat resulting from the regular widening of an artery in the body as blood flows through it 〈Feel your wrist for a *pulse.*〉

pul•ver•ize \'pəl-və-ˌrīz\ *vb* **pul•ver•ized; pul•ver•iz•ing**
to beat or grind into a powder or dust

pu•ma \'pyü-mə, 'pü-\ *n*
COUGAR

pum•ice \'pə-məs\ *n*
► a very light porous volcanic glass that is used in powder form for smoothing and polishing

pum•mel \'pə-məl\ *vb* **pum•meled** *also* **pum•melled; pum•mel•ing** *also* **pum•mel•ling**
1 to hit repeatedly
2 to defeat badly

[1]pump *n*
a device for raising, moving, or compressing liquids or gases

[2]pump \'pəmp\ *vb* **pumped; pump•ing**
1 to raise, move, or compress by using a pump 〈*pump* water〉
2 to fill by using a pump 〈*pump* up tires〉
3 to move or force onward like a pump 〈The heart *pumps* blood through the body.〉
4 to question again and again to find out something 〈They *pumped* me for details.〉
5 to move (something) up and down or in and out quickly and repeatedly 〈He *pumped* his fist in the air.〉
6 to remove (a liquid or gas) from by using a pump 〈We *pumped* the boat dry.〉

pum•per•nick•el \'pəm-pər-ˌni-kəl\ *n*
a dark rye bread

pump•kin \'pəmp-kən\ *n*
▼ a usually large round orange fruit that grows on a vine, is related to the squash and cucumber, and is used for food or decoration

[1]pun \'pən\ *n*
a form of joking in which a person uses a word in two senses

pumpkins

[2]pun *vb* **punned; pun•ning**
to make a joke by using a word in two senses

[1]punch \'pənch\ *vb* **punched; punch•ing**
1 to strike with the fist
2 to sharply press or poke 〈She *punched* the keys on her computer.〉
3 to make (a hole) by pressing into or through something
4 to make a hole in with a punch

[2]punch *n*
a drink usually containing different fruit juices

pumice

[3]punch *n*
a blow with or as if with the fist

[4]punch *n*
a tool for piercing, stamping, or cutting

punc•tu•al \'pəŋk-chə-wəl\ *adj*
arriving or acting at the right time : not late
punc•tu•al•ly *adv*

punc•tu•ate \'pəŋk-chə-ˌwāt\ *vb* **punc•tu•at•ed; punc•tu•at•ing**
1 to add punctuation marks to writing
2 to interrupt or occur in repeatedly 〈Her speech was *punctuated* by applause.〉
3 to give emphasis to 〈He pounded the table with his fist to *punctuate* his point.〉

punc•tu•a•tion \ˌpəŋk-chə-'wā-shən\ *n*
1 the act of adding punctuation marks to writing
2 a system of using punctuation marks

punctuation mark *n*
any one of the marks (as a period, comma, or question mark) used in writing to make the meaning clear and separate parts (as clauses and sentences)

[1]punc•ture \'pəŋk-chər\ *n*
1 an act of piercing with something pointed
2 a hole or wound made by piercing with something pointed

[2]puncture *vb* **punc•tured; punc•tur•ing**
1 to pierce with something pointed
2 to weaken or damage as if by piercing a hole in 〈Failure *punctured* my self-esteem.〉

pun•gent \'pən-jənt\ *adj*
having a strong or sharp taste or smell
pun•gent•ly *adv*

pun•ish \ˈpə-nish\ *vb* **pun•ished**; **pun•ish•ing**
1 to make suffer for a fault or crime ⟨The child was *punished* for lying.⟩
2 to make someone suffer for (as a crime) ⟨The law *punishes* theft.⟩

▶ **Synonyms** PUNISH and DISCIPLINE mean to put a penalty on someone for doing wrong. PUNISH means giving some kind of pain or suffering to the wrongdoer often rather than trying to reform the person. ⟨The criminals were *punished* with life imprisonment.⟩ DISCIPLINE is used of punishing the wrongdoer but usually includes an effort to bring the person under control. ⟨Parents must *discipline* their children.⟩

pun•ish•able \ˈpə-ni-shə-bəl\ *adj*
deserving to be punished ⟨a *punishable* offense⟩

pun•ish•ment \ˈpə-nish-mənt\ *n*
1 the act of making a wrongdoer suffer : the state or fact of being made to suffer for wrongdoing
2 the penalty for a wrong or crime

punk \ˈpəŋk\ *n*
a rude and violent young man

[1]punt \ˈpənt\ *vb* **punt•ed**; **punt•ing**
to drop and kick a ball before it hits the ground
punt•er *n*

[2]punt *n*
an act or instance of dropping and kicking a ball before it hits the ground

pu•ny \ˈpyü-nē\ *adj* **pu•ni•er**; **pu•ni•est**
1 small and weak in size or power
2 not very impressive or effective ⟨My boss gave me a *puny* raise.⟩

▶ **Word History** In medieval French *puisné*, literally, "born afterward," was used to mean "younger" when talking about two people. Borrowed into English, *puisne* and the phonetic spelling *puny* came to be used of anyone in a position of less importance than another. By the time of the playwright William Shakespeare *puny* no longer suggested relative rank, but had come to mean "weak" or "feeble"—a meaning the word retains today.

pup \ˈpəp\ *n*
1 PUPPY
2 ▶ a young animal ⟨seal *pups*⟩

pu•pa \ˈpyü-pə\ *n, pl* **pu•pae** \-ˌpē\ *or* **pupas**
an insect (as a bee, moth, or beetle) in an intermediate inactive stage of its growth in which it is enclosed in a cocoon or case

[1]pu•pil \ˈpyü-pəl\ *n*
a child in school or under the care of a teacher

[2]pupil *n*
the opening in the iris through which light enters the eye

▶ **Word History** If you look into another person's eyes, you see reflected within the iris a tiny image of your own face. The Romans, comparing this image of a miniature human to a doll, called the opening in the iris that seems to hold the image *pupilla*, which is derived from *pupa*, meaning "doll." This Latin word, by way of medieval French *pupille*, was borrowed into English as *pupil*.

pup•pet \ˈpə-pət\ *n*
1 a doll moved by hand or by strings or wires
2 someone or something (as a government) whose acts are controlled by another

pup•py \ˈpə-pē\ *n, pl* **puppies**
▶ a young dog

[1]pur•chase \ˈpər-chəs\ *vb* **pur•chased**; **pur•chas•ing**
to get by paying money : BUY

[2]purchase *n*
1 an act of buying ⟨the *purchase* of supplies⟩
2 something bought
3 a firm hold or grasp or a safe place to stand ⟨I could not get a *purchase* on the slippery ledge.⟩

pure \ˈpyu̇r\ *adj* **pur•er**; **pur•est**
1 not mixed with anything else : free from everything that might injure or lower the quality ⟨*pure* water⟩ ⟨*pure* silk⟩
2 free from sin : INNOCENT, CHASTE
3 nothing other than : TOTAL ⟨*pure* nonsense⟩
pure•ly *adv*

pure•bred \ˈpyu̇r-ˈbred\ *adj*
bred from ancestors of a single breed for many generations ⟨*purebred* horses⟩

[1]purge \ˈpərj\ *vb* **purged**; **purg•ing**
1 to get rid of ⟨Ineffective workers were *purged* from the company.⟩
2 to rid of unwanted things or people

[2]purge *n*
1 an act or instance of ridding of what is unwanted
2 the removal of members thought to be treacherous or disloyal ⟨a *purge* of party leaders⟩

pu•ri•fi•ca•tion \ˌpyu̇r-ə-fə-ˈkā-shən\ *n*
an act or instance of freeing from impurities or of being freed from impurities

pu•ri•fy \ˈpyu̇r-ə-ˌfī\ *vb* **pu•ri•fied**; **pu•ri•fy•ing**
to make pure : free from impurities

puppy

pu•ri•tan \ˈpyu̇r-ə-tᵊn\ *n*
1 *cap* a member of a 16th and 17th century Protestant group in England and New England opposing formal customs of the Church of England
2 a person who practices, preaches, or follows a stricter moral code than most people

pup 2: a seal pup

A B C D E F G H I J K L M N O P Q R S T U V W X Y Z

pu•ri•ty \'pyu̇r-ə-tē\ *n*
1 freedom from dirt or impurities
2 freedom from sin or guilt

pur•ple \'pər-pəl\ *n*
a color between red and blue

pur•plish \'pər-plish\ *adj*
somewhat purple

pur•pose \'pər-pəs\ *n*
something set up as a goal to be achieved : INTENTION, AIM
on purpose PURPOSELY

pur•pose•ful \'pər-pəs-fəl\ *adj*
having a clear intention or aim
pur•pose•ful•ly \-fə-lē\ *adv*
pur•pose•ful•ness *n*

pur•pose•ly \'pər-pəs-lē\ *adv*
with a clear or known aim

[1]purr \'pər\ *vb* **purred**; **purr•ing**
to make the low murmuring sound of a contented cat or a similar sound

[2]purr *n*
the low murmuring sound of a contented cat or a similar sound ⟨the *purr* of the engine⟩

[1]purse \'pərs\ *n*
1 ► a bag or pouch for money
2 HANDBAG
3 the amount of money that a person, organization, or government has available for use
4 a sum of money offered as a prize or collected as a present

[2]purse *vb* **pursed**; **purs•ing**
to form into a tight circle or line ⟨She *pursed* her lips.⟩

pur•sue \pər-'sü\ *vb* **pur•sued**; **pur•su•ing**
1 to follow after in order to catch or destroy : CHASE ⟨A dog *pursued* the fleeing cat.⟩
2 to follow up or proceed with ⟨He won't answer, so why *pursue* it?⟩
3 to try to get or do over a period of time ⟨I've decided to *pursue* a degree in geography.⟩
synonyms see CHASE
pur•su•er *n*

pur•suit \pər-'süt\ *n*
1 the act of chasing, following, or trying to obtain ⟨the *pursuit* of wealth⟩
2 ACTIVITY 2, OCCUPATION ⟨the *pursuit* of teaching⟩

pus \'pəs\ *n*
a thick yellowish substance that is produced when a part of the body or a wound becomes infected

[1]push \'pu̇sh\ *vb* **pushed**; **push•ing**
1 to press against with force so as to drive or move away ⟨He helped *push* a car out of the snow.⟩
2 to force forward, downward, or outward ⟨The tree is *pushing* its roots deep in the soil.⟩
3 to go or make go ahead ⟨I had to *push* to finish the swim.⟩
4 to pressure to do something or work hard at something ⟨The teacher *pushed* her students to succeed.⟩

[2]push *n*
1 a sudden thrust : SHOVE ⟨Pa gave the rotten tree a *push* and it fell over.⟩
2 a steady applying of force in a direction away from the body from which it comes ⟨We gave the car a *push* up the hill.⟩

push button *n*
a small button or knob that when pushed operates something usually by closing an electric circuit

push•cart \'pu̇sh-,kärt\ *n*
a cart pushed by hand

[1]purse 1

push•over \'pu̇sh-,ō-vər\ *n*
1 an opponent that is easy to defeat ⟨They thought our team would be a *pushover*.⟩
2 someone who is easy to persuade or influence ⟨He asked his grandmother for a loan knowing she was a *pushover*.⟩
3 something easily done ⟨The exam was a *pushover*.⟩

push–up \'pu̇sh-,əp\ *n*
an exercise performed while lying with the face down by raising and lowering the body with the straightening and bending of the arms

pushy \'pu̇-shē\ *adj* **push•i•er**; **push•i•est**
too aggressive : FORWARD

pussy willow *n*
► a willow with large furry flower clusters

put \'pu̇t\ *vb* **put**; **put•ting**
1 to place in or move into a particular position ⟨She *put* the book on a table.⟩ ⟨*Put* your hand up.⟩
2 to bring into a specified state or condition ⟨The charity *puts* the money to good use.⟩ ⟨He *put* the room in order.⟩
3 to cause to undergo something ⟨Our class *puts* them to shame.⟩
4 to give expression to ⟨I can't *put* my fear into words.⟩ ⟨This book *puts* the idea clearly.⟩
5 to devote to or urge to an activity ⟨They can improve if they *put* their minds to it.⟩ ⟨The coach is *putting* us to work.⟩
6 to think of as worthy of : ATTRIBUTE ⟨The candidate *puts* a high value on peace.⟩
7 to begin a voyage ⟨The ship *put* to sea.⟩
put away to take in food and drink ⟨She *put away* a big dinner.⟩
put down
1 to bring to an end by force ⟨Police *put down* the riot.⟩
2 CRITICIZE 2
put forward PROPOSE 1 ⟨The committee *put forward* a new plan.⟩
put in
1 to ask for ⟨She *put in* for a job.⟩
2 to spend time in a place or activity ⟨I *put in* two hours of work.⟩
put off to hold back to a later time : DEFER ⟨I *put off* my appointment.⟩
put on
1 to dress in ⟨He *put* a new jacket *on*.⟩
2 PRETEND 2 ⟨She *put on* a show of anger.⟩
3 [1]PRODUCE 4 ⟨The senior class *put on* a play.⟩

pussy willow: a branch from a pussy willow

[1]putty: putty being trimmed with a putty knife

put out
1 EXTINGUISH 1 ⟨Be sure to *put out* the light.⟩
2 IRRITATE 1, ANNOY ⟨I was *put out* by their behavior.⟩
3 [1]MAKE 1 ⟨The factory *puts out* tires.⟩
4 to cause to be out (in baseball)
5 to make use of ⟨The team *put out* a real effort.⟩
put together
1 to create as a whole : CONSTRUCT
2 to consider as a single unit

pyramid 1: pyramids in the desert at Giza, Egypt

put up
1 [1]BUILD 1 ⟨The town plans to *put up* a new school.⟩
2 to make (as food) ready for later use ⟨I *put* vegetables *up* for the winter.⟩
3 to give or get shelter and often food ⟨They often *put* tourists *up*.⟩
4 to make by action or effort ⟨They *put up* a good fight.⟩
put up to to urge or cause to do something wrong or unexpected ⟨Those kids *put* me *up to* the prank.⟩
put up with to stand for : TOLERATE

put•out \'pu̇t-ˌau̇t\ *n*
[4]OUT

pu•trid \'pyü-trəd\ *adj*
1 ROTTEN 1 ⟨*putrid* meat⟩
2 coming from or suggesting something rotten ⟨a *putrid* smell⟩

put•ter \'pə-tər\ *vb* **put•tered; put•ter•ing**
to act or work without much purpose ⟨She enjoys *puttering* around the garden.⟩

[1]**put•ty** \'pə-tē\ *n, pl* **putties**
◀ a soft sticky substance that hardens as it dries and is used for holding glass in a window frame or filling holes

[2]**putty** *vb* **put•tied; put•ty•ing**
to seal up with putty

[1]**puz•zle** \'pə-zəl\ *vb* **puz•zled; puz•zling**
1 CONFUSE 1, PERPLEX ⟨The mysterious phone call *puzzles* me.⟩
2 to solve by thought or by clever guessing ⟨She tried to *puzzle* out the crime.⟩

[2]**puzzle** *n*
1 a question, problem, or device intended to test skill or cleverness
2 JIGSAW PUZZLE
3 something that perplexes : MYSTERY

puz•zle•ment \'pə-zəl-mənt\ *n*
the state of being perplexed

pyg•my \'pig-mē\ *adj*
smaller than the usual size ⟨a *pygmy* goat⟩

pyr•a•mid \'pir-ə-ˌmid\ *n*
1 ▲ a large structure built especially in ancient Egypt that usually has a square base and four triangular sides meeting at a point and that contains tombs
2 a shape or structure with a polygon for its base and three or more triangles for its sides which meet to form the top

pyre \'pīr\ *n*
a heap of wood for burning a dead body

py•thon \'pī-ˌthän\ *n*
▼ a large nonpoisonous snake of Africa, Asia, and Australia that squeezes and suffocates its prey

python: an Indian python

Qq

Sounds of Q: The letter **Q** is almost always followed by the letter **U**. Most often, **Q** and **U** together make a sound like **KW**, as in ***quack*** and ***banquet***. In some words, **QU** sounds like a **K** alone, as in *conquer* and *bouquet*.

q \'kyü\ *n, pl* **q's** *or* **qs** \'kyüz\ *often cap*
the 17th letter of the English alphabet

QC *abbr* Quebec

qt. *abbr* quart

[1]quack \'kwak\ *vb* **quacked**; **quack•ing**
to make the cry of a duck

[2]quack *n*
a cry made by a duck

[3]quack *n*
a person who pretends to have medical knowledge and skill

[4]quack *adj*
1 relating to or being a person who pretends to have medical knowledge and skill ⟨a *quack* doctor⟩
2 pretending to cure disease ⟨*quack* remedies⟩

quad•ran•gle \'kwäd-,raŋ-gəl\ *n*
QUADRILATERAL

quad•rant \'kwä-drənt\ *n*
1 one-fourth of a circle
2 any of the four parts into which something is divided by two imaginary or real lines that intersect each other at right angles

quadri- \'kwä-drə\ *or* **quadr-** *or* **quadru-** \'kwä-drə\ *prefix*
1 four
2 fourth

quad•ri•lat•er•al \,kwä-drə-'la-tə-rəl\ *n*
a flat geometric figure of four sides and four angles

quad•ru•ped \'kwä-drə-,ped\ *n*
an animal having four feet

[1]qua•dru•ple \kwä-'drü-pəl\ *vb* **qua•dru•pled**; **qua•dru•pling**
to make or become four times as great or many

[2]quadruple *adj*
1 having four units or parts
2 being four times as great or as many

qua•dru•plet \kwä-'drü-plət, -'drə-\ *n*
▼ one of four offspring born at one birth

quag•mire \'kwag-,mīr\ *n*
1 soft spongy wet ground
2 a difficult situation

[1]quail \'kwāl\ *n, pl* **quail** *or* **quails**
▶ a small plump bird (as a bobwhite) that feeds mostly on the ground and is sometimes hunted for food or sport

[2]quail *vb* **quailed**; **quail•ing**
to lose courage **:** draw back in fear

quaint \'kwānt\ *adj* **quaint•er**; **quaint•est**
pleasingly old-fashioned or unfamiliar ⟨a *quaint* town⟩ ⟨*quaint* customs⟩
quaint•ly *adv*
quaint•ness *n*

[1]quake \'kwāk\ *vb* **quaked**; **quak•ing**
1 to shake violently ⟨houses *quaking*⟩
2 to tremble usually from cold or fear

[2]quake *n*
EARTHQUAKE

[1]quail:
a Japanese quail

qual•i•fi•ca•tion \,kwä-lə-fə-'kā-shən\ *n*
1 a special skill, knowledge, or ability that makes someone suitable for a particular job or activity
2 a condition or requirement that must be met ⟨*qualifications* for membership⟩
3 something that is added to a statement to limit or change its meaning

qual•i•fy \'kwä-lə-,fī\ *vb* **qual•i•fied**; **qual•i•fy•ing**
1 to give the training, skill, or ability needed for a special purpose
2 to have or show the skill or ability needed for a special purpose or event
3 to narrow down or make less general in meaning ⟨I *qualify* my statement.⟩

quadruplets

[1]qual•i•ty \'kwä-lə-tē\ *n, pl* **qual•i•ties**
1 What sets a person or thing apart : CHARACTERISTIC ⟨The water has a salty *quality.*⟩
2 how good or bad something is ⟨The food is of excellent *quality.*⟩
3 a high standard : EXCELLENCE ⟨His skill shows in the *quality* of his work.⟩

[2]quality *adj*
very good : EXCELLENT ⟨*quality* work⟩

qualm \'kwäm, 'kwälm\ *n*
a feeling of doubt or uncertainty especially in matters of right and wrong

quan•da•ry \'kwän-də-rē, -drē\ *n, pl* **quan•da•ries**
a state of doubt or confusion ⟨I was in a *quandary* about what to do.⟩

quan•ti•ty \'kwän-tə-tē\ *n, pl* **quan•ti•ties**
1 [2]AMOUNT, NUMBER ⟨There's a small *quantity* of fuel left.⟩
2 a large number or amount ⟨*quantities* of money⟩ ⟨We buy food in *quantity.*⟩

[1]quar•an•tine \'kwȯr-ən-ˌtēn\ *n*
1 isolation of people, animals, or things (as plants) out of a certain area to prevent the spread of disease or pests
2 a period during which a person or animal with a contagious disease is isolated
3 a place (as a hospital) where a person or animal with a contagious disease is isolated

► **Word History** Centuries ago people in Europe did not have a good understanding of infectious diseases. But experience taught them that when ships arrived in port and brought strangers, illness would sometimes follow. In Venice, a port in Italy, the practice developed of holding a ship in the harbor for forty days if the passengers were suspected of carrying disease, especially plague. If no one developed signs of illness, the passengers were let ashore. The word for this period of forty days was in Italian *quarantena,* a derivative of *quaranta,* "forty," and it is a source of the English word *quarantine.*

[2]quarantine *vb* **quar•an•tined; quar•an•tin•ing**
to put or hold in isolation to prevent the spread of disease or pests

[1]quar•rel \'kwȯr-əl\ *n*
1 an angry argument or disagreement
2 a cause of disagreement or complaint

[2]quarrel *vb* **quar•reled** *or* **quar•relled; quar•rel•ing** *or* **quar•rel•ling**
1 to argue angrily
2 to find fault ⟨No one *quarreled* with his decision.⟩

[2]quarry: a stone quarry

quar•rel•some \'kwȯr-əl-səm\ *adj*
usually ready to disagree or argue ⟨a *quarrelsome* person⟩

[1]quar•ry \'kwȯr-ē\ *n, pl* **quar•ries**
an animal or bird hunted as game or prey

► **Word History** *Quarry* in the meaning "game" or "prey" can be traced to a hunting ritual from medieval times. At the end of a successful hunt the hounds used in the pursuit were rewarded with a part of the slain animal's entrails. Traditionally the entrails were spread out on the animal's hide. The word for the hounds' feast in medieval French was *cuiree,* a derivative of *cuir,* meaning "skin, hide." *Cuiree* was borrowed into English as *querre* or *quirre.* Over time the meaning of the word shifted from the slain animal's entrails to the live animal itself, seen as the object of a hunt.

[2]quarry *n, pl* **quar•ries**
▲ an open pit usually for obtaining building stone, slate, or limestone

► **Word History** The origin of this word is completely different from that of the *quarry* meaning "prey." The word *quadrus* in Latin meant "hewn stone" and is related to Latin *quadrum,* "square," and *quadri-,* "four" (as in English *quadrilateral*). From a derivative of *quadrum* came Old French *quarrere,* "pit for cutting stone," which was borrowed into English and eventually altered to *quarry.*

[3]quarry *vb* **quar•ried; quar•ry•ing**
1 to dig or take from or as if from a quarry ⟨Stone was *quarried* from the hillside.⟩
2 to make a quarry in ⟨A crew *quarried* a rocky slope.⟩

quart \'kwȯrt\ *n*
a measure of liquid capacity that equals two pints (about .95 liter)

quarter horse

[1]quar•ter \ˈkwȯr-tər\ *n*
1 one of four equal parts into which something can be divided 〈a *quarter* of an hour〉 〈Cut the pie into *quarters*.〉
2 a United States coin worth 25 cents
3 someone or something (as a place, direction, or group) not clearly identified 〈Complaints came from all *quarters*.〉
4 a particular division or district of a city 〈the city's historic *quarter*〉
5 **quarters** *pl* a dwelling place 〈living *quarters*〉
6 MERCY 1 〈The soldiers showed no *quarter* to the enemy.〉

[2]quarter *vb* **quar•tered**; **quar•ter•ing**
1 to divide into four usually equal parts 〈Peel and *quarter* an orange.〉
2 to provide with lodgings or shelter

[3]quarter *adj*
consisting of or equal to one fourth of 〈Give it a *quarter* turn.〉

quar•ter•back \ˈkwȯr-tər-ˌbak\ *n*
a football player who leads a team's attempts to score usually by passing the ball to other players

quarter horse *n*
▲ a stocky muscular saddle horse capable of running fast for short distances

[1]quar•ter•ly \ˈkwȯr-tər-lē\ *adv*
four times a year 〈Interest is compounded *quarterly*.〉

[2]quarterly *adj*
coming or happening four times a year 〈They hold *quarterly* meetings.〉

[3]quarterly *n, pl* **quar•ter•lies**
a magazine published four times a year

quar•ter•mas•ter \ˈkwȯr-tər-ˌma-stər\ *n*
1 an army officer who provides clothing and supplies for troops
2 an officer of a ship (as in the navy) in charge of navigation

quar•tet *also* **quar•tette** \kwȯr-ˈtet\ *n*
1 a piece of music for four instruments or voices
2 ▼ a group of four singers or musicians who perform together
3 a group or set of four

quartet 2

▶ quartz
While typical quartz rocks are colorless, others may be white, gray, red, purple, pink, yellow, green, brown, or black. Quartz is often used in making jewelry.

quartz \ˈkwȯrts\ *n*
▲ a common mineral often found in the form of colorless transparent crystals but sometimes (as in amethysts, agates, and jaspers) brightly colored

[1]qua•ver \ˈkwā-vər\ *vb* **qua•vered**; **qua•ver•ing**
to sound in shaky or unsteady tones 〈My voice *quavered* nervously.〉

[2]quaver *n*
a sound that trembles or is unsteady 〈a *quaver* in his voice〉

quay \ˈkē, ˈkwā\ *n*
▶ a structure built along the bank of a waterway (as a river) for use as a landing for loading and unloading boats

quea•sy \ˈkwē-zē\ *adj* **quea•si•er**; **quea•si•est**
1 somewhat nauseated 〈The boat ride made me *queasy*.〉
2 full of doubt : UNEASY
quea•si•ness \-nəs\ *n*

queen \'kwēn\ *n*
1 a woman who rules a country or kingdom
2 the wife or widow of a king
3 a woman or girl who is highly respected or well-known within a field 〈the *queen* of the blues〉
4 ▶ the most powerful piece in the game of chess
5 a playing card bearing the figure of a queen
6 a fully developed adult female insect (as a bee, ant, or termite) that lays eggs
queen•ly *adj*

queer \'kwir\ *adj* **queer•er**; **queer•est**
oddly unlike the usual or normal 〈a *queer* smell〉
queer•ly *adv*

quell \'kwel\ *vb* **quelled**; **quell•ing**
1 to stop or end by force 〈Police *quelled* a riot.〉
2 [4]QUIET, CALM 〈He *quelled* their fears.〉

quench \'kwench\ *vb* **quenched**; **quench•ing**
1 to end by satisfying 〈The drink *quenched* my thirst.〉
2 to put out (as a fire)

quer•u•lous \'kwer-yə-ləs, -ə-ləs\ *adj*
having or showing a complaining attitude 〈a *querulous* voice〉

[1]**que•ry** \'kwir-ē, 'kwer-ē\ *n, pl* **queries**
[1]QUESTION 1

queen 4: a queen from a modern ornamental chess set

[2]**query** *vb* **que•ried**; **que•ry•ing**
1 to put as a question 〈"Can I come?" she *queried.*〉
2 to ask questions about especially in order to clear up a doubt 〈They *queried* his decision.〉
3 to ask questions of 〈I'll *query* the professor.〉

quest \'kwest\ *n*
1 an effort to find or do something 〈a *quest* for answers〉
2 a usually adventurous journey made in search of something 〈a *quest* for lost treasure〉

[1]**ques•tion** \'kwes-chən\ *n*
1 something asked 〈Please answer my *question.*〉
2 a topic discussed or argued about 〈The book raises several *questions.*〉
3 OBJECTION 1 〈He obeyed without *question.*〉
4 doubt or uncertainty about something 〈I trust him without *question.*〉
5 POSSIBILITY 1, CHANCE 〈There was no *question* of escape.〉

[2]**question** *vb* **ques•tioned**; **ques•tion•ing**
1 to ask questions of or about 〈Lawyers *questioned* the witness.〉
2 to have or express doubts about 〈They *questioned* his loyalty.〉

ques•tion•able \'kwes-chə-nə-bəl\ *adj*
1 not certain or exact : DOUBTFUL
2 not believed to be true, sound, or proper 〈Her motives are *questionable.*〉

question mark *n*
a punctuation mark ? used chiefly at the end of a sentence to indicate a direct question

quay: passengers waiting for a ferry at Queen's Quay in Toronto, Canada

a b c d e f g h i j k l m n o p q r s t u v w x y z

ques•tion•naire \ˌkwes-chə-ˈner\ *n*
a set of questions to be asked of a number of people usually in order to gather information or opinions

[1]queue \ˈkyü\ *n*
1 PIGTAIL
2 ▶ a waiting line ⟨There's a *queue* at the ticket window.⟩

[2]queue *vb* **queued**; **queu•ing** *or* **queue•ing**
to form or wait in a line ⟨People are *queuing* up for tickets.⟩

[1]quib•ble \ˈkwi-bəl\ *vb* **quib•bled**; **quib•bling**
to argue or complain about small and unimportant things

[2]quibble *n*
a small and usually unimportant complaint, criticism, or argument

[1]quick \ˈkwik\ *adj* **quick•er**; **quick•est**
1 done or taking place in a very short period of time ⟨a *quick* look⟩ ⟨a *quick* nap⟩
2 very swift : SPEEDY ⟨*quick* steps⟩
3 fast in learning or understanding : mentally alert ⟨a *quick* mind⟩
4 easily stirred up ⟨a *quick* temper⟩
quick•ly *adv*
quick•ness *n*

▶ **Word History** The word *quick* first meant "alive." Most animals that are alive can move and run, so *quick* came to mean "moving" or "running." From this sense came the sense of *quick* that is most familiar today: "fast." New senses have come from this common sense. *Quick* can mean "alert," which is "fast in understanding," or "reacting fast."

▶ **Synonyms** QUICK, PROMPT, and READY mean able to respond right away. QUICK is used when the response is immediate and often when the ability is part of a person's nature. ⟨He has *quick* reflexes.⟩ PROMPT is used when the ability to respond right away is the product of training and discipline. ⟨The store gives *prompt* service.⟩ READY is used when the response comes easy or is smooth. ⟨He always had a *ready* answer to every question.⟩

[2]quick *n*
1 a very tender area of flesh (as under a fingernail)
2 someone's innermost feelings ⟨She was hurt to the *quick* by the remark.⟩

[3]quick *adv* **quick•er**; **quick•est**
in a quick manner : FAST

[1]queue 2: queues for tickets at Grand Central train station in New York City

quick•en \ˈkwi-kən\ *vb* **quick•ened**; **quick•en•ing**
1 to make or become faster : HASTEN ⟨They *quickened* their steps.⟩
2 to make or become stronger or more active ⟨Curiosity *quickened* my interest.⟩

quick•sand \ˈkwik-ˌsand\ *n*
a deep area of loose sand mixed with water into which heavy objects sink

quick•sil•ver \ˈkwik-ˌsil-vər\ *n*
MERCURY 1

▶ **Word History** The metal mercury has a color like silver. Most metals are solid but mercury is liquid at ordinary temperatures. It moves and flows and acts almost as if it were alive. The word *quick* once meant "alive" or "moving." This is why mercury was given the name *quicksilver.*

quick–tem•pered \ˈkwik-ˈtem-pərd\ *adj*
easily made angry

[1]qui•et \ˈkwī-ət\ *n*
the quality or state of being calm or without noise ⟨Can we please have some *quiet*?⟩

[2]quiet *adj* **qui•et•er**; **qui•et•est**
1 free from noise or uproar ⟨a *quiet* classroom⟩
2 marked by little or no motion or activity : CALM ⟨*quiet* seas⟩
3 not disturbed : PEACEFUL ⟨a *quiet* lunch⟩
4 tending not to talk or show excitement much ⟨a *quiet* child⟩ ⟨a *quiet* disposition⟩
5 not shown in an obvious way ⟨*quiet* determination⟩
6 away from public view : SECLUDED ⟨a *quiet* corner⟩
qui•et•ly *adv*
qui•et•ness *n*

[3]quiet *adv*
in a quiet manner : QUIETLY

[4]quiet *vb* **qui•et•ed**; **qui•et•ing**
to make or become calmer or less noisy ⟨She tried to *quiet* the crowd.⟩

quill \ˈkwil\ *n*
1 a large stiff feather of a bird's wing or tail
2 the hollow tubelike part of a feather
3 a hollow sharp spine of a porcupine or hedgehog
4 ▶ a pen made from a feather

shaft

quill 4

[1]quilt \ˈkwilt\ *n*
a bed cover made of two layers of cloth with a filling of wool, cotton, or down held together by patterned stitching

[2]quilt *vb* **quilt•ed**; **quilt•ing**
to stitch or sew together as in making a quilt

quince \'kwins\ *n*
a hard sour yellow fruit that resembles an apple, grows on a shrubby Asian tree, and is used especially in jams and jellies

qui•nine \'kwī-,nīn\ *n*
a bitter drug obtained from cinchona bark and used to treat malaria

quin•tet \kwin-'tet\ *n*
1 a piece of music for five instruments or voices
2 a group of five singers or musicians who perform together
3 a group or set of five

quin•tu•plet \kwin-'tə-plət, -'tü-\ *n*
1 one of five offspring born at one birth
2 a combination of five of a kind

quirk \'kwərk\ *n*
1 an odd or unusual characteristic or habit
2 something strange that happens by chance 〈Their meeting was a *quirk* of fate.〉

quirky \'kwər-kē\ *adj* **quirk•i•er**; **quirk•i•est**
unusual especially in an interesting way

quit \'kwit\ *vb* **quit**; **quit•ting**
to leave or stop doing something 〈*quit* a job〉 〈*quit* smoking〉

quite \'kwīt\ *adv*
1 beyond question or doubt : COMPLETELY 〈I was *quite* alone.〉 〈Are you *quite* sure?〉
2 to a considerable extent 〈That's *quite* interesting.〉 〈We're *quite* near.〉

quit•ter \'kwi-tər\ *n*
a person who gives up too easily

[1]quiv•er \'kwi-vər\ *n*
▶ a case for carrying arrows

[2]quiver *vb* **quiv•ered**; **quiv•er•ing**
to move with a slight trembling motion 〈The leaves *quivered* in the breeze.〉

[3]quiver *n*
the act or instance of trembling 〈She felt a *quiver* of excitement.〉

[1]quiz \'kwiz\ *n*, *pl* **quiz•zes**
a short test

[2]quiz *vb* **quizzed**; **quiz•zing**
to ask a lot of questions of 〈We *quizzed* him about his trip.〉

quiz•zi•cal \'kwi-zi-kəl\ *adj*
showing doubt, puzzlement or curiosity 〈a *quizzical* look〉
quiz•zi•cal•ly \-zi-klē, -zi-kə-lē\ *adv*

quoit \'kȯit, 'kwȯit, 'kwāt\ *n*
a ring (as of rope) tossed at a peg in a game (**quoits**)

[1]quiver

quo•rum \'kwȯr-əm\ *n*
the smallest number of people who must be present at a meeting in order for business to be carried on

quo•ta \'kwō-tə\ *n*
1 a limit on the number or amount of people or things that are allowed 〈a *quota* on imported goods〉
2 a share assigned to each member of a group 〈Each colony received its *quota* of troops.〉
3 a specific amount or number of things that is expected to be achieved 〈She sold her *quota* of candy bars.〉

quo•ta•tion \kwō-'tā-shən\ *n*
material (as a sentence or passage from a book) that is repeated exactly by someone else

quotation mark *n*
one of a pair of punctuation marks " " or ' ' used chiefly to indicate the beginning and end of a quotation

[1]quote \'kwōt\ *vb* **quot•ed**; **quot•ing**
to repeat (someone else's words) exactly 〈I *quoted* my favorite poem.〉

▶ **Word History** Sometimes passages in books are numbered. The English word *quote* came from a medieval Latin word *quotare* that meant "to refer to a passage by number." English *quote* means "to repeat the words of a passage exactly." The idea of number has been lost.

[2]quote *n*
QUOTATION

quo•tient \'kwō-shənt\ *n*
the number obtained by dividing one number by another 〈Dividing 10 by 5 gives a *quotient* of 2.〉

A B C D E F G H I J K L M N O P Q R S T U V W X Y Z

Rr

Sounds of R: The letter **R** makes only one sound, the sound heard in *rat* and *arm*. When **R** appears with an **H**, only the **R** is heard, as in *rhyme*. The vowels that people pronounce before an **R** often sound very different from the vowels that they pronounce in other situations. This is why we list these vowels separately in the Pronunciation Symbols list. Additionally, some people may not pronounce an **R** at all when it occurs after a vowel and before a consonant or pause.

r \ˈär\ *n, pl* **r's** *or* **rs** \ˈärz\ *often cap*
the 18th letter of the English alphabet

R *abbr* regular

r. *abbr* right

R. *abbr* rabbi

rab•bi \ˈra-ˌbī\ *n, pl* **rab•bis**
a person educated in Jewish law and able to lead a Jewish congregation

rabbit

rab•bit \ˈra-bət\ *n*
▲ a short-tailed mammal that has soft fur and long ears and hind legs and digs burrows

rab•ble \ˈra-bəl\ *n*
1 a crowd that is noisy and hard to control : MOB
2 a group of people looked down upon as ignorant and hard to handle

ra•bid \ˈra-bəd, ˈrā-\ *adj*
1 very angry : FURIOUS
2 having or expressing a very extreme opinion about or interest in something 〈a *rabid* fan〉
3 affected with rabies 〈a *rabid* dog〉
ra•bid•ly *adv*

ra•bies \ˈrā-bēz\ *n*
a deadly disease of the nervous system that affects animals and can be passed on to people by the bite of an infected animal

rac•coon \ra-ˈkün\ *n*
a small North American animal that is mostly gray with black around the eyes, has a bushy tail with black rings, is active mostly at night, and eats small animals, fruits, eggs, and insects

► **Word History** Like *hickory, moccasin,* and *tomahawk,* the word *raccoon* comes from an American Indian language that was spoken around the Jamestown settlement in Virginia. The English colonist John Smith—famous for having his life spared by Pocahontas—first recorded the name for the unfamiliar animal as *aroughcun, rarowcun,* and *raugroughcun.*

¹race \ˈrās\ *vb* **raced**; **rac•ing**
1 to go, move, function, or drive at top speed
2 to take part in a contest of speed
3 to cause an engine of a motor vehicle in neutral to run fast

²race *n*
1 a contest of speed
2 a contest involving progress toward a goal 〈the *race* for mayor〉
3 a strong or rapid current of water

³race *n*
1 any one of the groups that human beings can be divided into based on shared distinctive physical traits
2 a group of individuals who share a common culture or history 〈the English *race*〉
3 a major group of living things 〈the human *race*〉

race•course \ˈrās-ˌkȯrs\ *n*
a place where races are held

race•horse \ˈrās-ˌhȯrs\ *n*
▼ a horse bred or kept for racing

racehorse: racehorses on a racetrack

rac•er \ˈrā-sər\ *n*
1 a person, animal, or vehicle that participates in or is used for participation in races
2 a long slender active snake (as the blacksnake)

race•track \ˈrās-ˌtrak\ *n*
a usually oval course on which races are run

ra•cial \ˈrā-shəl\ *adj*
of, relating to, or based on race ⟨a *racial* group⟩
ra•cial•ly *adv*

rac•ism \ˈrā-ˌsi-zəm\ *n*
1 belief that certain races of people are by birth and nature superior to others
2 discrimination or hatred based on race

rac•ist \ˈrā-sist\ *adj*
based on or showing racism ⟨a *racist* comment⟩
racist *n*

[1]rack \ˈrak\ *n*
a frame or stand for storing or displaying things ⟨a magazine *rack*⟩ ⟨a hat *rack*⟩

[2]rack *vb* **racked**; **rack•ing**
1 to cause to suffer torture, pain, or sorrow ⟨He was *racked* by a cough.⟩
2 to force to think hard ⟨I *racked* my brain for an answer.⟩

[1]rack•et \ˈra-kət\ *n*
1 a loud confused noise
2 a dishonest scheme for obtaining money

[2]racket *or* **rac•quet** *n*
▶ a piece of sports equipment consisting of a handle and a frame with strings stretched tightly across it

[2]racket

rack•e•teer \ˌra-kə-ˈtir\ *n*
a person who gets money or advantages by using force or threats

ra•dar \ˈrā-ˌdär\ *n*
▶ a radio device for detecting the position of things in the distance and the direction of moving objects (as distant airplanes or ships)

ra•di•ance \ˈrā-dē-əns\ *n*
warm or vivid brightness

ra•di•ant \ˈrā-dē-ənt\ *adj*
1 giving out or reflecting rays of light ⟨the *radiant* sun⟩
2 glowing with love, confidence, or joy ⟨a *radiant* smile⟩
3 transmitted by radiation
synonyms see BRIGHT

radiant energy *n*
energy sent out in the form of electromagnetic waves ⟨Heat, light, and radio waves are forms of *radiant energy*.⟩

ra•di•ate \ˈrā-dē-ˌāt\ *vb* **ra•di•at•ed**; **ra•di•at•ing**
1 to send out rays : SHINE
2 to come forth in the form of rays ⟨Light *radiates* from shining bodies.⟩
3 to go out in a direct line from a center ⟨Spokes *radiate* from the center of the wheel.⟩
4 to spread around from or as if from a center
5 to show very clearly ⟨She *radiates* confidence.⟩

ra•di•a•tion \ˌrā-dē-ˈā-shən\ *n*
1 the process of giving off energy in the form of waves or particles
2 something that is radiated (as light or X-rays)

ra•di•a•tor \ˈrā-dē-ˌā-tər\ *n*
▶ a device to heat air (as in a room) or to cool an object (as an automobile engine) by heating the surrounding air

[1]rad•i•cal \ˈra-di-kəl\ *adj*
1 very new and different from the usual or ordinary : EXTREME ⟨a *radical* change⟩
2 of or relating to people who favor rapid and sweeping changes in laws and government
rad•i•cal•ly *adv*

[2]radical *n*
a person who favors rapid and sweeping changes especially in laws and government

radii *pl of* RADIUS

[1]ra•dio \ˈrā-dē-ˌō\ *n, pl* **ra•di•os**
1 the process that is used for sending or receiving signals by means of electromagnetic waves without a connecting wire
2 a device that receives signals sent by radio
3 programs that are broadcast by radio
4 a device used to both send and receive messages by radio
5 the radio broadcasting industry

[2]radio *adj*
1 of or relating to radio waves
2 of, relating to, or used in radio broadcasting

[3]radio *vb* **ra•di•oed**; **ra•di•o•ing**
to communicate or send a message to by radio

radiator

ra•dio•ac•tive \ˌrā-dē-ō-ˈak-tiv\ *adj*
caused by or exhibiting radioactivity ⟨a *radioactive* element⟩

▶ **radar**
Radio waves transmitted from a radar antenna strike a distant object, such as the airplane shown below, and are reflected back to the source. A computer then calculates the speed and distance of the airplane by the delay in the signal's return.

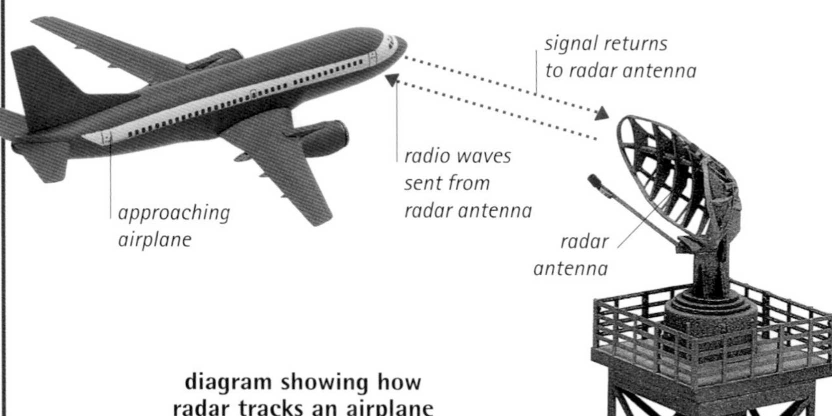

diagram showing how radar tracks an airplane

ra•dio•ac•tiv•i•ty \ˌrā-dē-ō-ak-ˈti-və-tē\ *n*
1 the giving off of rays of energy or particles by the breaking apart of atoms of certain elements (as uranium)
2 the rays or particles that are given off when atoms break apart

radio wave *n*
an electromagnetic wave used in radio, television, or radar communication

rad•ish \ˈra-dish\ *n*
▶ a small roundish crisp root that has a sharp flavor and is usually eaten raw as a vegetable

radish

ra•di•um \ˈrā-dē-əm\ *n*
a strongly radioactive element found in very small quantities in various minerals (as pitchblende) and used in the treatment of cancer

ra•di•us \ˈrā-dē-əs\ *n*, *pl* **ra•dii** \-dē-ˌī\
1 a straight line extending from the center of a circle to the outside edge or from the center of a sphere to the surface
2 an area that extends in all directions from a place ⟨Most students live within a *radius* of five miles from the school.⟩
3 the bone on the thumb side of the arm between the wrist and the elbow

[1]raf•fle \ˈra-fəl\ *n*
a contest for a prize in which people buy tickets and which is won by the person whose ticket is picked at a drawing

[2]raffle *vb* **raf•fled**; **raf•fl•ing**
to give (something) as a prize in a raffle

[1]raft \ˈraft\ *n*
▶ a flat structure (as a group of logs fastened together) for support or transportation on water

[1]raft: model of a primitive fishing raft

[2]raft *n*
a large amount or number ⟨*rafts* of birds⟩

raf•ter \ˈraf-tər\ *n*
one of the usually sloping timbers that support a roof

rag \ˈrag\ *n*
1 a worn piece of cloth
2 **rags** *pl* shabby or very worn clothing ⟨The child is dressed in *rags*.⟩

rag•a•muf•fin \ˈra-gə-ˌmə-fən\ *n*
a poorly clothed and often dirty child

[1]rage \ˈrāj\ *n*
1 very strong and uncontrolled anger : FURY ⟨I was filled with *rage*.⟩
2 a fit of anger ⟨The rude remark sent him into a *rage*.⟩
3 violent action (as of wind or sea)
4 FAD
synonyms see ANGER

[2]rage *vb* **raged**; **rag•ing**
1 to feel or show extreme or uncontrolled anger
2 to continue out of control ⟨The fire *raged* for hours.⟩

rag•ged \ˈra-gəd\ *adj*
1 having a rough or uneven edge or outline ⟨*ragged* cliffs⟩
2 very worn-out : TATTERED ⟨*ragged* clothes⟩
3 wearing very worn-out clothes
4 done in an uneven way ⟨a *ragged* performance⟩
rag•ged•ly *adv*
rag•ged•ness *n*

rag•gedy \ˈra-gə-dē\ *adj*
1 RAGGED 2
2 RAGGED 3

rag•tag \ˈrag-ˌtag\ *adj*
not well organized or put together

rag•time \ˈrag-ˌtīm\ *n*
music that has a lively melody and a steady rhythm like a march

rag•weed \ˈrag-ˌwēd\ *n*
a common weed with pollen that irritates the eyes and noses of some people

[1]raid \ˈrād\ *n*
a sudden attack or invasion

[2]raid *vb* **raid•ed**; **raid•ing**
1 to enter (a place) to look for something or someone or to steal or take something ⟨Let's *raid* the cookie jar.⟩
2 to make a sudden attack
raid•er *n*

[1]rail \ˈrāl\ *n*
1 a bar extending from one support to another and serving as a guard or barrier
2 a bar of steel forming a track for wheeled vehicles
3 RAILROAD 1 ⟨They travel across Canada by *rail*.⟩

[2]rail *vb* **railed**; **rail•ing**
to provide with a railing

[3]rail *n*
▼ a small or medium-sized wading bird related to the crane that has very long toes for walking on the soft mud of marshes

[3]rail

[4]rail *vb* **railed**; **rail•ing**
to scold or complain in harsh or bitter language ⟨Students *railed* about a longer school year.⟩

rail•ing \ˈrā-liŋ\ *n*
1 a barrier (as a fence) made up of vertical bars and their supports
2 material for making rails

rail•lery \ˈrā-lə-rē\ *n*
an act or instance of making fun of someone in a good-natured way

rail•road \ˈrāl-ˌrōd\ *n*
1 a permanent road that has parallel steel rails that make a track for train cars
2 a company that owns and operates trains

rail•way \ˈrāl-ˌwā\ *n*
RAILROAD 1

rai•ment \ˈrā-mənt\ *n*
CLOTHING

[1]rain \ˈrān\ *n*
1 water falling in drops from the clouds
2 a fall of water in drops from the clouds
3 rainy weather
4 a heavy fall of objects

[2]rain *vb* **rained**; **rain•ing**
1 to fall as water in drops from the clouds
2 to send down rain ⟨The clouds *rained* for days.⟩
3 to fall in large amounts ⟨Ashes *rained* from the volcano.⟩

4 to give in large amounts ⟨Friends *rained* advice on me.⟩
rain cats and dogs POUR 2

rain•bow \'rān-,bō\ *n*
an arc of colors that appears in the sky opposite the sun and is caused by the sun shining through rain, mist, or spray

rain•coat \'rān-,kōt\ *n*
a coat of waterproof or water-resistant material

rain•drop \'rān-,dräp\ *n*
a drop of rain

rain•fall \'rān-,fȯl\ *n*
1 [1]RAIN 2
2 amount of precipitation ⟨Their average annual *rainfall* is 80 centimeters.⟩

rain forest *n*
▼a woodland with a high annual rainfall and very tall trees and that is often found in tropical regions

5 to bring to notice ⟨No one *raised* any objection.⟩
6 [1]INCREASE ⟨They're *raising* the rent.⟩
7 to make louder ⟨Don't *raise* your voice.⟩
8 to give life to : AROUSE ⟨The children made enough noise to *raise* the dead.⟩
9 to set upright by lifting or building ⟨A monument was *raised*.⟩
10 PROMOTE 1, ELEVATE ⟨She was *raised* to captain.⟩
11 to give rise to : PROVOKE ⟨The joke *raised* a laugh.⟩
12 to make light and airy ⟨Yeast can *raise* dough.⟩
13 to cause to form on the skin ⟨The burn *raised* a blister.⟩
synonyms see LIFT
rais•er *n*

[2]**raise** *n*
an increase in amount (as of pay)

[1]**ral•ly** \'ra-lē\ *vb* **ral•lied; ral•ly•ing**
1 to bring or come together for a common purpose
2 to publicly support or oppose ⟨The whole school *rallied* behind the principal.⟩
3 to rouse from low spirits or weakness ⟨The patient *rallied* and survived.⟩ ⟨The team *rallied* to win the game.⟩

[2]**rally** *n, pl* **rallies**
1 a sudden improvement in performance or condition ⟨The team's late *rally* helped them win.⟩
2 a big meeting held to rouse enthusiasm

[1]**ram** \'ram\ *vb* **rammed; ram•ming**
1 to strike or strike against with violence
2 to force in, down, or together by driving or pressing ⟨He *rammed* clothes into a suitcase.⟩
3 [2]FORCE 2 ⟨The law was *rammed* through Congress.⟩

rain forest: tropical rain forest vegetation

rain•proof \'rān-'prüf\ *adj*
not letting in rain

rain•storm \'rān-,stȯrm\ *n*
a storm of or with rain

rain•wa•ter \'rān-,wȯ-tər, -,wä-\ *n*
water from rain

rainy \'rā-nē\ *adj* **rain•i•er; rain•i•est**
having much rain ⟨a *rainy* season⟩

[1]**raise** \'rāz\ *vb* **raised; rais•ing**
1 to cause to rise : LIFT ⟨Please *raise* your hand.⟩
2 COLLECT 1 ⟨The school is trying to *raise* money.⟩
3 to look after the growth and development of : GROW ⟨The farmer *raised* hogs.⟩
4 to bring up a child : REAR ⟨He was *raised* by his grandmother.⟩

rai•sin \'rā-zᵊn\ *n*
a sweet dried grape used for food

ra•ja *or* **ra•jah** \'rä-jə\ *n*
an Indian prince

[1]**rake** \'rāk\ *n*
a garden tool with a long handle and a bar with teeth or prongs at the end

[2]**rake** *vb* **raked; rak•ing**
1 to gather, loosen, or smooth thoroughly with or as if with a rake ⟨*rake* leaves⟩ ⟨We *raked* together money to buy pizza.⟩
2 to search through
3 to sweep the length of with gunfire

rak•ish \'rā-kish\ *adj*
JAUNTY, DASHING ⟨He wears his hat at a *rakish* angle.⟩

[2]**ram** *n*
1▼ a male sheep
2 BATTERING RAM

RAM \'ram\ *n*
a computer memory that provides the main storage available to the user for programs and data

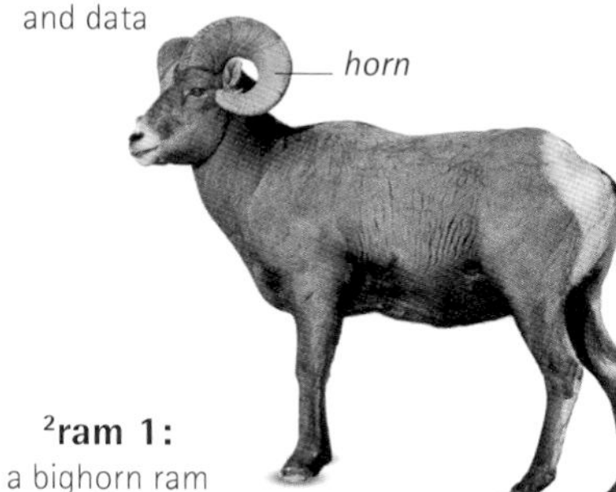

[2]**ram 1:** a bighorn ram

Ram•a•dan \'rä-mə-,dän, ,rä-mə-'dän\ *n*
the ninth month of the Islamic calendar observed as sacred with fasting practiced daily from sunrise to sunset

[1]ram•ble \'ram-bəl\ *vb* **ram•bled; ram•bling**
1 to go aimlessly from place to place : WANDER ⟨She spent a year *rambling* around the country.⟩
2 to talk or write without a clear purpose or point
3 to grow or extend in many directions ⟨a *rambling* vine⟩
synonyms see WANDER

[2]ramble *n*
a long stroll with no particular destination

ram•bunc•tious \ram-'bəŋk-shəs\ *adj*
not under control in a way that is playful or full of energy ⟨The schoolyard was filled with *rambunctious* kids.⟩

ramrod

ram•i•fi•ca•tion \,ra-mə-fə-'kā-shən\ *n*
something that is the result of something else ⟨Our committee will study the *ramifications* of the change.⟩

ramp \'ramp\ *n*
a sloping passage or roadway connecting different levels ⟨a highway exit *ramp*⟩

ram•page \'ram-,pāj\ *n*
a period or instance of violent action or behavior

ram•pant \'ram-pənt\ *adj*
existing or growing greatly and quickly ⟨Fear was *rampant* in the town.⟩

ram•part \'ram-,pärt\ *n*
a broad bank or wall raised as a protective barrier

[1]range 3: a large range with two ovens

ram•rod \'ram-,räd\ *n*
◀ a rod for forcing the charge down the barrel in a firearm that is loaded through the muzzle

ram•shack•le \'ram-,sha-kəl\ *adj*
ready to fall down ⟨a *ramshackle* barn⟩

ran *past of* RUN

[1]ranch \'ranch\ *n*
1 a large farm for the raising of livestock (as cattle)
2 a farm devoted to a special crop

> ► **Word History** In the Spanish language of the 1500s the verb *rancharse* was used by soldiers in the sense "to be camped" someplace. The conquistadors who took this verb to the Americas also were familiar with a derivative noun *rancho,* referring originally to a camp or temporary dwelling such as a hut. Both the general sense "dwelling" and the specifically Mexican sense "small farm" were adopted into American English in the 1800s—as *rancho* and the more English-sounding *ranch.* By the late 1800s *ranch* was most often not a small farm but a large piece of land devoted to raising livestock—a meaning the word still maintains.

[2]ranch *vb* **ranched; ranch•ing**
to live or work on a large farm where livestock are raised
ranch•er *n*

ran•cid \'ran-səd\ *adj*
having a strong disagreeable smell or taste from no longer being fresh ⟨*rancid* butter⟩

ran•cor \'raŋ-kər\ *n*
deep hatred

ran•cor•ous \'raŋ-kə-rəs\ *adj*
showing deep hatred ⟨He gave a *rancorous* answer.⟩

ran•dom \'ran-dəm\ *adj*
lacking a clear plan, purpose, or pattern ⟨I read a *random* selection of poems.⟩
ran•dom•ly *adv*
ran•dom•ness *n*

ran•dom–ac•cess \,ran-dəm-'ak-,ses\ *adj*
permitting access to stored data in any order the user desires

random–access memory *n*
RAM

rang *past of* [3]RING

[1]range \'rānj\ *n*
1 a series of things in a line ⟨a *range* of mountains⟩
2 the distance over which someone or something can be seen, heard, or reached
3 ◀ a cooking stove
4 open land over which livestock may roam and feed
5 a variety of choices within a scale ⟨a *range* of colors⟩
6 the difference between the least and the greatest of a set of values
7 the distance a gun will shoot
8 a place where shooting is practiced

[2]range *vb* **ranged; rang•ing**
1 to arrange in a particular place or order
2 to roam over or through
3 to come within an upper and a lower limit ⟨Prices *range* from three to ten dollars.⟩

rang•er \'rān-jər\ *n*
1 FOREST RANGER
2 a soldier specially trained in close-range fighting and in raiding tactics

rangy \'rān-jē\ *adj* **rang•i•er; rang•i•est**
tall and slender

[1]rank \'raŋk\ *n*
1 [2]ROW 1, SERIES ⟨*ranks* of houses⟩
2 a line of soldiers standing side by side
3 ranks *pl* the body of enlisted persons in an army
4 position within a group ⟨Who is highest in *rank* in this office?⟩
5 high social position
6 official grade or position ⟨the *rank* of major⟩

[2]rank *adj*
1 strong and active in growth ⟨*rank* weeds⟩
2 [2]OUTRIGHT 1 ⟨*rank* dishonesty⟩
3 having an unpleasant smell

[3]rank *vb* **ranked; rank•ing**
1 to take or have a certain position in a group ⟨He *ranks* near the top of the class.⟩
2 to arrange in a classification
3 to arrange in lines or in a formation

ran•kle \'raŋ-kəl\ *vb* **ran•kled; ran•kling**
to cause anger, irritation, or bitterness

ran•sack \'ran-,sak\ *vb* **ran•sacked; ran•sack•ing**
to search through in a way that causes disorder or damage ⟨A burglar *ransacked* the house.⟩

[1]ran•som \'ran-səm\ *n*
1 something paid or demanded for the freedom of a captured person
2 the act of freeing from captivity by paying a price

[2]ransom *vb* **ran•somed; ran•som•ing**
to free from captivity or punishment by paying a price

rant \'rant\ *vb* **rant•ed; rant•ing**
to talk loudly and wildly

[1]rap \'rap\ *vb* **rapped; rap•ping**
to give a quick sharp blow

[2]rap *n*
1 a sharp blow or knock

2 the blame or punishment for something

[3]rap *vb* **rapped**; **rap•ping**
1 to talk freely and informally
2 to perform rap music

[4]rap *n*
1 an informal talk : CHAT
2 a type of music that usually has a fast rhythm and in which words are spoken instead of sung

ra•pa•cious \rə-ˈpā-shəs\ *adj*
1 very greedy
2 PREDATORY
ra•pa•cious•ly *adv*
ra•pa•cious•ness *n*

rape \ˈrāp\ *n*
▶ a plant related to the mustard that is grown for animals to graze on, for its seeds which are fed to birds, and as a source of oil

rape

rap•id \ˈra-pəd\ *adj*
very fast 〈a *rapid* current〉 〈*rapid* progress〉
synonyms see FAST
rap•id•ly *adv*

ra•pid•i•ty \rə-ˈpi-də-tē\ *n*
the quality or state of being rapid

rap•ids \ˈra-pədz\ *n pl*
▼ a part of a river where the current flows very fast usually over rocks

ra•pi•er \ˈrā-pē-ər\ *n*
a straight sword with a narrow blade having two sharp edges

rap•pel \rə-ˈpel, ra-\ *vb* **rap•pelled**; **rap•pel•ling**
to move down a steep slope (as a cliff) by pushing the feet against its surface and sliding down a rope

rapids: rapids on a river

rap•per \ˈra-pər\ *n*
a person who performs rap music

rap•port \ra-ˈpȯr\ *n*
a friendly relationship

rapt \ˈrapt\ *adj*
showing complete delight or interest 〈They listened with *rapt* attention.〉

rap•tor \ˈrap-tər\ *n*
BIRD OF PREY

rap•ture \ˈrap-chər\ *n*
a strong feeling of joy, delight, or love

[1]rare \ˈrer\ *adj* **rar•er**; **rar•est**
1 very uncommon 〈*rare* old coins〉
2 very fine : EXCELLENT 〈a *rare* June day〉
3 not thick or compact : THIN 〈The atmosphere is *rare* at high altitudes.〉

▶ **Synonyms** RARE, SCARCE, and UNCOMMON mean being in short supply. RARE is usually used for an object or quality of which only a few examples are to be found and which is therefore especially appreciated. 〈He found a *rare* gem.〉 SCARCE is used for something that for a while is in too short supply. 〈Food was *scarce* that winter.〉 UNCOMMON can be used of anything which is not often found, but usually there is no suggestion that more is desired. 〈Identical twins are *uncommon*.〉

[2]rare *adj* **rar•er**; **rar•est**
cooked so that the inside is still red 〈*rare* roast beef〉

rare•ly \ˈrer-lē\ *adv*
not often : SELDOM 〈He *rarely* speaks.〉

rar•ing \ˈrer-ən, -iŋ\ *adj*
very eager 〈*raring* to go〉

rar•i•ty \ˈrer-ə-tē\ *n, pl* **rar•i•ties**
1 the quality or state of being rare
2 something that is uncommon

ras•cal \ˈra-skəl\ *n*
1 a usually young mischievous person
2 a mean or dishonest person

[1]rash \ˈrash\ *adj*
done or made quickly and without thought of the likely result 〈a *rash* decision〉
rash•ly *adv*
rash•ness *n*

[2]rash *n*
1 a breaking out of the skin with red spots (as from illness or an allergic reaction)
2 a series of bad things that happen in a short time 〈a *rash* of fires〉

[1]rasp \ˈrasp\ *vb* **rasped**; **rasp•ing**
1 to say with or make a harsh sound
2 to rub with or as if with a rough object or substance 〈I *rasped* off the rough edges.〉

[2]rasp *n*
1 a harsh sound or sensation
2 a coarse file used for smoothing

rasp•ber•ry \ˈraz-ˌber-ē\ *n, pl* **rasp•ber•ries**
▼ a sweet juicy red, black, or purple berry of a prickly plant

raspberries

raspy \ˈras-pē\ *adj* **rasp•i•er**; **rasp•i•est**
having a harsh sound 〈a *raspy* voice〉

[1]rat \ˈrat\ *n*
1 a gnawing animal with brown, black, white, or grayish fur that looks like but is larger than a mouse
2 a person who betrays friends

[2]rat *vb* **rat•ted**; **rat•ting**
to betray a friend

[1]rate \ˈrāt\ *n*
1 a price or charge set according to a scale or standard 〈hotel *rates*〉
2 the amount of something measured in units of something else or in comparison with others 〈a high success *rate*〉
at any rate in any case 〈Maybe it's not ten miles, but *at any rate* it's far.〉

[2]**rate** *vb* **rat•ed; rat•ing**
1 to be placed in comparison with others : RANK ⟨Our school *rates* high in math scores.⟩
2 CONSIDER 3, REGARD ⟨You are *rated* an expert.⟩
3 to have a right to : DESERVE ⟨He *rates* a promotion.⟩

rath•er \'ra-t͟hər\ *adv*
1 [2]SOMEWHAT ⟨It's a *rather* cold day.⟩
2 more willingly ⟨I would *rather* stay home.⟩
3 more correctly or truly ⟨It's just ten minutes away, or *rather* nine and a half.⟩
4 INSTEAD ⟨The meals were not better but *rather* worse.⟩

rat•i•fi•ca•tion \ˌra-tə-fə-'kā-shən\ *n*
the act or process of giving legal approval to

rat•i•fy \'ra-tə-fī\ *vb* **rat•i•fied; rat•i•fy•ing**
to give legal approval to (as by a vote)

rat•ing \'rā-tiŋ\ *n*
a position within a grading system ⟨credit *rating*⟩

ra•tio \'rā-shō, -shē-ˌō\ *n, pl* **ra•tios**
the relationship in number or quantity between two or more things ⟨the *ratio* of teachers to students⟩

[1]**ra•tion** \'ra-shən, 'rā-shən\ *n*
1 a food allowance for one day
2 rations *pl* [1]PROVISION 1
3 the amount each person is allowed by an authority ⟨a gas *ration*⟩ ⟨The government set a gas *ration*.⟩

[2]**ration** *vb* **ra•tioned; ra•tion•ing**
1 to control the amount an individual can use ⟨The government *rationed* gas.⟩
2 to use sparingly ⟨*Ration* your water on the hike.⟩

ra•tio•nal \'ra-shə-nᵊl\ *adj*
1 having the ability to reason ⟨Humans are *rational* creatures.⟩
2 based on or showing reason ⟨*rational* thinking⟩ ⟨a *rational* decision⟩
ra•tio•nal•ly *adv*

ra•tio•nale \ˌra-shə-'nal\ *n*
a basic explanation or reason for something ⟨What is the *rationale* behind your decision?⟩

ra•tio•nal•ize \'ra-shə-nə-ˌlīz\ *vb* **ra•tio•nal•ized; ra•tio•nal•iz•ing**
to find an excuse for something that seems reasonable or believable

rational number *n*
a number that can be expressed as a whole number or the quotient of two whole numbers

rat•ter \'ra-tər\ *n*
a dog or cat that catches rats

[1]**rat•tle** \'ra-tᵊl\ *vb* **rat•tled; rat•tling**
1 to make or cause to make a rapid series of short sharp sounds ⟨Wind *rattled* the windows.⟩
2 to move with a clatter ⟨A wagon *rattled* down the road.⟩
3 to speak or say quickly or without stopping ⟨He *rattled* off the answers.⟩
4 to disturb the calmness of : UPSET ⟨The question *rattled* the speaker.⟩

[2]**rattle** *n*
1 a series of short sharp sounds ⟨the *rattle* of dishes⟩
2 ▶ a toy that makes a rattling sound
3 a part at the end of a rattlesnake's tail that makes a buzzing rattle when shaken

rat•tler \'rat-lər\ *n*
RATTLESNAKE

rat•tle•snake \'ra-tᵊl-ˌsnāk\ *n*
▼ a poisonous American snake with a rattle at the end of its tail

rattlesnake: a western diamondback rattlesnake

rat•ty \'ra-tē\ *adj* **rat•ti•er; rat•ti•est**
in bad condition : SHABBY ⟨a *ratty* old sweater⟩

rau•cous \'rò-kəs\ *adj*
1 loud and harsh ⟨*raucous* laughter⟩
2 behaving in a rough and noisy way ⟨a *raucous* crowd⟩
rau•cous•ly *adv*

[1]**rav•age** \'ra-vij\ *n*
destructive action or effect ⟨the *ravages* of disease⟩

[2]**ravage** *vb* **rav•aged; rav•ag•ing**
to attack or act upon with great violence ⟨The forest was *ravaged* by fire.⟩

rave \'rāv\ *vb* **raved; rav•ing**
1 to talk wildly or as if crazy
2 to talk with great enthusiasm ⟨He *raved* about the new play.⟩

rav•el \'ra-vəl\ *vb* **rav•eled** *or* **rav•elled; rav•el•ing** *or* **rav•el•ling**
UNRAVEL 1 ⟨We *raveled* the net for fishing.⟩

[1]**ra•ven** \'rā-vən\ *n*
▶ a large shiny black bird that is larger than the related crow

[2]**raven** *adj*
shiny and black like a raven's feathers

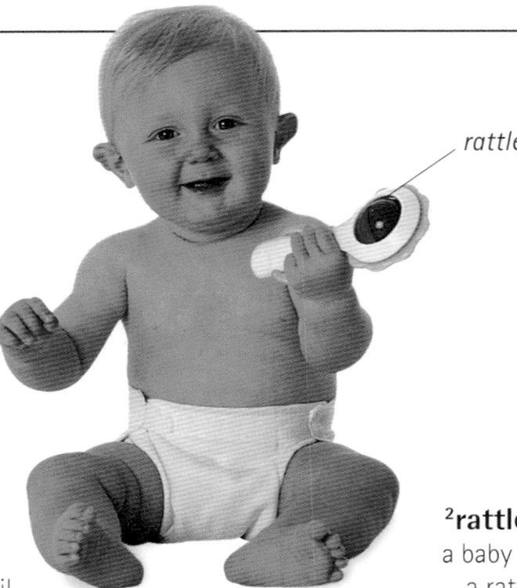

[2]**rattle 2:** a baby with a rattle

rav•en•ous \'ra-və-nəs\ *adj*
very hungry
rav•en•ous•ly *adv*

ra•vine \rə-'vēn\ *n*
a small narrow valley with steep sides that is larger than a gully and smaller than a canyon

rav•ish \'ra-vish\ *vb* **rav•ished; rav•ish•ing**
1 to seize and take away by force
2 to fill with joy or delight

rav•ish•ing \'ra-vi-shiŋ\ *adj*
very beautiful

raw \'rò\ *adj* **raw•er; raw•est**
1 not cooked ⟨*raw* fish⟩
2 having the skin scraped or roughened ⟨She had *raw* red hands.⟩
3 being in or nearly in the natural state : not treated or prepared ⟨*raw* sewage⟩
4 not trained or experienced ⟨*raw* recruits⟩
5 unpleasantly damp or cold ⟨a *raw* day⟩
6 lacking a normal or usual finish ⟨the *raw* edge of a seam⟩
raw•ness *n*

raw•hide \'rò-ˌhīd\ *n*
cattle skin before it has been made into leather

[1]**raven**

[1]ray \ˈrā\ *n*
1 one of the lines of light that appear to be given off by a bright object ⟨*rays* of sunlight⟩
2 a thin beam of radiant energy (as light)
3 light cast in rays
4 a tiny bit : PARTICLE ⟨a *ray* of hope⟩
5 any of a group of lines that spread out from the same center
6 a straight line extending from a point in one direction only
7 a slender plant or animal structure

[2]ray *n*
▶ a flat broad fish (as a skate or stingray) related to the shark that has its eyes on the top of its head and often winglike fins

ray•on \ˈrā-ˌän\ *n*
a cloth made with fibers produced chemically from cellulose

raze \ˈrāz\ *vb* **razed**; **raz•ing**
to destroy completely by knocking down or breaking to pieces : DEMOLISH

ra•zor \ˈrā-zər\ *n*
a sharp cutting instrument used to shave off hair

razz \ˈraz\ *vb* **razzed**; **razz•ing**
to make fun of : TEASE

rd. *abbr*
1 road
2 rod

re \ˈrā\ *n*
the second note of the musical scale

re- *prefix*
1 again ⟨*re*fill⟩
2 back : backward ⟨*re*call⟩

[1]reach \ˈrēch\ *vb* **reached**; **reach•ing**
1 to extend the arm far enough to touch or grab ⟨I can't *reach* the top shelf.⟩
2 to arrive at : COME ⟨We should *reach* the border before noon.⟩
3 to extend or stretch to ⟨Their land *reaches* the river.⟩
4 to communicate with ⟨I tried to *reach* you by phone.⟩
5 to grow, develop, or increase ⟨The temperature *reached* a record high.⟩

▶ **Synonyms** REACH, GAIN, and ACHIEVE mean to arrive at a point or end by work or effort. REACH is used for arriving at something or some place by any amount of effort. ⟨They *reached* the city after many days.⟩ GAIN is used of a struggle to arrive at a goal. ⟨The slaves *gained* their freedom.⟩ ACHIEVE is used when skill or courage is involved. ⟨The artist *achieved* greatness.⟩

[2]reach *n*
1 the distance within which something can be touched or grabbed
2 the act of stretching especially to take hold of something ⟨Make a *reach* for my hand.⟩
3 the probability that something can be achieved ⟨Success is within *reach*.⟩
4 an unbroken stretch (as of a river)
5 ability to stretch (as an arm) so as to touch something ⟨She has a long *reach*.⟩

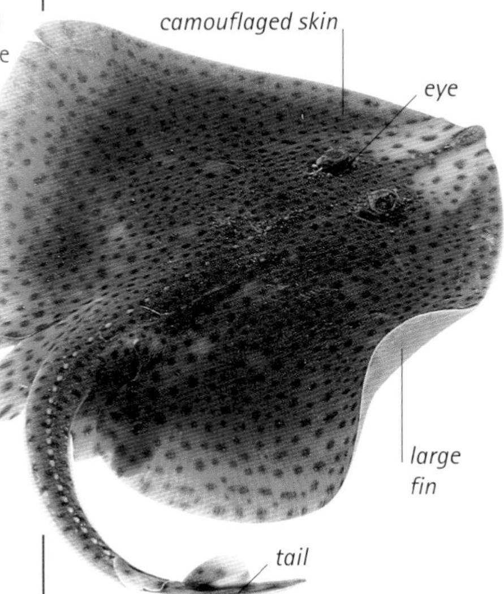

[2]ray: a spotted ray

re•act \rē-ˈakt\ *vb* **re•act•ed**; **re•act•ing**
1 to act or behave in response to something ⟨Firefighters *reacted* quickly to the situation.⟩
2 to oppose a force or influence
Hint: In this sense, *react* is usually used with against. ⟨Workers *reacted* against unfair treatment.⟩
3 to go through a chemical reaction ⟨Acids *react* with bases to form salt.⟩

re•ac•tion \rē-ˈak-shən\ *n*
1 behavior or attitude in response to something ⟨What was your *reaction* to the news?⟩
2 a response of the body to a stimulus ⟨He had an allergic *reaction* to peanuts.⟩
3 a chemical change that is brought about by the action of one substance on another and results in a new substance being formed

re•ac•tor \rē-ˈak-tər\ *n*
a device using atomic energy to produce heat

read \ˈrēd\ *vb* **read** \ˈred\; **read•ing** \ˈrē-diŋ\
1 to understand language through written symbols for speech sounds
2 to speak aloud written or printed words ⟨I *read* a poem to the class.⟩
3 to learn from information provided in writing or printing ⟨We bought a newspaper to *read* about the fire.⟩
4 to discover something about by looking at certain characteristics or behavior ⟨*read* palms⟩ ⟨On his face I *read* boredom.⟩
5 to show by letters or numbers ⟨The thermometer *reads* zero.⟩
6 to explain what something is
7 to interpret stored data (as on a computer drive or optical disk) ⟨The DVD player has to *read* the disk.⟩

read•able \ˈrē-də-bəl\ *adj*
able to be read easily

read•er \ˈrē-dər\ *n*
1 ▼ a person who reads or has the ability to read
2 a book for learning or practicing reading

read•i•ly \ˈre-də-lē\ *adv*
1 quickly and easily ⟨The lid *readily* came off.⟩
2 without hesitation or complaint ⟨He *readily* agreed to help.⟩

read•ing \ˈrē-diŋ\ *n*
1 the act of reading ⟨a poetry *reading*⟩
2 something read or available to be read
3 the number or fact shown on an instrument ⟨Take a *reading* from the thermometer.⟩

read–only memory \ˈrēd-ˈōn-lē-\ *n*
ROM

reader 1: a child reading a book

read•out \'rēd-au̇t\ *n*
1 information from an automatic device (as a computer) that is recorded (as on a disk) or presented in a form that can be seen
2 an electronic device that presents information in a form that can be seen ⟨a calculator's *readout*⟩

[1]**ready** \'re-dē\ *adj* **read•i•er; read•i•est**
1 prepared for use or action ⟨Dinner is *ready.*⟩ ⟨I'm *ready* to eat.⟩
2 likely to do something ⟨I was *ready* to cry.⟩
3 WILLING 1 ⟨I'm *ready* to help.⟩
4 needing or wanting something as soon as possible ⟨I'm *ready* for some sleep.⟩
5 showing ease and promptness ⟨a *ready* smile⟩
6 available right away : HANDY ⟨*ready* money⟩
synonyms see QUICK
read•i•ness \'re-dē-nəs\ *n*

[2]**ready** *vb* **read•ied; ready•ing**
to prepare for use or action

ready–made \,re-dē-'mād\ *adj*
made beforehand in large numbers ⟨*ready-made* clothes⟩

[1]**re•al** \'rē-əl, 'rēl\ *adj*
1 not imaginary : ACTUAL ⟨Blondie's *real* name is Ashley.⟩
2 not artificial : GENUINE ⟨*real* leather⟩ ⟨He's a *real* gentleman.⟩

► **Synonyms** REAL, ACTUAL, and TRUE mean agreeing with known facts. REAL is used when a thing is what it appears to be. ⟨This is a *real* diamond.⟩ ACTUAL means that someone or something does or did occur or exist. ⟨Is Santa Claus an *actual* person?⟩ TRUE may be used of something that is real or actual. ⟨It's a *true* story.⟩ It may also be used of something that agrees with a standard. ⟨A whale is not a *true* fish.⟩

[2]**real** *adv*
[1]VERY 1 ⟨I had a *real* good time.⟩

real estate *n*
property consisting of buildings and land

re•al•ism \'rē-ə-,li-zəm\ *n*
willingness to face facts or to give in to what is necessary

re•al•is•tic \,rē-ə-'li-stik\ *adj*
1 true to life or nature ⟨a *realistic* painting⟩
2 ready to see things as they really are and to deal with them sensibly
re•al•is•ti•cal•ly \-ti-kə-lē\ *adv*

re•al•i•ty \rē-'a-lə-tē\ *n, pl* **re•al•i•ties**
1 the way things actually are ⟨Our trip is over. Now it's back to *reality.*⟩
2 someone or something that is real or actually exists ⟨He made his dream a *reality.*⟩

re•al•i•za•tion \,rē-ə-lə-'zā-shən\ *n*
1 the state of understanding or becoming aware of something
2 the act of accomplishing something planned or hoped for

[1]rear 1: a horse rearing

re•al•ize \'rē-ə-,līz\ *vb* **re•al•ized; re•al•iz•ing**
1 to be aware of : UNDERSTAND ⟨Do they *realize* the danger?⟩
2 to bring into being : ACCOMPLISH ⟨*realize* a lifelong ambition⟩
3 to get as a result of effort : GAIN ⟨Will your business *realize* a profit?⟩

re•al•ly \'rē-ə-lē, 'rē-lē\ *adv*
1 in fact ⟨She didn't *really* mean it.⟩
2 without question ⟨It's a *really* fine day.⟩

realm \'relm\ *n*
1 KINGDOM 1
2 field of activity or influence ⟨He's important in the *realm* of law.⟩

real time *n*
the actual time during which something takes place ⟨We chatted online in *real time.*⟩
real–time *adj*

re•al•ty \'rē-əl-tē\ *n*
REAL ESTATE

ream \'rēm\ *n*
1 a quantity of paper that may equal 480, 500, or 516 sheets
2 **reams** *pl* a great amount ⟨I took *reams* of notes in class.⟩

reap \'rēp\ *vb* **reaped; reap•ing**
1 to cut (as grain) or clear (as a field) with a sickle, scythe, or machine
2 [2]HARVEST 1 ⟨*reap* a crop⟩
3 to get as a result ⟨You'll *reap* the benefit of your hard work.⟩

reap•er \'rē-pər\ *n*
a worker or machine that harvests crops

re•ap•pear \,rē-ə-'pir\ *vb* **re•ap•peared; re•ap•pear•ing**
to appear again after not being seen for a while

[1]**rear** \'rir\ *vb* **reared; rear•ing**
1 ◄ to rise up on the hind legs ⟨The horse *reared* in fright.⟩
2 to bring up ⟨They wanted to *rear* children in the country.⟩
3 to rise high
4 to take care of the breeding and raising of ⟨*rear* cattle⟩

[2]**rear** *n*
1 the space or position at the back ⟨Go to the *rear* of the building.⟩
2 the part (as of an army) or area farthest from the enemy
3 the human buttocks

[3]**rear** *adj*
being at the back ⟨a *rear* tire⟩

re•ar•range \,rē-ə-'rānj\ *vb* **re•ar•ranged; re•ar•rang•ing**
to arrange again usually in a different way

[1]**rea•son** \'rē-zᵊn\ *n*
1 a statement given to explain a belief or an act ⟨My parents gave a *reason* for my absence.⟩
2 a fact that makes something right or fair to do ⟨I have *reasons* for what I did.⟩
3 [1]CAUSE 1 ⟨The child wanted to know the *reason* for rain.⟩
4 the power to think and understand in a logical way
5 a fair and sensible way of thinking about something ⟨He won't listen to *reason.*⟩

[2]**reason** *vb* **rea•soned; rea•son•ing**
1 to think in a logical way
2 to talk with another in a sensible way so as to influence his or her actions or opinions
3 to state or ask logically ⟨How, I *reasoned,* could such a thing happen?⟩

rea•son•able \'rēz-nə-bəl, 'rē-zᵊn-ə-bəl\ *adj*
1 fair and sensible ⟨I'm willing to compromise, but her demands are not *reasonable.*⟩
2 not too expensive
3 fairly or moderately good
rea•son•able•ness *n*
rea•son•ably \-blē\ *adv*

re•as•sur•ance \,rē-ə-'shu̇r-əns\ *n*
something that is said or done to make someone feel less afraid, upset, or doubtful

re•as•sure \ˌrē-ə-ˈshu̇r\ *vb* **re•as•sured**; **re•as•sur•ing**
to make (someone) feel less afraid, upset, or doubtful

rebate *n*
the return of part of a payment or of an amount owed ⟨Mail in your receipt and get a *rebate.*⟩

¹reb•el \ˈre-bəl\ *n*
1 a person who opposes or fights against a government
2 a person who does not obey authority or follow usual standards

²re•bel \ri-ˈbel\ *vb* **re•belled**; **re•bel•ling**
1 to be or fight against authority and especially the authority of a person's government
2 to feel or show anger, strong dislike, or disapproval

³reb•el \ˈre-bəl\ *adj*
opposing or fighting against a government or ruler

re•bel•lion \ri-ˈbel-yən\ *n*
1 open opposition to authority ⟨The strict rules caused *rebellion* in their class.⟩
2 an open fight by citizens against their government

re•bel•lious \ri-ˈbel-yəs\ *adj*
1 taking part in rebellion ⟨*rebellious* troops⟩
2 fighting against or refusing to obey authority ⟨a *rebellious* teenager⟩
re•bel•lious•ly *adv*
re•bel•lious•ness *n*

re•birth \ˌrē-ˈbərth, ˈrē-ˌbərth\ *n*
1 a period in which something becomes popular again
2 a period of new life or growth ⟨Spring brings signs of *rebirth.*⟩

re•born \ˌrē-ˈbȯrn\ *adj*
born again

¹re•bound \ˌrē-ˈbau̇nd\ *vb* **re•bound•ed**; **re•bound•ing**
1 to bounce back after hitting something
2 to get over a disappointment
3 to catch a basketball after a player has thrown it at the basket and has not scored a point

²re•bound \ˈrē-ˌbau̇nd\ *n*
1 the action of bouncing back after hitting something
2 an immediate reaction to a loss or disappointment
3 the act of catching a basketball after a player has thrown it at the basket and missed

¹re•buff \ri-ˈbəf\ *vb* **re•buffed**; **re•buff•ing**
to refuse (something) in a sharp or rude way ⟨His suggestion was *rebuffed.*⟩

²rebuff *n*
a sharp or rude refusal of something (as an offer)

re•build \ˌrē-ˈbild\ *vb* **re•built** \-ˈbilt\; **re•build•ing**
1 to make important repairs to or changes in ⟨I'm *rebuilding* an old house.⟩
2 to construct again

¹re•buke \ri-ˈbyük\ *vb* **re•buked**; **re•buk•ing**
to criticize severely ⟨She was *rebuked* for being late.⟩

²rebuke *n*
an expression of strong disapproval

re•bus \ˈrē-bəs\ *n*
a riddle or puzzle made up of letters, pictures, and symbols whose names sound like the syllables and words of a phrase or sentence ⟨I C U is a *rebus.*⟩

re•but \ri-ˈbət\ *vb* **re•but•ted**; **re•but•ting**
to prove to be wrong by argument or by proof

¹re•call \ri-ˈkȯl\ *vb* **re•called**; **re•call•ing**
1 to bring back to mind : REMEMBER ⟨I don't *recall* the address.⟩
2 to ask or order to come back ⟨Soldiers recently sent home were *recalled.*⟩

²re•call \ri-ˈkȯl, ˈrē-ˌkȯl\ *n*
1 the ability to remember or an instance of remembering
2 a command to return

re•cap•ture \ˌrē-ˈkap-chər\ *vb* **re•cap•tured**; **re•cap•tur•ing**
1 to regain possession of
2 to experience again ⟨I wish I could *recapture* my youth.⟩

rec'd. *abbr* received

re•cede \ri-ˈsēd\ *vb* **re•ced•ed**; **re•ced•ing**
1 to move back or away ⟨Floodwaters are *receding.*⟩
2 to become smaller or weaker

re•ceipt \ri-ˈsēt\ *n*
1 a written statement saying that money or goods have been received
2 RECIPE
3 the act of receiving ⟨I acknowledged *receipt* of the letter.⟩
4 **receipts** *pl* something received ⟨Put the *receipts* from the sale in a safe place.⟩

re•ceive \ri-ˈsēv\ *vb* **re•ceived**; **re•ceiv•ing**
1 to take or get something that is given, paid, or sent ⟨Did you *receive* the money I sent?⟩
2 ²EXPERIENCE ⟨*receive* a shock⟩
3 to accept as a visitor or member : WELCOME ⟨She's too ill to *receive* friends.⟩
4 to change incoming radio waves into sounds or pictures

re•ceiv•er \ri-ˈsē-vər\ *n*
1 a device for changing electricity or radio waves into light or sound ⟨a radio *receiver*⟩
2 a football player who catches passes thrown toward the opponent's goal

re•cent \ˈrē-sᵊnt\ *adj*
1 of or relating to a time not long past ⟨*recent* history⟩
2 having lately appeared to come into being : NEW, FRESH ⟨*recent* events⟩
re•cent•ly *adv*

re•cep•ta•cle \ri-ˈsep-tə-kəl\ *n*
something used to receive and hold smaller objects ⟨a trash *receptacle*⟩

re•cep•tion \ri-ˈsep-shən\ *n*
1 the act or manner of welcoming ⟨We got a warm *reception* from our new neighbors.⟩
2 a social gathering to celebrate something or welcome someone ⟨a wedding *reception*⟩
3 the ability to receive a radio or television broadcast
4 the act of catching a pass thrown toward the opponent's goal

re•cep•tion•ist \ri-ˈsep-shə-nist\ *n*
▼ an office employee who deals with callers or visitors

receptionist: a woman with her child talking to a receptionist behind the counter

re•cep•tive \ri-ˈsep-tiv\ *adj*
willing to consider new ideas

re•cep•tor \ri-ˈsep-tər\ *n*
a cell that receives a stimulus (as light or heat) and activates an associated nerve to send a message to the brain and that may be grouped into a sense organ (as a taste bud)

¹re•cess \ˈrē-ˌses, ri-ˈses\ *n*
1 a brief period for relaxation between work periods ⟨The students play ball at *recess.*⟩
2 a secret or hidden place
3 a hollow cut or built into a surface (as a wall) ⟨The room has a *recess* lined with books.⟩
4 a brief time off from the activity of a court

²recess *vb* **re•cessed**; **re•cess•ing**
1 to put into a hollow space ⟨The light fixture was *recessed* into the ceiling.⟩
2 to interrupt for or take a brief time off

re•ces•sion \ri-ˈse-shən\ *n*
a period of reduced business activity

re•ces•sive \ri-ˈse-siv\ *adj*
being or produced by a form of a gene whose effect can be hidden by a dominant gene and which can produce a noticeable effect only when two copies of the gene are present ⟨Blue eye color is a *recessive* trait.⟩

rec•i•pe \ˈre-sə-pē\ *n*
► a set of instructions for making something (as a food dish) by combining various things

► **Word History** In the Middle Ages, a doctor's instructions for taking a drug would begin with the Latin word *recipe*, literally, "take!" *Recipe* is a form used in commands of the verb *recipere*, meaning "to take" or "to receive." The verb *receive* itself comes from Latin *recipere*, but through French—as does the word *receipt*, which was once commonly used to mean "recipe." From its use as a name for a drug prescription, *recipe* extended its meaning to cover instructions for making other things we consume, such as prepared food.

re•cip•i•ent \ri-ˈsi-pē-ənt\ *n*
someone who receives something

re•cip•ro•cal \ri-ˈsi-prə-kəl\ *n*
one of a pair of numbers (as 9 and 1/9, 2/3 and 3/2) whose product is one

re•cit•al \ri-ˈsī-tᵊl\ *n*
1 ► a public performance of music or dance given by one or more people ⟨a piano *recital*⟩
2 an act of describing something usually in great detail

recital 1: a man giving a piano recital

20 MINUTES SERVES 4

HOT DOGS WITH SALSA

You will need
Large saucepan • Colander • Chopping board • Bread knife • Sharp knife
Spoon • Bowl • Lemon squeezer

For the hot dogs
4 Frankfurter sausages
4 hot-dog rolls

For the salsa
½ small onion
225 g (8 oz) tomatoes
½ lime
A few drops Tabasco sauce
Salt and pepper

Making the hot dogs

1 Heat a large saucepan of water until it *simmers*, then add the sausages. Cook them for 5 minutes, then drain them.

2 Warm the rolls in the oven for a few minutes, then split each one down the middle. Put a cooked sausage in each roll.

Making the salsa

1 *Chop* the onion finely. Cut the tomatoes in half, then scoop out and discard the seeds. Chop the tomato flesh finely.

2 Put the chopped tomato in a bowl. Add the onion, the juice of half a lime, the Tabasco, and the *seasoning* and mix well.

Serve the salsa in a small bowl.

This hot dog has a squiggle of mustard on top.

This one is topped with tomato ketchup.

This hot dog is topped with tomato salsa.

20

recipe: a recipe for making hot dogs with salsa

rec•i•ta•tion \ˌre-sə-ˈtā-shən\ *n*
1 the act or an instance of saying something out loud
2 the act of saying something in a particular order

re•cite \ri-ˈsīt\ *vb* **re•cit•ed**; **re•cit•ing**
1 to repeat from memory ⟨Please *recite* your poem.⟩
2 to tell about in detail ⟨He *recited* his experiences.⟩

reck•less \ˈre-kləs\ *adj*
showing lack of caution : engaging in wild careless behavior
reck•less•ly *adv*
reck•less•ness *n*

reck•on \ˈre-kən\ *vb* **reck•oned**; **reck•on•ing**
1 to believe that something is true or possible ⟨I *reckon* we're lost.⟩
2 CALCULATE 1 ⟨They *reckon* the distance to be a mile.⟩
3 to regard or think of as : CONSIDER ⟨She was *reckoned* among the leaders.⟩

re•claim \ri-ˈklām\ *vb* **re•claimed**; **re•claim•ing**
1 to get back (something that was lost or taken away) ⟨The skater *reclaimed* her championship.⟩
2 to restore to an original state ⟨*reclaim* a swamp⟩
3 to obtain from a waste product or by-product ⟨The bottles are made from *reclaimed* plastic.⟩

rec•la•ma•tion \ˌre-klə-ˈmā-shən\ *n*
the act or process of recovering : the state of being recovered

re•cline \ri-ˈklīn\ *vb* **re•clined**; **re•clin•ing**
1 to lie down or sit back usually in a relaxed way
2 to lean backward ⟨Does that chair *recline?*⟩

rec•og•ni•tion \ˌre-kig-ˈni-shən\ *n*
1 the act of knowing and remembering upon seeing
2 the act of accepting the existence, truth, or importance of something ⟨*recognition* of past mistakes⟩
3 special attention or notice ⟨The writer's work won *recognition.*⟩

rec•og•nize \ˈre-kig-ˌnīz\ *vb* **rec•og•nized**; **rec•og•niz•ing**
1 to know and remember upon seeing ⟨I *recognized* an old friend.⟩
2 to be willing to accept ⟨I *recognized* my own faults.⟩
3 to take approving notice of ⟨They *recognized* his bravery with a medal.⟩

[1]**re•coil** \ri-ˈkȯil\ *vb* **re•coiled; re•coil•ing**
1 to draw back ⟨He *recoiled* in horror.⟩
2 to spring back to or as if to a starting position ⟨The rifle *recoiled* upon firing.⟩

[2]**recoil** *n*
a sudden backward movement or springing back (as of a gun just fired)

rec•ol•lect \ˌre-kə-ˈlekt\ *vb* **rec•ol•lect•ed; rec•ol•lect•ing**
to call to mind : REMEMBER ⟨Can you *recollect* what happened?⟩

rec•ol•lec•tion \ˌre-kə-ˈlek-shən\ *n*
1 the act or power of remembering : MEMORY ⟨a good *recollection*⟩
2 something remembered ⟨*recollections* of childhood⟩

rec•om•mend \ˌre-kə-ˈmend\ *vb* **rec•om•mend•ed; rec•om•mend•ing**
1 to present or support as worthy or fit ⟨We *recommended* her for the job.⟩ ⟨Can you *recommend* a hotel?⟩
2 to make a suggestion : ADVISE ⟨I *recommend* that the matter be dropped.⟩
3 to make acceptable ⟨The plan has many points to *recommend* it.⟩

rec•om•men•da•tion \ˌre-kə-mən-ˈdā-shən\ *n*
1 the act of presenting or supporting as worthy or fit
2 a thing or course of action suggested as suitable or appropriate ⟨The doctor's *recommendation* was to rest.⟩
3 something (as a letter) that explains why a person is appropriate or qualified

[1]**rec•om•pense** \ˈre-kəm-ˌpens\ *vb* **rec•om•pensed; rec•om•pens•ing**
to pay for or pay back ⟨He was *recompensed* for his loss.⟩

[2]**recompense** *n*
something given in return for damage or suffering

rec•on•cile \ˈre-kən-ˌsīl\ *vb* **rec•on•ciled; rec•on•cil•ing**
1 to make friendly again ⟨She helped to *reconcile* friends who had been quarreling.⟩
2 to settle by agreement : ADJUST ⟨You'll have to *reconcile* your differences.⟩
3 to make agree ⟨His story cannot be *reconciled* with the facts.⟩
4 to cause to give in or accept ⟨I *reconciled* myself to the loss.⟩

rec•on•cil•i•a•tion \ˌre-kən-ˌsi-lē-ˈā-shən\ *n*
the act of becoming friendly again (as after a disagreement)

re•con•di•tion \ˌrē-kən-ˈdi-shən\ *vb* **re•con•di•tioned; re•con•di•tion•ing**
to restore to good condition

re•con•nais•sance \ri-ˈkä-nə-zəns\ *n*
a survey (as of enemy territory) to get information

re•con•sid•er \ˌrē-kən-ˈsi-dər\ *vb* **re•con•sid•ered; re•con•sid•er•ing**
to think carefully about again especially with the possibility of change or reversal

re•con•sid•er•a•tion \ˌrē-kən-ˌsi-də-ˈrā-shən\ *n*
the act of thinking carefully about again especially with the possibility of change or reversal

re•con•struct \ˌrē-kən-ˈstrəkt\ *vb* **re•con•struct•ed; re•con•struct•ing**
to make or form again : REBUILD

[1]**re•cord** \ri-ˈkȯrd\ *vb* **re•cord•ed; re•cord•ing**
1 to set down in writing
2 to show a measurement of
3 to change sound or visual images into a form (as on an optical disk or hard drive) that can be listened to or watched at a later time

[2]**rec•ord** \ˈre-kərd\ *n*
1 something written to give proof of something or tell about past events ⟨I read the historical *record*.⟩
2 something that recalls or tells about past events ⟨the fossil *record*⟩
3 a performance or achievement that is the best of its kind ⟨It's a new *record* for the fastest mile.⟩
4 the known or recorded facts about a person or thing ⟨He has a good school *record*.⟩
5 ▼ something on which sound or visual images have been recorded
of record made known in public documents
on record published in official documents

[2]**record 5:** a record on a record player

[3]**rec•ord** \ˈre-kərd\ *adj*
outstanding among other like things ⟨a *record* crop⟩ ⟨*record* high temperatures⟩

re•cord•er \ri-ˈkȯr-dər\ *n*
1 a person or device that records ⟨a digital video *recorder*⟩
2 a musical instrument like a long hollow whistle with eight holes for the fingers

re•cord•ing \ri-ˈkȯr-diŋ\ *n*
[2]RECORD 4

[1]**re•count** \ri-ˈkau̇nt\ *vb* **re•count•ed; re•count•ing**
to tell all about : NARRATE ⟨She *recounted* her adventures.⟩

[2]**re•count** \ˌrē-ˈkau̇nt\ *vb* **re•count•ed; re•count•ing**
to count again

[3]**re•count** \ˈrē-ˌkau̇nt, -ˈkau̇nt\ *n*
a counting again (as of election votes)

re•course \ˈrē-ˌkȯrs\ *n*
someone or something that can be turned to for help or protection

re•cov•er \ri-ˈkə-vər\ *vb* **re•cov•ered; re•cov•er•ing**
1 to get back : REGAIN ⟨I *recovered* my lost wallet.⟩
2 to regain or return to a normal or usual state (as of health or composure ⟨Have you *recovered* from the flu?⟩
3 to make up for ⟨We can't *recover* lost time.⟩

re•cov•ery \ri-ˈkə-və-rē, -ˈkəv-rē\ *n*, *pl* **re•cov•er•ies**
the act or process of regaining or returning to a normal or usual state ⟨She made a full *recovery*.⟩

rec•re•a•tion \ˌrek-rē-ˈā-shən\ *n*
something done for fun and relaxation ⟨We bike for *recreation*.⟩

[1]**re•cruit** \ri-ˈkrüt\ *vb* **re•cruit•ed; re•cruit•ing**
1 to enlist as a member of the armed forces
2 to get the services of ⟨The team *recruited* a new pitcher.⟩

[2]**recruit** *n*
1 a newly enlisted member of the armed forces
2 a newcomer to a group or field of activity

rect•an•gle \ˈrek-ˌtaŋ-gəl\ *n*
a flat geometric four-sided figure with right angles and with opposite sides parallel

rect•an•gu•lar \rek-ˈtaŋ-gyə-lər\ *adj*
shaped like a rectangle ⟨a *rectangular* building⟩

rec•ti•fy \ˈrek-tə-ˌfī\ *vb* **rec•ti•fied; rec•ti•fy•ing**
to set or make right ⟨She promised to *rectify* the problem.⟩

rec•tor \ˈrek-tər\ *n*
PASTOR

rec•tum \'rek-təm\ *n, pl* **rec•tums** *also* **rec•ta** \-tə\
the last part of the large intestine

re•cu•per•ate \ri-'kü-pə-,rāt, -'kyü-\ *vb* **re•cu•per•at•ed**; **re•cu•per•at•ing**
to regain health or strength

re•cu•per•a•tion \ri-,kü-pə-'rā-shən, -,kyü-\ *n*
a recovery of health or strength

re•cur \ri-'kər\ *vb* **re•curred**; **re•cur•ring**
to occur or appear again ⟨The fever *recurred.*⟩

re•cur•rence \ri-'kər-əns\ *n*
the state of occurring or appearing again or time after time

re•cur•rent \ri-'kər-ənt\ *adj*
happening or appearing again and again ⟨a *recurrent* infection⟩

recyclable: recyclable articles

re•cy•cla•ble \(,)rē-'sī-kə-lə-bəl\ *adj*
▲ able to be recycled ⟨*recyclable* plastic bottles⟩

re•cy•cle \,rē-'sī-kəl\ *vb* **re•cy•cled**; **re•cy•cling**
to process (as paper, glass, or cans) in order to regain or reuse materials

¹red \'red\ *adj* **red•der**; **red•dest**
1 of the color of blood : colored red ⟨a *red* light⟩
2 flushed with emotion (as embarrassment) ⟨His face was *red.*⟩
red•ness *n*

²red *n*
1 the color of blood or of the ruby
2 something red in color ⟨She's wearing *red.*⟩

red•bird \'red-,bərd\ *n*
any of several birds (as a cardinal) with mostly red feathers

red blood cell *n*
a tiny reddish cell of the blood that contains hemoglobin and carries oxygen from the lungs to the tissues

red•breast \'red-,brest\ *n*
a bird (as a robin) with a reddish breast

red cell *n*
RED BLOOD CELL

red•coat \'red-,kōt\ *n*
▼ a British soldier especially in America during the Revolutionary War

red•den \'re-dᵊn\ *vb* **red•dened**; **red•den•ing**
to make or become red ⟨The cold *reddened* our cheeks.⟩

red•dish \'re-dish\ *adj*
somewhat red

re•deem \ri-'dēm\ *vb*
1 to make up for ⟨The exciting ending *redeemed* the otherwise dull movie.⟩
2 to buy, get, or win back ⟨He *redeemed* his honor.⟩
3 to make good : FULFILL ⟨You must *redeem* your promise.⟩
4 to exchange for something of value ⟨I *redeemed* my tickets for a prize.⟩
5 to free from sin
re•deem•er *n*

redcoat: model of a redcoat

re•demp•tion \ri-'demp-shən\ *n*
1 the act of making up for ⟨The messy job was beyond *redemption.*⟩
2 an exchange for something of value ⟨*redemption* of empty soda cans⟩
3 the act of saving from sin

red–hand•ed \'red-'han-dəd\ *adv or adj*
in the act of doing something wrong ⟨I was caught *red-handed.*⟩

red•head \'red-,hed\ *n*
a person having reddish hair

red•head•ed \'red-,he-dəd\ *adj*
having reddish hair or a red head ⟨a *redheaded* girl⟩ ⟨*redheaded* birds⟩

red–hot \'red-'hät\ *adj*
1 glowing red with heat ⟨*red-hot* coals⟩
2 very active or successful ⟨a *red-hot* team⟩
3 extremely popular ⟨a *red-hot* fashion⟩

re•di•rect \,rē-də-'rekt, -dī-\ *vb* **re•di•rect•ed**; **re•di•rect•ing**
to change the course or direction of

re•dis•cov•er \,rē-dis-'kə-vər\ *vb* **re•dis•cov•ered**; **re•dis•cov•er•ing**
to discover again

red–let•ter \'red-'le-tər\ *adj*
of special importance : MEMORABLE ⟨This was a *red-letter* day in my life.⟩

re•do \,rē-'dü\ *vb* **re•did** \-'did\; **re•done** \-'dən\; **re•do•ing** \-'dü-iŋ\
to do over or again

re•dou•ble \rē-'də-bəl\ *vb* **re•dou•bled**; **re•dou•bling**
to greatly increase the size or amount of ⟨They *redoubled* their efforts.⟩

red panda *n*
▶ a long-tailed animal that is related to and resembles the raccoon, has long reddish brown fur, and is found from the Himalayas to southern China

re•dress \ri-'dres\ *vb* **re•dressed**; **re•dress•ing**
to set right : REMEDY ⟨The court will *redress* an injustice.⟩

red tape *n*
rules and regulations that seem unnecessary and prevent things from being done quickly and easily ⟨governmental *red tape*⟩

re•duce \ri-'düs, -'dyüs\ *vb* **re•duced**; **re•duc•ing**
1 to make smaller or less ⟨*reduce* expenses⟩ ⟨*Reduce* your speed ahead.⟩
2 to bring to a usually worse state ⟨The story *reduced* them to tears.⟩

3 to lower in grade or rank
4 to change to a simpler form ⟨*Reduce* a fraction to its lowest terms.⟩
5 to lose weight by dieting

re•duc•tion \ri-ˈdək-shən\ *n*
1 the act of making something smaller or less : the state of being made smaller or less ⟨a *reduction* in noise⟩
2 the amount by which something is made smaller or less

red•wood \ˈred-ˌwu̇d\ *n*
a very tall tree of California that bears cones and has light durable brownish red wood

reed \ˈrēd\ *n*
1 a tall slender grass that grows in wet areas
2 a stem or a growth or mass of reeds
3 a thin flexible piece of cane, plastic, or metal fastened to the mouthpiece of an instrument (as a clarinet) or over an air opening in an instrument (as an accordion) and made to vibrate by an air current

reef \ˈrēf\ *n*
▶ a chain of rocks or coral or a ridge of sand at or near the surface of water

[1]reek \ˈrēk\ *n*
a strong or unpleasant smell

[2]reek *vb* **reeked**; **reek•ing**
to have a strong or unpleasant smell

red panda

reef: an overhead view of part of the Great Barrier Reef, Australia

[1]reel \ˈrēl\ *n*
1 a device that can be turned round and round to wind up something flexible ⟨a fishing rod and *reel*⟩
2 ▶ a quantity of something wound on a reel ⟨a *reel* of film⟩

[2]reel *vb* **reeled**; **reel•ing**
1 to wind on a reel
2 to pull by the use of a reel ⟨I *reeled* in a fish.⟩
reel off to say or recite rapidly or easily ⟨He can *reel off* the answers.⟩

[3]reel *vb* **reeled**; **reel•ing**
1 to whirl or spin around
2 to be in a confused or dizzy state ⟨Our heads were *reeling* with excitement.⟩
3 to fall back suddenly (as after being hit)
4 to walk or move unsteadily : STAGGER

[4]reel *n*
a lively folk dance

re•elect \ˌrē-ə-ˈlekt\ *vb* **re•elect•ed**; **re•elect•ing**
to elect for another term

re•en•act \ˌrē-ə-ˈnakt\ *vb* **re•en•act•ed**; **re•en•act•ing**
to repeat the actions of (an earlier event) ⟨The group *reenacted* the battle.⟩

re•en•ter \ˌrē-ˈen-tər\ *vb* **re•en•tered**; **re•en•ter•ing**
to enter again

re•es•tab•lish \ˌrē-i-ˈsta-blish\ *vb* **re•es•tab•lished**; **re•es•tab•lish•ing**
to establish again : bring back into existence ⟨*reestablished* communication.⟩

ref \ˈref\ *n*
[1]REFEREE 1

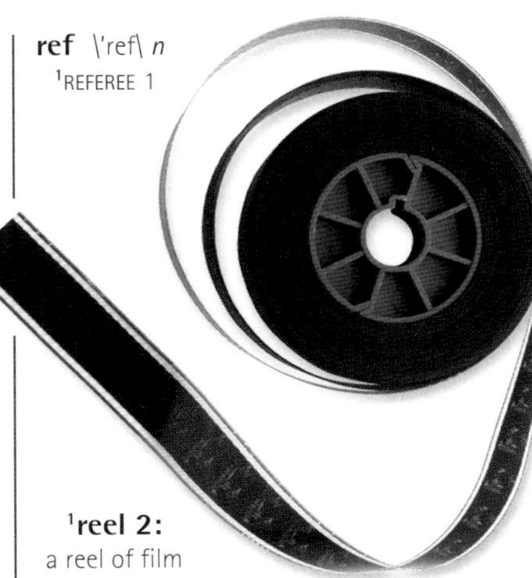
[1]reel 2: a reel of film

re•fer \ri-ˈfər\ *vb* **re•ferred**; **re•fer•ring**
1 to look at for information ⟨She kept *referring* to her notes.⟩
2 to send or direct to some person or place for treatment, aid, information, or decision ⟨The patient was *referred* to a specialist.⟩
3 to call attention ⟨The teacher *referred* to a story in the newspaper.⟩
4 to mention (something) in talking or writing

[1]ref•er•ee \ˌre-fə-ˈrē\ *n*
1 a sports official with final authority for conducting a game
2 a person who is asked to settle a disagreement

[2]referee *vb* **ref•er•eed**; **ref•er•ee•ing**
to act or be in charge of as referee ⟨I *referee* basketball games.⟩

a b c d e f g h i j k l m n o p q r s t u v w x y z

ref•er•ence \'re-fə-rəns, 'ref-rəns\ *n*
1 the act of looking at or in something for information
2 a relation to or concern with something ⟨I am writing in *reference* to your advertisement.⟩
3 the act or an instance of mentioning ⟨They made no *references* to my error.⟩
4 a work (as a dictionary) that contains useful information
5 something that refers a reader to another source of information
6 a person who can be asked for information about another person's character or ability
7 a written statement about someone's character or ability

ref•er•en•dum \,re-fə-'ren-dəm\ *n, pl* **ref•er•en•da** \-də\ *or* **ref•er•en•dums**
the practice of voting on an issue

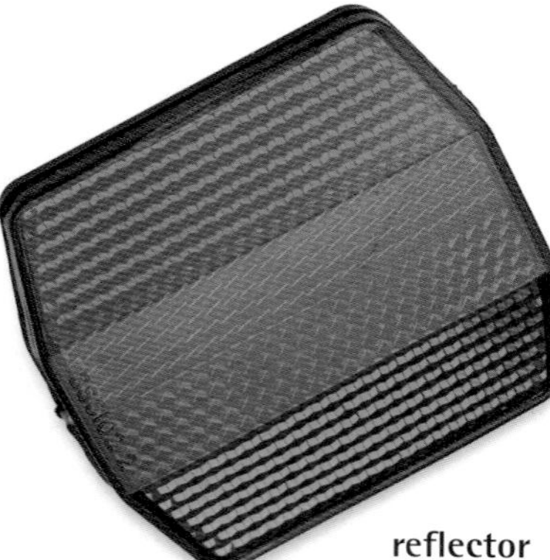
reflector

[1]**re•fill** \,rē-'fil\ *vb* **re•filled**; **re•fill•ing**
to fill or become filled again

[2]**re•fill** \'rē-,fil\ *n*
a new or fresh supply of something

re•fine \ri-'fīn\ *vb* **re•fined**; **re•fin•ing**
1 to bring to a pure state ⟨*refine* sugar⟩
2 to make better : IMPROVE ⟨He's *refining* his recipe.⟩

re•fined \ri-'fīnd\ *adj*
1 having or showing good taste or training ⟨She has *refined* manners.⟩
2 freed from impurities : PURE ⟨*refined* gold⟩

re•fine•ment \ri-'fīn-mənt\ *n*
1 the act or process of improving something or bringing something to a pure state ⟨*refinement* of sugar⟩
2 excellence of manners or tastes ⟨a person of *refinement*⟩
3 a small change meant to improve something

re•fin•ery \ri-'fī-nə-rē\ *n, pl* **re•fin•er•ies**
a building and equipment where something (as oil or metal) is made pure and ready for use

re•fin•ish \,rē-'fi-nish\ *vb* **re•fin•ished**; **re•fin•ish•ing**
to give (as furniture) a new surface

re•fit \,rē-'fit\ *vb* **re•fit•ted**; **re•fit•ting**
to make ready for use again ⟨*refit* a ship⟩

re•flect \ri-'flekt\ *vb* **re•flect•ed**; **re•flect•ing**
1 to bend or throw back (waves of light, sound, or heat) ⟨A polished surface *reflects* light.⟩
2 to give back an image or likeness of in the manner of a mirror ⟨The clouds were *reflected* in the water.⟩
3 to make known ⟨The book *reflects* her beliefs.⟩
4 to cause to be thought of in a specified way or in a bad way ⟨Your poor behavior *reflects* on the whole class.⟩
5 to think seriously and carefully about ⟨I *reflected* on the problem.⟩

re•flec•tion \ri-'flek-shən\ *n*
1 the return of light or sound waves from a surface
2 an image produced by or as if by a mirror
3 something that brings blame or disgrace ⟨It's a *reflection* on my honesty.⟩
4 careful thought ⟨After much *reflection*, I agreed.⟩
5 an opinion formed or a remark made after careful thought

re•flec•tor \ri-'flek-tər\ *n*
◀ a shiny surface for reflecting light or heat

re•flex \'rē-,fleks\ *n*
1 an action or movement that is made automatically without thinking as a reaction to a stimulus
2 **re•flex•es** *pl* the natural ability to react quickly ⟨A driver needs good *reflexes*.⟩

re•for•est \,rē-'fȯr-əst\ *vb* **re•for•est•ed**; **re•for•est•ing**
to renew forest growth by planting seeds or young trees

re•for•es•ta•tion \,rē-,fȯr-ə-'stā-shən\ *n*
the act of renewing forest growth by planting seeds or young trees

[1]**re•form** \ri-'fȯrm\ *vb* **re•formed**; **re•form•ing**
1 to make better or improve by removal of faults ⟨The program *reforms* prisoners.⟩ ⟨The law should be *reformed*.⟩
2 to stop engaging in bad habits or behavior ⟨He promised to *reform*.⟩
re•form•er \ri-'fȯr-mər\ *n*

[2]**reform** *n*
the improvement of something by removing faults or problems ⟨political *reform*⟩

ref•or•ma•tion \,re-fər-'mā-shən\ *n*
the act of changing something or someone for the better

re•fract \ri-'frakt\ *vb* **re•fract•ed**; **re•fract•ing**
to make (light) bend when it passes through at an angle

re•frac•tion \ri-'frak-shən\ *n*
the bending of a ray when it passes at an angle from one medium into another in which its speed is different (as when light passes from air into water)

re•frac•to•ry \ri-'frak-tə-rē\ *adj*
1 resisting control or authority : STUBBORN ⟨a *refractory* child⟩
2 capable of enduring very high temperatures ⟨*refractory* clays⟩

[1]**re•frain** \ri-'frān\ *vb* **re•frained**; **re•frain•ing**
to keep from giving in to a desire or impulse

[2]**refrain** *n*
a phrase or verse repeated regularly in a poem or song

re•fresh \ri-'fresh\ *vb* **re•freshed**; **re•fresh•ing**
to bring back to an original state or normal condition (as by restoring energy or making more active) ⟨Let me *refresh* your memory.⟩
re•fresh•er *n*

re•fresh•ment \ri-'fresh-mənt\ *n*
something (as food or drink) that refreshes — often used in pl.

re•frig•er•ate \ri-'fri-jə-,rāt\ *vb* **re•frig•er•at•ed**; **re•frig•er•at•ing**
to make or keep cold or cool especially by placing in a refrigerator

re•frig•er•a•tor \ri-'fri-jə-,rā-tər\ *n*
▼ a device or room for keeping articles (as food) cool

refrigerator:
a refrigerator full of food

re•fu•el \ˌrē-ˈfyü-əl\ *vb* **re•fu•eled**; **re•fu•el•ing**
to provide with or take on more fuel

ref•uge \ˈre-fyüj\ *n*
1 shelter or protection from danger or distress ⟨We took *refuge* in a nearby barn.⟩
2 a place that provides shelter or protection ⟨a wildlife *refuge*⟩

ref•u•gee \ˌre-fyu̇-ˈjē\ *n*
a person who flees for safety (as from war) usually to a foreign country

¹re•fund \ri-ˈfənd\ *vb* **re•fund•ed**; **re•fund•ing**
to return (money) as repayment ⟨If you are not satisfied the purchase price will be *refunded.*⟩

²re•fund \ˈrē-ˌfənd\ *n*
an amount of money that is returned as repayment

re•fus•al \ri-ˈfyü-zəl\ *n*
the act of showing unwillingness to do, give, or allow something

¹re•fuse \ri-ˈfyüz\ *vb* **re•fused**; **re•fus•ing**
1 to express unwillingness to accept : turn down (something) ⟨I *refused* the job.⟩
2 to express or show unwillingness to do, give, or allow something ⟨They *refused* to help.⟩

²ref•use \ˈre-ˌfyüs\ *n*
TRASH 1, RUBBISH

re•fute \ri-ˈfyüt\ *vb* **re•fut•ed**; **re•fut•ing**
to say or prove that something is wrong or untrue

reg. *abbr*
1 region
2 regular

re•gain \ri-ˈgān\ *vb* **re•gained**; **re•gain•ing**
1 to gain or get again : get back ⟨I *regained* my health.⟩
2 to get back to : reach again ⟨The swimmer *regained* the shore.⟩

re•gal \ˈrē-gəl\ *adj*
relating to or suitable for a king or queen : ROYAL
re•gal•ly *adv*

re•gale \ri-ˈgāl\ *vb* **re•galed**; **re•gal•ing**
to give pleasure or amusement to ⟨He *regaled* his guests with stories.⟩

¹re•gard \ri-ˈgärd\ *n*
1 CONSIDERATION 2 ⟨She shows no *regard* for others.⟩
2 a feeling of respect ⟨She was held in high *regard.*⟩
3 **regards** *pl* friendly greetings ⟨Give them my *regards.*⟩
4 a point to be considered ⟨Be careful in this *regard.*⟩
5 ²LOOK 1 ⟨a tender *regard*⟩
in regard to in relation to
with regard to in relation to

²regard *vb* **re•gard•ed**; **re•gard•ing**
1 to think of in a particular way : CONSIDER ⟨He *regarded* them as friends.⟩
2 to look at ⟨The police *regarded* them with suspicion.⟩
3 to give consideration to

re•gard•ing \ri-ˈgär-diŋ\ *prep*
relating to : ABOUT ⟨She talked with them *regarding* their behavior.⟩

re•gard•less \ri-ˈgärd-ləs\ *adv*
in spite of something that might be a problem ⟨It may rain, but I will go *regardless.*⟩

regardless of *prep*
in spite of ⟨He jogs every day *regardless of* the weather.⟩

re•gat•ta \ri-ˈgä-tə, -ˈga-\ *n*
▼ a race or a series of races between sailboats, speedboats, or rowing boats

regatta: a sailing regatta in Australia

re•gen•er•ate \ri-ˈje-nə-ˌrāt\ *vb* **re•gen•er•at•ed**; **re•gen•er•at•ing**
to grow (as a lost body part) once more

re•gent \ˈrē-jənt\ *n*
a person who temporarily governs a kingdom in place of a monarch

re•gime \rā-ˈzhēm, ri-\ *n*
1 a form or system of government ⟨a military *regime*⟩
2 REGIMEN

reg•i•men \ˈre-jə-mən\ *n*
a systematic course of action ⟨a daily exercise *regimen*⟩

reg•i•ment \ˈre-jə-mənt\ *n*
a military unit made up usually of a number of battalions

re•gion \ˈrē-jən\ *n*
1 an area having no definite boundaries ⟨darker *regions* of the night sky⟩
2 a broad geographic area
3 VICINITY 1 ⟨He felt pain in the *region* of the heart.⟩

re•gion•al \ˈrē-jə-nᵊl\ *adj*
of, relating to, or characteristic of a certain geographic area ⟨a *regional* newspaper⟩

¹reg•is•ter \ˈre-jə-stər\ *n*
1 an official list or book for keeping records of something ⟨Guests signed the hotel *register.*⟩
2 a mechanical device (as a cash register) that records items
3 a device for regulating ventilation or the flow of heated air from a furnace

²register *vb* **reg•is•tered**; **reg•is•ter•ing**
1 to enter or enroll in an official list or book of public records ⟨I *registered* to vote.⟩
2 to record automatically ⟨The thermometer *registered* 15 degrees.⟩
3 to show by expression and bodily movements ⟨Her face *registered* surprise.⟩
4 to make known officially and publicly ⟨I'd like to *register* a complaint.⟩
5 to be recognized or remembered ⟨His name didn't *register* with me.⟩
6 to get special protection for (something mailed) by paying extra postage

reg•is•tra•tion \ˌre-jə-ˈstrā-shən\ *n*
1 the act of entering on an official list ⟨Kindergarten *registration* begins today.⟩
2 a document showing that something is registered ⟨a car *registration*⟩

reg•is•try \ˈre-jə-strē\ *n, pl* **reg•is•tries**
a place where registration takes place ⟨a *registry* of motor vehicles⟩

¹re•gret \ri-ˈgret\ *vb* **re•gret•ted**; **re•gret•ting**
to be sorry for ⟨She *regrets* her rash decision.⟩

²regret *n*
1 sadness or disappointment caused especially by something beyond a person's control
2 an expression of sorrow or disappointment
3 **regrets** *pl* a note politely refusing to accept an invitation ⟨I send my *regrets.*⟩

re•gret•ful \ri-'gret-fəl\ *adj*
feeling or showing regret
re•gret•ful•ly \-fə-lē\ *adv*

re•gret•ta•ble \ri-'gre-tə-bəl\ *adj*
causing sorrow or disappointment ⟨a *regrettable* mistake⟩
re•gret•ta•bly \-blē\ *adv*

re•group \,rē-'grüp\ *vb* **re•grouped**; **re•group•ing**
1 to form into a group again ⟨The students *regrouped* after recess.⟩
2 to form into a new group ⟨To subtract 129 from 531 *regroup* 531 into 5 hundreds, 2 tens, and 11 ones.⟩

reg•u•lar \'re-gyə-lər\ *adj*
1 steady in practice or occurrence : happening on or as if on a schedule ⟨a *regular* routine⟩ ⟨The club holds *regular* meetings.⟩
2 following established usages or rules ⟨*regular* procedures⟩
3 ¹NORMAL 1 ⟨Practice will be at the *regular* time.⟩ ⟨The *regular* price is $15.⟩
4 following the usual manner of inflection ⟨"Talk" is a *regular* verb, but "say" is not.⟩
5 having all sides equal and all angles equal ⟨a *regular* polygon⟩
reg•u•lar•ly *adv*

▶ **Synonyms** REGULAR, NORMAL, and TYPICAL mean being of the sort that is considered to be usual, ordinary, or average. REGULAR is used of something that follows a rule, standard, or pattern. ⟨The team has *regular* afternoon practice.⟩ NORMAL is used of something that does not vary from what is the most usual or expected. ⟨That's *normal* behavior for a two-year-old.⟩ TYPICAL is used of something that shows all the important characteristics of a type or group. ⟨Ours is a *typical* small town.⟩

reg•u•lar•i•ty \,re-gyə-'ler-ə-tē\ *n*
the quality or state of happening on or as if on a schedule

reg•u•late \'re-gyə-,lāt\ *vb* **reg•u•lat•ed**; **reg•u•lat•ing**
1 to bring under the control of authority : make rules concerning ⟨Laws *regulate* water quality.⟩
2 to control the time, amount, degree, or rate of ⟨The dam *regulates* water flow.⟩
3 to bring order or method to ⟨The program is *regulated* well.⟩
reg•u•la•tor \-,lā-tər\ *n*

reg•u•la•tion \,re-gyə-'lā-shən\ *n*
1 a rule or law telling how something is to be done ⟨safety *regulations*⟩
2 the act of controlling or bringing under control

re•gur•gi•tate \rē-'gər-jə-,tāt\ *vb* **re•gur•gi•tat•ed**; **re•gur•gi•tat•ing**
to bring food that has been swallowed back to and out of the mouth

re•hears•al \ri-'hər-səl\ *n*
a private performance or practice session in preparation for a public appearance

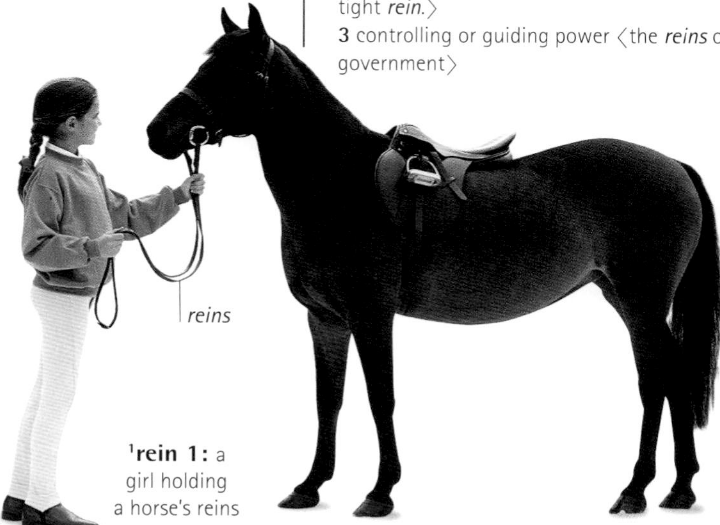

¹rein 1: a girl holding a horse's reins

re•hearse \ri-'hərs\ *vb* **re•hearsed**; **re•hears•ing**
to practice in private in preparation for a public performance ⟨We *rehearsed* our play.⟩

▶ **Word History** A device called a harrow is used to break up and smooth soil. Sometimes the first run with the harrow does not break up all the lumps of earth, and the farmer has to take the harrow over the ground more than once. The medieval French verb *rehercer* (from *herce*, "harrow") meant "to go over again with a harrow." English borrowed this verb as *rehersen*, later *rehearse.* When we rehearse something we are, so to speak, going over the same ground again and again.

¹reign \'rān\ *n*
1 the authority or rule of a monarch
2 the time during which a monarch rules

²reign *vb* **reigned**; **reign•ing**
1 to rule as a monarch
2 to be usual or widespread ⟨Enthusiasm *reigned* in the classroom.⟩
3 to be the best or most powerful ⟨the *reigning* champions⟩

re•im•burse \,rē-əm-'bərs\ *vb* **re•im•bursed**; **re•im•burs•ing**
to pay back : REPAY
re•im•burse•ment \-mənt\ *n*

¹rein \'rān\ *n*
1 ▼ a line or strap that is attached at either end of the bit of a bridle and is used to control an animal — usually used in pl.
2 an influence that slows, limits, or holds back ⟨The parents kept their child under a tight *rein.*⟩
3 controlling or guiding power ⟨the *reins* of government⟩

²rein *vb* **reined**; **rein•ing**
to check, control, or stop by or as if by reins

re•in•car•na•tion \,rē-,in-,kär-'nā-shən\ *n*
rebirth of the soul in a new body after death

rein•deer \'rān-,dir\ *n, pl* **reindeer**
CARIBOU

re•in•force \,rē-ən-'fȯrs\ *vb* **re•in•forced**; **re•in•forc•ing**
1 to strengthen with new supplies or more people
2 to strengthen by adding more material for support ⟨The wall needs to be *reinforced.*⟩

re•in•force•ment \,rē-ən-'fȯr-smənt\ *n*
1 people or things (as supplies) sent to help or support
2 the act of making something stronger or able to last longer

re•in•state \,rē-ən-'stāt\ *vb* **re•in•stat•ed**; **re•in•stat•ing**
to place again in a former position or condition ⟨The fired employee was *reinstated.*⟩
re•in•state•ment \-mənt\ *n*

re•it•er•ate \rē-ˈi-tə-ˌrāt\ *vb* **re•it•er•at•ed; re•it•er•at•ing**
to repeat something said or done ⟨I *reiterated* my warning.⟩

[1]re•ject \ri-ˈjekt\ *vb* **re•ject•ed; re•ject•ing**
to refuse to accept, believe, or consider ⟨Dad *rejected* my excuse.⟩ ⟨He *rejected* their offer.⟩

[2]re•ject \ˈrē-ˌjekt\ *n*
a person or thing not accepted as good enough for some purpose

re•jec•tion \ri-ˈjek-shən\ *n*
the act of not accepting, believing, or considering something : the state of being rejected

re•joice \ri-ˈjȯis\ *vb* **re•joiced; re•joic•ing**
to feel or show joy or happiness ⟨We *rejoiced* over their good luck.⟩

re•join \ri-ˈjȯin\ *vb* **re•joined; re•join•ing**
1 to join again : return to ⟨I *rejoined* my family after the trip.⟩
2 to reply often in a sharp or critical way

re•join•der \ri-ˈjȯin-dər\ *n*
[2]REPLY

re•kin•dle \ˌrē-ˈkin-dᵊl\ *vb* **re•kin•dled; re•kin•dling**
to cause to be active again ⟨*rekindle* a fire⟩ ⟨*rekindle* hope⟩

[1]re•lapse \ri-ˈlaps, ˈrē-ˌlaps\ *n*
1 a return of illness after a period of improvement
2 a return to a former and undesirable state or condition ⟨a *relapse* into bad habits⟩

[2]re•lapse \ri-ˈlaps\ *vb* **re•lapsed; re•laps•ing**
to return to a former state or condition (as of illness or bad behavior) after a change for the better

re•late \ri-ˈlāt\ *vb* **re•lat•ed; re•lat•ing**
1 to give an account of : NARRATE ⟨*related* their experiences⟩
2 to show or have a relationship to or between : CONNECT ⟨The events are *related.*⟩ ⟨The lesson *relates* to history.⟩

re•lat•ed \ri-ˈlā-təd\ *adj*
1 sharing some connection ⟨painting and the *related* arts⟩
2 connected by common ancestry or by marriage ⟨We call her "auntie," but we're not actually *related.*⟩
3 connected by a usually distant common ancestor and typically sharing similar characteristics ⟨Horses and zebras are *related.*⟩

re•la•tion \ri-ˈlā-shən\ *n*
1 CONNECTION 2, RELATIONSHIP ⟨Doctors studied the *relation* between sleep and health.⟩
2 a related person : RELATIVE
3 REFERENCE 2, RESPECT ⟨He'll speak in *relation* to this matter.⟩
4 **relations** *pl* the interaction between two or more people, groups, or countries ⟨foreign *relations*⟩

re•la•tion•ship \ri-ˈlā-shən-ˌship\ *n*
1 the state of being related or connected
2 connection by common ancestry or marriage
3 the state of interaction between two or more people, groups, or countries ⟨The sisters have a close *relationship.*⟩

[1]rel•a•tive \ˈre-lə-tiv\ *n*
a person connected with another by ancestry or marriage

[2]relative *adj*
1 existing in comparison to something else ⟨What is the *relative* value of the two houses?⟩
2 RELEVANT ⟨Please ask questions *relative* to the topic.⟩
rel•a•tive•ly *adv*

re•lax \ri-ˈlaks\ *vb* **re•laxed; re•lax•ing**
1 to make or become loose or less tense ⟨*Relax* your muscles.⟩ ⟨She *relaxed* her grip on the reins.⟩
2 to make or become less severe or strict ⟨Mom *relaxed* the rules for the summer.⟩
3 to become calm and free from stress
4 to seek rest or enjoyment ⟨You can *relax* at the beach.⟩

re•lax•a•tion \ˌrē-ˌlak-ˈsā-shən\ *n*
1 the act or fact of being or becoming rested, calm, or less tense or severe
2 a way of becoming rested or calm and free from stress ⟨I listen to music for *relaxation.*⟩

[1]re•lay \ˈrē-ˌlā\ *n*
1 ▼ a race between teams in which each team member covers a certain part of the course
2 the act of passing something from one person to the next
3 a fresh supply (as of horses or people) arranged to relieve others

[1]relay 1: a runner finishes her part of the relay by passing a stick called a baton to the next runner

[2]re•lay \ˈrē-ˌlā, ri-ˈlā\ *vb* **re•layed; re•lay•ing**
to pass along by stages ⟨Please *relay* the message to the others.⟩

[1]re•lease \ri-ˈlēs\ *vb* **re•leased; re•leas•ing**
1 to set free or let go of ⟨The fish was caught and *released.*⟩ ⟨He *released* his hold on the rope.⟩
2 to allow to escape ⟨The factory *released* chemicals into the river.⟩
3 to relieve from a duty, responsibility, or burden ⟨She *released* him from his promise.⟩
4 to give up or hand over to someone else ⟨I *released* my claim.⟩
5 to permit to be published, sold, or shown ⟨The movie will be *released* next month.⟩

[2]release *n*
1 the act of setting free or letting go ⟨*release* of a prisoner⟩
2 the act of allowing something to escape ⟨the *release* of smoke⟩
3 a discharge from an obligation or responsibility
4 relief or rescue from sorrow, suffering, or trouble ⟨*release* from pain⟩
5 a device for holding or releasing a mechanism
6 the act of making something available to the public
7 something (as a new product or song) that is made available to the public

re•lent \ri-ˈlent\ *vb* **re•lent•ed; re•lent•ing**
1 to become less severe, harsh, or strict ⟨The wind *relented* by evening.⟩
2 to give in after first resisting or refusing

re•lent•less \ri-ˈlent-ləs\ *adj*
showing no lessening of severity, intensity, or strength ⟨*relentless* heat⟩
re•lent•less•ly *adv*
re•lent•less•ness *n*

relief 6:
an ancient Greek relief

rel•e•vance \'re-lə-vəns\ *n*
relation to the matter at hand

rel•e•vant \'re-lə-vənt\ *adj*
having something to do with the matter at hand ⟨a *relevant* question⟩

re•li•abil•i•ty \ri-,lī-ə-'bi-lə-tē\ *n*
the quality or state of being fit to be trusted or relied on ⟨a car's *reliability*⟩

re•li•able \ri-'lī-ə-bəl\ *adj*
fit to be trusted or relied on : DEPENDABLE
re•li•ably \-blē\ *adv*

re•li•ance \ri-'lī-əns\ *n*
the act or state of depending on someone or something ⟨The nation's *reliance* on petroleum is growing.⟩

rel•ic \'re-lik\ *n*
1 something left behind after decay or disappearance ⟨They uncovered *relics* of an ancient city.⟩
2 an object that is considered holy because of its connection with a saint or martyr

re•lief \ri-'lēf\ *n*
1 the feeling of happiness that occurs when something unpleasant or distressing stops or does not happen ⟨What a *relief* to be home safe.⟩
2 removal or lessening of something painful or troubling ⟨I need *relief* from this headache.⟩
3 something that interrupts in a welcome way ⟨The rain was a *relief* from dry weather.⟩
4 release from a post or from performance of a duty ⟨*relief* of a guard⟩
5 WELFARE 2
6◀ a sculpture in which figures or designs are raised from a background
7 elevations of a land surface ⟨The map shows *relief*.⟩

re•lieve \ri-'lēv\ *vb* **re•lieved**; **re•liev•ing**
1 to free partly or wholly from a burden, pain, or distress ⟨The phone call *relieved* the worried parents.⟩
2 to bring about the removal or lessening of ⟨No words could *relieve* her sorrow.⟩
3 to release from a post or duty ⟨*relieve* a sentry⟩
4 to break the sameness of ⟨The dark red house was *relieved* by white trim.⟩
re•liev•er *n*

re•li•gion \ri-'li-jən\ *n*
1 the belief in and worship of God or gods
2 a system of religious beliefs and practices

re•li•gious \ri-'li-jəs\ *adj*
1 believing in God or gods and following the practices of a religion ⟨a *religious* person⟩
2 of or relating to religion ⟨*religious* books⟩
3 very devoted and faithful ⟨She's *religious* about wearing a seat belt.⟩
re•li•gious•ly *adv*

re•lin•quish \ri-'liŋ-kwish\ *vb* **re•lin•quished**; **re•lin•quish•ing**
to let go of : give up

[1]rel•ish \'re-lish\ *n*
1 great enjoyment ⟨He plays the game with *relish*.⟩
2► a highly seasoned food eaten with other food to add flavor

[1]relish 2:
a jar of corn and pepper relish

[2]relish *vb* **rel•ished**; **rel•ish•ing**
1 to be pleased by : ENJOY ⟨She *relishes* the attention she's been getting.⟩
2 to like the taste of

re•live \,rē-'liv\ *vb* **re•lived**; **re•liv•ing**
to experience again (as in the imagination)

re•luc•tance \ri-'lək-təns\ *n*
the quality or state of showing doubt or unwillingness

re•luc•tant \ri-'lək-tənt\ *adj*
showing doubt or unwillingness ⟨She was *reluctant* to go.⟩
re•luc•tant•ly *adv*

re•ly \ri-'lī\ *vb* **re•lied**; **re•ly•ing**
to trust in or depend on ⟨I *rely* on my family to help me out.⟩

re•main \ri-'mān\ *vb* **re•mained**; **re•main•ing**
1 to stay in the same place ⟨Please *remain* in your seats.⟩
2 to stay after others have gone ⟨Only one bus *remained* at school.⟩
3 to continue to be ⟨The weather *remained* cold.⟩ ⟨They *remained* friends.⟩
4 to be left after others have been removed, subtracted, or destroyed ⟨Little *remained* after the fire.⟩
5 to be something yet to be done or considered ⟨Her innocence *remains* to be proved.⟩

re•main•der \ri-'mān-dər\ *n*
1 a group or part that is left ⟨She took the *remainder* of the cake.⟩
2 the number left after a subtraction ⟨5 minus 3 leaves a *remainder* of 2.⟩
3 the number left over from the dividend after division that is less than the divisor

re•mains \ri-'mānz\ *n pl*
1 whatever is left over or behind ⟨the *remains* of a meal⟩
2 a dead body

re•make \,rē-'māk\ *vb* **re•made** \-'mād\; **re•mak•ing**
to make again or in a different form

[1]re•mark \ri-'märk\ *n*
1 a brief comment ⟨He made a rude *remark*.⟩
2 **remarks** *pl* a short speech

[2]remark *vb* **re•marked**; **re•mark•ing**
to make a comment : express as an observation ⟨"We've met before," I *remarked*.⟩

re•mark•able \ri-'mär-kə-bəl\ *adj*
worthy of being or likely to be noticed especially as being unusual ⟨You've made *remarkable* progress.⟩
re•mark•ably \-blē\ *adv*

re•match \'rē-,mach\ *n*
a second meeting between the same contestants

re•me•di•al \ri-'mē-dē-əl\ *adj*
intended to make something better ⟨He takes classes in *remedial* reading.⟩

[1]rem•e•dy \'re-mə-dē\ *n, pl* **rem•e•dies**
1 a medicine or treatment that cures or relieves
2 something that corrects a problem

[2]remedy *vb* **rem•e•died**; **rem•e•dy•ing**
to provide or serve as a cure or solution for

re•mem•ber \ri-ˈmem-bər\ *vb* **re•mem•bered**; **re•mem•ber•ing**
1 to bring to mind or think of again ⟨Do you *remember* my name?⟩
2 to keep in mind ⟨Please *remember* your promise.⟩
3 to pass along greetings from ⟨*Remember* us to your family.⟩

re•mem•brance \ri-ˈmem-brəns\ *n*
1 the act of thinking about again ⟨My *remembrance* of the party made me laugh.⟩
2 MEMORY 4
3 something that is done to honor the memory of a person or event
4 something (as a souvenir) that brings to mind a past experience

re•mind \ri-ˈmīnd\ *vb* **re•mind•ed**; **re•mind•ing**
to cause to remember ⟨I'm calling to *remind* you of your appointment.⟩
re•mind•er *n*

rem•i•nisce \ˌre-mə-ˈnis\ *vb* **rem•i•nisced**; **rem•i•nisc•ing**
to talk or think about things in the past

rem•i•nis•cence \ˌre-mə-ˈni-sᵊns\ *n*
1 the act of recalling or telling of a past experience
2 **reminiscences** *pl* a story of a person's memorable experiences

rem•i•nis•cent \ˌre-mə-ˈni-sᵊnt\ *adj*
being a reminder of something else

re•miss \ri-ˈmis\ *adj*
careless in the performance of work or duty ⟨I was *remiss* in paying my bills.⟩

re•mis•sion \ri-ˈmi-shən\ *n*
a period of time during a serious illness when there are few or no symptoms

re•mit \ri-ˈmit\ *vb* **re•mit•ted**; **re•mit•ting**
1 to send money (as in payment)
2 [2]PARDON 2

re•mit•tance \ri-ˈmi-tᵊns\ *n*
money sent in payment

rem•nant \ˈrem-nənt\ *n*
something that remains or is left over ⟨a *remnant* of cloth⟩

re•mod•el \ˌrē-ˈmä-dᵊl\ *vb* **re•mod•eled** *or* **re•mod•elled**; **re•mod•el•ing** *or* **re•mod•el•ling**
to change the structure or appearance of

re•mon•strate \ˈre-mən-ˌstrāt, ri-ˈmän-\ *vb* **re•mon•strat•ed**; **re•mon•strat•ing**
[1]PROTEST 1

re•morse \ri-ˈmȯrs\ *n*
deep regret for doing or saying something wrong ⟨She felt a pang of *remorse* after yelling.⟩
re•morse•ful \-fəl\ *adj*
re•morse•less \-ləs\ *adj*

[1]**re•mote** \ri-ˈmōt\ *adj* **re•mot•er**; **re•mot•est**
1 far off in place or time ⟨*remote* countries⟩ ⟨the *remote* past⟩
2 SECLUDED 1 ⟨a *remote* valley⟩
3 small in degree ⟨a *remote* possibility⟩
4 distant in manner : ALOOF
5 not closely connected or related ⟨*remote* ancestors⟩
re•mote•ly *adv*
re•mote•ness *n*

[2]**remote** *n*
REMOTE CONTROL 1

remote control *n*
1 a device for controlling something from a distance ⟨a *remote control* for a TV⟩
2 control (as by a radio signal) of operation from a distant point

re•mov•able \ri-ˈmü-və-bəl\ *adj*
possible to be taken off or gotten rid of ⟨The jacket comes with a *removable* lining.⟩

re•mov•al \ri-ˈmü-vəl\ *n*
the act of moving away or getting rid of : the fact of being moved away or gotten rid of ⟨snow *removal*⟩ ⟨*removal* of stains⟩

re•move \ri-ˈmüv\ *vb* **re•moved**; **re•mov•ing**
1 to move by lifting or taking off or away ⟨Please *remove* your hat.⟩ ⟨I had my tonsils *removed.*⟩
2 to get rid of ⟨Bleach will *remove* the stain.⟩
3 to dismiss from a job or office

re•mov•er \ri-ˈmü-vər\ *n*
something (as a chemical) used in getting rid of a substance ⟨paint *remover*⟩

re•nais•sance \ˌre-nə-ˈsäns\ *n*
1 ▼ *cap* the period of European history between the 14th and 17th centuries marked by a fresh interest in ancient art and literature and by the beginnings of modern science
2 the act of changing in a positive way : a period during which things are improving ⟨The city's downtown is experiencing a *renaissance.*⟩

Renaissance 1
The Renaissance movement began in Italy, and spread throughout western Europe. Explorers, scientists, inventors, and astronomers began to expand human knowledge, while writers, artists, and sculptors tried to portray or describe people and the natural world with greater accuracy.

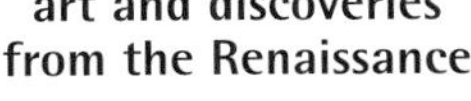
art and discoveries from the Renaissance

art
sculpture by Michelangelo \ˌmī-kə-ˈlan-jə-ˌlō\ (1475–1564)

copy of a 15th-century map

exploration
world map on a modern globe showing regions newly discovered by Europeans in the 15th century

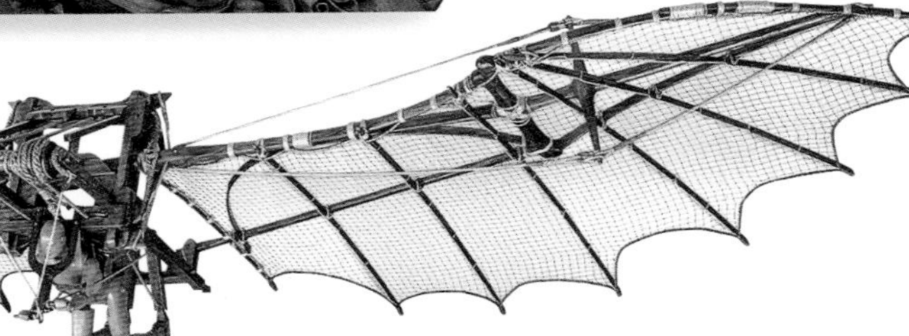

science
modern model of a flying machine designed by Leonardo da Vinci \ˌlē-ə-ˈnär-dō-də-ˈvin-chē\ (1452–1519)

re•name \rē-ˈnām\ *vb* **re•named; re•nam•ing** to give a new name to ⟨The street was *renamed.*⟩

rend \ˈrend\ *vb* **rent** \ˈrent\; **rend•ing** to tear apart by force

ren•der \ˈren-dər\ *vb* **ren•dered; ren•der•ing**
1 to cause to be or become ⟨He was *rendered* helpless by the blow.⟩
2 to furnish or give to another ⟨Passing drivers stopped to *render* aid.⟩
3 to officially report ⟨The jury *rendered* a verdict.⟩
4 to obtain by heating ⟨*render* lard from fat⟩
5 PERFORM 3 ⟨*render* a song⟩

ren•dez•vous \ˈrän-di-ˌvü, -dā-\ *n, pl* **ren•dez•vous** \-ˌvüz\
1 a place agreed on for a meeting
2 a planned meeting

ren•di•tion \ren-ˈdi-shən\ *n* an act or a result of performing ⟨He played his own *rendition* of a popular tune.⟩

ren•e•gade \ˈre-ni-ˌgād\ *n*
1 a person who deserts a faith, cause, or party
2 a person who does not obey rules

re•nege \ri-ˈnig, -ˈneg\ *vb* **re•neged; re•neg•ing** to go back on a promise or agreement

re•new \ri-ˈnü, -ˈnyü\ *vb* **re•newed; re•new•ing**
1 to make or become new, fresh, or strong again ⟨We *renewed* our friendship.⟩
2 to make, do, or begin again ⟨We *renewed* our efforts.⟩
3 to put in a fresh supply of ⟨*Renew* the water in the tank.⟩
4 to continue in force for a new period ⟨We *renewed* our lease.⟩

re•new•able \ri-ˈnü-ə-bəl, -ˈnyü-\ *adj* capable of being replaced by natural processes ⟨Forests are a *renewable* resource.⟩

re•new•al \ri-ˈnü-əl, -ˈnyü-\ *n*
1 the act of continuing in force for a new period ⟨the *renewal* of a magazine subscription⟩
2 the state of being made new, fresh, or strong again
3 something renewed ⟨license *renewals*⟩

re•nounce \ri-ˈnau̇ns\ *vb* **re•nounced; re•nounc•ing**
1 to give up, abandon, or resign usually by a public declaration ⟨The queen *renounced* the throne.⟩
2 to refuse to follow, obey, or recognize any longer ⟨They *renounced* the goals of the organization.⟩

ren•o•vate \ˈre-nə-ˌvāt\ *vb* **ren•o•vat•ed; ren•o•vat•ing** to put in good condition again ⟨The entire house is being *renovated.*⟩
ren•o•va•tor \-ˌvā-tər\ *n*

re•nown \ri-ˈnau̇n\ *n* the state of being widely and favorably known

re•nowned \ri-ˈnau̇nd\ *adj* widely and favorably known ⟨a *renowned* author⟩

[1]rent \ˈrent\ *n* money paid for the use of another's property
for rent available for use at a price

[2]rent *vb* **rent•ed; rent•ing**
1 to pay money in exchange for the use of someone else's property
2 to give the possession and use of in return for for an agreed upon amount of money ⟨The couple *rented* their cottage to friends.⟩
3 to be available for use at a price ⟨The house *rents* for $700 a month.⟩

[3]rent *past and past participle of* REND

[1]rent•al \ˈren-tᵊl\ *n* an amount paid or collected as rent

[2]rental *adj* relating to or available for rent

rent•er \ˈren-tər\ *n* a person who pays money for the use of something (as a place to live)

re•open \ˌrē-ˈō-pən\ *vb* **re•opened; re•open•ing** to open again

re•or•ga•nize \ˌrē-ˈȯr-gə-ˌnīz\ *vb* **re•or•ga•nized; re•or•ga•niz•ing** to organize differently ⟨She needs to *reorganize* her closet.⟩

rep. *abbr* representative

[1]re•pair \ri-ˈper\ *vb* **re•paired; re•pair•ing**
1 ▶ to put back in good condition : FIX ⟨Can you *repair* this broken toy?⟩
2 to make up for ⟨I can't *repair* the damage I did to our friendship.⟩
synonyms see MEND

[2]repair *n*
1 the act or process of putting back in good condition
2 [1]CONDITION 1 ⟨The house is in good *repair.*⟩

rep•a•ra•tion \ˌre-pə-ˈrā-shən\ *n*
1 the act of making up for a wrong
2 something paid by a country losing a war to the winner to make up for damages done in the war

re•past \ri-ˈpast\ *n* [1]MEAL

re•pay \rē-ˈpā\ *vb* **re•paid** \-ˈpād\; **re•pay•ing**
1 to pay back ⟨*repay* a loan⟩
2 to do or give something in return ⟨How can I *repay* the favor?⟩

re•pay•ment \rē-ˈpā-mənt\ *n* the act or an instance of paying back

re•peal \ri-ˈpēl\ *vb* **re•pealed; re•peal•ing** to do away with especially by legislative action ⟨The law was *repealed.*⟩

[1]re•peat \ri-ˈpēt\ *vb* **re•peat•ed; re•peat•ing**
1 to state or tell again ⟨Please *repeat* the question.⟩
2 to say from memory : RECITE ⟨I'll try to *repeat* what I heard that night.⟩
3 to make or do again ⟨I don't want to *repeat* a mistake.⟩

[2]repeat *n*
1 the act of happening or being done again
2 something happening or being done again

re•peat•ed \ri-ˈpē-təd\ *adj* done or happening again and again ⟨*repeated* attempts⟩
re•peat•ed•ly *adv*

re•pel \ri-ˈpel\ *vb* **re•pelled; re•pel•ling**
1 to drive back ⟨We tried to *repel* the enemy.⟩
2 to push away ⟨Two magnets can *repel* each other.⟩
3 to keep out : RESIST ⟨The cloth is treated to *repel* water.⟩
4 [2]DISGUST ⟨The sight *repelled* everyone.⟩

re•pel•lent \ri-ˈpe-lənt\ *n* a substance used to keep off pests (as insects)

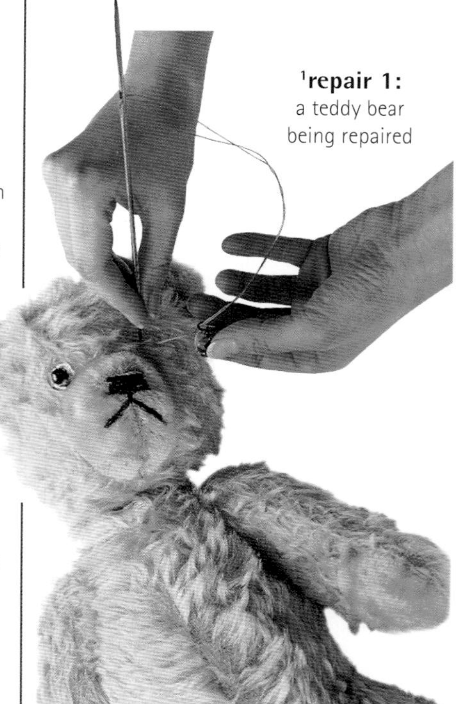

[1]repair 1: a teddy bear being repaired

re•pent \ri-ˈpent\ *vb* **re•pent•ed; re•pent•ing**
to acknowledge regret for having done something wrong ⟨He *repented* a life of crime.⟩

re•pen•tance \ri-ˈpen-tᵊns\ *n*
the action or process of acknowledging regret for having done something wrong

re•pen•tant \ri-ˈpen-tᵊnt\ *adj*
feeling or showing regret for something said or done
re•pen•tant•ly *adv*

re•per•cus•sion \ˌrē-pər-ˈkə-shən\ *n*
a widespread, indirect, or unexpected effect of something said or done ⟨Everyone felt the *repercussions* of the change.⟩

rep•er•toire \ˈre-pər-ˌtwär\ *n*
a list or supply of plays, operas, or pieces that a company or person is prepared to perform

rep•er•to•ry \ˈre-pər-ˌtȯr-ē\ *n, pl* **rep•er•to•ries**
REPERTOIRE

rep•e•ti•tion \ˌre-pə-ˈti-shən\ *n*
1 the act or an instance of stating or doing again
2 something stated or done again

re•place \ri-ˈplās\ *vb* **re•placed; re•plac•ing**
1 to put back in a former or proper place ⟨Please *replace* your book on the shelf.⟩
2 to take the place of ⟨DVDs have *replaced* videotape.⟩
3 to put something new in the place of ⟨I'll gladly *replace* the broken dish.⟩

re•place•ment \ri-ˈplās-mənt\ *n*
1 the act of putting back, taking the place of, or substituting : the state of being put back or substituted
2 ¹SUBSTITUTE

re•plen•ish \ri-ˈple-nish\ *vb* **re•plen•ished; re•plen•ish•ing**
to make full or complete once more ⟨We need to *replenish* our supplies.⟩

re•plete \ri-ˈplēt\ *adj*
well supplied ⟨The game was *replete* with thrills.⟩

rep•li•ca \ˈre-pli-kə\ *n*
▶ a very exact copy

¹re•ply \ri-ˈplī\ *vb* **re•plied; re•ply•ing**
to say or do in answer : RESPOND

²reply *n, pl* **re•plies**
something said, written, or done in answer ⟨I'm waiting for a *reply* to my request.⟩

¹re•port \ri-ˈpȯrt\ *n*
1 a usually complete description or statement ⟨a weather *report*⟩ ⟨a book *report*⟩
2 a written or spoken statement that may or may not be true ⟨There are *reports* of a breakthrough.⟩
3 REPUTATION 1 ⟨They're people of evil *report.*⟩
4 an explosive noise ⟨the *report* of a gun⟩

²report *vb* **re•port•ed; re•port•ing**
1 to give a written or spoken description of something ⟨A witness *reported* what happened.⟩
2 to make known to the proper authorities ⟨*report* a fire⟩
3 to complain about (someone) for misconduct ⟨He will *report* the bully to the principal.⟩
4 to make a statement that may or may not be true ⟨The man is *reported* to be all right.⟩
5 to prepare or present an account of something (as for television or a newspaper)
6 to show up ⟨He *reports* for work at noon.⟩
re•port•er *n*

replica:
a replica of the Statue of Liberty

▶ **synonyms** REPORT, DESCRIBE, and NARRATE mean to talk or write about something. REPORT is used of giving information to others often after some investigation has been done. ⟨Newspapers *report* important events.⟩ DESCRIBE is used of giving a clear mental picture of an event or situation. ⟨Students were asked to *describe* a day at school.⟩ NARRATE means to tell a story with a beginning and an end. ⟨The speaker *narrated* a tale about pirates.⟩

report card *n*
a written statement of a student's grades

¹re•pose \ri-ˈpōz\ *vb* **re•posed; re•pos•ing**
to lay or lie at rest ⟨I *reposed* my head on his shoulder.⟩ ⟨The dog is *reposing* on the couch.⟩

²repose *n*
1 a state of resting
2 freedom from disturbance or excitement : CALM

rep•re•hen•si•ble \ˌre-pri-ˈhen-sə-bəl\ *adj*
deserving criticism or condemnation ⟨*reprehensible* behavior⟩

rep•re•sent \ˌre-pri-ˈzent\ *vb* **rep•re•sent•ed; rep•re•sent•ing**
1 to present a picture, image, or likeness of : PORTRAY ⟨This picture *represents* a country scene.⟩
2 to be a sign or symbol of ⟨The flag *represents* our country.⟩
3 to act for or in place of ⟨We elect men and women to *represent* us in Congress.⟩

rep•re•sen•ta•tion \ˌre-pri-ˌzen-ˈtā-shən\ *n*
1 one (as a picture or symbol) that is a sign or portrayal of something else
2 the act of doing something on behalf of another or others : the state of doing something on behalf of another or others (as in a legislative body)

¹rep•re•sen•ta•tive \ˌre-pri-ˈzen-tə-tiv\ *adj*
1 serving to portray ⟨The painting is *representative* of a battle.⟩
2 carried on by people elected to act for others ⟨a *representative* government⟩
3 being a typical example of the thing mentioned ⟨This song is *representative* of the blues.⟩

²representative *n*
1 a typical example (as of a group or class)
2 a person who acts for others (as in a legislature and especially in the House of Representatives of the United States or of a state)

reptile
Related to the dinosaurs, modern reptiles live in habitats throughout the world, avoiding only cold regions and high altitudes. All have dry, scaly skin, which prevents water loss in hot, dry climates, and reproduce by laying eggs, which hatch into fully formed young. Most reptiles shed skin as they grow, and many lizards can lose their tail at will to escape a predator; the tail later grows again.

re•press \ri-ˈpres\ *vb* **re•pressed**; **re•press•ing**
to hold in check by or as if by pressure

[1]**re•prieve** \ri-ˈprēv\ *vb* **re•prieved**; **re•priev•ing**
1 to delay something (as the punishment of a prisoner sentenced to die)
2 to give relief to ⟨We were *reprieved* when school was cancelled on test day.⟩

[2]**reprieve** *n*
1 the act of postponing something
2 a temporary relief ⟨Rain brought a *reprieve* from the heat.⟩

[1]**rep•ri•mand** \ˈre-prə-ˌmand\ *n*
a severe or formal criticism : CENSURE

[2]**reprimand** *vb* **rep•ri•mand•ed**; **rep•ri•mand•ing**
to criticize (a person) severely or formally

re•pri•sal \ri-ˈprī-zəl\ *n*
an act in return for harm done by another : an act of revenge

[1]**re•proach** \ri-ˈprōch\ *vb* **re•proached**; **re•proach•ing**
to find fault with : BLAME

[2]**reproach** *n*
1 something that deserves blame or disgrace
2 an expression of disapproval
re•proach•ful \-fəl\ *adj*
re•proach•ful•ly \-fə-lē\ *adv*

re•pro•duce \ˌrē-prə-ˈdüs, -ˈdyüs\ *vb* **re•pro•duced**; **re•pro•duc•ing**
1 to produce another living thing of the same kind ⟨Many plants *reproduce* by means of seeds.⟩
2 to imitate closely ⟨Sound effects *reproduced* thunder.⟩
3 to make a copy of

re•pro•duc•tion \ˌrē-prə-ˈdək-shən\ *n*
1 the process by which living things produce offspring
2 the act or process of copying something ⟨*reproduction* of sound⟩
3 [1]COPY 1 ⟨photographic *reproductions*⟩

re•pro•duc•tive \ˌrē-prə-ˈdək-tiv\ *adj*
relating to or concerned with the production of offspring ⟨*reproductive* cells⟩

re•proof \ri-ˈprüf\ *n*
blame or criticism for a fault

re•prove \ri-ˈprüv\ *vb* **re•proved**; **re•prov•ing**
to express blame or disapproval of : SCOLD

rep•tile \ˈrep-təl, -ˌtīl\ *n*
▲ a cold-blooded animal (as a snake, lizard, turtle, or alligator) that breathes air and usually has the skin covered with scales or bony plates

Word History Most of the animals we call *reptiles* creep or crawl about. Some, like snakes, crawl about on their bellies. Some, like lizards, creep about on little, short legs. The English word *reptile* came from a Latin word *reptilis* that meant "creeping," which is derived from the verb *repere* meaning "to crawl."

re•pub•lic \ri-ˈpə-blik\ *n*
a country with elected representatives and an elected chief of state who is not a monarch and who is usually a president

[1]**re•pub•li•can** \ri-ˈpə-bli-kən\ *n*
1 a person who favors a form of government having elected representatives
2 *cap* a member of the Republican party of the United States

the **caiman** \'kā-mən\ of Central and South America is related to crocodiles and alligators

²republican *adj*
1 being a form of government having elected representatives
2 relating to a major political party in the United States that is associated with business interests and favors a limited government role in economic matters

re•pu•di•ate \ri-'pyü-dē-,āt\ *vb* **re•pu•di•at•ed**; **re•pu•di•at•ing**
1 to refuse to have anything to do with ⟨They *repudiated* their wayward son.⟩
2 to refuse to believe or approve of ⟨She *repudiated* the rumors.⟩

re•pug•nance \ri-'pəg-nənts\ *n*
a strong feeling of dislike or disgust

re•pug•nant \ri-'pəg-nənt\ *adj*
causing a strong feeling of dislike or disgust

¹re•pulse \ri-'pəls\ *vb* **re•pulsed**; **re•puls•ing**
1 to drive or beat back : REPEL ⟨The army *repulsed* their enemy.⟩
2 to reject in a rude or unfriendly way : SNUB ⟨He *repulsed* attempts to help him.⟩
3 to cause dislike or disgust in

²repulse *n*
1 ²REBUFF, SNUB
2 the action of driving back an attacker

re•pul•sive \ri-'pəl-siv\ *adj*
causing disgust ⟨a *repulsive* sight⟩
re•pul•sive•ly *adv*
re•pul•sive•ness *n*

rep•u•ta•ble \'re-pyə-tə-bəl\ *adj*
having a good reputation ⟨a *reputable* business⟩

rep•u•ta•tion \,re-pyə-'tā-shən\ *n*
1 overall quality or character as seen or judged by people in general ⟨This car has a good *reputation.*⟩
2 notice by other people of some quality or ability ⟨a *reputation* for shrewdness⟩

¹re•pute \ri-'pyüt\ *vb* **re•put•ed**; **re•put•ing**
CONSIDER 3 ⟨She is *reputed* to be rich.⟩

²repute *n*
1 REPUTATION 1 ⟨He has the *repute* of a liar.⟩
2 good reputation : HONOR

¹re•quest \ri-'kwest\ *n*
1 the act of asking for something
2 something asked for ⟨grant a *request*⟩
3 the condition of being asked for ⟨Tickets are available on *request.*⟩

²request *vb* **re•quest•ed**; **re•quest•ing**
1 to ask something of someone ⟨He *requested* them to sing.⟩
2 to ask for ⟨I'm *requesting* a loan.⟩

re•qui•em \'re-kwē-əm\ *n*
1 a mass for a dead person
2 a musical service or hymn in honor of dead people

re•quire \ri-'kwīr\ *vb* **re•quired**; **re•quir•ing**
1 to have a need for ⟨This trick *requires* skill.⟩
2 ¹ORDER 2, COMMAND ⟨The law *requires* drivers to wear seat belts.⟩

re•quire•ment \ri-'kwīr-mənt\ *n*
something that is necessary

¹req•ui•site \'re-kwə-zət\ *adj*
needed for reaching a goal or achieving a purpose ⟨*requisite* skills⟩

²requisite *n*
REQUIREMENT ⟨Previous experience is a *requisite.*⟩

re•read \'rē-'rēd\ *vb* **re•read** \-'red\; **re•read•ing**
to read again

res. *abbr* residence

¹res•cue \'re-skyü\ *vb* **res•cued**; **res•cu•ing**
to free from danger : SAVE
res•cu•er *n*

[2]rescue *n*
an act of freeing someone or something from danger

[1]re•search \ri-ˈsərch, ˈrē-ˌsərch\ *n*
careful study and investigation for the purpose of discovering and explaining new knowledge
re•search•er *n*

[2]research *vb* **re•searched**; **re•search•ing**
to search or investigate thoroughly ⟨Doctors *researched* the disease.⟩

re•sem•blance \ri-ˈzem-bləns\ *n*
the quality or state of being similar to another

re•sem•ble \ri-ˈzem-bəl\ *vb* **re•sem•bled**; **re•sem•bling**
to be like or similar to ⟨This house *resembles* mine.⟩

re•sent \ri-ˈzent\ *vb* **re•sent•ed**; **re•sent•ing**
to feel annoyance or anger at ⟨He *resents* his sister's laziness.⟩

re•sent•ful \ri-ˈzent-fəl\ *adj*
full of angry displeasure ⟨She's *resentful* at being treated like a baby.⟩

[1]re•serve \ri-ˈzərv\ *vb* **re•served**; **re•serv•ing**
1 to arrange to have set aside and held for someone's use ⟨I called to *reserve* a hotel room.⟩
2 to keep in store for special use
3 to keep from using until a future time ⟨We need to *reserve* our strength.⟩
4 to hold over to a future time or place ⟨*Reserve* judgment until you know the facts.⟩

[2]reserve *n*
1 **reserves** *pl* military forces held back or available for later use
2 an area of land set apart ⟨a nature *reserve*⟩
3 caution in words and behavior
4 something stored for future use ⟨oil *reserves*⟩
5 an act of setting something aside for future use

re•served \ri-ˈzərvd\ *adj*
1 cautious in words and actions
2 kept or set apart for future or special use

reservoir: a reservoir that provides water to a large city

re•sent•ment \ri-ˈzent-mənt\ *n*
a feeling of angry displeasure at a real or imagined wrong, insult, or injury

res•er•va•tion \ˌre-zər-ˈvā-shən\ *n*
1 an act of setting something aside for future use
2 an arrangement to have something (as seating in a restaurant) held for someone's use
3 something (as land) set aside for a special use ⟨a wildlife *reservation*⟩
4 an area of land set aside for American Indians to live
5 something that limits ⟨I can't agree without *reservations*.⟩

res•er•voir \ˈre-zər-ˌvwär\ *n*
▲ a place where something (as water) is kept in store for future use

re•set \ˌrē-ˈset\ *vb* **re•set**; **re•set•ting**
to set again

re•side \ri-ˈzīd\ *vb* **re•sid•ed**; **re•sid•ing**
1 to live permanently and continuously : DWELL
2 to have its place : EXIST ⟨The choice *resides* in the voters.⟩

res•i•dence \ˈre-zə-dəns\ *n*
1 the act or fact of living in a place
2 a building used for a home
3 the time during which a person lives in a place

residue of lemon pulp after a lemon is squeezed

[1]res•i•dent \ˈre-zə-dənt\ *n*
a person who lives in a place

[2]resident *adj*
1 living in a place for some length of time
2 serving in a full-time position ⟨a *resident* doctor⟩

res•i•den•tial \ˌre-zə-ˈden-shəl\ *adj*
1 used as a residence or by residents ⟨a *residential* hotel⟩
2 suitable for or containing residences ⟨a *residential* street⟩

res•i•due \ˈre-zə-ˌdü, -ˌdyü\ *n*
▲ whatever remains after a part is taken, set apart, or lost

re•sign \ri-ˈzīn\ *vb* **re•signed**; **re•sign•ing**
1 to give up (a job or position) by a formal or official act
2 to prepare to accept something unpleasant ⟨I *resigned* myself to the loss.⟩

res•ig•na•tion \ˌre-zig-ˈnā-shən\ *n*
1 an act of giving something up formally or officially
2 a letter or written statement that gives notice of giving something up ⟨I've handed in my *resignation*.⟩
3 the feeling of a person who is prepared to accept something unpleasant

re•signed \ri-ˈzīnd\ *adj*
showing acceptance of something unpleasant ⟨"I'll do it," he said in a *resigned* voice.⟩

res•in \ˈre-zᵊn\ *n*
1 ▶ a yellowish or brownish substance obtained from the gum or sap of some trees (as the pine) and used in varnishes and medicine
2 any of various manufactured products that are similar to natural resins in properties and are used especially as plastics

re•sist \ri-ˈzist\ *vb* **re•sist•ed**; **re•sist•ing**
1 to fight against : OPPOSE ⟨Students *resisted* the war.⟩
2 to avoid doing or having something ⟨I can't *resist* bragging.⟩ ⟨Who can *resist* chocolate?⟩

3 to withstand the force or effect of 〈These plants *resist* disease.〉

re•sis•tance \ri-ˈzi-stəns\ *n*
1 an act or instance of opposing
2 the ability to withstand the force or effect of 〈*resistance* to disease〉
3 an opposing or slowing force 〈The car's sleek design reduces wind *resistance*.〉
4 the opposition offered by a substance to the passage through it of an electric current

re•sis•tant \ri-ˈzis-tənt\ *adj*
capable of withstanding the force or effect of 〈The material is fire-*resistant*.〉

res•o•lute \ˈre-zə-ˌlüt\ *adj*
firmly determined
res•o•lute•ly *adv*

res•o•lu•tion \ˌre-zə-ˈlü-shən\ *n*
1 something decided on 〈a New Year's *resolution*〉
2 firmness of purpose : DETERMINATION
3 the act of solving 〈They went to court for *resolution* of the matter.〉
4 the solution to a problem 〈They found a *resolution* to the dispute.〉
5 a statement of the feelings, wishes, or decisions of a group

[1]re•solve \ri-ˈzälv\ *vb* **re•solved; re•solv•ing**
1 to find an answer to : SOLVE 〈They *resolved* the difficulty.〉
2 to reach a firm decision about something 〈I *resolve* to work hard.〉
3 to decide by a formal resolution and vote

[2]resolve *n*
firmness of purpose : DETERMINATION

res•o•nance \ˈre-zə-nəns\ *n*
a long loud, clear, and deep quality of sound

res•o•nant \ˈre-zə-nənt\ *adj*
making a long loud, clear, and deep sound 〈a *resonant* voice〉
res•o•nant•ly *adv*

[1]re•sort \ri-ˈzȯrt\ *n*
1 someone or something that is looked to for help 〈I asked for help as a last *resort*.〉
2 a place where people go on vacation 〈a ski *resort*〉

[2]resort *vb* **re•sort•ed; re•sort•ing**
to seek aid, relief, or advantage 〈The police had to *resort* to force.〉

re•sound \ri-ˈzau̇nd\ *vb* **re•sound•ed; re•sound•ing**
1 to become filled with sound : REVERBERATE 〈The hall *resounded* with cheers.〉
2 to sound loudly 〈The organ *resounds* through the hall.〉

re•sound•ing \ri-ˈzau̇n-diŋ\ *adj*
1 producing resonant sound
2 leaving no doubt 〈a *resounding* victory〉

re•source \ˈrē-ˌsȯrs\ *n*
1 **resources** *pl* a usable stock or supply (as of money or products)
2 NATURAL RESOURCE
3 the ability to meet and deal with situations

re•source•ful \ri-ˈsȯrs-fəl\ *adj*
clever in dealing with problems
re•source•ful•ness *n*

[1]re•spect \ri-ˈspekt\ *n*
1 high or special regard : ESTEEM
2 thoughtfulness or consideration 〈You must show *respect* for the privacy of others.〉
3 **respects** *pl* an expression of regard or courtesy 〈pay my *respects*〉
4 [1]DETAIL 2 〈Our trip was perfect in all *respects*.〉
5 relation to or concern with something specified 〈I'm writing with *respect* to your ad.〉

[2]respect *vb* **re•spect•ed; re•spect•ing**
1 to consider worthy of high regard : ESTEEM
2 to pay attention to 〈We *respected* their wishes.〉

re•spect•able \ri-ˈspek-tə-bəl\ *adj*
1 decent or correct in conduct : PROPER 〈They're *respectable* people.〉
2 fit to be seen : PRESENTABLE 〈Wear something *respectable*.〉
3 deserving high regard 〈She acted in a *respectable* manner.〉
4 fair in size or quantity 〈We collected a *respectable* amount.〉
re•spect•ably \-blē\ *adv*

re•spect•ful \ri-ˈspekt-fəl\ *adj*
showing high regard or courtesy 〈a *respectful* manner〉
re•spect•ful•ly \-fə-lē\ *adv*

re•spect•ing \ri-ˈspek-tiŋ\ *prep*
CONCERNING 〈I have news *respecting* your uncle.〉

re•spec•tive \ri-ˈspek-tiv\ *adj*
not the same or shared : SEPARATE 〈They hurried to their *respective* homes.〉
re•spec•tive•ly *adv*

res•pi•ra•tion \ˌre-spə-ˈrā-shən\ *n*
1 the act or process of breathing : the inhaling of oxygen and the exhaling of carbon dioxide
2 the process by which cells use oxygen to break down sugar and obtain energy

res•pi•ra•tor \ˈre-spə-ˌrā-tər\ *n*
1 a device covering the mouth or nose especially to prevent the breathing in of harmful substances (as dust or fumes)
2 a device used for helping a person to breathe

res•pi•ra•to•ry \ˈre-spə-rə-ˌtȯr-ē\ *adj*
of, relating to, or concerned with breathing or the parts of the body involved in breathing 〈a *respiratory* infection〉

respiratory system *n*
a system of the body used in breathing that in human beings consists of the nose, nasal passages, pharynx, larynx, trachea, bronchial tubes, and lungs

re•spire \ri-ˈspīr\ *vb* **re•spired; re•spir•ing**
BREATHE 1

res•pite \ˈre-spət\ *n*
1 a short delay
2 a period of rest or relief

re•splen•dent \ri-ˈsplen-dənt\ *adj*
shining brightly : SPLENDID
re•splen•dent•ly *adv*

re•spond \ri-ˈspänd\ *vb* **re•spond•ed; re•spond•ing**
1 to say something in return
2 to react in a way that shows some action was successful 〈Did the patient *respond* to surgery?〉

resin 1
Resins include amber, balsam, and rosin, as well as frankincense and myrrh. Prized since ancient times, frankincense and myrrh are fragrant resins still used in incense, perfumes, and cosmetics.

pellets of dried myrrh

pellets of dried frankincense

restaurant: a group of people having a meal at a restaurant

re•sponse \ri-ˈspäns\ *n*
1 an act or instance of replying : ANSWER ⟨There was no *response* to my question.⟩
2 words said or sung by the people or choir in a religious service
3 a reaction of a living being (as to a drug)

re•spon•si•bil•i•ty \ri-ˌspän-sə-ˈbi-lə-tē\ *n, pl* **re•spon•si•bil•i•ties**
1 the quality or state of being in charge of someone or something
2 the quality of being dependable ⟨Show *responsibility* by always doing your homework.⟩
3 something or someone for which someone has charge ⟨The children are my *responsibility*.⟩

re•spon•si•ble \ri-ˈspän-sə-bəl\ *adj*
1 getting the credit or blame for acts or decisions ⟨You are *responsible* for the damage.⟩
2 RELIABLE ⟨*responsible* teenagers⟩
3 needing a dependable person ⟨a *responsible* job⟩
re•spon•si•bly \-blē\ *adv*

re•spon•sive \ri-ˈspän-siv\ *adj*
1 showing interest ⟨He was not *responsive* to our invitation.⟩
2 quick to respond in a sympathetic way ⟨The store is *responsive* to its customer's needs.⟩
re•spon•sive•ly *adv*
re•spon•sive•ness *n*

[1]**rest** \ˈrest\ *vb* **rest•ed; rest•ing**
1 to relax, sleep, or refrain from taking part in work or an activity
2 to refrain from using for a short time
3 to sit or lie fixed or supported ⟨A house *rests* on its foundation.⟩
4 DEPEND 2 ⟨Success *rests* on your abilities.⟩
5 to lie dead
6 to fix or be fixed in trust or confidence ⟨My neighbors *rested* their hopes on their children.⟩

[2]**rest** *n*
something that is left over : REMAINDER

[3]**rest** *n*
1 a state of inactivity during which the body and mind become refreshed
2 freedom from activity or work ⟨I need a *rest* from work.⟩
3 a state of not moving or not doing anything ⟨The ball was at *rest*.⟩
4 a place for stopping or refraining from activity
5 a silence in music
6 ▼ a symbol in music that stands for a certain period of silence in a measure
7 something used for support ⟨a head *rest*⟩

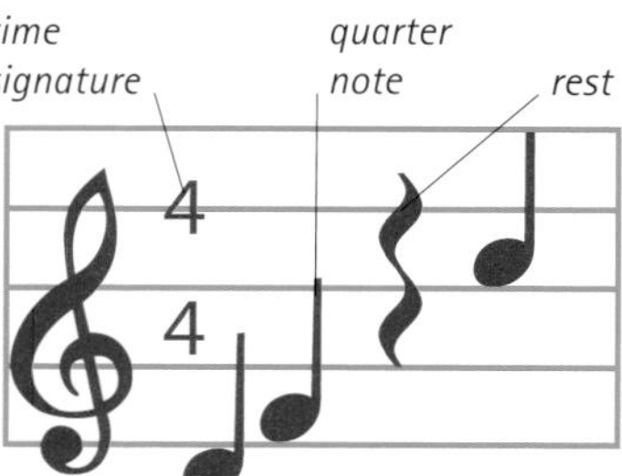

[3]**rest 6:** the musical notation for a one-beat rest

res•tau•rant \ˈre-stə-rənt, -ˌränt\ *n*
◀ a public eating place

rest•ful \ˈrest-fəl\ *adj*
giving a feeling of peace or relaxation : QUIET ⟨a *restful* scene⟩

res•tive \ˈre-stiv\ *adj*
showing impatience, nervousness, or discomfort ⟨a *restive* crowd⟩

rest•less \ˈrest-ləs\ *adj*
1 not relaxed or calm ⟨The waiting audience became *restless*.⟩
2 having or giving no rest ⟨a *restless* night⟩
rest•less•ly *adv*
rest•less•ness *n*

res•to•ra•tion \ˌre-stə-ˈrā-shən\ *n*
1 ▶ an act of returning something to its original condition : the result of having been returned to the original condition
2 something (as a building) that has been returned to its original condition

re•store \ri-ˈstȯr\ *vb* **re•stored; re•stor•ing**
1 to put or bring back to an earlier or original state
2 to put back into use or service ⟨Power has been *restored*.⟩
3 to give back ⟨Police *restored* the stolen car to its owner.⟩

re•strain \ri-ˈstrān\ *vb* **re•strained; re•strain•ing**
1 to keep from doing something ⟨I wanted to speak, but *restrained* myself.⟩

2 to keep back : CURB ⟨He couldn't *restrain* his laughter.⟩

re•straint \ri-'strānt\ *n*
1 the act of stopping or holding back : the state of being stopped or held back
2 a force or influence that stops or holds back
3 control over thoughts or feelings ⟨You're angry, but show *restraint.*⟩

re•strict \ri-'strikt\ *vb* **re•strict•ed; re•strict•ing**
to keep within bounds : set limits to

re•stric•tion \ri-'strik-shən\ *n*
1 something (as a law or rule) that limits ⟨There are *restrictions* on building.⟩
2 an act of limiting : the condition of being limited

re•stric•tive \ri-'strik-tiv\ *adj*
serving or likely to keep within bounds

rest•room \'rest-,rüm, -,ru̇m\ *n*
a room with a toilet and sink

[1]re•sult \ri-'zəlt\ *vb* **re•sult•ed; re•sult•ing**
1 to come about as an effect ⟨Flooding *resulted* from heavy rain.⟩
2 to end as an effect ⟨The storm *resulted* in tree damage.⟩

[2]result *n*
1 something that comes about as an effect or end ⟨the *results* of hard work⟩
2 a good effect ⟨This method gets *results.*⟩

re•sume \ri-'züm\ *vb* **re•sumed; re•sum•ing**
1 to begin again ⟨The teams *resumed* play.⟩
2 to take or occupy again ⟨Please *resume* your seats.⟩

re•sump•tion \ri-'zəmp-shən\ *n*
the act of starting again

res•ur•rect \,re-zə-'rekt\ *vb* **res•ur•rect•ed; res•ur•rect•ing**
1 to bring back to life
2 to bring to view or into use again ⟨The band *resurrected* an old song.⟩

res•ur•rec•tion \,re-zə-'rek-shən\ *n*
1 an instance of coming back into use or importance ⟨The style enjoyed a *resurrection.*⟩
2 *cap* the rising of Jesus Christ from the dead
3 *often cap* the act of rising again to life of all human dead before the final judgment

re•sus•ci•tate \ri-'sə-sə-,tāt\ *vb* **re•sus•ci•tat•ed; re•sus•ci•tat•ing**
to bring back from apparent death or unconsciousness

re•sus•ci•ta•tion \ri-,sə-sə-'tā-shən\ *n*
the act of bringing back from apparent death or unconsciousness

[1]re•tail \'rē-,tāl\ *vb* **re•tailed; re•tail•ing**
to sell in small amounts to people for their own use
re•tail•er *n*

[2]retail *n*
the sale of products or goods in small amounts to people for their own use

[3]retail *adj*
relating to or engaged in selling products in small amounts to people for their own use ⟨*retail* stores⟩

re•tain \ri-'tān\ *vb* **re•tained; re•tain•ing**
1 to keep or continue to use ⟨They *retain* old customs.⟩
2 to hold safe or unchanged ⟨Lead *retains* heat.⟩

re•tal•i•ate \ri-'ta-lē-,āt\ *vb* **re•tal•i•at•ed; re•tal•i•at•ing**
to get revenge by returning like for like

re•tal•i•a•tion \ri-,ta-lē-'ā-shən\ *n*
the act or an instance of getting revenge

re•tard \ri-'tärd\ *vb* **re•tard•ed; re•tard•ing**
to slow down : DELAY ⟨Bad weather *retarded* our progress.⟩

retch \'rech\ *vb* **retched; retch•ing**
to vomit or try to vomit

re•ten•tion \ri-'ten-shən\ *n*
1 the act of continuing to possess, control, or hold ⟨moisture *retention*⟩
2 the power or ability to keep or hold something ⟨memory *retention*⟩

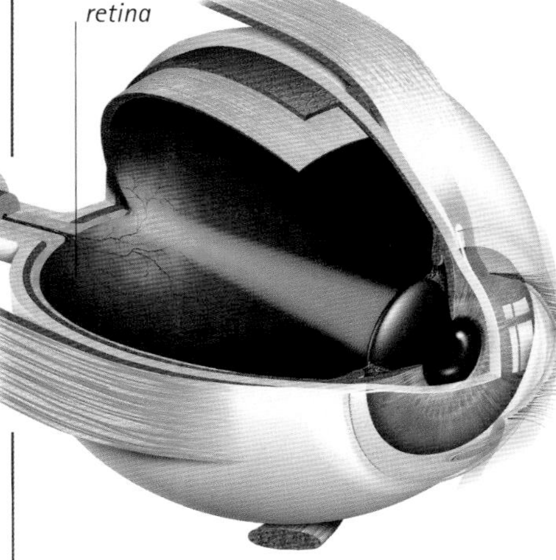

retina: cross-section model of a human eye showing the retina

ret•i•na \'re-tə-nə\ *n, pl* **retinas** *also* **ret•i•nae** \-,nē\
▲ the membrane that lines the back part of the eyeball, contains the rods and cones, and converts the images received by the lens into signals that are transmitted to the brain

re•tire \ri-'tīr\ *vb* **re•tired; re•tir•ing**
1 to give up a job permanently : quit working ⟨My grandfather *retired* at 65 years old.⟩
2 to go away especially to be alone ⟨I *retired* to my room.⟩
3 to go to bed ⟨I'm *retiring* for the night.⟩
4 to withdraw from use or service ⟨The navy *retired* an old ship.⟩
5 to get away from action or danger : RETREAT ⟨The army *retired* from the battlefield.⟩
re•tire•ment \-mənt\ *n*

restoration 1

Damaged paintings are often saved by restoration. With the technique of picture restoration shown here, an old painting is first strengthened by soaking with glue. When dry, it is cleaned with a solvent, which is painted onto the surface through a piece of cloth. The area is then covered with plastic film to prevent the liquid from evaporating. Finally, after further cleaning with turpentine, any places where paint has flaked away are carefully repainted.

restoration of a damaged 15th-century Russian painting

re·tired \ri-ˈtīrd\ *adj*
not working at active duties or business ⟨a *retired* teacher⟩

re·tir·ing \ri-ˈtīr-iŋ\ *adj*
[1]SHY 2, RESERVED

[1]**re·tort** \ri-ˈtȯrt\ *vb* **re·tort·ed**; **re·tort·ing**
1 to reply usually angrily or sharply
2 to reply with an argument against ⟨When Mom objected to ice cream as unhealthy, I *retorted* that it contained milk.⟩

[2]**retort** *n*
a quick, clever, or angry reply

re·trace \rē-ˈtrās\ *vb* **re·traced**; **re·trac·ing** to go over once more ⟨I *retraced* my steps.⟩

re·tract \ri-ˈtrakt\ *vb* **re·tract·ed**; **re·tract·ing**
1 to pull back or in ⟨A cat can *retract* its claws.⟩
2 to take back (as an offer or statement) : WITHDRAW

[1]**re·treat** \ri-ˈtrēt\ *n*
1 an act of going back or away especially from something dangerous, difficult, or disagreeable ⟨The enemy is in *retreat.*⟩
2 a military signal for turning away from the enemy ⟨He sounded the *retreat.*⟩
3 a place of privacy or safety ⟨a mountain *retreat*⟩
4 a period of time in which a person goes away to pray, think quietly, or study

[2]**retreat** *vb* **re·treat·ed**; **re·treat·ing**
1 to move back or away especially from something dangerous, difficult, or disagreeable ⟨The troops *retreated* at nightfall.⟩
2 to go to a place of privacy or safety

ret·ri·bu·tion \ˌre-trə-ˈbyü-shən\ *n*
PUNISHMENT 1

re·trieve \ri-ˈtrēv\ *vb* **re·trieved**; **re·triev·ing**
1 to get and bring back ⟨One of the players *retrieved* the ball.⟩
2 to find and bring back killed or wounded game ⟨The dog learned to *retrieve* birds.⟩

re·triev·er \ri-ˈtrē-vər\ *n*
► a dog that has a water-resistant coat and is skilled in retrieving game

ret·ro·spect \ˈre-trə-ˌspekt\ *n*
a looking back on things past ⟨In *retrospect,* I made the right decision.⟩

[1]**re·turn** \ri-ˈtərn\ *vb* **re·turned**; **re·turn·ing**
1 to come or go back again ⟨Birds *return* each spring.⟩
2 to bring, give, send, or put back ⟨Have you *returned* your library book?⟩
3 REPAY 1 ⟨She never *returned* the borrowed money.⟩
4 to respond in the same way ⟨I *returned* the compliment.⟩
5 to make an official report of ⟨The jury *returned* a verdict.⟩
6 [1]YIELD 4, PRODUCE ⟨The investment *returned* a profit.⟩

[2]**return** *n*
1 the act of coming or going back to a place or condition ⟨They await his *return* home.⟩ ⟨She hoped for a *return* to normal.⟩
2 RECURRENCE ⟨the *return* of spring⟩
3 the act of returning something (as to a former condition or owner) ⟨He thanked me for the *return* of his wallet.⟩
4 something given in payment or exchange ⟨She asked nothing in *return.*⟩
5 a report of the results of voting ⟨election *returns*⟩
6 a statement of income to be taxed
7 the profit from labor, investment, or business

[3]**return** *adj*
1 happening or done for the second time ⟨a *return* visit⟩
2 used for returning ⟨a *return* ticket⟩

re·union \rē-ˈyün-yən\ *n*
1 an act of coming or bringing together again after being apart ⟨the band's *reunion*⟩
2 an organized gathering of people who have not been together for some time ⟨a class *reunion*⟩

re·unite \ˌrē-yu̇-ˈnīt\ *vb* **re·unit·ed**; **re·unit·ing**
to come or bring together again after being apart

re·use \rē-ˈyüz\ *vb* **re·used**; **re·us·ing**
to use again

retriever:
a Labrador retriever

rev \ˈrev\ *vb* **revved**; **rev·ving**
to increase the number of revolutions per minute of (a motor) ⟨*rev* an engine⟩

Rev. *abbr* reverend

re·veal \ri-ˈvēl\ *vb* **re·vealed**; **re·veal·ing**
1 to make known ⟨*reveal* a secret⟩
2 to show clearly ⟨The opened door *revealed* a messy room.⟩

rev·eil·le \ˈre-və-lē\ *n*
a signal sounded at about sunrise on a bugle to call soldiers or sailors to duty

[1]**rev·el** \ˈre-vəl\ *vb* **rev·eled** *or* **rev·elled**; **rev·el·ing** *or* **rev·el·ling**
to take great pleasure ⟨He *reveled* in his success.⟩

[2]**revel** *n*
a noisy or merry celebration

rev·e·la·tion \ˌre-və-ˈlā-shən\ *n*
a secret or surprising fact that is made known

rev·el·ry \ˈre-vəl-rē\ *n, pl* **rev·el·ries**
wild and noisy celebration

[1]**re·venge** \ri-ˈvenj\ *vb* **re·venged**; **re·veng·ing**
to cause harm or injury in return for ⟨He'll *revenge* the insult.⟩

[2]**revenge** *n*
1 an act or instance of causing harm or injury in return for a wrong ⟨*revenge* against enemies⟩
2 a desire to cause harm or injury in return for a wrong ⟨She was motivated by *revenge.*⟩
3 a chance for getting satisfaction ⟨The team sought *revenge* through a rematch.⟩

rev·e·nue \ˈre-və-ˌnü, -ˌnyü\ *n*
1 money that is made by or paid to a business or organization ⟨sales *revenues*⟩
2 money collected by a government (as through taxes)

re·ver·ber·ate \ri-ˈvər-bə-ˌrāt\ *vb* **re·ver·ber·at·ed**; **re·ver·ber·at·ing**
to continue in or as if in a series of echoes ⟨My voice *reverberated* throughout the room.⟩

re·vere \ri-ˈvir\ *vb* **re·vered**; **re·ver·ing**
to have great respect for ⟨The town *reveres* him as a hero.⟩

rev·er·ence \ˈre-və-rəns, ˈrev-rəns\ *n*
honor and respect often mixed with love and awe

rev·er·end \ˈre-və-rənd, ˈrev-rənd\ *adj*
1 worthy of honor and respect
2 used as a title for a member of the clergy ⟨the *Reverend* John Doe⟩ ⟨the *Reverend* Jane Doe⟩

rev·er·ent \ˈre-və-rənt, ˈrev-rənt\ *adj*
very respectful ⟨*reverent* mourners⟩
rev·er·ent·ly *adv*

rev•er•ie \'re-və-rē\ *n, pl* **rev•er•ies**
the state of being lost in thought especially about pleasant things

re•ver•sal \ri-'vər-səl\ *n*
a change to an opposite or former state, condition, view, or direction

[1]**re•verse** \ri-'vərs\ *adj*
1 opposite to a previous, normal, or usual condition ⟨*reverse* order⟩
2 opposite to the front ⟨the *reverse* side⟩

[2]**reverse** *vb* **re•versed; re•vers•ing**
1 to turn completely around or upside down or inside out ⟨The jacket *reverses.*⟩
2 to change the order or position of ⟨*Reverse* the vowels to correctly spell the word.⟩
3 to change or cause to change to an opposite or former state, condition, or view ⟨The court *reversed* a decision.⟩
4 to go or cause to go in the opposite direction

[3]**reverse** *n*
1 something opposite to something else : CONTRARY ⟨The river flows west to east, not the *reverse.*⟩
2 an act or instance of changing to an opposite or former state, condition, view, or direction ⟨a *reverse* of plans⟩
3 the back part of something ⟨the *reverse* of a coin⟩
4 a gear that reverses something ⟨Put the car in *reverse.*⟩

re•vert \ri-'vərt\ *vb* **re•vert•ed; re•vert•ing**
to come or go back ⟨He *reverted* to bad habits.⟩

[1]**re•view** \ri-'vyü\ *n*
1 a look at or examination of ⟨a *review* of the year's major events⟩
2 a piece of writing about the quality of something (as a book, performance, or product) ⟨The film got rave *reviews.*⟩
3 a fresh study of material studied before
4 a formal inspection of troops by officers of high rank or an important person

[2]**review** *vb* **re•viewed; re•view•ing**
1 to look at or study again ⟨Let's *review* the lesson.⟩
2 to look at or examine carefully ⟨Let's *review* your record.⟩
3 to report on or evaluate the quality of ⟨Critics will *review* the book.⟩
4 to make an official inspection of (as troops)
re•view•er *n*

re•vile \ri-'vīl\ *vb* **re•viled; re•vil•ing**
to speak to or about in an insulting way

re•vise \ri-'vīz\ *vb* **re•vised; re•vis•ing**
to make changes that correct or improve ⟨I *revised* my book report.⟩

re•viv•al \ri-'vī-vəl\ *n*
1 a return of interest in ⟨a *revival* of jazz music⟩
2 a new production of an older play or movie
3 a return of strength or importance ⟨a *revival* of business⟩
4 a meeting or series of meetings led by a preacher to stir up religious feelings or to make converts

re•vive \ri-'vīv\ *vb* **re•vived; re•viv•ing**
1 to bring back or come back to life, consciousness, freshness, or activity ⟨Doctors *revived* the patient.⟩ ⟨Water will *revive* the flowers.⟩
2 to bring back into use or popularity ⟨The family *revived* an old custom.⟩

re•voke \ri-'vōk\ *vb* **re•voked; re•vok•ing**
to take away or cancel ⟨My driver's license was *revoked.*⟩

[1]**re•volt** \ri-'vōlt\ *vb* **re•volt•ed; re•volt•ing**
1 to rebel against a ruler or government
2 to be or cause to be disgusted or shocked ⟨I was *revolted* by the smell.⟩

[2]**revolt** *n*
violent action against a ruler or government : REBELLION

rev•o•lu•tion \,re-və-'lü-shən\ *n*
1 the action by a heavenly body of going round in a fixed course ⟨The *revolution* of the earth around the sun marks one year.⟩
2 a spinning motion around a center or axis : ROTATION ⟨A light push started the globe's *revolution.*⟩
3 a single complete turn (as of a wheel) ⟨The earth makes one *revolution* on its axis in 24 hours.⟩
4 a sudden, extreme, or complete change (as in manner of living or working)
5 the overthrow of a ruler or government by violent action

rev•o•lu•tion•ary \,re-və-'lü-shə-,ner-ē\ *adj*
1 relating to or involving rebellion against a ruler or government ⟨*revolutionary* leaders⟩
2 being or bringing about a big or important change ⟨a *revolutionary* invention⟩
3 *cap* of or relating to the American Revolution

rev•o•lu•tion•ize \,re-və-'lü-shə-,nīz\ *vb* **rev•o•lu•tion•ized; rev•o•lu•tion•iz•ing**
to change greatly or completely ⟨The invention of the airplane *revolutionized* travel.⟩

re•volve \ri-'välv, -'vȯlv\ *vb* **re•volved; re•volv•ing**
1 to move in an orbit ⟨Planets *revolve* around the sun.⟩
2 ROTATE 1

re•volv•er \ri-'väl-vər, -'vȯl-\ *n*
a pistol having a revolving cylinder holding several bullets all of which may be shot without loading again

re•vue \ri-'vyü\ *n*
a show in a theater consisting usually of short and often funny sketches and songs

re•vul•sion \ri-'vəl-shən\ *n*
a strong feeling of dislike or disgust

[1]**re•ward** \ri-'wȯrd\ *vb* **re•ward•ed; re•ward•ing**
1 to give something (as money) to in return for a service or accomplishment ⟨I always *reward* my pet for good behavior.⟩
2 to give something in return for ⟨The boss *rewarded* his efforts.⟩

[2]**reward** *n*
something (as money) given or offered in return for a service or accomplishment

re•wind \rē-'wīnd\ *vb* **re•wound** \-'wau̇nd\; **re•wind•ing**
to reverse the winding or direction of play of

re•word \,rē-'wərd\ *vb* **re•word•ed; re•word•ing**
to state in different words ⟨Let me *reword* the question.⟩

re•write \,rē-'rīt\ *vb* **re•wrote** \-'rōt\; **re•writ•ten** \-'ri-tᵊn\; **re•writ•ing** \-'rī-tiŋ\
to write over again especially in a different way ⟨*Rewrite* this confusing sentence.⟩

rhea \'rē-ə\ *n*
▶ a tall flightless South American bird that resembles but is smaller than the ostrich

rhea

rheu•mat•ic fever \rü-'ma-tik-\ *n*
a serious disease especially of children that causes fever, pain and swelling of joints, and sometimes heart damage

rheu•ma•tism \'rü-mə-,ti-zəm\ *n*
a condition in which muscles or joints are painful

rhine•stone \'rīn-,stōn\ *n*
a small imitation gem used in jewelry or for decoration

rhi•no \'rī-nō\ *n, pl* **rhino** *or* **rhi•nos**
RHINOCEROS

rhi•noc•er•os \rī-'nä-sə-rəs\ *n, pl* **rhi•noc•er•os•es** *also* **rhinoceros**
▶ a large plant-eating mammal of Africa and Asia with short legs, thick gray to brown skin with little hair, and one or two heavy upright horns on the snout

rhinoceros

▶ **Word History** The ancient Greeks were familiar with the African species of rhinoceros and called the animal in Greek *monokerōs*, "one-horned," and more commonly *rhinokerōs*, "nose-horned." "Nose-horned" is a more or less accurate description, because the horn does grow out of the nose, but "one-horned" is not, because both of the African species have two horns.

rho•do•den•dron \,rō-də-'den-drən\ *n*
▼ a shrub with leathery evergreen leaves and showy clusters of flowers

rhododendron

rhom•bus \'räm-bəs\ *n*
a parallelogram whose sides are equal in length

rhu•barb \'rü-,bärb\ *n*
▶ the thick juicy pink or red stems of a garden plant that have a tart flavor and are used cooked especially in jams and desserts

[1]rhyme \'rīm\ *n*
1 close similarity in the final sounds of two or more words or lines of writing
2 a piece of writing (as a poem) whose lines end in similar sounds

[2]rhyme *vb* **rhymed**; **rhym•ing**
1 to end with the same sound ⟨"Bug" *rhymes* with "rug."⟩
2 to have lines that end with the same sound ⟨Not all poems *rhyme*.⟩
3 to cause lines or words to end with a similar sound ⟨He *rhymed* "moon" with "June."⟩

rhythm \'ri-t͟həm\ *n*
a regular repeated pattern of beats, sounds, activity, or movements

rhyth•mic \'rit͟h-mik\ *or* **rhyth•mi•cal** \-mi-kəl\ *adj*
having a regular repeated pattern of beats, sounds, activity, or movements ⟨*rhythmic* drumming⟩
rhyth•mi•cal•ly *adv*

RI *abbr* Rhode Island

rib \'rib\ *n*
1 one of the curved bones of the chest that are joined to the backbone and help to stiffen the body wall and protect the organs
2 a piece of meat from an animal (as a cow or pig) that includes a rib and is used as food
3 something (as a piece of wire supporting the fabric of an umbrella) that is like a rib in shape or use
4 one of the parallel ridges in a knitted or woven fabric
ribbed \'ribd\ *adj*

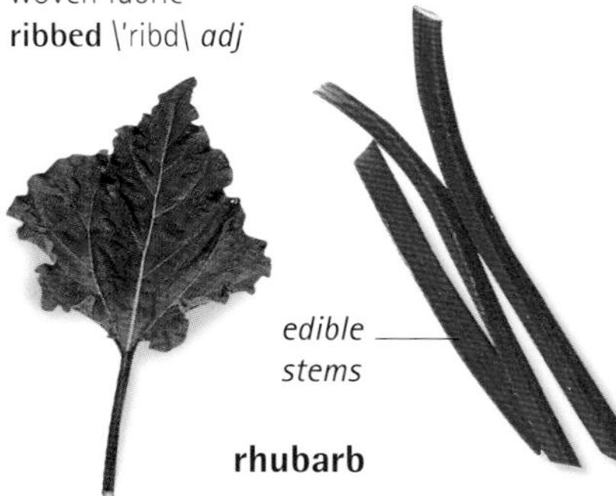

rhubarb

rib•bon \'ri-bən\ *n*
1 a narrow strip of usually colorful fabric used especially for decoration or to tie things
2 a ribbon that is given as an award
3 TATTER 1, SHRED — usually used in pl. ⟨The sails were torn to *ribbons*.⟩

rib cage *n*
the bony enclosing wall of the chest consisting of the ribs and their connecting parts

rice \'rīs\ *n*
the small seeds of a tall cereal grass widely grown in warm wet regions that are the chief food in many parts of the world

rich \'rich\ *adj* **rich•er**; **rich•est**
1 having a lot of money and possessions : WEALTHY ⟨*rich* people⟩
2 [1]VALUABLE 1, EXPENSIVE ⟨*rich* robes⟩
3 well supplied : ABUNDANT ⟨The city is *rich* in tradition.⟩
4 FERTILE 1 ⟨*rich* soil⟩

5 containing much sugar, fat, or seasoning ⟨*rich* food⟩
6 deep and pleasing in color or tone
rich•ly *adv*
rich•ness *n*

rich•es \'ri-chəz\ *n pl*
things that make someone rich

rick•ets \'ri-kəts\ *n*
a disease especially of children in which the bones are soft and deformed and which is caused by lack of vitamin D

rick•ety \'ri-kə-tē\ *adj*
in poor condition and likely to break ⟨*rickety* stairs⟩

rick•shaw *also* **rick•sha** \'rik-,shȯ\ *n*
▶ a small carriage with two wheels that is pulled by one person and was used originally in Japan

ric•o•chet \'ri-kə-,shā\ *vb* **ric•o•cheted**; **ric•o•chet•ing**
to bounce off at an angle

rid \'rid\ *vb* **rid** *also* **rid•ded**; **rid•ding**
to free from something : RELIEVE ⟨A shampoo *rid* the dog of fleas.⟩

¹rid•dle \'ri-dᵊl\ *n*
1 a puzzling question to be solved or answered by guessing
2 someone or something that is hard to understand ⟨His strange behavior was a *riddle*.⟩

²riddle *vb* **rid•dled**; **rid•dling**
1 to pierce with many holes
2 to fill with something unpleasant or unwanted ⟨The report is *riddled* with errors.⟩

rickshaw: a bicycle rickshaw in Thailand

¹ride \'rīd\ *vb* **rode** \'rōd\; **rid•den** \'ri-dᵊn\; **rid•ing** \'rī-diŋ\
1 to travel or move by sitting or standing on or in ⟨I *ride* the bus.⟩
2 to sit on and control so as to be carried along ⟨I learned to *ride* a bicycle.⟩
3 to be supported or carried on ⟨Surfers *rode* the waves.⟩
4 to travel over a surface ⟨The car *rides* well.⟩
5 to endure without great harm or damage ⟨We'll *ride* out the storm.⟩
6 DEPEND 2 ⟨Our hopes are *riding* on you.⟩
rid•er \'rī-dər\ *n*

²ride *n*
1 a trip on horseback or by vehicle
2 a mechanical device (as a merry-go-round) that moves around while people sit or stand on it for entertainment
3 a way of getting from one place to another ⟨She needs a *ride* to school.⟩

ridge \'rij\ *n*
1 ▼ a range of hills or mountains or its upper part
2 a raised strip ⟨The plow created a *ridge* of soil.⟩
3 the line made where two sloping surfaces come together ⟨the *ridge* of a roof⟩
ridged \'rijd\ *adj*

¹rid•i•cule \'ri-də-,kyül\ *n*
the act of making fun of someone or something in a cruel or harsh way : mean or unkind comments or behavior

²ridicule *vb* **rid•i•culed**; **rid•i•cul•ing**
to make fun of in a cruel or harsh way ⟨They *ridiculed* the idea.⟩

ri•dic•u•lous \rə-'di-kyə-ləs\ *adj*
causing or deserving ridicule : very silly or unreasonable
ri•dic•u•lous•ly *adv*

¹rif•fle \'ri-fəl\ *vb* **rif•fled**; **rif•fling**
1 to move lightly ⟨Wind *riffled* the bird's feathers.⟩
2 to look through quickly ⟨I *riffled* through a magazine.⟩

ridge 1: a moutain ridge on the island of Maui, Hawaii

²riffle *n*
1 a shallow area of a stream bed that causes ripples
2 ²RIPPLE 1

riff•raff \'rif-ˌraf\ *n*
a group of people who are not considered respectable or honest

¹ri•fle \'rī-fəl\ *vb* **ri•fled; ri•fling**
1 to search through quickly and roughly often to steal something
2 ¹STEAL 1

²rifle *n*
a gun that has a long barrel with spiral grooves on its inside

rift \'rift\ *n*
1 an opening made by splitting or separation : CLEFT ⟨a *rift* in the ice⟩
2 a break in friendly relations

¹rig \'rig\ *vb* **rigged; rig•ging**
1 to build or set up usually quickly and for temporary use ⟨We *rigged* up a shelter of branches.⟩
2 to provide (as a ship) with rigging
3 CLOTHE 1, DRESS
4 to provide with gear

²rig *n*
1 the shape, number, and arrangement of sails and masts of a ship that sets it apart from other types of ships
2 ▶ equipment or machinery for a certain purpose ⟨an oil-drilling *rig*⟩

rig•ging \'ri-giŋ\ *n*
lines and chains used on a ship to help support the masts and sails

¹right \'rīt\ *adj*
1 following or in accordance with what is just, good, or proper ⟨It's not *right* to lie.⟩
2 ACCURATE, CORRECT ⟨That's the *right* answer.⟩
3 SUITABLE, APPROPRIATE ⟨He's the *right* person for the job.⟩
4 located on the side of the body away from the heart ⟨the *right* arm⟩
5 located nearer to the right side of the body than to the left ⟨the chair's *right* arm⟩
6 being or meant to be the side on top, in front, or on the outside ⟨The box landed *right* side up.⟩ ⟨Turn the socks *right* side out.⟩
7 in a normal or healthy state or condition ⟨I don't feel *right* today.⟩ ⟨That milk doesn't smell *right*.⟩
8 ¹STRAIGHT 1 ⟨a *right* line⟩
right•ly *adv*
right•ness *n*

²right *n*
1 the ideal of what is just, good, or proper ⟨He hasn't learned *right* from wrong.⟩
2 something to which a person has a just claim ⟨the *right* to vote⟩ ⟨He has a *right* to be angry.⟩
3 the cause of truth or justice ⟨They fought for *right*.⟩
4 the right side : a part or location that is on or toward the right side ⟨My house is on the *right*.⟩

³right *adv*
1 according to what is just, good, or proper ⟨She lives *right*.⟩
2 in the exact location, position, or moment PRECISELY ⟨It's *right* where you left it.⟩
3 in a direct line or course : STRAIGHT ⟨Come *right* home.⟩
4 according to truth or fact ⟨You guessed *right*.⟩
5 in a suitable, proper, or desired way ⟨You're not doing it *right*.⟩
6 all the way ⟨We stayed *right* to the end of the game.⟩

right angle

right angle

7 without delay : IMMEDIATELY ⟨Let's go *right* after lunch.⟩
8 on or to the right ⟨turn *right*⟩
9 in a complete way ⟨He felt *right* at home here.⟩
right away without delay : IMMEDIATELY

▶ **²rig 2**
Drilling for oil requires the use of large rigs. Some oil-drilling rigs are built as platforms over the sea, supported by a steel frame attached to the floor of the sea. The platform holds machinery and pipes used to drill wells for oil, which is pumped back to the rig, before being piped ashore or transported by oil tanker. The people who work on the rig also live there, and work in shifts so that the rig is operated day and night. The only way to reach land or to receive supplies is by boat or helicopter.

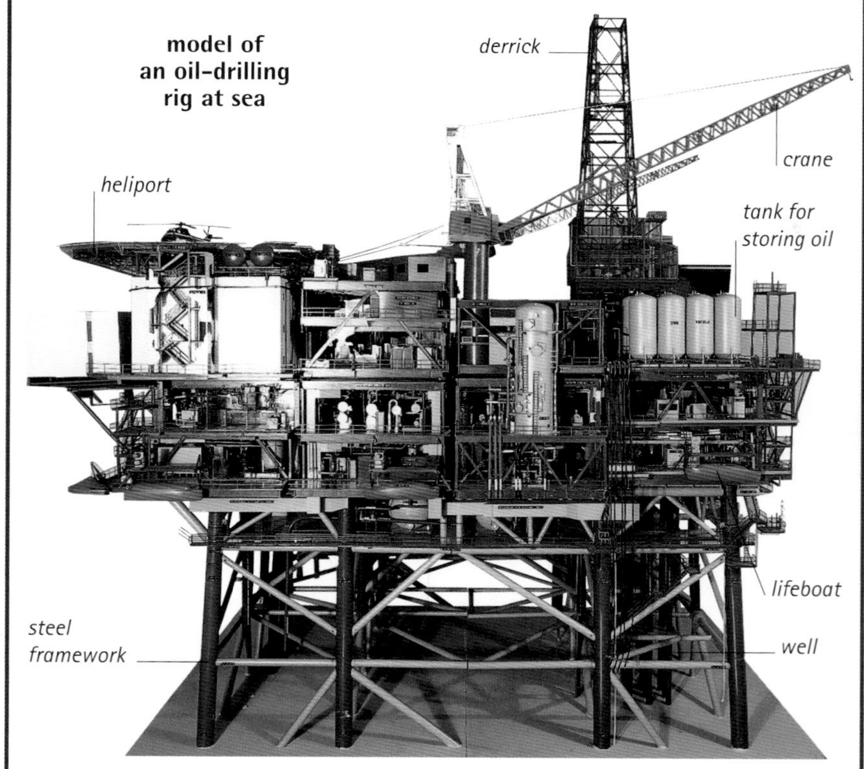

model of an oil-drilling rig at sea

[4]right *vb* **right•ed; right•ing**
1 to make better or more just ⟨If only we could *right* the world's wrongs.⟩
2 to adjust or restore to a proper state or condition
3 to bring or bring back to an upright position ⟨I *righted* the books.⟩
4 to become upright ⟨The ship slowly *righted* again.⟩

right angle *n*
◀ an angle formed by two lines that are perpendicular to each other : an angle of 90 degrees

righ•teous \'rī-chəs\ *adj*
1 doing or being what is just or proper ⟨*righteous* people⟩ ⟨a *righteous* action⟩
2 caused by an insult to what is believed to be just or proper ⟨*righteous* anger⟩
righ•teous•ly *adv*
righ•teous•ness *n*

right•ful \'rīt-fəl\ *adj*
LAWFUL 2, PROPER ⟨the *rightful* owner⟩
right•ful•ly \-fə-lē\ *adv*

right–hand \'rīt-,hand\ *adj*
1 located on the right side
2 RIGHT-HANDED 1
3 relied on most of all ⟨He's her *right-hand* man.⟩

right–hand•ed \'rīt-'han-dəd\ *adj*
1 using the right hand better or more easily than the left
2 done or made with or for the right hand ⟨a *right-handed* glove⟩

right–of–way \,rīt-əv-'wā\ *n*, *pl* **rights–of–way** \,rīt-səv-\
1 the legal right to pass over someone else's land
2 the right of some traffic to go before other traffic

right triangle *n*
a triangle having a right angle

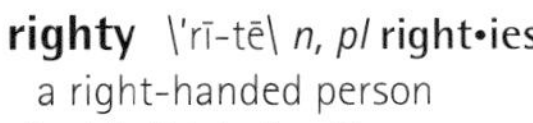

[1]ring 1: a napkin rolled into a napkin ring

righty \'rī-tē\ *n*, *pl* **right•ies**
a right-handed person

rig•id \'ri-jəd\ *adj*
1 not flexible : STIFF ⟨*rigid* plastic⟩
2 STRICT 2, SEVERE ⟨*rigid* discipline⟩
rig•id•ly *adv*

rig•ma•role \'rig-mə-,rōl\ *n*
1 a long and usually meaningless or uninteresting story
2 a complicated and often unnecessary procedure

rig•or \'ri-gər\ *n*
a harsh condition (as of discipline)

rig•or•ous \'ri-gə-rəs\ *adj*
1 very strict ⟨*rigorous* rules⟩
2 hard to endure because of extreme conditions : HARSH ⟨*rigorous* winters⟩
rig•or•ous•ly *adv*

rile \'rīl\ *vb* **riled; ril•ing**
to make angry : IRRITATE

rill \'ril\ *n*
a very small stream

[1]rim \'rim\ *n*
1 ▼ an outer edge especially of something curved ⟨the *rim* of a plate⟩
2 the part of a wheel that the tire is mounted on
rimmed \'rimd\ *adj*

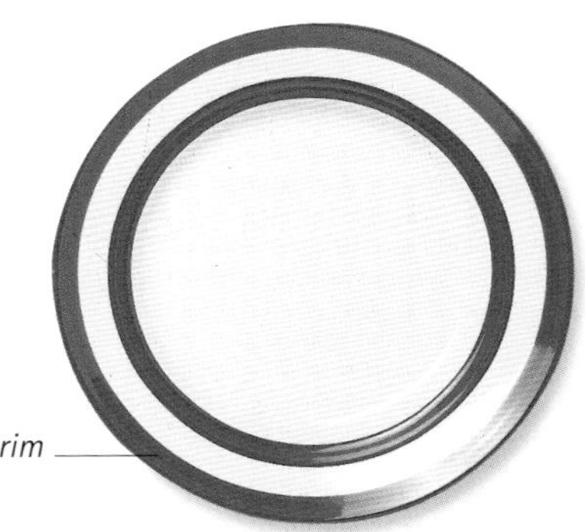

[1]rim 1: a plate with a blue rim

[2]rim *vb* **rimmed; rim•ming**
to form a rim around ⟨Rocks *rimmed* the lake.⟩

rime \'rīm\ *n*
[1]FROST 1

rind \'rīnd\ *n*
a tough outer layer ⟨watermelon *rind*⟩

[1]ring \'riŋ\ *n*
1 ▲ a circular band used for holding, fastening, or connecting ⟨a key *ring*⟩
2 a circular band usually of precious metal worn especially on the finger as jewelry
3 something circular in shape ⟨a smoke *ring*⟩
4 an often circular space for shows or contests ⟨a circus *ring*⟩
5 a group of people who work together for dishonest purposes
6 ANNUAL RING
ringed \'riŋd\ *adj*

[2]ring *vb* **ringed; ring•ing**
to place or form a ring around ⟨Tall trees *ring* the meadow.⟩

[3]ring *vb* **rang** \'raŋ\; **rung** \'rəŋ\; **ring•ing**
1 to make or cause to make a clear vibrating sound ⟨The bell *rang.*⟩ ⟨*Ring* the bell.⟩
2 to announce by or as if by striking a bell ⟨We'll *ring* in the new year.⟩
3 to sound loudly ⟨Cheers *rang* out.⟩
4 to fill or be filled with the sound of something ⟨The hall *rang* with laughter.⟩
5 to be filled with a humming sound ⟨His ears were *ringing.*⟩
6 to seem to be a certain way ⟨Their story *rings* true.⟩
7 to call for especially by ringing a bell ⟨I *rang* for the servants.⟩

[4]ring *n*
1 a clear sound made by or as if by vibrating metal ⟨the *ring* of a bell⟩ ⟨a telephone's *ring*⟩
2 a continuous or repeating loud sound
3 something that suggests a certain quality ⟨Their story had the *ring* of truth.⟩
4 a telephone call ⟨Give me a *ring* this afternoon.⟩

ring finger *n*
the third finger especially of the left hand when counting the index finger as the first

ring•lead•er \'riŋ-,lē-dər\ *n*
a leader especially of a group of people who cause trouble

ring•let \'riŋ-lət\ *n*
▼ a long curl of hair

ringlet: a woman in 19th-century costume with her hair in ringlets

rink: ice-skating rink at Rockefeller Center, New York

ring•tone \'riŋ-,tōn\ *n*
a sound made by a cell phone to signal that a call is coming in

ring•worm \'riŋ-,wərm\ *n*
a fungus infection that causes red ring-shaped patches to appear on the skin

rink \'riŋk\ *n*
▲ a place for ice-skating or roller-skating

[1]**rinse** \'rins\ *vb* **rinsed**; **rins•ing**
1 to wash lightly with water
2 to remove (something) with clean water ⟨I *rinsed* soap off the dishes.⟩

[2]**rinse** *n*
1 an act of washing with a liquid and especially with clean water
2 a liquid used for rinsing

[1]**ri•ot** \'rī-ət\ *n*
1 violent and uncontrolled public behavior by a group of people
2 a colorful display ⟨a *riot* of wildflowers⟩
3 someone or something that is very funny ⟨The movie was a *riot.*⟩

[2]**riot** *vb* **ri•ot•ed**; **ri•ot•ing**
to take part in violent and uncontrolled public behavior

[1]**rip** \'rip\ *vb* **ripped**; **rip•ping**
1 to cut or tear open : split apart
2 to remove quickly (as by tearing) ⟨He *ripped* a page out.⟩
rip•per *n*

[2]**rip** *n*
a usually long tear

ripe \'rīp\ *adj* **rip•er**; **rip•est**
1 fully grown and developed ⟨*ripe* fruit⟩
2 of advanced years ⟨a *ripe* old age⟩
3 [1]READY 1 ⟨They were *ripe* for action.⟩
ripe•ness *n*

rip•en \'rī-pən\ *vb* **rip•ened**; **rip•en•ing**
to make or become ripe

[1]**rip•ple** \'ri-pəl\ *vb* **rip•pled**; **rip•pling**
1 to move or cause to move in small waves ⟨The lion's muscles *rippled.*⟩ ⟨A breeze *rippled* the water.⟩
2 to pass or spread over or through ⟨Laughter *rippled* through the crowd.⟩

[2]**ripple** *n*
1 a very small wave on the surface of a liquid ⟨The rock made *ripples* in the pond.⟩
2 something that passes or spreads through ⟨a *ripple* of laughter⟩

[1]**rise** \'rīz\ *vb* **rose** \'rōz\; **ris•en** \'ri-zᵊn\; **ris•ing** \'rī-ziŋ\
1 to get up from lying, kneeling, or sitting
2 to get up from sleeping in a bed
3 to go or move up ⟨We saw smoke *rising.*⟩
4 to swell in size or volume ⟨The river was *rising.*⟩ ⟨Their voices *rose* as they argued.⟩
5 to increase in amount or number ⟨Prices are *rising.*⟩
6 to become encouraged or grow stronger ⟨Their spirits *rose.*⟩
7 to appear above the horizon ⟨The sun *rises* at six.⟩
8 to gain a higher rank or position ⟨He *rose* to colonel.⟩ ⟨The game *rose* in popularity.⟩
9 to come into being ⟨The river *rises* in the hills.⟩
10 to successfully deal with a difficult situation ⟨She *rose* to the challenge.⟩
11 to return from death
12 to launch an attack or revolt ⟨The people *rose* in rebellion.⟩
ris•er \'rī-zər\ *n*

[2]**rise** *n*
1 an increase in amount, number, or volume ⟨a *rise* in prices⟩
2 upward movement ⟨the *rise* and fall of waves⟩
3 the act of gaining a higher rank or position ⟨a *rise* to power⟩
4 BEGINNING 1, ORIGIN ⟨the *rise* of democracy⟩
5 an upward slope
6 a spot higher than surrounding ground
7 an angry reaction ⟨She's just saying that to get a *rise* out of you.⟩

[1]**risk** \'risk\ *n*
1 possibility of loss or injury ⟨This adventure involves *risks.*⟩
2 something or someone that may cause loss or injury ⟨Smoking is a health *risk.*⟩
synonyms see DANGER

[2]**risk** *vb* **risked**; **risk•ing**
1 to expose to danger ⟨He *risked* his life to save the children.⟩
2 to take the risk or danger of ⟨I'm not willing to *risk* hurting myself.⟩

risky \'ris-kē\ *adj* **risk•i•er**; **risk•i•est**
DANGEROUS 1

rite \'rīt\ *n*
an act performed in a ceremony

rit•u•al \'ri-chə-wəl\ *n*
a ceremony or series of acts that is always performed the same way

[1]**ri•val** \'rī-vəl\ *n*
someone or something that tries to defeat or be more successful than another

► **Word History** *Rival* is borrowed from Latin *rivalis.* As an adjective made from the noun *rivus,* "stream," *rivalis* meant "of a brook or stream." As a noun, *rivalis* was used to refer to those who use the same stream for water. Just as neighbors might dispute each other's rights to a common source of water, disagreement often arises when two people want something that only one can possess. Thus Latin *rivalis* also developed a sense relating to competition in other areas, and this sense came into English.

[2]**rival** *adj*
being equally good ⟨*rival* claims⟩

[3]**rival** *vb* **ri•valed** *or* **ri•valled**; **ri•val•ing** *or* **ri•val•ling**
to be as good as or almost as good as ⟨Her skills *rival* those of the champion.⟩

ri•val•ry \'rī-vəl-rē\ *n, pl* **ri•val•ries**
the state of trying to defeat or be more successful than another : COMPETITION

river 1: the Altmühl River winding through a valley in Lower Bavaria, Germany

riv•er \'ri-vər\ *n*
1 ▲ a natural stream of water larger than a brook or creek
2 a large stream or flow ⟨a *river* of mud⟩

[1]riv•et \'ri-vət\ *n*
a bolt with a head that is passed through two or more pieces and is hammered into place

[2]rivet *vb* **riv•et•ed**; **riv•et•ing**
1 to fasten with rivets
2 to attract and hold (as someone's attention) completely ⟨We were *riveted* by the story.⟩
3 to make (someone) unable to move because of fear or shock

riv•u•let \'ri-vyə-lət\ *n*
a small stream

roach \'rōch\ *n*
COCKROACH

road \'rōd\ *n*
1 a hard flat surface for vehicles, persons, and animals to travel on
2 a way to achieve something ⟨the *road* to success⟩

road•run•ner \'rōd-ˌrə-nər\ *n*
a long-tailed bird that is found in dry regions of the southwestern United States and is able to run very fast

road•side \'rōd-ˌsīd\ *n*
the strip of land beside a road

road•way \'rōd-ˌwā\ *n*
the part of a road used by vehicles

roam \'rōm\ *vb* **roamed**; **roam•ing**
to go from place to place with no fixed purpose or direction
synonyms see WANDER

[1]roan \'rōn\ *adj*
of a dark color (as black or brown) mixed with white ⟨a *roan* horse⟩

[2]roan *n*
an animal (as a horse) with a dark-colored coat mixed with white

[1]roar \'ròr\ *vb* **roared**; **roar•ing**
1 to make a long loud sound ⟨The engine *roared.*⟩
2 to laugh loudly
3 to say loudly ⟨"Goal!" the announcer *roared.*⟩
4 to move with a loud noise

[2]roar *n*
a long shout, bellow, or loud noise

roar•ing \'ròr-iŋ\ *adj*
very active or strong ⟨a *roaring* business⟩ ⟨a *roaring* fire⟩

[1]roast \'rōst\ *vb* **roast•ed**; **roast•ing**
1 to cook with dry heat (as in an oven)
2 to be or make very hot ⟨I *roasted* in the sun.⟩
roast•er *n*

[2]roast *adj*
cooked with dry heat ⟨*roast* beef⟩

[3]roast *n*
1 ▼ a piece of meat suitable for cooking with dry heat
2 an outdoor party at which food is cooked over an open fire

rob \'räb\ *vb* **robbed**; **rob•bing**
1 to unlawfully take something away from a person or place in secrecy or by force, threat, or trickery
2 to keep from getting something due, expected, or desired
rob•ber *n*

rob•bery \'rä-bə-rē, 'räb-rē\ *n, pl* **rob•ber•ies**
the act or practice of taking something unlawfully

[3]roast 1: a cooked beef roast

rodent
There are almost 2,000 species of rodents living in diverse environments around the world. Rodents are generally small, furry, plant-eating creatures with upper and lower pairs of sharp incisor teeth, which grow quickly to compensate for constant gnawing. Many rodents are nocturnal, preferring darkness to protect them from predators. Others are camouflaged or run quickly for cover when threatened.

capybara \ˌka-pi-ˈber-ə\ is a South American rodent often found in or near water

guinea pig

mouse

squirrel

rat

porcupine

[1]**robe** \ˈrōb\ *n*
1 a long loose or flowing garment ⟨a judge's *robe*⟩
2 a loose garment worn especially after bathing or while relaxing at home

[2]**robe** *vb* **robed**; **rob•ing**
to dress especially in a robe

rob•in \ˈrä-bən\ *n*
1 ▼ a large North American songbird with a grayish back and dull reddish breast
2 a small European songbird with an orange throat and breast

robin 1

ro•bot \ˈrō-ˌbät\ *n*
1 a machine that looks and acts like a human being
2 a machine that can do the work of a person automatically or under the control of a computer

▶ **Word History** In 1923 the play *R.U.R.*, by Karel Čapek, opened in London and New York. In the play "R.U.R." stands for "Rossum's Universal Robots," a company formed by an English scientist named Rossum to manufacture humanlike machines called "robots" to do hard, boring jobs. In Czech—the language of what is today the Czech Republic and the original language of the play—the word *robota* means "forced labor," and Čapek based his new coinage "robot" on this word. Čapek's play was popular, and soon the word became a general term for machines that can perform the tasks of a person.

ro•bust \rō-ˈbəst\ *adj*
strong and healthy
ro•bust•ly *adv*

[1]**rock** \ˈräk\ *vb* **rocked**; **rock•ing**
1 to move gently back and forth or side to side
2 to cause (something) to shake violently ⟨An earthquake *rocked* the town.⟩

[2]**rock** *n*
1 solid mineral deposits ⟨The bulldozer hit *rock.*⟩
2 a mass of stone

[3]**rock** *n*
1 a rocking movement
2 popular music played on instruments that are amplified electronically

rock and roll *or* **rock 'n' roll** *n*
[3]ROCK 2

rock dove *n*
1 a bluish gray dove of Europe and Asia that nests on rocky cliffs
2 a variety of the rock dove that is now found in cities throughout the world

rock•er \ˈrä-kər\ *n*
1 ROCKING CHAIR
2 a curving piece of wood or metal on which an object (as a cradle or rocking chair) rocks

[1]**rock•et** \ˈrä-kət\ *n*
1 a firework that is driven through the air by the gases produced by a burning substance
2 a jet engine that is driven by gases produced by a burning substance
3 a bomb, missile, or vehicle that is driven by gases produced by a burning substance

[2]rocket *vb* **rock•et•ed; rock•et•ing**
1 to rise swiftly ⟨Prices have *rocketed.*⟩
2 to travel rapidly in or as if in a rocket

rock•ing chair \'rä-kiŋ-\ *n*
a chair mounted on rockers

rocking horse *n*
▶ a toy horse mounted on rockers

rock salt *n*
common salt in large crystals

rocky \'rä-kē\ *adj* **rock•i•er; rock•i•est**
full of or consisting of rocks ⟨a *rocky* shore⟩ ⟨*rocky* cliffs⟩

rod \'räd\ *n*
1 a light flexible pole often with line and a reel attached used in fishing
2 a stick or bundle of twigs used in whipping a person
3 a straight slender stick or bar
4 a measure of length equal to 16½ feet (about 5 meters)
5 a cell of the retina of the eye that is shaped like a rod and is sensitive to faint light

rode *past of* RIDE

ro•dent \'rō-d^{ə}nt\ *n*
◀ a usually small mammal (as a squirrel, rat, mouse, or beaver) with sharp front teeth used in gnawing

ro•deo \'rō-dē-,ō, rə-'dā-ō\ *n, pl* **ro•de•os**
▼ an exhibition that features cowboy skills (as riding and roping)

roe \'rō\ *n*
the eggs of a fish especially while still held together in a membrane

rogue \'rōg\ *n*
1 a dishonest or evil person
2 a pleasantly mischievous person

rocking horse

rogu•ish \'rō-gish\ *adj*
showing mischievousness ⟨a *roguish* smile⟩
rogu•ish•ly *adv*

role \'rōl\ *n*
1 a character assigned or taken on
2 a part played by an actor or singer
3 [1]FUNCTION 1 ⟨The teacher plays an important *role* in education.⟩

role model *n*
a person whose behavior in a certain function is imitated by others

[1]roll \'rōl\ *vb* **rolled; roll•ing**
1 to move or cause to move by turning over and over on a surface
2 to shape or become shaped in rounded form ⟨She *rolls* the dough to make cookies.⟩
3 to sound with a full echoing tone or with a continuous beating sound ⟨*rolling* thunder⟩
4 to flow in or as if in a continuous stream ⟨The money was *rolling* in.⟩
5 to move or cause to move in a circular manner ⟨She *rolled* her eyes.⟩ ⟨He *rolled* over on his back.⟩
6 to go by : PASS ⟨Time *rolled* by.⟩
7 to move with a side-to-side sway ⟨The ship *rolled.*⟩
8 to make smooth, even, or firm with a roller ⟨He *rolls* out the dough.⟩
9 to move on rollers or wheels
roll around to happen again ⟨We'll go when Friday *rolls around.*⟩

[2]roll *n*
1 something or a quantity of something that is rolled up or rounded as if rolled ⟨a *roll* of tape⟩
2 a small piece of baked bread dough
3 a writing that may be rolled up : SCROLL
4 an official list of names

[3]roll *n*
1 a sound produced by rapid strokes on a drum
2 a heavy echoing sound ⟨the *roll* of thunder⟩
3 a movement or action that involves turning over and over or circling around

roll•er \'rō-lər\ *n*
1 a turning cylinder over or on which something is moved or which is used to press, shape, or smooth something
2 a rod on which something (as a map or hair) is rolled up
3 a small wheel
4 a long heavy wave on the sea

roller coaster *n*
an amusement park ride that is an elevated railway with sharp curves and steep slopes over which cars travel

rodeo: cowboys at a rodeo

a b c d e f g h i j k l m n o p q r s t u v w x y z

roller–skate *vb* **roller–skat•ed**; **roller–skat•ing**
to ride on roller skates

roller skate *n*
a skate that has wheels instead of a runner

rolling pin *n*
a cylinder (as of wood) used to roll out dough

romper:
a young boy in rompers

ROM \'räm\ *n*
a usually small computer memory that contains special-purpose information (as a program) which cannot be changed

[1]Ro•man \'rō-mən\ *n*
1 a person born or living in Rome
2 a citizen of an ancient empire centered on Rome
3 *not cap* upright letters or type

[2]Roman *adj*
1 of or relating to Rome or the Romans
2 *not cap* of or relating to a type style with upright characters (as in "these letters")

Roman Catholic *adj*
belonging to or relating to the Christian church led by the pope

ro•mance \rō-'mans\ *n*
1 an attraction or appeal to the emotions ⟨the *romance* of the sea⟩
2 a love story
3 a love affair
4 an old tale of knights and noble ladies
5 an adventure story

Ro•mance \rō-'mans\ *adj*
relating to or being the languages (as French, Italian, and Spanish) that are descended from Latin

Roman numeral *n*
a numeral in a system of figures based on the ancient Roman system ⟨In *Roman numerals* X equals 10.⟩

ro•man•tic \rō-'man-tik\ *adj*
1 stressing or appealing to the emotions or imagination
2 involving or showing feelings of love
3 not realistic : IMPRACTICAL
4 suitable for a love story
ro•man•ti•cal•ly \-ti-kə-lē\ *adv*

[1]romp \'rämp\ *vb* **romped**; **romp•ing**
to play in a rough and noisy way

[2]romp *n*
rough and noisy play : FROLIC

romp•er \'räm-pər\ *n*
◀ a young child's one-piece garment having legs that can be unfastened around the inside — usually used in pl.

[1]roof \'rüf, 'ru̇f\ *n, pl* **roofs**
1 the upper covering part of a building
2 something like a roof in form, position, or purpose
roofed \'rüft, 'ru̇ft\ *adj*

[2]roof *vb* **roofed**; **roof•ing**
to cover with a roof

roof•ing \'rü-fiŋ, 'ru̇-\ *n*
material for a roof

[1]rook \'ru̇k\ *n*
a crow of Europe and Asia that nests and sleeps in groups usually in the tops of trees

[2]rook *vb* **rooked**; **rook•ing**
[1]CHEAT 2, SWINDLE

[3]rook *n*
one of the pieces in the game of chess

rook•ie \'ru̇-kē\ *n*
BEGINNER, RECRUIT

[1]room \'rüm, 'ru̇m\ *n*
1 a divided part of the inside of a building
2 a bedroom in a home or hotel
3 the people in a room ⟨The whole *room* cheered.⟩
4 available space ⟨We had barely *room* to move.⟩
5 a suitable opportunity ⟨There's *room* for improvement.⟩

[2]room *vb* **roomed**; **room•ing**
to provide with or live in lodgings ⟨Our mothers *roomed* together in college.⟩

room•er \'rü-mər, 'ru̇-\ *n*
LODGER

rooming house *n*
a house having furnished rooms for rent to lodgers

room•mate \'rüm-,māt, 'ru̇m-\ *n*
one of two or more people sharing a room or dwelling

rooster

roomy \'rü-mē, 'ru̇-\ *adj* **room•i•er**; **room•i•est**
SPACIOUS ⟨The house has *roomy* closets.⟩
room•i•ness *n*

[1]roost \'rüst\ *n*
a place where birds rest or sleep

[2]roost *vb* **roost•ed**; **roost•ing**
to settle down for rest or sleep ⟨Sparrows *roost* in the trees.⟩

roost•er \'rü-stər\ *n*
▲ an adult male chicken

[1]root \'rüt, 'ru̇t\ *n*
1 ▼ the leafless underground part of a plant that absorbs water and minerals, stores food, and holds the plant in place
2 the part of something by which it is attached ⟨The tooth's *root* is anchored in bone.⟩

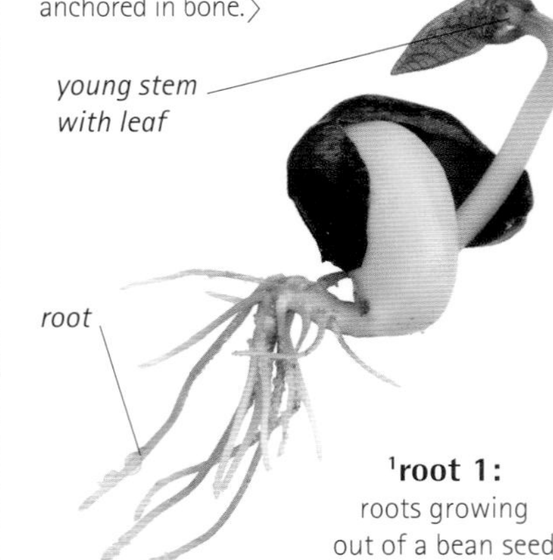

[1]root 1:
roots growing out of a bean seed

3 SOURCE 1 ⟨Money is the *root* of all evil.⟩
4 the ancestors of a person or group of people
5 a special relationship ⟨They have *roots* in the community.⟩
6 [1]CORE 3 ⟨We finally got to the *root* of the problem.⟩
7 a word or part of a word from which other

words are obtained by adding a prefix or suffix ⟨The word "hold" is the *root* of "holder."⟩
root•ed \'rü-təd, 'rú-\ *adj*

[2]root *vb* **root•ed; root•ing**
1 to form or cause to form roots ⟨The seedlings *rooted* quickly.⟩
2 to attach by or as if by roots ⟨He was *rooted* to his chair.⟩
root out to remove by or as if by pulling out the roots ⟨The mayor promised to *root out* crime.⟩

[3]root *vb* **rooted; rooting**
to turn up or dig with or as if with the snout ⟨She *rooted* in her desk for a pen.⟩

[4]root \'rüt\ *vb* **rooted; rooting**
to wish for the success of ⟨We're *rooting* for the underdog.⟩
root•er *n*

root beer *n*
a sweet drink flavored with extracts of roots and herbs

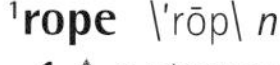

[1]rope 1: a length of rope

[1]rope \'rōp\ *n*
1 ▲ a strong thick cord of strands (as of fiber or wire) twisted or braided together
2 a number of similar things held together on a string

[2]rope *vb* **roped; rop•ing**
1 to bind, fasten, or tie with a cord
2 to set off or divide by a cord ⟨Police *roped* off a street.⟩
3 [1]LASSO
rop•er *n*

ro•sa•ry \'rō-zə-rē\ *n, pl* **ro•sa•ries**
► a string of beads used in counting prayers

rosary

[1]rose *past of* RISE

[2]rose \'rōz\ *n*
1 a showy and usually fragrant white, yellow, pink, or red flower that grows on a prickly shrub
2 a medium pink

rose•mary \'rōz-,mer-ē\ *n*
► a fragrant mint with needlelike leaves used as a seasoning in cooking

ro•sette \rō-'zet\ *n*
a badge or ornament of ribbon gathered in the shape of a rose

rose•wood \'rōz-,wu̇d\ *n*
a reddish or purplish wood streaked with black that is used especially for making furniture and musical instruments

Rosh Ha•sha•nah \,rōsh-hə-'shō-nə\ *n*
the Jewish New Year observed as a religious holiday in September or October

ros•in \'rä-zᵊn\ *n*
a hard brittle yellow to dark red substance obtained especially from pine trees and used in varnishes and on violin bows

ros•ter \'rä-stər\ *n*
an orderly list of people belonging to some group

ros•trum \'rä-strəm\ *n, pl* **ros•tra** \-trə\ *or* **rostrums**
a stage or platform for public speaking

rosy \'rō-zē\ *adj* **ros•i•er; ros•i•est**
1 having a pink color
2 PROMISING, HOPEFUL ⟨He's a good student with a *rosy* future.⟩

[1]rot \'rät\ *vb* **rot•ted; rot•ting**
1 to undergo decay
2 to go to ruin ⟨He was left to *rot* in jail.⟩

[2]rot *n*
1 the process of decaying : the state of being decayed
2 something that has decayed or is decaying

ro•ta•ry \'rō-tə-rē\ *adj*
1 turning on an axis like a wheel ⟨a *rotary* blade⟩
2 having a rotating part

ro•tate \'rō-,tāt\ *vb* **ro•tat•ed; ro•tat•ing**
1 to turn about an axis or a center
2 to go from one person to another or others in a cycle ⟨The staff *rotates* working weekends.⟩
3 to pass in a series ⟨The seasons *rotate.*⟩

ro•ta•tion \rō-'tā-shən\ *n*
1 the act of turning about an axis
2 the system of growing different crops in the same field usually in a regular order

rote \'rōt\ *n*
the act of repeating over and over often without attention to meaning ⟨I learned the poem by *rote.*⟩

ro•tor \'rō-tər\ *n*
1 the part of an electrical machine that turns
2 a system of spinning horizontal blades that support a helicopter in the air

rosemary

rot•ten \'rä-tᵊn\ *adj*
1 having rotted ⟨*rotten* wood⟩
2 morally bad
3 of poor quality ⟨They did a *rotten* job.⟩
4 very unpleasant ⟨I had a *rotten* day.⟩

ro•tund \rō-'tənd\ *adj*
1 somewhat round
2 [1]PLUMP

rouge \'rüzh\ *n*
a cosmetic used to give a red color to cheeks or lips

[1]rough \'rəf\ *adj* **rough•er; rough•est**
1 uneven in surface ⟨*rough* tree bark⟩ ⟨a *rough* road⟩
2 having many bumps and jolts ⟨a *rough* ride⟩
3 not calm ⟨*rough* seas⟩
4 being harsh or violent ⟨*rough* treatment⟩
5 difficult or unpleasant to deal with
6 coarse or rugged in nature or look ⟨a *rough* face⟩
7 having a harsh sound ⟨a *rough* voice⟩
8 not complete or exact ⟨a *rough* estimate⟩ ⟨a *rough* draft⟩
rough•ly *adv*
rough•ness *n*

[2]rough *n*
1 uneven ground covered with high grass, brush, and stones
2 something in a crude or unfinished state

[3]rough *vb* **roughed**; **rough•ing**
1 to handle violently : BEAT ⟨He was *roughed* up by bullies.⟩
2 to make or shape coarsely or unevenly
rough it to live without ordinary comforts

rough•age \ˈrə-fij\ *n*
1 FIBER 2
2 ▼ food (as bran) containing much indigestible material acting as fiber

roughage 2: a bowl of bran cereal

rough•en \ˈrə-fən\ *vb* **rough•ened**; **rough•en•ing**
to make or become rough

rough•neck \ˈrəf-ˌnek\ *n*
a rough aggressive person

[1]round \ˈrau̇nd\ *adj* **round•er**; **round•est**
1 having every part of the surface or circumference the same distance from the center : shaped like a circle or ball
2 shaped like a cylinder ⟨a *round* peg⟩
3 [1]PLUMP
4 having curves rather than angles ⟨*round* corners⟩
5 [1]COMPLETE 1, FULL ⟨a *round* dozen⟩
6 nearly correct or exact ⟨in *round* numbers⟩
7 LARGE ⟨a good *round* sum⟩
8 moving in or forming a circle
round•ish \ˈrau̇n-dish\ *adj*
round•ness *n*

[2]round *adv*
[1]AROUND

[3]round *n*
1 a regularly covered route
2 something (as a circle or globe) that is round
3 one shot fired by a soldier or a gun
4 a series or cycle of repeated actions or events ⟨a *round* of talks⟩
5 a song in which three or four singers sing the same melody and words one after another at intervals
6 a period of applause
7 an indirect path
8 ammunition for one shot
9 one of the parts into which a contest or game is divided
10 a cut of beef especially between the rump and the lower leg

[4]round *vb* **round•ed**; **round•ing**
1 to go or pass around ⟨I saw her house as I *rounded* the corner.⟩
2 to express as a round number ⟨He *rounded* 947 to 950.⟩
3 to bring to completion ⟨They'll *round* out the season with a win.⟩
4 to make or become round ⟨I *rounded* off the corners.⟩
round up
1 to collect (as cattle) by circling in vehicles or on horseback and forcing them in
2 to gather in or bring together

[5]round *prep*
[2]AROUND ⟨He travels *round* the world.⟩

round•about \ˈrau̇n-də-ˌbau̇t\ *adj*
not direct ⟨I took a *roundabout* route to get here.⟩

round•house \ˈrau̇nd-ˌhau̇s\ *n*, *pl* **round•hous•es** \-ˌhau̇-zəz\
a circular building where locomotives are kept or repaired

round trip *n*
a trip to a place and back usually over the same route

round•up \ˈrau̇nd-ˌəp\ *n*
1 the act of gathering together animals on the range by circling them in vehicles or on horseback and driving them in

rowboat: a father and his son in a rowboat

A B C D E F G H I J K L M N O P Q R S T U V W X Y Z

2 the act of gathering together scattered persons or things
3 ²SUMMARY ⟨Here's a *roundup* of the day's news.⟩

round•worm \'raůnd-,wərm\ *n*
a worm that has a round body with no segments and is sometimes a serious parasite of people and animals

rouse \'raůz\ *vb* **roused**; **rous•ing**
1 ¹AWAKE 1
2 to stir up : EXCITE ⟨The idea *roused* great interest.⟩

¹rout \'raůt\ *vb* **rout•ed**; **rout•ing**
1 to cause to run away
2 to defeat completely

²rout *n*
1 an easy or lopsided defeat ⟨We lost 44-0—it was a *rout.*⟩
2 wild confusion or disorderly retreat

¹route \'rüt, 'raůt\ *n*
a regular, chosen, or assigned course of travel

²route *vb* **rout•ed**; **rout•ing**
to send or transport by a selected course

¹rou•tine \rü-'tēn\ *n*
1 a usual order and way of doing something ⟨Taking a shower is part of my morning *routine.*⟩
2 a series of things that are repeated as part of a performance ⟨a dance *routine*⟩

²routine *adj*
1 done very often ⟨*routine* surgery⟩
2 done or happening in a standard or usual way ⟨He went to the doctor for a *routine* checkup.⟩
rou•tine•ly *adv*

rove \'rōv\ *vb* **roved**; **rov•ing**
to wander without definite plan or direction
rov•er *n*

¹row \'rō\ *vb* **rowed**; **row•ing**
1 to move a boat by using oars
2 to travel or carry in a rowboat

²row \'rō\ *n*
1 a series of persons or things lined up in an orderly arrangement ⟨a *row* of houses⟩ ⟨He sat in the first *row.*⟩
2 ¹WAY 10, STREET

³row \'raů\ *n*
noisy disturbance or quarrel

⁴row \'rō\ *n*
an act or instance of using oars to move a boat

row•boat \'rō-,bōt\ *n*
◀ a boat made to be moved by oars

¹row•dy \'raů-dē\ *adj* **row•di•er**; **row•di•est**
rough or noisy ⟨*rowdy* baseball fans⟩
row•di•ness *n*

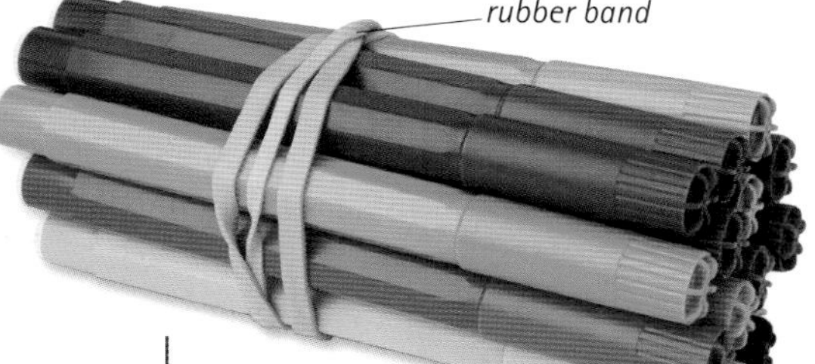

rubber band: pens bound together with a rubber band

²rowdy *n, pl* **rowdies**
a person who behaves coarsely or roughly

roy•al \'röi-əl\ *adj*
1 of or relating to a king or queen : REGAL ⟨a *royal* wedding⟩
2 fit for a king or queen ⟨We gave the team a *royal* welcome.⟩
roy•al•ly *adv*

roy•al•ty \'röi-əl-tē\ *n, pl* **roy•al•ties**
1 the status or power of a king or queen or his or her family
2 members of the royal family of a king or queen
3 a share of a product or profit (as of a mine) claimed by the owner for allowing another to use the property
4 payment made to the owner of a patent or copyright for the use of it

rpm *abbr* revolutions per minute

RR *abbr* railroad

R.S.V.P. *abbr* please reply
Hint: The abbreviation *R.S.V.P.* comes from the French phrase *répondez s'il vous plaît,* which means "please reply."

rt. *abbr* right

rte. *abbr* route

¹rub \'rəb\ *vb* **rubbed**; **rub•bing**
1 to move along the surface of something with pressure ⟨Kitty *rubbed* against my legs.⟩
2 to move back and forth against something in a way that causes pain or damage
3 to scour, polish, or smear by pressure and friction ⟨He *rubbed* oil on the wood.⟩
rub elbows with to meet and talk with in a friendly way
rub in to keep reminding someone of (something unpleasant) ⟨I know I looked silly. Don't *rub* it *in.*⟩
rub off to come off a surface and often stick to another surface by rubbing ⟨The ink *rubbed off* on my fingers.⟩
rub the wrong way to cause to be angry : IRRITATE

²rub *n*
1 the act of rubbing ⟨a back *rub*⟩
2 something that causes a problem

rub•ber \'rə-bər\ *n*
1 an elastic substance obtained from the milky juice of some tropical plants
2 something (as an overshoe) made of rubber
3 something used in rubbing
4 a synthetic substance like rubber
5 a flat white rectangle on which a baseball pitcher stands

rubber band *n*
◀ a continuous band made of rubber for holding things together : ELASTIC

rubber stamp *n*
▶ a stamp with a printing face of rubber

rubber stamp

rub•bery \'rə-bə-rē\ *adj*
weak, shaky, and unstable ⟨After getting off the roller coaster, my legs felt *rubbery.*⟩

rub•bish \'rə-bish\ *n*
1 TRASH 1
2 NONSENSE

rub•ble \'rə-bəl\ *n*
rough broken pieces of stone or brick from buildings

ru•ble \'rü-bəl\ *n*
a Russian coin or bill

ru•by \'rü-bē\ *n, pl* **rubies**
1 ▼ a gemstone of a deep red color
2 a deep purplish red

ruby 1

ruck•sack \'rək-,sak, 'rük-\ *n*
KNAPSACK

ruck•us \'rə-kəs\ *n*
a noisy disturbance or quarrel

rud•der \'rə-dər\ *n*
a movable flat piece attached at the rear of a ship or aircraft for steering

rud•dy \'rə-dē\ *adj* **rud•di•er**; **rud•di•est**
having a healthy reddish color

rude \'rüd\ *adj* **rud•er**; **rud•est**
1 IMPOLITE ⟨*rude* remarks⟩
2 not refined or cultured
3 roughly made ⟨a *rude* shelter⟩
rude•ly *adv*
rude•ness *n*

ru•di•ment \'rü-də-mənt\ *n*
a basic principle

ru•di•men•ta•ry \,rüd-ə-'men-tə-rē\ *adj*
1 ELEMENTARY, SIMPLE
2 not fully developed ⟨*rudimentary* wings⟩

rue \'rü\ *vb* **rued**; **ru•ing**
to feel sorrow or regret for

rue•ful \'rü-fəl\ *adj*
1 exciting pity or sympathy
2 MOURNFUL 1, REGRETFUL

ruff 1: a ruff worn by a man in 16th-century dress

ruff \'rəf\ *n*
1 ▲ a large round collar of pleated fabric worn by men and women in the 16th and 17th centuries
2 a fringe of long hairs or feathers growing around or on the neck of an animal

ruf•fi•an \'rə-fē-ən\ *n*
a violent and cruel person

[1]**ruf•fle** \'rə-fəl\ *vb* **ruf•fled**; **ruf•fling**
1 to move or lift so as to disturb the smoothness of ⟨She *ruffled* the boy's hair.⟩
2 [2]TROUBLE 1, VEX

[2]**ruffle** *n*
a strip of fabric gathered or pleated on one edge

rug \'rəg\ *n*
▶ a piece of thick heavy fabric usually with a nap or pile used especially as a floor covering

rug•ged \'rə-gəd\ *adj*
1 having a rough uneven surface ⟨*rugged* hills⟩
2 STRONG 3, TOUGH ⟨*rugged* pioneers⟩
3 involving hardship ⟨*rugged* training⟩
rug•ged•ly *adv*
rug•ged•ness *n*

[1]**ru•in** \'rü-ən\ *vb* **ru•ined**; **ru•in•ing**
1 to reduce to wreckage ⟨a *ruined* city⟩
2 to damage beyond repair

[2]**ruin 2:** the ruins of a 15th-century English abbey

rug: Turkish rugs on display

3 to have a very bad effect on the quality of (something) ⟨Losing my wallet *ruined* the trip.⟩
4 [2]BANKRUPT

[2]**ruin** *n*
1 complete collapse or destruction
2 ▼ **ruins** *pl* the remains of something destroyed ⟨the *ruins* of an ancient city⟩
3 the situation in which someone experiences loss of money, social status, or position ⟨They were on the brink of financial *ruin*.⟩
in ruins nearly or completely destroyed

ru•in•ous \'rü-ə-nəs\ *adj*
causing or likely to cause collapse or destruction ⟨a *ruinous* war⟩
ru•in•ous•ly *adv*

[1]rule \'rül\ *n*
1 a guide or principle for conduct or action ⟨To play this game, you need to follow the *rules.*⟩
2 an accepted or usual method, custom, or habit
3 the exercise of authority or control : GOVERNMENT
4 RULER 2

[2]rule *vb* **ruled; rul•ing**
1 to exercise authority over : GOVERN
2 [1]CONTROL 1, DIRECT ⟨Don't let emotions *rule* your decision.⟩
3 to be supreme or outstanding in ⟨He *rules* the tennis courts.⟩
4 to give or state as a considered decision
5 to mark with lines drawn along the straight edge of a ruler

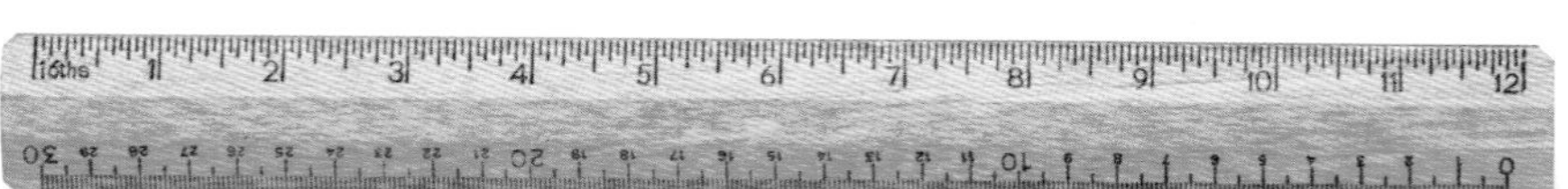

ruler 2

rul•er \'rü-lər\ *n*
1 a person (as a king or queen) having supreme power over a nation
2 ▲ a straight strip (as of plastic, wood, or metal) with a smooth edge that is marked off in units and used for measuring or as a guide in drawing straight lines

rul•ing \'rü-liŋ\ *n*
an official decision (as by a judge)

rum \'rəm\ *n*
an alcoholic liquor made from sugarcane or molasses

[1]rum•ble \'rəm-bəl\ *vb* **rum•bled; rum•bling**
to make or move with a low heavy continuous sound ⟨A truck *rumbled* by.⟩

[2]rumble *n*
a low heavy rolling sound

ru•mi•nant \'rü-mə-nənt\ *n*
► a hoofed animal (as a cow or sheep) that chews its cud and has a stomach with usually four chambers
ruminant *adj*

ruminant: a cow is a ruminant

ru•mi•nate \'rü-mə-ˌnāt\ *vb* **ru•mi•nat•ed; ru•mi•nat•ing**
to think carefully and deeply : MEDITATE

[1]rum•mage \'rə-mij\ *vb* **rum•maged; rum•mag•ing**
to search especially by moving and looking through the contents of a place or container ⟨His dog likes to *rummage* through the trash.⟩

[2]rummage *n*
a mixed up collection of different articles

rum•my \'rə-mē\ *n*
a card game in which each player tries to lay down cards in groups of three or more

[1]ru•mor \'rü-mər\ *n*
information or a story that is passed from one person to another but has not been proven to be true and has no known source

[2]rumor *vb* **ru•mored; ru•mor•ing**
to spread information or a story that has not been proven to be true

rump \'rəmp\ *n*
1 the back part of an animal's body where the hips and thighs join
2 a cut of beef between the loin and the round

rum•ple \'rəm-pəl\ *vb* **rum•pled; rum•pling**
to make (something) messy or wrinkled

rum•pus \'rəm-pəs\ *n*
a noisy disturbance or quarrel

[1]run \'rən\ *vb* **ran** \'ran\; **run; run•ning**
1 to go at a pace faster than a walk
2 to go rapidly or hurriedly ⟨She *ran* home to get her book.⟩
3 to take to flight ⟨They saw the police and *ran.*⟩
4 to pass over, across, or through ⟨She *ran* her fingers through her hair.⟩
5 [2]FUNCTION ⟨That old car is still *running.*⟩
6 to cause to function ⟨Can you *run* this machine?⟩
7 EXTEND 2 ⟨The trail *runs* from here to the border.⟩
8 to move freely about ⟨He let the animals *run* loose.⟩
9 [1]FLOW 1 ⟨A brook *runs* through the field.⟩
10 to be in charge of : MANAGE ⟨I *run* the book fair.⟩
11 to do something by or as if by running ⟨I'm *running* errands.⟩
12 to take part in a race
13 to move on or as if on wheels
14 to go back and forth often according to a fixed schedule ⟨The train *runs* between Boston and Chicago.⟩
15 to migrate or move in schools ⟨The salmon are *running* early this year.⟩
16 to continue in force ⟨The exhibit *runs* until the end of the month.⟩
17 to pass into a specified condition ⟨The well *ran* dry.⟩
18 to spread into another area ⟨The dyes are guaranteed not to *run.*⟩
19 to give off liquid ⟨My nose is *running.*⟩
20 to tend to develop a specified feature or quality ⟨The shirts *run* small.⟩
21 to slip through or past ⟨They *ran* the blockade.⟩
22 to cause to penetrate ⟨He *ran* a knife through the bread.⟩
23 to cause to go ⟨The sheriff *ran* them out of town.⟩ ⟨I *ran* my car off the road.⟩
24 to take on ⟨She *ran* the risk of being caught.⟩
25 to print or broadcast ⟨Every channel *runs* the ad.⟩
26 to be a candidate for office ⟨She *ran* for mayor.⟩
27 to occur again and again ⟨The condition *runs* in the family.⟩
run away to leave home secretly without intending to return
run into to meet by chance
run off to leave in a hurry
run out
1 to come to an end ⟨Time *ran out* before I finished.⟩
2 to become used up ⟨Supplies were *running out.*⟩
run out of to use up the available supply of ⟨We *ran out of* gas.⟩
run over [1]OVERFLOW 1

[2]run *n*
1 an act or the action of running ⟨He took the dog for a *run.*⟩
2 a score made in baseball by a base runner reaching home plate
3 an enclosure for animals where they may feed and exercise
4 the usual or normal kind ⟨It's like the usual *run* of shops.⟩
5 a continuous series especially of similar things ⟨We have had a long *run* of good luck.⟩
6 sudden heavy demands from depositors, creditors, or customers ⟨There was a *run* on the bank.⟩
7 the quantity of work turned out in a continuous operation
8 the distance covered in a period of continuous traveling
9 a regular course or trip
10 freedom of movement ⟨Our guests had the *run* of the house.⟩
11 a way, track, or path frequented by animals ⟨a deer *run*⟩
12 [1]SLOPE 1 ⟨a ski *run*⟩
13 a spot in knitted fabric that has unraveled ⟨My stocking has a *run* in it.⟩

[1]run•away \'rə-nə-,wā\ *n*
1 someone who leaves a place (as home) secretly without intending to return
2 a horse that is running out of control

[2]runaway *adj*
1 having left a place secretly with no intention of returning
2 escaping from control ⟨a *runaway* horse⟩

run–down \'rən-'daùn\ *adj*
1 in poor condition ⟨a *run-down* farm⟩
2 in poor health

[1]rung \'rəŋ\ *past participle of* [3]RING

[2]rung *n*
1 a rounded part placed as a crosspiece between the legs of a chair
2 ▶ one of the crosspieces of a ladder

rung

[2]rung 2: a ladder with six rungs

run–in \'rən-,in\ *n*
an angry argument

run•ner \'rə-nər\ *n*
1 a person or animal that runs
2 a thin piece or part on or in which something slides ⟨the *runners* on a sled⟩
3 MESSENGER
4 a slender creeping branch of a plant that roots at the end or at the joints to form new plants
5 a long narrow carpet (as for a hall)

run•ner–up \'rə-nə-,rəp\ *n*, *pl* **run•ners–up** \'rə-nər-,zəp\
the competitor in a contest who finishes second

run•ny \'rə-nē\ *adj* **run•ni•er; run•ni•est**
giving off or likely to give off liquid ⟨a *runny* nose⟩

runt \'rənt\ *n*
an unusually small person or animal

run•way \'rən-,wā\ *n*
1 a path beaten by animals in going to and from feeding grounds
2 a paved strip of ground on a landing field for the landing and takeoff of aircraft

ru•pee \rü-'pē\ *n*
▼ any of various coins (as of India or Pakistan)

rupee: a one-rupee coin from India

[1]rup•ture \'rəp-chər\ *n*
1 a break in peaceful or friendly relations
2 a breaking or tearing apart of body tissue ⟨*rupture* of an eardrum⟩
3 a crack or break in something ⟨a pipeline *rupture*⟩

[2]rupture *vb* **rup•tured; rup•tur•ing**
1 to part by violence : BREAK
2 to produce a break or tear in ⟨High water pressure *ruptured* the pipe.⟩
3 to have or develop a break or tear ⟨The blood vessel *ruptured.*⟩

ru•ral \'rür-əl\ *adj*
relating to the country, country people or life, or agriculture

ruse \'rüs, 'rüz\ *n*
[1]TRICK 3, ARTIFICE

[1]rush \'rəsh\ *vb* **rushed; rush•ing**
1 to move forward or act very quickly or in a way that shows eagerness or the need to hurry ⟨Police *rushed* to the scene.⟩
2 to perform in a short time or at high speed ⟨Don't *rush* your decision.⟩
3 to make (someone) act quickly ⟨Stop *rushing* me!⟩
4 to bring (someone) to a place quickly ⟨He was *rushed* to the hospital.⟩
5 [1]ATTACK 1, CHARGE

[3]rush: rush plants

[2]rush *n*
1 a quick strong forward motion ⟨A *rush* of air came from the vent.⟩
2 a burst of activity or speed ⟨She left in a *rush.*⟩
3 an eager migration of people usually to a new place in search of wealth ⟨the gold *rush*⟩

[3]rush *n*
▲ a grasslike marsh plant with hollow stems used in chair seats and mats

[4]rush *adj*
demanding special speed ⟨a *rush* order⟩

[1]Rus•sian \'rə-shən\ *adj*
of or relating to Russia, its people, or the Russian language

[2]Russian *n*
1 a person born or living in Russia
2 a language of the Russians

[1]rust \'rəst\ *n*
1 a reddish coating formed on metal (as iron) when it is exposed especially to moist air
2 ▶ a plant disease caused by fungi that makes spots on plants
3 a fungus that causes a rust

[2]rust *vb* **rust•ed; rust•ing**
to make or become rusty

[1]rus•tic \'rə-stik\ *adj*
1 relating to or suitable for the country
2 [1]PLAIN 7, SIMPLE
3 made from rough wood ⟨*rustic* furniture⟩

[2]rustic *n*
a person living or raised in the country

[1]rus•tle \'rə-səl\ *vb* **rus•tled; rus•tling**
1 to make or cause to make a quick series of small sounds ⟨Leaves *rustled* in the wind.⟩
2 to steal (as cattle) from the range
rus•tler \'rə-slər\ *n*

[1]rust 2: a leaf affected with rust

[2]rustle *n*
a quick series of small sounds

rusty \'rə-stē\ *adj* **rust•i•er; rust•i•est**
1 affected by rust ⟨a *rusty* nail⟩
2 less skilled and slow through lack of practice or use
rust•i•ness *n*

[1]rut \'rət\ *n*
1 a track worn by a wheel or by habitual passage
2 [1]ROUTINE 1

[2]rut *vb* **rut•ted; rut•ting**
to make a track in

ru•ta•ba•ga \'rü-tə-,bā-gə\ *n*
a turnip with a large yellow root

ruth•less \'rüth-ləs\ *adj*
having no pity : CRUEL
ruth•less•ly *adv*
ruth•less•ness *n*

-ry \rē\ *n suffix, pl* **-ries**
-ERY ⟨citizen*ry*⟩

rye \'rī\ *n*
a hardy cereal grass grown especially for its edible seeds that are used in flour and animal feeds

Sounds of S: The letter **S** most commonly makes the sound heard in ***sand, first,*** and ***streets.*** In some words, and especially at the ends of words, **S** sounds like a **Z**, as in ***easy, words,*** and ***dries.*** Combined with **H, S** makes the sound heard in ***share.*** **S** alone or with another **S** also sometimes makes this sound, as in ***sugar*** and ***pressure.*** Another sound is heard in words like ***measure*** and ***confusion.*** This sound is indicated by the symbol zh. In a few words, such as ***island,*** **S** is silent.

s \'es\ *n, pl* **s's** *or* **ss** \'e-səz\ *often cap*
1 the 19th letter of the English alphabet
2 a grade rating a student's work as satisfactory

S *abbr*
1 satisfactory
2 small
3 south
4 southern

[1]**-s** \s *after sounds* f, k, p, t, th; əz *after sounds* ch, j, s, sh, z, zh; z *after other sounds*\ *n pl suffix*
used to form the plural of most nouns that do not end in *s, z, sh, ch, x,* or *y* following a consonant ⟨head*s*⟩ ⟨book*s*⟩ ⟨belief*s*⟩ and with or without an apostrophe to form the plural of abbreviations, numbers, letters, and symbols used as nouns ⟨4*s*⟩ ⟨#*s*⟩ ⟨B'*s*⟩

[2]**-s** *adv suffix*
used to form adverbs showing usual or repeated action or state ⟨We are always at home Sunday*s.*⟩

[3]**-s** *vb suffix*
used to form the third person singular present of most verbs that do not end in *s, z, sh, ch, x,* or *y* following a consonant ⟨fall*s*⟩ ⟨take*s*⟩ ⟨play*s*⟩

-'s *n suffix or pron suffix*
used to form the possessive of singular nouns ⟨elephant*'s*⟩, of plural nouns not ending in *s* ⟨children*'s*⟩, and of some pronouns ⟨anyone*'s*⟩

Sab•bath \'sa-bəth\ *n*
a day of the week that is regularly observed as a day of rest and worship ⟨Jews observe the *Sabbath* from Friday evening to Saturday evening.⟩

sa•ber *or* **sa•bre** \'sā-bər\ *n*
▼ a long sword with a curved blade

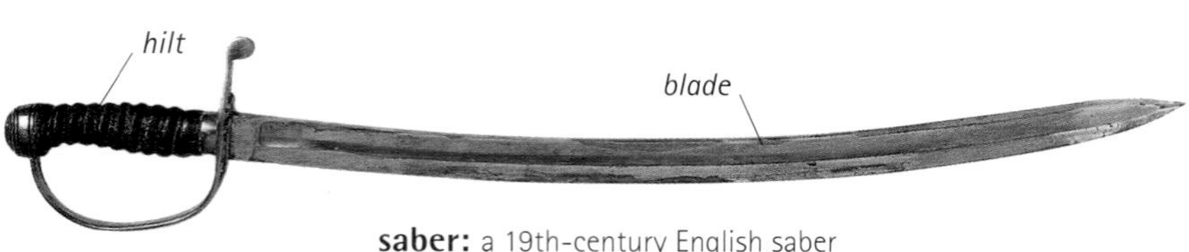

saber: a 19th-century English saber

sa•ber–toothed cat \'sā-bər-,tütht-\ *n*
SABER-TOOTHED TIGER

saber–toothed tiger *n*
a very large extinct cat of prehistoric times with long sharp curved upper canine teeth

sa•ble \'sā-bəl\ *n*
1 the color black
2 ▶ a meat-eating animal of northern Europe and Asia that is related to the weasel and has soft brown fur

sable 2

[1]**sab•o•tage** \'sa-bə-,täzh\ *n*
deliberate destruction of or damage to property ⟨Angry workers used *sabotage* to disable the factory's machinery.⟩

[2]**sabotage** *vb* **sab•o•taged; sab•o•tag•ing**
to damage or destroy on purpose **:** to engage in sabotage ⟨The country's water supply was *sabotaged* by the retreating enemy.⟩

sac \'sak\ *n*
a part of a plant or animal resembling a bag and often containing a liquid or air
sac•like \-,līk\ *adj*

sa•chem \'sā-chəm\ *n*
a North American Indian chief

[1]**sack** \'sak\ *n*
1 [1]BAG 1
2 a sack and its contents ⟨a *sack* of potatoes⟩

[2]**sack** *vb* **sacked; sack•ing**
1 to put into a sack ⟨I *sacked* my purchases.⟩
2 to fire from a job or position

[3]**sack** *vb* **sacked; sack•ing**
to loot after capture **:** PLUNDER ⟨The invading army *sacked* the city.⟩

sack•ing \'sa-kiŋ\ *n*
a strong rough cloth (as burlap) from which sacks are made

sac•ra•ment \'sa-krə-mənt\ *n*
a Christian religious act or ceremony that is considered especially sacred

sa•cred \'sā-krəd\ *adj*
1 HOLY 1 ⟨a *sacred* shrine⟩
2 RELIGIOUS 2 ⟨*sacred* songs⟩
3 deserving to be respected and honored ⟨Freedom is a *sacred* right.⟩

[1]**sac•ri•fice** \'sa-krə-,fīs\ *n*
1 the act or ceremony of making an offering to God or a god especially on an altar
2 something offered as a religious act
3 an act of giving up something especially for the sake of someone or something else ⟨We were happy to make a *sacrifice* of our time to help a friend in need.⟩
4 something given up especially for the sake of helping others

[2]**sacrifice** *vb* **sac•ri•ficed; sac•ri•fic•ing**
1 to offer or kill as a religious act ⟨The ancient ritual involved *sacrificing* an animal.⟩
2 to give up (something) especially for the sake of something or someone else ⟨They *sacrificed* their lives for their country.⟩

A B C D E F G H I J K L M N O P Q R S T U V W X Y Z

sad \'sad\ *adj* **sad•der**; **sad•dest**
1 feeling or showing sorrow or unhappiness ⟨I'm *sad* that you're leaving.⟩ ⟨The dog had *sad* eyes.⟩
2 causing sorrow or unhappiness ⟨*sad* news⟩
sad•ly *adv*
sad•ness *n*

► **Word History** The word *sad* goes far back into the past of the English language, though modern meanings such as "unhappy" or "causing sorrow" give us little idea of its history. It comes from the Old English word *sæd,* which meant "full, having had enough," a sense matched by related words in other languages, such as German *satt.* In Middle English, *sad* continued to mean "full," but it also developed many other senses, such as "firmly established, fixed," "solid, weighty," "sober, serious," "true, real," and "deep, intense (of a color)." The meaning "sorrowful" was in use fairly early, by about 1300, though strangely enough only this sense among all the others has lasted into modern English.

sad•den \'sa-dᵊn\ *vb* **sad•dened**; **sad•den•ing**
to make or become sad

[1]sad•dle \'sa-dᵊl\ *n*
1 a padded and leather-covered seat for a rider on horseback
2 something like a saddle in shape, position, or use

[2]saddle *vb* **sad•dled**; **sad•dling**
1 to put a saddle on ⟨I *saddled* my horse.⟩
2 to put a load on : BURDEN ⟨She *saddled* him with the hardest job.⟩

saddle horse *n*
a horse suited for or trained for riding

sa•fa•ri \sə-'fär-ē\ *n*
▼ a trip to see or hunt animals especially in Africa

[1]safe \'sāf\ *adj* **saf•er**; **saf•est**
1 free or secure from harm or danger ⟨I don't feel *safe* here.⟩
2 giving protection or security against harm or danger ⟨a *safe* neighborhood⟩
3 HARMLESS ⟨*safe* drinking water⟩
4 unlikely to be wrong or cause disagreement ⟨a *safe* answer⟩
5 not likely to take risks : CAREFUL ⟨a *safe* driver⟩
6 successful in reaching a base in baseball
safe•ly *adv*

► **Synonyms** SAFE and SECURE mean free from danger. SAFE is used of freedom from a present danger. ⟨I felt *safe* as soon as I crossed the street.⟩ SECURE is used of freedom from a possible future danger or risk. ⟨The locks on the door made us feel *secure.*⟩

[2]safe

[2]safe *n*
▲ a metal box with a lock that is used for keeping something (as money) safe

[1]safe•guard \'sāf-,gärd\ *n*
something that protects and gives safety ⟨Drink water as a *safeguard* against dehydration.⟩

[2]safeguard *vb* **safe•guard•ed**; **safe•guard•ing**
to make or keep safe or secure
synonyms see DEFEND

safe•keep•ing \'sāf-'kē-piŋ\ *n*
the act of keeping safe : protection from danger or loss

safe•ty \'sāf-tē\ *n*
freedom from danger or harm : the state of being safe

safety belt *n*
SEAT BELT

safety pin *n*
a pin that is bent back to form a spring and has a guard that covers the point

safari: tourists on a safari in Botswana, Africa

saf•fron \ˈsa-frən\ *n*
1 an orange spice that is made from the dried stigmas of a crocus and is used to color or flavor foods
2 an orange to orange yellow

[1]sag \ˈsag\ *vb* **sagged**; **sag•ging**
1 to sink, settle, or hang below the natural or right level 〈The roof *sags* in the middle.〉
2 to become less firm or strong 〈As all our efforts failed, our spirits *sagged*.〉

[2]sag *n*
a part or area that sinks or hangs below the natural or right level

sa•ga \ˈsä-gə\ *n*
1 a story of heroic deeds
2 a long and often complicated story

sa•ga•cious \sə-ˈgā-shəs\ *adj*
quick and wise in understanding and judging

[1]sage \ˈsāj\ *adj*
[1]WISE 1 〈She gave *sage* advice.〉
sage•ly *adv*

[2]sage *n*
a very wise person

[3]sage 1:
sage leaves

[3]sage *n*
1 ► a mint with grayish green leaves used especially to flavor foods
2 SAGEBRUSH

sage•brush \ˈsāj-ˌbrəsh\ *n*
a plant of the western United States that grows as a low shrub and has a bitter juice and strong smell

sag•gy \ˈsa-gē\ *adj*
hanging down too much : not firm 〈a *saggy* mattress〉

Sag•it•tar•i•us \ˌsa-jə-ˈter-ē-əs\ *n*
1 ► a constellation between Scorpio and Capricorn imagined as a centaur
2 the ninth sign of the zodiac or a person born under this sign

sa•gua•ro \sə-ˈwär-ə, -ˈwär-ō, -ˈgwär-ō\ *n*, *pl* **sa•gua•ros**
a giant cactus of the southwestern United States and Mexico

said *past and past participle of* SAY

[1]sail \ˈsāl\ *n*
1 a sheet of strong cloth (as canvas) used to catch enough wind to move boats through the water or over ice
2 the sails of a ship 〈They lowered *sail* as they approached the bay.〉
3 a trip in a ship or boat moved especially by the wind 〈We went for a *sail* on the lake.〉

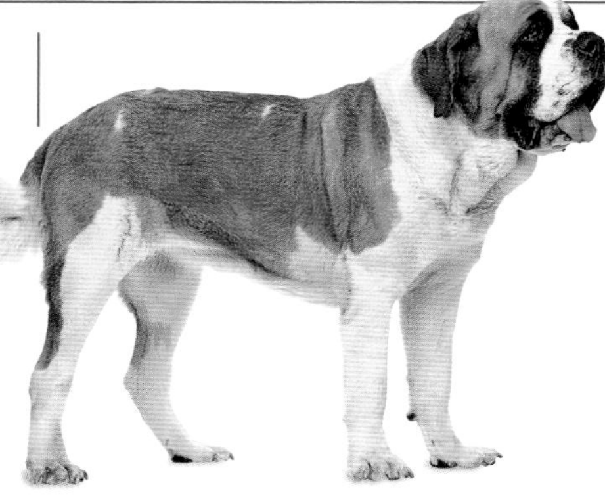

Saint Bernard

[2]sail *vb* **sailed**; **sail•ing**
1 to travel on a boat moved especially by the wind 〈He *sailed* around the world.〉
2 to travel on or by water 〈Boats *sailed* by.〉
3 to control the motion of (a ship or boat) while traveling on water
4 to move or proceed in a quick and smooth way

sail•boat \ˈsāl-ˌbōt\ *n*
a boat equipped with sails

sail•fish \ˈsāl-ˌfish\ *n*
a fish with a large fin like a sail on its back

sail•or \ˈsā-lər\ *n*
a person who works on or controls a boat or ship as part of the crew

saint \ˈsānt\ *n*
1 a good and holy person and especially one who in the Christian church is declared to be worthy of special honor
2 a person who is very good, helpful, or patient 〈You were a *saint* for helping me all day.〉

Saint Ber•nard \ˌsānt-bər-ˈnärd\ *n*
◄ a very large powerful dog originally of the Swiss Alps and used in the past to find and help lost travelers

saint•ly \ˈsānt-lē\ *adj*
like a saint or like that of a saint 〈a *saintly* deed〉
saint•li•ness *n*

sake \ˈsāk\ *n*
1 PURPOSE 〈Let's assume, for the *sake* of argument, that it was a mistake.〉
2 WELFARE 1, BENEFIT 〈for the *sake* of the country〉

sal•able *or* **sale•able** \ˈsā-lə-bəl\ *adj*
good enough to sell

sal•ad \ˈsa-ləd\ *n*
1 a mixture of raw usually green leafy vegetables (as lettuce) combined with other vegetables (as tomato and cucumber) and served with a dressing
2 a mixture of small pieces of food (as meat, fish, pasta, fruit, or vegetables) usually combined with a dressing

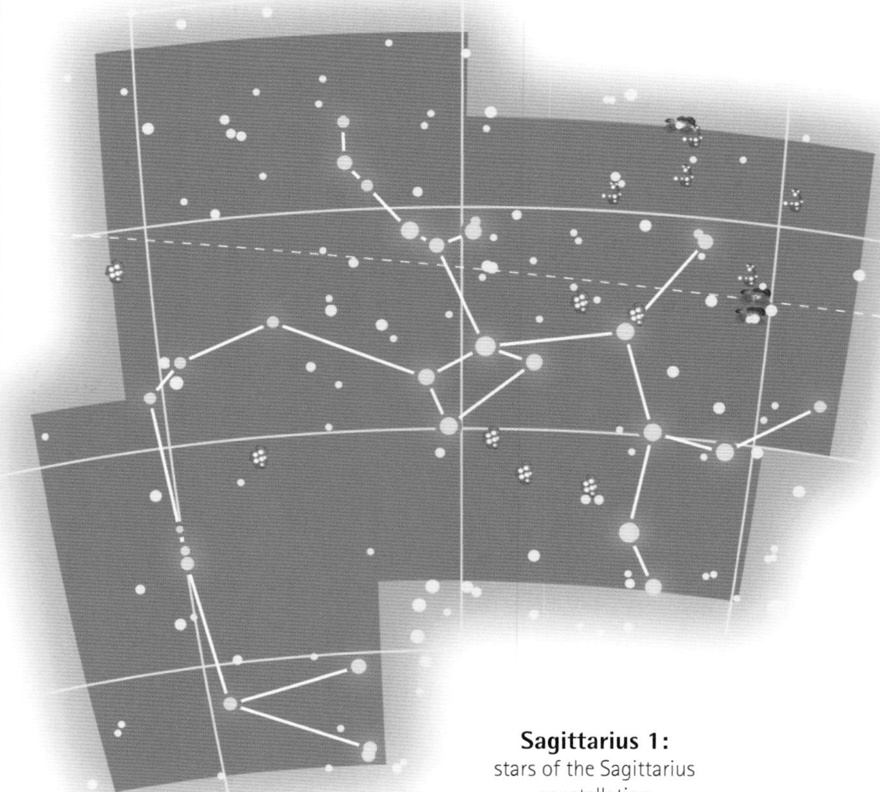

Sagittarius 1:
stars of the Sagittarius constellation

salamander
There are more than 300 species of salamander that live mainly in cool, temperate areas throughout Europe, North America, and Asia. They have adapted to many habitats, living among trees and shrubs, in crevices, or in water. Some salamanders have lungs, while others breathe through their skin and the lining of their mouth.

European fire salamander when threatened releases an irritating substance through special glands in the skin

spotted salamander lives underground in burrows or beneath fallen leaves

sal•a•man•der \'sa-lə-,man-dər\ *n*
▲ a small animal with smooth moist skin that is related to the frog but looks like a lizard

sa•la•mi \sə-'lä-mē\ *n*
a large highly seasoned sausage of pork and beef that is usually eaten cold

sal•a•ry \'sa-lə-rē, 'sal-rē\ *n, pl* **sal•a•ries**
a fixed amount of money paid at regular times for work done

sale \'sāl\ *n*
1 an exchange of goods or property for money
2 an event at which goods are sold at lowered prices
for sale available to be bought ⟨The house is *for sale*.⟩

sales•clerk \'sālz-,klərk\ *n*
a person who works in a store selling goods

sales•man \'sālz-mən\ *n, pl* **sales•men** \-mən\
a person who sells goods or services in a particular geographic area, in a store, or by telephone

sales•per•son \'sālz-,pər-sᵊn\ *n*
SALESMAN

sales tax *n*
a tax paid by the buyer on goods bought

sales•wom•an \'sālz-,wu̇-mən\ *n, pl* **sales•wom•en** \-,wi-mən\
a woman who sells goods or services in a particular geographic area, in a store, or by telephone

sa•li•va \sə-'lī-və\ *n*
a watery fluid that moistens chewed food and contains enzymes which break down starch and that is secreted into the mouth from three pairs of glands near the mouth

sal•i•vary \'sa-lə-,ver-ē\ *adj*
of, relating to, or producing saliva ⟨*salivary* glands⟩

sal•i•vate \'sa-lə-,vāt\ *vb* **sal•i•vat•ed**; **sal•i•vat•ing**
to produce or secrete saliva especially in large amounts

sal•low \'sa-lō\ *adj*
slightly yellow in a way that does not look healthy ⟨*sallow* skin⟩

[1]**sal•ly** \'sa-lē\ *n, pl* **sallies**
1 a sudden attack in which a group of soldiers rush out at the enemy
2 a clever and funny remark

[2]**sally** *vb* **sal•lied**; **sal•ly•ing**
1 to rush out ⟨Will he *sally* to their rescue?⟩
2 to set out (as from home)

salm•on \'sa-mən\ *n*
a fish with reddish or pinkish flesh that is often caught for sport or food and lives most of its life in the ocean but swims up rivers or streams as an adult to breed

sa•lon \sə-'län, 'sa-,län\ *n*
a business that offers beauty treatments

sa•loon \sə-'lün\ *n*
BAR

sal•sa \'sȯl-sə, 'säl-\ *n*
1 ▼ a spicy sauce of tomatoes, onions, and hot peppers

salsa 1

2 popular music of Latin American origin with characteristics of jazz and rock

[1]**salt** \'sȯlt\ *n*
1 a colorless or white substance that consists of sodium and chlorine and is used in seasoning foods, preserving meats and fish, and in making soap and glass
2 a compound formed by the combination of an acid and a base or a metal

[2]**salt** *vb* **salt•ed**; **salt•ing**
to flavor or preserve with salt

[3]**salt** *adj*
containing salt : SALTY ⟨*salt* water⟩

salt•wa•ter \'sȯlt-,wȯ-tər, -,wä-\ *adj*
relating to or living in salt water ⟨a *saltwater* fish⟩

salty \'sȯl-tē\ *adj* **salt•i•er**; **salt•i•est**
of, tasting of, or containing salt ⟨*salty* food⟩

sal•u•ta•tion \,sal-yə-'tā-shən\ *n*
1 an act or action of greeting
2 a word or phrase used as a greeting at the beginning of a letter

[1]**sa•lute** \sə-'lüt\ *vb* **sa•lut•ed**; **sa•lut•ing**
1 to give a sign of respect to (as a military officer) especially by a movement of the right hand to the forehead
2 to show or express respect for : HONOR ⟨She was *saluted* for her bravery.⟩

[2]**salute** *n*
1 the position taken or the movement made when bringing the right hand to the forehead in a sign of respect (as for a military officer)
2 an act or ceremony that is a show of respect or honor

[1]**sal•vage** \'sal-vij\ *n*
1 the act of saving a ship or its cargo
2 the saving or rescuing of possessions in danger of being lost (as from fire)
3 something that is saved (as from a wreck)

sanctuary 3: a wildlife sanctuary

²salvage *vb* **sal•vaged; sal•vag•ing**
to recover (something usable) especially from wreckage or ruin

sal•va•tion \sal-ˈvā-shən\ *n*
1 the saving of a person from sin or evil
2 something that saves from danger or difficulty ⟨The book was my *salvation* from boredom.⟩

¹salve \ˈsav, ˈsäv\ *n*
a healing or soothing ointment

²salve *vb* **salved; salv•ing**
to quiet or soothe with or as if with a salve

¹same \ˈsām\ *adj*
1 not another : IDENTICAL ⟨They lived in the *same* house all their lives.⟩
2 UNCHANGED ⟨His reaction is always the *same* no matter what we do.⟩
3 very much alike ⟨I eat the *same* breakfast every day.⟩

▶ **Synonyms** SAME, IDENTICAL, and EQUAL mean not different or not differing from one another. SAME is used when the things being compared are really one thing and not two or more things. ⟨We saw the *same* person.⟩ IDENTICAL usually is used when two or more things are just like each other in every way. ⟨The two jewels seemed *identical*.⟩ EQUAL is used when the things being compared are like each other in some particular way. ⟨The two baseball players are of *equal* ability.⟩

²same *pron*
something identical with or like another ⟨You had an ice cream cone, and I had the *same*.⟩

same•ness \ˈsām-nəs\ *n*
1 the quality or state of being identical or like another ⟨There was a *sameness* to his stories.⟩
2 MONOTONY

¹sam•ple \ˈsam-pəl\ *n*
1 a part or piece that shows the quality or character of the whole ⟨A water *sample* was taken to test for purity.⟩
2 a small amount of something that is given to people to try

²sample *vb* **sam•pled; sam•pling**
to judge the quality or character of by trying or examining a small part or amount ⟨We *sampled* the store's cheese.⟩

san•a•to•ri•um \ˌsa-nə-ˈtȯr-ē-əm\ *n*, *pl* **san•a•to•ri•ums** *or* **san•a•to•ria** \-ē-ə\
a place for the care and treatment usually of people recovering from illness or having a disease likely to last a long time

¹sanc•tion \ˈsaŋk-shən\ *n*
1 official approval or permission ⟨The soldiers' conduct did not have the king's *sanction*.⟩
2 an action (as the ending of financial aid) taken by one or more nations to make another nation comply with a law or rule

²sanction *vb* **sanc•tioned; sanc•tion•ing**
to officially accept or allow ⟨The coaches *sanctioned* the new rule.⟩

sanc•tu•ary \ˈsaŋk-chə-ˌwer-ē\ *n*, *pl* **sanc•tu•ar•ies**
1 a holy or sacred place
2 a building or room for religious worship
3 ▲ a place that provides safety or protection ⟨a wildlife *sanctuary*⟩
4 the protection from danger or a difficult situation that is provided by a safe place

¹sand \ˈsand\ *n*
1 loose material in grains produced by the natural breaking up of rocks
2 a soil made up mostly of sand

²sand *vb* **sand•ed; sand•ing**
1 to sprinkle with sand ⟨The snowy roads were plowed and *sanded*.⟩
2 to smooth or clean with sandpaper
sand•er *n*

san•dal \ˈsan-dəl\ *n*
a shoe consisting of a sole that is held in place by straps

san•dal•wood \ˈsan-dəl-ˌwu̇d\ *n*
the fragrant yellowish wood of an Asian tree

sand•bag \ˈsand-ˌbag\ *n*
a bag filled with sand and used as a weight (as on a balloon) or as part of a wall or dam

sand•bar \ˈsand-ˌbär\ *n*
a ridge of sand formed in water by tides or currents

sand•box \ˈsand-ˌbäks\ *n*
a large low box for holding sand especially for children to play in

sand dollar *n*
▶a flat round sea urchin

sand dollar

sand•pa•per \'sand-,pā-pər\ *n*
paper that has rough material (as sand) glued on one side and is used for smoothing and polishing

sand•pip•er \'sand-,pī-pər\ *n*
a small shorebird with long slender legs and bill

sand•stone \'sand-,stōn\ *n*
rock made of sand held together by a natural cement (as of calcium carbonate)

sand•storm \'sand-,stȯrm\ *n*
a desert storm with strong wind that blows clouds of sand

[1]**sand•wich** \'sand-,wich\ *n*
two or more slices of bread or a split roll with a filling (as meat or cheese) between them

▶ **Word History** John Montagu, the Earl of Sandwich, who lived from 1718 to 1792, was not a very distinguished figure in English history. According to stories told in the 1760s he was best known for gambling. The Earl is said to have once spent 24 hours at the gaming tables without eating anything but slices of cold beef between pieces of toast. If the story is correct, it describes the invention of what is called a *sandwich*, still one of the most popular of fast foods.

[2]**sandwich** *vb* **sand•wiched**; **sand•wich•ing**
to fit in between two or more things or people ⟨The children were *sandwiched* between their parents.⟩

sandy \'san-dē\ *adj* **sand•i•er**; **sand•i•est**
1 full of or covered with sand ⟨*sandy* soil⟩
2 of a yellowish gray color

sane \'sān\ *adj* **san•er**; **san•est**
1 having a healthy and sound mind
2 very sensible ⟨a *sane* policy⟩

sang *past of* SING

san•i•tar•i•um \,sa-nə-'ter-ē-əm\ *n*, *pl* **san•i•tar•i•ums** *or* **san•i•tar•ia** \-ē-ə\
SANATORIUM

san•i•tary \'sa-nə-,ter-ē\ *adj*
1 relating to health or hygiene ⟨poor *sanitary* conditions⟩
2 free from filth, infection, or other dangers to health ⟨*sanitary* hands⟩

san•i•ta•tion \,sa-nə-'tā-shən\ *n*
the act or process of making or keeping things free from filth, infection, or other dangers to health

san•i•ty \'sa-nə-tē\ *n*
the state of having a healthy and sound mind

sank *past of* SINK

San•ta Claus \'san-tə-,klȯz\ *n*
the spirit of Christmas as represented by a plump jolly old man with a white beard who is dressed in a red suit and delivers presents to good children

[1]**sap** \'sap\ *n*
a watery juice that circulates through a plant and carries food and nutrients

[2]**sap** *vb* **sapped**; **sap•ping**
to weaken or use up little by little ⟨The hard work *sapped* our strength.⟩

sap•ling \'sa-pliŋ\ *n*
a young tree

sap•phire \'sa-,fīr\ *n*
▼ a clear bright blue gemstone

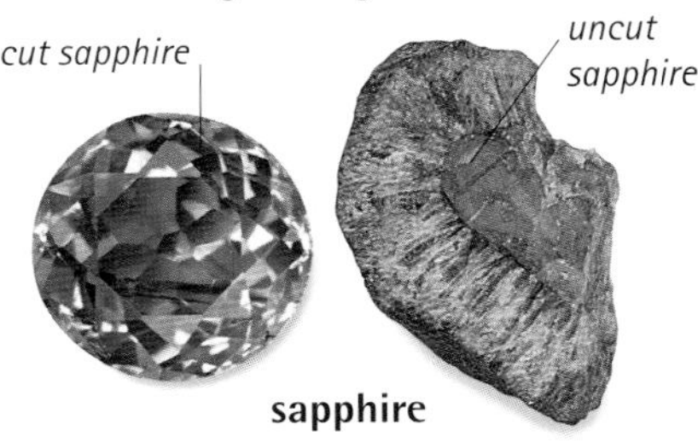

sapphire

sap•py \'sa-pē\ *adj* **sap•pi•er**; **sap•pi•est**
sad or romantic in a foolish or exaggerated way ⟨a *sappy* story⟩

sap•wood \'sap-,wu̇d\ *n*
young wood through which sap travels that is found just beneath the bark of a tree and is usually lighter in color than the heartwood

sar•casm \'sär-,ka-zəm\ *n*
the use of words that normally mean one thing to mean just the opposite usually to hurt someone's feelings or show scorn

sar•cas•tic \sär-'ka-stik\ *adj*
1 showing sarcasm ⟨a *sarcastic* reply⟩
2 being in the habit of using sarcasm ⟨a *sarcastic* person⟩
sar•cas•ti•cal•ly \-sti-kə-lē\ *adv*

sar•dine \sär-'dēn\ *n*
a young or very small fish often preserved in oil and used for food

sa•ri \'sä-rē\ *n*
a piece of clothing worn mainly by women of southern Asia that is a long light cloth wrapped around the body and head or shoulder

sar•sa•pa•ril•la \,sa-spə-'ri-lə, ,sär-\ *n*
a sweetened carbonated beverage that tastes somewhat like root beer

[1]**sash** \'sash\ *n*
a broad band of cloth worn around the waist or over the shoulder

[2]**sash** *n*
1 a frame for a pane of glass in a door or window
2 the movable part of a window

Sask. *abbr* Saskatchewan

[1]**sass** \'sas\ *n*
a rude or disrespectful reply

[2]**sass** *vb* **sassed**; **sass•ing**
to speak to in a rude or disrespectful way

sas•sa•fras \'sa-sə-,fras\ *n*
a tall tree of eastern North America whose dried root bark was formerly used in medicine or as a flavoring

sassy \'sa-sē\ *adj* **sass•i•er**; **sass•i•est**
having or showing a rude lack of respect ⟨*sassy* children⟩ ⟨a *sassy* answer⟩

sat *past and past participle of* SIT

Sat. *abbr* Saturday

Sa•tan \'sā-tᵊn\ *n*
DEVIL 1

satch•el \'sa-chəl\ *n*
a small bag (as for carrying clothes or books) that often has a shoulder strap

sat•el•lite \'sa-tə-,līt\ *n*
1 a smaller body that revolves around a planet
2 ▼ an object or vehicle sent out from the earth to revolve around the earth, moon, sun, or a planet

satellite 2:
a satellite revolving around the Earth

satellite dish *n*
a bowl-shaped antenna for receiving transmissions (as of television programs) from a satellite orbiting the earth

sat•in \'sa-tᵊn\ *n*
a cloth with a smooth shiny surface

sat•ire \'sa-,tīr\ *n*
1 humor that is used to make fun of and often show the weaknesses of someone or something
2 something (as a book or movie) that uses satire

sat•is•fac•tion \ˌsa-təs-ˈfak-shən\ *n*
1 a feeling of happiness or content with something **:** the condition of being satisfied
2 something that makes a person happy, pleased, or content

sat•is•fac•to•ry \ˌsa-təs-ˈfak-tə-rē\ *adj*
good enough for a particular purpose **:** causing satisfaction ⟨*satisfactory* work⟩
sat•is•fac•to•ri•ly \-rə-lē\ *adv*

sat•is•fy \ˈsa-təs-ˌfī\ *vb* **sat•is•fied**; **sat•is•fy•ing**
1 to make happy or contented ⟨Everyone was *satisfied* with the compromise.⟩
2 to meet the needs of ⟨The meal *satisfied* our hunger.⟩
3 CONVINCE ⟨We are *satisfied* the story is true.⟩
4 to do what has been agreed upon ⟨The contract has been *satisfied*.⟩

sat•u•rate \ˈsa-chə-ˌrāt\ *vb* **sat•u•rat•ed**; **sat•u•rat•ing**
to soak completely ⟨*Saturate* the sponge with water.⟩

Sat•ur•day \ˈsa-tər-dē\ *n*
the seventh day of the week

Saturn

Sat•urn \ˈsa-tərn\ *n*
▲ the planet that is sixth in distance from the sun and has a diameter of about 75,000 miles (120,000 kilometers)

sauce \ˈsȯs\ *n*
1 a usually thick liquid poured over or mixed with food ⟨spaghetti *sauce*⟩
2 boiled or canned fruit ⟨cranberry *sauce*⟩

sauce•pan \ˈsȯs-ˌpan\ *n*
a small deep cooking pan with a handle

sau•cer \ˈsȯ-sər\ *n*
a small shallow dish often with a slightly lower center for holding a cup

saucy \ˈsȯ-sē\ *adj* **sauc•i•er**; **sauc•i•est**
1 being rude and disrespectful **:** SASSY ⟨a *saucy* manner⟩
2 stylish in dress or appearance ⟨a *saucy* hat⟩
sauc•i•ly \-ə-lē\ *adv*

sau•er•kraut \ˈsau̇-ər-ˌkrau̇t\ *n*
finely cut cabbage soaked in a salty mixture

savanna: savanna grasslands

saun•ter \ˈsȯn-tər\ *vb* **saun•tered**; **saun•ter•ing**
to walk in a slow relaxed way **:** STROLL ⟨They *sauntered* along the beach.⟩

sau•sage \ˈsȯ-sij\ *n*
1 spicy ground meat (as pork) usually stuffed in casings
2 a roll of sausage in a casing

[1]sav•age \ˈsa-vij\ *adj*
1 not tamed **:** WILD ⟨*savage* beasts⟩
2 being cruel and brutal **:** FIERCE
sav•age•ly *adv*

► **Word History** In Latin the adjective *silvaticus*, (derived from the noun *silva*, "forest") meant "growing or living in the forest." Because forest life is wild rather than domesticated, the adjective easily took on the meaning "wild" in later Latin. Altered to *salvaticus*, the word passed into Old French as *sauvage*. When it was borrowed into Middle English, it kept the meanings "wild, uncultivated (of fruit)" and "untamed (of animals)." But *sauvage* could also be applied to humans, in which case its meanings could range from "not civilized, barbarous" to "fierce, cruel." It is mainly the last sense that modern English *savage* brings to mind.

[2]savage *n*
1 a person belonging to a group with a low level of civilization
2 a cruel or violent person

sav•age•ry \ˈsa-vij-rē\ *n, pl* **sav•age•ries**
1 an uncivilized condition or character
2 an act of cruelty or violence

sa•van•na *also* **sa•van•nah** \sə-ˈva-nə\ *n*
▲ land of warm regions (as Africa) that is covered with grass and only a few shrubs and trees

[1]save \ˈsāv\ *vb* **saved**; **sav•ing**
1 to free or keep from danger or harm ⟨He *saved* a child from drowning.⟩
2 to keep from being ruined **:** PRESERVE ⟨The group works to *save* the rain forests.⟩
3 to put aside for later use ⟨*Save* some milk for me.⟩
4 to put aside money ⟨*saving* for college⟩
5 to keep from being spent, wasted, or lost ⟨I'm *saving* my energy.⟩
6 to make unnecessary ⟨The shortcut *saves* an hour's driving.⟩
7 to store (data) in a computer or on a storage device so that it can be used later

[2]save *prep*
[1]EXCEPT 2 ⟨It rained every day *save* one.⟩

sav•ing \ˈsā-viŋ\ *n*
1 something that is not spent, wasted, or lost ⟨a *saving* in electricity⟩
2 **savings** *pl* money put aside (as in a bank)

sav•ior *or* **sav•iour** \ˈsāv-yər\ *n*
1 a person who saves someone or something from danger or harm
2 *cap* JESUS CHRIST

[1]sa•vor \ˈsā-vər\ *n*
the taste or smell of something ⟨the *savor* of fresh mint⟩

[2]savor *vb* **sa•vored**; **sa•vor•ing**
1 to taste or smell with pleasure ⟨I *savored* every bite of my meal.⟩
2 to delight in **:** ENJOY ⟨The team *savored* its victory.⟩

sa•vo•ry \'sā-və-rē\ *adj*
pleasing to the taste or smell ⟨*savory* sausages⟩

[1]sav•vy \'sa-vē\ *n*
practical knowledge or understanding ⟨She's admired for her business *savvy.*⟩

[2]savvy *adj*
having practical knowledge or understanding of something ⟨*savvy* buyers⟩

[1]saw *past of* SEE

[2]saw \'sȯ\ *n*
▶ a tool or machine with a blade having sharp teeth that is used for cutting hard material (as wood or metal)

[3]saw *vb* **sawed**; **sawed** *or* **sawn** \'sȯn\; **saw•ing**
to cut or shape with a saw

[4]saw *n*
a common saying : PROVERB

saw•dust \'sȯ-ˌdəst\ *n*
tiny bits (as of wood) which fall from something being sawed

saw•horse \'sȯ-ˌhȯrs\ *n*
a frame or rack on which wood is rested while being sawed

saw•mill \'sȯ-ˌmil\ *n*
a mill or factory having machinery for sawing logs

saw–toothed \'sȯ-'tütht\ *adj*
having an edge like the teeth of a saw

saxophone: a tenor saxophone

sax•o•phone \'sak-sə-ˌfōn\ *n*
▲ a woodwind instrument usually in the form of a curved metal tube with keys used to change pitch and a mouthpiece with a single reed

[1]say \'sā\ *vb* **said** \'sed\; **say•ing** \'sā-iŋ\
1 to express in words ⟨He *said* that she would be late.⟩ ⟨What does the card *say?*⟩
2 to state as an opinion or decision : DECLARE ⟨I *say* you are wrong.⟩
3 [1]REPEAT 2, RECITE ⟨I *said* my prayers.⟩
4 INDICATE 2, SHOW ⟨The clock *says* noon.⟩
5 to consider as a possibility or example ⟨Can you spare, *say,* 20 dollars?⟩

tooth-edged blade

[2]saw: a handsaw

[2]say *n*
1 an expression of opinion ⟨Everybody had a *say* at the meeting.⟩
2 the power to decide or help decide ⟨We had no *say* in making the plans.⟩

say•ing \'sā-iŋ\ *n*
PROVERB

SC *abbr* South Carolina

scab \'skab\ *n*
a crust mostly of hardened blood that forms over and protects a sore or wound as it heals

scab•bard \'ska-bərd\ *n*
a protective case or sheath for the blade of a sword or dagger

scab•by \'ska-bē\ *adj* **scab•bi•er**; **scab•bi•est**
covered with scabs ⟨*scabby* skin⟩

sca•bies \'skā-bēz\ *n, pl* **scabies**
an itch or mange caused by mites living as parasites under the skin

scaf•fold \'ska-fəld\ *n*
1 a raised platform built as a support for workers and their tools and materials
2 a platform on which executions take place

scal•a•wag *or* **scal•ly•wag** \'ska-li-ˌwag\ *n*
RASCAL 1

[1]scald \'skȯld\ *vb* **scald•ed**; **scald•ing**
1 a burn caused by hot liquid or steam
2 to bring to a temperature just below the boiling point ⟨*scald* milk⟩

[2]scald *n*
a burn caused by hot liquid or steam

scald•ing \'skȯl-diŋ\ *adj*
very hot ⟨*scalding* soup⟩

[1]scale \'skāl\ *n*
1 either pan of a balance or the balance itself
2 a device for weighing

[2]scale *n*
1 one of the small stiff plates that cover much of the body of some animals (as fish or snakes)
2 a thin layer or part suggesting a fish scale ⟨the *scales* on a butterfly's wing⟩
scaled \'skāld\ *adj*
scale•less \'skāl-ləs\ *adj*

[3]scale *vb* **scaled**; **scal•ing**
1 to remove the scales of ⟨*scale* a fish⟩
2 [2]FLAKE ⟨My dry skin was *scaling.*⟩

[4]scale *vb* **scaled**; **scal•ing**
1 to climb by or as if by a ladder ⟨Climbers *scaled* the cliff.⟩
2 to regulate or set according to a standard — often used with *down* or *up* ⟨We had to *scale* down our elaborate plans.⟩

[5]scale *n*
1 a series of musical tones going up or down in pitch in fixed steps
2 a series of spaces marked off by lines and used for measuring distances or amounts ⟨a thermometer's *scale*⟩
3 a series of like things arranged in order (as according to size or degree) ⟨a color *scale*⟩
4 the size of a picture, plan, or model of a thing compared to the size of the thing itself ⟨The *scale* of the model is 1/35.⟩
5 a standard for measuring or judging ⟨On a *scale* of one to ten, I give it an eight.⟩
6 the size or extent of something especially in comparison to something else

[1]scallop 1

[1]scal•lop \'skä-ləp, 'ska-\ *n*
1 ▲ an edible shellfish that is a mollusk with a ribbed shell in two parts
2 one of a series of half-circles that form a border on an edge (as of lace)

[2]scallop *vb* **scal•loped**; **scal•lop•ing**
1 to bake with crumbs, butter, and milk
2 to embroider, cut, or edge with half-circles ⟨I *scalloped* the skirt's hem.⟩

[1]scalp \'skalp\ *n*
the part of the skin of the head usually covered with hair

[2]scalp *vb* **scalped**; **scalp•ing**
to remove the scalp from

scaly \'skā-lē\ *adj* **scal•i•er**; **scal•i•est**
covered with scales or flakes ⟨*scaly* skin⟩

scamp \'skamp\ *n*
RASCAL 1

¹scam•per \'skam-pər\ *vb* **scam•pered**; **scam•per•ing**
to run or move quickly and often playfully about

²scamper *n*
a hurried and often playful run or movement

scan \'skan\ *vb* **scanned**; **scan•ning**
1 to examine or look over carefully ⟨He *scanned* the field with binoculars.⟩
2 to look through or over quickly ⟨I *scanned* the headlines of the newspaper.⟩
3 to examine with a special device (as a scanner) especially to obtain information ⟨My bag was *scanned* at the airport.⟩

scan•dal \'skan-dəl\ *n*
1 something that angers or shocks people because rules or standards of behavior are violated
2 talk that injures a person's good name

scan•dal•ous \'skan-də-ləs\ *adj*
1 containing shocking information ⟨*scandalous* rumors⟩
2 very bad or shocking ⟨*scandalous* behavior⟩

¹Scan•di•na•vian \,skan-də-'nā-vē-ən, -vyən\ *n*
a person born or living in Scandinavia

²Scandinavian *adj*
of or relating to Scandinavia or its people ⟨*Scandinavian* countries⟩

scan•ner \'ska-nər\ *n*
a device that converts a printed image (as text or a photograph) into a form a computer can display or alter

scant \'skant\ *adj*
1 barely enough ⟨a *scant* lunch⟩
2 not quite to a full amount, degree, or extent ⟨He poured a *scant* cup of milk.⟩

scanty \'skan-tē\ *adj* **scant•i•er**; **scant•i•est**
barely enough : lacking in size or quantity ⟨a *scanty* harvest⟩

¹scar \'skär\ *n*
1 a mark left on the skin after a wound heals
2 an ugly mark (as on furniture) showing damage
3 the lasting effect (as a feeling of sadness) of some unhappy experience

²scar *vb* **scarred**; **scar•ring**
1 to mark or become marked with a scar ⟨The accident *scarred* his left arm.⟩
2 to leave a lasting bad effect on ⟨The tragedy *scarred* her emotionally.⟩

scar•ab \'ska-rəb\ *n*
a large dark beetle used in ancient Egypt as a symbol of eternal life

scarecrow: a scarecrow in a wheat field

¹scarce \'skers\ *adj* **scarc•er**; **scarc•est**
not plentiful ⟨Food was *scarce* during the war.⟩
synonyms see RARE

²scarce *adv*
HARDLY, SCARCELY ⟨I could *scarce* believe what I was hearing.⟩

scarce•ly \'skers-lē\ *adv*
1 only just : BARELY ⟨They had *scarcely* enough to eat.⟩
2 certainly not

scar•ci•ty \'sker-sə-tē\ *n, pl* **scar•ci•ties**
a very small supply : the condition of being scarce ⟨a *scarcity* of water⟩

¹scare \'sker\ *vb* **scared**; **scar•ing**
to become or cause to become frightened ⟨Your stories *scare* the children.⟩
scare up to find or get with some difficulty ⟨She *scared up* something for us to eat.⟩

²scare *n*
1 a sudden feeling of fear : FRIGHT
2 a widespread state of alarm ⟨There was a *scare* that the disease would spread.⟩

scare•crow \'sker-,krō\ *n*
▲ an object made to look like a person and set up to scare birds away from crops

scarf \'skärf\ *n, pl* **scarves** \'skärvz\ *or* **scarfs**
1 a piece of cloth worn loosely on the shoulders, around the neck, or on the head
2 a long narrow strip of cloth used as a cover (as on a bureau)

¹scar•let \'skär-lət\ *n*
a bright red

²scarlet *adj*
colored bright red

scarlet fever *n*
a serious illness in which there is a sore throat, high fever, and red rash

scary \'sker-ē\ *adj* **scar•i•er**; **scar•i•est**
causing fright 〈a *scary* movie〉

scat \'skat\ *vb* **scat•ted**; **scat•ting**
to go away quickly
Hint: *Scat* is often used as a command to frighten away an animal. 〈*Scat*! Go away, cat.〉

scat•ter \'ska-tər\ *vb* **scat•tered**; **scat•ter•ing**
1 to toss, sow, or place here and there 〈He *scattered* his toys all around the house.〉
2 to separate or cause to separate and go in different ways 〈The crowd suddenly *scattered*.〉

scat•ter•brain \'ska-tər-,brān\ *n*
a person who is unable to concentrate or think clearly
scat•ter•brained \-,brānd\ *adj*

scav•enge \'ska-vənj\ *vb* **scav•enged**; **scav•eng•ing**
to search through and collect usable items especially from what has been thrown away

scav•en•ger \'ska-vən-jər\ *n*
1 a person who picks over junk or garbage for useful items
2 ▼ an animal (as a vulture) that feeds on dead or decaying material

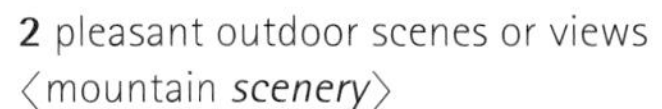

scavenger 2: a vulture

scene \'sēn\ *n*
1 a division of an act in a play
2 a single interesting or important happening in a play or story 〈a fight *scene*〉
3 the place of an event or action 〈the *scene* of a crime〉
4 a view or sight that resembles a picture 〈a winter *scene*〉
5 a display of anger or bad behavior

scen•ery \'sē-nə-rē, 'sēn-rē\ *n*
1 the painted scenes used on a stage and the furnishings that go with them
2 pleasant outdoor scenes or views 〈mountain *scenery*〉
3 a person's usual surroundings 〈I need a change of *scenery*.〉

sce•nic \'sē-nik\ *adj*
1 having views of pleasant natural features 〈We took a *scenic* drive in the country.〉
2 relating to stage scenery 〈*scenic* design〉

^{1}**scent** \'sent\ *n*
1 an odor that is given off by someone or something 〈the *scent* of flowers〉
2 power or sense of smell 〈The dog has a keen *scent*.〉
3 a course followed in search or pursuit of something 〈The reporter was on the *scent* of a story.〉
4 ^{1}PERFUME 1

^{2}**scent** *vb* **scent•ed**; **scent•ing**
1 to become aware of or follow through the sense of smell 〈The dog *scented* a rabbit.〉
2 to get a hint of
3 to fill with an odor : PERFUME 〈Roses *scent* the air.〉

scep•ter \'sep-tər\ *n*
► a rod carried by a ruler as a sign of authority 〈a royal *scepter*〉

^{1}**sched•ule** \'ske-jül, -jəl\ *n*
1 a plan of things that need to be done and the times they will be done 〈a construction *schedule*〉 〈I have a busy *schedule*.〉
2 a written or printed list of things and the time they will be done 〈my course *schedule*〉
3 a list of the times set for certain events 〈a baseball *schedule*〉
4 TIMETABLE 〈the bus *schedule*〉

^{2}**schedule** *vb* **sched•uled**; **sched•ul•ing**
to plan at a certain time 〈My arrival is *scheduled* for late morning.〉

^{1}**scheme** \'skēm\ *n*
1 a secret plan : PLOT
2 a plan of something to be done : PROJECT
3 an organized design 〈I like the room's color *scheme*.〉
synonyms see PLAN

^{2}**scheme** *vb* **schemed**; **schem•ing**
to form a secret plan
schem•er *n*

schol•ar \'skä-lər\ *n*
1 a student in a school : PUPIL
2 a person who knows a great deal about one or more subjects : a learned person

schol•ar•ly \'skä-lər-lē\ *adj*
like that of or suitable to learned persons

schol•ar•ship \'skä-lər-,ship\ *n*
1 money given a student to help pay for further education
2 serious academic study or research of a subject

scho•las•tic \skə-'la-stik\ *adj*
relating to schools, students, or education

^{1}**school** \'skül\ *n*
1 a place for teaching and learning
2 a session of teaching and learning 〈night *school*〉 〈You'll be late for *school*.〉
3 SCHOOLHOUSE
4 the teachers and pupils of a school 〈The entire *school* was at the rally.〉
5 a group of persons who share the same opinions and beliefs 〈a new *school* of philosophy〉

scepter: a 15th-century painting of Isabella I \,iz-ə-'bel-ə\ of Spain holding her scepter

► **Word History** You may not think of your education as relaxation, but, believe it or not, the word *school* can be traced back to a Greek word meaning "leisure." Ancient Greek *scholē*, "rest, leisure," came to be applied to the philosophical discussions in which the best of Greek society spent their free time (of which they had a great deal, since slaves did most of the real work). The meaning of *scholē* was extended to the groups who listened to a particular philosopher, and later to the set of beliefs held by such a group. When Latin *schola* was borrowed from Greek, the emphasis fell more on the place where a philosopher spoke, and it is the sense "place of instruction" that was ultimately passed to English.

A B C D E F G H I J K L M N O P Q R S T U V W X Y Z

²school *vb* **schooled; school•ing**
TEACH 2, TRAIN

³school *n*
▶ a large number of one kind of fish or water animals swimming together

▶ **Word History** A group of fish is called a *school* not because they resemble students in a classroom. The word *school* in this sense is borrowed from a Dutch word that means "crowd" or "throng."

school•bag \'skül-,bag\ *n*
a bag for carrying schoolbooks

school•book \'skül-,bu̇k\ *n*
TEXTBOOK

school•boy \'skül-,bȯi\ *n*
a boy who goes to school

school•girl \'skül-,gərl\ *n*
a girl who goes to school

school•house \'skül-,hau̇s\ *n*, *pl* **school•hous•es** \-,hau̇-zəz\
a building used as a place for teaching and learning

school•ing \'skü-liŋ\ *n*
EDUCATION 1

school•mas•ter \'skül-,ma-stər\ *n*
a man who is in charge of a school or teaches in a school

school•mate \'skül-,māt\ *n*
a fellow student

school•mis•tress \'skül-,mi-strəs\ *n*
a woman who is in charge of a school or teaches in a school

school•room \'skül-,rüm, -,ru̇m\ *n*
CLASSROOM

schooner:
a schooner at sea

³school: a school of parrot fish

school•teach•er \'skül-,tē-chər\ *n*
a person who teaches in a school

school•work \'skül-,wərk\ *n*
lessons done at school or assigned to be done at home

school•yard \'skül-,yärd\ *n*
the playground of a school

schoo•ner \'skü-nər\ *n*
◀ a ship usually having two masts with the mainmast located toward the center and the shorter mast toward the front

schwa \'shwä\ *n*
1 an unstressed vowel that is the usual sound of the first and last vowels of the English word *America*
2 the symbol ə commonly used for a schwa and sometimes also for a similarly pronounced stressed vowel (as in *cut*)

sci. *abbr* science

sci•ence \'sī-əns\ *n*
1 knowledge about the natural world that is based on facts learned through experiments and observation
2 an area of study that deals with the natural world (as biology or physics)
3 a subject that is formally studied ⟨the *science* of linguistics⟩
4 something that can be studied and learned ⟨Pitching is a *science*.⟩

science fiction *n*
made-up stories about the influence of real or imagined science on society or individuals

sci•en•tif•ic \,sī-ən-'ti-fik\ *adj*
1 relating to science or scientists ⟨*scientific* theories⟩
2 using or applying the methods of science ⟨*scientific* research⟩
sci•en•tif•i•cal•ly \-'ti-fi-kə-lē\ *adv*

sci•en•tist \'sī-ən-təst\ *n*
a person who studies, specializes in, or investigates a field of science and does scientific work

scis•sors \'si-zərz\ *n pl*
a cutting instrument with two blades fastened together so that the sharp edges slide against each other

scoff \'skäf, 'skȯf\ *vb* **scoffed; scoff•ing**
to show great disrespect with mocking laughter or behavior ⟨People once *scoffed* at the idea of space travel.⟩

¹scold \'skōld\ *vb* **scold•ed; scold•ing**
to find fault with or criticize in an angry way
scold•ing *n*

²scold *n*
a person who frequently criticizes and blames

[1]scoop \'sküp\ *n*
1 the amount held by a scoop ⟨I ate a *scoop* of ice cream.⟩
2 a kitchen utensil resembling a deep spoon and used for digging into and lifting out a soft substance ⟨an ice cream *scoop*⟩
3 a motion made with or as if with a scoop
4 a large deep shovel for digging, dipping, or shoveling

[2]scoop *vb* **scooped**; **scoop•ing**
1 to take out or up with or as if with a dipping motion
2 to make something (as a hole) by creating a hollow place

scoot \'sküt\ *vb* **scoot•ed**; **scoot•ing**
to go suddenly and quickly

scoot•er \'skü-tər\ *n*
1 a vehicle consisting of a narrow rectangular base mounted between a front and a back wheel, guided by a handle attached to the front wheel, and moved by the rider pushing off with one foot
2 MOTOR SCOOTER

scope \'skōp\ *n*
1 space or opportunity for action or thought
2 the area or amount covered, reached, or viewed ⟨That subject is beyond the *scope* of this book.⟩

scorch \'skȯrch\ *vb* **scorched**; **scorch•ing**
1 to burn on the surface
2 to dry or shrivel with or as if with intense heat
3 to produce intense heat

[1]score \'skȯr\ *n*
1 a record of points made or lost (as in a game)
2 the number of points earned for correct answers on a test
3 a group of 20 things : TWENTY
4 harm done by someone and kept in mind for later response ⟨I have a *score* to settle with you.⟩
5 DEBT 2
6 a line (as a scratch) made with or as if with something sharp
7 [1]GROUND 8, REASON ⟨We were tired but wouldn't leave on that *score*.⟩
8 the written or printed form of a musical composition
score•less \-ləs\ *adj*

[2]score *vb* **scored**; **scor•ing**
1 to make or cause to make a point or points in a game ⟨His brother *scored* a touchdown.⟩
2 to cut or mark with a line, scratch, or notch ⟨I *scored* the wood with a knife.⟩
3 ACHIEVE 1, WIN
4 [2]GRADE 1, MARK
5 to set down in an account : RECORD
6 to keep the score in a game

[1]scorn \'skȯrn\ *n*
1 a strong feeling of disgust and anger ⟨I have nothing but *scorn* for cheaters.⟩
2 an expression of disgust and anger ⟨They poured *scorn* on the idea.⟩

[2]scorn *vb* **scorned**; **scorn•ing**
to show disgust and anger for
synonyms see DESPISE

scorn•ful \'skȯrn-fəl\ *adj*
feeling or showing disgust and anger
scorn•ful•ly \-fə-lē\ *adv*

Scor•pio \'skȯr-pē-,ō\ *n*
1 a constellation between Libra and Sagittarius imagined as a scorpion
2 the eighth sign of the zodiac or a person born under this sign

scor•pi•on \'skȯr-pē-ən\ *n*
▼ an animal related to the spiders that has a long jointed body ending in a slender tail with a poisonous stinger at the end

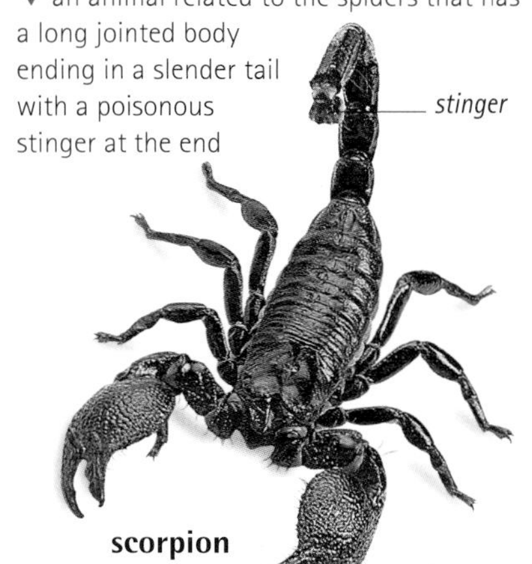

scorpion

Scot \'skät\ *n*
a person born or living in Scotland

[1]Scotch \'skäch\ *adj*
[1]SCOTTISH

[2]Scotch *n pl*
[2]SCOTTISH

scot–free \'skät-'frē\ *adj*
completely free from duty, harm, or punishment

[1]Scot•tish \'skä-tish\ *adj*
of or relating to Scotland or the Scottish people

[2]Scottish *n pl*
the people of Scotland

scoun•drel \'skaün-drəl\ *n*
a mean or wicked person

[1]scour \'skaür\ *vb* **scoured**; **scour•ing**
1 to rub hard with a rough substance or object in order to clean
2 to free or clear from impurities by or as if by rubbing

[2]scour *vb* **scoured**; **scouring**
to go or move swiftly about, over, or through in search of something ⟨Detectives *scoured* the records for a clue.⟩

[1]scourge \'skərj\ *n*
1 a cause of widespread or great suffering
2 [2]WHIP 1

[2]scourge *vb* **scourged**; **scourg•ing**
1 to cause trouble or suffering to : AFFLICT
2 to whip severely : FLOG

[1]scout \'skaüt\ *vb* **scout•ed**; **scout•ing**
1 to explore an area to find out information about it
2 to search an area for someone or something

[2]scout *n*
1 a person, group, boat, or plane that gathers information or searches an area
2 *often cap* BOY SCOUT
3 *often cap* GIRL SCOUT

scout•ing \'skaü-tiŋ\ *n*
1 the activity of gathering information or searching an area
2 *often cap* the general activities of Boy Scout and Girl Scout groups

scout•mas•ter \'skaüt-,ma-stər\ *n*
the leader of a troop of Boy Scouts

scow \'skaü\ *n*
a large boat with a flat bottom and square ends that is used chiefly for loading and unloading ships and for carrying rubbish

[1]scowl \'skaül\ *vb* **scowled**; **scowl•ing**
1 to make a look that shows anger
2 to say with an angry look

[2]scowl *n*
an angry look

scrag•gly \'skrag-lē, 'skra-gə-\ *adj* **scrag•gli•er**; **scrag•gli•est**
of rough or uneven outline : UNKEMPT ⟨a *scraggly* beard⟩

scram \'skram\ *vb* **scrammed**; **scram•ming**
to go away at once
Hint: *Scram* is often used as a command. ⟨*Scram*! Get out of here!⟩

[1]scram•ble \'skram-bəl\ *vb* **scram•bled**; **scram•bling**
1 to move or climb quickly and if necessary on hands and knees
2 to cook the mixed whites and yolks of eggs by stirring them while frying
3 to put in the wrong order ⟨The letters of the word are *scrambled*.⟩
4 to work hard to win or escape something ⟨She had to *scramble* to earn a living.⟩

[2]scramble *n*
a disorderly rush ⟨Players made a *scramble* for the loose ball.⟩

[1]scrap \'skrap\ *n*
1 a small bit ⟨a *scrap* of paper⟩ ⟨a *scrap* of evidence⟩
2 **scraps** *pl* pieces of leftover food
3 waste material (as metal) that can be made fit to use again

[2]**scrap** *vb* **scrapped**; **scrap•ping**
to abandon or throw away as worthless ⟨We ran out of money and the project had to be *scrapped.*⟩

[3]**scrap** *n*
[1]QUARREL 1, FIGHT

scrap•book \ˈskrap-ˌbu̇k\ *n*
a blank book in which clippings or pictures are kept

[1]**scrape** \ˈskrāp\ *vb* **scraped**; **scrap•ing**
1 to remove by repeated strokes with something sharp or rough
2 to clean or smooth by rubbing ⟨I *scraped* the windshield to clear off the ice.⟩
3 to rub or cause to rub so as to make a harsh noise ⟨The boat's keel *scraped* the stony bottom.⟩
4 to hurt or roughen by dragging against a rough surface ⟨I *scraped* my knee on the pavement.⟩
5 to get with difficulty and a little at a time ⟨She's trying to *scrape* together money.⟩

[2]**scrape** *n*
1 a sound, mark, or injury made by something being dragged or rubbed against something else
2 a difficult or unpleasant situation
3 the act of scraping

scrap•er \ˈskrā-pər\ *n*
▼a tool used to scrape something off a surface ⟨a paint *scraper*⟩

scraper: a paint scraper

[1]**scratch** \ˈskrach\ *vb* **scratched**; **scratch•ing**
1 to scrape or rub lightly ⟨*scratch* an itch⟩ ⟨He *scratched* his head.⟩
2 to injure by scraping with something sharp ⟨He *scratched* his thumb on a nail.⟩
3 to make a scraping noise ⟨The dog was *scratching* at the door.⟩
4 to erase by scraping ⟨I *scratched* out my mistake.⟩

[2]**scratch** *n*
a mark or injury made by scraping with something sharp

scratchy \ˈskra-chē\ *adj* **scratch•i•er**; **scratch•i•est**
1 likely to injure with something sharp ⟨a *scratchy* rosebush⟩
2 causing irritation ⟨a *scratchy* wool sweater⟩
3 COARSE 1 ⟨I shook his *scratchy* hand.⟩
4 somewhat sore ⟨a *scratchy* throat⟩

[1]**scrawl** \ˈskrȯl\ *vb* **scrawled**; **scrawl•ing**
to write quickly and carelessly ⟨The doctor *scrawled* a signature.⟩

[2]**scrawl** *n*
something written carelessly or without skill

scraw•ny \ˈskrȯ-nē\ *adj* **scraw•ni•er**; **scraw•ni•est**
poorly nourished : SKINNY ⟨a *scrawny* cat⟩

[1]**scream** \ˈskrēm\ *vb* **screamed**; **scream•ing**
to cry out (as in fright) with a loud and high-pitched sound
scream•er \ˈskrē-mər\ *n*

[2]**scream** *n*
a long cry that is loud and high-pitched

[1]**screech** \ˈskrēch\ *vb* **screeched**; **screech•ing**
1 to make a high-pitched harsh sound ⟨The car *screeched* to a stop.⟩
2 to utter with a high-pitched harsh sound
3 to cry out in a loud, high-pitched way (as in terror or pain)
synonyms see SHOUT

[2]**screech** *n*
1 a high-pitched harsh cry ⟨the *screech* of an owl⟩
2 a high-pitched harsh sound ⟨the *screech* of brakes⟩

[1]**screen** \ˈskrēn\ *n*
1 a frame that holds a usually wire netting and is used to let air in but keep pests (as insects) out ⟨a window *screen*⟩
2 a curtain or wall used to hide or to protect
3 the flat surface on which movies are projected
4 the surface on which the image appears in an electronic display (as on a television set or computer terminal)
5 a network of wire set in a frame for separating finer parts from coarser parts (as of sand)

[2]**screen** *vb* **screened**; **screen•ing**
1 to hide or protect with or as if with a curtain or wall
2 to separate or sift with a network of wire set in a frame
3 to look at carefully to select as suitable ⟨The committee *screened* job candidates.⟩

screen saver *n*
a computer program that usually displays images on the screen of a computer that is on but not in use so as to prevent damage to the screen

[1]**screw** \ˈskrü\ *n*
1 a nail-shaped or rod-shaped piece of metal with a winding ridge around its length used for fastening and holding pieces together
2 the act of twisting
3 PROPELLER

[2]**screw** *vb* **screwed**; **screw•ing**
1 to attach or fasten with a screw
2 to turn or twist on a winding ridge to attach ⟨Remember to *screw* the lid back on the jar.⟩
3 to twist out of shape ⟨Her face was *screwed* up with pain.⟩
4 to increase in amount ⟨He had to *screw* up his nerve to ask.⟩

screw•driv•er \ˈskrü-ˌdrī-vər\ *n*
▼ a tool for turning screws

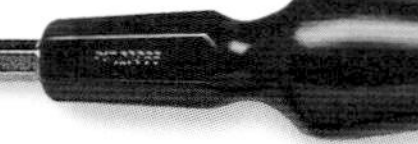
screwdriver

screwy \ˈskrü-ē\ *adj* **screw•i•er**; **screw•i•est**
1 oddly different and unfamiliar
2 CRAZY 1

[1]**scrib•ble** \ˈskri-bəl\ *vb* **scrib•bled**; **scrib•bling**
to write quickly or carelessly
scrib•bler \ˈskri-blər\ *n*

[2]**scribble** *n*
something written quickly or carelessly

scribe \ˈskrīb\ *n*
a person who copies writing (as in a book)

scrim•mage \ˈskri-mij\ *n*
1 the action between two football teams when one attempts to move the ball down the field
2 a practice game between two teams or between two groups from the same team

script \ˈskript\ *n*
1 the written form of a play or movie or the lines to be said by a performer
2 HANDWRITING

scrip•ture \ˈskrip-chər\ *n*
1 *cap* BIBLE 1
2 writings sacred to a religious group

[1]**scroll** \ˈskrōl\ *n*
a roll of paper or parchment on which something is written or engraved

[2]**scroll** *vb* **scrolled**; **scroll•ing**
to move words or images up or down a display screen as if by unrolling a scroll

[1]**scrub** \ˈskrəb\ *vb* **scrubbed**; **scrub•bing**
to rub hard in washing

[2]**scrub** *n*
a thick growth of small or stunted shrubs or trees

[3]**scrub** *n*
the act, an instance, or a period of rubbing hard in washing

scrub•by \'skrə-bē\ *adj* **scrub•bi•er; scrub•bi•est**
covered with a thick growth of small or stunted shrubs or trees

scruff \'skrəf\ *n*
the loose skin on the back of the neck

scruffy \'skrə-fē\ *adj* **scruff•i•er; scruff•i•est**
dirty or shabby in appearance

scrump•tious \'skrəmp-shəs\ *adj*
1 DELICIOUS
2 DELIGHTFUL

scrunch \'skrənch\ *vb* **scrunched; scrunch•ing**
1 to cause (as facial features) to draw together
2 [1]CROUCH, HUNCH
3 to draw or squeeze together tightly 〈She *scrunched* her fists.〉
4 CRUMPLE 1
5 [1]CRUSH 1

scru•ple \'skrü-pəl\ *n*
1 a sense of right and wrong that keeps a person from doing something bad
2 a feeling of guilt from doing something bad

scru•pu•lous \'skrü-pyə-ləs\ *adj*
careful in doing what is right and proper
scru•pu•lous•ly *adv*

scru•ti•nize \'skrü-tə-,nīz\ *vb* **scru•ti•nized; scru•ti•niz•ing**
to examine very closely

scru•ti•ny \'skrü-tə-nē, 'skrüt-nē\ *n*
a close inspection

scu•ba \'skü-bə\ *n*
equipment used for breathing while swimming underwater

scuba diver *n*
▼ a person who swims underwater with scuba gear

scuff \'skəf\ *vb* **scuffed; scuff•ing**
1 to scrape the feet while walking
2 to mark or scratch by scraping 〈Don't *scuff* your good shoes.〉

scuba diver

[1]scuf•fle \'skə-fəl\ *vb* **scuf•fled; scuf•fling**
1 to fight briefly and not very seriously
2 SCUFF 1

[2]scuffle *n*
1 a short fight that is not very serious
2 the sound of shuffling

scull \'skəl\ *n*
a boat driven by one or more pairs of short oars

sculpt \'skəlpt\ *vb* **sculpt•ed; sculpt•ing**
[2]SCULPTURE
sculp•tor \'skəlp-tər\ *n*

[1]sculp•ture \'skəlp-chər\ *n*
1 the action or art of making statues by carving or chiseling (as in wood or stone), by modeling (as in clay), or by casting (as in melted metal)
2 ▶ a work of art produced by sculpture

[2]sculpture *vb* **sculp•tured; sculp•tur•ing**
to make (a work of art) by shaping (as stone, wood, or metal)

scum \'skəm\ *n*
1 a film of matter that rises to the top of a boiling or fermenting liquid
2 a coating (as of algae) on the surface of still water
3 a loathsome person

[1]scur•ry \'skər-ē\ *vb* **scur•ried; scur•ry•ing**
to move quickly

[2]scurry *n, pl* **scur•ries**
the act of moving quickly

[1]scur•vy \'skər-vē\ *n*
a disease caused by a lack of vitamin C in which the teeth loosen, the gums soften, and there is bleeding under the skin

[2]scurvy *adj* **scur•vi•er; scur•vi•est**
[2]MEAN 1, CONTEMPTIBLE 〈a *scurvy* trick〉

[1]scut•tle \'skə-t^{ə}l\ *vb* **scut•tled; scut•tling**
to run rapidly from view

[2]scuttle *n*
a pail or bucket for carrying coal

[1]sculpture 2: marble sculptures

[3]scuttle *n*
a small opening with a lid or cover (as in the deck of a ship)

[4]scuttle *vb* **scut•tled; scut•tling**
to sink (a ship) by cutting holes through the bottom or sides

scythe \'sīth\ *n*
a tool with a curved blade on a long curved handle that is used to mow grass or grain by hand

SD, S. Dak. *abbr* South Dakota

SE *abbr* southeast

sea \'sē\ *n*
1 a body of salt water not as large as an ocean and often nearly surrounded by land
2 OCEAN 1
3 rough water 〈A high *sea* swept the deck.〉
4 something suggesting a sea's great size or depth 〈The speaker looked out on a *sea* of faces.〉

sea anemone *n*
a hollow sea animal that is related to the coral and has a cluster of tentacles around its mouth

sea•bird \'sē-,bərd\ *n*
a bird (as a gull or puffin) that lives on or near the open ocean

sea•coast \'sē-,kōst\ *n*
the shore of the sea

sea cucumber *n*
► a sea animal that is related to the starfish and has a flexible muscular body shaped like a cucumber

[1]sea•far•ing \'sē-,fer-iŋ\ *adj*
of or employed in sailing

[2]seafaring *n*
sailing on the sea as work or as recreation

sea•food \'sē-,füd\ *n*
saltwater fish and shellfish used as food

sea•go•ing \'sē-,gō-iŋ\ *adj*
suitable or used for sea travel ⟨a *seagoing* vessel⟩

sea•gull \'sē-,gəl\ *n*
a gull that lives near the sea

sea horse *n*
▼a small fish with a head which looks like the head of a horse

sea horse: a yellow sea horse

[1]seal \'sēl\ *n*
1 a sea mammal that swims with flippers, lives mostly in cold regions, bears young on land, feeds on fish and other sea animals (as squid), and is sometimes hunted for its fur, hide, or oil
2 the soft fur of a seal

[2]seal *n*
1 something that closes tightly ⟨The *seal* on the package is broken.⟩
2 the condition of having a tight seal ⟨Caulk gives the window a *seal.*⟩
3 ► an official mark stamped or pressed on something

sea cucumber

4 a device with a cut or raised design or figure that can be stamped or pressed into wax or paper
5 a stamp that may be used to close a letter or package ⟨Christmas *seals*⟩
6 something (as a pledge) that makes safe or secure ⟨The deal was made under *seal* of secrecy.⟩

[3]seal *vb* **sealed**; **seal•ing**
1 to close tightly or completely to prevent anyone or anything from moving in or out
2 to put an official mark on
seal•er *n*

sea level *n*
the surface of the sea halfway between the average high and low tides

sea lion *n*
a large seal of the Pacific Ocean

seal•skin \'sēl-,skin\ *n*
[1]SEAL 2

seam \'sēm\ *n*
1 the fold, line, or groove made by sewing together or joining two edges or two pieces of material
2 a layer in the ground of a mineral or metal

sea•man \'sē-mən\ *n, pl* **sea•men** \-mən\
1 a person who helps in the handling of a ship at sea : SAILOR
2 an enlisted person in the navy or coast guard ranking above a seaman apprentice

seaman apprentice *n*
an enlisted person in the navy or coast guard ranking above a seaman recruit

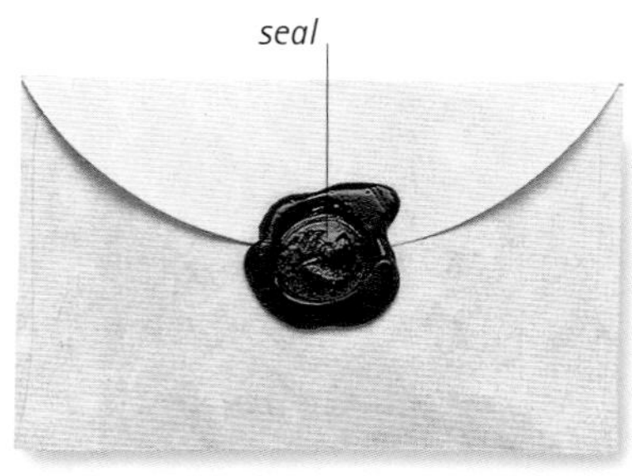

[2]seal 3:
a wax seal on an envelope

seaman recruit *n*
an enlisted person of the lowest rank in the navy or coast guard

seam•stress \'sēm-strəs\ *n*
a woman who sews especially for a living

sea•plane \'sē-,plān\ *n*
an airplane that can rise from and land on water

sea•port \'sē-,pȯrt\ *n*
a port, harbor, or town within reach of seagoing ships

sear \'sir\ *vb* **seared**; **sear•ing**
1 to burn, mark, or injure with or as if with sudden heat ⟨*searing* pain⟩ ⟨The sight was *seared* into my memory.⟩
2 to dry by or as if by heat : PARCH
3 to quickly cook the surface by high heat

[1]search \'sərch\ *vb* **searched**; **search•ing**
1 to go through or look around carefully and thoroughly in an effort to find something ⟨*search* the house⟩
2 to carefully look for someone or something
3 to look in the pockets or the clothing of (someone) for something hidden
4 to use a computer to find information (as in a database or on the Internet)
synonyms see SEEK

[2]search *n*
an act or instance of looking for someone or something

search engine *n*
computer software used to search data (as text or a database) for requested information

search•light \'sərch-,līt\ *n*
a lamp for sending a beam of bright light

sea•shell \'sē-,shel\ *n*
the shell of a sea animal

sea•shore \'sē-,shȯr\ *n*
the shore of a sea

sea•sick \'sē-,sik\ *adj*
sick in the stomach from the pitching or rolling of a ship
sea•sick•ness *n*

sea•side \'sē-,sīd\ *n*
SEACOAST

[1]sea•son \'sē-zᵊn\ *n*
1 one of the four quarters into which a year is commonly divided
2 a period of time associated with something special ⟨apple *season*⟩

[2]season *vb* **sea•soned**; **sea•son•ing**
1 to add flavor to (food) with spices and herbs
2 to make suitable for use (as by aging or drying) ⟨Has this wood been *seasoned*?⟩

sea•son•al \'sē-zᵊn-əl\ *adj*
happening, available, or used at a certain season ⟨*seasonal* foods⟩

sea•son•ing \'sē-zən-iŋ\ *n*
something added to food to give it more flavor

sea star *n*
STARFISH

[1]seat \'sēt\ *n*
1 something (as a chair) used to sit in or on
2 the part of something on which a person sits ⟨a chair *seat*⟩ ⟨There's a tear on the *seat* of my pants.⟩
3 the place on or at which a person sits ⟨Take your *seat*.⟩
4 a place that serves as a capital or center ⟨a *seat* of government⟩
seat•ed \'sēt-əd\ *adj*

[2]seat *vb* **seat•ed; seat•ing**
1 to place in or on a seat ⟨Ushers *seated* the guests.⟩
2 to have enough places to sit for ⟨The hall *seats* 500 people.⟩

seat belt *n*
a strap (as in an automobile or airplane) designed to hold a person in a seat

sea urchin *n*
▶ a small sea animal that is related to the starfish, lives on the sea bottom, and is enclosed in a roundish shell covered with spines that can move

sea•wall \'sē-,wȯl\ *n*
a bank or a wall to prevent sea waves from eroding the shore

sea•wa•ter \'sē-,wȯ-tər, -,wä-\ *n*
water in or from the sea

sea•weed \'sē-,wēd\ *n*
▶ an alga (as a kelp) that grows in the sea

sea•wor•thy \'sē-,wər-t͟hē\ *adj*
fit or safe for a sea voyage ⟨a *seaworthy* vessel⟩

sec. *abbr* second

se•cede \si-'sēd\ *vb* **se•ced•ed; se•ced•ing**
to end an association with an organization (as a country)

se•clud•ed \si-'klü-dəd\ *adj*
1 hidden from sight
2 living or kept away from others

se•clu•sion \si-'klü-zhən\ *n*
the condition of being hidden from sight or kept away from others

[1]sec•ond \'se-kənd\ *adj*
1 being next after the first in time or order ⟨a *second* child⟩ ⟨the *second* floor⟩
2 next lower in rank, value, or importance than the first ⟨*second* prize⟩
3 another of the same type ⟨a *second* car⟩ ⟨a *second* language⟩

[2]second *n*
1 a 60th part of a minute of time or of a degree
2 MOMENT 1, INSTANT ⟨I'll be with you in a *second*.⟩

[3]second *vb* **sec•ond•ed; sec•ond•ing**
to support a suggestion, motion, or nomination

[4]second *adv*
in the second place or rank

[5]second *n*
someone or something that is second ⟨Theirs is the first house, and mine is the *second*.⟩

sec•ond•ary \'se-kən-,der-ē\ *adj*
1 second in rank, value, or importance ⟨We need to find water. Food is *secondary*.⟩
2 derived from or coming after something original or primary ⟨a *secondary* effect⟩
3 relating to secondary school ⟨a *secondary* education⟩
4 relating to or being the second of three levels of stress in pronunciation

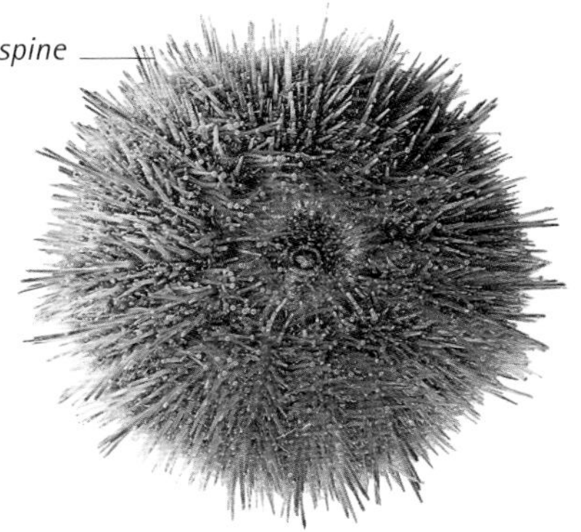

sea urchin: overhead view of a sea urchin

secondary school *n*
a school for students above elementary school level and below college level

sec•ond•hand \,se-kənd-'hand\ *adj*
1 not new : having had a previous owner ⟨a *secondhand* automobile⟩
2 selling used goods ⟨a *secondhand* shop⟩

second lieutenant *n*
a commissioned officer of the lowest rank in the army, air force, or marine corps

second person *n*
a set of words or forms (as pronouns or verb forms) referring to the person the speaker or writer is addressing

sec•ond–rate \,se-kənd-'rāt\ *adj*
of ordinary or second quality or value ⟨She buys *second-rate* clothing.⟩

se•cre•cy \'sē-krə-sē\ *n*
1 the act of keeping things secret ⟨I swore him to *secrecy*.⟩
2 the quality or state of being secret or hidden ⟨The meetings were held in *secrecy*.⟩

[1]se•cret \'sē-krət\ *adj*
1 hidden from the knowledge of others ⟨a *secret* staircase⟩ ⟨Keep your plans *secret*.⟩
2 done, made, or working in a way that no other or only a few other people know about ⟨a *secret* attack⟩ ⟨a *secret* agent⟩
se•cret•ly *adv*

▶ **seaweed**
The three most common types of seaweed are brown, red, and green. Seaweed can be found on the beach, in the sea, and in salty, rocky tide pools where it anchors itself onto rocks and solid surfaces.

[2]**secret** *n*
something kept or planned to be kept from others' knowledge

sec•re•tary \'se-krə-ˌter-ē\ *n, pl* **sec•re•tar•ies**
1 a person who is employed to take care of records, letters, and routine work for another person
2 an officer of a business corporation or society who is in charge of the letters and records and who keeps minutes of meetings
3 a government official in charge of a department ⟨the *secretary* of education⟩
4 ▼ a writing desk with a top section for books

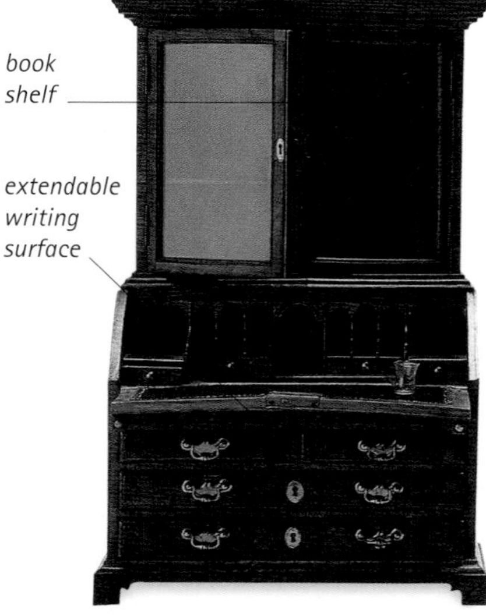

secretary 4: model of a secretary

[1]**se•crete** \si-'krēt\ *vb* **se•cret•ed**; **se•cret•ing**
to produce and give off as a secretion ⟨Some glands *secrete* mucus.⟩

[2]**secrete** *vb* **se•cret•ed**; **se•cret•ing**
to put in a hiding place

se•cre•tion \si-'krē-shən\ *n*
1 the act or process of giving off a substance ⟨the *secretion* of saliva by salivary glands⟩
2 a substance formed in and given off by a gland that usually performs a useful function in the body ⟨Digestive *secretions* contain enzymes.⟩

se•cre•tive \'sē-krə-tiv, si-'krē-\ *adj*
tending to act in secret or keep secrets

sect \'sekt\ *n*
a group within a religion which has a special set of teachings or a special way of doing things

[1]**sec•tion** \'sek-shən\ *n*
1 a division of a thing or place ⟨A *section* of the fence broke.⟩
2 a part cut off or separated ⟨a *section* of an orange⟩
3 a part of a written work ⟨the sports *section* of a newspaper⟩
4 CROSS SECTION 1
synonyms see PART

[2]**section** *vb* **sec•tioned**; **sec•tion•ing**
to cut into parts

sec•tor \'sek-tər\ *n*
a part of an area or of a sphere of activity ⟨the industrial *sector* of the economy⟩

sec•u•lar \'se-kyə-lər\ *adj*
1 not concerned with religion or the church ⟨*secular* society⟩ ⟨*secular* music⟩
2 not belonging to a religious order ⟨a *secular* priest⟩

[1]**se•cure** \si-'kyu̇r\ *adj* **se•cur•er**; **se•cur•est**
1 free from danger or risk ⟨Being home made me feel *secure*.⟩
2 strong or firm enough to ensure safety ⟨a *secure* lock⟩
3 free from worry or doubt : CONFIDENT ⟨He's *secure* in his abilities.⟩
4 [1]SURE 5, CERTAIN ⟨Victory is *secure*.⟩
synonyms see SAFE

[2]**secure** *vb* **se•cured**; **se•cur•ing**
1 to make safe ⟨Police *secured* the building.⟩
2 to fasten or put something in a place to keep it from coming loose ⟨*Secure* your belongings under the seat.⟩
3 to get hold of : ACQUIRE ⟨*secure* information⟩ ⟨She *secured* a job.⟩

se•cu•ri•ty \si-'kyu̇r-ə-tē\ *n, pl* **se•cu•ri•ties**
1 the state of being safe : SAFETY ⟨national *security*⟩
2 freedom from worry or anxiety ⟨financial *security*⟩
3 something given as a pledge of payment ⟨He gave *security* for a loan.⟩
4 something (as a stock certificate) that is evidence of debt or ownership

se•dan \si-'dan\ *n*
1 a closed automobile that has two or four doors and a permanent top and seats four or more people
2 SEDAN CHAIR

sedan chair *n*
▶ a chair made to hold one person and to be carried on two poles by two others

se•date \si-'dāt\ *adj*
quiet and steady in manner or conduct
se•date•ly *adv*

sed•a•tive \'se-də-tiv\ *n*
a medicine that calms or relaxes someone

sed•en•tary \'se-dᵊn-ˌter-ē\ *adj*
doing much sitting : not physically active

sedge \'sej\ *n*
a plant that is like grass but has solid stems and grows in tufts in marshes

sed•i•ment \'se-də-mənt\ *n*
1 the material from a liquid that settles to the bottom
2 material (as stones and sand) carried onto land or into water by water, wind, or a glacier

sed•i•men•ta•ry \ˌse-də-'men-tə-rē\ *adj*
relating to or formed from sediment ⟨Sandstone is a *sedimentary* rock.⟩

se•duce \si-'düs, -'dyüs\ *vb* **se•duced**; **se•duc•ing**
to persuade (someone) to do something and especially to do something wrong ⟨She was *seduced* into crime.⟩

[1]**see** \'sē\ *vb* **saw** \'sȯ\; **seen** \'sēn\; **see•ing**
1 to have the power of sight ⟨The book is in braille for those who cannot *see*.⟩
2 to view with the eyes ⟨Did you *see* me fall?⟩
3 to have experience of ⟨This motel has *seen* better days.⟩
4 to understand the meaning or importance of ⟨Do you *see* what I mean?⟩
5 to come to know : DISCOVER ⟨He'll be angry when he *sees* what you've done.⟩
6 to call on : VISIT ⟨He's going to *see* a friend.⟩
7 to form a mental picture of ⟨I can still *see* your father when he was a boy.⟩
8 to imagine as a possibility ⟨I can't *see* myself ever getting married.⟩
9 to make sure ⟨*See* that the job gets done.⟩
10 to attend to ⟨I'll *see* to your order at once.⟩
11 to meet with ⟨The doctor will *see* you now.⟩
12 ACCOMPANY 1, ESCORT ⟨I'll *see* you home.⟩

[2]**see** *n*
1 the city in which a bishop's church is located
2 DIOCESE

[1]**seed** \'sēd\ *n*
1 a tiny developing plant that is enclosed in a protective coat usually along with a supply of food and that is able to develop under suitable conditions into a plant like the one that produced it

sedan chair: porcelain model of a sedan chair made in Russia in the early 20th century

A B C D E F G H I J K L M N O P Q R S T U V W X Y Z

2 a small structure (as a spore or a tiny dry fruit) other than a true seed by which a plant reproduces itself
3 the descendants of one individual
4 a source of development or growth : GERM 〈The comment planted a *seed* of doubt in my mind.〉
seed•ed \'sē-dəd\ *adj*
seed•less \'sēd-ləs\ *adj*

[2]seed *vb* **seed•ed**; **seed•ing**
1 [2]SOW 2, PLANT 〈Farmers *seed* the fields with wheat.〉
2 to produce or shed seeds 〈The plant *seeds* early.〉
3 to take the seeds out of 〈You have to wash and *seed* the peppers.〉

seed•ling \'sēd-liŋ\ *n*
1 a young plant grown from seed
2 a young tree before it becomes a sapling

seed plant *n*
a plant that produces seed

seed•pod \'sēd-,päd\ *n*
POD

seedy \'sē-dē\ *adj* **seed•i•er**; **seed•i•est**
1 having or full of seeds 〈a *seedy* orange〉
2 poor in condition or quality 〈a *seedy* hotel〉

seek \'sēk\ *vb* **sought** \'sȯt\; **seek•ing**
1 to try to find 〈*seek* help〉
2 to try to win or get 〈He *sought* revenge.〉
3 to make an attempt 〈Doctors are *seeking* to find a cure.〉

▶ **Synonyms** SEEK, SEARCH, and HUNT mean to look for something. SEEK may be used in looking for either material or mental things. 〈She's always *seeking* new friends.〉 〈I *seek* the truth.〉 SEARCH is used when looking for something in a very careful, thorough way. 〈We *searched* all over the house for the letter.〉 HUNT is used for a long pursuit. 〈I *hunted* all day for the right present.〉

seem \'sēm\ *vb* **seemed**; **seem•ing**
1 to give the impression of being : APPEAR 〈They certainly *seemed* pleased.〉
2 used to make a statement less forceful or more polite 〈I can't *seem* to recall where we met.〉

seem•ing \'sē-miŋ\ *adj*
APPARENT 3 〈Mom was suspicious of our *seeming* enthusiasm for work.〉
seem•ing•ly *adv*

seen *past participle of* SEE

seep \'sēp\ *vb* **seeped**; **seep•ing**
to flow slowly through small openings 〈Water *seeped* into the basement.〉

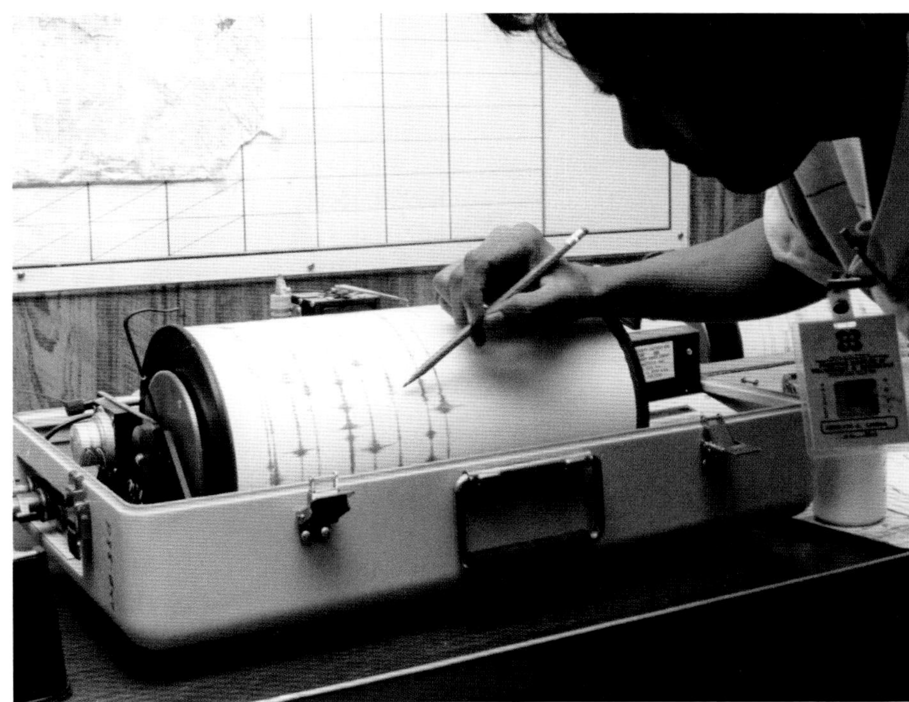

seismograph: a person checking a seismograph in order to monitor earth movements

seer \'sir\ *n*
a person who predicts events

[1]see•saw \'sē-,sȯ\ *n*
1 a plank for children to play on that is balanced in the middle on a raised bar with one end going up while the other goes down
2 a situation in which something keeps changing from one state to another and back again

[2]seesaw *vb* **see•sawed**; **see•saw•ing**
to keep changing from one state to another and back again

seethe \'sēth\ *vb* **seethed**; **seeth•ing**
1 to feel or show great excitement or emotion (as anger) 〈The unjust criticism caused me to *seethe*.〉
2 to move constantly and without order 〈Flies *seethed* around garbage.〉

seg•ment \'seg-mənt\ *n*
1 any of the parts into which a thing is divided or naturally separates
2 a part cut off from a figure (as a circle) by means of a line or plane
3 a part of a straight line included between two points

seg•re•gate \'se-gri-,gāt\ *vb* **seg•re•gat•ed**; **seg•re•gat•ing**
to separate a race, class, or group from the rest of society

seg•re•ga•tion \,se-gri-'gā-shən\ *n*
the practice or policy of separating a race, class, or group from the rest of society

seis•mo•graph \'sīz-mə-,graf, 'sīs-\ *n*
▲ a device that measures and records vibrations of the earth

seize \'sēz\ *vb* **seized**; **seiz•ing**
1 to take possession of by or as if by force 〈Invaders *seized* the castle.〉 〈He *seized* the lead.〉
2 to take hold of suddenly or with force
3 to take or use eagerly or quickly 〈She *seized* the opportunity to go.〉
synonyms see TAKE

sei•zure \'sē-zhər\ *n*
1 an act of taking suddenly or with force : the state of being taken suddenly or with force
2 an abnormal state in which a person usually experiences convulsions and may become unconscious

sel•dom \'sel-dəm\ *adv*
not often : RARELY 〈He *seldom* talks about his past.〉

[1]se•lect \sə-'lekt\ *vb* **se•lect•ed**; **se•lect•ing**
to pick out from a group 〈I *selected* a ripe peach.〉
synonyms see CHOOSE

[2]select *adj*
1 chosen to include the best or most suitable individuals 〈*select* committees〉 〈*Select* students participated in the program.〉
2 of special value or excellence 〈a *select* hotel〉

se•lec•tion \sə-'lek-shən\ *n*
1 the act or process of choosing
2 something that is chosen

se•lec•tive \sə-ˈlek-tiv\ *adj*
careful to choose or include only the best or most suitable individuals ⟨a *selective* college⟩

se•le•ni•um \sə-ˈlē-nē-əm\ *n*
a gray powdery chemical element used chiefly in electronic devices

self \ˈself\ *n, pl* **selves** \ˈselvz\
1 a person regarded as an individual apart from everyone else
2 a special side of a person's character ⟨He isn't his cheerful *self* today.⟩

self- *prefix*
1 someone's or something's self ⟨*self*-governing⟩
2 of or by someone's or something's self ⟨*self*-control⟩
3 to, with, for, or toward someone's or something's self ⟨*self*-respect⟩

self–ad•dressed \ˌself-ə-ˈdrest, -ˈa-ˌdrest\ *adj*
addressed for return to the sender ⟨a *self-addressed* envelope⟩

self–cen•tered \ˈself-ˈsen-tərd\ *adj*
SELFISH

self–con•fi•dence \ˈself-ˈkän-fə-dəns\ *n*
someone's confidence in himself or herself and in his or her own abilities

self–con•scious \ˈself-ˈkän-shəs\ *adj*
feeling uncomfortably nervous or embarrassed when in the presence of or when being observed by other people ⟨He's very *self-conscious* about his appearance.⟩
self–con•scious•ly *adv*
self–con•scious•ness *n*

self–con•trol \ˌself-kən-ˈtrōl\ *n*
someone's control over his or her own impulses, emotions, or actions

self–de•fense \ˌself-di-ˈfens\ *n*
someone's act of defending himself or herself or his or her property ⟨I acted in *self-defense*.⟩

self–es•teem \ˌself-ə-ˈstēm\ *n*
a feeling of satisfaction that someone has in himself or herself and his or her own abilities

self–ev•i•dent \ˈself-ˈe-və-dənt\ *adj*
clearly true and requiring no proof ⟨*self-evident* truths⟩

self–gov•ern•ing \ˈself-ˈgə-vər-niŋ\ *adj*
being governed by its own members or citizens ⟨a *self-governing* island⟩

self–gov•ern•ment \ˈself-ˈgə-vərn-mənt, -vər-mənt\ *n*
government by the people making up a group or community

self–im•por•tance \ˌself-im-ˈpȯr-tᵊns\ *n*
an attitude showing that someone has an overly high opinion of his or her own importance

self–im•por•tant \ˌself-im-ˈpȯr-tᵊnt\ *adj*
having or showing the attitude of someone who has too high an opinion of his or her own importance : showing self-importance

self•ish \ˈsel-fish\ *adj*
taking care of only a person's own needs and feelings without thought for others
self•ish•ly *adv*
self•ish•ness *n*

self•less \ˈsel-fləs\ *adj*
showing great concern for and willingness to give unselfishly to others
self•less•ly *adv*
self•less•ness *n*

self–pos•sessed \ˌself-pə-ˈzest\ *adj*
having or showing control of emotions or reactions

self–pro•pelled \ˌself-prə-ˈpeld\ *adj*
containing within itself the means for its own movement

self–re•li•ance \ˌself-ri-ˈlī-əns\ *n*
a feeling of trust that someone has in his or her own efforts and abilities

self–re•spect \ˌself-ri-ˈspekt\ *n*
someone's proper regard for himself or herself as a human being

self–re•straint \ˌself-ri-ˈstrānt\ *n*
proper self-control over actions or emotions

self–righ•teous \ˈself-ˈrī-chəs\ *adj*
having or showing the attitude of someone who strongly believes in the rightness of his or her own actions or opinions
self–righ•teous•ness *n*

self•same \ˈself-ˌsām\ *adj*
exactly the same

self–ser•vice \ˈself-ˈsər-vəs\ *adj*
allowing or requiring customers to serve themselves without help from workers

self–suf•fi•cient \ˌself-sə-ˈfi-shənt\ *adj*
able to live or function without the help of others

self–worth \ˈself-ˈwərth\ *n*
SELF-ESTEEM

sell \ˈsel\ *vb* **sold** \ˈsōld\; **sell•ing**
1 to exchange in return for money or something else of value ⟨He *sold* his bike to my brother.⟩
2 to make available for sale ⟨The store *sells* shoes.⟩
3 to be sold or priced ⟨The new product is *selling* well.⟩ ⟨These *sell* for a dollar apiece.⟩
sell•er *n*
sell out
1 to be bought until all are gone ⟨Tickets quickly *sold out*.⟩
2 to betray a person or duty ⟨They *sold out* their country.⟩

selves *pl of* SELF

sem•a•phore \ˈse-mə-ˌfȯr\ *n*
1 a device for sending signals that can be seen by the receiver
2 ▶a system of sending signals with two flags held one in each hand

sem•blance \ˈsem-bləns\ *n*
outward appearance

se•mes•ter \sə-ˈme-stər\ *n*
either of two terms that make up a school year

semi- *prefix*
1 half ⟨*semi*circle⟩
2 partly : not completely
3 partial

semi•cir•cle \ˈse-mi-ˌsər-kəl\ *n*
half of a circle

semi•co•lon \ˈse-mi-ˌkō-lən\ *n*
a punctuation mark ; that can be used to separate parts of a sentence which need clearer separation than would be shown by a comma, to separate main clauses which have no conjunction between, and to separate phrases and clauses containing commas

semi•con•duc•tor \ˌse-mi-kən-ˈdək-tər\ *n*
a solid substance that conducts electricity imperfectly

semi•fi•nal \ˈse-mi-ˌfī-nᵊl\ *n*
a match or game coming before the final round in a tournament

sem•i•nary \ˈse-mə-ˌner-ē\ *n, pl* **sem•i•nar•ies**
1 a private school at or above the high school level
2 a school for the training of priests, ministers, or rabbis

Sem•i•nole \ˈse-mə-ˌnōl\ *n, pl* **Sem•i•noles** *or* **Seminole**
a member of an American Indian people of Florida and Oklahoma

semi•sol•id \ˌse-mi-ˈsä-ləd\ *adj*
having the qualities of both a solid and a liquid

Sen. *abbr* senate, senator

sen•ate \ˈse-nət\ *n*
1 *cap* the upper house of a legislature (as the United States Congress)
2 a governing body

sen•a•tor \ˈse-nə-tər\ *n*
a member of a Senate

send \ˈsend\ *vb* **sent** \ˈsent\; **send•ing**
1 to cause to go ⟨The sick student was *sent* home.⟩ ⟨I'll *send* a message.⟩
2 to set in motion by physical force ⟨The hitter *sent* the ball out of the ballpark.⟩
3 to cause to move in a particular direction or manner ⟨The high demand *sent* prices up.⟩
4 to cause someone to pass a message on or do an errand ⟨Let's *send* out for pizza.⟩
5 to give an order or request to come or go ⟨Our principal *sent* for the child.⟩

semaphore 2: a series of semaphore signals that spell the word "Hello"

6 to bring into a certain condition ⟨His remarks *sent* me into a rage.⟩
send•er *n*

Sen•e•ca \'se-ni-kə\ *n, pl* **Seneca** *or* **Sen•e•cas**
1 a member of an American Indian people of western New York
2 the language of the Seneca people

[1]se•nior \'sēn-yər\ *n*
1 a person older or higher in rank than someone else
2 a student in the final year of high school or college
3 an elderly person

[2]senior *adj*
1 being older
Hint: This sense is often used to distinguish a father from a son with the same name. ⟨John Doe, *Senior*⟩
2 higher in rank or office ⟨Who is the *senior* partner of the law firm?⟩
3 relating to students in the final year of high school or college

senior airman *n*
an enlisted person in the air force who ranks above airman first class but who has not been made sergeant

senior chief petty officer *n*
a petty officer in the navy or coast guard ranking above a chief petty officer

senior master sergeant *n*
a noncommissioned officer in the air force ranking above a master sergeant

sen•sa•tion \sen-'sā-shən\ *n*
1 awareness (as of noise or heat) or a mental process (as seeing or smelling) resulting from stimulation of a sense organ ⟨I felt a tingling *sensation* in my leg.⟩
2 an indefinite awareness of a feeling or experience ⟨a *sensation* of flying⟩
3 a state of excited interest or feeling ⟨The rumor caused a *sensation*.⟩
4 a cause or object of excited interest ⟨The play was a *sensation*.⟩

sen•sa•tion•al \sen-'sā-shə-nᵊl\ *adj*
1 causing or meant to cause great interest ⟨a *sensational* crime⟩
2 very or unexpectedly excellent

[1]sense \'sens\ *n*
1 a specialized function or mechanism (as sight, taste, or touch) of the body that involves the action and effect of a stimulus on a sense organ
2 awareness arrived at through or as if through the senses ⟨He felt a *sense* of danger.⟩
3 a particular sensation or kind of sensation ⟨I lost my *sense* of balance.⟩
4 the ability to make wise decisions
5 an awareness or understanding of something ⟨a *sense* of humor⟩ ⟨a *sense* of pride⟩
6 a reason or excuse based on intelligence or good judgment ⟨There is no *sense* in continuing.⟩
7 a logical, sensible, or practical thing, act, or way of doing ⟨Saving money for the future makes *sense*.⟩
8 a meaning or one of a set of meanings a word, phrase, or story may have

[2]sense *vb* **sensed**; **sens•ing**
to be or become aware of ⟨My cat can *sense* the approach of a storm.⟩

sense•less \'sen-sləs\ *adj*
1 UNCONSCIOUS 2 ⟨I was knocked *senseless*.⟩
2 STUPID 2
sense•less•ly *adv*

sense organ *n*
a part of the body (as the eye or nose) that contains special cells that receive stimuli (as light) and activate associated nerves so that they carry impulses to the brain

sen•si•bil•i•ty \ˌsen-sə-'bi-lə-tē\ *n, pl* **sen•si•bil•i•ties**
1 the ability to receive or feel sensations
2 the ability to feel and understand emotions

sen•si•ble \'sen-sə-bəl\ *adj*
1 showing or containing good sense or judgment ⟨a *sensible* driver⟩
2 designed for a practical purpose rather than for appearance ⟨*sensible* shoes⟩
3 capable of feeling or perceiving ⟨The patient was *sensible* to pain.⟩
sen•si•bly \-blē\ *adv*

sen•si•tive \'sen-sə-tiv\ *adj*
1 easily or strongly affected, impressed, or hurt ⟨a *sensitive* child⟩
2 likely to affect, impress, or hurt ⟨a *sensitive* topic⟩
3 understanding of the feelings of others
4 capable of responding to stimulation ⟨*sensitive* structures of the ear⟩
5 readily affected or changed often in an unpleasant or negative way ⟨I have *sensitive* skin.⟩
sen•si•tive•ly *adv*

sen•si•tiv•i•ty \ˌsen-sə-'ti-və-tē\ *n*
1 an awareness and understanding of the feelings of others
2 the ability to express thoughts and feelings ⟨She sings with great *sensitivity*.⟩

sen•so•ry \'sen-sə-rē\ *adj*
of or relating to sensation or the senses ⟨*sensory* nerves⟩

sen•su•al \'sen-shə-wəl\ *adj*
relating to the pleasing of the senses

sent *past and past participle of* SEND

[1]sen•tence \'sen-tᵊns\ *n*
1 a group of words that makes a statement, asks a question, or expresses a command, wish, or exclamation
2 punishment set by a court ⟨He served a *sentence* for robbery.⟩
3 a mathematical statement (as an equation) in words or symbols

[2]sentence *vb* **sen•tenced**; **sen•tenc•ing**
to set the punishment of ⟨The judge *sentenced* the prisoner.⟩

sen•ti•ment \'sen-tə-mənt\ *n*
1 a thought or attitude influenced by feeling ⟨a strong religious *sentiment*⟩
2 OPINION 1
3 tender feelings of affection

sen•ti•men•tal \ˌsen-tə-'men-tᵊl\ *adj*
1 influenced strongly by feelings of affection or yearning ⟨She kept her old doll for *sentimental* reasons.⟩
2 primarily affecting the emotions ⟨a *sentimental* story⟩

sen•ti•nel \'sen-tə-nəl\ *n*
SENTRY

sen•try \'sen-trē\ *n, pl* **sentries**
a person (as a soldier) on duty as a guard

Sep. *abbr* September

se•pal \'sē-pəl, 'se-\ *n*
▼ one of the specialized leaves that form the calyx of a flower

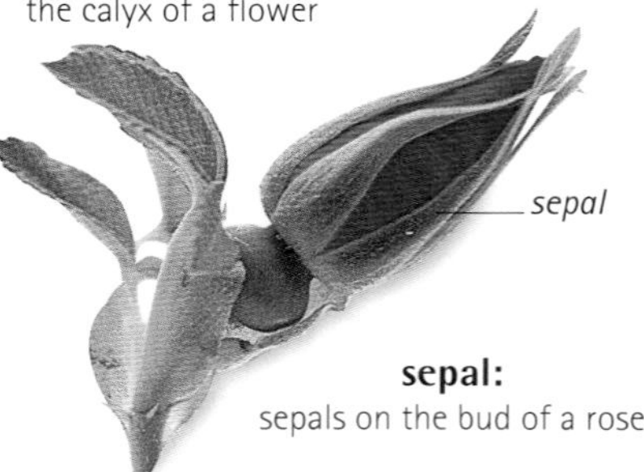

sepal:
sepals on the bud of a rose

¹sep•a•rate \'se-pə-,rāt\ *vb* **sep•a•rat•ed; sep•a•rat•ing**
1 to set or keep apart ⟨*Separate* the egg yolk from the white.⟩
2 to make a distinction between ⟨Be sure to *separate* fact from fiction.⟩
3 to cease to be together : PART

▶ **Synonyms** SEPARATE, PART, and DIVIDE mean to break into parts or to keep apart. SEPARATE may be used when things have been put into groups, or a thing has been removed from a group, or something has been inserted between like things. ⟨*Separate* the good eggs from the bad ones.⟩ ⟨A fence *separates* the two yards.⟩ PART is used when the things to be separated are closely joined in some way. ⟨Only death could *part* the two friends.⟩ DIVIDE means separating by cutting or breaking into pieces or sections. ⟨*Divide* the pie into six equal portions.⟩

²sep•a•rate \'se-pə-rət, 'se-prət\ *adj*
1 set apart ⟨The motel contains fifty *separate* units.⟩
2 not shared : INDIVIDUAL ⟨We were each busy with our *separate* projects.⟩
3 existing independently from each other ⟨The company broke up into three *separate* businesses.⟩

sep•a•rate•ly \'se-pə-rət-lē\ *adv*
apart from others or another ⟨The children eat *separately.*⟩

sep•a•ra•tion \,se-pə-'rā-shən\ *n*
1 the act of setting or pulling apart : the state of being set or pulled apart
2 a point or line at which something is divided
3 a space between ⟨The buildings have a narrow *separation.*⟩

Sept. *abbr* September

Sep•tem•ber \sep-'tem-bər\ *n*
the ninth month of the year

▶ **Word History** The earliest Roman calendar had only ten months and began with the month of March. The seventh month was called in Latin *September*, a word which combines the Latin words for "seven" (*septem*), "month" (*mens*), and a final word-forming element *-ri-*. The name was kept — and eventually borrowed by English — after September became the ninth of twelve Roman months.

sep•tet \sep-'tet\ *n*
a group or set of seven

sep•ul•chre *or* **sep•ul•cher** \'se-pəl-kər\ *n*
¹GRAVE, TOMB

se•quel \'sē-kwəl\ *n*
1 a book or movie that continues a story begun in another
2 an event that follows or comes afterward : RESULT

se•quence \'sē-kwəns\ *n*
1 the order in which things are or should be connected, related, or dated ⟨Follow the directions in *sequence.*⟩
2 a group of things that come one after another ⟨a *sequence* of numbers⟩

se•quin \'sē-kwən\ *n*
▼ a bit of shiny metal or plastic used as an ornament usually on clothing

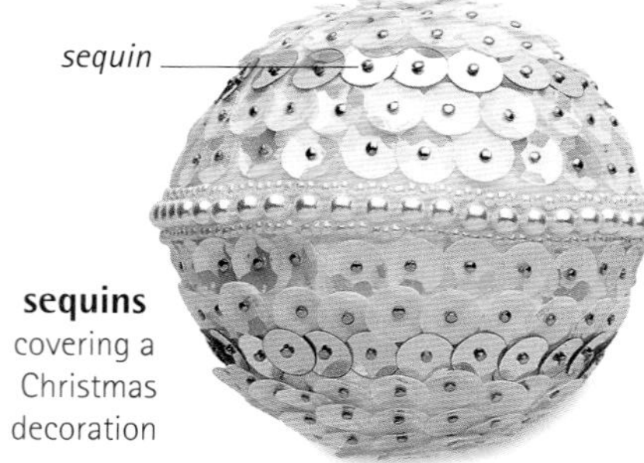

sequins covering a Christmas decoration

se•quoia \si-'kwȯi-ə\ *n*
1 GIANT SEQUOIA
2 REDWOOD

¹ser•e•nade \,ser-ə-'nād\ *n*
music sung or played at night for a woman

²serenade *vb* **ser•e•nad•ed; ser•e•nad•ing**
to entertain (a woman) with music sung or played at night

se•rene \sə-'rēn\ *adj*
1 being calm and quiet ⟨a *serene* manner⟩
2 ¹CLEAR 2 ⟨*serene* skies⟩
se•rene•ly *adv*

se•ren•i•ty \sə-'re-nə-tē\ *n*
the quality or state of being calm and peaceful

serf \'sərf\ *n*
a servant or laborer of olden times who was treated as part of the land worked on and went along with the land if it was sold

serge \'sərj\ *n*
a strong woolen cloth

ser•geant \'sär-jənt\ *n*
1 a noncommissioned officer in the army or marine corps ranking above a corporal or in the air force ranking above an airman first class
2 an officer in a police force

sergeant first class *n*
a noncommissioned officer in the army ranking above a staff sergeant

sergeant major *n*
1 the chief noncommissioned officer at a military headquarters
2 a noncommissioned officer in the marine corps ranking above a first sergeant

¹se•ri•al \'sir-ē-əl\ *adj*
arranged in or appearing in parts or numbers that follow a regular order ⟨a *serial* story⟩

²serial *n*
a story appearing (as in a magazine or on television) in parts at regular intervals

se•ries \'sir-ēz\ *n, pl* **series**
a number of things or events arranged in order and connected by being alike in some way ⟨the third book in the *series*⟩

se•ri•ous \'sir-ē-əs\ *adj*
1 not joking or funny ⟨a *serious* drama⟩
2 being such as to cause distress or harm ⟨a *serious* accident⟩
3 thoughtful or quiet in appearance or manner ⟨a *serious* person⟩
4 requiring much thought or work ⟨a *serious* task⟩
se•ri•ous•ness *n*

▶ **Synonyms** SERIOUS, SOLEMN, and EARNEST mean not funny or not playful. SERIOUS means being concerned or seeming to be concerned about really important things. ⟨He's a *serious* student.⟩ SOLEMN is used for dignity along with complete seriousness. ⟨The preacher is always very *solemn.*⟩ EARNEST means that someone is sincere and has serious intentions. ⟨She's an *earnest*, diligent student.⟩

se•ri•ous•ly \'sir-ē-əs-lē\ *adv*
1 in an earnest way ⟨He takes his job *seriously.*⟩

2 in a literal way ⟨Don't take me *seriously.* It was just a joke.⟩
3 to a large degree or extent ⟨*seriously* wounded⟩

ser•mon \ˈsər-mən\ *n*
1 a speech usually by a priest, minister, or rabbi for the purpose of giving religious instruction
2 a serious talk to a person about his or her conduct

ser•pent \ˈsər-pənt\ *n*
a usually large snake

ser•pen•tine \ˈsər-pən-ˌtēn, -ˌtīn\ *adj*
winding or turning one way and another ⟨a *serpentine* path⟩

se•rum \ˈsir-əm\ *n*
the clear liquid part that can be separated from coagulated blood and contains antibodies

ser•vant \ˈsər-vənt\ *n*
a person hired to perform household or personal services

[1]serve \ˈsərv\ *vb* **served; serv•ing**
1 to help people to food or drink or set out helpings of food or drink
2 to be of use : answer some purpose ⟨A tree *served* as shelter.⟩
3 to be a servant
4 to give the service and respect due ⟨*serve* God⟩
5 to be in prison for or during (a period of time)
6 to provide helpful services ⟨Our friendly staff will *serve* you.⟩
7 to be enough for ⟨The pie will *serve* eight people.⟩
8 to hold an office : perform a duty ⟨I *served* as club treasurer.⟩
9 to perform a term of service ⟨He *served* in the marines.⟩
10 to furnish with something needed or desired ⟨There is no grocery store to *serve* the area.⟩
11 to put the ball or shuttlecock in play (as in tennis, volleyball, or badminton)
serve someone right to be deserved ⟨You didn't study, so if you fail the test it will *serve you right.*⟩

[2]serve *n*
▶ an act of putting the ball or shuttlecock in play (as in tennis, volleyball, or badminton)

[1]ser•vice \ˈsər-vəs\ *n*
1 [2]HELP 1, USE ⟨Can I be of *service* to you?⟩
2 a religious ceremony ⟨the Sunday *service*⟩ ⟨a funeral *service*⟩
3 the occupation or function of serving or working as a servant
4 the work or action of helping customers ⟨This restaurant gives quick *service.*⟩
5 a helpful or useful act : good turn ⟨My neighbor did me a *service* by retrieving my dog.⟩
6 a set of dishes or silverware ⟨a silver tea *service*⟩
7 an organization that provides something to the public ⟨the postal *service*⟩
8 a nation's armed forces ⟨During the war, Dad was called into the *service.*⟩
9 an organization or business that supplies some public demand or provides maintenance and repair for something ⟨bus *service*⟩ ⟨television sales and *service*⟩
10 [2]SERVE

[2]service *vb* **ser•viced; ser•vic•ing**
to work on in order to maintain or repair ⟨It's time to have my vehicle *serviced.*⟩

ser•vice•able \ˈsər-və-sə-bəl\ *adj*
1 USEFUL 1
2 of adequate quality ⟨*serviceable* shoes⟩

[2]serve:
a player preparing to serve

ser•vice•man \ˈsər-vəs-ˌman\ *n, pl* **ser•vice•men** \-ˌmen\
a man who is a member of the armed forces

service station *n*
GAS STATION

ser•vice•wom•an \ˈsər-vəs-ˌwu̇-mən\ *n, pl* **ser•vice•wom•en** \-ˌwi-mən\
a woman who is a member of the armed forces

ser•vile \ˈsər-vəl\ *adj*
1 of or suitable to a slave ⟨*servile* work⟩
2 very obedient and trying too hard to please

serv•ing \ˈsər-viŋ\ *n*
a helping of food

ser•vi•tude \ˈsər-və-ˌtüd, -ˌtyüd\ *n*
the condition of being a slave or of having to obey another

ses•sion \ˈse-shən\ *n*
1 a meeting or period devoted to a particular activity ⟨The football team held a practice *session.*⟩
2 a single meeting (as of a court, lawmaking body, or school)
3 a whole series of meetings ⟨Congress was in *session* for six months.⟩
4 the time during which a court, congress, or school meets

[1]set \ˈset\ *vb* **set; set•ting**
1 to put or fix in a place or condition ⟨I *set* the box on a table.⟩
2 to cause to be, become, or do ⟨Police *set* the prisoner free.⟩
3 [1]START 4 ⟨He *set* a fire.⟩
4 to fix or decide on ⟨They *set* the wedding date.⟩ ⟨Have you *set* a price?⟩
5 to furnish as a model ⟨You should *set* an example for the others.⟩ ⟨She ran to the front and *set* the pace.⟩
6 to adjust or put in order for use ⟨Please *set* the table.⟩ ⟨Did you *set* the alarm?⟩
7 to fix firmly ⟨He *sets* his feet and takes aim.⟩
8 to pass below the horizon : go down ⟨The sun is *setting.*⟩
9 to begin some activity ⟨They *set* to work on the cleaning project.⟩
10 to cause to sit ⟨I *set* the baby in her chair.⟩
11 to arrange in a desired and especially a normal position ⟨Doctors *set* the broken bone.⟩
12 to become or cause to become firm or solid ⟨Wait for the cement to *set.*⟩
13 to cover and warm eggs to hatch them ⟨The hen *set* for days.⟩
14 to locate the plot of (a story)
15 to provide (as words or verses) with music
set aside to reserve for some purpose
set eyes on to catch sight of : SEE ⟨Though he lived nearby, I had never *set eyes on* him.⟩

a b c d e f g h i j k l m n o p q r s t u v w x y z

A B C D E F G H I J K L M N O P Q R S T U V W X Y Z

set in to make its appearance : BEGIN 〈They needed to leave arctic waters before winter *set in.*〉
set off
1 to start a journey 〈We *set off* for home.〉
2 EXPLODE 1 〈We *set off* fireworks.〉
3 to make noticeable 〈The phrase is *set off* by commas.〉
4 to cause to start 〈The story *set* them *off* laughing.〉
set out
1 to begin on a course or journey 〈We arrived a month after we *set out.*〉
2 to begin with a purpose 〈He *set out* to win.〉
set up
1 to place or secure in position 〈Help me *set up* the tables.〉
2 to put in operation 〈The community *set up* an animal shelter.〉

²set *n*
1 a number of persons or things of the same kind that belong together, are used together, or occur together 〈a model train *set*〉 〈a *set* of footsteps〉
2 the act or action of going below the horizon 〈the *set* of the sun〉
3 an electronic apparatus 〈a television *set*〉
4 a collection of mathematical elements
5 a group of tennis games that make up a match
6 the form or movement of the body or of its parts 〈the *set* of the shoulders〉
7 an artificial setting for a scene of a play or motion picture

³set *adj*
1 fixed by authority 〈a *set* rule〉
2 not very willing to change 〈The people he works with are *set* in their ways.〉
3 ¹READY 1 〈Are you all *set*?〉

set•back \'set-,bak\ *n*
a slowing of progress : a temporary defeat 〈Despite several *setbacks* we finished on schedule.〉

set•tee \se-'tē\ *n*
a long seat with a back

set•ter \'se-tər\ *n*
1 ▼ a large dog that has long hair and is used in hunting birds
2 someone or something that sets

setter 1: an Irish setter

set•ting \'se-tiŋ\ *n*
1 the act of someone or something that sets
2 that in which something is set or mounted 〈a gold *setting* for a ruby〉
3 the background (as time and place) of the action of a story or play

¹set•tle \'se-tᵊl\ *vb* **set•tled; set•tling**
1 to come to rest 〈Birds *settled* on a branch.〉 〈Dust *settled* on the table.〉
2 to make a home 〈I'd like to *settle* in the country.〉
3 to make quiet : CALM 〈The tea *settled* my nerves.〉
4 DECIDE 1 〈It's *settled* then—we'll each pay our own way.〉
5 to place so as to stay 〈I *settled* myself in a chair.〉
6 to sink gradually to a lower level 〈The foundations of the house *settled.*〉
7 to sink in a liquid
8 to give attention to 〈*Settle* down to work now.〉
9 to fix by agreement 〈They are hoping to *settle* the case out of court.〉
10 to put in order 〈They *settled* their affairs.〉
11 to complete payment on 〈Waiter, we're ready to *settle* our bill.〉
12 to bring to an end 〈They *settled* their argument.〉
13 to take up a stable life 〈You're not a kid anymore. It's time to *settle* down.〉
14 to be content with 〈He *settled* for his second choice.〉

²settle *n*
a long wooden bench with arms and a high solid back

set•tle•ment \'se-tᵊl-mənt\ *n*
1 a formal agreement that ends an argument or dispute
2 final payment (as of a bill)
3 the act or fact of establishing colonies 〈the *settlement* of New England〉
4 a place or region newly settled
5 ▼ a small village

set•tler \'set-lər\ *n*
a person who settles in a new region : COLONIST

¹sev•en \'se-vən\ *adj*
being one more than six

²seven *n*
1 one more than six : 7
2 the seventh in a set or series

¹sev•en•teen \,se-vən-'tēn\ *adj*
being one more than 16

²seventeen *n*
one more than 16 : 17

¹sev•en•teenth \,se-vən-'tēnth\ *adj*
coming right after 16th

²seventeenth *n*
number 17 in a series

¹sev•enth \'se-vənth\ *adj*
coming right after sixth

settlement 5: a remote settlement in Canada

[2]**seventh** *n*
1 number seven in a series
2 one of seven equal parts

[1]**sev•en•ti•eth** \'se-vən-tē-əth\ *adj*
coming right after 69th

[2]**seventieth** *n*
number 70 in a series

[1]**sev•en•ty** \'se-vən-tē, -dē\ *adj*
being seven times ten

[2]**seventy** *n*
seven times ten : 70

sev•er \'se-vər\ *vb* **sev•ered**; **sev•er•ing**
to cut off

[1]**sev•er•al** \'se-və-rəl, 'sev-rəl\ *adj*
1 consisting of more than two but not very many ⟨*several* people⟩ ⟨*several* minutes⟩
2 separate or distinct from others : DIFFERENT ⟨federal union of the *several* states⟩

[2]**several** *pron*
a small number : more than two but not many ⟨The new rules made *several* of us angry.⟩

se•vere \sə-'vir\ *adj* **se•ver•er**; **se•ver•est**
1 serious in feeling or manner
2 hard to bear or deal with ⟨*severe* suffering⟩ ⟨a *severe* test⟩
3 very strict : HARSH ⟨a *severe* ruler⟩
4 not using unnecessary ornament : PLAIN ⟨a *severe* style⟩
se•vere•ly *adv*

se•ver•i•ty \sə-'ver-ə-tē\ *n*
the quality or state of being severe ⟨They're determining the *severity* of the damage.⟩

sew \'sō\ *vb* **sewed**; **sewn** \'sōn\ *or* **sewed**; **sew•ing**
1 to join or fasten by stitches
2 to work with needle and thread

sew•age \'sü-ij\ *n*
waste materials carried off by sewers

[1]**sew•er** \'sü-ər\ *n*
a usually covered drain to carry off water and waste

[2]**sew•er** \'sō-ər\ *n*
someone that sews

sew•er•age \'sü-ə-rij\ *n*
1 the removal and disposal of waste materials by sewers
2 a system of sewers

sew•ing \'sō-iŋ\ *n*
1 the act, method, or occupation of someone or something that works with needle and thread
2 material being or to be worked with needle and thread

sex \'seks\ *n*
1 either of two divisions into which many living things can be divided according to their roles in reproduction and which consist of males or females
2 the state of being male or female ⟨The form asks for your name, age, and *sex*.⟩
3 sexual activity

sex•ism \'sek-,si-zəm\ *n*
distinction and especially unjust distinction based on gender and made against one person or group (as women) in favor of another

sex•ist \'sek-sist\ *adj*
based on or showing sexism ⟨a *sexist* remark⟩
sexist *n*

sex•ton \'seks-tən\ *n*
an official of a church who takes care of church buildings and property

sex•u•al \'sek-shə-wəl\ *adj*
1 of or relating to sex or the sexes
2 of, relating to, or being the form of reproduction in which germ cells from two parents combine in fertilization to form a new individual
sex•u•al•ly *adv*

Sgt. *abbr* sergeant

shab•by \'sha-bē\ *adj* **shab•bi•er**; **shab•bi•est**
1 faded and worn from use or wear ⟨*shabby* clothes⟩
2 in poor condition : DILAPIDATED ⟨a *shabby* house⟩
3 dressed in worn clothes
4 not fair or generous ⟨We received *shabby* treatment.⟩
shab•bi•ly \'sha-bə-lē\ *adv*
shab•bi•ness \'sha-bē-nəs\ *n*

shack \'shak\ *n*
HUT, SHANTY

[1]**shack•le** \'sha-kəl\ *n*
1 a ring or band that prevents free use of the legs or arms
2 something that prevents free action ⟨The country was freed from the *shackles* of oppression.⟩

[2]**shackle** *vb* **shack•led**; **shack•ling**
1 to bind or fasten with a ring or band placed on the legs or arms
2 to prevent free action

shad \'shad\ *n, pl* **shad**
a silvery ocean fish that swims up rivers to lay or fertilize eggs and is often used for food

[1]**shade** \'shād\ *n*
1 space sheltered from light or heat and especially from the sun ⟨I needed to sit in the *shade* of a tree.⟩
2 partial darkness ⟨The trees cast *shade*.⟩
3 something that blocks off or cuts down light ⟨a lamp *shade*⟩ ⟨a window *shade*⟩
4 the darkness or lightness of a color ⟨four *shades* of brown⟩
5 a very small difference or amount ⟨He's just a *shade* taller than me.⟩
6 GHOST, SPIRIT
7 the darkening of some objects in a painting or drawing to suggest that they are in shade

[2]**shade** *vb* **shad•ed**; **shad•ing**
1 to shelter from light or heat ⟨I *shaded* my eyes with a hand.⟩
2 to mark with or turn a darker color ⟨The *shaded* parts of the graph show growth.⟩ ⟨Her face *shaded* purple with embarrassment.⟩

[1]**shad•ow** \'sha-dō\ *n*
1 ▼ the dark figure cast on a surface by a body that is between the surface and the light ⟨My *shadow* stays with me.⟩
2 [1]SHADE 2 ⟨The valley was in *shadow*.⟩
3 PHANTOM
4 a very little bit : TRACE ⟨I believe his story beyond a *shadow* of doubt.⟩
5 something that causes a bad feeling ⟨The news cast a *shadow* over the party.⟩
6 **shadows** *pl* darkness caused by the setting of the sun

shadow

[1]**shadow 1:**
a boy looking at his shadow

[2]**shadow** *vb* **shad•owed**; **shad•ow•ing**
1 to cast a shadow upon ⟨Trees *shadowed* the ground.⟩
2 to follow and watch closely especially in a secret way

shad•owy \'sha-də-wē\ *adj*
1 full of shade ⟨a *shadowy* lane⟩
2 INDISTINCT

shady \'shā-dē\ *adj* **shad•i•er**; **shad•i•est**
1 sheltered from the sun's rays
2 producing shade ⟨a *shady* tree⟩
3 not right or honest ⟨*shady* business deals⟩

shaft \'shaft\ *n*
1 the long handle of a weapon, tool, or instrument ⟨the *shaft* of a spear⟩ ⟨the *shaft* of a golf club⟩
2 one of two poles between which a horse is hitched to pull a wagon or carriage
3 an arrow or its narrow stem
4 a narrow beam of light
5 a long narrow part or structure especially when round ⟨the *shaft* of a feather⟩
6 a mine opening made for finding or mining ore
7 an opening or passage straight down through the floors of a building ⟨an air *shaft*⟩ ⟨an elevator *shaft*⟩
8 a bar to support rotating pieces of machinery or to give them motion

shag•gy \'sha-gē\ *adj* **shag•gi•er; shag•gi•est**
covered with or made up of a long and tangled growth (as of hair) ⟨The dog has a *shaggy* coat.⟩

[1]shake \'shāk\ *vb* **shook** \'shu̇k\; **shak•en** \'shā-kən\; **shak•ing**
1 to make or cause to make quick movements back and forth or up and down ⟨The ground *shook*.⟩ ⟨Squirrels *shook* the branches.⟩
2 to tremble or make tremble : QUIVER ⟨She was so frightened her legs began to *shake*.⟩
3 to move from side to side ⟨I *shook* my head.⟩
4 to grasp and move up and down ⟨After reaching an agreement, they *shook* hands.⟩
5 to get away from ⟨She ran faster, but couldn't *shake* the dog.⟩
6 to make less firm : WEAKEN ⟨After being beaten badly their confidence was *shaken*.⟩
7 to cause to be, become, go, or move by or as if by using a quick back and forth motion ⟨We can *shake* apples from the tree.⟩

[2]shake *n*
a quick back and forth or up and down movement

shak•er \'shā-kər\ *n*
a container used to mix the contents or sprinkle out some of the contents ⟨a salt *shaker*⟩

shaky \'shā-kē\ *adj* **shak•i•er; shak•i•est**
1 characterized by quivering : not firm ⟨a *shaky* hand⟩ ⟨a *shaky* voice⟩
2 likely to fail or be insufficient : UNSOUND ⟨*shaky* arguments⟩
shak•i•ly \-kə-lē\ *adv*

shale \'shāl\ *n*
▶ a rock with a fine grain formed from clay, mud, or silt

shale

shall \shəl, 'shal\ *helping verb, past* **should** \shəd, 'shu̇d\; *present sing & pl* **shall**
1 am or are going to or expecting to : WILL ⟨I *shall* never mention it again.⟩
2 is or are forced to : MUST ⟨They *shall* not pass.⟩

[1]shal•low \'sha-lō\ *adj* **shal•low•er; shal•low•est**
1 not deep ⟨a *shallow* stream⟩
2 taking in small amounts of air ⟨*shallow* breaths⟩
3 showing little knowledge, thought, or feeling ⟨They're *shallow* people only interested in money.⟩
shal•low•ness *n*

[2]shallow *n*
a shallow place in a body of water — usually used in pl.

[1]sham \'sham\ *n*
1 something that deceives : HOAX
2 something that is claimed to be true or real but which is actually phony
3 a decorative covering for a pillow

[2]sham *adj*
not real : FALSE ⟨*sham* concern⟩

[3]sham *vb* **shammed; sham•ming**
to act in a deceiving way

sham•ble \'sham-bəl\ *vb* **sham•bled; sham•bling**
to walk in an awkward unsteady way

sham•bles \'sham-bəlz\ *n pl*
a place or scene of disorder or destruction ⟨After the party, the house was a *shambles*.⟩
Hint: *Shambles* can be used as a singular or a plural in writing and speaking.

[1]shame \'shām\ *n*
1 a painful emotion caused by having done something wrong or improper
2 ability to feel shame ⟨Have you no *shame*?⟩
3 [1]DISHONOR 1, DISGRACE
4 something that brings disgrace or causes painful emotion or strong regret ⟨It's a *shame* he couldn't join us.⟩

[2]shame *vb* **shamed; sham•ing**
1 to make ashamed ⟨I was *shamed* by my actions.⟩
2 [2]DISHONOR
3 to force by causing to feel shame ⟨They were *shamed* into confessing.⟩

shame•faced \'shām-'fāst\ *adj*
seeming ashamed

▶ **[1]shark**
There are about 200 species of shark worldwide. Sharks are cartilaginous fish that range in size from the small lantern shark to the enormous whale shark. They have excellent eyesight and a very good sense of smell, and can accelerate quickly through the water to catch their prey. Not all sharks are a threat to humans; the whale shark, for example, eats only plankton, and most sharks are too shy or live too deep in the ocean to bother people.

pointed snout
sharp teeth
dorsal fin
gill slit

features of a great white shark

examples of sharks

leopard shark eats mainly fish and shellfish from the sea floor

lantern shark is one of the smallest species of shark

shame•ful \'shām-fəl\ *adj*
bringing shame : DISGRACEFUL 〈*shameful* behavior〉
shame•ful•ly \-fə-lē\ *adv*
shame•ful•ness *n*

shame•less \'shām-ləs\ *adj*
having no shame 〈a *shameless* liar〉
shame•less•ly *adv*
shame•less•ness *n*

[1]**sham•poo** \sham-'pü\ *n, pl* **sham•poos**
1 a cleaner made for washing the hair
2 an act of washing the hair

[2]**sham•poo** *vb* **sham•pooed**; **sham•poo•ing**
to wash the hair and scalp

sham•rock \'sham-,räk\ *n*
a plant (as some clovers) that has leaves with three leaflets and is used as an emblem by the Irish

shank \'shaŋk\ *n*
1 the part of the leg between the knee and ankle
2 a cut of meat from the usually upper part of the leg 〈a lamb *shank*〉
3 the part of a tool that connects the working part with a part by which it is held or moved 〈the *shank* of a drill bit〉

shan't \'shant\
shall not

shan•ty \'shan-tē\ *n, pl* **shanties**
a small roughly built shelter or dwelling

[1]**shape** \'shāp\ *vb* **shaped**; **shap•ing**
1 to give a certain form or shape to 〈*Shape* the dough into loaves.〉
2 to plan out : DEVISE 〈We *shaped* a winning strategy.〉
3 to have great influence on the development of
shap•er *n*
shape up
1 to develop in a particular way 〈This is *shaping up* to be an exciting trip.〉
2 to improve in behavior or condition

[2]**shape** *n*
1 outward appearance : the form or outline of something 〈the *shape* of a pear〉 〈circles, squares, and other *shapes*〉
2 definite arrangement and form 〈The plan is finally taking *shape*.〉
3 [1]CONDITION 1 〈The car is in poor *shape*.〉
4 a physically fit condition 〈She keeps in *shape* by exercising.〉
shaped \,shāpt\ *adj*

shape•less \'shā-pləs\ *adj*
1 having no fixed or definite shape 〈a *shapeless* blob〉
2 lacking a pleasing or usual shape or form 〈a *shapeless* coat〉

shape•ly \'shā-plē\ *adj* **shape•li•er**; **shape•li•est**
having a pleasing shape or form

shard \'shärd\ *n*
a sharp piece or fragment of something

[1]**share** \'sher\ *n*
1 a portion belonging to, due to, or contributed by one person 〈I finished my *share* of the work.〉
2 the part given or belonging to one of a group of people owning something together 〈I sold my *share* of the business.〉
3 any of the equal parts into which a property or corporation is divided 〈100 *shares* of stock〉

[2]**share** *vb* **shared**; **shar•ing**
1 to divide and distribute in portions 〈We *shared* the last cookie.〉
2 to use, experience, or enjoy with others 〈I *share* a locker with my friend.〉
3 to have or take a part in 〈I *share* the blame for what happened.〉
4 to have in common 〈We *share* a love of music.〉

share•crop \'sher-,kräp\ *vb* **share•cropped**; **share•crop•ping**
to farm another's land for a share of the crop or profit
share•crop•per *n*

[1]**shark** \'shärk\ *n*
▼ a large usually gray saltwater fish that has sharp teeth and a skeleton of cartilage

[2]**shark** *n*
a person who cheats others out of money

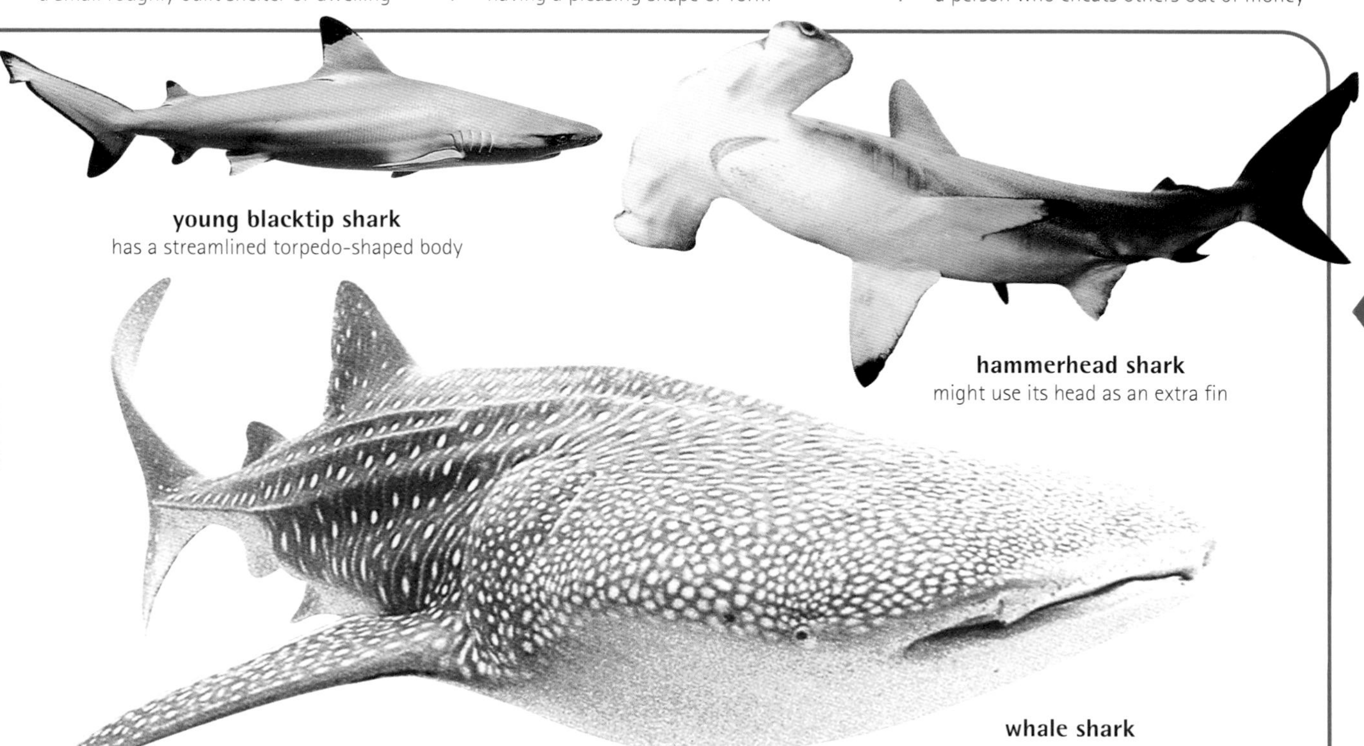

young blacktip shark
has a streamlined torpedo-shaped body

hammerhead shark
might use its head as an extra fin

whale shark
is the largest living fish

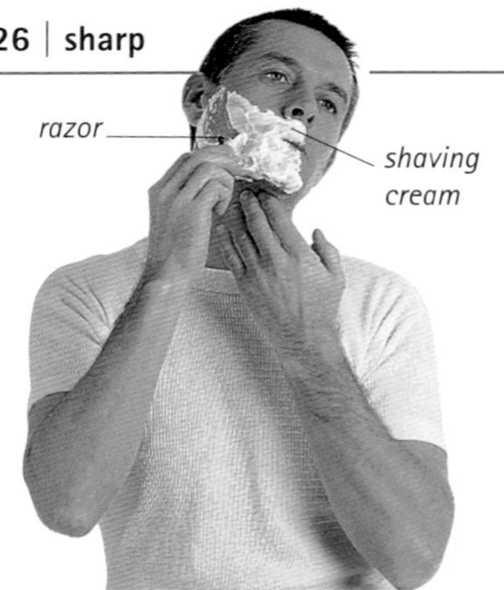

²shave 1: a man giving himself a shave

¹sharp \'shärp\ *adj* **sharp•er; sharp•est**
1 having a thin edge or fine point (as for cutting or piercing) 〈a *sharp* knife〉
2 brisk and cold 〈a *sharp* wind〉
3 very smart 〈a *sharp* student〉
4 ATTENTIVE 1 〈He kept a *sharp* watch.〉
5 having very good ability to see or hear 〈You have *sharp* eyes.〉
6 ENERGETIC, BRISK 〈We kept up a *sharp* pace.〉
7 showing anger or disapproval 〈a *sharp* reply〉
8 causing distress : SEVERE 〈a *sharp* pain〉 〈*sharp* criticism〉
9 strongly affecting the senses 〈a *sharp* taste〉
10 ending in a point or edge 〈a *sharp* mountain peak〉
11 involving a sudden and quick change 〈a *sharp* drop in the temperature〉 〈a *sharp* turn〉
12 clear in outline or detail : DISTINCT 〈a *sharp* image〉
13 raised in pitch by a half step 〈F *sharp*〉
14 higher than true pitch 〈Her singing was slightly *sharp*.〉
15 STYLISH 〈a *sharp* outfit〉
sharp•ly *adv*
sharp•ness *n*

²sharp *adv*
1 at an exact time 〈four o'clock *sharp*〉
2 at a higher than true pitch 〈He sang *sharp*.〉
3 in a stylish way 〈You look *sharp* in your new suit.〉

³sharp *n*
1 a musical note or tone that is a half step higher than the note named
2 a sign # that tells that a note is to be made higher by a half step

sharp•en \'shär-pən\ *vb* **sharp•ened; sharp•en•ing**
to make or become sharp or sharper
sharp•en•er *n*

shat•ter \'sha-tər\ *vb* **shat•tered; shat•ter•ing**
1 to break or fall to pieces 〈The window *shattered*.〉
2 to destroy or damage badly 〈The news *shattered* our hopes.〉

¹shave \'shāv\ *vb* **shaved; shaved** *or* **shav•en** \'shā-vən\; **shav•ing**
1 to cut or trim off a thin layer of (as with a sharp blade) 〈I *shaved* the wood from the tip of the pencil.〉
2 to cut off very close to the skin 〈He *shaved* the hair from his head.〉
3 to make bare or smooth by cutting the hair from 〈He *shaved* his face.〉

²shave *n*
1 ◀ an act of making bare or smooth by cutting the hair from
2 a narrow escape 〈a close *shave*〉

shav•ing \'shā-viŋ\ *n*
a thin slice or strip sliced or trimmed off with a cutting tool 〈wood *shavings*〉

shawl \'shȯl\ *n*
a square or oblong piece of cloth used especially by women as a loose covering for the head or shoulders

she \'shē\ *pron*
that female one 〈*She* is my mother.〉

sheaf \'shēf\ *n, pl* **sheaves** \'shēvz\
1 a bundle of stalks and ears of grain
2 a group of things fastened together 〈a *sheaf* of papers〉

shear \'shir\ *vb* **sheared; sheared** *or* **shorn** \'shȯrn\; **shear•ing**
1 to cut the hair or wool from : CLIP 〈*shear* sheep〉
2 to cut or clip (as hair or wool) from something
3 to strip of as if by cutting 〈The tyrants were *shorn* of their power.〉
4 to cut or break sharply 〈The sign was *sheared* off by a car.〉
shear•er *n*

shears \'shirz\ *n pl*
▼ a cutting tool like a pair of large scissors

shears: a pair of garden shears

sheath \'shēth\ *n, pl* **sheaths** \'shēthz\
1 a case for a blade (as of a knife)
2 a covering that surrounds and usually protects something

sheathe \'shēth\ *vb* **sheathed; sheath•ing**
1 to put into a sheath 〈*Sheathe* your sword.〉
2 to cover with something that protects 〈The ship's bottom is *sheathed* with copper.〉

sheath•ing \'shē-thiŋ\ *n*
material used as a protective covering 〈waterproof *sheathing*〉

sheaves *pl of* SHEAF

¹shed \'shed\ *vb* **shed; shed•ding**
1 to give off in drops 〈They *shed* tears of joy.〉
2 to get rid of 〈I'm trying to *shed* some extra pounds.〉
3 to give off or out 〈Your explanation *shed* light on the subject.〉
4 REPEL 3 〈Raincoats *shed* water.〉
5 to lose or cast aside (a natural covering or part) 〈The dog is *shedding* hair.〉

²shed *n*
a small simple building used especially for storage

she'd \'shēd\
she had : she would

sheen \'shēn\ *n*
a bright or shining condition : LUSTER

sheep \'shēp\ *n, pl* **sheep**
1 ▲ an animal related to the goat that is often raised for meat or for its wool and skin
2 a weak helpless person who is easily led

sheep•fold \'shēp-,fōld\ *n*
a pen or shelter for sheep

sheep•herd•er \'shēp-,hər-dər\ *n*
a person in charge of a flock of sheep

sheep•ish \'shē-pish\ *adj*
1 like a sheep (as in being meek or shy)
2 feeling or showing embarrassment especially over being discovered having done something wrong or foolish 〈a *sheepish* look〉
sheep•ish•ly *adv*

sheep•skin \'shēp-,skin\ *n*
the skin of a sheep or leather prepared from it

sheer \'shir\ *adj* **sheer•er; sheer•est**
1 very thin or transparent 〈*sheer* curtains〉
2 complete and total : ABSOLUTE 〈*sheer* nonsense〉

sheep 1: a flock of sheep

3 taken or acting apart from everything else 〈He won through *sheer* determination.〉
4 very steep 〈a *sheer* cliff〉

[1]sheet \'shēt\ *n*
1 a large piece of cloth used to cover something and especially to cover a bed
2 a usually rectangular piece of paper
3 a broad continuous surface 〈a *sheet* of ice〉
4 something that is very thin as compared with its length and width 〈a *sheet* of iron〉

[2]sheet *n*
a rope or chain used to adjust the angle at which the sail of a boat is set to catch the wind

sheikh *or* **sheik** \'shēk, 'shāk\ *n*
1 an Arab chief
2 a leader of a Muslim group

shek•el \'she-kəl\ *n*
a bill or coin used in Israel

shelf \'shelf\ *n, pl* **shelves** \'shelvz\
1 a flat piece (as of wood or metal) set above a floor (as on a wall or in a bookcase) to hold things
2 a flat area (as of rock)

[1]shell \'shel\ *n*
1 ▼ a stiff hard covering of an animal (as a turtle, oyster, or crab)
2 the tough outer covering of an egg
3 the outer covering of a nut, fruit, or seed especially when hard or tough 〈walnut *shells*〉
4 something like a shell (as in shape, function, or material) 〈a pastry *shell*〉
5 a narrow light racing boat rowed by one or more persons
6 a metal or paper case holding the explosive charge and the shot or object to be fired from a gun or cannon
shelled \'sheld\ *adj*

[2]shell *vb* **shelled**; **shell•ing**
1 to remove the shell or outer covering of 〈*shell* nuts〉
2 to remove the kernels of grain from (as a cob of corn)
3 to shoot shells at or upon

she'll \'shēl\
she shall : she will

[1]shel•lac \shə-'lak\ *n*
a varnish made from a material that is given off by an insect and that is dissolved usually in alcohol

[2]shellac *vb* **shel•lacked**; **shel•lack•ing**
to coat with shellac

shell•fish \'shel-,fish\ *n, pl* **shellfish**
an invertebrate animal (as a clam or lobster) that has a hard outer shell and lives in water

[1]shel•ter \'shel-tər\ *n*
1 something that covers or protects 〈We made a *shelter* from branches.〉
2 a place that provides food and housing to those in need 〈a homeless *shelter*〉 〈an animal *shelter*〉
3 the condition of being protected 〈I found *shelter* from the storm.〉

[2]shelter *vb* **shel•tered**; **shel•ter•ing**
1 to provide with a place that covers or protects : be a shelter for 〈A cave *sheltered* the climbers.〉
2 to find and use a shelter for protection 〈The boat *sheltered* near an inlet.〉

shelve \'shelv\ *vb* **shelved**; **shelv•ing**
1 to place or store on a shelf 〈*shelve* books〉
2 to put off or aside : DEFER 〈The plan has been *shelved* for now.〉

shelves *pl of* SHELF

[1]shell 1

Shells form a protective cover around the bodies of some animals. The shells of mollusks, such as those shown below, are arranged in a spiral around a central axis or have two halves joined by a hinge. Sometimes an empty shell is occupied by another creature, such as a crab.

tip of the central axis

hermit crab

a **triton** \'trī-t^{ə}n\ **shell** occupied by a hermit crab

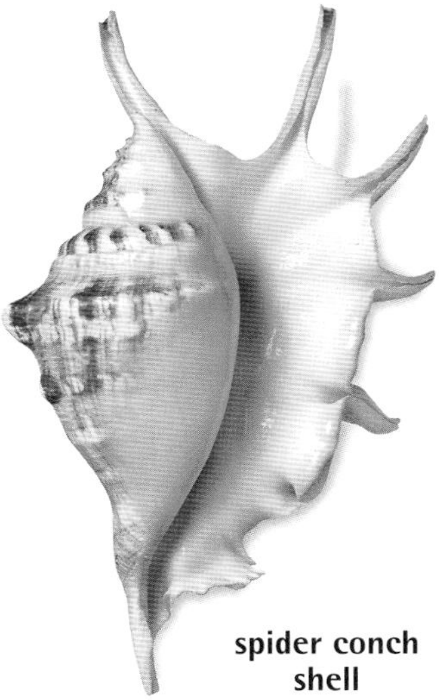

purple sea snail shell

spider conch shell

scallop shell

auger shell

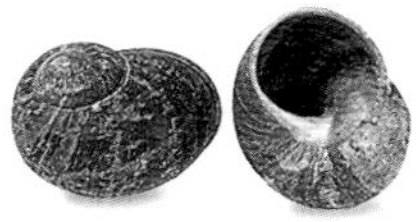

land snail shells

she•nan•i•gans \shə-ˈna-ni-gənz\ *n pl*
funny or mischievous activity or behavior

[1]shep•herd \ˈshe-pərd\ *n*
a person who takes care of and guards a flock of sheep

[2]shepherd *vb* **shep•herded; shep•herd•ing**
1 to take care of and guard a flock of sheep
2 to gather, lead, or move in the manner of a shepherd

shep•herd•ess \ˈshe-pər-dəs\ *n*
a woman who takes care of and guards a flock of sheep

sher•bet \ˈshər-bət\ *n*
a frozen dessert made of sweetened fruit juice and milk

sher•iff \ˈsher-əf\ *n*
the officer of a county who is in charge of enforcing the law

she's \ˈshēz\
she is : she has

Shetland pony

Shet•land pony \ˈshet-lənd-\ *n*
▲ a small stocky horse with a heavy coat and short legs

[1]shield \ˈshēld\ *n*
1 ► a broad piece of armor carried (as by a soldier) for protection
2 something that serves as a defense or protection ⟨the heat *shield* on a space shuttle⟩

[2]shield *vb* **shield•ed; shield•ing**
to cover or screen (as from danger or harm) : provide with protection

[1]shift \ˈshift\ *vb* **shift•ed; shift•ing**
1 to change or make a change in place, position, or direction ⟨She *shifted* the bag to her other shoulder.⟩
2 to go through a change ⟨Public opinion *shifted* in his favor.⟩
3 to change the arrangement of gears transmitting power (as in an automobile)
4 to get along without help : FEND ⟨I can *shift* for myself.⟩

[2]shift *n*
1 a change in place, position, or direction ⟨a *shift* in the wind⟩
2 a change in emphasis or attitude ⟨a *shift* in priorities⟩
3 a group of workers who work together during a scheduled period of time
4 the scheduled period of time during which one group of workers is working
5 GEARSHIFT

shift•less \ˈshift-ləs\ *adj*
LAZY 1

shifty \ˈshif-tē\ *adj* **shift•i•er; shift•i•est**
not worthy of trust : causing suspicion ⟨a *shifty* character⟩

shil•ling \ˈshi-liŋ\ *n*
an old British coin equal to 1/20 pound

[1]shim•mer \ˈshi-mər\ *vb* **shim•mered; shim•mer•ing**
to shine with a wavering light : GLIMMER ⟨Candlelight *shimmered* behind the windows.⟩

[2]shimmer *n*
a wavering light ⟨the *shimmer* of silver leaves⟩

shim•my \ˈshi-mē\ *vb* **shim•mied; shim•my•ing**
to move the body from side to side ⟨I *shimmied* into my jacket.⟩

[1]shin \ˈshin\ *n*
the front part of the leg below the knee

[2]shin *vb* **shinned; shin•ning**
SHINNY

[1]shine \ˈshīn\ *vb* **shone** \ˈshōn\ *or* **shined; shin•ing**
1 to give off light ⟨The sun is *shining.*⟩
2 to be glossy : GLEAM ⟨He polished the silver until it *shone.*⟩
3 to direct the light of ⟨*Shine* the flashlight in that corner.⟩
4 to be outstanding ⟨She *shines* in sports.⟩
5 to make bright by polishing ⟨*shine* shoes⟩

[1]shield 1:
a 19th-century warrior's shield from India

[2]shine *n*
1 brightness from light given off or reflected ⟨the *shine* of polished silver⟩
2 fair weather : SUNSHINE ⟨rain or *shine*⟩
3 [2]POLISH 1 ⟨My shoes need a *shine.*⟩

shin•er \ˈshī-nər\ *n*
a small silvery American freshwater fish

[1]shin•gle \ˈshiŋ-gəl\ *n*
1 a small thin piece of building material for laying in overlapping rows as a covering for the roof or sides of a building
2 a small sign

[2]shingle *vb* **shin•gled; shin•gling**
to cover with shingles

shin•ny \ˈshi-nē\ *vb* **shin•nied; shin•ny•ing**
to climb (as a pole) by grasping with arms and legs and moving upward by repeated jerks

shiny \ˈshī-nē\ *adj* **shin•i•er; shin•i•est**
having a smooth bright appearance ⟨a *shiny* new car⟩

[1]ship \ˈship\ *n*
1 a large boat designed for travel by sea
2 AIRSHIP, AIRPLANE
3 a vehicle for traveling beyond the earth's atmosphere ⟨a rocket *ship*⟩

[2]ship *vb* **shipped; ship•ping**
1 to cause to be transported ⟨The grain was *shipped* by rail.⟩
2 to put or receive on board for transportation by water
3 to send (someone) to a place ⟨They *shipped* her off to boarding school.⟩
4 to take into a ship or boat ⟨*ship* oars⟩ ⟨*ship* water⟩
5 to sign on as a crew member on a ship

-ship \ˌship\ *n suffix*
1 state : condition : quality ⟨friend*ship*⟩
2 office : rank : profession ⟨author*ship*⟩
3 skill ⟨penman*ship*⟩
4 something showing a quality or state of being ⟨champion*ship*⟩ ⟨town*ship*⟩
5 someone having a specified rank ⟨your Lord*ship*⟩

ship•board \ˈship-ˌbȯrd\ *n*
1 a ship's side
2 [1]SHIP 1 ⟨We met on *shipboard.*⟩

ship•ment \ˈship-mənt\ *n*
1 the act of shipping ⟨The order is ready for *shipment.*⟩
2 a package or goods shipped

ship•ping \ˈshi-piŋ\ *n*
1 the act or business of a person who ships goods
2 a group of ships in one place or belonging to one port or country

ship•shape \ˈship-ˈshāp\ *adj*
being neat and orderly : TIDY

A B C D E F G H I J K L M N O P Q R S T U V W X Y Z

[1]ship•wreck \'ship-,rek\ *n*
1 ▶a ruined or destroyed ship 〈Divers explored the *shipwreck.*〉
2 the loss or destruction of a ship 〈Only a few sailors survived the *shipwreck.*〉

[2]shipwreck *vb* **ship•wrecked; ship•wreck•ing**
1 to cause to experience destruction of a ship and usually be left stranded 〈The crew was *shipwrecked.*〉
2 to ruin or destroy (a ship) by crashing ashore or sinking

ship•yard \'ship-,yärd\ *n*
a place where ships are built or repaired

shirk \'shərk\ *vb* **shirked; shirk•ing**
to avoid doing something especially because of laziness, fear, or dislike

shirt \'shərt\ *n*
a piece of clothing for the upper part of the body usually with sleeves and often a collar

[1]shiv•er \'shi-vər\ *vb* **shiv•ered; shiv•er•ing**
to shake slightly (as from cold or fear)

[2]shiver *n*
a small shaking movement of the body (as from cold or emotion) 〈a *shiver* of delight〉

[1]shoal \'shōl\ *adj* **shoal•er; shoal•est**
[1]SHALLOW 1 〈*shoal* water〉

[2]shoal *n*
1 a place where a sea, lake, or river is shallow
2 a mound or ridge of sand just below the surface of the water

[3]shoal *n*
[3]SCHOOL 〈a *shoal* of mackerel〉

[1]shock \'shäk\ *n*
a bunch of sheaves of grain or stalks of corn set on end (as in a field)

[2]shock *n*
1 a sudden strong unpleasant or upsetting feeling 〈a *shock* of surprise〉
2 something that causes a sudden unpleasant or upsetting feeling 〈His resignation came as a *shock.*〉
3 a severe shake, jerk, or impact 〈an earthquake *shock*〉
4 the effect of a charge of electricity passing through the body of a person or animal
5 a serious bodily reaction that usually follows severe injury or large loss of blood

[3]shock *vb* **shocked; shock•ing**
1 to strike with surprise, horror, or disgust 〈Their behavior *shocked* us.〉
2 to affect by a charge of electricity
3 to move to action especially by causing upset, surprise, or disgust 〈The news *shocked* the public into protest.〉

[4]shock *n*
a thick bushy mass 〈a *shock* of red hair〉

[1]shipwreck 1: a shipwreck at the bottom of the sea

shock•ing \'shä-kiŋ\ *adj*
1 causing surprise, horror, or disgust 〈*shocking* news〉
2 being intense or bright in color 〈*shocking* pink boots〉
shock•ing•ly *adv*

shod•dy \'shä-dē\ *adj* **shod•di•er; shod•di•est**
poorly done or made 〈*shoddy* work〉
shod•di•ness \'shä-dē-nəs\ *n*

[1]shoe \'shü\ *n*
1 an outer covering for the human foot usually having a thick and somewhat stiff sole and heel and a lighter upper part
2 HORSESHOE 1

[2]shoe *vb* **shod** \'shäd\ *also* **shoed** \'shüd\; **shoe•ing**
to put a shoe or horseshoe on : furnish with shoes

shoe•horn \'shü-,hȯrn\ *n*
a curved piece (as of metal) to help in sliding the heel of the foot into a shoe

shoe•lace \'shü-,lās\ *n*
a lace or string for fastening a shoe

shoe•mak•er \'shü-,mā-kər\ *n*
a person who makes or repairs shoes

shoe•string \'shü-,striŋ\ *n*
SHOELACE

shone *past and past participle of* SHINE

shoo \'shü\ *vb* **shooed; shoo•ing**
to wave, scare, or send away 〈She *shooed* us out of the kitchen.〉
Hint: *Shoo* is often used as a command. 〈*Shoo*! Go outside.〉

shook *past of* SHAKE

[1]shoot \'shüt\ *vb* **shot** \'shät\; **shoot•ing**
1 to let fly or cause to be driven forward with force 〈He *shot* an arrow into the air.〉
2 to cause a projectile (as a bullet) to be driven out of 〈The guard *shot* a gun.〉
3 to cause a weapon to discharge a projectile 〈Aim and *shoot.*〉
4 to strike with a projectile from a bow or gun 〈He *shot* a deer.〉
5 to hit, throw, or kick (as a ball or puck) toward or into a goal
6 to score by shooting 〈The player *shot* a basket.〉
7 [1]PLAY 2 〈Let's *shoot* some pool.〉
8 to thrust forward swiftly 〈Lizards *shot* out their tongues.〉
9 to grow rapidly 〈The corn is *shooting* up.〉
10 to go, move, or pass rapidly 〈They *shot* past on skis.〉
11 to direct at quickly and suddenly 〈I *shot* them an angry look.〉
12 to stream out suddenly : SPURT 〈Blood was *shooting* from the wound.〉
13 to film or photograph 〈The movie was *shot* in Australia.〉
14 to pass swiftly along or through 〈We *shot* the rapids in a canoe.〉
shoot•er *n*

[2]shoot *n*
1 a stem or branch of a plant especially when young or just beginning to grow
2 a hunting party or trip 〈a duck *shoot*〉

A B C D E F G H I J K L M N O P Q R S T U V W X Y Z

shooting star *n*
▶ a meteor appearing as a temporary streak of light in the night sky

[1]shop \'shäp\ *n*
1 a place where goods are sold **:** a usually small store ⟨a flower *shop*⟩
2 a worker's place of business ⟨the blacksmith *shop*⟩
3 a place in which workers are doing a particular kind of work ⟨a repair *shop*⟩

[2]shop *vb* **shopped; shop•ping**
to visit stores or shops for the purpose of looking over and buying goods
shop•per *n*

shop•keep•er \'shäp-,kē-pər\ *n*
STOREKEEPER 1

shop•lift \'shäp-,lift\ *vb* **shop•lift•ed; shop•lift•ing**
to steal merchandise on display in stores
shop•lift•er \-,lif-tər\ *n*

[1]shore \'shȯr\ *n*
the land along the edge of a body of water

[2]shore *vb* **shored; shor•ing**
to keep from sinking, sagging, or falling by placing a support under or against ⟨We had to *shore* up a wall.⟩

shore•bird \'shȯr-,bərd\ *n*
▼ a bird (as a plover or sandpiper) that frequents the seashore

shorebird: a crowned plover

shore•line \'shȯr-,līn\ *n*
the line or strip of land where a body of water and the shore meet

shorn *past participle of* SHEAR

[1]short \'shȯrt\ *adj* **short•er; short•est**
1 not long or tall ⟨*short* hair⟩ ⟨a *short* boy⟩ ⟨*short* stories⟩
2 not great in distance ⟨a *short* trip⟩
3 not lasting long **:** brief in time ⟨a *short* delay⟩ ⟨a *short* memory⟩

shooting star

4 cut down to a brief length ⟨"Doc" is *short* for "doctor."⟩
5 less than the usual or needed amount ⟨Fruit was in *short* supply.⟩ ⟨We met on *short* notice.⟩
6 having less than what is needed **:** not having enough ⟨I'm *short* of money.⟩ ⟨The team was *short* two players.⟩
7 not reaching far enough ⟨The throw was *short.*⟩
8 easily stirred up ⟨a *short* temper⟩
9 rudely brief ⟨I didn't mean to be *short* with you.⟩
10 of, relating to, or being one of the vowel sounds \ə, a, e, i, u̇\ and sometimes \ä\ and \ȯ\
short•ness *n*

[2]short *adv*
1 with suddenness ⟨I stopped *short.*⟩
2 to or at a point that is not as far as expected or desired ⟨He threw the ball *short.*⟩

[3]short *n*
1 shorts *pl* pants that reach to or almost to the knees
2 shorts *pl* short underpants
3 something (as a movie) shorter than the usual or regular length
4 SHORT CIRCUIT

short•age \'shȯr-tij\ *n*
a condition in which there is not enough of something needed **:** DEFICIT ⟨a water *shortage*⟩

short•cake \'shȯrt-,kāk\ *n*
▶ a dessert made usually of rich biscuit dough baked and served with sweetened fruit

short circuit *n*
an electrical connection made between points in an electric circuit between which current does not normally flow

short•com•ing \'shȯrt-,kə-miŋ\ *n*
FAULT 1

short•cut \'shȯrt-,kət\ *n*
a shorter, quicker, or easier way

short•en \'shȯr-tᵊn\ *vb* **shor•tened; shor•ten•ing**
to make or become short or shorter ⟨I *shortened* my trip.⟩

short•en•ing \'shȯr-tᵊn-iŋ, 'shȯrt-niŋ\ *n*
a fat used in baking especially to make pastry flaky

short•horn \'shȯrt-,hȯrn\ *n*
a cow of a short-horned breed of beef and dairy cattle developed in England

short–lived \'shȯrt-'livd, -'līvd\ *adj*
living or lasting only a short time ⟨*short-lived* joy⟩

short•ly \'shȯrt-lē\ *adv*
1 in or within a short time **:** SOON ⟨They should arrive *shortly.*⟩
2 in a brief way that shows anger or disapproval ⟨She spoke *shortly.*⟩

short–sight•ed \'shȯrt-'sī-təd\ *adj*
1 made without thinking about what will happen in the future ⟨a *short-sighted* policy⟩
2 NEARSIGHTED

short•stop \'shȯrt-,stäp\ *n*
a baseball infielder whose position is between second and third base

Sho•shone \shə-'shōn, -'shō-nē; 'shō-,shōn\ *or* **Sho•sho•ni** \shə-'shō-nē\ *n, pl* **Sho•shones** *or* **Shoshoni**
1 a member of a group of American Indian peoples originally of California, Idaho, Nevada, Utah, and Wyoming
2 the language of the Shoshones

[1]shot \'shät\ *n*
1 the act of shooting ⟨The *shot* missed.⟩
2 *pl* **shot** a bullet, ball, or pellet for a gun or cannon
3 [2]ATTEMPT, TRY ⟨Take another *shot* at the puzzle.⟩
4 [1]CHANCE 3 ⟨You have a *shot* at winning.⟩
5 the flight of a projectile or the distance it travels **:** RANGE ⟨They were within rifle *shot.*⟩
6 a person who shoots ⟨That hunter is a good *shot.*⟩

shortcake: strawberry shortcake

7 a heavy metal ball thrown for distance in a track-and-field contest (**shot put**)
8 an act of hitting, throwing, or kicking a ball or puck toward or into a goal
9 an injection of something (as medicine) into the body
10 ¹PHOTOGRAPH

²shot *past and past participle of* SHOOT

shot•gun \'shät-,gən\ *n*
a gun with a long barrel used to fire shot at short range

should \shəd, 'shu̇d\ *past of* SHALL
1 ought to ⟨They *should* be here soon.⟩
2 happen to ⟨If you *should* see them, say hello for me.⟩
3 used as a more polite or less assured form of *shall* ⟨*Should* I turn the light out?⟩

¹shoul•der \'shōl-dər\ *n*
1 ▼ the part of the body of a person or animal where the arm or foreleg joins the body
2 the part of a piece of clothing that covers a person's shoulder
3 a part that resembles a person's shoulder in shape ⟨the *shoulder* of a hill⟩
4 the edge of a road

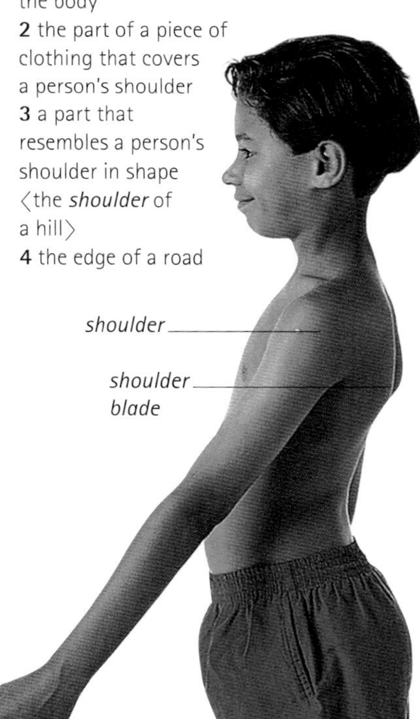

¹shoulder 1

²shoulder *vb* **shoul•dered; shoul•der•ing**
1 to push with the shoulder ⟨He *shouldered* his way through the crowd.⟩
2 to accept as a burden or duty ⟨You must *shoulder* the blame.⟩

shoulder blade *n*
the flat triangular bone of the back of the shoulder

shouldn't \'shu̇-dᵊnt\
should not ⟨You *shouldn't* go.⟩

¹shout \'shau̇t\ *vb* **shout•ed; shout•ing**
1 to make a sudden loud cry ⟨We *shouted* with joy.⟩
2 to say in a loud voice ⟨I *shouted* a warning.⟩

► **Synonyms** SHOUT, SHRIEK, and SCREECH mean to utter a loud cry. SHOUT means any kind of loud cry meant to be heard either far away or above other noise. ⟨We *shouted* to them across the river.⟩ SHRIEK means a high-pitched cry that is a sign of strong feeling. ⟨The children *shrieked* with excitement.⟩ SCREECH means an extended shriek that is usually without words and very harsh and unpleasant. ⟨The cats fought and *screeched*.⟩

²shout *n*
a sudden loud cry ⟨a *shout* of surprise⟩

¹shove \'shəv\ *vb* **shoved; shov•ing**
1 to push with steady force ⟨He *shoved* the box under the table.⟩
2 to push along or away carelessly or rudely ⟨She *shoved* me out of the way.⟩

²shove *n*
a forceful push

¹shov•el \'shə-vəl\ *n*
1 ▼ a tool with a long handle and broad scoop used to lift and throw loose material (as dirt or snow)
2 as much as a shovel will hold ⟨a *shovel* of sand⟩

¹shovel 1

²shovel *vb* **shov•eled** *or* **shov•elled; shov•el•ing** *or* **shov•el•ling**
1 to lift or throw with a shovel ⟨*shovel* snow⟩
2 to dig or clean out with a shovel ⟨I *shoveled* out the sheep pens.⟩
3 to move large amounts of into something quickly ⟨He *shoveled* food into his mouth.⟩

¹show \'shō\ *vb* **showed; shown** \'shōn\ *or* **showed; show•ing**
1 to place in sight : DISPLAY ⟨She *showed* everyone her pictures.⟩
2 REVEAL 2 ⟨They *showed* themselves to be cowards.⟩
3 to make known ⟨They *showed* their support.⟩
4 to give as appropriate treatment ⟨*Show* them no mercy.⟩ ⟨*Show* some respect.⟩
5 TEACH 1, INSTRUCT ⟨She *showed* him how to solve the problem.⟩
6 PROVE 1 ⟨That *shows* we're right.⟩
7 to lead to a place : DIRECT ⟨I *showed* them to the door.⟩
8 to point out to ⟨*Show* me where it hurts.⟩
9 to be easily seen or noticed ⟨The stain hardly *shows*.⟩ ⟨Determination *showed* in her face.⟩
show off to make an obvious display of a person's own abilities or possessions in order to impress others
show up APPEAR 2 ⟨He didn't *show up* for work today.⟩

► **Synonyms** SHOW, EXHIBIT, and PARADE mean to present something so that it will attract attention. SHOW is used of letting another see or examine. ⟨*Show* me a picture of your family.⟩ EXHIBIT is used of putting something out for public viewing. ⟨The children *exhibited* their drawings at the fair.⟩ PARADE is used of making a great show of something. ⟨Look at them *parading* their new bikes.⟩

²show *n*
1 a public performance intended to entertain people ⟨a puppet *show*⟩ ⟨a musical *show*⟩
2 a television or radio program
3 an event at which things of the same kind are put on display ⟨a fashion *show*⟩
4 a display to make known a feeling or quality ⟨a *show* of strength⟩ ⟨She answered with some *show* of alarm.⟩
5 an appearance meant to deceive ⟨He made a great *show* of friendship.⟩

show•boat \'shō-,bōt\ *n*
a river steamboat used as a traveling theater

show•case \'shō-,kās\ *n*
a protective glass case in which things are displayed

¹show•er \'shau̇-ər\ *n*
1 a short fall of rain over a small area
2 a large number of things that fall, are given off, or happen at the same time ⟨a *shower* of sparks⟩ ⟨a *shower* of praise⟩
3 a bath in which water is sprayed on the body or a device for providing such a bath
4 a party where gifts are given especially to a woman who is about to be married or have a baby

[2]shower *vb* **show•ered; show•er•ing**
1 to wet with fine spray or drops ⟨A passing car *showered* us with muddy water.⟩
2 to fall in or as if in a shower ⟨Sparks *showered* down on us.⟩
3 to provide in great quantity ⟨We *showered* them with gifts.⟩
4 to bathe in a shower

show•man \'shō-mən\ *n,* *pl* **show•men** \-mən\
a person having a special skill for presenting something in a dramatic way

show–off \'shō-,ȯf\ *n*
a person who tries to impress other people with his or her abilities or possessions

showy \'shō-ē\ *adj* **show•i•er; show•i•est**
1 attracting attention : STRIKING ⟨*showy* flower blossoms⟩
2 given to or being too much outward display : GAUDY ⟨*showy* jewelry⟩

shrank *past of* SHRINK

shrap•nel \'shrap-nᵊl\ *n*
small metal pieces that scatter outwards from an exploding bomb, shell, or mine

[1]shred \'shred\ *n*
1 a long narrow piece torn or cut off : STRIP ⟨*shreds* of cloth⟩
2 a small amount : BIT ⟨There is not a *shred* of evidence.⟩

[2]shred *vb* **shred•ded; shred•ding**
to cut or tear into small pieces

shrew 1: a common shrew

shrew \'shrü\ *n*
1 ▲ a small mouselike animal with a long pointed snout and tiny eyes that lives mostly on insects and worms
2 an unpleasant woman with a bad temper

shrewd \'shrüd\ *adj* **shrewd•er; shrewd•est**
showing quick practical cleverness ⟨a *shrewd* businessman⟩
shrewd•ly *adv*
shrewd•ness *n*

[1]shriek \'shrēk\ *vb* **shrieked; shriek•ing**
1 to make a loud high-pitched cry ⟨We *shrieked* with delight.⟩
2 to say in a loud high-pitched voice ⟨She *shrieked* my name.⟩
synonyms see SHOUT

[2]shriek *n*
a loud high-pitched cry or sound

[1]shrill \'shril\ *vb* **shrilled; shrill•ing**
1 to make a high-pitched usually piercing sound
2 to say in a loud high-pitched voice

[2]shrill *adj* **shrill•er; shrill•est**
having a high-pitched usually piercing sound ⟨a *shrill* whistle⟩
shrill•ness *n*
shril•ly \'shril-lē\ *adv*

shrimp \'shrimp\ *n*
1 a small shellfish of the sea that is related to the crabs and lobsters and is often used for food
2 a very small or unimportant person or thing

shrine \'shrīn\ *n*
1 a case or box for sacred relics (as the bones of saints)
2 ▶ a place connected with a holy person or event where people worship
3 a place that is considered sacred or regarded with great respect ⟨The Lincoln Memorial is a *shrine* to all lovers of freedom.⟩

shrink \'shriŋk\ *vb* **shrank** \'shraŋk\ *or* **shrunk** \'shrəŋk\; **shrunk** *or* **shrunk•en** \'shrəŋ-kən\; **shrink•ing**
1 to make or become smaller ⟨The sweater *shrank* when it got wet.⟩
2 to curl up or move back in or as if in fear or pain ⟨*shrink* in horror⟩
3 to refrain from doing something especially because of difficulty or unpleasantness ⟨He did not *shrink* from telling the truth.⟩

shrink•age \'shriŋ-kij\ *n*
the amount by which something shrinks or becomes less

shriv•el \'shri-vəl\ *vb* **shriv•eled** *or* **shriv•elled; shriv•el•ing** *or* **shriv•el•ling**
to shrink and become dry and wrinkled

[1]shroud \'shrau̇d\ *n*
1 the cloth placed over or around a dead body
2 something that covers or hides ⟨a *shroud* of secrecy⟩

[2]shroud *vb* **shroud•ed; shroud•ing**
to cover or hide with or as if with a shroud ⟨The road was *shrouded* in fog.⟩

shrub \'shrəb\ *n*
a woody plant that has several stems and is smaller than most trees

shrub•bery \'shrə-bə-rē\ *n,* *pl* **shrub•ber•ies**
a group of shrubs or an area where shrubs are growing

[1]shrug \'shrəg\ *vb* **shrugged; shrug•ging**
to raise and lower the shoulders usually to express doubt, uncertainty, or lack of interest

shrine 2: a Catholic shrine to the Virgin Mary in a Spanish church

[2]shrug *n*
an act of raising and lowering the shoulders

[1]shuck \'shək\ *n*
a covering shell or husk

[2]shuck *vb* **shucked; shuck•ing**
to remove the shell or husk from ⟨I helped *shuck* corn.⟩

[1]shud•der \'shə-dər\ *vb* **shud•dered; shud•der•ing**
1 to tremble especially with fear or horror or from cold
2 to move or sound as if being shaken ⟨The train slowed and *shuddered* to a halt.⟩

[2]shudder *n*
an act or instance of trembling or shaking ⟨a *shudder* of fear⟩

[1]shuf•fle \'shə-fəl\ *vb* **shuf•fled; shuf•fling**
1 to slide back and forth without lifting ⟨He *shuffled* his feet.⟩
2 to walk or move by sliding or dragging the feet ⟨I just *shuffled* along.⟩
3 to mix up the order of (as playing cards)
4 to push or move about or from place to place ⟨She *shuffled* the papers on her desk.⟩

[2]shuffle *n*
1 a sliding or dragging walk
2 an act of mixing up or moving so as to change the order or position
3 a confusing jumble ⟨The idea was lost in the *shuffle*.⟩

shun \'shən\ *vb* **shunned; shun•ning**
to avoid purposely or by habit ⟨He *shunned* noisy places.⟩

A B C D E F G H I J K L M N O P Q R S T U V W X Y Z

shunt \'shənt\ *vb* **shunt•ed; shunt•ing**
1 to turn or move off to one side or out of the way 〈Cattle were *shunted* into a corral.〉
2 to switch (as a train) from one track to another

shut \'shət\ *vb* **shut; shut•ting**
1 to close or become closed 〈She *shut* the book loudly.〉 〈The door *shuts* by itself.〉
2 to stop or cause to stop operation 〈She *shut* down the computer.〉 〈*Shut* off the TV.〉
3 to confine by or as if by enclosing or by blocking the way out 〈Guards *shut* the thieves in a jail cell.〉
4 to close by bringing parts together 〈Don't look! *Shut* your eyes!〉
shut out
1 to keep (something) from entering 〈Curtains *shut out* the sun.〉
2 to keep (an opponent) from scoring in a game
shut up to stop talking

shut•out \'shət-,au̇t\ *n*
a game in which one side fails to score

shut•ter \'shə-tər\ *n*
1 ▶ a usually movable cover for the outside of a window
2 a device in a camera that opens to let in light when a picture is taken

shutter 1: a window with wooden shutters

[1]**shut•tle** \'shə-tᵊl\ *n*
1 an instrument used in weaving to carry the thread back and forth from side to side through the threads that run lengthwise
2 a vehicle (as a bus or train) that goes back and forth over a short route
3 SPACE SHUTTLE

[2]**shuttle** *vb* **shut•tled; shut•tling**
to move or bring back and forth rapidly or often 〈The ferry *shuttled* travelers across the river.〉

shut•tle•cock \'shə-tᵊl-,käk\ *n*
▶ a light cone-shaped object that is used in badminton

shuttlecock

[1]**shy** \'shī\ *adj* **shi•er** *or* **shy•er; shi•est** *or* **shy•est**
1 not feeling comfortable meeting and talking to people 〈a *shy* awkward boy〉
2 easily frightened : TIMID 〈a *shy* kitten〉
3 showing a dislike of attention 〈a *shy* face〉
4 tending to avoid something or someone 〈I'm camera *shy.* Don't take my picture.〉
5 having less than a full or an expected amount or number 〈We were *shy* about ten dollars.〉
shy•ly *adv*
shy•ness *n*

▶ **Synonyms** SHY and BASHFUL mean feeling awkward around others. SHY is used of someone who doesn't want to meet or talk with people either by habit or for special reasons. 〈New students are often *shy.*〉 BASHFUL is used of someone who is shy and afraid like a very young child. 〈He was too *bashful* to ask for a dance.〉

[2]**shy** *vb* **shied; shy•ing**
1 to avoid or draw back in dislike or distaste 〈He *shied* from publicity.〉
2 to move quickly to one side in fright 〈The horse *shied* at the thunder.〉

sib•ling \'si-bliŋ\ *n*
a brother or sister 〈an older *sibling*〉

sick \'sik\ *adj* **sick•er; sick•est**
1 affected with disease or illness : not well
2 of, relating to, or intended for use in or during illness 〈*sick* pay〉
3 affected with or accompanied by nausea 〈The bobbing of the boat made me feel *sick.*〉
4 badly upset by strong emotion 〈I was *sick* with worry.〉
5 annoyed or bored of something from having too much of it 〈We were *sick* of his whining.〉
6 filled with disgust or anger 〈Such gossip makes me *sick.*〉

sick•bed \'sik-,bed\ *n*
a bed on which a sick person lies

sick•en \'si-kən\ *vb* **sick•ened; sick•en•ing**
1 to make or become sick or ill 〈Many of the colonists *sickened* on the long voyage.〉
2 to cause to feel disgusted or angry 〈We were *sickened* by his cruelty.〉

sick•en•ing \'si-kə-niŋ\ *adj*
causing sickness or disgust 〈a *sickening* smell〉
sick•en•ing•ly *adv*

sick•le \'si-kəl\ *n*
a tool with a sharp curved blade and a short handle used especially to cut grass and grain

sick•ly \'sik-lē\ *adj* **sick•li•er; sick•li•est**
1 somewhat sick : often ailing 〈I was *sickly* as a child.〉
2 caused by or associated with ill health 〈a *sickly* complexion〉
3 SICKENING 〈a *sickly* odor〉
4 appearing as if sick 〈The *sickly* plants withered away.〉

sick•ness \'sik-nəs\ *n*
1 ill health : ILLNESS
2 a specific disease 〈He came down with an unknown *sickness.*〉
3 NAUSEA 1

sideburns: a young man with sideburns

[1]**side** \'sīd\ *n*
1 the right or left part of the body from the shoulder to the hip ⟨I have a pain in my right *side.*⟩
2 a place, space, or direction away from or beyond a central point or line ⟨The statue was leaning to one *side.*⟩
3 a surface or line forming a border or face of an object ⟨A square has four *sides.*⟩
4 an outer surface or part of something considered as facing in a certain direction ⟨the upper *side*⟩
5 either surface of a thin object ⟨Write on both *sides* of the paper.⟩
6 a place next to something or someone ⟨the *side* of the road⟩ ⟨I stood at his *side.*⟩
7 an opinion or position viewed as opposite or different from another ⟨Listen to my *side* of the story.⟩
8 a group of people involved in a competition, dispute, or war ⟨Which *side* won?⟩
9 a line of ancestors traced back from either parent ⟨I'm French on my mother's *side.*⟩

[2]**side** *adj*
1 of or located on the side ⟨*side* pockets⟩ ⟨a *side* door⟩
2 going toward or coming from the side ⟨a *side* wind⟩
3 related to something in a minor or unimportant way ⟨a *side* remark⟩
4 being in addition to a main portion ⟨a *side* order of French fries⟩

[3]**side** *vb* **sid•ed; sid•ing**
to agree with or support the opinions or actions of ⟨We *sided* with our friend in the argument.⟩

side•arm \'sīd-ˌärm\ *adv*
with the arm moving out to the side ⟨She threw the ball *sidearm.*⟩

side•board \'sīd-ˌbȯrd\ *n*
a piece of furniture for holding dishes, silverware, and table linen

side•burns \'sīd-ˌbərnz\ *n pl*
◀ hair growing on the side of the face in front of the ears

▶ **Word History** During the American Civil War there was a Union general named Ambrose Burnside who grew long bushy whiskers on the sides of his face. His appearance first struck the people of Washington, D.C., as he led parades with his regiment of Rhode Island volunteers. Though his later military career had its ups and downs, the general's early popularity encouraged a fashion for such whiskers, which began to be called *burnsides.* By the 1880s the order of the two words making up *burnsides* was reversed to give *sideburns.*

sid•ed \'sī-dəd\ *adj*
having sides often of a stated number or kind ⟨a four-*sided* figure⟩

side•line \'sīd-ˌlīn\ *n*
1 a line marking the side of a playing field or court
2 a business or a job done in addition to a person's regular occupation

[1]**side•long** \'sīd-ˌlȯŋ\ *adj*
made to one side or out of the corner of the eye ⟨a *sidelong* look⟩

[2]**sidelong** *adv*
out of the corner of the eye ⟨The boy glanced *sidelong* at the pie on the table.⟩

side•show \'sīd-ˌshō\ *n*
a small show off to the side of a main show or exhibition (as of a circus)

side•step \'sīd-ˌstep\ *vb* **side•stepped; side•step•ping**
1 to take a sideways step
2 to avoid by a step to the side ⟨He *sidestepped* the punch.⟩
3 to avoid answering or dealing with ⟨She *sidestepped* the question.⟩

sieve: sifting flour with a sieve

side•track \'sīd-ˌtrak\ *vb* **side•tracked; side•track•ing**
to turn aside from a main purpose or direction ⟨His career got *sidetracked.*⟩

side•walk \'sīd-ˌwȯk\ *n*
a usually paved walk at the side of a street or road

side•ways \'sīd-ˌwāz\ *adv or adj*
1 from one side ⟨I looked at it *sideways.*⟩
2 with one side forward ⟨a *sideways* position⟩ ⟨He turned *sideways* to let me by.⟩
3 to one side ⟨a *sideways* move⟩ ⟨The statue fell *sideways.*⟩

side•wise \'sīd-ˌwīz\ *adv or adj*
SIDEWAYS

sid•ing \'sī-diŋ\ *n*
1 a short railroad track connected with the main track
2 material (as boards or metal pieces) used to cover the outside walls of frame buildings

si•dle \'sī-dᵊl\ *vb* **si•dled; si•dling**
to go or move with one side forward ⟨The crab *sidled* away.⟩

siege \'sēj\ *n*
the act of moving an army around a fortified place to capture it
lay siege to to attack militarily

si•er•ra \sē-'er-ə\ *n*
a range of mountains especially with jagged peaks

si•es•ta \sē-'e-stə\ *n*
a nap or rest especially at midday

▶ **Word History** The ancient Romans counted the hours of the day from sunrise to sunset, an average of about twelve hours. The sixth hour of the Roman day—in Latin, *sexta hora,* or simply *sexta*—fell around noon. The word *sexta* passed into Spanish as *siesta,* which referred first to the hot period around the middle of the day, and then to a nap taken during this period after the midday meal. English *siesta* comes from the Spanish word.

sieve \'siv\ *n*
◀ a utensil with meshes or holes to separate finer particles from coarser ones or solids from liquids

sift \'sift\ *vb* **sift•ed; sift•ing**
1 to pass or cause to pass through a sieve ⟨*sift* flour⟩
2 to separate or separate out by or as if by passing through a sieve ⟨I *sifted* the lumps.⟩

3 to test or examine carefully ⟨Police will *sift* through the evidence.⟩
sift•er *n*

[1]sigh \'sī\ *vb* **sighed**; **sigh•ing**
1 to take or let out a long loud breath often as an expression of sadness or weariness
2 to make a sound like sighing ⟨Wind was *sighing* in the branches.⟩
3 to say with a sigh ⟨"Oh, dear," she *sighed*.⟩

[2]sigh *n*
the act or a sound of taking or letting out a long loud breath ⟨She finished with a *sigh* of relief.⟩

[1]sight \'sīt\ *n*
1 the function, process, or power of seeing **:** the sense by which a person or animal becomes aware of the position, form, and color of objects
2 the act of seeing ⟨It was love at first *sight*.⟩
3 something that is seen **:** SPECTACLE
4 something that is worth seeing ⟨He showed us the *sights* of the city.⟩
5 something that is peculiar, funny, or messy ⟨You're a *sight*!⟩
6 the presence of an object within the field of vision ⟨I can't stand the *sight* of blood.⟩ ⟨She caught *sight* of an eagle.⟩
7 the distance a person can see ⟨A ship came into *sight*.⟩
8 a device (as a small metal bead on a gun barrel) that aids the eye in aiming or in finding the direction of an object

[2]sight *vb* **sight•ed**; **sight•ing**
1 to get a look at **:** SEE ⟨Their dog was *sighted* in a neighbor's garden.⟩
2 to look at through or as if through a device that aids the eye in aiming or in finding the direction of an object

sight•less \'sīt-ləs\ *adj*
lacking sight **:** BLIND

sight•see \'sīt-,sē\ *vb* **sight•saw**; **sight•see•ing**
to go about seeing places and things of interest
sight•se•er \-,sē-ər, -,sir\ *n*

[1]sign \'sīn\ *n*
1 a motion, action, or movement of the hand that means something ⟨The teacher made a *sign* for them to be quiet.⟩
2 a public notice that advertises something or gives information ⟨a stop *sign*⟩
3 something that indicates what is present or is to come ⟨the first *signs* of spring⟩
4 a symbol (as + or ÷) indicating a mathematical operation
5 one of the twelve parts of the zodiac

sign language
Sign language allows people who are deaf, hard of hearing, or unable to speak, to communicate. There is a sign for each letter of the alphabet to enable the spelling of individual words, as well as signs that represent whole words and names. Sometimes, even a whole sentence can be expressed through one or two signs.

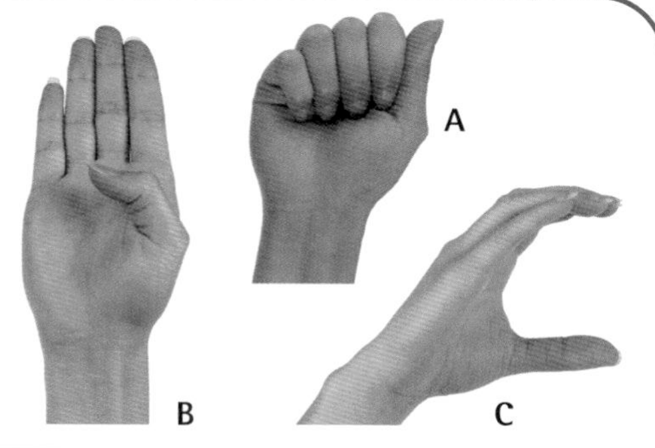

[2]sign *vb* **signed**; **sign•ing**
1 to put a signature on to show acceptance, agreement, or responsibility ⟨His boss *signed* the order form.⟩
2 to communicate by using sign language
3 to represent or show by a motion, action, or movement
4 to make or place a sign on
sign up to sign someone's name in order to get, do, or take something ⟨I *signed up* to go.⟩

[1]sig•nal \'sig-nᵊl\ *n*
1 a sign, event, or word that serves to start some action ⟨Wait for a *signal* to light the fires.⟩
2 a sound, a movement of part of the body, or an object that gives warning or a command ⟨The police officer made a *signal* with his hand.⟩ ⟨a traffic *signal*⟩
3 a radio wave that transmits a message or effect (as in radio or television)

[2]signal *vb* **sig•naled** *or* **sig•nalled**; **sig•nal•ing** *or* **sig•nal•ling**
1 to notify by a motion, action, movement, or sound
2 to communicate with motions, actions, movements, or sounds

[3]signal *adj*
1 unusually great ⟨a *signal* honor⟩
2 used for sending a message, warning, or command ⟨a *signal* light⟩

sig•na•ture \'sig-nə-,chu̇r, -chər\ *n*
1 the name of a person written by that person
2 a sign or group of signs placed at the beginning of a staff in music to show the key (**key signature**) or the meter (**time signature**)

sign•board \'sīn-,bȯrd\ *n*
a board with a sign or notice on it

sig•nif•i•cance \sig-'ni-fi-kəns\ *n*
1 MEANING 2
2 IMPORTANCE ⟨It's a subject of some *significance*.⟩

sig•nif•i•cant \sig-'ni-fi-kənt\ *adj*
1 having a special or hidden meaning ⟨The teacher gave them a *significant* smile.⟩
2 IMPORTANT 1 ⟨These changes are *significant*.⟩
3 large enough to be noticed

sig•ni•fy \'sig-nə-,fī\ *vb* **sig•ni•fied**; **sig•ni•fy•ing**
1 [1]MEAN 1, DENOTE ⟨A check mark *signifies* a correct answer.⟩
2 to show especially by a sign **:** make known ⟨She nodded to *signify* agreement.⟩
3 to have importance **:** MATTER

sign language *n*
▲ a system of hand movements used for communication (as by people who are deaf)

signpost: a signpost from the city of London

sign•post \'sīn-,pōst\ *n*
▲ a post with a sign or signs (as for directing travelers)

si•lage \'sī-lij\ *n*
fodder fermented (as in a silo) to produce a juicy feed for livestock

[1]si•lence \'sī-ləns\ *n*
1 the state of keeping or being silent ⟨The teacher motioned for *silence*.⟩
2 the state of there being no sound or noise **:** STILLNESS

[2]silence *vb* **si•lenced**; **si•lenc•ing**
1 to stop the noise or speech of **:** cause to be silent
2 SUPPRESS 1 ⟨The group tried to *silence* opposing views.⟩

si•lent \ˈsī-lənt\ *adj*
1 not speaking ⟨He stood *silent* for a moment, and then answered.⟩
2 not talkative ⟨a *silent* person⟩
3 free from noise or sound : STILL ⟨Except for a ticking clock the house was *silent.*⟩
4 done or felt without being spoken ⟨*silent* reading⟩ ⟨*silent* prayer⟩
5 making no mention ⟨They were *silent* about their plan.⟩
6 not in operation ⟨*silent* factories⟩
7 not pronounced ⟨The letter **e** in "came" is *silent.*⟩
8 made without spoken dialogue ⟨*silent* movies⟩
si•lent•ly *adv*

[1]silhouette 2: a silhouette of an oak tree

[1]sil•hou•ette \ˌsi-lə-ˈwet\ *n*
1 [1]OUTLINE 1 ⟨In the dim light, their faces were just *silhouettes.*⟩
2 ▲ a drawing, picture, or portrait of the outline of a person or object filled in with a solid usually black color

▶ **Word History** A man named Étienne de *Silhouette* was once in charge of the finances of France. He was a miser who did not like to spend his money or the country's money. According to one story he was too cheap to buy paintings for the walls of his mansion, and so he made simple outline drawings to hang in place of paintings. In French and in English *silhouette* still means "an outline drawing."

[2]silhouette *vb* **sil•hou•ett•ed; sil•hou•ett•ing**
to represent by an outline : show against a light background ⟨An airplane was *silhouetted* against the sky.⟩

sil•i•con \ˈsi-li-kən, ˈsi-lə-ˌkän\ *n*
a chemical element that next to oxygen is the most common element in the earth's crust and is used especially in electronic devices

silk \ˈsilk\ *n*
1 a fine fiber that is spun by many insect larvae usually to form their cocoon or by spiders to make their webs and that includes some kinds used for weaving cloth
2 ▶ thread, yarn, or fabric made from silk
3 the threadlike strands that are found over the kernels of an ear of corn

silk 2: twists of silk for use in sewing

silk•en \ˈsil-kən\ *adj*
1 made of or with silk ⟨a *silken* scarf⟩
2 having a soft and smooth look or feel ⟨*silken* hair⟩

silk•worm \ˈsilk-ˌwərm\ *n*
a yellowish caterpillar that is the larva of an Asian moth (**silk moth** or **silkworm moth**), is raised in captivity on mulberry leaves, and produces a strong silk that is the silk most used for thread or cloth

silky \ˈsil-kē\ *adj* **silk•i•er; silk•i•est**
1 soft and smooth ⟨*silky* fur⟩
2 agreeably smooth ⟨a *silky* voice⟩

sill \ˈsil\ *n*
1 a heavy horizontal piece (as of wood) that forms the bottom part of a window frame or a doorway
2 a horizontal supporting piece at the base of a structure

sil•ly \ˈsi-lē\ *adj* **sil•li•er; sil•li•est**
1 having or showing a lack of common sense : FOOLISH ⟨*Silly* me! I forgot again.⟩ ⟨What a *silly* mistake!⟩
2 not serious or important ⟨a *silly* reason⟩
3 playful and lighthearted ⟨*silly* jokes⟩
synonyms see ABSURD
sil•li•ness *n*

si•lo \ˈsī-lō\ *n, pl* **silos**
a covered trench, pit, or especially a tall round building in which silage is made and stored

[1]silt \ˈsilt\ *n*
1 particles of small size left as sediment from water
2 a soil made up mostly of silt and containing little clay

[2]silt *vb* **silt•ed; silt•ing**
to fill, cover, or block with silt

[1]sil•ver \ˈsil-vər\ *n*
1 a soft white metallic chemical element that can be polished and is used for money, jewelry and ornaments, and table utensils
2 coin made of silver
3 SILVERWARE ⟨table *silver*⟩
4 a medal made of silver that is given to someone who wins second place in a contest
5 a medium gray

[2]silver *adj*
1 made of, coated with, or yielding the soft white metallic chemical element silver ⟨a *silver* teapot⟩
2 having the medium gray color of silver ⟨*silver* hair⟩

[3]silver *vb* **sil•vered; sil•ver•ing**
to coat with or as if with silver

sil•ver•smith \ˈsil-vər-ˌsmith\ *n*
a person who makes objects of silver

sil•ver•ware \ˈsil-vər-ˌwer\ *n*
▶ things (as knives, forks, and spoons) made of silver, silver-plated metal, or stainless steel

sil•very \ˈsil-və-rē\ *adj*
shiny and medium gray ⟨a *silvery* fish⟩

sim•i•lar \ˈsi-mə-lər\ *adj*
having qualities in common ⟨The houses are *similar* in design.⟩
sim•i•lar•ly *adv*

sim•i•lar•i•ty \ˌsi-mə-ˈler-ə-tē\ *n, pl* **sim•i•lar•i•ties**
the quality or state of being alike in some way or ways

sim•i•le \ˈsi-mə-ˌlē\ *n*
a figure of speech comparing two unlike things using *like* or *as* ⟨"Their cheeks are like roses" is a *simile.* "Their cheeks are roses" is a metaphor.⟩

sim•mer \ˈsi-mər\ *vb* **sim•mered; sim•mer•ing**
1 to cook gently at or just below the boiling point
2 to be on the point of bursting out with violence or anger

sim•per \ˈsim-pər\ *vb* **sim•pered; sim•per•ing**
to smile or speak in a way that is not sincere or natural

sim•ple \ˈsim-pəl\ *adj* **sim•pler; sim•plest**
1 not hard to understand or solve ⟨a *simple* task⟩
2 [1]EASY 1, STRAIGHTFORWARD ⟨a *simple* explanation⟩
3 lacking in education, experience, or intelligence
4 not complex or fancy ⟨She wore *simple* clothing.⟩

A B C D E F G H I J K L M N O P Q R S T U V W X Y Z

5 INNOCENT 1, MODEST
6 not rich or important ⟨*simple* folk⟩
7 without qualification : SHEER ⟨the *simple* truth⟩

simple machine *n*
one of the fundamental devices that all machines were formerly thought to be made from ⟨The lever, axle, pulley, inclined plane, wedge, and screw are the classic *simple machines.*⟩

sim•ple•ton \'sim-pəl-tən\ *n*
a foolish or stupid person

sim•plic•i•ty \sim-'pli-sə-tē\ *n, pl* **sim•plic•i•ties**
1 the quality or state of being simple or plain and not complicated or difficult
2 SINCERITY
3 directness or clearness in speaking or writing

silverware

sim•pli•fy \'sim-plə-,fī\ *vb* **sim•pli•fied**; **sim•pli•fy•ing**
to make simple or simpler : make easier

sim•ply \'sim-plē\ *adv*
1 in a clear way ⟨The instructions are *simply* written.⟩
2 in a plain way ⟨They dressed *simply.*⟩
3 in a sincere and direct way ⟨He told the story as *simply* as a child would.⟩
4 [2]ONLY 1, MERELY ⟨May I ask a question *simply* out of curiosity?⟩
5 in actual fact : REALLY, TRULY ⟨The trip was *simply* wonderful.⟩

si•mul•ta•neous \,sī-məl-'tā-nē-əs\ *adj*
existing or taking place at the same time ⟨*simultaneous* events⟩
si•mul•ta•neous•ly *adv*

[1]**sin** \'sin\ *n*
1 an action that breaks a religious law
2 an action that is or is felt to be bad ⟨Wasting food is a *sin.*⟩

[2]**sin** *vb* **sinned**; **sin•ning**
to do something that breaks a religious law or is felt to be bad
sin•ner \'si-nər\ *n*

[1]**since** \'sins\ *adv*
1 from a definite past time until now ⟨He moved and hasn't returned *since.*⟩
2 before the present time : AGO ⟨The poet is long *since* dead.⟩
3 after a time in the past ⟨She has *since* become rich.⟩

[2]**since** *conj*
1 in the period after ⟨We've played better *since* you joined the team.⟩
2 BECAUSE ⟨*Since* you have finished your work, you may go.⟩

[3]**since** *prep*
1 in the period after ⟨I haven't seen them *since* last week.⟩
2 continuously from ⟨We have lived here *since* I was born.⟩

sin•cere \sin-'sir\ *adj* **sin•cer•er**; **sin•cer•est**
1 HONEST 1, STRAIGHTFORWARD ⟨a *sincere* person⟩
2 being what it seems to be : GENUINE ⟨*sincere* good wishes⟩
sin•cere•ly *adv*

sin•cer•i•ty \sin-'ser-ə-tē\ *n*
freedom from fraud or deception : HONESTY

sin•ew \'sin-yü\ *n*
TENDON

sin•ewy \'sin-yə-wē\ *adj*
1 STRONG 1, POWERFUL ⟨*sinewy* arms⟩
2 full of tendons : TOUGH, STRINGY ⟨a *sinewy* piece of meat⟩

sin•ful \'sin-fəl\ *adj*
being or full of sin : WICKED

sing \'siŋ\ *vb* **sang** \'saŋ\ *or* **sung** \'səŋ\; **sung**; **sing•ing**
1 to produce musical sounds with the voice ⟨He *sings* in the choir.⟩
2 to express in musical tones ⟨Will you *sing* a song?⟩
3 to make musical sounds ⟨The birds were *singing* at dawn.⟩
4 [1]CHANT 2 ⟨*sing* mass⟩
5 to make a small high-pitched sound ⟨Arrows went *singing* through the air.⟩
6 to speak with enthusiasm ⟨Their teacher is happy to *sing* their praises.⟩
7 to do something with song ⟨He *sang* the baby to sleep.⟩
sing•er *n*

sing. *abbr* singular

singe \'sinj\ *vb* **singed**; **singe•ing**
to burn lightly or on the surface : SCORCH ⟨The flame *singed* her hair.⟩

[1]**sin•gle** \'siŋ-gəl\ *adj*
1 being alone : being the only one
2 being a separate whole : INDIVIDUAL ⟨a *single* thread⟩
3 not married
4 made up of or having only one ⟨The word has a *single* syllable.⟩
5 made for only one person ⟨a *single* bed⟩

[2]**single** *vb* **sin•gled**; **sin•gling**
to select or distinguish (as one person or thing) from a number or group ⟨My sister was *singled* out for praise.⟩

[3]**single** *n*
1 a separate individual person or thing
2 a hit in baseball that enables the batter to reach first base

sin•gle–hand•ed \,siŋ-gəl-'han-dəd\ *adj*
1 done or managed by one person or with one hand
2 working alone : lacking help
single–handed *adv*
sin•gle–hand•ed•ly *adv*

sin•gly \'siŋ-gə-lē, 'siŋ-glē\ *adv*
one by one : INDIVIDUALLY

sing•song \'siŋ-,sȯŋ\ *n*
a way of speaking in which the pitch of the voice rises and falls in a pattern
singsong *adj*

[1]**sin•gu•lar** \'siŋ-gyə-lər\ *adj*
1 of, relating to, or being a word form used to show not more than one person or thing ⟨The *singular* form of "calves" is "calf."⟩
2 [1]SUPERIOR 2, EXCEPTIONAL ⟨He showed *singular* poise.⟩
3 of unusual quality ⟨We had a *singular* experience.⟩
4 STRANGE 2, ODD ⟨*singular* habits⟩

[2]**singular** *n*
a form of a word used to show that only one person or thing is meant

sin•is•ter \'si-nəs-tər\ *adj*
1 threatening evil, harm, or danger ⟨We heard *sinister* rumors.⟩
2 [1]EVIL 1, CORRUPT

[1]**sink** \'siŋk\ *vb* **sank** \'saŋk\ *or* **sunk** \'səŋk\; **sunk**; **sink•ing**
1 to move or cause to move downward so as to be swallowed up ⟨The ship *sank.*⟩
2 to fall or drop to a lower level ⟨She *sank* to her knees.⟩
3 to penetrate or cause to penetrate ⟨He *sank* an ax into the tree.⟩
4 to go into or become absorbed ⟨Water *sank* into the ground.⟩
5 to become known or felt ⟨She had to let the news *sink* in.⟩
6 to lessen in amount ⟨The temperature *sank.*⟩
7 to form by digging or boring ⟨We'll *sink* a well for water.⟩
8 to spend (money) unwisely
9 to descend into a feeling of sadness or dread

[2]**sink** *n*
a wide bowl or basin attached to a wall or floor and having water faucets and a drain

a b c d e f g h i j k l m n o p q r **s** t u v w x y z

sin•u•ous \'sin-yə-wəs\ *adj*
having a wavy or winding form

si•nus \'sī-nəs\ *n*
any of several spaces in the skull mostly connected with the nostrils

Sioux \'sü\ *n, pl* **Sioux** \'sü, 'süz\
DAKOTA

[1]**sip** \'sip\ *vb* **sipped**; **sip•ping**
to take small drinks of

[2]**sip** *n*
1 the act of taking a small drink
2 a small amount taken by sipping

[1]**si•phon** \'sī-fən\ *n*
1 a bent pipe or tube through which a liquid can be drawn by air pressure up and over the edge of a container
2 a tubelike part especially of a mollusk (as a clam) usually used to draw in or squirt out water

[2]**siphon** *vb* **si•phoned**; **si•phon•ing**
to draw off by or as if by a siphon

sir \'sər\ *n*
1 used without a name as a form of polite address to a man ⟨May I help you, *sir?*⟩
2 *cap* used as a title before the given name of a knight or a baronet ⟨*Sir* Walter Raleigh⟩
3 *cap* used without a name as a form of address at the beginning of a letter

[1]**sire** \'sīr\ *n*
1 *often cap* [1]FATHER 1
2 the male parent of a domestic animal
3 used in the past to address a man of rank (as a king) ⟨Your horses are ready, *sire.*⟩

[2]**sire** *vb* **sired**; **sir•ing**
to become the father of

si•ren \'sī-rən\ *n*
a device that makes a loud warning sound ⟨an ambulance *siren*⟩

sir•loin \'sər-,lȯin\ *n*
a cut of beef taken from the part just in front of the rump

si•sal \'sī-səl, -zəl\ *n*
► a long strong white fiber made from the leaves of a Mexican plant and used to make rope and twine

sisal: twine made of sisal

sis•sy \'si-sē\ *n, pl* **sis•sies**
a fearful or cowardly person

sis•ter \'si-stər\ *n*
1 a female person or animal related to another person or animal by having one or both parents in common
2 a member of a religious society of women : NUN
3 a woman related to another by a common tie or interest
sis•ter•ly *adj*

sis•ter•hood \'si-stər-,hu̇d\ *n*
1 the state of being a sister
2 women joined in a group

sis•ter–in–law \'si-stər-ən-,lȯ\ *n, pl* **sis•ters–in–law**
1 the sister of someone's husband or wife
2 the wife of someone's brother

sit \'sit\ *vb* **sat** \'sat\; **sit•ting**
1 to rest upon the part of the body where the hips and legs join : to rest on the buttocks or hindquarters ⟨We *sat* and waited on a bench.⟩ ⟨The dog *sat* by the fire.⟩
2 to put the buttocks down on a surface ⟨I *sat* down to write a letter.⟩
3 to cause to be seated ⟨He *sat* the baby in the chair.⟩
4 [2]PERCH ⟨The bird *sat* on a branch.⟩
5 to be located or stay in a place or position ⟨A vase *sits* on the table.⟩
6 to provide seats for ⟨The car *sits* five.⟩
7 to hold a place as a member of an official group ⟨She was elected to *sit* in Congress.⟩
8 to hold a session ⟨The court *sat* last month.⟩
9 to pose for a portrait or photograph
10 BABYSIT

site \'sīt\ *n*
1 the place where something (as a town or event) is found or took place ⟨a famous battle *site*⟩
2 the space of ground a building rests upon
3 WEB SITE

sit•ter \'si-tər\ *n*
BABYSITTER

sit•ting \'si-tiŋ\ *n*
1 a period during which someone poses for a portrait or photograph
2 SESSION 2 ⟨a *sitting* of the legislature⟩
3 a time when a meal is served to a number of people ⟨There will be two *sittings* for the dinner.⟩

sitting room *n*
LIVING ROOM

sit•u•at•ed \'si-chə-,wā-təd\ *adj*
1 having its place ⟨The town is *situated* on a hill.⟩
2 being in such financial circumstances ⟨They're not rich but comfortably *situated.*⟩

sit•u•a•tion \,si-chə-'wā-shən\ *n*
1 the combination of surrounding conditions ⟨The *situation* at school is better than it was.⟩
2 a state of affairs that is urgent or difficult ⟨We have a *situation* to deal with.⟩
3 [1]PLACE 5
4 position or place of employment : JOB

sit–up \'sit-,əp\ *n*
► an exercise done by lying on the back and rising to a sitting position

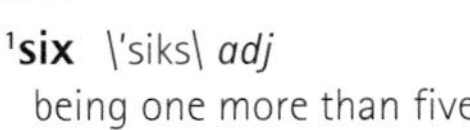

sit–up: a boy doing sit-ups

[1]**six** \'siks\ *adj*
being one more than five

[2]**six** *n*
1 one more than five : two times three : 6
2 the sixth in a set or series

six•pence \'siks-pens\ *n*
1 the sum of six pence
2 an old British coin worth six pence

six–shoot•er \'siks-,shü-tər\ *n*
a revolver having six chambers

[1]**six•teen** \sik-'stēn\ *adj*
being one more than 15

[2]**sixteen** *n*
one more than 15 : four times four : 16

[1]**six•teenth** \sik-'stēnth\ *adj*
coming right after 15th

[2]**sixteenth** *n*
number 16 in a series

[1]**sixth** \'siksth\ *adj*
coming right after fifth

[2]**sixth** *n*
1 number six in a series
2 one of six equal parts

[1]**six•ti•eth** \'sik-stē-əth\ *adj*
coming right after 59th

[2]**sixtieth** *n*
number 60 in a series

[1]**six•ty** \'sik-stē\ *adj*
being six times ten

[2]**sixty** *n*
six times ten : 60

siz•able *or* **size•able** \'sī-zə-bəl\ *adj*
fairly large

size \'sīz\ *n*
1 amount of space occupied by someone or something : how large or small someone or something is
2 the number or amount of people or things ⟨The population grows in *size.*⟩
3 one of a series of measures especially of manufactured articles (as clothing)

▶ **skeleton 1**
At birth the human skeleton has over 300 bones, some of which fuse together during growth, leaving 206 bones in the adult body. About half of these bones can be found in the hands and the feet. The largest bone in the human body is the femur, and the smallest are the group of three tiny bones in each ear.

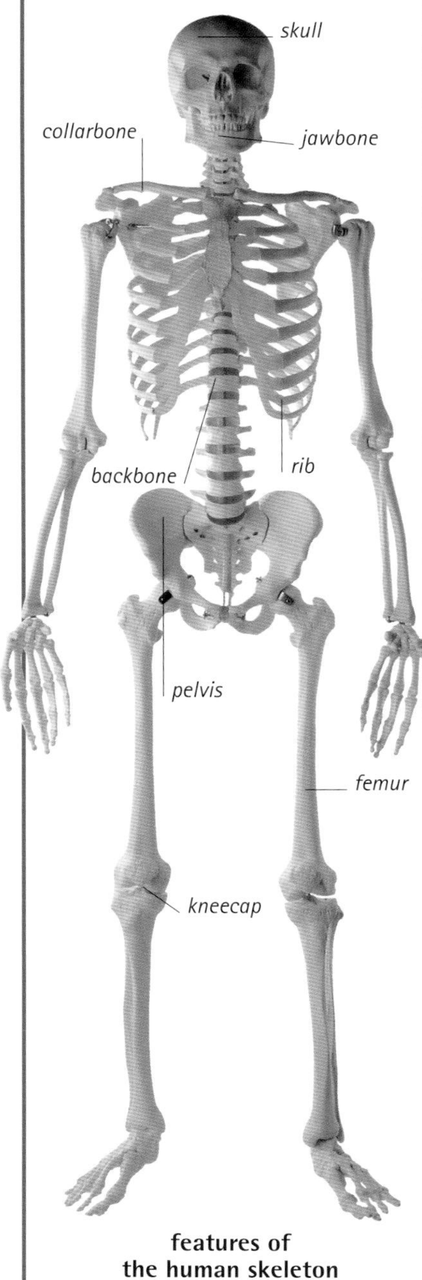

features of the human skeleton

sized \'sīzd, ˌsīzd\ *adj*
having a specified size

siz•zle \'si-zəl\ *vb* **siz•zled**; **siz•zling**
to make a hissing or sputtering noise in or as if in frying or burning

SK *abbr* Saskatchewan

[1]**skate** \'skāt\ *vb* **skat•ed**; **skat•ing**
1 to glide along on skates
2 to slide or glide along
skat•er *n*

[2]**skate** *n*
1 a metal blade fitting the sole of the shoe or a shoe with a permanently attached metal blade used for gliding on ice
2 ROLLER SKATE

[3]**skate** *n*
a flat fish related to the sharks that has large and nearly triangular fins

[1]**skate•board** \'skāt-ˌbȯrd\ *n*
a short board mounted on small wheels that is used for coasting and often for performing athletic stunts

[2]**skateboard** *vb* **skate•board•ed**; **skate•board•ing**
to ride or perform stunts on a skateboard
skate•board•er \'skāt-ˌbȯr-dər\ *n*

skein \'skān\ *n*
a quantity of yarn or thread arranged in a loose coil

skel•e•tal \'ske-lə-tᵊl\ *adj*
of or relating to a skeleton ⟨*skeletal* muscles⟩

skel•e•ton \'ske-lə-tən\ *n*
1 ◀ a firm structure or framework of a living thing that in vertebrates (as fish, birds, or humans) is typically made of bone and supports the soft tissues of the body and protects the internal organs
2 FRAMEWORK ⟨the steel *skeleton* of a building⟩

skep•tic \'skep-tik\ *n*
a person who has or shows doubt about something

skep•ti•cal \'skep-ti-kəl\ *adj*
having or showing doubt ⟨He thinks he'll make money, but I'm *skeptical*.⟩

[1]**sketch** \'skech\ *n*
1 a rough outline or drawing showing the main features of something
2 a short written work (as a story or essay)
3 a short comic performance

[2]**sketch** *vb* **sketched**; **sketch•ing**
1 to make a drawing, rough draft, or outline of
2 to describe or outline (something) briefly

sketchy \'ske-chē\ *adj* **sketch•i•er**; **sketch•i•est**
1 roughly outlined
2 lacking completeness or clearness ⟨a *sketchy* description⟩

[1]**ski** \'skē\ *n, pl* **skis**
one of a pair of narrow strips fastened one on each foot and used in gliding over snow or water

[2]**ski** *vb* **skied**; **ski•ing**
to glide on skis
ski•er *n*

[1]**skid** \'skid\ *vb* **skid•ded**; **skid•ding**
1 [1]SLIDE 1, SLIP ⟨He was tempted to *skid* across the ice.⟩
2 to slide sideways ⟨The car *skidded* off the road.⟩
3 to roll or slide on a platform of logs, planks, or rails

[2]**skid** *n*
1 a platform of logs, planks, or rails used to support a heavy object while it is being moved or stored
2 the act of sliding

skiff \'skif\ *n*
a small light rowboat

ski•ing \'skē-iŋ\ *n*
▼ the art or sport of gliding and jumping on skis

skiing: a skier enjoying skiing in the mountains of Norway

A B C D E F G H I J K L M N O P Q R S T U V W X Y Z

skill \'skil\ *n*
1 ability that comes from training or practice ⟨The band played with *skill*.⟩
2 a developed or acquired ability ⟨The *skill* of diving can be learned.⟩

skilled \'skild\ *adj*
1 having skill ⟨a *skilled* mason⟩
2 requiring skill and training ⟨a *skilled* trade⟩

skil•let \'ski-lət\ *n*
a frying pan

skill•ful \'skil-fəl\ *adj*
1 having or showing ability : EXPERT ⟨a *skillful* gardener⟩
2 done or made with ability ⟨a *skillful* dive⟩
skill•ful•ly \-fə-lē\ *adv*

skim \'skim\ *vb* **skimmed**; **skim•ming**
1 to clean a liquid of scum or floating substance : remove (as cream or film) from the top part of a liquid
2 to read or examine quickly and not thoroughly ⟨I *skimmed* the newspaper.⟩
3 to skip (a stone) along the surface of water
4 to pass swiftly or lightly over

skim milk *n*
milk from which the cream has been removed

skimp \'skimp\ *vb* **skimped**; **skimp•ing**
to give too little or just enough attention or effort to or money for

skimpy \'skim-pē\ *adj* **skimp•i•er**; **skimp•i•est**
very small in size or amount : SCANTY

[1]**skin** \'skin\ *n*
1 the usually flexible outer layer of an animal body that in vertebrate animals is made up of two layers of cells forming an inner dermis and an outer epidermis
2 the hide of an animal
3 an outer or surface layer ⟨potato *skins*⟩
skin•less \-ləs\ *adj*
skinned \'skind\ *adj*

[2]**skin** *vb* **skinned**; **skin•ning**
1 to strip, scrape, or rub off the skin of ⟨I *skinned* my knee.⟩
2 to remove an outer layer from (as by peeling)

skin–dive \'skin-,dīv\ *vb* **skin–dived**; **skin–div•ing**
to swim below the surface of water with a face mask and sometimes a portable breathing device
skin diver *n*

skin•ny \'ski-nē\ *adj* **skin•ni•er**; **skin•ni•est**
very thin ⟨*skinny* legs⟩
synonyms see LEAN

[1]**skip** \'skip\ *vb* **skipped**; **skip•ping**
1 to move by taking short light steps and jumps
2 to pass over or omit an item, space, or step ⟨I think you *skipped* a page.⟩
3 to leap over lightly and nimbly
4 to fail to attend or do ⟨She *skipped* the meeting.⟩
5 to bound or cause to bound off one point after another : SKIM ⟨We were *skipping* stones on the pond.⟩

[2]**skip** *n*
1 a light bounding step
2 a way of moving by hops and steps

skip•per \'ski-pər\ *n*
the master of a ship and especially of a fishing, trading, or pleasure boat

[1]**skir•mish** \'skər-mish\ *n*
1 a minor fight in war
2 a minor argument

[2]**skirmish** *vb* **skir•mished**; **skir•mish•ing**
to take part in a fight or dispute

[1]**skirt** \'skərt\ *n*
1 a piece of clothing or part of a piece of clothing worn by women or girls that hangs from the waist down
2 a part or attachment serving as a rim, border, or edging

[2]**skirt** *vb* **skirt•ed**; **skirt•ing**
1 [2]BORDER 2
2 to go or pass around or about the outer edge of
3 to avoid for fear of difficulty ⟨She *skirted* the issue.⟩

skit \'skit\ *n*
a brief sketch in play form

skit•ter \'ski-tər\ *vb* **skit•tered**; **skit•ter•ing**
to glide or skip lightly or quickly

skit•tish \'ski-tish\ *adj*
easily frightened ⟨a *skittish* horse⟩

skulk \'skəlk\ *vb* **skulked**; **skulk•ing**
to hide or move in a sly or sneaking way ⟨The thief *skulked* behind a fence.⟩

skull \'skəl\ *n*
the case of bone or cartilage that forms the skeleton of the head and face, encloses the brain, and supports the jaws

skunk \'skəŋk\ *n*
a North American animal related to the weasels that has coarse black-and-white fur and can squirt out a fluid with a very unpleasant smell

sky \'skī\ *n, pl* **skies**
1 the stretch of space over the earth
2 [1]WEATHER, CLIMATE ⟨sunny *skies*⟩

► **Word History** English owes a number of words to Old Norse, the language of the Viking raiders and settlers who came to England in the eighth to tenth centuries. The word *sky*, for example, though it dates to the Middle Ages, has its nearest relatives in modern Scandinavian languages (Danish and Swedish *sky*, "cloud") rather than in Old English. Other common words borrowed from Old Norse are *crawl, egg, kid, leg, root, seem, take, wing*, and *wrong*.

sky•div•ing \'skī-,dī-viŋ\ *n*
the sport of jumping from an airplane using a parachute

sky•lark \'skī-,lärk\ *n*
a European lark noted for its song

sky•light \'skī-,līt\ *n*
a window or group of windows in a roof or ceiling

sky•line \'skī-,līn\ *n*
1 the line where earth and sky seem to meet : HORIZON
2 ◄ an outline against the sky ⟨Tall buildings form the *skyline* of the city.⟩

sky•scrap•er \'skī-,skrā-pər\ *n*
a very tall building

slab \'slab\ *n*
a flat thick piece or slice ⟨a *slab* of stone⟩

skyline 2: the city skyline in Sydney \'sid-nē\, Australia

[1]slack \'slak\ *adj*
1 CARELESS 1, NEGLIGENT
2 not energetic : SLOW ⟨a *slack* pace⟩
3 not tight or firm ⟨a *slack* rope⟩ ⟨a *slack* jaw⟩
4 not busy or active ⟨Business is *slack*.⟩

[2]slack *vb* **slacked**; **slack•ing**
1 to make or become looser, slower, or less energetic
2 to avoid work
slack•er \'sla-kər\ *n*

[3]slack *n*
1 a part (as of a rope or sail) that hangs loose without strain
2 **slacks** *pl* dressy pants
3 a portion (as of work or resources) that is required but lacking ⟨He was hired to take up the *slack*.⟩
4 additional relief from pressure
Hint: This sense is usually used with *cut*. ⟨Can you cut me some *slack* on the schedule?⟩

slack•en \'sla-kən\ *vb* **slack•ened**; **slack•en•ing**
1 to make slower or less energetic ⟨The wind *slackened*.⟩
2 to make less tight or firm ⟨She *slackened* the reins.⟩

slag \'slag\ *n*
the waste left after the melting of ores and the separation of the metal from them

slain *past participle of* SLAY

slake \'slāk\ *vb* **slaked**; **slak•ing**
QUENCH 1 ⟨A drink of water *slaked* my thirst.⟩

[1]slam \'slam\ *vb* **slammed**; **slam•ming**
1 to shut with noisy force : BANG ⟨Don't *slam* the door.⟩
2 to strike or beat hard ⟨My sled *slammed* into a tree.⟩
3 to put or place with force ⟨He *slammed* down the money.⟩
4 to criticize harshly

[2]slam *n*
1 a severe blow ⟨The batter gave the ball a *slam*.⟩
2 the noise made by a violent act of closing : BANG ⟨She closed the book with a *slam*.⟩

[1]slan•der \'slan-dər\ *vb* **slan•dered**; **slan•der•ing**
to make a false and damaging statement against

[2]slander *n*
a false statement that damages another person's reputation

slang \'slaŋ\ *n*
very informal words used by a group of people

[1]slant \'slant\ *vb* **slant•ed**; **slant•ing**
to turn or incline diagonally from a straight line or level : SLOPE

[2]slant *n*
a direction, line, or surface that is not level or straight up and down : SLOPE

[3]slant *adj*
not level or straight up and down

slant•wise \'slant-,wīz\ *adv or adj*
at a slant : in a slanting position ⟨The boards were placed *slantwise*.⟩

[1]slap \'slap\ *vb* **slapped**; **slap•ping**
1 to strike with or as if with the open hand
2 to make a sound like that of slapping ⟨Waves *slap* on the rocky shore.⟩
3 to put, place, or throw with careless haste or force ⟨She *slapped* her report on the desk.⟩

[2]slap *n*
1 a quick sharp blow especially with the open hand
2 a noise like that made by a blow with the open hand ⟨the *slap* of waves⟩

[1]slash \'slash\ *vb* **slashed**; **slash•ing**
1 to cut or strike at with sweeping blows
2 to reduce sharply ⟨The store is *slashing* prices.⟩

[2]slash *n*
1 an act of cutting or striking with sweeping strokes
2 a long cut or slit made with sweeping blows

slat \'slat\ *n*
a thin narrow strip of wood, plastic, or metal

slate \'slāt\ *n*
1 a fine-grained usually bluish gray rock that splits into thin layers or plates and is used mostly for roofing and blackboards
2 a framed piece of slate used to write on

[1]slaugh•ter \'slȯ-tər\ *n*
1 the act of killing
2 the act of killing and preparing animals for food
3 destruction of many lives especially in battle

[2]slaughter *vb* **slaugh•tered**; **slaugh•ter•ing**
1 [2]BUTCHER 1
2 [2]MASSACRE

slaugh•ter•house \'slȯ-tər-,hau̇s\ *n*, *pl* **slaugh•ter•hous•es** \-,hau̇-zəz\
a building where animals are killed and prepared for food

Slav \'släv, 'slav\ *n*
a native speaker of a Slavic language

[1]slave \'slāv\ *n*
1 a person who is owned by another person and can be sold at the owner's will
2 a person who is strongly influenced and controlled by something ⟨a *slave* to fashion⟩
3 DRUDGE

[2]slave *vb* **slaved**; **slav•ing**
to work very hard, for long hours, or under difficult conditions

slave•hold•er \'slāv-,hōl-dər\ *n*
an owner of slaves

slav•ery \'slā-və-rē, 'slāv-rē\ *n*
1 the state of being owned by another person : BONDAGE
2 the custom or practice of owning slaves
3 hard tiring labor : DRUDGERY

Slav•ic \'slä-vik, 'sla-\ *adj*
of, relating to, or characteristic of the Slavs or their languages

slav•ish \'slā-vish\ *adj*
following, copying, or accepting something or someone without questioning ⟨*slavish* imitators⟩

slay \'slā\ *vb* **slew** \'slü\; **slain** \'slān\; **slay•ing**
[1]KILL 1
slay•er *n*

[1]sled \'sled\ *n*
1 ▼ a vehicle on runners for carrying loads especially over snow
2 a small vehicle used mostly by children for sliding on snow and ice

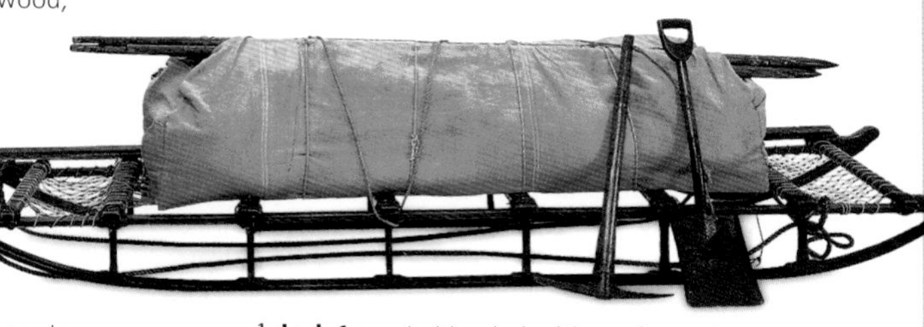
[1]sled 1: a sled loaded with equipment, as used in the early 1900s by Arctic explorers

[2]sled *vb* **sled•ded**; **sled•ding**
to ride or carry on a sled

sledge \'slej\ *n*
a strong heavy sled

sledge•ham•mer \'slej-,ha-mər\ *n*
a large heavy hammer usually used with both hands

sleek \'slēk\ *adj* **sleek•er**; **sleek•est**
1 smooth and glossy as if polished ⟨*sleek* dark hair⟩
2 having a healthy well-groomed look ⟨*sleek* cattle⟩
3 straight and smooth in design or shape ⟨a *sleek* jet⟩
4 stylish and elegant ⟨a *sleek* actress⟩

[1]sleep \'slēp\ *vb* **slept** \'slept\; **sleep•ing**
to rest with eyes closed in a temporary state of inactivity : be or lie in a state of sleep ⟨The baby is *sleeping*.⟩

[2]sleep *n*
1 a natural temporary state of rest during which an individual becomes physically inactive and unaware of the surrounding environment and many bodily functions (as breathing) slow
2 an inactive state (as hibernation) like true sleep
3 DEATH 3 ⟨The sick pet was put to *sleep.*⟩
sleep•less \'slēp-ləs\ *adj*
sleep•less•ness *n*

sleep•er \'slē-pər\ *n*
1 someone that sleeps ⟨I'm a light *sleeper.*⟩
2 a railroad car with berths for sleeping

sleeping bag *n*
a large fabric bag that is warmly lined for sleeping outdoors or in a camp or tent

sleep•over \'slēp-ō-vər\ *n*
an overnight stay at another's home

sleep•walk \'slēp-,wȯk\ *vb* **sleep•walked**; **sleep•walk•ing**
to walk about while asleep
sleep•walk•er \-,wȯ-kər\ *n*

sleepy \'slē-pē\ *adj* **sleep•i•er**; **sleep•i•est**
1 ready to fall asleep : DROWSY
2 not active, noisy, or busy ⟨a *sleepy* town⟩
sleep•i•ness *n*

[1]sleet \'slēt\ *n*
frozen or partly frozen rain

[2]sleet *vb* **sleet•ed**; **sleet•ing**
to shower sleet

sleeve \'slēv\ *n*
1 the part of a piece of clothing covering the arm
2 a part that fits over or around something like a sleeve
sleeved \'slēvd\ *adj*
sleeve•less \'slēv-ləs\ *adj*
up someone's sleeve held secretly in reserve ⟨Watch him. He's got something *up his sleeve.*⟩

sleigh \'slā\ *n*
▼ an open usually horse-drawn vehicle with runners for use on snow or ice

sleight of hand \,slī-təv-'hand\ *n*
skill and quickness in the use of the hands especially in doing magic tricks

slen•der \'slen-dər\ *adj* **slen•der•er**; **slen•der•est**
1 gracefully thin
2 narrow for its height or length ⟨a *slender* pole⟩ ⟨a *slender* rope⟩
3 very little ⟨a *slender* income⟩

slept *past and past participle of* SLEEP

slew *past of* SLAY

[1]slice \'slīs\ *vb* **sliced**; **slic•ing**
1 to cut with or as if with a knife
2 to cut into thin flat pieces ⟨I *sliced* a tomato.⟩

[2]slice *n*
a thin flat piece cut from something ⟨a *slice* of bread⟩

[1]slick \'slik\ *vb* **slicked**; **slick•ing**
to make sleek or smooth

[2]slick *adj*
1 having a smooth surface : SLIPPERY ⟨*slick* pavement⟩
2 TRICKY 2 ⟨a *slick* salesman⟩
3 having skill and cleverness ⟨She made some *slick* moves during the game.⟩

slick•er \'sli-kər\ *n*
a long loose raincoat

[1]slide \'slīd\ *vb* **slid** \'slid\; **slid•ing** \'slī-diŋ\
1 to move or cause to move smoothly over a surface : GLIDE ⟨Skaters *slid* over the ice.⟩
2 to move or pass smoothly and without much effort ⟨She *slid* into the seat.⟩
3 to get gradually worse over time ⟨Her grades began to *slide.*⟩

[2]slide *n*
1 the act or motion of moving smoothly over a surface
2 a movement to a lower or worse condition ⟨a *slide* in business⟩
3 a surface down which a person or thing slides
4 a loosened mass that moves swiftly : AVALANCHE
5 a glass or plastic plate for holding an object to be examined under a microscope
6 ▶ a transparent picture that can be projected on a screen
7 something that operates or adjusts by sliding

[2]slide 6

[1]slight \'slīt\ *adj* **slight•er**; **slight•est**
1 small of its kind or in amount ⟨a *slight* smell of gas⟩
2 thin and delicate ⟨a trim *slight* figure⟩
3 not important : TRIVIAL ⟨a *slight* wound⟩
4 FLIMSY, FRAIL
slight•ly *adv*

[2]slight *vb* **slight•ed**; **slight•ing**
to treat without proper respect or courtesy ⟨I didn't mean to *slight* her.⟩

[3]slight *n*
1 an act or an instance of treating without proper respect or courtesy
2 an instance of being treated without proper respect or courtesy

[1]slim \'slim\ *adj* **slim•mer**; **slim•mest**
1 SLENDER 1
2 very small ⟨a *slim* chance⟩

[2]slim *vb* **slimmed**; **slim•ming**
to make or become slender

slime \'slīm\ *n*
1 soft slippery mud
2 a soft slippery material (as on the skin of a slug or catfish)

slimy \'slī-mē\ *adj* **slim•i•er**; **slim•i•est**
1 having a slippery feel or look
2 covered with slime ⟨*slimy* rocks⟩

[1]sling \'sliŋ\ *vb* **slung** \'sləŋ\; **sling•ing**
1 to throw with a sudden sweeping motion : FLING ⟨She *slung* her backpack over her shoulder.⟩
2 to hurl with a sling

[2]sling *n*
1 a device (as a short strap with a string attached at each end) for hurling stones
2 a device (as a rope or chain) by which something is lifted or carried
3 a bandage hanging from the neck to hold up the arm or hand

[3]sling *vb* **slung** \'sləŋ\; **sling•ing**
1 to put in or move or support with a sling
2 to hang from two points ⟨*sling* a hammock⟩

sling•shot \'sliŋ-,shät\ *n*
a forked stick with an elastic band attached for shooting small stones

driver's seat
dashboard
attachment for hitching a horse to the sleigh
runner

sleigh: a traditional sleigh from Russia

slink \'sliŋk\ *vb* **slunk** \'sləŋk\; **slink•ing**
to move or go by or as if by creeping especially so as not to be noticed (as in fear or shame)

[1]slip \'slip\ *vb* **slipped**; **slip•ping**
1 to move easily and smoothly ⟨He *slipped* the ring on his finger.⟩
2 to slide into or out of place or away from a support ⟨Try to *slip* the bolt and open the door.⟩ ⟨The book *slipped* out of my hand.⟩
3 to slide on a slippery surface so as to lose balance ⟨I *slipped* on the wet floor.⟩
4 to pass or let pass or escape without being noted, used, or done ⟨Time *slipped* by.⟩
5 to move into or out of a place without being noticed ⟨She *slipped* from the room.⟩
6 to escape the attention or memory of ⟨It just *slipped* my mind.⟩
7 to put on or take off a piece of clothing quickly and easily ⟨The child *slipped* out of his coat.⟩
8 to make or become known by mistake
9 to go from one state or condition to an often worse one ⟨Your grades are *slipping*.⟩
10 to get away from ⟨One of the robbers *slipped* the police.⟩
slip up to make a mistake

[2]slip *n*
1 the act or an instance of sliding down or out of place ⟨a *slip* on the ice⟩
2 a secret or quick departure or escape ⟨Their prisoner gave them the *slip*.⟩
3 a small mistake : BLUNDER
4 a fall from some level or standard : DECLINE ⟨a *slip* in stock prices⟩
5 a place for a ship between two piers
6 an undergarment for women made in dress or skirt length

[3]slip *n*
1 a usually small piece of paper and especially one used for some record ⟨a permission *slip*⟩
2 a long narrow piece of material

slip•cov•er \'slip-,kə-vər\ *n*
a cover (as for a sofa or chair)

slip•knot \'slip-,nät\ *n*
a knot made by tying the end of a line around the line itself to form a loop so that the size of the loop may be changed by slipping the knot

slip•per \'sli-pər\ *n*
a light low shoe that is easily slipped on the foot and is made to be worn indoors

slip•pery \'sli-pə-rē\ *adj* **slip•per•i•er**; **slip•per•i•est**
1 having a surface smooth or wet enough to make holding onto or moving or standing on difficult ⟨a *slippery* fish⟩ ⟨A man fell on the *slippery* walk.⟩
2 not to be trusted : TRICKY ⟨a *slippery* politician⟩

slip•shod \'slip-'shäd\ *adj*
very careless ⟨Their work was *slipshod*.⟩

[1]slit \'slit\ *n*
a long narrow cut or opening

[2]slit *vb* **slit**; **slit•ting**
to make a long narrow cut in : SLASH

slith•er \'sli-thər\ *vb* **slith•ered**; **slith•er•ing**
[1]GLIDE ⟨The snake *slithers* along.⟩

slith•ery \'sli-thə-rē\ *adj*
having a slippery surface, texture, or quality

[1]sliv•er \'sli-vər\ *n*
1 a long slender piece of something cut or torn off : SPLINTER
2 a small amount ⟨a *sliver* of moon⟩ ⟨a *sliver* of doubt⟩

[2]sliver *vb* **sliv•ered**; **sliv•er•ing**
to cut or form into long slender pieces

slob \'släb\ *n*
1 a sloppy or lazy person
2 an ordinary person ⟨The poor *slob* didn't deserve such bad luck.⟩

[1]slob•ber \'slä-bər\ *vb* **slob•bered**; **slob•ber•ing**
to let saliva or liquid dribble from the mouth

[2]slobber *n*
dripping saliva

slo•gan \'slō-gən\ *n*
a word or phrase used by a party, a group, or a business to attract attention

sloop \'slüp\ *n*
a sailing boat with one mast and a fore-and-aft mainsail and jib

[1]slop \'släp\ *n*
1 thin tasteless drink or liquid food
2 food waste or gruel fed to animals
3 body waste
4 soft mud

[2]slop *vb* **slopped**; **slop•ping**
1 to spill or spill something on or over ⟨The toddler *slopped* gravy on the table.⟩
2 to feed slop to ⟨The farmer *slopped* the pigs.⟩

[1]slope \'slōp\ *n*
1 a piece of slanting ground (as a hillside) ⟨a steep *slope*⟩
2 upward or downward slant ⟨the *slope* of a roof⟩

[2]slope *vb* **sloped**; **slop•ing**
to take a slanting direction ⟨The bank *slopes* down to the river.⟩

slop•py \'slä-pē\ *adj* **slop•pi•er**; **slop•pi•est**
1 careless in work or in appearance
2 wet enough to spatter easily : containing a lot of moisture ⟨*sloppy* mud⟩

slosh \'släsh\ *vb* **sloshed**; **slosh•ing**
1 to walk with trouble through water, mud, or slush
2 to move with a splashing motion

[1]slot \'slät\ *n*
a narrow opening, groove, or passage

[2]slot *vb* **slot•ted**; **slot•ting**
to cut a narrow opening, groove, or passage in

sloth \'slȯth, 'slōth\ *n*
1 the quality or state of being lazy
2 ▼ an animal of Central and South America that hangs with its back downward and moves slowly along the branches of trees on whose leaves, twigs, and fruits it feeds

sloth 2: a three-toed sloth

[1]slouch \'slau̇ch\ *n*
1 a lazy worthless person ⟨He's no *slouch* as a worker.⟩
2 a way of standing, sitting, or walking with the head and shoulders bent forward

[2]slouch *vb* **slouched**; **slouch•ing**
to walk, stand, or sit lazily with the head and shoulders bent forward

[1]sluice 1: a sluice in a canal

slough \'slü, 'slau̇\ *n*
a wet marshy or muddy place
slov•en•ly \'slə-vən-lē\ *adj*
1 personally untidy
2 very careless
[1]slow \'slō\ *adj* **slow•er; slow•est**
1 moving, flowing, or going at less than the usual speed 〈*slow* music〉 〈Traffic was *slow.*〉
2 taking more time than is expected or desired 〈We had a *slow* start on the project.〉
3 not as smart or as quick to understand as most people
4 not active 〈Business was *slow.*〉
5 indicating less than is correct 〈My watch is five minutes *slow.*〉
6 not easily aroused or excited 〈Grandmother is *slow* to anger.〉
slow•ly *adv*
slow•ness *n*
[2]slow *vb* **slowed; slow•ing**
to go or make go less than the usual speed 〈The car *slowed* around the corner.〉
[3]slow *adv* **slow•er; slow•est**
in a slow way 〈Can you talk *slower*?〉
slow•poke \'slō-,pōk\ *n*
a very slow person
sludge \'sləj\ *n*
a soft muddy mass resulting from sewage treatment
[1]slug \'sləg\ *n*
a wormlike animal living mostly on land that is a mollusk related to the snails but that has an undeveloped shell or none at all
[2]slug *n*
1 BULLET
2 a metal disk often used in place of a coin
[3]slug *n*
a hard blow especially with the fist
[4]slug *vb* **slugged; slug•ging**
to hit hard with the fist or with a bat
slug•gard \'slə-gərd\ *n*
a lazy person
slug•ger \'slə-gər\ *n*
a boxer or baseball batter who hits hard
slug•gish \'slə-gish\ *adj*
slow in movement or reaction
slug•gish•ly *adv*
[1]sluice \'slüs\ *n*
1 ▲ a man-made channel for water with a gate for controlling its flow or changing its direction
2 a device for controlling the flow of water
3 a sloping trough for washing ore or for floating logs
[2]sluice *vb* **sluiced; sluic•ing**
1 to wash in a stream of water running through a sluice
2 [3]FLUSH 2, DRENCH
slum \'sləm\ *n*
a very poor crowded dirty section especially of a city
[1]slum•ber \'sləm-bər\ *vb* **slum•bered; slum•ber•ing**
[1]SLEEP 1
[2]slumber *n*
[2]SLEEP 1
[1]slump \'sləmp\ *vb* **slumped; slump•ing**
1 to drop or slide down suddenly : COLLAPSE 〈The tired woman *slumped* into a chair.〉
2 [2]SLOUCH 〈Don't *slump* when you walk.〉
3 to drop sharply 〈Sales *slumped.*〉
[2]slump *n*
a big or continued drop especially in prices, business, or performance
slung *past and past participle of* SLING
slunk *past and past participle of* SLINK
[1]slur \'slər\ *n*
an insulting remark
[2]slur *vb* **slurred; slur•ring**
to speak in a way that is difficult to understand
[3]slur *n*
a way of talking that is difficult to understand
[1]slurp \'slərp\ *vb* **slurped; slurp•ing**
to eat or drink noisily or with a sucking sound
[2]slurp *n*
a sucking sound made while eating and drinking
slush \'sləsh\ *n*
partly melted snow
slushy \'slə-shē\ *adj* **slush•i•er; slush•i•est**
covered with or resembling partly melted snow 〈*slushy* roads〉
sly \'slī\ *adj* **sli•er** *or* **sly•er; sli•est** *or* **sly•est**
1 both clever and tricky
2 tending to keep secrets and hide intentions
3 MISCHIEVOUS 2
sly•ly *adv*
sly•ness *n*
on the sly so as not to be seen or caught : SECRETLY
[1]smack \'smak\ *vb* **smacked; smack•ing**
1 to make or give a noisy slap
2 to close and open the lips noisily especially in eating
3 to kiss usually loudly or hard
[2]smack *n*
1 a noisy slap or blow
2 a quick sharp noise made by the lips (as in enjoyment of some taste)
3 a loud kiss
[3]smack *adv*
in a square and sharp manner : DIRECTLY
[4]smack *vb* **smacked; smacking**
to have a flavor, trace, or suggestion 〈This pizza *smacks* of garlic.〉
[5]smack *n*
a slight taste, trace, or touch of something
[1]small \'smȯl\ *adj* **small•er; small•est**
1 little in size 〈a *small* house〉
2 few in numbers or members 〈a *small* crowd〉
3 little in amount 〈a *small* supply〉
4 very young 〈a *small* child〉
5 not very much 〈*small* success〉
6 UNIMPORTANT 〈There are some *small* details to work out.〉
7 operating on a limited scale 〈*small* car dealers〉
8 very soft and quiet 〈a *small* voice〉 〈a *small* cry〉
9 not generous : MEAN
10 made up of units of little worth 〈*small* change〉
11 [1]HUMBLE 3, MODEST 〈She came from a *small* beginning.〉

12 lowered in pride ⟨After fumbling the ball, I felt pretty *small.*⟩
13 being letters that are not capitals
small•ness *n*

[2]small *n*
a part smaller and usually narrower than the rest ⟨the *small* of the back⟩

small intestine *n*
the long narrow upper part of the intestine in which food is mostly digested and from which digested food is absorbed into the body

small•pox \'smȯl-,päks\ *n*
a sometimes deadly disease in which fever and skin rash occur and which is believed to have been wiped out worldwide by vaccination

[1]smart \'smärt\ *adj* **smart•er; smart•est**
1 quick to learn or do : BRIGHT ⟨*smart* students⟩
2 showing wisdom ⟨a *smart* decision⟩
3 FRESH 8
4 stylish and fashionable ⟨a *smart* dresser⟩
5 BRISK 1 ⟨I was walking at a *smart* pace.⟩
6 controlled by computers and able to do things that seem intelligent ⟨a *smart* machine⟩
smart•ly *adv*
smart•ness *n*

[2]smart *vb* **smart•ed; smart•ing**
1 to cause or feel a sharp stinging pain ⟨My eyes were *smarting* from the smoke.⟩
2 to be upset about something

[3]smart *n*
a stinging pain usually in one spot

smart al•eck \'smärt-,a-lik\ *n*
a person who likes to show off in a clever but rude or annoying way

smart•phone \'smärt-,fōn\ *n*
a cell phone that includes additional functions (as e-mail or an Internet browser)

[1]smash \'smash\ *n*
1 a violent blow
2 the action or sound of shattering or hitting violently ⟨He broke the plate with a *smash.*⟩
3 a striking success

[2]smash *vb* **smashed; smash•ing**
1 to break in pieces : SHATTER
2 to hit or move violently ⟨The ball *smashed* through a window.⟩ ⟨He *smashed* a ball over the fence.⟩
3 to destroy completely ⟨Our best swimmer *smashed* the state record.⟩ ⟨He *smashed* the car.⟩

[1]smear \'smir\ *vb* **smeared; smear•ing**
1 to spread or soil with something oily or sticky ⟨The window was *smeared* with fingerprints.⟩
2 to spread over a surface ⟨Her makeup *smeared.*⟩
3 to harm the reputation of (someone) with false statements

[2]smear *n*
a spot or streak made by or as if by an oily or sticky substance : SMUDGE

[1]smell \'smel\ *vb* **smelled** \'smeld\ *or* **smelt** \'smelt\; **smell•ing**
1 to become aware of the odor of by means of special cells located in the nose ⟨Stop and *smell* the flowers.⟩
2 to notice (something) because of its smell ⟨I think I *smell* gas.⟩
3 to have or give off an odor ⟨My socks *smell* sweaty.⟩
4 to sense as if by smelling ⟨I *smell* trouble.⟩

[2]smell *n*
1 the sense by which a person or animal becomes aware of an odor
2 the sensation gotten through the sense of smell : ODOR, SCENT ⟨the *smell* of an onion⟩

smelly \'sme-lē\ *adj* **smel•li•er; smel•li•est**
having an odor and especially a bad odor

[1]smelt \'smelt\ *n, pl* **smelts** *or* **smelt**
▼ a small silvery fish that is sometimes used for food

[1]smelt

[2]smelt *vb* **smelt•ed; smelt•ing**
to melt (as ore) in order to separate the metal : REFINE

[1]smile \'smīl\ *vb* **smiled; smil•ing**
1 make the corners of the mouth turn up in an expression of amusement or pleasure
2 to look with amusement or pleasure ⟨She *smiled* at the picture.⟩
3 to express by a smile ⟨Both parents *smiled* approval.⟩

[2]smile *n*
▶ an expression in which the corners of the mouth turn upward especially to show amusement or pleasure

smirk \'smərk\ *vb* **smirked; smirk•ing**
to smile in an insincere manner
smirk *n*

smite \'smīt\ *vb* **smote** \'smōt\; **smit•ten** \'smi-tᵊn\; **smit•ing** \'smī-tiŋ\
1 to strike hard especially with the hand or a weapon
2 to kill or injure

smith \'smith\ *n*
1 a worker in metals
2 BLACKSMITH

smith•er•eens \,smi-t͟hə-'rēnz\ *n pl*
small broken pieces ⟨The target was blown to *smithereens.*⟩

smithy \'smi-thē\ *n, pl* **smith•ies**
the workshop of someone who works in metals and especially of a blacksmith

smock \'smäk\ *n*
a loose outer garment worn especially for protection of clothing ⟨an artist's *smock*⟩

smog \'smäg\ *n*
a fog made heavier and thicker by the action of sunlight on polluted air

[1]smoke \'smōk\ *n*
1 the gas given off by burning materials (as coal, wood, or tobacco) made visible by particles of carbon floating in it
2 the act of drawing in and blowing out the fumes of burning tobacco

[2]smoke *vb* **smoked; smok•ing**
1 to give out smoke ⟨The fire was still *smoking.*⟩
2 to draw in and blow out the fumes of burning tobacco (as in a cigarette)
3 to expose (as meat) to the fumes of burning materials to give flavor and keep from spoiling
smok•er *n*

smoke de•tec•tor \-di-'tek-tər\ *n*
a device that sounds an alarm automatically when it detects smoke

smoke•house \'smōk-,hau̇s\ *n, pl* **smoke•hous•es** \-,hau̇-zəz\
a building where meat or fish is smoked

smoke•stack \'smōk-,stak\ *n*
a large chimney or a pipe for carrying away smoke (as on a factory or ship)

smoky \'smō-kē\ *adj* **smok•i•er; smok•i•est**
1 giving off smoke especially in large amounts ⟨*smoky* stoves⟩
2 filled with or darkened by smoke ⟨a *smoky* room⟩
3 having a flavor, taste, or appearance of smoke

[2]smile:
a girl with a smile on her face

smol•der *or* **smoul•der** *vb* **smol•dered** *or* **smoul•dered; smol•der•ing** *or* **smoul•der•ing**
1 to burn slowly usually with smoke and without flame ⟨A fire was *smoldering.*⟩
2 to burn inwardly ⟨Her anger *smoldered.*⟩

[1]snake 1

There are over 2,500 species of snakes. Some snakes, such as the garter snake, eat their prey alive. Others kill or paralyze their prey before swalllowing. The diamondback rattlesnake and monocled cobra inject their prey with venom while the corn snake and Pacific island boa coil tightly around prey to cause death by suffocation.

examples of snakes

sidewinder snakes \ˈsīd-ˌwīn-dər\ are found in the southwestern US and move sideways across hot desert sands in a series of S-shaped curves

features of a diamondback rattlesnake

scaly skin

rattle

forked tongue

copperhead snakes use heat-sensitive pits on each side of the face to locate mice

milk snakes are harmless but have a color pattern similar to the deadly coral snakes

[1]smooth \ˈsmüth\ *adj* **smooth•er; smooth•est**
1 not rough or uneven in surface ⟨a *smooth* board⟩
2 not hairy ⟨a *smooth* face⟩
3 free from difficulties or things in the way ⟨a *smooth* path⟩ ⟨a *smooth* journey⟩
4 moving or progressing without breaks, sudden changes, or shifts ⟨a *smooth* stream⟩ ⟨*smooth* speech⟩
5 appearing to be friendly and flattering without really meaning it ⟨a *smooth* talker⟩
smooth•ly *adv*
smooth•ness *n*

[2]smooth *vb* **smoothed; smooth•ing**
1 to remove bumps, lumps, or wrinkles : make smooth
2 to free from trouble or difficulty ⟨Pioneers *smoothed* the way for us.⟩

smote *past of* SMITE

smoth•er \ˈsmə-thər\ *vb* **smoth•ered; smoth•er•ing**
1 to kill or injure by keeping from getting air or by exposing to smoke or fumes : SUFFOCATE
2 to become suffocated
3 to keep from growing or developing by or as if by covering ⟨*smother* a fire⟩ ⟨*smothering* hopes⟩
4 to keep from happening : SUPPRESS ⟨I tried to *smother* a yawn.⟩
5 to cover thickly ⟨The salad was *smothered* with dressing.⟩

[1]smudge \ˈsməj\ *n*
1 a blurred spot or streak : SMEAR
2 a smoky fire (as to drive away mosquitoes)

[2]smudge *vb* **smudged; smudg•ing**
to soil or blur by rubbing or smearing

smug \ˈsməg\ *adj* **smug•ger; smug•gest**
showing a superior attitude
smug•ly *adv*

smug•gle \ˈsmə-gəl\ *vb* **smug•gled; smug•gling**
1 to export or import secretly and unlawfully ⟨They *smuggled* stolen goods.⟩
2 to take or bring secretly
smug•gler \ˈsmə-glər\ *n*

snail

smut \ˈsmət\ *n*
1 something (as a particle of soot) that soils or blackens
2 a destructive disease of plants (as cereal grasses) that is caused by a fungus
3 a fungus that causes smut

[1]snack \ˈsnak\ *n*
a small amount of food eaten between meals

[2]snack *vb* **snacked; snack•ing**
to eat a small amount of food between meals

[1]snag \ˈsnag\ *n*
1 a rough or broken part sticking out from something
2 an unexpected difficulty ⟨Our plan hit a *snag.*⟩
3 a stump or stub of a tree branch especially when hidden under water

[2]snag *vb* **snagged; snag•ging**
1 to catch or damage on or as if on a part sticking up or out ⟨He *snagged* his sleeve on a nail.⟩
2 to catch or capture by or as if by reaching out quickly and grabbing

snail \ˈsnāl\ *n*
◀ a small slow-moving mollusk that has a spiral shell into which it can draw itself for safety and that can live either on land or in water

monocled cobras \'män-i-kəld\ from Thailand spread out bones in their neck to form a hood when threatened

corn snakes are common in the southeastern US, and eat mice

common garter snakes are widespread and live in many different habitats

Pacific island boas feed chiefly on frogs, lizards, and rodents

[1]**snake** \'snāk\ *n*
1 ▲ a limbless reptile that has a long body with scales and feeds usually on large insects or small animals and birds
2 a person who is mean or can't be trusted

[2]**snake** *vb* **snaked**; **snak•ing**
to crawl, wind, or move like a snake ⟨The parade *snaked* its way along Main Street.⟩

snaky \'snā-kē\ *adj* **snak•i•er**; **snak•i•est**
1 of or like a snake
2 full of snakes

[1]**snap** \'snap\ *vb* **snapped**; **snap•ping**
1 to break or break apart suddenly and often with a cracking noise ⟨The branch *snapped.*⟩
2 to grasp or grasp at something suddenly with the mouth or teeth
3 to speak or utter sharply or irritably ⟨*snap* out a command⟩
4 to make or cause to make a sharp or crackling sound ⟨*snap* a whip⟩
5 to close or fit in place with a quick movement ⟨The lid *snapped* shut.⟩
6 to put into or remove from a position suddenly or with a cracking sound ⟨She *snapped* on the light.⟩
7 to act or be acted on with energy ⟨The soldier *snapped* to attention.⟩
8 to grasp at something eagerly ⟨I *snapped* at the chance.⟩
9 to get, take, or buy at once ⟨Customers were hoping to *snap* up a bargain.⟩
10 to close by means of snaps or fasteners
11 to take a snapshot of
12 to make a short sharp sound by quickly moving the middle finger against the thumb

[2]**snap** *n*
1 a sudden short sharp sound
2 an act of moving the middle finger against the thumb to make a short sharp sound
3 something that is easy and presents no problems ⟨That job is a *snap.*⟩
4 a sudden change in weather ⟨a cold *snap*⟩
5 a catch or fastening that closes or locks with a click ⟨the *snap* on a purse⟩
6 SNAPSHOT
7 a short amount of time

[3]**snap** *adj*
1 made suddenly or without careful thought ⟨a *snap* decision⟩
2 closing with a click or by means of a device that snaps ⟨a *snap* lock⟩
3 very easy

snap•drag•on \'snap-,dra-gən\ *n*
a garden plant with stalks of usually white, pink, red, or yellow flowers with two lips

snap•per \'sna-pər\ *n*
1 SNAPPING TURTLE
2 an active fish of warm seas that is caught for sport and food

snap•ping tur•tle \,sna-piŋ-'tər-t^{ə}l\ *n*
▼ a large American turtle that catches its prey with a snap of the powerful jaws

snapping turtle: an alligator snapping turtle

snap•py \'sna-pē\ *adj* **snap•pi•er**; **snap•pi•est**
1 full of life : LIVELY ⟨*snappy* colors⟩
2 briskly cold : CHILLY
3 [1]QUICK 1 ⟨Come here, and make it *snappy.*⟩
4 STYLISH, SMART ⟨a *snappy* dresser⟩
5 clever and funny ⟨a *snappy* remark⟩

snap•shot \'snap-,shät\ *n*
a photograph taken usually with an inexpensive hand-held camera

[1]snare \'sner\ *n*
1 a trap (as a noose) for catching small animals and birds
2 something that traps or deceives

[2]snare *vb* **snared**; **snar•ing**
to catch or entangle by or as if by use of a trap for catching small animals

snare drum *n*
▼ a small drum with two heads that has strings stretched across its lower head to produce a rattling sound

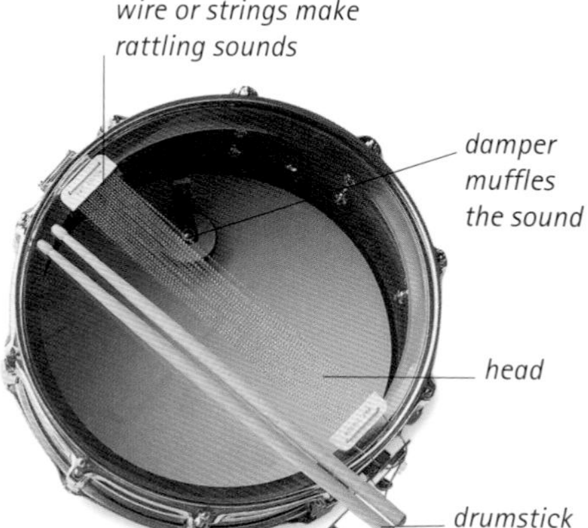

snare drum: the underside of a snare drum, with the bottom head removed.

[1]snarl \'snärl\ *vb* **snarled**; **snarl•ing**
1 to growl with a showing of teeth ⟨The dog *snarled* at the stranger.⟩
2 to speak in an angry way

[2]snarl *n*
an angry growl

[3]snarl *n*
1 a tangle usually of hairs or thread : KNOT ⟨She's combing out the *snarls*.⟩
2 a situation that makes movement difficult ⟨a traffic *snarl*⟩

[4]snarl *vb* **snarled**; **snarl•ing**
to get or become tangled

[1]snatch \'snach\ *vb* **snatched**; **snatch•ing**
to take hold of or try to take hold of something quickly or suddenly

[2]snatch *n*
1 something brief, hurried, or in small bits ⟨*snatches* of old songs⟩
2 an act of taking hold of something quickly
3 a brief period ⟨I slept in *snatches*.⟩

[1]sneak \'snēk\ *vb* **sneaked** \'snēkt\ *or* **snuck** \'snək\; **sneak•ing**
to move, act, bring, put, or take in a sly or secret way

[2]sneak *n*
a person who acts in a sly or secret way

sneak•er \'snē-kər\ *n*
a sports shoe with a rubber sole

sneaky \'snē-kē\ *adj* **sneak•i•er**; **sneak•i•est**
behaving in a sly or secret way or showing that kind of behavior ⟨a *sneaky* person⟩ ⟨a *sneaky* trick⟩

[1]sneer \'snir\ *vb* **sneered**; **sneer•ing**
1 to smile or laugh while making a face that shows disrespect
2 to speak or write in a disrespectful way

[2]sneer *n*
a disrespectful expression or remark

[1]sneeze \'snēz\ *vb* **sneezed**; **sneez•ing**
to force the breath out in a sudden and noisy way

[2]sneeze *n*
an act or instance of sneezing

[1]snick•er \'sni-kər\ *vb* **snick•ered**; **snick•er•ing**
to give a small and often mean or sly laugh

[2]snicker *n*
an act or sound of laughing in a mean or sly way

snide \'snīd\ *adj*
unkind or insulting in an indirect way ⟨*snide* remarks⟩

[1]sniff \'snif\ *vb* **sniffed**; **sniff•ing**
1 to smell by taking short breaths ⟨*sniff* perfume⟩
2 to draw air into the nose in short breaths loud enough to be heard
3 to say with scorn

[2]sniff *n*
1 the act or sound of drawing air into the nose in short breaths (as to smell something) ⟨He took a *sniff* of the pie.⟩
2 an odor detected through the nose ⟨a *sniff* of sea air⟩

snif•fle \'sni-fəl\ *vb* **snif•fled**; **snif•fling**
1 to sniff repeatedly
2 to speak with sniffs ⟨The child *sniffled* about where it hurt.⟩

snif•fles \'sni-fəlz\ *n pl*
a common cold in which the main symptom is a runny nose

[1]snig•ger \'sni-gər\ *vb* **snig•gered**; **snig•ger•ing**
[1]SNICKER

[2]snigger *n*
[2]SNICKER

[1]snip \'snip\ *n*
1 a small piece that is clipped off ⟨*snips* of paper⟩
2 an act or sound of clipping

[2]snip *vb* **snipped**; **snip•ping**
to cut or cut off with or as if with shears or scissors

[1]snipe \'snīp\ *n, pl* **snipes** *or* **snipe**
a bird that lives in marshes and has a long straight bill

[2]snipe *vb* **sniped**; **snip•ing**
1 to shoot from a hiding place (as at individual enemy soldiers)
2 to criticize someone in a harsh or unfair way
snip•er *n*

[1]snitch \'snich\ *vb* **snitched**; **snitch•ing**
[1]STEAL 1

[2]snitch *vb* **snitched**; **snitching**
INFORM 2, TATTLE

[3]snitch *n, pl* **snitch•es**
TATTLETALE

snob \'snäb\ *n*
a person who looks down on or avoids those felt to be less important

snob•bish \'snä-bish\ *adj*
being or characteristic of a snob ⟨a *snobbish* attitude⟩

snob•by \'snä-bē\ *adj* **snob•bi•er**; **snob•bi•est**
SNOBBISH

[1]snoop \'snüp\ *vb* **snooped**; **snoop•ing**
to look or search especially in a sneaking or nosy way
snoop•er *n*

[2]snoop *n*
a person who looks or searches in a sneaky or nosy way

snoot \'snüt\ *n*
[1]NOSE 1

snooty \'snü-tē\ *adj* **snoot•i•er**; **snoot•i•est**
rude and arrogant especially to people from a lower class

[1]snooze \'snüz\ *vb* **snoozed**; **snooz•ing**
to take a nap

[2]snooze *n*
a short sleep : NAP

[1]snore \'snȯr\ *vb* **snored**; **snor•ing**
to breathe with a rough hoarse noise while sleeping

[2]snore *n*
an act or sound of breathing with a rough hoarse noise while sleeping

[1]snor•kel \'snȯr-kəl\ *n*
▶ a tube used by swimmers for breathing with the head underwater

face mask
mouthpiece

[1]snorkel

[2]**snorkel** *vb* **snor•keled; snor•kel•ing**
to swim underwater using a tube for breathing

[1]**snort** \ˈsnȯrt\ *vb* **snort•ed; snort•ing**
1 to force air through the nose with a rough harsh sound
2 to say something with anger or scorn

[2]**snort** *n*
an act of or the rough harsh sound made by forcing air through the nose

snot•ty \ˈsnä-tē\ *adj* **snot•ti•er; snot•ti•est**
rude and arrogant

snout

snout 1

snout \ˈsnau̇t\ *n*
1 ▲ the projecting part of an animal's face that includes the nose or nose and mouth
2 a usually large and ugly human nose

[1]**snow** \ˈsnō\ *n*
1 small white crystals of ice formed directly from the water vapor of the air
2 a mass of snowflakes fallen to earth ⟨a foot of *snow*⟩

[2]**snow** *vb* **snowed; snow•ing**
to fall or cause to fall in or as snow ⟨It's *snowing* west of here.⟩

snow•ball \ˈsnō-ˌbȯl\ *n*
a round mass of snow pressed or rolled together

snow•bank \ˈsnō-ˌbaŋk\ *n*
a mound or pile of snow that results from clearing pavement

snow–blind \ˈsnō-ˌblīnd\ *adj*
having the eyes red and swollen and unable to see from the effect of glare reflected from snow

snow•blow•er \ˈsnō-ˌblō-ər\ *n*
a machine in which rotating parts pick up snow and throw it aside

snow•board \ˈsnō-ˌbȯrd\ *n*
▶ a board like a wide ski ridden in a surfing position over snow
snow•board•er \ˈsnō-ˌbȯr-dər\ *n*
snow•board•ing *n*

snow•bound \ˈsnō-ˈbau̇nd\ *adj*
shut in or blocked by snow ⟨*snowbound* mountain passes⟩

snow•drift \ˈsnō-ˌdrift\ *n*
a bank of drifted snow

snow•fall \ˈsnō-ˌfȯl\ *n*
1 a fall of snow
2 the amount of snow that falls in a single storm or in a certain period

snow•flake \ˈsnō-ˌflāk\ *n*
▶ a single snow crystal : a small mass of snow crystals

snow•man \ˈsnō-ˌman\ *n*, *pl* **snow•men** \-ˌmen\
snow shaped to look like a person

snow•mo•bile \ˈsnō-mō-ˌbēl\ *n*
a small motor vehicle designed for travel on snow

snow•plow \ˈsnō-ˌplau̇\ *n*
any of various devices used for clearing away snow

[1]**snow•shoe** \ˈsnō-ˌshü\ *n*
a light, wide frame (as of wood or aluminum) that is worn under a shoe to prevent sinking into soft snow

[2]**snowshoe** *vb* **snow•shoed; snow•shoe•ing**
to walk with snowshoes

snowboard: a boy holding a snowboard

snowflake:
magnified view of a snowflake

snow•storm \ˈsnō-ˌstȯrm\ *n*
a storm of falling snow

snow•suit \ˈsnō-ˌsüt\ *n*
a one-piece or two-piece warm outer garment for a child

snow thrower *n*
SNOWBLOWER

snowy \ˈsnō-ē\ *adj* **snow•i•er; snow•i•est**
1 having or covered with snow ⟨*snowy* mountains⟩
2 white like snow ⟨*snowy* clouds⟩

[1]**snub** \ˈsnəb\ *vb* **snubbed; snub•bing**
to ignore or treat rudely on purpose

[2]**snub** *n*
an act or an instance of ignoring or treating rudely on purpose

snub–nosed \ˈsnəb-ˈnōzd\ *adj*
having a stubby and usually slightly turned-up nose

snuck *past and past participle of* SNEAK

[1]**snuff** \ˈsnəf\ *n*
powdered tobacco that is chewed, placed against the gums, or drawn in through the nostrils

[2]**snuff** *vb* **snuffed; snuff•ing**
to draw through or into the nose with force

[3]**snuff** *vb* **snuffed; snuffing**
1 to cut or pinch off the burned end of the wick of a candle
2 to put an end to

[1]**snuf•fle** \ˈsnə-fəl\ *vb* **snuf•fled; snuf•fling**
to breathe noisily through a nose that is partly blocked

[2]**snuffle** *n*
the sound made in breathing through a nose that is partly blocked

snug \ˈsnəg\ *adj* **snug•ger; snug•gest**
1 fitting closely and comfortably ⟨a *snug* coat⟩
2 COMFORTABLE 1, COZY ⟨a *snug* corner⟩
3 offering protection or a hiding place ⟨a *snug* harbor⟩
snug•ly *adv*

snug•gle \'snə-gəl\ *vb* **snug•gled**; **snug•gling**
1 to curl up comfortably or cozily : CUDDLE
2 to pull in close to someone

[1]so \'sō\ *adv*
1 in the way indicated ⟨Do you think *so?*⟩
2 in the same way : ALSO ⟨They wrote well and *so* did you.⟩
3 [1]THEN 2 ⟨Wash your face and *so* to bed.⟩
4 to an indicated extent or way ⟨He had never felt *so* well.⟩ ⟨Don't be *so* rude!⟩
5 to a great degree ⟨She loved them *so.*⟩
6 to a definite but not specified amount ⟨A person can do only *so* much in a day.⟩
7 most certainly : INDEED ⟨You did *so* say it!⟩
8 THEREFORE ⟨I was tired, *so* I took a nap.⟩

[2]so *conj*
1 in order that ⟨Be quiet *so* I can sleep!⟩
2 and therefore ⟨We were hungry, *so* we ate.⟩

[3]so \'sō\ *pron*
1 the same : THAT ⟨They told me *so.*⟩
2 about that ⟨I was there an hour or *so.*⟩

so. *abbr* south

[1]soak \'sōk\ *vb* **soaked**; **soak•ing**
1 to lie covered with liquid ⟨He *soaked* in the tub.⟩
2 to place in a liquid to wet or as if to wet thoroughly ⟨*Soak* the beans in water.⟩
3 to make very wet ⟨The rain *soaked* us.⟩
4 to enter or pass through something by or as if by tiny holes : PERMEATE ⟨The water *soaked* into the ground.⟩
5 to draw in by or as if by absorption ⟨She *soaked* up the sunshine.⟩

[2]soak *n*
1 the act or process of letting something stay in a liquid for a long time to soften or clean it
2 a long bath

[1]soap \'sōp\ *n*
a substance that is used for washing

[2]soap *vb* **soaped**; **soap•ing**
to rub a cleaning substance over or into something

soap•stone \'sōp-,stōn\ *n*
a soft stone that has a soapy or greasy feeling

soapy \'sō-pē\ *adj* **soap•i•er**; **soap•i•est**
1 covered with soap ⟨a *soapy* face⟩
2 containing soap ⟨*soapy* water⟩
3 like soap ⟨a *soapy* feel⟩

soar \'sȯr\ *vb* **soared**; **soar•ing**
1 to fly or glide through the air often at a great height ⟨An eagle *soared* overhead.⟩
2 to increase quickly ⟨Prices were *soaring.*⟩
3 to rise quickly ⟨The ball *soared* out of the park.⟩ ⟨My spirits *soared* with the news.⟩
4 to rise to a great height ⟨Buildings *soared* above us.⟩

[1]sob \'säb\ *vb* **sobbed**; **sob•bing**
1 to cry noisily with short sudden breaths
2 to say while crying noisily ⟨She *sobbed* out the story.⟩

[2]sob *n*
an act or the sound of crying loudly with short sudden breaths ⟨He shook with *sobs.*⟩

[1]so•ber \'sō-bər\ *adj* **so•ber•er**; **so•ber•est**
1 not drinking too much : TEMPERATE
2 not drunk
3 having or showing a serious attitude : SOLEMN ⟨a *sober* child⟩ ⟨a *sober* voice⟩
4 having a plain color ⟨*sober* clothes⟩
5 carefully reasoned or considered : REALISTIC ⟨a *sober* reminder⟩

[2]sober *vb* **so•bered**; **so•ber•ing**
1 to make or become less drunk
2 to make or become serious or thoughtful

so–called \'sō-'kȯld\ *adj*
commonly or wrongly named ⟨a *so-called* friend⟩

soc•cer \'sä-kər\ *n*
▶ a game played between two teams of eleven players in which a round inflated ball is moved toward a goal usually by kicking

▶ **Word History** In the 1870s at Oxford University in England, it became a fad among students to make up slang by clipping words to a single syllable and adding *–er.* Most of these slang words, such as *fresher* for *freshman* and *brekker* for *breakfast*, are unfamiliar in North American English, if they have survived at all. However, one *–er* word succeeded in the United States: the word *soccer. Soccer* was shortened from *association* (or *assoc.*) *football*, which was the name for a game played according to the rules of the Football Association, founded in England in 1863.

so•cia•ble \'sō-shə-bəl\ *adj*
1 liking to be around other people : FRIENDLY
2 involving or encouraging friendliness or pleasant companionship with other people ⟨We enjoyed a *sociable* evening.⟩

[1]so•cial \'sō-shəl\ *adj*
1 enjoying other people : SOCIABLE ⟨a *social* person⟩
2 relating to interaction with other people especially for pleasure ⟨a busy *social* life⟩
3 of or relating to human beings as a group ⟨Marriage and family are *social* institutions.⟩
4 living naturally in groups or communities ⟨Bees are *social* insects.⟩
5 relating to or based on rank in a particular society ⟨*social* classes⟩
so•cial•ly *adv*

[2]social *n*
a friendly gathering usually for a special reason

so•cial•ism \'sō-shə-,li-zəm\ *n*
a social system or theory in which the government owns and controls the means of production (as factories) and distribution of goods

soccer: two players during a soccer match

so•cial•ist \'sō-shə-list\ *n*
a person who supports socialism

social media *n*
forms of electronic communication (as Web sites) through which people create online communities to share content (as information, personal messages, and video)

social net•work•ing \-'net-,wər-kiŋ\ *n*
the activity of creating and maintaining personal and business relationships especially online

social studies *n pl*
studies (as civics and history) that deal with human relationships and how society works

so•ci•ety \sə-'sī-ə-tē\ *n, pl* **so•ci•et•ies**
1 a community or group of people having common traditions, institutions, and interests ⟨medieval *society*⟩ ⟨western *society*⟩

2 all of the people of the world ⟨Medical advances help *society.*⟩
3 a group of persons with a common interest, belief, or purpose ⟨historical *societies*⟩
4 friendly association with others ⟨He avoided the *society* of other painters.⟩

[1]**sock** \'säk\ *n, pl* **socks** \'säks\
a knitted or woven covering for the foot usually reaching past the ankle and sometimes to the knee

[2]**sock** *vb* **socked; sock•ing**
[1]HIT 1, PUNCH

[3]**sock** *n*
[3]PUNCH

sock•et \'sä-kət\ *n*
a small opening or hollow part that forms a holder for something ⟨an eye *socket*⟩ ⟨an electric *socket*⟩

sod \'säd\ *n*
the upper layer of the soil that is filled with roots (as of grass)

so•da \'sō-də\ *n*
1 a powdery substance like salt used in washing and in making glass or soap
2 BAKING SODA
3 SODA WATER
4 SODA POP
5 a sweet drink made of soda water, flavoring, and often ice cream

soda pop *n*
a beverage containing soda water, flavoring, and a sweet syrup

soda water *n*
▶ water with carbon dioxide added

sod•den \'sä-dᵊn\ *adj*
SOGGY ⟨*sodden* fields⟩

so•di•um \'sō-dē-əm\ *n*
a soft waxy silver-white chemical element occurring in nature in combined form (as in salt)

soda water: a glassful of soda water and ice

sodium bicarbonate *n*
BAKING SODA

sodium chlo•ride \-'klȯr-,īd\ *n*
[1]SALT 1

so•fa \'sō-fə\ *n*
a long upholstered seat usually with a back and arms

[1]**soft** \'sȯft\ *adj* **soft•er; soft•est**
1 not hard, solid, or firm ⟨a *soft* mattress⟩
2 smooth or pleasant to touch ⟨a *soft* silk⟩
3 having a soothing or comfortable effect : not bright or glaring ⟨*soft* lights⟩ ⟨*soft* colors⟩

softwood: cross-section of a softwood log from a bishop pine tree

4 quiet in pitch or volume ⟨*soft* voices⟩
5 not strong or forceful : GENTLE ⟨*soft* breezes⟩ ⟨a *soft* touch⟩
6 involving little work or effort : EASY ⟨a *soft* job⟩
7 sounding like the letter *c* in *ace* and the letter *g* in *gem*
8 easily affected by emotions : sympathetic and kind ⟨a *soft* heart⟩
9 lacking in strength or fitness ⟨He had grown *soft* from good living.⟩
10 free from substances that prevent lathering of soap ⟨*soft* water⟩
11 not containing alcohol ⟨*soft* drinks⟩
soft•ness *n*

[2]**soft** *adv* **softer; softest**
SOFTLY ⟨You hit the ball too *soft.*⟩

soft•ball \'sȯft-,bȯl\ *n*
1 a game like baseball played with a larger ball thrown underhand
2 the ball used in softball

soft•en \'sȯ-fən\ *vb* **soft•ened; soft•en•ing**
1 to make or become soft or less firm ⟨Let the wax *soften* in the sun.⟩
2 to make or become gentler or less harsh ⟨Her expression *softened* when the children entered the room.⟩
soft•en•er *n*

soft•ly \'sȯft-lē\ *adv*
in a soft way : quietly or gently ⟨speak *softly*⟩ ⟨He walked *softly* across the room.⟩

soft•ware \'sȯft-,wer\ *n*
the programs and related information used by a computer

soft•wood \'sȯft-,wu̇d\ *n*
▲ the wood of a tree (as a pine or spruce) that has needles as distinguished from the wood of a tree (as a maple) with broad leaves

sog•gy \'sä-gē, 'sȯ-\ *adj* **sog•gi•er; sog•gi•est**
heavy with water or moisture ⟨*soggy* ground⟩

[1]**soil** \'sȯil\ *vb* **soiled; soil•ing**
to make or become dirty ⟨I *soiled* my shirt while cooking.⟩

[2]**soil** *n*
1 the loose surface material of the earth in which plants grow
2 COUNTRY 1, LAND ⟨my native *soil*⟩
soil•less \'sȯil-ləs\ *adj*

[1]**so•journ** \'sō-,jərn\ *n*
a temporary stay

[2]**sojourn** *vb* **so•journed; so•journ•ing**
to stay as a temporary resident ⟨He *sojourned* for a month at a desert inn.⟩

sol \'sōl\ *n*
the fifth note of the musical scale

so•lace \'sä-ləs, 'sō-\ *n*
1 comfort in times of sorrow or worry ⟨I'll seek *solace* in friends.⟩
2 something that gives comfort ⟨Books were his only *solace.*⟩

so•lar \'sō-lər\ *adj*
1 of or relating to the sun ⟨a *solar* eclipse⟩
2 measured by the earth's course around the sun ⟨a *solar* year⟩
3 produced or made to work by the action of the sun's light or heat ⟨*solar* energy⟩

▶ solar system
The sun lies at the center of the solar system, and is orbited by eight planets. Most of the planets are themselves circled by one or more moons. Millions of asteroids, meteors, and comets also orbit the sun.

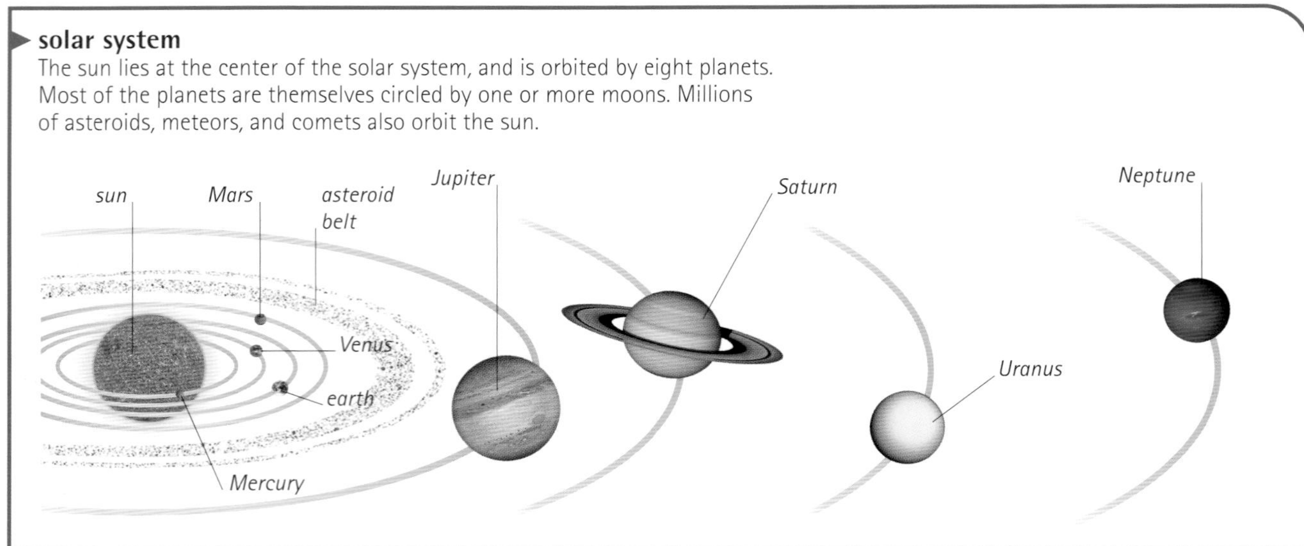

solar system *n*
▲ the sun and the planets, asteroids, comets, and meteors that revolve around it

sold *past and past participle of* SELL

[1]sol•der \'sä-dər\ *n*
a metal or a mixture of metals used when melted to join or repair surfaces of metal

[2]solder *vb* **sol•dered**; **sol•der•ing**
to join together or repair with solder

sol•dier \'sōl-jər\ *n*
▶ a person in military service and especially an enlisted person who is in the army

[1]sole \'sōl\ *n*
1 the bottom of the foot
2 the bottom of a shoe, slipper, or boot

[2]sole *vb* **soled**; **sol•ing**
to put a new sole on ⟨*sole* shoes⟩

[3]sole *n*
a flatfish that has a small mouth and small eyes set close together and is often used for food

[4]sole *adj*
1 [1]SINGLE 1, ONLY ⟨the *sole* heir⟩
2 limited or belonging only to the person or group mentioned ⟨The coach had *sole* authority over the team.⟩

sole•ly \'sōl-lē\ *adv*
1 without another involved : ALONE ⟨The decision is *solely* yours.⟩
2 [2]ONLY 2 ⟨Sort the blocks *solely* by color.⟩

sol•emn \'sä-ləm\ *adj*
1 very serious or formal in manner, behavior, or expression ⟨a *solemn* procession⟩ ⟨a *solemn* face⟩
2 done or made seriously and thoughtfully ⟨a *solemn* promise⟩
synonyms see SERIOUS
sol•emn•ly *adv*

soldier: a US Army soldier in camouflage uniform

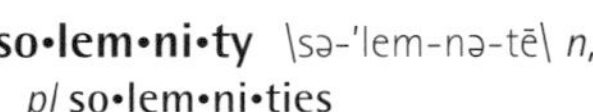

so•lem•ni•ty \sə-'lem-nə-tē\ *n*, *pl* **so•lem•ni•ties**
1 a serious or formal ceremony ⟨The important visitors were welcomed with fitting *solemnity*.⟩
2 formal dignity ⟨He spoke with *solemnity*.⟩

so•lic•it \sə-'li-sət\ *vb* **so•lic•it•ed**; **so•lic•it•ing**
1 to come to with a request or plea ⟨We *solicited* local businesses for donations.⟩
2 to try to get by asking or pleading ⟨They *solicited* the help of their neighbors.⟩

[1]sol•id \'sä-ləd\ *adj*
1 not hollow ⟨a *solid* ball of rubber⟩
2 not loose or spongy : COMPACT ⟨a *solid* mass of rock⟩
3 neither liquid nor gaseous ⟨The water turned to *solid* ice.⟩
4 made firmly and well ⟨a *solid* chair⟩
5 being without a break, interruption, or change ⟨a *solid* yellow line⟩ ⟨I practiced for a *solid* hour.⟩
6 UNANIMOUS 1 ⟨The candidate had the *solid* support of her party.⟩
7 RELIABLE, DEPENDABLE ⟨a *solid* citizen⟩ ⟨*solid* advice⟩
8 of one material, kind, or color ⟨*solid* gold⟩
synonyms see HARD
sol•id•ly *adv* ⟨He talked *solidly* for an hour.⟩

[2]solid *n*
1 something (as a cube) that has length, width, and thickness
2 a substance that keeps its size and shape : a solid substance

so•lid•i•fy \sə-'li-də-,fī\ *vb* **so•lid•i•fied**; **so•lid•i•fy•ing**
to make or become solid

A B C D E F G H I J K L M N O P Q R S T U V W X Y Z

sol•i•taire \'sä-lə-,ter\ *n*
a card game played by one person alone

sol•i•tary \'sä-lə-,ter-ē\ *adj*
1 all alone : without anyone or anything else ⟨a *solitary* traveler⟩
2 seldom visited : LONELY ⟨a *solitary* seashore⟩
3 growing or living alone : not one of a group or cluster ⟨*solitary* insects⟩
synonyms see ALONE

sol•i•tude \'säl-ə-,tüd, -,tyüd\ *n*
the quality or state of being alone or away from others : SECLUSION

[1]so•lo \'sō-lō\ *n, pl* **solos**
1 a piece of music performed by one singer or musician ⟨a piano *solo*⟩
2 an action done alone ⟨The pilot flew his first *solo*.⟩

[2]solo *adv or adj*
without another person : ALONE ⟨fly *solo*⟩ ⟨a *solo* dancer⟩

[3]solo *vb* **so•loed; so•lo•ing**
to do something (as perform music or fly an airplane) alone or without an instructor

so•lo•ist \'sō-lə-wist\ *n*
a person who performs a solo

sol•stice \'säl-stəs, 'sōl-, 'sȯl-\ *n*
the time of the year when the sun passes overhead the farthest north (**summer solstice**, about June 22) or south (**winter solstice**, about December 22) of the equator

sol•u•ble \'säl-yə-bəl\ *adj*
1 capable of being dissolved in liquid ⟨Sugar is *soluble* in water.⟩
2 capable of being solved or explained ⟨a *soluble* problem⟩

so•lu•tion \sə-'lü-shən\ *n*
1 the act or process of solving ⟨His *solution* to the problem was to wait.⟩
2 an answer to a problem : EXPLANATION ⟨The *solution* of the math problem is on the board.⟩
3 the act or process by which a solid, liquid, or gas is dissolved in a liquid
4 a liquid in which something has been dissolved ⟨a *solution* of sugar in water⟩

solve \'sälv, 'sȯlv\ *vb* **solved; solv•ing**
to find the answer to or a solution for ⟨Can you *solve* the riddle?⟩

sol•vent \'säl-vənt, 'sȯl-\ *n*
a usually liquid substance in which other substances can be dissolved or dispersed ⟨Turpentine is a *solvent* for paint.⟩

som•ber *or* **som•bre** \'säm-bər\ *adj*
1 very sad or serious ⟨a *somber* mood⟩ ⟨*somber* news⟩
2 being dark and gloomy : DULL ⟨*somber* colors⟩

som•bre•ro \səm-'brer-ō\ *n, pl* **som•bre•ros**
▼ a tall hat with a very wide brim worn especially in Mexico

sombrero: a 19th-century straw sombrero

[1]some \'səm\ *adj*
1 not known, named, or specified ⟨*Some* person called while you were out.⟩
2 being one, a part, or an unspecified number of something ⟨*Some* birds can't fly.⟩
3 being of an amount or number that is not mentioned ⟨Can you buy *some* apples?⟩

[2]some *pron*
a certain number or amount ⟨*Some* of the milk has spilled.⟩ ⟨*Some* of the paintings are sold.⟩

[1]-some \,səm\ *adj suffix*
distinguished by a specified thing, quality, state, or action ⟨trouble*some*⟩

[2]-some *n suffix*
group of so many members ⟨four*some*⟩

[1]some•body \'səm-,bä-dē, -bə-dē\ *pron*
a person who is not known, named, or specified ⟨*Somebody* was looking for you.⟩

[2]somebody *n, pl* **some•bod•ies**
a person of importance ⟨He wanted to be a *somebody*.⟩

some•day \'səm-,dā\ *adv*
at some future time ⟨*Someday* I'll travel.⟩

some•how \'səm-,hau̇\ *adv*
in a way that is not known or certain ⟨She *somehow* managed to get home.⟩

some•one \'səm-wən, -,wən\ *pron*
a person who is not known, named, or specified ⟨*Someone* has to do the job.⟩

[1]som•er•sault \'sə-mər-,sȯlt\ *n*
► a movement in which someone makes a complete turn by bringing the feet over the head

► **Word History** If you pay attention only to its sound, *somersault* is rather puzzling, because going head over heels has nothing to do with summer or salt. The spelling, however, suggests that the key to its history lies elsewhere. *Somersault* comes from a 16th-century French word *sombresaut*, made up of *sombre* or *sobre*, "over," and *saut*, "jump."

[2]somersault *vb* **som•er•sault•ed; som•er•sault•ing**
to perform a movement in which a person makes a complete turn by bringing the feet over the head

some•thing \'səm-thiŋ\ *pron*
1 a thing that is not known or named ⟨We'll have to do *something* about it.⟩
2 a thing or amount that is clearly known but not named ⟨I have *something* for you.⟩
3 SOMEWHAT ⟨She is *something* of an expert.⟩

some•time \'səm-,tīm\ *adv*
1 at a future time ⟨I'll repay you *sometime*.⟩
2 at a time not known or not specified ⟨It disappeared *sometime* yesterday.⟩

some•times \'səm-,tīmz\ *adv*
now and then : OCCASIONALLY ⟨*Sometimes* she walks to work.⟩

some•way \'səm-,wā\ *adv*
SOMEHOW

[1]some•what \'səm-,hwät, -,wät, -,hwət, -,wət\ *pron*
some amount or extent ⟨It came as *somewhat* of a surprise.⟩

[2]somewhat *adv*
to some extent ⟨The instructions were *somewhat* confusing.⟩

some•where \'səm-,hwer, -,wer\ *adv*
1 in, at, or to a place not known or named ⟨The boy ran off *somewhere*.⟩
2 rather close to ⟨They arrived *somewhere* around two o'clock.⟩

[1]somersault: a gymnast performing a somersault in midair

A B C D E F G H I J K L M N O P Q R S T U V W X Y Z

son \'sən\ *n*
1 a male child or offspring
2 a man or boy closely associated with or thought of as a child of something (as a country, race, or religion) 〈*sons* of liberty〉

so•nar \'sō-,när\ *n*
a device for detecting objects underwater using reflected sound waves

so•na•ta \sə-'nä-tə\ *n*
a musical composition for one or two instruments consisting of three or four separate sections in different forms and keys

song \'sȯŋ\ *n*
1 a short musical composition of words and music
2 the act or art of singing 〈He burst into *song.*〉
3 a series of usually musical sounds produced by an animal and especially a bird
4 a small amount 〈That old house can be bought for a *song.*〉

song•bird \'sȯŋ-,bərd\ *n*
▼ a bird that produces a series of usually musical sounds

songbird: a thrush is a songbird

son•ic \'sä-nik\ *adj*
using, produced by, or relating to sound waves

sonic boom *n*
a sound like an explosion that is made by an aircraft traveling faster than the speed of sound

son–in–law \'sən-ən-,lȯ\ *n, pl* **sons–in–law**
the husband of a person's daughter

son•ny \'sə-nē\ *n, pl* **son•nies**
a young boy
Hint: *Sonny* is used mostly by an older person to address a boy.

so•no•rous \sə-'nȯr-əs, 'sä-nə-rəs\ *adj*
loud, deep, or rich in sound : RESONANT 〈a *sonorous* voice〉

soon \'sün\ *adv* **soon•er; soon•est**
1 without delay : before long 〈The fog *soon* disappeared.〉
2 in a prompt way : QUICKLY 〈I'll call you as *soon* as possible.〉
3 before long 〈They *soon* learned the truth.〉
4 [1]EARLY 2 〈I wish you'd told me *sooner.*〉
5 RATHER 2 〈I would *sooner* walk than ride.〉

soot \'su̇t, 'sət\ *n*
a black powder formed when something is burned : the very fine powder that colors smoke

soothe \'sü<u>th</u>\ *vb* **soothed; sooth•ing**
1 to please by praise or attention 〈The waiter tried to *soothe* the angry customer.〉
2 RELIEVE 1 〈Lotion will *soothe* your sunburn.〉
3 to calm down : COMFORT 〈Music *soothed* the crying baby.〉

sooth•say•er \'süth-,sā-ər\ *n*
a person who claims to foretell events

sooty \'su̇-tē, 'sə-\ *adj* **soot•i•er; soot•i•est**
1 covered with soot 〈*sooty* hands〉
2 like soot in color 〈a *sooty* bird〉

sop \'säp\ *vb* **sopped; sop•ping**
1 to soak or dip in or as if in liquid 〈He *sopped* the bread in gravy.〉
2 to mop or soak up 〈The water was *sopped* up with rags.〉

so•phis•ti•cat•ed \sə-'fi-stə-,kā-təd\ *adj*
1 very complicated : COMPLEX 〈*sophisticated* electronic devices〉
2 having a lot of knowledge about the world especially through experience
3 appealing to a person's intelligence 〈a *sophisticated* novel〉

soph•o•more \'säf-,mȯr, 'sä-fə-,mȯr\ *n*
a student in his or her second year at a high school or college

sop•ping \'sä-piŋ\ *adj*
thoroughly wet

so•pra•no \sə-'pra-nō, -'prä-\ *n, pl* **so•pra•nos**
1 the highest part in harmony that has four parts
2 the highest singing voice of women or boys
3 a singer or an instrument having a soprano range or part

sor•cer•er \'sȯr-sə-rər\ *n*
a person who practices sorcery or witchcraft : WIZARD

sor•cer•ess \'sȯr-sə-rəs\ *n*
a woman who practices sorcery or witchcraft : WITCH

sor•cery \'sȯr-sə-rē\ *n, pl* **sor•cer•ies**
the use of magic : WITCHCRAFT

sor•did \'sȯr-dəd\ *adj*
1 very dirty : FILTHY 〈*sordid* surroundings〉
2 of low moral quality 〈a *sordid* life〉

[1]sore \'sȯr\ *adj* **sor•er; sor•est**
1 very painful or sensitive : TENDER 〈My muscles are *sore* from exercise.〉
2 hurt or red and swollen so as to be or seem painful 〈a *sore* throat〉
3 causing emotional distress 〈a *sore* subject〉
4 ANGRY 〈Are you still *sore* with me?〉
sore•ly *adv*
sore•ness *n*

[2]sore *n*
a sore or painful spot on the body usually with the skin broken or bruised and often with infection

sor•ghum \'sȯr-gəm\ *n*
1 a tall grass that is grown for forage and grain
2 a sweet syrup from the juice of sorghum stems

so•ror•i•ty \sə-'rȯr-ə-tē\ *n, pl* **so•ror•i•ties**
a club of girls or women especially at a college

[1]sor•rel \'sȯr-əl\ *n*
1 a light reddish brown horse often with a white mane and tail
2 a brownish orange to light brown

[2]sorrel *n*
any of several plants with sour juice

[1]sor•row \'sär-ō\ *n*
1 sadness felt after a loss (as of someone or something loved)
2 a cause of grief or sadness 〈He moved away to forget his *sorrows.*〉
3 a feeling of regret

▶ **Synonyms** SORROW, GRIEF, and WOE mean a feeling of great sadness. SORROW is used for a feeling that something has been lost and often feelings of guilt and regret. 〈He expressed *sorrow* for having caused the accident.〉 GRIEF is used for a feeling of great sorrow usually for a particular reason. 〈She felt *grief* over the death of her pet.〉 WOE is used for a feeling of hopelessness and misery. 〈All my troubles left me in a state of *woe.*〉

[2]sorrow *vb* **sor•rowed; sor•row•ing**
to feel or express sorrow : GRIEVE

sor•row•ful \'sär-ō-fəl, -ə-fəl\ *adj*
1 full of or showing sadness 〈a *sorrowful* face〉
2 causing sadness 〈a *sorrowful* tale〉

sor•ry \'sär-ē\ *adj* **sor•ri•er; sor•ri•est**
1 feeling sorrow or regret 〈I'm *sorry* I lied.〉
2 causing sorrow, pity, or scorn : PITIFUL 〈a *sorry* sight〉 〈a *sorry* excuse〉

[1]sort \'sȯrt\ *n*
1 a group of persons or things that have something in common : KIND 〈all *sorts* of people〉
2 PERSON 1, INDIVIDUAL 〈He was not a bad *sort.*〉
3 general disposition : NATURE 〈people of an evil *sort*〉

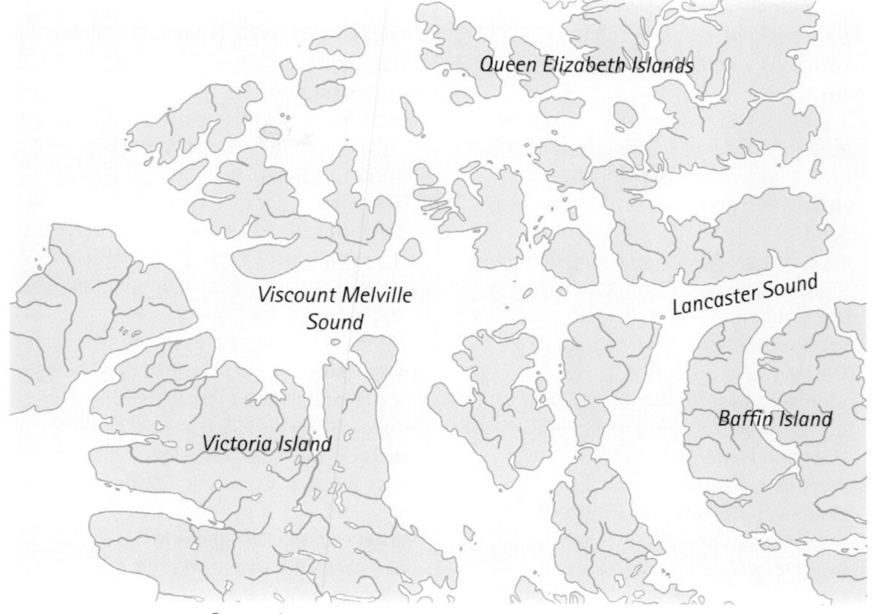

[5]sound: map showing sounds of northern Canada

out of sorts
1 not feeling well
2 easily angered : IRRITABLE

[2]sort *vb* **sort•ed; sort•ing**
1 to separate and arrange according to kind or class ⟨*Sort* the beads by color.⟩
2 [1]SEARCH 1 ⟨He *sorted* through a stack of papers.⟩

SOS \ˌes-ō-ˈes\ *n*
1 an international radio code distress signal used especially by ships and airplanes calling for help
2 a call for help

[1]so–so \ˈsō-ˈsō\ *adv*
fairly well ⟨She plays the violin just *so-so.*⟩

[2]so–so *adj*
neither very good nor very bad ⟨a *so-so* movie⟩

sought *past and past participle of* SEEK

soul \ˈsōl\ *n*
1 the spiritual part of a person believed to give life to the body
2 the essential or most important part of something ⟨This room is the *soul* of the house.⟩
3 a person who leads or stirs others to action : LEADER ⟨He was the *soul* of the campaign.⟩
4 a person's moral and emotional nature ⟨I felt my *soul* rebel against the injustice.⟩
5 human being : PERSON ⟨a kind *soul*⟩
6 a style of music expressing deep emotion that was created by African-Americans

[1]sound \ˈsau̇nd\ *adj* **sound•er; sound•est**
1 free from disease or weakness : HEALTHY ⟨a *sound* mind and body⟩
2 solid and strong ⟨a building of *sound* construction⟩
3 free from error ⟨a *sound* argument⟩ ⟨*sound* beliefs⟩
4 showing good sense : WISE ⟨*sound* advice⟩
5 SEVERE 2 ⟨a *sound* whipping⟩
6 deep and undisturbed ⟨a *sound* sleep⟩
sound•ly *adv*
sound•ness *n*

[2]sound *adv*
to the full extent ⟨*sound* asleep⟩

[3]sound *n*
1 the sensation experienced through the sense of hearing : an instance or occurrence of this ⟨the *sound* of laughter⟩
2 one of the noises that together make up human speech ⟨the *sound* of "s" in "sit"⟩
3 the suggestion carried or given by something heard or read ⟨The excuse had a suspicious *sound.*⟩
4 hearing distance : EARSHOT ⟨They are still within the *sound* of my voice.⟩
sound•less \ˈsau̇nd-ləs\ *adj*
sound•less•ly *adv*

[4]sound *vb* **sound•ed; sound•ing**
1 to make or cause to make a sound or noise ⟨*sound* a trumpet⟩ ⟨The buzzer *sounded.*⟩
2 PRONOUNCE 1 ⟨*Sound* each word clearly.⟩
3 to order, signal, or indicate by a sound ⟨*Sound* the alarm!⟩ ⟨The clock *sounded* noon.⟩
4 to make known : PROCLAIM ⟨*sound* praises⟩
5 to make or give an impression especially when heard ⟨It *sounds* too good to be true.⟩ ⟨The story *sounds* false.⟩

[5]sound *n*
◀ a long stretch of water that is wider than a strait and often connects two larger bodies of water or forms a channel between the mainland and an island

[6]sound *vb* **sounded; sounding**
1 to measure the depth of (as by a weighted line dropped down from the surface)
2 to try to find out the views or intentions of a person ⟨I *sounded* them out on the idea.⟩

sound•proof \ˈsau̇nd-ˈprüf\ *adj*
capable of keeping sound from entering or escaping

sound wave *n*
a wave that is produced when a sound is made and is responsible for carrying the sound to the ear

soup \ˈsüp\ *n*
a liquid food made by cooking vegetables, meat, or fish in a large amount of liquid

[1]sour \ˈsau̇r\ *adj* **sour•er; sour•est**
1 having an acid or tart taste ⟨a *sour* fruit⟩
2 having spoiled : not fresh ⟨*sour* milk⟩
3 suggesting decay ⟨a *sour* smell⟩
4 not pleasant or friendly ⟨a *sour* look⟩
sour•ly *adv* ⟨He spoke *sourly.*⟩
sour•ness *n*

[2]sour *vb* **soured; sour•ing**
1 to make or become acid or tart in taste (as by spoiling) ⟨The milk *soured.*⟩
2 to lose or cause to lose interest or enthusiasm ⟨He *soured* on trying new stunts following the mishap.⟩
3 to harm or damage ⟨The misunderstanding *soured* their friendship.⟩

source \ˈsȯrs\ *n*
1 a cause or starting point ⟨the *source* of a rumor⟩
2 the beginning of a stream of water ⟨the *source* of the Nile River⟩
3 someone or something that supplies information ⟨a reference *source*⟩
4 someone or something that provides what is needed ⟨a *source* of supplies⟩ ⟨a *source* of strength⟩

sou•sa•phone \ˈsü-zə-ˌfōn, -sə-\ *n*
▼ a large circular tuba designed to rest on the player's shoulder and used chiefly in marching bands

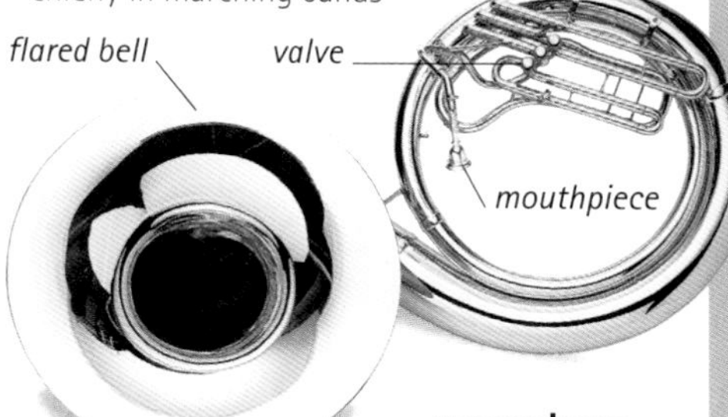

sousaphone

a b c d e f g h i j k l m n o p q r s t u v w x y z

[1]south \'sau̇th\ *adv*
to or toward the south ⟨The cabin faces *south.*⟩

[2]south *adj*
placed toward, facing, or coming from the south ⟨a *south* wind⟩

[3]south *n*
1 the direction to the right of someone facing east : the compass point opposite to north
2 *cap* regions or countries south of a point that is mentioned or understood

[1]South American *n*
a person born or living in South America

[2]South American *adj*
of or relating to South America or the South American people ⟨a *South American* plant⟩

south•bound \'sau̇th-,bau̇nd\ *adj*
going south ⟨a *southbound* train⟩

[1]south•east \sau̇th-'ēst\ *adv*
to or toward the direction between south and east ⟨We hiked *southeast.*⟩

[2]southeast *adj*
placed toward, facing, or coming from the southeast ⟨the *southeast* corner of town⟩

[3]southeast *n*
1 the direction between south and east
2 *cap* regions or countries southeast of a point that is mentioned or understood

south•east•er•ly \sau̇th-'ē-stər-lē\ *adv or adj*
1 from the southeast ⟨*southeasterly* gales⟩
2 toward the southeast ⟨a *southeasterly* direction⟩

south•east•ern \sau̇th-'ē-stərn\ *adj*
1 *often cap* of, relating to, or like that of the Southeast ⟨a *southeastern* city⟩
2 lying toward or coming from the southeast ⟨*southeastern* New York⟩

south•er•ly \'sə-t͟hər-lē\ *adj or adv*
1 from the south ⟨a *southerly* wind⟩
2 toward the south ⟨a *southerly* shore⟩ ⟨They sailed *southerly.*⟩

south•ern \'sə-t͟hərn\ *adj*
1 *often cap* of, relating to, or like that of the South ⟨a *southern* climate⟩
2 lying toward or coming from the south ⟨*southern* Asia⟩

south•paw \'sau̇th-,pȯ\ *n*
a person (as a baseball pitcher) who is left-handed

south pole *n, often cap S & P*
1 the most southern point of the earth : the southern end of the earth's axis
2 the end of a magnet that points toward the south when the magnet is free to swing

south•ward \'sau̇th-wərd\ *adv or adj*
toward the south

[1]south•west \sau̇th-'west\ *adv*
to or toward the direction between south and west ⟨The town is *southwest* of here.⟩

[2]southwest *adj*
placed toward, facing, or coming from the southwest ⟨*southwest* winds⟩

[3]southwest *n*
1 the direction between south and west
2 *cap* regions or countries southwest of a point that is mentioned or understood

south•west•er•ly \sau̇th-'we-stər-lē\ *adv or adj*
1 from the southwest ⟨*southwesterly* breezes⟩
2 toward the southwest ⟨a *southwesterly* direction⟩

south•west•ern \sau̇th-'we-stərn\ *adj*
1 *often cap* of, relating to, or like that of the Southwest ⟨*southwestern* art⟩
2 lying toward or coming from the southwest ⟨the *southwestern* part of the country⟩

sou•ve•nir \'sü-və-,nir\ *n*
something that serves as a reminder ⟨a *souvenir* from Hawaii⟩

[1]sov•er•eign \'sä-və-rən, 'sä-vrən\ *n*
1 a person (as a king or queen) having the highest power and authority
2 an old British gold coin

[2]sovereign *adj*
1 highest in power or authority ⟨a *sovereign* ruler⟩
2 having independent authority ⟨a *sovereign* state⟩
3 of the most important kind ⟨a *sovereign* duty⟩

sov•er•eign•ty \'sä-və-rən-tē, 'sä-vrən-\ *n, pl* **sov•er•eign•ties**
1 supreme power especially over a political unit (as a country)
2 a country's independent authority and right of self-control

[1]sow \'sau̇\ *n*
▼ an adult female pig

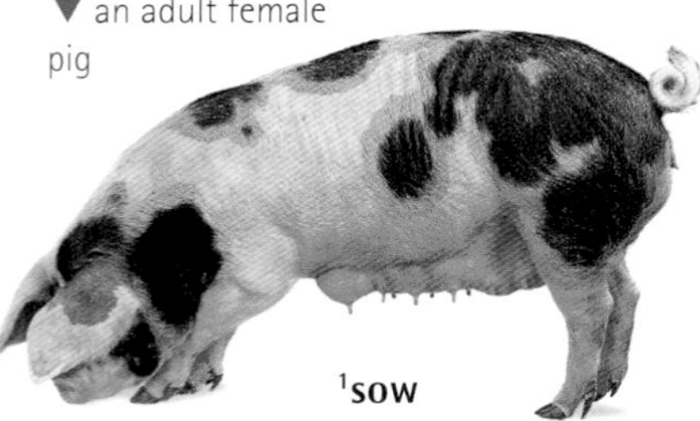
[1]sow

[2]sow \'sō\ *vb* **sowed**; **sown** \'sōn\ *or* **sowed**; **sow•ing**
1 to plant or scatter (as seed) for growing ⟨We *sow* corn every spring.⟩
2 to cover with or as if with scattered seed for growing ⟨The farmer *sowed* a field with oats.⟩
3 to set in motion : cause to exist ⟨Both groups are *sowing* bad feelings.⟩
sow•er *n*

sow bug \'sau̇-\ *n*
WOOD LOUSE

soy•bean \'sȯi-,bēn\ *n*
the edible seed of an Asian plant that is rich in protein

soy sauce \'sȯi-\ *n*
a brown sauce made from soybeans and used especially in Chinese and Japanese cooking

[1]space \'spās\ *n*
1 a part of a distance, area, or volume that can be measured ⟨a grassy open *space*⟩
2 a certain place set apart or available ⟨a parking *space*⟩ ⟨There's still some *space* in the cupboard.⟩
3 the area without limits in which all things exist and move ⟨endless *space* and time⟩
4 a period of time ⟨The phone rang five times within the *space* of 15 minutes.⟩
5 the region beyond the earth's atmosphere
6 an empty place ⟨Sit in the *space* between us.⟩

[2]space *vb* **spaced**; **spac•ing**
to place or separate with some distance or time between

space•craft \'spās-,kraft\ *n, pl* **spacecraft**
a vehicle for travel beyond the earth's atmosphere

space•ship \'spās-,ship\ *n*
SPACECRAFT

space shuttle *n*
a spacecraft designed to transport people and cargo between earth and space that can be used repeatedly

space station *n*
an artificial satellite designed to stay in orbit permanently and to be occupied by humans for long periods

space suit *n*
a suit that covers the entire body and is equipped to keep its wearer alive in space

spa•cious \'spā-shəs\ *adj*
having ample space ⟨a *spacious* room⟩

spade \'spād\ *n*
a digging tool with a long handle that has a flat blade which can be pushed into the ground with the foot

spa•ghet•ti \spə-'ge-tē\ *n*
pasta made in the shape of long thin strings

[1]spam \'spam\ *n*
e-mail sent to a large number of addresses and usually containing advertising

[2]spam *vb* **spammed**; **spam•ming**
to send spam to
spam•mer \'spa-mər\ *n*

[1]span \'span\ *n*
1 a limited portion of time ⟨*span* of life⟩ ⟨I learned to ski in the *span* of one hour.⟩
2 the spread (as of an arch or bridge) from one support to another
3 the width of something from one side to another

[2]span *vb* **spanned**; **span•ning**
1 to reach or extend across ⟨A bridge *spans* the river.⟩
2 to continue over a period of time ⟨The actor's career *spanned* five decades.⟩

span•gle \'spaŋ-gəl\ *n*
SEQUIN

Span•iard \'span-yərd\ *n*
a person born or living in Spain

span•iel \'span-yəl\ *n*
▶ a small or medium-sized dog with a thick wavy coat, long drooping ears, and usually short legs

[1]Span•ish \'spa-nish\ *adj*
of or relating to Spain, its people, or the Spanish language

[2]Spanish *n*
1 the language of Spain and the countries colonized by Spaniards
2 **Spanish** *pl* the people of Spain

spank \'spaŋk\ *vb* **spanked**; **spank•ing**
to strike on the buttocks with the open hand

[1]spank•ing \'spaŋ-kiŋ\ *adj*
fresh and strong or lively ⟨a *spanking* stallion⟩

[2]spanking *adv*
[1]VERY 1 ⟨a *spanking* new toy⟩

[1]spar \'spär\ *n*
a long rounded piece of wood or metal (as a mast) to which a sail is fastened

[2]spar *vb* **sparred**; **spar•ring**
1 to box or make boxing movements with the fists for practice or for fun
2 to argue often in a playful way

[1]spare \'sper\ *vb* **spared**; **spar•ing**
1 to keep from being punished or harmed : show mercy to ⟨The king promised to *spare* the prisoner.⟩
2 to free from having to go through something difficult ⟨He *spared* us from having to clean up.⟩
3 to keep from using or spending ⟨More pancakes, please, and don't *spare* the syrup.⟩
4 to give up especially as not really needed ⟨Can you *spare* a few minutes?⟩
5 to have left over ⟨I got there with time to *spare*.⟩

[2]spare *adj* **spar•er**; **spar•est**
1 held in reserve (as for an emergency) ⟨a *spare* tire⟩
2 being over what is needed ⟨*spare* time⟩
3 somewhat thin ⟨a *spare* figure⟩
4 SCANTY ⟨a *spare* diet⟩

[3]spare *n*
1 a replacement or duplicate piece or part
2 the knocking down of all ten bowling pins with the first two balls

spare•ribs \'sper-,ribz\ *n pl*
▶ a cut of pork ribs

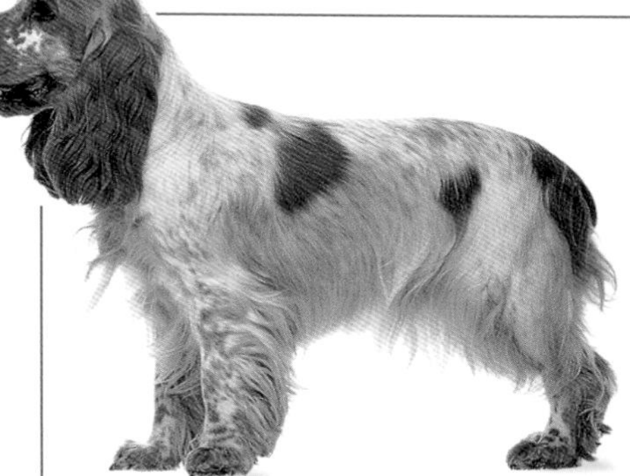

spaniel: an English cocker spaniel

spar•ing \'sper-iŋ\ *adj*
careful in the use of money or supplies ⟨The campers were *sparing* with the matches.⟩
synonyms see ECONOMICAL
spar•ing•ly *adv*

[1]spark \'spärk\ *n*
1 a small bit of burning material ⟨*Sparks* flew from a fire.⟩
2 a hot glowing bit struck from a mass (as by steel on flint)
3 a short bright flash of electricity between two points
4 [2]SPARKLE 1
5 [1]TRACE 2 ⟨He showed a *spark* of interest.⟩

[2]spark *vb* **sparked**; **spark•ing**
1 to give off or cause to give off small bits of burning material or short bright flashes of electricity ⟨The burning wood crackled and *sparked*.⟩ ⟨The wires made contact and *sparked*.⟩
2 to set off ⟨The question *sparked* a discussion.⟩

[1]spar•kle \'spär-kəl\ *vb* **spar•kled**; **spar•kling**
1 to give off small flashes of light ⟨The diamond *sparkled*.⟩
2 to be lively or bright ⟨The conversation *sparkled*.⟩ ⟨His eyes *sparkled*.⟩
synonyms see GLEAM

spareribs: a plate of cooked spareribs

[2]sparkle *n*
1 a little flash of light ⟨*sparkles* of red light⟩
2 the quality of being bright or giving off small flashes of light ⟨the *sparkle* of a diamond⟩ ⟨the *sparkle* of her eyes⟩

spar•kler \'spär-klər\ *n*
a small firework that throws off very bright sparks as it burns

spark plug *n*
a device used in an engine to produce a spark that ignites a fuel mixture

spar•row \'sper-ō\ *n*
a small songbird that has usually brownish or grayish feathers

sparrow hawk *n*
▼ a small hawk

sparrow hawk: a European sparrow hawk

sparse \'spärs\ *adj* **spars•er**; **spars•est**
not thickly grown or settled ⟨a *sparse* beard⟩
sparse•ly *adv*

spasm \'spa-zəm\ *n*
1 a sudden uncontrolled and often painful tightening of muscles ⟨back *spasms*⟩
2 a sudden, strong, and temporary effort, emotion, or outburst ⟨a *spasm* of coughing⟩ ⟨a *spasm* of guilt⟩

spas•mod•ic \spaz-'mä-dik\ *adj*
relating to or affected by spasm : involving spasms ⟨*spasmodic* jerking⟩
spas•mod•i•cal•ly \-di-kə-lē\ *adv*

[1]spat *past and past participle of* SPIT

[2]spat \'spat\ *n*
a cloth or leather covering for the instep and ankle men once wore over shoes

[3]spat *n*
a brief unimportant quarrel

spa•tial \'spā-shəl\ *adj*
of or relating to space

[1]spat•ter \'spa-tər\ *vb* **spat•tered**; **spat•ter•ing**
1 to splash with drops or small bits of something wet ⟨Don't *spatter* the floor with paint.⟩
2 to scatter by splashing ⟨A passing car *spattered* mud on my clothes.⟩

[1]spear 1: a medieval European spear used for hunting

[2]spat·ter *n*
1 the act or sound of something splashing in drops ⟨the *spatter* of rain on a roof⟩
2 a drop or splash spattered on something **:** a spot or stain due to spattering ⟨a grease *spatter*⟩

spat·u·la \ˈspa-chə-lə\ *n*
1 a tool resembling a knife with a broad flexible blade that is used mostly for spreading or mixing soft substances
2 a kitchen utensil with a long handle and a wide blade used for scraping batter from a bowl or for lifting and flipping food

[1]spawn \ˈspȯn\ *vb* **spawned; spawn·ing**
to produce or deposit a large number of eggs ⟨Salmon swim up rivers to *spawn*.⟩

[2]spawn *n*
the many small eggs of an animal (as a fish or frog) that are deposited in water

spay \ˈspā\ *vb* **spayed; spay·ing**
to remove the ovaries of (a female animal) ⟨a *spayed* cat⟩

speak \ˈspēk\ *vb* **spoke** \ˈspōk\; **spo·ken** \ˈspō-kən\; **speak·ing**
1 to utter words **:** TALK ⟨He *speaks* too fast.⟩
2 to utter in words ⟨Does he *speak* the truth?⟩
3 to mention in speech or writing ⟨She *spoke* of being ill.⟩
4 to use or be able to use in talking ⟨Can you *speak* Spanish?⟩
speak out to express an opinion openly
speak up
1 to speak loudly and clearly
2 to express an opinion openly

▶ **Synonyms** SPEAK, TALK, and CONVERSE mean to express in words. SPEAK is used of anything said, whether it is understood or not and whether it is heard or not. ⟨We didn't know what language they were *speaking*.⟩ TALK is used when there is a listener who understands what is said and often when both people do some speaking. ⟨We *talked* about school.⟩ CONVERSE is used for exchanging of thoughts and opinions. ⟨The scientists *conversed* about traveling in space.⟩

speak·er \ˈspē-kər\ *n*
1 a person who speaks
2 a person who conducts a meeting
3 LOUDSPEAKER

[1]spear \ˈspir\ *n*
1 ▲ a weapon with a long straight handle and sharp head or blade used for throwing or jabbing
2 an instrument with a sharp point and curved hooks used in stabbing fish

[2]spear *vb* **speared; spear·ing**
to strike or pierce with or as if with a spear

[3]spear *n*
a usually young blade or sprout (as of grass)

[1]spear·head \ˈspir-ˌhed\ *n*
1 the head or point of a spear
2 the person, thing, or group that is the leading force (as in a development or an attack)

[2]spearhead *vb* **spear·head·ed; spear·head·ing**
to serve as leader of ⟨She *spearheaded* a campaign for change.⟩

spear·mint \ˈspir-ˌmint\ *n*
▶ a common mint used for flavoring

spearmint

spe·cial \ˈspe-shəl\ *adj*
1 unusual and better in some way **:** EXTRAORDINARY ⟨a *special* occasion⟩
2 liked very well ⟨a *special* friend⟩
3 different from others **:** UNIQUE ⟨a *special* case⟩
4 [1]EXTRA ⟨a *special* edition⟩
5 meant for a particular purpose or occasion ⟨a *special* diet⟩
spe·cial·ly *adv*

special education *n*
classes or instruction designed for students with special educational needs

spe·cial·ist \ˈspe-shə-list\ *n*
1 a person who studies or works at a special occupation or branch of learning ⟨a *specialist* in animal behavior⟩ ⟨an eye *specialist*⟩
2 an enlisted person in the army with a rank similar to that of corporal

spe·cial·ize \ˈspe-shə-ˌlīz\ *vb* **spe·cial·ized; spe·cial·iz·ing**
1 to limit attention or energy to one business, subject, or study ⟨The factory will *specialize* in jet airplanes.⟩
2 to change and develop so as to be suited for some particular use or living conditions ⟨The front legs of a mole are *specialized* for digging.⟩

spe·cial·ty \ˈspe-shəl-tē\ *n, pl* **spe·cial·ties**
something for which a person or place is known ⟨Pancakes are my *speciality*.⟩ ⟨Good service is the restaurant's *specialty*.⟩

spe·cies \ˈspē-shēz, -sēz\ *n, pl* **species**
1 a group of similar living things that ranks below the genus in scientific classification and is made up of individuals able to produce offspring with one another ⟨The one-humped camel is a different *species* from the two-humped camel.⟩
2 a class of things of the same kind and with the same name **:** KIND, SORT

spe·cif·ic \spi-ˈsi-fik\ *adj*
1 relating to or being an example of a certain kind of thing ⟨a *specific* case⟩
2 relating to a particular individual or situation ⟨There are problems *specific* to this project.⟩
3 clearly and exactly presented or stated ⟨*specific* directions⟩
spe·cif·ic·al·ly \-ˈsi-fi-kə-lē\ *adv*

spec·i·fi·ca·tion \ˌspe-sə-fə-ˈkā-shən\ *n*
1 the act or process of mentioning exactly and clearly
2 a single item exactly and clearly mentioned
3 a description of work to be done or materials to be used — often used in pl. ⟨building *specifications*⟩

spec·i·fy \ˈspe-sə-ˌfī\ *vb* **spec·i·fied; spec·i·fy·ing**
1 to mention or name exactly and clearly ⟨Can you *specify* the cause of the crash?⟩
2 to include in a description of work to be done or materials to be used

spec·i·men \ˈspe-sə-mən\ *n*
1 something collected as a sample or for examination
2 a notable example of something ⟨The cathedral is a magnificent *specimen* of medieval architecture.⟩
3 an example of a type of person

speck \ˈspek\ *n*
1 a small spot or blemish
2 a very small amount **:** BIT ⟨a *speck* of dirt⟩

[1]speck·le \ˈspe-kəl\ *n*
a small mark (as of color)

[2]speckle *vb* **speck·led; speck·ling**
to mark or be marked with small spots

spec·ta·cle \ˈspek-ti-kəl\ *n*
1 an unusual or impressive public display (as a big parade)
2 **spectacles** *pl* GLASS 3
3 an object of curiosity or contempt ⟨Don't make a *spectacle* of yourself!⟩

spectator: spectators at a sports event

spec•tac•u•lar \spek-ˈta-kyə-lər\ *adj*
STRIKING, SHOWY ⟨a *spectacular* sunset⟩

spec•ta•tor \ˈspek-ˌtā-tər\ *n*
▲ a person who looks on (as at a sports event)

spec•ter *or* **spec•tre** \ˈspek-tər\ *n*
1 GHOST
2 something that haunts or bothers the mind ⟨the *specter* of starvation⟩

spec•trum \ˈspek-trəm\ *n, pl* **spec•tra** \-trə\ *or* **spec•trums**
the group of different colors including red, orange, yellow, green, blue, indigo, and violet seen when light passes through a prism and falls on a surface or when sunlight is affected by drops of water (as in a rainbow)

spec•u•late \ˈspe-kyə-ˌlāt\ *vb* **spec•u•lat•ed**; **spec•u•lat•ing**
1 to think or wonder about something
2 to come up with ideas or theories about something
3 to engage in a risky but possibly very profitable business deal

spec•u•la•tion \ˌspe-kyə-ˈlā-shən\ *n*
1 [2]GUESS
2 the taking of a big risk in business in hopes of making a big profit

SpEd, SPED *abbr* special education

speech \ˈspēch\ *n*
1 the communication or expression of thoughts in spoken words
2 something that is spoken : STATEMENT
3 a public talk
4 a form of communication (as a language or dialect) used by a particular group
5 a way of speaking ⟨her soft *speech*⟩
6 the ability to speak ⟨I was so surprised I lost my *speech.*⟩

speech•less \ˈspēch-ləs\ *adj*
unable to speak especially because of a strong emotion ⟨*speechless* with surprise⟩

[1]speed \ˈspēd\ *n*
1 quickness in movement or action
2 rate of moving or doing ⟨a *speed* of 100 miles an hour⟩

[2]speed *vb* **sped** \ˈsped\ *or* **speed•ed**; **speed•ing**
1 to move or cause to move fast : HURRY
2 to go or drive at too high a rate of movement ⟨I got a ticket for *speeding.*⟩
3 to increase the rate of an action or movement ⟨How can we *speed* this process?⟩
speed up to move more quickly

speed•boat \ˈspēd-ˌbōt\ *n*
a motorboat designed to go fast

speed bump *n*
a low ridge built across a roadway (as in a parking lot) to limit vehicle speed

speed•om•e•ter \spi-ˈdä-mə-tər\ *n*
an instrument that measures speed

speedy \ˈspē-dē\ *adj* **speed•i•er**; **speed•i•est**
moving or taking place fast ⟨She made a *speedy* recovery.⟩
speed•i•ly \ˈspē-də-lē\ *adv*

[1]spell \ˈspel\ *vb* **spelled**; **spell•ing**
1 to name, write, or print in order the letters of a word
2 to make up the letters of ⟨C-A-T *spells* the word "cat."⟩
3 to have (such) a spelling ⟨My name is Lynne *spelled* with an E.⟩
4 to amount to : MEAN ⟨Another drought would *spell* famine.⟩

[2]spell *n*
1 a spoken word or group of words believed to have magic power : CHARM
2 a very strong influence ⟨Their talking broke the music's *spell.*⟩

[3]spell *n*
1 a short period of time ⟨Come and sit a *spell.*⟩
2 a stretch of a specified kind of weather ⟨a dry *spell*⟩ ⟨a warm *spell*⟩
3 a period of bodily or mental distress or disorder ⟨fainting *spells*⟩
4 a person's turn at work or duty
5 a period spent in a job or occupation

[4]spell *vb* **spelled**; **spelling**
to take the place of for a time : RELIEVE ⟨*spell* a person at shoveling⟩

spell•bound \ˈspel-ˌbau̇nd\ *adj*
having the interest or attention held by or as if by magic power

sphinx: the Great Sphinx, a statue constructed in the third millennium B.C. in Egypt

spell–check•er \'spel-,che-kər\ *n*
a computer program that shows the user any words that might be incorrectly spelled

spell•er \'spe-lər\ *n*
1 a person who spells words
2 a book with exercises for teaching spelling

spell•ing \'spe-liŋ\ *n*
1 an exercise or the practice of forming words from letters
2 the letters composing a word ⟨What is the correct *spelling* of your name?⟩

spend \'spend\ *vb* **spent** \'spent\; **spend•ing**
1 to use (money) to pay for something
2 to cause or allow (as time) to pass ⟨He *spent* the night at a friend's house.⟩
3 to use wastefully : SQUANDER

spend•thrift \'spend-,thrift\ *n*
a person who uses up money wastefully

spent \'spent\ *adj*
1 used up ⟨a *spent* battery⟩
2 drained of energy ⟨By Fridays, I'm *spent*.⟩

sperm \'spərm\ *n*
SPERM CELL

sperm cell *n*
a male reproductive cell of animals and plants that can unite with an egg cell to form a new individual cell

sperm whale *n*
► a huge whale with a large head having a closed cavity that contains a mixture of wax and oil

spew \'spyü\ *vb* **spewed**; **spew•ing**
to pour out ⟨The volcano *spewed* lava.⟩

sphere \'sfir\ *n*
1 an object (as the moon) shaped like a ball
2 a figure so shaped that every point on its surface is an equal distance from its center
3 a field of influence or activity ⟨Electrical work is outside a plumber's *sphere*.⟩

spher•i•cal \'sfir-i-kəl, 'sfer-\ *adj*
relating to or having the form of a sphere

sphinx \'sfiŋks\ *n*
▲ a mythical figure of ancient Egypt having the body of a lion and the head of a man, a ram, or a hawk

[1]spice \'spīs\ *n*
1 a seasoning (as pepper or nutmeg) that comes from a dried plant part and that is usually a powder or seed
2 something that adds interest ⟨My boring routine needs some *spice*.⟩

[2]spice *vb* **spiced**; **spic•ing**
to add something that gives flavor or interest ⟨What did you *spice* the stew with?⟩ ⟨A new hairstyle *spiced* up her image.⟩

spick–and–span *or* **spic–and–span** \,spik-ən-'span\ *adj*
1 quite new and unused
2 very clean and neat

sperm whale

spicy \'spī-sē\ *adj* **spic•i•er**; **spic•i•est**
1 flavored with or containing spice ⟨a *spicy* sauce⟩
2 somewhat shocking or indecent ⟨a *spicy* story⟩
spic•i•ness *n*

spi•der \'spī-dər\ *n*
1 ► a wingless animal that is somewhat like an insect but has eight legs instead of six and a body divided into two parts instead of three and that often spins threads of silk into webs for catching prey
2 a cast-iron frying pan

spi•der•web \'spī-dər-,web\ *n*
the silken web spun by most spiders and used as a resting place and a trap for prey

spig•ot \'spi-gət, -kət\ *n*
1 a plug used to stop the vent in a barrel
2 FAUCET

[1]spike \'spīk\ *n*
1 a very large nail
2 something pointed like a nail
3 one of the metal objects attached to the heel and sole of a shoe (as a baseball shoe) to prevent slipping

[2]spike *vb* **spiked**; **spik•ing**
1 to fasten with large nails
2 to pierce or cut with or on a large nail
3 to hit or throw (a ball) sharply downward
4 to add alcohol or drugs to

[3]spike *n*
1 a tight mass of grain ⟨*spikes* of wheat⟩
2 a long usually rather narrow flower cluster in which the blossoms grow very close to a central stem

[1]spill \'spil\ *vb* **spilled** \'spild\ *also* **spilt** \'spilt\; **spill•ing**
1 to cause or allow to fall, flow, or run out so as to be wasted or scattered ⟨I knocked the glass over and *spilled* my milk.⟩
2 to flow or run out, over, or off and become wasted or scattered ⟨He filled the jar until it *spilled* over.⟩ ⟨The milk *spilled*.⟩
3 to cause (blood) to flow by wounding
4 to make known ⟨I accidentally *spilled* the secret.⟩

[2]spill *n*
1 an act of spilling
2 a fall especially from a horse or vehicle
3 something spilled ⟨Please mop up the *spill* on the floor.⟩

[1]spin \'spin\ *vb* **spun** \'spən\; **spin•ning**
1 to turn or cause to turn round and round rapidly : TWIRL ⟨He fell after *spinning* in circles.⟩

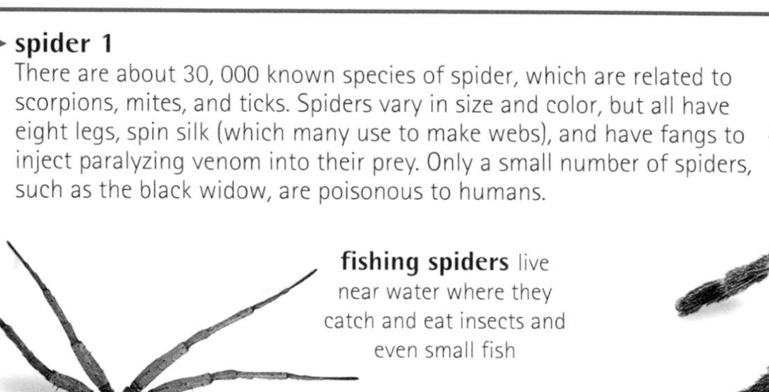

spider 1

There are about 30, 000 known species of spider, which are related to scorpions, mites, and ticks. Spiders vary in size and color, but all have eight legs, spin silk (which many use to make webs), and have fangs to inject paralyzing venom into their prey. Only a small number of spiders, such as the black widow, are poisonous to humans.

fishing spiders live near water where they catch and eat insects and even small fish

features of a tarantula

trap-door spiders build burrows lined with silk and topped with a hinged lid

crab spiders resemble crabs in having a flattened body and in being able to move sideways

2 to make yarn or thread from (fibers) 〈He *spun* the silk into thread.〉
3 to make (yarn or thread) from fibers 〈She was *spinning* yarn from wool.〉
4 to form threads or a web or cocoon by giving off a sticky fluid that quickly hardens 〈A spider was *spinning* its web.〉
5 to feel as if in a whirl 〈My head was *spinning*.〉 〈The room was *spinning*.〉
6 to make up and tell using the imagination 〈I listened to him *spin* a tale.〉
7 to move swiftly on wheels or in a vehicle 〈The car *spun* away.〉
8 to make, shape, or produce by or as if by whirling 〈The woman *spun* sugar as a demonstration.〉
spin•ner \'spi-nər\ *n*

²spin *n*
1 a rapid motion of turning around and around
2 a short trip in or on a wheeled vehicle

spin•ach \'spi-nich\ *n*
a garden plant with usually large dark green leaves that are eaten cooked or raw as a vegetable

spi•nal \'spī-nᵊl\ *adj*
of, relating to, or located near the backbone or the spinal cord 〈a *spinal* injury〉

spinal column *n*
BACKBONE 1

spinal cord *n*
a thick bundle of nerves that extends from the brain down through the cavity of the backbone and connects with nerves throughout the body to carry information to and from the brain

spin•dle \'spin-dəl\ *n*
1 a slender round rod or stick with narrowed ends by which thread is twisted in spinning and on which it is wound
2 something (as an axle or shaft) which has a slender round shape and on which something turns

spinet 1:
an 18th-century spinet from England

spin•dly \'spind-lē\ *adj*
being thin and long or tall and usually feeble or weak 〈*spindly* legs〉 〈a *spindly* plant〉

spine \'spīn\ *n*
1 BACKBONE 1
2 a stiff pointed part growing from the surface of a plant or animal

spine•less \'spīn-ləs\ *adj*
1 lacking spines 〈*spineless* stems〉
2 having no backbone 〈a *spineless* animal〉
3 lacking spirit, courage, or determination

spin•et \'spi-nət\ *n*
1 ◀ a harpsichord with one keyboard and only one string for each note
2 a small upright piano

spinning wheel *n*
a small machine driven by the hand or foot that is used to spin yarn or thread

spin•ster \'spin-stər\ *n*
an unmarried woman past the usual age for marrying

spiny \'spī-nē\ *adj* **spin•i•er; spin•i•est**
covered with spines

spiny lobster *n*
a sea animal that is related to and resembles the lobster

spi•ra•cle \'spir-ə-kəl\ *n*
an opening on the body (as of an insect) used for breathing

¹spiral 2: a spiral staircase in Vatican City

¹spi•ral \'spī-rəl\ *adj*
1 winding or circling around a center and gradually getting closer to or farther away from it ⟨the *spiral* seashell⟩
2 ▲ circling around a center like the thread of a screw ⟨a *spiral* staircase⟩

²spiral *n*
1 a single turn or coil in a spiral object
2 something having a form that winds or circles around a center

³spiral *vb* **spi•raled** *or* **spi•ralled**; **spi•ral•ing** *or* **spi•ral•ling**
to move in or as if in a winding or circular path ⟨Smoke *spiraled* from the chimney.⟩

spire \'spīr\ *n*
1 a pointed roof especially of a tower
2 STEEPLE

spi•rea *or* **spi•raea** \spī-'rē-ə\ *n*
▶ a shrub related to the rose that bears clusters of small white or pink flowers

¹spir•it \'spir-ət\ *n*
1 ¹MOOD ⟨I'm in good *spirits* today.⟩
2 a being (as a ghost) whose existence cannot be explained
3 a lively or brisk quality ⟨They sang with *spirit*.⟩
4 a force within a human being thought to give the body life, energy, and power : SOUL
5 an attitude or feeling ⟨It was said in a *spirit* of fun.⟩
6 PERSON 1 ⟨She was a bold *spirit*.⟩
7 an alcoholic liquor usually used in pl.
8 *cap* God in the form of a spirit in Christianity
9 **spirits** *pl* a solution in alcohol ⟨*spirits* of camphor⟩
10 real meaning or intention ⟨the *spirit* of the law⟩
spir•it•less \-ləs\ *adj*

²spirit *vb* **spir•it•ed**; **spir•it•ing**
to carry off secretly or mysteriously ⟨The jewels were *spirited* out of the country.⟩

spir•it•ed \'spir-ə-təd\ *adj*
full of courage or energy ⟨a *spirited* horse⟩ ⟨a *spirited* debate⟩

¹spir•i•tu•al \'spir-i-chə-wəl\ *adj*
1 of, relating to, or consisting of spirit : not bodily or material
2 of or relating to sacred or religious matters
spir•i•tu•al•ly *adv*

²spiritual *n*
a religious folk song developed especially among black people of the southern United States

¹spit \'spit\ *vb* **spit** *or* **spat** \'spat\; **spit•ting**
1 to force (saliva) from the mouth ⟨He *spat* on the ground.⟩
2 to force (something) from the mouth ⟨*Spit* out your gum.⟩
3 to express by or as if by spitting ⟨He was *spitting* an angry answer.⟩
4 to give off usually briskly : EMIT ⟨The fire is *spitting* sparks.⟩
5 to rain lightly or snow in flurries
spit up ²VOMIT ⟨The baby *spit up.*⟩

²spit *n*
1 SALIVA
2 a foamy material given off by some insects
3 perfect likeness ⟨The child was the *spit* and image of the parent.⟩

spirea: spirea flowers

³spit *n*
1 a thin pointed rod for holding meat over a fire
2 a small point of land that runs out into a body of water

¹spite \'spīt\ *n*
dislike or hatred for another person with a wish to torment, anger, or defeat
in spite of without being prevented by ⟨The club failed *in spite of* our efforts.⟩

²spite *vb* **spit•ed**; **spit•ing**
ANNOY, ANGER ⟨He did it to *spite* me.⟩

spite•ful \'spīt-fəl\ *adj*
filled with or showing spite : MALICIOUS
spite•ful•ly \-fə-lē\ *adv*

spitting image *n*
IMAGE 2

spit•tle \'spi-tᵊl\ *n*
1 SALIVA
2 ²SPIT 3

¹splash \'splash\ *vb* **splashed**; **splash•ing**
1 to hit (something liquid or sloppy) and cause to move and scatter roughly
2 to wet or soil by spattering with something wet (as water or mud) ⟨I got *splashed* by a passing car.⟩
3 to move or strike with a splashing sound ⟨Children like to *splash* through a puddle.⟩
4 to spread or scatter like a splashed liquid ⟨The sunset *splashed* the sky with red.⟩

²splash *n*
1 material that has been hit and made to scatter
2 a spot or smear from or as if from liquid that has been hit and made to scatter
3 the sound or action of liquid that has been hit and made to scatter

¹splat•ter \'spla-tər\ *vb* **splat•tered**; **splat•ter•ing**
to splash against something in large drops

²splatter *n*
²SPLASH 2

spleen \'splēn\ *n*
an organ near the stomach that destroys worn-out red blood cells and produces some of the white blood cells

splen•did \'splen-dəd\ *adj*
1 impressive in beauty, excellence, or magnificence ⟨You did a *splendid* job.⟩ ⟨a *splendid* palace⟩
2 having or showing splendor : BRILLIANT
3 EXCELLENT ⟨We had a *splendid* time.⟩
splen•did•ly *adv*

▶ **Synonyms** SPLENDID, GLORIOUS, and SUPERB mean very impressive. SPLENDID is used for something far above the ordinary in excellence or magnificence. ⟨What a *splendid* idea!⟩ ⟨She wore a *splendid* jewel.⟩ GLORIOUS is used for something that is radiant with light or beauty. ⟨I watched the *glorious* sunset.⟩ SUPERB is used of the highest possible point of magnificence or excellence. ⟨The food was *superb*.⟩

splen•dor \'splen-dər\ *n*
1 great brightness ⟨the *splendor* of the sun⟩
2 POMP, GLORY ⟨the *splendors* of ancient Rome⟩
3 an impressive feature ⟨The house has many *splendors*.⟩

[1]splice \'splīs\ *vb* **spliced**; **splic•ing**
1 to unite (as two ropes) by weaving together
2 to unite (as rails or pieces of film) by connecting the ends together

[2]splice *n*
the process of joining or a joint made by weaving or connecting the ends together

splint \'splint\ *n*
1 a thin flexible strip of wood woven together with others in making a chair seat or basket
2 a rigid device for keeping a broken or displaced bone in place while it heals

[1]splin•ter \'splin-tər\ *n*
a thin piece split or torn off lengthwise : SLIVER

[2]splinter *vb* **splin•tered**; **splin•ter•ing**
to break into slivers

[1]split \'split\ *vb* **split**; **split•ting**
1 to divide lengthwise or by layers ⟨*split* a log⟩
2 to separate into parts or groups ⟨Let's *split* up and search different areas.⟩
3 to burst or break apart or in pieces
4 to divide into shares or sections

[2]split *n*
1 a product or result of dividing, separating, or breaking apart : CRACK

[2]split 3: a gymnast performing a split

2 the act or process of dividing, separating, or breaking apart : DIVISION
3 ▲ an action or position in which a person's legs are extended in a straight line and in opposite directions

[3]split *adj*
divided by or as if by splitting ⟨We're *split* on what to do next.⟩

splurge \'splərj\ *vb* **splurged**; **splurg•ing**
to spend lavishly or give in to indulgence

splut•ter \'splə-tər\ *vb* **splut•tered**; **splut•ter•ing**
1 to make a noise as if spitting
2 to speak or say in haste or confusion

[1]spoil \'spȯil\ *vb* **spoiled** \'spȯild\ *or* **spoilt** \'spȯilt\; **spoil•ing**
1 to damage the character of by allowing too many things or not correcting bad behavior ⟨The boy's parents *spoiled* him.⟩

[1]sponge 2

2 to damage badly : RUIN ⟨Frost *spoiled* the crop.⟩
3 to damage the quality or effect of ⟨A quarrel *spoiled* the celebration.⟩
4 to decay or lose freshness, value, or usefulness by being kept too long ⟨The milk *spoiled*.⟩

[2]spoil *n*
stolen goods : PLUNDER

spoil•age \'spȯi-lij\ *n*
the process or result of the decay of food

spoil•er \'spȯi-lər\ *n*
1 a person or thing that spoils something
2 a device (as on an airplane or automobile) that controls the flow of air and lift
3 information about the plot of a book, movie, or television show that spoils the surprise or suspense for a reader or viewer

[1]spoke *past of* SPEAK

[2]spoke \'spōk\ *n*
▶ one of the bars or rods extending from the hub of a wheel to the rim

[1]spoken *past participle of* SPEAK

[2]spo•ken \'spō-kən\ *adj*
1 expressed in speech : ORAL
2 used in speaking ⟨the *spoken* language⟩
3 speaking in a specified manner ⟨soft-*spoken*⟩

spokes•man \'spōks-mən\ *n, pl* **spokes•men** \'spōks-mən\
a person who speaks for or represents someone or something

spokes•per•son \'spōks-,pər-sᵊn\ *n*
SPOKESMAN

spokes•wom•an \'spōks-,wu̇-mən\ *n, pl* **spokes•wom•en** \-,wi-mən\
a woman who speaks for or represents someone or something

[1]sponge \'spənj\ *n*
1 a water animal that lives permanently attached to a solid surface (as the ocean bottom) and has a simple body of loosely connected cells with a skeleton supported by stiff fibers or hard particles
2 ◀ a piece of springy material that forms the skeleton of sponges or is manufactured and is used for cleaning
3 a pad of folded gauze used in surgery and medicine

[2]sponge *vb* **sponged**; **spong•ing**
1 to clean or wipe with a sponge
2 to get something or live at the expense of another ⟨He *sponged* off me for dinner.⟩

spongy \'spən-jē\ *adj* **spong•i•er**; **spong•i•est**
springy and absorbent ⟨*spongy* ground⟩

[1]spon•sor \'spän-sər\ *n*
1 a person who takes the responsibility for some other person or thing ⟨He agreed to be our *sponsor* at the club.⟩
2 a person who represents someone being baptized and takes responsibility for his or her spiritual development : GODPARENT
3 a person or an organization that pays for or plans and carries out a project or activity
4 a person who gives money to someone participating in an event for charity
5 a person or an organization that pays the cost of a radio or television program
spon•sor•ship \-,ship\ *n*

[2]sponsor *vb* **spon•sored**; **spon•sor•ing**
to act as sponsor for

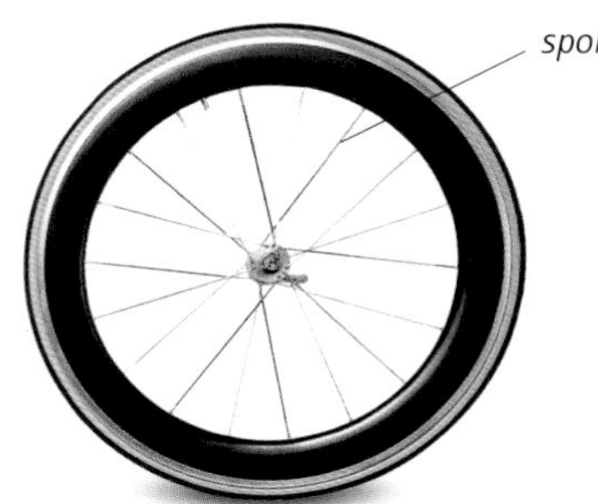

[2]spoke: spokes on a bicycle wheel

spon•ta•ne•ous \spän-'tā-nē-əs\ *adj*
1 done, said, or produced freely and naturally ⟨*spontaneous* laughter⟩
2 acting or taking place without outside force or cause ⟨a *spontaneous* fire⟩
spon•ta•ne•ous•ly *adv*

A B C D E F G H I J K L M N O P Q R S T U V W X Y Z

spontaneous combustion *n*
a bursting of material into flame from the heat produced within itself through chemical action

[1]spook \'spük\ *vb* **spooked**; **spook•ing**
to make or become frightened

[2]spook *n*
GHOST, SPECTER

spooky \'spü-kē\ *adj* **spook•i•er**; **spook•i•est**
1 scary and frightening ⟨a *spooky* story⟩
2 suggesting the presence of ghosts ⟨a *spooky* place⟩ ⟨a *spooky* noise⟩

spool: a spool of thread

spool \'spül\ *n*
► a small cylinder which has a rim or ridge at each end and a hole from end to end for a pin or spindle and on which material (as thread, wire, or tape) is wound

[1]spoon \'spün\ *n*
an eating and cooking utensil consisting of a small shallow bowl with a handle

[2]spoon *vb* **spooned**; **spoon•ing**
to take up in or as if in a spoon

spoon•bill \'spün-,bil\ *n*
▼ a wading bird having a bill which widens and flattens at the tip

spoonbill: a roseate \'rō-zē-ət\ spoonbill

spoon•ful \'spün-,fu̇l\ *n*, *pl* **spoon•fuls** \-,fu̇lz\ *also* **spoons•ful** \'spünz-,fu̇l\
as much as a spoon can hold

spore \'spȯr\ *n*
a reproductive body that is produced by fungi and by some plants and microorganisms and consists of a single cell that is able to produce a new individual
spored \'spȯrd\ *adj*

[1]sport \'spȯrt\ *n*
1 physical activity (as running or an athletic game) engaged in for pleasure or exercise ⟨Skating is my favorite *sport*.⟩
2 a person who shows good sportsmanship ⟨He's a *sport* and doesn't mind losing.⟩ ⟨Don't be a bad *sport*.⟩
3 PASTIME, RECREATION
4 [1]FUN 3 ⟨He made *sport* of their embarrassment.⟩

[2]sport *vb* **sport•ed**; **sport•ing**
to wear in a way that attracts attention ⟨She came to school *sporting* new shoes.⟩

sports•man \'spȯrts-mən\ *n*, *pl* **sports•men** \'spȯrts-mən\
a person who engages in or is interested in sports and especially outdoor sports (as hunting and fishing)

sports•man•ship \'spȯrts-mən-,ship\ *n*
fair play, respect for opponents, and gracious behavior in winning or losing

sports•wom•an \'spȯrts-,wu̇-mən\ *n*, *pl* **sports•wom•en** \-,wi-mən\
a woman who engages in or is interested in sports and especially outdoor sports

sport–utility vehicle *n*
an automobile similar to a station wagon but built on a light truck frame

[1]spot \'spät\ *n*
1 a small part that is different from the main part ⟨He has a bald *spot*.⟩
2 an area soiled or marked (as by dirt)
3 a particular place ⟨a good *spot* for a picnic⟩
4 [1]POSITION 3
5 FAULT 1 ⟨There's a *spot* on his good name.⟩
spot•ted \'spä-təd\ *adj*
on the spot
1 right away ⟨She was hired *on the spot*.⟩
2 at the place of action ⟨The reporter was reporting *on the spot*.⟩
3 in difficulty or danger ⟨The question put me *on the spot*.⟩

[2]spot *vb* **spot•ted**; **spot•ting**
1 to mark or be marked with spots
2 to single out : IDENTIFY ⟨I *spotted* him in the crowd.⟩

spot•less \'spät-ləs\ *adj*
1 free from spot or blemish ⟨*spotless* skin⟩
2 perfectly clean or pure ⟨a *spotless* bathroom⟩ ⟨a *spotless* record⟩
spot•less•ly *adv*

[1]spot•light \'spät-,līt\ *n*
1 a spot of light used to show up a particular area, person, or thing (as on a stage)
2 public notice ⟨She's a celebrity but doesn't like the *spotlight*.⟩
3 ► a lamp used to direct a narrow strong beam of light on a small area

[2]spotlight *vb* **spot•light•ed** *or* **spot•lit** \'spät-,lit\; **spot•light•ing**
1 to light up with or as if with a spotlight
2 to bring to public attention

spotted owl *n*
a rare brown owl with white spots and dark stripes that is found from British Columbia to southern California and central Mexico

spot•ty \'spä-tē\ *adj* **spot•ti•er**; **spot•ti•est**
1 having spots
2 not always the same especially in quality ⟨Your work has been *spotty*.⟩

spouse \'spau̇s\ *n*
a married person : HUSBAND, WIFE

[1]spout \'spau̇t\ *vb* **spout•ed**; **spout•ing**
1 to shoot out (liquid) with force ⟨Wells *spouted* oil.⟩
2 to speak with a long and quick flow of words so as to sound important ⟨He *spouted* his opinions at the meeting.⟩
3 to flow out with force : SPURT ⟨Blood *spouted* from the wound.⟩

[2]spout *n*
1 a tube, pipe, or hole through which something (as rainwater) shoots out
2 a sudden strong stream of fluid

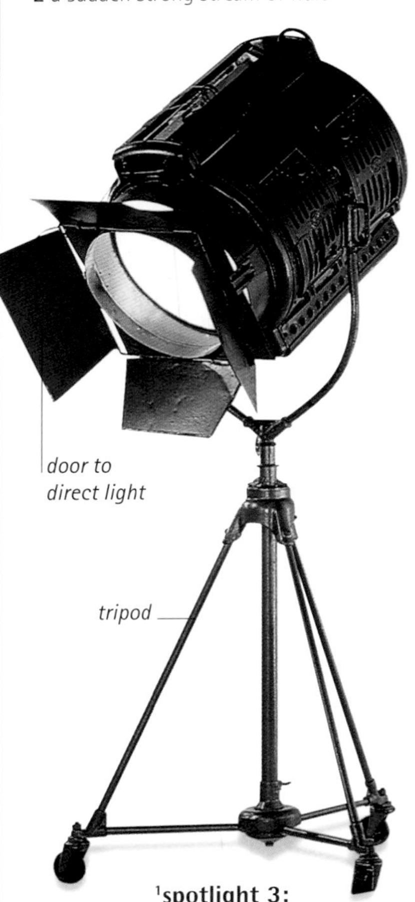

[1]spotlight 3: a spotlight used in a film studio

[1]sprain \ˈsprān\ *n*
an injury that results from the sudden or severe twisting of a joint with stretching or tearing of ligaments

[2]sprain *vb* **sprained**; **sprain•ing**
to injure by a sudden or severe twist 〈She fell and *sprained* her ankle.〉

sprang *past of* SPRING

[1]sprawl \ˈspról\ *vb* **sprawled**; **sprawl•ing**
1 to lie or sit with arms and legs spread out
2 to spread out unevenly

[2]sprawl *n*
the act or posture of spreading out

[1]spray \ˈsprā\ *vb* **sprayed**; **spray•ing**
1 to scatter or let fall in a fine mist 〈She *sprayed* paint on the boards.〉
2 to scatter fine mist on or into 〈I *sprayed* the boards with paint.〉
spray•er *n*

[2]spray *n*
1 liquid flying in fine drops like water blown from a wave
2 a burst of fine mist
3 a device for scattering fine drops of liquid or mist

[3]spray *n*
a green or flowering branch or a usually flat arrangement of these

[1]spread \ˈspred\ *vb* **spread**; **spread•ing**
1 to stretch out : EXTEND 〈I *spread* my arms wide.〉
2 to pass or cause to pass from person to person 〈The news *spread* rapidly.〉 〈Flies can *spread* disease.〉
3 to open or arrange over a larger area 〈The captain *spread* out a map.〉
4 to increase in size or occurrence 〈The fire keeps *spreading*.〉 〈Cell phone use *spread* quickly.〉
5 to scatter or be scattered 〈*spread* fertilizer〉
6 to give out over a period of time or among a group 〈The boss *spread* work to make it last.〉
7 to put or have a layer of on a surface 〈He *spread* butter on bread.〉
8 to cover something with 〈Mom *spread* a cloth on the table.〉
9 to stretch or move apart 〈I *spread* my fingers open.〉
10 to prepare for a meal : SET 〈The table was *spread* for dinner.〉

[2]spread *n*
1 the act or process of increasing in size, amount, or occurrence 〈the *spread* of education〉
2 the distance between two points that are farthest to each side 〈the *spread* of a bird's wings〉
3 a noticeable display in a magazine or newspaper
4 a food to be put over the surface of bread or crackers 〈cheese *spread*〉
5 a very fine meal : FEAST
6 a cloth cover for a table or bed

spree \ˈsprē\ *n*
an outburst of an activity 〈They went on a buying *spree*.〉

sprig \ˈsprig\ *n*
a small shoot or twig

spright•ly \ˈsprīt-lē\ *adj* **spright•li•er**; **spright•li•est**
full of spirit : LIVELY

[1]spring \ˈspriŋ\ *vb* **sprang** \ˈspraŋ\ *or* **sprung** \ˈsprəŋ\; **sprung**; **spring•ing**
1 to move suddenly upward or forward : LEAP 〈The lion crouched, waiting to *spring*.〉
2 to appear or grow quickly or suddenly 〈Weeds *sprang* up overnight.〉 〈Tears *sprang* from her eyes.〉
3 to have (a leak) appear
4 to move quickly by or as if by stretching and springing back 〈The lid *sprang* shut.〉
5 to cause to operate suddenly 〈He was planning to *spring* a trap.〉
6 to come into being : ARISE 〈Hope *springs* eternal.〉

[2]spring *n*
1 the season between winter and summer including in the northern hemisphere usually the months of March, April, and May
2 a twisted or coiled strip of material (as metal) that recovers its original shape when it is released after being squeezed or stretched
3 the ability of something to return to its original shape when it is compressed or stretched
4 a source of supply (as of water coming up from the ground)
5 the act or an instance of leaping up or forward
6 a bouncy or lively quality 〈She had a *spring* in her step.〉

spring•board \ˈspriŋ-ˌbȯrd\ *n*
▼a flexible board usually fastened at one end and used for jumping high in the air in gymnastics or diving

spring peeper

spring peep•er \-ˈpē-pər\ *n*
▲a small frog that makes a high peeping sound heard mostly in spring

spring•time \ˈspring-ˌtīm\ *n*
the season of spring

springy \ˈspriŋ-ē\ *adj* **spring•i•er**; **spring•i•est**
1 able to return to an original shape when twisted or stretched 〈a *springy* branch〉
2 having or showing a lively and energetic movement 〈He walks with a *springy* step.〉

[1]sprin•kle \ˈspriŋ-kəl\ *vb* **sprin•kled**; **sprin•kling**
1 to scatter in drops or particles 〈*sprinkle* water〉 〈*sprinkle* sand〉
2 to scatter over or in or among 〈*Sprinkle* the corn with salt.〉
3 to rain lightly
sprin•kler \-klər\ *n*

[2]sprinkle *n*
1 a light rain
2 SPRINKLING

sprin•kling \ˈspriŋ-kliŋ\ *n*
a very small number or amount

[1]sprint \ˈsprint\ *vb* **sprint•ed**; **sprint•ing**
to run at top speed especially for a short distance
sprint•er *n*

[2]sprint *n*
1 a short run at top speed
2 a race over a short distance

sprite \ˈsprīt\ *n*
ELF, FAIRY

springboard:
a springboard used in gymnastics

sprock•et \'sprä-kət\ *n*
▶ one of many points that stick up on the rim of a wheel (**sprocket wheel**) shaped so as to fit into the links of a chain

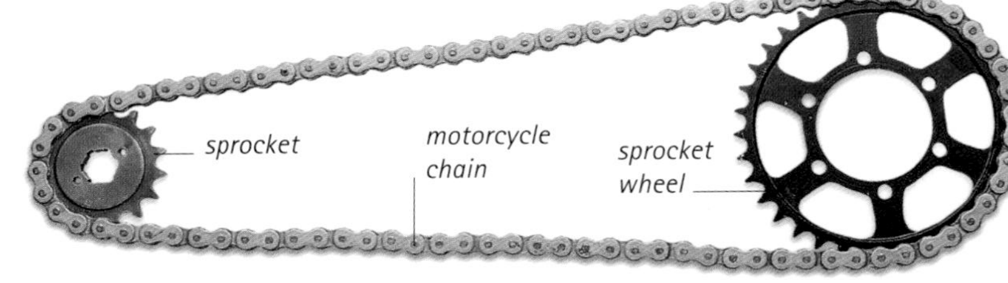

sprocket: sprockets on the sprocket wheels of a motorcycle

[1]**sprout** \'spraůt\ *vb* **sprout•ed; sprout•ing**
to produce or cause to produce new growth ⟨The seeds of corn were *sprouting*.⟩

[2]**sprout** *n*
a young stem of a plant especially when coming directly from a seed or root

[1]**spruce** \'sprüs\ *n*
an evergreen tree that has short needles for leaves, drooping cones, and light soft wood

[2]**spruce** *vb* **spruced; spruc•ing**
to make (someone or something) neat or stylish in appearance ⟨Fresh paint *spruced* up the room.⟩ ⟨Let me *spruce* up before we go.⟩

[3]**spruce** *adj* **spruc•er; spruc•est**
neat or stylish in appearance
spruce•ly *adv*

sprung *past and past participle of* SPRING

spry \'sprī\ *adj* **spri•er** *or* **spry•er; spri•est** *or* **spry•est**
LIVELY 1, ACTIVE ⟨My grandma is still *spry* at 80.⟩

spun *past and past participle of* SPIN

spunk \'spəŋk\ *n*
COURAGE, SPIRIT

▶ **Word History** The English word *spunk* comes from *spong*, a word in Scottish Gaelic (the traditional language of northern Scotland) that meant "tinder" or "sponge." This word, in turn, came from Latin *spongia*, "sponge." The English word at first meant "tinder," which is a spongy material that catches fire easily. Since the human spirit can also be thought of as catching fire, *spunk* came to mean "spirit."

spunky \'spəŋ-kē\ *adj* **spunk•i•er; spunk•i•est**
full of spirit and courage

[1]**spur** \'spər\ *n*
1 a pointed device fastened to the back of a rider's boot and used to urge a horse on
2 something that makes a person want to do something : INCENTIVE
3 a mass of jagged rock coming out from the side of a mountain
4 a short section of railway track coming away from the main line
5 a usually short pointed growth or projecting part (as a spine on the leg of a rooster)
spurred \'spərd\ *adj*
on the spur of the moment without thinking for a long time ⟨We decided to go *on the spur of the moment*.⟩
Hint: *Spur-of-the-moment* is often used as an adjective. ⟨a *spur-of-the-moment* decision⟩

[2]**spur** *vb* **spurred; spur•ring**
1 to urge a horse on with spurs
2 INCITE ⟨A promised reward *spurred* them to work.⟩

spurn \'spərn\ *vb* **spurned; spurn•ing**
to reject with scorn ⟨He *spurned* the offer.⟩

[1]**spurt** \'spərt\ *vb* **spurt•ed; spurt•ing**
to pour out or make pour out suddenly ⟨Water *spurted* from the leaky hose.⟩ ⟨His nose *spurted* blood.⟩

[2]**spurt** *n*
a sudden pouring out ⟨a *spurt* of venom⟩

[3]**spurt** *n*
a brief burst of increased effort, activity, or development

[1]**sput•ter** \'spə-tər\ *vb* **sput•tered; sput•ter•ing**
1 to spit noisily from the mouth ⟨She came out of the water coughing and *sputtering*.⟩
2 to speak in a hasty or explosive way in confusion or excitement ⟨Students *sputtered* out protests.⟩
3 to make explosive popping sounds ⟨The motor *sputtered* and died.⟩

[2]**sputter** *n*
the act or sound of sputtering

[1]**spy** \'spī\ *vb* **spied; spy•ing**
1 to watch secretly ⟨Agents *spied* on the enemy.⟩
2 to catch sight of : SEE ⟨They *spied* land from their ship.⟩

[2]**spy** *n, pl* **spies**
1 a person who watches the movement or actions of others especially in secret
2 a person who tries secretly to get information especially about a country or organization for another country or organization

spy•glass \'spī-ˌglas\ *n*
▼ a small telescope

spyglass

squab \'skwäb\ *n*
a young pigeon especially when ready for use as food

[1]**squab•ble** \'skwä-bəl\ *n*
a noisy quarrel usually over something unimportant

[2]**squabble** *vb* **squab•bled; squab•bling**
to quarrel noisily for little or no reason

squad \'skwäd\ *n*
1 a small group of soldiers
2 a small group working or playing together ⟨a football *squad*⟩

squad car *n*
CRUISER 1

squad•ron \'skwä-drən\ *n*
1 a group of soldiers, ships, or aircraft moving and working together
2 a large group ⟨A *squadron* of geese flew overhead.⟩

squal•id \'skwä-ləd\ *adj*
filthy or degraded from a lack of care or money ⟨They lived in *squalid* conditions.⟩

[1]**squall** \'skwȯl\ *vb* **squalled; squall•ing**
to let out a harsh cry or scream

[2]**squall** *n*
a harsh cry

[3]**squall** *n*
a sudden strong gust of wind often with rain or snow

squal•or \'skwä-lər\ *n*
the quality or state of being squalid ⟨The children had to live in *squalor*.⟩

squan•der \'skwän-dər\ *vb* **squan•dered; squan•der•ing**
to spend foolishly : WASTE ⟨She *squandered* her allowance.⟩ ⟨Don't *squander* this opportunity.⟩

[1]**square** \'skwer\ *n*
1 a flat geometric figure that has four equal sides and four right angles
2 something formed with four equal or roughly equal sides and four right angles ⟨the *squares* of a checkerboard⟩
3 the product of a number or amount multiplied by itself
4 an open place or area where two or more streets meet

A B C D E F G H I J K L M N O P Q R S T U V W X Y Z

5 ▼ a tool having at least one right angle and two or more straight edges used to mark or test right angles ⟨a carpenter's *square*⟩

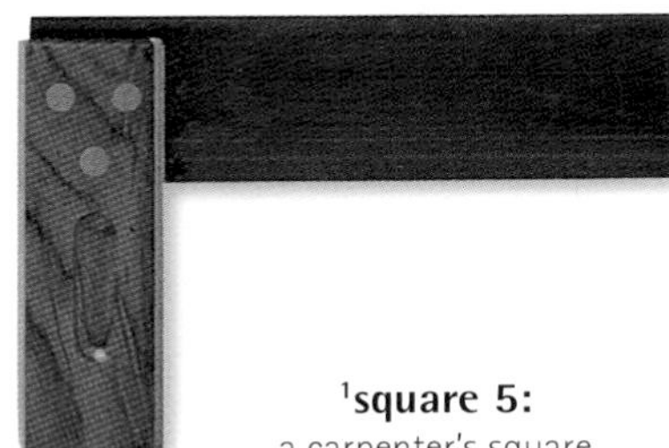

[1]square 5:
a carpenter's square

[2]square *adj* **squar•er; squar•est**
1 having four equal sides and four right angles ⟨a *square* room⟩
2 being a unit of area consisting of a figure with four right angles and four sides of a given length ⟨a *square* meter⟩
3 having a specified length in each of two equal dimensions ⟨The room is ten feet *square*.⟩
4 having outlines that suggest sharp corners rather than curves ⟨a *square* jaw⟩
5 forming a right angle ⟨a *square* corner⟩
6 [1]JUST 4, FAIR ⟨a *square* deal⟩
7 not owing anything **:** EVEN ⟨I paid you back so we're *square*.⟩
8 large enough to satisfy ⟨a *square* meal⟩
square•ly *adv*

[3]square *vb* **squared; squar•ing**
1 to form with right angles, straight edges, and flat surfaces ⟨I need to *square* off the boards.⟩
2 to make straight ⟨I sat before the boss and *squared* my shoulders.⟩
3 to multiply a number by itself
4 AGREE 4 ⟨Your story does not *square* with the facts.⟩
5 [1]SETTLE 11 ⟨Let's *square* our accounts.⟩

[4]square *adv*
in a direct, firm, or honest way ⟨She won fair and *square*.⟩ ⟨He looked me *square* in the eye.⟩

square dance *n*
a dance for four couples who form the sides of a square

square knot *n*
a knot made of two half-knots tied in opposite directions that does not come untied easily

square–rigged \'skwer-'rigd\ *adj*
having the principal sails extended on yards fastened in a horizontal position to the masts at their center

square root *n*
a number that when multiplied by itself equals a specified number ⟨The *square root* of 9 is 3.⟩

[1]squash \'skwäsh\ *vb* **squashed; squash•ing**
to beat or press into a soft or flat mass **:** CRUSH

[2]squash *n*
▶ the fruit of a plant related to the gourd that comes in many varieties and is usually eaten as a vegetable

[2]squash:
different varieties of squash

[1]squat \'skwät\ *vb* **squat•ted; squat•ting**
1 to crouch by bending the knees fully so as to sit on or close to the heels
2 to settle without any right on land that someone else owns
3 to settle on government land in order to become its owner

[2]squat *adj* **squat•ter; squat•test**
1 low to the ground
2 having a short thick body

[3]squat *n*
a position in which the knees are fully bent and the body sits on or close to the heels

[1]squawk \'skwȯk\ *vb* **squawked; squawk•ing**
1 to make a harsh short cry ⟨The bird *squawked* loudly.⟩
2 to complain or protest loudly or with strong feeling

[2]squawk *n*
1 a harsh short cry
2 a noisy complaint

[1]squeak \'skwēk\ *vb* **squeaked; squeak•ing**
1 to make a short high-pitched cry or sound
2 to barely get, win, or pass ⟨He *squeaked* through the fence.⟩

[2]squeak *n*
a short high-pitched cry or sound

squeaky \'skwē-kē\ *adj* **squeak•i•er; squeak•i•est**
making or likely to make a short high-pitched cry or sound ⟨a *squeaky* voice⟩ ⟨a *squeaky* door⟩

[1]squeal \'skwēl\ *vb* **squealed; squeal•ing**
1 to make a sharp long high-pitched cry or noise
2 INFORM 2

[2]squeal *n*
a sharp high-pitched cry or noise

squea•mish \'skwē-mish\ *adj*
hesitant because of shock or disgust ⟨I'm *squeamish* about giving blood.⟩

[1]squeeze \'skwēz\ *vb* **squeezed; squeez•ing**
1 to press together from the opposite sides or parts of **:** COMPRESS
2 to get by squeezing ⟨*Squeeze* the juice from a lemon.⟩
3 to force or crowd in by compressing ⟨We *squeezed* into the car.⟩

[2]squeeze *n*
an act or instance of compressing

squid \'skwid\ *n*
a sea mollusk that is related to the octopus and has a long thin soft body with eight short arms and two usually longer tentacles

[1]squint \'skwint\ *vb* **squint•ed; squint•ing**
1 to look or peer with the eyes partly closed ⟨She *squinted* to read the small print.⟩
2 to cause (an eye) to partly close

[2]squint *n*
the action or an instance of causing the eyes to partly close or of looking at something with the eyes partly closed

squire \'skwīr\ *n*
1 a person who carries the shield or armor of a knight
2 [1]ESCORT 1
3 an owner of a country estate

squirm \'skwərm\ *vb* **squirmed; squirm•ing**
to twist about because of nervousness or embarrassment or in an effort to move or escape ⟨The children got bored and began to *squirm*.⟩

A B C D E F G H I J K L M N O P Q R S T U V W X Y Z

squir•rel \'skwər-əl\ *n*
▼ a small gnawing animal that is a rodent usually with a bushy tail and soft fur and strong hind legs used especially for leaping among tree branches

▶ **Word History** When a squirrel sits up, its long tail curves up and over its head and sometimes casts a shadow. The English word *squirrel* comes ultimately from the Greek word for a squirrel, *skiouros*, which is thought to mean "shadow-tailed" (*skia*, "shadow," plus *oura*, "tail").

▶ **squirrel**
Squirrels are rodents with a long bushy tail and large eyes and ears. Like other rodents, they have teeth adapted for gnawing, and they usually feed on nuts and seeds.

gray squirrel

European red squirrel

¹squirt \'skwərt\ *vb* **squirt•ed**; **squirt•ing**
to shoot out liquid in a thin stream : SPURT

²squirt *n*
a small powerful stream of liquid : JET

Sr. *abbr*
1 senior
2 sister

st. *abbr* state

St. *abbr*
1 saint
2 street

¹stab \'stab\ *n*
1 a wound produced by or as if by a pointed weapon
2 ²THRUST 1 ⟨His first *stab* missed.⟩
3 ²TRY, EFFORT ⟨Take a *stab* at the answer.⟩

²stab *vb* **stabbed**; **stab•bing**
1 to wound or pierce with or as if with a pointed weapon
2 ¹DRIVE 4, THRUST ⟨She *stabbed* a fork into the meat.⟩

sta•bil•i•ty \stə-'bi-lə-tē\ *n, pl* **sta•bil•i•ties**
the condition of being reliable or unlikely to change suddenly or greatly

sta•bi•lize \'stā-bə-,līz\ *vb* **sta•bi•lized**; **sta•bi•liz•ing**
to make or become unlikely to change suddenly or greatly
sta•bi•liz•er *n*

¹sta•ble \'stā-bəl\ *n*
a building in which horses are housed and cared for

²stable *vb* **sta•bled**; **sta•bling**
to put or keep in a stable

³stable *adj* **sta•bler**; **sta•blest**
1 not easily changed or affected ⟨a *stable* government⟩
2 not likely to change suddenly or greatly ⟨a *stable* income⟩
3 LASTING ⟨a *stable* peace⟩

stac•ca•to \stə-'kä-tō\ *adj*
1 cut short so as not to sound connected ⟨*staccato* notes⟩
2 played or sung with breaks between notes

¹stack \'stak\ *n*
1 a neat pile of objects usually one on top of the other
2 a large number or amount ⟨We've got a *stack* of bills to pay.⟩
3 a large pile (as of hay) usually shaped like a cone
4 CHIMNEY 1, SMOKESTACK
5 a structure with shelves for storing books

²stack *vb* **stacked**; **stack•ing**
to arrange in or form a neat pile

sta•di•um \'stā-dē-əm\ *n, pl* **sta•di•ums** *or* **sta•dia** \'stā-dē-ə\
▲ a large usually outdoor structure with rows of seats for spectators at sports events

staff \'staf\ *n, pl* **staffs** *or* **staves** \'stavz\
1 a pole, stick, rod, or bar used as a support or as a sign of authority ⟨the *staff* of a flag⟩ ⟨a bishop's *staff*⟩
2 *pl* **staffs** a group of persons serving as assistants to or employees under a chief ⟨a hospital *staff*⟩ ⟨the administrative *staff*⟩
3 the five parallel lines with their four spaces on which music is written
4 something that is a source of strength ⟨Bread is the *staff* of life.⟩
5 *pl* **staffs** a group of military officers who plan and manage for a commanding officer

staff sergeant *n*
a noncommissioned officer in the army, air force, or marine corps ranking above a sergeant

stag \'stag\ *n*
an adult male deer

¹stage \'stāj\ *n*
1 a raised floor (as for speaking or performing)
2 a step forward in a journey, a task, a process, or a development : PHASE
3 the theatrical profession or art
4 a place where something important happens ⟨the political *stage*⟩
5 STAGECOACH

²stage *vb* **staged**; **stag•ing**
to produce or show to others on or as if on the stage ⟨The drama club *staged* two plays.⟩ ⟨The schools *staged* a track meet.⟩

stadium: a sports stadium

stage•coach \ˈstāj-ˌkōch\ *n*
a coach pulled by horses that runs on a schedule from place to place carrying passengers and mail

¹stag•ger \ˈsta-gər\ *vb* **stag•gered; stag•ger•ing**
1 to move or cause to move unsteadily from side to side as if about to fall : REEL ⟨He *staggered* under the load's weight.⟩
2 to cause or feel great surprise or shock ⟨The news *staggered* me.⟩
3 to arrange or be arranged in a zigzag but balanced way ⟨*Stagger* the nails along either edge of the board.⟩

²stagger *n*
a reeling or unsteady walk

stag•nant \ˈstag-nənt\ *adj*
1 not flowing ⟨a *stagnant* pool⟩
2 not active or brisk : DULL ⟨*stagnant* business⟩

stag•nate \ˈstag-ˌnāt\ *vb* **stag•nat•ed; stag•nat•ing**
to be or become inactive or still ⟨Business has *stagnated.*⟩

¹stain \ˈstān\ *vb* **stained; stain•ing**
1 to soil or discolor especially in spots
2 to use something (as a dye) to change the color of ⟨I spent the weekend *staining* the deck.⟩
3 ¹CORRUPT 1 ⟨Her conscience was *stained.*⟩
4 ¹DISGRACE ⟨The scandal *stained* his reputation.⟩

²stain *n*
1 ¹SPOT 2, DISCOLORATION ⟨Will this *stain* wash out?⟩
2 a mark of guilt or disgrace : STIGMA
3 something (as a dye) used in staining
stain•less \-ləs\ *adj*

stained glass *n*
pieces of colored glass used to make patterns in windows

stainless steel *n*
an alloy of steel and chromium that is resistant to stain, rust, and corrosion

stair \ˈster\ *n*
1 a series of steps or flights of steps for going from one level to another often used in pl. ⟨Children ran down the *stairs.*⟩
2 one step of a stairway

stair•case \ˈster-ˌkās\ *n*
a flight of steps with their supporting structure and railings

stair•way \ˈster-ˌwā\ *n*
one or more flights of steps usually with connecting landings

¹stake \ˈstāk\ *n*
1 a pointed piece (as of wood) that is driven into the ground as a marker or a support for something ⟨tent *stakes*⟩ ⟨A sign was nailed to a *stake.*⟩
2 a post to which a person is tied to be put to death by burning
3 something that is put up to be won or lost in gambling ⟨They play cards for high *stakes.*⟩
4 the prize in a contest
5 ¹SHARE 1, INTEREST ⟨She owns a *stake* in the business.⟩
at stake in a position to be lost if something goes wrong ⟨If you miss the deadline, your job is *at stake.*⟩

²stake *vb* **staked; stak•ing**
1 ²BET 1 ⟨I've *staked* my reputation on the new plan.⟩
2 to mark the limits of by stakes ⟨They *staked* out the yard.⟩
3 to fasten or support (as plants) with stakes
4 to give money to in order to help (as with a project)

sta•lac•tite \stə-ˈlak-ˌtīt\ *n*
▼ a deposit hanging from the roof or side of a cave in the shape of an icicle formed by the partial evaporation of dripping water containing minerals

sta•lag•mite \stə-ˈlag-ˌmīt\ *n*
a deposit like an upside down stalactite formed by the dripping of water containing minerals onto the floor of a cave

stale \ˈstāl\ *adj* **stal•er; stal•est**
1 having lost a good taste or quality through age ⟨*stale* bread⟩
2 used or heard so often as to be dull ⟨*stale* jokes⟩
3 not so strong, energetic, or effective as before ⟨He felt *stale* in his job.⟩

¹stalk \ˈstȯk\ *n*
1 a plant stem especially when not woody ⟨*stalks* of celery⟩
2 a slender supporting structure ⟨the *stalk* of a goblet⟩
stalked \ˈstȯkt\ *adj*

stalactite: stalactites in a cave

[1]stall 2: stalls for selling gifts and souvenirs in Shanghai, China

[2]stalk *vb* **stalked; stalk•ing**
1 to walk in a stiff or proud manner 〈He *stalked* angrily out of the room.〉
2 to hunt slowly and quietly 〈A cat *stalked* the bird.〉
stalk•er *n*

[1]stall \'stȯl\ *n*
1 a compartment for one animal in a stable or barn
2 ▲ a booth, stand, or counter where business may be carried on or articles may be displayed for sale
3 a seat in a church choir : a church pew
4 a small enclosed private compartment 〈a shower *stall*〉

[2]stall *vb* **stalled; stall•ing**
to distract attention or make excuses to gain time 〈Quit *stalling* and answer me.〉

[3]stall *vb* **stalled; stall•ing**
1 to stop or cause to stop usually by accident 〈The engine keeps *stalling*.〉
2 to put or keep in a stall 〈They *stalled* the horses for the night.〉

stal•lion \'stal-yən\ *n*
an adult male horse and especially one used for breeding

stal•wart \'stȯl-wərt\ *adj*
STURDY 1, RESOLUTE 〈a *stalwart* body〉 〈*stalwart* spirits〉

sta•men \'stā-mən\ *n*
▶ the part of a flower that produces pollen and is made up of an anther and a filament

stam•i•na \'sta-mə-nə\ *n*
the ability or strength to keep doing something for a long time

[1]stam•mer \'sta-mər\ *vb* **stam•mered; stam•mer•ing**
to speak with involuntary stops and much repeating

[2]stammer *n*
an act or instance of speaking with involuntary stops and much repeating

[1]stamp \'stamp\ *vb* **stamped; stamp•ing**
1 to bring the foot down hard and with noise 〈Don't *stamp* around in the house.〉
2 to put an end to by or as if by hitting with the bottom of the foot 〈We *stamped* out the fire.〉 〈The mayor promised to *stamp* out crime.〉
3 to mark or cut out with a tool or device having a design 〈The bill was *stamped* paid.〉 〈The mint *stamps* coins.〉
4 to attach a postage stamp to
5 CHARACTERIZE 1 〈Their acts *stamped* them as cowards.〉

stamen: a pink lily with long stamens

[2]stamp *n*
1 ▶ a small piece of paper or a mark attached to something to show that a tax or fee has been paid 〈a postage *stamp*〉
2 a device or instrument for marking with a design
3 the mark made by stamping
4 a sign of a special quality 〈the *stamp* of genius〉 〈She gave the idea her *stamp* of approval.〉
5 the act of bringing the foot down hard

[1]stam•pede \stam-'pēd\ *n*
1 a wild rush or flight of frightened animals or people
2 a sudden foolish action or movement of a large number of people

[2]stampede *vb* **stam•ped•ed; stam•ped•ing**
1 to run or cause to run away in fright or panic 〈People *stampeded* to the exits.〉
2 to act or cause to act together suddenly and without thought

stance \'stans\ *n*
way of standing : POSTURE

[1]stand \'stand\ *vb* **stood** \'stu̇d\; **stand•ing**
1 to be in or take an upright position on the feet 〈*Stand* for the pledge.〉
2 to take up or stay in a specified position or condition 〈*Stand* aside.〉 〈The judges *stood* firm.〉
3 to rest, remain, or set in a usually vertical position 〈A clock *stands* on the shelf.〉
4 to be in a specified place 〈Their house *stands* on the hill.〉
5 to put up with : ENDURE 〈He can't *stand* pain.〉
6 to have an opinion 〈How do you *stand* on the issue?〉
7 to stay in effect 〈The order still *stands*.〉
8 UNDERGO 〈*stand* trial〉
9 to perform the duty of 〈*stand* guard〉
stand by
1 to be or remain loyal or true to 〈I *stand by* my promise.〉 〈He *stood by* a friend.〉
2 to be present 〈We *stood by* and watched the fight.〉
3 to be or get ready to act 〈I'll *stand by* to help.〉
stand for
1 to be a symbol for : REPRESENT 〈What does your middle initial *stand for*?〉
2 to put up with : PERMIT 〈His teacher won't *stand for* any nonsense.〉
stand out to be easily seen or recognized
stand up
1 to stay in good condition 〈This type of watch *stands up* well under hard use.〉

A B C D E F G H I J K L M N O P Q R S T U V W X Y Z

[2]stamp 1

Stamps to show payment of postal charges were introduced in the mid-19th century. Most early stamps featured portraits of a country's ruler or its political leaders, but over the years it has become more common for countries to issue stamps showing a wide variety of other subjects as well. Countries occasionally issue stamps that have unusual shapes.

stamp from the US

stamp from the Netherlands

stamp from Sri Lanka

1960s stamp from Tonga

stamp from Japan

2 to fail to keep an appointment with ⟨You *stood* me *up* yesterday.⟩

stand up for DEFEND 2

stand up to to face boldly

[2]stand *n*

1 a structure containing rows of seats for spectators of a sport or spectacle

2 a stall or booth often outdoors for a small business ⟨a fruit *stand*⟩

3 [1]POSITION 2 ⟨They took a strong *stand* on the question.⟩

4 a group of plants growing near one another ⟨a *stand* of pine trees⟩

5 an act of stopping or staying in one place

6 a halt for defense or resistance ⟨Villagers made a *stand* against the enemy.⟩

7 a place or post which a person occupies : STATION ⟨The witness took the *stand*.⟩

8 a small structure (as a rack or table) on or in which something may be placed ⟨an umbrella *stand*⟩

9 a raised area (as for speakers or performers)

[1]stan•dard \'stan-dərd\ *n*

1 something set up as a rule for measuring or as a model ⟨a *standard* of weight⟩

2 the personal flag of the ruler of a state

3 an upright support ⟨a lamp *standard*⟩

4 a figure used as a symbol by an organized body of people

[2]standard *adj*

1 used as or matching a model or rule to compare against ⟨*standard* weight⟩

2 regularly and widely used ⟨It's a *standard* practice in the trade.⟩

3 widely known and accepted to be of good and permanent value ⟨The book is a *standard* reference work on grammar.⟩

stan•dard•ize \'stan-dər-ˌdīz\ *vb* **stan•dard•ized; stan•dard•iz•ing**

to make alike or matching a model

standard time *n*

the time established by law or by common usage over a region or country

[1]stand•ing \'stan-diŋ\ *adj*

1 [1]ERECT ⟨a *standing* position⟩

2 done while standing ⟨a *standing* ovation⟩

3 not flowing : STAGNANT ⟨a *standing* pool⟩

4 remaining at the same level or amount until canceled ⟨a *standing* offer⟩

5 PERMANENT ⟨a *standing* invitation⟩

[2]standing *n*

1 length of existence or service ⟨It's a custom of long *standing*.⟩

2 [1]POSITION 5, STATUS ⟨My friend had the highest *standing* in the class.⟩

stand•point \'stand-ˌpȯint\ *n*

a way in which things are thought about : POINT OF VIEW

stand•still \'stand-ˌstil\ *n*

the condition of not being active or busy : STOP ⟨Business was at a *standstill*.⟩

stank *past of* STINK

stan•za \'stan-zə\ *n*

a group of lines forming a division of a poem

[1]sta•ple \'stā-pəl\ *n*

1 a short thin wire with bent ends that is punched through papers and squeezed to hold them together or punched through thin material to fasten it to a surface

2 a piece of metal shaped like a U with sharp points to be driven into a surface to hold something (as a hook, rope, or wire)

[2]staple *vb* **sta•pled; sta•pling**

to fasten with staples

[3]staple *n*

1 a chief product of business or farming of a place

2 something that is used widely and often ⟨I went shopping for bread, milk, and other *staples*.⟩

3 the chief part of something ⟨Potatoes are the *staple* of their diet.⟩

[4]staple *adj*

1 much used, needed, or enjoyed usually by many people ⟨a *staple* plot in mystery novels⟩

2 [1]PRINCIPAL, CHIEF ⟨*staple* crops⟩

sta•pler \'stā-plər\ *n*

▼ a device that fastens using staples

stapler: a stapler stapling a piece of cloth

[1]star \'stär\ *n*

1 any of the heavenly bodies except planets which are visible at night and look like fixed points of light

2 a figure or object with five or more points that represents or suggests a star in the sky

3 a very talented or popular performer ⟨a movie *star*⟩

4 a planet that is believed in astrology to influence someone's life ⟨She was born under a lucky *star*.⟩

5 the principal member of a theater or opera company

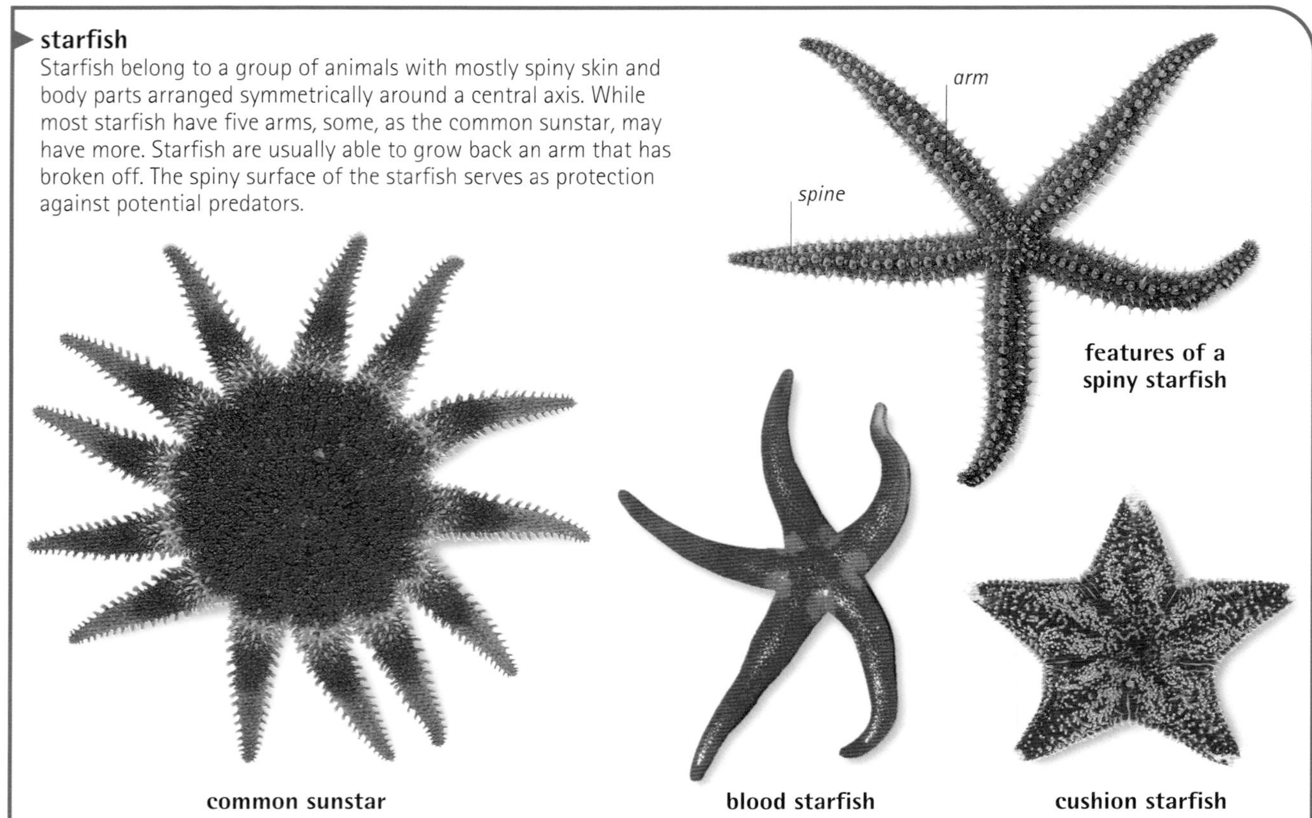

[2]star *vb* **starred; star•ring**
1 to mark with a star or an asterisk as being special or very good
2 to present in the role of a star ⟨The show *stars* my favorite actor.⟩
3 to play the most important role ⟨She will *star* in a new play.⟩
4 to perform in an outstanding manner

[3]star *adj*
1 being favored or very popular ⟨the teacher's *star* pupil⟩ ⟨a *star* athlete⟩
2 being of outstanding excellence ⟨a *star* chef⟩

star•board \'stär-bərd\ *n*
the right side of a ship or airplane looking forward

[1]starch \'stärch\ *n*
a white odorless tasteless substance that is the chief form in which carbohydrates are stored in plants, is an important component of many foods (as rice and bread), and has various uses (as for stiffening clothes)

[2]starch *vb* **starched; starch•ing**
to stiffen with starch

starchy \'stär-chē\ *adj* **starch•i•er; starch•i•est**
like or containing starch ⟨A potato is a *starchy* vegetable.⟩

[1]stare \'ster\ *vb* **stared; star•ing**
to look at hard and long often with wide-open eyes
synonyms see GAZE

[2]stare *n*
the act or an instance of looking at hard and long

star•fish \'stär-,fish\ *n*
▲ a sea animal that usually has five arms that spread out from a central disk and feeds mostly on mollusks

[1]stark \'stärk\ *adj* **stark•er; stark•est**
1 BARREN 2, DESOLATE ⟨a *stark* landscape⟩
2 clear and harsh ⟨She faced the *stark* reality of poverty.⟩
3 very obvious ⟨The differences were *stark*.⟩

[2]stark *adv*
COMPLETELY ⟨*stark* naked⟩

star•light \'stär-,līt\ *n*
the light given by the stars

star•ling \'stär-liŋ\ *n*
a dark brown or greenish black European bird that is now common in the United States

star•lit \'stär-,lit\ *adj*
lighted by the stars ⟨a *starlit* night⟩

star•ry \'stär-ē\ *adj* **star•ri•er; star•ri•est**
1 full of stars ⟨*starry* heavens⟩
2 shining like stars ⟨*starry* eyes⟩
3 having parts arranged like a star

Stars and Stripes *n*
▶ the flag of the United States

the Stars and Stripes

[1]start \'stärt\ *vb* **start•ed; start•ing**
1 to begin an activity ⟨I'm *starting* a new book.⟩
2 to come or bring into being or action ⟨Who *started* the rumor?⟩ ⟨Rain is likely to *start* soon.⟩
3 to begin to move toward a particular place or in a particular direction ⟨Let's *start* for home.⟩

A B C D E F G H I J K L M N O P Q R S T U V W X Y Z

4 to cause to move, act, or operate ⟨I'll try to *start* the motor.⟩
5 to give a sudden twitch or jerk (as in surprise)
6 to stick out or seem to stick out ⟨Their eyes *started* from the sockets.⟩

²start *n*
1 a sudden twitching or jerking movement ⟨a *start* of surprise⟩
2 a beginning of movement, action, or development ⟨I got an early *start.*⟩
3 a brief act, movement, or effort ⟨They work by fits and *starts.*⟩
4 a place of beginning (as of a race)

start•er \'stär-tər\ *n*
someone or something that starts something or causes something else to start ⟨a car's *starter*⟩ ⟨There were seven *starters* in the race.⟩

2 a body of people living in a certain territory under one government : the government of such a body of people
3 one of the divisions of a nation having a federal government ⟨the United *States* of America⟩

²state *vb* **stat•ed; stat•ing**
1 to express especially in words ⟨I'm just *stating* my opinion.⟩
2 to set by rule, law, or authority ⟨The rules of the contest are *stated* below.⟩

state•house \'stāt-,hau̇s\ *n*
the building where the legislature of a state meets

state•ly \'stāt-lē\ *adj* **state•li•er; state•li•est**
impressive in size or dignity ⟨*stately* oaks⟩ ⟨*stately* homes⟩
state•li•ness *n*

3 a collection of or the place that contains radio or television equipment for transmitting or receiving
4 ¹POSITION 5, RANK ⟨a person of high *station*⟩
5 the place or position where a person or thing stands or is assigned to stand or remain ⟨Don't leave your *station.*⟩
6 a post or area of duty ⟨military *station*⟩

²station *vb* **sta•tioned; sta•tion•ing**
to assign to or set in a post or position : POST ⟨Her father is *stationed* in Germany.⟩

sta•tion•ary \'stā-shə-,ner-ē\ *adj*
1 having been set in a certain place or post : IMMOBILE ⟨a *stationary* bike⟩
2 not changing : STABLE ⟨Their weekly income remained *stationary.*⟩

sta•tion•ery \'stā-shə-,ner-ē\ *n*
writing paper and envelopes

station wagon *n*
◀ an automobile that has a large open area in the back instead of a trunk and a back door for loading and unloading things

station wagon

stat•ue \'sta-chü\ *n*
an image or likeness (as of a person or animal) sculptured, modeled, or cast in a solid substance (as marble or bronze)

stat•ure \'sta-chər\ *n*
1 a person's height ⟨He's of rather small *stature.*⟩
2 quality or fame gained (as by growth or development) ⟨a writer of *stature*⟩

sta•tus \'stā-təs, 'sta-\ *n*
1 position or rank of a person or thing ⟨I lost my *status* as an amateur.⟩
2 state of affairs : SITUATION ⟨What is the patient's medical *status?*⟩

stat•ute \'sta-chüt\ *n*
LAW 4 ⟨a state *statute*⟩

staunch \'stȯnch, 'stänch\ *adj* **staunch•er; staunch•est**
1 strongly built : SUBSTANTIAL ⟨*staunch* foundations⟩
2 LOYAL, STEADFAST ⟨They were *staunch* supporters.⟩
staunch•ly *adv*

¹stave \'stāv\ *n*
1 one of the narrow strips of wood or iron plates that form the sides, covering, or lining of something (as a barrel)
2 a wooden stick : STAFF

²stave *vb* **staved** *or* **stove** \'stōv\; **stav•ing**
1 to break in the staves of ⟨*stave* a barrel⟩
2 to smash a hole in ⟨Waves *staved* the boat's hull.⟩
stave off to keep away : ward off ⟨A snack will *stave off* hunger.⟩

staves *pl of* STAFF

star•tle \'stär-tᵊl\ *vb* **star•tled; star•tling**
1 to move or jump (as in surprise or fear) ⟨The cat *startles* easily.⟩
2 to frighten suddenly but slightly

star•tling *adj*
causing a moment of fright or surprise ⟨a *startling* noise⟩ ⟨a *startling* discovery⟩

star•va•tion \stär-'vā-shən\ *n*
suffering or death caused by lack of food : the condition of being starved

starve \'stärv\ *vb* **starved; starv•ing**
1 to suffer or die or cause to suffer or die from lack of food
2 to suffer or cause to suffer from a lack of something other than food ⟨The dog was *starving* for affection.⟩

¹stash \'stash\ *vb* **stashed; stash•ing**
to store in a usually secret place for future use

²stash *n*
an amount of something stored secretly for future use

¹state \'stāt\ *n*
1 manner or condition of being ⟨Steam is water in the gaseous *state.*⟩ ⟨The room was in a *state* of disorder.⟩

state•ment \'stāt-mənt\ *n*
1 something written or said in a formal way : something stated ⟨The company issued a *statement* about the new game.⟩
2 a brief record of a business account ⟨a monthly bank *statement*⟩

state•room \'stāt-,rüm, -,ru̇m\ *n*
a private room on a ship or a train

states•man \'stāts-mən\ *n, pl* **states•men** \-mən\
a usually wise, skilled, and respected government leader

¹stat•ic \'sta-tik\ *n*
noise produced in a radio or television receiver by atmospheric or electrical disturbances

²static *adj*
1 showing little change or action ⟨a *static* population⟩
2 of or relating to charges of electricity (as those produced by friction) that do not flow

¹sta•tion \'stā-shən\ *n*
1 a regular stopping place (as on a bus, train, or subway line) : DEPOT
2 a place for specialized observation or for a public service ⟨weather *station*⟩ ⟨police *station*⟩

A B C D E F G H I J K L M N O P Q R S T U V W X Y Z

[1]stay \'stā\ *vb* **stayed; stay•ing**
1 to remain after others have gone ⟨She *stayed* after the party to help.⟩
2 to continue unchanged ⟨We *stayed* friends for many years.⟩
3 to stop going forward **:** PAUSE ⟨He instructed the dog to *stay.*⟩
4 to live for a while ⟨I'm *staying* with friends.⟩
5 to put a stop to **:** HALT ⟨The governor *stayed* the execution.⟩

[2]stay *n*
1 a period of living in a place ⟨Our *stay* in the country was too short.⟩
2 the action of bringing to a stop **:** the state of being stopped ⟨a *stay* of the execution⟩

[3]stay *n*
a strong rope or wire used to steady or brace something (as a mast)

[4]stay *n*
1 [2]PROP, SUPPORT
2 a thin firm strip (as of steel or plastic) used to stiffen a garment (as a corset) or part of a garment (as a shirt collar)

[5]stay *vb* **stayed; staying**
to hold up ⟨Supports *stayed* the sign.⟩

stead \'sted\ *n*
the place usually taken or duty usually carried out by the person or thing mentioned ⟨I'll work in your *stead.*⟩
stand someone *or* **something in good stead**
to be useful or helpful to someone or something ⟨Her problem-solving skills *stood her in good stead* as a computer programmer.⟩

stead•fast \'sted-,fast\ *adj*
1 not changing ⟨a *steadfast* refusal⟩
2 LOYAL ⟨*steadfast* friends⟩
stead•fast•ly *adv*
stead•fast•ness *n*

[1]steady \'ste-dē\ *adj* **steadi•er; steadi•est**
1 firmly fixed in position ⟨Make sure the ladder is *steady.*⟩
2 direct or sure in action ⟨She worked with *steady* hands.⟩ ⟨I took *steady* aim.⟩
3 lasting or continuing over time ⟨a *steady* flow of water⟩ ⟨I found a *steady* job.⟩
4 not easily upset ⟨*steady* nerves⟩
5 RELIABLE ⟨a *steady* worker⟩
stead•i•ly \'ste-də-lē\ *adv*
stead•i•ness \'ste-dē-nəs\ *n*

[2]steady *vb* **stead•ied; steady•ing**
to make, keep, or become steady ⟨He put on some music to *steady* his nerves.⟩

steak \'stāk\ *n*
1 ▶ a thick slice of meat and especially beef
2 a thick slice of a large fish (as salmon)

steam engine: a train powered by a steam engine at Puukolii Station, Hawaii

[1]steal \'stēl\ *vb* **stole** \'stōl\; **sto•len** \'stō-lən\; **steal•ing**
1 to take and carry away (something that belongs to another person) without permission and with the intention of keeping
2 to come or go quietly or secretly ⟨She *stole* out of the room.⟩
3 to draw attention away from others ⟨The puppy *stole* the show.⟩
4 to take or get secretly or in a tricky way ⟨He *stole* a nap.⟩
5 to reach the next base safely in baseball by running to it when the ball has not been hit in play

steak 1: grilled steak

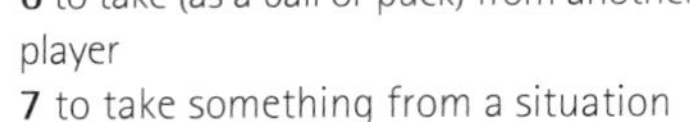

6 to take (as a ball or puck) from another player
7 to take something from a situation

[2]steal *n*
1 the act or an instance of stealing ⟨He leads the team in *steals.*⟩
2 [1]BARGAIN 2 ⟨At 20 dollars, these boots were a *steal.*⟩

stealth \'stelth\ *n*
sly or secret action

stealthy \'stel-thē\ *adj* **stealth•i•er; stealth•i•est**
done in a sly or secret manner
stealth•i•ly \-thə-lē\ *adv*

[1]steam \'stēm\ *n*
1 the vapor into which water is changed when heated to the boiling point
2 steam or the heat or power produced by it when kept under pressure ⟨Some houses are heated by *steam.*⟩
3 the mist formed when water vapor cools
4 driving force **:** POWER ⟨By the end of the day, I had run out of *steam.*⟩

[2]steam *vb* **steamed; steam•ing**
1 to give off steam or vapor
2 to rise or pass off as steam ⟨Heat *steamed* from the pipes.⟩
3 to move or travel by or as if by the power of steam ⟨The ship *steamed* out of the harbor.⟩
4 to expose to steam (as for cooking)

steam•boat \'stēm-,bōt\ *n*
a boat powered by steam

steam engine *n*
◀ an engine powered by steam

steam•er \'stē-mər\ *n*
1 a ship powered by steam
2 a container in which something is steamed 〈a vegetable *steamer*〉

steam•roll•er \'stēm-'rō-lər\ *n*
a machine that has wide heavy rollers for pressing down and smoothing roads

steam•ship \'stēm-,ship\ *n*
STEAMER 1

steam shovel *n*
a power machine for digging

steamy \'stē-mē\ *adj* **steam•i•er**; **steam•i•est**
1 hot and humid 〈a *steamy* day〉
2 producing or covered with steam 〈a *steamy* window〉

steed \'stēd\ *n*
a usually lively horse

[1]**steel** \'stēl\ *n*
1 a hard and tough metal made by treating iron with great heat and mixing carbon with it
2 an item (as a sword) made of steel

[2]**steel** *vb* **steeled**; **steel•ing**
to fill with courage or determination 〈I *steeled* myself for the struggle.〉

[3]**steel** *adj*
made of steel 〈a *steel* plow〉

steely \'stē-lē\ *adj* **steel•i•er**; **steel•i•est** like steel (as in hardness, strength, or color) 〈*steely* eyes〉

[1]**steep** \'stēp\ *adj*
steep•er; **steep•est**
1 having a very sharp slope : almost straight up and down 〈a *steep* hill〉
2 too great or high 〈*steep* prices〉
steep•ly *adv*
steep•ness *n*

[2]**steep** *vb* **steeped**; **steep•ing**
1 to soak in a hot liquid 〈*steep* tea〉
2 to fill with or involve deeply 〈The story is *steeped* with legend.〉

stee•ple \'stē-pəl\ *n*
1 a tall pointed structure usually built on top of a church tower
2 ▼ a church tower

stee•ple•chase \'stē-pəl-,chās\ *n*
1 a horse race across country
2 a race on a course that has hedges, walls, and ditches to be crossed

[1]**steer** \'stir\ *vb* **steered**; **steer•ing**
1 to make a vehicle move in a particular direction 〈*steer* a boat〉
2 to guide or change the direction of something 〈I tried to *steer* the conversation away from politics.〉
3 to follow a course of action 〈She *steers* clear of girls who gossip.〉

[2]**steer** *n*
a castrated bull usually raised for beef

steering wheel *n*
a wheel that allows a driver to control the direction of a vehicle

stego•sau•rus \,ste-gə-'sȯr-əs\ *n*
a large plant-eating dinosaur with bony plates along its back and tail and with spikes at the end of the tail

[1]**stem** \'stem\ *n*
1 the main stalk of a plant that develops buds and shoots and usually grows above ground
2 a thin plant part (as a leafstalk) that supports another part 〈a cherry's *stem*〉
3 the bow of a ship
4 the basic part of a word to which prefixes or suffixes may be added
5 something like a stalk or shaft 〈the *stem* of a goblet〉
from stem to stern in or to every part : THOROUGHLY

[2]**stem** *vb* **stemmed**; **stem•ming**
1 to make progress against 〈The boat was able to *stem* the current.〉
2 to check or hold back the progress of 〈New safety rules *stemmed* the increase in accidents.〉

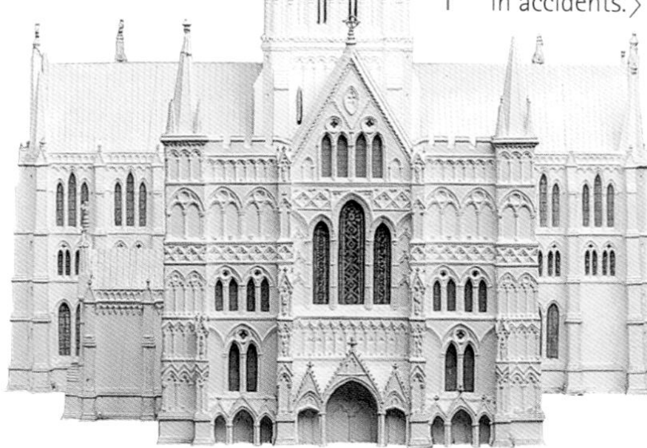

steeple 2: a model of a church with a steeple

[3]**stem** *vb* **stemmed**; **stem•ming**
1 to develop as a consequence of 〈His illness *stems* from an accident.〉
2 to come from : DERIVE 〈The word "misty" *stems* from "mist."〉
3 to remove the stem from 〈*stem* cherries〉

[4]**stem** *vb* **stemmed**; **stem•ming**
to stop or check by or as if by damming 〈We were able to *stem* the flow of blood.〉

[5]**STEM** *abbr*
science, technology, engineering, and mathematics

stemmed \'stemd\ *adj*
having a stem 〈long-*stemmed* roses〉

[1]**sten•cil** \'sten-səl\ *n*
1 a piece of material (as a sheet of paper or plastic) that has lettering or a design cut out and is used as a guide (as in painting or drawing)
2 a pattern, design, or print produced with a stencil

[2]**stencil** *vb* **sten•ciled** *or* **sten•cilled**; **sten•cil•ing** *or* **sten•cil•ling**
1 to mark or paint with a stencil 〈I *stenciled* a box with designs.〉
2 to produce with a stencil 〈*Stencil* the number on the paper.〉

[1]**step** \'step\ *n*
1 a movement made by lifting one foot and putting it down in another spot
2 a rest or place for the foot in going up or down : STAIR
3 a combination of foot and body movements in a repeated pattern 〈a dance *step*〉
4 manner of walking 〈a lively *step*〉
5 FOOTPRINT
6 the sound of a footstep 〈I heard *steps* in the hall.〉
7 the space passed over in one step 〈The garden was a few *steps* away.〉
8 a short distance 〈The house is only a *step* away.〉
9 the height of one stair
10 steps *pl* [1]COURSE 2 〈We directed our *steps* toward home.〉
11 one of a series of actions taken to achieve something 〈They took *steps* to correct the situation.〉
12 a stage in a process 〈What's the first *step* in assembling the toy?〉
13 a level, grade, or rank in a scale or series 〈His work was a *step* above average.〉
14 the distance from one tone of a musical scale or one note on a musical staff to another that is one tone away (**half step**) or two tones away (**whole step**)

[2]step *vb* **stepped; step•ping**
1 to move in a particular way or direction by lifting one foot and putting it down in another spot ⟨They *stepped* aside to let me pass.⟩
2 [1]DANCE 1 ⟨The couple *stepped* gracefully together.⟩
3 to go on foot : WALK ⟨He *stepped* slowly along the path.⟩
4 to move quickly ⟨They were really *stepping* along.⟩
5 to put or press the foot on or in ⟨I *stepped* on glass.⟩ ⟨Don't *step* in the puddle.⟩
6 to come or move as if at a step by the foot ⟨I *stepped* into a good job.⟩
7 to measure by steps ⟨*Step* off ten yards.⟩
step up to increase the amount, speed, or intensity of ⟨The factory *stepped up* production.⟩

step–by–step \ˌstep-bī-ˈstep\ *adj*
moving or happening by steps one after the other

step•fa•ther \ˈstep-ˌfä-t͟hər\ *n*
the husband of someone's mother after the death or divorce of his or her real father

step•lad•der \ˈstep-ˌla-dər\ *n*
a light freestanding ladder with broad flat steps and a hinged frame

step•moth•er \ˈstep-ˌmə-t͟hər\ *n*
the wife of someone's father after the death or divorce of his or her real mother

steppe \ˈstep\ *n*
land that is dry, rather level, mostly treeless, and covered with grass in regions (as parts of Asia and southeastern Europe) with usually hot summers and cold winters

step•ping–stone \ˈste-piŋ-ˌstōn\ *n*
1 ▼ a stone on which to step (as in crossing a stream)
2 something that helps in progress or advancement ⟨a *stepping-stone* to success⟩

-ster \stər\ *n suffix*
1 someone who does or handles or operates
2 someone who makes or uses ⟨song*ster*⟩
3 someone who is associated with or takes part in ⟨gang*ster*⟩
4 someone who is ⟨young*ster*⟩

ste•reo \ˈster-ē-ˌō, ˈstir-\ *n, pl* **ste•re•os**
a sound system that reproduces the effect of listening to the original sound
stereo *adj*

[1]ste•reo•type \ˈster-ē-ə-ˌtīp, ˈstir-\ *n*
a fixed idea that many people have about a thing or a group that may often be untrue or only partly true

[2]ste•reo•type *vb* **ste•reo•typed; ste•reo•typ•ing**
to form a fixed and often untrue or only partly true idea about ⟨It's unfair to *stereotype* people according to where they live.⟩

ste•reo•typed \ˈster-ē-ə-ˌtīpt, ˈstir-\ *adj*
following a pattern or stereotype : lacking originality ⟨The book had only *stereotyped* characters.⟩

ste•reo•typ•i•cal \ˌster-ē-ə-ˈti-pi-kəl\ *adj*
based on or characteristic of a stereotype ⟨a *stereotypical* sports fan⟩
ste•reo•typ•i•cal•ly \-pi-kə-lē\ *adv*

ster•ile \ˈster-əl\ *adj*
1 not able to produce fruit, crops, or offspring : not fertile ⟨*sterile* soil⟩
2 free from living germs ⟨a *sterile* bandage⟩

ster•il•ize \ˈster-ə-ˌlīz\ *vb* **ster•il•ized; ster•il•iz•ing**
to make sterile and especially free from germs

[1]ster•ling \ˈstər-liŋ\ *n*
1 British money
2 sterling silver : articles made from sterling silver

[2]sterling *adj*
1 of or relating to British sterling
2 being or made of a specific alloy that is mostly silver with a little copper ⟨*sterling* silver⟩
3 EXCELLENT ⟨a *sterling* example⟩

[1]stern \ˈstərn\ *adj* **stern•er; stern•est**
1 hard and severe in nature or manner : very strict and serious ⟨a *stern* judge⟩ ⟨a *stern* warning⟩
2 showing severe displeasure or disapproval ⟨a *stern* look⟩
3 firm and not changeable ⟨She showed *stern* determination to succeed.⟩
stern•ly *adv*

[2]stern *n*
the rear end of a boat

ster•num \ˈstər-nəm\ *n, pl* **ster•nums** *or* **ster•na** \-nə\
BREASTBONE

ste•roid \ˈstir-ˌȯid, ˈster-\ *n*
any of various chemical compounds that include many hormones (as anabolic steroids)

stetho•scope \ˈste-thə-ˌskōp\ *n*
▶ a medical instrument used for listening to sounds produced in the body and especially those of the heart and lungs

stethoscope

[1]stew \ˈstü, ˈstyü\ *n*
1 a dish of usually meat with vegetables prepared by slow boiling
2 a state of excitement, worry, or confusion ⟨He got in a *stew* over nothing.⟩

[2]stew *vb* **stewed; stew•ing**
1 to boil slowly : SIMMER ⟨*stew* tomatoes⟩
2 to become excited or worried

stepping-stone 1: stepping-stones over a stream

stew•ard \'stü-ərd, 'styü-\ *n*
1 a manager of a very large home, an estate, or an organization
2 a person employed to manage the supply and distribution of food and look after the needs of passengers (as on an airplane or ship)

stew•ard•ess \'stü-ər-dəs, 'styü-\ *n*
▶ a woman who looks after passengers (as on an airplane or ship)

[1]stick \'stik\ *n*
1 a cut or broken branch or twig
2 a long thin piece of wood
3 WALKING STICK 1
4 something like a stick in shape or use ⟨fish *sticks*⟩ ⟨a hockey *stick*⟩

[2]stick *vb* **stuck** \'stək\; **stick•ing**
1 to push into or through ⟨I *stuck* a needle in my finger.⟩
2 to stab or pierce with something pointed ⟨Ow! The thorn *stuck* me.⟩
3 to put in place by or as if by pushing ⟨She *stuck* candles in the cake.⟩
4 to push out, up, into, or under ⟨I *stuck* out my hand.⟩
5 to put in a specified place or position ⟨I *stuck* a cap on my head.⟩
6 to remain in a place, situation, or environment ⟨We decided to *stick* where we were.⟩
7 to halt the movement or action of ⟨The car was *stuck* in traffic.⟩
8 BAFFLE ⟨I got *stuck* on the first problem.⟩
9 to burden with something unpleasant ⟨She was *stuck* with paying the bill.⟩
10 to fix or become fixed in place by or as if by gluing ⟨*Stick* a stamp on the letter.⟩
11 to cling or cause to cling ⟨My wet clothes *stuck* to me.⟩
12 to become blocked or jammed ⟨The door is *stuck*.⟩

stick•er \'sti-kər\ *n*
something (as a slip of paper with glue on its back) that can be stuck to a surface

stick insect *n*
▶ a wingless long-legged insect that has a long body resembling a stick

stick•le•back \'sti-kəl-,bak\ *n*
a small scaleless fish with sharp spines on its back

sticky \'sti-kē\ *adj* **stick•i•er**; **stick•i•est**
1 tending to cling like glue : ADHESIVE ⟨*sticky* syrup⟩

stick insect

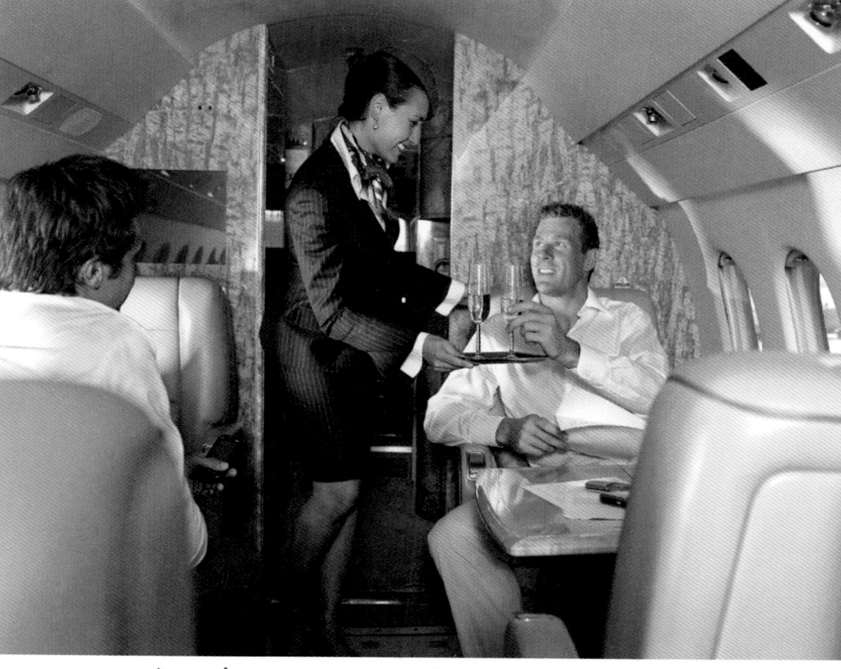

stewardess: a stewardess serving a passenger on an airplane

2 coated with a substance that sticks to things ⟨My fingers are *sticky*.⟩
3 MUGGY, HUMID ⟨a *sticky* day⟩
4 tending to become blocked or jammed ⟨*sticky* windows⟩
stick•i•ness *n*

stiff \'stif\ *adj* **stiff•er**; **stiff•est**
1 not easily bent ⟨a *stiff* collar⟩
2 not easily moved ⟨*stiff* muscles⟩
3 firm and not changeable ⟨*stiff* determination⟩
4 not friendly, relaxed, or graceful in manner ⟨a *stiff* salute⟩
5 POWERFUL, STRONG ⟨a *stiff* wind⟩
6 not flowing easily : THICK ⟨Beat the egg whites until *stiff*.⟩
7 SEVERE 3 ⟨a *stiff* penalty⟩
8 hard to do or deal with : DIFFICULT ⟨a *stiff* test⟩
stiff•ly *adv*
stiff•ness *n*

stiff•en \'sti-fən\ *vb* **stiff•ened**; **stif•fen•ing**
1 to make or become stiff or stiffer ⟨The paper *stiffened* as it dried.⟩
2 to become tense and still ⟨He *stiffened* with suspicion.⟩

sti•fle \'stī-fəl\ *vb* **sti•fled**; **sti•fling**
1 to cause or have difficulty in breathing ⟨The room was hot and *stifling*.⟩
2 to keep in check by effort ⟨I had to *stifle* a laugh.⟩

stig•ma \'stig-mə\ *n*, *pl* **stig•ma•ta** \stig-'mä-tə, 'stig-mə-tə\ *or* **stig•mas**
1 a mark of disgrace or dishonor
2 the upper part of the pistil of a flower which receives the pollen grains

stile \'stīl\ *n*
1 a step or set of steps for crossing a fence or wall
2 TURNSTILE

sti•let•to \stə-'le-tō\ *n*, *pl* **sti•let•tos** *or* **sti•let•toes**
▶ a knife with a slender pointed blade

[1]still \'stil\ *adj*
1 having no motion ⟨*still* water⟩
2 making no sound : QUIET ⟨The children were finally *still*.⟩
3 free from noise and commotion ⟨The streets were *still*.⟩
still•ness *n*

[2]still *vb* **stilled**; **still•ing**
1 to make or become motionless or silent ⟨The announcement *stilled* the chatter.⟩
2 to calm or make less intense ⟨He could not *still* their fears.⟩

stiletto: an 18th-century stiletto from Italy

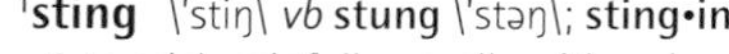

[3]still *adv*
1 without motion ⟨Please sit *still.*⟩
2 up to this or that time ⟨We *still* live there.⟩
3 NEVERTHELESS ⟨They know it's not true, but they *still* believe it.⟩
4 [2]EVEN 2 ⟨She ran *still* faster.⟩
5 in addition ⟨He won *still* more money.⟩

[4]still *n*
[1]QUIET, SILENCE ⟨the *still* of the night⟩

[5]still *n*
a device used in making alcoholic liquors

stilt \'stilt\ *n*
1 one of a pair of tall poles each with a high step or loop for the support of a foot used to lift the person wearing them above the ground in walking
2 a stake or post used as one of the supports of a structure (as a building) above ground or water level

stilt•ed \'stil-təd\ *adj*
not easy and natural ⟨a *stilted* speech⟩

[1]stim•u•lant \'sti-myə-lənt\ *n*
1 something (as a drug) that makes the body or one of its parts temporarily more active ⟨a heart *stimulant*⟩
2 STIMULUS 1

[2]stimulant *adj*
stimulating or tending to stimulate

stim•u•late \'sti-myə-,lāt\ *vb* **stim•u•lat•ed; stim•u•lat•ing**
1 to make active or more active : AROUSE ⟨The advertisements *stimulated* interest in the new product.⟩
2 to act on as a bodily stimulus or stimulant ⟨Caffeine *stimulates* the nervous system.⟩

stim•u•la•tion \,sti-myə-'lā-shən\ *n*
an act or result of making more active ⟨Puzzles provide intellectual *stimulation.*⟩

stim•u•lus \'sti-myə-ləs\ *n*, *pl* **stim•u•li** \-,lī, -,lē\
1 something that stirs or urges to action ⟨The reward was a *stimulus* for greater effort.⟩
2 an influence that acts usually from outside the body to partly change bodily activity (as by exciting a receptor or sense organ) ⟨Light, heat, and sound are common physical *stimuli.*⟩

[1]sting \'stiŋ\ *vb* **stung** \'stəŋ\; **sting•ing**
1 to prick painfully usually with a sharp or poisonous stinger ⟨A bee *stung* my hand.⟩
2 to suffer or affect with sharp quick burning pain ⟨Hail *stung* their faces.⟩
3 to hurt emotionally ⟨She was *stung* by the harsh criticism.⟩

[2]sting *n*
1 an act of pricking painfully usually with a sharp or poisonous stinger ⟨a bee's *sting*⟩
2 a wound or burning pain caused by the pricking of the skin with a stinger ⟨the *sting* of a bitter wind⟩
3 emotional pain ⟨the *sting* of criticism⟩
4 STINGER

sting•er \'stiŋ-ər\ *n*
a sharp part of an animal (as a bee or scorpion) that is used to wound and often poison prey or an enemy

sting•ray \'stiŋ-,rā\ *n*
▼ a flat fish with a sharp stinging spine on its long thin tail

eyes
fin
stinging spine
tail

stingray

stin•gy \'stin-jē\ *adj* **stin•gi•er; stin•gi•est**
1 not generous
2 very small in amount ⟨a *stingy* portion⟩
stin•gi•ness \-jē-nəs\ *n*

[1]stink \'stiŋk\ *vb* **stank** \'staŋk\ *or* **stunk** \'stəŋk\; **stunk; stink•ing**
1 to give off or cause to have a strong unpleasant smell ⟨The garbage *stinks.*⟩
2 to be very bad or unpleasant ⟨That news really *stinks.*⟩

[2]stink *n*
a strong unpleasant smell

stink•bug \'stiŋk-,bəg\ *n*
a bug that gives off a bad smell

stinky \'stiŋ-kē\ *adj* **stink•i•er; stink•i•est**
having a strong unpleasant smell ⟨*stinky* socks⟩

[1]stint \'stint\ *vb* **stint•ed; stint•ing**
to be stingy or sparing ⟨Don't *stint* on necessities.⟩

[2]stint *n*
1 an amount of work given
2 a period of time spent at a particular activity

[1]stir \'stər\ *vb* **stirred; stir•ring**
1 to make or cause to make a usually slight movement or change of position ⟨She heard the child *stir* in bed.⟩ ⟨The breeze *stirred* the tree's leaves.⟩
2 to make active ⟨A good book can *stir* the imagination.⟩
3 to mix, dissolve, or move about by making a circular movement in ⟨He *stirred* sugar into his coffee.⟩ ⟨*Stir* the gravy so it doesn't burn.⟩
4 to cause to arise or take place ⟨Don't *stir* up trouble.⟩

[2]stir *n*
1 a state of upset or activity ⟨The whole town is in a *stir.*⟩
2 a slight movement ⟨We heard the *stir* of leaves in the breeze.⟩
3 the act of making circular movements in ⟨Give the sauce a *stir.*⟩

stir•ring \'stər-iŋ\ *adj*
MOVING 2 ⟨a *stirring* speech⟩

stir•rup \'stər-əp\ *n*
▼ either of a pair of small light frames or loops often of metal hung by straps from a saddle and used as a support for the foot of a horseback rider

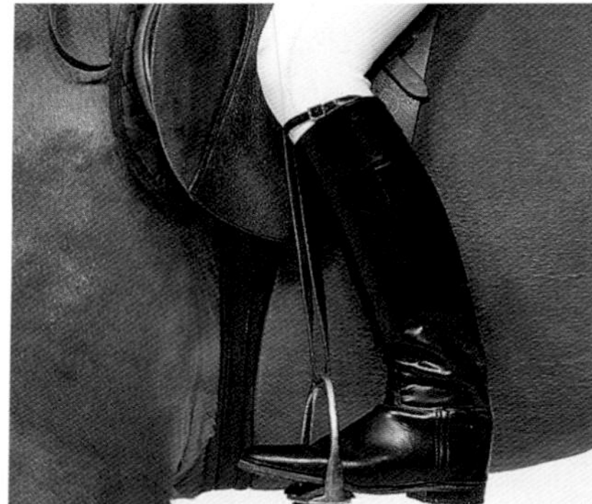

stirrup

[1]stitch \'stich\ *n*
1 one in-and-out movement of a threaded needle in sewing or in closing a wound : a portion of thread left after one such movement
2 a single loop of thread or yarn around a tool (as a knitting needle or crochet hook)
3 a type or style of stitching
4 a sudden sharp pain especially in the side

[2]stitch *vb* **stitched; stitch•ing**
1 to fasten or join by sewing ⟨*Stitch* the ends of the two strips together.⟩
2 to make, mend, or decorate by or as if by sewing ⟨My mother *stitched* up my torn pants.⟩
3 SEW 2

¹stock \ˈstäk\ *n*
1 the whole supply or amount on hand ⟨Our *stock* of food is running low.⟩
2 **stocks** *pl* a wooden frame with holes to hold the feet or the feet and hands once used to punish a wrongdoer publicly
3 the wooden part by which a rifle or shotgun is held against the shoulder during firing
4 the source from which others descend : ANCESTRY ⟨He is of Irish *stock*.⟩
5 farm animals : LIVESTOCK, CATTLE
6 a part ownership in a business that can be traded independently
7 liquid in which meat, fish, or vegetables have been simmered
in stock on hand : in the store and available for purchase

²stock *vb* **stocked**; **stock•ing**
1 to provide with or get supplies especially for future use ⟨I'm *stocking* up on groceries.⟩
2 to get or keep a supply of ⟨That store *stocks* only the best goods.⟩

³stock *adj*
1 kept regularly in supply especially for sale ⟨The window comes in *stock* sizes.⟩
2 commonly used : STANDARD ⟨He gave a *stock* answer.⟩

stock•ade \stä-ˈkād\ *n*
1 a line of strong posts set in the ground to form a defense
2 an enclosure usually formed by posts pounded into the ground

stock•bro•ker \ˈstäk-ˌbrō-kər\ *n*
a person who handles orders to buy and sell stocks

stock•hold•er \ˈstäk-ˌhōl-dər\ *n*
an owner of stock

stock•ing \ˈstä-kiŋ\ *n*
1 a close-fitting usually knit covering for the foot and leg
2 ¹SOCK

stock market *n*
a place where shares of stock are bought and sold

stocky \ˈstä-kē\ *adj* **stock•i•er**; **stock•i•est**
short, broad, and sturdy in build ⟨a *stocky* man⟩

stock•yard \ˈstäk-ˌyärd\ *n*
a yard for keeping livestock about to be slaughtered or shipped

¹stole *past of* STEAL

²stole \ˈstōl\ *n*
a long wide scarf worn across the shoulders

stolen *past participle of* STEAL

stol•id \ˈstä-ləd\ *adj*
having or showing little or no feeling ⟨a *stolid* person⟩
stol•id•ly *adv*

▶ Stone Age
Humans living in the Stone Age began to make tools from stone some two and a half million years ago. Hand-held axes, flint scrapers, and adzes were some of the tools early humans utilized for cutting, grinding, slicing, and preparing animal skins for use. In the later Stone Age, people began to make more sophisticated items, such as flint arrowheads and blades which were used in hunting for food, chopping wood, and carving bone and antler.

examples of tools from the Stone Age

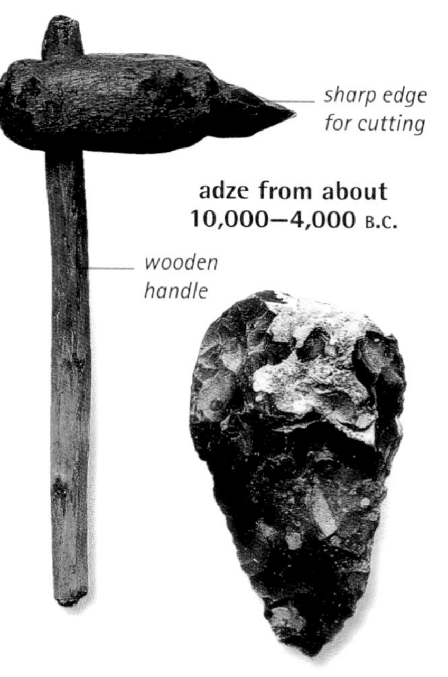

adze from about 10,000–4,000 B.C.

hand ax from about 300,000–70,000 B.C.

flint scraper from about 1,600,000–200,000 B.C.

¹stom•ach \ˈstə-mək\ *n*
1 the pouch into which food passes from the esophagus for mixing and digestion before passing to the small intestine
2 the part of the body that contains the stomach : ABDOMEN
3 ²DESIRE 1, LIKING ⟨She had no *stomach* for trouble.⟩

²stomach *vb* **stom•ached**; **stom•ach•ing**
to bear patiently : put up with ⟨I couldn't *stomach* their rude behavior.⟩

stomp \ˈstämp, ˈstȯmp\ *vb* **stomped**; **stomp•ing**
to walk heavily or noisily : STAMP ⟨He *stomped* angrily away.⟩

¹stone \ˈstōn\ *n*
1 earth or mineral matter hardened in a mass : ROCK
2 a piece of rock coarser than gravel ⟨Don't throw *stones*.⟩
3 GEM 1
4 a stony mass that sometimes forms in certain organs of the body ⟨a kidney *stone*⟩
5 the seed of a fruit (as a peach) in its hard case
6 *pl usually* **stone** an English measure of weight equaling 14 pounds (about 6.3 kilograms)

²stone *vb* **stoned**; **ston•ing**
1 to throw stones at
2 to remove the stony seeds of ⟨*stone* cherries⟩

³stone *adj*
relating to or made of stone ⟨a *stone* wall⟩

⁴stone *adv*
COMPLETELY, TOTALLY ⟨The soup was *stone*-cold.⟩

Stone Age *n*
▲ the oldest period in which human beings are known to have existed : the age during which stone tools were used

stony \ˈstō-nē\ *adj* **ston•i•er**; **ston•i•est**
1 full of stones ⟨*stony* soil⟩
2 hard as or like stone ⟨*stony* meteorites⟩
3 INSENSITIVE 1, UNFEELING ⟨a *stony* stare⟩

stood *past and past participle of* STAND

stool \ˈstül\ *n*
1 ▶ a seat without back or arms supported by three or four legs or by a central post
2 FOOTSTOOL
3 a mass of bodily waste discharged from the intestine

stool 1

¹stoop \'stüp\ *vb* **stooped; stoop•ing**
1 to bend down or over ⟨She *stooped* down to pick up the child.⟩
2 to stand or walk with the head and shoulders bent forward
3 to do something that is petty, deceitful, or morally wrong ⟨He would never *stoop* to lying.⟩

²stoop *n*
a forward bend of the head and shoulders ⟨She walks with a *stoop*.⟩

³stoop *n*
a porch, platform, or stairway at the entrance of a house or building

¹stop \'stäp\ *vb* **stopped; stop•ping**
1 to cease moving especially temporarily or for a purpose ⟨I *stopped* to catch my breath.⟩ ⟨The bus *stops* here.⟩
2 to halt the movement or progress of ⟨*Stop* the car!⟩
3 to keep from doing something ⟨I couldn't *stop* him from leaving.⟩
4 to come or bring (something) to an end ⟨The rain *stopped*.⟩ ⟨*Stop* that yelling.⟩
5 to cease operating or functioning ⟨The engine just *stopped*.⟩
6 to close or block up or become closed or blocked up : PLUG ⟨I *stopped* my ears with cotton.⟩ ⟨The drain was *stopped* up.⟩
7 to take time ⟨*Stop* to think first.⟩

²stop *n*
1 ¹END 2, FINISH ⟨Let's put a *stop* to the arguing.⟩
2 the act of bringing or coming to a halt : the state of being stopped ⟨The train came to a *stop*.⟩
3 a halt in a journey : STAY ⟨We made a brief *stop* in the mountains.⟩
4 a stopping place ⟨a bus *stop*⟩
5 something that delays, blocks, or brings to a halt ⟨a door *stop*⟩
6 STOPPER, PLUG
7 a set of organ pipes of one tone quality : a control knob for such a set

stop•light \'stäp-,līt\ *n*
1 TRAFFIC LIGHT
2 a light on the rear of a motor vehicle that goes on when the driver presses the brake pedal

stop•over \'stäp-,ō-vər\ *n*
a stop made during a journey

stop•page \'stä-pij\ *n*
²STOP 2

stop•per \'stä-pər\ *n*
something (as a cork or plug) used to close or block an opening

stop•watch \'stäp-,wäch\ *n*
▶ a watch that can be started and stopped for exact timing (as of a race)

stor•age \'stȯr-ij\ *n*
1 space or a place for putting things for future use or for safekeeping ⟨The house has plenty of *storage*.⟩
2 the act of putting things somewhere especially for future use : the state of being stored ⟨The boat is in *storage* until the spring.⟩

storage battery *n*
a battery that can be made capable of being used again by passing an electric current through it

¹store \'stȯr\ *vb* **stored; stor•ing**
1 to place or leave something in a location (as a warehouse, library, or computer memory) for later use, disposal, or safekeeping ⟨*Store* the old toys in the attic.⟩
2 to bring together or collect as a supply ⟨The body *stores* fat.⟩
3 to provide with what is needed : SUPPLY ⟨They *stored* a ship with goods.⟩

²store *n*
1 a place where goods are sold : SHOP ⟨a candy *store*⟩
2 a large quantity, supply, or number ⟨a *store* of natural resources⟩
3 **stores** *pl* something collected and kept for future use ⟨a ship's *stores*⟩
in store ¹READY 1 ⟨We have a big surprise *in store* for you.⟩

store•house \'stȯr-,hau̇s\ *n*, *pl* **store•hous•es** \-,hau̇-zəz\
1 a building for storing goods
2 a large supply or source

store•keep•er \'stȯr-,kē-pər\ *n*
1 an owner or manager of a store or shop
2 a person in charge of supplies (as in a factory)

store•room \'stȯr-,rüm, -,ru̇m\ *n*
a room for keeping things for future use

stork \'stȯrk\ *n*
a large wading bird that has a long heavy bill and long legs and builds large nests usually in trees or on the top of roofs and poles

¹storm \'stȯrm\ *n*
1 a heavy fall of rain, snow, or sleet often with strong winds

stopwatch

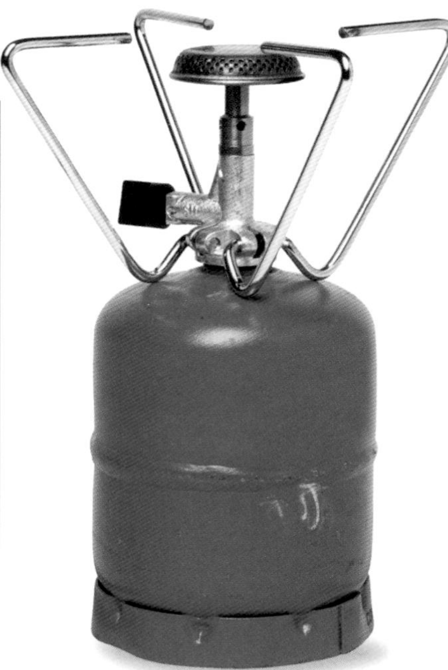
¹stove: a camping stove

2 a serious disturbance of any element of nature ⟨a dust *storm*⟩
3 a strong outburst ⟨a *storm* of protest⟩
4 a violent attack on a defended position ⟨The army took the fort by *storm*.⟩

²storm *vb* **stormed; storm•ing**
1 to blow hard and rain, snow, or sleet heavily
2 to make a sudden mass attack against ⟨Soldiers *stormed* the fort.⟩
3 to feel or express angry feelings : RAGE ⟨He *stormed* at the long delay.⟩
4 to rush about violently or angrily ⟨The mob *stormed* through the streets.⟩

stormy \'stȯr-mē\ *adj* **storm•i•er; storm•i•est**
1 relating to or affected by a storm ⟨a *stormy* sea⟩
2 displaying anger and strong emotions ⟨a *stormy* meeting⟩

¹sto•ry \'stȯr-ē\ *n*, *pl* **sto•ries**
1 a report about incidents or events : ACCOUNT ⟨Let's hear your *story* of what happened.⟩
2 a short often amusing tale ⟨My grandfather tells *stories* of his childhood.⟩
3 a fictional tale shorter than a novel
4 a widely told rumor
5 ³LIE, FALSEHOOD ⟨They made up a *story* of how the window got broken.⟩

[2]**sto•ry** *also* **sto•rey** \'stȯr-ē\ *n, pl* **sto•ries** *also* **sto•reys**
a set of rooms or an area making up one floor level of a building ⟨The building is 20 *stories* high.⟩

stout \'stau̇t\ *adj* **stout•er**; **stout•est**
1 of strong character : BRAVE, DETERMINED ⟨a *stout* general⟩
2 of a strong or lasting sort : STURDY, TOUGH ⟨*stout* timbers⟩ ⟨*stout* boots⟩
3 having a large body with much fat ⟨a *stout* gentleman⟩
4 wide and usually thick ⟨a *stout* bill⟩
stout•ly *adv*
stout•ness *n*

[1]**stove** \'stōv\ *n*
◀ a device usually of iron or steel that burns fuel or uses electricity to provide heat (as for cooking or heating)

[2]**stove** *past and past participle of* STAVE

stove•pipe \'stōv-ˌpīp\ *n*
1 a metal pipe to carry away smoke from a stove
2 a tall silk hat

stow \'stō\ *vb* **stowed**; **stow•ing**
1 to put away : STORE ⟨He *stowed* his belongings in the closet.⟩
2 [2]LOAD 1 ⟨The ship was *stowed* before the voyage.⟩
stow away to hide on a vehicle (as a ship) in order to travel without paying or being seen

stow•away \'stō-ə-ˌwā\ *n*
a person who hides on a vehicle (as a ship) to travel without paying or being seen

strad•dle \'stra-dᵊl\ *vb* **strad•dled**; **strad•dling**
1 to stand, sit, or walk with the legs spread wide apart
2 to stand, sit, or ride with a leg on either side of ⟨He *straddled* the horse.⟩
3 to seem to favor two opposite sides of ⟨Not wanting to offend anyone, she *straddled* the issue.⟩

strag•gle \'stra-gəl\ *vb* **strag•gled**; **strag•gling**
1 to walk or move in a slow and disorderly way ⟨The children finally *straggled* in from outside.⟩
2 to move away or spread out from others of the same kind ⟨The cabins *straggled* into the woods.⟩
strag•gler \'stra-glər\ *n*

strag•gly \'stra-glē, -gə-lē\ *adj* **strag•gli•er**; **strag•gli•est**
growing, hanging, or arranged in an untidy or scattered way ⟨*straggly* hair⟩

[1]**straight** \'strāt\ *adj* **straight•er**; **straight•est**
1 following the same direction throughout its length : not having curves, bends, or angles ⟨a *straight* line⟩
2 being perfectly vertical or horizontal ⟨Does the flagpole look *straight*?⟩
3 following one after the other in order ⟨We worked for five *straight* hours.⟩
4 not changing from an indicated pattern ⟨I got *straight* A's on my report card.⟩
5 not straying from what is right or honest ⟨a *straight* answer⟩
6 correctly ordered or arranged ⟨We set the kitchen *straight*.⟩
7 [2]CORRECT 1 ⟨Let's get the facts *straight*.⟩
8 not showing any feeling especially of amusement ⟨a *straight* face⟩
straight•ness *n*

[2]**straight** *adv*
1 without delay or hesitation ⟨I came *straight* home.⟩
2 in a direct and uninterrupted course : without turning or curving aside ⟨The library is *straight* ahead.⟩
3 in or into an upright position ⟨stand *straight*⟩
4 without interruption ⟨They have been working for three days *straight*.⟩
5 in a normal or correct way ⟨I can't think *straight*.⟩

straight•away \ˌstrā-tə-'wā\ *adv*
without delay : IMMEDIATELY ⟨She found the hidden note *straightaway*.⟩

straight•en \'strā-tᵊn\ *vb* **straight•ened**; **straight•en•ing**
1 to make or become straight ⟨The road *straightened* out.⟩
2 to put in order ⟨Please *straighten* up the room.⟩

straight•for•ward \strāt-'fȯr-wərd\ *adj*
being clear and honest : FRANK ⟨He gave a *straightforward* reply.⟩
straight•for•ward•ly *adv*

straight•way \'strāt-ˌwā\ *adv*
STRAIGHTAWAY

[1]**strain** \'strān\ *n*
1 a group of closely related living things that look similar but possess one or more unique characteristics ⟨Scientists are developing a new *strain* of wheat.⟩
2 a quality or disposition that runs through a family or group ⟨There's a *strain* of genius in that family.⟩
3 a small amount : TRACE ⟨There was a *strain* of sadness in his voice.⟩
4 MELODY 2, TUNE

[2]**strain** *vb* **strained**; **strain•ing**
1 to stretch or be stretched, pulled, or used to the limit ⟨My muscles *strained* under the load.⟩
2 to stretch beyond a proper limit ⟨The story *strains* the truth.⟩
3 to try very hard : make a great effort ⟨People in the back *strained* to hear.⟩
4 to injure or be injured by too much or too hard use or effort ⟨Don't *strain* your back.⟩
5 to press or pass through a strainer : FILTER ⟨*strain* juice⟩
6 to pour off liquid from by using a strainer ⟨Boil and then *strain* the pasta.⟩

[3]**strain** *n*
1 great worry and concern or physical effort
2 something that causes great worry and concern or physical effort ⟨Running the business was a *strain* on him.⟩ ⟨The heavy load was a *strain* on her back.⟩
3 bodily injury resulting from too much use or from a wrench or twist that stretches muscles and ligaments
4 a force that pulls or stretches something to its limit : STRESS

strained \'strānd\ *adj*
1 showing the effects of worry and concern ⟨a *strained* voice⟩
2 not easy or natural ⟨a *strained* smile⟩
3 not friendly or relaxed ⟨Relations between the countries are *strained*.⟩

strain•er \'strā-nər\ *n*
▼ a device (as a screen, sieve, or filter) to hold back solid pieces while a liquid passes through

strainer

strait \'strāt\ *n*
1 a narrow channel connecting two bodies of water
2 a situation of difficulty or distress often used in pl. ⟨The lost hikers were in dire *straits*.⟩

[1]**strand** \'strand\ *n*
the land bordering a body of water : SHORE, BEACH

[2]**strand** *vb* **strand•ed**; **strand•ing**
1 to run, drive, or cause to drift from the water onto land ⟨The storm *stranded* boats.⟩
2 to leave in a strange or unfavorable place especially without any way of leaving ⟨He's *stranded* in a strange city.⟩

[3]strand *n*
1 one of the fibers, threads, strings, or wires twisted or braided to make a cord, rope, or cable
2 something long or twisted like a rope 〈a *strand* of pearls〉

strange \ˈstrānj\ *adj* **strang•er**; **strang•est**
1 UNFAMILIAR 1 〈*strange* surroundings〉
2 different from what is usual, normal, or expected 〈a *strange* sight〉 〈*strange* behavior〉
3 not relaxed **:** UNEASY 〈I felt *strange* on the first day at school.〉
strange•ly *adv*
strange•ness *n*

strang•er \ˈstrān-jər\ *n*
1 a person in a new or unfamiliar place 〈She is a *stranger* here and does not know her way around.〉
2 a person whom another person does not know or has not met 〈Children should not talk to *strangers*.〉

stran•gle \ˈstraŋ-gəl\ *vb* **stran•gled**; **stran•gling**
1 to choke to death by squeezing the throat
2 to die or suffer from or as if from being choked
stran•gler \-glər\ *n*

[1]strap \ˈstrap\ *n*
a narrow strip of flexible material used especially for fastening, holding together, or wrapping

[2]strap *vb* **strapped**; **strap•ping**
1 to fasten with or attach by means of a strap
2 to whip with a strap

strap•ping \ˈstra-piŋ\ *adj*
strong and healthy 〈a *strapping* young man〉

strat•a•gem \ˈstra-tə-jəm\ *n*
a clever trick or plan

stra•te•gic \strə-ˈtē-jik\ *adj*
1 relating to or showing the use of a plan or method to achieve a goal 〈a *strategic* military retreat〉
2 useful or important in military strategy 〈*strategic* weapons〉

strawberries

strat•e•gy \ˈstra-tə-jē\ *n*, *pl* **strat•e•gies**
a carefully developed plan or method for achieving a goal or the skill in developing and undertaking such a plan or method 〈We learned *strategies* for improving business.〉

strato•sphere \ˈstra-tə-ˌsfir\ *n*
an upper portion of the atmosphere extending from about 6 miles (10 kilometers) to 30 miles (50 kilometers) upward where temperature changes little and clouds rarely form

[1]stream 1: a stream in the Scottish countryside

stra•tum \ˈstrā-təm, ˈstra-\ *n*, *pl* **stra•ta** \-tə\
[1]LAYER 1 〈a *stratum* of rock〉

stra•tus \ˈstrā-təs, ˈstra-\ *n*, *pl* **stra•ti** \ˈstrā-ˌtī, ˈstra-\
a cloud extending over a large area at an altitude of from 2,000 to 7,000 feet (600 to 2,100 meters)

straw \ˈstrȯ\ *n*
1 dry plant stems (as of grain after threshing) 〈a mat of *straw*〉
2 a slender tube for sucking up a beverage

straw•ber•ry \ˈstrȯ-ˌber-ē\ *n*, *pl* **straw•ber•ries**
◀ the juicy edible usually red fruit of a low-growing plant with white flowers and long slender runners

[1]stray \ˈstrā\ *n*
a domestic animal (as a cat or dog) that is lost or has no home

[2]stray *vb* **strayed**; **stray•ing**
1 to wander from a group or from the proper place **:** ROAM 〈The gate was left open and the cow *strayed*.〉
2 to go off from a direct or chosen route or the right course 〈We *strayed* from the path.〉
3 to become distracted from a topic or train of thought

[3]stray *adj*
1 lost or having no home 〈a *stray* dog〉
2 not in the proper or intended place 〈I found a few *stray* socks.〉
3 occurring here and there **:** RANDOM 〈a few *stray* hairs〉

[1]streak \ˈstrēk\ *n*
1 a line or mark of a different color or texture from its background 〈You left a *streak* of mud on the rug.〉
2 a narrow band of light 〈a *streak* of lightning〉
3 an amount of a quality 〈She's got a stubborn *streak*.〉
4 a short series of something 〈a winning *streak*〉
streaked \ˈstrēkt, ˈstrē-kəd\ *adj*

[2]streak *vb* **streaked**; **streak•ing**
1 to make or have a line or mark of color in or on 〈His hair is *streaked* with gray.〉
2 to move swiftly **:** RUSH 〈A jet *streaked* across the sky.〉

[1]stream \ˈstrēm\ *n*
1 ◀ a body of water (as a brook or river) flowing on the earth
2 a flow of liquid or gas 〈a *stream* of tears〉
3 a steady series (as of words or events) following one another 〈They kept up an endless *stream* of chatter.〉

[2]stream *vb* **streamed; stream•ing**
1 to flow in or as if in a stream ⟨Rain was *streaming* down the windows.⟩
2 to give out a bodily fluid in large amounts ⟨His face *streamed* sweat.⟩
3 to become wet with flowing liquid ⟨The windows are *streaming* with rain.⟩
4 to trail out at full length ⟨Her hair *streamed* in the wind.⟩
5 to pour, enter, or arrive in large numbers ⟨The people *streamed* into the hall.⟩ ⟨Complaints were *streaming* in.⟩
6 to transfer (data, as music or videos) in a continuous stream especially to be played immediately

stream•er \'strē-mər\ *n*
1 a flag that floats or moves in the wind **:** PENNANT
2 a long narrow strip (as of ribbon or paper) that is often hung for decoration
3 streamers *pl* AURORA BOREALIS

stream•lined \'strēm-,līnd\ *adj*
1 designed or constructed to make motion through water or air easier or as if for this purpose ⟨a *streamlined* automobile⟩
2 made shorter, simpler, or more efficient ⟨They developed a *streamlined* manufacturing process.⟩

street \'strēt\ *n*
1 a public road especially in a city, town, or village
2 the people living along a street ⟨The whole *street* was excited.⟩

streetcars in San Francisco

street•car \'strēt-,kär\ *n*
▲ a vehicle for carrying passengers that runs on rails and operates mostly on city streets

strength \'streŋth\ *n*
1 the quality or state of being physically strong ⟨He pushed with all his *strength.*⟩
2 power to resist force ⟨the *strength* of a rope⟩
3 ability to produce an effect ⟨maximum *strength* cough syrup⟩
4 degree of intensity ⟨The *strength* of the wind increased.⟩
5 power as measured in numbers ⟨The army is at full *strength.*⟩
6 a strong or positive quality ⟨What do you think are your *strengths* and weaknesses?⟩
7 the inner courage or determination that allows a person to face and deal with difficulties

strength•en \'streŋ-thən\ *vb* **strength•ened; strength•en•ing**
to make, grow, or become stronger or more powerful ⟨Exercises will *strengthen* your muscles.⟩

stren•u•ous \'stren-yə-wəs\ *adj*
1 showing or requiring much energy and effort ⟨a *strenuous* climb⟩
2 very active **:** ENERGETIC ⟨He leads a *strenuous* life.⟩
stren•u•ous•ly *adv*

strep throat \'strep-\ *n*
a sore throat that is accompanied by fever and caused by a bacterium

[1]stress \'stres\ *n*
1 a force that tends to change the shape of an object
2 something that causes physical or emotional tension **:** a state of tension resulting from a stress ⟨She felt the *stress* of working two jobs.⟩
3 special importance given to something ⟨The speaker laid *stress* on a particular point.⟩
4 relative loudness or force of a part of a spoken word or a beat in music ⟨"Finally" has the *stress* on the first syllable.⟩

[2]stress *vb* **stressed; stress•ing**
1 to subject to excessive use or to forces that cause a change in shape ⟨Hard use was *stressing* the equipment.⟩
2 to cause or experience physical or emotional tension ⟨All these changes are *stressing* me.⟩
3 to pronounce (part of a word) with relative loudness or force ⟨*Stress* the first syllable.⟩
4 to give special importance to **:** EMPHASIZE ⟨He *stressed* the need to save energy.⟩

stress mark *n*
a mark used to show what part or syllable of a written word should be stressed when spoken

[1]stretch \'strech\ *vb* **stretched; stretch•ing**
1 to reach out **:** EXTEND, SPREAD ⟨I *stretched* my neck to see better.⟩
2 to pull or draw out in length or width or both ⟨Don't *stretch* my sweater.⟩
3 to extend (as the body) in a flat position ⟨I *stretched* out on the bed.⟩
4 to extend the body or limbs ⟨You should *stretch* before exercising.⟩
5 to pull tight ⟨*Stretch* the canvas over a frame.⟩
6 to cause to reach or continue ⟨A wire was *stretched* between two posts.⟩
7 EXAGGERATE ⟨You're *stretching* the truth.⟩
8 to become extended without breaking ⟨Rubber *stretches* easily.⟩
9 to extend over a continuous period ⟨His fascination with dinosaurs *stretches* back to childhood.⟩

[2]stretch *n*
1 the act of extending or drawing out beyond ordinary or normal limits ⟨The story was a *stretch* of the imagination.⟩
2 the ability to be pulled or drawn out in length or width or both ⟨The fabric has a lot of *stretch.*⟩
3 the act or an instance of stretching the body or one of its parts
4 a continuous extent in length, area, or time ⟨a short *stretch* of beach⟩ ⟨a long *stretch* of silence⟩

stretch•er \'stre-chər\ *n*
▼ a device like a cot used for carrying sick or injured persons

strew \'strü\ *vb* **strewed; strewed** *or* **strewn** \'strün\; **strew•ing**
1 SCATTER 1 ⟨Toys were *strewn* about the yard.⟩
2 to spread by scattering ⟨I *strewed* crumbs for the birds.⟩
3 to cover by or as if by scattering something ⟨Drivers *strewed* the highway with litter.⟩

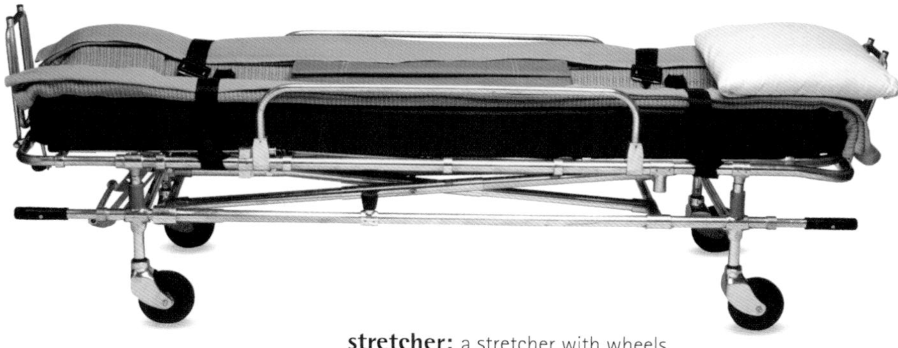

stretcher: a stretcher with wheels

strick•en \'stri-kən\ *adj*
1 showing the effect of disease, misfortune, or sorrow ⟨a grief-*stricken* look⟩
2 hit or wounded by or as if by an object that was shot or thrown

strict \'strikt\ *adj* **strict•er; strict•est**
1 not to be avoided or ignored : requiring obedience ⟨*strict* orders⟩
2 strongly enforcing rules and discipline ⟨a *strict* coach⟩
3 kept with great care : ABSOLUTE ⟨*strict* secrecy⟩
4 carefully observing something (as a rule or principle) ⟨a *strict* vegetarian⟩
5 [1]EXACT 1, PRECISE ⟨the *strict* sense of a word⟩
strict•ly *adv*
strict•ness *n*

[1]**stride** \'strīd\ *vb* **strode** \'strōd\; **strid•den** \'stri-dᵊn\; **strid•ing** \'strī-diŋ\
to walk or run with long even steps

[2]**stride** *n*
1 a long step or the distance covered by such a step ⟨She crossed the room in only a few *strides*.⟩
2 a step forward : ADVANCE ⟨We've made great *strides* toward a cure.⟩
3 a way of walking ⟨a bouncy *stride*⟩

strife \'strīf\ *n*
bitter and sometimes violent disagreement ⟨political *strife*⟩

[1]**strike** \'strīk\ *vb* **struck** \'strək\; **struck** *also* **strick•en** \'stri-kən\; **strik•ing** \'strī-kiŋ\
1 to touch, hit, or affect with force ⟨He *struck* the horse with a whip.⟩⟨The tree was *struck* by lightning.⟩
2 to come into contact or collision with ⟨The ship *struck* a rock.⟩
3 to attack or seize suddenly ⟨The snake *struck*.⟩
4 GO 1, PROCEED ⟨They *struck* off into the woods.⟩
5 to lower, take down, or take apart ⟨Let's *strike* camp.⟩
6 to make known by sounding : cause to sound ⟨The clock *struck* one.⟩
7 to affect usually suddenly ⟨She was *stricken* with a high fever.⟩
8 to produce by or as if by a blow ⟨We'll *strike* fear into the enemy.⟩
9 to happen with damaging force or effect ⟨The storm *struck* the island.⟩
10 to cause to ignite by scratching ⟨I *struck* a match.⟩
11 to agree on the arrangements of ⟨We *struck* a deal.⟩
12 to make an impression on ⟨The idea *struck* me as funny.⟩
13 to come to mind ⟨The answer *struck* me suddenly.⟩
14 to produce on a musical instrument ⟨*Strike* up a tune.⟩
15 to remove or cancel with or as if with the stroke of a pen ⟨*Strike* that name from the list.⟩
16 to come upon : DISCOVER ⟨Miners *struck* gold.⟩
17 to take on : ASSUME ⟨She *struck* a relaxed pose.⟩
18 to stop work in order to force an employer to meet demands regarding conditions of work
19 to produce by stamping ⟨The mint is *striking* a new coin.⟩
strike out to be out in baseball by getting three strikes during a turn at bat
strike up to cause to begin ⟨We *struck up* a conversation.⟩

string beans

[2]**strike** *n*
1 an act or instance of striking ⟨a lightning *strike*⟩ ⟨the *strike* of the clock⟩
2 a stopping of work by workers to force an employer to agree to demands
3 an unhelpful or undesirable characteristic : DISADVANTAGE ⟨Their poor attendance was a *strike* against them.⟩
4 a baseball pitch that is not hit fair or that passes through a certain area over home plate (**strike zone**) without being hit and that counts against the batter
5 the knocking down of all the pins with the first ball in bowling
6 a discovery of a valuable mineral deposit ⟨an oil *strike*⟩
7 a military attack ⟨The army launched a *strike* against the enemy.⟩

strike•out \'strīk-,au̇t\ *n*
an out in baseball that results from a batter getting three strikes during a turn at bat

strik•ing \'strī-kiŋ\ *adj*
attracting attention : REMARKABLE ⟨a *striking* resemblance⟩
strik•ing•ly *adv*

[1]**string** \'striŋ\ *n*
1 a thin cord used to bind, fasten, or tie
2 something that resembles a string ⟨potato *strings*⟩
3 the gut, wire, or plastic cord of a musical instrument that vibrates to produce a tone when touched ⟨a guitar *string*⟩
4 **strings** *pl* the stringed instruments of an orchestra
5 a group, series, or line of things threaded on a string or arranged as if strung together ⟨a *string* of lights⟩ ⟨a *string* of automobiles⟩
6 a series of events which follow each other in time ⟨a *string* of robberies⟩
7 **strings** *pl* requirements that are connected with something ⟨The agreement has no *strings* attached.⟩

[2]**string** *vb* **strung** \'strəŋ\; **string•ing**
1 to provide with strings ⟨*string* a violin⟩
2 [2]THREAD 4 ⟨*string* beads⟩
3 to tie, hang, or fasten with string ⟨She *strung* a key around her neck.⟩
4 to set or stretch out in a line ⟨Telephone lines were *strung* for miles.⟩
5 to remove the tough fibers of ⟨*string* peas⟩

string bass *n*
DOUBLE BASS

string bean *n*
◀ a bean with a long slender pod that is cooked and eaten as a vegetable

stringed instrument \'striŋd-\ *n*
▶ a musical instrument (as a violin, guitar, or harp) sounded by plucking or striking or by drawing a bow across its tight strings

stringy \'striŋ-ē\ *adj* **string•i•er; string•i•est**
containing, consisting of, or like string ⟨*stringy* meat⟩ ⟨*stringy* hair⟩

[1]**strip** \'strip\ *vb* **stripped; strip•ping**
1 to remove clothes : UNDRESS
2 to remove a covering or surface layer from ⟨I'm *stripping* furniture for refinishing.⟩
3 to make bare or clear ⟨The land was *stripped* of its trees.⟩
4 to take away all duties, honors, or special rights ⟨The soldiers were *stripped* of their rank.⟩
5 to remove all the contents (as equipment or accessories) from ⟨Thieves *stripped* the car.⟩
6 to tear or damage the thread of (as a screw or bolt)

stringed instrument

Some stringed instruments can be plucked or strummed, such as the balalaika, sitar, harp, and electric bass. Other instruments, such as the cello, violin, viola, and double bass, are sounded with a bow. The thinner and shorter the string, the higher the note it will produce. Larger instruments, such as the double bass, can produce lower notes.

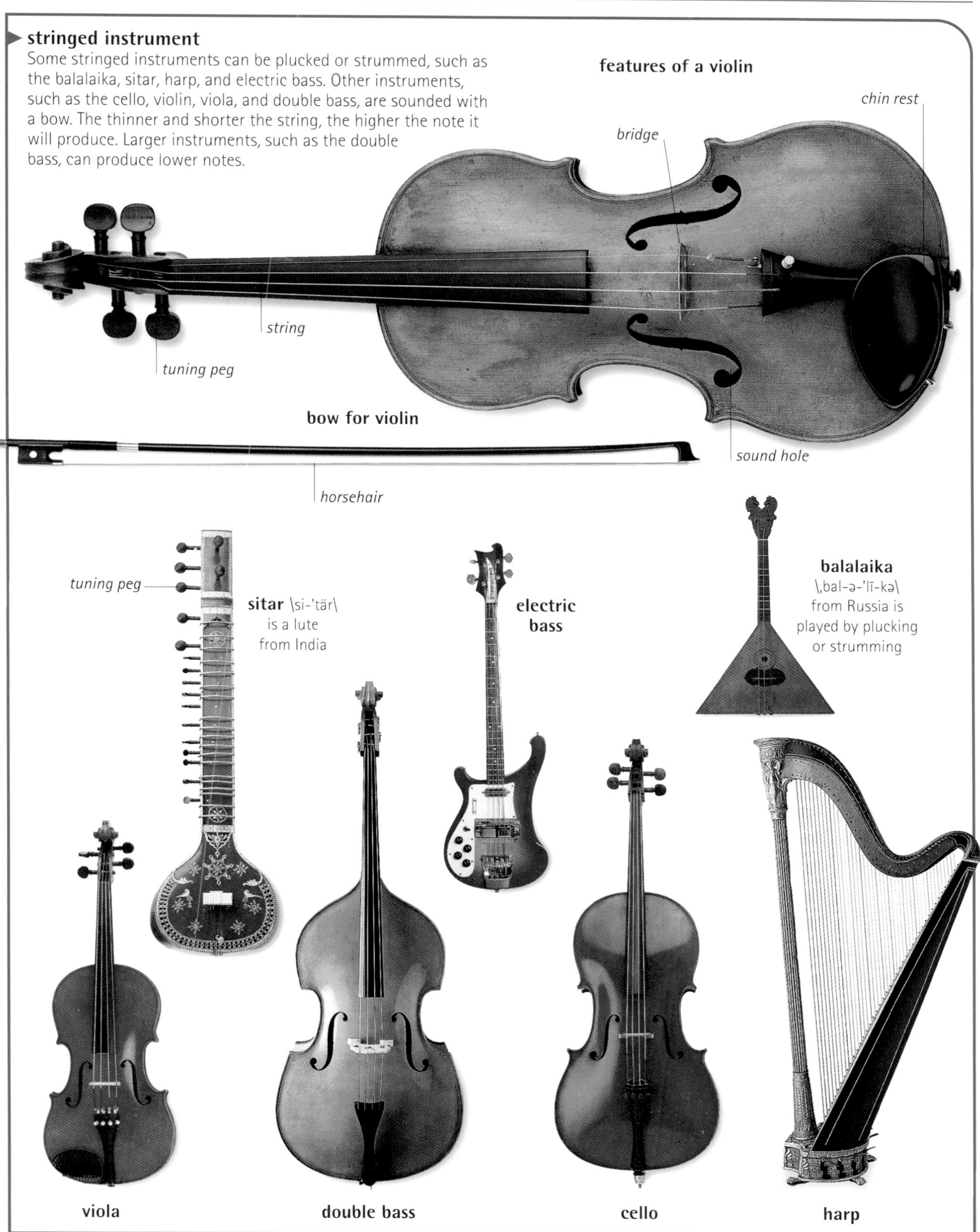

[2]strip *n*
a long narrow piece or area 〈*strips* of bacon〉 〈a *strip* of land〉

[1]stripe \ˈstrīp\ *vb* **striped**; **strip•ing**
to make stripes on

[2]stripe *n*
1 a line or long narrow section differing in color or appearance from the background 〈The shirt is black with red *stripes.*〉
2 ► a piece of material often with a special design worn (as on a sleeve) to show military rank or length of service 〈a sergeant's *stripes*〉

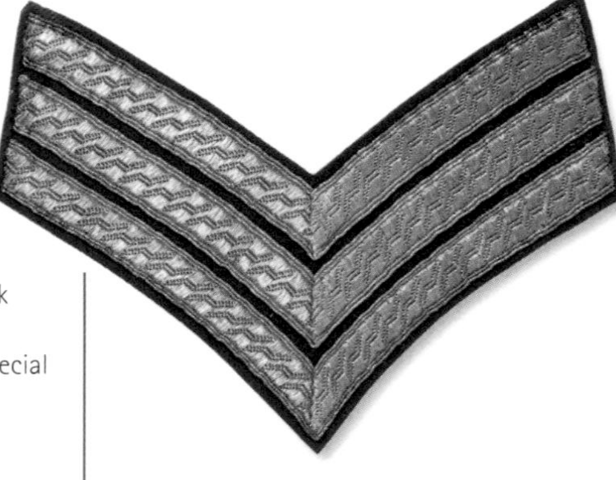

[2]stripe 2: stripes for the rank of sergeant

striped \ˈstrīpt, ˈstrī-pəd\ *adj*
having stripes

strive \ˈstrīv\ *vb* **strove** \ˈstrōv\; **striv•en** \ˈstri-vən\ *or* **strived**; **striv•ing** \ˈstrī-viŋ\
to try very hard 〈We will *strive* to win.〉

strode *past of* STRIDE

[1]stroke \ˈstrōk\ *vb* **stroked**; **strok•ing**
to rub gently in one direction 〈I *stroked* the dog's head.〉

[2]stroke *n*
1 the act of striking : BLOW 〈the *stroke* of a whip〉
2 one of a series of repeated movements (as in swimming or rowing)
3 a sudden serious illness caused by the breaking or blocking of an artery in the brain
4 the sound of striking (as of a clock or bell) 〈the *stroke* of midnight〉
5 the hitting of a ball in a game (as golf or tennis)
6 a sudden or unexpected example 〈a *stroke* of luck〉
7 a single movement or the mark made by a single movement of a brush, pen, or tool
8 a sudden action or process that results in something being struck 〈a *stroke* of lightning〉
9 effort by which something is done or the results of such effort 〈It was a *stroke* of genius.〉

[1]stroll \ˈstrōl\ *vb* **strolled**; **stroll•ing**
to walk in a leisurely manner

[2]stroll *n*
a leisurely walk

stroll•er \ˈstrō-lər\ *n*
a small carriage in which a baby can sit and be pushed around

strong \ˈstrȯŋ\ *adj* **stron•ger** \ˈstrȯŋ-gər\; **stron•gest** \ˈstrȯŋ-gəst\
1 having great power in the muscles
2 HEALTHY 1 〈She's young and *strong.*〉
3 not easy to injure, overcome, or resist : SOLID 〈a *strong* bridge〉 〈a *strong* opponent〉 〈a *strong* urge〉
4 ENTHUSIASTIC, ZEALOUS 〈a *strong* supporter〉
5 moving with speed and force 〈a *strong* wind〉
6 having much of some quality : INTENSE 〈*strong* coffee〉 〈*strong* light〉
7 having a great deal of power 〈a *strong* nation〉
8 of a specified number 〈an army 10,000 *strong*〉
9 PERSUASIVE 〈*strong* arguments〉
10 well established : FIRM 〈*strong* beliefs〉 〈*strong* traditions〉
11 having a powerful action or effect 〈*strong* medicine〉 〈*strong* discipline〉
12 very noticeable 〈a *strong* resemblance〉
strong•ly \ˈstrȯŋ-lē\ *adv*

► **Synonyms** STRONG, STURDY, and TOUGH mean showing the power to endure opposing force. STRONG is used of great physical or material power. 〈A *strong* person with a *strong* rope is needed to lift that.〉 STURDY is used for the ability to endure pressure or hard use. 〈The table is old but *sturdy.*〉 TOUGH means that something is very firm and able to stay together. 〈*Tough* fabric lasts for years.〉

strong•hold \ˈstrȯŋ-ˌhōld\ *n*
FORTRESS

strove *past of* STRIVE

struck *past and past participle of* STRIKE

struc•tur•al \ˈstrək-chə-rəl\ *adj*
relating to or affecting the way in which something is built 〈*structural* defects〉

struc•ture \ˈstrək-chər\ *n*
1 something built or arranged in a definite way 〈He entered a small brick *structure.*〉 〈We studied leaves and other plant *structures.*〉
2 the manner in which something is built, arranged, or organized 〈the *structure* of the body〉

[1]strug•gle \ˈstrə-gəl\ *vb* **strug•gled**; **strug•gling**
1 to make a great effort to do or achieve something or to overcome someone or something 〈I *struggled* with the burglar.〉 〈We're *struggling* with money problems.〉
2 to move with difficulty or with great effort 〈A woman *struggled* through the snow.〉

[2]struggle *n*
1 a difficult or violent effort
2 [2]FIGHT 1, CONTEST

strum \ˈstrəm\ *vb* **strummed**; **strum•ming**
to play on a stringed instrument by brushing the strings with the fingers 〈*strum* a guitar〉

strung *past and past participle of* STRING

[1]strut \ˈstrət\ *vb* **strut•ted**; **strut•ting**
to walk in a confident and proud way

[2]strut *n*
1 a stiff proud step or walk
2 a bar or brace used to resist pressure in the direction of its length

[1]stub \ˈstəb\ *n*
1 a short part remaining after the rest has been removed or used up 〈a pencil *stub*〉
2 a small part of a larger piece of printed paper (as a check or ticket) kept as a record of the purpose of the paper

[2]stub *vb* **stubbed**; **stub•bing**
to strike (as the toe) against an object

stub•ble \ˈstə-bəl\ *n*
1 a short growth of beard
2 the short ends of crops and especially cereal grasses remaining attached to the ground after harvest

stub•born \ˈstə-bərn\ *adj*
1 refusing to change an opinion or course of action in spite of difficulty or urging 〈She's too *stubborn* to ask for help.〉
2 PERSISTENT 〈a *stubborn* cough〉
3 difficult to handle, manage, or treat 〈a *stubborn* stain〉
stub•born•ly *adv*
stub•born•ness *n*

stub•by \ˈstə-bē\ *adj* **stub•bi•er**; **stub•bi•est**
short and thick like a stub 〈*stubby* fingers〉 〈a *stubby* tail〉

stuc•co \ˈstə-kō\ *n, pl* **stuc•cos** *or* **stuc•coes**
a plaster for coating walls

stuck *past and past participle of* STICK

stuck–up \ˈstək-ˈəp\ *adj*
VAIN 2, CONCEITED

[1]stud \ˈstəd\ *n*
1 one of the smaller vertical supports in the walls of a building to which the wall materials are fastened
2 a removable device like a button used for fastening or as an ornament 〈shirt *studs*〉

A B C D E F G H I J K L M N O P Q R S T U V W X Y Z

3 one of the metal cleats used on a snow tire to provide a better grip
4 a small piece of jewelry that is attached through a hole in part of a person's body

²stud *vb* **stud•ded; stud•ding**
to cover or be covered with many small items 〈water *studded* with islands〉

stu•dent \'stü-dᵊnt, 'styü-\ *n*
a person who studies especially in school : PUPIL

stu•dio \'stü-dē-,ō, 'styü-\ *n, pl* **stu•di•os**
1 ▶ the place where an artist, sculptor, or photographer works
2 a place for the study of an art
3 a place where movies are made
4 a place from which radio or television programs are broadcast

stu•di•ous \'stü-dē-əs, 'styü-\ *adj*
very serious about studying 〈a *studious* child〉
stu•di•ous•ly *adv*

¹study \'stə-dē\ *vb* **stud•ied; study•ing**
1 to make an effort to learn about something by reading, investigating, or memorizing
2 to give close attention to 〈She *studied* the request carefully.〉

²study *n, pl* **stud•ies**
1 the act of making an effort to learn by reading, practicing, or memorizing
2 a careful investigation or examination of something 〈the *study* of a disease〉
3 a room especially for study, reading, or writing

¹stuff \'stəf\ *n*
1 materials, supplies, or equipment that people need or use 〈We helped move his *stuff* to the new apartment.〉
2 writing, speech, sounds, actions, or ideas of little value 〈The speaker said a lot of *stuff* I didn't understand.〉
3 something mentioned or understood but not named 〈Wipe that *stuff* off your face.〉
4 basic part of something : SUBSTANCE 〈The floor is made of tough *stuff.*〉 〈She shows the *stuff* of greatness.〉

²stuff *vb* **stuffed; stuff•ing**
1 to force into something : THRUST 〈She *stuffed* the clothes into a drawer.〉
2 to fill by packing or crowding things in : CRAM 〈I *stuffed* the suitcases.〉
3 OVEREAT, GORGE
4 to fill with a stuffing 〈*stuff* a turkey〉
5 to block up : CONGEST 〈His nose is *stuffed.*〉
synonyms see PACK

stuff•ing \'stə-fiŋ\ *n*
1 ▶ a mixture (as of bread crumbs and seasonings) used to stuff a food (as meat or a vegetable)
2 material used in filling up something

▶ studio 1
Different artists, such as photographers and painters, have specially equipped studios suited to their work. For example, a photographer's studio has a range of lighting devices, camera accessories, and screens. This equipment gives the photographer control over the intensity and color of the lighting, camera angle and focus, and the subject's background.

a photographer's studio

stuffy \'stə-fē\ *adj* **stuff•i•er; stuff•i•est**
1 needing fresh air 〈a *stuffy* room〉
2 stuffed or blocked up 〈a *stuffy* nose〉
3 very formal and self-important

¹stum•ble \'stəm-bəl\ *vb* **stum•bled; stum•bling**
1 to trip in walking, running, or dancing
2 to walk unsteadily 〈She *stumbled* around in the dark.〉
3 to speak or act in a clumsy manner 〈The student *stumbled* through his presentation.〉
4 to come unexpectedly or accidentally 〈We *stumbled* onto a clue.〉

stuffing 1: vegetable stuffing in a sweet pepper

²stumble *n*
an act or instance of tripping or walking unsteadily

¹stump \'stəmp\ *n*
1 the part of a tree that remains in the ground after the tree is cut down
2 the part of something (as a tooth or a pencil) that remains after the rest has been removed, lost, or worn away : STUB

²stump *vb* **stumped; stump•ing**
1 PERPLEX, BAFFLE 〈My question *stumped* the experts.〉
2 to walk or walk over heavily, stiffly, or clumsily as if with a wooden leg

stun \'stən\ *vb* **stunned; stun•ning**
1 to make dizzy or senseless by or as if by a blow 〈The bird laid *stunned* after crashing into the window.〉
2 to affect with shock or confusion : fill with disbelief 〈He was *stunned* by the news.〉

stung *past and past participle of* STING

stunk *past and past participle of* STINK

stun•ning \'stə-niŋ\ *adj*
1 able or likely to make a person senseless or confused 〈a *stunning* blow〉 〈*stunning* news〉
2 unusually lovely or attractive : STRIKING

[1]stunt \'stənt\ *n*
1 an unusual or difficult performance or act 〈acrobatic *stunts*〉
2 something done for the purpose of gaining attention or publicity

[2]stunt *vb* **stunt•ed**; **stunt•ing**
to hold back the normal growth of

stu•pe•fy \'stü-pə-,fī, 'styü-\ *vb* **stu•pe•fied**; **stu•pe•fy•ing**
1 to make confused or unable to think clearly
2 ASTONISH, ASTOUND

stu•pen•dous \stü-'pen-dəs, styü-\ *adj*
amazing especially because of great size or height
stu•pen•dous•ly *adv*

stu•pid \'stü-pəd, 'styü-\ *adj* **stu•pid•er**; **stu•pid•est**
1 not intelligent : slow in understanding
2 not sensible : FOOLISH 〈a *stupid* mistake〉
3 not interesting or worthwhile 〈a *stupid* plot〉
stu•pid•ly *adv*

stu•pid•i•ty \stü-'pi-də-tē, styü-\ *n*, *pl* **stu•pid•i•ties**
1 the quality or state of being foolish or slow in understanding
2 a foolish thought, action, or remark

stu•por \'stü-pər, 'styü-\ *n*
a condition of being not alert or able to think normally

stur•dy \'stər-dē\ *adj* **stur•di•er**; **stur•di•est**
1 firmly built or made 〈The branch was *sturdy* enough to support his weight.〉
2 strong and healthy in body : ROBUST
3 RESOLUTE
synonyms see STRONG
stur•di•ly \'stər-də-lē\ *adv*
sturd•i•ness \'stər-dē-nəs\ *n*

stur•geon \'stər-jən\ *n*
a large fish that has tough skin and rows of bony plates and is often used for food

[1]stut•ter \'stə-tər\ *vb* **stut•tered**; **stut•ter•ing**
to speak or say with involuntary repetition or interruption of sounds

[2]stutter *n*
the act or an instance of speaking with involuntary repetition or interruption

[1]sty \'stī\ *n*, *pl* **sties**
PIGPEN

[2]sty *or* **stye** \'stī\ *n*, *pl* **sties** *or* **styes**
a painful red swelling on the edge of an eyelid

[1]style \'stīl\ *n*
1 a particular form or design of something 〈classical *style* of dance〉 〈Dinner was served buffet *style*.〉
2 a way of speaking or writing
3 an individual way of behaving or doing something 〈He changed his *style* of holding the bat and hit more balls.〉
4 a method, manner, or quality that is felt to be very respectable, fashionable, or proper : FASHION 〈They dine in *style*.〉 〈Dad's clothes are out of *style*.〉
5 an easy and graceful manner 〈She handled the situation with *style*.〉
6 the narrow middle part of the pistil of a flower
synonyms see FASHION

[2]style *vb* **styled**; **styl•ing**
1 to design and make in a known or new style 〈well-*styled* hats〉
2 to give a special shape to someone's hair
3 to identify by some descriptive term : CALL

styl•ish \'stī-lish\ *adj*
having style : FASHIONABLE 〈a *stylish* suit〉
styl•ish•ly *adv*

sty•lus \'stī-ləs\ *n*, *pl* **sty•li** \-,lī\ *also* **sty•lus•es**
▶ a pointed instrument used in ancient times for writing on wax tablets

stylus: a bronze stylus from Southeast Asia

[1]sub \'səb\ *n*
[1]SUBSTITUTE

[2]sub *vb* **subbed**; **sub•bing**
to act as a substitute

[3]sub *n*
SUBMARINE

sub- *prefix*
1 under : beneath : below 〈*sub*marine〉
2 lower in importance or rank : lesser
3 division or part of 〈*sub*set〉

sub•di•vide \,səb-də-'vīd\ *vb* **sub•di•vid•ed**; **sub•di•vid•ing**
1 to divide the parts of into smaller parts
2 to divide (a piece of land) into lots on which houses will be built

sub•di•vi•sion \,səb-də-'vi-zhən\ *n*
1 the act of dividing into smaller parts
2 one of the parts into which something is subdivided

sub•due \səb-'dü, -'dyü\ *vb* **sub•dued**; **sub•du•ing**
1 to bring under control 〈He *subdued* his fears.〉 〈Police *subdued* the angry man.〉
2 to overcome in battle 〈Troops *subdued* the enemy.〉

sub•dued \səb-'düd, -'dyüd\ *adj*
lacking in liveliness, intensity, or strength 〈a *subdued* voice〉

sub•head \'səb-,hed\ *n*
a heading under which one of the divisions of a subject is listed

sub•head•ing \'səb-,he-diŋ\ *n*
SUBHEAD

[1]sub•ject \'səb-jikt\ *n*
1 the person or thing discussed : TOPIC 〈She's the *subject* of rumors.〉 〈Let's change the *subject*.〉
2 an area of knowledge that is studied in school 〈Geography is my favorite *subject*.〉
3 a person who owes loyalty to a monarch or state
4 a person under the authority or control of another
5 the word or group of words about which the predicate makes a statement
6 a person or animal that is studied or experimented on

[2]subject *adj*
1 owing obedience or loyalty to another 〈The people were *subject* to their king.〉
2 possible or likely to be affected by 〈The schedule is *subject* to change.〉 〈The area is *subject* to flooding.〉
3 depending on 〈I'll send the samples *subject* to your approval.〉

[3]sub•ject \səb-'jekt\ *vb* **sub•ject•ed**; **sub•ject•ing**
1 to bring under control or rule 〈The Romans *subjected* much of Europe.〉
2 to cause to put up with 〈My parents are unwilling to *subject* us to embarrassment.〉

sub•jec•tive \səb-'jek-tiv\ *adj*
based mainly on opinions or feelings rather than on facts 〈a *subjective* report〉

sub•lime \sə-'blīm\ *adj*
1 grand or noble in thought, expression, or manner 〈*sublime* truths〉
2 beautiful or impressive enough to arouse a feeling of admiration and wonder 〈*sublime* scenery〉

sub•ma•rine \'səb-mə-,rēn, ,səb-mə-'rēn\ *n*
a naval ship designed to operate underwater

sub•merge \səb-'mərj\ *vb* **sub•merged**; **sub•merg•ing**
1 to put under or plunge into water
2 to cover or become covered with or as if with water 〈Floods *submerged* the town.〉

sub•mis•sion \səb-'mi-shən\ *n*
1 the act of putting forward something (as for consideration or comment)
2 the condition of being humble or obedient
3 the act of giving in to power or authority

sub•mis•sive \səb-'mi-siv\ *adj*
willing to give in to others
sub•mis•sive•ly *adv*

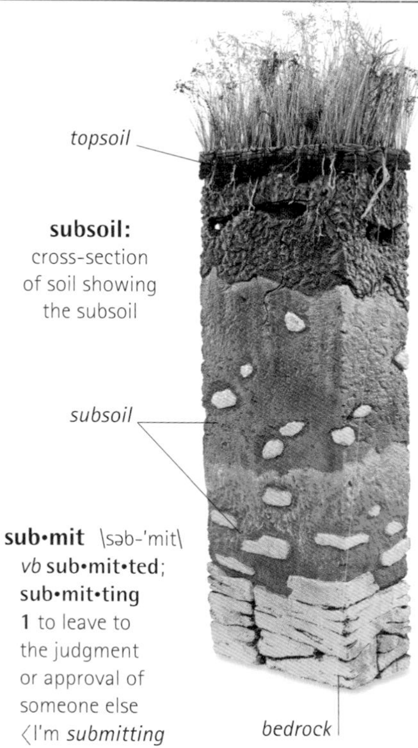

subsoil: cross-section of soil showing the subsoil

sub•mit \səb-'mit\ *vb* **sub•mit•ted**; **sub•mit•ting**
1 to leave to the judgment or approval of someone else ⟨I'm *submitting* a plan for consideration.⟩
2 to yield to the authority, control, or choice of another
3 to put forward as an opinion, reason, or idea ⟨I *submit* that computers have changed business.⟩

[1]**sub•or•di•nate** \sə-'bȯr-də-nət\ *adj*
1 being in a lower class or rank : INFERIOR ⟨a *subordinate* officer⟩
2 yielding to or controlled by authority

[2]**subordinate** *n*
someone who has less power or authority than someone else

[3]**sub•or•di•nate** \sə-'bȯr-də-ˌnāt\ *vb* **sub•or•di•nat•ed**; **sub•or•di•nat•ing**
to treat as inferior in rank or importance

sub•scribe \səb-'skrīb\ *vb* **sub•scribed**; **sub•scrib•ing**
1 to place an order for a publication or service which is delivered over a stated period
2 to agree with or support ⟨I *subscribe* to the idea that voting is a duty.⟩
sub•scrib•er *n*

sub•scrip•tion \səb-'skrip-shən\ *n*
an agreement to buy a publication or service for a stated period

sub•se•quent \'səb-si-kwənt\ *adj*
following in time, order, or place ⟨*subsequent* events⟩
sub•se•quent•ly *adv*

sub•ser•vi•ent \səb-'sər-vē-ənt\ *adj*
SUBMISSIVE

sub•set \'səb-ˌset\ *n*
a small division or portion

sub•side \səb-'sīd\ *vb* **sub•sid•ed**; **sub•sid•ing**
1 to become less strong or intense ⟨The pain *subsided.*⟩ ⟨The storm is beginning to *subside.*⟩
2 to become lower : SINK ⟨The flood *subsided.*⟩

sub•sist \səb-'sist\ *vb* **sub•sist•ed**; **sub•sist•ing**
to continue living or being ⟨They *subsisted* on bread and water.⟩

sub•sis•tence \səb-'sis-təns\ *n*
the smallest amount (as of food and clothing) necessary to support life

sub•soil \'səb-ˌsȯil\ *n*
◀ a layer of soil lying just under the topsoil

sub•stance \'səb-stəns\ *n*
1 material of a certain kind ⟨an oily *substance*⟩
2 the most basic or important part or quality ⟨The books differ in both style and *substance.*⟩
3 material belongings : WEALTH ⟨a person of *substance*⟩

sub•stan•dard \ˌsəb-'stan-dərd\ *adj*
lower in quality than expected

sub•stan•tial \səb-'stan-shəl\ *adj*
1 large in amount ⟨a *substantial* improvement⟩
2 IMPORTANT 1 ⟨a *substantial* difference⟩
3 firmly constructed ⟨*Substantial* walls surround the castle.⟩
4 ABUNDANT ⟨a *substantial* meal⟩
5 PROSPEROUS 1 ⟨a *substantial* farmer⟩
6 made up of or relating to substance : MATERIAL

[1]**sub•sti•tute** \'səb-stə-ˌtüt, -ˌtyüt\ *n*
a person or thing that takes the place of another

[2]**substitute** *vb* **sub•sti•tut•ed**; **sub•sti•tut•ing**
1 to put in the place of another
2 to take the place of another ⟨Honey can *substitute* for sugar in the recipe.⟩

sub•sti•tu•tion \ˌsəb-stə-'tü-shən, -'tyü-\ *n*
the act or process of putting in or taking the place of another

sub•ter•ra•nean \ˌsəb-tə-'rā-nē-ən, -nyən\ *adj*
being, lying, or operating under the surface of the earth ⟨a *subterranean* lake⟩

sub•tle \'sə-tᵊl\ *adj* **sub•tler** \'sət-lər\; **sub•tlest** \'sət-ləst\
1 difficult to perceive ⟨a *subtle* difference⟩
2 SHREWD, KEEN ⟨*subtle* questions⟩
3 DELICATE 1 ⟨a *subtle* fragrance⟩
sub•tly \'sət-lē\ *adv*

sub•top•ic \'səb-ˌtä-pik\ *n*
a topic (as in a composition) that is a division of a main topic

sub•tract \səb-'trakt\ *vb* **sub•tract•ed**; **sub•tract•ing**
to take away (as one part or number from another) : DEDUCT

sub•trac•tion \səb-'trak-shən\ *n*
the act or process of taking one number away from another

sub•urb \'sə-ˌbərb\ *n*
a smaller community close to a city
sub•ur•ban \sə-'bər-bən\ *adj*

sub•way \'səb-ˌwā\ *n*
▼ a usually electric underground railway

subway: subway in Barcelona, Spain

suc•ceed \sək-ˈsēd\ *vb* **suc•ceed•ed; suc•ceed•ing**
1 to achieve a desired result : be successful
2 to turn out well ⟨The plan *succeeded.*⟩
3 to come after : FOLLOW ⟨This new model of car *succeeds* the old one.⟩
4 to come next after another person in office or position

suc•cess \sək-ˈses\ *n*
1 satisfactory completion of something
2 the gaining of wealth, respect, or fame
3 a person or thing that succeeds ⟨The show was a *success.*⟩

suc•cess•ful \sək-ˈses-fəl\ *adj*
1 resulting or ending well or in success ⟨My attempt to swim across the harbor was *successful.*⟩
2 gaining or having gained success ⟨a *successful* business⟩
suc•cess•ful•ly \-fə-lē\ *adv*

sucker 4: a Chinese sailfin sucker

suc•ces•sion \sək-ˈse-shən\ *n*
1 a series of people or things that follow one after another ⟨A *succession* of police cars raced past.⟩
2 the order, act, or right of succeeding to a throne, title, or property

suc•ces•sive \sək-ˈse-siv\ *adj*
following in order and without interruption ⟨The family became more powerful with each *successive* generation.⟩
suc•ces•sive•ly *adv*

suc•ces•sor \sək-ˈse-sər\ *n*
a person who succeeds to a throne, title, property, or office

suc•cor \ˈsə-kər\ *n*
²HELP 1, RELIEF

suc•cu•lent \ˈsə-kyə-lənt\ *adj*
JUICY ⟨*succulent* fruits⟩

suc•cumb \sə-ˈkəm\ *vb* **suc•cumbed; suc•cumb•ing**
1 to yield to force or pressure ⟨Don't *succumb* to temptation.⟩
2 ¹DIE 1

¹**such** \ˈsəch\ *adj*
1 of a kind just specified or to be specified ⟨a bag *such* as a doctor carries⟩
2 of the same class, type, or sort : SIMILAR ⟨We've opened three *such* stores.⟩
3 so great : so remarkable ⟨I've never seen *such* a crowd.⟩

²**such** *pron*
that sort of person, thing, or group ⟨boards and nails and *such*⟩

suck \ˈsək\ *vb* **sucked; suck•ing**
1 to draw something (as liquid or air) into the mouth ⟨He *sucked* chocolate milk through a straw.⟩
2 to draw liquid from by action of the mouth ⟨He *sucked* an orange.⟩
3 to allow to dissolve gradually in the mouth ⟨*suck* a lollipop⟩
4 to put (as a thumb) into the mouth and draw on as if drawing liquid
5 to take in by or as if by absorption or suction ⟨Plants *suck* moisture from the soil.⟩

suck•er \ˈsə-kər\ *n*
1 a person easily fooled or cheated
2 a part of an animal's body used for sucking or for clinging by suction
3 LOLLIPOP
4◀ a freshwater fish related to the carp that has thick soft lips for sucking in food
5 a new stem from the roots or lower part of a plant
6 SUCKLING

suck•le \ˈsə-kəl\ *vb* **suck•led; suck•ling**
▶ to feed from the breast or udder

suck•ling \ˈsə-kliŋ\ *n*
a young mammal still sucking milk from its mother

su•crose \ˈsü-ˌkrōs\ *n*
a sweet usually crystalline substance found in many plants that is obtained especially from sugarcane and sugar beets for use in sweetening foods and beverages

suc•tion \ˈsək-shən\ *n*
1 the act or process of sucking
2 the process of drawing something into a space (as in a pump) by removing air from the space
3 the force caused by suction ⟨The vacuum cleaner has strong *suction.*⟩

sud•den \ˈsə-dᵊn\ *adj*
1 happening or coming quickly and unexpectedly ⟨a *sudden* shower⟩
2 met with unexpectedly ⟨We came to a *sudden* turn in the road.⟩
3 HASTY 2 ⟨He made a *sudden* decision.⟩
sud•den•ly *adv*
sud•den•ness *n*
all of a sudden sooner than was expected : SUDDENLY ⟨*All of a sudden* I saw him.⟩

suds \ˈsədz\ *n pl*
1 soapy water especially when foamy
2 the foam on soapy water

sue \ˈsü\ *vb* **sued; su•ing**
to seek justice or right by bringing legal action

suede \ˈswād\ *n*
leather tanned and rubbed so that it is soft and has a nap

su•et \ˈsü-ət\ *n*
the hard fat around the kidneys in beef and mutton from which tallow is made

suf•fer \ˈsə-fər\ *vb* **suf•fered; suf•fer•ing**
1 to feel or endure pain, illness, or injury ⟨She *suffers* from arthritis.⟩
2 to experience something unpleasant ⟨*suffer* a defeat⟩
3 to bear loss or damage ⟨Business *suffered* during the storm.⟩
4 to become worse ⟨His grades are *suffering.*⟩
5 ¹PERMIT 1
suf•fer•er \ˈsə-fər-ər\ *n*

suf•fer•ing \ˈsə-fə-riŋ, ˈsə-friŋ\ *n*
pain experienced during an injury or loss

suf•fice \sə-ˈfīs\ *vb* **suf•ficed; suf•fic•ing**
to satisfy a need : be enough ⟨I'm hungry, but just a snack will *suffice.*⟩

suf•fi•cient \sə-ˈfi-shənt\ *adj*
enough to achieve a goal or fill a need ⟨*sufficient* evidence⟩
suf•fi•cient•ly *adv*

suckle: a cat suckling her kittens

suf•fix \ˈsə-ˌfiks\ *n*
a letter or group of letters that comes at the end of a word and has a meaning of its own

suf•fo•cate \ˈsə-fə-ˌkāt\ *vb* **suf•fo•cat•ed; suf•fo•cat•ing**
1 to kill by stopping the breathing of or by depriving of oxygen to breathe
2 to die from being unable to breathe
3 to be or become choked or smothered ⟨Weeds are *suffocating* the flowers we planted.⟩
4 to suffer from lack of fresh air

suf•fo•ca•tion \ˌsə-fə-ˈkā-shən\ *n*
the act of killing by or dying from lack of air : the state of being killed by lack of air

suf•frage \ˈsə-frij\ *n*
the right to vote

[1]sug•ar \ˈshu̇-gər\ *n*
1 a sweet material that consists essentially of sucrose obtained from sugarcane or sugar beets, is typically colorless or white when pure, and is commonly used to sweeten foods and beverages
2 any of numerous soluble and usually sweet carbohydrates (as glucose or sucrose) that occur naturally especially in plants

[2]sugar *vb* **su•gared**; **su•gar•ing**
to mix, cover, or sprinkle with sugar ⟨The baker *sugared* the doughnuts.⟩

sugar beet *n*
a large beet with white roots that is grown as a source of sugar

sug•ar•cane \ˈshu̇-gər-ˌkān\ *n*
a tall strong grass with jointed stems widely raised in tropical regions for the sugar it yields

sugar maple *n*
▼ a maple tree of the northeastern United States with hard strong wood and a sweet sap that is used to make maple syrup and maple sugar

sug•gest \səg-ˈjest, sə-ˈjest\ *vb* **sug•gest•ed**; **sug•gest•ing**
1 to put (as a thought or desire) into a person's mind ⟨Are you *suggesting* I'm wrong?⟩
2 to recommend as being worthy of accepting or doing ⟨Can I *suggest* a dessert?⟩
3 to call to mind through close connection or association ⟨Smoke *suggests* fire.⟩

sug•ges•tion \səg-ˈjes-chən, sə-ˈjes-\ *n*
1 a thought or plan that is offered or proposed ⟨I have a *suggestion*. Let's get pizza.⟩
2 the act or process of putting a thought in someone's mind ⟨At his *suggestion* we left.⟩
3 [1]HINT 2 ⟨She wore just a *suggestion* of a smile.⟩

sug•ges•tive \səg-ˈje-stiv, sə-ˈje-\ *adj*
1 giving a hint ⟨The furniture is *suggestive* of the past.⟩
2 full of suggestions ⟨I read a *suggestive* book about decorating.⟩
3 suggesting something improper or indecent

sui•cide \ˈsü-ə-ˌsīd\ *n*
1 the act of someone who kills himself or herself purposely
2 a person who kills himself or herself purposely

sugar maple: leaves of a sugar maple in fall

sug•ary \ˈshu̇-gə-rē, ˈshu̇-grē\ *adj*
1 containing a lot of sugar ⟨*sugary* breakfast cereals⟩
2 too sweetly sentimental ⟨a *sugary* song⟩

[1]suit \ˈsüt\ *n*
1 a set of clothing having matching top and bottom pieces
2 a set of clothes or protective coverings worn for a special purpose or under particular conditions ⟨a gym *suit*⟩ ⟨a *suit* of armor⟩
3 an action in court to settle a disagreement or enforce a right or claim
4 all the playing cards of one kind (as spades, hearts, diamonds, or clubs) in a pack

[2]suit *vb* **suit•ed**; **suit•ing**
1 to be suitable or satisfactory ⟨The time of the meeting *suits* my schedule.⟩
2 to make suitable : ADAPT ⟨You should *suit* your speech for your audience.⟩
3 to be proper for or pleasing with ⟨That scarf does not *suit* the dress.⟩
4 to meet the needs or desires of

suit•able \ˈsü-tə-bəl\ *adj*
being fit or right for a use or group ⟨The movie is *suitable* for children.⟩
suit•abil•i•ty \ˌsü-tə-ˈbi-lə-tē\ *n*
suit•ably \-blē\ *adv*

suit•case \ˈsüt-ˌkās\ *n*
▶ a rectangular case used to carry clothing and belongings when traveling

suitcase

suite \ˈswēt, ˈsüt\ *n*
1 a number of connected rooms (as in a hotel)
2 a set of matched furniture for a room

suit•or \ˈsü-tər\ *n*
a man who tries to get a woman to marry him

sul•fur *also* **sul•phur** \ˈsəl-fər\ *n*
a yellow chemical element that is found widely in nature and is used in making chemicals and paper

sul•fu•rous *also* **sul•phu•rous** \ˈsəl-fə-rəs\ *adj*
containing or suggesting sulfur ⟨a *sulfurous* odor⟩

[1]sulk \ˈsəlk\ *vb* **sulked**; **sulk•ing**
to be angry or irritable about something but childishly refuse to talk about it

[2]sulk *n*
1 the state of a person who is sullenly silent or irritable ⟨He has a case of the *sulks*.⟩
2 a sulky mood ⟨She's in a *sulk*.⟩

[1]sulky \ˈsəl-kē\ *adj* **sulk•i•er**; **sulk•i•est**
1 angry or upset by something but refusing to discuss it
2 often angry or upset

[2]sulky *n, pl* **sulk•ies**
a light vehicle with two wheels, a seat for the driver only, and usually no body

A B C D E F G H I J K L M N O P Q R S T U V W X Y Z

summit: a view of Licancabur Volcano showing its summit

sul•len \'sə-lən\ *adj*
1 not sociable : SULKY
2 GLOOMY 1, DREARY ⟨a *sullen* sky⟩
sul•len•ly *adv*

sul•tan \'səl-t^{ə}n\ *n*
a ruler especially of a Muslim state

sul•ta•na \,səl-'ta-nə\ *n*
the wife, mother, sister, or daughter of a sultan

sul•try \'səl-trē\ *adj* **sul•tri•er**; **sul•tri•est**
very hot and humid ⟨*sultry* summer weather⟩

[1]**sum** \'səm\ *n*
1 the result obtained by adding numbers ⟨The *sum* of 4 and 5 is 9.⟩
2 a problem in arithmetic
3 a quantity of money ⟨We donated a small *sum.*⟩
4 the whole amount ⟨Two trips is the *sum* of my travel experience.⟩

[2]**sum** *vb* **summed**; **sum•ming**
to find the total number of by adding or counting
sum up to tell again in a few words : SUMMARIZE

su•mac *also* **su•mach** \'shü-,mak, 'sü-\ *n*
► a tree, shrub, or woody vine that has leaves with many leaflets and loose clusters of red or white berries

sum•ma•rize \'sə-mə-,rīz\ *vb* **sum•ma•rized**; **sum•ma•riz•ing**
to tell in or reduce to a short statement of the main points

[1]**sum•ma•ry** \'sə-mə-rē\ *adj*
1 expressing or covering the main points briefly : CONCISE ⟨a *summary* account⟩
2 done without delay ⟨*summary* punishment⟩

[2]**summary** *n, pl* **sum•ma•ries**
a short statement of the main points (as in a book or report)

[1]**sum•mer** \'sə-mər\ *n*
1 the season between spring and autumn which is in the northern hemisphere usually the months of June, July, and August
2 one of the years of a person's lifetime ⟨a youth of sixteen *summers*⟩

flowers

sumac: a branch of a staghorn \'stag-horn\ sumac

[2]**summer** *vb* **sum•mered**; **sum•mer•ing**
to pass the summer ⟨We *summered* at the shore.⟩

sum•mer•time \'sə-mər-,tīm\ *n*
the summer season

sum•mery \'sə-mə-rē\ *adj*
relating to or typical of summer ⟨*summery* weather⟩ ⟨a *summery* outfit⟩

sum•mit \'sə-mət\ *n*
▲ the highest point (as of a mountain) : TOP

sum•mon \'sə-mən\ *vb* **sum•moned**; **sum•mon•ing**
1 to call or send for : CONVENE
2 to order to appear before a court of law
3 to call into being : AROUSE ⟨She tried to *summon* up courage.⟩

sum•mons \'sə-mənz\ *n, pl* **sum•mons•es**
1 the act of calling or sending for
2 a call by authority to appear at a place named or to attend to some duty ⟨a royal *summons*⟩
3 a written order to appear in court

sump•tu•ous \'səmp-chə-wəs\ *adj*
very expensive or luxurious ⟨a *sumptuous* meal⟩ ⟨a *sumptuous* fabric⟩

[1]**sun** \'sən\ *n*
1 the heavenly body in our solar system whose light makes our day and around which the planets revolve
2 SUNSHINE 1 ⟨I'm going outside to get some *sun.*⟩
3 a heavenly body like our sun

[2]sun *vb* **sunned; sun•ning**
to expose to or lie or sit in the rays of the sun

Sun. *abbr* Sunday

sun•bathe \'sən-,bāth\ *vb* **sun•bathed; sun•bath•ing**
to sit or lie in the rays of the sun to get a tan

sun•beam \'sən-,bēm\ *n*
a ray of sunlight

sun•block \'sən-,bläk\ *n*
a preparation applied to the skin to prevent sunburn usually by blocking the sun's ultraviolet radiation

sun•bon•net \'sən-,bä-nət\ *n*
a bonnet with a wide curving brim that shades the face and usually a ruffle at the back that protects the neck from the sun

[1]sun•burn \'sən-,bərn\ *n*
a sore red state of the skin caused by too much sunlight

[2]sunburn *vb* **sun•burned** \-,bərnd\ *or* **sun•burnt** \-,bərnt\; **sun•burn•ing**
to burn or discolor by exposure to the sun

sun•dae \'sən-dā, -dē\ *n*
▶ a serving of ice cream with a topping (as fruit, syrup, whipped cream, nuts, or bits of candy)

sundae: an ice cream sundae

Sun•day \'sən-dā, -dē\ *n*
the first day of the week

Sunday school *n*
a school held on Sunday in a church for religious education

sun•di•al \'sən-,dī-əl\ *n*
▶ a device that shows the time of day by the position of the shadow cast onto a marked plate by an object with a straight edge

sun•down \'sən-,daủn\ *n*
SUNSET 2

sun•dries \'sən-drēz\ *n pl*
various small articles or items

sun•dry \'sən-drē\ *adj*
more than one or two : VARIOUS ⟨We disagreed for *sundry* reasons.⟩

sun•fish \'sən-,fish\ *n, pl* **sunfish** *or* **sun•fish•es**
a small and brightly colored North American freshwater fish related to the perch

sunset 1: a sunset as seen from the shore

sun•flow•er \'sən-,flaủ-ər\ *n*
a tall plant often grown for its large flower heads with brown center and yellow petals or for its edible oily seeds

sung *past and past participle of* SING

sun•glass•es \'sən-,gla-səz\ *n pl*
glasses worn to protect the eyes from the sun

sunk *past and past participle of* SINK

sunk•en \'səŋ-kən\ *adj*
1 fallen in : HOLLOW ⟨*sunken* cheeks⟩
2 lying at the bottom of a body of water ⟨*sunken* ships⟩
3 built or settled below the surrounding or normal level ⟨a *sunken* garden⟩

sun•less \'sən-ləs\ *adj*
being without sunlight : DARK ⟨a *sunless* day⟩ ⟨a *sunless* cave⟩

sun•light \'sən-,līt\ *n*
SUNSHINE 1

sun•lit \'sən-,lit\ *adj*
lighted by the sun ⟨*sunlit* fields⟩

sundial: an 18th-century brass sundial

sun•ny \'sə-nē\ *adj* **sun•ni•er; sun•ni•est**
1 bright with sunshine ⟨a *sunny* day⟩ ⟨a *sunny* room⟩
2 MERRY 1, CHEERFUL ⟨a *sunny* smile⟩

sun•rise \'sən-,rīz\ *n*
1 the apparent rise of the sun above the horizon
2 the light and color of the rise of the sun above the horizon
3 the time at which the sun rises

sun•screen \'sən-,skrēn\ *n*
a preparation applied to the skin to prevent sunburn usually by chemically absorbing the sun's ultraviolet radiation

sun•set \'sən-,set\ *n*
1 ▲ the apparent passing of the sun below the horizon
2 the light and color of the passing of the sun below the horizon
3 the time at which the sun sets

sun•shade \'sən-,shād\ *n*
something (as a parasol) used to protect from the sun's rays

sun•shine \'sən-,shīn\ *n*
1 the sun's light or direct rays : the warmth and light given by the sun's rays
2 something that spreads warmth or happiness ⟨You are my *sunshine.*⟩

sun•stroke \'sən-,strōk\ *n*
an illness that is marked by high fever and weakness and is caused by exposure to too much sun

sun•tan \'sən-,tan\ *n*
a browning of skin from exposure to the sun

sun•up \'sən-,əp\ *n*
SUNRISE 2

sun•ward \'sən-wərd\ *adv or adj*
toward or facing the sun

sup \'səp\ *vb* **supped**; **sup•ping**
to eat the evening meal

su•per \'sü-pər\ *adj*
1 very great ⟨*super* strength⟩
2 very good

super– *prefix*
1 more than ⟨*super*human⟩
2 extremely : very

su•perb \sů-'pərb\ *adj*
outstandingly excellent, impressive, or beautiful
synonyms see SPLENDID

su•per•com•put•er \'sü-pər-kəm-,pyü-tər\ *n*
a large very fast computer used especially for scientific computations

su•per•fi•cial \,sü-pər-'fi-shəl\ *adj*
1 of or relating to the surface or appearance only ⟨a *superficial* cut⟩
2 not thorough or complete ⟨He has only *superficial* knowledge of the subject.⟩
su•per•fi•cial•ly *adv*

su•per•flu•ous \sů-'pər-flə-wəs\ *adj*
going beyond what is enough or necessary : EXTRA ⟨Her story was filled with *superfluous* details.⟩

su•per•he•ro \'sü-pər-,hir-ō, -,hē-rō\ *n*
a fictional hero having extraordinary or superhuman powers

su•per•high•way \,sü-pər-'hī-,wā\ *n*
an expressway for high-speed traffic

su•per•hu•man \,sü-pər-'hyü-mən, -'yü-mən\ *adj*
going beyond normal human power, size, or ability

su•per•in•tend \,sü-pər-in-'tend\ *vb* **su•per•in•tend•ed**; **su•per•in•tend•ing**
to have or exercise the charge of

su•per•in•ten•dent \,sü-pər-in-'ten-dənt\ *n*
a person who looks after or manages something (as schools or a building)

[1]**su•pe•ri•or** \sů-'pir-ē-ər\ *adj*
1 situated higher up : higher in rank, importance, numbers, or quality
2 excellent of its kind : BETTER ⟨a *superior* athlete⟩
3 showing the feeling of being better or more important than others : ARROGANT ⟨a *superior* smirk⟩

[2]**superior** *n*
1 a person who is higher than another in rank, importance, or quality
2 the head of a religious house or order

su•pe•ri•or•i•ty \sů-,pir-ē-'ór-ə-tē\ *n*
the state or fact of being better, more important, or higher in rank than others

[1]**su•per•la•tive** \sů-'pər-lə-tiv\ *adj*
1 being the form of an adjective or adverb that shows the greatest degree of comparison ⟨"Best" is the *superlative* form of "good."⟩
2 better than all others : SUPREME ⟨*superlative* work⟩

[2]**superlative** *n*
the superlative degree or a superlative form in a language

su•per•mar•ket \'sü-pər-,mär-kət\ *n*
▼ a store selling foods and household items

su•per•nat•u•ral \,sü-pər-'na-chə-rəl, -'nach-rəl\ *adj*
of or relating to something beyond or outside of nature or the visible universe

su•per•sede \,sü-pər-'sēd\ *vb* **su•per•sed•ed**; **su•per•sed•ing**
to take the place or position of ⟨These instructions *supersede* those you received earlier.⟩

su•per•son•ic \,sü-pər-'sä-nik\ *adj*
1 above the normal range of human hearing
2 having a speed from one to five times that of sound ⟨a *supersonic* airplane⟩

supermarket: a man shopping at a supermarket

A B C D E F G H I J K L M N O P Q R S T U V W X Y Z

su•per•sti•tion \ˌsü-pər-ˈsti-shən\ *n*
a belief or practice resulting from ignorance, fear of the unknown, or trust in magic or chance

su•per•sti•tious \ˌsü-pər-ˈsti-shəs\ *adj*
showing or influenced by superstition

su•per•vise \ˈsü-pər-ˌvīz\ *vb* **su•per•vised**; **su•per•vis•ing**
to coordinate and direct the activities of ⟨Who will *supervise* the workers while you are away?⟩

su•per•vi•sion \ˌsü-pər-ˈvi-zhən\ *n*
the act of overseeing : MANAGEMENT

su•per•vi•sor \ˈsü-pər-ˌvī-zər\ *n*
1 a person who is in charge of others
2 an officer in charge of a unit or an operation of a business, government, or school

sup•per \ˈsə-pər\ *n*
1 the evening meal especially when dinner is eaten at midday
2 refreshments served late in the evening especially at a social gathering

sup•plant \sə-ˈplant\ *vb* **sup•plant•ed**; **sup•plant•ing**
to take the place of another

sup•ple \ˈsə-pəl\ *adj* **sup•pler** \ˈsə-plər\; **sup•plest** \ˈsə-pləst\
1 capable of bending or of being bent easily without stiffness, creases, or damage ⟨a *supple* body⟩ ⟨*supple* leather⟩
2 ADAPTABLE ⟨a *supple* mind⟩

[1]**sup•ple•ment** \ˈsə-plə-mənt\ *n*
something that supplies what is needed or adds to something else ⟨a food *supplement*⟩

[2]**sup•ple•ment** \ˈsə-plə-ˌment\ *vb* **sup•ple•ment•ed**; **sup•ple•ment•ing**
to add to : COMPLETE ⟨Many workers *supplement* their incomes by doing odd jobs.⟩

sup•ple•men•ta•ry \ˌsə-plə-ˈmen-tə-rē\ *adj*
added to something else : ADDITIONAL ⟨*supplementary* income⟩

sup•pli•cate \ˈsə-plə-ˌkāt\ *vb* **sup•pli•cat•ed**; **sup•pli•cat•ing**
to ask or beg in a humble way : BESEECH

sup•pli•ca•tion \ˌsə-plə-ˈkā-shən\ *n*
the act of asking or begging in a humble way

[1]**sup•ply** \sə-ˈplī\ *vb* **sup•plied**; **sup•ply•ing**
1 to provide for : SATISFY ⟨There is enough to *supply* the demand.⟩
2 to make available : FURNISH ⟨The tree *supplies* shade.⟩

[2]**supply** *n, pl* **sup•plies**
1 the amount of something that is needed or can be gotten ⟨medical *supplies*⟩
2 [2]STORE 3 ⟨I keep a *supply* of pencils in my desk.⟩
3 the act or process of providing something ⟨The company is engaged in the *supply* of raw materials.⟩

[1]**sup•port** \sə-ˈpȯrt\ *vb* **sup•port•ed**; **sup•port•ing**
1 to hold up or in position : serve as a foundation or prop for ⟨Posts *support* the porch roof.⟩
2 to take sides with : FAVOR ⟨Which candidate do you *support*?⟩
3 to provide evidence for : VERIFY ⟨They cannot *support* this claim.⟩
4 to pay the costs of : MAINTAIN ⟨His income *supports* a large family.⟩
5 to keep going : SUSTAIN ⟨There is not enough air to *support* life.⟩
6 to provide help or encouragement to ⟨My friends *supported* me while I was sick.⟩
sup•port•er *n*

[2]**support** *n*
1 the act of supporting : the condition of being supported
2 someone or something that supports

sup•pose \sə-ˈpōz\ *vb* **sup•posed**; **sup•pos•ing**
1 to think of as true or as a fact for the sake of argument ⟨Let's *suppose* you won.⟩
2 BELIEVE 2, THINK ⟨I *suppose* that's true.⟩
3 [1]GUESS 1 ⟨Who do you *suppose* won?⟩

sup•posed \sə-ˈpōzd\ *adj*
1 forced, expected, or required ⟨I am *supposed* to be home early.⟩
2 believed or claimed to be true or real ⟨the *supposed* murderer⟩
3 given permission ⟨I'm not *supposed* to stay out after dark.⟩
sup•pos•ed•ly \-ˈpō-zəd-lē\ *adv*

sup•press \sə-ˈpres\ *vb* **sup•pressed**; **sup•press•ing**
1 to put down (as by authority or force) : SUBDUE ⟨Police *suppressed* a riot.⟩
2 to hold back : REPRESS ⟨The girls could hardly *suppress* a smile.⟩

sup•pres•sion \sə-ˈpre-shən\ *n*
an act or instance of putting down or holding back : the state of being put down or held back

su•prem•a•cy \sü-ˈpre-mə-sē\ *n, pl* **su•prem•a•cies**
the highest rank, power, or authority

su•preme \sü-ˈprēm\ *adj*
1 highest in rank, power, or authority
2 highest in degree or quality ⟨I have *supreme* trust in you.⟩
3 most extreme or great ⟨They made the *supreme* sacrifice.⟩
su•preme•ly *adv*

Supreme Being *n*
GOD 1

supreme court *n, often cap*
the highest court of law in the United States or in many of its states

[1]**sure** \ˈshu̇r\ *adj* **sur•er**; **sur•est**
1 having no doubt : CERTAIN ⟨I'm *sure* of it.⟩
2 true without question
3 firmly established ⟨a *sure* grip⟩
4 RELIABLE, TRUSTWORTHY ⟨a *sure* remedy⟩
5 bound to happen ⟨*sure* disaster⟩
6 bound as if by fate ⟨You are *sure* to win.⟩

[2]**sure** *adv*
1 SURELY 1
2 SURELY 2 ⟨*Sure*, we'll be there.⟩

sure•ly \ˈshu̇r-lē\ *adv*
1 without doubt ⟨It's a book you will *surely* enjoy.⟩
2 beyond question : REALLY ⟨I *surely* do miss them.⟩
3 with confidence : CONFIDENTLY ⟨He answered their questions *surely*.⟩

[1]**surf** \ˈsərf\ *n*
1 the waves of the sea that splash on the shore
2 the sound, splash, and foam of breaking waves

[2]**surf** *vb* **surfed**; **surf•ing**
1 to ride the incoming waves of the sea (as on a surfboard)
2 to scan a wide range of offerings (as on television or the Internet) for something that is interesting or fills a need

[1]**sur•face** \ˈsər-fəs\ *n*
1 the outside or any one side of an object ⟨She floated on the water's *surface*.⟩
2 the outside appearance ⟨On the *surface* the idea seems good.⟩

[2]**surface** *adj*
not deep or real ⟨a *surface* wound⟩ ⟨a *surface* friendship⟩

[3]**surface** *vb* **sur•faced**; **sur•fac•ing**
1 to come to the surface ⟨The submarine *surfaced*.⟩
2 to become obvious ⟨Their dislike of one another began to *surface*.⟩
3 to give a new top layer to : make smooth (as by sanding or paving)

surf•board \ˈsərf-ˌbȯrd\ *n*
a long narrow board that floats and is ridden in surfing

surf•ing \ˈsər-fiŋ\ *n*
▶ the sport of riding waves toward the shore usually while standing on a surfboard

[1]**surge** \ˈsərj\ *vb* **surged**; **surg•ing**
1 to rise suddenly and greatly 〈Prices have *surged* recently.〉
2 to move suddenly and quickly in a particular direction 〈Crowds were *surging* through the streets.〉

[2]**surge** *n*
1 a rush like that of a wave 〈She felt a *surge* of anger.〉
2 a large wave 〈*surges* of water〉

sur•geon \ˈsər-jən\ *n*
a doctor who performs surgery

sur•gery \ˈsər-jə-rē\ *n, pl* **sur•ger•ies**
▼ medical treatment (as of disease, injury, or physical abnormality) that involves cutting into the body usually to expose internal parts 〈She had *surgery* to remove her appendix.〉

sur•gi•cal \ˈsər-ji-kəl\ *adj*
of, relating to, or associated with surgery or surgeons 〈*surgical* instruments〉

sur•ly \ˈsər-lē\ *adj* **sur•li•er**; **sur•li•est**
mean and rude : UNFRIENDLY 〈a *surly* neighbor〉

▶ **Word History** To a noble person it might seem natural to link together high birth and good manners, but the word *surly* is evidence that other people have not always thought this way. In Middle English the word was spelled *sirly*, which made more obvious its derivation from *sir*, the traditional title of respect. *Sirly* had much the same meaning as *lordly* does today, that is, "proud, haughty." Although its meaning has evolved to "rude" or "unfriendly," *surly* still refers to a way of acting that is quite the opposite of good-mannered.

surfing: a man engaged in surfing

[1]**sur•mise** \sər-ˈmīz\ *n*
a thought or idea based on very little evidence : GUESS

[2]**surmise** *vb* **sur•mised**; **sur•mis•ing**
to form an idea on very little evidence : GUESS

sur•mount \sər-ˈmau̇nt\ *vb* **sur•mount•ed**; **sur•mount•ing**
1 OVERCOME 1 〈He'll have to *surmount* difficulties to win.〉
2 to get to the top of
3 to be at the top of 〈A castle *surmounts* the cliff.〉

sur•name \ˈsər-ˌnām\ *n*
the name that comes at the end of someone's full name 〈James Smith's *surname* is Smith.〉

sur•pass \sər-ˈpas\ *vb* **sur•passed**; **sur•pass•ing**
1 to be greater, better, or stronger than : EXCEED
2 to go beyond the reach or powers of 〈The task *surpassed* their strength.〉

[1]**sur•plus** \ˈsər-pləs\ *n*
an amount left over : EXCESS

[2]**surplus** *adj*
left over : EXTRA 〈*surplus* wheat〉

[1]**sur•prise** \sər-ˈprīz, sə-ˈprīz\ *n*
1 something that is unexpected 〈I have a *surprise* for you.〉
2 ASTONISHMENT, AMAZEMENT 〈To my *surprise*, his plan worked.〉
3 an act or instance of coming upon without warning 〈They were taken by *surprise*.〉

[2]**surprise** *vb* **sur•prised**; **sur•pris•ing**
1 to cause to feel wonder or amazement because of being unexpected

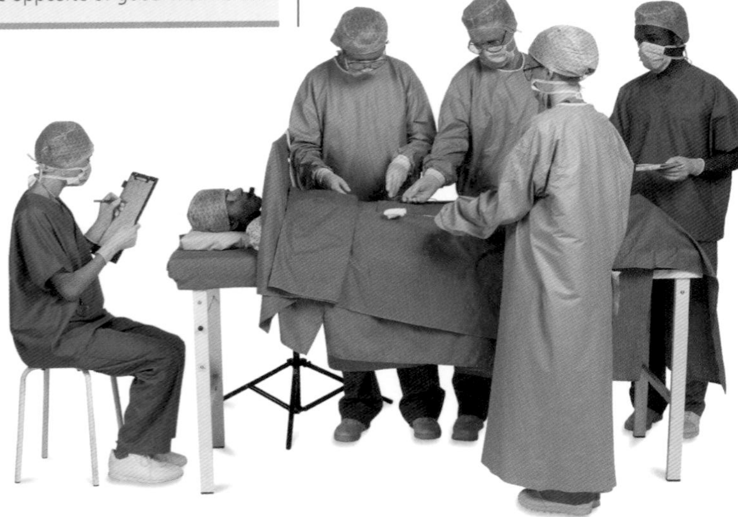

surgery: doctors performing surgery on a patient

2 to come upon without warning ⟨The robbers were *surprised* by police.⟩
3 to attack without warning : capture by an unexpected attack

▶ **Synonyms** SURPRISE, ASTONISH, and AMAZE mean to impress forcibly by being unexpected, startling, or unusual. SURPRISE is used when something is unexpected even though it by itself is not startling. ⟨A sudden storm *surprised* the hikers.⟩ ASTONISH means to surprise very much with something that is hard or impossible to believe. ⟨The first airplanes *astonished* people.⟩ AMAZE is used when something causes a person to wonder and puzzle over it. ⟨The magician *amazed* the children.⟩

sur•pris•ing \sər-ˈprī-ziŋ, sə-ˈprī-ziŋ\ *adj*
causing astonishment : UNEXPECTED ⟨*surprising* news⟩
sur•pris•ing•ly *adv*

[1]**sur•ren•der** \sə-ˈren-dər\ *vb* **sur•ren•dered**; **sur•ren•der•ing**
1 to give up after a struggle ⟨The soldiers *surrendered.*⟩ ⟨We'll never *surrender* the fort.⟩
2 to let go of : RELINQUISH ⟨We *surrendered* our place in line.⟩

[2]**surrender** *n*
1 the act of giving up after a struggle
2 the act of giving something over to the possession or control of someone else

sur•rey \ˈsər-ē\ *n, pl* **surreys**
a pleasure carriage that has two wide seats and four wheels and is drawn by horses

sur•round \sə-ˈraůnd\ *vb* **sur•round•ed**; **sur•round•ing**
1 to enclose on all sides : ENCIRCLE ⟨A fence *surrounds* the property.⟩
2 to be closely related or connected to

sur•round•ings \sə-ˈraůn-diŋz\ *n pl*
the circumstances, conditions, or things around an individual : ENVIRONMENT

[1]**sur•vey** \sər-ˈvā\ *vb* **sur•veyed**; **sur•vey•ing**
1 to look over : EXAMINE ⟨The governor *surveyed* damage caused by the flood.⟩
2 to find out the size, shape, or boundaries of (as a piece of land)
3 to gather information from : ask questions of ⟨We *surveyed* students to find out who was the most popular teacher.⟩

[2]**sur•vey** \ˈsər-ˌvā\ *n, pl* **surveys**
1 the action or an instance of gathering information or examining something
2 something that is examined
3 a history or description that covers a large subject briefly

sur•vey•ing \sər-ˈvā-iŋ\ *n*
1 the act or occupation of a person who determines the size, shape, or boundaries of a piece of land
2 a branch of mathematics that teaches how to measure the earth's surface and record these measurements accurately

sur•vey•or \sər-ˈvā-ər\ *n*
▼ a person whose occupation is determining the size, shape, or boundaries of pieces of land

instrument for surveying an area of land

surveyor

sur•viv•al \sər-ˈvī-vəl\ *n*
the continuation of life ⟨Our *survival* depended on finding water.⟩

sur•vive \sər-ˈvīv\ *vb* **sur•vived**; **sur•viv•ing**
1 to remain alive : continue to exist ⟨No creature can *survive* without water.⟩ ⟨The tradition *survives* to this day.⟩
2 to live or exist longer than or past the end of ⟨The house *survived* the flood.⟩
sur•vi•vor \sər-ˈvī-vər\ *n*

sus•cep•ti•ble \sə-ˈsep-tə-bəl\ *adj*
1 of such a nature as to permit ⟨The words are *susceptible* of being misunderstood.⟩
2 having little resistance (as to infection or damage) ⟨I am *susceptible* to colds.⟩
3 easily affected or impressed by ⟨You're so *susceptible* to flattery.⟩

[1]**sus•pect** \sə-ˈspekt\ *vb* **sus•pect•ed**; **sus•pect•ing**
1 to suppose to be true or likely ⟨I hid the money where no one would *suspect.*⟩
2 to have doubts of : DISTRUST ⟨I *suspect* his reasons for helping.⟩
3 to imagine to be guilty without proof

[2]**sus•pect** \ˈsə-ˌspekt\ *n*
a person who is thought to be guilty of something

[3]**sus•pect** \ˈsə-ˌspekt, sə-ˈspekt\ *adj*
thought of with suspicion ⟨Her honesty is *suspect.*⟩

sus•pend \sə-ˈspend\ *vb* **sus•pend•ed**; **sus•pend•ing**
1 to force to give up some right or office for a time ⟨The cheater was *suspended* from school.⟩
2 to hang especially so as to be free except at one point ⟨A light bulb was *suspended* from the ceiling.⟩
3 to stop or do away with for a time ⟨The principal is *suspending* a rule.⟩
4 to stop operation or action for a time ⟨All business *suspended* during the storm.⟩

sus•pend•er \sə-ˈspen-dər\ *n*
one of a pair of straps that are attached to pants or a skirt and go over the shoulders

sus•pense \sə-ˈspens\ *n*
uncertainty, worry, or excitement in wondering about the result of something

sus•pen•sion \sə-ˈspen-shən\ *n*
1 the act of stopping, removing, or making someone or something ineffective for a time
2 the state of being stopped, removed, or made ineffective for a time ⟨*suspension* of a game⟩
3 the period during which someone or something is stopped, removed, or made ineffective ⟨a two week *suspension* from school⟩
4 the act of hanging : the state of being hung
5 the system of springs that support the upper part of a vehicle on the axles

sus•pi•cion \sə-ˈspi-shən\ *n*
1 an act or instance of suspecting or the state of being suspected ⟨The elderly man was above *suspicion.*⟩
2 a feeling that something is wrong : DOUBT ⟨I have my *suspicions* about him.⟩

sus•pi•cious \sə-ˈspi-shəs\ *adj*
1 likely to arouse suspicion ⟨*suspicious* actions⟩
2 likely to distrust or be distrustful ⟨People in town are *suspicious* of strangers.⟩
3 showing distrust ⟨a *suspicious* glance⟩

sus•tain \sə-ˈstān\ *vb* **sus•tained**; **sus•tain•ing**
1 to provide with what is needed ⟨Food *sustains* life.⟩
2 to keep up the spirits of ⟨Hope *sustained* us.⟩
3 to keep up : PROLONG ⟨This author's books *sustain* my interest.⟩
4 to hold up the weight of ⟨The roof couldn't *sustain* the weight of the snow.⟩
5 [2]EXPERIENCE ⟨The army *sustained* heavy losses.⟩
6 to allow or uphold as true, legal, or fair ⟨The judge *sustained* the motion to dismiss the case.⟩

sus•te•nance \ˈsə-stə-nəns\ *n*
1 [2]LIVING 3, SUBSISTENCE
2 the act of supplying with the necessities of life
3 [2]SUPPORT 2 ⟨God is our *sustenance* in time of trouble.⟩

SUV \ˌes-ˌyü-ˈvē\ *n, pl* **SUVs**
SPORT-UTILITY VEHICLE

SW *abbr* southwest

[1]swab \ˈswäb\ *n*
1 a yarn mop especially as used on a ship
2 a wad of absorbent material usually wound around the end of a small stick and used for applying or removing material (as medicine or makeup)

[2]swab *vb* **swabbed**; **swab•bing**
1 to clean with or as if with a mop ⟨A boy *swabbed* the ship's deck.⟩
2 to apply medication to with a wad of absorbent material ⟨A nurse *swabbed* the wound with iodine.⟩

[1]swag•ger \ˈswa-gər\ *vb* **swag•gered**; **swag•ger•ing**
to walk with a proud strut

[2]swagger *n*
an act or instance of walking with a proud strut

[1]swal•low \ˈswä-lō\ *n*
a small bird that has long wings and a forked tail and feeds on insects caught while in flight

[2]swallow *vb* **swal•lowed**; **swal•low•ing**
1 to take into the stomach through the mouth and throat ⟨Chew your food well before you *swallow*.⟩
2 to perform the actions used in swallowing something ⟨Clear your throat and *swallow* before answering.⟩
3 to completely surround : ENGULF ⟨A ship was *swallowed* by the waves.⟩
4 to accept or believe without question ⟨You *swallow* every story you hear.⟩
5 to keep from expressing or showing : REPRESS ⟨I *swallowed* my pride and asked for help.⟩

[3]swallow *n*
1 an act of taking something into the stomach through the mouth and throat : an act of swallowing ⟨He ate the cupcake in one *swallow*.⟩
2 an amount that can be swallowed at one time ⟨She took a *swallow* of water.⟩

swam *past of* SWIM

[1]swamp \ˈswämp\ *n*
▼ wet spongy land often partly covered with water

[1]swamp: a forested swamp

[2]swamp *vb* **swamped**; **swamp•ing**
1 to fill or cause to fill with water : sink after filling with water ⟨High waves *swamped* the boat.⟩ ⟨The boat *swamped*.⟩
2 OVERWHELM 1 ⟨She was *swamped* with work.⟩

swampy \ˈswäm-pē\ *adj* **swamp•i•er**; **swamp•i•est**
consisting of or like a swamp

swan \ˈswän\ *n*
a usually white waterbird that has a long neck and large body and is related to but larger than the goose

[1]swap \ˈswäp\ *vb* **swapped**; **swap•ping**
to give in exchange : make an exchange : TRADE

[2]swap *n*
[1]EXCHANGE 1, TRADE

[1]swarm \'swȯrm\ *n*
1 a large number of bees that leave a hive together to form a new colony elsewhere
2 a large number grouped together and usually in motion ⟨a *swarm* of mosquitoes⟩ ⟨a *swarm* of tourists⟩

[2]swarm *vb* **swarmed**; **swarm•ing**
1 to form a swarm and leave the hive ⟨*swarming* bees⟩
2 to move or gather in a large number ⟨Shoppers *swarmed* into the stores.⟩
3 to be filled with a great number : TEEM

swar•thy \'swȯr-t͟hē, -thē\ *adj* **swar•thi•er**; **swar•thi•est**
having a dark complexion

[1]swat \'swät\ *vb* **swat•ted**; **swat•ting**
to hit with a quick hard blow ⟨I *swatted* a fly.⟩

[2]swat *n*
a hard blow

swath \'swäth\ *or* **swathe** \'swät͟h\ *n*, *pl* **swaths** *or* **swathes**
1 an area of grass or grain that has been cut or mowed
2 a long broad strip or belt

[1]sway \'swā\ *vb* **swayed**; **sway•ing**
1 to swing slowly back and forth or from side to side ⟨Tree branches were *swaying* in the wind.⟩
2 to change or cause to change between one point, position, or opinion and another ⟨The lawyer tried to *sway* the jury.⟩

[2]sway *n*
1 the act of slowly swinging back and forth or from side to side
2 a controlling influence or force : RULE ⟨The country is under the *sway* of a tyrant.⟩

swear \'swer\ *vb* **swore** \'swȯr\; **sworn** \'swȯrn\; **swear•ing**
1 to use bad or vulgar language : CURSE
2 to make a statement or promise with sincerity or under oath : VOW ⟨I *swear* to tell the truth.⟩
3 to give an oath to ⟨The witness was *sworn*.⟩
4 to bind by an oath ⟨He *swore* them to secrecy.⟩
5 to be or feel certain ⟨I *swear* I saw it a minute ago.⟩

[1]sweat \'swet\ *vb* **sweat** *or* **sweat•ed**; **sweat•ing**
1 to give off salty moisture through the pores of the skin : PERSPIRE
2 to collect moisture on the surface ⟨A pitcher of ice water *sweats* on a hot day.⟩
3 to work hard enough to perspire ⟨She *sweat* over the lesson.⟩

[2]sweat *n*
1 PERSPIRATION 2
2 moisture coming from or collecting in drops on a surface
3 the condition of a person or animal perspiring ⟨We worked up a *sweat*.⟩

sweat•er \'swe-tər\ *n*
▼ a knitted or crocheted piece of clothing for the upper body

sweater:
a colorful sweater with stripes

sweat gland *n*
a small gland of the skin that gives off perspiration

sweat•shirt \'swet-ˌshərt\ *n*
a loose pullover or jacket without a collar and usually with long sleeves

sweaty \'swe-tē\ *adj* **sweat•i•er**; **sweat•i•est**
wet with, stained by, or smelling of sweat

Swede \'swēd\ *n*
a person born or living in Sweden

[1]Swed•ish \'swē-dish\ *adj*
of or relating to Sweden, the Swedes, or Swedish

[2]Swedish *n*
the language of the Swedes

[1]sweep \'swēp\ *vb* **swept** \'swept\; **sweep•ing**
1 to remove with a broom or brush ⟨Please *sweep* up the dirt.⟩
2 to clean by removing loose dirt or small trash with a broom or brush ⟨I need to *sweep* the floor.⟩
3 to move over or across swiftly often with force or destruction ⟨Fire *swept* the village.⟩
4 to move or gather as if with a broom or brush ⟨I *swept* the money from the table.⟩
5 to move the eyes or an instrument through a wide curve ⟨They *swept* the hill for some sign of the enemy.⟩
6 to touch a surface of quickly ⟨The musician's fingers *swept* the piano keys.⟩
7 to drive along with steady force ⟨Debris was *swept* away by the tide.⟩
8 to become suddenly very popular throughout ⟨It's a show that is *sweeping* the nation.⟩
9 to achieve a complete or easy victory
sweep•er *n*

[2]sweep *n*
1 a curving movement, course, or line ⟨I brushed it away with a *sweep* of my hand.⟩
2 an act or instance of cleaning with a broom or brush
3 a wide stretch or curve of land
4 something that sweeps or works with a sweeping motion
5 a complete or easy victory
6 [1]RANGE 2, SCOPE ⟨The island was outside the *sweep* of our vision.⟩
7 CHIMNEY SWEEP

[1]sweep•ing \'swē-piŋ\ *adj*
1 moving or extending in a wide curve or over a wide area ⟨a *sweeping* glance⟩ ⟨a *sweeping* driveway⟩
2 EXTENSIVE ⟨*sweeping* changes⟩

[2]sweeping *n*
1 an act of cleaning an area with a broom or brush
2 **sweepings** *pl* things collected by sweeping

sweep•stakes \'swēp-ˌstāks\ *n pl*
a contest in which money or prizes are given to winners picked by chance (as by drawing names)
Hint: *Sweepstakes* can be used as a singular or a plural in writing and speaking.

[1]sweet \'swēt\ *adj* **sweet•er**; **sweet•est**
1 containing or tasting of sugar ⟨*sweet* muffins⟩
2 having a pleasant sound, smell, or appearance ⟨a *sweet* fragrance⟩ ⟨*sweet* voices⟩
3 very gentle, kind, or friendly ⟨a *sweet* personality⟩ ⟨It was *sweet* of you to remember.⟩
4 pleasing to the mind or feelings : AGREEABLE ⟨*sweet* memories⟩
5 much loved : DEAR ⟨my *sweet* child⟩
6 agreeable to oneself but not to others ⟨You took your *sweet* time!⟩
7 not sour, stale, or spoiled ⟨*sweet* milk⟩
8 not salt or salted ⟨*sweet* butter⟩
9 having a mild taste : not sharp ⟨*sweet* peppers⟩
sweet•ly *adv*
sweet•ness *n*
sweet on in love with

[2]sweet *n*
1 something (as candy) that contains or tastes of sugar
2 [1]DARLING 1, DEAR

a b c d e f g h i j k l m n o p q r s t u v w x y z

sweet corn *n*
▼ corn with kernels rich in sugar that is cooked and eaten as a vegetable while young

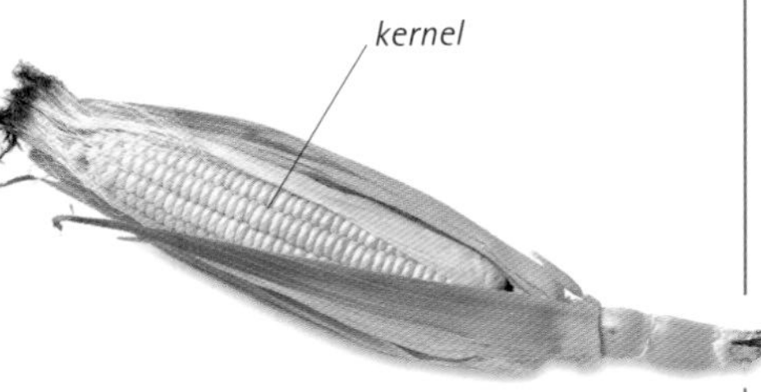

sweet corn: an ear of sweet corn

sweet•en \'swē-tᵊn\ *vb* **sweet•ened**; **sweet•en•ing**
to make or become sweet or sweeter

sweet•en•ing \'swē-tᵊn-iŋ\ *n*
1 the act or process of making sweet
2 something that sweetens

sweet•heart \'swēt-,härt\ *n*
a person whom someone loves

sweet•meat \'swēt-,mēt\ *n*
a food (as a piece of candy or candied fruit) rich in sugar

sweet pea *n*
► a climbing plant that is grown for its fragrant flowers of many colors

sweet potato

sweet potato *n*
▲ the large sweet edible root of a tropical vine that is cooked and eaten as a vegetable

[1]**swell** \'swel\ *vb* **swelled**; **swelled** *or* **swol•len** \'swō-lən\; **swell•ing**
1 to enlarge in an abnormal way usually by pressure from within or by growth ⟨Her sprained ankle is *swelling* up.⟩
2 to grow or make bigger (as in size or value) ⟨The town's population *swelled*.⟩
3 to stretch upward or outward : BULGE
4 to fill or become filled with emotion ⟨His heart *swelled* with pride.⟩

[2]**swell** *n*
1 a gradual increase in size, value, or volume ⟨a *swell* of laughter⟩
2 a long rolling wave or series of waves in the open sea
3 the condition of bulging ⟨the *swell* of big muscles⟩
4 a rounded elevation

[3]**swell** *adj*
EXCELLENT, FIRST-RATE ⟨We had a *swell* time.⟩

swell•ing \'swe-liŋ\ *n*
a swollen lump or part

swel•ter \'swel-tər\ *vb* **swel•tered**; **swel•ter•ing**
to suffer, sweat, or be faint from heat

swel•ter•ing \'swel-tər-iŋ\ *adj*
oppressively hot

swept *past and past participle of* SWEEP

[1]**swerve** \'swərv\ *vb* **swerved**; **swerv•ing**
to turn aside suddenly from a straight line or course ⟨The van *swerved* to avoid an oncoming car.⟩

[2]**swerve** *n*
an act or instance of turning aside suddenly

sweet pea: sweet pea flowers

[1]**swift** \'swift\ *adj* **swift•er**; **swift•est**
1 moving or capable of moving with great speed ⟨a *swift* river⟩ ⟨a *swift* runner⟩
2 occurring suddenly ⟨a *swift* kick⟩ ⟨a *swift* descent⟩
synonyms see FAST
swift•ly *adv*
swift•ness *n*

[2]**swift** *adv*
in a swift manner ⟨a *swift*-flowing stream⟩

[3]**swift** *n*
a small usually black bird that is related to the hummingbirds but looks like a swallow

swig \'swig\ *n*
the amount drunk at one time : GULP

[1]**swill** \'swil\ *vb* **swilled**; **swill•ing**
to eat or drink greedily

[2]**swill** *n*
1 [1]SLOP 2
2 GARBAGE 1, REFUSE

[1]**swim** \'swim\ *vb* **swam** \'swam\; **swum** \'swəm\; **swim•ming**
1 ► to move through or in water by moving arms, legs, fins, or tail
2 to cross by swimming ⟨He *swam* the river.⟩
3 to float on or in or be covered with or as if with a liquid ⟨The corn was *swimming* in butter.⟩
4 to be dizzy : move or seem to move in a dizzying way ⟨My head *swam* in the hot room.⟩
swim•mer *n*

[2]**swim** *n*
an act or period of swimming

swimming pool *n*
a tank (as of concrete or plastic) made for swimming

swim•suit \'swim-,süt\ *n*
a garment for swimming or bathing

[1]**swin•dle** \'swin-dəl\ *vb* **swin•dled**; **swin•dling**
to get money or property from dishonestly : CHEAT

[2]**swindle** *n*
an act or instance of getting money or property from someone dishonestly

swin•dler \'swind-lər\ *n*
a person who swindles

► **Word History** It's hard to imagine that someone whose head is whirling could be convincing enough to swindle you. However, the original meaning of the German noun *Schwindler*—the source of our word *swindler*—was "giddy person." In the same way that *giddy* has been extended in English to describe someone who is frivolous or foolish, *Schwindler* was extended to persons given to flights of fancy. The Germans applied the word as well to a fantastic schemer, then to a participant in shaky business deals, and finally to a cheat.

swine \'swīn\ *n, pl* **swine**
a wild or domestic pig

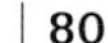

[1]swim 1

Swimmers combine different movements of the arms, legs, and torso to propel themselves through water in four basic competitive swimming strokes — the crawl, backstroke, breaststroke, and butterfly.

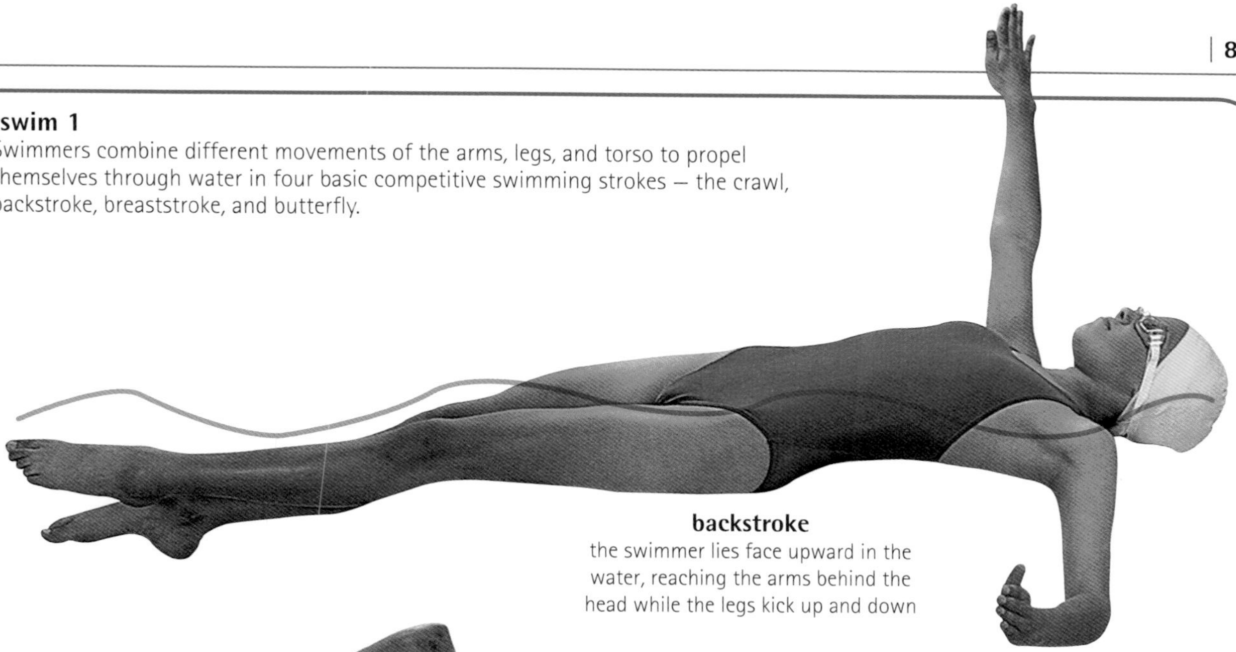

backstroke
the swimmer lies face upward in the water, reaching the arms behind the head while the legs kick up and down

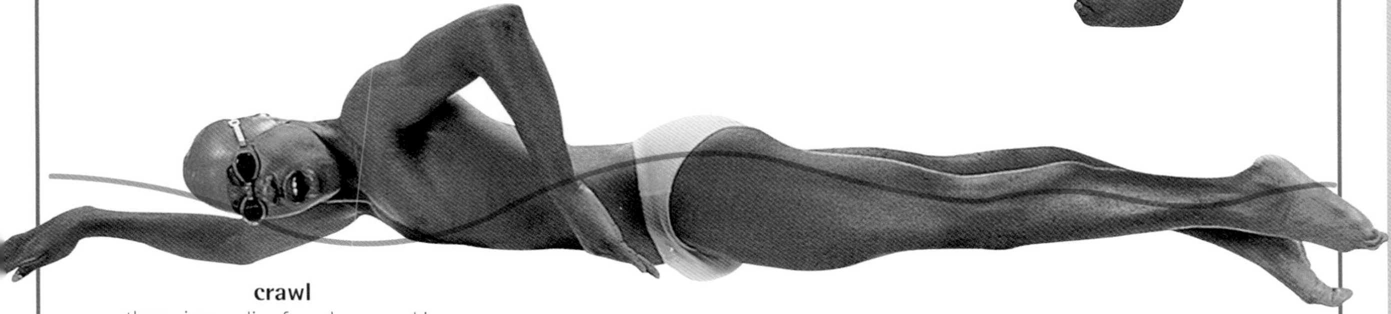

crawl
the swimmer lies face downward in the water, moving the arms over the head and kicking the legs up and down

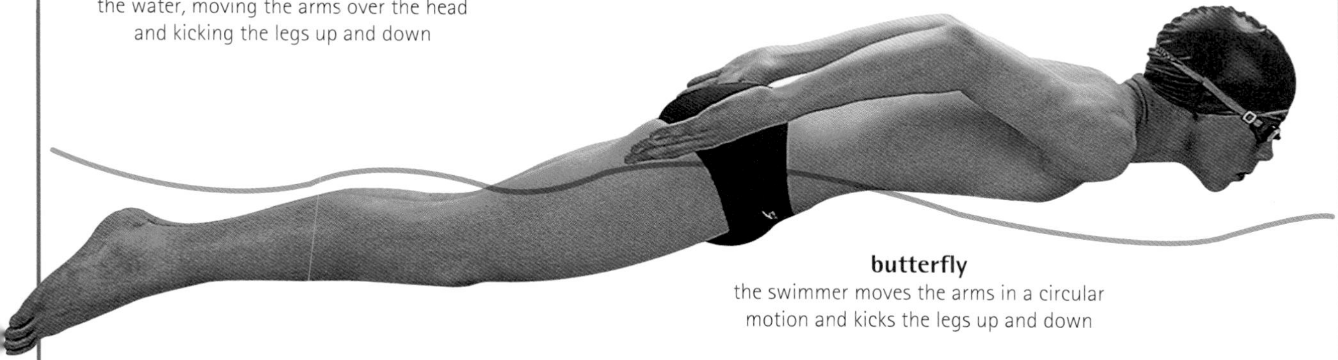

butterfly
the swimmer moves the arms in a circular motion and kicks the legs up and down

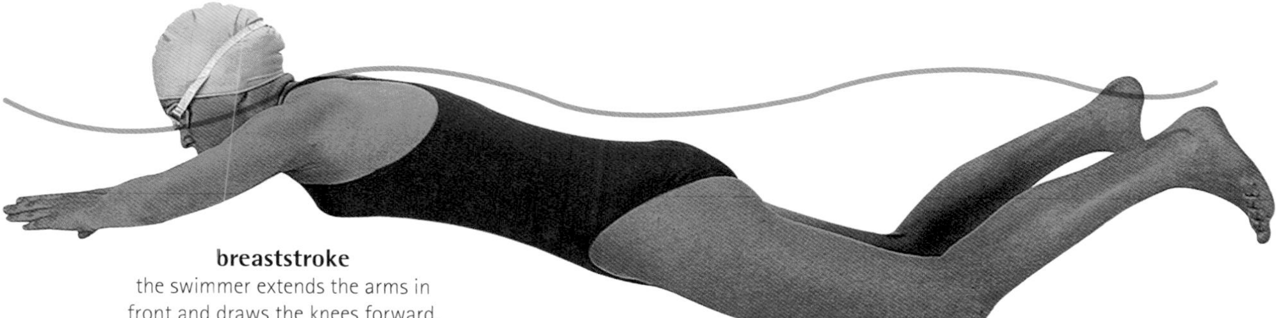

breaststroke
the swimmer extends the arms in front and draws the knees forward, then sweeps the arms back while kicking the legs backward

a b c d e f g h i j k l m n o p q r s t u v w x y z

[1]swing \'swiŋ\ *vb* **swung** \'swəŋ\; **swing•ing**
1 to move rapidly in a sweeping curve ⟨I *swung* the bat.⟩
2 to turn on a hinge or pivot ⟨The door *swung* open.⟩
3 to move with a curving motion ⟨Monkeys can *swing* from branch to branch.⟩ ⟨She *swung* her legs up on the bed.⟩
4 to turn or move quickly in a particular direction ⟨He *swung* the light in the direction of the noise.⟩
5 to move back and forth or from side to side while hanging from a fixed point ⟨Sheets *swung* on the clothes line.⟩
6 to move back and forth in or on a swing
7 to manage or handle successfully ⟨I'll work two jobs if I can *swing* it.⟩

[2]swing *n*
1 ► a seat usually hung by overhead ropes and used to move back and forth
2 an act of moving something (as a bat) rapidly in a sweeping curve
3 a sweeping movement, blow, or rhythm
4 the distance through which something sways to and fro ⟨The class measured the *swing* of a pendulum.⟩
5 a style of jazz marked by lively rhythm and played mostly for dancing

[1]swipe \'swīp\ *n*
a strong sweeping movement ⟨He took a *swipe* at the ball.⟩

[2]swipe *vb* **swiped**; **swip•ing**
1 [1]STEAL 1 ⟨Someone *swiped* my pen.⟩
2 to make a strong sweeping movement ⟨The cat *swiped* at the dog.⟩

[1]swirl \'swərl\ *vb* **swirled**; **swirl•ing**
to move with a spinning or twisting motion

[2]swirl *n*
1 a spinning mass or motion : EDDY ⟨a *swirl* of water⟩
2 busy movement or activity ⟨She got caught up in the *swirl* of events.⟩
3 ► a twisting shape or mark ⟨The ice cream has chocolate *swirls*.⟩

[2]swirl 3: a yellow lollipop with orange swirls

[2]swing 1: children on swings

[1]swish \'swish\ *vb* **swished**; **swish•ing**
to make, move, or strike with a soft sweeping or brushing sound ⟨The horse *swished* its tail.⟩

[2]swish *n*
1 a soft sweeping or brushing sound
2 a movement that produces a sweeping or brushing sound

[1]Swiss \'swis\ *n, pl* **Swiss**
a person born or living in Switzerland

[2]Swiss *adj*
of or relating to Switzerland or the Swiss

[1]switch \'swich\ *n*
1 a device for making, breaking, or changing the connections in an electrical circuit
2 a change from one thing to another ⟨a *switch* in plans⟩
3 a narrow flexible whip, rod, or twig
4 an act of switching
5 a device for adjusting the rails of a track so that a train or streetcar may be turned from one track to another

[2]switch *vb* **switched**; **switch•ing**
1 to turn, shift, or change by operating a device that makes, breaks, or changes the connections in an electrical circuit ⟨Remember to *switch* off the light.⟩
2 to move quickly from side to side ⟨The cow was *switching* its tail.⟩
3 to make a shift or change ⟨He *switched* to a new barber.⟩
4 to strike with or as if with a whip, rod, or twig

switch•board \'swich-ˌbȯrd\ *n*
a panel for controlling the operation of a number of electric circuits

[1]swiv•el \'swi-vəl\ *n*
a device joining two parts so that one or both can turn freely (as on a bolt or pin)

[2]swivel *vb* **swiv•eled** *or* **swiv•elled**; **swiv•el•ing** *or* **swiv•el•ling**
to turn on or as if on a swivel ⟨He *swiveled* around to see who was behind him.⟩

swollen *past participle of* SWELL

[1]swoon \'swün\ *vb* **swooned**; **swoon•ing**
[2]FAINT

[2]swoon *n*
[3]FAINT

[1]swoop \'swüp\ *vb* **swooped**; **swoop•ing**
to rush down or pounce suddenly

[2]swoop *n*
an act or instance of rushing down or pouncing suddenly

sword \'sȯrd\ *n*
► a weapon having a long blade usually with a sharp point and edge

sword•fish \'sȯrd-,fish\ *n, pl* **swordfish** *or* **sword•fish•es**
a large ocean fish that has a long pointed bill formed by the bones of the upper jaw and is often used for food

swords•man \'sȯrdz-mən\ *n, pl* **swords•men** \-mən\
a person who fights with a sword

swore *past of* SWEAR

sworn *past participle of* SWEAR

swum *past participle of* SWIM

swung *past and past participle of* SWING

syc•a•more \'si-kə-,mȯr\ *n*
1 a fig tree of Egypt and the Middle East
2 a large tree of the United States with round hard fruits and bark that peels off in flakes

syl•lab•ic \sə-'la-bik\ *adj*
relating to or being syllables

syl•lab•i•cate \sə-'la-bə-,kāt\ *vb* **syl•lab•i•cat•ed**; **syl•lab•i•cat•ing**
SYLLABIFY

syl•lab•i•ca•tion \sə-,la-bə-'kā-shən\ *n*
the forming of syllables : the dividing of words into syllables

syl•lab•i•fi•ca•tion \sə-,la-bə-fə-'kā-shən\ *n*
SYLLABICATION

syl•lab•i•fy \sə-'la-bə-,fī\ *vb* **syl•lab•i•fied**; **syl•lab•i•fy•ing**
to form or divide into syllables

syl•la•ble \'si-lə-bəl\ *n*
1 a unit of spoken language that consists of one or more vowel sounds alone or with one or more consonant sounds coming before or following
2 one or more letters (as *syl*, *la*, and *ble*) in a written word (as *syl•la•ble*) usually separated from the rest of the word by a centered dot or a hyphen and used as guides to the division of the word at the end of a line

sym•bol \'sim-bəl\ *n*
1 ▶ something that stands for something else : EMBLEM ⟨The eagle is a *symbol* of the United States.⟩
2 a letter, character, or sign used instead of a word to represent a quantity, position, relationship, direction, or something to be done ⟨The sign + is the *symbol* for addition.⟩
synonyms see EMBLEM

sym•bol•ic \sim-'bä-lik\ *also* **sym•bol•i•cal** \-li-kəl\ *adj*
of, relating to, or using symbols or symbolism ⟨Lighting the candles has a *symbolic* meaning.⟩

sym•bol•ism \'sim-bə-,li-zəm\ *n*
1 the use of symbols to represent an idea or quality ⟨The story was filled with *symbolism.*⟩
2 the meaning of a symbol ⟨What is the *symbolism* of the lion and lamb in this picture?⟩

symbol 1: a badge showing an eagle as the symbol of the US

sym•bol•ize \'sim-bə-,līz\ *vb* **sym•bol•ized**; **sym•bol•iz•ing**
to serve as a representation of ⟨A lion *symbolizes* courage.⟩

▶ **sword**
There are two main types of sword: cutting swords, such as those used by medieval knights, and stabbing swords, such as the rapier. Cutting swords were widely used by armies until the 19th century, when the rapier became more popular. Today, swords are mainly used in the sport of fencing.

features of a 17th-century German rapier

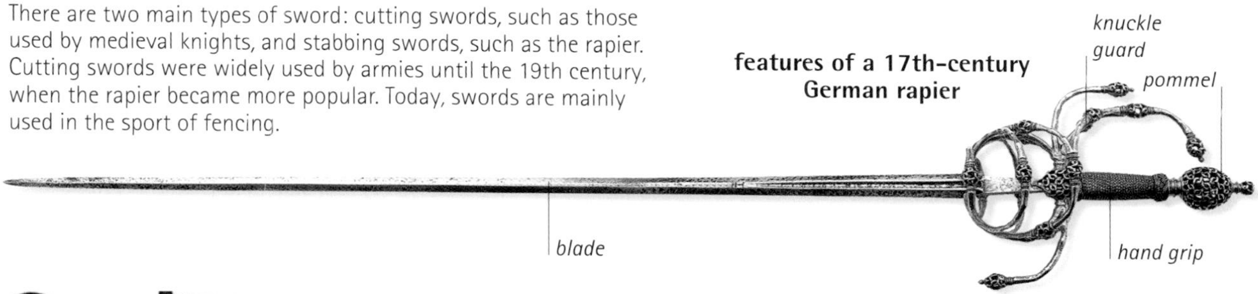

knuckle guard
pommel
blade
hand grip

14th-century French knight's sword

17th-century Japanese sword

17th-century German cavalry sword

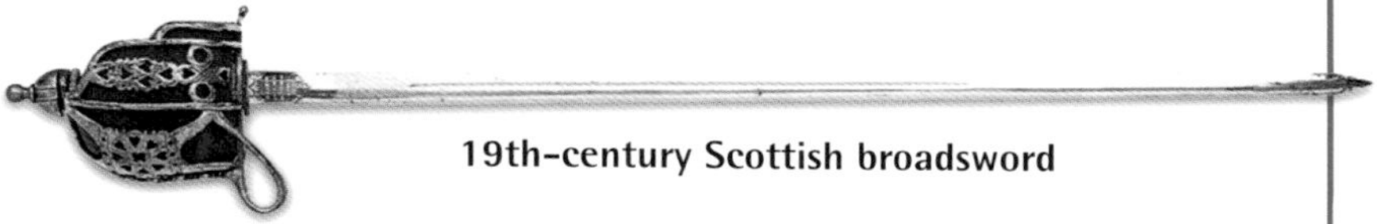

19th-century Scottish broadsword

a b c d e f g h i j k l m n o p q r s t u v w x y z

sym•met•ri•cal \sə-ˈme-tri-kəl\ *or* **sym•met•ric** \-rik\ *adj*
having or showing symmetry ⟨a *symmetrical* shape⟩

sym•me•try \ˈsi-mə-trē\ *n, pl* **sym•me•tries**
close agreement in size, shape, and position of parts that are on opposite sides of a dividing line or center : an arrangement involving regular and balanced proportions ⟨the *symmetry* of the human body⟩

sym•pa•thet•ic \ˌsim-pə-ˈthe-tik\ *adj*
1 feeling or showing care or understanding ⟨I received help from *sympathetic* friends.⟩
2 feeling favorable ⟨They're not *sympathetic* to the idea.⟩
sym•pa•thet•i•cal•ly \-ti-kə-lē\ *adv*

sym•pa•thize \ˈsim-pə-ˌthīz\ *vb* **sym•pa•thized**; **sym•pa•thiz•ing**
1 to feel or show pity or care and understanding for ⟨We *sympathize* with the family in its sorrow.⟩
2 to be in favor of something ⟨I *sympathize* with my friend's ambitions.⟩

sym•pa•thy \ˈsim-pə-thē\ *n, pl* **sym•pa•thies**
1 sorrow or pity for another ⟨She felt *sympathy* for the poor lost puppy.⟩
2 readiness to favor or support ⟨He expressed *sympathy* for the protesters.⟩
3 a relationship between people or things in which whatever affects one similarly affects the other

sym•phon•ic \sim-ˈfä-nik\ *adj*
relating to a symphony

sym•pho•ny \ˈsim-fə-nē\ *n, pl* **sym•pho•nies**
1 a usually long musical composition for a full orchestra
2 a large orchestra of wind, string, and percussion instruments
3 harmonious arrangement (as of sound or color)

symp•tom \ˈsimp-təm\ *n*
1 a noticeable change in the body or its functions that indicates the presence of a disease or other disorder
2 INDICATION 2, SIGN ⟨Loss of jobs is a *symptom* of a weakening economy.⟩

syn. *abbr* synonym

syn•a•gogue *also* **syn•a•gog** \ˈsi-nə-ˌgäg\ *n*
a Jewish house of worship

syn•apse \ˈsi-ˌnaps\ *n*
the point at which a nerve impulse passes from one nerve cell to another

syn•co•pa•tion \ˌsiŋ-kə-ˈpā-shən\ *n*
an instance of temporarily accenting a normally weak beat in music to vary the rhythm

syn•o•nym \ˈsi-nə-ˌnim\ *n*
a word having the same or almost the same meaning as another word in the same language

syn•on•y•mous \sə-ˈnä-nə-məs\ *adj*
alike in meaning

syn•tax \ˈsin-ˌtaks\ *n*
the way in which words are put together to form phrases, clauses, or sentences

syn•the•size \ˈsin-thə-ˌsīz\ *vb* **syn•the•sized**; **syn•the•siz•ing**
to produce from the combination of simpler materials ⟨Plants *synthesize* starch from molecules of glucose.⟩

syn•thet•ic \sin-ˈthe-tik\ *adj*
produced artificially especially by chemical means : produced by human beings ⟨*synthetic* diamonds⟩

sy•ringe \sə-ˈrinj\ *n*
▶ a device used to force fluid into or withdraw it from the body or its cavities

syringe

syrup 1: maple syrup poured over pancakes

syr•up \ˈsər-əp, ˈsir-\ *n*
1 ▲ a thick sticky solution of sugar and water often containing flavoring or a medicine ⟨chocolate *syrup*⟩ ⟨cough *syrup*⟩
2 the juice of a fruit or plant with some of the water removed ⟨maple *syrup*⟩

sys•tem \ˈsi-stəm\ *n*
1 a group of parts combined to form a whole that works or moves as a unit ⟨a park *system*⟩ ⟨a heating *system*⟩
2 a body that functions as a whole ⟨The disease weakened his entire *system*.⟩
3 a group of organs that together perform an important function in the body ⟨the nervous *system*⟩
4 an orderly way of managing, controlling, organizing, or doing something ⟨a democratic *system* of government⟩ ⟨Dad has a *system* for planting a garden.⟩

sys•tem•at•ic \ˌsi-stə-ˈma-tik\ *adj*
using a system or a regular and orderly method ⟨She works in a *systematic* way.⟩
sys•tem•at•i•cal•ly \-ti-kə-lē\ *adv*

sys•tem•ic \si-ˈste-mik\ *adj*
of or relating to the body as a whole ⟨*systemic* disease⟩

Tt

Sounds of T: The letter **T** most commonly makes the sound heard in *time* and *cat*. **T** is sometimes silent, as in *bouquet* and *whistle*. The letters **T** and **H** together make two different sounds. One is the sound heard in *think* and *tooth*. The other is the sound heard in *there* and *bother*. This sound is indicated by the symbol th. In some words, especially when **T** is followed by ION, **T** makes an SH sound, as in *potion*. In other words, such as *equation*, **T** followed by ION makes a sound indicated by the symbol zh. And in some words, especially when **T** is followed by URE, **T** sounds like a CH, as in *future* and *creature*.

t \'tē\ *n, pl* **t's** *or* **ts** \'tēz\ *often cap*
the 20th letter of the English alphabet
to a T just fine : EXACTLY ⟨My house suits me *to a T.*⟩

T *abbr* true

tab \'tab\ *n*
1 a short flap or tag attached to something for filing, pulling, or hanging
2 a careful watch ⟨Let's keep *tabs* on the weather.⟩

tab•by \'ta-bē\ *n, pl* **tabbies**
▶ a domestic cat with a striped and spotted coat

tabby

▶ **Word History** A silk cloth with a wavy pattern was once made in a part of the city of Baghdad, now the capital of the modern nation of Iraq. In Arabic the cloth was known as *'attābī*, from *Al-'Attābīya*, the name of its place of origin. The name for the cloth passed into medieval Latin as *attabi* and then into French as *tabis*. When the word was borrowed into English as *tabby* in the 1600s, it only referred to a kind of silk with a wavy, mottled pattern. Before long, however, people noticed a resemblance between the cloth and the striped or mottled markings on their domestic cats. *Tabby* has been the name for this type of cat since then.

tabernacle 1: the Mormon Tabernacle in Salt Lake City, Utah

tab•er•na•cle \'ta-bər-,na-kəl\ *n*
1 ▲ a place of worship
2 *often cap* a tent used as a place of worship by the ancient Israelites during their wanderings in the wilderness with Moses

¹ta•ble \'tā-bəl\ *n*
1 a piece of furniture having a smooth flat top on legs ⟨the kitchen *table*⟩ ⟨a picnic *table*⟩
2 food to eat ⟨Grandma sets a good *table.*⟩
3 the people around a table ⟨The whole *table* ordered fish.⟩
4 a short list ⟨a *table* of contents⟩
5 an arrangement in rows or columns for reference ⟨multiplication *tables*⟩

²table *vb* **ta•bled; ta•bling**
1 TABULATE
2 to put on a table

tab•leau \'ta-,blō\ *n, pl* **tab•leaux** *also* **tab•leaus** \-,lōz\
a scene or event shown by a group of persons who remain still and silent

ta•ble•cloth \'tā-bəl-,klȯth\ *n*
a covering spread over a dining table before the places are set

ta•ble•land \'tā-bəl-,land\ *n*
PLATEAU

ta•ble•spoon \'tā-bəl-,spün\ *n*
1 ▶ a large spoon used mostly for dishing up food
2 a unit of measure used in cooking equal to 1/2 fluid ounce (about 15 milliliters)

tablespoon 1

tableware: tableware set on a table

ta•ble•spoon•ful \ˌtā-bəl-ˈspün-ˌfu̇l\ *n, pl* **tablespoonfuls** \-ˌfu̇lz\ *also* **ta•ble•spoons•ful** \-ˈspünz-ˌfu̇l\
1 as much as a tablespoon will hold
2 TABLESPOON 2

tab•let \ˈta-blət\ *n*
1 a thin flat slab used for writing, painting, or drawing
2 a number of sheets of writing paper glued together at one edge
3 a small usually round mass of material containing medicine ⟨aspirin *tablets*⟩
4 a flat, rectangular computing device that is used especially for connecting to the Internet, watching videos, playing games, and reading e-books

table tennis *n*
▶ a game played on a table by two or four players who use paddles to hit a small hollow plastic ball back and forth over a net

ta•ble•ware \ˈtā-bəl-ˌwer\ *n*
▲ utensils (as of china, glass, or silver) for use at the table

tab•u•late \ˈta-byə-ˌlāt\ *vb* **tab•u•lat•ed**; **tab•u•lat•ing**
to count and record in an orderly way ⟨*tabulate* votes⟩

tac•it \ˈta-sət\ *adj*
understood or made known without being put into words
tac•it•ly *adv*

[1]tack \ˈtak\ *n*
1 a small nail with a sharp point and usually a broad flat head
2 the direction a ship is sailing as shown by the position the sails are set in
3 a course or method of action ⟨Since I wasn't getting any answers, I decided to try a different *tack*.⟩
4 a temporary stitch used in sewing

[2]tack *vb* **tacked**; **tack•ing**
1 to fasten with tacks
2 to attach or join loosely or quickly ⟨At the end of the report, she *tacked* on her own complaints.⟩
3 to change from one course to another in sailing
4 to follow a zigzag course

table tennis: paddle and ball used to play table tennis

[1]tack•le \ˈta-kəl\ *vb* **tack•led**; **tack•ling**
1 to seize and throw (a person) to the ground
2 to begin working on ⟨I decided to *tackle* the job.⟩

[2]tackle *n*
1 ▼ a set of special equipment ⟨fishing *tackle*⟩
2 an arrangement of ropes and wheels for hoisting or pulling something heavy
3 an act of seizing and throwing a person to the ground
4 a football player positioned on the line of scrimmage

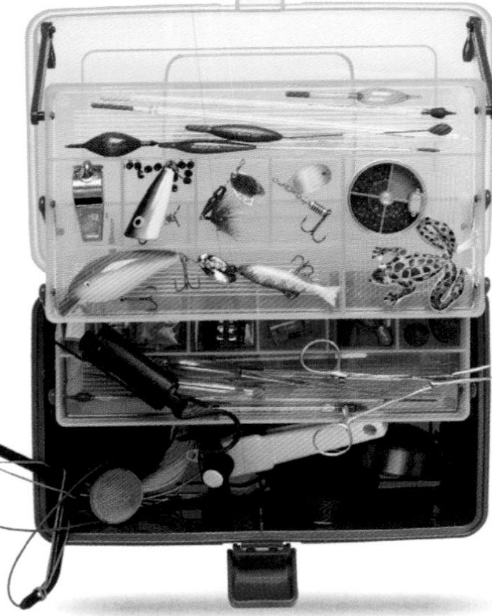

[2]tackle 1: fishing tackle

ta•co \ˈtä-kō\ *n, pl* **tacos**
▶ a corn tortilla usually folded and fried and filled with a spicy mixture (as of ground meat and cheese)

tact \ˈtakt\ *n*
the ability to do or say things without offending other people ⟨She settled the argument with *tact*.⟩

tact•ful \ˈtakt-fəl\ *adj*
having or showing the ability to do or say things without offending other people
tact•ful•ly \-fə-lē\ *adv*
tact•ful•ness *n*

tac•tic \ˈtak-tik\ *n*
a planned action for some purpose

tac•tics \ˈtak-tiks\ *n pl*
1 the science and art of arranging and moving troops or warships for best use
2 a system or method for reaching a goal

Hint: *Tactics* can be used as a singular or a plural in writing and speaking.

tac•tile \ˈtak-təl\ *adj*
relating to the sense of touch

tact•less \ˈtakt-ləs\ *adj*
having or showing no tact
tact•less•ly *adv*
tact•less•ness *n*

tad•pole \ˈtad-ˌpōl\ *n*
▶ the larva of a frog or toad that has a long tail, breathes with gills, and lives in water

tail
developed leg
tadpole

▶ **Word History** A young tadpole, which looks like a large head with a tail, will in time become a toad or a frog. The English word *tadpole* comes from a Middle English compound word *taddepol,* made up from *tadde,* "toad," and *pol,* "head."

taf•fy \ˈta-fē\ *n, pl* **taffies**
a candy made usually of molasses or brown sugar boiled and pulled until soft

[1]**tag** \ˈtag\ *n*
a small flap or tab fixed or hanging on something ⟨a price *tag*⟩ ⟨a name *tag*⟩

taco: a plate of tacos

[2]**tag** *vb* **tagged; tag•ging**
1 to follow closely and continually
2 to put a tab or label on
tag along to follow another's lead in going from one place to another

[3]**tag** *n*
a game in which one player who is it chases the others and tries to touch one of them to make that person it

[4]**tag** *vb* **tagged; tag•ging**
1 to touch in or as if in a game of tag
2 to touch a runner in baseball with the ball and cause the runner to be out

[1]**tail** \ˈtāl\ *n*
1 ▶ the rear part of an animal or a usually slender flexible growth that extends from this part
2 something that in shape, appearance, or position is like an animal's tail ⟨the *tail* of a coat⟩
3 the back, last, or lower part of something ⟨the *tail* of an airplane⟩
4 the side or end opposite the head
tailed \ˈtāld\ *adj*
tail•less \ˈtāl-ləs\ *adj*

[2]**tail** *vb* **tailed; tail•ing**
to follow closely to keep watch on ⟨Police *tailed* the suspect.⟩

tail•gate \ˈtāl-ˌgāt\ *n*
a panel at the back end of a vehicle that can be lowered for loading and unloading

[1]**tai•lor** \ˈtā-lər\ *n*
a person whose business is making or making adjustments in clothes

[2]**tailor** *vb* **tai•lored; tai•lor•ing**
1 to make or make adjustments in (clothes)
2 to change to fit a special need ⟨They *tailored* their plans to suit the weather.⟩

tail•pipe \ˈtāl-ˌpīp\ *n*
the pipe carrying off the exhaust gases from the muffler of an engine in a car or truck

tail•spin \ˈtāl-ˌspin\ *n*
a dive by an airplane turning in a circle

[1]**taint** \ˈtānt\ *vb* **taint•ed; taint•ing**
1 to rot slightly ⟨*tainted* meat⟩
2 to affect slightly with something bad

[2]**taint** *n*
a trace of decay

[1]**take** \ˈtāk\ *vb* **took** \ˈtu̇k\; **tak•en** \ˈtā-kən\; **tak•ing**
1 to get hold of : GRASP ⟨You should *take* it by the handle.⟩ ⟨He *took* my hand.⟩
2 to carry or go with from one place to another ⟨I'll *take* you home.⟩ ⟨This bus will *take* us there.⟩
3 to get control of : CAPTURE ⟨*took* the fort⟩
4 to receive into the body ⟨Don't forget to *take* your medicine.⟩
5 to get possession or use of ⟨She *took* the book from the table.⟩ ⟨We will *take* a cottage by the shore for the summer.⟩
6 to begin to perform the responsibilities of : ASSUME ⟨She *took* charge.⟩ ⟨A new mayor *took* office.⟩
7 to do the action of ⟨Let's *take* a walk.⟩
8 to use as a way of going from one place to another ⟨I *take* the bus.⟩ ⟨We'll *take* the highway.⟩

[1]**tail 1:** a kangaroo has a muscular tail
tail

9 REQUIRE 1 ⟨It will *take* a long time.⟩ ⟨I *take* a size ten.⟩
10 to put up with : ENDURE ⟨I don't have to *take* that from you.⟩
11 to come upon ⟨We *took* them by surprise.⟩
12 to adopt or accept ⟨He *took* my side in the argument.⟩ ⟨She *took* all the credit.⟩
13 [1]WIN 2 ⟨My essay *took* second prize.⟩
14 CHOOSE 1, SELECT ⟨I'll *take* the red one.⟩
15 to sit in or on ⟨Please *take* a seat.⟩
16 to find out by testing or examining ⟨Let me *take* your temperature.⟩
17 to save in some permanent form ⟨He *took* down every word of the speech.⟩ ⟨Will you *take* a picture?⟩
18 BELIEVE 2 ⟨I *took* it to be the truth.⟩ ⟨You can *take* my word for it.⟩
19 to be guided by : FOLLOW ⟨He refused to *take* my advice.⟩
20 to become affected suddenly ⟨She *took* sick just before the holiday.⟩
21 UNDERSTAND 4, INTERPRET ⟨I *took* it to mean something different.⟩
22 to react in a certain way ⟨They *take* pleasure in music.⟩ ⟨Don't *take* offense.⟩
23 SUBTRACT ⟨*take* 2 from 4⟩
24 CONSIDER 1
25 to have effect : be successful ⟨The vaccination *took*.⟩
26 to be formed or used with ⟨Prepositions *take* objects.⟩
27 CAPTIVATE, DELIGHT ⟨We were *taken* with its beauty.⟩
tak•er *n*

a b c d e f g h i j k l m n o p q r s **t** u v w x y z

take advantage of
1 to make good use of ⟨*Take advantage of* your free time.⟩
2 to treat (someone) unfairly

take after RESEMBLE ⟨Many children *take after* their parents.⟩

take back to try to cancel (as something said) ⟨I *take* it *back.* I really don't hate you.⟩

take care to be careful

take care of to do what is needed : look after

take charge to assume care or control

take effect
1 to go into existence or operation ⟨The new rate *takes effect* Monday.⟩
2 to have an intended or expected result ⟨Wait for the medicine to *take effect.*⟩

take for granted to assume as true, real, or expected

take hold to become attached or established ⟨The tree I planted never *took hold.*⟩

take in
1 to make smaller ⟨She *took* the dress *in.*⟩
2 to receive as a guest ⟨We *took in* travelers for the night.⟩
3 to allow to join ⟨The club is not *taking in* new members.⟩
4 to receive and do at home for pay ⟨She *takes in* washing.⟩
5 to have within its limits ⟨The tour *takes in* both museums.⟩
6 to go to ⟨Let's *take in* a movie.⟩
7 to get the meaning of ⟨He *took in* the situation at a glance.⟩
8 [1]CHEAT 1 ⟨They were *taken in* by an old trick.⟩

talc: a rock of talc

take off
1 to take away (a covering) : REMOVE ⟨You can *take* your shoes *off.*⟩
2 DEDUCT ⟨I'm willing to *take off* ten percent.⟩
3 to leave a surface in beginning a flight or leap ⟨The plane is *taking off* now.⟩

take on
1 to begin (a task) or struggle against (an opponent) ⟨She *took on* the champion.⟩
2 to gain or show as or as if a part of oneself ⟨The city *took on* a carnival mood.⟩
3 [1]EMPLOY 1 ⟨The business will *take on* more workers.⟩
4 to make an unusual show of grief or anger ⟨Don't *take on* so.⟩

take over to get control of ⟨Military leaders *took over* the government.⟩

take part to do or join in something together with others ⟨Come *take part* in the fun.⟩

take place to come about or occur : HAPPEN ⟨The meeting *took place* yesterday.⟩

take up
1 to get together from many sources ⟨We'll *take up* a collection for the gift.⟩
2 to start something for the first time or after a pause ⟨I'd like to *take up* painting.⟩ ⟨Our class *took up* the lesson where we left off.⟩
3 to change by making tighter or shorter ⟨She needs to *take up* the dress in the back.⟩

▶ **Synonyms** TAKE, SEIZE, and GRASP mean to get a hold on with or as if with the hand. TAKE can be used of any way of getting possession or control of something. ⟨Please *take* this gift.⟩ ⟨You *took* more food than you can use.⟩ SEIZE is used for an act of taking something suddenly and by force. ⟨A police officer *seized* the thief in the act of escaping.⟩ GRASP is used for taking something in the hand and keeping it there firmly. ⟨*Grasp* my arm and walk slowly.⟩

[2]take *n*
1 the number or quantity of animals or fish killed, captured, or caught
2 money received ⟨His *take* from the sale was half the price.⟩

take•off \ˈtāk-ˌȯf\ *n*
1 an act or instance of leaving the ground (as by an airplane)
2 an imitation especially to mock the original
3 a spot at which something leaves the ground

talc \ˈtalk\ *n*
◀ a soft mineral that has a soapy feel and is used especially in making talcum powder

tal•cum powder \ˈtal-kəm-\ *n*
▶ a usually perfumed powder for the body made of talc

tale \ˈtāl\ *n*
1 something told ⟨He told a *tale* of woe.⟩
2 a story about an imaginary event ⟨fairy *tales*⟩
3 [3]LIE
4 a piece of harmful gossip

tal•ent \ˈta-lənt\ *n*
1 unusual natural ability
2 a special often creative or artistic ability
3 a person or group of people having special ability
synonyms see ABILITY
tal•ent•ed \ˈta-lən-təd\ *adj*

▶ **Word History** *Talent* was the name of a unit of weight and money in the ancient world. The Christian Bible has a story about a man who gave three servants talents to keep for him while he was away. The first two servants invested their money and doubled it. The third hid the talent he had been given in the ground. When the master returned, he praised the first two servants. But he scolded the third, who could give back only what he had been given. The meaning of the story is that people should make good use of their natural gifts. From this story came a new meaning of *talent* : "special gift."

tal•is•man \ˈta-lə-smən\ *n, pl* **tal•is•mans**
▶ a ring or stone carved with symbols and believed to have magical powers : CHARM

[1]talk \ˈtȯk\ *vb* **talked; talk•ing**
1 to express in speech : SPEAK ⟨You're *talking* too fast.⟩
2 to speak about : DISCUSS ⟨They're *talking* business.⟩
3 to cause or influence with words ⟨I *talked* them into agreeing.⟩
4 to use a certain language ⟨They were *talking* Spanish.⟩
5 to exchange ideas by means of spoken words : CONVERSE ⟨Let's sit and *talk.*⟩
6 to pass on information other than by speaking ⟨Can you *talk* with your hands?⟩

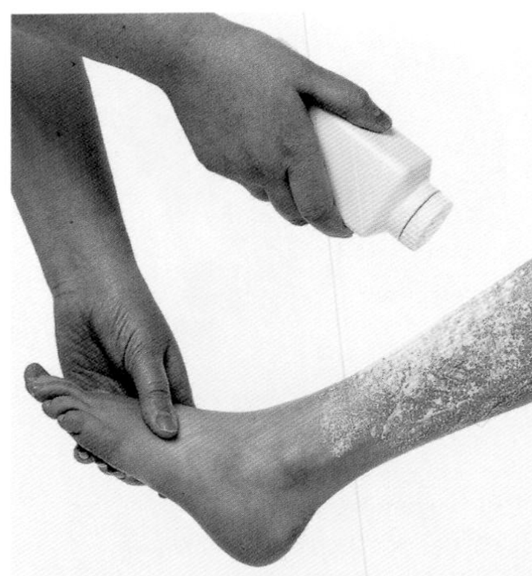

talcum powder: talcum powder being sprinkled on a person's leg

7 [2]GOSSIP ⟨If you act that way, people will *talk.*⟩
8 to reveal secret information ⟨Officials forced the spy to *talk.*⟩
synonyms see SPEAK
talk•er *n*
talk over DISCUSS 2 ⟨We need to *talk over* our vacation plans.⟩

[2]talk *n*
1 the act or an instance of speaking with someone ⟨We had a *talk.*⟩
2 a way of speaking : LANGUAGE
3 CONFERENCE
4 [1]RUMOR ⟨Has there been *talk* of war?⟩
5 the topic of comment or gossip ⟨The President's visit is the *talk* of the town.⟩
6 an informal address ⟨The coach gave us a *talk* to raise our spirits.⟩

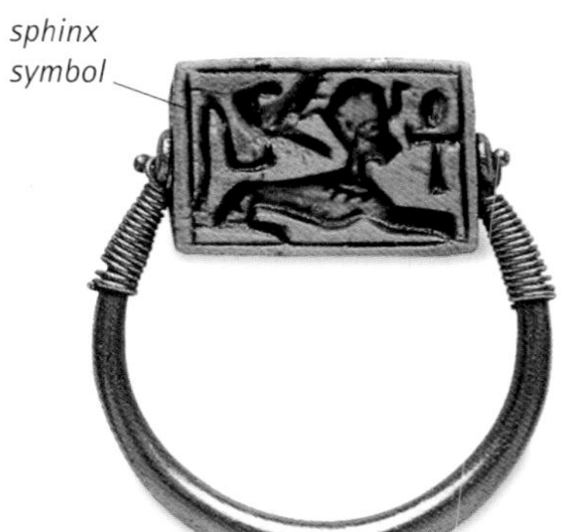

talisman: an ancient Egyptian ring serving as a talisman

talk•a•tive \'tȯ-kə-tiv\ *adj*
fond of talking
talk•a•tive•ness *n*

talk•ing–to \'tȯ-kiŋ-,tü\ *n*
an often wordy scolding

[1]tall \'tȯl\ *adj* **tall•er; tall•est**
1 having unusually great height
2 of a stated height ⟨ten feet *tall*⟩
3 made up ⟨a *tall* tale⟩
synonyms see HIGH
tall•ness *n*

[2]tall *adv*
so as to be or look tall ⟨Stand *tall* and straight.⟩

tal•low \'ta-lō\ *n*
a white solid fat of cattle and sheep used mostly in making candles and soap

[1]tal•ly \'ta-lē\ *n, pl* **tallies**
1 a recorded count
2 a score or point made (as in a game)

[2]tally *vb* **tal•lied; tal•ly•ing**
1 to keep a count of
2 to make a tally : SCORE
3 to match or agree : CORRESPOND

talon

talon of an eagle

Tal•mud \'täl-,mu̇d, 'tal-məd\ *n*
a collection of writings on Jewish law and custom and religious practice

tal•on \'ta-lən\ *n*
▲ the claw of a bird of prey
tal•oned \-ənd\ *adj*

ta•ma•le \tə-'mä-lē\ *n*
seasoned ground meat rolled in cornmeal, wrapped in corn husks, and steamed

tam•bou•rine \,tam-bə-'rēn\ *n*
► a small shallow drum with only one head and loose metal disks around the rim that is played by shaking or hitting with the hand

[1]tame \'tām\ *adj* **tam•er; tam•est**
1 changed from the wild state so as to become useful and obedient to people : DOMESTIC ⟨a *tame* elephant⟩
2 not afraid of people ⟨The chipmunks at the park are very *tame.*⟩
3 not interesting : DULL ⟨a *tame* movie⟩
tame•ly *adv*

[2]tame *vb* **tamed; tam•ing**
to make or become gentle or obedient ⟨They *tamed* the lion.⟩
tam•er *n*

tamp \'tamp\ *vb* **tamped; tamp•ing**
to press down or in by hitting lightly ⟨She *tamped* down the soil.⟩

tam•per \'tam-pər\ *vb* **tam•pered; tam•per•ing**
to interfere or change in a secret or incorrect way
synonyms see MEDDLE

[1]tan \'tan\ *vb* **tanned; tan•ning**
1 to change animal hide into leather especially by soaking in a tannin solution
2 to make or become brown in color ⟨She doesn't *tan.* Instead, she gets a sunburn.⟩
3 [1]BEAT 1, THRASH

[2]tan *adj* **tan•ner; tan•nest**
of a light yellowish brown color

tambourine

[3]tan *n*
1 a brown color given to the skin by the sun or wind
2 a light yellowish brown : the color of sand

tan•a•ger \'ta-ni-jər\ *n*
▼ a brightly colored mostly tropical bird that feeds on insects and fruit

tanager: a scarlet tanager

tandem bicycle: a couple riding a tandem bicycle

[1]tan•dem \'tan-dəm\ *n*
1 a carriage pulled by horses hitched one behind the other
2 TANDEM BICYCLE

[2]tandem *adv*
one behind another

tandem bicycle *n*
▲ a bicycle for two people sitting one behind the other

tang \'taŋ\ *n*
a sharp flavor or smell 〈the *tang* of salt air〉
tangy \'taŋ-ē\ *adj*

tan•ger•ine \'tan-jə-ˌrēn\ *n*
a Chinese orange with a loose skin and sweet pulp

tan•gi•ble \'tan-jə-bəl\ *adj*
1 possible to touch or handle : MATERIAL
2 easily seen or recognized 〈*tangible* benefits〉
tan•gi•bly \-blē\ *adv*

[1]tan•gle \'taŋ-gəl\ *vb* **tan•gled; tan•gling**
to twist or become twisted together into a mass that is hard to straighten out again 〈I *tangled* my comb in my hair.〉

[2]tangle *n*
a mass that is twisted together and hard to straighten 〈a *tangle* of yarn〉 〈a *tangle* of branches〉
2 a complicated or confused state

tank \'taŋk\ *n*
1 an often large container for a liquid 〈water *tank*〉 〈fish *tank*〉
2 ▼ an enclosed combat vehicle that has heavy armor and guns and a tread which is an endless belt

tan•kard \'taŋ-kərd\ *n*
a tall cup with one handle and often a lid

tank•er \'taŋ-kər\ *n*
a vehicle or ship with tanks for carrying a liquid 〈oil *tankers*〉

tan•ner \'ta-nər\ *n*
a person who tans hides into leather

tan•nery \'ta-nə-rē\ *n, pl* **tan•ner•ies**
a place where hides are tanned

tan•nin \'ta-nən\ *n*
a substance often made from oak bark or sumac and used in tanning animal hides, dyeing fabric and yarn, and making ink

tan•ta•lize \'tan-tə-ˌlīz\ *vb* **tan•ta•lized; tan•ta•liz•ing**
to tease or excite by or as if by showing, mentioning, or offering something desirable but keeping it out of reach

▶ **Word History** There was once, so Greek mythology tells us, a king named Tantalus who was not a good man. He murdered his own son and served him as food to the gods. For this the king was punished by being made to stand underneath a fruit tree in water up to his chin. If he bent his head to drink, the water got lower and he could not reach it. If he lifted his head to bite into a fruit, the bough went higher and he could not reach it. He was made miserable by food and drink kept just out of reach. The word *tantalize* comes from the name of this mythical king.

tan•trum \'tan-trəm\ *n*
an outburst of bad temper

tank 2: an army tank from the former Soviet Union

¹tap \'tap\ *vb* **tapped; tap•ping**
to hit lightly
tap•per *n*

²tap *n*
a light blow or its sound ⟨There was a *tap* at the window.⟩

³tap *n*
FAUCET, SPIGOT
on tap coming up ⟨What's *on tap* for the weekend?⟩

⁴tap *vb* **tapped; tap•ping**
1 to let out or cause to flow by making a hole or by pulling out a plug ⟨He *tapped* water from a barrel.⟩
2 to make a hole in to draw off a liquid ⟨We *tap* maple trees for sap.⟩
3 to draw from or upon ⟨I *tapped* the last of my savings.⟩
4 to connect into (a telephone wire) to listen secretly
tap•per *n*

tap–dance \'tap-,dans\ *vb* **tap–danced; tap–danc•ing**
to perform a tap dance
tap–danc•er *n*

tap dance *n*
a kind of dance featuring loud tapping sounds from shoes with metal plates on the heels and toes

¹tape \'tāp\ *n*
1 a narrow strip of material that is sticky on one side and is used to stick one thing to another
2 MAGNETIC TAPE
3 ¹VIDEOTAPE 2
4 TAPE RECORDING
5 a narrow band of cloth or plastic ⟨He broke the *tape* and won the race.⟩

²tape *vb* **taped; tap•ing**
1 to fasten, cover, or hold up with sticky tape
2 to make a recording of ⟨She *taped* their conversation.⟩

tape deck *n*
a device used to play back and often to record on magnetic tapes

tape measure *n*
▼ a flexible piece of material marked off for measuring

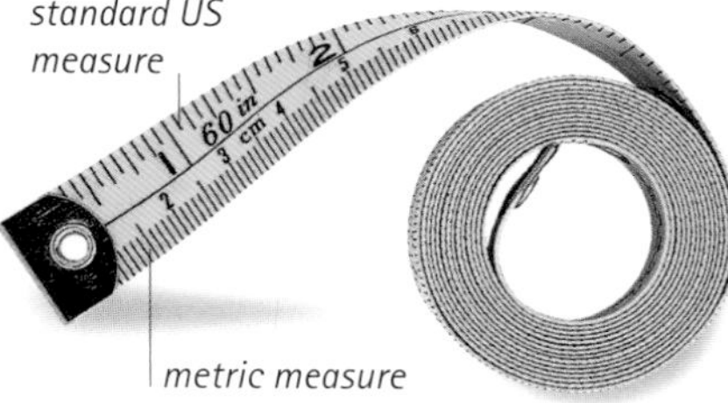

tape measure

tapestry: an ancient tapestry depicting birds

¹ta•per \'tā-pər\ *n*
1 a slender candle
2 a gradual lessening in thickness or width in a long object

²taper *vb* **ta•pered; ta•per•ing**
1 to make or become gradually smaller toward one end ⟨The leaves *taper* to a point.⟩
2 to grow gradually less and less ⟨The rain *tapered* off.⟩

tape recorder *n*
a device for recording on and playing back magnetic tapes

tape recording *n*
a recording made on magnetic tape

tap•es•try \'ta-pə-strē\ *n, pl* **tap•es•tries**
▲ a heavy cloth that has designs or pictures woven into it and is used especially as a wall hanging
tap•es•tried \-strēd\ *adj*

tape•worm \'tāp-,wərm\ *n*
a worm with a long flat body that lives as a parasite in the intestines of people and animals

tap•i•o•ca \,ta-pē-'ō-kə\ *n*
small pieces of starch from roots of a tropical plant used especially in puddings

ta•pir \'tā-pər\ *n*
a large hoofed plant-eating animal of tropical America and southeastern Asia that has short thick legs, a short tail, and a long flexible snout

tap•root \'tap-,rüt, -,ru̇t\ *n*
a main root of a plant that grows straight down and gives off smaller side roots

taps \'taps\ *n pl*
the last bugle call at night blown as a signal to put out the lights
Hint: *Taps* can be used as a singular or a plural in writing and speaking.

¹tar \'tär\ *n*
1 a thick dark sticky liquid made from wood, coal, or peat
2 a substance (as one formed by burning tobacco) that resembles tar

²tar *vb* **tarred; tar•ring**
to cover with or as if with tar

ta•ran•tu•la \tə-'ran-chə-lə\ *n*
▼ a large hairy spider of warm regions of North and South America whose bite may be painful but is usually not serious to humans except for a few South American species

tar•dy \'tär-dē\ *adj* **tar•di•er; tar•di•est**
not on time : LATE
tar•di•ness \'tär-dē-nəs\ *n*

tar•get \'tär-gət\ *n*
1 a mark or object to shoot at or attack
2 a person or thing that is talked about, criticized, or laughed at
3 a goal to be reached

tarantula: a Mexican red-kneed tarantula

tar•iff \'ter-əf\ *n*
1 a list of taxes placed by a government on goods coming into a country
2 the tax or the rate of taxation set up in a tariff list

[1]**tar•nish** \'tär-nish\ *vb* **tar•nished**; **tar•nish•ing**
1 to make or become dull, dim, or discolored
2 to bring disgrace or ruin ⟨The scandal *tarnished* his reputation.⟩

[2]**tarnish** *n*
a surface coating formed during tarnishing

tarp \'tärp\ *n*
TARPAULIN

tar•pau•lin \tär-'pò-lən, 'tär-pə-lən\ *n*
a sheet of waterproof canvas

[1]**tar•ry** \'ter-ē\ *vb* **tar•ried**; **tar•ry•ing**
1 to be slow in coming or going
2 to stay in or at a place

tassel 1:
a tassel on an ornament

[2]**tar•ry** \'tär-ē\ *adj*
like or covered with tar ⟨*tarry* smoke⟩ ⟨*tarry* boots⟩

[1]**tart** \'tärt\ *adj* **tart•er**; **tart•est**
1 pleasantly sharp or sour to the taste ⟨a *tart* apple⟩
2 having an unkind quality ⟨a *tart* manner⟩
tart•ly *adv*
tart•ness *n*

[2]**tart** *n*
▶ an often small pie usually with no top crust

tar•tan \'tär-t[ə]n\ *n*
a woolen cloth with a plaid design originally made in Scotland

tar•tar \'tär-tər\ *n*
a crust that forms on the teeth and consists of plaque that has become hardened by the deposit of calcium-containing salts

tar•tar sauce *or* **tar•tare sauce** \'tär-tər-\ *n*
a sauce made chiefly of mayonnaise and chopped pickles

task \'task\ *n*
a piece of work that has been assigned, needs to be done, or presents a challenge ⟨Passing this course will not be an easy *task.*⟩

> ▶ **Synonyms** TASK, DUTY, and JOB mean a piece of work assigned or to be done. TASK is used for work given by a person in a position of authority. ⟨The boss used to give me every difficult *task.*⟩ DUTY is used when a person has responsibility to do the work. ⟨The *duty* of police is to protect people.⟩ JOB may mean that the work is necessary, hard, or important. ⟨We all have to do our *job.*⟩

tas•sel \'ta-səl\ *n*
1 ▼ a hanging ornament (as on clothing) made of a bunch of cords of the same length fastened at one end
2 the male flower cluster on the top of some plants and especially corn

[1]**taste** \'tāst\ *vb* **tast•ed**; **tast•ing**
1 to find out the flavor of something by taking a little into the mouth ⟨He has never *tasted* mango.⟩
2 to have a certain flavor ⟨The milk *tastes* sour.⟩

[2]**tart:**
a strawberry and blueberry tart

[2]**tattoo:**
a New Zealand man with a tribal tattoo

3 to recognize by the sense of taste ⟨I can *taste* salt in the soup.⟩
4 to eat or drink usually in small amounts ⟨May I *taste* your dessert?⟩
5 [2]EXPERIENCE ⟨She has the opportunity to *taste* big city life.⟩
tast•er *n*

[2]**taste** *n*
1 the sense by which sweet, sour, bitter, or salty flavors are detected through sense organs (**taste buds**) in the tongue
2 the quality of something recognized by the sense of taste or by this together with smell and touch : FLAVOR ⟨The fruit had a bitter *taste.*⟩
3 a small amount tasted ⟨Do you want a *taste* of the ice cream?⟩
4 a personal liking ⟨My sister has very expensive *tastes.*⟩
5 the ability to choose and enjoy what is good or beautiful ⟨He has good *taste* in clothes.⟩
6 a sample of what something is like

taste•ful \'tāst-fəl\ *adj*
having or showing the ability to choose what is good, beautiful, or proper ⟨a *tasteful* color combination⟩
taste•ful•ly \-fə-lē\ *adv*

taste•less \'tāst-ləs\ *adj*
1 having little flavor ⟨a *tasteless* stew⟩
2 not having or showing the ability to choose what is good, beautiful, or proper ⟨a *tasteless* remark⟩
taste•less•ly *adv*

tasty \'tā-stē\ *adj* **tast•i•er**; **tast•i•est**
pleasing to the taste ⟨a *tasty* dessert⟩
tast•i•ness *n*

tat•ter \'ta-tər\ *n*
1 a part torn and left hanging : SHRED
2 **tatters** *pl* ragged clothing

tat•tered \'ta-tərd\ *adj*
1 torn in or worn to shreds ⟨*tattered* clothes⟩
2 dressed in ragged clothes

tat•tle \ˈta-tᵊl\ *vb* **tat•tled**; **tat•tling**
to tell on someone
tat•tler \ˈtat-lər\ *n*

tat•tle•tale \ˈta-tᵊl-ˌtāl\ *n*
a person who tells on someone

[1]**tat•too** \ta-ˈtü\ *vb* **tat•tooed**; **tat•too•ing**
to mark the body with a picture or pattern by using a needle to put color under the skin

[2]**tattoo** *n, pl* **tat•toos**
◀ a picture or design made by putting color under the skin

taught *past and past participle of* TEACH

[1]**taunt** \ˈtȯnt\ *n*
a mean insulting remark

[2]**taunt** *vb* **taunt•ed**; **taunt•ing**
to make fun of or say insulting things to

Tau•rus \ˈtȯr-əs\ *n*
1 a constellation between Aries and Gemini imagined as a bull
2 ▼ the second sign of the zodiac or a person born under this sign

Taurus 2: a representation of the sign of the zodiac Taurus

taut \ˈtȯt\ *adj* **taut•er**; **taut•est**
1 tightly stretched ⟨The rope was pulled *taut.*⟩
2 very tense ⟨Her nerves were *taut* with excitement.⟩
3 firm and not flabby ⟨*taut* muscles⟩
taut•ly *adv*

tav•ern \ˈta-vərn\ *n*
1 a place where beer and liquor are sold and drunk
2 INN

taw•ny \ˈtȯ-nē\ *adj* **taw•ni•er**; **taw•ni•est**
of a brownish orange color

[1]**tax** \ˈtaks\ *n*
money collected by the government from people or businesses for public use

[2]**tax** *vb* **taxed**; **tax•ing**
1 to require to pay money to a government for public use
2 to cause a strain on ⟨Fighting to survive the storm *taxed* their strength.⟩

tax•able \ˈtak-sə-bəl\ *adj*
subject to tax ⟨*taxable* income⟩

tax•a•tion \tak-ˈsā-shən\ *n*
1 the action of taxing
2 money gotten from taxes

[1]**taxi** \ˈtak-sē\ *n, pl* **tax•is** \-sēz\
TAXICAB

[2]**taxi** *vb* **tax•ied**; **taxi•ing**
1 to run an airplane slowly along the ground under its own power
2 to go by taxicab

taxi•cab \ˈtak-sē-ˌkab\ *n*
▼ a vehicle that carries passengers for a fare usually based on the distance traveled

taxi•der•my \ˈtak-sə-ˌdər-mē\ *n*
the practice or job of preparing, stuffing, and mounting the skins of animals

tax•on•o•my \tak-ˈsä-nə-mē\ *n*
classification of living things (as plants and animals) using a system that is usually based on natural relationships

tax•pay•er \ˈtaks-ˌpā-ər\ *n*
a person who pays or is responsible for paying a tax

TB \tē-ˈbē\ *n*
TUBERCULOSIS

T–ball \ˈtē-ˌbȯl\ *n*
baseball for young children in which the ball is batted from a tee rather than being pitched

tbs., tbsp. *abbr* tablespoon

tea \ˈtē\ *n*
1 the dried leaves and leaf buds of a shrub widely grown in eastern and southern Asia

tea 2: a cup of tea

2 ▲ a drink made by soaking tea in boiling water
3 refreshments often including tea served in late afternoon
4 a party at which tea is served
5 a drink or medicine made by soaking plant parts (as dried roots) ⟨ginger *tea*⟩

teach \ˈtēch\ *vb* **taught** \ˈtȯt\; **teach•ing**
1 to help in learning how to do something : show how ⟨He *taught* me to swim.⟩
2 to guide the studies of ⟨A substitute is *teaching* the class today.⟩
3 to give lessons in ⟨She *teaches* math.⟩
4 to cause to know the unpleasant results of something ⟨That will *teach* you to talk back.⟩

▶ **Synonyms** TEACH, INSTRUCT, and TRAIN mean to cause to gain knowledge or skill. TEACH can be used of any method of passing on information or skill so that others may learn. ⟨She agreed to *teach* me how to play.⟩ INSTRUCT is used when the teaching is done in a formal or orderly manner. ⟨Teachers will *instruct* all students in the sciences.⟩ TRAIN is used for instruction with a particular purpose in mind. ⟨An engineer *trained* workers to operate the new machines.⟩

teach•er \ˈtē-chər\ *n*
a person who passes on information or skill

taxicab

teaching *n*
1 the duties or profession of a teacher
2 something taught ⟨We studied the philosopher's *teachings.*⟩
tea•cup \'tē-ˌkəp\ *n*
a cup used with a saucer for hot drinks
teak \'tēk\ *n*
the hard yellowish-brown wood of a tall Asian tree that resists decay
tea•ket•tle \'tē-ˌke-tᵊl\ *n*
a covered pot that is used for boiling water and has a handle and spout
teal \'tēl\ *n*
a small wild duck of America and Europe
[1]team \'tēm\ *n*
1 ▶ a group of persons who work or play together ⟨a *team* of scientists⟩ ⟨a football *team*⟩
2 two or more animals used to pull the same vehicle or piece of machinery
[2]team *vb* **teamed**; **team•ing**
to form a team ⟨They *teamed* up to get the job done.⟩
team•mate \'tēm-ˌmāt\ *n*
a person who belongs to the same team as someone else
team•ster \'tēm-stər\ *n*
a worker who drives a team or a truck
team•work \'tēm-ˌwərk\ *n*
the work of a group of persons acting together ⟨Cleaning up the neighborhood will require *teamwork.*⟩
tea•pot \'tē-ˌpät\ *n*
▼ a pot for making and serving tea

teapot

[1]tear \'tir\ *n*
1 a drop of the salty liquid that moistens the eyes and the inner eyelids and that flows from the eyes when someone is crying
2 *pl* an act of crying ⟨I burst into *tears.*⟩
[2]tear \'ter\ *vb* **tore** \'tȯr\; **torn** \'tȯrn\; **tear•ing**
1 to pull into two or more pieces by force ⟨This paper is easy to *tear.*⟩
2 to wound or injure by or as if by tearing : LACERATE ⟨Use an ointment where you *tore* the skin.⟩

[1]team 1: players from two teams in a soccer game

3 to remove by force ⟨I *tore* the notice from the wall.⟩
4 to move powerfully or swiftly ⟨A car *tore* up the street.⟩
tear down to knock down and break into pieces ⟨The old school was *torn down.*⟩
[3]tear \'ter\ *n*
damage from being torn ⟨This blanket has a *tear* in it.⟩
tear•drop \'tir-ˌdräp\ *n*
[1]TEAR
tear•ful \'tir-fəl\ *adj*
flowing with, accompanied by, or causing tears ⟨a *tearful* goodbye⟩
tear•ful•ly \-fə-lē\ *adv*
[1]tease \'tēz\ *vb* **teased**; **teas•ing**
1 to make fun of
2 to annoy again and again ⟨Stop *teasing* the dog.⟩
synonyms see ANNOY
teas•er *n*
[2]tease *n*
1 the act of making fun of or repeatedly bothering a person or animal
2 a person who makes fun of people usually in a friendly way
tea•spoon \'tē-ˌspün\ *n*
1 a small spoon used especially for stirring drinks
2 a unit of measure used in cooking equal to 1/6 fluid ounce or 1/3 tablespoon (about 5 milliliters)

tea•spoon•ful \'tē-ˌspün-ˌfu̇l\ *n*, *pl* **teaspoonfuls** \-ˌfu̇lz\ *also* **tea•spoons•ful** \-ˌspünz-ˌfu̇l\
1 as much as a teaspoon can hold
2 TEASPOON
teat \'tit, 'tēt\ *n*
NIPPLE 1 — used mostly of domestic animals
tech•ni•cal \'tek-ni-kəl\ *adj*
1 having special knowledge especially of a mechanical or scientific subject ⟨a *technical* expert⟩
2 relating to a practical or scientific subject ⟨a *technical* book on electronics⟩
3 according to a strict explanation of the rules or facts ⟨a *technical* knockout in boxing⟩
tech•ni•cal•ly *adv*
tech•ni•cal•i•ty \ˌtek-nə-'ka-lə-tē\ *n*, *pl* **tech•ni•cal•i•ties**
something that is understood only by a person with special training ⟨a legal *technicality*⟩

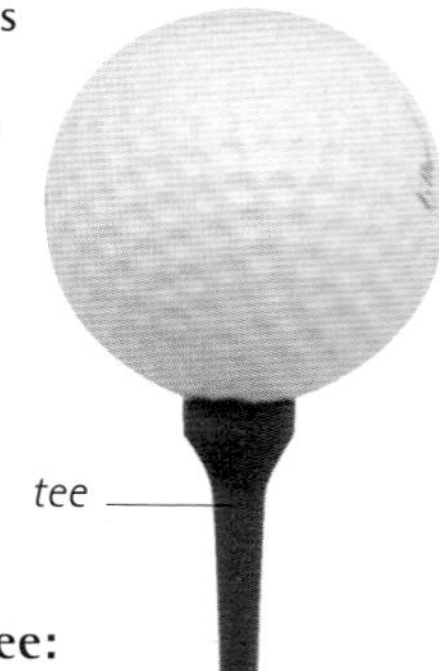

tee: a golf ball on its tee

technical sergeant *n*
a noncommissioned officer in the air force ranking above a staff sergeant

tech•ni•cian \tek-'ni-shən\ *n*
a person skilled in the details or techniques of a subject, art, or job ⟨A dental *technician* helps the dentist.⟩

tech•nique \tek-'nēk\ *n*
1 the way in which basic physical movements or skills are used ⟨The players practiced basic *techniques.*⟩
2 the ability to use basic physical movements and skills ⟨The pianist is admired for her *technique.*⟩
3 a way of doing something using special knowledge or skill ⟨Here's a good *technique* to help you relax.⟩

tech•no•log•i•cal \,tek-nə-'lä-ji-kəl\ *adj*
of or relating to technology

tech•nol•o•gist \tek-'nä-lə-jəst\ *n*
a person who specializes in technology

tech•nol•o•gy \tek-'nä-lə-jē\ *n, pl* **tech•nol•o•gies**
1 the use of science in solving problems (as in industry or engineering)
2 a method of or machine for doing something that is created by technology

teddy bear

ted•dy bear \'te-dē-\ *n*
▲ a stuffed toy bear

te•dious \'tē-dē-əs, 'tē-jəs\ *adj*
tiring because of length or dullness ⟨a *tedious* explanation⟩ ⟨a *tedious* job⟩
te•dious•ly *adv*
te•dious•ness *n*

tee \'tē\ *n*
◀ a device (as a post or peg) on which a ball is placed to be hit or kicked in various sports ⟨a golf *tee*⟩ ⟨a football *tee*⟩

teem \'tēm\ *vb* **teemed; teem•ing**
to be full of something ⟨The streams *teemed* with fish.⟩

teen•age \'tēn-,āj\ *or* **teen•aged** \-,ājd\ *adj*
being or relating to teenagers ⟨*teenage* styles⟩

teen•ag•er \'tēn-,ā-jər\ *n*
a person between the ages of 13 and 19

teens \'tēnz\ *n pl*
the years 13 through 19 in a person's life

tee•ny \'tē-nē\ *adj* **tee•ni•er; tee•ni•est**
TINY

tee shirt *variant of* T-SHIRT

tee•ter \'tē-tər\ *vb* **tee•tered; tee•ter•ing**
to move unsteadily back and forth or from side to side

tee•ter–tot•ter \'tē-tər-,tä-tər\ *n*
[1]SEESAW 1

teeth *pl of* TOOTH

teethe \'tēth\ *vb* **teethed; teeth•ing**
to experience the growth of teeth through the gums

TEFL *abbr* teaching English as a foreign language

tele- *or* **tel-** *prefix*
1 at a distance ⟨*tele*gram⟩
2 television
3 using a telephone ⟨*tele*marketing⟩

tele•gram \'te-lə-,gram\ *n*
a message sent by telegraph

[1]**tele•graph** \'te-lə-,graf\ *n*
▼ an electric device or system for sending messages by a code over connecting wires

[2]**telegraph** *vb* **tele•graphed; tele•graph•ing**
1 to send by code over connecting wires
2 to send a telegram to

tele•mar•ket•ing \,te-lə-'mär-kə-tiŋ\ *n*
the act of selling goods or services by telephone

te•lep•a•thy \tə-'le-pə-thē\ *n*
a way of communicating thoughts directly from one mind to another without speech or signs

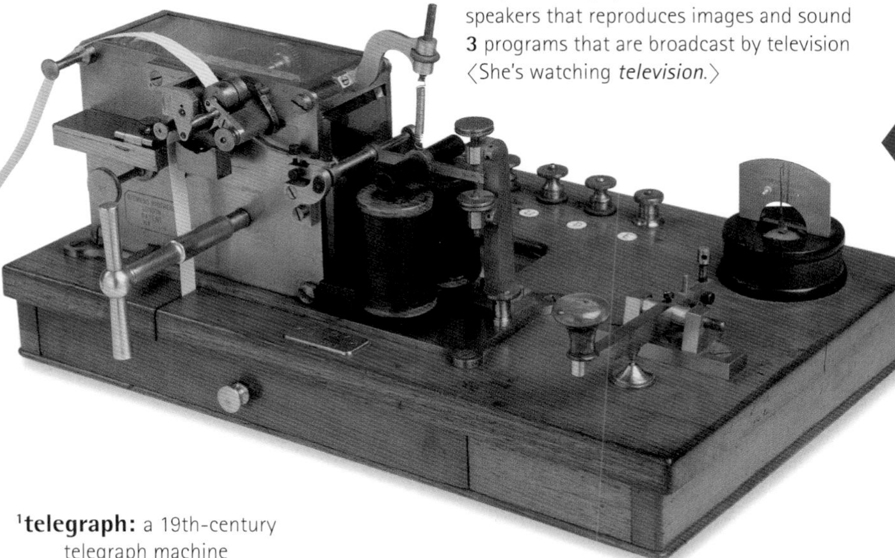
[1]**telegraph:** a 19th-century telegraph machine

[1]**telephone**

[1]**tele•phone** \'te-lə-,fōn\ *n*
▲ a device for transmitting and receiving sounds over long distances

[2]**telephone** *vb* **tele•phoned; tele•phon•ing**
to speak to by telephone

[1]**tele•scope** \'te-lə-,skōp\ *n*
a piece of equipment shaped like a long tube that has lenses for viewing objects at a distance and especially for observing objects in outer space

[2]**telescope** *vb* **tele•scoped; tele•scop•ing**
to slide or force one part into another

tele•vise \'te-lə-,vīz\ *vb* **tele•vised; tele•vis•ing**
to send (a program) by television

tele•vi•sion \'te-lə-,vi-zhən\ *n*
1 an electronic system of sending images and sound over a wire or through space by devices that change light and sound into electrical signals and then change these back into light and sound
2 a piece of equipment with a screen and speakers that reproduces images and sound
3 programs that are broadcast by television ⟨She's watching *television.*⟩

teller 2: a teller (right) dealing with a customer

tell \'tel\ *vb* **told** \'tōld\; **tell•ing**
1 to let a person know something : to give information to ⟨*Tell* them the news.⟩
2 [1]ORDER 2 ⟨The policeman *told* us to wait.⟩
3 to find out by observing ⟨My little brother has learned to *tell* time.⟩
4 [1]SAY 1 ⟨Don't *tell* a lie.⟩
5 to describe in detail ⟨*tell* a story⟩
6 to make known ⟨*tell* a secret⟩
7 to bring the bad behavior of to the attention of an authority ⟨Don't *tell* on me.⟩
8 [1]COUNT 1 ⟨All *told* there were 27 of us.⟩
9 to have a noticeable result ⟨The pressure began to *tell* on them.⟩
10 to act as evidence ⟨They had smiles *telling* of success.⟩
11 to see or understand the differences between two people or things ⟨Can you *tell* right from wrong?⟩
12 to see or know (something) with certainty ⟨It's hard to *tell* if he's serious.⟩

tell•er \'te-lər\ *n*
1 a person who tells stories : NARRATOR
2 ▲ a bank employee who receives and pays out money
3 a person who counts votes

tell•tale \'tel-,tāl\ *adj*
indicating or giving evidence of something

[1]**temper** \'tem-pər\ *n*
1 characteristic state of feeling ⟨She has a very even *temper.*⟩
2 calmness of mind ⟨I lost my *temper.*⟩
3 a tendency to become angry ⟨Try to control your *temper.*⟩
4 the hardness or toughness of a substance (as metal)

[2]**temper** *vb* **tem•pered**; **tem•per•ing**
1 to make less severe or extreme : SOFTEN ⟨Mountains *temper* the wind.⟩
2 to heat and cool a substance (as steel) until it is as hard, tough, or flexible as is wanted

tem•per•a•ment \'tem-pə-rə-mənt, -prə-mənt\ *n*
a person's attitude as it affects what he or she says or does ⟨a nervous *temperament*⟩

tem•per•a•men•tal \,tem-pə-rə-'men-tᵊl, -prə-'men-tᵊl\ *adj*
1 likely to become angry or upset
2 unpredictable in behavior or performance ⟨a *temperamental* car⟩
tem•per•a•men•tal•ly *adv*

tem•per•ance \'tem-pə-rəns, -prəns\ *n*
1 control over actions, thoughts, or feelings
2 the use of little or no liquor

tem•per•ate \'tem-pə-rət, -prət\ *adj*
1 keeping or held within limits : not extreme or excessive ⟨*temperate* pride⟩
2 not drinking much liquor
3 showing self-control ⟨Though angry, he used *temperate* language.⟩
4 having a mild climate that is not too hot or too cold

tem•per•a•ture \'tem-pə-rə-,chu̇r, -prə-,chu̇r, -pə-,chu̇r, -chər\ *n*
1 degree of hotness or coldness as measured on a scale
2 abnormally high body heat : FEVER

tem•pest \'tem-pəst\ *n*
1 a strong wind often accompanied by rain, hail, or snow
2 UPROAR

tem•pes•tu•ous \tem-'pes-chə-wəs\ *adj*
very stormy

[1]**tem•ple** \'tem-pəl\ *n*
a building for worship

[2]**temple** *n*
▶ the flattened space on either side of the forehead

tem•po \'tem-pō\ *n, pl* **tem•pi** \-,pē\ *or* **tempos**
the rate of speed at which a musical composition is played or sung

tem•po•rary \'tem-pə-,rer-ē\ *adj*
not permanent ⟨We performed on a *temporary* stage.⟩
tem•po•rar•i•ly \,tem-pə-'rer-ə-lē\ *adv*

tempt \'tempt\ *vb* **tempt•ed**; **tempt•ing**
to consider or cause to consider doing something wrong or unwise ⟨Sometimes in nice weather, she is *tempted* to skip school.⟩ ⟨He *tempted* me to cheat.⟩
tempt•er *n*

temp•ta•tion \temp-'tā-shən\ *n*
1 the act of considering or causing to consider doing something wrong or unwise
2 a strong desire ⟨a *temptation* for candy⟩
3 something that causes a strong desire ⟨The money was a *temptation.*⟩

[1]**ten** \'ten\ *adj*
being one more than nine

[2]**ten** *n*
1 one more than nine : two times five : 10
2 the tenth in a set or series

te•na•cious \tə-'nā-shəs\ *adj*
1 PERSISTENT ⟨a *tenacious* fighter⟩
2 not easily pulled apart

te•nac•i•ty \tə-'na-sə-tē\ *n*
the quality or state of being persistent ⟨The dog held his bone with *tenacity.*⟩

[1]**ten•ant** \'te-nənt\ *n*
a person or business that rents property from its owner

[2]**tenant** *vb* **ten•ant•ed**; **ten•ant•ing**
to hold or live in as a renter

[1]**tend** \'tend\ *vb* **tend•ed**; **tend•ing**
1 to take care of ⟨She *tends* the garden.⟩
2 to pay attention ⟨*tend* to business⟩
3 to manage the operation of ⟨Who's *tending* the store?⟩

[2]**tend** *vb* **tended**; **tending**
1 to be likely ⟨She *tends* to sleep late.⟩
2 to move or turn in a certain direction ⟨The road *tends* to the right.⟩

temple

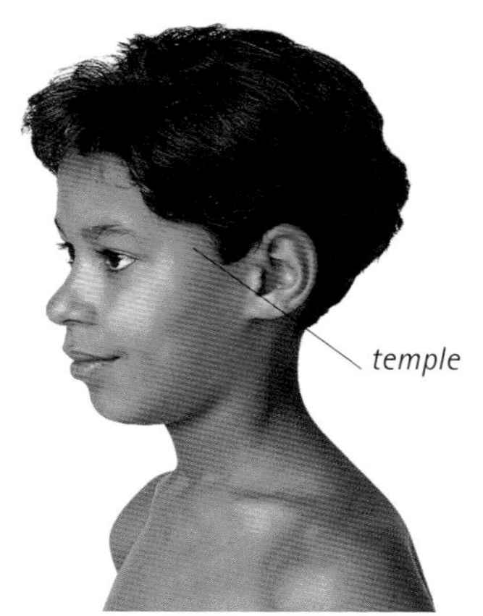

[2]temple

ten•den•cy \'ten-dən-sē\ *n, pl* **ten•den•cies**
1 a leaning toward a particular kind of thought or action ⟨He has a *tendency* to ask a lot of questions.⟩
2 a way of doing something that is becoming more common : TREND

[1]ten•der \'ten-dər\ *adj* **ten•der•er; ten•der•est**
1 not tough ⟨a *tender* steak⟩
2 DELICATE 4 ⟨*tender* plants⟩
3 [1]YOUNG 1 ⟨He left home at a *tender* age.⟩
4 feeling or showing love ⟨a *tender* look⟩
5 very easily hurt ⟨a *tender* scar⟩
ten•der•ly *adv*
ten•der•ness *n*

[2]tender *vb* **ten•dered; ten•der•ing**
1 to offer in payment
2 to present for acceptance ⟨She *tendered* her resignation.⟩

support
tendril

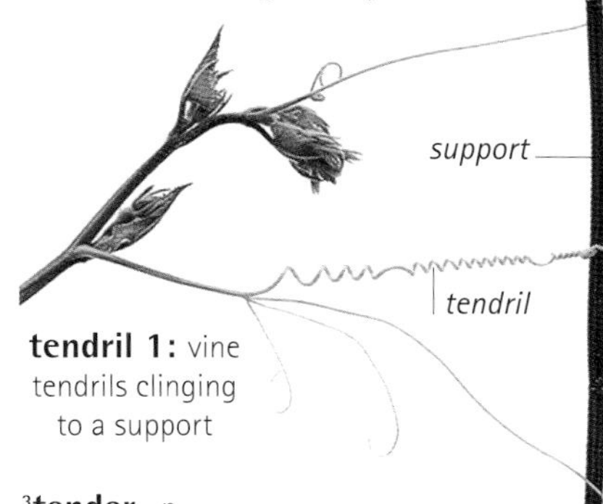

tendril 1: vine tendrils clinging to a support

[3]tender *n*
1 [2]OFFER 3
2 something (as money) that may be offered in payment

[4]tend•er \'ten-dər\ *n*
1 a boat that carries passengers or freight to a larger ship
2 a car attached to a locomotive for carrying fuel or water

ten•der•heart•ed \,ten-dər-'här-təd\ *adj* easily affected with feelings of love, pity, or sorrow

ten•don \'ten-dən\ *n* a band of tough white fiber connecting a muscle to another part (as a bone)

ten•dril \'ten-drəl\ *n*
1 ◀ a slender leafless winding stem by which some climbing plants attach themselves to a support
2 something that winds like a plant's tendril ⟨*tendrils* of hair⟩

ten•e•ment \'te-nə-mənt\ *n* a building divided into separate apartments for rent

Tenn. *abbr* Tennessee

ten•nis \'te-nəs\ *n* ▼ a game played on a level court by two or four players who use rackets to hit a ball back and forth across a low net dividing the court

ten•or \'te-nər\ *n*
1 the next to the lowest part in harmony having four parts
2 the highest male singing voice
3 a singer or an instrument having a tenor range or part

tennis

Played indoors and outdoors, tennis is a popular racket sport in which a tennis ball is hit between players on a court using strokes such as the forehand or backhand. A player wins a point when his or her opponent fails to return a ball in bounds.

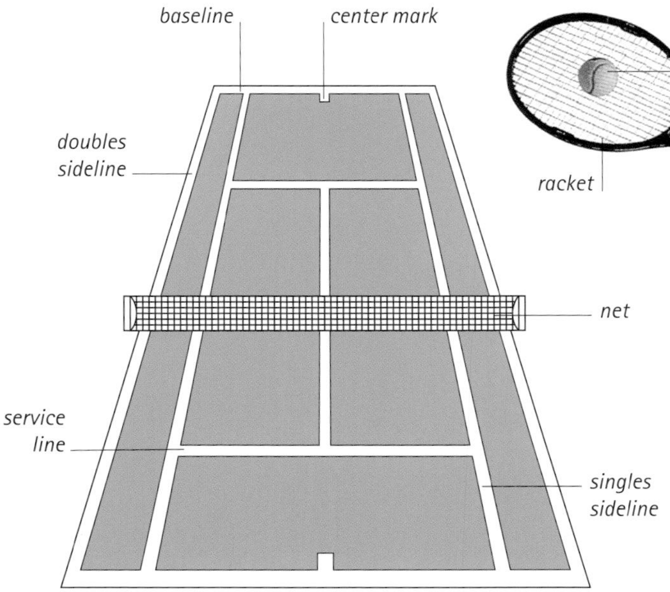

baseline
center mark
doubles sideline
net
service line
singles sideline

diagram of a tennis court

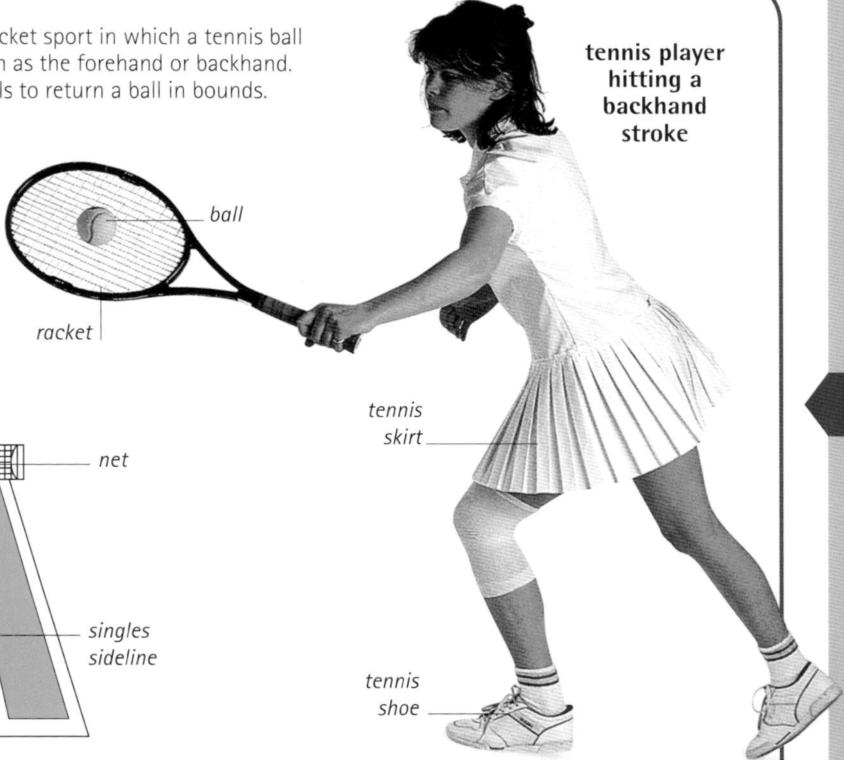

ball
racket
tennis skirt
tennis shoe

tennis player hitting a backhand stroke

a b c d e f g h i j k l m n o p q r s t u v w x y z

[1]**tense** \ˈtens\ *n*
a form of a verb used to show the time of the action or state

[2]**tense** *adj* **tens•er; tens•est**
1 feeling or showing worry or nervousness **:** not relaxed ⟨a *tense* smile⟩
2 marked by strain or uncertainty ⟨a *tense* moment⟩
3 stretched tight ⟨*tense* muscles⟩
tense•ly *adv*
tense•ness *n*

[3]**tense** *vb* **tensed; tens•ing**
1 to make or become worried or nervous ⟨She *tensed* as the deadline grew near.⟩
2 to make (a muscle) hard and tight ⟨She *tensed* her shoulders.⟩

ten•sion \ˈten-shən\ *n*
1 the act of straining or stretching **:** the condition of being strained or stretched ⟨I adjusted the strap's *tension.*⟩
2 a state of worry or nervousness
3 a state of unfriendliness

tent

tent \ˈtent\ *n*
▲ a portable shelter (as of canvas) stretched and supported by poles

ten•ta•cle \ˈten-tə-kəl\ *n*
one of the long thin flexible parts that stick out around the head or the mouth of an animal (as a jellyfish or sea anemone) and are used especially for feeling or grasping

ten•ta•tive \ˈten-tə-tiv\ *adj*
1 not final ⟨*tentative* plans⟩
2 showing caution or hesitation
ten•ta•tive•ly *adv*

tent caterpillar *n*
a caterpillar that lives in groups which spin a large silken web resembling a tent

[1]**tenth** \ˈtenth\ *adj*
coming right after ninth ⟨*tenth* grade⟩

[2]**tenth** *n*
1 number ten in a series
2 one of ten equal parts

te•pee \ˈtē-ˌpē\ *n*
► a tent shaped like a cone and used as a home by some American Indians

tep•id \ˈte-pəd\ *adj*
LUKEWARM 1 ⟨*tepid* water⟩

[1]**term** \ˈtərm\ *n*
1 a word or expression that has an exact meaning in some uses or is limited to a subject or field ⟨legal *terms*⟩
2 a period of time fixed especially by law or custom ⟨a school *term*⟩
3 terms *pl* conditions that limit the nature and scope of something (as a treaty or a will) ⟨the *terms* of a contract⟩
4 terms *pl* relationship between people ⟨I'm on good *terms* with the neighbors.⟩
5 any one of the numbers in a series
6 the numerator or denominator of a fraction

[2]**term** *vb* **termed; term•ing**
to call by a particular name ⟨He *termed* them liars.⟩

[1]**ter•mi•nal** \ˈtər-mə-nᵊl\ *adj*
relating to or forming an end ⟨branches with *terminal* buds⟩

[2]**terminal** *n*
1 either end of a transportation line or a passenger or freight station located at it ⟨the bus *terminal*⟩
2 a device (as in a computer system) used to put in, receive, and display information ⟨He typed his request into the *terminal.*⟩
3 a device at the end of a wire or on a machine for making an electrical connection

ter•mi•nate \ˈtər-mə-ˌnāt\ *vb* **ter•mi•nat•ed; ter•mi•nat•ing**
[2]END, CLOSE ⟨I *terminated* my membership.⟩

ter•mi•na•tion \ˌtər-mə-ˈnā-shən\ *n*
1 the end of something
2 the act of ending something

abdomen

antenna

termite: model of a termite

ter•mi•nus \ˈtər-mə-nəs\ *n, pl* **ter•mi•ni** \-ˌnī, -ˌnē\ *or* **ter•mi•nus•es**
1 an ending point
2 the end of a travel route
3 a station at the end of a travel route

ter•mite \ˈtər-ˌmīt\ *n*
▲ a chewing insect resembling an ant that lives in large colonies and feeds on wood

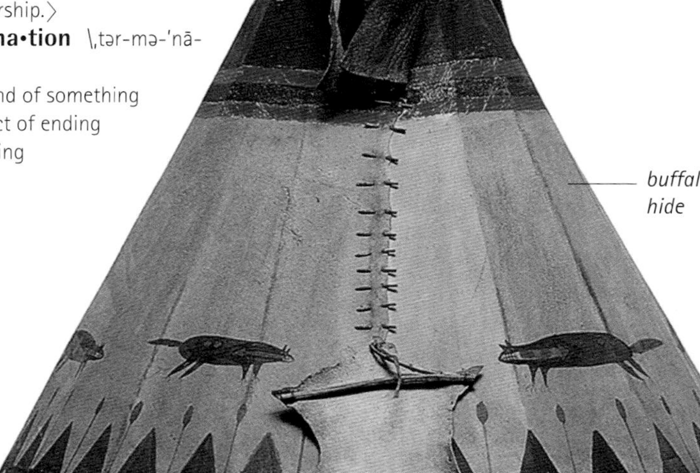

tepee: model of a traditional tepee

A B C D E F G H I J K L M N O P Q R S T U V W X Y Z

▶ **terrier**
There are many breeds of terrier. They are often found exploring and digging tunnels, and make spirited and loyal pets.

tern \'tərn\ *n*
a small slender seagull with black cap, white body, and narrow wings

[1]ter•race \'ter-əs\ *n*
1 a level area next to a building
2 a raised piece of land with the top leveled ⟨Rice is planted in *terraces* on sides of the hill.⟩
3 a row of houses on raised ground or a slope

[2]terrace *vb* **ter•raced; ter•rac•ing**
to form into a terrace or supply with terraces ⟨Rice growers *terrace* hillsides.⟩

ter•rain \tə-'rān\ *n*
▶ the features of the surface of a piece of land ⟨hilly *terrain*⟩ ⟨swampy *terrain*⟩

ter•ra•pin \'ter-ə-pən\ *n*
▼ a North American turtle that lives in or near fresh or somewhat salty water

terrapin: a red-eared terrapin

ter•rar•i•um \tə-'rer-ē-əm\ *n, pl* **ter•rar•ia** \-ē-ə\ *or* **ter•rar•i•ums**
a usually glass container used for keeping plants or small animals (as turtles) indoors

ter•res•tri•al \tə-'re-strē-əl\ *adj*
1 relating to the earth or its people
2 living or growing on land ⟨*terrestrial* birds⟩

ter•ri•ble \'ter-ə-bəl\ *adj*
1 very great in degree ⟨a *terrible* fright⟩ ⟨a *terrible* mess⟩
2 very bad ⟨I got a *terrible* grade on the test.⟩
3 causing great fear ⟨a *terrible* monster⟩
ter•ri•bly \-blē\ *adv*

ter•ri•er \'ter-ē-ər\ *n*
◀ a usually small dog originally used by hunters to force animals from their holes

▶ **Word History** Terriers were first used in hunting. Their job was to dig for small animals and force them from their holes. The word *terrier* comes from a medieval French phrase *chen terrer* (or *chien terrier*), literally, "earth dog." The *terr-* in *terrier* comes ultimately from Latin *terra*, "earth."

ter•rif•ic \tə-'ri-fik\ *adj*
1 EXCELLENT ⟨That's a *terrific* idea.⟩
2 very unusual : EXTRAORDINARY ⟨The car was going at *terrific* speed.⟩
3 causing terror : TERRIBLE ⟨The storm caused *terrific* damage.⟩

ter•ri•fy \'ter-ə-,fī\ *vb* **ter•ri•fied; ter•ri•fy•ing**
to cause (someone) to become very frightened

ter•ri•to•ri•al \,ter-ə-'tòr-ē-əl\ *adj*
1 of or relating to a territory ⟨a *territorial* government⟩
2 displaying behavior associated with defending an animal's territory ⟨My dog is very *territorial.*⟩

terrain: rocky and sandy terrain in Death Valley, California

A B C D E F G H I J K L M N O P Q R S T U V W X Y Z

ter•ri•to•ry \'ter-ə-ˌtȯr-ē\ *n, pl* **ter•ri•to•ries**
1 a geographical area belonging to or under the rule of a government
2 a part of the United States not included within any state but organized with a separate governing body
3 REGION 1, DISTRICT
4 an area that is occupied and defended by an animal or group of animals

ter•ror \'ter-ər\ *n*
1 a state of great fear ⟨They fled in *terror.*⟩
2 a cause of great fear

ter•ror•ism \'ter-ər-ˌi-zəm\ *n*
the use of violence as a means of achieving a goal

ter•ror•ist \'ter-ər-ist\ *n*
someone who engages in terrorism

ter•ror•ize \'ter-ər-ˌīz\ *vb* **ter•ror•ized**; **ter•ror•iz•ing**
1 to fill with fear
2 to use terrorism against

terse \'tərs\ *adj* **ters•er**; **ters•est**
being brief and to the point ⟨a *terse* statement⟩
terse•ly *adv*

[1]**test** \'test\ *n*
1 a set of questions or problems by which a person's knowledge, intelligence, or skills are measured
2 a means of finding out the nature, quality, or value of something ⟨Separation was a *test* of their friendship.⟩

► **Word History** The English word *test* first meant "a small bowl used in analyzing metals." It came from a Latin word *testum* that meant "a bowl or pot made of clay." The bowl called a *test* was used to examine things. That is why the word *test* came to mean "examination."

[2]**test** *vb* **test•ed**; **test•ing**
1 to measure a person's knowledge, intelligence, or skills
2 to find out the nature, quality, or value of something

tes•ta•ment \'te-stə-mənt\ *n*
1 either of two main parts (**Old Testament** and **New Testament**) of the Bible
2 [2]WILL 4

tes•ti•fy \'te-stə-ˌfī\ *vb* **tes•ti•fied**; **tes•ti•fy•ing**
to make a formal statement of something sworn to be true ⟨Two witnesses *testified* in court.⟩

tes•ti•mo•ny \'te-stə-ˌmō-nē\ *n, pl* **tes•ti•mo•nies**
a statement made by a witness under oath especially in a court

tes•tis \'te-stəs\ *n, pl* **tes•tes** \'te-ˌstēz\
a male reproductive gland that produces sperm

test tube *n*
► a plain tube of thin glass closed at one end and used especially in chemistry and biology

sulfur
iron

test tube containing iron and sulfur

tet•a•nus \'te-tə-nəs, 'tet-nəs\ *n*
a serious disease that is marked by spasms of the muscles especially of the jaws and that is caused by poison from a bacterium that usually enters the body through a wound

[1]**teth•er** \'te-t͟hər\ *vb* **teth•ered**; **teth•er•ing**
to fasten by a line that limits range of movement

[2]**tether** *n*
a line by which something is fastened so as to limit where it can go

Tex. *abbr* Texas

[1]**text** \'tekst\ *n*
1 the actual words of an author's work
2 the main body of printed or written matter on a page
3 TEXTBOOK
4 a passage from the Bible chosen as the subject of a sermon
5 TEXT MESSAGE

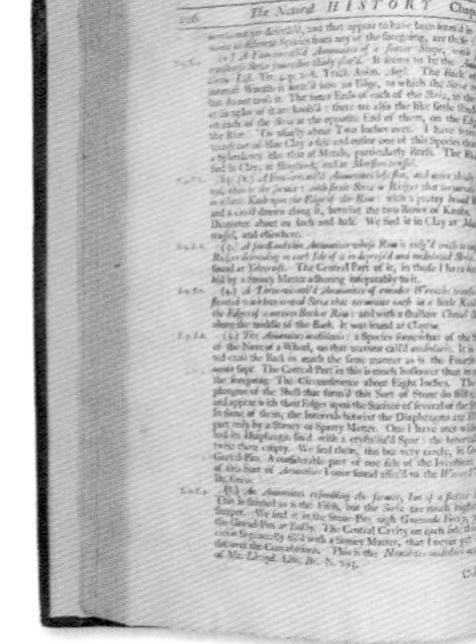

textbook: an old textbook with illustrations of shells

[2]**text** *vb* **text•ed**; **text•ing**
1 to send (someone) a text message
2 to communicate by text messaging

text•book \'tekst-ˌbu̇k\ *n*
▼ a book used in the study of a subject

text message *n*
a short message that is sent electronically to a cell phone or other device

text messaging \-'me-si-jiŋ\ *n*
the sending of messages electronically usually from one cell phone to another

tex•tile \'tek-ˌstīl, 'tek-stəl\ *n*
a woven or knit cloth

tex•ture \'teks-chər\ *n*
the structure, feel, and appearance of something

-th \th\ *or* **-eth** \əth\ *adj suffix*
used to form numbers that show the place of something in a series ⟨hundred*th*⟩ ⟨forti*eth*⟩

than \t͟hən, 't͟han\ *conj*
when compared to the way in which, the extent to which, or the degree to which ⟨You are older *than* I am.⟩

thank \'thaŋk\ *vb* **thanked**; **thank•ing**
1 to express gratitude to
2 to hold responsible

thank•ful \'thaŋk-fəl\ *adj*
1 feeling or showing thanks : GRATEFUL
2 GLAD 1
thank•ful•ly \-fə-lē\ *adv*
thank•ful•ness *n*

theater 1: actors performing in an open-air theater at Theodore Roosevelt National Park, North Dakota

thank•less \'thaŋk-ləs\ *adj*
1 UNGRATEFUL
2 not appreciated 〈a *thankless* job〉

thanks \'thaŋks\ *n pl*
1 GRATITUDE 〈Let me express my *thanks*.〉
2 an expression of gratitude (as for something received)
thanks to
1 with the help of
2 because of

thanks•giv•ing \thaŋks-'gi-viŋ\ *n*
1 *cap* THANKSGIVING DAY
2 a prayer or an expression of gratitude

Thanksgiving Day *n*
the fourth Thursday in November observed as a legal holiday for giving thanks

[1]**that** \'that\ *pron, pl* **those** \'thōz\
1 the person or thing seen, mentioned, or understood 〈I'm sure *that* is my book.〉
2 the time, action, or event mentioned 〈Wash up, and after *that*, you can eat.〉
3 the one farther away 〈This is an elm, *that* is a hickory.〉
4 the one : the kind 〈The richest ore is *that* found higher up.〉

[2]**that** \thət, 'that\ *conj*
1 used to introduce a clause that modifies a noun or adjective 〈I'm sure *that* it is so.〉
2 used to introduce a clause that modifies an adverb or adverbial expression 〈He'll go anywhere *that* he is invited.〉
3 used to introduce a noun clause serving especially as the subject or object of a verb 〈He said *that* he wasn't afraid.〉
4 [2]SO 1 〈She shouted *that* all might hear.〉
5 used to introduce a clause naming a result 〈I was so hungry *that* I fainted.〉
6 BECAUSE 〈He is glad *that* you came.〉

[3]**that** *adj, pl* **those**
1 being the one mentioned, indicated, or understood 〈*that* boy〉 〈*those* people〉
2 being the one farther away 〈this book or *that* one〉 〈these crayons or *those*〉

[4]**that** \thət, 'that\ *pron*
1 WHO 2, WHOM, WHICH 〈the person *that* won the race〉 〈the people *that* you saw〉 〈the food *that* I like〉
2 in, on, or at which 〈the year *that* I moved〉

[5]**that** \'that\ *adv*
to the extent or degree shown (as by the hands) 〈The table is about *that* high.〉

[1]**thatch** \'thach\ *n*
a plant material (as straw) for use as roofing

[2]**thatch** *vb* **thatched; thatch•ing**
to cover (a roof) with dried plant material

[1]**thaw** \'thȯ\ *vb* **thawed; thaw•ing**
1 to melt or cause to melt
2 to grow less unfriendly or quiet in manner

[2]**thaw** *n*
1 a period of weather warm enough to melt ice and snow
2 the action, fact, or process of becoming less hostile or unfriendly

[1]**the** *especially before consonant sounds* thə, *before vowel sounds* thē, *4 is often* 'thē\ *definite article*
1 that or those mentioned, seen, or clearly understood 〈I'll take *the* red one.〉
2 that or those near in space, time, or thought 〈What's *the* news?〉
3 [1]EACH 〈There are 40 cookies to *the* box.〉
4 that or those considered best, most typical, or most worth singling out 〈She is *the* person for this job.〉
5 any one typical of or standing for the entire class named 〈Here are useful tips for *the* beginner.〉
6 all those that are 〈*the* British〉

[2]**the** *adv*
1 than before 〈I'm none *the* wiser for it.〉
2 to what extent : by how much 〈*The* faster you go, the sooner you'll finish.〉
3 to that extent : by that much 〈The more you think, *the* more you'll learn.〉

the•ater *or* **the•atre** \'thē-ə-tər\ *n*
1 ▲ a building in which plays, motion pictures, or shows are presented
2 the art or profession of producing plays
3 plays or the performance of plays
4 a place or area where some important action is carried on 〈a *theater* of war〉

a b c d e f g h i j k l m n o p q r s t u v w x y z

the•at•ri•cal \thē-ˈa-tri-kəl\ *adj*
for or relating to the presentation of plays ⟨a *theatrical* production⟩ ⟨*theatrical* costumes⟩

thee \ˈthē\ *pron, objective case of* THOU
⟨"my country, 'tis of *thee*"⟩

theft \ˈtheft\ *n*
the act of stealing

their \thər, ˈther\ *adj*
of or relating to them or themselves especially as owners or as agents or objects of an action ⟨*their* clothes⟩ ⟨*their* deeds⟩

theirs \ˈtherz\ *pron*
that which belongs to them ⟨The red house is *theirs*.⟩

them \thəm, ˈthem\ *pron*
objective case of THEY

theme \ˈthēm\ *n*
1 a subject of a work of art, music, or literature
2 a specific quality, characteristic, or concern ⟨The room is decorated in a tropical *theme*.⟩
3 a written exercise : ESSAY

theme park *n*
▼ an amusement park in which the rides and buildings are based on a central subject

them•selves \thəm-ˈselvz\ *pron*
their own selves ⟨They enjoyed *themselves*.⟩ ⟨The students did it *themselves*.⟩

[1]then \ˈthen\ *adv*
1 at that time ⟨People *then* believed in dragons.⟩
2 soon after that : NEXT ⟨Go two blocks, *then* turn left.⟩
3 in addition : BESIDES ⟨*Then* there are the dishes to wash.⟩
4 in that case ⟨Take it, *then*, if you want it so badly.⟩
5 as an expected result ⟨If you were there, *then* you must have seen me.⟩

[2]then *n*
that time ⟨Wait until *then*.⟩

[3]then *adj*
existing or acting at that time ⟨the *then* president⟩

thence \ˈthens\ *adv*
1 from that place ⟨First go home, and *thence* to the hospital.⟩
2 from that fact ⟨The answer follows *thence*.⟩

thence•forth \ˈthens-ˌfȯrth\ *adv*
from that time on

the•ol•o•gy \thē-ˈä-lə-jē\ *n, pl* **the•ol•o•gies**
the study and explanation of religious faith, practice, and experience

the•o•ry \ˈthē-ə-rē, ˈthir-ē\ *n, pl* **the•o•ries**
1 an idea or opinion that is presented as true ⟨Nobody knows where he went, but each of us has a *theory*.⟩
2 a general rule offered to explain a scientific phenomenon ⟨the *theory* of gravity⟩
3 the general rules followed in a science or an art ⟨music *theory*⟩

ther•a•peu•tic \ˌther-ə-ˈpyü-tik\ *adj*
MEDICINAL

ther•a•pist \ˈther-ə-pəst\ *n*
a person specializing in treating disorders or injuries of the body or mind especially in ways that do not involve drugs and surgery

ther•a•py \ˈther-ə-pē\ *n, pl* **ther•a•pies**
treatment of a disorder or injury of the body or mind

[1]there \ˈther\ *adv*
1 in or at that place ⟨Stand over *there*.⟩
2 to or into that place ⟨Take the basket *there* and leave it.⟩
3 in that situation or way ⟨*There* I disagree with you.⟩
4 used to show satisfaction, soothing, or defiance ⟨*There, there*, it's all right.⟩ ⟨So *there*!⟩
5 used to attract attention ⟨*There*, look at that!⟩

[2]there *pron*
used to introduce a sentence in which the subject comes after the verb ⟨*There* is a person outside.⟩

theme park: visitors at a dinosaur theme park in Hollywood, California

[3]there *n*
that place ⟨Get away from *there.*⟩

there•abouts \ˌther-ə-ˈbau̇ts\ *also* **there•about** \-ˈbau̇t\ *adv*
1 near that place or time ⟨There was a cabin *thereabouts.*⟩
2 near that number, degree, or amount ⟨The temperature reached 100 degrees or *thereabouts.*⟩

there•af•ter \ther-ˈaf-tər\ *adv*
after that

there•by \ther-ˈbī\ *adv*
by that ⟨He tripped and *thereby* lost the race.⟩

there•fore \ˈther-ˌfȯr\ *adv*
for that reason ⟨She is sick and *therefore* will be absent.⟩

there•in \ther-ˈin\ *adv*
in or into that place, time, or thing ⟨He owns the house and all that is *therein.*⟩

there•of \ther-ˈəv, -ˈäv\ *adv*
of that or it ⟨Our teacher explained the problem and the solution *thereof.*⟩

there•on \ther-ˈȯn, -ˈän\ *adv*
on that ⟨The road and the signs *thereon.*⟩

there•to \ther-ˈtü\ *adv*
to that

there•up•on \ˈther-ə-ˌpȯn, -ˌpän\ *adv*
1 on that thing ⟨They found the tree and *thereupon* the tree house.⟩
2 for that reason ⟨I apologized and *thereupon* we made up.⟩
3 immediately after that : at once ⟨They ate and *thereupon* left.⟩

there•with \ther-ˈwith, -ˈwith\ *adv*
with that ⟨Here's the letter and the picture enclosed *therewith.*⟩

ther•mal \ˈthər-məl\ *adj*
of, relating to, or caused by heat ⟨*thermal* insulation⟩

ther•mom•e•ter \thər-ˈmä-mə-tər, thə-ˈmä-\ *n*
▶ an instrument for measuring temperature

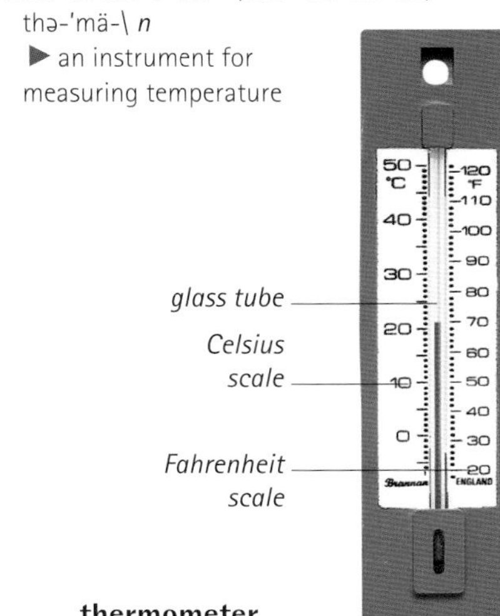

thermometer

ther•mos \ˈthər-məs\ *n*
a container (as a bottle or jar) that has a vacuum between an inner and an outer wall and is used to keep liquids hot or cold for several hours

ther•mo•stat \ˈthər-mə-ˌstat\ *n*
a device that automatically controls temperature

the•sau•rus \thi-ˈsȯr-əs\ *n, pl* **the•sau•ri** \-ˈsȯr-ˌī, -ˌē\ *or* **the•sau•rus•es** \-ˈsȯr-ə-səz\
a book of words and their synonyms

these *pl of* THIS

the•sis \ˈthē-səs\ *n, pl* **the•ses** \-ˌsēz\
1 a statement that a person wants to discuss or prove
2 an essay presenting results of original research

they \ˈthā\ *pron*
those individuals : those ones

they'd \ˈthād\
they had : they would ⟨*They'd* be glad to let you stay.⟩

they'll \ˈthāl\
they shall : they will ⟨*They'll* be here soon.⟩

they're \thər, ˈther\
they are ⟨*They're* my friends.⟩

they've \ˈthāv\
they have ⟨*They've* left me.⟩

thi•a•mine *also* **thi•a•min** \ˈthī-ə-mən\ *n*
a type of vitamin B that is used by the body to convert carbohydrates into energy and to maintain normal nerve function

[1]thick \ˈthik\ *adj* **thick•er; thick•est**
1 having great size from one surface to its opposite ⟨a *thick* wall⟩
2 closely packed together ⟨*thick* hair⟩ ⟨a *thick* clump of bushes⟩
3 heavily built ⟨a *thick* neck⟩
4 not flowing easily ⟨a *thick* milk shake⟩
5 measuring a certain amount in the smallest of three dimensions ⟨two millimeters *thick*⟩
6 producing speech that is hard to understand ⟨She speaks with a *thick* accent.⟩
7 STUPID 1
8 occurring in large numbers : NUMEROUS ⟨Mosquitoes were *thick* in the swamp.⟩
9 having haze, fog, or mist ⟨The air was *thick.*⟩
10 too intense to see in ⟨*thick* darkness⟩
synonyms see DENSE
thick•ly *adv*

[2]thick *n*
1 the most crowded or active part ⟨The soldier was in the *thick* of the battle.⟩
2 the part of greatest thickness ⟨the *thick* of the thumb⟩

thicket: a thicket of canes

thick•en \ˈthi-kən\ *vb* **thick•ened; thick•en•ing**
to make or become thick ⟨Wait for the pudding to *thicken.*⟩
thick•en•er *n*

thick•et \ˈthi-kət\ *n*
▲ a thick usually small patch of bushes or low trees

thick•ness \ˈthik-nəs\ *n*
1 the quality or state of being thick
2 the smallest of three dimensions ⟨length, width, and *thickness*⟩

thick•set \ˈthik-ˌset\ *adj*
STOCKY

thief \ˈthēf\ *n, pl* **thieves** \ˈthēvz\
a person who steals : ROBBER

thieve \ˈthēv\ *vb* **thieved; thiev•ing**
[1]STEAL 1, ROB

thiev•ery \ˈthē-və-rē\ *n*
THEFT

thigh \ˈthī\ *n*
the part of a leg between the hip and the knee

thim•ble \ˈthim-bəl\ *n*
▶ a cap or cover used in sewing to protect the finger that pushes the needle

thimble

[1]thin \'thin\ *adj* **thin•ner; thin•nest**
1 having little body fat
2 having little size from one surface to its opposite : not thick 〈a *thin* board〉
3 having the parts not close together 〈*thin* hair〉
4 flowing very easily 〈a *thin* soup〉
5 having less than the usual number 〈Attendance was *thin.*〉
6 not very convincing 〈a *thin* excuse〉
7 somewhat weak or high 〈a *thin* voice〉
8 having less oxygen than normal 〈*thin* air〉
synonyms see LEAN
thin•ly *adv*
thin•ness *n*

[2]thin *vb* **thinned; thin•ning**
to make or become smaller in thickness or number 〈The crowd was beginning to *thin.*〉

thine \'thīn\ *pron*
YOURS
Hint: *Thine* is a very old word that still appears in books and sayings from long ago. People also use it today especially to imitate that old way of speaking. *Thine* can be used as a singular or a plural.

thing \'thiŋ\ *n*
1 an act or matter that is or is to be done 〈I have a *thing* or two to take care of.〉 〈You did the right *thing.*〉
2 something that exists and can be talked about 〈Nouns name people and *things.*〉 〈Say the first *thing* that pops into your mind.〉 〈How do you work this *thing?*〉
3 **things** *pl* personal possessions 〈Pack your *things,* we're leaving.〉
4 [1]DETAIL 2 〈He checks every little *thing.*〉
5 **things** *pl* existing conditions and circumstances 〈*Things* are improving.〉
6 EVENT 1 〈The accident was a terrible *thing.*〉
7 [1]DEED 1, ACHIEVEMENT, ACT 〈We expect great *things* from them.〉
8 a piece of clothing 〈not a *thing* to wear〉
9 what is needed or wanted 〈It's just the *thing* for a cold.〉
10 an action or interest especially that someone enjoys very much 〈Music is my *thing.*〉
11 [2]INDIVIDUAL 1 〈She's a cute little *thing.*〉
12 a spoken or written observation or point

think \'thiŋk\ *vb* **thought** \'thȯt\; **think•ing**
1 to have as an opinion or belief 〈I *think* you can do it.〉
2 to form or have in the mind 〈We were afraid to even *think* what had happened.〉
3 REMEMBER 1 〈I didn't *think* to ask.〉
4 to use the power of the mind to understand, find out, or decide 〈You're just not *thinking.*〉
5 to consider for some time : PONDER 〈I'm still *thinking* it over.〉
6 to invent something by thinking 〈She tried to *think* up an excuse.〉
7 to hold a strong feeling 〈They *think* highly of you.〉
8 to have as a plan 〈I *think* I'll call first.〉
9 to care about 〈I must *think* first of my family.〉
think•er *n*

thin•ner \'thi-nər\ *n*
a liquid used to thin paint

[1]third \'thərd\ *adj*
coming right after second

[2]third *n*
1 number three in a series
2 one of three equal parts

third person *n*
a set of words or forms (as pronouns or verb forms) referring to people or things that are not being addressed directly

[1]thirst \'thərst\ *n*
1 a feeling of dryness in the mouth and throat that accompanies a need for liquids
2 the bodily condition that produces thirst 〈die of *thirst*〉
3 a strong desire 〈a *thirst* for knowledge〉

[2]thirst *vb* **thirst•ed; thirst•ing**
1 to feel a need for liquids
2 to have a strong desire 〈They *thirst* for freedom.〉

thirsty \'thər-stē\ *adj* **thirst•i•er; thirst•i•est**
1 feeling a need for liquids
2 needing moisture 〈*thirsty* crops〉
3 having a strong desire : EAGER 〈The stray dog was *thirsty* for affection.〉
thirst•i•ly \'thər-stə-lē\ *adv*

[1]thir•teen \,thər-'tēn\ *adj*
being one more than twelve

[2]thirteen *n*
one more than twelve : 13

[1]thir•teenth \,thər-'tēnth\ *adj*
coming right after twelfth

[2]thirteenth *n*
number 13 in a series

[1]thir•ti•eth \'thər-tē-əth\ *adj*
coming right after 29th

[2]thirtieth *n*
number 30 in a series

[1]thir•ty \'thər-tē\ *adj*
being three times ten

[2]thirty *n*
three times ten : 30

[1]this \'this\ *pron, pl* **these** \'thēz\
1 the one nearer 〈I believe *this* is your book and that is mine.〉
2 the person, thing, or idea that is present or near in place, time, or thought or that has just been mentioned 〈*This* is where it happened.〉 〈*This* is your last chance.〉

[2]this *adj, pl* **these**
1 being the one present, near in place, time, or thought or that has just been mentioned 〈*this* morning〉 〈We've been friends all *these* years.〉
2 being the one nearer 〈Are you reading *this* book or that one?〉

[3]this \'this\ *adv*
1 to the degree suggested by something in the present situation 〈I didn't expect to wait *this* long.〉
2 to the extent shown (as with the hands) 〈I need a nail *this* long.〉

this•tle \'thi-səl\ *n*
▼ a prickly plant that has usually purplish often showy heads of flowers

thistle

thith•er \'thi-thər\ *adv*
to that place : THERE 〈We walked *thither* and back.〉

thong \'thȯŋ\ *n*
1 a strip of leather used especially for fastening something
2 a sandal held on by straps that run across the foot and between the big and second toe

tho•rax \'thȯr-,aks\ *n, pl* **tho•rax•es** *or* **tho•ra•ces** \'thȯr-ə-,sēz\
1 the part of the body of a mammal that lies between the neck and the abdomen and contains the heart and lungs
2 the middle of the three main divisions of the body of an insect

thorn \'thȯrn\ *n*
1 ▶ a hard sharp leafless point on the stem or branch of a plant (as a rose bush)
2 a bush or tree that has thorns

thorny \'thȯr-nē\ *adj* **thorn•i•er**; **thorn•i•est**
1 full of or covered with thorns
2 full of difficulties ⟨a *thorny* situation⟩

thor•ough \'thər-ō\ *adj*
1 being such to the fullest degree : COMPLETE ⟨a *thorough* search⟩
2 careful about little things ⟨a *thorough* worker⟩
thor•ough•ly *adv*
thor•ough•ness *n*

[1]**thor•ough•bred** \'thər-ō-ˌbred\ *adj*
PUREBRED

[2]**thoroughbred** *n*
1 *cap* a speedy horse of an English breed kept mainly for racing
2 a purebred animal
3 a very educated or skilled person

thor•ough•fare \'thər-ō-ˌfer\ *n*
1 a street or road open at both ends
2 a main road

thor•ough•go•ing \ˌthər-ə-'gō-iŋ\ *adj*
THOROUGH 1

those *pl of* THAT

thou \'t͟hau̇\ *pron*
YOU
Hint: *Thou* is a very old word that still appears in books and sayings from long ago. People also use it to imitate that old way of speaking.

[1]**though** \'t͟hō\ *conj*
ALTHOUGH 1 ⟨*Though* it was raining, we went out.⟩

[2]**though** *adv*
HOWEVER 3, NEVERTHELESS ⟨He's been quiet. Not for long, *though.*⟩

[1]**thought** *past and past participle of* THINK

[2]**thought** \'thȯt\ *n*
1 the act or process of thinking ⟨She was deep in *thought.*⟩
2 something (as an idea or opinion) formed in the mind ⟨What are your *thoughts* on the matter?⟩
3 serious attention ⟨Give *thought* to the future.⟩

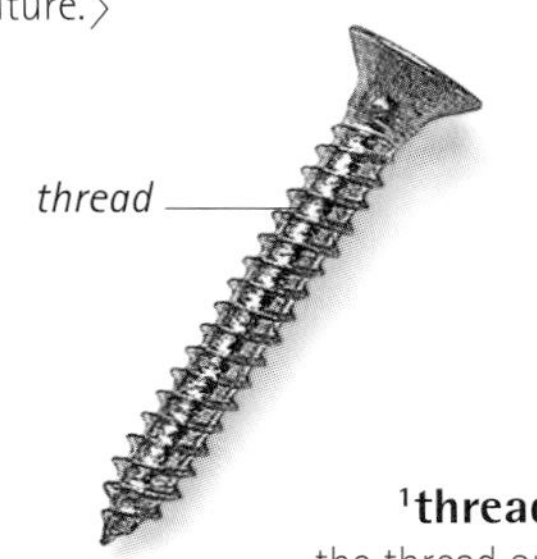

[1]**thread 3:**
the thread on a screw

thorn 1:
a twig with thorns

thought•ful \'thȯt-fəl\ *adj*
1 considerate of others
2 deep in thought
3 showing careful thinking ⟨a *thoughtful* essay⟩
thought•ful•ly \-fə-lē\ *adv*
thought•ful•ness *n*

thought•less \'thȯt-ləs\ *adj*
1 not considerate of others ⟨*thoughtless* behavior⟩
2 not careful and alert
3 done without thinking ⟨*thoughtless* actions⟩
thought•less•ly *adv*
thought•less•ness *n*

[1]**thou•sand** \'thau̇-zᵊnd\ *n*
1 ten times one hundred : 1000
2 a very large number ⟨*thousands* of things to do⟩

[2]**thousand** *adj*
being 1000

[1]**thou•sandth** \'thau̇-zᵊnth\ *adj*
coming right after 999th

[2]**thousandth** *n*
number 1000 in a series

thrash \'thrash\ *vb* **thrashed**; **thrash•ing**
1 to beat very hard
2 to move about violently ⟨Something was *thrashing* wildly in the brush.⟩
3 THRESH 1

thrash•er \'thra-shər\ *n*
an American bird (as the common reddish brown **brown thrasher**) related to the mockingbird and noted for its song

[1]**thread** \'thred\ *n*
1 a thin fine cord formed by spinning and twisting short fibers into a continuous strand
2 a thin fine line or strand of something ⟨a *thread* of light⟩
3 ◀ the ridge or groove that winds around a screw
4 a train of thought that connects the parts of something (as an argument or story)
thread•like \-ˌlīk\ *adj*

[2]**thread** *vb* **thread•ed**; **thread•ing**
1 to put a thread in working position (as in a needle)
2 to pass something through another thing ⟨*Thread* the film through the camera.⟩
3 to make a way through or between
4 to put together on a thread : STRING

thread•bare \'thred-ˌber\ *adj*
1 worn so much that the thread shows : SHABBY
2 not effective because of overuse ⟨a *threadbare* excuse⟩

threat \'thret\ *n*
1 the act of showing an intention to do harm
2 someone or something that threatens ⟨the *threat* of punishment⟩

threat•en \'thre-tᵊn\ *vb* **threat•ened**; **threat•en•ing**
1 to show an intention to do harm or something unwanted ⟨He *threatened* to quit.⟩
2 to give warning of by an indication ⟨The clouds *threatened* rain.⟩
threat•en•ing•ly *adv*

[1]**three** \'thrē\ *adj*
being one more than two

[2]**three** *n*
1 one more than two : 3
2 the third in a set or series

3–D \'thrē-'dē\ *adj*
THREE-DIMENSIONAL 2 ⟨a *3-D* movie⟩

three–dimensional *adj*
1 ▼ relating to or having the three dimensions of length, width, and height ⟨A cube is *three-dimensional.*⟩
2 giving the appearance of depth or varying distances ⟨a *three-dimensional* movie⟩

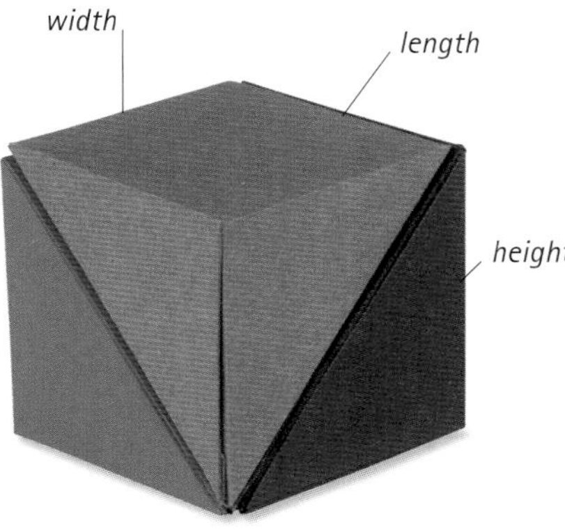

three-dimensional 1:
a cube is a three-dimensional object

three•fold \'thrē-ˌfōld\ *adj*
being three times as great or as many

three•score \'thrē-ˌskȯr\ *adj*
[1]SIXTY

thresh \'thrash, 'thresh\ *vb* **threshed**; **thresh•ing**
1 to separate the seed from a harvested plant by beating ⟨*threshing* wheat⟩
2 THRASH 2

thresh•er \'thra-shər, 'thre-\ *n*
THRESHING MACHINE

threshing machine *n*
a machine used to separate grain from harvested plants

thresh•old \'thresh-ˌhōld\ *n*
1 the sill of a door
2 a point or place of beginning or entering ⟨She is at the *threshold* of an adventure.⟩

threw *past of* THROW

thrice \'thrīs\ *adv*
three times

thrift \'thrift\ *n*
careful management especially of money

thrifty \'thrif-tē\ *adj* **thrift•i•er**; **thrift•i•est**
carefully and wisely managing money
synonyms see ECONOMICAL

[1]**thrill** \'thril\ *vb* **thrilled**; **thrill•ing**
to have or cause to have a sudden feeling of excitement or pleasure
thrill•er *n*

► **Word History** In the 1300s a person who was *thrilled* might not live long enough to tell about it, because the Middle English verb *thrillen*—the ancestor of our word *thrill*—meant literally "to pierce" or "stab," as with a sword or spear. *Thrillen* was a variant of *thirlen,* which continued Old English *thyrlian,* derived from *thyrel,* "hole." (The word *thyrel* also entered into Old English *nosthyrl,* literally, "nose hole," the ancestor of modern English *nostril.*) Because the feeling of being pierced is a little like the experience of being moved by a strong emotion, *thrill* came to mean "to cause someone to feel excited."

[2]**thrill** *n*
1 a sudden strong feeling especially of excitement or happiness ⟨the *thrill* of victory⟩
2 something that produces a feeling of excitement ⟨The boys went into town in search of *thrills.*⟩

thrive \'thrīv\ *vb* **thrived** *or* **throve** \'thrōv\; **thrived** *also* **thriv•en** \'thri-vən\; **thriv•ing** \'thrī-viŋ\
to grow or develop very well : FLOURISH ⟨Cacti *thrive* in dry conditions.⟩ ⟨Business is *thriving.*⟩

throat \'thrōt\ *n*
1 the passage through the neck from the mouth to the stomach and lungs ⟨a sore *throat*⟩
2 the front part of the neck on the outside

throaty \'thrō-tē\ *adj* **throat•i•er**; **throat•i•est**
uttered or produced in deep low tones ⟨a *throaty* whisper⟩

[1]**throb** \'thräb\ *vb* **throbbed**; **throb•bing**
1 to feel repeated pangs of pain ⟨My head is *throbbing.*⟩
2 to beat hard or fast ⟨Our hearts *throbbed* from fright.⟩
3 to beat or rotate in a normal way ⟨The motor *throbbed* quietly.⟩

[2]**throb** *n*
1 [2]BEAT 2, PULSE
2 pain that comes in repeated pangs

throne \'thrōn\ *n*
1 ▼ the chair used by a monarch or bishop for ceremonies
2 the position of king or queen

throne 1:
a 19th-century throne from Portugal

[1]**throng** \'thrȯŋ\ *n*
a large group of people : CROWD

[2]**throng** *vb* **thronged**; **throng•ing**
[1]CROWD 4

[1]**throt•tle** \'thrä-tᵊl\ *vb* **throt•tled**; **throt•tling**
1 to strangle or choke (someone)
2 to reduce the speed of (an engine) by closing the throttle valve

[2]**throttle** *n*
a valve or a lever that controls the valve for regulating the flow of steam or fuel in an engine

[1]**through** \'thrü\ *prep*
1 into at one side and out at the other side of ⟨He drove a nail *through* the wood.⟩
2 from one side or end to another of ⟨We rode *through* town.⟩
3 by way of ⟨I got in *through* the window.⟩
4 AMONG 1 ⟨There's a path *through* the trees.⟩
5 by means of ⟨She succeeded *through* hard work.⟩
6 over the whole of ⟨The rumor swept *through* school.⟩
7 during the whole of ⟨The baby slept *through* the night.⟩
8 to and including ⟨We're open Monday *through* Friday.⟩
9 into and out of ⟨I'm *through* the worst of it.⟩

[2]**through** *adv*
1 from one end or side to the other ⟨The nail went *through.*⟩
2 from beginning to end ⟨He read the book *through* in one evening.⟩
3 to completion ⟨I plan to see the job *through.*⟩
4 in or to every part ⟨Heat the sauce *through.*⟩

[3]**through** *adj*
1 having reached an end ⟨We're *through* with the job.⟩
2 allowing free or continuous passage : DIRECT ⟨a *through* road⟩
3 going from point of origin to destination without changes or transfers ⟨*through* trains⟩
4 coming from and going to points outside a local zone ⟨*through* traffic⟩

[1]**through•out** \thrü-'au̇t\ *adv*
1 EVERYWHERE ⟨The apartments are of one color *throughout.*⟩
2 from beginning to end ⟨He remained loyal *throughout.*⟩

[2]**throughout** *prep*
1 in or to every part of ⟨We spent a year traveling *throughout* the country.⟩
2 during the whole period of ⟨It rained *throughout* the day.⟩

throve *past of* THRIVE

[1]**throw** \'thrō\ *vb* **threw** \'thrü\; **thrown** \'thrōn\; **throw•ing**
1 to send through the air with a quick forward motion of the arm ⟨*Throw* me a ball.⟩
2 to put suddenly in a certain position or condition ⟨Don't *throw* trash on the ground.⟩ ⟨They *threw* him in prison.⟩
3 to cause to fall ⟨The horse *threw* its rider.⟩
4 to put on or take off in a hurry ⟨Let me *throw* on a coat.⟩

A B C D E F G H I J K L M N O P Q R S T U V W X Y Z

5 to move (the body or part of the body) in a certain way ⟨I *threw* myself on the bed.⟩ ⟨He *threw* his arms around her.⟩
6 to move (as a window or switch) to an open or closed position
7 to give by way of entertainment ⟨Let's *throw* a party!⟩
throw•er *n*
throw away
1 to get rid of : DISCARD
2 SQUANDER, WASTE ⟨Don't *throw away* your money.⟩
throw out
1 to get rid of ⟨Did you *throw out* the newspaper?⟩
2 to remove from a place, position, or participation ⟨The ref *threw out* two players.⟩
3 to give off ⟨The wire *threw out* sparks.⟩
4 to cause to project : EXTEND ⟨He *threw out* his arms.⟩
throw up ^{2}VOMIT

▶ **Synonyms** THROW, TOSS, and HURL mean to cause something to move swiftly through space often by using the arm. THROW is the broadest word and can be used of almost any motion and driving force. ⟨The graduates *threw* their caps in the air.⟩ ⟨A crash *threw* the driver from the car.⟩ TOSS is used for a light or careless throwing of something. ⟨Let's *toss* a coin.⟩ ⟨He *tossed* the paper into the wastebasket.⟩ HURL is used when throwing with strong force. ⟨An angry mob *hurled* rocks.⟩

^{2}**throw** *n*
1 an act of causing something to move with a motion of the arm
2 the distance something is or may be sent with a motion of the arm

thrum \ˈthrəm\ *vb* **thrummed**; **thrum•ming**
to play a stringed instrument idly : STRUM

thrush \ˈthrəsh\ *n*
a usually brown bird that has a spotted breast and a melodious song

^{1}**thrust** \ˈthrəst\ *vb* **thrust**; **thrust•ing**
1 to push with force : SHOVE
2 PIERCE 1, STAB
3 EXTEND 1 ⟨He *thrust* out his arm.⟩
4 to press the acceptance of on someone ⟨New responsibilities were *thrust* on her.⟩

^{2}**thrust** *n*
1 a push or jab with a pointed weapon
2 a military attack
3 a forward or upward push

thru•way \ˈthrü-ˌwā\ *n*
EXPRESSWAY

Thu. *abbr* Thursday

^{1}**thud** \ˈthəd\ *n*
a dull sound : THUMP

^{2}**thud** *vb* **thud•ded**; **thud•ding**
to move, strike, or pound so as to make a dull sound

thug \ˈthəg\ *n*
a violent person or criminal

^{1}**thumb** \ˈthəm\ *n*
1 the short thick finger next to the forefinger
2 the part of a glove covering the thumb

^{2}**thumb** *vb* **thumbed**; **thumb•ing**
1 to turn the pages of quickly with the thumb
2 to seek or get (a ride) in a passing automobile by signaling with the thumb

thumb•tack \ˈthəm-ˌtak\ *n*
a tack with a broad flat head for pressing into a board or wall with the thumb

^{1}**thump** \ˈthəmp\ *vb* **thumped**; **thump•ing**
1 to strike or beat with something thick or heavy so as to cause a dull sound
2 to beat hard : POUND

^{2}**thump** *n*
1 a blow with something blunt or heavy
2 the sound made by or as if by a blow with something blunt or heavy

^{1}**thun•der** \ˈthən-dər\ *n*
1 the loud sound that follows a flash of lightning
2 a loud noise ⟨the *thunder* of drums⟩

^{2}**thunder** *vb* **thun•dered**; **thun•der•ing**
1 to produce thunder
2 to make a loud sound
3 ^{1}ROAR 1, SHOUT ⟨The audience *thundered* its approval.⟩

thun•der•bolt \ˈthən-dər-ˌbōlt\ *n*
▼ a flash of lightning and the thunder that follows it

thun•der•cloud \ˈthən-dər-ˌklau̇d\ *n*
a dark storm cloud that produces lightning and thunder

thun•der•head \ˈthən-dər-ˌhed\ *n*
a rounded mass of dark cloud with white edges often appearing before a thunderstorm

thun•der•show•er \ˈthən-dər-ˌshau̇-ər\ *n*
a shower with thunder and lightning

thun•der•storm \ˈthən-dər-ˌstȯrm\ *n*
a storm with thunder and lightning

thunderbolt: a thunderbolt over northwest England

thun•der•struck \'thən-dər-ˌstrək\ *adj*
stunned as if struck by a thunderbolt ⟨They were *thunderstruck* by the news.⟩

Thur., Thurs. *abbr* Thursday

Thurs•day \'thərz-dā, -dē\ *n*
the fifth day of the week

thus \'t͟həs\ *adv*
1 in this or that way
2 to this degree or extent : SO ⟨It's a mild winter *thus* far.⟩
3 because of this or that : THEREFORE ⟨He worked hard and *thus* succeeded.⟩

thwart \'thwȯrt\ *vb* **thwart•ed; thwart•ing**
to stop from happening or succeeding ⟨Police *thwarted* the crime.⟩

thy \'t͟hī\ *adj*
YOUR
Hint: *Thy* is a very old word that still appears in books and sayings from long ago. People also use it today to imitate that old way of speaking.

thyme \'tīm\ *n*
▼ a mint with tiny fragrant leaves used especially in cooking

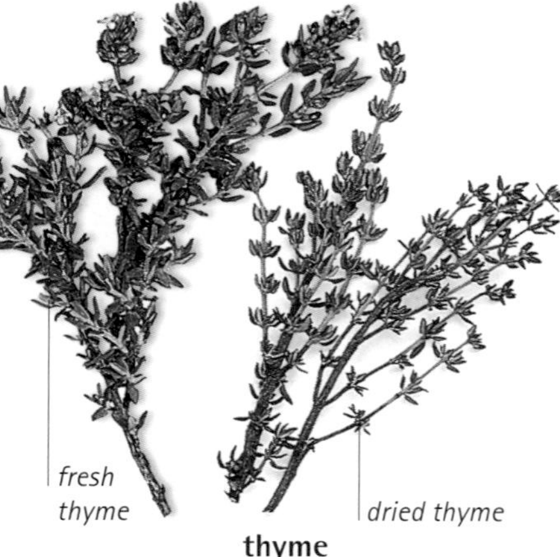

thyme

thy•roid \'thī-ˌrȯid\ *n*
a gland at the base of the neck that produces hormones which affect growth, development, and the rate at which the body uses energy

thy•self \t͟hī-'self\ *pron*
YOURSELF
Hint: *Thyself* is a very old word that still appears in books and sayings from long ago. People also use it today to imitate that old way of speaking.

ti \'tē\ *n*
the seventh note of the musical scale

tib•ia \'ti-bē-ə\ *n, pl* **tib•i•ae** \'ti-bē-ˌē, -bē-ˌī\ *also* **tib•i•as**
the inner and larger of the two bones between the knee and ankle

[1]tick \'tik\ *n*
1 a light rhythmic tap or beat (as of a clock)
2 a small mark used chiefly to draw attention to something or to check an item on a list

[2]tick *vb* **ticked; tick•ing**
1 to make a light rhythmic tap or a series of light rhythmic taps ⟨a *ticking* clock⟩
2 to mark, count, or announce by or as if by light rhythmic taps ⟨A meter *ticked* off the cab fare.⟩
3 [2]CHECK 5 ⟨She *ticked* off each item in the list.⟩
4 OPERATE 1, FUNCTION ⟨The old car is still *ticking*.⟩

[3]tick *n*
a tiny animal with eight legs that is related to the spider and attaches itself to humans and animals from which it sucks blood

[1]tick•et \'ti-kət\ *n*
1 a document or token showing that a fare or a fee for admission or participation has been paid ⟨a round trip *ticket*⟩ ⟨movie *tickets*⟩ ⟨a lottery *ticket*⟩
2 a summons or warning issued to a person who breaks a traffic law ⟨a speeding *ticket*⟩
3 a list of candidates for nomination or election
4 a slip or card recording a sale or giving information
5 the correct or desirable thing ⟨When school ended, a trip was just the *ticket*.⟩

[2]ticket *vb* **tick•et•ed; tick•et•ing**
1 to attach a tag to : LABEL
2 to give a traffic ticket to

[1]tick•le \'ti-kəl\ *vb* **tick•led; tick•ling**
1 to have a tingling or prickling sensation ⟨My nose *tickles*.⟩
2 to touch (a body part) lightly so as to cause laughter or jerky movements ⟨I *tickled* the baby's feet.⟩
3 to excite or stir up agreeably ⟨This food *tickles* my taste buds.⟩
4 AMUSE 2 ⟨We were *tickled* by his antics.⟩

[2]tickle *n*
a tingling or prickling sensation

tick•lish \'ti-klish\ *adj*
1 sensitive to tickling
2 calling for careful handling ⟨a *ticklish* situation⟩

tid•al \'tī-dᵊl\ *adj*
of or relating to tides : flowing and ebbing like tides

tidal wave *n*
1 a very high sea wave that sometimes follows an earthquake
2 an unusual rise of water along a shore due to strong winds

tid•bit \'tid-ˌbit\ *n*
1 a small tasty piece of food
2 a small interesting but unimportant bit (as of news)

[1]tide \'tīd\ *n*
1 the rising and falling of the surface of the ocean caused twice daily by the attraction of the sun and the moon
2 something that rises and falls or rushes in a mass ⟨The *tide* of public opinion often changes.⟩

▶ **Word History** The English word *tide* at first meant "time" or "a space of time." Later the word was used for the space of time between the rising and falling of the sea's surface. Then *tide* came to mean "the rising and falling of the sea." This is the most common meaning of the word today.

tiger

[2]tide *vb* **tid•ed; tid•ing**
to help to overcome or put up with a difficulty ⟨A snack will *tide* me over until dinner.⟩

tide pool *n*
a pool of salt water that is left behind when the tide goes out and in which small sea animals (as snails, crabs, and barnacles) are often found

tid•ings \'tī-diŋz\ *n pl*
NEWS 4

[1]ti•dy \'tī-dē\ *adj* **ti•di•er; ti•di•est**
1 well ordered and cared for : NEAT
2 LARGE, SUBSTANTIAL ⟨a *tidy* sum⟩
synonyms see NEAT
ti•di•ness *n*

▶ **Word History** The English word *tidy* comes from the word *tide*. *Tide* first meant "time," and *tidy* first meant "timely, at the proper time." Soon *tidy* came to mean "in good condition." The current meaning "neat" developed from this sense.

A B C D E F G H I J K L M O P Q R S T U V W X Y Z

²tidy *vb* **ti•died; ti•dy•ing**
to make things neat

¹tie \'tī\ *n*
1 NECKTIE
2 an equality in number (as of votes or scores) 〈The game ended in a *tie*.〉
3 a contest that ends with an equal score 〈They finished the season with six wins and two *ties*.〉
4 one of the cross supports to which railroad rails are fastened
5 a connecting link : BOND 〈family *ties*〉
6 a line, ribbon, or cord used for fastening, joining, or closing
7 a part (as a beam or rod) holding two pieces together

²tie *vb* **tied; ty•ing** \'tī-iŋ\ *or* **tie•ing**
1 to fasten, attach, or close by means of a tie
2 to form a knot or bow in
3 to bring together firmly : UNITE 〈They are *tied* by marriage.〉
4 to hold back from freedom of action 〈Obligations *tied* her down.〉
5 to make or have an equal score with in a contest

tier \'tir\ *n*
a row, rank, or layer usually arranged in a series one above the other

tiff \'tif\ *n*
a minor quarrel

ti•ger \'tī-gər\ *n*
◀ a large Asian meat-eating animal of the cat family that is light brown with black stripes

¹tight \'tīt\ *adj* **tight•er; tight•est**
1 very closely packed or compressed 〈a *tight* bundle〉 〈a *tight* fist〉
2 fixed or held very firmly in place 〈a *tight* jar cover〉
3 fitting too closely 〈*tight* shoes〉
4 firmly stretched or drawn : TAUT 〈Pull the rope until it's *tight*.〉
5 difficult to get through or out of 〈I'm in a *tight* spot.〉
6 firm in control 〈She keeps a *tight* hand on affairs.〉
7 STINGY 1
8 low in supply : SCARCE 〈Money is *tight* until I get paid.〉
9 painfully or uncomfortably tense 〈a *tight* throat〉
10 barely allowing enough time 〈a *tight* schedule〉
tight•ly *adv*
tight•ness *n*

²tight *adv*
1 in a firm, secure, or close manner 〈Shut the door *tight*.〉 〈Hold on *tight*.〉
2 in a deep and uninterrupted manner : SOUNDLY 〈Sleep *tight*.〉

tightrope: a street performer walking a tightrope in Mexico City, Mexico

tight•en \'tī-tᵊn\ *vb* **tight•ened; tight•en•ing**
to make or become tight 〈He *tightened* his grip.〉

tight•rope \'tīt-ˌrōp\ *n*
▲ a rope or wire stretched tight on which an acrobat performs

tights \'tīts\ *n pl*
a garment closely fitted to the body and covering it usually from the waist down

tight•wad \'tīt-ˌwäd\ *n*
a stingy person

ti•gress \'tī-grəs\ *n*
a female tiger

til•de \'til-də\ *n*
a mark ˜ placed especially over the letter *n* (as in Spanish *señor*) to indicate a sound that is approximately \nyə\

¹tile \'tīl\ *n*
1 a thin piece of material (as plastic, stone, or clay) used for roofs, walls, floors, or drains
2 a small flat piece used in a game

²tile *vb* **tiled; til•ing**
to cover with tiles

¹till \'til\ *prep or conj*
UNTIL 〈Wait *till* later.〉

²till *vb* **tilled; till•ing**
to work by plowing, sowing, and raising crops on 〈Farm workers *till* the fields.〉

³till *n*
a drawer for money

till•age \'ti-lij\ *n*
the practice of working land by plowing, sowing, and raising crops on

¹til•ler \'ti-lər\ *n*
▶ a lever used to turn the rudder of a boat from side to side

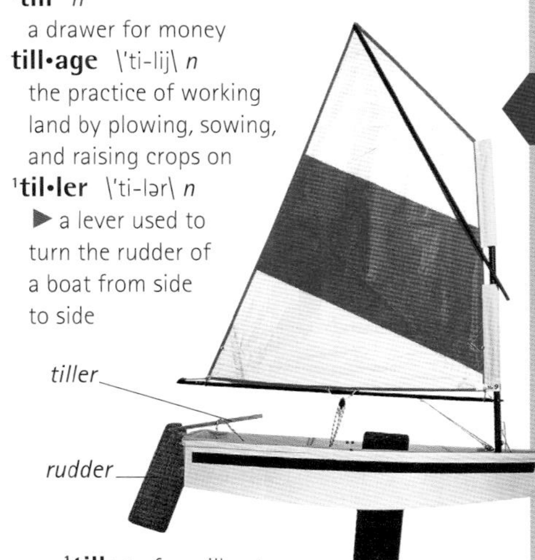

¹tiller of a sailboat

[2]tiller *n*
someone or something that tills land

[1]tilt \'tilt\ *vb* **tilt•ed**; **tilt•ing**
to move or shift so as to slant or tip ⟨She *tilted* her head to one side.⟩

[2]tilt *n*
1 [2]SLANT
2 [1]SPEED 2 ⟨We were traveling at full *tilt.*⟩

tim•ber \'tim-bər\ *n*
1 wood suitable for building or for carpentry
2 a large squared piece of wood ready for use or forming part of a structure

tim•ber•land \'tim-bər-,land\ *n*
▶ wooded land especially as a source of timber

tim•ber•line \'tim-bər-,līn\ *n*
the upper limit beyond which trees do not grow (as on mountains)

[1]time \'tīm\ *n*
1 a period during which an action, process, or condition exists or continues ⟨We've been friends for a long *time.*⟩
2 a point or period when something occurs : OCCASION ⟨Remember the *time* I helped you?⟩
3 one of a series of repeated instances or actions ⟨They visited him many *times.*⟩
4 a moment, hour, day, or year as shown by a clock or calendar ⟨What *time* is it?⟩
5 a set or usual moment or hour for something to occur ⟨We arrived on *time.*⟩ ⟨It's *time* to take your medicine.⟩
6 a historical period : AGE ⟨in ancient *times*⟩
7 conditions of a period — usually used in pl. ⟨hard *times*⟩
8 times *pl* added quantities or examples ⟨five *times* greater⟩
9 a person's experience during a certain period ⟨She had a good *time.*⟩
10 a part of the day when a person is free to do as he or she pleases ⟨I found *time* to read.⟩
11 rate of speed : TEMPO
12 a system of determining time ⟨solar *time*⟩
13 RHYTHM
at times SOMETIMES ⟨We were, *at times,* very happy.⟩
for the time being for the present
from time to time once in a while
in time
1 soon enough
2 as time goes by : EVENTUALLY ⟨The missing items will reappear *in time.*⟩
3 at the correct speed in music
time after time over and over again
time and again over and over again

[2]time *vb* **timed**; **tim•ing**
1 to arrange or set the point or rate at which something happens ⟨The dryer was *timed* to run for half an hour.⟩

timberland: trees being sawed in a timberland

2 to measure or record the point at which something happens, the length of the period it takes for something to happen, or the rate at which certain actions take place ⟨All the racers were *timed.*⟩
tim•er *n*

time capsule *n*
a container holding records or objects representative of a current culture that is put in a safe place for discovery in the future

time•keep•er \'tīm-,kē-pər\ *n*
an official who keeps track of the time in a sports contest

time•less \'tīm-ləs\ *adj*
not restricted to a certain historical period ⟨a *timeless* story⟩

time•ly \'tīm-lē\ *adj* **time•li•er**; **time•li•est**
1 coming early or at the right time ⟨a *timely* payment⟩
2 especially suitable to the time ⟨a *timely* book⟩

time–out \'tīm-'au̇t\ *n*
1 a short period during a game in which play is stopped
2 a quiet period used as a way to discipline a child

time•piece \'tīm-,pēs\ *n*
a device (as a clock or watch) to measure the passing of time

times \'tīmz\ *prep*
multiplied by ⟨2 *times* 4 is 8⟩

time•ta•ble \'tīm-,tā-bəl\ *n*
a table telling when something (as a bus or train) is scheduled to leave or arrive

time zone *n*
a geographic region within which the same standard time is used

tim•id \'ti-məd\ *adj*
feeling or showing a lack of courage or self-confidence : SHY ⟨a *timid* deer⟩ ⟨a *timid* smile⟩
tim•id•ly *adv*
tim•id•ness *n*

tim•ing \'tī-miŋ\ *n*
the time when something happens or is done especially when it is thought of as having a good or bad effect on the result

tim•o•rous \'ti-mə-rəs\ *adj*
easily frightened : FEARFUL
tim•o•rous•ly *adv*

tin \'tin\ *n*
1 a soft bluish white metallic chemical element used chiefly in combination with other metals or as a coating to protect other metals
2 something (as a can or sheet) made from tinplate ⟨a *tin* of cookies⟩

tin•der \'tin-dər\ *n*
material that burns easily and can be used as kindling

tin•foil \'tin-ˌfȯil\ *n*
a thin metal sheeting usually of aluminum or an alloy of tin and lead

[1]**tinge** \'tinj\ *n, pl* **ting•es**
a slight coloring, flavor, or quality ⟨The walls were gray with a bluish *tinge.*⟩

[2]**tinge** *vb* **tinged; tinge•ing**
to color or flavor slightly

[1]**tin•gle** \'tiŋ-gəl\ *vb* **tin•gled; tin•gling**
to feel or cause a prickling or thrilling sensation

[2]**tingle** *n*
a prickling or thrilling sensation or condition

tin•ker \'tiŋ-kər\ *vb* **tin•kered; tin•ker•ing**
to repair or adjust something in an unskilled or experimental manner

[1]**tin•kle** \'tiŋ-kəl\ *vb* **tin•kled; tin•kling**
to make or cause to make short high ringing or clinking sounds

[2]**tinkle** *n*
a short high ringing or clinking sound

tin•plate \'tin-'plāt\ *n*
thin steel sheets covered with tin

tin•sel \'tin-səl\ *n*
1 ▼ a thread or strip of metal or plastic used for decoration
2 something that seems attractive but is of little worth

tinsel 1: a decoration made of strips of tinsel

tin•smith \'tin-ˌsmith\ *n*
a worker in tin or sometimes other metals

[1]**tint** \'tint\ *n*
1 a slight or pale coloring
2 a shade of a color

[2]**tint** *vb* **tint•ed; tint•ing**
to give a tint to : COLOR

ti•ny \'tī-nē\ *adj* **ti•ni•er; ti•ni•est**
very small

[1]**tip** \'tip\ *n*
1 the usually pointed end of something ⟨the *tip* of a knife blade⟩
2 a small piece or part serving as an end, cap, or point ⟨the *tip* of an arrow⟩

[2]**tip** *vb* **tipped; tip•ping**
1 to turn over ⟨They *tipped* the canoe.⟩
2 to bend from a straight position : SLANT ⟨She *tipped* her head to the side.⟩
3 to raise and tilt forward ⟨He *tips* his hat.⟩

[3]**tip** *n*
a piece of useful or secret information

[4]**tip** *n*
a small sum of money given for a service

[5]**tip** *vb* **tipped; tip•ping**
to give a small sum of money for a service ⟨We *tipped* the waiter.⟩

[6]**tip** *vb* **tipped; tip•ping**
1 to attach an end or point to
2 to cover or decorate the tip of

[1]**tip•toe** \'tip-ˌtō\ *n*
► the position of being balanced on the balls of the feet and toes with the heels raised — usually used with *on* ⟨He stood on *tiptoe.*⟩

[2]**tiptoe** *adv or adj*
on or as if on the balls of the feet and toes with the heels raised ⟨I walked *tiptoe* past the dog.⟩

[3]**tiptoe** *vb* **tip•toed; tip•toe•ing**
to walk on the balls of the feet and toes with the heels raised

[1]**tip•top** \'tip-'täp\ *adj*
EXCELLENT, FIRST-RATE ⟨I'm in *tiptop* shape.⟩

[2]**tiptop** *n*
the highest point

[1]**tire** \'tīr\ *vb* **tired; tir•ing**
1 to make or become weary
2 to lose or cause to lose patience or attention : BORE

[2]**tire** *n*
▼ a rubber cushion that usually contains compressed air and fits around a wheel (as of an automobile)

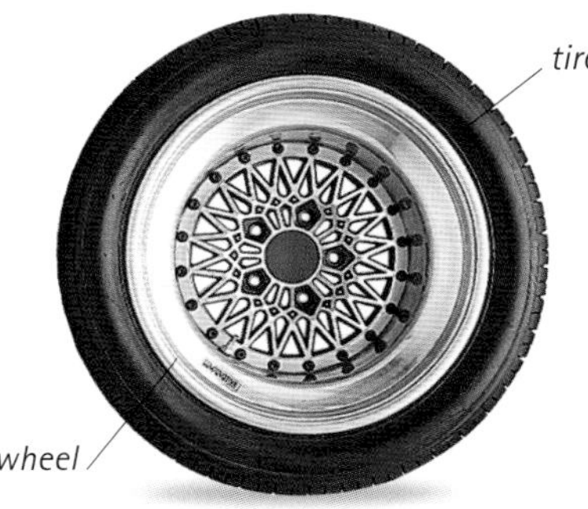

[2]**tire:** an automobile tire

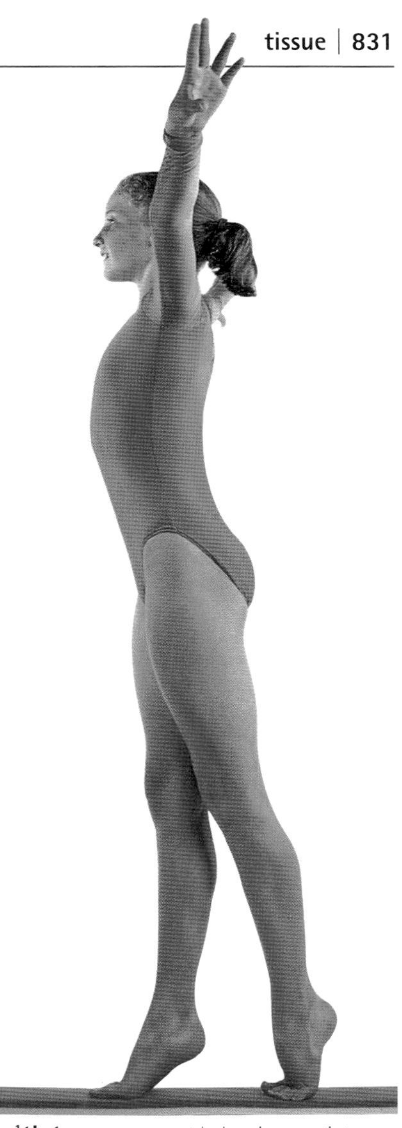

[1]**tiptoe:** a gymnast balancing on tiptoe

tired \'tīrd\ *adj*
needing rest : WEARY

tire•less \'tīr-ləs\ *adj*
able to work or persist a long time without becoming tired
tire•less•ly *adv*

tire•some \'tīr-səm\ *adj*
causing boredom, annoyance, or impatience because of length or dullness ⟨a *tiresome* lecture⟩

'tis \'tiz\
it is

tis•sue \'ti-shü\ *n*
1 a fine lightweight fabric
2 a piece of soft absorbent paper ⟨She dabbed at her nose with a *tissue.*⟩
3 a mass or layer of cells usually of one kind that perform a special function and form the basic structural material of an animal or plant body ⟨muscle *tissue*⟩

a b c d e f g h i j k l m n o p q r s t u v w x y z

▸ toad

Toads are carnivorous amphibians that live throughout most of the world, mainly on land, although they do move to streams, ponds, and rivers during the breeding season. Toads have dry warty skin, squat bodies, and short stout legs.

green toad flattens itself to the ground when threatened

cane toad was introduced to Australia from South America, and has become a pest

red-spotted toad lives mostly in rocky areas near a stream or river

ti•tan•ic \tī-ˈta-nik\ *adj*
enormous in size, force, or power

ti•tle \ˈtī-tᵊl\ *n*
1 the name given to something (as a book, song, or job) to identify or describe it
2 a word or group of words attached to a person's name to show an honor, rank, or office ⟨With her promotion came a new *title*.⟩
3 a legal right to the ownership of property
4 CHAMPIONSHIP 1 ⟨My brother won the batting *title*.⟩

tit•mouse \ˈtit-ˌmau̇s\ *n*, *pl* **tit•mice** \-ˌmīs\
▶ a small active usually gray bird that feeds mostly on seeds and insects

titmouse

¹tit•ter \ˈti-tər\ *vb* **tit•tered**; **tit•ter•ing**
to laugh in a quiet and nervous way

²titter *n*
a nervous laugh

Tlin•git \ˈtliŋ-kət, -gət\ *n*, *pl* **Tlingit** *or* **Tlin•gits**
1 a member of a group of American Indian peoples of the islands and coast of southern Alaska
2 the language of the Tlingit people

TN *abbr* Tennessee

TNT \ˌtē-ˌen-ˈtē\ *n*
an explosive used in artillery shells and bombs and in blasting

¹to \tə, ˈtü\ *prep*
1 in the direction of ⟨I'm walking *to* school.⟩
2 AGAINST 4, ON ⟨Apply salve *to* the burn.⟩
3 as far as ⟨It fell from the top *to* the bottom.⟩ ⟨Water was up *to* my waist.⟩
4 so as to become or bring about ⟨You broke it *to* pieces!⟩
5 ²BEFORE 2 ⟨Meet me at ten *to* six.⟩
6 ¹UNTIL ⟨The café is open from six *to* noon.⟩
7 fitting or being a part of or response to ⟨I found a key *to* the lock.⟩ ⟨What do you say *to* that?⟩
8 along with ⟨Skip *to* the music.⟩
9 in relation to or comparison with ⟨This one is similar *to* that one.⟩ ⟨We won ten *to* six.⟩
10 in agreement with ⟨It's made *to* order.⟩
11 within the limits of ⟨There's no more *to* my knowledge.⟩
12 contained, occurring, or included in ⟨There are two pints *to* a quart.⟩
13 used to show the one or ones that an action is directed toward ⟨He spoke *to* my parents.⟩ ⟨I gave it *to* them.⟩
14 for no one except ⟨We had the room *to* ourselves.⟩
15 into the action of ⟨We got *to* talking.⟩
16 used to mark an infinitive ⟨I like *to* swim.⟩

²to \ˈtü\ *adv*
1 in a direction toward ⟨They ran *to* and fro.⟩
2 to a conscious state ⟨The driver came *to* an hour after the accident.⟩

toad \ˈtōd\ *n*
▲ a tailless leaping animal that is an amphibian and differs from the related frog by having rough dry skin and by living mostly on land

toad•stool \ˈtōd-ˌstül\ *n*
a mushroom especially when poisonous or unfit for food

¹toast \ˈtōst\ *vb* **toast•ed**; **toast•ing**
1 to make (food) crisp, hot, and brown by heat ⟨*toast* bread⟩ ⟨*toast* cheese⟩
2 to warm completely

²toast *n*
1 sliced bread made crisp, hot, and brown by heat
2 an act of drinking in honor of a person
3 a person in whose honor other people drink
4 a highly admired person ⟨He's the *toast* of the town.⟩

³toast *vb* **toast•ed**; **toast•ing**
to drink in honor of

toast•er \ˈtō-stər\ *n*
▼ an electrical appliance for making slices of bread crisp, hot, and brown

toaster

toasty \'tō-stē\ *adj* **toast•i•er; toast•i•est**
comfortably warm

to•bac•co \tə-'ba-kō\ *n, pl* **to•bac•cos**
the usually large sticky leaves of a tall plant related to the potato that are dried and prepared for use in smoking or chewing or as snuff

to•bog•gan \tə-'bä-gən\ *n*
▼ a long light sled made without runners and curved up at the front

▶ **Word History** *Toboggan,* a name for a kind of sled without runners, is borrowed from the languages of American Indians living in eastern Canada and the northeast United States. In Micmac, for example, a language spoken in Nova Scotia, New Brunswick, and Quebec, the word is ***tepaqan***, and in Maliseet, spoken in New Brunswick, ***tapakon***. These words go back to an older word in Algonquian, the language from which Micmac and Maliseet developed. The Micmac and Maliseet words were formed from ***wetapye-***, "to drag with a cord" and ***-kan***, "implement, thing for doing something."

toboggan: a child riding a toboggan

[1]**to•day** \tə-'dā\ *adv*
1 on this day ⟨Do it *today*.⟩
2 at the present time

[2]**today** *n*
the present day, time, or age

tod•dler \'täd-lər\ *n*
a small child

[1]**toe** \'tō\ *n*
1 one of the separate parts of the front end of a foot
2 the front end or part of a foot or hoof
3 the front end of something worn on the foot
toed \'tōd\ *adj*

[2]**toe** *vb* **toed; toe•ing**
to touch, reach, or kick with the toes

toe•nail \'tō-,nāl\ *n*
the hard covering at the end of a toe

tofu

to•fu \'tō-fü\ *n*
▲ a soft food product prepared from soybeans

to•ga \'tō-gə\ *n*
▶ the loose outer garment worn in public by citizens of ancient Rome

to•geth•er \tə-'ge-thər\ *adv*
1 in or into one group, body, or place ⟨We gathered *together*.⟩
2 in touch or in partnership with ⟨They are in business *together*.⟩
3 with or near someone or something else ⟨Let's walk *together*.⟩
4 at one time ⟨They gave the same answer *together*.⟩
5 in or by combined effort ⟨Members of the team worked *together* to win.⟩
6 in or into agreement ⟨We need to get *together* on a plan.⟩
7 considered as a whole ⟨My father gave more than all the others *together*.⟩
8 in or into contact ⟨She bangs the pots *together*.⟩
9 as a single unit or piece ⟨Tape holds it *together*.⟩

[1]**toil** \'tȯil\ *n*
long hard labor

[2]**toil** *vb* **toiled; toil•ing**
1 to work hard and long
2 to go on with effort ⟨They were *toiling* up a steep hill.⟩

toi•let \'tȯi-lət\ *n*
1 a device for getting rid of body waste that consists usually of a bowl that is flushed with water
2 BATHROOM
3 the act or process of getting dressed and groomed

toga: a man dressed in a toga

toilet paper *n*
a thin soft sanitary absorbent paper usually in a roll for bathroom use

to•ken \'tō-kən\ *n*
1 an outer sign : PROOF ⟨a *token* of friendship⟩
2 a piece like a coin that has a special use ⟨a bus *token*⟩
3 an object used to suggest something that cannot be pictured ⟨This ring is a *token* of my affection.⟩
4 SOUVENIR
5 INDICATION 2
synonyms see EMBLEM

told *past and past participle of* TELL

tol•er•a•ble \'tä-lə-rə-bəl\ *adj*
1 capable of being put up with ⟨I still have pain, but it's *tolerable*.⟩
2 fairly good ⟨*tolerable* weather⟩
tol•er•a•bly \-blē\ *adv*

tol•er•ance \'tä-lə-rəns\ *n*
1 ability to put up with something harmful, bad, or annoying
2 sympathy for or acceptance of feelings or habits which are different from someone's own

tol•er•ant \'tä-lə-rənt\ *adj*
showing tolerance
tol•er•ant•ly *adv*

tol•er•ate \'tä-lə-,rāt\ *vb* **tol•er•at•ed; tol•er•at•ing**
1 to allow something to be or to be done without making a move to stop it
2 to stand the action of 〈These plants *tolerate* drought well.〉

[1]toll \'tōl\ *n*
1 a tax paid for a privilege (as the use of a highway or bridge)
2 a charge paid for a service
3 the cost in life or health

[2]toll *vb* **tolled; toll•ing**
1 to announce or call by the sounding of a bell 〈The clock *tolled* midnight.〉
2 to sound with slow strokes 〈Bells *tolled* solemnly.〉

[3]toll *n*
the sound of a bell ringing slowly

tom•a•hawk \'tä-mi-,hȯk\ *n*
▶ a light ax used as a weapon by North American Indians

tomahawk: a ceremonial Dakota tomahawk

to•ma•to \tə-'mā-tō, -'mä-\ *n, pl* **to•ma•toes**
the usually red juicy fruit of a plant related to the potato that is eaten raw or cooked as a vegetable

tomb \'tüm\ *n*
1 [1]GRAVE
2 a house or burial chamber for dead people

tom•boy \'täm-,bȯi\ *n*
a girl who enjoys things that some people think are more suited to boys

tomb•stone \'tüm-,stōn\ *n*
GRAVESTONE

tom•cat \'täm-,kat\ *n*
a male cat

tome \'tōm\ *n*
a big thick book

tom•fool•ery \,täm-'fül-rē, -'fü-lə-\ *n*
playful or foolish behavior

[1]to•mor•row \tə-'mär-ō\ *adv*
on the day after today 〈Meet me *tomorrow.*〉

[2]tomorrow *n*
the day after today

tom–tom \'täm-,täm\ *n*
a drum (as a traditional Asian, African, or American Indian drum) that is beaten with the hands

ton \'tən\ *n*
a measure of weight equal either to 2000 pounds (about 907 kilograms) (**short ton**) or 2240 pounds (about 1016 kilograms) (**long ton**) with the short ton being more frequently used in the United States and Canada

[1]tone \'tōn\ *n*
1 an individual way of speaking or writing especially when used to express an emotion 〈He replied in a friendly *tone.*〉
2 common character or quality 〈There was a polite *tone* to the discussions.〉
3 quality of spoken or musical sound
4 a sound on one pitch
5 a shade of color 〈The room is decorated in soft *tones.*〉
6 a color that changes another 〈It's gray with a blue *tone.*〉
7 a healthy state of the body or any of its parts 〈He has good muscle *tone.*〉

[2]tone *vb* **toned; ton•ing**
to give a healthy state to : STRENGTHEN 〈She exercised to *tone* up her muscles.〉
tone down to soften or blend in color, appearance, or sound 〈Can you *tone down* the music?〉

tongs \'täŋz, 'tȯŋz\ *n pl*
a tool for taking hold of or lifting something that consists usually of two movable pieces joined at one end or in the middle

tongue \'təŋ\ *n*
1 ▶ a fleshy movable part of the mouth used in tasting, in taking and swallowing food, and by human beings in speaking
2 a particular way or quality of speaking 〈Keep a polite *tongue.*〉
3 LANGUAGE 1 〈Many *tongues* are spoken in a big city.〉
4 something that is long and fastened at one end 〈a *tongue* of land〉

tongue–tied \'təng-,tīd\ *adj*
unable to speak clearly or freely (as from shyness)

ton•ic \'tä-nik\ *n*
1 a medicine or preparation for improving the strength or health of mind or body
2 SODA POP
Hint: This sense of *tonic* is used mostly in New England.
3 the first note of a scale

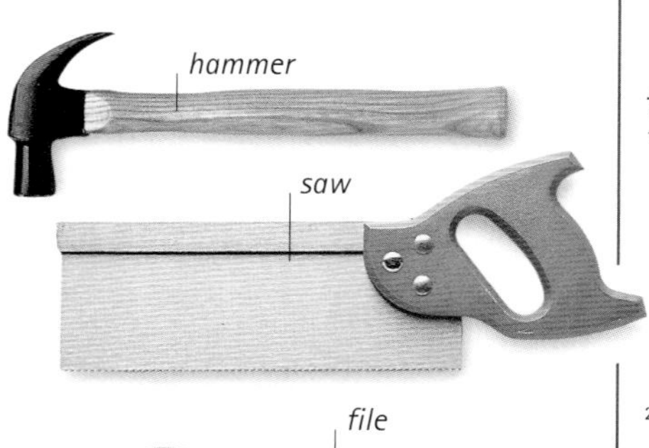

[1]tool 1: a selection of carpentry tools

[1]to•night \tə-'nīt\ *adv*
on this present night or the night following this present day 〈It's cold *tonight.*〉

[2]tonight *n*
the present or the coming night

ton•nage \'tə-nij\ *n*
1 ships in terms of the total number of tons that are or can be carried
2 total weight in tons shipped, carried, or mined

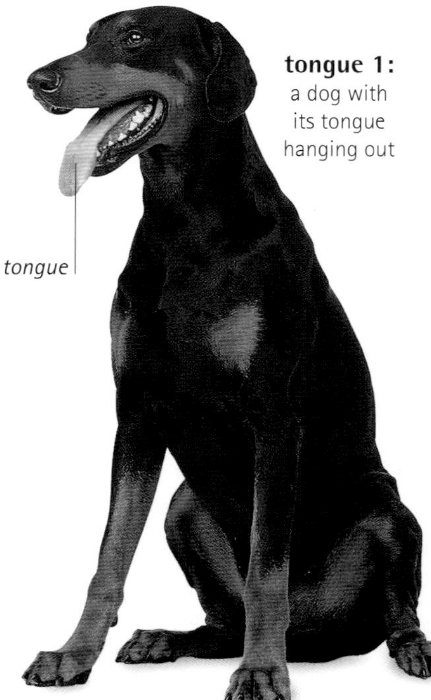

tongue 1: a dog with its tongue hanging out

ton•sil \'tän-səl\ *n*
either of a pair of masses of spongy tissue at the back of the mouth

ton•sil•li•tis \,tän-sə-'lī-təs\ *n*
a sore reddened state of the tonsils

too \'tü\ *adv*
1 in addition : ALSO 〈I'm a student *too.*〉
2 to a greater than wanted or needed degree 〈The load was *too* heavy.〉
3 [1]VERY 1 〈He's not *too* upset.〉

took *past of* TAKE

[1]tool \'tül\ *n*
1 ◀ an instrument (as a saw, file, knife, or wrench) used or worked by hand or machine to perform a task
2 something that helps to gain an end
3 a person used by another : DUPE
synonyms see INSTRUMENT

[2]tool *vb* **tooled; tool•ing**
1 to drive or ride in a vehicle
2 to shape, form, or finish with a tool
3 to equip a plant or industry with machines and tools for production

tool•box \'tül-ˌbäks\ *n*
a box for storing or carrying tools

tool•shed \'tül-ˌshed\ *n*
a small building for storing tools

[1]**toot** \'tüt\ *vb* **toot•ed; toot•ing**
1 to sound a short blast (as on a horn)
2 to blow or sound an instrument (as a horn) especially in short blasts

[2]**toot** *n*
a short blast (as on a horn)

tooth \'tüth\ *n, pl* **teeth** \'tēth\
1 one of the hard bony structures set in sockets on the jaws of most vertebrates and used especially to chew and bite
2 something like or suggesting an animal's tooth in shape, arrangement, or action ⟨the *teeth* of a comb⟩
3 one of the projections around the rim of a wheel that fit between the projections on another part causing the other part to move as the wheel turns
tooth•less \'tüth-ləs\ *adj*

tooth•ache \'tüth-ˌāk\ *n*
pain in or near a tooth

tooth•brush \'tüth-ˌbrəsh\ *n*
a brush for cleaning the teeth

toothed \'tütht\ *adj*
having or showing teeth especially of a particular kind ⟨sharp-*toothed*⟩

tooth•paste \'tüth-ˌpāst\ *n*
a paste for cleaning the teeth

tooth•pick \'tüth-ˌpik\ *n*
a pointed instrument for removing bits of food caught between the teeth

tooth•some \'tüth-səm\ *adj*
pleasing to the taste : DELICIOUS

toothy \'tü-thē\ *adj* **tooth•i•er; tooth•i•est**
having or showing many usually large teeth ⟨a *toothy* grin⟩

[1]**top** \'täp\ *n*
1 the highest point, level, or part of something ⟨the *top* of the hill⟩
2 the upper end, edge, or surface ⟨The glass was filled to the *top*.⟩
3 an upper piece, lid, or covering ⟨Put the *top* on the jar.⟩
4 the highest position ⟨She ranks at the *top* of her class.⟩
5 a garment worn on the upper part of the body
6 the stalk and leaves of a plant and especially of one with roots that are used for food ⟨beet *tops*⟩

[2]**top** *vb* **topped; top•ping**
1 to cover with or be covered with ⟨ice cream *topped* with chocolate sauce⟩
2 to go over the top of ⟨After *topping* the hill we needed a rest.⟩
3 to be better than or exceed ⟨Some odd things have happened, but this *tops* all.⟩
4 to remove or cut the top of ⟨Workers *topped* the tree.⟩

[3]**top** *adj*
relating to or being at the top ⟨*top* students⟩

[4]**top** *n*
a child's toy with a tapering point on which it can be made to spin

topaz: a cut topaz

to•paz \'tō-ˌpaz\ *n*
▲ a clear yellow crystal that is used as a gem

top•coat \'täp-ˌkōt\ *n*
a lightweight overcoat

top•ic \'tä-pik\ *n*
the subject of something that is being discussed or has been written or thought about

topic sentence *n*
a sentence that states the main thought of a paragraph

top•knot \'täp-ˌnät\ *n*
a tuft of feathers or hair on the top of the head

top•mast \'täp-ˌmast, -məst\ *n*
the second mast above a ship's deck

top•most \'täp-ˌmōst\ *adj*
highest of all ⟨I can't reach the *topmost* shelf.⟩

top•ple \'tä-pəl\ *vb* **top•pled; top•pling**
to fall or cause to fall from an upright position

top•sail \'täp-ˌsāl, -səl\ *n*
1 the sail next above the lowest sail on a mast in a square-rigged ship
2 the sail above the large sail on a mast in a ship with a fore-and-aft rig

top•soil \'täp-ˌsȯil\ *n*
the rich upper layer of soil in which plants have most of their roots

top•sy–tur•vy \ˌtäp-sē-'tər-vē\ *adv or adj*
1 upside down ⟨The wagon lay *topsy-turvy* at the bottom of the hill.⟩
2 in complete disorder

To•rah \'tȯr-ə\ *n*
1 the Jewish Bible and especially the first five books of writings
2 a scroll containing the first five books of the Jewish Bible that is used in religious services

torch \'tȯrch\ *n*
1 ▼ a flaming light that is made of something which burns brightly and that is usually carried in the hand
2 something that gives light or guidance ⟨She passed the *torch* of family traditions to her children.⟩
3 a portable device for producing a hot flame ⟨a welder's *torch*⟩

tore *past of* TEAR

[1]**tor•ment** \tȯr-'ment\ *vb* **tor•ment•ed; tor•ment•ing**
1 to cause severe suffering of body or mind to ⟨Flies *tormented* the cattle.⟩
2 VEX 1, HARASS

torch 1: runners bearing a torch to signal the start of the 1996 Olympic Games in Atlanta

tortoise 1
There are about 40 species of tortoise found in warm climates around the world. They can all retract their limbs and heads into their shell for protection from predators. Some species lay as many as 160 eggs at a time.

African hinge-back tortoise has a hinged rear section that closes for extra protection from predators

leopard tortoise is so called because of its spots

[2]**tor•ment** \'tȯr-ˌment\ *n*
1 extreme pain or distress of body or mind
2 a cause of suffering in mind or body

torn *past participle of* TEAR

tor•na•do \tȯr-'nā-dō\ *n, pl* **tor•na•does** *or* **tor•na•dos**
a violent whirling wind accompanied by a cloud that is shaped like a funnel and moves overland in a narrow path

[1]**tor•pe•do** \tȯr-'pē-dō\ *n, pl* **tor•pe•does**
a long narrow self-propelled underwater weapon used for blowing up ships

► **Word History** In 1776, David Bushnell, a supporter of the American cause in the Revolutionary War, built a wooden submarine with a detachable container of gunpowder that could be hooked to an enemy ship and set to explode after the submarine steered clear. Bushnell is believed to have dubbed the container with the Latin word *torpedo*, "electric ray," that is, a fish that delivers an electric shock. Though Bushnell's submarine and explosive device never damaged a British vessel, the name *torpedo* was later applied to modern weapons used to attack ships.

[2]**torpedo** *vb* **tor•pe•doed; tor•pe•do•ing**
to hit with or destroy by a torpedo

tor•rent \'tȯr-ənt\ *n*
1 a rushing stream of liquid
2 a large amount of something especially that is released suddenly ⟨a *torrent* of rain⟩

tor•rid \'tȯr-əd\ *adj*
very hot and usually dry

tor•so \'tȯr-sō\ *n*
the human body except for the head, arms, and legs

tor•ti•lla \tȯr-'tē-ə\ *n*
a round flat bread made of corn or wheat flour and usually eaten hot with a filling

tor•toise \'tȯr-təs\ *n*
1 ▲ a usually large turtle that lives on land
2 TURTLE

tor•toise•shell \'tȯr-təs-ˌshel\ *n*
1 a hard brown and yellow material that covers the shell of a sea tortoise used especially in the past for ornamental objects
2 a brightly colored butterfly

tor•tu•ous \'tȯr-chə-wəs\ *adj*
having many twists and turns ⟨a *tortuous* path⟩

[1]**tor•ture** \'tȯr-chər\ *n*
1 the act of causing great pain especially to punish or to obtain a confession
2 distress of body or mind ⟨Waiting is just *torture* for me.⟩

[2]**torture** *vb* **tor•tured; tor•tur•ing**
1 to punish or force someone to do or say something by causing great pain
2 to cause great suffering to
tor•tur•er *n*

[1]**toss** \'tȯs\ *vb* **tossed; toss•ing**
1 to throw with a quick light motion
2 to lift with a sudden motion ⟨The horse *tossed* its head.⟩
3 to throw or swing back and forth or up and down ⟨Waves *tossed* the ship about.⟩
4 to be thrown about rapidly ⟨A canoe was *tossing* on the waves.⟩
5 to move about restlessly ⟨Instead of sleeping, he *tossed* in his bed.⟩
6 to stir or mix lightly ⟨*tossed* salad⟩
synonyms see THROW

[2]**toss** *n*
1 an act or instance of throwing something
2 the act of lifting with a sudden motion ⟨a *toss* of the head⟩

tot \'tät\ *n*
a young child

[1]**to•tal** \'tō-tᵊl\ *adj*
1 being such to the fullest degree ⟨*total* ruin⟩
2 making up the whole ⟨I collected the *total* amount.⟩
3 of or relating to the whole of something ⟨a *total* eclipse of the sun⟩
4 making use of every means to do something ⟨*total* war⟩
to•tal•ly *adv*

[2]**total** *n*
the entire number or amount counted
: SUM

[3]**total** *vb* **to•taled** *or* **to•talled; to•tal•ing** *or* **to•tal•ling**
1 to add up ⟨Did you *total* the scores?⟩
2 to amount to : NUMBER ⟨Donations *totaled* five hundred dollars.⟩

A B C D E F G H I J K L M N O P Q R S T U V W X Y Z

tote \'tōt\ *vb* **tot•ed**; **tot•ing**
CARRY 1, HAUL ⟨He *totes* a heavy backpack.⟩

to•tem \'tō-təm\ *n*
1 an object (as an animal or plant) serving as the emblem of a family or clan
2 a carving or picture representing such an object

totem pole *n*
► a usually wooden pole or pillar carved and painted with totems and set up by American Indian tribes of the northwest coast of North America

tot•ter \'tä-tər\ *vb* **tot•tered**; **tot•ter•ing**
1 to sway or rock as if about to fall
2 to move unsteadily : STAGGER

tou•can \'tü-,kan\ *n*
▼ a brightly colored tropical bird that has a very large beak and feeds mostly on fruit

toucan

[1]touch \'təch\ *vb* **touched**; **touch•ing**
1 to feel or handle (as with the fingers) especially so as to be aware of ⟨I *touched* the rabbit's soft fur.⟩
2 to be or cause to be in contact with something ⟨Lightly *touch* the paintbrush to your paper.⟩
3 to hit lightly ⟨Be careful not to *touch* the walls.⟩
4 [2]HARM ⟨No one will dare to *touch* you.⟩
5 to make use of ⟨She never *touches* meat.⟩
6 to refer to in passing ⟨The report *touched* upon many topics.⟩
7 to affect the interest of ⟨This matter *touches* all of us.⟩
8 to have an influence on ⟨As a teacher, he *touched* many lives.⟩
9 to move emotionally ⟨I was *touched* by your kindness.⟩

totem pole: a totem pole from British Columbia, Canada

[2]touch *n*
1 a light stroke or tap ⟨Stop crying. It was only a *touch* and couldn't have hurt.⟩
2 the act or fact of touching or being touched ⟨I felt a gentle *touch* on my shoulder.⟩
3 the sense by which light pressure on the skin is felt ⟨The substance is soft to the *touch.*⟩
4 an impression gotten through the sense of touch ⟨the soft *touch* of silk⟩
5 a state of contact or communication ⟨It is important to keep in *touch* with friends.⟩
6 a small amount : TRACE ⟨a *touch* of humor⟩
7 a small detail ⟨We put the finishing *touches* on the decorations.⟩

touch•down \'təch-,dau̇n\ *n*
a score made in football by carrying or catching the ball over the opponent's goal line

touch•ing \'tə-chiŋ\ *adj*
causing a feeling of tenderness or pity ⟨a *touching* story⟩

touch pad *n*
a flat surface on an electronic device (as a microwave oven) divided into several differently marked areas that are touched to make choices in controlling the device

touch screen *n*
a display screen (as for a computer) on which the user selects options by touching the screen

touch–tone \'təch-'tōn\ *adj*
relating to or being a telephone with push buttons that produce tones corresponding to the numbers

touchy \'tə-chē\ *adj* **touch•i•er**; **touch•i•est**
1 easily hurt or insulted ⟨She's *touchy* about her weight.⟩
2 calling for tact or careful handling ⟨a *touchy* subject⟩

tough \'təf\ *adj* **tough•er**; **tough•est**
1 strong or firm but flexible and not brittle ⟨*tough* fibers⟩ ⟨*tough* leather⟩
2 not easily chewed ⟨*tough* meat⟩
3 physically or emotionally strong enough to put up with strain or hardship
4 very strict, firm, or determined ⟨a *tough* coach⟩ ⟨*tough* rules⟩
5 very difficult to do or deal with ⟨We've had some *tough* times.⟩ ⟨The math test was *tough.*⟩
6 LAWLESS 2 ⟨a *tough* neighborhood⟩
synonyms see STRONG
tough•ness *n*

tough•en \'tə-fən\ *vb* **tough•ened**; **tough•en•ing**
to make or become tough ⟨Going barefoot *toughened* my feet.⟩

[1]tour \'tu̇r\ *n*
1 a trip usually involving a series of stops and ending at the point where it started ⟨a *tour* of the city⟩
2 a fixed period of duty
synonyms see JOURNEY

[2]tour *vb* **toured**; **tour•ing**
to make a tour of : travel as a tourist

tour•ist \'tu̇r-ist\ *n*
a person who travels for pleasure

tour•na•ment \'tu̇r-nə-mənt\ *n*
1 a series of contests played for a championship ⟨a golf *tournament*⟩ ⟨a chess *tournament*⟩
2 a contest between knights wearing armor and fighting with blunted lances or swords

tour•ni•quet \'tu̇r-ni-kət\ *n*
a device (as a bandage twisted tight) for stopping bleeding or blood flow

tou•sle \'tau̇-zəl\ *vb* **tou•sled**; **tou•sling**
to put into disorder by rough handling ⟨She *tousled* my hair.⟩

[1]tow \'tō\ *vb* **towed**; **tow•ing**
to draw or pull along behind

[2]tow *n*
an act or instance of drawing or pulling along behind : the fact or state of being drawn or pulled along behind

town 1: a panoramic view of the town of Monthermé by the Meuse River in the Champagne region of France

[3]tow *n*
short broken fiber of flax, hemp, or jute used for yarn, twine, or stuffing

to•ward \'tō-ərd, tə-'wȯrd\ *or* **to•wards** \'tō-ərdz, tə-'wȯrdz\ *prep*
1 in the direction of ⟨We're heading *toward* town.⟩
2 along a course leading to ⟨They made efforts *toward* peace.⟩
3 in regard to ⟨I like his attitude *toward* life.⟩
4 so as to face ⟨Their backs were *toward* me.⟩
5 [2]NEAR ⟨I awoke *toward* morning.⟩
6 as part of the payment for ⟨She put money *toward* a new car.⟩

tow•el \'tau̇-əl\ *n*
a cloth or piece of absorbent paper for wiping or drying

[1]tow•er \'tau̇-ər\ *n*
a building or structure that is higher than its length or width, is higher than most of what surrounds it, and may stand by itself or be attached to a larger structure

[2]tower *vb* **tow•ered**; **tow•er•ing**
to reach or rise to a great height

tow•er•ing \'tau̇-ər-iŋ\ *adj*
1 rising high : TALL
2 very powerful or intense ⟨a *towering* rage⟩
3 going beyond proper bounds ⟨*towering* ambition⟩

tow•head \'tō-ˌhed\ *n*
a person with very light blond hair

town \'tau̇n\ *n*
1 ▲ a thickly settled area that is usually larger than a village but smaller than a city
2 the people of a town ⟨The whole *town* came out to watch the parade.⟩

town hall *n*
a public building used for offices and meetings of town government

town•ship \'tau̇n-ˌship\ *n*
1 a unit of local government in some northeastern and north central states
2 a division of territory in surveys of United States public lands containing 36 square miles (about 93 square kilometers)

tox•ic \'täk-sik\ *adj*
containing, being, or caused by poisonous or dangerous material ⟨*toxic* waste⟩ ⟨*toxic* effects⟩

► **Word History** Sometimes people put poison on the points of arrows. Even a slight wound from such an arrow can be fatal. The ancient Greeks referred to arrow poison as *toxikon*, short for *toxikon pharmakon*, literally, "bow drug" (from *toxos*, "bow"). As Latin *toxicum*, the word was applied more generally to any poison. The English word *toxic* comes from this Latin word.

tox•in \'täk-sən\ *n*
a poison produced by a living thing (as an animal or bacterium)

[1]toy \'tȯi\ *n*
1 something for a child to play with
2 something of little or no value
3 something small of its kind

[2]toy *vb* **toyed**; **toy•ing**
1 to fidget or play with without thinking
2 to think about something briefly and not very seriously
3 to flirt with

[1]trace \'trās\ *n*
1 a mark left by something that has passed or is past
2 a very small amount ⟨He speaks with a *trace* of an accent.⟩

[2]trace *vb* **traced**; **trac•ing**
1 [2]SKETCH 1
2 to form (as letters) carefully
3 to copy (as a drawing) by following the lines as seen through a transparent sheet placed over the thing copied
4 to follow the footprints, track, or trail of
5 to study or follow the development of in detail ⟨This book *traces* the history of art through the ages.⟩
6 to follow something back to its cause or beginning

[3]trace *n*
either of the two straps, chains, or ropes of a harness that fasten a horse to a vehicle

tra•chea \ˈtrā-kē-ə\ *n, pl* **tra•che•ae** \-kē-ˌē\
1 a stiff-walled tube of the respiratory system that connects the pharynx with the lungs
2 a breathing tube of an insect that connects with the outside of the body and carries oxygen directly to the cells

trac•ing \ˈtrā-siŋ\ *n*
a copy of something traced from an original

[1]track \ˈtrak\ *n*
1 a mark left by something that has gone by
2 PATH 1, TRAIL
3 the rails of a railroad
4 a course laid out for racing
5 awareness of things or of the order in which things happen or ideas come ⟨I've lost *track* of the time.⟩ ⟨Keep *track* of your expenses.⟩
6 either of two endless metal belts on which a vehicle (as a tank) travels
7 ▶ track-and-field sports

[2]track *vb* **tracked**; **track•ing**
1 to follow the marks or traces of : to search for someone or something
2 to bring indoors on the bottom of the shoes, feet, or paws

track-and-field \ˌtrak-ən-ˈfēld\ *adj*
relating to or being sports events (as racing, throwing, and jumping contests) held on a running track and on the enclosed field

[1]tract \ˈtrakt\ *n*
1 an indefinite stretch of land ⟨a large *tract* of forest⟩
2 a defined area of land ⟨40 acre *tracts*⟩
3 a system of body parts or organs that serve some special purpose ⟨The kidneys are part of the urinary *tract*.⟩

[2]tract *n*
a pamphlet of political or religious ideas and beliefs

trac•tion \ˈtrak-shən\ *n*
the force that causes a moving thing to slow down or to stick against the surface it is moving along ⟨The wheels get more *traction* when the road is dry.⟩

trac•tor \ˈtrak-tər\ *n*
1 ▶ a vehicle that has large rear wheels or moves on endless belts and is used especially for pulling farm implements
2 a short truck for hauling a trailer

[1]trade \ˈtrād\ *n*
1 the business or work in which a person takes part regularly : OCCUPATION
2 the business of buying and selling items : COMMERCE
3 an occupation requiring manual or mechanical skill : CRAFT
4 an act of trading : TRANSACTION
5 the persons working in a business or industry
6 a firm's customers

[2]trade *vb* **trad•ed**; **trad•ing**
1 to give in exchange for something else
2 to take part in the exchange, purchase, or sale of goods ⟨Our country *trades* in many parts of the world.⟩
3 to deal regularly as a customer

trade•mark \ˈtrād-ˌmärk\ *n*
a device (as a word) that points clearly to the origin or ownership of merchandise to which it is applied and that is legally reserved for use only by the owner

trad•er \ˈtrā-dər\ *n*
1 a person who trades
2 a ship engaged in commerce

trades•man \ˈtrādz-mən\ *n, pl* **trades•men** \-mən\
1 a person who runs a retail store
2 CRAFTSMAN 1

trades•peo•ple \ˈtrādz-ˌpē-pəl\ *n pl*
people engaged in occupations requiring manual or mechanical skill

trade wind *n*
a wind blowing steadily toward the equator from an easterly direction

trading card *n*
a card that usually has pictures and information about someone or something and that is part of a set collected by trading with other people

trading post *n*
a store set up in a thinly settled region

tra•di•tion \trə-ˈdi-shən\ *n*
1 the handing down of information, beliefs, or customs from one generation to another
2 a belief or custom handed down from one generation to another

tra•di•tion•al \trə-ˈdi-shə-nᵊl\ *adj*
1 handed down from age to age ⟨a *traditional* story⟩
2 based on custom : CONVENTIONAL ⟨the *traditional* Thanksgiving dinner⟩ ⟨a *traditional* artist⟩
tra•di•tion•al•ly *adv*

▶ **[1]track 7**
Competition in track usually takes place in a stadium, with a central field area for throwing sports such as shot put, long strips for jumping sports such as long jump, and an oval racetrack for running and hurdling sports.

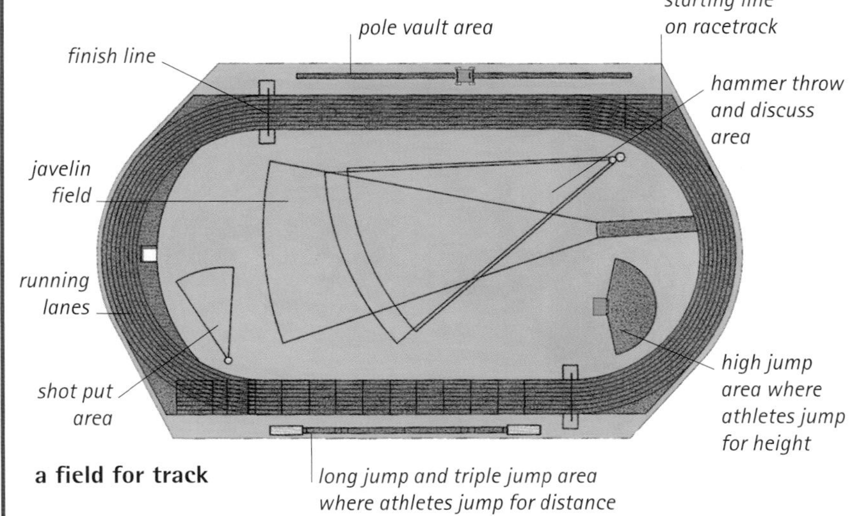

a field for track

tractor 1

[1]traf•fic \'tra-fik\ *n*
1 the movement (as of vehicles or pedestrians) along a route
2 the people or goods carried by train, boat, or airplane or passing along a road, river, or air route
3 the business of carrying passengers or goods 〈the tourist *traffic*〉
4 the business of buying and selling : COMMERCE
5 exchange of information 〈They had no *traffic* with the enemy.〉

[2]traffic *vb* **traf•ficked; traf•fick•ing**
[2]TRADE 2

traffic light *n*
▶ a visual signal (as a set of colored lights) for controlling the flow of vehicles

traffic light

trag•e•dy \'tra-jə-dē\ *n, pl* **trag•e•dies**
1 a disastrous event
2 a serious play that has a sad or disastrous ending

trag•ic \'tra-jik\ *adj*
1 very unfortunate 〈a *tragic* mistake〉
2 of or relating to tragedy 〈a *tragic* drama〉

[1]trail \'trāl\ *vb* **trailed; trail•ing**
1 to drag or draw along behind 〈The horse *trailed* its reins.〉
2 to become weak, soft, or less 〈The sound *trailed* off.〉
3 to follow in the tracks of : PURSUE 〈Police *trailed* the robbers.〉
4 to hang down, rest on, or creep over the ground 〈*trailing* vines〉
5 to lag behind

[2]trail *n*
1 a trace or mark left by something that has passed or been drawn along 〈The dog left a *trail* of mud on the carpet.〉
2 a beaten path
3 a path marked through a forest or mountainous region 〈hiking *trails*〉

trail•er \'trā-lər\ *n*
1 a platform or frame with wheels that is pulled behind a vehicle and used to transport something (as a boat)
2 a vehicle designed to serve wherever parked as a dwelling or a place of business
3 PREVIEW

[1]train \'trān\ *n*
1 a connected series of railway cars usually hauled by a locomotive
2 ▶ a part of a gown that trails behind the wearer
3 a connected series 〈*train* of thought〉 〈a *train* of events〉
4 a moving line of persons, vehicles, or animals 〈a wagon *train*〉
5 the followers of an important person

[2]train *vb* **trained; train•ing**
1 to give or receive instruction, discipline, or drill
2 to teach in an art, profession, or trade 〈I was never formally *trained* as a chef.〉
3 to make ready (as by exercise) for a test of skill 〈He's *training* for the race.〉
4 to teach (an animal) to obey
5 to make (a plant) grow in a particular way usually by bending, trimming, or tying
6 to aim something at a target 〈We *trained* our eyes on the horizon.〉
synonyms see TEACH
train•er *n*

train•ing \'trā-niŋ\ *n*
1 the course followed by a person or animal who trains or is being trained
2 the skill, knowledge, or experience acquired by a person or animal who has trained

training wheels *n pl*
a pair of small wheels connected to the rear axle of a bicycle to help a beginning rider keep balance

traipse \'trāps\ *vb* **traipsed; traips•ing**
to walk or wander about

trait \'trāt\ *n*
a quality that makes one person, animal, or thing different from another : CHARACTERISTIC

trai•tor \'trā-tər\ *n*
1 a person who is not loyal or true to a friend, duty, cause, or belief or is false to a personal duty
2 a person who betrays his or her country : a person who commits treason

trai•tor•ous \'trā-tə-rəs\ *adj*
1 guilty or capable of treason
2 amounting to treason 〈*traitorous* acts〉
synonyms see FAITHLESS

[1]tramp \'tramp\ *vb* **tramped; tramp•ing**
1 to travel or wander through on foot 〈*tramp* the woods〉
2 to walk heavily

[2]tramp *n*
1 a person who wanders from place to place, has no home or job, and often lives by begging or stealing

[1]train 2: the train on a dress in 1900s style

2 the sounds made by the beat of marching feet
3 [2]HIKE

tram•ple \'tram-pəl\ *vb* **tram•pled; tram•pling**
1 to tramp or tread heavily so as to bruise, crush, or injure something 〈She *trampled* on the flowers.〉
2 to crush under the feet 〈Don't *trample* the flowers.〉
3 to treat as if worthless or unimportant 〈You can't just *trample* other people's dreams for the future.〉

tram•po•line \,tram-pə-'lēn\ *n*
a canvas sheet or web supported by springs in a metal frame used for springing and landing in acrobatic tumbling

trance \'trans\ *n*
1 a condition like sleep (as deep hypnosis)
2 a state of being so deeply absorbed in thought about something as to be unaware of anything else
3 STUPOR

tran•quil \'trang-kwəl\ *adj*
very calm and quiet : PEACEFUL 〈a *tranquil* sea〉 〈a *tranquil* life〉
synonyms see CALM

tran•quil•iz•er \'traŋ-kwə-ˌlī-zər\ *n*
a drug used to make someone calm and relaxed

tran•quil•li•ty *or* **tran•quil•i•ty** \tran-'kwi-lə-tē\ *n*
the state of being calm : QUIET

trans. *abbr* transitive

trans– *prefix*
1 on or to the other side of : across : beyond ⟨*trans*atlantic⟩
2 so as to change or transfer ⟨*trans*plant⟩

trans•act \tran-'zakt\ *vb* **trans•act•ed**; **trans•act•ing**
to carry on : MANAGE, CONDUCT ⟨*transacting* business⟩

trans•ac•tion \tran-'zak-shən\ *n*
1 a business deal
2 **transactions** *pl* the record of the meeting of a club or organization

trans•at•lan•tic \ˌtran-zət-'lan-tik\ *adj*
crossing or being beyond the Atlantic Ocean

tran•scend \tran-'send\ *vb* **tran•scend•ed**; **tran•scend•ing**
1 to rise above the limits of ⟨The music *transcends* cultural boundaries.⟩
2 to do better or more than ⟨The poem *transcended* all others in its beauty.⟩

trans•con•ti•nen•tal \ˌtrans-ˌkän-tə-'nen-tᵊl\ *adj*
crossing, extending across, or being on the farther side of a continent

tran•scribe \tran-'skrīb\ *vb* **tran•scribed**; **tran•scrib•ing**
to make a copy of

tran•script \'tran-ˌskript\ *n*
1 [1]COPY 1
2 an official copy of a student's school record

[1]**trans•fer** \trans-'fər\ *vb* **trans•ferred**; **trans•fer•ring**
1 to move from one person or place to another ⟨*Transfer* the cookies to a rack to cool.⟩
2 to pass or cause to pass from one person, place, or condition to another ⟨If only he could *transfer* his thoughts to her mind.⟩
3 to move to a different place, region, or job ⟨I'm *transferring* to a smaller college.⟩
4 to give over the possession or ownership of ⟨He *transferred* the house to the new owners.⟩
5 to copy (as by printing) from one surface to another by contact
6 to change from one vehicle or transportation line to another

[2]**trans•fer** \'trans-ˌfər\ *n*
1 the act of giving over right, title, or interest in property to another person or other persons
2 an act or process of moving someone or something from one place to another
3 someone who has changed schools
4 a ticket allowing a passenger on a bus or train to continue the journey on another route without paying more fare

trans•fix \trans-'fiks\ *vb* **trans•fixed**; **trans•fix•ing**
to hold motionless by or as if by piercing through with a pointed weapon

trans•form \trans-'fȯrm\ *vb* **trans•formed**; **trans•form•ing**
to change completely ⟨*transform* waterpower into electric power⟩

trans•for•ma•tion \ˌtrans-fər-'mā-shən\ *n*
the act or process of changing completely : a complete change

trans•form•er \trans-'fȯr-mər\ *n*
a device for changing the voltage of an electric current

trans•fu•sion \trans-'fyü-zhən\ *n*
1 the process of passing a fluid (as blood) into a vein of a person or animal
2 the act of giving something a fresh supply ⟨The club needs a *transfusion* of new members.⟩

trans•gres•sion \trans-'gre-shən\ *n*
a violation of a command or law

[1]**tran•sient** \'tran-shənt\ *adj*
not lasting or staying long ⟨a *transient* illness⟩ ⟨*transient* workers⟩

[2]**transient** *n*
a person traveling about usually in search of work

tran•sis•tor \tran-'zi-stər\ *n*
a small solid electronic device used for controlling the flow of electricity

tran•sit \'tran-sət, -zət\ *n*
1 the act of passing through or across ⟨the *transit* of a satellite's signals⟩
2 the act or method of carrying things from one place to another ⟨The goods were lost in *transit*.⟩
3 local transportation of people in public vehicles
4 a surveyor's instrument for measuring angles

tran•si•tion \tran-'si-shən, -'zi-\ *n*
an act or the process of passing from one state, stage, place, or subject to another : CHANGE

tran•si•tive \'tran-sə-tiv, -zə-\ *adj*
having or containing a direct object ⟨*transitive* verbs⟩

trans•late \trans-'lāt\ *vb* **trans•lat•ed**; **trans•lat•ing**
1 to turn from one language into another
2 to change from one form to another ⟨Let's *translate* words into action.⟩
trans•lat•or \-'lā-tər\ *n*

trans•la•tion \trans-'lā-shən\ *n*
the act, process, or result of changing from one form or language into another

trans•lu•cent \trans-'lü-sᵊnt\ *adj*
not transparent but clear enough to allow rays of light to pass through

trans•mis•sion \trans-'mi-shən\ *n*
1 an act or process of transmitting, spreading, or passing along ⟨the *transmission* of a disease⟩
2 the gears that pass power from the engine to the axle that gives motion to a motor vehicle

trans•mit \trans-'mit\ *vb* **trans•mit•ted**; **trans•mit•ting**
1 to transfer, pass, or spread from one person or place to another ⟨*transmit* information⟩ ⟨*transmit* a disease⟩
2 to pass on by or as if by inheritance ⟨Parents *transmit* traits to their offspring.⟩
3 to pass or cause to pass through space or through a material ⟨Glass *transmits* light.⟩
4 to send out (a signal) by means of radio waves

trans•mit•ter \trans-'mi-tər\ *n*
1 someone or something that transmits something
2 the part of a telephone that includes the mouthpiece and a device that picks up sound waves and sends them over the wire
3 a device that sends out radio or television signals

tran•som \'tran-səm\ *n*
1 ▼ a piece that lies crosswise in a structure (as in the frame of a window or of a door that has a window above it)
2 a window above a door or another window

transom 1:
the transom of a doorway

a b c d e f g h i j k l m n o p q r s **t** u v w x y z

trans•par•en•cy \trans-ˈper-ən-sē\ *n, pl* **trans•par•en•cies**
1 the quality or state of being transparent
2 a picture or design on glass or film that can be viewed by shining a light through it

trans•par•ent \trans-ˈper-ənt\ *adj*
1 clear enough or thin enough to be seen through
2 easily detected 〈a *transparent* lie〉
trans•par•ent•ly *adv*

trans•pi•ra•tion \ˌtrans-pə-ˈrā-shən\ *n*
the process by which plants give off water vapor through openings in their leaves

trans•pire \trans-ˈpīr\ *vb* **trans•pired**; **trans•pir•ing**
1 to come to pass : HAPPEN 〈Important events *transpired* that day.〉
2 to become known or apparent 〈It *transpired* that they had met before.〉
3 to give off water vapor through openings in the leaves

[1]trans•plant \trans-ˈplant\ *vb* **trans•plant•ed**; **trans•plant•ing**
1 to dig up and plant again in another soil or location 〈*transplant* seedlings〉
2 to remove from one place and settle or introduce elsewhere 〈The beavers were *transplanted* to another part of the forest.〉
3 to transfer (a body organ or tissue) from one part or individual to another

[2]trans•plant \ˈtrans-ˌplant\ *n*
1 something or someone planted or moved elsewhere
2 the process or act of planting or moving elsewhere 〈a heart *transplant*〉

[1]trans•port \trans-ˈpȯrt\ *vb* **trans•port•ed**; **trans•port•ing**
1 to carry from one place to another
2 to fill with delight 〈The beautiful music *transported* me.〉

[2]trans•port \ˈtrans-ˌpȯrt\ *n*
1 the act of carrying from one place to another : TRANSPORTATION
2 a ship for carrying soldiers or military equipment
3 a vehicle used to carry people or goods from one place to another
4 a state of great joy or pleasure

trans•por•ta•tion \ˌtrans-pər-ˈtā-shən\ *n*
1 an act, instance, or means of carrying people or goods from one place to another or of being carried from one place to another
2 public carrying of passengers or goods especially as a business

trans•pose \trans-ˈpōz\ *vb* **trans•posed**; **trans•pos•ing**
1 to change the position or order of 〈*Transpose* the letters in "tow" to spell "two."〉
2 to write or perform in a different musical key

trapeze: an acrobat about to jump holding on to a trapeze

trans•verse \trans-ˈvərs\ *adj*
lying or being across : placed crosswise
trans•verse•ly *adv*

[1]trap \ˈtrap\ *n*
1 a device for catching animals
2 something by which someone is caught or stopped by surprise 〈Police set a *trap* for the criminal.〉
3 a light one-horse carriage with springs
4 a device that allows something to pass through but keeps other things out 〈a *trap* in a drain〉

[2]trap *vb* **trapped**; **trap•ping**
1 to catch or be caught in a trap 〈Hunters were *trapping* game.〉 〈The animal was *trapped.*〉
2 to put or get in a place or position from which escape is not possible
synonyms see CATCH
trap•per *n*

trap•door \ˈtrap-ˈdȯr\ *n*
a lifting or sliding door covering an opening in a floor or roof

tra•peze \tra-ˈpēz\ *n*
▲ a short horizontal bar hung from two parallel ropes and used by acrobats

trap•e•zoid \ˈtra-pə-ˌzȯid\ *n*
▼ a flat geometric figure with four sides but with only two sides parallel

trapezoid

trap•pings \ˈtra-piŋz\ *n pl*
1 ornamental covering especially for a horse
2 outward decoration or dress

trash \ˈtrash\ *n*
1 something of little or no value that is thrown away
2 people who deserve little respect

[1]trav•el \ˈtra-vəl\ *vb* **trav•eled** *or* **trav•elled**; **trav•el•ing** *or* **trav•el•ling**
1 to journey from place to place or to a distant place

A B C D E F G H I J K L M N O P Q R S T U V W X Y Z

2 to get around : pass from one place to another 〈The news *traveled* fast.〉
3 to journey through or over 〈We're *traveling* the countryside.〉
trav•el•er *or* **trav•el•ler** *n*

► **Word History** For many of us travel is usually for pleasure, so that we are unlikely to associate travel with hard labor or torture. However, the ultimate source of *travel* is a spoken Latin verb *trepaliare*, "to torture," derived from *trepalium*, a name for an instrument of torture. *Trepaliare* developed into medieval French *travailler*, which meant "to torture or torment," as well as "to suffer or labor." Middle English borrowed the French verb as *travailen* with the same sense. But the difficulties of getting from place to place in the Middle Ages, when any journey was an exhausting effort, led medieval speakers of English to apply *travailen* to making a trip. We still use the word, though travel is now much easier.

[2]travel *n*
1 the act or a means of journeying from one place to another 〈Air *travel* is fast.〉
2 [1]JOURNEY, TRIP — often used in pl. 〈I've collected many souvenirs from my *travels.*〉
3 the number journeying 〈There is heavy *travel* around Thanksgiving.〉

tra•verse \trə-'vərs\ *vb* **tra•versed**; **tra•vers•ing**
to pass through, across, or over

[1]trawl \'trȯl\ *vb* **trawled**; **trawl•ing**
to fish or catch with a large net dragged along the sea bottom

[2]trawl *n*
a large net in the shape of a cone dragged along the sea bottom in fishing

trawl•er \'trȯ-lər\ *n*
► a boat used for fishing with a large net dragged along the sea bottom

trawler:
model of a fishing trawler

tray \'trā\ *n*
► an open container with a flat bottom and low rim for holding, carrying, or showing articles 〈a waiter's *tray*〉 〈a *tray* of ice cubes〉

treach•er•ous \'tre-chə-rəs\ *adj*
1 not safe because of hidden dangers 〈a *treacherous* place for boats〉
2 not trustworthy : guilty of betrayal or likely to betray 〈a *treacherous* enemy〉
treach•er•ous•ly *adv*

treach•ery \'tre-chə-rē\ *n, pl* **treach•er•ies**
1 the behavior of a person who betrays trust or faith 〈a tale of *treachery* and revenge〉
2 an act or instance of betraying trust or faith 〈She was hurt by her friend's *treacheries.*〉

[1]tread \'tred\ *vb* **trod** \'träd\; **trod•den** \'trä-dᵊn\ *or* **trod**; **tread•ing**
1 to step or walk on or over
2 to beat or press with the feet
3 to move on foot : WALK
tread water to keep the body upright in water and the head above water by moving the legs and arms

[2]tread *n*
1 the action, manner, or sound of stepping or walking
2 a mark made by a tire rolling over the ground
3 the part of something (as a shoe or tire) that touches a surface
4 the part of a step that is stepped on 〈stair *treads*〉

trea•dle \'tre-dᵊl\ *n*
a device worked by the foot to drive a machine

tray:
a tray for making ice cubes

tread•mill \'tred-,mil\ *n*
1 a device having an endless belt on which an individual walks or runs in place for exercise
2 a tiresome routine

trea•son \'trē-zᵊn\ *n*
the crime of trying or helping to overthrow the government of the criminal's own country or cause its defeat in war

[1]trea•sure \'tre-zhər\ *n*
1 wealth (as money or jewels) stored up or held in reserve
2 something of great value 〈The park is one of the city's *treasures.*〉

[2]treasure *vb* **trea•sured**; **trea•sur•ing**
to treat as precious : CHERISH 〈I *treasure* your friendship.〉
synonyms see APPRECIATE

trea•sur•er \'tre-zhər-ər\ *n*
a person (as an officer of a club or business) who has charge of the money

trea•sury \'tre-zhə-rē\ *n, pl* **trea•sur•ies**
1 a place in which money and valuable objects are kept
2 a place where money collected is kept and paid out
3 *cap* a government department in charge of finances

[1]treat \'trēt\ *vb* **treat•ed**; **treat•ing**
1 to handle, deal with, use, or act toward in a usually stated way 〈*Treat* these flowers gently.〉 〈*Treat* this as secret.〉
2 to pay for the food or entertainment of 〈I'll *treat* you to dinner.〉
3 to give medical or surgical care to : use medical care on 〈The patient was *treated* for fever.〉 〈Doctors sometimes *treat* cancer with drugs.〉
4 to expose to some action (as of a chemical) 〈Gardeners *treat* soil with lime.〉

[2]treat *n*
1 an often unexpected or unusual source of pleasure or amusement 〈The day at the park was a *treat.*〉
2 a food that tastes very good and is not eaten very often
3 an instance of paying for someone's food or entertainment 〈Dinner is my *treat.*〉

▶ [1]**tree 1**
Trees grow in many different environments around the world. Each tree has anchoring roots which pass water and nutrients up the trunk to the branches, to nourish the leaves, flowers, seeds, or cones. The tallest trees — sequoias — can grow to a height of more than 360 feet.

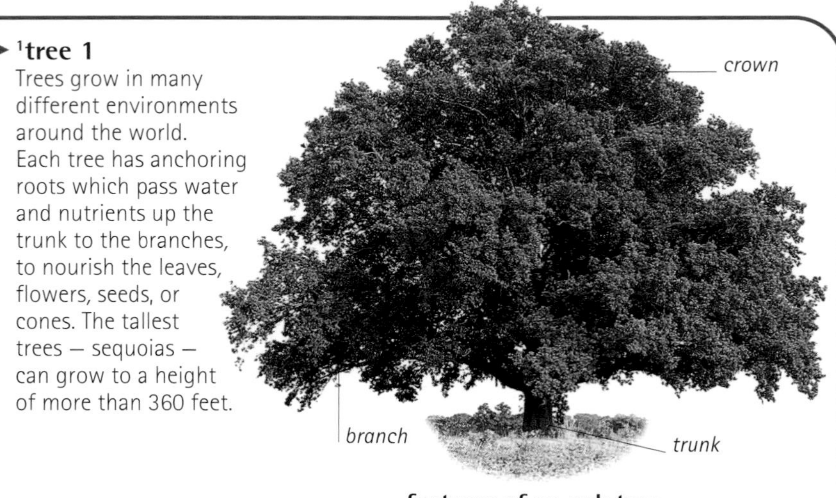

features of an oak tree

treat•ment \'trēt-mənt\ *n*
1 the act or manner of treating someone or something ⟨The dog received rough *treatment* by his previous owners.⟩
2 medical or surgical care ⟨The accident victim required immediate *treatment.*⟩
3 a substance or method used in treating ⟨a *treatment* for acne⟩ ⟨waste *treatment*⟩

trea•ty \'trē-tē\ *n, pl* **trea•ties**
an agreement between two or more states or sovereigns ⟨a peace *treaty*⟩

tree fern

[1]**tre•ble** \'tre-bəl\ *n*
1 the highest part in harmony having four parts : SOPRANO
2 an instrument having the highest range or part
3 a voice or sound that has a high pitch
4 the upper half of the musical pitch range

[2]**treble** *adj*
1 being three times the number or amount
2 relating to or having the range of a musical treble

[3]**treble** *vb* **tre•bled; tre•bling**
to make or become three times as much

[1]**tree** \'trē\ *n*
1 ▲ a long-lived woody plant that has a single usually tall main stem with few or no branches on its lower part
2 a plant of treelike form ⟨a banana *tree*⟩
3 something shaped like a tree ⟨a clothes *tree*⟩
tree•less \-ləs\ *adj*
tree•like \-,līk\ *adj*

[2]**tree** *vb* **treed; tree•ing**
to force to go up a tree ⟨A dog *treed* their cat.⟩

tree fern *n*
◀ a tropical fern with a tall woody stalk and a crown of often feathery leaves

tree house *n*
a structure (as a playhouse) built among the branches of a tree

tree•top \'trē-,täp\ *n*
the highest part of a tree

tre•foil \'trē-,fȯil\ *n*
1 a clover or related plant having leaves with three leaflets
2 a fancy design with three leaflike parts

[1]**trek** \'trek\ *vb* **trekked; trek•king**
to walk a long way with difficulty

[2]**trek** *n*
a slow or difficult journey

trel•lis \'tre-ləs\ *n*
▶ a frame of lattice used especially as a screen or a support for climbing plants

[1]**trem•ble** \'trem-bəl\ *vb* **trem•bled; trem•bling**
1 to shake without control (as from fear or cold) : SHIVER
2 to move, sound, or happen as if shaken ⟨The building *trembled.*⟩ ⟨My voice *trembled.*⟩
3 to have strong fear or doubt ⟨I *tremble* to think of what might happen.⟩

[2]**tremble** *n*
the act or a period of shaking

tre•men•dous \tri-'men-dəs\ *adj*
1 astonishingly large, strong, or great ⟨The boy has a *tremendous* appetite.⟩
2 very good or excellent ⟨We had a *tremendous* time.⟩
tre•men•dous•ly *adv*

trem•or \'tre-mər\ *n*
1 a trembling or shaking especially from weakness or disease
2 a shaking motion of the earth during an earthquake

trem•u•lous \'tre-myə-ləs\ *adj*
1 marked by trembling or shaking ⟨a *tremulous* voice⟩
2 FEARFUL 2, TIMID

trench \'trench\ *n*
a long narrow ditch

trend \'trend\ *n*
general direction taken in movement or change ⟨a down *trend* in the business⟩ ⟨new *trends* in fashion⟩

trendy \'tren-dē\ *adj* **trend•i•er; trend•i•est**
currently fashionable or popular ⟨a *trendy* restaurant⟩

trellis: an ivy plant climbing up a trellis

trep•i•da•tion \ˌtre-pə-ˈdā-shən\ *n*
a state of alarm or nervousness ⟨The boys approached the abandoned house with *trepidation.*⟩

[1]**tres•pass** \ˈtres-pəs, -ˌpas\ *n*
1 unlawful entry upon someone's land
2 [1]SIN, OFFENSE

[2]**trespass** *vb* **tres•passed**; **tres•pass•ing**
1 to enter upon someone's land unlawfully
2 to do wrong : SIN
tres•pass•er *n*

tress \ˈtres\ *n*
a long lock of hair

tres•tle \ˈtre-səl\ *n*
1 a braced frame consisting usually of a horizontal piece with spreading legs at each end that supports something (as the top of a table)
2 a structure of timbers or steel for supporting a road or railroad over a low place

T. rex \tē-ˈreks\ *n*
TYRANNOSAUR

tri- *prefix*
three ⟨*tri*angle⟩

tri•ad \ˈtrī-ˌad\ *n*
a chord made up usually of the first, third, and fifth notes of a scale

tri•al \ˈtrī-əl\ *n*
1 the hearing and judgment of something in court
2 a test of someone's ability to do or endure something
3 an experiment to test quality, value, or usefulness
4 the action or process of trying or testing

tri•an•gle \ˈtrī-ˌaŋ-gəl\ *n*
1 a flat geometric figure that has three sides and three angles
2 something that has three sides and three angles ⟨a *triangle* of land⟩
3 ▼ a musical instrument made of a steel rod bent in the shape of a triangle with one open angle

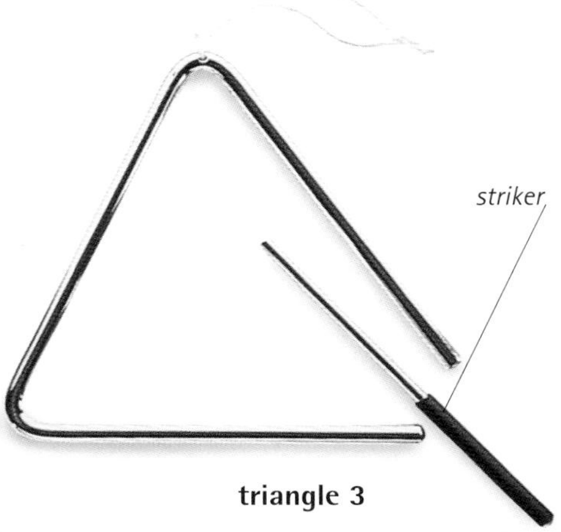

triangle 3

triceratops:
a model of a triceratops

tri•an•gu•lar \trī-ˈaŋ-gyə-lər\ *adj*
1 having three angles, sides, or corners ⟨a *triangular* sign⟩
2 of, relating to, or involving three parts or persons

trib•al \ˈtrī-bəl\ *adj*
relating to a tribe ⟨a *tribal* custom⟩

tribe \ˈtrīb\ *n*
1 a group of people including many families, clans, or generations ⟨an American Indian *tribe*⟩
2 a group of people who are of the same kind or have the same occupation or interest

tribes•man \ˈtrībz-mən\ *n*, *pl* **tribes•men** \-mən\
a member of a tribe

trib•u•la•tion \ˌtri-byə-ˈlā-shən\ *n*
1 an experience that is hard to bear ⟨He suffered many trials and *tribulations.*⟩
2 distress or suffering resulting from cruel and unjust treatment or misfortune ⟨Her son's illness has been a source of *tribulation.*⟩

tri•bu•nal \trī-ˈbyü-nᵊl\ *n*
a court of justice

trib•u•tary \ˈtri-byə-ˌter-ē\ *n*, *pl* **trib•u•tar•ies**
a stream flowing into a larger stream or a lake ⟨The river has several *tributaries.*⟩

trib•ute \ˈtri-byüt\ *n*
1 something done, said, or given to show respect, gratitude, or affection
2 a payment made by one ruler or state to another especially to gain peace

tri•cer•a•tops \trī-ˈser-ə-ˌtäps\ *n*, *pl* **triceratops**
▲ a large plant-eating dinosaur with three horns, a large bony crest around the neck, and hoofed toes

[1]**trick** \ˈtrik\ *n*
1 an action intended to deceive or cheat
2 a mischievous act : PRANK
3 an action designed to puzzle or amuse ⟨a card *trick*⟩
4 a quick or clever way of doing something ⟨I know a *trick* for remembering names.⟩
5 the cards played in one round of a game

[2]**trick** *vb* **tricked**; **trick•ing**
to deceive with tricks

[3]**trick** *adj*
relating to or involving actions intended to deceive or puzzle ⟨We scored a touchdown on a *trick* play.⟩

trick•ery \ˈtri-kə-rē\ *n*
the use of actions intended to deceive or cheat

[1]**trick•le** \ˈtri-kəl\ *vb* **trick•led**; **trick•ling**
1 to run or fall in drops
2 to flow in a thin slow stream
3 to move slowly or in small numbers ⟨Customers *trickled* in.⟩

[2]**trickle** *n*
a thin slow stream

trick or treat *n*
a children's Halloween practice of going around usually in costume asking for treats

trick•ster \ˈtrik-stər\ *n*
a person who uses tricks

tricky \'tri-kē\ *adj* **trick·i·er; trick·i·est**
1 requiring special care and skill ⟨Opening the lock is *tricky*.⟩
2 likely to use tricks

tri·cy·cle \'trī-sə-kəl\ *n*
▼ a vehicle with three wheels that is usually moved by pedals

tricycle: a boy on his tricycle

tri·dent \'trī-dᵊnt\ *n*
a spear with three prongs

tried *past and past participle of* TRY

tried–and–true *adj*
found good or trustworthy through experience or testing ⟨a *tried-and-true* remedy⟩

[1]**tri·fle** \'trī-fəl\ *n*
something of little value or importance

[2]**trifle** *vb* **tri·fled; tri·fling**
to treat (someone or something) as unimportant

tri·fling \'trī-fliŋ\ *adj*
1 not serious : FRIVOLOUS ⟨He worries about *trifling* details.⟩
2 of little value ⟨We paid a *trifling* amount.⟩

trig·ger \'tri-gər\ *n*
the part of the lock of a gun that is pressed to release the hammer so that it will fire

[1]**trill** \'tril\ *n*
1 [1]WARBLE 1
2 the rapid vibration of one speech organ against another (as the tongue against the teeth) ⟨She pronounces *r*'s with a *trill*.⟩
3 a quick movement back and forth between two musical tones one step apart

[2]**trill** *vb* **trilled; trill·ing**
to utter as or with a trill

tril·lion \'tril-yən\ *n*
a thousand billions

tril·li·um \'tri-lē-əm\ *n*
► a plant related to the lilies that has three leaves and a single flower with three petals and that blooms in the spring

[1]**trim** \'trim\ *vb* **trimmed; trim·ming**
1 to put decorations on : ADORN ⟨The dress is *trimmed* in lace.⟩
2 to make neat especially by cutting or clipping ⟨He *trimmed* his beard.⟩
3 to free of unnecessary matter ⟨We need to *trim* our expenses.⟩
4 to adjust (as a sail) to a desired position
trim·mer *n*

[2]**trim** *adj* **trim·mer; trim·mest**
neat and compact in line or structure
synonyms see NEAT
trim·ly *adv*

[3]**trim** *n*
1 material used for ornament or trimming
2 the woodwork in the finish of a building especially around doors and windows
3 an act or instance of cutting or clipping ⟨I'm going to the barber for a *trim*.⟩

trim·ming \'tri-miŋ\ *n*
something that ornaments, seasons, or completes ⟨turkey with all the *trimmings*⟩

trin·ket \'triŋ-kət\ *n*
a small object of little value

trio \'trē-ō\ *n, pl* **tri·os**
1 a group or set of three
2 a group of three musicians who perform together

[1]**trip** \'trip\ *vb* **tripped; trip·ping**
1 to catch the foot against something so as to stumble : cause to stumble
2 to make or cause to make a mistake ⟨Their tricky questions *tripped* us up.⟩
3 to move (as in dancing) with light quick steps ⟨She *tripped* lightly around the room.⟩
4 to release (as a spring) by moving a catch

[2]**trip** *n*
1 an instance of traveling from one place to another ⟨a *trip* to Europe⟩
2 a brief errand having a certain aim or being more or less regular ⟨a *trip* to the dentist⟩
3 the action of releasing something mechanically
4 a device for releasing something by tripping a mechanism
synonyms see JOURNEY

tripe \'trīp\ *n*
a part of the stomach of a cow used for food

[1]**tri·ple** \'tri-pəl\ *vb* **tri·pled; tri·pling**
to make or become three times as great or as many ⟨I *tripled* my savings.⟩

[2]**triple** *n*
1 a sum, amount, or number that is three times as great

trillium

2 a combination, group, or series of three
3 a hit in baseball that lets the batter reach third base

[3]**triple** *adj*
1 having three units or parts
2 being three times as great or as many
3 repeated three times

trip·let \'tri-plət\ *n*
1 a combination, set, or group of three
2 one of three offspring born at one birth

tri·pod \'trī-,päd\ *n*
1 something (as a container or stool) resting on three legs
2 a stand (as for a camera) having three legs

trite \'trīt\ *adj* **trit·er; trit·est**
so common that the newness and cleverness have worn off : STALE ⟨*trite* remarks⟩

[1]**tri·umph** \'trī-əmf\ *n*
1 the joy of victory or success
2 an outstanding victory
synonyms see VICTORY

[2]**triumph** *vb* **tri·umphed; tri·umph·ing**
1 to celebrate victory or success in high spirits
2 to gain victory : WIN

tri·um·phal \trī-'əm-fəl\ *adj*
following or in celebration of victory ⟨a *triumphal* return⟩ ⟨a *triumphal* parade⟩

tri·um·phant \trī-'əm-fənt\ *adj*
1 VICTORIOUS, SUCCESSFUL
2 rejoicing for or celebrating victory
tri·um·phant·ly *adv*

triv·ia \'tri-vē-ə\ *n pl*
interesting facts that are not well-known
Hint: *Trivia* can be used as a singular or a plural in writing and speaking.

triv·i·al \'tri-vē-əl\ *adj*
of little worth or importance ⟨Don't get angry about *trivial* matters.⟩

trod *past and past participle of* TREAD

trodden *past participle of* TREAD

[1]**troll** \'trōl\ *n*
1 a dwarf or giant of folklore living in caves or hills
2 a person who tries to cause problems on an Internet message board by posting messages that cause arguments or anger

[2]**troll** *vb* **trolled; troll·ing**
1 to sing the parts of (a song) in succession

2 to fish with a hook and line pulled along through the water

[3]troll *n*
a lure or a line with its lure and hook drawn through the water in fishing

trol•ley \'trä-lē\ *n, pl* **trolleys**
1 a passenger car that runs on tracks and gets its power through electricity
2 a wheeled cart

trom•bone \träm-'bōn\ *n*
▶ a brass musical instrument made of a long bent tube that has a wide opening at one end and one section that slides in and out to make different tones

[1]troop \'trüp\ *n*
1 a group of soldiers
2 **troops** *pl* armed forces : MILITARY
3 a group of beings or things 〈*Troops* of fans turned out for the game.〉
4 a unit of boy or girl scouts under a leader

[2]troop *vb* **trooped; troop•ing**
to move or gather in groups

troop•er \'trü-pər\ *n*
1 a soldier in a cavalry unit
2 a state police officer

tro•phy \'trō-fē\ *n, pl* **trophies**
1 something given to celebrate a victory or as an award for achievement 〈I won the bowling *trophy*.〉
2 something taken in battle or conquest especially as a memorial

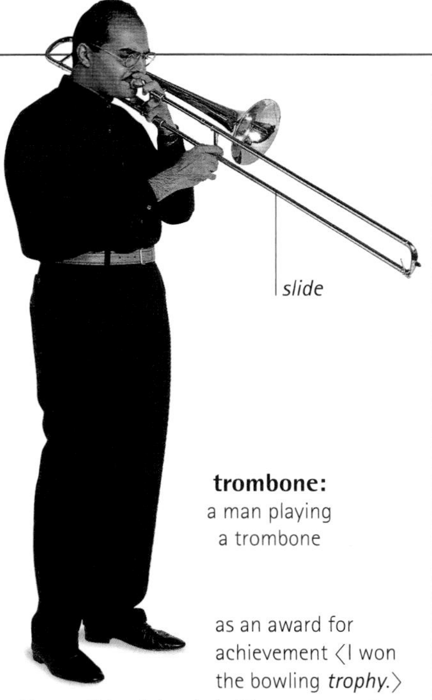

trombone: a man playing a trombone

trop•ic \'trä-pik\ *n*
1 either of two parallels of the earth's latitude of which one is about 23½ degrees north of the equator and the other about 23½ degrees south of the equator
2 **tropics** *pl, often cap* the region lying between the Tropic of Cancer and the Trop ic of Capricorn

trop•i•cal \'trä-pi-kəl\ *adj*
of, or occurring in the tropics 〈*tropical* fruit〉 〈a *tropical* island〉

tropical fish *n*
▼ a small often brightly colored fish kept in aquariums

tropical storm *n*
a storm that begins in the tropics with winds that are not as strong as those of a hurricane

[1]trot \'trät\ *n*
1 a gait of an animal with four feet that is faster than walking but slower than galloping and in which a front foot and the opposite hind foot move as a pair
2 a human jogging pace between a walk and a run

[2]trot *vb* **trot•ted; trot•ting**
1 to ride, drive, go, or cause to go at a trot 〈A horse *trotted* by.〉
2 to go along quickly : HURRY 〈He *trotted* off to school.〉

▶ **tropical fish**
Tropical fish kept in aquariums are bred from species that live in the warm water of coral reefs and coastal parts of the tropics. As shown below, they exist in a huge variety of shapes, sizes, and colors.

clownfish lives among stinging sea anemones

damselfish lives above tropical Atlantic reefs

butterfly fish hides among the coral at night

angelfish feeds on coral with its powerful jaws

lionfish has fins containing a powerful venom

porcupine fish inflates itself when frightened

a b c d e f g h i j k l m n o p q r s t u v w x y z

trout: a lake trout

[1]trou•ble \'trə-bəl\ *n*
1 something that causes worry or distress : MISFORTUNE 〈I've suffered many *troubles.*〉
2 an instance of distress or disturbance 〈Don't make *trouble.*〉
3 extra work or effort 〈They took the *trouble* to write.〉
4 ill health : AILMENT
5 failure to work normally 〈He had *trouble* with the engine.〉

[2]trouble *vb* **trou•bled; trou•bling**
1 to become or make worried or upset
2 to produce physical disorder in : AFFLICT 〈He's *troubled* with weak knees.〉
3 to put to inconvenience 〈Don't *trouble* yourself, I can do it.〉
4 to make an effort 〈Do not *trouble* to write.〉

trou•ble•some \'trə-bəl-səm\ *adj*
1 giving distress or anxiety 〈*troublesome* news〉
2 difficult to deal with 〈a *troublesome* child〉

trough \'trȯf\ *n*
1 a long shallow open container especially for water or feed for livestock
2 a channel for water : GUTTER
3 a long channel or hollow

trounce \'trau̇ns\ *vb* **trounced; trounc•ing**
1 to beat severely : FLOG
2 to defeat thoroughly

troupe \'trüp\ *n*
a group especially of performers who act or work together 〈a *troupe* of acrobats〉

trou•sers \'trau̇-zərz\ *n pl*
PANTS

trout \'trau̇t\ *n, pl* **trout**
◀ a freshwater fish related to the salmon that is often caught for food or sport

trow•el \'trau̇-əl\ *n*
1 a small hand tool with a flat blade used for spreading and smoothing mortar or plaster
2 a small hand tool with a curved blade used by gardeners

tru•an•cy \'trü-ən-sē\ *n, pl* **tru•an•cies**
an act or an instance of staying out of school without permission

tru•ant \'trü-ənt\ *n*
1 a student who stays out of school without permission
2 a person who neglects his or her duty

truce \'trüs\ *n*
an agreement between enemies or opponents to stop fighting for a certain period of time

[1]truck \'trək\ *n*
▼ a vehicle (as a strong heavy wagon or motor vehicle) for carrying heavy articles or hauling a trailer

[2]truck *n*
close association 〈He wanted no *truck* with criminals.〉

[3]truck *vb* **trucked; truck•ing**
to transport on or in a truck

trudge \'trəj\ *vb* **trudged; trudg•ing**
to walk or march steadily and usually with much effort 〈She *trudged* through the snow.〉

[1]true \'trü\ *adj* **tru•er; tru•est**
1 agreeing with the facts : ACCURATE 〈a *true* story〉
2 completely loyal : FAITHFUL 〈You are a *true* friend.〉
3 consistent or in accordance with 〈The movie is *true* to the book.〉
4 properly so called : GENUINE 〈Mosses have no *true* seeds.〉
5 placed or formed accurately : EXACT 〈*true* pitch〉
6 being or holding by right : LEGITIMATE 〈the *true* owner〉
7 fully realized or fulfilled 〈It's a dream come *true.*〉
synonyms see FAITHFUL, REAL

[2]true *adv*
1 in agreement with fact : TRUTHFULLY 〈She speaks *true.*〉
2 in an accurate manner : ACCURATELY 〈The arrow flew straight and *true.*〉

[3]true *n*
the quality or state of being accurate (as in alignment) 〈The door is out of *true.*〉

[4]true *vb* **trued; true•ing** *also* **tru•ing**
to bring to exactly correct condition as to place, position, or shape

true–blue \'trü-'blü\ *adj*
very faithful

tru•ly \'trü-lē\ *adv*
in a manner that is actual, genuine, honest, or without question 〈I am *truly* grateful for your help.〉

[1]trumpet 1: a man playing a trumpet

[1]trum•pet \'trəm-pət\ *n*
1 ▲ a brass musical instrument that consists of a tube formed into a long loop with a wide opening at one end and that has valves by which different tones are produced
2 something that is shaped like a trumpet 〈the *trumpet* of a lily〉

[1]truck: a trailer truck

[2]**trumpet** *vb* **trum•pet•ed; trum•pet•ing**
1 to blow a trumpet
2 to make a sound like that of a trumpet 〈The elephant *trumpeted* loudly.〉
3 to praise (something) loudly and publicly
trum•pet•er *n*

trun•dle \'trən-dəl\ *vb* **trun•dled; trun•dling**
to roll along : WHEEL 〈She *trundled* her suitcase into the room.〉 〈Buses *trundle* through town.〉

trundle bed *n*
a low bed on small wheels that can be rolled under a taller bed

trunk 2: a 19th-century trunk

trunk \'trəŋk\ *n*
1 the thick main stem of a tree not including the branches and roots
2 ▲ a box or chest for holding clothes or other articles especially for traveling
3 the enclosed space in the rear of an automobile for carrying articles
4 the long round muscular nose of an elephant
5 **trunks** *pl* a swimsuit for a man or boy
6 the body of a person or animal not including the head, arms, and legs

[1]**truss** \'trəs\ *vb* **trussed; truss•ing**
1 to bind or tie firmly
2 to support, strengthen, or stiffen by a framework of beams

[2]**truss** *n*
a framework of beams or bars used in building and engineering

[1]**trust** \'trəst\ *vb* **trust•ed; trust•ing**
1 to rely on or on the truth of : BELIEVE 〈I wouldn't *trust* anything he says.〉
2 to place confidence in someone or something 〈She doesn't *trust* the car to get us home.〉
3 to be confident : HOPE 〈I *trust* you had a good time.〉

[2]**trust** *n*
1 firm belief in the character, strength, or truth of someone or something 〈He placed his *trust* in me.〉
2 a person or thing in which confidence is placed
3 confident hope 〈I waited in *trust* of their return.〉
4 a property interest held by one person or organization (as a bank) for the benefit of another
5 a combination of firms or corporations formed by a legal agreement and often held to reduce competition
6 an organization in which money is held or managed by someone for the benefit of another or others
7 responsibility for safety and well-being 〈I left my cat in the *trust* of neighbors.〉

trust•ee \ˌtrə-'stē\ *n*
a person who has been given legal responsibility for someone else's property

trust•ful \'trəst-fəl\ *adj*
full of trust
trust•ful•ness *n*

trust•ing \'trə-stiŋ\ *adj*
having or showing faith, confidence, or belief in someone or something

trust•wor•thy \'trəst-ˌwər-t͟hē\ *adj*
deserving faith and confidence
trust•wor•thi•ness *n*

trusty \'trə-stē\ *adj* **trust•i•er; trust•i•est**
worthy of being depended on

truth \'trüth\ *n, pl* **truths** \'trüt͟hz\
1 the body of real events or facts 〈He'll keep investigating until he finds the *truth.*〉
2 the quality or state of being true 〈There is no *truth* in what she told you.〉
3 a true or accepted statement or idea 〈I learned some hard *truths* about life.〉
in truth in actual fact : REALLY

truth•ful \'trüth-fəl\ *adj*
telling or being in the habit of telling facts or making statements that are true
truth•ful•ly \-fə-lē\ *adv*
truth•ful•ness *n*

[1]**try** \'trī\ *vb* **tried** \'trīd\; **try•ing**
1 to make an effort or attempt at 〈He *tries* to remain calm.〉 〈*Try* calling her.〉
2 to put to a test 〈Have you ever *tried* artichokes?〉 〈You might *try* this key in the lock.〉
3 to examine or investigate in a court of law 〈They were *tried* for murder.〉
4 to conduct the trial of 〈An experienced judge will *try* the case.〉
5 to test to the limit 〈The children are *trying* my patience.〉
try on to put on (a garment) to test the fit
try out to compete to fill a part (as on an athletic team or in a play)

[2]**try** *n, pl* **tries**
an effort to do something : ATTEMPT 〈It took several *tries,* but I finally scored.〉

try•ing \'trī-iŋ\ *adj*
hard to bear or put up with

try•out \'trī-ˌau̇t\ *n*
a test of the ability (as of an athlete or an actor) to fill a part or meet standards

T-shirt *also* **tee shirt** \'tē-ˌshərt\ *n*
a shirt with short sleeves and no collar and usually made of cotton

tsp. *abbr* teaspoon

tsu•na•mi \su̇-'nä-mē\ *n*
a large sea wave produced especially by an earthquake or volcanic eruption under the sea : TIDAL WAVE

Tu. *abbr* Tuesday

tub \'təb\ *n*
1 a wide low container
2 BATHTUB
3 an old or slow boat
4 the amount that a tub will hold 〈We used a whole *tub* of margarine.〉

tu•ba \'tü-bə, 'tyü-\ *n*
▼ a brass musical instrument of lowest pitch with an oval shape and valves for producing different tones

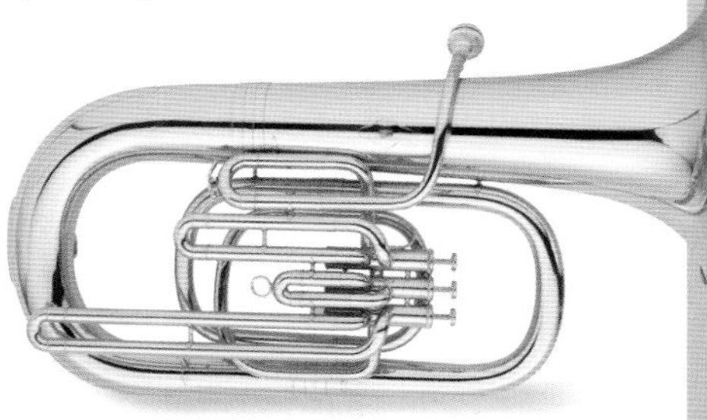
tuba

tub•by \'tə-bē\ *adj* **tub•bi•er; tub•bi•est**
short and somewhat fat

tube \'tüb, 'tyüb\ *n*
1 a long hollow cylinder used especially to carry fluids
2 a long soft container whose contents (as toothpaste or glue) can be removed by squeezing
3 a slender channel within a plant or animal body : DUCT
4 a hollow cylinder of rubber inside a tire to hold air
5 ELECTRON TUBE
6 TELEVISION 2
tube•like \'tüb-ˌlīk, 'tyüb-\ *adj*

tug–of–war 1: children having a tug-of-war

tu•ber \'tü-bər, 'tyü-\ *n*
a short thick fleshy usually underground stem (as of a potato plant) having buds that can produce new plants

tu•ber•cu•lo•sis \tu̇-,bər-kyə-'lō-səs, tyu̇-\ *n*
a serious disease that mostly affects the lungs and in which there is fever, cough, and difficulty in breathing

tu•bu•lar \'tü-byə-lər, 'tyü-\ *adj*
1 having the form of or made up of a tube ⟨*tubular* flowers⟩
2 made with tubes

^{1}**tuck** \'tək\ *vb* **tucked**; **tuck•ing**
1 to put or fit into a snug or safe place
2 to push in the edges of ⟨Remember to *tuck* in your shirt.⟩
3 to pull up into or as if into a fold ⟨She *tucked* her hair up to cook.⟩
4 to cover by pushing in the edges of bedclothes ⟨Grandma *tucked* the children in for the night.⟩
5 to eat or drink with obvious pleasure
6 to make stitched folds in

^{2}**tuck** *n*
a fold stitched into cloth usually to alter it

tuck•er \'tə-kər\ *vb* **tuck•ered**; **tuck•er•ing**
to cause to tire ⟨The long hike *tuckered* me out.⟩

Tue., Tues. *abbr* Tuesday

Tues•day \'tüz-dē, 'tyüz-\ *n*
the third day of the week

tuft \'təft\ *n*
1 a small bunch of long flexible things (as hairs or blades of grass) growing close together
2 ^{1}CLUMP 1
tuft•ed *adj*

^{1}**tug** \'təg\ *vb* **tugged**; **tug•ging**
1 to pull hard ⟨I *tugged* at the rope.⟩
2 to move by pulling hard **:** DRAG
3 to tow with a tugboat

^{2}**tug** *n*
1 an act of pulling hard **:** a hard pull ⟨She gave him a *tug*.⟩
2 TUGBOAT
3 a strong pulling force ⟨the *tug* of gravity⟩
4 a struggle between two people or forces

tug•boat \'təg-,bōt\ *n*
a small powerful boat used for towing ships

tug–of–war \,təg-əv-'wȯr\ *n*, *pl* **tugs–of–war**
1 ▲ a contest in which two teams pull against each other at opposite ends of a rope
2 a struggle to win ⟨The racers were in a *tug-of-war* for the championship.⟩

tu•ition \tu̇-'i-shən, tyu̇-\ *n*
money paid for instruction (as at a college)

tu•lip \'tü-ləp, 'tyü-\ *n*
▼ a plant related to the lily that grows from a bulb and has a large cup-shaped flower in early spring

tulips

^{1}**tum•ble** \'təm-bəl\ *vb* **tum•bled**; **tum•bling**
1 to fall suddenly and helplessly ⟨He *tumbled* off the bridge.⟩
2 to fall while rolling or bouncing ⟨Boxes *tumbled* down the stairs.⟩
3 to move or go in a hurried or confused way ⟨The children *tumbled* out of the bus.⟩
4 to toss together into a confused mass
5 to perform gymnastic feats of rolling and turning
6 to suffer a sudden downward turn or defeat ⟨The value of gold *tumbled*.⟩

^{2}**tumble** *n*
1 an act or instance of falling often while rolling or bouncing
2 a messy state or collection

tum•ble•down \'təm-bəl-,dau̇n\ *adj*
DILAPIDATED ⟨a *tumbledown* old house⟩

tum•bler \'təm-blər\ *n*
1 a person (as an acrobat) who tumbles
2 a drinking glass
3 a movable part of a lock that must be adjusted (as by a key) before the lock will open

tum•ble•weed \'təm-bəl-,wēd\ *n*
a plant that breaks away from its roots in autumn and tumbles about in the wind

tum•my \'tə-mē\ *n*, *pl* **tummies**
1 ^{1}STOMACH 1 ⟨an ache in the *tummy*⟩
2 ^{1}STOMACH 2 ⟨She tickled my *tummy*.⟩

tu•mor \'tü-mər, 'tyü-\ *n*
an abnormal growth of body tissue

tu•mult \'tü-,məlt, 'tyü-\ *n*
1 UPROAR ⟨A great *tumult* arose in the audience.⟩
2 great confusion of mind

tu•mul•tu•ous \tu̇-'məl-chə-wəs, tyu̇-\ *adj*
characterized by uproar ⟨a *tumultuous* welcome⟩

tu•na \'tü-nə, 'tyü-\ *n*, *pl* **tuna** *or* **tunas**
a large sea fish caught for food and sport

tun•dra \'tən-drə\ *n*
a treeless plain of arctic regions having a permanently frozen layer below the surface of the soil

^{1}**tune** \'tün, 'tyün\ *n*
1 a series of pleasing musical tones **:** MELODY
2 correct musical pitch or key ⟨We were singing out of *tune*.⟩
3 AGREEMENT 1, HARMONY ⟨Your feelings are in *tune* with mine.⟩

4 general attitude ⟨They changed their *tune* when they knew all the facts.⟩
tune•ful \-fəl\ *adj*

2tune *vb* **tuned**; **tun•ing**
1 to adjust a radio or television so that it receives clearly
2 to adjust in musical pitch ⟨I *tuned* my guitar.⟩
3 to come or bring into harmony
4 to put (as an engine) in good working order **Hint:** This sense is often used with *up*.
tun•er *n*
tune out to ignore what is happening or being said

tung•sten \ˈtəŋ-stən\ *n*
a grayish-white hard metallic chemical element used especially for electrical parts (as for the fine wire in an electric light bulb) and to make alloys (as steel) harder

tu•nic \ˈtü-nik, ˈtyü-\ *n*
1 a usually knee-length belted garment worn by ancient Greeks and Romans
2 a shirt or jacket reaching to or just below the hips

tuning fork *n*
▶ a metal instrument that gives a fixed tone when struck and is useful for tuning musical instruments

tuning fork

1tun•nel \ˈtə-nᵊl\ *n*
a passage under the ground

2tunnel *vb* **tun•neled** *or* **tun•nelled**; **tun•nel•ing** *or* **tun•nel•ling**
to make a passage under the ground

tun•ny \ˈtə-nē\ *n, pl* **tun•nies**
TUNA

tur•ban \ˈtər-bən\ *n*
1 a head covering worn especially by Muslims and made of a long cloth wrapped around the head or around a cap
2 a woman's small soft hat with no brim

tur•bid \ˈtər-bəd\ *adj*
dark or discolored with sediment ⟨a *turbid* stream⟩

tur•bine \ˈtər-bən\ *n*
an engine whose central driving shaft is fitted with a series of winglike parts that are spun by the pressure of water, steam, or gas

tur•bu•lence \ˈtər-byə-ləns\ *n*
irregular movements of air currents ⟨The ride got rough when the plane hit *turbulence*.⟩

tur•bu•lent \ˈtər-byə-lənt\ *adj*
causing or being in a state of unrest, violence, or disturbance ⟨*turbulent* protests⟩ ⟨*turbulent* weather⟩

tu•reen \tə-ˈrēn\ *n*
▶ a deep bowl from which food (as soup) is served

turf \ˈtərf\ *n*
1 the upper layer of soil bound into a thick mat by roots of grass and other plants
2 land covered with grass
3 an area that is or is felt to be under an individual's control ⟨Fluffy won't allow any other dogs on his *turf*.⟩

Turk \ˈtərk\ *n*
a person born or living in Turkey

tur•key \ˈtər-kē\ *n, pl* **turkeys**
▼ a large North American bird related to the chicken and widely raised for food

▶ **Word History** The plump, chicken-like birds called guinea fowl are of African origin. However, they were introduced into Europe from Mediterranean lands controlled by Turkey, so that in English they were frequently called *turkey-cocks* or *turkey-hens* in the 1500s. When the North American birds that we call turkeys entered Europe, they were at first thought to be varieties of guinea fowl and so were also called *turkey-cocks*, later shortened to *turkeys*. This name fell out of use for guinea fowl—whose current name more accurately reflects their origin, since *Guinea* is an old name for West Africa—but it has been kept for the American bird.

turkey

1Turk•ish \ˈtər-kish\ *adj*
of or relating to Turkey, the Turks, or Turkish

2Turkish *n*
the language of the Turks

tureen: a tureen of soup

tur•moil \ˈtər-ˌmȯil\ *n*
a very confused or disturbed state or condition ⟨A shortage of fuel left the country in *turmoil*.⟩

1turn \ˈtərn\ *vb* **turned**; **turn•ing**
1 to change in position usually by moving through an arc of a circle ⟨They *turned* and walked away.⟩ ⟨*Turn* the pancakes over.⟩
2 to change course or direction ⟨The road *turns* to the left.⟩
3 to move or direct toward or away from something ⟨We *turned* toward home.⟩
4 to become or cause to become a certain way ⟨The weather *turned* leaves red.⟩
5 1CHANGE 1, TRANSFORM ⟨*turn* lead into gold⟩
6 to move or cause to move around a center : ROTATE ⟨The earth *turns* on its axis.⟩
7 to twist so as to bring about a desired end ⟨*Turn* the key to unlock the door.⟩
8 to go around ⟨We *turned* the corner.⟩
9 to reach or pass beyond ⟨Soon she will *turn* ten.⟩
10 to become or make very unfriendly ⟨We were friends until she *turned* on me.⟩
11 to pass from one state to another : BECOME ⟨The weather *turned* cold.⟩
12 EXECUTE 2, PERFORM ⟨*turn* somersaults⟩
13 to set in another and especially an opposite direction ⟨It's difficult to *turn* the car on such a narrow street.⟩
14 1WRENCH 2 ⟨*turn* an ankle⟩
15 1UPSET 2 ⟨His behavior *turns* my stomach.⟩
16 to make an appeal ⟨He *turned* to a friend for help.⟩
17 to make or become spoiled ⟨The milk *turned*.⟩
18 TRANSLATE 1
19 to give a rounded form to (as on a lathe)
turn down
1 to lower by using a control ⟨*Turn down* the heat.⟩
2 1REFUSE 1, REJECT ⟨I *turned down* the offer.⟩
3 to fold back or under ⟨*Turn down* the sheets.⟩

A B C D E F G H I J K L M N O P Q R S T U V W X Y Z

turn off
1 to stop by using a control ⟨Remember to *turn off* the alarm.⟩
2 to change direction ⟨They *turned off* onto another road.⟩
turn on to make work by using a control ⟨*Turn on* the light.⟩

turnips

turn out
1 to prove to be ⟨The noise *turned out* to be from mice.⟩
2 to turn off
turn over to give control or responsibility of to someone
turn tail to turn so as to run away
turn up
1 to be found or happen unexpectedly ⟨Don't worry, the key will *turn up.*⟩
2 to raise by or as if by using a control ⟨*Turn up* the volume.⟩
3 ARRIVE 1

[2]**turn** *n*
1 the act of moving about a center ⟨Give the crank another *turn.*⟩
2 a change or changing of direction, course, or position ⟨Make a left *turn.*⟩
3 a place at which something changes direction ⟨a *turn* in the road⟩
4 a period of action or activity : SPELL ⟨I had my *turn* as guard.⟩
5 proper place in a waiting line or time in a schedule ⟨Take your *turn.*⟩
6 a change or changing of the general state or condition ⟨Business took a *turn* for the better.⟩
7 an act affecting another ⟨Do a friend a good *turn.*⟩
8 a short walk or ride ⟨They took a *turn* through the park.⟩
9 a special purpose or need ⟨That will serve the *turn.*⟩
10 special quality ⟨a nice *turn* of phrase⟩
11 the beginning of a new period of time ⟨the *turn* of the century⟩
12 a single circle or loop (as of rope passed around an object)
13 natural or special skill ⟨She has a *turn* for writing.⟩
at every turn all the time : CONSTANTLY, CONTINUOUSLY ⟨She has managed to succeed *at every turn.*⟩
by turns one after another
in turn one after the other in order
to a turn precisely right ⟨The turkey was cooked *to a turn.*⟩

turn•about \ˈtərn-ə-ˌbau̇t\ *n*
a change from one direction or one way of thinking or acting to the opposite ⟨In a complete *turnabout,* he admitted that he had lied.⟩

tur•nip \ˈtər-nəp\ *n*
◀ the thick white or yellow root of a plant related to the cabbage that is cooked and eaten as a vegetable

turn•out \ˈtərn-ˌau̇t\ *n*
a gathering of people for a special reason ⟨We had a good *turnout* for the meeting.⟩

turn•over \ˈtərn-ˌō-vər\ *n*
a filled pastry with one half of the crust turned over the other

turn•pike \ˈtərn-ˌpīk\ *n*
a road that people must pay a toll to use

turn•stile \ˈtərn-ˌstīl\ *n*
a post having arms that turn around which is set at an entrance or exit so that people can pass through only on foot one by one

tur•pen•tine \ˈtər-pən-ˌtīn\ *n*
an oil made from resin and used as a solvent and as a paint thinner

turquoise

tur•quoise \ˈtər-ˌkȯiz, -ˌkwȯiz\ *n*
▲ a blue to greenish gray mineral used in jewelry

tur•ret \ˈtər-ət\ *n*
1 ▼ a little tower often at a corner of a building
2 a low usually rotating structure (as in a tank, warship, or airplane) in which guns are mounted

tur•tle \ˈtər-tᵊl\ *n*
a reptile that lives on land, in water, or both and has a toothless horny beak and a shell of bony plates which covers the body and into which the head, legs, and tail can usually be drawn

tur•tle•dove \ˈtər-tᵊl-ˌdəv\ *n*
a small wild pigeon that has a low soft cry

tur•tle•neck \ˈtər-tᵊl-ˌnek\ *n*
1 a high turned-over collar
2 a garment having a high turned-over collar

turret 1: a Spanish castle with turrets

tusk \'təsk\ *n*
a very long large tooth (as of an elephant or walrus) that sticks out when the mouth is closed and is used especially in digging and fighting

[1]tus•sle \'tə-səl\ *n*
1 a short fight or struggle
2 a rough argument or a struggle against difficult odds

[2]tussle *vb* **tus•sled; tus•sling**
1 to struggle roughly : SCUFFLE
2 to argue or compete with

[1]tu•tor \'tü-tər, 'tyü-\ *n*
a teacher who works with an individual student

[2]tutor *vb* **tu•tored; tu•tor•ing**
to teach usually individually

tu•tu \'tü-,tü\ *n, pl* **tu•tus**
▼ a short skirt that extends out and is worn by a ballerina

tutu: a ballerina's tutu

tux•e•do \,tək-'sē-dō\ *n, pl* **tux•e•dos** *or* **tux•e•does**
a formal suit for a man

TV \'tē-'vē\ *n*
TELEVISION

twain \'twān\ *n*
[2]TWO 1

[1]twang \'twaŋ\ *n*
1 a harsh quick ringing sound
2 speech that seems to be produced by the nose as well as the mouth

[2]twang *vb* **twanged; twang•ing**
to sound or cause to sound with a harsh quick ringing noise ⟨He *twanged* his guitar.⟩

'twas \'twəz, 'twäz\
it was

[1]tweak \'twēk\ *vb* **tweaked; tweak•ing**
to pinch and pull with a sudden jerk and twist ⟨Grandpa *tweaked* my nose.⟩

[2]tweak *n*
an act of pinching and pulling with a sudden jerk and twist

tweed \'twēd\ *n*
1 a rough woolen cloth
2 **tweeds** *pl* clothing (as a suit) made of rough woolen cloth

[1]tweet \'twēt\ *n*
1 a chirping sound
2 a post made on the Twitter online message service

[2]tweet *vb* **tweet•ed; tweet•ing**
1 [2]CHIRP
2 to post a message to the Twitter online message service

tweezers

tweez•ers \'twē-zərz\ *n pl*
▲ a small instrument that is used like pincers in grasping or pulling something

[1]twelfth \'twelfth\ *adj*
coming right after eleventh ⟨December is the *twelfth* month of the year.⟩

[2]twelfth *n*
number twelve in a series

[1]twelve \'twelv\ *adj*
being one more than eleven

[2]twelve *n*
one more than eleven : three times four : 12

twelve•month \'twelv-,mənth\ *n*
YEAR

[1]twen•ti•eth \'twen-tē-əth\ *adj*
coming right after 19th

[2]twentieth *n*
number 20 in a series

[1]twen•ty \'twen-tē\ *adj*
being one more than 19 ⟨One dollar equals *twenty* nickels.⟩

[2]twenty *n*
one more than 19 : four times five : 20

twice \'twīs\ *adv*
two times ⟨He knocked at the door *twice*.⟩

twid•dle \'twi-dᵊl\ *vb* **twid•dled; twid•dling**
[1]TWIRL ⟨I *twiddled* my thumbs.⟩

twig \'twig\ *n*
a small shoot or branch

twi•light \'twī-,līt\ *n*
1 the period or the light from the sky between full night and sunrise or between sunset and full night
2 a period of decline ⟨She is in the *twilight* of her career.⟩

twill \'twil\ *n*
a way of weaving cloth that produces a pattern of diagonal lines

[1]twin \'twin\ *n*
1 ▼ either of two offspring produced at one birth
2 one of two persons or things closely related to or very like each other ⟨On the opposite side of the river is the city's *twin*.⟩

[2]twin *adj*
1 born with one other or as a pair at one birth ⟨my *twin* brother⟩
2 made up of two similar, related, or connected members or parts ⟨a *twin*-engine airplane⟩
3 being one of a pair

[1]twine \'twīn\ *n*
a strong string of two or more strands twisted together

[2]twine *vb* **twined; twin•ing**
1 to twist together ⟨We *twined* the branches into a wreath.⟩
2 to coil around a support ⟨A vine *twines* around the pole.⟩

[1]twinge \'twinj\ *n*
a sudden sharp stab (as of pain or emotion) ⟨She felt a *twinge* of envy.⟩

[2]twinge *vb* **twinged; twing•ing** *or* **twinge•ing**
to affect with or feel a sudden sharp pain or emotion

[1]twin 1: identical twins

[1]twin•kle \'twiŋ-kəl\ *vb* **twin•kled**; **twin•kling**
1 to shine or cause to shine with a flickering or sparkling light 〈Stars *twinkle* in the sky.〉
2 to appear bright with amusement 〈His eyes *twinkled* at the joke.〉
3 to move or flutter rapidly

[2]twinkle *n*
1 [2]SPARKLE 1, FLICKER
2 a very short time

twin•kling \'twiŋ-kliŋ\ *n*
[2]TWINKLE 2

[1]twirl \'twərl\ *vb* **twirled**; **twirl•ing**
to turn or cause to turn rapidly 〈a *twirling* windmill〉
twirl•er *n*

[2]twirl *n*
an act of turning or causing to turn rapidly

[1]twist \'twist\ *vb* **twist•ed**; **twist•ing**
1 to turn a part of the body around 〈She *twisted* in her seat.〉
2 to follow a winding course 〈The path *twisted* between the trees.〉
3 to form into an unnatural shape : CONTORT 〈The girl *twisted* her face.〉
4 to unite by winding one thread, strand, or wire around another
5 [2]TWINE 2
6 to turn so as to sprain or hurt 〈He *twisted* his ankle.〉
7 to pull off, rotate, or break by a turning force 〈*Twist* the flower from its stem.〉
8 to turn (something) in a circular motion with the hand 〈*Twist* off the cap.〉
9 to change the meaning of 〈You're *twisting* my words.〉

[2]twist *n*
1 something that has been turned upon itself, coiled, or rotated 〈*twists* of rope〉
2 ► an act of turning with force, coiling, or rotating : the state of being turned with force, coiled, or rotated
3 a spiral turn or curve
4 a turn or development that is both surprising and strange
5 an act of changing the meaning

twist•er \'twi-stər\ *n*
1 TORNADO
2 WATERSPOUT 2

[1]twitch \'twich\ *vb* **twitched**; **twitch•ing**
1 to move or cause to move with a slight trembling or jerky motion : QUIVER 〈The rabbit *twitched* its ears.〉
2 to move or pull with a sudden motion : JERK 〈She *twitched* the blanket aside.〉

[2]twitch *n*
1 a slight tremble or jerk of a muscle or body part 〈a *twitch* of the tail〉
2 a short sudden pull or jerk 〈I gave the fishing pole a *twitch*.〉

[1]twit•ter \'twi-tər\ *vb* **twit•tered**; **twit•ter•ing**
1 to make a series of chirping noises
2 to talk in a chattering fashion

[2]twitter *n*
1 the chirping of birds
2 a light chattering or laughing
3 a nervous upset state 〈We were all of a *twitter*.〉

[1]two \'tü\ *adj*
being one more than one

typewriter

key

[2]two *n*
1 one more than one : 2
2 the second in a set or series

two–dimensional *adj*
having the two dimensions of length and width 〈A square is *two-dimensional*.〉

two–faced \'tü-'fāst\ *adj*
not honest or sincere : saying different things to different people in order to gain their approval instead of speaking and behaving honestly

two•fold \'tü-,fōld\ *adj*
being twice as great or as many

two–way *adj*
1 moving or acting or allowing movement or action in either direction 〈*two-way* traffic〉 〈a *two-way* street〉
2 involving two persons or groups 〈Communication is a *two-way* process.〉
3 made to send and receive messages 〈a *two-way* radio〉

TX *abbr* Texas

ty•coon \tī-'kün\ *n*
a very powerful and wealthy business person

tying *present participle of* TIE

[1]type \'tīp\ *n*
1 a particular kind or group of things or people : VARIETY 〈a seedless *type* of orange〉
2 a set of letters or figures that are used for printing or the letters or figures printed by them
3 the special qualities or characteristics by which members of a group are set apart from other groups 〈plants grouped by *type*〉

[2]type *vb* **typed**; **typ•ing**
1 to write with a keyboard (as on computer)
2 to identify as belonging to a certain group

type•writ•er \'tīp-,rī-tər\ *n*
◄ a machine that prints letters or figures when a person pushes its keys down

type•writ•ing \'tīp-,rī-tiŋ\ *n*
1 the use of a typewriter
2 writing done with a typewriter

ty•phoid \'tī-,fȯid\ *n*
TYPHOID FEVER

typhoid fever *n*
a disease that spreads through contaminated food and water and in which there is fever, diarrhea, and great weakness

[2]twist 2: a man performing a yoga twist

typhoon: a satellite photo of a typhoon

ty•phoon \tī-ˈfün\ *n*
▲ a tropical cyclone in the region of the Philippines or the China Sea

ty•phus \ˈtī-fəs\ *n*
a disease spread especially by body lice and in which there is high fever, delirium, severe headache, and a dark red rash

typ•i•cal \ˈti-pi-kəl\ *adj*
combining or showing the special characteristics of a group or kind ⟨a *typical* Sunday dinner⟩
synonyms see REGULAR
typ•i•cal•ly *adv*

typ•i•fy \ˈti-pə-ˌfī\ *vb* **typ•i•fied**; **typ•i•fy•ing**
1 REPRESENT 2 ⟨The cathedral *typifies* architecture of this period.⟩
2 to have the usual characteristics of **:** be a typical part of ⟨The heavy beat *typifies* the band's music.⟩

typ•ist \ˈtī-pist\ *n*
a person who uses a typewriter

ty•ran•ni•cal \tə-ˈra-ni-kəl\ *adj*
relating to or like that of tyranny or a tyrant ⟨*tyrannical* acts⟩

ty•ran•no•saur \tə-ˈra-nə-ˌsȯr, tī-\ *n*
▶ a very large North American meat-eating dinosaur that had small forelegs and walked on its hind legs

ty•ran•no•sau•rus \tə-ˌra-nə-ˈsȯr-əs, tī-\ *n*
TYRANNOSAUR

tyr•an•ny \ˈtir-ə-nē\ *n, pl* **tyr•an•nies**
1 an act or the pattern of harsh, cruel, and unfair control over other people
2 a government in which all power is in the hands of a single ruler

ty•rant \ˈtī-rənt\ *n*
1 a ruler who has no legal limits on his or her power
2 a ruler who exercises total power harshly and cruelly
3 a person who uses authority or power harshly ⟨My boss is a real *tyrant.*⟩

tyrannosaur: model of a tyrannosaur

Sounds of U. The letter **U** makes a number of sounds. The long **U** is heard in words like *rule* and *sue*. It is indicated by the symbol ü. The long **U** is also often pronounced as if there is a **Y** in front of it, as in *mule* and *unit*. The sound heard in the words *cut* and *bump* is the short **U**. Letter **U** can also make the schwa sound, in words like *support* or *circus*. Both this sound and the short **U** sound are indicated by the symbol ə. The letter **U** makes another sound, which is heard in *put* and *full*. This sound is indicated by the symbol u̇. In *busy*, **U** sounds like a short **I**. In *bury*, **U** sounds like a short **E**. **U** often sounds like a **W**, usually after **Q** in words like *quick* and *quote*, but also in other words such as *persuade*. **U** makes a variety of sounds when combined with other letters, such as in *scout*, *haul*, and *feud*.

u \ˈyü\ *n, pl* **u's** *or* **us** \ˈyüz\ *often cap*
1 the 21st letter of the English alphabet
2 a grade rating a student's work as unsatisfactory

ud•der \ˈə-dər\ *n*
a large bag-shaped organ (as of a cow) enclosing two or more milk-producing glands each draining into a separate nipple on the lower surface

ugh \ˈəg\ *interj*
used to express disgust or horror

ug•ly \ˈə-glē\ *adj* **ug•li•er**; **ug•li•est**
1 unpleasant to look at : not attractive ⟨an *ugly* color⟩
2 [1]OFFENSIVE 1 ⟨*ugly* habits⟩
3 likely to cause bother or discomfort : TROUBLESOME ⟨an *ugly* situation⟩
4 showing a mean or quarrelsome disposition ⟨an *ugly* temper⟩
ug•li•ness *n*

UK *abbr* United Kingdom

uku•le•le \ˌyü-kə-ˈlā-lē\ *n*
▶ a musical instrument like a small guitar with four strings

▶ **Word History** In the Hawaiian language *'ukulele* means literally "jumping flea," a creature with little resemblance to a small guitar. It is likely that this peculiar name became attached to the instrument in a roundabout way. Edward Purvis, a former British army officer living at the court of the Hawaiian king, is said to have been given the nickname *'ukulele* because he was a small, lively man. In 1879 Portuguese immigrants to Hawaii brought with them a small four-stringed guitar called a *machete*. Purvis was taken with the instrument and soon learned to play it. When the *machete* became a Hawaiian favorite, it took on Purvis's nickname, *'ukulele*, and its Portuguese name was soon forgotten.

ul•cer \ˈəl-sər\ *n*
a slow-healing open painful sore (as of the lining of the stomach) in which tissue breaks down

ul•na \ˈəl-nə\ *n, pl* **ul•nas** *or* **ul•nae** \-nē\
the bone on the little-finger side of the arm between the wrist and elbow

ul•te•ri•or \ˌəl-ˈtir-ē-ər\ *adj*
kept hidden usually on purpose ⟨*ulterior* motives⟩

ul•ti•mate \ˈəl-tə-mət\ *adj*
1 last in a series : FINAL
2 most extreme ⟨the *ultimate* sacrifice⟩
3 relating to or being the chief or most important ⟨She has *ultimate* responsibility for the accident.⟩
ul•ti•mate•ly *adv*

ul•ti•ma•tum \ˌəl-tə-ˈmā-təm\ *n, pl* **ul•ti•ma•tums** *or* **ul•ti•ma•ta** \-ˈmā-tə\
a final condition or demand that if rejected could end future negotiations and lead to forceful or undesirable action

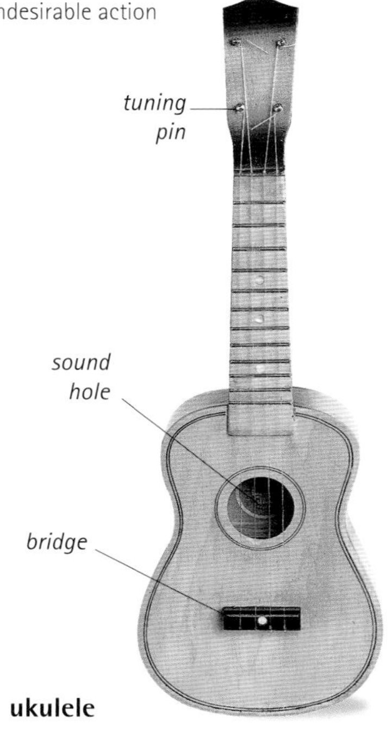

ukulele

ul•tra \ˈəl-trə\ *adj*
[1]EXTREME 1 ⟨*ultra* plush chair⟩

ultra- *prefix*
1 beyond in space : on the other side ⟨*ultra*violet⟩
2 beyond the limits of : SUPER-
3 beyond what is ordinary or proper

ul•tra•vi•o•let \ˌəl-trə-ˈvī-ə-lət\ *adj*
relating to, producing, or being energy that is like light but has a slightly shorter wavelength and lies beyond the violet end of the spectrum

um•bil•i•cal cord \ˌəm-ˈbi-li-kəl-\ *n*
a cord that contains blood vessels and connects a developing fetus with the placenta of the mother

um•brel•la \ˌəm-ˈbre-lə\ *n*
a fabric covering stretched over a circular folding frame of rods attached to a pole and used as a protection against rain or sun

▶ **Word History** We most often think of an umbrella as something that protects us from the rain. However, its shade can protect us from the hot sun, too. The English word *umbrella* came from Italian *ombrella*, which itself is taken from Latin *umbella*, literally, "little shade." *Umbella* is derived from *umbra*, meaning "shade" or "shadow."

um•pire \ˈəm-ˌpīr\ *n*
▶ an official in a sport (as baseball) who enforces the rules

UN *abbr* United Nations

[1]**un-** \ˌən, ˈən\ *prefix*
1 not : IN-, NON- ⟨*un*skilled⟩
2 opposite of : contrary to ⟨*un*constitutional⟩

[2]**un-** *prefix*
1 do the opposite of : DE-, DIS- ⟨*un*dress⟩
2 remove a specified thing from or free or release from ⟨*un*leash⟩
3 completely ⟨*un*loose⟩

un•able \ˌən-ˈā-bəl\ *adj*
not able ⟨I am *unable* to attend.⟩

A B C D E F G H I J K L M N O P Q R S T U V W X Y Z

un•ac•cept•able \ˌən-ik-ˈsep-tə-bəl, -ak-\ *adj*
not pleasing or welcome : not acceptable ⟨*unacceptable* behavior⟩

un•ac•count•able \ˌən-ə-ˈkau̇n-tə-bəl\ *adj*
not to be explained : STRANGE ⟨*unaccountable* noises⟩
un•ac•count•ably \-blē\ *adv*

un•ac•cus•tomed \ˌən-ə-ˈkə-stəmd\ *adj*
not used to something ⟨He was *unaccustomed* to strenuous work.⟩

un•af•fect•ed \ˌən-ə-ˈfek-təd\ *adj*
1 not influenced or changed ⟨My concentration was *unaffected* by the constant noise.⟩
2 free from false behavior intended to impress others : GENUINE ⟨an *unaffected* manner⟩

un•afraid \ˌən-ə-ˈfrād\ *adj*
not afraid

un•aid•ed \ˌən-ˈā-dəd\ *adj*
without help : not aided ⟨The star is visible to the *unaided* eye.⟩

un•al•loyed \ˌən-ə-ˈlȯid\ *adj*
PURE 1

unan•i•mous \yu̇-ˈna-nə-məs\ *adj*
1 having the same opinion : agreeing completely ⟨They were *unanimous* in their choice.⟩
2 agreed to by all ⟨a *unanimous* vote⟩

un•armed \ˌən-ˈärmd\ *adj*
having no weapons or armor

un•as•sum•ing \ˌən-ə-ˈsü-miŋ\ *adj*
MODEST 1

un•at•trac•tive \ˌən-ə-ˈtrak-tiv\ *adj*
not attractive : PLAIN

un•avoid•able \ˌən-ə-ˈvȯi-də-bəl\ *adj*
not preventable : INEVITABLE ⟨an *unavoidable* accident⟩
un•avoid•ably \-blē\ *adv*

[1]**un•aware** \ˌən-ə-ˈwer\ *adv*
UNAWARES

[2]**unaware** *adj*
not having knowledge : not aware ⟨They're *unaware* of the danger.⟩

un•awares \ˌən-ə-ˈwerz\ *adv*
1 without warning : by surprise ⟨They were taken *unawares*.⟩
2 without knowing : UNINTENTIONALLY

un•bear•able \ˌən-ˈber-ə-bəl\ *adj*
seeming too great or too bad to put up with ⟨*unbearable* pain⟩
un•bear•ably \-blē\ *adv*

un•be•com•ing \ˌən-bi-ˈkə-miŋ\ *adj*
not suitable or proper : not becoming ⟨*unbecoming* clothes⟩ ⟨*unbecoming* behavior⟩

un•be•knownst \ˌən-bi-ˈnōnst\ *also* **un•be•known** \-ˈnōn\ *adj*
happening without someone's knowledge : UNKNOWN ⟨*Unbeknownst* to him, we were planning a surprise party.⟩

umpire: a tennis player arguing with the chair umpire during a match

un•be•liev•able \ˌən-bə-ˈlē-və-bəl\ *adj*
1 too unlikely to be believed ⟨an *unbelievable* excuse⟩
2 very impressive or amazing ⟨an *unbelievable* catch⟩
un•be•liev•ably \-blē\ *adv*

un•bi•ased \ˌən-ˈbī-əst\ *adj*
free from bias

un•bind \ˌən-ˈbīnd\ *vb* **un•bound** \-ˈbau̇nd\; **un•bind•ing**
1 to remove a band from : UNTIE
2 to set free

un•born \ˌən-ˈbȯrn\ *adj*
not yet born

un•bound•ed \ˌən-ˈbau̇n-dəd\ *adj*
having no limits ⟨*unbounded* enthusiasm⟩

un•break•able \ˌən-ˈbrā-kə-bəl\ *adj*
not easily broken

un•bri•dled \ˌən-ˈbrī-dᵊld\ *adj*
not controlled or restrained ⟨*unbridled* anger⟩

un•bro•ken \ˌən-ˈbrō-kən\ *adj*
1 not damaged : WHOLE
2 not interrupted : CONTINUOUS ⟨*unbroken* sleep⟩
3 not tamed for use ⟨an *unbroken* colt⟩

un•buck•le \ˌən-ˈbə-kəl\ *vb* **un•buck•led**; **un•buck•ling**
to unfasten the buckle of (as a belt)

un•bur•den \ˌən-ˈbər-dᵊn\ *vb* **un•bur•dened**; **un•bur•den•ing**
to free from a burden and especially from something causing worry or unhappiness

un•but•ton \ˌən-ˈbə-tᵊn\ *vb* **un•but•toned**; **un•but•ton•ing**
to unfasten the buttons of ⟨I *unbuttoned* my shirt.⟩

un•called–for \ˌən-ˈkȯld-ˌfȯr\ *adj*
not needed or wanted : not proper ⟨*uncalled-for* remarks⟩

un•can•ny \ˌən-ˈka-nē\ *adj*
1 strange or unusual in a way that is surprising or mysterious ⟨an *uncanny* resemblance⟩
2 suggesting powers or abilities greater than normal ⟨an *uncanny* sense of direction⟩
un•can•ni•ly \-ˈka-nə-lē\ *adv*

un•cer•tain \ˌən-ˈsər-tᵊn\ *adj*
1 not exactly known or decided on ⟨an *uncertain* amount⟩
2 not sure ⟨They were *uncertain* of the rules.⟩
3 not known for sure ⟨an *uncertain* claim⟩
4 likely to change : not dependable ⟨*uncertain* weather⟩
un•cer•tain•ly *adv*

un•cer•tain•ty \ˌən-ˈsər-tᵊn-tē\ *n, pl* **un•cer•tain•ties**
1 lack of certainty : DOUBT ⟨He began his new task without hesitation or *uncertainty.*⟩
2 something that is doubtful or unknown

un•change•able \ˌən-ˈchān-jə-bəl\ *adj*
not changing or capable of being changed ⟨*unchangeable* facts⟩

un•changed \ˌən-ˈchānjd\ *adj*
not changed ⟨Our plans remained *unchanged.*⟩

un•chang•ing \ˌən-ˈchān-jiŋ\ *adj*
not changing or able to change ⟨an *unchanging* pattern of lights⟩

un•char•ac•ter•is•tic \ˌən-ˌker-ək-tə-ˈri-stik\ *adj*
not typical or characteristic ⟨an *uncharacteristic* outburst of temper⟩
un•char•ac•ter•is•ti•cal•ly \-sti-klē, -kə-lē\ *adv*

un•civ•il \ˌən-ˈsi-vəl\ *adj*
IMPOLITE

un•civ•i•lized \ˌən-ˈsi-və-ˌlīzd\ *adj*
1 having, relating to, or being like a culture that is not advanced
2 not having or showing good manners : RUDE

un•cle \ˈəŋ-kəl\ *n*
1 the brother of a person's father or mother
2 the husband of a person's aunt

un•clean \ˌən-ˈklēn\ *adj*
1 DIRTY 1, FILTHY
2 not pure and innocent
3 not allowed for use by religious law

un•clear \ˌən-ˈklir\ *adj*
difficult to understand or make sense of ⟨Your directions are *unclear.*⟩

un•cleared \ˌən-ˈklird\ *adj*
not cleared especially of trees or brush

un•clothed \ˌən-ˈklōthd\ *adj*
not wearing or covered with clothes

un•com•fort•able \ˌən-ˈkəm-fər-tə-bəl, -ˈkəmf-tər-bəl\ *adj*
1 causing discomfort or uneasiness ⟨an *uncomfortable* chair⟩ ⟨an *uncomfortable* silence⟩
2 feeling discomfort or uneasiness ⟨His staring made me *uncomfortable.*⟩
un•com•fort•ably \-blē\ *adv*

un•com•mon \ˌən-ˈkä-mən\ *adj*
1 not often found or seen : UNUSUAL ⟨an *uncommon* bird⟩
2 not ordinary : REMARKABLE ⟨*uncommon* ability⟩ ⟨*uncommon* courage⟩
synonyms see RARE
un•com•mon•ly *adv*

un•com•pro•mis•ing \ˌən-ˈkäm-prə-ˌmī-ziŋ\ *adj*
not willing to give in even a little
un•com•pro•mis•ing•ly *adv*

un•con•cern \ˌən-kən-ˈsərn\ *n*
lack of care or interest

un•con•cerned \ˌən-kən-ˈsərnd\ *adj*
1 free of worry ⟨She was *unconcerned* about the test.⟩
2 not involved or interested ⟨I'm *unconcerned* with winning or losing.⟩

un•con•di•tion•al \ˌən-kən-ˈdi-shə-nᵊl\ *adj*
without any special exceptions ⟨an *unconditional* surrender⟩
un•con•di•tion•al•ly *adv*

un•con•quer•able \ˌən-ˈkäŋ-kə-rə-bəl\ *adj*
not capable of being beaten or overcome ⟨an *unconquerable* spirit⟩

un•con•scious \ˌən-ˈkän-shəs\ *adj*
1 not aware ⟨He was *unconscious* of being watched.⟩
2 having lost consciousness ⟨I was knocked *unconscious* by the fall.⟩
3 not intentional or planned ⟨an *unconscious* error⟩
un•con•scious•ly *adv*
un•con•scious•ness *n*

un•con•sti•tu•tion•al \ˌən-ˌkän-stə-ˈtü-shə-nᵊl, -ˈtyü-\ *adj*
not according to or agreeing with the constitution of a country or government

un•con•trol•la•ble \ˌən-kən-ˈtrō-lə-bəl\ *adj*
hard or impossible to control ⟨an *uncontrollable* rage⟩
un•con•trol•la•bly \-blē\ *adv*

un•con•trolled \ˌən-kən-ˈtrōld\ *adj*
not being controlled

un•co•op•er•a•tive \ˌən-kō-ˈä-pə-rə-tiv\ *adj*
not showing a desire to act or work with others in a helpful way

un•couth \ˌən-ˈküth\ *adj*
impolite in conduct or speech : CRUDE ⟨*uncouth* manners⟩ ⟨*uncouth* people⟩

> ▶ **Word History** The word *uncouth* first meant "unknown" or "strange." It goes back to Old English *uncūth,* made up of *un-,* "not," and *cūth,* "known," which is related to modern English *can* and *know.*

un•cov•er \ˌən-ˈkə-vər\ *vb* **un•cov•ered**; **un•cov•er•ing**
1 to make known usually by investigation ⟨Police *uncovered* a crime.⟩
2 to make visible by removing some covering
3 to remove the cover from

un•curl \ˌən-ˈkərl\ *vb* **un•curled**; **un•curl•ing**
to make or become straightened out from a curled position

un•cut \ˌən-ˈkət\ *adj*
1 not cut down or cut into ⟨*uncut* forests⟩
2 not shaped by cutting ⟨an *uncut* diamond⟩

un•daunt•ed \ˌən-ˈdȯn-təd\ *adj*
not discouraged or afraid to continue

un•de•cid•ed \ˌən-di-ˈsī-dəd\ *adj*
1 not yet settled or decided ⟨The date for the picnic is still *undecided.*⟩
2 not having decided : uncertain what to do ⟨We are still *undecided* about where to stay.⟩

un•de•clared \ˌən-di-ˈklerd\ *adj*
not made known : not declared ⟨an *undeclared* war⟩

un•de•feat•ed \ˌən-di-ˈfē-təd\ *adj*
having no losses

un•de•ni•able \ˌən-di-ˈnī-ə-bəl\ *adj*
clearly true : impossible to deny ⟨an *undeniable* fact⟩
un•de•ni•ably \-blē\ *adv*

[1]**un•der** \ˈən-dər\ *adv*
1 in or into a position below or beneath something ⟨The dog squeezed *under* the fence.⟩
2 below some quantity or level ⟨ten dollars or *under*⟩

[2]**under** *prep*
1 lower than and topped or sheltered by ⟨*under* a tree⟩
2 below the surface of ⟨*under* the sea⟩
3 in or into such a position as to be covered or hidden by ⟨I wore a sweater *under* my jacket.⟩
4 commanded or guided by ⟨Many soldiers served *under* George Washington.⟩
5 controlled or managed by ⟨The restaurant is *under* new management.⟩
6 affected or influenced by the action or effect of ⟨The disease is *under* treatment.⟩
7 within the division or grouping of ⟨That information is *under* this heading.⟩
8 less or lower than (as in size, amount, or rank) ⟨The candy costs *under* a dollar.⟩ ⟨The package weighs *under* two pounds.⟩

[3]**under** *adj*
1 lying or placed below or beneath
2 lower in position or authority
Hint: The adjective *under* is often used in combination with other words. ⟨*under*side⟩

un•der•arm \ˈən-dər-ˌärm\ *n*
ARMPIT

un•der•brush \ˈən-dər-ˌbrəsh\ *n*
shrubs and small trees growing among large trees

un•der•clothes \ˈən-dər-ˌklōz, -ˌklōthz\ *n pl*
UNDERWEAR

un·der·cooked \ˌən-dər-ˈku̇kt\ *adj*
not cooked enough

un·der·cur·rent \ˈən-dər-ˌkər-ənt\ *n*
1 a flow of water that moves below the surface
2 a hidden feeling or tendency often different from the one openly shown ⟨She sensed an *undercurrent* of dissatisfaction.⟩

un·der·dog \ˈən-dər-ˌdȯg\ *n*
a person or team thought to have little chance of winning (as an election or a game)

un·der·foot \ˌən-dər-ˈfu̇t\ *adv*
1 under the feet ⟨The rocks were slippery *underfoot*.⟩
2 close about a person's feet **:** in the way ⟨My puppy is always *underfoot*.⟩

un·der·gar·ment \ˈən-dər-ˌgär-mənt\ *n*
a garment to be worn under another

un·der·go \ˌən-dər-ˈgō\ *vb* **un·der·went** \-ˈwent\; **un·der·gone** \-ˈgȯn\; **un·der·go·ing** \-ˈgō-iŋ\
to experience or endure (something) ⟨I have to *undergo* an operation.⟩ ⟨He *underwent* a change of feelings.⟩

[1]**un·der·ground** \ˌən-dər-ˈgrau̇nd\ *adv*
1 below the surface of the earth
2 in or into hiding or secret operation

[2]**un·der·ground** \ˈən-dər-ˌgrau̇nd\ *n*
1 SUBWAY
2 a secret political movement or group

[3]**un·der·ground** \ˈən-dər-ˌgrau̇nd\ *adj*
1 located under the surface of the ground ⟨*underground* pipes⟩
2 done or happening secretly ⟨an *underground* revolt⟩

un·der·growth \ˈən-dər-ˌgrōth\ *n*
▼ low growth on the floor of a forest that includes shrubs, herbs, and saplings

[1]**un·der·hand** \ˈən-dər-ˌhand\ *adv*
with an upward movement of the hand or arm ⟨She threw *underhand*.⟩

[2]**underhand** *adj*
1 done in secret or so as to deceive ⟨*underhand* dealings⟩
2 made with an upward movement of the hand or arm ⟨an *underhand* throw⟩

un·der·hand·ed \ˌən-dər-ˈhan-dəd\ *adj*
[2]UNDERHAND 1

un·der·lie \ˌən-dər-ˈlī\ *vb* **un·der·lay** \-ˈlā\; **un·der·lain** \-ˈlān\; **un·der·ly·ing** \-ˈlī-iŋ\
1 to lie or be located under ⟨A tile floor *underlies* the rug.⟩
2 to form the foundation of **:** SUPPORT ⟨What ideals *underlie* democracy?⟩

un·der·line \ˈən-dər-ˌlīn\ *vb* **un·der·lined**; **un·der·lin·ing**
1 to draw a line under
2 EMPHASIZE ⟨The poor results *underline* our need to try harder.⟩

un·der·mine \ˌən-dər-ˈmīn\ *vb* **un·der·mined**; **un·der·min·ing**
1 to dig out or wear away the supporting earth beneath ⟨Erosion *undermined* the wall.⟩
2 to weaken secretly or little by little ⟨Their criticisms *undermine* my confidence.⟩

[1]**un·der·neath** \ˌən-dər-ˈnēth\ *prep*
directly under ⟨We wore our bathing suits *underneath* our clothes.⟩

[2]**underneath** *adv*
1 below a surface or object **:** BENEATH ⟨She lifted the log and found ants crawling *underneath*.⟩
2 on the lower side ⟨The pot was scorched *underneath*.⟩

un·der·nour·ished \ˌən-dər-ˈnər-isht\ *adj*
given too little food for proper health and growth

un·der·pants \ˈən-dər-ˌpants\ *n pl*
underwear worn on the lower part of the body

un·der·part \ˈən-dər-ˌpärt\ *n*
► a part lying on the lower side (as of a bird or mammal)

underpart

underpart: a weasel showing its white underpart

un·der·pass \ˈən-dər-ˌpas\ *n*
a road or passage that runs under something (as another road)

un·der·priv·i·leged \ˌən-dər-ˈpri-və-lijd\ *adj*
having fewer advantages than others especially because of being poor

un·der·rate \ˌən-dər-ˈrāt\ *vb* **un·der·rat·ed**; **un·der·rat·ing**
to rate too low **:** UNDERVALUE

un·der·score \ˈən-dər-ˌskȯr\ *vb* **un·der·scored**; **un·der·scor·ing**
1 UNDERLINE 1
2 EMPHASIZE

un·der·sea \ˈən-dər-ˈsē\ *adj*
1 being or done under the sea or under the surface of the sea ⟨an *undersea* volcano⟩
2 used under the surface of the sea ⟨an *undersea* vessel⟩

undergrowth: undergrowth on the floor of a forest

a b c d e f g h i j k l m n o p q r s t u v w x y z

un•der•shirt \'ən-dər-ˌshərt\ *n*
a collarless garment with or without sleeves that is worn as an undergarment

un•der•side \'ən-dər-ˌsīd\ *n*
the side or surface lying underneath ⟨the *underside* of a leaf⟩

un•der•stand \ˌən-dər-'stand\ *vb* **un•der•stood** \-'stu̇d\; **un•der•stand•ing**
1 to get the meaning of ⟨Do you *understand* my instructions?⟩
2 to know thoroughly ⟨I *understand* Spanish.⟩ ⟨She *understands* the situation.⟩
3 to have reason to believe ⟨I *understand* that they will come today.⟩
4 to take as meaning something not clearly made known ⟨I *understand* the letter to be a refusal.⟩
5 to have a sympathetic attitude ⟨Don't worry, I *understand* how you feel.⟩
6 to accept as settled ⟨It is *understood* that I will pay.⟩

un•der•stand•able \ˌən-dər-'stan-də-bəl\ *adj*
1 possible or easy to get or realize the meaning of : capable of being understood ⟨The teacher made a difficult subject quite *understandable.*⟩
2 normal and reasonable for a particular situation ⟨an *understandable* reaction⟩
un•der•stand•ably \-blē\ *adv*

[1]**un•der•stand•ing** \ˌən-dər-'stan-diŋ\ *n*
1 ability to get the meaning of and judge
2 an agreement of opinion or feeling ⟨We've come to an *understanding* about how to proceed.⟩
3 a willingness to show kind or favorable feelings toward others
4 the particular way in which someone understands something ⟨It's my *understanding* that they're coming.⟩

[2]**understanding** *adj*
having or showing kind or favorable feelings toward others : SYMPATHETIC

un•der•state•ment \ˌən-dər-'stāt-mənt\ *n*
a statement that makes something seem smaller or less important or serious than it really is

un•der•study \'ən-dər-ˌstə-dē\ *n, pl* **un•der•stud•ies**
an actor who is prepared to take over another actor's part if necessary

un•der•take \ˌən-dər-'tāk\ *vb* **un•der•took** \-'tu̇k\; **un•der•tak•en** \-'tā-kən\; **un•der•tak•ing**
1 to plan or try to accomplish ⟨They *undertook* a trip around the world.⟩
2 to take on as a responsibility : AGREE ⟨I *undertake* to deliver your package.⟩

un•der•tak•er \'ən-dər-ˌtā-kər\ *n*
a person whose business is to prepare the dead for burial and to take charge of funerals

un•der•tak•ing \'ən-dər-ˌtā-kiŋ\ *n*
an important or difficult task or project ⟨Creating a mural is a big *undertaking.*⟩

un•der•tone \'ən-dər-ˌtōn\ *n*
1 a low or quiet voice ⟨They spoke in *undertones.*⟩
2 a partly hidden feeling or meaning ⟨There was an *undertone* of anger in the answer.⟩

un•der•tow \'ən-dər-ˌtō\ *n*
a current beneath the surface of the water that moves away from or along the shore while the surface water above it moves toward the shore

un•der•val•ue \ˌən-dər-'val-yü\ *vb* **un•der•val•ued**; **un•der•valu•ing**
to value below the real worth

[1]**un•der•wa•ter** \'ən-dər-'wȯ-tər, -'wä-\ *adj*
lying, growing, worn, performed, or operating below the surface of the water ⟨an *underwater* cave⟩ ⟨*underwater* somersaults⟩

[2]**un•der•wa•ter** \ˌən-dər-'wȯ-tər, -'wä-\ *adv*
under the surface of the water ⟨I like to swim *underwater.*⟩

un•der•wear \'ən-dər-ˌwer\ *n*
clothing worn next to the skin and under other clothing

un•der•weight \ˌən-dər-'wāt\ *adj*
weighing less than what is normal, average, or necessary

underwent *past of* UNDERGO

un•der•world \'ən-dər-ˌwərld\ *n*
the world of crime

un•de•sir•able \ˌən-di-'zī-rə-bəl\ *adj*
having qualities that are not pleasing or wanted ⟨an *undesirable* effect⟩

un•de•vel•oped \ˌən-di-'ve-ləpt\ *adj*
1 not used for farming or building on ⟨*undeveloped* land⟩
2 having few large industries and a simple economic system ⟨an *undeveloped* country⟩
3 not fully grown or matured

un•dig•ni•fied \ˌən-'dig-nə-ˌfīd\ *adj*
lacking proper seriousness or self-control in behavior or appearance : not showing dignity ⟨*undignified* conduct⟩

un•dis•cov•ered \ˌən-di-'skəv-ərd\ *adj*
not discovered

un•dis•put•ed \ˌən-di-'spyüt-əd\ *adj*
not disputed : UNQUESTIONABLE ⟨the *undisputed* leader⟩

un•dis•turbed \ˌən-di-'stərbd\ *adj*
1 not moved, interrupted, or interfered with ⟨an *undisturbed* sleep⟩ ⟨*undisturbed* snow⟩
2 not upset ⟨She was *undisturbed* by the change.⟩

un•di•vid•ed \ˌən-də-'vī-dəd\ *adj*
complete or total ⟨I want your *undivided* attention.⟩

un•do \ˌən-'dü\ *vb* **un•did** \-'did\; **un•done** \-'dən\; **un•do•ing** \-'dü-iŋ\; **un•does** \-'dəz\
1 UNTIE 2, UNFASTEN ⟨Can you *undo* this knot?⟩
2 to cancel the effect of : REVERSE ⟨The damage cannot be *undone.*⟩
3 to cause the ruin or failure of ⟨He was *undone* by greed.⟩

un•do•ing \ˌən-'dü-iŋ\ *n*
a cause of ruin or failure ⟨My quick temper was my *undoing.*⟩

un•done \ˌən-'dən\ *adj*
not done or finished

un•doubt•ed \ˌən-'dau̇-təd\ *adj*
definitely true or existing : not doubted ⟨*undoubted* proof of guilt⟩

un•doubt•ed•ly \ˌən-'dau̇-təd-lē\ *adv*
without doubt : SURELY ⟨She's *undoubtedly* the school's best athlete.⟩

un•dress \ˌən-'dres\ *vb* **un•dressed**; **un•dress•ing**
to remove the clothes or covering of

un•du•late \'ən-jə-ˌlāt, -də-, -dyə-\ *vb* **un•du•lat•ed**; **un•du•lat•ing**
to move in or as if in a wavy or flowing way ⟨The field of grass *undulated* in the breeze.⟩

un•dy•ing \ˌən-'dī-iŋ\ *adj*
lasting forever : IMMORTAL ⟨*undying* devotion⟩

un•earth \ˌən-'ərth\ *vb* **un•earthed**; **un•earth•ing**
1 to bring up from underground : dig up ⟨Pirates *unearthed* the buried treasure.⟩
2 to bring to light : UNCOVER ⟨Reporters *unearthed* a scandal.⟩

un•easy \ˌən-'ē-zē\ *adj* **un•eas•i•er**; **un•eas•i•est**
1 not comfortable in manner : AWKWARD ⟨Their staring made me *uneasy.*⟩
2 showing or filled with worry : APPREHENSIVE ⟨He was *uneasy* before the test.⟩
un•eas•i•ly \-zə-lē\ *adv*
un•eas•i•ness \-zē-nəs\ *n*

un•ed•u•cat•ed \ˌən-'e-jə-ˌkā-təd\ *adj*
1 lacking in education and especially schooling
2 based on little or no knowledge or fact ⟨an *uneducated* guess⟩

un•em•ployed \ˌən-im-'plȯid\ *adj*
having no job : not employed ⟨*unemployed* workers⟩

un•em•ploy•ment \ˌən-im-'plȯi-mənt\ *n*
1 the state of being out of work
2 the number of people who do not have jobs

un•end•ing \ˌən-'en-diŋ\ *adj*
having no ending : ENDLESS

un•equal \ˌən-ˈē-kwəl\ *adj*
1 not alike (as in size or value)
2 badly balanced or matched ⟨an *unequal* fight⟩
3 not having the needed abilities ⟨They proved *unequal* to the task.⟩
un•equal•ly *adv*

un•equaled \ˌən-ˈē-kwəld\ *adj*
having no equal or match

un•even \ˌən-ˈē-vən\ *adj*
1 ODD 3 ⟨*uneven* numbers⟩
2 not level, straight, or smooth ⟨an *uneven* surface⟩
3 IRREGULAR 4 ⟨*uneven* breathing⟩
4 varying in quality ⟨an *uneven* performance⟩
5 UNEQUAL 2 ⟨an *uneven* competition⟩
un•even•ly *adv*
un•even•ness *n*

un•event•ful \ˌən-i-ˈvent-fəl\ *adj*
having nothing exciting, interesting, or important happening : not eventful ⟨an *uneventful* vacation⟩
un•event•ful•ly \-fə-lē\ *adv*

un•ex•pect•ed \ˌən-ik-ˈspek-təd\ *adj*
not expected : UNFORESEEN ⟨an *unexpected* visit⟩
un•ex•pect•ed•ly *adv*

un•fail•ing \ˌən-ˈfā-liŋ\ *adj*
not failing or likely to fail : CONSTANT ⟨*unfailing* support⟩
un•fail•ing•ly *adv*

un•fair \ˌən-ˈfer\ *adj*
not fair, honest, or just ⟨an *unfair* trial⟩
un•fair•ly *adv*
un•fair•ness *n*

un•faith•ful \ˌən-ˈfāth-fəl\ *adj*
not faithful : DISLOYAL

un•fa•mil•iar \ˌən-fə-ˈmil-yər\ *adj*
1 not well-known : STRANGE ⟨an *unfamiliar* sight⟩
2 lacking good knowledge of something ⟨I'm *unfamiliar* with this subject.⟩

un•fas•ten \ˌən-ˈfa-sᵊn\ *vb* **un•fas•tened**; **un•fas•ten•ing**
to make or become loose ⟨He *unfastened* the buckle.⟩

un•fa•vor•able \ˌən-ˈfā-və-rə-bəl\ *adj*
1 expressing or showing disapproval ⟨an *unfavorable* comment⟩
2 likely to make difficult or unpleasant ⟨We had *unfavorable* weather for our trip.⟩
un•fa•vor•ably \-blē\ *adv*

un•feel•ing \ˌən-ˈfē-liŋ\ *adj*
having no kindness or sympathy : CRUEL ⟨an *unfeeling* joke⟩

un•fin•ished \ˌən-ˈfi-nisht\ *adj*
not finished

un•fit \ˌən-ˈfit\ *adj*
1 not suitable ⟨The food was *unfit* to eat.⟩
2 not qualified ⟨He is *unfit* for this job.⟩
3 physically unhealthy

un•fold \ˌən-ˈfōld\ *vb* **un•fold•ed**; **un•fold•ing**
1 to open the folds of : open up ⟨Carefully *unfold* the map.⟩
2 to lay open to view or understanding : REVEAL ⟨*unfold* a plan⟩
3 to develop gradually

un•fore•seen \ˌən-fōr-ˈsēn\ *adj*
not known beforehand : UNEXPECTED ⟨*unforeseen* problems⟩

un•for•get•ta•ble \ˌən-fər-ˈge-tə-bəl\ *adj*
not likely to be forgotten : lasting in memory ⟨an *unforgettable* experience⟩
un•for•get•ta•bly \-blē\ *adv*

un•for•giv•able \ˌən-fər-ˈgi-və-bəl\ *adj*
not to be forgiven or pardoned ⟨an *unforgivable* crime⟩
un•for•giv•ably \-blē\ *adv*

un•for•tu•nate \ˌən-ˈfȯr-chə-nət\ *adj*
1 not fortunate : UNLUCKY ⟨the *unfortunate* victim⟩ ⟨an *unfortunate* incident⟩
2 accompanied by or resulting in bad luck ⟨an *unfortunate* decision⟩
3 not proper or suitable ⟨an *unfortunate* remark⟩
un•for•tu•nate•ly *adv*

un•found•ed \ˌən-ˈfau̇n-dəd\ *adj*
not based on facts or proof : GROUNDLESS ⟨*unfounded* suspicions⟩

un•friend•ly \ˌən-ˈfrend-lē\ *adj* **un•friend•li•er**; **un•friend•li•est**
1 not friendly or kind ⟨an *unfriendly* glance⟩
2 not agreeable : UNFAVORABLE ⟨*unfriendly* conditions⟩

un•furl \ˌən-ˈfərl\ *vb* **un•furled**; **un•furl•ing**
to open out from a rolled or folded state ⟨*unfurl* a flag⟩

un•gain•ly \ˌən-ˈgān-lē\ *adj* **un•gain•li•er**; **un•gain•li•est**
CLUMSY 1, AWKWARD ⟨an *ungainly* walk⟩

un•god•ly \ˌən-ˈgäd-lē\ *adj* **un•god•li•er**; **un•god•li•est**
1 SINFUL, WICKED
2 not normal or bearable ⟨I got up at an *ungodly* hour.⟩

un•gra•cious \ˌən-ˈgrā-shəs\ *adj*
not kind or polite

un•grate•ful \ˌən-ˈgrāt-fəl\ *adj*
not feeling or showing thanks ⟨an *ungrateful* child⟩

un•gu•late \ˈəŋ-gyə-lət\ *n*
► a usually plant-eating animal (as a cow, horse, or sheep) with hooves

un•hap•py \ˌən-ˈha-pē\ *adj* **un•hap•pi•er**; **un•hap•pi•est**
1 not cheerful : SAD ⟨an *unhappy* person⟩
2 not pleased or satisfied ⟨We were *unhappy* with the hotel room.⟩
3 full of or showing feelings of sadness or misery ⟨an *unhappy* childhood⟩ ⟨an *unhappy* face⟩
4 not fortunate : UNLUCKY ⟨an *unhappy* coincidence⟩
5 not suitable : INAPPROPRIATE ⟨an *unhappy* choice⟩
un•hap•pi•ly \-ˈha-pə-lē\ *adv*
un•hap•pi•ness \-ˈha-pē-nəs\ *n*

un•healthy \ˌən-ˈhel-thē\ *adj* **un•health•i•er**; **un•health•i•est**
1 not good for someone's health : promoting a state of poor health ⟨Smoking is an *unhealthy* habit.⟩
2 not in good health : SICKLY
3 HARMFUL, BAD ⟨an *unhealthy* situation⟩
un•health•i•ly \-thə-lē\ *adv*

un•heard \ˌən-ˈhərd\ *adj*
not heard ⟨I entered the room *unheard*.⟩

un•heard–of \ˌən-ˈhərd-ˌəv, -ˌäv\ *adj*
not known before

un•hin•dered \ˌən-ˈhin-dərd\ *adj*
not kept back : proceeding freely ⟨*unhindered* progress⟩

un•hitch \ˌən-ˈhich\ *vb* **un•hitched**; **un•hitch•ing**
to free from being hitched ⟨*Unhitch* the horses.⟩

un•ho•ly \ˌən-ˈhō-lē\ *adj* **un•ho•li•er**; **un•ho•li•est**
1 not holy : WICKED
2 UNGODLY 2 ⟨Stop that *unholy* racket!⟩

ungulate: sheep are ungulates

a b c d e f g h i j k l m n o p q r s t **u** v w x y z

un•hook \ˌən-ˈhu̇k\ *vb* **un•hooked; un•hook•ing**
1 to remove from a hook ⟨He *unhooked* the fish.⟩
2 to unfasten the hooks of ⟨I *unhooked* my belt.⟩

un•horse \ˌən-ˈhȯrs\ *vb* **un•horsed; un•hors•ing**
to cause to fall from or as if from a horse

un•hur•ried \ˌən-ˈhər-ēd\ *adj*
not in a rush

uni- \ˈyü-ni\ *prefix*
one : single

uni•corn \ˈyü-nə-ˌkȯrn\ *n*
▼ an imaginary animal that looks like a horse with one horn in the middle of the forehead

unicorn: a statue of a unicorn

un•iden•ti•fi•able \ˌən-ī-ˌden-tə-ˈfī-ə-bəl\ *adj*
impossible to identify : not recognizable ⟨*unidentifiable* sounds⟩

un•iden•ti•fied \ˌən-ī-ˈden-tə-ˌfīd\ *adj*
having an identity that is not known or determined ⟨an *unidentified* person⟩

uni•fi•ca•tion \ˌyü-nə-fə-ˈkā-shən\ *n*
the act, process, or result of bringing or coming together into or as if into a single unit or group ⟨*unification* of a divided nation⟩

[1]**uni•form** \ˈyü-nə-ˌfȯrm\ *adj*
always the same in form, manner, appearance, or degree throughout or over time ⟨a *uniform* temperature⟩ ⟨*uniform* procedures⟩
uni•form•ly *adv*

[2]**uniform** *n*
▶ special clothing worn by members of a particular group (as an army)

uni•formed \ˈyü-nə-ˌfȯrmd\ *adj*
dressed in uniform

uni•for•mi•ty \ˌyü-nə-ˈfȯr-mə-tē\ *n, pl* **uni•for•mi•ties**
the quality or state of being the same in form, manner, appearance, or degree

uniform resource lo•ca•tor \-ˈlō-ˌkā-tər, -lō-ˈkā-\ *n*
URL

uni•fy \ˈyü-nə-ˌfī\ *vb* **uni•fied; uni•fy•ing**
to bring or come together into or as if into a single unit or group : UNITE

un•imag•in•able \ˌən-ə-ˈma-jə-nə-bəl\ *adj*
not possible to imagine or understand ⟨*unimaginable* treasures⟩

un•im•por•tant \ˌən-im-ˈpȯr-tᵊnt\ *adj*
not important ⟨*unimportant* details⟩

un•in•hab•it•ed \ˌən-in-ˈha-bə-təd\ *adj*
not lived in or on ⟨an *uninhabited* island⟩

un•in•tel•li•gi•ble \ˌən-in-ˈte-lə-jə-bəl\ *adj*
impossible to understand ⟨*unintelligible* speech⟩

un•in•ten•tion•al \ˌən-in-ˈten-shə-nᵊl\ *adj*
not done on purpose : not intentional ⟨an *unintentional* error⟩
un•in•ten•tion•al•ly *adv*

un•in•ter•est•ed \ˌən-ˈin-trə-stəd, -ˈin-tə-rə-\ *adj*
not interested ⟨He was *uninterested* in watching the parade.⟩

un•in•ter•est•ing \ˌən-ˈin-trə-stiŋ, -ˈin-tə-rə-\ *adj*
not attracting or keeping interest or attention

un•in•ter•rupt•ed \ˌən-ˌin-tə-ˈrəp-təd\ *adj*
not interrupted : CONTINUOUS ⟨My sleep was *uninterrupted.*⟩

un•in•vit•ed \ˌən-ˌin-ˈvī-təd\ *adj*
not having been invited ⟨an *uninvited* guest⟩

union \ˈyün-yən\ *n*
1 an act or instance of uniting or joining two or more things into one ⟨The river is formed by the *union* of two tributaries.⟩
2 something (as a nation) formed by a combining of parts or members
3 *cap* the United States
4 *cap* the group of states that supported the United States government in the American Civil War
5 a device for connecting parts (as pipes)
6 LABOR UNION

▶ [2]**uniform**

One of the purposes of a uniform is to make a group of people immediately recognizable. Most uniforms are also designed to be comfortable and helpful for the wearers while they work. This is especially important for workers like firefighters and members of the armed forces.

US police officer | British nurse | Australian firefighter

Union *adj*
relating to the group of states that supported the United States government in the American Civil War 〈*Union* soldiers〉

union suit *n*
an undergarment with shirt and pants in one piece

unique \yu̇-ˈnēk\ *adj*
1 being the only one of its kind 〈Every snowflake is *unique.*〉
2 very unusual : NOTABLE 〈a *unique* talent〉
unique•ly *adv*
unique•ness *n*

uni•son \ˈyü-nə-sən\ *n*
the state of being tuned or sounded at the same pitch or at an octave
in unison
1 in exact agreement 〈They are *in unison* as to what to do next.〉
2 at the same time 〈We recited the alphabet *in unison.*〉

unit \ˈyü-nət\ *n*
1 a single thing, person, or group forming part of a whole
2 the least whole number : ONE
3 a fixed quantity (as of length, time, or value) used as a standard of measurement 〈An inch is a *unit* of length.〉
4 a part of a school course with a central theme

unite \yu̇-ˈnīt\ *vb* **unit•ed**; **unit•ing**
1 to put or come together to form a single unit
2 to bind by legal or moral ties 〈This treaty will *unite* our nations.〉
3 to join in action 〈The two groups *united* to improve schools.〉

unit•ed \yu̇-ˈnī-təd\ *adj*
1 made one 〈*United* States of America〉
2 having the same goals, ideas, and principles

uni•ty \ˈyü-nə-tē\ *n, pl* **uni•ties**
1 the quality or state of being one
2 the state of those who are in full agreement : HARMONY 〈Why can't we live in *unity*?〉

uni•ver•sal \ˌyü-nə-ˈvər-səl\ *adj*
1 including, covering, or taking in all or everything 〈*universal* medical care〉
2 present or happening everywhere 〈*universal* celebration〉
uni•ver•sal•ly *adv*

universal resource lo•ca•tor \-ˈlō-ˌkā-tər, -lō-ˈkā-\ *n*
URL

uni•verse \ˈyü-nə-ˌvərs\ *n*
all created things including the earth and heavenly bodies viewed as making up one system

uni•ver•si•ty \ˌyü-nə-ˈvər-sə-tē\ *n, pl* **uni•ver•si•ties**
an institution of higher learning that gives degrees in special fields and where research is performed

un•just \ˌən-ˈjəst\ *adj*
not just : UNFAIR 〈an *unjust* decision〉
un•just•ly *adv*

un•kempt \ˌən-ˈkempt\ *adj*
1 not combed 〈*unkempt* hair〉
2 not neat and orderly : UNTIDY 〈an *unkempt* room〉

un•kind \ˌən-ˈkīnd\ *adj* **un•kind•er**; **un•kind•est**
not kind or sympathetic 〈an *unkind* remark〉
un•kind•ly *adv*
un•kind•ness *n*

[1]**un•known** \ˌən-ˈnōn\ *adj*
not known 〈*unknown* lands〉

[2]**unknown** *n*
one (as a quantity) that is unknown

un•lace \ˌən-ˈlās\ *vb* **un•laced**; **un•lac•ing**
to undo the laces of 〈*unlace* a shoe〉

un•latch \ˌən-ˈlach\ *vb* **un•latched**; **un•latch•ing**
▶ to open by lifting a latch

un•law•ful \ˌən-ˈlȯ-fəl\ *adj*
not lawful : ILLEGAL
un•law•ful•ly \-fə-lē\ *adv*

un•learned *adj*
1 \ˌən-ˈlər-nəd\ not educated
2 \-ˈlərnd\ not based on experience : INSTINCTIVE

un•leash \ˌən-ˈlēsh\ *vb* **un•leashed**; **un•leash•ing**
to free from or as if from a leash 〈A storm *unleashed* its fury.〉

un•less \ən-ˈles\ *conj*
except on the condition that 〈You can't have dessert *unless* you finish your dinner.〉

un•lik•able \ˌən-ˈlī-kə-bəl\ *adj*
difficult to like

[1]**un•like** \ˌən-ˈlīk\ *prep*
1 different from 〈You are *unlike* the rest.〉
2 unusual for 〈It's *unlike* them to be so late.〉
3 differently from 〈I behave *unlike* the others.〉

[2]**unlike** *adj*
DIFFERENT 1, UNEQUAL

un•like•ly \ən-ˈlī-klē\ *adj* **un•like•li•er**; **un•like•li•est**
1 not likely 〈an *unlikely* story〉
2 not promising 〈This is an *unlikely* place for fishing.〉

un•lim•it•ed \ˌən-ˈli-mə-təd\ *adj*
1 having no restrictions or controls 〈*unlimited* freedom〉
2 BOUNDLESS, INFINITE 〈*unlimited* possibilities〉

un•load \ˌən-ˈlōd\ *vb* **un•load•ed**; **un•load•ing**
1 to take away or off : REMOVE 〈Workers *unloaded* cargo.〉
2 to take a load from 〈Help me *unload* the car.〉
3 to get rid of or be freed from a load or burden 〈The ship is *unloading.*〉

un•lock \ˌən-ˈläk\ *vb* **un•locked**; **un•lock•ing**
1 to unfasten the lock of
2 to make known 〈Scientists are *unlocking* the secrets of nature.〉

un•looked–for \ˌən-ˈlu̇kt-ˌfȯr\ *adj*
not expected 〈an *unlooked-for* treat〉

unlatch: a person unlatching a door by foot

a b c d e f g h i j k l m n o p q r s t **u** v w x y z

A B C D E F G H I J K L M N O P Q R S T U V W X Y Z

un•loose \ˌən-ˈlüs\ *vb* **un•loosed**; **un•loos•ing**
1 to make looser : RELAX ⟨I *unloosed* my grip.⟩
2 to set free

un•lucky \ˌən-ˈlə-kē\ *adj* **un•luck•i•er**; **un•luck•i•est**
1 not fortunate : having bad luck ⟨He's been *unlucky* in love.⟩
2 marked by bad luck or failure ⟨an *unlucky* day⟩
3 likely to bring misfortune ⟨Are black cats really *unlucky*?⟩
4 causing distress or regret
un•luck•i•ly \-ˈlək-ə-lē\ *adv*

un•man•age•able \ˌən-ˈma-ni-jə-bəl\ *adj*
hard or impossible to handle or control ⟨an *unmanageable* child⟩

un•man•ner•ly \ˌən-ˈma-nər-lē\ *adj*
not having or showing good manners

un•mar•ried \ˌən-ˈmer-ēd\ *adj*
not married : SINGLE

un•mis•tak•able \ˌən-mə-ˈstā-kə-bəl\ *adj*
impossible to mistake for anything else ⟨We smelled the *unmistakable* odor of a skunk.⟩
un•mis•tak•ably \-blē\ *adv*

un•moved \ˌən-ˈmüvd\ *adj*
1 not being stirred by deep feelings or excitement ⟨The music left me *unmoved*.⟩
2 staying in the same place or position

un•nat•u•ral \ˌən-ˈna-chə-rəl, -ˈnach-rəl\ *adj*
1 different from what is found in nature or happens naturally
2 different from what is usually considered normal behavior
3 not genuine ⟨an *unnatural* smile⟩
un•nat•u•ral•ly *adv*

un•nec•es•sary \ˌən-ˈne-sə-ˌser-ē\ *adj*
not needed
un•nec•es•sar•i•ly \ˈən-ˌne-sə-ˈser-ə-lē\ *adv*

un•nerve \ˌən-ˈnərv\ *vb* **un•nerved**; **un•nerv•ing**
to cause to lose confidence, courage, or self-control

un•no•tice•able \ˌən-ˈnō-tə-sə-bəl\ *adj*
not easily noticed

un•num•bered \ˌən-ˈnəm-bərd\ *adj*
1 not numbered ⟨an *unnumbered* page⟩
2 INNUMERABLE

un•ob•served \ˌən-əb-ˈzərvd\ *adj*
not noticed ⟨She left the room *unobserved*.⟩

un•oc•cu•pied \ˌən-ˈä-kyə-ˌpīd\ *adj*
1 ▶ not being used, filled up, or lived in : EMPTY ⟨an *unoccupied* seat⟩
2 not busy

un•of•fi•cial \ˌən-ə-ˈfi-shəl\ *adj*
not official
un•of•fi•cial•ly *adv*

un•pack \ˌən-ˈpak\ *vb* **un•packed**; **un•pack•ing**
1 to separate and remove things that are packed ⟨Will you *unpack* the groceries?⟩
2 to open and remove the contents of ⟨I *unpacked* my suitcase.⟩

un•paid \ˌən-ˈpād\ *adj*
not paid ⟨*unpaid* bills⟩

un•par•al•leled \ˌən-ˈper-ə-ˌleld\ *adj*
having no counterpart or equal ⟨an *unparalleled* celebration⟩

un•pleas•ant \ˌən-ˈple-zᵊnt\ *adj*
not pleasing or agreeable ⟨an *unpleasant* smell⟩
un•pleas•ant•ly *adv*
un•pleas•ant•ness *n*

un•pop•u•lar \ˌən-ˈpä-pyə-lər\ *adj*
not widely favored or approved ⟨an *unpopular* rule⟩ ⟨an *unpopular* teacher⟩

un•prec•e•dent•ed \ˌən-ˈpre-sə-ˌden-təd\ *adj*
not done or experienced before ⟨The event was *unprecedented*.⟩

un•pre•dict•able \ˌən-pri-ˈdik-tə-bəl\ *adj*
impossible to predict ⟨*unpredictable* hazards of travel⟩

un•prej•u•diced \ˌən-ˈpre-jə-dəst\ *adj*
not resulting from or having a bias for or against ⟨The judge gave an *unprejudiced* opinion.⟩

un•pre•pared \ˌən-pri-ˈperd\ *adj*
not being or made ready

un•prin•ci•pled \ˌən-ˈprin-sə-pəld\ *adj*
not having or showing high moral principles ⟨*unprincipled* behavior⟩

un•prof•it•able \ˌən-ˈprä-fə-tə-bəl\ *adj*
not producing a profit

un•ques•tion•able \ˌən-ˈkwes-chə-nə-bəl\ *adj*
being beyond doubt
un•ques•tion•ably \-blē\ *adv*

un•ques•tion•ing \ˌən-ˈkwes-chə-niŋ, -ˈkwesh-\ *adj*
accepting without thinking or doubting ⟨*unquestioning* obedience⟩

un•rav•el \ˌən-ˈra-vəl\ *vb* **un•rav•eled** *or* **un•rav•elled**; **un•rav•el•ing** *or* **un•rav•el•ling**
1 to separate the threads of : UNTANGLE
2 SOLVE ⟨She *unraveled* the mystery.⟩

un•re•al \ˌən-ˈrē-əl\ *adj*
not actual or genuine

un•rea•son•able \ˌən-ˈrē-zᵊn-ə-bəl\ *adj*
not fair, sensible, appropriate, or moderate ⟨an *unreasonable* schedule⟩ ⟨*unreasonable* behavior⟩ ⟨an *unreasonable* fear⟩
un•rea•son•ably \-blē\ *adv*

un•re•lent•ing \ˌən-ri-ˈlen-tiŋ\ *adj*
1 not giving in or softening in determination : STERN
2 not letting up or weakening in energy or pace
un•re•lent•ing•ly *adv*

un•re•li•able \ˌən-ri-ˈlī-ə-bəl\ *adj*
not worthy of trust

un•rest \ˌən-ˈrest\ *n*
a disturbed or uneasy state ⟨political *unrest*⟩

unoccupied 1: the middle seat is unoccupied

un•ripe \ˌən-ˈrīp\ *adj*
▶ not ripe or mature

un•ri•valed *or* **un•ri•valled** \ˌən-ˈrī-vəld\ *adj*
having no rival

un•roll \ˌən-ˈrōl\ *vb* **un•rolled**; **un•roll•ing**
1 to unwind a roll of
2 to become unrolled

un•ruf•fled \ˌən-ˈrə-fəld\ *adj*
1 not upset or disturbed
2 ¹SMOOTH 4 〈*unruffled* water〉

un•ruly \ˌən-ˈrü-lē\ *adj* **un•rul•i•er**; **un•rul•i•est**
difficult to control 〈*unruly* hair〉
un•rul•i•ness *n*

un•safe \ˌən-ˈsāf\ *adj*
exposed or exposing to danger 〈People are *unsafe* on the streets.〉 〈The bridge is *unsafe* for heavy trucks.〉

un•san•i•tary \ˌən-ˈsa-nə-ˌter-ē\ *adj*
likely to cause sickness or disease : dirty or full of germs

un•sat•is•fac•to•ry \ˈən-ˌsa-təs-ˈfak-tə-rē\ *adj*
not what is needed or expected 〈His behavior in class has been *unsatisfactory.*〉
un•sat•is•fac•to•ri•ly \-rə-lē\ *adv*

un•sat•is•fied \ˌən-ˈsa-təs-ˌfīd\ *adj*
1 not fulfilled 〈an *unsatisfied* ambition〉
2 not pleased

un•scathed \ˌən-ˈskāthd\ *adj*
completely without harm or injury 〈They emerged from the wreckage *unscathed.*〉

un•schooled \ˌən-ˈsküld\ *adj*
not trained or taught

un•sci•en•tif•ic \ˌən-ˌsī-ən-ˈti-fik\ *adj*
not using or applying the methods or principles of science : not scientific 〈an *unscientific* explanation〉

un•scram•ble \ˌən-ˈskram-bəl\ *vb* **un•scram•bled**; **un•scram•bling**
to make orderly or clear again 〈If you *unscramble* the letters they spell a word.〉

un•screw \ˌən-ˈskrü\ *vb* **un•screwed**; **un•screw•ing**
1 to loosen or withdraw by turning 〈*Unscrew* the light bulb.〉
2 to remove the screws from

un•scru•pu•lous \ˌən-ˈskrü-pyə-ləs\ *adj*
not having or showing regard for what is right and proper 〈an *unscrupulous* salesman〉
un•scru•pu•lous•ly *adv*

un•seal \ˌən-ˈsēl\ *vb* **un•sealed**; **un•seal•ing**
to break or remove the seal of : OPEN

un•sea•son•able \ˌən-ˈsē-zᵊn-ə-bəl\ *adj*
happening or coming at the wrong time 〈*unseasonable* weather〉
un•sea•son•ably \-blē\ *adv*

unripe: a bunch of unripe bananas

un•sea•soned \ˌən-ˈsē-zᵊnd\ *adj*
not made ready or fit for use (as by the passage of time) 〈*unseasoned* lumber〉

un•seat \ˌən-ˈsēt\ *vb* **un•seat•ed**; **un•seat•ing**
1 to remove from a position of authority 〈The mayor was *unseated* in the election.〉
2 to cause to fall from a seat or saddle

un•seem•ly \ˌən-ˈsēm-lē\ *adj* **un•seem•li•er**; **un•seem•li•est**
not polite or proper 〈*unseemly* behavior〉

un•seen \ˌən-ˈsēn\ *adj*
not seen : INVISIBLE

un•self•ish \ˌən-ˈsel-fish\ *adj*
not selfish
un•self•ish•ly *adv*
un•self•ish•ness *n*

un•set•tle \ˌən-ˈse-tᵊl\ *vb* **un•set•tled**; **un•set•tling**
to disturb the quiet or order of : UPSET 〈Spicy food *unsettles* my stomach.〉 〈Social changes can *unsettle* old beliefs.〉

un•set•tled \ˌən-ˈse-tᵊld\ *adj*
1 not staying the same 〈*unsettled* weather〉
2 feeling nervous, upset, or worried
3 not finished or determined 〈*unsettled* business〉 〈an *unsettled* question〉
4 not paid 〈an *unsettled* account〉
5 not lived in by settlers 〈*unsettled* territory〉

un•sheathe \ˌən-ˈshēth\ *vb* **un•sheathed**; **un•sheath•ing**
to draw from or as if from a sheath

un•sight•ly \ˌən-ˈsīt-lē\ *adj*
not pleasant to look at : UGLY

un•skilled \ˌən-ˈskild\ *adj*
1 not having skill 〈*unskilled* workers〉
2 not needing skill 〈*unskilled* jobs〉

un•skill•ful \ˌən-ˈskil-fəl\ *adj*
not skillful : not having skill
un•skill•ful•ly \-fə-lē\ *adv*

un•sound \ˌən-ˈsau̇nd\ *adj*
1 not based on good reasoning or truth 〈an *unsound* argument〉 〈*unsound* advice〉
2 not firmly made or placed 〈an *unsound* building〉
3 not healthy or in good condition 〈*unsound* teeth〉
4 being or having a mind that is not normal

un•speak•able \ˌən-ˈspē-kə-bəl\ *adj*
1 impossible to express in words 〈*unspeakable* beauty〉
2 extremely bad 〈*unspeakable* conduct〉
un•speak•ably \-blē\ *adv*

un•spec•i•fied \ˌən-ˈspe-sə-ˌfīd\ *adj*
not mentioned or named 〈She resigned for *unspecified* reasons.〉

un•spoiled \ˌən-ˈspȯild\ *adj*
not damaged or ruined 〈*unspoiled* milk〉 〈an *unspoiled* view〉

un•sta•ble \ˌən-ˈstā-bəl\ *adj*
not stable 〈an *unstable* boat〉

un•steady \ˌən-ˈste-dē\ *adj* **un•stead•i•er**; **un•stead•i•est**
not steady : UNSTABLE 〈Her legs are so *unsteady* she needs help walking.〉
un•stead•i•ly \-ˈste-də-lē\ *adv*

un•strap \ˌən-ˈstrap\ *vb* **un•strapped**; **un•strap•ping**
to remove or loosen a strap from

un•stressed \ˌən-ˈstrest\ *adj*
not accented 〈an *unstressed* syllable〉

un•suc•cess•ful \ˌən-sək-ˈses-fəl\ *adj*
not ending in or having gained success 〈an *unsuccessful* attempt〉
un•suc•cess•ful•ly \-fə-lē\ *adv*

un•suit•able \ˌən-ˈsü-tə-bəl\ *adj*
not fitting : INAPPROPRIATE 〈*unsuitable* clothing〉 〈*unsuitable* behavior〉

un•sup•port•ed \ˌən-sə-ˈpȯr-təd\ *adj*
1 not proved 〈*unsupported* claims〉
2 not held up 〈The roof is *unsupported* in places.〉

un•sur•passed \ˌən-sər-ˈpast\ *adj*
not exceeded (as in excellence)

un•sus•pect•ing \ˌən-sə-ˈspek-tiŋ\ *adj*
without suspicion

un•tan•gle \ˌən-ˈtaŋ-gəl\ *vb* **un•tan•gled**; **un•tan•gling**
1 to remove a tangle from
2 to straighten out 〈You need to *untangle* your money situation.〉

un•think•able \ˌən-ˈthiŋ-kə-bəl\ *adj*
not to be thought of or considered as possible or reasonable 〈The idea of quitting school is *unthinkable.*〉

un•think•ing \ˌən-ˈthiŋ-kiŋ\ *adj*
not thinking about actions or words and how they will affect others 〈*unthinking* remarks〉

un•ti•dy \ˌən-ˈtī-dē\ *adj* **un•ti•di•er**; **un•ti•di•est**
not neat
un•ti•di•ly \-ˈtī-də-lē\ *adv*
un•ti•di•ness \-ˈtī-dē-nəs\ *n*

un•tie \ˌən-ˈtī\ *vb* **un•tied**; **un•ty•ing** *or* **un•tie•ing**
1 to undo the knots in ⟨I can't *untie* my shoelaces.⟩
2 to free from something that fastens or holds back ⟨He *untied* the horse.⟩

[1]un•til \ən-ˈtil\ *prep*
up to the time of ⟨I worked *until* noon.⟩

[2]until *conj*
up to the time that ⟨Wait *until* I call.⟩

un•time•ly \ˌən-ˈtīm-lē\ *adj*
1 happening or done before the expected, natural, or proper time ⟨The game came to an *untimely* end.⟩
2 coming at the wrong time ⟨an *untimely* joke⟩

un•tir•ing \ˌən-ˈtī-riŋ\ *adj*
not becoming tired

un•to \ˈən-tü\ *prep*
[1]TO

un•told \ˌən-ˈtōld\ *adj*
1 not told or made public ⟨*untold* secrets⟩
2 too great or too numerous to be counted : VAST ⟨*untold* resources⟩

un•touched \ˌən-ˈtəcht\ *adj*
1 not tasted ⟨Her dinner sat on the tray *untouched*.⟩
2 not affected ⟨I was *untouched* by the turmoil.⟩

un•to•ward \ˌən-ˈtō-ərd\ *adj*
unexpected and unpleasant or improper ⟨an *untoward* accident⟩

un•trou•bled \ˌən-ˈtrə-bəld\ *adj*
not troubled : free from worry

un•true \ˌən-ˈtrü\ *adj*
1 not correct : FALSE
2 not faithful : DISLOYAL

un•truth \ˌən-ˈtrüth\ *n*
1 the state of being false
2 [3]LIE

un•truth•ful \ˌən-ˈtrüth-fəl\ *adj*
not containing or telling the truth : FALSE
un•truth•ful•ly \-fə-lē\ *adv*

un•used \ˌən-ˈyüzd, *1 often* -ˈyüst *before "to"*\ *adj*
1 not accustomed ⟨I'm *unused* to this heat.⟩
2 not having been used before ⟨fresh *unused* linen⟩
3 not being used ⟨an *unused* chair⟩

un•usu•al \ˌən-ˈyü-zhə-wəl\ *adj*
not done, found, used, experienced, or existing most of the time ⟨an *unusual* job⟩ ⟨an *unusual* odor⟩
un•usu•al•ly *adv*

un•veil \ˌən-ˈvāl\ *vb* **un•veiled**; **un•veil•ing**
to show or make known to the public for the first time ⟨The statue was *unveiled*.⟩ ⟨The mayor *unveiled* a new plan.⟩

un•voiced \ˌən-ˈvȯist\ *adj*
VOICELESS 2

un•want•ed \ˌən-ˈwȯn-təd, -ˈwän-\ *adj*
not desired or needed

un•wary \ˌən-ˈwer-ē\ *adj* **un•war•i•er**; **un•war•i•est**
easily fooled or surprised ⟨*unwary* buyers⟩

un•washed \ˌən-ˈwȯsht, -ˈwäsht\ *adj*
▼ not having been washed : DIRTY ⟨*unwashed* grapes⟩ ⟨*unwashed* dishes⟩

unwashed carrots

un•well \ˌən-ˈwel\ *adj*
being in poor health

un•whole•some \ˌən-ˈhōl-səm\ *adj*
not good for bodily, mental, or moral health ⟨*unwholesome* food⟩

un•wieldy \ˌən-ˈwēl-dē\ *adj*
hard to handle or control because of size or weight ⟨an *unwieldy* class⟩ ⟨The package is not heavy, but it is *unwieldy*.⟩
un•wield•i•ness *n*

un•will•ing \ˌən-ˈwi-liŋ\ *adj*
not willing : RELUCTANT
un•will•ing•ly *adv*
un•will•ing•ness *n*

un•wind \ˌən-ˈwīnd\ *vb* **un•wound** \-ˈwau̇nd\; **un•wind•ing**
1 to uncoil a strand of ⟨I *unwound* yarn from a ball.⟩ ⟨The fishing line *unwound* from the reel.⟩
2 RELAX 4

un•wise \ˌən-ˈwīz\ *adj*
FOOLISH ⟨an *unwise* decision⟩
un•wise•ly *adv*

un•wor•thy \ˌən-ˈwər-t͟hē\ *adj* **un•wor•thi•er**; **un•wor•thi•est**
1 not deserving someone or something ⟨He's *unworthy* of such praise.⟩
2 not appropriate for a particular kind of person or thing ⟨That behavior is *unworthy* of you.⟩
un•wor•thi•ness \-t͟hē-nəs\ *n*

un•wrap \ˌən-ˈrap\ *vb* **un•wrapped**; **un•wrap•ping**
to remove the wrapping from

un•writ•ten \ˌən-ˈri-tᵊn\ *adj*
not in writing : followed by custom ⟨*unwritten* law⟩

un•yield•ing \ˌən-ˈyēl-diŋ\ *adj*
1 not soft or flexible : HARD
2 showing or having firmness or determination ⟨an *unyielding* belief⟩

[1]up \ˈəp\ *adv*
1 in or to a high or higher place or position ⟨She put her hand *up*.⟩
2 in or into a vertical position ⟨Stand *up*.⟩
3 from beneath a surface (as ground or water) ⟨Come *up* for air.⟩
4 with greater force or to a greater level ⟨Speak *up*.⟩ ⟨Turn the heat *up*.⟩
5 so as to make more active ⟨Stir *up* the fire.⟩
6 so as to appear or be present ⟨The missing ring turned *up*.⟩
7 COMPLETELY ⟨Use it *up*.⟩
8 so as to approach or be near ⟨He walked *up* and said "hello."⟩
9 from below the horizon ⟨The sun came *up*.⟩
10 out of bed ⟨What time did you get *up*?⟩
11 in or into a better or more advanced state ⟨He worked his way *up* in the company.⟩ ⟨She grew *up* on a farm.⟩
12 for consideration or discussion ⟨I brought *up* the issue.⟩
13 into the control of another ⟨I gave myself *up*.⟩
14 used to show completeness ⟨Fill *up* the gas tank.⟩
15 so as to be closed ⟨Seal *up* the package.⟩
16 in or into pieces ⟨The puppy tore it *up*.⟩
17 to a stop ⟨Pull *up* at the curb.⟩
18 into a working or usable state ⟨I set *up* the computer.⟩

[2]up *adj*
1 risen above the horizon or ground ⟨The sun is *up*.⟩
2 being out of bed
3 unusually high ⟨Gas prices are *up*.⟩
4 having been raised or built ⟨The windows are *up*.⟩ ⟨The house is *up*.⟩
5 moving or going upward ⟨an *up* elevator⟩
6 being busy and moving about ⟨He likes to be *up* and doing things.⟩
7 well prepared ⟨Are you *up* for this challenge?⟩
8 happy or excited ⟨The team was *up* after their win.⟩
9 going on ⟨Find out what's *up*.⟩
10 at an end ⟨Time is *up*.⟩
11 well informed ⟨I'm not *up* on the latest news.⟩
12 functioning correctly ⟨The computer system is *up*.⟩

A B C D E F G H I J K L M N O P Q R S T U V W X Y Z

[3]up *prep*
1 to, toward, or at a higher point of ⟨He climbed *up* a ladder.⟩
2 to or toward the beginning of ⟨We paddled *up* a river.⟩
3 [1]ALONG 1 ⟨Let's walk *up* the street.⟩
up to
1 as far as ⟨We found ourselves in mud *up to* our ankles.⟩
2 in accordance with ⟨The game was not *up to* our standards.⟩
3 to the limit of ⟨The car holds *up to* six people.⟩

[4]up *n*
a period or state of doing well ⟨You've had your *ups* and downs.⟩

[5]up *vb* **upped; up•ping**
1 to act suddenly or surprisingly ⟨The teenager *upped* and left home.⟩
2 to make or become higher ⟨Coffee producers *upped* prices.⟩

up–and–down \ˌəp-ənd-ˈdau̇n\ *adj*
1 switching between upward and downward movement or action
2 [1]PERPENDICULAR 1 ⟨an *up-and-down* post⟩

[1]up•beat \ˈəp-ˌbēt\ *n*
a beat in music that is not accented and especially one just before a downbeat

[2]upbeat *adj*
cheerful and positive ⟨an *upbeat* story⟩

up•braid \ˌəp-ˈbrād\ *vb* **up•braid•ed; up•braid•ing**
to criticize or scold severely

up•bring•ing \ˈəp-ˌbriŋ-iŋ\ *n*
the process of raising and training

up•com•ing \ˈəp-ˌkə-miŋ\ *adj*
coming soon

[1]up•date \ˌəp-ˈdāt\ *vb* **up•dat•ed; up•dat•ing**
1 to give or include the latest information
2 to make more modern

[2]up•date \ˈəp-ˌdāt\ *n*
something that gives or includes the latest information

up•draft \ˈəp-ˌdraft\ *n*
an upward movement of air

up•end \ˌəp-ˈend\ *vb* **up•end•ed; up•end•ing**
to set, stand, or rise on end

up•grade \ˈəp-ˌgrād, əp-ˈgrād\ *vb* **up•grad•ed; up•grad•ing**
1 to raise to a higher grade or position
2 to improve or replace old software or an old device

up•heav•al \ˌəp-ˈhē-vəl\ *n*
a period of great change or violent disorder

[1]up•hill \ˈəp-ˈhil\ *adv*
in an upward direction

[2]up•hill \ˈəp-ˌhil\ *adj*
1 going up ⟨an *uphill* trail⟩
2 DIFFICULT 1 ⟨His recovery will be an *uphill* battle.⟩

up•hold \ˌəp-ˈhōld\ *vb* **up•held** \-ˈheld\; **up•hold•ing**
1 to give support to ⟨Judges swear to *uphold* the Constitution.⟩
2 to lift up

up•hol•ster \ˌəp-ˈhōl-stər\ *vb* **up•hol•stered; up•hol•ster•ing**
to provide with or as if with upholstery
up•hol•ster•er *n*

up•hol•stery \ˌəp-ˈhōl-stə-rē\ *n, pl* **up•hol•ster•ies**
▼ materials used to make a soft covering for a seat

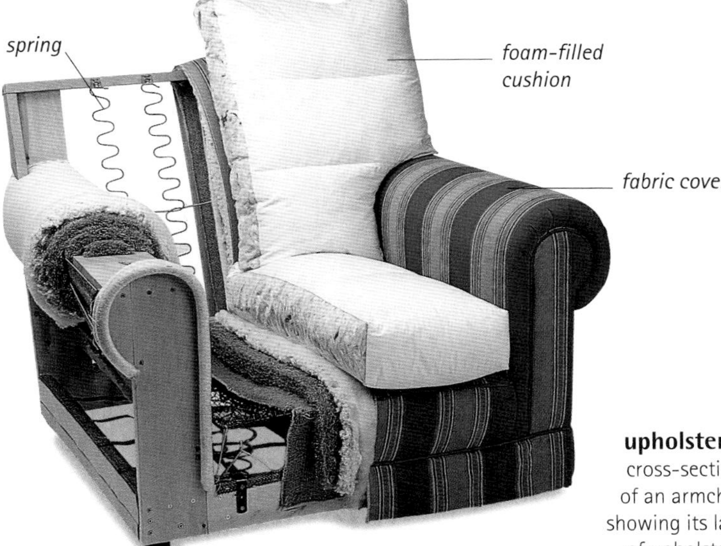

upholstery: cross-section of an armchair showing its layers of upholstery

up•keep \ˈəp-ˌkēp\ *n*
the act or cost of keeping something in good condition

up•land \ˈəp-lənd, -ˌland\ *n*
high land usually far from a coast or sea

[1]up•lift \ˌəp-ˈlift\ *vb* **up•lift•ed; up•lift•ing**
1 to lift up
2 to make feel happy or hopeful ⟨The music *uplifted* us.⟩

[2]up•lift \ˈəp-ˌlift\ *n*
an increase in happiness or hopefulness

up•on \ə-ˈpȯn, ə-ˈpän\ *prep*
[1]ON ⟨I put the plate *upon* the table.⟩

[1]up•per \ˈə-pər\ *adj*
1 higher in position or rank ⟨the building's *upper* stories⟩ ⟨the *upper* classes⟩
2 farther inland ⟨the region of the *upper* Mississippi River⟩

[2]upper *n*
▼ something (as the parts of a shoe above the sole) that is upper

[2]upper: a shoe showing the upper

up•per•case \ˌə-pər-ˈkās\ *adj*
having the form A, B, C rather than a, b, c
uppercase *n*

upper hand *n*
ADVANTAGE 2

up•per•most \ˈə-pər-ˌmōst\ *adj*
1 farthest up ⟨the *uppermost* branches of a tree⟩
2 being in the most important position ⟨The thought is *uppermost* in my mind.⟩

up•raise \ˌəp-ˈrāz\ *vb* **up•raised; up•rais•ing**
to raise or lift up

[1]up•right \ˈəp-ˌrīt\ *adj*
1 [1]VERTICAL ⟨an *upright* post⟩
2 straight in posture
3 having or showing high moral standards
up•right•ly *adv*

► **Synonyms** UPRIGHT, HONEST, and JUST mean having or showing a great concern for what is right. UPRIGHT means having high moral standards in all areas of life. ⟨She's an *upright* person and an example to us all.⟩ HONEST means dealing with others in a fair and truthful way. ⟨He is an *honest* merchant who wouldn't cheat anyone.⟩ JUST is used when a person's fairness comes from both conscious choice and habit. ⟨The principal is *just* to all students.⟩

²upright *adv*
in or into a vertical position

up•rise \ˌəp-ˈrīz\ *vb* **up•rose** \-ˈrōz\; **up•ris•en** \-ˈri-zᵊn\; **up•ris•ing** \-ˈrī-ziŋ\
1 to rise to a higher position
2 to get up from sleeping or sitting

up•ris•ing \ˈəp-ˌrī-ziŋ\ *n*
REBELLION 2

up•roar \ˈəp-ˌrȯr\ *n*
a state of commotion, excitement, or violent disturbance

► **Word History** In spite of appearances, the *-roar* part of the word *uproar* has no historical connection with the sound made by some animals. In Dutch *oproer* means "revolt, uprising," having been compounded from *op*, "up," and *roer*, "motion." When the word was taken into English, its Dutch meaning was kept at first, but its spelling was altered to fit already familiar English words. English speakers assumed that the *-roar* in *uproar* did indeed refer to loud cries, and so the word went from meaning "uprising" to "a state of commotion."

up•root \ˌəp-ˈrüt, -ˈru̇t\ *vb* **up•root•ed**; **up•root•ing**
1 to take out by or as if by pulling up by the roots 〈Many trees were *uprooted* by the storm.〉
2 to take, send, or force away from a country or a traditional home 〈Taking the job would mean moving and *uprooting* the family.〉

¹up•set \ˌəp-ˈset\ *vb* **up•set**; **up•set•ting**
1 to worry or make unhappy 〈The bad news *upset* us all.〉
2 to make somewhat ill 〈Pizza *upsets* my stomach.〉
3 to force or be forced out of the usual position : OVERTURN 〈Sit down before you *upset* the canoe.〉
4 to cause confusion in 〈Rain *upset* our plans.〉
5 to defeat unexpectedly

²up•set \ˈəp-ˌset\ *n*
1 an unexpected defeat
2 a feeling of illness in the stomach
3 a period of worry or unhappiness 〈an emotional *upset*〉

³up•set \ˌəp-ˈset\ *adj*
emotionally disturbed or unhappy

up•shot \ˈəp-ˌshät\ *n*
the final result

up•side–down \ˈəp-ˌsīd-ˈdau̇n\ *adj*
1 having the upper part underneath and the lower part on top 〈The letter "u" is an *upside-down* "n."〉
2 showing great confusion 〈*upside-down* logic〉

up•side down \ˈəp-ˌsīd-\ *adv*
1 in such a way that the upper part is underneath and the lower part is on top 〈A curious cat turned the box *upside down*.〉
2 in or into great confusion 〈The injury turned her life *upside down*.〉

uranium:
a lump of uranium ore

¹up•stairs \ˌəp-ˈsterz\ *adv*
up the stairs : on or to an upper floor 〈Go *upstairs* to your room!〉

²up•stairs \ˈəp-ˈsterz\ *adj*
being on or relating to an upper floor 〈*upstairs* bedrooms〉

³up•stairs \ˌəp-ˈsterz\ *n*
the part of a building above the ground floor

up•stand•ing \ˌəp-ˈstan-diŋ\ *adj*
HONEST 1

up•start \ˈəp-ˌstärt\ *n*
a person who gains quick or unexpected success and shows off that success

up•stream \ˈəp-ˈstrēm\ *adv*
at or toward the beginning of a stream 〈She rowed *upstream*.〉

up•swing \ˈəp-ˌswiŋ\ *n*
a great increase or rise 〈an *upswing* in business〉

up•tight \ˈəp-ˈtīt, ˌəp-\ *adj*
being tense, nervous, or uneasy

up–to–date \ˌəp-tə-ˈdāt\ *adj*
1 including the latest information 〈an *up-to-date* map〉
2 knowing, being, or making use of what is new or recent 〈My dentist uses the most *up-to-date* equipment.〉

up•town \ˈəp-ˈtau̇n\ *adv*
to, toward, or in what is thought of as the upper part of a town or city

¹up•turn \ˈəp-ˌtərn, ˌəp-ˈtərn\ *vb* **up•turned**; **up•turn•ing**
to turn upward or up or over

²up•turn \ˈəp-ˌtərn\ *n*
an upward turning (as toward better conditions)

¹up•ward \ˈəp-wərd\ *or* **up•wards** \-wərdz\ *adv*
1 in a direction from lower to higher 〈The balloon floated *upward*.〉
2 toward a higher or better state
3 toward a greater amount or a higher number or rate
4 toward the head

²upward *adj*
turned toward or being in a higher place or level 〈an *upward* gaze〉 〈an *upward* movement of prices〉
up•ward•ly *adv*

up•wind \ˈəp-ˈwind\ *adv or adj*
in the direction from which the wind is blowing

ura•ni•um \yu̇-ˈrā-nē-əm\ *n*
◄ a radioactive metallic chemical element used as a source of atomic energy

Ura•nus \ˈyu̇r-ə-nəs, yu̇-ˈrā-nəs\ *n*
▼ the planet that is seventh in order of distance from the sun and has a diameter of about 32,000 miles (51,000 kilometers)

Uranus

ur•ban \'ər-bən\ *adj*
of, relating to, or being a city ⟨*urban* life⟩

ur•chin \'ər-chən\ *n*
1 a mischievous or disrespectful youngster
2 SEA URCHIN

▶ **Word History** The English word *urchin* first meant "hedgehog." In the 1500s some people seem to have compared mischievous children to hedgehogs and began calling them *urchins.* The sea urchin got its name because it has spines like a hedgehog.

-ure *suffix*
1 act : process ⟨expos*ure*⟩
2 office : duty
3 body performing an office or duty ⟨legislat*ure*⟩

urea \yu̇-'rē-ə\ *n*
a compound of nitrogen that is the chief solid substance dissolved in the urine of a mammal and is formed by the breaking down of protein

[1]**urge** \'ərj\ *vb* **urged; urg•ing**
1 to try to get (something) accepted : argue in favor of ⟨She's always *urging* reform.⟩
2 to try to convince ⟨He *urged* his guests to stay.⟩
3 [2]FORCE 1, DRIVE ⟨His dog *urged* the sheep onward.⟩

[2]**urge** *n*
a strong desire ⟨She had the *urge* to laugh.⟩

ur•gen•cy \'ər-jən-sē\ *n*
the quality or state of requiring immediate action or attention ⟨"Let's get out of here!" he said with a sense of *urgency.*⟩

ur•gent \'ər-jənt\ *adj*
1 calling for immediate action ⟨an *urgent* need⟩
2 having or showing a sense of requiring immediate action ⟨She spoke in an *urgent* voice.⟩
ur•gent•ly *adv*

uri•nary \'yu̇r-ə-,ner-ē\ *adj*
▶ of or relating to urine or the parts of the body through which it passes ⟨the *urinary* bladder⟩

uri•nate \'yu̇r-ə-,nāt\ *vb* **uri•nat•ed; uri•nat•ing**
to pass urine out of the body

uri•na•tion \,yu̇r-ə-'nā-shən\ *n*
the act of urinating

urine \'yu̇r-ən\ *n*
the yellowish liquid produced by the kidneys and given off from the body as waste

URL \,yü-,är-'el, 'ərl\ *n*
the address of a computer or a document on the Internet

urn \'ərn\ *n*
1 ▶ a container usually in the form of a vase resting on a stand
2 a closed container with a faucet used for serving a hot beverage ⟨a coffee *urn*⟩

us \əs, 'əs\ *pron, objective case of* WE

US *abbr* United States

USA *abbr* United States of America

us•able \'yü-zə-bəl\ *adj*
suitable or fit for use ⟨He saves things that might someday be *usable.*⟩

us•age \'yü-sij, -zij\ *n*
1 usual way of doing things ⟨a business *usage*⟩
2 the way in which words and phrases are actually used
3 the action of using : USE ⟨The book was worn from long *usage.*⟩

[1]**use** \'yüz\ *vb* **used** \'yüzd, *in the phrase "used to" usually* 'yüst\; **us•ing** \'yü-ziŋ\
1 to put into action or service : make use of ⟨*use* tools⟩ ⟨*use* good English⟩
2 used with *to* to show a former custom, fact, or state ⟨Grandma said winters *used* to be harder.⟩
3 to take into the body ⟨people who *use* drugs⟩ ⟨I don't *use* sugar in tea.⟩
4 to do something by means of ⟨Be sure to *use* care.⟩
5 to behave toward : TREAT ⟨He *used* the children kindly.⟩
us•er *n*
use up to make complete use of : EXHAUST ⟨We *used up* the supply of firewood within a week.⟩

urn 1: a ceramic urn

▶ **urinary**
The urinary system eliminates some waste from the human body through a process that involves the kidneys and the bladder. The kidneys regulate water levels inside the body and filter waste from the blood. This liquid waste travels through a duct called the ureter \'yu̇r-ə-tər\ from each kidney to the bladder and then passes out of the body in the form of urine.

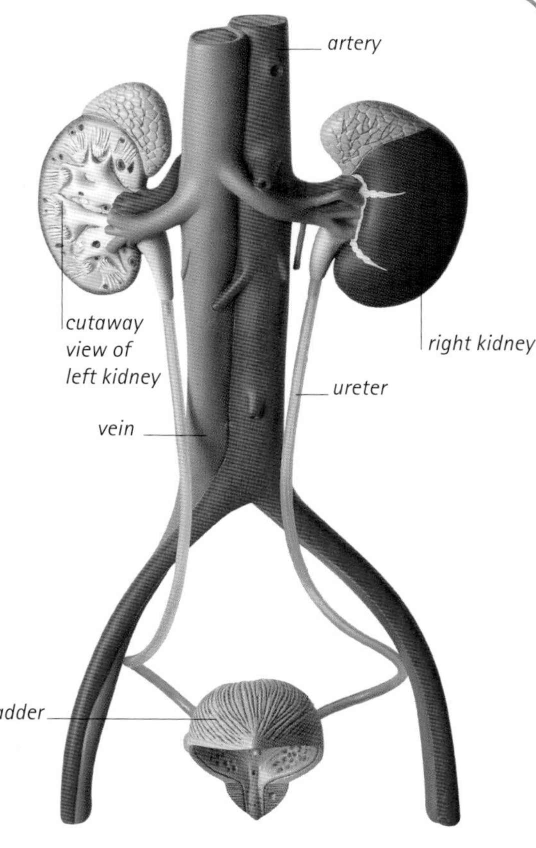

diagram of the human urinary system

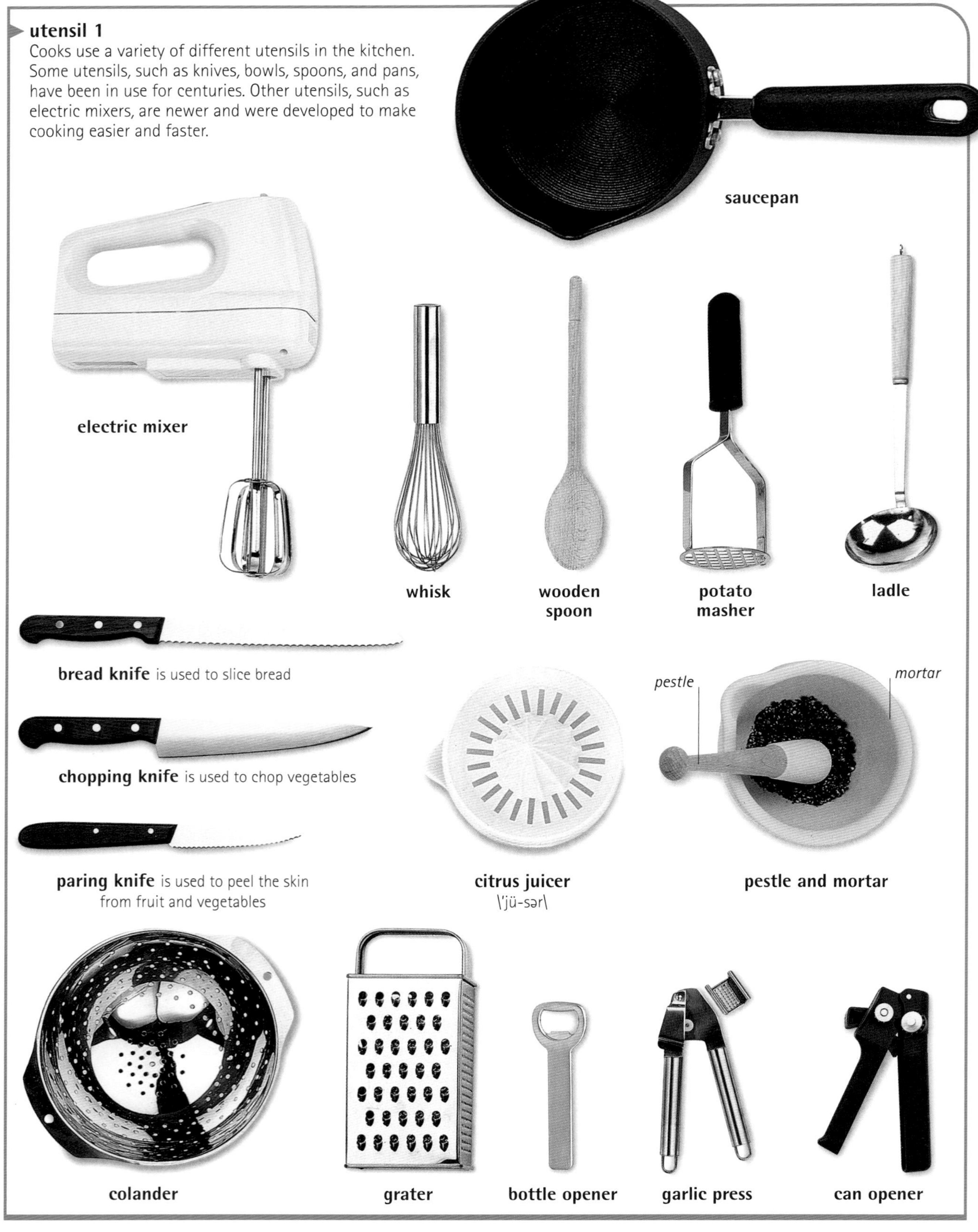
utensil 1
Cooks use a variety of different utensils in the kitchen. Some utensils, such as knives, bowls, spoons, and pans, have been in use for centuries. Other utensils, such as electric mixers, are newer and were developed to make cooking easier and faster.
saucepan
electric mixer
whisk
wooden spoon
potato masher
ladle
bread knife is used to slice bread
chopping knife is used to chop vegetables
paring knife is used to peel the skin from fruit and vegetables
citrus juicer \'jü-sər\
pestle
mortar
pestle and mortar
colander
grater
bottle opener
garlic press
can opener

²use \'yüs\ *n*
1 the act of putting something into action or service 〈put knowledge to *use*〉
2 the fact or state of being put into action or service 〈a book in daily *use*〉
3 way of putting into action or service 〈the proper *use* of tools〉
4 the ability or power to put something into action or service 〈It's a blessing to have the *use* of one's legs.〉
5 the quality or state of being useful
6 a reason or need to put into action or service 〈I've no *use* for it.〉
7 LIKING 〈We have no *use* for mean people.〉

used \'yüzd, *2 often* 'yüst *before "to"*\ *adj*
1 SECONDHAND 1 〈Dad bought a *used* car.〉
2 having the habit of doing or putting up with something 〈He's *used* to flying.〉

use•ful \'yüs-fəl\ *adj*
1 capable of being put to use : USABLE 〈*useful* scraps of material〉
2 helpful in doing or achieving something 〈a *useful* tool for gardening〉
use•ful•ly \-fə-lē\ *adv*
use•ful•ness *n*

use•less \'yüs-ləs\ *adj*
being of or having no use
use•less•ly *adv*
use•less•ness *n*

us•er–friend•ly \ˌyü-zər-'frend-lē\ *adj*
easy to learn, use, understand, or deal with
user–friendliness *n*

us•er•name \'yü-zər-ˌnām\ *n*
a combination of letters and often numbers that identifies a user when logging on to a computer or website

¹ush•er \'ə-shər\ *n*
a person who shows people to seats (as in a theater, at a game, or at a wedding)

²usher *vb* **ush•ered**; **ush•er•ing**
1 to show or be shown to a place
2 to come before as if to lead in or announce 〈We had a party to *usher* in the new year.〉

usu. *abbr*
1 usual
2 usually

usu•al \'yü-zhə-wəl\ *adj*
done, found, used, or existing most of the time 〈This is the *usual* state of the house.〉
usu•al•ly *adv*

usurp \yu̇-'sərp, -'zərp\ *vb* **usurped**; **usurp•ing**
to take and hold unfairly or by force 〈The traitors *usurp* power from the king.〉
usurp•er *n*

USVI *abbr* United States Virgin Islands

UT *abbr* Utah

uten•sil \yu̇-'ten-səl\ *n*
1◀ a tool or container used in a home and especially a kitchen
2 a useful tool
synonyms see INSTRUMENT

uter•us \'yü-tə-rəs\ *n, pl* **uter•us•es** *or* **uteri** \'yü-tə-ˌrī\
the organ of a female mammal in which the young develop before birth

util•i•ty \yu̇-'ti-lə-tē\ *n, pl* **util•i•ties**
1 the quality or state of being useful
2 a business that supplies a public service (as electricity or gas) under special regulation by the government

uti•li•za•tion \ˌyü-tə-lə-'zā-shən\ *n*
the action of making use of : the state of being used

uti•lize \'yü-tə-ˌlīz\ *vb* **uti•lized**; **uti•liz•ing**
to make use of especially for a certain job 〈We had to *utilize* our navigation skills to find our way.〉

¹ut•most \'ət-ˌmōst\ *adj*
of the greatest or highest degree or amount 〈The message is of the *utmost* importance.〉

²utmost *n*
the greatest or highest degree or amount 〈She stretched her arm to the *utmost*.〉

¹ut•ter \'ə-tər\ *adj*
in every way : TOTAL 〈*utter* nonsense〉 〈*utter* strangers〉
ut•ter•ly *adv*

²utter *vb* **ut•tered**; **ut•ter•ing**
1 to send forth as a sound 〈The injured animal *uttered* a short cry.〉
2 to express in usually spoken words 〈She wanted to *utter* an angry protest.〉

ut•ter•ance \'ə-tə-rəns\ *n*
1 something said
2 the act of saying something

Vv

Sounds of V. The letter **V** makes only one sound, heard in *very* and *love*.

v \'vē\ *n, pl* **v's** *or* **vs** \'vēz\ *often cap*
1 the 22nd letter of the English alphabet
2 five in Roman numerals

v. *abbr* verb

VA, Va. *abbr* Virginia

va•can•cy \'vā-kən-sē\ *n, pl* **va•can•cies**
1 something (as an office or hotel room) that is vacant
2 empty space
3 the state of being vacant

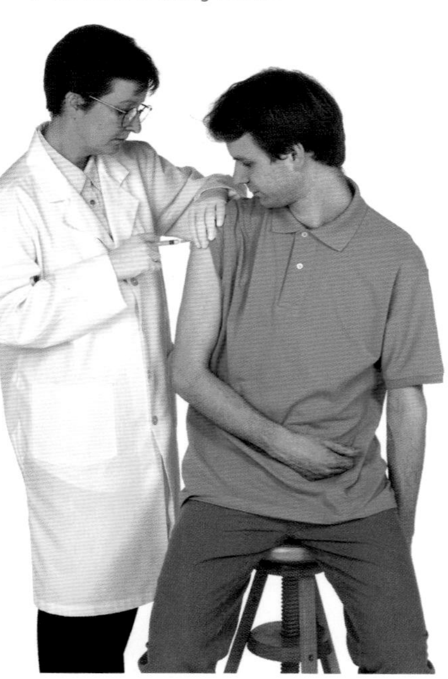

vaccination:
a patient receiving a vaccination

va•cant \'vā-kənt\ *adj*
1 not filled, used, or lived in ⟨a *vacant* house⟩ ⟨a *vacant* lot⟩ ⟨a *vacant* job position⟩
2 showing a lack of thought or expression ⟨*vacant* eyes⟩
3 free from duties or care ⟨*vacant* hours⟩
synonyms see EMPTY
va•cant•ly *adv*

va•cate \'vā-,kāt\ *vb* **va•cat•ed; va•cat•ing**
to leave empty or not used ⟨The tenants *vacated* the house.⟩

[1]**va•ca•tion** \vā-'kā-shən\ *n*
1 a period during which activity (as of a school) is stopped for a time
2 a period spent away from home or business in travel or amusement

[2]**vacation** *vb* **va•ca•tioned; va•ca•tion•ing**
to take or spend a period away from home or business in travel or amusement
va•ca•tion•er *n*

vac•ci•nate \'vak-sə-,nāt\ *vb* **vac•ci•nat•ed; vac•ci•nat•ing**
to give a vaccine to usually by injection

vac•ci•na•tion \,vak-sə-'nā-shən\ *n*
◄ the act of vaccinating

vac•cine \vak-'sēn, 'vak-,sēn\ *n*
a preparation containing usually killed or weakened microorganisms (as bacteria or viruses) that is given usually by injection to increase protection against a particular disease

► **Word History** In the late 1700s the English doctor Edward Jenner investigated the old belief that people who contracted a mild disease called cowpox from cows thereby became immune to smallpox, a much more dangerous disease. Jenner documented 23 such cases, where people inoculated with matter from cowpox sores came down with cowpox but then did not contract smallpox. Because *variolae vaccinae*, literally, "cow pustules," was the medical Latin name for cowpox, the virus-containing material used for inoculations eventually came to be called *vaccine*.

vac•il•late \'va-sə-,lāt\ *vb* **vac•il•lat•ed; vac•il•lat•ing**
to hesitate between courses or opinions : be unable to choose

[1]**vac•u•um** \'va-,kyüm\ *n, pl* **vac•u•ums** *or* **vac•ua** \-kyə-wə\
1 a space completely empty of matter
2 a space from which most of the air has been removed (as by a pump)
3 VACUUM CLEANER

[2]**vacuum** *vb* **vac•u•umed; vac•u•um•ing**
to use a vacuum cleaner on ⟨She's *vacuuming* the carpet.⟩

vacuum cleaner *n*
► an electrical appliance for cleaning (as floors or rugs) by suction

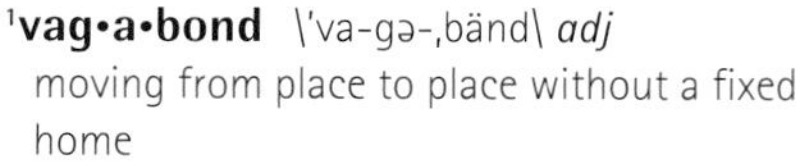

vacuum cleaner

[1]**vag•a•bond** \'va-gə-,bänd\ *adj*
moving from place to place without a fixed home

[2]**vagabond** *n*
a person who moves from place to place without a fixed home

va•gi•na \və-'jī-nə\ *n*
a canal that leads from the uterus to the outside of the body

[1]**va•grant** \'vā-grənt\ *n*
a person who has no steady job and wanders from place to place

[2]**vagrant** *adj*
1 wandering about from place to place
2 having no fixed course ⟨*vagrant* breezes⟩

vague \'vāg\ *adj* **vagu•er; vagu•est**
1 not clearly expressed ⟨a *vague* answer⟩
2 not clearly understood or sensed ⟨They knew in a *vague* way what they wanted.⟩
3 not clearly outlined ⟨We saw *vague* figures in the fog.⟩
vague•ly *adv*
vague•ness *n*

valentine 1:
a valentine of roses

vain \'vān\ *adj* **vain•er; vain•est**
1 having no success ⟨He made a *vain* effort to escape.⟩
2 having or showing the attitude of a person who thinks too highly of his or her looks or abilities
vain•ly *adv*
in vain
1 without success ⟨I searched *in vain* for my key.⟩
2 in an unholy way

vale \'vāl\ *n*
VALLEY

val•e•dic•to•ri•an \ˌva-lə-ˌdik-'tȯr-ē-ən\ *n*
a student usually of the highest standing in a class who gives the farewell speech at the graduation ceremonies

val•en•tine \'va-lən-ˌtīn\ *n*
1 ▲ a greeting card or gift sent or given on Valentine's Day
2 a sweetheart given something as a sign of affection on Valentine's Day

Valentine's Day *n*
February 14 observed in honor of Saint Valentine and as a time for exchanging valentines

va•let \'va-lət, 'va-lā, va-'lā\ *n*
1 a person who parks cars for guests (as at a restaurant)
2 a male servant or hotel employee who takes care of a man's clothes and does personal services

val•iant \'val-yənt\ *adj*
1 boldly brave ⟨*valiant* knights⟩
2 done with courage : HEROIC
val•iant•ly *adv*

val•id \'va-ləd\ *adj*
1 having legal force or effect ⟨a *valid* driver's license⟩
2 based on truth or fact ⟨She had a *valid* excuse for missing practice.⟩
val•id•ly *adv*

val•i•date \'va-lə-ˌdāt\ *vb* **val•i•dat•ed; val•i•dat•ing**
1 to have legal force or effect
2 to prove to be true, worthy, or justified

va•lid•i•ty \və-'li-də-tē\ *n*
the quality or state of being true or legally in force or effect

va•lise \və-'lēs\ *n*
SUITCASE

val•ley \'va-lē\ *n, pl* **valleys**
▼ an area of lowland between ranges of hills or mountains

valley in Yosemite \yō-'se-mə-tē\ National Park, California

val•or \'va-lər\ *n*
COURAGE

val•or•ous \'va-lə-rəs\ *adj*
having or showing courage : BRAVE
val•or•ous•ly *adv*

[1]**valu•able** \'val-yə-wə-bəl, 'val-yə-bəl\ *adj*
1 worth a large amount of money
2 of great use or service ⟨*valuable* skills⟩

[2]**valuable** *n*
a personal possession of great value

[1]**val•ue** \'val-yü\ *n*
1 a fair return in goods, services, or money for something exchanged
2 worth in money
3 worth, usefulness, or importance in comparison with something else ⟨The letter is of great historical *value*.⟩
4 a principle or quality that is valuable or desirable ⟨They shared many goals and *values*.⟩
5 a numerical quantity that is assigned or found by calculation or measurement ⟨What is the *value* of *x*?⟩

[2]**value** *vb* **val•ued; val•u•ing**
1 to estimate the worth of ⟨The necklace is *valued* at 200 dollars.⟩
2 to think highly of ⟨I *value* your friendship.⟩

valve \'valv\ *n*
1 a structure in the body that temporarily closes to prevent passage of material or allow movement of a fluid in one direction only ⟨a heart *valve*⟩
2 ▶ a mechanical device by which the flow of liquid, gas, or loose material may be controlled by a movable part
3 a device on a brass musical instrument that changes the pitch of the tone
4 one of the separate pieces that make up the shell of some animals (as clams) and are often hinged

valve 2

vam•pire \'vam-ˌpīr\ *n*
the body of a dead person believed to come from the grave at night and suck the blood of sleeping people

vampire bat *n*
a bat of tropical America that feeds on the blood of birds and mammals

van \'van\ *n*
a usually closed wagon or truck for moving goods or animals

va•na•di•um \və-'nā-dē-əm\ *n*
a metallic chemical element used in making a strong alloy of steel

van•dal \'van-dəl\ *n*
a person who destroys or damages property on purpose

▶ **Word History** When the Roman Empire ended there was a great movement of peoples in and around Europe. Tribes that we call "Germanic" settled in many areas; some, as the Angles, Saxons, Franks, and Bavarians, became ancestors of the people of modern England, France, and Germany. Another such tribe was the Vandals, who swept through Europe, crossed the Strait of Gibraltar, and seized the Roman province of Africa in the year 429, finally disappearing from history in the 500s and 600s. Though the Vandals were no worse than other tribes in a violent age, they became the model of the destructive barbarian, and their name became attached to anyone who willfully defaces public property.

vapor 2: thermal geysers emitting vapor

van•dal•ism \ˈvan-də-ˌli-zəm\ *n*
intentional destruction of or damage to property

van•dal•ize \ˈvan-də-ˌlīz\ *vb* **van•dal•ized**; **van•dal•iz•ing**
to destroy or damage property on purpose

vane \ˈvān\ *n*
1 WEATHER VANE
2 a flat or curved surface that turns around a center when moved by wind or water 〈the *vanes* of a windmill〉

van•guard \ˈvan-ˌgärd\ *n*
1 the troops moving at the front of an army
2 FOREFRONT

va•nil•la \və-ˈni-lə, -ˈne-\ *n*
a substance extracted from vanilla beans and used as a flavoring especially for sweet foods and beverages

vanilla bean *n*
▼ the long pod of a tropical American orchid from which vanilla is extracted

vanilla beans

van•ish \ˈva-nish\ *vb* **van•ished**; **van•ish•ing**
to pass from sight or existence : DISAPPEAR

van•i•ty \ˈva-nə-tē\ *n, pl* **van•i•ties**
1 the quality or fact of being vain
2 something that is vain
3 a small box for cosmetics

van•quish \ˈvaŋ-kwish\ *vb* **van•quished**; **van•quish•ing**
OVERCOME 1

va•por \ˈvā-pər\ *n*
1 fine bits (as of fog or smoke) floating in the air and clouding it
2 ▲ a substance in the form of a gas 〈water *vapor*〉

va•por•ize \ˈvā-pə-ˌrīz\ *vb* **va•por•ized**; **va•por•iz•ing**
to turn from a liquid or solid into vapor
va•por•iz•er \-ˌrī-zər\ *n*

var. *abbr* variant

[1]**var•i•able** \ˈver-ē-ə-bəl\ *adj*
1 able to change : likely to be changed : CHANGEABLE 〈a *variable* climate〉
2 having differences
3 different from what is normal or usual
var•i•ably \-blē\ *adv*

[2]**variable** *n*
1 something that changes or can be changed
2 a symbol (as *x* or *) used in mathematics in the place of a numeral : PLACEHOLDER

[1]**var•i•ant** \ˈver-ē-ənt\ *adj*
differing from others of its kind or class 〈*variant* strains of disease〉 〈*variant* spellings〉

[2]**variant** *n*
1 one of two or more things that show slight differences 〈A new *variant* of the disease has appeared.〉
2 one of two or more different spellings or pronunciations of a word

var•i•a•tion \ˌver-ē-ˈā-shən\ *n*
1 a change in form, position, or condition 〈Our routine could use some *variation.*〉
2 amount of change or difference 〈*variations* in temperature〉
3 departure from what is usual to a group 〈The poodle's offspring show no *variation* from the breed.〉

var•ied \ˈver-ēd\ *adj*
having many forms or types 〈*varied* interests〉

var•ie•gat•ed \ˈver-ē-ə-ˌgā-təd, ˈver-i-ˌgā-\ *adj*
1 having patches, stripes, or marks of different colors 〈*variegated* leaves〉
2 full of variety

va•ri•ety \və-ˈrī-ə-tē\ *n, pl* **va•ri•et•ies**
1 a collection of different things ⟨This store sells a *variety* of items.⟩
2 the quality or state of having different forms or types ⟨My diet lacks *variety.*⟩
3 something (as a plant or animal) that differs from others of the same general kind or of the group to which it belongs ⟨a *variety* of tulip⟩
4 entertainment made up of performances (as dances and songs) that follow one another and are not related

var•i•ous \ˈver-ē-əs\ *adj*
1 of different kinds ⟨They sell *various* flavors of ice cream.⟩

vat: a wooden vat in a winery

2 different one from another : UNLIKE ⟨The projects are in *various* stages of completion.⟩
3 made up of an indefinite number greater than one

[1]var•nish \ˈvär-nish\ *n*
a liquid that is spread on a surface and dries into a hard coating

[2]varnish *vb* **var•nished; var•nish•ing**
to cover with or as if with a liquid that dries into a hard coating

var•si•ty \ˈvär-sə-tē\ *n, pl* **var•si•ties**
the main team that represents a school or club in contests

vary \ˈver-ē\ *vb* **var•ied; vary•ing**
1 to make a partial change in ⟨He *varied* the rhythm of the poem.⟩
2 to make or be of different kinds ⟨She *varies* her exercise routine.⟩
3 to show or undergo change ⟨The sky constantly *varies.*⟩
4 to differ from the usual members of a group
synonyms see CHANGE

vas•cu•lar \ˈva-skyə-lər\ *adj*
of, relating to, containing, or being bodily vessels that carry fluid (as blood in an animal or sap in a plant) ⟨a tree's *vascular* system⟩

vase \ˈvās, ˈvāz\ *n*
▶ an often round container of greater depth than width used chiefly for ornament or for flowers

vas•sal \ˈva-səl\ *n*
a person in the Middle Ages who received protection and land from a lord in return for loyalty and service

vast \ˈvast\ *adj*
very great in size or amount ⟨*vast* stretches of land⟩ ⟨She has *vast* experience.⟩
vast•ly *adv*
vast•ness *n*

vat \ˈvat\ *n*
◀ a large container (as a tub) especially for holding liquids in manufacturing processes

vaude•ville \ˈvȯd-vəl\ *n*
theatrical entertainment made up of songs, dances, and comic acts

[1]vault \ˈvȯlt\ *n*
1 a room or compartment for storage or safekeeping
2 something like a vast ceiling ⟨the *vault* of sky⟩
3 ▼ an arched structure of stone or concrete forming a ceiling or roof
4 a burial chamber

vase: flowers in a glass vase

[2]vault *vb* **vault•ed; vault•ing**
to leap with the aid of the hands or a pole

[3]vault *n*
[2]LEAP 1

vb. *abbr* verb

VCR \ˌvē-ˌsē-ˈär\ *n*
a device for recording (as television programs) on videocassettes and playing them back

veal \ˈvēl\ *n*
the meat of a young calf used for food

vec•tor \ˈvek-tər\ *n*
a living thing (as a mosquito, fly, or tick) that carries and passes on a disease-causing microorganism

vee•jay \ˈvē-ˌjā\ *n*
an announcer of a program (as on television) that features music videos

[1]vault 3: the vault over the central aisle in the Cathedral of Constance, Germany

veer \ˈvir\ *vb* **veered; veer•ing**
to change direction

[1]veg•e•ta•ble \ˈvej-tə-bəl, ˈve-jə-tə-\ *adj*
containing or made from plants or parts of plants ⟨*vegetable* oil⟩

[2]vegetable *n*
1 ▼ a plant or plant part (as lettuce, broccoli, or peas) grown for use as food and eaten raw or cooked usually as part of a meal
2 [2]PLANT 1

veg•e•tar•i•an \ˌve-jə-ˈter-ē-ən\ *n*
a person who does not eat meat

veg•e•ta•tion \ˌve-jə-ˈtā-shən\ *n*
plant life or cover (as of an area) ⟨The valley was green with *vegetation.*⟩

veg•e•ta•tive \ˈve-jə-ˌtā-tiv\ *adj*
of, relating to, or functioning in nutrition and growth rather than reproduction ⟨*vegetative* cells⟩

ve•he•mence \ˈvē-ə-məns\ *n*
the quality or state of being vehement

ve•he•ment \ˈvē-ə-mənt\ *adj*
1 showing great force or energy ⟨a *vehement* wind⟩
2 highly emotional ⟨*vehement* patriotism⟩
3 expressed with force ⟨a *vehement* denial⟩
ve•he•ment•ly *adv*

ve•hi•cle \ˈvē-ˌi-kəl, -ˌhi-\ *n*
1 something used to transport people or goods
2 a means by which something is expressed, achieved, or shown ⟨She used the show as a *vehicle* to display her talent.⟩

[1]veil \ˈvāl\ *n*
1 ▼ a piece of cloth or net worn usually by women over the head and shoulders and sometimes over the face
2 something that covers or hides like a veil ⟨a *veil* of secrecy⟩

[1]veil 1: a woman wearing a veil

[2]veil *vb* **veiled; veil•ing**
to cover with or as if with a piece of cloth or net for the head and shoulders or face

vein \ˈvān\ *n*
1 one of the blood vessels that carry the blood back to the heart
2 a long narrow opening in rock filled with a specific mineral ⟨a *vein* of gold⟩
3 a streak of different color or texture (as in marble)
4 a style of expression ⟨in a witty *vein*⟩
5 one of the bundles of fine tubes that make up the framework of a leaf and carry food, water, and nutrients in the plant
6 one of the slender parts that stiffen and support the wing of an insect
veined \ˈvānd\ *adj*

ve•loc•i•ty \və-ˈlä-sə-tē\ *n, pl* **ve•loc•i•ties**
quickness of motion : SPEED

[1]vel•vet \ˈvel-vət\ *n*
a fabric with short soft raised fibers

[2]velvet *adj*
1 made of or covered with velvet
2 VELVETY

vel•vety \ˈvel-və-tē\ *adj*
soft and smooth ⟨*velvety* skin⟩

vend \ˈvend\ *vb* **vend•ed; vend•ing**
to sell or offer for sale

ven•dor *also* **vend•er** \ˈven-dər\ *n*

▶ [2]vegetable 1
Vegetables come in a wide range of types. These include roots, such as carrots and radishes; tubers, such as potatoes; bulbs, such as onions and garlic; leaves, such as lettuce and cabbage; stems, such as celery; flowers, such as broccoli and cauliflower; and fruits, such as tomatoes, corn, peas, and peppers.

carrots
peas
celery
corn
potatoes
garlic
lettuce
sweet pepper
broccoli
tomatoes

vending machine *n*
a machine for selling merchandise operated by putting money into a slot

ve•neer \və-ˈnir\ *n*
a layer of material that provides a finer surface or a stronger structure

ven•er•a•ble \ˈve-nə-rə-bəl\ *adj*
1 deserving to be venerated
Hint: *Venerable* is often used as a religious title.
2 deserving honor or respect

ven•er•ate \ˈve-nə-ˌrāt\ *vb* **ven•er•at•ed**; **ven•er•at•ing**
1 to consider holy
2 to show deep respect for

ven•er•a•tion \ˌve-nə-ˈrā-shən\ *n*
1 the act of showing respect for **:** the state of being shown respect
2 a feeling of deep respect

ve•ne•tian blind \və-ˈnē-shən-\ *n*
▶ a blind having thin horizontal slats that can be adjusted to keep out light or to let light come in between them

venetian blind: a living room fitted with venetian blinds

ven•geance \ˈven-jəns\ *n*
harm done to someone usually as punishment in return for an injury or offense
with a vengeance
1 with great force or effect
2 to an extreme or excessive degree

venge•ful \ˈvenj-fəl\ *adj*
wanting revenge

ven•i•son \ˈve-nə-sən, -zən\ *n*
the meat of a deer used for food

Venn diagram \ˈven-\ *n*
a diagram that shows the relationship between two groups of things by means of overlapping circles

ven•om \ˈve-nəm\ *n*
poison produced by an animal (as a snake or scorpion) and passed to a victim usually by biting or stinging

ven•om•ous \ˈve-nə-məs\ *adj*
having or producing venom **:** POISONOUS ⟨*venomous* snakes⟩

[1]**vent** \ˈvent\ *vb* **vent•ed**; **vent•ing**
1 to provide with an outlet ⟨Dangerous gases were *vented* to the outside.⟩
2 to serve as an outlet for ⟨Chimneys *vent* smoke.⟩
3 [1]EXPRESS 1 ⟨He needs to *vent* his anger.⟩

[2]**vent** *n*
1 an opening for the escape of a gas or liquid or for the relief of pressure
2 an opportunity or means of release ⟨His writing gives *vent* to his anger.⟩

ven•ti•late \ˈven-tə-ˌlāt\ *vb* **ven•ti•lat•ed**; **ven•ti•lat•ing**
1 to let in air and especially a current of fresh air ⟨Windows *ventilate* the room.⟩
2 to provide with fresh air ⟨Keep the plants *ventilated.*⟩
3 to discuss freely and openly ⟨You should *ventilate* your complaints.⟩

ven•ti•la•tion \ˌven-tə-ˈlā-shən\ *n*
1 the act or process of ventilating
2 a system or means of providing fresh air

ven•ti•la•tor \ˈven-tə-ˌlā-tər\ *n*
a device for letting in fresh air or driving out bad or stale air

ven•tral \ˈven-trəl\ *adj*
of, relating to, or being on or near the surface of the body that in human beings is the front but in most animals is the lower surface ⟨a fish's *ventral* fins⟩

ven•tri•cle \ˈven-tri-kəl\ *n*
the part of the heart from which blood passes into the arteries

ven•tril•o•quist \ven-ˈtri-lə-kwəst\ *n*
a person skilled in speaking in such a way that the voice seems to come from a source other than the speaker

[1]**ven•ture** \ˈven-chər\ *vb* **ven•tured**; **ven•tur•ing**
1 to offer at the risk of being criticized ⟨She wouldn't *venture* an opinion.⟩
2 to go ahead in spite of danger ⟨When I heard the noise again, I *ventured* into the cave.⟩
3 to face the risks and dangers of
4 to expose to risk ⟨She *ventured* her fortune on the deal.⟩

[2]**venture** *n*
1 a task or an act involving chance, risk, or danger ⟨a space *venture*⟩
2 a risky business deal

ven•ture•some \ˈven-chər-səm\ *adj*
1 tending to take risks
2 involving risk
synonyms see ADVENTUROUS

ven•tur•ous \ˈven-chə-rəs\ *adj*
VENTURESOME

Ve•nus \ˈvē-nəs\ *n*
▼ the planet that is second in order of distance from the sun and has a diameter of about 7,500 miles (12,100 kilometers)

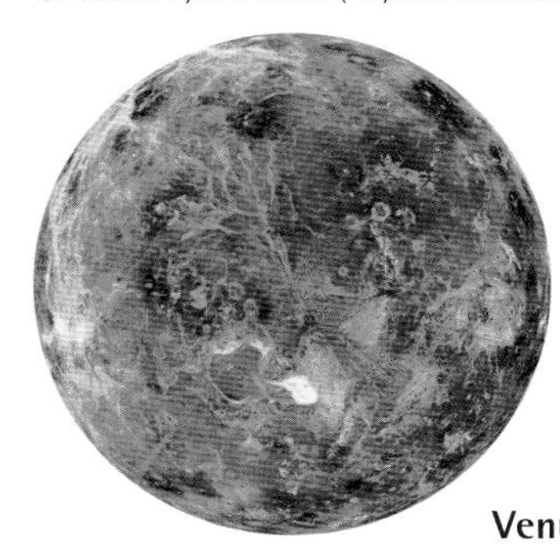

Venus

veranda: the veranda of a house

ve•ran•da *or* **ve•ran•dah** \və-ˈran-də\ *n*
a long porch extending along one or more sides of a building

verb \ˈvərb\ *n*
a word that expresses an act, occurrence, or state of being

ver•bal \ˈvər-bəl\ *adj*
1 of, relating to, or consisting of words ⟨*verbal* communication⟩
2 spoken rather than written ⟨*verbal* testimony⟩
3 of, relating to, or formed from a verb ⟨a *verbal* adjective⟩
ver•bal•ly *adv*

ver•dant \ˈvər-dᵊnt\ *adj*
green with growing plants ⟨a *verdant* landscape⟩

ver•dict \ˈvər-dikt\ *n*
1 the decision reached by a jury
2 JUDGMENT 2, OPINION ⟨What's your *verdict* on his proposal?⟩

ver•dure \ˈvər-jər\ *n*
green vegetation

[1]**verge** \ˈvərj\ *n*
1 THRESHOLD 2, BRINK ⟨They're on the *verge* of bankruptcy.⟩
2 something that borders, limits, or bounds : EDGE ⟨the *verge* of a road⟩

[2]**verge** *vb* **verged**; **verg•ing**
to come near to being ⟨This *verges* on madness.⟩

ver•i•fi•ca•tion \ˌver-ə-fə-ˈkā-shən\ *n*
the act or process of confirming or checking the accuracy of : the state of being confirmed or having the accuracy of checked

ver•i•fy \ˈver-ə-ˌfī\ *vb* **ver•i•fied**; **ver•i•fy•ing**
1 to prove to be true or correct : CONFIRM
2 to check or test the accuracy of

ver•i•ta•ble \ˈver-ə-tə-bəl\ *adj*
ACTUAL, TRUE
Hint: *Veritable* is often used to emphasize similarity to something else. ⟨He is a *veritable* encyclopedia of facts.⟩

ver•min \ˈvər-mən\ *n, pl* **vermin**
small common harmful or objectionable animals (as fleas or mice) that are difficult to get rid of

ver•nal \ˈvər-nᵊl\ *adj*
marking the beginning of spring ⟨the *vernal* equinox⟩

ver•sa•tile \ˈvər-sə-tᵊl\ *adj*
1 able to do many different kinds of things
2 having many uses ⟨a *versatile* tool⟩

ver•sa•til•i•ty \ˌvər-sə-ˈti-lə-tē\ *n*
the quality or state of having many uses or being able to do many different kinds of things

verse \ˈvərs\ *n*
1 a portion of a poem or song : STANZA
2 writing in which words are arranged in a rhythmic pattern
3 one of the short parts of a chapter in the Bible

versed \ˈvərst\ *adj*
having knowledge or skill as a result of experience, study, or practice ⟨He is *versed* in art.⟩

ver•sion \ˈvər-zhən\ *n*
1 an account or description from a certain point of view ⟨The jury heard several different *versions* of the incident.⟩
2 a translation especially of the Bible
3 a form of a type or original

ver•sus \ˈvər-səs\ *prep*
AGAINST 1 ⟨our football team *versus* theirs⟩

ver•te•bra \ˈvər-tə-brə\ *n, pl* **ver•te•brae** \-ˌbrā, -brē\
one of the bony sections making up the backbone

[1]**ver•te•brate** \ˈvər-tə-brət\ *adj*
having vertebrae or a backbone ⟨Mammals are *vertebrate* animals.⟩

[2]**vertebrate** *n*
▶an animal (as a fish, amphibian, reptile, bird, or mammal) that has a backbone extending down the back of the body

ver•tex \ˈvər-ˌteks\ *n, pl* **ver•ti•ces** \ˈvər-tə-ˌsēz\ *also* **ver•tex•es**
1 the point opposite to and farthest from the base of a geometrical figure
2 the common endpoint of the sides of an angle

[1]**ver•ti•cal** \ˈvər-ti-kəl\ *adj*
rising straight up and down from a level surface
ver•ti•cal•ly *adv*

[2]**vertical** *n*
something (as a line or plane) that rises straight up and down

ver•ti•go \ˈvər-ti-ˌgō\ *n, pl* **ver•ti•goes** *or* **ver•ti•gos**
a feeling of dizziness

[1]**very** \ˈver-ē\ *adv*
1 to a great degree : EXTREMELY ⟨It was *very* hot.⟩
2 in actual fact : TRULY ⟨That's the *very* best chocolate you can buy.⟩

[2]**very** *adj*
1 [1]EXACT, PRECISE ⟨the *very* heart of the city⟩
2 exactly suitable or necessary ⟨That's the *very* tool for this job.⟩
3 MERE, BARE ⟨The *very* thought frightened them.⟩
4 exactly the same ⟨That's the *very* story I told.⟩

ves•pers \ˈve-spərz\ *n pl, often cap*
a late afternoon or evening church service

ves•sel \ˈve-səl\ *n*
1 a craft larger than a rowboat for navigation of the water
2 a hollow utensil (as a cup or bowl) for holding something
3 a tube (as an artery) in which a body fluid is contained and carried or circulated

A B C D E F G H I J K L M N O P Q R S T U V W X Y Z

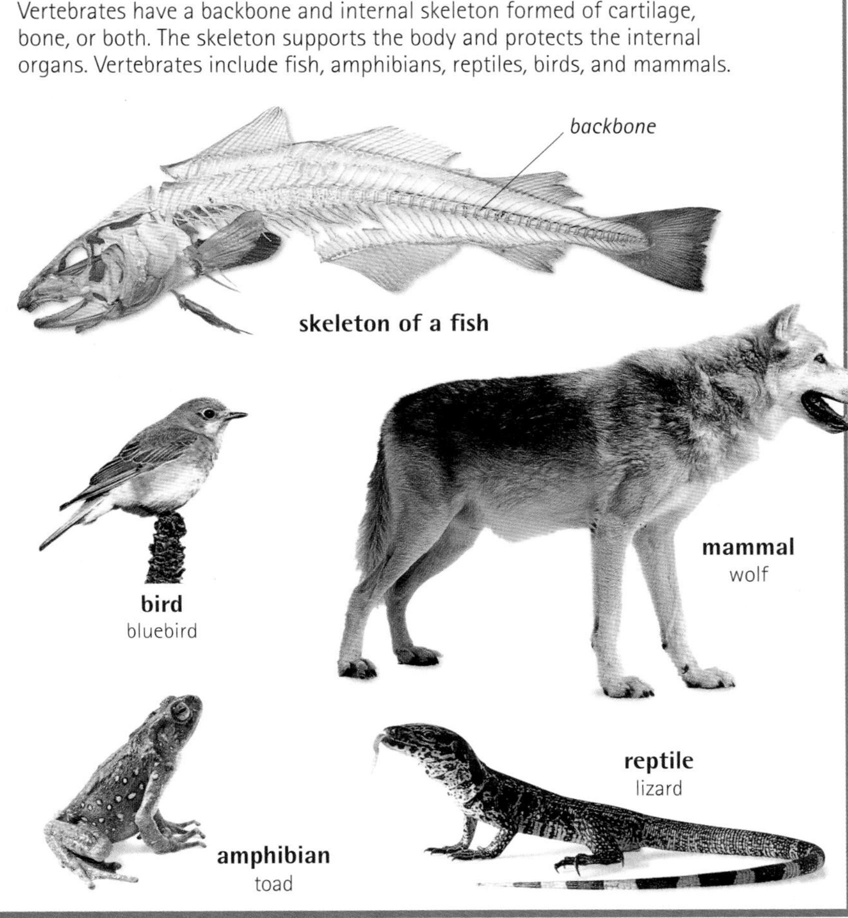

[1]**vest** \'vest\ *n*
a sleeveless garment usually worn under a suit coat

[2]**vest** *vb* **vest•ed**; **vest•ing**
1 to place or give into the possession or control of some person or authority ⟨The Constitution *vests* the Congress with certain powers.⟩
2 to clothe in vestments

ves•ti•bule \'ve-stə-,byül\ *n*
a hall or room between the outer door and the inside part of a building

ves•tige \'ve-stij\ *n*
a tiny amount or visible sign of something lost or vanished : TRACE ⟨We stayed outside to enjoy the last *vestiges* of daylight.⟩

ves•ti•gial \ve-'sti-jē-əl, -'sti-jəl\ *adj*
of, relating to, or being the last remaining amount or visible sign of something lost or vanished

vest•ment \'vest-mənt\ *n*
an outer garment especially for wear during ceremonies or by an official

[1]**vet** \'vet\ *n*
VETERINARIAN

[2]**vet** *n*
[1]VETERAN

[1]**vet•er•an** \'ve-tə-rən, 've-trən\ *n*
1 a person who has had long experience
2 a former member of the armed forces especially in war

[2]**veteran** *adj*
having gained skill through experience ⟨She is a *veteran* dog trainer.⟩

vet•er•i•nar•i•an \,ve-tə-rə-'ner-ē-ən\ *n*
► a doctor who gives medical treatment to animals

[1]**vet•er•i•nary** \'ve-tə-rə-,ner-ē\ *adj*
of, relating to, specializing in, or being the medical care of animals ⟨a *veterinary* surgeon⟩

[2]**veterinary** *n, pl* **vet•er•i•nar•ies**
VETERINARIAN

[1]**ve•to** \'vē-tō\ *n, pl* **vetoes**
1 the act of forbidding something by a person in authority
2 the power of a president, governor, or mayor to prevent something from becoming law

[2]**veto** *vb* **ve•toed**; **ve•to•ing**
1 FORBID, PROHIBIT ⟨We wanted to stay up, but Dad *vetoed* the idea.⟩
2 to prevent from becoming law by use of the power to do so

vex \'veks\ *vb* **vexed**; **vex•ing**
1 to bring trouble, distress, or worry to ⟨He was *vexed* by thoughts of what might have been.⟩
2 to annoy by small irritations ⟨Flies *vexed* the cows.⟩

vex•a•tion \vek-'sā-shən\ *n*
1 the quality or state of being annoyed by small irritations
2 the act of bringing trouble, distress, or worry to
3 a cause of trouble or worry

VG *abbr* very good

VI *abbr* Virgin Islands

v.i. *abbr* verb intransitive

via \'vī-ə, 'vē-ə\ *prep*
by way of ⟨Our bus went *via* the northern route.⟩

vi•a•ble \'vī-ə-bəl\ *adj*
1 capable of living or growing ⟨*viable* seeds⟩
2 possible to use or apply ⟨a *viable* plan⟩

veterinarian: a veterinarian examining a dog

via•duct \'vī-ə-,dəkt\ *n*
▶ a bridge for carrying a road or railroad over something (as a gorge or highway)

vi•al \'vī-əl\ *n*
a small container (as for medicines) that is usually made of glass or plastic

vi•brant \'vī-brənt\ *adj*
having or giving the sense of life, vigor, or action ⟨a *vibrant* personality⟩
vi•brant•ly *adv*

vi•brate \'vī-,brāt\ *vb* **vi•brat•ed**; **vi•brat•ing**
to move or cause to move back and forth or from side to side very quickly

vi•bra•tion \vī-'brā-shən\ *n*
1 a rapid motion (as of a stretched cord) back and forth
2 the action of moving or causing to move back and forth or from side to side very quickly : the state of being swung back and forth
3 a trembling motion

vic•ar \'vi-kər\ *n*
a minister in charge of a church who serves under the authority of another minister

vi•car•i•ous \vī-'ker-ē-əs\ *adj*
sharing in someone else's experiences through the use of imagination or sympathetic feelings ⟨She got *vicarious* enjoyment from her sister's travels.⟩
vi•car•i•ous•ly *adv*
vi•car•i•ous•ness *n*

vice \'vīs\ *n*
1 evil conduct or habits
2 a moral fault or weakness

vice– \'vīs\ *prefix*
one that takes the place of

vice pres•i•dent \'vīs-'pre-zə-dənt\ *n*
an official (as of a government) whose rank is next below that of the president and who takes the place of the president when necessary

vice ver•sa \,vī-si-'vər-sə, 'vīs-'vər-\ *adv*
with the order turned around ⟨Go here to there, not *vice versa*.⟩

vi•cin•i•ty \və-'si-nə-tē\ *n, pl* **vi•cin•i•ties**
1 a surrounding area : NEIGHBORHOOD ⟨There is a school in the *vicinity*.⟩
2 the state of being close ⟨It cost in the *vicinity* of 500 dollars.⟩

vi•cious \'vi-shəs\ *adj*
1 very dangerous ⟨a *vicious* dog⟩
2 filled with or showing unkind feelings ⟨*vicious* gossip⟩
3 violent and cruel ⟨a *vicious* attack⟩
4 very severe ⟨a *vicious* storm⟩
vi•cious•ly *adv*
vi•cious•ness *n*

viaduct: a viaduct carrying a railroad over a valley

vic•tim \'vik-təm\ *n*
1 a person who is cheated, fooled, or hurt by another
2 an individual injured or killed (as by disease, violence, or disaster)
3 a living being offered as a religious sacrifice

vic•tim•ize \'vik-tə-,mīz\ *vb* **vic•tim•ized**; **vic•tim•iz•ing**
to make a victim of

vic•tor \'vik-tər\ *n*
someone who defeats an enemy or opponent : WINNER

vic•to•ri•ous \vik-'tȯr-ē-əs\ *adj*
having won a victory
vic•to•ri•ous•ly *adv*

vic•to•ry \'vik-tə-rē\ *n, pl* **vic•to•ries**
1 the act of defeating an enemy or opponent
2 success in a struggle against difficulties

▶ **Synonyms** VICTORY, CONQUEST, and TRIUMPH mean a success in a competition or struggle. VICTORY is used for a win over an opponent or over difficult problems. ⟨Doctors won a *victory* over disease.⟩ CONQUEST means the act of overcoming someone or something that is brought under control. ⟨We're studying Rome's *conquests* in Britain.⟩ TRIUMPH is used of an especially great victory that brings honor and glory. ⟨The outcome of the battle was a *triumph* for the general.⟩

vict•uals \'vi-tᵊlz\ *n pl*
food and drink

vi•cu•ña *or* **vi•cu•na** \vi-'kün-yə, vī-'kü-nə\ *n*
▼ an animal of the Andes that is related to the llama and has long soft woolly hair

vicuña: a vicuña standing in a grassland

[1]vid•eo \'vi-dē-,ō\ *n*
1 TELEVISION 1
2 the visual part of television ⟨Our broken TV showed the *video* but we couldn't hear the audio.⟩
3 [1]VIDEOTAPE 1
4 a recorded performance of a song ⟨a rock *video*⟩
5 a digital recording of an image or set of images

[2]video *adj*
1 relating to or used in the sending or

receiving of television images ⟨a *video* channel⟩
2 being, relating to, or involving images on a television screen or computer display

video camera

video camera *n*
▲ a camera (as a camcorder) that records video and usually also audio

vid•eo•cas•sette \ˌvi-dē-ō-kə-ˈset\ *n*
1 a case containing videotape for use with a VCR
2 a recording (as of a movie) on a videocassette

videocassette recorder *n*
VCR

video game *n*
a game played with images on a video screen

[1]**vid•eo•tape** \ˈvi-dē-ō-ˌtāp\ *n*
1 a recording of visual images and sound (as of a television production) made on magnetic tape
2 the magnetic tape used for such a recording

[2]**videotape** *vb* **vid•eo•taped**; **vid•eo•tap•ing**
to make a videotape of

videotape recorder *n*
a device for recording on videotape

vie \ˈvī\ *vb* **vied**; **vy•ing**
COMPETE ⟨Players *vie* for prizes.⟩

[1]**Viet•nam•ese** \vē-ˌet-nə-ˈmēz, ˌvē-ət-\ *n*
1 a person born or living in Vietnam
2 the language of the Vietnamese

[2]**Vietnamese** *adj*
of or relating to Vietnam, the Vietnamese people, or their language

[1]**view** \ˈvyü\ *n*
1 OPINION 1 ⟨In his *view*, the plan will fail.⟩
2 all that can be seen from a certain place ⟨The house has a *view* of the lake.⟩
3 range of vision ⟨There is no one in *view*.⟩
4 PURPOSE ⟨She studies with a *view* to passing.⟩
5 a picture that represents something that can be seen ⟨The postcard shows a beach *view*.⟩

[2]**view** *vb* **viewed**; **view•ing**
1 to look at carefully ⟨We'll *view* the museum's exhibits.⟩

Viking: a man dressed as a 10th-century Viking

2 [1]SEE 1 ⟨A large audience *viewed* the movie.⟩
3 [2]REGARD 1 ⟨I've always *viewed* him as a friend.⟩
view•er *n*

view•find•er \ˈvyü-ˌfīn-dər\ *n*
a device on a camera that shows the view to be included in the picture

view•point \ˈvyü-ˌpȯint\ *n*
POINT OF VIEW, STANDPOINT

vig•il \ˈvi-jəl\ *n*
an act of keeping watch especially when sleep is usual

vig•i•lance \ˈvi-jə-ləns\ *n*
the quality or state of staying alert especially to possible danger ⟨The guards maintained their *vigilance* in watching for intruders.⟩

vig•i•lant \ˈvi-jə-lənt\ *adj*
alert especially to avoid danger ⟨a *vigilant* guard⟩

vig•i•lan•te \ˌvi-jə-ˈlan-tē\ *n*
a member of a group of volunteers who are not police but who decide on their own to stop crime and punish criminals

vig•or \ˈvi-gər\ *n*
1 strength or energy of body or mind ⟨the *vigor* of youth⟩
2 active strength or force ⟨He argued with great *vigor*.⟩

vig•or•ous \ˈvi-gə-rəs\ *adj*
1 very healthy and strong ⟨a *vigorous* plant⟩
2 done with force and energy ⟨*vigorous* exercise⟩
vig•or•ous•ly *adv*

Vi•king \ˈvī-kiŋ\ *n*
◀ one of the Scandinavians who raided or invaded the coasts of Europe in the eighth to tenth centuries

vile \ˈvīl\ *adj* **vil•er**; **vil•est**
1 WICKED 1 ⟨a *vile* deed⟩
2 very bad or unpleasant ⟨a *vile* smell⟩

vil•i•fy \ˈvi-lə-ˌfī\ *vb* **vil•i•fied**; **vil•i•fy•ing**
to speak of harshly and often unfairly ⟨The newspaper *vilified* him for his opinions.⟩

vil•la \ˈvi-lə\ *n*
▼ a large house or estate usually in the country

villa: an 18th-century villa overlooking Lake Como in Lombardy, Italy

vil•lage \ˈvi-lij\ *n*
1 a place where people live that is usually smaller than a town
2 the people living in a village ⟨The entire *village* turned out for the parade.⟩

vil•lag•er \ˈvi-li-jər\ *n*
a person who lives in a village

vil•lain \ˈvi-lən\ *n*
1 a wicked person
2 a character in a story or play who opposes the hero or heroine

vil•lain•ous \ˈvi-lə-nəs\ *adj*
WICKED 1

vil•lainy \ˈvi-lə-nē\ *n, pl* **vil•lain•ies**
bad or evil behavior or actions

vil•lus \ˈvi-ləs\ *n, pl* **vil•li** \ˈvi-ˌlī, -lē\
one of the tiny extensions shaped like fingers that line the small intestine and are active in absorbing nutrients

vim \ˈvim\ *n*
great energy and enthusiasm

vin•di•cate \ˈvin-də-ˌkāt\ *vb* **vin•di•cat•ed**; **vin•di•cat•ing**
1 to free from blame or guilt ⟨The evidence will *vindicate* her.⟩
2 to show to be true or correct ⟨Later discoveries *vindicated* their claim.⟩

vin•dic•tive \vin-ˈdik-tiv\ *adj*
1 likely to seek revenge ⟨a *vindictive* person⟩
2 meant to be harmful ⟨*vindictive* remarks⟩

vine: red and green tomatoes on vines

vine \ˈvīn\ *n*
▲ a plant whose stem requires support and which climbs by tendrils or twining or creeps along the ground
vine•like \-ˌlīk\ *adj*

vineyard in Napa Valley, California

vin•e•gar \ˈvi-ni-gər\ *n*
a sour liquid made from cider, wine, or malt and used to flavor or preserve foods

► **Word History** The English word *vinegar* came from the medieval French words *vin egre* with the same meaning. The literal meaning of *vin egre* is "sour wine," reflecting the fact that vinegar was often made from old wine in which the alcohol has oxidized.

vine•yard \ˈvin-yərd\ *n*
▲ a field of grapevines

[1]**vin•tage** \ˈvin-tij\ *n*
1 the grapes grown or wine made during one season
2 the time when something started or was made ⟨He uses slang of recent *vintage*.⟩

[2]**vintage** *adj*
1 produced in a particular year ⟨a *vintage* wine⟩
2 of old and continuing interest, importance, or quality ⟨*vintage* cars⟩

vi•nyl \ˈvī-nᵊl\ *n*
a substance or product (as a fiber) made from an artificial plastic

[1]**vi•o•la** \vī-ˈō-lə, vē-\ *n*
a garden plant that looks like but is smaller than a pansy

[2]**vi•o•la** \vē-ˈō-lə\ *n*
a stringed musical instrument like a violin but slightly larger and lower in pitch

vi•o•late \ˈvī-ə-ˌlāt\ *vb* **vi•o•lat•ed**; **vi•o•lat•ing**
1 to fail to keep : BREAK ⟨Students who *violate* the rules are punished.⟩
2 to treat in a very disrespectful way ⟨Vandals *violated* the shrine.⟩
3 DISTURB 1 ⟨Don't *violate* their privacy.⟩
vi•o•la•tor \-ˌlā-tər\ *n*

vi•o•la•tion \ˌvī-ə-ˈlā-shən\ *n*
an act or instance of violating something and especially a failure to do what is required or expected by a law, rule, or agreement ⟨a traffic *violation*⟩

vi•o•lence \ˈvī-ə-ləns\ *n*
1 the use of force to harm a person or damage property
2 great force or strength especially of a kind that involves destruction ⟨the *violence* of a storm⟩

vi•o•lent \ˈvī-ə-lənt\ *adj*
1 showing very strong force ⟨a *violent* earthquake⟩
2 [1]EXTREME 1, INTENSE ⟨*violent* pain⟩
3 using or likely to use harmful force ⟨a *violent* person⟩
4 caused by force ⟨a *violent* death⟩
vi•o•lent•ly *adv*

vi•o•let \ˈvī-ə-lət\ *n*
1 a wild or garden plant related to the pansies that has small often fragrant white, blue, purple, or yellow flowers
2 a bluish purple

vi•o•lin \ˌvī-ə-ˈlin\ *n*
► a stringed musical instrument with four strings that is usually held against the shoulder under the chin and played with a bow

vi•o•lin•ist \ˌvī-ə-ˈli-nist\ *n*
a person who plays the violin

vi•per \ˈvī-pər\ *n*
a poisonous heavy-bodied snake with long hollow fangs

vir•eo \ˈvir-ē-ˌō\ *n, pl* **vir•e•os**
a small songbird that eats insects and is olive-green or grayish in color

[1]**vir•gin** \ˈvər-jən\ *n*
a person who has not had sexual intercourse

[2]**virgin** *adj*
not yet disturbed or changed by human activity 〈*virgin* forests〉

Vir•go \ˈvər-gō, ˈvir-\ *n*
1 a constellation between Leo and Libra imagined as a young woman
2 the sixth sign of the zodiac or a person born under this sign

vir•ile \ˈvir-əl, ˈvir-ˌīl\ *adj*
having qualities generally associated with men

vir•tu•al \ˈvər-chə-wəl\ *adj*
being in effect but not in fact or name : close to but not quite something 〈Rain is a *virtual* certainty today.〉
vir•tu•al•ly *adv*

virtual reality *n*
an artificial environment which is experienced through sights and sounds provided by a computer and in which a person's actions partly decide what happens in the environment

vir•tue \ˈvər-chü\ *n*
1 morally good behavior or character 〈We were urged to lead lives of *virtue*.〉
2 a good, moral, or desirable quality 〈Patience is a *virtue*.〉
3 the good result that comes from something 〈I learned the *virtue* of hard work.〉
by virtue of because of : through the force of 〈She succeeded *by virtue of* persistence.〉

► **Word History** From the Latin word *vir*, meaning "man," the Romans formed the word *virtus* to describe such so-called "manly" qualities as firmness of purpose and courage. Gradually this word was used for any good qualities in males or females. The English word *virtue* came by way of French from Latin *virtus*.

bow
string

violin: a girl playing a violin

vir•tu•o•so \ˌvər-chə-ˈwō-sō, -zō\ *n, pl* **vir•tu•o•sos** *or* **vir•tu•o•si** \-sē, -zē\
a person who is an outstanding performer especially in music 〈a piano *virtuoso*〉

vir•tu•ous \ˈvər-chə-wəs\ *adj*
morally good : having or showing virtue
vir•tu•ous•ly *adv*

vir•u•lent \ˈvir-ə-lənt\ *adj*
spreading quickly and causing serious harm 〈a *virulent* disease〉

vi•rus \ˈvī-rəs\ *n*
1 a disease-causing agent that is too tiny to be seen by the ordinary microscope, that may be a living organism or may be a very special kind of protein molecule, and that can only multiply when inside the cell of an organism
2 a disease caused by a virus
3 a usually hidden computer program that causes harm by making copies of itself and inserting them into other programs

vis•count \ˈvī-ˌkau̇nt\ *n*
a British nobleman ranking below an earl and above a baron

vis•count•ess \ˈvī-ˌkau̇n-təs\ *n*
1 the wife or widow of a viscount
2 a woman who holds the rank of a viscount in her own right

vise \ˈvīs\ *n*
► a device with two jaws that can be opened and closed by a screw or lever for holding or clamping work

vis•i•bil•i•ty \ˌvi-zə-ˈbi-lə-tē\ *n*
the ability to see or be seen 〈The bad weather caused poor *visibility* on the roads.〉 〈Bright clothing increased the hunter's *visibility*.〉

vis•i•ble \ˈvi-zə-bəl\ *adj*
1 capable of being seen 〈The sky was cloudy and no stars were *visible*.〉
2 easily seen or understood : OBVIOUS 〈Her anger was quite *visible*.〉
vis•i•bly \-blē\ *adv*

vi•sion \ˈvi-zhən\ *n*
1 the sense by which the qualities of an object (as color) that make up its appearance are perceived through a process in which light rays entering the eye are transformed into signals that pass to the brain
2 the act or power of seeing : SIGHT
3 something dreamt or imagined 〈She had *visions* of discovering great treasures.〉
4 exceptional ability to know or believe what should happen or be done in the future 〈a leader with *vision*〉

vi•sion•ary \ˈvi-zhə-ˌner-ē\ *n, pl* **vi•sion•ar•ies**
a person who has an exceptional ability to plan or have ideas for the future

[1]**vis•it** \ˈvi-zət\ *vb* **vis•it•ed**; **vis•it•ing**
1 to go to see for a particular purpose 〈*visit* a friend〉 〈*visit* a doctor〉 〈*visit* the zoo〉
2 to stay with for a time as a guest 〈I am *visiting* with relatives.〉
3 to come to or upon 〈We were *visited* by many troubles.〉

[2]**visit** *n*
1 an act of going to see a person, place, or thing for a particular purpose 〈a *visit* with friends〉 〈our *visit* to the museum〉
2 a stay as a guest 〈a weekend *visit* with relatives〉

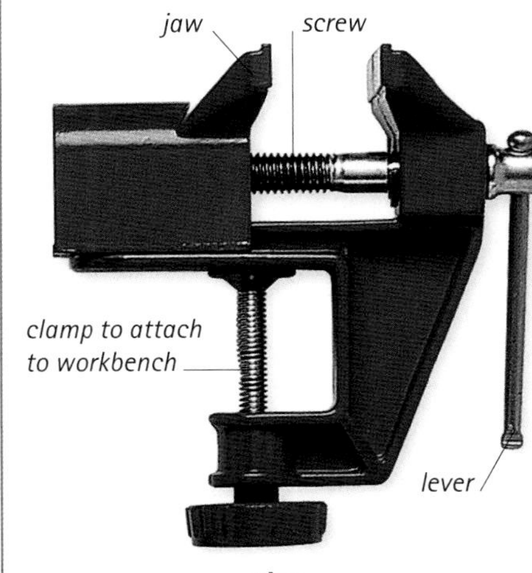

vise

vis•i•tor \ˈvi-zə-tər\ *n*

vi•sor \ˈvī-zər\ *n*
1 the movable front upper piece of a helmet that is brought down to protect the face
2 ▼ a part (as on a cap) that sticks out to protect or shade the eyes

visor 2

vis•ta \ˈvi-stə\ *n*
a large and scenic view in the distance ⟨a breathtaking mountain *vista*⟩

vi•su•al \ˈvi-zhə-wəl\ *adj*
1 obtained by the use of sight ⟨a *visual* impression⟩
2 of, relating to, or used in seeing ⟨the *visual* organs⟩
3 appealing to the sense of sight ⟨Charts, drawings, and other *visual* aids can enhance a presentation.⟩
vi•su•al•ly *adv*

vi•su•al•ize \ˈvi-zhə-wə-ˌlīz\ *vb*
vi•su•al•ized; vi•su•al•iz•ing
to see or form a mental image : IMAGINE

vi•tal \ˈvī-tᵊl\ *adj*
1 concerned with or necessary to the continuation of life ⟨The heart and lungs are *vital* organs.⟩
2 full of life and energy ⟨At 80, he's still an active and *vital* man.⟩
3 very important ⟨a *vital* clue⟩
vi•tal•ly *adv*

vi•tal•i•ty \vī-ˈta-lə-tē\ *n, pl* **vi•tal•i•ties**
1 capacity to live and develop ⟨the *vitality* of a seed⟩
2 ENERGY 1, VIGOR ⟨She's a woman of great *vitality*.⟩

vi•tals \ˈvī-tᵊlz\ *n pl*
the bodily organs (as the brain, heart, lungs, and liver) that are needed to stay alive

vi•ta•min \ˈvī-tə-mən\ *n*
any of a group of substances that are found naturally in many foods, are necessary in small quantities for good health and normal development and functioning, and are designated by a capital letter and sometimes a number ⟨*vitamin* B_6⟩ ⟨*vitamin* C⟩

vi•va•cious \və-ˈvā-shəs, vī-\ *adj*
full of energy and good spirits ⟨a *vivacious* personality⟩

vi•vac•i•ty \və-ˈva-sə-tē, vī-\ *n*
the quality or state of being full of energy and good spirits

viv•id \ˈvi-vəd\ *adj*
1 producing strong mental images ⟨a *vivid* description⟩
2 very strong or bright ⟨*vivid* red⟩
3 acting clearly and powerfully ⟨a *vivid* imagination⟩
4 seeming full of life and freshness ⟨a *vivid* painting⟩
viv•id•ly *adv*
viv•id•ness *n*

vix•en \ˈvik-sən\ *n*
a female fox

vo•cab•u•lary \vō-ˈka-byə-ˌler-ē\ *n, pl* **vo•cab•u•lar•ies**
1 a list or collection of words and their meanings
2 the words used in a language, by a group or individual, or in relation to a subject

vo•cal \ˈvō-kəl\ *adj*
1 uttered by the voice : ORAL ⟨*vocal* communication⟩
2 composed or arranged for or sung by the human voice ⟨the *vocal* parts of a song⟩
3 speaking freely or loudly : OUTSPOKEN ⟨a *vocal* critic⟩
4 relating to or involved in producing the voice ⟨the *vocal* organs⟩
vo•cal•ly *adv*

vocal cords *n pl*
a pair of folds of tissue that extend across the inside of the larynx and that produce the voice when air exhaled from the lungs causes them to tighten and vibrate

vo•cal•ist \ˈvō-kə-list\ *n*
a person who sings : SINGER

vo•ca•tion \vō-ˈkā-shən\ *n*
1 a strong desire for a certain career or course of action ⟨It was her *vocation* to be an actress.⟩
2 the work in which a person is regularly employed : OCCUPATION

vo•ca•tion•al \vō-ˈkā-shə-nᵊl\ *adj*
1 of, relating to, or concerned with an occupation ⟨*vocational* opportunities⟩
2 relating to or providing training in a skill or trade to be pursued as a career ⟨a *vocational* school⟩

vod•ka \ˈväd-kə\ *n*
a colorless alcoholic liquor

vogue \ˈvōg\ *n*
1 the quality or state of being popular at a certain time ⟨Portable electronic devices are in *vogue*.⟩
2 something that is in fashion at a certain time ⟨Baggy clothes are the *vogue*.⟩

¹voice \ˈvȯis\ *n*
1 sound that passes out of the mouth and throat of vertebrates and especially human beings and is produced mainly by the vibration of the vocal cords within the larynx (as in speaking or shouting)
2 musical sounds produced by singing ⟨We love listening to her beautiful *voice*.⟩
3 the power to use the voice ⟨I had a sore throat and lost my *voice*.⟩
4 a sound similar to vocal sound ⟨the cheerful *voice* of a cricket⟩
5 the right to express a wish, choice, or opinion ⟨Everyone has a *voice* in the decision.⟩
6 a means of expression ⟨The newspaper was the *voice* of optimism.⟩

²voice *vb* **voiced; voic•ing**
to express in words ⟨I *voiced* a complaint.⟩

voice box *n*
LARYNX

voiced \ˈvȯist\ *adj*
1 having a voice of a specified kind ⟨loud-*voiced*⟩
2 spoken with vibration of the vocal cords : not silent ⟨the *voiced* consonants \b\, \d\, and \th\⟩

voice•less \ˈvȯis-ləs\ *adj*
1 having no voice
2 spoken without vibration of the vocal cords ⟨the *voiceless* consonants \p\, \t\, and \th\⟩

voice mail *n*
an electronic communication system in which spoken messages are recorded to be played back later

¹void \ˈvȯid\ *adj*
1 containing nothing : EMPTY ⟨*void* space⟩
2 being without : DEVOID ⟨a person *void* of common sense⟩
3 having no legal effect ⟨a *void* contract⟩

²void *n*
empty space ⟨the great *void* between planets⟩ ⟨Her departure left a *void* in my life.⟩

vol. *abbr*
1 volume
2 volunteer

vol•a•tile \ˈvä-lə-tᵊl\ *adj*
1 easily becoming a gas at a fairly low temperature ⟨*volatile* solvents⟩
2 likely to change suddenly ⟨a *volatile* temper⟩

volcano 1

vol•ca•nic \väl-'ka-nik, vȯl-\ *adj*
of, relating to, or produced by a volcano ⟨*volcanic* ash⟩

vol•ca•no \väl-'kā-nō, vȯl-\ *n, pl* **vol•ca•noes** *or* **vol•ca•nos**
1 ▲ an opening in the earth's crust from which hot or melted rock and steam erupt
2 a hill or mountain composed of material thrown out in a volcanic eruption

▶ **Word History** Before Columbus, Europeans knew only the handful of active volcanoes long familiar to sailors in the Mediterranean, such as Vesuvius in Italy. There was no general word to describe a mountain that emitted fire. his situation changed in the 1500s, however, when the Spanish conquistadors came upon the great volcanic peaks of Mexico, Central America, and the Andes. The writings of the conquistadors used for these mountains the word *volcán*, whose roots lie in the ancient world. *Vulcanus*, the Roman god of fire, was particularly associated with the volcanic Lipari Islands off the coast of Sicily, one of which is still called *Vulcano* in Italian. Through Arabic, Latin *Vulcanus* was brought to Spanish as a name for fiery peaks, and from Spanish to Italian, French, and English.

vole \'vōl\ *n*
a small animal that is a rodent which looks like a fat mouse or rat and is sometimes harmful to crops

vo•li•tion \vō-'li-shən\ *n*
the act or power of making choices or decisions without being influenced by other people : WILL ⟨I chose to go on my own *volition.*⟩

[1]**vol•ley** \'vä-lē\ *n, pl* **volleys**
1 a group of missiles (as arrows or bullets) passing through the air
2 the firing of many weapons (as rifles) at the same time
3 a bursting forth of many things at once ⟨a *volley* of questions⟩
4 a hit or kick of the ball while it is in the air before it touches the ground ⟨The player hit a *volley* over the net.⟩

[2]**volley** *vb* **vol•leyed; vol•ley•ing**
to hit an object (as a ball) while it is in the air before it touches the ground

vol•ley•ball \'vä-lē-ˌbȯl\ *n*
1 ▼ a game played by two teams that hit a ball filled with air over a net without letting the ball touch the ground
2 the ball used in volleyball

volt \'vōlt\ *n*
a unit for measuring the force that moves an electric current

▶ **volleyball 1**
Volleyball is played with two teams, usually of six players each. Once the ball is served, it is volleyed back and forth across the net, each team trying to return it to the opponent's side in three or fewer hits. The first team that fails to do this loses the round. If the serving team is the one that loses, the opposing team serves next. Otherwise, the serving team scores and continues serving.

volleyball court

volleyball player striking the ball

volleyball

a b c d e f g h i j k l m n o p q r s t u v w x y z

volt•age \'vōl-tij\ *n*
electric force measured in volts ⟨the *voltage* of a current⟩

vol•ume \'väl-yəm, -yüm\ *n*
1 [1]BOOK 1
2 one of a series of books that together form a complete work or collection
3 an amount of space that can be measured in cubic units ⟨The *volume* of the box is three cubic feet.⟩
4 [2]AMOUNT ⟨a high *volume* of sales⟩
5 a large amount ⟨He received *volumes* of mail.⟩
6 the degree of loudness of a sound ⟨Turn up the *volume* of the radio.⟩

► **Word History** The earliest books were not like the books we read today. Instead of having pages that turn, they were written on rolls of papyrus. The Latin word for such a scroll, *volumen*, came from the verb *volvere*, meaning "to roll." English *volume* came by way of French from Latin *volumen*. At first *volume* meant "scroll" or "book," but later it came to mean "the size of a book" as well. This sense led to the more general meaning of "size" or "amount" as in the volume of a jar or the volume of sales. From this sense came still another meaning: "loudness or intensity of sound."

vo•lu•mi•nous \və-'lü-mə-nəs\ *adj*
1 of great size or amount **:** LARGE ⟨a *voluminous* stamp collection⟩
2 [1]FULL 5 ⟨a *voluminous* robe⟩

vol•un•tary \'vä-lən-,ter-ē\ *adj*
1 done, given, or acting of free choice ⟨a *voluntary* confession⟩ ⟨a *voluntary* participant⟩
2 done or acting with no expectation of payment ⟨a *voluntary* job⟩
3 relating to or controlled by the will ⟨*voluntary* muscle movements⟩
vol•un•tar•i•ly \,vä-lən-'ter-ə-lē\ *adv*

► **Synonyms** VOLUNTARY, INTENTIONAL, and DELIBERATE mean done or brought about by choice. VOLUNTARY is used of an act that results from freedom of will. ⟨Joining the club is *voluntary.*⟩ It can also be used of an act that is controlled by the will. ⟨Blinking the eyes can be a *voluntary* movement.⟩ INTENTIONAL is used of something that is done for a reason and only after some thought. ⟨Her neglect of the task was *intentional.*⟩ DELIBERATE is used of an act that is done purposefully and with full understanding of the likely results. ⟨It was a *deliberate* insult.⟩

[1]**vol•un•teer** \,vä-lən-'tir\ *n*
a person who does something by free choice usually with no payment expected or given ⟨*Volunteers* painted the town hall.⟩

[2]**volunteer** *adj*
relating to or done by volunteers ⟨a *volunteer* fire department⟩

[3]**volunteer** *vb* **vol•un•teered; vol•un•teer•ing**
to offer or give without being asked or forced and usually with no expectation of payment ⟨We *volunteered* to help clean up.⟩ ⟨I *volunteered* my services.⟩

[1]**vom•it** \'vä-mət\ *n*
material from the stomach brought up suddenly through the mouth

[2]**vomit** *vb* **vom•it•ed; vom•it•ing**
to bring up the contents of the stomach through the mouth

vo•ra•cious \vȯ-'rā-shəs, və-\ *adj*
1 very hungry **:** having a huge appetite
2 very eager ⟨a *voracious* reader⟩
vo•ra•cious•ly *adv*

[1]**vote** \'vōt\ *n*
1 ▼ a formal expression of opinion or choice (as by ballot in an election)
2 the decision reached by voting ⟨The *vote* is in favor of the amendment.⟩
3 the right to vote ⟨In 1920, American women won the *vote.*⟩
4 the act or process of voting ⟨The question came to a *vote.*⟩
5 a group of voters with some common interest or quality ⟨the farm *vote*⟩

[1]**vote 1:** residents of El Paso, Texas, casting their votes in an election

[2]**vote** *vb* **vot•ed; vot•ing**
1 to express a wish or choice by a vote 〈We *voted* by raising our hands.〉
2 to elect, decide, pass, defeat, grant, or make legal by a vote 〈The group *voted* down the proposal.〉
3 to declare by general agreement 〈She was *voted* student of the month.〉
4 to offer as a suggestion 〈I *vote* we go home.〉

vot•er \'vō-tər\ *n*
a person who votes or who has the legal right to vote

vouch \'vau̇ch\ *vb* **vouched; vouch•ing**
to give a guarantee 〈The teacher *vouched* for their honesty.〉

vouch•safe \vau̇ch-'sāf\ *vb* **vouch•safed; vouch•saf•ing**
to give or grant as a special favor

[1]**vow** \'vau̇\ *n*
a solemn promise or statement

[2]**vow** *vb* **vowed; vow•ing**
to make a solemn promise : SWEAR 〈He *vowed* to follow all the rules.〉

vow•el \'vau̇-əl\ *n*
1 a speech sound (as \ə\, \ā\, or \ȯ\) produced without obstruction in the mouth
2 a letter (as *a, e, i, o, u*) representing a vowel

[1]**voy•age** \'vȯi-ij\ *n*
a journey especially by water to a distant or unknown place

[2]**voyage** *vb* **voy•aged; voy•ag•ing**
to take a long trip usually by boat 〈The explorers *voyaged* to distant lands.〉
voy•ag•er *n*

VP *abbr* vice president

vs. *abbr* versus

VT, Vt. *abbr* Vermont

v.t. *abbr* verb transitive

vul•ca•nize \'vəl-kə-,nīz\ *vb* **vul•ca•nized; vul•ca•niz•ing**
to treat rubber with chemicals in order to give it more strength or flexibility

vul•gar \'vəl-gər\ *adj*
1 having or showing poor taste or manners : COARSE 〈*vulgar* table manners〉
2 offensive in language or subject matter 〈a *vulgar* joke〉

vul•gar•i•ty \,vəl-'ger-ə-tē\ *n, pl* **vul•gar•i•ties**
1 the quality or state of having or showing poor taste or manners
2 rude or offensive language or behavior

vul•ner•a•ble \'vəl-nə-rə-bəl\ *adj*
1 capable of being easily hurt or injured 〈The patient is *vulnerable* to infection.〉
2 open to attack or damage 〈The troops were in a *vulnerable* position.〉

vul•ture \'vəl-chər\ *n*
▼ a large bird related to the hawks and eagles that has a head bare of feathers and feeds mostly on dead animals

vying *present participle of* VIE

vulture:
an African vulture

a b c d e f g h i j k l m n o p q r s t u v w x y z

Ww

Sounds of W: The letter **W** makes the sound heard in ***wind*** and ***forward***. **W** is sometimes silent, as in ***write*** and ***two***. The letters **W** and **H** together make three different sounds. In one, the **W** is silent, as in ***who***. In another, the **H** is silent, as in the way many people say ***when*** and ***which***. Some people, however, pronounce these words with an **H** sound before the **W** sound, so that they sound like \hwen\ and \hwich\. The letter **W** can also be used in combination with other letters to form vowel sounds in words such as ***cow***, ***law***, or ***new***.

w \'də-bəl-yü\ *n, pl* **w's** *or* **ws** \-yüz\ *often cap*
the 23rd letter of the English alphabet

W *abbr*
1 west
2 western

WA *abbr* Washington

wacky \'wa-kē\ *also* **whacky** \'hwa-kē, 'wa-\ *adj* **wack•i•er** *also* **whack•i•er**; **wack•i•est** *also* **whack•i•est**
CRAZY 2, INSANE

[1]**wad** \'wäd\ *n*
1 a small mass or lump of soft material ⟨a *wad* of tissues⟩ ⟨a *wad* of chewing gum⟩
2 a thick pile of folded money

[2]**wad** *vb* **wad•ded**; **wad•ding**
to crush or press into a small tight mass

[1]**wad•dle** \'wä-dᵊl\ *vb* **wad•dled**; **wad•dling**
to walk with short steps swaying like a duck

[2]**waddle** *n*
a way of walking by taking short steps and swaying from side to side

wade \'wād\ *vb* **wad•ed**; **wad•ing**
1 to walk through something (as water, snow, or a crowd) that makes it hard to move
2 to pass or cross by stepping through water ⟨We decided to *wade* the stream.⟩
3 to proceed with difficulty ⟨She's *wading* through paperwork.⟩

wading bird *n*
▼ a bird (as a heron) with long legs that wades in water in search of food

wading bird: a grey heron

waffle

wa•fer \'wā-fər\ *n*
a thin crisp cake or cracker

waf•fle \'wä-fəl\ *n*
▲ a crisp cake of batter baked in a waffle iron and often indented with a pattern of small squares

waffle iron *n*
a cooking utensil with two hinged metal parts that come together for making waffles

[1]**waft** \'wäft, 'waft\ *vb* **waft•ed**; **waft•ing**
to move or be moved lightly by or as if by the action of waves or wind

[2]**waft** *n*
a slight breeze or puff of air

wagon: a traditional wooden wagon

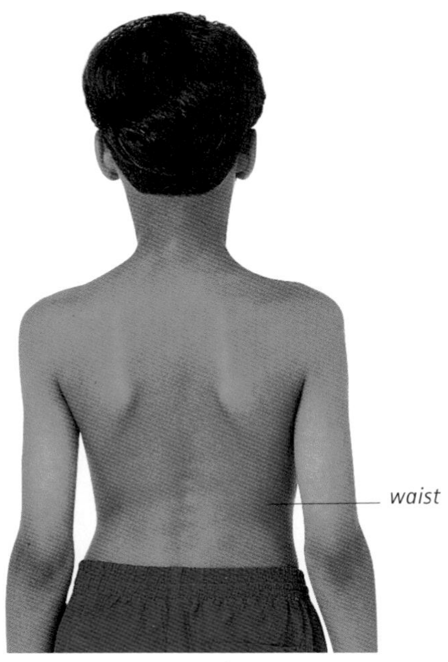

waist 1

[1]**wag** \'wag\ *vb* **wagged**; **wag•ging**
to swing to and fro or from side to side 〈The dog *wagged* her tail.〉

[2]**wag** *n*
a movement back and forth or from side to side

[3]**wag** *n*
a person full of jokes and humor

[1]**wage** \'wāj\ *n*
payment for work done especially when figured by the hour or day

[2]**wage** *vb* **waged**; **wag•ing**
to engage in : carry on 〈The new police chief vowed to *wage* a fight against crime.〉

[1]**wa•ger** \'wā-jər\ *n*
1 [1]BET 2
2 the act of betting

[2]**wager** *vb* **wa•gered**; **wa•ger•ing**
to bet on the result of a contest or question

wag•gish \'wa-gish\ *adj*
showing or done in a spirit of harmless mischief

wag•gle \'wa-gəl\ *vb* **wag•gled**; **wag•gling**
to move backward and forward, from side to side, or up and down

wag•on \'wa-gən\ *n*
◀ a vehicle having four wheels and used for carrying goods

waif \'wāf\ *n*
a homeless child

[1]**wail** \'wāl\ *vb* **wailed**; **wail•ing**
1 to make a long, loud cry of pain or grief
2 to complain with a loud voice

[2]**wail** *n*
a long cry of grief or pain

wain•scot \'wān-skət, -ˌskōt, -ˌskät\ *n*
the bottom part of an inside wall especially when made of material different from the rest

wain•scot•ing *or* **wain•scot•ting** \'wān-ˌskō-tiŋ, -ˌskä-\ *n*
WAINSCOT

waist \'wāst\ *n*
1 ◀ the part of the body between the hips and chest or upper back
2 the part of a garment that fits around a person's waist

[1]**wait** \'wāt\ *vb* **wait•ed**; **wait•ing**
1 to stay in a place looking forward to something that is expected to happen
2 to stop moving or doing something 〈*Wait* at the door.〉 〈*Wait* a second—I have a better idea.〉
3 to remain not done or dealt with 〈The chore can *wait.*〉 〈There's a package *waiting* for you.〉
4 to serve food as a waiter or waitress

[2]**wait** *n*
1 an act or period of waiting 〈We had a long *wait.*〉
2 a hidden place from which a surprise attack can be made
Hint: This sense of *wait* is usually used in the expression *lie in wait.*

wait•er \'wā-tər\ *n*
a person who serves food to people at tables

waiting room *n*
a room (as in a station or an office) for the use of people waiting

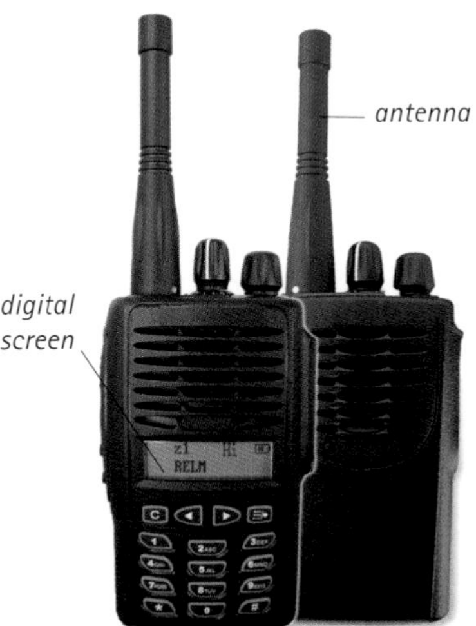

walkie-talkie: a pair of walkie-talkies

wait•ress \'wā-trəs\ *n*
a girl or woman who serves food to people at tables

waive \'wāv\ *vb* **waived**; **waiv•ing**
to give up claim to

[1]**wake** \'wāk\ *vb* **woke** \'wōk\ *also* **waked**; **wo•ken** \'wō-kən\ *or* **waked** *also* **woke**; **wak•ing**
1 to arouse from sleep : AWAKE
Hint: This sense of *wake* is often used with *up.* 〈*Wake* us up at six.〉
2 to become alert or aware

[2]**wake** *n*
a watch held over the body of a dead person before burial

[3]**wake** *n*
a track or mark left by something moving especially in the water 〈a motorboat's *wake*〉

wake•ful \'wāk-fəl\ *adj*
not sleeping or able to sleep
wake•ful•ness *n*

wak•en \'wā-kən\ *vb* **wak•ened**; **wak•en•ing**
[1]WAKE 1 〈The sound of thunder *wakened* me.〉

[1]**walk** \'wȯk\ *vb* **walked**; **walk•ing**
1 to move or cause to move along on foot at a natural slow pace 〈I *walk* to school.〉
2 to cover or pass over on foot 〈We *walked* 20 miles.〉
3 to go with (a person or animal) by walking 〈Will you *walk* me home?〉
4 to go or cause to go to first base after four balls in baseball
walk•er *n*
walk out
1 to leave suddenly and unexpectedly
2 to go on strike

[2]**walk** *n*
1 the act of moving along on foot at a natural slow pace
2 a place or path for walking 〈My dog ran up the *walk* to greet me.〉
3 distance to be walked often measured in time required by a walker to cover 〈Her house is a long *walk* from here.〉
4 way of walking 〈He approached with a confident *walk.*〉
5 an advance to first base after four balls in baseball
6 position in life or the community
7 a slow way of moving by a horse

walk•ie–talk•ie \ˌwȯ-kē-'tȯ-kē\ *n*
◀ a small portable radio set for receiving and sending messages

walking stick *n*
1 ▶ a stick used to maintain balance when walking
2 STICK INSECT

walk•out \'wȯk-ˌau̇t\ *n*
1 a labor strike
2 the act of leaving a meeting or organization to show disapproval

walking stick 1: a stick used for hiking

¹wall 2: the Great Wall of China was built to protect the northern borders of the Chinese empire, and is the longest man-made structure in the world

¹wall \'wȯl\ *n*
1 one of the sides of a room or building
2 ▲ a solid structure (as of stone) built to enclose or shut off a space ⟨The property is surrounded by a brick *wall*.⟩
3 something that separates one thing from another ⟨a *wall* of mountains⟩
4 a layer of material enclosing space ⟨the heart *wall*⟩ ⟨the *wall* of a pipe⟩
walled \'wȯld\ *adj*

²wall *vb* **walled**; **wall•ing**
to build or have a wall in or around

wall•board \'wȯl-ˌbȯrd\ *n*
a building material (as of wood pulp) made in large stiff sheets and used especially inside walls and ceilings

wal•let \'wä-lət\ *n*
a small flat case for carrying paper money and personal papers

wall•eye \'wȯl-ˌī\ *n*
a large North American freshwater fish that has large glassy eyes and is caught for food and sport

¹wal•lop \'wä-ləp\ *vb* **wal•loped**; **wal•lop•ing**
to hit hard

²wallop *n*
a hard blow

¹wal•low \'wä-lō\ *vb* **wal•lowed**; **wal•low•ing**
1 to roll about in or as if in deep mud
2 to seem to want to be unhappy

²wallow *n*
a muddy or dust-filled area where animals roll about

wall•pa•per \'wȯl-ˌpā-pər\ *n*
decorative paper for covering the walls of a room

wal•nut \'wȯl-ˌnət\ *n*
▶ a wrinkled edible nut that comes from a tall tree with hard strong wood

▶ **Word History** Walnut trees grew in southern Europe for a long time before they were grown in England. As a result the English gave the walnut a name which showed plainly that it was not an English nut. The Old English name for this southern nut was *wealhhnutu,* from *wealh,* "foreigner," and *hnutu,* "nut." The modern English word *walnut* comes from the Old English name.

wal•rus \'wȯl-rəs\ *n*
a large animal of northern seas that is related to the seal and has long ivory tusks, a tough wrinkled hide, and flippers used in swimming, diving, and moving about on land

¹waltz \'wȯlts\ *n, pl* **waltz•es**
a dance in which couples glide to music having three beats to a measure

²waltz *vb* **waltzed**; **waltz•ing**
to dance a waltz

walnut: a branch and the dried nuts from an English walnut tree

Wam•pa•noag \'wäm-pə-,nȯg\ *n, pl* **Wampanoag** *or* **Wam•pa•noags**
a member of an American Indian people of eastern Rhode Island and neighboring parts of Massachusetts

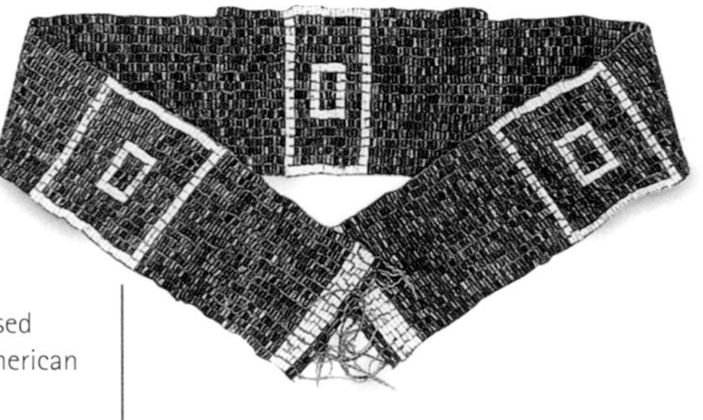

wampum: wampum woven into an Iroquois belt

wam•pum \'wäm-pəm\ *n*
▶ beads made of shells and once used for money or ornament by North American Indians

wan \'wän\ *adj* **wan•ner; wan•nest**
1 having a pale or sickly color
2 showing little effort or energy ⟨a *wan* smile⟩
wan•ly *adv*

wand \'wänd\ *n*
▼ a slender rod ⟨a magic *wand*⟩

wand: a magician's wand

wan•der \'wän-dər\ *vb* **wan•dered; wan•der•ing**
1 to move about without a goal or purpose : RAMBLE
2 to get off the right path or leave the right area : STRAY
3 to lose concentration ⟨My mind began to *wander.*⟩
4 to follow a winding course
wan•der•er *n*

> ▶ **Synonyms** WANDER, ROAM, and RAMBLE mean to move about from place to place without a reason or plan. WANDER is used for moving about without following a fixed course. ⟨The tribes *wandered* in the desert for forty years.⟩ ROAM is used for the carefree act of wandering over a wide area often for the sake of enjoyment. ⟨I *roamed* over the hills and through the meadows.⟩ RAMBLE is used for wandering in a careless way. ⟨Horses *rambled* over the open range.⟩

wane \'wān\ *vb* **waned; wan•ing**
1 to grow smaller or less ⟨His interest in the game was *waning.*⟩ ⟨The moon *wanes.*⟩
2 to grow shorter ⟨The day is *waning.*⟩

[1]**want** \'wȯnt, 'wänt\ *vb* **want•ed; want•ing**
1 to desire, wish, or long for something ⟨I *want* to go home.⟩
2 to feel or suffer the need of something ⟨After a long run I badly *wanted* a drink of water.⟩
3 to be without : LACK ⟨Luckily, my family does not *want* much.⟩

[2]**want** *n*
1 [2]LACK, SHORTAGE ⟨His actions show a *want* of common sense.⟩
2 the state of being very poor ⟨They died in *want.*⟩
3 a wish for something : DESIRE

want•ing \'wȯn-tiŋ, 'wän-\ *adj*
falling below a standard, hope, or need ⟨The plan was found *wanting.*⟩

wan•ton \'wȯn-t^{ə}n\ *adj*
1 not modest or proper : INDECENT
2 showing no thought or care for the rights, feelings, or safety of others ⟨*wanton* cruelty⟩
wan•ton•ly *adv*
wan•ton•ness *n*

[1]**war** \'wȯr\ *n*
1 a state or period of fighting between states or nations
2 a struggle between opposing forces or for a particular end ⟨the *war* on poverty⟩

[2]**war** *vb* **warred; war•ring**
to engage in a series of battles

[1]**war•ble** \'wȯr-bəl\ *n*
1 low pleasing sounds that form a melody (as of a bird)
2 the action of making low pleasing sounds that form a melody

[2]**warble** *vb* **war•bled; war•bling**
to sing a melody of low pleasing sounds

war•bler \'wȯr-blər\ *n*
1 an Old World bird related to the thrush and noted for its musical song
2 a brightly colored American bird having a song that is usually weak and not musical

[1]**ward** \'wȯrd\ *n*
1 a large room in a hospital where a number of patients often needing similar treatment are cared for
2 one of the parts into which a town or city is divided for management
3 a person under the protection of a guardian

[2]**ward** *vb* **ward•ed; ward•ing**
to avoid being hit or affected by ⟨Wear a sweater to *ward* off the cold.⟩

[1]**-ward** \wərd\ *also* **-wards** \wərdz\ *adj suffix*
1 that moves, faces, or is pointed toward ⟨wind*ward*⟩
2 that is found in the direction of

[2]**-ward** *or* **-wards** *adv suffix*
1 in a specified direction ⟨up*ward*⟩
2 toward a specified place

war•den \'wȯr-d^{ə}n\ *n*
1 a person who sees that certain laws are followed ⟨game *warden*⟩
2 the chief official of a prison

ward•robe \'wȯr-,drōb\ *n*
1 ▼ a room, closet, or large chest where clothes are kept
2 the clothes a person owns

wardrobe 1: a freestanding wardrobe

warehouse: cardboard boxes holding goods stored in a warehouse

ware  \ˈwer\ *n*
1 manufactured articles or products of art or craft — often used in combination ⟨silver*ware*⟩
2 items (as dishes) of baked clay : POTTERY
3 an article of merchandise ⟨Merchants were selling their *wares.*⟩

ware•house \ˈwer-ˌhau̇s\ *n, pl* **ware•hous•es** \-ˌhau̇-zəz\
▲ a building for storing goods and merchandise

war•fare \ˈwȯr-ˌfer\ *n*
1 military fighting between enemies
2 conflict between opposing forces or for a particular end

war•like \ˈwȯr-ˌlīk\ *adj*
1 fond of war ⟨*warlike* people⟩
2 fit for or characteristic of war ⟨*warlike* aggression⟩

war•lock \ˈwȯr-ˌläk\ *n*
a man who practices witchcraft

[1]warm \ˈwȯrm\ *adj* **warm•er; warm•est**
1 somewhat hot ⟨*warm* milk⟩
2 giving off a little heat ⟨a *warm* stove⟩
3 making a person feel heat or experience no loss of body heat ⟨*warm* clothing⟩
4 having a feeling of warmth ⟨His hands are *warm.*⟩
5 showing strong feeling ⟨a *warm* welcome⟩
6 newly made : FRESH ⟨a *warm* scent⟩
7 near the object sought ⟨Keep going, you're getting *warm.*⟩
8 of a color in the range yellow through orange to red
warm•ly *adv*

[2]warm *vb* **warmed; warm•ing**
1 to make or become warm
2 to give a feeling of warmth
3 to become more interested than at first ⟨They began to *warm* to the idea.⟩
warm up
1 to exercise or practice lightly in preparation for more strenuous activity or a performance
2 to run (as a motor) at slow speed before using

warm–blood•ed \ˈwȯrm-ˈblə-dəd\ *adj*
able to keep up a relatively high constant body temperature that is independent of that of the surroundings

warmth \ˈwȯrmth\ *n*
1 gentle heat
2 strong feeling

warm–up \ˈwȯrm-ˌəp\ *n*
◀ the act or an instance of preparing for a performance or a more strenuous activity

warn \ˈwȯrn\ *vb* **warned; warn•ing**
1 to put on guard : CAUTION
2 to notify especially in advance

warm–up: a woman doing warm-ups before exercising

warn•ing \'wȯr-niŋ\ *n*
▶something that cautions of possible danger or trouble 〈storm *warnings*〉

¹warp \'wȯrp\ *n*
1 the threads that go lengthwise in a loom and are crossed by the woof
2 a twist or curve that has developed in something once flat or straight

²warp *vb* **warped**; **warp•ing**
1 to curve or twist out of shape
2 to cause to judge, choose, or act wrongly 〈Their thinking is *warped* by greed.〉

¹war•rant \'wȯr-ənt\ *n*
1 a reason or cause for an opinion or action 〈There is no *warrant* for such behavior.〉
2 a document giving legal power

²warrant *vb* **war•rant•ed**; **war•rant•ing**
1 to be sure of or that 〈I'll *warrant* they know the answer.〉
2 ²GUARANTEE 1 〈The toaster is *warranted* for 90 days.〉
3 to call for : JUSTIFY 〈The report *warrants* careful study.〉

warrant officer *n*
an officer in the armed forces in one of the grades between commissioned officers and noncommissioned officers

war•ren \'wȯr-ən\ *n*
a place where rabbits live or are kept

war•rior \'wȯr-yər, 'wȯr-ē-ər\ *n*
a person who is or has been in warfare

war•ship \'wȯr-,ship\ *n*
a ship armed for combat

wart \'wȯrt\ *n*
a small hard lump of thickened skin caused by a virus

wart•hog \'wȯrt-,hȯg, -,häg\ *n*
a wild African hog with pointed tusks and in the male thick growths of skin on the face which resemble warts

wary \'wer-ē\ *adj* **war•i•er**; **war•i•est**
very cautious
war•i•ly \'wer-ə-lē-\ *adv*
war•i•ness \'wer-ē-nəs\ *n*

was *past first person & third person sing of* BE

¹wash \'wȯsh, 'wäsh\ *vb* **washed**; **wash•ing**
1 to cleanse with water and usually a cleaning agent (as soap) 〈*Wash* your hands and face.〉
2 to wet completely with liquid 〈The flowers were *washed* with raindrops.〉
3 to flow along or overflow against 〈Waves *wash* up on the shore.〉
4 to remove or carry away by the action of water
5 to stand being cleansed without injury 〈Linen *washes* well.〉

²wash *n*
1 articles (as clothes, sheets, and towels) in the laundry

warning: a warning for flash floods

2 an act or instance of cleansing or of being cleansed
3 the flow, sound, or action of water
4 a backward flow of water (as made by the motion of a boat)
5 material carried or set down by water

Wash. *abbr* Washington

wash•able \'wȯ-shə-bəl, 'wä-\ *adj*
capable of being cleansed without damage 〈a *washable* jacket〉

wash•bowl \'wȯsh-,bōl, 'wäsh-\ *n*
a large bowl for water to wash the hands and face

wash•cloth \'wȯsh-,klȯth, 'wäsh-\ *n*
a small towel for washing the face and body

wash•er \'wȯ-shər, 'wä-\ *n*
1 WASHING MACHINE
2 a ring (as of metal) used to make something fit tightly or to prevent rubbing

washing machine *n*
a machine used for washing clothes and household linen

wash•out \'wȯsh-,au̇t, 'wäsh-\ *n*
1 a place where earth has been washed away
2 a complete failure

wash•tub \'wȯsh-,təb, 'wäsh-\ *n*
a tub for washing clothes or for soaking them before washing

wasn't \'wə-zᵊnt, 'wä-\
was not

wasp \'wäsp, 'wȯsp\ *n*
▼ a winged insect related to the bee and ant that has a slender body with the abdomen attached by a narrow stalk and that in females and workers is capable of giving a very painful sting

▶ **wasp**
There are thousands of different types of wasps around the world. Some live in large nesting colonies, while others are solitary, sometimes laying their eggs on other live insects. The developing larvae then gradually eat their host's body.

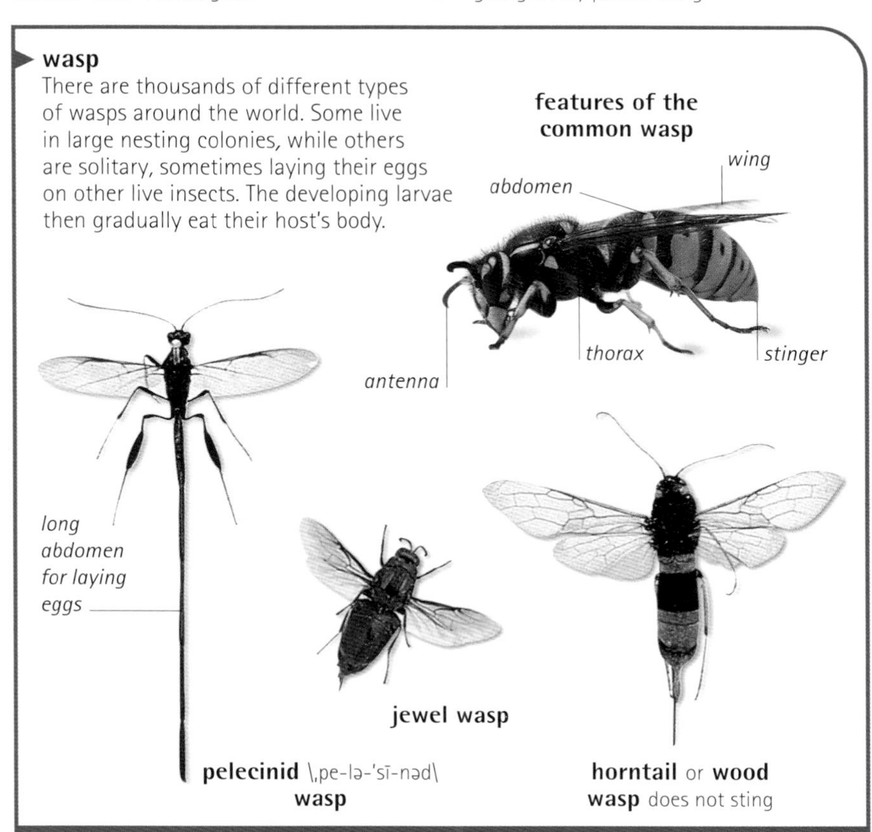

wasp•ish \'wäs-pish, 'wȯs-\ *adj*
³CROSS 1, IRRITABLE
wasp•ish•ly *adv*

¹**waste** \'wāst\ *n*
1 the action of spending or using carelessly or uselessly : the state of being spent or used carelessly or uselessly ⟨a *waste* of time⟩
2 material left over or thrown away
3 material (as carbon dioxide in the lungs or urine in the kidneys) produced in and of no further use to the living body
4 a large area of barren land : WASTELAND

²**waste** *vb* **wast•ed**; **wast•ing**
1 to spend or use carelessly or uselessly
2 to lose or cause to lose weight, strength, or energy
3 to bring to ruin

³**waste** *adj*
1 being wild and without people or crops : BARREN ⟨*waste* areas⟩
2 of no further use

waste•bas•ket \'wāst-ˌba-skət\ *n*
an open container for odds and ends to be thrown away

waste•ful \'wāst-fəl\ *adj*
spending or using in a careless or foolish way
waste•ful•ly \-fə-lē\ *adv*
waste•ful•ness *n*

waste•land \'wāst-ˌland\ *n*
land that is barren or not fit for crops

¹**watch** \'wäch\ *vb* **watched**; **watch•ing**
1 to keep in view ⟨Did you *watch* the game?⟩
2 to be on the lookout ⟨I'm *watching* for a signal.⟩
3 to take care of : TEND ⟨*Watch* the house until I get back.⟩
4 to be careful of ⟨*Watch* your step.⟩
5 to keep guard ⟨*Watch* outside the door.⟩
6 to stay awake
watch•er *n*
watch out to be aware of and ready for ⟨Remember to *watch out* for broken glass.⟩

²**watch** *n*
1 ▶ a small timepiece worn on the wrist or carried
2 close observation
3 ¹GUARD 1
4 the time during which someone is on duty to guard or be on the lookout
5 an act of keeping awake to guard or protect

²watch 1: a watch with a clear face that shows its mechanics

watch•dog \'wäch-ˌdȯg\ *n*
a dog kept to guard property

waterfall: Lower Yosemite \yō-'se-mə-tē\ Falls, California

watch•ful \'wäch-fəl\ *adj*
ATTENTIVE 1, VIGILANT
watch•ful•ly \-fə-lē\ *adv*
watch•ful•ness *n*

watch•man \'wäch-mən\ *n, pl* **watch•men** \-mən\
a person whose job is to guard property at night or when the owners are away

watch•tow•er \'wäch-ˌtau̇-ər\ *n*
a tower for a guard or watchman

watch•word \'wäch-ˌwərd\ *n*
PASSWORD

¹**wa•ter** \'wȯ-tər, 'wä-\ *n*
1 the liquid that comes from the clouds as rain and forms streams, lakes, and seas
2 a body of water or a part of a body of water

²**water** *vb* **wa•tered**; **wa•ter•ing**
1 to wet or supply with water ⟨I'm *watering* the plants.⟩
2 to fill with liquid (as tears or saliva)
3 to add water to ⟨Someone *watered* down the punch.⟩

wa•ter•bird \'wȯ-tər-ˌbərd, 'wä-\ *n*
a swimming or wading bird

water buffalo *n*
a buffalo of Asia with large curving horns that is often used as a work animal

wa•ter•col•or \'wȯ-tər-ˌkə-lər, 'wä-\ *n*
1 a paint whose liquid part is water
2 ▶ a picture painted with watercolor
3 the art of painting with watercolor

wa•ter•course \'wȯ-tər-ˌkȯrs, 'wä-\ *n*
1 a channel in which water flows
2 a stream of water (as a river or brook)

wa•ter•cress \'wȯ-tər-ˌkres, 'wä-\ *n*
a plant that grows in or near water and has sharp-tasting leaves used especially in salads

wa•ter•fall \'wȯ-tər-ˌfȯl, 'wä-\ *n*
◀ a fall of water from a height

water flea *n*
a tiny often brightly colored freshwater animal related to the crab and lobster

wa•ter•fowl \'wȯ-tər-ˌfau̇l, 'wä-\ *n*
1 a bird that is typically found in or near water
2 a swimming bird (as a duck or goose) often hunted as game

wa•ter•front \'wȯ-tər-ˌfrənt, 'wä-\ *n*
land that borders on a body of water

water hyacinth *n*
a floating water plant that often clogs streams in the southern United States

water lily *n*
▶ a water plant with rounded floating leaves and showy often fragrant flowers

wa•ter•line \'wȯ-tər-ˌlīn, 'wä-\ *n*
any of several lines marked on the outside of a ship that match the surface of the water when the ship floats evenly

wa•ter•logged \'wȯ-tər-ˌlȯgd, 'wä-, -ˌlägd\ *adj*
so filled or soaked with water as to be heavy or hard to manage

wa•ter•mark \'wȯ-tər-ˌmärk, 'wä-\ *n*
1 a mark that shows a level to which water has risen
2 a mark made in paper during manufacture that is visible when the paper is held up to the light

watercolor 2: a watercolor by contemporary artist Jane Gifford

wa•ter•mel•on \'wȯ-tər-,me-lən, 'wä-\ *n*
a large edible fruit with a hard rind and a sweet red juicy pulp

water moccasin *n*
a poisonous snake of the southern United States that lives in or near water

water lilies

water park *n*
an amusement park with pools and wetted slides

wa•ter•pow•er \'wȯ-tər-,pau̇-ər, 'wä-\ *n*
the power of moving water used to run machinery

[1]**wa•ter•proof** \,wȯ-tər-'prüf, ,wä-\ *adj*
not letting water through ⟨a *waterproof* tent⟩

[2]**waterproof** *vb* **wa•ter•proofed**; **wa•ter•proof•ing**
to make something resistant to letting water through

wa•ter•shed \'wȯ-tər-,shed, 'wä-\ *n*
1 a dividing ridge (as a mountain range) separating one drainage area from others
2 the whole area that drains into a lake or river

wa•ter–ski \'wȯ-tər-,skē, 'wä-\ *vb* **wa•ter–skied**; **wa•ter–ski•ing**
to ski on water while being pulled by a speedboat

water ski *n, pl* **water skis**
a ski used in water-skiing

wa•ter•spout \'wȯ-tər-,spau̇t, 'wä-\ *n*
1 a pipe for carrying off water from a roof
2 a slender cloud that is shaped like a funnel and extends down to a cloud of spray torn up from the surface of a body of water by a whirlwind

water strid•er \-'strī-dər\ *n*
▶ a bug with long legs that skims over the surface of water

wa•ter•tight \,wȯ-tər-'tīt, ,wä-\ *adj*
so tight as to be waterproof ⟨The pipe's joints are *watertight.*⟩

wa•ter•way \'wȯ-tər-,wā, 'wä-\ *n*
a channel or a body of water by which ships can travel

wa•ter•wheel \'wȯ-tər-,hwēl, 'wä-, -,wēl\ *n*
a wheel turned by a flow of water against it

wa•ter•works \'wȯ-tər-,wərks, 'wä-\ *n pl*
a system of dams, reservoirs, pumps, and pipes for supplying water (as to a city)

wa•tery \'wȯ-tə-rē, 'wä-\ *adj*
1 full of or giving out liquid ⟨*watery* eyes⟩
2 containing or giving out water or a thin liquid ⟨a *watery* mixture⟩
3 like water especially in being thin, soggy, pale, or without flavor ⟨*watery* soup⟩
4 lacking in strength or determination ⟨a *watery* smile⟩

watt \'wät\ *n*
a unit for measuring electric power

wat•tle \'wä-t^{ə}l\ *n*
▼ a fleshy flap of skin that hangs usually from the neck (as of a bird)

[1]**wave** \'wāv\ *vb* **waved**; **wav•ing**
1 to move (as the hand) to and fro as a signal or in greeting
2 to move (something) back and forth
3 to curve slightly ⟨Her hair *waves* naturally.⟩
4 to flutter with a rolling movement

[2]**wave** *n*
1 a moving ridge on the surface of water
2 a waving motion ⟨a *wave* of the hand⟩

wattle: wattle on a turkey

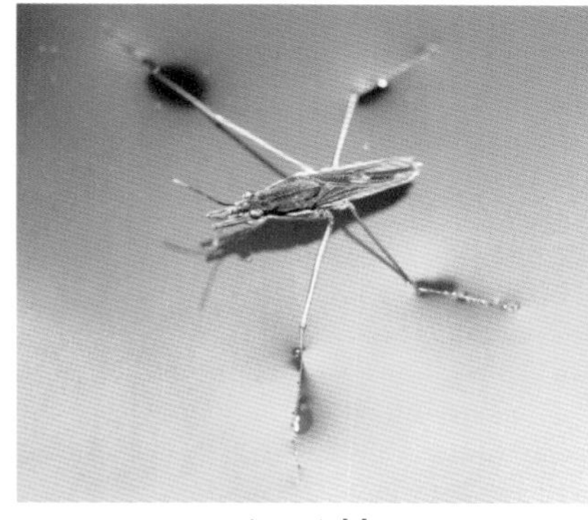
water strider: a water strider on water

3 something that swells and dies away ⟨A *wave* of anger came over her.⟩
4 a rolling movement passing along a surface or through the air ⟨*waves* of grain⟩
5 a curving shape or series of curving shapes ⟨hair with *waves*⟩
6 a sudden increase in something ⟨a crime *wave*⟩
7 a motion that is somewhat like a wave in water and transfers energy from point to point ⟨sound *waves*⟩

wave•length \'wāv-,leŋth\ *n*
the distance in the line of advance of a wave from any one point to the next similar point

wa•ver \'wā-vər\ *vb* **wa•vered**; **wa•ver•ing**
1 to be uncertain in opinion
2 to move unsteadily or to and fro
3 to give an unsteady sound

wavy \'wā-vē\ *adj* **wav•i•er**; **wav•i•est**
like, having, or moving in waves ⟨*wavy* hair⟩
wav•i•ness *n*

[1]**wax** \'waks\ *n*
1 a yellowish sticky substance made by bees and used in building the honeycomb : BEESWAX
2 a material (as paraffin) that resembles the wax made by bees (as by being soft and easily molded when warm)

[2]**wax** *vb* **waxed**; **wax•ing**
to treat or polish with wax

[3]**wax** *vb* **waxed**; **waxing**
1 to grow larger or stronger ⟨The moon *waxes* and then wanes.⟩
2 BECOME 1, GROW ⟨She *waxed* nostalgic at the reunion.⟩

wax bean *n*
a string bean with yellow waxy pods

wax•en \'wak-sən\ *adj*
lacking vitality or animation : PALE

wax myrtle *n*
a shrub or small tree that has bluish gray waxy berries and is related to the bayberry

wax•wing \'waks-,wiŋ\ *n*
► a crested mostly brown bird having yellow on the tip of the tail and often a waxy substance on the tip of some wing feathers

waxwing: a Bohemian \bō-'hē-mē-ən\ waxwing

waxy \'wak-sē\ *adj* **wax•i•er; wax•i•est**
1 being like wax ⟨a *waxy* material⟩
2 made of or covered with wax
3 marked by smooth or shiny whiteness ⟨*waxy* skin⟩

¹way \'wā\ *n*
1 the manner in which something is done or happens
2 the course traveled from one place to another : ROUTE ⟨Do you know the *way* to my house?⟩
3 a noticeable point ⟨In some *ways* I wish I lived closer to school.⟩
4 ¹STATE 1 ⟨That's the *way* things are.⟩
5 distance in time or space ⟨You're a long *way* from home.⟩ ⟨The wedding is still a long *way* off.⟩
6 a special or personal manner of behaving ⟨Being quiet is just my *way*.⟩
7 a talent for handling something ⟨He has a *way* with words.⟩
8 room to advance or pass ⟨Make *way*—coming through!⟩
9 DIRECTION 1 ⟨I paid full fare each *way*.⟩
10 a track for travel : PATH, STREET
11 a course of action ⟨He chose the easy *way*.⟩
12 personal choice as to situation or behavior : WISH ⟨She insists on getting her *way*.⟩
13 progress along a course ⟨I'm working my *way* through college.⟩
14 a particular place ⟨The weather has been nice out our *way*.⟩
15 CATEGORY, KIND ⟨I had little in the *way* of help.⟩
by the way apart from that ⟨*By the way*, did you hear what happened?⟩
by way of
1 for the purpose of ⟨I mentioned it *by way of* example.⟩
2 by the route through ⟨We drove *by way of* back roads.⟩
in someone's way *also* **in the way** in a position to hinder or obstruct
out of the way
1 in or to a place away from public view
2 done fully ⟨He got his homework *out of the way*.⟩

²way *adv*
1 ¹FAR 1 ⟨The sleeves hung *way* down.⟩
2 ¹FAR 2 ⟨He eats *way* too much candy.⟩

way•far•er \'wā-,fer-ər\ *n*
a traveler especially on foot

way•lay \'wā-,lā\ *vb* **way•laid** \-,lād\; **way•lay•ing**
to attack from hiding

-ways \,wāz\ *adv suffix*
in such a way, direction, or manner ⟨side*ways*⟩

way•side \'wā-,sīd\ *n*
the edge of a road
by the wayside into a condition of neglect or disuse

way•ward \'wā-wərd\ *adj*
1 DISOBEDIENT
2 not following a rule or regular course of action ⟨A *wayward* throw broke the window.⟩

we \'wē\ *pron*
I and at least one other

We. *abbr* Wednesday

weak \'wēk\ *adj* **weak•er; weak•est**
1 lacking strength of body, mind, or spirit ⟨a *weak* smile⟩ ⟨a *weak* patient⟩
2 not able to stand much strain or force ⟨a *weak* rope⟩
3 easily overcome ⟨a *weak* argument⟩
4 not able to function well ⟨a *weak* heart⟩
5 not rich in some usual or important element ⟨*weak* tea⟩
6 lacking experience or skill ⟨He's a good reader, but is *weak* in math.⟩
7 not loud or forceful ⟨a *weak* voice⟩
8 relating to or being the lightest of three levels of stress in pronunciation
weak•ly *adv*

► **Synonyms** WEAK, FEEBLE, and FRAIL mean not strong enough to stand pressure or hard effort. WEAK can be used of either a temporary or permanent loss of strength or power. ⟨I felt *weak* after the operation.⟩ ⟨I have *weak* eyes.⟩ FEEBLE implies very great and pitiful weakness. ⟨A *feeble* dog wandered in the streets.⟩ FRAIL can be used of a person who since birth has had a delicate body. ⟨Being a *frail* child I was always getting sick.⟩

weak•en \'wē-kən\ *vb* **weak•ened; weak•en•ing**
to make or become weak or weaker

weak•ling \'wē-kliŋ\ *n*
a person or animal that lacks strength

weak•ness \'wēk-nəs\ *n*
1 lack of strength
2 a weak point : FLAW
3 a special fondness or the object of a special fondness ⟨Chocolate is my *weakness*.⟩

wealth \'welth\ *n*
1 a large amount of money or possessions
2 a great amount or number ⟨a *wealth* of ideas⟩

wealthy \'wel-thē\ *adj* **wealth•i•er; wealth•i•est**
having a lot of money or possessions : RICH

wean \'wēn\ *vb* **weaned; wean•ing**
1 to get a child or young animal used to food other than its mother's milk
2 to make someone stop desiring a thing he or she has been fond of ⟨I *weaned* myself off sweets.⟩

weap•on \'we-pən\ *n*
something (as a gun, knife, or club) to fight with

weap•on•ry \'we-pən-rē\ *n*
a particular grouping of weapons

¹wear \'wer\ *vb* **wore** \'wȯr\; **worn** \'wȯrn\; **wear•ing**
1 to use as an article of clothing or decoration
2 to carry or use on the body ⟨Do you *wear* glasses?⟩ ⟨I am *wearing* perfume.⟩
3 ¹SHOW 1 ⟨He always *wears* a smile.⟩
4 to damage, waste, or produce by use or by scraping or rubbing ⟨The carpet has been badly *worn*.⟩
5 to make tired
6 to last through long use ⟨The cloth *wears* well.⟩
7 to diminish or fail with the passing of time ⟨The day *wore* on.⟩
wear•er *n*
wear out
1 to make useless by long or hard use
2 ¹TIRE 1

²wear *n*
1 the act of wearing : the state of being worn
2 clothing for a particular group or for a particular occasion ⟨children's *wear*⟩ ⟨rain *wear*⟩
3 the result of wearing or use ⟨This dictionary is showing signs of *wear*.⟩

wea•ri•some \'wir-ē-səm\ *adj*
TEDIOUS, DULL

¹wea•ry \'wir-ē\ *adj* **wea•ri•er; wea•ri•est**
1 having lost strength, energy, or freshness : TIRED ⟨*weary* eyes⟩
2 having lost patience, pleasure, or interest ⟨I'm growing *weary* of their quarreling.⟩

3 causing a loss of strength or interest ⟨a *weary* journey⟩
wea•ri•ly \'wir-ə-lē\ *adv*
wea•ri•ness \'wir-ē-nəs\ *n*

[2]**weary** *vb* **wea•ried**; **wea•ry•ing**
to make or become weary

wea•sel \'wē-zəl\ *n*
a small slender active animal related to the mink that feeds on small birds and animals

[1]**weath•er** \'we-thər\ *n*
the state of the air and atmosphere in regard to how warm or cold, wet or dry, or clear or stormy it is

[2]**weather** *vb* **weath•ered**; **weath•er•ing**
1 to expose to the weather
2 to change (as in color or structure) by the action of the weather
3 to be able to last or come safely through

weath•er•man \'we-thər-,man\ *n, pl* **weath•er•men** \-,men\
a person who reports and forecasts the weather : METEOROLOGIST

weath•er•per•son \'we-thər-,pər-sᵊn\ *n*
a person who reports and forecasts the weather : METEOROLOGIST

weather vane *n*
▼ a movable device usually attached to a roof to show which way the wind is blowing

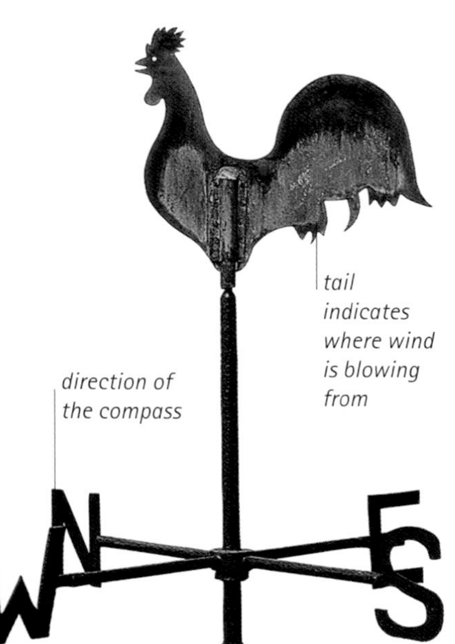

weather vane shaped like a rooster

[1]**weave** \'wēv\ *vb* **wove** \'wōv\; **wo•ven** \'wō-vən\; **weav•ing**
1 to move back and forth, up and down, or in and out
2 to form (as cloth) by lacing together strands of material
3 [1]SPIN 4
4 to make by or as if by lacing parts together ⟨He proceeds to *weave* a tale of adventure.⟩
weav•er \'wē-vər\ *n*

[2]**weave** *n*
a method or pattern of lacing together strands of material

[1]**web** \'web\ *n*
1 SPIDERWEB, COBWEB
2 a network of threads spun especially by the larvae of certain insects (as tent caterpillars) and usually serving as a nest or shelter
3 something that catches and holds like a spider's web ⟨He was caught in a *web* of lies.⟩
4 a complex pattern like something woven
5 a layer of skin or tissue that joins the toes of an animal (as a duck)
6 *cap* WORLD WIDE WEB

[2]**web** *vb* **webbed**; **web•bing**
to join or surround with strands woven together

webbed \'webd\ *adj*
having or being toes joined by a layer of skin or tissue ⟨the *webbed* feet of ducks⟩

web•cam \'web-,kam\ *n*
a small video camera that is used to show live images on a Web site

web–foot•ed \'web-'fu̇-təd\ *adj*
having toes joined by a layer of skin or tissue ⟨a *web-footed* gecko⟩

Web page *n*
a page of written material and pictures that is shown on a Web site

Web site *or* **web•site** *n*
a group of World Wide Web pages usually containing links to each other and made available online by an individual, company, or organization

wed \'wed\ *vb* **wed•ded** *also* **wed**; **wed•ding**
1 MARRY
2 to connect closely

Wed. *abbr* Wednesday

we'd \wēd\
we had : we should : we would

wed•ding \'we-diŋ\ *n*
a marriage ceremony

[1]**wedge** \'wej\ *n*
1 a piece of wood or metal that tapers to a thin edge and is used for splitting logs or for tightening by being forced into a space
2 something with a triangular shape ⟨a *wedge* of cake⟩

[2]**wedge** *vb* **wedged**; **wedg•ing**
1 to crowd or squeeze in
2 to fasten, tighten, or separate with a triangular piece of wood or metal

wed•lock \'wed-,läk\ *n*
MARRIAGE 1

[1]**weed:**
a weed growing between two curb stones

Wednes•day \'wenz-dā, -dē\ *n*
the fourth day of the week

wee \'wē\ *adj*
very small : TINY

[1]**weed** \'wēd\ *n*
▲ a plant that grows where not wanted often crowding out more desirable plants

[2]**weed** *vb* **weed•ed**; **weed•ing**
1 to remove weeds from ⟨*weed* a garden⟩
2 to get rid of what is not wanted ⟨She's *weeding* out the old computer files.⟩

weedy \'wē-dē\ *adj* **weed•i•er**; **weed•i•est**
1 full of or consisting of weeds
2 like a weed especially in having strong rapid growth ⟨a *weedy* vine⟩
3 very skinny ⟨a *weedy* horse⟩

week \'wēk\ *n*
1 seven days in a row especially beginning with Sunday and ending with Saturday
2 the working or school days that come between Sunday and Saturday

week•day \'wēk-,dā\ *n*
a day of the week except Sunday or sometimes except Saturday and Sunday

week•end \'wēk-,end\ *n*
the period between the close of one work or school week and the beginning of the next

[1]**week•ly** \'wē-klē\ *adj*
1 happening, done, or produced every week ⟨a *weekly* meeting⟩ ⟨a *weekly* newspaper⟩
2 figured by the week ⟨*weekly* wages⟩

[2]**weekly** *n, pl* **weeklies**
a newspaper or magazine published every week

weep \'wēp\ *vb* **wept** \'wept\; **weep•ing**
to shed tears : CRY

weep•ing \'wē-piŋ\ *adj*
having slender drooping branches

weeping willow: weeping willows around a pond

weeping willow *n*
▲ a willow originally from Asia that has slender drooping branches

wee•vil \'wē-vəl\ *n*
a small beetle that has a long snout and often feeds on and is harmful to plants or plant products (as nuts, fruit, and grain)

weigh \'wā\ *vb* **weighed**; **weigh•ing**
1 to have weight or a specified weight ⟨It *weighs* one pound.⟩
2 to find the weight of ⟨Use a scale to *weigh* the apples.⟩
3 to think about as if weighing ⟨He *weighed* their chances of winning.⟩
4 to lift an anchor before sailing
weigh down to cause to bend down

[1]weight \'wāt\ *n*
1 the amount that something weighs ⟨Her *weight* is 115 pounds.⟩
2 the force with which a body is pulled toward the earth
3 a unit (as a pound) for measuring weight
4 ▶ an object (as a piece of metal) of known weight for balancing a scale in weighing other objects
5 a heavy object used to hold or press down something
6 a heavy object lifted during exercise
7 [1]BURDEN 2
8 strong influence ⟨The mayor threw his *weight* behind the proposal.⟩

[2]weight *vb* **weight•ed**; **weight•ing**
1 to load or make heavy with a weight
2 to trouble with a burden

weight•less \'wāt-ləs\ *adj*
1 having little or no weight
2 not affected by gravity

weighty \'wā-tē\ *adj* **weight•i•er**; **weight•i•est**
1 having much weight : HEAVY
2 very important ⟨a *weighty* discussion⟩

[1]weight 4: weights on a scale

weird \'wird\ *adj* **weird•er**; **weird•est**
very unusual : STRANGE ⟨That's a *weird* way to cook an egg!⟩

▶ **Word History** The adjective *weird* came from an earlier noun *weird,* which meant "fate." In Scotland *weird* was used as an adjective in the phrase "the Weird Sisters," a name for the Fates, three goddesses who set human destinies. In his play *Macbeth,* William Shakespeare adapted this phrase for the eerie sisters who tell Macbeth his fate. So well-known was Shakespeare's usage that the original meaning of *weird* was forgotten and people assumed that it meant "strange, fantastic"—which accurately described the sisters in the play.

weirdo \'wir-dō\ *n, pl* **weird•os**
a very strange person

[1]wel•come \'wel-kəm\ *vb* **wel•comed**; **wel•com•ing**
1 to greet with friendship or courtesy
2 to receive or accept with pleasure ⟨We *welcomed* the opportunity to travel.⟩

[2]welcome *adj*
1 greeted or received gladly ⟨a *welcome* rain⟩ ⟨Visitors are *welcome.*⟩

2 giving pleasure ⟨a *welcome* sight⟩
3 willingly permitted to do, have, or enjoy something ⟨You're *welcome* to come along.⟩
4 used in the phrase "You're welcome" as a reply to an expression of thanks

[3]welcome *n*
a friendly greeting

[1]weld \'weld\ *vb* **weld•ed**; **weld•ing**
1 to join two pieces of metal or plastic by heating and allowing the edges to flow together
2 to be capable of being joined by heating and allowing the edges to flow together ⟨Some metals *weld* easily.⟩
3 to join closely
weld•er *n*

[2]weld *n*
▶ a joint made by heating and allowing the edges to flow together

wel•fare \'wel-,fer\ *n*
1 the state of being or doing well especially in relation to happiness, well-being, or success
2 aid in the form of money or necessities for people in need

[1]well \'wel\ *adv* **bet•ter** \'be-tər\; **best** \'best\
1 in a skillful or expert manner ⟨He plays the guitar *well.*⟩
2 by as much as possible : COMPLETELY ⟨We are *well* aware of the problem.⟩
3 in such a way as to be pleasing : as wanted ⟨Everything went *well.*⟩
4 EASILY 1 ⟨We could *well* afford the cost.⟩
5 in a thorough manner ⟨Shake *well.*⟩
6 in a familiar manner ⟨I know them *well.*⟩
7 by quite a lot ⟨*well* over a million⟩
8 so as to be right : in a satisfactory way ⟨The plan worked *well.*⟩
9 in a complimentary or generous way ⟨They always speak *well* of you.⟩
10 with reason or courtesy ⟨I cannot *well* refuse.⟩
as well
1 in addition : ALSO
2 with the same result ⟨might *as well* try⟩

[2]well *interj*
1 used to express surprise or doubt
2 used to begin a conversation or remark or to continue one that was interrupted

[3]well *n*
1 a hole made in the earth to reach a natural deposit (as of water, oil, or gas)
2 a source of supply ⟨He was a *well* of news.⟩
3 something like a deep hole

[4]well *adj*
1 being in a satisfactory or good state ⟨All is *well.*⟩
2 free or recovered from ill health : HEALTHY
3 FORTUNATE 1 ⟨It was *well* that we left.⟩

[5]well *vb* **welled**; **well•ing**
to rise to the surface and flow out ⟨Tears *welled* up in her eyes.⟩

we'll \'wēl\
we shall : we will

well–be•ing \'wel-'bē-iŋ\ *n*
WELFARE 1

well–bred \'wel-'bred\ *adj*
having or showing good manners : POLITE

well–done \'wel-'dən\ *adj*
1 done right ⟨a *well-done* job⟩
2 cooked thoroughly

well–known \'wel-'nōn\ *adj*
known by many people

well–nigh \'wel-'nī\ *adv*
ALMOST

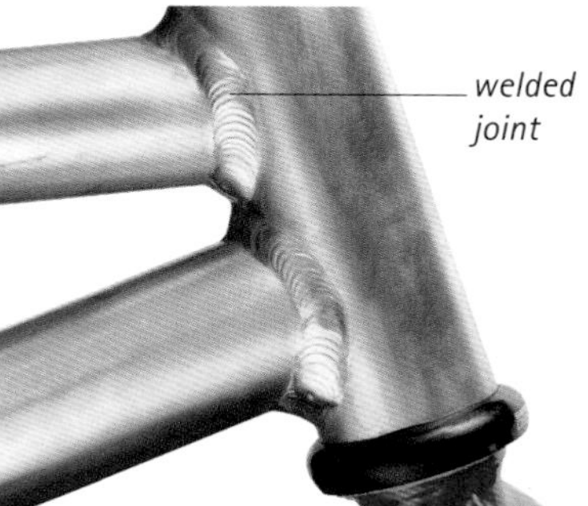

[2]weld: welds on a bicycle frame

well–off \'wel-'ȯf\ *adj*
1 being in good condition or in a good situation
2 WELL-TO-DO

well–to–do \,wel-tə-'dü\ *adj*
having plenty of money and possessions

[1]Welsh \'welsh\ *adj*
of or relating to Wales or the people of Wales

[2]Welsh *n*
the people of Wales

welt \'welt\ *n*
a ridge raised on the skin (as by a blow)

wel•ter \'wel-tər\ *n*
a confused jumble ⟨a *welter* of emotions⟩

wend \'wend\ *vb* **wend•ed**; **wend•ing**
to go from one place to another

went *past of* GO

wept *past and past participle of* WEEP

were *past second person sing, past pl, or past subjunctive of* BE

we're \'wir, 'wər\
we are

weren't \'wərnt\
were not

were•wolf \'wer-,wu̇lf, 'wər-\ *n, pl* **were•wolves** \-,wu̇lvz\
a person in folklore who is changed or is able to change into a wolf

▶ **Word History** The modern English word *werewolf* came from an Old English word *werwulf* that was formed from *wer,* "man," and *wulf,* "wolf."

[1]west \'west\ *adv*
to or toward the direction of sunset

[2]west *adj*
located in, facing, or coming from the direction of sunset ⟨the *west* side of the house⟩

[3]west *n*
1 the direction of sunset : the compass point opposite to east
2 *cap* regions or countries west of a point that is mentioned or understood

west•bound \'west-,bau̇nd\ *adj*
going west

west•er•ly \'we-stər-lē\ *adj or adv*
1 toward the west ⟨the lake's *westerly* shore⟩
2 from the west ⟨a *westerly* wind⟩

[1]west•ern \'we-stərn\ *adj*
1 *often cap* of, relating to, or like that of the West
2 lying toward or coming from the west

[2]western *n, often cap*
a story, film, or radio or television show about life in the western United States especially in the last part of the 19th century

west•ward \'west-wərd\ *adv or adj*
toward the west

[1]wet \'wet\ *adj* **wet•ter**; **wet•test**
1 containing, covered with, or soaked with liquid (as water) ⟨a *wet* cloth⟩
2 RAINY ⟨*wet* weather⟩
3 not yet dry ⟨*wet* paint⟩
wet•ness *n*

[2]wet *vb* **wet** *or* **wet•ted**; **wet•ting**
to make wet ⟨*Wet* the cloth before wiping.⟩

[3]wet *n*
rainy weather : RAIN

wet•land \'wet-,land, -lənd\ *n*
a wet area of land (as a marsh or swamp) having soil filled with or covered by water all or part of the year
Hint: *Wetland* is usually used in the plural form *wetlands.*

we've \'wēv\
we have

[1]whack \'hwak, 'wak\ *vb* **whacked**; **whack•ing**
to hit with a hard noisy blow ⟨The batter *whacked* the ball.⟩

[2]whack *n*
1 a hard noisy blow ⟨I gave the ball a *whack.*⟩
2 the sound of a hard noisy blow
out of whack not in good working order or shape

a b c d e f g h i j k l m n o p q r s t u v w x y z

[1]whale

There are two main types of whale inhabiting the world's oceans — toothed and baleen whales. Toothed whales, such as the dolphin and killer whale, hunt fish, squid, and other sea animals. Baleen whales, such as the blue whale and humpback whale, strain small fish and plankton from huge gulps of water. Whales have a sleek and powerful body, and a thick layer of blubber keeps them warm and provides a reserve supply of energy. The baleen whale shown below is a blue whale, which is the largest whale and can grow up to 100 ft (30 m) in length and weigh up to 150 tons (140 metric tons). When born, a blue whale is already the size of an elephant.

features of a blue whale

flipper

a blowhole \'blō-ˌhōl\ *is a nostril in the top of the whale's head*

eye

a fluke \'flük\ *is one of the lobes of a whale's tail*

whacky *variant of* WACKY

[1]whale \'hwāl, 'wāl\ *n*
▲ a very large sea mammal that has flippers and a flattened tail and breathes through an opening on the top of the head

[2]whale *vb* **whaled**; **whal•ing**
to hunt whales

whale•bone \'hwāl-ˌbōn, 'wāl-\ *n*
BALEEN

whal•er \'hwā-lər, 'wā-\ *n*
a person or ship that hunts whales

wharf \'hwȯrf, 'wȯrf\ *n, pl* **wharves** \'hwȯrvz, 'wȯrvz\ *also* **wharfs**
a structure built on the shore for loading and unloading ships

[1]what \'hwät, 'hwət, 'wät, 'wət\ *pron*
1 which thing or things ⟨*What* happened?⟩
2 which sort of thing or person ⟨*What* is this?⟩ ⟨*What* are they, doctors?⟩
3 that which ⟨Do *what* you're told.⟩
4 used to ask someone to repeat something ⟨You did *what*?⟩
5 [1]WHATEVER 1 ⟨Take *what* you need.⟩
what for [1]WHY
what if
1 what would happen if ⟨*What if* they find out?⟩
2 what does it matter if ⟨So *what if* they do? I don't care.⟩

[2]what *adv*
1 in what way : HOW ⟨*What* does it matter?⟩
2 used before one or more phrases that tell a cause ⟨*What* with the school and sports, she's busy.⟩

[3]what *adj*
1 used to ask about the identity of a person, object, or matter ⟨*What* books do you read?⟩
2 how remarkable or surprising ⟨*What* an idea!⟩
3 [2]WHATEVER 1 ⟨I don't know *what* else to say.⟩

[1]what•ev•er \hwät-'e-vər, hwət-, wät-, wət-\ *pron*
1 anything or everything that ⟨Take *whatever* you need.⟩
2 no matter what ⟨*Whatever* you do, don't cheat.⟩
3 what in the world ⟨*Whatever* made you do that?⟩

[2]whatever *adj*
1 any and all : any . . . that ⟨Take *whatever* money you need.⟩
2 of any kind at all ⟨There's no food *whatever*.⟩

what•so•ev•er \ˌhwät-sə-'we-vər, ˌhwət-, ˌwät-, ˌwət-\ *pron or adj*
WHATEVER

wheat \'hwēt, 'wēt\ *n*
▼ a cereal grain that grows in tight clusters on the tall stalks of a widely cultivated grass, that is typically made into fine white flour used mostly in breads, baked goods (as cakes and crackers), and pasta, and that is also used in animal feeds

wheat: stalks of wheat

wheat•en \'hwē-tᵊn, 'wē-\ *adj*
containing or made from wheat ⟨*wheaten* bread⟩

whee•dle \'hwē-dᵊl, 'wē-\ *vb* **whee•dled**; **whee•dling**
1 to get (someone) to think or act a certain way by flattering : COAX

2 to gain or get by coaxing or flattering ⟨He's trying to *wheedle* money out of them.⟩

[1]wheel \'hwēl, 'wēl\ *n*
1 a disk or circular frame that can turn on a central point
2 something that is round ⟨a *wheel* of cheese⟩
3 STEERING WHEEL
4 something having a wheel as its main part ⟨a spinning *wheel*⟩
5 **wheels** *pl* moving power : necessary parts ⟨the *wheels* of government⟩
wheeled \'hwēld, wēld\ *adj*

[2]wheel *vb* **wheeled**; **wheel•ing**
1 to carry or move on wheels or in a vehicle with wheels
2 ROTATE 1 ⟨Seagulls *wheeled* above the boat.⟩
3 to change direction as if turning on a central point ⟨I *wheeled* and faced them.⟩

wheel•bar•row \'hwēl-,ber-ō, 'wēl-\ *n*
a cart with two handles and usually one wheel for carrying small loads

wheel•chair \'hwēl-,cher, 'wēl-\ *n*
▼ a chair with wheels used especially by sick, injured, or disabled people to get about

[1]wheeze \'hwēz, 'wēz\ *vb* **wheezed**; **wheez•ing**
1 to breathe with difficulty and usually with a whistling sound
2 to make a whistling sound like someone having difficulty breathing

wheelchair

[2]wheeze *n*
a whistling sound like that made by someone having difficulty breathing

whelk \'hwelk, 'welk\ *n*
► a large sea snail that has a spiral shell and is sometimes used for food in Europe

whelp \'hwelp, 'welp\ *n*
one of the young of an animal (as a dog) that eats flesh

[1]when \'hwen, 'wen, hwən, wən\ *adv*
1 at what time ⟨*When* did you leave?⟩
2 the time at which ⟨I was not sure of *when* they'd come.⟩
3 at, in, or during which

[2]when *conj*
1 at, during, or just after the time that ⟨She wants to leave *when* I do.⟩
2 in the event that : IF ⟨*When* you have a question, raise your hand.⟩
3 ALTHOUGH 1 ⟨Why do you tease, *when* you know it's wrong?⟩
4 the time at which ⟨Tomorrow is *when* we leave.⟩

[3]when *pron*
what or which time ⟨Since *when* have you been an expert?⟩

whence \'hwens, 'wens\ *adv*
1 from what place, source, or cause ⟨*Whence* come all these questions?⟩
2 from or out of which ⟨We knew little of the land *whence* they came.⟩

when•ev•er \hwen-'e-vər, wen-, hwən-, wən-\ *conj or adv*
at whatever time ⟨You may go *whenever* you want.⟩

whelk

[1]where \'hwer, 'wer\ *adv*
1 at, in, or to what place ⟨*Where* are they?⟩
2 at or in what way or direction ⟨*Where* does this plan lead?⟩ ⟨*Where* am I wrong?⟩

[2]where *conj*
1 at, in, or to the place indicated ⟨Sit *where* the light's better.⟩
2 every place that ⟨They go *where* they want to.⟩

[3]where *n*
what place, source, or cause ⟨I don't know *where* that came from.⟩

[1]where•abouts \'hwer-ə-,bau̇ts, 'wer-\ *adv*
near what place ⟨*Whereabouts* did you lose it?⟩

[2]whereabouts *n pl*
the place where someone or something is
Hint: *Whereabouts* can be used as a singular or plural in writing and speaking. ⟨I discovered his *whereabouts*.⟩

where•as \hwer-'az, wer-\ *conj*
1 since it is true that
2 while just the opposite ⟨Water quenches fire, *whereas* gasoline feeds it.⟩

where•by \hwer-'bī, wer-\ *adv*
by or through which ⟨We made a deal *whereby* we each took turns.⟩

where•fore \'hwer-,fȯr, 'wer-\ *adv*
[1]WHY

where•in \hwer-'in, wer-\ *adv*
1 in what way
2 in which

where•of \hwer-'əv, wer-, -'äv\ *conj*
of what : that of which ⟨I know *whereof* I speak.⟩

where•up•on \'hwer-ə-,pȯn, 'wer-, -,pän\ *conj*
and then : at which time ⟨They failed, *whereupon* they tried harder.⟩

[1]wher•ev•er \hwer-'ev-ər, wer-\ *adv*
1 where in the world ⟨*Wherever* have you been?⟩
2 any place at all ⟨Just put it *wherever*.⟩

[2]wherever *conj*
1 at, in, or to whatever place ⟨We can have lunch *wherever* you like.⟩
2 in any situation in which : at any time that ⟨I help *wherever* possible.⟩

whet \'hwet, 'wet\ *vb* **whet•ted; whet•ting**
1 to sharpen the edge of by rubbing on or with a stone
2 to make (as the appetite) stronger

wheth•er \'hwe-thər, 'we-\ *conj*
1 if it is or was true that ⟨See *whether* they've left.⟩
2 if it is or was better ⟨I wondered *whether* to stay or go home.⟩
3 used to introduce two or more situations of which only one can occur ⟨The game will be played *whether* it rains or shines.⟩

whet•stone \'hwet-,stōn, 'wet-\ *n*
► a stone on which blades are sharpened

whetstone: an ancient flint whetstone

whew *often read as* 'hwü, 'wü, 'hyü\ *n*
a sound almost like a whistle made as an exclamation chiefly to show amazement, discomfort, or relief

whey \'hwā, 'wā\ *n*
the watery part of milk that separates from the curd after the milk sours and thickens

[1]which \'hwich, 'wich\ *adj*
what certain one or ones ⟨*Which* hat should I wear?⟩

[2]which *pron*
1 which one or ones ⟨*Which* is the right answer?⟩
2 used in place of the name of something other than people at the beginning of a clause ⟨The suggestion *which* you made was a good one.⟩

[1]which•ev•er \hwich-'e-vər, wich-\ *adj*
being whatever one or ones : no matter which ⟨Take *whichever* book you want.⟩

[2]whichever *pron*
whatever one or ones ⟨Buy the sweater or the coat, *whichever* you like better.⟩

[1]whiff \'hwif, 'wif\ *n*
1 a small gust
2 a small amount (as of a scent or a gas) that is breathed in
3 [1]HINT 2 ⟨His tone had a *whiff* of anger.⟩
4 STRIKEOUT

[2]whiff *vb* **whiffed; whiff•ing**
1 to blow out or away in small amounts
2 to breathe in an odor
3 to fail to hit ⟨*whiff* a ball⟩

[1]while \'hwīl, 'wīl\ *conj*
1 during the time that ⟨Someone called *while* you were out.⟩
2 ALTHOUGH 1 ⟨*While* the book is famous, it is seldom read.⟩

[2]while *n*
1 a period of time ⟨Let's rest a *while*.⟩
2 time and effort used in doing something ⟨I'll make it worth your *while* to help out.⟩

[3]while *vb* **whiled; whil•ing**
to cause to pass especially in a pleasant way ⟨We *whiled* away the time with games.⟩

whim \'hwim, 'wim\ *n*
a sudden wish, desire, or decision

[1]whim•per \'hwim-pər, 'wim-\ *vb* **whim•pered; whim•per•ing**
to cry in low broken sounds : WHINE

[2]whimper *n*
a whining cry

whim•si•cal \'hwim-zi-kəl, 'wim-\ *adj*
1 full of whims
2 unusual in a playful or amusing way

[1]whine \'hwīn, 'wīn\ *vb* **whined; whin•ing**
1 to make a high-pitched troubled cry or a similar sound ⟨The saw *whined* through knots in the wood.⟩
2 to complain by or as if by whining ⟨"I always get blamed," she *whined*.⟩
whin•er \hwī-nər, 'wī-\ *n*

[2]whine *n*
a high-pitched troubled or complaining cry or sound

[1]whin•ny \'hwi-nē, 'wi-\ *vb* **whin•nied; whin•ny•ing**
to neigh usually in a low gentle way

[2]whinny *n, pl* **whinnies**
a low gentle neigh

whiny *also* **whin•ey** \'hwī-nē, 'wī-\ *adj* **whin•i•er; whin•i•est**
1 having a tendency to whine
2 characterized by whining ⟨*whiny* remarks⟩

[1]whip \'hwip, 'wip\ *vb* **whipped; whip•ping**
1 to move, snatch, or jerk quickly or with force ⟨She *whipped* out a camera.⟩
2 to hit with something long, thin, and flexible : LASH
3 to defeat thoroughly
4 to beat into foam ⟨*whip* cream⟩
5 to cause a strong emotion (as excitement) in ⟨The speaker *whipped* up the crowd.⟩
6 to move back and forth in a lively way ⟨Flags *whipped* in the breeze.⟩
7 to make in a hurry ⟨I'll *whip* up dinner.⟩

[2]whip *n*
1 ◄ a long thin strip of material (as leather) used in punishing or urging on
2 a dessert made by whipping some part of the mixture

[2]whip 1: a leather whip

whip•poor•will \'hwi-pər-,wil, 'wi-\ *n*
a bird of eastern North America that is active at night and has a loud call that sounds like its name

[1]whir \'hwər, 'wər\ *vb* **whirred; whir•ring**
to fly, operate, or turn rapidly with a buzzing sound

[2]whir *n*
a buzzing sound made by something spinning or operating quickly

[1]whirl \'hwərl, 'wərl\ *vb* **whirled; whirl•ing**
1 to turn or move in circles rapidly
2 to feel dizzy ⟨After the ride my head *whirled*.⟩
3 to move or carry around rapidly

[2]whirl *n*
1 a rapid movement in circles
2 something that is or seems to be moving in circles ⟨a *whirl* of dust⟩
3 a state of busy movement : BUSTLE
4 a brief or experimental try ⟨I've never tried, but I'll give it a *whirl*.⟩

whirl•pool \'hwərl-,pül, 'wərl-\ *n*
a rapid swirl of water with a low place in the center which draws in floating objects

whirl•wind \'hwərl-,wind, 'wərl-\ *n*
a small windstorm in which the air turns rapidly in circles

[1]whisk \'hwisk, 'wisk\ *vb* **whisked; whisk•ing**
1 to move suddenly and quickly ⟨She *whisked* us into her office.⟩
2 to brush with or as if with a whisk broom
3 to stir or beat with a whisk or fork

[2]whisk *n*
1 a quick sweeping or brushing motion
2 ▼ a kitchen utensil of wire used for whipping (as eggs or cream)

[2]whisk 2

whisk broom *n*
a small broom with a short handle

whis•ker \'hwi-skər, 'wi-\ *n*
1 whiskers *pl* the hair that grows on a man's face
2 one hair of the beard
3 a long bristle or hair growing near the mouth of an animal (as a cat)

whis•key *or* **whis•ky** \'hwi-skē, 'wi-\ *n, pl* **whis•keys** *or* **whis•kies**
a strong alcoholic drink usually made from grain (as of rye or barley)

[1]**whis•per** \'hwi-spər, 'wi-\ *vb* **whis•pered; whis•per•ing**
1 to speak softly and quietly
2 to tell by speaking softly and quietly
3 to make a low rustling sound ⟨The wind *whispered* in the trees.⟩

[2]**whisper** *n*
1 a soft quiet way of speaking that can be heard only by people who are near
2 the act of speaking softly and quietly
3 something said softly and quietly
4 [1]HINT 2 ⟨a *whisper* of smoke⟩

[1]**whis•tle** \'hwi-səl, 'wi-\ *n*
1 ▼ a device by which a loud high-pitched sound is produced
2 a high-pitched sound (as that made by forcing the breath through puckered lips)

[1]**whistle 1**

[2]**whistle** *vb* **whis•tled; whis•tling**
1 to make a high-pitched sound by forcing the breath through the teeth or lips
2 to move, pass, or go with a high-pitched sound ⟨The arrow *whistled* past.⟩
3 to produce a high-pitched sound by forcing air or steam through a device ⟨The kettle *whistled*.⟩
4 to express by forcing breath through the teeth or lips ⟨I *whistled* my surprise.⟩

whit \'hwit, 'wit\ *n*
a very small amount ⟨The boy had not a *whit* of sense.⟩

[1]**white** \'hwīt, 'wīt\ *adj* **whit•er; whit•est**
1 of the color of fresh snow : colored white
2 light or pale in color ⟨*white* wine⟩ ⟨Her face was *white* with fear.⟩
3 pale gray : SILVERY
4 belonging to a race of people having light-colored skin
5 [1]BLANK 1 ⟨Don't write in the *white* spaces.⟩
6 not intended to cause harm ⟨*white* lies⟩
7 SNOWY 1 ⟨a *white* Christmas⟩
white•ness *n*

[2]**white** *n*
1 the color of fresh snow : the opposite of black
2 the white part of something (as an egg)
3 white clothing ⟨She is dressed in *white*.⟩
4 a person belonging to a race of people having light-colored skin

white blood cell *n*
one of the tiny colorless cells of the blood that help fight infection

white•board \'hwīt-,bȯrd-, 'wīt-\ *n*
a large board with a smooth white surface that can be written on with special markers

white•cap \'hwīt-,kap, 'wīt-\ *n*
the top of a wave breaking into foam

white cell *n*
WHITE BLOOD CELL

white•fish \'hwīt-,fish, 'wīt-\ *n*
a freshwater fish related to the trout that is greenish above and silvery below and is sometimes used for food

white flag *n*
a flag of plain white raised in asking for a truce or as a sign of surrender

whit•en \'hwī-tᵊn, 'wī-\ *vb* **whit•ened; whit•en•ing**
to make or become white or whiter ⟨Bleach *whitens* sheets.⟩

white–tailed deer \'hwīt-,tāld, 'wīt-\ *n*
▶ a common North American deer with the underside of the tail white

white-tailed deer: an adult male white-tailed deer

[1]**white•wash** \'hwīt-,wȯsh, 'wīt-, -,wäsh\ *vb* **white•washed; white•wash•ing**
1 to cover with a mixture that whitens
2 to try to hide the wrongdoing of ⟨The company didn't *whitewash* their acts.⟩

[2]**whitewash** *n*
a mixture (as of lime and water) for making a surface (as a wall) white

whith•er \'hwi-thər, 'wi-\ *adv*
to what place or situation

whit•ish \'hwī-tish, 'wī-\ *adj*
somewhat white

whit•tle \'hwi-tᵊl, 'wi-\ *vb* **whit•tled; whit•tling**
1 to cut or shave off chips from wood : shape by cutting or shaving off chips from wood
2 to reduce little by little ⟨They are trying to *whittle* down their spending.⟩

[1]**whiz** *or* **whizz** \'hwiz, 'wiz\ *vb* **whizzed; whiz•zing**
to move, pass, or fly rapidly with a buzzing sound

[2]**whiz** *or* **whizz** *n, pl* **whizz•es**
a buzzing sound ⟨the *whiz* of passing traffic⟩

[3]**whiz** *n, pl* **whizzes**
WIZARD 2 ⟨a math *whiz*⟩

who \'hü\ *pron*
1 what or which person or people ⟨*Who* is that?⟩ ⟨We know *who* did it.⟩
2 used to stand for a person or people at the beginning of a clause ⟨Students *who* need help should ask for it.⟩

whoa \'wō, 'hō, 'hwō\ *vb*
used as a command to an animal carrying a rider or pulling a load to stop

who•ev•er \hü-'e-vər\ *pron*
whatever person ⟨*Whoever* wants a snack must tell me now.⟩

[1]**whole** \'hōl\ *adj*
1 made up of all its parts : TOTAL, ENTIRE ⟨the *whole* family⟩
2 all the ⟨the *whole* week⟩
3 not cut up or ground ⟨a *whole* onion⟩
4 not scattered or divided ⟨I gave it my *whole* attention.⟩
5 having all its proper parts : COMPLETE ⟨*whole* milk⟩
6 completely healthy or sound in condition
whole•ness *n*

[2]whole *n*
1 something that is full or complete 〈The *whole* of my day was spent working.〉
2 a sum of all the parts and elements 〈the *whole* of creation〉
on the whole
1 all things considered
2 in most cases

whole•heart•ed \'hōl-'här-təd\ *adj*
not holding back 〈a *wholehearted* effort〉
whole•heart•ed•ly *adv*

whole number *n*
a number that is zero or any of the natural numbers

[1]whole•sale \'hōl-,sāl\ *n*
the sale of goods in large quantities to dealers

[2]wholesale *adj*
1 of, relating to, or working at selling to dealers
2 done or happening on a large scale 〈*wholesale* panic〉

[3]wholesale *vb* **whole•saled; whole•sal•ing**
to sell to dealers usually in large quantities
whole•sal•er *n*

whole•some \'hōl-səm\ *adj*
1 helping to improve or keep the body in good condition 〈*wholesome* food〉
2 healthy for the mind or morals 〈*wholesome* entertainment〉
whole•some•ness *n*

whole wheat *adj*
made from or containing wheat kernels that were ground in their entirety

whol•ly \'hō-lē\ *adv*
to the limit : COMPLETELY 〈a *wholly* honest person〉

whom \'hüm\ *pron, objective case of* WHO

whom•ev•er \hü-'me-vər\ *pron, objective case of* WHOEVER

[1]whoop \'hüp, 'hu̇p\ *vb* **whooped; whoop•ing**
1 to shout or cheer loudly and strongly
2 to make the high-pitched gasping sound that follows a coughing attack in whooping cough

[2]whoop *n*
a loud strong shout or cheer

whooping cough *n*
a bacterial disease especially of children in which severe attacks of coughing are often followed by a high-pitched gasping intake of breath

whooping crane *n*
a large white nearly extinct North American crane that has a loud trumpeting call

[1]whoosh \'hwüsh, 'wüsh, 'hwu̇sh, 'wu̇sh\ *vb* **whooshed; whoosh•ing**
to pass or move along with a sound like that of something moving quickly

[2]whoosh *n, pl* **whoosh•es**
the sound created by something moving quickly

whop•per \'hwä-pər, 'wä-\ *n*
1 something huge of its kind 〈She won a *whopper* of a prize.〉
2 a big lie

whorl \'hwȯrl, 'wȯrl, 'hwərl, 'wərl\ *n*
1 a row of parts (as leaves or petals) encircling a stem
2 something that whirls or winds 〈a *whorl* of smoke〉

[1]whose \'hüz\ *adj*
of or relating to whom or which 〈*Whose* bag is it?〉 〈This is the book *whose* cover is torn.〉

[2]whose *pron*
that or those belonging to whom

[1]why \'hwī, 'wī\ *adv*
for what cause or reason 〈*Why* did you do it?〉

[2]why *conj*
1 the cause or reason for which 〈We know *why* you did it.〉
2 for which 〈Here's the reason *why* I did it.〉

[3]why *interj*
used to express surprise, uncertainty, approval, disapproval, or impatience 〈*Why*, how did you know that?〉

WI *abbr* Wisconsin

wick \'wik\ *n*
▶ a cord, strip, or ring of loosely woven material through which a liquid (as oil) is drawn to the top in a candle, lamp, or oil stove for burning

wick

wick: a wick in a candle

wick•ed \'wi-kəd\ *adj* **wick•ed•er; wick•ed•est**
1 bad in behavior, moral state, or effect : EVIL 〈a *wicked* laugh〉
2 DANGEROUS 2 〈a *wicked* storm〉
3 of exceptional quality or degree 〈He threw some *wicked* pitches.〉
synonyms see BAD
wick•ed•ly *adv*
wick•ed•ness *n*

[1]wick•er \'wi-kər\ *n*
1 a flexible twig (as of willow) used especially in making baskets or furniture
2 WICKERWORK

[2]wicker *adj*
made of wicker 〈*wicker* furniture〉

wick•er•work \'wi-kər-,wərk\ *n*
▶ something (as a basket or chair) made of wicker

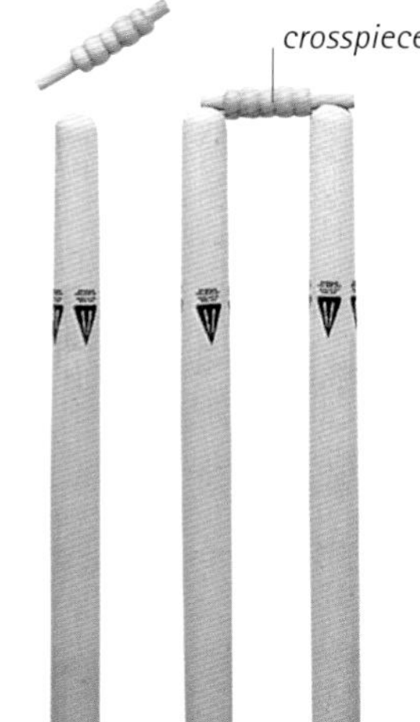

wicket 4: a player is sent off the field when the ball knocks a crosspiece off the wicket

wick•et \'wi-kət\ *n*
1 an arch (as of wire) through which the ball is hit in the game of croquet
2 a small gate or door in or near a larger gate or door
3 a small window (as in a bank) through which business is conducted
4 ▲ either of the two sets of three rods topped by two crosspieces at which the ball is bowled in cricket

[1]wide \'wīd\ *adj* **wid•er; wid•est**
1 having a large measure across : BROAD 〈a *wide* street〉 〈a *wide* grin〉
2 opened as far as possible 〈Her eyes were *wide* with wonder.〉
3 covering a very large area
4 measured across or at right angles to length 〈The cloth is three feet *wide*.〉
5 not limited : having a large extent 〈There's a *wide* range of choices.〉
6 to the side of : away from 〈The shot was *wide* of the goal.〉
wide•ly *adv*
wide•ness *n*

wickerwork: a wicker basket

[2]**wide** *adv* **wid•er; wid•est**
1 over a wide area ⟨He's traveled far and *wide.*⟩
2 to the limit : COMPLETELY ⟨The door was *wide* open.⟩

wide–awake \ˌwīd-ə-ˈwāk\ *adj*
1 fully awake
2 very alert

wid•en \ˈwī-dᵊn\ *vb* **wid•ened; wid•en•ing**
to make or become wide or wider ⟨The road is being *widened.*⟩

wide•spread \ˈwīd-ˈspred\ *adj*
1 widely stretched out ⟨*widespread* wings⟩
2 widely scattered ⟨*widespread* public interest⟩

[1]**wid•ow** \ˈwi-dō\ *n*
a woman whose spouse is dead

[2]**widow** *vb* **wid•owed; wid•ow•ing**
to make a widow or widower of

wid•ow•er \ˈwi-də-wər\ *n*
a man whose spouse is dead

width \ˈwidth\ *n*
1 the measurement of the shortest or shorter side of an object : BREADTH
2 a measured piece of something ⟨a *width* of cloth⟩

wield \ˈwēld\ *vb* **wield•ed; wield•ing**
1 to use (as a tool) in an effective way ⟨The knights *wielded* swords.⟩
2 [2]EXERCISE 1 ⟨The banker *wields* great influence.⟩

wie•ner \ˈwē-nər\ *n*
FRANKFURTER

wife \ˈwīf\ *n, pl* **wives** \ˈwīvz\
a female partner in a marriage
wife•ly *adj*

wig \ˈwig\ *n*
a manufactured covering of natural or artificial hair for the head

[1]**wig•gle** \ˈwi-gəl\ *vb* **wig•gled; wig•gling**
1 to move up and down or from side to side with quick short motions ⟨She *wiggled* her toes.⟩
2 to proceed with twisting and turning movements

[2]**wiggle** *n*
a twisting turning motion

wig•gly \ˈwi-glē\ *adj* **wig•gli•er; wig•gli•est**
1 constantly moving with twisting turning motions ⟨a *wiggly* worm⟩
2 WAVY ⟨*wiggly* lines⟩

wig•wam \ˈwig-ˌwäm\ *n*
a dome-shaped hut formerly used as a house or shelter by some American Indians

[1]**wild** \ˈwīld\ *adj* **wild•er; wild•est**
1 living in a state of nature and not under human control and care : not tame ⟨*wild* animals⟩
2 growing or produced in nature : not cultivated by people ⟨*wild* honey⟩ ⟨*wild* grapes⟩
3 not civilized : SAVAGE
4 not kept under control : not restrained ⟨*wild* rage⟩ ⟨a *wild* party⟩
5 made without knowledge ⟨a *wild* guess⟩
6 done without accuracy ⟨a *wild* throw⟩
7 going beyond what is usual ⟨*wild* colors⟩
8 ENTHUSIASTIC ⟨*wild* applause⟩
wild•ly *adv*
wild•ness *n*

[2]**wild** *n*
WILDERNESS

wild boar *n*
a wild pig of Europe and Asia that is the ancestor of the domestic pig

wild•cat \ˈwīld-ˌkat\ *n*
a wild animal (as an ocelot or lynx) of the cat family that is of small or medium size

wil•de•beest \ˈwil-də-ˌbēst\ *n*
▼ a large African antelope with a head like that of an ox, curving horns, a short mane, and long tail

[1]**will** \wəl, ˈwil\ *helping verb, past* **would** \wəd, ˈwu̇d\; *present sing & pl* **will**
1 wish to ⟨They *will* have milk.⟩
2 am, is, or are willing to ⟨I *will* go if you ask me.⟩
3 am, is, or are determined to ⟨We *will* go in spite of the storm.⟩
4 am, is, or are going to ⟨Everyone *will* be there.⟩
5 is or are commanded to ⟨You *will* obey.⟩
6 is or are able to ⟨The car *will* hold six people.⟩
7 is or are likely or bound to ⟨The truth *will* come out.⟩

[2]**will** \ˈwil\ *n*
1 a firm desire or determination ⟨They have the *will* to win.⟩
2 the power to decide or control emotions or actions
3 a particular person's decision or choice ⟨It's the king's *will* that he be jailed.⟩
4 a legal paper in which a person states to whom his or her property is to be given after death

wildebeest: a mother wildebeest with her two calves

wil•der•ness \ˈwil-dər-nəs\ *n*
an area in its natural state in which few or no people live

wild•fire \ˈwīld-ˌfīr\ *n*
an uncontrollable fire that destroys a wide area

wild•flower \ˈwīld-ˌflau̇-ər\ *n*
the flower of a wild plant or the plant bearing it

wild•life \ˈwīld-ˌlīf\ *n*
wild animals living in their natural environment

[1]**wile** \ˈwīl\ *n*
a trick meant to trap or deceive

[2]**wile** *vb* **wiled; wil•ing**
[2]LURE

[3]**will** \ˈwil\ *vb* **willed; will•ing**
1 to intend or order ⟨It will happen if God *wills* it.⟩
2 to bring to a certain condition by the power of the will ⟨*will* yourself to sleep⟩
3 to decide on by choice ⟨Go where you *will.*⟩
4 to leave by will ⟨They *willed* the house to me.⟩

will•ful *or* **wil•ful** \ˈwil-fəl\ *adj*
1 STUBBORN 1 ⟨*willful* children⟩
2 INTENTIONAL ⟨*willful* disobedience⟩
will•ful•ly \-fə-lē\ *adv*
will•ful•ness *n*

wil•lies \ˈwi-lēz\ *n pl*
a fit of nervousness ⟨That scary movie gives me the *willies.*⟩

will•ing \'wi-liŋ\ *adj*
1 feeling no objection ⟨I'm *willing* to go.⟩
2 not slow or lazy ⟨She's a *willing* worker.⟩
3 made, done, or given by choice : VOLUNTARY ⟨a *willing* sacrifice⟩
will•ing•ly *adv*
will•ing•ness *n*

wil•low \'wi-lō\ *n*
►a tree or bush with narrow leaves, catkins for flowers, and tough flexible stems sometimes used in making baskets

willow: a branch of a white willow

will•pow•er \'wil-ˌpau̇-ər\ *n*
strong determination ⟨It takes *willpower* to get yourself in shape.⟩

[1]wilt \'wilt\ *vb* **wilt•ed**; **wilt•ing**
1 to lose freshness and become limp ⟨The roses are *wilting.*⟩
2 to lose strength

[2]wilt *n*
a plant disease (as of tomatoes) in which wilting and browning of leaves leads to death of the plant

wily \'wī-lē\ *adj* **wil•i•er**; **wil•i•est**
full of tricks : CRAFTY

[1]win \'win\ *vb* **won** \'wən\; **win•ning**
1 to achieve the victory in a contest ⟨She likes to *win.*⟩
2 to obtain by victory ⟨I *won* the trophy.⟩
3 to be the victor in ⟨I hope you *win* the race.⟩
4 to get by effort or skill : GAIN ⟨The performance *won* praise.⟩
5 to ask and get the favor of ⟨He *won* over the voters.⟩
win•ner *n*

[2]win *n*
an act or instance of winning

wince \'wins\ *vb* **winced**; **winc•ing**
to draw back (as from pain)

windmill: a windmill in a field in East Anglia, England

winch \'winch\ *n*
a machine that has a roller on which rope is wound for pulling or lifting

[1]wind \'wind\ *n*
1 a natural movement of the air ⟨northerly *winds*⟩
2 power to breathe ⟨Falling down knocked the *wind* out of me.⟩
3 limited knowledge especially about something secret ⟨They got *wind* of our plans.⟩
4 **winds** *pl* wind instruments of a band or orchestra

[2]wind *vb* **wind•ed**; **wind•ing**
to cause to be out of breath

[3]wind \'wīnd\ *vb* **wound** \'wau̇nd\; **wind•ing**
1 to move in or be made up of a series of twists and turns ⟨The trail *winds* through the trees.⟩
2 to twist around ⟨The machine *winds* thread on a spool.⟩
3 to cover with something twisted around : WRAP ⟨*Wind* your arm with a bandage.⟩
4 to make the spring of tight ⟨I *wound* my watch.⟩
wind up
1 to bring to an end : CONCLUDE ⟨Let's *wind up* the meeting.⟩
2 to reach a place or situation that was not expected ⟨How did we *wind up* back here?⟩
3 to swing the arm before pitching a baseball

wind•break \'wind-ˌbrāk\ *n*
something (as a growth of trees and shrubs) that reduces the force of the wind

wind•fall \'wind-ˌfȯl\ *n*
1 something (as fruit from a tree) blown down by the wind
2 an unexpected gift or gain

wind•ing \'wīn-diŋ\ *adj*
1 having a course made up of a series of twists and turns ⟨a *winding* path⟩
2 having a curved or spiral form ⟨a *winding* staircase⟩

wind instrument *n*
a musical instrument (as a clarinet, harmonica, or trumpet) sounded by the vibration of a stream of air and especially by the player's breath

wind•mill \'wind-ˌmil\ *n*
◄ a mill or a machine (as for pumping water) worked by the wind turning sails or vanes at the top of a tower

win•dow \'win-dō\ *n*
1 an opening in a wall to let in light and air
2 the glass and frame that fill a window opening
3 any of the areas into which a computer

display may be divided and on which different types of information may be shown
win•dow•less *adj*

► **Word History** To people living in cold regions around the world, a window in a house was only practical when glass became available to provide light while sealing out the weather. As a result, in English and other languages of northern Europe, words for "window" appear relatively late, after glass was introduced from southern Europe. In Old English, "window" was *ēagduru*, literally "eye-door," or *ēagthyrel*, "eye-hole"—since a window, like an eye, is a means of seeing out. The word *window* itself comes from a word *vindauga* in Old Norse (the language of the Vikings) that means literally "wind-eye."

win•dow•pane \ˈwin-dō-ˌpān\ *n*
a pane in a window

win•dow•sill \ˈwin-dō-ˌsil\ *n*
SILL 1

wind•pipe \ˈwind-ˌpīp\ *n*
TRACHEA 1

wind•proof \ˈwind-ˈprüf\ *adj*
protecting from the wind

wind•shield \ˈwind-ˌshēld\ *n*
a clear screen (as of glass) attached to the body of a vehicle (as a car) in front of the riders to protect them from the wind

wind•storm \ˈwind-ˌstȯrm\ *n*
a storm with strong wind and little or no rain

wind•up \ˈwīnd-ˌəp\ *n*
1 the last part of something : FINISH
2 a swing of a baseball pitcher's arm before the pitch is thrown

[1]**wind•ward** \ˈwind-wərd\ *adj*
moving or placed toward the direction from which the wind is blowing

[2]**windward** *n*
the side or direction from which the wind is blowing ⟨Sail to the *windward.*⟩

windy \ˈwin-dē\ *adj* **wind•i•er**; **wind•i•est**
having much or strong wind ⟨a *windy* day⟩ ⟨a *windy* city⟩

wine \ˈwīn\ *n*
1 an alcoholic beverage made from the fermented juice of grapes
2 an alcoholic beverage made from the usually fermented juice of fruits (as peaches) other than grapes

win•ery \ˈwī-nə-rē\ *n, pl* **win•er•ies**
a place where wine is made

[1]**wing** \ˈwiŋ\ *n*
1 ► one of the paired moveable feathered or membranous parts with which a bird, bat, or insect flies
2 something like a wing in appearance, use, or motion ⟨the *wings* of an airplane⟩
3 a part (as of a building) that sticks out from the main part
4 a division of an organization
5 wings *pl* an area just off the stage of a theater
wing•less \-ləs\ *adj*
wing•like \-ˌlīk\ *adj*
on the wing in flight

[2]**wing** *vb* **winged**; **wing•ing**
1 to move by means of wings : FLY
2 [1]THROW 1

winged \ˈwiŋd, ˈwiŋ-əd\ *adj*
having wings or winglike parts ⟨*winged* insects⟩

wing•span \ˈwiŋ-ˌspan\ *n*
the distance from the tip of one wing to the tip of the other wing

[1]**wink** \ˈwiŋk\ *vb* **winked**; **wink•ing**
1 to close and open one eye quickly as a signal or hint
2 to close and open the eyelids quickly : BLINK

[2]**wink** *n*
1 a hint or sign given by closing and opening one eye quickly
2 a brief period of sleep
3 an act of closing and opening usually one eye quickly
4 a very short time ⟨I'll be back in a *wink.*⟩

[1]**win•ning** \ˈwi-niŋ\ *n*
1 the act of a person or people who win
2 something won especially in gambling — often used in pl.

[2]**winning** *adj*
1 being someone or something that wins, has won, or wins often ⟨a *winning* candidate⟩ ⟨a *winning* ticket⟩
2 tending to please or delight ⟨a *winning* smile⟩

win•now \ˈwi-nō\ *vb* **win•nowed**; **win•now•ing**
1 to remove (as waste from grain) by a current of air
2 to sort or separate from a larger group

[1]**wing 1:**
the wing of a pigeon

win•some \ˈwin-səm\ *adj*
[2]WINNING 2

[1]**win•ter** \ˈwin-tər\ *n*
1 the season between autumn and spring (as from December to March in the northern half of the earth)
2 one of the years of a person's life ⟨a person of seventy *winters*⟩

[2]**winter** *vb* **win•tered**; **win•ter•ing**
1 to pass the winter ⟨We *wintered* in Florida.⟩
2 to keep, feed, or manage during the winter ⟨The farmer *winters* livestock on silage.⟩

win•ter•green \ˈwin-tər-ˌgrēn\ *n*
a low evergreen plant with shiny leaves which produce an oil used in medicine and flavoring

win•ter•time \ˈwin-tər-ˌtīm\ *n*
the winter season

win•try \ˈwin-trē\ *adj* **win•tri•er**; **win•tri•est**
1 marked by or characteristic of winter ⟨a *wintry* landscape⟩ ⟨*wintry* weather⟩
2 not friendly : COLD ⟨a *wintry* welcome⟩

[1]**wipe** \ˈwīp\ *vb* **wiped**; **wip•ing**
1 to clean or dry by rubbing ⟨Will you *wipe* the dishes?⟩
2 to remove by or as if by rubbing ⟨*Wipe* away your tears.⟩
wip•er *n*
wipe out to destroy completely

[2]**wipe** *n*
an act of wiping : RUB

[1]**wire** \ˈwīr\ *n*
1 metal in the form of a thread or slender rod
2 a number of strands grouped together and used to send or receive electrical signals
3 TELEGRAM

[2]**wire** *vb* **wired**; **wir•ing**
1 to provide or equip with wire ⟨An electrician *wired* the house.⟩
2 to bind with wire
3 to send or send word to by telegraph

[1]**wire•less** \ˈwīr-ləs\ *adj*
relating to communication by electromagnetic waves but without connecting wires : RADIO

[2]**wireless** *n*
a computer, telephone, or network that uses radio waves to send and receive electronic signals

wiry \ˈwīr-ē\ *adj* **wir•i•er**; **wir•i•est**
1 being slender yet strong and muscular
2 coarse and stiff ⟨*wiry* hair⟩

Wis., Wisc. *abbr* Wisconsin

wis•dom \ˈwiz-dəm\ *n*
1 knowledge or learning gained over time
2 good sense
3 a wise attitude, belief, or course of action

wisteria: wisteria growing up a wall

wisdom tooth *n*
the last tooth of the full set of teeth on each side of the upper and lower jaws

[1]wise \'wīz\ *adj* **wis•er; wis•est**
1 having or showing good sense or good judgment : SENSIBLE ⟨a *wise* woman⟩ ⟨a *wise* decision⟩
2 having knowledge or information ⟨I was *wise* to their trick.⟩
3 rude or insulting in speech
wise•ly *adv*

[2]wise *n*
MANNER 2, WAY
Hint: This meaning of *wise* is used in such phrases as *in any wise*, *in no wise*, or *in this wise*.

-wise \,wīz\ *adv suffix*
1 in the manner of
2 in the position or direction of ⟨clock*wise*⟩
3 with regard to

wise•crack \'wīz-,krak\ *n*
a clever and often insulting statement usually made in joking

[1]wish \'wish\ *vb* **wished; wish•ing**
1 to have a desire for : WANT
2 to form or express a desire concerning ⟨He *wished* them both good luck.⟩
3 to request by expressing a desire ⟨I *wish* you to go now.⟩
synonyms see DESIRE

[2]wish *n*
1 an act or instance of having or expressing a desire usually in the mind ⟨Close your eyes and make a *wish*.⟩
2 something wanted ⟨I got my *wish*.⟩
3 a desire for happiness or luck ⟨Send them my best *wishes*.⟩

wish•bone \'wish-,bōn\ *n*
a bone in front of a bird's breastbone that is shaped like a V

wish•ful \'wish-fəl\ *adj*
having, showing, or based on a wish

wishy–washy \'wi-shē-,wȯ-shē, -,wä-\ *adj*
lacking spirit, courage, or determination : WEAK

wisp \'wisp\ *n*
1 a thin piece or strand ⟨*wisps* of hair⟩
2 a thin streak ⟨*wisps* of smoke⟩
3 a small amount of something

wispy \'wi-spē\ *adj* **wisp•i•er; wisp•i•est**
being thin and light ⟨a *wispy* moustache⟩

wis•te•ria \wi-'stir-ē-ə\ *also* **wis•tar•ia** \-'stir-ē-ə, -'ster-\ *n*
◀ a woody vine that is grown for its long clusters of violet, white, or pink flowers

wist•ful \'wist-fəl\ *adj*
feeling or showing a quiet longing especially for something in the past
wist•ful•ly \-fə-lē\ *adv*
wist•ful•ness *n*

wit \'wit\ *n*
1 normal mental state usually used in pl. ⟨He scared me out of my *wits*.⟩
2 power to think, reason, or decide ⟨He had the *wit* to leave.⟩ ⟨The chess player matched *wits* with a computer.⟩
3 clever and amusing comments, expressions, or talk
4 a talent for making clever and usually amusing comments
5 a person with a talent for making clever and amusing comments

witch \'wich\ *n*
1 a person and especially a woman believed to have magic powers
2 an ugly or mean old woman

witch•craft \'wich-,kraft\ *n*
the use of sorcery or magic

witch doctor *n*
a person who uses magic to cure illness and fight off evil spirits

witch•ery \'wi-chə-rē\ *n, pl* **witch•er•ies**
1 WITCHCRAFT
2 power to charm or fascinate

witch ha•zel \'wich-,hā-zəl\ *n*
1 a shrub with small yellow flowers in late fall or early spring
2 a soothing alcoholic lotion made from the bark of the witch hazel

▶ **Word History** The *witch* in *witch hazel* has nothing to do with sorcery, but is rather a now uncommon word meaning "shrub with pliable branches." It goes back to Old English *wice*, which may be related to modern English *weak*. As for the better-known *witch* meaning "sorceress," it goes back to Old English *wicce*, a counterpart to the masculine noun *wicca*, "sorcerer."

with \'with, 'with\ *prep*
1 in the company of ⟨I went to the show *with* a friend.⟩
2 by the use of ⟨I measured *with* a ruler.⟩
3 having in or as part of it ⟨coffee *with* cream⟩
4 in regard to ⟨He is patient *with* children.⟩
5 in possession of ⟨animals *with* horns⟩ ⟨Dad arrived *with* good news.⟩
6 AGAINST 1 ⟨The boy fought *with* his brother.⟩
7 in shared relation to ⟨I like to talk *with* friends.⟩
8 compared to ⟨This sock is identical *with* the rest.⟩
9 in the opinion or judgment of ⟨Is the party all right *with* your parents?⟩
10 so as to show ⟨Her mother spoke *with* pride.⟩
11 as well as ⟨She hits the ball *with* the best of them.⟩
12 FROM 2 ⟨I hated to part *with* my books.⟩
13 because of ⟨I was pale *with* anger.⟩
14 DESPITE ⟨*With* all your tricks you failed.⟩
15 if given ⟨*With* your permission, I'll leave.⟩
16 at the time of or shortly after ⟨We'll need to get up *with* the dawn.⟩ ⟨*With* that, I paused.⟩
17 in support of ⟨I'm *with* you all the way.⟩
18 in the direction of ⟨Sail *with* the tide.⟩

with•draw \with-'drȯ, with-\ *vb* **with•drew** \-'drü\; **with•drawn** \-'drȯn\; **with•draw•ing**
1 to draw back : take away ⟨I *withdrew* money from the bank.⟩
2 to take back (as something said or suggested)
3 to go away especially for privacy or safety

with•draw•al \with-'drȯ-əl, with-\ *n*
an act or instance of withdrawing

with•er \'wi-thər\ *vb* **with•ered; with•er•ing**
to shrivel or cause to shrivel from or as if from loss of moisture : WILT

with•ers \'wi-thərz\ *n pl*
the ridge between the shoulder bones of a horse

with•hold \with-'hōld, with-\ *vb* **with•held** \-'held\; **with•hold•ing**
to refuse to give, grant, or allow ⟨The teacher *withheld* permission.⟩

[1]with•in \with-'in, with-\ *adv*
[2]INSIDE ⟨Sounds came from *within*.⟩

[2]within *prep*
1 [4]INSIDE 1 ⟨Stay *within* the house.⟩
2 not beyond the limits of ⟨You should live *within* your income.⟩
3 before the end of ⟨I'll be there *within* a week.⟩

[1]with•out \with-ˈau̇t, with-\ *prep*
1 not accompanied by or showing ⟨Don't leave *without* your key.⟩ ⟨He spoke *without* thinking.⟩
2 completely lacking ⟨They're *without* hope.⟩
3 [4]OUTSIDE 1
4 not using something ⟨Do the math *without* a calculator.⟩

[2]without *adv*
1 on the outside
2 not having something

with•stand \with-ˈstand, with-\ *vb* **with•stood** \-ˈstu̇d\; **with•stand•ing**
1 to hold out against ⟨This house is able to *withstand* the worst weather.⟩
2 to oppose (as an attack) successfully

wit•less \ˈwit-ləs\ *adj*
lacking in wit or intelligence

[1]wit•ness \ˈwit-nəs\ *n*
1 a person who sees or otherwise has personal knowledge of something ⟨*witnesses* of an accident⟩
2 a person who gives testimony in court
3 a person who is present at an action (as the signing of a will) so as to be able to say who did it
4 TESTIMONY ⟨He gave false *witness* in court.⟩

[2]witness *vb* **wit•nessed**; **wit•ness•ing**
1 to see or gain personal knowledge of something
2 to act as a witness to
3 to be or give proof of ⟨Their actions *witness* their guilt.⟩

wit•ted \ˈwi-təd\ *adj*
having wit or understanding — used in combination ⟨quick-*witted*⟩ ⟨slow-*witted*⟩

wit•ty \ˈwi-tē\ *adj* **wit•ti•er**; **wit•ti•est**
having or showing cleverness ⟨a *witty* person⟩ ⟨a *witty* remark⟩

wives *pl of* WIFE

wiz•ard \ˈwi-zərd\ *n*
1 SORCERER, MAGICIAN
2 a very clever or skillful person ⟨a carpentry *wizard*⟩

wiz•ard•ry \ˈwi-zər-drē\ *n*
the art or practice of a sorcerer

wk. *abbr* week

[1]wob•ble \ˈwä-bəl\ *vb* **wob•bled**; **wob•bling**
to move from side to side in a shaky manner
wob•bly \ˈwä-blē\ *adj*

[2]wobble *n*
a rocking motion from side to side

woe \ˈwō\ *n*
1 great sorrow, grief, or misfortune : TROUBLE
2 something that causes a problem
synonyms see SORROW

woe•ful \ˈwō-fəl\ *adj*
1 full of grief or misery ⟨a *woeful* heart⟩ ⟨a *woeful* tale⟩
2 bringing woe or misery ⟨a *woeful* day⟩
3 very bad
woe•ful•ly *adv*

woke *past of* WAKE

woken *past participle of* WAKE

[1]wolf \ˈwu̇lf\ *n, pl* **wolves** \ˈwu̇lvz\
1 ▶ a large bushy-tailed wild animal that resembles the related domestic dog, eats meat, and often lives and hunts in packs
2 a crafty or fierce person
wolf•ish \ˈwu̇l-fish\ *adj*

[1]wolf 1: a gray wolf

[2]wolf *vb* **wolfed**; **wolf•ing**
to eat fast or greedily

wolf dog *n*
1 WOLFHOUND
2 the offspring of a wolf and a domestic dog

wolf•hound \ˈwu̇lf-ˌhau̇nd\ *n*
a large dog used especially in the past for hunting large animals

wol•fram \ˈwu̇l-frəm\ *n*
TUNGSTEN

wol•ver•ine \ˌwu̇l-və-ˈrēn\ *n*
a mostly dark brown wild animal with shaggy fur that resembles a small bear but is related to the weasel, eats meat, and is found chiefly in the northern forests of North America

wolves *pl of* WOLF

wom•an \ˈwu̇-mən\ *n, pl* **wom•en** \ˈwi-mən\
1 an adult female person
2 women considered as a group

wom•an•hood \ˈwu̇-mən-ˌhu̇d\ *n*
1 the state of being a woman
2 womanly characteristics
3 WOMAN 2

wom•an•kind \ˈwu̇-mən-ˌkīnd\ *n*
WOMAN 2

wom•an•ly \ˈwu̇-mən-lē\ *adj*
having the characteristics typical of a woman

womb \ˈwüm\ *n*
UTERUS

wom•en•folk \ˈwi-mən-ˌfōk\ *or* **wom•en•folks** \-ˌfōks\ *n pl*
women especially of one family or group

won *past and past participle of* WIN

[1]won•der \ˈwən-dər\ *vb* **won•dered**; **won•der•ing**
1 to be curious or have doubt ⟨I *wonder* if we're lost.⟩
2 to feel surprise or amazement

[2]wonder *n*
1 something extraordinary : MARVEL ⟨the *wonders* of nature⟩
2 a feeling (as of astonishment) caused by something extraordinary

won•der•ful \ˈwən-dər-fəl\ *adj*
1 causing marvel : MARVELOUS
2 very good or fine ⟨She had a *wonderful* time.⟩
won•der•ful•ly \-fə-lē\ *adv*

won•der•ing•ly \ˈwən-də-riŋ-lē\ *adv*
in or as if in astonishment ⟨The child looked at them *wonderingly*.⟩

won•der•land \ˈwən-dər-ˌland\ *n*
a place of wonders or surprises ⟨a vacation *wonderland*⟩

won•der•ment \ˈwən-dər-mənt\ *n*
AMAZEMENT

won•drous \ˈwən-drəs\ *adj*
WONDERFUL 1

[1]wont \ˈwȯnt, ˈwōnt\ *adj*
being in the habit of doing ⟨I slept longer than I was *wont*.⟩

[2]wont *n*
HABIT 3 ⟨I slept longer than was my *wont*.⟩

won't \ˈwōnt\
will not ⟨He *won't* listen.⟩

woo \ˈwü\ *vb* **wooed**; **woo•ing**
1 to try to gain the love of
2 to try to gain ⟨The candidates *wooed* votes.⟩

[1]wood \ˈwu̇d\ *n*
1 a thick growth of trees : a small forest — often used in pl. ⟨We hiked in the *woods*.⟩
2 a hard fibrous material that makes up most of the substance of a tree or shrub beneath the bark and is often used as a building material or fuel

[2]wood *adj*
1 WOODEN 1 ⟨a *wood floor*⟩
2 used for or on wood ⟨a *wood* chisel⟩
3 *or* **woods** \ˈwu̇dz\ living or growing in woodland ⟨*woods* herbs⟩

a b c d e f g h i j k l m n o p q r s t u v w x y z

wood•chuck \'wu̇d-,chək\ *n*
a reddish brown burrowing animal that is a plant-eating rodent that hibernates during the winter : GROUNDHOG

wood•cock \'wu̇d-,käk\ *n*
a brownish bird that has a long bill and feeds chiefly on earthworms

wood•cut•ter \'wu̇d-,kə-tər\ *n*
a person who cuts wood especially as an occupation

wood•ed \'wu̇-dəd\ *adj*
covered with trees ⟨a *wooded* lot⟩

wood•en \'wu̇-dᵊn\ *adj*
1 made of wood
2 lacking spirit, ease, or charm ⟨a *wooden* manner⟩

wood•land \'wu̇d-lənd, -,land\ *n*
land covered with trees and shrubs : FOREST

wood•lot \'wu̇d-,lät\ *n*
a small area of trees that is set aside to be used for firewood or to provide wood for building things

wood louse *n*
a tiny flat gray animal that is a crustacean usually found living under stones or bark

wood•peck•er \'wu̇d-,pe-kər\ *n*
▼a bird that climbs trees and drills holes in them with its bill in search of insects

woodpecker: a woodpecker pecking at a tree

wood•pile \'wu̇d-,pīl\ *n*
a pile of wood and especially firewood

wood•shed \'wu̇d-,shed\ *n*
a shed for storing firewood

woods•man \'wu̇dz-mən\ *n, pl* **woods•men** \-mən\
a person who works in the forest and who is knowledgeable about trees and wood

woodsy \'wu̇d-zē\ *adj* **woods•i•er**; **woods•i•est**
being, located in, or suggesting woodland ⟨a *woodsy* smell⟩

woodwind: a bassoon is a woodwind instrument

wood•wind \'wu̇d-,wind\ *n*
▲ one of the group of wind instruments consisting of the flutes, oboes, clarinets, bassoons, and sometimes saxophones

wood•work \'wu̇d-,wərk\ *n*
work (as the edge around doorways) made of wood

wood•work•ing \'wu̇d-,wər-kiŋ\ *n*
the art or process of shaping or working with wood

woody \'wu̇-dē\ *adj* **wood•i•er**; **wood•i•est**
1 having or covered with trees ⟨*woody* land⟩
2 of or containing wood or wood fibers ⟨a *woody* stem⟩
3 very much like wood ⟨a *woody* texture⟩

[1]woof \'wu̇f\ *n*
a deep harsh sound made by a dog

[2]woof *vb* **woofed**; **woof•ing**
to make the deep harsh sound of a dog

[3]woof \'wu̇f, 'wüf\ *n*
1 the threads that cross the warp in weaving a fabric
2 a woven fabric or its texture

wool \'wu̇l\ *n*
1 soft wavy or curly usually thick hair especially of the sheep
2 a substance that looks like a mass of wavy hair ⟨steel *wool*⟩
3 a material (as yarn) made from wool

wool•en *or* **wool•len** \'wu̇-lən\ *adj*
1 made of wool
2 producing cloth made of wool ⟨a *woolen* mill⟩

wool•ly \'wu̇-lē\ *adj* **wool•li•er**; **wool•li•est**
made of or resembling wool ⟨a *woolly* sweater⟩ ⟨a *woolly* wig⟩

woolly mammoth *n*
►an extinct mammal that was a heavy-coated mammoth of cold northern regions

woo•zy \'wü-zē, 'wu̇-\ *adj* **woo•zi•er**; **woo•zi•est**
slightly dizzy, nauseous, or weak

[1]word \'wərd\ *n*
1 a sound or combination of sounds that has meaning and is spoken by a human being
2 a written or printed letter or letters standing for a spoken word
3 a brief remark or conversation ⟨I'd like a *word* with you.⟩
4 [2]COMMAND 1, ORDER
5 NEWS 1 ⟨Has there been any *word* on how they are?⟩
6 [1]PROMISE 1 ⟨I give you my *word*.⟩
7 **words** *pl* remarks said in anger or in a quarrel ⟨We had *words* yesterday.⟩

[2]word *vb* **word•ed**; **word•ing**
to express in words : PHRASE

word•ing \'wər-diŋ\ *n*
the way something is put into words

word processing *n*
the production of printed documents (as business letters) with automated and usually computerized equipment

word processor *n*
1 a computer used for creating, storing, and printing text
2 software designed to perform word processing

wordy \'wər-dē\ *adj* **word•i•er**; **word•i•est**
using or containing many words or more words than are needed ⟨She left a *wordy* message.⟩
word•i•ness *n*

wore *past of* WEAR

woolly mammoth: model of a woolly mammoth with its baby

[1]work \'wərk\ *n*
1 the use of a person's physical or mental strength or ability in order to get something done or get some desired result ⟨Cleaning the playground was a lot of *work.*⟩
2 OCCUPATION 1, EMPLOYMENT
3 the place where someone works ⟨I left my coat at *work.*⟩
4 something that needs to be done or dealt with : TASK, JOB ⟨I have *work* to do.⟩
5 [1]DEED 1, ACHIEVEMENT ⟨The principal will honor the club for its good *works.*⟩
6 something produced by effort or hard work ⟨an author's latest *work*⟩ ⟨a researcher's *work*⟩
7 **works** *pl* a place where industrial labor is done : PLANT, FACTORY ⟨a locomotive *works*⟩
8 **works** *pl* the working or moving parts of a mechanical device ⟨the *works* of a watch⟩
9 the way someone performs labor : WORKMANSHIP ⟨The job was spoiled by careless *work.*⟩
10 **works** *pl* everything possessed, available, or belonging ⟨She ordered a hamburger with the *works.*⟩
synonyms see LABOR

[2]work *vb* **worked** *or* **wrought** \'ròt\; **work•ing**
1 to do something that involves physical or mental effort especially for money or because of a need instead of for pleasure : labor or cause to labor
2 to have a job ⟨I haven't *worked* in three years.⟩
3 to perform or act or to cause to act as planned : OPERATE ⟨The plan *worked* well.⟩ ⟨How do you *work* this thing?⟩
4 to force to do something that involves physical or mental effort ⟨The coach really *works* the team.⟩
5 to move or cause to move slowly or with effort ⟨*Work* the liquid into a cloth.⟩ ⟨The screw *worked* loose.⟩
6 to cause to happen ⟨I can't *work* miracles.⟩
7 [1]MAKE 1, SHAPE ⟨The vase is beautifully *wrought.*⟩
8 to make an effort especially for a long period ⟨She *worked* hard to make the dinner a success.⟩
9 EXCITE 1, PROVOKE ⟨You're going to *work* yourself into a rage.⟩
10 to carry on an occupation in, through, or along ⟨Two agents *worked* the city.⟩
work out
1 to invent or solve by effort ⟨Let's see if we can *work out* an arrangement.⟩
2 to go through an exercise routine

work•able \'wər-kə-bəl\ *adj*
capable of being worked or done ⟨a *workable* plan⟩ ⟨Is this radio *workable?*⟩

work•bench \'wərk-ˌbench\ *n*
▼ a bench on which work is done (as by mechanics)

workbench: a woman sawing wood on a workbench

work•book \'wərk-ˌbu̇k\ *n*
a book made up of a series of problems or practice examples for a student to use as part of a course of study

worked up *adj*
emotionally excited and especially angry or upset

work•er \'wər-kər\ *n*
1 a person who works ⟨cafeteria *workers*⟩ ⟨He's a good *worker.*⟩
2 one of the members of a colony of bees, ants, wasps, or termites that do most of the work of the colony

work•ing \'wər-kiŋ\ *adj*
1 doing work especially for a living ⟨*working* people⟩
2 relating to work ⟨*working* hours⟩
3 good enough to allow work or further work to be done ⟨a *working* agreement⟩

work•ing•man \'wər-kiŋ-ˌman\ *n*, *pl* **work•ing•men** \-ˌmen\
a person who works for wages usually at manual labor

work•man \'wərk-mən\ *n*, *pl* **work•men** \-mən\
1 WORKINGMAN
2 a skilled worker (as a carpenter)

work•man•ship \'wərk-mən-ˌship\ *n*
1 the art or skill of a workman
2 the quality of a piece of work ⟨They take pride in their good *workmanship.*⟩

work•out \'wərk-ˌau̇t\ *n*
an exercise or practice to test or improve ability or performance

work•shop \'wərk-ˌshäp\ *n*
a shop where work and especially skilled work is carried on

work•sta•tion \'wərk-ˌstā-shən\ *n*
1 an area with equipment for the performance of a particular task usually by one person
2 a computer usually connected to a larger network

world \'wərld\ *n*
1 EARTH 1 ⟨They sailed around the *world.*⟩
2 people in general : HUMANITY
3 a state of existence ⟨a future *world*⟩
4 a great number or amount ⟨a *world* of troubles⟩
5 a part or section of the earth ⟨Antarctica is a unique *world.*⟩
6 an area of interest or activity ⟨the *world* of politics⟩

▶ **Word History** The original meaning of *world,* which goes back to Old English *weorold,* was "lifetime," which makes sense in view of the word's makeup: it was a compound of Old English *wer,* "man," and an element *-old* that meant "age" or "period of time" and is related to modern English *old.* Already in Old English, though, the word had extended meanings, such as "human life in general," or "the earth and everything living on it." These are some of its most common meanings today.

world•ly \'wərld-lē\ *adj* **world•li•er**; **world•li•est**
1 of or relating to the affairs of life rather than with spiritual affairs
2 WORLDLY-WISE
world•li•ness *n*

world•ly–wise \'wərld-lē-ˌwīz\ *adj*
aware of and having knowledge about the things and ways of this world

[1]world•wide \'wərld-'wīd\ *adj*
extending over or involving the entire world ⟨She received *worldwide* attention.⟩

[2]worldwide *adv*
throughout the world

World Wide Web *n*
a part of the Internet designed to allow easier navigation of the network through the use of text and graphics that link to other documents

[1]worm \ˈwərm\ *n*
1 a usually long creeping or crawling animal (as a tapeworm) that has a soft body
2 EARTHWORM
3 a person hated or pitied
4 **worms** *pl* infection caused by parasitic worms living in the body ⟨a dog with *worms*⟩
worm•like \-ˌlīk\ *adj*

[2]worm *vb* **wormed; worm•ing**
1 to move slowly by creeping or wriggling ⟨She had to *worm* through thick brush.⟩
2 to get hold of or escape from by trickery ⟨I tried to *worm* my way out of trouble.⟩
3 to rid of parasitic worms

wormy \ˈwər-mē\ *adj* **worm•i•er; worm•i•est**
containing worms ⟨*wormy* flour⟩

worn *past participle of* WEAR

worn–out \ˈwȯrn-ˈau̇t\ *adj*
1 useless from long or hard wear ⟨*worn-out* sneakers⟩
2 very weary

wor•ri•some \ˈwər-ē-səm\ *adj*
1 worrying a lot ⟨a *worrisome* parent⟩
2 causing worry

[1]wor•ry \ˈwər-ē\ *vb* **wor•ried; wor•ry•ing**
1 to feel or express great concern ⟨I *worry* about Grandma's health.⟩
2 to make anxious or upset ⟨The child's illness *worried* his parents.⟩
3 to shake and tear with the teeth ⟨The puppy was *worrying* an old shoe.⟩
wor•ri•er \-ē-ər\ *n*

[2]worry *n, pl* **worries**
1 concern about something that might happen : ANXIETY
2 a cause of great concern ⟨Her poor grades are a *worry* to her parents.⟩

[1]worse \ˈwərs\ *adj, comparative of* BAD *or of* ILL
1 more bad or evil ⟨Is cheating *worse* than lying?⟩
2 being in poorer health ⟨The child was *worse* the next day.⟩
3 more unfavorable, difficult, or unpleasant ⟨a *worse* punishment⟩
4 of poorer quality, value, or condition ⟨This car is *worse* than that one.⟩
5 less skillful
6 less happy ⟨She made me feel *worse.*⟩
7 more faulty or unsuitable ⟨His idea was even *worse.*⟩

[2]worse *n*
something worse ⟨I suffered insults and *worse.*⟩

[3]worse *adv, comparative of* BADLY *or of* ILL
not as well : in a worse way ⟨I hate getting lost *worse* than anything.⟩

wors•en \ˈwər-sᵊn\ *vb* **wors•ened; wors•en•ing**
to get worse ⟨His fever is *worsening.*⟩

[1]wor•ship \ˈwər-shəp\ *n*
1 deep respect toward God, a god, or a sacred object
2 too much respect or admiration

[2]worship *vb* **wor•shipped** *also* **wor•shiped; wor•ship•ping** *also* **wor•ship•ing**
1 to honor or respect as a divine being
2 to regard with respect, honor, or devotion ⟨She *worships* her son.⟩
3 to take part in worship or an act of worship
wor•ship•per *or* **wor•ship•er** *n*

[1]worst \ˈwərst\ *adj, superlative of* BAD *or of* ILL
1 most bad, ill, or evil
2 most unfavorable, difficult, or unpleasant ⟨This is the *worst* day of my life.⟩
3 least appropriate or acceptable ⟨You came at the *worst* time.⟩
4 least skillful ⟨the *worst* player⟩
5 most troubled ⟨That is the *worst* part of the city.⟩

[2]worst *adv, superlative of* ILL *or of* BADLY
in the worst way possible ⟨He was hurt *worst.*⟩

[3]worst *n*
a person or thing that is worst

[4]worst *vb* **worst•ed; worst•ing**
to get the better of : DEFEAT

worsted 2: samples of worsted cloth

wor•sted \ˈwu̇s-təd, ˈwərs-\ *n*
1 a smooth yarn spun from long fibers of wool
2 ▲ fabric woven from a worsted yarn

[1]worth \ˈwərth\ *prep*
1 equal in value to ⟨The painting is *worth* thousands of dollars.⟩
2 having possessions or income equal to ⟨She is *worth* millions.⟩
3 deserving of ⟨This project is *worth* the effort.⟩
4 capable of ⟨I ran for all I was *worth.*⟩

[2]worth *n*
1 the value or usefulness of something or someone
2 value as expressed in money or in amount of time something will last ⟨a week's *worth* of groceries⟩
3 EXCELLENCE ⟨a man of *worth*⟩

worth•less \ˈwərth-ləs\ *adj*
1 lacking worth ⟨Play money is *worthless.*⟩
2 USELESS ⟨*worthless* junk⟩

worth•while \ˈwərth-ˈhwīl, -ˈwīl\ *adj*
being worth the time spent or effort used ⟨a *worthwhile* trip⟩

wor•thy \ˈwər-t͟hē\ *adj* **wor•thi•er; wor•thi•est**
1 having worth or excellence ⟨a *worthy* goal⟩
2 having enough value or excellence ⟨These students are *worthy* of praise.⟩
wor•thi•ness *n*

would \wəd, ˈwu̇d\ *vb, past of* [1]WILL
1 used as a helping verb to show that something might be likely or meant to happen under certain conditions ⟨They *would* come if they could.⟩ ⟨If I were you, I *would* save my money.⟩
2 used to describe what someone said, expected, or thought ⟨She said she *would* help me.⟩ ⟨I thought it *would* take an hour.⟩
3 used as a politer form of *will* ⟨*Would* you please stop?⟩
4 prefers or prefer to ⟨They *would* die rather than surrender.⟩
5 was or were going to ⟨We wish that you *would* go.⟩
6 is or are able to : COULD ⟨No stone *would* break that window.⟩
7 strongly desire : WISH ⟨I *would* that I were home.⟩

wouldn't \ˈwu̇-dᵊnt\
would not

[1]wound \ˈwünd\ *n*
1 an injury that involves cutting or breaking of bodily tissue ⟨a knife *wound*⟩
2 an injury or hurt to a person's feelings or reputation

[2]wound *vb* **wound•ed; wound•ing**
1 to hurt by cutting or breaking bodily tissue
2 to hurt the feelings or pride of

[3]wound \ˈwau̇nd\ *past and past participle of* WIND

wove *past of* WEAVE

woven *past participle of* WEAVE

[1]wran•gle \ˈraŋ-gəl\ *vb* **wran•gled; wran•gling**
1 to argue angrily
2 to care for and herd livestock and especially horses

[2]wrangle *n*
[1]QUARREL 1

wran•gler \'raŋ-glər\ *n*
1 a person who quarrels
2 a worker on a ranch who tends horses or cattle

[1]wrap \'rap\ *vb* **wrapped**; **wrap•ping**
1 to cover by winding or folding ⟨I'll *wrap* the baby in a blanket.⟩
2 to enclose in a package
3 to wind or fold around ⟨She *wrapped* her arms around me.⟩
4 to involve the attention of completely ⟨He was *wrapped* up in his work.⟩
wrap up
1 to bring to an end ⟨Let's *wrap up* this meeting.⟩
2 to put on warm clothing

[2]wrap *n*
a warm loose outer garment (as a shawl, cape, or coat)

wrap•per \'ra-pər\ *n*
1 ▼ a protective covering ⟨candy *wrappers*⟩
2 a person who wraps merchandise
3 a garment that is worn wrapped about the body

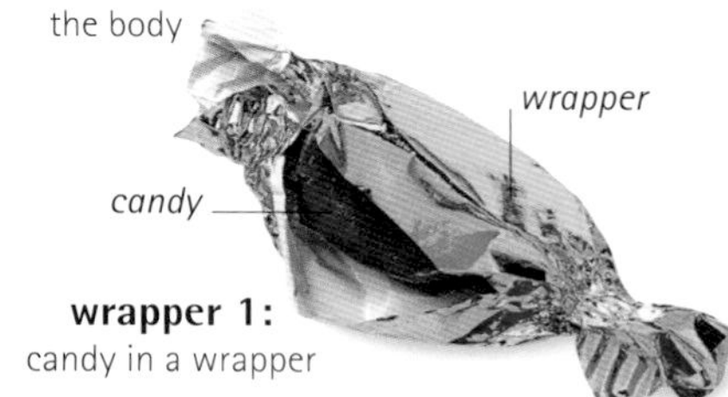

wrapper 1: candy in a wrapper

wrap•ping \'ra-piŋ\ *n*
something used to wrap something else : WRAPPER

wrath \'rath\ *n*
violent anger : RAGE

wrath•ful \'rath-fəl\ *adj*
1 full of wrath
2 showing wrath

wreak \'rēk\ *vb* **wreaked**; **wreak•ing**
to bring down as or as if punishment ⟨The storm *wreaked* destruction.⟩

wreath \'rēth\ *n, pl* **wreaths** \'rēthz, 'rēths\
▶ something twisted or woven into a circular shape ⟨a *wreath* of flowers⟩ ⟨a *wreath* of smoke⟩

wreathe \'rēth\ *vb* **wreathed**; **wreath•ing**
1 to form into wreaths ⟨Evergreen branches were *wreathed* and hung.⟩
2 to crown, decorate, or cover with or as if with a wreath ⟨The hill was *wreathed* with mist.⟩

[1]wreck \'rek\ *n*
1 the remains (as of a ship or vehicle) after heavy damage usually by storm, collision, or fire
2 a person who is very tired, ill, worried, or unhappy ⟨I'm a nervous *wreck*.⟩
3 the action of damaging or destroying something ⟨A lower speed limit will reduce *wrecks*.⟩
4 something in a state of ruin ⟨The house is a *wreck*.⟩

[2]wreck *vb* **wrecked**; **wreck•ing**
1 to damage or destroy by or as if by force or violence ⟨I *wrecked* my car.⟩
2 to bring to ruin or an end ⟨Our picnic was *wrecked* by the rain.⟩
3 [2]SHIPWRECK 2

wreck•age \'re-kij\ *n*
1 the remains of a wreck
2 the act of wrecking : the state of being wrecked

wreck•er \'re-kər\ *n*
1 a truck for removing wrecked or broken-down vehicles
2 a person who wrecks something

wren \'ren\ *n*
a small brown songbird with a short tail that points upward

[1]wrench \'rench\ *vb* **wrenched**; **wrench•ing**
1 to pull or twist with sudden sharp force ⟨He *wrenched* a branch from the tree.⟩
2 to injure by a sudden sharp twisting or straining ⟨I *wrenched* my knee.⟩

[2]wrench *n*
1 ▶ a tool used in turning nuts or bolts
2 a violent twist to one side or out of shape
3 an injury caused by twisting or straining : SPRAIN

wrest \'rest\ *vb* **wrest•ed**; **wrest•ing**
1 to pull away by twisting or wringing
2 to obtain only by great and steady effort

wreath: a decorative wreath

[1]wres•tle \'re-səl\ *vb* **wres•tled**; **wres•tling**
1 to fight by grasping and attempting to turn, trip, or throw down an opponent or to prevent the opponent from being able to move
2 to struggle to deal with ⟨He's *wrestling* with a problem.⟩
wres•tler \'re-slər\ *n*

[2]wrestle *n*
[2]STRUGGLE 1

wres•tling \'re-sliŋ\ *n*
a sport in which two opponents wrestle each other

wretch \'rech\ *n*
1 a miserable unhappy person
2 a very bad person ⟨You're an ungrateful *wretch*.⟩

wretch•ed \'re-chəd\ *adj*
1 very unhappy or unfortunate : suffering greatly
2 causing misery or distress ⟨*wretched* living conditions⟩
3 of very poor quality : INFERIOR ⟨*wretched* food⟩ ⟨I have a *wretched* memory.⟩
wretch•ed•ly *adv*
wretch•ed•ness *n*

wrig•gle \'ri-gəl\ *vb* **wrig•gled**; **wrig•gling**
1 to twist or move like a worm : SQUIRM, WIGGLE
2 to advance by twisting and turning

[2]wrench 1: a pipe wrench

wrig•gler \'ri-glər\ *n*
1 someone or something that squirms
2 a mosquito larva

wring \'riŋ\ *vb* **wrung** \'rəŋ\; **wring•ing**
1 to twist or press so as to squeeze out moisture ⟨*Wring* out your bathing suit.⟩
2 to get by or as if by twisting or pressing ⟨Police *wrung* a confession from the criminal.⟩
3 to twist with a forceful or violent motion ⟨He *wrung* the chicken's neck.⟩
4 to affect as if by wringing ⟨The bad news *wrung* our hearts.⟩
5 to twist (hands) together as a sign of anguish

wring•er \'riŋ-ər\ *n*
a machine or device for squeezing liquid out of something (as laundry)

[1]wrin•kle \'riŋ-kəl\ *n*
1 a crease or small fold (as in the skin or in cloth)
2 a clever notion or trick ⟨She thought up a new *wrinkle* for the game.⟩
3 a surprise in a story or series of events

a b c d e f g h i j k l m n o p q r s t u v w x y z

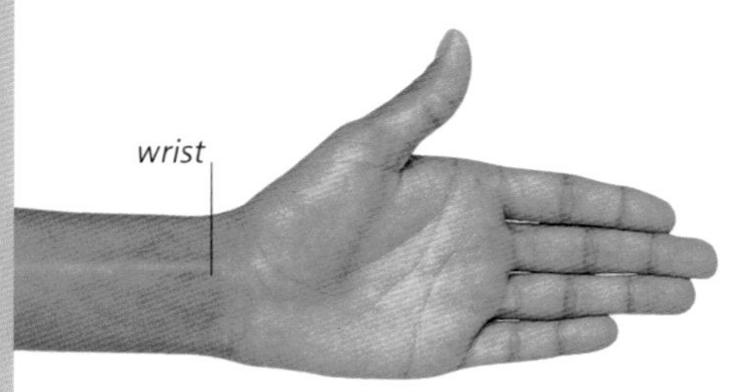

wrist

[2]**wrinkle** *vb* **wrin•kled**; **wrin•kling**
to develop or cause to develop creases or small folds

wrist \'rist\ *n*
▲ the joint or the region of the joint between the hand and arm

wrist•band \'rist-,band\ *n*
1 the part of a sleeve that goes around the wrist
2 a band that goes around the wrist (as for support or to absorb sweat)

wrist•watch \'rist-,wäch\ *n*
a watch attached to a bracelet or strap and worn on the wrist

writ \'rit\ *n*
an order in writing signed by an officer of a court ordering someone to do or not to do something

write \'rīt\ *vb* **wrote** \'rōt\; **writ•ten** \'ri-t^{ə}n\; **writ•ing** \'rī-tiŋ\
1 ► to form letters or words with pen or pencil ⟨The kindergartners are learning to *write*.⟩
2 to form the letters or the words of (as on paper) ⟨*Write* your name.⟩
3 to put down on paper ⟨For homework, *write* about your vacation.⟩
4 to make up and set down for others to read ⟨I'm *writing* a novel.⟩
5 to compose music
6 to communicate with someone by sending a letter

writ•er \'rī-tər\ *n*
a person who writes especially as a business or occupation

writhe \'rīth\ *vb* **writhed**; **writh•ing**
to twist and turn from side to side ⟨She was *writhing* in pain.⟩

writ•ing \'rī-tiŋ\ *n*
1 the act of a person who writes
2 HANDWRITING ⟨I can't read his *writing*.⟩
3 something (as a letter or book) that is written

[1]**wrong** \'ròŋ\ *adj*
1 not the one wanted or intended ⟨I took the *wrong* train.⟩
2 not correct or true : FALSE ⟨Your addition is *wrong*.⟩
3 not right : SINFUL, EVIL ⟨It is *wrong* to lie.⟩
4 not satisfactory : causing unhappiness ⟨You're upset. What's *wrong*?⟩
5 not suitable ⟨This coat is the *wrong* size.⟩

write 1:
a girl using a pencil to write

6 made so as to be placed down or under and not to be seen ⟨the *wrong* side of cloth⟩
7 not proper ⟨He swallowed something the *wrong* way.⟩
8 not working correctly ⟨Something's *wrong* with the car.⟩
wrong•ly *adv*

[2]**wrong** *n*
something (as an idea, rule, or action) that is not right

[3]**wrong** *adv*
in the wrong direction, manner, or way ⟨I answered *wrong*.⟩

[4]**wrong** *vb* **wronged**; **wrong•ing**
to treat badly or unfairly

wrong•do•er \'ròŋ-'dü-ər\ *n*
a person who does wrong and especially a moral wrong

wrong•do•ing \'ròŋ-'dü-iŋ\ *n*
bad behavior or action

wrong•ful \'ròŋ-fəl\ *adj*
1 [1]WRONG 3, UNJUST
2 UNLAWFUL

wrote *past of* WRITE

[1]**wrought** *past and past participle of* WORK

[2]**wrought** \'ròt\ *adj*
1 beaten into shape by tools ⟨*wrought* metals⟩
2 much too excited ⟨Don't get all *wrought* up over the test.⟩

wrung *past and past participle of* WRING

wry \'rī\ *adj* **wry•er**; **wry•est**
1 funny in a clever or ironic way ⟨a *wry* remark⟩
2 expressing irony ⟨a *wry* smile⟩

wt. *abbr* weight

WV, W.Va. *abbr* West Virginia

www *abbr* World Wide Web

WY, Wyo. *abbr* Wyoming

Sounds of X: The letter **X** usually sounds like **KS**. You can hear this sound in *ax* and *extra*. It also frequently sounds like **GZ** in words like *exact*. **X** can also sound like **K** followed by **SH** in words like *complexion*, or like **G** followed by the sound we write as **ZH** in some pronunciations of words like *luxurious*. In the few words that begin with it, the letter **X** usually sounds like a **Z**, as in *xylophone*. In even fewer words that begin with **X**, the letter says its own name, as in *X-ray*.

x \'eks\ *n, pl* **x's** *or* **xs** \'ek-səz\ *often cap*
1 the 24th letter of the English alphabet
2 ten in Roman numerals
3 an unknown quantity

x–ax•is \'eks-,ak-səs\ *n*
a line of reference usually stretching horizontally on a graph

XL *abbr* extra large

Xmas \'kri-sməs\ *n*
CHRISTMAS

► **Word History** Some people dislike the use of *Xmas* for *Christmas*, saying it is wrong to take *Christ* out of *Christmas*. Really, they are the ones who are wrong, for the *X* in *Xmas* stands for the Greek letter *chi* that looks just like our *X* and is the first letter of *Christ* in Greek. For many centuries this letter has been used as an abbreviation and a symbol for Christ.

x–ray \'eks-,rā\ *vb* **x–rayed**; **x–ray•ing** *often cap X*
to examine, treat, or photograph with X-rays

X–ray \'eks-,rā\ *n*
1 a powerful invisible ray made up of very short waves that is somewhat similar to light and that is able to pass through some solids and acts on photographic film like light
2 ► a photograph taken by the use of X-rays <an *X-ray* of the lungs>

► **Word History** In November, 1895, the German scientist Wilhelm Röntgen was conducting an experiment on the properties of electron tubes. He noticed that a fluorescent surface in the vicinity of the tube would light up even if shielded from the tube's direct light. A thick metal object would block some of the rays, while a less dense object such as wood would cast only a weak shadow. Röntgen's explanation was that the tube produced some type of invisible radiation that could pass through substances that blocked ordinary light. Because he did not know the nature of this radiation, he named it *X-Strahl*—translated into English as *X-ray*—based on the mathematical use of *x* to indicate an unknown quantity.

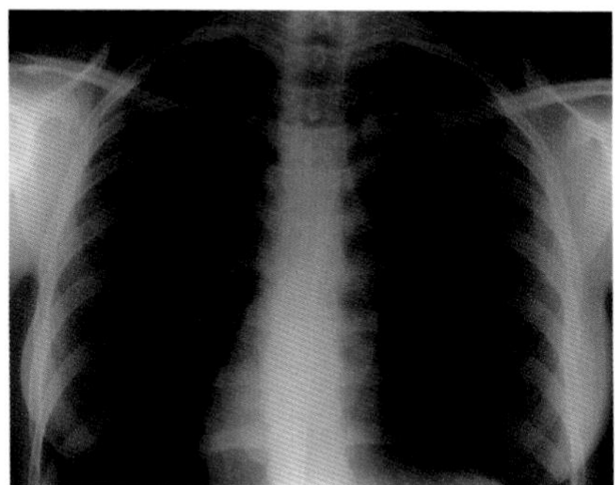

X–ray 2: an X-ray of a human chest

xy•lo•phone \'zī-lə-,fōn\ *n*
▼ a musical instrument consisting of a series of wooden bars of different lengths that are struck by special mallets to produce musical notes

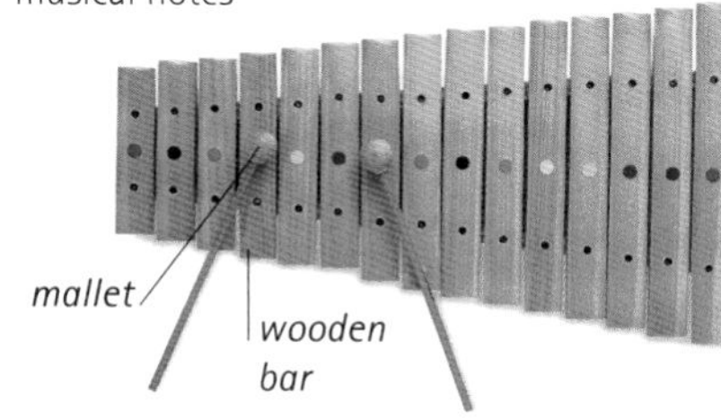

xylophone: a toy xylophone

Yy

Sounds of Y: The letter **Y** makes the sound heard in the words *yes* and *layer*. But **Y** often makes vowel sounds. It sounds like a long **E** in words like *silly* and *wavy*. It sounds like a long **I** in words like *sky* and *myself*. It sounds like a short **I** in words like *mystic* and *rhythm*. It can also make the schwa sound, indicated by the symbol ə, in words such as *polymer*. When following a vowel, **Y** is often silent, as in *way* and *key*. It can also combine with vowels to make other sounds, as in *prey*, *boy*, and *buy*.

y \ˈwī\ *n, pl* **y's** *or* **ys** \ˈwīz\ *often cap*
the 25th letter of the English alphabet

[1]**-y** *also* **-ey** \ē\ *adj suffix* **-i•er; -i•est**
1 showing, full of, or made of ⟨dirty⟩ ⟨muddy⟩ ⟨icy⟩
2 like ⟨wintry⟩
3 devoted to : enthusiastic about
4 tending to ⟨sleepy⟩
5 somewhat : rather ⟨chilly⟩

[2]**-y** \ē\ *n suffix, pl* **-ies**
1 state : condition : quality ⟨jealousy⟩
2 activity, place of business, or goods dealt with ⟨laundry⟩
3 whole body or group

[3]**-y** *n suffix, pl* **-ies**
occasion or example of a specified action ⟨entreaty⟩ ⟨inquiry⟩

[4]**-y** see -IE

yacht \ˈyät\ *n*
a small ship used for pleasure cruising or racing

▶ **Word History** In the 1500s the Dutch developed a kind of fast-moving sailing ship for use in coastal waters and river mouths. These vessels were called by the name *jaght*, short for *jachtschip* or *jageschip* in Dutch and German dialects —literally, "hunting ship" or "pursuit ship." The word was soon borrowed into English as *yoath* or *yaught*. The spelling *jacht* or *yacht* became widespread after 1660, when the English king Charles II was given such a boat, dubbed the *Mary*, by the Dutch East India Company. The king chose to use the boat for excursions and racing, and the word *yacht* became attached to other vessels used for the same purposes.

yacht•ing \ˈyä-tiŋ\ *n*
the activity or recreation of racing or cruising in a yacht

yak \ˈyak\ *n*
▶ a wild or domestic ox of the uplands of central Asia that has very long hair

yam \ˈyam\ *n*
1 ▶ the starchy thick underground tuber of a climbing plant that is an important food in many tropical regions
2 a sweet potato with a moist and usually orange flesh

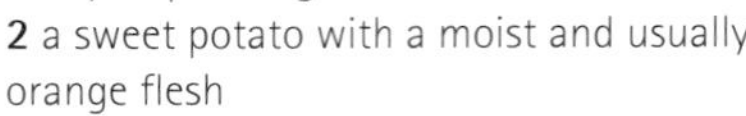

yam 1

[1]**yank** \ˈyaŋk\ *n*
a strong sudden pull : JERK

[2]**yank** *vb* **yanked; yank•ing**
to pull suddenly or forcefully ⟨She *yanked* the drawer open.⟩

Yan•kee \ˈyaŋ-kē\ *n*
1 a person born or living in New England
2 a person born or living in the northern United States
3 a person born or living in the United States

[1]**yap** \ˈyap\ *vb* **yapped; yap•ping**
1 to bark often continuously with quick high-pitched sounds
2 to talk continuously and often loudly : CHATTER

[2]**yap** *n*
a quick high-pitched bark

[1]**yard** \ˈyärd\ *n*
1 an outdoor area next to a building that is often bordered (as by shrubs or fences) ⟨Children played in the *yard*.⟩
2 the grounds of a building ⟨a prison *yard*⟩
3 a fenced area for livestock ⟨a chicken *yard*⟩
4 an area set aside for a business or activity ⟨a navy *yard*⟩
5 a system of railroad tracks especially for keeping and repairing cars

[2]**yard** *n*
1 a measure of length equal to three feet or 36 inches (about 0.91 meter)
2 a long pole pointed toward the ends that holds up and spreads the top of a sail

yard•age \ˈyär-dij\ *n*
1 a total number of yards
2 the length or size of something measured in yards ⟨a sail's square *yardage*⟩

yard•arm \ˈyärd-ˌärm\ *n*
either end of the yard of a square-rigged ship

yard•stick \ˈyärd-ˌstik\ *n*
1 a measuring stick a yard long

yak: a wild yak grazing on a rocky land

2 a rule or standard by which something is measured or judged ⟨His story by any *yardstick* was dull.⟩

yarn \'yärn\ *n*
1 ▶ a natural or manufactured fiber (as of cotton, wool, or rayon) formed as a continuous thread for use in knitting or weaving
2 an interesting or exciting story

yaw \'yȯ\ *vb* **yawed**; **yaw•ing**
to turn suddenly from a straight course ⟨The boat *yawed* in heavy seas.⟩

yawl \'yȯl\ *n*
a sailboat having two masts with the shorter one behind the point where the stern enters the water

[1]yawn \'yȯn\ *vb* **yawned**; **yawn•ing**
1 to open the mouth wide and take a deep breath usually as an involuntary reaction to being tired or bored
2 to open wide ⟨A deep chasm *yawned* below.⟩

[2]yawn *n*
▼ an opening of the mouth while taking a deep breath usually as an involuntary reaction to being tired or bored

[2]yawn: a puppy letting out a yawn

y–ax•is \'wī-,ak-səs\ *n*
a line of reference usually stretching vertically on a graph

yd. *abbr* yard

ye \'yē\ *pron*
YOU 1
Hint: *Ye* is a very old word that still appears in books and sayings from long ago. People also use it today to imitate that old way of speaking.

[1]yea \'yā\ *adv*
[1]YES 1
Hint: The word *yea* is used when a person is voting aloud for something.

[2]yea *n*
1 a vote in favor of something ⟨We counted 13 *yeas* and 15 nays.⟩
2 a person casting a yea vote

year \'yir\ *n*
1 the period of about 365¼ days required for the earth to make one complete trip around the sun

yarn 1: a ball of yarn

2 a period of 365 days or in leap year 366 days beginning January 1
3 a fixed period of time ⟨the school *year*⟩
4 the age of a person ⟨a six-*year* old⟩
5 a long time ⟨We've been standing in line for a *year*.⟩

year•book \'yir-,bu̇k\ *n*
1 a book published once a year especially as a report or summary of a certain topic (as new discoveries in science)
2 a publication that shows a school's current students and staff and the activities that took place during the school year

year•ling \'yir-liŋ\ *n*
an animal that is between one and two years old

year•ly \'yir-lē\ *adj*
occurring, made, or done every year : ANNUAL ⟨I had my *yearly* checkup.⟩

yearn \'yərn\ *vb* **yearned**; **yearn•ing**
to desire very much

▶ **Synonyms** YEARN, LONG, and PINE mean to desire something very much. YEARN is used of a very eager desiring along with restless or painful feelings. ⟨They're *yearning* for freedom.⟩ LONG is used when someone truly wants something and often tries very hard to get it. ⟨She *longed* to become a successful writer.⟩ PINE is used when someone is growing weak while continuing to want something that is impossible to get. ⟨She was *pining* away for her long lost friend.⟩

yearn•ing \'yər-niŋ\ *n*
an eager desire

year–round \'yir-'rau̇nd\ *adj*
active, present, or done throughout the entire year

yeast \'yēst\ *n*
1 a single-celled fungus that ferments sugar to produce alcohol and carbon dioxide
2 a commercial product containing living yeast cells that is used in baking to make dough rise and in the making of alcoholic beverages (as wine)

[1]yell \'yel\ *vb* **yelled**; **yell•ing**
to speak, call, or cry out loudly (as in anger or to get someone's attention)

[2]yell *n*
a loud call or cry : SHOUT

[1]yel•low \'ye-lō\ *adj*
1 of the color of a lemon : colored yellow ⟨a *yellow* raincoat⟩
2 COWARDLY 1

[2]yellow *n*
1 the color of a lemon
2 something (as the yolk of an egg) yellow in color

[3]yellow *vb* **yel•lowed**; **yel•low•ing**
to turn yellow

yellow fever *n*
a disease carried by mosquitoes in parts of Africa and South America

yel•low•ish \'ye-lə-wish\ *adj*
somewhat yellow

yellow jacket *n*
▶ a small wasp with yellow markings that usually nests in colonies in the ground and can sting repeatedly and painfully

yellow jacket

[1]yelp \'yelp\ *n*
a quick high-pitched bark or cry

[2]yelp *vb* **yelped**; **yelp•ing**
to make a quick high-pitched bark or cry ⟨A dog was *yelping* in pain.⟩

yen \'yen\ *n*
a strong desire : LONGING

yeo•man \'yō-mən\ *n*, *pl* **yeo•men** \-mən\
1 a petty officer in the navy who works as a clerk
2 a person who owns and cultivates a small farm

-yer see [2]-ER

[1]yes \'yes\ *adv*
1 used to express agreement in answer to a question, request, or offer or with an earlier statement ⟨"Are you ready?" "*Yes*, I am."⟩ ⟨*Yes*, I think you are right.⟩
2 used to introduce a phrase with greater emphasis or clearness ⟨We are glad, *yes*, very glad to see you!⟩
3 used to show uncertainty or polite interest ⟨*Yes*? Who's there?⟩ ⟨*Yes*, what can I do for you?⟩
4 used to indicate excitement ⟨*Yes*! We won!⟩

[2]yes *n*
a positive reply ⟨I received a *yes* to my request.⟩

[1]yes•ter•day \'ye-stər-dē\ *adv*
on the day before today ⟨I mailed the letter *yesterday*.⟩

[2]yesterday *n*
1 the day before today ⟨*Yesterday* was my birthday.⟩
2 the past in general ⟨Actors were dressed in the fashions of *yesterday*.⟩

yes•ter•year \ˈye-stər-ˌyir\ *n*
a time in the past

[1]yet \ˈyet\ *adv*
1 in addition ⟨They made up *yet* another excuse.⟩
2 [2]EVEN 2 ⟨We reached *yet* higher speeds.⟩
3 up to now **:** so far ⟨He hasn't done much *yet*.⟩
4 at this time ⟨Has the newspaper arrived *yet*?⟩
5 up to the present **:** STILL ⟨It is *yet* a new country.⟩
6 at some later time ⟨She may *yet* decide to go.⟩
7 NEVERTHELESS

[2]yet *conj*
in spite of the fact that ⟨I was sick *yet* I went to school.⟩

yew \ˈyü\ *n*
▶ a tree or shrub with stiff needlelike evergreen leaves and seeds having a red juicy covering

yew: a branch of a yew

Yid•dish \ˈyi-dish\ *n*
a language related to German that was originally spoken by Jews of central and eastern Europe

[1]yield \ˈyēld\ *vb* **yield•ed; yield•ing**
1 to give (something) over to the power or control of another **:** SURRENDER
2 to give in ⟨He *yielded* to temptation.⟩
3 to produce as a natural product ⟨These trees *yield* fruit.⟩
4 to produce or give back as interest or profit ⟨The investment *yielded* eight percent annually.⟩
5 to be productive **:** bring good results ⟨The studies *yielded* proof of the theory.⟩
6 to stop opposing or objecting to something ⟨I *yielded* to a friend's plea.⟩
7 to give way under physical force so as to bend, stretch, or break ⟨The rope *yielded* under the strain.⟩
8 to allow another person or vehicle to go first

[2]yield *n*
1 the amount produced or returned ⟨The high *yield* of wheat per acre increased.⟩
2 [2]RETURN 7 ⟨The *yield* on government bonds is five percent.⟩

[1]yip \ˈyip\ *vb* **yipped; yip•ping**
[1]YAP 1

[2]yip *n*
[2]YAP

YK *abbr* Yukon Territory

[1]yo•del \ˈyō-dᵊl\ *vb* **yo•deled** *or* **yo•delled; yo•del•ing** *or* **yo•del•ling**
to sing or call with frequent sudden changes from the natural voice range to a higher range and back
yo•del•er *n*

[2]yodel *n*
a song or call made by yodeling

yo•gurt \ˈyō-gərt\ *n*
a thick soft food that is made of milk soured by the addition of bacteria and that is often flavored and sweetened

[1]yoke \ˈyōk\ *n*
1 a wooden bar or frame by which two work animals (as oxen) are harnessed at the heads or necks for drawing a plow or load
2 a frame fitted to a person's shoulders to carry a load in two equal parts
3 a clamp that holds or connects two parts
4 *pl usually* **yoke** two animals yoked together
5 something that brings about pain, suffering, or a loss of freedom ⟨the *yoke* of tyranny⟩
6 SLAVERY 1
7 a fitted or shaped piece at the shoulder of a garment or at the top of a skirt

[2]yoke *vb* **yoked; yok•ing**
1 to put a yoke on
2 to attach a work animal to ⟨*Yoke* the horse to the wagon.⟩

yo•kel \ˈyō-kəl\ *n*
a person from a small town or the country who has little education or experience

yolk \ˈyōk\ *n*
▶ the yellow inner part of the egg of a bird or reptile containing stored food material for the developing young

eggshell

yolk of a chicken's egg

▶ **Word History** The word *yolk* goes back to Old English *geoloca* (a spelling that seems less strange when you know that *ge-* in Old English could stand for the sound /y/). *Geoloca*, in turn, is a derivative of *geolu*, the ancestor of our word *yellow*. This makes perfect sense given the color of a yolk, but changes in pronunciation over the course of centuries no longer make the relationship of the words obvious.

Yom Kip•pur \ˌyōm-ki-ˈpu̇r, ˌyȯm-, -ˈki-pər\ *n*
a Jewish holiday observed in September or October with fasting and prayer

[1]yon \ˈyän\ *adj*
[2]YONDER

[2]yon *adv*
1 [1]YONDER
2 THITHER ⟨I ran hither and *yon*.⟩

[1]yon•der \ˈyän-dər\ *adv*
at or in that place ⟨Look *yonder* down the hill.⟩

[2]yonder *adj*
1 more distant ⟨the *yonder* side of the hill⟩
2 being at a distance within view ⟨*yonder* hills⟩

yore \ˈyȯr\ *n*
time long past ⟨I heard stories of *yore*.⟩

you \ˈyü, yə\ *pron*
1 the person, thing, or group these words are spoken or written to
2 anyone at all ⟨*You* never know what will happen next.⟩

you'd \ˈyüd, ˈyəd\
you had **:** you would

you'll \ˈyül, ˈyəl\
you shall **:** you will

[1]young \ˈyəŋ\ *adj* **youn•ger** \ˈyəŋ-gər\; **youn•gest** \ˈyəŋ-gəst\
1 being in the first or an early stage of life, growth, or development ⟨*young* children⟩
2 lacking in experience ⟨That reporter is still *young* and naive.⟩
3 recently formed, produced, or come into being **:** NEW ⟨a *young* company⟩
4 YOUTHFUL 1

[2]young *n pl*
1 young people ⟨It's a story for *young* and old.⟩
2 immature or recently born offspring ⟨a bear and her *young*⟩

youn•gest \ˈyəŋ-gəst\ *n, pl* **youngest**
the least old member especially of a family ⟨His *youngest* is a toddler.⟩

young•ster \ˈyəŋ-stər\ *n*
1 a young person **:** YOUTH
2 CHILD 3 ⟨Her *youngsters* clung to her dress.⟩

your \yər, ˈyu̇r, ˈyȯr\ *adj*
1 relating to or belonging to you ⟨This is *your* book.⟩ ⟨The door will be on *your* right.⟩
2 by or from you ⟨Thank you for *your* gifts.⟩
3 relating to people in general ⟨Exercise is good for *your* health.⟩
4 used before a title of honor in addressing a person ⟨*your* Majesty⟩

you're \yər, ˈyu̇r, ˈyȯr\
you are

yours \ˈyu̇rz, ˈyȯrz\ *pron*
that which belongs to you ⟨The bike is *yours*.⟩ ⟨*Yours* is the empty glass.⟩

yo-yo

your•self \yər-ˈself\ *pron, pl* **your•selves** \-ˈselvz\
1 your own self ⟨Be careful or you might hurt *yourself.*⟩ ⟨You are responsible *yourselves* for the problem.⟩
2 your normal or healthy self ⟨You're not *yourself* today.⟩

youth \ˈyüth\ *n, pl* **youths** \ˈyüthz, ˈyüths\
1 the time of life between being a child and an adult ⟨He spent his *youth* in Europe.⟩
2 a young man ⟨an imaginative *youth*⟩
3 young people ⟨the *youth* of today⟩
4 the quality or state of being young

youth•ful \ˈyüth-fəl\ *adj*
1 belonging to, relating to, or characteristic of youth ⟨*youthful* optimism⟩
2 not old or mature
3 having the appearance, spirit, or energy of youth ⟨a *youthful* face⟩ ⟨*youthful* grandparents⟩
youth•ful•ness *n*

you've \ˈyüv, yəv\
you have

[1]yowl \ˈyau̇l\ *vb* **yowled**; **yowl•ing**
to utter a loud long cry (as of pain or suffering)

[2]yowl *n*
a loud long cry (as of pain or suffering)

yo–yo \ˈyō-yō\ *n, pl* **yo–yos** *also* **yo–yoes**
◀ a small round toy that has two flattened disks with a string attached to the center and that is made to fall and rise to the hand by unwinding and rewinding on the string

▶ **Word History** *Yo-yo* comes from a similar sounding word in languages of the Philippine Islands, where it is the name for a toy similar to our yo-yo. Though toys like the yo-yo have a long history in Europe and the Americas—a disk on a string called a ***whirligig*** was patented in 1866—the modern yo-yo dates from 1928, when a Philippine immigrant named Pedro Flores began to manufacture the toys in California based on the yo-yos he had known in his youth.

yr. *abbr* year

YT *abbr* Yukon Territory

yuc•ca \ˈyə-kə\ *n*
▶ a plant that grows in warm dry regions and has stiff pointed leaves at the base and a tall stiff stalk of usually whitish flowers

yucky \ˈyə-kē\ *adj* **yuck•i•er**; **yuck•i•est**
causing discomfort, disgust, or a strong feeling of dislike ⟨a *yucky* smell⟩

yule \ˈyül\ *n, often cap*
CHRISTMAS

yule log *n, often cap Y*
a large log once put in the fireplace on Christmas Eve as the foundation of the fire

yule•tide \ˈyül-ˌtīd\ *n, often cap*
the Christmas season

yum•my \ˈyə-mē\ *adj* **yum•mi•er**; **yum•mi•est**
very pleasing especially to the taste ⟨a *yummy* dessert⟩

yucca

a b c d e f g h i j k l m n o p q r s t u v w x y z

Zz

Sounds of Z: The letter **Z** makes the sound heard in the words *zipper* and *maze*. It can also sound like an **S** in words like *pretzel* or *quartz*. Sometimes, especially when there are two **Z**s together, **Z** can sound like a **T** followed by an **S**, as in *pizza*. In a few words, **Z** makes sound indicated by the symbol \zh\, such as *seizure*.

z \ˈzē\ *n, pl* **z's** *or* **zs** \ˈzēz\ *often cap*
the 26th letter of the English alphabet

za•ny \ˈzā-nē\ *adj* **za•ni•er; za•ni•est**
very strange and silly 〈a *zany* plan〉

zap \ˈzap\ *vb* **zapped; zap•ping**
to hit with or as if with a jolt of electricity 〈Lightning *zapped* the tree.〉

zeal \ˈzēl\ *n*
eager desire to get something done or see something succeed 〈I started on my chores with great *zeal*.〉

zeal•ous \ˈze-ləs\ *adj*
1 filled with or showing a strong and energetic desire to get something done or see something succeed
2 marked by passionate support for a person, cause, or ideal 〈a *zealous* fan〉
zeal•ous•ly *adv*

ze•bra \ˈzē-brə\ *n*
► an African animal that is related to the horse and has a hide striped in black and white or black and buff

zebra

ze•bu \ˈzē-byü\ *n*
▼ an Asian domestic ox that has a large hump over the shoulders and loose skin with hanging folds

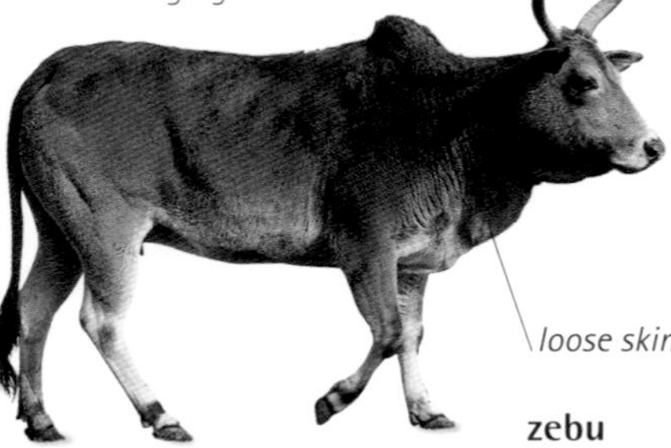

zebu

ze•nith \ˈzē-nəth\ *n*
1 the point in the sky directly overhead
2 the highest point or stage

zeph•yr \ˈze-fər\ *n*
a gentle breeze

zep•pe•lin \ˈze-pə-lən\ *n*
an airship resembling a huge long balloon that has a metal frame and is driven through the air by engines carried on its underside

ze•ro \ˈzē-rō, ˈzir-ō\ *n, pl* **zeros** *or* **zeroes**
1 the numerical symbol 0 meaning the absence of all size or quantity
2 the point on a scale (as on a thermometer) from which measurements are made
3 the temperature shown by the zero mark on a thermometer
4 a total lack of anything : NOTHING 〈His contribution was *zero*.〉

► **Word History** The word *zero* was taken into English through French from Italian. In Italian *zero* appears to have been shortened from *zefiro* or *zefro*, itself a borrowing from Arabic *ṣifr*. In the Middle Ages Italian merchants and mathematicians learned from the Arabs of a way of writing numbers different from the traditional Roman numerals. The new numbers had a symbol that Roman numerals lacked, which was called by the Arabs *ṣifr*, literally "empty." Our word *cipher* also comes ultimately from Arabic *ṣifr*.

zest \ˈzest\ *n*
1 a piece of the peel of a citrus fruit (as an orange or lemon) used to flavor foods
2 an enjoyable or exciting quality
3 keen enjoyment 〈They ate with *zest*.〉

► **Word History** The English word *zest* came from a French word *zeste* that means "the peel of an orange or a lemon." Because their flavor made food more tasty and enjoyable, lemon and orange peels were used to season food. In time the word *zest* came to mean any quality that made life more enjoyable.

[1]**zig•zag** \ˈzig-ˌzag\ *n*
1 one of a series of short sharp turns or angles in a line or course
2 ► a line, path, or pattern with a series of short sharp angles

[1]**zigzag 2:** a zigzag of toy blocks

[2]**zigzag** *adv*
in or by a line or course that has short sharp turns or angles 〈He ran *zigzag* across the field.〉

[3]**zigzag** *adj*
having short sharp turns or angles

[4]**zigzag** *vb* **zig•zagged; zig•zag•ging**
to form into or move along a line or course that has short sharp turns or angles 〈The bicycle rider *zigzagged* down the road.〉

zil•lion \ˈzil-yən\ *n*
an extremely large number 〈*zillions* of ants〉

zinc \ˈziŋk\ *n*
a bluish white metal that tarnishes only slightly in moist air and is used mostly to make alloys and to give iron and steel a protective coating

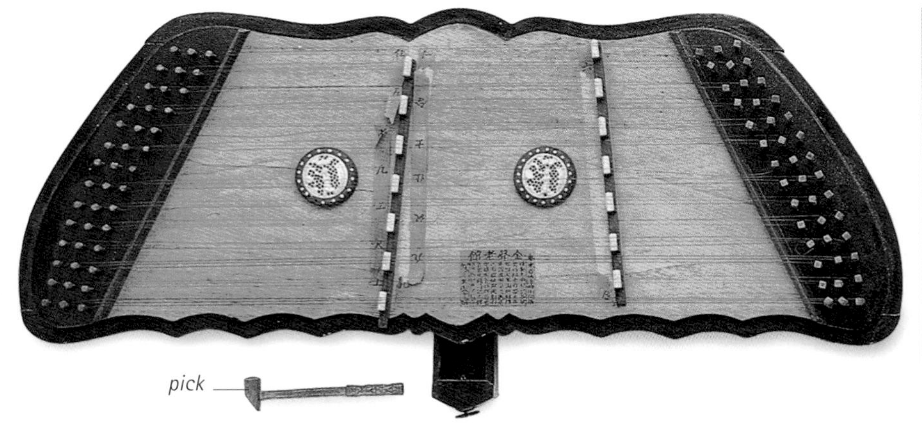

zither: a Chinese zither

[1]zing \'ziŋ\ *n*
1 a high-pitched humming sound 〈the *zing* of an arrow〉
2 a lively or energetic quality 〈It's a musical with lots of *zing.*〉
3 a sharp or spicy flavor

[2]zing *vb* **zinged; zing•ing**
to move very quick with a high-pitched humming sound

zin•nia \'zi-nē-ə, 'zin-yə\ *n*
▼ a garden plant grown for its long-lasting colorful flowers

zinnia

[1]zip \'zip\ *vb* **zipped; zip•ping**
to move or act quickly and often with energy and enthusiasm

[2]zip *n*
energy and enthusiasm 〈He performs with *zip.*〉

[3]zip *vb* **zipped; zip•ping**
to close or open with a zipper

zip code *n*
a number that identifies each postal delivery area in the United States

zip•per \'zi-pər\ *n*
a fastener (as for a jacket) consisting of two rows of metal or plastic teeth and a sliding piece that closes an opening by bringing the teeth together
zip•pered \-pərd\ *adj*

zip•py \'zi-pē\ *adj* **zip•pi•er; zip•pi•est**
1 SPEEDY 〈*zippy* cars〉
2 full of energy : LIVELY 〈a *zippy* song〉

zith•er \'zi-thər, -thər\ *n*
◀ a musical instrument with usually 30 to 40 strings that are plucked with the fingers or with a pick

zo•di•ac \'zō-dē-ˌak\ *n*
▼ an imaginary belt in the sky that includes the paths of the planets and is divided into twelve constellations or signs each with a special name and symbol

zom•bie *also* **zom•bi** \'zäm-bē\ *n*
a person who is believed to have died and been brought back to life without speech or free will

[1]zone \'zōn\ *n*
1 a region or area set off or characterized as different from surrounding or neighboring parts 〈The United States is located in one of earth's temperate *zones.*〉
2 one of the sections of an area created for or serving a particular use or purpose 〈a town's business *zone*〉

zodiac
Each constellation of the zodiac is made up of a pattern of stars that are imagined to represent an animal or character from ancient Greek myth. The twelve signs of the zodiac are used in astrology to identify different types of personality and to tell fortunes.

diagram showing the 12 signs of the zodiac

zoo: polar bears in their zoo enclosure

[2]zone *vb* zoned; zon•ing
to divide into sections for different uses or purposes

zoo \'zü\ *n, pl* zoos
▲ a place where living usually wild animals are kept for showing to the public

zoo•keep•er \'zü-,kē-pər\ *n*
a person who cares for animals in a zoo

zoo•log•i•cal \,zō-ə-'lä-ji-kəl\ *adj*
of or relating to zoology ⟨*zoological* classification⟩

zoological garden *n*
zoo

zoological park *n*
zoo

zo•ol•o•gist \zō-'ä-lə-jəst\ *n*
a person who specializes in zoology

zo•ol•o•gy \zō-'ä-lə-jē\ *n*
1 a branch of biology concerned with the study of animals and animal life
2 animal life (as of a region) ⟨the *zoology* of Australia⟩

[1]zoom \'züm\ *vb* **zoomed**; **zoom•ing**
1 to move quickly often with a loud low hum or buzz ⟨They got in the car and *zoomed* away.⟩
2 to move upward quickly ⟨The airplane *zoomed* into the sky.⟩

[2]zoom *n*
1 an act or process of moving quickly along or upwards
2 a loud low humming or buzzing sound

zuc•chi•ni \zü-'kē-nē\ *n*
a smooth cylinder-shaped green-skinned vegetable that is a type of squash

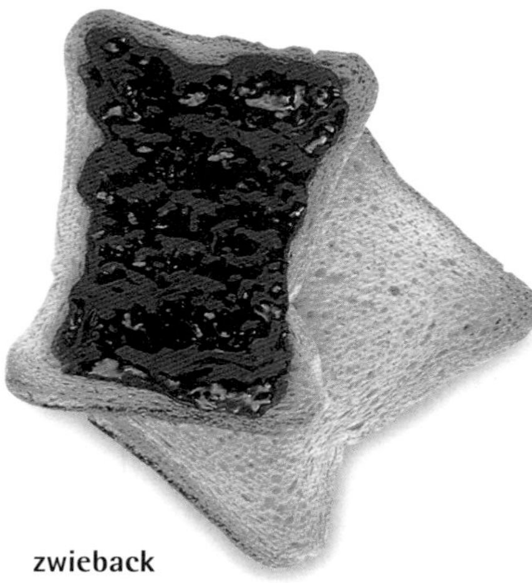

zwieback

zwie•back \'swē-,bak, 'swī-\ *n*
▲ a usually sweetened bread made with eggs that is baked and then sliced and toasted until dry and crisp

zy•gote \'zī-,gōt\ *n*
the new cell formed when a sperm cell joins with an egg cell

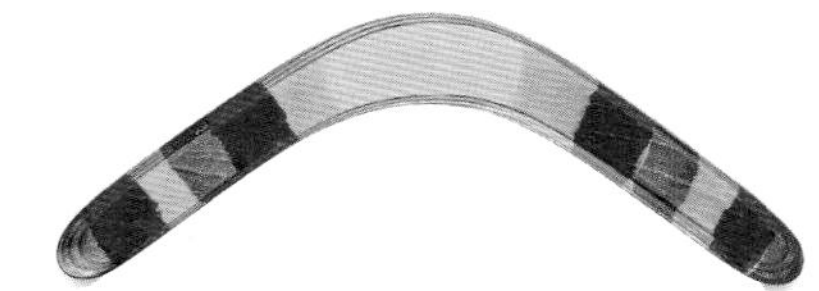

REFERENCE SECTION

4,590 miles
3,540 miles

Extent of North American lands

North America

STRETCHING FROM THE WARM Caribbean islands to icy Greenland, North America is the third-largest continent. Along each side of the mainland are mountain ranges – the Appalachians in the east and the giant Rocky Mountains in the west – that run parallel to one another. Between them lies a vast, flat landscape that includes the Great Plains and the freshwater Great Lakes.

Population: 587,580,611
No. of countries: 23

Ancient Civilizations

Centuries before European explorers set foot on North America, the continent was home to a series of advanced civilizations that traded and fought with each other. While some of these civilizations, such as the Adena and Hopewell cultures, flourished and died out, others, such as the Maya and Aztec, built vast empires.

Rocky Mountains

The snow-capped Rocky Mountains run down the length of the west side of North America, stretching from Alaska in the north to beyond Mexico in the south. Moraine \mə-'rān\ Lake, in the Canadian part of the Rockies, is one of many lakes and rivers that run from the mountain range. Rivers flowing east from the Rockies deposit silt on the Great Plains, which helps to develop fertile soil.

Native Peoples

The Inuit are the original people of Arctic Canada. The children shown here are from a town on the coast of Baffin Island in the Arctic Ocean. It snows here for eight months of the year and children keep warm using a combination of traditional and modern winter clothing.

Extreme Climates

Hottest place (Highest recorded temperature)	Death Valley, USA 134°F (56.7°C)
Driest place (Lowest average rainfall)	Bataques, Mexico 1.2 in (30.5 mm)
Coldest place (Lowest recorded temperature)	North Ice, Greenland -87°F (-66.1°C)
Wettest place (Highest average rainfall)	Henderson Lake, Canada 276 in (7,010 mm)

City Life

More than three quarters of all Americans live in cities or their suburbs, and the population is made up of people from many different ethnic backgrounds. San Francisco, shown here, is one of the oldest cities, renowned for its attractive 19th-century buildings.

Fact File

Largest country	Canada
Smallest country	St. Kitts & Nevis
Largest city	New York City
Largest lake	Lake Superior
Longest river	Mississippi-Missouri

NORTH AMERICA (see opposite page)
ATLANTIC OCEAN
Gulf of Mexico
NASSAU
THE BAHAMAS
HAVANA
CUBA
Turks & Caicos Islands (to UK)
British Virgin Islands (to UK)
Virgin Islands (to US)
Puerto Rico (to US)
Anguilla (to UK)
ST KITTS & NEVIS
ANTIGUA & BARBUDA
ST JOHN'S
BASSETERRE
Guadeloupe (to France)
DOMINICAN REPUBLIC
HAITI
PORT-AU-PRINCE
SANTO DOMINGO
Montserrat (to UK)
DOMINICA
ROSEAU
Martinique (to France)
CASTRIES
ST LUCIA
BARBADOS
BRIDGETOWN
KINGSTOWN
ST VINCENT & THE GRENADINES
GRENADA
ST. GEORGE'S
Cayman Islands (to UK)
JAMAICA
KINGSTON
Navassa Island (to US)
Caribbean Sea
Aruba (to Neth.)
Curaçao (to Neth.)
PORT OF SPAIN
TRINIDAD & TOBAGO
Bonaire (to Neth.)
SOUTH AMERICA
0 km 500
0 miles 250 500

Caribbean Islands

Characterized by long, sandy beaches, sunny weather, and warm waters, the islands of the Caribbean Sea attract many tourists every year. They are, however, prone to hurricanes, and volcanic eruptions.

United States of America

THE UNITED STATES is the world's largest economy, centered on service industries like retailing and banking. Known for its natural beauty and dramatic scenery, the US also has some of the world's best known city landscapes, such as San Francisco, New York, Los Angeles, and Chicago.

Grand Canyon

Over the last five million years, the Colorado River has carved its way through the rocky land of northern Arizona. At the same time, plateaus have risen. The largest land gorge in the world – known as the Grand Canyon – has formed as a result of these combined actions. The Canyon is the region's main attraction and is visited by millions of people every year.

Hawaiian Islands

Characterized by miles of coastline and a tropical climate, the Hawaiian Islands have a thriving tourist industry. Some of the islands are formed by volcanoes that rise out of the sea.

Mount Rushmore

Carved into Mount Rushmore are the heads of four great presidents: Washington, Jefferson, Theodore Roosevelt, and Lincoln. Completed in 1941, the monument has had millions of visitors.

Heads are sculpted into the rock face

Capitol building

Center of Government

Impressive marble buildings, such as the Capitol building, dominate Washington, DC. The city became the capital of the USA and seat of the federal government in 1800.

New York City

In the 19th century, New York was the second-largest city in the world and the business center of the USA. A fast-growing population resulted in New York's skyline moving upward to accommodate the extra people, and this remains one of New York's distinguishing features.

South America

ONE OF THE WORLD'S last great intact natural areas – the Amazonian rain forest – is found in South America, the fourth-largest continent. Bordering the western coast are the high peaks of the Andes, which are lined with numerous volcanoes. West of the Andes, the climate is dry with arid deserts, while by contrast the Amazon Basin and the Guiana Highlands in the north are humid and tropical.

Extent of South American lands

Population: 430,457,604
No. of countries: 12

Colombian emerald

Precious Stones
The emeralds found in Colombia are often considered to be of the best quality, and more than half of the world's emeralds are mined here.

Extreme Climates

Hottest place (Highest recorded temperature)	**Rivadavia, Argentina** 120°F (48.9°C)
Driest place (Lowest average rainfall)	**Arica, Chile** 0.03 in (0.76 mm)
Coldest place (Lowest recorded temperature)	**Sarmiento, Argentina** -27°F (-32.8°C)
Wettest place (Highest average rainfall)	**Quibdó, Colombia** 354 in (8,990 mm)

Inca sun god

Incas
The Incas were a group of Native American peoples whose empire in 15th-century Peru encompassed most of the Andes and large areas of desert and rain forest. Made of gold and inlaid with turquoise, the sun god shown above once formed the handle of a ceremonial knife.

Volcanic Andes

The Andes run the entire length of South America along a narrow strip of land bordering the Pacific Ocean. Many of the peaks are active or formerly active volcanoes. Despite the intense heat within these lava-filled mountains, the highest are covered in snow all year round.

Fact File

LARGEST COUNTRY	Brazil
SMALLEST COUNTRY	Suriname
LARGEST CITY	São Paulo \,sä-ō-'pau̇-lō\
LARGEST LAKE	Lake Titicaca \,lāk-,tit-i-'käk-ə\
LONGEST RIVER	Amazon

Flag bearer

Carnival Time

One of the world's largest and most spectacular carnivals is held in Brazil, with dancers from different clubs parading along one of the wide avenues of Rio de Janeiro \'rē-ō-,dā-zhə-'neər-ō\. The dancers wear elaborate costumes and every club has a flag bearer.

Amazon winds through rain forest

Amazon

From its source in the Andes Mountains of Peru, the Amazon River flows through a vast depression in the north of the continent and empties into the Atlantic Ocean. The Amazon, with its tributaries, nearby lakes, and swamps forms a network of fresh water that supports a huge area of tropical rain forest. The Amazon floods and deposits fertile silt on surrounding land. For more than half of its length, the Amazon flows through Brazil and is used by large boats to transport cargo inland.

Buenos Aires

Nearly half of all Argentinians live in or near the capital city of Buenos Aires. One of the major cities in the southern half of the world, it has wide avenues, a subway system, and popular shops. To the west of Buenos Aires, there are vast areas of open prairie known as pampas, where Argentinean cowboys called *gauchos* graze their cattle.

Plaza in Buenos Aires

Extent of European lands

Europe

ABOUT A QUARTER of the size of Asia and less than half the size of North America, Europe is the second-smallest continent. Irregularly shaped, it has many interlocking areas of land and sea. A vast curve of mountain ranges that include the Pyrenees and the Alps divides the north from the south. Europe's climate is generally temperate, with only a few places affected by extreme weather conditions. Most notable is the area around the Baltic Sea, which freezes over in winter. By contrast, countries along the Mediterranean Sea have milder weather and long, hot summers.

Fact File

LARGEST COUNTRY	Russia (European part)
SMALLEST COUNTRY	Vatican City
LARGEST CITY	Moscow
LARGEST LAKE	Lake Ladoga
LONGEST RIVER	Volga

Population: 747,182,751
No. of countries: 48

Swiss Alps

Europe's highest mountains, the Alps form a massive wall that separates northern Europe from the Mediterranean countries. The Swiss Alps are a popular ski resort and attract millions of tourists each year. Clustered in valleys, at the foot of the towering Alps, are picturesque villages and peaceful lakes. On the lower slopes are meadows where dairy cattle graze.

Folk Art

Made in Eastern Europe for centuries, nesting dolls can represent famous characters, but are mostly painted figures in traditional costumes. This form of folk art reflects the rural lifestyle of much of the population.

Nesting doll

Historic Cities

Italy has some of the world's most beautiful cities. One of the most remarkable is Venice, built on low-lying islands in a lagoon. Many Venetian houses are more than 400 years old and face on to canals, which take the place of roads.

Dutch Tulips

The largest producer of flowers in Europe is the Netherlands – particularly those grown from bulbs, such as tulips. In spring, the fields of flowers attract many tourists.

Mediterranean

Near the Mediterranean Sea, the climate is sunny and dry. Fields of lavender are characteristic of the South of France, where crops of fruit and cereal are also widely grown. By contrast, the climate in the north of France is cool and wet.

Extreme Climates

	Hottest place (Highest recorded temperature)	Seville, Spain 122°F (50°C)
	Driest place (Lowest average rainfall)	Astrakhan, Russia 8.5 in (217 mm)
	Coldest place (Lowest recorded temperature)	Ust' Shchugor, Russia -67°F (-55°C)
	Wettest place (Highest average rainfall)	Crkvice, Bosnia 183 in (4,658 mm)

Scandinavian ice-hockey players

Winter Sports

Scandinavia has deep fjords, lakes, and valleys that were gouged out by glaciers in past ice ages. During the long, cold winters, many of the lakes freeze up and ice hockey can be played outdoors. Long-distance, cross-country skiing is another popular winter sport here, as for many months much of the land becomes covered with deep snowfall.

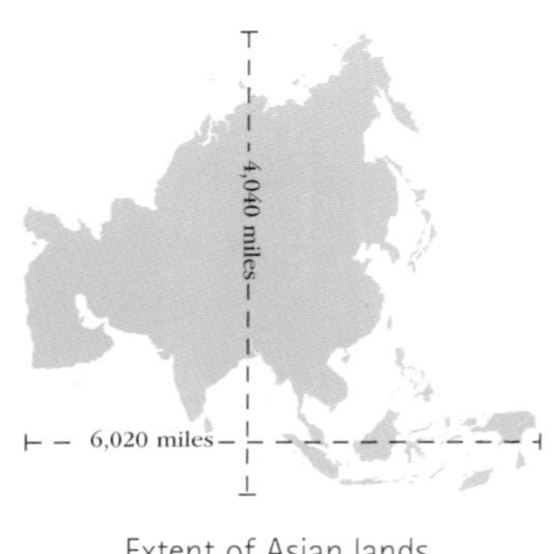

Extent of Asian lands

Asia

THE LARGEST CONTINENT, Asia has a rich variety of landscapes, climates, and traditions. Two out of every three people in the world live in Asia, and the most populated countries are China and India. In the Himalayas, Mount Everest is the highest place in the world, and the Dead Sea on the border of Israel and Jordan is the lowest. Climates vary from the frozen wastelands of Siberia in the north to the baking hot deserts of the Arabian Peninsula in the south. Toward the center of the continent, the climate is one of extreme contrasts – dry, hot summers and bitterly cold winters.

Dome of the Rock

Jerusalem
Jerusalem is a holy city for Christianity, Islam, and Judaism. Sacred buildings include the Islamic monument called Dome of the Rock.

Population: 4,601,371,198
No. of countries: 47

Siberia

This vast region – mostly in Asian Russia – is bitterly cold in winter. To the north of Siberia lies the tundra, where part of the soil has been frozen since the end of the Ice Age.

Mongolian family in traditional dress

Mongolia

Mongolia is a remote, sparsely populated country whose rulers once dominated China, central Asia, and eastern Europe. Genghis Khan was a famous Mongol leader.

Tokyo

Japan has huge economic power, with investments in land and property around the world. Many of its major banks and businesses are found in Tokyo. This busy city is hemmed in by mountains and built around Tokyo Bay.

Fact File

Largest country	Russia (Asian part)
Smallest country	Maldives
Largest city	Tokyo
Largest lake	Caspian Sea
Longest river	Yangtze

Extreme Climates

	Hottest place (Highest recorded temperature)	Tirat Zevi, Israel 129°F (53.9°C)
	Driest place (Lowest average rainfall)	Aden, Yemen 1.8 in (45.7mm)
	Coldest place (Lowest recorded temperature)	Verkhoyansk, Russia -90°F (-67.8°C)
	Wettest place (Highest average rainfall)	Cherrapunji, India 100 in (2,540 mm)

Himalayas

Forming a natural border between Tibet and India, the peaks of the Himalayas are permanently snow-capped. Himalaya is thought to mean "home of the snows" in the ancient language called Sanskrit.

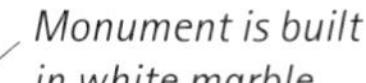

Monument is built in white marble

India

The world's second most populous country, India is a land of contrasts. While many people live in villages and farm small plots of land, India also has huge cities where office blocks stand next to ancient temples and monuments. The most famous monument is the Taj Mahal in northern India, built in the 17th century by an emperor as a tomb for his wife.

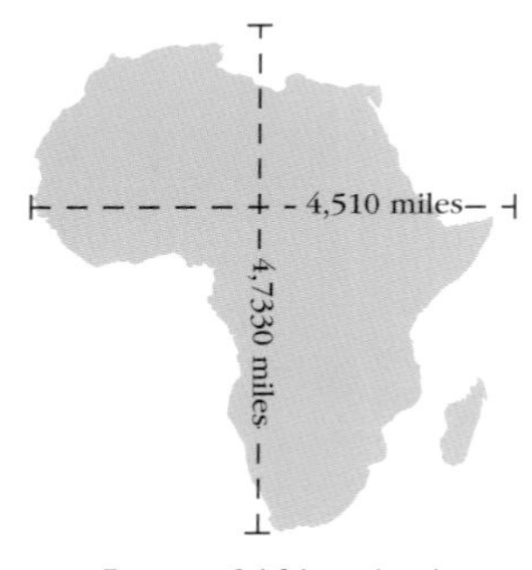

Extent of African lands

Africa

RAIN FORESTS AND ARID DESERTS dominate much of Africa, which is the world's second-largest continent. The landscapes of northern and southern Africa are hot and dry, with vast deserts stretching over raised platforms of rock. In these deserts – most famously the Sahara – the world's highest-ever temperatures have been recorded. By contrast, large tropical rain forests near to the Equator are home to a wide variety of animal and bird life. In East Africa, the landscape is made distinctive by steep-sided valleys, many of which contain enormous lakes.

Population: 1,308,064,195
No. of countries: 54

Extreme Climates

Hottest place (Highest recorded temperature)	Al 'Aziziyah, Libya 136°F (57.8°C)
Driest place (Lowest average rainfall)	Wadi Halfa, Sudan >0.1 in (2.54mm)
Coldest place (Lowest recorded temperature)	Ifrane, Morocco -11°F (-23.9°C)
Wettest place (Highest average rainfall)	Cape Debundscha, Cameroon 405 in (10,287 mm)

Mining

The mining industry is one of Africa's most important employers, and is crucial to many of its economies. The continent has large natural reserves of chromium, diamonds, gold, manganese, and platinum.

Colors vary

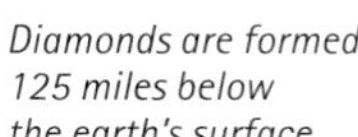

Diamonds are formed 125 miles below the earth's surface

Fact File

LARGEST COUNTRY	Algeria
SMALLEST COUNTRY	Seychelles
LARGEST CITY	Lagos
LARGEST LAKE	Lake Victoria
LONGEST RIVER	Nile

Sphinx is 187 ft (57 m) long and 66 ft (23 m) high

Ancient Egypt

Africa is home to one of the world's most ancient civilizations in Egypt. Between 3,000 B.C. and 30 B.C. the Egyptians built the first large stone buildings and invented one of the earliest forms of writing. Today, tourists flock to Egypt to see ancient monuments such as the pyramids and the Sphinx.

Equatorial Rain Forest

Near the Equator, dense tropical rain forests grow. Containing many plant and animal species, such as mountain gorillas and chimpanzees, the forests are threatened by overuse, hunting, and logging.

Sahara

The largest of Africa's deserts is the Sahara, which covers most of the northern part of the continent. One quarter of this desert land is sandy dunes, while the rest is made up of bare, rocky plains. The northern coast has a hot, dry climate, while further inland the Sahara is swept by strong winds.

Staff shows elder status

Type of bead necklace shows the wearer's age

Nomadic Herders

The quality of Africa's land is dependent on the amount of rainfall a particular area receives, and this has a great impact on the type of farming that takes place there. At the southern edge of the Sahara cultivation and nomadic herding are widely practiced. People from the Masai tribe, shown here, are nomads, moving from place to place in search of water and fresh grass for their cattle.

Australasia and Oceania

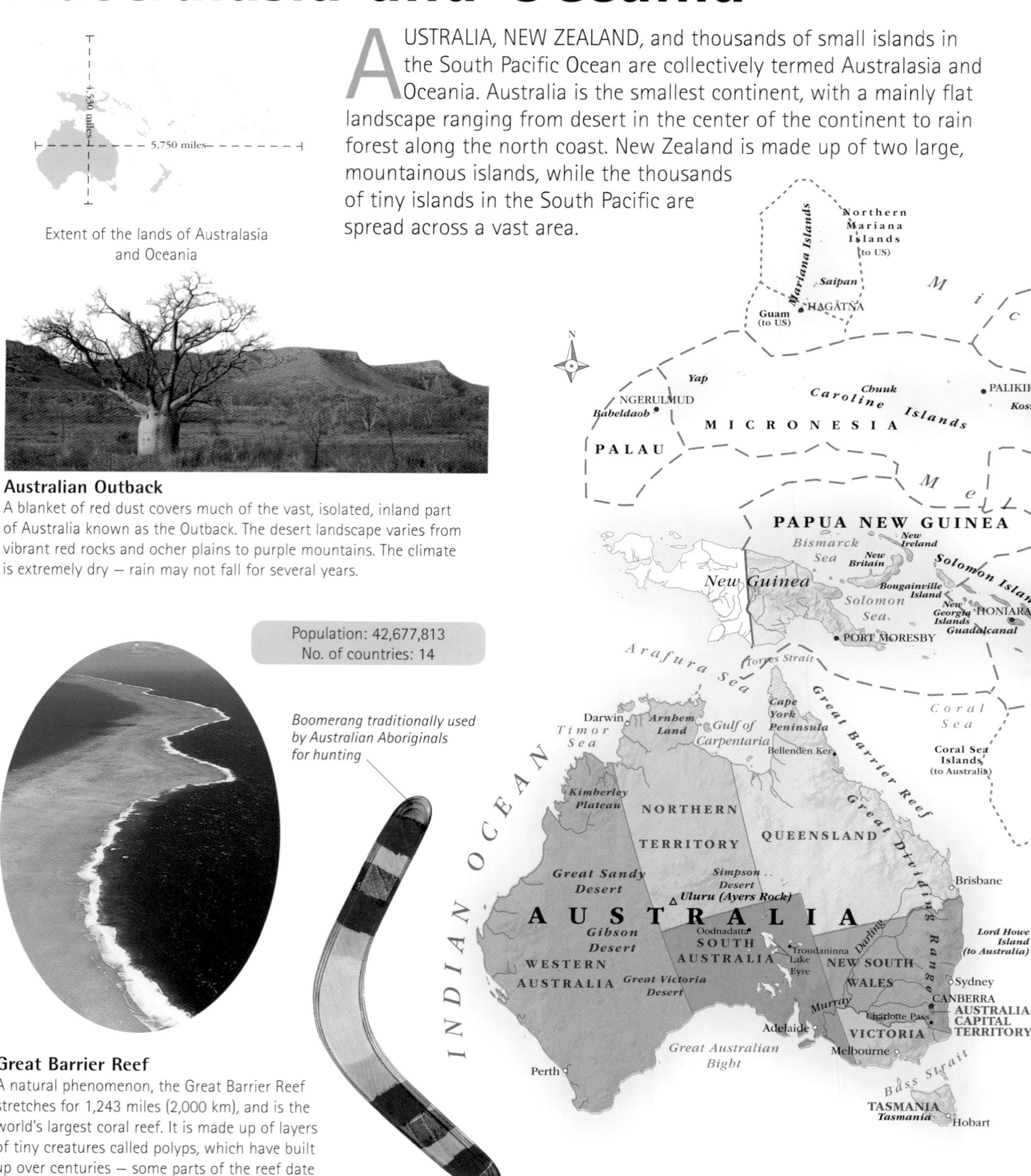

Extent of the lands of Australasia and Oceania

AUSTRALIA, NEW ZEALAND, and thousands of small islands in the South Pacific Ocean are collectively termed Australasia and Oceania. Australia is the smallest continent, with a mainly flat landscape ranging from desert in the center of the continent to rain forest along the north coast. New Zealand is made up of two large, mountainous islands, while the thousands of tiny islands in the South Pacific are spread across a vast area.

Australian Outback
A blanket of red dust covers much of the vast, isolated, inland part of Australia known as the Outback. The desert landscape varies from vibrant red rocks and ocher plains to purple mountains. The climate is extremely dry — rain may not fall for several years.

Population: 42,677,813
No. of countries: 14

Boomerang traditionally used by Australian Aboriginals for hunting

Great Barrier Reef
A natural phenomenon, the Great Barrier Reef stretches for 1,243 miles (2,000 km), and is the world's largest coral reef. It is made up of layers of tiny creatures called polyps, which have built up over centuries — some parts of the reef date back to 25 million years ago.

Cook Islands

There are chains of islands along the northern and western edges of the Pacific Ocean. Among these, the Cook Islands are made up of 15 coral and volcanic islands. Citrus fruit and copra production have developed alongside tourism.

Extreme Climates

Hottest place (Highest recorded temperature)	Oodnadatta, Australia 123°F (50.7°C)
Driest place (Lowest average rainfall)	Troudaninna, Australia 4.05 in (103 mm)
Coldest place (Lowest recorded temperature)	Charlotte Pass, Australia -9.4°F (-23°C)
Wettest place (Highest average rainfall)	Bellenden Ker, Australia 316.3 in (8,034 mm)

Fact File

Largest country	Australia
Smallest country	Nauru
Largest city	Sydney
Largest lake	Lake Eyre
Longest river	Murray-Darling

Wake Island (to US)
0 km 300 600
0 miles 300 600
International Date Line
MARSHALL ISLANDS
Bikini Atoll
Ratak Chain
lik Chain
Majuro Atoll
PACIFIC OCEAN
Kingman Reef (to US)
Palmyra Atoll (to US)
Teraina
Tabuarean (Fanning Island)
Kiritimati (Christmas Island)
Jarvis Island (to US)
Line Islands
Tarawa Atoll
Gilbeart Islands
Howland Island (to US)
Baker Island (to US)
NAURU
KIRIBATI
Phoenix Islands
Malden Island
Starbuck Island
TUVALU
Funafuti Atoll
Tokelau (to NZ)
Northern Cook Islands
Manihiki
Penrhyn
Millennium Island (Caroline Island)
Flint Island
OLOMON ISLANDS
Santa Cruz Islands
Banks Islands
piritu Santo
VANUATU
alekula
Efate
PORT-VILA
Erromango
Tanna
New Caledonia
NOUMÉA
New Caledonia (to France)
Wallis and Futuna (to France)
SAMOA
APIA
American Samoa (to US)
Samoa
PAGO PAGO
Vanua Levu
SUVA
Viti Levu
Lau Group
FIJI
TONGA
NUKU'ALOFA
Niue (to NZ)
Cook Islands (to NZ)
Southern Cook Islands
AVARUA
Rarotonga
Marquesas Islands
Society Islands
Tuamotu Islands
PAPEETE
Tahiti
French Polynesia (to France)
Mururoa
Îles Australes
Îles Gambier
Pitcairn, Henderson, Ducie & Oeno Islands (to UK)
PACIFIC OCEAN
Norfolk Island (to Australia)
Kermadec Islands (to NZ)
Polynesia
North Island
Tasman Sea
WELLINGTON
South Island
Southern Alps
NEW ZEALAND
Chatham Islands (to NZ)
Stewart Island
Auckland Islands (to NZ)

New Zealand

Two large mountainous islands form New Zealand's main land areas. The North Island, shown right, and the South Island are rich in grasslands, which are used for rearing sheep. Volcanoes are found on both islands, and many of them are still active.

Flags of the World

THE MAIN COUNTRIES and territories of the world have their own national flags, with a design relevant to that country. For example, the stars on the American flag represent the number of its member states.

Afghanistan
Asia

Albania
Europe

Algeria
Africa

Andorra
Europe

Angola
Africa

Antigua & Barbuda
North America

Argentina
South America

Armenia
Asia

Australia
Australasia & Oceania

Austria
Europe

Azerbaijan
Asia and Europe

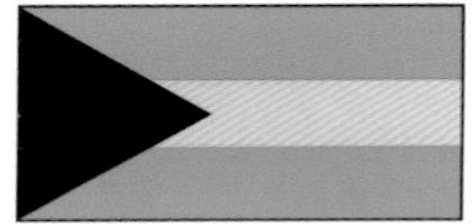

Bahamas
North America

Bahrain
Asia

Bangladesh
Asia

Barbados
North America

Belarus
Europe

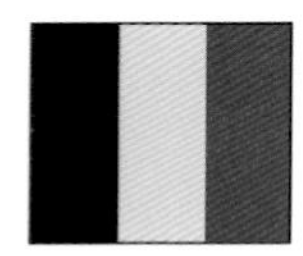

Belgium
Europe

Belize
North America

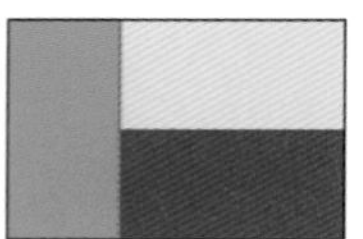

Benin
Africa

Bhutan
Asia

Bolivia
South America

Bosnia & Herzegovina
Europe

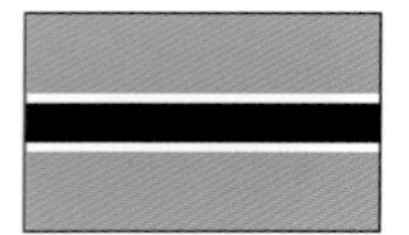

Botswana
Africa

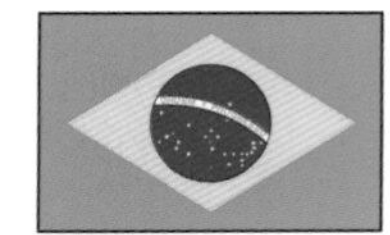

Brazil
South America

Brunei
Asia

Bulgaria
Europe

Burkina Faso
Africa

Burundi
Africa

Cabo Verde
Africa

Cambodia
Asia

Cameroon
Africa

Canada
North America

Central African Republic
Africa

Chad
Africa

Chile
South America

China
Asia

Colombia
South America

Comoros
Africa

Congo, Democratic Republic of the
Africa

Congo, Republic of the
Africa

Costa Rica
North America

Cote d'Ivoire
Africa

Croatia
Europe

Cuba
North America

Cyprus
Europe

Czechia
Europe

Denmark
Europe

Djibouti
Africa

Dominica
North America

Dominican Republic
North America

Ecuador
South America

Egypt
Africa

El Salvador
North America

Equatorial Guinea
Africa

Eritrea
Africa

Estonia
Europe

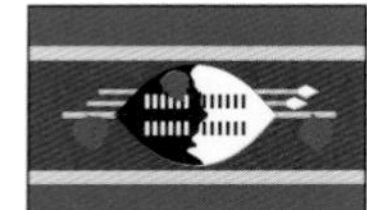
Eswatini
Africa

Ethiopia
Africa

Fiji
Australasia & Oceania

Finland
Europe

France
Europe

Gabon
Africa

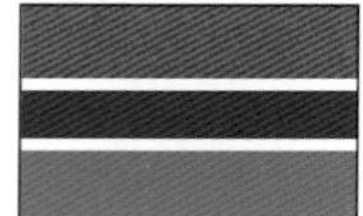
Gambia, The
Africa

Georgia
Asia

Germany
Europe

Ghana
Africa

Greece
Europe

Grenada
North America

Guatemala
North America

Guinea
Africa

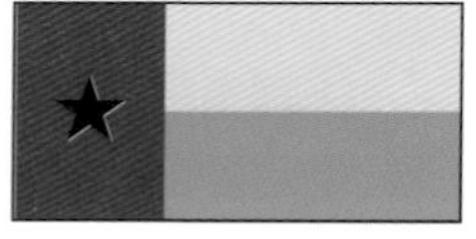
Guinea-Bissau
Africa

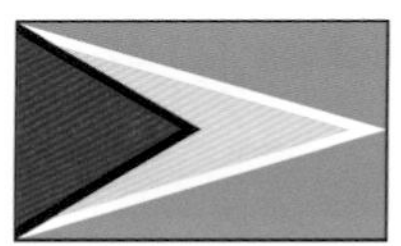
Guyana
South America

Haiti
North America

Honduras
North America

Hungary
Europe

Iceland
Europe

India
Asia

Indonesia
Asia

Iran
Asia

Iraq
Asia

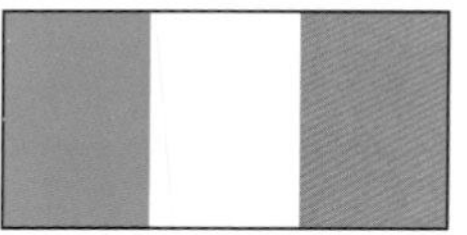
Ireland
Europe

Israel
Asia

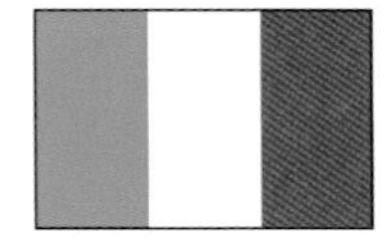
Italy
Europe

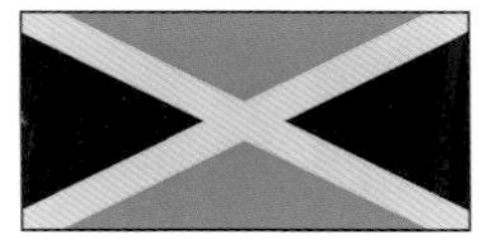
Jamaica
North America

Japan
Asia

Jordan
Asia

Kazakhstan
Asia

Kenya
Africa

Kiribati
Australasia & Oceania

Kosovo (disputed)
Europe

Kuwait
Asia

Kyrgyzstan
Asia

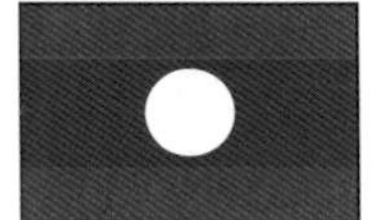
Laos
Asia

Latvia
Europe

Lebanon
Asia

Lesotho
Africa

Liberia
Africa

Libya
Africa

Liechtenstein
Europe

Lithuania
Europe

Luxembourg
Europe

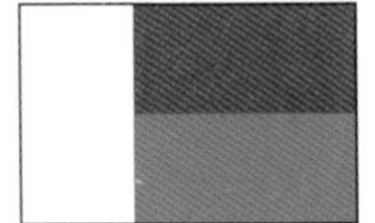
Madagascar
Africa

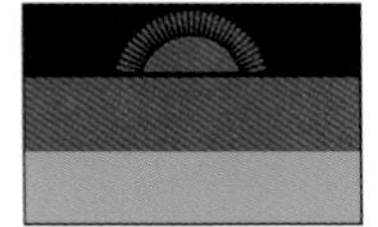
Malawi
Africa

Malaysia
Asia

Maldives
Asia

Mali
Africa

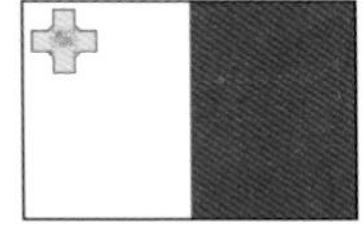
Malta
Europe

Marshall Islands
Australasia & Oceania

Mauritania
Africa

Mauritius
Africa

Mexico
North America

Micronesia
Australasia & Oceania

Moldova
Europe

Monaco
Europe

Mongolia
Asia

Montenegro
Europe

Morocco
Africa

Mozambique
Africa

Myanmar (Burma)
Asia

Namibia
Africa

Nauru
Australasia & Oceania

Nepal
Asia

Netherlands
Europe

New Zealand
Australasia & Oceania

Nicaragua
North America

Niger
Africa

Nigeria
Africa

North Korea
Asia

North Macedonia
Europe

Norway
Europe

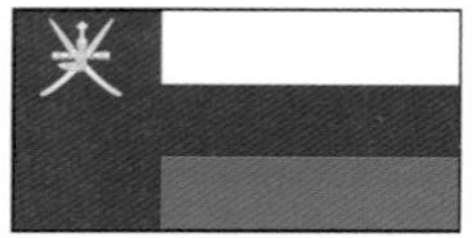
Oman
Asia

Pakistan
Asia

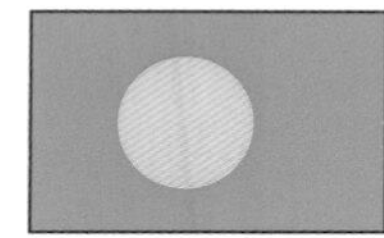
Palau
Australasia & Oceania

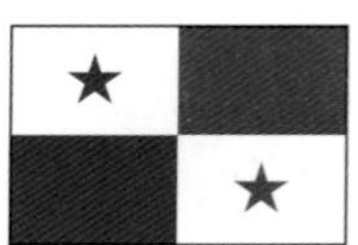
Panama
North America

Papua New Guinea
Australasia & Oceania

Paraguay
South America

Peru
South America

Philippines
Asia

Poland
Europe

Portugal
Europe

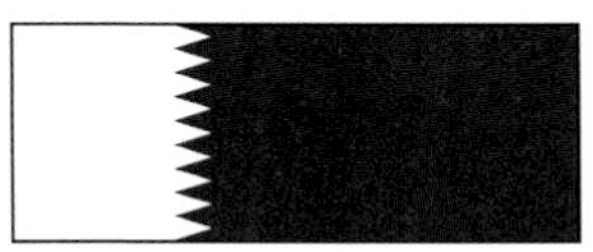

Qatar
Asia

Romania
Europe

Russia
Europe and Asia

Rwanda
Africa

St. Kitts & Nevis
North America

St. Lucia
North America

St. Vincent & the Grenadines
North America

Samoa
Australasia & Oceania

San Marino
Europe

São Tomé & Principe
Africa

Saudi Arabia
Asia

Senegal
Africa

Serbia
Europe

Seychelles
Africa

Sierra Leone
Africa

Singapore
Asia

Slovakia
Europe

Slovenia
Europe

Solomon Islands
Australasia & Oceania

Somalia
Africa

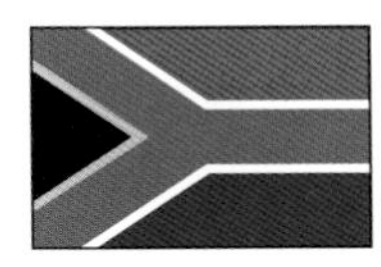

South Africa
Africa

South Korea
Asia

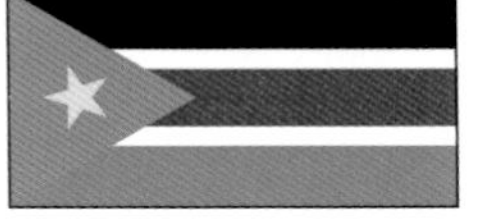

South Sudan
Africa

Spain
Europe

Sri Lanka
Asia

Sudan
Africa

Suriname
South America

Sweden
Europe

Switzerland
Europe

Syria
Asia

Tajikistan
Asia

Tanzania
Africa

Thailand
Asia

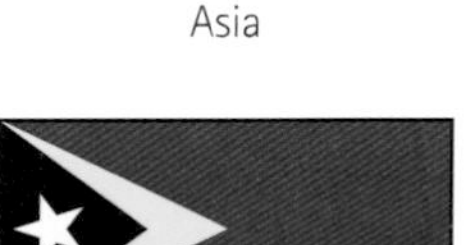
Timor-Leste
Asia

Togo
Africa

Tonga
Australasia & Oceania

Trinidad & Tobago
North America

Tunisia
Africa

Turkey
Asia and Europe

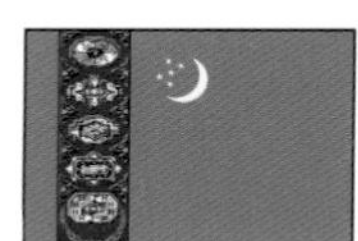
Turkmenistan
Asia

Tuvalu
Australasia & Oceania

Uganda
Africa

Ukraine
Europe

United Arab Emirates
Asia

United Kingdom
Europe

United States of America
North America

Uruguay
South America

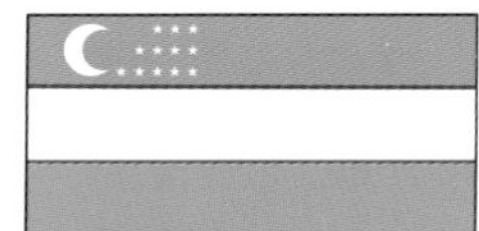
Uzbekistan
Asia

Vanuatu
Australasia & Oceania

Vatican City
Europe

Venezuela
South America

Vietnam
Asia

Yemen
Asia

Zambia
Africa

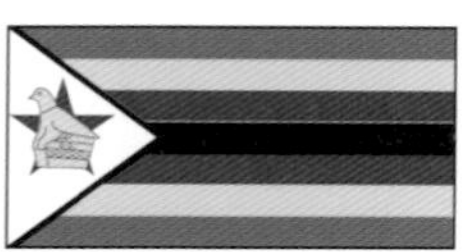
Zimbabwe
Africa

State Flags

Alabama

Alaska

Arizona

Arkansas

California

Colorado

Connecticut

Delaware

Florida

Georgia

Hawaii

Idaho

Illinois

Indiana

Iowa

Kansas

Kentucky

Louisiana

Maine

Maryland

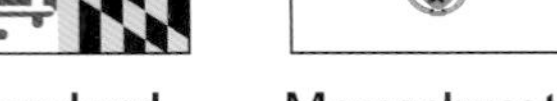

Massachusetts

Michigan

Minnesota

Mississippi

Missouri

Montana

Nebraska

Nevada

New Hampshire

New Jersey

New Mexico

New York

North Carolina

North Dakota

Ohio

Oklahoma

Oregon

Pennsylvania

Rhode Island

South Carolina

South Dakota

Tennessee

Texas

Utah

Vermont

Virginia

Washington

West Virginia

Wisconsin

Wyoming

District of Columbia

States of the USA

THE UNITED STATES OF AMERICA is made up of 50 states, including Alaska in the far north and Hawaii in the Pacific Ocean. The original 13 states on the East Coast were governed by Britain until independence in 1776. Today, each state has its own laws, but is ruled by the national government in Washington, DC.

States of the USA

(* indicates one of the original 13 states)

State	Capital	Date of entry into Union
Alabama \\,al-ə-'bam-ə\\	Montgomery \\mənt-'gəm-ə-rē, mänt-\\	1819
Alaska \\ə-'las-kə\\	Juneau \\'jü-nō, jü-'nō\\	1959
Arizona \\,ar-ə-'zō-nə\\	Phoenix \\'fē-niks\\	1912
Arkansas \\'är-kən-,sȯ\\	Little Rock \\'lit-l-,räk\\	1836
California \\,kal-ə-'fȯr-nyə\\	Sacramento \\,sak-rə-'ment-ō\\	1850
Colorado \\,käl-ə-'rad-ō, -'räd-\\	Denver \\'den-vər\\	1876
*Connecticut \\kə-'net-i-kət\\	Hartford \\'härt-fərd\\	1788
*Delaware \\'del-ə-,waər, -,weər\\	Dover \\'dō-vər\\	1787
Florida \\'flȯr-əd-ə\\	Tallahassee \\,tal-e-'has-ē\\	1845
*Georgia \\'jȯr-jə\\	Atlanta \\ət-'lant-ə, at-\\	1788
Hawaii \\hə-'wä-ē, -'wȯ-ē\\	Honolulu \\,hän-l-'ü-,lü, ,hōn-\\	1959
Idaho \\'īd-ə-,hō\\	Boise \\'bȯi-sē, -zē\\	1890
Illinois \\,il-ə-'nȯi\\	Springfield \\'spriŋ-,fēld\\	1818
Indiana \\,in-dē-'an-ə\\	Indianapolis \\,in-dē-ə-'nap-ə-ləs\\	1816
Iowa \\'ī-ə-wə\\	Des Moines \\di-'mȯin\\	1846
Kansas \\'kan-zəs\\	Topeka \\tə-'pē-kə\\	1861
Kentucky \\kən-'tək-ē\\	Frankfort \\'fraŋk-fərt\\	1792
Louisiana \\lü-,ē-zē-'an-ə, ,lü-ə-zē-\\	Baton Rouge \\,bat-n-'rüzh\\	1812
Maine \\'mān\\	Augusta \\ȯ-'gəs-tə, ə-\\	1820
*Maryland \\'mer-ə-lənd\\	Annapolis \\ə-'nap-ə-ləs\\	1788
*Massachusetts \\,mas-ə-'chü-səts, -zəts\\	Boston \\'bȯ-stən\\	1788
Michigan \\'mish-i-gən\\	Lansing \\'lan-siŋ\\	1837
Minnesota \\,min-ə-'sōt-ə\\	Saint Paul \\sānt-'pȯl, sənt-\\	1858
Mississippi \\,mis-ə-'sip-ē\\	Jackson \\'jak-sən\\	1817
Missouri \\mə-'zu̇r-ē, -'zu̇r-ə\\	Jefferson City \\,jef-ər-sən-\\	1821
Montana \\män-'tan-ə\\	Helena \\'hel-ə-nə\\	1889
Nebraska \\nə-'bras-kə\\	Lincoln \\'liŋ-kən\\	1867
Nevada \\nə-'vad-ə, -'väd-\\	Carson City \\,kärs-n-\\	1864
*New Hampshire \\-'hamp-shər, -,shir\\	Concord \\'käŋ-kərd\\	1788
*New Jersey \\-'jər-zē\\	Trenton \\'trent-n\\	1787
New Mexico \\-'mek-si-,kō\\	Santa Fe \\,sant-ə-'fā\\	1912
*New York \\-'yȯrk\\	Albany \\'ȯl-bə-nē\\	1788
*North Carolina \\-,kar-ə-'lī-nə\\	Raleigh \\'rȯ-lē, 'räl-ē\\	1789
North Dakota \\-də-'kōt-ə\\	Bismarck \\'biz-,märk\\	1889
Ohio \\ō-'hī-ō\\	Columbus \\kə-'ləm-bəs\\	1803
Oklahoma \\ō-klə-'hō-mə\\	Oklahoma City	1907
Oregon \\'ȯr-i-gən, 'är-\\	Salem \\'sā-ləm\\	1859

Glacier in Alaska

Arizona desert

Volcano in Hawaii

States of the USA

State	Capital	Date of entry into Union
*Pennsylvania \ˌpen-səl-ˈvān-yə\	Harrisburg \ˈhar-əs-ˌbərg\	1787
*Rhode Island \rō-ˈdī-lənd\	Providence \ˈpräv-ə-dəns, -ˌdens\	1790
*South Carolina \-ˌkar-ə-ˈlī-nə\	Columbia \kə-ˈləm-bē-ə\	1788
South Dakota \-də-ˈkōt-ə\	Pierre \ˈpiər\	1889
Tennessee \ˌten-ə-ˈsē\	Nashville \ˈnash-ˌvil, -vəl\	1796
Texas \ˈtek-səs, -siz\	Austin \ˈȯ-stən\	1845
Utah \ˈyü-ˌtȯ, -ˌtä\	Salt Lake City	1896
Vermont \vər-ˈmänt\	Montpelier \mänt-ˈpēl-yər, -ˈpil-\	1791
*Virginia \vər-ˈjin-yə\	Richmond \ˈrich-mənd\	1788
Washington \ˈwȯsh-iŋ-tən, ˈwäsh-\	Olympia \e-ˈlim-pē-ə\	1889
West Virginia \-vər-ˈjin-yə\	Charleston \ˈchärl-stən\	1863
Wisconsin \wis-ˈkän-sən\	Madison \ˈmad-ə-sən\	1848
Wyoming \wī-ˈō-miŋ\	Cheyenne \shī-ˈan, -ˈen\	1890

Farmland in Pennsylvania

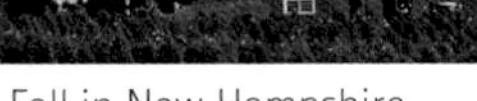
Fall in New Hampshire

Cattle drive in Texas

Devil's Tower, Wyoming

Provinces and Territories of Canada

Canada is the second-largest country in the world, occupying two-fifths of the North American continent. Divided into 10 provinces and three territories, Canada borders Alaska and the Pacific Ocean to the west, and the Atlantic Ocean to the east. Most of the population lives near the US border, around the Great Lakes.

Province or Territory	Capital
Alberta \al-ˈbert-ə\	Edmonton \ˈed-mən-tən\
British Columbia \-kə-ˈləm-bē-ə\	Victoria \vik-ˈtōr-ē-ə\
Manitoba \ˌman-ə-ˈtō-bə\	Winnipeg \ˈwin-ə-ˌpeg\
New Brunswick \-ˈbrənz-wik\	Fredericton \ˈfred-rik-tən\
Newfoundland and Labrador \ˈnü-fənd-lənd,-ənd-ˈlab-rə-ˌdȯr, ˈnyü-, -ˌland\	Saint John's \sānt-ˈjänz, sənt-\
Northwest Territories	Yellowknife \ˈyel-ə-ˌnīf\
Nova Scotia \ˌnō-və-ˈskō-shə\	Halifax \ˈhal-ə-ˌfaks\
Nunavut \ˈnu̇n-ə-vət\	Iqaluit \i-ˈkal-ü-it\
Ontario \än-ˈter-ē-ō, -ˈtar-\	Toronto \tə-ˈränt-ō\
Prince Edward Island \-ˌed-wərd-\	Charlottetown \ˈshär-let-ˌtau̇n\
Quebec \kwi-ˈbek, ki-\	Quebec
Saskatchewan \se-ˈskach-ə-wən, -ˌwän\	Regina \ri-ˈjī-nə\
Yukon \ˈyü-ˌkän-\	Whitehorse \ˈhwīt-ˌhȯrs, ˈwīt-\

Harbor in Quebec

Presidents of the USA

Presidents of the USA

Number	Name and Pronunciation of Surname	Life Dates	Birthplace	Term
1	George Washington \'wósh-iŋ-tən, 'wäsh-\	1732–1799	Virginia	1789–1797
2	John Adams \'ad-əmz\	1735–1826	Massachusetts	1797–1801
3	Thomas Jefferson \'jef-ər-sən\	1743–1826	Virginia	1801–1809
4	James Madison \'mad-ə-sən\	1751–1836	Virginia	1809–1817
5	James Monroe \mən-'rō\	1758–1831	Virginia	1817–1825
6	John Quincy Adams \'ad-əmz\	1767–1848	Massachusetts	1825–1829
7	Andrew Jackson \'jak-sən\	1767–1845	South Carolina	1829–1837
8	Martin Van Buren \van-'byu̇r-ən\	1782–1862	New York	1837–1841
9	William Henry Harrison \'har-ə-sən\	1773–1841	Virginia	1841
10	John Tyler \'tī-lər\	1790–1862	Virginia	1841–1845
11	James Knox Polk \'pōk\	1795–1849	North Carolina	1845–1849
12	Zachary Taylor \'ta-lər\	1784–1850	Virginia	1849–1850
13	Millard Fillmore \'fil-,mōr\	1800–1874	New York	1850–1853
14	Franklin Pierce \'pirs\	1804–1869	New Hampshire	1853–1857
15	James Buchanan \byü-'kan-ən\	1791–1868	Pennsylvania	1857–1861
16	Abraham Lincoln \'liŋ-kən\	1809–1865	Kentucky	1861–1865
17	Andrew Johnson \'jän-sən\	1808–1875	North Carolina	1865–1869
18	Ulysses Simpson Grant \'grant\	1822–1885	Ohio	1869–1877
19	Rutherford Birchard Hayes \'hāz\	1822–1893	Ohio	1877–1881
20	James Abram Garfield \'gär-,fēld\	1831–1881	Ohio	1881
21	Chester Alan Arthur \'är-thər\	1829–1886	Vermont	1881–1885
22	Grover Cleveland \'klēv-lənd\	1837–1908	New Jersey	1885–1889
23	Benjamin Harrison \'har-e-sen\	1833–1901	Ohio	1889–1893
24	Grover Cleveland \'klēv-lənd\	1837–1908	New Jersey	1893–1897
25	William McKinley \mə-'kin-lē\	1843–1901	Ohio	1897–1901
26	Theodore Roosevelt \'rō-zə-,velt\	1858–1919	New York	1901–1909
27	William Howard Taft \'taft\	1857–1930	Ohio	1909–1913
28	Woodrow Wilson \'wil-sən\	1856–1924	Virginia	1913–1921
29	William Gamaliel Harding \'härd-iŋ\	1865–1923	Ohio	1921–1923
30	Calvin Coolidge \'kü-lij\	1872–1933	Vermont	1923–1929
31	Herbert Clark Hoover \'hü-vər\	1874–1964	Iowa	1929–1933
32	Franklin Delano Roosevelt \'rō-zə-,velt\	1882–1945	New York	1933–1945
33	Harry S. Truman \'trü-mən\	1884–1972	Missouri	1945–1953
34	Dwight David Eisenhower \'īz-n-,hau̇-ər\	1890–1969	Texas	1953–1961
35	John Fitzgerald Kennedy \'ken-ə-dē\	1917–1963	Massachusetts	1961–1963
36	Lyndon Baines Johnson \'jän-sən\	1908–1973	Texas	1963–1969
37	Richard Milhous Nixon \'nik-sən\	1913–1994	California	1969–1974
38	Gerald Rudolph Ford \'fōrd\	1913–2006	Nebraska	1974–1977
39	Jimmy Carter \'kärt-ər\	1924–	Georgia	1977–1981
40	Ronald Wilson Reagan \'rā-gən\	1911–2004	Illinois	1981–1989
41	George Herbert Walker Bush \'bu̇sh\	1924–	Massachusetts	1989–1993
42	William Jefferson Clinton \'klin-tən\	1946–	Arkansas	1993–2001
43	George Walker Bush \'bu̇sh\	1946–	Connecticut	2001–2009
44	Barack Hussein Obama \ō-'bä-mə\	1961–	Hawaii	2009–2017
45	Donald John Trump \'trəmp\	1946–	New York	2017–

George Washington

Theodore Roosevelt

Woodrow Wilson

Barack Obama

\ə\ abut \ᵊ\ kitten \ər\ further \a\ mat \ā\ take \ä\ cot, cart \au̇\ out \ch\ chin \e\ pet \ē\ easy \g\ go \i\ tip \ī\ life \j\ job

Vice Presidents of the USA

Number	Name and Pronunciation of Surname	Life Dates	Birthplace	Term
1	John Adams \ˈad-əmz\	1735–1826	Massachusetts	1789–1797
2	Thomas Jefferson \ˈjef-ər-sən\	1743–1826	Virginia	1797–1801
3	Aaron Burr \ˈbər\	1756–1836	New Jersey	1801–1805
4	George Clinton \ˈklint-n\	1739–1812	New York	1805–1812
5	Elbridge Gerry \ˈger-ē\	1744–1814	Massachusetts	1813–1814
6	Daniel D. Tompkins \ˈtämp-kənz\	1774–1825	New York	1817–1825
7	John C. Calhoun \kal-ˈhün\	1782–1850	South Carolina	1825–1832
8	Martin Van Buren \van-ˈbyür-ən\	1782–1862	New York	1833–1837
9	Richard M. Johnson \ˈjän-sən\	1780–1850	Kentucky	1837–1841
10	John Tyler \ˈtī-lər\	1790–1862	Virginia	1841
11	George M. Dallas \ˈdal-əs\	1792–1864	Pennsylvania	1845–1849
12	Millard Fillmore \ˈfil-ˌmōr\	1800–1874	New York	1849–1850
13	William R. King \ˈkiŋ\	1786–1853	North Carolina	1853
14	John C. Breckinridge \ˈbrek-ən-rij\	1821–1875	Kentucky	1857–1861
15	Hannibal Hamlin \ˈham-lən\	1809–1891	Maine	1861–1865
16	Andrew Johnson \ˈjän-sən\	1808–1875	North Carolina	1865
17	Schuyler Colfax \ˈkōl-ˌfaks\	1823–1885	New York	1869–1873
18	Henry Wilson \ˈwil-sən\	1812–1875	New Hampshire	1873–1875
19	William A. Wheeler \ˈhwē-lər-, ˈwē\	1819–1887	New York	1877–1881
20	Chester A. Arthur \ˈär-thər\	1830–1886	Vermont	1881
21	Thomas A. Hendricks \ˈhen-driks\	1819–1885	Ohio	1885
22	Levi P. Morton \ˈmȯrt-n\	1824–1920	Vermont	1889–1893
23	Adlai E. Stevenson \ˈstē-vən-sən\	1835–1914	Kentucky	1893–1897
24	Garret A. Hobart \ˈhō-ˌbärt\	1844–1899	New Jersey	1897–1899
25	Theodore Roosevelt \ˈrō-zə-ˌvelt\	1858–1919	New York	1901
26	Charles W. Fairbanks \ˈfaər-ˌbaŋks, ˈfeər-\	1852–1918	Ohio	1905–1909
27	James S. Sherman \ˈshər-mən\	1855–1912	New York	1909–1912
28	Thomas R. Marshall \ˈmär-shəl\	1854–1925	Indiana	1913–1921
29	Calvin Coolidge \ˈkü-lij\	1872–1933	Vermont	1921–1923
30	Charles G. Dawes \ˈdȯz\	1865–1951	Ohio	1925–1929
31	Charles Curtis \ˈkərt-əs\	1860–1936	Kansas	1929–1933
32	John N. Garner \ˈgär-nər\	1868–1967	Texas	1933–1941
33	Henry A. Wallace \ˈwäl-əs\	1888–1965	Iowa	1941–1945
34	Harry S. Truman \ˈtrü-mən\	1884–1972	Missouri	1945
35	Alben W. Barkley \ˈbär-klē\	1877–1956	Kentucky	1949–1953
36	Richard M. Nixon \ˈnik-sən\	1913–1994	California	1953–1961
37	Lyndon B. Johnson \ˈjän-sən\	1908–1973	Texas	1961–1963
38	Hubert H. Humphrey \ˈhəm-frē\	1911–1978	South Dakota	1965–1969
39	Spiro T. Agnew \ˈag-nü, -nyü\	1918–1996	Maryland	1969–1973
40	Gerald R. Ford \ˈfōrd\	1913–2006	Nebraska	1973–1974
41	Nelson A. Rockefeller \ˈräk-i-ˌfel-ər\	1908–1979	Maine	1974–1977
42	Walter F. Mondale \ˈmän-ˌdāl\	1928–	Minnesota	1977–1981
43	George H. W. Bush \ˈbu̇sh\	1924–	Massachusetts	1981–1989
44	James Danforth Quayle \ˈkwāl\	1947–	Indiana	1989–1993
45	Albert Gore, Jr. \ˈgōr\	1948–	Washington, DC	1993–2001
46	Richard B. Cheney \ˈchē-nē\	1941–	Nebraska	2001–2009
47	Joseph R. Biden \ˈbī-dᵊn\	1942–	Pennsylvania	2009–2017
48	Michael R. Pence \ˈpens\	1959–	Indiana	2017–

John C. Calhoun

Hannibal Hamlin

Henry A. Wallace

James D. Quayle

Abbreviations

Abbreviations

Most of these abbreviations are shown in one form only. Variation in use of periods, in kind of type, and in capitalization is frequent and widespread (as mph, MPH, m.p.h., Mph).

abbr	abbreviation
AD	in the year of our Lord
adj	adjective
adv	adverb
AK	Alaska
AL, Ala.	Alabama
alt.	alternate, altitude
a.m., A.M.	before noon
Am., Amer.	America, American
amt.	amount
anon.	anonymous
ans.	answer
Apr.	April
AR	Arkansas
Ariz.	Arizona
Ark.	Arkansas
assn.	association
asst.	assistant
atty.	attorney
Aug.	August
ave	avenue
AZ	Arizona
Azerb	Azerbaijan
B.C.	before Christ
bet.	between
bldg.	building
blvd	boulevard
Br., Brit.	Britain, British
bro	brother
bros	brothers
bu.	bushel
c.	carat, cent, centimeter,century, chapter, cup
C	Celsius, centigrade
CA, Cal., Calif.	California
Can., Canad.	Canada, Canadian
cap.	capital, capitalize, capitalized
Capt.	captain
ch.	chapter, church
cm	centimeter
co.	company, county
CO	Colorado
COD	cash on delivery, collect on delivery
col.	column
Col.	colonel, Colorado
conj	conjunction
Conn.	Connecticut
ct.	cent, court
CT	Connecticut
cu.	cubic
CZ	Canal Zone
DC	District of Columbia
DDS	doctor of dental surgery
DE	Delaware
Dec.	December
Del.	Delaware
dept.	department
DMD	doctor of dental medicine
doz.	dozen
Dr.	doctor
DST	daylight saving time
E	east, eastern, excellent
ea.	each
e.g.	for example
Eng.	England, English
esp.	especially
etc.	et cetera
f.	female
F	Fahrenheit, false
FBI	Federal Bureau of Investigation
Feb.	February
fem.	feminine
FL, Fla.	Florida
Fri.	Friday
ft.	feet, foot, fort
g.	gram
G	good
Ga., GA	Georgia
gal.	gallon
GB	gigabyte
gen.	general
geog.	geographic, geographical, geography
gm	gram
gov.	governor
govt.	government
gt.	great
GU	Guam
HI	Hawaii
Herz.	Herzegovina
hr.	hour
H.S.	high school
ht.	height
Ia., IA	Iowa
ID	Idaho, identification
i.e.	that is
IL, Ill.	Illinois
in.	inch
IN	Indiana
inc.	incorporated
Ind.	Indian, Indiana
interj	interjection
intrans.	intransitive
Jan.	January
Jr., jun.	junior
Kan., Kans.	Kansas
KB	kilobyte
kg	kilogram
km	kilometer
KS	Kansas
Ky., KY	Kentucky
L	large, left, liter
La., LA	Louisiana
lb	pound
Lt.	lieutenant
ltd.	limited
m.	male, meter, mile
MA	Massachusetts
Maj.	major
Mar.	March
masc.	masculine

Mass.	Massachusetts
MB	megabyte
Md.	Maryland
MD	doctor of medicine, Maryland
Me., ME	Maine
Mex.	Mexican, Mexico
mg	milligram
MI, Mich.	Michigan
min.	minute
Minn.	Minnesota
Miss.	Mississippi
ml	milliliter
mm	millimeter
MN	Minnesota
mo.	month
Mo., MO	Missouri
Mon.	Monday
Mont.	Montana
mpg	miles per gallon
mph	miles per hour
MS	Mississippi
mt.	mount, mountain
MT	Montana
n	noun
N	north, northern
NC	North Carolina
ND, N. Dak.	North Dakota
NE	Nebraska, northeast
Neb., Nebr.	Nebraska
Nev.	Nevada
NH	New Hampshire
NJ	New Jersey
NM, N. Mex.	New Mexico
no.	north, number
Nov.	November
NV	Nevada
NW	northwest
NY	New York
NZ	New Zealand
O.	Ohio
obj.	object, objective
Oct.	October
off.	office
OH	Ohio
OK, Okla.	Oklahoma
OR, Ore., Oreg.	Oregon
oz.	ounce, ounces
p.	page
Pa., PA	Pennsylvania
part.	participle
pat.	patent
Penn., Penna.	Pennsylvania
pg.	page
pk.	park, peck
pkg.	package
pl.	plural
p.m., P.M.	afternoon
P.O.	post office
poss.	possessive
pp.	pages
pr.	pair
PR	Puerto Rico
prep	preposition
pres.	present, president
prof.	professor
pron	pronoun
P.S.	postscript, public school
pt.	pint, point
PTA	Parent-Teacher Association
PTO	Parent-Teacher Organization
qt.	quart
r.	right
rd.	road, rod
rec'd.	received
reg.	region, regular
res.	residence
Rev.	reverend
RFD	rural free delivery
RI	Rhode Island
rpm	revolutions per minute
RR	railroad
R.S.V.P.	please reply
rt.	right
rte.	route
Russ Fed	Russian Federation
S	south, southern, small, satisfactory
Sat	Saturday
SC	South Carolina
sci.	science
SD, S. Dak.	South Dakota
SE	southeast
sec.	second
Sept.	September
SI	International System of Units
sing.	singular
so.	south
sq	square
Sr.	senior, sister
SS	steamship
st.	state
St.	saint, street
Sun.	Sunday
SW	southwest
T	true
tbs., tbsp.	tablespoon
TD	touchdown
Tenn.	Tennessee
Tex.	Texas
Thurs., Thu.	Thursday
TN	Tennessee
trans.	transitive
tsp.	teaspoon
Tue., Tues.	Tuesday
TX	Texas
UN	United Nations
US	United States
USA	United States of America
USSR	Union of Soviet Socialist Republics
usu.	usual, usually
UT	Utah
v	verb
Va., VA	Virginia
var.	variant
vb.	verb
VG	very good
v.i.	verb intransitive
VI	Virgin Islands
vol.	volume, volunteer
VP	vice president
vs.	versus
v.t.	verb transitive
Vt., VT	Vermont
W	west, western
WA, Wash.	Washington
Wed.	Wednesday
WI, Wis., Wisc.	Wisconsin
wk.	week
wt.	weight
WV, W. Va.	West Virginia
www	World Wide Web
WY, Wyo.	Wyoming
yd.	yard
yr.	year

Pronunciation Guides

Continents and Nations of the World

Continent

Africa \ˈa-fri-kə\
Antarctica \ant-ˈärk-ti-kə, -ˈär-ti-\
Asia \ˈā-zhə, -shə\
Australia \ȯ-ˈstrāl-yə\
Europe \ˈyu̇r-əp\
North America \ˈnȯrth-ə-ˈmer-ə-kə\
South America \ˈsau̇th-ə-ˈmer-ə-kə\

Ocean

Arctic \ˈärk-tik, ˈärt-ik\
Atlantic \ət-ˈlan-tik, at-\
Indian \ˈin-dē-ən\
Pacific \pə-ˈsi-fik\
Southern \ˈsə-t͟hərn\

North America

Nation	Capital
Antigua and Barbuda \an-ˈtē-gə-ənd-bär-ˈbü-də\	Saint John's \sānt-ˈjänz, sənt-\
Bahamas \bə-ˈhä-məz\	Nassau \ˈna-ˌsȯ\
Barbados \bär-ˈbā-dōs\	Bridgetown \ˈbrij-ˌtau̇n\
Belize \bə-ˈlēz\	Belmopan \ˌbel-mō-ˈpän\
Canada \ˈka-nə-də\	Ottawa \ˈä-tə-ˌwä, -wə\
Costa Rica \ˌkȯ-stə-ˈrē-kə, ˌkō-\	San Jose \ˌsa-nə-ˈzā, -hō-ˈzā\
Cuba \ˈkyü-bə\	Havana \hə-ˈva-nə\
Dominica \dä-mə-ˈnē-kə\	Roseau \rō-ˈzō\
Dominican Republic \də-ˈmi-ni-kən-\	Santo Domingo \ˌsan-tə-də-ˈmiŋ-gō\
El Salvador \el-ˈsal-və-ˌdȯr\	San Salvador \san-ˈsal-və-ˌdȯr\
Grenada \grə-ˈnā-də\	Saint George's \sānt-ˈjȯr-jez, sənt-\
Guatemala \ˌgwä-tə-ˈmä-lə\	Guatemala City
Haiti \ˈhā-tē\	Port-au-Prince \ˌpȯrt-ō-ˈprins, -ˈprans\
Honduras \hän-ˈdu̇r-əs, -ˈdyu̇r-\	Tegucigalpa \tə-ˌgü-sə-ˈgal-pə\
Jamaica \jə-ˈmā-kə\	Kingston \ˈkiŋ-stən\
Mexico \ˈmek-si-ˌkō\	Mexico City
Nicaragua \ˌni-kə-ˈrä-gwə\	Managua \mə-ˈnä-gwä\
Panama \ˈpa-nə-ˌmä, -ˌmȯ\	Panama City
Saint Kitts & Nevis \sānt-ˈkits-ənd-ˈnē-vəs, sənt-\	Basseterre \bas-ˈter, bäs-\
Saint Lucia \sānt-ˈlü-shə, sənt-\	Castries \ˈkas-ˌtrēz, -ˌtrēs\
Saint Vincent and the Grenadines \sānt-ˈvin-sənt-ənd-t͟hə-ˌgre-nə-ˈdēnz, sənt-\	Kingstown \ˈkiŋz-ˌtau̇n\
Trinidad and Tobago \ˈtri-nə-ˌdad-ᵊn-tə-ˈbā-gō\	Port of Spain \-ˈspān\
United States of America \-ə-ˈmer-ə-kə\	Washington \ˈwȯ-shiŋ-tən, ˈwä-\

Bay

Gulf of Alaska \ˈgəlf, ə-ˈlas-kə\
Baffin Bay \ˈba-fən-ˌbā\
Hudson Bay \ˈhəd-sən-ˌbā\
Gulf of Mexico \ˈgəlf, ˈmek-si-ˌkō\

Islands

Aleutian Islands \ə-ˈlü-shən-ˌī-landz\
Anguilla \aŋ-ˈgwi-lə\
Aruba \ə-ˈrü-bə\
Baffin Island \ˈba-fən-ˌī-land\
Bonaire \bə-ˈner\
British Virgin Islands \ˈbri-tish-ˌvər-jən-ˌī-landz\
Cayman Islands \ˈkā-ˈman-ˌī-landz\
Curaçao \ˈkyu̇r-ə-ˌsō\
Ellesmere Island \ˈelz-ˌmir-ˈī-land\
Greenland \ˈgrēn-lənd\
Guadeloupe \ˈgwä-də-ˌlüp\
Martinique \ˌmär-tə-ˈnēk\
Montserrat \ˌmänt-sə-ˈrat\
Navassa Island \nə-ˈva-sə-ˌī-land\
Puerto Rico \ˌpȯr-tə-ˈrē-kō\
Queen Charlotte Islands \ˈkwēn-ˈshär-lət-ˌī-landz\
St Pierre and Miquelon \ˈsānt-ˈpir-and-ˈmi-kə-ˌlän\
Turks and Caicos Islands \ˌtərk-sən-ˈkā-kəs-ˌī-landz\
Vancouver Island \van-ˈkü-vər-ˌī-land\

Lakes

Great Bear Lake \ˈgrāt-ˈber-ˌlāk\
Great Slave Lake \ˈgrāt-ˈslāv-ˌlāk\
Lake Erie \ˈlāk-ˈir-ē\
Lake Huron \ˌlāk-ˈhyu̇r-ən\
Lake Michigan \ˌlāk-ˈmi-shi-gən\
Lake Nicaragua \ˌlāk-ˌni-kə-ˈrä-gwə\
Lake Ontario \ˌlāk-än-ˈter-ē-ō\
Lake Superior \ˌlāk-sü-ˈpir-ē-ər\
Lake Winnipeg \ˈlāk-ˈwi-nə-ˌpeg\

Rivers

Colorado \ˌkä-lə-ˈra-(ˌ)dō\
Mackenzie \mə-ˈken-zē\
Mississippi \ˌmi-sə-ˈsi-pē\
Missouri \mə-ˈzu̇r-ē\
Rio Grande \ˌrē-ō-ˈgrand\
St Lawrence \ˈsānt-ˈlȯr-ənts\

Seas

Beaufort \ˈbō-fərt\
Bering Sea \ˈbir-iŋ-ˌsē\

Strait

Davis Strait \ˈdā-vəs-ˌstrāt\

South America

Nation	Capital
Argentina \ˌär-jən-ˈtē-nə\	Buenos Aires \ˌbwā-nəs-ˈa-rēz\
Bolivia \bə-ˈli-vē-ə\	La Paz \lə-ˈpaz, -ˈpäz\
	Sucre \ˈsü-krā\
Brazil \brə-ˈzil\	Brasília \brə-ˈzil-yə\
Chile \ˈchi-lē\	Santiago \ˌsan-tē-ˈä-gō, ˌsän-\
	Valparaiso \ˌväl-pä-rä-ˈē-sō\
Colombia \kə-ˈləm-bē-ə\	Bogotá \ˌbō-gə-ˈtȯ, -ˈtä\
Ecuador \ˈek-wə-ˌdȯr\	Quito \ˈkē-tō\
Guyana \gī-ˈa-nə\	Georgetown \ˈjȯrj-ˌtau̇n\
Paraguay \ˈper-ə-ˌgwī, -ˌgwā\	Asunción \ə-ˌsün-sē-ˈōn\
Peru \pə-ˈrü\	Lima \ˈlē-mə\
Suriname \ˈsu̇r-ə-ˌnä-mə\	Paramaribo \ˌpa-rə-ˈma-rə-ˌbō\
Uruguay \ˈyu̇r-ə-ˌgwī, -ˌgwā\	Montevideo \ˌmän-tə-və-ˈdā-ō, -ˈvi-dē-ō\
Venezuela \ˌve-nə-ˈzwā-lə\	Caracas \kə-ˈra-kəs, -ˈrä-\

Europe

Nation	Capital
Albania \al-ˈbā-nē-ə\	Tirane \ti-ˈrä-nə\
Andorra \an-ˈdȯr-ə\	Andorra la Vella \-lä-ˈve-lə\
Austria \ˈȯ-strē-ə\	Vienna \vē-ˈe-nə\
Belarus \ˌbē-lə-ˈrüs, ˌbye-lə-\	Minsk \ˈminsk\
Belgium \ˈbel-jəm\	Brussels \ˈbrə-səlz\
Bosnia and Herzegovina \ˈbäz-nē-ə-ənd-ˌhert-sə-gō-ˈvē-nə\	Sarajevo \ˌsa-rə-ˈyā-vō\
Bulgaria \ˌbəl-ˈger-ē-ə\	Sofia \ˈsō-fē-ə, ˈsȯ-, sō-\
Croatia \krō-ˈā-shə\	Zagreb \ˈzä-ˌgreb\
Cyprus \ˈsī-prəs\	Nicosia \ˌni-kə-ˈsē-ə\
Czechia \ˈche-kē-ə\	Prague \ˈpräg\
Denmark \ˈden-ˌmärk\	Copenhagen \ˌkō-pən-ˈhā-gən, -ˈhä-\
Estonia \e-ˈstō-nē-ə\	Tallinn \ˈta-lən, ˈtä-\
Finland \ˈfin-lənd\	Helsinki \ˈhel-ˌsiŋ-kē, ˌhel-ˈ\
France \ˈfrans\	Paris \ˈpa-rəs\
Germany \ˈjər-mə-nē\	Berlin \bər-ˈlin\
Greece \ˈgrēs\	Athens \ˈa-thənz\
Hungary \ˈhəŋ-gə-rē\	Budapest \ˈbü-də-ˌpest\
Iceland \ˈīs-lənd, -ˌland\	Reykjavik \ˈrā-kyə-ˌvik, -ˌvēk\
Ireland \ˈīr-lənd\	Dublin \ˈdə-blən\
Italy \ˈi-tə-lē\	Rome \ˈrōm\
Kosovo (disputed) \ˈkȯ-sȯ-ˌvō, ˈkä-\	Pristina \ˈprēsh-tē-ˌnä, ˈprēsh-tē-nə\
Latvia \ˈlat-vē-ə\	Riga \ˈrē-gə\
Liechtenstein \ˈlik-tən-ˌstīn\	Vaduz \vä-ˈdüts\
Lithuania \ˌli-thə-ˈwā-nē-ə\	Vilnius \ˈvil-nē-əs\
Luxembourg \ˈlək-səm-ˌbərg\	Luxembourg
Malta \ˈmȯl-tə\	Valletta \və-ˈle-tə\
Moldova \mȯl-ˈdō-və\	Chisinau \ˌkē-shē-ˈnau̇\
Monaco \ˈmä-nə-ˌkō\	Monaco
Montenegro \ˌmän-tə-ˈnē-grō\	Podgorica \ˈpȯd-ˌgȯr-ēt-sä\
Netherlands \ˈne-t͟hər-ləndz\	Amsterdam \ˈam-stər-ˌdam\
	The Hague \t͟hə-ˈhāg\
North Macedonia \ˈnȯrth-ˌma-sə-ˈdō-nē-ə\	Skopje \ˈskȯp-ˌyā, -yə\
Norway \ˈnȯr-ˌwā\	Oslo \ˈäz-lō, ˈäs-\
Poland \ˈpō-lənd\	Warsaw \ˈwȯr-ˌsȯ\
Portugal \ˈpȯr-chi-gəl\	Lisbon \ˈliz-bən\
Romania \ru̇-ˈmā-nē-ə, rō-\	Bucharest \ˈbü-kə-ˌrest\
Russia \ˈrə-shə\	Moscow \ˈmäs-ˌkō, -ˌkau̇\
San Marino \ˌsan-mə-ˈrē-nō\	San Marino
Serbia \ˈsər-bē-ə\	Belgrade \ˈbel-ˌgrād, -ˌgräd\
Slovakia \slō-ˈvä-kē-ə\	Bratislava \ˌbrä-tə-ˈslä-və\
Slovenia \slō-ˈvē-nē-ə\	Ljubljana \lē-ˌü-blē-ˈä-nə\
Spain \ˈspān\	Madrid \mə-ˈdrid\
Sweden \ˈswē-dᵊn\	Stockholm \ˈstäk-ˌhōm, -ˌhōlm\
Switzerland \ˈswit-sər-lənd\	Bern \ˈbərn, ˈbern\
Ukraine \yü-ˈkrān, ˈyü-ˌ\	Kiev \ˈkē-ˌef, -ˌev\
United Kingdom	London \ˈlən-dən\
Vatican City \ˈva-ti-kən-\	

Islands
Aland \'ō-,län\
Balearic Islands \,ba-lē-'a-rik-'ī-ləndz\
Channel Islands \'cha-nəl-,ī-ləndz\
Corsica \'kȯr-si-kə\
Crete \'krēt\
Faroe Islands \'fer-(,)ō-'ī-ləndz\
Gotland \'gȯt-,länt\
Ibiza \ē-'vē-thä\
Ionian Islands \ī-'ō-nē-ən\
Isle of Man \'īl-əv-'man\
Majorca \mə-'jȯr-kə\
Minorca \mə-'nȯr-kə\
Orkney Islands \'ȯrk-nē-,ī-ləndz\
Outer Hebrides \'au̇-tər-'he-brə-,dēz\
Sardinia \sär-'di-nē-ə\
Shetland Islands \'shet-lənd-,ī-ləndz\
Sicily \'si-sə-lē\

Lakes
Ladoga \'la-də-gə\
Onega \,ə-'nye-gə\
Vanern \'va-nərn\

Rivers
Danube \'dan-yüb\
Dnieper \'nē-pər\
Dniester \'nē-stər\
Ebro \'ā-,brō\
Elbe \'el-bə\
Loire \lə-'wär\
Northern Dvina \'nȯr-thərn-dvē-'nä\
Rhone \'rōn\
Seine \'sān\
Volga \'väl-gə\

Seas
Azov \ə-'zȯf\
Baltic \'bȯl-tik\
Barents \'ba-rənts\
Ionian \ī-'ō-nē-ən\
Norwegian \nȯr-'wē-jən\
Tyrrhenian \tə-'rē-nē-ən\

Also on the map of Europe:
Basque Country \'bäsk-,kən-trē\
Bay of Biscay \'bā-əv-'bis-,kā\
Caucasus \'kȯ-kə-səs\
Ceuta \'thā-ü-,tä\
Gibraltar \jə-'brȯl-tər\
Gulf of Bothnia \'gəlf-əv-'bäth-nē-ə\
Kaliningrad \kə-'lē-nən-,grad\

Asia

Nation	Capital
Afghanistan \af-'ga-nə-,stan\	Kabul \'kä-bəl, kə-'bül\
Armenia \är-'mē-nē-ə\	Yerevan \,yer-ə-'vän\
Azerbaijan \,a-zər-,bī-'jän\	Baku \bä-'kü\
Bahrain \bä-'rān\	Manama \mə-'na-mə\
Bangladesh \,bän-glə-'desh, ,baŋ-\	Dhaka \'da-kə, 'dä-\
Bhutan \bü-'tan, -'tän\	Thimphu \thim-'pü\
Brunei \bru̇-'nī, 'brü-,nī\	Bandar Seri Begawan \,bən-dər-,ser-ē-bə-'gä-wən\
Cambodia \kam-'bō-dē-ə\	Phnom Penh \'nȯm-'pen, pə-'näm-\
China \'chī-nə\	Beijing \'bā-'jiŋ\
Georgia, Republic of \-'jȯr-jə\	Tbilisi \tə-'blē-sē\
India \'in-dē-ə\	New Delhi \-'de-lē\
Indonesia \,in-də-'nē-zhə, -shə\	Jakarta \jə-'kär-tə\
Iran \i-'ran, i-'rän, ī-'ran\	Tehran \,tā-ə-'ran, te-'ran, -'rän\
Iraq \i-'räk, i-'rak\	Baghdad \'bag-,dad\
Israel \'iz-rē-əl\	Jerusalem \jə-'rü-sə-ləm, -zə-\
Japan \jə-'pan, ji-, ja-\	Tokyo \'tō-kē-ō\
Jordan \'jȯr-dᵊn\	Amman \a-'män, -'man\
Kazakhstan \,ka-zak-'stan, ,kä-zäk-'stän\	Nur-Sultan \,nu̇r-su̇l-'tän\
Korea, North \-kə-'rē-ə\	Pyongyang \pē-'ȯŋ-'yäŋ\
Korea, South	Seoul \'sōl\
	Sejong City \'sā-'jȯŋ\
Kuwait \kə-'wāt\	Kuwait
Kyrgyzstan \,kir-gi-'stan, -'stän\	Bishkek \bish-'kek\
Laos \'lau̇s, 'lä-,ōs, 'lä-ōs\	Vientiane \vyen-'tyän\
Lebanon \'le-bə-nən, -,nän\	Beirut \bā-'rüt\
Malaysia \mə-'lā-zhə, -shə\	Kuala Lumpur \,kwä-lə-'lu̇m-,pu̇r, -'ləm-\
	Putrajaya \,pü-trə-'jī-ə\
Maldives \'mȯl-,dēvz, -,dīvz\	Male \'mä-lē\
Mongolia \män-'gōl-yə, mäŋ-\	Ulaanbaatar \,ü-,län-'bä-,tȯr\
Myanmar (Burma) \'myän-,mär\	Nay Pyi Taw \'ne-pyē-,dȯ\
Nepal \ne-'pȯl, -'päl, -'pal\	Kathmandu \,kat-,man-'dü\
Oman \ō-'män, -'man\	Muscat \'məs-,kat, -kət\
Pakistan \,pa-ki-'stan, ,pä-ki-'stän\	Islamabad \is-'läm-ə-,bad\
Philippines \,fi-lə-'pēnz\	Manila \mə-'ni-lə\
Qatar \'kä-tər, 'gä-, 'gə-\	Doha \'dō-hä\
Saudi Arabia \,sau̇-dē-ə-'rā-bē-ə, ,sȯ-, sä-,ü-\	Riyadh \rē-'äd\
Singapore \,siŋ-ə-,pȯr, -gə-\	Singapore
Sri Lanka \srē-'läŋ-kə, shrē-\	Colombo \kə-'ləm-bō\
	Sri Jayewardenepura Kotte \,srē-,jä-yä-wär-,dā-nā-'pü-rə-'kō-tā\
Syria \'sir-ē-ə\	Damascus \də-'ma-skəs\
Tajikistan \tä-,jē-ki-'stan, -'stän\	Dushanbe \dü-'sham-bə, -'shäm-\
Thailand \'tī-,land, -lənd\	Bangkok \'baŋ-,käk\
Timor-Leste \'tē-,mȯr-'lesh-,tā\	Dili \'di-lē\
Turkey \'tər-kē\	Ankara \'aŋ-kə-rə\
Turkmenistan \tərk-,me-ni-'stan, -'stän\	Ashgabat \'ash-gə-,bät\
United Arab Emirates \-'e-mər-əts, -,āts\	Abu Dhabi \,ä-,bü-'dä-bē\
Uzbekistan \u̇z-,be-ki-'stan, -'stän\	Tashkent \tash-'kent, 'täsh-\
Vietnam \vē-'et-'näm, ,vē-ət-, -'nam\	Hanoi \ha-'nȯi, hə-\
Yemen \'ye-mən\	Sanaa \sa-'nä\

Desert
Gobi \'gō-bē\

Islands
Andaman Islands \'an-də-mən-'ī-ləndz\
Borneo \'bȯr-nē-,ō\
Flores \'flȯr-əs\
Hainan \'hī-'nän\
Luzon \lü-'zän\
Mindanao \,min-də-'nä-ō\
Moluccas \mə-'lə-kəz\
Nicobar Islands \'ni-kə-,bür-'ī-ləndz\
Sakhalin \'sa-kə-,lēn\
Socotra \sə-'kō-trə\
Sumatra \su̇-'mä-trə\

Mountain ranges
Himalayas \,him-ə-'lā-əz\
Kunlun Mountains \'kün-'lün-,mau̇n-tᵊnz\

Rivers
Aldan \al-'dün\
Amur \ä-'mu̇r\
Angara \ən-,gə-'rä\
Argun \'är-'gün\
Brahmaputra \,bräm-ə-'pü-trə\
Euphrates \yu̇-'frā-tēz\
Ganges \'gan-,jēz\
Godavari \gō-'dä-və-rē\
Indigirka \,in-də-'gir-kə\
Irrawaddy \,ir-ə-'wäd-ē\
Irtysh \ir-'tish\
Kolyma \,kə-lə-'mü\
Krishna \'krish-na\

Rivers contd.
Lena \'lē-nə\
Mekong \'mā-'kȯŋ\
Narmada \nər-'mə-də\
Ob \'äb\
Salween \'sal-,wēn\
Syr Darya \sir-dər-'yä\
Tarim He \'dä-'rēm-,hē\
Tigris \tī-grəs\
Ural \'yu̇r-əl\
Vitim \və-'tēm\
Yangon \,yän-gōn\
Yangtze \'yaŋ-'sē\
Yenisey \,yi-ni-'sā\

Seas
Aral Sea \'a-rəl-,sē\
Kara Sea \'kär-ə-,sē\
Laptev Sea \'lap-,tēf-,sē\
Sulawesi \,sü-lə-'wā-sē\

Also on the map of Asia:
Arabian Peninsula \ə-'rā-bē-ən-pə-nin-sə-lə\
Bay of Bengal \,bā-əv-ben-'gȯl\
Gulf of Aden \'gəlf-əv-'ä-dᵊn\
Hong Kong \'häŋ-,käŋ, -'käŋ; 'hȯŋ-,kȯŋ,-'kȯŋ\
Macao \mə-'kau̇\
Gulf of Oman \'gəlf-əv-ō-män\
Kamchatka \kam-'chat-kə\
Plateau of Tibet \pla-'tō-əv-tə-'bet\
West Papua

Africa

Nation	Capital
Algeria \al-'jir-ē-ə\	Algiers \al-'jirz\
Angola \aŋ-'gō-lə, an-\	Luanda \lü-'an-də\
Benin \be-'nin, -'nēn\	Porto-Novo \,pȯr-tə-'nō-vō\
Botswana \bät-'swän-ə\	Gaborone \,gä-bə-'rōn\
Burkina Faso \bu̇r-'kē-nə-'fäs-ō\	Ouagadougou \,wä-gä-'dü-(,)gü\
Burundi \bu̇-'rün-dē\	Gitega \gē-'tā-gä\
Cabo Verde \,kä-bü-'ver-də\	Praia \'prī-ə\
Cameroon \,kam-ə-'rün\	Yaoundé \yau̇n-'dā\
Central African Republic	Bangui \bäŋ-'gē\
Chad \'chad\	N'Djaména \ən-jä-'mā-nä\
Comoros \'kä-mə-,rōz\	Moroni \mȯ-'r ō-nē\
Congo, Democratic Republic of \-'käŋ-gō\	Kinshasa \kin-'shä-sə\
Congo, Republic of the	Brazzaville \'bra-zə-,vil\
Cote d'Ivoire \,kōt-dē-'vwär\	Yamoussoukro \,yä-mə-'sü-krō\
Djibouti \jə-'bü-tē\	Djibouti
Egypt \'ē-jəpt\	Cairo \'kī-rō\
Equatorial Guinea \-'gi-nē\	Malabo \mä-'lä-bō\
Eritrea \,er-i-'trē-ə, -'trā-\	Asmara \az-'mä-rə, -'ma-\
Eswatini \,e-swä-'tē-nē\	Mbabane \,em-bə-'bän\
	Lobamba \lō-'bäm-bə\
Ethiopia \,ē-thē-'ō-pē-ə\	Addis Ababa \'ä-dis-'ä-bä-,bä\
Gabon \ga-'bōn\	Libreville \'lē-brə-,vil, -,vēl\
The Gambia \thə-'gam-bē-ə\	Banjul \'bän-,jül\
Ghana \'gä-nə, 'ga-\	Accra \ə-'krä\
Guinea \'gi-nē\	Conakry \'kä-nə-krē\
Guinea-Bissau \,gi-nē-bi-'sau̇\	Bissau \bi-'sau̇\
Kenya \'ken-yə, 'kēn-\	Nairobi \nī-'rō-bē\
Lesotho \lə-'sō-tō\	Maseru \'ma-zə-,rü\
Liberia \lī-'bir-ē-ə\	Monrovia \mən-'rō-vē-ə\
Libya \'li-bē-ə\	Tripoli \'tri-pə-lē\
Madagascar \,ma-də-'ga-skər\	Antananarivo \,an-tə-,na-nə-'rē-vō\
Malawi \mə-'lä-wē\	Lilongwe \li-'lȯŋ-wā\

Mali \'mä-lē, 'ma-\	Bamako \,bä-mə-'kō\
Mauritania \,mȯr-ə-'tā-nē-ə\	Nouakchott \nu̇-'äk-,shät\
Mauritius \mȯ-'ri-shē-əs\	Port Louis \-'lü-əs, -lü-ē, -lu̇-'ē\
Morocco \mə-'rä-kō\	Rabat \rə-'bät\
Mozambique \,mō-zəm-'bēk\	Maputo \mä-'pü-tō\
Namibia \nə-'mi-bē-ə\	Windhoek \'vint-,hu̇k\
Niger \'nī-jər\	Niamey \'nyä-mā\
Nigeria \nī-'jir-ē-ə\	Abuja \ä-'bü-jä\
Rwanda \ru̇-'än-də\	Kigali \ki-'gä-lē\
São Tomé and Príncipe \,sau̇-tə-'mā-ənd-'prin-sə-pə\	São Tomé
Senegal \,se-ni-'gȯl\	Dakar \'da-,kär\
Seychelles \sā-'shelz, -'shel\	Victoria \vik-'tȯr-ē-ə\
Sierra Leone \sē-,er-ə-lē-'ōn\	Freetown \'frē-,tau̇n\
Somalia \sō-'mä-lē-ə\	Mogadishu \,mō-gə-'dē-shü, -'di-\
South Africa, Republic of \-'a-fri-kə\	Pretoria \pri-'tȯr-ē-ə\
	Cape Town \'kāp-,tau̇n\
	Bloemfontein \'blüm-fən-,tān, -,fän-\
South Sudan	Juba \'jü-bə, -,bä\
Sudan \sü-'dan, -'dän\	Khartoum \kär-'tüm\
Tanzania \,tan-zə-'nē-ə\	Dodoma \dō-'dō-mä\
Togo \'tō-gō\	Lomé \lō-'mā\
Tunisia \tü-'nē-zhə, tyü-\	Tunis \'tü-nəs, 'tyü-\
Uganda \yü-'gan-də, -'gän-\	Kampala \käm-'pä-lə\
Zambia \'zam-bē-ə\	Lusaka \lü-'sä-kə\
Zimbabwe \zim-'bä-bwē\	Harare \hə-'rä-,rā\

Lakes	Rivers
Albert \'al-bərt\	Benue \'bā-nwā\
Chad \'chad\	Limpopo \lim-'pō-'pō\
Nasser \'nä-sər\	Niger \nī-jər\
Nyasa \nī-'a-sə\	Nile \'nīl\
Tanganyika \,tan-gə-'nyē-kə\	Senegal \,se-ni-'gȯl\
Victoria \vik-'tȯr-ē-ə\	Ubangi \ü-'baŋ-gē\
Volta \'väl-tə\	Zambezi \zam-'bē-zē\

Australasia and Oceania \'ō-shē-'an-ē-ə, -'än-\
(group of islands in the Pacific)

Nation	Capital
Australia \ȯ-'strāl-yə\	Canberra \'kan-bə-rə, -,ber-ə\
State	
New South Wales \'nü-,sau̇th-'wālz\	Sydney \'sid-nē\
Queensland \'kwēnz-land\	Brisbane \'briz-bən\
South Australia \sau̇th-ȯ-'strāl-yə\	Adelaide \'a-də-,lād\
Tasmania \taz-'mā-nē-ə\	Hobart \'hō-,bärt\
Victoria \vik-'tȯr-ē-ə\	Melbourne \'mel-bərn\
Western Australia \,we-stərn-ȯ-'strāl-yə\	Perth \'pərth\
Territory	
Australian Capital Territory	
Northern Territory	Darwin \'där-wən\
New Zealand \'nü-'zē-lənd\	Wellington \'we-liŋ-tən\

South Pacific Islands	Capital
American Samoa \-sə-'mō-ə\	Pago Pago \'päŋ-ō-'päŋ-ō\
Auckland Islands \'ȯ-klənd-,ī-ləndz\	
Austral Islands \'ȯ-strəl-,ī-ləndz\	
Babelthuap \,bä-bəl-'tü-,äp\	
Baker and Howland Islands \'bā-kər-ənd-,hau̇-lənd-ī-ləndz\	
Bikini Atoll \bi-'kē-nē-,a-tȯl\	
Bougainville Island \'bü-gən-,vil-'ī-lənd\	
Caroline Islands \'ka-rə-,līn-,ī-ləndz\	
Chatham Islands \'cha-təm-,ī-ləndz\	
Chuuk \'chu̇k\	
Cook Islands	Avarua \,ä-vä-'rü-ä\
Éfaté \ā-'fä-tā\	
Erromango \,er-ō-'mäŋ-gō\	
Fiji \'fē-,jē\	Suva \'sü-və\
French Polynesia \'french-,pä-lə-'nē-zhə\	
Gambier Islands \'gam-,bir-'ī-ləndz\	
Kermadec Islands \ker-'ma-dək-,ī-ləndz\	
Kiribati \'kir-ə-,bas\	Tarawa \tə-'rä-wə\
Kiritimati \kə-'ri-sməs\	
Kosrae \'kȯs-,rī\	
Lau Group \'lau̇-,grüp\	
Lord Howe Islands \'lȯrd-,hau̇-,ī-ləndz\	
Malden Island \'mȯl-dən-,ī-lənd\	
Malekula \,mä-lā-'kü-lä\	
Manihiki \,mä-nē-'hē-kē\	
Mariana Islands \,mer-ē-'a-nə-,ī-ləndz\	
Marshall Islands \'mär-shəl-\	Majuro \mə-'ju̇r-ō\
Melanesia \,me-lə-'nē-zhə\	
Micronesia \,mī-krə-'nē-zhə\	Palikir \,pä-lē-'kir\
Mururoa \,mü-rü-'rō-ä\	
Nauru \nä-'ü-rü\	
Norfolk Island \'nȯr-fək-,ī-lənd\	
Northern Mariana Islands \'nȯr-t͟hərn-,mer-ē-'a-nə-,ī-ləndz\	
Palau \pə-'lau̇\	Ngerulmud \ne-'ru̇l-mu̇d\
Palmyra Atoll \pal-'mī-rə-,a-tȯl\	
Papua New Guinea \'pa-pyə-wə-nü-'gi-nē, 'pä-pə-wə-, -nyü-\	Port Moresby \-'mȯrz-bē\
Penrhyn \'pen-,rin\	
Phoenix Islands \'fē-niks-,ī-ləndz\	
Pitcairn Island \'pit-,kern-'ī-lənd\	
Pohnpei \'pōn-,pā\	
Ralik Chain \'rä-lik-,chān\	
Rarotonga \,ra-rə-'täŋ-gə\	
Ratak Chain \'rä-,täk-,chān\	
Saipan \sī-'pan\	
Samoa \sə-'mō-ə\	Apia \ə-'pē-ə\
Santa Cruz Islands \,san-tə-'krüz-,ī-ləndz\	
Solomon Islands \'sä-lə-mən-'ī-ləndz\	Honiara \,hō-nē-'är-ə\
Starbuck Island \'stär-,bək-,ī-lənd\	
Stewart Island \'stü-ərt-,ī-lənd\	
Tabuaeran \tə-,bü-ə-'er-ən\	
Tahiti \tə-'hē-tē\	Papeete \,pä-pā-'ā-tā\
Tanna \'tä-nä\	
Teraina \te-'rī-nə\	
Tokelau \'tō-kə-,lau̇\	
Tonga \'täŋ-gə\	Nuku'alofa \,nü-kü-ä-'lō-fə\
Tuvalu \tü-'vä-lü\	Funafuti \,fü-nə-'fü-tē\
Vanua Levu \,vän-,wä-'lā-,vü\	
Vanuatu \,van-,wä-'tü\	Port-Vila \pȯrt-'vē-lə\
Viti Levu \'vē-tē-'lā-,vü\	
Wallis and Futuna \'wä-ləs-ənd-fə-'tü-nə\	
Yap \'yap\	

Deserts

Gibson Desert \gib-sən-'de-zərt\
Great Sandy Desert \'grāt-,san-dē-'de-zərt\
Great Victoria Desert \'grāt-vik-,tȯr-ē-ə-'de-zərt\
Simpson Desert \'simp-sən-,de-zərt\
Tanami Desert \tə-'nä-mē-,de-zərt\
Nullarbor Plain \'nəl-ə-,bȯr-'plān\

Also on the map of Australasia and Oceania:

Arnhem Land \'är-nəm-,land\
Bairiki \'bī-,rē-kē\
Cape York Peninsula \'kāp-yȯrk-pe-'nin-sə-lə\
Espiritu Santo \e-'spē-rē-,tü-'san-tō\
Fongafale \,fōŋ-gä-'fä-lā\
Foveaux Strait \'fō-vō-,strāt\
Great Australian Bight \'grāt-ȯ-'strāl-yən-,bīt\
Great Barrier Reef \'grāt-,ber-ē-ər-,rēf\
Gulf of Carpentaria \'gəlf-əv-,kär-pən-'ter-ē-ə\
Hamersley Range \'ha-mərz-lē-,rānj\
Kimberly Plateau \'kim-bər-lē-pla-,tō\
Murray \'mər-ē\
New Caledonia \,nü-,ka-lə-'dō-nyə\
Nouméa \nü-'mā-ə\
Torres Strait \'tȯr-əs-,strāt\
Uluru \ü-'lü-rü\

Signs and Symbols

Mathematics

+	plus; positive ⟨a+b=c⟩
−	minus; negative
±	plus or minus ⟨the square root of $4a^2$ is ±2a⟩
×	multiplied by; times ⟨6×4=24⟩ — also indicated by placing a dot between the numbers ⟨6 . 4=24⟩
÷ *or* :	divided by ⟨24÷6=4⟩— also indicated by writing the divisor under the dividend with a line between ⟨$\frac{24}{6}$ =4⟩ or by writing the divisor after the dividend with a diagonal between ⟨3/8⟩
=	equals ⟨6+2=8⟩
≠ *or* ≠	is not equal to
>	is greater than ⟨6>5⟩
<	is less than ⟨3<4⟩
≧ *or* ≥	is greater than or equal to
≦ *or* ≤	is less than or equal to
≯	is not greater than
≮	is not less than
≈	is approximately equal to
:	is to; the ratio of
∴	therefore
∞	infinity
∠	angle; the angle ⟨∠ABC⟩
∟	right angle ⟨∟ABC⟩
⊥	the perpendicular; is perpendicular to AB⊥CD⟩
∥	parallel; is parallel to ⟨AB∥CD⟩
⊙ *or* ○	circle
⌒	arc of a circle
△	triangle
□	square
▭	rectangle
√	square root ⟨ as in √4=2⟩
( )	parentheses — indicate that the quantities enclosed by them are to be taken together
[ ]	brackets — indicate that the quantities enclosed by them are to be taken together
{ }	braces — indicate that the quantities enclosed by them are to be taken together
π	pi; the number 3.14159265+; the ratio of the circumference of a circle to its diameter
°	degree ⟨60°⟩
′	minute(s); foot (feet) ⟨30′⟩
″	second(s); inch(es) ⟨30″⟩
^{2}, ^{3}, etc.	— used as exponents placed above and at the right of an expression to indicate that it is raised to a power indicated by the figure ⟨a^2 is the square of a⟩
∪	union of two sets
∩	intersection of two sets
⊂	is included in, is a subset of
⊃	contains as a subset
∈ or ∊	is an element of
∉	is not an element of
Λ or 0 or ∅ or { }	empty set

Astronomy

⊙	the sun; Sunday
◐, ☾, ☽	the moon; Monday
●	new moon
☽, ◐, 🌛	first quarter
○, 🌝	full moon
☾, ◑, 🌜	last quarter
☿	Mercury; Wednesday
♀	Venus; Friday
⊕, ⊖, ♁	the earth
♂	Mars; Tuesday
♃	Jupiter; Thursday
♄	Saturn; Saturday
⛢	Uranus
♆	Neptune
♇	Pluto
☄	comet
✻	fixed star

Miscellaneous

&	and
&c	et cetera; and so forth
/	diagonal *or* slant; used to mean "or" (as in *and/or*), "per" (as in *meters/second*); indicates end of a line of verse; separates the figures of a date (9/29/99)
†	died — used especially in genealogies
f/ or *f*:	relative aperture of a photographic lens
☠	poison
℞	take — used on prescriptions
♀	female
♂	male
☮	peace
×	by ⟨3×5 cards⟩

Business

@	at; each ⟨4 apples @ 25¢ = $1.00⟩
c/o	care of
#	number if it precedes a numeral ⟨track #3⟩; pound(s) if it follows ⟨a 5# sack of sugar⟩
lb	pound; pounds
%	percent
‰	per thousand
$	dollar(s)
¢	cent(s)
£	pound(s)
©	copyrighted
®	registered trademark

Reference Marks

These marks are often placed in written or printed text to direct attention to a footnote:

*	asterisk or star
†	dagger
‡	double dagger
§	section *or* numbered clause
∥	parallels
¶	paragraph

Picture Index

Page numbers in **bold** refer to entries with additional information

PICTURE INDEX

Acknowledgments

Merriam-Webster, Inc., wishes to thank: Emily B. Arsenault, Daniel B. Brandon, Robert D. Copeland, Kathleen M. Doherty, Adam Groff, G. James Kossuth, Rose Martino, Joan I. Narmontas, Roger W. Pease, Jr., Thomas F. Pitoniak, Donna L. Rickerby, Michael D. Roundy, Maria A. Sansalone, Adrienne M. Scholz, Peter A. Sokolowski, Kory L. Stamper, Mark A. Stevens, and Karen L. Wilkinson for additional editorial and research assistance; Carol A. Fugiel as Senior Clerk

Dorling Kindersley would like to thank: Latha Anantharaman, Maggie Crowley, and Jacqueline Jackson for editorial assistance; Pauline Clarke, Darren Holt, Mahipal Singh, Kathryn Thomas, and Olivia Triggs for design assistance; Surya Sarangi for picture research, Aoitha Dare, Marie Ducos, Robert Graham, Nicholas Schonberger, and Dipali Singh for additional research; John Plumer for cartography; Vikram Singh, Umesh Aggarwal, Nicola Erdpresser, Andrew O'Brien, Claudia Shill, and Mabel Wu for additional DTP design; Chuck Wills as US consultant; Dr Michael Goodman as geography consultant; Simon Mumford and Ed Merritt for cartography

Dorling Kindersley would also like to thank the following organizations for their help with research or photography for this dictionary. Unless otherwise stated all are located in the UK: All Saints Church, York; Angels & Bermans, London; Audifon UK Ltd. Hearing Systems, Horley, Surrey; Blists Hill and Jackfield Tile Museum, Telford, Shropshire; Boosey & Hawkes Music Publishers Ltd, London; British Telecom; Brooking Collection, University of Greenwich, London; Pat Buckler, Canada/Mr Starpasser; Bureau, London; Cambridge Botanic Garden; The Civil War Library and Museum, Philadelphia, Pennsylvania; Danish National Museum, Copenhagen, Denmark; Detmold Open Air Museum, Germany; David Edge; Elvax Door Entry Systems, Rayleigh, Essex; Gables Travel; Glasgow Museums; Alex Gunn; Hamleys Toy Store, London; Mrs Hampton, Briar Stud, Herts./Chatsworth Belle; Harrods Department Store, London; Mrs G. Harwood, Wychwood Stud/Wychwood Dynascha; Highly Sprung, High Wycombe, Bucks.; The History Museum, Moscow, Russia; Horniman Museum, New York; Miss M. Houlden, Amoco Park, Spruce Meadows, Canada; Instituto Incremento Ippico Di Crema/ Weaner; Janet Fitch and Juliet Sheath, London; Eileen Trippier at Kensington Lighting Company Ltd, London; Lady Fischer, Kentucky Horse Park, USA/Roy, Patrick, and Pegasus Of Kilverstone; Sam Tree at Keygrove Marketing Ltd; Bill Leonard; Jim Lockwood/Duke; London Underground; Manchester Museums; David and Jon Maughan; Pat and Joanna Maxwell, Lodge Farm/Altruista; Lyn Moran and John Goddard Fenwick/Neopolitano Dubowina IV; Musée de Saint Malo, France; Musée de l'Empéri, Salon de Provence, France; National Army Museum, London; National Railway Museum, York; Norfolk Rural Life Museum, Gressenhall; Odds Farm Park, High Wycombe, Bucks.; Ministry of Defence, Pattern Room, Nottingham; Pegasus Stables, Newmarket; Anthony Pozner at Hendon Way Motors, London; Purves & Purves, London; Peter Ray; RNLI; Science Museum, London; Shelleys Shoes Ltd., London; Stephen Jones Millinery, London; Texas Instruments; University Marine Biological Station, Millport, Isle of Cumbrae, Scotland; Van Cortlandt Museum, New York; Weald and Downland Open Air Museum, Chichester, West Sussex; West One, London; Whitbread Plc; Cecil Williamson Collection,Witheridge, London; Worthing Art Gallery and Museum; Yorkshire Museum, York; Xerox Corporation, New York

Illustrators While all efforts have been made to acknowledge all illustrators, Dorling Kindersley will be pleased to add any missing credits in future editions: Joanna Cameron; Luciano Corbello; John Hutchinson; Kenneth Lilly; Chris Orr; Daniel Pyne; Peter Serjeant

Model-makers: Mark Beesley; Roby Braun; Peter Minister, Model FX; Chris Reynolds and the team at BBC Visual Effects; Thorp Modelmakers; Thurston Watson

Commissioned photography While all efforts have been made to acknowledge all photographers, Dorling Kindersley will be pleased to add any missing credits in future editions: Max Alexander; Peter Anderson; Dennis Avon; Patrick Baldwin; Geoff Brightling; Paul Bricknell; Jane Burton; Martin Cameron; Peter Chadwick; Tina Chambers; Gordon Clayton; Joe Cornish; Andy Crawford; Geoff Dann; Tom Dobbie; Christine M. Douglas; Philip Dowell; Peter Downs; Mike Dunning; Andreas Einsiedel; David Exton; Neil Fletcher; Jo Foord; Lynton Gardiner; John Garrett; Peter Gathercole; Philip Gatward; Ann George Marsh; John Glover; Paul Goff; Steve Gorton; Christi Graham; Frank Greenaway; Derek Hall; Mark Hamilton; Finbar Hawkins; Peter Hayman; Stephen Haywood; Tim Hayward; John Hepver; Marc Henrie; Norman Hollands; Jacqui Hurst; James Jackson; David Johnson; Colin Keates; Alan Keohane; Gary Kevin; Barnabas and Anabel Kindersley, 'Children Just Like Me'; Dave King; Cyril Laubscher; Richard Leeney; Liz McAulay; Andrew McRobb; Maslowski Photo; Neil Mersh; Graham Miller; Ray Moller; Michael Moran; Tracy Morgan; David Murray; Nick Nicholls; Stephen Oliver; Gary Ombler; Roger Phillips; Susanna Price; Howard Rice; Tim Ridley; Kim Sayer; Philippe Sebert; Tim Shepard; Karl Shone; Steve Shott; Gary Staab; James Stevenson; Clive Streeter; Steve Tanner; Harry Taylor; Kim Taylor; Andreas Von Einsiedel; Colin Walton; David Ward; Matthew Ward; Alan Williams; Alex Wilson; Jerry Young; Michel Zabé

Agency Photography

Dorling Kindersley would like to thank the following for their kind permission to reproduce their photographs. Unless otherwise stated all are located in the UK.

a=above; b=below; c=center; l=left; r=right; t=top

AKG London Ltd: 709r. **Action Plus**: Chris Barry 885cr. **Allsport UK Ltd**: Steven Babineau 401bl, Vincent Laforet 401tr, Mike Powell 636cb, Richard Saker 468br. **American Museum of Natural History, New York**: 818br, 900t. **Alamy**: 33t, 73c, 82cl, 175cc, 254b, 446b, 596tr, Cornstock 840cl, Hemera Technologies 701tr. **Ardea London Ltd**: M. Iijima 700trt, 459cr. **Angus Beare**: 42tl. **Bridgeman Art Library, London**: Ashmolean Museum, Oxford 56tr, Private Collection 716br. **British Library, London**: 788c. © **The Trustees of the British Museum:** 539crb, 539br. **J. Allan Cash**: 333bl, 345tc, 659bl, 744, 931t, 933cr. **Charlestown Shipwreck and Heritage Centre, Cornwall**: 430t. **Bruce Coleman Collection**: Jonathan Blair 519cc, Nigel Blake 349c, Jeff Foott 234bl, 398bl, Dr. Scott Nielsen 106br, Allan G. Potts 510bc, Marie Read 450bl, Hans Reinhard 215tl, John Shaw 507tl. **Corbis**: 50cr, 71b, 77cr, 252br, 343cr, 362b, 451b, 470b, 525tc, 579b, 717t, 729t, 750c, 759t, 772cc, 821tr, 892t. 948cb, 949cb, Archivo Iconografico, S.A. 470tc, William A. Bake 596tr, Tom Bean 308tc, Neil Beer 606tr, Bettmann 948ct, 949ct, S. Carmona 330bl, Roger Chester/Eye Ubiquitous 516br, W. Cody 947t, The Corcoran Gallery of Art 949t, The Corcoran Gallery of Art/Bequest of Mrs. Benjamin Taylor 948t, Philip James Corwin 925c, Macduff Everton 947cc, Kevin Fleming 437br, 678cl, Franz-Marc Frei 762tl, J.D. Griggs 946b, Historical Picture Archive 640b, Wolfgang Kaehler 933t, George Lepp 514br, Wally MacNamee 835br, Lawrence Manning 313cr, Gunter Marx 591tl, Joe McDonald 527bc, Marc Muench 39bl, Amos Nachoum 724cr, Gianni Dagli Orti 928br, Christine Osborne 932l, Greg Probst 937b, Progressive Image/Bob Rowan 427cr, 469tr, Roger Ressmeyer 566tl, Bill Ross 947cr, Galen Rowell 536b, 657b, 946c, Ken Schafer 922t, Phil Schermeister 947cl, Michael T. Sedam 122c, Vince Streano 337cl, Ted Streshinsky 882tr, Jim Sugar Photography 885tl, Adam Woolfitt 927c, Michael S. Yamashita 489cl, Yogi, Inc. 946. **ESA / Hubble:** NASA , ESA, and A. Simon (GSFC) 457clb. **James Davis Travel Library**: 776b. **Denoyer-Geppert**: Geoff Brightling/ESPL/Dorling Kindersley 411cr, Dorling Kindersley/Geoff Brightling 869br. **Edinburgh/SUSM**: 700tr. **Philip Dowell** 49tc, c, 72cl, 101bc, 120cl, acr, b, 158tr, 164tl, 341ctl, ctc, 449cr, 466tr, 480tr, 502ctr, 529ctr, 549t, 553cl, 562cr, 570br, 572cl, 585cr, 602tl, cr, bc, 611cr, 656tl, 748cl, 876b. **Dudley Edmondson** 541cb. **The Eurospace Centre, Transinne, Belgium**: 141t. **Getty Images**: 60cr, 87br, 183b, 219b, 226cr, 248c, 342cr, 356tr, 385b, 439b, 467br, Bloomberg 293br, 740bl, Thomas Northcut/Photodisc 180c, Marc Serota 226cr, Stocktrek RF 752tl, Image Source 515c, 547t, 567t, 573br, 585cl, 614bl, 649t, 690b, 695b, 696tr, 701b, 734tl, 777tr, 805tr, 809br, 816t, 822b, 829tr, 830t, 833cc, 842tr, 857b, 886b. **Brooking Collection, University of Greenwich**: 473br. **Rough Guides**: 208cb, 769rb, 789rb, 806tl. **Robert Harding Picture Library**: Martyn Chillmaid 862bc. **Hibbert/Ralph**: 179c. **Graham High (model-maker)**: 855r. **Rose Horridge** 897tr. **Hugh McManners** 719t. **The Hutchison Library**: J.G. Fuller 812tr. **Imperial War Museum**: 371tl. **The Jewish Museum, London**: 393b. **Dorling Kindersley**: 381t, Guy Ryecart 591br, Dan Bannister 564b, Ken Findlay 710tr, Steve Gorton/Roby Braun - modelmaker 246clb, Jamie Marshall 792t, Peter Minister, Digital Sculptor 246bl, 246br, 247cr, 247bl, 247br, 845tr, Demetrio Carrasco 862cl, Demetrio Carrasco 862tl, The Trustees of the British Museum 54cb, 125tr, 216tc, 216ca, 308cr, 396cr, 497r, 497tr, 519tr, 672tl, 809l, 599br. **Dreamstime.com:** Bambi L. Dingman 948br, Oleksiy Mark 238br, Pancaketom 175br (One cent), Radlovskyaroslav 175br, Matthew Trommer 293br (Coins). **Fotolia:** dundanim 752cla. **Frank Lane Picture Agency**: 59ta, S.C. Brown 656r, Robin Chittenden 598br, Eric & David Hosking 764bl, 768bl, Gerard Lecz 507tc, Chris Mattison 765tr, Mark Newman 589b, Leonard Lee Rue 903cr, H. Schrempp 757r, Silvestris 667t, G. Stewart 832bl, R. Tidman 935bl, Larry West 639r, 749tr. **Melbourne Zoo, Australia**: 502cc. **Mexican Museum Authority**: 924l. **Motorcycle Heritage Museum, Westerville, Ohio**: 535ctr. **Musée Marmottan**: Dorling Kindersley/Susanna Price 218cl. **Museum of English Rural Life**: 420bl. **Museum of London**: 779c. **Museum of Mankind, London**: 190c, 891l. **The Museum of the Moving Image, London**: 764r. **Museum of the Revolution, Moscow, Russia**: 321l. **NASA** 348, JHUAPL / SwRI 619c, 705cr, Damian Peach, Amateur Astonomer 752ca (Jupiter), JPL 752tc, 752tc (Venus), 752tr, 752ca, Solar Dynamics Observatory 752cla (Sun), JPL 877br. **National Maritime Museum, Greenwich**: Tina Chambers 212b, 123b, 170cr, 260b, 457tr, 482r, 673bl, 741c, 793cb, 212cr, Tina Chambers and James Stevenson/Dorling Kindersley 656cb. **National Motor Museum, Beaulieu**: 442c. **National Museums of Scotland**: 139c, 447r, 786t. **Natural History Museum, London**: 64cr, 335br, 466cr, 529cb, 534l, 545l, 695br, 928cl, 935tl. **Natural History Picture Agency**: Nigel J. Dennis 502ctl, Pavel German 507ct, Martin Harvey 502t, Derek Karp 502bl, John Shaw 106tcr. **Oceanwideimages** 724cr. **Stephen Oliver** 802lb. **Order of the Black Prince** 457cr. **Oxford Scientific Films**: Alan Root/Survival Anglia 177c, DK 131, 404l, Max Gibbs 496l. **Pictor International**: 80, 837l, 880tr, 925br, 927t, b, 929tl, cl. **Pictures:** David Henderson 852br. **Pitt-Rivers Museum, Oxford**: 233cr, 728cb. **Planet Earth Pictures**: Doug Perrine 725l, Marty Snyderman 724tr, James D. Watt 725b. **PunchStock**: 648b, 695ta, 794b, 802ta. **Rex Features**: 217cr, Peter Brookes 949b, Sipa Press/Trippet 948b. **The Board of Trustees of the Royal Armouries**: 231br. **Royal Artillery Trust**: 70br. **Royal College of Music, Junior Department**: 848cr. **Science Museum, London**: 442bl, 442t, 442ca, 639r. **Science Photo Library**: Petit Format Nestlé 283b, Stammers/Thompson 915l. **Science Picture Library**: 376t, 517b, 575t. **South of England Rare Breeds Centre**: 756cr, 898crb. **The Stock Market**: 583. **Tony Stone Images**: 797, James Balog 598br, Paul Chesley 936bc, Florence Douyrou 509b, Chad Ehlers 937t, Robert Frerck 929b, Andy Sacks 303t, Oliver Strewe 936tl. **Telegraph Colour Library**: Bavaria Bildagentur 850t, 933cl, Colorific/Wayne Sorce/Visions 458tr, M. Trigalon 783l. **Vatican Museums**: 673tr. **Rollin Verlinde**: 154cl, 528br. **The Wallace Collection, London**: 200cr, 211tcr, 803cr, cl. **Warwick Castle**: 351r. Barrie Watts: 262cl. **Westminster Cathedral**: 693bl. **Wildlifeimages** 327cl. **Chris Wilkinson Architects Ltd, London**: 122tcr. **Paul Wilkinson** 150r. **The Earl of Pembroke & the Trustees of Wilton House**: 742tr. **Winchcombe Folk & Police Museum**: Ross Simms 700b. **Jerry Young**: 37b, 49b, 61br, 67tr, 70tr, 92bl, cr, 106cbr, tc, tl 114l, 204t, 206br, 210c, 280c, 319ctc, ,cbl, 327cr, 336br, 405bl, 409cr, 454b, 488cl, br, 530tr, 558bl, 584cr, 677tr, c, 684t, 743b, 746tl, tr, 747tl, 761tl, cl, cr, 832tr, cr, 836t, 879c, 909t.

Jacket images: *Front:* **Alamy Images:** eddie toro tr. **Dorling Kindersley:** Andrew Kerr br. **NASA:** JPL cla. *Back:* **Dorling Kindersley:** Rough Guides c. **Dreamstime.com:** Oleksiy Mark br, Pakhnyushchyy cr. **Fotolia:** dundanim tl.